D0152472

PRESSER LEARNING CENTER
Boyer College of Music
Temple University
Philadelphia, PA 19122-6079

The New Handbook of Research
on Music Teaching and Learning

THE NEW HANDBOOK OF RESEARCH ON MUSIC TEACHING AND LEARNING

A Project of the
Music Educators National Conference

Editors
Richard Colwell
Carol Richardson

PRESSER LEARNING CENTER
Boyer College of Music
Temple University
Philadelphia, PA 19122-0079

OXFORD
UNIVERSITY PRESS
2002

OXFORD

UNIVERSITY PRESS

Oxford   New York
Auckland   Bangkok   Buenos Aires   Cape Town   Chennai
Dar es Salaam   Delhi   Hong Kong   Istanbul   Karachi   Kolkata
Kuala Lumpur   Madrid   Melbourne   Mexico City   Mumbai   Nairobi
São Paulo   Shanghai   Singapore   Taipei   Tokyo   Toronto

and an associated company in Berlin

Copyright © 2002 by MENC: The National Association for Music Education

Published by Oxford University Press, Inc.
198 Madison Avenue, New York, New York 10016

www.oup.com

Oxford is a registered trademark of Oxford University Press

All rights reserved. No part of this publication may be reproduced,
stored in a retrieval system, or transmitted, in any form or by any means,
electronic, mechanical, photocopying, recording, or otherwise,
without the prior permission of Oxford University Press.

Library of Congress Cataloging-in-Publication Data
The new handbook of research on music teaching and learning: A Project of the Music Educators
National Conference / [edited by] Richard Colwell, Carol Richardson.
        p. cm.
     Includes bibliographical references and index.
     ISBN 0-19-513884-8
     1. Music—Instruction and study.   I. Colwell, Richard.   II. Richardson, Carol P.   III.
  Music Educators National Conference (U.S.)
MT1 .S44 2002
780'.71—dc21   2001036516

9 8 7 6 5 4 3 2 1

Printed in the United States of America
on acid-free paper

Preface

In the preface to the first *Handbook of Research on Music Teaching and Learning*, Richard Colwell suggested that music education was one of the broadest subjects in the school curriculum. In 2002, the profession has extended its programs and services even further. This Handbook reflects this increased diversity, introducing topics that have often been marginalized in music education research. This volume is not an update of the first handbook; rather, it complements and extends that publication. Change in music education has been brought about not only by the voluntary national standards but by monumental shifts in the field of education and in American society. Education and its priorities are no longer neutral topics, of interest only in the local faculty lounge; they are part of the national political process and political agenda. John Mahlmann, the executive director of MENC—the National Association for Music Education, has skillfully positioned not only music education but the arts education profession to take advantage of these changes. He has not been timid in seizing opportunities to promote and support the profession, to provide space for innovation and advocacy, and to voice the profession's concerns in educational and political circles. The authors of Handbook chapters have attempted to emulate his leadership by addressing many of the topics on Mahlmann's agenda, often going beyond the profession's present agenda. Thus, the Handbook breaks new ground in discussing topics that range from policy to partnerships, and in securing the contribution of outstanding scholars in many fields, scholars who are in a position to influence and enrich music pedagogy, its research, and its place in the larger cultural/educational scene.

The profession is challenged in that change has not replaced most of the cherished objectives that have long guided instructional practices. Stability is provided by performance practices, excellent private and group instruction, and rich performing ensembles that sustain the importance of excellence as a significant instructional outcome. The Handbook contains a chapter on studio instruction.

The first Handbook met with wide acceptance and unanticipated sales to a broad audience; it became virtually a required text for doctoral students and those professionals interested in teaching and research. One early review of the first Handbook criticized its unevenness, saying that the promises made in the preface were not fulfilled by all of the chapters. An accurate criticism. A project of this magnitude engenders frustrations and disappointments, and those occurred with this Handbook as well. Important chapters failed to materialize, word limits prevented authors from discussing everything projected in their outlines, and the quality of available research in some areas was disappointing. Still, the new Handbook is longer and more complete than the first Handbook. When planning was begun in 1995, there was a "wide awakeness" that the profession was evolving. There were new national issues: arts education as opposed to music education and accompanying it the major fields of arts advocacy, arts administration, and arts-based research; qualitative research techniques; and a renewed emphasis on the functional aspects of music, promoting the value of the many "spin-offs" that derive from music participation. Confirming recognition of this interest in the broadest of outcomes, the meta-analysis of Ellen Winner and Lois Hetland, two individuals outside the field of music education, published in volume 34 (2000) of the *Journal of Aesthetic Education*, was a study most often cited.

Any history of such a large project is always incomplete. Following acceptance of a tentative outline by MENC and Oxford University Press, a meeting of section editors and interested scholars was held in Baltimore in 1997 to refine chapter descriptions, set priorities, and identify potential authors. Prior to this meeting, comments were solicited from authors of the first handbook, a poll taken of the research priorities of leaders in the profession, and research issues coordinated with AERA, ASCD, and ERS, professional organizations involved with research issues in the arts. Two open planning meetings were held at the MENC in-service conference in Phoenix, attended by individuals interested in shaping the Handbook. Two years later at the Washington, DC, in-service meeting, two additional meetings—a regular open convention session and an assessment session by section leaders—helped solidify the final form of the Handbook. A clear message from these preliminary meetings was that the behavioral research training received by doctoral students had peaked in the 1970s and subsequently had been dropped by many institutions, leaving many young Ph.Ds and Ed.Ds with scant research competency. Although the Handbook could not remedy that situation, it could portray a research agenda that matched to some extent the interests of the profession.

It seems unusual to present a handbook with no part on "methods," a topic that often defines an undergraduate music education department. (Serious attention was given to philosophical considerations of the pedagogy of Zoltán Kodály, particularly because the projected author argued that it was being misrepresented: The Kodály method was designed for a Marxist educational system, and U.S. practitioners were not always aware of the changes necessary to make it compatible with democratic educational systems.) The alternative option was taken, however, to devote space to issues in curriculum, where researchers minimize the connection between curriculum and courses of instruction and focus on a broad definition of education, one that could engender and motivate considerable research in music education.

The involvement of educators and education supporters in political issues has been a major recent development, and the extent to which such issues will become research topics in music education is unknown. Certainly the priority of music in the curriculum will be affected by these political issues. The strength and importance of music to most students and teachers makes it as appropriate as a subject in after-school programs as it is as a curricular subject. Concerns for social justice underlie many of the curricular issues concerning the priorities of education. Education has always taken its cue from forces outside the discipline, most often from the church. Principles from the Judaic-Christian philosophies dominated education into the 20th century. With the secularization of society and education, there are conservative and liberal views and premises stemming from business, globalization, diversity, and individual and community rights/obligations. The critical theorists argue that research as well as curriculum has been based on illegitimate, dominatory, and repressive factors that reinforce the status quo. The issue is power. Researchers cannot be neutral when a primary purpose of education is to transform individuals to conform to the obligations of social democracy. For Jurgen Habermas, our interests are socially constructed. His argument is that the educational system has been constructed to favor those individuals and institutions presently in power, and to determine what counts as worthwhile knowledge and worthwhile research. When interests are socially constructed, the role of research is to clarify the meaning of all communication, verbal and nonverbal. These ideas have seeped into several Handbook chapters and are becoming part of the milieu of music education.

A major outcome of research in music education should be to interpret any data in terms of how they support theory or apply to the task of building a better educational system that upholds American or Western democracy. Data interpretation is understood in terms of one's philosophy. With new and expanded philosophies of education, data interpretation is more complex, not restricted only to positivism. The revolt against positivism had begun as early as the second half of the 19th century, with William Blake arguing that the universe was an organism, not a mechanism. Many of the goals of music education, including quality of life, cannot be weighed. The anti-positivist movement stemming from sociology includes the research techniques of phenomenology, ethnomethodology, and symbolic interactionism. We mention these philosophical influences not only because of their role in qualitative research but because they support research in feminist scholarship, one of the new chapters in this Handbook. Power and values, two important ideas stemming from the feminist movement, are cause for reflection on the educational enterprise. Positivist knowledge is often primarily technical knowledge, leading to a trivialization of the curriculum. Some argue that the emphasis on educational technology is an example of reinforcing the status quo by making education more efficient rather than transformative. Philosophy and theory become essential to the research enterprise: The positivists begin with a theory and seek to disprove it but they often suggest problems that are only tangentially related to philosophy or theory, whereas the purpose of qualitative research is to arrive at theory from the data, and the power of qualitative research is dependent upon the integrity, completeness, and coherence of the derived theory.

The research agenda has been and will continue to be strongly influenced by the type of educational system that is adopted to support an evolving definition of democracy, equity, excellence, and fairness. When Nel Noddings suggests that instilling a sense of caring, civility, and cooperation is more important than teaching and classrooms, researchers must take note of what meanings they derive from their efforts, as meaning is accepted by all parties as being socially constructed. A preface is no place for an extended philosophical discussion; suffice it to say that one must be free of all preconceptions before one can appropriately reflect on research outcomes in terms of the purpose or goal sought.

Credit for this *New Handbook of Research on Music Teaching and Learning* deservedly rests on the shoulders of the part editors, who have wrestled for the past four years with the multitude of issues required in producing scholarly chapters that will serve the profession for at least the next ten years. These editors, who have earned the respect of the profession, are Janet Barrett, Nicholas DeCarbo, John Flohr, Hildegard Froehlich, Jack Heller, Andreas Lehmann, Marie McCarthy, Michael Mark, David Myers, John Richmond, Peter Webster, Nancy Whitaker, and Lizabeth Wing. In addition, we had access to prepublication chapters of the fourth *AERA Handbook of Research on Teaching* through the generosity of editor Virginia Richardson; these chapters were especially helpful in the teacher education part of this Handbook.

The most vexing problem faced was the relationship of the Handbook to the first Handbook, in that, though much of the content of the first Handbook was still appropriate, the book was out of print. Despite the temptation to update the material in the first Handbook, the decision was made to produce an essentially new Handbook and address primarily those topics that had not been covered in the first Handbook and that were identified by a survey of music education researchers as important issues in music teaching and learning in the 21st century. The assumption is that the first Handbook is available in most libraries, where individuals interested in research can access the material without undue difficulty. Consideration was given to reprinting those chapters most salient in the 21st century but we found that most of the chapters remained pertinent. Only the areas of technology and early childhood education are updated, and these because of the progress and change of emphasis during the past decade.

Particular recognition must be accorded to the many reviewers of the chapters in this volume. We doubt that any music publication has been so extensively reviewed prior to publication. Each author outline was reviewed by five to ten professionals, as were the draft chapters. What has to be satisfying is the professionalism of the authors in reflecting upon these reviews; not only did they accommodate the suggestions but several authors began afresh. Such accommodation must be unusual when writing a substantive chapter *gratis*, where the only reward is the satisfaction of assisting teachers, students, and researchers who will come in contact with this publication. There is no single view in the Handbook, although all research topics are not treated equally. More leeway, and also guidance, was given to the authors of those chapters where there was a lack of substantive research in the field. Authors were asked to include only the better research and to critique studies when the critique would be helpful. They were asked to hypothesize and to suggest problems and trends. The task became complex when the research in question

had no problem statement and there was no interpretation at the conclusion as to the effect.

There continues to be a lack of appreciation for rigorous research in music education despite a century of sporadic efforts. Any historical review indicates not only peaks and valleys in quality but the remarkable influence of non-music educators with an interest in topics musical. The research work of music educators is uneven; further, those who evaluate our work either have little confidence in our products or are unable to critique them. A poster session at the MENC convention may be as valuable on one's vita as a substantive essay formally presented at a conference on music cognition. We, of course, have done little to police our own efforts or to discuss and establish research priorities. The source of a research agenda for the profession has been top-down, driven by two gatekeepers: doctoral advisors and the MENC leadership. A wide diversity exists in the ability of doctoral programs to produce skilled and insightful researchers who ask the important questions that lead to a career-length program of research. There is also a lack of consensus among doctoral advisors about what constitutes "quality" in dissertation-level research products. A source of confusion is the numerous calls for more "kinds" of research and the suggestions that our journals should publish more historical, more qualitative, more quantitative, or whatever, research. The kind of research should be dictated by the problem or question whose solution will make a difference. Most substantive research topics require competence in more than "kind" of research; when a research report begins with a statement categorizing it as a specific "kind," the knowledgeable reader reacts with "caveat emptor." Contemporary research texts minimize the distinction between kinds of research. There is always tension in research, but the existence of identifiable centers of kinds of research could be unfortunate. We would not expect numerical equality in the kinds of research in music teaching and learning because the research issues are defined by the nature of the profession and its particular needs at a particular time. We have found that there is no agreement on what qualifies as research. Some of this confusion may be due to long lists of references, exclusively in APA style, which does not distinguish between op-ed pieces and substantive research. Volume 30, number 2 (March 2001), of *Educational Researcher* contains an article by Mike Rose and Karen McClafferty, "A Call for the Teaching of Writing in Graduate Education," where the writers assert, "It's my belief that you can have too many citations. Too often, we see an over reliance on citation to establish authority in academic writing, a shopping bag of sources rather than building an argument. It's true that citation is the coin of the realm, but ask yourself what you're trying to achieve with your citations, what's your purpose?" (p. 27). The overuse of citations reminds one that, for most of our intellectual history, empirical evidence of proof was superseded by authority, and the more authorities one could quote, the stronger one's position. In the 16th century, Francis Bacon restored faith in reasoning, hypothesizing that if enough data were collected, the meaning of the data could be grasped by the alert observer. The nod to "kinds" of research in this Handbook occurs in the part edited by Jack Heller and Nicholas DeCarbo, where the approach is not one of advocacy or methodology but one that is descriptive, historical, inspirational, and perhaps provocative. One solution to the dismal trend of less-than-stellar research would be to have MENC sponsor research training in-service sessions for doctoral advisors at national meetings of MENC. This model has served the AERA well by providing extended training seminars on specific aspects of selected research methodologies, offered on the days preceding or following their annual meeting. MENC did initiate at the 1966 Seattle meeting a rigorous in-service education program for selected doctoral advisors that was continued at the Chicago meeting, taught by "experts" in research procedures and research design. It could be argued that this was a high point in MENC's involvement with research and that the impact on the quality of research was substantive and lasted for nearly two decades.

Organization of the Volume

Many editors convinced us that numerous topics could not be adequately covered within our original estimate of length for this volume. One part thus sacrificed is policy and philosophical research, where substantive issues should be raised as U.S. education becomes more political than it has ever been. We have excellent chapters in this part but should have had many more as the political spectrum influencing education has become enormous. Whereas John Dewey emphasized the connection between education and American democracy, today's educators such as William Pinar describe curriculum exclusively in political terms stemming from not only Paulo Freire but the entire body of critical theory. Individual rights, so strongly advocated by Emerson and Thoreau, often take precedent over the welfare of the community. Countering this view, the importance of the community is promoted by Amitai Etzioni, Richard Rorty, and sociologists like Pierre Bourdieu. Bourdieu's *habitas* that arises during adolescence, when individuals can draw upon their acquired knowledge and skills to derive meaning for their world, contributes to today's emphasis on deriving meaning from research knowledge. The ideas of democracy held by Dewey and George Herbert Mead are now foundational

for thinking about the relationship between contemporary democracy and education by such persons as John Goodlad, Roger Soder, and Timothy McMannon. Goodlad (Soder, Goodlad, and McMannon, 2001, p. 1) cites George Will's statement that the first half of the 20th century belonged to physicists and the second half to biologists, but without good philosophy this would bring calamity in the 21st century. These issues are affecting the priority of music education in schooling and in education. Researchers in visual arts are much more sophisticated in addressing policy issues than are we in music education; however, not only making policy but implementing it is critical to the long-term health of the profession. To heighten its importance, the Handbook begins with the part on policy and philosophy.

To undergird the part on curriculum, we turned to Ian Westbury, a leading scholar in the field and editor of the premier journal in the field. The curriculum is critical to reconstructionist education; the way in which a society selects, classifies, distributes, transmits, and evaluates public educational knowledge reflects both the distribution of power and the principles of social control. Goodlad suggests that crippling school budgets to ensure computer literacy makes no sense and is equivalent to a school's emphasizing the ability to ride a bicycle in the 1940s and 50s. For Goodlad, education is about the building of our humanity. He recognizes the importance of enculturating the young in a social and political democracy but notes that what is missing from discussions about teacher education is its mission (Soder, Goodlad, and McMannon, 2001, p. xvii). Ethics would loom large in any such curriculum, but the internet has no ethic, and the guiding ethic of the workplace is profit. Westbury, beginning with Dewey, carefully outlines the dilemma faced by those interested in curriculum research. Chapters in this part address issues in music education not covered in the first handbook: improvisation, critical thinking, distance learning, studio instruction, and the theoretical bases.

Musical learning continues to be a major field and it was necessary to select pressing issues in the field for this part. Education specialists Laurie Taetle, Barak Rosenshine, and Barry Zimmerman were co-authors with music educators on three of the chapters. We also turned to external writers who are well known in the field of motivation, Marty Maehr, Paul Pintrich, and Elizabeth Linnenbrink, as this was an area with scant substantive research in music education. We searched for theory, as there is a tendency for some researchers to hide behind the method and ignore the crucial area of theoretical development (Brown and Dowling, 1998, p. 83). Theory, for the positivist, is the ultimate aim of science.

Likewise for musical cognition and development, we secured the cooperation of topical experts, mostly outside the United States, with strong research interests in music. Special thanks go to Andreas Lehmann, whose intimate knowledge of the field assisted in identifying topics and identifying appropriate research-oriented authors in psychology and related fields.

The sociology of music is an emerging field with an encyclopedic number of possible topics. Sociology of music has for too long been associated with the relatively unimportant topic of preferences. Marie McCarthy involved sociologists and music educators from the United States, Canada, and Europe in assembling the most comprehensive body of research literature available to the profession.

To address teacher education, we determined that it would be necessary to pair professional educators and music educators in order to fairly represent the research problems in contemporary education. This was not an easy task but was handled adroitly by Lizabeth Wing and Janet Barrett. The lack of research in music teacher education is surprising; few of the curricular beliefs have been challenged in eight decades, and there is little agreement on a successful teacher. The collaborative efforts in each part were a learning experience for everyone; we found differences in meaning in many of the most common concepts, an important finding for researchers in music teaching and learning. Teacher education, like curriculum, was represented by single chapters in the first Handbook whereas complete parts on these topics are present in this Handbook.

Three parts are completely new and represent some of the areas that John Mahlmann has explored on behalf of the profession. The idea of partnerships and connections to the other arts was developed by David Myers, who reached out beyond the music education profession (true connections) to identify scholars in the field. John Flohr broached the field of music and medicine, which required physicians and researchers in the health fields to review the research and identify topics in music education. Michael Mark undertook the formidable task of reporting on research-based competencies that are spin-offs from an exacting teaching of music objectives such as those represented in the national standards. Again, Mark was able to identify individuals from outside music education to team with music education scholars, assuring a more objective approach to the topics.

The Handbook concludes with the expected part on research techniques although, again, bypassing the traditional approach to such topics. Refuting the idea that there is a substantive difference between qualitative and quantitative research, the chapters on data acquisition and assessment inspect potentials in these two areas while the chapter on contemporary issues in qualitative research is written knowing that the most substantive research in the profession during the past century has been of individuals or small populations (often called qualitative research to-

day), including Seashore's studies on vibrato, Moorehouse and Pond's on children's creativity, Revesz's study of musical genius, Rubin-Rabson on musical memory, and Serafine's research in musical cognition.

Despite a large number of stimulus-response research studies under controlled situations, there has long been consensus that the ultimate outcome of teaching and learning is for students to achieve competence in deriving musical meaning. There is agreement that enhancing musical meaning is an objective of instruction and that here the interactionists of the research community have taken the lead. With symbolic interaction, an individual has to construct, assemble, select, evaluate, and interpret perceived musical stimuli, stimuli that occur within a social context. The Frankfurt school is critical of our present interpretation of what these stimuli mean; the members contend that too much is presupposed—the situation, the relationships, and the structure—with little consideration of the ideological context, especially when these stimuli are placed in an artificial research configuration.

These suppositions affect the feasibility of new types of research. Among the new types are several that deserve mention here. Professor Raths entitles his introduction to the part on teacher education *fuzzy logic*. Fuzzy logic is a research technique that attempts to ascertain the extent to which a particular measure conforms to a semantic ideal (Fourali, 1997). Fuzzy logic recognizes that musical terms such as loud-soft, high-low, and good-bad vary depending upon the situation and suggests that measurement be more precise. The fuzzy logic technique relies on feedback to continually modify the meaning, to be sensitive to appropriateness and effectiveness in relationship to shifting standards.

Chaos theory has forced a more careful and thoughtful interpretation of results, recognizing that similar conditions can produce different outcomes, that repetition of a treatment may not work the same way a second time, that long-term prediction is difficult, and that much of what occurs in the classroom is largely unpredictable.

Acknowledgments

Any project of this scope requires the support of numerous behind-the-scene individuals. Maribeth Payne, general music editor for Oxford University Press, supported the publication of the first Handbook and willingly undertook this second project, providing excellent guidance. John Mahlmann, executive director of the Music Educators National Conference, and Peggy Senko Wang, executive editor, were enthusiastic about the project from the outset and were there when needed during the long gestation process. Paul Boylan, dean emeritus of the School of Music at the University of Michigan, volunteered financial and staff support, which was continued by Dean Karen Wolfe, and the project could not have been completed without this "home office," an office cheerfully presided over by Marionette Cano, who was the primary coordinator of the copious details generated by a project that involved well over 100 authors and some 500 reviewers. Recognition must be given to Richard Scerbo, who assisted Dr. Marie McCarthy with part V, and Chris Casazza and Stephanie Kish, who assisted Dr. Liz Wing with part VI. Two graduate assistants, Donna Emmanuel and Kristi Bishop, helped launch the project.

R.J.C
C. R.

REFERENCES

Brown, A., and Dowling, P. (1998). *Doing research/reading research: A mode of interrogation for education*, London: Falmer Press.

Fourali, C. (1997). Using fuzzy logic in educational measurement: the case of portfolio assessment. *Evaluation and Research in Education, 11* (3), 129–148.

Soder, R., Goodlad, J., & McMannon T. (Eds). (2001). *Developing character in the young*. San Francisco: Jossey-Bass.

Contents

Contributors

HAROLD ABELES is Professor and Coordinator of the Program in Music and Music Education at Teachers College, Columbia University, where he also serves as the co-director of the Center for Arts Education Research. He has conducted program evaluations for arts partnerships in Baltimore, Cleveland, Detroit, Hartford, New York, and Philadelphia. He recently completed a study with Judith Burton and Robert Horowitz on learning in and through the arts.

CHRISTOPHER D. AZZARA is Associate Professor of Music Education at the Hartt School of the University of Hartford. A freelance pianist and arranger, he often performs as a soloist and as a member of various ensembles. After receiving his bachelor's degree in music from George Mason University, he taught instrumental music in Fairfax County, Virginia, public schools and freelanced in the Washington, D.C., area. He later received a master of music and a Ph.D. in music education from the Eastman School of Music. Azzara is the author of numerous articles and books including *Creativity in Improvisation, Concert Selections for Winds and Percussion*, and *Jump Right In: The Instrumental Series*.

JEANNE BALLANTINE is Professor of Sociology at Wright State University, Dayton, Ohio. She is the author of several books, including two textbooks in sociology and education, *The Sociology of Education: A Systematic Approach* (2001) and *Schools and Society* (with Joan Spade, 2001). Her teaching and research areas include sociology of education, cross-cultural women's issues, and pedagogy and scholarship of teaching and learning.

JANET R. BARRETT is Professor of Music Education and Chair of the Music Department at the University of Wisconsin, Whitewater. She serves on the editorial committees for the *Bulletin of the Council of Research in Music Education and General Music Today*. Barrett is co-author of *Sound Ways of Knowing: Music in the Interdisciplinary Curriculum* and *Looking in on Music Teaching*. She earned her B.M. and M.A. degrees at the University of Iowa and her Ph.D. at the University of Wisconsin, Madison. She is currently serving as the president of the Wisconsin Music Educators Association.

LEE R. BARTEL is Associate Professor of Music Education at the University of Toronto and is Director of the Canadian Music Education Research Center. His primary research interests include research methods, response to music, and aspects of social psychology. Bartel is an associate of the Centre for Health Promotion, on the research staff at the Bloorview MacMillan Rehabilitation Centre, and a research associate of the John Adaskin Project. He is a former editor of the *Canadian Journal of Research in Music Education* and currently edits *Canadian Music Educator*.

WAYNE BOWMAN is Professor of Music and Chair of Music Education at Brandon University in Manitoba, Canada. Chief among his areas of scholarly expertise are philosophy of music and of music education. Bowman is author of numerous articles and book chapters and of *Philosophical Perspectives on Music* (Oxford University Press, 1988).

ALICE BRANDFONBRENNER received her M.D. from Columbia University's College of Physicians and Surgeons and received subsequent training in medicine and anesthesiology at Lenox Hill Hospital in New York, Northwestern Medical School, and Evanston Hospital in Chicago. She is currently Director of the Medical Program for Performing Artists at the Rehabilitation Institute of Chicago and Assistant Professor of Medicine at Northwestern University Medical School. Since 1999, she has also served as an Adjunct Professor of Performance studies at Northwestern's Music School, where she teaches "Medical Aspects of Performance."

LIORA BRESLER is a Professor at the College of Education at the University of Illinois at Urbana Champaign, where she also held positions at the Center for Instructional Research and Curriculum Evaluation and at the Bureau of Educational Research. She holds degrees in piano performance, philosophy, and musicology from Tel-Aviv University and a degree in education from Stanford. Her research interests include arts and aesthetic education and qualitative research methodology. She is co-editor of *Arts and Learning Journal* and the electronic *International Journal for Education and Arts*, and guest edits for *International Issues in Arts Education Policy Review*,

Educational Theory, Research Studies in Music Education, and *Visual Art Research.*

ARTHUR BROOKS is an Associate Professor of Public Administration at the Maxwell School of Citizenship and Public Affairs at Syracuse University, where he teaches courses on economics for public policy and nonprofit management. His research focuses on arts management and the economics of the entertainment industry.

JUDITH M. BURTON directs the Program in Art and Art Education at Teachers College, Columbia University. She also serves as the Co-director of the Center for Arts Education Research at Teachers College. Her professional interests include artistic-aesthetic development in childhood and adolescence. Her research on the transfer of learning forms the basis of "Learning in and through the Arts: The Issue of Transfer" in *Studies in Art Education* (2000); her study on the role of teaching in arts partnerships formed the basis of "Natural Allies: Children, Teachers, and Artists" in *Beyond Enrichment* (1998).

KRIS CHESKY is Director of Research and Education for the Texas Center of Music and Medicine. He holds a joint faculty appointment as Research Assistant Professor in the Department of Medicine at the University of North Texas Health Science Center in Fort Worth and at the University of North Texas College of Music in Denton.

DONALD COFFMAN is Associate Professor and Head of Music Education at the University of Iowa. With more than 20 years of teaching experience at all levels, he currently teaches courses in conducting, methods for teaching instrumental methods in schools, psychology of music, and techniques for researching and measuring musical behaviors. Coffman also directs the Iowa City/Johnson County Senior Center New Horizons Band. He holds degrees from Wichita State University (M.M.E.) and the University of Kansas (B.M.E., Ph.D.).

MICHELLE COLLAY is Visiting Associate Professor of Education at Pacific Lutheran University in Tacoma, Washington. A former music teacher, she is a teacher-scholar who seeks to improve teaching and scholarship in higher education and K–12 schools through collaboration with educators. Her research interests include new-teacher socialization, school-university partnerships, and creation of classroom communities. She is lead author of *Learning Circles: Creating Conditions for Professional Development* and co-author of *Designing for Learning: Six Elements in Constructivist Classrooms* (with George Gagnon, Jr.).

RICHARD COLWELL is Emeritus Professor of Music and Education at the University of Illinois. He was a Guggenheim Fellow and founder and editor of the Council for Research in Music Education and the *Quarterly*. His most recent publication is the 3rd edition of *Teaching Instrumental Music* with Thomas Goolsby, published by Prentice Hall in 2002.

GORDON COX is Director of the International Research Centre for Research in Music Education at the University of Reading. After studying at the Royal Academy of Music, London, he taught for some years in schools and colleges in England and Canada. He was a graduate student in the Department of Folklore at the Memorial University of Newfoundland, and received his Ph.D. in Music Education from the University of Reading. His current research focuses on music education history. Cox is the author of *Folk Music in a Newfoundland Outport* (1980) and *A History of Music Education in England, 1872–1928* (1993).

CHERYL CRAIG is currently an Associate Professor in the Curriculum and Instruction Department at the University of Houston. Formerly a Science Science and Humanities Research of Canada doctoral fellow, Craig conducts research in teachers' knowledge, school contexts, and narrative methodologies.

ROBERT CUTIETTA is Professor and Director of the School of Music and Dance at the University of Arizona. His research focuses on concept development in middle school children and hearing loss in adult musicians.

RICHARD J. DEASY has been the Director of the national Arts Education Partnership since its founding in 1995. He has served as an assistant state superintendent of Schools for Maryland and as an executive assistant to the secretary of Education for Pennsylvania. He has also served as president and CEO of an international educational and cultural exchange organization. He is an award-winning journalist and former teacher of high-school English.

LORI ANNE DOLLOFF is Associate Professor and Coordinator of Music Education at the University of Toronto. Her research interests include elementary music education, choral conducting, and teacher education. Her recent studies have focused on the development of self in music teacher education.

INSHAD FAKHOURI received her bachelor's degree in mathematics with a music minor from Florida State University. She is currently working toward her master's degree in music education at the University of North Texas. She serves as a graduate assistant for the music education department.

ALLAN FELDMAN is an Associate Professor of Science Education at the University of Massachusetts at Amherst. He taught middle and high-school science for 17 years before beginning his doctoral studies at Stanford University, where he received his Ph.D. in 1993. His research pertains to the nature of teaching and the use of action research for professional development.

DAVID J. FLINDERS is an Associate Professor of Education at Indiana University, Bloomington. His professional interests focus on qualitative research and curriculum theory. His own qualitative research was first published as a monograph, *Voices from the Classroom* (1989). He has also co-authored *Responsive Teaching* (1990) with C. A. Bowers, and co-edited

Theory and Concepts in Qualitative Research (1993) with Geoffrey Mills and the *Curriculum Studies Reader* (1997) with Stephen Thornton.

JOHN W. FLOHR received his doctorate in music education from the University of Illinois–Urbana. He has performed as a professional musician and taught at the college, public school, and preschool level. He is Professor of Music at Texas Women's University–Denton and specializes in early childhood music education. He has authored research papers, books, videos, audio recordings, and computer programs in music and music education. His recent research efforts have involved neonates and brain-imaging studies of young children.

HILDEGARD FROEHLICH is Professor of Music Education in the College of Music of the University of North Texas, Denton, where she also serves as the Coordinator of the Music Education Ph.D. Program. She has authored, co-authored, and edited several books, book chapters, and articles and has been a keynote speaker at a number of national and international conferences on a wide variety of topics in music education.

LYNN GALBRAITH, Ph.D., is Associate Professor of Art at the University of Arizona. Her recent research examines issues related to preparing pre-service teachers and the working lives of faculty teacher educators. Her work is also informed by an interest in case study methods and interactive technology within visual art education. She is the author of several book chapters and editor of the anthology *The Preservice Classroom: Issues and Practice.* She has published widely in such journals as *Studies in Art Education, Art Education, The Journal of Art and Design Education,* and *The Journal of Multicultural and Cross-cultural Research in Art Education.* In 1998, she received the National Art Education Association's National Higher Educator of the Year Award.

CONSTANCE BUMGARNER GEE is an Associate Professor of Public Policy and Education at the Peabody College of Vanderbilt University. She has written extensively on the impact and consequences of public policy and programming on elementary and secondary arts education. She earned her Ph.D. in arts education, with an emphasis in policy analysis and program evaluation, from Pennsylvania State University in 1993. She is an executive editor of *Arts Education Policy Review,* a board member of the First Center for the Visual Arts in Nashville, Tennessee, and a member of the Nashville Metropolitan Arts Commission.

MERRYL R. GOLDBERG is an Associate Professor of Visual and Performing Arts at California State University at San Marcos, where she teaches courses on arts and learning and music. She is a professional saxophonist and recording artist who toured internationally for 13 years with the Klezmer Conservatory Band. Her published works include *Arts and Learning: An Integrated Approach to Teaching and Learning in Multicultural and Multilingual Settings* (Longman), *Arts as Education* (Harvard Educational Review), and several articles. She re-

ceived the Spencer and John D. and Catherine T. MacArthur grants and the Fulbright-Hays Foundation grant for her work on arts in the schools.

MARY HAFELI is Assistant Professor and Director of the Arts Education Program at the State University of New York at New Paltz. She has directed community education programs at the Ann Arbor Art Association and Maryland Hall for the Creative Arts, and has conducted education program evaluations for arts partnerships in Hartford, Baltimore, Cleveland, Detroit, and Philadelphia. Her work in assessment includes presentations and workshops at the American Symphony Orchestra League and the Massachusetts Art Education Association.

BETTY HANLEY teaches music education in the Faculty of Education at the University of Victoria. She earned a B.A. in music from the University of Western Ontario, an M. Mus. from Wayne State University, and a Ph.D from the University of Minnesota. She co-organized the 1989 symposium Rethinking Music Education in British Columbia, chaired the second National Symposium on Arts Education (NSAE), Victoria 1998, and has published articles in the *Canadian Music Educator,* the *Canadian Journal of Education,* the *Journal of Music Teacher Education,* and the *British Journal of Music Education.* She is a co-author of *Making Music Meaningful: A Sourcebook for Beginning Teachers* (1991) and *The State of the Arts: Arts Literacy in Canada* (1993) and author of *Foundations for Music Education* (1995).

DAVID HARGREAVES is Professor of Child Development and Director of the Centre for Advanced Studies in Music Education at the University of Surrey, Roehampton. He is also Visiting Professor of Research in Music Education at the University of Gothenburg, Sweden, and Visiting Professor at the Inter-University Institute of Macau. He is a Fellow of the British Psychological Society, and has held visiting research fellowships at the University of Illinois, Chicago, and at Florida State University. His publications include *The Developmental Psychology of Music* (1986), *Children and the Arts* (1989), *The Social Psychology of Music* (with Adrian North, 1997), and *Musical Learning and Development: The International Perspective* (with Adrian North, 2001).

JACK HELLER is Professor of Music at the University of South Florida, Tampa, and Music Director of the Tampa Bay Symphony and Spanish Lyric Theater of Tampa. He received his undergraduate training at the Juilliard School, his M.Mus. from the University of Michigan, and his Ph.D. from the University of Iowa. He has held postdoctoral fellowships at Ohio State and Yale Universities. He taught in the public schools of Ohio and Iowa and was concertmaster of the Toledo Orchestra for several years. He has served on the editorial committees of the *Council for Research in Music Education Bulletin,* the *Journal of Research in Music Education, Research Perspectives in Music Education,* and *Psychomusicology.*

MIRIAM HENOCH is a Research Associate of the Texas Center for Music and Medicine, where she investigates hearing loss among musicians. She is Associate Professor of Audiology at the Department of Speech and Hearing Sciences at the University of North Denton, Texas.

MAUD HICKEY is Assistant Professor of Music Education and Technology in the School of Music at Nortwestern University. She teaches courses in curriculum development, music education methods, creative thinking in music, research, and technology. Hickey received her bachelor's degree in music education from Indiana University, her M.S. in educational psychology from the University of Wisconsin at Madison, and a Ph.D. in music education from Northwestern University. Her research interests include the development of creative musical thinking in children, assessment, and computer technology as an aid to music instruction.

JOHN HIPPLE is a Research Associate of the Texas Center for Music and Medicine where he investigates mental health issues among musicians. He is Senior Staff Counselor for the University of North Texas and Associate Professor in the University's College of Education in Denton.

NIKOLA G. HOBBEL is a teacher and teacher educator currently working on her doctorate at the University of Wisconsin–Madison. Her research interests include the intersections of language, power, and policy in teacher education.

DONALD HODGES is Professor of Music and Director of the Institute for Music Research at the University of Texas at San Antonio. He received his doctorate from the University of Texas at Austin. He is contributing editor of the *Handbook of Music Psychology*, along with the accompanying *Multimedia Companion*. His recent research addresses brain-imaging studies of musicians.

MARY HOOKEY is an independent scholar and researcher who retired from the Faculty of Education of Nipissing University, Ontario, in 2000. She is currently active as a researcher, writer, and instructor in the master of education program. She holds an Ed.D. from the Ontario Institute for Studies in Education, University of Toronto, and a gold medal for the ARCT diploma in voice. Her research interests include music education, teacher development, and instructional supervision. Her articles appear in *The Recorder, The Canadian Music Education Research Journal*, and several ISME publications.

SAMUEL HOPE is Executive Director of the National Association of Schools of Music, the national accrediting agency for institutions and programs providing professional education in music. He is also executive director of the accrediting agencies for art and design, dance, and theater, and of the Higher Education Arts Data Services. He is an executive editor of *Arts Education Policy Review* magazine, an editorial consultant to the *Journal of Aesthetic Education*, and trustee of the American Academy of Liberal Education. He holds degrees in composition from the Eastman School of Music and Yale University, and was a composition pupil of Nadia Boulanger in Paris.

ROBERT HOROWITZ is Associate Director of the Center for Arts Education Research at Teachers College, Columbia University, and is consultant to arts organizations, schools, school districts, and foundations. He has helped to develop many arts partnerships throughout the country. He is author of *From Service Provider to Partnership: A Manual for Planning, Developing and Implementing Collaborations with the New York City Public Schools*. He has co-written *Institutionalizing Arts Education for the New York City Public Schools*, the blueprint for a $36 million Annenberg Arts Education Initiative.

SANDRA WIELAND HOWE is an independent scholar in Wayzata, Minnesota, where she teaches piano and theory. She has degrees from Wellesley College (A.B. in music history), Harvard Graduate School of Education (A.M.T. in music), and the University of Minnesota (M.A. in musicology and Ph.D. in music education). She is the musicologist for the Minnesota Public Radio High School Music Listening Contest and the author of *Luther Whiting Mason: International Music Educator* (1997). She has published numerous articles on the history of music education and women in music.

JOYCE JORDAN-DECARBO is Professor and Chair of Music Education and Music Therapy at the University of Miami School of Music. Since 1982, she has primarily been involved in the teacher-training program. She is an active researcher in the area of early childhood music and coordinates and teaches a music enrichment outreach program in Miami. She serves as a member of the editorial committees of the journals *Early Childhood Connections* and *Research Perspectives in Music Education*. She is past president of the Early Childhood Music and Movement Association.

ESTELLE JORGENSEN is Professor of Music Education at Indiana University in Bloomington. She obtained her terminal degree from the University of Calgary. She founded the *Philosophy of Music Education Review* and continues as its editor. She is the author of *Transforming Music Education* (2002).

RICHARD KENNELL currently serves as Interim Dean of the College of Musical Arts at Bowling Green State University. He holds bachelor's and master's degrees from Northwestern University and a doctorate from the University of Wisconsin–Madison. Before coming to Bowling Green in 1980, he was a member of the Chicago Saxophone Quartet and Coordinator of Music Admissions at DePaul University in Chicago. At Bowling Green, Kennell is a member of the performance studies department, where he specializes in studio instruction research and teaches a graduate research class for performance majors.

GEORGE KONDRASKE is a Research Associate at the Texas Center for Music and Medicine. He is Director of the Human Performance Institute (HPI) and Professor of Electrical and Biomedical Engineering at the University of Texas at Arlington.

ROBERTA LAMB is Associate Professor at the School of Music, Queen's University at Kingston, Canada. She holds cross-appointments to the Institute of Women's Studies and Faculty of Music Education. She teaches music education courses and courses on women, gender, and music in the School of Music.

RICHARD LEDERMAN received his M.D. and Ph.D. degrees from the State University of New York at Buffalo. Subsequent training included two years of internal medicine at Bronx Municipal Hospital Center, two years at the National Institutes of Health, and a residency in Neurology at the Massachusetts General Hospital. Since 1973, he has been a member of the Department of Neurology at the Cleveland Clinic Foundation. He is the director of the Medical Center for Performing Artists at the Cleveland Clinic and was founding vice-president of the Performing Arts Medicine Association. He plays chamber music as a violinist/violist.

MARY LEGLAR is Chair of Music Education at the University of Georgia School of Music. She is editor of the *Southeastern Journal of Music Education* and the *Georgia Music News*, and is currently serving on the editorial board of the *Journal of Music Teacher Education*. Her areas of interest include choral music education, early field experiences, and applications of technology to teacher education.

ELIZABETH A. LINNENBRINK is currently a doctoral candidate in the Combined Program in Education and Psychology at the University of Michigan. She received her B.A. in psychology and music and her M.A. in cognitive psychology from the University of Michigan. She studies the interplay between achievement and affect as well as the relation of achievement motivation and affect to cognitive processing.

BARBARA REEDER LUNDQUIST is Professor Emerita at the University of Washington. She received an outstanding Achievement Award from the National Black Music Caucus of MENC in 1981, was Stauffer Professor at San Diego State in 1988, gave the Springfield Music Lecture at Rhodes College in 1993, and has been visiting professor at many U.S. colleges and universities, including the University of Pittsburgh's Semester at Sea. She has publications in the areas of music education, sociomusicology, and music in general studies, and is past president of the College Music Society.

MARTIN L. MAEHR, Professor of Education and Psychology at the University of Michigan, received his Ph.D. from the University of Nebraska, Lincoln. He was formerly Professor of Educational Psychology and Director of the Institute for Health and Human Development at the University of Illinois. He has also held special appointments at Tehran University (Iran), the University of Queensland (Australia), and Leuven University (Belgium). His research and scholarly work, focusing on sociocultural influences on motivation and achievement, has appeared in *Sociocultural Origins of Achievement, The Motivation Factor: Toward a Theory of Personal Investment*, and *Transforming School Cultures*.

JOHN MAHLMANN, Ed.D., has served as executive director of MENC since 1983. He has been a vigorous advocate for school music education not only through his leadership role with MENC but also through MENC's constitutive roles in the National Coalition for Arts Education and the Consortium of National Arts Education Organizations, which developed the *National Standards for Arts Education* (1994).

MICHAEL L. MARK is Professor of Music, Emeritus, at Towson University, where he also served as Dean of the Graduate School. He formerly taught at the Catholic University of America and Morgan State University. He is a Fulbright scholar who has published several books and research articles on the history of music education.

MARIE MCCARTHY is Associate Professor and Chair of Music Education at the University of Maryland. She is a general music specialist and teaches courses on music in the elementary and middle school, music learning theory, world music in the classroom, and research methods in music education. She is author of the book *Passing It On: The Transmission of Music in Irish Culture* and has edited *Music Education as Praxis* and *Cross Currents: Setting an Agenda for Music Education in Community Culture*, both published by the University of Maryland.

GARY MCPHERSON studied music education at the Sydney Conservatorium of Music before completing a masters degree in music education at Indiana University and Ph.D. at the University of Sydney. He is Associate Professor of Music Education at the University of New South Wales and former treasurer for the International Society of Music Education and national president of the Australian Society for Music Education. His published research addresses visual, aural, and creative aspects of musical performance in young developing musicians.

RENATE MUELLER has been Professor of Sociology of Culture and Education, Ludwigburg University of Education, since 1991. Between 1979 and 1991 she was a music educator in elementary and junior high schools, during which one pedagogical focus, among others, was rock dance in music education. She was a member of the Curriculum Music Committee in Hamburg (1983–85). She holds a master's degree in sociology and a doctoral degree in music education, Her research interests include the sociology of music, the study of youth cultures and computer-assisted research of aesthetic behavior.

DAVID MYERS is Professor of Music and Associate Director of the School of Music at Georgia State University. He has been associated with education programs of arts organizations since 1978, when he hosted a composer residency for his middle school music program. A frequent writer and presenter on collaborative music education programs, he has presented sessions for MENC, NASM, ASOL, the National Guild of Community Schools of the Arts, and the International Society for Music Education. In 1995–96, he conducted a national study of orchestra education partnerships for the NEA, the findings of which were published as *Beyond Tradition: Partnerships Among Orchestras, Schools, and Communities.* Myers is founding director of the Center for Educational Partnerships in Music at Georgia State.

GLENN E. NIERMAN is currently Professor and Chair of the Music Education Division and Interim Associate Director of the School of Music at the University of Nebraska–Lincoln. He has authored numerous journal articles, given presentations at MENC conventions, and delivered addresses at world congresses of the International Society for Music Education. His research interests include assessment, teacher education, and instructional strategies. He has received an award for outstanding undergraduate teaching (1997) and the Steinhart Distinguished Endowed Professorship in Music Education (1998).

JO ANN NEVILLE NELSON worked with rural families and children as an extension agent in Minnesota. She later earned a master's degree in child development and a Ph.D. in educational psychology/human development at the University of Illinois, where she taught naturalistic observation and assessment of children for many years. With a lifelong interest in children's musical development, she collected children's folksongs from international students. Recent publications include articles on worldwide lullabies, Reggio Emilia, and children's "multiple literacies." She is a member of NAEYC, ECMMA, MENC, OASA, the Word Organization for Early Childhood Education, and the Balalaika and Domra Association. She has served as vice president of the Illinois Association for the Education of Young Children.

ADRIAN NORTH is a Lecturer in Psychology at the University of Leicester, United Kingdom. His research interests are the social psychology of music, with particular concern for interactions between musical preference and the listening environment, effects of music on consumer behavior, music and the zeitgeist, and the role of music in adolescence. He has published in *Nature,* the *Journal of Applied Psychology,* and the *British Journal of Psychology.* He edited *The Social Psychology of Music* for Oxford University Press with David Hargreaves.

EDWARD J. P. O'CONNOR is Professor Emeritus at the University of Connecticut, where he taught courses in music education, research, and world music. He served as evaluator for more than a dozen schools and special music programs. His primary area of research has been in multicultural music education. He co-authored "Czech Republic and Slovakia" in *the Garland Encyclopedia of World Music: Europe,* and held an International Research and Exchanges Board fellowship to Czechoslovakia. He received his B.M.E. and M.M. degrees from Northwestern University and his Ed.D. from Teachers College, Columbia University.

BENGT OLSSON holds an M.A. in music education and history and a Ph.D. in musicology. He is currently Professor in Research of Music Education and Dean of the Faculty of Fine and Applied Arts at Göteborg University, Sweden. He has re-

cently been involved in research projects about musical knowledge and aesthetic discourses. His articles about the social psychology of music education and musical teaching and learning in Scandinavia appear in international journals.

STEPHEN J. PAUL (deceased) was Coordinator of Music Education at the University of Arizona. His research specialties included sociology of music education, and instrumental music. He held a B.A. degree in English literature and mathematics from Westminster College, Fulton, Missouri, and M.M.E. and Ph.D. degrees in music education from the University of North Texas. He formerly taught on the faculties of the University of North Texas, the University of Oregon, and the University of Oklahoma. His research and writing are published in major music education publications.

RANDALL G. PEMBROOK received his bachelors and masters degrees in music education and piano performance at Southern Illinois University at Edwardsville. His doctoral work was completed at Florida State University. He is currently Dean of the Conservatory of Music of the University of Missouri at Kansas City. He has served on the editorial boards of *The Journal of Research in Music Education, Symposium, Psychomusicology,* and the *Quarterly Journal of Music Teaching and Learning,* among others. His research interests include music perception, aural skills, teacher training, and theory pedagogy.

PAUL R. PINTRICH is Professor of Education and Psychology and Chair of the Combined Program in Education and Psychology at the University of Michigan. His research focuses on the development of motivation, epistemological thinking, and self-regulated learning in adolescence. He has published more than 100 articles, book chapters, and books. He is the past editor of the American Psychology Association journal for Division 15–Educational Psychology, *Educational Psychologist.*

JAMES RATHS is currently Professor in the School of Education at the University of Delaware, where he has also served as a department chair. He earned his B.S. from Yale in mathematics and his master's in teaching and history from Yale University. His Ph.D. in education research, evaluation, and statistics is from New York University. Raths has served on the faculty at the University of Illinois at Urbana-Champaign, the University of Maryland, the University of Vermont, the University of North Carolina at Chapel Hill, and the University of Wisconsin at Milwaukee. He is executive editor of the *Journal of Education Research* and has published widely in books and journals.

RUDOLF E. RADOCY received his B.S. from Ohio State University, his M.M. from the University of Michigan, and his Ed.D. from Pennsylvania State University. After teaching instrumental and vocal music in Michigan public schools, he joined the faculty in Music Education and Music Therapy at the University of Kansas. He co-authored *Psychological Foundations of Musical Behavior and Measurement and Evaluation of Musical Experiences* and has edited the *Journal of Research in Music Education.* He was named Outstanding Alumnus by

Ohio State and Penn State, received the MENC Senior Researcher Award, and was elected to the Kansas Music Educators' Association Hall of Fame.

FRANCES H. RAUSCHER is Associate Professor of cognitive development at the University of Wisconsin, Oshkosh. She holds two bachelor's degrees (in cello performance and in psychology), and earned her Ph.D. at Columbia University. Her research involves the relationship between music exposure and spacial intelligence in children, adults, and animals. As a recipient of the William T. Grant Faculty Scholars Award, Rauscher is currently investigating the longitudinal effects of keyboard, singing, and rhythm instrument instruction on Head Start students' spacial and perceptual abilities.

CAROL P. RICHARDSON is Associate Professor and Chair of Music Education at the School of Music, University of Michigan. She currently chairs the Music Education SIG of the American Educational Research Association and serves on the Editorial Committee of the *Bulletin of the Council for Research in Music Education*. She received a National Academy of Education/Spencer postdoctoral fellowship for her 1995 study of Cambodian children's music-listening processes. Her most recent book, *Music Every Day: Transforming the Elementary Classroom*, with co-author Betty Atterbury, was published by McGraw-Hill in 2001.

JOHN W. RICHMOND is Professor of Music Education in the School of Music at the University of South Florida. He teaches undergraduate and graduate courses in choral music education, choral conducting, arts education administration, and aesthetics. He publishes in the areas of arts education policy, music education philosophy, choral music, chamber music, and curriculum. He also consults internationally in the areas of music in higher education and program evaluation.

ROGER RIDEOUT is Professor of Music Education at the University of Massachusetts at Amherst, where he coordinates the music education program and teaches graduate courses in research, history, and philosophy of music education.

BARAK ROSENSHINE is an Emeritus Professor of Educational Psychology at the University of Illinois at Urbana. His specialties are research on classroom instruction and cognitive strategy instruction.

BERNARD RUBIN is a Medical Director of the Texas Center for Music and Medicine. He is Professor of Medicine and Chief of Rheumatology at the University of North Texas Health Science Center, Fort Worth.

MARIA RUNFOLA is a member of the music education faculty at the State University of New York at Buffalo. Formerly Chair of the Department of Music and Associate Dean of the Graduate School, she is currently serving the New York State Education Department as Music Chair for the ASSETS (Assessment, Standards, Staff Education and Technology Systems) project. She teaches music to newborns and toddlers in the University's Fisher Price Endowed Early Childhood Research Center in order to investigate the first three stages of preparatory audiation.

ED SARATH is Professor and Chair of the Department of Jazz and Contemporary Improvisation at the University of Michigan School of Music. His work as performer (flugelhornist) and composer is documented on several recordings with such leading artists as David Liebman, Joanne Brackeen, Cecil McBee, Billy Hart, Mick Zgoodrick, Harvie Swartz, Marvin Smitty Smith, and Karl Berger. Sarath's writings on the cognitive, aesthetic, and pedagogical aspects of music appear in the *Journal of Music Theory, International Society for Music Educators Journal,* and *Jazz Educators Journal.*

E. GLENN SCHELLENBERG is an Associate Professor in the Department of Psychology at the University of Toronto at Mississauga. His research focuses on how perceptual and cognitive predispositions affect musical structures, and, conversely, how exposure to music affects perception and cognition. Participants in his experiments include infants, children, and younger and older adults. He is consulting editor for *Music Perception.*

CAROL SCOTT-KASSNER received her Ph.D. from the University of Washington in Psychomusicology with an emphasis on musical growth in young children. She served as a professor of music education at Seattle Pacific University and at the University of Central Florida. She currently works as a consultant in music education. She co-authored *Music in Childhood: From Preschool through the Elementary Years* (Schirmer 1995) and *Making Music* (Silver Burdett Ginn 2001). She has also published many articles in national and international journals and has served as a consultant, speaker, and clinician.

KENT SEIDEL serves as Executive Director of the Alliance for Curriculum Reform, a collaborative project of 26 national education organizations. He is also on the faculty at the University of Cincinnati Graduate School of Education. He consults with the university's Evaluation Services Center regarding evaluation and research design. His content specialty is theater and performing arts eduction.

PATRICIA SINK earned B.M. and M.M. degrees in music education from the University of North Carolina at Greensboro and a Ph.D. from the University of Kansas. She is a registered music therapist and has taught choral and general music in the North Carolina and Iowa public schools. She has published in the *Journal of Research in Music Education*, the *Bulletin of Historical Research in Music Education,* and the *Southeastern Journal of Music Education.* She is active in MENC and the North Carolina Music Educators Association.

RALPH A. SMITH is Professor Emeritus of Cultural and Educational Policy at the University of Illinois, Urbana-Champaign. He did his undergraduate and graduate work in liberal studies and fine arts at Columbia University and taught courses in art history and art education at state universities in Ohio, Wisconsin, and New York before settling in Illinois.

He founded the *Journal of Aesthetic Education* in 1966 and was its sole editor until 2000. He authored the *Sense of Art: A Study in Aesthetic Education, Excellence II: The Continuing Quest in Art Education, General Knowledge and Arts Education*, and *Art Education: A Critical Necessity*, with A. W. Levi.

KEITH SWANWICK, GRSM, LRAM, ARCO, MEd, Ph.D., is Dean of Research and Professor of Music Education at the Institute of Education, University of London. He graduated with distinction from the Royal Academy of Music, where he studied trombone, piano, organ, composition, and conducting. He has extensive experience as a choral and orchestral conductor and has also been an orchestral musician, church organist, and choirmaster. His books include *Popular Music and the Teacher* (1968), *A Basis for Music Education* (1979), *Discovering Music* (with Dorothy Taylor, 1982), *Music, Mind, and Education* (1988), and *Teaching Music Musically* (1999).

KATI SZEGO received an M.A. in Ethnomusicology from the University of Hawaii and a Ph.D. in Systematic Musicology from the University of Washington and is presently Assistant Professor at Memorial University of Newfoundland, Canada. Szego, who is co-editor and author of *Musics of the World's Cultures: A Source Book for Music Educators* (1998), is interested in musical transmission and learning especially as it involves issues of cultural boundary-crossing and colonization.

LAURIE TAETLE graduated with her bachelors and masters degrees in music education from the University of Michigan and Northwestern University. After more than 20 years of public school vocal music teaching in kindergarten through 12th grade, Taetle recently received her Ph.D. in music education from the University of Arizona. Her dissertation on active music learning and spatial cognition in kindergarten children was awarded an American Dissertation Fellowship from the American Association of University Women. She has served as fine arts and research coordinator for the University of Arizona College of Education DISCOVER Projects, a U.S. Department of Education grant promoting curriculum grounded in problem-solving through the arts.

MARK TARRANT is a Lecturer in Psychology at the University of Leicester, United Kingdom. He researches the social psychology of music and is currently investigating how young people use music to distinguish between social groups. Other interests include the relationship between group membership and social development and the impact of the school environment on self-concept. His research has been published in *Social Development, Journal of Adolescence*, and *the Journal of Psychology*.

DENNIS THIESSEN is Professor and Associate Chair in the Curriculum, Teaching, and Learning Department at the Ontario Institute for Studies in Education of the University of Toronto.

His research interests include teacher development, school improvement, and educational change. His recent publications include four books: *Making a Difference About Difference: The Lives and Careers of Racial Minority Immigrant Teachers* with Nina Basca and Ivor Goodson; *Children and Their Curriculum: The Perspectives of Primary and Elementary School Children* with Andrew Pollard and Ann Filer; *Agents, Provocateurs: Reform-Minded Leaders for Schools of Education* with Ken Howey; and *Getting into the Habit of Change: The Cross-Case Study of 12 Transforming Learning Communities* with Stephen Anderson.

WILLIAM FORDE THOMPSON is an Associate Professor in the Department of Psychology, York University, Toronto, where he is cross-appointed to the Department of Music. His research includes studies of music and emotion, memory for music, and music performance. He is a consulting editor for the journals *Psychomusicology* and *Music Perception* and is on the board of the Society for Music Perception and Cognition. His current research includes studies of cognitive links between melody and speech prosody.

BRUCE TORFF is Assistant Professor of Education at Hofstra University. He has published numerous books and articles on topics including intuitive conceptions, implicit learning, intelligence, and musical cognition. He co-edited *Understanding and Teaching the Intuitive Mind* and is currently preparing *The Teacher's Guide to the Mind*. He earned a doctorate from Harvard University, where he worked with Howard Gardner.

RENA UPITIS is a Professor of Arts Education at Queen's University, Kingston, Ontario. She teaches courses on music and mathematics curriculum methods integrating art and technology, and research methodologies. She has worked as a music teacher in inner-city schools in Canada and the United States and has been a studio teacher of piano and music theory for more than 25 years. Her two books on music teaching explore possibilities for teaching music through children's improvisation and composition in regular classroom settings (*This Too Is Music*, 1990, Heinemann; *Can I Play You My Song? The Compositions and Invented Notations of Children*, 1992, Heinemann).

IAN WESTBURY is Professor of Curriculum and Instruction at the University of Illinois at Urbana-Champaign. He is co-editor of *Teaching as a Reflective Practice; The German Didaktik Tradition* (2000) and general editor of the *Journal of Curriculum Studies*. His research interests focus on curriculum theory, cross-national studies of curriculum policy, and urban education.

SUSAN WILCOX is a Senior Instructional Development Associate in the Instructional Development Centre and Associate Professor in the Faculty of Education at Queen's University, Kingston, Ontario. Her daily work focuses on the development of educational knowledge in the higher education setting. Her scholarship is concerned with the role of dialogue and critical self-reflection in emancipatory adult education, self-directed learning and research in higher education, transformative models of continuing professional education, and alternative approaches to inquiry in education.

PAUL WOODFORD is Associate Professor of Music Education at the University of Western Ontario in London, where he teaches courses in the philosophy of music education and wind conducting. His articles on philosophical topics have appeared in the *Philosophy of Music Education Review, Quarterly Journal of Music Teaching and Learning, Music Educators Journal,* and the *Canadian Music Educator.*

BETTY ANNE YOUNKER is Assistant Professor in the School of Music at the University of Michigan. Prior to university appointments, she taught music in the public schools system for 10 years. Her research areas include pedagogy of music education, critical thinking about music, and musical thinking. In addition to her university and research activities, she adjudicates at various music festivals and teaches flute at summer music camps. Currently, she continues to make music as a member of the Ann Arbor Cantata Singers in Ann Arbor, Michigan.

KEN ZEICHNER is Hoefs-Bascom Professor of Teacher Education and Associate Dean for Teacher Education and Undergraduate Education at the University of Wisconsin–Madison. He has been principal investigator in the National Centers for Research on Teacher Education and Teacher Learning at Michigan State University and is currently involved in the Carnegie Foundation for the Advancement of Teaching's Study of Teachers. He has published widely on issues of teacher education in North America, Australia, Africa, and Latin America.

BARRY J. ZIMMERMAN received his Ph.D. from the University of Arizona and is Distinguished Professor of Educational Psychology and Head of the Learning, Development, and Instruction Concentration at the Graduate School and University Center of the City University of New York. He has written more than 200 research articles, book chapters, and conference papers, and has written and edited 7 books on social and self-regulatory processes in the learning of children and youth. He received the Senior Scientist Award of the American Psychological Association Division 16 for sustained and exceptional program of scholarship and the Sylvia Scribner Award of the American Educational Research Association for exemplary research in learning and instruction.

Reviewers

Advisory Reviewers

Bradley Almquist
Eckart Altenmuller
Deborah Atkins
Wolfgang Auhagen
James Austin
Chris Azzara
Janet Barrett
Nancy Barry
William Bauer
Carol Beynon
Wayne Bowman
Alice Brandfonbrener
David Brinkman
Andrew Brown
Herbert Bruhn
Jeffrey Bush
David Butler
Mark Campbell
William Clark
Irma Collins
Mihayi Csikszentmihalyi
Nicolas DeCarbo
George DeGraffenreid
Christopher Doane
Susan Duffy
Karen Faaborg
Todd Fallis
Lawrence Ferrara
Harold Fiske
Donna Fox
Hildegard Froehlich
Darla Funk
Alf Gabrielsson
Lynn Galbraith
Sue Gamble
Scott Goble
Norman Goldberg
Thomas Goolsby
Joyce Gromko
Sandra Guerard

Donald Hamann
Robert Harding
David Hargreaves
Lee Harris
Eve Harwood
Jan Hemming
Warren Henry
Richard Hoppmann
Sondra Howe
Allen Howell
Jere Humphreys
Williiam Jones
Michelle Kaschub
Mary Kennedy
Jody Kerchner
Patricia Kim
Carl King
John Kratus
Judith Kritzmire
Paul Larson
William Lee
Andreas Lehmann
Karel Lidral
Scott Lipscomb
John Loughran
Ralph Manchester
Michael Mark
Walter Mayo
Philip McClintock
Gerard McKenna
Sarah McKoin
Sam Miller
Charlene Morton
Alicia Mueller
David Myers
Edward O'Connor
Ken Philips
JoAnn Phillion
Rudolf Radocy
Sam Reese
Thomas Regelski
Mary Reichling

Roger Rideout
Brian Roberts
Mitchell Robinson
Debbie Rohwer
Eric Rombach
Pamela Rossi
Lois Schleuter
Margaret Schmidt
James Sherbon
James Shugert
Carolee Stewart
Eleanor Stubley
Daniel Stufflebeam
Susan Tarnowski
Keith Thompson
Kathy Tosolini
James Undercofler
Darrel Walters
Peter Webster
Jackie Wiggins
David Williams
Paul Woodford
Robery Woody

Reviewers

Frank Abrahams
William Anderson
Anthony Barresi
Lee Bartel
Mary Belz
Peggy Bennett
Martin Bergee
Linda Berger
J. David Betts
Ann Blombach
Peter Boonshaft
Chelcy Bowles
Judith Bowman
Paul Boylan
Manny Brand

Donna Brink Fox
Walter Britt
Andrew Brown
Verna Brummett
Vernon Burnsed
Karyl Carlson
Karen Carter
Linda Damer
Douglas DiBianco
Jon Dugle
Roy Ernst
Lawrence Ferrara
Richard Fiese
Harold Fiske
John Flohr
Mark Fonder
Guy Forbes
William Fredrickson
Donald Gephardt
Sylvia Gholson
Robert Gillespie
Merryl Goldberg
Lucy Green
Gary Greenberg
Mitzi Groom
Richard Grunow
Louie Hall
Sue Hallam
Albert Harrison
Robert Hartwell
William Hazard
June Hinckley
Don Hodges
Charles Hoffer
Janet Jensen
Eddie Jones
Polly Kahn
Vincent Kantorski

Edward Kvet
David Lapin
Paul Lehman
Carolyn Livingston
John Loughran
Richard Maag
Joseph Manfredo
Wendy March
W. Stephen Mayo
Peter McAllister
Kevin McCarthy
Marie McCarthy
Ken McGuire
Harold McNiel
Gary McPherson
Margaret Merrion
Dan Miller
Beth Ann Miller
Janet Mills
Hafez Modirzadeh
William Moody
Marvelene Moore
Brian Moore
Mark Munson
Joy Nelson
Katherine Norman
Ruth Nott
Giacomo Oliva
David Osterlund
Judy Palac
Richard Parncutt
Ken Phillips
William Pinar
Aaryn Post
Rosalie Pratt
Rudolf Radocy
Darhyl Ramsey
Rudolf Rauch

Fred Rees
Virginia Richardson
Edith Roebuck
Franz Roehmann
Robert Rumbelow
Joanne Rutkowski
Charles Ruzicka
Rosita Sands
Richard Sang
Ed Sarath
Alenoush Saroyan
Deborah Scesa
Lois Schleuter
Stan Schleuter
James Scholten
Patricia Shand
Scott Shuler
Camille Smith
Ralph Smith
Katharine Smithrim
Dee Spencer
James Stivers
Cynthia Taggart
Donald Tanner
Mark Taylor
Rena Upitis
Loren Waa
Linda Walker
Robert Walker
Roger Warner
Robert Washut
Rosemary Watkins
Norman Weinberger
Jackie Wiggins
Joan Wildman
Liz Wing
David Woods
Iris Yob

Part I
POLICY AND PHILOSOPHY

John W. Richmond
Editor

Introduction

JOHN W. RICHMOND

This opening part of our research Handbook deals with issues of policy and philosophy in the music education professions. It is hard to imagine a more appropriate way to begin a volume of this sort. Music education—especially as practiced in educational institutions—is entrenched deeply in traditions of *activity*. The pace of professional life for the music educator in the classroom/rehearsal hall can be frenetic and the opportunities for "reflective practice" are simply much too rare.

The fields of music education policy and philosophy then become twin acolytes for the music educator in the field, helping him or her to scrutinize trends in the profession and practices in the classroom in the critical light of careful, deliberate analysis. Indeed, policy and philosophy can be understood as complementary systems of examining and directing our complex, multifaceted work from prekindergarten to postdoctoral study in music. Both systems of inquiry ponder core values and their manifestations in professional practice. Both systems explore the contexts in which these core values then are carried out. And, recently, both systems reflect real debate and even rancor as competing ideologies strive to gain primacy in the value systems of our field. If ever they were boring in the past, recent writings in the policy and philosophy of our field are anything but dull today.

How then are policy and philosophy different? Are they completely redundant? Not at all. As the reader will discover shortly, policy studies are linked tightly to issues of decision making and resource allocation to a far greater degree than is required or appropriate in basic philosophical inquiry. At its best, policy can be the social and institutional vehicle by which enlightened philosophy is carried out. Sometimes, however, policy is something less—a re-

flection of untested traditions, old habits, persistent prejudices, or political compromises. Regardless, policies in music education specify the conditions in which music education is carried out and the kinds of persons responsible for that work. They determine the nature of musical engagements students enjoy, which students will enjoy them, and the kinds of accountability measures to which music students, instructors, institutions, and the curricula will be subject.

Philosophy, by contrast, addresses broader questions of meaning and value. The traditional branches of classical Western philosophy illustrate this breadth. Logic, epistemology, ethics, metaphysics, and, more recently, aesthetics, all attempt to clarify what we *mean* when we speak of such things as reasoning, knowing, virtue, being, and art, respectively. Because values change and the language that attends to such issues changes, each generation is obliged to take up these questions of meaning for their own time, place, and culture. At its most helpful, philosophy critically sorts out the actions implied by espoused values and the values implied by human actions. The symbiotic implications for policy are obvious.

In the following chapters, the reader will explore the importance of both policy and philosophy for the ongoing work of the music educator in the classroom and for the music education researcher in the field or lab. She or he likely will be struck by the range of issues that these two disciplines seek to address and the considerable work yet to be done in both arenas. Finally, I suspect the reader will leave this section inspired, as I was, by the promise that research in philosophy and policy holds for us as we pursue an increasingly enlightened and informed practice of professional music education.

Policy Frameworks, Research, and K–12 Schooling

SAMUEL HOPE

Looking back over the last 100 years, one sees a clear overall advance for music in the schools. The expertise and dedication of professional music teachers have produced regular expansions of substance and scope. Policies supporting school music programs that demand the work of such professionals have been a resounding success for education, the art of music, and culture more generally. However, many other forces are at work developing ideas and values in society as a whole. All these forces are constituted and reconstituted into policy frameworks that wield powerful influences on decision making. Aspirations, content, expert and lay personnel, organizational structures, funding patterns, and many other elements combine and recombine over time. A policy framework is a constellation of such forces and resources moving together or in parallel to fulfill a common purpose. The influences of various policy frameworks are as complex as life itself, and as difficult to understand. It is easy to be blinded by simplicity, to get lost in complexity, and to be so involved in one policy framework that the others are obscure, unreal, or beyond reasonable engagement. All these positions are dangerous. Each can thwart or stop a progressing cause. Indeed, some forces and frameworks have hurt or destroyed specific music education programs, thus slowing, but not stopping, the aggregate development of the field.[1]

Most readers of this Handbook are professionally committed to continuing the long advance of music education in the schools. Working toward this goal means connecting with numerous issues, sorting priorities as one goes. Using frameworks as a tool to simplify complexity and to make sense of specific policy forces can help keep the focus required to succeed.

It also is important to stop from time to time and remind ourselves of what we are advancing. It is possible to build huge conceptual and operational systems associated with music education and, in the process, lose sight of the fundamental goal: providing individual students with the opportunity to gain musical knowledge and skills. This chapter explores potential and future relationships among policy frameworks and this supreme goal. It concludes with suggestions for future policy research.

Policy

A policy is a decision about how to proceed, based in part on knowledge or research and in part on values and opinion. Its existence presupposes potential action aligned with the decision reached. Policy is made because of a perceived need to act.

Individuals set policies for themselves. Policies are developed for groups from the family unit to the nation and beyond. Some policies are set by the force of tradition, others by deep strategic thought, and others by decisions not to think but, rather, to act using one or more ideas or techniques that seem to be working at a given time. Definitions and examples of policy notwithstanding, music education in the schools is caught up in an interlocking web of policies and policy making at all levels. From the values of families, to the decisions of governments, to the choices and marketing strategies of corporations, to the preferences of various kinds of music presenters, policies and decisions based on them are ubiquitous, inescapable, and continuously evolving. What makes policy change? What are the roles of value and principle, information and analysis, financial interest and political will, cultural missions and spiritual responsibility? How do the answers to these questions affect decision making for music education?

5

Frameworks

There are many ways to categorize the policy frameworks influencing decision making in the United States today. In 1996, Mark Gerzon published a book entitled *A House Divided*. Understandably, the book received little attention—too honest, too revealing, too pointed. Gerzon identified six policy frameworks that he called the "divided states of America." He showed how these states compete, even war with each other. He noted that each has a set of core beliefs, sacred texts, channels of communication, language, and leaders. Gerzon's analysis documents, demonstrates, and compares these differences. His six states are:

- Patria—its core belief is that faith in Jesus Christ as Lord and Savior should shape every aspect of American life.[6]
- Corporatia—its core belief is that economic growth enriches society and makes progress possible.
- Disia—its core belief is that the exploitation and oppression in American society must be resisted by any means necessary.
- Media—its core belief is that society is liberated from ignorance and parochialism through freedom of communication.
- Gaia—its core belief is that social action based on higher consciousness will save the world.
- Officia—its core belief is that government represents the people and should have ultimate authority in all cases. (Gerzon, 1996, p. 4)

Of course, a number of other divisions come to mind based on sets of core beliefs. For example, we in education live in the state of academia where the core belief is, or at least used to be, that society improves through constant individual learning. But many academics now appear to be citizens of Disia, Gaia, or Officia. Gerzon shows how each of the six states he identifies works to turn its core values into public policies. He explains why people centered in one of these policy frameworks have complete contempt for or disinterest in those in the others, even though they make temporary alliances to promote their own cause. There seems to be a good deal of truth here. For example, major news media figures regularly act as though they are far more important public policy makers than elected officials. In the state of Media, they are.

My own analysis is that none of these six states, or most other major policy frameworks that could be identified, have much room at their cores for such values as learning for learning's sake, art for art's sake, or learning for art's sake.[7] They all have room for art for learning's sake as long as the learning is associated with something that supports the growth and power of their policy framework. Gerzon considers the potential meaning of these divisions for the future of wise decision making, and, ultimately, to

the kind of shared community that underlies democracy at all levels. These issues are beyond the scope of this chapter, although the way they evolve will have an impact on values influencing decisions about music education.

Whether one likes or accepts Gerzon's particular states or set of policy frameworks, it is impossible to deny that there are huge systems operating in our society centered around fundamentally different values, policies, and operational means. Competition and conflict among these systems are constant. Even music education involves a wide variety of interests. In policy discussions, it does not take long for divergences to reveal themselves. Although teachers and the music industry share many common goals, core values are often quite different. The public relations goals of politicians at all levels of leadership, including school superintendents and principals, often reveal values about music that are inconsistent with those held by committed teachers who seek to raise individual competence in the discipline itself. Huge differences appear over questions of relationship between entertainment and education; between mass media and mass psychological action on the one hand, and individual knowledge and skill development on the other. The policy frameworks represented by corporations of various kinds constitute a complex array in and of themselves. For example, those focused on selling computers, those seeking a workforce with basic three-R skills, those engaged in exploiting the teenage market, and those engaged in the sale of music and instruments to school-based music programs are not always in the same place on the subject of music education, although they are all corporations. The same is true within the education establishment, where there are tremendous arguments over curricular content, teaching methods, and ways to gain public support.

Policy frameworks and their influences constitute one of the less studied subjects in music education research. When music teachers enter their classrooms now, what is the greatest counterforce they face? Is it the policies of the federal, state, or local government, or the values about music created by an entertainment industry that uses mass psychological action to concentrate interests on fads of the moment, or the technology-dominated values tied to economic growth, or some other set of ideas and actions? Even if the answer is one, or the other, or a mixture, and even though the answer can change from time to time, it is clear that the policies of the entertainment and commercial industries targeting children and youth, and policies emanating from fears of losing the technological race, have an enormous impact (Hymowitz, 2000b). Although music education cannot necessarily change these policy frameworks, it can act with more sophistication about what these frameworks mean for continuing to provide opportunities for individual achievement. Policy-oriented research is a key to this capability.

Structures and Complexities

No matter what particular set of policy frameworks one considers, there is more going on in society as a whole than groups engaged in obvious, heated competition. More typically, each policy framework shares structures and complexities with all the others within a given society. Although core values may be different, there can be considerable commonality on specific points. Fortunately, most of us agree to stop when a traffic light is red. We agree that murder is wrong, that education is important, and that music is enjoyable. Indeed, we share access to various organizational styles—democratic, autocratic, corporate, religious, educational, governmental, and so forth. We share economic necessities and funding structures, including overall societal values placed on specific kinds of work and a tax system. We share communications systems and networks, value-creation techniques, and means of changing the balance of power in various situations. We may not agree on these things, or the ends to which they should be put, but we share means and general outcomes, nevertheless.

We also share an important result: Our separate actions produced in our own interests continuously reinforce sets of the most common values. Each policy framework uses values it doesn't want to change or doesn't care about, to promote itself and argue for changes it finds desirable. For example, almost every policy framework takes decisions that reinforce science and math as the most important ways of knowing and doing. Justification and promotion on scientific grounds are ubiquitous. This tendency applied across a range of subjects and beliefs produces a tremendous stabilizing force. Advertisers and propagandists use the elements maintaining this stability to reduce the credibility of others in favor of their own cause. The math justification for music study is a current example (Hetland, 2000a, 2000b; Vaughn, 2000; Winter & Cooper, 2000; see also Weiss, 1999).

When the nature of policy, its governmental and nongovernmental sources, the many competing and interlocking policy frameworks, and the common structures shared by all are considered together, it is clear why the whole is so difficult to perceive, and why understanding and wise decision making is so hard to achieve. In addition, the vast number of variables in motion creates evolutions in values and ideas. These in turn create policy forces that often are invisible until they flow together and form a set of propositions or achievements that compel attention.

A major issue here is the nature of power-seeking and the structure of reward systems. New policy has its greatest chance to transcend the continuous reinforcement of tradition, as discussed earlier in this chapter, when there is some kind of unusual or critical need. This fact leads naturally to all sorts of adventurism in identifying, developing attention to, or even creating illusions about critical needs. In the electronic media age, it is easy to create mass attention to a real or imaginary problem, at least for a short period. Those working for the interests of any policy framework usually try to create as much urgency as possible to develop a force for change in their favor. If one believes that the natural human tendency is to increase powers on behalf of one's own interests, it is easy to understand why Gerzon's six states of America, or any other policy frameworks one cares to identify, are regularly calling attention to a national or global crisis. Thus, the current policy arena in the United States has become a snake-pit of competing crises, each alleged to be greater than the next and each requiring emergency policy attention, usually of a draconian nature.[8] Constant crisis development has become central to doing business in the United States. Billions are spent annually on this activity. This practice, in turn, produces more complexity. How does one sort among all these crises to develop a wise, thoughtful, and prudent way forward? Another problem: When every interest cries wolf constantly, attention spans diminish and policy work becomes viewed primarily as manipulative.[9] Crises, real or contrived, are ignored.

In order to deal with this labyrinth, several strategic issues are critical to any field working with the various policy frameworks that affect it: understanding, engagement, values, investment, expertise, working room, funding, and sustained will. This is only one formulation of these qualities, but whatever formulation is used, a loss in any one begins to affect all the others. For example, the field of music education has an enormous interest in maintaining policies that produce respect for expertise. If expertise is not respected, then understanding of the field is diminished because expert opinion is not heard and valued. Then, anyone can decide what music education is and should be.[10]

Attention to these strategic issues—understanding, values, investments, and so forth—is one way to keep one's head clear in addressing the policy ideas and forces that are thrown out by the various policy frameworks operating in our society. Music education will pay a great price for strategic failures where the simple is made too complex, or the complex made too simple.[11] An understanding of complexity and how it evolves is essential to avoid becoming entangled in the follies of any particular time. The ability to create and promulgate fantasies about reality is greater now than at any time in history. These abilities played out through the values of different frameworks are producing vast collisions in the policy arena. Fantasies are colliding both with each other and with basic realities of the human condition. History, myth, and common sense teach us that mendacity does not work. Continuing collisions of contrived crisis fantasies produce an atmosphere that is culturally explosive, and politically dangerous to music education and all other serious arts endeavors.

Policy Forces and Techniques

As described earlier in this chapter, policy forces regularly coalesce into policy frameworks centered in core values or basic beliefs. Our analysis now turns to values influencing music education policy. American mass youth culture is our primary example. Many policy frameworks we have identified contribute in some way to the reinforcement of one or more values present in and powering this culture. Here are several primary messages: Everything must be fun; everything must be sensational; everything must be simple; everything must be new; everything must change constantly; everything must be fast; everything must be easy; everything is essentially about me.[12]

Of course, there are many other views held by some young people. There are always countervailing forces. But there is no question that these messages and their high level of acceptance by youth and parents alike produce a problematic policy climate for schooling and music education. Over the last 40 years, commercial and governmental entrepreneurialism have changed common views of possibilities and responsibilities. Lifestyles now come and go by design. The standard of living, at least in economic terms, has risen substantially. The culture of instant gratification and adolescent tendencies toward rebellion are actively promoted both separately and in noxious mixtures. Music both alone and videoed has become a carrier of mass youth culture. If music teachers are so disposed, they can counter instant gratification, rebellion, and so forth in various ways, but it is hard to conceive of anything beyond cataclysm that would reverse the continuous reinforcement of mass youth culture values. Too many people in too many policy frameworks benefit.

What about the adult world? In intellectual life, emphasis has moved from content to process, and now to context; from subject matter to method, and now to personality and social group. In education, both context and process regularly trump content. Backlashes produce struggles over such matters as phonics versus whole language, new math versus traditional math, and education as social action versus knowledge and skills in basic disciplines.

Another extremely strong value is to believe in only that which has scientific proof. The methods of science are preeminent, and every discipline or activity seeking public approbation attempts to present itself and its reason for being along scientific lines. Too often disciplines and groups demean their own nature in order to promote their work as science-based. The verbal and mathematical thus retain their preeminence. As a result, most individuals do not conceive of any other means of doing intellectual work.

Focus on the scientific approach has also nurtured the rise of theory. In many nonscientific fields, accepted theories often represent a triumph of what sounds good over what works. Theories come and go. In a theory-based environment, failure is never taken seriously because failure produces grounds for a new theory, just like science. The connection between the rise of faith in the theoretical and its impact on music education represents an important policy analysis area for the profession.

Unquestioning faith in the scientific approach also creates deep-seated belief that technologies, techniques, and systems can be developed for universal application. This view is regularly derided as a one-size-fits-all philosophy. But neither derision nor failure has changed the belief of many, in systems of centralized control for every area of human action, especially education.[13] This approach is supported by various policy forces working through various policy frameworks. Providing education as a means for developing individual intellectual competence is lost as a major value. Serious discipline-centered teachers fight constantly against tendencies to turn all of education toward indoctrination or vocationalism.

Faith in systems also leads to vast amounts of policy energy being spent on attempting to transfer systems from one arena to another. These transfers often are imposed irrespective of their applicability in the new situation, and in practice, they often illustrate Matheson's Law: "Structure commands function. If you could raise an oyster the size of a horse, it would not win the Kentucky Derby no matter who rode it" (Dixon, 1980, p. 134). The concept of building systems specifically to fit goals is increasingly lost when education is seen only instrumentally, and never as a value in and of itself.[14]

Many other values constitute policy forces in our society. Not all are negative, but K–12 education is faced with a particularly difficult set of conditions. It confronts values that are problematic not so much because they are wrong, but because they are not balanced with equally important values and qualities. For example, some things are fun, but some require effort; the technical way of knowing and acting is only one of several basic ways for working in the world; speed makes money (and messes) large and small. Education does not fare best in a policy arena in which so many forces narrow perspective by crafting manipulative messages that suggest that personal liberation, social advance, and economic bounty can be obtained with little effort.

All of the policy forces just presented have access to techniques for advancing their cause. No technique remains secret for long. Over thousands of years, human beings have had plenty of time to create and perfect techniques for developing, promulgating, and imposing policy. Since direct manipulation is almost always resented once it is sensed, policy development often proceeds indirectly or by stealth. There are many techniques for leading a group to think that a certain policy is its own idea. Other techniques produce senses of inevitability and the futility of opposition or the need to join in. There are techniques for distorting or lying about opposing positions; some produce the awesome damage of the continuous subtle negative. And, of course, there is the vast and constant construction and destruction of buzz words, buzz concepts, and bandwagons.

Propaganda techniques are called forth, blended, and refined to move agendas forward. The idea is to bypass reason, thoughtful consideration, factual evidence, and the natural sense of humility in front of great natural, psychological, and spiritual forces. Propaganda's purpose is to lead to a massive discounting of these realities in favor of an emotional knee-jerk reaction. The arts provide immediate access to the emotions. They bypass the verbal and mathematical without appearing to do so.

While many of the greatest works of art are filled with all the qualities that much current propaganda usually seeks to obscure, most can be enjoyed without direct reference to these qualities. For example, details of reason and balance in a Mozart symphony are not readily apparent to the untrained listener. The music is simply beautiful. This is one reason why art can be used against people as well as for them. It can be used both to encourage and discourage thinking. It can be a powerful propaganda or policy-shaping tool. All the techniques of all the arts are available for every purpose—from the educational to the social, to the avocational to the propagandistic. Mass spectacle, for example, can be as harmless as an American marching band show at halftime, or as sinister as a Nazi rally or a Soviet May Day demonstration in Red Square.[15]

Music education is conducted in an arena that is full of policy and propaganda techniques. In this arena, and through these techniques, the term "arts education" has been so broadened that it no longer denotes serious, sequential study exclusively. To the extent a term means everything, to the same extent, it means nothing. But as long as a term or phrase is current, it can hold symbolic power and act as a cover for all sorts of agendas. When one calls for specificity, or makes contrasts for purposes of clarity, it is normal to be accused of destroying unity or being uncooperative. The music and arts education communities have been down this path many times, primarily when dealing with the federal government.[16]

Such policy and propaganda techniques are even more apparent in the large national discussion on education now flying under the flag of education reform. Reform has become permanent and thus oxymoronic. It constantly devalues the role of professional expertise by creating impressions that teachers and administrators are to blame for everything. Often, reform is a means for centralizing power in Washington or in state capitals. But this agenda has run into another viewpoint focused on decentralization and devolution of power to the local level. Support for local control is present in much more than education. Policy development for music education must analyze and attend to both centralizing and decentralizing forces, for neither will prevail entirely.

Policy and the Nature of Music Study

The policy environment depicted here is complex. With work, it can be understood sufficiently to make thoughtful strategic and tactical decisions. It contains great opportunity, but also grave danger. Success depends on knowing and understanding where danger really lies. This is the function of intelligence services of all kinds, including the efforts of policy analysts working to support music education. When effective, analysis is able to separate the irritating from the truly threatening. It is able to forewarn. Policy research for music education is important and necessary because of this need to understand vulnerabilities and opportunities in a sense that attends to but goes beyond immediate concerns, regnant fads, contrived crises, and propaganda circuses. Indeed, a more comprehensive understanding makes it possible to make better decisions about immediate concerns.

Policy analysis is never useful for taking action unless it is centered in reality. The military commander seeking comforting information rather than the true facts is likely to make decisions that will cost many their lives. There are times when any group is outnumbered, or outmaneuvered. The question then is how and when to retreat without losing a fundamentally strategic position. Or, if a strategic position must be lost temporarily, what are the next steps toward regaining it?

The most critical factor in creating a usable analysis is clear understanding about the natures of policy frameworks and forces in the arena of action. There is an old Finnish saying that wisdom begins with a clear understanding of the facts. Here are some basic facts associated with music education. Music has a specific nature. If it did not, it would not be music. There are things in the nature of music that are shared with other fields. There are also things unique to music. The same is true for music study. The same sequence is true for other disciplines in K–12 schooling. And the same is true for various ideas, concepts, programs, systems, techniques, and values that are in the policy arena. If we apply the meaning of this sequence in policy analyses, we will find immediately that the nature of music study is inconsistent with the natures of many other policy forces. Let us look at a few examples.

The fundamental goal of most music teachers should be to give students a rich gift: a body of knowledge and skills that can be the basis of lifelong engagement. Music teachers introduce their students to a world of artistic action, great achievement, and civilizing power. The national voluntary K–12 standards are based primarily on this premise (Consortium of National Arts Education Associations, 1994). In contrast, much prevailing intellectual opinion sees the arts as a tool for cultural, social, or political engineering. The art of music is not to be given to students with the hope that they will become enriched and engaged as individuals in its artistic, intellectual, cultural, and spiritual dimensions but, rather, as a direct or indirect means of achieving other ends. Commercial interests have yet another role in mind for music. They see it as a means of reinforcing the natural rebelliousness of the teenage years with a powerful emotional tool to create an immediacy culture, and to support the kind of forced fadding that churns markets in consumer goods.

It is important to remember that we are not talking about people and corporations but, rather, sets of ideas that produce policy forces that in turn energize policy frameworks. Of course, music is an important ingredient in cultural formation and socialization. Of course, music has commercial tie-ins and applications and is important as an industry. Problems come when there is an illusion that these purposes are the same as educational ones, based on the acquisition of individual knowledge and skills. They are not the same, they do not accomplish the same things, and to pretend, act, or promote as though they do is to take a strategic decision that hobbles the traditional teaching and learning mission of music education by sowing confusion about its purposes. Within the scope of this chapter, the important point is that these differences exist. Providing a deep analysis or weighing priorities among these differences should be a major goal of music and arts education policy analyses. The question is not whether to interact with other forces, but how, with what content, and on what terms.

As an example, how should educators deal with the contrast between the messages regularly delivered in our culture and the nature of music study? To accept and reinforce the notion that everything must be fun goes absolutely counter to the struggle most people have in learning to play an instrument or sing proficiently. For most, the acquisition of musical knowledge and skills is hard work. Composition, performance, analysis, and history are all challenges. The hard work produces pleasure, fun, and fulfillment, but there are usually difficulties along the way. A society that tells its young that there should be no difficulties is not a society that is supporting music study. The notion that everything must oppose the values and styles of the older generation, or that knowledge of the past is useless—that only the narrow choices of the peer-pressured

now are important—runs counter to learning about or having personal access to the vast richness of musical expression. The culture of rebellion against all that has gone before is anti-intellectual, anti-art, anti-diversity, and certainly, anti-music study. So is the notion that everything must be new. Constant newness can be a manipulation technique that destroys an individual's or organization's command of its own time. It creates the illusion that everything must be new, while the truth is that in any complex situation, some things are new and some are not. Thus, total constant newness is a recipe for continuous self-deception. The notion that everything must change all the time is a formula for accomplishing nothing but constant reorganization. In music and the other arts, the new does not drive out the old but, rather, comes alongside it. Furthermore, everything that is new is not better. Change can be for the worse.

The notion that everything must be simple is profoundly counter to the nature of music study. In contrast, music study teaches lessons about the nature of complexity; about the relationships of parts to wholes; about balance, proportion, interweaving of elements, structure, and design. The notion that everything must be fast and easy could not be more in contrast to the nature of music study. Patience with difficulty and willingness to work in the short term toward long-term goals are essential. The rehearsal/performance sequence teaches how many hours of mental and physical labor must be dedicated to produce a few minutes of excellence.

The contrasts we have been making are accompanied by many others: the overvaluing of the verbal and mathematical as the primary or only means of knowing the world, confusion between education and indoctrination or advertising, the loss of distinctions between various agendas for the arts, and in arts education, the massive push to obscure differences between music experience and music study. These provide abundant evidence that a large number of policy forces at work today are, by their very nature, counter to the nature of music education, at least the kind that leads to individual competence at some level.

These notions in the general culture have tremendous influence on decision making about music in the schools. They sculpt the values of parents and students. They shape individual and group concepts about what various constituencies want. In many ways, they are far more powerful than governmental policy making at any level, because the ebb and flow of these values has tremendous influence on decisions made everywhere from the local school board, to the state capitol, to Washington; and from national music organizations to local organizations, to colleges and universities engaged in teacher preparation, to decisions of individual teachers in the K–12 classrooms. The research questions here involve knowing and understanding basic differences in the natures of various forces in the policy arena. This understanding is essential when making strategic decisions intended to support teaching and learning.

Tremendous influences on music education also come from the large K–12 public school establishment. This arena itself is the scene of policy wars over centralization versus decentralization. Methodologies and content are mercilessly pitted against one another in a struggle which the establishment seems to be losing little by little. At its best, music education is about giving students power *in* a discipline. So much policy effort in the larger K–12 arena seems to be devoted to struggles about who will have symbolic, bureaucratic, or assessment power *over* something. It is essential for music educators to work within these power struggles, while keeping the supreme strategic goal of teaching and learning music in mind. Needs to understand the evolving nature of these struggles and the natures of the forces engaged in them produce essential continuing research issues for the music education profession.

Another huge area is the enterprise focused primarily on arts creation, presentation, and their funding. This sector is a looser policy framework than it used to be. Purposes, types and levels of commitment, definitions of art and what it is for, and educational connections vary. In music, some presenting organizations such as the St. Louis Symphony Orchestra have been deeply engaged in operating community schools of music that provide serious sequential instruction. But there are many efforts in this sector that by their very nature are not consistent with the nature of music study. There is little problem here as long as these distinctions are understood. As has been said many times, experience and study reinforce each other. But experience alone is not a substitute for study. Future research can illuminate the natures of this rich and varied sector so that mutually supportive work can be undertaken whenever possible, and the terms of engagement between teaching and presenting functions can be clear.

Foundations are another source of policy influence. Today, many foundations establish their own specific goals rather than support the work of others. Coercive philanthropy is a policy reality, as is highly funded, heavily publicized, short-term support. The centrality or the relationships of arts and education-oriented philanthropies to other policy frameworks are central policy analysis questions for music education. Philanthropy, too, will evolve as new wealth is created and new foundations take on some of the values and styles of their benefactors.

The nature and thrust of higher education policy also needs careful attention. American higher education is so vast that it is hard to generalize about prevailing values. Since the sensational is most often reported, it is hard to find where consensus truly lies. However, there is no question that many current theories sweeping through the humanities—including studies of the arts—are, by their nature, inconsistent with the nature of music study. When the first and only filter for everything is race, class, gender, ethnicity, or sexual preference, there is a narrowing of cultural perspective that masks under the guise of openness and liberation. Of course, race, class, gender, ethnicity, and sexual preference are influential in culture. As such, they deserve thorough study. But these concerns, as illuminating as they are, do not lead to basic acquisition of musical knowledge and skills. In other words, musical knowledge and skills are far more than these concerns alone or together. Equally problematic are deconstructionist theories that attempt to use speech logic to prove that speech logic is not logical, and that set a high value on themselves as a basis for proving that all expression is equal and that valuing is elitist. Such self-imposed intellectual constraints reinforce the vapidities of mass youth culture, although not by using the same terms. Music education needs to be wise enough to learn what it can from all intellectual movements, without doing strategic or long-term damage to its central purpose. Anti- any civilization, Western or otherwise, is a profoundly anti-music education agenda.

The university culture of research and scholarship also needs attention, particularly the reward systems that drive so much individual decision making about the content and direction of professional work. Research and scholarship can be broadly or narrowly conceived. A research question for music education is the extent to which current graduate program policies are sufficiently broad to embrace the large number of research questions that the field needs to address, including policy itself. To what extent would higher education reward and respect research efforts associated with the kind of questions chapters in this part of this Handbook are raising?

A last example is targeted marketing. This promotional technique is extremely effective. It uses psychological and purchasing-pattern analysis to divide the population into groups likely to make certain decisions. It then targets those groups with messages that reinforce previous beliefs and, if possible, creates barriers through psychological pressure to stay within certain social, style, and consumption boundaries. The result is a society of many lifestyles, each with boundaries carefully drawn and reinforced. These boundaries may be those of the six states Gerzon posited in *A House Divided*, or they may demarcate other territory. Targeted marketers have far more subdivisions than six. Advancing computer technology has increased the power of this psychological reinforcement tool, but such an approach is profoundly contrary to the traditional goals of music education, which make no distinctions with regard to background, taste, purchasing power and pattern, culture, or talent. The traditional policy goal of music education remains to provide the gift of musical knowledge and skills to all by providing opportunity for serious sequential instruction in the public and private schools. The conflict between the nature of targeted marketing and the nature of music education can be managed, but not if it is ignored or insufficiently understood. Music education seeks to broaden cultural experience; targeted marketing works to narrow it. Music education wants to bring art from all over the world to everyone. Targeted marketing seeks to use what is known and liked to sell more of the same. Because targeted marketing is so prevalent in support of everything from commercial sales to political ideas, intellectual discourse, and advertising design, the music education field has a significant policy job ahead. Targeted marketing is affecting every person who makes a decision about music education. It has already broken down aspirations for common culture, and done far more than deconstruction to isolate and demean connoisseurship. Targeted marketing positions music as a matter of cultural preference, not a means of knowing and doing that should be available to all. It could be the most anti-diversity influence in American culture today.[17]

Research Questions

The foregoing analysis concentrates on multiple forces influencing decision making for music education. To this point, it has all but ignored a critical influence on policy: the music education profession itself. Over many decades, dedicated music teachers have been primarily responsible for building and sustaining music education programs in the schools. The expert teacher can work miracles transcending the local context and all the negative forces we have been discussing. This fact is worth remembering, and a critical matter for future policy development. Can it be that protecting and advancing the field's capabilities to produce qualified teachers is its foremost strategic policy issue? Is it possible to create systems for the purpose of improvement that undermine the continuing provision of excellent individual teachers, because the systems themselves produce unattractive and unprofessional environments? As we have shown, many forces in the arena are producing a vast devaluation of education centered on study and disciplinary mastery. Mass culture broken into pieces by targeted marketing has far more influence on education than education is having on culture. To what extent is education in charge of its own destiny? Is there one education any more? If yes or no, what roles do music teachers play? To what extent are they cultural leaders?

A good first policy research question for music educators is: *Do we know enough now to teach music well?* If to any extent the answer is no, then what do we need to know? If we are not sure that we know enough to teach music well and do not in every way exude confidence that we can, we are severely disadvantaged in working with all the policy frameworks that affect K–12 schooling.

Therefore, it is critical to make distinctions between knowing how to do something well, and wanting to do it even better. It is a vast strategic error to accept a general charge of failure from anyone. The issue is how to demonstrate competence and promote substantive educational values to decision makers either influenced by, or members of, various policy frameworks.

This policy question is related to but not the same as field-specific internal issues such as:

1. the relative capabilities of music teachers in such areas as composition, improvisation, analysis, and history;
2. the will and ability of teachers to base improvements on research;
3. the roles of various mechanisms such as graduate study, clinics, methods affiliation, independent work, and so forth, in continuing education; or
4. the content to be addressed in professional development.

It is a major strategic mistake to pursue such important internal questions in ways that produce the public impression that music teachers do not know how to teach music. Making this mistake creates a vacuum that others with far less competence as musicians and teachers seem anxious to fill.

A follow-up question is: *Do we know enough to lead others to understand why music is worth teaching in the schools?* Policy research clearly is needed here, because our success in this area is mixed. If we don't know enough, what do we need to know in order to address both neutral and hostile audiences? What do we need to know beyond the ability to understand and imitate the propaganda techniques of those successful in creating favor for their cause or product? Which of these techniques and messages undermine our fundamental effort to nurture individual learning? If we cannot answer these questions with clear understanding of facts, conditions, and ramifications, we are disadvantaged in working for our cause within the various policy frameworks that affect us.

What are the major policy frameworks influencing music education? What are their respective core beliefs, sacred texts, channels of communication, sectors of influence, language, and leaders? How can changes within these frameworks be monitored or influenced in favor of music education? How can positions and changes in each framework influence the delivery of substantive music education? (See Brazil, 1999; Hymowitz, 2000; Sewall, 2000.)

The next question involves a resource dimension: *Do we have a sufficient early warning system about potential external or internal dangers to music education?* How quick are we to understand what may evolve from policy directions that we or others do or do not control? For example, what kinds of messages about technology support music study and what kinds hurt it? What about messages that everything must be fast, easy, new, and fun? Without the ability to analyze ideas and where they might lead in policy development, music education is left reacting to ideas and contrived urgencies emanating from various policy frameworks and, at times, repeating messages that work contrary to music education's long-term goals.[18]

Are we able to address the negatives we regularly encounter? Over years of effort, music educators have faced many standard arguments for and against their work. Policy research could help find the various sources of negative arguments and help formulate messages to counter them. For example, how well is the music education profession prepared to proclaim its differences from other activities and points of view? To what extent is it willing to claim that the study of music seriously on its own terms is an important element in producing multiple perspectives on ways to think and work in the world? To be ineffective here is to feel forced to jump on every policy-influencing bandwagon that comes along, irrespective of its consistency with the nature of music study and the goals for it in schooling espoused by music educators. Over time, rationale-jumping produces a general view that music has no sustaining purpose in K–12 education (Gee, 1999).

Do we have a grand strategic goal for music learning? And do we have the means to pursue this goal with a clear understanding of the distinctions and connections between being mission-driven and market-driven?[19]

As scientific discoveries about music are presented, are we able to use them judiciously? Are we able to move these ideas as policy influences, keeping distinctions between science that supports the cause of music study, and scientism that regularly opposes it (Reimer, 1999)?

Are we sufficiently able to work with the concepts and realities of markets and market formation? What level of sophistication do we have in making decisions about whether to ignore, play with, play into, create, or change a market? How can we make the best decisions and guesses about the results of marketing decisions? More fundamentally, what are our criteria for marketing success? What specific weights and balances among positions and values produce success in qualitative and quantitative terms? What about ideas that the boundaries between disciplines are arbitrary, that everything is interdisciplinary and ultimately converging?[20]

What levels of understanding of music study, its purposes, and values can we expect to develop in various populations over the next two decades? Are all equally critical? If not, what are the most critical populations? How can they be reached and brought from interest to understanding, to commitment? Does music education need its own targeted marketing? What would the impacts be (Best, 2000)?

How shall music education influence government, particularly local and state government? What policies, strategies, and tactics can advance music in the schools on its own terms—that is, music study as music study? How can a more sophisticated understanding of policy frameworks influence values and decisions of government policy makers, and thus become the basis for greater success, especially at the local level?

How can music education work with delivery systems that, to some extent, bypass traditional policy-making structures for schools? What about charter schools, distance learning, private institutions, community music schools, private instruction, and so forth?

What is the long-term policy impact of various positions regarding the extent to which music education has a responsibility to teach and promote aspirations for the highest art, no matter what its cultural source? This is a difficult question, presently uncomfortable for many, but working on answers to it can reveal significant information and new insight. Addressing the question can put us in a better position to deal with the adverse policy results of this position: People enjoy, consume, and use music without studying it. Music seems to choose them. Why should everyone study it? Why should taxpayers fund music study in the schools? An associated question is: *What are the policy ramifications of various public postures on music as a way of knowing, as a form of mental training and development?* What does one learn when one learns to think in music? To what extent can this learning be explained to those who have never experienced it?[21]

Can the field of music education build more sophisticated and systematic data-gathering systems to keep accurate size, scope, and content information available for policy development? It is virtually impossible to produce trustworthy intelligence without good numerical data. Numbers available today do not provide authoritative answers about the rise or fall of access or participation in school-based music education. Nor do available data correlate specific kinds of study with specific results over the long term. Without such data and analysis, the field does not have fundamental indications of its status or progress in a national sense.

Can the field of music education research support the kind of work that synthesizes and integrates from various areas of current research and study? This capability is likely to be increasingly important if we are to address the complexities of various policy frameworks that influence direction and funding for the field. Can the field develop such a capability, and how rapidly?

These questions do not have permanent answers. The answers change from time to time and place to place. Effective policy analysis produces intelligent answers to these questions in different situations and as issues evolve. This kind of analysis helps us to consider our answers as we work with various policy frameworks influencing decision making on K–12 schools.

Music education has a powerful ally: the force of music itself. Music is an emotional dynamo and a large majority naturally gravitates toward it.[22] Channeling natural attraction into support for music study in the schools is the primary tactical goal for achieving the field's strategic mission of individual competence. Music education continues to be fortunate to have leaders at all levels who are able to maintain the force of their professional activities, while protecting and advancing their cause. Over the last 35 years, there has been increasing sophistication about policy frameworks and their general dispositions toward music education. Tremendous energy has been spent protecting and advancing music education in various governmental initiatives and policies. Gerzon's state of Officia is much better understood. This growing sophistication is essential and the results are laudable. But if music education is to move from the margins to a place in the center of K–12 schooling, the same kind of strategic understanding that has begun to evolve with respect to government policies needs to expand into other policy frameworks that have equal if not greater influence. No legislation or regulation can make up for the loss of individual valuing. In the field as a whole, attention to both framework and individual values in combination with other, more established branches of music education research will be essential to give the field the full complement of tools that it needs to fulfill its destiny on behalf of music learning for K–12 students.

NOTES

1. Public acceptance and funding are continuing problems for music education. The justification struggle and the messages it produces often obscure the historical gains of the profession. To acknowledge long-term growth and development is not to hide serious problems in locale after locale. Successes and problems are both part of the truth about music education.

2. For example, actions of the federal government in both Democratic and Republican administrations attempt to increase federal powers over elementary and secondary education. The Tenth Amendment to the Constitution states: "The powers not delegated to the United States by the Constitution, nor prohibited by it to the States, are reserved to the States respectively, or to the people." For an overview of this issue, see DeMuth (2000).

3. An opposite view is promoted by analysts who bring class-struggle perspectives to persistent educational problems, often suggesting that inequalities in educational opportunity are the result of malicious intent. For example, see Kozol (1991) and Spring (1989).

4. According to the U.S. Constitution, the states have the authority, but the degree of centralized control over education varies significantly among the states. The amount of control determines the degree to which state policies matter.

5. Voter apathy, general cynicism, and increasing perceptions that government is a spoils game seem to be increasingly obscuring the importance of government in the minds of many citizens. The result is that while government can still make and enforce laws and regulations, its pronouncements are no longer widely accepted simply because the government is speaking. In elementary and secondary education there are numerous large movements to bypass traditional governmental systems: vouchers, charter schools, the growth of private education, and so forth.

6. Gerzon's choice here recognizes the power of Christian affiliation in American life and the way it is focused at present in a significant number of citizens who constitute a policy framework. However, his choice of words is interesting, because fundamentalists in each of the other frameworks also believe that their viewpoint should shape every aspect of American life. To be fair, many devout Christians believe that their relationship with Jesus Christ should shape every aspect of *their* lives. They seek social improvement more by developing an aggregation of individual believers than by ideology imposed through political action. Jesus himself said, "My kingdom is not of this world." (See John 18:36.)

7. This is not to say that individuals centered in or associated with these belief systems cannot value learning or art for their own sake. It is to suggest, however, that when these frameworks promote policies in the political arena, their first interests are elsewhere. To be fair, it is neither necessary nor appropriate that in all times and in all places learning and art be considered purely for their own sake. But in educational settings, failure to acknowledge the primacy of these values turns learning and art away from their own natures and thus diminishes their power to illuminate themselves and thus also to serve other purposes.

8. Consider, for example, education reform. Negative rhetoric is constantly used to set the stage for proposals to alter the way power flows in the educational delivery system. Reform began with the focus on disciplinary outcomes, but over time has evolved to a focus on assessment, then to accountability, and now to accounting.

9. See Wolterstorff (1995). "When a single boy too often cries 'wolf,' in the absence of wolves, we disregard *his* speech. When it becomes a habit of many to cry 'wolf' in the absence of wolves, our system of speaking itself is undermined."

10. The issue of expertise is also central to the question of who teaches. Over the last 35 years, several policy frameworks have sought more emphasis on the general classroom teacher as the leader of arts instruction, even in an education reform period where there is significant rhetoric supporting high levels of teacher competence in the subject being taught. Often, when budget or other pressures intervene, school boards are tempted to pass responsibilities for arts instruction from specialists who have spent many years gaining expertise in their fields to generalists who do not have equal or even any expertise. As these ideas and practices continue, it is extremely hard to keep the debate focused on expertise rather than who gets paid.

11. Oversimplification is particularly prevalent now with respect to information technology. Both technology and music

study are complex issues. There are some simple relationships, however. For example, the power of music and the power of technology are each so strong that neither obviates the necessity of learning the other. Technology and music have many relationships, but in basic terms, one does not validate the other.

12. For an analysis of the views of youth and their impact on education, see Ruggiero (2000).

13. Centralization appears as a logical end when one pursues such qualities as efficiency, equal opportunity, system-wide accountability, and reciprocity of educational credentials. It is interesting, however, how little rhetoric in K–12 education is devoted to the ideas of professionalism centered in high levels of autonomy for individual practitioners after they have proved that they are worthy of professional credentials. Education reform has inexorably removed authority from classrooms where instruction is actually delivered and moved it beyond educational institutions and systems into legislatures or other bodies.

14. Instrumentalism in a period of rapid change produces two major dysfunctions. First, it provides students with time-specific learning that is quickly outmoded. Second, it produces an ever-changing set of priorities that prevent the stability and space necessary for comprehensive knowledge and skill acquisition. Thus, instrumentality and educational fad chasing seem to go together.

15. For a magisterial view of the principles involved, see Ellul (1965).

16. For a specific example, see Gee (1999).

17. For a view of targeting applied in extreme form to elementary/secondary education, see Wellner (2000).

18. For a current analysis of technology's impact on life and learning, see Gelernter (2001).

19. For an example of what is at stake, see Healy (1998).

20. See Big Issue 4 (1999). This publication contains many articles exploring various sides of the convergence issue. For a succinct overview of the contextual difficulties, see Gabler (1999).

21. For a hopeful view of the future of the arts, see Johnson (2000).

22. The magic of music's impact is a subject of intensifying interest. See Sulit (2000a, 2000b).

REFERENCES

Best, H. M. (2000). Art, words, intellect, emotion. *Arts Education Policy Review, 101*(6), 3–11; *102*(1), 3–10.

Big Issue 4, The great convergence, *Forbes ASAP* (October 4, 1999).

Brazil, J. (1999). Play dough. *American Demographics* (December), 57–61.

Bumgarner [Gee], C. M. (1994). Artists in the classrooms: The impact and consequences of the National Endowment for the Arts' artists residency program on K–12 education. *Arts Education Policy Review, 95*(3, 4), 14–29, 8–31.

Consortium of National Arts Education Associations. (1994). *National standards for arts education*. Reston, VA: Music Educators National Conference.

DeMuth, C. C. (2000). Why the era of big government isn't over. *Commentary 109*(4) (April), 23–29.

Dixon, P. (1980). *The official explanations*. New York: Delacorte Press.

Ellul, J. (1965). *Propaganda*. New York: Alfred A. Knopf.

Gabler, N. (1999). The republic of entertainment. *AIGA Journal of Graphic Design: 1999, 17*(2), 16–19.

Gee, C. B. (1999). For you dear—anything! *Arts Education Policy Review, 100*(4), 3–17.

Gelernter, D. (2001). Computers and the pursuit of happiness. *Commentary 111*(1) (January), 31–35.

Gerzon, M. (1996). *A house divided: Six belief systems struggling for America's soul*. New York: Most/Tarcher, Putnam Publishing Group.

Healy, J. M. (1998). *Failure to connect: How computers affect our children's minds—for better and worse*. New York: Simon & Schuster.

Hetland, L. (2000a). Learning to make music enhances spatial reasoning. *The Journal of Aesthetic Education 34*(3–4), 179–238.

Hetland, L. (2000b). Listening to music enhances spatial/temporal reasoning: Evidence for the "Mozart effect." *The Journal of Aesthetic Education 34*(3–4), 105–148.

Hymowitz, K. S. (2000a). The sex and violence show. *Commentary 110*(5) (December), 52–65.

Hymowitz, K. S. (2000b). The teening of childhood. *American Educator 24*(1), 20–25, 45–47.

Johnson, P. (2000). Toward recovery. *The National Review* (January 24), 37–41.

Kozol, J. (1991). *Savage inequalities*. New York: Crown Publishers.

Reimer, B. (1999). Facing the risks of the "Mozart Effect." *Music Educators Journal 86*(1), 37–43.

Ruggiero, V. R. (2000). Bad attitude: Confronting the views that hinder students' learning. *American Educator 24*(2), 10–48.

Sewall, G. T. (2000). Lost in action. *American Educator 24*(2), 4–9, 42–43.

Sulit, A. (2000a). Feels so good: Music, morale and marketing. *Executive Update* (June), 88–91.

Sulit, A. (2000b). The biology of music. *The Economist* (February 12), 83–85.

Spring, J. H. (1989). *The sorting machine revisited: National educational policy since 1945*. New York: Longman.

Vaughn, C. (2000). Music and mathematics: Modest support for the oft-claimed relationship. *The Journal of Aesthetic Education, 34*(3–4), 149–166.

Weiss, R. (1999). Mozart sonata's IQ impact: Eine kleine oversold? *The Washington Post* (August 30), AO9.

Wellner, A. S. (2000). Generation Z. *American Demographics 22*(9), 60–64.

Winner, E., & Cooper, M. (2000). Mute those claims: No evidence (yet) for a causal link between arts study and academic achievement. *The Journal of Aesthetic Education, 34*(3–4), 11–75.

Wolterstorff, N. (1995). *Divine discourse*. New York: Cambridge University Press.

MENC: A Case in Point

2

JOHN J. MAHLMANN

Samuel Hope's essay elsewhere in this Handbook (chap. 1) provides a useful map of the territory that organizations generally refer to as "policy." In it, Hope explores a variety of contexts, frameworks, and variables that define the systems of decision making operating in our society impinging on education. Along the way, he points to a number of values, belief systems, interests, and operational structures that shape policy perspectives and are thus influential in shaping policy at "street level."

This chapter takes up the discussion where Hope leaves off. I am interested here in tightening his focus, in narrowing the broad perspective he has outlined, by looking at four core points of the policy process that are essential to association life, and to one association in particular: MENC—The National Association for Music Education. Along the way, I want to give special attention to two factors: (1) the research dimension that informs each of the four policy areas; and (2) how policy making in a particular organization is established, influenced, and evaluated. Overall, the thread tying these elements together is the importance of research to the policy process.

Four Core Points about Policy

Policy Is a Means of Organizational Orientation

For most associations (and this is true of MENC) policy is not, at least in the first instance, a set of specific rules the association follows; rather, policy is a way of describing an association's orientation to the world. Put differently, policy is a way of talking about how an association steers its way through the currents of the world around it. Unexpectedly, this way of looking at policy means that its primary function is *de*scriptive, not *pre*scriptive; that is, policy does not dictate organizational behavior but pro-

vides a description of what its behavior looks like when the association remains true to its core identity and aims. To maintain the nautical metaphor, policy is more about responding to wind, weather, and current than it is about the rules for steering the vessel. In today's climate, the wind is more variable than ever. That requires more aggressive responses and adjustments in policy than have previously been necessary. As the adage has it, "If you can't change the wind, adjust your sails."

Thus, policy, like most religious creeds, is actually designed more to defend against heresy than to define orthodoxy; it keeps association staffs moving in the right direction in a continual process of building fences, rather than trying to shape behavior with goads and sanctions. There is, of course, good reason for this approach. Policy frameworks that try to nail things down too tightly all too often wind up cutting off the circulation of both thought and energy.

In the case of MENC, this task of self-orientation works itself out in everyday practice as we carry out a relatively new mission statement: "The mission of MENC is to advance music education by encouraging the study and making of music by all." Not coincidentally, MENC's policy perspective has been accompanied by a change in name. Until 1999, MENC's official name was the "Music Educators National Conference." The old name underscored a mission that had school music teachers foremost in mind. But in recent years, as MENC has begun to see its mission in broader terms, a more inclusive name was needed. We now call ourselves "MENC—The National Association for Music Education," a title that honors our past while reaching out to the nation as a whole. It no longer refers to educators only.

On a day-to-day basis, that broader reach naturally means continuing to provide leadership, information, materials, support, and professional development resources to our teacher members. But we also see ourselves providing guidance, support, and resources for parents, students, businesses, community partners, and others who want to work with us in advocating and advancing music education.

These services, which we provide as a matter of *policy*, both stem from, and continually lead us back toward, our core identity as a professional organization. We come to know ourselves by what we *do*; that is, we are as we act. In MENC, to take an obvious but far from trivial example, we expand our reach not just to honor inclusiveness as a matter of morality and law, which is primary, but also as a way of recognizing that this policy is the best possible alignment we can make with the prevailing currents in American society and culture. It is, quite simply, a way of keeping in touch.

In the first instance, then, MENC's policies help it to define its place in the greater scheme of things, giving the organization a lens through which to look at what the world offers up, as events and trends affect our own agenda. Thus, policy becomes a primary tool for helping MENC deal with change. It grows out of our ever-changing understanding of the forces that act on us, reinforcing or altering our worldview, sustaining or challenging our perspective.

Research becomes significant precisely at this interface between MENC and the world. Without a solid grounding in the data that describe the shifting priorities of American education in general, and of school reform in particular, we could not carry out our mission. Without holding a well-moistened finger to the cultural wind, MENC would not know how to set its organizational sails. In terms of the membership example, MENC establishes its policies by asking (which is what research basically is) what the attitudes of both education decision makers and the general public are about music education—how they value it, what they are willing to spend on it, and how music and music education rank in terms of the nation's educational priorities. Aligning MENC's orientation in the currents of education thus requires a solid research base.

Policy Keeps an Organization Focused on Its Core Values

Put differently, policy is the operational dimension of what the organization believes—about itself, about its goals, about the world—and about how those three interact. In MENC's case, arising as it does from the strong traditions of both the arts and the humanities, music education espouses a wide range of values (some manifest, some latent) to which MENC members are professionally and personally committed. One of these, for example, is the ideal that persons on their way to adulthood are well served devel-

opmentally when they have music as a part of their lives, and, indeed, are better served than if they do not. MENC members believe that music nourishes each new generation's cognitive, educational, emotional, social, and cultural development in ways that enrich both the child and the society at large.

This belief has continuing policy implications. For example, MENC gave renewed attention in 2000 to early childhood education as a high-priority area of organizational involvement and support. As a matter of policy, we amplified our efforts in early childhood music education research, for example, and we moved to strengthen our ties to professional organizations of teachers and caregivers in this field, such as the National Association for the Education of Young Children (NAEYC).

In this same values context, policy also helps MENC define desired relationships between means and ends, keeping the association aware of the value and power of this dynamic. Here, policy expresses the way MENC traverses the distance between the "is" and the "ought," between the legacy of the past and the promise of the future, in its organizational life. Exploring the dynamic between means and ends is more a matter of astute observation and careful reflection than of overt research. The research part comes in continual measurement of the gap between MENC's objectives and the real-world outcomes of its efforts—a kind of formative evaluation. Any organization interested in the means-ends question therefore takes its cues about its own values from its membership, because the relationship between means and ends breaks down and its members are treading whenever an organization no longer has its ear to the ground. If there is to be a legitimate correspondence between values and action, the values perspectives of the membership as a whole will find their expression here.

Policy Provides an Association with a Place to Start in Achieving Outcomes

This is a place for an association to begin realizing its mission. In practical terms, policy gives the association a handle on its problems and how to go to work on them. Policy is therefore not a road map but a compass, not a scorecard but a benchmark. Without a policy perspective, any organization will be blown hither and yon by every wind of doctrine and will wind up achieving very little. The ship may have sails, but if the rudder of policy is either absent altogether or supplied by someone else, the association cannot hold its own course.

Policy thus helps to establish the correspondence between the association's ideals and what is feasible, which means wrestling with real-world conditions. To learn what is doable, organizations have to ask their members what they think, and more important, find out what they are willing to commit themselves to do. MENC members may believe, for example, that they should, as a matter of state or local chapter policy, work to convince school boards that music is a vital part of "basic" education. But the effectiveness of that effort will depend on assembling a case based on research and study, an effort to which local members may be reluctant to devote time.

Policy Helps an Association Allocate Its Resources, Achieve Its Outcomes, and Work on Problems

This is the tricky part, because here is where judgments about time, talent, and treasure converge in the service of organizational ends. Without firm *organizational* commitments to policy objectives, idiosyncratic circumstances can too easily be interpreted as "emergencies" and quickly override planning. The issue of organizational resources quickly becomes an exercise in defining *terms of agreement* in three areas: (1) agreement on our direction ("Where are we going?"); (2) agreement on how resources should be allocated ("What are our priorities?"); and (3) agreement on measurable results ("How will we know when we have achieved our objectives?"). Thus, when plans are translated into policies, they very soon acquire the weight of a higher level of commitment, precisely because here is where plans and resources mesh gears. Here, too, an alert is sounded. If taking a particular action involves going against established policy, associations are bound to exercise more care in their decision making.

At a bare minimum, any association/organization has to establish and attend to policies in six major areas to sustain its life. These are presented here in hierarchical order, that is, in the order of their lack of susceptibility to change:

1. First, every organization must have a *mission statement* that expresses, in succinct fashion, what the organization is setting out to accomplish. Mission statements are often Janus-faced, looking in two directions. In MENC, for example, our mission statement already expresses a relationship between means and ends: "The mission of MENC is to advance music education by encouraging the study and making of music by all." In other organizations, the mission statement looks simultaneously outward toward the world the organization wants to change, and inward at the task of equipping its members to bring that change about. However it is structured, the mission statement is the seedbed for all other policies, which must be tied to it.

2. The next most important policy every organization has to have relates to its *governance*, that is, how the organization is to be organized and run. There are, of course, many governance models, almost always codified in the form of a constitution and by-laws. Both of these are deliberately constructed so as to be difficult to change; that is, basic structures and relationships can be tweaked but

not toppled. Associations also can lose precious energy via reorganization as communication channels, lines of responsibility and accountability, personal relationships, and individual loyalties are disrupted. The hard truth is that not every new organizational initiative requires a new organization chart. Of primary importance in association governance, then, is fixing accountability for policy making and its consequences, as well as for assigning responsibility for carrying them out without turning the exercise into a game of Uproar.

A further caveat here, especially for associations operating nationally, is the potential for organizational structures of long standing to wind up at odds with mission. MENC provides an example. A few states have long had MENC chapters that are not organized geographically but by professional interest area, for example, band, orchestra, chorus, jazz, general music, and so forth. When it comes to executing a national advocacy strategy for school music education, states with these alternative forms of organization are automatically misaligned with the efforts of other states and the national strategic effort. Where does a high school band director go in his own state organization to become involved? Adjustments have to be made, a process that always depletes organizational energy.

3. Third, every association needs to express itself in policy terms on *financial issues*, that is, how it supports its activities, allocates and manages its resources, and spends its money. Financial policy is almost always conservative because it is at this point that the association's self-preservation is most nakedly at stake.

It is worth pointing out a conundrum that emerges at this point. Rarely, if ever, in any association, does its mission actually drive its budget. Why? Because annual budgets are almost never constructed on the basis of the question that puts mission first. They should ask: "Assuming that these are the ends we want to accomplish, what resources are required, and how do we generate them?" Rather, most associations' annual budgets are actually structured to place their mission in a derivative position. So instead, they ask: "Given dollar resources that we can reliably estimate, what part of our mission can (should) we achieve with those resources?" An interesting set of research questions for any organization is which of these two questions really drive its budget process, why, and whether some change in orientation is in order.

4. The fourth area of policy construction involves *personnel and internal management*, that is, how the organization manages the staff members who carry out its mission and sets procedures for getting the work done. The issues here revolve around hiring and firing, salaries and benefits, working conditions, safety, and the internal organization required to accomplish the mission. Internal organization is usually subject to great change over time, as different departments, projects, personnel and initiatives

come and go. The most common areas of internal association management in which constancy of policy is of paramount importance are: membership, meetings, publications, finance, information, and governmental relations. In associations that operate according to long-range planning cycles, this management function (which cuts across all others) often has organizational standing of its own. What is most important here is that lines of authority, accountability, and reporting are clear.

5. The fifth area of policy is how the association puts on its public face, that is, how it conducts its relationships with the rest of the world. In short, it is *public affairs and governmental relations*. Included here are clear policy statements about who speaks for the organization, approval processes for public statements, and the like.

Increasingly, the agenda of any association involved in education and the arts is becoming politicized and the recognition has dawned that political measures are required to deal with public policy. This awakening brings both bad news and good news. The bad news is that as associations choose to become more deeply enmeshed in the political issues that shape their mission and members' interests, the more likely it is that the political agenda will cloud the association's view of its own mission. Winning tactical battles begins to override long-range strategies and obscure the goal of winning the war. The good news is that a heightened political consciousness opens up totally new arenas and avenues for working on old problems. What was formerly seen as a problem can be recast as a challenge.

Again, MENC is a case in point. In 1989, MENC, the (then-called) National Association of Music Merchants (NAMM), and the National Academy of Recording Arts and Sciences (NARAS) together recognized that music and the other arts were being excluded from discussions about school reform; for example, the arts were at first omitted from the Goals 2000 education initiative. The role of the arts in public education was being underfunded and short-changed. The three organizations determined to do something about it. They successfully rallied support to the cause of music education in the schools through a jointly established National Coalition for Music Education, an organization that remains active 11 years later.

6. Finally, there is *research* itself. There are two major issues at stake here: the organization's ability to support its mission and the ongoing activities of its members on the one hand, and its long-range ability to find and explore the cutting edge of its own concerns *as an organization* on the other. The latter realm is seldom examined, except in times of organizational crisis, when it may be too late to be either creative or responsive. The relationship of an organization to its own organizational needs should be a subject of continual inquiry, that is, research.

Whereas every association must keep a continual finger on its own organizational pulse, doing so costs money. But this is the only way to acquire the necessary information (e.g., by telephone polling, e-mail solicitations, mailed questionnaires, etc.) needed to steer a straight course, especially in tumultuous times. It is often also the best way to keep the association from shooting itself in the foot.

There are two main points at which things can go wrong in crafting a research policy. First, an association's research agenda is often shaped, by default, by either its academic members or its frontline practitioners, who are both driven by their own interests and concerns. Content with validation from "the field," they pursue their research interests with little or no reference to long-range aims of the association itself. A second, equally distracting danger is the myopic focus that can develop among association staff that transforms the structural survival of the organization into an issue that focuses research concerns. Research policy must take both these threats to the research agenda into account in achieving a balanced approach.

Factors Shaping the Policy Arena for MENC

What influences play a role in establishing MENC's policies? Among the enduring influences in MENC's policy environment is, first, the perpetual wrangle between two areas of interest that contend for members' attention and continually shape the "tenor of the times" for MENC.

On the one hand, the vast majority of our members are school music teachers; they have a perpetual concern with and commitment to music *performance*—in the form of their marching band, school orchestra, annual Christmas concert, glee club tour, and the like. On the other, the environment within which school music programs have to vie for resources has in recent years been one of (sometimes acrimonious) advocacy, as teacher and parents band together to convince decision makers to support school music—almost always at the expense of some other priority and its supporters.

Within the ongoing institutional life of MENC itself, this tension works its way out every year in the form of decisions that have to be made about what kind of "air time" each of these concerns gets at our annual convention. The tug-of-war gets waged as we decide such issues as whether to fill a "prime time" convention slot with a performance by, say, Wynton Marsalis, who will talk about teaching music, or by the secretary of education, who will talk about education policy issues for music educators.

Second, in determining how MENC evaluates the success of its policy making, many criteria are brought to bear, not the least of which is arriving at some definition of "success." In the case of one of our most visible programs, the annual "World's Largest Concert" broadcast over PBS every year, "success" tends to boil down to the size of the program's viewership, the media response to the concert itself, the number of outlets broadcasting the concert, and the new or renewed memberships that MENC can trace directly to the broadcast.

A third factor shaping policy is highly idiosyncratic. It is found in the answer to the question, "Who sets program policy at MENC?" In our case, program policy, in the sense of MENC's short-term priorities, is largely set by the elected president, who serves for 2 years. The president is hugely influential in determining the theme and agenda of our biennial convention. He or she is also a key player in deciding what kinds of initiatives MENC will undertake, and in establishing association priorities.

This kind of presidential clout has impact in two ways. On the one hand, it ensures that new ideas and fresh perspectives are injected into our policies and priorities. On the other, a too-narrow focus, a too-loose or too-tight rein, or a number of other factors can create problems with program. This presidential system, which is followed by many associations, does have the distinct advantage of creating a "policy laboratory," as new short-term projects are launched that wind up becoming long-term programs. As this way of creating policy "on the fly" works itself out, it is held in check by the checks and balances of permanent staff (who can, after all, simply wait a president out), while simultaneously rejuvenating the association with new funds, new ideas, and new life.

Sometimes this "new life" can be a long time coming, however. In 1994, MENC took a leadership role in developing the *National Standards for Arts Education*. But from our perspective, by then music education standards was already a 70-year-old idea; we had devised learning standards for music education as a result of a policy initiative taken in the 1920s. We had to wait for the "*kairos of the times*" to catch up with us—for a critical mass of support for the idea of education standards to take shape in other academic disciplines.

Policy and Policy Making at MENC

Orientation

MENC's orientation is directed at two fundamental overlapping worlds and constituencies. The fundamental context is to the world of education and MENC's allegiance is to teachers and their students. But MENC has another, broader allegiance as well—to the qualitative dimensions of music itself as an art form, as expressed in the *National Standards for Music Education*.

The bedrock issue is this context is: How does MENC deal with conflict and change on these issues? As it turns out, the operational answer to this question is "relatively conservatively." Put differently, MENC is fairly open to *questions* about its mission, but is less so when it comes to initiatives or policy perspectives that might pose a *threat*

to its mission. Predictably, as with many associations, a number of the initiatives MENC takes have a polarizing effect. This shows up in interesting ways.

Recently, for example, we and two of our advocacy partners paid a public relations firm to conduct a poll to determine the "100 best American communities in which to conduct a school music program." We thought the results would be "good PR" for music education in those places. We did the research and got some good press. But of unsuspected value to MENC was the discovery of a division among our members on whether they thought conducting the poll itself was a good idea or a bad one. Those denigrating the idea thought that it was a strong negative to associate school music education—which they viewed as an intrinsic education good—with public opinion. Those favoring the poll taking thought it did what we suspected—boosted school music in the eyes of the communities concerned. The lesson: Try to find alternative ways to collect similar information in the future.

Values and Outcomes

MENC espouses three basic values (ends) as an association: (1) it is an advocacy organization that promotes the worth of music education for every American and seeks to deliver that worth via the activities of its members; (2) it insists on the intrinsic value of music as an art form and holds out its enduring worth as essential to individuals and civilization itself; and (3) it promotes the beneficial dimensions of music for youth as a part of learning by providing services to its members that promote those benefits. Our members believe that MENC is truest to itself when it pursues the ends that are beyond itself, for example, music as an art form and teaching as a way of shaping the lives of children.

As an association, therefore, MENC seeks to achieve a number of basic outcomes related to its values. But how do those ends shape the way MENC works (i.e., its choice of means) in the policy arena? An interesting test of our members' musical values as they relate to educational outcomes arose recently when MENC became involved in the question of sorting out the use of religious music as part of the performance repertoire of school choruses during religious holiday seasons. The policy stance we had traditionally taken—and the stance that was argued legally—was that there is no way to keep high-quality school music programs of this kind from being "religious," any more than you can teach the art of the Renaissance without using "religious" paintings. Besides, we also argued, eliminating such pieces would eliminate about 90% of the choral music repertoire, surely an undesirable outcome. The issue was finally decided along the lines of allowing teachers to teach the *music* so long as the *words* were basically ignored. The policy brief we subsequently prepared for our members turned out to be one of our most asked-for publications. An interface with the importance of research was also evident here, as a good deal of legal research went into our involvement.

Resources

MENC brings four distinct resources to the policy-making arena: (1) a commitment to music and children; (2) a strong advocacy base; (3) a clear picture of what it wants to accomplish; and (4) alliances with others of like mind.

A good illustration of the policy ramifications in this area arises with (4). In recent years, MENC has made a conscious policy choice to construct "useful" alliances with other associations whose missions and objectives align well with ours. A major arena for working on this policy choice has been the biannual "music summit" conferences MENC has sponsored on issues concerning music education. These meetings can involve upward of 70 people from almost as many organizations and businesses.

The impact on MENC's own policy perspectives stemming from these "summits" has been powerful. Several new organizational alliances, including those with associations such as NAEYC and the New York Philharmonic, as well as with corporations such as Texaco, Pepsi, and Disney, have been formed on such divergent issues as:

- the relation of music to physical health and wellness;
- the educational potential of music for preschool youngsters, and the consequent broadening of MENC's interests beyond the K–12 school curriculum to include early childhood education; and
- a continuing interest in the interface between musical activity and learning, as demonstrated from music/brain research.

Thus, MENC's policy to pursue alliances has paid off as the interests of other associations and corporations have been aligned with our own.

The basic value of any alliances or partnerships is largely strategic—in terms of the different constituencies brought together, the interests coalesced, and the resources redirected from other organizational business. MENC's 10-year alliance with NAMM and NARAS in the National Coalition for Music Education is a strong case in point. Although the mission and orientation of each of the three organizations is very different (MENC's mission is oriented toward the professional concerns of music teachers; NAMM's is toward the economic concerns of music store owners, instrument manufacturers, and music publishers; NARAS's is toward the health of the recording industry), the constituents of all three associations have a long-term, strategic stake in banding together to *create more music makers*. Their jointly supported advocacy efforts therefore focus on legislation, education policy at all levels, research into the value and importance of music education for learning across the board, and generating support for school music programs.

Alliances like the coalition necessarily involve give-and-take among potentially competitive interests of their members, and those who create such alliances have to be prepared not to get everything they want. Here, as everywhere, interorganizational politics is part vision, part acrobatics, but mostly shoe leather. Logistical relationships among the alliance members sometimes break down. When they do, strong communication and more tightly focused staff attention must be brought to bear. A strong commitment from the top organizational leadership composing the alliance is utterly essential to the success of any alliance.

Conclusion

The process of information gathering, analysis, and evaluation is vitally important to the policy process as conceived and carried out at MENC. Indeed, the connections are so obvious they scarcely bear repeating. It is no overstatement to say that the association that does not engage in research as a full-time enterprise in support of its mission is setting itself up for failure. A simple example from MENC's recent history will illustrate what I mean.

A few years ago, we began receiving complaints from our members that our flagship journal, *Music Educators Journal*, was not really meeting the needs of teachers. Like many such journals in the association world, it was devoted to publishing peer-reviewed research—articles largely written by professors for professors, or for the few teachers involved with the theme of a given issue.

Some careful research revealed that the teachers wanted not something else but something more. They wanted a journal devoted to classroom concerns, the nuts and bolts (or the resin and bows, I should say) of teaching music to kids in grades K–12, administering school music programs, and teaching tips. In response, we launched *Teaching Music*, a practitioner's journal devoted to teachers' issues. It has been a great success—not just because the articles in it are good ones, although they are, and not just because the layout, design, and pictures are good, although they are. *Teaching Music* has succeeded because we had sense enough to do the research we needed to do to determine what our policy should be. We asked our members what they needed, and had the good sense to listen to what they told us.

We changed a policy that had been to say, in effect, "Our professional communications to our members will be of the highest academic caliber," to one that said, "In addition, we will speak to our members in a voice they all understand about issues that affect their professional lives *as teachers*." And that, for us, is what policy is all about.

Recent Trends and Issues in Policy Making

3

RALPH A. SMITH

Discussions of policy making in the first Handbook addressed various aspects of policy for arts education (Smith, 1992). Essays ranged over such topics as the definition of policy, descriptions of particular policy decisions, the role of professional associations, the involvement of federal and private agencies, and questionable instances of policy formulation and implementation. My own contribution discussed a few of the latter. One of the flaws of policy making stemmed from inadequate considerations of the nature and value of art, without which policies can have little direction. Another consisted of limited visions of arts education that were inadequate for an effective understanding and appreciating of works of art. Yet another was attributing to both art and arts education inordinate measures of instrumental efficacy. A surfeit of benefits, for example, was believed to derive from simply having "art experiences," a phrase characteristically left undefined. Also noted were examples of bad faith, which is to say the undertaking of purportedly unbiased and objective studies and research that were in fact intended to advance particular agendas. Termed "advocacy research," this tendency came under strong scrutiny by critics. Advocacy, of course, is necessary and can be pursued responsibly, but in too many instances the motives and statements of advocates begged credibility. Moreover, there was a tendency to glamorize advocacy by showcasing figures from the worlds of entertainment and business whose contributions usually consisted of little more than sound bites.

Another feature of policy making was a consequence of the growing number of groups committed to promoting the arts. A plethora of agencies, organizations, councils, centers, and institutes, often devoted to securing their own survival and growth, tended to encourage the substitution of bureaucratic process for substantive implementation—endless meetings and conferences that recommended more meetings and conferences, research calling for more research that was not always related to art and arts education, salaries and expense budgets that improved the status of professionals and bureaucrats more than that of teachers of art or art programs, and so forth. Such shortcomings were and continue to be characteristic aspects of institutions comprising a new cultural and educational complex that after almost 40 years is still searching for a coherent policy.

The policy decisions just discussed were summed up as the sentimentalizing, the bureaucratizing, the politicizing, and the glamorizing of policy for the arts and arts education. A major instance exemplifying these trends was what was commonly referred to as the Rockefeller report. Titled *Coming to Our Senses: The Significance of the Arts for American Education* (Arts, Education, and Americans Panel, 1977), the document was characterized by serious critics as a monument to the nonserious study of arts education (Lipman, 1992). In contrast, *Toward Civilization: A Report on Arts Education* (National Endowment for the Arts, 1988), provided a more substantive alternative. It understood art as a serious subject that was worth studying and cherishing for its inherent values and the sense of civilization such study and cherishing can engender. The emergence of the Getty Center for Education in the Arts (later renamed the Getty Institute for Education in the Arts) in the early 1980s and its notion of discipline-based art education—an interpretation that featured the grounding of the study of art in the four interrelated disciplines of aesthetics, art making, art criticism, and art history—was another significant step in establishing solid foundations for arts education (Getty Center for Education in the Arts, 1985). Limited mostly to the improvement of visual art education, including art museum education, in its later phases it supported disciplined-based music education as well (Patchen, 1996). Getty policy makers, to be sure, were not immune to some of the flaws of policy thinking and implementation, as were for that matter the authors of *Toward Civilization*. Worth noting, however, is that its emphasis on the development of a sense of civilization and the Getty's stress on complementing creative activities with historical and critical studies suggested that the study of the arts was assuming a more traditional humanities cast.[1] The discussion of policy trends and issues in the first Handbook concluded with observations about some of the problems posed by the increasing interest in multiculturalism, especially the issue created by advocates of either cultural particularism or cultural pluralism, the former stressing separateness and multiple enclaves and the latter a diverse yet unified common culture.

Policy Developments Between the Two Handbooks

Have matters significantly changed since the publication of the first Handbook? Yes and no. Inflated rhetoric and overstatement of claims, excessive bureaucracy, interest groups pressing social and political agendas, the use of celebrities to promote the arts, and the mixed consequences of multiculturalism are still evident and just as harmful to serious thinking about the arts and arts education. Since I assume other chapters in this part provide accounts of what has transpired in policy making for music education since the first Handbook, it might be asked why an outsider was once more invited to record observations. Perhaps it was because the editors thought it worthwhile to have the views of a generalist who has written critically about the problems of defining cultural and educational relations and edited an interdisciplinary journal of arts education for over three decades.

Four developments that have recently influenced thinking about policy for arts education deserve scrutiny: the promulgation by a coalition of national art education associations of national standards for the arts, further educational activities of the Getty Institute for Education in the Arts, research purporting to show positive effects of the study of the arts on academic achievement, and challenges presented by the social sciences to conventional interpretations of arts education.

National Standards for Arts Education

This major policy document sets down what every young American should know about and be able to do in the arts of dance, music, theater, and the visual arts. The introduction prefaces discussions of the various standards by saying that

People unfamiliar with the arts often mistakenly believe that excellence and quality are merely matters of opinion ("I know what I like"), and that one opinion is as good as another. The standards say that the arts have "academic" standing. They say there is such a thing as achievement, that knowledge and skills matter, and that mere willing participation is not the same thing as education. They affirm that discipline and rigor are the road to achievement. And they state emphatically that all these things can in some way be measured if not always on a numerical scale, then by informed critical judgment. (Consortium of National Arts Education Associations, 1994, p. 15)

These are some of the document's best words. They say that, in addition to being substantive and demanding, the study of art should be devoted to cultivating a taste for excellence that is grounded in critical discernment. Such assumptions are congruent with those of the excellence-in-education movement of the 1980s, the major goal of which was to make school learning more demanding. It is also possible to find in the introduction a worthwhile definition of art as a special form of communication whose history of outstanding achievement reveals a strong sense of cultural continuity and civilization. In an attempt to appear objective and fair, the authors of the document further assert that the standards espouse no particular philosophy of education or aesthetic point of view. The standards do, however, tend to favor the creative and performing arts. Whenever historical and critical studies are mentioned they are typically integrated into creative and performing activities. Such integration has the effect of dampening interest in historical and critical study in their own right or in knowledge of art historical chronology that is indispensable for an appreciation of cultural continuity and change. Similarly, little attention is given to critical dialogue that is required to address puzzles that arise in interpreting and evaluating works of art. Once more in the spirit of fairness, impartiality, and inclusiveness, the cultural accomplishments of all civilizations are considered worth studying, again a praiseworthy commitment but one that does raise problems of curriculum selection and accommodation. Such observations notwithstanding, the accomplishment of a coalition-crafted consensus about national standards for arts education represents a unique achievement and constitutes a milestone in policy formulation.

Most important, by stressing that the arts have academic standing, the authors of the standards encourage a way of thinking about arts education that significantly contrasts with earlier discussions that were cool to the academic side of arts study. In this respect, the case for arts education exemplified by the standards bears significant resemblance to the arts endowment report *Toward Civilization* and its recommendation to cultivate a sense of civilization by restoring historical memory of artistic excellence and critical judgment. The standards further reveal the influence of the Getty Institute for Education in the Arts, to be discussed in the next section.

Yet, there are some reservations. The first one centers on typical utopianism and excessive estimates of the benefits to be derived from arts education. Second, a discrepancy occasionally exists between the rhetoric of the introduction and the phrasing of the content and achievement standards, not to mention examples given to illustrate standards. And, third, as mentioned, there is the problem of inclusiveness. How should these matters be addressed?

A few suggestions. First, there must be a considerable paring down of expectations. For example, consider the sorts of things the young should know and be able to do: communicate at a basic level in each of the four arts (dance, music, theater, and visual art); communicate proficiently in at least one of them; perform structural, historical, cultural, and critical analyses of works of art in each art; acquire an informed acquaintance with exemplary works of art from a variety of cultures and historical periods; understand historical development not only in each art but also across the arts; relate knowledge and skills within an art form, across the arts, and from the arts to the rest of the subjects in the curriculum; and so on. Achieving these objectives would exceed the capacities of a lifetime and can hardly be expected to be the responsibility of the schools, especially when arts education exists principally in the margins of the curriculum and not as a basic subject. Nor is there, or is there likely to be, a professionally trained teacher corps that could implement such a range of activities.

One of the standards that if widely adopted could possibly derail the basic purpose of the whole enterprise—the cultivating of excellence grounded in critical judgment—is devoted to cross-disciplinary learning, not just across the arts but across other disciplines and subjects in the curriculum. Such a recommendation expresses confidence in the value and power of integration. Yet, thoughtful reflection reveals some difficulties that should not be ignored. Interdisciplinary studies of different kinds are difficult enough in their own right and are not likely to go very far unless those involved are competent in their respective disciplines or areas of specialization. But when one of these disciplines—the arts, in this case—is relegated to serving instrumentally the attainment of the objectives of other subjects, then arts education as a subject in its own right in the curriculum must be given short shrift. There can, of course, be no objection to teachers wanting to enliven their efforts by making references to the arts or by including them in the study of themes that integrate material from different disciplines. Pedagogical choices such as these become an issue only when they are considered a substitute for the serious study of art itself. To permit such substitution would amount to saying that art is really not worth valuable curriculum time, since everything that needs to be

said or done about it can be accomplished in other contexts. But a serious comprehension and appreciation of the arts cannot be attained in this way; an outreach mission to other subjects is questionable as a basic purpose of arts education. A more significant function is that of familiarizing the young with a distinctive way of knowing that has a history of outstanding achievement and basic problems of understanding and evaluating.

One promising kind of interdisciplinary teaching of the arts is an approach that features teams of art specialists. Before proceeding in this direction, however, important cognitive, psychological, and institutional obstacles should be taken into account. Ponder some of the conditions that must be met. Such conditions were set out in an interesting study undertaken by Hugh Petrie several years ago that still has relevance.[2] On the assumption that interdisciplinary study implies the careful coordination of all team members, the first condition is that team members bring to their task a firm grasp of their own disciplines and be able to communicate them to others in comprehensible ways. This is more difficult than often realized. Although teachers in a field of study usually have an intuitive or practical grasp of it, they may not always have a good conceptual understanding of it and thus have difficulty in conveying its basic concepts and modes of inquiry to other specialists. A shakedown period is usually necessary before different kinds of specialists can effectively communicate with one another at a level that is efficacious for teaching. Part of the problem is that specialists feel more comfortable in their own subject-area niches and are therefore reluctant to enter onto unfamiliar ground, especially when doing so demands a degree of curiosity and adventuresomeness for which they may not be rewarded as well as for work in their own subject area. Furthermore, institutional support for such projects may be withdrawn if signs of success are not forthcoming early in the undertaking. As such cognitive, psychological, and institutional considerations are adequately addressed, the prospects for effective interdisciplinary study will become greater.

The Getty Venture

A reform venture lasting almost two decades cannot be adequately described in a few pages, but an effort will be made to condense its principal policy viewpoint. The major educational efforts of the Getty extended from the early 1980s to the late 1990s, with some limited activities being carried over into the 21st century. At the outset of this period, representatives of what was then called the Getty Center for Education in the Arts announced their intention to support the general purpose of the excellence-in-education movement of the early 1980s, which was to make schooling more substantive and rigorous. Concentrating primarily on the teaching of the arts in the public schools and museum education, Getty policymakers were guided by a strong belief that a serious sense of art is best developed in the young when instruction is grounded in the content and methods of inquiry of four overlapping disciplines: art making, art history, art criticism, and aesthetics (by which was usually meant the philosophy of art) (Clark, Day, & Greer, 1989; Smith, 1989a). In other words, building a well-developed sense of art involves instruction in historical and critical studies as well as creative activities. This approach went by the name of discipline-based art education, although the term *comprehensive education* was sometimes used to suggest the broader, holistic interpretation of art education that the Getty was striving to attain. In this respect, the Getty venture is best understood as the combination of some of the leading ideas being articulated in the field of art education at the time the Getty arrived on the educational scene, the ideas the Getty generated as its activities evolved, and the impact of its policies on the field of arts education.

The criteria for assessing the successes and failures of the Getty undertaking were in effect articulated by its educational director, Leilani Lattin Duke, when she spoke about the role of private institutions in attempts to accomplish educational reform (Duke, 1986). Private institutions must first of all be aware of their own strengths and limitations, particularly of what they can hope to accomplish in a democratic society committed largely to state and local control of schools. This realization ruled out any idea of bringing about reform by fiat or imposition. Effective change, it was believed, can be achieved only by working cooperatively with schools and other agencies interested in similar goals. Ideally, such cooperation will be a result of synergism, that is, the achievement of a total result greater than that which can be attained by any single effort. The potential of private institutions to reach their goals resides in the resources they can bring to bear and the risks they can afford to take. In the case of the Getty, examples of such risks were uncertainty over the acceptance of its recommendations by practitioners in the field and over the ability of endorsed policies to be sufficiently productive of anticipated reform. Yet, as an affluent and prestigious private institution, the Getty had the capacity to confer status on innovative efforts that might otherwise be met with resistance, for example, the notion of discipline-based art education.

What grade can be given to the Getty venture? On a pass-fail basis, certainly "pass," and then some. In a presentation to the National Art Education Association, the Getty's educational director summarized what she considered to be the Getty's successes and failures during her 17-year tenure (Duke, 1999). The summary reveals Getty involvement in practically every major policy development in art education during the 1980s and 1990s. Most obvi-

ous was the Getty's support of the paradigm shift in the theory of art education mentioned earlier. Its regional staff development institutes and numerous publications and conferences were vivid testimonials to its influence, as is a comprehensive bibliography of over 600 annotated entries devoted to various aspects of the Getty's activities.[3] Not insignificant was the Getty's ability to persuade many in the field of art education and related academic areas to accept the general premises of its policies. As stated in its second guidebook (Dobbs, 1998, pp. 5–6), these policies—in addition to arguing for a substantive study of art grounded in the four interrelated disciplines of the arts—prescribed a written curriculum, the use of certified teachers of art, school-sponsored and community-based learning opportunities, assessment of learning, integration of art with the general curriculum, coordinated administration of programs, and the incorporation of new technology. Consistent with a commitment to synergism and cooperation, the Getty was conspicuously successful in forming coalitions and partnerships with public and private agencies, professional associations, organizations in charge of testing and admissions, and business and parent groups, among others. As Duke said, the Getty's "fingerprints" can be found on efforts to include the arts in the statement of the national educational goals, on the formulation of the national standards for the arts, on the criteria used in assessing national progress in the arts, and on the statement of professional teaching standards.[4] That is to say, advocacy for the arts was furthered through the powers of what was believed to be a critical mass of organizations.

Significant accomplishments notwithstanding, the education director also spoke forthrightly about disappointments and failures, some of them of such a nature as to inhibit seriously the attainment of the Getty's objectives. One disappointment was the inability to develop an acceptable children's television program despite a heavy investment of funds; another and more important one was the failure to exert sufficient influence on the preservice education of teachers of art. This failure was attributed largely to faculty turnover in preservice education programs and shifting ideological priorities. While the nature of these priorities was not mentioned, it may be assumed that among them were the ideological viewpoints espoused by a new cadre of educational theorists who became more interested in teaching the arts to achieve a range of social and political objectives than in developing an understanding and appreciation of the arts for the sake of their inherent values. The evolution of the Getty venture was arrested when, after a period in which the Getty had established an important leadership role in art education, a change in the chief administrative officers of the Getty Trust resulted in the slowdown of Getty's educational activities, reduction of its staff, and the cancellation of some of its programs.

One issue referred to by the former educational director in her summary involves the distinction between the noninstrumental and instrumental uses of art, that is, the study of art for its inherent values in contrast to its use to achieve nonarts outcomes. Duke acknowledged that the instrumental claim often served as a "hook" to convince others of the importance of art education but, in truth, the instrumental benefits of the arts became overemphasized to such an extent that even those partial to the Getty venture recommended paring them down. In retrospect, however, Duke ultimately repudiated the expedient of justifying art education in terms of questionable nonarts outcomes.

The Getty's commitment to inclusiveness also can be questioned. By inclusiveness is not meant the number of disciplines drawn on by discipline-based arts education. Any adequate sense of art requires for its development some experience in creative, historical, and critical studies for which the disciplines of DBAE are important resources. Nor by a commitment to inclusiveness is intended the Getty's support of multiculturalism. Rather, the use of the term pertains to both the variety of curriculum options encouraged and a catholic view of art that was open-ended and made no distinction between fine, popular, and applied art. Local needs and interests were to be determinants in deciding the content of art instruction so long as it was meaningful, interesting, and engaging for students and in compliance with the guidelines mentioned above. In short, by the time the Getty approach had evolved into the 1990s, it wore several different faces. The massive Getty report *The Quiet Evolution*, which describes the activities of the Getty's regional institutes, outlines a number of such options.[5]

The disappointments and failures noted by Duke plus the observations made here do not, however, in any way diminish the extraordinary leadership exemplified by Duke during her tenure or the quite tangible impact the Getty venture has had on the theory, literature, and practice of art education, and—to a lesser extent—on music education. The Getty's limitations were not of the same magnitude as those of previous reform efforts that in their adversarial attitude toward the field of art education often tried to sidestep that field altogether. The Getty undertaking produced a far greater interest in the history, aesthetics, and criticism of art than previous ventures had and lent support to making art education more substantive and academic—and that represents genuine progress.

The Arts and Academic Achievement

The claim that the study of the arts contributes notably to the improvement of higher-level cognitive skills and academic achievement is less obviously an advance in policy thinking.[6] Widespread acceptance of such claims could affect not only the ways in which the case for arts education is argued but also the nature of preservice education and research and development priorities. The issue once more is whether to emphasize the more immediate values experienced in the creation, performance, and appreciation of art or more remote or distant values to the realization of which the study of the arts is believed to be instrumental. There is also some confusion not only about the benefits purportedly being transferred from one domain to another but also about the instrumentalities by means of which such values, whatever they may be, are being transmitted and internalized in learning. The terminology in which the difference between the two types of value are discussed is part of the problem.

Among the contrasting terms are two purportedly different kinds of values, aesthetic and extra-aesthetic values, instrumental and noninstrumental values, utilitarian and nonutilitarian values, primary and secondary values, intrinsic and extrinsic values, direct and indirect values, art-based, art-related, and ancillary values, and so forth. Another problem is the nature of the conditions that effect transfer. Do they consist of any kind of arts activity, arts education in general, creative activities, perceptual and appreciative experiences, historical and critical studies associated with the arts, the pedagogy favored, a school's atmosphere, the attitudes of teachers, students' socioeconomic background, parental expectations, the Hawthorne effect, or some combination of these? There is the further question regarding which aesthetic activities of what duration contribute to which nonaesthetic outcomes of what duration. Uncertainties like these indicate the complexity of identifying relevant variables. The apparent interest of policy makers and advocates in the possibility of such transfer is also worth noting in light of the marginal place of the arts in the curriculum and the lack of agreement in the field about its aims, purposes, and pedagogy.

It would seem, then, that in order to clarify what benefits are derivable from arts instruction and what kind of values might prove transferable, the first order of business should be the establishment of arts education as a substantive and challenging subject in its own right, that is, as a subject characterized by distinctive content, history of accomplishment, and problems of understanding and appreciation. This, however, is difficult to achieve without a theory about the nature and value of art, for it is only if the arts have unique inherent values that any serious case can be made for art education as an important, even indispensable, domain of learning. Statements about the nature and magnitude of art's values abound in the literature of arts education, but they fail to cohere into a theory that delineates clearly the relationships between different kinds of value. It will therefore be instructive to look at one interpretation of art's function that has been systematically worked out and has policy ramifications. The discussion deserves the space given to it because it is a key to understanding several other issues.

The theory in question is Monroe C. Beardsley's instrumental theory of aesthetic value.[7] Beardsley's conception of art's characteristic function—simply put, its capacity to induce a high level of aesthetic experience—was articulated and refined in a number of books, articles, and essays that spanned a period from the late 1950s to the early 1980s, a period also referred to as the Beardsleyan period in American aesthetics. Interest in his writings waned during the 1970s and 1980s as the interest of theorists centered more on the ideological than on the aesthetic features of art. But, as often happens, a pendulum swing in opinion seems to be occurring, which is believed to be the result of an awareness that something important is lost when aesthetic considerations are too often sacrificed to extra-aesthetic considerations.[8]

The bare essentials of Beardsley's theory posit that regardless of the intentions of artists or the various functions that works of art perform, what works of art are good for, what they do better than anything else, is to provide opportunities for a special kind of experience called aesthetic experience. The aesthetic value of a work of art, then, is its capacity to provide occasions for such experience. This is why his theory is called an instrumental theory. Persons do not experience works of art for their own sakes but rather for the sake of the kind of experience they can induce. Whatever inherent values works of art have are a function of the close and careful attention paid to art's characteristic features. But what are inherent values?

In Beardsley's theory, inherent values consist of two kinds: the more direct and immediately felt values of the experience of art itself and the more indirect and longer-range values to which such experience may contribute. Because of its peculiar configuration of expressive significance, art has the capacity to contribute to both kinds of value. Consider first the nature of the more immediately felt features of aesthetic experience. Beardsley believes that experience has an aesthetic character when it consists of a cluster of feelings, not just one so-called aesthetic emotion: the feelings of object directedness, detached affect, felt freedom, active discovery, and wholeness or integration. This is to say that during aesthetic experience a person's mental states willingly submit to direction from the qualities, relations, and meanings of works of art, reassured by a feeling, sometimes with exhilarating effect, that things are working out or have worked themselves out fittingly. Since the experience is freely undergone, there occurs a feeling of uncoerced involvement with an object or with what is presented or semantically invoked by it. Consequently, antecedent concerns about past and future are suppressed in favor of establishing rapport with the phenomena under

view. Important for maintaining control over awareness is a certain detachment of affect that discourages percipients' letting attention drift away from a work's components or their becoming too emotionally involved with it. Keeping feelings and emotions in check is especially important when a work of art presents dark and disturbing aspects of human experience that could easily give rise to negative and distracting feelings. The aesthetic experience of a work of some substance and complexity also may produce a feeling of active discovery, that is, a feeling that the constructive powers of the mind are being activated by challenges to perception and comprehension. A sense of active discovery may in turn bring about a state of excitement of the kind that normally accompanies the discovery of something new and worthwhile. The act of discerning connections between percepts and meanings in effect results in a feeling of intelligibility. The pedagogical implications of this feature of aesthetic experience are perhaps obvious. An aesthetic experience that has the foregoing characteristics, or at least most of them, may additionally induce a feeling of wholeness or personal integration. Not all of the features of aesthetic experiences just mentioned need be present for experience to have aesthetic character, although the first one is indispensable, and Beardsley acknowledged that further analysis of aesthetic experience might reveal it to have more or fewer such features.

Digressing for a moment, Beardsley's persuasive analysis makes implausible the belief that there is no such thing as aesthetic experience or that the idea of the aesthetic attitude is a myth. The term *aesthetic* and its cognates came into the language to serve a special purpose—to describe certain kinds of values and experiences that the arts and their counterparts in nature are especially well suited to realize. In contrast to the skepticism of critics, defenders of aesthetic experience have in fact elevated it to one of life's central goals and see it as an important part of a moral and rational existence. Such experience can not only provide a high degree of pleasure and delight but also sensitize, vitalize, and inspire human beings. Unfortunately, experiences worthy of being called aesthetic are all too rare. How often in the course of a day, or even a lifetime for some people, does experience have an aesthetic character? How often is something freely and willingly entertained for the sheer gratification of experiencing its configuration of components and its inherent values? The disposition to seek aesthetic experiences must therefore be carefully nurtured, which involves instruction in the perceptual and intellectual skills that are preconditions for having rich instances of them.

So much for the direct or immediate inherent values of aesthetic experience. What about the indirect, longer-range benefits to which a disposition to have aesthetic experiences might conceivably contribute? Returning now to

Beardsley, based on some evidence and reasonable speculation at the time he wrote he suggests that four basic values can be hypothesized which in turn suggest still others. Psychologically, the disposition to have aesthetic experiences may help relieve tensions and quiet destructive impulses, offer a surrogate for violence, and satisfy the human need for excitement. Or, as intimated earlier, aesthetic experience may facilitate the amelioration of inner conflicts; it may, for example, provide for integration and harmonization within the personality by clearing the mind and making it more decisive. Such a result can be called the tonic effect of aesthetic experience.

More obviously perhaps, the sustained attention imperative for aesthetic experiences can refine perception and discrimination generally. The inclination to perceive the subtle nuances of human qualities and relationships in works of art might conceivably translate into a readiness to forge sympathetic relations with other persons and perhaps with nature and the humanly made environment. Closely related to the refinement of perception and discrimination is the development of imagination. This conjecture, continuing with Beardsley's account, is based on the fact that the experience of works of art often requires projecting oneself into a range of situations, not just into the fictional relationships of literature and drama but in many other instances of art as well. Consequently, routine ways of thinking and feeling might be altered, minds could become more open and flexible, and ideas might be gained for resolving dilemmas and responding more appropriately to novel situations and contingencies. These possibilities bespeak the capacity of aesthetic experiences to foster mutual respect, sympathy, and understanding among individuals.

Assuming such indirect effects are realizable, Beardsley goes on to say, a disposition to experience things aesthetically could be recommended as an aid to mental health. A daily ingestion of aesthetic value might well decrease the occurrence or lessen the severity of the neuroses and psychoses rampant in society. Aesthetic values could thus enhance the amplitude of life itself. Finally, one of the inherent values of aesthetic experience lies in its providing an ideal for human existence; it encourages shaping a human career so that it has some of the qualities of aesthetic experience favored so much by John Dewey. In view of all the factors that make human existence so empty and unfulfilling, it should be easy to appreciate how the inherent values of art can provide clues to what life might be like.

What makes Beardsley's thinking about the inherent values of art so important is the contrast it presents to much of the contemporary literature and research associated with the arts and academic achievement. His instrumental theory of aesthetic value derives the extra-aesthetic benefits of art from what is distinctive about the components of an aesthetic situation. Without such a theory,

the search for relationships between art education and other educationally desirable outcomes is rudderless and can easily result in unsupportable claims and, hence, in poor policy making. It is from careful investigations guided by theories of art that research and policy making should take their lead.

The Challenge of the Social Sciences

The challenge arises because of the increasing attention policymakers and theorists of art education are paying to the social and political dimensions of the field. Earlier discussion suggested that the idea of the field's being discipline-based in effect located art education within the domain of the humanities. Yet, views emerging from recent theoretical writing recommend a more prominent role for the social sciences.[9] These writings range from an unobjectionable concern for rounding out the historical, philosophical, and psychological foundations of arts education with the insights of the social sciences to beliefs that arts education should in effect transform itself into social science.

A spectrum of opinion as wide as this raises a number of issues that need addressing. It is beyond question that the creation and experience of the arts occur within social settings that affect and influence the form, content, and style of works of art. Consequently, the development of some understanding of the relations of art and society has a proper place in the teaching of art. The field of arts education needs to be aware of its social foundations as much as it does of its historical, philosophical, and psychological foundations. A social science approach to arts education becomes a policy problem only when the study of social and cultural relationships receives inordinate emphasis, when, for example, programs are excessively energized by political and social-reform agendas. Widespread endorsement of these tendencies could possibly have the consequence of jettisoning the disciplines traditionally associated with the study of the arts. Such displacement would in turn result in reducing, or even in eliminating, the central role that art's inherent values should play in policy deliberations for arts education. This outcome could even signal the end of arts education and render moot any argument for establishing it as a separate area of instruction in the curriculum. Discussion of art would probably become the responsibility of social studies courses. Other consequences might follow, with the absorption of arts education by the social sciences. Changes in teacher education and professional membership could happen. To be sure, it is unlikely that changes of such magnitude would occur easily and without considerable resistance, given the difficulty of effecting educational reform of any kind. But inevitably there would result a noticeable transformation in the ethos of art education, one that would result in a lessening of interest in the inherent values of art and would thus constitute a major policy issue.

The relations of arts education and the social sciences, however, can be adjudicated without the consequences of some of the extreme changes just mentioned. It is possible to see the two fields, the humanities and the social sciences, as complementary rather than antagonistic. Granting that a philosophy of art education should include a discussion of the social context of art education, that is not necessarily saying that works of art are clearly and primarily manifestations of the power relations and the viewpoints of dominant groups in a society, or that being expressions of such beliefs is the most important thing about them. Such conclusions are controversial to say the least and are not the kind that traditionally theorists and practitioners of art education have assumed. Social science as a set of disciplines is less committed to understanding and appreciating works of art, which is a standard and conventional goal of arts education, than in undertaking critical analyses that issue in generalizations about art and society. What needs emphasizing are the empowering notions of the traditional disciplines of the humanities, though in ways different from those of the social sciences. Anita Silvers (1999) puts it well when she says that "aesthetics, art criticism, and art history all guide our celebrations in art, while social science helps to understand the practice of aesthetics, art criticism, and art history in providing such guidance" (pp. 100–101). There is a place for both, then, the humanities and the social sciences, provided that the arts receive a proportionately weightier emphasis because of their inherent values. These values, however, cannot be encompassed by reductive conceptions of art that see works of art essentially as symptomatic of oppressive social relations. Silvers points out that the sheer complexity of works of art makes them unfit vehicles for unambiguously expressing political and power relations that can act as a stimulus for social action. Works of art, she says, have the power to transcend social and political realities, not least because of their capacity to transcend the commonplace even while engaging it.

Other reasons can be given for questioning the adoption of critical theories that have extreme social and political dimensions, reasons that, although they can merely be mentioned here, are valid not only for art education but also for education generally. In important respects, certain new critical theories are inherently anti-educative, anarchical, and antihumanistic. Certain versions of deconstruction, postmodernist thinking, and theories underlying cultural studies attempt to discredit such traditional humanistic ideas and ideals as communication, value, meaning, and objectivity.[10] But it is difficult to see how without such concepts education, and even society itself, can function.

Conclusion

If this chapter has not been concerned with formal definitions of policy, it is because the general meaning of the term is well known. A policy is a statement about an overall plan for the purpose of managing wisely a course of action or set of procedures that presumably was agreed on after serious consideration of alternatives. Policies may be the high-level policies of governments or of any group that decides some oversight of matters is necessary. Failure to observe policies may result in more or less severe sanctions or none at all if a policy merely makes recommendations, the acceptance of which is voluntary. Practically all of the policy recommendations discussed in this chapter fall into the latter category. No one is likely to be imprisoned or fined for failing to implement the national standards for the arts or the approach known as discipline-based art education. Yet, even policies voluntarily adopted obviously have effects, as this chapter has tried to show. It is the task of policy analysis and criticism to understand and assess such policies and to suggest alternatives. In the first Handbook, the suggestion was made to soften the sentimentalizing, politicizing, bureaucratizing, and glamorizing of policy thinking and implementation. This suggestion is still relevant but, as this chapter has indicated, policy thinking has made significant strides by conceiving arts education in more substantive and academic terms. If policy grows out of conditions existing at a given time and addresses old as well as new challenges, then the most important challenge facing policy formulation and implementation at this time is one that concerns the definition and status of the field of arts education. An important part of such a definition is a much better understanding of the relations of art, society, and art education.

I once more turn to Beardsley's thought. In his later writings, he concedes that he had overemphasized the value of aesthetic criticism in order to return interest to the object of art and its inherent values after a period of overemphasis on the biographical, psychological, and historical aspects of art. Beardsley subsequently called for a coherent and judicious account of the relations of art and other components or segments of culture. Such an account would recognize art as one strand of social interaction that has close connections with other central functions, practices, and institutions of society, while recognizing the special contribution art makes to the goodness and preciousness of human life. Acknowledging the increasing interest in cultural criticism, he nonetheless reminded that "cultural criticism does not eliminate or replace aesthetic criticism, but embraces and builds upon it; its own enterprise must acknowledge, make room for, and preserve the distinctively aesthetic point of view" (Beardsley, 1982b). Policymakers and theorists need to be reminded of this from time to time if the arts are to play a vital role in human experience and become a standard subject of learning.

Overall, writings about policy during the last decade of the 20th century exhibited a significant trend that takes into account the major components of the aesthetic complex: creation and performance, object, experience, criticism, and cultural context. The *National Standards* are a forward step in recognizing the interrelationships of these components. The task for a philosophy of arts education for the future is the harmonization of these components and the task of research studies is to provide support for policy-making decisions.

NOTES

1. See Levi and Smith (1991) for a humanities interpretation of discipline-based art education. This is a volume in the Getty-sponsored series, Disciplines in Art Education: Contexts of Understanding (1991–1997).

2. See Petrie (1976). Although written a quarter of a century ago, Petrie's analysis is still relevant and helps to appreciate the difficulty of implementing interdisciplinary ventures at whatever level of learning.

3. See Smith (2000), a selection of articles and excerpts from a project that identified the sources and topics of DBAE. At the time of this writing (fall 2000), the whole bibliography can be located on the Getty website ArtsEdNet. Also see the five coauthored volumes in the Getty series.

4. For Getty's cooperation with the College Board, see Boston (1996).

5. See Wilson (1997). Cf. Wilson and Rubin (1997), which discusses what was learned about the difficulties of bringing about change.

6. The discussion draws on a special issue of the *Journal of Aesthetic Education* (Winner & Hetland, 2000). Devoted to the topic "The Arts and Academic Achievement: What the Evidence Shows," the issue reviews relevant literature and reports the results of an extensive research project carried out under the umbrella of Harvard Project Zero. A major finding of the research was a failure to distinguish clearly between correlation and causation.

7. The discussion follows the analyses in Beardsley (1981, 1982a).

8. See Carroll (2000) and Eaton (1989). These writers represent a continuing interest in both the concept of aesthetic experience and, in the case of Carroll, in Beardsley's writings.

9. Representative is Chalmers (1996).

10. See Wilsmore (1987) for a systematic critique of deconstruction, Shaw (1989) for a discussion of the antihumanism of deconstruction, and Smith (1989b) for discussions of policy, culture, ideology, and deconstruction.

REFERENCES

Arts, Education, and Americans Panel (1977). *Coming to our senses: The significance of the arts for American edu-cation.* New York: McGraw-Hill. Introduction by D. Rockefeller, Jr.

Beardsley, M. C. (1981). *Aesthetics: Problems in the philosophy of criticism,* 2nd ed. (pp. 571–77). Indianapolis: Hackett.

Beardsley, M. C. (1982a). Aesthetic experience. In M. J. Wreen & D. M. Callen (Eds.), *The aesthetic point of view: Selected essays* (pp. 288–97). Ithaca, NY: Cornell University Press.

Beardsley, M. C. (1982b). Art and its cultural context. In M. J. Wreen and D. M. Callen (Eds.), *The aesthetic point of view: Selected essays* (pp. 352–70). Ithaca, NY: Cornell University Press.

Boston, B. O. (1996). *Connections: The arts and the integration of the high school curriculum.* Los Angeles and New York: College Board and Getty Center for Education in the Arts.

Carroll, N. (2000). Art and the domain of the aesthetic. *British Journal of Aesthetics, 40*(2), 191–208.

Chalmers, F. G. (1996). *Celebrating pluralism: Art, education, and cultural diversity.* Los Angeles: J. Paul Getty Trust.

Clark, G. A., Day, M. D., & Greer, W. D. (1989). Discipline-based art education: Becoming students of art. In R. A. Smith (Ed.), *Discipline-based art education: Origins, meaning, development* (pp. 129–193). Urbana: University of Illinois Press.

Consortium of National Arts Education Associations. (1994). *National standards for arts education.* Reston, VA: Music Educators National Conference.

Dobbs, S. M. (1998). *Learning in and through the arts: A guide to discipline-based art education.* Los Angeles: Getty Institute for Education in the Arts.

Duke, L. L. (1999). Looking back, looking forward. *Keynote addresses, 1999.* Reston, VA: National Art Education Association.

Duke, L. L. (1986). The role of private institutions in art education. *Journal of Aesthetic Education, 20*(4), 48–49.

Eaton, M. (1989). *Aesthetics and the good life.* Rutherford, NJ: Farleigh University Press.

Getty Center for Education in the Arts. (1985). *Beyond creating: The place of art in America's schools.* Los Angeles: Getty Center for Education in the Arts. [Foreword by H. M. Williams. Preface by L. L. Duke.]

Getty series. (1991–1997). *Disciplines in art education: Contexts of understanding.* (R. H. Smith, gen. series ed.) Urbana: University of Illinois Press.

Levi A. W., and Smith, R. A. (1991). *Art education: A critical necessity.* Urbana: University of Illinois Press.

Lipman, S. (1992). The NEA: Looking back, looking ahead. In R. A. Smith & R. Berman (Eds.), *Public policy and the aesthetic interest: Critical essays on defining cultural and educational relations* (pp. 168–178). Urbana: University of Illinois Press. First published in 1984, *The New Criterion, 3,* 7–15.

National Endowment for the Arts. (1988). *Toward civilization: A report on arts education.* Washington, DC: National Endowment for the Arts. Foreword by F. Hodsoll.

Patchen, J. (1996). Overview of discipline-based music education. *Music Educators Journal, 83*(2), 19–26, 44.

Petrie, H. (1976). Do you see what I see: The epistemology of interdisciplinary inquiry. *Journal of Aesthetic Education, 10*(1), 29–43.

Shaw, P. (1989). The dark age of the humanities. In *The war against intellect: Episodes in the decline of discourse* (pp. 155–70). Iowa City: University of Iowa Press.

Silvers, A. (1999). Multiculturalism and the aesthetics of recognition: Reflections on celebrating pluralism. *Journal of Aesthetic Education, 33*(1), 100–101. [Essay review of Chalmers's book.]

Smith, R. A. (Ed.). (1989a). *Discipline-based art education: Origins, meaning, development.* Urbana: University of Illinois Press.

Smith, R. A. (1989b). *The sense of art: A study in aesthetic education.* New York: Routledge.

Smith, R. A. (1992). Trends and issues in policy-making for arts education. In R. Colwell (Ed.), *Handbook of research on music teaching and learning* (pp. 749–59). New York: Macmillan.

Smith, R. A. (Ed.) (2000). *Readings in discipline-based art education. A literature of educational reform.* Reston, VA: National Art Education Association.

Wilsmore, M. J. (1987). Scepticism and deconstruction. *Man and World, 20,* 437–55.

Wilson, B. (1997). *The quiet evolution: Changing the face of art education.* Los Angeles: Getty Education Institute for the Arts.

Wilson, B., & Rubin, B. (1997). DBAE and educational change. *Visual Arts Research, 23,* 89–97.

Winner, E., & Hetland, L. (Eds.). (2000). The arts and academic achievement: What the evidence shows. *Journal of Aesthetic Education, 34*(3–4).

Law Research and Music Education

4

JOHN W. RICHMOND

The history of music education as formal curriculum in America's public schools is now nearly 170 years old, tracing to Lowell Mason's efforts with the Boston public schools in the 1830s. Legislation making provision for public school music education and litigation pertaining to its provision and practice are nearly that old. Bennett Boyles identifies one of the earliest music education lawsuits (*Bellmeyer v. Independent School District of Marshalltown*; Boyles, 1981, p. 46) as having been decided by the Iowa Supreme Court in 1876—more than 120 years ago. Throughout music education's public school history, the significance and power of the law—both in terms of legislation and litigation—have become increasingly important considerations as vehicles for music education policy formation. The range and scope of education issues touched by our nation's laws are extensive, and a chronic naivete about the power of the law to shape our professional lives can only mean an increasingly perilous state of affairs at best for American music education. Any discussion of policy in music education would be incomplete without a least a modest, cursory examination of our laws and their impact on our field.

Some law research topics are likely to be more familiar than others to readers of this Handbook. Copyright law, for example, is sure to be one of the most familiar, as it has received considerable attention in our journals, newsletters, and convention programs during the last four decades. Advancing technologies and the economy of the photocopy machine have had much to do with this. Frankly put, the ease teachers now have in gaining access to these copy technologies has made their use too convenient, too expedient, too tempting, and too often suspect. More recently, the emergence of the Worldwide Web has made this issue even more complex, and created a need for new and updated legal definitions of such terms as broadcasting, personal use, and fair use. As we shall see later in this chapter, this ex-

tremely important area of the law continues to evolve in dramatic and sometimes contentious ways.

Some choral and general music educators will recognize the topic of "separation of church and state" because it is relevant to the study and programming of music with sacred texts. The U.S. Constitution expressly forbids the "establishment of religion" by our government (First Amendment). This issue surfaces for music educators when we choose sacred music for study or public performance. What this "Establishment Clause" means for public education policy can be a matter of highly rancorous debate so that there is no small amount of case law (decisions of judges in lawsuits) surrounding this question. As a matter of professional concern, it has received more than modest attention in our refereed journal publications and convention programs.[1]

Ever since William Hazard published his now famous book for music educators on issues of tort liability (1979b), our profession has had at least some acquaintance with the calamitous impact such lawsuits can have on teachers. Because music educators spend so much more time with students during the course of a work week, the likelihood of being the defendant in such a grievance is greater than it is for teachers of more traditional, academic subjects that see students in such limited contexts. Standard procedures that music teachers now use routinely (permission slips for field trips, etc.) are a product, at least in part, of lessons learned "the hard way" in the light of tort liability grievances.

While these topics are reasonably familiar, many other matters of law remain vital to our work, although veiled (sometimes in a kind of blissful ignorance) from our sight until a challenge to current policies and practices arises. These include matters of constitutional importance (such as freedom of speech and equal protection), matters of federal law (such as PL 94-142), and matters of state law (including the curricular provisions for arts instruction).

In this chapter, I examine briefly certain law-related issues that have emerged from the research literature of American public music education and related fields (education law, legal theory, etc.). First, I outline the legal standing of public education generally and music education specifically in an attempt to situate our work in the larger public policy arena. Second, I summarize what we know about what I believe to be the most salient legal issues facing our profession today. Finally, I close with a brief discussion of the many important questions for which we have very few answers in an attempt to suggest the general parameters of a future research agenda for our profession in this area. The limited space available in this volume does not permit an exhaustive treatment of any of the topics in this chapter. Therefore, the reader will be referred often to more complete sources in which each of the topics surveyed is considered more fully. Sources for this chapter included selected theses and dissertations, refereed journal articles, law review articles, the language of case law, and certain selected books and monographs. This chapter cannot, and does not, aspire to comprehensiveness, but rather it intends to focus and provide perspective.

Two final caveats seem fitting. First, I am not an attorney. I am a professor of music education with a keen interest in arts education policy. I have been writing about music education and the law for some time. It is important for the reader to remember, however, that I am constrained by law from offering legal advice. Nothing in this chapter should be so construed. *Teachers needing legal counsel should consult an attorney.*

Second, the meaning of legislation drafted by our nation's lawmakers is determined, that is, *interpreted*, by our nation's courts. It is a feature of the "balance of powers" established by the framers of our U.S. Constitution. Our nation's courts convene daily to hear cases argued before them. Likewise, these courts render decisions that shape, revise, and sometimes even *reverse* our understanding of the meaning of our statutes and constitutions (federal and state). Hence, it seems prudent to remind the reader that American jurisprudence is always, and quite appropriately, in a state of evolution and flux. The reader will want to keep in mind that court decisions reported in the paragraphs that follow are not immutable and fixed but, rather, only the status quo. In the days and months that follow the publication of this Handbook, court opinions reported here can, and likely will, be revised.

Public Education as a Function of State Government

The reasonable and common assumption among citizens of the United States is that public education is a matter of local governance. We speak routinely of our *local* school, our *local* school board, and our *local* property taxes that are used often to finance public education. These labels reinforce the impression that public education in America is a matter of local governmental concern.

It is true that in the United States education certainly is not governed at the national level. We do not have a national ministry of education as do most countries in the industrialized world. We do not require that all children in all schools subscribe to a mandatory national curriculum, nor that they undergo nationalized testing (although one could argue that the SAT and ACT examinations serve just such a de facto function).[2]

However, to understand American public education policy generally, and music education policy in the context of American public schools, the first step is to understand that *education is a function not of local, but rather state, government.* Tyll van Geel (1987) notes that:

> Abundant judicial opinions support the proposition that *it is the state legislature that enjoys the preeminent authority to control public elementary, secondary, and higher education* [italics added] in the state by setting up a system of public educational institutions and arranging for its financing and regulation. It is important to stress that while the federal Constitution assumes state authority over education, *it does not impose an affirmative obligation on the states to establish a public school system* [italics added]; however, the people of all states, except Connecticut have, through the states' own constitutions, imposed just such a duty. (p. 66)

States are not obliged by any language in the U.S. Constitution to provide public education for the children living in that state. The word "education" appears nowhere in it. States embrace such a duty by virtue of the language of their own state constitutions. Because nearly all states make such provisions for public education in their respective state constitutions, state government can be understood to be the real locus for public education policy formation. Local education authorities (LEAs—school districts) are technically branches of state government, brought into being by state legislatures. Confusion about this matter often is exacerbated by the use of conterminous boundaries for school districts and other "local" governmental units. In Florida, for example, the school districts of the state have precisely the same boundaries as the counties of the state. One should not regard public education in Florida, however, as a county government matter. By contrast, schools in Hawaii are administered without benefit of LEAs. The state administers the schools within it directly from the state level. "Local" property taxes, still used in many states to support public schools, are actually taxes that are brought into being by state law, and revised or eliminated by the actions of state legislators. Even the provision for LEAs to levy additional tax burdens on themselves is a discretion bestowed on them by *state* legislatures and adjudicated when challenged in *state* courts. Public education in the United States is a matter of state governance.

This understanding is crucial because it determines how and where education policy decisions are made. *State legislatures* are extremely important in the formulation of education policy, and in the last decade, *state courts* (especially state supreme courts) have become pivotal in adjudicating arguments about the just and proper provision of education to the children of the public schools. This is not to suggest that education lawsuits are no longer filed in federal court. They certainly are. It is to suggest, however, that music educators need to understand how important state *policies* and state *politics* are in the organization, administration, and funding of public schools.

Status of Copyright Law as It Pertains to Music Education

If featured articles published in our professional literature and presentations scheduled at professional conferences are useful indicators of importance, then it seems fair to suggest that copyright is perhaps the most important legal topic in music education. This has not always been the case. Copyright protection became an important topic for the teaching professions as the photocopy machine and the tape recorder became more widely available and affordable. These emerging technologies became more commonplace in American schools in the 1960s. They created real opportunities for music educators to serve students as never before, but they also presented some unfortunate temptations with respect to copyright infringements as well. Early publications addressing the importance of copyright compliance surfaced in the mid-1960s, but it very likely was the monthly, 11-part series by Lee Eliot Berk, published in the *Music Educators Journal* (February 1971–March 1972), that raised copyright to the level of national importance for music teachers. From that time to the present, the stream of articles, presentations, booklets, and books pertaining to music educators and copyright has been reasonably steady.

New and emerging technologies today continue this tradition of creating both opportunities and temptations for music educators in the performance of their professional duties. While it may have been true that our profession was naive about the requirements of copyright law in mid-century, there may be good reason to believe today that copyright noncompliance can no longer be attributed solely to ignorance of the law.

Principal Features of Copyright Protection

The term "copyright" refers to the legal means by which individuals and corporations protect intellectual property.

> Copyright is a form of protection provided by the laws of the United States (Title 17, U.S. Code) to authors of "original works of authorship," including literary, dramatic, musical, artistic, and certain other intellectual works. This protection is available to both published and unpublished works.[3]

Copyright laws restrict the use of protected material by providing the copyright owner with the *exclusive* right:

- To *reproduce* the work in copies and phonorecords;
- To prepare *derivative works* based upon the work;
- To *distribute copies or phonorecords* of the work to the public by sale or other transfer of ownership, or by rental, lease, or lending;
- To *perform the work publicly*, in the case of literary, musical, dramatic, or choreographic works, pantomimes, and motion pictures and other audiovisual works;
- To *display the copyrighted work publicly*, in the case of literary, musical, dramatic, and choreographic works, pantomimes, and pictorial, graphic, or sculptural works, including the individual images of a motion picture or other audiovisual work; and
- In the case of *sound recordings, to perform the work publicly* by means of a *digital audio transmission*. (U.S. Copyright Office, 2000, §106)

In large measure, only the copyright holder may engage in any of these activities as they pertain to his or her "intellectual property." All others must obtain permission from, and often compensate, the copyright owner.

Fair Use

These copyright protections are not limitless, however. Copyright law recognizes that scholars, educators, and others need reasonable access to protected works in the interest of our common good (research, teaching, criticism, news reporting, etc.). This provision of the law is called "fair use" and it has been the subject of much discussion, debate, legislation, and litigation in the last decade.

The provisions for fair use are found in Title 17, §107 of the U.S. Code. The language of the statute outlines four general considerations when determining if any given action is covered by fair use provision. These are:

1. the purpose and character of the use, including whether such use is of a commercial nature or is for nonprofit educational purposes;
2. the nature of the copyrighted work;

3. the amount and substantiality of the portion used in relation to the copyrighted work as a whole; and

4. the effect of the use upon the potential market for or value of the copyrighted work. (Title 17 U.S.C. §107)

As the reader can see, these considerations are framed in broad language. This breadth, while a strength in many respects, also provides less specific direction than many practitioners in the music professions would prefer. In an attempt to respond to this need for specificity, several sets of guidelines were developed in 1976 by representatives from across the education and music professions.[4] One such set of guidelines, entitled *Guidelines for Educational Uses of Music*, offers 10 brief policy statements outlining recommended "permissible uses" for both photocopying and sound recording, and also suggesting the "prohibitions" against unauthorized copying. Please note that ". . . virtually all exemptions granted to educators for the fair use of music are limited to *nondramatic* musical works" (Woody & Woody, 1994, p. 16). Musicals, operas, and other dramatic musical works are not covered by these guidelines, so that permissions must be secured and royalties must be paid by schools. The guidelines read as follows:

A. Permissible Uses
1. Emergency copying to replace purchased copies which for any reason are not available for an imminent performance provided purchased replacement copies shall be substituted in due course.

2. For academic purposes other than performance, single or multiple copies of excerpts of works may be made, provided that the excerpts do not comprise a part of the whole which would constitute a performable unit such as a section, movement or aria, but in no case more than 10 percent of the whole work. The number of copies shall not exceed one copy per pupil.

3. Printed copies which have been purchased may be edited or simplified provided that the fundamental character of the work is not distorted or the lyrics, if any, altered or lyrics added if none exist.

4. A single copy of recordings of performances by students may be made for evaluation or rehearsal purposes and may be retained by the educational institution or individual teacher.

5. A single copy of a sound recording (such as a tape, disc, or cassette) of copyrighted music may be made from sound recordings owned by an educational institution or an individual teacher for the purpose of constructing aural exercises or examinations and may be retained by the educational institution or individual teacher. (This pertains only to the copyright of the music itself and not to any copyright which may exist in the sound recording.)

B. Prohibitions
1. Copying to create or replace or substitute for anthologies, compilations or collective works.

2. Copying of or from works intended to be "consumable" in the course of study or of teaching such as workbooks, exercises, standardized tests and answer sheets and like material.

3. Copying for the purpose of performance, except as in A(1) above.

4. Copying for the purpose of substituting for the purchase of music, except as in A(1) and A(2) above.

5. Copying without inclusion of the copyright notice which appears on the printed copy. (Music Publishers' Association of the United States, 1976)

A second set of guidelines, entitled *Agreement on Guidelines for Classroom Copying in Not-for-Profit Educational Institutions with Respect to Books and Periodicals*, outlines recommended "permissions and prohibitions" both for single copies made by teachers/professors for their own scholarly uses and for multiple copies for classroom use. Permissions for single copies, made by teachers in the context of scholarly research and teaching preparation, are broader in scope than those for multiple copies. Generally, the *Guidelines* allow single copies of a book chapter, an article from a periodical or newspaper, a short story, short essay, or short poem, or a chart graph, diagram, drawing, cartoon, or picture from a book, periodical, or newspaper (Ad Hoc Committee on Copyright Law Revision, 1976). The provisions for multiple copies for classroom use are far more complex and involved. In every case, multiple copies may not exceed one copy per pupil per course, *and* three "tests" must be met in order for fair use to be established: "A. The copying meets the tests of brevity and spontaneity as defined below; and B. Meets the cumulative effect test as defined below; and C. Each copy includes a notice of copyright" (Ad Hoc Committee, 1976). While space here does not allow a full reporting of these definitions, certain excerpts from them will be of great interest to music teachers and professors reading this Handbook. First, under "Brevity," the *Guidelines* permit "(a) Either a complete article, story or essay of less than 2,500 words, or (b) an excerpt from any prose work of not more than 1,000 words or 10% of the work, whichever is less, but in any event a minimum of 500 words." Second, under "Spontaneity," the *Guidelines* permit multiple copying under fair use, provided that: "(i) The copying is at the instance and inspiration of the individual teacher [and] (ii) The inspiration and decision to use the work and the moment of its use for maximum teaching effectiveness are so close in time that it would be unreasonable to expect a timely reply to a request for permission." Third, under "Cumulative Effect," the *Guidelines* restrict multiple copying as follows: "(i) The copying of the material is for only one course in the school in which the copies are made [and] (ii) Not more than one short poem, article, story, essay or two excerpts may be copies from the same author, nor more than three from the sane [sic] collective work or periodical volume during one class term [and] (iii) there shall not be more than nine instances of such multiple copying for one course during one class term." The *Guidelines* also prohibit copying that is "used to create or replace or substitute for anthologies" and also to prohibit the copying of "consumable" course items, such as workbooks, and so forth. Finally, the *Guidelines* remind teachers that copying should not substitute for purchasing published copyrighted items, and no charge to a student should exceed the actual costs of photocopying (Ad Hoc Committee, 1976).

Two common music copyright issues are not addressed in either of these guidelines, however. They are matters pertaining to performance rights and to making recordings with the intent to sell them. Both such rights are protected by Title 17, §106 of the U.S. Code. Certain fair use provisions are made for performing in §110 of the law. Again, these provisions are for nondramatic musical works only. They allow for musical performances of copyrighted works in classrooms as a part of face-to-face instruction. They also allow for performances for the public as a part of religious services and in school and other nonprofit contexts, so long as no one is paid to perform or produce the event, *and* (1) there is no direct or indirect admission charge, *or* (2) "the proceeds, after deducting the reasonable costs of producing the performance, are used exclusively for educational, religious, or charitable purposes and not for private financial gain" (U.S.C. §110). Even if these conditions are met, however, the law also provides for means by which the copyright holder may expressly object to the performance of his/her copyrighted work (U.S.C. §110).

Provisions for what are called "compulsory licenses for making and distributing phonorecords" are found in Title 17, §110 of the U.S. Code. In summary, the law states that the right to record a musical composition belongs exclusively to the copyright holder, but that once a piece has been recorded and sold in the United States then other performers also may record the piece and the copyright owner is "compelled" to grant permission, provided that the copyright holder is paid a license fee at the "statutory rate," as outlined in Title 17, §115 of the U.S. Code. The rates in U.S. dollars per pressed CD sound recording at the time of this writing are as follows: 7.55 cents per song of 5 minutes or less, 1.45 cents per minute or fraction thereof for all songs over 5 minutes (Statutory Royalty Rates, 2000). It should be noted, however, that this compulsory license provision is qualified early in the language of the section with the phrase "by complying with the pro-

visions of this section . . ." and these provisions are considerable. Music educators planning to record their students and press CDs or other formats of recording are advised strongly to seek the counsel of professionals current in these laws in order to ensure that they are in compliance and not vulnerable to legal action. Many educators find it both prudent and convenient to employ the services of the Harry Fox Agency or other specialists to manage the copyright issues pertaining to the recording projects.[5] Readers of this Handbook are encouraged strongly to seek counsel before proceeding with recording projects.

To some reading the many "permissions" and "prohibitions" found in the guideline documents reviewed earlier— perhaps for the first time—there may be a raised eyebrow or two. Strict conformity to these copyright provisions is less commonplace than one might hope in American schools. In fact, recent research on the question of copyright compliance (or rather noncompliance) by American music educators has produced some interesting and, at times, disturbing findings that we will consider shortly.

This noncompliance may explain, in part, the reason that so many articles have appeared and so many conference presentations have been offered. The music industry has an enlightened self-interest in keeping copyright compliance before the music education profession. There is an important symbiosis between school music educators and music publishers. Music educators need to have access to music, workbooks, figuring charts, vocabulary sheets, and so on. Publishers need to maintain pleasant working relationships with their principal customers. Enforced compliance may achieve some short-term remedies but may alienate the music industry from their public school constituency. It seems highly likely that no one publisher wants to be the first to sue a school or school district for copyright infringement. Thus, it makes sense for the music industry to keep this issue in the minds of music teachers.

Recent Legislation Revising Copyright Protections: Implications for Music Education

Judith L. Marley identified three recent, significant revisions to copyright law that have implications for academic institutions. All were passed in October 1998 (Marley, 1999). These included the Digital Millennium Copyright Act (1998), the Sonny Bono Copyright Term Extension Act (1998), and the Fairness in Music Licensing Act (1998). These new laws are important to education policy because they affect the role of fair use in educational contexts. The Digital Millennium Copyright Act (DMCA) amended the Copyright Act of 1976. It guarantees that "copyright holders can legally protect their electronic creations through encryption, passwords, or other devices, [but] nevertheless allows limited fair use for digital preservation,

Questions of change and evolution lead us directly to government and governmental policies. The governmental structure affecting music education programs in the schools is clear. The federal government is prohibited by the Tenth Amendment to the U.S. Constitution, by the Elementary/Secondary Education Act, the Arts and Humanities Act establishing the two Endowments, and other pieces of legislation from direct control over the curriculum and management of schools. The states ultimately have statutory authority, but the primary governmental units are local school boards. This structure is consistent with American values that support dispersions of power. The counterforce is another American value: entrepreneurialism. Applied in government, it produces the will and energy to acquire and centralize power.[2]

In general, education in the United States is structured to provide as much opportunity as possible for as many students as possible, and thus sufficient commonality to enable mobility.[3] These goals produce policies that favor a certain amount of standardization. A teacher educated in one state should be able to teach in the others. A student completing third grade in Texas should be able to enter fourth grade in Maine. The knowledge and skills of the entering high school junior in Missouri should not be significantly different from those of a colleague in Oregon. There are many other policy forces that promote standardization. These include the success of the industrial corporation, the easy linkage of standardization to simplistic kinds of accountability, and the consistency of standardization with concepts of centralized government control valued almost universally until the end of the 20th century.

Unquestionably, local government policy in favor of music study as part of the school curriculum is a make-or-break variable for the future of K–12 music education. The century-long advance of the field has been punctuated by significant disasters and reversals. These are sufficiently known and experienced firsthand to maintain constant fear throughout the profession that support for music study is always on the verge of being withdrawn or redefined to remove substance. This fear places tremendous energy behind monitoring, attending to, and influencing government policies. In order to secure policy continuity at the local level, it is essential to maintain policy influence at the state level. Recognizing that although the states can mandate but only local school boards can fund substantially, state mandates remain important as a verifier of music education's value, both legally and promotionally.[4] Efforts at the federal level are once again removed from local decision making. Here, however, the first concern is that federal arts and arts education policies remain clear about distinctions and connections between arts experience and study of the arts disciplines (Bumgarner, 1994). The primary impact of federal policy is its influence on state and local policy. A complete removal of all federal funding for arts education would change almost nothing in the overall delivery of music education. A significant question is the extent to which this is a problem or, rather, constitutes an important insurance policy.

The obvious power of government action, as an influence on the existence and health of music education, can produce a dangerous myopia. Regular engagements with government policy at any level can obviate the time necessary to look at policy frameworks beyond government that influence music education. Some of these nongovernmental frameworks create the values and opinions from which government policy is formed. What government does at any level is important, but it is not everything. All illusions to the contrary, government cannot legislate, regulate, or produce individuals that will value either music or music study. Governments cannot legislate or regulate excellence, although they can have some impact on setting expectations for basic levels of competence. Clearly, governmental policy and action are powerful, but limited, and, in our society, increasingly mistrusted.[5]

Music education is always under enormous pressure to justify itself. However, in most cases, unless a local school board determines that music study is important enough to provide the requisite set of resources—including qualified personnel, sequential curricula, and sufficient time—all policy and rhetoric at federal, state, or even local levels will not deliver music education to students. This fact produces a continuing research and analysis question that should be asked at local, state, and national levels. What are the policy frameworks that influence local school board decisions? How much do local school board members think this question through for themselves as they make their decisions? How much difference does it make what a federal official announces, structures, or funds? What about the state level? What about ideas and slogans repeated incessantly in the echo chamber of our mass media? What about local parents and citizens? What about personal values about what counts in society, what is deemed prestigious, valuable, economically important, and so forth? Looking at the values foundation about music education operating at the most critical decision-making points, it is clear that government is one factor, and that often it is following as much as it is leading, even though it always pretends to be leading. Naturally, around Washington or a state capitol during legislative season, or in any government office, the atmosphere crackles with "we are in charge." But, in reality, to consider policy in terms of governmental decisions alone is to impose debilitating restrictions on policy work for music education. It is possible to act on the fact that governmental policy is extremely important, while building recognition of the fact that nongovernmental policy frameworks have at least equal, if not greater, influence.

electronic loan, and distance-education purposes" (Marley, 1999, p. 367). Michael Milone argues that the most important aspect of DMCA is its provision of liability limits for nonprofit educational institutions when students or staff use school computers or other devices to copy protected materials illegally (Milone, 1999). This likely will provide important protection to schools when students or faculty copy CDs and DVDs illegally. DMCA allows a plaintiff to pursue any person (student, faculty, staff) alleged to be responsible for pirating the recordings. It protects the school from legal exposure, however. It also encourages the U.S. Copyright Office to "make recommendations to Congress on how to promote distance education through digital technologies" (Milone, 1999, p. 60). Given the anxiety in some quarters of the profession about the intellectual property issues attendant to Web instruction, and so forth, this legislation demonstrates an interest, at least, on the part of Congress to manage these issues in ways that, once again, inform the common good.

The Sonny Bono Copyright Term Extension Act (SBCTEA) lengthens the term of a copyright before it passes into the public domain from life plus 50 years to life plus 70 years for works of individual authors (Marley, 1999, p. 367). It also "includes an exemption that permits libraries and other nonprofit educational institutions to treat a work in its last 20 years of protection as if it were in the public domain, for noncommercial purposes, provided that a reasonable investigation has determined the work is not subject to normal commercial exploitation" (Marley, 1999, p. 367). It also extends the duration of copyright in anonymous or pseudonymous works or "works made for hire" on or after such date to 95 years (previously 75 years) from the year of the first publication, or 120 years (previously 100 years) from the year of creation, whichever expires first. This provision for works made for hire has considerable bearing on academics, especially those working in colleges and universities.

Georgia Holmes and Daniel Levin, in an extended analysis, consider ownership/copyright questions when university professors create instructional materials as a part of their professional responsibilities (2000). The primary question, of course, is who owns these materials—the professor or the university for whom he or she works? Holmes and Levin explain that while the usual appropriation of ownership goes to the person who actually creates the work, that Section 101 of the Copyright Act of 1976 makes explicit provision for "works made for hire." Either of two conditions can satisfy the conditions necessary for a work to be so classified:

(1) a work may be prepared by an employee within the scope of his or her employment; or (2) a work specially ordered or commissioned for use as a contribution to a collective work, as a part of a motion picture or other audiovisual work as a sound recording, as a translation, as a supplementary work, as a compilation, as an instructional text, as a test, as answer material for a test, or as an atlas, *if the parties expressly agree in a written instrument signed by them that the work shall be considered a work made for hire* [italics added]. (Title 17 U.S.C. §101)

When a work is classified as "made for hire," the employer or hiring party becomes the owner of the copyright. Holmes and Levin (2000) suggest that at least three of the categories of works cited in (2) above would concern academics: instructional texts, tests, and answer material for tests. The researchers examined relevant case law and found that "All reported cases . . . have either held, or stated in dictum, that the copyright to the materials at issue in those cases belonged to the faculty member, at least in the absence of an explicit agreement to the contrary between the institution and the faculty member" (p. 186).

What then of course materials created by faculty to be placed on the Web when the university serves as the Internet Service Provider (ISP) or for distance learning applications? Here, Holmes and Levin turn to DMCA for guidance. In summary, they suggest that "unless course materials are clearly prepared as works for hire, the DMCA would seem to grant additional protection to teachers and professors in claiming ownership rights in Internet course materials and in exchange grant schools, colleges and universities immunity from liability for copyright infringement claims of professors and publishers" (Holmes & Levin, 2000, p. 184).

The third and final piece of legislative reform identified by Marley is the Fairness in Music Licensing Act, which exempts certain small businesses that use music from broadcast sources (restaurants, bars and retail stores that meet certain requirements of size, square footage, numbers of speakers and televisions, etc.) from having to pay license fees to the producers of that music (songwriters, composers, publishers, performers, and others). While there is no question that this legislation has had a dramatic impact on the question of fair use and may represent new directions the U.S. Congress will pursue in the future, it appears to have less direct bearing on the practice of the music education profession in its daily work.

Music Educators and Copyright Compliance: A Case of "Civil Disobedience"?

Much of the discussion in this chapter examines statutes and case law as a way of understanding current music education policy and recommending the best practices for compliance in light of that policy. In a recent study, Kenneth Hilliard took a different research perspective. Hilliard chose to examine how music educators respond to the law—in this case, copyright law—and more specifically the various justifications music educators use to justify photocopying music when such photocopying may infringe on copyright protections, that is, when music educators knowingly engage in willful noncompliance (Hilliard, 1998). He surveyed 600 music educators located in 20 states from the membership of MENC: The National Association for Music Education. The survey instrument sought to determine the degree to which music educators were aware of copyright prohibitions, the degree to which teachers complied with these prohibitions, and the justifications used by teachers when they willfully transgressed these prohibitions. The results were striking.

> This study concluded that although an overwhelming majority of music educators were aware of existing copyright laws and the consequences for copyright infringement, the duplication of copyrighted works on photocopying machines occurs. This study further concluded that there were many factors that influence this decision to photocopy. Among them were: fiscal constraints, student accountability for replacing lost music, and the time, cost, and frequency of photocopying. (Hilliard, 1998, abstract)

The reason this is striking is because the "consequences for copyright infringement" to which Hilliard refers at the time he conducted his study included $100,000 in fines for each copyrighted work a teacher has copied (Hilliard, 1998, p. 82). Presently, Title 17, §504 of the U.S. Code provides for maximum fines of up to $150,000. This is not an inconsequential risk tolerance within the music profession, if his research is correct and can be replicated. Hilliard proceeds then to posit the question of the moral dilemma created by the photocopy constrictions. He argues that there likely is no profit motive behind the illegal copying in which music educators indulge. Certain instructional materials simply are out of the reach of present education budgets when compliance means that every "t" is crossed and every "i" is dotted regarding the copyright laws of the United States. Perhaps in the minds of music educators, the benefits such careful compliance would produce are too meager and the educational losses such compliance would mean for students are too dear to defend present policies embedded in these statutes. This suggests the possibility that current, widespread copyright infringement practices may be an expression of civil disobedience.[6]

Of course, another explanation is that music educators are in a kind of collective denial about the risks they take as they willfully disregard copyright prohibitions about which they are reasonably well aware. They may not believe they will get caught, or believe that if caught, the outcome will be little more than a "slap of the hand." The statutory language of 17 U.S.C. §105 certainly suggests far more than a modest reprimand, however. Other explanations of this music educator behavior also come to mind. Perhaps music educators do not know how simply and

inexpensively they can secure copyright permissions, or perhaps they simply do not know where to begin such an effort. Perhaps music educators already feel too beleaguered to take the time to learn how the copyright laws can be managed effectively. In any case, the profession could benefit from replication of Hilliard's work, coupled with well-crafted studies that extend this line of inquiry.

Conspicuous Case Law of Interest to Music Educators

Space here precludes a discussion of much of the relevant copyright case law that would be of interest to music educators. Readers would do well to review the seven case summaries provided by Robert Henley Woody III and Robert Henley Woody II.[7] Of particular importance there is the last case covered, that of *Basic Books, Inc. v. Kinko's Graphics Corp.*, 758 F.Supp 1522 (S.D.N.Y. 1991). In this case, a group of eight textbook publishers sued Kinko's, a photocopy chain, for producing course packets of photocopied articles, book chapters, and other copyrighted materials at the request of college professors for use by their students in their classes. Kinko's did not pay royalties for these photocopied materials, claiming fair use protection. The court denied fair use protection to Kinko's, however, even though the materials were being used for educational purposes. Kinko's paid a settlement of nearly $2 million and then withdrew completely from the course packet preparation business (Marley, 1999). While the obvious commercial context of this case would suggest, at first glance, that it has little direct relevance to music educators in public schools, nevertheless it also seems reasonable to suspect that such a conspicuous and celebrated case will have something of a chilling effect on the disposition of academic administrators in the management of photocopying in the public school and university arenas.

The recent history of copyright litigation in music education contexts traces back nearly half a century. In *Wihtol v. Crow*, 309 F.2d 777 (8th Cir. 1962), a case older than those reported by Woody and Woody and predating the explicit provisions of fair use found in the Copyright Act of 1976, a music teacher was sued for copyright infringement after adapting a musical composition for choir use and distributing 48 copies of the adaptation to his students for use in music class.[8] Although a lower court was willing to allow the teacher's claim of fair use, this decision was reversed on appeal. The Eighth Circuit said that copying/revising all or nearly all of a copyrighted song without permission could not be construed to be fair use, regardless of the fact that it was being used in an educational context and that there was no profit intent by the teacher.

The copyright case that has received much national attention in the months immediately preceding the writing of this chapter is the case of *A & M Records, et al. v.*

Napster, Inc. (114 F.Supp. 2d 896 [2000]). Napster, the defendant in this case, was accused by 18 record companies of violating copyright protections by making possible the duplication and transmission (downloading and uploading) of copyrighted professional recordings on the Internet. Napster sought to expand the "fair use doctrine" as articulated in an earlier law suit (*Sony Corp. of America v. Universal City Studios, Inc.*, 464 U.S. 417 [1984]) to encompass the prodigious downloading of music files (MP3s) by Napster users. The court found in favor of the plaintiffs, and enjoined Napster from continuing to make possible the trading of MP3s without the expressed permission of the copyright owner. It also ordered the plaintiffs (the record companies) to post a bond of $5 million to compensate the defendant (Napster) for lost revenue in the event that the injunction would be reversed on appeal. Such appeals are ongoing at this writing.

Closing Remarks Concerning Copyright

Given the complexities and rapid expansion of copy technologies, the complexities and rapid revisions of copyright legislation, and the proliferation of copyright litigation, there are several observations about copyright research that can be made with confidence. First, this area of the law will continue to be of vital interest to the music education profession. Second, ongoing research regarding both legislative reforms and case law will be crucial if our profession hopes to remain current about this topic. Third, new research may be required that addresses the ethical tensions that exist for music educators in this area. Clearly, conflicts of interest are at work here and music educators are dealing with these tensions in ways that might rise to the standard of pseudo-"civil disobedience" *or* stoop to the level of expedience and theft *or* something in between these extremes.

Separation of Church and State: Implications for Music Educators

If copyright is the most familiar legal question for music educators, the issue of separation of church and state must be nearly as familiar. It certainly is a point of concern for all general and choral music educators. The reason, of course, relates to the issue of lyrics. General and choral educators select, rehearse, and present compositions in which the lyrics are drawn from sacred sources. Especially popular in Western art music are the scriptures of the Old and New Testaments of the Bible. The issue that has been brought before the courts pertains to this issue. Plaintiffs claim that by selecting music for obligatory study in one of these settings (general music class or school choir rehearsal), students enrolled in these courses are placed in the position of singing these sacred texts and thereby are forced to participate in state-sponsored religious activities.

The U.S. Constitution has language that expressly forbids our governments (state and local) from engaging in activities that establish religion. The First Amendment reads, in part, that "Congress shall make no law respecting an establishment of religion, or prohibiting the free exercise thereof." The phrase concerning the "establishment of religion" has been the guiding force historically in determining whether practices of schools and other public institutions have violated constitutional protections.

A brief history of the case law of this issue will help frame the most recent litigation to address these questions in federal court. The early case law concerning the Establishment Clause pertained to the public support of sectarian education, that is, of public money supporting church-sponsored private schools. The controlling case for this issue continues to be, in part, the famous 1971 case of *Lemon v. Kurtzman* (403 U.S. 602 [1971]). In this landmark U.S. Supreme Court case, plaintiffs objected to the use of Pennsylvania and Rhode Island public school dollars to pay the salaries and instructional materials costs of faculty teaching secular subjects in sectarian schools. Teachers whose salaries were paid with public funds then were restricted by statute to teach only nonreligious, secular subjects.

In the decision of this case, Chief Justice Warren Burger outlined a three-part test—now known as the "Lemon Test"—by which to determine if certain policies or statutes violate the Establishment Clause of the First Amendment:

> Every analysis in this area must begin with consideration of the cumulative criteria developed by the Court over many years. Three such tests may be gleaned from our cases. First, the statute must have a secular legislative purpose; second, its principal or primary effect must be one that neither advances nor inhibits religion; finally, the statute must not foster "an excessive government entanglement with religion." (*Lemon v. Kurtzman*, 403 U.S. 602, at 612)

The high court ruled that the laws of Pennsylvania and Rhode Island failed the third part of the Lemon Test by creating an unavoidable and "excessive government entanglement with religion" in their statutes that provide public funds to assist sectarian education in this way.

As is often the case, such a major decision rendered by our nation's highest court has an impact on subsequent decisions and shapes policies across a broad range of activities, including public education. In music education, the Lemon Test has been cited repeatedly as the guiding principle by which to determine if the programming of sacred music is a legal practice in American public schools.[9] This is so despite the fact that the study of sacred music was not at issue in the Lemon case. A more recent federal case examined the practice of programming sacred music more directly, however.

In the case of *Bauchman v. West High School* (900 F. Supp. 254 [1995]), a 15-year-old Jewish girl claimed that the Establishment Clause of the First Amendment was violated by her high school choir because of the "perceived overly Christian religious content of songs in the choir repertoire and singing of choir songs in religious venues." In addition, the plaintiff alleged that her teacher openly berated her for her objections to these practices, and that her classmates harassed her for her objections. While space here does not permit a detailed retelling of the background of this case, interested readers are encouraged to read the court opinion, which provides this background in greater detail. It provides considerable material for future study not only in terms of education law but also in terms of professional ethics standards for our profession.

The District Court ruled that the singing of choral music with sacred texts is not necessarily a violation of the Establishment Clause. In their discussion of the case, the court said that

> Singing of songs is not an "explicit religious exercise," like the graduation prayer was deemed to be by the Supreme Court in *Lee v. Weisman*, or like other prayers and singing in cases cited by plaintiff. Music has a purpose in education beyond the mere words or notes in conveying a feeling or mood, teaching culture and history, and broadening understanding of art. In this regard, A'Cappella [*sic*] singing often contains religious sentiment. Despite reference in some songs to "God" and the "Lord," as well as language in the songs reflecting a supplication to deity, the songs with religious content are not ipso facto the equivalent of prayers. Neither does the fact that the lyrical source of some songs is scriptural automatically render those songs violative of the Establishment Clause.[10]

The most recent and widely publicized U.S. Supreme Court case dealing with the Establishment Clause was a school prayer case, much like the *Lee v. Weisman* case mentioned above. In the case of *Santa Fe Independent School District v. Jane Doe* (530 U.S. 290 [2000]), the U.S. Supreme Court considered a challenge to the policy in certain Texas public schools in which "the school district had allowed students to read overtly Christian prayers at graduation ceremonies and home football games." The school district included in this policy a host of provisions that attempted to insure that students felt no obligation to participate and that the language of the prayer was ecumenical in nature.

The Supreme Court ruled this practice to be unconstitutional under the Establishment Clause. The decision was framed in the context of *Lee v. Weisman*. It reinforced the principle that formal prayer activities in school, including school-sponsored extracurricular activities, violated constitutional protections separating church and state. It is worth noting that the courts, in recent decisions, have drawn a distinction between school prayer and the study and performance of sacred music. It also is worth noting that, to date, the Supreme Court is silent on the matter of sacred music performance. In the *Bauchman* case (argued at the District Court level), the plaintiff asserted that sacred texts often are in the form of a prayer. If such texts could not be spoken in school, why then should they be sung in school? Thus far, the District Court did not find such arguments persuasive. It is clear, however, that the current Supreme Court is not willing to tolerate certain religious observances as a part of the public school experience. The music education profession, especially those members of the general and choral music education communities, will need to continue to monitor these questions as they surely will continue to be challenged in our nation's courts. The history of litigation and the Supreme Court's willingness to interpret school prayer, and so forth, as constitutionally infirm creates a climate of fear and apprehension in schools for all religious content. For extensive examinations of these issues, the reader is encouraged to consult two excellent law review discussions of this topic by Faith D. Kasparian in the *Duke Law Journal* and Lisa Ness Seidman in the *George Washington Law Review*.[11]

Tort Liability and the Music Educator

Definitions and Conditions for Tort Liability

William Hazard is credited with introducing the music education profession to the precepts of tort law. His book on the topic and his article in the *Music Educators Journal* that same year (1979a) brought national attention and focus to what had been a long overlooked and underdiscussed area of professional life. This area of the law remains somewhat less considered in the music education professional literature than other topics.

Hazard defines a tort as "a private or civil wrong (other than a breach of trust or contract) for which the law requires compensation" (Hazard, 1978, p. 594). Civil wrongs can be contrasted with criminal wrongs. In civil court, the alleged wrong is committed by one person or group against another person or group. In a crime, the alleged wrong is committed by one person or group against the state. Hence, the state is represented in criminal court by the "state's attorney." Remedies for crimes include fines and imprisonment. Remedies for libelous actions include damages (money)—both compensatory (i.e., reimbursement for losses) and punitive (i.e., payment as punishment). The most common types of tort action are misfeasance (well meaning, but libelously inept, acts) and nonfeasance (a libelous failure to act appropriately). Malfeasance (a libelous and deliberately hurtful act) is far less common in education law settings.

The American public in general became acquainted with the distinctions between criminal prosecutions and liability suits in the O. J. Simpson cases. There, Simpson was found "not guilty" of the crime of murdering his ex-wife, but "liable" for her wrongful death. The successful criminal prosecution of Simpson would have resulted in imprisonment at the very least. The successful liability action against Simpson did result in a very large monetary judgment against him.

In order for a person (plaintiff) to bring a tort liability case to court, a series of conditions must be established to the satisfaction of the court. These conditions must be met in order to sustain a tort liability grievance.

First, the plaintiff (typically the student) must show that the defendant (typically the teacher) had a "duty of care"— a responsibility to attend to the well-being—for the student. For example, a student might sue every faculty member of his or her school (a "shotgun" approach to litigation) when hurt during a school physical education class. The music teacher would ask the court to dismiss charges on the grounds that music teachers have no duty of care for students when they are participating in physical education. That duty belongs to the physical education faculty. Second, the plaintiff must show that the defendant "breached this duty of care." That is, the student must show that the teacher not only had a responsibility for the student's welfare, but failed to address that responsibility in some way. Third, the student must suffer a loss of some kind in order for tort liability to be determined. Fourth, the loss must be a direct, causal result of the breach of duty. Tort liability cannot be a product of coincidence. Fifth, it must be possible to assess a dollar value to the loss. Civil actions are subject to damages—monetary reparations for losses suffered. Finally, the courts require the plaintiff to demonstrate that the loss they suffered was "foreseeable." They must show that a normal person would have been able to anticipate the consequences of their actions or failure to act, and would have been able to avoid the loss altogether.

Illustrative Tort Liability Case Law

While there are a number of cases that illustrate issues of tort liability in the context of music teachers in the workplace, some are a bit sensational, pertaining to allegations of sexual misconduct, for example.[12] At the risk of disappointing the reader, those will be tabled for another discussion. It makes more sense to me to examine sample cases in which the most ordinary of circumstances surface suddenly in such a way as to lead to tort litigation. Two such cases are summarized below.

In the case of *Christopher (Chris) Albers v. Community*

Consolidated (155 Ill. App. 3d 1083 [1987]), the Appellate Court of Illinois, Fifth District, considered an appeal from a student challenging a jury verdict in favor of the defendant school and defendant teacher in a tort liability action. The original claim was based on severe injuries the student suffered from physical aggression by a fellow student when his music teacher was absent from the room. It seems that the music class of fourth-grade students had just completed rehearsal for the annual Christmas program in the gymnasium. The music teacher dismissed the class, telling the students to get a drink, use the washroom, and then return to the music classroom. The teacher positioned herself halfway between the washrooms and the classroom in an effort to give the best supervision possible under the circumstances. The plaintiff testified that when he returned to the classroom, the boys and girls were on opposite sides of the room. One member of the class, another boy, was standing in front of the girls. When the plaintiff approached him, the boy hit him. The boy testified, however, that the plaintiff had had a piece of aluminum foil that he had thrown at another student. This other student picked up the foil and then began to chase the plaintiff. The plaintiff tripped and was hit in the eye by the first boy's pencil. The plaintiff eventually lost all sight in the injured eye.

The plaintiff and his parents sought tort liability relief, suggesting that the absence of the teacher from the room constituted "wilful and wanton misconduct" by the teacher. In Illinois at that time, "wilful and wanton misconduct" was the necessary standard of law required for the appellate court to reverse the decision of the trial court. Otherwise, Illinois law declared school officials and school districts to be immune from tort liability for personal injuries that students sustain during school activities.

In their decision, the court ruled that "To impose liability upon defendants, plaintiff must show . . . that when defendants acted, or failed to act, it was with knowledge that such conduct posed a high probability of serious physical harm to others." The court ruled that the plaintiff failed to do this. The court therefore affirmed the decision of the trial court and sided with the defendant.

In a more recent case, a plaintiff (fifth-grade girl) sued her music teacher, her school district, the individual members of the school board, the principal of the school, and the town in which the school district was located for injuries she suffered at school.[13] The plaintiff and several of her classmates were asked by the music teacher to assist him in moving an upright piano. In the course of the move, the piano fell off of the dolly on which it was riding and the plaintiff's knee was hurt.

In her suit, the plaintiff alleged that the teacher

failed to properly supervise his students; he failed to instruct or warn Ashley (the plaintiff) of the hazards of moving the piano; he inappropriately requested Ashley's assistance in conducting a dangerous activity; he failed to issue a policy regarding moving the piano; and he failed to organize the activity in a safe manner. (*Ashley Grimes, et al. v. Steven Houser, et al.*, per n. 13)

The plaintiff alleged that the principal was liable for all of these failures as well, and also that he was negligent in maintaining school equipment as required by Connecticut law.

The final disposition of this appeal is unknown (see note 13), but the language of the court opinion suggests that the complaints against the town, the school district, and the board members were dismissed by the court. The language of the opinion left open the door for further action with regard to the music teacher and the principal, however. Connecticut law required that the court determine if the duties of care of the teacher and the principal were, in this case, "discretionary" or "ministerial." Because that was not possible at the time of this decision, the summary judgment requested of the court by the teacher and the principal was denied.

Other Law Research Topics Relating to Music Education

Music Education and Equal Educational Opportunity

Because public education is a responsibility of the state, it has come under legal scrutiny in the light of the "Equal Protection Clause" found in the Fourteenth Amendment to the U.S. Constitution. This Amendment reads, in part, "No state shall . . . deprive any person of life, liberty, or property, without due process of law; nor deny to any person within its jurisdiction the equal protection of the laws." This provision for equal protection is relevant to public education policies precisely because public education is a function of state government. Therefore, gross disparities in the provision of education have been challenged in the courts (both federal and state), alleging that such gross disparities are a violation of equal protection.[14]

The controlling case from the federal perspective on this matter is a 1973 United States Supreme Court case, *San Antonio Independent School District v. Rodriguez* (411 U.S. 1 [1973]). In this case, the plaintiffs challenged the public education funding scheme in Texas, which permitted gross disparities in per pupil funding between districts within the state. The Court held that such disparities do not offend the U.S. Constitution because education is not a fundamental right for the purposes of constitutional law. The U.S. Constitution makes no mention of education anywhere in the document.

Subsequent litigation continues to challenge the gross disparities in education funding by applying the logic of the *Rodriguez* decision in the context of state constitutional law. In this sense, then, the state as the locus of education policy evolution has become even more crucial. This state-based argument goes like this: Although the U.S. Constitution makes no explicit provision for public education, all state constitutions do make explicit provision for the education of all resident children at the public expense. All state constitutions also have language that parallels the sentiments of the Equal Protection Clause found in the U.S. Constitution. Therefore, although education is not a fundamental right under the terms of the U.S. Constitution, it is a fundamental right under the provisions of the state constitution. The grossly disparate provision of educational opportunities to children living in different districts within the state, as manifested in grossly differences in per-pupil spending, constitutes a violation of the equal protection provisions found within the state constitutions. Thus, gross disparities in intrastate, interdistrict public school funding are unconstitutional. This argument is known as the *Rodriguez Syllogism* (*Fair School Finance Council of Oklahoma, Inc. v. State*, 746 P.2d at 1148 [1987]). Seventeen of 43 such challenges to state education financing schemes, argued in the state's highest court, have invalidated such disparities by way of this argument and related arguments (Swenson, 2000). Twenty-six upheld the school funding scheme, however. "Their reasoning has varied, but typically includes notions that school finance policy is best left to state legislatures or to local prerogative" (Swenson, 2000).

Most challenges to public education policy of this sort have challenged the per-pupil spending as a violation of equal protection. Not all cases have approached the problem in this way, or solely in this way, however. Some court decisions have mentioned not only spending but also the impact on curriculum as a symptom of constitutionally infirm policy (*Pauley v. Kelly*, 255 S.E. 2d 859 [1979]). I examined these issues at some length in my doctoral dissertation, and published a shorter, article-length summary of these issues, as well.[15] What is interesting to me in the evolution of this case law is that there is language in legal opinions available to plaintiffs and their attorneys by which to make the case for a challenge to gross disparities between districts within a state as manifest in gross disparities in arts curricular offerings. When one district elects to remove the arts completely from the curriculum while a neighboring district within the same state provides robust instruction in the arts, such removal of the arts by the first school district may be challengeable by way of *Rodriguez*-type arguments. Clearly, it remains a question worth pursuing in the future.

Court Challenges Regarding the Music Curriculum

Curriculum, including music curriculum, is not immune from litigation challenges. In fact, the history of music curriculum litigation is nearly as old as the history of public school music itself. As reported in the opening paragraph of this chapter, the first lawsuit addressing music education issues directly was argued and decided in 1876 and pertained to the provision of music as curriculum in the public schools of Iowa. In this case, the plaintiff (parent) challenged the right of a school district to use public funds to hire a music teacher, something of which he clearly did not approve. The court found in favor of the school district (Boyles, 1981). A few years later, a father in another state challenged certain required school music activities for his son. The son refused to participate in these required activities and was expelled. The father sued. The court upheld the expulsion, declaring that, "absent a sufficient excuse," the school had "discretionary power conferred by law."[16] By 1909, however, the court ruled in an Oklahoma case that a parent had the right to have their child excluded from required school singing lessons, declaring that "the right of the parent . . . is superior to that of the school."[17]

Not all cases are argued in the legal (or curricular) context in which they come to have importance. One need think back only to the now infamous U.S. Supreme Court case of *Plessy v. Ferguson*—in which the high court approved of racially "separate but equal" railway cars, thereby giving those disposed to maintain racially segregated schools the legal "shelter" by which to do so—to appreciate the legal symbiosis in which we live in the United States (163 U.S. 537 [1896]). So it is with cases having great importance to music curriculum. While some important cases have been argued specifically in the context of music education policy and practice, there are several important cases pertaining to curriculum which affect music education, although they have been argued in other contexts.[18] Space permits the discussion here of only one such case.

In the case of *Hazelwood School District, et al. v. Kuhlmeier, et al.* (484 U.S. 260 [1988]), the U.S. Supreme Court upheld a decision by a St. Louis–area high school to censor certain content in the high school newspaper. In rendering this verdict, the U.S. Supreme Court outlined a set of legal principles by which to guide lower courts and inform school officers interested in the policy implications of their decision. In this regard, it is an approach not unlike the approach in the *Lemon* case. In the *Hazelwood* case, the high court outlined the following four legal principles:

(a) First Amendment rights of students in the public schools are not automatically coextensive with the rights of adults in other settings, and must be applied in light of the special characteristics of the school environment.

(b) The school newspaper here cannot be characterized as a forum for public expression . . . and school officials may impose reasonable restrictions on the speech of students, teachers, and other members of the school community.

(c) The standard for determining when a school may punish student expression that happens to occur on school premises is not the standard for determining when a school may refuse to lend its name and resources to the dissemination of student expression (*Tinger v. Des Moines Independent Community School Dist.*, 393 U.S. 503, distinguished). Educators do not offend the First Amendment by exercising editorial control over the style and content of student speech in school-sponsored expressive activities so long as their actions are reasonably related to legitimate pedagogical concern.

(d) The school principal acted reasonably in this case in requiring the deletion of the pregnancy article, the divorce article, and the other articles that were to appear on the same pages of the newspaper.[19]

In elaborating on the intentions of item (c) above, Justice White said that

a school may in its capacity as publisher of a school newspaper or producer of a school play "disassociate itself" (*Fraser*, 478 U.S., at 685) not only from speech that would "substantially interfere with (its) work . . . or impinge upon the rights of other students" (*Tinker*, 393 U.S., at 509), but also from speech that is, for example, ungrammatical, poorly written, inadequately researched, *biased or prejudiced, vulgar or profane, or unsuitable for immature audiences* [italics added]. (*Hazelwood v. Kuhlmeier*, 484 U.S. 271 [1988])

The emphasized text at the end of this quote underscores the broad latitude that the high court conferred on school officers when it rendered this verdict. First Amendment protections seem to be largely curtailed for school students if school officers may suppress speech that is alleged to be "unsuitable for immature audiences." This seems on its face to be an enormously promiscuous legal standard that offers students little recourse when they sense a need to challenge what they believe to be unwarranted censorship. Nor is it difficult to apprehend the immediate implications for school music programs. Choral educators who choose to study and present to the public certain selected choruses from Orff's *Carmina Burana* could easily find their concerts canceled and their job security compromised when a principal or superintendent (or parent or local journalist) reads the text translations of this secular oratorio. Elementary music educators could find their lesson plans that call for a field trip experience to see and hear a performance of Mozart's *Marriage of Figaro* challenged. Such suggestions would have been silly and comical before the 1988 *Hazelwood* decision. Education law scholars do not find them so comical now.

Indeed, the many controversies about publicly sponsored "vulgar" art (consider the Robert Mapplethorpe sensation) have fueled the fires of artistic censorship. Regardless of the reader's point of view about these matters, it is clear that administrative discretion and power expanded with the *Hazelwood* case, and the implications of this expansion are profoundly relevant for our work.

Closing Remarks and Implications for Future Research

A number of areas of education law and music education law remain unreported in this chapter. It simply is not possible to address, even briefly, the rich array of issues important to our profession in anything short of a book-length narrative. In fact, such a book would be prodigious, to be sure. Instead, this chapter has focused largely on familiar law topics, with an interest in providing updates and exploring new issues. There is nothing remotely comprehensive about this chapter.

Clearly, however, there is important research that needs to be done in this field, even among these familiar areas. The laws change daily, as do the interpretations of their meanings by our nation's courts. Principles of law evolve rapidly. Our recent U.S. presidential election experience taught us that, if nothing else. The ongoing vigilance of music education scholars is required to help the profession understand its obligations and opportunities. Understanding is necessary, but insufficient, if our profession aspires to function at its potential. Hilliard's study of copyright law compliance shows this. Something may be "going on" within the music education community in the area of copyright law, but many subsequent studies will be required to understand the range of implications here. As the technological means by which to copy and broadcast become ever more available (democratized), so do the opportunities by which to comply or violate the protections we have developed to encourage intellectual property.

Fresh topics are required in our work, as well. We do not know as much as we need to know about the legal implications of providing music instruction in schools for special-needs students. Interesting dissertation studies have helped us begin this work of addressing the "street-level" needs of music educator compliance with PL 94-142 (the Education for All Handicapped Children Act of 1975), for example.[20] What happens when parents of handicapped students challenge the audition procedures of local music educators, especially if these procedures effectively predict the systematic exclusion of their children? We know, for example, that normal children and their parents have challenged youth orchestra audition procedures in court (*Tse-Ming Cheung, M.D. v. Youth Orchestra Foundation of Buffalo, Inc., et al.*, 906 F.2d 59 [1990]). What does this case law imply, if anything, about the claims of special-needs students?

Finally, are the courts a domain for aggressive, proactive, arts education policy advancement? Is it reasonable to speculate about the ways in which the place of arts in the schools might be strengthened by litigious activism? Can strategies like the *Rodriguez Syllogism* play a role in such efforts in our state courts? Is there reason to speculate on the influence such litigation might have in influencing the behavior of state legislators? Might they be inclined to draft legislation designed to anticipate and manage such court claims, fearful that jurists will prescribe remedies more extreme than what might otherwise be politically viable and affordable?

Our work has barely begun. It is clear, however, that it is work worth doing. Our policy functions are incomplete at best, and highly exposed at worst, without it.

NOTES

1. For examples, see Aquino (1976); Grier (1979, 1984, 1996). There are a number of articles of this sort also available in the general education literature.

2. It is somewhat ironic to note that education is not situated as a federal governmental issue, inasmuch as a national election in the United States was ongoing at the time of this writing, and many candidates for national office were making education one of the spotlighted issues about which they frequently speak and make recommendations.

3. U.S. Copyright Office, *Copyright Basics (Circular 1)*. [Online] Rev. May 2000. Available: http://www.loc.gov/copyright/circs/cirs1.html [November 28, 2000]. The reader should note that the entire text of the *Copyright Law of the United States of America and Related Laws Contained in Title 17 of the United States Code* is available on the Internet at http://www.loc.gov/copyright/title 17/ [November 30, 2000]. These provisions can be found in §106 of that law.

4. Developed and approved by the Music Publishers' Association of the United States, Inc., the National Music Publishers' Association, Inc., the Music Teachers National Association, the Music Educators National Conference, the National Association of Schools of Music, and the Ad Hoc Committee on Copyright Law Revision, *Guidelines for Educational Uses of Music* [On-line] Rev. April 1976. Available: http://www.musiclibraryassoc.org/Copyright/guidemus.htm [November 30, 2000]; see also Ad Hoc Committee on Copyright Law Revision (by Sheldon Elliott Steinbach), Author-Publisher Group and Authors League of America (by Irwin Karp, Counsel), and Association of American Publishers, Inc. (by Alexander C. Hoffman, Chairman, Copyright Committee), *Agreement on Guidelines for Classroom Copying in Not-for-Profit Educational Institutions with Respect to Books and Periodicals* [On-line] Rev. March 19, 1976. Available: http://

www.musiclibraryassoc.org/Copyright/guidebks.htm [December 4, 2000].

5. To contact the Harry Fox Agency, write or call: NMPA/HFA, 711 Third Avenue, New York, NY 10017; Tel: 212-370-5330, Fax: 212-953-2384.

6. Readers may want to revisit the tenets of Thoreau's classic essay, "Civil Disobedience." See Thoreau (1966).

7. Woody and Woody (1994). These cases include *Basic Books, Inc. v. Kinko's Graphics Corp.*, 758 F.Supp. 1522 (S.D.N.Y. 1991); *Bright Tunes Music Corp. v. Harrison Music Ltd.*, 420 F.Supp. 177 (1976); *Encyclopaedia Brittanica Educational Corp. v. Crooks*, 542 F.Supp. 1156 (W.D.N.Y. 1982), and 558 F.Supp. 1246 (W.D.N.Y. 1983); *Gaste v. Kaiserman*, 863 F.2d 1061 (2d Cir. 1988); *Krofft Television Productions, Inc. v. McDonald's Corp.*, 562 F.2d 1157 (9th Circ. 1977); *Marcus v. Rowley*, 695 F.2d 1171 (9th Cir. 1983); *Selle v. Gibb*, 567 F.Supp. 1173 (N.D. Ill. 1983), *Aff'd*, 741 F.2d 896 (7th Cir. 1984). As a matter of historical interest, readers also might wish to examine *Wihtol v. Crow*, 309 F.2d 777 (8th Cir. 1962).

8. As reported in Bartow (1998).

9. See, for example, "Religious Music in the Schools." *Music Educators Journal* 83 (Nov. 1996), supp. 1–4. This article outlines the provisions of the Lemon Test generally, and also refers to the Bauchman case.

10. *Bauchman v. West High School*, 900 F.Supp. 254 (1995). *Lee v. Weisman*, 505 U.S. 577 (1992) refers to the case in which the U.S. Supreme Court ruled unconstitutional the practice of Providence, RI, policy of inviting a member of the local clergy to provide an invocation and benediction at the schools' graduation ceremonies.

11. Kasparian (1997); Seidman (1997). It is notable that both of these fine essays were published in the same month.

12. See, for example, *Sharon Ominski v. Dung Ba Tran*, 1997 U.S. Dist. LEXIS 13177 (1997).

13. *Ashley Grimes, et al. v. Steven Houser, et al.*, 1993 Conn. Super. LEXIS 2107 (1993). Lexis/Nexis reports in the record of this decision that "This decision is unreported and may be subject to further appellate review. Counsel is cautioned to make an independent determination of the status of this case." That was not possible at this writing.

14. For one of the more influential studies of this issue, see Wise (1968); for a recent update on the progress nationally to equalize public education funding, see *School Finance [microform]: State Efforts to Equalize Funding Between Wealthy and Poor School Districts: Report to Congressional Requesters* (1998).

15. Richmond (1990). For a shorter treatment of these issues, see also Richmond (1992).

16. Boyles (1981), 47; citing *State ex rel. Andrews v. Webber*, 108 ind. 31, 8 NE 708 (1886).

17. Boyles (1981), 48; citing *School Board District No. 18 v. Thompson*, 24 Okla. 1, 103 Pac. 578 (1909).

18. For an extended treatment of this subject, see Richmond (1994).

19. Richmond (1994), citing Hazelwood at "Syllabus."

20. For examples, see Sheridan (1979); Nelson (1980); and Brown (1981).

REFERENCES

Aquino, J. (1976). Can we still sing Christmas carols in public schools? *Music Educators Journal, 63*(3), 70–73.

Bartow, A. (1998). Educational fair use in copyright: Reclaiming the right to photocopy freely. *U. Pitt. L. Rev., 60,* 149.

Boyles, N. B. (1981). *The legal aspects of the public school academic curriculum.* Unpublished Ed.D. dissertation, University of North Carolina at Greensboro.

Brown, M. C. (1981). *Problems in mainstreaming programs in the Los Angeles Unified School District as perceived by junior high school music teachers.* Unpublished M.A. dissertation, University of Southern California.

Grier, R. (1979). Sacred music in the schools: An update. *Music Educators Journal, 66*(3), 48–51.

Grier, R. (1984). Religious music in the schools. *Music Educators Journal, 71*(3), 28–30.

Grier, R. (1996). Religious music in the schools. *Music Educators Journal, 83*(3), s1–s4.

Hazard, W. R. (1978). *Education and the law: Cases and materials on public schools,* 2nd ed. New York: The Free Press.

Hazard, W. R. (1979a). A tort is not a piece of cake: Teachers' legal responsibilities. *Music Educators Journal, 65*(8), 26–33, 62–65.

Hazard, W. R. (1979b). *Tort liability and the music educator.* Reston, VA: Music Educators National Conference.

Hilliard, K. B. (1998). *Music copyright laws: Implications for music educators.* Unpublished Ed.D. dissertation, Teacher's College, Columbia University.

Holmes, G., & Levin, D. A. (2000). Who owns course materials prepared by a teacher or professor? The application of copyright law to teaching materials in the Internet age. *BYU Educ. & L.J.,* 165.

Kasparian, F. D. (1997). The constitutionality of teaching and performing sacred choral music in public schools. *Duke Law Journal, 46,* 1111.

Marley, J. L. (1999). Guideline favoring fair use: An analysis of legal interpretations affecting higher education. *Journal of Academic Librarianship, 25*(5), 367–371.

Milone, M. (1999). Digital millennium act revises copyright legislation. *Technology & Learning, 19*(6), 60.

Nelson, B. M. (1980). *Music educators' attitudes toward interaction with specific handicapped students in compliance with public law 94–142.* Unpublished M.M. thesis, Michigan State University.

Richmond, J. W. (1992). Arts education as equal educational opportunity: The legal issues. *Journal of Research in Music Education, 40,* 236–52.

Richmond, J. W. (1990). *Equal opportunity for aesthetic development: The arts, the schools, and the law.* Unpublished Ph.D. dissertation, Northwestern University.

Richmond, J. W. (1994). The litigation engine: Influence and control of K–12 arts education policy. *Arts Education Policy Review, 95,* 31–37.

School finance [microform]: State efforts to equalize funding between wealthy and poor school districts: Report to congressional requesters. (1998). Washington, DC: United States General Accounting Office.

Seidman, L. N. (1997). Religious music in the public schools: Music to establishment clause ears? *Geo. Wash. L. Rev., 65,* 406.

Sheridan, W. F. (1979). Public Law 94–142 and the development of the Oregon plan for mainstreaming in music. Unpublished Ph.D. dissertation, University of Oregon.

Statutory royalty rates effective January 1, 2000. (2000). [Online] Rev. Dec. 19, 2000. Available: http://www.nmpa.org/hfa/ratecurrent.html [Dec. 19, 2000].

Swenson, K. (2000). School finance reform litigation: Why are some state supreme courts activists and others restrained? *Alb. L. Rev., 63,* 1147.

Thoreau, H. D. (1966). *Walden, and civil disobedience: Authoritative texts, background, reviews, and essays in criticism.* Ed. O. Thomas. New York: W. W. Norton.

van Geel, T. (1987). *The courts and American education law.* Buffalo, NY: Prometheus Books.

Wise, A. E. (1968). *Rich schools, poor schools: The promise of equal educational opportunity.* Chicago: University of Chicago Press.

Woody, III, R. H., & Woody, II, R. H. (1994). *Music copyright law in education.* No. 368 of the Phi Delta Kappan FASTBACK Series. Bloomington, IN: Phi Delta Kappa Education Foundation.

5

Philosophical Issues in Curriculum

ESTELLE R. JORGENSEN

What is meant by the word "curriculum"?[1] Conceptual problems abound where clarification is lacking and it is not surprising to see the curriculum field described as "moribund" and "fraudulent."[2] In addressing this question, rather than attempt an exhaustive survey of this terrain and drawing on representative literature along the way I sketch a conceptual map of ways of thinking about curriculum generically.[3] My objective is to show that the concept of curriculum needs to be clarified, describe ways in which it can be envisaged, and suggest that such clarification can result in sharpening the focus of music teaching and learning research and practice.

The outline of images that follows is not intended to be exhaustive but provides a framework for and exemplifies a useful approach to conceptualizing curriculum that can be expanded on or modified in subsequent research in music education. I move beyond William Schubert's trilogy of historical curricular paradigms—the theoretical, practical, and reconceptualist—to formulate my own list of "images" of curriculum described with reference to examples from music education. These images are curriculum as instructional content, system, process, realm of meaning, and discourse. Each curricular image contributes to our understanding, yet is limited or flawed in one way or another. None suffices as the ultimate, only, or best way of conceiving of curriculum. I conclude this chapter with brief remarks on the implications of this analysis for research and practice in music teaching and learning.[4]

Conceptualizing Curriculum

The word "curriculum" is used variously as noun, verb ("currere"), adjective ("curricular"), in the singular or plural ("curriculum" or "curricula"), in the abstract or phenomenal sense (as "anticipated" or "resultant" curriculum,

respectively), descriptively and prescriptively, and literally and figuratively. So first one has to be clear in which particular sense the word is being used in this given instance.[5] For example, does it refer to the doing of curriculum as a practical process or activity or to an "essence" or product somehow separate from the practitioner? Is this notion of curriculum contingent on some other conception be it "content" as in the phrase "curricular content," "evaluation" as in the phrase "curricular evaluation," or "instruction" as in the phrase "curricular instruction"? Is it construed as a conceptually independent entity or variable, where content, instruction, curriculum, and evaluation are conceived to be mutually exclusive?

When one concept is dependent on another in order for the distinction to be made, if differences between the concepts have not been clearly articulated in the first place, they dissolve when the analysis is pressed backward. Even when a clean theoretical distinction can be made between what curriculum is and what it is not, distinctions are sometimes difficult to maintain because of the practical interrelatedness of aspects of education. Take, for example, the words "curriculum and instruction," which often are spoken more or less in the same breath because of their interconnectedness in educational thought and practice. If one is going to get to the bottom of curriculum and instruction, it will be necessary to clarify the differences between them and determine the specific respects in which curriculum differs from instruction, evaluation, or any of the other attributes with which it is often associated by educators. Even though Ralph Tyler dodges this conceptual problem in his foray into curricular and instructional theory, his analysis has not prompted a subsequent and concerted philosophical attempt to clarify exactly where curriculum ends and instruction begins or vice versa.[6]

Ambiguity arises when curriculum is viewed as a "weak syndrome" in which one concept overlaps, gradually melds, or phases into another between two theoretically extreme positions.[7] Assuming that curriculum is a weak syndrome seems justified, practically speaking, because the various elements of education—curriculum, instruction, evaluation, teaching, learning, and administration—seem interconnected to those involved in its work. Allowing for fuzzy boundaries and ambiguity may be desirable, because it presumes and fosters intuitive and imaginative thought. However, one of the purposes of philosophical analysis is to examine and clarify concepts, observe important discontinuities, and make fine distinctions where possible. If the achievements of a particular study are to be clearly shown, the philosopher and empirical researcher of curriculum are duty bound to clarify the specific nature of the object under study. Suppose curriculum and instruction are considered to be weak syndromes, that is, it is difficult to say exactly where curriculum ends and instruction begins, or vice versa, and a researcher studies a particular curriculum. It is fair to ask if she or he has clarified the concept sufficiently or distinguished between curriculum and instruction so that the reader may conclude with reasonable confidence that this is indeed a study of curriculum and not instruction or something else. In the absence of this distinction, a reader may be unsure what specific entity is under study, because the characteristic differences have not been clearly drawn. For example, suppose one analyzes three empirical studies relating to the general area of curriculum and instruction with the object of comparing them. If one study seems to focus on curriculum, another seems to apply to instruction, and still another seems to concern both curriculum and instruction, the validity of these studies may be questioned because their specific objects are unclear. Although some ambiguity is likely, practically speaking, the researcher still needs to carefully distinguish between the things under study insofar as possible.

Curriculum is grounded on philosophical assumptions about the purposes and methods of education. As such, it relates fundamentally to educational values and is justified philosophically rather than verified or refuted scientifically (Scheffler, 1973). Many music curricula focus on instructional approaches and frameworks that are often presented with little justification, or justified on experiential and practical rather than systematic and logical grounds. For example, the *National Standards for Arts Education* (modeled on earlier formulations such as *The School Music Program* [1974, 1986]) are justified briefly with reference to "commonplaces." Among those that are justified more extensively, one thinks of Émile Jaques-Dalcroze's defense of "rhythmique gymnastique" (later termed "eurhythmics") (1976), Percy Scholes's defense of music appreciation (1935), Bennett Reimer's defense of comprehensive arts programs and aesthetic education (1978), Thomas Regelski's defense of an action learning approach to the secondary school general music curriculum (1981), and Patricia Shehan Campbell's (1991), Susan Wolf's (1996), and Therese Volk's (1998) defenses of multicultural approaches to music education.

Music teachers sometimes disagree strongly about the underlying values of music instruction, for example, the appropriate role of popular music in the school music curriculum, specific objectives or methods of musical instruction, or various aesthetics and their associated values. In such cases, there may be a tendency to think that value difficulties will dissipate if one can draw music and curriculum sufficiently broadly or inclusively. If there is room for many points of view, one does not have to negotiate values in tension if not outright conflict but can simply sidestep them by choosing those with which one agrees. This view is flawed, because greater inclusiveness renders a curriculum even more problematic than one that is narrow. In the case of the broader curriculum, many more things can conflict, blunt, prevent, and undermine other aspects, and many more possibilities need to be considered in coming to a decision about what to do in practice. Discussing and taking into account the many differences and conflicts in value systems becomes even more crucial in building a solid foundation for a broader curriculum than in a narrower one. Rather than solving the problem of what values are to underlie it and how these are to be negotiated, a broader curriculum makes the work of music education even more difficult to justify and practice.

Seeing that it straddles the theoretical and phenomenal worlds of philosophical assumption and practical realization, curriculum is inherently dialectical, in the sense of some conceptions, elements or aspects being in tension or conflict with others.[8] As a practical entity, it expresses the philosophical assumptions of its maker(s) much as an art work expresses the ideas and feelings of its creator(s) and performer(s). It refers both to the shape of things hoped for and those that come to pass. Embodying the assumptions that comprise it, practically speaking, one cannot separate the curriculum from the assumptions that ground it any more than one might separate the work of art from its meanings to composer, performer, and listener alike. Tying together theory and practice is also more problematical than is commonly supposed, because the worlds of practice and theory are discontinuous. Although they overlap, there is not a one-to-one correspondence between them (Scheffler, 1973). As a result, a theory can be realized in several different practices just as a practice may follow from any one of several different assumptive sets.[9] So an investigator needs take into account this dialectic between theory and practice—two elements in tension with each other and for which there is no easy solution. For example, the desired or intended curriculum is distinct from yet interrelated with the actual or resultant curriculum (Jorgensen, 1988). A nest of other dialectics also emerges, including the dynamic and static qualities of curriculum, its processual and product orientation, claims on intellect and feeling, subjective and objective qualities, descriptive and normative properties, and conservative and transformative purposes. And these dialectics reinforce an already ambiguous construct, thereby complicating and problematizing the idea/practice of curriculum.

Another and also interrelated matter is the level of generality at which the notion of curriculum is cast. The descriptor "curriculum" is typically used at various levels of integrative analysis or causation. It may be construed psychologically, institutionally, culturally, or historically, to depict a particular lesson, course of study, program, or a generalization covering an array of instances that more or less exemplify certain characteristic features.[10] For example, one might describe a Suzuki curriculum with regard to a particular lesson or segment of lesson taught by a particular exponent, an overall course of study for this student devised by this teacher, or a generalization of what different exponents of the approach tend to do over an extended period of time. On this continuum between micro- and macro-level conceptions or increasing levels of generalization, one might plot instances of curriculum. It is therefore important for the researcher to specify where this particular instance of curriculum falls within the range of levels of generality in order to avoid the fallacy of equating conceptions of curriculum at differing levels of generality. And, for this reason, it may be important to make some distinctions between the terms curriculum, program, and lesson plan.

With these preliminary points in mind, what are some of the images of curriculum, and what are their respective contributions and detractions? After sketching each of the images in turn and showing that all have something to offer and are limited in one way or another, I suggest that they are all in dialectic or tension one with another. In order to ground the analysis, each image is illustrated by several music curricula. This approach is challenging for at least four reasons. First, there are notable differences among the ideas of proponents of each image and a danger in reductionistic thinking, that is, ascribing greater coherence in the viewpoint than is warranted. Second, there is the inherent ambiguity of theory and practice and a danger of confusing the two. For this reason, only some of the prominent features of each image are sketched, and it should not be assumed that writers cited in regard to particular points would agree with every aspect described. Third, the examples associated with each image are intended only to suggest prominent aspects or emphases in curricula as I see them, and may invoke other images as well. Images may intersect and overlap. Seeing that each image potentially spawns an array of different interpretations and music curricula supports the already observed ambiguity of theory and practice and serves to caution against reductive thinking that would underestimate the

variety and diversity of curricula associated with a particular curricular image. And, fourth, it is important to be wary of drawing too simplistic a conclusion that the more images invoked in any particular curriculum the better, there is no "middle way" that avoids extreme positions, or the ideal solution is simply to combine uncritically this image with that. On the contrary, some curricula may draw mainly from one or a few images, and can do so with integrity, and it is not always easy to find the appropriate overlaps, correspondences, and continuities between multiple images. Rather, my point is to show that all of the following curricular images are provocative and helpful, flawed and limited in one way or another. And they should not be foreclosed prematurely without considering how they illumine a particular set of circumstances.

Curriculum as Instructional Content

Traditionally, curriculum refers to the subject matter or content of instruction, that is, what is taught by teachers, or the raison d'être and focus of the student and teacher pedagogical interaction. This is the notion of curriculum generally employed in state and professional guidelines concerning what should be taught, published course catalogs and descriptions, and the like. Here, the teacher's function is to transmit the wisdom of the past, that is, those beliefs, values, mores, and practices valued personally or by the institution responsible for education. Content, in this view, can be systematically described in terms of particular ideas and practices and one can distinguish between the body of knowledge to be communicated and the means whereby it is transmitted to others; or, the content of a subject is regarded as distinct from the manner of its presentation. Not only is the focus on instructional content contingent on the notion of instruction but there is the additional implicit assumption that subject matter is something "out there," objectified and separate from the human experience of it. As such, it can be rationalized as a logical system of tightly articulated abstract propositions or concepts that are or should be taught and learned and it can be generalized to describe courses or programs of study.

The notion of instruction is particularly interesting. Vernon Howard (1992) is at pains to distinguish between instructions given by teachers that are often specific, procedural, and technical, and instruction signifying more generally what the teacher seeks to pass on to the student. In contrast to Howard's notion of instruction having primarily to do with what teachers do, my own view of instruction is more dialectical and interactive in that it necessitates an interaction between teacher and student in situations where knowledge is being transmitted and transformed (Jorgensen, 1980). Such an interactive definition enables me to more clearly distinguish the terms *teaching* and *learning* from instruction, and to apply the term *instruction* in a more systematic and rigorous way. Instruction is inherently ambiguous, however, because music teaching and learning are also informal in that they occur in situations that are not explicitly or intentionally pedagogical but are serendipitous and happen within the frameworks and rituals of ordinary life. This being the case, it is often difficult in practice to define the limits of instruction as that which is formal or intentionally pedagogical.

Of course, purposeful instruction enables the communication of certain knowledge that is procedural as well as propositional,[11] and curriculum conceived as the subject matter of instruction focuses on that knowledge. As it goes to the heart of what goes on in the instructional process, such a focus prompts the teacher and student to defend the nature of the subject matter, in this case, music and its specific claims in general and professional music education. Regarding musical subject matter within the social context of music instruction enables one to see it contextually, situated with regard to particular assumptions about musical beliefs and practices. This wisdom is forged within communities that David Elliott (1995) describes as "music practices," I (1997a) denote as "spheres of musical validity," and Christopher Small (1998) describes as social rituals, each of which is understood in terms of a particular aesthetic perspective.[12] The differing aesthetic systems underlying or accompanying these musics help to explain why various beliefs are held and the particular meanings that musics have for their exponents and publics. Allowing an overlap between aims and methods of music education,[13] where the subject matter and method of or approach to its presentation are construed as a weak syndrome, blurs the lines between curriculum and instruction. It also enables curriculum to be conceived dynamically in terms of the sorts of dialectics already alluded to.

On the other side of the coin, it is tempting to view curriculum conceived as content or subject matter as a static body of knowledge, periodically updated when educational reform occurs or students do poorly on standardized tests. In this view, the curriculum becomes the object of study and the subject (student or teacher) is distanced (even alienated) from it. This view presumes that certain knowledge is universally acknowledged as worthy of study, privileged, and tested through time. Not only is this wisdom fixed but it presents a stock of knowledge independent of the knower. As such, it polarizes the knower and the known, the subject and the experience of it—a state of affairs that constitutes a false dichotomy. It takes insufficient account of the powerful cultural, social, and psychological forces in the construction of knowledge. As well, seeing that the subject is articulated rationally, logical thought is privileged over intuition, imagination, and feeling, implying yet another false dichotomy between intellect and emotion. In its emphasis on formal and didactic instruction over the informal and serendipitous activities that typically comprise a part of the educational program construed broadly, it downplays the latter as peripheral to the purposes and ends of music education. This artificial separation of curriculum as instructional content from assessment, teaching, learning, instruction, and administration fails to emphasize sufficiently that curriculum is at best a weak syndrome. The precise distinctions between these elements are impossible to sustain in the phenomenal world. It is difficult to separate the subject matter from the manner of its presentation, especially since the medium constitutes the message (at least in part). Also, in taking this view, one is apt to be speaking about an inherently ambiguous content or subject matter in which the articulation proceeds more or less contemporaneously at different levels of generality. One may refer either to the broad program of educational studies, a particular subject taken for credit, or a particular aspect of that subject. All these concepts qualify as descriptions of the content although stated more or less specifically and abstractly. There is also the difficulty that the subject matter tends to be conceived theoretically and abstractly in terms of concepts to be learned rather than practically in terms of the activities that learners undertake. This difficulty seems unavoidable especially seeing that, when used in this way, the notion of curriculum seems to refer more to normative questions relating to the desired ends of its study rather than to descriptive matters having to do with what actually happens in the instructional process and how those ends are achieved.

While the notion of curriculum as subject matter offers important advantages, it is also flawed. It clearly does not suffice as the only useful image of curriculum because it fails to take sufficient account of the interrelatedness and dynamic quality of the various aspects of education and the inherent ambiguity between educational aims and methods. And it does not encompass sufficiently the complex process whereby subject matter and learner meet and are engaged, the dialectics and dilemmas this process presents for teacher and student alike, the learner's construction of knowledge, and the social context in which this process takes place.[14]

Curriculum as System

Tyler set out his basic curricular and instructional principles as a quartet of questions—"What educational purposes should the school seek to attain?" "How can learning experiences be selected which are likely to be useful in attaining these objectives?" "How can these educational experiences be effectively organized?" and "How can we determine whether these purposes are being attained?"

Since then, it has become fashionable to employ systems theory as a way of depicting the "flow" of activities from the formulation of objectives to the design of educational experiences that meet these objectives, the organization of instruction around these objectives, and the assessment of the process and each of its elements.[15] Even though Tyler sets forth his questions in a less systemic manner than some of his followers, his questions also can be asked within the context of a closed system that flows from one element to the other or from one question set to the next. The logical appeal of Tyler's rationale also fits nicely with economic metaphors of education that emphasize values such as efficiency, control, least resistance to learning, optimization of flow, achievement of predicted results, assessment and documentation of results, and evaluation of each system element to improve and ensure its efficient functioning. In this view, curriculum becomes one of the elements in the educational system in which precise movements from one element to the next can be predicted and represented graphically in a flow chart.

The production process that constitutes the metaphor for this view of curriculum assumes a closed system in which one stage in the process leads logically and inexorably to the next, where the learner does not come upon the next stage until the one before it or on which it is contingent is satisfied or complete. The manufacturer is able to predict which elements are required in production with a high degree of certainty, rationalize the production process, achieve economies of scale, and more or less guarantee that the objectives can and will be met. Curriculum is therefore interpreted as a means of production whereby the objectives to be attained are clearly articulated in advance and the outcomes are assessed objectively. The flow process masks the mechanistic assumptions required in order to make the system work and complete. It also hides the closed nature of the process, which is systematically articulated and inherently rational. This curricular image is exemplified in competency-based music education approaches and their variants.[16]

Among the potential contributions of this view, because the various system elements are clarified, specific distinctions can be made between and among such things as curriculum, instruction, and assessment, and the dynamic "flow" of the process can be represented. In a world in which economic and production considerations predominate, this conceptualization of curriculum has a wide appeal to business people and the public at large. It emphasizes educational accountability, particularly the importance of analyzing educational objectives and rationalizing education as an efficient system. Its systematic standardization and predictability appeal in an age in which mass production promises economies of scale. The prospect of verifiability and refutation makes it particularly appealing to those who wish to study it. And its commitment to observable outcomes, behaviors, and dispositions resonates with practitioners who are then in a position to demonstrate the effectiveness of their own particular contributions to the process. In a world in which reason and logic prevail, a systemic view of curriculum offers the ultimate rationalization for instruction and a way to see curriculum as a discrete element in a unified system in which all of the parts are conceptually independent.

This view of curriculum is also problematic. The metaphor of the closed system cannot account fully for the inherently open educational system of which curriculum forms a part. In practice, all educational outcomes cannot be specified in advance of the instruction. Some are found to be flawed while the system is in operation. And teachers do not always move logically but also intuitively, sometimes quite unsure what they should do or what the ends will turn out to be. One of the points of Howard's analysis of arts teaching is to show that teachers (like artists) both know and do not know what they are up to.[17] The ends they think might be achieved at the outset of instruction seem to change along the way as ends become means to yet other ends.[18] As they go along, teachers may change their minds or adjust their objectives and methods to fit particular students' experiences. All of this activity, commonly understood by practicing teachers, suggests that the assumptions required to justify a closed system such as the production metaphor implies simply do not hold in the phenomenal world. The distinctions between the system elements inevitably turn out to be theoretical generalizations, abstract even fictional accounts of practical realities. And the system takes little account of the nonrational or irrational elements of education that play an important role in educational experience. A purely mechanistic and technical approach to teaching is required, and there is no room for serendipity, coalescence, and chaos—features important in new views of science.[19] Seeing that the system's actors—students, teachers, administrators, and others—are presumably devoid of feeling presupposes a false dichotomy between reason and emotion as elements of cognition and is unrealistic when compared with ordinary human experience. And where emotion, passion, surprise, and humanity are excluded from the system and where there is no room for free will on the part of learners and their teachers, a sense of alienation, disconnectedness, and dehumanization results.

Curriculum as Process

A related though arguably less mechanistic metaphor is that of curriculum as process. Among the early champions of this view, Jerome Bruner (1963) posits that organizing themes underlie the subject matter and serve as its logical and conceptual structure or framework. These themes can be examined at progressively higher levels of sophistication and complexity. The result is a dynamic process from the most elementary or necessary first principles of a subject to its highest levels. Beliefs and practices that constitute the subject matter are organized conceptually and introduced systematically as ways of thinking and acting. In Bruner's earlier thinking, such an approach yielded a spiral curriculum, applied in music in examples such as the Manhattanville Music Curriculum Project, June Boyce-Tillman's and Keith Swanwick's curricular spiral, and, in different vein, Boyce-Tillman's work on a holistic approach to music education and music education for purposes of healing (2000a, 2000b). Unlike the metaphor of curriculum as system—oriented toward the creation of particular educational products or achievement of specific results—the end of education is the undergoing of the educational process as teacher and student interact around and in the midst of the subject matter. In this view, education is conceived primarily as a journey or pilgrimage to a destination where the traveling to that place is as important as arriving at it (Yob, 1989). The learner is in the process of becoming, and the curriculum describes that journey. In his more recent writing, Bruner focuses on the process whereby the learner makes meaning within a cultural context (1986, 1990, 1996). The learner intuitively, imaginatively, emotionally, and logically grasps the subject's articulated and organizing structures as unified wholes. The subject matter is not independent or separate from the learner as an objective reality but is engaged, known, and experienced by the learner subjectively. This stance presumes that when thinking of content and its meaning, it is essential to focus on the constructive quality of knowledge and on the interaction between the learner and that to be learned, and to see knowledge and meaning-making as inherently social and psychological processes. One never escapes a dynamic sense of becoming as one gradually comes to know the subject more intimately. And qualities of movement, fluidity, or process constitute a focus and principal characteristic of curriculum.

The emphasis on the process whereby humans make meaning and the structures that organize knowledge focuses attention on the essentially human qualities of learning, the necessary interconnectedness of logical structure with individual personality and perception, and the frames of society and culture in which people live and that partly shape the ways they think and feel. In more recent writing, Bruner has moved away from the spiral curriculum (with its presumption of causal linearity and the contingency of one level on another), toward a looser, less hierarchical, and more complex view of the interrelationships, coincidences, correspondences, and interconnections that typify human life and to which the spiral cannot do justice. Focusing on the organizing structures of the subject matter also reveals the interrelationships among all of its constit-

uent elements, and evidences the application of reason to education. Recognizing the contingency of learning on the person's readiness to learn also highlights the role of sensory perceptions and intellectual processes in the ways in which learner and subject matter come together. The dynamic nature of this process of becoming suggests that curriculum is not a static object but a fluid movement from one point to another that mirrors common experience. And taking into account the meaning-making by the learner highlights the fact that a curriculum does not consist of objective subject matter distinct from the learner's understanding of it but is subjectively known, experienced, and constructed by each learner at progressively more sophisticated levels of understanding.

By contrast, reason remains primary, because it is the learner's responsibility to come to the subject and gradually master it. And the hierarchy of ever "higher," abstract, and more valued understandings reflecting the progressive development of human reason privileges mind over heart, and logical thought over intuition. The idea of building a curriculum on the progressive and rational organization of the subject matter is challenged by Dewey, who urges quite a different stance—starting with the learner's psychological constructs and perspectives and gradually moving toward an emphasis on the logical organization of subject matter at advanced levels of instruction (Dewey, 1956). In the theory of music education curriculum, if not its practice, curriculum is designed principally with reference to the rational development of musical concepts rather than in terms of the particular mind-sets and perspectives of students' musical development. Witness the appeal to national standards and concepts that fit them in recently published basal series (Beethoven et al., 2000; Bond et al., 2000). Such musical curricula remain profoundly conceptual notwithstanding Bruner's acknowledgment of the many different ways humans make meaning in their lives and the cultural constructions that reflect and reinforce these ways of meaning-making. Following developmental models and strategies also invites a prescriptive and technical approach to music instruction that overlooks the emotional and physical selves of learners. It also fails to take into account the sense of discovery and individual differences among and between students and teachers or the role of imagination and creative thoughts and acts suggesting divergent rather than convergent educational ends. Through the process of coming to know the discipline of music education (or any other subject), one eventually comes to see it objectified, distanced from personal reality and the subjective self, and thereby alienated from oneself and others. Such a curriculum focuses on the individual learner rather than the educational community of which she is a part, and the deemphasis on educational ends fails to shoulder public responsibility for one's actions and accountability for one's efforts. Thus, while seemingly more humane and less mechanistic than the system approach, curriculum as process masks an undercurrent of forces that threaten to undermine humanity while also avoiding accountability. Seeing that educational process and product are distinct and understanding how something is made do not necessarily explain what has been created or vice versa (Scheffler, 1991). One without the other cannot suffice. Both process and product are essential for a broad grasp of the subject in question.

Curriculum as Realm of Meaning

Philip Phenix (1986) is among the curriculum thinkers to mine philosophical writing about symbol systems and their role in meaning-making by Ernst Cassirer (1944) and Susanne Langer (1957a). Phenix notes the centrality of symbolic thinking in human meaning-making and offers a provisional classification of different sorts of symbol systems as a basis for organizing a general education curriculum.[20] Allowing the prospect of various sorts of symbol systems suggests that there are also corresponding realms of meaning-making, each with its own perspectives, practices, and publics, all of which should be included in the curriculum. For Phenix, the general education curriculum ought to comprise all of the following realms of meaning—symbolics (language and mathematics), empirics (science, biology, psychology, and social science), aesthetics (music, visual arts, dance, and literature), synnoetics (or personal knowledge), ethics (moral knowledge), and synoptics (history, religion, and philosophy), and no general education is complete without the study of them all. To understand a realm of meaning, one needs to come to know its underlying symbolic system, not only what it is but how it works and how to do it or go on in it. That is, one needs to acquire propositional and procedural knowledge about it. To accomplish these ends, one requires an intimate and deep understanding of a realm of meaning. Rather than learners being distanced from the subject matter, they need to dig into it deeply in order to understand how it works practically as well as theoretically. In this vein, Eisner and Reimer are among those to posit the value of the arts as modes of knowing distinct from the sciences. Goodman proposes a theory of art that articulates some of the differences among the various realms of meaning. And drawing on Langer's work regarding the various sorts of symbols and ways of symbolic transformation that humans employ, Gardner proposes discrete human intelligences, all of which, presumably, should be developed in general education.

Construed as realms of meaning, symbol systems are explored and learners come to know about them, how they function, and their role in organizing and communicating human thought and practice. They may also employ them expressively. Seeing that these symbol systems are cultural as well as biological or psychological constructs opens the door to thinking about curriculum as a social and cultural construct. In this view, symbolic transformation is mediated and driven by, as it also impacts, individual thought and action (Bruner, 1990, 1996). And music educators need to write the stories of and construct philosophies that emerge from within their own cultural and political milieus. Making arguments for the legitimate place of various realms of meaning in general education also raises the question of which realms will be emphasized and how the claims of each will be adjudicated. The idea that including various realms of meaning constitutes a good can be applied specifically within a particular subject such as music so that composing, performing, and listening are characterized as distinct if also interrelated musical perspectives or realms of meaning. This idea also can be applied to the different musical systems evident throughout the world, each of which might be considered a theoretically distinct realm of meaning. Among examples of this approach to music curriculum, one thinks of the Comprehensive Musicianship Program and its successors, comprehensive arts programs such as the "Education for Aesthetic Awareness" program led by Bennett Reimer, and world music curricula urged by such writers as Campbell, Philomena Brennan, Mary Hookey, Volk, and Mary Goetze.[21]

Among its insights, this view of curriculum recognizes many differences in the ways in which people know the world and the variety of systems or realms of meaning-making that they invent and commonly practice. One realm cannot be judged according to the rules for another. Each of the symbol systems in which these various realms are based has its own distinctive attributes. Moreover, symbols mediate between the knower and known. Even within the arts, Langer and others in her train show that while the arts share commonalities, they also exhibit notable differences, so one art cannot substitute for another because each is a distinctive way of knowing.[22] This, in spite of Langer's point that in times past the arts were once more unified than they now are. Eisner, by contrast, is more inclined to group the arts together for the sorts of common attributes that they share and to view the arts in contrast to the sciences among other subjects studied in school.[23] The ideal, in this view, is a curriculum that represents the sum of all the important realms of meaning-making on the grounds that if one realm is lacking, the entire education suffers by its exclusion. Fewer writers are willing to go further to determine the specific criteria for inclusion and the relative importance of each realm. Instead, it is generally assumed that education ought by definition to be comprehensive of human culture, all the realms of meaning can and should be studied in school, and all are good and important. Herbert Read is one of the few to accord the arts primacy in the school curriculum as the "unifying principle" in general education, invert the traditional curriculum, and organize all the school subjects into departments of art.[24]

By contrast, the notion of a realm of meaning is ambiguous. It can be applied at various levels of generality across general education and human culture to groups of subjects that share common characteristics such as the arts or the sciences, to a particular art, and within an art to the many ways in which it is made and taken around the world. The assumption that each of these realms is equally important, efficacious, and good eventually expands and clutters the traditional school curriculum with a multitude of goods. In this case, more seems better than less, comprehensiveness is regarded as a virtue even at the expense of superficiality, and the difficult questions concerning how one practically evaluates a multiplicity of goods or balances often conflicting ends is sidestepped. Aside from the tensions, discontinuities, and conflicts between things that may have merit when taken alone, or those things that may not be defensible, teachers need to make judgments about what things to omit or downplay and which to include or emphasize. Things that may seem to constitute a good when taken alone may turn out not to be so when judged in the light of the whole. Teachers have to decide what not to include as much as what to include, what to treat in passing as much as what to emphasize among these realms of meaning. So the claim that each realm is of equal although different value to the others and that all are required in general education is unrealistic and impractical. It does not provide a basis for making the difficult practical decisions, especially when realms and value systems conflict and time—among other resources—is limited. And in its focus on belief and meaning-making, curriculum as realm of meaning focuses on the intellectual dimensions of education rather than on its more holistic or person-centered imperatives and practices.

Curriculum as the Practical Application of Reason

Israel Scheffler (1973), Paul Hirst (1974; Hirst & Peters, 1970), R. S. Peters (1967), and Robin Barrow (1984) are among those who regard curriculum as applied philosophy, where ideas and concepts analyzed logically are applied within the phenomenal world to educational practice. The assumptions that undergird practice are articulated, amplified, and organized through philosophical analysis, deconstructed or analyzed into their constituent elements, constructed or reconstructed within a coherent and consistent whole, and defended logically (Scheffler, 1973). As such,

curriculum is simply the outworking in practice of thoughts, desires, and beliefs about what ought to take place in education. It is therefore incumbent on teachers to explain and defend their assumptions about what ought to be before going the further step of deciding how these imperatives can be realized practically. One cannot fully understand curriculum in its practical manifestation without grasping the underlying assumptions that drive the practice. When curriculum is regarded as inherently philosophical, having to do with the working out in practice of value judgments, it is appropriately defended with regard to underlying philosophical assumptions that constitute moral, logical, and aesthetic or artistic imperatives. In this view, curriculum is closer to philosophy than to science and should be studied accordingly. Seeing curriculum as the application of philosophy assumes that a study of the practical instance provides insight into the philosophical assumptions that presumably undergird it and are exemplified by or expressed in it. However, the evident discontinuity between the worlds of theory and practice makes the process of translating ideas into practice or attributing practices to particular ideas that give rise to them somewhat problematic. As such, curriculum is situated between the worlds of theory and practice and exemplifies the tension or dialectic between them. In music education, the Mountain Lake group commits to working out in practice the "curricular commonplaces" derived directly from Schwab's work.[25] Others include the music education as aesthetic education view exemplified in the *Silver Burdett Music* basal series, Carlotta Parr's philosophical principles as a basis for educating music teachers as "reflective practitioners" that remain to be elaborated practically, Doreen Rao's *Choral Music Experience* program presaged in her doctoral dissertation, Thomas Regelski's "action learning" approach to general music, and Christoph Richter's musical workshop approach drawn from the philosophies of Martin Heidegger, Hans-Georg Gadamer, and Karl Ehrenforth.[26]

This view of curriculum has much to recommend it. Its emphasis on an articulated structure of assumptions focuses on the sources rather than results of action, and goes beneath a superficial view of practical characteristics to explain why and how these beliefs and practices are created, fostered, and sustained. Not only does it establish a rational basis for practical endeavor in its appeal to logical, ethical, and aesthetic rules, but also it recognizes the tension in every curriculum between the theoretical and phenomenal worlds, the desirable and the possible. In emphasizing justification more than refutation, it defends particular beliefs and practices, links intellectual and practical endeavor, and avoids a narrow focus on knowledge as an intellectual construct on the one hand and as a practice on the other. Its focus on values as central to the curriculum provides the means to logically examine their respective merits and offers a way to adjudicate conflicting educational claims. And in drawing on philosophical rules and insights, it offers a means of thinking critically about what teachers and students do in the course of musical instruction.

By contrast, this very logical and rational view of curriculum may take insufficient account of the emotional and irrational aspects of music teaching and learning. Other fields besides philosophy—for example, sociology, critical theory, psychology, anthropology, ethnology, and history—also offer perspectives that complement and conflict with those of philosophy. Basing curriculum on philosophical insights alone may provide too narrow a basis for practice. Given that music education is an interdisciplinary enterprise, various fields of study afford important and differing insights on its work, and regarding curriculum as applied philosophy may not take sufficient account of these other perspectives. Ambiguity arises because curriculum is situated between philosophical assumption on the one hand and practice on the other. Practically speaking, philosophical ideas are often realized differently than philosophers intend or in varying degree, and there is considerable leakage between assumption and application.[27] Difficult questions remain, such as "How accurately and to what extent should a philosophy be applied in the phenomenal world before it can count as curriculum in the sense of applied philosophy?"

Curriculum as Discourse

The most radical view of curriculum during the past quarter-century is offered by William Pinar and his colleagues drawing on the work of other "reconceptualists" including Michael Apple, Maxine Greene, Dwayne Huebner, and Herbert Kliebard, to name a few.[28] The notion of discourse draws on postmodern ideas in education and the social sciences about the frames of reference in which individuals and institutions construct realities that encompass ways of conceptualizing and talking about ideas and the variety of practices that exemplify, flow from, and reinforce them. For Pinar and his colleagues (1995), curriculum as text is alternatively historical, political, racial, gendered, post-structuralist, de-constructed, postmodern, autobiographical, biographical, aesthetic, theological, institutionalized, and international. Whether regarding politics, gender, postmodernism, aesthetics, social psychoanalysis, or identities, these writers criticize traditional curriculum ideas and practices. They suggest alternatives that are more inclusive, affirm diverse perspectives and peoples, and reconstitute educational purposes and procedures in ways that are more inclusive, egalitarian, and pluralistic.[29] They all seek to subvert the establishment's traditional beliefs and practices.

The purpose of curriculum in this view is to unmask and deconstruct practice and transform it through becoming aware or "wide awake" about what is happening,[30] and working for change toward a better world. Curriculum is therefore avowedly ideological. It challenges students to act to change the present state of affairs and construct new identities. This transformative vision of curriculum is praxial in the liberatory sense articulated by Paulo Freire, Maxine Greene, Henry Giroux, Ira Shor, bell hooks, and Thomas Popkewitz, among others, of signifying the theory-practice that criticizes traditional ideas and practices and struggles toward a more humane world.[31] This explicitly subversive emphasis is shown in its commitment to unmask and unseat dogma and transform practice rather than simply transmit traditions from one generation to the next. And the notion of curriculum as "text" suggests that a situation is examined systematically, systemically, and specifically with the benefit of particular perspectives that assist the learning community in clarifying what would otherwise be hidden from view, be they perspectives of gender, race, sexuality, politics, postmodern thought, theology, or aesthetics. Among the music and arts curricula to take this tack are those advocated by Murray Schafer, Claire Detels, and members of the Mayday Group.[32]

This view of curriculum as an exercise in transforming tradition contributes important insights. It actively engages, challenges, criticizes, and supplants past ideas and practices, and attends directly to the dialectic between thought and action. Also, it necessitates teachers and students being actively involved in the educational enterprise, thinking critically about the things that they are teaching and learning, and working to improve the human situation. There is a commitment to explicit ideologies that replace those of the past and take account of the imperative of different value judgments as a basis for building curriculum. And insights from fields beyond philosophy broaden the conceptual basis on which the curriculum is built and focus not only on the explanation of philosophical premises but also on the articulation and derivation of its practices. The workings of political and other social processes within educational institutions internationally is of as much interest as the theoretical ideas they exemplify. This is not so much a matter of digging beneath the practice to see the underlying philosophy as on focusing on the practice itself, seeking to understand it, asking how it should be changed in the future, and attempting to change it. In understanding the particularities as well as commonalities among and between practices, it reveals the many ways in which humans are alike and different from each other and the importance of the things they do together and alone in helping to shape and contextualize knowledge and experience. And in the multiplicity of discourses and perspectives on curriculum, this image reveals the multifaceted nature of knowledge and the partiality, incompleteness, even fallibility of any one perspective as the best or only way to understand self, world, and whatever lies beyond.

Still, the emphasis on practice may pay insufficient attention to the dialectic between philosophy and practice, and the ideas that give rise to practices. In focusing on the many specific differences among people, one may too quickly dismiss or fail to grasp sufficiently the many commonalities that they share.[33] Subversion also risks the loss of tradition, especially if the criticisms mounted of it are unwarranted or ill considered. Seeing that unexpected consequences follow from actions, it is possible that one's present perceptions and understandings may turn out in the long run to have been misguided, because one sees the present differently than with the benefit of historical perspective. The avowedly ideological purposes of curriculum in exposing evil and righting past wrongs also raise the central question of whose purposes are to prevail in education and how conflicting purposes are to be adjudicated. Having displaced philosophical reflection to the borders of the curriculum to be replaced by insights from other fields, there also is the possibility of espousing unwarranted assumptions and failing to expose error sufficiently—tasks that philosophers typically fulfill. And once one moves beyond philosophical thought to embrace an ideology, there is the risk that in becoming more committed to and less critical of an idea, one may become doctrinaire and refuse to brook criticism of this ideology or curriculum. From the perspective of an adherent of, or believer in, an ideology and for whom it is truth, challenging the ideology reveals one's ignorance of truth or commits heresy. When ideologues are uncritical of their own beliefs, it becomes very difficult to dialogue with them without meeting strong resistance or ridicule. They may see the blind spots in others but they cannot see their own.

Conclusion

In sum, notions of curriculum as content of instruction, system, process, realm of meaning, application of reason, and discourse all offer important insights and are flawed or limited in one way or another. No one suffices as the best or only image. Rather, they are like actors playing on a stage, the one or other coming to the fore when the role demands.[34] They may all be useful for different purposes and yet they are all problematic.

Clarifying the particular sense in which the word curriculum is being used, whether as a reference to the subject matter of instruction, the systemic and processual qualities of curriculum, the particular perspectives or lenses through which ideas and practices are studied, or the imperatives for curricular transformation, discloses and elucidates the positions of observer and participant. It also offers a

sounder basis on which to interpret curricular research and practice than in the absence of these images. The likelihood of partial and fallible understanding requires caution in constructing, interpreting, and evaluating curriculum theoretically and practically. And the presence of dialectics between these images suggests the possibility of tension and conflict between them, focuses on confronting apparent paradoxes as a central educational concern, and raises sometimes difficult theoretical and practical questions for the music teacher who draws on one or another image as the need arises.[35]

I see this "both/and" dialectical view of multiple images of curriculum as inevitable and useful. Mapping the images of curriculum enables researchers of music teaching and learning to more rigorously situate the concepts of curriculum they invoke, sharpen and better defend the focus of their research, and thereby improve the validity of curriculum studies in music education. And it facilitates teachers reflecting systematically on their purposes of and plans for music instruction, about what and how they and their students should and will study. This approach suggests that teachers should not prematurely foreclose their options but think through and reflect on the merits and detractions of each image for their particular situations before, in the midst of, and after instruction.[36]

In such a view, no one curricular image when taken alone suffices or is without its detractions. Images may overlap with others, for example, curriculum as realm of meaning and practical application of reason exemplified in the case of Reimer's approach to music education as aesthetic education. The resulting dialectics suggest that the work of music teaching and learning takes place in the "eye of paradox."[37] Teachers are faced with deciding how to bring together those aspects they see as overlapping, and reconciling those aspects that are in tension, conflict, or logically incompatible. Such an approach requires critical thinking on the part of teachers and their students. One never seems to arrive at a perfect practical solution, and there is no "high road" for all time. Far from being a debilitating result, such a situation requires imaginative and critical thought and practical skill on the part of teacher and student. It offers the prospect of mutuality, whereby aspects of each image may be combined or melded with others. And in allowing for and respecting differences, tensions, and even conflicts between images, and invoking imaginative and critical thought in negotiating between them, this dialectical approach opens up the possibility of many ways to teach and learn music with integrity.

NOTES

1. I am indebted to Mary J. Reichling, Iris M. Yob, Richard J. Colwell, Peter Webster, Nancy Whitaker, anonymous reviewers, and doctoral students in my curriculum in music

class at Indiana University—Dennis Ballard, Elizabeth Bauer, Brenda Graham, Eva Kwan, and Anne Sinclair—for comments on this essay.

2. Schwab (1978); Degenhardt (1989). Degenhardt may overstate the case and overlook the work of curricular reconceptualists and writers such as Henry Giroux and Ira Shor who have tackled some of these value-related issues from the field of cultural studies or the margins of education. See, for example, William Pinar (1975); Giroux (1983, 1992, 2000); Shor (1992). However, Martha C. Nussbaum's (1997) critique of the postmodern defense of educational plurality and diversity, especially regarding identity politics, suggests the need to revisit the theoretical underpinnings of curriculum—especially its underlying values—in a philosophically rigorous way. For example, Shor's sketch of values in dialogical education in his *Empowering Education* requires further philosophical analysis and criticism.

3. For more exhaustive and comparative surveys of the literature in curriculum, see Pinar, Reynolds, Slattery, and Taubman (1995), especially pp. 869–1034.

4. Schubert (1986), 169–187. This approach is similar to that regarding organizations in Morgan (1986).

5. This ambiguity is noted in Barrow and Milburn (1986). On the narrative mode in curriculum, see Doll (1993), pp. 168–169. On curriculum as metaphor, see Kliebard (1992), pp. 202–216.

6. Ralph W. Tyler's *Basic Principles of Curriculum and Instruction* (1949) is regarded as one of the foundational studies in American curricular theory.

7. On the ambiguity of art and craft, see Howard (1982), pp. 17–19. A weak syndrome suggests that there is overlap between things being compared, and ambiguity between or leakage from one to another. In comparing art and craft, for example, Howard points to notions of "arty craft" and "crafty art" that lie between the theoretical archetypes of art and craft.

8. Specific notions of dialectics vary from one writer to another. For example, while John Dewey (1916) is more sanguine about the possibility of resolving dialectics in synthesis, other later educational writers, for example, Paulo Freire (1993) and Maxine Greene (1988), see the situation as more complex. Discontinuities, tensions, conflicts, and logical incompatibilities may arise that make it difficult if not inappropriate to achieve synthesis. The practical dilemmas of dealing with dialectics may render music teaching paradoxical. For a discussion of my notion of dialectics, see Jorgensen (1997a, 1997b); Yob (1996); Bogdan (1998); Jorgensen (in press b).

9. Even if Israel Scheffler is right that the disparity between the two may not be as wide as Joseph Schwab would have us believe, both writers concur that a disjunction still persists; see Schwab (1970, 1971).

10. On "integrative levels of analysis" see Taylor (1975).

11. For a discussion of propositional and procedural knowledge in the context of education in music and the arts, see Howard (1982, 1992).

12. David J. Elliott (1995); Jorgensen (1997a); Christopher Small (1998). Elliott (pp. 29–33) argues against an "aesthetic concept" of music and music education referring specifically to notions of "music-as-object, aesthetic experience, and aesthetic perception" that underpin his view of Bennett Reimer's notion of "music education as aesthetic education" (p. 29). Here, I use the word "aesthetic" in its broader, philosophical reference to characteristic philosophical perspectives and expectations that refer to and undergird practices that constitute what we call, in the West, musical traditions.

13. Koopman (1997) faults music educators for failing to distinguish sufficiently between aims and methods. In reply, I argue that they overlap, practically speaking; see Jorgensen (in press a).

14. Dewey (1956) points to the dialectic between the student and the subject matter of instruction in his *The Child and the Curriculum*, originally published in 1902. Also, see Bergman and Luckmann (1990).

15. Tyler (1949), 1. For an early systems approach to curriculum, see Johnson (1967), pp. 127–140, especially Figure 1, "A model showing curriculum as an output of one system and an input of another" (133).

16. One such approach is that of Yarbrough and Madsen (1980). See Jorgensen (1988), p. 95, on "intended" and "resultant" curriculum.

17. See Howard (1982), ch. 5, on the nature of artistic foresight.

18. The interrelatedness of ends as means to yet other ends is integral to Dewey's theory of experience (1963), particularly chs. 2, 3.

19. On cognitive emotions, see Scheffler (1991), pp. 3–17. On chaos theory, see Gleick (1987); Kiel and Elliott (1996). On the potential of chaos theory for music education philosophy, see Yob (2000).

20. His ideas are reinforced in the writings of Nelson Goodman, Vernon Howard, Howard Gardner, Elliot Eisner, and, in music education, Bennett Reimer; see Goodman (1976); Howard (1982); Gardner (1983); Eisner (1985, 1994); Reimer (1989).

21. In the case of these examples, there is a wide variety in the sophistication of the philosophical bases for curricula. Too often, influential music teachers have not devoted the same attention to the defense of their curricular assumptions as they have to creating, buttressing, and illustrating their practical plans and materials. Among the better defended curricula, the Contemporary Music Project for Creativity in Music Education (CMP) recommended tenets for comprehensive musicianship. For a description of the historical events surrounding this project and a sketch of its recommendations and uses see Michael L. Mark (1996), pp. 28–34, 161–166. On aesthetic education, see Reimer (1978). An example of the work undertaken under the aegis of the CMP is found in Warren Benson (1967). The thought behind this project is illustrated in the anthology of writings prepared by the CMP (1971). And on world music curricula, see Campbell (1991), Philomena S. Brennan (1992), pp. 221–225, one of several practical approaches to multicultural music curricula in the same issue: Mary Hookey (1994); Volk (1998); Mary Goetze (2000).

22. Langer (1957), pp. 13, 14, suggests that despite these

differences between the arts there is a fundamental "unity" between them or a point at which all dissimilarities disappear.

23. Although Eisner (1994) emphasizes the sensory basis of artistic cognition, he acknowledges the various forms of artistic representation. His point is to demonstrate the contributions of the arts to cognition within general education rather than highlight specific differences between them.

24. Read (1958, 1966). Read's approach resonates with that of Nelson Goodman (1984), pp. 168–172, where the arts rather than sciences are preeminent in university education.

25. Hookey (1999) builds on Schwab's curricular commonplaces to develop her own list of five commonplaces: people, processes, perspectives, musics, and contexts.

26. For an application of Bennett Reimer's philosophy, see *Silver Burdett Music* (1981). Along with coauthors Elizabeth Crook, David W. Walker, Mary E. Hoffman, and Albert McNeil, Reimer designed a conceptual framework based on the activities of perceiving and reacting, producing, conceptualizing, analyzing, evaluating, and integrative learning toward realizing the stated objectives of perceiving, reacting, producing, conceptualizing, analyzing, evaluating, and valuing. Doreen Rao (1987–1991) outlines principles of choral music education that are exemplified in Doreen Rao with Lori-Anne Dolloff and Sandra Prodan (1993). N. Carlotta Parr (1999) outlines principles of teacher education drawn from the ideas of Jerome Bruner, Vernon Howard, and Maxine Greene that she believes should be implemented in preservice and in-service teacher education programs. Also, see Doreen Rao (1988). Thomas A. Regelski outlines principles for a praxial music curriculum, including an emphasis on the doing of music through practical (or practicum) experiences in his as yet unpublished essay, "Implications of Aesthetic vs. Praxial Philosophies of Music for Curriculum Theory in Music Education," and in his book in progress, *Musicianship Laboratory: An Action Learning Approach to Intermediate and Middle School General Music*. Christoph Richter's ideas are available in English in his essay, "The Didactic Interpretation of Music" (1996), pp. 33–49, and his forthcoming essay, "Musical Workshop-Activity as an Aspect of Hermeneutic Understanding and as a Way of Didactic Interpretation of Music" (in press).

27. Estelle R. Jorgensen, "What are the roles of philosophy in music education?" (in press b).

28. These authors are represented in Pinar (1975) and Pinar et al. (1995).

29. See Apple (2000) on politics and curriculum; Grumet (1988) and bell hooks (1994) on gender and curriculum; Doll (1993) on postmodernism and curriculum; Eisner (1994) on aesthetics and curriculum; Kincheloe and Pinar (1991) on social-psychoanalysis and curriculum; and Pinar (1998) on identities and curriculum.

30. In her notion of what it is to be "wide awake," Greene (1978), ch. 11, draws on Schutz (1967). For a discussion of Greene's notion of the importance of becoming "wide awake," see Parr (1996), pp. 125–132.

31. Carr (2001) draws on Aristotelian notions of praxis in examining jazz. Regelski (1998) sketches the Aristotelian

roots of praxis from the perspective of a critical pedagogy. Notions of music education espoused by Allsup (in press), and Jorgensen, *Renewing Education Through Music*, unpublished monograph available from the author, jorgense@indiana.edu are avowedly liberatory. A radically democratic and liberatory view of education is evident in Freire (1993); Greene (1988); Giroux (1993, 1996, 1997, 2000); Shor (1992); hooks (1994); Thomas S. Popkewitz (1998).

32. Schafer (1988); Detels (1999). For example, the May Day group of music educators has committed to particular "regulative ideals," and is devoted to unmasking the errors of traditional practice, articulating and forging a new plan, raising support for it, and eventually implementing it institutionally. One of the founders of the May Day group, Regelski, criticizes the status quo and urges change in music education belief and practice in his essay "Scientism in Experimental Music Research" (1996), pp. 3–19, and his paper "Sociology of Knowledge, Critical Theory and 'Methodolatry' in Music Education" (1995). Interestingly, two decades ago, Reimer (1978), p. 66, saw The Cleveland Area Project for the Arts in the Schools, "Education for Aesthetic Awareness," which he led for several years, as seeking "nothing less than a *transformation of arts education* [italics mine] from the traditional music and visual arts offerings found in most schools to total arts programs embodying the most advanced thinking about what aesthetic education might be and how major changes can take place in schooling." While his views are now considered as a foil for self-described praxialists Elliott and Regelski, nevertheless Reimer attempted to implement an ambitious program that he saw as a transformative vision of music education for his time.

33. Nussbaum (1997), p. 138, notes the importance in academic education of noticing these "common human problems."

34. Yob (1997) coined this metaphor in her response to Jorgensen (1997b). Such a dialectical approach while giving rise to problems and paradoxes, as Bogdan observes (1998), is worth pursuing because it is true to the nature of teaching. Others who concur with this dialectical view of teaching include Greene (1988); Palmer (1998).

35. For example, an eclectic music curriculum is proposed in Carder (c. 1990), notwithstanding that the philosophical assumptions and curricular images upon which these approaches draw differ in sometimes significant and conflicting ways.

36. Of particular interest to the education of artists is the notion of "reflection-in-action" described in Schön (1987).

37. Bogdan (1998), p. 73. This view resonates with Palmer's focus on recapturing the "hidden wholeness" beneath the dialectics and paradoxes of teaching. See Palmer (1998), ch. 3.

REFERENCES

Allsup, R. E. (in press). Music education as liberatory practice: Exploring the ideas of Milan Kundera. *Philosophy of Music Education Review*.

Apple, M. (2000). *Democratic education in a conservative age.* 2nd ed. New York: Routledge.

Barrow, R. (1984). *Giving teaching back to teachers: A critical introduction to curriculum theory.* Totowa, NJ: Barnes and Noble.

Barrow, R., & Milburn, G. (1986). *A critical dictionary of educational concepts: An appraisal of selected ideas and issues in educational theory and practice.* New York: St. Martin's Press.

Beethoven, J., et al. (2000). *Music connection.* Glenview, IL: Scott Foresman/Silver Burdett Ginn.

Benson, W. (1967). Creative projects in musicianship: A report of pilot projects sponsored by the Contemporary Music Project at Ithaca College and Interlochen Arts Academy. Washington, DC: Contemporary Music Project, Music Educators National Conference.

Bergman, P. L., & Luckmann, T. (1990). *The social construction of reality: A treatise in the sociology of knowledge.* New York: Anchor Books.

Bogdan, D. (1998). Book review. *Philosophy of Music Education Review,* 6(1), 171–73.

Bond, J., et al. (2000). *Share the music.* New York: Macmillan/McGraw-Hill School Division.

Boyce-Tillman, J. (2000a). *Constructing musical healing: Wounds that sing.* London: Jessica Kingsley.

Boyce-Tillman, J. (2000b). Promoting well-being through music education. *Philosophy of Music Education Review,* 8(2), 89–98.

Brennan, P. S. (1992). Design and implementation of curricula experiences in world music. In H. Lees (Ed.) *Music education: Sharing musics of the world. Proceedings of the 20th World Conference of the International Society for Music Education held in Seoul, Korea* (pp. 221–225). Christchurch, New Zealand: International Society for Music Education.

Bruner, J. S. (1963). *The process of education.* New York: Vintage Books.

Bruner, J. (1986). *Actual minds, possible worlds.* Cambridge, MA: Harvard University Press.

Bruner, J. (1990). *Acts of meaning.* Cambridge, MA: Harvard University Press.

Bruner, J. (1996). *The culture of education.* Cambridge, MA: Harvard University Press.

Campbell, P. S. (1991). *Lessons from the world: A cross-cultural guide to music teaching and learning.* New York: Schirmer.

Carder, P. (Ed.) (1990). *The eclectic curriculum in American music education: Contributions of Dalcroze, Kodály and Orff.* Reston, VA: Music Educators National Conference.

Carr, D. (2001). Can white men play the blues? Music, learning theory, and performance knowledge. *Philosophy of Music Education Review* 9(1), 23–31.

Cassirer, E. (1944). *An essay on man: An introduction to a philosophy of culture.* New Haven and London: Yale University Press.

Consortium of National Arts Education Associations. (1994). *National standards for arts education: What every young American should know and be able to do in the arts.* Reston, VA: Music Educators National Conference.

Contemporary Music Project for Creativity in Music Education. *Comprehensive musicianship: An Anthology of evolving thought.* Washington, DC: Music Educators National Conference.

Degenhardt, M. A. B. (1989). Curriculum as fraud. *Unicorn,* 15(2) 96–99.

Detels, C. (1999). *Soft boundaries: Re-visioning the arts and aesthetics in American education.* Westport, CT: Bergin and Garvey.

Dewey, J. (1916). *Democracy and education: An introduction to the philosophy of education.* New York: Macmillan.

Dewey, J. (1956). *The child and the curriculum and the school and society.* Chicago and London: University of Chicago Press.

Dewey, J. (1963). *Experience and education.* New York: Collier Books.

Doll, Jr., W. E. (1993). *A post-modern perspective on curriculum.* New York: Teachers College Press.

Dolloff, L. A., & Prodan, S. (1993). *We will sing! Choral music experience for classroom choirs.* New York: Boosey & Hawkes.

Eisner, E. (Ed.). (1985). *Learning and teaching the ways of knowing. Eighty-fourth Yearbook of the National Society for the Study of Education, Part 2.* Chicago: National Society for the Study of Education.

Eisner, E. W. (1994). *Cognition and curriculum reconsidered.* 2nd ed. New York: Teachers College Press.

Elliott, D. J. (1995). *Music matters: A new philosophy of music education.* New York: Oxford University Press.

Freire, P. (1993). *Pedagogy of the oppressed.* New rev. 20th-anniversary ed., trans. Myra Bergman Ramos. New York: Continuum.

Gardner, H. (1983). *Frames of mind: The theory of multiple intelligences.* New York: Basic Books.

George, W. E., Hoffer, C. R., Lehman, P. R., & Taylor, R. G. (1986). *The school music program: Description and standards,* 2nd ed. Reston, VA: Music Educators National Conference.

Giroux, H. A. (1983). *Theory and resistance in education: A pedagogy for the opposition.* New York: Bergin and Garvey.

Giroux, H. A. (1992). *Border crossings: Cultural workers and the politics of education.* New York: Routledge.

Giroux, H. A. (1993). *Living dangerously: Multiculturalism and the politics of difference.* New York: Peter Lang.

Giroux, H. A. (1996). *Fugitive cultures: Race, violence, and youth.* New York: Routledge.

Giroux, H. A. (1997). *Pedagogy and the politics of hope: Theory, culture, and schooling: A critical reader.* Boulder, CO: Westview Press.

Giroux, H. A. (2000). *Impure acts: The practical politics of cultural studies.* New York: Routledge.

Gleick, J. (1987). *Chaos: Making a new science.* New York: Penguin Books.

Goetze, M. (2000). Challenges of performing diverse cultural music. *Music Educators Journal,* 87(1), 23–30.

Goodman, N. (1976). *Languages of art: An approach to a theory of symbols*. Indianapolis: Hackett.

Goodman, N. (1984). *Of mind and other matters*. Cambridge, MA: Harvard University Press.

Greene, M. (1978). *Landscapes of meaning*. New York: Teachers College Press.

Greene, M. (1988). *The dialectic of freedom*. New York: Teachers College Press.

Grumet, M. R. (1988). *Bitter milk: Women and teaching*. Amherst, MA: University of Massachusetts Press.

Hirst, P. H. (1974). *Knowledge and the curriculum: A collection of philosophical papers*. London: Routledge and Kegan Paul.

Hirst, P. H., & Peters, R. S. (1970). *The logic of education*. London: Routledge and Kegan Paul.

Hookey, M. (1994). Culturally responsive music education: Implications for curriculum development and implementation. In H. Lees (Ed.), *Musical connections: Tradition and change. Proceedings of the 21st World Conference of the International Society for Music Education held in Tampa, Florida, U.S.A.* (pp. 84–91). Auckland, New Zealand: International Society for Music Education.

Hookey, M. (1999). Charting the conceptual terrain in music teacher education: Roles for maps and models, metaphors and mirrors. *The Mountain Lake Reader* (Spring), 40–49.

hooks, b. (1994). *Teaching to transgress: Education as the practice of freedom*. New York: Routledge.

Howard, V. A. (1982). *Artistry: The work of artists*. Indianapolis: Hackett.

Howard, V. A. (1992). *Learning by all means: Lessons from the arts*. New York: Peter Lang.

Jaques-Dalcroze, É. (1976). *Rhythm, music and education*. Trans. H. F. Rubinstein. New York: Arno Press.

Johnson, Jr., M. (1967). Definitions and models in curriculum theory. *Educational Theory, 17*(2), 127–140.

Jorgensen, E. R. (1980). On the development of a theory of musical instruction. *Psychology of Music, 8*, 25–30.

Jorgensen, E. R. (1988). The curriculum design process in music. *The College Music Symposium, 28*, 94–105.

Jorgensen, E. R. (1997a). *In search of music education*. Urbana: University of Illinois Press.

Jorgensen, E. R. (1997b). "Justifying music in general education: Belief in search of reason." In F. Margonis (Ed.), *Philosophy of education 1996* (pp. 228–236). Urbana, IL: Philosophy of Education Society.

Jorgensen, E. R. (2001a). What does it mean to transform education? In L. Stone (Ed.), *Philosophy of education, 2000* (pp. 242–252). Urbana, IL: Philosophy of Education Society.

Jorgensen, E. R. (2001b) *Transforming music education*. Unpublished monograph available from the author, jorgense @ indiana.edu.

Jorgensen, E. R. (in press-a). The aims of music education: A preliminary excursion. *Journal of Aesthetic Education*.

Jorgensen, E. R. (in press-b). What are the roles of philosophy in music education? *Research Studies in Music Education*.

Kiel, L. D., & Elliot E. (Eds.). (1996). *Chaos theory in the social sciences: Foundations and applications*. Ann Arbor: University of Michigan Press.

Kincheloe, J. L., & Pinar, W. F. (Eds.). (1991). *Curriculum as social psychoanalysis: The significance of place*. Albany: State University of New York Press.

Kliebard, H. M. (1992). *Forging the American curriculum: Essays in curriculum history and theory*. New York: Routledge.

Koopman, C. (1997). Aims in music education: A conceptual study. *Philosophy of Music Education Review, 5*(2), 63–79.

Langer, S. K. (1957a). *Philosophy in a new key: A study in the symbolism of reason, rite, and art*. 3rd ed. Cambridge, MA: Harvard University Press.

Langer, S. K. (1957b). *Problems of art: Ten philosophical lectures*. New York: Charles Scribner's Sons.

Mark, M. L. (1996). *Contemporary music education*. 3rd ed. New York: Schirmer Books.

Morgan, G. (1986). *Images of organization*. Beverly Hills, CA: Stage Publications.

Nussbaum, M. C. (1997). *Cultivating humanity: A classical defense of reform in liberal education*. Cambridge, MA: Harvard University Press.

Palmer, P. J. (1998). *The courage to teach: Exploring the inner landscape of a teacher's life*. San Francisco: Jossey-Bass Publishers.

Parr, N. C. (1996). *Towards a philosophy of music teacher education: Applications of the ideas of Jerome Bruner, Maxine Greene, and Vernon A. Howard*. Unpublished doctoral dissertation, Indiana University.

Parr, N. C. (1999). Towards a philosophy of music teacher preparation. *Philosophy of Music Education Review, 7*(1), 55–64.

Peters, R. S. (Ed.). (1967). *The concept of education*. London: Routledge and Kegan Paul.

Phenix, P. H. (1964). *Realms of meaning: A philosophy of the curriculum for general education*. New York: McGraw-Hill.

Pinar, W. (Ed.) (1975). *Curriculum theorizing: The reconceptualists*. Berkeley, CA: McCutchan Publishing Corporation.

Pinar, W. F. (Ed.). (1998). *Curriculum: Toward new identities*. New York: Garland.

Pinar, W. F., Reynolds, W. M., Slattery, P., & Taubman, P. M. (1995). *Understanding curriculum: An introduction to the study of historical and contemporary curriculum discourses*. New York: Peter Lang.

Popkewitz, T. S. (1998). *Struggling for the soul: The politics of schooling and the construction of the teacher*. New York: Teachers College Press.

Rao, D. (1988). *Craft, sing craft and musical experience: A philosophical study with implications for vocal music education as aesthetic education*. Unpublished doctoral dissertation, Northwestern University.

Rao, D. (1987–1991). *Choral music experience—Education through artistry*. 5 vols. New York: Boosey & Hawkes.

Read, H. (1958). *Education through art*. London: Faber and Faber.

Read, H. (1966). *The redemption of the robot: My encounter with education through art*. New York: Trident Press.

Regelski, T. A. (1981). *Teaching general music: Action learning for middle and secondary schools*. New York: Schirmer Books.

Regelski, T. A. (1995, April). Sociology of knowledge, critical theory and "Methodolatry" in music education. Paper presented at the Indiana Symposium in Interdisciplinary Perspectives on Music Education, Indiana University, Bloomington, Indiana.

Regelski, T. A. (1996). Scientism in experimental music research. *Philosophy of Music Education Review*, 4(1), 3–19.

Regelski, T. A. (1998). The Aristotelian bases of praxis for music and music education as praxis. *Philosophy of Music Education Review*, 6(1), 22–59.

Reimer, B. (1978). Education for aesthetic awareness: The Cleveland Area Project. *Music Educators Journal*, 64(6), 66–69.

Reimer, B. (1989). *A philosophy of music education*. 2nd ed. Englewood Cliffs, NJ: Prentice Hall.

Reimer, B., Crook, E., Walker, D. W., Hoffman, M. E., & McNeil, A. (1981). *Silver Burdett Music*. 8 vols., teacher's ed. Morristown, NJ: Silver Burdett.

Richter, C. (1996). The didactic interpretation of music. *Philosophy of Music Education Review*, 4(1), 33–49.

Richter, C. (in press.) Musical workshop-activity as an aspect of hermeneutic understanding and as a way of didactic interpretation of music. *Philosophy of Music Education Review*.

Schafer, R. M. (1988). *The thinking ear: Complete writings on music education*. (Toronto, ON: Arcana Editions.

Scheffler, I. (1973). *Reason and teaching*. Indianapolis: Bobbs-Merrill.

Scheffler, I. (1991). *In praise of the cognitive emotions and other essays in the philosophy of education*. New York: Routledge.

Scholes, P. (1935). *Music, the child and the masterpiece: A comprehensive handbook of aims and methods in all that is usually called musical appreciation*. London: Oxford University Press.

Schön, D. A. (1987). *Educating the reflective practitioner: Towards a new design for teaching and learning in the professions*. San Francisco: Jossey-Bass.

Schubert, W. H. (1986). *Curriculum: Perspective, paradigm, and possibility*. New York: Macmillan.

Schutz, A. (1967). *Collected papers, I: The problem of social reality*. 2nd ed. The Hague: Nijoff.

Schwab, J. J. (1970). *The practical: A language for curriculum*. Washington, DC: National Education Association.

Schwab, J. J. (1971). The practical: Arts of eclectic. *School Review*, 79, 493–542.

Schwab, J. J. (1978). *Science, curriculum and liberal education*. Chicago: University of Chicago Press.

Shor, I. (1992). *Empowering education: Critical teaching for social change*. Chicago: University of Chicago Press.

Small, C. (1998). *Musicking: The meanings of performance and listening*. Hanover and London: Wesleyan University Press.

Swanwick, K. (1988). *Music, mind, and education*. London: Routledge.

Taylor, A. (1975). Systems approach to the political organization of space. *Social Science Information, International Social Science Council*, 14, 7–40.

Thomas, R. B. (Ed.). (1970). *MMCP synthesis*. (1986). Elnora, NY: Media.

Tyler, R. W. (1949). *Basic principles of curriculum and instruction*. Chicago: University of Chicago Press.

Volk, T. (1998). *Music, education, and multiculturalism: Foundations and principles*. New York: Oxford University Press.

Wolf, S. R. (1996). A pitch for multiculturalism. In M. McCarthy (Ed.), *Cross currents: Setting an agenda for music education in community culture: A colloquium in music education with Patricia Shehan Campbell and Susan R. Wolf, Michael L. Mark, and Paddy B. Bowman, University of Maryland, College Park, April 22, 1995* (pp. 35–45). College Park: University of Maryland.

Yarbrough, C., & Madsen, C. (1980). *Competency-based music education*. Englewood Cliffs, NJ: Prentice Hall.

Yob, I. M. (1989). The pragmatist and pilgrimage: Revitalizing an old metaphor for religious education. *Religious Education* 84(4), 521–537.

Yob, I. M. (1997). Can the justification of music education be justified? In F. Margonis (Ed.), *Philosophy of education, 1996* (pp. 237–240). Urbana, IL: Philosophy of Education Society.

Yob, I. M. (2000, March). Response to Estelle Jorgensen, "Aims of music education: A preliminary excursion." Philosophy Special Research Interest Group, Music Educators National Conference, Washington, DC.

Educating Musically

6

WAYNE BOWMAN

It is from playing the lyre that both good and bad lyre players are produced.

Aristotle, Nicomachean Ethics

Is it even always an advantage to replace an indistinct picture by a sharp one? Isn't the indistinct one often exactly what we need?

Wittgenstein, Philosophical Investigations

"The most crucial clarification about teaching occurs at the level at which we decide what kind of interaction it is," writes Joseph Dunne (1997, p. 367). "A decision at this level has the heaviest consequences not only for how we understand but also how we go about doing it." Dunne is right, of course. What kind of endeavor we understand music education to be—and more specifically, of what kind of *interactions* it should consist—has profound importance for the way music educators teach. It is also crucial to how we structure curriculum, to the kinds of experiences in which we expect students to engage, to the ways we evaluate student progress, and to how we orient and conduct our professional research. At first gloss, there is nothing particularly noteworthy or controversial about this. The "interactions" in which music educators are engaged are straightforwardly concerned with teaching their subject, music. Music education is, self-evidently, the business of helping students develop musically: to understand, appreciate, respond to, create, and to engage meaningfully in music. The concerns of music education are coextensive with the concerns of musical instruction, and musical instruction consists of the techniques and methods for developing things like musicianship, literacy, or appreciation. In short, music education is the means to ends that are specifically musical. That being the case, the most important guidance as to the nature of the discipline and its in-

structional concerns flows from a proper understanding of music's intrinsic nature and value.

Or is this right? There are a number of difficulties in starting with music, its nature and its value, and conceiving of music education as the machinery for teaching and learning about it, or developing proficiency in it. One such difficulty is that music's nature is not enough in itself to establish that it should be taught to or learned by all. Suggestive though it may be for many aspects of instructional method, curricular choices and priorities generally stem from considerations not immediately addressed by music's intrinsic nature. Furthermore, music's value is radically plural and diverse, and capable therefore of orienting instruction and curriculum in quite a variety of potentially disparate directions.[1] And finally, however unique the nature of music, however much we may value it, the troublesome facts remain that it is not essential to life and that many of the putative outcomes of musical study are not highly valued by society at large.[2]

Music is without question a ubiquitous presence in human societies, and musical propensities are clearly among the more remarkable and distinctive attributes of the human animal. Music also affords us experience that is unlike any other, extending to us humanly unique ways of being in the world. However, striking and indisputable though these facts about music may be, they do not in themselves establish a need for education in it, particularly where time and resources are finite and in short supply.

One strategic counter to such concerns is that, inessential though music may be to life, it is indispensable to a life lived well, or to a life worth living. It can, taught and learned well, impart rich meaning and purpose to people's lives.[3] Music, and therefore education in it, is crucial to human flourishing, or *eudaimonia* as the ancient Greeks called it. Music teaches us things about our common humanity[4] that are worth knowing, and renders us less vulnerable to forces that subvert or compromise human well-being. Studying and making music changes who we are and what we expect from life.

There are important elements of potential truth in such claims. However, it is also true that none of them follows automatically, unconditionally, or absolutely from musical instruction and musical experience. Each is profoundly contingent, dependent on such concerns as what music is taught, in what context, and how. Nor are these putative outcomes strictly musical: They are functional or utilitarian, concerned less with education *in* music or *about* music than with *education through music*, and interested in what use that might be. Our understandings of music's nature and value of music are necessary, indeed crucial, to music education. They are not, however, sufficient.

In this chapter, I ask what it may mean to become educated through music, or to become *musically educated* as opposed to being taught music or being musically trained. I am interested in discerning, in other words, what kind of interaction music teaching might be when undertaken with fully and specifically educational intent.[5] Using the educational lens in the designation "music education" brings concerns and insights into focus that have far-reaching consequences for the way we conceptualize our instructional, curricular, and research efforts.[6] I begin by exploring what the educational commitment implicit in the phrase music *education* entails: what, beyond the effective delivery of instruction or the transmission of sophisticated skills and knowledge, the word "educate" implies. Among my conclusions is that education is distinctively ethical in character, concerned ultimately with the development of character and identity. In the second major section, I explore the nature of the ethical mode of being and its significance for our understandings of education more broadly and music education more narrowly. A distinction between technical rationality and practical wisdom figures prominently in these deliberations, as I argue the inadequacy of technical means to educational ends. I conclude by offering a few suggestions as to how the issues explored here might, taken seriously, transform musical instructional practices, understandings of the music education profession, and through these, implicitly, assumptions about the presumed range and focus of music education research.

Musical Education, Instruction, Schooling, and Training

What does it mean to be or become educated? What essential characteristics distinguish it from formative experience that is not educative? What attributes, dispositions, or virtues do we hope to find in educated individuals that we do not necessarily expect to find in those who are trained, perhaps quite effectively, yet not educated? This last way of putting the question begins to draw what to me is an interesting and important distinction: a distinction between instruction carried out with educational intent and instruction whose primary concern is to train. Although this distinction should not be pushed too far, I suggest it is a useful conceptual tool for refining our understanding of what educating musically entails.[7]

The position I advance here is that the designation "music education" brings with it commitments, values, and obligations that have not always been at the forefront of our professional consciences, and for reasons related to the subordinate role "education" has played to "music" in defining our professional identity. It is entirely possible to teach and to make music *well* while failing to achieve its educative potential. Roberta Lamb's stinging indictment of musical performance suggests just how egregious such oversights can be. "Musical performance," she alleges, "is untheorized practice. It is not praxis; it is what we musicians do because it is what we do. . . . Performance is about control by a master, a conductor, usually male, usually white."[8] These assertions raise quite a number of issues, on levels too numerous to explore here. The primary point I wish to underscore is that this failure to "theorize practice," to reflect critically on the ends to which our musical and instructional practices may lead, leaves open the very real possibility that our musical engagements miseducate rather than educate. Now obviously, musical performance is not inherently or invariably about power and control. Nor is teaching. Yet both may be, and often are. Music making and musical instruction may indeed be constructive, but what they construct is not desirable inherently or automatically. Approached without due consideration for what besides "the music" is being learned, the skilled performance of beautiful music may even be harmful. Musical instruction can humanize, but it can and arguably often does dehumanize. Thus, as David Best has persuasively argued, education in the arts has an utterly inescapable moral dimension: "No teacher," he writes, "can avoid the moral responsibility of deciding what to teach and how to teach it."[9]

Focusing so closely on the musical part of the "music education" equation leads music educators to gloss the educational side, with consequences not just potentially troublesome, but at times highly undesirable.[10] When we neglect the distinction between education and training, we risk conflating the two and accepting the latter as an acceptable substitute for the former. This potential is particularly worrisome in North American societies that valorize technical reason and the development of "practical" skill above other forms of mindfulness and expertise.[11] Exclusive reliance on music's allegedly intrinsic nature and value for our understanding of music education thus elides concerns that belong at the very heart of the latter.

The reasons for this preponderant emphasis on music in conceptualizing music education are many and varied. Some have to do with institutional arrangements, the historical influence of the music conservatory for instance,[12] and the typical location of music education curricula within schools of music rather than faculties and colleges of education. Others have to do with the highly practical or instrumental nature of North American musical instruction since its early days in the singing school.[13] Others may be traced to the uncritical equation of education with schooling, wherein music education's role is simply "to school" children in musical "subject-matter,"[14] and all teaching/learning activities directed to that end are deemed casually to be instances of music education. These institutional and historical influences lead us to speak of music education, musical instruction, and schooling, as if they were the same, and as though any instance of musical teaching and learning were an instance of music education.

Other reasons for our emphasis on music to the detriment of education stem from the politics of schooling, where advocacy efforts struggle to persuade skeptical others that music brings things to the instructional table that no other school subject can. Such efforts have often encouraged us to draw a sharp distinction between music's "insides" (attributes and capacities presumed to follow from its intrinsic, or properly musical, nature and value) and its "outsides" (its extrinsic values). These well-intended strategies often lead advocates to valorize the properly or wholly musical values of music over its lesser, supposedly "extramusical" ones.[15] Because educational ends and aims are wrongly regarded as extramusical in this narrowly dualistic scheme, many of the features that distinguish instructional processes and outcomes that are properly educative from those that are not have been neglected in our philosophical and research efforts, as well as in our understandings of what music education is and why it is important. Indeed, efforts to establish our uniqueness in the instructional milieu of public schooling often come precariously close to situating music outside that milieu altogether. So utterly distinctive is a music education defined exclusively by music's intrinsic nature and value that it appears to fall outside what many people are inclined to regard as education.

Ironically, school-based music education often eludes close scrutiny on such grounds precisely because of the preponderantly technical orientation of modern schools, and their pathetically narrow vision of human purposes. It is relatively easy to demonstrate, after all, that music students are developing concrete skills and understandings, and that we are therefore "adding value" just like the "other" disciplinary areas.[16] However, to return to the main point, this fails to address the larger concern of what kind of value is being added, or whether that value is educationally positive or negative. It fails to distinguish education from training, or to distinguish musical instruction with educational intent from musical instruction whose impact extends no further than training.

Indoctrinating, Training, and Educating

Again, what is education, and what might music in particular have to contribute to instructional efforts dedicated to specifically educational outcomes? How might our collective professional efforts differ if we were to take up the explicitly educational claim in the label "music education"? It may help to frame the conception of education I want to advance if we consider the other end of the instructional continuum: the indoctrination implicit in Lamb's indictment of musical performance as control. The potentially adverse effects of indoctrinative instruction are well expressed in Pink Floyd's "We don't need no education, We don't need no mind control . . ." and in this poignant admonition by Doris Lessing:

Ideally, what should be said to every child, repeatedly, throughout his or her school life is something like this: "You are in the process of being indoctrinated. We have not yet evolved a system of education that is not a system of indoctrination. We are sorry, but it is the best we can do. What you are being taught here is an amalgam of current prejudice and the choices of this particular culture. The slightest look at history will show how impermanent these must be. You are being taught by people who have been able to accommodate themselves to a regime of thought laid down by their predecessors. It is a self-perpetuating system. Those of you who are more robust and individual than others will be encouraged to leave and find ways of educating yourself—educating your own judgment. Those that stay must remember, always and all the time, that they are being molded and patterned to fit into the narrow and particular needs of this particular society."[17]

Mind control and education lie at opposite ends of an instructional continuum, with training variably situated somewhere between the two. Like indoctrination, training is highly directive. Control and management of the learner may not be total, as is implicitly the case for indoctrination, yet to be trained is to be prepared to execute a specific task or tasks. Education has different ends in mind.

Training, as Peter Abbs (1994) points out,

invariably involves a narrowing down of consciousness to master certain techniques or skills. These . . . are known in advance and can be unambiguously imparted by the trainer and assimilated by the learner. What is transmitted is functional and predetermined, a set of skills matching a set of operations. (p. 15)

Thus, training seeks to impart skills or techniques designed to serve some aspect of the status quo; it seeks to shape behaviors to prespecified ends. Education, by contrast, involves what Abbs describes as "an opening out of the mind that transcends detail and skill and whose movement cannot be predicted." It does not have, he continues, "a direct utilitarian purpose; it leads to a certain mode of consciousness, a delicate, sustained reflective disposition toward experience, an openness toward potential truth and possible meaning, though it generally presupposes the internalization of various skills and techniques" (Abbs, 1994, p. 15). The essential dynamics of education, observes Abbs, always take the student "beyond the status quo into what is not fully known, fully comprehended, fully formalized. Education is the expression and development of a primary impulse for truth, a deep epistemic instinct that we inherit as part of our biological nature" (Abbs, 1994, p. 16).

The product of this process, the educated person, is one who has acquired in the learning process not just a set of skills and understandings but complex sets of values as well: values that are held neither lightly nor dogmatically. The educated person is also one who is capable of acting and thinking both cooperatively and independently, able to judge when circumstances warrant "going with the flow" and where they require the courage to stand out from what Northrop Frye (1988) called "the uniform bleating of the herd" (p. 18). To be educated is to be responsive to the needs of others yet capable of self-reliance, able to think and act on one's own, guided by one's own sense of rightness. Accordingly, the educated person approaches new experience open-mindedly, with a capacity to weigh rival claims judiciously and to examine issues from alternative points of view and value orientations. Part of what it means to be educated is to be resourceful, agile, and flexible, to be able to discern what is important in novel or unfamiliar circumstances and to adapt where necessary.

Education, Growth, and Identity

In short, and in rather strong contrast to training whose efficacy is gauged by the successful execution or application of transmitted skills and understandings, education has an open texture. Indeed, education always "takes its chances," as the range of things the educated person may question or challenge extends even to the specific skills and understandings initially part of one's own educational experience. Education, then, does not just equip people to execute specific tasks. It empowers them to transform tasks where necessary, to judge when or whether such interventions are appropriate, and even to question or reject things deemed incontrovertible in previous instruction. Clearly,

we are talking now not so much about what a person knows or can do as the kind of person one has become as a result of those knowings and doings, the attitudes and dispositions that orient and motivate an individual. Education creates people who have not only the capacity but the inclination to question, to look at things from various perspectives, and who are aware of the partiality and fallibility of all such perspectives, their own included.

This last claim may sound like a weakness, but it is one of the distinguishing strengths of an educated individual. While training has relatively clear-cut ends and determinate points of arrival, education does not. This is because education consists, as Dewey maintained, in an open process of growth and becoming that requires as a fundamental condition of its possibility the revision of one's beliefs and desires in light of new information and experiences. Education habituates inquiry, and nurtures experimental dispositions. It does not teach us what to see but how to look; not what to do but how to refine and improve our doings. Richard Rorty (1989) brings these points together this way:

> This notion of a species of animals gradually taking control of its own evolution by changing its environmental conditions leads Dewey to say, in good Darwinian language, that "growth itself is the moral end" and that to "protect, sustain, and direct growth is the chief *ideal* of education." Dewey's conservative critics denounced him for fuzziness, for not giving us a criterion of growth. But Dewey rightly saw that any such criterion would cut the future down to the size of the present. Asking for such a criterion is like asking a dinosaur to specify what would make a good mammal or asking a fourth-century Athenian to propose forms of life for the citizens of a twentieth-century industrial democracy. (p. 201)

On this view, education fails if it prepares people to deal with unchanging circumstances in a static social order, for such states of affairs are seldom if ever found in the world of human endeavor (Dewey, 1934).

Thus, instruction with educational intent always takes its chances. Its outcomes are multiple, potentially divergent, and even indeterminate in the sense that we cannot stipulate beforehand what specific form they may take. As Hannah Arendt writes, in educating, we prepare people for "the task of renewing a common world" and in doing so extend to them the "chance of undertaking something new, something unforeseen by us" (1961, p. 196). We can thus characterize what it means to be musically educated in general terms only, not in terms of objective requisite musical skills or understandings. This is because what we are ultimately concerned with as educators are the attitudes, propensities, and dispositions acquired through study that is musically educative. Our educational concern has to do with how to approach life and living (and others engaged in those same processes) as a result of having engaged in musical studies and experiences of certain kinds, not with the studies themselves or what they explicitly impart about music. This is not to suggest that these latter are somehow dispensable to becoming musically educated. Clearly, they are not. But necessary though they undoubtedly are, they are not sufficient. And among the vast array of skills, understandings, and experiences that are properly musical, not all are equally suited to educational ends.

If education is not primarily concerned with the transmission of skills and knowledge, how does it work, when it works, and how can we tell when it has? One of John Dewey's answers that is particularly relevant to music education focuses on the quality of experience and its transformative potential: education works by changing in fundamental ways what we expect of life and experience. Experience is not all of a piece, Dewey shows: some has within it qualities and conditions that impart a marked sense of wholeness, unity, self-sufficiency, and vividness. Undergoing experiences of this kind changes who we are by setting more elevated standards for all kinds of subsequent experience. In *Democracy and Education* (1916), Dewey describes the arts as "organs of vision." They "arouse discontent with conditions that fall below their measure; they create a demand for surroundings to come up to their level. They reveal a depth and range of meaning in experience which otherwise might be mediocre and trivial." As such, he asserts, "They are not luxuries of education, but emphatic expressions of that which makes any education worthwhile" (Dewey, 1916, p. 279). What makes education worthwhile, and presumably an important part of what distinguishes the educated, are experiences whose vividness and richness fundamentally change who we are by elevating what we expect of experience, of life, of each other. Education works through experiences that transform our expectations of the world and, consequently, who we are.

However, such experiences cannot be summoned at will and dispensed like medicines in preordained dosages and with reasonable confidence in specific, predictable outcomes by which their efficacy can be gauged. Another way of characterizing what education develops is "practical wisdom," a capacity that consists not so much in what one knows and can do as in how such knowings and doings orient one to new experience. The wise person is one who has become a fairly fluent judge of what is important to attend to in novel situations. The point I wish to stress, however, is that there are no technical means to assure attainment of such fluency, no formulas for identifying what is salient. There can be no rules for right action.[18] There can be no training for wisdom. A person who is trained is equipped with skills and concepts to be deployed

and applied in more or less the manner in which they were acquired, and in situations for which the skills and concepts are specifically designed—which is to say, technically. Training and technique are highly useful, but often not outside the specific domain within which they are crafted. The concrete particulars of novel situations call for something more flexible, improvisatory, and amenable to reformulation than technique, something less susceptible to "method" than training.[19] Hence, another characteristic of the educated individual is a tendency to hold to specific ideas and skills provisionally, in recognition of their potential limitations and their contingency.[20]

If and when education succeeds, it does so by changing who we are: no change, no educational outcome. We become educated as we come to recognize the fallibility of what once seemed irrefutable; as we become more discerning of what we expect of subsequent knowledge and experience; as we become more fluent and agile at assessing things around us; and as we become more passionate about things that manage to surpass the level of the mundane. Such capacities cannot be dispensed technically, methodologically, step by step, and in clear succession toward a clearly delineated, preordained goal. Nor can they be measured by standardized tests because of the diverse and unpredictable ways in which they may manifest themselves. These capacities are not so much things the educated person "has" as they are things he or she has become. They are part, in other words, of one's character or identity.[21]

Now, if our concern is not so much what one knows and can do as who one becomes through educative processes and experiences, education is clearly concerned with identity, the construction of selfhood of a certain kind, and the formation of fundamental dispositions.[22] That being the case, education is a doubly ethical undertaking: double because decisions to cultivate certain habits and dispositions and to suppress others have unavoidable ethical implications; and because the kinds of dispositions one hopes to cultivate and nurture are themselves ethical in important ways. Abbs puts it this way: "Education exists primarily to engender *virtue—a thinking that actually works through and on existence and which therefore develops the personality*. Teaching is an ethical activity and education is, in part, the act and art of releasing a critical-ethical process in the other, the final outcome of which cannot be known in advance."[23]

Let us turn then to the pivotal question of the nature of this ethical domain that figures so prominently in the distinction I want to draw between training and education. Without that, we shall be at a loss to understand what it might mean to be musically educated, and what if anything there is in music that might make it an appropriate vehicle for a distinctly educational enterprise.

The "Between-ness" of Ethical Encounter

The word "ethics" conjures up all manner of confusion and controversy, and its philosophical terrain defies easy navigation.[24] So I will proceed here by advancing a particular view rather than conducting a comprehensive survey. I will draw on a thoughtful essay by Geraldine Finn in which she explores what she calls "the question which *is* ethics,"[25] and the relationships between ethical thought and practical or political action. In a statement that resonates richly with the kinds of distinctions I have been attempting to tease out between education and training, Finn declares that,

> an ethics which relies on the (political) categories of established thought and/or seeks to solidify or cement them— into institutionalized rights and freedoms, rules and regulations, and principles of practice, for example—is not so much an ethics . . . as an abdication of ethics for politics under another description. As it exchanges the undecidability, the an-archy, the responsibility of the space-between of the ethical encounter with others for the security, the hier-archy, of the pre-scribed and prescriptive places of the categories.[26]

Crucial to this account of practical ethics is the point that a great deal of what is conventionally called ethics simply is not. Formulation and adherence to rules of conduct, for instance, is not at all "ethical" in the sense Finn advocates. The truly ethical encounter takes place only when categorical assumptions are bracketed, when one sets aside the comfort and security of preordained rules, regulations, and procedures, in an effort to encounter the other *as concrete other* rather than simply as an instance of something already familiar. Such an act requires openness and puts one in a position of vulnerability. And importantly for our purposes here, it cannot be executed by adhering to explicit procedures or methods.

Central to Finn's account of the ethical encounter, properly so-called, is the "space-between" where it is situated.[27] This is the phenomenal space between category and experience, between language and life, between representation and reality. In it, one regards who or what one encounters (the other) not as an exotic variant of something familiar and subsumable under a categorical label already at hand, or amenable to treatment along lines suggested in some abstract regulative ideal. It is imperative, as Finn sees it, that in a truly ethical encounter the other be recognized as a concrete, unique particularity. Failure to do so distorts the other, treats it as "more of the Same," reducing the potentially ethical encounter to a merely technical one. More to the point, an ethical encounter that fails to question the political status quo that frames it, the particular vision of the "good life" in which the issue at hand is en-

meshed (and by which it is to some degree defined), implicitly endorses that vision's adequacy. She explains,

> Ethical praxis which merely rearticulates the values and goals of the status quo realities identified as problematic for it, seems to me to consist not so much in *ethical* interventions directed towards fundamental issues of right and wrong and the constitution of the good life, as *technical*— and for that reason, *political*—interventions directed towards the fine tuning of norms and procedures already in place to accommodate new realities within the system which might otherwise disturb its hierarchies of power and control or its appearance of Reason and Right. Thus, much of what passes for "ethical" . . . is not really ethical at all from this point of view, but technical-political in the given sense.[28]

In other words, by accepting a system's premises and basic categorical assumptions, the parties in potentially ethical situations unwittingly preempt the transformative power of genuinely ethical inquiry. They tinker with symptoms rather than addressing the problems that give rise to them. Their resistance only serves to reinforce and sustain the status quo. If the existing norms and values of society were adequate to experience, if language were commensurate with life, or representations were adequate to reality, there would be no dissent or disaffection. However, Finn says, "the contingent and changing world always exceeds the ideal categories of thought within which we attempt to express and contain it. And the same is true of people. We are always both more and less than the categories which name and divide us." People's lives leave remainders ("say more than they mean") just as categories leave residues ("mean more than they say"), says Finn.[29]

In an authentically ethical encounter, one encounters things in their concrete particularity rather than as instances of the familiar. Subsuming a person or a thing within an existing scheme "relieves us of the ethical responsibility of attending to the particularity of the other and inventing our relationship with it." By contrast, the between-ness of the ethical encounter "puts me in the presence of that which has never been there before: the other in all its singularity . . . an epiphany, an absolute exteriority which cannot without violence be integrated into the Same" (Finn, 1994, p. 108).

The categorical schemas of institutionalized discourses channel the "affective anarchical ethical residues and remainders of experience . . . into authorised categorical hierarchical meanings, intentionalities, and desires compatible with and amenable to the controlling interests of prevailing political powers" (Finn, 1994, p. 109). The substitution of technique for ethical encounter, an act that carries within it an implicit endorsement of the integrity of the status quo, is an important part of the machinery by which prevailing power is sustained. Hence, to reject the certainty and security of technical rationality for the between-ness and openness of the ethical orientation is often denigrated as irrational or soft-headed by those privileged within a given order. The ethical attitude is regarded as aberrant, confused, a kind of experience that needs to be cleaned up and perfected by reason.[30] Thus, while the between-ness of the ethical encounter makes it the only encounter that "makes a difference and demands a responsibility from me which is not already pre-scribed" (Finn, 1994, p. 111) that transformative potential often goes unrealized. Such is the hegemony of technical rationality, the impersonal manipulation of ideas, whose advocates would have us believe its rules and methods are our only reliable epistemic resources.[31]

My concern is to emphasize the liberative and transformational potentials of the ethical mode of being. Ethical presence-to-the-other makes profound demands on its agents. It requires that they accept and embrace personal responsibility for constructing their relationship to the other, and, concomitantly, that they be willing to yield something of themselves as formerly constituted. In Finn's words, ethical presence to the other requires one "to think and be anew: to risk being-otherwise-than-being what I have already become" (Finn, 1994, p. 111). It "puts me into question, which challenges and changes me, as well as the other . . . and the socius/the system which contains and sustains us." The ethical is, in short, "a praxis which will cost me something if it is effective. A praxis of the absolutely particular for which there can be no rules, no principles and no guarantees. A praxis of risk and response-ability in which, I believe, lies our only hope for real political change."[32]

The uncertainty and between-ness of this ethical mode of knowing/being contrasts starkly with the sovereignty and control assumed by technical rationality, the de facto norm by which the worth of instruction is so widely gauged. But the point is, technical reason does not comprise the whole of our rational powers and clearly has its limits. The ethical encounter deploys a rationality of its own, and is not just potentially educative, but in a pivotal sense, considerably more so than the theoretical and technical enterprises in which instruction invests so overwhelmingly. Finn points to another way of knowing, one deployed and at home in the realm of practical human interactions, and one that draws demandingly on our full powers of creative consciousness. The ethical encounter is grounded in commitment, caring, and responsibility. The question that lies at its heart (the question which is ethics) arises in the confrontation of good with good.[33]

Episteme, Techne, Praxis, and Phronesis

Since it has potentially far-reaching implications for the way we conceptualize education and, hence, musical in-

struction with educational intent, I want to pursue further this intriguing account of ethical engagement and the kind of knowledge required of the ethical agent, and to do so through Aristotle. While we often associate his name with the syllogism and its logical rules, Aristotle explicitly acknowledged the existence and importance of three distinct kinds of knowledge, or three ways of knowing.[34] Theory (episteme), or pure contemplative knowledge, was concerned with timeless universals. By contrast, there are ways of knowing that are practical and more personal in nature, the kinds of knowing deployed and exercised in the changing situations of human makings and doings. This domain of practical knowledge or personal know-how takes two distinct forms: techne, the technical/procedural know-how exemplified by the making-actions of the skilled craftsman;[35] and praxis, the experiential resourcefulness (or wisdom, perhaps) by which people navigate the social/political world. In other words, Aristotle described two kinds of know-how, of personal or action knowledge: techne and praxis.[36] Part of what distinguishes the latter from the former is the kind of situation in which it is deployed. The other distinguishing feature of praxis, and the one in which I am primarily interested here, is what one might call its guidance system. Praxis is grounded in and takes its guidance from phronesis, an ethic concerned with right action in the variable and unpredictable realm of human interactions. Praxis is tightly tethered to the concreteness and particularity of experience on the one hand, and to one's identity or selfhood. Thus, praxical know-how is fundamentally reliant on the processual monitoring of this personal ethical fluency called phronesis.[37] Techne, on the other hand, is more akin to what we sometimes call "method," a kind of knowledge that, though practical, can be detached from the person whose knowledge it is and transferred or taught to others. It has a kind of generality that renders it "portable" between different situations and contexts.

Let us set Aristotle's episteme aside, concentrating for the moment on the distinctions between his two modes of practical knowledge. Recall that it is the conflation of these two modes of knowing, the reduction of ethics to technique, that concerns Finn. That is my concern as well, for the distinction has important consequences for our effort to shed light on the educational significance of musical studies and musical experience. If, as I believe they are, education and music are praxes (instances of praxis), they are fundamentally reliant on guidance by this ethical/phronetic fluency; and if that is so, then approaching them technically threatens to neutralize the mode of encounter essential to the realization of truly educational outcomes. Useful though techniques and methods are within certain spheres of activity, they lack the characteristic between-ness of ethical space. The problem is captured vividly in a passage from Wittgenstein:

The more narrowly we examine actual language, the sharper becomes the conflict between it and our requirement. (For the crystalline purity of logic was, of course, not a *result of investigation*: it was a requirement.) The conflict becomes intolerable; the requirement is now in danger of becoming empty.—We have got onto slippery ice where there is no friction and so in a certain sense the condition is ideal, but also, just because of that, we are unable to walk. We want to walk: so we need *friction*. Back to the rough ground![38]

The difference between logic's "crystalline purity" and the messiness of ordinary conversation, between the slipperiness of ice and the sure footing afforded by rough ground, parallels that between techne and praxis in interesting ways.[39] Technical rationality is perfectly fine in its domain, as ice is fine for skating. However, talking and walking require grounds better suited to those ways of getting around. We need language that lends itself to our practical discursive needs, and footing whose "grip" enables us to change direction as necessary. The point that began to emerge in our consideration of Finn can now be made more fully explicit. The ethical attitude she describes is the means by which we maintain our bearings in the concrete, ever-changing world of everyday experience. And because that is so, the kind of fully engaged presence it demands can hardly be regarded as an educational luxury. Such experience is, to borrow a phrase from Gadamer, "perhaps the fundamental form of experience compared with which all other experience represents a denaturing."[40]

Techne, in contrast, is a practical knowledge applied to making-actions instead of human interactions. Its end, envisioned at the outset, guides one's actions and provides a relatively stable measure for gauging successful action. Dunne (1997) argues, further, that even though techne is not theoretical in the purely contemplative sense of *episteme*, it nonetheless has many of the hallmarks Aristotle attributed to theory: "a concern not so much with particular instances as with a knowledge that is explanatory, generalized, systematic, and transmissible, and is at the same time a source of reliable control over the facts that it brings within its ambit" (1997, p. 228). To the extent techne is more interested in generality, replication or reliability than particularity and concreteness, more interested in controlled accuracy than in qualitative richness, it gravitates more toward the theoretical pole than the practical one.

However, Dunne continues, "Much in the conduct of practical affairs depends on singular judgments which cannot be derived from, and answer to epistemic conditions different from those of, idealized [technical, abstractive] discourse" (1997, p. 381). Praxis is not some vague, deficient version of episteme or techne, then. It is not just well suited, it is utterly essential to "right action" in the here-and-now, real-time, human social world. And importantly for our purposes here, it is an experiential, personal knowledge, rooted in one's sense of who one is. Phronesis requires presence or close attunement to the particular occasion, an attunement which assures one's actions are directed to the "right person, to the right extent, at the right time, with the right aim, and in the right way."[41]

We might say, then, that praxis is unavoidably contextual. It is a situation-specific knowledge and is therefore finite and contingent by nature. It has an inescapable element of hazard, which it retains no matter how proficient one becomes, because each new start is in crucial ways a new action/event. It is also vulnerable or fallible, Hannah Arendt observes, in its dependency "upon the unreliable and only temporary agreement of many wills and intentions," because of which it cannot "be possessed like strength or applied like force."[42] Thus, praxis demands of the agent/knower a deep engagement or involvement, a high level of alertness, and a flexible responsiveness to changes in the experiential field.

Praxis is "lighter on its feet" than the making-knowledge that guides techne, because its terrain is that of human interaction where unpredictability, complexity, and change are norms. Unlike technical know-how, praxis has no clear-cut, preordained outcome to which it can turn for guidance or validation. Praxis takes its bearings from a phronetic sense of what is important and appropriate as the experience unfolds in time. Because of the particularity and unpredictability of its terrain and its requisite responsiveness and flexibility, phronesis is talk-like, conversational. It holds its convictions provisionally, reassessing and revising them in light of what other participants contribute.[43] As experiential knowledge, praxis is not just at home with the possibility of surprise; its comfort with the unexpected is central to effective guidance within fluid, here-and-now circumstances. Among the distinctive traits of phronesis is openness to the unforeseen, comfort with being-in-play, improvisatory quickness.[44] An important part of what distinguishes an "experienced" person is precisely a "readiness for" and openness to further experience. In Dunne's words, "To be experienced does not mean to have had one's surprises so that one is now proof against any new ones but, on the contrary, to have learned to be at home with the possibility of surprise as a permanent possibility inseparable from historical existence itself."[45]

As we have been seeing, because phronesis is not instrumental and because it is concerned with concreteness, experience and perceptiveness are the primary assets of praxis, *not formulated knowledge*. The root of phronesis is a "refined sense of the contingencies of a particular situation," an ineffable yet reliable sense for what Sparshott calls "the nerve of a practice."[46] Phronesis enables one to discern what is significant and how to act rightly in diverse and fluid situations, fields of action for whose demands one can never be fully prepared.

The Corporeal Root of Practical Knowledge

The words I am using to describe phronesis resist my desire to portray it as a processual fluency rather than an inert "thing" or abstract "capacity." So I must reassert the crucial point that phronesis, this ethical disposition on which praxis relies so fundamentally, is not some "thing" one first possesses, then applies. It is part of one's very character, inseparable from one's identity. "Phronesis is not a cognitive capacity that one has at one's disposal but is, rather, very closely bound up with the kind of person that one is," comments Dunne (1997, p. 273). "All genuine phronesis," he remarks elsewhere, "is absorbed into action—action as an ineluctable movement that a person can never step out of" (1997, p. 268). One does not so much deploy phronesis as enact it. Nor is the identity or character to which it is so inextricably linked abstract and disembodied. This ethical mode of being present to otherness does not take its guidance from some detached intellectual regulatory mechanism but from one's entire being. One's corporeality or embodiment is thus a profoundly important dimension of phronesis. One's sense of how best to make one's way in unfamiliar situations is mediated by the body, and not casually. As one feels one's way forward, the sense that finds one lead or possibility compelling, and another barren, is deeply rooted in the body. Einstein's claim that his sense of discovery was muscular in character is a case in point.

Pierre Bourdieu puts it this way:

Practical belief is not a state of mind, still less a kind of arbitrary adherence to a set of instituted dogmas and doctrines (beliefs), but rather a state of the body. Doxa is . . . the pre-verbal taking-for-granted of the world that flows from practical sense. Enacted belief, instilled by the childhood learning that treats the body as a living memory pad, an automaton that leads the mind unconsciously along with it, and as a repository for the most precious values . . . is the product of quasi-bodily dispositions, operational schemes, analogous to the rhythm of a line of verse whose words have been forgotten, or the thread of a discourse that is being improvised. . . . Practical sense, social necessity turned into nature, converted into motor schemes and body automatisms, is what causes practices . . . to be *sensible*, that is, informed by a common sense. It is because agents never know completely what they are doing that what they do has more sense than they know.

Every social order systematically takes advantage of the disposition of the body and language to function as depositories of deferred thoughts that can be triggered off at a distance in space and time by the simple effect of replacing the body in an overall posture which recalls the associated thoughts and feelings, in one of the inductive states of the body which, as actors know, give rise to states of mind.[47]

The body, Bourdieu continues, "does not represent what it performs, it does not memorize the past, it *enacts* the past, bringing it back to life. What is 'learned by the body' is not something that one has, like knowledge that can be brandished, but something that one is."[48] This bodily basis of practical sense or know-how, the ineffable feel for which course of action may be "right" in novel circumstances, lies at the heart of phronesis.[49]

It is well worth noting that what we are discussing here is not "human instinct" in any transcendental or universal sense, and that the identity with which this bodily dimension is so intimately intertwined is a contingent one that is always under construction. Our bodily actions build on habits and on the firing of neural pathways whose routing depends on the contingencies of personal experience. Phronesis is thus borne of the habits, needs, purposes, and actions of each of us individually, and the kind of guidance it affords is, although grounded in human bodies that are alike in many ways, deeply personal because of the uniqueness of each individual's experience. This personal nature of phronesis is a central reason it cannot be passed directly or mechanically from one person to the next. To the extent it is deeply personal, such knowledge is both "subjective" and tacit. Yet, as Michael Polanyi demonstrated so compellingly, such knowledge must not be regarded for those reasons as unreliable or somehow dispensable to human endeavor.[50]

Finally, because embodiment, action, and agency are crucial components of phronesis, it is a fundamentally social phenomenon. Phronesis, comments Dunne, is "an enactment through which [people] constitute themselves as persons in a historical community. It is through praxis that a person comes to have an individual identity, but at the same time it always transpires within an intersubjective medium."[51] Thus, phronesis is no less than a "medium for becoming through action" (1997, p. 263). It is, one might say, a prime instance of *a doing, that constitutes a being.*[52]

Education and Phronesis

This chapter began by examining differences between education and training. I trust that the parallels between that discussion and the techne/praxis contrast are sufficiently evident that they require no elaboration. But before turning directly to music education, let us return briefly to the aims of education, examining them against the background of the ethical/phronetic strand of action/knowledge I have been attempting to illuminate. How does our acknowledgment of the between-ness of practical judgment refine or qualify what we might want to claim for the educated person, the human needs and tendencies to which education ministers?

First, I hope we might be inclined to grant that one of the central aims of education should be that phronesis become an abiding disposition, that phronetic dispositions become features of one's identity. Flexibility and openness to experience, convictions held provisionally and sustained by experimental attitudes, discernment and acceptance of what is unique in a given situation: Surely these are educational virtues. They are educational virtues in no small part because of the ballast they provide against the human tendency to dogmatism and stereotype. It is easier to see what is familiar than what is distinctive, far easier to use the perceptual and conceptual tools that are in wide circulation than to construct and reconstruct one's own in cooperation with others. But stereotype and dogma are fundamental obstacles to transformation and progressive change. They are tools of oppression, and deliver a view of human possibilities as all-or-none, black-or-white. The realm of human meaning is, as Dewey insisted, wider, more urgent, and more fertile (1958, p. 410). The person for whom phronesis has become an abiding disposition is one who recognizes and appreciates the urgency and fertility of knowledge that may not conform to logic's crystalline structure.

That is not to say that logic, reason, and generalizable knowledge do not have their legitimate place. They do, of course. But it is an important educational advance when fascination with their remarkable rigor is balanced by awareness of their restricted sphere of validity. The point of emphasizing phronetic dispositions is not to dispute the efficacy of theory and technique but to remind us of their limitations and consequences, and to reassure us of the integrity of a way of knowing and living beyond the jurisdiction of technical discourse.

Second, capacities like improvisatory resourcefulness and agility, the creative and constructive impulses at work in phronesis, are important reminders of the fluidity and malleability of human knowledge and of the necessity for openness and flexibility in human affairs. They alert us to the essential role the knower plays in all knowing, and of the intersubjective ground on which all knowing ultimately rests. The nerve of phronetic action is, as we suggested earlier, conversational. It is inseparable from the ethos in which it arises, and is never available to us as a technique. It has neither a preordained structure nor outcome. It arises and is carried forward by a "lack" on both sides.

Third, phronetic experience is proof of the integrity of action. Neither creativity nor discovery can know its outcome at outset, and both are guided by what Michael Polanyi describes as a "deepening gradient of coherence,"[53] not by rules. In an ever-increasingly "managed" society,[54] it is crucial we recognize that such profoundly important things as conversations and creativity and discovery cannot be perfected through management, they must be ministered to. An education that nurtures and sustains our trust in phronetic dispositions may be our best hope of preserving such essential capacities as these.

Fourth, a commitment to educating for phronetic dispositions has significant implications for the way instruction occurs and for the kind of interaction we understand it to be. If our aim is to foster ethical awareness, appreciation of the importance of the between-ness of the ethical encounter, the power and authority vested in teachers as purveyors of knowledge and judges of skill must somehow be softened and decentered.[55] Since phronesis is not the kind of disposition that can be technically dispensed or "managed," it must be exemplified in teachers' attitudes and relationships to students. Fallibilism and openness to unexpected outcomes would need to become prominent features of instructional style, as would such ethical concerns as commitment to justice, mutuality of respect, and so on. Moreover, learners would have to be given rights of intellectual disagreement, provided they are first able to state views they oppose in ways acceptable to those who hold them. In other words, deliberate steps would need to be taken to assure that the power and authority that come of knowledge are not abused, but wielded lightly. Teachers would have to be seen not as dogmatic authorities, but as members of the community of learners.[56]

If we take as given that technical and theoretical rationality are constitutive of reason, then phronesis, itself neither technical nor theoretical, is, by syllogistic logic, irrational.[57] But it is precisely the point here that "reason" so construed does not exhaust the rational capacities of which humans routinely avail themselves. In fact, if we look at people's everyday deeds and actions, we see that they are engaged extensively in undertakings that, while not irrational, proceed entirely without recourse to theoretical or technical rationality. The problem with "reason" and the "logocentrism" with which it is closely allied is that we have placed inordinate emphasis on reason's "epistemic functions," writes Nicholas Burbules, and neglected the "moral and political dimensions that are actually at the heart of decisions about what to believe and how to act" (1995, p. 83). The postmodern "rage against reason," while justified in certain respects, is really directed at reason conceived as a narrow, rigid, and exclusively logical instrument—or in the terminology I have been using here, a technique or method. However, reason can be reconstructed in ways that avoid the evils attributed to it by postmodern critics without capitulating to abject relativism or nihilism. What is needed, Burbules argues, is a more inclusive and flexible understanding of reason, one more accommodating of such things as pluralism and diversity, and one more modest in its presumed sphere of validity. Drawing from Charles Taylor and Richard Rorty, respectively, Burbules points out that rationality involves more than avoiding inconsistency, and that reason "names a set of moral virtues: tolerance, respect for the opinions of those around one, willingness to listen, reliance on persuasion, not force."[58] What we require, Burbules concludes, is a character-driven view of reason, one distinguished not for its strict adherence to logic but for its qualities of reasonableness.

"A person who is reasonable wants to make sense, wants to be fair to alternative points of view, wants to be careful and prudent in the adoption of important positions in life, is willing to admit when he or she has made a mistake, and so on" (Burbules, 1995, p. 86). A reasonable person is also one who is able to engage others in debate about beliefs and values, but conversationally rather than in an adversarial manner, and with the objective of reaching understanding rather than winning. In contrast to the individualism of Cartesian reasoning, reasonableness is very much an intersubjective, socially interactive achievement.

However, and this is particularly important in light of the emphasis on tolerance and plurality I have been advancing here, reasonableness requires a fundamental critical strain as well. By failing to resist the status quo when required, one becomes part of the machinery that perpetuates it. Thus, where circumstances are unreasonable, as they often are, it may be unreasonable to act reasonably. After all, to be reasonable does not mean one's mind is so open one's brain falls out; and tolerance for "many" cannot mean just "any."[59] The educated person, like the human agent guided by phronesis, is at once open and discriminating, at once tolerant and critical, at once patient and passionate, at once cooperative and independent, and at once confident and humble. If the proper balance between and among these is not something amenable to formula or rule, that is precisely the point we have been pursuing. Because of commitment to principles like fairness, equality and justice the educated person is tolerant of ambiguity, complexity, and diversity. Yet not infinitely so: the educated person is trusting, but not gullible. And so, an educated person is one who, while respectful of and open to the views and values of others, also has the courage and means to think and act independently where necessary. Many of the virtues of education are, as Frye reminded us, social vices: the tendency, for instance, to question "received wisdom," "common sense," and authority. It is therefore imperative that education allow learners the latitude to pull away from "the kind of well-adjusted social behavior that leads to security, popularity, and the death of the free mind" (Frye, 1988, p. 72).

Musical Education as Ethical Interaction

I have suggested from a number of perspectives now that education requires Wittgenstein's "rougher ground" as a fundamental condition of its possibility. While my arguments may have been suggestive, though, we have yet to ask explicitly what all this has to do with music, or how music may fit into such a scheme. How might the idea of educating through music, and of teaching for ends like those described here, reorient our conception of music education and the kinds of interactions of which it should consist?[60] How might recognition of music education's moral and ethical dimensions alter our views of what curricular practices and experiences are desirable? In what ways might an educational emphasis reorient our assumptions about the proper focus of musical instruction and research? In what ways is musical experience well suited to the ethical and educational aims discussed here? Under what circumstances is it not? Reasonable though it may be to conceive of education as an ethical undertaking, is it right to think of musical experience itself as an ethical encounter—and particularly well suited to developing the kinds of dispositions we have suggested characterize the educated? Is the act of making music itself ethical in some sense, or do such acts only *resemble* the ethical encounter in certain interesting ways?[61]

Because the scope of this essay does not permit full treatment of each of these issues, some of them must await exploration elsewhere. My conviction, however, is that music and music education are indeed ethically significant enterprises[62] and I want to suggest some ways in which it may be fruitful to consider them so. Because many regard the distinction between "moral value"[63] and musical value (apparently synonymous, for some, with "aesthetic" value) to be a crucial philosophical advance, however, several preliminary points are necessary. First, ascribing an ethical or moral dimension to musical experience does not entail reducing all musical value to moral or ethical value, any more than acknowledging that music is fundamentally social means it is nothing but social. I am not proposing the reduction of musical value to moral value. Rather, I am urging recognition of a musical dimension obscured by historically formalistic philosophical enterprises. Second, to say music is an ethical space or constitutes an ethical encounter is not to claim that engaging in music makes one morally good or upright. Such a claim would entail the very means-ends relationship whose absence distinguishes practical ethics from technique.[64] Nor is it being suggested that curricular decisions be guided by some explicit, identifiable moral character supposedly implicated in music.

I do think it may be reasonable, however, to suggest that certain musical endeavors and experiences can develop dispositions that are potentially useful in other ethical situations. Musical experience has the potential to impart ethical dispositions, and to exercise the kind of phronetically guided experience that is the *sine qua non* of practical wisdom. It can achieve this, however, only if it is experienced or learned in ways that foreground betweenness and nurture the attitudes on which practical judgment relies. There are musics, modes of instruction, and ways of experiencing music that are poorly suited to nurturing and sustaining such dispositions, and still others that threaten to extinguish them. Just as lyre playing begets both good and bad lyre players, music can be taught and experienced in ways that subvert its ethical potential or divert its unique power to undesired ends. Engaging in musical instruction with educational intent requires we attend to what is being performed, experienced, taught, or learned besides the "music itself." In particular, it should make us wary of the idea that "if it sounds right it is right."[65] Surely, one of the important insights attending recognition of music's ethical capacity is that sounding right and "being right" do not necessarily go hand in hand.

Our concern in this chapter is to formulate an understanding of music education by asking not what music is, but by asking first what we want or need education to do for our children and society, and then asking what musical experience has to offer. The question becomes, then, in what ways may particular musics and instructional practices be well suited to ends that are specifically educational? The desire to share one's passion for music with others is both laudable and crucial to musical instruction. But it is important to remember that this passion is a function not just of what music is, but of our experiences with it, and what and who we have become through such experiences.[66] Likewise, although it is defensible and pedagogically sound to urge that music be taught and experienced in ways that enable people to know it authentically, it is equally important to recall that knowing about music or making it well does not automatically constitute educational outcomes.

To illustrate the potential significance of this point, consider David Elliott's argument that music education should be multicultural. The ground for his claim is that since music is multiple and culturally situated, musical instruction must make these musical facts apparent. "If [music] consists in a diversity of musical cultures, then [music] is inherently multicultural. And if [music] is inherently multicultural, then music education ought to be multicultural in essence."[67] Only, these facts about music's nature are, even if valid, insufficient to establish either that music should be taught or that it should be taught multicultur-

ally. That is because a descriptive claim (music is . . .) does not in itself implicate a normative one (education about it should be . . .). Perhaps, then, *music education* need not be multicultural even if we are in agreement that *music* is. And perhaps the more important consideration as to how music education should be conceived and conducted lies in "oughts" or normative considerations that may be, for educational purposes, prior to music's nature.

Let us examine several issues here. If music has an essence and that music is indeed multicultural, then it would seem to follow that the truer musical instruction and curriculum are to this essence, the more radically multiple must be the musics studied and experienced. But this authentic grasp of music's multicultural nature would obviously entail unacceptable sacrifices to meaningful engagement in a single music. Perhaps, then, limited instructional time and resources might be better invested in efforts to nurture students' capacities to experience one music deeply and meaningfully, regardless of music's multiplicity. Or perhaps the abundant diversity of Western art music is sufficient to sustain an authentic grasp of music's inherent multiplicity. It might even be argued that music's diversity is so radically multiple that it can neither be taught nor fully grasped, and that instructional priorities should be guided by more manageable concerns.

I am not disputing the validity of multicultural approaches to music education. I only want to point out that "ought" claims rely on our aspirations for education, on the kind of interaction we understand it to be, and on the kind of people and societies we hope to foster through those interactions. A multicultural claim for music education follows more compellingly from a transformative vision rooted in convictions about who we ought to become through musical experiences than from ontological claims, however justified, about what music is. In other words, musical multiculturalism as an educational ideal emerges more convincingly from concerns about people, oppression, tolerance, diversity, understanding, and sharing, than from an interest in knowing music adequately. Because education is concerned with selective cultivation, it cannot be infinitely inclusive. Therefore, educational philosophy is inescapably normative. One must choose, for instance, between the liberal ideal of breadth and the conservative ideal of depth. One must choose between the kind of knowledge that comes with diverse musical experiential roots and that which can only come from deep, sustained immersion in a particular practice.[68] It is unlikely that both can be achieved in the same program.

The insufficiency of music's nature and value to educational ends does not mean that music is ill suited to the attainment of such ends. It means that the attainment of educational ends through musical experience is contingent rather than automatic. And it means that music education must be guided by discriminating judgment as to what musical and instructional practices do or do not constitute right action toward educational aims. Such instructional and curricular decisions comprise the most conspicuously ethical dimension of music education, because they concern the cultivation of habits, preferences, and dispositions, and ultimately, what kind of people our students become.

The implications are clear. Musical instructional arrangements and experiences should move students deliberately toward the attributes we have predicated of educational experience, while arrangements and experiences that nurture things like dependency and dogmatism should be avoided. It is difficult to imagine a music educator taking issue with these claims. And, yet, we need not look far to find musical and instructional practices that exhibit considerable tension with educational aims. The master-apprentice mode of applied music instruction, for instance, too often focuses on the imitative repetition to the detriment of educational ideals like independence, or the refinement of technical skills at the expense of curiosity, flexibility, and experimental-mindedness. Large ensembles where most musical decisions are made by a director may be better suited to nurturing conformity and submission to authority than self-reliance and creativity. Instructional approaches to music theory or history that dispense black-and-white answers and single points of view may neglect inquisitiveness and fail to help learners take initiative and responsibility for their own learning. Overreliance on the written score may cause students' imaginations to atrophy. Music programs devoted predominantly to appreciative listening or aesthetic responsiveness may inadvertently train people for lives devoted to receptivity and consumption rather than action and production.

How Is Music Suited to Educational Aims?

Concerns like those I have just raised can be countered by modifying instructional practices, of course. They are not inherent in music, after all, only functions of the way it is taught and experienced. Music can be taught in ways that either support or subvert educational aims. But that is not a very strong case for music education, as presumably the same is true of most things. We can and should take our lead from education, then, but we need to return to music's nature, and to ask what there is about music and musical experience that make them particularly likely candidates for instruction with specifically educational intent. When we turn to that task, several musical facts seem particularly salient. Music is a fundamentally social activity grounded in sonorous experience. It consists, furthermore, in ritualistic enactments of certain kinds of social relatedness. And the phenomenal character of musical engagements is unlike any other, as the musically engaged person becomes one with the music, or becomes what one writer memorably

describes as a "body in a state of music."[69] These facts suggest a number of ways in which music, taught and experienced properly, may be particularly well suited to the educational aims we have been exploring in this chapter.

In the first place, musical engagement is in many respects a perfect example of the between-ness of the ethical encounter, because it consists in a process of becoming without a point of arrival. It is resistant, complex, fragile, elusive, and therefore deeply engaging. Sustaining it demands our full presence and the deployment of all the powers at our disposal. It requires an attitude of caring and commitment, an investment on our part. And because of this, it is not so much something done or attended to as it is a vital part of who we are. To the extent it is successful, musical experience stands as vivid evidence of the integrity of the nontechnical kind of knowing on which the educated person draws in copious amounts and with relative fluency.

Second, making music draws on the kind of experiential knowledge that is one with action and human agency. It requires and nurtures the kind of improvisational resourcefulness and agility that makes the educated person comfortable with the unforeseen and open to change, confident that the resources at hand can somehow be made adequate to the challenges presented by a novel situation or unanticipated circumstances.

Musical experience is, further, a fundamentally social phenomenon,[70] which makes it well suited to exercising the cooperative and intersubjective understandings so crucial to attributes like tolerance, compassion, patience, and the ability to attend closely and empathetically to others. It is, as Charles Keil (Keil & Feld, 1994) urges, "our last and best source of participatory consciousness" (p. 20), a state sustained in important ways by the inevitable "participatory discrepancies" among players in the musical field and sounds they generate. However, it is not only social in this sense of being made with others, thereby satisfying what Keil calls the "urge to merge" (p. 217), it is also a potent tool in constructing and maintaining social identity. Musical activities are themselves ritual enactments of human social order.[71] Therefore, musical experience offers us vivid evidence of the moral desirability of engaging with others in the creation of intersubjective, participatory meanings, and of our mutual reliance on one another in all human endeavors.

Music's nature as ritual becomes crucial when we turn to what may be the most pivotal claim I want to make for music's ethical and educational significance. This claim is that we are what we do, and do repeatedly. Music's ritualistic actions and the dispositions that undergird them are fundamental to the formation of character, both collective and individual. More strongly still, music plays a fundamental role in the social production and regulation of identity. If music is an important part of the machinery by which people's individual and collective identities are constructed, reconstructed, maintained, and regulated, music education becomes something dramatically more momentous and problematic than an act of overseeing the development of musical skills, musicianship, or "aesthetic sensibilities." The view on which this claim is based is performative, one that sees identities not as natural facts, but cultural performances. However, "performances" must be understood here not as pretences, but as actions that actually generate what they enact: "doings" that constitute states of "being."

Music and Performativity

One of the best-known advocates of this performative account of identity is Judith Butler, who first developed her argument in a provocative book entitled *Gender Trouble* (1990). Although I will not pursue the matter extensively here, it is important to acknowledge at the outset that this reference to gender is not merely incidental to the idea of performative identity. For among other things, identity comes in genders. If music is involved in the production and regulation of identity, and if such identity is gendered, it is possible to construe musical experience as variously implicated in the formation and management of gender, and thus enmeshed in issues of power and politics. This is not the place to argue these points, but it is important that we see the extent and significance of the terrain potentially opened up by the idea of music's involvement in identity.

The main point of Butler's theory is that identity is not so much given as created. And what is thus created is not a permanent, unchanging self, but a fluid self that is constantly being re-created, refashioned, and redefined. Identity is always a doing, then, but it is not the achievement of a human subject that may be said to exist prior to the deed (1990, p. 25). Instead, the agent, the self, or the doer (one's identity) is variably constructed in and through its deeds and actions.[72] Accordingly, what we consider "the 'coherence' and 'continuity' of 'the person' are not logical or analytical features of personhood, but, rather, socially instituted and maintained norms of intelligibility" (1990, p. 17).

So selfhood and identity do not reside in some durable or essential substrate. They are created, rather, through our actions, our interactions, and our language. Put differently, people's identities are socially and discursively constituted. On this view, language "is not an *exterior medium or instrument* into which I pour a self and from which I glean a reflection of that self" (1990, pp. 143–44). Instead, the self is constituted in and through social and linguistic activity. Selfhood is "a sedimented effect of a reiterative or ritual practice" (Butler, 1993, p. 10).

The same claims may be made, I submit, for music. Music making and music listening are not mere exteriorities, activities in which a preexistent self engages, catching occasional glimpses of that self so engaged. Musicking does not give us insights into the patterns of human subjectivity so much as it shapes and molds subjective awareness and identity. As Eleanor Stubley shows so well, music making consists in "an ongoing tuning process in which the self is experienced as an identity in the making" (1998, p. 98). In nontrivial ways, selfhood and identity are created in and through musical activity. And to an extent far more significant than commonly acknowledged, people's identities are sedimented effects of reiterative or ritual musical action. Self-growth is not music's purview so much as self-creation.[73]

Thinking of musical engagements as ritual enactments of different modes of subjectivity, of different kinds of community, and so on, takes us well beyond the borders of "music proper" as discursively constituted by aesthetic formalism. It obliges music educators to inquire what, besides "the music" (construed as expressive sonorous patterns), is being performed, enacted, and taught. Once we grant that the idea of "music alone" represents a kind of false consciousness, it becomes imperative to ask whether what is being ritually enacted in musical settings is ethically, morally, or educationally desirable. If personal and social meanings are not mere contextual variables but are themselves part of musical content, segregating musical meanings from personal or social ones is no longer something we can do in good conscience. It is concerns like these that lead Suzanne Cuzick to wonder if her faithful performance of an art song might serve as an "act of public obedience to a culturally prescribed script," an enactment of self-suppression, obedience, and submission (1994, pp. 80–81). "Might my real work," she wonders, "be that of demonstrating for you how submission may be most beautifully performed? Might I always be performing the role of a subaltern who knows her place?" (1994, p. 92). If, in short, identity is performative, and if repeated musical acts (including, incidentally, the act of listening appreciatively) become part of the fabric of our very selves, it is incumbent upon us as educators to ask whether sounding good is all there is to being good musically, and to remain ever vigilant about what in addition to expressive sonorous patterns is produced in our musical doings. This dialectically interactive tension between music's formal and moral "goodness," between actions that are technically or even musically successful and actions that serve important human needs, makes of music education an endeavor considerably more complex than the development of musicianship or proficiency. But that complexity and the demands it makes on educator, listener, and music maker alike are precisely what makes music so well suited to developing the phronetic dispositions so central to education.

These accounts present powerful testimony to the potential of music to contribute significantly to the attainment of educational aims, with all the complexity we have seen that entails. But music is not just another option, just another means to such ends. Its material groundedness in the body makes musical experience momentous, gripping, and compelling to a degree few other human endeavors can claim. The uniquely corporeal dimension of musical experience and its remarkable capacity to engage a unified mind-body suggest that music is exceptionally suited to educational ends. The elusiveness of the border between music's capacity to sooth and noise's capacity to disturb, and the necessity that the musically engaged person monitor that ever-elusive border make of musical experience a prime example of ethical presence-to-the-other: a here-and-now experience for which there are no absolute rules, no guarantees, and no safety nets. Musical experience may be our most vividly compelling proof of the necessity for non-technical experience to the human life well lived.

Again we must acknowledge the contingency of all this. The fact that we are involved in making or responding to or learning about music actualizes none of these potentials automatically. What we are talking about is music taught, engaged in, and experienced in ways ethically desirable and educationally fruitful. The features that make music such a potentially powerful educational tool also can be deployed to ends that are undesirable. There exist at least two kinds of impediment to the successful realization of the educational potentials claimed here for music. First, there are impediments that deprive music of the richness, complexity, and wonder of ethical between-ness. The seductive lure of technique threatens to reduce education to training, teaching to "method," thought to formula, creativity to recipe, spontaneity to calculation, agency to consumption, and action to mere activity. Equally serious are those untheorized musical practices that deploy music's potency to ends incompatible with education. Such impediments to music's educational potential should be among the music education profession's most pressing concerns.

What Might These Points Mean for Music Education and Research?

It remains to say, in closing, how conceptualizing music education along the lines advanced here might change things. What real differences does it make? In the first place, it renders less obvious what music and music education are. It puts the disciplinary "self" into question in a way that blurs boundaries and raises a host of issues where remarkably few currently seem to exist. It demands that we seriously reexamine the focus and scope of our instructional, curricular, and research efforts. Without such

questioning and reexamination, professional growth is scarcely possible.

It also suggests a dramatic shift in the kind of question that interests us. It leads us away from our currently technical ("how-to") preoccupation, and toward questions like "whether," "when," "whose," and "why." It necessitates thinking of musical goodness in ways more complex and educationally relevant than those to which we have grown accustomed, and thinking of music in terms that extend well beyond the condition of its sounds. It strongly suggests that musicianship does not exhaust what the name "music education" commits us to developing. It requires that we learn to see musical instruction not as technical means to ends wholly musical, but as a process that exemplifies phronesis, and that provides students with experiences replete with opportunities to exercise such dispositions themselves. It requires that we become more attentive to much of what we are currently and mistakenly inclined to regard as "context" or "extramusical," and that we become much more resistant to attempts to separate music from the social ecology to which it owes its very existence.[74]

It suggests disenchantment with instructional and musical circumstances presided over by charismatic but dogmatic leaders, and it strongly implies an increased interest in musical processes like improvisation and creativity.[75] It requires a more explicit acknowledgment of the limitations of schooling and how these impinge on our ability to educate there. It means drawing the disciplinary boundary for music education much more openly and inclusively than is currently the case, in recognition of the fact that much music education, properly so-called, goes on in places other than schools.

Most important, it demands a concerted collective effort to recover the profoundly important potential of musical experience to facilitate ends truly educational: to nurture the character and dispositions people need to thrive in unpredictable or unforeseeable circumstances; to cultivate the openness, inquisitiveness, and resourcefulness essential to the life lived well; and to assure that people recognize such a life is possible only where justice and fairness are carefully and tightly woven into the fabric of which it is comprised.

Coda

I began this chapter with a distinction between musical instruction designed to train and musical instruction whose intent is educational. Some will criticize this distinction for its perceived black-and-whiteness: for setting up a rigid dichotomy that misrepresents training and is inconsistent with the themes developed later in my chapter. I think a close reading will show that such criticisms misconstrue my point. I have not argued that training is inevitably or invariably linked to dependence and inflexibility but, rather, that these are among its potentials, particularly when instruction is pursued without explicit commitment to (and systematic provision for) ends that are specifically educational. To train is not necessarily to educate.

The danger of misrepresenting training must be weighed, I submit, against the dangers of neglecting the distinction between training and education. The consequences of the latter are more grievous: the reduction of education to training; the substitution of technical fluency for ethical deliberation; the replacement of the practical knowledge at the heart of music making, teaching, and creativity with technical skill and theoretical understanding. My concern has not been to vilify training but to show that educational results do not follow automatically from musical instruction—even from musical instruction that is highly skilled or proficient. It all depends.

This contingency needs to be more salient in the conceptual frameworks that orient our research efforts, in the instructional concerns and practices we seek to illuminate through those efforts, and in our philosophical inquiry as well. It matters, and profoundly, what we mean when we presume to conduct research in the area of music education—where the boundaries of that disciplinary focus are drawn, what they are presumed to include or to exclude.

Research methods are only ways of investigating questions. Our research, therefore, can be no better than the questions we choose to explore. I hope I have shown that an explicit commitment to educating musically implicates a broader range and a different order of questions than have conventionally occupied our attention. The nature of educational commitments necessitates a concern with concrete situations and relations, an interest in the particularity of meanings, and a renewed recognition of the fundamentally ethical nature of music education.

NOTES

I wish to acknowledge, with gratitude, the many penetrating and challenging criticisms of an early draft of this chapter by numerous anonymous and semianonymous reviewers. I learned a great deal from them and the chapter is much better for their helpful insights.

1. This plurality and diversity of musical value may be reduced somewhat by restricting one's purview to "the art" of music. However, the precise nature and range of musical activity such a restriction entails, and whether such an exclusion is justified, remain contentious issues. If music is whatever people say or believe it is when engaging in it, its natures and values may well be innumerable.

2. Or in any case, they are not valued as highly as the outcomes promised by "other subjects of study." Here one

thinks, for instance, of music education's traditional claims to develop the life of feeling, or awareness of the patterns of human sentience. Part of the problem with this is that contemporary society codes feeling as feminine, and confers upon such concerns a status profoundly subordinate to masculine reason. See Morton (1996).

3. It is well worth noting that this is true not just of music, but of an immense potential range of human endeavors, such that this claim by itself is rather insubstantial. Also needed are arguments about how the kind of meaning and purpose music potentially provides is more desirable or durable than other contenders. That is one of the objectives of this chapter, which should become apparent eventually.

4. This is a conventional claim. It is important to add, however, that it also teaches us about those things that make us different. I am indebted to one of the reviewers of this chapter for this important point.

5. The underlying point here is one that many thoughtful music educators and scholars have attempted to express for years: As a profession, we must be concerned with education *through* music more than instruction *in* or *about* music. What might be distinctive in my treatment is the idea that this unavoidably implicates an ethical obligation for musical instruction, an "ethical turn" for music education philosophy. The formalistic predilections of our conventional philosophical orientations have led, I submit, to serious neglect of what some might wish to characterize as the human side of music education.

6. While some readers might fund this essay an "odd fit" for a research handbook, it is really not odd at all: The issues I will raise go right to the very heart of what music education is, what the "proper" object and range of music education research might be, and what means are best suited to the conduct of research in a discipline so construed.

7. An important caveat here. This distinction does not mean the differences between the two are insurmountable or absolute, or that drill and training are invariably negative, or that they are unavoidably opposed to education. Clearly, education relies and builds on training in important ways. But the fact that they are potentially interrelated does not mean that they are coextensive or that important distinctions cannot and should not be drawn. My point is that necessary though training may be to education, it is not sufficient. At issue is whether drill and training leave students better able to exercise independent judgment, or whether they ultimately give students more control over their lives or the skills and dispositions necessary to lives lived well. There is nothing wrong with an individual who is more knowledgeable or skilled telling or showing others what to do. Teaching involves cultivation, after all. The difficulty is that external constraints have a way of becoming internalized. We drill, train, or otherwise burden students legitimately and educatively if their freedom in the long term is enhanced by doing so. Drill and training contain an unavoidable coercive component, though, and instruction involves power and authority. The problem is to avoid subjecting students to arbitrary and excessive authority, making them dependent upon us for dependency's sake alone. A commitment to educating requires that the dependency as-

sociated with training and drill be temporary, and that the power and authority inherent in the instructional relationship be wielded lightly. The point, again, is that musical instruction is not automatically or necessarily educational. The advance or transition from training to education does not happen on its own: it needs to be the object of deliberate and strategic planning.

8. Lamb (1995), p. 126. It is worth noting that the term "praxis" is used here to designate "theorized practice" or practical engagement dialectically informed by critical/theoretical reflection.

9. 1992, pp. 180–81. Best goes on to assert that the decision to restrict one's purview to the development of technical skills "is itself a great responsibility" (182).

10. This possibility is made all the more disturbing by the often overwhelming beauty of musical experience. This is a point made vividly by Cuzick (1994).

11. In Peter Abbs's view, our neglect of true education and emphasis on technology have "erase[d] the thinker from the thought and ended in a landscape of dispossessed objects, systems without spirit, products without human purposes, closed questions unsupported by existential quests" (1994, p. 22). Part of what motivates this chapter is a conviction that, too often, musical instruction unwittingly serves these very ends.

12. Schools of music within North American colleges and universities evolved from music conservatories whose missions were straightforwardly to train professional musicians. This, along with the music education's close alliance with the music schools into which these conservatories eventually evolved, has been an important formative influence.

13. Wherein training for specific performing and reading skills was the norm.

14. In which case "school music" would be a more appropriate name for the discipline. Although the point that schooling and education are not synonymous is fairly commonplace, for most intents and purposes "music education" in North America denotes "school music." A broader conception of education would probably yield music education curricula substantially different from current configurations.

15. This in order to avoid the appearance of saying no more than "me, too," and to advance the position that music has something unique to offer, rather than being just another way of achieving outcomes rightly claimed by studies in other areas. The danger, I obviously am implying, is that many of the things that may best secure the argument for music education fall within the territory thus characterized as extramusical, as less-than-musical.

16. My use of quotation marks here is in the first instance to signal the irony of the view that what education does is, like business, add value—surely indicative of technicist assumptions. In the second instance, my intent is to question the adequacy of the assumption that music is properly regarded as a disciplinary area. Both seem to me highly reductive.

17. Waters/Pink Floyd (1979). Lessing (1962), xxiii–xxiv. I found both in an insightful essay by Bennett (1995), pp. 73–81. I hasten to add that overt indoctrination may not be the limit case after all, since the kinds of injustice and inequity

perpetuated systemically but remaining invisible and out of critical reach are probably more insidious.

18. Of practical knowledge, Bourdieu (1990, pp. 103–104) writes, "This practical sense, which does not burden itself with rules or principles (except in cases of misfiring or failure), still less with calculations or deductions . . . is what makes it possible to appreciate the meaning of the situation instantly, at a glance, in the heat of the action and to produce at once the opportune response. Only this kind of acquired mastery, functioning with the automatic reliability of an instinct, can make it possible to respond instantaneously to all the uncertain and ambiguous situations of practice."

19. This is not to say that education and the wisdom with which it is concerned cannot be cultivated, of course; only that they are not amenable to technical development. Best (1992, p. 182) points to one of the basic ways in which such cultivation diverges from training when he writes, "[The teacher] must try progressively to avoid indoctrination, the imposition, even inadvertently, of his [sic] own prejudices. He [sic] must stimulate and encourage the progressive development of the student's own attitudes, conceptions, feelings."

20. Such recognitions are themselves without criteria, defy technical transmission, and are functions of character or identity.

21. I see these as intimately related, and will use them more or less interchangeably. Those who think of identity as foundational or essential rather than constructed may wish to maintain that character and identity are different on that count. Since I do not find essentialist accounts of identity persuasive, I see the notion of character as closely related.

22. Interestingly, Dewey (1916, p. 383) says that "If we are willing to conceive education as the process of forming fundamental dispositions, intellectual and emotional, toward nature and fellow men [sic], philosophy may even be defined as the general theory of education."

23. Abbs, 1994, p. 18. Italics in the original.

24. Although his project differs from mine in many ways, John Richmond's "Beyond Aesthetics and Meaning: Ethics and the Philosophy of Music Education" (1996) provides a useful overview of schools of ethical thought and their applicability to music education.

25. Finn (1994), pp. 101–116. The specific point of Finn's essay is that feminists resist the temptation to debate ethical issues using rules and systems derived from and incorporating the values and assumptions of a patriarchal status quo—in particular, "the values of liberal individualism upon which the contemporary *polis* relies for its legitimation, reproduction and control" (p. 106). The point, in Audre Lorde's memorable words (1984), is that "The Master's tools will never dismantle the Master's house." Or as Judith Butler puts it, "[T]he feminist subject turns out to be discursively constituted by the very political system that is supposed to facilitate its emancipation. This becomes problematic if that system can be shown to produce gendered subjects along a differential axis of domination or to produce subjects who are presumed to be masculine. In such cases, an uncritical appeal to such a system for the emancipation of 'women' will be clearly self-defeating" (1990, p. 2). Although I have chosen to side-step

the political point of the argument in my treatment here, I encourage readers to pursue it on their own. I would be irresponsible were I not to acknowledge that many features of my essay are informed by feminist convictions and deeply indebted to feminist theory, which has greatly challenged, broadened, and humanized my thinking and writing.

26. From the perspective of its critics, this act of suspending presuppositions can only result in nihilism. But as Judith Butler writes (in another context), "To call a presupposition into question is not the same as doing away with it altogether; rather it is to free it from its metaphysical lodgings in order to understand what political interests were secured in and by that metaphysical placing, and thereby permit the term to occupy and to serve very different aims. . . . [A] loss of certainty is not the same as political nihilism. On the contrary, such a loss may well indicate a significant and promising shift in political thinking" (1993), p. 30.

27. Eleanor Stubley (1996, 1998) has explored closely and sensitively the notion of an ethical, in-between space as it relates specifically to musical performance in certain settings. Indeed, her poetic treatment is more successful in many respects than the prosaic exposition I undertake here. The concept of between-ness also figures in her essay (1999) "Modulating Identities and Musical Heritage: Improvisation as a Site for Self and Cultural Re-Generation."

28. Finn (1994, p. 104). There is interesting resonance between some of what Finn advances here and Theodor Adorno's comment in *Negative Dialectics* (1973) that "The power of the status quo puts up facades into which our consciousness crashes. It must seek to crash through them" (p. 17).

29. Finn (1994, p. 107). Again, Adorno's *Negative Dialectics* comes to mind: "Objects do not go into their concepts without leaving a remainder. Aware that the conceptual totality is mere appearance, I have no way but to break immanently . . . through the appearance of total identity. Since that totality is structured to accord with logic, however, whose core is the principle of the excluded middle, whatever will not fit this principle, whatever differs in quality, comes to be designated as a contradiction. Contradiction is nonidentity under the aspect of identity; the dialectical primacy of the principles of contradiction makes the thought of unity the measure of heterogeneity. As the heterogeneous collides with its limit, it exceeds itself. What we differentiate will appear divergent, dissonant, and negative for just as long as the structure of our consciousness obliges it to strive for unity" (p. 5).

30. Gadamer (1975, p. 324) calls this the "illusion of experience perfected and replaced by knowledge."

31. My intent is not to deny the validity of technical reason within its proper realm, but to urge against its sufficiency or suitability (particularly in light of its ideals of objective detachment, abstract universality, and control) to the conduct of life more generally.

32. Finn (1994, pp. 113–114). The political change to which she alludes here is concerned with social justice. If music educators are hard-pressed to see the relevance of such issues to their professional practice I hope the remainder of this chapter may offer some strong suggestions. Note that

Finn's use of "praxis" differs subtly from Lamb's cited earlier; nor is it the precisely same as the Aristotelian sense I will explore later. Advocates and critics of praxis-based accounts of music education would do well to recognize the diversity of meanings the term "praxis" carries. While that diversity is not nearly as radical as the semantic baggage that accompanies the term "aesthetic" it is no less important in discussions of praxis to stipulate in what sense the term is being used.

33. My choice of these words was inspired by a passage in Alasdair McIntyre's *After Virtue* (1984).

34. These receive a close and highly lucid treatment in Joseph Dunne's *Back to the Rough Ground*, on which I shall rely extensively in what follows. My primary concern here is to stress the contrasts between *techne* and *praxis*, the insufficiency of *techne* to *praxis*, and the potential educational consequences of failing to recognize such distinctions. As such, I will not explore the important relationships between and among theory, technique, and praxis. The idea of praxis is one of the orienting ideas for David Elliott's *Music Matters* (1995). An inductive approach to puzzling out the distinctive features of praxially informed music education can be found in my "The Limits and Grounds of Musical Praxialism," forthcoming in Elliott's *Critical Matters*. The most detailed and thorough analyses of the idea of praxis as it pertains to music education can be found in Thomas Regelski's recent work (1996, 1998a, 1998b).

35. It is worth noting that music was considered a *techne* in this scheme—a view, I submit, that must be regarded as misguided unless one restores to *techne* the integrity of which it is deprived when skill is regarded as mere manual dexterity. I believe praxis may be better suited to music, especially in light of its inextricably social nature.

36. The distinction between knowing-that and knowing-how is Ryle's, and is used extensively by David Elliott in his philosophical accounts of music education. I draw attention to the fact that know-how includes both *techne* and *praxis*.

37. Please note that ethical here does not mean "moral" or refer to the sets of rules and codes that have become substitutes for ethical engagement in much of the modern world. The application of such rules approximates more closely what I call "technical rationality" here. In an important sense, recourse to rules amounts to an evasion of ethical responsibility.

38. Wittgenstein (1976), §107 (p. 46). This passage is the source of Dunne's title, obviously.

39. I have been reminded by Eleanor Stubley that *techne* as Aristotle conceived it was not merely technical: it, like *praxis*, was personal and changing. The "mereness" of technique or technical rationality is not inherent in the making-actions of *techne*, then. It has, however, become a marked attribute of modern conceptions of technique.

40. Quoted in Dunne (1997), p. 127.

41. Aristotle, *Nicomachean Ethics*, quoted in Dunne (1997), p. 368. I make no claim to present a purely or authentically Aristotelian account of phronesis here. Rather, I draw my claims more broadly from the broad resources Dunne brings to bear on it in his book. It would probably be wise to distance the understanding of praxis/phronesis being advanced here from the Marxist view which, in portraying

moral life as a mere reflection of material production, develops what Jurgen Habermas argues convincingly is a highly reductive concept of *praxis* (Dunne, pp. 178–80).

42. Quoted in Dunne, p. 93.

43. Dunne explores Godamer's use of conversational metaphor on pages 117–21.

44. Please note that "improvisatory" does not here mean anything like capricious, or hastily thrown together. Rather, it points to the skillful making of numerous decisions and developing their implications "on the fly," in the midst of ever-changing circumstances. To improvise is to act without absolute foreknowledge, to work without a safety net. These are, I submit, necessary conditions of the ethical encounter.

45. Dunne (1997), p. 133, interpreting Gadamer. In these respects, Gadamer asserts that the experienced individual is quite unlike the person "captivated by dogma."

46. This reference to contingencies comes from Martha Nussbaum's *The Fragility of Goodness* (1968), p. 318, and is applied to phronesis by Dunne (1997), p. 102. Sparshott's useful phrase "the nerve of a practice" appears in his "Aesthetics of Music—Limits and Grounds" (1986), p. 53.

47. Pierre Bourdieu (1990), pp. 68–69. Mark Johnson (1987) and George Lakoff and Mark Johnson (1999) provide fascinating accounts of the embodied nature of cognition that are useful in showing how embodiment functions beyond the realm of practical reason with which Bourdieu is primarily concerned in the passage quoted here.

48. Bourdieu (1990, p. 73). Musicians will find the passage from which this quotation is drawn particularly cogent, since it goes on to speculate about the "disincarnation" or bodily disengagement that occurs when music is objectified.

49. My treatment of corporeality here can be justifiably criticized as an overly brief and passing gesture. I invite the reader to consult Stubley's work for outstanding examples of writing that keeps musical/ethical experience more fully and properly embodied. I argue the centrality of corporeality to musical experience in Bowman (2000).

50. Polyani (1958) does not address phronesis or the between-ness of the ethical encounter per se, nor does he stress the corporeal dimension. He does, however, advance a cogent account of the personal and tacit foundations of knowledge and the profound importance of such knowledge. See also my "Tacit Knowing, Musical Experience, and Music Instruction: The Significance of Michael Polanyi's Thought for Music Education" (1981).

51. These are Dunne's words, as he explores Habermas's account of praxis (p. 176). The distinction between technique and praxis is at the core of Habermas's critical philosophy.

52. Put differently, it is an action that generates what it enacts. This idea of "performativity" will be examined more directly in the final section of this paper, specifically with regard to the musical construction of identity.

53. Again, I suggest this deepening gradient is extensively mediated by the body.

54. Adorno often described modern society as "totally managed."

55. This is particularly true of an undertaking like music instruction, one might argue. Joyce Bellous (2000) of Mc-

Master University writes: "The problem with talent and identity in the musical arena has to do with the totality of the teacher's involvement over the learner—body, mind, and spirit. To be musical, and to develop the gift, the child's body is taken over by someone else who knows how the body should stand, look, posture itself, move, when and where. The influence of the musical teacher over the musical student is far more intrusive than the math teacher over the math student. Music didn't used to be the only discipline that did this. The English teacher, and every other teacher, had something to say about how the learner sat, held a pencil, looked toward the front and conveyed attentiveness. I think it is fair to suggest that only music remains in the domain of body management in this sense, and to the extreme that it does. Surely this must be seen as radically intrusive" (p. 39).

56. This is true in part because ethical attitudes and dispositions cannot be mechanically transmitted: they are not so much taught as caught.

57. In much the same way Maurice Merleau-Ponty's phenomenological effort to ground philosophy in bodily experience was called a philosophy of irrationalism by his critics.

58. Taylor is quoted on page 87 of "Reasonable Doubt" (Burbules, 1995). Rorty's statement comes from "Science and Solidarity," in Nelson, Megill, and McCloskey (1987), p. 40.

59. These phrases are Rorty's, I believe, although I can no longer recall where I encountered them. Both describe the "abject relativism" to which I referred earlier.

60. Musical performance and the connection between ethical thought and the construction of identity are given cogent treatment by Eleanor Stubley (1995), pp. 55–69. Indeed, these are important recurrent themes in Stubley's work.

61. Jane O'Dea, for instance, writes specifically of phronesis in music, but seems to stop short of the position being advanced here. "Excellence in musical performance requires the exercise of a species of reasoning and judgment *analogous* to Aristotelian practical wisdom," she writes (1993 p. 233), emphasis mine. O'Dea's reluctance to recognize music as itself-ethical stems, I believe, from a narrow, practice-specific view of "performance" and of "score" (wherein what performers do is *interpret scores*) and a failure to recognize music as itself social. Similarly, Elliott (1995, p. 167) suggests that "actions in musical performing parallel our actions in moral affairs." He comes closer than O'Dea to recognizing the ethical nature of music, indicating that "the self-other dialogue that we find at the center of music making is continuous with all other forms of ethical existence" (p. 168), but stops short of finding music itself an ethical encounter—this, one suspects, because of a failure to conceive of music as always also social. Stubley, by contrast, writes of the ". . . ethical tension experienced as the performer weighs the value of alternative courses of action" (1995, p. 62).

62. Of course there is nothing particularly "new" about this, except, perhaps, that these ideas have validity in the modern world. Both Plato and Aristotle attributed immensely important ethetic power for music, which was why it was deemed fundamental to *paideia*, or character education.

63. Although "the ethical" and "the moral" are not the same, I will mix references to the two in the latter part of this

essay. I am not entirely comfortable doing so. I would prefer to reserve "moral" for issues of right and wrong, or for conventional codes and standards of conduct, and "ethical" for the particular kind of encounter that has been characterized here as between-ness. In speaking about music's moral value in this sentence, I mean simply music's capacity to help or to harm, and have in mind the conventional codes mentioned above. Were I to speak of its ethical value, by contrast, I would hope to point to the distinctive capacity of music to situate people in the state of between-ness that has here been called ethical, the space opened up in the confrontation of good with good. Notes 37 and 64 may help clarify the distinction I want to make.

64. Conventional morality is, in this sense, technical rather than ethical.

65. Indeed, a phronesis of right action requires that we ask in what ways (plural) musical experience and musical instruction may or may not be "good," what they may be "good for" as well as "bad for," and then to ask critically whether musical experience or instruction actually delivers the goods. The point is crucial because of the unfortunate assumption, implicit in much conventional musical discourse, that being musically good or right is a strictly intramusical concern. That can only be true if music is reduced to its sonorous patterns. On the view being advanced here, people can be attracted to and perhaps even take deep satisfaction in musical activities with negative educational or ethical value.

66. It is equally important to note that "who we have become" through musical engagement is a function, in part, of its resistance and elusiveness, the ever escalating challenges that prevent us from "coasting" or "idling" with gears disengaged. Who we become through music is tightly bound up in its nature as a profoundly nontechnical mode of action-embedded knowing that demands of us full engagement of all our powers of knowing, doing, and being.

67. Elliott (1995, p. 207). I have changed Elliott's uppercase MUSIC to "music" in this passage because that distinction is not germane to the point at hand here. My intent is not to discredit Elliott or to dispute his conclusion. Indeed, I think a strong case for multicultural music education can be made. I only want to suggest that a stronger case seems to follow from normative educational considerations than from ontological/epistemological considerations about the nature of music.

68. Note that despite his claim to music's multicultural essence and insistence that music education be multicultural, Elliott ultimately endorses experiential richness and depth over breadth of exposure.

69. The quoted phrase appears in a discussion on Barthes in Middleton (1990, p. 181). Similar points appear in T. S. Eliot's (1988) reference to music experienced so deeply that "you are the music while the music lasts" and in Thomas Clifton's claim, "Music is what I am when I experience it" (1983, p. 297).

70. One anticipates the objection that music need not be social, since one can listen to it in private. But this overlooks the point that there can be no musical experience devoid of the social traditions and institutions by which it becomes mu-

sic. Even our most private musical experiences are social in that they rest on a physiological and culturally inflected constitution shared by normal individuals. Put in Deweyan terms, experience is always interaction of an organism with its environment, an environment that (especially in music's case) is human as well as physical, inclusive of materials shaped by human traditions. Music is shaped profoundly by the social contexts in which it is embedded, the social means of its production, and the social requirements of its reception. A musical experience devoid of social significance would not be musical, merely sonorous.

71. That all such enactments are not equally desirable is made abundantly clear by Jacques Attali (1985). R. Murray Schafer's (1976) characterization of the concert band as a purveyor of "herdesque happiness" puts still another spin on this.

72. Butler (1990, p. 142) denies this is simply a rehashing of the existentialist claim that existence precedes essence and that the self is constituted through its acts: "For existential theory maintains a prediscursive structure for both the self and its acts. It is precisely the discursively variable construction of each in and through the other that has interested me here," she adds.

73. The claim to insights into human subjectivity is Langer's. The claim to self growth is Elliott's. (Stubley, by the way, writes of self-discovery, self-definition, and identity-in-making—ideas that seem to point in the direction of the claim I make here.)

74. Joseph Kerman (1985, p. 73), writes, "By removing the bare score from its context . . . the analyst removes that organism from the ecology that sustains it."

75. In view of the widespread contemporary reduction of improvisation and composition to formula or technique, it is probably necessary for me to indicate emphatically that such approaches are not what I refer to here.

REFERENCES

Abbs, P. (1994). *The educational imperative: A defence of socratic and aesthetic learning.* London: Falmer Press.

Adorno, T. (1973). *Negative dialectics.* New York: Seabury Press.

Arendt, H. (1961). *Between past and future.* London: Faber and Faber.

Aristotle (1915). *Ethica Nicomachea.* Trans. W. D. Ross. In *The works of Aristotle translated into English.* London: Oxford University Press.

Attali, J. (1985). *Noise: The political economy of music.* Trans. B. Massumi. Minneapolis: University of Minnesota Press.

Bellous J. (2000). Talent and identity. *Orbit, 31*(1), 39. Excerpted from "Thoughts on Shaping Talent and Identity" by L. Bartel, J. Bellous, W. Bowman, & K. Peglar, in *Orbit, 31*(1) 2000 on-line edition [http://www.oise.utoronto.ca/orbit/vol31no1/tosti/index.html].

Bennett, P. (1995). Permit them to flourish. In W. Kohli (Ed.), *Critical conversations in philosophy of education* (pp. 73–81). New York: Routledge.

Best, D. (1992). *The rationality of feeling*. London: Falmer Press.

Bourdieu, P. (1990). *The logic of practice*. Stanford, CA: Stanford University Press.

Bowman, W. (1981). *Tacit knowing, musical experience, and music instruction: The significance of Michael Polanyi's thought for music education*. Unpublished Ed.D. dissertation, University of Illinois.

Bowman, W. (2000). A somatic, "Here and Now" semantic: Music, body, and self. *Council for Research in Music Education Bulletin 144*, 55–60.

Bowman, W. (forthcoming). The limits and grounds of musical praxialism. In D. Elliott (Ed.), *Critical matters in music education*. New York: Oxford University Press.

Burbules, N. (1995). Reasonable doubt: Toward a postmodern defense of reason as an educational aim. In W. Kohli (Ed.), *Critical conversations in philosophy of education* (pp. 82–102). New York: Routledge.

Butler, J. (1990). *Gender trouble: Feminism and the subversion of identity*. New York: Routledge.

Butler, J. (1993). *Bodies that matter: On the discursive limits of "Sex."* New York: Routledge.

Clifton, T. (1983). *Music as heard: A study in applied phenomenology*. New Haven: Yale University Press.

Cuzick, S. (1994). Gender and the cultural work of a classical music performance. *Repercussions, 3*(1), 77–110.

Dewey, J. (1916). *Democracy and education: An introduction to the philosophy of education*. New York: Macmillan.

Dewey, J. (1934). *Education and the social order*. New York: League for Industrial Democracy.

Dewey, J. (1958). *Experience and nature*. New York: Dover.

Dunne, J. (1997). *Back to the rough ground: Practical judgment and the lure of technique*. Notre Dame, IN: University of Notre Dame Press.

Eliot, T. S. (1988). The dry salvages: "V." *Four quartets*. New York: Harcourt Brace Jovanovich.

Elliott, D. (1995). *Music matters*. New York: Oxford University Press.

Finn, G. (1994). The space-between ethics and politics: Or, more of the same? In E. Godway & G. Finn (Eds.), *Who is this we? Absence of community* (pp. 101–115). Montreal: Black Rose Books.

Frye, N. (1988). *On education*. Markham, ON: Fitzhenry and Whiteside.

Gadamer, H.-G. (1975). *Truth and method*. Trans. G. Barden and J. Cumming. London: Sheed and Ward.

Johnson, M. (1987). *The body in the mind: The bodily basis of meaning, imagination, and reason*. Chicago: University of Chicago Press.

Kerman, J. (1985). *Contemplating music: Challenges to musicology*. Cambridge, MA: Harvard University Press.

Keil, C., & Feld, S. (1994). *Music grooves*. Chicago: University of Chicago Press.

Kohli, W. (1995). *Critical conversations in philosophy of education*. New York: Routledge.

Lakoff, G., & Johnson, M. (1999). *Philosophy in the flesh: The embodied mind and its challenge to Western thought*. New York: Basic Books.

Lamb, R. (1995). Tone deaf/symphonies singing: Sketches for a musicale. In Jane Gaskell & John Willinsky (Eds.), *Gender in/forms curriculum: From enrichment to transformation* (pp. 109–135). New York: Teachers College Press.

Lessing, D. (1962). *The golden notebook*. New York: McGraw-Hill.

Lorde, A. (1984). *Sister outsider*. Santa Cruz, CA: Crossing Press.

McIntyre, A. (1984). *After virtue*. Notre Dame, IN: University of Notre Dame Press.

Middleton, R. (1990). *Studying popular music*. Milton Keynes, UK: Open University Press.

Morton, C. (1996). *The "status problem": The feminized location of school music and the burden of justification*. Unpublished Ph.D. dissertation, University of Toronto.

Nelson, J., Megill, A., and McCloskey, D. (1987). *The rhetoric of the human sciences*. Madison: University of Wisconsin Press.

Nussbaum, M. (1968). *The fragility of goodness*. Cambridge: Cambridge University Press.

O'Dea, J. (1993). Phronesis in musical performance. *Journal of Philosophy of Education, 27*(2), 233–243.

Polanyi, M. (1958). *Personal knowledge: Towards a postcritical philosophy*. Chicago: University of Chicago Press.

Regelski, T. (1996). Prolegomenon to a praxial philosophy of music education. *Finnish Journal of Music Education, 1*(1), 23–38.

Regelski, T. (1998a). Schooling for musical praxis. *Finnish Journal of Music Education, 3*(1), 7–37.

Regelski, T. (1998b). The Aristotelian bases of praxis for music and music education as praxis. *Philosophy of Music Education Review, 6*(1), 22–59.

Richmond, J. (1996). Beyond aesthetics and meaning: Ethics and the philosophy of music education. In L. Bartel and D. Elliott (Eds.), *Critical reflections on music education: Proceedings of the Second International Symposium on the Philosophy of Music Education*, (pp. 1–22). Toronto: Canadian Music Research Centre.

Rorty, R. (1989). Education without dogma. *Dissent* (Spring), 198–204.

Schafer, R. M. (1976). *Creative music education: A handbook for the modern music teacher*. New York: Schirmer.

Sparshott, F. (1986). Aesthetics of music—Limits and grounds. In P. Alperson (Ed.), *What is music?* (pp. 33–100). New York: Haven Press.

Stubley, E. (1995). The performer, the score, the work: Musical performance and transactional reading. *Journal of Aesthetic Education, 29*(3), 55–69.

Stubley, E. (1996). Play and the field of musical performance. In L. Bartel and D. Elliott (Eds.), *Critical reflections on music education: Proceedings of the Second International Symposium on the Philosophy of Music Education*, (pp. 358–76). Toronto: Canadian Music Education Research Centre.

Stubley, E. (1998). Being in the body, being in the sound: A tale of modulating identities. *Journal of Aesthetic Education, 32*(4), 93–105.

Stubley, E. (1999). *Modulating identities and musical heritage: Improvisation as a site for self and cultural re-generation.* Unpublished paper presented at Canadian University Music Society and at Guelph Jazz Festival.

Waters, R., and Pink Floyd. (1979). Another brick in the wall, Part II. *The wall.* Columbia Records PC2-36183.

Wittgenstein, L. (1976). *Philosophical investigations.* Trans. G. E. M. Anscombe. New York: Macmillan.

Philosophical Perspectives on Research

7

DAVID J. ELLIOTT

Philosophy is the sustained, systematic and critical examination of belief. This chapter offers a critical examination of the beliefs underlying several types of research employed by music educators past and present. (Note: This chapter does not provide a philosophy of research; it offers a critique or meta-analysis of the assumptions anchoring various modes of "research.") The rationale for doing so is that to ignore the foundations of a given research framework is to risk applying it (or teaching it) inappropriately and narrowly, as a simplistic exercise in methods, procedures, or technologies. Put another way, a full understanding of "research" includes understanding the *why* of each form of inquiry as well as its *what* and *how*.

This kind of probe is not unusual. Historically, philosophers have continuously scrutinized the assumptions underpinning all forms of educational research, as one can see from critical discussions in the *Educational Researcher*, the *International Journal of Educational Research* and many similar publications. Unfortunately, research textbooks tend to focus narrowly on research designs, methods of data collection and procedures of data analysis (e.g., Best & Kahn, 1993; Borg & Gall, 1989). Their main purpose is to explain *how* to implement a limited range of research "tools." Although such texts may provide introductory remarks on the nature of research, these discussions are often restricted, uncritical, and acontextual. Consequently, the literature of music education research also tends to neglect the deep interdependencies among research modes, ideological convictions, and cultural values.

Another reason for this chapter, then, is to alert music educators to the social-cultural nature of research. Indeed, the rich variety of research frameworks we enjoy today reflects fundamental differences among scholars concerning the most basic issues and concepts of human culture. Examples of these contested concepts include the following: the objectivity/subjectivity of our world; the lawfulness or cause-effect nature of phenomena; the validity of concepts such as determinacy, rationality, impersonality, and prediction; the belief (or faith) in "scientific" methods as the ultimate model for all inquiries; and so forth.

Each form of inquiry, including scientific research, is embedded in a web of cultural and social beliefs. Regardless of the research problems involved, each type of inquiry rests on a particular version of reality (an *ontology*), a particular way of knowing the world (an *epistemology*), and a specific way of judging and justifying things in the world (an *axiology*). Note, also, that because model-building and theory-development are central to the conduct and interpretation of all research, investigators who fail to understand the grounding assumptions of their chosen form of research place their models in jeopardy from the outset.

The main body of this chapter examines the conceptual foundations of Empiricism, Positivism, Postpositivism, Interpretivism, Critical Theory, Gender Studies, and Postmodernism. (Note: Each of these categories of research subdivides into several subcategories I cannot address fully here. Also, I will not discuss historical and philosophical research since these are critically examined elsewhere in this volume.)

Before discussing each of these in turn, it is important to step back for a "wide-angle" perspective on the axioms that underpin these several forms of inquiry. Two concepts will help us greatly in building this perspective: *modernity* and *postmodernity*. (Note: I will follow the majority of scholars in making a basic distinction in this chapter between *postmodernity* as an era and *"postmodern-ism"* as distinct artistic and intellectual movements.) As we shall see, the nature of contemporary Western society, educational research and music education research are tied directly to issues and values inherent in these two concepts.

Research in Cultural Context

The word "modernity" is used in two ways: it names a period of history and it names the belief-system underlying this epoch. Historically, the origins of modernity trace back to the 18th-century European Enlightenment that reached maturity at the end of the 19th century (Kumar, 1995; Turner, 1991). The defining characteristics and institutions of contemporary Western societies trace their roots to Enlightenment beliefs. The belief-system called "modernity" rests on the following assumptions: The natural world can be transformed for the benefit of individuals and society-at-large through applications of scientific thinking to all aspects of intellectual, social, cultural, and economic life. The aims of modernity, says David Harvey (1989), were "to develop objective science, universal morality and law and autonomous art according to their inner logic or internal structure" (p. 9).

Fueled by enormous faith in the power of science, the advance of industrialization, the growth of secularism, and the potential of "rational" bureaucratic hierarchies, Enlightenment leaders set out to "modernize" the world. How? By boosting the productivity and prosperity of work and social life through scientific research and means-ends (input-output) forms of organization. However, like most human constructs, "modernization" and its guiding belief system (modernity) produced positive and negative results.

For example, the modernization of work achieved economic prosperity for many. Industrial and bureaucratic systems of organization increased Western productivity and prosperity enormously. Jobs became more plentiful and more secure over many decades. By contrast, the costs of modernity have been high. Employees of modernist industries have been routinely dehumanized through the strict standardization and fragmentation of tasks, the suppression of individual initiative and responsibility, strict supervision, long hours, and the rigorous "quality control" (or monitoring) of "work output."

We begin to see how modernity shaped Western education as we know it. In fact, mass education through public schooling is a cornerstone of modernity and the modern nation-state. On the one hand, schools and universities make cultural capital and economic success accessible and achievable for many. On the other hand, the public tends to assume it is natural to educate all children in factory-like settings based on modernity's scientific-industrial concepts, including standardized curricula, standardized achievement tests, teacher-centered methods, restricted instructional time, and age-segregated or ability-segregated classes. Even the design, look, feel, smell, and supervision of many institutions of mass education mimic modernist bureaucratic institutions where standardization, centrali-

zation, mass production and mass consumption are the norm (Hargreaves, 1994).

Modernity began to lose its grip on Western society toward the middle of the 20th century. Many "new" characteristics of Western societies that we experience today—the era of postmodernity—began to emerge in the late 1960s when major technological innovations fueled the globalization of communications, finance, politics, and most other aspects of our world. In the realms of work and finance, the 1970s marked a time of Western economic collapse. This economic crisis, in turn, precipitated political and social crises. Blame for these developments included a gradual loss of public faith in the rational-scientific bases of bureaucratic organizations: governments, corporations, hospitals, universities, and schools.

In other words, the basic assumption of modernity—that humans can find the "right" solutions to economic, organizational, social, and educational problems through scientific research—was challenged formally by intellectuals and questioned increasingly by public consumers. These challenges were part of broader crises that paved the way for postmodern alternatives to longstanding modernist assumptions about social norms and values, human "being" and the nature and generation of knowledge (Fornas, 1995; Hargreaves, 1994; Kumar, 1995).

Scholars today suggest we are living in the middle of a tense tug-of-war between two powerful social forces: the end of modernity and the advance of the postmodern world. Nowhere is this disunity more evident than in the worlds of education and research. A major difficulty in trying to understand the breadth and depth of our current situation is the paradoxical nature of postmodernity.

For example, a major feature of our times is flexibility. New forms of work and study have emerged. The inflexible standardization of the factory system has given way to integrated, overlapping or rotating tasks and job descriptions. More and more, then, schools are being forced to rethink their traditional assumptions about strict subject-matter divisions, inflexible scheduling and the "proper" length of time students should take to finish qualifications. But to what extent will demands for flexibility compromise the quality of education and our social commitment to the "true aims of education" as each one of us conceives these notions from our modernist or postmodern (or some other) belief system?

Indeed, given the tension between local and global forces, the increasing cultural diversity of "national" populations and the free flow of information via new technologies, it is not surprising that our postmodern world is brimming with competing beliefs. Only 20 years ago, scholars, researchers, teachers, and students still dealt in a fairly manageable range of knowledge, cultural, and religious assumptions, and so forth. Nowadays, however, every premise, every expert, and every "solution" is open to scrutiny from multiple directions. On the one hand, today's plurality of perspectives holds enormous potential for individual growth, collaborative research, and democratic development; on the other hand, the pluralism and ambiguity of our postmodern situation means bewilderment, frustration, or conflict for many.

Another feature of our era is the advance of digital technologies. In addition to providing many innovations affecting all aspects of life, computer technologies allow individuals and organizations to cut across borders and time zones instantly. Cyberspace challenges, compromises, or eradicates many important aspects of people's geographic, national, historic and cultural "space." With this comes personal disorientation, loss of identity, and fear, for many. Accordingly, and paradoxically, many communities worldwide are responding to digital globalization by "retreating inward" to defend their local ways of life (linguistic, cultural, religious) against the advance of (what they conceive to be) a digital-technological form of imperialism or colonialism.

Let us connect several points from the above to details of educational and music education research.

Educational Research in Context

The growth of the natural sciences in Europe cleared the way for the birth of educational research as an empirical discipline toward the end of the nineteenth century. In parallel with the aims and methods of experimental psychology (as developed by Wundt in 1880), "experimental pedagogy" (as it was known then) got underway around 1900 in Germany, France, the United States, and Switzerland (Landsheere, 1999).

The period of 1900–1930 was the heyday of empirical and early positivist research in education built primarily around behaviorist psychology. In line with the ideals of modernity, Thorndike (1901, 1903), among other thinkers (e.g., Watson, 1919), was intent on making education an exact science through empirical research. In his seminal book, *Educational Psychology* (1903), Thorndike rejected research based on "speculative opinions" in favor of a narrowly behaviorist conception of learning that revolved around stimuli, responses, and connections between them. This empirical-behaviorist view was taken up and advanced by the Harvard psychologist B. F. Skinner (1938, 1953, 1968), one of the most eminent educational researchers of the 20th century. Skinner's conceptions of research and behaviorism were positivistic to the core (positivism is a modified form of empiricism). Due to Skinner's influence, the behaviorist conception remained a dominant force in education and a testament to the continuance of

modernist thinking in education (e.g., Drumheller, 1971; Gronlund, 1970; Tanner, 1972) and music education (e.g., Madsen & Madsen, 1974; Madsen & Yarbrough, 1980).

Between 1900 and 1960, four other approaches to educational research emerged gradually as background to the dominant foreground of empirical-behaviorist research. These four were: (1) the "child study" movement, otherwise known as "child psychology"; (2) the New Education strand, or the "progressive" movement, which flowed from philosophical thinkers such as John Dewey; (3) the "new" scientific approach based on positivist assumptions; and (4) beginning in the later 1960s, interpretivist or qualitative approaches, which draw from several research traditions including sociology, anthropology, and philosophy.

In parallel with the gradual decline of modernity and the rise of postmodern thinking, educational research between (roughly) 1945 and 1970 became less dominated by empiricist-positivist approaches. Early postmodern thinking began to appear in educational research at the onset of the "cognitive revolution" in the 1960s. It has continued to do so steadily as a large body of critical scholarship has accumulated to challenge the basic assumptions of empiricism and positivism and the atomistic nature of such research in all areas of education.

Coincidentally, humanistic and postmodern scholars argued persuasively for more inclusive and socially sensitive ways of investigating educational issues. Indeed, the strict "cognitive" focus of much research in the 1960s and 1970s caused scholars (aware of postmodern thinking) to emphasize the paucity of research on human subjectivity, personal identity formation and gender issues. As part of this emphasis on the "whole person," educational research broadened to include Action Research, Ethnography, Narrative Inquiry, Critical Theory, Feminist Inquiry, and Postmodernism.

Paradigms

Although the history and realities of educational research are exceedingly complex, people tend to reduce this richness to a simple split between two main research paradigms: the quantitative (or rationalistic) paradigm and the qualitative (interpretive, humanistic, or naturalistic) paradigm.

A "paradigm" is a cluster of related beliefs; it is a particular way of defining, selecting, conceptualizing and investigating problems. "The paradigm determines how a problem is formulated and methodologically tackled" (Husen, 1999, p. 33). In the world of academe, professors mentor young scholars in the sense that they initiate, immerse, and socialize their students in the beliefs, values, and methods of the prevailing ways (paradigms) of doing research. In other words, says Husén, a paradigm is a "cultural artifact" (p. 31) which scholars employ to justify and guide their own (and their students') research.

Thomas Kuhn introduced the "paradigm" idea in his influential book *The Structure of Scientific Revolutions* (1962). Kuhn used the paradigm-concept as a tool to examine how different kinds of scientific thinking emerged, developed and became rooted in the minds of scholars. More important, the paradigm-concept enabled Kuhn to explain important changes, crises, revolutions, or *paradigm shifts* that had taken place in the world of science. Husén (1999) explains:

> A 'revolution' . . . occurs when one or several researchers at a given time encounter anomalies, for instance, make observations, which in a striking way do not fit the prevailing paradigm. Such anomalies can give rise to a crisis after which the universe under study is perceived in an entirely new light. Previous theories and facts become subject to thorough rethinking and reevaluation. (p. 31)

The familiar distinction between quantitative and qualitative paradigms has its roots in a much older distinction between the natural sciences and the humanities. In the 1890s, Dilthey offered a useful way of thinking about these differences in terms of *Erklaren* (to explain) and *Verstehen* (to understand). Dilthey (1890) said that the sciences seek to *explain* (to generalize and make predictions about) reality through empirical and quantifiable observations. In contrast, the humanities seek to *understand* reality by means of their own forms of logic linked to a deep concern for the uniqueness of the individual *in situ* (in place, or in context).

Broadly speaking, the conventional distinction people tend to make between quantitative and qualitative research paradigms in educational and music education research corresponds to the contrasting belief systems we know as modernity and postmodernity. The modernist, quantitative paradigm assumes it is possible and desirable to construct objective, rational, verifiable, "means-ends" understandings of education. For the most part, modernist researchers exclude personal, social, subjective, contextual, and cultural variables from their inquiries. By contrast, interpretive (or qualitative) approaches, which evince many characteristics of postmodernity, hold that it is not only possible but necessary to investigate educational topics through forms of inquiry that employ holistic, personal, social, subjective, contextual, cultural, collaborative, or consensual approaches.

Should music educators lean toward one research mode rather than another? As I suggested earlier, contemporary research in education and music education includes a wide variety of complementary and competing forms of inquiry.

This complexity renders the old quantitative-qualitative split obsolete. What is the message of this complexity? Have one or more forms of inquiry emerged as more logical, valid, reliable, or appropriate for music education than others? Is it reasonable to combine approaches? If so, why? If not, why not? These are just some of the questions that the following sections of this chapter may help to answer.

Empiricism

Since the end of the 19th century, "research" in the Anglo-Saxon world has been dominated by "scientific" research, which is based on Empiricism and its offspring Positivism.

Empiricism, in turn, is a form of Foundationalism. As Phillips and Burbules (2000) explain, the shared assumption among these "isms" is that in order to be counted as "knowledge," one must demonstrate that a belief or knowledge claim has a *secure foundation*. To John Locke (1690 [1959]), this secure foundation is the experience of the world we derive (see, hear, and so forth) from our human senses.

More specifically, three basic beliefs underpin empiricism (and positivism). The first belief is that human knowledge originates from sensory experience. Empiricism regards sensory data as solid, reliable information. Empiricism is "any of a variety of views to the effect that either our concepts or our knowledge are, wholly or partly, based on experience through the senses and introspection" (Lacey, 1976, p. 55).

The second belief is that knowledge claims must be justified or "warranted" in terms of sensory experience (e.g., observational data or measurements) rather than on theory. (This is called "ontological privilege" because ontology concerns the "being" or essence of things.) In the absence of observable evidence, says the empiricist, a claim is merely an "unwarranted" speculation.

Implicit in these first two beliefs is the third. Empiricists assume that justifying claims via observations is a value-neutral or objective means of explaining phenomena. Indeed, many scholars in music education (and educational research) today still maintain or imply that because empirical researchers are free of personal biases, their observations and experimental results are more valid and reliable than all other forms of investigation.

At this point, it may be instructive to examine Jack Heller's definition of "research" (chap. 58). Heller suggests that reliable knowledge is derived through systematic observations related to "very specific" questions carried out in "unbiased" ways and "supported by empirical evidence" (p. 1089). Based on this definition, Heller avers (for example) that he does "not consider philosophy as research" (p. 1090).

Notice, first, that Heller's definition of research is not a verifiable (observable, warranted, unbiased) fact itself. It is a belief. Heller believes in a concept of research that traces its roots to John Locke's modernist, Enlightenment assumptions about the nature of the human mind, the reliability of human sensory experience, and the ability of the latter to produce securely founded knowledge. So, Heller's definition of research is a social-cultural construction. It rests on a specific ideology. Let us unpack more details of this common ideology now.

On the surface, empirical methods of investigating the origins of phenomena or justifying claims about such origins seem unassailable. How could anyone dispute that knowledge of the world follows from the way the world *is*, or appears to be, according to our "unbiased" eyes, ears and so forth?

In fact, numerous eminent thinkers past and present (including Wittgenstein, Dewey, Popper, Hanson, and Kuhn) argue that the foundations of empirical research are illogical. The first problem is that human sensory experiences are not natural, pure, or unbiased. Instead, all forms of human observation—all gathering of empirical evidence— is judgmental, conceptual, or theory-laden. "What is seen (or felt or heard or tasted or smelled), and how it is seen (or felt . . .), is influenced by the knowledge the experiencer already possesses" (Phillips, 1999, p. 252).

The second problem is that empirical research pivots on specific observations of the singular kind, "This water boiled when heated to a temperature of 100° Celsius." Investigators test and justify (or warrant) the truth of this kind of observation (or not) by replicating the same experimental processes many times, as precisely as possible. In other words, the results of empirical observation statements apply to specific details and circumstances of the kind, "*This* (boiling) happened to *this* thing (pure water) under these precise conditions (normal pressure and heat of 100° Celsius) at this time and place."

But as thinkers have argued since the time of Hume (1748), even a very large number of observation statements do not add up to "knowledge" in the sense of infallible theories, guarantees, laws, or statements of the general sort that empiricists like to make (such as "Water boils at 100° Celsius"). In other words, empiricists always cross a bridge from (a) a restricted number of observations to (b) general claims about an infinite set of all possible situations. This "bridge" is the process called "*induction.*" To reason inductively is to make general claims (inferences) to situations beyond our current experience—to past events, future events, or events in distant galaxies—from a restricted set of observations here and now.

But, what makes empiricists believe that inductive reasoning is sound, reliable, or logically justified? Indeed, there is no guarantee that the next pot of water will boil when heated to 100° Celsius. It might not. In fact, human experience shows that our inferences do not always hold for every situation. Besides, as Clarke (1997) asks, "can induction be justified by induction?" That is, if induction works in some situations (e.g., the case of boiling water), can we conclude rationally that it will always work for all other materials, events, or situations everywhere? No. Accordingly, Sir Karl Popper (1976) concludes that induction is irrational:

> As for induction (or inductive logic, . . .) I assert that there is no such thing. If I am right then this solves, of course, the problem of induction. . . . The point is that there is no rule of inductive inference—inference leading to theories of universal laws—ever proposed which can be taken seriously for even a minute. (pp. 145–147)

Another nail in the coffin of empiricism follows from the above: There will always be a variety of possible explanations for whatever data empiricists gather. In other words, and in the jargon of research—theories are always *underdetermined*. To use a simple example, suppose a person claims to "know" there is a baseball sitting on a table in front of her and attempts to warrant the truth of her claim by saying that she "knows" this because she actually sees the ball. Is this the end of the story? No, because it is very possible for someone else to claim that this thing he sees is not a baseball but an exact porcelain replica of a baseball. Then again, another person might claim, by the same means (his eyes), that what he sees is not a "real" baseball, but a soft, rubber toy (Phillips, 1999).

Finally, and to anticipate a related weakness of positivism (explained later), if we accept the empirical-observational (Heller) definition of research, then we must exclude many types of current inquiry. For example, we will have to inform contemporary physicists working in the new field of "string theory" that their efforts do not count as "research" because "strings" cannot be observed and, therefore, cannot be "supported by empirical evidence," as Heller insists. (Strings are conjectures, or "convenient fictions"; they are *believed* to be vibrating entities smaller than a trillionth of a trillionth the size of an atom). In reality, however, the verifiable fact is that string theorists today are garnering an enormous number of research grants, research awards, and university research appointments.

In summary, the foundations of empiricism (and the Heller-type definition of research) are deeply flawed. There is no rational basis for asserting that the term "research" applies only to investigations focused on "very specific" entities examined in "unbiased ways" that can be "supported by empirical evidence." This is akin to claiming that the term "law" applies only to British "law." Likewise, as we shall see by the end of this chapter, there is no basis for the frequent assumption that empirical-positivistic research (which still dominates the *Journal of Research in*

Music Education, for example), or any other form of investigation, is more valid or reliable than any other form of inquiry done well.

In summary, empiricism (like all forms of research) is, itself, a human construct based on assumptions about the ends, means and values of human understanding. In other words, a person's decision to investigate a topic empirically and feel confident about the results is an act of believing in a particular philosophy of reality, knowledge, and value.

Positivism

During the first half of the 20th century, some educational researchers began to accept the inadequacies of empiricism. Accordingly, they also began the search for a more satisfactory concept of scientific inquiry. Positivism, another form of empiricism (with several internal subdivisions of its own), was the chosen successor. One form of positivism, called logical positivism (e.g., Ayer, 1936; Reichenbach, 1953), had the greatest impact on educational research in the years following World War II. (Ayer's writings were a major source of Skinner's conviction that psychology should limit itself to the study of observable behavior.)

The logical positivists, like their fellow empiricists, held that knowledge rests on our sensory experiences of objects in the external world. On this view, sense data are the bedrock of science and the ultimate foundations of all "certain" knowledge that science produces. But the logical positivists went a step further. They introduced the *verifiability principle of meaning*, which imposed a strict separation between statements of *fact* and statements of *value*. Positivists held that science should focus exclusively on empirically verifiable *facts* or on statements that are true by definition—on things as they *are* (as opposed to things as they appear). They sought to anchor science securely, which (to them) meant removing any possibility that human subjectivity would contaminate scientific inquiry. In other words, positivists insist that if we cannot see or measure something (e.g., the "superstrings" of string theory), then it is not meaningful (Phillips, 1999). (Clearly and unacceptably, this positivist view of knowledge excludes all fields involving matters of value judgments, including education.)

To strengthen science even further, positivists (in the 1930s) sought a way to escape the problem of induction explained long ago by Hume (discussed earlier). The strategy they devised was called *hypothetico-deduction*. In plain English, hypothetico-deduction means that after selecting a problem for inquiry a researcher formulates a precise hypothesis (or theory) that might (reasonably) explain the issue under investigation. Next, the researcher tests his or her hypothesis by deducing an observation statement that, in turn, is verified (or not) by accumulating observations in repeated experimental trials.

In an effort to make their research as scientifically rigorous (and prestigious) as possible, a majority of scholars in education and music education embraced positivism enthusiastically and uncritically. By the 1970s, however, positivism had been discredited by compelling criticisms. The most embarrassing weakness of the positivist view is the "principle of verifiability," which says that a statement is true if and only if it is empirically verifiable or true by definition. But, of course, this statement, itself, is neither empirically verifiable nor true by definition. In other words, positivism "falls on its own sword." In reality, science and social science deal in all sorts of problems (e.g., weightlessness, quarks, superstrings, intelligence, creativity, music aptitude) that are neither directly observable nor true by definition. Positivistic researchers miss the point that they often proceed on the basis of conjectures and speculative concepts. So, for positivists to claim that these concepts (and theories about these concepts) are meaningless is to negate the essence of their own procedures.

The same criticism applies to hypothetico-deduction. Hypotheses are not neutral, objective, or uninformed guesses; they are statements, assumptions, or questions put forth by informed, educated, experienced researchers who live in particular times and places. So, hypotheses (null or affirmative) are influenced by personal and professional ideologies about the nature of human knowledge, being, and significance.

The positivistic credo that observable, quantifiable evidence is the essence of "serious" research has influenced music education dramatically and, arguably, deleteriously. For example, as Regelski (1996) argues, because musical phenomena are complex, "internal," and, therefore, unobservable states of mind (e.g., music aptitude, or a person's experience of a symphony), positivistic researchers have no choice but to reduce these phenomena to "operational definitions" (Phillips & Burbules, 2000, p. 10) or quantifiable data (e.g., measures of music aptitude, divergent thinking, or changes in brain activity) that "fit" their experimental tools. The upshot is that in the quest to discover "laws" of music cognition, design measures of music aptitude, or test for musical creativity, positivistic researchers atomize and reduce these complex phenomena to bits of numeric data that are (surely) distortions of the "whole" they purport to represent. Regelski (1996) sums the problem:

> In seeking the "exact observation and strict correlation of data" more suitable to the inanimate subject matter of the physical sciences, many music researchers have disintegrated the subject matter of music—its musical integrity, its human interest—to the degree that their results are irrelevant and of no theoretical interest or pragmatic use. (p. 12)

Because of its profound weaknesses, the consensus among many scholars today is that positivism, as an organized movement, and as a philosophy [of science], is dead" (Clarke, 1997, p. 21). Still, many music education researchers continue to support and practice this form of inquiry.

This is not to say, however, that scientific experiments should be discarded. Not at all. Experimental inquiries are essential for revealing factors involved in all sorts of cause-effect situations. For example, as a means of determining what elements may be responsible for an illness or disease, experiments are indispensable.

Postpositivism

The transition from a positivist to a postpositivist concept of science in the 1960s and 1970s paralleled and reflected the larger social transition from modernity to postmodernity (outlined earlier). Put another way, the advent of postpositivism marked a major shift away from educational research dominated by quantification and measurement to a much more pluralistic view of epistemology, ontology, and axiology.

As the term implies, postpositivist is not a form of foundationalism, empiricism, or positivism. Also, it is not one unified position. There are several alternative conceptions of postpositivist (e.g., Feyerabend, 1975; Kuhn, 1979; Lakatos, 1974; Popper, 1965). It seems right to say, however, postpositivist is a concept of science that views knowledge as conjectural. As Popper (1965) says: "There are no ultimate sources of knowledge . . . every source, every suggestion, is open to critical examination" (p. 27).

So, in regard to any sort of claim, postpositivists take the view that researchers should examine every form of evidence it is possible to gather about a claim (arguments, calculations, experiments, interviews, whatever)—past and present; pro and con; positive and negative—regardless of where or how it originated. On these bases, the task of the investigator is to build a case for his or her claim or viewpoint with the understanding that this view will be revisited for future confirmation or refutation by herself or himself or others. Here is another key tenet of postpositivism: The case one makes for a claim must always be seen as provisional.

Phillips and Burbules (2000) use the analogy of a detective (e.g., Sherlock Holmes) to explain the point. Based on whatever he can find, a detective gathers evidence and attempts to build a circumstantial case. If he succeeds in making a "good" (warranted) case against a suspect, then his evidence, arguments, and so forth might lead to the arrest, trial, and conviction of his suspect. Of course, if further contrary evidence is found later (e.g., DNA evi-

dence), then the original arrest and conviction of the suspect are overturned; the original conclusion (based on the best evidence available to the investigators at the time) is now seen to be erroneous or unwarranted.

Phillips and Burbules (2000) add this:

This acceptance of the possible imperfection and fallibility of evidence is one of the central tenets of postpositivism, but it does not entail that we have to give up the idea that evidence is pertinent to our judgments about the truth or warrantability of our conjectures. (p. 31)

Does this warning point to a basic problem with postpositivism? After all, and at the least for some people, there is a sense of hopelessness in the view that all knowledge is elusive, fragile, temporary, or conjectural, and that there is no such thing as "truth" in the completely reliable sense. If claims can always been overthrown, say critics, why believe in anything or investigate anything?

The answer is that humans must make decisions and take actions to survive and live. Decisions and actions require beliefs about what is safe, or best, or right to do (or not). Research attempts to offer reasons, evidence, and justifications for making the best decisions possible at a given time and place. In other words, just because it is impossible to have certain knowledge of something is no reason to abandon our actions to whims, impulses or fantasies. We can do better; that is, we can do the best we can with the best available knowledge. For example, would it be reasonable and prudent to eat food that researchers believe to be contaminated with "mad cow disease" because researchers cannot explain completely or "truly" how the disease develops, mutates, and so forth? No. We may not know the whole truth about mad cow disease, now or ever, but the *beliefs* of those who specialize in researching such things, and the community of knowledge-builders who function as judges of how well such research is carried out, provide "good enough" reasons for not eating suspicious meat at this time.

Also, postpositivism argues there are an infinite number of potentially "true" statements that can be developed about any event or situation. Thus, no one instance or form of research can possibly account for the complete "truth" or reality of anything.

In sum, postpositivists tell us to make an important distinction between *truth* and *belief*. Why, how, and whether to believe a knowledge claim is the key issue. The goal of research, then, is continuously to seek relevant descriptions and explanations of a phenomenon based on the best and most complete knowledge we can garner about that phenomenon. This much more open concept of knowledge, being, value, and research liberated several forms of inquiry from the margins of serious investigation. Let us consider these now.

Interpretivism

The origins of interpretive research trace back to the work of Immanuel Kant, who rejected science as a legitimate approach to social inquiry. To Kant, knowledge was constructed by a knowing "eye" (or I) and not merely copied from the "real" world through neutral observation. This realization (reflected in critics' views of empiricism and positivism, above) paved the way for a separation between the social sciences and the physical sciences. Over time, some educational scholars acknowledged that the social world is inherently "mental" in the sense that social reality pivots on the ways people interpret and act in their worlds in relation to their tacit beliefs and interpretations. From this perspective, human believing, interpreting, thinking, and acting are often unpredictable, because human consciousness is always involved in continuous, integrated processes of attention, cognition, emotion, intention, and memory. Thus, it is difficult, if not impossible, to posit causal laws to explain human behaviors.

As these views gained currency among educational researchers in the 1960s, and as positivists in education took up more sophisticated methods of "control" to exclude details of context, intersubjectivity, and the social nature of knowledge, a cadre of scholars began to engage in interpretive forms of inquiry, by which I mean phenomenology, action research, ethnography, narrative inquiry and others we cannot address in this space. As noted above, this expansion or "shift" in educational research paralleled the larger societal movement away from the ideals of modernity and toward the ideals of postmodernity—epistemological, ontological, axiological, and ethical.

In terms of epistemology, interpretive scholars hold that knowledge is socially and culturally constructed; it is "open," fluid, and rooted in its contexts of development and application. In terms of ontology, interpretivists believe there is no "external" reality lying "outside" the shared meanings of a social group. Human meanings and values are intrinsic to specific communities—professional, artistic, social, and so forth.

It is important to emphasize, however, that within the domain of "interpretive research" there is a division (or continuum) between moderates and strict advocates of this approach. Moderates believe that social life can be investigated more deeply and comprehensively by combining scientific methods with interpretative approaches. Members of the strict camp argue against any such combination on the grounds that positivistic research is only appropriate for the physical sciences. In education and music education, we know this "split" best as the "quantitative versus qualitative" debate (see earlier discussion).

Similarly, while strict positivists hold that scientific inquiry is both necessary and sufficient for investigating issues in the physical and social sciences, moderate positivists and postpositivists acknowledge that while "science" as traditionally conceived is necessary and useful for many types of problems, it is neither necessary nor sufficient for investigating many aspects of social life, especially the subjective and experiential aspects of teaching and learning.

It terms of aims and "methods," then, interpretive researchers seek to build our knowledge of complex social phenomena (e.g., teaching, learning, music making) by grasping the meanings and values that educational experiences have for various groups of people. Doing so requires that interpretive researchers often take the stance of empathetic observer-participants or fully involved participant-observers. Researchers in the United Kingdom often use the term "case study" instead of "interpretive research" to name these kinds of holistic, in-depth investigations. The aim of these studies is to explain the "interdependencies of parts and of the patterns that emerge" from these whole-part relations (Sturman, 1999, p. 103).

Specifically, doing interpretive research as an ethnographer, action researcher, or narrative inquirer requires taking a stance that is simultaneously insider-outsider, critically reflective, empathetic, narrative, cognitive-affective, and diagnostic-interpretive. The researcher's focus is on human *actions* that are meaningful to people in their social transactions with others. He or she also seeks out and probes the contextual "rules" that may be influencing self-other relations in a community. The goal of interpretive inquiry is to discover the beliefs, values, motivations, and attitudes of people's actions in educational contexts. Why? Because to discover people's subjective meanings (beliefs, values, and so on) is to gain deeper insights into individual and group actions (Clark, 1997, p. 38).

As one would expect from a research paradigm that values human interactions and "community" so highly, interpretive investigators usually make their findings and interpretations available (as a matter of research protocol) to the participants in their studies for their feedback, use, and (possible) enlightenment. This is especially important in ethnography and action research.

Philosophically, then, interpretive forms of inquiry rest on views of epistemology, ontology, and axiology that honor competing viewpoints, intersubjectivity, personal wisdom, self-reflection, personal experience, and "local" criteria of worth.

Critics have several objections to interpretivism. First and fundamentally, without criteria of credibility, how do we judge the merit, "truth," or relevance of one investigator's account of a group or phenomenon versus another researcher's account (e.g., the informal acquisition of songs among Innuit children)? Or, in a related vein, suppose a researcher receives conflicting accounts of a process, situation, or phenomenon from small groups of participants within the group she is investigating. The answer given by defenders of interpretive research is that all "truth" or knowledge is *relative* (or "locally" applicable) to individual social groups.

In an effort to counter the problem of relativism and strengthen the validity of interpretive research, its defenders argue that a researcher's account of why and how a community believes, acts, values, and creates the way they do must include several components. An account must include a coherent and coordinated discussion of the range of meanings uncovered during the investigation; a reflective comparison of the researcher's views with the evaluation criteria of the specific type of interpretive research community involved; and "the evaluation criteria of the research participants, that is, it [the researcher's account] must be accepted by them as being a plausible account of their lived experience" (e.g., Carr & Kemmis, 1986, p. 92).

But this kind of defense fails to acquit the fundamental problem of "relativism," which is self-contradictory. How so? Because if we accept the claim that all statements are true relative to the group that states them (instead of being true for all people), then any conclusions made by interpretive researchers only apply locally—to other interpretive researchers—and not (as they assume) to their study's participants, or to other researchers, or to anyone else beyond their scholarly community. In other words, interpretive researchers cannot have their cake and eat it, too; if they want to be logical, they cannot insist that for everyone everywhere, universally and absolutely, all knowledge is relative (Clark, 1997; Smith, 1983). This is self-refuting.

Second, by conceptualizing communities and individuals as *unique*, interpretive studies are prone to overlook important similarities across situations (e.g., middle school settings). Third, by focusing on the reasons and motivations underlying participants' actions, there is a danger of overlooking the consequences of their unreasoned or unintended actions. Fourth, consider the problem of what happens if a researcher's conclusions are ruled invalid because they do not match the participants' views of their situation. As Clark (1997) points out, "If the participants have a false or distorted or partial view, then the researcher's acceptance of their accounts simply perpetuates their self-deception" (p. 41). Fifth, if interpretive researchers fail to involve themselves empathetically in their chosen communities of interest, then (some critics suggest) they are no different from "distanced" positivists and just as unlikely to improve the lives of their participants (Carr & Kemmis, 1986).

Scholars' attempts to solve the problems of interpretive inquiry in the mid-twentieth century ranged widely from a purely relativistic, "no-possible-decision" view at one end of the continuum, to positivistic analyses of interpretive data at the other end. Some thinkers continue to debate the problem of how to determine which reports or interpretations are true, or not. Others accept that it is illogical

to purse this question due to the inevitable lack of objective, universal criteria for deciding such questions. As Smith (1983) says, "There is no special, privileged way to distinguish genuine knowledge from false claims to knowledge and objective knowledge from biased research" (pp. 118–19). All we can do is to explain the theoretical or practical educational consequences of selecting one interpretation over another.

Yet another view from Guba and Lincoln (1989) emphasizes that it is much too early to expect interpretive researchers to have methods of "trustworthiness" equal to those in the sciences. Interpretive scholars have had very little time to evolve their approaches; empiricists "have had centuries of experience to shape their standards" (Guba & Lincoln, 1989, p. 147). At present, interpretivists are working to develop standards equivalent to validity and reliability under the headings of "credibility, transferability, dependability, and confirmability" (Guba & Lincoln, 1989, p. 147).

Critical Theory

Critical Theory is an interdisciplinary form of inquiry. It is a distinctive way of conceptualizing and investigating problems. (Think of "Critical Theory" as a verb, not a noun. Critical Theory is not a specific theory, as the term implies.)

Critical Theory originated in the aftermath of World War I. Germany lay in ruins; communism was taking hold in Russia; and the economic and political systems of Europe were heading toward depression and fascism in the 1930s. In these circumstances, a small group of European intellectuals gathered at the Institute of Social Research (at the University of Frankfurt, Germany) in 1923 with the purpose of contributing to human justice through critical theory. The name "Frankfurt School" refers to the efforts of this group and their original members (including Horkheimer, Marcuse, Adorno, Benjamin, and Fromm). Jurgen Habermas (who became director of the Social Institute in 1964) reworked the foundations of the Frankfurt founders "to produce what is now recognized as a remarkable intellectual endeavor spanning politics, sociology, psychology, linguistics and philosophy" (Clark, 1997, p. 45).

Indeed, there is no unitary method of doing Critical Theory. Critical theorists pursue solutions to theory-practice dilemmas through a synthesis of perspectives. Some theorists work by connecting quantitative and qualitative approaches; however, the majority reject positivistic research in favor of combining interpretive approaches within an intensely self-critical concept of philosophical research.

A major reason for calling this approach "critical" theory is to emphasize that these scholars work by continuously monitoring their own presuppositions and the "agendas" implicit in their research paradigms (Morrow & Brown, 1994). Habermas held that critical self-reflection was the key to achieving insights that could liberate people from false beliefs and lead to "concrete proposals for overcoming oppression" (Lakomski, 1999, p. 175). As Kellner (1989) says, Critical Theory involves:

> a collective, supra-disciplinary synthesis of philosophy, the sciences and politics, in which critical social theory is produced by groups of theorists and scientists from various disciplines working together to produce a critical theory of the present age aimed at radical social-political transformation. (p. 7)

Not surprisingly, critical theorists were among the first to point out that "scientific method" is a social ideology tied to a particular period of Western history—modernity—which, in turn, promotes a particular set of values and priorities. Thus, warned Habermas (1973), to question scientific inquiry is to risk being called a lunatic or heretic by the uncritical majority, including professors for whom scientific research is a faith as much as a method. Habermas held that if people challenged the dominant epistemology of our time (that "knowledge = scientific knowledge"), and the concepts of human reality and significance implicit in this assumption, then society would gain opportunities to achieve greater self-understanding, emancipation, democracy, self-actualization, and institutional change.

Habermas believed that "knowledge" included but went far beyond empirical-analytic knowledge. To Habermas (1971), scholars also must pursue knowledge through communicative and cultural forms of inquiry. These pathways enable us to explain how humans communicate and formulate personal meanings (thoughts, feelings, hopes, desires, fears) and how language shapes and is shaped by social life.

In terms of education, critical theorists share a deep concern for the political, social, economic, gender, and power issues of teaching, learning, and research. "Critical theory addresses the relations among schooling, education, culture, society, economy, and governance" (Popkewitz & Fendler, 1999, p. xiii). Critical theorists insist that teaching and learning are deeply related to social practices, "and that it is the task of the critical intellectual to identify and address injustices in these practices" (Lakomski, 1999, p. 175). Their quest is to improve the efforts and outcomes of educational theorists, policy makers, teachers, learners, and others involved in education.

Critical theorists have been active in mainstream educational research for more than fifty years. In music education, one of the only examples of Critical Theory is the work of the "Mayday Group" (Gates and Regelski), which has been ongoing since 1991.

Specifically, Critical Theory aims to achieve accords among reasonable people about theory/practice problems and solutions by means of rational discussion. Critical Theory, then, is a procedural model of negotiation. Through negotiation, critical thinkers develop "true statements" that lead to "prudent decisions" (Habermas, 1973). Habermas assumed that communities of rational thinkers were capable of creating "ideal speech" situations through disciplined interchanges based on "communicative competence," which means the ability to utter statements that are comprehensible, true, sincere, and appropriate (Habermas, 1973).

But what happens when we think carefully and critically about Critical Theory? Does it stand up to tests of logic and common sense? No. Critical Theory is flawed for several related reasons. First, there is no way for anyone to determine if an "ideal speech" situation exists, or if critical negotiators possess "communicative competence," and, therefore, no way to determine whether a "consensus" reached is rationally "founded" (Clark, 1997; Lakomski, 1999).

Habermas tried to counter these criticisms by arguing that we *can* determine whether the conditions of an "ideal speech" situation exist (or existed) by using postdiscussion self-reports by participants to evaluate the nature and quality of their negotiations. But this defense also fails because there is no way of determining the veracity of thinkers' self-reports (these may be false, or misleading, depending on personal motives). Again, then, we can never know with confidence that the statements of "rational" participants are true. But for the sake of argument, let us suppose that we did find good reasons to question a consensus in retrospect. How do we know when we have achieved a better or "true" rational consensus? Through more talk? If so, how do we stop the infinite regress? Where do we find the ultimate criteria we need to achieve confidence in any rational consensus reached in the future? Besides, the governing ideal of Critical Theory—"truth as rational consensus"—is too distant from reality-as-experience (or "real-world" problems) to distinguish the practical "truth" of Critical Theory from the conclusions of any other kind of inquiry. In sum, the claim that Critical Theory is more likely to unite theory and practice is baseless.

Gender Studies

A key force in the decline of modernity and the rise of postmodernity has been the gradual rise of a "feminist consciousness": an awareness of society's ingrained discrimination against women, past and present, and a (very slowly) growing societal commitment to guarantee women full access to all human rights.

One result of this major development occurred in the 1960s, when women researchers began to challenge the ways in which male priorities and perspectives continuously dictated the nature and conduct of research. This challenge first appeared in the form of studies that focused exclusively on women and topics related to women's lives for the benefit of other women. Included in these studies were descriptions, explanations, and interpretations of female experiences, including the location and revelation of patriarchal prejudices in traditional research. However, research foci expanded quickly to embrace many issues surrounding the social and cultural construction of gender and identity.

It is extremely difficult to categorize "feminist" or "gender" research neatly. For one thing, most scholars in this field reject the notion of a distinctly feminist research methodology (Clegg, 1985; Harding, 1989). Indeed, people who identify themselves as feminist scholars (for example) employ a wide range of research modes to examine many issues. Still, gender research exhibits several characteristic features.

First, gender scholars usually oppose positivist forms of educational research. This rejection ranges from efforts to develop a distinctly feminist positivism, to the amalgamation of positivistic and interpretive approaches, to the recommendation that gender scholars will be served best by an exclusive use of interpretive or postmodern approaches.

Another characteristic is the frequent focus on questions of why and how powerful male interests have dominated all aspects of Western culture (including research), while female interests have been ignored. The most obvious example is the Western world's ceaseless prejudice against women's research interests, by which I mean that until very recently "women were rarely researched and rarely researchers" (Clark, 1997, p. 124).

Third, feminist-gender research emphasizes the human value-bounded nature of research. That is, because research is a social endeavor, it cannot be objective; research reflects the values of the people and institutions who do it. So, feminist-gender scholars not only reject traditional claims about "objective science" and "factual knowledge," they identify these notions as elements of the patriarchal *status quo* that trivializes and oppresses women's efforts in the "workplace" of research.

A fourth characteristic follows directly from the last. Feminist-gender inquiries often place a high priority on employing research resources and results for the emancipation of people victimized by many forms of neglect and discrimination so they can recognize, understand, and liberate themselves from their oppressive circumstances.

To summarize this (much too) brief discussion of feminist-gender research, let us simply point out the following. There is no unity among scholars in this realm about which concept(s) of knowledge, being, or values

should ground or direct their inquiries. All that is clear is that feminist-gender scholars share many views that have developed since the demise of modernity and positivism, including these: knowledge is socially and culturally constructed; there is no such thing as value-free research; viewpoints alter in relation to social hierarchies and gender identities; gender issues are implicit in all research methods and interpretations; emotion is an important research construct; an investigator's biography and intentions are appropriate issues in all facets of research (Clark, 1997, pp. 126–27).

In conclusion, feminist-gender researchers have made an enormous contribution to educational research generally and music education particularly by focusing our attention on and exposing the complexities of the "gendered" nature of all aspects of teaching and learning.

Postmodernism

"Postmodern" research is impossible to define neatly. Attempts to do so have spawned huge debates in a growing literature covering a wide range of disciplines (e.g., Bauman, 1992; Connor, 1989; Lash, 1990; Marshall & Peters, 1999; Rosenau, 1992; Smart, 1992; Usher & Edwards, 1994).

Perhaps a good way to begin is to say what postmodern research is *not*. Postmodernism does not refer to a systematic set of premises and strategies; it is not a cohesive philosophy; it is not a method of inquiry; it is not an identifiable cultural movement.

A major reason why postmodernism eludes simple definitions is because most postmodern thinkers oppose the basic assumption underlying the idea of "definition" itself. Postmodernism rejects any effort to provide a single unified explanation of anything (Usher & Edwards, 1994). More broadly, postmodern scholars deny the basic premise grounding all forms of "rational" Anglo-Saxon inquiry; they reject the belief that humans have the ability to "know" or "explain" anything with any degree of certainty, which includes knowing how to investigate problems systematically and rationally. (Notice that in defiance of postmodern ideals I am attempting to explain postmodernism.)

At the very least, then, postmodernism is an intellectual paradigm that breaks radically with traditional Enlightenment beliefs in causality, objective certainty, rationality, and universal narratives (Rosenau, 1992). Postmodern thinkers reject the basic belief (social theme, or "grand narrative") promoted by modernity that Westerners often accept on pure faith: that science is the highest form of human thought such that scientific thinking has the power to lead society out of social darkness to some kind of rationally explained "promised land." In other words, postmodern scholarship disputes the foundations of science, social science, interpretivism, and philosophy, not to mention the most cherished beliefs and assumptions of scholars who value conventional concepts of education, schooling, or music.

Postmodern researchers argue that (a) any belief in "reason" is a belief in the supremacy and universality of some rules (e.g., scientific or interpretive rules) over all others, and that (b) arguments that make such claims have no basis beyond personal opinion. Whereas the dominant Western ideology of knowledge presumes that scientific and analytic reasoning is "effective" and applicable to all countries and cultures, the postmodernist argues that each situation is different and calls for multiple, local understandings.

Implicit in postmodern thinking, then, is a profound concern with the social nature and consequences of "knowledge." As Toulmin (1990) puts it, the Western assumption that "rational" inquiry leads to the "best" answers negates intellectual diversity and tolerance that, in turn, leads to unfairness and oppression for others. In fact, say postmodernists, rational forms of thought have only delivered "progress" to a very *small* upper class. The mass of humanity remains trapped in poverty, illness, and oppression. In his seminal book, *The Postmodern Condition: A Report on Knowledge*, Lyotard (1984) emphasizes that a characteristic of modernity is the concept of knowledge as a commodity. To possess certain kinds of knowledge in the "modern" world is to hold the keys to economic and military domination. In short, postmodern thinkers view knowledge and power as two sides of the same coin.

What this means in practice is that postmodern thinkers take an "agnostic" view of language and communication. They question strongly that any form of communication can transmit reliable messages. At best, says Foucault (1984), human languages only yield unreliable exchanges because there is no single, universal meta-language—no universal epistemology. Thus, humans have no universal set of rules for evaluating the "truth" of statements made in one particular language or research jargon.

Not surprisingly, postmodernists reject the idea of "method" altogether. To accept that there is one supreme form of inquiry is to believe in "closed" practices and unfounded notions of "rational" knowing and believing. Postmodern scholars hold that there are no rules of procedure they must follow and no "right" procedures of investigation because, again, there is no externally verifiable meta-system of knowledge and reference for the whole world.

Still, as one might predict, there is a range of positions within postmodernism. At one end of the continuum, moderate or "affirmative" postmodernists use introspection, anti-objectivist (individualized) interpretation and "deconstruction" (discussed later). The topics of postmodern

research are human paradoxes, enigmas, and ambiguities. In approaching such problems, scholars invariably make use of their individual feelings, intuitions, judgments, imaginations, and creative strategies. Postmodern thinkers do not aim to produce the "best" theory of this-or-that because, to them, there are no "truths," only an infinite number of more-and-less useful viewpoints and interpretations. At the other end of the continuum, extreme, "skeptical" postmodernists argue that "anything goes" in terms of scholarly procedures. In sum, if postmodern scholars share anything in common, it is a critical, freethinking, cynical, or heretical mindset (Rosenau, 1992).

Now a word about the word "deconstruction." This term identifies an important postmodern concept put forth by Derrida, who holds that "texts" (in the broadest possible sense, including the conclusions of science and philosophy) cannot and do not have one true, coherent meaning. Instead, the meanings of anything in life—research, education, music—are not to be found in some different, objective, "external" reality to which a discussion or event refers. Instead, meanings lie "inside" texts (discussions, institutions and events) in the stories (or narratives) that people tell for and about these things.

So, a text always presents an infinite range of meanings to the postmodern investigator, some of which may contradict the original author's basic claims, intentions and beliefs. Because there are many ways of interpreting a text, scholars say that texts can be "deconstructed" in terms of their hidden meanings, metaphors, subtexts, political agendas, and so forth. Deconstruction sets out to demystify a text by unpacking its internal, arbitrary priorities and assumptions, and by revealing what it does not say, what it excludes or conceals (Rosenau, 1992). As Culler (1982) says: "Deconstruction attempts to undo, reverse, displace, and resituate the hierarchies involved in polar opposites [which traditional Western narratives tend to employ], such as object-subject, right-wrong, good-bad, pragmatic-principled" (p. 150).

Accordingly, postmodern thinkers reject all other forms of research, including Critical Theory. This is so because a major tenet of Critical Theory is the belief that there is an "ideal speech community" of rational thinkers who can achieve some form of consensus about how to address theory-practice issues effectively (Peters, 1995). Also, and contrary to postmodern ideals, all other forms of inquiry, including Critical Theory, pursue verifiable knowledge in the modernist belief (or hope) that this pursuit will yield reasonable answers.

Postmodern thinking has had a major impact on educational research because it calls into question the meta-narratives that investigators have always accepted and used to justify their research practices, institutions, and educational planning. More deeply still, postmodernism undercuts the idealism of many teachers and scholars who view themselves as dedicated, humanistic, knowledge-builders working for the good of all. Postmodern scholars argue, instead, that if we open our eyes, we will see that our dominant beliefs about education and educational research are actually modernity's ways and means of benefiting certain members of society and oppressing others. Education, in this view, is a tool of modernity's peculiar values (Rosenau, 1992, p. 24; Lyotard, 1992, p. 97). Foucault (1984) holds that "rational" Western societies seek to "construct" individuals through systems of knowledge management, control, and power. For example, school examinations, test measurements, and subject "disciplines" serve to "normalize" people into lives of obedient, practical work (Marshall & Peters, 1999). Viewed with these thoughts in mind, we see that Small's recent concept (1998) of "music" as social-cultural interactions (as opposed to "musical works") has an important postmodern point to make: consider carefully whether and how "music education" may function to liberate, normalize, or oppress people of different kinds.

Together, the works of Derrida, Foucault, and Lyotard have focused many people's attention on the use and abuse of power in education and the ways knowledge can be conceptualized, commodified, packaged, limited, or prioritized to suit the aims of special interests. In their view, intellectuals today should seek to develop alternative theories and understandings of local issues. In terms of education, these three scholars argue that we should recognize and accommodate plural realities, diverse viewpoints, and multiple layers of meaning because, in fact, there is no certainty, at all.

Critics of postmodernism begin with its extreme relativism. For example, although postmodernists claim that no single interpretation is more defensible than another, it is easy to defeat this claim with any example that has a finite range of appropriate interpretations. For example, a text like the Declaration of Independence is the product of modernity (it is "located" in an interpretable sociopolitical context). Obviously, then, it is a political document, not a manual for operating a computer (Rosenau, 122).

Other critics add that by concentrating so much on the languages of texts, postmodern deconstruction is as "logocentric" as the modernist epistemologies it attacks. So, in the end, deconstruction is just another form of conventional critique that reduces everything to the same form of "trivial," linguistic residue (Donoghue, 1989). Indeed, Habermas (1987) argues that deconstruction is destructive, not constructive, because it reduces all texts in the same way toward the same conclusions.

Most damaging of all are the self-contradictions at the heart of postmodernism. On the one hand, postmodernists claim that no single view has more privilege than any other; on the other hand, postmodernists have decided that their way of investigating problems has more merit than

others and that some social and political movements they support (e.g., feminism, or environmentalism) are superior to others (Rosenau, 1992).

Many "moderate" postmodern scholars defend themselves with the reply that if one looks carefully at deconstruction one sees an orderly and rigorous system of analysis with its own underlying logic. If so, then this is another self-contradiction. For how can postmodernists deny the existence of rational thought and, at the same time, employ their own system of logic to unpack the meanings (inconsistencies, contradictions) of a text? Presumably, they also sift and sort the meanings of texts (contradictions, inconsistencies, inner subtexts) in relation to some "external," hierarchical system of thought, just like the modernists they oppose.

After an exhaustive study of postmodernism, Rosenau (1992) concludes the following:

It is far from evident that replacing conventional social science methodology with postmodern methods of interpretation and deconstruction constitutes any improvement in the social sciences. If adopted without modification, postmodern methodology leaves social science with no basis for knowledge claims and no rationale for choosing between conflicting interpretations. (p. 124)

Theory and Model Building

To conclude this chapter, let us discuss the construction of research models and theories in general terms first and, then, in relation to the themes examined earlier.

As I said at the beginning, our powers of observation are not neutral. So, to call something a "problem" is to view it in a certain way and to assume it may have a solution. The next crucial step is to *structure* (formulate, organize, shape, delimit, or configure) the problem. That is, a researcher must develop a guiding hypothesis, model, or theory of the problem. This model must be sufficiently detailed that a researcher can decide whether there is a good "fit" or logical correspondence between key elements of the model and key elements of the problem. If there is a good fit, then we say the model and the problem share a "systematic structure" (Kaplan, 1999).

Suppose, for example, that an automobile engineer begins by drawing a blueprint for a ("hypothetical") car. Based on the blueprint, the engineer then makes a model car. Next, the engineer creates a series of test conditions to simulate actual driving conditions (e.g., a wind tunnel). The aim is to study and predict what may happen to a real car (having the same elements as the model car) driving in the same conditions. In this case, there is a highly structured relationship between most details of the model car and most details of the hypothetical car that remains to be built.

When a conception of a problem is sufficiently structured that it yields significant deductions and interpretations, or shows strong relationships between its claims and a corresponding problem, it deserves to be called a "theory" or a "model." The term "theory" usually refers to a logical progression of arguments and data-based claims (e.g., Einstein's theory of relativity) that do not correspond exactly with real situations. Of course, a non-physical model expressed in terms of analytic reasoning or other symbolic procedures (e.g., a philosophical or psychological theory of a problem) cannot possibly correspond to reality with the exactitude of a model car. The term "model" usually means something like a close physical approximation of a real object (e.g., a model car).

Let us summarize to this point. From one perspective, the journey from an initial hunch to a highly developed theory takes the form of a highly individual, creative process. This process moves progressively (e.g., stepwise, circular, back-and-forth, or some combination) toward complexity (Kaplan, 1999; Phillips, 1987). An investigator (scientist, philosopher, interpretive researcher, feminist scholar, critical theorist, postmodernist, or some combination) may move from (a) an informed guess (hunch, intuition, feeling, or opinion), to (b) an initial "map" of possible correspondences, to (c) a metaphorical level of thinking (the researcher posits a small system of correspondences between an idea and a problematic situation), to (d) an extended metaphor (a more explicit concept of a structured match of elements), to (e) an analogy (even more explicit and detailed but still inexact), to (f) a highly structured model or theory.

Legitimate strategies for use during this creative phase include visual, kinesthetic, intuitive, rational-symbolic, or any other means of generating and selecting hunches, metaphors, analogies, or tentative models. Another strategy researchers often use is to consult other fields of research for theories that address problems that run parallel to their own. For example, a theory developed in the field of semiotics may be useful (in whole or part) for developing a theory of musical meaning (e.g., Nattiez, 1990); or a theory of knowledge developed in cognitive psychology may be beneficial for building a model of what music listeners need to know (e.g., Elliott, 1995).

From another perspective, theory building is a highly context-dependent process. This is so because other investigators have pursued similar problems along similar roads before. Indeed, as we now understand, each type of inquiry has its own standards and traditions of practice. Every form of inquiry and every paradigm is embedded in a rich history and deep philosophical attachments (e.g., epistemological and ontological beliefs). Naturally, then, this "baggage" of beliefs influences the nature and construction of theories and models in a researcher's *preferred* paradigm.

Indeed, most researchers carry out all or most of their work in the paradigm they know best. This means that most investigators do not work in an "ideal" way: They do not formulate a problem and then select a research paradigm to fit their problem. They do the reverse. Accordingly, the theories and models researchers develop are shaped (restricted or dictated) from the outset by the investigator's context of research.

For example, empirical researchers insist that research must be preceded and guided by a priori theories. Otherwise, an investigation is mindless. Some philosophers and sociologists also follow the a priori approach. For example, Bennett Reimer (1970/1989) selects a theory of music a priori (Langer 1942, 1953) to anchor his philosophy of music education. Similarly, Christopher Small's sociological view of music (1998) rests on the a priori theory of Bateson (1972, 1979).

In contrast, many philosophers and most interpretive researchers reject a priori theory. Their reasons trace to their beliefs about knowledge, reality and value that, in turn, are reflected in their chosen forms of philosophical and interpretive inquiry. For example, interpretive researchers hold that theories can and should emerge gradually in the process of an investigation as (say) an ethnographer records and reflects on her field notes, amends them and interprets them with the "eyes" of other collaborators and informants. In addition, many scholars hold that the a priori approach is problematic because it can introduce "slants" or biases that cause researchers to overlook or dismiss details not accounted for by their guiding theory.

Because researchers differ about the nature and source of theories (a priori, or not), they also differ about the nature of research *designs*. So, because empiricists insist on a priori theory to guide their research, they also insist on a priori design. Some even claim that "good design" is the key to good research. These beliefs motivate some dissertation advisors to insist that all forms of research carried out by doctoral students must follow the positivist a priori approach. But this practice cannot be justified because it ignores the fundamental philosophical differences (concerning knowledge, reality and values) that differentiate these paradigms.

To complete this chapter, let us continue this examination of how basic "paradigm beliefs" influence theory and model building in several other ways. In terms of *reality*, empiricists assume there is a single, tangible, observable reality that can be broken into parts (e.g., independent variables) and studied separately. In contrast, interpretive theorists assume that reality is pluralistic, divergent, and intangible because people construct their own realities. If so, then empirical models are inadequate to address many problems (especially in music and music education) because they fail to acknowledge and investigate human phenomena conceived as multidimensional, subjective, cultural, and social.

Also in terms of reality, empirical investigators believe it is both possible and necessary to maintain an "objective distance" with a problem. In opposition, most other researchers doubt the possibility of subject-object independence. The upshot is that qualitative investigators view reality as being infused with subjective interactivity. Interpretivists and their "subjects" always (and should) influence each other. This mutuality is a major key to formulating theories that are realistic and holistic. Of course, the "proper" amount of influence depends on each researcher's beliefs about limiting or exploiting this mutuality.

Beliefs about the nature of reality and knowledge also have a direct link to the kinds of "truth" researchers seek. Scientific researchers seek knowledge in the sense of "truth statements of enduring value that are context free" (Guba & Lincoln, 1999, p. 142). Because theorists in this paradigm believe in cause-effect relationships, they model problems and select research designs that match these priorities. Their goal is "knowledge" in the form of value-free generalizations. Most other researchers eschew cause-effect models in the belief that human experiences are always tied to webs of unpredictable influences. Thus, generalizations (if these are possible) are of limited value. So, qualitative researchers tend to construct theories in the form of "working hypotheses." They assume their theories will evolve in complexity as they grow to understand the individual differences, unique circumstances and varied stances of their informants. Also, qualitative researchers and philosophers deny the "myth of objectivity" underlying empirical research. As argued above, human values are always present in human minds. This is clearly evident from the selections empiricists make among all possible problems, theories, data analyses, and so forth. These selections, in turn, reflect a deep faith in the tenets and values of modernity.

Based on these values, scientific researchers usually express their theories in the most economical forms of linguistic and mathematical communication. In contrast, scholars in philosophy, feminism, postmodernism, and all forms of interpretive research place great emphasis on formulating and reporting their theories in rich (even poetic) forms of expression. For some time now, formulations and articulations of interpretive theories have included audio and video recordings. Here is another example of the interactions between culture, values, and research: Postmodernity influences and is influenced by investigators who see themselves as "human instruments" engaged in probing a wide range of human experience and knowledge—procedural, propositional, experiential, intuitive, and meta-cognitive. Most of these forms of knowing cannot be captured in numbers or simple language, but they are still "known" and applied in complex ways by research participants.

These points also hold for the contexts in which research takes place. That is to say, scientists develop theories in "controlled," restricted conditions (e.g., laboratories) with the result that their findings only generalize to these same conditions. Interpretive studies occur in situ because interpretive researchers aim to theorize in relation to what actually happens (as opposed to what might happen outside the laboratory).

At this point, it is essential to note the obvious: Theories/models have a "dark side" (Phillips, 1987). They can mislead us because they use means (e.g., linear statements, one-dimensional diagrams, unexamined assumptions, and inappropriate metaphors) that distort the phenomena they seek to explain. Consider the frequent use of metaphors and diagrams to "model" cognitive processes in terms of (say) knowledge "storage," or "input and output"; computer hardware and software; electrical wiring; or spider webs. The nature (and danger) of these models of human thinking—as one-dimensional, autonomous, unemotional lines-on-paper—is that they impress but misinform readers at the same time because the details they show (and omit) amount to "negative analogies" (Phillips, 1987).

This brings us back, again, to the issue of validity. The first criterion of a good model or theory is its coherence with the best theory available at the time investigators begin their research. In other words, a new theory should do justice to what previous theories already account for well. Second, a theory must relate well to reality or practice, including the reality of ongoing research. Third, a theory should explain (not simply describe) a problem. The value of such explanations in the empirical paradigm is related to the predictions a researcher deduces from the premises of a theory; in the interpretive paradigm, validity is related to how well a theory identifies patterns and relationships in a holistic context of human actions.

Of course, no theory or model can be complete in itself. Every explanation is partial and provisional because no human or group of humans can ever provide the "whole truth and nothing but the truth." Researchers make one or more contributions to an ongoing, evolving body of knowledge; nothing more, nothing less. Empirical studies are approximate and indeterminate because empirical validity is only statistical. Interpretive, philosophical, and other forms of theorizing are also approximate and indeterminate because nonempirical validity is subjective.

The last point to make is this. Given the rise of postmodernity and the concomitant evolution of research modes that reflect postmodern beliefs and values, we should expect to see new forms of theory and research arise that go beyond the traditions and standards of existing research. In fact, at the time of this writing, "arts-informed research" or "artistic scholarship" is underway. The assumption of arts-informed research is that "knowledge" can also take the form of what artists know how to do. The goal is to infuse qualitative research and the expression of qualitative theories with artistic forms of expression. As Richardson (1994) argues, "The core of postmodernism is the doubt that any method or theory, discourse or genre, tradition or novelty, has a universal and general claim as the 'right' or privileged form of authoritative knowledge" (p. 517).

Eisner (1997) agrees:

> One of the basic questions scholars are now raising is how we perform the magical feat of transforming the contents of our consciousness into public form that others can understand. The assumption that the language of the social sciences—propositional language and number—are the exclusive agents of meaning is becoming increasingly problematic, and as a result, we are exploring the potential of other forms of representation for illuminating the educational worlds we wish to understand. (p. 4)

These "other forms" are musical compositions, novels, paintings, films and other forms of artistic expression. As Slattery (1997) avers, "Traditional social science research in either quantitative or qualitative form is no more rigorous or insightful than informed eclectic postmodern alternatives" (p. 1). Slattery's logic is dubious, of course. Still, the validity of works of art as "research" and research "theory" is now being discussed in relation to what Eisner (1994) calls "referential adequacy" and "structural corroboration." In this vein, some universities have now approved the writing of a novel as a legitimate "research-methodology" and document for the doctoral dissertation in education (Eisner, 1996). Madness? I think not. Just one more step beyond modernity and postmodernity to . . . who knows what?

REFERENCES

Ayer, A. J. (1936). *Language, truth and logic.* London: V. Gollancz.

Bailey, R. M. (2000). *Visiting the music classroom through the use of the case method in the preparation of senior-level music teacher education students: A study of reflective judgment.* Unpublished doctoral dissertation, University of Cincinnati.

Bateson, G. (1972). *Steps to an ecology of mind.* New York: Chandler.

Bateson, G. (1979). *Mind and nature.* London: Wildwood House.

Bauman, Z. (1992). *Modernity and ambivalence.* Ithaca, NY: Cornell University Press.

Best, J. W., & Kahn, J. V. (1993). *Research in education.* Boston: Allyn and Bacon.

Borg, R. B., & Gall, M. D. (1989). *Educational research: An introduction.* New York: Longman.

Burgess, R. G. (Ed.). (1985). *Issues in educational research: Qualitative methods.* London: Falmer Press.

Caputto, V. (1996). *Musical matters: Performativity, gender and culture in an anthropology of urban Canadian childhoods.* Unpublished doctoral dissertation, York University (Canada).

Carr, W., & Kemmis, S. (1986). *Becoming critical: education, knowledge, and action research.* Victoria: Deakin University.

Chen, C. (2000). *Constructivism in general music education: A music teacher's lived experience.* Unpublished doctoral dissertation, University of Illinois at Urbana-Champaign.

Clark, J. (1997). *Educational research: Philosophy, politics, ethics.* Palmerston North, NZ: ERDC Press.

Clegg, M. (1985). *Research partnerships: a feminist approach.* Ottawa: Canadian Research Institute for the Advancement of Women.

Connor, S. (1989). *Postmodernist culture: An introduction to theories of the contemporary.* Oxford: Blackwell.

Culler, J. (1982). *On deconstruction.* Ithaca, NY: Cornell University Press.

Derrida, J. (1981). *Positions.* Chicago: University of Chicago Press.

Dilthey, W. (1890[1988]). *Introduction to the human sciences.* Detroit: Wayne State University.

Donoghue, D. (1989). The strange case of Paul de Man. *New York Review of Books, 29,* 32–37.

Drumheller, S. (1971). *Handbook of curriculum design.* Englewood Cliffs, NJ: Educational Technology Publications.

Dunlop, R. (1999). *"Boundary Bay": A novel as educational research.* Unpublished doctoral dissertation, University of British Columbia (Canada).

Eisner, E. (1994). *The educational imagination: On the design and evaluation of school programs.* New York: Macmillan.

Eisner, E. (1996). Yes, but is it research? The conversation continues: Should a novel count as a dissertation in education. Chicago: AERA Session 5.25.

Eisner, E. (1997). The promise and perils of alternative forms of data representation. *Educational researcher, 22*(7), 5–11.

Elliott, D. J. (1995). *Music matters: A new philosophy of music education.* New York: Oxford.

Feyerabend, P. (1975). *Against method: Outline of an anarchistic theory of knowledge.* London: NLB.

Fornas, J. (1995). *Cultural theory and late modernity.* London: Sage.

Foucault, M. (1984). What is enlightenment? In P. Rabinow (Ed.), *The Foucault reader* (pp. 32–50). New York: Pantheon.

Gates, J. T., & Regelski, T. A. (1997). *Action for change in music education: the guiding ideals of the "MayDay Group."* [Online]. http://members.aol.com/jtgates/maydaygroup

Giroux, H. (1983). *Critical theory and educational practice.* Geelong: Deakin University Press.

Gronlund, N. (1970). *Sociometry in the classroom.* Bath: Chivers.

Guba, E., & Lincoln, Y. (1989). *Fourth generation evaluation.* Newbury Park, CA: Sage.

Habermas, J. (1970). *Toward a rational society*. Boston: Beacon Press.

Habermas, J. (1971). *Knowledge and human interests*. Boston: Beacon Press.

Habermas, J. (1973). *Theory and practice*. Boston: Beacon Press.

Habermas, J. (1987). *The theory of communicative action*. Boston: Beacon Press.

Harding, S. (1989). *The science question in feminism*. Ithaca, NY: Cornell University Press.

Hargreaves, A. (1994). *Changing teachers, changing times*. Toronto: OISE Press.

Harvey, D. (1989). *The condition of postmodernity*. Oxford: Blackwell.

Heshusius, L., & Ballard, K. (Eds.). (1996). *From positivism to interpretivism and beyond*. New York: Teachers College Press.

Hume, D. (1748[1955]). *Enquiry concerning human understanding*. Chicago: Regency.

Husén, T. (1999). Research paradigms in education. In J. P. Keeves & G. Lakowski (Eds.), *Issues in educational research* (pp. 31–39). Amsterdam: Pergamon.

Imada, T. (1999). *Exteriority and deconstruction: Against counterfeit nineteenth-century European ideas on music education*. Unpublished doctoral dissertation, University of British Columbia (Canada).

Kaplan, A. (1999). Scientific methods in educational research. In J. P. Keeves & G. Lakomski (Eds.), *Issues in educational research* (pp. 79–91). Amsterdam: Pergamon.

Keeves, J. P., & G. Lakowski (Eds.). (1999). *Issues in educational research*. Amsterdam: Pergamon.

Kellner, D. (1989). *Critical theory, Marxism and modernity*. Cambridge, MA: Polity.

Kemmis, S. (1999). Action research. In J. P. Keeves & G. Lakowski (Eds.), *Issues in educational research* (pp. 150–159). Amsterdam: Pergamon.

Koshy, A. A. (1995). *Transformation through music: Experiences in music education*. Unpublished master's thesis, University of Manitoba (Canada).

Kuhn, T. (1962). *The structure of scientific revolutions*. Chicago: University of Chicago Press.

Kuhn, T. S. (1977). *The essential tension: Selected studies of scientific tradition and change*. Chicago: University of Chicago Press.

Kumar, K. (1995). *From post-industrial to post-modern society*. Oxford: Blackwell.

Lacey, A. R. (1976). *A dictionary of philosophy*. New York: Scribner's.

Lakatos, I. (1978). *Mathematics, science, and epistemology*. London: Cambridge University Press.

Lakomski, G. (1999). Critical theory and education. In J. P. Keeves & G. Lakowski (Eds.), *Issues in educational research* (pp. 174–183). Amsterdam: Pergamon.

Lamb, R. K. (1987). *Including women composers in music curricula: Development of creative strategies for the general music class, grades 5–8*. Unpublished doctoral dissertation, Columbia University Teachers College.

Landsheere, G. D. (1999). History of educational research. In J. P. Keeves & G. Lakowski (Eds.), *Issues in educational research*. (pp. 15–30). Amsterdam: Pergamon.

Langer, S. K. (1942). *Philosophy in a new key*. Cambridge: Harvard University Press.

Langer, S. K. (1953). *Feeling and form*. New York: Scribner's.

Lash, S. (1990). Postmodernism as humanism? In B. S. Turner (Ed.), *Theories of modernity and postmodernity*. Newbury Park, CA: Sage.

Lather, P. (1986). Research as praxis. *Harvard Educational Review, 56*(3), 257–274.

Lengel, L. B. (1995). *Empowering stages: Contemporary women performers, music and the mass media in Tunisia*. Unpublished doctoral dissertation, Ohio University.

Lewin, K. (1946). Action research and minority problems. *Journal of Social Issues, 2*(4), 34–46.

Locke, J. (1690 [1959]). *An essay concerning the human understanding*. London: Dent/Everyman Library.

Long, V. A. (1997). *Playing the piano by ear: A critical analysis of pathways and processes from life stories*. Unpublished doctoral dissertation, University of Wisconsin–Madison.

Lyotard, J.-F. (1984). *The post modern condition: A report of knowledge*. Minneapolis: University of Minnesota Press.

Lyotard, J. F. (1997). *Postmodern fables*. Minneapolis, MN: University of Minnesota Press.

Madsen, C. H., & Madsen, C. K. (1974). *Teaching/discipline: A positive approach for educational development*. (2nd ed). Boston: Allyn and Bacon.

Madsen, C. K., & Yarbrough, C. (1980). *Competency-based music education*. Englewood Cliffs, NJ: Prentice Hall.

Marshall, J. D., & Peters, M. A. (Eds.). (1999). *Education policy*. Palmerston North, NZ: Dunmore Press.

McCormick, T. (1989). The effects of feminist approaches on research methodologies. In W. Tomm (Eds.), *Feminism and the new crisis in methodology*. Waterloo, Ontario: Wilfred Laurier University Press.

McLaren, P. L., & Giarelli, J. M. (Eds.). (1995). *Critical theory and educational research*. Albany: State University of New York Press.

Miller, B. A. (1995). *Integrating elementary music instruction with a whole language first-grade classroom*. Unpublished doctoral dissertation, University of Illinois at Urbana-Champaign.

Morrow, R. A., & Brown, D. D. (1994). *Critical theory and methodology*. London: Thousand Oaks.

Morton, C. A. (1996). *The "status problem": The feminized location of school music and the burden of justification*. Unpublished doctoral dissertation, University of Toronto (Canada).

Nattiez, J.-J. (1990). *Music and discourse: Toward a semiology of music*. Princeton: Princeton University Press.

O'Toole, P. A. (1994). *Redirecting the choral classroom: A feminist poststructural analysis of power relations within three choral settings*. Unpublished doctoral dissertation, University of Wisconsin–Madison.

Parr, N. C. (1996). *Toward a philosophy of music teacher education: Applications of the ideas of Jerome Bruner, Max-*

ine Greene, and Vernon A. Howard. Unpublished doctoral dissertation, Indiana University.

Peters, M. A. (Ed.). (1995). *Education and the postmodern condition.* Westport, CT: Bergin & Garvey.

Phillips, D. C. (1987). *Philosophy, science and social inquiry.* Oxford: Pergamon Press.

Phillips, D. C. (1999). Postivism, antipositivism, and empiricism. In J. P. Keeves & G. Lakowski (Eds.), *Issues in educational research* (pp. 249–155). Amsterdam: Pergamon.

Phillips, D. C., & Burbules, N. C. (2000). *Postpositivism and educational research.* New York: Rowan and Littlefield.

Popkewitz, T. S., & Fendler, L. (Eds.). (1999). *Critical theories in education: Changing terrains of knowledge and politics.* New York: Routledge.

Popper, K. (1965). *Conjectures and refutations.* New York: Basic Books.

Regelski, T. (1996). Scientism in experimental music research. *Philosophy of Music Education Review, 4*(1), 3–19.

Reichenbach, H. (1953). *The rise of scientific philosophy.* Berkeley: University of California Press.

Reimer, B. (1970/1989). *A Philosophy of music education.* Englewood Cliffs, NJ: Prentice Hall.

Richardson, L. (1994). Writing: a method of inquiry. In N. K. Denzin & Y. Lincoln (Eds.), *Handbook of qualitative research* (pp. 516–529). Thousand Oaks, CA: Sage.

Robinson, M. (1999). *A theory of collaborative music education between higher education and urban public schools.* Unpublished doctoral dissertation, University of Rochester, Eastman School of Music.

Rose, A. M. (1990). *Music education in culture: A critical analysis of reproduction, production and hegemony.* Unpublished doctoral dissertation, University of Wisconsin–Madison.

Rosenau, P. M. (1992). *Post-modernism and the social sciences: Insights, inroads, and intrusions.* Princeton, NJ: Princeton University Press.

Ross-Hammond, A. N. (1999). *A historical narrative of the West African Bush schools: Implications for contemporary music education curricula.* Unpublished doctoral dissertation, University of Denver.

Scott, D., & Usher, R. (Eds.). (1996). *Understanding educational research.* London: Routledge.

Skinner, B. F. (1938). *The behavior of organisms.* New York: Appleton-Century-Crofts.

Skinner, B. F. (1953). *Science and human behavior.* New York: Macmillan.

Skinner, B. F. (1968). *The technology of teaching.* New York: Appleton-Century-Crofts.

Slattery, P. (1997). *Postmodern curriculum research and alternative forms of data presentation.* Paper presented to the Curriculum and Pedagogy Institute, University of Alberta.

Small, C. (1998). *Musicking: The meanings of performing and listening.* Hanover, NH: University Press of New England.

Smart, B. (1992). *Modern conditions: postmodern controversies.* London: Routledge.

Smith, J. K. (1983). Quantitative versus qualitative research: An attempt to clarify the issue. *Educational Researcher, 12* (3), 6–13.

Stronach, I., & MacLure, M. (1997). *Educational research undone: The postmodern embrace.* Buckingham, UK: Open University Press.

Sturman, A. (1999). *Social justice in education.* Melbourne: Australian Council for Educational Research.

Tanner, D. (1972). *Using behavioral objectives in the classroom.* New York: Macmillan.

Thorndike, E. (1901). *Notes on child-study.* New York: Arno Press.

Thorndike, E. (1903). *Educational psychology.* New York: Lemeke & Buechner.

Toulmin, S. (1990). *Cosmopolis: The hidden agenda of modernity.* New York: Free Press.

Townsend, R. D. (2000). *Extra-musical association and the Freedom Farm Senior Saints: The process of music philosophy.* Unpublished doctoral dissertation, Michigan State University.

Tsisserev, A. (1998). *An ethnography of secondary school student composition in music: A study of personal involvement within the compositional process.* Unpublished doctoral dissertation, University of British Columbia (Canada).

Turner, B. (1991). Periodization and politics in the postmodern. In B. Turner (Ed.), *Theories of modernity and postmodernity* (pp. 1–13). London: Sage.

Usher, R., & Edwards, R. (1994). *Postmodernism and education.* London: Routledge.

Veblen, K. K. (1991). *Perceptions of change and stability in the transmission of Irish traditional music: An examination of the music teacher's role.* Unpublished doctoral dissertation, University of Wisconsin–Madison.

Watson, J. B. (1919). *Psychology from the standpoint of a behaviorist.* Philadelphia: Lippincott.

Wendel-Caraher, E. (1999). *Feeling silenced as a woman in music education.* Unpublished master's thesis, University of Western Ontario (Canada).

Part II

EDUCATIONAL CONTEXT AND THE CURRICULUM

Peter Webster
Nancy Whitaker
Editors

Toward an Understanding of the "Aims" of Music Education

IAN WESTBURY

I began emphasizing aesthetic education more than thirty years ago . . . with an article entitled "Music Education: Aesthetic Education."

At the time of publication of that article and during the intervening years, I never anticipated that the concept of aesthetic education would come to be used as the major tenet in the justification of music education. That has, however, happened. As a result, the profession has been sated with vague esoteric statements of justification that no one understands, including, I suspect, most of the people who make those statements.

Charles Leonhard, A Realistic Rationale for Teaching Music

Although the chapters that make up this section of the Handbook are concerned centrally with the curriculum of music education, several of these chapters also look outward to the idea of education, to the larger context of the curriculum, and to the field of curriculum studies. In doing so they bring into the already complex discussions of the curriculum of music education the additional complexities that surround all discussions around the ideas of education, schooling, and curricula, and the contemporary "curriculum field." My goal in this introduction is to provide a map that can offer, hopefully, a way of navigating such discussions of the curriculum as they bear both on music education and the larger curriculum field. I also will be seeking to extend the range of conventional discussion by introducing two perspectives from outside conventional curriculum theorizing that would seem to have a special applicability to music education.

But let me begin close to the beginning. In her masterful chapter in the first Handbook, Wing (1992) observes that the curriculum is the point of mediation between an idea of education and practice and, as such, "provide[s] a central point of departure for considering, first, what schools are intentionally about and, second, how these intents are

realized" (p. 196). Wing's observation is a telling one, highlighting as it does the central link between ideas of intentionality and the curriculum. The curriculum is the inevitable focus of all efforts to "improve" schooling. It is a central issue for those who want to see a different culture and society represented in the school. It is, necessarily, a fundamental issue in the education of teachers as the focus of their induction into the traditions of education and to the alternative possibilities around teaching that inhere in that tradition. But how we think about the curriculum in the light of these purposes has become quite complicated.

Thus, as seen most clearly in chapters 5 and 8, the exploration both of the curriculum and of ways of discussing the curriculum has become, over the past 20 or so years, a veritable industry on the part of ideologues of all stripes, political, social and cultural "leaders," policy makers, and academic theorists and researchers from many disciplines. This industry has led to the far-reaching extension of the boundaries of traditional curriculum discourse, but it has also had the result, as Philip Jackson (1996) concluded in his introductory chapter to the authoritative *Handbook of Research on Curriculum*, that:

> The variety of intellectual pursuits available to those who wish to contribute to an understanding of educational matters in general or curricular matters in particular is truly vast in number and therefore a bit daunting. . . . To some, that condition is troublesome; to others it is exhilarating; to all, it can become confusing at times. (p. 37)

For Jackson, the question was one of finding a way to secure some firm ground in this daunting and confusing, but nevertheless central, discussion.

Jackson's search for a place from which to begin thinking about the curriculum is also my search here. The range of old and emergent issues around both the curriculum itself *and* the theory of the curriculum cries out for some ground on which we can confidently stand in order to look across the territory being mapped. What is this thing "the curriculum," and how do curricula express or embody "intentions," "aims," and "rationales" for the schools? Whose "intentions," "aims," and "rationales" should be embedded in a curriculum? What are educational "intentions," "aims," and "rationales"? Indeed, what is curriculum discourse, research, and scholarship about? I will seek to make an argument around these questions here that offers a perspective grounded in a view of general curriculum theory. I will leave it to my readers to assess its usefulness for thinking in a sustained way about music education. I will be suggesting that much that passes as curriculum discussion or policy making can be seen as shadow boxing that derives from the political and cultural tensions that circle around the school but does not get at what we ask, or might ask, our students to do in their music or other classrooms.

A conventional approach to considering the curriculum starts, as do several of the following chapters, with an examination of various ideas about "curriculum"—with the implication that one or another such idea is the appropriate one—or with an argument, in the postmodern manner, that the curriculum is simply a set of "texts" that can be "read" in different ways. The conclusions that result usually express a confusing mélange of understandings of the curriculum—ranging from the idea of the curriculum as a formal course of study, which implies issues around how such a course of study might be developed and introduced to schools and teachers, with what effect, to the idea that the "real" curriculum is always, in some sense, emergent from the interactions between students and teachers, with the implication that that curriculum cannot be directed, and can only be characterized after the event by an observer. Likewise, understandings of theorizing around the curriculum range from a search for explicit prescriptions about how courses of study should best be developed and introduced, to sketches of better worlds that should come into being, to, as Wing (1992) suggests, the idea of curriculum theorizing and activity as a form of deliberative conversation around "educational aims, objectives, materials, scope and sequence, articulation, teaching strategies, learner activities, and outcomes" (p. 196).

But if we are to secure a perspective from which we can come to terms with the set of *all* of these starting points, we need to begin our reconnaissance in a different place. I will look for this place here by arguing that the idea of curriculum is best looked for in the pervasive web of beliefs and understandings about what schooling is that is to be found embedded in any society or culture.[1] In modern states, this framework of cultural beliefs becomes instantiated organizationally, and thus politically, in the form of the policies, curricula, and programs of state-organized and managed school systems. However, such organizational manifestations are always interpreted in the light of a culture's more or less firm understanding of the proper nature and appropriate character of education and schooling. The curriculum in its organized form is always measured against an underlying curriculum-as-idea, although the organized, reified curriculum-as-a-thing also contributes in important ways to the curriculum-as-an-idea. It is this culturally embedded curriculum-as-an-idea that gives the organizational form of the school and curriculum its significance—in a way that is analogous to what Peter Berger (1967; see also Luckmann, 1967) called the "sacred canopy" of religious belief, the imagined reality that gives meaning to all formal religious practice.

This invisible, imagined curriculum-as-canopy or curriculum-as-idea should be seen, first and foremost, as a body of implicit—but well-understood—principles that order and legitimate the webs of activity that define the role of schooling as a pathway from childhood to adulthood. It gives us *our* understandings of what should be happening to, and on behalf of, *our* children and young people as they attend school. This "power" of the curriculum-as-an-idea to direct beliefs about and behavior around schools is not mediated by organizations and structures but is directly apprehended by every person in a culture. It is, to use another image, an *exo*skeleton that structures the culture of any society or community. Thus, it is common understandings of the American curriculum-as-an-idea, an understanding that is shared by teachers, students, parents, and communities, which makes fourth grades, bands, orchestras, or algebra 1 classes from Bangor, Maine, to San Diego, California, more or less similar in character and meaning, *despite* the decentralized governance of the American school. It is this invisible curriculum that sets out, and even prescribes, the categories of experience that schools of this or that type must offer, for example, math, art, band, orchestra, and so forth, and that gives the work done within those categories its social and cultural significance. It is the larger framework that links "band," "algebra II," "shop," "U.S. history," "jazz ensemble," as categories, to the various pasts of families and communities, and to the imagined futures of their children.

As I have been suggesting, as *the* meaning-giving frame for the school experience, this invisible curriculum does not have any immediately tangible form, although it might find a cathexis around ideas like the centrality of algebra or geometry to an "appropriate" high school experience, or around activities like the Christmas concert or Friday-night football. It is a collective *imaging* of the school experience and of the functions and role of that experience in the pathway to a responsible, appropriate adulthood. As such, this curriculum-as-an-idea has great social and cultural valence; it is an object of significant societal, communal, and individual investment, *and* of individual and collective consumption.

Such cultural images of the curriculum and its relationship to adulthood are the outcome of the enculturating processes of societies and communities. They reflect the commonality, and the diversity, of imagined pasts and imagined futures of the societies and communities that they define. And, in different contexts, such images can be more or less fixed in all of their particulars or they may be somewhat open, with a perceived nonnegotiable core and a negotiable periphery. Thus, Americans would question the legitimacy of a high school that did not teach a required course in U.S. history. Most Americans would be puzzled by a large public high school that did not have an orchestra, band, and choir; they might regard it as desirable that their school also have a jazz ensemble, undertake an annual performance of Gilbert and Sullivan, or initiate a chorale, but they would accept it if it did not. By contrast, Americans are very conflicted about including the discussion of abortion as a routine procedure for fertility control in a middle school health course or a school nurse's office. But, in the main, conflict between and within communities around like issues such as fertility control and its place in the school occurs on the margin of the substantial consensus about what the overall curriculum is and should be and how that curriculum relates to the pathway to adulthood.

As John Meyer and his colleagues have emphasized in their development of the view of the curriculum I have been offering here, this invisible curriculum-as-an-idea is profoundly embedded in the imagery that defines nations and communities. Thus, both images of the appropriate national culture and society and its future, and of the ways in which the nation's institutions are seen as organized, have come to include understandings around the role of education and schooling in the national culture. In modern states, the curriculum as an idea melds with ideas around the school as an organization, and in understandings of the forms of authoritative governance and organization that are appropriate for the nation's institutions.

As a result of these processes, formal organized curricula have emerged as frameworks laid out by authoritative centers outlining the set of subject offerings (and requirements) that schools deliver, along with formal statements about what these categories are believed to do for children. Such curricula-as-a-thing in turn require administrators who manage the agency, the "delivery" of the curriculum, and who can provide reassurance to elites, the public at large, and parents and students that all is well with the work of the school, that what is done mirrors what should be being done. And, of course, the agency requires agents, teachers who know what they should be doing to work within both the curriculum-as-a-thing and, more important perhaps, the curriculum-as-an-idea—and, thus, an appropriate socialization of teachers.

But, as we also know, much of the organized framework, and the organizing work, around the school and curriculum is symbolic. Schools are "loosely-coupled" (Weick, 1976) or "decoupled" (Meyer & Rowan, 1977) organizations in which macrolevel frameworks are often only weakly reflected (or not at all reflected) in day-to-day practice. This is well understood by "insiders": teachers do what they do, they reenact their understanding of the curriculum-in-the-culture; administrators, policy makers, academics do what they do, they work around public and professional images of the curriculum. And if we are to make sense of much of this work, we must always wonder: Who is being addressed? For what purpose? Was, for example, his advocacy of "music as aesthetic education" as a "rationale" for music education that Charles Leonhard reflected on in the epigraph to this introduction meant to change teachers' work in the private spaces of their classrooms? Or was it an attempt to address symbolically, in terms of a new image encapsulated in a slogan, a dissonance that he perceived between public ideas around music-education-as-a-thing and an underlying music-education-as-an-idea?

Seen in this way, the "confusing" intellectual pursuit around the curriculum that concerned Jackson (1996), and that surfaces in this section of the Handbook, is largely an epiphenomenon around the curriculum-as-a-thing—and has little immediate connection to the curriculum-as-an-idea. More often than not the pursuit is, as I have been suggesting, a form of symbolic "work" that is undertaken most aggressively when there is a tension between the curriculum-as-a-thing and the curriculum-as-an-idea. Such work seeks to rearticulate, in visible rhetorical or organizational ways, aspects of the invisible world that gives schools their meaning and legitimacy—and to underline, through utterance and administrative action, the commitment of the visible school system to this invisible world. In teacher education, the pursuit communicates rhetorical forms and practices that can be used to symbolize the public and professional legitimacy of the curriculum-as-a-thing. And, in its "critical" aspect, the pursuit reflects, and projects, the tensions and ambiguities around different understandings of the correct, legitimate pathway to an imagined adulthood.

In other words, the varied and vexing forms of the visible pursuit of, for example, aims or rationales for music, math, or whatever are not significant in any straightforward way. Aims, rationales, curricula express—but never direct—what schools might do. They are symbols of the invisible curriculum, and a reaction to the conflicts and contention that circle around that invisible curriculum as it becomes visible. Whether it is creating a new music curriculum-as-a-document or a new curriculum-as-program, or laying the "aims" for an education in music, such work is best seen as being undertaken for specific expressive purposes within specific contexts. It is a form, following Hess (1999), to be judged in terms of its appropriateness to a task, situation, and context.

All such visible activity directed at the curriculum draws on the rhetorical and organizational resources of its culture (Westbury, 1993). Thus, it was the socially available organizational forms of 19th-century American society, and their rationales, which were drawn on to create the organization and rhetorical forms of, for example, formal curricula and courses of study. The "Tyler rationale" became the symbol of the mid-20th-century form of such work and of its organizational assumptions and, as such, became both a symbolic resource for, and a justification of, a particular form of visible curriculum work, *and* a symbol of the "technical rationality" that was seen to inhere in this 19th-century organizational form. The contemporary activity around such enterprises as the "MENC Performance Standards" (Music Educators National Conference) are latter-day manifestations of the same underlying symbols and, needless to say, provokes the same responses pro and con. But all such action and reaction, claim and counterclaim, presume the myth that the program outlined in this or that seemingly authoritative document, movement, or ideology has some directive significance in the day-to-day work of the schools—which, of course, it does not have. Likewise, the perennial "pursuit," pro and con, of "managerialism" versus "reconceptualism," "training" versus "education," "vocationalism" versus "liberal education," and so forth, has little practical impact on the underlying curriculum-as-an-idea or the working practices of teachers. However, such debates can define symbolically the axes around which social mobilizations directed at recalibrating the ideological relationship between the organizational and the institutional curriculum can and do occur. But more often than not, as we saw Charles Leonhard suggesting, such debates peter out to become a ritual reiteration of vague or esoteric symbols, the stuff of keynote addresses at one or another kind of gathering.

But what does such a background analysis of the "curriculum" imply for how we might think about curriculum theory and practice? More immediately, what does it imply for the ways in which we might think about the curriculum of music education?

In their recent essay reviewing their "institutionalist" project on the cross-cultural sociology of the curriculum, McEneaney and Meyer (2000) summarize their view of the trajectory of arts education in the "modern" school in the following way:

> Emphasis on canonical sacred tradition declines, and cultural emphases become eclectic and organized around the interests and participation of the student. The student is to understand a broad range of national and cultural forms,

and is to do so in a way that emphasizes participation and interest. Paralleling curricular treatments of literature, the expressive possibilities of art and culture are themselves worthy of consideration. (p. 206)

This abstracted view of the trajectory of arts education reflects McEneaney and Meyer's understanding that modern "educational systems are fundamentally engaged in a project of constructing *individuals* who understand themselves and others as having interests and the capacity to act on them" (p. 193; emphasis in original). The animation of this modern project, which affects all subject areas and the overall curriculum itself, emerges from a pervasive, cross-cultural image of modern nations which are "thoroughly manageable and rationalized, [and] composed of agentic individuals" (p. 197) who participate individually and collectively in a global order.

As McEneaney and Meyer (2000) see it, there are two major implications that give clear direction to the aims and intentions of the school and curriculum-as-an-idea in this image of the modern nation-state, society, and culture: first, the incorporation of the population in a *common* experience of the "school," and, second, the redirection of the curriculum to, on the one hand, facilitate this incorporation or participation of all, and, on the other hand, instill the understandings that reflect the "modern" image of the order. The trends that McEneaney and Meyer (2000) see as the characteristics of "modern" arts education reflect these "tasks" of the school and curriculum in the pathway to a "modern" adulthood. Through her experience in the "modern" school, she is/will be "scripted to be an empowered member and participant in a very broad society and nature, not to be subordinated to an exogenously authoritative elite culture" (p. 207). In McEneaney and Meyer's view, transcending traditions, whether religious, cultural, musical, or whatever, have faded as objects of the school's work in the light of such intentions. Likewise, they see a concern for local traditions, local content, and local languages diminishing in the face of the needs of the imagined *nation*. At the same time, the child or youth, with his or her diverse interests, is being recognized and acknowledged, with the implication that school, curricula, and teaching must be relevant, and appealing. As the logical consequence of all of these trends, the curriculum across all subjects is becoming what McEneaney and Meyer (2000) call a form of "cultural tourism designed to eliminate disliking, rather than instilling particular commitments or technical expertise" (p. 201). "Progressivism" in one or another of its guises becomes the visible *epiphenomenal* symbolic manifestation of this project.

It is important to note that McEneaney and Meyer's (2000) characterization of the direction of the modern school, and of arts education within it, is not normative, but it is an empirically based characterization of what they see as a century-long development seen across all modern and modernizing societies. Their research seeks to describe and to understand the trajectory, and the source, of the phenomena they see as associated with a pervasive, cross-national curricular form. They acknowledge, of course, "resistance" to this project—often initiated in response to school or curricular "reforms" that emerge as fleeting shifts in aspects of the images of society (and that become crystallized in the media) interact with images of the seemingly inappropriate, unreformed practices of the school. Such resistance is, in its turn, reflected symbolically in the idea of a "traditionalist discourse" evoking different (usually older) images of the curriculum. However, as McEneaney and Meyer note, such resistance, and the related traditionalist discourse, has had little long-term impact on the increasingly routine "modernization" of the institutional, invisible curriculum: "[T]he main evolution goes quite the other way, towards more expansive, participatory, and broadened conception of knowledge, involving the development and interests of the student rather than the authority of received knowledge" (p. 204).

McEneaney and Meyer's (2000) thesis is important to all *thinking* about the curriculum. It offers a perspective on the nature of the contemporary curriculum which, in contrast to most accounts, embeds its view of the curriculum as a real-world social phenomenon. Second, it offers a perspective that suggests how the historical changes and new directions in, say, music education, *as a social phenomenon*, might be understood. They offer what is, in a sense, an empirical "rationale" for the music program, and for a changing music curriculum, which highlights the question of whose aims, intentions, and rationales for music education we should be considering.

Thus, for reasons that can only be guessed at, American music education traditionally has been one of the paradigmatic instances of the modernizing project around the curriculum and the school. Music education has long been open to the culture in a way that few other areas of the curriculum have been. As a result, music education has embraced an ever-expanding variety of musical forms and cultures while maintaining its commitment to the traditional forms—a reflection perhaps of the changing structure of musical taste in the larger culture (see, for example, Bryson, 1996). It has been an area that has most actively linked the school with the broad national cultures of music, and musical taste, in enjoyable, participatory and accessible ways. As students successfully reenact the form of the marching band, gospel choir, swing band, a Gershwin or Rodgers and Hammerstein musical, banjo choir, madrigal group, and the like, they begin, and publicly celebrate, their authentic participation in the larger national culture and, as I will suggest later, their parents and communities are able to participate with them in that celebration of larger culture.

However, McEneaney and Meyer (2000), writing as macrosociologists, look at trends across the curriculum from the outside, in ways that do not yield any immediate, particular insight into the educationally and pedagogically important questions around the cultures that are being *enacted*, and thus reflected, within the classroom. This is, of course, the central question for any teacher. We can well understand that the overall purpose of our teaching has been and is a form of McEneaney and Meyer's "cultural tourism," but what do we mean when we ask whether a particular curriculum or a pattern of teaching has an educational justification *within this frame*? Curricular discussion within music education clearly needs a way of addressing this issue that avoids the emptiness of the "rationales" and "aims" that we saw Charles Leonhard reflecting on as he discussed the reception of his exploration of the idea of music as aesthetic education. When we bring together McEneaney and Meyer's overall understanding of the curriculum with the perspective offered by Peter Menck (2000), work that reflects the very different "curricular" perspective found within the German "Didaktik" tradition,[2] we perhaps have a way of thinking that goes to the heart of this educational concern.

Menck's essays start with the idea that the school's central task is to form children to the norms and values of a culture. As he sees it, this task is at the heart of the carefully contrived signs of the living culture that are presented to students in the school, and expressed in everything it does. In chapter after chapter of *Looking in Classrooms*, Menck asks his readers to consider what this "axiom" (as he terms it) means—to think about and ponder the ways in which the dimensions of a culture are mirrored and articulated in the world of the classroom:

> "The Hallelujah Chorus," with the whole *Messiah* thrown in, is performed much better by a professional choir than by the school orchestra with Alexander playing solo. And yet . . . we go along to the school's Christmas recital, although we really do not have the time. Why? Surely not for the utility value of these things. No, we go because the products are *signs* that our children have acquired something and, at the same time, have made something of themselves. Crooked and off-key they may be, but we are prepared to accept what we would never accept from a carpenter or a virtuoso, as long as we are sure that our children have worked as though the future of the world depended on it, in other words, seriously and with dedication. (Menck, 2000, p. 78)

For Menck, the fundamental curricular questions are "What image of the world is *produced* [italics added] by the work done in the classroom?" and "What is the image we expect the pupils to adopt *as their own* [italics added]?" (p. 78). Although they might express it differently, this is also the assumption, and the question, at the heart of the project of John Meyer and his colleagues.

In Menck's view, a music classroom is, like all classrooms, a contrived and protected place in which children are presented with signs of music as a complex cultural form. They are invited to work on and appropriate these signs. As they do this, more or less seriously, they put themselves into a relationship with the world that is embedded in and signed by the form and the repertoire of their ensemble and by the tasks that they engage in while they are in the music classroom. They learn to interpret this classroom world as what it is, a symbolic mirror of a larger world with its ways of listening, thinking and playing, thinking about playing, responses, values, and so forth—and, in so doing, they internalize the forms and values of the larger world outside the small, protected world of the school.

This work of the school might be commonplace and self-evident. But to get at the heart of Menck's thinking, we need to recognize that the school is not "the world" but a place that presents its students with an *image* of the world. Moreover, we need to recognize that any effective working pedagogy is necessarily artful and contrived. The teacher must project the culture of the curriculum to his students, *and* at the same time represent their needs—because they are, when all is said and done, only faintly aware of what they are doing and where they are going. *It is the task of pedagogy to make the world that is being mirrored in the classroom compelling and accessible.* Thus the pictures, stories, works, settings, and pedagogies of the school serve, in Menck's (2000) words, to:

- Represent this order in symbolic way;
- [Present this order] in a didactical context in such a way that pupils are able to recognize themselves in the stories and the pictures. They can place themselves therein, and find themselves introduced to this order without force; and they:
- Demand validity for the underlying order and the behavioral norms embedded in that order. (p. 122)

Like McEneaney and Meyer (2000), Menck's viewpoint is *not* normative, and he is not focused in any immediate sense on the "improvement" of what is being done in classrooms and schools. The world that a curriculum renders into symbols and signs, the imagined world that is mirrored in the school, is not under direct organizational or administrative control in other than marginal ways. Furthermore, any "culture," and thus any school, has elements of both the "good" and the "bad," but overall schools and classrooms successfully mirror complex, ongoing cultures in all of their complexity, but mostly for the good. Outsiders cannot change what schools and teachers do because, in a sense, their task is a cultural given that overrides any short-term mandates. The practices, whatever they might be, that are found in classrooms and schools, and have persisted, have emerged out of social, cultural, and pedagogical histories and inevitably reflect a total culture. Fresh possibilities for pedagogies can be offered to teachers and schools—but more often than not these are older ways that have been forgotten, or maybe not known in this setting.

In other words, we must acknowledge that orchestras and choirs, or recorder groups and spring musicals, as persisting activities within the didactical and pedagogical order of the school, are educationally significant—for otherwise the forms would not persist. It is the work that is being done in such settings that educational and curriculum research should, as its central task, seek to understand. It must attempt to penetrate the cultural meanings and pedagogical forms of these settings in their own terms, as manifestations of the formation of new members in an ongoing culture, *not* in terms of the shadow boxing of ideological dualisms and grand schemes of the visible and epiphenomenal public and professional cultures that surround that work of formation.

As we do this, we might hypothesize that we will see music educators fully engaged in the agenda McEneaney and Meyer (2000) saw as controlling developments in arts education—but we also might see other patterns, and we might wonder, as good empiricists, what cultures or subcultures they mirror. We should also expect to see and understand the means by which schools differentiate students into groups in which one or another kind of specialized formation takes place, and we should ask what signs are found in which such settings, what the pedagogy of such formation might be, and how they might be different from the signs and pedagogies of other settings—and what cultures are being expressed by such differential formation.

In summary, the aims of music education are cultural givens, and do not emerge from formal curriculum or curriculum policies. They reside in the ground of the school. They are, moreover, ethical, not technical and not cognitive or skill-based in any narrow sense; the school is about the business of creating, through its signing and symbolizing of the culture, the dispositions and attitudes of students who will live in and contribute to that culture in their adulthoods. Schools cannot change that culture, that imagined nation; they can only reflect them. The "aims of education" reside outside the world of curriculum offices and documents, however well intentioned those offices and documents might be. Instead, they are found in the imagings, understandings, and dispositions of students, parents, communities, and teachers as members and agents of a living, albeit invisible *Weltbild*. We can, like

Charles Leonhard, articulate our rationales and hope, wistfully, that others may listen in some serious way. But no visible agent or agency can legislate educational aims and rationales.

What, then, are we seeking to do in and with any discussion of the curriculum of music education? What audience are we addressing? for what end? Thus Hanley and Montgomery (chapter 8) quote Wing (1992) to the effect that:

> The bulk of [curriculum work in music education] relates to having good ideas (comprehensive musicianship, sequential organization of concepts to the learned, quality literature and so on), being able to create curricula based on these ideas, getting teachers to use these programs in various degrees for a period of time, and seeing some evidence that students learned what was intended from these programs. (p. 211)

For Wing, such activity was just "doing curriculum" (p. 211) in that it lacked a framework of significant questions, a framework of theory. The work of teacher education requires the prescriptions and recommendations that Wing's "doing curriculum" entails. But while the use of prescriptions, recommendations, and scripts does not necessarily lead to either good or bad teaching, dependence on them does tend to restrict those who advocate or follow one or another approach to see it as the only way. "Theory," Menck writes, "should show a way out of such restrictions" (p. 40). But what is the nature of the curriculum theory that meets the test that Menck implies? How might curriculum theorizing in general, or curriculum theorizing within music education, show ways out of what restrictions? In other words, what are discussions of the curriculum of music education, that is, of curriculum policies, of programs, of the aims and rationales of music education, seeking to *do*?

NOTES

1. This view of the curriculum in the following paragraphs draws heavily on the writing of John Meyer of Stanford University. For a recent discussion of the understanding of the curriculum being developed by Meyer and his colleagues, see McEneaney and Meyer (2000). I will be returning to McEneaney and Meyer's thesis later in this introduction.

2. For a discussion of this German tradition of thinking about the curriculum, see Westbury, Hopmann, and Riquarts (2000).

REFERENCES

Berger, Peter L. (1967). *The sacred canopy: Elements of a sociological theory of religion.* Garden City, NY: Doubleday.

Bryson, B. (1996). "Anything but heavy metal": Symbolic exclusion and musical dislikes. *American Sociological Review, 61,* 884–899.

Hess, F. (1999). *Spinning wheels: The politics of urban school reform.* Washington, DC: Brookings Institution.

Jackson, P. W. (1996). Conceptions of curriculum and curriculum specialists. In P. W. Jackson (Ed.), *Handbook of research on curriculum* (pp. 34–40). New York: Macmillan.

Leonhard, C. (1985). *A realistic rationale for teaching music.* Reston, VA: Music Educators National Conference.

Luckmann, Thomas. (1967). *The invisible religion: The problem of religion in modern society.* New York: Macmillan.

McEneaney, E. H., & Meyer, J. W. (2000). The content of the curriculum: An institutionalist perspective. In M. T. Hallinan (Ed.), *Handbook of the sociology of education* (pp. 189–211). New York: Kluwer.

Menck, P. (2000). *Looking into classrooms: Papers on didactics.* Stamford, CT: Ablex.

Meyer, J. W., & Rowan, B. (1977). Institutionalized organizations: Formal structure as myth and ceremony. *American Journal of Sociology, 83,* 340–363.

Music Educators National Conference, Committee on Performance Standards. (1996). *Performance standards for music: Strategies and benchmarks for assessing progress towards the national standards, grades pre-K–12.* Reston, VA: Music Educators National Conference.

Weick, K. (1976) Educational organizations as loosely coupled systems. *Administrative Science Quarterly, 21*(1), 1–19.

Westbury, I. (1993). Curriculum studies in the United States: Reflections on a conversation with Ulf Lundgren. In D. Broady (Ed.), *Education in the late 20th century: Essays presented to Ulf P. Lundgren on the occasion of his fiftieth birthday* (pp. 117–140). Stockholm, Sweden: Stockholm Institute of Education Press.

Westbury, I., Hopmann, S., & Riquarts, K. (Eds.). (2000). *Teaching as a reflective practice: The German Didaktik tradition.* Mahwah, NJ: Lawrence Erlbaum.

Wing, L. N. (1992). Curriculum and its study. In R. Colwell (Ed.), *Handbook of research on music teaching and learning: A project of the Music Educators National Conference* (pp. 196–217). New York: Schirmer Books.

Contemporary Curriculum Practices and Their Theoretical Bases

8

BETTY HANLEY

JANET MONTGOMERY

The particular domain of curriculum research is not in its method(s) but rather in its questions, questions that appreciate the continually shifting coalescence of all its parts.

L. B. Wing, "Curriculum and Its Study"

Although the practical issues that surround the teaching of music have always been important, the field of curriculum study has not historically received a high priority in North American music education. For example, Wing's (1992) review of curriculum conversations in the *Journal of Research in Music Education* and the *Bulletin of the Council for Research in Music Education* from 1953 to 1988 revealed only 88 articles related to curriculum, 61% of which were dissertations. Applying Wing's criteria to the same sources between 1989 and 2000, we found 44 articles, 77% of which were dissertations. It seems that music educators are demonstrating some sign of increased interest in curriculum studies. This chapter provides an account of this interest.

Context of Curriculum Issues

After establishing a context for the discussion of curriculum issues, we begin the chapter with an overview of curriculum theory from Tyler (1949) to the present. We then examine the research related to contemporary music education curriculum from two perspectives: (1) curriculum research in the positivistic mode and (2) reconceptualized curriculum work. We conclude by revisiting some of the questions raised throughout the chapter and looking to the future.

What Is Curriculum?

There are many possible definitions of curriculum, with some focusing on content and others on form. We have selected a few to demonstrate the scope of the discussion. Fowler (1984, p. 33), for example, identified curriculum as the content of a subject or discipline. Eisner (1994) described curriculum as "the program of activities and opportunities provided to the young" (p. 61). Doyle (1992) relied on what he described as the way curriculum is "usually understood": "Curriculum refers to the substance or content of schooling, the course of study (literally, a racecourse)" (p. 486). Runfola and Rutkowski (1992) adopted an operational definition by Pratt (1980): Curriculum "refers to an organized set of formal educational and/or training intentions" (p. 697). Foshay (2000) conceived of curriculum as "a plan for action by students and teachers" that required clarity of goals, content, and practice (p. xv). Wing (1992) avoided a single definition of curriculum but suggested that curriculum involves conversations that surround "educational aims, objectives, materials, scope and sequence, articulation, teaching strategies, learner activities, and outcomes" (p. 196). Jackson (1992) traced historical changes in curriculum definitions, identifying different focuses and the importance of interpretation in definition making: Is curriculum what teachers plan? What students experience? The course of studies? The unplanned/hidden/undelivered curriculum?

There is a difference in the scope of these approaches to defining curriculum. The first six direct us to classroom practice. The last one asks us to think about the meaning of definitions and to examine the underlying assumptions. Definitions are "pieces of arguments" (Jackson, 1992,

113

p. 12) that present a point of view. Given the value-laden nature of definitions, Jackson emphasized the need to consider a number of questions when considering curriculum definitions and issues: What is the purpose of the proposed idea? Where does it come from and why? Why should anyone urge us to believe that it is so? Whose interests would be served? What impact would the ideas have on our beliefs? What actions might ensue? (p. 11). Jackson's questions themselves represent a particular way of seeing the world.

Jackson (1992) divided the many possible definitions of curriculum into two categories: (1) those "narrowly focused" concerns that deal with the development and implementation of specific subjects or topics within a school or set of schools and (2) those "more broadly focused" concerns that deal with theoretical issues such as "the construction of general theories and principles of curriculum development or broad perspectives on the curriculum as a whole or on the status of curriculum as a field of study" (p. 3). We will use this twofold conceptualization as our framework for discussing curriculum and direct the reader to Jackson (1992) for a detailed account of the historical evolution of curriculum.

What is important at this point is to acknowledge the complexity and many meanings of curriculum. As Pinar (1995) stated, definitions can be both beginnings and endings "dependent upon the discourse and its functions" (p. 28).

Curriculum Practice and Research

How have curriculum practice and research interacted in music education? Music educators have typically approached curriculum from the perspective of specialists who are interested in the subject matter (cf. Gary, 1967; Thomas, 1970) and in specialized topics such as the teaching of singing (Phillips, 1992) or the acquisition of music-reading skills (Hodges, 1992) rather than in what Jackson (1992) called "curriculum in general or curriculum improvement across the board" (p. 37). Discussing the factors that influenced curriculum decisions before there were curriculum specialists, Jackson identified custom and tradition, usefulness, authority, and textbooks (p. 22). These factors remain influential in contemporary music education. Curriculum in music education has been developed more on the basis of tradition and rigorous evaluation than on systematic research (Colwell, 1990a, 1990b).

There has been, moreover, concern that research has not significantly impacted on classroom practice. In *What Works: Instructional Strategies for Music Education*, a compilation of research-based strategies, Merrion (1989) wrote: "Although it may appear obvious that researched strategies would prove useful to teachers, there do not

seem to be many practitioners who use or highly value such information" (p. i). In the minds of practitioners, research has often been equated with theory, with both considered largely irrelevant.

Where Does Theory Fit?

If practitioners have been reluctant to use research, they have not been any more eager to engage in theory building. Reminiscing on his early years in the profession, LeBlanc (1996), who later in his career developed and tested a theory of music performance anxiety and a theory of music preference acquisition, described his reluctance to develop theories on which to base his research. This reluctance is shared by many music educators who consider theory to be esoteric. Whatever the reason, the quality of much research has suffered from a lack of solid theory building. Referring to research methodology in music education, Costanza and Russell (1992) concluded:

> There has been a good deal of research regarding the techniques, methods, and curricula used in the field of music education; however, because of the absence of a philosophical basis and a foundation of research for many of these techniques, methods, and curricula, there have not been many exemplary studies dealing with music education methodologies. (p. 505)

Beall (1991), however, questioned the value of unified theories "to guide all of our efforts in music teaching and learning" (p. 96), while Plummeridge (1985, 1999) discussed the limitations of theory. Are theory and practice unrelated? Does theory influence practice, or does practice generate theory? Or is practice theoretical (Pinar, Reynolds, Slatter, & Taubman, 1995, p. 586)? These questions will be examined in this chapter in the context of curriculum research in music education.

What Constitutes Curriculum Research?

In her seminal article, "Curriculum and Its Study," Wing (1992) drew together the literature and research from a number of disciplines to help clarify the field of curriculum study in music education. After providing a summary of the history of curriculum, she examined the relationship between curriculum conversation and teaching practice, the conceptions of curriculum implied in program evaluation models, and the challenges to curriculum. Wing noted a reluctance to conduct thorough curriculum studies, the emphasis on and inadequacy of the "scientific" study of curriculum, and the importance of the interrelationship of context, teachers, and learners in the curriculum. She emphasized the importance of asking the right questions, not "just 'doing' curriculum" (p. 211), and the need to determine what knowledge is of most value. She concluded that

> the bulk of it [curriculum knowledge in music education] relates to having good ideas (comprehensive musicianship, sequential organization of concepts to be learned, quality literature, and so on), being able to create curricula based on these ideas, getting teachers to use these programs in varying degrees for a period of time, and seeing some evidence that students learned what was intended from these programs. The profession knows itself largely from the standpoints of stated values and scientifically conducted, quantitative inquiry into some of its curriculum efforts. (p. 211)

Much depends on the definition of curriculum employed. Discussing curriculum ideologies or belief systems and their impact on curriculum, Eisner (1992) recognized three areas of possible research: studies of the social and intellectual sources of the ideology, historical studies of the consequences of ideology on the content and form of schooling, and assessments of the effect of a particular ideology on "the processes and outcomes of schooling" (p. 319).

Identifying a number of issues that had not been addressed in research, D. F. Walker (1992) defined curriculum research as "any research that illuminates a curriculum problem or advances our ability to deal with it" (p. 109). He suggested the following research questions:

- How do we study curriculum practices in relation to their contexts rather than as isolated independent factors?
- How do we do justice in research to the differing values, interests, and perspectives of all those involved in curriculum practice?
- How do we reconcile research that meets the practical need for detailed studies of specific curriculum practices with traditional methodological standards and the institutional structures and procedures of the research community?
- How do we identify purposes when studying curriculum practice? (p. 112)

Curriculum research includes historical, analytical, descriptive, experimental, action-research, ethnographic, phenomenological, critical theory, and narrative models, each with its own criteria for excellence and assumptions about the nature of reality. The answer you get depends on the questions you ask.

The following critical observations have been made about curriculum research in music education:

1. There has been a lack of rigor in determining the effectiveness of innovation through evaluation (Costanza & Russell, 1992; Leonhard & Colwell 1976; Shuler, 1991a) and in music curriculum research in general (Wing, 1992).
2. There has been an absence of philosophical bases and research foundations for music education methodologies (Costanza & Russell, 1992, p. 505).
3. There has been a tendency to base curriculum on activities and techniques rather than carefully developed models (Runfola & Rutkowski, 1992, p. 700; Shuler, 1991a) and to neglect the study of the merits of teaching strategies/methods (Colwell, 1990a, p. 47).
4. There are few replications of research studies undertaken (Wing, 1992, p. 210).
5. There is a need for longitudinal and large-scale studies (Costanza & Russell, 1992; Reimer, 1985).
6. There is a lack of knowledge about what students are actually doing in classrooms (Wing, 1992, p. 212). Furthermore, researchers have noted a discrepancy between policy and practice (Shepherd & Vulliamy, 1994, p. 37), between the ideas behind curriculum and their actual implementation (Reimer, 1989, p. 161; Stake & Easley, 1978), between beliefs and practice (Hanley, 1989; Robinson, 1996; Stake, Bresler, & Mabry, 1991), between what teachers report they do and what they are observed doing (Swanwick, 1992, p. 5), and between what researchers and teachers consider to be ideal and what is presented in textbooks (Prawat, 1993).

Overview of the Chapter

In this chapter we will focus on developments in music curriculum in U.S. and Canadian and to some extent English and Australian K–12 schools since the publication of the first *Handbook of Research on Music Teaching and Learning* (Colwell, 1992). Mirroring Jackson's (1992) categories, our overall intention is twofold: (1) to examine practice and theory in music curriculum research from a "broad focus" in order to interpret the theoretical perspectives evident in curriculum research in music education and situate this research in the context of the general curriculum field and (2) to examine the more "narrowly focused" theoretical basis of music education practice and curriculum research.

In undertaking this chapter we realized that, given the magnitude of our purpose and the relative brevity of this chapter, we would have to be very selective in the research cited and focus more on the research literature than the practical realization of the ideas. We begin with the broad focus.

Curriculum Theory

Music education does not exist in a vacuum. While music educators are sometimes happy to be left alone, we are also eager to jump on the latest educational bandwagon so that music education is perceived to be an integral part of the whole educational enterprise. Indeed, as we endeavor to maintain a place for music in the school timetable, it is becoming increasingly important to consider how music education fits into the broader framework of curriculum theory. In this section, we begin with the Tylerian Rationale, which underpins a generation of curriculum work described as prototypical of current school-based curriculum (Pinar et al., 1995). We next consider a decade of change and conclude the section with a look at the reconceptualized curriculum field.

Tylerian Rationale

The Tylerian Rationale has remained influential in curriculum development, implementation, and evaluation in the schools since the publication of Ralph Tyler's *Basic Principles of Curriculum and Instruction* in 1949. Tyler proposed putting curriculum on a scientific footing by asking four questions to guide curriculum work:

1. What educational purposes should the school seek to attain? [setting objectives]
2. What educational experiences can be provided that are likely to attain these purposes? [designing learning experiences]
3. How can these educational experiences be effectively organized? [determining scope and sequence]
4. How can we determine whether these purposes are being attained? [evaluating student learning] (p. 1)

The Tylerian model developed and implemented by practitioners over 50 years is linear and hierarchical, with the teacher's role that of implementing the given curriculum. The model may sound quite familiar; its principles continue to form the basis for curriculum practice in North American schools. In this traditional conception of curriculum, the focus is on schooling. Researchers in this curriculum model adopt the positivist assumption "that human experience can only be understood via research methods modeled after those employed in the natural sciences" (Pinar, 1995, p. 52). Thus such curriculum researchers value validity, reliability, and generalizability and rely on the statistical analysis of data in what is called quantitative research.

The Tylerian Rationale has been heavily criticized. Doyle (1992) saw it as a production-system conception of education, a way of controlling teachers through the imposition of curriculum: "The knowledge of most worth—that is, practical knowledge—tended to be that which administrators could use to control how schooling was conducted" (pp. 491–492). An interest in curriculum implementation rather than in classroom experience was one outcome of this model (p. 492). Phrases such as *curriculum*

policy, *planning*, and *supervision* feature prominently in the applications of this model. The Rationale supported a "technical rationality" that focused on teacher effectiveness and grounded research in behavioral psychology. Pinar et al. (1995) argued that the Rationale was atheoretical and ahistorical because it was "procedural, and this bureaucratic interest has little need to consult history" (p. 42).

A Decade of Change

In the early 1970s the curriculum field was at a crossroads. Jackson (1992) considered the problem to be a matter of direction and saw two emerging trends. The first trend was a rapprochement of curriculum specialists to the *practice* of education by becoming consultants rather than distant experts. This view was supported, for example, by Schwab (1969, 1970, 1973, 1983), who thought the weaknesses of the curriculum field would be addressed by considering the practical over unsubstantiated theory. The second trend was a move "toward the academy," with the curriculum specialist serving as a "critic of educational affairs in general" (Jackson, 1992, p. 34) removed from the daily life of schooling. This latter trend may have contributed to the "ivory tower" label attached to academics in faculties of education. Pinar et al. (1995), however, saw this period as the beginning of a "paradigm change" (chap. 4 in Pinar) that was to shake the foundations of curriculum studies and also lead to a "balkanization" of the field.

Meanwhile, positivist research was increasingly being criticized because it tended to rely on the following assumptions:

1. In the same circumstances many people will have the same experience.
2. The majority dictates reality.
3. The individual is omitted in understanding a situation.
4. There is a tendency to treat subjects as means to ends.
5. Quantitative research pretends that objectivity, including political neutrality, is possible by eradicating subjectivity and ideology. (Pinar, 1995, p. 53)

The purpose of positivist researchers is to seek the Truth (the right answer), predict, and control through the application of criteria more appropriate to the natural sciences than to human subjects. The Tylerian approach to curriculum and curriculum research was very influential, but change was imminent.

A Reconceptualized Curriculum Field

In *Understanding Curriculum*, a landmark synoptic text, Pinar et al. (1995) described a reconceptualized view of the curriculum field they thought had successfully emerged in the 1980s. In the reconceptualized view, a quest for understanding and meaning making replaced a desire for improvement, collaboration replaced hierarchy, and inquiry replaced an emphasis on action and results: "The field had been reconceived from one with an essentially institutionalized aim to maintain practice (by improving it incrementally) to one with a critical hermeneutical goal of understanding practice and experience" (Pinar, 1995, p. xvi). According to Pinar, this view of the curriculum field prevails at the writing of this chapter, with the addition of the "relatively sudden and influential appearance of 'cultural studies' in curriculum, emphasizing popular culture" (personal communication, October 7, 2000). In the reconceptualized field, "why" became more important than "how." Proponents of this view were united mainly by their opposition to the Tylerian tradition (p. xvii), their belief in use of "eclectic traditions" such as phenomenology, and their "left-wing political bias" (Pinar, 1995, p. 39).

The contemporary curriculum field focuses on discourse as text and as words and ideas. *Discourse* refers to "a particular discursive practice, or a form of articulation that follows certain rules and which constructs the very objects it studies" (Pinar, 1995, p. 7). In the reconceptualized curriculum field, curriculum specialists are interested in understanding curriculum as political, racial, gender, autobiographical/biographical, phenomenological, postmodern, theological, institutionalized (in practice), and international texts. The interest in school-based curriculum research continues, but as only one of a number of discourses and with an important change in perspective: The difference between traditional (Tylerian) curriculum research and curriculum as institutionalized text is the search for understanding evident in the latter.

Addressing the theory/practice issue, Pinar concluded that "contemporary scholars are simultaneously closer to both 'practice' and closer to 'theory'" (p. 40). In the reconceptualized curriculum field, the distinction between theory and practice is one of appearance; the lines have blurred: "In the contemporary field practice *is* theoretical" (Pinar et al., 1995, p. 586). What has changed, in the authors' view, is the relationship between researcher and practitioner from one between expert and subject to one of collaboration. Nevertheless, to date, contemporary curriculum specialists have focused on what most would call theoretical issues, such as who is disenfranchised in curriculum decision making or whose values are being imposed (issues of hegemony). These issues are not always directly applicable to the classroom (cf. Jackson, 1992, p. 35, for research by curriculum generalists). The role of theory is to promote inquiry (Pinar, 1995, pp. 8–9). Referring to the early 1990s, Pinar stated that the majority of the ideas generated have not yet permeated elementary and secondary schools (p. 39). We note, however, that some inroads have been made in classroom practice in the past few years (e.g., in racism, ecology, and gender discourses).

Pinar proposed a more relevant definition of curriculum, one in which the point of view is made explicit: "Curriculum understood as a symbolic representation [rather than school materials] refers to those institutional and discursive practices, structures, images, and experiences that can be identified and analyzed in various ways" (p. 16). Curriculum is seen to be a "conversation" (Pinar et al., 1995, p. 848).

Not surprisingly, given this definition, the research methodology has broadened to encompass qualitative methods (for example, case studies, ethnographic research, action research, and critical and theoretical research). The map of the curriculum field includes classroom practice as one of the interests, but the focus in classroom research has changed to one of understanding—"understanding curriculum as it functions bureaucratically" (Pinar et al., 1995, p. 661). The role of the researchers, too, has changed: "The traditional role of the 'expert' which implied a relationship of 'theory' *into* 'practice' has been altered to a smaller, more modest role of consultant" (p. 662).

Commenting on the nature of contemporary curriculum research, Oberg suggested that in the conservative tradition research consisted of psychological effectiveness studies—an input/process/output model to determine the impact of a treatment on learning. In the ethnographic approach, the interest is in what actually happens in the classroom. In Oberg's view, curriculum research can be more expansive than has been previously acknowledged. Newer research focuses on the learner's experience as seen from the learner's perspective, and theory seeks the political implications of decisions, programs, and teacher actions (personal communication, Victoria, February 17, 2000).

One consequence of the reconceptualized curriculum has been a move away from subject specialization to an interest in issues that go across or beyond the curriculum. Another has been a new way of thinking about research that has led to the use of qualitative methods. In a postmodern world, there is no longer one Truth, one external point of judgment, one narrative. Reality is socially constructed and, therefore, multiple (Natoli, 1997). Curriculum is "a process—not of transmitting what is (absolutely) known but of exploring what is unknown" (Doll, 1993, p. 155).

Where does music education fit in this bigger picture? We address this question in the remainder of the chapter.

Music Education Practice and Theory in the Broader Theoretical Curriculum Context

Music education is facing a profound disparity between theory and practice forced on us by the emergence of a postmodern society.

R. Rideout, On Leadership in American Music Education

The first purpose of this chapter was to examine practice and theory in music curriculum research from a "broad focus" in order to interpret the theoretical perspectives evident in curriculum research in music education and situate this research in the context of the general curriculum field. We are now prepared to address this purpose.

Music education research followed the path traced earlier with a small time lag. It was only in 1953, when the American *Journal of Research in Music Education* (*JRME*) first appeared, that music education research had "gained sufficient stature to be considered a serious aspect of the profession" (Mark, 1986, p. 287). By 1972, most of the articles in *JRME* were descriptive or experimental, with some historical research. The second major American research publication, the *Bulletin of the Council for Research in Music Education*, first appeared in 1963. It was established to report on funded research and critique research studies, not all of which were quantitative. Nevertheless, these journals reflected an interest in experimental research that continues to the present in some streams of music education research (Schmidt, 1996, p. 80). In 1985 Reimer acknowledged this predominance: "If we were to eliminate from the research literature in music education all the studies using statistical tests of significance . . . what do you think we'd be left with?" (p. 15) and commented on the isolated, unrelated, and disconnected nature of the experiments. Until recently music education curriculum research typically adopted mainstream quantitative models. What about curriculum in the classroom?

Although many music educators resisted what they considered a mechanistic model inappropriate to music, music curriculum documents were designed with a focus on development, implementation, and the use of increasingly specific behavioral objectives. The focus of this "conventional" curriculum (Elliott, 1995) was on program delivery rather than on teaching and learning. A number of authors supported the assumptions of the Tylerian Rationale in their curriculum writing (e.g., Boyle, 1974; Greer, 1980; Labuta, 1974; Madsen, Greer, & Madsen, 1975; Madsen & Madsen, 1970).

Elliott (1995) explained that "a softer variation on Tyler's scheme" developed in the 1960s. This variation was based on the work of Bruner and others who supported a structure-of-disciplines approach "based on the assumption that every subject has a foundational pattern of verbal concepts that, when understood by teachers and students, enables all other aspects of that subject to fall into place" (Elliott, 1995, p. 244). For Elliott, the result of this approach in music education was the use of verbal concepts about music to organize curriculum rather than the "procedural essence of musicianship" (p. 246). Although Bruner did not emphasize language as the main focus of conceptual understanding (1960, p. 31; 1993, p. 138), music

education curricula used verbal concepts as labels to identify the concepts of nonverbal musical sounds. These verbal concepts were then used to organize the music curriculum. According to Elliott, both behavioral objectives and the concept approach had a profound impact on music education: "Separately, and in combination, the Tylerian concept and the structure-of-disciplines approach resulted in a steady stream of 'teacher-proof' curricula that continues to flow to the present day" (p. 244).

This traditional curriculum thinking continued to be the basis for "real" research until the late 1980s when the "paradigm change" started to infiltrate music education curriculum research. Eisner, Reimer, and Plummeridge, among others, saw the need for new ways of doing research. Eisner (1985) explored the idea of research as "educational criticism," and Reimer (1985) invoked the richness of qualitative research in addressing human experience. Plummeridge (1985) stressed the need to replace the emphasis on methodology and resources with "increased 'understanding' of curricula and a clearer sense of direction in music teaching" (p. 49).

One sign of change was the initiation of a number of new English music education research journals that allowed for greater diversity and representation: the *British Journal of Music Education* (1984), the *Canadian Journal of Research in Music Education* (1987), the *Quarterly Journal of Music Teaching and Learning* (1990), *Research Studies in Music Education* (1993), and *Music Education Research* (1999). Another significant step was the acceptance of qualitative research methodology by the *Bulletin of the Council for Research in Music Education* (see particularly issues no. 123 in 1994/95 and no. 130 in 1996). Further signs of changing research practice were evident in the chapter on qualitative methodology by Bresler and Stake (1992) in the first *Handbook of Research on Music Teaching and Learning* (Colwell, 1992) and journal articles by Bresler (1992, 1994, 1996a). The establishment of the *Philosophy of Music Education Review* in 1993 was yet another indication of a growing interest in "why" questions. As a synopsis of research in music education, the chapters related to curriculum in the 1992 Handbook are revealing. Most authors reported on past research (largely experimental); the tone and assumptions were traditional. Wing's chapter, however, represented a transitional stage in which the identification of curriculum conversation and the importance of questions hinted at the future yet did not identify completely with the reconceptualized contemporary curriculum field.

Since the 1990s, music education curriculum research related to the schools (curriculum as institutional text) has been undergoing a transformation. The increased frequency of qualitative research models, the search for understanding in both quantitative and qualitative work, and the tendency to look at the experience rather than the delivery are all signs that at least part of the music education research community is adopting a reconceptualized view of curriculum. As Pinar (1995) wrote: "The point of contemporary curriculum research is to stimulate self-reflection, self-understanding, and social change. Simply put, practical or theoretical research is intended as much to provoke questions as it is to answer questions" (p. 56).

Commenting on the gap between researchers and teachers, Colwell (1985) pointed out that "one reason thinking and research have had little impact on music education is the high importance teachers attach to the information that comes through daily, first-hand experience" (p. 32). One benefit of the newer type of curriculum research is that it may resonate better with practitioners, some of whom are engaging in this type of research as initiators or partners. Perhaps contemporary research practice will put an end to the researcher/practitioner dichotomy that has so troubled the research community and alienated teachers.

Meanwhile, experimental researchers have moved away from the seemingly esoteric and atomistic kinds of research that have characterized the field to more subtle and connected studies (Gouzouasis, 1992; McDonald, 1991; Shuler, 1991b). As might be suspected of a postmodern age where multiple viewpoints are expected, experimental research still has its place:

> Experimental research, when directly related to a growing set of coherent understandings, can be undertaken with the kind of precision that it requires but also with the kind of meaningfulness that can only exist when an experiment is guided by a larger need. (Reimer, 1985, p. 16)

In spite of the changing times, traditional thinking still lingers in high places. In MENC's *Thinking Ahead: A Research Agenda for Music Education* (Lindeman, Flowers, Jellison, Kaplan, & Price, 1998), the wording in the section about curriculum clearly reflects a traditional viewpoint:

> The National Standards for Music Education identify what students should know and be able to do as they progress from kindergarten through grade 12.... Now the challenge is to find ways to implement and study the outcomes of the standards and examine emerging curricular issues in a time of education reform. (p. 7)

This wording is consistent with the nature of the standards themselves, which, in spite of the consensus-building process used in their development, are traditional in that one size fits all. Two of the suggestions for research in *Thinking Ahead* provide further evidence of this view:

- How can content listed in the national standards be communicated to and implemented by persons responsible for local curriculum development? To what extent are the standards being implemented, by whom, and with what result?
- Is there a core of songs that can and should be learned by all American school children? (p. 7)

The thinking behind these statements is hierarchical, implying that there is a right answer, and positivist—numbers will tell the tale. These underlying assumptions may be partially responsible for the reluctance of some music educators to "embrace" the standards. Schmidt (1996) commented: "The very act of establishing national standards presupposes that there is a body of knowledge and/or skills that is identifiable by some authority as true and valuable and that the acquisition of such may be measured" (p. 77). She considers the standards to be more of an advocacy tool than a vehicle for change. Her conclusion may prove to be ironically inaccurate if states opt to develop standardized tests in music that in turn drive the curriculum.

Have government curriculum policies and documents for the schools changed? The short answer is a qualified no. The emphasis on national standards (USA) and national curricula (England and Australia) suggests that, at the political level, the model is still Tylerian. Rideout (1998) proposed that the leadership in American music education is operating from a modernist worldview (emphasizing universal goals, hierarchical achievement, and peer comparisons) in a postmodern society (with multiple realities, socially constructed meaning, and collaboration) (p. 7). At the same time, there have also been attempts to develop research-based, learner-centered curricula with greater decision making given to teachers (Saskatchewan Education, 1995). Has curriculum in classrooms changed? The short answer is a qualified yes. Teachers have had to adapt to rapidly changing cultural and social expectations and technological advances. In some locations (e.g., the province of Ontario), teachers are expected to be curriculum developers, with single textbooks no longer accepted as the source of all knowledge. What will become of music textbook series in such a climate, you might ask? To paraphrase Mark Twain, the news of their demise is premature. Not so long ago, Gordon's use of coded cards with activities that teachers could coordinate with his learning sequence in *Jump Right In* (Gordon & Woods, 1985) was one of the reasons the series was not well received (Shuler, 1991a, p. 53); the new series (Bolton et al., 2000) has textbooks. In addition, in 1996 McLellan found that only 11 of 112 K–6 music teacher respondents indicated they did not use textbooks.

So far in looking at change we have addressed curriculum as institutionalized text. Is there also evidence of increased interest in theoretical issues in music education? The MayDay Group (Gates, 1999), an international think tank formed in 1993, provides an example of a discourse based on critical theory. There are also examples of feminist scholars (Green, 1993; Koza, 1994a, 1994b; Lamb, 1993) and cultural studies scholars (Shepherd & Wicke, 1997). These researchers work more in the area of theory, although their ideas could have significant impact on music education in the future, as will become evident in the discussion of a reconceptualized view of curriculum.

Having provided a quick overview of educational trends and situated music education within the broader enterprise, we will now progress to our second purpose: to examine the more "narrowly focused" theoretical basis of music education practice and curriculum research. We begin with school-based music curriculum research and theory development based on the Tylerian view of music curriculum practice. We then examine how a reconceptualized field of curriculum is emerging in music education.

Music Curriculum Theory and Research in the Tylerian Tradition

Most of us formed opinions on the worth of CMP, Manhattanville, programed learning, CEMREL, and the Rolland string materials on what we would like to believe, not on the basis of student readiness or any evaluation of the effectiveness of the materials.

  R. J. Colwell, "Program Evaluation in Music Teacher Education"

In most cases the innovators who developed the methods were almost entirely concerned with helping children to learn music and worked from the basis of the music rather than from psychological theory.

  M. L. Mark, Contemporary Music Education

The methods/approaches used to teach music in the classrooms have been many. Mark (1986) identified nine: the Dalcroze Method, the Orff Approach, the Kodály method, Orff and Kodály combined, the Manhattanville Music Curriculum Program (MMCP), teaching music through learning theory (Gordon), the Carabo-Cone Method, Suzuki Talent Education, and Comprehensive Musicianship. Costanza and Russell (1992) would add music textbooks to the list. We would include Discipline-Based Music Education (DBME), Education Through Music (ETM), and the Generative Approach (Boardman, 1988a, 1988b, 1989). In addition, music education exists in different instructional settings, such as general, instrumental, choral, keyboard, elementary, secondary, middle school, and early childhood (Colwell, 1992), and is sometimes required and sometimes an elective. Sometimes music is supposed to be taught by classroom teachers (elementary grades) and sometimes by specialist teachers (elementary and secondary grades). The 1992 Handbook reviewed research about many of these approaches and settings. The

research cited was predominantly quantitative or descriptive, operating within a positivistic framework.

Rather than address each of the approaches/methods/instructional settings in turn, we will examine (1) the theoretical sources of classroom practice at a time when the Tyler Rationale prevailed and (2) the research generated within the positivistic perspective under six categories identified by Wing (1992) in her review of curriculum literature:

1. position statements and curriculum guidelines,
2. status studies (surveys/analyses),
3. development of curriculum/curricular materials,
4. curriculum development and trial,
5. evaluation of existing curricula, and
6. curriculum development and comparative study (p. 210)

Theoretical Bases of Music Teaching in the Schools—Positivist Views

There have been strong trends in education which have always resulted from some viewpoint or standpoint originating within an influential personality or group, and spreading first to the leaders then to the grassroots of the profession. These trends seemingly constitute the philosophy of the profession.

  R. J. Colwell, "Music Education and Experimental Research"

Historically, music education curriculum has been somewhat lacking in the area of philosophical discussion, favoring the identification of what works based on common sense and experience: the WHAT and HOW rather than the WHY. Although Costanza and Russell (1992) considered the Kodály, Orff, Dalcroze, and Suzuki approaches to be methodologies, meaning "a body of techniques, methods, and curricula . . . based on a philosophical system and a foundation of research" (p. 498), other writers are less convinced about the philosophical and research foundations of these approaches (Atterbury, 1991; Dolloff, 1993; Gouzouasis, 1991; Reimer, 1989, pp. 159–160; Shuler, 1991a, p. 39). Even though the approaches listed previously along with choral music, instrumental music, and so on, could claim to have underlying learning principles and philosophical assumptions, questioning and clarifying these underlying principles have not been a priority. Historically, improving practice and, in some cases, proving the worth of an approach have been the major concerns. Is music education still guided by "influential personalities" or do we have a more reasoned approach to curriculum? We will examine two examples of well-developed theoretical foundations for music education. The first is based on psychological learning principles, the second on philosophical method. Both have impacted on classroom practice.

Psychology.   Psychology has dominated educational thinking in music education (Rideout, 1997a). The most developed model of music education with a psychological base is Gordon's music-learning theory. For over 40 years, Gordon has remained committed to developing and refining a theory of music learning and teaching and a method that he characterizes as sequential and comprehensive (Gordon, 1993, p. 46).

Music-learning theory "refers to the specific sequential taxonomies for skills and for tonal and rhythm content that Gordon formulated, as well as to his general theories of musical development" (Shuler, 1991a, p. 40). Learning theory is "an explanation of how we learn when we learn music" (Gordon, 1993, p. 33) and implies how students should be taught:

> Proper methodology in music is based on an understanding of music learning theory. Music learning theory provides a teacher with the basis for establishing sequential objectives in a music curriculum, in accord with his/her own teaching styles and beliefs, that are sensitive to individual musical differences among students. (p. iv)

Gordon addresses students' readiness in terms of melodic and rhythmic aptitude. Individual differences are identified through the use of psychometric music aptitude tests developed by Gordon (the *Musical Aptitude Profile*, 1965, for stabilized aptitude; the *Primary Measures of Music Audiation*, 1979; and *Intermediate Measures of Music Audiation*, 1982, for developmental aptitude).

Gordon presented his theory most recently in *A Music Learning Theory for Newborn and Young Children* (1990) and *Learning Sequences in Music* (1993), in which he also explained the importance of the development of audiation (the process of assimilating and comprehending music in our minds) to both music aptitude and music achievement. For Gordon, audiation is the key to musical understanding, and understanding is the goal of music education (1993, pp. 33–35). Gordon's music-learning theory is operationalized in *Jump Right In: The Music Curriculum* (Gordon & Woods, 1985), *Jump Right In: The Instrumental Series* (Grunow & Gordon, 1989), and *Jump Right In: General Music Series* (Bolton et al., 2000).

Gordon's work can be described as positivistic because his approach is atomistic and skills-based; his method is prepackaged; meaning is externally imposed rather than constructed by the learner (Woodford, 1996, p. 88); he neglects the context of music; much of his research involves the development and use of psychometric tests; and he operates within a quantitative understanding of what research can be (Gordon, 1992, pp. 62–63). In 1991, while acknowledging Gordon's important contributions to music education in theory development and in his development of aptitude measurement, Colwell and Abrahams (1991) claimed "there is no research which is sufficiently definitive to indicate the degree of truthfulness or error in the research of Gordon and his writings" (p. 19). Shuler (1991a) reinforced the need for research that supported Gordon's theories, and Stokes (1996) wrote that Gordon's learning theory had more internal than external validity. Gordon's major contribution to curriculum has been in the application of his music-learning theory to classroom practice.

We now move to Reimer, a philosopher who may, at first glance, seem to fit poorly under the heading of positivism. After all, Reimer aligned himself with cognitive psychology, not behaviorism; he criticized isolated experimental research and did not engage in it himself. Why is his work included in this section? There is some justification, if not a sterling match.

Philosophy.   Stokes (1996) summarized seven aspects of curriculum identified by Reimer "for responsible curriculum enterprise":

> Curriculum theorists must base educational choices on a sound philosophy, relevant psychological research and educational practice and research, effective short- and long-term sequencing of learning, professional teacher interpretation of materials, experienced teacher/student operations in the classroom, what students undergo and bring to the learning situation, and what educators and society expect from the educational process. (p. 96)

Reimer (1989) argued that "practice must be grounded in a secure philosophy" (p. 10). He was not impressed with the rationales for music education presented in the past: "On the philosophy side, music education has offered rationales so puny, so unessential, so political, so tied to values not unique to music, as to convince many that music is little more than a pleasant, recreational hobby" (1989, p. 149). Reimer also did not think that psychological theory alone provides a sufficient foundation for curriculum development, because it does not address questions of value (pp. 149–150); psychology comes into play to bring philosophy to life. Reimer developed a philosophy of music education based on "the nature and value of the art of music" (1989, p. 1). At the core of the philosophy was the importance of sensitivity to the expressive qualities of music. Called absolute expressionism and, in practice, aesthetic music education, Reimer's philosophy was made available to practitioners in the elementary music series *Silver Burdett Music* (Crook, Walker, & Reimer, 1974, 1978, 1981, 1985; Reimer, Hoffman, & McNeil, 1974, 1978, 1981, 1985). In the introduction (Crook et al., 1981, Grade 5), the authors claimed consistency with developmental learning theory because the series "provides opportunities for gradual, progressive, consistent growth" and high levels of success and challenge (p. vi) and a spiral mode of organization. So Reimer coherently addressed both philosophical and psychological concerns in his curriculum development work.

Reimer's work is important because aesthetic music education arguably became the "bedrock upon which our self-concept, as a profession, rests" (Reimer, 1989, p. xi). Reimer was accurate in describing the considerable influence of aesthetic music education on the field for nearly 30 years (Mark & Gary, 1999, p. xviii), even if its ideas were imperfectly understood and implemented (Elliott, 1995, p. 29; Hanley, 1989; Reimer, 1989, p. xi).

It is on the basis of the *Silver Burdett Music* series that the case for a positivist designation can be made. Reimer's work can certainly not be classified as Tylerian, but it is an example of the "soft variation" noted by Elliott (1995, p. 244). There are two reasons for this conclusion. First, *Silver Burdett Music* portrayed a structure-of-disciplines organizational approach with the content organized around verbally mediated concepts related to music (what Elliott called verbal concepts, 1995) as determined by experts (even though these concepts were in service of the student's perception of and response to music). Second, the series is a commercial curriculum and therefore an attempt to develop a "teacher-proof" package. Although *Silver Burdett Music* has been used for control groups in comparative studies (Byrd, 1989), we have located no published research about its efficacy in terms of student learning, in spite of the competency tests developed for the series (Colwell, 1979).

Trends.   In addition to the two preceding examples, there are other indications of a greater interest in the theoretical underpinnings (both philosophical and psychological) of music education methods. One example is Dolloff's (1993) study of Orff's *Schulwerk* to identify the cognitive, musical, and artistic foundations that the approach provides for the development of children. A second is represented by Montgomery's (1997; in press) decision to use the unifying principle of sound before symbol in her work, focusing on a process with a strong basis in research rather than on more experientially based methods. Her view is that research efforts that attempted to test/justify a whole method have been futile and have merely reinforced unproductive competition among Dalcroze, Orff, and Kodály proponents. The focus on sound before symbol that is common to the three methods (as well as to Gordon's approach) provides a more fruitful foundation for music education (personal communication, June 13, 2000). So, the answer to the question "Is music education still guided by 'influential personalities' or do we have a more reasoned approach to curriculum?" is (arguably) that, as a profession, we are showing a greater understanding of the need for theoretical bases and becoming better at applying what we are learning.

Research about Curriculum Practice

We will now examine the research related to classroom practice using Wing's six categories as organizers. Our purpose is to examine the research mindful of both current practice and theoretical bases while focusing mainly on the past decade.

1. Position statements and curriculum guidelines. We have selected two sources of guidelines: The first is a collaboration among arts organizations, a university, foundations, and the schools; the second looks at national initiatives. When it exists, research in this category comes from an examination of guidelines and their implementation.

Discipline-Based Music Education.

There is a recent curriculum initiative based on a structure-of-disciplines approach that is quite different from the concept-driven model of the 1970s and 1980s. Rather than using music concepts as curriculum organizers, in DBME music instruction is based on works of music (Patchen & Harris, 1996). DBME is modeled on the Getty Institute for the Arts' development of Discipline-Based Art Education (DBAE) under way since the 1980s and was evaluated by Wilson (1997) in his model study, *The Quiet Evolution: Changing the Face of Arts Education.* DBAE grew out of the reform efforts of the 1960s (Wilson, 1997) and the work of Bruner (1960). From Bruner's emphasis on disciplines arose the four-discipline perspective—production, history, aesthetics, and criticism. DBME was an extension of DBAE undertaken by the University of Tennessee at Chattanooga, where local funding established the Southeast Institute for Education in Music (SIEME) to engage in research, development, and implementation.

Patchen (1996), an early director of the center, noted that the discipline-based approach is "reflected in the new *National Standards for Arts Education*" (p. 17) and that because it is "a conceptual framework and not a curriculum or methodology, it is compatible with the major methodologies in music education such as Orff, Kodály, and Dalcroze" (p. 18). SIEME undertook an extensive evaluation of DBME from 1989 to 1994 conducted by Asmus. The positive findings of the annual reports and site observations are summarized in *A Discipline-Based Music Education Handbook* (Patchen & Harris, 1996, "Conceptual Framework," p. 12). The practice of DBME was enhanced by an emphasis on team building, in-service delivery, and, as of 1993, a required course on the discipline-based approach for elementary music majors at the University of Tennessee at Chattanooga. This teacher education program implements discipline-based instruction in all four arts over a nine-state area (Kim Wheetley, personal correspondence, June 1, 2000). Others have also shown an interest in DBME (e.g., developing a theoretical framework

[Sibbald, 1989]; determining the frequency of component use [Townsend, 1998]).

National Curricula.   We proceed to examine four cases of national curriculum development: one in a small country where government control is more manageable and the curriculum is imposed and inspected; one in a large country where standards have been developed through "consensus-building" (see Schmidt, 1996, for a critique of this process) and adoption by states is voluntary; one in a large country where the provincial jurisdiction of education is enshrined and interprovincial partnerships have been slow to build; and the last in a large country where state and territories administer education and teachers have maintained professional independence.

First, to England. Following the 1988 Education Reform Act, *Music in the National Curriculum* (Department of Education, 1992, 1995) was adopted in England. The National Curriculum represents "national priorities for learning and assessment," a "framework for school inspection," and a "basis of the National Standards for Initial Teacher Training" (National Advisory Committee on Creative and Cultural Education, 1999, p. 72). The music curriculum documents identified two Attainment Targets: (1) performing and composing and (2) listening and appraising. The National Curriculum replaced a system in which music teachers were autonomous and had no obligation to respond to calls for a common direction (Plummeridge, 1996, p. 29) and had a politically conservative agenda (Cox, 1993; Shepherd & Vulliamy, 1994). In the new system, "what 'counts' as music is now firmly determined by the government through the School Curriculum and Assessment Authority. . . . There is now an 'official' view of music education" (Plummeridge, 1996, pp. 30–31). Kushner (1999) commented on the limiting nature of the National Curriculum:

> It imposes a logic of "simple to complex," it insists on a theory of iteration, it assumes that the only worthwhile learning is that which follows teaching, it demands universal treatment of pupils, it subjugates individual professional knowledge to the theories of professional "tribal elders." (p. 213)

Some (Gane, 1996; Preston, 1994; Stowasser, 1993) saw opportunities in the National Curriculum because of the potential for expanded encounters with music. Major (1996), however, critiqued the concept basis of the secondary curriculum, calling for more attention to neglected skill development.

The implementation of the music curriculum is checked by HM Inspectors of Schools (HMI). Official reports of the quality of music teaching use public criteria for assessment (OFSTED, 1993a), and early studies indicated that

implementation was more successful in the primary years (ages 5 to 10) than in the secondary years (ages 11 to 14) (Mills, 1994, 1997; OFSTED, 1993b). Mills (Clay, Hertrich, Jones, Mills, & Rose, 1998) noted that, in spite of overall positive results, "continuity and progression," "exploiting pupils' musical creativity and developing their musical imagination," and "participation in music at school" in Key Stage 4 remained areas of concern (pp. 60–61).

Non-government-affiliated researchers were, however, more critical of the early implementation of the curriculum. Lawson, Plummeridge, and Swanwick (1994) found that the teaching of listening and appraising was weak and the teaching of literacy and sound exploration was neglected. Writing about the National Curriculum, Paynter (1993) concluded that while national guidelines may be useful, "it is impossible to legislate for universally good education" (p. 176); it is innovative and inventive teaching that makes the difference.

Second, the American National Standards for Arts Education (Consortium of National Arts Education Associations, 1994) include standards for music, which "have quickly become accepted as the basis for most state and local music standards and frameworks" (Music Educators National Conference, 1996, p. 1). The standards were a response to those who believed that the quality of student learning had degenerated to the point that the nation was at risk. The music standards were developed by a coalition led by the Music Educators National Conference (MENC) that wanted to ensure that the arts were included in the Goals 2000 Project and were thus part of the national education agenda. The standards provide a common foundation for curriculum development by presenting nine content and achievement standards for students in K–4, 5–8, and 9–12. To date, 44 states have adopted some form of the standards, with development and implementation at different stages of completion (American Music Conference News, 1996). Given the voluntary nature of the standards and the regulation of education by individual states, not the federal government, this level of collaboration is an indication of considerable success (possibly related to funding).

The National Assessment of Educational Progress (NAEP) recently completed its 1997 report card in music and the other arts for Grade 8 students (Persky, Sandene, & Askew, 1998). The content of the assessment "was designed in conjunction with the newly developed voluntary" standards (p. 11), taking advantage of the opportunity to coordinate curriculum and evaluation at a national level. Although the NAEP results show a high level of achievement by some young people, they also show that "too many young people lack the skills and knowledge that are necessary to experience the satisfaction, fulfillment, and enrichment that music can bring to the life of every citizen"

(Lehman, 1999, p. 37). The gap between standards and student achievement seems considerable.

Third, in Canada there has been an attempt to develop a Pan-Canadian protocol for arts education similar to the Pan-Canadian Science Project developed by the Council of Ministers of Education (CMEC) in 1997 (Sandner, 1999). Favaro (1999) explained the process and lack of success for the arts project at a political level, and Hanley (1998a) addressed grassroots discomfort with the idea of a national curriculum framework or standards in the arts. Provincial governments, for their part, are watchful of their jurisdictional prerogatives. There has been some headway toward consolidation in that, since 1993, the western provinces and territories have agreed to collaborate on the development of common curriculum frameworks in mathematics, language arts, and social studies (mathematics was completed in 1995), but the arts are not on the agenda. Meanwhile, the four Atlantic (eastern) provinces have produced *Foundation for the Atlantic Canada Arts Education Curriculum* (Atlantic Provinces Education Foundation, 2000), a framework for elementary arts education. There appears to be a different interest in the arts on each coast. In an attempt to address the dilution of elementary music programs, the Coalition for Music Education in Canada and the Canadian Music Educators Association (CMEA) have collaborated to produce *Achieving Musical Understanding: Concepts & Skills Pre-Kindergarten to Grade 8* (2001) independent of any government affiliation. The impact of this resource, if any, is yet to be determined. There has been no recent attempt to assess student learning in music either nationally or provincially.

Fourth, in the late 1980s in Australia there was an attempt to develop a national framework for curriculum development that identified eight core areas of learning, one of which was the arts. The result was *The Arts—A Curriculum Profile for Australian Schools* (Curriculum Corporation, 1994). Education in Australia is administered by state and territory systems. Although the curriculum framework is in place, "more than a decade of continuing efforts to standardize pedagogical practices around Australia" has not resulted in homogeneous practice across the country: "Australians have always resisted a top-down approach by governments and education systems which prescribes a central curriculum" (McPherson & Dunbar-Hall, 2001). McPherson and Dunbar-Hall present a view of music education that they described as postmodern in the questioning of tradition, in adopting the view that "the student is the source of knowledge rather than the teacher," in the increased use of technology, and in adopting an ethnological foundation for music education with curriculum more inclusive of aboriginal music systems.

Four stories, four political contexts. Many questions arise. Why is there a trend to national curriculum initiatives at this time? What agenda do standards and frame-

works mask? What evidence supports the validity of national curricula? Who decides what will be included? How is the assessment of student learning integrated into the planning? Clearly there are issues of development and control when national curriculum initiatives appear (Plummeridge, 1996, p. 27).

2. Status studies (surveys/analyses). These studies include surveys and curriculum analyses that are intended to inform decision making. They differ in scale from more local to national projects.

On a smaller scale, Finter (1995) examined the elementary music curricula in Nevada to see whether they conformed to authoritative sources. On the basis of percentage of agreement, the author concluded that the best match was in "psychomotor/manipulative" objectives and the least congruency existed in the area of "cognitive/elemental" objectives. Finter evidently assumed that the authorities he cited knew what is required to construct a valid music curriculum.

National studies provide large databases, and the comparison across districts can be instructive. Brown (1993) examined the status of elementary music education in Canada through a comparison of provincial curriculum guidelines and questionnaire responses from administrators and music teachers with the MENC *School Music Program: Description and Standards.* Not surprisingly, recommendations included more specialist teachers, more in-service, more time, and better facilities. Given provincial jurisdiction over education, Brown's recommendation for the development of national standards for music education in Canada was more unexpected.

Siverson (1990) developed a questionnaire that undertook a national study in the United States to determine the degree to which utilitarian versus aesthetic goals were pursued in high school band programs. The results supported the researcher's belief that band teachers would prefer to teach for aesthetic outcomes but are required to spend more time on utilitarian objectives. The study, unfortunately, had only a very low return rate and used a rather simplistic questionnaire.

Demonstrating an increased interest in music curriculum across Canada, Shand and Bartel (1993) described in considerable detail 74 provincial music curriculum documents published between 1980 and 1992. The topics addressed in the reference tool were document characteristics, program orientation, characteristics of the recommended repertoire, and methodology. This study provides a helpful source for researchers.

Status reports are useful because they inform us about the state of affairs and provide a baseline for more local studies. These studies, however, are costly and time-consuming. Three examples are reports about the number of states that have adopted or are working toward implementing the American National Standards for Arts Education (American Music Conference, 1996), the state of arts education in American elementary schools (Carey, 1995), and the status of adoption, implementation, and assessment of the standards in visual arts, music, theater, and dance in 176 school districts in Colorado (Colorado Alliance for Arts Education, 2000).

3. Development of curriculum/curricular materials. This kind of research has been most directly relevant to practitioners. It involves the development of theoretical models, curriculum, and music textbooks.

In addition to Gordon's music-learning theory, examples of theory development include Kuehmann's (1987) survey and review of the literature and design of a general music curriculum model for fundamentalist Christian elementary schools (based on Bandura, Skinner, Gagné, and Piaget); Musoleno's (1990) identification of 12 essential elements in a model middle school music program that addressed placement, operation, and content based mainly on responses from "experts"; Bourne's (1990) curriculum model for children's choirs based on observed instructional techniques used in rehearsals and interviews of six exemplary directors; and Clausel's (1998) music curriculum model for kindergarten and first-grade children that uses Cambourne's model of literacy learning and the Orff-Schulwerk method. These models have had only limited application.

Music textbooks continue to impact on music education at all levels, but especially in the elementary grades. Examples of curriculum and curriculum materials developed to assist teachers include:

- textbooks for elementary general music (*Holt Music* [Meske, Andress, Pautz, & William, 1988], *Share the Music* [Bond et al., 1995], *The Music Connection* [Silver Burdett Ginn, 1995], and *Jump Right In* [Bolton et al., 2000]);
- programs for choral music (*We Will Sing! Choral Music Experience for Classroom Choirs* [Rao, 1993]); and
- methods books for instrumental music classes (*The Comprehensive Music Instructor* [Froseth, 1986], *Jump Right In: The Instrumental Series* [Grunow & Gordon, 1989], *Essential Elements: A Comprehensive Band Method* [Rhodes, Bierschenk, Lautzenheiser, & Higgins, 1991], *Strictly Strings* [Dillon, Kjelland, & O'Reilly, 1992], *Standards of Excellence* [Pearson, 1993], and *Essential Elements for Strings* [Allen, Gillespie, & Hayes, 1994]).

In a current trend, the major publishers of elementary music textbooks have opted for reaching the greatest market over program coherence and a unified philosophy. The use of multiple authors may have contributed to this trend.

McLellan (1996) surveyed K–6 elementary music teachers about their use of and the effectiveness of elementary music series. Most teachers reported satisfaction with their series and found them compatible with mastery learning theory and their school system's curriculum. These teachers wanted to continue using their textbooks. McLellan advised further research about the effectiveness of these series and alternative approaches.

What research informs music textbook development? In recent years, publishers have conducted marketing research that relies on information gathered from experts in the field; however, very few research studies on the effectiveness of music textbooks have been published. In an exemplary and critical study of Silver Burdett & Ginn's *World of Music* (Culp, Eisman, & Hoffman, 1988) that was based on a common set of framing questions across subjects, May (1993) concluded that research that informs the "design, structure, or content" of music textbooks is sparse, as is research about teachers' use of music texts (p. 17). Furthermore, "publishers' decisions most often rely on intuition, not on research" (p. 14). May also pointed out how little we know about the use of music textbooks in the classroom. Her remarks could apply equally well to instrumental and choral textbooks.

4. Curriculum development and trial. It is in curriculum implementation that the gap between the theory and practice is most evident. The piloting of curriculum and planned implementation research are ways of bridging this gap.

Byo (1999) examined Florida music specialist and Grade 4 classroom teachers' perceptions of their ability to implement the U.S. national standards. She concluded that specialist teachers should be responsible for the delivery of some of the standards and share responsibility with classroom teachers for others. Her findings showed a clear support for specialist music teachers at the elementary level.

Technology presents both challenges and opportunities to music education curriculum. Over 3 years, Nelson (1988) developed and piloted a middle school general music program that taught orchestration and music composition with the incorporation of computer-assisted instruction (CAI) and aspects of Gordon's music-learning theory. Nelson concluded that the computer can be used successfully at a Grade 7 level. Clarkson and Pegley (1991) developed and piloted the Technology in Music Programme (TIMP), a program of creative activities for Grades 7 and 8 students that included improvising, arranging, composing, sound production, performing, and listening. The teaching context was collaborative, and discovery was encouraged. In the pilot, 52% of the educational objectives were achieved, and students were very enthusiastic about the program. Replication studies are needed to determine whether it is novelty or something else that contributes to student enthusiasm when technology is used in the music classroom.

Comprehensive music education is an American contribution to the field. The next example illustrates a large-scale, recursive, big-budget curriculum development and implementation process. The Hawaii Music Program was inspired by the Yale Seminar Report (Arberg & Palisca, 1964) and the documentary report of the Tanglewood Symposium (Choate, 1968). The research and development of the K–12 program involved "rethinking music as a discipline of knowledge" (Burton, 1990, p. 68). The result was the development and implementation of curriculum and materials organized around music concepts that promoted the principles of comprehensive music (Burton & Thompson, 1982; Thompson, 1974). In the Hawaii program, *comprehensive musicianship* referred to "the belief that a program of music education should be all-inclusive and all-embracing within the context of music as a discipline of knowledge" (Burton, 1990, p. 69), meaning that students should participate in music as performers, composers, and musicologists. A curriculum research and development group (CRDG) was formed; one of its purposes was to "conduct major curriculum evaluation projects" that assisted in "extensive evaluations, and a revision cycle that results in new editions" (p. 70). Burton, a director of the project since 1969, mentioned opportunities for longitudinal studies, but the focus seemed to have been on the use of research to develop new textbooks and implement the program successfully rather than the publication of research to show its effectiveness. Twenty years after the project originated, Burton wrote that many projects "were successfully tested . . . but were never used or known widely due to the lack of an ongoing implementation plan" (p. 72). According to Burton, the project published the only complete set of curriculum based on comprehensive musicianship, but the interest in comprehensive musicianship has not been limited to Hawaii (Johnson, 1992; Strange, 1990; Whitener, 1980).

5. Evaluation of existing curricula. Runfola and Rutkowski (1992) suggested that music education curriculum research has focused on "proving" rather than "improving" (p. 704). Perhaps that is one explanation for the small number of studies in this category and the lack of research on curriculum effectiveness.

Ardrey (1999) observed 20 middle school music teachers to identify teachers who best met the needs of adolescents and the extent to which they applied Dalcroze, Orff, and Kodály methodologies to solve some of the problems inherent in middle school teaching. During the observations, common problems in the teaching of 16 teachers were identified and solutions were drawn from the 4 teachers whose practice was deemed exemplary. Ardrey did not find the comprehensive application of any of the methodologies she had targeted but was reluctant to abandon her theory. She noted that the better teachers "naturally" applied the pedagogical principles of the methodologies she had targeted. A stronger theoretical basis would have made for a more valuable study.

Sweeney (1993) investigated the impact of the National Curriculum in England, particularly its assessment features, through a survey of existing practice and a case study examination of the implementation of material at Key Stages 1, 2, 3, and 4. He concluded that assessment and attendant lessons were not well developed in practice.

The lack of replication of studies has been one of the criticisms of music education curriculum research. Munsen's (1986) and Martin's (1992) studies are two exceptions. One of the Orff *Schulwerk*'s goals is to nurture student creativity and musical independence (Choksy, Abramson, Gillespie, & Woods, 1986, p. 97). Does the approach succeed? Munsen (1986) investigated the effectiveness of an Orff-*Schulwerk* program in developing melodic and rhythmic improvisation in students in Grades 1, 3, and 5. She concluded that the improvisation tasks peaked at Grade 3 and the attitude to music and music class became increasingly negative. Martin (1992) replicated Munsen's study with modifications. Her findings reinforced the negative view of music class as children got older. In the 1992 study, Grade 1 students were rated highest for melodic improvisation and Grade 5 students for rhythmic improvisation. More replication studies that establish a pattern of research are needed.

6. Curriculum development and comparative study. One area of research interest has involved comparing the effectiveness of one approach to teaching music with that of another. This debate has been particularly strong concerning the efficacy of the Kodály, Orff, and Dalcroze approaches compared with a variety of traditional methods, including music textbooks. As Swanwick (1999) explains:

> Teaching methodologies seem to shape the curriculum in different ways and there are often competing claims for the musical high ground by followers of Orff, Kodály, and Dalcroze, or the users of schemes published by Silver Burdett, MacMillan, and so on. (p. 103)

After an extensive review of the research about elementary general education methods, Costanza and Russell (1992) concluded that

> the studies that have compared various techniques or methods with each other or with a "traditional method" have found no differences between experimental and control groups, but have reported increases (some significant, some not) in gain scores for the experimental group. (p. 501)

Gordon (1992) questioned the value of comparative studies and outlined the problems with this type of research, including the difficulty of finding teachers equally skilled in both methods and of finding similar students and contexts (p. 63). In addition, the objectivity of many of the researchers engaged in comparative studies could be questioned, since the hope is generally to prove the efficacy of the method they champion (Joseph, 1982; Madhosingh, 1984; Siemens, 1969). Has there been any change in the past decade?

Ironically, a number of studies have investigated the benefits of using Gordon's learning sequences. In a carefully designed study, McDonald (1991) applied Gordon's learning sequence to teaching recorder to third-grade students. The control group received a traditional note-reading method; the experimental group received a sound-before-symbol approach consistent with Gordon's sequence. McDonald found Gordon's sound-before-symbol approach was more effective in terms of superior performance and student enthusiasm. She also found support for Gordon's initial isolation of the tonal and rhythmic components of music.

In 1987 Shuler noted variations in how teachers incorporate Gordon's learning theory. A second study supported this conclusion. Shuler (1991b) used an experimental design to study the vocal performance achievements of a class of Grade 3 children. Using Gordon's learning sequence activities for 25% of the music class was compared with traditional classroom activities. No conclusions could be drawn regarding the effectiveness of the treatment. In spite of teacher expertise with Gordon's sequence, the teacher was the significant variable: "The effectiveness of the experimental treatment appeared to vary dramatically from one teacher to the other" (p. 127).

Stevens (1992) compared a small beginning instrumental class that used a technical skill development approach with one that used Gordon's skill-learning sequence to determine which method would result in better playing by ear. She found no significant difference in her results, a finding she attributed to flaws in her research design rather than to possible differences in the effectiveness of the methods.

Gouzouasis (1992) studied the effects of two types of tonal and rhythm pattern instruction on beginning Grade 6 guitar players. The first type of instruction used Gordon's pattern sequences from *Jump Right In: The Music Curriculum*, "Learning Sequence Activities"; the second used patterns selected from *Tonal and Rhythm Pattern Audiation Cassettes* but was not taught in a hierarchy of audiation difficulty. Hierarchically ordered rhythm pattern instruction did result in better guitar performance, but hierarchically sequential melodic patterns did not contribute to better melodic performance on the guitar. Gouzouasis was also interested in the effectiveness of the two approaches on students with high and low levels of tonal aptitudes. He concluded that the level of students' music aptitude was responsible for the level of their performance. These studies related to Gordon's work seem to reinforce the difficulties inherent in this type of research.

Comparative studies continue to appeal to researchers. For example, Holmes (1997) compared the relationship between music and academic achievement and instrumental music programs. The 3-year study, which involved 389 Grade 5 students in nine schools, had the experimental group taking instrumental classes while the control group did not. Participation in instrumental music classes produced no significant difference in academic achievement; according to the data, the more academically proficient students chose instrumental programs.

Johnson (1992) used qualitative techniques to compare the Wisconsin Comprehensive Musicianship through Performance (WCMP) approach to choral teaching at two middle schools and two high schools in Wisconsin with traditional rehearsal techniques. The conclusions of the study were muddied because the non-WCMP teachers demonstrated WCMP attributes. The conclusions might have been more valuable had a phenomenological or hermeneutic study been undertaken.

Summary

The publication years of the works cited in this section provide evidence that the Tylerian Rationale remains an important factor in music education curriculum. Statistics and their use have become more sophisticated, but how well have researchers addressed the criticisms identified earlier? Some headway has been made, particularly toward attempts to provide theoretical bases and research foundations for curriculum and methodologies. There have also been a few more longitudinal and large-scale studies. In spite of small victories, however, much remains the same, including the difficulty of being truly objective (open) when trying to prove a pet theory and the need for more replication studies to build a credible body of knowledge. The literature still consists mainly of isolated studies, with little interest in what students or teachers are experiencing in classrooms. One notable exception to the isolation problem is the research generated by Gordon's music-learning theory. Assembling research in one issue, as the *Quarterly* did for Gordon's work (vol. 2, no. 1/2, 1991), may be a useful way of encouraging researchers to modify, support, or refute earlier findings. Without this larger vision we will be like the blind men who do not get beyond their limited experience of the elephant's tail or trunk (in Forsythe, 1993).

Music Curriculum Theory and Practice—A Reconceptualized View

In uncertain times the urge to simplify is often as strong as it is brutal; complexity, subtlety and doubting wisely all take courage, sophistication and intelligence.
  M. Ross and M. Kamba,
  The State of the Arts in Five English Secondary Schools

Given the earlier introduction to this view, what ideas would you expect to encounter in this section about re-conceptualized curriculum? Look for a critical examination of issues, a focus on understanding and meaning making, recognition of a variety of discourses and multiple realities, a tension among competing values, an interrelated view of theory and practice, a valuing of personal experience, an acceptance of paradox (not "either/or" but "and"), reality as a social construction, and challenges to the legitimacy of any privileged social order. Expect new ways of thinking about curriculum and curriculum issues. Bowman (2000), for example, commented on the "kind of inconsequential curriculum restructuring project with which music educators are all too familiar. We need to be wary of structural approaches to problems that require systemic, transformative solutions." These characteristics are consistent with a postmodern paradigm (Natoli, 1997). Qualitative research methods are one of the strategies used to promote understanding.

Pinar (1995) identified a number of texts (social realities) presented in the reconceptualized curriculum field. Four of these discourses have emerged in music education. Although the boundaries are fuzzy and in flux, we will seek to understand music education curriculum as institutionalized text, gender text, cultural studies text, and political text. Once again, space limitation necessitated selectivity in order to represent the scope of the issues and quality of the work.

Understanding Music Curriculum as Institutionalized Text

The emergent foci on values, processes and multiple perspectives promoted the development of new paradigms and methods [in research] attentive to the process rather than the product of teaching, and that were capable of capturing the voices of school practitioners, teachers and students.

L. Bresler, "Traditions and Change across the Arts"

Ideal curricula should provide students not only with instruction, but also with opportunities to actively process information and construct meaning.

W. T. May, "Teaching for Understanding in the Arts"

While understanding is an issue in this discourse, there is still considerable interest in school improvement and maintenance. "There are still those of us liberal enough to believe that curriculum theory can also serve a somewhat more traditional purpose: that is, to be more directly helpful to practitioners in planning and using actual curricula" (Barone, 2000, p. 51). Some writers attempt to understand the bureaucratic system by examining hidden assumptions. Issues include the changing role of the expert to a more

consultative role, the changing status of the teacher to an empowered decision maker, and an emphasis on collaboration. Whereas the main focus is on the schools, theory continues to play an important role in this discourse. We examine four areas of institutionalized text: generating curriculum, curriculum as lived experience, how we are doing, and policy issues.

Generating Curriculum.   Curriculum development and theoretical frameworks are still needed. We look at two examples of school-based curriculum thinking in this discourse: E. Boardman's generative approach and Swanwick's curriculum model.

Although Boardman's generative theory of musical learning is realized in a music series textbook (*Holt Music* [Meske et al., 1988]), her discussion and application of the theory (1988a, 1988b, 1989) place her within this discourse. Boardman used philosophical theories (including aesthetic music education) and psychological theories (including Bruner's emphasis on structure and the spiral curriculum) to develop a theory of instruction. The generative theory was based on many years of classroom practice rather than on experimental research, which had not produced what Boardman thought was needed—information about how individuals respond to a musical whole. The generative approach seeks to encourage more learning in both teacher and students and fosters student independence. Boardman and Landis had addressed these philosophical and psychological concerns in curriculum development in the elementary music series *Exploring Music* as early as 1966. The hierarchical relationship of both music skills and concepts and of teacher and student is replaced by a view of music and music education that is holistic, relational, and synergistic. Music and music education are integrated systems (1988a, p. 27). Boardman identified six components for "a holistic learning environment": content, context, behavior, mode of knowledge representation, cognitive skill, and attitudinal climate (1988b). Boardman's language reads less like that of an expert and more like that of a collaborator in learning, but she is, nevertheless, traditional in her view of curriculum as specifying "the sequential development of the socially approved behaviors, values, and cognitive skills" (1988a, p. 27). With *Holt Music* no longer in publication, will the generative approach continue to evolve? Perhaps some of its tenets are already being absorbed by the field.

Swanwick's work harkens to the 1970s, when his *A Basis for Music Education* (1979) appeared, and he proposed a model for music education based on the acronym *C(L)A(S)P* (Composition, Literature study, Audition, Skill acquisition, and Performance). Since that time, Swanwick has continued to refine and support his theory using research to develop a sequence of musical development; this sequence subsequently has become a framework for understanding student development in composition (Swanwick, 1988; Swanwick & Tillman, 1986), performance (Swanwick, 1994, pp. 108–111), and listening (1994, pp. 112–117). The overall curriculum implication of the developmental sequence is that "we should focus our musical curriculum activities towards broad aspects of musical development" such as identified in the sequence (Swanwick & Tillman, 1986, p. 335). The 1986 Swanwick/Tillman study was replicated in Cyprus (Swanwick, 1991), with the data supporting the earlier sequence of developmental levels. Swanwick employs a combination of quantitative and qualitative methods in his research. One of Swanwick's major contributions to music education is the way he convincingly interweaves research, theory, and their implications for practice, especially in *Musical Knowledge* (1994). Musical understanding has become a unifying idea in Swanwick's work (1997; Swanwick & Franca, 1999). Swanwick and Franca's research (1999) demonstrated the need to integrate composition, performing, and audience listening since each activity reveals different levels of musical understanding.

There has been further corroborating quantitative and qualitative research that supports the developmental sequence. Hentschke and Oliveira (1999) used Swanwick's theoretical framework to develop and evaluate curriculum in Brazil. Hentschke (1993) tested a model of audience-listening development to examine the relationship between how English students construct their musical experience and Swanwick's developmental theory. Hentschke and Del Ben (1999) tested the application of the developmental sequence to the assessment of audience listening in Brazil with suggestions for ways of expanding the model to include opinions of the piece, style- or genre-related responses, and extramusical associations.

Swanwick's theories are evident in versions of the National Curriculum in England (Swanwick, 1992). His *A Basis for Music Education* (1979) was influential in all the versions of the curriculum in that "the musical activities of composing, performing, and audience-listening (curiously called appraising) are intended to be integrated," and in the latest incarnation (DfEE & QCA, 1999) there is "a kind of muddled version of the Swanwick/Tillman sequence" (personal correspondence, June 5, 2000). Addressing the problem of Key Stage descriptions in formative evaluation, Swanwick (1997) developed a model for assessing quality in the National Curriculum that integrates his sequence with general criteria for musical understanding, "the actual *quality* of what is learned" (p. 208). Swanwick's approach encourages teacher decision making; there is no textbook series, just anecdotes about practice in particular circumstances.

Curriculum as Lived Experience.   The studies in this section build on the research and type of questions that seek to

discover children's development of music cognition by observing and listening to children as they construct musical meaning (Bamberger, 1982, 1991; Upitis, 1987, 1992). The research is based on children's understanding instead of an adult conception of knowledge and how knowledge is constructed. The implications for teaching and learning are many, including questions about when to introduce the expert's knowledge of a discipline and how to bridge the gap between intuitive and formal knowledge (see also Gardner, 1991). As Stowasser (1993) noted:

> Researches which are focused upon the way in which children perceive and respond to music are replacing the old preoccupation with testing children's musical abilities. Researchers are now more interested in what music can do for children than the other way round (p. 16).

MacInnis (1996) undertook an autoethnographic study of how 3 students experienced and understood a computer-based curriculum. She concluded that the old type of curriculum designed around the music elements of melody, rhythm, harmony, forms, texture, and dynamics may no longer be adequate. Curriculum should be built instead on students' understandings.

Kushner (1991), an educational researcher, was commissioned to study a performing-musicians-in-schools project that involved the City of Birmingham Symphony Orchestra and the Birmingham Local Education Authority. *The Children's Music Book* strove to give an account of the children's experience from their perspective while also presenting the teachers' and musicians' voices. Kushner makes us privy to the problems of undertaking this kind of research and focuses more on whether "connectedness to lived experience" was encouraged during musicians' visits rather than on musical learning. The responses of children from different cultures to the music experiences offered to them revealed some of the difficulties music teachers face when encountering conflicting cultural beliefs, difficulties that may not usually be voiced by students. Kushner noted that most musicians do not have "educational theories of their arts in schools activities," and he raised questions about the educational value of their visits (p. 81).

A study by Wiggins and Bodoin (1998) was a collaborative effort between a university researcher and a second-grade music teacher. Data were collected about teacher expertise and "the way students made sense out of musical ideas" (p. 285). The title of the article, "Painting a Big Soup," acknowledged the "messiness" of classroom practice. The study had the greatest (known) impact on Bodoin, who became more aware of the decisions she made when she taught as she uncovered that she, too, often misread what was occurring in her classroom and that "children needed to be able to establish their own contexts for understanding" (p. 297).

Brand (1998) asked 6-, 9-, and 12-year-olds to learn a short Zulu song on their own. Her purpose was to find out how children learn a song, noting errors as ways of understanding the mind: "The real way to improve accuracy may be to recognize and point out the *validity* of the inaccuracy, and only then to find ways to correct it" (p. 33). Some findings were that children can learn independently and that errors are revealing about how the children are thinking. Both findings have significant bearing on methodology and curriculum decisions.

Campbell (1998) used nonparticipant observation to reveal music and its meaning in children's lives. Through conversations reported as narrative tales, Campbell provided rich insight into what music means to 15 children. The implications of her study for the music curriculum are many, including that music is natural to children and more than exposure programs are needed to nurture the musical impulse; that the experience of music, rather than the sound alone, provides personal meaning; that "children are drawn to music for its personal and social uses" (p. 178); and that some children benefit more from enculturative instruction than from formal, sequential, didactic teaching.

The focus on how learners construct meaning is compatible with a recent theory of learning and knowing called constructivism. Constructivism is based on the work of Bruner (1986, 1996), Feuerstein (1990), and Vygotsky (1962, 1978), and can be recognized from the following principles:

1. Knowledge and beliefs are formed within the learner.
2. Learners personally imbue experiences with meaning.
3. Learning activities should cause learners to gain access to their experiences, knowledge, and beliefs.
4. Learning is a social activity that is enhanced by shared inquiry.
5. Reflection and metacognition are essential aspects of constructing knowledge and meaning.
6. Learners play an essential role in assessing their own learning.
7. The outcomes of the learning process are varied and often unpredictable. (D. Walker & Lambert, 1995, pp. 17–19)

Music educators have been slowly showing an increased interest in the principles of constructivism. The Mountain Lake Colloquium held in Virginia is one example of a discussion forum for these ideas (Wing, 1999). A second is found in Wiggins's new textbook, *Teaching for Musical Understanding* (2001), which clearly espouses a constructivist view of learning.

How We Are Doing. The studies in this section involve multiple locations and are larger in scope. More studies of this kind are needed. Swanwick (1989) reported on a study undertaken by the Music Department of the Institute of Education, London, to "map out the current context and practice of music teaching" (p. 155). A small section of England was selected, questionnaires were distributed, and in-depth multiple case studies undertaken. Swanwick's C(L)A(S)P model was used in the observation schedules. The researchers concluded that music in the schools was not in as unhealthy a state as some of the publicity had claimed but that music teachers needed opportunities "to expand their horizons" beyond their own classrooms (p. 170).

M. Ross and Kamba (1997) replicated on a smaller scale a 1971 study on the state of the arts in England. Using multiple assessment strategies, the researchers identified five schools and administered questionnaires to teachers and students. Students were also asked to create a timetable and fill in subject profiles. Of interest was the low ranking of music in both the 1971 and 1996 studies (11th of 11 subjects), although the general conclusion was that support for music is increasing (cf., however, Harland et al.'s conclusion that music was "the most problematic and vulnerable" of the arts in their large-scale 3-year study of English and Welsh schools [2000]). Ross and Kamba presented 25 conclusions and recommendations about arts education, which ranged from full parity for the arts to the need for political involvement by arts teachers.

In 1997–1998, Saskatchewan Education (1998) hired an independent research firm and a university research unit to undertake an evaluation of the implementation of its K–9 arts education curriculum, a process that began in 1990. The researchers used quantitative and qualitative methods to gather evidence from education partners, administrators, teachers, students, and the local arts communities. Saskatchewan Education had developed a curriculum organized around three components (creative/productive, critical/responsive, and cultural/historical) and four strands (art, dance, drama, and music), with classroom teachers often charged with the delivery. The research findings reflected misunderstandings of the new philosophy, lack of teacher expertise, and criticisms by a "minority group" (music teachers) of ineffective implementation (especially in music). That the study happened at all is remarkable. That it is thorough and available for public scrutiny and acknowledges diverse views makes it a model for large-scale government curriculum evaluation.

One research project that involves all the arts is a model of "service-oriented" case study and its value to education. For *Custom & Cherishing*, Stake et al. (1991) selected 8 schools that were not representative of any population or special arts schools for a holistic study of the school, the community, the school and community, and society. Real accounts of happenings in real schools were reported: "Ordinary classrooms are understudied, often misunderstood. . . . Effective reform is seldom born of goal-setting and standards-raising but rather of intensive analysis of problems and careful delineation of areas susceptible to improvement" (p. 6). The researchers' purpose was not to explain but to seek "understanding of particular situations" (p. 6). The eight in-depth portraits of school practice were realistic, honest, and sometimes distressing. The analysis of the data was revealing, addressing such issues as the contrast between beliefs and practice, teacher expertise (or lack thereof) in the different arts, and the need for leadership. The study is a rich source of insight about music education.

Policy Issues.   Reinterpreting data from the 1991 study (Stake et al.), Bresler identified (1) three curriculum orientations in elementary school music programs (1993); (2) three orientations to teaching the arts in the primary grades (1995/1996); (3) a look at traditions and change across the arts, in which she concluded that "these traditions are not mutually exclusive and can be integrated in different ways" (1996b, p. 33); and (4) the meso (institutional), micro (teachers' beliefs and backgrounds), and macro (larger cultural and societal) contexts of school music (1998b). In the latter study, Bresler discussed the differing institutional contexts of classroom teachers and music specialists. In another study, Bresler noted that "the advocacies of arts educators and administrative reforms are not translated into public school curricula" because teachers are left out of the equation (1996b, p. 31). Her writing has increasingly focused on policy analysis. Bresler (1998a) also examined the concepts of "child art" (art created by children), "fine art" (masterworks), and "art for children" (art created for children). Each conceptualization impacts on what happens in the classroom. She noted that child art was rarely evident in music classes while art for children prevailed.

As music education is "expanding its horizons," policy analysis as it pertains to curriculum is becoming more important. Harris (1991) used a case study of 3 Canadian settings to examine music education in the broad school context, including philosophy, action, and educational policy. Questioning unexamined assumptions, she identified seven myths that underlie school music programs: the myth that there is a relationship between musical aptitude and high academic achievement, the myth of talent, the myth of taste, the myth of the prima donna, the myth that classroom teachers can teach anything, the myth of music for fun, and the myth that "children share equal access to musical opportunities in school" (pp. 251–258). Harris suggested that school music too often reproduces a musical elite.

Two other studies indicate an increased interest in policy. Dunsmore (1994) investigated the impact of government policy on choral music education programs in Newfoundland particularly in view of the (then) pending proposal for interdenominational schools and the possible effects on choral repertoire. Russell-Bowie (1993) examined the development and implementation of the *Music (K–6) Syllabus* (New South Wales Department of Education, 1984) 7 years after its implementation to see how well deficiencies identified when the curriculum was launched had been addressed. Policy suggestions were made to address identified problems.

Summary.   While schooling remains a central interest as in the past, the ways of thinking about teaching and learning are changing, as is the role of the teacher, the student, the researcher, and understandings of the school context. The accepted "structure" of music is also being questioned (MacInnis, 1996; May, 1990, p. 9).

Not all recent music education thinking and research, however, expresses the strong reconceptualized view evident in the work selected. As noted previously, there are many studies that maintain the traditional stance and a goodly number that use qualitative research techniques without adopting a questioning of underlying assumptions (cf. Menczel, 1997; Scott, 1990). A postmodern view acknowledges multiple ways of seeking understanding; music education is benefiting from the conversation.

Understanding Music Curriculum as Gender Text

To engage in this discourse is to engage in "the ways we construct and are constructed by the prevailing system of gender" (Pinar et al., 1995, p. 359). Since the gender discourse is addressed more fully in part V, chapter 6, we examine only a few of the studies that relate to music curriculum.

Green (1997) considered gender from the point of view of ideology, "a collective mental force which both springs from and perpetuates pre-existing relationships of economic and cultural dominance or subservience between social classes" (p. 3). After giving a review of historical gender that affirmed and threatened ideology, Green described a questionnaire distributed to teachers in 78 secondary schools to examine their beliefs about gender. The assumption was that their underlying beliefs about gender significantly influenced how they interacted with boys and girls—their practice. She then interviewed boys and girls in secondary music classes, asking them some intriguing questions like: "Do you think that boys/girls feel the same way about music lessons as you do?" (p. 150). Green acknowledged that, at first, no problems were evident: "Like a *trompe l'oeil*, first one sees no gender issues, then one sees them" (p. 230). Among many other startling findings, Green reported that

it is the very *fact* of girls' hard work that *proves their lack* of the attribute which history has made possessable only by males. But it is not only that girls are seen to lack the cerebral qualities that are necessary for genuine attainment: more than that, this lack *constitutes* their femininity. (p. 228)

Green's teacher questionnaire was replicated by Hanley (1998b) in British Columbia, Canada, with similar findings.

Koza performed two gender studies related to public schools. In the first (1994a), she examined the way females were represented in the illustrations in music textbooks series for sixth, seventh, and eighth grades. Koza selected the current music textbooks *Holt Music* (Meske et al., 1988), *Music and You* (Staton, Staton, Lawrence, Jothen, & Knorr, 1988), and *World of Music* (Culp et al., 1988). In spite of existing equity guidelines, Koza's quantitative analysis indicated that females were underrepresented in these books: "Unequal power relations persist in society and are manifested in cultural artifacts such as textbooks" (p. 166). In another study, Koza's (1994b) examination of choral methods textbooks revealed that in order to keep boys in the choir, girls are neglected and their interests overlooked.

Morton (1996) examined the place of music education in the curriculum and drew analogies between the low status of music and its perception as a feminine pursuit. She further attributed music's low status in the curriculum to the "ascendancy, in traditional Western thought, of mind over body and labour over leisure" (p. ii). Morton thinks it important for music educators to "address the politics of knowledge" if they are to achieve a higher status in the education system.

In a study somewhat related to Koza's (1994b) examination of choral textbooks, Costley (1993) realized an action research project in her secondary music class. The school had an equity policy, and students were aware that racist and sexist remarks were unacceptable. The research focused on the lyrics of songs and making students conscious of some of the issues that arise in the vocal repertoire. For example, girls sang boys' songs without obvious protest, but boys did not want to sing girls' songs unless the words were changed to apply to males. Both teacher and students became more aware of the way lyrics convey hidden messages as they negotiated a resolution to the issue.

Feminist scholars politicize gender relationships. There are many ways that gender impacts on curriculum decisions both positively and negatively. Becoming aware of underlying ideologies and socially constructed gender dynamics is a step to assuring equitable education for all students.

Understanding Music Curriculum as Cultural Studies Text

The practice of art is at one and the same time an essentially *social* practice.

J. Shepherd and P. Wicke, Music and Cultural Theory

To engage in curriculum as cultural studies text is to examine issues of cultural hegemony (see Apple, 1977, 1979a, 1979b, 1979c, for an early discussion of reproduction theory that maintains that education systems support the social and corporate status quo). The idea of a single, universal norm for music that has been a widespread legacy of Western dominance has been seriously challenged (Haughton, 1984; Martin, 1995; Shepherd & Vulliamy, 1994; R. Walker, 1996). The substantial history of this discourse harks back to Shepherd, Virden, Vulliamy, and Wishart's *Whose Music?* (1977). In their book the authors shattered many assumptions about the universal nature of classical music in an attempt to reform music teaching. More recently, Shepherd and Wicke (1997) sought links between music and cultural theory, while Small (1998) continues to challenge the assumptions of the Western musical tradition, stressing that music is an activity, not a thing. The cultural studies discourse is addressed more fully in chapter 34. We have selected a few studies related to curriculum to provide an example of the areas of understanding sought in this discourse.

Two dissertations articulate some of the major concerns. Using "grounded theory" and analytic induction, Haughton (1984) studied how cultural reproduction was legitimized in curriculum development in Ontario, resulting in the exclusion of minorities and reaffirmation of Western cultural hegemony, a particularly disconcerting finding given Canada's official stance on multiculturalism. Using critical theory and ethnographic interviews, Rose (1990) examined music education's role in cultural production and reproduction. According to Rose, music education has historically played a reproductive function. Rose sees the possibility of transforming music educators to change agents in the production of music and culture.

Part of the hegemony issue has involved the place of popular music in the curriculum. After a long struggle, popular music has generally won a reluctant legitimacy in the schools, sometimes as a way into the classics, sometimes in its own right. Green (in press) interviewed popular musicians to gain insight into how they learn music, their attitudes about what they do, and how they fit into traditional music education. She concluded that the informal learning practices of popular musicians could well have the potential to invigorate formal music education: "I believe that popular music will play an important part in the future of vernacular music learning practices, and that its role in this respect should not remain beyond the limits of formal music education" (chap. 1).

Multiculturalism, although it spans both the racism and cultural studies discourses, originated in music education through cultural studies issues. One consequence of this discourse at the school level has been the discussion about whose music should be included as part of the repertoire and, increasingly, how cultural issues can be respectfully addressed (Volk, 1998). R. Walker (1990) established the importance of underlying assumptions about music and the need to acknowledge belief systems if cultural understanding is to occur. Implementation issues have extended beyond token approaches to multiculturalism that sampled repertoire and instruments to a deeper examination of cultural issues, authenticity, and belief systems (Barbour, 1994; Campbell, 1993; Damm, 1998; Lea-McKeown, 1987; Morton, 2000b; Robinson, 1996). For example, Morton (2000a) seeks to replace what she calls liberalist and pluralist views of multiculturalism that allow educators to accept the status quo with a critical multiculturalism that

> retains a pedagogical commitment to challenge students to examine and appreciate the contingency of identity, and to question how people, their cultural ideologies and institutions, and even their art, shape the good life as well as the bad, the just as well as the unjust. (p. 118)

Examining time, metaphor, and the importance of worldview, Boyea's (1999) article about Native American musics in the curriculum is a fine example of how cultural beliefs and music interrelate.

The issues extend beyond what is taught in music classes. In a pluralist worldview, how music should be taught is also of concern. The assumption that concepts should be the basis for all music teaching may need to be reexamined. Commenting that "awareness of and response to the cultural origins of teaching approaches is rare in music education" (p. 137), Dunbar-Hall (2000) examined universalist and pluralist approaches to teaching music. He concluded that there is no single right way to teach music and that "a focus on the implications of music pedagogy for the construction of attitudes to music and the people who produce it becomes the impetus for rethinking the approaches through which music is taught" (p. 137).

One offshoot of cultural studies is the increased interest in issues of sovereignty. Brand and Ho (1999) examined the effect of the 1997 "recolonialisation" of Hong Kong by the People's Republic of China after many years of British colonial rule. They asked whose values and whose music were being fostered in music classes? Was "one country, two systems" being honored? The authors observed that "most schools avoid music with an emphasis on political or democratic dimensions as a means of guarding against involvement in social conflicts and political tensions" (p. 232). While there was more emphasis on encouraging Chinese music in the curriculum, a great shift from Western practice was not yet evident in their study. Music literature reflected neither democratic, political freedom nor "revolutionary or communist party content." Brand and Ho's observation of the apolitical nature of music education in Hong Kong is strongly reinforced by the absence of political references in Ng and Morris's (1999) description of music curriculum in Hong Kong secondary schools.

Whose music should be experienced in the schools is not only a question for non-European countries. Shepherd and Vulliamy (1994), building on earlier work that applied critical sociology to music education (Vulliamy & Shepherd, 1984), explored the ideological basis of the heated debate about "what should count as school music" that surrounded the English National Curriculum, with the conservative Thatcher government supporting an "Englishness" based on a classical European heritage and the Working Group that developed the curriculum supporting a multicultural perspective. The public nature of the debate brought national media attention to music education, catapulting the issues out of the academic closet. Understanding the curriculum as cultural studies text can only become more important in the years ahead as greater cultural understanding becomes an imperative.

Understanding Music Curriculum as Political Text

The emphasis of study upon a particular aspect of music is in itself ideological because it contains implications about the music's value.

L. Green, "Ideology"

The schooling system operates in such a way as to help perpetuate the social class structure of our capitalist society.

G. Vulliamy and J. Shepherd,
"The Application of a Critical Sociology to Music Education"

Understanding curriculum as political text means looking at curriculum in social, economic, and political contexts. Apple (1990b) claimed that "decisions about the curriculum, about whose knowledge is to be made 'official,' are *inherently* matters of political and cultural power" (p. 348). Ideologies are important in shaping beliefs and guiding action. Both the content and practice of curriculum are ideological, with the values of the dominant culture being promoted (Apple, 1990a). One concern in this text is the analysis of culture to determine whose ideas prevail and whose ideas are marginalized. This discourse as it is developing in music education presents a challenge to the status quo. Three examples will illustrate this curriculum discourse.

Green (1988) critiqued the elitist classical Western view of music, what she calls the ideology of autonomy (chap. 7). She developed a theory of "the inherent meaning (how 'notes' relate to each other) and delineated meaning (how the music relates to various social contexts), arguing that all music experience must engage dialectically with both types of meaning" (personal communication, December 12, 2000). Green criticized school music in England because "the demands of fetishised establishment music have led straight to alienation, ambiguity, and mystification for many children" (p. 143). Explaining that what counts as music is a political issue, Green has contributed to a growing chorus that supports a movement away from "bourgeois" musical choices to an openness to diversity and multiple worldviews. In a chapter on the subject, she wrote that the ideology of music education has served to "perpetuate existing social relations" by rewarding those who share certain musical values (1999).

In addition to lambasting aesthetic music education as "the ethnocentric ideology of a bygone age" (p. 33), Elliott (1995) criticized the conventional music curriculum for "placing too much emphasis on the verbal specifications of teaching plans and too little emphasis on the procedural and situational nature of teaching" (p. 253) and for its linear rather than cyclical, interactive structure. He advocated a practical curriculum and proposed that teachers as reflective practitioners should be at the center of curriculum development. His model acknowledges seven interactive "commonplaces," open categories that teachers fill— aims, knowledge, learners, teaching-learning processes, teacher(s), evaluation, and learning context (p. 254)—and focuses on the process of curriculum making. Elliott argued against using verbal concepts as curriculum organizers; instead, musicianship should be at the core of music education. Drawing on developmental psychology and curriculum theory, he proposed a praxial orientation to music curriculum that is "interactive (not linear), context-dependent (not abstract), and flexible (not rule-bound)" (p. 256). For Elliott, curriculum is something that is experienced by teachers and students.

A group of music educators who were concerned about the social and political contexts of music education formed the MayDay Group in 1993. This group seeks

> (a) to apply critical theory and critical thinking to the purposes and practices of music education and (b) to affirm the central importance of musical participation in human life and, thus, the value of music in the general education of all people. (Gates, 1999, p. 15)

The name as well as the international appeal of the agenda signal that "the education-based preservation system of music in 'western civilization' is headed for serious, systemic trouble and knowledgeable music educators sense something's wrong" (p. 24). Seven ideals guide the dialogue and explain the agenda of the group:

1. Musical action that is fully mindful of musical results is the necessary condition of music making and, therefore, of an effective music education.
2. The social and cultural contexts of musical action are integral to musical meaning and cannot be ignored or minimized in music education.
3. Since human musical actions create, sustain, and reshape musical cultures, music educators can and should formally channel this cultural process, influencing the directions in which it develops and the individual and collective human values it serves.
4. The contributions made by schools, colleges, and other musical institutions are important to musical culture, but these need to be systematically examined and evaluated in terms of the directions and extent of their influence.
5. In order to be effective, music educators must establish and maintain contact with ideas and people from other disciplines.
6. The research and theoretical bases for music education must simultaneously be refined and radically broadened . . . in terms of [both] their theoretical interest and practical relevance.
7. An extensive and intensive consideration of curriculum for music education is needed as a foundation to greater professional unity and must be guided by a sound philosophical process. (pp. 17–23)

Regelski has written voluminously on MayDay issues, especially those related to curriculum (e.g., 1998a, 1998b, 1999). In "Critical Theory and Music Education" (1998b), he raised a number of issues, some of which are listed here to illustrate the provocative tone of his writing: the need to be more critical of the beliefs that have guided us (e.g., modernist/positivist thinking); the need to reject theory that disempowers people; the need to see meaning as "personally constituted"; a rejection of "methodolatry," "taken-for-granted recipes," and the "endullment" of students; the importance of good results rather than merely good teaching or good materials; a reduced need for advocacy if music education actually delivered what it promised; an inclusive view of music education; and the need for curriculum theory in music education. Regelski sees the need to be aware of ideologies—the "system of seemingly rational ideas, practices, and paradigms that serve to justify or legitimate the values, vested interests, and beliefs of a particular group of people"—and to take action. Regelski supports an "action-learning" music curriculum (1998a) that is context-based, a curriculum that examines what is "good" for students in terms of what will be of personal and social benefit to students rather than what is deemed to be good for them, and a curriculum that involves students in and with music.

Curriculum as political text is a relatively recent discourse in music education. The purpose of this discourse is to ask questions and seek greater understanding. Its impact on classroom practice is yet to be determined.

Summary. Have those operating from the reconceptualized curriculum stance addressed the criticisms of curriculum research listed earlier? While some of the criticisms are being addressed (larger scale and longitudinal studies, exploring student experience in the classroom, and the search for theoretical foundations), other criticisms do not relate to the way curriculum is being reconceptualized. Indeed, the very questions being asked about curriculum are changing.

Conclusion

We are at the edge of history.
    R. Rideout, On Leadership in American Music Education

The purpose of this chapter was (1) to examine practice and theory in music curriculum research from a "broad focus" in order to interpret the theoretical perspectives evident in curriculum research in music education and situate this research in the context of the general curriculum field and (2) to examine the more "narrowly focused" theoretical basis of music education practice and curriculum research. The complexity of the curriculum field is evident. What trends have emerged in the past 10 years? There is a growing interest in sociology (Horner & Swiss, 1999; Rideout, 1997b) as well as philosophy in providing theoretical foundations for music curriculum. There is greater emphasis on the need to understand curriculum theory and practice and therefore the importance of questioning assumptions. The use of qualitative research in conjunction with quantitative methods is providing a better portrait of what happens in teaching and learning. Collaboration is becoming the modus operandi for research as theory and practice are more closely linked.

Has music education moved beyond the having of "good ideas" to asking good questions (Wing, 1992)? At theoretical and research levels, the answer is a qualified yes: we are moving in this direction. The focus on understanding and identifying and questioning assumptions has generated new interest in curriculum and healthy international dialogue about the meaning of curriculum practice (Hargreaves & North, 2001; Leong, 1997).

What broad curriculum issues, challenges, and opportunities face music education? The issues are not new, but they are coming more sharply into focus: (1) the need to examine and understand music curriculum from a more global perspective, recognizing and learning from diversity (Leong, 1997; Lundquist & Szego, 1998); (2) the need to connect music curriculum research to general educational research (National Advisory Committee on Creative and Cultural Education, 1999; J. Ross, 1990); and (3) the need to integrate music into the general curriculum (Detels, 1999; Livermore & McPherson, 1998; McPherson,

1995; Stowasser, 1993), without a loss of identity and integrity (see Colwell, 1995, regarding the impact of changing priorities). The last point is particularly significant at a time when arts education models and research and integrated curriculum models are favorably viewed by educational policy and decision makers (see Abbs, 1994, for a defense of a generic community of the arts and Detels, 2000, for a proposal that addresses what she views as the excessive specialization of music). And finally, there is the need to examine the politically motivated trend toward national (centralized) curriculum and its implications for music education (Hargreaves & North, 2001), encompassing student assessment and curriculum effectiveness.

There are also three areas of practical challenges and opportunities that face contemporary music educators as they make curriculum decisions. What content should be included—Western traditional music, national music, world music? What approaches should be used—universalist or pluralist (Dionyssiou, 2000; Dunbar-Hall, 2000), general or specialist (Hargreaves & North, 2001)? Who should be teaching music in the school—musicians, classroom teachers, music teachers (Lawson et al., 1994; Stowasser, 1993)? Who should be making curriculum decisions in music education—textbook developers, national consortia, teachers? These issues are increasingly being viewed from a reconceptualized perspective. Even the multiple authorship of elementary music textbooks could be seen as an attempt to address diversity (even though sales are the priority). As for curriculum planning, too often it seems that considerable effort is put into the development, less on the implementation, and even less on the impact of curriculum on student learning.

Curriculum issues are multiple and complex. Where should future curriculum research be focused? The needs and challenges identified in this chapter provide a research agenda for the future in terms of both understanding and implementing curriculum. A greater understanding of the big education issues but also of music teaching and learning is essential. The dialogue has begun; the conversation must continue. At the level of practice (necessarily embedded in theory), if music education is to be constructed on more than an intuitive level, then we need to work harder at developing a coherent body of knowledge that will inform our educational choices.

How should music curriculum research be conducted? We need to address Colwell's (1995) criticism that "the emphasis on qualitative research brings us rich descriptions of inadequate programs and no convincing data about which way to turn and how" (p. 23). Both quantitative and qualitative research methodologies can play a role; it all depends on the research question (Carlsen, 1994). As Geringer (2000) wrote: "We must be aware of each other's work, talk with each other, and learn to make transfers across methodological borders" (p. 204).

We began by asking: "What is curriculum?" The answer depends on underlying assumptions about schooling. It is the question that is most important.

REFERENCES

Abbs, P. (1994). *The educational imperative: A defence of Socratic and aesthetic learning.* London: Falmer Press.

Allen, M., Gillespie, R., & Hayes, P. T. (1994). Essential elements for strings. Milwaukee, WI: Hal Leonard.

American Music Conference News. (1996). Standards implementation marches forward: Special report of the American Music Conference. *Arts Education Policy Review, 98*(2), 10–16.

Apple, M. (1977). *The curriculum and cultural reproduction.* Milton Keynes, UK: Open University Press.

Apple, M. (1979a). Curriculum and reproduction. *Curriculum Inquiry, 9*(3), 231–252.

Apple, M. (1979b). *Ideology and curriculum.* London: Routledge & Kegan Paul.

Apple, M. (1979c). On analyzing hegemony. *Journal of Curriculum Theory, 1*(1), 10–27.

Apple, M. (1990a). *Ideology and curriculum* (2nd ed.). New York: Routledge & Kegan Paul.

Apple, M. (1990b). Is there a curriculum voice to reclaim? In D. J. Flinders & S. J. Thornton (Eds.), *The curriculum studies reader* (pp. 342–349). New York: Routledge & Kegan Paul.

Arberg, H., & Palisca, C. V. (1964). Implications of the government sponsored Yale Seminar in Music Education. *College Music Symposium, 4,* 113–124.

Ardrey, C. M. (1999). *Middle school general music: Kodály, Dalcroze, Orff and the developmental needs of adolescents.* Unpublished doctoral dissertation, Temple University, Philadelphia.

Atlantic Provinces Education Foundation. (2000). *Foundation for the Atlantic Canada arts education curriculum.* Halifax, Nova Scotia, Canada: Author.

Atterbury, B. W. (1991). Some directions for research in elementary general education. *Bulletin of the Council for Research in Music Education, 109,* 37–45.

Bamberger, J. (1982). Revisiting children's descriptions of simple rhythms: A function for reflection-in-action. In S. Strauss (Ed.), *U-shaped behavioral growth* (pp. 191–226). New York: Academic Press.

Bamberger, J. (1991). *The mind behind the musical ear: How children develop musical intelligence.* Cambridge, MA: Harvard University Press.

Barbour, G. M., Sr. (1994). *An exploration into the acceptance and approbation of African and multicultural music into the standard music curriculum of three large public school systems of Atlanta (Georgia).* Unpublished doctoral dissertation, Walden University, Minneapolis, Minnesota.

Barone, T. (2000). *Aesthetics, politics, and educational inquiry: Essays and examples.* New York: Peter Lang.

Beall, G. (1991). Learning sequence and music learning. *Quarterly Journal of Music Teaching and Learning, 2*(1/2), 87–96.

Boardman, E. (1988a). The generative theory of musical learning. Part I: Introduction. *General Music, 2*(1), 4–5, 26–31.

Boardman, E. (1988b). The generative theory of musical learning. Part II. *General Music, 2*(2), 3–6, 28–32.

Boardman, E. (1989). The generative theory of musical learning. Part III: Planning for learning. *General Music, 2*(3), 11–16.

Boardman, E., & Landis, B. (1966). *Exploring music 5.* New York: Holt, Rinehart & Winston.

Bolton, B. M., Taggart, C. C., Reynolds, A. M., Valerio, W. H., Woods, D. G., & Gordon, E. E. (2000). *Jump right in: General music series.* Chicago: GIA.

Bond, J., Copeland Davidson, M., Goetze, M., Lawrence, V. P., & Snyder, S. (1995). *Share the music.* New York: Macmillan/McGraw-Hill.

Bourne, P. A. S. (1990). *Instructional techniques for children's choirs: A curricular model.* Unpublished doctoral dissertation, Arizona State University, Tempe.

Bowman, W. (2000). *Déjà vu all over again: A critical response to Claire Detel's Helsinki Discussion paper.* Retrieved July 15, 2000, from http://members.aol.com/jtgates/maydaygroup/bowmandetels.html

Boyea, A. (1999). Encountering complexity: Native musics in the curriculum. *Philosophy of Music Education Review, 7*(1), 31–48.

Boyle, D. (Comp.). (1974). *Instructional objectives in music—Resources for planning instruction and evaluating achievement.* Vienna, VA: Music Educators National Conference.

Brand, E. (1998). Children's learning: Implications for music teacher education. In R. R. Rideout & S. J. Paul (Eds.), *Innovations in music teacher education* (pp. 30–42). Norman: University of Oklahoma.

Brand, M., & Ho, W-C. (1999). China recaptures Hong Kong: A study of change for music education. *British Journal of Music Education, 16*(3), 227–236.

Bresler, L. (1992). Qualitative paradigms in music research education. *Quarterly Journal of Music Teaching and Learning, 3*(1), 64–79.

Bresler, L. (1993). Three orientations to arts in the primary grades: Implications for curriculum reform. *Arts Education Policy Review, 94*(6), 29–34.

Bresler, L. (1994). Formative research in music education. *Quarterly Journal of Music Teaching and Learning, 5*(3), 11–24.

Bresler, L. (1995/96). Curriculum orientations in elementary school music: Roles, pedagogies and values. *Bulletin of the Council for Research in Music Education, 127,* 22–27.

Bresler, L. (1996a). Ethnography, phenomenology, and action research in music education. *Quarterly Journal of Music Teaching and Learning, 6*(3), 6–18.

Bresler, L. (1996b). Traditions and change across the arts: Case studies of arts education. *International Journal of Music Education, 27,* 24–35.

Bresler, L. (1998a). "Child art," "fine art," and "art for children": The shaping of school practice and implications for change. *Arts Education Policy Review, 100*(1) 3–10.

Bresler, L. (1998b). The genre of school music and its shaping by meso, micro, and macro contexts. *Research Studies in Music Education, 11,* 2–18.

Bresler, L., & Stake, R. (1992). Qualitative research methodology in music education. In R. J. Colwell (Ed.), *Handbook of research on music teaching and learning: A project of the Music Educators National Conference* (pp. 75–90). New York: Schirmer Books.

Brown, E. A. (1993). *Elementary music education curricula in the public schools of Canada.* Unpublished doctoral dissertation, Northwestern University, Chicago.

Bruner, J. S. (1960). *The process of education.* Cambridge, MA: Harvard University Press.

Bruner, J. S. (1986). *Actual minds, possible worlds.* Cambridge, MA: Harvard University Press.

Bruner, J. S. (1996). *The culture of education.* Cambridge, MA: Harvard University Press.

Burton, L. H. (1990). Comprehensive musicianship—The Hawaii music curriculum project. *Quarterly Journal of Music Teaching and Learning, 1*(3), 67–76.

Burton, L. H., & Thompson, W. (Eds.). (1982). *Music: Comprehensive musicianship program.* Honolulu: Hawaii University.

Byo, S. J. (1999). Classroom teachers' and music specialists' perceived ability to implement the national standards for music education. *Journal of Research in Music Education, 47*(2), 111–123.

Byrd, M. E. (1989). *A comparative analysis of Edwin Gordon's approach to sequential musical learning and learning sequences found in three elementary general music series.* Unpublished doctoral dissertation, University of Illinois at Urbana-Champaign.

Campbell, P. S. (1993). Cultural issues and school music participation: The new Asians in American schools. *Quarterly Journal of Music Teaching and Learning, 4*(2), 45–56.

Campbell, P. S. (1998). *Songs in their heads: Music and its meaning in children's lives.* New York: Oxford University Press.

Carey, N. (1995). *Arts education in public elementary and secondary schools* (Statistical Analysis Report). Rockville, MD: Westat, Inc. (ERIC Document Reproduction Service No. ED388607)

Carlsen, J. C. (1994). The need to know: 1994 Senior Researcher Award acceptance address. *Journal of Research in Music Education, 42,* 181–189.

Choate, R. A. (1968). *Documentary report of the Tanglewood Symposium.* Washington, DC: Music Educators National Conference.

Choksy, L., Abramson, R. M., Gillespie, A. E., & Woods, D. (1986). *Teaching music in the twentieth century.* Englewood Cliffs, NJ: Prentice Hall.

Clarkson, A. E., & Pegley, K. (1991). *An assessment of a technology in music programme* (Technical Report 91–2). North York, Ontario, Canada: York University. (ERIC Document Reproduction Service No. ED341364)

Clausel, S. L. S. (1998). *Applications of Cambourne's model of literacy learning and the Orff-music method to the development of a curriculum model for Mississippi music education, K–1.* Unpublished doctoral dissertation, University of Mississippi, Lafayette County.

Clay, G., Hertrich, J., Jones, P., Mills, J., & Rose, J. (1998). *The arts inspected.* Oxford, England: Heinemann.

Coalition for Music Education in Canada & Canadian Music Educators Association. (2001). *Achieving musical understanding: Concepts & skills pre-kindergarten to grade 8.* Toronto, Ontario, Canada: Author. Available from P.O. Box 52635, 1801 Lakeshore Rd., W., Mississauga, ON, Canada L2J 4S6.

Colorado Alliance for Arts Education. (2000). *Survey on the status of arts education in Colorado public school districts, 1999–2000.* Available from CAAE, 200 Grant Street, Denver, CO 80203 (email caae@artstozoo.org).

Colwell, R. J. (1979). *Silver Burdett competency tests.* Morristown, NJ: Silver Burdett.

Colwell, R. J. (1985). Program evaluation in music teacher education. *Bulletin of the Council for Research in Music Education, 81,* 18–64.

Colwell, R. J. (1990a). The posture of music education research. *Design for Arts in Education, 91*(5), 42–52.

Colwell, R. J. (1990b). Research findings: Shake well before using. *Music Educators Journal, 77*(3), 29–34.

Colwell, R. J. (Ed.). (1992). *Handbook of research on music teaching and learning: A project of the Music Educators National Conference.* New York: Schirmer Books.

Colwell, R. J. (1995). Voluntary national standards and teacher education. *Bulletin of the Council for Research in Music Education, 125,* 20–31.

Colwell, R. J. & Abrahams, F. (1991). Edwin Gordon's contributions: An appraisal. *Quarterly Journal of Music Teaching and Learning, 2*(1/2), 19–36.

Consortium of National Arts Education Associations. (1994). *National Standards for Arts Education: What every young American should know and be able to do in the arts.* Reston, VA: Music Educators National Conference.

Costanza, P., & Russell, T. (1992). Methodologies in music education. In R. J. Colwell (Ed.), *Handbook of research on music teaching and learning: A project of the Music Educators National Conference* (pp. 498–508). New York: Schirmer Books.

Costley, C. (1993). Music and gender at Key Stage Three (11–14): An action research project. *British Journal of Music Education, 10,* 197–203.

Cox, G. (1993). Music in the National Curriculum: Some historical perspectives. *Curriculum Journal, 4*(3), 351–362.

Crook, E., Walker, D., & Reimer, B. (1974, 1978, 1981, 1985). *Silver Burdett music* [Grades 1–6]. Morristown, NJ: Silver Burdett.

Culp, C. E., Eisman, L., & Hoffman, M. E. (1988). *World of music.* Morristown, NJ: Silver Burdett & Ginn.

Curriculum Corporation. (1994). *The arts—A curriculum profile for Australian schools.* Melbourne, Australia: Author.

Damm, R. J. (1998). *American Indian music in elementary school music programs of Oklahoma: Repertoire, authenticity and instruction.* Unpublished doctoral dissertation, University of North Texas, Denton.

Department of Education. (1992). *Music in the National Curriculum (London).* London: HMSO.

Department of Education. (1995). *Music in the National Curriculum.* London: HMSO.

Detels, C. (1999). *Soft boundaries: Revisioning the arts and aesthetics in American education.* Westport, CT: Bergin & Garvey.

DfEE & QCA. (1999). *The National Curriculum for England: Music.* London: Author.

Dillon, J., Kjelland, J., & O'Reilly, J. (1992). *Strictly strings.* Van Nuys, CA: Alfred.

Dionyssiou, Z. (2000). The effects of schooling on the teaching of Greek traditional music. *Music Education Research, 2*(2), 141–163.

Doll, W. E. (1993). A post-modern perspective on curriculum. New York: Teachers College Press, Columbia University.

Dolloff, L. (1993). *Das Schulwerk: A foundation for the cognitive, musical, and artistic development of children* (Monograph No. 1, *Research perspective in music education*, L. Bartel [Ed.]). Toronto, Ontario, Canada: University of Toronto.

Doyle, W. (1992). Curriculum and pedagogy. In P. W. Jackson (Ed.), *Handbook of research on curriculum* (pp. 486–516). New York: Macmillan.

Dunbar-Hall, P. (2000). Concept or context? Teaching and learning Balinese gamelan and the universalist-pluralist debate. *Music Education Research, 2*(2), 127–139.

Dunsmore, D. A. (1994). *The effect of Newfoundland government policy on choral music education: Voices and opinions about the past, present and future.* Unpublished doctoral dissertation, University of Wisconsin, Madison.

Eisner, E. (1985). *The educational imagination: On the design and evaluation of education programs* (2nd ed.). New York: Macmillan.

Eisner, E. (1992). Curriculum ideologies. In P. W. Jackson (Ed.), *Handbook of research on curriculum* (pp. 302–326). New York: Macmillan.

Eisner, E. (1994). *Cognition and curriculum reconsidered* (2nd ed.). New York: Teachers College Press, Columbia University.

Elliott, D. J. (1995). *Music matters: A new philosophy of music education.* New York: Oxford University Press.

Favaro, E. (1999). Looking back: An action plan revisited. In B. Hanley (Ed.), *Leadership, advocacy, communication* (pp. 7–10). Victoria, British Columbia: Canadian Music Educators Association.

Feuerstein, R. (1990). The theory of structural cognitive modifiability. In B. Z. Presseisen (Ed.), *Learning and thinking styles: Classroom interaction* (pp. 68–134). Washington, DC: National Education Association.

Finter, L. A. (1995). *A study of elementary music curricula in Nevada as they conform to authoritative opinions (curriculum objectives).* Unpublished doctoral dissertation, Walden University, Minneapolis, Minnesota.

Forsythe, J. L. (1993). The blind musicians and the elephant. In C. K. Madsen & C. Pricket (Eds.), *Research in music behavior: Applications and extensions* (pp. 329–338). Tuscaloosa: University of Alabama Press.

Foshay, A. W. (2000). *The curriculum: Purpose, substance, practice.* New York: Teachers College Press, Columbia University.

Fowler, C. B. (1984). *Arts in education/Education in arts.* Washington, DC: National Endowment for the Arts.

Froseth, J. O. (1986). *The comprehensive music instructor: Listen, move, sing, and play.* Chicago: GIA.

Gane, P. (1996). Instrumental teaching and the National Curriculum: A possible partnership? *British Journal of Music Education, 13*(1), 49–65.

Gardner, H. (1991). *The unschooled mind: How children think and how schools should teach.* New York: Basic Books.

Gary, C. L. (Ed.). (1967). *The study of music in the elementary school—A conceptual approach.* Washington, DC: Music Educators National Conference.

Gates, T. J. (1999). Action for change in music education: The MayDay Group agenda. In M. McCarthy (Ed.), *Music education as praxis: Reflecting on music-making as human action* (pp. 14–25). The 1997 Charles Fowler Colloquium on Innovation in Arts Education, April 18–19, 1997. College Park: University of Maryland.

Geringer, J. M. (2000). Senior researcher acceptance address: On publishing, pluralism, and pitching. *Journal of Research in Music Education, 48,* 191–205.

Gordon, E. E. (1965). *Musical aptitude profile.* Chicago: GIA.

Gordon, E. E. (1979). *Primary measures of music audiation.* Chicago: GIA.

Gordon, E. E. (1982). *Intermediate measures of music audiation.* Chicago: GIA.

Gordon, E. E. (1990). *A music learning theory for newborn and young children.* Chicago: GIA.

Gordon, E. E. (1992). A response to volume II, numbers 1 & 2, of the *Quarterly Journal of Music Teaching and Learning. Quarterly Journal of Music Teaching and Learning, 2*(4), 62–72.

Gordon, E. E. (1993). *Learning sequences in music: Skill, content, & patterns.* Chicago: GIA.

Gordon, E. E., & Woods, D. G. (1985). *Jump right in: The music curriculum.* Chicago: GIA.

Gouzouasis, P. (1991). A progressive developmental approach to the music education of preschool children. *Canadian Music Educator, 32*(3), 45–53.

Gouzouasis, P. (1992). The comparative effect of two tonal pattern systems and two rhythm pattern systems for learning to play the guitar. *Quarterly Journal of Music Teaching and Learning, 3*(4), 10–18.

Green, L. (1988). *Music on deaf ears: Musical meaning, ideology, and education.* New York: St. Martin's Press.

Green, L. (1993). Music, gender, and education. *British Journal of Music Education, 10*(3), 219–253.

Green, L. (1997). *Music, gender, education.* New York: Cambridge University Press.

Green, L. (1999). Ideology. In B. Horner & T. Swiss (Eds.), *Key terms in popular music and culture* (pp. 5–17). Malden, MA: Blackwell.

Green, L. (In press). *How popular musicians learn: A way ahead for music education.* London: Ashgate Press.

Greer, R. D. (1980). *Design for music learning.* New York: Teachers College Press, Columbia University.

Grunow, R. F., & Gordon, E. E. (1989). *Jump right in: The instrumental series.* Chicago: GIA.

Hanley, B. (1989). Educators' attitudes to philosophies of music education. *Canadian Music Educator Research Edition, 31*(1), 1–23.

Hanley, B. (1998a). Creating a national vision for arts education in Canada. *Canadian Music Educator, 40*(1), 9–13.

Hanley, B. (1998b). Gender in secondary music education in British Columbia. *British Journal of Music Education, 15*(1), 51–69.

Hargreaves, D. J., & North, A. C. (Eds.). (2001). *Musical development and learning: The international perspective.* London: Continuum International.

Harland, J., Kinder, K., Lord, P., Stott, A., Schagen, I., & Haynes, J. (2000). *Arts education in secondary schools: Effects and effectiveness.* Berkshire, UK: National Foundation for Educational Research.

Harris, C. (1991). *Administering school music in three Canadian settings: Philosophy, action, and educational policy.* Unpublished doctoral dissertation, University of Toronto, Ontario, Canada.

Haughton, H. S. (1984). *Social and cultural reproduction in the (music) curriculum guideline process in Ontario education: Ethnic minorities and cultural exclusion.* Unpublished doctoral dissertation, University of Toronto, Ontario, Canada.

Hentschke, L. (1993). *Musical development: Testing a model in the audience-listening setting.* Unpublished doctoral dissertation, University of London.

Hentschke, L., & Del Ben, L. (1999). The assessment of audience-listening: Testing a model in the educational setting of Brazil. *Music Education Research, 1*(2), 127–146.

Hentschke, L., & Oliveira, A. (1999). Music curriculum development and evaluation based on Swanwick's theory. *International Journal of Music Education, 34*, 14–29.

Hodges, D. (1992). The acquisition of music reading skills. In R. J. Colwell (Ed.), *Handbook of research on music teaching and learning: A project of the Music Educators National Conference* (pp. 466–471). New York: Schirmer Books.

Holmes, D. M. (1997). *An examination of fifth grade instrumental music programs and their relationship with music and academic achievement.* Unpublished doctoral dissertation, University of Washington, Seattle.

Horner, B., & Swiss, T. (Eds.). (1999). *Key terms in popular music and culture.* Malden, MA: Blackwell.

Jackson, P. W. (1992). Conceptions of curriculum and curriculum specialists. In P. W. Jackson (Ed.), *Handbook of research on curriculum* (pp. 3–40). New York: Macmillan.

Johnson, J. P. (1992). *An investigation of four secondary level choral directors and their application of the Wisconsin comprehensive musicianship through performance approach: A qualitative study.* Unpublished doctoral dissertation, University of Wisconsin, Madison.

Joseph, A. S. (1982). *A Dalcroze Eurhythmics approach to music learning in kindergarten through rhythmic movement, ear training, and improvisation.* Unpublished doctoral dissertation, Carnegie-Mellon University, Pittsburgh, Pennsylvania.

Koza, J. E. (1994a). Females in 1988 middle school textbooks: An analysis of illustrations. *Journal of Research in Music Education, 42*(2), 145–171.

Koza, J. E. (1994b). Getting a word in edgewise: A feminist critique of choral methods texts. *Quarterly Journal of Music Teaching and Learning, 5*(3), 68–77.

Kuehmann, K. M. (1987). *A theoretical model for curriculum development in general music for fundamentalist Christian elementary schools.* Unpublished doctoral dissertation, Arizona State University, Tempe.

Kushner, S. (1991). *The children's music book.* London: Calouste Gulbenkian Foundation.

Kushner, S. (1999). Fringe benefits: Music education out of the National Curriculum. *Music Education Research, 1*(2), 209–218.

Labuta, J. (1974). *Guide to accountability in music instruction.* West Nyack, NY: Parker.

Lamb, R. (1993). The possibilities of/for feminist music criticism in music education. *British Journal of Music Education, 10*(3), 169–180.

Lawson, D., Plummeridge, C., & Swanwick, K. (1994). Music and the National Curriculum in primary schools. *British Journal of Music Education, 11*(1), 3–14.

Lea-McKeown, M. Y. (1987). *The importance of native music culture in education at a Manitoba Ojibwa reserve from an ethnological perspective.* Unpublished doctoral dissertation, University of Alberta, Edmonton, Canada.

LeBlanc, A. (1996). Building theory in music education: A personal account. *Philosophy of Music Education Review, 4*(2), 107–116.

Lehman, P. R. (1999). National assessment of arts education: A first look. *Music Educators Journal, 85*(4), 34–37.

Leong, S. (Ed.). (1997). *Music in schools and teacher education: A global perspective.* Nedlands, WA: Callaway International Resource Centre for Music Education.

Leonhard, C. E., & Colwell, R. J. (1976). Research in music education. *Bulletin of the Council for Research in Music Education, 49*, 1–30.

Lindeman, C. A., Flowers, P. J., Jellison, J. A., Kaplan, P. R., & Price, H. E. (1998). *Thinking ahead: A research agenda for music education.* Reston, VA: Music Educators National Conference.

Livermore, J., & McPherson, G. E. (1998). Expanding the role of the arts in the curriculum: Some Australian initiatives. *Arts Education Policy Review, 99*(3), 10–15.

Lundquist, B., & Szego, C. K. (1998). *Musics of the world's cultures: A source book for music educators.* Reading, UK: International Society for Music Education.

MacInnis, P. (1996). *Experiencing and understanding a computer-based music curriculum: A teacher's story.* Unpublished doctoral dissertation, University of Toronto, Ontario, Canada.

Madhosingh, D. F. (1984). *An approach to developing comprehensive musicianship in the intermediate grades using the voice and ukulele.* Unpublished doctoral dissertation, University of British Columbia, Vancouver, Canada.

Madsen, C., Greer, R. D., & Madsen, C. (1975). *Research in music behavior: Modifying music behavior in the classroom.* New York: Teachers College Press, Columbia University.

Madsen, C., & Madsen, C. (1970). *Experimental research in music.* Englewood Cliffs, NJ: Prentice Hall.

Major, A. (1996). Reframing curriculum design. *British Journal of Music Education, 13*(3), 183–193.

Mark, M. L. (1986). *Contemporary music education* (2nd ed.). New York: Schirmer.

Mark, M. L., & Gary, C. L. (1999). *A history of American music education* (2nd ed.). Reston, VA: Association for Music Education.

Martin, M. A. (1992). *An examination of the Orff-Schulwerk approach to music education in a public elementary school: A replication study.* Unpublished doctoral dissertation, University of North Carolina, Chapel Hill.

Martin, P. (1995). *Sounds & society: Themes in the sociology of music.* Manchester, UK: Manchester University Press.

May, W. T. (1990). Teaching for understanding in the arts: The Elementary Subjects Center at Michigan State University. *Quarterly Journal of Music Teaching and Learning, 1*(1/2), 5–16.

May, W. T. (1993). *What in the world is music in "World of Music"? A critique of a commonly used textbook series* (Elementary Subjects Center Series No. 76). East Lansing: Michigan State University Institute for Research on Teaching. (ERIC Document Reproduction Service No. ED355155)

McDonald, J. C. (1991). The application of Gordon's empirical model of learning sequence to teaching the recorder. *Quarterly Journal of Music Teaching and Learning, 2*(1/2), 110–117.

McLellan, N. D. (1996). *Music teachers' opinions regarding the use and effectiveness of elementary music series books in Missouri public schools.* Unpublished doctoral dissertation, University of Missouri, Kansas City.

McPherson, G. E. (1995). Integrating the arts into the general curriculum: An Australian perspective. *Arts Education Policy Review, 97*(1), 25–31.

McPherson, G. E., & Dunbar-Hall, P. (2001). Music education in Australian schools. In D. J. Hargreaves & A. C. North (Eds.), *Musical development and learning: The international perspective* (pp. 14–16). London: Continuum International.

Menczel, V. (1997). *The application of the Suzuki method in Israel and the United States: A comparative case study.* Unpublished doctoral dissertation, New York University, New York.

Merrion, M. (Ed.). (1989). *What works: Instructional strategies for music education.* Reston, VA: Music Educators National Conference.

Meske, E. B., Andress, B., Pautz, M. P., & William, F. (1988). *Holt music* [Grades 1–8]. New York: Holt, Rinehart & Winston.

Mills, J. (1994). Music in the National Curriculum: The first year. *British Journal of Music Education, 11*(3), 191–196.

Mills, J. (1997). A comparison of the quality of class music teaching in primary and secondary schools in England. *Bulletin of the Council for Research in Music Education, 133,* 72–76.

Montgomery, A. (1997). Orff or Kodály: What's all the fuss? *Canadian Music Educator, 39*(1), 11–13.

Montgomery, A. (In press). *Teaching musical understanding: From sound to symbol.* Don Mills, Ontario, Canada: Pearson.

Morton, C. (1996). *The "status problem": The feminized location of school music and the burden of justification.* Unpublished doctoral dissertation, University of Toronto, Ontario, Canada.

Morton, C. (2000a). Addressing bias in music: A Canadian case study. *Music Education Research, 2*(2), 111–125.

Morton, C. (2000b). In the meantime: Finding a vision for multicultural music education in Canada. In B. Hanley & B. A. Roberts (Eds.), *Looking forward: Challenges to Canadian music education* (pp. 251–272). Victoria, British Columbia: Canadian Music Educators Association.

Munsen, S. C. (1986). *A description and analysis of an Orff-Schulwerk program of music education.* Unpublished doctoral dissertation, University of Illinois at Urbana-Champaign.

Music Educators National Conference. (1996). *Performance standards for music.* Reston, VA: Author.

Musoleno, R. R. (1990). *A model for a curriculum suited to exemplary practices of middle school education.* Unpublished doctoral dissertation, University of Kansas, Lawrence.

National Advisory Committee on Creative and Cultural Education. (1999). *All our futures: Creativity, culture, and education.* Retrieved January 12, 2001, from http://www.dfee.gov.uk/nacce/index1.htm

Natoli, J. (1997). *A primer to postmodernity.* Oxford: Blackwell.

Nelson, B. J. P. (1988). *The development of a middle school general music curriculum: A synthesis of computer-assisted instruction and music learning theory.* Unpublished doctoral dissertation, University of Rochester, Eastman School of Music, New York.

New South Wales Department of Education. (1984). *Music (K–6) syllabus and support statements.* Sydney, Australia: Government Printing Office.

Ng, F. Y-F., & Morris, P. (1999). The music curriculum in Hong Kong secondary schools—Intentions and constraints. *Arts Education Policy Review, 100*(5), 29–40.

OFSTED [Office for Standards in Education]. (1993a). *Handbook for the inspection of schools.* London: HMSO.

OFSTED. (1993b). *Music: Key Stages, 1, 2, and 3. First year 1992–1993.* London: HMSO.

Patchen, J. (1996). Overview of discipline-based music education. *Music Educators Journal, 83*(2), 19–26.

Patchen, J. H., & Harris, L. D. (Eds.). (1996). *A discipline-based music education handbook*. Chattanooga: University of Tennessee at Chattanooga.

Paynter, J. (1993). Open peer commentary: Musical knowledge. *Psychology of Music, 20*, 175–177.

Pearson, B. (1993). *Standards of excellence*. San Diego, CA: Neil A. Kjos.

Persky, H. R., Sandene, B. A., & Askew, J. M. (1998). *The NAEP 1997 arts report card*. Washington, DC: U.S. Department of Education.

Phillips. K. (1992). Research on the teaching of singing. In R. J. Colwell (Ed.), *Handbook of research on music teaching and learning: A project of the Music Educators National Conference* (pp. 568–576). New York: Schirmer Books.

Pinar, W. F. (1995). Understanding curriculum: An introduction. In W. F. Pinar, W. M. Reynolds, P. Slattery, & P. M. Taubman (Eds.), *Understanding curriculum: An introduction to the study of historical and contemporary curriculum discourses* (pp. 3–65). New York: Peter Lang.

Pinar, W. F., Reynolds, W. M., Slattery, P., & Taubman, P. M. (1995). *Understanding curriculum: An introduction to the study of historical and contemporary curriculum*. New York: Peter Lang.

Plummeridge, C. (1985). Curriculum development in music education: The limitation of theory. *Psychology of Music, 13*(1), 49–57.

Plummeridge, C. (1996). Curriculum development and the problem of control. In C. Plummeridge (Ed.), *Music education: Trends and issues* (pp. 27–40). London: Institute of Education, University of London.

Plummeridge, C. (1999). Aesthetic education and the practice of music teaching. *British Journal of Music Education, 16*(2), 115–122.

Pratt, D. (1980). *Curriculum design and development*. New York: Harcourt Brace Jovanovich.

Prawat, R. S. (1993). *Commonalities and differences in views about ideal and actual curriculum in six subject matter domains* (Elementary Subjects Center Series No. 101). East Lansing: Michigan State University Institute for Research on Teaching. (ERIC Document Reproduction Service No. ED356901)

Preston, H. (Ed.). (1994). Listening, appraising and composing: Case studies in music. *British Journal of Music Education, 11*(1), 15–55.

Rao, D. (1993). *We will sing! Choral music experience for classroom choirs*. New York: Boosey & Hawkes.

Regelski, T. A. (1998a). The Aristotelian bases of praxis for music and music education as praxis. *Philosophy of Music Education Review, 6*(1), 22–59.

Regelski, T. A. (1998b). *Critical theory and music education*. Retrieved September 17, 2000, http://member.aol.com/jtgates/maydaygroup/crittheory.html

Regelski, T. A. (1999). Action learning: Curriculum and instruction as and for praxis. In M. McCarthy (Ed.), *Music education as praxis: Reflecting on music-making as human action* (pp. 99–120). The 1997 Charles Fowler Colloquium on Innovation in Arts Education, April 18–19, 1997. College Park: University of Maryland.

Reimer, B. (1985). Toward a more scientific approach to music education. *Bulletin of the Council for Research in Music Education, 83*, 1–21.

Reimer, B. (1989). *A philosophy of music education* (2nd ed.). Englewood Cliffs, NJ: Prentice Hall.

Reimer, B., Hoffman, M., & McNeil, A. (1974, 1978, 1981, 1985). *Silver Burdett Music* [Grades 7–8]. Morristown, NJ: Silver Burdett.

Rhodes, T. C., Bierschenk, D., Lautzenheiser, T., & Higgins, J. (1991). *Essential elements: A comprehensive band method*. Milwaukee, WI: Hal Leonard.

Rideout, R. (1997a). Antecedents to a sociology of music education. In R. Rideout (Ed.), *On the sociology of music education* (pp. 65–70). Norman: University of Oklahoma.

Rideout, R. (Ed.). (1997b). *On the sociology of music education*. Norman: University of Oklahoma.

Rideout, R. (1998). *On leadership in American music education*. Unpublished manuscript, University of Oklahoma, Norman.

Robinson, K. M. (1996). *Multicultural general music education: An investigation and analysis in Michigan's public elementary schools, K–6*. Unpublished doctoral dissertation, University of Michigan, Lansing.

Rose, A. M. (1990). *Reproduction, production, and hegemony*. Unpublished doctoral dissertation, University of Wisconsin, Madison.

Ross, J. (1990). The National Arts Education Research Center at New York University: Challenging tradition. *Quarterly Journal of Music Teaching and Learning, 1*(1/2), 17–21.

Ross, M., & Kamba, M. (1997). *The state of the arts in five English secondary schools*. Exeter: University of Exeter.

Runfola, M., & Rutkowski, J. (1992). General music curriculum. In R. J. Colwell (Ed.), *Handbook of research on music teaching and learning: A project of the Music Educators National Conference* (pp. 697–709). New York: Schirmer Books.

Russell-Bowie, D. E. (1993). *Policy and practice in music education in New South Wales state primary schools (Australia)*. Unpublished doctoral dissertation, University of Wollongsong, Australia.

Sandner, L. (1999). Pan-Canadian projects. In B. Hanley (Ed.), *Leadership, advocacy, communication* (pp. 1–6). Victoria, British Columbia: Canadian Music Educators Association.

Saskatchewan Education. (1995). *Arts education: A curriculum guide for Grades 1 to 5*. Regina, Saskatchewan, Canada: Author.

Saskatchewan Education. (1998). *Arts education: Grades 1–9 curriculum evaluation report*. Regina, Saskatchewan, Canada: Author.

Schmidt, A. M. (1996). Who benefits? Music education and the national standards. *Philosophy of Music Education Review, 4*(2), 71–82.

Schwab, J. J. (1969). The practical: Arts of eclectic. *School Review, 79* (4), 493–542.

Schwab, J. J. (1970). *The practical: A language for curriculum*. Washington, DC: National Education Association.

Schwab, J. J. (1973). The practical 3: Translation into curriculum. *School Review, 81*(4), 501–522.

Schwab, J. J. (1983). The practical 4: Something for curriculum professors to do. *Curriculum Inquiry, 13* (3), 239–265.

Scott, S. S. C. (1990). *An ethnographic study of choral music education in two selected small school districts of Mississippi*. Unpublished doctoral dissertation, University of Southern Mississippi, Hattiesburg.

Shand, P. M., & Bartel, L. R. (1993). *A guide to provincial music curriculum documents since 1980*. Toronto, Ontario, Canada: University of Toronto.

Shepherd, J., Virden, P., Vulliamy, G., & Wishart, T. (1977). *Whose music? A sociology of musical languages*. London: Latimer.

Shepherd, J., & Vulliamy, G. (1994). The struggle for culture: A sociological case study of the development of a national music curriculum. *British Journal of Sociology of Education, 15*(1), 27–40.

Shepherd, J., & Wicke, P. (1997). *Music and cultural theory*. Cambridge, UK: Policy Press.

Shuler, S. C. (1987). *The effects of Gordon's learning sequence activities on music achievement*. Unpublished doctoral dissertation, Eastman School of Music, University of Rochester.

Shuler, S. C. (1991a). A critical examination of the contributions of Edwin Gordon's music learning theory to the music education profession. *Quarterly Journal of Music Teaching and Learning, 2*(1/2), 37–58.

Shuler, S. C. (1991b). The effects of Gordon's learning sequence activities on vocal performance achievement of primary music students. *Quarterly Journal of Music Teaching and Learning, 2*(1/2), 118–129.

Sibbald, M. J. M. (1989). *A humanistic approach to Discipline-Based Music Education*. Unpublished doctoral dissertation, University of Illinois at Urbana-Champaign.

Siemens, M. T. (1969). A comparison of Orff and traditional instructional methods in music. *Journal of Research in Music, 17*(3), 272–285.

Silver Burdett & Ginn. (1995). *The music connection*. Parsippany, NJ: Author.

Siverson, G. W. (1990). *An examination of the extent to which senior high school band programs reflect aesthetic and utilitarian goals*. Unpublished doctoral dissertation, University of Miami, Coral Gables, Florida.

Small, C. (1998). *Musicking: The meanings of performing and listening*. Hanover, NH: Wesleyan University Press.

Stake, R., Bresler, L., & Mabrey, L. (1991). *Custom & cherishing: The arts in elementary schools*. Urbana: University of Illinois at Urbana-Champaign.

Stake, R., & Easley, J. (Eds.). (1978). *Case studies in science education*. Urbana: Center for Instructional Research and Curriculum Evaluation, University of Illinois at Urbana-Champaign.

Staton, B., Staton, M., Lawrence, V., Jothen, M., & Knorr, J. (1988). *Music and you*. New York: Macmillan.

Stevens, M. H. (1992). The comparative effectiveness of a traditional approach versus an approach based on Gordon's skill learning sequence on beginning wind instrumentalists' ability to play a song by ear. *Pennsylvania Bulletin of Research in Music Education, 18,* 50–64.

Stokes, A. A. (1996). Is Edwin Gordon's learning theory a cognitive one? *Philosophy of Music Education Review, 4*(2), 96–106.

Stowasser, H. (1993). Some personal observations of music education in Australia, North America and Great Britain. *International Journal of Music Education, 22,* 14–28.

Strange, C. M. (1990). *The development of a beginning violin curriculum integrating a computer station with the principles of comprehensive musicianship*. Unpublished doctoral dissertation, Columbia University Teachers College, New York.

Swanwick, K. (1979). *A basis for music education*. Windsor, UK: NFER.

Swanwick, K. (1988). *Music, mind and education*. London: Routledge & Kegan Paul.

Swanwick, K. (1989). Music in schools: A study of context and curriculum practice. *British Journal of Music Education, 6*(2), 155–171.

Swanwick, K. (1991). Further research on the musical development sequence. *Psychology of Music, 19*(1), 22–32.

Swanwick, K. (1992). *Music education and the National Curriculum*. London: Tufnell Press.

Swanwick, K. (1994). *Musical knowledge: Intuition, analysis, and music education*. London: Routledge & Kegan Paul.

Swanwick, K. (1997). Assessing musical quality in the National Curriculum. *British Journal of Music Education, 14*(3), 205–215.

Swanwick, K. (1999). *Teaching music musically*. London: Routledge & Kegan Paul.

Swanwick, K., & Franca, C. C. (1999). Composing, performing and audience-listening as indicators of musical understanding. *British Journal of Music Education, 16*(1), 5–19.

Swanwick, K., & Tillman, J. (1986). The sequence of musical development: A study of children's compositions. *British Journal of Music Education, 3*(3), 305–339.

Sweeney, S. E. (1993). *Music in the national curriculum: Implications of assessment for pupils, teachers and schools*. Unpublished doctoral dissertation, University of Bath, United Kingdom.

Thomas, R. B. (1970). Rethinking the curriculum. *Music Educators Journal, 56*(6), 70.

Thompson, W. (1974). *Comprehensive musicianship through classroom music*. Belmont, CA: Addison-Wesley.

Townsend, K. C. (1998). *The beginning string class: Exemplary curricular content and processes in selected Indiana middle/junior high schools*. Unpublished doctoral dissertation, Ball State University, Muncie, Indiana.

Tyler, R. W. (1949). *Basic principles of curriculum and instruction*. Chicago: University of Chicago Press.

Upitis, R. (1987). Toward a model for rhythm development. In J. C. Peery, I. W. Peery, & T. W. Draper (Eds.), *Music and child development* (pp. 54–79). New York: Springer-Verlag.

Upitis, R. (1992). *Can I play you my song? The compositions and invented notation of children*. Portsmouth, NH: Heinemann Educational Books.

Volk, T. (1998). *Music, education, and multiculturalism*. New York: Oxford University Press.

Vulliamy, G., & Shepherd, J. (1984). The application of a critical sociology to music education. *British Journal of Music Education, 1*(3), 247–266.

Vygotsky, L. S. (1962). *Thought and language*. (E. Hanfmann & G. Vaker, Trans.). Cambridge, MA: MIT Press.

Vygotsky, L. S. (1978). *Mind in society*. Cambridge, MA: Harvard University Press.

Walker, D., & Lambert, L. (1995). Learning and leading theory: A century in the making. In L. Lambert, D. Walker, D. P. Zimmerman, J. E. Cooper, M. D. Lambert, M. E. Gardner, & P. J. Ford Slack (Eds.), *The constructivist reader* (pp. 1–27). New York: Teachers College Press.

Walker, D. F. (1992). Methodological issues in curriculum research. In P. W. Jackson (Ed.), *Handbook of research on curriculum* (pp. 98–118). New York: Macmillan.

Walker, R. (1990). *Musical beliefs: Psychoacoustic, mythical, and educational perspectives*. New York: Teachers College Press.

Walker, R. (1996). Music education freed from colonialism: A new praxis. *International Journal of Education, 27*, 2–15.

Whitener, W. T. (1980). *An experimental study of a comprehensive approach to beginning instruction in instrumental music*. Unpublished doctoral dissertation, Indiana University, Bloomington.

Wiggins, J. (2001). *Teaching for musical understanding*. New York: McGraw-Hill.

Wiggins, J., & Bodoin, K. (1998). Painting a big soup: Teaching and learning in a second-grade general music classroom. *Journal of Research in Music Education, 46*(2), 281–302.

Wilson, B. (1997). *The quiet evolution: Changing the face of arts education*. Los Angeles: Getty Education Institute for the Arts.

Wing, L. B. (1992). Curriculum and its study. In R. J. Colwell (Ed.), *Handbook of research on music teaching and learning: A project of the Music Educators National Conference* (pp. 196–217). New York: Schirmer Books.

Wing, L. B. (Ed.). (1999). *Mountain Lake reader: Conversations on the study and practice of music teaching*. Manhattan, KS: AG Press.

Woodford, P. (1996). Evaluating Edwin Gordon's music learning theory from a critical thinking perspective. *Philosophy of Music Education Review, 4*(2), 83–95.

9 Theory, Research, and the Improvement of Music Education

IAN WESTBURY

The quest to identify a kind of knowledge that enjoys a privileged status over commonsense perceptions and understandings of the world has been pursued since the very beginnings of reflections about how we know. The record of responses to that quest provides a capsule summary of the major moments in the history of human speculation. The idea of the Good, the authority of Revelation, the clear and distinct truths of geometry, the controlled outcomes of investigation, the self-understandings by humans of human projects, the demystified grasp of real historic forces, the quantification of metric operations, the analysis of unconscious expressions, the enlightenment that follows disciplined meditation—these are some of the well-known candidates for that privileged position.

Donald N. Levine,
"The Forms and Functions of Social Knowledge"

Theoretical knowledge of how children develop continues to grow but just how to relate this knowledge to the practical contexts in which adults intentionally and systematically intervene to foster this development, in a word, educate, remains almost as mysterious as when such efforts first began.

David R. Olson and Jerome S. Bruner,
"Folk Psychology and Folk Pedagogy"

Like their colleagues in the other fields of educational theory and research, most researchers and theorists in music education assume that as the knowledge and insights that they provide the field become incorporated as best practices in schools, the improvement or at least the enhancement of music education will result. They believe that their work offers, to use the term from the epigraph from Levine's (1986) essay, a *privileged* foundation for better curricula and ways of teaching.[1] This chapter will seek to problematize that assumption. I will take as my starting point and as my given that neither the basic or applied research of education nor the theory building of the field

has had or is having any discernible systemic effects on music teaching in either schools or studios. And how theory and research might have such an impact remains, as Olson and Bruner (1998) remind us, "almost as mysterious as when such efforts first began." I will be arguing here that this situation is inevitable because the vision of a foundational theory and research that lead to a better practice within schooling is *in principle* unrealizable.

My argument is grounded in the *praxial* movement within educational theory, which has been well outlined for music educators by, for example, McCarthy (1999). However, I will not be seeking here to extend or develop the base for the praxial perspective insofar as it bears on music education. Instead I will direct the perspective toward both the metatheory of educational theory and research and the school, the institution that hosts much of the work of music education. I will be arguing, with Elliott (1994), that without a clear understanding of the school and schooling and its context, the seeming implications for practice of any "old" or "new" philosophy of music education, body of findings from empirical research, ambitious curriculum projects, or national curricula will run headlong into the brick wall of the institution.[2] I will be arguing that it is only as we have an appropriate understanding of the school and its people, the enveloping context of any program, that we will be in a position to engage in realistic improvement and reform in music education, science education, or whatever—and that that improving work will not be theoretical or research-based in any traditional way.

There are, of course, many discussions of the research–practice relationship that begin with the (proper) character and (proper) methods of educational theory and research, with their problems and possibilities, or with their potential role in improving practice. This chapter will start in a different place, by privileging *practice* by way of an examination of John Dewey's turn-of-the-20th-century framing of the problem of curriculum improvement. With that analysis in hand we can then go on to ask—at the turn of the 21st century—how our understanding of the problems Dewey raised a century earlier has shifted, changed, or developed and what the conclusions of such an analysis might mean for our understanding of a contemporary educational theory and research.

John Dewey's *The Educational Situation*

Dewey's question in *The Educational Situation* (1902, 1976) centered on our problem, why the then-curriculum did not seem to change despite earnest and persistent advocacy of a new vision of education, new subjects, and new ways of learning and teaching *and* the near-total acceptance of the desirability and necessity of the "reform" this acceptance foreshadowed among the leaders of teachers. As he wrote:

> The question is just this: Why do the newer studies, drawing, music, nature study, manual training, and the older studies, the three R's, practically conflict with instead of reinforcing one another? Why is it that the practical problem is so often one of outward annexation or mechanical compromise? Why is it that the adjustment of the conflict is left to the mere push and pull of contending factors, to the pressure of local circumstances and of temporary reactions? (p. 266)

The task Dewey undertook in *The Educational Situation* was to spell out his understanding of this problem. As he explored this issue, he covered a vast territory. All that can be done here is pick out some of the central arguments of one chapter of this short book, his treatment of the elementary school. My discussion will seek to highlight the reality that, 100 years later, Dewey's analysis of "the educational situation as concerns the elementary school" still holds in virtually every respect and could be readily extended to the contemporary high school. But today's modes of analysis of this same problem within curriculum research and theory—and I include here music education research and theory—are arguably less sophisticated than were Dewey's arguments of 100 years ago.

The Educational Situation begins with a trenchant analysis of the disjunction that Dewey saw between the turn-of-the-century "theory" and "practice":

> Horace Mann and the disciples of Pestalozzi did their peculiar missionary work so completely as intellectually to crowd the conservative to the wall. For half a century after their time the ethical emotion, the bulk of exhortation, the current formulae and catchwords, the distinctive principles of theory have been on the side of progress, of what is

known as reform. The supremacy of self-activity . . . the priority of character to information, the necessity of putting the real before the symbol, the concrete before the abstract . . . ; all these ideas, at the outset so revolutionary, have filtered into the pedagogical consciousness and become the commonplace of pedagogic writing and of gatherings where teachers meet for inspiration and admonition.

> It is, however, sufficiently obvious that while the reformer took possession of the field of theory and enthusiasm and preaching, the conservative . . . was holding his own pretty obstinately in the region of practice. He could afford to neglect all these sayings: nay, he could afford to take a part in a glib reiteration of the shibboleths because as a matter of fact his own work remained so largely untouched. . . . So the "great big battle" was fought with mutual satisfaction, with each side having an almost complete victory in its own field. (pp. 260–261)

However, as Dewey saw it, in the last years of the 19th century,

> The unconscious insincerity in continually turning the theory over and over in terms of itself, the unconscious self-deceit in using it simply to cast an idealized and emotional halo over a mechanical school routine with which it was fundamentally at odds, became somewhat painfully apparent. (p. 26)

As a result, new subjects had been introduced into the elementary school—for example, music, nature study, and such—but these subjects had become *additive* to the curriculum, and stood in an uneasy and fragile relationship with the traditional three R's. As a result, their priority waxed and waned depending on transitory political considerations.

The Educational Situation identifies three conditions around the curriculum of the elementary school that created this instability around the new subjects: (1) the "machinery" of the school, (2) the hold of the symbols that this machinery had created on the community's understanding of the "school," and (3) the vested interests that lived on those structures and understandings. The most important of these conditions, because it influenced community understandings of what school should be, was Dewey's "machinery," "the conditions that underlie and regulate [the contact of teacher and child and] dominate the educational situation" (p. 268), that is, the structures of the school, the graded classes, the consequent need for a concept of curricular progression, and so forth, and the resulting standards and expectations for the ordered and orderly accomplishment of learning, the "mechanics of examination and promotion," and external supervision.

As Dewey saw it, the omnipresence of this machinery created a situation in which students, teachers, and communities could never sense or experience the inherent "unity" of a truly educative encounter. And without any sense of a whole that might develop all of the powers, the three R's and what they stood for had come to define the school. They had come to represent that which was central to the work of the school, while music, art, nature study, and so forth, were at best "recreations" that could relieve the stress of the hard, but real, work of learning.[3]

However, Dewey also develops a further and very significant argument out of his observations about the absence of professional or public understanding of the unity of the truly educative experience. Because of this situation, curricula and courses of study had had to be put in place in order to coordinate from the outside the work of the school. But within such a system of coordination teachers necessarily became *agents* of the curriculum and, as agents, did not have to work through for themselves the "educative bearing" of what they were required to teach. Teachers did not have to recognize what they were: the points of contact between the forms of an evolving, integrated culture and *their* children.

Thus, while it was easy, Dewey suggested, "to fall into the habit of regarding the mechanics of school organization and administration as something comparatively external and indifferent to educational purposes and ideals" (p. 267), these mechanics defined the "school." And as he saw it, the ideologies of "reform" and "progress" collided with the school as the organized agency that "delivered" the formal curriculum. In this context these ideologies served only to give "a halo of sentiment . . . about it [i.e., the traditional curriculum], or a great wish-wash of superficiality covering up the residuum of grind" (p. 280).

Dewey concluded his chapter with an expression of his hope: "With our minds possessed by a sane and coherent view of the whole situation, we may attempt such gradual, yet positive modification of existing procedures as will enable us to turn theory into practice" (p. 280). But at the same time we must not be "too precipitate . . . in demanding light upon what to do next" (p. 280). We need *enlightened* experimentation; we need to attack the problem as reformers—"not at large and all over the entire field, but at the most promising point . . . and concentrate all . . . efforts upon educating alike the community, the teacher and the child" (p. 281). Later "blind experimentation might give way to something more directed" (p. 281).

The Educational Situation was published in 1902. One hundred years later it seems appropriate to ask (1) how the school and the public understanding of "education" that Dewey observed might have changed and (2) how our sense of appropriate strategies for educational improvement might have advanced over the cautious pragmatic experimentation that Dewey advocated. The analysis that these questions imply is, of course, the raison d'être of the study of education. But most objective contemporary observers are as pessimistic as Dewey was about what the 20th century's curricular reforms have brought in the way

of real change in the educational significance of the school experience.[4] And most objective observers are equally pessimistic both about what educational research's analyses of the educational situation have yielded and about the efficacy of its understandings about the improvement of education. How might we understand this situation?

Research and Theory as Foundation for Practice

[This book] has attempted to develop a philosophy that explains the nature and significance of music education. . . .
    The next main question is this: How can music educators organize music programs that are congruent with the nature and values of MUSIC as a diverse human practice?
    Implicit in this praxial philosophy is a distinctive concept of curriculum . . . *all* music programs . . . ought to be organized and taught as reflective musical practicums.
            David J. Elliott, Music Matters: A New Philosophy
            of Music Education *(emphasis in original)*

Dewey's perspective in *The Educational Situation* reflected his philosophical pragmatism, with its rejection of both privileged starting points for analysis and "certainty," and its concern for experimentalism in a world. Thought and knowledge did not yield, for Dewey, privileged and necessary starting points, or "foundations," for a practice that stood outside the immediate world of practical action. Instead thinking is itself an action and is found within all problem solving. Thought as a particular form of action is an instrument of what he termed *enlightenment*, and a source of perspective within every practice. It is then curious, although given Dewey's own analysis in *The Educational Situation* not surprising, that "Dewey" as a foundational icon, a symbol of a body of ideas outside of but foundational to action, was to come to replace his icons of Horace Mann and Pestalozzi as *the* 20th-century symbol for progressive educational "reform" and "progress." Today, of course, Dewey's iconic place remains, but he has been joined by social theorists such as Jürgen Habermas, Michel Foucault, and Paolo Freire, psychologists such as Jerome Bruner, Jean Piaget, and Lev Vygotsky, aestheticians and philosophers of art such as Suzanne Langer and Harry Broudy, and others—as well as by a host of those who advocate the foundational facticity of music, learning, skills, intelligence(s), aptitude(s), motivation, class, race/ethnicity, gender, sexuality, culture, and so on.

The 20th-century assimilation of "Dewey" as a "foundational theorist" who offers a starting point for educational thinking reflects the kind of understanding of educational theory and research illustrated in the epigraph to this section.[5] All through the century's educational thinking, a first-theory/then-practice model has defined theorists and researchers', and the research university's, self-understanding of their fundamental contribution to educational improvement. Within this understanding, "theory," whether psychological, philosophic, socioeconomic, musicological, sociocultural, and so forth, serves as the starting point for all significant and potentially fundamental thinking about curricula, teaching, and learning. As Abeles, Hoffer, and Klotman (1994) put it: "From the *basic* [italics added] academic disciplines of history, philosophy, psychology and sociology, music teachers utilize and synthesize information and beliefs to come up with what they think is the *best* [italics added] way to teach a song or instrumental work" (p. 2).

The process by which "theory" and its companion "research" attained this sense of legitimate privilege as ways of thinking about "practice"—as well as the contests over which theory and which field had a "true" foundational status in relation to practice—can be seen in different ways. However, in her historical exploration of this issue Cruikshank (1998) points to the central consequences of the distinction that Grace Bibb, one the first professors of pedagogy in the United States, made in 1882 between an approach to thinking about education and teacher education based on the "science" side of education, that is, "a grasp of all the conditions of the problem of education," and the "art" side, that is, the basing of teaching on the results of experience. Reflecting the world of education in the 19th-century university, Bibb saw the "art side" as the limited sphere of the then-normal school, with the "science" of education being the concern of the university and of university-prepared teachers. Abbott's (1988) understanding of the professions suggests that we see Bibb's preoccupation with theory as a reflection of the search by university-based teacher educators for a distinct "jurisdiction," that is, a sphere of professional authority grounded in a legitimated expertise. But as Abbott emphasizes, such a claim for a jurisdiction has to be accepted by the "relevant publics." Such acceptance has been the sticking point for the practitioners of research and theory; the publics of educational theory and research, including teachers, have not accepted the claim that research and theory offer a distinctively powerful way of thinking about the practice or the improvement of schools and curricula.

But in addition to the professionalizing issues Abbott's analysis suggests lay behind advocacy like Bibb's of a science of education, there is also an important set of more explicitly epistemological preoccupations that circled around this late-19th-century idea of a "science" of education and remain with us today to lie behind the contemporary theory/action "problem."

When one views curricular thought in terms of the grand sweep of history, the conventional approach is to see its beginnings in the world of antiquity. As this tradition of curricular thought became elaborated, it came to offer a habitual and largely unexamined intellectual form for thinking about education and schooling (see Hopmann, 1999). An ideal curriculum is imagined, constructed, sketched, and so forth, on the basis of one or another authoritative starting point, and this ideal then becomes a template or standard against which the actual work of schools can be measured and judged and which it can be expected to mirror. It is this form, as a starting point for educational thought, that gives the idea of curriculum its special importance and significance in educational discourse. The curriculum becomes the point of mediation between an idea of education and practice. As Wing (1992) puts it, the curriculum and curriculum thinking "provide a central point of departure for considering, first, what schools are intentionally about and, second, how these intents are realized" (p. 196). As education emerged as a discipline in the 19th century, particularly in Germany, this idealistic and idealizing tradition of discourse was to define the subject. This model of education as a field entered the U.S. university in the second half of the 19th century—to be reflected in Grace Bibb's view of the "science" of education—and, as I have been suggesting, mutations of this transplant continue to define educational theory and research.

We can see the character of this "scientific," foundational approach to thinking about education in William Torrey Harris's edition of J. K. F. Rosenkranz's *Philosophy of Education*[6] (1892). Thus Harris (the volume includes many of his glosses on the translation of Rosenkranz's text) sets out what he sees as the proper scope of rationale for the "science" in the following way. After presenting Rosenkranz's statement that "the formulae of teaching are admirable material upon which to apply the science, but are not the science itself," Harris adds the gloss that

> the science of education distinguished from the art of education: the former containing the abstract general treatment, and the latter taking into consideration all the conditions of concrete individuality, e.g., the peculiarities of the teacher and the pupil. . . .
>
> *The special conditions and peculiarities considered in education as an art may be formulated and reduced to system, but they should not be introduced as a part of the science of education* [italics added]. (p. 13)[7]

It is Harris's conception that is reflected in the epigraph to this section from *Music Matters*. And as seen in Table 9.1, this framework is also mirrored in the emphases, the structure, and the sequence of topics in the first *Handbook of Research on Music Teaching and Learning* (Colwell, 1992). Dewey's concern for the "machinery" of education has only a marginal place in such a conception of education as a scholarly field. It is a surface *outside* the scope of the "science," that is, educational theory and research.

Table 9.1. Conceptual and rhetorical structure of the *Handbook of Research on Music Teaching and Learning: A Project of the Music Educators National Conference* (Colwell, 1992).

Section A: Conceptual Framework

Section B: Research Modes and Techniques

Section C: Evaluation

Section D: Perception of Cognition

Section E: Teaching and Learning Strategies

Section F: The Teaching of Specific Musical Skills and Knowledge in Different Instructional Settings

Section G: Schools/Curriculum

Section H: Social and Institutional Contexts

Cruikshank (1998) observes that the turn-of-the-20th-century debate between Harris and the American Herbartians about the nature of the appropriate theory of education centered on whether or not there would be one approach—that is, Harris's—or several approaches. The debate did not question the nature or special place of educational theory and research or the implication that they could and should yield a "standard" against which the "art" of schooling might be measured. Harris's position lost the debate, and, as a result, the child study, Herbartianism, behaviorism, progressivism, and social reconstructionism of the prewar years and the contemporary cognitivism, reconceptualism, postmodernism, feminism, race theory, and such have contested among themselves within the academy. *But the proponents of all of these theoretical schools shared, and share, the common vision that theirs is the standard-setting and privileged understanding that is foundational to the "mere" surface of the art or craft of teaching.*

As I have suggested, we see this perspective well expressed in the structure of David Elliott's (1995) *Music Matters,* a "philosophical *foundation* [italics added] for educating people towards the fullest understanding and enjoyment of music making and music listening" (p. vii). *Music Matters* is built around music as the starting point for thinking about music teaching and learning and begins by setting out its questions:

- What is music? Is music significant in human life? If so, why?
- What is music education? Does music education deserve a secure place in general education? Why?
- If cogent answers to these questions could be developed, what would this mean for the organization and conduct of music teaching and learning? (p. 3)

The answers to the first and second cluster of these questions define Elliott's standard for music education, which

will, or should, find expression in "the organization and conduct of music teaching and learning," that is, in what Bibb and Harris termed the *art* of teaching.

But in order to secure a critical perspective on the intellectual tradition Elliott's questions mirror we need to recognize the underlying assumptions of the form and order of argument they reflect. Thus Hopmann (1999) points out that the idea of a curriculum-as-a-standard requires three premises:

- teaching can and should be planned, and schools can bring about the planned outcome;
- what is known can be taught, and what is taught can be learned; and
- what is learned corresponds to its effects.

He demonstrates that, despite their centrality to the standard-seeking form of curriculum argument, none of these premises has been realizable!

There is yet another presumption that lurks behind discourse around the role of theory and research in education and must also be highlighted. But to see the force of this presumption, we need to acknowledge the sociotechnical complexity and thus significance of the day-by-day routines of teaching and learning, of, say, singing and choral music, gospel, orchestra, band, jazz, musical theater, composition, improvisation, or whatever. The situational inventiveness and entrepreneurship required for the development, enhancement, and diffusion of such now-routine forms created, of course, most, if not all, of what happens in the school (see Abeles, Hoffer & Klotman, 1994: chap. 1; Britton, 1991). But such inventiveness and entrepreneurship do not require a "theory" of education or a body of empirical results to give its outcomes a justification or rationale within the schools or their communities. They emerge from the tradition and culture of school music and from the narratives of the teachers and communities concerned; the ideas and technologies that emerge are tested and survive, or die, depending on how the stories that surround these initiatives are received and accepted in the worlds of the schools (see Clandinin & Connelly, 1995). *But within the foundational perspective such inventiveness and entrepreneurship reflect ways of thinking that, in the absence of the specification of a theoretical rationale, lack any real significance.*[8] And by virtue of this denial of significance, a vast stream of activity falls into invisibility from within the perspective of educational research and theory. I will return to this theme later in this chapter.

In short, as it has been defined within the university, the theory/practice problem that is the concern of this chapter has not been seen as one of incorporating an understanding of either Dewey's "machinery" of the school or the landscape of "practice" *within* theory. Instead the curriculum-oriented work of the theory and research communities has been (self-)imaged as the export of foundational curriculum or instructional theory(ies) *to* the surface of practice. However, this presumes that the "theories" or the "standards" to be exported do and can fit the context of practice. As Hopmann (1999) emphasizes, they do not. Let us turn to some of the problems that this idea of the export of the theory of the researcher into practice encounters in the world of the schools.

Exploring Curriculum Practice

Much, if not most, theory building and research within curriculum studies and music education can still be seen either as what Dewey termed exhortation and the articulation of ethical emotion or as attempts to spell out or debate one or another understanding of a curriculum-as-a-standard. However, there are important strands within the field that are not normative and that seek, from historical or empirical points of view, to understand the school and the curriculum as phenomena. Rather than simply accepting conventional, often normative, conceptions of the curriculum and the school, such work seeks an analytic perspective on schooling as a social and cultural institution and of the place of the curriculum within schooling. And we must always remember that with the historical absence of systems of schools that perfectly or imperfectly embody any curriculum standard, it is the interaction of real-world students with this real-world institutional surface, warts and all, that has always brought about, and brings about, the values we associate with the idea of education.

The best-known stream of such work has sought to understand the relationship between the curriculum and its school, social, and cultural environments, most typically focusing on the ways in which the people-processing function/task of the school as an institution intersects with the cultural-processing function/task. This perspective accepts the fact that parents and students always use the school for their own ends and assumes that social reproduction, that is, the reproduction of social and economic structures, is related to an accompanying cultural reproduction.

In the English-speaking world, such work has had its most characteristic expression in the research of the British "new sociology of education." And in music education this tradition had a distinguished instantiation in the 1970s and 1980s in the important work of Graham Vulliamy and his colleagues (see Shepherd & Vulliamy, 1983; Vulliamy, 1977, 1978; Vulliamy & Shepherd, 1984, 1985). The tradition has been extended and developed more recently in an important but very different way by Swanwick (1993, 1998).

The initial concern of the "new" sociology of the curriculum was, to use a contemporary term, "deconstruc-

tionist"—it sought to demystify the high-status English grammar school, that is, academic secondary school, and its curriculum, along with the presumption that the grammar school was a socially neutral, meritocratic institution accessible to anyone who had the appropriate "ability." In particular, this project sought to see the "curriculum" as an instrumentality for social and cultural reproduction by examining the phenomenology of the classroom. Curricula and teaching practices were seen as the products of highly structured interactions on the part of students and teachers within the hidden curriculum of the classroom.

Thus, as Vulliamy (1977) pointed out, what counted as music in the schools he observed instantiated a host of taken-for-granted cultural assumptions about what counted as "good" music and what constituted an "appropriate" response to such music. And he saw an unexamined emphasis on musical "literacy" rather than "sounds" converting music into a cultural discipline rather than a creative *activity*. This embedding of musical literacy in an honored tradition of listening to "serious" music also excluded many students from active engagement with music—and many such students became discipline problems in the music classroom as a result of their nonresponsiveness to the "legitimate" classroom activities. The music program was, in other words, profoundly implicated with issues of social and cultural control and, by extension, reproduction.[9]

In a fundamentally important essay that reflected this tradition, Basil Bernstein (1971) sought to order and systematize Vulliamy's kind of interest in the embedded "hidden" structures of classroom by distinguishing the ways in which school knowledge was (1) "classified," that is, the boundaries, that is, "strong" or "weak," between bodies of knowledge, such as serious and pop music, and (2) "framed," that is, who has control of the modes of acquisition of this knowledge, that is, teachers or students. Given the sociology of the time, Bernstein saw the patterns of classroom work that derived from this typology as reflections of social and class cultures—seeing, in particular, the preference for "weak classification" and "weak framing" that was and is the hallmark of educational progressivism as a preference of a "modern" knowledge-using cultural élite. However, classification and framing are distinct concepts in Bernstein's formal typology, with the implication that all combinations of his categories can be observed. Bernstein's scheme has, in other words, implications for thinking about cultural *production* as well as reproduction.

For example, writing some 20 years after the publication of Bernstein's classic essays his colleague Keith Swanwick (1993) drew on his typology to highlight and extend the inevitability of classification and framing in the institutionalized setting of the school:

When music making and music taking are abstracted from everyday psychological and cultural life, becoming institutionalized in schools and colleges, it becomes necessary to make decisions as to *what* music is included or excluded and *how* teaching and learning are to be managed. . . . The issue is, therefore, not *whether* but *how* musical knowledge might be classified and framed. (pp. 148, 151, emphasis in original)

The ways in which classification and framing are ordered within particular places reflect both the preferences of the social and cultural communities (and subcommunities) that engage with both schools at large and each school—the thrust of Bernstein's (1971) original analysis—and, as Swanwick highlights, the inherent needs for a workable classification and framing that derive from the institutional "needs" of the school situation itself. Public performance by bands and choirs, which communities might expect, will almost inevitably involve strong classification in terms of repertoire and strong framing in terms of rehearsal as a directed practice[10]—which can work against the internalization of musical understanding or appreciation (Swanwick, 1998). The impulse of teachers to make music "relevant" leads to experiments with popular music—but such music must be "fitted" to the school. The musical and social form of popular music must be abstracted and analyzed—and given a school and curricular interpretation: "The loudness levels (and the impact) is reduced, dancing is impractical and the cultural context is shorn away" (Swanwick, 1998). In other words, the viewpoint Swanwick draws from Bernstein (1971) gives the "surface" of the school a significance that it does not have in the foundational perspective and, as he suggests, yields very different basic curriculum questions than the traditional and foundational "What music is of most worth?": "Is it possible to structure a music curriculum without neutralizing musical experience?" "How can musical knowledge be classified and framed?" (Swanwick, 1993, pp. 148, 151; see also Wolf, 1992, p. 955).

Governance of the Curriculum

As Dewey emphasized in *The Educational Situation*, the curriculum has become the necessary instrument of coordination of the work of the public systems of schools. In that U.S. public schools are governed by public authorities, these authorities, by definition, have the right and the obligation to direct this curriculum in the public interest. Furthermore, it is assumed that public and political decision making about the curriculum, that is, curriculum policy making, directs and in a sense *animates* the work of schools. This overt public control of the curriculum is, of course, largely symbolic. However, the idea of an authoritative curriculum has had considerable significance for the

theory and research community: If theory and research are to have any practical significance for schools, the assumption of a (professionally) directed curriculum that mediates between a theory and a practice is a convenient, and some would say necessary, starting point.

This view of the curriculum as directing the work of teachers in the classroom finds its clearest expression in notions like the distinction between *intended* and *implemented* curricula and the all too common gap between the two (see Regelski, 1999). Thus sometimes—some would say more often than not—teachers and schools fail to do what policy-making elites and experts expect or direct them to do. This can be seen as the results of either an unfortunate "slippage" between intention and realization or "resistance" by communities, schools, and teachers. Slippage is then seen as the result of a failure in the methods of implementation of the curriculum or a curriculum policy, of a lack of "capacity" to realize the curriculum on the part of communities, teachers, and schools, and so forth, or of failures in the larger system of policy implementation, which better approaches can overcome. Resistance is seen as an unfortunate nuisance, largely attributable to teachers' lack of commitment to or understanding of their organizational obligations. However, the existence of such slippage and resistance has not been seen as a reason to question the idea of a (potentially) authoritative curriculum as a formally mandated standard or prescription.

Over the past decade, however, in reaction to the failures of virtually all curriculum reform movements in the three decades from the 1960s to the 1980s,[11] the assumption of a simple hierarchical relationship between an authoritative curriculum and school practice has been exposed to sustained conceptual and empirical analysis. This analysis has resulted in attempts to explore what curricula are, along with a parallel concern for how they relate to school practice.[12] One outcome is the awareness of the pervasively symbolic nature of curricula and the related national curriculum projects.

A similar and parallel shift in understandings has affected discussions of curriculum policy making by elites and experts. And as the focus of discussion has moved from the factors that surround the implementation, or nonimplementation, of discrete reforms to the more global notion of the effectiveness of schools, the analytic web has widened. With this widening a new awareness has emerged about the ranges of meaning associated with the ideas of curriculum, curriculum policy, and curriculum policy making.[13]

Nevertheless, the organizational assumption that if a range of appropriate policy instruments[14] could be engaged by the appropriate centers in the appropriate ways improvement in curricula and teaching practices could result continues, as seen in the contemporary political and academic advocacy, and the related policy making, around, say, "diversity" and/or multiculturalism or systemic, standards-based reform (see, e.g. Colwell, 1999; Daugherty, 1995). In other words, the turn-of-the-century assumption that Dewey identified in *The Educational Situation*—that what happens in the school can be and should be directed, animated, and coordinated by the policies of governing or expert centers—persists. But do curricula or policy in fact direct teaching in practice?

If they do, how do they do so?[15] As Cuban (1999) suggests, the first question is what is a "curriculum"?

Doyle (1992) has sought to disentangle and order the idea of curriculum and contends that "curriculum" and curricular discussion can be seen occurring at two distinct levels of schooling: (1) at *institutional* levels and (2) at the *classroom* level. At the institutional level curricular discussions emerge in two distinct arenas:

- at the intersection between schooling, culture and society, that is, the *policy level,* and
- in the specification of "content" for and in schools, school types, and tracks with their subject elements, cores and electives, credits, and so forth, and then in the construction of appropriate "content" for classroom use within these subjects, that is, the *programmatic level.*

At the *classroom level,* a quite different kind of curriculum and curricular reflection, discussion, and argument is seen as the programmatic curriculum is elaborated and then connected to the worlds of real, flesh-and-blood students and events of the classroom.

Doyle observes—and this observation is critical to his understanding of curriculum discourses—that discussion of curricula at the *policy level* centers on images, metaphors, and narratives as reified typifications of what is thought to happen in a school, what McEneaney and Meyer (2000) call the "ideal norms of an *imagined* social enterprise" (p. 195, emphasis added). However, such idealizing reifications are fundamentally important because they embody conceptions of what is thought to be desirable in a social and cultural order, what is and should be valued and sought after by members of a community. Discussion, debate, and planning around curriculum "policies," and the public and professional processes involved in such planning, are a social form for clarifying social, cultural, and professional norms and for considering the role schooling as an idea should play in realizing social and cultural images. Within the school system, the varied typifications around the institutional curriculum that are available at any time provide, as one or another language is embraced, languages that school people and publics can use to redefine the images of the school and the curriculum that they present to meet changing social and cultural circumstances.[16]

The *programmatic* or *organizational curriculum,* the framework for organizing the routine delivery of the service of schooling, involves political and cultural processes through which an educational and curricular vision is translated into an operational framework for systems of schools and into an understanding of what social, cultural, and educational images mean for the character of work in classrooms. At this level the process of constructing curricula-as-programs is grounded in socially embedded arguments and presumptions that rationalize the selection and deployment of subjects and their elements, that is, performance, musical appreciation, and so forth, for schools and classes of particular types as well as the transformation of that content into school subjects appropriate to those schools or school types. But the link between such organizational curricula and actual classroom teaching continues to remain indirect. This organizational and programmatic work addresses an image of teaching rather than teaching itself. Teaching is still characterized as dependent on a reified organizational ideology or program.

At the *classroom level,* the curriculum is quite different. Like work of an artist with a score, it is a sequence of events, initiated by the teacher and jointly developed by teachers and students, that reflects an understanding on the part of teachers, students, and parents of the potential for them of the programmatic curriculum. At this level teachers are not so much "agents" as interpreters of the institutional and programmatic curriculum-as-text. They shape the views of that curriculum that are allowed, they guide students through the topics and experiences that constitute *their* curriculum, and, importantly, they define the tasks that students are to accomplish in their classes. Teachers' classroom curricula and their understandings of what they are doing may or may not be well articulated with the curriculum at the policy and programmatic levels.

Hopmann (1999) has extended Doyle's emphasis on the loose coupling of curricular discourse by offering the important additional insight, drawn from contemporary systems theory, that these discourses occur in autonomous and self-referential domains, *not* at nested higher and lower "levels." Thus Hopmann emphasizes the extent to which discussion and decision making at the policy level define only negatively—by offering or withholding resources, and so forth—the degrees of freedom at the programmatic and classroom levels. Policy work does not direct affirmatively what is done there.

However, as Hopmann emphasizes (and this insight is central to his analysis), the myth that policy is directive does make it possible for managers of public school systems to use curricula and curriculum policy making to order the often-turbulent interface among the cultures around the school, the school as an institution that is subject to political forces, and the day-to-day work of classrooms. And he goes on to suggest that it is the central task of institutionalized curriculum making at state and central district levels to draw on this myth to manage these interfaces in ways that, when successful, maintain both the necessary equilibrium around the school and stability within the school. In this view, the essential task or function of central, that is, national, state, and district, curriculum making is to put a culturally salient (symbolic) gloss on the ("unreformed") day-to-day work of the schools. This is done via curricula and courses of study that present ongoing practice in ways that are culturally and politically appropriate. In arguing in this way, Hopmann is emphasizing what he sees as the reality that schools and teachers do not and cannot accept or accommodate frequent fundamental changes in the content and forms of teaching. Curriculum makers know this and, as agents of school systems, work to preserve the legitimacy of the stable, routine practices of their schools by, paradoxically, asserting the symbolic reality of change and reform!

Theory to Practice or Practice to Theory?

The contemporary understanding of the political, cultural, and institutional web that constitutes the idea and institution of the school, the inevitability of its pervasive role in both social and cultural reproduction, and the complexities around the idea of curriculum making vitiate any simple understanding of the relationship between a philosophy and theory of, say, music education or research and practice. The relationships and links between a theory and practice can never be direct; there are no clear distinctions to be made between interdependent basic, technological, and applied levels of work that map onto real phenomena. The conclusions of theory and the findings of research are never (and can never be) exported in any straightforward way from the world of studies to the world of policy and then to the world of practice—because there is no curriculum and no directed practice to be changed in any simple way. Indeed, the curriculum is not a thing but a pervasive symbolic web that holds the institution of the school together in political and organizational mythology.

But if this is the case, what might be the alternative to the foundational theory/research tradition that might promise what that now-dominant tradition has failed to achieve, the capacity to change *in fact* what schools do? That task remains. What role might "thought," that is, theory and research, play in that alternative?

In a landmark essay, first published in 1969, Joseph J. Schwab (1978) opened up this problem by pointing to what he saw as the irrelevance of educational research and educational theory to the enhancement or improvement of schooling. As he saw it, if the idea that research and theory contributes to the systemic improvement of schools pro-

vides the raison d'être of the enterprise, this irrelevance constitutes a crisis for educational research and theory.

Schwab attributed the failure of the projects of both educational theory and research to their overwhelmingly "theoretical" perspective, to what I have described here as their idealizing and foundational, that is, standard-seeking, characters. The necessary concern of any theoretical project for the "essential," the "universal"—with the resulting need for the "science" of education to abstract away both the surface of teaching and schools and the complexity that inheres in their inevitably artful and sociotechnical character—rendered the traditional project irrelevant to what he saw as the fundamentally local character of school improvement. If it is to have any local impact, educational improvement must focus on the experience of, in his words, "this student, in that school, on the south side of Columbus, with Principal Jones during the present mayoralty of Ed Tweed and in view of the probability of his reelection" (p. 289). As an alternative to foundational research and theory building, Schwab argued for a conceptualization of educational and curriculum research that, following the Aristotelian tradition, he termed practical and deliberative, and which has been termed *praxial* in the philosophies around contemporary music education.[17]

In other words, Schwab claimed, as Eraut (1989) puts it, "*on epistemological grounds* [italics added] that a scientific [i.e., theory and research] approach to curriculum development is *impossible*" [italics added] (p. 321). In this sense, his paper was a fundamental critique of the entire 20th-century tradition of educational research and theory, and one that struck at its very heart. But Schwab's thesis can be also seen as predicting and as formalizing the contemporary leading edge of thinking about the improvement of schooling. His project, for example, foreshadowed the praxial turn in the philosophy of music education in every respect, albeit without its "critical" cast, but did this in a way that Bowman (in press–b) identifies as *the* need within the praxial movement in music education, to address the systemic and local complexities of schooling as the context of all (school) music teaching with the same zeal that the movement has given the task of understanding music.[18]

We can see what such a development and extension of the philosophy of music praxialism might imply by drawing on the parallels that Gravemeijer and Terwel (2000) describe between Schwab's conception of a practical/praxial curriculum theory and research and the project of his near-contemporary the distinguished Dutch mathematics educator Hans Freudenthal. As Gravemeijer and Terwel write, like "but independently from" Schwab, Freudenthal

stressed the practical character of curriculum work and the process of dialogue between curriculum specialists and teachers. [He] was against any fixed curricular system, and he fiercely opposed content being bottled and funneled into schemes and structures. (p. 791)

Describing his approach as *developmental research* or *educational development*, Freudenthal focused on the prototyping, developing, and testing of materials and approaches that could foster actual and immediate change in ongoing classroom teaching. Although his overall project was animated by a perspective, or platform, on mathematics that he termed the mathematizing of everyday activity, *theory* in mathematics education was for Freudenthal only a by-product of local, practical work. His *research* program was, in effect, a program of formative evaluation, emphasizing qualitative/interpretative approaches to understanding what happened in teaching experiments in individual classrooms. Gravemeijer and Terwel (2000) suggest that Freudenthal's work did in fact change the teaching of mathematics in Dutch schools.

The movement into naturalistic learning environments within the cognitivist paradigm has also moved toward a position that might be thought of as reminiscent of a "practical" reconceptualization of the theory–practice relationship. Moving from an enhanced awareness of the distributed nature of cognition (J. S. Brown, Collins, & Duiguid, 1989; Engeström & Middleton, 1996; Starr, 1996) and its situated, interactive character, the cognitivist community has begun to emphasize that learning is necessarily a process of internalizing patterns of action, ways of thinking, and such, which are initially practiced in interaction with others at the complex social and organizational surface of the purposeful action that is found in the classroom and school. In this view, curriculum development and change become situated, distributed, interactive processes by which researchers and teachers jointly assume responsibility for instantiating platforms for new curricula and teaching practices in real contexts. This "new" paradigm is also termed *developmental* research: "the kind of research that includes developmental work in designing learning environments, formulating curricula, and assessing achievements of cognition and learning, and simultaneously, efforts to contribute to fundamental scientific understanding" (Greeno, Collins, & Resnick, 1996, p. 41; see also A. L. Brown, 1992; Greeno et al., 1999).

Van den Akker, Branch, Gustafson, Nieveen, and Plomp (1999; see also Walker, 1992) have sought to draw the threads of all of these contemporary movements together under the overall rubric of *design research*.[19] Curriculum research becomes, in their view, a *design science* that informs the decision-making process during the development of a product or program. Such a design science seeks to develop ways to improve both an immediate product or program as well as the developer's *capabilities*. Like the developmental research of Freudenthal and the cognitivists, the design science of van den Akker et al. (1999) puts at the center of attention the "surfaces" of the program and school that the traditional theory and research project had abstracted away. And rather than seeing research and theory as offering a foundation for what Grace Bibb and William Torrey Harris called the *art* of teaching, real-world and real-time teaching and schooling come to the fore, with "theory," providing a *platform*[20] or starting point for reflection within the ongoing context of purposeful, relevant, and situated action.

In addition to their focus on design-centered, evaluation-based principles for curriculum and program design, van den Akker et al. (1999) also draw on Schwab's *deliberative* understanding of curriculum work to emphasize the communicative nature of all curriculum development and improvement, that is, the need to achieve a real, working consensus among the immediate community around any curriculum or program about what the problem is that a proposed program is meant to address. Thus Visscher-Voerman, Gustafson, and Plomp (1999; see also Kessels & Plomp, 2000) highlight Walker's (1990) emphasis on the need to "develop sensitivity to the moral and legal rights and obligations of all affected by a decision and [to] learn to arrange deliberation in ways that consider the particular human and institutional context without undue threat to those involved" (pp. 19–20). In other words, the vision of a design science outlined by van den Akker and his colleagues also includes a concern for the understandings of the potential users of a program about why this project is or might be needed in this organization or context at this time.

A New Paradigm for Research

Dewey's life project centered on articulating a view of "intelligence" as a means for harnessing resources for improving human experience. There is, Dewey would have emphasized, no meaningful "standard" for or "foundation" of music education external to practice, merely the possibility of an intelligent quest for a resolution of problematic situations. "Design," with its focus on addressing this problem in this situation, captures part of this notion.

But what might a response along these lines to the cluster of problems within traditional educational theory and research, and school improvement, mean in practice? Does a nonfoundational, design-based, praxial view inevitably lead to a rejection of an image of the music educator built on ideas of basic research or foundational scholarship? Does this view favor "craft" or "artistic," or design-based and developmental, images of the work of the music educators as practitioners, albeit practitioners who, like their colleagues who teach performance, are master practitioners? Is it the implication of this view that the core activity of the music educator should be a form of tinkering toward local and immediate improvement based in each person's or community's sense of the musicianship that is appropriate for their students? Such work would begin with a sense of the traditions, practice, and possibilities of music education and its potential for students and a strong sense of the realities of the school, *not* with an elaborated philosophy and theory of music education.

A craft-based image of the work of the music educator built on these lines is attractive. It captures the sense of workmanship involved in bringing together a commitment to an idea or possibility, the necessary resources, a repertoire, the teaching of the skills and understandings that are needed to bring the idea off, and the notion that all concerned are going to get something quite tangible (for themselves) out of it. It was this model, when all is said and done, that lay behind such historical developments in music education as the emergence of school bands, and so forth, and such exemplary leaders as Lowell Mason. While the articulation of principles would be part of such work, the core of the work, as in, say, architectural design, would center on the design or development, and then deployment, of real-world approaches and methods. The skills and knowledge involved in such a practice would be transmitted through apprenticeship, in a studio, an atelier, or school(s), not in a formal university or college classroom. Writing, that is, research and theory, would only serve to articulate and perhaps systematize practices that could be seen or heard, with the implication that the articulation would not be independent of the practice. Schön (1985) makes a powerful case for such a model in the context of the design professions, and his arguments could readily be extended to designing for music education. The designing practices that Schön describes are, of course, based on well-understood standards that define a good and poor, or a better or worse, design, but these standards do not have the form of foundations *for* practice. They find their meaning *within* the practice of design.

However, as Dewey so clearly recognized in *The Educational Situation*, schooling is a complex institution. A concept of design does not give a clear direction for thinking about the improvement of music education organizationally and systemically. Furthermore, a reformulation of curriculum research as design research does not eliminate the fundamental institutional problem that Dewey also addressed in *The Educational Situation*: how does the face-to-face work of a local community become incorporated within the ongoing conceptions of appropriate schooling and education held within the larger environing community? It was these conceptions that Dewey saw as defining what schools could in fact undertake and as legitimating what was central and what was peripheral to the core curriculum.

These issues have their greatest force as we recognize that over the past half-century the work of schools has been marked by fundamental changes in its scope, significance, and mission. For teachers in the aggregate, these changes have brought what Carlgren (1999) has called a sequence of major "ruptures" in their professional lives, with each rupture implying a loss in the self-evident quality of the curriculum and a "loss of competence . . . which makes the accumulation of knowledge difficult" (pp. 44–45). While an individual professional life might not be affected by any particular rupture, like, for example, the emergence of mass college-preparatory secondary education in the 1950s and 1960s in the United States and mass post–compulsory education in Europe in the 1980s and 1990s, racial integration in the United States, the contemporary concern for multiculturalism in Europe, and so forth, the lives and careers of a cohort of teachers and students will be. In such contexts, old skills and patterns become discounted. There is a need for new ways of thinking and new regulative ideas to govern the classroom curriculum along with new skills, new working patterns, and sometimes new kinds of people. It is such ruptures that create the greatest challenge to the idea of curriculum work as purposeful design.

The tradition of theory-derived responses to the need for such fundamental curriculum change has seen this complex of issues in terms of changes directed in terms of one or another variant of the research, development, and dissemination (RD&D) model. Research and theory, which provide answers/solutions to the issues in question, constitute a privileged foundation for derived and then engineered policy "solutions"—which are then implemented (somehow) by a center. To use Burk's (1991) words, this model assumes that, in principle at least, "it is possible (through 'basic' research) to identify specific cause–effect relationships, knowledge of which provides definite answers to particular questions to be 'applied' in solving problems" (p. 28).

But as Elmore, Sykes, and Spillane (1992) make clear, the RD&D model has not proven useful for thinking about the sustained improvement of schooling. As they observe, much of the activity undertaken within the RD&D framework is symbolic; that is, research and development is set in train by policy makers as a way of giving the appearance of purposeful action while avoiding the necessary policy making (and of course researchers all too willingly collaborate in this evasion because they benefit from it). But the power of the RD&D model as symbol also reaches outside government as is seen, for example, in the Getty Center's Discipline-Based Arts Education (DBAE), which not only is built around an RD&D model but also, in a way that reflects its foundational external starting point, privileges the disciplines of art historians, art critics, aestheticians, and others (see Wolf, 1992). Within the world of DBAE, the surface of ongoing work in, say, music education, which is criticized but not examined, lacks legitimacy in the light of the deeper understandings of the DBAE foundation.

It is here that the difference between the view of large-scale research-inspired change directed and managed by the "system" and the practical or praxial and deliberative view of institutional change emerges most clearly. If the school system and its parts and the enveloping culture and society are imaged in terms of praxialism's metaphor of a changing ecological system with a typically unpredictable course, we have to ask how ordered, "intelligent" responses to the pervasive problematic situations created by such ruptures might be possible. The necessary adaptations and responses to the changing environment will be framed by the curriculum debates of the larger context. But the response to the change can only emerge piecemeal, as local adaptations, responses, and changes in understandings. In a kind a feedback loop, it is only as these local adaptations accumulate that significant changes can become registered, and thus available as possibilities that might alter the larger community's understandings of school.

In this perspective, organization building, social mobilization, and local experimentation become the key concepts that must be used in thinking about educational and curriculum change within the school seen as a social institution—and particularly the major social change required in the context of rupture (see Janowitz, 1991). The entrepreneurs and reformers who engage in such work understand their markets and how their messages relate to their markets. They can distinguish symbolic action from "real" action; they understand the landscape of teaching and the schools; they know what teachers and schools can and cannot do, and want to do and do not want to do. They know that the hard work of designing solutions to the new problems they are facing must be undertaken in protected contexts and then, as the part of the process of managing the hoped-for social change, diffused slowly to other places by way of processes of institution and organization building. Their focus is, therefore, not, for example, music education as such but rather the "local" institutions and organizations of music educators, because in contexts of rupture it is these organizations and institutions that must be rebuilt to support the new ways.[21] In such work, theory and research are resources, *not* foundations or starting points. They provide the initiating platforms for social experimentation. They offer perspectives that can be used to secure a reflective understanding of what we might be doing in such experimentation and how we might be doing it.

Theory, Research, and the Vision of Mindful Practice

This chapter has sought to make a case for a nonfoundational view of theory and research in music education that has, at its center, first, a view of how the curriculum functions within the web of forces in the environment of the school and, second, a perspective that sees curriculum work as local, "practical"—that is, praxial—and deliberative (Regelski, 1998a, 1998b, 1999; Reid, 1992, 1999). It has sought to make an argument for replacing foundational questions like "What is the 'essential' nature of music?" "Whose music should we teach?" "What are the 'best' approaches to teaching and instruction?" and "What should the curriculum be?" as the core questions of theory and research in music education with different questions: "What do *we* want to do?" and "How do *we* do it?" in the institution of schooling and in classrooms. Let me now move toward closure by outlining (too briefly) some of the dimensions of a possible "solution" to the thought-action problem that seem to follow this argument and have the promise of avoiding the pitfalls of the traditional model.

It could be argued that I have been making a case for abandoning values, philosophy, research, and theory in music education in favor of both a renewed emphasis on the craft tradition of music education and collaborative and concrete action and doing in schools and classrooms, albeit with systematic evaluation added. Such an interpretation of the argument would not be inappropriate. To the extent that empirical research has a role in a world in which its tasks were seen in terms of a renewed concern for the enhancement of the day-to-day practice of music education, much of that research should be one or another form of "evaluation"—the attempt to judge what works and does not work and why. The goal of such work would be the development of a prudential understanding of the possibilities and the conditions around the work of music education.

Thus problems, possibilities, and ideas present themselves as societies, cultures, and technologies change and throw up new possibilities; "I" and then "we" move to explore one or another of these possibilities. We succeed or don't succeed in the way we wanted, or we succeed in a way that we did not intend. I/we want to understand why, in concrete terms, this or that came about from our efforts, so that next time we can move in a different way. A "handbook" of such research would offer a discussion of small- and large-scale experiments and programs in music education in ongoing settings, some "traditional," some "experimental," along with an analysis of what they yielded in the way of outcomes, and a discussion of the larger understandings that emerge from the record (see Elmore et al., 1992). The metatheory would emerge from the theory of evaluation (see, for example, Scriven, 1980; Stufflebeam, Madaus, & Kellaghan, 2000). The theory that informed the analysis would derive from the available and emergent languages[22] within the terms of which curricula and teaching in music can and might be thought about and from examined experience in the development and design of programs—and, of course, the development of such languages would be an important outcome of such research. But as with Schön's (1985) design professions and all analyses of performance and all making of art, these languages would find their meaning in action, in the thoughtful, mindful praxis of ongoing activity of curriculum making and teaching.

However, I have also been implying that the community of music educators, as "leaders" with a mandate and the freedom to look beyond the demands of Monday morning, should also be engaging actively with the larger social systems of the working teachers of music and must, as a result, know other things. We must, for example, have the data we need for an appreciation of the situation we want to address as a basis for discerning where the work of improvement might begin. We must, in other words, move on the basis of an analysis of what is happening in the music classrooms and what is being "achieved" in the system of classrooms we are working with (see, for example, Stake, Bresler, & Mabry, 1991). Following Clandinin and Connelly (1992) and Schwab (1978; see also Drake, Spillane, & Hufferd-Ackles, 2001), we must know what teachers we work with want to do and can do, and do not want to do and cannot do and why. It is teachers with their priorities and their ambitions, as Doyle (1992) and Clandinin and Connelly (1995) emphasize, not curricula or policies, who animate the work of the schools.[23]

I acknowledge that the agenda for theory building and research in music education implied by the practical/praxial understanding of educational theory and research I have been advocating here can (and has been) criticized for its absence of a clear vision of what music education might be. It might also be said that this sketch gives no appropriate role for the research community and its work. These are, of course, real reservations—but they must be asked in the light of the situation Dewey described 100 years ago and the subsequent experience with both the idea of the curriculum as a standard and failure of the theory- and research-based paradigm. All agree that radical, foundational visions that derived from outside the ongoing practice of schooling have *not* entered the practice—at least in the ways theorists and researchers hoped for and policy makers and curriculum makers planned for. The platforms that have become actualized emerged as practice engaged reflectively with its own traditions and its own possibilities, as it related to other practices and as it interacted with the cultural and social worlds that circle around school practice. One activity of traditional research and theory has been highlighting just those points of tension within and around practice and spelling out—typically from the point of view of a standard—what they might mean for an enhanced practice. But such all-too-characteristic criticism of schools and classrooms, with its failure to articulate a real-world practice that can concretely remedy the problems

that are identified, has had little directive power within practice.

In the case of music education, it is relatively easy to meet these reservations. Music education is almost unique inasmuch as it represents a pervasive social practice that has found its way into the school and what is done can be recognized by everyone as mirroring at least something of the real worlds of music making, listening, and such. As school music has engaged with music as a social practice, it has also engaged with both social and cultural orders in both productive and reproductive senses. Like all areas of the arts within the school, school music has expanded its range and scope, enthusiastically and successfully, bringing into the school the marching band, jazz, musical theater, and the like—and, in doing so, changed in a way that most other school subjects have not. The big problem, of course, is and has been the "schooling" of music, with the accompanying routinization and the related loss of connection to the whole world of music itself. But, paradoxically, this "schooling" of music is, as Swanwick (1993) emphasizes, at the very heart of mindful practice of music education and, as he suggests, the place where the most interesting puzzles arise.

Given this, we can ask if music education in fact needs a larger vision than the one of a mindful situated and local practice of music in all of its forms and manifestations. Our ambition should be to maintain an open mind toward music as a social form, and we should look carefully at the machinery of schooling and at the social and cultural movements in and around our local worlds for ways in which we can expand and change the experience of school music. At the same time, we must recognize with Swanwick (1993, 1998) that what emerges from our reflection on music must be closed, bounded, and systematized if it is to serve the sociotechnical purposes of music education and if it is to work for teachers in their local worlds of classrooms and communities.

Conclusion

Traditional educational theory and research must be regarded as a failed project, at least when seen from the viewpoint of improving schooling in a sustained and sustaining way. If such improvement is the task of theory and research, we have to ask if we should persist with the form of that work we have inherited, or do we reenvision the field? This chapter has presented an argument for such a reenvisioning of the understanding of theory and research in music education along praxial lines, that is, in terms of the needs of a mindful, situated enlightened practice of music education, which recognizes, with the Dewey of *The Educational Situation*, the centrality of the school as an organization and institution in any conceptualization of music education and the work of the music educator. It is, when all is said and done, the organizations and institutions that host school music that theory and research around music education must hope to affect.

Within such a perspective, theory building and research in music education would seek to offer the grounds for a mindful immediate action rather than seek to develop universalizing prescriptions for the correct standards of an abstracted "best practice." In this view, practitioners of theory and research in music education would embrace experimentalism rather than certainty, the local rather than the general, and limit their sights to the practice of music education rather than search for the utopian and unrealizable. The "vision" or platform that might animate such a project would derive from music and the traditions of music education. We would be constantly asking what experience of what music we want our students to encounter, following through with designs to reflect our answers, and then aggressively seeking the feedback that evaluation provides in order to refine our initial designs—or to suggest that they were misconceived or unrealizable.

NOTES

I must acknowledge the generous assistance given me as I wrote and rewrote this chapter by Wayne Bowman, Richard J. Colwell, Margery Osborne, Tom A. Regelski, William A. Reid, Bennett Reimer, Decker F. Walker, Peter Webster, Nancy Whitaker, and the Handbook's anonymous reviewers of the first versions of the chapter. I have to particularly thank Richard Colwell and Tom Regelski. They offered me short courses in recent developments around the philosophy of music education when it became clear that, as an outsider to the field, I had not gotten hold of the fascinating recent thinking.

1. Gates (1998) articulates well the conventional view I am calling foundational while at the same time distinguishing the conventional image of the nested arenas within which research sees itself playing a role: "Most large fields—medicine, psychology, social work, management, even manufacturing—recognize at least three different but intentionally articulated levels of research activity: Let's call them basic research, engineering and technology. Researchers at one level ground their work on other work at the same level, but they also use the findings of researchers at other levels. A person who is working in technology knows the engineering research related to what he or she is working on, and may even know the basic research on which the engineering is based" (p. 11).

2. In saying this, I am taking aim at the assumptions of much, if not most, of the empirical research, philosophizing, and theory building within education. And I include within these terms modern and postmodern—i.e., Deweyan, feminist, critical, and such—philosophies and theories, as well as most empirical research!

3. For a contemporary commentary on this observation, see Eckel (1997).

4. In assessing the impact of research and reform on the schools, we must distinguish, following McEneaney and Meyer (2000), between those educational and curricular changes that reflect the responses of the institution to larger social and cultural change and those changes that might have emerged from educational research and theory or the formal machinery of educational policy making. This chapter is concerned with this latter set—which, as I argued earlier, is nearly empty.

5. I am using the quotation from Elliott's *Music Matters* (1995) to illustrate a form of argument that I see as conventional, *not* to criticize the significance of his perspective—although, as I will make clear, I do have reservations about what the impact of his proposals might be for the practice of music education in schools.

6. The title of Rosenkranz's work, *Die Pädagogik als System*, is more accurately translated as "Theory of Education as a System."

7. Harris's use of the word *science* here reflects the German word *Wissenschaft*, which refers to scholarly, systematic study. However, the connotations of "science" within English were to come to the fore with G. Stanley Hall's later claim for psychology as the foundational science for education.

8. It is, therefore, very unusual to read paragraphs such as the following within research literature around music education, indeed in the research literature around any school subject:

> Music education in the United States, on the whole and speaking generally, is truly something splendid, something to be encouraged and preserved largely in its present aspects. . . .
>
> The general condition of music education has continued, despite occasional setbacks, to improve gradually during all the course of my lifetime. Many of the things that used to bother me can no longer do so because they have disappeared from the scene. For example, the musical content of elementary school songbooks no longer features the specially composed songs and the artificial folk songs that used to fill the books when I was at school. Our heightened awareness and appreciation of ethnic and cultural differences have permitted us to fill our books with real songs from real countries, intended to be performed with faithfulness to their origins.
>
> The very aims of elementary school music have been transformed. Children are no longer subjected to hours of drill on the so-fa syllables. (Britton, 1991, pp. 175, 176–177)

We might ask how such significant changes in music education occurred and became accepted as legitimate by music educators, teachers, and schools. Did the theory building and research of music education play any significant part in these changes?

Note also, for example, Keith Swanwick's (1988) description of his early musical training (such a craft-based approach to music education has no legitimacy in the research literature). "I am reminded of my own experiences a boy in a Midlands village brass band. Music was to some extent learned in the context of other social activities. . . . I mastered the technique of the E flat tenor horn quite informally, without instruction—the band master never quite got round to *instruction*. Most of the playing was of whole pieces or long sections with very little fragmentation into part-learning or analysis of particular difficulties. . . . It was also considered vital to be playing with others. Few members of the band seemed to practice at home very often and most technical aspects seemed to be achieved mainly when playing together. I suspect that this pattern of learning is still prevalent today in church choirs, amateur orchestras, rock bands, folk groups, the Salvation Army, steel bands and many other variations of our rich musical culture" (p. 128, emphasis in original).

For a diverse sampling of historical "practice," largely uninformed by "research," see the file of the UK-based journal of research on textbooks *Paradigm*: http://www.ed.uiuc.edu/Paradigm/

9. See also Shepherd and Vulliamy (1983) and Vulliamy (1977); for comments on this work see Shepherd (1991), Swanwick (1984a, 1984b), and Vulliamy and Shepherd (1984, 1985) for reactions to Swanwick's critique.

10. Where, to use Tom Regelski's metaphor, the students act as "organ pipes."

11. For brief but authoritative reviews see, from a contemporary policy-making perspective, Elmore et al. (1992) and, from a historical perspective, Cuban (1992).

12. One outcome of this work has been a bewildering proliferation of definitions and classifications of *curriculum* as a term and a conception. L. Cuban (1999), for example, has distinguished the *recommended curriculum*, the *official curriculum*, the *taught curriculum*, the *tested curriculum*, and the *learned curriculum*.

13. Cuban (1999) reflects such confusion around the idea of policy by distinguishing *policy talk, policy action,* and *policy implementation*. He notes that that confusion has often arisen "because highly publicized discourse (*policy talk*) over which policies to adopt (*policy action*) encouraged researchers and policy makers to assume that teachers had put into practice (*policy implementation*) new courses and programs. When evidence eventually emerged that some teachers were faithfully observing the adopted policy while most of their colleagues continued with traditional practices, policy makers and researchers expressed disappointment with teachers and curriculum reform. That disappointment, however, was anchored in confusing what appeared in the recommended and official curricula with what teachers did every day" (p. 70).

14. For a discussion of the range of such policy instruments, see Cohen and Spillane (1992). The instruments Cohen and Spillane discuss reflect the range of considerations around the idea of "systemic reform."

15. Fullan (1999) reflected the views of many when he wrote that "we are in the very early stages of appreciating the nature and complexity of educational reform on a large scale" (p. 66). For discussions of the problems and paradoxes in this topic, see, for example, Kirk and MacDonald (2001) and Page (2001).

16. Thus Reimer (1989) can be read as a discussion, at a consciously "political" level, of the one set of "images" for music education at the policy level.

17. Schwab's "practical" starting points and approach have been well articulated by those who advocate a praxial perspective on school music (see, e.g., Regelski, 1998b). As Bowman (in press–a) puts it: "The praxial [i.e. practical] realm shared with techne an interest in the execution of tasks (in 'doing'), and shared with theoria an emphasis upon what we might characterize as mindfulness." Schwab (1978) used the term *deliberation* to capture the method of such work. William Reid's *Curriculum as Institution and Practice: Essays in the Deliberative Tradition* (1999) offers one view of the development of Schwab's deliberative curriculum theory.

18. Bowman (in press–a) writes that "praxial convictions and loyalties do not in themselves address or answer questions like Whose? or Which? or How Many? Such issues are at least as political and ideological as they are philosophical, and may need to be addressed by means other than an appeal to praxis. It is not so much that praxial convictions fail to resolve issues like these as they are largely indifferent to them. Praxialism offers to empirically orient and ground music philosophy, and although that is no small achievement, its basic instincts appear to be pluralistic and non-normative, providing no clear basis for sustaining one practice's claim for ultimacy or privilege over another. . . . [Praxialism's] descriptive commitment provides a rather awkward fit to the inherently normative concerns of an undertaking like education."

I would argue that the questions Bowman suggests are left open by the philosophy of music praxialism can be answered by drawing on the topics or commonplaces of students, teachers, subject matter, that is, music, curriculum making, and milieu, wielded eclectically (see Reid, 1999). Within Schwab's viewpoint (1978; see also Reid, 1999), it is the task of the "eclectic" and "deliberation" to effect a resolution of the competing claims of these commonplaces—as they manifest themselves in a Deweyan "situation."

19. For both Walker (1992) and van den Akker (1999) design research embraces the kind of work associated with formative evaluation—and, as such, represents what van den Akker (1999) sees as an "emerging trend, characterized by a proliferation of terminology and a lack of consensus on definitions" (p. 3).

20. This term was introduced into the curriculum literature by Decker Walker (1971, 1975), although in his original use a platform was the starting place for the deliberations of a group charged with a curriculum development project. As I use the term here, a platform is the starting point of a social mobilization, which may include major curriculum development projects as well as small-scale adaptations that are not centrally organized or supported but, rather, have peer support—as well as local experiments by an individual asking what can happen musically for my/our students within, say, a ukulele choir. Elliott (1995) and Swanwick (1988, 1993), to take two instances, offer systematic "philosophies" for a contemporary music education that can be seen as exemplars for thinking about what a platform for music education might look like. Other examples of starting points for such platforms would include Freudenthal's philosophy of the "mathematizing" of everyday activity, music praxialism's emphasis on real-life music, cognitive theory's emphasis on the situated nature of cognition, an applied music theory that can serve

the needs of jazzers, rockers, folk musicians, and others. The MayDay Group (Gates, 1998, 1999) has offered a "platform" for theory and research in music education as a framework for the social mobilization of those concerned with the theory of music education

21. Although many would argue that such a perspective should be obviously central to all action and thought about large-scale curriculum change, curriculum theory and research, and theory and research in music education, have given it little or no systematic attention. I have argued here for why, both epistemologically and politically, this has been the case. But is it possible that in an area like music education, which does not arouse strong political and cultural interest and, as a result, receives little research and development funding—with its implications for how developmental and research agendas and ways of thinking are set by centers—there is much to be learned about the larger task of large-scale curriculum enhancement (see Sarason, 1995).

22. See, for example, Regelski's (1986) and Swanwick's (1993) discussions of music education's "concept language" and Swanwick's (1993) discussion of a "musical feature" language.

23. The central topic for an action-centered music education research must be "teachers." They are, as Doyle (1992) has emphasized, the primary curriculum makers. It is their curriculum theory that is instantiated in their classrooms. But what is known about music teachers? Are they, like Lortie's (1975) generalist elementary teachers, heterogeneous in their self-understandings and little influenced by their education in education? Are they, like most teachers, limited in their sense of the possibilities of music education in that their ambitions have developed almost solely out of their own school experiences? Or are they committed, "talented," entrepreneurial, and so forth, with active lives with and around music outside the school? Do the contacts that music teachers might have with music making and listening give them a sense of possibilities that other teachers do not have—because of, say, the relatively inaccessible nature of math, history, or whatever, to those who work in schools?

Models for such work are found in the work of Clandinin (1986), Clandinin and Connelly (1992, 1995), Connelly and Clandinin (1999), Drake, Spillane, and Hufferd-Ackles (2001), F. Elbaz (1983), and S. Gudmundsdottir (in press), to name just a few examples. See Fenstermacher (1994) and Cochran-Smith and Lytle (1999) for reviews of recent work on teachers' "knowledge."

REFERENCES

Abbott, A. (1988). *The system of professions: An essay on the division of expert labor.* Chicago: University of Chicago Press.

Abeles, H. F., Hoffer, C. F., & Klotman, R. H. (1994). *Foundations of music education.* New York: Schirmer Books.

Bernstein, B. (1971). On the classification and framing of knowledge. In M. White (Ed.), *Knowledge and control: New directions for the sociology of education* (pp. 47–69). London: Collier-Macmillan.

Bowman, W. (in press–a). The limits and grounds of musical praxialism. In D. Elliott (Ed.), *Critical matters in music education.* New York: Oxford University Press.

Bowman, W. (in press–b). What should the music education profession expect of philosophy? *Arts and Learning.*

Britton, A. P. (1991). American music education: Is it better than we think? A discussion of the roles of performance and repertory, together with a brief mention of certain other problems. In R. Colwell (Ed.), *Basic concepts in music education* (Vol. 2, pp. 175–188). Niwot: University Press of Colorado.

Brown, A. L. (1992). Design experiments: Theoretical and methodological challenges in creating complex interventions in classroom settings. *Journal of the Learning Sciences, 2,* 141–178.

Brown, J. S., Collins, A., & Duiguid, P. (1989). Situated cognition and the culture of learning. *Educational Researcher, 18,* 32–42.

Burk, J. (1991). Introduction: A pragmatic sociology. In M. Janowitz, *On social organization and social control* (J. Burk, Ed.) (pp. 1–56). Chicago: University of Chicago Press.

Carlgren, I. (1999). Professionalism and teachers as designers. *Journal of Curriculum Studies, 31,* 43–56.

Clandinin, D. J. (1986). *Classroom practices: Teacher images in action.* London: Falmer Press.

Clandinin, D. J., & Connelly, F. M. (1992). Teachers as curriculum maker. In P. W. Jackson (Ed.), *Handbook of research on curriculum* (pp. 363–401). New York: Macmillan.

Clandinin, D. J., & Connelly, F. M. (1995). *Advances in contemporary educational thought*: Vol. 4. *Teachers' professional knowledge landscapes.* New York: Teachers College Press.

Cochran-Smith, M., & Lytle, S. L. (1999). Relationships of knowledge and practice: Teacher learning in communities. In A. Iran-Nejad & D. P. Pearson (Eds.), *Review of research in education* (Vol. 24, pp. 249–306). Washington, DC: American Educational Research Association.

Cohen, D. K., & Spillane, J. P. (1992). Policy and practice: The relations between governance and instruction. In G. Grant (Ed.), *Review of research in education* (Vol. 18) (pp. 3–49). Washington, DC: American Educational Research Association.

Colwell, R. J. (Ed.). (1992). *Handbook of research on music teaching and learning: A project of the Music Educators' National Conference.* New York: Schirmer Books.

Colwell, R. (1999). *Visual and performing arts: A chapter of the Curriculum Handbook.* Alexandria, VA: Association for Supervision and Curriculum Development.

Connelly, F. M., & Clandinin, D. J. (1999). *Shaping a professional identity: Stories of educational practice.* New York: Teachers College Press.

Cruikshank, K. (1998). The prelude to education as an academic discipline: American Herbartianism and the emergence of a science of pedagogy. *Paedagogica Historica, Supplementary Series: Vol. 3 History of Educational Studies,* 99–120.

Cuban, L. (1992). Curriculum stability and change. In P. W.

Jackson (Ed.), *Handbook of research on curriculum* (pp. 216–249). New York: Macmillan.

Cuban, L. (1999). The integration of modern sciences into the American secondary school, 1890–1990s. *Studies in Philosophy and Education, 18,* 67–87.

Daugherty, E. (Ed.). (1995). National standards in music education. *Quarterly Journal of Music Teaching and Learning, 6*(2), whole issue.

Dewey, J. (1902). *The Educational Situation. Contributions to Education: No. III.* Chicago: University of Chicago Press.

Dewey, J. (1976). The educational situation. In J. A. Boydston (Ed.), *John Dewey: The middle works, 1899–1924, Vol. 1. 1899–1901* (pp. 257–313). Carbondale: Southern Illinois University Press.

Doyle, W. (1992). Curriculum and pedagogy. In P. W. Jackson (Ed.), *Handbook of research on curriculum* (pp. 486–516). New York: Macmillan.

Drake, C., Spillane, J. P., & Hufferd-Ackles, K. (2001). Storied identities: Teacher learning and subject-matter context. *Journal of Curriculum Studies, 33,* 1–23.

Eckel, S. L. (1997). Student opinions speak volumes: Value statements regarding performance music courses. *Dialogue in Instrumental Music Education, 21,* 46–62.

Elbaz, F. (1983). *Teacher thinking.* London: Croom Helm.

Elliott, D. J. (1994). Music, education and schooling. In M. McCarthy (Ed.), *Winds of change: A colloquium in music education with Charles Fowler and David J. Elliott: University of Maryland at College Park, April 3, 1993* (pp. 24–45). New York: American Council for the Arts in cooperation with the University of Maryland at College Park.

Elliott, D. J. (1995). *Music matters: A new philosophy of music education.* New York: Oxford University Press.

Elmore, R., Sykes, G., & Spillane, J. P. (1992). Curriculum policy. In P. W. Jackson (Ed.), *Handbook of research on curriculum* (pp. 185–215). New York: Macmillan.

Engeström, Y., & Middleton, D. (Eds.). (1996). *Cognition and communication at work.* Cambridge: Cambridge University Press.

Eraut, M. (1989). Design contexts and approaches. In M. Eraut (Ed.), *The international encyclopedia of educational technology* (pp. 317–322). Oxford: Pergamon Press.

Fenstermacher, G. (1994). The knower and the known: The nature of knowledge in research on teaching. In L. Darling-Hammond (Ed.), *Review of research in education* (Vol. 20) (pp. 3–56). Washington, DC: American Educational Research Association.

Fullan, M. (1999). *Change forces: The sequel.* London: Falmer Press.

Gates, J. T. (1998). *The MayDay Group and its agenda.* Retrieved December 15, 2000, from http://members.aol.com/jtgates/maydaygroup/agenda2.html

Gates, J. T. (1999). Action for change in music education: The MayDay Group agenda. In M. McCarthy & K. A. Martin (Eds.), *Music education as praxis: Reflecting on music-making as human action: The 1997 Charles Fowler Colloquium on Innovation in Arts Education, University of*

Maryland, April 18–19, 1997 (pp. 12–25). College Park: University of Maryland.

Gravemeijer, K., & Terwel, J. (2000). Hans Freudenthal: A mathematician on didactics and curriculum theory. *Journal of Curriculum Studies, 32,* 777–796.

Greeno, J. G., Collins, A., & Resnick, L. B. (1996). Cognition and learning. In D. C. Berliner & R. Calfee (Eds.), *Handbook of educational psychology* (pp. 15–46). New York: Macmillan.

Greeno, J. G., McDermott R., Cole, K., Engle, R., Goldman, S., Knudsen, J., Lauman, B., & Linde, C. (1999). Research, reform, and aims of education: Modes of action in search of each other. In E. C. Lagemann & L. S. Shulman (Eds.), *Issues in education research: Problems and possibilities* (pp. 299–335). San Francisco: Jossey-Bass.

Gudmundsdottir, S. (in press). Narrative research on practice. In V. Richardson (Ed.), *Handbook of research on teaching* (4th ed.). New York: Macmillan.

Hopmann, S. (1999). The curriculum as a standard in public education. *Studies in Philosophy and Education, 18,* 89–105.

Janowitz, M. (1991). Theory and policy: Engineering or enlightenment models. In M. Janowitz, *On social organization and social control* (J. Burk, Ed.) (pp. 86–95). Chicago: University of Chicago Press.

Kessels, J., & Plomp, T. (2000). A systematic and relational approach to obtaining curriculum consistency in corporate education. *Journal of Curriculum Studies, 31,* 679–709.

Kirk, D., & MacDonald, D. (2001). Teacher voice and the ownership of curriculum change. *Journal of Curriculum Studies, 32,* 551–568.

Levine, D. N. (1986). The forms and functions of social knowledge. In D. W. Fiske & R. A. Shweder (Eds.), *Metatheory in social science: Pluralisms and subjectivities* (pp. 271–283). Chicago: University of Chicago Press.

Lortie, D. C. (1975). *Schoolteacher: A sociological study.* Chicago: University of Chicago Press.

McCarthy, M. (Ed.). (1999). *Music education as praxis: Reflecting on music-making as human action.* The 1997 Charles Fowler Colloquium on Innovation in Arts Education, April 18–19, 1997 (pp. 12–25). College Park: University of Maryland.

McEneaney, E. H., & Meyer, J. W. (2000). The content of the curriculum: An institutionalist perspective. In M. T. Hallinan (Ed.), *Handbook of the sociology of education* (pp. 189–211). New York: Kluwer.

Olson, D. R., & Bruner, J. S. (1998). Folk psychology and folk pedagogy. In D. R. Olson & N. Torrance (Eds.), *The handbook of education and human development* (pp. 9–27). Malden, MA: Blackwell.

Page, R. N. (2001). Common sense: A form of teacher knowledge. *Journal of Curriculum Studies, 32,* 525–534.

Regelski, T. A. (1986). Concept-learning and action-learning in music education. *British Journal of Music Education, 3,* 185–216.

Regelski, T. A. (1998a). The Aristotelian bases of praxis for music and music education as praxis. *Philosophy of Music Education Review, 6*(1) 22–59.

Regelski, T. A. (1998b). Critical theory as a foundation for critical thinking in music education. *Studies in Music from the University of Western Ontario, 17*, 1–21.

Regelski, T. A. (1999). Action learning: Curriculum and instruction as and for praxis. In M. McCarthy (Ed.), *Music education as praxis: Reflecting on music-making as human action*. The 1997 Charles Fowler Colloquium on Innovation in Arts Education, April 18–19, 1997 (pp. 99–120). College Park: University of Maryland.

Reid, W. A. (1992). *The pursuit of curriculum: Schooling and the public interest*. Norwood, NJ: Ablex.

Reid, W. A. (1999). *Curriculum as institution and practice: Essays in the deliberative tradition*. Mahwah, NJ: Erlbaum.

Reimer, B. (1989). *A philosophy of music education* (2nd ed.). Englewood Cliffs, NJ: Prentice Hall.

Rosenkranz, J. K. F. (1892). *The philosophy of education* (A. C. Brackett, Trans., W. T. Harris, Ed.). New York: D. Appleton.

Sarason, B. S. (1995). *Parental involvement and the political principle: Why the existing governance structure of schools should be abolished*. San Francisco: Jossey-Bass.

Schön, D. (1985). *The design studio: An exploration of its traditions and potential*. London: RIBA.

Schwab, J. J. (1978). The practical: A language for curriculum. In J. J. Schwab, *Science, curriculum, and liberal education: Selected essays* (I. Westbury & N. J. Wilkof, Eds.) (pp. 287–321). Chicago: University of Chicago Press.

Scriven, M. (1980). *The logic of evaluation*. Inverness, CA: Edgepress.

Shepherd, J. (1991). *Music as social text*. Cambridge: Polity Press.

Shepherd, J., & Vulliamy, G. (1983). A comparative sociology of school knowledge. *British Journal of Sociology of Education, 4*, 3–18.

Stake, R., Bresler, L., & Mabry, L. (1991). *Custom and cherishing: The arts in elementary schools: Studies of U.S. elementary schools portraying the ordinary problems of teachers teaching music, drama, dance and the visual arts in 1987–1990*. Urbana: National Arts Education Research Center, University of Illinois at Urbana-Champaign.

Starr, S. L. (1996). Working together: Symbolic interactionism, activity theory, and information systems. In Y. Engeström & D. Middleton (Eds.), *Cognition and communication at work* (pp. 296–318). Cambridge: Cambridge University Press.

Stufflebeam, D. L., Madaus, G. F., & Kellaghan, T. (Eds.). (2000). *Evaluation models: Viewpoints on educational and human services evaluation* (2nd ed.). Boston: Kluwer.

Swanwick, K. (1984a). A further note on the sociology of music education. *British Journal of Sociology of Education, 5*, 303–307.

Swanwick, K. (1984b). Problems of a sociological approach to pop music in schools. *British Journal of Sociology of Education, 5*, 49–56.

Swanwick, K. (1988). *Music, mind and education*. London: Routledge & Kegan Paul.

Swanwick, K. (1993). Music curriculum development and the concept of feature. In E. R. Jorgensen (Ed.), *Philosopher, teacher, musician: Perspectives on music education* (pp. 143–162). Urbana: University of Illinois Press.

Swanwick, K. (1998). Music as culture. Retrieved January 3, 2001, from http://members.aol.com/jtgates/maydaygroup/calls2b.html.

van den Akker, J. (1999). Principles of methods of developmental research. In J. van den Akker, R. M. Branch, K. Gustafson, N. Nieveen, & T. Plomp (Eds.), *Design approaches and tools in education and training* (pp. 1–14). Dordrecht, The Netherlands: Kluwer.

van den Akker, J., Branch, R. M., Gustafson, K., Nieveen, N., & Plomp, T. (Eds.). (1999). *Design approaches and tools in education and training*. Dordrecht, The Netherlands: Kluwer.

Visscher-Voerman, I., Gustafson, K., & Plomp, T. (1999). Educational design and development: An interview of paradigms. In J. van den Akker, R. M. Branch, K. Gustafson, N. Nieveen, & T. Plomp (Eds.), *Design approaches and tools in education and training* (pp. 15–28). Dordrecht, The Netherlands: Kluwer.

Vulliamy, G. (1977). Music as a case study in the "New sociology of education." In J. Shepherd, P. Virden, G. Vulliamy, & T. Wishart, *Whose music? A sociology of musical languages* (pp. 201–232). London: Latimer.

Vulliamy, G. (1978). Culture clash and school music: A sociological analysis. In L. Barton & R. Meighan (Eds.), *Sociological interpretations of schooling and classrooms: A reappraisal* (pp. 115–127). Driffield, UK: Nafferton Books.

Vulliamy, G., & Shepherd, J. (1984). Sociology and music education: A response to Swanwick. *British Journal of Sociology of Education, 5*, 57–76.

Vulliamy, G., & Shepherd, J. (1985). Sociology and music education: A further response to Swanwick. *British Journal of Sociology of Education, 6*, 225–229.

Walker, D. F. (1971). The process of curriculum development: A naturalistic model. *School Review, 80*, 51–65.

Walker, D. F. (1975). Curriculum development in an art project. In W. A. Reid & D. F. Walker (Eds.), *Case studies in curriculum change: Great Britain and the United States* (pp. 91–135). London: Routledge & Kegan Paul.

Walker, D. F. (1990). *Fundamentals of curriculum*. Fort Worth, TX: Harcourt Brace.

Walker, D. F. (1992). Methodological issues in curriculum research. In P. W. Jackson (Ed.), *Handbook of research on curriculum* (pp. 98–118). New York: Macmillan.

Wing, L. N. (1992). Curriculum and its study. In R. Colwell (Ed.), *Handbook of research on music teaching and learning: A project of the Music Educators National Conference* (pp. 196–217). New York: Schirmer Books.

Wolf, D. P. (1996). Becoming knowledge: The evolution of the art education curriculum. In P. W. Jackson (Ed.), *Handbook of research on curriculum* (pp. 945–963). New York: Macmillan.

Critical Thinking

10

BETTY ANNE YOUNKER

In the previous *Handbook of Research on Music Teaching and Learning*, Richardson and Whitaker (1992) concluded their chapter on critical thinking in music education by stating that there is a need to explore the musical implementation of a single theoretical base (p. 556). The authors suggest that to clarify meanings, refine conceptions, and make clear connections between critical thinking and musical thinking we must investigate philosophical studies. It would seem logical to use these directives as organizers for this chapter to provide continuity of thought between past and present and provide direction for further implications. Another means of continuity is provided by presenting brief summaries of those areas in Richardson and Whitaker's chapter that are relevant to the sections in this chapter, specifically definitions of critical thinking and the issue of generalizability as related to critical thinking.

This chapter begins with definitions of critical thinking, first presenting a summary of Richardson and Whitaker's descriptions and critiques of definitions of critical thinking as offered by John Dewey, John McPeck, Robert Ennis, and Richard Paul. I will then examine more recent thoughts offered by Paul and examine views on critical thinking as offered by Harvey Siegel and Stephen Norris, philosophers whose views are representative of contemporary thought on critical thinking in education. After comparing the various definitions, I will identify similarities and frame two broad components of critical thinking that may be applicable to music education.

The rest of the chapter will be organized around the following topics: the issue of generalizability, empirical research on critical thinking in music, critical-thinking processes in music, and implications for future research.

Descriptions of Critical Thinking

A Summary of Richardson and Whitaker's Descriptions and Critiques

Richardson and Whitaker (1992) organized their chapter around the following areas of consideration: How is critical thinking defined? What is the relationship of critical thinking to subject or content area? How can critical thinking be evaluated? Two bodies of literature that were considered included research on critical thinking in education and research on musical thinking in music education (p. 546).

Richardson and Whitaker (1992) provided the views of John Dewey, John McPeck, Robert Ennis, and Richard Paul with respect to definitions of critical thinking, relationships between critical thinking and subject matter, and the evaluation of critical thinking. Of these three areas, the first two will be summarized in what follows. This summary will provide a context for the additional definitions that will be examined and conclusions that will be offered about defining critical thinking.

As a point of reference for the terms *reflective* and *critical thinking*, Dewey (1991; originally published 1933) used the term *reflective thinking* and identified the critical aspect of thinking as that which occurs before adoption of action or belief upon reaching a conclusion. McPeck, Ennis, and Paul use the term *critical thinking*. For the purposes of this chapter, the terms will be viewed synonymously. In the following summaries, Dewey's thinking will receive the most attention because of the significance of his writing, from a historical perspective, on the contemporary educational philosophers who think about critical thinking and whose thinking is examined in subsequent paragraphs.

Dewey

Dewey has had a profound influence on writers of educational, moral, and social issues, but, in particular, Dewey's thoughts on reflective thinking have provided foundations for contemporary writers of critical thinking in education (Richardson & Whitaker, 1992). Richardson and Whitaker explained Dewey's definitions of four types of thinking that are not reflective and his definition of reflective thinking. Dewey's (1991) underlying belief was that learning improves to the degree that it arises out of the process of reflection. Reflective thinking involves active and persistent consideration of any belief or knowledge by examining the grounds upon which they are based. As the grounds are examined, we locate and define any felt difficulty. In an attempt to resolve the felt difficulty, solutions are explored and critically examined as a means to determine the effectiveness of each. Through observation and experimentation, we accept or reject those possibilities and thus accept or reject the initial belief (Dewey, 1991, p. 72). Dewey envisioned a dialogue, although representative of a systematic inquiry, in an environment that guided and fueled inquiry (Woodford, in progress).

Inseparably tied to the individuality of reflective thinking is the concept of funding (Dewey, 1991). One person, because of previous experiences, may encounter a situation in which no element of doubt is found, while another may encounter the situation and, because of lack of relevant experiences from which to draw, experience a doubt or perplexity. As a result, depth and scope of thinking would differ for each person. Funded experience allows us to make sense of a situation and gives a context for the situation in which the experience appears. A person who is experiencing doubt or perplexity will think reflectively in an attempt to arrive at a solution. As a person makes sense of an experience, his or her fund of intellectual, emotional, and imaginative experience comes into play. The uniqueness of the situation and the individual's perception of the problem are further individualized by the experiences each person brings to that situation (Richardson & Whitaker, 1992).

Dewey (1991) viewed the ability to think reflectively as a natural inclination that could be nurtured. We are inclined to be curious, spontaneous, and satisfied with order. Dewey also discussed dispositions in terms of readiness, in that people approach the task thoughtfully rather than making judgments based on tradition, custom, or prejudice. In a later writing, Dewey (1938) emphasized the important point of including students in the formation of the purposes that direct their activities in the learning process (p. 67), a point reflective of progressive education. Including students results in their active cooperation while formulating the purposes that are involved in their studies. It is crucial that the students understand what a purpose is, how it is formulated, and how it functions in an experience. The students' involvement in these processes can, according to Dewey (1938), fuel a desire and nurture a value to think reflectively.

McPeck, Ennis, and Paul

McPeck (1981) defined critical thinking as "the propensity and skill to engage in an activity with reflective skepticism" (p. 9). For McPeck, critical thinking includes the inclination and skill to think critically, the delay of decisions until solutions are considered, and reflection at a level that results in a reasonable solution. Critical thinking differs from creative and imaginative thinking and from logic but does include the affective and cognitive domains. The affect is involved by acquiring a disposition to think critically when a problem is encountered. Thinking critically involves more than analyzing arguments; it involves evaluating data, information, and supposed facts (McPeck 1984). It is subject-specific, thus not generalizable; there are no general skills or abilities in critical thinking. Knowledge about the subject area is needed to identify a problem and skillfully question about and evaluate the problem, aspects of the situation, and possible solutions.

Confusion arises from Ennis's writing as he interchangeably uses the terms *higher order thinking, reflective thinking*, and *critical thinking* and uses the term *informal logic* as something connected with critical thinking in a limited fashion (Richardson & Whitaker, 1992, p. 548). Ennis (1987) does, however, define critical thinking as "reasonable reflective thinking that is focused on deciding what to believe or do" (p. 10). There are various components to his definition, the first involving some form of reasoning; the second "reflective," for which he offers no clarification; and the remaining involving decisions about belief or action (Richardson & Whitaker, 1992). There are two taxonomies, the first for reasoning abilities and the second for dispositions. Richardson and Whitaker note that it is unclear whether or not one must move through all of the abilities and use all of the dispositions to think critically. Ennis suggests that there is a general approach to critical thinking and therefore it is not subject-specific.

Paul (1987) offers two types of disciplines and two types of thinking. The two types of disciplines are monological or technical and multi- or dialogical. The former include mathematics, physics, and chemistry, while the latter include history, psychology, sociology and anthropology, economics, and philosophy. The two types of thinking are aligned with each of the disciplines. Technical disciplines are atomistic and involve monological thinking, while dialogical disciplines involve more than one logical system and thinking that may involve multiple, possibly conflicting, viewpoints or frames of reference (Richardson & Whitaker, 1992, pp. 548–550). Paul does not refer to the arts; hence one must speculate about the feasability of teaching for dialogical thinking in music. He does, however, support a general approach to critical thinking.

Definitions of Critical Thinking

This section will examine the thinking of Paul, Siegel, and Norris with regard to critical thinking and then compare and contrast their definitions of critical thinking.

Paul

Paul (1993) suggests that critical thinking involves relearning, recritiquing, and reevaluating, processes that do not involve habituation. He suggests that in a rapidly changing world it is imperative that we think critically, find and solve problems, adapt, resolve issues, and take initiative and responsibility. When we are thinking critically we do not know just what to think but also how and why to think. Critical thinking is a systematic way to form and shape one's thinking. It is purposeful and exacting. It is thought that is disciplined, comprehensive, based on intellectual standards, and, as a result, well-reasoned (p. 20). Paul's emphasis on the "how" and "why" aspects of thinking as a systematic approach that involves evaluation and reason is the antithesis of habituation and acceptance without reflection.

Paul (1993) offers five dimensions of critical thinking: elements of reasoning, intellectual abilities, modes of reasoning, traits of mind, and intellectual standards. The various elements of reasoning include the purpose, problem, empirical/conceptual dimension, assumptions, conclusions, implications, point of view or frame of reference, and reasons. When one is thinking about these various elements with respect to a specific subject or task, the following questions can be used to operationalize the elements: "What is the purpose of my thinking?" "What precise question am I trying to answer?" "What point of view am I thinking?" "What information am I using?" "How am I interpreting that information?" "What concepts or ideas are central to my thinking?" "What conclusions am I coming to?" "What assumptions am I making?" "If I accept the conclusions, what are the implications?" (p. 22). While these opening questions are not subject- or task-specific, the content of the answers and further questions may be relevant to that subject or task at hand and would require specific knowledge and skills of that subject area.

Paul's second dimension, intellectual abilities, involves those abilities that enable students to identify and recognize, apply, analyze, synthesize and evaluate, and create or generate. These abilities empower students to do something with information or materials of a given product and of an original product. Questions, among others, that

would engage these abilities include: Does this solution apply to any other situation, and if so, which one and why? What knowledge or skills are applicable to this problem? What are the relationships, if any, between and among the solutions? Would these relationships be the same in other situations? What solutions are most appropriate and why? Again, while these questions are not subject-specific, the content of the answers and thus further questions would be subject-specific and require knowledge and skills of that subject area.

Paul's third dimension is the modes of reasoning: reading, writing, speaking, and listening critically; questioning Socratically; learning collaboratively; and engaging in role-playing. Involving students through Socratic discussions can enhance their understanding of intellectual discipline and thoroughness, develop their appreciation of the strengths of logic and logical thinking, and inform them about how thoughts can be followed in at least four directions: (1) their origin in terms of how the thoughts evolved and in what context; (2) their support in terms of why one would believe and the strengths of that belief as a result of examining evidence, assumptions, and reasons; (3) their conflicts with other thoughts in terms of the what, how, and why of objections; and (4) their implications and consequences in terms of identifying those implications and examining them in a context and identifying the implications for the thoughts (Paul, 1993, pp. 296–301). Collaborative learning can encourage dialogical thinking (that which involves a dialogue between differing points of view or frames of reference) and dialectical thinking (that which is initiated to test the strengths and weaknesses of opposing points of view). Role-playing can allow students to experience alternative points of view while, among other things, involving them in presenting points of view, justifying those points of view, analyzing and evaluating those and alternative views, and examining consequences and implications of those and alternative points of view. These methods of procedure are of concern from a pedagogical perspective but might not be of concern, specifically, within a musical context. Are all required for critical thinking to be experienced? If so, are they all present at some time or other when thinking critically about music?

Paul's fourth dimension, traits of mind, includes, among others, the following characteristics: intellectual independence, humility, courage, and good faith. To actively engage in critical thought, one must have various dispositions of mind to seek out problems and solutions in an evaluative manner. Possessing intellectual abilities does not guarantee the desire to put those abilities into practice, nor does it imply that one values the pursuit of intellectual inquiry. Paul (1993) suggests that critical thinking can develop traits such as intellectual integrity, intellectual humility, fair-mindedness, intellectual empathy, and intellectual courage (p. 21).

The fifth dimension that Paul offers is intellectual standards, which assess thinking. To establish standards, criteria such as the level of accuracy, relevancy, clarity, precision, plausibility, consistency, completeness, adequacy, and fairness must be identified. From a standards perspective, determining relationships between two constructs is different from determining the *significance* of the relationships between the two constructs.

Paul targets what critical thinking involves and why critical thinking is a crucial aspect of education. He defines critical thinking and describes five dimensions of critical thinking. He emphasizes that critical thinking involves unavoidable self-improvement that comes from the ability to use standards by which thinking is appropriately assessed.

Siegel

Siegel (1997) offers a volume of essays that represent the development and defense of his views on critical thinking that were presented in *Educating Reason* (Siegel, 1988). This development and defense evolved since his 1988 publication in response to a variety of issues, one being the "anti-Enlightenment" thinking that has occurred in philosophy and philosophy of education since the 1988 publication. In his 1997 publication, Siegel included the thinking of those who support approaches of narrative, contextualism, feminism, multiculturalism, and postmodernism (p. 1) and his response to those authors' thinking.

Siegel (1988, 1997) refers to critical thinking as rationality's "educational cognate." His basic view of a critical thinker is one "who is *appropriately moved by reasons*" (p. 2, emphasis in original). For Siegel, a role of education is to facilitate students' growth of dispositions, skills, and attitudes to reason and to facilitate their understanding about the role reason plays in actions and beliefs.

Siegel's (1997) two dimensions of critical thinking involve (1) skills and abilities and (2) dispositions, habits of mind, and character traits. The first dimension, which he refers to as the "*reason assessment* component" (p. 2, emphasis in original), involves evaluating reasons and arguments. When "moved by reasons" (p. 2), we believe, judge, and act in agreement with the power of proof with which our reasons support our beliefs, judgments, and actions. The desire to be moved to reason and evaluate is a notion he terms *felt* reasons. The skills and abilities to think critically involve understanding the principles of assessing reason and having the ability to use that understanding necessary to evaluate beliefs, actions, and judgments and the reasons deemed supportive of them.

Siegel (1990), within the context of the Informal Logic Movement (ILM), which attempts to clarify the nature of reasoning and argument and advocates empowering critical thought, differentiates between skills and abilities when he considers the teachableness of students' reasoning ability. Siegel refers to teaching critical thinking as enhancing students' reasoning skills and offers the following as examples of these skills: identifying assumptions, tracing relationships between premises and conclusions, and identifying standard fallacies (p. 77).

The second dimension, which Siegel (1997) refers to as the "critical spirit" component, includes attitudes, disposition, habits of mind, and character traits (p. 3), namely, characteristics that habituate a person to think critically. The desire to think critically is in one's nature; it is a routine habit to actively engage in assessing reasons that support beliefs, judgments, and actions. The person, then, is moved by reasons to believe, judge, and act in certain fashions and values those reasons and the basis they provide (p. 2).

For Siegel (1997), critical thinking forms a fundamental educational ideal, with the underlying justification being a moral one: Empowering students to think critically is equal to treating them with the respect they deserve as human beings and, therefore, treating them in a moral and acceptable way. In addition, it contributes to their self-sufficiency, prepares them for adulthood, initiates them into the rational traditions, and engages them in a democratic lifestyle (p. 4).

Norris

As Norris (1990) addresses thinking about critical thinking, he challenges the philosophers of education to not only read existing scientific research more extensively but also think about how this body of research can contribute to the thinking of critical thinking. As he examines how critical thinking should be defined and whether or not it is generalizable across subject areas, he acknowledges the relevancy of philosophical considerations but also suggests that those considerations are inadequate by themselves.

Norris provides a brief explanation about how philosophers have traditionally provided "conceptual analyses" (p. 68) of various concepts of education, including teaching, learning, and education. As an example of a conception of good thinking, Norris refers to a set of criteria put forth by Robert Ennis (1980) for defining critical thinking. He offers an explanation for why those in education are encouraged to adopt Ennis's view of critical-thinking competence in general "because of its conceptual soundness and usefulness to education" (p. 68). Norris then provides McPeck's (1981) opposition to Ennis's views of and approaches to critical thinking. Norris refers to Ennis's and McPeck's thinking to make the point that the approaches advocated by Ennis and McPeck were inadequate to resolve issues about critical thinking, including a definitive definition.

In order to determine what additional information is needed to make a decision, we need to understand the meaning of the assertion "someone has critical thinking ability" (Norris, 1990, p. 68). Claiming that someone has critical thinking ability asserts something about a person's mental power. Mental powers, in turn, evolve from mental structures and "processes in the same way that physical powers (magnetism is an example) arise from the internal structures and processes of physical objects" (p. 68). For Norris, defining critical-thinking ability begins with making a claim "at the *generic* level of existence of *some* mental ability, a claim based on the observable behaviors of people" (p. 69, emphasis in original). Stopping our investigation at this stage would prevent us from stating how many abilities were involved and describing the nature of those abilities in terms of many things, including their nature, relationships to one another, and development. Without further investigation, there is uncertainty about ascribing specific mental abilities to the observable behaviors. In order to do this, empirical research is needed to provide a lens through which we can view the nature of the mental structures and mechanisms. This may shed light on what mental processes were used to solve problems, how these processes were related to other processes, and how the mental processes evolved from the structures. Then we can ascertain what it means to have an ability to do a specific task.

Paul, Siegel, and Norris Compared and Contrasted

When one compares and contrasts Paul and Siegel, many similarities surface. Of Paul's five dimensions, there are two that bear resemblance to Siegel's two dimensions. Both authors offer one dimension that includes abilities that are necessary to understand and assess reasons, claims, and arguments and another dimension that includes dispositions, attitudes, or character traits that suggest a value and desire for critical thought.

The intellectual abilities Paul lists are not inert characteristics but enabling abilities. Siegel targets the operative aspect of understanding that is involved when assessing reasons, claims, and judgments. The question that begs to be answered is expressed as the need for empirical research in order to identify what mental abilities are involved when we think critically and to determine the nature of those abilities and the relationships that exist among those abilities.

Based on the analysis of Paul and Siegel, two broad dimensions or, as Siegel (1992) suggests, components of critical thinking can be identified. The first encompasses abilities that are necessary to think critically. These include: (1) identifying or recognizing a problem (Paul) or identifying assumptions and standard fallacies (Siegel, 1990), (2) evaluating various possibilities and suspending judg-

ment until possibilities are weighed (Paul) or assessing reasons for belief, judgments, and actions (Siegel), (3) synthesizing (Paul, Siegel), (4) concluding (Paul, Siegel), and (5) tracing relationships between premises and conclusions (Siegel).

The second dimension includes attitudes, dispositions, and traits of mind that are identified as intellectual independence, humility, courage, and good faith (Paul); and habits, moved to reason, and values (Siegel).

The Issue of Generalizability

Before the 1980s, there was an implicit assumption that critical thinking was generalizable. During the 1980s and into the 1990s, however, those who advocated generalizability were faced with criticisms and challenges. Psychologists examined how experts and novices solved problems within specific subjects and noted that knowledge of subject and not some general ability to think well differentiated experts and novices (Norris, 1992). From the philosophical field, it was argued by some that what may count as a good reason in one field may not count as a good reason in another field, hence different thinking for different fields (McPeck, 1981, 1989).

The question of generalizability in the critical-thinking literature has received as much attention, if not more, since the previous Handbook publication. The issue that remains is whether or not critical thinking is generalizable and, if it is, to what extent. Are there non-subject-specific abilities and skills employed while thinking critically that can be taught? Are there dispositions and attitudes associated with critical thinking that can be nurtured? Of the possible definitions of defining critical thinking described earlier, I will examine Siegel's and Norris's application of generalizability.

To distinguish between generalizability and specificity with regards to critical thinking, Siegel (1997) offers two principles of reason assessment: general or subject-neutral principles and subject-specific principles. The former are those that apply and are relevant to many contexts and therefore not confined to specific subjects. Principles that would be taught in a critical-thinking course, that is, formal and informal principles of logic, are not subject-specific. Skills and abilities of reason assessment such as recognizing weak reasoning, using statistical evidence in an appropriate manner, and justifying choices made with logical thought are subject-neutral and can be taught in a variety of contexts.

Principles that are subject-specific guide the assessment of reasons for a particular domain. In order to judge, evaluate, and make decisions, one must have some knowledge that is subject-specific in order to assess reasons. Siegel suggests, then, that students can strengthen their general critical-thinking skills and abilities, but to think critically about a certain subject students need to have some knowledge about the specific subject.

In discussions about generalizability, Norris (1992) links people's perception of generalizability with how they define critical thinking. He suggests that the following four conditions have to be satisfied in order for critical thinking to be considered generalizable: (1) the idea of thinking in general makes sense; (2) some commonality exists across fields, subjects, topics, concerns; (3) critical thinking provides a significant store of resources for dealing with the variety of fields, subjects, topics, and concerns; and (4) the ability to think critically in one field, subject, topic, and concern has a positive influence on thinking critically about another field, subject, topic, and concern (p. 1). The first is a question for conceptual analysis and the fourth a question for psychology. While debate about whether the second and third are met is an epistemological or empirical psychological issue, Norris suggests that the issue raises conceptual, epistemological, and empirical questions and thus requires research outside of the philosophical field.

In addition to the needed empirical research results as suggested by Norris (1990), educators may profit from what the psychological field can offer. Historically there has been a separation of the logical question and the psychological question. The former question addresses the rightness of an answer, while the latter addresses the processes through which the mind goes in finding the right answer (McDaniel & Lawrence, 1990). Those concerned with the logical question focus on procedures involved in analyzing reasoning, while those concerned with the psychological question focus on the processes of thought. Differing from the traditional view of thinking as right reasoning, McDaniel and Lawrence view thinking primarily as the selection, organization, and transformation of information as the individual makes sense of situations (p. 1). The traditional view holds that formal reasoning involves a highly defined problem situation to which rules of reasoning are applied that lead to an answer that is in agreement with the facts. There are, however, problems encountered in everyday life for which there are clearly no correct answers and no procedures for solving the problems and for which premises may or may not be implicit. When one perceives, defines, and supports the point of view, accumulated knowledge and experiences are used (a concept supported by Siegel, 1997). Problems are quite often of personal relevance and are examined as a means for other goals. Integral to this everyday reasoning is the process in which the information is selected, organized, and interpreted, a process that is consistent with one's values, attitudes, and understandings of the way the world works (McDaniel & Lawrence, 1990).

Empirical Research on Critical Thinking in Music

I will first present recent research on critical thinking in music. I will then extract those abilities identified in the research and described by Paul and Siegel and present them in this section.

As I reviewed the major research journals in music education, it became clear that since the last Handbook publication there have been few studies in which critical thinking about music has been investigated. What follows is a representation of research in which critical thinking in music has been examined and has been conducted since the publication of the previous Handbook.

Colley, Banton, Down, and Pither (1992) were interested in the differences of strategies between novice and expert musicians when given a composing task. Data were in the form of verbal reports, scores, and verbal responses collected in an interview setting. The expert, who was the only one to complete the task, approached it with an overall viewpoint while considering the strategic plans and utilized a variety of procedures when applying specific rules. The novices approached the task by completing each component of the task utilizing knowledge of basic theory.

Bundra (1993) examined children's music-listening processes that occurred while listening to extended examples of music. Data were collected by asking the children to think aloud and by questioning them during the think-aloud procedure. Bundra considered the effect of age, gender, and musical background when analyzing the verbal protocols and examined the children's own reflections on listening. Most important, Bundra concluded that children were capable of describing their thoughts while listening to music and after listening were able to articulate ideas about their listening processes. Findings, among others, revealed that qualitative and quantitative differences in terms of what was heard were age-specific. Older children more frequently exhibited processes reported by Richardson (1988), specifically, prediction, comparison, evaluation, preferences, reflection, and recognition. As well, they were more willing to express judgments about the music (Bundra, 1993, p. 367).

Richardson (1996) found that musically trained children, while listening to music of many styles and genres, articulated statements that revealed similar cognitive skills to those reflected in her model of the adult music expert's thinking (Richardson, 1988). In another study, Richardson (1998) found common thinking skills (cognitive skills) across participants, from three diverse populations, who were asked to think aloud while listening to a piece of music. These commonalities included classifying, elaborating, comparing, predicting, and evaluating. She suggested a need for asking students questions that require them to not only label, identify, and describe but also express their thinking and speculate about musical decisions. The results, when compared across studies, indicate that the ability to think critically while listening to music is related to factors other than age, a finding that differs from one of Bundra's results.

Based on a study by Davidson and Welsh (1988), Younker and Smith (1996) asked 4 subjects, an adult expert, an adult novice, a high school expert, and a high school novice, to think aloud while completing a compositional task. Smith and I were interested in how thought processes were used during a music composition task and wanted to investigate possible developmental patterns that may emerge based on the subjects' experiences and backgrounds. The adult expert was a doctoral composition student, the adult novice was a master of music education student, the high school expert was a student who had moderately high composition background, and the high school novice was a student who had never composed but had written a brief arrangement. Four distinct approaches across the four subjects were revealed through a comparative analysis. The following describes those approaches: The adult expert approached the task from an overall perspective, outlining possible solutions to problems inherent in the task and identified by him. There was evidence of exploration as well as an ability to arrive quickly at a decision. The high school expert began by exploring and improvising. The initial melody was quickly written, but then time was spent revising and evaluating what was written. This subject struggled between applying theoretical knowledge and making the melody sound right. The adult novice began notating immediately and improvising after some notation occurred. She explored possibilities but had difficulty converging on a solution. The high school novice approached the task sequentially by notating note-by-note throughout the procedure. There was minimal exploration and use of minimal time to complete the task.

In a later work (Younker, 2000), I examined whether or not strategies exhibited by university music majors who had not studied composition in a formal setting would resemble strategies as exhibited by the experts or novices in the previous (Younker & Smith, 1996) study. Based on the definition used in the 1996 study, these students would be novice composers. Verbal reports were collected through the think-aloud procedure while students composed a piece of music. An analysis of the verbal protocols revealed distinctive approaches similar to those found in the previous study. These approaches included: (1) proceeding without formulating a plan of action and composing in a step-by-step fashion with minimal analysis, synthesis, or evaluation; (2) formulating a framework for the composition, composing with minimal analysis, synthesis, and evaluation, and maintaining the framework even when problems were encountered that were related to that framework; (3) formulating a framework for the composition, composing with an increased amount of analysis, synthesis, and evaluation, and maintaining the framework even when problems were encountered that were related to that framework; and (4) exploring possibilities before converging on a framework, composing with an increased amount of analysis, synthesis, and evaluation, and changing the framework when problems were encountered that were related to the original framework.

Critical-Thinking Processes in Music

The purpose of the preceding studies was to identify thought processes that occurred while interacting with music. This research represents one of the kinds of research advocated by Norris (1990) as a means to identify processes that are involved in critical thinking. In an attempt to make identifiable those thoughts that occurred while interacting with music, the studies examined the subjects' thought processes. In the following paragraph, critical-thinking abilities as identified by Paul (1993) and Siegel (1997) will be compared with abilities identified in the studies that were examined in the previous section.

Colley, Banton, Down, and Pither (1992) revealed differences of abilities between the novices and expert that signify the need for knowledge that is subject-specific in order to think critically about that subject area (Siegel, 1997). The processes of comparing, evaluating, reflecting, and judging, as identified by Bundra (1993), and classifying, elaborating, comparing, predicting, and evaluating, as identified by Richardson (1998), are included in the abilities given by Paul (1993) and Siegel (1997). Within four distinct approaches, Younker and Smith (1996) and Younker (2000) identified the following abilities as found in Paul's second dimension of critical thinking: identifying, applying, generating, analyzing, synthesizing, and evaluating.

Implications for Further Research

While some questions have been answered as a result of Richardson and Whitaker's (1992) directives, many remained unanswered. In addition to those posed by Richardson and Whitaker, the following implications are offered for further research:

First, we have only begun to identify abilities that are associated with thinking critically in music. Further research is needed to reveal the presence or absence of those abilities as identified by philosophers of education who write about critical thinking and then address the relationships among those abilities that have been identified.

Second, the task for music educators is to identify, if any, those aspects of critical thinking that are used in all musical interactions regardless of the specific area of expertise and those that are specific to an area of expertise (composing, listening, performing, and improvising). Next we need to identify what specific knowledge is needed to think critically while composing, performing, listening, and improvising. What would those bodies of knowledge be and how can we determine them through empirical research?

Third, are there developmental aspects of critical thinking in music, or is it an ability that is either present or absent? If the former, then what are those developmental levels when thinking about music? Does thinking critically mean we need to acquire all of the abilities as outlined by the various philosophers, or does our growth as critical thinkers evolve over time as we acquire the abilities and accumulate related knowledge?

When one is formulating research designs to identify abilities of novice and expert thinkers, there is a need to involve subjects who would qualify as novices and determine similarities and differences of abilities across those subjects. There is also a need to involve subjects who would qualify as experts and determine similarities and differences across those subjects. Investigating how experts think critically about music can guide our understanding when making inferences about musical thinking. Thought has to be given, however, to what constitutes an expert. Bereiter and Scardamalia (1993) suggest that experts do not perform tasks in an attempt to solve the problem (and thinking that by performing them, the problem will be solved) but rise to the level of the problem presented to them and address the problem. If we adopt Bereiter and Scardamalia's thinking, then we need to rethink the purpose of replicating studies like Younker and Smith (1996) and Colley et al. (1992).

There appears to be a misunderstanding about what it means to identify or recognize or sense or encounter a problem. Can we assume that Paul, Siegel, and Norris mean the same thing as Dewey when they include identifying or recognizing a problem as an aspect of critical thinking? Can we formulate research studies that require students to identify the problem when they experience a doubt or perplexity and then require them to analyze, synthesize, and evaluate plausible solutions? Or should we propose research studies that require students to identify a problem that has been formulated by the researcher? The same questions need to be addressed from a pedagogical perspective. If we value critical thinking, then we need to formulate opportunities that allow the students to identify problems that are meaningful to them.

Another area of research to consider is capturing students' thought processes as they compose using computer software programs. While some work has been done in exploring aspects of creative thinking (Hickey, 1995) and critical thinking, further investigation is needed on aspects of research design.

Assessment of critical thinking is another area of research that needs attention. How can we assess students' ability to analyze solutions to musical problems, to synthesize and evaluate musical solutions? Would the assessment tool be the same across composing, listening, performing, and improvising?

As we continue to design research studies based on theoretical models and definitions, we can further our knowledge about what constitutes critical thinking in music. This knowledge can guide us as we develop the curricula that in turn will inform us about pedagogical practices, methodologies, and assessment issues related to critical thinking in music.

REFERENCES

Bereiter, C., & Scardamalia, M. (1993). *Surpassing ourselves: An inquiry into the nature and implications of expertise.* Chicago: Open Court.

Bundra, J. (1993) A study of music listening processes through the verbal reports of school-aged children. *Dissertation Abstracts International,* (UMI No. 9415701)

Colley, A., Banton, L., Down, J., & Pither, A. (1992). An expert–novice comparison in musical composition. *Psychology of Music, 20,* 124–137.

Davidson, L., & Welsh, P. (1988). From collections to structure: The developmental path of tonal thinking. In J. A. Sloboda (Ed.), *Generative processes in music: The psychology of performance, improvisation, and composition* (pp. 260–285). New York: Oxford University Press.

Dewey, J. (1938). *Experience and education.* New York: Collier Books.

Dewey, J. (1991). *How we think.* Buffalo, NY: Prometheus Books. (Original work published 1933)

Ennis, R. H. (1980). A conception of rational thinking. In J. R. Coombs (Ed.), *Philosophy of education 1979* (pp. 3–30). Normal, IL: Philosophy of Education Society.

Ennis, R. H. (1987). A taxonomy of critical thinking dispositions and abilities. In J. B. Baron and R. J. Sternberg (Eds.), *Teaching thinking skills: Theory and practice* (pp. 9–26). New York: Freeman.

Hickey, M. (1995). *Qualitative and quantitative relationships between children's creative musical thinking processes and products.* Unpublished doctoral dissertation, Northwestern University, Evanston, Illinois.

McDaniel, E., & Lawrence, C. (1990). *Levels of cognitive complexity: An approach to the measurement of thinking.* New York: Springer.

McPeck, J. E. (1981). *Critical thinking and education.* New York: St. Martin's Press.

McPeck, J. E. (1984). Stalking beasts but swatting flies: The teaching of critical thinking. *Canadian Journal of Education, 9*(1), 28–44.

McPeck, J. E. (Ed.). (1990). *Teaching critical thinking*. New York: Routledge & Kegan Paul.

Norris, S. P. (1990). Thinking about critical thinking: Philosophers can't go it alone. In J. E. McPeck (Ed.), *Teaching critical thinking* (pp. 67–74). New York: Routledge & Kegan Paul.

Norris, S. P. (1992). Introduction: The generalizability question. In S. P. Norris (Ed.), *The generalizability of critical thinking: Multiple perspectives on an educational ideal* (pp. 1–15). New York: Teachers College Press.

Paul, R. W. (1987). Dialogical thinking: Critical thought essential to the acquisition of rational knowledge and passions. In J. B. Baron & R. J. Sternberg (Eds.), *Teaching thinking skills: Theory and practice* (pp. 127–148). New York: Freeman.

Paul, R. W. (1993). Chapters 3–5. In J. Willsen & A. J. A. Binker (Eds.), *Critical thinking: How to prepare students for a rapidly changing world* (pp. 37–100). Santa Rosa, CA: Foundations for Critical Thinking.

Richardson, C. P. (1988). *Musical thinking as exemplified in music criticism*. Unpublished doctoral dissertation, University of Illinois at Urbana-Champaign.

Richardson, C. P. (1996). A theoretical model of the connoisseurs' musical thought. *Bulletin of the Council for Research in Music Education, 128,* 15–24.

Richardson, C. P. (1998). The roles of the critical thinker in the music classroom. *Studies in Music from the University of Western Ontario, 17,* 107–120.

Richardson, C. P., & Whitaker, N. L. (1992). Critical thinking and music education. In R. J. Colwell (Ed.), *Handbook of research on music teaching and learning: A project of the Music Educators National Conference* (pp. 546–557). New York: Schirmer Books.

Siegel, H. (1988). *Educating reason: Rationality, critical thinking, and education*. New York: Routledge & Kegan Paul (Philosophy of Education Research Library).

Siegel, H. (1990). McPeck, informal logic, and the nature of critical thinking. In J. E. McPeck (Ed.), *Teaching critical thinking* (pp. 75–85). New York: Routledge & Kegan Paul.

Siegel, H. (1992). The generalizability of critical thinking skills, dispositions, and epistemology. In S. P. Norris (Ed.), *The generalizability of critical thinking: Multiple perspectives on an educational ideal* (pp. 97–108). New York: Teachers College Press.

Siegel, H. (1997). *Rationality redeemed? Further dialogues on an educational ideal*. New York: Routledge & Kegan Paul.

Woodford, P. G. (2001). *Democracy and music education*. Unpublished manuscript.

Younker, B. A. (2000). Composing with voice: Students' strategies, thought processes, and reflections. In B. A. Roberts (Ed.), *The phenomenon of singing: Proceedings of the international symposium* (pp. 247–260). St. Johns, Newfoundland, Canada: Memorial University.

Younker, B. A., & Smith, W. H., Jr. (1996). Comparing and modeling musical thought processes of the expert and novice composers. *Bulletin of the Council for Research in Music Education, 128,* 25–36.

Improvisation

11

CHRISTOPHER D. AZZARA

Many music educators have advocated the development of students' creativity and improvisation skills in music classrooms (Biasini, Thomas, & Pogonowski, 1970; Consortium of National Arts Education Associations, 1994; Contemporary Music Project, 1966, 1971; National Association of Schools of Music, 1999; Richmond, 1989). Despite such advocacy, much of the literature on the topic of improvisation in music education points to the fact that it is rarely part of the core of music education curricula (e.g., Azzara, 1993; Kratus, 1989; Schmidt & Sinor, 1986; Webster, 1987a). With the publication of *National Standards for Arts Education* (Consortium of National Arts Education Associations, 1994), music educators have become increasingly aware of the importance of the art of improvisation as a valuable musical skill for all music students. Researchers have continued to articulate the need for improvisation instructional materials, teacher education in improvisation, and, in general, emphasis on improvisation as a vital part of music curricula (e.g., Azzara, 1999; Bitz, 1999; Brown, 1991; Della Pietra & Campbell, 1995; Gregory, 1996; Jorgensen, 1998; Lubart, 1998; Richmond, 1989; Riveire, 1998; Rosfeld, 1989; Townsend, 1998).

The purpose of this chapter is to discuss the nature of improvisation and its role in the music teaching and learning process. Included are significant studies on improvisation in music and music education, interpretation of this research, and suggestions and questions for research and practice. The chapter has two sections: "Components of Improvisation" is a discussion of several components of improvisation: definition; social and cultural and psychological aspects; and historical significance and performance practice in world music and Western music. "Pedagogy Research and Practice" is a discussion of improvisation pedagogy research, implications for teaching practice, and im-

provisation's role in the music curriculum. This section includes discussions of improvisation research and practice in vocal, general, and instrumental music, technology, and jazz pedagogy.

Components of Improvisation

Definition

Improvisation has been an essential component of music throughout history, yet its manifestation in contemporary music classrooms is not clearly defined. In most cases, comprehensive improvisation skill development is absent from music curricula. When improvisation has been incorporated into music curricula, it appears in a variety of ways and consensus regarding a definition for improvisation or emerging improvisation skills is difficult to find. With a deeper understanding of what it means to improvise, music educators may begin to come to terms with its role in the teaching and learning process.

In much of the research, the definition of improvisation involves an ability to make music spontaneously within specified musical parameters. Kratus (1990) differentiates between exploration and improvisation: "A person who is improvising is able to predict the sounds that result from certain actions, whereas a person who is exploring cannot" (p. 35). Spontaneity and interaction also are central ingredients to most definitions of improvisation found in the related research. Studying the features of creative improvisation, Briggs (1987) notes that there are certain universal components in all creative improvisation. Briggs refers to improvisation as "musical dialogue" and states that model sound patterns and processes of interaction were common to each improvisation investigated. Briggs also points to extramusical factors such as context, environment, background, and experience of the improvisers as contributing factors to the content and form of the music.

In a study of fifth-grade instrumentalists' ability to improvise (Azzara, 1992), I defined improvisation as a manifestation of musical thought. In this research, *improvisation* means that an individual has internalized a music vocabulary and is able to understand and to express musical ideas spontaneously, in the moment of performance. Improvisation is often compared to speaking and conversation in language. B. Dobbins (1980) compares the improvisation process to language:

> Full proficiency in a verbal language must include the ability to command a considerable vocabulary with equal facility at the reading, conversational, and intuitive levels. The development of proficiency in a music "language" involves the same general process. The ability to play a Beethoven sonata or an Art Tatum solo is, by itself, no more an indication of musical creativity than is the ability to read a Shakespeare play an indication of the ability to use the English language creatively. (p. 37)

In this context, improvisation skill allows individuals to express musical thoughts and ideas from an internal source, with meaning, and it also promotes the acquisition of higher order thinking skills.

A variety of viewpoints exist that regard the relationship between improvisation and composition. S. Nachmanovitch (1990) writes:

> In improvisation there is only one time . . . the time of inspiration, the time of technically structuring and realizing the music, the time of playing it, and the time of communicating with the audience, as well as ordinary clock time, are all one. Memory and intention (which postulate past and future) and intuition (which indicates the eternal present) are fused. (p. 18)

Sarath (1996) contrasts improvisation and composition "from the standpoint of temporal perception" in a model with the central premise "that the improviser experiences time in an inner-directed, or 'vertical,' manner, where the present is heightened and the past and future are perceptually subordinated" (p. 1). Detailing the importance of "inner-directedness," ideas that sound in the localized present, and spontaneity, Sarath outlines an analytical and aesthetic framework for improvised music. M. Pelz-Sherman (1999) also presents a framework for analyzing improvised music. This model describes the structural analysis of music created by a group of improvising musicians as being distinct from the structural analysis of traditionally composed music. He notes that improvised music relies on the interactions among the musicians performing in the moment as compared to a sole composer making mu-

sical decisions outside of real time. The three "building blocks" of the analysis framework are soloing/accompanying, sharing, and not-sharing. According to Pelz-Sherman, musicians must develop high levels of communication skill using these building blocks in order to interact successfully.

Several themes that appear in the literature help to define improvisation. Key factors for defining improvisation include a process of (1) spontaneously expressing musical thoughts and feelings, (2) making music within certain understood guidelines, and (3) engaging in musical conversation (Azzara, 1999; Dobbins, 1980; Kratus, 1990; Sawyer, 1999). P. Nardone (1997) conducted a phenomenological psychological analysis in an attempt to understand the meaning of improvisation as a distinct form of artistic activity in the life-world of musicians. Nardone reports the findings of this analysis as "lived meanings" that constitute the psychological experience of improvisation and the musical context in which improvisation takes place. These include: (1) ensuring spontaneity while yielding to it; (2) being present and not present to musical processes; (3) exploring familiar and unfamiliar musical terrain; (4) drawing from a corporeal and incorporeal source of musical inspirations; (5) having trust and confidence in oneself and musical others in musical risk taking; (6) extending toward the listening other in musical risk taking; (7) perceiving temporality as altered; and (8) attending moment to moment to temporality.

Several educators (Abramson, 1980; Aebersold, 1988; Azzara, 1999; & Kratus, 1991) urge that improvisation can and should be a meaningful part of every person's life and education. Nachmanovitch (1990) states: "When we think *improvisation,* we tend to think first of improvised music or theater or dance; but beyond their own delights, such art forms are doors into an experience that constitutes the whole of everyday life. We are all improvisers" (p. 17).

Social Aspects, the Role of Community, and the Importance of an Improvisation Culture

Much of the improvisation literature recommends the importance of creating a culture that embraces and encourages improvisation, creativity, and risk taking. Csikszentmihalyi (1996) describes creativity as a systemic phenomenon and notes that creativity happens in the interaction between a person's thoughts and a sociocultural context. He writes: "Creativity is any act, idea, or product that changes an existing domain, or that transforms an existing domain into a new one" (p. 28). Improvisation takes place in a social context, with various individuals interacting with one another to create the music.

Leavell (1997) studied social aspects of secondary students' jazz band experience, remarking that student perspectives in improvisation have for the most part been ignored. He investigated students' views about improvising, playing individualized parts, and interpreting and articulating swing rhythms and reported that several students felt anxious when improvising alone in front of their peers and that group improvisation and rhythmic embellishment of familiar tunes were helpful in alleviating their concerns. The students also were aware of the environmental differences between jazz band and concert band and felt they had more "freedom of expression" in the jazz band setting of this study. Demonstrating another outcome of this freer environment, Leavell observed that the more eager student improvisers forged friendships with one another.

Montello (1990) examined the effect of "holistic group music therapy" that incorporated clinical musical improvisation, musical performance, awareness techniques, and verbal processing as a treatment for the fear and anxiety aspect of performance stress. This intervention was found to be an effective way to reduce performance stress and help musicians become more aware of the issues related to performance anxiety, experience a safe environment, transform stress through creativity, and bond in the spirit of community.

The role of community, interaction, and the aural learning process in folk (Adler, 1980), jazz (Berliner, 1994; Collier, 1996; Monson, 1992, 1996), and world music (Brinner, 1986; Thompson, 1995) traditions has been examined. Improvisation and playing by ear are central to folk, jazz, and world music. In a study of the learning and "traditionalizing" process of amateur bluegrass banjo players, Adler suggests that a person's involvement in the tradition of bluegrass is a progressive sequence of "intentional" stages as "auditor," "competent listener," "inceptor," "beginner," and "competent banjoist." Adler continues that in the process of becoming a competent bluegrass banjo player an individual proceeds through a series of important encounters with the music, model players, and an instrument. The author notes that competent players express themselves by connecting their musical thoughts to sounds.

Monson (1992) examined the musical interaction in modern jazz and comments that the musical and social context of the jazz ensemble is fundamental for explaining the musical events and choices that occur during improvisation. From research with professional jazz musicians Monson found that individual instrumentalists stressed the importance of musical interaction. They also spoke of the need for players to develop keen listening skills in order to anticipate and respond to one another's musical ideas.

Interaction among musicians is an important aspect of musical expression in the performance of the Solonese *pathetan* repertoire (Brinner, 1986). *Pathetan* are short, ametrical, rhythmically free polyphonic pieces performed on four of the elaborating instruments of the Central Javanese gamelan with or without male chorus or vocal soloist. Rather than learn a specific part, musicians learn the process for creating their part. Various melodies interact and are coordinated in an ametrical context. Skill in playing *pathetan* depends on a musician's ability to play smaller patterns in response to other musicians within the context of larger patterns that make up a *pathetan*. The interaction among musicians is based on a set of cues, the role of instruments in the ensemble, and the personality, experience, age, and status of the ensemble members. In a study of the Mandinka drummers in the Gambia, Thompson (1995) explored the process by which rhythmic structures and improvisation were used to create music and social life. In this setting, the lead drummer plays a critical role in the development of musical dialogue and social interaction through the rhythmic, melodic, and communicative aspects of the drumming.

A necessary element for creating an improvisation culture is the letting go of fear. Nachmanovitch (1990) writes of "five fears" the Buddhists describe that are obstacles to our freedom to create: fear of loss of life, fear of loss of livelihood, fear of loss of reputation, fear of unusual states of mind, and fear of speaking before an assembly. Fear of speaking before an assembly is taken to mean "stage fright," or fear of performing. Fear of performing is "profoundly related to fear of foolishness, which has two parts: fear of being thought a fool (loss of reputation) and fear of actually being a fool (fear of unusual states of mind)" (p. 135). To these fears Nachmanovitch adds the fear of ghosts, that is, being overcome by teachers, authorities, parents, or great masters. Werner (1996) also discusses the aspect of fear—fear-based practicing, fear-based teaching, fear-based listening, and fear-based composing. Werner writes that improvisation and self-expression require "the taming of the mind, the dissolution of the ego, and the letting go of all fears" (p. 75). Both Nachmanovitch and Werner cite Aaron Copland (1952), who said: "Inspiration may be a form of super-consciousness, or perhaps of subconsciousness—I wouldn't know. But I am sure that it is the antithesis of self-consciousness" (Nachmanovitch, 1990, p. 51).

Psychological Aspects and Mental Processes

Individuals such as Elliot (1995), Gordon (1997a), Kratus (1991), Pressing (1988), Sarath (1996), Serafine (1988), Sloboda (1985, 1988), and Webster (1988, 1991) attempt to describe the mental processes that enable persons to create meaning in music. Elliot (1995) writes that musical creativity, that is, a performance, improvisation, composition, or arrangement, exists in the context of musical practice and is the result of both musical intelligence ("enabling" abilities) and musicianship ("promoting" abilities).

Webster (1988, 1991) describes the creative process as beginning with an intended product, for example, improvisation/performance or composition. The nature of creativity, according to Webster, depends on "enabling skills" (e.g., music aptitudes, conceptual understanding, craftsmanship, and aesthetic sensitivity) and is influenced by "enabling conditions" (e.g., motivation, subconscious imagery, personality, and environment). Webster proposes that through a process of divergent and convergent thinking skills these enabling skills and conditions ultimately come together in the creation of a product.

Kratus (1991) and Hargreaves, Cork, and Setton (1991) note that differences in approach are apparent when one compares the experiences of novice and expert improvisers. Kratus (1991, 1996) developed a multilevel sequential model for understanding the improvisation process. His theory describes seven levels of development. In the *exploration* level, the student tries out sounds and combinations of sounds in a loosely structured context. The student produces more cohesive patterns in *process-oriented improvisation* and then becomes conscious of structural principles such as tonality and meter in *product-oriented improvisation. Fluid improvisation* occurs when the student manipulates his or her voice or instrument in a more automatic and more relaxed manner. In *structural improvisation,* the student is aware of the overall structure and develops a repertoire of strategies for shaping an improvisation. *Stylistic improvisation* involves the skillful incorporation of melodic, harmonic, and rhythmic characteristics of a musical style. At the highest level, *personal improvisation,* individuals are capable of transcending recognized improvisation styles and developing a new style.

Improvisation is a skill and level of learning in Gordon's music-learning sequence (1997a). In the development of his music-learning theory, Gordon coined the term *audiation.* Audiation offers a more precise definition of musical imagery, that is, aural perception and kinesthetic reaction, and a definition of how persons understand and create meaning in music. In the current definition, Gordon describes several types and stages of audiation. He defines audiation as hearing and comprehending in one's mind the sound of music that is no longer or may never have been physically present (1997a). Audiation is to music what thinking is to language. Gordon states that we audiate music we have heard, as well as the music we are predicting; individuals audiate music when reading, writing, creating, improvising, listening, and performing. The abilities to retain, recall, compare, and predict are recognized as primary mental functions in Gordon's definition of audiation. Gordon suggests that for meaningful improvisation to take place, an individual must audiate what he or she is going to create or improvise (Gordon, 1997a; Richmond, 1989). He also suggests that "perhaps only the readiness to learn to improvise can be taught, and improvisation itself has to be learned" (2000, p. 35). Gordon (1997b, 2000) has studied the "readiness" for harmonic and rhythmic improvisation and has designed two tests, the Harmonic Improvisation Readiness Record and the Rhythm Improvisation Readiness Record, for helping teachers adapt instruction to students' individual needs. For tonal improvisation, Gordon (1997b) recommends that students should

> hear a variety of tonal patterns, imitate (echo) a variety of tonal patterns, audiate tonal patterns, produce tonal patterns, and improvise tonal patterns. For harmonic improvisation, students should hear a variety of harmonic progressions, imitate (echo) a variety of harmonic progressions, audiate harmonic progressions, produce harmonic progressions, and improvise harmonic progressions. (p. 10)

Sloboda (1988) edited a textbook that contains contributions from various authors interested in generative processes in music, that is, the psychology of performance, improvisation, and composition. The editor notes the "inextricable connection" of generative and receptive processes in music as a recurring theme of the book. He comments on researchers' neglect of generative processes in music and cites three concerns: cultural bias, problems of measurement, and problems of control. Based on the findings of the contributors, Sloboda provides a supposition that the impulse to generate and perform music is as intrinsically a part of being human as is the impulse to generate language. Contributors Sagi and Vitanyi (1988) studied the spontaneous improvisation of untrained, "ordinary" Hungarians and emphasized the features of style and structure inherent in their improvisations. Similarly, Dowling (1988) provides evidence to demonstrate that young children produce "spontaneous songs which incorporate but by no means mimic elements of adult productions" (p. vi). Dowling notes that children's songs contain both the elements of reproduction and improvisation "intertwined." Sloboda also cites the work of Swanwick and Tillman (1986) as an example to support the idea that when given opportunities for self-directed musical productivity "children demonstrate an impressively varied yet ordered progression of compositional strategies right through the school ages" (p. vii).

Pressing (1988) surveyed the modeling tools from a number of different disciplines in an attempt to understand how people improvise and how improvisational skill is learned and taught. He presents a cognitive model for the process of improvisation and relates this model to improvisation skill acquisition. His theory of improvisation focuses on the moment-to-moment choices within the structure of an improvisation. The model is "reductionist" in the sense that the cognitive construction of mental processing is broken down into "aspects" and then into "types of analytical representation" and these into "characterizing elements." Pressing suggests that the improvisation process develops as a series of choices of "event clusters" that either continue or interrupt the context of the stream of elements.

These models for understanding the improvisation process provide researchers with several points of departure for continued investigations. Many of the conclusions drawn here need to be substantiated by evidence in research and practice. With a better understanding of the creative processes involved in improvisation, music teachers will be able to improve instruction and provide environments conducive to creativity and improvisation.

Historical Significance: World and Western Music Performance Research and Practice

World Music. Improvisation plays an important role in music from all over the world. For example, the gamelan music of Java and Bali involves high levels of group improvisation performance (Brinner, 1986). Park (1986) provides an example of improvisation's role in Korean music. Park studied Korean creative musicians, the *tanggol,* and their accompanists, the *koin.* This author examined how these musicians function as individual performers and as integrated groups in the process of improvisation. Displaying much skill and intuitive ability, these musicians invent melody and poetry to meet the specific circumstances of particular rituals.

Other examples of improvisation can be found in the music of Turkey, China, Yugoslavia, and Iran and throughout sub-Saharan Africa (Campbell, 1990; Stubbs, 1995). The Persian system of improvisation is taught by the learning of the *radif,* a large repertoire of mostly nonmetric music. The *radif* forms the basis for improvisation and composition. Throughout Africa, improvisation plays a vital role in the music-making process. In West Africa, certain traditions require the spontaneous creation of new melodies, rhythms, and song texts during the act of performance (Campbell, 1990).

In South India, musicians improvise passages and variations in the performances of a repertory of composed songs (Cormack, 1992; Reck, 1983). Cormack documented and analyzed *svara kalpana,* one of several improvised forms performed in a South Indian classical Carnatic concert. Reck studied the music of South India through the life and performances of a South Indian musician. He notes that South Indian musicians learn and perform music by ear and that improvisation skill is developed in the process of teaching and learning. This work also defines the concepts of raga (mode) and tala (meter) and, in particular, provides an understanding of the raga and tala of the performances studied.

Booth (1987) presents a case study of the oral transmission practices of tabla performers in transition. Tabla are the drums of North Indian art music that accompany both instrumental and vocal performance. Booth observed tabla lessons and interviewed tabla performers, teachers, and students in five urban centers of northern India. He found contrasts in the philosophy and pedagogy between the more "traditional" teachers, who believed that teaching was an obligation of their art and the more "contemporary" teachers who thought of teaching as a source of income. Improvisation was a goal of the more traditional, oral transmission of the music; memorization was a goal associated with the more contemporary, literate transmission of the music. Booth offers a comparison to the "oral–literate" dichotomy present in the development of music education in the United States.

Western Music. Improvisation has also been a prevalent part of music making throughout the history of Western music. In recent years, many performers, especially performers of music from the 18th century and before, have developed skill and understanding for improvisation in the interest of authentic performance. For example, the art of improvisation was important to the development of melismatic types of liturgical chant. Other examples of improvisation in early music are found in the performance of discant, in the performance of medieval songs such as *cantus coronatus,* and in *faburden*—an English technique of polyphonic vocal improvisation performed in the 15th and 16th centuries (Ferand, 1961).

Improvisation was essential to the performance practice of the music in the Baroque and Classical eras of Western music history (Candelaria, 1987; Ferand, 1961; Greenan, 1997; Weiss & Taruskin, 1984). Many of the composers of the Western canon, for example, Bach, Handel, Mozart, and Beethoven, were exuberant improvisers and teachers (Bellman, 1991; David & Mendel, 1972; Mann, 1987; Schonberg, 1987; Weiss & Taruskin, 1984). Improvisation, active performance, and teaching were all closely related and played a vital role in these great composers' lives. Mann points out, for instance, that Bach's and Handel's attitude toward teaching

> is evident, on the one hand, from the fact that the study of composition was invariably linked to skill in active performance, and on the other hand, from the fact that both composers constantly rewrote their own works—as well as the works of others—with a view to changing performance requirements. (p. 7)

Researchers such as Lamott (1980), Harrison (1995), and Nutting (1989) have examined the field of organ improvisation teaching and practice. For example, Lamott provides a detailed examination of *Nova Instruction Pro Pulsandis Organis,* a 17th-century keyboard treatise designed for the systematic teaching of preludial improvisation. *Nova Instruction* was written by a German Carmelite and was published in three parts in 1670 and 1672 and circa 1675–1677. Lamott (1980) describes this treatise as an extensive practical method for teaching improvisation through the partimento-style realization of figured bass progressions. It particularly addressed organists and choirmasters in monasteries who, because of liturgical requirements, improvised daily. Another researcher, Harrison (1995), studied an 18th-century pedagogical treatise on beginning keyboard playing written by organist Michael Wiedeburg. Harrison writes of Wiedeburg's life, musical career, and improvisation pedagogy. Weideburg's method for improvisation instruction can be found in the third volume of this large three-volume treatise. It begins with explanations of harmony and simple patterns for chorale improvisations and progresses to the improvisation of free fantasies and other 18th-century forms not based on chorales. Volume 3 also includes Weideburg's pedagogical ideas for how to improvise chorale harmonizations, simple variations, and interludes. In 1989, Nutting wrote a technical manual based on hymn tunes for the purpose of developing specific improvisation techniques such as (1) varying a melody; (2) developing motives; (3) playing common harmonic progressions; (4) playing hymn settings by supplying one or more voice and/or placing the melody in the alto, tenor, or bass voice; (5) reharmonizing hymn tunes; (6) extending and creating phrases; and (7) improvising complete hymn settings that included introduction, interludes, and coda.

Greenan (1997) states that improvisation is vital to the identity of the Classical style. The cadenza is a well-known vehicle for improvisation in music for soloists, especially in the concerto or other work with accompanying ensemble. Greenan's study contributes a more comprehensive understanding of the music of the Classical period by identifying the role of a structurally important means of improvisation: the *Eingang*. An *Eingang* is a short, cadenza-like passage for the soloist that precedes and leads into a solo section in a work. The study cites references to the *Eingang* in treatises that range from Quantz to Czerny. Greenan argues that the Eingang of the Classical period may be seen as a transitional vehicle between the Baroque musical aesthetic, in which the performer(s) completed the melodic progression through improvisational melodic ornamentation and figured bass realization, and the Romantic musical aesthetic, where the composer permanently completed an individually expressive, quasi-improvisatory melodic progression (p. 5).

In the 19th century, Carl Czerny (1836, 1836/1983) wrote a comprehensive treatise on the subject of piano improvisation, which is considered to be the first attempt to present such a work on this topic to the public (Goertzen, 1996, p. 301). Johann Nepomuk Hummel, an influential composer and one of the greatest improvisers of his time, also wrote a method for piano that had a significant effect

on piano pedagogy in the first half of the 19th century. Hummel's thoughts on the importance of improvisation in music education are expressed in this instructional book:

> I close by recommending free improvisation in general and in every respectable form to all those for whom [music] is not merely a matter of entertainment and practical ability, but rather principally one of inspiration and meaning in their art. This recommendation, to be sure, has never been so urgent now, because the number of people whose interest belong to the former category and not to the latter has never been so great. Even if a person plays with inspiration, but always from a written score, he or she will be much less nourished, broadened, and educated than through the frequent offering of all of his or her powers in a free fantasy practiced in the full awareness of certain guidelines and directions, even if this improvisation is only moderately successful. (Hummel, 1828/1829, p. 468; Goertzen, 1996, p. 305)

Chopin, Mendelssohn, Liszt, Bruckner, Saint-Saëns, and Franck were well known for improvising in the style of their own compositions. Bellman (1991) presents historical research on Fredric Chopin's performance style and suggests parameters for improvisation in Chopin's Nocturnes. Goertzen (1996) studied the history of improvised piano preludes in the 18th and 19th centuries. This author states that improvising preludes was a common part of piano performance at this time in history, but that it is not a part of current performance practice because of the absence of notation. Goertzen also notes that Hummel and Czerny outlined the guidelines for constructing preludes in their method books. This study provides examples of improvised piano preludes of Mozart, Clementi, Mendelssohn, Clara Schumann, and Robert Schumann.

While some 20th-century and now 21st-century classical composers have included improvisation sections in their pieces, improvisation's role in Western classical music has decidedly declined since the middle of the 19th century. Currently the art of improvisation thrives in jazz. Schuller (1968) writes: "Improvisation is the heart and soul of jazz" (p. 58). Through a process of chronicling jazz musicians' experiences with improvisation as the centerpiece of their art form, Berliner (1994) describes the nature of jazz improvisation. His text includes firsthand accounts from musicians who describe the preparation and process for improvising jazz. Significant to Berliner's model for jazz improvisation are the concepts of early musical environments, the jazz community as an educational system, developing a jazz repertoire, developing a jazz vocabulary, interaction, musical conversation, jazz as a way of life, thinking jazz, and making music in the moment.

Since the 1940s, researchers in music education have investigated the nature of improvisation and have developed and examined instructional materials to teach improvisation. The section that follows considers this research.

Pedagogy Research and Practice

Improvisation is defined and incorporated into music education curricula in a variety of ways. Researchers have used various criteria for understanding improvisation skill, ranging from exploration and free improvisation to improvisations based on form and harmonic progression. This review of the literature is organized by research that relates to: (1) preschool/classroom improvisation, (2) improvisation in instrumental music, and (3) jazz improvisation in vocal and instrumental settings.

Preschool/Classroom Improvisation Research

Particular attention has been given to the improvisation of young children. Moorhead and Pond (1978) published one of the first studies of children's improvisations. The research took place during the 1940s at the Pillsbury Foundation School in Santa Barbara, California. Moorhead and Pond observed 2- to 6-year-old students chanting improvisations and playing improvisations on instruments. The researchers found that with guidance and experience children could improvise as they explored tonal and rhythmic patterns. The initial improvisation experiences involved the exploration of tone and timbre. Improvisations included patterns within a steady beat and asymmetrical patterns. In 1981 Pond reflected upon his work at the Pillsbury school, noting the importance of community:

> Music making, as I observed, became an integral part of the community's life—there were few activities that were not spontaneously accompanied by *their* appropriate music. In this regard I found, again, my studies of the music of primitive peoples instructive. (p. 11)

The Pillsbury Foundation School began operation in Santa Barbara in February 1937 and continued until 1948. The Pillsbury Foundation School Archives are now housed at the Music Educators National Conference Historical Center, University of Maryland. Wilson (1981) comments that "somewhat like the belated discovery of Charles Ives' music, music researchers and teachers are perhaps more ready for a knowledge of the Pillsbury Foundation School now than they were when it was a contemporary institution" (p. 13). In a project similar to Pond's work, Cohen (1980) spent 3 years observing kindergarten children. In addition to making detailed personal observations, Cohen videotaped the kindergartners, in particular the interactions of two children. Cohen found that the children explored with instruments and musical sounds, developed mastery with certain skills, and produced "musical gestures" (musical ideas a few notes in length or longer) as a part of the improvisation process.

Dalcroze and Orff Schulwerk curricula emphasize improvisation in the music learning process. Dalcroze improvisation activities include spontaneous movement, vocal performance, and instrumental performance. With regard to Dalcroze and music education, Abramson (1980) states: "To improvise is to speak the musical language of motion and pitch, without text, but clearly, expressively and memorably. Jaques-Dalcroze thought of improvisation as basic to life, as an expression of life, and as life itself" (p. 68). Joseph (1983) studied a Dalcroze Eurhythmics approach to learning music for kindergarten children. Music classes involved activities that incorporated ear training, rhythmic movement, and improvisation. This research compared three groups of kindergarten students. Group 1 received "informal" music instruction, group 2 received Eurhythmics with improvisation, and group 3 received Eurhythmics without improvisation. In the course of 1 year, the students involved in the Eurhythmics program participated in 44 lessons that incorporated ear training, movement exploration, rhythmic movement, rhythmic games, relaxation, improvisation, and a "concert time." As a result of this research, Joseph concludes that Dalcroze Eurhythmics that incorporates improvisation should be included in early childhood music education in order to enrich children's musical lives. Joseph (1983) states:

> In Dalcroze Eurhythmics, movement is not an end in itself; it is a means for heightening music perception and clarifying abstract concepts by relating physical motion to musical motion. Vocal and instrumental improvisation are the synthesis of rhythmic movement and ear-training; innate creativity and accumulated experiences interact to produce one's personal musical statement. (p. 59)

An important goal of Orff Schulwerk teachers is to establish "an environment conducive to nurturing the creative ability and musical independence of students" (Martin, 1993). Munsen (1987) and Martin (1993), who replicated the study, analyzed and described selected aspects of an Orff Schulwerk program of music education. Orff Schulwerk activities involve singing, the use of *bordurs*, improvised rhythms, improvised movement, and improvised pitches from the pentatonic scale. More advanced Orff Schulwerk improvisation activities incorporate the church modes, diatonic scales with functional harmony, and more chromatic materials.

Flohr (1979) cites the Manhattanville Music Curriculum Project (MMCP) definitions for improvisation and incorporates a hierarchy of "exploratory improvisation," "free exploration," and "guided exploration." He asked 4-, 6-, and 8-year-old children to improvise on a xylophone using a two-octave pentatonic scale. Flohr made the following conclusions: (1) young children are able to improvise patterns that are related to musical stimuli; (2) young children are able to form musical images in response to verbal stimuli; and (3) as children mature, tonal orientation and a sense of cohesiveness in improvisation improve. In a second study, Flohr (1985) confirmed that young children could use musical patterns to unify their improvisations.

Reinhardt (1990) examined the rhythmic improvisations of 3-, 4-, and 5-year-old children. While accompanied by a *bordun* played on a bass xylophone, children improvised songs playing a diatonic alto xylophone. Reinhardt found that nearly all of the students in the study were able to improvise with a steady beat and a consistent meter to the *bordun* accompaniment. The researcher also found that older children used a greater variety of rhythm patterns in their songs than the younger students. T. S. Brophy (1999) examined age-related differences in the melodic improvisations of 6- through 12-year-old children that might be developmental in nature. The children in this study improvised three eight-measure melodies drawn from the C-pentatonic scale on an alto xylophone. These melodies were performed as the B, C, and D sections of a seven-part rondo for Orff Schulwerk instrumentation. The entire rondo was accompanied by a broken *bordun* played on the bass xylophone. The findings of this study indicate that developmental trends were present for the rhythmic and structural dimensions of improvisation performances but not the melodic dimension. Also, age and facility with mallets appear to be significant predictors of the improvisation characteristics researched in this study. The combined characteristics of the improvisations change significantly with age independently from mallet facility. Brophy considers this change developmental in nature. The improvisations grow to include more formally organized content, the creation of more rhythm patterns, and increased motivic development. Changes were particciularly evident from ages 6 through 9, followed by a period of stasis from ages 9 through 11. The developmental trends seem to continue at age 12.

In a study that combined Gordon's audiation-learning sequence techniques and Orff Schulwerk–based rhythm improvisation activities, Jessen (1993) examined the effect of audiation on sixth-grade students' ability to improvise rhythmically. Jessen concluded that (1) audiation and improvisation techniques must be developed slowly; (2) a correlation exists between rhythm aptitude, as measured by Gordon's *Intermediate Measures of Music Audiation*, and three dimensions of rhythm performance: completeness of beats, steadiness of pulse, and sense of finality; and (3) understanding steady beat is a prerequisite to audiating rhythm.

Freundlich (1978) investigated the development of musical thinking by examining a child's spontaneous solution to a musical problem. He worked with two fifth-grade stu-

dents, asking them to improvise on a diatonic xylophone within the musical "frame" of a standard 12-bar blues. The improvisations were transcribed and analyzed using three dimensions: (1) conformity to the frame, (2) coherence within the improvised line, and (3) enrichment of musical material. The results indicated that the children could produce "authentic" musical ideas without notation. The musical concepts provided by the improvisation procedure were found to be logically organized and feasible for improvisation study. In his work with children 4 to 10 years of age, Ott (1996) found that formal instruction contributed significantly to the prediction of improvisation skill when students were provided with a harmonic context in root position.

Children from three schools in Budapest participated in a study of improvisation ability by Laczó (1981). Laczó examined the improvisations of children of different ages and musical education and found that the amount of students' music experience and music education does have an effect on their ability to improvise. Kalmár and Balasko (1987) studied the melodic improvisations sung by children from two nursery schools in Budapest. An examination of these children's improvisations revealed evidence of a "musical mother tongue." That is, many of the improvisations appeared to be "creative transformations" of learned musical material. Kalmar and Balasko write: "Many of the typical features of the Hungarian folk children's songs, in respect to volume, tonality, intervals, structure, phrases and rhythm patterns, are identifiable in the children's improvisations" (p. 81). Both the amount and quality of the child's musical experience are evident in the improvisations. An important finding of this research is that children who demonstrated the highest levels of creative music performance were taught in a setting where the teacher was musically well educated and creative.

Daignault (1997) provides an example of research that incorporates computer technology and improvisation in the process of composition. Students, aged 10–11, were asked to record three to eight improvisations onto a sequencer as an initial step in the composition of a piece of music. The children were then asked to select one improvisation for further development with notation.

The diversity of means in which improvisation in preschool and classroom general music is defined and measured compounds the nature of interpretation and application of this research. Common threads to much of the research are that, when given the opportunity, children will improvise to varying degrees; improvisation skill is developmental in nature; and as children mature, their improvisations become more consistent and integrated. More research is needed that deals with how these improvisation skills connect and transfer to music making outside of the general music class, that is, in the students' home music culture. Additional research should also be conducted to (1) investigate the relationship between improvisation skill in preschool/classroom general music and performance on a band/orchestra instrument and (2) investigate the relationship between improvisation skill in preschool/classroom general music and more advanced improvisation skills.

Instrumental Music Improvisation Research

Another setting for the study of improvisation in music education is in instrumental music instruction. Several researchers in this field are interested in studying the relationship between improvisation and the ability to read music as a criterion measure of musical achievement (Azzara, 1992; McPherson, 1993; Montano, 1983; J. Wilson 1971). The results of these studies suggest that while improvisation is a valuable skill in its own right, it appears that improvisation ability transfers to a student's clearer comprehension of music performed from notation. Montano, for example, examined the effect of improvisation of given rhythms on rhythmic accuracy in sight-reading achievement by college elementary group piano students. The problem of this study was to assess whether those college elementary group piano students who have regular practice improvising specific pitches for pieces within various meters, rhythmic notations, and textures would show greater achievement of rhythmic accuracy in sight-reading than similar students who did not have that practice. Montano used an experimental pretest/posttest control group design with 32 undergraduate students from elementary group piano classes. The data from this research indicated that students who had the improvisation practice demonstrated significantly greater achievement of rhythmic accuracy in sight-reading than the control group who did not have that practice.

In my 1992 work, I discuss the relationship between improvisation and music reading in my research on elementary school–aged instrumentalists. The purpose of this research was to develop and to examine an improvisation curriculum designed to improve the music achievement of elementary school instrumental music students. The researcher-designed curriculum used in this study included (1) learning to sing and to play a repertoire of melodies and bass lines by ear, (2) chanting, playing, and improvising rhythm patterns and series of rhythm patterns in the context of duple and triple meter, (3) singing, playing, and improvising tonal patterns and series of tonal patterns in the context of harmonic progressions in major and minor tonalities, (4) learning solfège that defines harmonic function and learning rhythm syllables that define rhythm movement, (5) improvising rhythm patterns to familiar bass lines and improvising rhythms on specific harmonic

tones, (6) improvising melodies by choosing notes that outline the harmonic functions of the progression, and (7) combining improvised rhythm patterns and improvised tonal patterns to improvise a melody. Music achievement was measured in terms of the instrumental performance of three etudes I composed: a student-prepared etude, a teacher-assisted etude, and a sight-read etude. The specific problems of this study were to investigate the effect of improvisation study on the music achievement of fifth-grade wind and percussion music students and to investigate the differential effects of levels of aptitude on the music achievement of fifth-grade wind and percussion music students. Four judges independently rated the performances using a rating scale with 5-point continuous criteria tonal and rhythm dimensions designed by the researcher and a 5-point expression dimension. Results indicated that students who received instrumental music instruction that included an improvisation curriculum had significantly higher composite etude performance scores than those students who received instrumental music instruction without an emphasis on improvisation. Significant differences were also found among aptitude levels.

I concluded that improvisation study improves the music achievement of elementary instrumental music students and that with improvisation skill students can express their musical thoughts spontaneously. This expression is possible when students comprehend the tonal and rhythm patterns of a musical line within a larger context. In other words, when students understand tonal and rhythm patterns and can combine and sequence them in a syntactic manner they internalize a sense of tonality and meter. This kind of understanding engenders an understanding of harmonic progression. Harmonic progression is defined here in a linear sense by *how* the harmony changes (tonal function) and *when* the harmony changes (harmonic rhythm). Based on this research, I concluded that when asked to improvise in this fashion, students express what they are thinking in terms of tonality, meter, and expressive performance; furthermore, students who have the skills to improvise enhance their performance of notated music. I suggest in my 1999 work that to begin the improvisation process, individuals should listen to improvised music, learn a repertoire of tunes by ear, learn melodies and bass lines by ear, learn harmony and counterpoint by ear, learn the vocabulary of the genre by ear, and take risks.

The effects of group improvisation on the musical development of selected high school instrumental music students was examined by J. Wilson (1971). Wilson employed a method of improvisation originated by Lukas Foss and Richard Duffalo that was adapted for secondary use by Silverman (Silverman, 1962; Gould, 1963). In this study, students became familiar with a hierarchy of intervals and their relationships to their guide tone, that is, the note selected as the tonal center. The results indicated that students with improvisation experience made greater improvements than the control group in aural recognition of melodic elements and idioms, aural recognition of rhythmic elements and idioms, and sight-reading.

Many investigators have used Guilford's four basic divergent production abilities—fluency, flexibility, elaboration, and originality (Guilford & Hoepfner, 1971)—as a point of departure for measuring musical creativity (Gorder, 1980; Hassler & Feil, 1986; McPherson, 1993, 1995, 1996; Vaughan, 1977; Vaughan & Meyers, 1971; Webster, 1977, 1987b). Torrance (1966) also researched and developed creativity tests using these constructs. In research on the construction of a test of musical creativity in school instrumental music students, W. Gorder (1980) defined musical divergent production abilities that directly paralleled Guilford's definitions of the four constructs. This test, titled Measures of Musical Divergent Production (MMDP), was based on models of Guilford and Torrance. Tests were scored for the number of improvised phrases produced (fluency), shifts of musical content (flexibility), varied use of musical content (elaboration), rarely used content (originality), and a fifth ability of musical appeal that Gorder calls music quality. In a study with high school instrumental and choral students, Webster (1977) developed a scoring approach similar to Gorder's, translating Guilford's four constructs into musical terms. Webster asked students to perform increasingly difficult musical tasks on melody bells. This involved the performance of the melody "Twinkle, Twinkle, Little Star" and three variations of the tune. Each successive variation was to "move further away from the original." Ultimately, the students composed an original tune, played it from memory, and then merged it with "Twinkle." Webster's further research led to the development of the Measures of Creative Thinking in Music (1987b), a measure that can be given to younger children. A revised version of this measure has been developed that incorporates the use of MIDI (Hickey & Webster, 1999). For discussion of the literature that regards research on the assessment of creative thinking in music, refer to Webster (1992).

Based on Gorder's and Webster's work, Feil developed a model for the assessment of improvisations and compositions performed by public and grammar school students who were able to play at least one instrument (Hassler & Feil, 1986). In this study, the boys had an average of 5.14 years of training and the girls had an average of 5.33 years of training. Feil used the following criteria: (1) first impression, (2) originality, (3) imaginativeness: (a) melodic, (b) sound space, (c) varying and ornamenting, (d) within variations, (e) harmonic, (f) rhythmic, (g) sensitivity, and expression; (4) general impression; and (5) final appraisal (summary of all performances of each individual).

McPherson (1993) designed the Test of Ability to Improvise for use in a study of high school instrumentalists. This researcher noted that the criteria used to assess the improvised responses expanded the work of Gorder and Webster and included dimensions of instrumental fluency, musical syntax, creativity, and musical quality. McPherson writes about the results of this study:

> As a musician develops skill on an instrument and enters a more advanced stage of development, performance proficiency and improvisational ability become much more intertwined. It is possible that learning another instrument, mentally rehearsing music, and participating in various forms of singing activities all act to strengthen an ability to "think in sound" and thereby to improvise musically. (p. 19)

In 1996 McPherson examined the degree of correlation and developmental differences among five visual, aural, and creative aspects of performance: sight-reading, performing rehearsed music, playing from memory, playing by ear, and improvising. Results showed significant moderate correlations between (1) an ability to sight-read and perform rehearsed music and (2) an ability to sight-read and improvise. An important finding revealed that an ability to sight-read correlated higher with an ability to play by ear, to play from memory, and to improvise than with an ability to perform rehearsed music. Also, results indicated moderate to strong correlations between an ability to play by ear and to improvise. Other interesting findings were the nonsignificant correlations between playing from memory and playing by ear and between playing from memory and improvising. McPherson concludes:

> The weaker pattern of correlations between the ability to perform rehearsed music and the other four skills reinforces the need for the profession to recognize the importance of other skills in developing an ability to perform music in its widest sense. (p. 121)

The results of this study and other studies indicate that performing a repertoire of rehearsed music from notation represents only one aspect of musical performance. Future research should continue to examine the relationships among listening, improvising, reading, composing, and analyzing music. There is also a need for further understanding the connection between improvisation in general music and improvisation in instrumental music.

Jazz Improvisation Research

Improvisation is the essence of jazz. Several researchers have developed and examined the effects of various instructional materials and methods for teaching jazz improvisation (e.g., Bash, 1984; Carlson, 1981; Paulson, 1986; Schenkel, 1980; Zwick, 1987). These researchers studied different approaches to jazz improvisation with implications for improving music instruction, curricula, and jazz improvisation skills. Many of these studies and curricula for improvisation focus primarily on teaching improvisation through imitation and music theory. For example, Bash (1984) studied the effectiveness of three instructional methods on the acquisition of jazz improvisation skills in high school instrumentalists. The results of this study suggest the viability of incorporating an aural perspective—which in this study includes vocal rote responses to blues patterns, vocalization of blues improvisation, and instrumental echo responses to patterns taught by rote—along with the more "traditional" format that emphasizes scales and chordal activities. In a review of a representative sampling of research completed in jazz pedagogy from 1972 through 1986, Bowman (1988) recommended that further research, comprising higher standards, should be done in order to understand more deeply the content of improvisation study and the relationship between improvisation and music education.

Both Coy (1990) and Alibrio (1988) examined jazz improvisation at the middle school level. The results of Coy's work with middle school band students with 2 to 3 years of instrumental music instruction suggest that these students could develop fundamental skills in jazz improvisation in a relatively short period of time. Alibrio implemented a jazz improvisation curriculum as a possible solution to the problem of attrition in the middle school string program. The author commented that many of the instructional materials available at this level center on the development of technical skills and exclude creativity. This investigation incorporated a curriculum guide to develop improvisational skills with middle school string musicians. Alibrio concluded that a creative approach to music instruction that included improvisation might lessen attrition and provide a more positive approach toward string playing.

L. Porter (1983) and Moorman (1985) are examples of individuals who have analyzed performances of jazz musicians in their attempts to understand further the nature of improvisation in jazz. Studying the music of John Coltrane, Porter provides information on Coltrane's personal style and concepts and gives a detailed examination of a sample of Coltrane's work. After analyzing selected jazz improvisation compositions, Moorman made specific recommendations for improvisational performance. He surveyed existing literature on jazz improvisation and analyzed 25 selected jazz improvisations of artists, including Louis Armstrong, Coleman Hawkins, Leon "Bix" Beiderbecke, Thelonious Monk, Clifford Brown, Theodore "Fats" Navarro, Donald Byrd, Charlie Parker, John Coltrane, Oscar Peterson, Miles Davis, Earl "Bud" Powell, Kenny Dorham, Woody Shaw, John Birks "Dizzy" Gillespie, Teddy Wilson, Dexter Gordon, and Lester Young. The researcher noted that all methods he surveyed emphasized the importance of melodic, rhythmic, and harmonic study as the foundation for jazz improvisation. Moorman also recommended that the ii–V chord progression should be an integral part of harmony study in jazz improvisation.

Fern (1996) made use of jazz solo transcriptions and chordal/scalar analytical techniques in an interactive computer program designed for jazz improvisation instruction. This research attempted to determine the efficacy of such a computer program and to develop an understanding of the attitudes of students who used the courseware. College student volunteers with varied amounts of improvisation skill participated in the study and were interviewed about their experience using this computer program. The data indicated that students found the program to be comprehensive in content, nonthreatening, and motivating. The students were enthusiastic about using an interactive computer program but thought that the program's weakness was the absence of human feedback.

Concerning the need for understanding the criteria for predicting and measuring improvisation skills, Madura (1993, 1995, 1996) investigated the relationships among tonal, rhythmic, and expressive dimensions of vocal jazz improvisation achievement and selected predictor variables. The independent variables included jazz theory achievement, jazz experience, imitative ability, instrumental lessons, voice lessons, general creativity, and gender. The subjects were college students enrolled in vocal jazz courses. The tonal, rhythmic, and expressive dimensions were measured using 5-point rating scales for performances of a blues progression and a ii–V7–I progression. Madura found strong significant correlations between vocal jazz improvisation achievement and jazz theory knowledge, imitative ability, and jazz experience. Tonality, rhythm, and divergence were identified as underlying factors of vocal jazz improvisation. In 1995 Greenngel examined the extent to which certain variables operate as predictors of vocal jazz improvisation achievement. The subjects for this study were jazz vocal majors. The two variables that accounted for the greatest proportion of variance in this research were (1) the ratings of subjects' creativity as determined by a researcher-designed creativity assessment and (2) the subjects' self-ratings as improvisers. Greenngel found significant correlations for self-rating, hours spent listening to jazz, prior ensemble experience, creativity, instrumental lessons, and frequency of listening to jazz.

Pfenninger's (1991) and Horowitz's (1995) work focused on the development of rating scales to measure jazz improvisation achievement. Pfenninger constructed and investigated the validity of a rating scale that contained tonal, rhythm, and expression dimensions. Ten jazz performers and teachers helped to construct the criteria used for the rating scale. Six performers and teachers independently rated improvised performances of 20 university jazz majors. Pfenninger found that the tonal and rhythm dimensions of the rating scale operated as objective, valid measures of jazz improvisation skill; however, the results from the expressive dimension were influenced by subjectivity. Horowitz utilized a facet-factorial approach in the construction of a rating scale for jazz guitar improvisation. He found that a facet-factorial approach to rating-scale construction could provide a reliable and valid measurement tool for improvisation. Factor analysis of the data indicated that there should be three dimensions to the rating scale: musicianship, expression, and overall structure. Ten criteria were chosen for each of the three dimensions to form the 30-item rating scale. Horowitz recommended that additional research be conducted in order to develop a curriculum for teaching improvisation based on the dimensions and criteria used in this study.

Several issues important to understanding improvisation arise as a result of this body of jazz research. For example, what is the relationship of jazz improvisation skills to overall improvisation skills? Which aspects of jazz improvisation skill can be generalized to the understanding of music in various styles? Much of the research concerns the skills of secondary school and college-aged students and has been divided into examining either instrumental jazz or vocal jazz pedagogy. Many studies have used music theory and imitation as a means to develop improvisation skill. What are the underlying principles associated with developing the mental, aesthetic, and social aspects of all improvisers, regardless of performance medium? What models can be developed and presented for nurturing jazz improvisation in a cultural, sequential, and developmental fashion that begins in early childhood and proceeds through adulthood?

Summary and Suggestions for Further Research

Several common themes appear throughout this research, including (1) the importance of developing an improvisation culture and community; (2) the importance of establishing an environment where improvisation, spontaneity, and interaction are nurtured; (3) understanding improvisation as a lifestyle, not only an activity; (4) the belief that improvisation skill acquisition is developmental in nature and all students have some potential to improvise; (5) the importance of improvisation as part of a comprehensive music curriculum that can affect achievement in other music skill areas such as listening, performing, reading, composing, and analyzing; and (6) the importance of incorporating a model for improvisation skill assessment in order to help teachers attend to students' individual needs.

The research suggests that students should be provided with opportunities to make music spontaneously in a meaningful way through improvisation. Improvisation allows students to express themselves individually, to develop higher order thinking skills, and to develop a more comprehensive and intimate relationship with music, performing with and without notation. These objectives may be accomplished when students comprehend the deeper levels of the tonal and rhythmic architecture in the music. Aural comprehension of music in the context of this larger framework comes from grouping notes into patterns, patterns into phrases, and phrases into the context of the overall tonal and rhythmic form of the music. When putting content into context, students begin to attain the skills necessary to improvise with meaning.

Research on the topic of improvisation in music education is relatively young and in need of replication and expansion. The most fundamental issues that face music educators concern an improved understanding of the improvisation process and the inclusion of improvisation in comprehensive music education curricula. To help speak to these concerns, specific research questions should be systematically addressed and further studies that relate to models for improvisation will need to be examined by future researchers. Particular questions include: What are the appropriate levels of understanding and skill development for students as they progress through their music education from preschool to adulthood? What skills are associated with various levels of development? Are there critical periods for the development of certain skills or dispositions necessary for improvisation? What are the necessary ingredients for the creation of an improvising culture?

While many music educators have advocated the inclusion of creativity and improvisation in music curricula, the research literature indicates that aside from jazz and beyond some elementary general music classes it is rare to find a music class setting where improvisation is a central part of the curriculum. Even in jazz settings at the secondary school level, it is uncommon to find a developmentally sequential curriculum for preparing all students to improvise. Also, there appears to be a gap between the criteria used for children's improvisation in general music settings and the criteria used for improvising in secondary settings, postsecondary settings, and jazz settings. Giving improvisation a more prominent role in music education will necessitate change in current music curricula, communication among teachers in the various music education disciplines, and music teacher education. Nearly all of the researchers cited in this chapter request, and indeed the research requires, further study. Continued research will further illuminate improvisation's importance to a comprehensive music education.

REFERENCES

Abramson, R. M. (1980). Dalcroze-based improvisation. *Music Educators Journal 66*(5), 62.

Adler, T. (1980). The acquisition of a traditional competence: Folk-musical and folk-cultural learning among bluegrass banjo players (Doctoral dissertation, Indiana University). *Dissertation Abstracts International, 41*(3), 1165A.

Aebersold, J. (1988). Music is for life. *Instrumentalist, 43*(9), 108.

Alibrio, F. J. (1988). Addressing the problem of attrition in the middle school string program by implementing jazz improvisation: A curriculum guide to develop improvisational skills with the middle school musician. (Master's thesis, University of Lowell). *Masters Abstracts International, 27*(1), 21.

Azzara, C. D. (1992). The effect of audiation-based improvisation techniques on the music achievement of elementary instrumental music students (Doctoral dissertation, Eastman School of Music, University of Rochester). *Dissertation Abstracts International, 53*(4), 1088A.

Azzara, C. D. (1993). Audiation-based improvisation techniques and elementary instrumental students' music achievement. *Journal of Research in Music Education, 41*(4), 328–342.

Azzara, C. D. (1999). An aural approach to improvisation. *Music Educators Journal, 86*(3), 21–25.

Bash, L. (1984). The effectiveness of three instructional methods on the acquisition of jazz improvisation skills (Doctoral dissertation, State University of New York at Buffalo). *Dissertation Abstracts International, 44*(7), 2079A.

Bellman, J. D. (1991). Improvisation in Chopin's nocturnes: Some suggested parameters (Poland) (Doctoral dissertation, Stanford University). *Dissertation Abstracts International, 51*(8), 2558A.

Berliner, P. (1994). *Thinking in jazz.* Chicago: University of Chicago Press.

Biasini, A., Thomas, R., & Pogonowski, L. (1970). *MMCP interaction* (2nd ed.). Bardonia, NY: Media Materials.

Bitz, M. (1999). A description and investigation of strategies for teaching classroom music improvisation (Doctoral dissertation, Columbia University Teachers College). *Dissertation Abstracts International, 59*(10), 3386A.

Booth, G. (1987). The oral tradition in transition: Implications for music education from a study of North Indian tabla transmission (*India*) (Doctoral dissertation, Kent State University). *Dissertation Abstracts International, 47*(9), 3348A.

Bowman, W. (1988). Doctoral research in jazz improvisation pedagogy: An overview. *Bulletin of the Council for Research in Music Education 96,* 47–76.

Briggs, N. L. (1987). Creative improvisation: A musical dialogue (Doctoral dissertation, University of San Diego). *Dissertation Abstracts International, 47*(8), 2787A.

Brinner, B. (1986). Competence and interaction in the performance of "Pathetan" in central Java (Indonesia, Gamelan, Improvisation) (Doctoral dissertation, University of California, Berkeley), *Dissertation Abstracts International, 47*(3), 704A.

Brophy, T. S. (1999). The melodic improvisations of children ages six through twelve: A developmental perspective (Doctoral dissertation, University of Kentucky, 1998). *Dissertation Abstracts International, 59*(9), 3386A.

Brown, T. (1991). An investigation of the effectiveness of a piano course in playing by ear and aural skills development for college students (Doctoral dissertation, University of Illinois at Urbana-Champaign). *Dissertation Abstracts International, 51*(12), 4052A.

Campbell, P. (1990). Cross-cultural perspectives of musical creativity. *Music Educators Journal, 76*(9), 43–46.

Candelaria, L. (1987). An overview of performance practices relating to seventeenth-and eighteenth-century trumpet music: Consideration for modern performance (Doctoral dissertation, Northwestern University). *Dissertation Abstracts International, 47*(12), 4225A.

Carlson, W. (1981). A procedure for teaching jazz improvisation based on an analysis of the performance practice of three major jazz trumpet players: Louis Armstrong, Dizzy Gillespie, and Miles Davis (Doctoral dissertation, Indiana University). *Dissertation Abstracts International, 42*(3), 1042A.

Cohen, V. (1980). The emergence of musical gestures in kindergarten children (Doctoral dissertation, University of Illinois at Urbana-Champaign). *Dissertation Abstracts International, 41*(11), 4637A.

Collier, G. (1996). *Interaction: Opening up the jazz ensemble.* Berlin: Advance Music.

Consortium of National Arts Education Associations. (1994). *National Standards for Arts Education.* Reston, VA: Music Educators National Conference.

Contemporary Music Project. (1966). *Experiments in musical creativity.* Washington, DC: Music Educators National Conference.

Contemporary Music Project. (1971). *Comprehensive musicianship: An anthology of evolving thought.* Washington, DC: Music Educators National Conference.

Copland, A. (1952). *Music and imagination.* Cambridge, MA: Harvard University Press.

Cormack, J. (1992). Svara kalpana: Melodic/rhythmic improvisation in karnatak music (Doctoral dissertation, Wesleyan University). *Dissertation Abstracts International, 53*(5), 1438A.

Coy, D. (1990). A multisensory approach to teaching jazz improvisation to middle school band students (Doctoral dissertation, University of Oregon). *Dissertation Abstracts International, 50*(11), 3508A.

Csikszentmihalyi, M. (1996). *Creativity.* New York: Harper Collins.

Czerny, C. (1836). *Complete theoretical and practical piano forte school, op. 500, 3 volumes.* London: R. Cocks, pp. 166–123.

Czerny, C. (1983) *A systematic introduction to improvisation on the pianoforte,* Op. 200 (A. L. Mitchell, Trans. and

Ed.). New York: Longman. (Original work published 1836)

Daignault, L. (1997). Children's creative musical thinking within the context of a computer-supported improvisational approach to composition (Doctoral dissertation, Northwestern University). *Dissertation Abstracts International, 57*(11), 4681A.

David, H. T., & Mendel, A. (1972). *The Bach reader.* New York: W. W. Norton.

Della Pietra, J. D., & Campbell, P. S. (1995). An ethnography of improvisation training in a music methods course. *Journal of Research in Music Education, 43*(2), 112–126.

Dobbins, B. (1980). Improvisation: An essential element of musical proficiency. *Music Educators Journal, 66*(5), 62–68.

Dowling, W. J. (1988). Tonal structure and children's early tonal learning of music. In J. Sloboda (Ed.), *Generative processes in music: The psychology of performance, improvisation and composition* (pp. 113–128). New York: Oxford University Press.

Elliot, D. J. (1995). *Music matters: A new philosophy of music education.* New York: Oxford University Press.

Ferand, E. (1961). *Improvisation in nine centuries of Western music.* Cologne: Arno Volk Verlag, Hans Gerig KG.

Fern, J. (1996). The effectiveness of a computer-based courseware program for teaching jazz improvisation (Doctoral dissertation, University of Southern California). *Dissertation Abstracts International, 57*(1), 144A.

Flohr, J. (1979). Musical improvisation behavior of young children (Doctoral dissertation, University of Illinois). *Dissertation Abstracts International, 40*(10), 5355A.

Flohr, J. (1985) Young children's improvisations: Emerging creative thought. *Creative Child and Adult Quarterly, 10*(2), 79–85.

Freundlich, D. (1978). The development of musical thinking: Case studies in improvisation (Doctoral dissertation, Harvard University, 1978). *Dissertation Abstracts International, 39*(11), 6617A.

Goertzen, V. (1996). By way of introduction: Preluding by 18th- and 19th-century pianists. *Journal of Musicology—A Quarterly Review of Music History, Criticism, Analysis, and Performance Practice, 14*(3), 299–337.

Gorder, W. (1980). Divergent production abilities as constructs of musical creativity. *Journal of Research in Music Education, 28*(1), 34–42.

Gordon, E. (1997a). *Learning sequences in music: Skill, content, and patterns.* Chicago: GIA.

Gordon, E. (1997b). Preparing young children to improvise at a later time. *Early Childhood Connection, 3*(4), 6–12.

Gordon, E. (2000). Studies in readiness for harmonic and rhythmic improvisation. *GIML Monograph III.* Chicago: GIA.

Gould, O. A. (1963). [Critique of M. Silverman's *Ensemble improvisation as a creative technique in the secondary instrumental program*]. *Bulletin of the Council for Research in Music Education, 1,* 59–61.

Greenan, A. (1997). The instrumental eingang in the Classical era (improvisation) (Doctoral dissertation, University of

Maryland, College Park). *Dissertation Abstracts International, 58*(11), 2201A.

Greennagel, D. (1995). A study of selected predictors of jazz vocal improvisation skills (Doctoral dissertation, University of Miami). *Dissertation Abstracts International, 55*(8), 2201A.

Gregory, J. (1996). Improvisation and integration of the arts at the Pecs Free School of Arts in Hungary (Doctoral dissertation, University of Northern Colorado). *Dissertation Abstracts International, 57*(2), 617A.

Guilford, J. P., & Hoepfner, R. (1971). *The analysis of intelligence.* New York: McGraw-Hill.

Hargreaves, D. J., Cork, C. A., & Setton, T. (1991). Cognitive strategies in jazz improvisation: An exploratory study. *Canadian Journal of Research in Music Education, 33,* 47–54.

Harrison, E. (1995). Michael Wiedeburg's "der sich selbst informirende clavierspieler" and his pedagogy of improvisation (Germany) (Doctoral dissertation, Stanford University). *Dissertation Abstracts International, 56*(6), 2035A.

Hassler, M., & Feil, A. (1986). A study of the relationship of composition improvisation to selected personal variables. *Bulletin of the Council for Research in Music Education 87,* 26–34.

Hickey, M., & Webster, P. (1999). MIDI-based adaptation and continued validation of the measures of creative thinking in music. *Bulletin of the Council for Research in Music Education 142,* 93–94 (Abstract).

Horowitz, R. (1995). The development of a rating scale for jazz guitar improvisation performance (Doctoral dissertation, Columbia University Teachers College). *Dissertation Abstracts International, 55*(11), 3443A.

Hummel, J. (1829). *Ausführliche theoretisch-practische Anweisung zum Piano-Forte-Speil* (2nd ed.). Vienna: Tobias Haslinger. (Original work published 1828)

Jessen, P. (1993). The effect of audiation on elementary students' rhythm improvisations (Master's thesis, University of Manitoba-Canada). *Masters Abstracts International 31*(4), 1460.

Jorgensen, M. (1998). An analytical comparison of the kindergarten through fourth-grade sections of the California music educators association music education K–6 scope and sequence with the kindergarten through fourth-grade section of the National Standards for Arts Education (Doctoral dissertation, University of the Pacific). *Dissertation Abstracts International, 58*(8), 3058A.

Joseph, A. (1983). A Dalcroze Eurhythmics approach to music learning in kindergarten through rhythmic movement, ear training and improvisation (Doctoral dissertation, Carnegie-Mellon University). *Dissertation Abstracts International, 44*(2), 420A.

Kalmár, M., & Balasko, G. (1987). Musical mother tongue and creativity in preschool children's melody improvisations. *Bulletin of the Council for Research in Music Education, 91,* 77–86.

Kratus, J. (1989). A time analysis of the compositional processes used by children ages 7–11. *Journal of Research in Music Education, 37*(1), 5–20.

Kratus, J. (1990). Structuring the Music Curriculum for Creative Learning. *Music Educators Journal, 76*(9), 33–37.

Kratus, J. (1991). Growing with improvisation. *Music Educators Journal, 78*(4), 35–40.

Kratus, J. (1996). A developmental approach to teaching music improvisation. *International Journal of Music Education, 26,* 27–38.

Laczó, Z. (1981). A psychological investigation of improvisation abilities in the lower and higher classes of the elementary school. *Bulletin of the Council for Research in Music Education, 66 & 67,* 39–45.

Lamott, B. (1980). Keyboard improvisation according to "Nova Instructio Pro Pulsandis Organis" (Doctoral dissertation, Stanford University). *Dissertation Abstracts International, 41*(5), 1828A.

Leavell, B. (1997). "Making the change": Middle school band students' perspectives on the learning of musical-technical skills in jazz performance (Doctoral dissertation, University of North Texas). *Dissertation Abstracts International, 57*(7), 2931A.

Lubart, A. (1998). Teaching percussion ensemble improvisation and composition: A teacher training manual for the non–music specialist (Doctoral dissertation, Columbia University Teachers College). *Dissertation Abstracts International, 59*(1), 117A.

Madura, P. (1993). Relationships among vocal jazz improvisation achievement, jazz theory knowledge, imitative ability, previous musical experience, general creativity, and gender (Doctoral dissertation, Indiana University). *Dissertation Abstracts International, 53*(12), 4245A.

Madura, P. (1995). An exploratory investigation of the assessment of vocal jazz improvisation. *Psychology of Music, 23*(1), 48–62.

Madura, P. (1996). Relationships among vocal jazz improvisation achievement, jazz theory knowledge, imitative ability, musical experience, creativity, and gender. *Journal of Research in Music Education, 44*(3), 252–267.

Mann, A. (1987). *Theory and practice: The great composers as teachers and students.* New York: W. W. Norton.

Martin, M. A. (1993). An examination of the Orff-Schulwerk approach to music education in a public elementary school: A replication study (Doctoral dissertation, University of North Carolina at Chapel Hill). *Dissertation Abstracts International, 53*(8), 2728A.

McPherson, G. (1993). Evaluating improvisational ability of high school instrumentalists. *Bulletin of the Council for Research in Music Education, 119,* 11–20.

McPherson, G. (1995). The assessment of musical performance: Development and validation of five new measures. *Psychology of Music, 23*(2), 142–161.

McPherson, G. (1996). Five aspects of musical performance and their correlates. *Bulletin of the Council for Research in Music Education, 127,* 115–121.

Monson, I. (1992). Musical interaction in modern jazz: An ethnomusicological perspective (Doctoral dissertation, New York University). *Dissertation Abstracts International, 53*(1), 15A.

Monson, I. (1996). *Saying something: Jazz improvisation and interaction.* Chicago: University of Chicago Press.

Montano, D. R. (1983). The effect of improvising in given rhythms on piano students' sight reading rhythmic accuracy achievement (Doctoral dissertation, University of Missouri–Kansas City). *Dissertation Abstracts International, 44*(6), 1720A.

Montello, L. (1990). Utilizing music therapy as a mode of treatment for the performance stress of professional musicians (Doctoral dissertation, New York University). *Dissertation Abstracts International, 50*(10), 3175A.

Moorhead, G., & Pond, D. (1978). *Music for young children.* Santa Barbara, CA: Pillsbury Foundation for the Advancement of Music Education. (Originally published as four separate papers: 1941, 1942, 1944, 1951)

Moorman, D. (1985). An analytic study of jazz improvisation with suggestions for performance (Doctoral dissertation, New York University). *Dissertation Abstracts International, 45*(7), 2023A

Munsen, S. (1987). A description and analysis of an Orff-Schulwerk program of music education (improvisation) (Doctoral dissertation, University of Illinois at Urbana-Champaign). *Dissertation Abstracts International, 47*(9), 3351A

Nachmanovitch, S. (1990). *Free play: The power of improvisation in life and the arts.* Los Angeles: Jeremy P. Tarcher.

Nardone, P. (1997). The experience of improvisation in music: A phenomenological psychological analysis (Doctoral dissertation, Saybrook Institute). *Dissertation Abstracts International, 57*(11), 7246B

National Association of Schools of Music. (1999). *National Association of Schools of Music 1999–2000 handbook.* Reston, VA: National Association of Schools of Music.

Nutting R. (1989). A method of elementary improvisation for church organists (Doctoral dissertation, Southern Baptist Theological Seminary). *Dissertation Abstracts International, 50*(2), 381A.

Ott, D. (1996). Effects of musical context on the improvisations of children as a function of age, training, and exposure to music (Doctoral dissertation, University of Alabama). *Dissertation Abstracts International, 57*(2), 1469B.

Park, M. (1986). Music and shamanism in Korea: A study of selected "ssikkum-gut" rituals for the dead (Doctoral dissertation, University of California, Los Angeles). *Dissertation Abstracts International, 46*(7), 1775A.

Paulson, J. (1986). The development of an imitative instructional approach to improvising effective melodic statements in jazz solos (Doctoral dissertation, University of Washington). *Dissertation Abstracts International, 46*(10), 2957A.

Pelz-Sherman, M. (1999). A framework for the analysis of performer interactions in Western improvised contemporary art music (Doctoral dissertation, University of California, San Diego). *Dissertation Abstracts International, 59*(11), 4007A

Pfenninger, R. (1991). The development and validation of three rating scales for the objective measurement of jazz improvisation achievement (Doctoral dissertation, Temple

University). *Dissertation Abstracts International, 51*(8), 2674A.

Pond, D. (1981). A composer's study of young children's innate musicality. *Bulletin of the Council for Research in Music Education, 68,* 1–12.

Porter, L. (1983). John Coltrane's music of 1960 through 1967: Jazz improvisation as composition (Doctoral dissertation, Brandeis University). *Dissertation Abstracts International, 44*(6), 1622A.

Pressing, J. (1988). Improvisation: Methods and models. In J. Sloboda (Ed.), *Generative processes in music: The psychology of performance, improvisation and composition* (pp. 129–178). New York: Oxford University Press.

Reck, D. (1983). A musician tool-kit: A study of five performances by Thirugokarnam Ramachandra Iyer. Volume I: Text. Volume II: Transcriptions, extended musical examples, appendices, cassette tape recording (Doctoral dissertation, University of Maryland, Baltimore County). *Dissertation Abstracts International, 54*(1), 22A.

Reinhardt, D. (1990). Preschool children's use of rhythm in improvisation. *Contributions to Music Education 17,* 7–19.

Richmond, J. (Ed.). (1989). *The proceedings of the suncoast music education forum on creativity.* Tampa: University of South Florida.

Riveire, J. (1998). California string teachers' curricular content and attitudes regarding improvisation and the national standards (Doctoral dissertation, University of Southern California). *Dissertation Abstracts International, 59*(5), 1504A.

Rosfeld, M. (1989). The development of a series of instructional units for teaching improvisational principles to pianists (Doctoral dissertation, University of Oklahoma). *Dissertation Abstracts International, 50*(6), 1478A.

Sagi, M., & Vitanyi, I. (1988). Experimental research into musical generative ability. In J. Sloboda (Ed.), *Generative processes in music: The psychology of performance, improvisation and composition* (pp. 179–194). New York: Oxford University Press.

Sarath, E. W. (1996). A new look at improvisation. *Journal of Music Theory, 40*(1), 1–38.

Sawyer, R. K. (1999). Improvised conversations: Music, collaboration, and development. *Psychology of Music, 27*(2), 192–205.

Schenkel, S. (1980). A guide to the development of improvisational skills in the jazz idiom (Doctoral dissertation, Washington University). *Dissertation Abstracts International, 41*(3), 847A.

Schmidt, C., & Sinor, J. (1986). An investigation of the relationships among music audiation, musical creativity, and cognitive style. *Journal of Research in Music Education. 34*(3), 160–172.

Schonberg, H. (1987). *The great pianists.* New York: Simon & Schuster.

Schuller, G. (1968). *Early jazz: Its roots and musical development.* New York: Oxford University Press.

Serafine, M. L. (1988). *Music as cognition: The development of thought in music.* New York: Columbia University Press.

Silverman, M. L. (1962). Ensemble improvisation as a creative technique in the secondary instrumental music program. (Doctoral dissertation, Stanford University). *Dissertation Abstracts International, 23*(5), 1562.

Sloboda, J. (1985). *The musical mind.* New York: Oxford University Press.

Sloboda, J. (Ed.). (1988). *Generative processes in music: The psychology of performance, improvisation and composition.* New York: Oxford University Press.

Stubbs, F. (1995). The art and science of Taksim: An empirical analysis of traditional improvisation from 20th century Istanbul (Doctoral dissertation, Wesley University). *Dissertation Abstracts International, 55*(7), 1865A.

Swanwick, K., & Tillman, J. (1986). The sequence of musical development: A study of children's compositions. *British Journal of Music Education 3*(3), 305–339.

Thomas, R. (1970a). *Manhattanville music curriculum project: Final report* (Report No. BR6-1999). Purchase, NY: Manhattanville College of the Sacred Heart. (ERIC Document Reproduction Service No. ED 045 865)

Thomas, R. B. (1970b). *MMCP synthesis.* Bardonia, NY: Media Materials.

Thompson, R. (1995). Calloused hands and a drummer's toolkit: Mandinka drumming in the Gambia (Doctoral dissertation, Indiana University). *Dissertation Abstracts International, 56*(2), 612A.

Torrance, E. P. (1966). *The Torrance tests of creative thinking.* Princeton, NJ: Personal Press.

Townsend, K. (1998). The beginning string class: Exemplary curricular content and processes in selected Indiana middle/junior high schools (Doctoral dissertation, Ball State University). *Dissertation Abstracts International, 59*(10), 3769A.

Vaughan, M. (1977). Musical creativity: Its cultivation and measurement. *Bulletin of the Council for Research in Music Education, 50,* 72–77.

Vaughan, M., & Meyers, R. (1971). An examination of musical process as related to creative thinking. *Journal of Research in Music Education, 19*(3), 337–341.

Webster, P. (1977). A factor of intellect approach to creative thinking in music (Doctoral dissertation, University of Rochester). *Dissertation Abstracts International, 38*(6), A3136.

Webster, P. (1979). Relationship between creative behavior in music and selected variables as measured in high school students. *Journal of Research in Music Education, 27*(4), 227–242.

Webster, P. (1987a). Conceptual bases for creative thinking in music. In J. C. Perry, I. W. Peery, & T. W. Draper (Eds.), *Music and child development* (pp. 158–174). New York: Springer.

Webster, P. (1987b). Refinement of a measure of creative thinking in music. In C. K. Madsen & C. A. Prickett (Eds.), *Applications of research in music education* (pp. 257–271). Tuscaloosa: University of Alabama Press.

Webster, P. (1988). Creative thinking in music: Approaches to research. In J. Gates (Ed.), *Music education in the United States: Contemporary issues* (pp. 66–81) Tuscaloosa: University of Alabama Press.

Webster, P. (1991). Creativity as creative thinking. In D. Hamann (Ed.), *Creativity in the classroom: The best of MEJ* (pp. 25–34). Reston, VA: Music Educators National Conference. (Original work published 1990)

Webster, P. (1992). Research on creative thinking in music: The assessment literature. In R. Colwell (Ed.), *Handbook of research on music teaching and learning: A project of the Music Educators National Conference* (pp. 266–279). New York: Schirmer Books.

Werner, K. (1996). *Effortless mastery: Liberating the master musician within.* New Albany, IN: Jamey Aebersold Jazz.

Weiss, P., & Taruskin, R. (1984). *Music in the Western world: A history in documents.* New York: Schirmer Books.

Wilson, B. (1981). Implications of the Pillsbury Foundation School of Santa Barbara in perspective. *Bulletin of the Council for Research in Music Education, 68,* 13–25.

Wilson, J. (1971). The effects of group improvisation on the musical growth of selected high school instrumentalists (Doctoral dissertation, New York University). *Dissertation Abstracts International, 31*(7), 3589A.

Zwick, R. (1987). Jazz improvisation: A recommended sequential format of instruction (Doctoral dissertation, University of North Texas). *Dissertation Abstracts International, 48*(3), 592A.

Improvisation and Curriculum Reform

12

EDWARD SARATH

Despite appeals by NASM, MENC, and UNESCO's International Music Council for greater diversity in musical study, strategies for reform remain elusive for many college and university music departments. Conventional curricular models filled to the brim with requirements in interpretive performance and analysis of European repertory leave little room for experiences in improvisation, composition, technology, and multiethnic musicianship—to list some of the areas most commonly cited to be lacking. As a result, many students graduate with little or no training in skill domains that will be important to their professional careers. If substantive strides toward reform are to be made, change must take place at the core level, where the seeds of diverse musicianship are planted early on in students' development.

In this chapter, I propose that improvisation, particularly when studied from what I call a trans-stylistic perspective, is uniquely equipped to address these needs and therefore warrants a significant place in the core music curriculum. The creative, integrative, eclectic, and hands-on qualities of improvisational experience promote the development of both conventional and contemporary skills, foster in students an all-important self-sufficiency, and also open up pathways to emerging educational areas such as consciousness and contemplative studies. Moreover, as these inherent qualities in improvisation point to new types of educational models, they also illuminate new reform strategies through which these models may be achieved.

In presenting these ideas, I will depart somewhat from the general tone of the Handbook as a commentary on existing research, and instead use existing research as a point of departure for personal viewpoints on the role of improvisation in the curriculum reform process.

What Is Improvisation?

The marginalized status of improvisation in the curriculum appears to be consistent with, and possibly a result of, its marginalized status as a research topic. Bruno Nettl (1998, p. 4) points out that "among the activities and processes studied by music historians and ethnomusicologists, improvisation plays a small part." This remark echoes Derek Bailey's (1980, p. 1) comment that "improvisation enjoys the curious distinction of being both the most widely practised of musical activities and the least acknowledged and understood." While one might be tempted to cite as an exception to these observations the burgeoning body of jazz literature that has appeared in recent years, the fact that this literature is either pedagogical and largely formulaic (e.g., focusing on idiomatic patterns, chord-scale theory, etc.) or historical in nature still leaves exploration of the cognitive, interactive, and inventive aspects of the improvisation process—aspects that one would expect to be essential to any substantive ontological inquiry—largely untouched. That the same claims might be directed at existing literature on baroque improvisation (Bach, 1759/1949; Czerny 1836/1983; Quantz, 1752/1966) support the contention (Sloboda, 1987) that musical scholarship has neglected inventive processes at large in favor of either finished works or replication of style features.

A small but growing body of work that deals with aesthetic and cognitive concerns of improvised music makes modest attempts at filling this gap. Pressing (1987) makes one of the very few attempts at delineating a cognitive foundation for the improvisation process, and later he explores improvisatory skill from the standpoint of expertise theory (1998). Nachmanovitch's (1990) poetic treatise *Free Play* illuminates connections between improvisation and overall human creativity. Elliott (1987) probes the interplay between emotion and the basic elements of music in a jazz improvisation context, and in *Music Matters* (1995) he grounds his advocacy of improvisation as a central component of musical study in the rich cognitive foundations of the process.

Lewis's (1997) exploration of jazz and its offshoots in the latter half of the 20th century and Collier's (1996) consideration of interactive aspects of jazz performance also illuminate insights into a more general understanding of the improvisation process. Belgrad (1998) and Monson (1996) frame their inquiries into the interactive and spontaneous aspects of jazz within the context of postmodern critical theories, in attempts at revealing links between improvisatory strategies and overall cultural behaviors. Alperson (1984), Gioia (1988), and Nettl (1974) offer aesthetic reflections that in one way or another seek to illuminate distinctions between improvised and composed music. However, while the need for improvised music to be evaluated according to different criteria from those used for composed music is an implicit theme in much of this literature, the lack of a compelling means for differentiating the two processes continues to relegate improvisation to a subcategory of composition, where it is presumed that the improviser in a single moment seeks to pursue the same strategies carried out by the composer over weeks or months.

Elsewhere (Sarath, 1996), I challenge this viewpoint. My central premise is that because improvisation and the composition process are undertaken within contrasting creative conditions or environments, the two processes promote differing cognitive, expressive, and aesthetic pathways. Improvisation is undertaken in a single, continuous format, with no provisions for revising or editing; creation occurs simultaneously with performance and reception, and ideas in collective improvising formats are the product of multiple input and interaction (among players and listeners).

Composition is undertaken in a discontinuous format where extensive reworking of ideas is possible, creation occurs in a different time and place from performance and reception, and, because composers usually work alone, the ideas generated are not shaped by collective input of other artists or listeners present during the time of creation.

Extending from these contrasting conditions are contrasting modes of cognitive functioning, particularly in the way time is experienced. Improvisation is rooted in an inner-directed temporal conception, where the current moment is heightened and relationships to past and future moments are subordinated. Composition is driven by an expanding conception, in which the relationships between any moment and its past and future within a work are intensified. While both conceptions, when realized optimally, have the capacity to invoke transcendent states of consciousness (which I will go into in greater detail later) they do so in contrasting manners.

The inner-directed conception of improvisation invokes transcendence through a collapse of the "inner boundaries of the localized present" (Sarath, 1996, p. 18), which is central to the realization of the interactive demands of the music. Transcendence is also associated with the cyclic pitch and rhythmic structures (e.g., jazz time feels and chord progressions, Hindustani raga and tala frameworks) central to much improvised music (Berliner, 1994, pp. 391–392; Olsen-Sorflaten, 1995). These cyclic structures, due to their very recurring nature, further undermine temporal projections, promote heightened sense of the moment, and also promote a realization or enlivenment of the transcendent qualities associated with these underlying formats.[1]

In composition, an expanding conception prevails and promotes transcendence through the "collapse of the outer boundaries of the present moment" (Sarath, 1996, p. 18), leading to realization of large-scale formal relationships possible in composed music. Transcendence in improvisation can thus be thought of as more process-mediated, driven by spontaneous interactions and enlivenment of underlying cyclical formats, and in composition more structure-driven, as the ever-evolving form places demands on consciousness to shift from ordinary to heightened states. These distinctions appear to be supported by descriptions of transcendent moments offered by improvisers and composers.

Nachmanovitch (1990, p. 100,1) talks of an "entrainment" in peak improvisations, which he equates to the "trance states in the sama dances of the Sufis," where "the audience, the environment, and the players link into a self-organizing whole." Melba Liston (Berliner, 1994, p. 392) describes moments when "everybody can feel what each other is thinking and everything. You breathe together, you swell together, you just do everything together, and a different aura comes over the room." While spontaneity and interactive concerns are the focus of these and other improvisers' testimonies (see also Leonard, 1987; Milano, 1984; Monson, 1998; Racy, 1998), structural parameters tend to be much more predominant in composers' testimonies. Brahms (Harmon, 1984, p. 46) cited "rare, inspired moods" where "measure by measure the finished product is revealed to me . . . clothed in the right forms, harmonies and orchestration." Mozart mused over experiences where (Harmon, p. 33) "the whole, though long, stands almost complete and finished in my mind, so that I can survey it, like a fine picture or a beautiful statue, at a glance."

While the limitations of improvised music in fostering the same architectural results as composition generally underlie notions that it is a less sophisticated process, this perspective may be the result of a lack of awareness of the underlying cognitive principles that are unique to improvisation and enable expressive results—spontaneous invention, interaction, and enlivenment of cyclic pitch-rhythmic frameworks unattainable through composition. The point, however, is not to cast one process over the other but to recognize their differences and unique and complementary roles in the contemporary landscape. As Steve Lacy (1994, p. 21) reflects, "There is a music which must be composed, there is another music which can only be improvised." Efforts at grounding this aesthetic viewpoint in an underlying theoretical-cognitive model are essential not only for extricating improvisation from classification as a possibly less evolved form of composing but also for understanding the educational value of improvisation. Whether or not the temporal distinctions I propose fulfill the former need, the premise that improvisation is a central aspect of musical and possibly human creative and transpersonal development (Maslow, 1971; Nachmanovitch, 1990) points to an underlying educational richness that can be harnessed in music curricula.

Improvisation, Creativity, and Transcendence

While many of the educational attributes of improvisation are also shared by composition, improvisation is unique in two important ways. First, it is the most integrative of musical operations, including (unlike composition) real-time performance on the principal instrument in addition to (like composition) invention, theory, aural skills, and historical and aesthetic considerations.

Second, because improvisation is intrinsic to many of the world's musical traditions, it is a primary tool for assimilation of certain practices that have emerged as a result of the merging of these traditions in today's world. A primary example is the variety of time-feel-based musical styles that have originated in drumming traditions from Asia including the Mideast, Africa, Europe, and South America and are manifested in a rich array of contemporary offshoots. While composers can capture surface features of these time feels, improvisation provides the interactive context through which they can be more comprehensively realized.

Figure 12.1 represents three levels of creative awareness accessible through the improvisation process. When awareness is confined to the surface level, creativity and transcendent awareness are minimal; when awareness is rooted in the foundational level, creativity and transcendent awareness are optimal. An important aspect of this scheme is its inclusivity; penetration to underlying levels of awareness subsumes, rather than bypasses, awareness of overlying levels. Thus the range of influences that can affect creative expressions increases with depth of creative experience. In addition, because the deeper the penetration, the less the awareness is attached to surface perceptions, an all-levels experience promotes heightened spontaneity and interactive skills.

At each level, two complementary forces interact to uphold awareness at that level: structures and processes. Structural or craft elements are formations that have crystallized over time into established norms within a discipline; in jazz, for example, these include the idiom's standard repertory and characteristic technical, harmonic, rhythmic, and melodic aspects. Processes are the fluid, searching, at times risky, inventive excursions in which structural elements are manipulated and transformed. Development of both structural and processual skills is necessary for an all-levels creative experience, which we will see requires a balance between contrasting types of learning modalities. Structural knowledge is gained through replicative study: emulation, transcription, even rote learning. There is nothing "anticreative" about these learning modalities. In fact, they are essential for assimilation of certain kinds of skills. The problem is when a structural emphasis dominates at the expense of processual study, which requires exploratory, stylistically open formats, where students are able to shape their own creative destinations. An all-levels type of creative development requires the coexistence of the replicative modalities necessary for structural mastery and the exploratory experiences central to processual development. Conventional musical study, with little or no improvisation at all, and jazz improvisation models strictly confined to mainstream jazz syntax are two examples of overly structural approaches that impede all-levels creative growth. I advocate a trans-stylistic approach to improvisation study, which includes both rigorous structural parameters (e.g., improvising with jazz chord changes and time feels, with corresponding theoretical, technical studies) and rich, exploratory process-based formats, where style destinations manifest as a by-product of creative exploration rather than specified in advance. We will see that the latter exploratory aspect enables students to not only fathom deeper strata of the process–structure interplay but also work with hybrid forms, which is important in today's eclectic world.

Creative Awareness Level III

Structural Features: Syntactic and Nonsyntactic Musical Parameters.   Figure 12.1 shows that the structural features of Creative Awareness Level III are the basic building blocks of music, which can be categorized, roughly according to concepts of theorist Leonard Meyer (1989, p. 340), into two types of parameters. *Syntactic* parameters (Level IIIA) are harmony, melody, and rhythm; *nonsyntactic* parameters (Level IIIB) are density, dynamics, silence, texture and harmony, melody, and rhythm. It is important

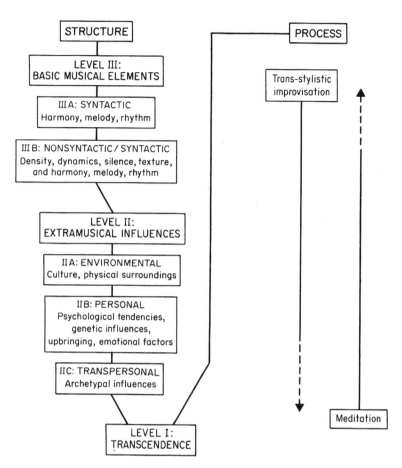

Figure 12.1. Levels of creative awareness accessible through the improvisation process and meditation.

to reiterate the inclusivity principle stated earlier, which tells us that Level IIIB awareness subsumes awareness of Level IIIA parameters. From this standpoint, IIIB awareness is more creative than IIIA awareness because the former places syntactic concerns (IIIA) within a broader, more fluid perspective. Harmony, melody, and rhythm are perceived along with a heightened sense of density, dynamics, and so forth. The artist is freer from conditioned responses to harmonic, melodic, and rhythmic contexts and is able to discover new configurations that lead to new ideas.

Process Features: Stylistic and Trans-Stylistic Improvising. For each awareness level we can identify corresponding processes that most directly promote access to that level. As indicated in figure 12.1, the prevailing process element at Levels IIIA and IIB is "trans-stylistic" improvising, which refers to a palette of improvisatory experiences that include both syntactic formats where style features are delineated in advance and more open formats where style is a by-product of process. The defining principle of trans-stylistic improvisation is not the use of multistylistic frameworks, where students, say, improvise

using jazz chord changes, Turkish *maqam*, and Indian ragas. Rather, *trans-stylistic* simply means that within the spectrum of improvisatory experiences students at times work in formats where—instead of preordained style parameters—they are enabled to draw freely from the complete range of style influences they have assimilated and consequently fashion their own. When students are enabled to transcend stylistic boundaries and draw upon their entire reservoir of style resources, they "deconstruct"[2] the syntactic formations (IIIA) into constituent nonsyntactic elements and thus perceive the syntactic–nonsyntactic (IIIB) spectrum in a more fluid manner, where basic elements can be molded into an array of style formations.

In my teaching, I use nonsyntactic elements (density, dynamics, silence, texture, and so forth) as improvisatory catalysts, as well as interactive strategies (e.g., player A states an idea, player B plays contrasting material, and then the two gradually switch roles during the improvisation), and completely open improvisatory formats as complements to syntactic (tonal, modal, rhythmic parameters delineated in advance) improvising models to achieve the trans-stylistic spectrum.

Creative Awareness Level II

Structural Features: Extramusical Influences. At Level II, the awareness extends beyond musical elements to access an underlying domain of extramusical, interior content. This content includes the totality of influences assimilated from one's life experiences—one's dreams, feelings, relationships, studies, travels, and such. Artists commonly describe tapping into an internal reservoir comprising life experiences (Berliner, 1994, p. 202). This inner reservoir is also shaped by inherited physical and psychological tendencies, as well as transcendent/transpersonal influences, and is what makes each individual unique. Perhaps the most comprehensive vision of the range of influences that might feed into this reservoir is found in philosopher Ken Wilber's (1999, p. 494) four-quadrant model of consciousness, in which he acknowledges the interplay of interior subjective influences ("I," levels of awareness, or states of consciousness, that range from waking and dreaming to transpersonal or spiritual domains), exterior subjective influences (physiological correlates to interior levels of consciousness), interior intersubjective influences ("We"; social, cultural influences), and exterior intersubjective influences (ecosystems, social institutions, villages, tribes, and so forth) in human development. I propose that from this spectrum of influences three levels of extramusical imagery can be distilled that inform the improvisation process: environmental (IIA), personal (IIB), and transpersonal (IIC) influences. Environmental influences include one's familial, social, cultural, political, economic, geographical, climatic, and other circumstances that play a role in shaping personality and, by extension, artistic creativity. Personal influences include physiological and psychological tendencies; while some tendencies within these categories will be genetic, others will be environmentally shaped, so we need to keep in mind that the boundaries between levels are not always crystal clear.

Transpersonal (IIC) influences include content from deep within the psyche that transcends genetic or environmental origins. Psychologist Carl Jung (1960) elaborated on concepts rooted in Eastern and Western philosophical traditions in postulating that archetypes—primordial patterns—emerge from the collective consciousness (or what he called unconscious) and manifest in dreams, artworks, mythology, and other expressions. When artists access Awareness Level IIC, they combine archetypal imagery with personal and environmental imagery. Jung (1961, p. 82) states that "the creative process consists in the unconscious activation of the archetypal image. . . . By giving it shape, the artist translates it into the language of the present, and so makes it possible for us to find our way back to the deepest springs of life."[3]

Process Features: Trans-Stylistic Improvising and Meditation. Trans-stylistic improvising plays a key role in promoting Level IIA, IIB, and IIC awareness. Meditative practices, which serve to deconstruct (and thus render more assimilable to awareness) content from the foundational angle of transcendent experiences, can complement this degree of penetration. Whereas trans-stylistic improvising works from the surface downward, meditation works from the foundation upward in cultivating an all-levels awareness.

Creative Awareness Level I: Transcendence

At Level I, structure and process unite. Note that, as illustrated in figure 12.1, structures and process come increasingly closer to each other, the deeper the probing of creative awareness. As content toward underlying levels is increasingly perceived as fluid and integrated, the boundaries that sustain perception of overlying quantities as rigid and discrete begin to give way to unified awareness of musical and extramusical elements. At Level I, this union of structure and process culminates in a cognitive synthesis, where being and becoming are part of an unbroken wholeness, which we call transcendence.

By *transcendence*, I refer to exceptional instances of human experience, where the ordinary consciousness that governs most of everyday life is transformed into a peak emotional, intuitive, and physical experience. While commonly associated with meditative states, transcendent experiences—whose features include include inner well-being, communion with environment, flow—can also be invoked in virtually all types of human activity (Alexander, 1990; Csikszentmihaly, 1990; Maslow, 1971). Wilber (1999) cites parallels for transcendent experience and corresponding levels of development across widely divergent cultural boundaries, and he also integrates the related transpersonal perspective of human development within conventional psychological models of human growth. Neurophysiological research into transcendent states in recent decades (Austin, 1998; Wallace, 1991) further supports the notion that these experiences are far more than subjective musings but are in fact objectively verifiable modes of consciousness that, even if elusive in terms of willful access and sustainability, are inherent in the structure of the human nervous system.

Process Features. While transcendent experiences have been reported in a wide variety of human activities, a common thread in much of the literature is that the experiences are difficult to invoke at will (Csikszentmihalyi, 1990; Maslow, 1971; Murphy & White, 1995). Meditation techniques are widely thought to be vehicles that enhance the consistency of such experiences. Murphy and White (1995) cite athletes who, having glimpsed heightened states in their respective sports, turn to meditation and yoga in quest of more systematic and consistent access to these states. Therefore, whereas trans-stylistic improvising can give glimpses of Level I transcendent experiences, meditation can serve to promote more consistent access to these states.

A curriculum that includes both trans-stylistic improvising and meditation is therefore ideal for promoting an all-levels type of creative growth. Trans-stylistic improvising promotes creative penetration from the surface to the core, through the deconstruction of structural parameters at each level, in so doing giving access to underlying perceptual levels, while meditation promotes deconstruction of inner content from the opposite direction. By tapping into experiences of inner calm, meditation renders fluid deep psychic content so that it can be expressed in musical formats. While some time may elapse before many schools are able to implement the meditation component, considerable strides may be made with a curriculum grounded in trans-stylistic improvising due to the depth of creative penetration this process promotes.

Here it should be emphasized that trans-stylistic improvising is not the only pathway to transcendence or creativity in music but, rather, that it is unique in the cognitive breadth it brings to these domains and thus the resultant type of musical understanding. When strictly stylistic improvisers and interpretive performers invoke transcendence, they do so not by integrating Awareness Levels IIIB and IIA, B, or C into their experience but instead through inspired immersion in IIIA activity, which serves as a direct conduit for Level I experience. Recall that when style parameters are ordained in advance, contact with basic musical elements in fluid forms (IIIB), which would then enable Level II infusion of environmental, personal, and transpersonal influences on the route to transcendent experiences, is limited. Interpretive performers and strictly stylistic improvisers bypass these levels and contact with corresponding influences, and thus, while their transcendent experiences represent peak aesthetic episodes and perhaps deeply intimate connections with the repertory or styles involved, a foundation is lacking for cultivation of the type of awareness necessary for the broader musical landscape of today's world.

The value of a curriculum grounded in trans-stylistic improvising is that its processual and structural breadth, combined with its all-levels penetration, lays cognitive groundwork for the assimilation of a wide diversity of musical influences, which enhances study of both the multiethnic expanse of our times and the traditional style areas that have comprised conventional curricula. The trans-stylistic model is thus uniquely inclusive from both horizontal (breadth of musical genres and processes) and vertical (all-levels depth of penetration) standpoints.

Educational Ramifications of the Creativity–Transcendence Relationship: Toward a New Core Curriculum

The task of music-learning institutions is to harness the full range of the preceding scheme within educational models, so that students may experience music as a vehicle for a broader type of creative and transpersonal growth than conventional curricula provide. As stated earlier, the trans-stylistic foundation enables this kind of development through its juxtaposition of stylistically open and closed inventive formats, where students work within both precisely proscribed constraints (e.g., jazz harmonic and rhythmic sequences) and open, exploratory formats where style features are by-products of the creative process. When the individual penetrates beyond the surface syntactic configurations of music and accesses syntactic and nonsyntactic elements in more fluid forms and infuses subsequent interior Level II content, entirely new educational principles are accessed that redefine the notion of curricular core. Looking at these principles and the resultant learning model from a systems perspective, we will see that they not only support a broad spectrum of skill development but also bring strong self-organizing elements to the educational scenario that allow the diverse and creative growth initiated within students to manifest in the entire learning environment and then be transmitted to the society at large.

Alignment of Invention and Craft

Creative development is driven by the interplay of process and structure or invention and craft. Optimal assimilation of any given craft area depends upon the existence of a corresponding inventive or expressive outlet. Craft areas include instrumental technique, theory, aural skills, history, and style influences. The closest expressive outlet for instrumental technique is interpretive performance, and thus it is no surprise that interpretive students generally excel in this type of development. The necessary expressive outlets for areas such as theory, aural skills, multiethnic influences, rhythmic training, and technology are improvisation and composition. Here the lack of alignment between the respective craft and expressive outlets give us reason for concern. The problem with the conventional curriculum is not only its narrow structural and processual range, which limits its ability to address contemporary musical horizons, but also the fact that even assimilation of much conventional content/craft is limited by the absence of corresponding processes/expressive outlets. The trans-stylistic improvisation foundation, because it supports a wide breadth of processes and style elements, supports this diversity of craft-expression alignments necessary for these areas to be assimilated.

Autotelic Experiences Through the Intimate Connection with Elements of Music

When the study of craft is aligned with a corresponding expressive outlet, craft elements are perceived as intimate extensions of the psyche. This can be analyzed in the context of the all-levels penetration considered earlier, where students penetrate to underlying levels of creative and transcendent experience and subsequent musical expressions are directly informed by environmental, personal, and transpersonal influences, resulting in the experience of music as a deeply personal and meaningful commentary on one's inner self. Because surface statements generated are linked to interior psychoemotional impulses, music is seen as a direct extension of the self and musical study is seen as a means to further self-knowledge. The incentive for further study takes on what Csikszentmihalyi (1990, p. 67) calls *autotelic* qualities—where one is driven internally and does not require external rewards—to pursue a task. The deep immersion in the learning process characteristic of autotelic experience is a powerful factor in assimilation of knowledge.

Teleonomic Qualities

Closely related to the autotelic experience is the enlivenment of an inner intelligence that directs students toward areas of study necessary for integration of consciousness. Csikszentmihalyi (1988, pp. 24–28) identifies *teleonomic*, or goal-seeking, qualities of the self, where the self possesses intrinsic drives toward certain types of experiences for its evolution. The ramifications of this concept for musical study are compelling in light of the scope of the knowledge base our students confront. When creative processes penetrate deep into the psyche or self and stir up subtle, transpersonal/archetypal content, the self seeks corresponding expressive outlets through which this content might manifest and thus be realized. Otherwise, transpersonal content lies dormant, unintegrated into awareness, and the urge to create is left unfulfilled.

Teleonomic experience is educationally valuable in that it represents an internal mechanism that directs students toward a particular musical terrain at a particular time. When inner content is aligned with the appropriate external framework for its expression, the self exerts a pull toward the corresponding skill areas that need to be developed for this expression to occur and evolve. This is not to say that the enlivenment of the self-directing qualities of the psyche, which will guide students toward what to study and when, will render institutional requirements un-

necessary. Rather, as we will examine shortly, the coexistence of carefully considered institutional requirements and increased curricular flexibility, which will enable the enlivened teleonomic qualities in trans-stylistic improvising students to motivate the learning process, give rise to an optimal educational environment.

Diversity: A New, Internally Regulated Approach

While schools are rightly urged to diversify the training they provide, the challenge of mapping the ever-growing range of skills of today's world onto an unchanging curricular base remains one of the most elusive challenges of our times. This problem is all the more difficult when it comes to multiethnic musicianship, where we confront three daunting questions: What degree of mastery within another musical tradition can realistically be expected given the lifelong task of mastering the music of one's own culture? As an alternative, can superficial skimming of diverse elements from various cultures fulfill today's multiethnic imperative? How, in either case, will institutions equip themselves with the staffing and material resources to deal with the enormous range of multicultural streams that informs today's musical world?

The preceding analysis points to interior solutions to these challenges. The enlivenment of autotelic and teleonomic qualities through trans-stylistic improvisation directs students toward those style areas needed at a given time in their growth. The extent of access to a given tradition will be determined internally; one student may be drawn to spend time abroad for intensive immersion in a foreign musical culture, while another's multiethnic needs may be fulfilled through personalized integration of particular elements (e.g., the strong movement in contemporary jazz circles to incorporate Mid-Eastern and Indian rhythmic influences) that may be available in his or her surroundings. In either case, if whatever multicultural access occurs is rooted in the autotelic, teleonomic experience, then groundwork is established for the fulfillment of three important goals of multicultural study.

The first is the experience of an intimate, personal/transpersonal relationship to another musical tradition, which is the basis for genuine respect and appreciation for the ethnic diversity of the entire musical landscape. The second and third goals are more practical: the ability to access cultural diverse elements for one's own creative purposes and the ability to interact with musicians of diverse backgrounds. As for the latter goal, a point of emphasis: Trans-stylistic improvising skills will not enable an American musician to perform Carnatic music, but they will enable an American musician to collaborate with a Carnatic musician who also extends beyond his or her syntactic boundaries into a trans-stylistic middle zone where musicians from all backgrounds can unite.

The task of the institution regarding multiethnic training is thus twofold: first, to provide forums for trans-stylistic improvisatory experiences and development, which will serve to engender a receptivity to multiethnic influences; and second, to provide as wide an array of cultural resources as is possible given available resources. A robust program rooted in the former can serve as a guide to the latter, as students, when allowed the opportunity to create, will bring wide-ranging influences to the learning environment.

Pathways to Reform

The preceding commentary points to a new curricular core, one that includes the conventional areas associated with musical rigor, along with the interior domains of integrative, creative, autotelic, teleonomic, and stylistically diverse musical experiences, which warrant also being associated with a new, expanded concept of rigor (Gardner, 1993). Among the distinguishing features of this core is that it is grounded in levels of musical perception where the surface divisions that prevail at the curricular surface (e.g., separate courses and administrative departments in theory, performance, history, etc.) are transcended. In other words, the trans-stylistic improviser consistently accesses a level of creative penetration in which boundaries between idioms and processes simply do not exist and, instead, the totality of the musical landscape is perceived as a source of potential expressive resources. In that conventional music-learning models are rooted in very different principles—that is, noncreative, fragmented, specialized, monocultural, institution-driven versus self-driven learning—the task of educators is to find new frameworks through which the emergent qualities can manifest. Let us consider three conditions necessary to reform.

The first is the design of new learning models that not only incorporate trans-stylistic improvisation experiences but also integrate these experiences into the overall fabric of musical study. The second condition for change is a streamlined core curriculum in which students are given latitude, within reasonable constraints, to determine what they study and when. The third condition is institutional initiatives (e.g., incentives for faculty diversification, new course design, new promotion and hiring criteria) that promote the integration of improvisation in the overall culture of the music school.

Design of New Core Musicianship Models

A major challenge to reform is the sheer breadth of the knowledge base, and an important way of addressing this challenge will be the design of new courses that selectively retain essential conventional knowledge and integrate it

with essential contemporary knowledge. At the University of Michigan School of Music, I have designed an improvisation-based alternative to the second-year theory and aural skills track along these lines.

The course integrates a trans-stylistic approach to improvisation, composition, keyboard skills, harmony, melody, aural skills, rhythm, and analysis within a hands-on format that utilizes resources from diverse musical traditions. Students bring their principal instruments to class; they improvise, compose, sing, and play all concepts covered at the keyboard. Rhythmic training utilizes principles from African, South Indian, and Brazilian music. Improvisation is undertaken in jazz, globally influenced, contemporary classical, and figured bass styles. Harmonic training draws from jazz and European classical music, with keyboard realization as the primary learning vehicle. Students learn to be pianistically "bilingual"—able to play contemporary jazz/pop chord symbols and Baroque figured bass chord changes. This integration of jazz and classical sources is also central to the writing component of the class, where, as an alternative to the four-part chorale context that is central to much theory training, my class uses a keyboard-style written approach that, in fact, is linked to both Baroque and jazz traditions.

The advantage of this trans-stylistic and multistylistic approach is twofold. First, by drawing from diverse styles, we not only integrate a greater expanse of the musical landscape but also are forced to identify critical underlying principles that are common to multiple styles and bypass details that may be unique to one genre but not necessarily essential for, at least at the core level, a basic foundation. Students do not need to know about vocal ranges, spacing, four-part voice leading, and other details idiosyncratic of four-part chorale writing in order to understand the harmonic structure of a Beethoven sonata or an Ellington work, let alone create tonal music of their own. What they do need is an understanding of the basic structure and function of these chords and the ability to play them (even if using reconfigured voicings/notations for students who are non-keyboard principals) and manipulate them within formats of their own design or those encountered in their musical travels.

A second advantage of the multistylistic approach is that its expanded breadth of content and processes enables more efficient means for skill assimilation to emerge. For example, instead of looking at a single genre as the sole source of tonal materials, I first identified what skills would be needed and then sought the most effective means for gaining those skills, regardless of style source. Thus the harmonic component of the class begins with jazz due to the idiom's ability to cultivate strong skills in basic chord structure, progression, and voice-leading principles. We turn to European common practice for the study of chord inversion and additional voice-leading principles. The class then returns to jazz for chord extension and covers modal mixture, altered chords, and other nondiatonic strategies through a combination of the two traditions.

In this way, we are able to make strides toward diversity as an organic outgrowth of the pursuit of creative skills, rather than as a politically mandated component of the learning environment. The value of this approach in the quest for multicultural curriculum is particularly evident in the rhythmic component of the class. Again, I began by considering what rhythmic skills would be needed and then sought the richest source I could find for those skills. For inner pulse development, I had found over the years that South Indian *konnekol*, a kind of rhythm solfège, is ideal, and so this found its way into the class. For time feels, African and Brazilian concepts are used. For mixed meters, contemporary concert music sources are most ideal. By stepping back and recognizing the entire landscape as a source of tools we can in a single stroke better prepare our students for the contemporary world while also exposing them to diverse musical traditions.

Institutional Role in Reform Process

An important component of this reform scenario is the necessity for administrations to create the conditions that promote faculty creativity. This means that incentives must be established for faculty to design courses that embody the integrative, diverse, and creative values sought. And if these values are to manifest in the classroom, they must also manifest in the professional profiles of faculty members. Administrations must begin to recognize integrative, diverse, and creative skill development as important criteria for promotion and tenure. Moreover, a conscious effort to hire these types of individuals must be made.

Options

As we examined earlier, when students begin to see music as intimately related to self-growth they begin to evolve as self-driven learners. Craft is seen not as drudgery but as a source of tools for further self-expression. Students naturally reflect on what areas they need to move toward and how this material needs to be learned. Students begin to become aware of their particular learning styles, which of their multiple intelligences (Gardner, 1993) are dominant, and which courses and experiences promote the inner–outer alignment of interior imagery and surface musical outlet described earlier. Options are necessary to harness and cultivate the autotelic, integrative thrust initiated in all-levels creative experiences.

A possible reform approach here is to have four areas of the curriculum—theory, history, private instruction, and ensembles—each "donate" two of their required terms to

a pool of options, which would also include courses in composition, improvisation, technology, and world musics, so that students may either choose to take what were previously required areas or choose alternatives. In other words, theory and history donate two of their generally required four terms, and ensembles and private lessons donate two of their eight terms to this pool. This would be a strategy that most schools could implement immediately, and when this is done concurrently with design of new, trans-stylistic based models, it would begin to serve both the external and internal needs of students.

Another institutionwide benefit that results from the provision for options is the enlivening of a quality- and currency-regulating mechanism within the learning environment. Faculty who previously taught core courses for which there were no alternatives now must face the prospect of reduced enrollment and must attend to the relevance of what they teach in a new way in order to ensure full classes. While on one hand this might seem to foster competition among faculty—which in itself could be very healthy—on the other hand it also encourages faculty creativity and collaboration. The point is that students could only benefit from faculty who are given the latitude to create.

Conclusion

In 1997 the American Council of Learned Societies launched the Contemplative Practice Fellowship, whose goal is to promote the use of meditation in university classrooms in order to promote heightened mental clarity, calm, compassion, self-knowledge, and other benefits. Over 75 institutions nationwide, including Yale and Columbia Law School, have participated in this program. At the University of Michigan School of Music, a BFA in Jazz and Contemplative Studies curriculum was recently approved, where the interplay between trans-stylistic improvising and meditation can be fully explored. Perhaps the greatest significance of this curriculum is in the possibility, currently being discussed, of making improvisation and meditation experiences available to a wider student population.

While these sorts of initiatives will be rejected by some as untested deviations from tradition and applauded by others as at the vanguard of educational thought, advocates of both perspectives need be reminded that these developments represent a return to, rather than a departure from, tradition. Improvisation has been a core music-making process in most of the world's music, and meditative practices have been central to exploration and cultivation of human potential in cultures across the globe. That the keys to curriculum reform may be found in the musical and knowledge traditions educational institutions pay homage to yet have not harnessed to their full extent both illuminates the shortcomings of existing models and points to blueprints for the future.

Possibilities for Further Research

1. The temporality of improvisation and composition: Might there be ways of objectively measuring the temporal distinctions I propose, perhaps through neurophysiological connections?
2. Qualitative research on motivational aspects of trans-stylistic improvisers, versus mainstream jazz improvisers versus interpretive specialists.
3. Longitudinal research on educational benefits of meditation in education and in musical study.
4. Effectiveness of pilot theory compared to conventional theory class.
5. Systematic learning methodologies for trans-stylistic improvisation.

NOTES

1. The use of underlying pitch and rhythmic structures (e.g., jazz chord sequences and time feels, Hindustani raga and tala cycles) at first glance may seem to promote the broader formal relationships attributed to composition. However, they produce the opposite result; the cyclic nature of these forms actually undermines the sense of large-scale temporal projections necessary to the overall architecture achieved in composition and instead promote a heightened sense of moment-to-moment development (Sarath, 1996).

2. My use of the term *deconstruct* differs from that conventional postmodern/poststructural discourse. Whereas the latter sources posit that when readers deconstruct texts they infer personal interpretations rather than gleaning some transcendent meaning, which is claimed to not exist, I suggest that artists deconstruct internal imagery by breaking it down into constituent structures of awareness, thereby allowing transcendence, which is a source of meaning, to permeate the creative experience. My usage, therefore, shifts the focus from the perceiver/listener to the inventing artist and, instead of rejecting underlying transcendental values, embraces them. However, my framework does not preclude but rather also subsumes the notion that personal, cultural, and environmental influences can also inform meaning. In essence, creative experience involves all of these influences.

3. I am well aware of the unfashionable status of "universals," of which Jung's archetypal principle would be a prime embodiment, in today's postmodern climate. While a critique of this aspect of postmodernism lies beyond the scope of this chapter, I concur with Wilber's (1999) illumination of the narrow and self-contradicting features of academic postmodernism (e.g., categorical rejection of transcendental, universal connections that might manifest across cultural boundaries, while positing this very rejection as a universal premise), as well as its significant contributions to contemporary

thought (e.g., illumination of the role of cultural influences as important components in shaping human experience).

REFERENCES

Alexander, C. (1990). Growth of higher stages of human consciousness: Maharishi's Vedic psychology of human development. In C. Alexander & E. Langer (Eds.), *Higher stages of human development* (pp. 286–341). New York: Oxford University Press.

Alperson, P. (1984). Thoughts on improvisation. *Journal of Aesthetics and Art Criticism, 43,* 17–29.

Austin, J. (1998). *Zen and the brain.* Cambridge, MA: MIT Press.

Bach, C. P. E. (1949). *Essay on the true art of playing keyboard instruments* (W. J. Mitchell, Trans.). New York: W. W. Norton. (Original work published 1759)

Bailey, D. (1980). *Musical improvisation.* Englewood Cliffs, NJ: Prentice Hall.

Belgrad, D. (1998). *The culture of spontaneity: Improvisation and the arts in postwar America.* Chicago: University of Chicago Press.

Berliner, P. (1994). *Thinking in jazz.* Chicago: University of Chicago Press.

Collier, G. (1996). *Interaction: Opening up the jazz ensemble.* Berlin: Advance Music.

Csikszentmihalyi, M. (1990). *Flow: The psychology of optimal experience.* New York: Harper & Row.

Csikszentmihalyi, M., & Csikszentmihalyi, I. (Eds.). (1988). *Optimal experience: Psychological studies of flow in consciousness.* New York: Cambridge University Press.

Czerny, C. (1983). *A systematic introduction to improvisation on the pianoforte,* Op. 200 (A. L. Mitchell, Trans. and Ed.). New York: Longman. (Original work published 1836)

Elliott, D. J. (1987). Structure and feeling in jazz: Rethinking philosophical foundations. *Bulletin of the Council for Research in Music Education, 95,* 3–38.

Elliott, D. J. (1995). *Music matters: A new philosophy of music education.* New York: Oxford University Press.

Gardner, H. (1993). *Multiple intelligences.* New York: Basic Books.

Gioia, T. (1988). *The imperfect art.* New York: Oxford University Press.

Harmon, W. (1984). *Higher creativity.* Los Angeles: Jeremy P. Tarcher.

Jung, C. G. (1960). *On the nature of the psyche.* Princeton, NJ: Princeton University/Bollingen Foundation.

Jung, C. G. (1961). *The spirit in man, art and literature.* Princeton: Princeton University/Bollingen Foundation.

Lacy, S. (1994). *Findings: My experience with the soprano saxophone.* Paris: CMAP, Outre Mesure.

Leonard, N. (1987). *Jazz: Myth and religion.* New York: Oxford University Press.

Lewis, G. (1997). Improvised music after 1950: African and European perspectives. *Black Music Research.*

Maslow, A. (1971). *The farther reaches of human nature.* New York: Penguin.

Meyer, L. (1989). *Style and music theory, history; ideology.* Philadelphia: University of Philadelphia Press.

Milano, D. (1984). The psychology of improvisation. *Keyboard Magazine, 10*(10), 30–35.

Monson, I. (1996). *Saying something: Jazz improvisation and interaction.* Chicago: University of Chicago Press.

Monson, I. (1998). On freedom: George Russell, John Coltrane and modal jazz. In B. Nettl (Ed.), *In the course of performance: Studies in the world of musical improvisation* (pp. 149–168). Chicago: University of Chicago Press.

Murphy, M., & White, R. (1995). *In the zone: Transcendent experience in sports.* New York: Penguin.

Nachmanovitch, S. (1990). *Free play: The power of improvisation in life and the arts.* Los Angeles: Jeremy P. Tarcher.

Nettl, B. (1974). Thoughts on improvisation: A comparative approach. *Musical Quarterly 60*(1), 1–19.

Nettl, B. (Ed.). (1998). *In the course of performance: Studies in the world of musical improvisation.* Chicago: University of Chicago Press.

Olsen-Sorflaten, T. (1995). *Increased personal harmony and integration as effects of Maharishi Gandharvaveda music on affect, physiology, and behavior: The psychophysiol-ogy.* Unpublished doctoral dissertation, Maharishi International University.

Pressing, J. (1987). Improvisation: Methods and models. In J. Sloboda (Ed.), *Generative processes in music* (pp. 129–176). London: Oxford University Press.

Pressing, J. (1998). Psychological constraints on improvisational expertise and communication. In B. Nettl (Ed.), *In the course of performance: Studies in the world of musical improvisation* (pp. 47–68). Chicago: University of Chicago Press.

Quantz, J. J. (1966). *On playing the flute* (E. R. Reilly, Trans.). New York: Schirmer Books. (Original work published 1752.)

Racy, J. (1998). Improvisation, ecstasy, and performance dynamics in Arabic music. In B. Nettl (Ed.), *In the course of performance: Studies in the world of musical improvisation.* Chicago: University of Chicago Press.

Sarath, E. W. (1996). A new look at improvisation. *Journal of Music Theory, 40*(1), 1–38.

Sloboda, J. (Ed.). (1987). *Generative processes in music.* London: Oxford University Press.

Wallace, R. K. (1991). *The neurophysiology of enlightenment.* Fairfield, IA: MIU Press.

Wilber, K. (1999). Integral psychology. In *The collected works of Ken Wilber* (vol. 4). Boston: Shambala.

Adult Education

13

DON D. COFFMAN

American adults now outnumber those younger than 18 for the first time ever. They report having accumulated more years of education and are more culturally and ethnically diverse (U.S. Census Bureau, 2000). The demands of a global economy and the shift to an information society have established a need for continuous learning and updating. These forces have contributed to an increased awareness of the need to view learning as lifelong.

What is an adult? What are the characteristics of adulthood? Based on age-related issues of physical maturation, our society has established legal definitions for certain adult privileges and responsibilities. However, adults also undergo psychological and social maturation and do not necessarily progress at the same rate. This suggests that adults who are at different levels of cognitive or emotional maturity may learn differently.

Furthermore, specialists in adult development and education are aware that descriptions of physical, cognitive, and emotional maturity do not completely account for what it means to be considered an adult. Sociocultural roles are influential because adults deal with issues of earning a living, sexual partnership, parenting, citizenship, and retirement. Thus it appears that there are at least two broad perspectives of adulthood, one emphasizing biological and psychological development and the other focusing on particular functions within a culture.

What is adult education? Based on the developmental and social function issues already noted, adult education has been defined as those systematic processes used to foster changes in the knowledge, skills, and attitudes of persons whose dominant social roles are characteristic of adulthood (Darkenwald, 1992). These persons have ended their continuous formal schooling and have taken on adult social roles. This is an admittedly subjective construct, for it excludes all full-time education of adolescents and young

adults in secondary and tertiary education but does include part-time education for out-of-school individuals, be they youths or young adults, workers or unemployed. Nevertheless, this narrowed definition provides useful boundaries and is congruent with adult education philosophy, which emphasizes the importance of social roles in defining adulthood (Tuijnman, 1996).

This chapter is divided into three sections. It begins with an overview of the basic concepts of adult development, adult participation in education, and principles of adult learning. This first section provides a framework for organizing and evaluating the research in the second section, which reviews music education research with adults. The chapter ends with conclusions and recommendations for future research. The body of research on adults within the field of music education is only emerging, so a substantial portion of the chapter presents research and theory from the adult education and development literature.

Basic Concepts

Adult Development

The term *adult development* implies orderly, sequential change over time. The body reaches its maximum physical maturity between the ages of 19 and 26 and then begins to experience some gradual deterioration, which affects the senses, the cardiovascular and neuromuscular systems, the brain, and internal organs. Nevertheless, these aging effects need not interfere with the capacity to learn if simple corrective measures such as eyeglasses, nonglare surfaces, hearing aids, speaking louder and enunciating carefully, or more serious corrections, such as cataract surgery, are utilized. However, other aspects of adult development are not so sequential, which could lead one to question whether adulthood constitutes a single coherent stage of development at all. This section summarizes research in cognitive and psychosocial adult development.

Cognitive Development. Researchers who examined how adults receive, store, transform, and retrieve information have documented age-related decrements. Older adults require more time to encode and select information, sustain attention, and divide attention between tasks (Cavanaugh, 1997). One noticeable change is in reaction time, which typically slows after age 65 (Bee, 1996) and is influenced by task complexity. Reaction time deficits can be minimized through task familiarity, sufficient structuring of information, and regular exercise (Cavanaugh, 1997).

Primary mental abilities proposed by theorists (e.g., number and word fluency, vocabulary, inductive reasoning, spatial orientation, closure factors) have been observed to decline with age, usually affecting performance in everyday life after age 60, more noticeably after the mid-70s (Schaie, 1996). However, higher order secondary mental abilities (fluid intelligence, crystallized intelligence, idea production, visual intelligence, auditory intelligence, memory, and speed) do not exhibit uniform declines.

Fluid and crystallized intelligences have received substantial attention (Horn, 1982). Fluid intelligence (flexible, abstract, analytic reasoning that is relatively independent of experience and education) is theorized to develop earlier in life and decline with age. Crystallized intelligence (culturally based knowledge and reasoning acquired through life experience and education) is thought to increase with age. The increased reliance on crystallized intelligence may explain how older adults are able to compensate for decreases in cognitive speed.

Cognitive scientists observe that individuals are rarely experts in multiple areas, perhaps due to the large amount of domain-specific knowledge required to become an expert. It is therefore reasonable to suppose that adults experience some deterioration of general cognitive ability with age but may maintain or even increase mental abilities in areas of expertise (Pieters, 1996). Gardner's (1983) theory of multiple intelligences and Goleman's (1995) emotional intelligence theory are two examples of attempts to explain areas of human expertise.

Piaget's concept of cognitive development has served as the basic point of departure for adult cognition theorists, who generally acknowledge that his formal operations stage cannot be considered an end point in development. They believe that Piaget's logical, hypothetico-deductive reasoning (which is aimed at finding correct solutions) is only one kind of thinking for adults. Post–formal operational thinking recognizes that "truth" varies with situations, that solutions must be tempered by real-world constraints, that ambiguity and contradiction prevail, and that emotion and subjective factors impact thinking. In short, adults coordinate logical/formal thought systems with emotional and interpersonal thought systems. Many theories of adult development typically extend Piaget's framework, theorizing that one or more subsequent stages exist in a hierarchy that moves from absolutist to relativistic to dialectical thinking (King & Kitchener, 1994; Kramer, 1983; Labouvie-Vief, 1984; Perry, 1981; Sinnott, 1994).

Psychosocial Development. Adult educational psychology has long been dominated by personal growth theory (Allport, Maslow) and ego psychology (Jung, Erikson). Subsequent researchers typically have combined these internal and external perspectives, yielding psychosocial theories of development. These theories parallel to some degree cognitive development theories, generally asserting that humans move from childhood dependency, relying on external authorities, toward adult-oriented dilemmas, relying on internal belief structures that integrate personal and social issues.

Some theorists (Levinson, 1986; Sheehy, 1995) propose age brackets to demarcate sequential life experience stages, while others (Schlossberg, 1989; Sugarman, 1986) use major life events (marriage, child rearing, divorce, empty-nest syndrome, retirement, etc.) to define particular life phases. For them, the life course is a succession of tasks and social roles; personal growth occurs as we move from disequilibrium to equilibrium during the transitions between life phases.

Adult Participation in Education

Adult education can be observed in a variety of formal, nonformal, and informal settings (Colletta, 1996). *Formal education* refers to the deliberate, systematic delivery of knowledge, skills, and attitudes with well-defined specifications for space, time, materials, and teacher qualifications. It often leads to degrees or credit of some sort and is most typically found in colleges and schools but also can be observed elsewhere (e.g., workplace training programs, libraries, and museums). *Nonformal education* is like formal education in being deliberate and systematic, but it occurs outside of formal educational institutions and often emphasizes social action. Flexible, less structured, less regulated, and more responsive to localized needs, it can be seen when people gather (e.g., in churches and community centers) to address a specific concern. *Informal education* can refer either to learner-initiated learning, which includes hobbies and self-help efforts, or to the incidental learning implicit in interacting with family, coworkers, and community members. Acknowledging the vast array of human activities that can be placed in this last category has prompted many adult educators to assert that most adult learning is informal and self-directed (Brookfield, 1983).

A number of closely related conceptions of adult education have been proposed. These can be differentiated by examining the degree of continuous education through the life span and can be placed on a continuum (Sutton, 1996). At one end is lifelong learning, which assumes free access to learning for all persons, embraces a variety of delivery systems, and requires dramatic restructuring of resources to allow for such continuous learning. Recurrent education proponents (located at the midpoint of the continuum) consider the constraints of existing resources by advocating cyclical, discontinuous periods of learning that alternate with work and leisure activities. Early advocates proposed delaying parts of secondary and tertiary learning so that recurrent education could be influenced by work experience. At the far end of the continuum is continuing education, conceived as a furthering of initial education and occasional retraining. These programs are often found in higher education extension programs and often have vocational or functional goals.

Principles of Adult Learning

A number of authors (e.g., Brookfield, 1986; Titmus, 1996) have acknowledged a failure to find a general theory of adult learning. Although Knowles (1984) did popularize the term *andragogy* in the United States to differentiate instruction designed for adults from "pedagogy" for children, andragogy is not so much a learning theory as it is a set of assumptions about adult learners. Brookfield (1986) offered six characteristics of adult learners, which incorporate and extend Knowles's list. According to Brookfield, adults (1) learn throughout life as they adjust to life phase transitions, (2) display a variety of learning styles, (3) prefer problem-centered learning that readily applies to specific personal concerns, (4) are influenced (aided and hampered) by prior experiences, (5) need to view themselves as learners if learning is to occur, (6) tend to be self-directed learners.

This learner-centered perspective views adults as mutual partners or primary designers of their learning, as long as they feel competent or committed to the process. Brookfield (1987) views adult learning as largely voluntary, requiring mutual respect among learners, often collaborative, and aiming toward developing critically reflective, self-directed learners. However, one should not naively assume that adult learning is always enjoyable, self-directed, unique in style, and based on adults' perceptions of their own needs (Brookfield, 1992). (For a review of other andragocial models, see Merriam & Caffarella, 1999.)

Self-directed learning has received considerable attention from theorists, researchers, and practitioners. Acknowledged as perhaps more of a goal than a defining characteristic of adult learners (Brookfield, 1986), it requires a redefinition of the role of a teacher, particularly in formal educational settings. Grow (1991) proposed a four-stage model based on situational leadership theory (Hersey & Blanchard, 1988). In Grow's model, the teacher's role shifts from teacher to facilitator based on the adult's skill in learning, familiarity with the subject matter, sense of personal competence, and commitment to learning.

Music Education Research

The research literature on educating adults in music is not extensive. This section's order of topics parallels the topics of the chapter's first section by presenting first studies of adult musical development, then studies of participation in music, and finally studies of the learning process. Because the majority of music education research with adults has occurred within the past 20 years, this review is limited to that time span.

Adult Musical Development

Recent efforts to define musical development in adulthood have relied on retrospective interviews of adults. For example, Sloboda and Howe (1991) reported that adults with a lifelong commitment to music often had childhood memories that involved supportive conditions for musical activities and strong positive emotions. Adults not involved with music more often reported strong negative emotions to the context of the musical activity (for example, teacher criticism). Parents, siblings, peers, professional musicians, and teachers have been reported as influencing the early and sustained development of a musician (Davidson, Howe, & Sloboda, 1997).

Sloboda (1994) proposed a three-stage theory of musical development, observing that many nonmusicians seem to have missed the first stage of engagement, which is based in pleasure. His second and third stages described increasing levels of commitment and achievement. Surveys of career symphony musicians (Bernstein, 1986; Marty, 1982) and professional singers (Rexroad, 1985) revealed the importance that these individuals placed on their enjoyment of making music. Bernstein (1986) used flow theory (Csikszentmihalyi, 1975) to analyze self-reports of the intrinsically motivating psychological states that career musicians repeatedly achieved and sustained.

Researchers have used survey and interview techniques to document the vast amount of time required to achieve mastery in musical performance. Studies reveal that experts accumulate three to four times as many hours of practice as less skilled musicians of comparable age (Ericsson, Krampe, & Tesch-Romer, 1991; Ericsson, Tesch-Romer, & Krampe, 1990; Sloboda, Davidson, Howe, & Moore, 1996). This deliberate practice needs to be maintained throughout one's life if skills are to be maintained (Krampe & Ericsson, 1995, cited in Davidson et al., 1997). Professional musicians can maintain their skills well into old age, but little is known about the strategies used to compensate for physiological or cognitive slowing. Perhaps the processes of thinking (attention, memory, logical reasoning) become increasingly linked to products of thinking (for example, piano performance), so that experts are less affected by age-related declines in information processing and intelligence (Rybash, Hoyer, & Roodin, 1986).

Simonton (1997) has examined the creative lifetime output of composers through use of an extensive computer database of the initial melodic patterns of thousands of musical compositions. He has observed that composers' output rates peak in their thirties or forties, then decline gradually, although the peak for smaller musical forms (arts songs, piano pieces) is earlier than that for larger forms (symphonies, operas). The melodic originality of these melodic fragments increased until around age 56.

Adult Participation in Music

Much of the research on adult musicians examines their participation in community musical organizations. This body of research does not test theories of adult development, educational methods, or adult learning. Nonetheless, the findings do provide information about adult musicians (demographics, musical backgrounds, musical preferences, motivations) and details of organizational structure. Community bands, choruses, orchestras, and music school organizations can be considered examples of nonformal (out-of-school) adult education. The research relies almost exclusively on descriptive methods (surveys, interviews), although a few have written histories of specific musical organizations (Carson, 1992; Engelson, 1994; Wilhjelm, 1998). Surveys of adult programs in community music guild schools (Graessle, 1999; Pflieger, 1985) report that about 15 to 20% of the students are adults. Smith (1991, 1998) examined the Elderhostel courses for adults and observed that about 10% of all courses were in music.

Researchers have surveyed members of brass bands (Hosler, 1992), community bands (Bowen, 1995; Heintzelman, 1989; Martin, 1983; Patterson, 1986; Spencer, 1996), senior citizen bands and choruses (Black, 1997; Coffman, 1996; Coffman & Adamek, 1999; Darrough, 1990), community choirs (Spell, 1990; Tipps, 1992; Vincent, 1997), church choirs (Seago, 1993), and adult piano classes (Johnson, 1983). There have been surveys of older adults who were living independently or in retirement centers and nursing homes (Bowles, 1991; Edgington, 1992; McCullough, 1981) to document their preferences for particular music activities and classes as well as the music ed-

ucation opportunities available to them (Patchen, 1986; Robertson, 1992; Tatum, 1985).

Last, researchers have surveyed music participants and nonparticipants to contrast possible differences in behavior and attitude. The approach has been to survey high school graduates of particular communities or regions, identify music participants and nonparticipants based on self-reports, and then describe group differences (Dregalla, 1994; Frakes, 1985).

These studies have relied on quantitative techniques to analyze the data, which range from simple percentages to multivariate analyses. Participants in the community groups were typically middle- to upper-middle-class college-educated professionals. Choruses were predominantly female (Spell, 1990; Tipps, 1992; Vincent, 1997), while bands were predominantly male (Bowen, 1995; Coffman & Schilf, 1998; Martin, 1983; Spencer, 1996), and most members viewed themselves as amateur musicians, although a proportion (e.g., 33% in the Bowen sample and 10% in Spencer's) reported some professional experience as a music teacher or performer.

Reasons for participating in these music experiences can be grouped into three categories: (1) personal motivations, such as self-expression, recreation, self-improvement, and use of leisure time; (2) musical motivations, such as professed love of music, performing for one's self and others, and learning more about music; and (3) social motivations, such as meeting new people, being with friends, and having a sense of belonging. No single reason consistently emerges as the most important one, although more able performers tend to report personal and musical reasons more frequently than less able performers.

In general, one finds that adults who participate in music activities typically had musical parents or music in the home when they were children and were also making music themselves, either in the home or at school, particularly in high school musical groups. These findings probably reveal more about where researchers have focused their attention than it does about describing the "typical" adult who is involved in active music making. Nonetheless, as a whole, this body of music research reflects one of the characteristics of adult learners in general, namely, the importance of prior experience to future participation.

A Theory of Participation.   Gates (1991) reviewed the literature on music participation and proposed a model to account for different levels of adult involvement and to provide a theoretical framework for further research, policy making, and practice. He first observed that members of our society, examined with respect to involvement in music, could be viewed as either participants, spectators, or not involved. Furthermore, he noted that people are socialized into one of these groups and that it is difficult to change groups.

Drawing from theorists in leisure sociology, Gates presented a typology that classified six kinds of participants, defined as

> those who directly or indirectly produce musical events for an audience, even if the audience is the performer him/herself, and even if the audience is not yet present as when an individual learns or composes music for an upcoming performance. (p. 6)

These six kinds of participants were dabblers, recreationists, hobbyists, amateurs, apprentices, and professionals. Dabblers and recreationists view music as play, hobbyists and amateurs view it as serious leisure, and apprentices and professionals view it as work.

One of Gates's conclusions was that community music ensembles largely consisted of amateurs, apprentices, and professionals, persons who were validated by public performance. He also concluded that participation rates in music ensembles will improve only to the extent that music educators identify the dabblers, recreationists, and hobbyists and tailor programs to their interests, which are typically individualistic.

At least three researchers have relied on Gates's ideas, especially his call for qualitative research methods. Belz (1995) and Holmquist (1995) surveyed, observed, and interviewed chorus members, while Chiodo (1998) interviewed a range of amateur and professional adult musicians from various instrumental groups. All three investigators observed the shared values of these adult musicians (who could arguably be placed in Gates's amateur category) and concluded that adult participation was often an extension of childhood and adolescent music participation. Larson's (1983) case studies of 12 lifelong amateur musicians also found that interest in music began early in life, expanded in adolescence, and frequently increased in retirement. Prior to this typology's appearance, Hinkle (1988) used a Q-sort technique to classify chorus members into three motivation categories. One category of singer that emerged from Hinkle's analysis and does not readily fit the typology contained singers who participated for spiritual reasons.

Outcomes of Participation.

Few studies have examined the benefits of music making and learning for physical and mental well-being. Parr (1985) asked pianists to perform strenuous piano exercises. Her measurements found that playing the piano stressed the whole body, not just the forearms, and put a stress on the heart equivalent to that produced by a brisk walk. Swedish researchers (Bygren, Konlaan, & Johansson, 1996) surveyed nearly 13,000 adults about their cultural activities and then followed them up with respect to survival 8 years later. Statistically controlling for a number of confounding variables, the researchers observed that persons who attended cultural events, read books or periodicals, made music, or sang in a choir had lower mortality rates.

Other researchers have surveyed (Coffman & Adamek, 1999; Vanderark, Newman, & Bell, 1983; Wise, Hartmann, & Fisher, 1992) and interviewed (Kahn, 1998) older adults involved in music groups to find that making music contributes favorably to their perceived health, quality of life, and mental well-being. Music ensembles also contribute to social development by providing senior citizens a venue to make friends (Coffman & Adamek, 2001). A handful of studies have shown that there are social and musical benefits from intergenerational music activities (i.e., mixing children, teenagers, or college students with senior citizens; see Bowers, 1998; Darrow, Johnson, & Ollenberger, 1994; Leitner, 1982).

Adult Learning in Music

While a number of music researchers have reviewed adult education and development theories in establishing the context for their studies, relatively few have sought to validate aspects of these theories directly. Some have developed instructional programs, others have examined learning processes, and still others have measured the products of learning.

Curriculum Development and Implementation.

Studies that have involved designing, implementing, and evaluating instructional programs span a variety of topics: music listening and appreciation (Bernhart, 1991; Mullee, 1997), voice (Astrup, 1991), band instruments (Burley, 1980), choruses (Green, 1998), keyboard instruments (Curran, 1982; Keenan, 1995; Turner, 1987), orchestral strings (Rosenthal, 1987), guitar (Simmons, 1995), and multifaceted music programs especially designed for elderly adults (Edgington, 1992; Janowitz, 1986; Kellmann, 1985). These researchers have usually designed programs based to varying degrees on adult educational theory combined with commercially available musical materials. Some researchers have undertaken needs/interests surveys of the intended clientele before developing a program (Edgington, 1992; Kellmann, 1985). At the end of the instructional program, the researchers generally have evaluated the success of the curriculum based not on objective measures of achievement but on participant self-perceptions of achievement and enjoyment. The participants in these studies report enjoying the classes and believing that they improved their musical skills.

Mullee's study (1997) is a good example of designing music instruction firmly based on andragogical principles. Two of her recommendations, based on her efforts to design and evaluate a music-listening workshop, are to: (1) encourage adult learners to take responsibility for their learning and, in turn, incorporate their ideas; and (2) use strategies such as small group projects and discussions that allow adults to be resources for one another, because they bring a wealth of prior experiences to learning.

Studies of adults in music that have employed an experimental design with treatment and control groups are exceedingly rare. Myers (1986) conducted an experimental study that used a cross-sectional design to test the outcomes of a music program (based on Edwin Gordon's music-learning theory) among musically unskilled young, middle-aged, and older adults. Myers found no evidence for age-related declines in learning rate and in fact found higher posttest achievement and enjoyment scores for singing melodies in the older adults. Furthermore, while older adults began the study with lower kinesthetic response scores, they overcame this deficit over the course of instruction. Finally, older adults displayed higher levels of participation during the study, perhaps because they had more available time to practice and attend class sessions. Myers's study is a sensible approach to testing for developmental effects without resorting to longitudinal studies.

Mack (1983), in another experimental study, examined the effect of one semester of weekly music instruction on musical achievement, self-concept, and perceived musical ability. She compared scores of chorus members, newly admitted members, and a no-contact control group of adult nonmusician volunteers. Chorus members demonstrated an increase in cognitive musical achievement and perceived musical ability but no change in self-concept when compared to the no-contact control.

Descriptions of Teaching and Learning. There are fewer studies of music teaching and learning processes. The researchers interested in processes usually have relied on naturalistic approaches to data collection. Alperson (1995) observed and videotaped 4 classes and interviewed teachers and participants in a Dalcroze Eurhythmics class. Her analysis revealed a student-centered approach and a cyclical flow of idea into action by the participants.

Chen (1996), using structured interviews of adult piano learners, observed that self-concept did not automatically increase with improved musical achievement. Furthermore, he observed that self-directedness was not present during lessons, noting that adults often deferred to the teacher's expertise and relied on teacher evaluation of their achievements. Chen recommended that teachers who wanted to foster self-directed learning should incorporate improvisation into lessons.

Monrouzeau (1993) examined 5 musically untrained adults' transcription and performance of a simple melody using invented musical notations in an attempt to describe changes in their apprehension of pitch and rhythm over successive interactions. Over a period of 3 weeks, subjects were asked to transcribe the melody, then sing/play the melody from their notation, and, last, explain their system of notions. Pitch and rhythm relationships were reflected in the invented notations according to how pitch relationships were experienced, while singing and rhythm relationships were experienced while clapping.

Irish (1993) examined how adults with a strong interest in music construct meaning while listening to music, drawing on theories of learning, aesthetics, and music cognition. She collected quantitative data from surveys and rating scales to measure learning style and music-listening preferences and collected qualitative data from interviews. She found adults' cognitive and affective responses were individualistic but that adults with similar education and experience exhibited similar response patterns. Using videotapes, audiotapes, and structured interviews of skilled pianists, McCollum (1990) analyzed varying music memorization strategies to conclude that visual memory was more important than auditory memory, tactile memory, and cognitive analysis ability.

Rybak (1996) applied Csikszentmihalyi's revised flow theory in analyzing the components of successful group music making. She observed, interviewed, and gave questionnaires to four groups of players with intermediate–advanced skill levels. Findings showed evidence of clear goals, concentration, and absence of self-consciousness in these groups. Conda (1997) grounded her observations of a "teacherless" piano performance club for "late bloomers" by using a number of motivation theories to explain why adults joined and continued in the bimonthly club. Childhood musical experiences and recent life-changing events were among the motivations to join the club. The level of a member's commitment to the club was linked to issues of self-confidence, prior experience, and relationships with other group members.

The study most clearly centered in the philosophical goals of advocates for nonformal adult education is Kaltoft's (1990) documentation of music's role in helping adults in three community education programs move toward sociopolitical transformation. This research is not so much about learning to make music as it is about how people use music to enhance their learning, gain cultural empowerment, and effect social change.

Conclusion

The array of musical activities available to adults is diverse: making music in amateur, semiprofessional, and professional community groups; attending lectures, concerts, and folk festivals; listening to radios and recordings; enrolling in music programs through Elderhostel and institutions of higher education; and engaging in self-directed music study. Yet despite this diversity, all these activities can be considered forms of music education, according to adult education experts, because they can be viewed as examples of formal, nonformal, or informal education. As long as one recognizes that music teaching and learning can occur outside of teacher-led classrooms, then virtually no activities need to be excluded. This observation highlights the fact that music researchers and educators have much to explore.

This chapter has presented a brief overview of the major aspects of adult development and learning to provide a framework for viewing a selective body of music research with adults. The majority of the music studies with adults have been in the areas of music participation or curriculum development. Far fewer studies have sought to describe processes of teaching and learning or explore music development in adults.

Further research is needed in many areas (many excellent questions are posed by Myers, 1989, 1995). In order to see if music learning is influenced by adult development, researchers will need to employ more cross-sectional and longitudinal designs. In order to examine more closely aspects of adult learning, researchers will need to gather field-based data through use of qualitative approaches. In order to validate instructional techniques, researchers will need to use more experimental designs. This chapter closes with a review of some principles of adult education, coupled with issues that warrant further investigation.

Adulthood is a process of change. This unremarkable statement is presented because music researchers have rarely explored the variations among adult learners. Not only does the physical body change, but the processes of thinking and the content of thinking apparently shift as well. Adult development has been characterized as a shift from childhood dependence to adult autonomy, a continual reconciling of inner goals with social expectations. Young adults differ from middle-aged and older adults, and each group embodies a different set of perspectives and strategies for living. Are particular life phases more conducive to particular forms of music participation? What adaptive strategies do skilled older musicians use to cope with physical aging effects? Music researchers should consider that adult learners' cognitive and psychosocial development may influence what they choose to learn, when they choose to learn it, and how they wish to learn.

Adult learners often pursue learning voluntarily. They are motivated by meaningful challenges, which can arise from life events. Music researchers have examined the broad motivations for participation in music performance groups and documented the high levels of commitment and

enjoyment among members of these groups. Gates's typology (1991) provides a coherent framework for exploring reasons for adult music participation. Assuming that music educators wish to reach all levels of participants, from dabblers to professionals, what are effective ways to provide instruction to these different types of individuals? In exploring the motivations of these participants, music researchers should pursue designs and data collection techniques that are more qualitative and allow us to observe in detail music understanding from the learner perspective.

Self-directed learning is viewed both as a defining characteristic of adult learners and as a goal of adult education. While acknowledging that self-directedness is more a desired characteristic than an empirically observed one, advocates of this goal want to develop adults who are reflective about their learning, think critically, and engage in self-directed learning activities, given sufficient command of the subject matter. Music teachers often employ prescriptive or authoritarian approaches to both one-on-one instruction and direction of musical ensembles (i.e., "do it this way"). This is clearly efficient and reflects a master–apprentice model of instruction. Perhaps there is no reason to do otherwise. Yet based on this perspective, there seems to be no difference between teaching music to children and teaching music to adults. What kinds of music instruction are more appropriate for adult learners? Are there ways to modify traditional instructional approaches in music education that encourage self-direction? Field-based studies are needed to assess effective instructional strategies.

Adults' prior experiences are valuable resources for subsequent learning. Music researchers know that experience in a musical organization during adolescence is a good predictor of musical involvement as an adult. Mullee's (1997) use of small group projects and discussions in a music appreciation course is one example of how to allow adults to be learning resources for one another, because they possess a wealth of prior experiences. What other ways can be devised to draw upon adult resources?

Collaboration and mutual respect among learners are key elements of adult education. Music studies have reported that the need for socializing was a strong motivator for joining and continuing in musical groups. Participants in intergenerational music programs enthusiastically attest to musical and interpersonal benefits from interacting across generations. Researchers have documented participants' self-perceptions of the mental, physical, and emotional health benefits they attribute to music activity. Continued efforts to obtain objective and subjective measures of these nonmusical benefits will help us understand music's effect on the whole person. How does the role of the group influence music teaching and learning? Research that explores the social component of music making (such as Conda, 1997; Rybak, 1996) is needed to help us better understand the dynamics of group learning.

Adults display a variety of learning styles. Successfully meeting life's challenges often requires some creativity. Myers (1995), observing that to be creative is to be human, ventured that music was a means of providing adults with opportunities to be creative. Does the creativity displayed in the practical intelligence of adulthood have any bearing on the creative and re-creative processes and products of music? Researchers have typically focused on group music making. Much less is known about the adults who are self-taught or self-directed.

Judging from the increasing number of studies and efforts such as the formation of the Adult and Community Special Research Interest Group by the Society for Research in Music Education, music educators and researchers no longer need convincing that lifelong learning of music outside of formal education is an important endeavor. Three responses are needed:

1. Music educators need to start training future teachers to teach adults, not just children. Ideally, this training would involve working in community music activities.
2. Music educators need to increase the availability of appropriate entry points for music instruction. Efforts by the music industry to support New Horizons concert bands for senior citizens (Coffman & Levy, 1997; Ernst & Emmons, 1992) and by the National Endowment for the Arts to provide exemplary arts programs for senior citizens (Terry, 2000) are laudable and should be extended.
3. Music researchers need to apply sufficient rigor in the research to help music educators understand music learning across the life span.

REFERENCES

Alperson, R. (1995). A qualitative study of Dalcroze Eurhythmics classes for adults. *Dissertation Abstracts International, 56*(10), 3875A. (UMI No. AAT96-03274)

Astrup, M. F. (1991). Vocal pedagogy: A comprehensive course in vocal musicianship for the adult beginner. *Dissertation Abstracts International, 52*(10), 3551A. (UMI No. AAT91-36350)

Bee, H. L. (1996). *Journey of adulthood* (3rd ed.). Englewood Cliffs, NJ: Prentice Hall.

Belz, M. J. D. (1995). The German Gesangverein as a model of life long participation in music (Doctoral dissertation, University of Minnesota, 1994). *Dissertation Abstracts International, 56,* 485A.

Bernhart, J. H. L. (1991). A project in the teaching of guided music listening lessons to older adults. *Dissertation Abstracts International, 52*(2), 458A. (UMI No. AAT91-20780)

Bernstein, C. M. (1986). Experiential factors influencing choice of career for orchestral musicians: An exploratory study (Doctoral dissertation, University of Colorado, 1986). *Dissertation Abstracts International, 47,* 2021A.

Black, M. F. (1997). The status of beginning/intermediate concert band programs for mature adults: A national survey. *Dissertation Abstracts International, 58*(6), 2125A. (UMI No. AAT97-38215)

Bowen, C. K. (1995). Adult community bands in the southeastern United States: An investigation of current activity and background profiles of the participants. *Dissertation Abstracts International, 56*(4), 1172A. (UMI No. AAT95-26740)

Bowers, J. (1998). Effects of an intergenerational choir for community-based seniors and college students on age-related attitudes. *Journal of Music Therapy, 35,* 2–18.

Bowles, C. (1991). Self-expressed adult music education interests and music experiences. *Journal of Research in Music Education, 39,* 191–205.

Brookfield, S. (1983). *Adult learners, adult education and the community.* New York: Teachers College Press.

Brookfield, S. (1986). *Understand and facilitating adult learning.* San Francisco: Jossey-Bass.

Brookfield, S. (1987). *Developing critical thinkers.* San Francisco: Jossey-Bass.

Brookfield, S. (1992). Why can't I get this right: Myths and realities in facilitating adult learning. *Adult Learning, 3* (6), 12–15.

Burley, J. M. (1980). A feasibility study of structured instruction in instrumental music for the adult beginner (Doctoral dissertation, University of Illinois at Urbana-Champaign, 1979). *Dissertation Abstracts International, 40,* 5354A.

Bygren, L. O., Konlaan, B. B., & Johansson, S. (1996). Attendance at cultural events, reading books or periodicals, and making music or singing in a choir as determinants for survival: Swedish interview survey of living conditions. *British Medical Journal, 313* (7072), 1577–1580.

Carson, W. S. (1992). A history of the Northshore Concert Band, Wilmette, Illinois, 1956–1986: The first thirty years. *Dissertation Abstracts International, 53*(7), 2150A. (UMI No. AAT92-37242)

Cavanaugh, J. C. (1997). *Adult development and aging* (3rd ed.) Pacific Grove, CA: Brooks/Cole.

Chen, H. (1996). An investigation of self-directed learning among non-music major adult piano learners in one-to-one piano instruction. *Dissertation Abstracts International, 57* (7), 2929A. (UMI No. AAT96-35962)

Chiodo, P. A. (1998). The development of lifelong commitment: A qualitative study of adult instrumental music participation (Doctoral dissertation, State University of New York at Buffalo, 1997). *Dissertation Abstracts International, 58*(7), 2578A.

Coffman, D. D. (1996). Musical backgrounds and interests of active older adult band members. *Dialogue in Instrumental Music Education, 20*(1), 25–34.

Coffman, D. D., & Adamek, M. (1999). The contributions of wind band participation to quality of life of senior adults. *Music Therapy Perspectives, 17*(1), 27–31.

Coffman, D. D., & Adamek, M. (2001). Perceived social support of New Horizons Band participants. *Contributions to Music Education, 28*(1), 27–40.

Coffman, D. D., & Levy, K. M. (1997). Senior adult bands: Music's new horizon. *Music Educators Journal, 84*(3), 17–22.

Coffman, D. D., & Schilf, P. (1998). *Band instrument gender associations by senior citizen musicians*. Paper presented at Southeastern Music Education Symposium, Athens, GA.

Colletta, N. J. (1996). Formal, nonformal and informal education. In A. C. Tuijnman (Ed.), *International encyclopedia of adult education and training* (2nd ed., pp. 22–27). New York: Elsevier Science.

Conda, J. M. (1997). The late bloomers piano club: A case study of a group in progress (Doctoral dissertation, University of Oklahoma, 1997). *Dissertation Abstracts International, 58,* 409A.

Csikszentmihalyi, M. (1975). *Beyond boredom and anxiety.* San Francisco: Jossey-Bass.

Curran, J. M. (1982). A design for the development and implementation of a beginning group piano for leisure age adults. *Dissertation Abstracts International, 43,* 391A. (UMI No. AAT82-15903)

Darkenwald, G. G. (1992). Adult education. In M. C. Alkin (Ed.), *Encyclopedia of education research* (6th ed., pp. 30–35). New York: Macmillan.

Darrough, G. P. (1990). Older adult participants in selected retirement community choruses. *Dissertation Abstracts International, 51*(8), 2559A. (UMI No. AAT91-01869)

Darrow, A. A., Johnson, C. M., & Ollenberger, T. (1994). The effect of participation in an intergenerational choir on teens' and older persons' cross-age attitudes. *Journal of Music Therapy, 31,* 119–134.

Davidson, J. W., Howe, M. J. A., & Sloboda, J. A. (1997). Environmental factors in the development of musical skill over the life span. In D. J. Hargreaves & A. C. North (Eds.), *The social psychology of music* (pp. 188–206). Oxford: Oxford University Press.

Dregalla, D. M. (1994). A descriptive study of the post-secondary musical/cultural behaviors and attitudes of participants and non-participants of instrumental music ensembles from two secondary schools in eastern Massachusetts (Doctoral dissertation, Ohio State University, 1993). *Dissertation Abstracts International, 54,* 2786A.

Edgington, D. V. (1992). The process of deriving a structure for a program of music education for senior citizens. *Dissertation Abstracts International, 53*(6), 1835A. (UMI No. AAT92-32686)

Engelson, R. A. (1994). A history of adult community choirs in Charlotte, North Carolina: 1865–1918. *Dissertation Abstracts International, 54*(11), 3922A. (UMI No. AAT94-10962)

Ericsson, K. A., Krampe, R. T., & Tesch-Romer, C. (1991). *The role of deliberate practice in the acquisition of expert performance* (Technical Rep. No. 91-06). Boulder: Institute of Cognitive Sciences, University of Colorado at Boulder.

Ericsson, K. A., Tesch-Romer, C., & Krampe, R. T. (1990). The role of practice and motivation in the acquisition of expert-level performance in real life. In M. J. A. Howe (Ed.), *Encouraging the development of exceptional skills and talents* (pp. 109–130). Leicester: British Psychological Society.

Ernst, R. E., & Emmons, S. (1992). New horizons for senior adults. *Music Educators Journal, 79*(4), 30–34.

Frakes, L. (1985). Differences in music achievement, academic achievement, and attitude among participants, dropouts, and non-participants in secondary school music. (Doctoral dissertation, University of Iowa, 1984). *Dissertation Abstracts International, 46,* 370A.

Gardner, H. (1983). *Frames of mind.* New York: Basic Books.

Gates, J. T. (1991). Music participation: Theory, research, and policy. *Bulletin of the Council for Research in Music Education, 109,* 1–35.

Goleman, D. (1995). *Emotional intelligence: Why it can matter more than IQ.* New York: Bantam Books.

Graessle, R. K. (1999). Adult music programming in member schools of the National Guild of Community Schools of the Arts (Doctoral dissertation, University of Oklahoma, 1998). *Dissertation Abstracts International, 59,* 3387A.

Green, V. B. (1998). Enhanced musical literacy through participation in the adult amateur/volunteer chorus: A descriptive study. *Dissertation Abstracts International, 59*(7), 2411A. (UMI No. AAT98-39071)

Grow, G. (1991). Teaching learners to be self-directed: A stage approach. *Adult Education Quarterly, 41,* 125–149.

Heintzelman, T. D. (1989). Adult concert band participation in the United States (Doctoral dissertation, Indiana University, 1988). *Dissertation Abstracts International, 50,* 381A.

Hersey, P., & Blanchard, K. (1988). *Management of organizational behavior: Utilizing human resources* (5th ed.). Englewood Cliffs, NJ: Prentice Hall.

Hinkle, L. B. (1988). The meaning of choral experience to the adult membership of the German singing societies comprising the United Singers Federation of Pennsylvania (Doctoral dissertation, Pennsylvania State University, 1987). *Dissertation Abstracts International, 48,* 2568A.

Holmquist, S. P. (1995). A study of community choir members' school experiences (Doctoral dissertation, University of Oregon, 1995). *Dissertation Abstracts International, 56,* 1699A.

Horn, J. L. (1982). The aging of human abilities. In B. B. Wolman (Ed.), *Handbook of developmental psychology* (pp. 847–870). Englewood Cliffs, NJ: Prentice-Hall.

Hosler, N. M. (1992). The brass band movement in North America: A survey of brass bands in the United States and Canada. *Dissertation Abstracts International, 53*(5), 1316A. (UMI No. AAT92-27288)

Iguina Monrouzeau, J. R. (1993). Adults' representation of pitch and rhythm relationships in invented notations: A study of intuitive apprehension and meaningful learning. *Dissertation Abstracts International, 54*(5), 1717A. (UMI No. AAT93-27370)

Irish, B. M. (1993). Meaning in music: Cognitive and affective response in adults (Doctoral dissertation, Cornell University, 1993). *Dissertation Abstracts International, 54,* 1198A.

Janowitz, J. L. (1986). Using a learning activity package for general music with older adults attending senior centers.

Dissertation Abstracts International, 47(3), 775A. (UMI No. AAT86-11872)

Johnson, R. G. (1983). An investigation of the initiating interests of two sub-groups of adult beginning pianists participating in a class piano teaching environment (Doctoral dissertation, Ohio State University, 1982). *Dissertation Abstracts International, 43,* 2589A.

Kahn, A. P. (1998). Healthy aging: A study of self-perceptions of well-being. *Dissertation Abstracts International, 58,* 4740B. (UMI No. AAT98-10054)

Kaltoft, G. (1990). Music and emancipatory learning in three community education programs. *Dissertation Abstracts International, 51*(7), 2239A. (UMI No. AAT90-33861)

Keenan, K. J. (1995). Opinions, attitudes, music skills, and acquired knowledge of older adults using an adapted version of a technology-assisted music education curriculum. *Dissertation Abstracts International, 56*(6), 2161A. (UMI No. AAT95-34003)

Kellmann, R. H. (1985). The development of a music education program for older adults suitable for use in senior citizens centers, retirement homes, or other sites (Doctoral dissertation, 1984). *Dissertation Abstracts International, 46,* 95A.

King, P. M., & Kitchener, K. S. (1994). *Developing reflective judgment.* San Francisco: Jossey-Bass.

Knowles, M. S. (1984). *The adult learner: A neglected species* (3rd ed.). Houston, TX: Gulf.

Kramer, D. A. (1983). Post-formal operations? A need for further conceptualization. *Human Development, 26,* 91–105.

Krampe, R., & Ericsson, K. A. (1995). *Acquisition and maintenance of high-level skills in violinists and pianists: The role of deliberate practice.* Paper presented at 7th European Conference on Developmental Psychology, Krakow.

Labouvie-Vief, G. (1984). Logic and self-regulation from youth to maturity: A model. In M. L. Commons, F. A. Richards, & C. Armon (Eds.), *Beyond formal operations: Late adolescent and adult cognitive development* (pp. 158–179). New York: Praeger.

Larson, P. (1983). An exploratory study of lifelong musical interest and activity: Case studies of twelve retired adults (Doctoral dissertation, Temple University, 1982). *Dissertation Abstracts International, 44,* 100A.

Leitner, M. J. (1982). The effects of intergenerational music activities on senior day care participant and elementary school children. *Dissertation Abstracts International, 42*(8), 3752A. (UMI No. AAT82-02620)

Levinson, D. J. (1986). A conception of adult development. *American Psychologist, 41*(1), 3–13.

Mack, L. S. (1983). Self-concept and musical achievement in the adult learner (Doctoral dissertation, University of Illinois at Urbana-Champaign, 1982). *Dissertation Abstracts International, 43,* 3533A.

Martin, P. J. (1983). A status study of community bands in the United States. *Dissertation Abstracts International, 44*(9), 2703A. (UMI No. AAT84-00706)

Marty, Q. G. (1982). Influences of selected family background, training, and career preparation factors on the career development of symphony orchestra musicians: A pilot study. *Dissertation Abstracts International, 43*(5), 1464A. (UMI No. AAT82-24354)

McCollum, J. P. (1990). The process and function of melodic memory systems among adult performers (Doctoral dissertation, University of South Dakota, 1989). *Dissertation Abstracts International, 50,* 1899A.

McCullough, E. C. (1981). An assessment of the musical needs and preferences of individuals 65 and over. *Dissertation Abstracts International, 42*(3), 909A. (UMI No. AAT81-18455)

Merriam, S. B., & Caffarella, R. S. (1999). *Learning in adulthood: A comprehensive guide* (2nd ed.). San Francisco: Jossey-Bass.

Mullee, M. A. (1997). Development of a workshop to improve adult music listening skills (Doctoral dissertation, Columbia University Teachers College, 1996). *Dissertation Abstracts International, 57,* 2932A.

Myers, D. E. (1986). An investigation of the relationship between age and music learning in adults (Doctoral dissertation, University of Michigan, 1986). *Dissertation Abstracts International, 47,* 2071A.

Myers, D. E. (1989). Principles of learning and the older adult music student. *Southeastern Journal of Music Education, 1,* 137–151.

Myers, D. E. (1995). Lifelong learning: An emerging research agenda for music education. *Research Studies in Music Education, 4,* 21–27.

Parr, S. M. (1985). The effects of graduated exercise at the piano on the pianist's cardiac output, forearm blood flow, heart rate, and blood pressure. *Dissertation Abstracts International, 46*(6), 1436A. (UMI No. AAT85-18673)

Patchen, J. H. (1986). The relationships among current activity level and selected musical and demographic variables within an elderly population. *Dissertation Abstracts International, 48*(1), 73A. (UMI No. AAT87-10539)

Patterson, F. C. (1986). Motivational factors contributing to participation in community bands of the Montachusett region of north central Massachusetts (Doctoral dissertation, University of Connecticut, 1985). *Dissertation Abstracts International, 46,* 1776A.

Perry, W. G. (1981). *Forms of intellectual and ethical development in the college years.* Austin, TX: Holt, Rinehart & Winston.

Pflieger, D. B. (1985). Community schools of the arts: Outreach, scholarship, and financial assistance programs (Doctoral dissertation, Louisiana State University and Agricultural and Mechanical College, 1985). *Dissertation Abstracts International, 46,* 1551A.

Pieters, J. M. (1996). Psychology of adult education. In A. C. Tuijnman (Ed.), *International encyclopedia of adult education and training* (2nd ed., pp. 150–158). New York: Elsevier Science.

Rexroad, E. F. (1985). Influential factors on the musical development of outstanding professional singers. *Dissertation Abstracts International, 46*(4), 921A. (UMI No. AAT85-11664)

Robertson, W. D. (1992). A survey of music education programs for senior citizens in Mecklenburg County, North

Carolina. *Dissertation Abstracts International, 53*(10), 3468A. (UMI No. AAT93-03945)

Rosenthal, L. J. (1987). A comprehensive curriculum for adult string players (Doctoral dissertation, Union for Experimenting Colleges and Universities, 1986). *Dissertation Abstracts International, 48,* 329A.

Rybak, C. A. (1996). Older adults and "flow": Investigating optimal experience in selected music leisure activities (Doctoral dissertation, Arizona State University, 1995). *Dissertation Abstracts International, 56,* 4695A.

Rybash, J. M., Hoyer, W. J., & Roodin, P. A. (1986). *Adult cognition and aging.* New York: Pergamon Press.

Schaie, K. W. (1996). Intellectual functioning in adulthood. In J. E. Birren & K. W. Schaie (Eds.), *Handbook of the psychology of aging* (4th ed., pp. 266–286). San Diego, CA: Academic Press.

Schlossberg, N. K. (1989). *Overwhelmed: Coping with life's ups and downs.* San Francisco: Lexington Books.

Seago, T. (1993). Motivational factors influencing participation in selected Southern Baptist Church choirs. *Dissertation Abstracts International, 54*(5), 1718A. (UMI No. AAT93-20319)

Sheehy, G. (1995). *New passages: Mapping your life across time.* New York: Random House.

Simmons, D. A. (1995). The development and evaluation of an instructional guide for the guitar teacher of the adult student (Doctoral dissertation, Columbia University Teachers College, 1994). *Dissertation Abstracts International, 55,* 3387A.

Simonton, D. K. (1997). Products, persons, and periods: Historiometric analyses of compositional creativity. In D. J. Hargreaves & A. C. North (Eds.), *The social psychology of music* (pp. 107–122). Oxford: Oxford University Press.

Sinnott, J. D. (1994). The relationship of postformal thought, adult learning, and lifespan development. In J. D. Sinnott (Ed.), *Interdisciplinary handbook of adult lifespan learning* (pp. 105–119). Westport, CT: Greenwood Press.

Sloboda, J. A. (1994). Music performance: Expression and the development of excellence. In R. Aiello (Ed.) with J. A. Sloboda, *Musical perceptions* (pp. 152–169). Oxford: Oxford University Press.

Sloboda, J. A., Davidson, J. W., Howe, M. J. A., & Moore, D. G. (1996). The role of practice in the development of expert musical performance. *British Journal of Psychology, 87,* 287–309.

Sloboda, J. A., & Howe, M. J. A. (1991). Biographical precursors of musical excellence: An interview study. *Psychology of Music, 19,* 3–21.

Smith, D. S. (1987). Preferences for differentiated frequency loudness levels in older adult music listening (Doctoral dissertation, Florida State University, 1987). *Dissertation Abstracts International, 48,* 1693A.

Smith, D. S. (1991). Elderhostel music courses: An exploratory study. *Southeastern Journal of Music Education, 3,* 79–88.

Smith, D. S. (1998). *Lifelong general music: A longitudinal investigation of music in the Elderhostel program.* Paper presented at the Music Educators National Conference research poster session, Phoenix, AZ.

Spell, G. M. (1990). Motivational factors and selected sociodemographic characteristics of Georgia community chorus participants as measured by the Education Participation Scale, the Community Chorus Participation Scale, and the Personal Inventory Form (Doctoral dissertation, University of Georgia, 1989). *Dissertation Abstracts International, 51,* 445A.

Spencer, W. D. (1996). An attitude assessment of amateur musicians in adult community bands. *Dissertation Abstracts International, 57*(11), 4684A. (UMI No. AAT97-14061)

Sugarman, L. (1986). *Life-span development: Concepts, theories and interventions.* New York: Methuen.

Sutton, P. J. (1996). Lifelong and continuing education. In A. C. Tuijnman (Ed.), *International encyclopedia of adult education and training* (2nd ed., pp. 27–33). New York: Elsevier Science.

Tatum, M. E. (1985). A descriptive analysis of the status of music programs in selected retirement residences and senior citizens' centers in the southeastern United States. *Dissertation Abstracts International, 47*(2), 460A. (UMI No. AAT86-08958)

Terry, P. (2000). *Opening doors to lifelong learning in the arts.* Retrieved October 9, 2000, from http://arts.endow.gov/partner/Accessibility/Monograph/Terry.html

Tipps, J. W. (1992). Profile characteristics and musical backgrounds of community chorus participants in the southeastern United States. *Dissertation Abstracts International, 53*(7), 2288A. (UMI No. AAT92-34255)

Titmus, C. J. (1996). Adult education: Concepts and principles. In A. C. Tuijman (Ed.), *International encyclopedia of adult education and training* (2nd ed., pp. 9–71). New York: Elsevier Science.

Tuijnman, A. C. (1996). Concepts, theories, and methods. In A. C. Tuijnman (Ed.), *International encyclopedia of adult education and training* (2nd ed., pp. 3–8). New York: Elsevier Science.

Turner, S. C. (1987). A guide to hymn playing for the inexperienced adult pianist. *Dissertation Abstracts International, 48*(7), 1694A. (UMI No. AAT87-22662)

U.S. Census Bureau. (2000). *Table A-1. Years of school completed by people 25 years old and over, by age and sex: Selected years 1940 to 2000.* Retrieved January 22, 2001, from http:www.census.gov/population/socdemo/education/tableA-1.txt

Vanderark, S., Newman, I., & Bell, S. (1983). The effects of music participation on quality of life of the elderly. *Music Therapy, 3,* 71–81.

Vincent, P. M. (1997). A study of community choruses in Kentucky and implications for music education. *Dissertation Abstracts International, 58*(6), 1982A. (UMI No. AAT97-35637)

Wilhjelm, C. C. (1998). A case study of the Ridgewood concert band, a New Jersey community band dedicated to lifelong learning. *Dissertation Abstracts International, 59*(7), 2413A. (UMI No. AAT98-39135)

Wise, G. W., Hartmann, D. J., & Fisher, B. J. (1992). Exploration of the relationship between choral singing and successful aging. *Psychological Reports, 70,* 1175–1183.

Music and Early Childhood Education

JOYCE JORDAN-DECARBO
JO ANN NELSON

This chapter is designed to provide current information regarding the philosophical and theoretical bases of the field of early childhood education that is most relevant to issues underpinning music education for children, from birth to age 8. In addition, it will summarize existing music research, as well as interdisciplinary research supporting the major issues in early childhood music education.

The studies selected represent a body of research published in major journals and books from approximately the mid- to late 1980s to the present that provides the reader with some understanding of the emerging issues and questions about musical development in young children. Generally, efforts were made to focus only on the target ages, birth to 8. However, some studies incorporating a wider age span are cited if results related to the younger ages have been deemed important for inclusion.

The organization of the chapter consists of four sections: research and theories on the development of young children, research on specific nonmusical and musical abilities, curricular practices in early childhood classrooms, and recommendations for research. The first section consists of research on development in early childhood education and music education, beginning with an overview of the conceptualizations of childhood in today's society that have guided both researchers and practitioners in the field. Much emphasis is devoted in this section to cognitive development: the neurological findings resulting from brain research and their relevance to spatial ability and issues related to musical development are briefly highlighted. The second section includes research focused on musical abilities, including aural discrimination, vocal abilities and song acquisition, and movement and rhythmic

skills. The third section includes a summary of various ideological positions governing current practice both in education and music education, as well as comparisons of specific models and approaches and the contributions they have made to the profession. The chapter concludes with directions for the future in terms of research and practice and recommendations for many of the unanswered questions that remain about how children learn, perform, and understand music.

The Development of Young Children

Conceptions of Childhood

The concept of childhood as socially constructed was introduced by Aries (1962). Through history, the meaning of "child" has changed from the ideal child as totally obedient to adults, to the modern child guided by wise and benevolent adults, to the autonomous independent postmodern child. Kessen (1979) described influences on changing notions of childhood and pervading themes that are being reexamined: the commitment to a scientific view of the child, belief in the importance of early experience, and belief in the individual, self-contained child. As each of these themes is reexamined, confidence in a positivist scientific view of children's development has opened up to postmodern questioning of the universality of development. The illusion of scientific objectivity and the issue of whose interests are being served are questioned by Kessler and Swadener (1992). Vygotsky has shown the child interacting within a social context. The image of the child as a continuous creation of biological and sociocultural forces is far more complex than the image of a maturing individual child.

Romanticized views of childhood give support to two versions of childhood: "the child as savior" and the "child to be saved" (Goffin, Wilson, Hill, & McAninch, 1997), suggesting that middle-class children from idealized self-sufficient families are "saviors," while in recurring periods of history, policies for children of the poor are based upon the *need* to *be saved* and rescued from an "at-risk" status. As a legacy of the 1960s, a concern for human capital has permitted the evaluation of programs for young children in economic terms and in their potential for reducing disruption to society (Goffin et al., 1997). In the belief in the child as savior *or* saved, early childhood education carries with it a moral imperative for society to create a better future through children.

Elkind (1994) described changes in families from the modern to the postmodern; in both cases an imbalance between needs of children and adults was likely to create an advantage for children in the modern era and for adults in the postmodern. (In the premodern era, few distinctions were made between children and adults; childhood had not been invented.) The modern nuclear family, with clear-cut boundaries between public and private lives, was considered beneficial to children; well-defined standards meant that children could devote their energies to growing up. In the more flexible, permeable postmodern family, parents cannot control the flow of adult information to children. As there is an increase in the skills needed for adulthood, so there is a decrease in the support and guidance offered to the young. Authority in the family is likely to be mutual between parent and child rather than unilateral. Postmodern benefits, too, are seen for children; with the expectations to be independent at a young age, children may show competencies and abilities that were unrecognized in an earlier period. The establishment of early childhood education as a field of study and service to children and families is seen as a benefit to the changed lives of children and parents throughout the industrialized world (Elkind, 1994).

Many children lead fragmented lives, participating in disconnected settings during the course of a day (Hills, 1987). To travel from home to prekindergarten, to Head Start, to after school childcare and then home again is not unusual for a preschool child; similar arrangements exist for some primary school children. Although each of the settings may be of high "quality," the discontinuities may add up to stress for children, parents, and teachers. Hills (1987) recommends that early childhood programs should make up a comprehensive system of education that supports the interests of all participants and that "conserves childhood."

Demographic changes in the present generation of parents mean that many parents have little time for children but money to spend on them and anxious expectations for their achievement (Gallagher & Caché, 1987). Among middle-class parents, the need to structure children's stimulation may result from children being status symbols of leisure class. Children's clothing, toys, education, and structured leisure serve as indicators of parental success; children become depersonalized agents of competition. Behind the "hurried child" (Elkind, 1994) is the hurried parent, in a hurried society. Sigel (1987) describes "hothousing" as the process of inducing children to acquire knowledge that typically is acquired at a later level of development. Does it rob children of their childhood? Sigel describes the difference between rote acquisition of pieces of information versus the ability to understand how that information fits into a broader scheme of knowledge. Children can be taught bits of information, but Siegel questions why it should be done until children have developed understanding that would enable them to use information meaningfully. Hothousing tends to lead to anxiety about achievement and to a belief by children that they are valued for what they produce. In other words, children's disposition to learn for its own sake is damaged.

How corporate America has revolutionized childhood is described by Steinberg and Kincheloe (1997); childhood is a contemporary crisis. The authors examine the corporate production of popular *kinderculture* and its impact on children in pedagogical sites such as schools and media, games, and sports. Steinberg and Kincheloe reveal the "footprints of power left by the corporate producers of kinderculture and their effects on the psyches of our children" via Disney movies, revisions of history, Barbie, and MTV and other images (p. 7). The blurred boundaries of business, education, and entertainment mean that corporate producers of *kinderculture* are influential pedagogues, undermining previous conceptions of childhood. From the view of a music educator, Hornyak (1996) describes America as a "culture at risk"; he advocates a cultural renaissance of the human spirit and intellect. "Cultural decay" can be combated through "aesthetic teaching" that focuses on "arts, sciences, and human dignity" (1996, p. 36).

Conceptualizations of Development

Development is commonly recognized as a process of qualitative change, a set of transformations and transitions occurring through lives, in contrast to learning, which is considered quantitative change. The relationship between these processes has been a topic of debate for decades. Cole (1998) summarizes three 20th-century conceptualizations or frameworks of development and a contemporary fourth alternative. Each of the three positions is based on combinations of biological/maturational factors, environmental/learning factors, and interaction between these major contributors. The three frameworks are commonly described as follows.

Biological factors are represented in Gesell's (1940) view of inherent maturational mechanisms determining the progression of behavioral development. This view was predominant until the 1950s, when cognitive-developmental/constructivist ideas became more influential.

Environmental factors are represented in the most extreme case by B. F. Skinner's belief that operant conditioning shapes behavior as a sculptor shapes a lump of clay. Throughout the process of shaping, nothing new emerges, so the final product is a sum—an added-on copy—rather than a transformation of forces from the environment. Learning is incremental and cumulative, changing qualitatively. For example, vocabulary grows from 10 to 20 to 50 comprehensible words.

The *constructivist/interactionist* position, most often referred to as "constructivist," is represented largely by Piaget and, more recently, Vygotsky. Cognition tends to evolve as a function of biological maturity in interaction with experience (Sigel, 1987). The interaction involves both ontogenetic (individual and social) factors and phylogenetic (species) factors, resulting in transformations of mental structures that make possible the construction of new knowledge and new kinds of interaction with the physical and social environment. The social environment and interpersonal relationships modify an individual's responses, and these responses may in turn modify the mental structures that constitute development.

A chief characteristic of interactionist/constructivist positions is the active role the developing person plays in constructing knowledge from the interplay of a changing mental structure and daily encounters. For example, Trevarthen (1998) describes the child's accommodations to events around her and her assimilation of new information with "increasing strategic wisdom," which includes seeking insights into other persons' thoughts and feelings. Vygotsky (1962) describes the child attempting tasks slightly beyond his reach and seeking adult support in order to accomplish them. Vygotsky recognized the child's constructive use of language (including talking to oneself) in controlling actions, creating new thoughts, and taking in knowledge and points of view of other people.

Current understandings of interactionist/constructivist theories show the significance of the child's active tendencies within a sociocultural and interpersonal environment. In the current field of early childhood education, developmental knowledge is derived from current understandings of Piaget's construction of knowledge in a social setting of equal peers and from Vygotsky's guided participation with more skilled partners in culturally relevant activities. The "zone of proximal development" is derived from Vygotsky's depiction of the area of development between an area in which the child has achieved competence and a higher level in which the child is not yet competent. The "zone" is the in-between area from which the child may reach out to an adult for help in understanding or may give cues to a perceptive teacher that indicate that the child is ready for something more. The teacher's recognition of the zone and her planning of activities that specifically support children's development in that area is considered "scaffolding," a term also derived from Vygotsky (Berk, 1994; Berk & Winsler, 1995). For example, the use of self-chosen musical play in a child-centered music room as described by Turner (2000) is based on Vygotsky-inspired constructivist principles. Centers and activities include singing games, sound exploration, musical play, books that encourage musical imagination or improvisation, and listening, which may involve fantasy play or movement. Observing children's interactions with materials and peers in such activities provides an opportunity to observe children in the "zone of proximal development," as well as more familiar activities. Adults have an opportunity to scaffold children's learning on an individual basis in self-chosen activities within a community of learners (Stremmel & Fu, 1993; Vygotsky, 1978).

A *cultural context* position, the fourth framework for understanding development, is proposed by Cole (1998). This position views the interaction of biology and environment as mediated through culture. Trevarthen (1998) considers culture as a natural human product that communities endow with meaning, which is coconstructed by people sharing, comparing, and negotiating their interests with others. All human inventions, knowledge, beliefs, art, law, and customs function to coordinate human beings with the physical world and with each other. The emphasis on culture as the context for development cuts across the usual distinctions of cognitive, social, and affective aspects of the system in which children develop. Rogoff (1990) suggests that it is useful to focus on the mutual involvement of a child within a social world in which the child is an "apprentice to thinking."

According to Bredekamp and Copple (1997), some issues concerning cognitive development have become unnecessarily polarized. In Piaget's view, development precedes learning; particular learnings are possible when prerequisite cognitive structures have been attained. Vygotsky, on the other hand, maintained that learning precedes development—that learning particular concepts may advance more mature cognitive structures. Contemporary developmentalists suggest that each perspective is correct in explaining the course of development during early childhood and in recognizing the effectiveness of strategic teaching, or scaffolding, when it is attuned to the child's level.

Learning and development are complex concepts; no one theory can explain all; both perspectives are needed (Sameroff & McDonough, 1994; Seifert, 1993).

The psychodynamic Bank Street approach, based on the child-centered and experience-centered philosophy of John Dewey, also influences contemporary meanings of development. All of these psychological, cultural, and philosophical approaches contribute to developmental educational practice. In addition, development encompasses concerns for health, safety, and nutrition, individual special needs, and the potential effects of violence and abuse (Isenberg & Brown, 1997).

Musical Development

Zimmerman (1993) provides an overview of research related to music development spanning from midcentury through the mid-1980s. Other important collections of writings or extensive research reviews are *The Developmental Psychology of Music* (Hargreaves, 1986), *Musical Beginnings* (Deliege & Sloboda, 1996), *Music and Child Development* (Peery, Peery, & Draper, 1987), *Handbook of Music Psychology* (Hodges, 1996), and *Music and Child Development* (Wilson & Roehmann, 1990).

Musical Development Processes

Research on fetal development has suggested that processing of information may begin once sensory systems have emerged and are functioning (Fifer & Moon, 1989). From an extensive review of research related to prenatal auditory experience, Lecanuet (1996) concludes that the auditory system is fully functional 3 to 4 months prior to birth and that the fetus is stimulated by environmental sounds, the mother's voice and speech patterns, and musical sounds. Prenatal familiarization with sound patterns or classes of sounds may predispose the infant for preference for the maternal voice and her cultural language or specific musical stimuli. It is possible that the mechanical and neurological structures of human audition may be predisposed toward efficient processing of particular configurations of auditory information (Schellenberg & Trehub, 1994). Six-month-olds perceive segmental organization in musical passages, preferring those that are interrupted at phrase boundaries as opposed to random breaks (Krumhansl & Jusczyk, 1990). Some psychologists believe there is growing support for a theory that views education in the early years as a necessary support for existing capacities rather than a mandate for building new perceptual and cognitive structures (Kessen, Levine, & Wendrick, 1979).

Humans respond to so many different kinds of musical stimuli in so many diverse situations that studies on behavioral responses are scattered throughout various areas of psychology, music, and education (Konecni, in Hargreaves, 1986, p. 105). Hargreaves provides a scope of relevant studies utilizing varying methodological approaches of both naturalistic and experimental design (see Hargreaves, 1986) that is comprehensive but beyond the scope of this chapter. For this chapter, only a few representative studies related to young children have been reviewed.

The influence of musical exposure during the prenatal period or infancy has been the focus of a number of recent studies. Fetuses exposed daily to specific types of music for 38 weeks had greater fetal movements and heart rate decelerations than the control group. Tested again at 6 weeks after birth, the same babies were more receptive to music and more active in response to music stimuli than the control babies (Wilkin, 1995). Premature infants exposed to vocal music, including lullabies and children's repertoire, retained a higher percentage of birth weight, had a lower formula intake (but not a lower caloric intake), and exhibited lower stress symptoms, resulting in shorter hospital stays (Caine, 1991). Sedative and stimulative musical selections also affected the physiological responses, including systolic blood pressure, heart rate, and respiratory rate of premature infants (Lorch, Lorch, Diefendorf, & Earl, 1994).

When normal infants were exposed to the mother's voice (reading), an unfamiliar female voice (reading), and music, babies preferred the mother's voice to music. When music was compared to the other female voice, babies preferred music (Standley & Madsen, 1990). Infants were mostly silent during auditory stimuli and tended to listen intently and decrease other gross motor activity during music, as compared to the other auditory stimuli.

Three studies have suggested that infants are able to exhibit adultlike patterns of discrimination and categorization with respect to perception of culturally familiar versus culturally unfamiliar musical stimuli (Cohen, Thorpe, & Trehub, 1987; Lynch & Eilers, 1992; Trehub, Thorpe, & Trainor, 1990). Lynch and Eilers (1992) suggested that progression toward this pattern occurs between 6 and 12 months of age.

Lynch, Short, and Chua (1995), in an effort to investigate musical processing that was crosscultural and crosssectional with regard to age sampling, employed healthy premature infants matched with full-term infants in relative perception of culturally familiar versus unfamiliar musical structure. The results of the first three experiments suggested that processing of musical pitch relations is affected by typical musical exposure during the first year of life, a similar age period for the development of perceptual knowledge about speech. The comparisons of full-term and premature infants in Experiment 4 supported the hypothesis that infants' musical processing was influenced by experience. The conclusion that training makes a difference is not surprising.

Gordon (1997a) describes his music learning theory in stages that are roughly similar to language development. He refers to these stages as acculturation, imitation, and assimilation. The first stage involves acculturation or absorption of musical sounds (birth to age 2–4), which become the basis for music babble, and this absorption stage is most stable prior to the onset of language. Subsequent stages in preparatory audition are dependent on the richness and variety of exposure (tonalities, harmonies, and meters) during acculturation. The imitative stage (ages 2–4 to 3–5) initiates awareness of similarities and differences in sound patterns. During the assimilation stage (ages 3–5 to 4–6) children increase their awareness of their own performance (tonally and rhythmically) and are able to coordinate physical movements and vocal skills with that performance. At this point accommodations for accurateness become easier to achieve.

A musical development sequence was developed through an extensive analysis of the original compositions of children (ages 3 to 11). Musical examples were recorded nine times each year, yielding 745 compositions from 48 children over 4 years (Swanwick & Tillman, 1986). The analysis resulted in eight levels of development corresponding to an age at which a child's musical composition exhibits certain characteristics assigned to that level. Younger children generally fall into Levels 1–3, where there is pleasure in the sensory aspects of sound exploration and experimentation. Children may even exhibit some control in the music-making process through devices of repetition, pulse, and management, to a degree, of simple instruments. In spite of the lack of structural development, children seem to demonstrate elements of expressiveness through changes of loudness and speed, along with efforts to create atmosphere or mood. Two different populations were utilized to verify typical age assessments with regard to this model (Swanwick, 1991). Both populations revealed that the sensory, manipulative, and personal expression levels are already in place by age 4–5 (See chapter 22 for a more detailed explanation.)

Sloboda (1988) suggests that a cognitive representation of tonality and meter is developed through the process of enculturation. He believes that enculturation is the dominant process in Western culture until the child is approximately 10 years old.

Of several musical behaviors that appear in the early years of a child's life, that is, singing, instruments in the home, dancing, and so on, only singing was evident significantly earlier in the most competent musicians, with the onset of the behavior occurring generally around 6 months old (Howe, Davidson, Moore, & Sloboda, 1995).

In an analysis of the behavior of children (age 4 and 5) in a naturalistic setting, Custodero (1997) sought to determine the types of musical activities that seemed to contribute most to "flow" experiences, based on the theories of Csikszentmihalyi and Csikszentmihalyi (1988). Data revealed a total of 142 observable events coded for between 1 and 11 children, yielding a total of 472 entries. Out of nine affective indicators and eight behavioral indicators identified as appropriate for young children, the following indicators significantly predicted flow experience. Affective indicators were alertness, involvement, activity, satisfaction and success; behavioral indicators were skill, anticipation, expansion, extension, challenge, and adult awareness. Methodological issues of what constituted appropriate behaviors for young children and the claim that a behavior could be generalized based on one child limit the importance of this study.

M. R. Campbell (1991) reviews the theoretical framework, psychological processes, and operations that underlie the perception and cognition of musical understanding as proposed by Serafine (1983a, 1983b, 1988), Sloboda (1985), Gardner (1982, 1983), and Zimmerman (1982, 1986). Following a discussion of the major ideas of these writers, Campbell provides implications for teaching and learning music that may serve as a basis for curricular development and the sequencing of music activities.

Before there is a visible increase of systematic music programs in early childhood centers, documentation is needed to identify the benefits of music for total child development. A recent study (Jordan-DeCarbo & Galliford, 2001) investigating the effect of a systematic and integrated program using music with disadvantaged children (106 subjects 3 months–4 years old) found that the experimental group scored significantly higher than the control group on the motor, cognitive, expressive language, and social-emotional subtests of the Preschool Evaluation Scale (McCarney, 1992). While this kind of study has inherent problems with external validity, the results were dramatic for the short period of time for the music intervention (10 weeks).

Hargreaves (1986) suggests that renewed interest in child development in the last 20 years has three major features: (a) the view of the child as an "active" agent in his or her own socialization with parents and child, each influencing the behavior of the other; (b) a shift from a behaviorist's psychological view of growth to an attempt by contemporary cognitive psychologists to get at internal responses; and (c) the enhanced and sophisticated methodological research techniques, strategies, and measurement devices that are prompting investigative ventures heretofore not possible.

Brain Research and Musical Development.   In the last 2 decades there has been an explosive beginning of information based on brain research. Magnetic resonance imaging (MRI) machines and other variations—functional MRI and nuclear MRI—allow researchers to measure the sequence of thinking across sections of the brain. (For a more detailed explanation of music learning and music cognition as affected by brain research, see chapter 25.) Other devices, such as electroencephalograms (EEGs), positron emission tomography (PET), and spectrometers have contributed to this information about brain function.

Developmental psychologists continue to believe that the first 5 years lay the foundation for learning and responding. Chugani (1997) describes these years as the "critical" period and the developmental period of the brain's systems. PET scans of children during different stages of development traced high levels of activity in the cortical and subcortical regions (sensorimotor functions) at 1 month of age; increased cortical activity during the second and third months (supporting visual and auditory stimulation); and increased frontal cortex metabolic activity at 8 months of age (indicating that bonding with the caregiver supports emotional self-regulation).

Hodges (2000) discusses five areas of interest in what he terms "neuromusical" studies—the increasing evidence that (a) music is a biological right for human beings; (b) the human being responds to musical stimuli from the womb through old age; (c) training in musical skills causes different brain transformations from those of persons who have not received musical training; (d) the musical brain is modularized, with specific structures in the brain carrying out specific musical tasks; and (e) for persons with disabilities or diseases, musical pursuits of some kind remain possible because of the brain's resilience.

The malleability of the brain (Diamond, 1967) and the potential power of enriched environments to affect subsequent neural connections are realities, and the fact that not just gifted children have access to this "window of opportunity" has fostered a great deal of interest in early childhood education and the power of the arts to enhance learning. Music training, as monitored through EEGs (Flohr, Miller, & deBeus, 2000), may even affect the brain's efficiency in working on certain tasks. Books directed to parents and educators on how the brain works and the importance of early experiences to overall child development provide them with nontechnical yet informed explanations, whether such persons are working closely with children in the home, the school, or the community (Goleman, 1995; Gopnik, Meltzoff, & Kuhl, 1999; Greenspan & Benderly, 1997; Hannaford, 1995; Healey, 1990; Heath, 1983; Jensen, 1998; Kranowitz, 1998; Sylvester, 1995).

Music and Social Development. Activation of children's cultural potential takes place in different types of social activities during the course of socialization. The effect of music on socialization skills has really been neglected. For young children, activities fostering socialization are most often nested in play. Vygotsky's theory suggests that children will not become able to function independently in a culture without learning from other social agents. Three case studies by Kelly and Sutton-Smith (1987), Adachi (1994), and Umezawa (1990) support applications of this theory to children's development in a music culture achieved in a home setting. In all three studies, the adult roles contributed to the children's internalization of musical signs through social processes, which are, according to Vygotsky, the foundation of children's cultural thinking. While these studies make inferences from a very small number, they are included because they represent one of the few applications in music that are based on the theories of Vygotsky.

Other studies that recognize the elements of music and socialization of young children are geared to situations involving exceptional populations or children who experience different types of learning delays (Davis, 1990; Gunsberg, 1988; Jellison, Brooks, & Huck, 1984). Humpal (1991) implemented a music mainstreaming program for improved socialization skills of children in a preschool. Results indicated that intervention strategies were followed by a trend of increased interaction, and the handicapped children benefited from the positive peer role models and demonstrated improved social skills. It was determined that the music intervention not only facilitated this outcome but was necessary for the end result. The effect of background music that consisted of folk songs or rock-and-roll increased preschool children's social interactions with each other and decreased such interactions with the classroom teacher (Godeli, Santana, Souza, & Marquetti, 1996).

Doxey and Wright (1990) examined the relationships between children's musical ability and the physical and social environments of the home and school as well as the child characteristics of creativity and cognition. Sixty children, aged 4 to 6, and their parents participated in this well-designed study. While mothers in general provided a more musical environment, it was the fathers' involvement in music activities which may have been more influential in relation to children's musical aptitude (as tested by Gordon's *Primary Measures of Music Audiation* [PMMA]). Cognitive ability was the only significant predictor of musical aptitude. However, when parent and teacher ratings were used as a measure of children's musical ability, the social home environment was the significant predictor variable.

Music and Language Development

Gradually, we are beginning to discover more and more about how humans process acoustical information in the environment. Such research has determined the sensitivity of the auditory system to the temporal aspects of sounds and tones, as well as the auditory grouping and segregation process of language acquisition, including prosodic contours, phrases, words, phonemes, and vowels. Even more important is the process of attaching meaning to these perceptual units. Much of the research in this field is being done by psychologists or through corroborative efforts across disciplines. The studies are well designed and are a valuable source of data for the music researcher. For an in-depth review of literature related to these processes, see Fassbender (1996). Such research is of much interest because of the commonalities between speech and music. "In the beginning, perceptions of speech and music seem to arise from the same basis, but they may take different developmental courses when meaning becomes attached to specific acoustical information in the social interaction of intuitive parenting" (p. 80).

In speech to newborns and young infants, the most salient prosodic adjustments concern melodic contours (pitch contours), often referred to as "motherese." Parents typically use a small repertoire of simple, expanded, highly repetitive, and distinctive melodic prototypes in mostly nonlinguistic utterances (Papousek, Papousek, & Haekel, 1987). Infants (aged 18–30 weeks) exhibited greater attentiveness to both male and female parents when scripts were delivered in motherese than in normal adult speaking styles (Werker & McLeod, 1989). Further, infants (aged 7–10 months old) focused longer on speech that was segmented at phrase breaks than to speech interrupted at within-phrase locations (Hirsh-Pasek et al., 1987). Hirsh-Pasek et al. (1987), in contrast to earlier studies, focused on the ability of infants to recognize and isolate segments of input, thus revealing perceptual units that relate to the building blocks of grammar. Then and only then can learners use the input syntactically in the target language. Such a finding supports the notion that the exaggerated prosody characteristic of motherese speech patterns may facilitate language acquisition. The acoustic properties of melodic contours and the modes in which they are displayed (repetitiveness, slow tempo, contingency on infant behaviors) can help the infant to detect, categorize, and abstract elementary holistic units in the flow of speech (Trehub, 1990).

Maternal speech patterns represent crosslinguistic universals that function as unconscious support for preverbal communication for infants. Analysis of the functions and meaning of melodic contours in motherese when parents spontaneously interact with infants, that is, encouraging attention, encouraging imitation, encouraging play, and so on, was conducted and compared across two cultures, one with a stress language (English) and one with a tone language (Mandarin Chinese). Maternal melodies were analyzed into contour types and each contour profiled by its acoustic characteristics. While American mothers raised their pitch more than Chinese mothers, both cultural groups used the same kinds of pitch contours to convey the same kinds of meanings in relation to most interaction contexts (Papousek, Papousek, & Symmes, 1991).

When an adult male or female face was matched with either an approving sound contour or a disapproving sound contour, approving contours controlled infants' attention and disapproving contours inhibited attention. Results also indicated infant preference for female contours compared to male contours (Papousek, Bornstein, Nuzzo, Papousek, & Symmes, 1990).

A surprising number of mothers sing to infants, contrary to their claims that they sing infrequently and have little involvement with music (Trehub et al., 1997). Both mothers' and fathers' song performances were affected by the presence of an infant, and they utilized a full complement of song adjustments characterized by specific emotional features that were not detected in simulated instances when infants were absent. When singing to infants both fathers and mothers tended to sing at a higher pitch level and slower tempo and were more emotionally engaged than when singing in simulated instances. These adjustments were perceived by mothers of young children, male and female college students with relatively limited childcare experience, and members of the local community. Extensive musical training did facilitate the identification of infant-directed singing. While immigrant listeners were able to successfully identify infant-directed singing, same-culture listeners outperformed them in accuracy. Listeners' accuracy of distinguishing the two singing versions was highly correlated with ratings (a 9-point Likert scale from "very low" to "total" emotional engagement) of an independent sample of 50 men and 50 women who also listened to the paired singing examples. Surprisingly, the parents, who were all untrained singers, used a considerable range of features to achieve emotionally expressive performances. Fathers, like mothers, produced perceptible adjustments in their infant-directed singing despite their secondary involvement in caregiving, produced similar vocal changes in pitch and tempo, and were judged by listeners to be as emotionally engaging as mothers.

Five groups of independent listeners rated recordings of mothers singing a song of choice to their infants and again in the absence of their infants (Trainor, 1996). Raters were very accurate in distinguishing the two versions and perceived the songs sung to infants as more loving in character. Raters were able to consistently determine whether the intent of the singer was to lull an infant to sleep or to rouse and play with an infant. Playsong types were rated as more rhythmic, and lullaby types were rated as less rhythmic. Based on these ratings, six infant-present/infant-absent pairs of recordings, three highly rated as playsongs and three as lullabies, were systematically presented to 60 infants between the ages of 5 and 6 months old. Using infant's head-turning behavior as a measure of attention, infants preferred listening to infant-directed (5 out of the 6 pairs) over infant-absent singing.

In a follow-up study, acoustic differences between infant-directed and non-infant-directed singing were examined in several playsong and lullaby pairs recorded in the Trainor (1996) study. For both playsongs and lullabies the tempo was slower, there was relatively more energy at lower frequencies, interphrase pauses were lengthened, and the pitch and jitter factor (variation in the fundamental frequency at the smallest time period) were higher in the infant-directed over the infant-absent versions. Pitch variability was higher and the rhythm more exaggerated in playsongs compared to lullabies (Trainor, Clark, Huntley, & Adams, 1997).

Studies illustrating the benefits of music instruction for preschool and primary learners found that the implementation of music programs by the classroom teacher was enhanced by access to appropriate materials (Clark, 1989) and that such implementation boosted language levels of bilingual classes by one to two levels (Ray, 1997). Teachers indicated they would use music to a greater extent if they had more confidence in their skills, if they were supported in their efforts, and if they had sufficient equipment, time, and space (Allen, 1996). Conditions that most related to actual music practices in the classroom were positive perceptions about music, music teaching skills, and undergraduate coursework that emphasized a holistic curricular approach (Moore, 1990; Saunders & Baker, 1991).

Bygrave (1994) examined whether the implementation of a music program, a storytelling program, or the combination of both would contribute to improvement of listening skills and associated language skills for problem readers. The Peabody Picture Vocabulary Test–Revised (Dunn & Dunn, 1981) was used to measure students' receptive vocabulary skills. The subjects, aged 7–9 years, who were involved in the music program for 2 semesters scored significantly higher but only on the post-posttest (administered 7 weeks after the posttest), suggesting that the effect of a music program on children experiencing difficulties in reading is a long-term prospect.

Music and Affective Development

Relatively little is known about emotional communication in music (Juslin, 1997) and even less about its development. Juslin outlines a review of research regarding a functionalist approach denoting a possible link between emotional expression and performance. Adachi and Trehub (1998) provide a substantial review of literature on those aspects related to their study. Children (160 children 4 to 12 years old) were asked to sing a familiar song in a way that would make the listener feel happy (or sad). In a second performance they were asked to sing it again and

make the listener feel sad (or happy). Audio and video recordings permitted access to vocal and gestural means of emotional expression. According to set criteria, half the children at each level were "good" singers; the remaining were "ordinary" singers. Results for noncategorical data (tempo, dynamics, and pitch) indicated that regardless of age and singing ability, children sang their songs faster, louder, and at a higher pitch level for happy versions than for sad versions. Only age was significant, and that was true for tempo only. Children 8–10 years old used significantly greater tempo changes across emotional contexts than did the other children. Tempo changes were used less by 4- and 5-year-olds than the other age groups. Overall, regardless of age or singing skill, children relied primarily on expressive devices used in interpersonal communication and made little use of music-specific devices. More devices were used for sad performances than happy performances.

Children as young as 5 responded to mood in classical music no differently from 9-year-olds (Giomo, 1993). The finding concurs with Gardner's theory of artistic development, which stipulates that after the age of 2, children are proficient users of the art symbol, and that after the age of 7 there is no fundamental qualitative change in the child but rather continued refinement and differentiation of skills. Similarly, the theoretical construct of Swanwick and Tillman (1986) and Swanwick (1991), based on children's compositions, indicates that children between the ages of 4 and 9 actively deal with the concept of mood in music. Findings of this study support the theories that postulate that musical development may follow a different timeline from cognitive development as theorized by Piaget and others.

Cognition and Development

Over the past quarter-century, art education came to be understood increasingly as a cognitive activity. What had previously, under the sway of behaviorism, been relegated to the intuitive, affective, and creative realm is now understood as cognitive, which includes the process and content of nonobservable thinking (Parsons, 1992).

Howard Gardner (1982) advocated an expansion of cognitive theory to examine the nature of artistic thinking in human development. Gardner suggests that the arts make use of several symbol systems and that each is worthy of separate inquiry. Gardner's extensive observations over time of 12 preschool children in Harvard's Project Zero showed children's development in use of language, music, and drawing media in a variety of tasks. Children exhibited broad individual differences in personal styles: for example, self-starters versus completers of each task. Gardner suggests investigating each kind of symbol use separately; he cites the need to integrate cognitive and affective domains, for in reality these cannot be separated. He suggests too that systematic changes over time reveal developmental change in children, while relatively stable features of children's behavior indicate more enduring qualities of affect. Gardner points out that the early Project Zero study revealed the value of observing not only what the child does spontaneously but also what the child does in a series of tasks that, for example, involve completion or assembly. In the administration of different kinds of tasks in each symbolic medium, it is possible to determine a child's relationship to a particular medium as well as consistency across kinds of tasks.

Davis and Gardner (1993) describe both Piaget's and Vygotsky's influences on cognitive approaches to children's development in the arts; both were concerned with children's interactions with realities in the outside world as well as with children's internal constructions of these realities, which tend to change with development. Such approaches are contrasted with the behaviorism of the 1950s, which was preoccupied solely with children's observable external behavior, and psychoanalytic approaches, which assumed that creative behavior was motivated by unconscious inner forces. In contrast, Piaget focused attention on internal mental structures that make possible children's changing constructions; Vygotsky showed how children use carefully chosen symbols as "building blocks" to convey their thought processes. Cognitive approaches thus enable us to view the child from inside out; expressive behavior is conceptualized as active meaning-making rather than the release of emotion or the result of reward and reinforcement. Examples from the work of Turner (2000) and Young (1998) have already been cited.

Within the cognitive point of view, two contrasting approaches are prevalent. Information processing focuses on children's choices of problem-solving strategies. On the other hand, in the symbol systems approach, a variation of cognitive theory devoted specifically to the arts, a distinction is made between presentational symbols, such as dance gestures or shapes in a drawing, which embody meaning as properties of the symbol itself, and discursive symbols, such as words or musical notation, which are intentionally chosen to refer to meaning. Davis and Gardner (1993) suggest that presentational symbols may be more expressive, while discursive or notational ones may be more precise. A major question is whether performance in a specific symbolic language represents general cognitive processes (a view consistent with Piaget's developmental theory) or whether competence in one symbolic domain is independent of competence in other domains. Gardner and Wolf (cited in Davis & Gardner, 1993, p. 205) offer longitudinal evidence that symbol users encounter system-specific problems that demand system-specific solutions, for example, pitch relationships within a musical scale; these kinds of problems are considered *streams*. *Waves*, on

the other hand, refer to forms of "analogical mapping"; waves include the kinds of symbolic uses that have analogies that are not specific to one domain but have meaning across symbolic domains, for example, body gestures as symbolic of musical pitch. Parsons (1992) suggests that thinking is intrinsic to a particular art form; artistry consists of thinking in a medium, such as paint or sound, and the discrimination and manipulations of those media as well as the qualities of their varied combinations. To respond aesthetically means being able to "read the medium."

Goodman (1976) considered that symbols that have aesthetic significance are ordinary symbols that in a certain context are used in expressive ways that demand attention. For children, this means developing the ability to exploit the expressive (aesthetic) qualities of symbols in order to create meaning.

In a classroom example of children's uses of multiple symbol systems in a naturalistic study of her own diverse first grade, Gallas (1991) describes children's uses of the "arts as epistemology" over the course of a school year. Children wondered, questioned, researched, and discussed a range of subjects, using a variety of art forms to discover and express their growing knowledge and understandings. For example, during the study of insects many children sketched the action they were observing as a butterfly struggled to break free from the chrysalis. As they wondered together whether the butterfly would ever come out, one child began to sing, "I'll sing it out." Others improvised a song about the emerging butterfly, while some continued to sketch. Gallas documented that children show what they know and how they learn best. Expressing their knowledge in art materials, they revisit, clarify, and revise their understanding. Gallas concluded that participation in arts-based education makes it possible for children to transcend individual limitations, such as language, culture, or life experience that is outside the mainstream; such education enables children to find new means of communication and expression and to "recognize the breadth and depth of their learning" (Gallas, 1991, p. 30).

Development of Creativity

Howard Gardner (1982) characterizes the preschool years as a time abounding in artistic creativity. He and his colleagues, as a result of numerous experiments with children, are inclined to believe that artistic development follows children's overall patterns of development. The earliest experiences are centered around getting to know the world directly through the senses. From age 2 to 7, the child gradually begins to function with various levels of symbolic understandings. Exploration is free from convention, is fun, and, if encouraged, is generally extensive in output. Following this stage children enter into the "literal" stage, a time for mastering the rules, an intense focus on realism. It is not until sixth grade that students can once again sustain the exploratory phase similar to their preschool years, undaunted by convention and seeking out the novel.

The literature on creativity is not clear on its definition. Creative products by young children have been referred to as *musical utterances* (Sundin, 1998), *compositions* (Swanwick & Tillman, 1986) or *nonverbal expressions* of children's aesthetic decisions (Barrett, 1998). Sundin (1998) argues against the separation of process and product, indicating that for children 3 to 7 years old, the interactional aspect, often associated with children's creative output, might be a more effective direction for analysis of developmental processes of children than a "before and after" measurement of a creative product. Researchers have differed greatly in their assessment of children's original music, and, given the absence of a standard that was dominated by the child's world, the standard adopted by the adult's world became the norm. Stefani (1987) suggests that the existence of musical competence rests in the ability of the child composer to make musical sense through the traditional social and cultural traditions made available to him or her. To date very few studies have focused on the situational, social, and environmental factors that impact on the act of making music (McPherson, 1998). If the pleasure for young children resides in the sheer active "doing" then the focus for researchers might best be on the "musical thinking" aspect of the creative process as described by Webster (1987).

The more creative children monitor their performance and initiate appropriate task-related strategies as they engage in activities (Daugherty & Logan, 1996). Based on information-processing theory and Vygotsky's theory that specific qualities reflected in private speech significantly predict creative potential, Garren (1997) found that private speech assessment is a feasible tool for examining creative thought development and processes during preschool years. Parents of kindergartners who were tolerant and allowed free thinking and independence fostered creativity in children, according to theories based on Amabile (1989) and Gardner (1983). The limitations of the sample of this study preclude any extensive generalization of the findings.

Given the established relationship of creativity to divergent thinking behavior, Wittmer and Honig (1991) investigated the types of questions that teachers ask in daycare centers serving primarily low-income families. Out of a total of 667 "true" questions asked during approximately 70 hours of observation, 88% of the questions were convergent (solicits either a "yes" or "no" answer or one correct response) and 12% were divergent (answer is open-ended). The divergent questions required 3-year-old children to reason in order to generate, organize, and express ideas. Sigel (1970) found that often children from disadvantaged backgrounds were able to perform cognitively in response to divergent-type questions at the same level as children reared in a more advantaged learning climate.

In a musical problem-solving task that required children aged 5 to 7 to arrange four phrases of a familiar song, Nordlund (1995) was able to document 12 different strategies used by the children. Those aged 5 and 6 tended to use lower level strategies to solve the problem; 7-year-olds were inclined to use the more cognitively advanced strategies. Their constructions revealed some rather sophisticated logical resolutions, which may have been more meaningful to them than the correct version of the song. The sampled children were the total enrollment of children 5 to 7 years old in a Montessori school (73 subjects). Videotaping techniques allowed for careful analysis of students' problem-solving strategies.

Music and Spatial Abilities

Two theories proposed to account for enhanced performance on spatial tasks as a result of music instruction are "neural connections" theories (Huttenlocher, 1984) and "near transfer" theory (Gardner, 1983). Shaw (2000) has suggested that musical and spatial processing centers in the brain overlap and that because of neurological connections in the cortex, the development of certain kinds of musical and spatial abilities is interrelated, especially spatial-temporal abilities (the Trion model). Cognitive psychologists have been critical of the model because of two related theories: (1) modularity, which postulates that the mind is comprised of separate units that generate different kinds of information; and (2) cognitive transfer, which postulates that two kinds of learning generally are independent if the kinds of resultant performances are different, which is the case for music and spatial processing (in Hetland, 2000b). The second theory, "near transfer," proposes that several kinds of thinking are required to learn and make music. Because music-making and spatial abilities are both multidimensional processes, it is logical that a range of spatial skills might be improved because of the practice required in the music-making process.

A team of researchers, through a series of meta-analyses, investigated the effects of arts study on academic achievement (Winner & Hetland, 2000). The reports cover a range of art forms (music, drama, visual art, and dance) and examine possible links between one or more art forms and outcomes in a number of learning areas, such as verbal achievement, mathematical achievement, spatial reasoning, nonverbal reasoning, and visual thinking.

Several of the reports include studies involving young subjects; one report was devoted exclusively to studies with young children and investigated possible links between active music instruction and preschool and elementary students' performance on spatial tasks (Hetland, 2000a). An extensive search identified 553 potentially relevant studies for music's effects on nonmusical cognitive outcomes but only 15 specifically related to spatial reasoning. It seems that active instruction in music does appear to enhance spatial-temporal performance for preschool and elementary-aged children for up to 2 years or perhaps as long as instruction continues. Hetland (2000a) reported that while the effect was moderate, it was remarkably consistent across the population of the studies included, and that of the "Mozart effect" could not be explained away by a Hawthorne effect, nonequivalence of experimental groups, experimenter bias, or study quality. One problematic factor in the collection of studies reviewed was the persistently low reliabilities of the measures employed across the various studies (p. 203). Hetland advocates caution in interpreting the results.

Studies with preschool children establishing a connection between spatial ability and keyboard training (Rauscher, 1996; Rauscher, Shaw, & Ky, 1993; Rauscher et al., 1997) are promising but not conclusive. In all these studies the effects of music training were very short-lived or persisted only as long as the training continued. In a more recent study (Rauscher & Zupan, 2000) featuring classroom music instruction on the keyboard, 62 kindergarten children were pre- and posttested on two spatial-temporal tasks and one pictorial memory task. The keyboard group of children when retested at two 4-month intervals scored higher on both spatial-temporal tasks but not on the pictorial tasks. The difference was greater after 8 months of lessons. Studies utilizing a more diverse music training (Gromko & Poorman, 1998; Persellin, 2000) also found that the music groups scored better than the control groups but that the effects were not sustained over time. The use of a variety of measures of spatial reasoning is a methodological issue impacting the findings of these studies that investigate the connection between music and spatial reasoning abilities.

A study by Nelson, Barresi, and Barrett (1992), based on scores of three tests—musical analogy test, a spatial analogy test, and Gordon's PMMA—indicated that children (111 ranging in age from preschool to 11 years old) employed similar strategies for the music and spatial analogy tests. This study reinforced findings from an earlier study by Nelson and Barresi (1989) that indicated a relationship between age and the development of children's intellectual strategies when problem-solving in analogical tasks either in a musical (auditory) or a spatial (visual) context. Specific mean comparisons on the musical tasks in the aptitude and musical analogy measures indicated that children between kindergarten and second grade do not obtain significantly higher scores until they are in fourth grade and that there is not a significant difference in performance on the tasks thereafter up to sixth grade.

Between the ages of 2 and 6 the frontal lobes undergo a major growth spurt, and the linkage of other brain regions to this region is important for later cognitive development (Coulter, 1996). Coulter, a neuroscience educator, discusses the benefit of music enrichment in the early years as nourishment for the mind. "The frontal lobes thrive on rhythm and are invited to become the brain's 'executive headquarters' only in those children who have established a measure of rhythmicity, grace, and 'motor flow' " (Coulter, 1996, p. 32).

Research on Musical Abilities

Researchers have focused on the identification and development of musical abilities either in isolation or as connected to other nonmusical abilities developing in the infant or young child. The musical abilities include auditory discrimination, vocal abilities, song acquisition, movement, rhythmic skills, music literacy, and conceptual development.

Auditory Discrimination

While aural discrimination ability falls under the category of auditory perception, it is only one aspect of that broader collection of human properties. Generally, aural discrimination is thought of as the ability to recognize two auditory patterns of sound stimuli as being the same or different.

When 5- and 6-year-olds were asked to recognize and reproduce various melodic contours, findings indicated a higher percentage of correct responses for the 10-tone melodies as compared to 5-tone melodies, except for the undulating melody. One-direction contours were easier than multidirection contours, and descending contours were easier than ascending ones. The undulating contour was the most difficult to recognize. Further investigations indicated that the ability of 5-year-olds to detect differences between paired melodic patterns in which the contours were altered was affected both by contour distinctiveness and by the magnitude of the intervallic change (Fyk, 1995).

Children as young as age 5 are able to discriminate major versus minor mode changes but need cues to help them maintain attention. Associated labels for sound discriminations increased accuracy more than nonverbal responses (Costa-Giomi, 1996).

The relationship between aural discrimination ability and vocal performance ability continues to be investigated. A substantive study by Feierabend and Saunders (1998), in an effort to determine sequencing of tonal content, investigated the relationship between discrimination of aural tonal patterns and the ability to perform orally the same tonal patterns among children in first, second, and third grades (69 subjects). Tonal patterns were rank ordered from simple to complex for both the aural discrimination measure and the singing performance measure. With a few exceptions, the pattern ranking for the aural discrimination measure remained at similar difficulty levels for all three grades. With regard to sung tonal patterns, embedded intervals had an impact on difficulty, with thirds being the easiest to sing accurately, fourths and fifths more difficult, and intervals of the sixth and octave most difficult. Overall, vocal accuracy increased with grade level, and no meaningful relationship was found between the aural and oral skills, although a relationship between the two skills began to emerge by the age of 8 (third grade).

Vocal Abilities

The primary changes that characterize early vocal development are the changing structure of vocal fold tissues, an increase in vocal fold length, and the resultant changes in the speaking fundamental frequency (Titze, 1992). At birth a child's fundamental frequency averages about 500 Hz and lowers gradually as the child develops to around 275 Hz at age 8 (Sataloff & Spiegel, 1989). Physiologically, children's vocalizations are not simply scaled-down versions of adult vocalizations because of aerodynamic (pressure-flow) events. Children attempt to match the vocal loudness of adults by taking frequent breaths during speech and singing. Asking children to sing adult-length phrases, for example, is a disservice to their developing respiratory system. Further, between the ages of 6 and 16, the important change is not in range but in improved control, efficiency, and quality.

Infants (7 to 30 months) responded to prompts from either family members or the researcher, including individual pitches, intervals, musical motifs, and whole songs, in a study of infants' musical responses (Ries, 1987). Collectively, only 9% of the children's singing responses were tonally unrelated; the responses demonstrated selective use of pitch in a tonal framework. Infant expressiveness was characterized by vocal manipulations. While the overall upward range was nearly three octaves, 95% of the notes sung were in a range of a ninth (A# or B below middle C and up); D, D#, E, F, or F# were in first, second, or third place for the most frequently sung tone in the various age groups. Of ascending, descending, or unison intervals (repeated notes), the most frequently sung were descending (40%), followed by unison (33%), with ascending the least frequent (27%). Although generally static, the incidence of rhythmic patterns increased for the 19-month-old children and even more for the 30-month-old children. Duple meter was by far the most dominant meter. The 30-month-old children usually sang upon request; only a few 19-month-olds were inclined to do so. Combined results of the more holistic "songs" revealed that 91% of the responses were either an exact match or related tonally to the prompt.

Spontaneous or original songs were sung by all the age groups (Ries, 1987).

In comparing the pitch abilities of Cantonese children who speak a complicated tonal language with those of English children, Chen-Hafteck (1998) focused on the melody-text contrasts, since in tonal languages the text sound is only meaningful if the pattern of linguistic tones matches the melodic contour. The pitch accuracy of Cantonese-speaking children was not affected by either text-matched or text-mismatched conditions, but when asked to sing a Western song in Cantonese, they achieved significantly higher pitch accuracy than the English-speaking children singing it in English.

Similarly, a dominating characteristic in Japanese children's singing is speech melody—a melody arising naturally from speech that embodies the musical pitches and rhythms embedded in the language (Minami & Umezawa, 1990). Fujita (1990) found that Japanese children, although exposed primarily to Western-style songs in the schools, enjoyed them more when the style reflected speech melody; he believes this style plays an important role in the intuitive learning of music and movement among Japanese children.

The relationship of vocal production to a vocal model is especially important for the younger children. A head-voice model, compared to a chest-voice model, increased children' ability to sing in head voice after treatment (Rupp, 1993). Children (grades 1–6) more easily match a child voice, followed by a female model; male vocal models singing in the lower octave produced the most incorrect responses (Green, 1990). Incorrect responses were likely to be flat for the female and male models and sharp for the child model. Tatem (1992) found that out of the six timbres (oboe, piano, resonator bells, soprano voice, trumpet, and violin) used as stimuli, the soprano voice prompted the most accurate responses and the resonator bells prompted the least accurate responses. When asked to match single tones, melodic intervals, and tonal patterns, single tones were the most difficult for children to match.

Yarbrough, Bowers, and Benson (1992) compared vocal responses to a child vocal model, a female adult model singing without vibrato, and a female adult model singing with vibrato. Children responded best to the female adult model singing without vibrato; they also found that singing with vibrato was more problematic with uncertain singers than with certain singers.

Song Acquisition

Welch (1986) described children's singing behaviors as a developmental sequence through five stages. Later, as a result of a long-range project to identify singing competencies of children aged 5–8, the model was changed to four stages (Welch, Sergeant, & White, 1994). Strategies utilized in the schools affected competency profiles. There is support for teaching words and music separately and for breaking songs into smaller phrases, which seem to hold more meaning for young singers. Children respond first to the words of a song; following this chantlike stage there is an increasing awareness of pitch and an approximation of the melodic contour. The results of the study confirmed the developmental sequence projected at the outset, specifically that 5-year-olds tend to focus on the words and, as a result, sing melodic fragments more accurately than songs.

Children (4- and 5-year-olds) who were taught a repertoire of songs in which half included text and half were without words sang a criterion song without words more accurately than the song with words (Levinowitz, 1987). The most effective of three cues (speech rhythm, melody, and movement) for helping children (age 3–5) identify familiar songs was movement (Dunne-Sousa, 1988). Seven-year-olds had fewer performance errors when taught by immersion procedures, as opposed to breaking the songs into phrases (Klinger, Shehan, & Goolsby, 1998).

Adachi and Carlsen (1995) investigated the feasibility of assessing melodic expectancy in children (ages 3–12). They confirmed that the sung continuation procedure (upon hearing an interrupted melody, the subject was asked to sing what he or she believed the continuation of that melody would be) could be used as a melodic expectancy measure, but only with children identified as musical.

Through an ethnographic study of children and their invented music, Campbell (1998) found that children are music-makers and are resourceful in how they utilize music in the unfolding of their daily lives. She writes that "we may be most effective as teachers when we consider children less as blank slates for us to fill than as thoughtful minds—musical minds, already taking shape through the process of enculturation" (p. ix). P. S. Campbell (1991) summarizes the distinctive features of songs *by* children (5–7 years old) that were gathered from playgrounds in seven schools in the Midwest, in contrast to traditional songs *for* children: the former had substantially tighter range and greater use of repetition as a structural device. Some songs were rhythmic chants or a combination of song and speech rhythms and were rhythmically more complex than Anglo-American children's songs, or children's songs of Hispanic, Native American, and most other world cultures, and incorporated a greater use of movement, including gesture, handclaps, and dance, than traditional songs (pp. 21–22).

Movement

As part of a study of the initial stages of preparatory audiation, Hicks (1993) videotaped eight toddlers' responses to a familiar song and an unfamiliar song without text during the fifth, tenth, fifteenth, and twentieth lessons. The responses that were tallied were looking responses, non-

pulsating responses, pulsating responses, miscellaneous responses, vocal responses, and responses of anticipation. The majority of responses were looking responses. Other conclusions were that (1) during the acculturation period children will often anticipate music and respond physically during the silence, (2) upon hearing music accompanied by movement activities, children will respond without encouragement to do so, (3) the movement responses made by young children are developmental in nature and dependent on physical maturation, and (4) children tend to make purposeful movement responses to music before they make purposeful vocal responses to music (Hicks, 1993).

Given opportunities to move to chants in duple and triple meters, children (18 months) and their caregivers performed slightly more movement responses to duple meter chants as compared to triple. Simple rhythmic chant elicited immediate movement responses that tended to decrease over time, while complex rhythm patterns elicited a steady increase of movement responses (Reynolds, 1995).

Children (3 and 4 years old) asked to respond to changes in dynamics, timbre, tempi, pitch (register), texture, and articulation in a musical whole, using either body movement or a prop, all responded correctly most frequently to changes in tempi, followed by articulation; the least accurate responses were to changes in timbre. Except for the youngest 3-year-olds, children responded more accurately to changes when using a prop. There was little difference in correct response whether prop or body movement was used first (Morris, 1992). The effects of visual and auditory stimuli on a movement behavior of children aged 3 to 5 years confirmed that the highest on-task behavior occurred for the conditions involving the processing of only one sensory stimulus at a time (Donich, 1992).

Introduced to 3 weeks of specialized child-centered movement instruction versus a more broad-based music instruction, kindergarten and first-grade girls were found to be more musical than boys. Children identified with high musical aptitude (as tested by the PMMA; Gordon, 1979) were able to respond to elemental changes in the music and tended to engage the whole body in an expressive personal style (O'Hagin, 1997).

Rhythmic Skills

Despite its importance to the process of understanding and enjoying music, very little is known about how children develop a "sense" of rhythm (Upitis, 1987). Rhythmic organization is based on a developing understanding of two interrelated aspects of temporal sound phenomena—the rhythmic figure and meter. The figure is perceived as a cluster of sounds (five or less); the meter is an organization that underlies the surface or figural events.

Working with children 5 to 7 years old, Davidson and Colley (1987) investigated what effect text, complexity, and length of pattern have on children's production, notation, and rhythmic reading. Children aged 5 and 6 found it more difficult than 7-year-olds did to separate text from rhythmic structure. Items without a text were notated more accurately than those with text, yet the older children tended to use the words of the song in their notations, seeming to rely more on linguistic than musical memory. Younger children tended to be somewhat more accurate in their notations, probably because they relied on memory of the song. When recalling rhythm patterns in a familiar song, the younger children seemed to be able to attend to only one rhythmic feature at a time, either the pulse or the pattern. Most 7-year-olds (75%), however, were able to recall both. Notating patterns was more difficult than recalling patterns, and decoding patterns was more difficult than notating patterns. Regardless of text influence, children's accuracy of rhythmic perception decreased as the length of patterns increased.

Children's ability to perform selected rhythm patterns, under several conditions involving the three modes of presentation and their combinations, indicated that for the youngest children (first-graders), the visual icons alone proved tedious; when icons were coupled with auditory or kinesthetic modalities, scores were much improved. For the older children (third and fifth grade), icons seemed to aid memory for the patterns. Multimodal treatments did not seem to hinder performance (Persellin, 1992).

Emergence of Music Literacy

Upitis (1992) uses a "whole language" approach to facilitating children's development of musical literacy through invented notation of their own compositions, as "whole music." Her illustrations incorporate the work of Davidson and Scripp (1988), as well as reflecting her own teaching and research. She illustrates a 4-year-old's knowledge of words versus musical notes through "scribbles" that differentiate the two kinds of symbols. Her many examples of how children 5 to 9 years old represent melody, timbre, dynamics, and figural and metric aspects of rhythm show individual differences in children's construction of musical knowledge. Upitis suggests that the order of notational development seems to be predictable but with wide variation in the age at which such abilities emerge. Her examples are rich with narratives of individual children expressing and representing their ideas. Upitis found that some 5-year-olds could notate melodic contour if they were involved in composition, but if they were not involved in composition, the ability to notate was delayed until age 10. She believes that what matters is the nature of development that occurs when children begin to notate the sounds they create. Musical training makes a difference, along with children's "home musical diets" and the quality of their own compositions. Upitis reminds us of how much children can do

and how much adults can learn from watching children at *their* work as explorers and inventors.

Influenced by the work of Upitis, Poorman (1996) investigated early symbolic representation of musical sounds among 6 3- and 4-year-old children who invented ways to "write the way the song goes" using materials of different shapes, colors, and textures. Three different tasks involved children's representations of loud/soft and high/low perceptions and visual and tactile representation of sound. Analysis of the videotaped tasks revealed three qualitative levels of musical understanding: (a) the sensorimotor stage of fluent explorations; (b) early use of symbols with a mentoring teacher; (c) symbolic use that linked sound-producing actions with a representational image.

Domer and Eastlund Gromko (1996) studied 4- and 5-year-olds' qualitative changes in invented notations representing melodic contour, following 12 weeks of music instruction. Twenty-eight children were pretested with Gordon's PMMA and a test of visual contours in which they "wrote the way the song goes," resulting in four line drawings made on "high-low" charts while singing each of four folk songs. The drawings were classified in three types: scribbles unrelated to musical contour, enactive line drawings, and lines that indicated awareness of the contour of melody. After 12 weeks of singing more songs, drawing them in the air, and drawing melodies, the children again took the test of visual contours. Half of the children showed qualitative improvement in invented notation. Children who initially had low PMMA test scores showed little improvement, while those with high PMMA scores showed significant ($p < .05$) change. The ability to gain in notational ability appears to be mediated by aural perception ability.

Conceptual Development in Music

Kalmar (1989) investigated the effect of music training in fostering the acquisition of certain attribute-concepts in language development by 3- and 4-year-old Hungarian children. Forty children were tested for their understanding of the terms and then randomly assigned to an experimental and a control group. The language treatment involved eight adjective pairs, defining the following dimensions: length, height, depth, hardness, weight, strength, speed, and liveliness. The music treatment was based on structured activity that integrated singing, rhythmic movement, and symbolic play. The pretest took place at the time children entered nursery school, and the posttest took place approximately 2½ years later when children were 5½ to 6½ years old. The pre- and posttest consisted of two tasks. The first task required each child to select from three pictures that were characterized by a particular attribute, for example, height in a mountain, a tree, and a flower. The child was then asked to select two pictures that represented the best positive and negative examples for that particular word. The second task was to list as many objects or things that the child believed fit the word indicated by the experimenter. Task 1 proved to be very easy for 3- and 4-year-olds, with responses nearly 100% correct. Performance on Task 2 by the music group was significantly better than the control group at the posttest, indicating that music may foster semantic-conceptual development for children 3 to 6 years old.

Brand (2000) deduced a mental model of children's musical organization processes based on the strategies they employed to teach themselves a song. Given an unfamiliar African Zulu song, they were given a number of options to learn the song—play the tape over and over, play it on the xylophone or small drum, draw a picture of it, and so on. Vocal or instrumental renditions indicated a number of organizational devices, the most common being making boundaries and recognizing repetition and change. Older children used more organizations than the younger children and learned the song in less time. Playing an instrument seemed less of a determining factor than age.

The relationship of discrimination ability to conceptual development has received some attention in research literature, indicating that discrimination of contrasting musical elements generally precedes concept formation. When given single and double discrimination tasks (Sims, 1988), children's (32 subjects aged 4–6 years and 64 subjects aged 7–9 years) movement behaviors indicated age-related differences that could somewhat be explained according to Piaget's developmental age continuum. However, there were a surprising number of instances of first and second graders responding correctly or nearly correctly that were more difficult to explain.

In a follow-up study (Sims, 1991), training to boost musical discrimination ability was introduced to see if developmental patterns would emerge similar to those of conceptual development. Preschool children (30 subjects aged 4–5 years) in the experimental group were able to identify and label musical characteristics significantly better than those in the control group on single discriminations, but neither group performed well on double discrimination tasks. Children, as indicated by Piaget, tend to concentrate on only one characteristic at a time. Leu (1997) replicated a similar study but with Taiwanese subjects 4 to 6 years old. Again, children were able to identify and verbally label single musical characteristics, but most were unsuccessful with double concept discrimination tasks even after short-term instruction. The concept of tempo was easier for children to discriminate than that of articulation (smooth versus choppy).

Eliciting verbal labels from young children presents problems for researchers since it is difficult to determine a child's understanding of the label. Investigating children's difficulty with the labels high/low and up/down, Durkin and Townsend (1997) tested children's (42 subjects aged 5.7 to 6.8) understanding on the terms in both spatial and musical contexts. Training in both was anticipated to boost gains on the pitch task, a more difficult task. Children were much better, however, at the spatial meaning of the terms than the pitch meanings. In this study, training involved the simultaneous introduction of sound and label. Gordon (1997a) believes that experience with sound should precede labeling and that labeling should precede symbolic references. By contrast, Costa-Giomi (1994) utilized training to sensitize children aurally to harmonic changes in two presentations—harmonic progressions alone or harmonic progressions with melodic material. She found that 5-year-olds in a sample of 167 4- and 5-year-olds, enrolled in two preschools in Argentina and two preschools in Ohio, could detect chord changes when given aural presentations of chord progressions without melodic material; 4-year-olds were unable to do so.

Advanced organizer instruction seems to be more effective than more traditional approaches in fostering children's (4-year-olds) learning of four musical concepts—dynamics, pitch, tempo, and rhythm (Lawton & Johnson, 1992). Based on the theories of Ausubel, advanced organizer instruction supports a sequence of learning in which general concepts are presented first, followed by less general concepts and more specific information. Following the initial lesson, "related learning activities" to clarify the general concepts are presented to assist in the retention of the information in the memory. In this particular study the objective of each advance organizer lesson was to teach the defining properties of a musical concept. Subsequent related learning activities provided children with the opportunities to focus on the defining properties and to relate them to the general musical concept. By contrast, the children in the control group received instruction focused on the same objectives, but activities focusing on defining properties of each musical concept were not used. Results indicated that the experimental group children demonstrated superior understanding of pitch and rhythm concepts and performed significantly better on all three modes of representation (enactive, iconic, and symbolic). Both groups performed equally well regardless of the methods of presentation (using a single sound or a song accompanied by a piano or by a piano alone) on tests involving the understanding of dynamic and tempo musical concepts.

Gouzouasis (1993) contends that the audiation of rhythm and tonal patterns, regardless of the similarities and differences that occur across diverse cultural groups, may be considered a conceptual ability because of the musical meaning implied in the process of recognition and performance of those patterns.

Curricular Issues in Early Childhood Education

The field of early childhood education is growing, both in the number of programs for children and in public awareness, nationally and internationally. In the United States, the demands for accessibility, especially for children of low-income parents, and for high-quality education for all children are issues in political campaigns, in budget committees, and in the daily lives of children, families, and teachers of young children (Bredekamp, 1996). The majority of states now offer state-sponsored prekindergarten programs for 3- and 4-year-olds considered "at risk" of academic failure; elementary schools are thus expanded to serve children of younger ages. Care for infants and toddlers, after-school care for preschool and primary children, expanded care for preschoolers, and developmentally appropriate methods for primary school children: all of these are part of early childhood education. It is recognized, therefore, that early education is a diverse field, encompassing an age range from birth through 8 years, in public and private settings that go beyond traditional school boundaries, with varying regulatory agencies and standards, and a range of differing professional roles that demand varying kinds and levels of preparation (Bredekamp, 1996).

The notion of education for young children arouses a set of commonly held and conflicting beliefs about the purposes and value of educational programs for young children. Differing ideologies and conceptions of the nature and nurture of children and societal expectations for the outcomes of education all compete for salience in the education of the young. What should be taught, how, when, to whom, and why are crucial questions that enliven the profession (Bredekamp & Copple, 1997).

The nation's largest professional organization devoted exclusively to educational and developmental needs in early childhood is the National Association for the Education of Young Children (NAEYC), with 102,000 members in 2000. The NAEYC defines early childhood as the years from birth to age 8; this decision is based on the assumption that learning and development during this age period share characteristics such as vulnerability, dependence on family and adults, and concrete thinking. Experiences during this time are considered the foundation for later experiences. Children's interrelated learning and development in physical, social, cognitive, aesthetic, and emotional domains means that educational programs attempt to provide children's integrated experience in these areas, in order to address needs of the "whole child" (Bredekamp, 1996).

In order to understand the growth of early childhood

programs in the 20th century, we need to distinguish childcare programs that grew out of the child welfare movement from nursery schools, which were part of the child study movement. The former provided service for children of employed mothers or low-income families; their chief emphasis was on health, safety, and "maternal" care. In contrast, many nursery schools (or preschools) grew out of university departments of home economics as a laboratory for children's development and parent education. Since the mid-1960s, when Head Start and other experimental programs began, the childcare and child study movements have grown closer together. As a federally funded comprehensive program of child education, Head Start also offered health and social services for low-income families. One consequence of the Head Start involvement was increased emphasis on academic and intellectual performance, in contrast to earlier emphases on social development in the context of play. Since the mid-1980s, state departments of education, in cooperation with local districts, have initiated prekindergarten programs for children considered to be "at risk" from either individual or environmental factors (Day, 1988). Program emphases have changed to keep abreast with changing understandings of all children.

Trends in kindergarten education in the 1960s and 1970s paralleled trends in preschool education, changing from private sponsorship to inclusion in the public school. (Mississippi in 1987 was the last state to begin to offer public kindergarten in the United States [Bredekamp, 1996]). The demand for all-day care for young children of employed mothers has increased steadily during the past three decades, resulting in increasing diversity of services and settings. At present the dichotomy between care and education is beginning to close. Educational experiences commensurate with children's developmental levels are considered an essential part of quality care (Bredekamp, 1996).

The changes from the 1960s to the present were accompanied by the development of new knowledge of developmental theory and research, based largely on Piaget and Vygotsky, a renewal of John Dewey's educational theory, and recognition of Erik Erikson's stages of psychosocial development. The experimental model of direct instruction, direct instruction system for teaching (DISTAR), suggested another form of intervention for children of low-income families (Bereiter & Englemann, 1966). The growing knowledge base of child development and research and practice in early childhood pedagogy made possible the emerging field of early childhood education. Diversity in the profession is said to be held together by a shared base of knowledge that informs its practitioners (Bredekamp & Copple, 1997) and arouses alternative views and criticism. Current intellectual and philosophical knowledge bases for early childhood education are derived from many sources, predominantly the cognitive-developmental, constructivist/interactionist approach (Bredekamp & Copple, 1997; Raines, 1997; Rogoff, 1990).

Katz (1977) observed that academic disciplines seem to be marked by an inverse relationship between a large reliable database and the number of charismatic leaders and contending ideologies. One could speculate that the field of early childhood education is characterized by ideologies that reflect basic philosophical differences and a knowledge base that is broad but limited, because of ethical considerations that prohibit definitive experiments. Many issues have been argued from ideological positions that are resistant to change. For example, the question of "hothousing" represents divided and deeply felt opinion about the desirability of acquiring knowledge as early as possible, even though knowledge of child development suggests that hothousing may damage children's disposition for learning.

The nature of education for young children is influenced by social, political, and historical forces (Isenberg & Jalongo, 1997). What is considered worthwhile for children to know reflects sociocultural realities. Katz (1995) distinguishes four kinds of learning: knowledge, skills, dispositions, and feelings. For the young child, *knowledge* includes facts, stories, concepts, schemas. *Skills* are observable actions and abilities. *Dispositions* are "relatively enduring habits of mind, across varied situations such as curiosity, thoughtfulness, willingness or unwillingness to try something new" (p. 103). *Feelings* may be learned from experience or may reflect specific situations, such as competence or lack of it or peer rejection or acceptance. Katz suggests that these four kinds of learning need to be addressed equally and simultaneously in classroom practice.

Dweck (1986) and Dweck and Leggett (1988) provide research support for distinguishing patterns of cognitive-affective behavior as "mastery-oriented" responses versus maladaptive "helpless" responses, each characterized by differing approaches to challenging tasks. Situational and dispositional factors are both considered to play a role in producing goals and behavior patterns; dispositions are viewed as inclinations to act in one way or another, individual differences that influence the likelihood that a child will choose one set of goals rather than another. Dispositions are seen as a significant link to either task-involvement or helpless orientation. In a similar vein, Ames (1992) has demonstrated that different achievement goals of children produce "qualitatively different motivational patterns"; the learning environments of classrooms vary in expectations for instruction and result in "qualitatively different motivational patterns" (p. 262). For example, learning goals, mastery, and task involvement (comparable to Dweck and Leggett's mastery) focus on the intrinsic aspects of learning. In contrast, performance and ego-involvement goals emphasize one's ability, sense of worth in the eyes of others, recognition that one has performed better than others, and avoidance of challenging tasks. Learning goals are fostered by tasks in which children feel able to manage their own learning and that create "cognitive engagement patterns" (p. 264) in the social organization of the class and by evaluation that is perceived as informative rather than controlling. Dweck and Leggett (1988) point out that when performance goals are dominant, children who lack confidence in ability are especially at risk for developing helpless response patterns.

Developmentally Appropriate Practice (DAP)

Among the burgeoning number of educational programs for young children initiated since the 1960s, many emphasized academic skills in teacher-directed settings (Bereiter & Englemann, 1966). The growth of state-supported programs for 3- and 4-year-olds in public schools in the 1980s raised the question: What is appropriate education for young children? (Day, 1988). Decisions about what should be taught and how it can be learned depend on teachers' knowledge of the learner's developmental level as well as understanding of the relationships between experience and later developmental outcomes (Katz, 1995). Parental expectations may also influence what shall be taught.

The rationale for advocating "developmentally appropriate practice" (DAP) comes from several considerations: (1) claims for the long-term positive and lasting effects of high-quality early childhood programs (Schweinhart & Weikart, 1997); (2) large-scale, nationwide evaluations of early childhood programs that found that approximately 15% met standards for "good quality"; and (3) shifting academic expectations from elementary school to preschool. Developmentally appropriate practice is a set of principles that are based on knowledge of child development and learning, "age-related human characteristics that permit predictions about what activities, materials, interactions and experiences will be safe, healthy, interesting, achievable, and also challenging to children" (Bredekamp & Copple, 1997, p. 9). Guidelines also consider individual interests, strengths, and needs as well as awareness of the social and cultural worlds in which children live. The DAP guidelines include children from birth through 8 years from diverse cultural and linguistic backgrounds. Guidelines make accommodations for children with disabilities and developmental delays so that they may be served in the same settings as their peers. Early childhood settings function as a "community of learners"; the context for learning supports relationships between children and adults, among children, and between families and school (p. 16).

Criteria for excellence that are included in accreditation standards for high-quality programs are provided by

NAEYC's National Academy of Early Childhood Programs (1998). Guidelines for music and movement say "encourage expression, representation, and appreciation for the arts" and give recommendations for each age group. For infants "occasionally use music for movement, singing, or listening; sing to baby; appreciate infants' vocalizations and sound; provide time and space for movement and play." For preschool "provide time and space for dancing, movement activities, creative dramatics; do musical activities such as singing, listening, and playing instruments; provide visits by artists, materials representative of a variety of cultures; develop appreciation for the arts by taking trips to galleries, concerts, cultural events." For kindergarten and school-age care, "provide opportunities for children to represent ideas and feelings and learn fundamental concepts and skills in the fine arts" (NAEYC, 1998, p. 40).

Guidelines are also provided by some states for early childhood programs that convey an understanding of child development. For example, Illinois is piloting early learning standards for children 3 to 5 years (Henderson, 2000), intended for all children in group settings, regardless of sponsorship. In the fine arts section, standards are as follows: "Understand the sensory elements, organizational principles and expressive qualities of the arts" and "understand the similarities, distinctions, and connections in and among the arts." For music, the standards are as follows: "Investigate the elements of music" (p. 92) and "describe or respond to their own creative work or the creative work of others" (p. 94). The guidelines acknowledge that learning and development are interconnected within and across domains; curriculum is integrated and reflects a conceptual organization that enables children to make sense of their experience.

Young (1998) recommends that music educators value the early stages of child-initiated music-making, appreciating the rich competencies that children reveal in a wide range of activity in which music is "one interconnecting part." Turner's (2000) musical learning centers respect the innate musical abilities of every child and give opportunity for specialist and child to interact as a community of learners. Observing children's learning in the zone of proximal development provides for authentic assessment as well. Gunn (1996) describes music experiences that reflect DAP criteria for meeting individual and developmental needs of children from birth to age 8 in group settings. Features include active involvement with sensory materials and supportive adults; experiences with steady beat and the versatile human voice; a prepared environment that encourages exploration of sound and movement as individuals or small groups; "composing" using invented symbols; and an integrated curriculum in the primary school. Gunn suggests that many schools do not reflect current understandings of how children learn.

Criticism of developmentally appropriate practice comes from postmodern social theorists and curriculum reconceptualists (Block, 1992; Canella, 1997; Kessler, 1991; Kessler & Swadener 1992; Lubeck, 1996) who examine early childhood curriculum from feminist, critical, and interpretive points of view and who question the universality of the developmental paradigm. Critics fear that early childhood curricula perpetuate differences between poor and minority children and those of the middle class. Reconceptualists ask what knowledge is most important, whose interests are being served in the curriculum, and what vision of the future is implied in curriculum. Raines (1997) describes four common misconceptions of developmentally appropriate practice: that teachers have abandoned responsibility and are not "in charge"; that there is no classroom structure; that few skills are taught; and that DAP is one set curriculum. Raines counters each of these misconceptions with information about classroom practice. Teachers do organize predictable learning environments in which children have choices of stimulating activities and materials; a balance of teacher-led and child-motivated activity is sought. Structure is inherent in the organization of time, space, materials, and "conceptual framework" as themes, units, and projects that focus children's active involvement and learning in meaningful contexts and provide for children's social, cognitive, affective, physical, and aesthetic development. Children construct knowledge through interaction with materials and people and refine their skills and concepts over time, in "authentic instruction and assessment cycles" (p. 77).

Block (1992), Lubeck (1996), and Canella (1997) question the relevance of developmental psychology as a foundation for early childhood education. Block suggests that an emphasis on the individual or family ignores the complexity of influences on groups and constraints on opportunity and achievement; we tend to blame individuals rather than their circumstances. Block suggests that emphasis on an empirical-analytic paradigm limits researchers from taking other perspectives. Lubeck questions the assumptions that underlie all knowledge, since knowledge itself is constructed in power relationships. For example, Piaget's constructivism "reflects the dominant culture" and a "stratified social order," as shown in the class systems and tracking in Western education (p. 156). Canella suggests that the present knowledge base ignores the lives of many children, families, and teachers. As she reconceptualizes the field, she advocates three main values as the core of professionalism: social justice and equity for the young, hearing and responding to the young, and the development of "critical dispositions" in the search for social justice.

It is evident that DAP has generated critical analysis and discourse among theorists, expressing concerns for cultural sensitivity and questioning the developmental paradigm. It should be noted that recent criticism is largely based on the earlier position paper (Bredekamp, 1987). The newer Bredekamp and Copple (1997) edition recognizes the social and cultural context for learning; they acknowledge that children differ in learning styles and that children need a sense of psychological safety within school and community. Bowman (1994) responds to voices of concern with the reminder that in reflective practice, teachers adapt their teaching to children with diverse needs. Using a single teaching method for a diverse group of children is likely to result in mixed levels of success.

What are the outcomes of developmentally appropriate practice with minority children of low-income parents and children often considered "at-risk"? Huffman and Speer (2000), suggesting the need for early intervention strategies that meet the needs of an expanding urban underclass, report that DAP has been associated with positive outcomes for children in academic achievement as well as in social and behavioral domains. Bryant, Burchinal, Lau, and Sparling (1994), in a study of Head Start children, found DAP to be related to measures of cognitive development and school readiness. Observation of preschool children's stress showed significantly fewer stress behaviors in developmentally appropriate classrooms than in less developmentally appropriate settings (Burts et al., 1992). The High/Scope curriculum, known for its child-initiated constructivist approach, has demonstrated gains in cognitive skills by the first grade and long-term positive "social responsibility" behavior such as graduation from high school and fewer arrests for misconduct (Schweinhart & Weikart, 1997).

In a study of 113 mainly African American and Hispanic children involved in the Head Start/Public School Transition Project, Huffman and Speer (2000) studied the relationship between low and moderate levels of classroom appropriateness and performance on subscales of the Woodcock and Johnson *Psycho-educational Battery Tests of Achievement* across 28 Psycho-educational Battery classrooms. Developmental appropriateness was measured using the Assessment Profile for Early Childhood Programs (Abbott-Shim & Sibley, 1992). The sample of children represented a population considered at "exceptional risk for academic underachievement" (Huffman & Speer, 2000, p. 179). Significant gains were observed in kindergarten and first-grade children in letter-word recognition and applied problems, from the fall to the spring semester, in classrooms that were rated moderate (rather than low) in developmental appropriateness.

The authors consider the study significant in its demonstration of effectiveness of DAP with children in high-risk environments. However, the measurements presented limitations in the standardized skills-based assessment and in the "measurement" of classroom appropriateness. The authors write that although settings rated "low" and "moderate" differed appreciably, the cutoff points were close. Settings rated "moderate" were possibly weak examples of developmental appropriateness, and the environments rated "low" tended to be either regimented or disordered. The positive academic effects in the "moderate" classrooms could be attributed to the lack of regimentation or disorder that would hinder children's learning. The Huffman and Speer study points up the need for measures of children's achievement that are likely to reveal more realistic results of DAP. The authors suggest that the assessment of classroom practices should indicate the impact of classroom practices on learning and make clear that settings that limit exploration, initiative, and peer interaction may result in isolation and alienation for children. Emotional well-being is an important indicator of learning potential.

Models and Approaches in Early Childhood Education

Saracho and Spodek (1997) suggest that models of curriculum should follow from foundational principles such as those for developmentally appropriate practice. In contrast to principles, particular models offer choices for teachers' adoption. Some educators believe that a curriculum model constrains teachers' autonomy and therefore advocate an eclectic model of teachers' choice. Others maintain that if teachers are well educated in child development and education they have the judgment necessary to make their own eclectic decisions (Goffin, 1993). Descriptions follow of relevant models and examples of research that are compatible. It should be noted that all of these models "follow from foundational principles" and would be considered "developmentally appropriate."

Constructivist/Interactionist.   As developed by DeVries and Kohlberg (1987), this approach is built on Piaget's cognitive-developmental constructivist position that children actively construct knowledge of physical reality and also of social and moral understanding from mental action and interaction with the social and physical environment. The aim of education is development; the authors suggest that critics have interpreted "cognitive" in a limited way without acknowledging the cognitive bases of social, affective, and aesthetic knowledge. Constructivist theory provides a basis for children's development in the symbol systems that emerge during the "golden years of creativity," as Gardner (1982) described early childhood; symbol systems include language, music, and drawing. To represent experiences in symbolic form in art media is considered a prerequisite for artistic development and expression.

Three kinds of knowledge, according to Kamii and Ewing (1996), include: (1) social (conventional) knowledge, which is derived directly from other people; (2) physical knowledge, gained partly through experience with materials and partly from the child's own mental constructs; and (3) logico-mathematical knowledge, which is constructed by the child in thoughtful interaction with materials and people. For example, to be able to say that two blocks are similar (or the same or different) in shape depends partly on observation of physical objects and also on the concept of similar or different. This logical classificatory framework is constructed by the child; it cannot be taught directly. Constructivist teachers play an active role in preparing an environment with conditions that encourage children's discovery and creation of knowledge, based on what they can do, and in responding to children's errors with further opportunities for self-correction.

The Project Approach.   The project approach is a longstanding tradition in early childhood, including John Dewey's progressive education and other approaches that recognize that learning begins with interests of the learner. Katz and Chard (1989) propose that project work is one among several kinds of classroom activities, supporting children's intellectual development by "engaging their minds fully in the quest for knowledge, understanding, and skill" (p. xi). Developmentally appropriate education cultivates the life of the child's mind, emotionally, morally, and aesthetically. A project involves in-depth study that enables children to make sense of their experience; it involves children's active participation with the environment and community and with the people and objects within it that have significance for children. For example, how houses are built, how a marching band works and what music they play, and how insects live may all be studied by individual children, small groups, or an entire class. During preschool years projects may comprise a major portion of the program; during primary grades they may be one kind of learning that is available, along with academic activities. In each case, the project is likely to take children out of the classroom to observe, listen, question, interview, and sketch and then back to their room to discuss, create, reconstruct, and extend their learnings.

An integrated music and whole language project approach is described by Whitaker (1994) as *thematic cycles*, which she contrasts with thematic *units*. In a unit, the teacher generates ideas for a general theme. In a *thematic cycle*, students generate ideas from their intrinsic interest and involvement; they apply skills and knowledge from their areas of interest such as writing, composing, arranging, or notating. Music, art, and literature are valued for the aesthetic and cultural phenomena that they are rather than vehicles to teach math or word recognition; symbolic skills and tools support art content. The music teacher

serves as a resource who "nurtures the musical life of the class" (p. 28).

The Reggio Emilia Approach.   What has come to be called the Reggio approach began in Reggio Emilia, a city in northern Italy, at the close of World War II when parents picked up war rubble and began to create a future for their children by building schools (Edwards, Gandini, & Forman, 1993). The educational philosopher Loris Malaguzzi provided intellectual guidance for teachers, families, and the community, who together forged an educational philosophy based on strengths of the child rather than deficits and the rights of the child rather than needs and founded on the relationships among children, teachers, and community (Malaguzzi, 1993). Social and technological change after World War II provided the social context in which young children were viewed as worthy, competent, and deserving of the highest quality of early experience. The schools and the educational philosophy that developed from the endeavors of Malaguzzi, teachers, and the community have astonished educators throughout the world, with "extraordinary work done by ordinary children." *Newsweek* in 1991 awarded the Reggio schools highest honors for early childhood education. Reggio Emilia administers schools for children from 6 weeks to 6 years old in 30 schools across the city. Katz (1994) observed that if an American school can be compared to a factory, then Reggio Emilia schools are families.

The Reggio approach is a constructivist project approach and emergent curriculum based on teachers' abilities to attend carefully and thoughtfully to children's interests and curiosity. Projects consist of detailed and complex investigations that may extend from one day to several months of activity in small groups. The term "coconstructivist" refers to teachers' involvement as partners in learning, in listening to children's wonderings, and as coteachers, planning the projects that are richest in potential for multiple learning.

One of the defining features is an emphasis on the "one hundred languages of children," referring to symbolic languages in many media: painting, sculpture, shadow play, words, music, drawing, movement, block construction, and other ways that children symbolically represent their knowing, feeling, and imagining. "Materials have the power to engage children's minds, bodies, and emotions. Their evocative power calls the children into the processes of weaving what they have already experienced in the world with their new perceptions and sensibilities" (Cadwell, 1997, p. 27). Malaguzzi (1993) is often quoted as saying that "children have a hundred languages, yet the schools recognize only one." Gardner (1998) suggests that the "one hundred languages" approach nurtures the development of multiple intelligences. An educational program is rooted in local conditions. Without romanticizing the Reggio Emilia community, Gardner refers to it as a "sustained apprenticeship in humanity."

Other characteristics help to explain the extraordinary work of Reggio children.

- The teacher's role as *provocateur*, one who challenges and questions children's thinking, is to "get others to think about something in a new and compelling way" (New, 1994, p. 26). What would happen if—? How do you know? Do you still think that? are questions the *provocateur* teacher may ask. From the Vygotsky point of view, teachers use open-ended problem-solving and discovery to lead children beyond their comfort zone. The use of materials remains with the children; children are the artists, designers, composers, authors, and inventors.
- Representations in several media, or "crossmodal" representation, are part of project work. "Children learn more deeply when they represent the same concept in different media" (Forman, 1994, p. 41). Children are encouraged to revisit and revise their earlier representations.
- Looking at things, talking, arguing about them, are part of discovering other points of view and are a crucial part of the coconstructivist approach (Nelson, 1997).
- Belief in the right of children to the highest quality of education and belief in the strength, worth, and competence of children form the bases for an emergent curriculum.
- Rather than formal assessment, documentation of children's work tells the story of individual and group accomplishments. The stunning beauty created by children is organized and displayed by teachers on walls, ceilings, and floor. Parents and visitors review children's project work through art, photographs, reflections by teachers, and recorded and transcribed conversations of children. In these ways, teachers are also researchers; as coteachers in each classroom they plan together each week, teach, review, and reflect on the work of children.
- "The environment is the third teacher," including space, light, and organization of materials that shows their beauty and invites involvement with them.

The program has attracted thousands of visitors from all over the world and has sponsored traveling exhibits and seminars. In ways of their own, teachers have adapted Reggio ideas for their classrooms and communities, motivated by the desire to do what they believe is best for children. Throughout the United States, the Reggio approach has inspired varying adaptations in different kinds of early childhood settings—in primary schools and public prekindergartens, in private schools, and in Head Start. In St. Louis, for example, 10 public and private schools received funding between 1992 and 1995 to observe in Italy and to adapt Reggio ideas in their home sites.

Cadwell's book *Bringing Reggio Emilia Home* (1997) documents the creation of a Reggio-inspired program in the College School in St. Louis. Cadwell describes teachers learning how to listen, how to have conversations with children, and how to "read" a conversation. She describes how teachers learned to involve children with materials, illustrated with examples of children's work in many media. Teachers reexamined how they used time, organization, and relationships with colleagues, parents, and community. The teachers studied school space and transformed environments into spaces for caring and learning, the kind of environment that expressed their values. Cadwell's account is an excellent example of qualitative research in teaching.

High/Scope.   Developed in the 1960s and 1970s by the High/Scope Educational Foundation under the leadership of David Weikart (Schweinhart & Weikart, 1997; D. Weikart, 1996), the High/Scope curriculum (Schweinhart & Epstein, 1997) was originally known as the Perry Preschool Project. The focus was initially on the effects of a high-quality preschool program for low-income African American children but has expanded to encompass all types of early childhood centers. Two randomly selected samples of children were assigned to conditions of either no preschool or to a half-day curriculum. The longitudinal sample consisted of 123 African American children, now in their early forties. Data from participants include not only academic records but social responsibility factors such as income, welfare assistance, and contact with law enforcement. Results have consistently shown that participants in the early educational program have outperformed those without preschool in terms of educational attainment, income, and "socially responsible" behavior (Schweinhart & Weikart, 1997).

It is estimated that approximately 25% of all preschool programs around the world are influenced to some extent by the High/Scope model (Carlton, 2000). High/Scope emphasizes active, child-initiated learning based on cognitive-developmental, constructivist theory in a developmentally appropriate open framework. The curriculum consists of well-defined key experiences in cognitive, social, and physical developmental areas that provide a framework for planning, guiding, and evaluating children's initiatives. Learning centers consisting of books, blocks, computer, housekeeping and pretend, art, music, and sensory materials provide optimal opportunities for children's choices and for problem solving, social interaction, and independent thinking. The plan-do-review process enables children to make thoughtful choices, carry them out, and reflect on them. In addition to meeting NAEYC's standards for developmentally appropriate practice, the High/Scope program meets Head Start criteria for a curriculum based on principles of child development and for classroom arrangement, materials, teacher-child interaction, and parent involvement.

Music and movement have a central place throughout the day in a High/Scope curriculum, as part of circle time activities, in small groups, and when individual children use instruments or singing with a cassette and picture. Music and movement goals are described as key experiences that "represent basic music concepts that must be acted upon by each learner in developmentally-appropriate ways in order to construct a meaningful music knowledge-base" (Carlton, 2000, p. 18). Preschool key experiences in music are as follows: moving to music, exploring and identifying sounds, exploring the singing voice, developing melody, singing songs (acquiring a singing repertoire and sense of anchor pitch); feeling and expressing steady beat; and playing simple instruments. Guided by the key experiences, teachers are able to gauge children's developmental status and plan activities that expand their understanding. Musical concepts that are supported by key experiences include: intuitive responses and purposeful movement choices; aural discrimination of instrument and other sounds; vocal range from high to low; singing voice versus speaking voice; melodic direction and patterns and tuneful singing; steady beat versus rhythm and awareness of different kinds of steady beats; microbeat, macrobeat, and tonal memory (Carlton, 2000, p. 19).

The High/Scope consultant Phyllis Weikart provides leadership in purposeful movement, which promotes kinesthetic intelligence by developing the link between action, thought, and language (Carlton, 2000; P. Weikart, 1995). Children are encouraged to make and carry out a movement plan, to choose and think about their specific movement, and then to recall and talk about it. Key experiences in movement, which are appropriate for children up to second grade, are grouped into three broad goals that are further specified in terms of behavior.

High/Scope's Child Observation Record (COR) is used to assess the developmental status of children aged 2½ to 6 years, based on teachers' observation and brief narrative accounts of children's behavior in the following areas: initiative, social relations, creative representation, movement and music, language and literacy, and mathematics and logic. Teachers later use their written notes to classify each child's behavior on a checklist representing all these areas of learning, The COR can be used in any developmentally appropriate setting to make systematic periodic assessments of naturally occurring child behavior. As an assessment tool, the COR directly reflects the entire curriculum.

Waldorf Schools. The foundation of Waldorf education is the belief in the child as a spiritual being, born with a soul that exists before birth and continues after birth (Juul &

Maier, 1992). Waldorf schools are based on the anthroposophic beliefs of Rudolf Steiner, an Austrian scientist, educator, and artist. The role of teachers is to exercise children's soul faculties of Goodness, Beauty, and Truth, which correspond to the unfolding of children's development, encouraging curiosity, reverence, and wonder. During the first 7 years children occupy a "dream state," absorbing the environment and learning through imitation and sensory experience as their minds, bodies, and speech mature. When formal schooling begins at age 7, children cultivate the imagination and emotion through artistic experiences; artistic media are the vehicle for learning. During the intellectual awakening of adolescence the maturing person develops a sense of ethical judgment as he or she confronts abstract ideas. These verities underpin our civilization and in turn represent the main areas of human activity: religion, art, and science, which comprise the elements of human evolution (Childs, 1999). Juul and Maier (1992) describe the values of Waldorf education for children with physical and mental disabilities. Art experiences, including weaving, woodworking, and eurythmy, are an important focus, as they involve the whole child, head, heart, and hands. Although as of 1992 there were about 200 schools for curative education around the world, and perhaps some 350 schools in all, their influence is (unfortunately, the authors believe) not widespread in the United States.

Smithrim (2000) describes Waldorf kindergarten classrooms in New Hampshire and Ontario as filled with "beauty and respect" and nurturing the imagination, which is central to understanding. She cites several unique features of Waldorf music that are in contrast with most deeply held beliefs about young children's musical development. Waldorf teachers deemphasize the beat and steady pulse because, it is believed, a steady beat "pulls children to earth and grounds them prematurely, rather than helping them to live in dream consciousness" (Smithrim, 2000, p. 11). Based on metaphysical and esoteric explanations, the approach to tonality also differs from more traditional approaches. It is believed that the interval of the fifth became important during the Egyptian time in human history when human consciousness reoriented from the spiritual to the earthly world. Since this historical period corresponds to the first 7 years of a child's life, songs in the mood of the fifth are presented. Such songs center around A and extend to D a fifth below and to E a fifth above; these tones create the mood of the fifth; the interval of the ninth becomes the child's tonal realm. Smithrim gives examples of several songs in this tonality that kindergarten children are able to sing and that are described as having a calming, healing effect.

Eurythmy, a form of bodily movement that incorporates music and speech, was developed by Steiner and is a significant feature of Waldorf schooling. Based on the philosophical belief that such movement creates a place where "spirit and body meet," eurythmy is a way to make speech and music visible through dance (Reinsmith, 1989). Rhythmic exercises and movement in geometric patterns help children to attain control of body and breath and harmonize their bodies with other forces in life.

Smithrim compares Waldorf practices with currently held beliefs about music for children. In terms of high correlations previously found between beat competency and reading, Smithrim suggests that perhaps the timing of beat competency experiences in relation to reading is an open question. In addition, she points out that in both Orff and Kodaly approaches, the earliest sol-mi-la songs are without a tonal center; songs next in sequence change to pentatonic, in which there is a pull to the tonic. Edwin Gordon's approach, however, considers that the development of tuneful singing depends on children's feel for and memory of the tonal center. In spite of differences in musical belief and practice, the Waldorf approach raises worthy questions.

Montessori.   Maria Montessori (1870–1952) is known for her design of a prepared learning environment that respects children's unfolding development and gives opportunity for rich aural and sensory experience (Robinson, 2000). Montessori's sequential music materials include pairs of sound cylinders and bells for comparison and seriation tasks. Montessori principles include the absorbent mind, sensitive periods, the child's activity as work, concentration, and didactic materials that are self-correcting and permit control of error. It is believed that children go through a predictable series of changes from birth to young adulthood, between active and passive planes of development. Critics suggest that Montessori's natural unfolding view of development tends to negate individual differences and the influence of gender and culture (Hallquist, 1995). As a Montessori-trained teacher and music teacher, Robinson (2000) suggests that today's holistic and integrated early childhood curriculum is a useful addition to the Montessori model. Robinson's adaptations include a theme-based circle time with singing, moving, listening, and playing instruments, which may involve multicultural materials or nature study. Individual work time provides for exploration of materials, composition of rhythm patterns using notation cards, and play with rhythm sticks and resonator bars. Children repeat activities as often as they wish, since repetition is necessary for mastery of skills.

Heyge and Sillick (1997) describe Montessori's use of manipulatives for writing, applying Montessori's belief that written language gives a stable form to spoken language and is a means for better understanding of what is spoken. Reading comes later. Writing involves use of manipulative graphic symbols. Applying these beliefs to music, Heyge and Sillick suggest that the language of music must be experienced and assimilated as sound patterns within a repertoire of songs. Manipulative cards illustrate these sound patterns; in symbolic form they involve the eye, hand, and ear, and they can be rearranged and remembered.

The curriculum models described here tend to have in common a belief in the child as an active learner in an interactive environment who is constructing and revising her versions of the world and finding multiple means to interpret and express them.

Organizations

A number of organizations provide professional leadership. In early childhood education the NAEYC and the Association for Childhood Education International both support research and professional development opportunities for teachers of young children, at local, regional, and national levels. The Early Childhood Music and Movement Association has as its primary purpose the advocacy of music and movement for children from birth to age 7 and sponsors teacher certification that allows for three levels of progressive training. The International Society for Music Education has made a tremendous contribution in providing a journal and conference forums worldwide for the dissemination of research by the international community. The early childhood component of that organization, the Early Childhood Commission, has been very active in efforts to encourage, recognize, and disseminate research related specifically to young children. The Early Childhood Special Research Interest Group (SRIG)—the special interest group of the Music Educators National Conference (MENC)—has also given impetus to research issues of interest and importance to not only the research community but also the greater music education community.

MENC was instrumental in supporting standards for preschool age children, as presented in *Prekindergarten Music Education Standards* (1995). The MENC also has other publications related to the teaching of young children (Sims, 1995) and sponsored a conference in 2000. *Early Childhood Connections* (first issue 1995) is the only journal related to establishing connections among those who work with and for children through music, movement, and language. *Starting Points: Meeting the Needs of Our Youngest Children* (1994) and the *White House Conference on Early Child Development and Learning* (1997) were both public forums to create awareness regarding the importance of the early years in child development.

A growing grassroots movement of paraprofessionals provides early childhood music classes in private studios or community outreach programs. Curricula are varied: Some teachers develop their own materials; others use commercial programs developed by early childhood and/

or music specialists. Many of these early childhood proponents provide research-based curricular materials and support extensive teacher training programs (Jordan-DeCarbo, 1999).

Directions for the Future: Research and Assessment

Overall, there is little literature to indicate that the majority of music curricula for young children are theoretically based or participate in any meaningful assessment. Few early childhood centers have systematic music instruction. There are, however, some that reflect theoretical applications. Andress's (1998) approach is strongly aligned with Piagetian principles. Many commercially oriented curricula for ages birth to 6 are available as part of university or community outreach programs. Many of these businesses have well-integrated music curricula based on sound principles of child development. All are designed for parent/child participation, but the target population that has access to such instruction is very select because of the cost. Gordon's (1997a, 1997b) principles of musical sequencing for rhythm and melodic development have been adapted by many of these programs and are central to the *Jump Right In* series for both preschool (Valerio, Reynolds, Bolton, Taggart, & Gordon, 1998) and elementary age children (Gordon & Woods, 1985). Virtually no research exists to document if and how much benefit results from this early exposure to music.

It is important that music education researchers not only keep informed about the latest research connected with brain development but try to be more directly involved with such research whenever opportunities arise. Corroborative research brings together experts from more than one discipline and perspective. We wait in anticipation for research to document more substantially the impact of enriched environments on brain development, specifically those environments supporting the arts (Hodges, 2000, p. 21). The contributions of neuroscience will be increasingly important, not only in enhancing our understanding of musical processing but also in providing us with insights into the capacities of the musical mind. As the profession gains increasing access to technology, investigating how the brain processes all types of musical activity, by subjects of varying ages, will continue to inform the profession and the public at large of the place of music in the life of human development and behavior. Research is needed to help us understand more clearly the auditory processes involved in music processing, music performance, and the association of meaning to musical sound. While the importance of movement and motor development as it relates to music development has received some attention and is generally accepted as valid, research that connects such activity to specific brain functions is virtually nonexistent.

Research with infants has been accumulating throughout the past decade with respect to parallels across music and language development. There is a need to continue this research with children throughout the preschool years, especially up to 3 years old, when the window for language begins to close.

Good research is said to ask or find good questions (Walsh & King, 1993; Zimiles, 1993). Both qualitative and quantitative researchers focus on questions that appropriately use their favored methods, while being aware of limitations imposed by those methods. Gordon (2000) cautions researchers to distinguish the purpose of research from the specific problem to be studied. The results of a study should relate back to its problem, and conclusions should relate to its purpose. Gordon cites the need for researchers to understand clearly what measurement is; to recognize the "necessary readiness" children must have to respond to research questions; and to acknowledge children's individual differences. Understanding the difference between statistical and practical significance is essential; not all statistical significance is "significant." Walsh and King (1993) suggest that the insights of teachers and practitioners may provide valuable information that should be considered in a rigorous and systematic way by researchers.

Observational strategies continue to be used in examining children in a naturalistic setting. Bergen (1997) points out that in testing or experimental conditions an effort is made to eliminate extraneous variables, while in contextual observational studies it is important to become aware of environmental influences such as specific settings, situations, and interactions among children, peers, and adults.

Qualitative research depends on the ability to clarify the understandings that participants in a particular setting use to make sense of their world. What is taken for granted by participants is likely to be obscure to researchers. Interviewing informants is an important way to identify meaning-making structures, but interviewing children under 7 presents its own set of problems to the researcher-informant relationship. Hatch (1990) describes how to overcome problems that threaten the interview data from young children. Graue and Walsh (1998) provide suggestions on how to maintain focus on children during qualitative research in environments that are specific to children's lives. Graue and Walsh emphasize finding meaning within the context of children's lives, the significance of children's interactions, and practical suggestions for developing questions and methods pertinent to the setting.

The performance of children (6–10 years old) in testing situations may be influenced by more than their cognitive abilities. Children self-reporting low confidence in their abilities experienced more performance deterioration than children reporting high confidence. While it was acknowledged that the study was limited in terms of the musical skills tested, low confidence may contribute to helpless behavior patterns, regardless of actual ability (O'Neill & Sloboda, 1997). Documentation is needed to investigate the role of music exposure and experience, both formal and informal, to overall musical development; to investigate music's relationship to overall child development; to validate curricular issues; and to develop adequate assessment tools. Documentation is needed that validates the value of enriching environments on child development and the kinds of enrichment that benefit children the most.

Guidelines (Bredekamp & Rosegrant, 1992) for assessment for children aged 3 to 8 suggest that assessments should bring about some benefit to children, such as (a) planning for instruction that is relevant to the curriculum; (b) identification of children with special needs, without subjecting all children to measures that may be necessary for children with severe learning problems; and (c) evaluation of the effectiveness of early childhood programs, both locally and nationally, on the basis of shared curriculum goals. Hills (1993) calls for assessments that identify what children know and can do, focusing on strengths, in familiar environments. Structured assessments make use of predetermined tasks or open-ended questions that require analysis and synthesis of ideas. The younger the child, however, the more important nonstructured tasks are.

The "misassessment" of young children is built on a misunderstanding of educational process and outcome goals (Schweinhart, 1993). Criteria for assessment include developmental appropriateness, reliability, validity, and user-friendliness. Schweinhart recommends systematic observation for its ecological validity, nonintrusiveness, and ability to take account of all dimensions of development. The COR provides for teacher observation and narrative accounts of child achievement and behavior in six areas: initiative, creative representation, social relations, music and movement, language and literacy, and logic and mathematics. Reliability, validity, and feasibility were established by 64 Head Start teaching teams over a 2-year period (Schweinhart, McNair, Barnes, & Larner, 1993). As an integral part of the High/Scope program, such observation throughout the year is consistent with early childhood process and outcome goals.

Bergan and Feld (1993) suggest that the creation of developmental assessment systems has come about at a time of tension between measurement and instructional goals. The National Commission on Testing and Public Policy (1990) indicated that standardized tests tend not to reflect what children have learned in school. The authors describe the Measurement and Planning System (MAPS), widely used in Head Start, for observation of preschool and kindergarten cognitive and socioemotional development and fine and gross motor development. The authors advocate for assessment to be responsive to the changing needs and diversity of society.

Meisels (1993) describes how the pressure to show accountability through children's performance on standardized tests changes what and how teachers teach and robs teachers of their judgment. Meisels (2000) describes conventional tests as a barrier to learning and not a basis for policy. He suggests that what researchers choose to study "holds potential that must not be squandered by unfounded policies or procedures" (p. 18). Alternatively, the work sampling system (Meisels, 1993; Meisels, Liaw, Dorfman, & Nelson, 1995) is a form of performance assessment for children 3 to 8 years old that evaluates skills, knowledge, behavior, and accomplishments in an integrated way, on areas of learning and development that standardized tests cannot measure. The work sampling system has shown strong reliability and predictive validity (Meisels et al., 1995). There are three components. A developmental checklist consists of seven domains: personal and social development, language and literacy, mathematical thinking, scientific thinking, social studies, art and music, and physical development. Other components are a portfolio and summary for each child. Portfolios are a systematic collection of items of work in several domains, all documenting change in children's work. In demonstrating how children learn, portfolios integrate instruction and assessment; they show children, teachers, parents, and administrators the range and depth of children's learning and the activities that support learning. Periodic summary reports can reflect the rich information available from observations and portfolios. Gullo (1997) recommends two separate portfolios, one for work in progress and one for current and permanent work of items the children have selected for inclusion. The process of choosing enables children to reflect on their own learning.

The systematic development and assessment of environmental conditions and theory-based music curricula that are culturally connected to the population served is a critical shortfall in early childhood education today. Without ongoing guidance from the research community, early childhood music programs will develop more in tune with the latest popular versions of musical pursuit than with musical directions grounded by the nature of the growing child. Research is needed to investigate the current practices in public schools. School administrators will not recognize the musical needs of young children without research data that support change. The development and assessment of model curricula with a focus on cognitive development and the engagement of children's thinking will be needed if music education is to have an impact on early childhood educational practices.

REFERENCES

Abbott-Shim, M., & Sibley, A. (1992). *Assessment profile for early childhood programs, research version.* Atlanta, GA: Quality Assist.

Adachi, M. (1994). The role of the adult in the child's early musical socialization: A Vygotskian perspective. *Quarterly Journal of Music Teaching and Learning, 5*(3), 26–35.

Adachi, M., & Carlsen, J. C. (1995). Measuring melodic expectancies with children. *Bulletin of the Council for Research in Music Education, 127,* 1–7.

Adachi, M., & Trehub, S. E. (1998). Children's expression of emotion in song. *Psychology of Music, 26,* 133–153.

Allen, M. A. (1996). The role of music and rhyme in emergent literacy: Teacher perspectives (Doctoral dissertation, University of Texas, Austin, 1996). *Dissertation Abstracts International, 57*(6A), 2413.

Amabile, T. M. (1989). *The social psychology of creativity.* New York: Springer-Verlag.

Ames, C. (1992) Classrooms: Goals, structures, and student motivation. *Journal of Educational Psychology, 84*(3), 261–271.

Andress, B. (1998). *Music for young children.* Fort Worth, TX: Harcourt Brace.

Aries, P. (1962). *Centuries of childhood.* New York: Knopf.

Barrett, M. (1998). Children composing: A view of aesthetic decision making. In B. Sundin, G. E. McPherson, & G. Folkestad (Eds.), *Musikpedagogik: Children composing* (pp. 57–81). Malmo, Sweden: Lunds University.

Bereiter, C., & Englemann, S. (1966). *Teaching disadvantaged children in the preschool.* Englewood Cliffs, NJ: Prentice-Hall.

Bergan, J., & Feld, J. (1993). Developmental assessments: New directions. *Young Children, 48*(5), 41–47.

Bergen, D. (1997). Using observational techniques for evaluating children's learning. In B. Spodek & O. Saracho (Eds.), *Issues in early childhood educational evaluation and assessment* (pp. 108–128). New York: Teachers College Press.

Berk, L. (1994). Vygotsky's theory: The importance of make-believe play. *Young Children, 50*(1), 30–39.

Berk, L., & Winsler, A. (1995). *Scaffolding children's learning: Vygotsky and early childhood education.* Washington, DC: National Association for the Education of Young Children.

Block, M. (1992). Critical perspectives on the historical relationship between child development and early childhood education research. In S. Kessler & B. Swadener (Eds.), *Reconceptualizing the early childhood curriculum* (pp. 3–20). New York: Teachers College Press.

Bowman, B. (1994). The challenge of diversity. *Phi Delta Kappan, 76*(3), 218–224.

Brand, E. (2000). Children's mental musical organizations as highlighted by their singing errors. *Psychology of Music, 28,* 62–80.

Bredekamp, S. (1987). *Developmental appropriate practice in early childhood programs serving children birth to age 8* (Expanded ed.). Washington, DC: National Association for the Education of Young Children.

Bredekamp, S. (1991). Redeveloping early childhood education: A response to Kessler. *Early Childhood Research Quarterly, 6*(2), 199–209.

Bredekamp, S. (1996). Early childhood education. In J. Sikula (Ed.), *Handbook of research on teacher education* (2nd ed., chap. 16, pp. 323–347). New York: Macmillan.

Bredecamp, S., & Copple, C. (Eds.). (1997). *Developmentally appropriate practice in early childhood programs* (Rev. ed.). Washington, DC: National Association for the Education of Young Children.

Bredecamp, S., & Rosegrant, T. (Eds.). (1992). *Reaching potentials: Appropriate curriculum and assessment for young children: Vol. 1.* Washington, DC: National Association for the Education of Young Children.

Bryant, D. M., Burchinal, M., Lau, L. B., & Sparling, J. J. (1994). Family and classroom correlates of Head Start's developmental outcomes. *Early Childhood Research Quarterly, 9,* 289–309.

Burts, D. C., Hart, C. H., Charlesworth, R., Fleege, P. O., Mosley, J., & Thomasson, R. H. (1992). Observed activities and stress behaviors of children in developmentally appropriate and inappropriate kindergarten classrooms. *Early Childhood Research Quarterly, 7,* 297–318.

Bygrave, P. L. (1994). Development of listening skills in students in special education settings. *International Journal of Disability, Development and Education, 41*(1), 51–60.

Cadwell, L. (1997). *Bringing Reggio Emilia home: An innovative approach to early childhood education.* New York: Teachers College Press.

Caine, J. (1991). The effects of music on the selected stress behaviors, weight, caloric and formula intake, and length of hospital stay of premature and low birth weight neonates in a newborn intensive care unit. *Journal of Music Therapy, 28*(4), 180–182.

Campbell, M. R. (1991). Musical learning and the development of psychological processes in perception and cognition. *Bulletin of the Council of Research in Music Education, 107,* 35–48.

Campbell, P. S. (1991). The child-song genre: A comparison of songs by and for children. *International Journal of Music Education, 17,* 14–23.

Campbell, P. S. (1998). *Songs in their heads: Music and its meaning in children's lives.* New York: Oxford University Press.

Canella, G. S. (1997). *Deconstructing early childhood education: Social justice and revolution.* New York: Lang.

Carlton, E. (2000). Music and movement in High/Scope preschools. *Early Childhood Connections, 6*(2), 16–23.

Chen-Hafteck, L. (1998). Pitch abilities in music and language of Cantonese-speaking children. *International Journal of Music Education, 31,* 14–24.

Childs, G. (1999). *Truth, beauty, and goodness: Steiner-Waldorf education as a demand of our time.* London: Temple Lodge.

Chugani, H. T. (1997). Neuroimaging of developmental non-linearity and developmental pathologies. In R. W. Thatcher, G. R. Lyon, J. Rumsey, & N. Krasnegor (Eds.), *Developmental neuroimaging: Mapping the development of brain and behavior.* San Diego: Academic Press.

Clark, P. C. (1989). A sourcebook of musical experiences for caregivers in daycare centers (Doctoral dissertation, Columbia University Teachers College, 1989). *Dissertation Abstracts International, 52,* 4A.

Cohen, A. J., Thorpe, L. A., & Trehub, S. E. (1987). Infants' perception of musical relations in short transposed tone sequences. *Canadian Journal of Psychology, 41,* 33–47.

Cole, M. (1998). Culture in development. In M. Woodhead, D. Faulkner, & K. Littleton (Eds.), *Cultural worlds of early childhood* (pp. 11–33). London: Open University Press.

Costa-Giomi, E. (1994). Recognition of chord changes by 4- and 5-year-old American and Argentine children. *Journal of Research in Music Education, 42*(1), 68–45.

Costa-Giomi, E. (1996). Mode discrimination abilities of preschool children. *Psychology of Music, 24,* 184–198.

Coulter, D. J. (1996). Defending the magic: Current issues in early childhood education. *Early Childhood Connections, 2*(2), 30–35.

Csikszentmihalyi, M., & Csikszentmihalyi, I. S. (Eds.). (1988). *Optimal experience: Psychological studies of flow in consciousness.* New York: Cambridge University Press.

Custodero, L. A. (1997). An observational study of flow experience in young children's music learning (Doctoral dissertation, University of Southern California, 1997). *Dissertation Abstracts International, 59,* 5A.

Daugherty, M., & Logan, J. (1996). Private speech assessment: A medium for studying the cognitive processes of young creative children. *Early Child Development and Care, 115,* 7–17.

Davidson, L., & Colley, B. (1987). Children's rhythmic development from age 5 to 7: Performance, notation, and reading of rhythmic patterns. In J. C. Peery, I. W. Peery, & T. W. Draper (Eds.), *Music and child development* (pp. 107–136). New York: Springer-Verlag.

Davidson, L., & Scripp, L. (1988). Education and development in music from a cognitive perspective. In C. Hargreaves (Ed.), *Children and the arts* (pp. 59–86). London: Open University Press.

Davis, J., & Gardner, H. (1993). The arts and early childhood education: A cognitive developmental portrait of the young child as an artist. In B. Spodek (Ed.), *Handbook of research on the education of young children* (pp. 191–206). New York: Macmillan.

Davis, R. (1990). A model for the integration of musical therapy within preschool classrooms for children with physical disabilities or language delays. *Music Therapy Perspectives, 8,* 82–84.

Day, B. (1988). What's happening in early childhood programs across the United States? In *Resource guide to public schools early childhood programs* (pp. 3–31). Alexandria, VA: Association for Supervision and Curriculum Development.

Deliege, I., & Sloboda, J. (1996). *Musical beginnings: Origins and development of musical competence.* Oxford: Oxford University Press.

DeVries, R., & Kohlberg, L. (1987). *Constructivist early education: Overview and comparison with other programs.* Washington, DC: National Association for the Education of Young Children.

Diamond, M. C. (1967). Extensive cortical depth measurements and neuron size increases in the cortex of environmentally enriched rats. *Journal of Comparative Neurology, 131,* 357–364.

Domer, J., & Eastlund Gromko, J. (1996). Qualitative changes in preschoolers' invented notations following music instruction. *Contributions to Music Education, 23,* 62–78.

Donich, D. M. (1992). The effects of visual and auditory stimuli on the movement behavior of pre-school children (Master's thesis, Florida State University, 1992). *Masters Abstracts International, 31*(1), 0023.

Doxey, C., & Wright, C. (1990). An exploratory study of children's music ability. *Early Childhood Research Quarterly, 5,* 425–440.

Dunn, L., & Dunn, L. (1981). *Peabody picture vocabulary test–revised.* Circle Pines, MN: American Guidance Service.

Dunne-Sousa, D. (1988). The effect of speech rhythm, melody, and movement on the song identification and performance of preschool children (Doctoral dissertation, Ohio State University, 1988). *Dissertation Abstracts International, 49* (8A), 2140.

Durkin, K., & Townsend, J. (1997). The influence of linguistic factors on young school children's responses to musical pitch tests: A preliminary test. *Psychology of Music, 25*(2), 186–191.

Dweck, C. (1986). Motivational processes affecting learning. *American Psychologist, 41*(10), 1040–1048.

Dweck, C., & Leggett, E. (1988). A social-cognitive approach to motivation and personality. *Psychological Review, 95* (2), 256–273.

Edwards, C., Gandini, L., & Forman, G. (Eds.). (1993). *The hundred languages of children: The Reggio Emilia approach to early childhood education.* Norwood, NJ: Ablex.

Elkind, D. (1994). *Ties that stress: The new family imbalance.* Cambridge: Harvard University Press.

Fassbender, C. (1996). Infants' auditory sensitivity towards acoustic parameters of speech and music. In I. Deliege & J. Sloboda (Eds.), *Musical beginnings: Origins and development of musical competence* (pp. 56–87). Oxford: Oxford University Press.

Feierabend, J. M., & Saunders, T. C. (1998). The relationship between aural and oral musical abilities in first, second, and third grade students. *Early Childhood Connections, 4* (3), 10–18.

Fifer, W. P., & Moon, C. (1989). Psychobiology of newborn auditory preferences. *Seminars in Perinatology, 13,* 430–433.

Flohr, J. W., Miller, D. C., & deBeus, R. (2000). EEG studies with young children. *Music Educators Journal, 87*(2), 28–32.

Forman, G. (1994). Different media, different languages. In L. G. Katz & B. Cesarone (Eds.), *Reflections on the Reggio Emilia approach* (pp. 41–53). Urbana, IL: ERIC.

Fujita, F (1990). The intermediate performance between talking and singing—From an observational study of Japanese children's music activities in nursery school. In J. Dobbs

(Ed.), *Music education: Facing the future; Conference proceedings of the nineteenth ISME World Conference* (pp. 140–146). Christchurch, New Zealand: International Society for Music Education.

Fyk, J. (1995). Musical determinants of melodic contour recognition: Evidence from experimental studies of preschoolers. *Bulletin of the Council for Research in Music Education, 127,* 72–79.

Gallagher, J., & Caché, J. (1987). Hothousing: The clinical and educational concerns over pressuring young children. *Early Childhood Research Quarterly, 2,* 203–210.

Gallas, K. (1991). Arts as epistemology: Enabling children to know what they know. *Harvard Educational Review, 61* (1), 41–50.

Gardner, H. (1982). *Art, mind and brain: A cognitive approach to creativity.* New York: Basic Books.

Gardner, H. (1983). *Frames of mind: The theory of multiple intelligences.* New York: Basic Books.

Gardner, H. (1998). Foreword: Complimentary perspectives on Reggio Emilia. In C. Edwards, L. Gandini, & G. Forman (Eds.), *The hundred languages of children: The Reggio Emilia approach: advanced reflections* (pp. xv–viii). Greenwich, CT: Ablex.

Garren, B. A. (1997). The influence of parental attitudes toward child-rearing and creativity in relation to children's creative functioning (Doctoral dissertation, University of South Carolina, 1997). *Dissertation Abstracts International, 58*(11A), 4180.

Gesell, A. (1940). *The first five years of life.* New York: Harper and Row.

Giomo, C. (1993). Experimental study of children's sensitivity to mood in music. *Psychology of Music, 21*(2), 141–162.

Godeli, M. R., Santana, P. R., Souza, V. H. P., & Marquetti, G. P. (1996). Influence of background music on preschoolers' behavior: A naturalistic approach. *Perceptual and Motor Skills, 82,* 1123–1129.

Goffin, S., Wilson, C., Hill, J., & McAninch, S. (1997). Policies of the early childhood field and its public: Seeking to support young children and their families. In J. Eisenberg and M. R. Jalongo (Eds.), *Major trends and issues in early childhood education* (pp. 13–28). New York: Teachers College Press.

Goffin, S. G. (1993). *Curriculum models and early childhood education: Appraising the relationship.* New York: Merrill.

Goleman, D. (1995). *Emotional intelligence: Why it can matter more than IQ.* New York: Bantam Books.

Goodman, N. (1976). *The languages of art.* Indianapolis: Hackett.

Gopnik, A., Meltzoff, A. N., & Kuhl, P. K. (1999). *The scientist in the crib.* New York: Morrow.

Gordon, E. E. (1979). *Primary measures of music audiation.* Chicago: GIA.

Gordon, E. E. (1997a). *A music learning theory for newborn and young children.* Chicago: GIA.

Gordon, E. E. (1997b). *Study guide for learning sequences in music.* Chicago: GIA.

Gordon, E. E. (2000). Contemplating objective research in music education. *Early Childhood Connections, 6*(1), 30–36.

Gordon, E. E., & Woods, D. G. (1985). *Jump right in.* Chicago: GIA.

Gouzouasis, P. (1993). Music audiation: A comparison of music abilities of kindergarten children of various ethnic backgrounds. *Quarterly Journal of Music Teaching and Learning, 4*(2), 70–76.

Graue, E., & Walsh, D. (1998). *Studying children in context: Theories, methods, and ethics.* Thousand Oaks, CA: Sage.

Green, G. (1990). The effect of vocal modeling on pitch-matching accuracy of elementary school children. *Journal of Research in Music Education, 38*(3), 225–231.

Greenspan, S. I., & Benderly, B. L. (1997). *The growth of the mind and the endangered origins of intelligence.* New York: Addison-Wesley.

Gromko, J. E., & Poorman, A. S. (1998). The effect of music training on preschoolers' spatial-temporal task performance. *Journal of Research in Music Education, 46*(2), 173–181.

Gullo, D. (1997). Assessing student learning through the analysis of pupil products. In C. Spodek & O. Saracho (Eds.), *Issues in early childhood educational assessment and evaluation* (pp. 129–148). New York: Teachers College Press.

Gunn, M. (1996). Meeting their needs: Developmentally appropriate music for young children. *The Orff Echo, 28*(3), 10–12.

Gunsberg, A. (1988). Improvised musical play: A strategy for fostering social play between developmentally delayed and nondelayed preschool children. *Journal of Music Therapy, 25,* 178–191.

Hallquist, M. (1995). Maria Montessori: Glossary of terms and ideas. *Early Childhood Connections, 1*(3), 26–37.

Hannaford, C. (1995). *Smart moves: Why learning is not all in your head.* Arlington, VA: Great Ocean.

Hargreaves, D. J. (1986). *The developmental psychology of music.* New York: Cambridge University Press.

Hatch, A. (1990). Young children as informants in classroom studies. *Early Childhood Research Quarterly, 5,* 251–264.

Healey, J. M. (1990). *Endangered minds.* New York: Simon and Schuster.

Heath, S. B. (1983). *Ways with words: Language, life, and work in communities and classrooms.* New York: Cambridge University Press.

Henderson, K. (2000). *Illinois early learning standards* (Draft). Springfield, IL: Illinois State Board of Education.

Hetland, L. (2000a). Learning to make music enhances spatial reasoning. In E. Winner & L. Hetland (Eds.), *Journal of Aesthetic Education, 34*(3, 4), 179–238.

Hetland, L. (2000b). Listening to music enhances spatial-temporal reasoning: Evidence for the "Mozart Effect." In E. Winner & L. Hetland (Eds.), *Journal of Aesthetic Education, 34*(3, 4), 105–148.

Heyge, L., & Sillick, A. (1997). When is the right time? Montessori and the season for writing and reading. *Early Childhood Connections, 3*(4), 13–20.

Hicks, W. K. (1993). An investigation of the initial stages of preparatory audiation (music audiation, young children) (Doctoral dissertation, Temple University, 1993). *Dissertation Abstracts International, 54*(4A), 1277.

Hills, T. (1987). Children in the fast lane. *Early Childhood Research Quarterly, 2*, 265–273.

Hills, T. (1993). Assessment in context: Teachers and children at work. *Young Children, 48*(5), 20–28.

Hirsh-Pasek, K., Nelson, D. G., Jusczyk, P. W., Cassidy, K. W., Druss, B., & Kennedy, L. (1987). Clauses are perceptual units for young infants. *Cognition, 26*, 269–286.

Hodges, D. A. (Ed.). (1996). Neuromusical research: A review of the literature In *Handbook of music psychology* (pp. 197–284). San Antonio, TX: IMR Press.

Hodges, D. A. (2000). Implications of music and brain research. *Music Educators Journal, 87*(2), 17–22.

Hornyak, I. (1996). America: A culture at risk. *Early Childhood Connections, 2*(3), 30–37.

Howe, M. J., Davidson, J. W., Moore, J. G., & Sloboda, J. (1995). Are there early childhood signs of musical ability? *Psychology of Music, 23*, 162–176.

Huffman, L., & Speer, P. (2000). Academic performance among at-risk children: The role of developmentally appropriate practice. *Early Childhood Research Quarterly, 15*(2), 167–184.

Humpal, M. (1991). The effects of an integrated early childhood music program on social interaction among children with handicaps and their typical peers. *Journal of Music Therapy, 28*(3), 161–177.

Huttenlocher, P. R. (1984). Synapse elimination and plasticity in developing human cerebral cortex. *American Journal of Mental Deficiency, 88*, 488–496.

Isenberg, J., & Brown, D. L. (1997). Development issues affecting children. In J. Isenberg & M. R. Jalongo (Eds.), *Major trends and issues in early childhood education* (pp. 29–42). New York: Teachers College Press.

Isenberg, J., & Jalongo, M. R. (1997). *Major trends and issues in early childhood education.* New York: Columbia University.

Jellison, J., Brooks, B., & Huck, A. (1984). Structuring small groups and music reinforcement to facilitate positive interactions and acceptance of severely handicapped students in the regular music classroom. *Journal of Research in Music Education, 32*, 243–264.

Jensen, E. (1998). *Teaching with the brain in mind.* Alexandria, VA: Association for Supervision and Curriculum Development.

Jordan-DeCarbo, J. A. (1999). Early childhood music education: The professional landscape. In *National Association of Schools of Music proceedings: The seventy-fourth annual meeting 1998, 87*, 13–21. Reston, VA: National Association of Schools of Music.

Jordan-DeCarbo, J. A., & Galliford, J. (2001). The effects of a sequential music program on the motor, cognitive, expressive language, social/emotional, and musical movement abilities of preschool disadvantaged children. *Early Childhood Connections, 7*(3), 30–42.

Juslin, P. N. (1997). Emotional communication in music performance: A functionalist perspective and some data. *Music Perception, 14*(4), 383–418.

Juul, K., & Maier, M. (1992). Teacher training in curative education. *Teacher Education and Special Education, 15*(3), 211–218.

Kalmar, M. (1989). The effects of music education on the acquisition of some attribute-concepts in preschool children. *Canadian Journal of Research in Music Education, 30*, 51–59.

Kamii, C., & Ewing, J. K. (1996). Basing teaching on Piaget's constructivism. *Childhood Education, 72*(5), 261–264.

Katz, L. G. (Ed.). (1977). Early childhood programs and ideological disputes. In *Talks with teachers* (pp. 69–74). Washington, DC.: National Association for the Education of Young Children.

Katz, L. G. (1994). Images from the world. In L. G. Katz & B. Cecarone (Eds.), *Reflections on the Reggio Emilia approach* (pp. 1–17). Urbana, IL: ERIC.

Katz, L. G. (1995). *Talks with teachers of young children.* Norwood, NJ: Ablex.

Katz, L. G., & Cesarone, B. (Eds.). (1994). *Reflections on the Reggio Emilia approach.* Urbana, IL: ERIC.

Katz, L. G., & Chard, S. (1989). *Engaging children's minds: The project approach.* Norwood, NJ: Ablex.

Kelly, L., & Sutton-Smith, B. (1987). A study of infant musical productivity. In J. C. Peery, I. W. Peery, & T. W. Draper (Eds.), *Music and child development* (pp. 35–53). New York: Springer-Verlag.

Kessen, W. (1979). The American child and other cultural inventions. *American Psychologist, 34*(10), 815–820.

Kessen, W., Levine, J., & Wendrick, K. A. (1979). The imitation of pitch in infants. *Infant Behavior and Development, 2*, 93–99.

Kessler, S. (1991). Alternative perspectives on early childhood education. *Early Childhood Research Quarterly, 6*, 183–197.

Kessler, S., & Swadener, B. (1992). *Reconceptualizing the early childhood curriculum: Beginning the dialogue.* New York: Teachers College Press.

Klinger, R., Shehan, P. C., and Goolsby, T. (1998). Approaches to children's song acquisition: Immersion and phrase-by-phrase. *Journal of Research in Music Education, 46*(1), 24–34.

Kranowitz, C. S. (1998). *The out-of-sync child.* New York: Putnam.

Krumhansl, C. L., & Jusczyk, P. W. (1990). Infants' perception of phrase structure in music. *Psychological Science, 1*, 70–73.

Lawton, J. T., & Johnson, A. (1992). Effects of advance organizer instruction on preschool children's learning of musical concepts. *Bulletin of the Council for Research in Music Education, 111*, 35–48.

Lecanuet, J. (1996). Prenatal auditory experience. In I. Deliege and J. Sloboda (Eds.), *Musical beginnings: Origins and development of musical competence* (pp. 3–34). Oxford: Oxford University Press.

Leu, J. C. (1997). An investigation of Taiwanese kindergartners' ability to discriminate musical concepts in listening, singing, and movement (Doctoral dissertation, Columbia University Teachers College, 1997). *Dissertation Abstracts International, 59*(10A), 3768.

Levinowitz, L. M. (1987). An experimental study of the comparative effects of singing songs with words and without words on children in kindergarten and first grade (Doctoral dissertation, Temple University, 1987). *Dissertation Abstracts International, 48* (1987), 863A.

Lorch, C. A., Lorch, V., Diefendorf, A. O., & Earl, P. W. (1994). Effect of stimulative and sedative music on systolic blood pressure, heart rate, and respiratory rate in premature infants. *Journal of Music Therapy, 31*(2), 105–118.

Lubeck, S. (1996). Deconstructing "child development knowledge" and "teacher preparation." *Early Childhood Research Quarterly, 11,* 147–167.

Lynch, M. P., & Eilers, R. E. (1992). A study of perceptual development for musical tuning. *Perception and Psychophysics, 52,* 599–608.

Lynch, M. P., Eilers, R. E., & Bornstein, M. H. (1992). Speech, vision, and music perception: Windows on the ontogeny of mind. *Psychology of Music, 20,* 3–14.

Lynch, M. P., Short, L. B., & Chua, R. (1995). Contributions of experience to the development of musical processing in infancy. *Developmental Psychobiology, 28*(7), 377–398.

Malaguzzi, L. (1993). History, ideas, and basic philosophy. In C. Edwards, L. Gandini, & G. Forman (Eds.), *The hundred languages of children* (pp. 41–89). Norwood, NJ: Ablex.

McCarney, S. B. (1992). *The preschool evaluation scale.* Columbia, MO: Hawthorne Educational Services.

McPherson, G. E. (1998). Creativity and music education: Broader issues—wider perspectives. In B. Sundin, G. E. McPherson, & G. Folkestad, *Musikpedagogik: Children composing* (pp. 135–156). Malmo, Sweden: Lunds University.

Meisels, S. (1993). Remaking classroom assessment with the work sampling system. *Young Children, 48*(3), 34–40.

Meisels, S. (2000). On the side of the child: Personal reflections on testing, teaching, and early childhood education. *Young Children, 55*(6) 16–19.

Meisels, S., Liaw, F., Dorfman, A., & Nelson, R. F. (1995). The work sampling system: Reliability and validity of a performance assessment for young children. *Early Childhood Research Quarterly, 10,* 277–296.

Minami, Y., & Umezawa, Y. (1990). The situation in which a child sings an original song. In J. Dobbs (Ed.), *Music education: Facing the future; conference proceedings of the nineteenth ISME World Conference* (pp. 131–134). Christchurch, New Zealand: International Society for Music Education.

Moore, T. L. E. C. (1990). Perceptions and practices of kindergarten teachers regarding the role of music in the kindergarten curriculum (Doctoral dissertation, Indiana State University, 1990). *Dissertation Abstracts International, 52*(2A), 0421.

Morris, G. M. (1992). Movement as an indication of musical understanding in preschool children (Doctoral dissertation, University of Illinois at Urbana-Champaign, 1992). *Dissertation Abstracts International, 53*(7A), 2286.

Morrongiello, B. (1992). Effects of training on children's perception of music: A review. *Psychology of Music, 20*(1), 29–41.

National Association for the Education of Young Children. (1998). *Guide to accreditation* (rev. ed.). National Academy of Early Childhood Programs. Washington, DC: Author.

National Commission on Testing and Public Policy. (1990). *From gatekeeper to gateway: Transforming testing in America.* Chestnut Hill, MA: Author.

Nelson, D., & Barresi, A. (1989). Children's age-related intellectual strategies for dealing with musical and spatial analogical tasks. *Journal of Research in Music Education, 37*(2), 93–103.

Nelson, D., Barresi, A., & Barrett, J. (1992). Musical cognition within an analogical setting: Toward a cognitive component of musical aptitude in children. *Psychology of Music, 20*(1), 70–79.

Nelson, J. N. (1997). The Reggio Emilia approach: Creativity in a hundred languages. *Early Childhood Connections, 3* (1), 25–29.

New, R. (1994). Reggio Emilia: Its vision and its challenges for educators in the United States. In L. G. Katz & B. Cesarone (Eds.), *Reflections on the Reggio Emilia approach* (pp. 33–40). Urbana, IL: ERIC.

Nordlund, M. L. (1995). *Music problem-solving strategies of five-to seven-year-olds.* Unpublished doctoral dissertation, University of Alabama, Tuscaloosa, 1995.

O'Hagin, I. B. (1997). *The effects of a discovery approach to movement instruction on children's responses to musical stimuli.* Unpublished doctoral dissertation, University of Arizona, Tucson.

O'Neill, S. A., & Sloboda, J. A. (1997). The effects of failure on children's ability to perform a musical test. *Psychology of Music, 25,* 18–34.

Ormond, G., & Miller, L. (1999). Cognitive, musical, and environmental correlates of early music instruction. *Psychology of Music, 27,* 18–37.

Papousek, H. (1996). Musicality in infancy research: Biological and cultural origins of early musicality. In I. Deliege & J. Sloboda (Eds.), *Musical beginnings: Origins and development of musical competence.* Oxford: Oxford University Press.

Papousek, M., Bornstein, M. H., Nuzzo, C., Papousek, H., & Symmes, D. (1990). Infant responses to prototypical melodic contours in parental speech. *Infant Behavior and Development, 13,* 539–545.

Papousek, M., Papousek, H., & Haekel, M. (1987). Didactic admustments in fathers' and mothers' speech to their three-month-old infants. *Journal of Psycholinguistic Research, 16,* 491–516.

Papousek, M., Papousek, H., & Symmes, D. (1991). The meanings of melodies in motherese in tone and stress languages. *Infant Behavior and Development, 14,* 415–440.

Parsons, M. (1992). Cognition as interpretation in art education. In B. Reimer & R. A. Smith (Eds.), *The arts, education, and aesthetic knowing* (pp. 70–91). Chicago: University of Chicago Press.

Peery, J. C., Peery, I. W., & Draper, T. W. (1987). *Music and child development.* New York: Springer-Verlag.

Persellin, C. C. (1992). Responses to rhythm patterns when

presented to children through auditory, visual, and kinesthetic modalities. *Journal of Research in Music Education, 40*(4), 306–315.

Persellin, C. C. (2000). The effect of activity-based music instruction on spatial-temporal task performance of young children. *Early Childhood Connections, 6*(4), 21–29.

Poorman, A. (1996). The emergence of symbol use: Prekindergarten children's representations of musical sound. *Contributions to Music Education, 23,* 31–45.

Prekindergarten music education standards. (1995). Reston, VA: Music Educators National Conference.

Raines, S. (1997). Developmental appropriateness: Curriculum revisited and challenged. In J. Isenberg & M. R. Jalongo (Eds.), *Major trends and issues in early childhood education* (pp. 75–89). New York: Teachers College Press.

Rauscher, F. H. (1996). What educators must learn from science: The case for music in the schools. *Early Childhood Connections, 2,* 17–21.

Rauscher, F. H., Shaw, G. L., & Ky, K. N. (1993). Music and spatial task performance. *Nature, 365,* 611.

Rauscher, F. H., Shaw, G. L., Levine, L. J., Wright, E. L., Dennis, W. R., & Newcomb, R. L. (1997). Music training causes long-term enhancement of preschool children's spatial-temporal reasoning. *Neurological Research, 10,* 2–8.

Rauscher, F., & Zupan, M. (2000). Classroom keyboard instruction improves kindergarten children's spatial-temporal performance: A field experiment. *Early Childhood Research Quarterly, 15*(2), 215–228.

Ray, J. J. (1997). For the love of children: Using the power of music in "English as a second language" program (arts integration) (Doctoral dissertation, University of California at Los Angeles, 1997). *Dissertation Abstracts International, 58*(7A), 2571.

Reinsmith, W. (1989). The whole in every part: Steiner and Waldorf schooling. *The Educational Forum, 54*(1), 78–91.

Reynolds, A. M. (1995). An investigation of the movement responses performed by children 18 months to three years of age and their caregivers to rhythm chants in duple and triple meters (audiation, eighteen-month-old, three-year-old) (Doctoral dissertation, Temple University, 1995), *Dissertation Abstracts International, 56*(4A), 1283.

Ries, N. L. (1987). An analysis of the characteristics of infant-child singing expressions: Replication report. *Canadian Music Educator, 29*(1), 5–20.

Robinson, L. (2000). Music in the Montessori primary classroom: Traditional experiences support a new holistic approach to music education. *Early Childhood Connections, 6*(2), 24–29.

Rogoff, B. (1990). *Apprenticeship in thinking.* New York: Oxford University Press.

Rupp, C. E. (1993). The effects of vocal modeling and melodic direction on development of head voice placement in four-year-old, nonsinging children. *Bulletin of the Council for Research in Music Education, 120,* 84–86.

Sameroff, A., & McDonough, S. (1994). Educational implications of developmental transitions: Revisiting the 5- to 7-year shift. *Phi Delta Kappan, 76*(3), 188–193.

Saracho, O., & Spodek, B. (Eds.). (1997). *Issues in early childhood educational evaluation and assessment.* New York: Teachers College Press.

Sataloff, R. T., & Spiegel, J. R. (1989). The young voice. *NATS Journal, 45*(3), 35–37.

Saunders, T. C., & Baker, D. S. (1991). In-service classroom teachers' perceptions of useful music skills and understandings. *Journal of Research in Music Education, 39*(3), 248–261.

Schellenberg, E. G., & Trehub, S. E. (1994). Frequency rations and the perception of tone patterns. *Psychonomic Bulletin and Review, 1,* 191–201.

Schweinhart, L. (1993). Observing young children in action: The key to early childhood assessment. *Young Children, 48*(5), 29–33.

Schweinhart, L., & Epstein, A. (1997). Curriculum and evaluation in early childhood education. In O. Saracho & B. Spodek (Eds.), *Issues in early childhood educational evaluation and assessment* (pp. 48–59). New York: Teachers College Press.

Schweinhart, L., McNair, S., Barnes, H., & Larner, M. (1993) Observing young children in action to assess their development.: The High/Scope Child Observation Record study. *Educational and Psychological Measurement, 53*(2), 445–455.

Schweinhart, L., & Weikart, D. (1997). The High/Scope preschool curriculum comparison study through age 23. *Early Childhood Research Quarterly, 12*(2), 117–143.

Seifert, K. L. (1993). Cognitive development and early childhood education. In B. Spodek (Ed.), *Handbook of research on the education of young children* (pp. 9–23). New York: Macmillan.

Serafine, M. L. (1983a). Cognition in music. *Cognition, 14,* 119–183.

Serafine, M. L. (1983b). Cognitive processes in music: Discoveries vs. definitions. *Bulletin of the Council for Research in Music Education, 73,* 1–14.

Serafine, M. L. (1988). *Music as cognition: The development of thought in sound.* New York: Columbia University Press.

Shaw, G. (2000). *Keeping Mozart in mind.* San Diego: Academic Press.

Sigel, I. (1970). The distancing hypothesis: A causal hypothesis for the acquisition of representational thought. In M. R. Jones (Ed.), *Miami symposium on the prediction of behavior, 1968, effect of early experiences.* Coral Gables, FL: University of Miami Press.

Sigel, I. (1987). Does hothousing rob children of their childhood? *Early Childhood Research Quarterly, 2,* 211–225.

Sims, W. L. (1988). Movement responses of preschool children, primary grade children, and pre-service classroom teachers to characteristics of musical phrases. *Psychology of Music, 16,* 110–127.

Sims, W. L. (1991). Effects of instruction and task format on preschool children's music concept discrimination. *Journal of Research in Music Education, 39*(4), 298–310.

Sims, W. L. (1995). *Strategies for teaching prekindergarten music.* Reston, VA: Music Educators National Conference.

Sims, W. L., & Cassidy, J. W. (1997). Verbal and operant responses of young children to vocal versus instrumental song performances. *Journal of Research in Music Education, 45*(2), 234–244.

Sloboda, J. A. (1985). *The musical mind: The cognitive psychology of music.* Oxford: Clarendon Press.

Sloboda, J. A. (Ed.). (1988). *Generative processes in music: The psychology of performance, improvisation, and composition.* New York: Oxford University Press.

Smithrim, K. (2000). Music in the Waldorf kindergarten. *Early Childhood Connection, 6*(2), 9–15.

Standley, J. M., & Madsen, C. K. (1990). Comparison of infant preferences and responses to auditory stimuli: Music, mother, and other female voice. *Journal of Music Therapy, 27*(2), 54–97.

Starting points: Meeting the needs of our youngest children. (1994). New York: Carnegie Corporation of New York (www.carnegie.org/starting_points/index.html).

Stefani, G. (1987). A theory of musical competence. *Semiotica, 66,* 7–22.

Steinberg, S., & Kincheloe, J. (1997). Introduction: No more secrets—Kinderculture, information saturation, and the postmodern childhood. In S. Steinberg & J. Kincheloe (Eds.), *The corporate construction of childhood* (pp. 1–30). Boulder, CO: Westview Press.

Stremmel, A. J., & Fu, V. R. (1993). Teaching in the zone of proximal development: Implications for responsive teaching practice. *Child and Youth Care Forum, 22*(5), 337–350.

Sundin, B. (1998). Musical creativity in the first six years: A research project in retrospect. In B. Sundin, G. E. McPherson, & G. Folkestad, *Musikpedagogik: Children composing.* Malmo, Sweden: Lunds University.

Swanwick, K. (1991). Further research on the musical development sequence. *Psychology of Music, 19,* 22–32.

Swanwick, K., & Tillman, J. (1986). The sequence of musical development. *British Journal of Music Education, 3*(3), 305–339.

Sylvester, R. (1995). *A celebration of neurons: An educator's guide to the human brain.* Alexandria, VA: Association for Supervision and Curriculum Development.

Tatem, F. L. (1992). Effects of selected timbres, tasks, grade level, and gender on vocal pitch-matching accuracy of kindergarten through third-grade children. *Bulletin of the Council for Research in Music Education, 114,* 78–80.

Titze, I. (1992). Critical periods of vocal change: Early childhood. *NATS Journal, 49*(2), 16–17.

Trainor, L. J. (1996). Infant preferences for infant-directed versus non-infant-directed play songs and lullabies. *Infant Behavior and Development, 19,* 83–92.

Trainor, L. J., Clark, E. D., Huntley, A., & Adams, B. (1997). The acoustic basis of infant preferences for infant-directed singing. *Infant Behavior and Development, 20,* 383–396.

Trehub, S. E. (1990). The perception of musical patterns by their parents. In W. C. Stebbins & M. Berkley (Eds.), *Comparative perception: Vol. 1. Discrimination* (pp. 429–59). New York: Wiley.

Trehub, S. E., Thorpe, L. A., & Trainor, L. J. (1990). Infants' perception of good and bad melodies. *Psychomusicology, 9,* 5–15.

Trehub, S. E., Unyk, A. M., Kamenetsky, S. B., Hill, D. S., Trainor, L. J., Henderson, J. L., & Saraza, M. (1997). Mothers' and fathers' singing to infants. *Developmental Psychology, 33,* 500–507.

Trevarthen, C. (1998). The child's need to learn a culture. In M. Woodhead, D. Faulkner, & F. Littleton (Eds.), *Cultural worlds of early childhood* (pp. 87–100). London: Open University.

Turner, M. E. (2000). A child-centered music room. *Early Childhood Connections, 6*(2), 30–34.

Umezawa, Y. (1990). Ongakuteki-taiwa to shite no "kyoen": Haha-oya to kodomo no "kyoen" o tegakara ni ["Duet" as a musical dialogue: Based upon the mother-child "duet"]. *Aichikyoiku-daigaku Kenkyu Hokoku (geijutsu hoken-taiiku, kasei, gijutsu-kagaku hen), 39,* 1–15.

Upitis, R. (1987). Children's understanding of rhythm: The relationship between development and music training. *Psychomusicology, 7,* 41–60.

Upitis, R. (1992). *Can I play you my song?* Portsmouth, NH: Heinemann.

Valerio, W. H., Reynolds, A. M., Bolton, B. M., Taggart, C. C., & Gordon, E. E. (1998). *Music Play.* Chicago: GIA.

Vygotsky, L. S. (1962). *Thought and language.* Cambridge, MA: MIT Press.

Vygotsky, L. S. (1978). *Mind in society: The development of higher psychological processes.* Cambridge, MA: Harvard University Press.

Walsh, D., & King, G. (1993). Good research and bad research: Extending Zimiles's criticism. *Early Childhood Research Quarterly, 8*(3), 397–400.

Webster, P. (1987). Conceptual bases for creative thinking in music. In J. C. Peery, I. W. Peery, & T. W. Draper (Eds.), *Music and child development* (pp. 158–174). New York: Springer-Verlag.

Weikart, D. (1996). The High/Scope Perry Preschool Project. *Early Childhood Connections, 2*(3), 20–23.

Weikart, P. (1995). Purposeful movement: Have we overlooked the base? *Early Childhood Connections, 1*(4), 6–15.

Weinberger, N. M. (1998). Brain, behavior, biology, and music: Some research findings and their implications for educational policy. *Arts Education Policy Review, 99*(3), 28–36.

Welch, G., Sergeant, D. C., & White, P. J. (1994). The singing competencies of five-year-old developing singers. In *1994 Fifteenth International Research Seminar in University of Miami, Coral Gables, FL* (pp. 155–62). International Society for Music Education.

Welch, G. F. (1986). A developmental view of children's singing. *British Journal of Music Education, 3,* 295–302.

Werker, J. F., & McLeod, P. J. (1989). Infant preference for both male and female infant-directed talk: A developmental study of attentional and affective responsiveness. *Canadian Journal of Psychology, 43,* 230–246.

Whitaker, N. (1994). Whole language and music education. *Music Educators Journal, 81*(1), 24–28.

White House Conference on Early Childhood Development

and Learning. (1997, April 17). *What new research on the brain tells us about our youngest children.* Retrieved November 28, 2000, from www.naeye.org/public_affairs/policy/4-25-97b.htm

Wilkin, P. E. (1995). Comparison of fetal and newborn responses to music and sound stimuli with and without daily exposure to a specific piece of music. *Bulletin of the Council for Research in Music Education, 127,* 163–169.

Wilson, F. R., & Roehmann, F. L. (Eds.). (1990). *Music and child development.* St. Louis, MO: MMB Music.

Winner, E., & Hetland, L. (Eds.). (2000). The arts and academic achievement: What the evidence shows [Special issue]. *Journal of Aesthetic Education, 34*(3 & 4).

Wittmer, D. S., & Honig, A. S. (1991). Convergent or divergent? Teacher questions to three-year-old children in day care. *Early Childhood Development and Care, 68,* 141–147.

Yarbrough, C., Bowers, J., & Benson, J. (1992). The effect of vibrato on the pitch-matching accuracy of certain and uncertain singers. *Journal of Research in Music Education, 40*(1), 30–38.

Yarbrough, C., Green, G. A., Benson, W., & Bowers, J. (1991). Inaccurate singers: An exploratory study of variables affecting pitch-matching. *Bulletin for the Council for Research in Music Education, 107,* 23–34.

Young, S. (1998) Just making a noise? Reconceptualizing the music-making of 3 and 4-year-olds in a nursery setting. *Early Childhood Connections, 4*(1), 14–22.

Zenatti, A. (1981). *L'Enfant et son environnement musical: Etude expérimentale des mécanismes psychologigues d'assimilation musicale.* Issy-les-Moulineaux, France: Editions scientifiques et psychologiques.

Zenatti, A. (1991). Aesthetic judgements and musical cognition: A comparative study in samples of French and British children and adults. *Psychology of Music, 19,* 65–73.

Zimiles, H. (1993). In search of a realistic research perspectivee: A response to Fein and Walsh and King. *Early Childhood Research Quarterly, 8*(3), 401–405.

Zimmerman, M. P. (1982). Developmental processes in music learning. In R. Colwell (Ed.), *Symposium in music education: A festschrift for Charles Leonhard* (pp. 25–44). Urbana: University of Illinois Press.

Zimmerman, M. P. (1986). Music development in middle childhood: A summary of selected research studies. *Bulletin of the Council for Research in Music Education, 86,* 18–35.

Zimmerman, M. P. (1993). An overview of developmental research in music. *Council for Research in Music Education, 116,* 1–21.

Systematic Research in Studio Instruction in Music

15

RICHARD KENNELL

In his 1985 study *Developing Talent in Young People*, Benjamin Bloom identified one-on-one instruction as a particularly effective instructional context that is found across several disciplines. Results from his study suggested that the private music studio might be a fascinating laboratory for the study of teaching and learning. The importance of this study was that educational researchers began to take notice of this special context, which previously had been considered a deviant educational tradition (Schön, 1983) and outside the bounds of traditional educational research. There is a growing professional interest in applying the tools of systematic research to the context of studio instruction in music education research. Madsen (1985) and Yarbrough (1996) identified the potential of this research area. A special issue of the *Quarterly Journal of Music Teaching and Learning*, edited by Manny Brand (1992), was dedicated to studio instruction. The report of research that follows represents the work of a growing number of individuals who have found studio instruction a compelling area of investigation even though it presents a special research challenge: Within this simple expert-novice dyad is a complex world of human cultural evolution, including the use of language, symbol systems, tools, and many aspects of human psychology.

While our professional practice of teaching music one on one extends from beginning instruction to the most advanced levels of professional study, this review will focus on practices and research dealing with advanced applied instruction such as is found in collegiate music education. The studies included in this review include: (1) topics grounded in interests that relate to the professional community; (2) topics driven by theory, either theory-seeking or theory-evaluating; (3) projects that employ a methodology in gathering data objectively with appropriate controls for researcher bias; and (4) projects designed to add

to our existing body of professional knowledge or to generalize this knowledge to other contexts. While an extensive professional literature exists based on personal musical expertise, it is beyond the scope of this article.

The researcher who studies studio instruction is faced with the immediate challenge of straddling two competing musical communities: the world of the performer and the world of the researcher. In the 19th century, it was easier to identify the participants in these two communities because they existed in separate cultural institutions. Performers were members of the performance culture and resided in separate cultural institutions called conservatories. Conservatories were built on an epistemology of practice, or expertise. In contrast, researchers were members of a totally different institution, the modern research university. University culture was built on the philosophy of positivism, in which the methods of science, for example, observation, could be applied to solve all of humanity's problems. Human phenomena that could not be observed or measured were not worth pursuing (Schön, 1983). Over the past century, however, the modern American research university has included both music practitioners and researchers.

Embedded in the simple phrase "systematic research in studio instruction" is the assumption that members of one community (the empirically based scholar/researcher community) are aiming their powerful research lens on the practices of the other community (the community of performers). This assumption represents both challenge and opportunity, because the implicit goal of conducting systematic research is to show the practitioners, the members of the performance world, how to discern effectiveness, quality, and truth. Consider the vocabulary researchers use to describe the practitioner's knowledge: *anecdotal, experiential, autobiographical*. The practitioners' knowledge is limited. The researchers' knowledge is positive, powerful, and generalizable. As a result, the literature of these two groups varies according to epistemological stance. The literature from the performance tradition consists of biography, personal opinion, and successful experience related prescriptively (Gipson, 1978, p. 30). The testimony of expert teachers, also known as "methods," lies in epistemological contrast with positivistic investigative tools that search for global truths.

Expert-Novice Apprenticeship Models

In a sense, all music instruction can be reduced to the classic dyad of teacher and student. Conductors constantly shift their attention from the entire ensemble to a section and then to an individual performer. In all of these situations, the basic unit of instruction is the expert-novice dyad. Jones (1975) conceives of this dyad as a continuation of the parent-child relationship:

> The one-to-one relationship of the teacher and music student is only duplicated in one's life by the kinship of parent and child. A student often experiences a relationship with his teacher as personal as any in his life and is profoundly influenced musically and otherwise. (p. 46)

Patricia Shehan Campbell (1991) offers a useful view of the dyad by placing this professional practice in a world context:

> The making of a performing musician in the West is the result of events that transpire between student and teacher in the privacy of the studio lesson. For a period of thirty minutes or an hour each week, the student has the undivided personal attention of the teacher. As transmitters of their own musical heritage, teachers shape the musicianship of their students, demonstrating through their own performance the standards for tone quality and technique. They listen to students and respond to their individual needs regarding sound production, phrasing and articulation. They offer ways to improve students' literacy skills including sight reading ability, and define new symbols as they occur in the notated repertoire. They recommend methods of practice, advise means of memorizing a work, and suggest opportunities for the creative expression and interpretation of a piece. Teachers are the musical agents, the models, and the motivating forces for their students. (p. 276)

Campbell locates the study of studio instruction in a specific cultural context, the Western European tradition. She indicates that while other world cultures also employ one-on-one instruction, Western music is an art that is based primarily on literacy and the symbolic representation of ideas and procedures. This is in contrast with other world cultures, whose music is conceived holistically and is transmitted orally. Campbell's conception of studio instruction from a world perspective locates this review of studio instruction in the tradition of Western European art music, a tradition that has evolved within a larger context of human relationships called apprenticeships.

We know that apprenticeships have existed for thousands, perhaps even tens of thousands, of years. Dawkins (1976) attributed the success of the human apprenticeship to three factors: longevity, fecundity, and copy fidelity. In the apprenticeship, the teacher received compensation for his work and was able to engage in the endeavor over long periods of time. As a result, the master was able to interact with many different students and supervise each novice's development over time. The rules required that students did not leave the apprenticeship until the requisite skills were mastered to the satisfaction of the master teacher. Dawkins's view of apprenticeships provides a useful background from which to explore our knowledge of studio instruction in music. "Studio music instruction" is therefore a deceptively simple term that represents an extremely complicated professional practice. A conception of studio instruction must include the elements of teacher knowledge and the rise of expertise, student characteristics and development, and the interactive strategies that ensure faithful replication of these desired capabilities from one generation of musicians to the next.

The Evolution of a Theory of Studio Instruction

Over the years, various members of the music research community have focused their attention on the professional practices of teaching performance through one-on-one instruction. As music educators' conceptions of studio instruction and research tools have changed, so has the focus of systematic investigations.

Efficacy of Private Instruction

Some of the earliest interest in research concerning private music instruction compared the efficacy of private instruction with group instruction. Thompson Brandt (1986) has traced the literature concerned with private and group instruction to the 1930s. Brandt concluded: "These investigations have produced inconclusive and divided results which have failed to suggest which type of instruction appears best suited for individual students" (1986, p. 48). Other comparative studies include Hutcherson (1955), Sims (1961), Waa (1965), Manley (1967), Shugert (1969), Gipson (1978), Keraus (1973), and Seip (1976). Some of these researchers have suggested that a combination of private and group instruction would be better than either one alone, but this hypothesis has not yet been evaluated. Class instruction may offer advantages in the utilization of time and money and may encourage competition, social development, and ensemble performance. Private instruction, however, allows the teacher to focus on every aspect of the individual student's performance (Brandt, 1986, p. 53).

Many researchers were frustrated that this line of investigation failed to reveal conclusive evidence in support of either class or private instruction. Over time, however, we have come to a new conceptualization. Group instruction is not a teaching strategy; it is a teaching context. Likewise, private music teaching is a context and not a strategy. This conceptualization compels the researcher to seek new understandings about the component instructional strategies that teachers might employ in either private or group contexts.

Evaluation of Instruction

Several early studies focusing on the qualities of effective teachers learning (see Grant & Drafall, 1991) led to research intended to provide a more systematic evaluation of teaching. Perhaps the best example of this approach to the study of studio instruction is Hal Abeles's construction of a 30-item scale to evaluate applied music instruction (Abeles, 1975). The Abeles instrument was designed for the special context of studio instruction. The Applied Faculty Student Evaluation scale consisted of statements concerning teacher behaviors in five areas: rapport, instructional systemization, instructional skill, musical knowledge, and general musical competence.

The next investigations were derived from various theoretical conceptualizations about the effectiveness of studio instruction. Rosenthal (1984) conceived of the studio lesson as consisting of three different teaching behaviors: teacher model, teacher verbal guide, or a combination of the teacher's verbal guide plus model. She reported that the model-only strategy was the most effective of these three teaching strategies. Hepler (1986) evaluated teacher field dependence/field independence as an instructional variable: He observed that the lessons of relatively field-dependent teachers evidence more student vocal behavior than the lessons of relatively field-independent teachers.

Two studies focused on aspects of teacher personality in relationship to teaching behaviors. Schmidt (1989) investigated the relationship between applied teacher personality type, as measured by the *Myers-Briggs Type Indicator*, and applied teaching behaviors. He reported that teacher personality variables may be important factors underlying four applied teaching strategies: approvals, rate of reinforcement, teacher model/performance, and pace of instruction (p. 266). Donovan (1994) studied the effect of combinations of teacher personality and student personality as factors influencing student's musical achievement. After using the *Myers-Briggs Type Indicator* instrument to categorize both applied teachers and students, he reported that students with extrovert-type teachers made more progress than those with introvert-type teachers.

Expert-Novice Problem Solving

More recently, research in cognitive psychology has brought renewed attention to the role of expert problem solving. The role of the teacher-as-expert was to actively solve the problems of the student through interaction, and the cognitive processes of teachers are reconstructed or inferred from the observable outcomes. The teacher temporarily supported the student like a scaffold. A brief review of the research on the role of scaffolding in problem solving includes the work of Wood, Bruner, and Ross (1976); Bruner (1985); and Wood, Wood, and Middleton (1978).

Wood, Bruner, and Ross (1976) studied a very common expert-novice teaching-learning context and identified six different strategies that experts employ to support the performance of novices. Wood, Bruner, and Ross studied parents interacting with their infant children. The six basic scaffolding categories they described in 1976 are listed here in a slightly modified form, as appropriate examples of teacher interactions in a music lesson.

Recruitment: synchronizes attention and action between teacher and student. "Let's start at letter B."

Marking Critical Features: highlights existing elements of the task or its execution. "That note is an F♯ not an F♮."

Task Manipulation: Temporarily changes the difficulty of the task to make it easier or more difficult. "Play each note of the melody as whole notes" or "Just clap the rhythm for me."

Demonstration: The teacher offers a model performance (positive or negative) for the student. Teacher plays for the student.

Direction Maintenance: This strategy has a future orientation. It sets a goal for future student performance. "Bring an accompanist with you to your next lesson" or "Let's play this movement in recital class next week."

Frustration Control: Prolongs teacher-student interaction by reducing student frustration. "I know this is section is difficult, just keep trying!"

Two educational researchers articulated different scaffolding theories that might explain and predict teacher choices: Jerome Bruner (1985, pp. 29–30) proposed an order of presentation theory and suggested that teachers always start with demonstration, then manipulate the task, and finally mark critical features until the assigned task was mastered. Wood, Wood, and Middleton (1978, pp. 132–133) advanced a hierarchical rule theory and proposed that the teacher's selection of a scaffolding strategy was based on the simple rule: If the student makes progress, the teacher gets less involved. In observing this rule, demonstration will be followed by task manipulation *or* task manipulation will be followed by marking critical features. The rule continues: If the student does not make progress, the teacher gets more involved. This suggests that task manipulation will be followed by demonstration or marking critical features will be followed by task manipulation.

Kennell (1989) evaluated these existing scaffolding theories as possible theoretical lenses with which to study studio instruction in music. He reported that observations of studio lessons did not seem to follow either of these scaffolding theories. Instead, he formulated a third scaffolding theory, the teacher attribution scaffolding theory. In the attribution scaffolding theory, the teacher's choice of a scaffolding strategy is not based on a prescribed order of intervention strategies or on the simple assessment of student improvement. Instead, the teacher's preferred intervention strategy is based on the teacher's attribution of why the student's performance succeeded or failed. The student's performance results from the match between the requirements of the task and the existing capabilities of the student. Each scaffolding strategy was linked to the teacher's understanding of the student's performance, as shown in table 15.1. Kennell modified previously existing expert-novice theories derived from interactions between parents and their children.

The consideration of context informed a study by Sylvia Gholson (1998). Gholson attempted to generate a more environmentally valid theory of studio music instruction. She conducted a qualitative case study of the renowned string pedagogue Dorothy DeLay, utilizing lesson observations, field notes, audiotapes, and contextual artifacts. From this intense observation, Gholson articulated a theory of proximal positioning. She grouped teacher interventions into two categories of strategies: preparatory and facilitative. Gholson described the development and use of preparatory strategies as precursors to activities of direct instructional intervention. Gholson further described two different types of preparatory strategies, the "get acquainted strategy" and the "superordinate goals of teaching practice." Facilitative strategies include establishing a comfortable lesson atmosphere, magnifying critical features of details of lesson content, the use of metaphor, and focusing on obvious areas of weakness (Gholson, 1998, pp. 539–540).

Methodological Issues

In conducting systematic research in studio instruction, we must start with a theoretical basis for what it is we hope to observe, measure, and describe. Then we must be able to unobtrusively make our observations and convert these into usable data. There are a wide variety of time-sampling observation instruments designed to record specific aspects of teacher and student behavior and instruction progress (Duke & Madsen, 1991; Madsen & Madsen, 1974; Madsen & Yarbrough, 1980). Forms of data have included audio- and videotape recordings. A number of studio instruction studies have relied on the analysis of videotape-recorded lessons. The sampling frame has ranged from

Table 15.1 Teacher Attribution Scaffolding Theory

Pedagogical Context: The Teacher's Attribution of the Problem	If a Conceptual Deficit, the Teacher Employs:	If a Skill Deficit, the Teacher Employs:
A. The teacher knows a deficit condition exists—the student does not yet have this ability or understanding. The teacher must build this understanding or skill.	*Demonstration* to build a new conceptual understanding	*Task Manipulation* to build a new skill capability
B. The teacher knows that the student is familiar with this problem but has not yet attained mastery. The teacher must remind the student of what she already knows.	*Mark a critical feature* using a statement or a gesture to remind the student.	*Mark a critical feature* using a statement or a gesture to remind the student.
C. The teacher does not know what the student's capabilities are. The teacher must assess the student's capabilities before one of the other contexts can be determined. The results of this evaluation will lead to the teacher's attribution of the student-task context (A or B above).	*Mark a critical feature* by asking a question: What does this mean?	*Mark a critical feature* by issuing a command: Play this for me.

From "Three Teacher Scaffolding Strategies in College Applied Music Instruction," by R. Kennell, 1989, unpublished doctoral dissertation, University of Wisconsin–Madison, p. 47.

a single lesson to a semester-long set of weekly lessons. While the presence of video cameras is more common in our everyday environment, we must continue to ask how the presence of recording equipment changes the teaching interactions we intend to study. The consistent recording of every private music lesson between a teacher and student reduces the potential Hawthorne effect, while recording a single lesson increases it.

The documentation and categorization of student and teacher actions and interactions from audio and video data from studio lessons have been done in a variety of ways. A number of recent studies of studio instruction have utilized computer-assisted categorization and measurement strategies. The Simple Computer Recording Interface for Behavioral Evaluation, or SCRIBE (Duke & Farra, 1994), allows the researcher to define observation categories as buttons on the computer screen. While reviewing a videotape, the observer can use a mouse to click on the button that corresponds with the action on the tape. The SCRIBE program automatically calculates durations and frequencies of observations. Several recent studies of studio instruction have employed the SCRIBE software, such as Buckner (1997), Colprit (1998), and Kennell (1998).

Another major problem in the examination of studio music instruction is time: the interval of time and the temporal unit of analysis. Robert Duke (1994) suggests that the "rehearsal frame" is the appropriate unit of analysis in studies of studio instruction interaction. The rehearsal frame begins when the teacher identifies a target performance goal through modeling or verbalization. The frame ends when the teacher identifies a different target performance goal. The construct of the rehearsal frame is useful in focusing on teacher interventions from moment to moment in applied music lessons. At the other extreme, other studies were interested in very large units of analysis. For example, Kennell (1998) was interested in summarizing the interventions of one voice teacher working with one student over an entire semester. This study combined a random interval sampling or "experience sampling" strategy (see Larson & Csikszentmihalyi, 1983) with SCRIBE's capabilities of capturing teacher behavior categorizations. The resulting summary of randomly sampled observations of voice teaching was generalized to the entire population of teacher-student interactions during the semester.

Representative Descriptive Research

Over the years, researchers have employed different research strategies that are appropriate for the questions they frame (see Duke, Prickett, & Jellison, 1998). Descriptive studies have attempted to provide baseline data for many of the professional practices that comprise studio instruction. Estelle Jorgensen (1986) completed in-depth interviews with 15 private piano teachers. She surveyed professional practices in London utilizing 16 professional decisions in four policy areas: administrative decisions, student-related decisions, curricular decisions, and instructional decisions. Perhaps the most extensive study of private piano instruction was completed in 1997 with a sample of 124 teachers and 663 students (Duke, Flowers, & Wolfe, 1997). This broad study offers a useful benchmark on how students allocate their time among competing activities. It also presents the perceptions of teachers, parents, and students regarding the benefits of piano study. Piano study produces perceived benefits among students, teachers, and parents beyond the acquisition of music skills (p. 78).

Other descriptive studies have attempted to quantify teacher and student behaviors in studio lessons. Many of these approaches have employed an observational protocol following the Flanders System of Interaction Analysis (Flanders, 1970). Gipson (1978) developed such an observational system specifically for studio instruction. In this study, he sampled three 30-minute lessons from 3 students working with 3 different applied music teachers over one semester. Gipson reported reliability of intraobserver coefficients of agreement computed on multiple codings of randomly selected lesson tapes throughout the study to range from .75 to .84 (p. 162). Gipson reported, however, that the 37 categories of discrete behavior proved at times to be unwieldy, and he suggested that valid and reliable indices of lesson behavior may be obtainable through random observation of shorter segments of lessons (p. 164). To Gipson, the average lesson consisted primarily of musical behavior, with the student participating actively in the teaching-learning process over 50% of the time (p. 165). Musical behavior is the principal component of the private wind instrument music lesson. Individual teachers, however, vary as to the emphasis placed on certain instructional behaviors (p. 167). He also noted that older students, seniors, and graduate students engaged in more verbal behavior than did the freshmen students, and as the lessons progressed, teacher musical behavior decreased while student musical behavior increased. Finally, teachers used less negative appraisal, and the extended behavior of the student increased (p. 168). Results showed musical behavior to be the dominant behavior of the lessons, with verbal behavior and appraisal maintaining lesser totals. Teacher behavior outnumbered student behavior and shared behavior.

Kostka (1984) sampled 14 minutes (42 20-second intervals from the beginning, middle, and end of audio-recorded private lessons) of instruction from 96 piano lessons (2 students each for 48 studio teachers). She reported that 57% of lessons consisted of student performance and 42% consisted of teacher talk. Younger students received more frequent teacher approvals (54%) than older students and adults (41%).

Hepler (1986) developed a modified version of the Flanders instrument specifically for applied music lessons. His modification, entitled the Observational System for Applied Music (OSAM), included both affective and cognitive aspects of applied instruction (p. 107). Hepler's summary (pp. 310–311) of 20 studio teachers, each teaching 3 students, included:

- Applied music lessons are highly dominated by teacher behavior.
- Applied teacher behavior is highly dominated by vocal behavior.
- Teacher vocal behavior is highly dominated by statements. Questioning represents a small proportion of applied teaching methodology.
- Applied teachers of undergraduate level, non-music-major students emphasize conceptual and technical concerns over expressive concerns.
- Applied teachers spend about three times more time giving positive vocal appraisal than giving negative vocal appraisal.
- Student behavior is dominated by performance in the medium. Very little diversity of student behavior is indicated.
- The students did not contribute their own sustained verbal behavior to the lesson interaction, nor were they observed using notable amounts of body movement or on-task analysis.
- Teacher-student conversations within applied lessons are characterized by short exchanges. The foci of these exchanges vary widely.

A number of more recent studies have identified the pace of instruction as an important factor in studio teaching. Seibenaler (1997) reported that faster pace of instruction was associated with more effective teaching, and Buckner (1997) reported that "the five most successful [applied] teachers had higher rates of directives, information statements, positive and negative feedback, and questions" than less successful teachers in her study. Seibenaler asked an expert panel to evaluate teaching excerpts, 8- to 12-minute segments containing work on a piece in progress from 78 lessons (videotapes of three consecutive lessons with 13 teachers working with 1 adult and 1 child student). Buckner examined 40 piano lessons taught by 20 excellent teachers, each teaching 2 intermediate students. In her study, one segment of 8–12 minutes of teaching was extracted from each lesson videotape. These excerpts were further reduced into "rehearsal frames," units of analysis based on each teacher's specific goals.

L'Hommidieu (1992) conducted three case studies in which selected master teachers were profiled. Teacher effectiveness in his study was attributed to (a) student selection, (b) high level of subject area expertise, (c) intuitively effective management of the quality of instruction varia-

bles, and (d) an extremely high level of consistency in the teacher's characteristic management of the quality of instruction variables. He reported that there was little extant research on the sequence of instruction and goal formulation by master teachers (p. 307).

Kennell (1997) produced written transcripts from videotapes of seven successive 30-minute studio lessons in a study of lesson discourse seeking instances of teacher scaffolding strategies. Scaffolding strategies were considered to be examples of joint problem solving. But Kennell identified a number of teacher behaviors found in these lessons that were self-problem-solving interventions. These strategic behaviors functioned to familiarize the teacher with details concerning the student's specific problems or difficulties. They were informative to the teacher and not directed to the attention of the student.

A unique case study was reported by Ruth Gustafson (1986). Gustafson utilized Freud's theory of *defense mechanisms* in providing a psychoanalytic interpretation of student behaviors as observed in videotapes of lessons with 4 Suzuki violin students working with 4 teachers. She suggests that lesson behaviors for both teachers and students are dominated by the unconscious aims of the lesson participants.

The wide range of sample sizes, forms of data, intervals of sampling, and analytical decisions suggests that descriptive research on studio instruction has included examination of a wide variety of teacher and student actions and involved inference of teacher cognitive strategies from behaviors.

Representative Experimental Research

An influential study of studio instruction was reported by Roseanne Rosenthal (1984). She evaluated the effectiveness of three instructional contexts in college music instruction: a verbal guide only, a model guide only, and a combination of model guide and verbal guide. She reported that the model-guide-only treatment produced the greatest gains in student achievement as measured by the number of correctly performed measures. As a result, many considered Rosenthal's study to suggest that demonstration or modeling was a globally effective teaching strategy.

Kennell (1989) used a similar approach to evaluate aspects of the teacher attribution scaffolding model. He created three experimental treatments based on the instructional scaffolding strategies: a demonstration group, a task manipulation group, and a marking critical features group. The practice-only group served as the control. He ran this experiment three times with three different musical tasks. Each task was selected to produce a unique context of student deficit: Task 1, an easy selection in traditional notation, created no conceptual or skill deficit. Task 2, a simple piece employing graphic notation, created a conceptual deficit but no skill deficit. Task 3, a more challenging selection in traditional notation, created a context of no conceptual deficit but a skill deficit. Kennell's hypothesis was that different teacher scaffolding strategies would be selectively effective, as follows.

Task 1: *Marking critical features* would be most effective in reminding students of capabilities they already had learned.

Task 2: *Demonstration* would be most effective in building new concepts.

Task 3: *Task manipulation* would be most effective in building new skills.

The highest scores of student improvement as measured by the number of correctly performed measures followed this prediction. However, significant differences were identified in both Task 2 and Task 3 (pp. 250–254). The lack of significance associated with Task 1 was attributed to a ceiling effect, due to the students' ability to achieve mastery of the prescribed material in the practice-only control group. These results suggest the effectiveness of a teaching strategy might be dependent on the context of different pedagogical conditions.

The Rosenthal (1984) and Kennell (1989) studies differ in their conceptualization of the basic structure of teacher interaction yet utilize similar experimental designs. Rosenthal sorts teacher strategies into three categories: teacher talk, teacher demonstration, and combined teacher talk and demonstration. Kennell also utilized teacher demonstration as a treatment group, but he separated "teacher talk" into two functional categories: marking critical features and task manipulation.

The scarcity of experimental studies dealing with the instructional techniques of studio instruction demonstrates that our understanding of studio music instruction is in its infancy. Through these early investigations, we can glimpse the complexity of the teaching and learning process that is revealed by intensive study of the important context of one-on-one instruction.

The Studio Instruction System

Studio instruction is a cultural system interlocking with other cultural systems, including school music instruction, university music training, and the world of professional performance. Understanding this system involves studying our artifacts, the procedures for manipulating these artifacts, and the strategies we employ to teach others how to benefit from them. This section describes four component parts of the studio instructional system and identifies representative research for each: the novice, musical artifacts, teacher knowledge, and lesson interactions.

The Novice

Researchers are interested in the intellectual, physical, technical, and communicative skills of the novice student involved in a dyad. Fundamental skills in technical ability and communication are expected for the dyad to function properly (Olsson, 1997, p. 113).

While the lesson involves periodic interaction between the teacher and the student, student progress is facilitated by individual practice that occurs between lesson meetings. It is expected that students will practice assignments on their own from one lesson meeting to the next, and the frequency and duration of the practice sessions may have an impact of instruction and achievement. It is expected that between lessons the student has access to appropriate means to practice the weekly assignments.

Various practice strategies have been the focus of investigations. Ross (1985) and Coffman (1990) experimentally evaluated the comparative effectiveness of mental and physical practice. Their results suggest that combinations of mental and physical practice can shorten the time needed to reach a performance goal. Descriptive studies have also contributed to our understanding of practice. Barry and McArthur (1994) surveyed teacher knowledge and attitudes concerning practice. Geringer and Kostka (1984) directly observed actual student practice behaviors, while Hamann, Lucas, McAllister, and Teachout (1998) propose that student satisfaction derived from the practice experience is important to student persistence.

Depending on when lessons start, studio instruction may coincide with different stages in human development. Task appropriateness and instructional technique, therefore, may be dependent on the student's developmental stage. The study of pedagogy in universities today largely consists of the matching of musical repertoire/methods and/or instructional strategies to developmentally specific student stages: beginner, intermediate, and advanced (see Hargreaves, 1989; Zimmerman, 1993). Important student characteristics include goals, motivation, flexibility, and quickness. As a result of these qualities, in interaction with their teachers, some students will decide to separate themselves from the lesson and seek another teacher. The conditions that produce lesson breakdown have not yet been studied.

Musical Artifacts

Music lessons in the Western European art music tradition typically involve the study of music literature, or artifacts, appropriate for a specific instrument. Etudes are composed works intended to focus on various musical elements, such as technique or interpretation. Solos are complete cultural artifacts composed with the potential or intention of public performance. Each artifact offers a set of technical and stylistic opportunities that must be realized in order to display the desired level of mastery. Musical tasks are typically studied over several lessons. Some tasks, etudes for example, may take only 1 week of practice to achieve the teacher's desired level of mastery, while larger works will typically require several consecutive weeks of study. Most Western European musical artifacts represent the composer's musical ideas through symbolic notation. It is therefore the task of the applied music teacher to teach both the instructions represented in the notation as well as the production techniques specific to the instrument. A notable exception might be instruction in jazz as an oral art form. We currently, however, do not have systematic studies that compare the instructional strategies of these different traditions, for example, jazz lessons with classical lessons.

Some lesson material may not be notated but is described orally by the teacher. Examples include scales, vocalises, drills, and improvisations that teachers may request/require of the student at various points in the lesson. Moments in the music lesson interaction that depart from the study of the printed music may contain cultural procedures or lesson practices of interest to the researcher.

The lesson includes the use of musical tools, or instruments. The student brings an instrument to the lesson or uses one provided by the teacher. In the case of voice, the "instrument" is an approach to the use of the voice that is significantly different from that of normal speech. The instrument is an invented cultural device that offers certain advantages such as greater range, loudness, accuracy, or distinctive tone quality.

In the studio, the teacher's tools are carefully arranged to facilitate learning in a unique setting that may be considered an instructional laboratory. The studio includes the various technologies the teacher might employ in the process of instruction: a piano, a library of music, a metronome, a tape or video recorder, collections of music, a desk, telephone, and computer. Around the studio are typically found personal artifacts that reflect the expert teacher's former students or her professional history: photographs, posters, awards, certificates, and diplomas. This is a space dedicated to one purpose, teaching music one on one. The specific arrangement and configuration of tools in the learning environment is called a "constellation" (Keller & Keller, 1996). How the arrangement of the learning environment facilitates learning has not been studied.

Teacher Expertise

The teacher's expertise includes both experience in performance on a specific instrument and instructional expertise.

The applied teacher's knowledge includes experience beyond the classroom. The teacher's knowledge of the professional world, "an insider's knowledge that came from decades of performing with the best ensembles and under the world's great conductors" (L'Hommidieu, 1992, p. 299), is an important part of the teacher's knowledge base in meeting expectations of advanced students.

The expert has the responsibility of expanding or increasing the capabilities of the novice during the time that they work together, a process that involves acquisition of important information about the specific student and comparison of that information with previous teaching experience. The teacher projects a trajectory of satisfactory progress for the student by setting goals from one lesson to the next. There is a stated assignment or set of expectations that the student will meet by the next lesson through individual and independent practice based on high expectations for the student. To facilitate optimum student progress, the teacher selects repertoire that will not be too easy or too difficult for the specific student. Experienced teachers also acquire an understanding of the process of instruction. For example, mastery is not achieved on the first time through (L'Hommidieu, 1992, p. 303).

The professional practice of studio teachers includes many examples of decision-making. These include: what to assign, what to attend to, how to promote change, when to advance, and when to repeat. Such questions demonstrate the cognitive dimension to the teacher's participation in the lesson. Some teachers allow their students to help choose works they would like to study. Through lesson interactions, the teacher helps the student solve the various performance problems represented in the work, then assigns the student specific sections or details to practice on his own during the week. Elements of teacher decision-making direct the flow of the typical lesson. There is an expectation of reasonable progress from one studio lesson to the next. Students whose progress does not meet the teacher's expectations may be dropped from the private lesson schedule and replaced with other students. Again, how such breakdown occurs in contemporary music institutions has not yet been studied formally.

Within a given lesson, the in-flight decision making of the expert teacher has been linked to the aspect of timing (Duke, Prickett, & Jellison, 1998). Duke et al. suggested that "the mean duration of each activity episode (i.e. student performance or teacher verbalization) and the corresponding rates of alternation between teacher and student activities," what is commonly referred to as pacing, was an important factor (p. 268). L'Hommidieu (1992) suggests that teacher experience, the quality of instruction, and the effectiveness of the teacher's work are related to effectiveness with educational process variables, as seen in this excerpt from a case study.

He provided clear instructional cues in a manner and style that was appropriate for both the student and the instructional goal. He also provided reinforcement to individual students at appropriate intervals and in a way that provided informational feedback and the necessary boost to student motivation. Finally, he was extraordinarily effective and doggedly persistent in diagnosing problems and formulating instructional correctives for remediation of the problem. (p. 301)

The master teacher offers consistency in her approach to the lesson. This aspect of studio instruction applies to both teacher and student, as seen in this quotation from the student of a master teacher: "It was characteristic of this teacher that his personal interactions with students, his instructional interactions, his standards of preparation and performance, and the level of musical and technical detail remained virtually invariant from lesson to lesson" (p. 302). Teachers in a community of musicians will exhibit different levels of effectiveness: "There is a small number of unusually effective studio teachers (i.e. master teachers) with the subject area expertise and pedagogical skill to stimulate the highest levels of accomplishment in exceptionally talented students" (p. 8). Because of its one-on-one context, there is an expectation that any given studio music teacher has a finite and limited number of possible students at any given time. This reality may add the element of competition for openings among well-known and highly respected teachers.

Lesson Interactions

The applied music studio is simultaneously a location in which teaching takes place and a community of students working with one studio teacher. While lessons are taught individually, the studio is a community of selected students who share one teacher, who has actively decided who will be allowed to study and for how long (L'Hommidieu, 1992). Through this teacher they may come to share common expectations, experiences, and values. The lesson assumes that there is a common objective or goal, something in common that brings these individuals together. The intent is for the expert to pass along some specific capability to the novice.

The lesson includes important dimensions of time. Lessons are discrete units of time in which the expert and the novice interact. There is a starting and stopping point to each lesson. The typical duration and frequency of applied music lessons in the United States is 60 minutes, once a week (Campbell, 1991, p. 277). But some applied music teachers offer variants of this: two 30-minute lessons per week or lessons on demand (Kafer & Kennell, 1999). The succession of weekly lessons typically produces a long period of study. The duration of applied music study can be several years. It is common for the expert and novice to work together for more than just a semester or a year. The length of study shared between an expert and novice musician is an important characteristic of this mode of instruction. The professional practice of teaching music one on one frequently produces powerful relationships between teacher and student similar to parent-child relationships. It is not uncommon for the teacher to continue professional and personal relationships with former students after the apprenticeship period has concluded (Jones, 1975). Dysfunctional teacher-student relationships exist in anecdotes but have not been studied formally.

Teacher interventions over a succession of lessons do change: teacher musical behavior decreases, and teacher negative appraisal decreases (Gipson, 1978, p. 168). The length of student musical behaviors increases, thus showing the increasing mastery of the task by the student and further independence from the teacher in the performance of the task.

Discourse. The lesson involves a particular use of social language, a unique teacher-student discourse. These interactions employ the use of special professional language, both verbal and gestural. While the teacher directs this discourse, the student is also a full participant in the social exchange. As revealed by a number of descriptive studies of applied music lessons, most frequently teachers talk and students respond through performance. We assume that these interactions are systematic, even though they may possibly be unconscious, and thus can be observed and analyzed (L'Hommidieu, 1992, p. 9). The use of language to represent a multidimensional phenomenon such as music is problematic. What are the limits of language as a linear means of communication in representing the simultaneities involved with music? Is it possible that our atomistic approach to studying music is an accommodation to our use of language?

The teacher discourse in the studio lesson appears to be spontaneous. The prelesson production of elaborate teaching plans is not typically a part of the studio lesson tradition. Furthermore, the teacher's comments are directed to one specific student in studio instruction. In contrast, the master class represents a different social context. While related to the studio lesson, the master class directs the teacher's comments to the benefit of an audience as well as the individual student. By observing the teacher-student discourse in studio instruction, the structure of the music lesson is revealed. A music lesson is not one interaction; it consists of a succession of subcomponents the nature of which continues to be a major focus of investigation in studio teaching (Kennell, 2000).

Memory.   The cultural practice of performing music from memory has received a great deal of attention over the years. Grace Rubin-Rabson evaluated the effectiveness of different strategies for memorizing piano music: analytic pre-study (1937), hands alone versus hands together (1939), distributed versus massed practice time (1940a), and the whole-versus-part approach (1940b). These studies are the foundation for our professional knowledge of memorization of piano music. More recently, Schlaback (1974) revisited these issues and reported that "the ability to benefit from specific memorization methods depends on particular skills and talents" (p. 228). Each method has its advantages according to the subject's skills. Even more recently, Jones (1990) attempted to explore the discrepancies between the work of Rubin-Rabson and of Schlaback. Jones criticized previous research studies that had separated memory for piano music into four parts (visual, aural, intellectual, and kinesthetic). To him, "this is an artificial separation, since all of these are combined. . . . [T]hey are inexplicably intertwined during any performance, and so must be measured as a single skill" (p. 106). Williamson (1999) reported benefits from memorization: (a) performing from memory was superior to playing from the score, (b) the visibility of the performer positively influenced audiences' ratings of performances, (c) the extra time spent preparing for memorized performances was beneficial, and (d) musicians seemed biased in favor of performances without a music stand.

Evaluation.   Within our social music institutions, we find occasions to rate, compare, and rank students' efforts. These occasions include juries, auditions, and competitions offering members of the musical community an opportunity to compare student achievement within the same studio as well as across different studios, or schools. There is a social expectation that music students will publicly display their mastery of their musicianship in a public recital, master class, or other suitable event. There is an associated professional teacher decision that allows students who have reached a desired level to proceed with the public display of their mastery.

In the studio instruction system, the recital serves multiple purposes. It brings the composer's musical ideas to life for the audience. The occasion of a public appearance motivates the students to practice, and the teacher's success in promoting student achievement is on public display. Future music students and their parents may be introduced to the benefits of private music through attendance at a public recital or concert. Some students exhibit inordinate fear of performing in public. Performance anxiety detracts from the student's ability to perform and is an increasing area of study (Hamann, 1982; Lehrer, 1987).

Our professional knowledge of the studio instructional system is complex. In addition to our knowledge of the student, our knowledge of our musical artifacts, and our knowledge of teacher expertise, we also must understand how these system components interact in time and are mediated by the studio teacher in the context of the lesson.

Summary

The music apprenticeship serves as a crucible for teaching music to each new generation of students. A crucible is a durable vessel with finite dimensions, just as the lesson is defined by a fixed duration. Into the crucible, separate ingredients are added. In studio lessons, these ingredients include the teacher, the student, and various cultural artifacts. These artifacts include language, our musical literature, our musical tools (instruments), and our accepted procedures for employing all of these. In this conception of the studio lesson as a crucible, different ingredients combine to produce a desired change. The student is the object of that change. It is interesting to consider that as in a chemical change, external means such as heat or pressure might be employed to promote the permanence of these changes. The cultural tools of language, literature, and instructional process become the means for stimulating change.

The metaphor of the crucible enables us to conclude that the lesson as time interval or special location may promote or facilitate change but may not by itself produce change in the student. It is the experience of interacting with musical artifacts under the guidance of the teacher within the lesson that actually produces desired change in the student. Today, human interaction is perhaps the most crucial aspect of studio instruction that attracts the attention of music researchers. For hundreds of years, music practitioners have successfully passed along the cultural practices of performing and teaching to each new generation. The music studio offers the music researcher an opportunity to study the process of interaction between teacher and student with little distraction. As researcher, one has an opportunity to collaborate with the world of the performer/practitioner. This world is full of exciting, potential research questions: What is the best composition to assign to this student? When is the best time to teach? What is best pace to deliver instruction? What is the best way to teach this specific student? Is the student's progress satisfactory? How much responsibility should I allow the student? What can I do to help facilitate learning? What is the role of sight reading, rote learning, and scaffolding in relation to particular artifacts or task structures? These questions generated from the literature on collegiate studio experiences may also have applicability to younger students, and there may be important links to the development of expertise not only in the student but also in the studio teacher.

These are important questions that are central to music-making and music teaching, yet there is relatively little extant research on the dyad relationship in music. The lack of research is problematic if we purport to link instruction to a comprehensive theoretical base. Practitioners face these questions and answer them from moment to moment drawing on their own experience. This is the spontaneous application of personal professional knowledge to assist others that Donald Schön identified and referred to as "reflection in action" (Schön, 1983). It is important to understand how this professional knowledge is created and how this professional practice works. Studio instruction in music offers a convenient albeit problematic laboratory to study reflection in action.

There are several developments supporting increasing professional interest in studio music instruction as a research area:

- *The focus on culture.* The growing acceptance of qualitative research methods has allowed researchers to focus on rich detail as a balance to quantitative studies that generalize to larger populations. New research methods have emerged from the study of cultures and may be more appropriate for the study of the complex context of the music studio.
- *Analytical tools.* The wide use of the microcomputer to assist in data collection and analysis has facilitated the conversion of observations into useful, manageable, and accessible data.
- *Interest in human cognition.* Increased efforts to understand human problem solving take advantage of naturalistic settings and situations. The study of music as cognition connects researchers' professional practices with the wider field of educational inquiry. Teaching in the music studio offers an ideal laboratory to study expert problem solving.

There are considerable difficulties to be addressed. The paradigmatic conflict that exists between the research community and the performance community continues to be a barrier to future research efforts, because practitioners in studio teaching simply do not trust or value knowledge generated from systematic research. As Kuhn suggests, the opportunity to pursue these questions through a variety of methodologies is supported by the lack of a dominant theoretical view in the research community (Kuhn, 1962).

The private context of studio lessons raises two methodological questions: How can we study one-on-one instruction in music in such a way that our observations do not change the phenomenon itself? And does our existing knowledge of studio instruction allow us to be unbiased observers? Does previous extensive experience in studio instruction blind music professionals to important aspects of their professional practice?

There is great potential for future investigations. We need to understand the basic components of the music lesson in greater detail. How does the music teacher use language to promote change in student thinking and behavior? Why do teachers talk more often than they offer demonstrations in lessons? What tools are in the pedagogical toolbox? How do teachers use them and where did they come from? From future studies of one-on-one instruction we may learn more about human attention and how experts manipulate the novice's attention from holistic to atomistic human perceptions. In turn, we may learn more about how to teach students to listen. From a basic theoretical understanding of the dynamics of teacher-student lesson interactions, we can design new descriptive studies to contrast and compare different music teachers, across performance media as well as within a medium. So far, our knowledge is very specific. We are unable to describe the professional practices of "the typical studio teacher." There is excellent potential to conduct large-scale descriptive studies of applied teachers.

As we compare the pedagogy of Western music with other world cultures, we may learn more about the benefits as well as the costs of literacy in human society. Contrasting the professional practices of oral cultures and literate cultures, as Michael Bakan (1991) suggests, may help us to expand the orality of music and improve the applied music experience.

We need to consider the possibility that the effectiveness of any teaching strategy may be relative, dependent on relationships among multiple variables. We need to learn more about the mental comparisons embedded in the processes of making assignments, arriving at diagnoses, employing prescriptive interventions, and making professional judgments.

We need to explore the interface between the human artifact and the human being. Music lesson interaction is a four-way conversation among the student, the musical artifact, the instrumental artifact, and the teacher. We need to better understand how language mediates this conversation.

Future research into studio instruction must accommodate the musical dimension as well as the mechanical dimensions. After all, we ultimately teach more than correct notes and fingerings. We teach students to express complex musical ideas. How do teacher lesson interventions promote the acquisition of musicality? And how do master teachers go beyond the limitations of language to express the subtleties of musical expression?

We have an opportunity to view pedagogy in a historical if not anthropological context. Jones (1990) suggests that "the methodology of teaching piano may have changed enough over the last half-century that the pianists used in the early study may have had very different approaches to studying music" (p. 108). This notion raises the possibility that pedagogies change over time. What are the historical origins of our teaching strategies? Are they specific to the study of music, or can they be traced to broader, more universal aspects of human cultural evolution, such as parenting?

The study of studio instruction forces us to consider our knowledge as being socially situated. We may need to consider that the unit of cultural replication is the community of musicians rather than the individual musician. Hargreaves and North (1999) challenge us to rethink our research in studio instruction. Moving our research focus from the individual to the social dyad "forces us to acknowledge that the study of musical behaviour and experience is an interdisciplinary enterprise which must necessarily draw upon theories, insights, perspectives of other disciplines, and this crossfertilization can only serve to promote its healthy development" (p. 80). This observation has implications for the professional preparation of future music researchers. Other interdisciplinary approaches to the study of human culture exist. The evolution of Soviet psychology was founded on social interaction rather than individual trait psychology. More recently, Soviet activity theory draws on interdisciplinary application of anthropology, psychology, and sociology in the study of human culture (see Leonti'ev, 1981; Engstrom, 1999) and may represent potentially useful approaches for future research into studio instruction as a cultural system. A future research agenda that employs a methodology appropriate to the study of human culture may provide a bridge between the empirical researcher and the music practitioner. By documenting the professional knowledge of studio music teachers, we will learn more about how professional knowledge is applied in practical contexts.

We also need to adjust our thinking. Rather than looking for deficits within the professional practice of performance teachers, we might seek to explain why this professional practice works so well. For example, many studio teachers comment on the aesthetics of private lessons. How do lesson interactions employ or produce human emotions? How do teachers manipulate student emotions to promote learning in the studio? And how is teacher personality revealed through the discourse of the studio lesson?

We may even want to reconsider the role of the lesson itself. Is the lesson more than a static crucible that facilitates teaching? We might consider the possibility that studio lesson interventions function like miniature single case research studies. Each teacher intervention tests an unstated hypothesis. Accumulated results from such informal single case research studies may constitute a source of new knowledge for the practitioner. The studio instruction system might offer an epistemology of practice that now exists alongside the dominant positivistic paradigm, empiricism.

There is a growing discussion in higher education today concerning the high costs of studio instruction. As we expand our understanding of studio instruction as a cultural system, we will have the opportunity to join this discussion with new information. We may be able to counter concerns about the high cost of studio instruction with new details about the unique benefits derived from one-on-one instruction.

There are also indications that members of the performance tradition are seeking a more systematic approach. For decades, performance faculty have argued that their performance *is* their research. A new generation of performance professionals is revisiting this long-term stance by publishing as well as performing. It may be time to include some basic qualitative research methods in the professional preparation of future performer-practitioners.

There is much evidence that systematic research in studio instruction is in its infancy. There is great opportunity to document the variance in professional practices, but this effort would benefit from a more secure theoretical foundation. The profession values studio teaching. Yet only a few existing studies have attempted to evaluate theories about studio instruction. A number of descriptive studies have been completed, but the field is so vast that we still do not know if applied instruction follows one set of rules for all instruments or if different rules exist for teaching different instruments. In the search for such rules, much recent work consists of exploratory case studies.

The professional practice of teaching music through private lessons appears at first to be deceptively simple. In reality, the Western tradition of studio instruction is extremely complex. The studio lesson is the interface between the professional community and the individual who aspires to join that community. The studio teacher is the mediator between that professional community and the student. The challenge of studio instruction is that all of the cultural history of the professional community may be presented to the student through the medium of the weekly music lesson. As we advance our understanding of how this fundamental cultural replication unit works, we advance our understanding of the most basic teaching-learning process. This knowledge is important for our understanding not just of how we learn music but of how humans learn anything.

REFERENCES

Abeles, H. F. (1975). Student perceptions of characteristics of effective applied music instructors. *Journal of Research in Music Education, 23,* 147–154.

Bakan, M. (1991). Lessons from a world: Balinese applied music instruction and the teaching of western "art" music. *College Music Symposium, 33–34,* 1–20.

Barry, N. H., & McArthur, V. (1994). Teaching strategies in the music studio: A survey of applied teachers. *Psychology of Music and Music Education, 22*, 44–55.

Bloom, B. S. (1985). *Developing talent in young people.* New York: Ballantine Books.

Brand, M. (1992). Voodoo and the applied music studio [Special issue]. *Quarterly Journal of Music Teaching and Learning, 3*(2), 3–4.

Brandt, T. (1986). A review of research and literature concerned with private and class instruction in instrumental music. *Journal of Band Research, 22*(1), 48–55.

Bruner, J. S. (1985). Vygotsky: A historical and conceptual perspective. In J. V. Wertsch (Ed.), *Culture, communication and cognition: Vygotskian perspectives* (pp. 21–35). Cambridge, England: Cambridge University Press.

Buckner, J. L. (1997). *Assessment of teacher and student behavior in relation to the accomplishment of performance goals.* Unpublished doctoral dissertation, University of Texas, Austin.

Campbell, P. S. (1991). *Lessons from the world.* New York: Schirmer Books.

Chelton, C. M. (1968, September/October). Changing times. *The American Music Teacher, 18*, 36.

Coffman, D. D. (1990). Effects of mental practice, physical practice, and knowledge of results on piano performance. *Journal of Research in Music Education, 38*(3), 187–196.

Colprit, E. (1998). *Observation and analysis of Suzuki violin teaching.* Unpublished doctoral dissertation, University of Texas, Austin.

Dawkins, R. (1976). *The selfish gene.* Oxford: Oxford University Press.

Donovan, A. J. (1994). The interaction of personality traits in applied music teaching (Doctoral dissertation, University of Southern Mississippi, 1994). *Dissertation Abstracts International, 55*, 1499A.

Duke, R. A. (1994). Bringing the art of rehearsing into focus: The rehearsal frame as a model for prescriptive analysis of rehearsal conducting. *Journal of Band Research, 30*(1), 78–95.

Duke, R. A., & Farra, Y. (1994). *SCRIBE: Simple computer recording interface for behavioral evaluation.* Austin, TX: Learning and Behavioral Resources.

Duke, R. A., Flowers, P. J., & Wolfe, D. E. (1997). Children who study piano with excellent teachers in the United States. *Bulletin of the Council for Research in Music Education, 132*, 51–84.

Duke, R. A., & Madsen, C. (1991). Proactive vs. reactive teaching focusing observation on specific aspects of instruction. *Bulletin for the Council of Research in Music Education, 35*(1), 27–37.

Duke, R. A., Prickett, C. A., & Jellison, J. A. (1998). Empirical description of the pace of music instruction. *Journal of Research in Music Education, 46*(2), 265–280.

Engstrom, Y. (1999). Activity theory and individual and social transformation. In Y. Engstrom, R. Miettinen, & R. Punamaki (Eds.), *Perspectives on activity theory* (pp. 19–38). Cambridge, England: Cambridge University Press.

Flanders, N. A. (1970). *Analyzing teaching behavior.* Reading, MA: Addison-Wesley.

Geringer, J. M., & Kostka, M. J. (1984). An analysis of practice room behavior of college music students. *Contributions to Music Education, 11*, 24–27.

Gholson, S. A. (1998). Proximal positioning: A strategy of practice in violin pedagogy. *Journal of Research in Music Education, 46*(4), 535–545.

Gipson, R. C. (1978). *An observational analysis of wind instrument private lessons,* Unpublished doctoral dissertation, Pennsylvania State University, University Park.

Grant, J. W., & Drafall, L. E. (1991). Teacher effectiveness research: A review and comparison. *Bulletin for the Council for Research in Music Education, 108*, 31–48.

Gustafson, R. I. (1986). Effects of personal dynamics in the student-teacher dyads on diagnostic and remedial content of four private violin lessons. *Psychology of Music, 14*, 130–139.

Hamann, D. L. (1982). An assessment of anxiety in instrumental and vocal performances. *Journal of Research in Music Education, 30*(2), 77–90.

Hamann, D. L., Lucas, K. V., McAllister, P., & Teachout, D. (1998). An investigation into the factors contributing to individual practice. *Journal of Band Research, 34*, 59–68.

Hargreaves, D. J. (Ed.). (1989). *Children and the arts.* Philadelphia: Open University Press.

Hargreaves, D. J., & North, A. C. (1999). The functions of music in everyday life: Redefining the social in music psychology. *Psychology of Music, 27*(1), 71–83.

Hepler, L. E. (1986). *The measurement of teacher-student interaction in private music lessons and its relationship to teacher field dependence/field independence.* Unpublished doctoral dissertation, Case Western Reserve University, Cleveland, OH.

Hutcherson, R. J. (1955). *Group instruction in piano: An investigation of the relative effectiveness of group and individual piano instruction at the beginning level.* Unpublished doctoral dissertation, State University of Iowa, Ames.

Jones, A. R. (1990). *The role of analytical prestudy in the memorization and retention of piano music with subjects of varied aural/kinesthetic ability.* Unpublished doctoral dissertation, University of Illinois, Champaign-Urbana.

Jones, W. J. (1975). Games studio teachers play. *Music Journal, 33*, 46.

Jorgensen, E. R. (1986). Aspects of private piano teacher decision-making in London, England. *Psychology of Music, 14*, 111–129.

Kafer, H., & Kennell, R. (1999). 1998 national survey of high school pianists. *American Music Teacher, 49*(1), 34–38.

Keller, C. M., & Keller, J. D. (1996). *Cognition and tool use: The blacksmith at work.* Cambridge, England: Cambridge University Press.

Kennell, R. (1989). *Three teacher scaffolding strategies in college applied music instruction.* Unpublished doctoral dissertation, University of Wisconsin, Madison.

Kennell, R. (1997). Teaching music one-on-one. *Dialogue in Instrumental Music Education, 27*(1), 69–81.

Kennell, R. (1998). Toward a methodology of vocal pedagogy research. In B. A. Roberts (Ed.), *Proceedings of the international symposium: The phenomenon of singing* (pp. 129–137). St. Johns, Newfoundland: Memorial University.

Kennell, R. (2000). Improvisation in teaching: The constellation of scaffolding. In R. R. Rideout & S. J. Paul (Eds.), *On the sociology of music education: Vol. 2. The Music Education Symposium at the University of Oklahoma*, (pp. 113–120). Amherst, MA: University of Massachusetts.

Keraus, R. K. (1973). *An achievement study of private and class Suzuki violin instruction.* Unpublished doctoral dissertation, University of Rochester, Rochester, NY.

Kostka, M. (1984). An investigation of reinforcements, time use, and student attentiveness in piano lessons. *Journal of Research in Music Education, 32*(2), 113–122.

Kuhn, T. S. (1962). *The structure of scientific revolutions.* Chicago: Chicago University Press.

Larson, R., & Csikszentmihalyi, M. (1983). The experience sampling method. In H. T. Reis (Ed.), *Naturalistic approaches to studying social interaction* (pp. 41–56). New Directions for Methodology of Social and Behavioral Science, no. 15. San Francisco: Jossey-Bass.

Lehrer, P. M. (1987). A review of the approaches to the management of tension and stage fright in music performance. *Journal of Research in Music Education, 35*(3), 143–152.

Leonti'ev, A. N. (1981). The problem of activity in psychology. In J. V. Wertsch (Ed.), *The concept of activity in Soviet psychology* (pp. 37–71). Armonk, NY: Sharpe.

L'Hommidieu, R. L. (1992). *The management of selected educational variables by master studio teachers in music performance.* Unpublished doctoral dissertation, Northwestern University, Evanston, IL.

Madsen, C. (1985). Developing a research agenda: Issues concerning implementation. In *Proceedings: The sixtieth annual meeting of the National Association of Schools of Music* (pp. 37–43). Reston, VA: National Association of Schools of Music.

Madsen, C. H., & Madsen, C. K. (1974). *Teaching/discipline: A positive approach for educational development.* Boston: Allyn and Bacon.

Madsen, C. K., & Yarbrough, C. (1980). *Competency-based music education.* Englewood Cliffs, NJ: Prentice-Hall.

Manley, R. R. (1967). *A comparative analysis of the vocal intensity developed through beginning class and individual voice instruction of university students.* Unpublished doctoral dissertation, Indiana University, Bloomington.

Olsson, B. (1997). Is musical knowledge aesthetic or social? A pilot study of knowledge formation in music. *Bulletin for the Council for Research in Music Education, 133*, 110–114.

Rosenthal, R. (1984). The relative effects of guided model, model only, guide only and practice only treatments on the accuracy of advanced instrumentalists' musical performance. *Journal of Research in Music Education, 32*(4), 265–273.

Ross, S. L. (1985). The effectiveness of mental practice in improving the performance of college trombonists. *Journal of Research in Music Education, 33*(4), 221–230.

Rubin-Rabson, G. (1937). The influence of analytic pre-study in memorizing piano music. *Archives of Psychology, 30*, 1–53.

Rubin-Rabson, G. (1939). Studies in the psychology of memorizing piano music: 1. A comparison of the unilateral and the co-ordinated approach. *Journal of Educational Psychology, 30*, 321–345.

Rubin-Rabson, G. (1940a). Studies in the memorization of piano music: 2. A comparison of massed and distributed practice. *Journal of Educational Psychology, 31*, 270–284.

Rubin-Rabson, G. (1940b). Studies in the memorization of piano music: 3. A comparison of the whole and the part approach. *Journal of Educational Psychology, 31*, 460–475.

Schlaback, E. (1974). *The role of auditory memory in memorization at the piano.* Unpublished doctoral dissertation, University of Illinois, Urbana.

Schmidt, C. P. (1989). Applied music teaching behavior as a function of selected personality variables. *Journal of Research in Music Education, 37*, 258–271.

Schön, D. A. (1983). *The reflective practitioner: How professionals think in action.* New York: Basic Books.

Seibenaler, D. J. (1997). Analysis of teacher-student interactions in the piano lessons of adults and children. *Journal of Research in Music Education, 45*(1), 6–20.

Seip, N. F. (1976). *A comparison of class and private music instruction.* Unpublished doctoral dissertation, West Virginia University, Morgantown.

Shugert, J. M. (1969). *An experimental investigation of heterogeneous class and private methods of instruction with beginning instrumental music students.* Unpublished doctoral dissertation, University of Illinois, Urbana.

Sims, F. J. (1961). *An experimental investigation of the relative effects of group and individual voice instruction at the beginning level to high school students.* Unpublished doctoral dissertation, University of Oklahoma, Norman.

Sloboda, J., & Davidson, J. (1996). The young performing musician. In I. Deliege & J. Sloboda, *Musical beginnings.* Oxford: Oxford University Press.

Waa, L. R. (1965). *An experimental study of class and private methods of instruction in instrumental music.* Unpublished doctoral dissertation, University of Illinois, Urbana.

Williamson, A. (1999). The value of performing from memory. *Psychology of Music, 27*, 84–95.

Wood, D., Wood, H., & Middleton, D. (1978). An experimental evaluation of four face-to-face teaching strategies. *International Journal of Behavioral Development, 1*, 131–147.

Wood, D. J., Bruner, J. S., & Ross, G. (1976). The role of tutoring in problem solving. *Journal of Child Psychology and Psychiatry, 17*, 89–100.

Yarbrough, C. (1996). The future of scholarly inquiry in music education: 1996 senior researcher award acceptance address. *Journal of Research in Music Education, 44*(3), 190–203.

Zimmerman, M. P. (1993) An overview of developmental research in music. *Bulletin for the Council for Research in Music Education, 116*, 1–22.

Distance Learning and Collaboration in Music Education

FRED J. REES

Electronic information technology is altering the ways that teaching and research are being undertaken in education.[1] Computer-based multimedia resources, course management systems, videoconferencing, and web-based instruction are providing opportunities and challenges for the educator who seeks additional or alternative means to facilitate music learning.

Increased emphasis by the educational community on student-centered learning and access to education for everyone has given rise to investigating new ways in which teaching and learning can occur. In order to address these issues, accommodating diverse learning styles and personal schedules of students have become priorities. Traditional classroom teaching, with its tendency to treat students as a homogenous body of learners that meet at set times, cannot easily meet individual needs. However, the growing availability of internet-based resources that facilitate student acquisition of knowledge using different learning modes has precipitated ways of learning that are no longer restricted by time and place. Technology is also enabling people to work cooperatively on initiatives that transcend hour and location. Teachers, researchers, and students can form cohorts that instantaneously transmit information, share expertise, and focus on problems or projects of mutual interest at any moment, from anywhere in the world. These seemingly divergent directions, in which individual and group interests may be served through technology, suggest new opportunities for learning and scholarship that were not previously available. In recent years, two processes have been used by professionals to exploit technology in these ways that are attracting a lot of attention in education: distance learning and collaboration.

Distance learning is intended to facilitate instruction when the teacher and student are not meeting at the same time or place.[2] Government agencies, educational institutions, and businesses are increasingly viewing distance learning as a means of reaching students whose personal time constraints and geographical remoteness from centers of knowledge obviate opportunity to take courses traditionally delivered in public school settings and on collegiate campuses (Cunningham et al., 2000; Moore & Kearsley, 1996).

Collaboration is a process that seeks to engage parties with common interests to work cooperatively on some endeavor toward mutually agreed goals or outcomes. Collaborations can range from educational partnerships between collegiate institutions, public schools, and community groups to international consortia or teams of researchers engaged in high-level scholarship.

Most of the expansion in distance learning and collaboration has occurred since the early 1990s, when increasingly powerful computers, access to interactive televised instructional networks (ITV), and the proliferation of the internet enabled teachers, students, and researchers to utilize these resources for their respective purposes (Jeffries, 2001; Moore & Kearsley, 1996).

The music education community has been slow in adopting these processes, probably because of a combination of skepticism, lack of access to the technology, and discomfort with learning how to use computer-based applications. However, new generations of more accommodating music hardware and software, more powerful computers, and improved audio/visual resources over the internet are addressing some of the concerns that may have kept music educators from employing them. In addition, ITV and Web-based, easy-to-use course management systems (e.g., WebCT [http://www.webct.com/] and Blackboard [http://www.blackboard.net]) are providing avenues for teacher/student communication that can compensate for the lack of proximity and spontaneity associated with

257

in-person discourse. Coincidentally, such ever-improving technological resources have begun to spawn research studies and programing activities in music education that seek to further the educational interests of colleagues and their constituencies (e.g., Rees & Downs, 1995; Reese, 2001).

These early efforts reflect the youth of contemporary practice and scholarship in distance learning and collaboration. Like the greater corpus of educational literature, they do not yet yield exemplars of pedagogy or enduring research. Their activities and findings can be bound by the limits of the technology they employ and be subject to obsolescence as new technologies neutralize their significance. Nevertheless, they are providing insights that could lead eventually to a better understanding of how distance learning and collaboration work for music education.

Several caveats affect this chapter's content and design. Distance learning is now being subsumed under the classification of distributed learning. Increasingly, the same technologies and pedagogical approaches for reaching students off-campus are being employed for those on-campus, particularly outside of scheduled class meeting times. As the technology and pedagogy blur distinctions between how students in these populations receive instruction, so will distance learning lose much of its identity as a discrete mode of instructional delivery. A similar neutralization of identity will probably apply to collaboration as it becomes an integral tool for education and research. Nevertheless, both processes have distinct histories that provide the contexts for their current employment. An examination of their initial identities can help to explain why their respective evolutions seem to point toward assimilation with other aspects of education and scholarship.

Distance learning is inherently dependent on collaboration, as there is almost no aspect of its operation that does not involve third parties who provide technological infrastructure and educational services. While the reverse is not always true, the practice of using technologies shared with distance learning like the internet is enabling even locally designed collaborative initiatives to function outside of formal meeting and work schedules. The difference between these processes is that the focus is on learning for one and on whatever is the subject content of the cooperative endeavor for the other. In reviewing the literature, it is not necessarily apparent whether a given project or study involving distance learning places greater emphasis on this process or on collaboration.

Another consideration is that current music education literature involving distance learning or collaboration does not necessarily have either as its purpose. Employment of distance learning elements or technologies and collaborative activity can be more coincidental than intentional, as the primary interest is in using these processes to enhance music instruction and learning between participants rather than investigating how distance learning and/or collaboration enhances the music teaching and learning experience. There is no demarcation line between coincidental and intentional use of distance learning and collaboration in the literature. Rather than try to contrive one, project and research reports will be classified under these processes on the basis of which one seems to predominate in a given project or publication.

Finally, almost all of the program development and research in distance learning and collaboration involving current technologies are new. The relatively recent availability of the internet for music instruction and learning is only now yielding seminal studies. These early initiatives are few in number and scattered in focus and content. However, they reflect a growing interest in aspects of distance learning and collaboration in music education. They are reported here to provide evidence of such interest and to highlight some of the ways these processes have been applied in our profession.

This chapter will begin with separate discussions of distance learning and collaboration as they have evolved independently of each other and music education, followed by a review of the literature that examines their applications and research in general education. Music education programs and studies involving distance learning and collaboration are then discussed. Concerns about research that arise from the literature are then presented. The chapter concludes with new directions that could be taken for music education research.

Introduction

Distance learning and collaboration have become two of the most prominent areas of focus in contemporary education. Spurred on by the availability of technologies that facilitated rapid and interactive communication across time and distance, these processes have come to converge in pedagogical practice and research. Efforts during the past 10 years to openly discuss the process of collaboration have revealed its many facets, some of which have been evident in distance learning but not formally recognized. Likewise, some of the priorities of communication and information sharing, long a tradition for distance learning and now enhanced through the conduits of ITV and the internet, are revealing qualities shared with collaboration.

Both processes require a continuous level of communication between participants. Distance learning is dependent on the ability of the teacher to provide effective learning experiences for students, with opportunity for ongoing interaction between them regardless of location and, in some cases, time. Collaboration requires reliable and effective means for sharing information between parties, even when geographical distance and time obviate in-person meetings or extended periods of being in close physical proximity with one another. Distance learning necessitates collaboration between teacher and student as mutual investors in the educational process and often enlists the cooperation of school technology and library services or collegiate continuing education units to enhance the quality of service. Collaboration in educational and research settings involves organizational planning to structure and implement partnership activities that share attributes of course and lesson preparation that are employed by distance learning instructors. Both fields may exploit the same technologies to facilitate rapid transmission of information and interactive communication.

Yet another attribute shared by distance learning and collaboration is the opportunity to connect people who have complementary interests but with little option to act upon them in person. For distance learning, the challenge is bringing together teachers who want to convey their educational messages with the students who want access to them but are constrained by time schedules and geographical isolation. Collaborators can face a similar obstacle and, if they are involved in research, must also be able to send and receive information quickly and respond interactively at a distance. To address these issues, some context of distance learning and collaboration needs to be presented.

Learning at a Distance

Initially called correspondence education, distance learning was conceived as a service for students who lived too far from local schools or from educational institutions that could provide desired expertise. In the United States, distance learning programs can be traced back to the 1700s (Jeffries, 2001). According to Dirr (1999), they reflected one of four generations of distance education (rural education, televised instruction, the internet, and the virtual program of study). Taylor (2001) offers a more global version of a five-generation process of distance learning development that parallels the information technologies (print media, 1970s-style multimedia with computer-aided instruction, interactive telecommunications in its various guises, a flexible learning model using multimedia and the internet, and automated computer-based communications and campus portal systems). Historically, distance learning has been dismissed by the higher education community as a second-rate substitute for in-class teaching. Commonly held criticisms were concerns over quality of course content and delivery as well as the lack of direct contact between teacher and student (Lee, Armitage, Groves, & Stevens, 1999). The available technologies did not necessarily compensate for the dialogue or immediacy that the live teaching situation provided.

By the mid-1980s, however, technological developments were underway that would overcome some of these obstacles. One of them was the advent of audiographics conferencing, which used telephone lines to transmit two-way voice, graphic, and text data through a microcomputer. Another was slow-scan television, in which still images of users were transmitted two-way during transmission, with two-way audio. However, it was ITV that provided instantaneous student/teacher interaction. It also simulated live classroom teaching through the capacity for learner and instructor to see and hear each other.

Some of the earlier ITV efforts involved consortia of public schools, industry, and universities for teaching courses in rural areas that could not afford to employ teaching specialists in subjects mandated by state education departments (e.g., Kansas State Board of Education, 1993; Sullivan, Jolly, & Foster, 1993). The ITV systems can be expensive to construct and maintain, particularly those using satellite and optic fiber. To conserve on costs, many systems use compressed video, which generates inferior two-way images but satisfactory sound for transmitting the human voice. Some systems use *full-motion* television or enough bandwidth and speed to provide fluid movement of video images. One example is the Iowa Communication Network, which operates over 700 ITV classrooms in public schools, universities, libraries, medical schools, and civic offices, in what amounts to a giant statewide closed-circuit television system (http://www3.iptv.org/). Classrooms can be connected to the internet and have access to a range of computer and audiovisual equipment for instruction, immediate transfer of information by a dedicated telephone system, and connection of musical devices like a MIDI keyboard.

Another important development for distance learning has been the evolution of the internet. It is most often used to complement information provided by printed course materials, textbooks, prerecorded media, public television broadcasts, and ITV, as well as serving as a medium for text-based teacher-student and student-student communication. There is some evidence of employing the internet as the primary vehicle for distance instruction (World Lecture Hall [http://www.utexas.edu/world/lecture]). Video-streaming, desktop videoconferencing, file-sharing, web-based course management systems, chat rooms, threaded discussion groups, and on-line testing are among the resources that are being utilized.

The flexibility and availability of the internet relative to other distance learning technologies facilitate two types of instruction. One is called *synchronous*, in which student and teacher, regardless of location, meet at the same time. The ITV networks operate in this mode as well, providing the closest proximity to in-class instruction. In the other, called *asynchronous*, there is no common meeting schedule of classes, and instruction is delivered in some archived form (e.g., printed documents, prerecorded materials, internet downloadable or streamed files).

The Current State of Distance Learning

Distance learning, though relatively new to many parts of the United States, has had a strong tradition in other parts of the world (Harry, 1999; Moore & Kearsley, 1996; International Centre for Distance Learning [http://www-icdl. open.ac.uk/icdl/literatu/distance.htm]). Excluding the use of the internet for email and access to course requirements and assignments, most distance learning programs are still designed around textbooks, printed materials, prerecorded audiovisual media mailed to students, and radio or television broadcasts. Many countries do not have the economic resources to maintain ITV systems or the level of computer technology to distribute audio and video information over the internet that is available in North America, western Europe, and parts of Australasia. The United States, with its high priority on communications technology and current economic prosperity, is at the forefront of new developments in distance learning. Well over half of the internet users internationally are from the United States, with less than 1% in the Middle East or Africa (Scolaro, 1998). For example, Hezel Associates (1996) identified at least 190 televised instructional systems in the United States, many with two-way video and audio capacity. Such networks connect K–12 school districts in local or regional networks, collegiate institutions with satellite campuses, for-profit distance education companies, and even entire states. One of the largest federally supported distance learning projects that utilized telecommunications to reach over a million and a half K-12 learners was the U.S. Department of Education's Star Schools Program (http://www.ed.gov/prog_info/StarSchools/whatis. html). Begun in 1988, the project worked with coalitions of partners from the public and private sectors around the country to deliver instruction and provide learning opportunities in mathematics, science, foreign languages, and other subjects to students who had learning disabilities or were geographically isolated. It opened the door to use of new and evolving distance learning technologies and provided opportunity for curricular and pedagogy reconceptions that working with the technologies often imposed on users.

In addition to programs designed and maintained by educational institutions dedicated to distance learning, many collegiate institutions are now offering programs at a distance, with some leading to postgraduate degrees. Furthermore, a new generation of distance learning entities have surfaced that differ greatly in purpose, design, or operation from the traditional campus-based collegiate program. Cunningham et al. (2000) identify four new providers: (a) corporate universities (e.g., McDonald Hamburger, Microsoft, or Motorola University), (b) transnational or borderless providers (e.g., Universitas 21), (c) publicly driven virtual universities (e.g., Western Governors Conference), and (d) for-profit universities (e.g., University of Phoenix). Common to all are a focus on niche student markets and an emphasis on vocational training.

Farrell (1999) provides a perspective on the current world status of distance learning, with a distinctive focus on *virtual learning* and an emphasis on asynchronous instruction. Nine regions or countries covering five continents are represented in the report, with common themes of reaching more learners than campus-based collegiate institutions can accommodate and providing flexible educational alternatives for learners at a distance.

Some distance learning programs enroll large numbers of students, in what Daniel (1999) refers to as megauniversities. For example, the Sukhothai Thammathirat Open University in Thailand has about 200,000 students. Moore (1992) reported that two private institutions in Norway had approximately 140,000 distance education students in their programs. The United Kingdom's Open University claims that over 200,000 students participate in its courses (http://www.open.ac.uk). Between 1994 and 1998 in the United States, Lewis et al. estimated increases of distance learning collegiate-level course grew from 25,730 to 54,270 and student enrollments in these courses as expanding from 753,640 to 1,661,100 (Lewis, Alexander, Farris, & Greene, 1997; Lewis, Snow, Farris, Levin, & Greene, 1999). The number of collegiate degree programs offered at a distance increased from 690 in 1995 to 1,190 in 1997–98. The 1999 report also indicated that more collegiate institutions were intending to use ITV and internet-based instruction for distance learning into the year 2001.

Not all large-scale distance learning initiatives have been successful. Poorly conceived organizational infrastructure and misguided leadership forced the California Virtual University, essentially a clearinghouse for distance learning courses offered by California colleges and universities, to close after less than 2 years of operation (Downes, 1999). Another American consortium, the Western Governors University (WGU), which enrolled only about 200 students initially, became eligible for candidacy status with a major accreditation group in December 2000 (Carnevale, 2000). This step gave some credibility to the WGU as a legitimate entity in higher education. Through a network of universities, it offers several associate and bachelor's and one master's degree. However, it is unclear to what extent enrollments are growing or in what programs students are participating.

The ever-evolving internet is spawning new initiatives for distance learning, including the use of streaming video or audio and desktop videoconferencing. In recent years, course management systems (i.e., internet-based software that contains templates for course materials and different avenues for student-teacher and student-to-student interaction, like electronic mail or threaded discussion groups) have begun to appear. Some come from third-party vendors, and some have been designed by universities to operate on their networks.

Research on Distance Learning

Much of the research in distance learning involves effectiveness studies, comparing factors like teaching, student attitudes, and grades of distance learning versus on-campus student populations (Jeffries, 2001; Phipps & Merisotis, 1999; Rekkedal, 1994; Schlosser & Anderson, 1994; Trier, 1995). A substantial proportion of the literature on distance learning is anecdotal (Hanson et al., 1997) and, given the rapid changes in distance learning, dated (Phipps & Merisotis, 1999). Russell (1999) identifies hundreds of distance learning studies whose outcomes for learning were similar between on-campus and off-campus students. Overall, they suggest that attitudes and satisfaction of distance learning students were positive. Schlosser and Anderson's review of distance education research (1994) concluded that it was an effective mode of teaching and learning. Phipps, Wellman, and Merisotis (1998), upon review of the literature, were not convinced that student learning outcomes were necessarily higher or better than those among on-campus students.

Taking into account developments in ITV, Wetzel, Radtke, and Stern (1994) concluded that there was little difference in student achievement between televised and conventional classroom instruction. Cyrs and Conway (1997) cited 22 studies or literature reviews that indicated little difference in student achievement between televised and conventional classroom instruction.

Particularly lacking in this literature are research studies that provide baseline information on effective teaching practice or how students learn at a distance, although there are many small studies reported in distance learning journals that evaluate teaching of a specific course or using an ITV or internet-based technology in a distance learning context. There are also numerous instructional guides for learning at a distance. However, their findings and recommendations seem primarily to come from teaching and program development experience rather than through systematic inquiry.

The literature does reveal ongoing efforts to use new and evolving technologies for distance learning. In addition, the topical literature reports on the considerable amount of time and effort expended by authors in program development and implementation.

Collaboration

A precise definition of collaboration is elusive, as its applications throughout the literature vary considerably. A common thread that seems to appear in projects and models employing collaboration is the process of cooperative human involvement in some endeavor that supports interests of its participants toward mutually desired goals. On the surface, there is nothing new about collaboration, which has probably been a tool for human action since the dawn of our species. However, since the late 1980s, collaborative activities in business, research, and education have almost become *de rigueur*.

One of the reasons may have been identified by Schrage (1990, p. 40), for whom collaboration is "the process of *shared creation*: two or more individuals with complementary skills interacting to create a shared understanding that none had previously possessed or could have come to on their own." This idea of being able to generate something new that people working in isolation from each other would not be able to accomplish has plausibility. He cites the teams of the composers Rodgers and Hart and the scientists Watson and Crick as examples of collaboration. It would not be difficult to set up an exhaustive list in many fields of human endeavor that would add strong testimony to his point. Schrage also sees collaboration as a discipline, not just a process of cooperation. This perspective suggests that there are aspects of collaboration that can be formalized and studied. Roshelle and Teasley (1995, p. 70) see collaboration as a "coordinated, synchronous activity that is the result of a continued attempt to construct and maintain a shared conception of a problem."

Collaborative activities have participants who work collectively through casually constructed networks to enhance communication and learning or in specially designed environments that share technology to facilitate teaching, learning, and research. The role of electronic information technology plays a pivotal role in collaboration because of its capacity to connect people and share information quickly with those who need to have access to it, regardless of place, geographical distance, or time.

Unlike distance learning, collaboration is not bound by a specific purpose. Collaborative activities are not necessarily educational in nature. Their participants may not even be aware that they are working cooperatively. An example of this kind of collaboration in music education is the performing ensemble and the relationship that the conductor has with its members. The concept of collaboration could be extended to include the tacit involvement of its audience, the parents of the students who perform, and other teachers and administrators who might provide varying degrees of support. The often-rewarding outcomes on the day of performance are only attainable through the shared focus of all parties. The problem with viewing collaboration in this way is the lack of intention of its participants to consciously work cooperatively toward shared goals. While the conductor is likely to have a clear purpose and objectives leading to a performance, there is no reason to believe that the performers have the same agenda unless there has been expressed agreement between all parties from the first rehearsal.

Almost any effort by two or more people to work together on some task as basic as sharing the chore of washing dishes or adjudicating a music jury with peers could be classified as collaborative. This description makes the meaning of the term so broad that it becomes almost meaningless. To give it more of an identity, evidence of mutual intention and conscious participation in a cooperative endeavor leading to common goals will be considered essential to the definition of collaboration for this chapter.

Many prevailing alliances seem to fall into two categories: (1) informal collaboration, in which participants have come together to address a particular problem or issue, with no conceptual or organizational model driving the endeavor, and (2) formal collaboration, in which participants either operate within a conceptual model or generate one as a result of their work. These categories have been constructed to differentiate the two groups of collaborative activities that arise in the education literature. Most informal collaborations are either not research based or conduct research as a by-product of their activities. Formal collaborations will have a research component either evaluating them or their activities. The education literature offers some examples of these processes.

Informal Collaboration

Most collaborative activity falls under this category, with plenty of examples of team-teaching, interdisciplinary cooperation, school-community projects, and research studies involving multiple authors to illustrate its meaning. For example, the Concord Consortium (1997) cites numerous collaborations between students and teachers ranging from intraschool district classes to courses transmitted interstate, as well as its own participation in the Center for Innovative Learning Technologies, a consortium of businesses and universities focused on interdisciplinary development and research in these areas. Another illustration is the National Network of Regional Educational Laboratories (http://www.nwrel.org/cfc/frc/resrch.html#develop), which serves 10 sectors of the United States to foster research and program development assistance across disciplines for students of all ages. The International Links and Frontera Projects connected faculty at seven universities located in four countries in order to address matters involving culture and new media technologies (Lengel, 1998; Peacock & Lengel, 1998).

There are examples of collaborations that connect teachers, schools, and communities to enhance education. One of the largest of this kind is the TeleLearning Network of Centres of Excellence in Canada (http://www.telelearn.ca/), with over 121 international partners and 24 universities involved in program development and research for lifelong learning.

Formal Collaboration

Given the nature of formal collaboration, the presence or attainment of some conceptual framework or model suggests a more rigorously designed project or research study. Many academic fields have collaborations of this kind, and most of these are driven by some discipline-specific attribute as the conceptual underpinning for a given project or study. Some emerging and recurring fields that exploit formal collaboration include artificial intelligence, cognitive science, informatics, intelligent tutoring, new media, and robotics. If a common trait can be identified across them, it is that they provide different lenses to look at some of the same problems that may not or are not being resolved in traditionally accepted ways. The greatest validation, the arbiter of time, serves as the judge for what useful knowledge these fields will provide and how, since they are relatively new.

Among collaborations in education, a learning theory, pedagogical technique, or extension of work from another discipline generally serves as focus for a given endeavor, not the electronic means of information transmittal or study of pedagogical context that pervades distance learning research and much of informal collaboration.

As matters of example, Treadwell et al. (1999) discuss positive and negative factors surrounding several aspects of a collaborative learning project between four collegiate institutions that employ a collaborative distance learning model. Its basis is to transcend being used simply as locations of information transfer and knowledge acquisition and instead to move toward enabling active learning among students.

An exploratory research project examined methods of enhancing learning for engineering students at a distance using audio/video conferencing, a chat tool, and multimedia databases (Gay & Lentini, 1995). An intelligent collaborative learning system (ICLS) model is designed and tested to determine if it would aid students in acquiring collaborative skills in a cooperative learning environment (McManus & Aiken, 1996). Dillenbourg, Traum, and Schneider (1996) investigated the process of grounding as an essential component for collaboration and communication among learners.

One domain that seems to persistently surface is collaborative learning and, with it, the concept of *constructivism*. Elements of constructivism can be found in the work of Jean Piaget, Lev Vygotsky, Jerome Bruner, Seymour Papert, and Howard Gardner. It is set in a context where a student and one or more other learners work to solve a formal problem and in the process foster cognitive development built on their respective experiences and knowledge. Self-critiquing and constructive criticism are part of the collaborative learning process. Children who work in collaborative pairs on planning and problem solving are more successful than children who work alone (Blaye, Light, Joiner, & Sheldon, 1991).

Kumar (1996) identifies at least 14 computer-supported collaborative learning systems (CSCL), in which collaborative partners (fellow students) can facilitate learning and acquisition of subject knowledge with each other.

Scardamalia and Bereiter, working with other colleagues, schoolteachers, and their students, designed the Computer Supported Intentional Learning Environment (CSILE), an interactive computer-based learning tool, to facilitate student collaboration and communication. One of its most important features was the utilization of a communal database accessible to students and their teachers, in which their interactive responses with each other enabled collective knowledge-building to occur. This process capitalized on a finding from cognitive science that learning is an outcome of thinking rather than information transmittal (Scardamalia & Bereiter, 1992, 1994; Scardamalia, Bereiter, & Steinbach, 1984). Another hallmark of Scardamalia and Bereiter's work is its longevity, since CSILE began in 1986. Thus a rich body of data and experience has been generated that underscores the credibility of the researchers' findings.

An extension of collaboration is the *collaboratory*, a term first defined by William A. Wulf in 1988, when he was assistant director of the National Science Foundation, that he describes as a "computing environment that supports research among scientists and engineers that are not collocated" (Wulf, 1999, pp. 9–10). A critical component in collaboratories is the use of electronic information technologies for sharing data and working cooperatively at a distance.

Examples include the University of Michigan's Upper Atmospheric Research Facility, which employs a user-centered design, with behavioral and computer scientists working together (Finholt, 1995), and the Spectro-Microscopy Collaboratory at the University of Wisconsin–Milwaukee (Agarwal, 1999).

In education, the Collaborative Visualization (CoVis) Project used a variety of electronic communication tools through a process of scientific visualization (SciV) for high school–age students in a collaboration with professors from two universities, public school teachers, a science mu-seum, and a telecommunications company (Gordin & Pea, 1995; Pea, 1993a; Pea & Gomez, 1992). They also employed some of the cognitive tools, like scaffolding, that were developed to teach mathematics (Pea, 1985) and collaborative tools to support individual learning (Pea, 1993b; Resnick, 1987).

The Collaboratory Project at Northwestern University hosts a variety of initiatives and serves as a medium through which they can be undertaken, as opposed to being a topic- or discipline-based entity (Greenberg, 1998). Under a 4-year grant sponsored by Ameritech, this project supports educational programs using the technological infrastructure of the Collaboratory in the public school community and with other educational institutions.

Cargile (1997) describes a collaboratory designed for students in an inner-city Chicago high school. A virtual space that was shared by students was created for generating group projects and facilitating collaboration, itself a new and hard-to-manage process in the public school environment. Learning by doing, built on a constructivist approach, was another highlight of this initiative.

Distance Learning and Collaboration in Music Education

The music education community's involvement with distance learning and collaboration is quite recent. Excluding countries like Australia, where the need to reach remotely located students has made distance learning a priority for some time, interest in teaching or conducting research in this area has been minimal until recently. Although there were radio programs in the earlier part of the 20th century and numerous television series that addressed various aspects of music learning throughout the 1950s and 1960s in the United States, the impetus for using these media was not sustained. Undoubtedly, cost of production and quality of instruction were two factors that undermined their effectiveness. However, the greatest hurdle that could not be overcome was the problem of timely interaction between teacher and student. Opportunity to address this concern came with the advent of ITV and its capacity to provide immediate, two-way audiovisual information; for the first time music educators would be able to emulate in-class instruction. By the mid-1990s, reports on early uses of ITV for teaching music at a distance began to appear. Ongoing improvements and accessibility to the internet have attracted the interest of music practitioners and researchers. Some of the first studies on its use in distance learning are emerging in the literature.

Since collaboration is implicit in distance learning, virtually all work involving music instruction at a distance has some level of cooperative activity. Often collaboration is not discussed in a given report or, if mentioned, is given minimal attention in deference to coverage of the initiative or study content. In a sense, this approach signifies a preference on the part of an investigator for using distance learning resources to facilitate some aspect of music learning rather than to legitimize distance learning or collaboration. In the long term, the currency of these processes will probably gain greater value through their ability to facilitate the learning outcomes that music educators are wishing to accomplish through them rather than through research validation of their impact on the music learning process. This viewpoint is not without some difficulties, since distance learning and collaboration, as in all human processes, have impact on the participant. Nevertheless, the natural tendency of human beings to employ new tools that hold promise, particularly if they seem convenient for executing tasks that either previously involved the expending of greater personal time and energy or were not possible, does give these processes some currency.

For this reason, the following discussion concentrates less on the value of distance learning and collaboration to music education than on the ways they have been used to facilitate music learning. Issues that arise from this perspective will be treated later.

Teaching Music at a Distance

In the 1990s, one of the first initiatives for teaching music at a distance using current technology included isolated ITV workshops and music lessons (e.g., Downs, 1993; Fallin, 1996), conducting pedagogy (Henderson, 1996), and student teacher supervision (McCloud & Rose, 1995). The ITV systems usually consist of an origination site from which the course instructor delivers instruction to any number of classrooms. The host site is a regular classroom (albeit equipped with television broadcasting equipment) and may have on-campus students present, thus preserving an element of live instruction. The remote site or sites would be similarly equipped and usually capable of instantaneous send/receive video and audio. The University of Northern Iowa put two thirds of its master's of music degree coursework (music education emphasis) on the statewide ITV system in 1993—a program that is still in operation (Rees, 1996; Rees & Downs, 1995). Pinchas Zukerman has used videoconferencing to give music lessons between the Manhattan School of Music and Albuquerque, New Mexico (Smith, 1996).

While reports of the use of ITV for music education programming are generally positive, Ward's (1998) ITV experience with teaching a large collegiate music appreciation class cited problems of interacting with 300 enrolled students, low test scores from students at the one remote site, poor student attendance, and maintaining a sense of community within the class. Simonson (1993) described instru-

mental master classes being broadcast from Iowa State University to public school students at various classroom sites across the state.

Beyond these efforts, there has been little expansion in the use of ITV for music teaching. Broadcasting costs, wide variability in transmission standards between systems, inaccessibility to some ITV facilities, technical incompatibility between ITV networks, and faculty hesitation to embrace a technology that eliminates the physical proximity of teacher and student may be factors.

The internet, by comparison, is receiving more attention as a source for music instruction. Its continual improvement, relatively low cost for the user, and availability even without high-quality interactive video is making it the preferred tool for distance learning in music. Many music educators are already using it as an information resource, and some have created websites that complement their courses. There is growing evidence of institutions designing music courseware that is completely web based. One of the earliest examples was a 2-semester course in multimedia design and music technology developed by David B. Williams at Illinois State University, offered for the first time in 1996. It was the first internet-based course in music to incorporate all instructional materials, projects, and exams in a paperless environment. Other examples include designing and implementing a 20th-century music theory course (Clifford, 1998); use of the course management system, TopClass, for web-based teaching (Mayo, 1998); delivery of a music appreciation course (Christy, 1999); and teaching music history (Brandon, 1999). Duquesne University has a part of its graduate program in music education on the internet (http://www.home.duq.edu/%7Ebowmanj/musinfo.htm), and the Indiana University School of Music at Indiana University–Purdue University, Indianapolis, has committed to having its master's degree in music technology being delivered over the internet and with ITV (http://www.music.iupui.edu). Brigham Young University, through the WGU, is teaching courses in jazz history and applied organ at a distance (http://ce.byu.edu/is/univweb.htm).

In addition to these efforts, there is a growing list of websites established by private enterprises that are attempting to provide instrumental and vocal instruction and interactive courses in keyboard harmony, music theory, jazz theory, and music history and appreciation (e.g., http://www.fulltiltmusic.com; http://www.onlineconservatory.com). The educational quality and effectiveness of these efforts have yet to be evaluated. They do reflect, however, an optimism about using the internet for teaching music at a distance.

Two examples of collaboration in practice that used distance learning as the vehicle for creative music-making are the Composers in Electronic Residence (CIER) and the Vermont MIDI projects. A Canadian endeavor launched by David Beckstead in 1995, CIER included music faculties at York and Simon Frazer universities, the Canadian Music Centre, five public schools, and two composers to bring composition into the domain of the school-aged learner (http://www.edu.yorku.ca/CIER/Page2.html). Students can either meet with composers online to discuss their work or submit their own compositional efforts to a composer for feedback and direction. In 1997, the program expanded to include 15 schools and five composers.

The Vermont MIDI Project (Cosenza & MacLeod, 1998; http://www.vtmidi.org/) was initiated in 1995 with funding from the state's legislature and currently connects 60 schools in the state in an online music mentoring project for children grades 1–12. Learners could submit musical compositions that they created at the school MIDI workstations to composers, teachers, and other students for evaluation. The project's focus on meeting state educational benchmarks and the National Arts Education Standards has provided a framework around which its activities could be evaluated.

The Cassandra Project features an ongoing series of web-based collaborations among actors, dancers, and musicians at universities in New York City and Canada (Gilbert, 2000). They are seeking insights into collaborative models for making, teaching, and learning music.

Ruippo (1999), with technical assistance from the Sibelius Academy and the Helsinki Telephone Corporation, reported using the internet and NetMeeting to instruct musicians and music teachers from around Finland in music arranging.

The common thread of creative music-writing or composition that is emerging in these endeavors is heartening. The capacity of the internet to link composers with teachers and students in ongoing dialogue and musical information exchanges, regardless of location, capitalizes on this aspect of distance learning in a way that was not available previously. In addition, given the limited compositional training of most music educators, the opportunity to gain access to composers' expertise for students, as well as themselves (including training workshops, as in the case of the Vermont MIDI Project), provides another learning dimension that has not been available through traditional classroom instruction since the Contemporary Music Project of the 1960s. This point has not been lost on music education researchers. Among some of the current studies are initiatives in student music composition and music mentoring. Inevitably, they involve collaboration among university-based researchers, music teachers in the field, and their students (e.g., Reese & Hickey, 1999).

Most of the recent initiatives involving teaching music at a distance have not been subject to systematic inquiry. Time-intensive involvement with developing and using distance learning technology, the need for users to continually adopt new pedagogical approaches as the technology evolved during a given project or program, small or widely dispersed student populations, variation in multiple learning environments for students with different abilities, a disparity of music technology available in the schools, and little opportunity to conduct on-campus/off-campus comparative studies have probably contributed to a lack of scholarly activity to date. Nevertheless, a small body of research is starting to emerge that is investigating how music educators can further their interests in music learning through distance learning and collaborative arrangements.

Music Education Research Involving Distance Learning and Collaboration

In general, scholarship in music education that utilizes aspects of distance learning and collaboration falls into three areas. There are surveys that seek user evaluation of technologies like the internet, music learning initiatives that assess the technology and processes of teaching at a distance, and music discipline–based studies that employ, de facto, distance learning and collaboration processes. Studies follow the chronological availability of the two principal developments that have had impact on distance learning: ITV followed by the internet. Notable trends even at this early stage of scholarship involving music-based distance learning and collaboration are (1) the integral use of information and music technology for teaching at a distance and (2) researchers building on information they generated from their earlier studies.

Three music educators conducted separate teaching studies over the Iowa Communications Network (ICN) for music, one of the most sophisticated ITV systems available in the United States. Kerr (1997) surveyed 200 teachers regarding their attitudes toward using ITV to teach music in Iowa. The majority of teachers were undecided about teaching over the ICN. Teachers in the 20–29, 50–59, and 60–69 age brackets tended to have the most positive attitudes toward using the ICN, with the 60–69 age group scoring the most positive. Teachers from the 30–39 and 40–49 age groups were largely undecided. Voice teachers tended to be less enthusiastic about employing the ICN for teaching, and middle school teachers held the most positive attitudes toward the ICN, as did teachers with master's degrees. Downs (1993) reported on findings from the teaching of harp to four high school students in Cedar Falls by a teacher instructing from Des Moines. The harp teacher saw the use of ITV as a viable, temporary solution to the absence of a harp teacher resident in Cedar Falls (a basis for initiating the study) but favored live instruction. Student responses were generally positive.

Applying findings on how students verbally interact with teachers and each other using television-mediated observation (McDonald, 1996), Rees and Fanelli (1997) reported evidence of effectiveness in using ITV and a resident television production unit at the campus laboratory school to foster teacher observation skills among undergraduate music education majors, while a string instructor worked with middle school string students. The team of music professor, string educator, and camera crew planned and implemented broadcasts over several years in which lesson content, student population, and camera usage varied with each broadcast, yielding fruitful information about the use of the ITV mode for this kind of teaching. This initiative, which ran from 1994 until 1999, was recognized by its participants as an example of a productive collaboration between two music educators with different expertise, a media specialist, and two student populations.

One of the biggest challenges for conducting research in teaching music at a distance is structuring studies with enough of the elements that are commonly recognized as essential to good research design. The ambitious music education researcher will be challenged to generate a critical mass of subjects to form comparative assessments for study treatments. In cases where distance learning sites are geographically far apart from each other, there is little opportunity to monitor or direct the behavior of subjects unless they are mature and motivated or there is a proctor or teacher to supervise them—a confounding variable. Depending on the topic of a given study, the broad range of subjects' music and technological backgrounds can negate any standardized approach to treatment and invalidate evaluation efforts. Finding populations of subjects with access to the similar levels of MIDI-based computer technology and software can also be difficult. Even with ongoing improvements in distance technology, there are chronic connection problems and differing communications standards between computing systems that cause loss or nontransmission of information. Misconceived expectations by subjects of instantaneous communication over the internet can affect user attitudes and consequently their performance in a study.

Laboratory models for conducting research in distance learning and collaboration are not likely to be useful in gathering generalizable information until many aspects of electronic technology become standardized, infrastructures for delivering information (let alone instruction) at a distance are stabilized, and most learners can be expected to possess the same body of musical and technological information. This status is not likely to be achieved in the near future. However, there may be ways that information can be gleaned through systematic inquiry that would provide insight to processes of teaching music at a distance and collaboratively through technology. There are music education researchers who are looking for ways to provide this information.

Chizmar and Williams (1996, 1998, 1999, 2001) have used their teaching of courses in econometrics and arts technology to study a number of issues related to internet delivery of instruction, distance education, learning strategies, and faculty development activities. They employed a variety of distance learning tools, with implications for best teaching practice and hurdles involving course administration. The initiative is one of the first series of studies that reports the employment of the internet for music-related instruction. Chizmar and Williams also are among the first collaborative interdisciplinary teams to have conducted several studies involving teaching over the internet. This process has enabled them to ascertain some findings that have surfaced in their studies. Among those is the use of a constructivist approach toward learning in order to address disparate learning environments, the importance of technology being driven by pedagogy, and the employment of an assembly of student learning and assessment tools that include projects, portfolios, formal tests, and frequent teacher/student feedback mediated through technological resources like a course management system.

Reese (1999) presented data on participant responses from the Network for Technology, Composing, and Music Mentoring project (NETCOMM) using MIDI-based music composition over the internet through telementoring (guiding student learning online).

Repp (1998) and Bauer (1999) used surveys to determine attitudinal responses to inquiries about using the internet for music learning. Repp's study, which focused on the McClosky technique for vocal relaxation, noted that participants who interacted with the web-based presentation associated with the technique reflected a positive change of attitude toward the educational technology. Bauer surveyed 70 music educators from 27 states in the United States and in 4 foreign countries about their use of the internet and related technologies (e.g., email, FTP, listservs, Worldwide Web). He found that there was a strong interest among respondents in learning how to use the internet as part of music instruction. A majority of respondents wanted to see more music content and continuing education or professional development opportunities (e.g., methods instruction, lesson planning, music technology, jazz, administrative credentialing) on the web.

Formal collaborative research is beginning to surface as a tool for generating new knowledge. One example is the study of student composition for music learning, with the aid of computer-based technology and systematic student assessment (Hickey & Reese, 2001; Reese & Hickey, 1999).

Music Internet Connections (MICNet) links music teachers and their students with others from around the United States to work with composition using music technology at Northwestern University (Hickey, 1998). This initiative functions under the Northwestern University Collaboratory Project and, as such, represents the only current example of a collaboratory model being employed in music education.

Reese (2001) investigated the process of learning to teach composition at a distance by studying the feasibility of integrating online mentoring of music composition into the music teacher education process. This work is a continuation of earlier studies he initiated and builds as well on information gleaned from the CIER and Vermont MIDI projects. Reese raised eight research questions, six of which looked at feasibility issues involving technical, organizational, and instructional variables and two of which assessed influences on preservice teachers' ability and attitudes toward teaching composition and using technology and secondary students' attitudes toward working with online mentors (preservice teachers). Collegiate music education students (17 subjects) taking a music education technology program served as mentors to students grades 7–12 (43 subjects) studying music theory and composing with music technology at three Chicago secondary schools.

This study had to address numerous concerns that affect distance learning research. It serves as a good example of some of the challenges and some of the ways a researcher can address data gathering and evaluation while maintaining the integrity of teaching and learning contexts and accommodating students' different educational backgrounds.

The topic of mentoring students in composition is a new one for public education in the United States. Most experienced music educators or prospective music teachers do not have experience in composition and arranging unless professional circumstances or personal interest have motivated them to acquire such skills. There is no comparable alternative offered for public school students who do not have access to studying composition privately or attending college preparatory programs. Therefore, an approach to the teaching of composition by collegiate music education students through the internet to others who may not have much background in this area seems to be an appropriate application of distance learning. The collaborative nature of the enterprise provides an opportunity for the university music student mentors to exercise their pedagogical skills while learning about compositional process, with a student population that they may one day teach.

In terms of research procedure, Reese (1999) first conducted a pilot study to ascertain the viability of this kind of endeavor and work out problems that could undermine the validity of the primary study. He used standard music sequencing software (Musicshop) and an accessible conferencing tool (First Class) for written interaction and transmission of sound files between mentors and students. There was a plan for communication between mentors and students during the course of a semester.

The data collection and analysis section reflects the exploratory nature of this study and the apparent desire of the researcher to work with students in realistic educational contexts. Although all participated in 4 hours of workshops with a professional composer, the historical preparation in teaching and composition varied among student mentors. High school subjects also had differing capabilities with composition.

Two surveys, two written narratives, a 30- and 60-minute interview, logs, and review of all electronic messages and music files were employed to gather data for Research Questions 1–6. Descriptive data and frequency distributions were computed for surveys, logs, and message/file counts. Interview and narrative information was subjected to content analysis, coded, and categorized by research question.

Data for Questions 7–8 were generated by a time-sensitive pre- and postwriting test of mentors evaluating a middle school student's musical composition. Their responses were subject to evaluation by four independent judges, using a rating scale with an interrater reliability coefficient of .74, designed by Hickey and Reese (2001). Mentors also completed a pre and post 10-item scale assessing their attitudes toward confidence in teaching composing and using technology, the importance of composition in school music, the role of technology in learning composition, and internet-based teaching. Secondary school students completed a pre- and posttest four-item scale that assessed attitudes toward learning to compose and online mentoring, as well as an open-ended attitude survey. All scale results were computed using t-tests for paired means.

Statistically, the mentors' pre- and postwriting tests revealed improvement in their ability to provide instructive feedback on student compositions (t [16] = 2.29, p = .04, alpha level of .05), based on a combination of in-class instruction on mentoring and online mentoring practice. Mentor attitude scale results indicated significant improvement of confidence in teaching composition and using technology. Student scale results showed no change in attitude as a result of the mentoring experience (which they started positively), although positive responses to working with a mentor did decrease significantly. Reese infers reasons like the initial high expectations of the high school students about participating in this kind of endeavor compared with the realities of experiencing it.

Numerous other comments surfaced from the narratives and surveys, about matters such as time limitations for communicating between participants, technical problems, and lack of response from high school subjects to mentors yet enjoyment on the part of the students of working with the mentors. Frequency of mentor/student communication seemed to surface as a major factor for consideration in teaching and learning at a distance. Other findings supported the technical feasibility of using the internet and project software for this mode of learning. There were technical problems with internet connections, but they did not seem to undermine the progress of the study.

The study contains findings based on a variety of informational sources. This process provides an opportunity for generating statistical, narrative, recorded (through logs and electronic entries), categorized (through itemized survey choices), and externally judged information. Any findings here may surface in other earlier studies, thus providing a starting point for building a baseline of information about aspects of teaching composition at a distance.

An important point to reiterate is that this is not Reese's first study. Reese, Chizmar, and Williams; Hickey (who collaborated in studies with Reese); and Bauer are pursuing a succession of research in their areas of interest involving music technology, distance learning, and possibly collaboration, all of which reflect their own evolution of conducting research and generating information.

These authors appear to take distance learning and collaboration for granted, less out of a presumption that they are valuable than lack of awareness of what they are and how they function. They are not alone in their ignorance, as there is little information in the distance learning or collaboration literature to provide guidance. Given the current fascination in the greater educational community with both of these areas, there is good reason for skeptics to feel cautious about integrating either of these processes into their professional work, let alone employing technology through them.

A baseline of information for teaching music at a distance and working collaboratively is essential to the further growth of these areas. Some of the basic questions that need to be answered are as follows.

1. What learning takes place in teaching music at a distance?
2. What changes occur within students and instructors as they work in the distance learning environment?
3. What are effective pedagogical techniques for teaching music at a distance, regardless of prevailing technology?
4. What learners work well in the distance learning setting?
5. What technology is needed to facilitate teaching music at a distance?
6. What techniques are available to compensate for the differences of time and place in teaching music at a distance?
7. What conceptual frameworks can be employed to foster teaching music at a distance?
8. What areas of music can be taught effectively at a distance?
9. What is the process of collaboration in practice?
10. What constitutes effective collaboration in music teaching and research?
11. What impact on participants does collaboration have?
12. What kinds of effective collaboration are replicable?
13. What are the limitations of collaboration?

Most music educators have neither the time nor the expertise to answer these questions. The focus on music and pedagogy through various alternative processes of informational delivery and cooperative work is an understandable one for our profession. However, music education researchers have long understood that interaction with disciplines outside our field can be informative and generate new avenues of inquiry. It is for this reason that an earlier discussion of distance learning and collaboration has been provided. There may be colleagues in other fields who share some of the same interests in distance learning and collaboration that could appeal to music educators.

Crossdisciplinaray Interests with Music

Much of the same technology that has been enabling students to learn and colleagues to communicate with each other at a distance is also benefiting crossdisciplinary initiatives. Members of the artificial intelligence community have long since engaged in various kinds of inquiry relating to music (e.g., Coleman, 1995). The construction of computational models to explain some aspect of music perception is a common avenue of investigation (e.g., Desain, Honig, van Thienen, & Windsor, 1998). A growing tendency is for research to incorporate elements of different disciplines in the examination of some musical phenomenon, thus blurring disciplinary boundaries, in some cases for fields that were never clearly defined. For example, a project team involved with a study of neural networks and music may comprise individuals with backgrounds in artificial intelligence, cognitive science, intelligent tutoring, computer science, and music theory.

Another development is the introduction of new disciplines, one of the more recent being *informatics*. One definition of informatics that seems to encapsulate varied descriptions of this term is "the study of the structure, behavior, and interactions of natural and artificial computational systems" (http://www.informatics.ed.ac.uk/about/vision.html). Many disciplines have informatics programs including music. The universities of Edinburgh and Copenhagen already have music informatics groups, and Indiana University has a music component in its informatics program (Brandão, 1999; DIKU, 1998; Shiffrin, 1998). The Wilhelm Ostwald Schule (Gymnasium) in Leipzig, Germany, teaches informatics as a subject for its students (http://www.uni-leipzig.de/~sma/main_e.htm).

As a field, music education has not demonstrated substantial involvement with computer technology. Much interdisciplinary work remains within the fields of music composition and music theory. The diffuseness of research activity in artificial intelligence and cognitive science, with subspecializations like neural networks and intelligent tutoring, may contribute to this lack of participation, since much of it is initiated by colleagues who are not engaged in professional training of musicians or teachers.

From the technology side, a network called Internet2 (I2) by those collegiate institutions that have access to it might resolve some of the current concerns about interaction between teacher and student that truncate the capabilities of the internet that are generally available. Full-screen, full-motion video, stereo-quality sound, and two-way communication are among the immediate benefits. Indiana University (http://www.music.iupui.edu/), the University of Oklahoma, the University of Alabama at Birmingham (http://archives.internet2.edu/guest/archives/I2-NEWS/log0010/msg00008.html), New York University, and Rensselaer Polytechnic Institute (http://www.academy.rpi.edu/projects/technophobe/) have engaged in a variety of activities through I2 for creative, interactive music performance.

The Future of Distance Learning and Collaboration for Music Education Research

Two factors that surface repeatedly in the literature as bases for credibility are *need* and program or project *longevity*. Many reported initiatives had some recognizable grounds for existence beyond intellectual curiosity or opportunism. In the case of distributed education, such need might be to bolster student enrollments in programs or service special student populations who do not have ready access to the instruction they require. Collaborations usually involve some mutually recognized problem or goal(s) that participants with complementary skills and knowledge wish to address. Distance learning programs that continue to grow after several generations of students have participated in them and collaborations that have generated substantive information during their life span and either are still in operation or have extended their work to other locations might warrant greater stature in terms of their academic worth.

As a profession, music education seems to be engaging new avenues of teaching, learning, and research cautiously. Distance learning is expanding rapidly, but music instruction has a very small presence in it. Research in distance learning, beyond that which compares on-campus and off-campus instruction, is limited. There do not appear to be baseline studies that reveal effective teaching practice or processes of student learning at a distance, leaving the topical literature on the subject to serve as the basis for judgment in these matters. Until the late 1990s, there were a handful of reports on teaching music at a distance with the new electronic technologies. In the last year, research studies in this area have begun to appear, with formal elements of testing and evaluation. This may be marking the next step in the evolution of research in teaching music at a distance, as scholars seek more substantive information in the field.

Music education's involvement with collaborative endeavors is also quite small. Most collaborative networks do not incorporate music instruction, including those dedicated to teaching practice. This may be because of music education's historical tradition, which generally focuses on cultivating student musicianship and group performance rather than interdisciplinary endeavors with other colleagues. However, collaboration as a technology does have a history of generating new knowledge for all participants. It may provide an alternative model for teaching and research in some of the areas of music learning that have been addressed only recently, like student composition.

Researchers in distance learning need to be encouraged to provide more information on effective teaching practice and student learning processes. Music education researchers involved in distance learning may want to shift attention away from examining the applicability and effectiveness of its technology toward more conceptually based studies built on applying contemporary theories of learning through distance learning resources. Colleagues may want to consider formal collaborations with colleagues in fields like psychology, education, computer science, and informatics who possess expertise relating to music perception, information processing, computer-based expert systems that emulate patterns of student learning, and learning theories that seem to generate effective results in other disciplines.

This chapter has presented some of the vanguard efforts in areas of education and research that are expanding rapidly and has identified initiatives all of which, in some way, are being examined by music education researchers. While their initiatives may seem modest in print, they do reflect authentic initiatives by individuals to use new and emerging technologies to further the course of music education.

It is hard not to share the enthusiasm expressed by Webster (1998) as he looks at the growth in music education research over the past decade, and to know that colleagues in the field are continuing to look for new ways to teach and enable students to learn music. A large part of this activity is based on the availability of new electronic technologies that hold potential for innovation. The rest resides with us, and the combination of intellectual curiosity, academic rigor, and creative spirit that generates new knowledge.

NOTES

1. The term *electronic information technology* refers to all means by which information is gathered, processed, and delivered using electronic media (e.g. television, computer, MIDI

synthesizer). It will be referred to as *technology* hereafter in this chapter.

2. Distance learning is also referred to as *distance education, learning at a distance, open learning*, or *flexible learning* in the literature.

REFERENCES

Agarwal, D. (1999). *The spectro-microsopy collaboratory at the advanced light source* [On-line]. *Project report*. Available: http://www-itg.lbl.gov/~deba/ALS.DCEE/project.html).

Bauer, W. (1999). Music educators and the Internet. *Contributions to Music Education, 26*(2), 51–63.

Blaye, A., Light, P. H., Joiner, R., & Sheldon, S. (1991). Joint planning and problem solving on a computer-based task. *British Journal of Developmental Psychology, 9,* 471–483.

Brandão, M. (1999). *The music informatics research group* [On-line]. Available: http://www.dai.ed.ac.uk/groups/aimusic/aim.html.

Brandon, S. (1999). Pedagogical solutions for web-based music history courses. In S. Lipscomb (Ed.), *Proceedings of the Fifth International Technological Directions in Music Education Conference* (pp. 114–117). San Antonio, TX: Institute for Music Research.

Cargile, A. (1997). *The Collaboratory: A virtual, collaborative learning environment* [On-line]. *CHI 97 Electronic publications: Formal video program*. Available: http://www.acm.org/sigchi/chi97/proceedings/video/ajc.htm.

Carnevale, D. (2000). Accrediting committee grants candidate status to Western Governors University. *Chronicle of Higher Education*. [On-line]. Available: http://www.chronicle/com/free/2000/11/200012801u.htm.

Chizmar, J. F., & Williams, D. B. (1996). Altering time and space through network technologies in enhance learning. *Cause/Effect 19*(3), 14–21.

Chizmar, J. F., & Williams, D. B. (1998). Internet delivery of instruction: Issues of best teaching practice, administrative hurdles, and old-fashioned politics. *Campus-wide Information Systems 15*(5), 169–173. [On-line]. Available: http://www.orat.ilstu.edu/CAUSE/webteach.html.

Chizmar, J. F., & Williams, D. B. (1999). *Deconstructing classroom technology in practice: What our Web technologies suggest about what faculty want* at CAUSE99, Long Beach.

Chizmar, J. F., & Williams, D. B. (2001). What do faculty want? *Educause Quarterly, 24*(1). [On-line]. Available: http://www.educause.edu/pub/eq/eqm01/eqm011w.html.

Christy, W. (1999). Kamien, Intermuse, Pagemill and Quicktime: An Internet quartet. In S. Lipscomb (Ed.), *Proceedings of the sixth international Technological Directions in Music Education Conference* (pp. 108–109). San Antonio, TX: Institute for Music Research.

Clifford, R. (1998). Web-based instruction for fundamental musical concepts. In S. Lipscomb (Ed.), *Proceedings of the fifth international Technological Directions in Music Education conference* (pp. 109–113). San Antonio, TX: Institute for Music Research.

Coleman, E. B. (1995). Learning by explaining: Fostering collaborative progressive discourse in science. In Beun, R-J., Baker, M., and Reiner, M. (Eds.), *Series F: Computer and systems sciences: Vol. 142. Dialogue and instruction: Modeling interaction in intelligent tutoring systems* (pp. 122–135). Heidelberg, Germany: Springer-Verlag.

Concord Consortium, The. (1997). *Realizing the educational promise of technology* [On-line]. Available: http://www.concord.org/pubs/review6.html.

Cosenza, G., & MacLeod, S. (1998). Vermont MIDI distance learning network: A model for technology in classroom music. In S. D. Lipscomb (Ed.), *Proceedings of the fifth international Technological Directions in Music Learning conference* (pp. 137–138). San Antonio, TX: Institute for Music Research.

Cunningham, S., Ryan, Y., Stedman, L., Tapsall, S., Bagdon, K., Flew, T., & Coaldrake, P. (2000). *The business of borderless education*. Canberra, Australia: Department of Education, Training and Youth Affairs.

Cyrs, T. E., & Conway, E. D. (1997). *Teaching at a distance with merging technologies: An instructional systems approach*. Las Cruces, NM: New Mexico State University.

Daniel, J. (1999). *Technology is the answer: What was the question?* [On-line]. Available: http://www.open.ac.uk/vcs-speeches/teched99.htm.

Desain, P., Honig, H., van Thienen, H., & Windsor, L. (1998). Computational modeling of music cognition: Problem or solution? *Music Perception, 16*(1), 151–166. [On-line]. Available: http://www.nici.kun.nl/mmm/publications.html.

DIKU. (1998). *The music informatics group* [On-line]. Available: http://www.diku.dk/research-groups/musinf/index.html.

Dillenbourg, P., Traum, D. R., & Schneider, D. (1996). Grounding in multi-modal task-oriented collaboration [On-line]. Available: http://tecfa.unige.ch/tecfa/research/cscps/euroaied/murder-1.html.

Dirr, P. J. (1999). Distance and virtual learning in the United States. In G. M. Farrell (Ed.), *The development of virtual education: A global perspective* (pp. 23–46). Vancouver, Canada: Commonwealth of Learning. [On-line]. Available: http://www.col.org.virtualed/index/htm. (ED432668)

Downes, S. (1999). *What happened at California Virtual University?* [On-line]. Available: http://www.atl.ualberta.ca/downes/threads/column041499.htm.

Downs, D. (1993). Cedar Falls harp project: Music instruction on the fiber optic telecommunications network. In M. R. Simonson, C. Schlosser, & M. Anderson (Eds.), *Encyclopedia of distance education research in Iowa* (pp. 108–111). Ames, IA: Teacher Education Alliance of the Iowa Distance Education Alliance. (ED399314)

Fallin, J. (1996). Concerts for children via distance learning. In K. Walls (Ed.), *Proceedings of the second international Technological Directions in Music Education conference* (pp. 29–30). San Antonio, TX: Institute for Music Research.

Farrell, G. M. (1999). *The development of virtual education: A global perspective*. Vancouver, Canada: The Commonwealth of Learning. [On-line]. Available: http://www.col.org.

Finholt, T. (1995). *Evaluation of electronic work: Research on collaboratories at the University of Michigan* [On-line]. Available: http://edfu.lis.uiuc.edu/allerton/95/s5/finholt.html.

Gay, G., & Lentini, M. (1995). *Use of communication resources in a networked collaborative design environment* [On-line]. Available: http://jcmc.huji.ac.il/vol1/issue1/IMG_JCMC/ResourceUse.html.

Gilbert, J. (2000). *Cassandra 2000* [On-line]. Available: http://www.nyu.edu/classes/gilbert/cassandra/cass2000.html.

Gordin, D. N., & Pea, R. D. (1995). Prospects for scientific visualization as an education technology. *Journal of the Learning Sciences, 4*(30), 249–279.

Greenberg, G. (1998). *The Collaboratory: A regional network-based collaborative environment to support education and research* [On-line]. Available: http://collaboratory.nunet.net/cwebdocs/intro/coldesc.html.

Hanson, D., Maushak, N., Schlosser, C., Anderson, M., Sorensen, C., & Simonson, M. (1997). *Distance education: Review of the literature* (2nd ed.). Washington, DC: Association for Educational Communications and Technology and Research Institute for Studies in Education.

Harry, K. (Ed.). (1999). *Higher education through open and distance learning: World review of distance education and open learning: Vol. I.* London: Routledge.

Henderson, A. C. (1996). Teaching conducting long distance. In K. Walls (Ed.), *Proceedings of the second international Technological Directions in Music Education conference* (pp. 31–33). San Antonio, TX: Institute for Music Research.

Hezel Associates. (1996). *Educational telecommunications: The state-by-state analysis 1996–97.* Syracuse, NY: Hezel.

Hickey, M. (1998). *MICNet* [On-line]. Available: http://collaboratory.acns.nwu.edu/micnet/index.html.

Hickey, M., & Reese, S. (2001). The development of a rating scale for judging constructive feedback for student compositions. *Journal of Technolgy in Music Learning, 1*(1), 10–19.

Jeffries, M. (2001). *IPSE: Research in distance education* [On-line]. Available: http://www.ihets.org/consortium/ipse/dhandbook/resrch.html.

Kansas State Board Of Education. (1993). *ITV, interactive television: The future is now: Sharing our resources through communication.* Topeka: Kansas State Board of Education. (ED364213)

Kerr, B. (1997) Do music teachers feel that the Iowa Communications Network is a valid platform for the delivery of music instruction? And where is music teaching in the innovation-decision making process? In M. R. Simonson, C. Schlosser, & M. Anderson (Eds.), *Encyclopedia of distance education research in Iowa* (pp. 126–129). Ames, IA: Teacher Education Alliance of the Iowa Distance Education Alliance.

Kumar, V. S. (1996). *Computer-supported collaborative learning: Issues for research* [On-line]. Available: http://www.cs.usask.ca/grads/vsk719/academic/890/project2/project2.html.

Lee, D. L., Armitage, S., Groves, P., & Stevens, C. (1999). *Online teaching tools and projects* [On-line]. *On-line teaching tools and projects. Joint Information Systems Committee Technology Application Program.* Available: http://info.ox.ac.uk/jtap/reports/teaching/.

Lengel, L. (1998). *The Frontera Project: Technology and pedagogy for the future* [On-line]. *Frontiers of new technologies, education, research, and activism.* Available: http://www.richmond.ac.uk/intllinks/FaclaraF.htm.

Lewis, L., Alexander, D., Farris, E., & Greene, B. (1997). *Distance education in higher education institutions.* Washington, D.C.: U.S. Department of Education, National Center for Education Statistics.

Lewis, L., Snow, K., Farris, E., Levin, D., & Greene, B. (1999). *Distance education at postsecondary education institutions: 1997–98.* Washington, DC: U.S. Department of Education, National Center for Education Statistics. [On-line]. http://nces.ed.gov/pubs2000/200013.pdf. (ED 437 879)

MacLeod, S. (2000). *The Vermont MIDI project* [On-line]. Available: http://www.vtmidi.org/.

Mayo, S. (1998). Music courses over the internet: Demonstration of web-based course management system—TopClass. In S. Lipscomb (Ed.), *Proceedings of the fifth International Technological Directions in Music Education Conference* (pp. 130–132). San Antonio, TX: Institute for Music Research.

McCloud, W., & Rose, E. (1995). Impact NC; Impact on education: Impact on life. In K. Walls (Ed.), *Proceedings of the second International Technological Directions in Music Education Conference* (pp. 38–40). San Antonio, TX: Institute for Music Research.

McDonald, T. (1996). *Direct and television-mediated observation of verbal interaction in the classroom.* Unpublished doctoral dissertation, University of Northern Iowa, Cedar Falls.

McManus, M. M., & Aiken, R. M. (1996). Teaching collaborative skills with a group leader computer tutor. *Education and Information Technologies, 1*, 75–96.

Moore, M. G. (1992). Distance education at postsecondary level. In *Encyclopedia of Higher Education: Vol. 2* (pp. 1097–1106). Oxford: Pergamon Press.

Moore, M. G., & Kearsley, G. (1996). *Distance Education: A Systems View.* Belmont, CA: Wadsworth.

National Research Council. (1993). *National collaboratories: Applying information technology for scientific research.* Washington, DC: National Academy Press.

Pea, R. D. (1985). Beyond amplification: Using computers to reorganize human mental functioning. *Educational Psychologist, 20*, 167–182.

Pea, R. D. (1993a). Distributed multimedia learning environments: The Collaborative Visualization Project. *Communications of the ACM, 36*(5), 60–63.

Pea, R. D. (1993b). Learning scientific concepts through material and social activities: Conversational analysis meets conceptual change. *Educational Psychologist, 28*(3), 265–277.

Pea, R. D., & Gomez, L. (1992). Learning through collaborative visualization: Shared technology learning environments for science. *Proceedings of SPIE '92 (International Society of Photo-Optical Instrumentation Engineers): En-*

abling technologies for high-bandwidth applications, 1785, 253–264.

Peacock, S., & Lengel, L. (1998). *The International Links Project: Pedagogical collaboration through the Internet* [On-line]. Available: http://www.richmond.ac.uk/intllinks/Faculty9.htm.

Phipps, R., & Merisotis, J. (1999). *What's the difference? A review of contemporary research on the effectiveness of distance learning in higher education.* Washington, DC: Institute for Higher Education Policy. [On-line]. Available: http://www.ihep.com/difference.pdf.

Phipps, R., Wellman, J., & Merisotis, J. (1998). *Assuring quality in distance learning: A preliminary review. A report prepared for the Council of Higher Education Accreditation.* Washington, DC: Institute for Higher Education Policy. [On-line]. Available: http://www.ihep.com/PUB.html.

Rees, F. J. (1996). A preliminary evaluation of the University of Northern Iowa's Master of Music Program in Music Education on the Iowa Communications Network. In K. Walls (Ed.), *Proceedings of the second International Technological Directions in Music Education Conference* (pp. 34–38). San Antonio, TX: Institute for Music Research.

Rees, F. J., & Downs, D. (1995). Interactive television and distance learning. *Music Educators Journal, 82*(2), 21–25.

Rees, F. J., & Fanelli, M. (1997). ITVI as a tool for cultivating teacher observation skills. *American String Teacher, 47*(3), 35–37.

Reese, S. (1999). Potential and problems of Internet-based music composition mentoring. *Southeast Journal of Music Education, 11,* 1–11.

Reese, S. (2001). Integration of on-line composition mentoring into music teacher education. *Contributions to Music Education, 28*(1), 9–26.

Reese, S., & Hickey, M. (1999). Internet-based music composition and music teacher education. *Journal of Music Teacher Education, 9*(1), 25–32.

Rekkedal, T. (1994). *Research in distance education—Past, present, and future* [On-line]. Available: http://www.nettskolen.com/alle/in_english.

Repp, R. S. (1998). Pre-service music teacher attitudes toward an Internet-based presentation of the McClosky Technique for vocal relaxation. In S. Lipscomb (Ed.), *Proceedings of the fifth international Technological Directions in Music Education conference* (pp. 14–19). San Antonio, TX: Institute for Music Research.

Resnick, L. B. (1987). *Education and learning to think.* Committee on Mathematics, Science, and Technology Education, Commission on Behavioral and Social Sciences and Education, National Research Council. Washington, DC: National Academy Press. [On-line]. Available: http://www.nap.edu.

Roshelle, J., & Teasley, S. D. (1995). The construction of shared knowledge in collaborative problem solving. In C. O'Malley (Ed.), *Computer supported collaborative learning* (pp. 69–197). Berlin: Springer-Verlag.

Ruippo, M. (1999). *Net conferencing in music distance education: Observations on a pilot project* [On-line]. Available: http://www.pedanet.jyu.fi/cato/calive/musdista.html.

Russell, T. L. 1999. *The no significant difference phenomenon.* Chapel Hill, NC: Office of Instructional Telecommunications, North Carolina State University. [On-line]. Available: http://cuda.teleeducation.nb.ca/nosignificantdifference/index.cfm.

Scardamalia, M., & Bereiter, C. (1992). Collaborative knowledge building. In E. D. Corte, M. C. Linn, H. Mandl, & L. Verschaffel (Eds.), *Computer-based learning environments and problem solving* (pp. 44–66). Berlin: Springer-Verlag.

Scardamalia, M., & Bereiter, C. (1994). Computer support for knowledge-building communities. *Journal of the Learning Sciences, 3*(3), 265–283.

Scardamalia, M., Bereiter, C., & Steinbach, R. (1984). Teachability of reflective processes in written composition. *Cognitive Science, 8,* 173–190.

Schlosser, C. A., & Anderson, M. L. (1994). *Distance education: Review of the literature.* Ames, IA: Research Institute for Studies in Education, Iowa State University.

Schrage, M. (1990). *Shared minds: The new technologies of collaboration.* New York: Random House.

Scolaro, A. (1998). *Internet Statistics* [On-line]. Available: http://www.geocities.com/Eureka/Enterprises/6930/enstat.html.

Shiffrin, R. M. (1998). *Advancing into the information age: A school of informatics for Indiana University* [On-line]. Available: http://www.extreme.indiana.edu/~gannon/informatics/shiffin.html.

Simonson, D. (1993). The Iowa Communications Network as a vehicle for the delivery of applied instrumental music instruction. In M. R. Simonson, C. Schlosser, & M. Anderson (Eds.), *Encyclopedia of distance education research in Iowa* (pp. 185–188). Ames, IA: Teacher Education Alliance of the Iowa Distance Education Alliance.

Smith, K. (1996). Virtual teaching. *The Strad, 107*(1277), 912–915.

Sullivan, M., Jolly, D., & Foster, D. (1993). *Implementing two-way interactive video in rural, small, schools.* (ED 359002)

Taylor, J. C. (2001). *The future of learning—learning for the future: Shaping the transition.* 20th International Council on Distance Education World Conference, Düsseldorf, Germany. [On-line]. Available: http://www.fernuni-hagen.ed/ICDE/D-2001/final/keynote_speeches/wednesday/taylor_keynote.pdf.

Treadwell, T., Barimani, A., Ashcraft, D., Mittan, B., Arsenault, P., & Lewis, R. (1999). *Collaborative inter-class teaching and research over the Internet: Faculty and students' perspectives on the research and learning process* [On-line]. Available: http://albie.wcupa.edu/ttreadwell/99educ/99Edu1Causepaper.html.

Trier, V. (1995). *Guide no. 10. Distance education: Research* [On-line]. Available: www.uidaho.edu/evo/dist10.html.

Ward, L. F. (1998). Stay tuned for Music 110: Experiments in music appreciation and interactive television. In S. Lipscomb (Ed.), *Proceedings of the fifth international Tech-*

nological Directions in Music Education conference (pp. 114–120). San Antonio, TX: Institute for Music Research.

Webster, P. R. (1998). The new music educator. *Arts Education Policy Review, 100*(2), 2–21.

Wetzel, C. D., Radtke, P. H., & Stern, H. W. (1994). *Instructional effectiveness of video media.* Hillsdale, NJ: Erlbaum.

Wulf, W. A. (1999). Improving research capabilities through collaboratories. In North Carolina Board of Science and Technology and National Research Council, *Improving research capabilities in chemical and biomedical sciences* (pp. 9–12) [On-line]. Available: http://www.nap.edu/readingroom/books/collaboratories.

Part III
MUSICAL DEVELOPMENT AND LEARNING

Hildegard Froehlich
Editor

Introduction: Looking Multiple Ways in Research

ROSAMUND SHUTER-DYSON

The essence of the psychology of music has always been related to the development and acquisition of competencies in music. Much of this research has been focused on individuals who were special in some respect. To learn about musical memory was to think about and study those who had phenomenal musical memories like Mozart and Liszt. Revesz (1933) identified a musical prodigy and documented his progress from his fifth to his thirteenth year. Our knowledge of music and the blind and deaf was initiated through research on individuals who just happened to possess the characteristics of interest to the researcher. This qualitative research, advocated by Carl Seashore in his *Psychology of Music* in 1938, continued through much of the 20th century with Donald Pond's observation of the creative activities of young children, the identification of vocal ranges, and Seashore's research on vibrato, trills, and tone quality of outstanding artists. The seminal research of Marilyn Zimmerman, Jeanne Bamberger, and Mary Louise Serafine was with individuals of specified ages or with those who had been individually observed but could be classified into descriptive groups. The most influential behavioral-oriented research was completed by these musician-scholars, who would not think of themselves as behaviorists.

The increasing importance of school music in the 20th century may have prompted an interest in developmental musical characteristics of children that could aid in teaching children by grade levels, or it may have been the progress in child development and child psychology that prompted music education researchers to determine to what extent these ideas applied to music. Part 2 of the Shuter text of the *Psychology of Musical Ability* (1968) attempted to portray musical ability in a developmentally appropriate way. This was updated by Shuter-Dyson and Gabriel in 1981 and followed in 1986 by David Hargreave's ground-breaking text focused exclusively on issues in the developmental psychology of music.

Isaac Newton acknowledged that if he saw a bit farther it was because he stood on the shoulders of the giants who had preceded him. Hargreaves and Shuter-Dyson could focus on musical development in the last half of the 20th century because of the research on development that was conducted or observations that were documented earlier in the 20th century. Charles Spearman (Mursell & Glenn, 1931, p. 16) critiqued the Seashore *Measures of Musical Talents* (Seashore, 1938), finding no unitary factor; and of course Seashore himself made no such claim. This agreement on the lack of a single factor of musicality was supported by child study scholars such as Sophie Belaiew-Exemplarsky, whose careful observations revealed that tone was the first musical element of interest to children, followed by the motor element. The lack of interest in harmony was attributed by Moore and Valentine to training and not a factor closely related to maturation as were tone, movement (rhythm and meter), and eventually contour. The gradual coming-together of musical elements allowed James Mursell and other early psychologists to define music in terms of self-expression, emotional release, and creative impulses (Mursell & Glenn, 1931, p. 21). There was a role for natural learning as well as for focused instruction in the schools. Mursell could claim (a) the importance of the initial synthesis of the musical experience and (b) that any study phase needed to be related to the initial synthesis as well as to the final synthesis, thus justifying his developmental principle of synthesis-analysis-synthesis. Given natural learning and a reasonable developmental sequence, any blockages in learning were the result of inadequate earlier learning. The importance of musical experiences in early childhood continues to be confirmed by researchers at the beginning of the 21st century, with the work of Edwin Gordon and psychologists such as Shaw, Gruhn, Rauscher, Hodges, and Flohr who explore brain development and the effects resulting from musical stimuli, experiences, and instruction. One of the major differences between the early research and that presently being conducted is the emphasis on relating research to theory, an emphasis exemplified by chapters 17, 20, 21, and 22. The confirmation of the connection between theory and research occurs not only with respect to musical development but also bears upon pedagogical elements such as motivation. Mursell suggested in the 1930s that if little is expected little will be achieved, and this idea was confirmed by Maehr and his colleagues through lengthy and sophisticated research.

Systematic research with young children in music was stimulated by the 1970s findings of Paul Michel in East Germany and followed by Helmut Moog's research with more than 400 preschool children, the largest research study to date. Moog's use of 10 different age levels, from 6 months to 5½ years, and the help of some 1,000 parents established not only the importance but the potential of developmental research in music education.

The field virtually exploded with Petzold's 5-year study of children between the ages of 6 and 11 and Pflederer-Zimmerman's (also with Lee Sechrest) attempts to confirm Piaget's stage theory in which she found it impossible to reverse the stimuli, a requirement to replicate Piaget's work in music. Howard Gardner's research confirmed a presymbolic period, a period of symbol use from ages 2 to 7, and an absence of stages from age 8 onward as students gained the ability to fully engage in musical experiences. Mursell had been cautious about the presence of any stages; he found students too individualistic to fit into music experiences that conformed to age-level stages. Gardner brought cognitive psychology to the arts, a rather late entry to developmental research in music education. Similarly, Lev Vygotsky, a Russian psychologist who regarded education as central to the development of children, suggested that private speech is an important self-regulatory function and that adults play an important role in a child's intellectual development. These European advances in developmental psychology were compatible with advances being made in America. Barbara Rogoff suggested that the term "guided participation" described the mutual involvement between children and their social partners in collective activities (Meece, 1997, p. 158). Jerome Bruner had been using the term "scaffolding" to describe the process used when adults help children learn. It was a small but important step to apply these ideas of Vygotsky and others in the classroom as reciprocal teaching, an application credited to Annemarie Palinscar and Ann Brown. Heterogeneous instruction could be justified as cooperative learning techniques allowed less competent students to perform slightly above their present level of competence or in their "zone of proximal development." The chapters in this part of the handbook suggest the importance of applying these interesting theories to teaching and learning in music education. There has been limited confirmatory work on how Vygotsky's ideas, if applied to music, relate to the instructional strategies of Piaget, Bruner, Ausubel, Gagne, and other psychologists whose learning theories have been explored by music educators.

Our knowledge of music teaching and learning is also based on nondevelopmental research where investigators have explored the importance of immediate reinforcement (Lundin, 1967, p. 134), the value of prestudy in memorizing (Rubin-Rabson), the relationship of music to heart rate and blood pressure, Kemp's research on the musical temperament, and the role of music in therapy. Substantive research in several areas has made it possible for the authors in this part to move us into a new realm of thinking about the possibilities of research to improve music education. Developmental research has been largely focused on the youngest members of our society; the research on adolescents has been directed more toward the sociology of music than toward issues in development, sequencing, and ordering of performing, listening, or creating.

REFERENCES

Gardner, H. (1973). *The arts and human development*. New York: Wiley.

Hargreaves, D. (1986). *The developmental psychology of music*. London: Cambridge University Press.

Lundin, R. (1967). *An objective psychology of music* (2nd ed.). New York: Ronald Press.

Meece, J. (1997). *Child and adolescent development for educators*. New York: McGraw-Hill.

Mursell, J., & Glenn, M. (1931). *The psychology of school music teaching*. New York: Silver Burdett.

Revesz, G. (1933). *Introduction to the psychology of music* (G. I. C. deCourcy, Trans.). London: Longmans, Green.

Seashore, C. (1938). *Psychology of music*. New York: McGraw-Hill.

Shuter-Dyson, R. (1968). *The psychology of musical ability* (2nd ed.). London: Methuen. Reprint: with Clive Gabriel. (1981).

Learning Theories as Roots of Current Musical Practice and Research

17

LAURIE TAETLE

ROBERT CUTIETTA

Numerous theories ground research and practice in the broad domain of music. Theories of psychoacoustics guide the construction of a concert hall, theories of information and expectancy suggest to composers a listener's capacity for music appreciation, theories of musical preference affect a concert programmer's decision making, and theories of measurement influence the construction of a musical aptitude test.

In music education, theories of learning have contributed to an understanding of how the learner processes information and, through corresponding instructional theories, have caused change in instructional practice. Theories of motivation and recent theories of intelligence (Dweck, 1997) assist teachers in eliciting student productivity. Theories of child development govern the construction of age-appropriate subject matter. As both instructional and motivation theories are addressed elsewhere in this part of the Handbook, they have been excluded from the discussion in this chapter.

Learning theories, the topic this chapter is concerned with, have contributed to advances in thinking about educating and teaching the child in settings of formal schooling. Some of these theories have found acceptance and application in research on music learning as well, and they have impacted music educators' thought on how to sequence instruction in the classroom. Some learning theories also have guided sequencing in computer-assisted music instruction. However, depending on the philosophical perspective underlying any particular theory, different degrees of emphasis on behavioral, cognitive, or constructivist thinking have shaped the models used to explain how a child learns and hence to sequencing the instructional steps deemed necessary for effectively teaching a child.

Learning theories specifically derived from behavioral and cognitive psychology have appeared as roots of music education research since the 1960s. Developed outside the field of music, the theories seek to describe, explain, and possibly predict musical behavior. This "outside-in" approach continues to influence music education research and practice today, as many of the constructs used to describe nonmusic behavior also are widely accepted as valid descriptors of music behavior. Music educators have embraced the theories with the argument that musical behavior, as a part of human behavior in general, is subject to the same laws that govern all of learning. Conversely, there are researchers working to create theories of learning unique to music. Unfortunately, these theories of musical learning conceived from "inside" the musical domain continue to be less prevalent though they may have the potential to help music educators better understand the unique process of music learning. This chapter contains two broad sections: (1) a review of how theories from the general field of psychology have been applied to music education, and (2) an examination of research attempting to create learning theories unique to music.

Learning Theories and Their Application to Music

A Brief Chronology

Many important events guided by educators, psychologists, theorists, and researchers have contributed to the prevalence of general learning theories as roots of music education research and practice. These contributions, mostly influenced by educational psychologists, began with the educational and societal transitions of the 1960s. Interest in learning theories gathered momentum during the years of the Ann Arbor Symposia and continue to be impacted by technological advances, the resurgence of interest in "learning through doing," and—related to it—the application of "situated learning" to the study of music learning.

Prior to the 1960s, little evidence supports learning theories as important foundations of hypothesis-driven research in music education. The decade of the 1960s, however, focused on how learning theories could serve in the improvement of curriculum development and instruction. For example, Bruner (e.g., 1960, 1966) introduced theories of conceptual learning that led to a call for developmentally sequenced curricula. Bruner, influenced by the translation of Jean Piaget's research into English, theorized his own developmental stages of learning, which have found wide acceptance in a number of subject matters, including music. At the same time, behaviorist theories focused on the application of stimulus-response learning to the improvement of instructional strategies.

As Mark (1986) observed, the Tanglewood Symposium in 1967 and the resulting Music Educators National Conference (MENC) Goals and Objective (GO) Project in 1969 promoted the "application of significant new developments in curriculum (and) teaching-learning patterns" (p. 59). Bruner's spiral curriculum and emphasis on conceptual learning became the foundation of an elemental approach to teaching music. Aesthetic education (Reimer, 1970) gained momentum as music educators sought to secure the value of the arts in education. Here, too, Bruner's model of learning served as the basis for developing teaching strategies that would reach the goals of aesthetic education.

In the late 1970s and early 1980s, the Ann Arbor Symposia on the Applications of Psychology to the Teaching and Learning of Music reinforced the relationship between learning theories and music education research and practice. Leading music education researchers met with psychologists to determine how knowledge and expertise from both domains could improve scientific inquiry in music education. The original title of the Ann Arbor Symposia, "Implications of Learning Theory to the Teaching and Learning of Music," reveals one of the symposia's purposes: to strengthen the case for research and teaching grounded in learning theory.

In 1978, MENC and the Music Educators Research Council (MERC) created the Special Research Interest Groups (SRIGs). The titles of two of these original interest groups—Perception and Cognition; Learning and Development—indicated the interest in the community of music education researchers to make cognitive learning theories

integral components of their work. Since then, the accessibility of the computer has added to the practice of using learning theories as a theoretical basis not only for research on music learning but also for seeking to improve instruction. Programmed instruction based on behavioral learning theories has evolved into computer-assisted instruction (CAI). More recently, computer programmers have created a form of artificial intelligence (AI) that simulates human cognition or thinking; the impact of AI has broadened research involving the learning theory of human information processing (HIP) as well as the constructionist school of thought, which uses interactive models to explain learning. In fact, the renewed interest in Bruner's writings (1990, 1996) as well as recent translations of Vygotsky's teachings from Russian to English (1997a, 1997b) suggest a stronger focus on cognition and constructivism as theoretical bases for explaining the nature of how an individual learns than seems to have been the case for the 1970s and 1980s. Nonetheless, as has been the case with behaviorist learning models, they were always readily and quickly applied to instructional practice, regardless of how systematically their construct validity had been tested.

Major Theoretical Constructs

In this chapter, learning theories are restricted to those identified as behavioral, cognitive, and constructivist. The behavioral model has as its base the linear connection between stimuli that trigger responses. This model allows the researcher to look for those external forces that increase the likelihood of desired behaviors. These models are useful when one studies group or individual behavior in a variety of instructional settings.

Cognitive models describe learning behaviors from a more internal, developmental perspective, in that age, maturation, and perceptual experiences in combination make a learner take in new information in a stepwise process of exposure, reaction to the exposure, examination of the experience, and adjustment of previous experiences to new ones. Such theories stress the description and examination of appropriate internal stimuli on the readiness for new ones. Furthermore, the models seek to explain how an individual negotiates old and new information in relationship to each other. Such an approach requires study of learners as they respond individually to specific tasks.

Constructivist models of learning focus on describing in detail the many relationships that connect the learner to his or her internal as well as external environments. The environments include experiences and contacts with both the physical and the mental world by the learner both as an individual and as a member in a particular group. As the interactive nature of all experiences together results in learning, constructivist theories tend not to separate either internal or external stimuli or what constitutes a stimulus or a response. Similarly, it is not always clear what sets a constructivist theory apart from an instructional theory or, because of the close connection between any such theories and motivation theories, either of the former from the latter.

Constructs of Behavioral Learning Theories. Behavioral learning theories emerged from an effort to move away from the humanistic tradition of analysis through introspection and interpretation. To make research more robust and scientific, directly observable behaviors were to lead to laws of behavior. For behaviorists, learning is

> change in a subject's behavior or behavior potential to a given situation brought about by the subject's repeated experiences in that situation, provided that behavior change cannot be explained on the basis of the subject's native response tendencies, maturation or temporary states. (Bower & Hilgard, 1981, p. 11)

Although goals of behaviorism realize a close relationship between environment and organism and emphasize active learning (Wilson & Myers, 2000), action is ultimately determined by environment rather than by self. There are several theoretical subsets of behaviorism. Of those, *operant conditioning* influenced music education researchers who sought to develop instructional theories derived from behaviorist models.

The theory of *classical conditioning* introduced by Pavlov (1927) claims that a natural emotional response is associated with a neutral stimulus to the extent that the neutral stimulus alone will elicit the response. Building on Pavlov's theory, Thorndike (1932) maintained that a stimulus-response (S-R) connection constituted the basic learning unit. His connectionism included (1) the law of readiness, which maintained that one must be physically and motivationally ready in order to learn; (2) the law of effect, which says that responses followed by satisfaction will be strengthened; and (3) the law of exercise, which regards rewarded practice (as opposed to blind repetition) as key to learning. Watson (1925) defined the mind as a tabula rasa (a blank slate) and postulated both the law of frequency and recency to describe effective reinforcement. Guthrie (1935), via his contiguity theory, asserted that the last or most recent association between stimulus and response is the one that is retained (principle of postremity). He claimed that a single connection between stimulus and response constituted learning. Hull (1951) introduced characteristics of the organism as intervening variables in his stimulus-organism-response (S-O-R) model. Spence (1956) extended Hull's ideas through concepts such as habit strength, drive, and incentive motivation.

The theory of operant conditioning, developed by Skinner (e.g., 1948, 1953, 1968), says that reinforcements strengthen responses, and his law of extinction says the opposite: that lack of reinforcement weakens response. While he came to acknowledge mental events as real and measurable, Skinner consistently held that causes of mental change (learning) lie ultimately in the environment. Nonetheless, rather than a response elicited by the environment, the individual organism (operant) acts on the environment, emitting a response that alters it in some way. Skinner applied these laws extensively to research on instructional practice. He believed that students should enjoy and want to learn, that reinforcement should be consistent and positive, and that because students learn at different paces, instruction should be individualized (Schunk, 2000). Skinner argued that the proper arrangement of reinforcement contingencies (presentation of appropriately broken-down and sequenced material, active student response, immediate and appropriate feedback, individual pacing) are central to effective learning. Theorists building on Skinner's ideas have advocated curricula based on behavioral objectives, programmed instruction, contingency contracts, and personalized systems of instruction.

Applications to the Study of Music Learning. Much of the research of Clifford Madsen, Robert Duke, Harry Price, and Cornelia Yarbrough follows the operant conditioning model of learning. Their research has focused on instructional principles that guide "good" or "successful" teaching. Here, the role of appropriate and inappropriate reinforcement is integral to understanding learning behaviors. In this regard, researchers in music education have looked at a wide variety of issues regarding the effect of reinforcement (praise) and feedback (verbal corrections) on musical discrimination, attitude, and performance. More recent reviews of literature are by Duke and Henninger (1998), Taylor (1997), and Madsen and Duke (1985). In addition, the use of music itself serving as a mechanism of reinforcement has been studied, among others, by Greer (1981) and Madsen (1981). (For more information, also see chapters 18 and 19.)

The behaviorist learning model has significantly impacted music researchers' interest in programmed instruction and CAI. Programmed instruction, for the most part, involves programmed sequential patterns. The general idea is that a teaching machine (ranging from sequences of worksheets to CAI) can provide appropriate stimuli in the form of digestible bits of information, elicit responses in the form of easily accessible questions, and provide feedback/reinforcement through additional information and/or praise. Initially, programs were linear in that all students went through the same process, though at varying speeds; later programs were branched, allowing for more advanced students to skip material. Reviews of programmed instruction and the use of CAI in music education practice are provided by Orman (1998) and Higgins (1992). A related area of research, personalized systems of instruction (PSI, the Keller Plan), has been explored by Jumpeter's (1985) study in which he demonstrated PSI to be an effective mode of instruction in college music appreciation courses.

Constructs of Cognitive Learning Theories. Cognitive theories focus on efforts to map an individual's learning processes as new information is integrated with already familiar knowledge. Often viewed as the antithesis of behavioral theories, cognitive learning theories developed as reactions to and/or extensions of behaviorism, although today the constructs tend to emphasize aspects of self-determination in the learning process. Learners actively construct knowledge on the basis of their reactions to sensory stimuli. Critical to cognitive theories in music education is an understanding of major constructs inherent in Gestalt psychology as the latter describes cognitive development. Beyond that, constructs of cognitive theories have found application in theories on HIP and the phenomenon of "connectionism" as applied to brain research.

Gestalt psychology is a theoretical subset of Gestalt theory, an early theory of perception developed by Koffka (1935), Kohler (1929, 1969), and Wertheimer (1959). Their theory maintains that learning is insightful and relies on an active process of problem-solving strategies rather than on reactions (responses) to random trial-and-error experiences. Gestalt laws state that a person will impose order on perceived disorder according to the laws of similarity, proximity, closure, continuation, and common fate. As the terms suggest, similarity refers to an individual matching observed objects with others of similar form or color; proximity makes an individual relate a perception to another one that comes closest to it. Closure indicates an individual's tendency to want to complete imperfect wholes; similarly, good continuation means that natural successors will complete an incomplete series of observations or sensations. Finally, "common fate" is the term used to describe an individual attributing characteristics of the whole or of parts of the whole to individual parts, based again on "best match." This means that the individual seeks to place component parts of a new experience into the already familiar context of previous, familiar experiences.

Studies in *cognitive development* gained in popularity among educators as a result of Piaget's (e.g., 1928, 1952, 1972) observation of young children's learning processes. His resultant theory was both cognitive and developmental in that it sought to explain (1) how children process information and (2) how those processes change with age. His proposed stages are well known. They have been described as sensorimotor learning, or learning through motor activity and manipulation of objects (age 0 to 2), to preoperational learning, which is the transformation of

sensorimotor to symbolic learning (ages 2 to 7), to concrete operations, manifested by increasing ability to classify objects and events (ages 7–11), to formal operations, manifested by thought processes typical of an adult (age 11 onward). Influenced by Piaget, Bruner (1960; Bruner, Goodnow, & Austin, 1956) studied how people actively select, retain, and transform information inductively relative to three developmental modes of assimilating knowledge: enactive (experiential), iconic (visual or mental pictures), and symbolic (symbolic systems such as language, mathematics, or musical notation). Bruner's (1966) spiral curriculum, another construct influential for music education research, proposed to structure learning, and thus teaching, in such a way that any subject, no matter how complex, may be introduced at appropriate levels and periodically with greater levels of complexity. Piaget also influenced Gardner, who in 1973 began his quest for understanding the arts from a developmental perspective and influenced the research conducted for the past several decades by Project Zero.

A number of cognitive theorists developed their ideas in response to behavioral learning theories. Chomsky (1957) responded to Skinner's ideas about verbal behavior by arguing that language learning is too complex to be explained by behavioral theories. He described language development as a cognitive process involving structuralism: surface structures (individual words as they are spoken or read) and deep structures (grouping of individual words into phrases). Transition from surface structures to deep structures and vice versa are made possible through what Chomsky called transformational rules. Tolman (1932), a behaviorist with cognitive ideas, postulated that learning can occur without reinforcement or changes in behavior, that there may be intervening variables and individual differences, that behavior is purposeful and goal-oriented, and that learning results in an organized body of information. Ausubel (1968) disagreed with Skinner's claim that an individual must emit an active response in order to learn; he claimed that a student might be cognitively active without overt physical action and that expository instruction has its place as long as information is meaningful and can be applied to previous learning. Associated with the idea that learning involves a hierarchy of instructional steps, Gagné (1977, 1985) believed that simpler (behavioral) principles are taught first and then lead to the development of higher order (cognitive) principles.

Information-processing theories utilize metaphors from computer science to explain how the mind works. A precursor to information processing was information theory, developed by Shannon (Shannon & Weaver, 1949); he showed that information could be measured as binary digits representing yes/no alternatives, which became the fundamental basis of today's telecommunications. Miller, Gallanter, and Pribram (1960) developed an early information-processing model of learning: TOTE (test-operate-test-exit), a feedback circuit whereby behavior is organized according to assessment; TOTE determines whether the state of affairs is personally followed, if necessary, by actions to reach an optimal state. Well known for his idea of chunking, Miller (1956) believed that short-term memory (attention span) can only hold seven (plus or minus two) chunks of information. Atkinson and Shiffrin (1968, 1971) originally developed the dual-storage model of memory: Input enters the brain via the sensory register and is processed by the working (or short-term) memory; long-term memory influences the working memory and stores perceptions that have relevance and impact (Schunk, 2000).

A subset of information-processing theories includes *connectionism* and related theoretical constructs that allow the study of artificial neural nets as potential models of brain function. As a theory, connectionism offers an alternate paradigm to information processing in that it frees cognitive models from dependence on symbolic/metaphoric language. As documented by Beach, Hebb, Morgan, and Nissen (1960), Lashley (1929) demonstrated that neural connections are distributed and that cortical areas can substitute for each other. Hebb (1949), a student of Lashley, postulated that learning is based on modification of synaptic connections between neurons. Extending these ideas, Rumelhart, McClelland, and the Parallel Distributed Processing Research Group (1986) introduced their theory of parallel distributed processing. In another study of neural mechanisms, Posner and Keele (1968) wrote about how neural mechanisms underlie selective attention. The theory of Schmidt (1975) posited schemas as abstract sets of rules for determining movement, as, for example, in motor learning. Witkin, Moore, Goodenough, and Cox (1977) studied field dependence-independence that "refers to the extent that one depends on or is distracted by the context or perceptual field in which a stimulus or event occurs" (Schunk, 2000, p. 422).

Applications to the Study of Music Learning. The application of cognitive theories to the study of musical learning has been most prevalent in the use of Gestalt psychology to explain processing of musical information. Thus, the laws of similarity, proximity, and closure have been used to describe and distinguish between processes of music perception, development, and cognition. Wang and Sogin (1990) reviewed the study of Gestalt organizational principles in music. Gestalt concepts also are implicit in Karma's (1985) exposition of hierarchical music concepts.

Lehrdahl and Jackendoff (1983) formulated a generative theory of musical grammar based on the linguistic theories of Chomsky. According to Lehrdahl and Jackendorff, acoustic information triggers mental operations that impose order onto input. If there is sufficient exposure to music, musical understanding will occur through enculturation rather than formal training.

Research employing cognitive theories to describe the musical development of children has received the widest attention and emphasis since the 1960s. Detailed reviews of those efforts have been offered, among others, by Funk and Whiteside (1981), Hargreaves (1986), Hargreaves and Zimmerman (1992), Scott-Kassner (1992), and Zimmerman (1986). According to Hargreaves and Zimmerman, Piaget's theory has impacted at least three areas of research in music learning: developmental stages; development of symbolic function made manifest through language, drawings, and make-believe; and the concept of conservation "according to which young children gradually acquire the understanding that two properties of a concrete object can covary to produce an invariant third property" (p. 378). Zimmerman (née Pflederer, 1964, 1966, 1967; Pflederer & Sechrest, 1968) is generally acknowledged as a pioneer in studying conservation in music. Swanwick and Tillman's (1986) spiral model of creative musical development also draws on Piaget and Bruner. Their model builds on four developmental stages: (1) mastery (age 0–4) during which children develop a sense of and respond to sounds; (2) imitation (4–9) during which children include the use of sounds to represent event or objects; (3) imaginative play (10–15) during which children combine sounds creatively; and (4) metacognition (15 and up), during which adolescents reflect on their own thinking about and experience with music.

Bruner's three modes, enactive, iconic, and symbolic representation, were also the foundation for all of the research and publications of Eunice Boardman Meske. Gromko (1996) investigated children's invented descriptions of songs relative to Bruner's modes of learning and wrote a detailed review of developmental literature, particularly as it evolved from Gardner's (1983) earlier work, including Davidson and Scripp (1988, 1992) and Upitis (1990, 1992). A similarly neo-Piagetian approach was taken by Elmer (1997), while the "discovery method" advocated by Bruner was investigated in a musical context by Hewson (1966).

As early as in the 1970s, Andrews and Deihl (1970) reviewed the ideas of Bruner and Hebb in music education. Much of the research in concept learning has centered on student vocabularies, a topic summarized by Flowers (2000) and Chen-Hafteck (1999). Cutietta (1985) described and applied the hypothesis-testing model of Bruner and others to the development of musical concepts. Booth and Cutietta (1991) explored the possibility that cognition can be divided according to Tulving's (1972) theory into episodic and semantic memory (verbal processing versus concept formation). Carlsen (1987) and Adachi and Carlsen (1995) discussed and outlined research according to the theory of expectancy, which proposes that previous musical experiences and concepts shape how new information is perceived and processed. Thorisson (1997) compared the utility of prototype versus exemplar theory in the development of musical style concepts in music appreciation texts.

Four theories of motor learning have had varying degrees of application in research on music learning: closed-loop theory, open-loop or motor program theory, schema theory (mental knowledge), and the Bernstein approach (Gabrielsson, 1999). Applications of the first three have been reviewed by LaBerge (1981) and Sidnell (1981a). Two major studies conducted by Ross (1985) and Coffman (1990) have focused on mental practice in music learning. Both give informative reviews of related literature and discuss the positive effect of combined mental and physical practice and the theoretical roots of mental practice in the writings of Tolman (1932) and Kohler (1929, 1969). DeLorenzo (1989) investigated creative thinking from a problem-solving/problem-finding perspective and gives an extensive overview of related cognitive studies in musical creativity.

Research on hemispheric dominance, cognitive style, and field dependence/independence in music education has seen a proliferation of studies since the 1970s. Baumgarte and Franklin (1981) reviewed studies related to right or left-brain dominance in musical information processing; they concluded that a number of factors determine where music is processed in the brain and that musical processing is neither completely right- nor left-brain situated. Hemispheric dominance was also related to learning style in the research of Zalanowski (1990). Scheid and Eccles (1975) provided an extensive historical overview of brain hemisphere research and applications in music cognition studies. Strong (1992) examined hemispheric laterality as it related to disabled students' learning. Perhaps the most extensive discussion to date regarding cerebral hemispheric dominance and/or roles was made by Marin and Perry (1999). Barry (1992) reviewed studies that looked at field dependence/independence in music performance and perception. (For a more in-depth discussion of field dependence/independence that includes cognitive style, see Ellis and McCoy, 1990.)

Information theory for music was initially explicated by Abraham Moles and served as the foundation for the musical understanding theory of Leonard B. Meyer. The application of information theory to music education research was discussed by Krumhansl (1990) in the context of developing a hierarchical model of musical cognition. These efforts were reviewed by Coffman (1990) in a study measuring musical originality and creativity. Information-processing theory also was advocated by Williams (1981, 1982) and Williams and Peckham (1975), who developed a music information-processing model based on the work

of Atkinson and Shiffrin (1968) in verbal-auditory processing and concept development. Tallarico (1974) described a three-phase concept of memory and how it might be implemented in the study of music cognition. In his discussion, he drew from a wide array of sources in information processing, including the writing of Norman, Rumelhart et al. (1986), and Hebb (1949). Cutietta and Booth (1996) provided an overview of research related to categorization of musical information in memory. In this regard, Miller's (1956) idea of "chunking" has found frequent acknowledgment in music cognition research. Probably the most extensive and recent discussion of music processing and memory was presented by Deutsch (1999).

Regarding the application of "connectionism" and neuroscientific processes to the study of music learning, Fiske (1984) reviewed the controversy between serial and parallel processing and established a background for connectionist theory, primarily drawing from Posner and Keele (1968). Fiske (1992) proposed that musical information processing involved the brain's ability to construct three patterns from auditory information: a given pattern, a variation of a given pattern, and a distinctly different pattern. The brain classifies or encodes information according to cognitive processing rules and then compares patterns in order to determine their function. This connectionist model became apparent in subsequent studies by Fiske (1995, 1997). His research is central to the work of Bharucha (1999), who has collaborated with Krumhansl in developing a music learning theory. Leng, Shaw, and Wright's (1990) theory of neural firing patterns, based on Hebbian learning principles, has been reviewed and tested by Rauscher (1999). Neurological studies in music education that do not rely on computer simulation were reviewed by Gruhn, Altenmüller, and Babler (1997).

Constructs of Constructivist Learning Theories. These theories acknowledge the interconnections between the learner and his or her environment as crucial for understanding the process of learning itself. Therefore, the study of learning is approached from a more holistic perspective. Interactive theories acknowledge the multifaceted, multidimensional complexity that ensues when an individual encounters and responds to musical stimuli not only in the context of the group(s) of which he or she is a part but also in the context that is created by the mental and physical environments surrounding the interactions. As with connectionism, a cognitively based perspective, learning is viewed as a complex serial process without any clear and identifiable beginning and end points.

Lewin (Lewin, Lippitt, & White, 1939), considered by some writers the father of social psychology, derived his field theory of learning from Gestalt theory, an approach that emphasizes context familiarity as an important descriptor of how individuals learn and process information. However, similar thoughts were expressed before him by Mead (1934) and again in 1941 by Dollard (Miller & Dollard, 1941) when they argued that all social interactions lead to learning. As individuals interact with others in any social setting (even the interaction of two people with each other is considered such a social setting), they take on "behavioral" roles that are articulated to them by other members in the group or by people they hold important ("significant other"). According to Buttram (1996), this "imitative" approach to learning in social contexts was first applied to the study of formal learning by Miller and Dollard. Through their work in social psychology, the stimulus-response-reinforcement model of the behaviorists was widened to include inner processes, such as drives, in guiding responses. Bandura (1986) also stressed the place of personal awareness of one's social context in any stimulus-response model of learning, and he introduced the idea of observational learning, whereby individuals learn because they emulate the behaviors of those with whom they wish to identify.

Connected to this social interactionist model is Dewey's model of experiential learning. In fact, a resurgence of interest in Dewey's social constructivist thinking can be observed in the renewed focus on reflective practice and "learning through doing." Another social constructivist, Vygotsky (e.g., 1962, 1987, 1997a, 1997b), has received renewed attention as well, especially his theory of the social nature of knowledge and of the zone of proximal development (ZPD) that reflects a child's current abilities and knowledge.

Similar to any if not all of these approaches toward explaining learning from a constructivist perspective is the assumption that learning is most successful in the context of apprenticeships and "communities of practice." This and other types of "situated learning" have been outlined and described by Bredo (1997); Brown, Collins, and Duguid (1989); Rogoff (1996); Wenger (1999); and Lave and Wenger (1991). In this context, the work of Schön and Argyris (Argyris & Schön, 1974; Schön, 1987) needs to be mentioned. They developed a theory of reflective practice that argues that learning takes place as a result of both reflection-in-action (the "doing") and reflection-on-action (the post facto analysis of "doing"). Also known as the double-loop theory, it argues that learning requires both processes if it is to lead to conceptual, that is, personally owned, knowledge.

Applications to Music Education Research and Practice. Although advocated by some music educators since the 1960s and 1970s, the application of constructivist constructs of learning to the study of music learning has only more recently begun to enter the mainstream of pub-

lications in American music education. (For an in-depth discussion of sociology in music education, see chap. 31 of this Handbook). Two recent symposia on a sociology of music education contained papers and addresses that reiterated the usefulness of social constructivism and situated learning as constructs for the study of music learning (Rideout, 1997; Rideout & Paul, 2000). In addition, a renewed interest in applying John Dewey's theoretical constructs to music research can be observed and has been documented by a number of recent studies. For example, Whitaker (1996) applied Dewey's idea of reflective thinking to expert listening and teacher training. Elmer (1997) applied Piaget's epistemology as well as social constructivist ideas to a microanalysis of song learning. Campbell (1999) enlisted Dewey's idea of learning by experience in building a social constructivist framework for teacher development. Younker and Smith (1996) focused on Dewey's emphasis of process over product in studying musical composition.

Wiggins (1994b) drew together ideas of Gardner, Vygotsky, and Rogoff in a social constructivist study on teacher research. Later (2000) she integrated an overview of social constructivist theories, including the idea of distributed intelligence, in her study of shared musical understandings. Della Pietra and Campbell (1995) explored and reviewed social constructivism in improvisation, and Davidson and Scripp (1992), drawing from a large number of nonmusic researchers, proposed the idea of a situated music cognition model.

Implications for applying constructs of social interactionism to music teacher training were outlined by Olsson (1997). Gholson (1998) developed a strategy for practice in violin pedagogy (mentoring) that builds on Schön's "communities of practice" and similar ideas of Vygotsky. Schön's reflective practice is discussed by Barrett and Rasmussen (1996) and Brand (1998), along with ideas for "theories-in-action." Brown, Collins, and Duguid's (1989) situated cognition model was used by Wiggins (1994b) and Bresler (1993) in studies about action research by teachers.

Critique: Learning Theories and Their Application to Music

The adaptation of general, a priori learning theories to explain musical learning has served music education well. By building a research base that is derived from educational and general psychology, a wide array of studies have sought to answer complex questions, and their answers have been translated into music education practice. Research articles between 1960 and 2000 make it evident that general theories of behaviorism adapt directly and successfully to music teaching. Behavioral learning theories in particular have led to research not just on music learning but also on teaching techniques, instructional strategies, sequencing of instruction, and student motivation and attitudes in the classroom.

Historically, behavioral research has examined behaviors of groups of learners. Insofar as music teachers work with larger classes whose success depends on techniques affecting the "majority," implications for practice-derived behavioral learning models will continue to serve music education well. Cognitive and interactive theories, in contrast, focus more on the individual because learning is defined by the relationship between subject matter and each individual learner. While teachers facilitate scholarship and instructional guidance, actual learning depends upon a wide variety of influences that act upon the learner in different ways than they do on the teacher. For this reason, research literature built on the application of cognitive and interactive learning theories has produced somewhat less concrete instructional results.

The focus on practical results, then, requires attention if the relative impact of behavioral, cognitive, and constructivist research related to learning theories is to be assessed. At present, the validity of a particular learning theory appears to depend on how quickly it can be translated into instructional practice. Without any question, learning theories derived from behaviorism have had the greatest effect in that regard. Yet some strides in translating cognitive research into music education practice, especially in the organization of material to enhance learning, have been made. Not only has the use of concept maps and advanced organizers become popular, but there is an increased awareness of the need to individualize instruction, work with each student's strengths, and provide different sequences of instruction for different groups of learners.

The greater question, however, is what renders a learning theory valid—that we can adjust our teaching methods quickly and efficiently, or that the constructs accurately describe what actually is going on when musical stimuli are processed and responded to either by an individual learner or by an entire group? This means that we need to know the purpose for which we want to study learning processes in music: to make instruction as efficient as possible or to learn more about the field of music itself. One requires that we find expedient ways for the student to reach predefined instructional objectives and learning gains; the other means to map learning processes in music for the sake of comparing them to other learning processes.

Learning Theories Unique to Music

This section emphasizes a review of studies and writings whose findings may be useful in the construction of a theory of music learning derived from the observation of musical behaviors themselves. This approach, though not nec-

essarily informed but certainly supported by constructivist thinking, embraces the notion of leaving already established, nonmusic constructs behind and acknowledging musical behavior as its own "domain," situated in a context uniquely its own.

Ruttenberg (1994) defined music learning as an extended musical activity that is comprised of a progression of musical mental functions that go from sensation to perception, to cognition, to creativity. This progression has value in explaining musical processing as well as learning and thinking. Building upon Ruttenberg's (1994) definition, musical learning will be described for the purposes of this chapter as moving from sensation to perception to cognition, including a change in mental structure. This progression also may have value as a theoretical frame into which to place the many diverse studies in music education that address the nature of music learning from a music-specific vantage point. A few of these studies will be referred to later, but for the most part the work of five specific researchers will be highlighted: Edwin Gordon's efforts to develop a theory of music learning; Bamberger's work toward understanding how musical intelligence develops; Gardner's musical intelligence theory; and, finally, Cutietta's research, as well as Regelski's proposed praxis of music teaching, both of which may lead to a theory of music learning. In some instances, these perspectives have influenced research agendas of others, offer unique approaches toward researching musical thinking and learning, and contain commonalities as well as differences that may serve as the basis for an improved understanding of how music learning takes place. Eventually, the commonalities among the works may become the constructs for valid theories of music learning.

Edwin Gordon's initial research, beginning with the observation of individual students involved in the process of learning music, sought to develop a theory of music learning and not necessarily a measure of musical aptitude. After determining that individual students seemed to begin the music learning process at different stages, Gordon was "sidetracked [as he was] forced to embark on the study of the nature, development, and measurement of musical aptitudes" (Gordon, 1971, p. 8) rather than focusing solely on the development of a music learning theory. Though Gordon's contributions to music education are numerous, for the purpose of this chapter only his efforts at developing a theory of music learning unique to music education will be discussed. (For a more thorough review of Gordon's work, see chapter 22.)

Gordon's research into a theory of music learning, begun in the 1960s, derives from a search for a basic "key word" vocabulary of music. Unlike other educational thinkers, he focused his attention on aural rather than theoretical aspects of music. Thus, rather than follow educators who extracted from written music the conceptual elements of pitch, rhythm, dynamics, form, and timbre as basic components or "key words" of music, Gordon identified aural pitch and rhythmic patterns as the basic vocabulary of music. He arranged these key musical "words" in his learning sequences by identifying the most basic patterns, teaching them first, and then following them with increasingly more complex patterns as learning continued. Gordon believed that learning music resulted from building a musical vocabulary (aural pitch and rhythmic patterns) through repetition, rote learning, and drill.

A second feature of Gordon's approach was the parallel he drew to language development, in which thinking without sound can involve learning; thinking is conceived as "internally talking" with the use of words or the "voice in our heads." Gordon's music learning theory incorporates audiation or the process of thinking musically, as in hearing without sounds the "song in our heads." According to Gordon, children developmentally prepare to "audiate" by experiencing acculturation (a premature awareness of sound); imitation (some aural recognition of sounds); and assimilation (a more precise aural recognition of sounds).

On the basis of this chapter's definition of music learning, Gordon promoted the idea of internalizing musical patterns out of musical context so that the patterns may facilitate perception and change in mental structures within the context of music. By drilling and practicing predetermined, cumulative, and sequential pitch and rhythmic patterns (Gordon's theory of music learning translated into practice) learning occurs. As the musical vocabulary becomes ingrained in the learner, perceptual abilities grow, vocabulary becomes richer, ability to audiate becomes refined, and musical perception and learning is consequently enhanced.

Jeanne Bamberger's research investigating the development of musical intelligence began in the early 1970s. Her book *The Mind Behind the Musical Ear: How Children Develop Musical Intelligence* (1991) is the culmination of many years of observation of primary school children. Bamberger believed it was important to study musical behavior as it occurred in social context.

During individual or group sessions with young children, Bamberger observed and questioned them about their musical knowledge. Most of her work was concerned with how children reproduced music: They notated, primitively, what they heard and taught it to others using their original notation. Bamberger used as musical examples so-called simples, common pitch-time relations of tunes and rhythms that individuals can be presumed to have sung as children. Children learned about music through their own discovery and focused primarily on rhythm patterns and tune-building (pitch).

Bamberger described the children's inclination to hear, explain, and notate rhythm and pitch patterns figurally or formally. Figural hearing was motivic, as rhythm and pitch patterns were grouped according to what "goes together." Formal hearing attended to actual rhythmic durations or standard musical notation. For example, a familiar nursery rhyme appears (1) linguistically, (2) figurally, (3) formally, and then in (4) standard notation:

1. Five, six, pick up sticks, seven, eight, lay them straight
2. O, O, o o o, O, O, o o o
3. O, O, o o O, o o, O, o o O
4. Quarter, quarter, eighth, eighth, quarter; eighth, eighth, quarter; eighth, eighth, quarter

Notations 2 and 3 have 10 shapes derived from the 10 separate beats in the nursery rhyme; however, the figural representation (2) shows graphically the first two longer sounds and the following shorter sound, while the formal representation reflects the standard notation, as represented by the series of eighth and quarter notes (4). Formal hearing attends to duration, meter, and classifying rhythm and pitch patterns according to standard musical notation, while figural hearing is more motivic or graphic in nature. Because all children's drawings of rhythm and pitch patterns, regardless of developmental age, either involve figural hearing, formal hearing, or a combination of the two, Bamberger maintains that figural and formal hearing are inherent in perception.

Understanding and learning music is described by Bamberger as perceptual problem solving: Perception and cognition are intertwined and not discrete quantities (1982). Musical "hearings" (Bamberger, 1991, p. 3) are repeated hearings of the same piece of music and factor into perceptual problem solving; they are the same piece of music heard again and again, only differently each time as the learner accommodates new hearings. Bamberger therefore emphasizes the importance of multiple hearings in music learning: An individual can listen again to the same piece of music, perceive it differently the second or third time, and cognitively and conceptually reorganize the music before it is learned.

Bamberger believes music learning to be developmental, although it does not necessarily follow Piaget's stage development theory; rather, different ways of representing musical knowledge interact with each other in an ongoing multidimensional manner. For instance, as children create musical representations (both figural and formal) of what they hear, they create written material that "holds still" (Bamberger, 1991, p. 52) so that children can reflect on it. A conversation develops between the child's thinking and reflection about what is on the paper. This interactive component depends to some extent on reflection-in-action (Bamberger, 1991; Bamberger & Schön, 1991; Schön, 1987), which is the learner's ability (often with the help of the teacher) to move back and forth between reflection *of* experience and reflection *on* experience (Bamberger, 1991,

p. 52). Like other domains of learning, a child's musical learning is developmental: It is dependent on age or experience.

Music learning is a generative and sensorimotor process. "Generative," a term borrowed from linguistics, means that, like language learning, music learning is an active process whereby individuals organize sound/time phenomena as they occur (Bamberger, 1991). Organization of sound/time phenomena involves sensorimotor experiences, such as gestures, sequences of periodic movement, equilibrium, tension, and relaxation. These various sequences of motion in turn become "felt paths" (p. 10), which are akin to a performer's ability to play complex musical passages from memory: Felt paths or action paths become internalized in the learner.

Bamberger does not posit a *theory* of music learning; instead she describes the earliest stages of what summarily tends to be referred to as music cognition, meaning that a particular mental challenge leads to a change in mental structure. This transitional process is developmental; involves multiple hearings; includes sensorimotor experiences, reflection, and internalization (felt paths); and involves the ability to move from *figural* to *formal* hearings, descriptions, and constructions of music.

Developing Musical Intuitions (Bamberger, 2000) is an example of research evolving into practice. This book, a culmination of her life's work, is subtitled *A Project-Based Introduction to Making and Understanding Music.* Interactive computer software applications expose students to melodic structure, rhythm, and meter (i.e., duple and triple meter, scales, major and minor mode, I–IV–V harmonizations) that are derived from Bamberger's methodologies (1982, 1991). Students draw on what they know and create musical representations (in this case on the computer) that are derived from "chunks" (i.e., phrases) of musical material. These "chunks" come from figural and formal hearings, from subsequent drawings or representations of these hearings, and from figures that generate structural hierarchies (figures or motives that become part of phrases, which become part of sections) and metric hierarchies (a regenerating, living constituent as a piece of music moves through time).

Included in this interactive CAI journey described by Bamberger is reflection-in-action. The process of learning in *Musical Intuitions* (2000) depends on a "conversation," which is

> the usually silent conversations we have with materials as we are building, fixing, or inventing. As we handle these materials, arranging and rearranging them, watching them take shape even as we shape them, we learn. The materials "talk back" to us, remaking our ideas of what is possible. The back-talk leads to new actions on our material objects in a spiral of inner and outer activity; our inner intentions

are reflected back by the results of our actions, leading to new outer actions and often to changing of our intentions. It is a kind of "re-search"—one that is as familiar to the scientist designing a theory as to the painter or composer designing an artifact. (p. 2)

Evan Zipoyrn writes in the foreword to Bamberger (2000) that Bamberger's greatest innovation is her ability to "get people to pay attention to what they already know and how they come to know it" (p. x). Bamberger believes the way to deepen musical understanding is to examine what is already known and reflect on what is being heard.

Howard Gardner, author of *Frames of Mind* (1983) and the theory of multiple intelligences (1999), contributes to the development of a theory unique to music learning through his many writings about artistic expression (e.g., 1980) and musical intelligence (1973/1994, 1983, 1999). He believes that humans possess varying degrees of seven "original" intelligences (1983) and possibly three or more additional intelligences (1999). In *Frames of Mind* (1983), musical intelligence is defined as skills in the "performance, composition and appreciation of musical patterns" (p. 42). Gardner supports his claim that musical intelligence is separate and unique with case studies of brain-damaged and brain-altered individuals; musical ability is located in specific spheres of the brain and can remain unaltered in individuals with brain impairment.

Though Gardner focuses on musical *intelligence* and not on musical *learning*, explanations of how individuals learn music are implicit in his writings. Like Bamberger, Gardner's hypothetical theory of music learning is developmental: Children involved in sensorimotor experiences move their bodies to music and babble songs and melodies. These innate responses are, in some instances, not distinguishable from the animal kingdom: Birds "babble" songs and chimpanzees respond physically to music. However, beyond the sensorimotor response, the differences between humans and animals are distinguishable as humans move into stages of concrete operations and formal knowledge.

In 1999, Gardner updated his definition of intelligence as: "a bio-psychological potential to process information that can be activated in a cultural setting to solve problems or create products that are of value in a culture" (p. 33–34). This definition implies an "intelligence" required for music *learning* that even the most "humanlike" chimpanzee does not possess: the ability to solve musical problems or create musical products. Inherent in the ability to solve musical problems is the "susceptibility to encoding in a symbol system" (Gardner, 1999, p. 37). Musical symbol systems include predictable genres: written language, musical notation, musical pictures, musical drawings, iconic musical notation, and so on, as well as unpredictable elements or materials that may but "need not be a physical object" (Gardner, 1973/1994, p. 128), as in musical sounds.

Implicit in Gardner's hypothetical theory of music learning is modal-vectoral sensitivity (1973/1994, p. 126). The latter is a humanlike quality that contributes to the transition of responding innately to musical stimuli in the sensorimotor plane, to responding to musical stimuli in the symbolic plane, that is, as musical stimuli having reference to something outside oneself. This transitional process allows individuals to move from sensation and perceptual experiences (innate responses) to cognitive experiences (outside referencing, remembering, recalling an experience or picture after seeing an object, and so on).

Modal-vectoral sensitivity involves the ability to feel bodily sensations (i.e., holding on, letting go, envelopment, intrusion) and perceptions (i.e., intensity, roughness, smoothness); these responses promote in humans the ability to organize sensations and perceptions into remembered experiences. Within the musical domain, symbols (i.e., notation, visual representations of instruments, aural motifs) arouse modal-vectoral experiences and continue to do so as humans transition developmentally from the sensorimotor to the symbolic plane.

> Far from being merely a feeling experienced by the individual, an act made, or a discrimination perceived, modes become schemes for organizing all experience, be it perceived, felt, or made; modes invoke discrimination, involve feelings, and are manifested in motoric activity. Indeed, persons can classify in terms of these categories in perception, produce instances of the categories in making (i.e. constructing), and experience these categories as affect. The modes and vectors provide both form and content for the child's earlier experiences. They are drawn on as the child proceeds from the sensorimotor to the symbolic stage, and remain as a backdrop and substratum for all later experience. (Gardner, 1973/1994, p. 111)

Like Bamberger, Gardner has focused three decades of his life on the development of intelligence and educational reform, specifically that which operates in artistic domains. His theory of general intelligence focuses not only on problem-solving abilities but on the ability to create products as manifestations of understanding and learning. Undoubtedly, his interpretation of a theory of learning unique to music would include: sensation, perception, cognition, and a change in mental structure, followed by the ability to use tools (symbols) that demonstrate learning through problem solving and the creating of products.

Other research in the field of music education parallels Gardner's and Bamberger's interest in music learning through the acquisition of musical representations of sound. Though this research does not hypothesize a theory of music learning, research agendas have been built on the acquisition of musical representations of sound, the use of invented musical notation, and their contribution to musical understanding. A summary of some of these research efforts follows.

Gardner, Bamberger, and other researchers who have built research agendas on their work (i.e., Davidson & Scripp, 1988) were early members of Gardner's Harvard Project Zero team, which investigated the development of children's musical symbolic intelligence (Gromko, 1994, 1996a, 1996b) and children's use of symbols in artistic domains. A common thread in much of Project Zero's work and other research agendas built on this work is that children's invented notation is a means of "assessing their understanding of the musical features of songs or instrumental compositions" (Barrett, 1999, p. 14). Given that this chapter's focus is on the development of a theory unique to music "learning" and not on a theory of music "making, creating, or performing" (i.e., the creation of songs and instrumental compositions), children's invented musical notation is discussed as a "window" into understanding musical learning and not into understanding musical creativity and performance. Research investigating invented musical notation is presented insofar as it contributes to furthering an understanding of what happens when a change in mental structure produces music learning.

Bamberger proposed that children's invented musical notation progresses from figural to formal as children's invented drawings mature from "figurative" musical examples (i.e., motivic examples or drawing the way the music goes) to "formal" musical drawings that depict actual rhythmic duration or even standard music notation. Davidson and Scripp (1988) took Bamberger's work one step further by suggesting that children's invented musical notation moves progressively through five distinct types of invented notational systems or "strategies" (Barrett, 1999, p. 14): pictorial, abstract patterning, rebus, text, and combination/elaboration.

The *pictorial* system involves use of invented musical notation represented by pictures. The *abstract patterning* system includes lines and dots that "represent melodic units of the song and record the rhythmic groupings, underlying pulse, melodic contour or phrase structure" (Davidson & Scripp, 1988, p. 204). The *rebus* system uses icons, conventional signs, and words; the *text* system uses words, letters, or imitations of conventional language symbols that often depict the graphic layout of direction of pitch and rhythmic groupings in the music; and the *combination/elaboration* system includes both abstract symbols in combination with text that show how the text is to be sung (melodically and rhythmically). Children's invented musical notation matures from pictures, to more abstract visual representations, to more symbolic depictions of music.

Davidson and Scripp (1988) looked at children's musical cognitive processing through the use of song text, perhaps because it is easier for young children to follow musical progressions of sound when defined by words as well as music. Regardless of the use of text, it is apparent from this research that music learning is a temporal (ongoing) and generative process, whereby individuals are organizing sound/time phenomena as they are occurring (Bamberger, 1991). For the purpose of this chapter, Davidson and Scripp might concur that a theory of music learning involves sensation, perception, and cognition, processes that produce an ongoing change in mental structure as individuals continually add and modify musical knowledge. (A thorough summary of the work of Davidson and Scripp has been outlined in the first edition of the *Handbook of Research on Music Teaching and Learning* [Hargreaves & Zimmerman, 1992]).

The research agenda of Gromko (1994, 1996a, 1996b; Domer & Gromko, 1996) focuses on an emerging musical intelligence in young children, manifested by their ability to use musical icons and symbols. Though she is not a member of the Harvard Project Zero team, Gromko's hypotheses were derived from both Gardner's and Bamberger's investigations into the theory and development of musical intelligence. Gromko's research investigating children's use of invented musical notation does not include the development of a theory of music learning; however, her work expands on the cognitive processes described in Gardner's and Bamberger's work that may produce a change in mental structure and, subsequently, musical learning.

Like Bamberger and Gardner, Gromko believes that music learning is developmental. The nature of change in children's invented musical notation as a measure of their musical understanding suggests a

developmental progression that moves from: (a) scribbles not systematically associated with sound to (b) uninterrupted lines that account for the entire duration of the musical event and its regular pulsations, to (c) a melodic line drawing that accounts for the entire duration of the musical event and the highs and lows of its melody. (Domer & Gromko, 1996, p. 72)

Gromko (1994) also found that children notate pitch before rhythm and that their ability to represent pitch with lines and icons corresponds to their performance on the *Primary Measures of Musical Audition* (PMMA) (Gordon, 1979). She concluded (Gromko, 1995) that musical learning is enhanced by sensorimotor experiences. Like Bamberger, Gromko believes in studying children in a social, experiential context. Children who worked with tangible materials (i.e., colored blocks, glitter, felt) and made these materials correspond to the "way the music goes" were subsequently better able to construct symbols that repre-

sented music than children who did not. Concurrently, Gromko found that more developmentally advanced children were less dependent on sensory actions as an intermediate step between their perception and construction of musical representations. She, too, strongly believes in the process of reflection-in-action. Much of her research depends on a dialogue between the student and teacher about the music: "The process of invention may contribute to building understanding because the children's visual representations are images to be evaluated in a process of reflection" (p. 6).

Like Gardner, Gromko might concur that a hypothetical theory of music learning would include sensation, perception, and cognition, followed by a change in mental structure, and the subsequent ability to transform invented musical representations into musical symbols: "Invention, Piaget believed, is the inevitable result of understanding: to understand is to invent" (1994, p. 22). Much of Gromko's work traces the development of musical symbols in children (1994, 1995, 1996a, 1996b; Gromko & Poorman, 1998a, 1998b). She believes that

[s]ymbolically fluent children are capable of more than imitation or reproduction, for they have fixed references that allow them to represent an event symbolically and, abstractly. Symbolically fluent individuals, those for whom symbols are meaningful conveyors of information, have internalized the properties that symbols embody. (1995, p. 5)

If Gromko were to formally turn her research into instructional practice, she would recommend the necessity and importance of a music curriculum rich in sensory experiences (i.e., moving, playing, creating, reflecting) in order to create a symbolically fluent child. Especially for young children, Gromko would advocate an environment filled with manipulatives, colors, sounds, and textures and would encourage not only activity-oriented musical experiences but thoughtful discussions with children about the music they are making.

Hypothesizing that understanding and learning music require perceptual problem solving (Bamberger, 1991) may be *Cutietta's* (1985, Cutietta & Haggerty, 1987; Booth & Cutietta, 1991) position that the mind "categorizes" musical sounds in a nonelemental (pitch, rhythm, timbre, harmony, and form), more holistic fashion. When Bamberger and Gromko asked children to initially "draw the way the music goes" their representations were abstract, holistic, and figural and not representational of pitch and rhythm. More formal representations evolved as children's musical minds became more "cognitive." Cutietta suggests that the mind perceives and hears music differently from how music theorists presume it does and that in order to produce a change in mental structure, musical practice might need to adopt a nonelemental approach.

Cutietta's (1985) research focuses on the nature of categories used by children and adults when classifying music and the musical features used to place music into chosen categories. When middle school students were asked to describe what was "the same" about diverse pieces of music heard in sequence, Cutietta found that students classified music in a "holistic" manner. Students forced a wide array of music into small mental categories related to musical styles of rock, opera, television, and church, and the only category used appropriately was rock. Other categorizations (i.e., opera, television, and church) related more to style of performance than actual music. For example, anything performed on an organ, regardless of music, was classified as "church." Likewise, any music performed vocally with vibrato was classified as opera, even if the song was a popular song.

Building on Cutietta's work, Zwink (1988) explored categories used by preschool children to classify music prior to musical training. After hearing a wide variety of music, children were asked, through age-appropriate questions and activities, to verbally describe what they heard; certain categories were used with regularity by a substantial number of children. Again, a consistency in the category of "rock" was used in musically accurate ways by both preschoolers and middle schoolers. Similarly, Cutietta and Haggerty (1987) investigated whether similar categorizations were common among an even broader age span (from age 3 to 80) by determining an individual's ability to categorize music according to nonmusical attributes such as color. Results showed the ease and consistency of categorizations across types of music and age groups.

Another study of categorization processes (Booth & Cutietta, 1991) involved college students being asked to place music into "types of music." Two pieces of music chosen to confound the task contained musical elements that dictated one style (played in an arpeggio style on a solo acoustical guitar with identical meters, tempos, and tonal structure) while more holistic characteristics favored a different style (one was from a Christmas carol and the other was a popular rock-and-roll song). These two pieces were never placed in similar categories but instead were classified with other pieces with little musical similarity (i.e., the popular song was placed in the category with loud and driving electric guitars and drums while the Christmas song was placed in categories with choirs and orchestras). Other examples within the study demonstrated that it was common and easy for listeners to ignore elemental musical characteristics in favor of more holistic characteristics (i.e., style). Another study (Cutietta & Booth, 1996) examined the order of melodies remembered in a free-recall task by musicians and nonmusicians. Melodies were created that systematically paired elemental cues, such as meter and mode, with more global cues, such as melodic contour and melodic flow. Consistently elemental aspects of the music

(meter and mode) were discounted in favor of more global characteristics of music.

Several researchers have expanded on the work started by Cutietta. Lineburgh (1994) showed the ease with which students placed music into categories. Using first graders as subjects, she designed a task that encouraged students to place recordings of piano music into one of three categories, based on composer. Students were able to place music into a Chopin, Mozart, or Joplin category after minimal instruction. Furthermore, children were able to transfer this knowledge to unheard pieces by the same composer after just five instructional periods. Thus, she concluded "the act of classifying music is one that is readily undertaken by these children despite the fact that they do not seemingly have the knowledge base which one might assume necessary to undertake such fine discriminations. Clearly, the brain is eager to do the task" (p. 79).

Lineburgh's (1994) findings argue that other musically "correct" categories should be learned in early childhood besides those of the high/low (pitch) and slow/fast (meter). Berke (2000) presented preschoolers with instruction in the "holistic" task of anticipating harmonic changes in songs despite the fact that the students were untrained in more basic "preliminary skills" such as pitch height or pitch direction: After several months of training, 3- through 5-year-olds were able to anticipate and predict I–IV–V^7 chord changes, despite the fact that more "basic" skills of recognizing pitch direction were not mastered. O'Hagin (1997) designed a study using movement activities to ascertain the musical focus of preschool children using music that had inherent conflicts between traditional elements of music and more holistic characteristics of style and mood. Despite months of movement training in responding to elemental aspects of the music, the majority of children consistently favored holistic over elemental aspects of the music in interpreting the music through movement.

These three studies point to the fact that children can readily either learn to classify music using classifications such as jazz, rock, classical, and swing or respond to harmonic progressions before learning isolated pitch. Further, the studies suggest that discriminations usually reserved for more advanced study, such as the difference between classical and romantic solo piano works, are readily learned by young children if they are consistently encouraged to classify these correctly at an early age. The results of these studies open a discussion as to what musical characteristics children use to place music into categories if they have not yet learned to identify the "elements" of pitch, duration, rhythm, form, and timbre.

Cutietta (1993), in discussing implications of this line of research for music education practice, proposed changes not in instructional theory but instead in curriculum development. Commonly, music educators teach music according to its conceptual elements: melody (high/low), rhythm (fast/slow), harmony, timbre, dynamics (loud/soft), and form. These categories help musicians understand musical rudiments and impart musical knowledge to beginning musicians. Traditional curricula in series books and curriculum guides start with teaching basic building blocks of music from a theoretical standpoint, following models established for disciplines such as chemistry that begin with elemental components of a stimulus. Research findings on children's ability to categorize music according to prescribed criteria advocate reliance on the skills the child brings to the task of learning. The latter are primary learning tools and determine how musical information presented to the child is organized. This organizing principle could become the basis of any theory of music learning.

Cutietta (1993) suggests that curricula be structured in such a way that learning capitalizes on basic processes that are observable when learners make musical choices. Thus, before a change in mental structure can occur, it may be necessary to determine existing mental structures. While his research has not yet identified such structures in detail, it has demonstrated that fine discriminations, such as tempo or pitch height, may be not only unnecessary but not useful to young children who try to make sense of their musical world. Instead, it seems that holistic categorizations, based on musical styles or moods, are important first steps from a learning standpoint.

Regelski's (1982) work, too, is based on the observation of children involved in the music learning process. Believing that, too often, the child is told the "meaning" of knowledge as society sees it and not as the child sees it, he advocated that children must be encouraged to construct and create personal meaning from musical experiences in order for learning to occur. Theoretically, this view can be validated as a constructionist perspective. However, Regelski's concern about fostering a form of music learning that moves away from verbal learning models and toward an understanding of the child's own processes of "meaning making" in music reflects a more music-intrinsic approach toward developing a theory of music learning. This view is supported by Elliot's (1995) later proposed construct of "musicing," which means that the "doing" of music through performance and active listening is more important than the verbalization of learned concepts. According to Regelski (1982), too much of music learning is based on verbal models that lead to

> unhealthy states of mind among students in general music classes in the middle and secondary years. . . . Public school education has largely been a matter of acquiring verbal control over one's interaction with the environment. . . . Words, thus have come to stand between a person's perceptions and their actions. They have formed a semantic web that filters raw or pure experience. (p. 6)

Rather than base music learning on verbal models, Regelski believes that students should become more actively involved with making, creating, and manipulating musical sounds. However, he does not diminish the "verbalization" process, advocating that musicing must be accompanied by thoughtful and thought-provoking activity. Verbal learning does have a place in music education, but "it should be placed after the experience, not before it. And it should progress in the student's own terms. [If verbalization] is placed between the child and the reality, especially when the reality is music, all kinds of problems arise" (p. 10).

Regelski's model of music learning, which is, at the same time, his model of music education practice, does not differ essentially from those of other theorists seeking to develop constructs of music learning from within the field of music itself. Similar to Gromko's research, Regelski endorses initial musical learning as sensorimotor and as active, nonverbal musical experiences; Regelski warns that language is not needed before learning and that it can actually decrease learning. Comparable to Bamberger's research, Regelski relies on reflection as a means of facilitating learning; children construct personal meaning and understanding from experience based on past knowledge. Akin to Gordon's work, Regelski's work advocates aural rather than written or language-based musical experiences. As a way of furthering learning, Regelski recommends, as does Cutietta, beginning the instructional process with what the child perceives or knows.

Critique: Learning Theories Unique to Music

Any one theory of music learning derived from observing musical behaviors is likely to be the result of the work of not one but many individuals. Learning music is a complex and interwoven matrix of skills, knowledge, affect, and beliefs. To this end, it will take an array of researchers and scholars to bring these together.

The researchers reviewed here have made strides toward articulating what it means to learn and think musically. As is the case with any learning theory of any philosophical persuasion, categorizing sound is an essential first step in that regard. This is the commonality among them. How a learner is asked to describe musical experiences and group them, however, sets the researchers apart.

When looked at from a wider perspective, explorations such as the ones described begin to take on meaning beyond specific results yielded by any one study alone. Each contribution, while approaching the study of music learning from a different angle, becomes part of a larger whole. Gordon and Bamberger focused on how to make visible, without the use of words, what a learner does when presented with musical stimuli. Much, if not the majority, of research derived from learning theories outside of music makes the assumption that words are needed to document such processes. The inner "voice" that attempts to figure out something, or the fact that most of what is learned is mediated by words (either through reading, hearing, or speaking language), argues in favor of such an assumption. However, Gordon and Bamberger clearly reject the assumption that music involves verbal-type processes. Once this assumption is rejected, the first task toward creating a theory of music learning is to find what replaces the verbal foundation.

Gordon and Bamberger each took a different route to explore this fundamental question. Gordon looked within music, and Bamberger looked within the child. In Gordon's case, he found basic patterns within music that he believed represented the basic vocabulary of music. These pitch and rhythm patterns could be added together over a canvas of repeating beat patterns to represent music. In this way, sound patterns become the musical vocabulary for the inner "voice," but instead of talking, the voice sings. Since no word existed for this nonvocal singing, Gordon called it audiation.

Bamberger found that the children heard patterns similar to those proposed by Gordon. However, the patterns were not static, as Gordon suggested, but changed with each musical hearing. Because the child changed and evolved with each hearing, the musical patterning perceived by the child constantly changed and evolved.

Like Bamberger and Davidson and Scripp, Gromko explored this changing perspective and concurred that the perception of patterns is developmental. As children grow, their musical "encoding" grows with them. Gromko found that the earliest representations were holistic, while grouping of patterns appeared as the child got older. The work of Cutietta and others has concerned itself with *how* and *why* children select patterns. As the child starts to acquire musical patterns in the form of songs or pieces of music, he or she must find a place to store them for recall. It is clear from this research that children and adults group music together in memory. What causes them to group patterns and musical experiences in particular ways is still the question. Some say the answer lies in the affective nature of music; others argue that affect is the result of experience, exposure, and context.

Conclusion

The goal of scientific inquiry is the establishment or refinement of theory (Carlsen, 1987). Researchers in the behavioral, social, and "hard" sciences observe facts or data in their respective fields, seek answers to questions or problems arising from these facts, attempt to reason or hypothesize the origin of data on the basis of established or spec-

ulative theories, and measure and test these hypotheses in subsequent research. The end result is an attempt to unify the why and wherefore of phenomena as well as build a body of cohesive research in a given field. As Sidnell (1981b) wrote:

> Believing that music education is a study of the nature of, and modification of, human musical abilities, I am thoroughly convinced that we need to fashion a rational framework upon which a fabric of process can be woven to effect well-directed change in the people we teach. It is all about theory. (p. 175)

The use and creation of theories as the basis for research is the sign of a mature profession. Theories provide guidance and direction to research efforts and have allowed researchers to begin to build a body of literature that interrelates and collectively has the potential for making an impact. It requires an examination of the findings of seemingly diverse studies in the broader context of constructs that may explain the nature of music learning during different ages, developmental levels, and levels of experience with and exposure to music. It requires an understanding of learning both as a formal and as an informal endeavor and viewing the learner both as an individual and the member of a group. In both cases, the individual seeks to make meaning of and respond to internal and external stimuli, but the response may be different.

Over the 30-year period reviewed, there has been an ebb and flow of learning theories in the literature; clearly, some have been "in vogue" and then have become more obscure. It is not uncommon for a researcher to justify a particular study as a critical response to another study that utilized a different theoretical stance. In music education, this approach has often been somewhat naïve. Instead of showing a true, healthy skepticism toward theories or engaging in scholarly discourse over the relative merit of specific theoretical constructs, it too often has been the practice to "pit" one approach against the other or, worse, one researcher against the other. Far too many examples within the music education profession exist where justifying a study from a cognitive standpoint is based on the premise that all earlier research was behavioral or on the assumption that behavioral studies are tested with quantitative and cognitive theories with qualitative methodologies. Thus, learning theories are confused with research methodologies and constructs with design.

Instead, theories need to match the hypothesis tested. A study of improving trill speed in clarinetists or increasing practice time for band members might benefit from constructs derived from behavioral theories. Conversely, a study exploring how individual students approach the act of practicing might best involve variables more commonly found in cognitive or constructivist models.

Likewise, it is just as important to continue researching the creation of a learning theory unique to music as it is to examine the usefulness of importing theories from other disciplines to the music classroom. The profession is multifaceted enough to need a variety of diverse theories to explain different phenomena inherent in music learning.

In the future, the profession would be well-guided to increase the practice of grounding research in theory. Far too many studies still stand alone in the field with little or no relationship to the body of literature available. Greater strides will be achieved in translating research into practice when learning theories are used as the guiding and unifying force behind research efforts.

NOTE

We wish to acknowledge Vincent Bates's help with and contributions to this chapter.

REFERENCES

Adachi, M., & Carlsen, J. C. (1995). Measuring melodic expectancies with children. *Bulletin of the Council for Research in Music Education, 127,* 1–7.

Andrews, F. M., & Deihl, N. D. (1970). Development of a technique for identifying elementary school children's musical concepts. *Journal of Research in Music Education, 18* (3), 214–222.

Argyris, C. J., & Schön, D. (1974). *Theory in practice: Increasing professional effectiveness.* San Francisco: Jossey-Bass.

Atkinson, R. C., & Shiffrin, R. M. (1968). Human memory: A proposed system and its control processes. In K. W. Spence and J. T. Spence (Eds.), *Advances in the psychology of learning and motivation research and theory: Vol. 2.* New York: Academic Press.

Atkinson, R. C., and Shiffrin, R. M. (1971). The control of short-term memory. *Scientific American, 225,* 82–90.

Ausubel, D. P. (1968). *Educational psychology: A cognitive view.* New York: Holt, Rinehart and Winston.

Bamberger, J. (1982). Revisiting children's drawings of simple rhythms: A function for reflection-in-action. In S. Strauss (Ed.), *U-shaped behavioral growth* (pp. 191–226). New York: Academic Press.

Bamberger, J. (1991). *The mind behind the musical ear: How children develop musical intelligence.* Cambridge, MA: Harvard University Press.

Bamberger, J., and Schön, D. (1991). Learning as reflective conversation with materials. In F. Steier (Ed.) *Research and reflexivity* (p. 186–209). London: Sage.

Bamberger, J. (2000). *Developing music intuitions: A project-based introduction to making and understanding music.* New York: Oxford University Press.

Bandura, A. (1986). *Social foundations of thought and action: A social cognitive theory.* Englewood Cliffs, NJ: Prentice-Hall.

Bara, B. G. (1995). *Cognitive science: A developmental approach to the simulation of the mind* (J. Douthwaite, Trans.). Sussex, England: Erlbaum.

Barret, M. (1999). Modal dissonance: An analysis of children's invented notations of known songs, original songs, and instrumental compositions. *Bulletin for the Council for Research in Music Education, Special Edition. 141,* 14–22.

Barrett, J. R., & Rasmussen, N. S. (1996). What observation reveals: Videotaped cases as window to pre-service teachers' beliefs about music teaching and learning. *Bulletin of the Council for Research in Music Education, 130,* 75–88.

Barry, N. H. (1992). The effects of practice strategies, individual differences in cognitive style, and gender upon technical accuracy and musicality of student instrumental performance. *Psychology of Music, 20,* 112–123.

Baumgarte, R., & Franklin, E. (1981). Lateralization of components of melodic stimuli: Musicians versus nonmusicians. *Journal of Research in Music Education, 29*(3), 199–208.

Beach, F. A., Hebb, D. O., Morgan, C. T., & Nissen, H. W. (1960). *The neuropsychology of Lashley: Selected papers of K. S. Lashley.* New York: McGraw-Hill.

Berke, M. K. (2000). *The ability of preschool children to recognize chord changes and audiate implied harmony.* Unpublished doctoral dissertation, University of Arizona, Tucson.

Bharucha, J. J. (1999). Neural nets, temporal composites, and tonality. In D. Deutsch (Ed.), *Psychology of music* (2nd ed., pp. 413–441). San Diego: Academic Press.

Booth, G. D., & Cutietta, R. A. (1991). The applicability of verbal processing strategies to recall of familiar songs. *Journal of Research in Music Education, 39*(2), 121–131.

Bower, G. H., & Hilgard, E. (1981). *Theories of learning* (5th ed.). Englewood Cliffs, NJ: Prentice-Hall.

Brand, M. (1998). Process of identifying children's mental model of their own learning as inferred from learning a song. *Bulletin of the Council for Research in Music Education, 138,* 47–61.

Bredo, E. (1997). The social construction of learning. In G. D. Phye (Ed.), *Handbook of academic learning: Construction of knowledge.* New York: Academic Press.

Bresler, L. (1993). Teacher knowledge in music education research. *Bulletin of the Council for Research in Music Education, 118,* 1–20.

Brown, J. S., Collins, A., & Duguid, P. (1989). Situated cognition and the culture of learning. *Educational Researcher, 18*(1), 32–42.

Bruner, J. S. (1960). *Process of education.* New York: Vintage Books.

Bruner, J. S. (1966). *Toward a theory of instruction.* Cambridge, MA: Harvard University Press.

Bruner, J. S. (1990). *Acts of meaning.* Cambridge, MA: Harvard University Press.

Bruner, J. S. (1996). *The culture of education.* Cambridge, MA: Harvard University Press.

Bruner, J. S., Goodnow, J. J., and Austin, G. A. (1956). *A study of thinking.* New York: Wiley.

Buttram, J. B. (1996). Learning theory and related developments: Overview and applications in music education and music therapy. In D. A. Hodges (Ed.), *Handbook of music psychology* (pp. 401–467). San Antonio, TX: IMR Press.

Campbell, M. R. (1999). Learning to teach music: A collaborative ethnography. *Bulletin of the Council for Research in Music Education, 139,* 12–35.

Carlsen, J. C. (1987). Framework for research: An international perspective. *Bulletin of the Council for Research in Music Education, 90,* 15–24.

Chen-Hafteck, L. (1999). Discussing text-melody relationship in children's song-learning and singing: A Cantonese-speaking perspective. *Psychology of Music, 27,* 55–70.

Chomsky, N. (1957). *Syntactic structures.* The Hague: Mouton.

Coffman, D. D. (1990). Effects of mental practice, physical practice and knowledge of results on piano performance. *Journal of Research in Music Education, 38*(3), 187–196.

Cutietta, R. A. (1985). An analysis of musical hypotheses created by the 11–16 year-old recall of familiar learner. *Bulletin of the Council for Research in Music Education, 84,* 1–11.

Cutietta, R. A. (1991). The applicability of verbal processing strategies to songs. *Journal of Research in Music Education, 39*(2), 121–131.

Cutietta, R. A. (1993). The musical elements: Are they right? *Music Educators Journal, 79*(9), 48–53.

Cutietta, R. A., & Booth, G. D. (1996). The influence of metre, mode, interval type, and contour in repeated melodic free recall. *The Psychology of Music, 24*(2), 222–236.

Cutietta, R. A., & Haggarty, K. (1987). A comparative study of color associations with music at various age levels. *Journal of Research in Music Education, 35*(2), 78–91.

Davidson, L., & Scripp, L. (1988). Young children's musical representations: Windows on music cognition. In J. Sloboda (Ed.), *Generative processes in music: The psychology of performance, improvisation and composition* (pp. 195–230). New York: Oxford University Press.

Davidson, L., & Scripp, L. (1992). Surveying the coordinates of cognitive skills in music. In R. Colwell (Ed.), *Handbook of research on music teaching and learning* (pp. 392–413). New York: Schirmer Books.

Della Pietra, C. J., & Campbell, P. S. (1995). An ethnography of improvisation training in a music methods course. *Journal of Research in Music Education, 43*(2), 112–126.

DeLorenzo, L. C. (1989). A field study of sixth-grade students' creative music problem-solving processes. *Journal of Research in Music Education 37*(3), 188–200.

Deutsch., D. (1999). *The psychology of music.* New York: Academic Press.

Domer, J., & Gromko, J. (1996). Qualitative changes in preschoolers' invented notations following music instruction. *Contributions to Music Education, 23,* 62–78.

Duke, R. A., & Henninger, J. C. (1998). Effects of verbal corrections on student attitude and performance. *Journal of Research in Music Education, 46*(4), 482–495.

Dweck, C. S. (1999). *Self-theories: Their role in motivation, personality and development.* Philadelphia: Psychology Press.

Elliot, D. (1995). *Music matters.* New York: Oxford University Press.

Ellis, M. C., & McCoy, C. W. (1990). Field dependence/independence in college non-music majors and their ability to discern form in music. *Journal of Research in Music Education, 38*(4), 302–310.

Elmer, S. S. (1997). Approaching the song acquisition process. *Bulletin of the Council for Research in Music Education, 133,* 129–135.

Fiske, H. E. (1984). Music cognition: Serial processes or parallel processes. *Bulletin for the Council of Research in Music Education, 80,* 13–26.

Fiske, H. E. (1995). A connectionist model of musical learning. *Bulletin of the Council for Research in Music Education, 10,* 20–24.

Fiske, H. E. (1997). Categorical perception of musical patterns: How different is "different." *Bulletin of the Council for Research in Music Education, 10,* 20–24.

Flowers, P. J. (2000). The match between music excerpts and written descriptions by fifth and sixth graders. *Journal of Research in Music Education, 48*(3), 262–277.

Funk, J., & Whiteside, J. (1981). Developmental theory and the psychology of music. *Psychology of Music, 9*(2), 44–53.

Gabrielsson, A. (1999). The performance of music. In D. Deutsch (Ed.), *Psychology of music* (pp. 501–602). New York: Academic Press.

Gagné, R. M. (1977). *Conditions of learning* (3rd ed.). New York: Holt, Rinehart, and Winston.

Gagné, R. M. (1985). *The conditions of learning and theory of instruction.* (4th ed.). New York: Holt, Rinehart, and Winston.

Gardner, H. (1980). *Artful scribbles: The significance of children's drawings.* New York: Basic Books.

Gardner, H. (1983). *Frames of mind.* New York: Basic Books.

Gardner, H. (1994). *The arts and human development.* New York: Wiley. (Original work published 1973).

Gardner, H. (1999). *Intelligence reframed: Multiple intelligences for the twenty-first century.* New York: Basic Books.

Gholson, S. A. (1998). A proximal positioning: A study of practice in violin pedagogy. *Journal of Research in Music Education, 46*(4), 535–545.

Gordon, E. (1971). *The psychology of music teaching.* Englewood Cliffs, NJ: Prentice-Hall.

Gordon, E. (1997a). In dialogue: Edwin Gordon responds to "Evaluating Theory from a Critical Thinking Perspective," by Paul G. Woodford and "Is Edwin Gordon's Learning Theory a Cognitive One?" by Ann Stokes. *Philosophy of Music Education Review, 5*(1), 57–58.

Gordon, E. (1997b). *Learning sequences in music: Skill, content, and patterns.* Chicago: GIA.

Greer, R. D. (1981). An operant approach to motivation and affect: Ten years of research in music learning. In J. A. Mason (Ed.), *Documentary report of the Ann Arbor Symposium.* Reston, VA: Music Educators National Conference.

Gromko, J. E. (1994). Children's invented notations as measures of musical understanding. *Psychology of Music, 22,* 136–147.

Gromko, J. E. (1995). *Origins of symbolic intelligence*. Paper presented at Symposium for Research in General Music. University of Arizona, Tucson, AZ.

Gromko, J. (1996). In a child's voice: An interpretive interaction with young composers. *Bulletin of the Council for Research in Music Education, 128*, 37–51.

Gromko, J., & Poorman, A. (1998a). Developmental trends and relationships in children's aural perception and symbol use. *Journal of Research in Music Education, 46*(1), 16–23.

Gromko, J., & Poorman, A. (1998b). Does perceptual-motor performance enhance perception of patterned art music? *Musicæ Scientiæ: The Journal of the European Society for the Cognitive Sciences of Music, 2*(2), 157–170.

Gruhn, W., Altenmüller, E., & Babler, R. (1997). The influence of learning on cortical activation patterns. *Bulletin of the Council for Research in Music Education, 133*, 25–30.

Guthrie, E. R. (1935). *The psychology of learning*. New York: Harper and Row.

Hargreaves, D. J. (1986). *The development psychology of music*. New York: Cambridge University Press.

Hargreaves, D. J., & Zimmerman, M. P. (1992). Developmental theories of music learning. In R. Colwell (Ed.), *Handbook of research in music teaching and learning* (pp. 377–391). New York: Schirmer Books.

Hebb, D. O. (1949). *The organization of behavior*. New York: Wiley.

Hewson, A. T. (1966). Music reading in the classroom. *Journal of Research in Music Education, 14*(4), 289.

Higgins, W. (1992). Technology. In R. Colwell (Ed.), *Handbook of research on music teaching and learning* (pp. 480–497). New York: Schirmer Books.

Hull, C. L. (1951). *Essentials of behavior*. New Haven, CT: Yale University Press.

Jumpeter, J. (1985). Personalized system of instruction versus the lecture-demonstration method in a specific area of a college music appreciation course. *Journal of Research in Music Education, 33*(2), 113–122.

Karma, K. (1985). Components of auditive structuring: Towards a theory of musical aptitude. *Bulletin of the Council for Research in Music Education, 82*, 1–13.

Koffka, K. (1935). *Principles of Gestalt psychology*. New York: Harcourt, Brace.

Kohler, W. (1929). *Gestalt psychology*. New York: Liveright.

Kohler, W. (1969). *The task of Gestalt psychology*. Princeton, NJ: Princeton University Press.

Kostka, M. J. (1997). Effects of self-assessment and successive approximations on "knowing" and "valuing" selected keyboard skills. *Journal of Research in Music Education, 45*(2), 273–281.

Krumhansl, C. L. (1990). *Cognitive foundations of musical pitch*. New York: Oxford University Press.

LaBerge, D. (1981). Perceptual and motor schemas in the performance of musical pitch. In J. A. Mason (Ed.), *Documentary report of the Ann Arbor Symposium* (pp. 68–76). Reston, VA: Music Educators National Conference.

Lashley, K. S. (1929). *Brain mechanisms and intelligence: A quantitative study of injuries to the brain*. University of Chicago Press.

Lave, J., & Wenger, E. (1991). *Situated learning: Legitimate peripheral participation*. Cambridge, England: Cambridge University Press.

Lehrdahl, F., & Jackendoff, R. (1983). *A generative theory of tonal music*. Cambridge, MA: MIT Press.

Leng, X., Shaw, G. L., & Wright, E. L. (1990). Coding of musical structure and the trion model of the cortex. *Music Perception, 8*, 49–62.

Lewin, K., Lippitt, R., & White, R. K. (1939). Patterns of aggressive behavior in experimentally created "social climates." *Journal of Social Psychology, 10*, 271–299.

Lineburgh, N. E. (1994). *The effects of incidental exposure to musical prototypes on the stylistic discrimination ability of kindergarten and second grade children*. Unpublished doctoral dissertation, Kent State University, Kent, OH.

Madsen, C. K. (1981). Music lessons and books as reinforcement alternatives for an academic task. *Journal of Research in Music Education, 29*(2), 103–110.

Madsen, C. K., & Duke, R. A. (1985). Perception of approval/disapproval in music education. *Bulletin of the Council for Research in Music Education, 85*, 119–130.

Marin, O. S., & Perry, D. W. (1999). Neurological aspects of music perception and performance. In D. Deutsch (Ed.), *Psychology of music* (2nd ed.). San Diego: Academic Press.

Mark, M. (1986). *Contemporary music education* (2nd ed.). New York: Schirmer Books.

Mead, G. H. (1934). *Mind, self, and society: From the standpoint of a social behaviorist*. Chicago: University of Chicago Press.

Miller, G. A. (1956). The magical number seven, plus or minus two: Some limits on our capacity for processing information. *Psychological Review, 63*, 81–97.

Miller, G. A., Galanter, D., & Pribam, K. H. (1960). *Plans and structure of behavior*. New York: Holt, Rinehart & Winston.

Miller, N. E., & Dollard, J. (1941). *Social learning and imitation*. New Haven, CT: Yale University Press.

O'Hagin, B. (1997). *The effects of a discovery approach to movement instruction on children's responses to musical stimuli*. Unpublished doctoral dissertation, University of Arizona, Tucson.

Olsson, B. (1997). The social psychology of music education. In D. J. Hargreaves & A. C. North (Eds.), *The social psychology of music education* (pp. 290–306). New York: Oxford University Press.

Orman, E. K. (1998). Effect of interactive multimedia computing on young saxophonists' achievement and attitude. *Journal of Research in Music Education, 46*(1), 62–74.

Pavlov, I. P. (1927). *Conditioned reflexes* (G. V. Anrep, Trans.). London: Oxford University Press.

Pflederer, M. (1964). The responses of children to musical tasks embodying Piaget's principle of conservation. *Journal of Research in Music Education, 12*(4), 251–268.

Pflederer, M. (1966). How children conceptually organize musical sounds. *Bulletin of the Council for Research in Music Education, 7*, 1–12.

Pflederer, M. (1967). Conservation law as applied to the development of musical intelligence. *Journal of Research in Music Education, 15*, 215–223.

Pfledererer, M., & Sechrest, L. (1968). Conservation-type responses of children to musical stimuli. *Bulletin of the Council for Research in Music Education, 13,* 19–36.

Piaget, J. (1928). *Judgment and reasoning in the child* (M. Warden, Trans.). New York: Harcourt, Brace.

Piaget, J. (1952). *The origins of intelligence in children.* New York: International University Press.

Piaget, J. (1972). *The principles of genetic epistemology* (W. Mays, Trans.). New York: Basic Books.

Posner, M. I., & Keele, S. W. (1968). On the genesis of abstract ideas. *Journal of Experimental Psychology, 83,* 304–308.

Rauscher, F. H. (1999). Music exposure and the development of spatial intelligence in children. *Bulletin of the Council for Research in Music Education, 142,* 35–47.

Regelski, T. (1982). *Teaching music.* New York: Schirmer Books.

Reimer, B. (1970). *A philosophy of music education.* Englewood Cliffs, NJ: Prentice-Hall.

Rideout, R. R. (Ed.). (1997). *On the sociology of music education.* Norman, OK: University of Oklahoma Press.

Rideout, R. R., & Paul, S. J. (Eds.). (2000). *On the sociology of music education: vol. 2. Papers from the music education symposium at the University of Oklahoma.* Amherst: University of Massachusetts Press.

Rogoff, B. (1996). *Apprenticeship in thinking: Cognitive development in social context.* New York: Oxford University Press.

Ross, S. L. (1985). The effectiveness of mental practice in improving the performance of college trombonists. *Journal of Research in Music Education, 33*(4), 221–230.

Rumelhart, D. E., McLelland, J. L., & Research Group. (1986). *Parallel distributed processing: Explorations in the microstructure of cognition: Vol. 1. Foundations.* Cambridge, MA: MIT Press.

Ruttenberg, A. (1994). *Review and discussion of a generative theory of tonal music* [on-line]. Available: http://alanr.www.media.mit.edu/people/alanr/Jackendoff & LerdahlFinal.

Scheid, P., & Eccles, J. C. (1975). Music and speech: Artistic functions of the human brain. *Psychology of Music, 3*(1), 21–35.

Schmidt, R. A. (1975). A schema theory of discrete motor skill learning. *Psychological Review, 7,* 351–371.

Schön, D. A. (1987). *Educating the reflective practitioner: Toward a new design for teaching and learning in the professions.* San Francisco: Jossey-Bass.

Schunk, D. H. (2000). *Learning theories: An educational perspective* (3rd ed.). Upper Saddle River, NJ: Prentice-Hall.

Scott-Kassner, C. (1992). Research on music in early childhood. In R. Colwell (Ed.), *Handbook of research on music teaching and learning* (pp. 633–650). New York: Schirmer Books.

Shannon, C., & Weaver, W. (1949). *The mathematical theory of communication.* Urbana: University of Illinois Press.

Sidnell, R. G. (1981a). Motor learning in music education. In J. A. Mason (Ed.), *Documentary report of the Ann Arbor Symposium* (pp. 28–34). Reston, VA: Music Educators National Conference.

Sidnell, R. G. (1981b). Response (to R. N. Shepard paper). In J. A. Mason (Ed.), *Documentary report of the Ann Arbor Symposium* (pp. 174–179). Reston, VA: Music Educators National Conference.

Skinner, B. F. (1948). *Walden two.* New York: Macmillan.

Skinner, B. F. (1953). *Science and human behavior.* New York: Macmillan.

Skinner, B. F. (1968). *The technology of teaching.* New York: Appleton-Century-Crofts.

Spence, K. W. (1956). *Behavior theory and conditioning.* New Haven, CT: Yale University Press.

Strong, A. D. (1992). The relationship between hemispheric laterality and perception of musical and verbal stimuli in normal and learning disabled subjects. *Psychology of Music, 20,* 138–153.

Swanwick, K., & Tillman, J. (1986). The sequence of musical development: A study of children's composition. *British Journal of Music Education, 3,* 305–339.

Tallarico, P. T. (1974). A study of the three phase concept of memory: Its musical implications. *Bulletin of the Council for Research in Music Education, 39,* 1–15.

Taylor, O. (1997). Student interpretations of teacher verbal praise in selected seventh- and eighth-grade choral classes. *Journal of Research in Music Education, 45*(4), 536–546.

Thorisson, T. (1997). Effects of prototype and exemplar learning and four musical dimensions of the formation of musical style concepts. *Bulletin of the Council for Research in Music Education, 133,* 136–142.

Thorndike, E. L. (1932). *The fundamentals of learning.* New York: Teachers College Press.

Tolman, E. C. (1932). *Purposive behavior in animals and men.* New York: Century.

Tulving, E. (1972). Episodic and semantic memory. In E. Tulving & W. Donaldson (Eds.), *Organization of memory* (pp. 381–403). New York: Academic Press.

Upitis, R. (1990). *This too is music.* Portsmouth, NH: Heinemann.

Upitis, R. (1992). *Can I play you my song?* Portsmouth, NH: Heinemann.

Vygotsky, L. S. (1962). *Thought and language.* Cambridge, MA: MIT Press.

Vygotsky, L. S. (1987). *Thinking and speech.* New York: Plenum.

Vygotsky, L. S. (1997a). *The collected works of L. S. Vygotsky: Vol. 3. Problems of the theory and history of psychology* (R. W. Rieber & A. S. Carton, Eds.; R. Van Der Veer, Trans.) New York: Plenum.

Vygotsky, L. S. (1997b). *Educational psychology* (V. V. Davydow & R. Silverman, Trans.) New York: Plenum.

Wang, C. C., & Sogin, D. W. (1990). The recognition of melodic fragments as components of tonal patterns. *Psychology of Music 18,* 140–149.

Watson, J. B. (1925). *Behaviorism.* New York: Norton.

Wenger, E. (1999). *Communities of practice: Learning, meaning, and identity.* Cambridge: Cambridge University Press.

Wertheimer, M. (1959). *Productive thinking* (Michael Wertheimer, Ed., enl. ed.). New York: Harper.

Whitaker, N. L. (1996). A theoretical model of the musical problem solving and decision making of performers, arrangers, conductors, and composers. *Bulletin of the Council for Research in Music Education, 128,* 1–14.

Wiggins, J. H. (1994a). Children's strategies for solving compositional problems with peers. *Journal of Research in Music Education, 42*(3), 232–252.

Wiggins, J. H. (1994b). Teacher-research in a general music classroom: Effects on the teacher. *Bulletin of the Council for Research in Music Education 123,* 31–35.

Wiggins, J. H. (2000). The nature of shared musical understanding and its role in empowering independent musical thinking. *Bulletin of the Council for Research in Music Education, 143,* 65–90.

Williams, D. B. (1981). Music information processing and memory. In J. A. Mason (Ed.), *Documentary report of the Ann Arbor Symposium* (pp. 87–93). Reston, VA: Music Educators National Conference.

Williams, D. B. (1982). Auditory cognition: A study of the similarities in memory processing for music tones and spoken words. *Bulletin of the Council for Research in Music Education, 71,* 30–44.

Williams, D. B., & Peckham, P. D. (1975). The development of a computer simulation model for the investigation of music concept formation. *Psychology of Music, 3*(2), 37–54.

Wilson, B. G., & Myers, K. M. (2000). Situated cognition in theoretical and practical context. In D. H. Jonassen & S. M. Lund (Eds.), *Theoretical foundations of learning environments* (pp. 57–88). Mahwah, NJ: Erlbaum.

Witkin, H. A., Moore, C. A., Goodenough, D. R., & Cox, P. W. (1977). Field-dependent and field-independent cognitive styles and their educational implications. *Review of Educational Research, 47,* 1–64.

Younker, B. A., & Smith, W. H. (1996). Comparing and modeling musical thought processes of expert and novice composers. *Bulletin of the Council for Research in Music Education, 128,* 25–36.

Zalanowski, A. H. (1990). Music appreciation and hemispheric orientation: Visual versus verbal involvement. *Journal of Research in Music Education, 38*(3), 197–205.

Zimmerman, M. P. (1986). Music development in middle childhood: A summary of selected research studies. *Bulletin of the Council for Research in Music Education, 86,* 18–35.

Zwink, C. S. (1988). *Verbal categorization of holistic musical stimuli by preschool children: Implications for cognitive categorization.* Unpublished master's thesis, Kent State University, Kent, OH.

Systematic Instruction

18

BARAK ROSENSHINE

HILDEGARD FROEHLICH

INSHAD FAKHOURI

The past 40 years have witnessed a great deal of research on "effective teaching." A number of observational, correlational, and experimental studies were conducted in order to, first, identify those teachers whose classes made larger-than-expected test score gains and, then, identify the instructional procedures that were used more often by those same teachers. This research, mostly based on observations in the teaching of reading or mathematics, has revealed a pattern that might be called a systematic method of teaching. The pattern includes presenting material in small steps, pausing to check for student understanding, and requiring active and successful participation from all students.

Although initially derived from research in reading and mathematics instruction in elementary and middle schools, the results also are applicable to any other systematic or "well-structured" (Simon, 1973) subject matter in which the objectives are to teach skilled performance and the mastery of a body of knowledge. Clearly, and as shown in this chapter, music has such a body of knowledge with a definable content and explicit skills, and music education has an equally compelling body of research to support systematic instruction as a viable teaching model.

To assess the value of measures of instructional effectiveness as used in research on music teaching published between 1972 and 1997, Duke (1999) reviewed 86 selected experimental and descriptive studies published in leading music education journals. Common to all selected articles was "a specific measure of instructional variables that are under the control of a teacher during the process of instruction" (p. 3). The analysis of the studies focused on a comparison of (1) study purpose; (2) participants; (3) the independent variables; (4) the dependent measures; (5) the

evaluators/observers/raters/judges; and (6) the unit of measurement in each analysis.

Under "descriptive research," Duke found 15 studies that had allocated instructional time to specific music activities. Eighteen studies had described all three dimensions, that is, verbalization, gestures, *and* activities, while within the total of all studies only 7 studies had sought to determine the effect of multiple components of teaching on specific student behavior. Twenty-seven studies had been designed, as Duke termed it, to improve teaching.

In describing the findings of this comprehensive analysis, Duke only spoke to those findings "that were observed in multiple investigations" (p. 4). In terms of relating instructional activities to the teaching of tangible objectives and/or musical goals, Duke found that out of 5 studies reviewed, only 1 had reported "consistent relationships between the behavior of teachers and student performance quality (p. 5). It should be noted, however, that of the 86 studies under review, only a total of 13 had measured student achievement. This underrepresentation of student achievement as a dependent measure caused Duke to call for an expansion of research that includes "the systematic measurement of teaching effectiveness in relation to the accomplishment of instructional goals" (p. 1).

Research on Systematic Teaching

In general, researchers have found that when effective teachers teach well-defined concepts and skills, they do the following:

- Begin a lesson with a short review of previous, prerequisite learning

- Present new material in small steps, with student practice after each step
- Guide students during initial practice
- Give clear and detailed instructions and explanations
- Provide a high level of active practice for all students
- Provide systematic feedback and corrections
- Provide systematic instruction and practice for seatwork exercises and, when necessary, monitor students during seatwork
- Continue practice until students are independent and confident

Detailed plans for music lessons that follow these principles have been provided by such textbook authors as Campbell and Scott-Kassner (1995) for elementary general music, Phillips (1992) for elementary level singing, Collins (1993) for secondary choral instruction, and Colwell and Goolsby (2002) for instrumental music instruction. These authors provide step-by-step lesson plan examples of how music teachers should state instructional goals and objectives, review previously learned skills and knowledge, and present new materials and skills in small steps that are replete with ongoing, student-involved practice and continuous teacher feedback. All of the model lesson plans suggest that mastery requires time for the students to practice on their own, with or without the teacher's supervision.

From the textbook examples, the following principles of effective music teaching in school settings emerge.

- Previous skills and knowledge are reviewed in warm-ups, new material is rehearsed in incremental steps, and previously learned selections are polished.
- Instructions are directed to individuals, sections, and the entire group for the purpose of improving specific musical or technical challenges encountered in the situation.
- Student performance, including solos, is carefully guided, often at slow tempos, and the performance is interspersed with brief instructional comments by the teacher.
- Rehearsal of individuals and sections is limited and the focus of the music class is directed to all students to improve their performance.
- Feedback is provided through conducting, other nonverbal gestures, or verbal communication. In student-initiated, cooperative learning situations, section leaders and peers often provide verbal and nonverbal feedback through modeling. Additional verbal teacher feedback is provided at the end of a piece or the rehearsal, by listening to a recording and providing an outline of priorities that are to be practiced and mastered before the next rehearsal.
- Musical independence is aided when the conductor can leave the podium and listen from the back of the auditorium. A measure of success is evident when independent performance becomes possible. Successful public performances by the large ensemble and jazz band or small ensemble are further examples of the success of direct instruction in music.

Table 18.1 lists the teaching practices in music that meet the demands of direct instruction, translated into six instructional steps.

Research supports these practices. Casey's (1993) compilation of "tried and true" teaching strategies by experienced conductors and music teachers suggests that the teachers purposely planned learning steps rather than relying on them to happen (p. 79). Colprit (2000) affirmed the importance of having a clear, single focus in each lesson. Goolsby (1996) reported that the more effective teachers divided rehearsal time to allow for more warm-up time and to focus on two musical selections. Experienced teachers spent more than half of the period on performance, used the most nonverbal modeling, got the ensembles on task the quickest, and focused their own comments so that they talked the least during rehearsals (p. 286). Price (1992) portrayed "sequential patterns" of music instruction in which the teacher presented a task to be learned, the students then interacted with the teacher-conductor through performance and verbal communication, followed by corrective feedback specific to the task at hand. In this regard, some research to be discussed later in the chapter points to the importance of students experiencing success when performing.

The same principle of students experiencing success in learning through sequential instruction can be found in Gordon's (1997) sequences of discrimination and inference skills as well as rhythmic and tonal patterns. When the skills sequence is applied to the mastery of rhythmic and tonal patterns, both sequences together form the foundation for systematic music instruction in general music settings from early childhood to young adulthood. Theoretically, this is accomplished because the patterns, once internalized through audiation, provide the student with a repertoire of musical patterns that facilitates the learning of new musical materials.

Time Studies

In a series of studies, Goolsby (1996, 1997, 1999) analyzed the use of instructional time in instrumental rehearsals and compared the findings across differentially experienced teachers as well as student teachers. Of interest was how teachers used the available time. Instruction was devoted to verbal instruction, nonverbal modeling, verbally disciplining the students, and guiding practice/performance. Noteworthy among the findings of the 1996 study is that experienced teachers not only followed the steps of direct instruction but "stopped more frequently . . . and addressed several performance variables during a single stop" (p. 29). They also drilled short passages more frequently than did either the novice or student teachers, and their questions were designed to reinforce musically appropriate answers. The findings of the 1997 study showed that ex-

Table 18.1 Six Functions of Direct Teaching in Music

Band	Choral	General
1. Review of previously learned skills and materials		
1. Scales	1. Basic chordal patterns in chromatic modulation upward and downward motions	1. Greeting patterns based on sol-mi pitches
2. Unison passages		2. Clap rhythmic patterns based on familiar words and names of class members
3. Breathing exercises	2. Breathing exercises	3. Previously learned songs are polished
4. Chorales	3. Stretching exercises	
5. Harmonization of familiar tunes	4. Exercises focusing on resonance	
6. Previously learned selections are polished	5. Exercises focusing on vocal range	
	6. Previously learned selections are polished	
2. State lesson objectives and give instructions to achieve those objectives		
1. Explain the purpose of the objectives.	1. Explain the purpose of the objectives.	1. Teacher leads the class in a few activities that introduce the lesson's objectives.
2. Explain how these objectives fit into the week's/month's goals.	2. Explain how these objectives fit into the week's/month's goals to be achieved.	2. Teacher states the lesson's objectives by giving specific number of errors permitted in one try.
3. Provide subobjectives for individual sections.	3. Provide subobjectives for individual sections.	
4. Give brief instructions on how to achieve these goals, keeping the pace of the class moving.	4. Give brief instructions on how to achieve these goals by reminding students of what to focus on and what to be aware of before they start rehearsing.	
3. Lead the students in guided practice to achieve objectives		
1. Includes teacher modeling and student imitating	1. Teacher guides students through difficult phrases, passages, or note patterns by means of conducting gestures, by mouthing/articulation of the text sections or words, or by speaking over the music.	1. Teacher guides students through modeling.
2. Teacher guides the students in practice by teaching them by rote.		2. General discussions about songs are guided by the teacher.
3. Teacher guides the students in practice by teaching them a certain piece at a slower tempo.	2. Teacher demonstrates through modeling.	
4. Provide feedback that aids in the achievement of the stated objectives		
1. Feedback is provided through conducting, other nonverbal gestures, or verbal communication.	1. Feedback is provided through conducting, other nonverbal gestures, or verbal communication.	1. Feedback is provided through praising correct answers and allowing students to try again for wrong answers.
2. Feedback is provided in an objective rather than hateful manner.	2. Feedback is provided in an objective rather than hateful manner.	
3. Feedback is given on musical skills and demands rather than personal skill level.	3. Feedback is given on musical skills and demands rather than personal skill level.	
5. Independent practice		
1. Musical independence is aided when the conductor leaves the podium and listens to the ensemble from the back of the auditorium.	1. Musical independence is aided when the conductor leaves the podium and listens to the ensemble from the back of the auditorium.	1. Worksheets are handed out, for independent practice, in order to see whether the objectives were met.
2. A measure of success is evident when independent performance becomes possible.	2. A measure of success is evident when independent performance becomes possible.	2. A measure of success is evident when independent performance becomes possible.
6. Weekly and monthly reviews		
1. Teacher reviews the achievement of old objectives and learned skills by incorporating them into new lesson plans.	1. Teacher reviews the achievement of old objectives and learned skills by incorporating them into new lesson plans.	1. Teacher reviews the achievement of old objectives and learned skills by incorporating them into new lesson plans.

perienced teachers spent more time on attaining high-level standards on ensemble sound through demonstration/modeling and through verbal explanations as well as guided listening. The more experienced teachers also focused on patterns or short sections in the music that caused the students trouble either because the passage was difficult or unfamiliar or because it had not been practiced sufficiently in previous rehearsals. The 1999 study described how experienced teachers spent more time on guided practice than on verbal instructions, suggesting that experienced teachers are aware of the importance of the actual performance experience as the most engaging teaching activity in music.

Use and Limits of Systematic Instruction

In practice, a systematic approach is varied according to the level and ability of the students. It is most successful when the material to be taught is new and hierarchical. In this case, each presentation is relatively short and is followed by immediate student practice. In the middle of a unit, the steps are larger—that is, the presentations are longer, less time is spent in checking for understanding or in guided practice, and more of the independent practice can be done as homework or individual practicing because the students do not need as much help and supervision. But even in these situations, it is necessary to return to small-step instruction when the material becomes difficult.

Small-step instruction in music occurs most frequently when specific passages need "drilling." Goolsby's (1996) findings suggest that experienced teachers drilled short passages more frequently than novice teachers or student teachers. To do this efficiently, teachers need to approach their score study by identifying and isolating probable trouble spots and finding interesting and varied ways of rehearsing them. An experienced teacher can do this task quickly and with ease.

Information-Processing Research

Related to systematic teaching is recent research on human information processing. The results of these studies identified three principles: the limits of our working memory, the importance of practice, and the importance of continuing practice until the students are fluent.

First, current information-processing theories suggest that we are "limited-capacity processors." That is, there are limits to the amount of information one can attend to and process effectively. Most individuals can only process a few pieces of information (about seven) in their working memory at one time. When too much information is presented at once or when the processing demands are too great, the working memory becomes swamped, confusion results, and the material being read is not processed (Tobias, 1982). This is why, when teaching new or difficult

material, a teacher should teach only a small amount and arrange for student practice after each part. In this way, the amount taught at any time is manageable for working memory. Further, a teacher can help students by reviewing relevant learning and by providing an outline that helps the students to focus more readily on major points.

Second, we have to process new material in order to transfer it from our working memory to our long-term memory. That is, we have to elaborate on, review, rehearse, or summarize the material. This suggests that a teacher should provide active practice for all students. Such practice is facilitated if the teacher guides student processing and supervises students as they practice new steps in a skill, because extensive practice and frequent review are needed for effortless and automatic recall of skills and knowledge in the future. When prior learning is automatic, space is left free in our working memory to be used for application and higher level thinking.

We might summarize the points by saying that it is important for the teacher to provide "instructional support" when teaching students new material (see Tobias, 1982). Such support occurs when the teacher: (1) breaks the material or the music into small steps in order to reduce possible confusion; (2) structures learning by giving the behavioral or performance objectives for the day's rehearsal; (3) provides historical information about the music to be performed; (4) gives the learner active practice in each step in order to move the new learning or skill into long-term memory; and (5) provides for additional practice and "overlearning" so that the students can use the new material or skills effortlessly.

Six Teaching Functions

In analyzing the studies on systematic teaching, we have divided the results into six teaching functions: (1) review, (2) presentation of new material, (3) guided practice, (4) feedback and corrections, (5) independent practice, and (6) weekly and monthly reviews. Similar functions are also summarized in table 18.2. Obviously, the functions are not new; in fact, all teachers use some of the functions some of the time, but effective teachers apply these functional behaviors consistently and systematically while the less effective teachers, indeed, use each function less effectively.

Even though the findings came from the study of actual classrooms, a great deal of deliberation is required in order to apply these findings to daily lessons: Teachers have to make decisions on (1) the amount of material that will be presented at one time, (2) the way it will be presented, (3) how guided practice will be conducted, (4) how specific errors made by specific students will be corrected, (5) how to correct them with different students, and (6) the pace as well as time allotment for specific activities in a lesson.

Table 18.2 Teaching Functions

1. Review
   Review homework and practiced material
   Review relevant previous learning
   Review prerequisite skills and knowledge for the lesson

2. Presentation
   State lesson goals or provide outline
   Teach in small steps
   Model procedures
   Provide concrete positive and negative examples
   Use clear language
   Check for student understanding
   Avoid digressions

3. Guided practice
   More time
   High frequency of questions or guided practice
   All students respond and receive feedback
   High success rate
   Continue practice until students are fluent

4. Corrections and feedback
   Give process feedback when performance or answers are correct but hesitant
   Give sustaining feedback, clues, or reteaching when performance or answers are incorrect
   Reteach when necessary

5. Independent practice
   Students receive help during initial steps, or overview
   Practice continues until students are automatic (where relevant)
   Teacher provides active supervision (where possible)
   Routines are used to give help to slower students

6. Weekly and monthly reviews

See also similar ideas in Good and Grouws (1979) and Russell and Hunter (1981).

Thus a great deal of thought, creativity, and flexibility is needed to apply these results to specific music lessons.

Teaching Function 1: Daily Review

In academic subjects, effective teachers begin the lesson with a 5- to 8-minute review of previously covered material, correction of homework, and review of prior knowledge that is relevant to the day's lesson. The sequence is similar in music; however, demonstration of practiced material is substituted for correction of homework. The goal is to ensure that the students have a firm grasp of the prerequisite skills for this lesson. The daily review in music instruction includes doing the warm-up and physical exercises for good posture, relaxation, breathing, and tuning and letting the students know the order in which different pieces of music are to be rehearsed.

Familiar warm-up patterns are used to review intonation, scales, patterns, and a variety of comparable experiences. The first piece in the rehearsal is a less challenging piece that the group knows or has nearly mastered in the previous rehearsal. In addition, the director reminds the

students of particular performance challenges they encountered the day before.

In a general music class at the elementary school level, the music teacher facilitates review by greeting her students with sol-mi-la pitch patterns as a routine exercise. Introductions of this type set a personal tone for the class and facilitate the review of previously learned material. Daily review in rehearsal occurs when reviewing practice assignments or having sectionals. In both instances, the objectives to be accomplished by the sections or the individual students must be clear, concise, and deliberate (Ericsson, 1997).

Daily review is particularly important for teaching material that will be used in subsequent learning. Examples in instrumental music instruction include the following.

Review and drill of pattern vocabulary. In teaching tonality, the teacher asks the students questions about what tonality is and asks them to define the functions of different tonalities and key relationships (Schleuter, 1997, pp. 137–142).

Teaching new rhythm patterns. With the use of the metronome, the teacher begins with the performance of familiar patterns before engaging the students, through modeling and student response, in the clapping of more complex patterns. For example, the rhythm pattern quarter–quarter–quarter–rest is performed before the half-note value is introduced in a pattern of quarter–quarter–half.

Technique training. The teacher should ask the students to play a familiar song on their instruments written in a familiar key before they then are asked to transpose the song to a new (unfamiliar) key.

Examples of daily review in choral rehearsals include the review of proper posture and warm-up exercises, followed by breathing exercises or those that focus on proper production of vowels. Or the teacher uses the exercises to remind the singers of techniques involved in moving from high-register to low-register singing (Phillips, 1992). In elementary music teaching, daily review consists of the regular practice and performance of all song materials so that the students are comfortable with the songs before they are asked to analyze them according to alike-different patterns, repetition and contrast, form, or content of text. In any type of rehearsal setting, a particularly effective use of daily review lies in preparing students for difficult passages in a piece by incorporating the key elements of those passages into the warm-up exercises. The directors then alert the students to the appearance of these passages in the scores or parts. When presenting new material, the main point to remember is that students become confused when too much material is presented at once. Hence it is better to proceed in small steps, pause to check for student understanding, and allow students to process the new material. Digressions should be avoided, however interesting they may be, because they can frequently confuse the students by giving them too much information to process. Teachers should avoid giving directions too quickly or to assume that everyone understands because there are no questions. The introduction of more complex material should wait until the students have mastered earlier material.

Teaching Function 2: Stating Lesson Goal(s) and Objective(s)

At the start of any presentation, effective teachers focus the students' attention on what they are to do and learn. This is done by providing the students with a short behavioral objective such as "At the end of this lesson, you will be able to distinguish among metaphor, simile, and personification" or "Today you will be able to do problems using two-digit multiplication." These objectives help to focus the students and reduce the complexity of what is being presented. In addition, such objectives help the teacher to stick to the subject matter and avoid confusing digressions.

Stating lesson goals in music lessons seems superfluous to some directors as, in their own mind, the goal of any rehearsal lies in improving performance. In addition, different pieces that are part of the same rehearsal may have different objectives, ranging from technical accuracy to interpretation. However, a good director points out where the focus for each rehearsed piece lies. For example, in a middle school band setting, one piece to be worked on may be the *Gavorkna Fanfare* by Jack Stamp. After the warm-up exercises that include double-tonguing technique, the director says, "Today we need to focus our attention on the accurate execution of all double-tonguing passages in this piece." On another day, the objective in that piece may be to focus on phrasing, balance, and blend. In each class, the specific stating of an objective for a certain composition guides the teacher in focusing on what is important in that particular rehearsal. It prevents the director from seeking to correct or fix too many problems at the same time. In nonperformance settings, especially in general music, teachers may assume that students do not need to know or would not understand the "real" objectives. The teacher announces the lesson's goals by telling the students that their task is to find word patterns in a familiar song and that those patterns must match the notated rhythmic patterns on the board. Suggestions for stating instructional objectives systematically in a beginning elementary choir have been made by Schleuter (1997, pp. 144–145).

Modeling. By long tradition, music teachers have practiced and relied on the master-apprentices, imitative model of learning. It implies that the teacher sets the example through performance and behavior that the pupil is to follow as closely as possible. Many textbooks in music make this point when they speak to the need of the music teacher/conductor to provide examples of modeling and exemplary performance (e.g., Brinson, 1996; Haasemann & Jordan, 1991; Pfautsch, 1973; Rudolph, 1994; Shuller, 1997; see also Harwood, 1993; Madsen, Greer, & Madsen, 1975). Imitative by nature, modeling in music therefore implies nonverbal rote teaching as the first step of instruction. Often done through vocal demonstration (through singing or performing on one's instrument), this type of modeling is to be set apart from providing verbal explanations. Green's (1990) study is of note, as she investigated the effects of adult female, adult male, and child vocal modeling on the pitch-matching accuracy of 282 children in grades 1 through 6. Her results indicated that "vocal modeling had an effect on the subjects' pitch matching accuracy" (p. 225). A number of studies described and/or compared different conductors in their approaches toward modeling and demonstration (e.g., Dickey, 1991; Overturf, 1985; Thurman, 1977; Tyson, 1988).

Verbal explanations follow when the teacher determines that the students' imitation of the nonverbal or vocal model has not been successful. At times, verbal explanations contain verbal modeling (as opposed to vocal modeling) when a teacher uses metaphors and images to describe a desired performance outcome (e.g., Gonzo, 1977; Watkins, 1986). For example, a choral director might explain the singing of legato lines as "think of your voice as a ribbon of smooth velvet that connects the different pitches to each other."

Despite the prominent role that modeling plays in music instruction (Wolverton, 1993), a surprisingly small body of research exists that systematically has addressed modeling as a variable in music education. A review of its status was published in 1992 by Dickey. Before him, Sang (1987) documented the direct relationship between instrumental music teachers' modeling skills and pupil performance behavior and promoted interest in exploring the relationship further. Speer (1994) identified specific patterns of instruction when he analyzed 47 applied piano lessons taught by a total of 25 instructors. He reported that, while most of the time spent during a piano lesson was centered around student performance (participation), verbal teacher contributions on musical information preceded modeling and coaching, both of which were observed less often, that is, no more than 20% of the entire observation time (p. 23).

More recently, research on modeling has tended to be a part of systematic observation studies in music education that included teacher demonstration (verbal and nonverbal) as a category of observable behavior (see chapter 19). Three types of studies, then—studies on modeling, studies that investigate behavioristic constructs of direct music instruction, and descriptive "time-use and frequency" studies—have shown teacher modeling and demonstration to be an important category of successful music teaching.

Teaching in "Small Steps." Perhaps the most important finding from research in music and nonmusic settings is the importance of teaching in "small steps." Evertson, Emmer, and Brophy (1980) found that the most effective mathematics teachers spent more time in a combination of short presentations followed by guided practice. During this cycle, the more effective teachers gave explanations as well as many examples, checked for student understanding, and provided sufficient instruction so that the students practiced independently with minimal difficulty. In contrast, the less effective teachers gave much shorter presentations and explanations and then asked the students to practice independently. Under these conditions, the students made too many errors and had to be retaught.

There is little research on what constitutes the appropriate length of task presentations in teaching. When one teaches explicit skills, such as two-digit multiplication or determining least common multiples, the guided practice might begin after a short teacher presentation. Then a continued pattern of short presentations and guided practice shapes the remainder of the presentation phase. In other cases, where more explanation is given, there might be presentations of 8 to 10 minutes before guided practice begins. One might expect, on the basis of these results, that with younger or slower students, or when the material is new or different, that shorter segments of presentation are more effective.

The use of short presentations followed by practice is a major part of music instruction. Goolsby's (1997) work on comparing verbal, direct instructional patterns of expert, novice, and student teachers partially confirms that assumption. Although expert teachers "stopped more frequently," they also "addressed several performance variables during a single stop" (p. 29). These findings are comparable to those in other subject matter areas, in that the expert teachers were found to drill short passages more frequently than either the novice or student teachers. Goolsby also found expert teachers' questions to be more specific and focused. He further reported that expert teachers spent most of their instructional time on demonstrating and explaining intonation in a broader context, whereas the less experienced teachers spent their time simply on tuning or on correcting individual notes. Experienced teachers also provided more instruction on guided/focused listening (Goolsby, 1999). Price (1989) had reported similar findings in the context of studying rehearsals that had been conducted by differentially experienced directors.

Teaching in small steps and supporting students in each step is particularly important when students encounter specific sections of music beyond their immediate skill level—as is the case with the execution of a complex rhythmic pattern in music not written as pedagogical material and, thus, not strictly sequenced. Here the director can help the students by clapping the pattern and asking the students to repeat that pattern through clapping. After that the director might sing the pattern and asks the students to sing it or to repeat it by using the same "tonguing" (i.e., articulation) that they would use when they play that pattern on their instruments. After that, the director asks the students to tongue the pattern on their instruments on a single note; finally, he or she asks them to play that pattern with the written notes. If the students are still having difficulty with the pattern, then the director should assign the section as homework. Singing is often employed by the entire group to encourage the perception of unusual intervals and intricate rhythmic phrases. In this example, the director breaks the skill into a series of steps and provides models and guidance as the students move from simple practice to complex performance.

Checking for Understanding. Effective teachers stop to check for student understanding. They ask questions, have students summarize the presentation up to that point, and have them perform or repeat directions or procedures. An effective teacher often invites the students to agree or disagree with other students' answers or to match the performance. This checking tells the teacher whether material needs to be retaught. The wrong way to check for understanding is to ask "Are there any questions?" and to assume that what is taught has been learned when no student asks anything. Another error is to ask a few questions, call on volunteers to hear their (usually correct) answers, and then assume that the class understands and has learned from the volunteers. Many students study music outside of school and/or perform in other ensembles; thus the response of a few students does not reveal class understanding.

The process of performing itself affords the director as many opportunities to check for understanding as there are notes in the piece itself. These opportunities are limited only by the director's ability to diagnose and detect performance errors. Beyond that and in reference to systematic music teaching, effectiveness can be both verbal and nonverbal. Checking is followed by additional practice when appropriate.

Many music directors who want their students to achieve flawless musical performances achieve this goal by beginning their rehearsal with a one-time "run-through" of the music to be rehearsed. Then, to increase student competence, the director first focuses on the performance of smaller themes, phrases, sections, and specific details in the work, sometimes section by section. As a third step, the entire ensemble places the "learned" details back into larger phrases, sections, and movements, reconstructing the entirety of the composition. A final, full "play-through" ends the lesson. This pattern allows the students to hear the specific details in context of the musical phrases and themes that give the piece meaning. It also ensures that students have some sort of musical experience each day, as opposed to rehearsing only technical details.

Effective music teachers use this procedure with a broad range of activities. There is, on one hand, the typical band rehearsal, where once the piece has been "played through" the teacher identifies trouble spots, comments on them, and corrects them prior to moving on. Here, immediate rather than delayed feedback is important. It is also best that this feedback be brief, in order to avoid student off-task behavior (Dunn, 1997). There may be other situations in which a director chooses to have students give comments on what went well and what did not (Casey, 1993, p. 65) and to make suggestions of how to improve the performance. Audiotape recordings of rehearsal segments and a student's own playing also encourage student feedback and active involvement in musical learning.

In sum, the following suggestions, from both the music and nonmusic literature, are useful for aiding in effective task presentations.

- Organize material so that one point can be mastered before the next point needs to be introduced.
- State rehearsal/lesson goals.
- Give step-by-step directions.
- Focus on one thought (point, direction) at a time, completing one point and checking for understanding before proceeding to the next.
- Model behaviors.
- Avoid digressions.
- Make use of verbal as well as nonverbal gestures to communicate appropriate feedback throughout a performance.
- Avoid verbal interruptions that lead to student off-task behavior.

Teaching Function 3: Conducting Guided Practice

After the presentation of the material to be learned, the teacher conducts guided practice. Major purposes of this activity are to supervise students' initial practice of a skill and to provide the active practice, enhancement, and elaboration that are necessary to move new learning from working memory into long-term memory. Research on information processing has revealed that in order to learn new material we have to spend a lot of time processing it—that is, rephrasing, rehearsing, and summarizing the new material so that we can readily retrieve it from our long-term memory when applying it to new situations. Guided practice provides for this necessary processing.

An example of guided practice and checking for understanding in music occurs when one begins with short passages and then moves to lengthier episodes of music performance that are interspersed with immediate feedback on specific errors. These new episodes are followed by a repeat performance of the now-corrected passage. In this regard, Colprit's (2000) findings in string instruction, which suggest that teachers check for understanding by having students repeat a performance at least twice, are important. In only 15% of all the rehearsal frames studied did the students successfully complete two consecutive performance trials, even though 61% of all frames ended with one successful trial. This suggests that a one-time response is not sufficient to determine that actual learning or understanding took place.

Frequent Questions.   During guided practice, students actively participate by working problems or answering teacher questions. A number of correlational studies have shown that teachers who are more effective in obtaining student achievement growth ask a large number of questions (Coker, Lorentz, & Coker, 1980; Soar, 1973; Stallings & Kaskowitz, 1974; Stallings, Gory, Fairweather, & Needels, 1977). Two types of questions are usually asked: questions that call for specific answers and questions that call for an explanation of how an answer was found.

Recent research literature in music (e.g., daCosta, 1999; Hargreaves, 1996; Jorgensen & Lehmann, 1997; Nielsen, 1999; Sloboda, Davidson, Howe, & Moore, 1996) has discussed the place of purposeful, guided, and systematic practice in musical learning. However, most of the research on practicing has occurred either in the context of individual studio settings or with college-level students. Unfortunately, other than having some anecdotal knowledge of music educators using traditional practice cards or communicating with their students' parents through email, little systematic research exists on how music teachers provide guidance for individual student practice in group instructional settings or how teachers monitor home practice.

In a correlational study of junior high school mathematics instruction (Evertson, Anderson, Anderson, & Brophy, 1980), the most effective teachers asked an average of 24 questions during the 50-minute period, whereas the least effective teachers asked only 8.6 questions. The most effective teachers asked 6 process questions (questions about how students do their tasks) per period, whereas the least effective teachers asked only 1.3. In two other experimental studies (Anderson, Evertson, & Brophy, 1979; Good & Grouws, 1979), teachers were taught to follow the presentation of new material with guided practice, using a high frequency of questions. In both studies, the students of teachers in the experimental groups achieved more than the students of teachers in the control groups. In music, having one or more students in a section play their part is the music education equivalent of questioning. This practice is also a form of checking for understanding.

Hamblen (1984) suggested that the development of questions for the purpose of promoting student interest and sharpening of their analytical skills requires specific questioning strategies. Most types of questions in music instruction, she asserted, elicit memory-recall responses only. To foster abilities related to art criticism and higher order thinking skills, she proposed a series of different types of questions, ordered according to Bloom's taxonomic categories, that would lead to more conceptual learning than is commonly the case in most music instructional settings.

Teacher questioning can encourage students to make musical and interpretive decisions when they are engaged in guided listening or in examining a performance problem. When listening to a group performance, students might be asked to listen for a particular section and/or for individual parts. The students are then asked to describe what they heard in terms of balance, tone color, and overall effect and to make suggestions on how the performance might be improved.

Frequent Practice.   In all of the nonmusic studies cited, the frequency of practice is important. Students need a good deal of practice when learning new material, and effective teachers find ways to provide this practice. For example, when teaching concepts—such as metaphor, simile, and personification—the guided practice could consist of the teacher giving examples: "Is the statement 'My love is like a red, red rose' a metaphor, simile, or personification?" The students would respond and explain their answers; later students could be asked to give their own examples. At each step, the guided practice continues until the students are fluent. Only if the teacher feels them to be ready are the students to proceed to the next step. If they are not, then additional practice must be provided. In either case, one should only move to the next step once sufficient practice on the previous step has occurred and repeatedly has resulted in the desired learning outcome defined and articulated by the teacher from the onset of the lesson.

When teaching a more elaborate skill, such as dissecting a frog, using a computer package, or solving a geometry problem, students might first be asked to restate the steps that were taught. If the material is difficult, it might be best for the teacher to ask the students to state the steps one at a time, in order to resolve any confusion. The steps might be repeated until all students are fluent. Then the teacher can supervise the students as they begin the actual

practice, guiding them through each procedure until they can perform each step without errors.

All teachers spend time in guided practice. However, the most effective teachers spend more time in guided practice, more time asking questions, more time correcting errors, and more time having students work out problems with teacher guidance.

Asking students to match patterns and motives is an example of guided practice in performance settings. This guidance occurs in general music instruction when students are asked to match notated rhythm patterns within those in specific songs. Similarly, in a choral rehearsal the director may ask the members to identify similar and exact motives and phrases within the entirety of a score and sing them in sequence throughout all of the parts.

Music performance as the essence of active participation deals with all three aspects at once—frequent practice, high percentage of correct student performance, and active participation (e.g., Casey, 1993; Merrion, 1989). Most observational research confirms that student on-task behavior correlates with a high percentage of student performance in all types of music instructional settings.

Playing one's instrument (including singing) is the best prevention for student boredom. It is easy to see why in nonmusic settings, students need to practice and process new learning actively. This is particularly important in music-listening lessons and those that are dedicated to the development of music appreciation for the nonperformer. Here, active involvement of all students is of the essence while they are engaged in acute listening tasks. The tasks must be designed in such a way that they require (1) problem solving; (2) the active classification and categorization of differential musical styles, genres, and instruments; and (3) hands-on experiences with performing and discriminating between different rhythmic and tonal phrases, motives, and patterns.

High Percentage of Correct Answers.   Not only is the frequency of teacher questions important, but the percentage of correct student responses is also significant. Effective teachers have a high success rate of student responses (Anderson et al., 1979; Fisher et al., 1978; Gerstein, Carnine, & Williams, 1981). For example, in a study of fourth-grade mathematics, Good and Grouws (1979) found that 82% of the answers were correct in the classrooms of the most successful teachers, whereas the least successful teachers had a success rate of 73%. The optimal success rate appears to be about 75–80% during guided practice, suggesting that the effective teachers combine both success and sufficient challenge. The most effective teachers obtained this success level by combining short presentations with supervised student practice and by giving sufficient practice on each part before proceeding to the next step.

In 1994, Duke suggested viewing the entirety of a rehearsal as a purposeful effort to meet specific performance goals. All rehearsal episodes, he asserted, carry specific functions that need to be followed in order to aid students in intentional learning. In his study (cited earlier), he documented the underrepresentation of student achievement as a dependent measure and called for the expansion of music research that includes "the systematic measurement of teaching effectiveness in relation to the accomplishment of instructional goals" (p. 1). Those studies, he asserted, should focus on specific rehearsal frames by which to study music teaching. Each frame is identified by a specific "target" of learning that is characterized by smaller subgoals. Each of those goals by themselves requires "correct answers" by the students in order to determine the success rate of each rehearsal frame as a teaching unit. It also requires the stating of clear and unambigious learning objectives. Here, the previously mentioned rehearsal pattern of moving from the performance of the entire piece to the practice of isolated sections, measures, and patterns in the score becomes relevant. No longer does the accurate performance of an entire piece indicate success of teaching; now the success rate of each rehearsal frame being executed correctly by each student during rehearsal becomes the determining factor of effective music teaching. Similarly, overall ratings in contests and festivals would cease to serve as the deciding factor in teaching excellence. Rather, good teaching in music would be judged by the degree to which a music teacher manages to engage the students in the successful execution of specific musical tasks that are embedded within the musical composition itself and contribute to its overall effect.

Teaching Function 4: Providing Feedback and Correctives

During guided practice, checking for understanding, or any recitation or demonstration, how should a teacher respond to a student's answer? Research results indicate that if a student is correct and confident, then the teacher can simply ask another question or give a short statement of praise (such as "Very good") while maintaining the momentum of practice.

However, if the student is correct but hesitant, then it is important to tell the student that the answer is correct. In such cases, it is also useful to give "process feedback." This term, developed by Good and Grouws (1979), refers to the teacher saying "Yes, that's right, because . . ." and then proceeding to reexplain the process one goes through to arrive at the correct answer. Process feedback gives the student the additional explanation he or she needs when correct but hesitant.

When students make an error, it is appropriate to help them by simplifying the question, providing hints, or reteaching the material. Whether one uses hints or reteaches, the important point is that errors should not go uncorrected. When a student makes an error, it is inappropriate simply to give the correct answer and then move on.

In their review of effective college teaching, Kulik and Kulik (1979) found that instruction was more effective when students (1) received immediate feedback on their examinations and (2) had to study further and take another test when their quiz scores did not reach the set criterion. Both points seem relevant to this discussion: students learn better with feedback given as soon as possible; errors should be corrected before they become habitual.

Hendel (1995) conducted a quantitative and qualitative analysis of 9 experienced elementary school music specialists from culturally diverse environments. She reported that these teachers "included feedback in over 50% of their instruction. When the newly extended definitions of sequential patterns were used, more than 89% of their patterns were complete; that is, they included reinforcement" (p. 196).

Dunn (1997) conducted a study "to observe performance improvement of 10 choral music concepts after sequential, structured task presentations across a series of choral rehearsals" (p. 549). He reported that "students receiving feedback had higher performance ratings [and] recorded a more positive attitude [but also] were observed off-task a larger percentage of instructional time than students receiving no feedback" (p. 547). This finding is plausible because being engaged in performance prohibits students from being off-task. The performance itself is defined as "on-task." Teacher talk, on the other hand, invites attention away from performance, thereby easily resulting in the observation of off-task behavior.

Student, or peer, feedback is most useful when the music is being "polished," when it serves the purpose of introducing the students to general musical concepts, or when stylistic issues need to be reviewed that contribute to work interpretation. Few directors are likely to use peer feedback for "fixing" notes or specific errors because such interruption impedes the flow of the entire performance and leads to risk of off-task behavior. Rather than using verbal feedback, an effective music teacher singles out students or a section and provides nonverbal feedback or asks them to perform identified trouble spots.

Teaching Function 5: Conducting Independent Practice

Independent practice refers to both unassisted practice in class and to subsequent practice as homework. There is no need, of course, to mention the importance of this activity in music. It is helpful to look at the rationale and procedure for independent practice and homework that have been developed in nonmusic settings. In both music and nonmusic settings, students may be expected to perform the task steps correctly, if hesitantly, at the end of guided practice. This next step, independent practice, provides the additional review that students need to become fluent in a skill and to work without the cues present during guided practice. This need for fluency applies to many of the nonmusic procedures that are taught in school: using a rule to measure widths, adding decimals, reading a map, conjugating a regular verb in a foreign language, proofreading copy for errors, completing and balancing a chemical equation, operating equipment, and applying safety procedures. This need for fluency also applies to knowledge of facts, concepts, and discriminations that must be used in subsequent learning. The objective of this substantial practice is to help students reach a stage where they perform rapidly, successfully, and automatically—a stage where they no longer have to think through each step (Anderson, 1983; Bloom, 1986). Students who reach this stage can devote their full attention to comprehension and application.

Independent practice involves the same material as the guided practice. That is, if the guided practice dealt with identifying types of sentences, then the independent practice should deal with the same topic or, perhaps, with creating individual compound and complex sentences. It would be inappropriate to follow this example of guided practice with an independent practice assignment that asked students to write a paragraph using two compound and two complex sentences, because the students have not been adequately prepared for such an activity.

Similarly, if a nonmusic teacher is teaching students how to add decimals through the thousandths place, then the guided practice and the independent practice should include such activity with specific instructions to practice. In other words, students need guided practice in an activity before they are assigned independent practice. For example, it may be appropriate for a teacher to devote time to practice in-class homework problems (guided practice) before the students leave for home (independent practice). When the material to be learned is difficult, more time should be spent in supervised independent practice; when easier, independent practice is done as homework.

This need for fluency and independence particularly applies to all skill learning in music. In a music rehearsal, it is not uncommon for a director to assign individual practice by making a comment to a quiet and transparent section that the particular spot "requires a veiled and delicate tone. If you practice long tone scales at a *ppp* dynamic level, it will help you understand the idea. Try it for a few days, and we will check it again next Wednesday." In addition, as a rehearsal draws to a close, the director may review the progress of the students and subsequently identify certain areas that still need improvement. The director then encourages students to practice difficult passages at home and provides strategies that may help maximize the students' chances of actually doing it.

Research on detailed processes of independent practice in one-on-one music learning situations and studio settings is extensively reviewed elsewhere in this handbook. Far less research exists on how teachers encourage and incorporate independent student practice as an integral part of school music instruction. In general, music teachers assume that independent practice takes place at home. In that regard, Hallam (1997) identified a handful of procedures music teachers used to encourage and monitor their students' home practice. Wagner (1975) had found that requiring written practice reports led to more reported practice time by the students who had filled out the reports but not necessarily to better performance. Spradling (1979) reported that practice time was increased when students negotiated and then contracted with the teacher for specific amounts of practice periods as well as practice schedules. Wolfe (1987) confirmed that individual contracts between student and teacher were effective for increasing daily practice.

On the basis of this research, it appears that practice at home is facilitated if the teacher gives specific instructions about what needs to be worked on, how to do it, and what the result should sound like. Subsequently, the teacher not only needs to keep a log of such practice assignments but also needs to check for the relative success of such practice sessions and provide systematic feedback about the accomplished task. The more effective teachers were those who specifically prepared students for their home practice.

Independent practice during a lesson or rehearsal is less common in music, unless of course students have assigned worksheets, a practice more common in general music instruction than in rehearsal settings. In some instances, secondary performance music programs in larger school districts allow for students to be taken out of the ensemble to receive individual coaching and tutoring on their instrument. Beyond that, it would be the teacher's decision whether the physical environment of the rehearsal setting and the students' maturity would allow them to work together in small groups or as individuals to polish specific sections or passages in a work. Sectional rehearsals are common and are conducted by the student section leaders under the supervision of the music teacher.

A recent development in music education practice has seen an increase in small ensemble instruction as a part of the overall music program. Chamber music and the performer-led decisions in that process encourage and even require student independent practice as an integral part of the instructional process. Some research exists, by Carmody (1988) and Zorn (1969) and more recently by Berg (2000), who, for two high school student ensembles (winds and strings, respectively) examined the interactions of the players in the ensemble. While her focus was on issues concerning cooperative learning and "meaning making" in music, some of her findings are relevant. The students underwent a sequence of musical thought and action that "included four qualitatively different activities: initiating, performing, orienting, and assisted-learning" (p. 95). The objectives on which the ensembles chose to focus ranged from "intonation, dynamics, and articulation to rhythmic accuracy of individual parts as well as the ensemble" (p. 96). While this particular research did not include the role of the teacher in the rehearsal process, it is easy to see how the teacher could play a pivotal role in establishing step-by-step rehearsal goals even for a small ensemble, thereby directing the performers' attention from one to the other goal in a sequential manner.

Managing Independent Practice.   For nonmusic settings, investigators found that teachers who spent more time in guided practice had students who are more engaged during seatwork (Fisher et al., 1978). This suggests the importance of adequately preparing students. In contrast, when teachers have to give a great deal of explanation during seatwork, student error rates rise (Fisher et al., 1978). Having to provide abundant explanations during seatwork indicates that the initial explanation and guided practice were not sufficient. In summary, students are more engaged during independent practice when the teacher circulates and when there has been sufficient beforehand explanation in guided practice. Investigators also have found that students are more engaged during seatwork when their teacher circulates around the room and monitors and supervises their work (Fisher et al., 1978). This type of mobility is advisable when one works with beginners or young learners. Moving from student to student is necessary to better listen for intonation, correct student posture, give the students a sense of personal attention, and observe as well as control signs of off-task behavior. In large ensembles where, by instrumentation requirements alone, certain students are always in the back, the teacher should occasionally get away from the podium and personalize instruction.

There are few elementary general music teachers who do not know the importance and value of mobility in the classroom to monitor student learning and behavior. Ensemble rehearsal rooms discourage teacher mobility because of not only ensemble size but also room setup, which may include fixed or mobile risers. Teachers in beginning band and string instruction move from player to player to adjust posture and comment on embochure. Later, the director conducts those checks from the podium. Choral directors know the value of moving from section to section

and row to row, because it is nearly the only way to determine each individual student's contribution to the effort of the group. In the context of what she termed magnitude of behavior, Yarbrough (1975) included mobility as one of the defining variables. Although not decisive as a contributor to effective teaching, its presence is a defining teacher characteristic.

Students Helping Students.   Some investigators have developed procedures by which students help each other during seatwork (see Johnson & Johnson, 1975; Sharan, 1980; Slavin, 1980a). Research shows that all students tend to achieve more in these settings than in regular settings (Slavin, 1980a); a manual (Slavin, 1980b) explains how these procedures can be used in classrooms.

Student-guided sectional rehearsals, the mentoring of younger students by more experienced ones, and the creation of an environment in which small ensembles work under the supervision of the teacher on an ongoing basis are examples of this practice in music. Another example is class work where the stronger students are asked to coach weaker students on clearly identified learning objectives. Finally, intense and rigorous teacher preparation is required for instructional processes that make use of peer assessment. In this approach the teacher teams students at a similar level of performance skills and knowledge and sets up procedures by which these students evaluate each other's performance, compositions, or other musical processes or products. Again, the evaluative criteria must be concise and commensurate with the objectives that govern the rehearsal process.

Researchers (e.g., Hunter, 1999; Hunter & Russ, 1996; Searby & Ewers, 1996) investigated peer assessment procedures in learning settings of higher education—not all, however, in performance. It appears that peer work in music works better in one-on-one situations, as well as in such academic areas as music theory, composition, and history. In these disciplines, which require academic study and concept learning, many of the same principles of peer and team teaching are as applicable and appropriate as they are for math, science, and reading. Finally, Berg's (2000) earlier cited research on students teaching each other in small ensemble settings suggests that peer instruction is complicated and time-consuming if it is not carefully planned. Although it is a common practice in music, little research exists in music education that addresses this topic.

Presumably, the advantage in peer tutoring and assessment comes from having to explain the material to someone else and/or having someone else (other than the teacher) explain the material to the student (Webb, 1982). Cooperative/competitive settings are also valuable for helping slower students in a class by providing extra instruction for them during seatwork.

Teaching Function 6: Providing Weekly and Monthly Review

Successful programs in elementary schools provide for frequent review. For example, Good and Grouws (1979) recommend that teachers review the previous week's work every Monday and the previous month's work every fourth Monday. These reviews and assessments provide the additional practice that students need to become skilled, successful performers who can apply their knowledge and skills to new areas. Kulik and Kulik (1979) found that, even at the college level, classes that had weekly quizzes scored better on final exams than classes that had only one or two quizzes per term.

In sum, systematic review is an approach used by the more effective teachers. It exemplifies a process in which the teacher initially takes full responsibility for performing a task but gradually relinquishes responsibility to the students (Lohman, 1985; Pearson & Gallagher, 1983). This progression is a continuum that begins with full teacher control and progressively allows the teacher to diminish control throughout the lesson so that at the end students are working independently. This progression moves from teacher modeling, through guided practice using prompts and cues, to independent and fluent performance by the students.

Depending on the different type of learners in a class setting, modifications are needed on the time spent in the six functions just outlined (see table 18.3). When students are faster or older or when the material is less difficult, less time needs to be spent in review, and more time can be spent on new material (although music teachers often overestimate how much new material can be learned at a given time). In such cases, there is less need for guided and independent practice in class. More of the independent practice can be done as homework because the students do not need as much help and supervision. When the learners are younger and slower or when the material is difficult for all

students, more time ought to be spent in review, less time in presentation of new material, and more time in both guided and independent practice. During independent practice, there is close supervision and a greater emphasis on all students becoming quick and accurate. When material is particularly difficult, some teachers (Evertson, 1982) use a series of cycles of short presentation, guided practice, and independent practice.

Conclusion

Current research on teaching in systematic, well-structured disciplines such as music has shown that it is most effective to teach in an explicit and systematic manner, providing appropriate instructional support for the students at each stage of learning. The effective teacher begins with a review of prerequisite skills, relating the current material to past learning, and then teaches the new material in small steps. He or she uses short presentations and follows each presentation with questions. After the presentation, the teacher guides the students as they practice the new skill and continues this guidance until all students have been checked and received clear feedback. Guided practice is followed by independent practice, which is continued until students can perform the new skill independently and fluently. There is now a research base that draws on experimental studies conducted in average classrooms with nonselect teachers teaching important subject matter. The results have consistently shown that when teachers modify their instruction so that they teach systematically, student achievement improves. A related outcome frequently is that student attitudes toward self and school improve. Therefore, and because the direct teaching functions described here are derived from informed practice as well as research, they are recommended for consideration and full implementation in music.

NOTE

Thanks go to Al Corley, Ph.D. candidate in music education at the University of North Texas, who provided a number of the music teaching examples contained in this chapter.

Table 18.3 Modifications to Suit Different Students

Slower students	Faster students
More review	Less review
Less presentation	More presentation
More guided practice	Less guided practice
More independent practice	Less independent practice

Modification for difficult material

Presentation
↓
Guided practice
↓
Supervised independent practice ⌐

REFERENCES

Anderson, L. M., Evertson, C. M., & Brophy, J. E. (1979). An experimental study of effective teaching in first-grade trading groups. *Elementary School Journal, 79,* 193–222.

Berg, M. H. (2000). Thinking for yourself: The social construction of chamber music experience. In R. R. Rideout & S. J. Paul (Eds.), *On the sociology of music: Vol. 2. Papers from the Music Education Symposium at the Uni-*

versity of Oklahoma (pp. 91–112). Amherst: University of Massachusetts Press.

Bloom, B. S. (1986). Automaticity. *Educational Leadership, 56,* 70–77.

Brinson, B. A. (1996). *Choral music methods and materials: Developing successful choral programs (grades 5 to 12).* New York: Schirmer Books.

Campbell, P. S., & Scott-Kassner, C. (1995). *Music in childhood: From preschool through elementary grades.* New York: Schirmer Books.

Carmody, W. J. (1988). *The effects of chamber music experience on intonation and attitudes among junior high school string players.* Unpublished doctoral dissertation, University of Southern California, Los Angeles.

Casey, J. L. (1993). *Teaching techniques and insights for instrumental music educators* (rev. ed.). Chicago: GIA.

Coker, H., Lorentz, C. W., & Coker, J. (1980, April). *Teacher behavior and student outcomes in the Georgia study.* Paper presented to the annual meeting of the American Educational Research Association, Boston, MA.

Collins, D. (1993). *Teaching choral music.* Englewood Cliffs, NJ: Prentice-Hall.

Colprit, E. J. (2000). Observation and analysis of Suzuki string teaching. *Journal of Research in Music Education, 48*(3), 206–221.

Colwell, R., & Goolsby, T. W. (2002). *The teaching of instrumental music* (3rd ed.). Upper Saddle River, NJ: Prentice-Hall.

daCosta, D. D. (1999). An investigation into instrumental pupils' attitudes to varied, structured practice: Two methods of approach. *British Journal of Music Education, 16*(1), 65–77.

Dickey, M. R. (1991). A comparison of verbal instruction and nonverbal teacher-student modeling in instrumental ensembles. *Journal of Research in Music Education, 39*(2), 132–142.

Dickey, M. R. (1992). A review of research on modeling in music teaching and learning. *Bulletin: Council for Research in Music Education, 113,* 27–40.

Duke, R. A. (1994). Bringing the art of rehearsing into focus: The rehearsal frame as a model for prescriptive analysis of rehearsal conducting. *Journal of Band Research, 30*(1), 78–95.

Duke, R. A. (1999). Measures of instructional effectiveness in music research. *Bulletin of the Council for Research in Music Education, 143,* 1–48.

Dunn, D. E. (1997). Effect of rehearsal hierarchy and reinforcement on attention, achievement, and attitude of selected choirs. *Journal of Research in Music Education, 45*(4), 547–567.

Ericsson, K. A. (1997). Deliberate practice and the acquisition of expert performance: An overview. In H. Jorgensen & A. C. Lehmann (Eds.), *Does practice make perfect* (pp. 9–51). Oslo, Norway: Norges musikkhogskole og forfatterne.

Evertson, C. E. (1982). Differences in instructional activities in higher- and lower-achieving junior high English and math classes. *Elementary School Journal, 4,* 329–350.

Evertson, C. E., Anderson, C., Anderson, L., & Brophy, J. (1980). Relationship between classroom behaviors and student outcomes in junior high mathematics and English classes. *American Educational Research Journal, 17,* 43–60.

Evertson, C. E., Emmer, E. T., & Brophy, J. E. (1980). Predictors of effective teaching in junior high mathematics classrooms. *Journal of Research in Mathematics Education, 11,* 167–178.

Fisher, C. W., Filby, N. M., Marliave, R., Cohen, L. S., Dishaw, M. M., Moore, J. E., & Berliner, D. C. (1978). *Teaching behaviors, academic learning time, and student achievement: Final report of Phase III-B, Beginning Teacher Evaluation Study.* San Francisco: Far West Educational Laboratory for Educational Research and Development.

Gerstein, R. M., Carnine, D. W., & Williams, P. B. (1981). Measuring implementation of a structured educational model in an urban school district. *Educational Evaluation and Policy Analysis, 4,* 56–63.

Gonzo, C. L. (1977). Metaphoric behavior in choral conducting. *The Choral Journal, 17*(7) 8–12.

Good, T. L., & Grouws, D. A. (1979). The Missouri mathematics effectiveness project. *Journal of Educational Psychology, 71,* 143–155.

Goolsby, T. W. (1996). Time use in instrumental rehearsals: A comparison of experienced, novice, and student teachers. *Journal of Research in Music Education, 44*(4), 286–303.

Goolsby, T. W. (1997). Verbal instruction in instrumental rehearsals: A comparison of three career levels in pre-service teachers. *Journal of Research in Music Education, 45*(1), 21–40.

Goolsby, T. W. (1999). A comparison of expert and novice music teachers' preparing identical band compositions: An operational replication. *Journal of Research in Music Education, 47*(2), 174–187.

Gordon, E. E. (1997). *Learning sequences in music: Skill contentent and patterns: A music learning theory.* Chicago: GIA.

Green, G. A. (1990). The effect of vocal modeling on pitch-matching accuracy of elementary schoolchildren. *Journal of Research in Music Education, 38*(3), 225–231.

Haasemann, F., & Jordan, J. (1991). *Group vocal technique.* Chapel Hill, NC: Hinshaw Music.

Hallam, S. (1997). What do we know about practising? Towards a model synthesising the research literature. In H. Jorgensen & A. C. Lehmann (Eds.), *Does practice make perfect* (pp. 179–231). Oslo, Norway: Norges musikkhogskole og forfatterne.

Hamblen, K. A. (1984). An art criticism questioning strategy within the framework of Bloom's taxonomy. *Studies in Art Education, 26*(1), 41–50.

Hargreaves, D. (1996). The development of artistic and musical competence. In I. Deliege & J. Sloboda (Eds.), *Beginnings: Origins and development of musical competence* (pp. 145–170). Oxford: Oxford University Press.

Harwood, E. (1993). A study of apprenticeship learning in music. *General Music Today, 6*(3), 4–8.

Hendel, C. (1995). Behavioral characteristics and instructional patterns of selected music teachers. *Journal of Research in Music Education, 47,* 174–187.

Hunter, D. (1999). Developing peer-learning programmes in music: Group presentations and peer assessment. *British Journal of Music Education, 16*(1), 51–63.

Hunter, D., & Russ, M. (1996). Peer assessment in performance studies. *British Journal of Music Education, 13,* 67–78.

Johnson, D., & Johnson, R. (1975). *Learning together and alone.* Englewood Cliffs, NJ: Prentice-Hall.

Jorgensen, H., & Lehmann, A. C. (Eds.). (1997). *Does practice make perfect.* Oslo, Norway: Norges musikkhogskole og forfatterne.

Kulik, J. A., & Kulik, C. C. (1979). College teaching. In P. L. Peterson & H. J. Walberg (Eds.), *Research on teaching: Concepts, findings, and implications.* Berkeley, CA: McCutchan.

Lohman, D. F. (1985). *Teacher higher-order thinking skills.* Elmhurst, IL: North Central Laboratory for Educational Research and Development.

Madsen, C. K., Greer, R. D., & Madsen, C. H., Jr. (Eds.). (1975). *Research in music behavior: Modifying music behavior in the classroom.* New York: Teachers College Press.

Merrion, M. (Ed.). (1989). *What works: Instructional strategies for music education.* Reston, VA: Music Educators National Conference.

Nielsen, S. G. (1999). Learning strategies in instrumental music practice. *British Journal of Music Education, 16*(3), 277–287.

Overturf, M. S. (1985). *Implementing concepts of vocal sound: Rehearsal approaches of four conductors of outstanding high school choirs.* Unpublished doctoral dissertation, Florida State University, Tallahassee.

Paris, S. (1986). Teaching children to guide their reading and learning. In T. E. Raphael (Ed.), *The context of literacy.* New York: Random House.

Pearson, D. P., & Gallagher, M. C. (1983). The instruction of reading comprehension. *Contemporary Educational Psychology, 8,* 317–344.

Pfautsch, L. (1973). The choral conductor and the rehearsal. In H. A. Decker & J. Herford (Eds.), *Choral conducting: A symposium* (pp. 56–92). New York: Appleton-Century-Crofts.

Phillips, K. H. (1992). *Teaching kids to sing.* New York: Schirmer Books.

Price, H. E. (1989). An effective way to teach and rehearse: Research supports using sequential patterns. *Update, 8,* 42–46.

Price, H. E. (1992). Sequential patterns of music instruction and learning to use them. *Journal of Research in Music Education, 40*(1), 14–29.

Rudolph, M. (1994). *The grammar of conducting: A comprehensive guide to baton technique and interpretation* (3rd ed.). New York: Schirmer Books.

Russell, D., & Hunter, M. (1981). Planning for effective instruction: Lesson design. In *Increasing your teaching effectiveness* (pp. 63–69). Palo Alto, CA: Learning Institute.

Sang, R. C. (1987). A study of the relationship between instrumental music teachers' modeling skills and pupil performance behaviors. *Bulletin of the Council for Research in Music Education, 91,* 155–159.

Schleuter, S. L. (1997). *A sound approach to teaching instrumentalists: An application of content and learning sequences* (2nd ed.). New York: Schirmer Books.

Searby, M., & Ewers, T. (1996). Peer assessing composition in higher education. *British Journal of Music Education, 13,* 155–163.

Sharan, S. A. (1980). Cooperative learning in small groups. *Review of Educational Research, 50,* 241–271.

Shuller, G. (1997). *The complete conductor.* New York: Oxford University Press.

Simon, H. A. (1973). The structure of ill-structured problems. *Artificial Intelligence, 4,* 181–201.

Slavin, R. E. (1980a). Cooperative learning. *Review of Educational Research, 50,* 317–343.

Slavin, R. E. (1980b). *Using student team learning* (rev. ed.). Baltimore: Center for Social Organization of Schools, Johns Hopkins University.

Sloboda, J. A., Davidson, J. W., Howe, M., & Moore, D. G. (1996). The role of practice in the development of performing musicians. *British Journal of Psychology, 87,* 287–309.

Soar, R. S. (1973). *Follow-through classroom process measurement and pupil growth (1970-71): Final report.* Gainesville, FL: College of Education, University of Florida.

Speer, D. R. (1994). An analysis of sequential patterns of instruction on piano lessons. *Journal of Research in Music Education, 42,* 14–26.

Spradling, R. L. (1979). *The use of contingency contracting to increase the efficiency of practice time management in instrumental music majors.* Research presented to the National Association for Music Therapy National Convention, Dallas, Texas.

Stallings, J. A., Gory, R., Fairweather, J., & Needels, M. (1977). *Early childhood education classroom evaluation.* Menlo Park, CA: SRI International.

Stallings, J. A., & Kaskowitz, D. (1974). *Follow-through classroom observation.* Menlo Park, CA: SRI International.

Thurman, V. L. (1977). *The frequency and time description of selected rehearsal behaviors used by five choral conductors.* Unpublished doctoral dissertation, University of Illinois, Urbana-Champaign.

Tobias, S. (1982). When do instructional methods make a difference? *Educational Researcher, 11,* 4–10.

Tyson, T. L. (1988). *A descriptive case study of a master teacher's verbal behavior in a high school choral rehearsal.* Unpublished doctoral dissertation, University of Illinois, Urbana-Champaign.

Wagner, M. J. (1975). The effect of a practice report on practice time and musical performance. In C. K. Madsen, R. D. Greer, & C. H. Madsen Jr. (Eds.), *Research in music behavior* (pp. 125–130). New York: Teachers College Press.

Watkins, R. E. (1986). *A descriptive study of high school choral directors' use of modeling, metaphorical language, and musical/technical language related to student attentiveness.* Unpublished doctoral dissertation, University of Texas, Austin.

Webb, N. (1982). Student interaction and learning in small groups. *Review of Educational Research, 52,* 421–446.

Wolfe, D. E. (1987). The use of behavioral contracts in music instruction. In C. K. Madsen & C. A. Prickett (Eds.), *Applications of research in music behaviour* (pp. 43–50). Tuscaloosa, AL: University of Alabama Press.

Wolverton, J. L. (1993). Identifying relevant competencies for choral music teachers. *Southeastern Journal of Music Education, 5,* 50–61.

Yarbrough, C. (1975). Effect of magnitude of conductor behavior on students in selected mixed choruses. *Journal of Research in Music Education, 23*(2), 134–146.

Zorn, J. D. (1969). *The effectiveness of chamber music ensemble experience for members of ninth grade band learning certain aspects of music and musical performance.* Unpublished doctoral dissertation, Indiana University,

Behavioral Research on Direct Music Instruction

19

PATRICIA E. SINK

Behavioral research in music education has taken an *instructivist* rather than a *constructivist* approach. While the former stresses a teacher-centered instructional model and purposeful change of behavior, the latter emphasizes problem solving, holistic activities, visual formats, cooperative and collaborative learning, exploratory and discovery learning, and "authentic" assessment (von Glaserfeld, 1995). In instructivist models, the teacher leads and directs students to acquire and generate specific, clearly defined knowledge in the form of concepts (i.e., knowledge of), propositions (i.e., why), strategies (i.e., how), and operations (i.e., how to). Instructional processes that involve carefully constructed sequences to achieve explicit learning outcomes have been subsumed under the term *direct instruction* (Becker & Carnine, 1981; Becker, Engelman, & Thomas, 1971; Bereiter & Englemann, 1966; Rosenshine, 1976).

During the past 30 years, numerous studies have contributed to understanding the applications of the principles of behavioral psychology to music education. Most of these studies provide evidence of the efficacy of direct instruction in music. Many of these studies have been designed to systematically observe identifiable components of music instruction, control specific teaching behaviors, and determine effects of teacher behaviors on student attentiveness, attitudes, and at times, achievements.

In discussing systematic observation purposes and techniques, Rainbow and Froehlich (1987) grouped studies as those that: (1) were derived from Flanders's (1970) rationale for *Interaction Analysis* and determined teacher-centered ("direct") and student-centered ("indirect") instruction; (2) were conducted within the framework of behavior modification; and (3) sought to correlate observed behaviors with specific constructs of effectiveness in

the music classroom (pp. 217–218). For any of these three purposes, many different observation systems have been developed that not only differ in their respective constructs but also in the number of observational categories and coding procedures. Regardless of these differences, early studies tended to focus on the documentation of recorded times and frequencies of instructional behaviors during music lessons. One such example is the work by Wagner and Strul (1979), whose observational schema is presented in table 19.1.

In her review of selected observation systems specific to music education, Froehlich-Rainbow (1984) presented and described 26 different observation forms. Ten of those forms are included in Madsen and Madsen's (1981) collection of observation forms for the analysis of teacher behaviors, student behaviors and teacher-student interactions for groups and for individual students, student on-task and off-task behaviors, and interpersonal relationships. Many but not all of the findings reported in this chapter were derived from the schemata first presented by Madsen and Madsen (1981). This approach often has compelled music educators to associate the term "direct instruction" less with measuring classroom climates than with describing a behaviorial model of specific patterns of teacher-student interactions in music instructional settings. This chapter focuses on this approach.

In 1981, Yarbrough and Price defined direct instruction in music as a three-step sequence in which: the teacher presents a task, students respond to the task, and the teacher provides feedback to students in a manner that stresses positive learning experiences. This model has since become a dominant component of numerous published observational research studies during the past 20 years.

Table 19.1 Observed Teacher Behaviors in Wagner and Strul (1979, pp. 116–117)

Teaching Activities

Academic Instruction: Clarifying subject matter; teacher questions requiring short answers; lecturing . . .

Discussion: An on-task conversation period in which students and teachers participate and interact.

Written Assignments: Seat work requiring writing during the class period. The teacher acts as supervisor.

Directions: Teacher explaining rules or assignments and giving directions to students.

Music Activities

Singing: Vocal music performance . . . in which students participate, with or without the teacher.

Playing Instruments: Performance on musical instruments in which students participate, with or without the teacher . . .

Rhythm: Students participating in activities related to rhythm, with or without the teacher . . .

Movement: Movements related to music performed by students, with or without the teacher . . .

Listening: Attending to music that is [aurally presented].

Combinations: Certain combinations of music teaching activities, for example singing and moving or talking and seat work.

Nonteaching Activities

Preparation: Teacher-directed activity where the teacher is getting ready to do something, such as passing out materials, waiting for student attention, and arranging equipment or students before activity commences.

Talk: Teacher-directed conversation that is off task or irrelevant to the classroom subject matter.

Interruption: Unavoidable distraction caused by external environment . . .

Lost Control: Chaos. Normal student/teacher interactions no longer function contingently.

Teacher Reinforcement: Approvals

Academic: Approval for appropriate academic behavior.

Social: Approval for appropriate social behavior, such as on-task behavior.

Academic Mistake: Approval for inappropriate academic behavior.

Social Mistake: Approval for inappropriate social behavior.

Teacher Reinforcement: Disapprovals

Academic: Disapproval for incorrect academic response.

Social: Disapproval for inappropriate social behavior.

Academic Mistake: Disapproval for correct academic response.

Social Mistake: Disapproval for appropriate social behavior.

Elements in the Three-Step Instructional Sequence: Task Presentation, Student Response, and Teacher Feedback

Task Presentation

In the research on teacher presentations of tasks, the findings have produced descriptions of behaviors, such as "getting-ready" activities, providing directions, and talking about specific academic (music) or social (student atten-tion) goals either through review of previously presented materials or presentation of new materials. Wagner and Strul (1979) found that observed teachers talked about 50% of a music lesson or rehearsal; a finding that was confirmed later by other researchers (Colprit, 2000; Moore, 1981; Yarbrough and Price, 1981, 1989). Experienced teachers, however, spent less time giving directions to their music classes and talked less than other teacher groups. This finding was confirmed by Goolsby (1996, 1997, 1999). Wagner and Strul's reported use of teachers' class time also confirmed Forsythe's (1977) earlier conclusion that students' attending behaviors were affected positively by active participation in music making.

Students and classroom observers prefer presentations of explicit academic information rather than directions that do not include academic information (e.g., Yarbrough & Hendel, 1993; Yarbrough, Price, & Hendel, 1994). *Academic information* is defined as teachers talking about music concepts and skills, whereas *directions* are defined as teacher instructions about what to do, such as "turn to page five, and let's sing this section again." Music teachers spend a notable amount of time giving directions and getting ready. Yarbrough (1988) also has reported that shorter rather than longer instructional segments result in increased student attention.

Studies on the effectiveness of subject matter presentation include those by Hargiss (1965), Porter (1969), Froehlich (1977, 1979), and Yarbrough and Price (1981, 1989). Researchers who addressed the selection of subject matter include Greer, Dorrow, Wachhaus, and White (1973), Greer, Dorow, and Randall (1974), and Sheldon (2000). Types of reinforcement used during teacher presentations have been investigated by Madsen and Madsen (1972), Madsen, Moore, Wagner, and Yarbrough (1975), and Murray (1975).

Descriptions of effective music teaching have contributed to establishing common tenets, which are: (1) knowledge of the subject matter is a prerequisite of effective teaching; (2) modeling is necessary to develop effective teaching skills; and (3) the mastery of verbal and nonverbal rehearsal/presentation skills and analytical skills are essential to presenting the subject matter in an understandable and logical manner. Extracting these tenets has led researchers to report on the specific types of teacher-student interactions and feedback approaches that characterize the communicative patterns in instructional settings.

Student and Teacher Interactions

Student-teacher interactions in music instructional processes are multifaceted. Research results have focused on three facets, including: types of modeling and practice; levels of intensity in which teachers present themselves as music leaders; and attention teachers command from the students in terms of on-task and off-task behavior. Researchers have not always separated these three categories in their studies; in fact, often the findings are reported in relationship to each other.

Modeling and Practice.   Modeling is the presentation of live or recorded examples to be imitated by the learner (Madsen, Greer, & Madsen, 1975). Aural and visual models are associated with modeling that is used to help students understand a music skill or concept and to facilitate practice. Musicians recognize such practice as essential to improving and maintaining music skills (Radocy & Boyle, 1997).

One would assume that teacher modeling is integral to and most prominent during the time in which students are given the opportunity to practice specific skills. Yarbrough and Price (1989), however, reported that even though over half of the observed teaching sessions were devoted to practice, the sessions contained little teacher modeling. Rather, teachers gave directions about where to begin and who should play, and set the tempo by counting one or more measures aloud; and then, students played or drilled a music phrase or pattern until the teacher stopped the response often without providing feedback regarding the practice. Yarbrough and Price hypothesized that the efficacy of practice would be enhanced by teachers providing feedback.

Rosenthal (1984) investigated the effects of four modeling conditions on instrumentalists' performance achievements. The conditions were: guided model (combined aural and visual performances of a complex music selection); model only (aural performances only); guide only (verbal explanation of desired performance); and practice only. Rosenthal found that the "model only" group attained higher scores than the other groups. Students using the "guided model" performed better than the "guide only" and "practice only" groups. In 1988, Rosenthal, Wilson, Evans, and Greenwalt published findings of the effects of three experiences on performance accuracy, which were listening to performance models, singing, and practicing. The report suggested that listening to performance models and continuously imitating the model improved performance accuracy.

Prior to the Rosenthal et al. (1988) study, Sang (1987) reported that learning improved when a teacher presented contrasting models of performance. Students apparently learned to differentiate skills when both correct and incorrect models of the skills were presented rather than correct models only. The contrast between correct and incorrect models seemed to limit dimensions of the tasks involving music instruction and skills acquisition. Research on modeling supports that using contrasting models to teach con-

cepts and skills is an effective music teaching tool (Byo, 1990; Haack, 1972; Jetter & Wolff, 1985; Sang, 1987).

General music teachers often use visual cues to help students understand music concepts. Minimal research has been conducted on the effects of music teachers' visual and spatial gestures on students' acquisition of music concepts. Forsythe and Kelly (1989) made this the subject of their research. They reported that visual and spatial gestures associated with melodic phrases enhanced aural discrimination skills.

Dickey (1991) examined the effects of verbal instruction compared to modeling instruction on ear-to-hand skills, kinesthetic response skills, and music discrimination skills. The subjects of this study were students of four middle school bands. Two bands were taught using verbal instruction, and the other two bands were taught by modeling instruction. There was no significant difference in music discrimination between the groups receiving verbal or modeling instruction ($p > .05$). According to posttest analyses, however, the groups that were taught by means of modeling scored higher on ear-to-hand and kinesthetic tasks than the groups that received verbal instruction. Similarly, Linklater (1997) investigated the comparative effects of clarinet students' independent practice at home using audiotape-recorded and videotape-recorded models. He reported that students using a videotape-recorded model during independent practice scored higher on a performance achievement test than did the students who used the audiotape-recorded model.

Coffman's (1990) research focused on the importance of physical and mental practice techniques as essential components in the acquisition of music skills. He found that physical practice and alternating physical and mental practice significantly improved students' piano performance skills ($p < .05$). Ross (1985) also found that physical practice and combined mental and physical practice techniques produced higher performance achievements among trombonists than mental practice only.

Teaching Intensity.   Yarbrough (1975) investigated eight variables as indicators of the magnitude of conducting behaviors. She defined magnitude as the ability of a conductor to "change behavior dramatically in all defined categories [of behavior] at precisely the right time during the rehearsal" (p. 144). The behaviors associated with magnitude of conducting were body movement, voice loudness (referred to as voice volume), voice pitch, speed, activity, eye contact, gestures, and facial expression. Yarbrough focused her research on the effect of high and low magnitude conducting behaviors on performance, attention, and attitudes of students in mixed choruses. She found no significant difference between "high" and "low magnitude" conductor behaviors on performance and attention ($p >$

Table 19.2 Operational Definitions of High and Low Teaching Intensity (Yoder-White, 1993, p. 37)

Eye Contact
High: Maintains eye contact with group and/or individuals throughout lesson.
Low: Looks at group and individuals infrequently, focuses attention on a single student, [or looks at music, ceiling, or piano]. (Yarbrough, 1975, p. 138)

Proximity
High: Frequently walks toward or stands near group and/or individuals.
Low: Remains in front of classroom, maintaining distance between teacher and student, [or stands behind music stand at all time]. (Yarbrough, 1975, p. 138)

Voice Loudness
High: Utilizes firm, strong voice with varying loudness level; reflects vitality.
Low: Displays audible, yet quiet voice which maintains constant loudness level; reflects little vitality.

Voice Inflection
High: Exhibits wide range of pitch fluctuation in speaking voice.
Low: Displays little variation in pitch of speaking voice.

Gestures
High: Uses arms and hands frequently; [uses extensive variety of movements]. (Yarbrough, 1975, p. 138)
Low: Rarely uses arms and hands; maintains strict body posture and position; [performs exact movements]. (Yarbrough, 1975, p. 138)

Facial Expression
High: Displays animated expression incorporating a variety of facial expressions showing approval and disapproval (e.g., smiling, laughing, raising eyebrows, widening eyes, frowning, knitting brow, pursing lips, and/or narrowing eyes).
Low: Displays neutral facial expressions exhibiting little variety in expression [e.g., no frowns or smiles].

Pace
High: Maintains fast, exciting pace characterized by concise instruction, minimal talking, rapid speech, provision of immediate and constant [contingent] feedback (often while students are involved in activity), and absence of lag time between activities (less than one second between activities).
Low: Displays slow, methodical pace characterized by meticulous detail in instructions, much lag time between activities, and provision of feedback only when students are not involved in activity; [always stops group to give instructions]. (Yarbrough, 1975, p. 138)

.05). Increased student attention seemed attributable to high amounts of: (1) group and individual eye contact, (2) approving body movements, and (3) approving feedback.

Hendel (1995) replicated Yarbrough's study with elementary general music teachers. She found that elementary music teachers changed behaviors quickly, including body movements, voice loudness, pitch, pace, type of activity, eye contact, gestures, and facial expressions. The observed teachers spent 91% of the observed instructional time in eye contact with individual students or the entire class.

Teacher proximity to students was varied in two ways: (1) circling the perimeter of the class or moving to the center of the instructional environment, and (2) approaching and moving among students. The teachers used "normal" facial expressions 55% of the time; approving expressions (44%) far exceeded disapproving expressions (4%). With 22 changes per minute in eye contact, proximity, voice qualities, gestures, and facial expressions, the instruction was characterized as high teaching intensity. The teachers used 44% of their class time presenting specific academic (music) information and providing feedback to student responses at a rapid pace. Data on music learning outcomes were not provided.

Madsen's (1990) definition of teaching intensity is a global attribute that involves: "(1) *sustained* control of the student/teacher interaction, (2) efficient, accurate presentation of subject matter, and (3) enthusiastic affect and pacing" (Madsen, 1990, p. 38). Table 19.2 lists operational definitions of teacher intensity. Based on these variables, researchers have shown that teaching intensity can be taught (Byo, 1990; Cassidy, 1990, 1993; Madsen, Standley, & Cassidy, 1989).

Byo (1990) created an intensity-contrast videotape recording that illustrated differences between high and low intensity models of conducting gestures. High school students, nonmusic majors, and undergraduate and graduate music majors were taught to recognize high and low teaching intensity by studying pairs of positive and negative models of high and low intensity conducting gestures. Byo's subjects learned to discriminate accurately between high and low teaching intensity. The contrasting models clearly delineated the nature of the tasks by making demonstrated variations in intensity more noticeable than noncontrasting models.

Most of the research on teaching intensity has emphasized the importance of the interaction between knowledge of subject matter, effective delivery, and sequencing of the subject matter. The studies do not focus as much on music achievements as on student attentiveness and attitudinal measures of instructional outcomes. Teaching effectiveness has been defined as a teacher's knowledge of subject matter, enthusiasm, and sense of timing. An appropriate sense of timing and "doing the right thing at the right moment" is determined by a teachers' ability to hold students' attention through both high and low teaching intensity. Duke and Madsen (1991) maintain that a good sense of timing evolves from a teacher's awareness of student potentials and needs, and of how much and in what order the subject matter must be presented.

Student Attention—On-task and Off-task Behavior. Sims (1986) cites William James as one of the first authors to emphasize the importance of student attention. James

(1890) described attention as an active process of selecting a stimulus on which to focus. Behavioral researchers have examined the issue of attention by asking how student and teacher interactions and behaviors in music classes affect students' on-task and off-task behaviors. Active involvement increases student on-task behavior and, thus, student attention. Performance activities lead to higher on-task behavior than nonperformance activities (Brendel, 1996; Forsythe, 1975, 1977; Madsen & Geringer, 1983; Murray, 1975; Witt, 1986; Yarbrough, 1975). A high percentage of off-task behaviors occurs when teachers and students are involved in "getting-ready" activities and in verbal interactions not specifically related to music learning objectives (Forsythe, 1977; Madsen & Geringer, 1983). In her research on choral music teachers' use of time, Brendel (1996) found students tend to be more on task during activities requiring active responses (e.g., sight-reading, physical and vocal warm-ups, and music performance) as opposed to talking about the music. For music experiences that are not inherently reinforcing, music teachers may find it beneficial to use high levels of approving feedback and to make presentations of high involvement activities contingent on participation in low involvement activities.

Madsen and Madsen (1981) maintain that academic learning suffers when off-task behaviors in classrooms exceed 20%. Few studies, however, have shown that increased student attention results in significant increases in music achievement ($p < .05$). High student attention occurs, in part, because of the nature of participating in music making, and the activity of performing music *may* positively affect music achievement and attitudes.

Teacher Reinforcement—Feedback

Music performance (e.g., scale singing and choral performance) improves regardless of teacher approvals/disapprovals (Greer, Randall, & Timberlake, 1971; Madsen, Wolfe, & Madsen, 1969; Murray, 1975). Similarly, variations of approving and disapproving feedback do not seem to affect music performance. Specific feedback (contingent reinforcement), however, *may* positively affect achievements, attitudes, and attention (Forsythe, 1975, 1977; Madsen & Geringer, 1983; Moore, 1981; Wagner & Strul, 1979). For example, Madsen and Madsen (1972) found that students achieved significantly more accurate intonation when contingent reinforcement was used than when teacher reinforcement did not occur ($p < .05$).

High approval reinforcement improves student attention, reduces inappropriate social behaviors (Forsythe, 1975; Madsen & Alley, 1979), and increases students' positive attitudes toward music (Greer, Dorow, Wachhaus, & White, 1973). Additionally, students and teachers prefer teaching segments that end with approval rather than disapproval (Yarbrough & Hendel, 1993; Yarbrough, Price, & Hendel, 1994). Taylor (1997), however, found that students were able to detect when a teacher's praise was deserved and directed toward a good performance, and when praise was "instructional" with purposes of encouraging and gaining student cooperation.

Teacher feedback characterized as 80% approving has been shown most effective for maintaining student attention (Forsythe, 1975; Madsen & Alley, 1979). Kuhn (1975) investigated the effects of teacher approvals and disapprovals on fifth- and sixth-grade music students' attention, achievement, and attitudes. He found in classes with 80% teacher-approval behaviors that students followed classroom rules more than students who received high teacher disapproval. Kuhn, however, did not detect any systematic relationships among student attention, achievement, and attitudes. Murray (1975) reported that students who received 80% contingent approval expressed more positive attitudes toward their music rehearsals than students who rehearsed primarily with teacher disapproval. Similarly, Forsythe (1977) found that approval rates above 75% produced increased attention among elementary music students as compared to 75% disapproval rates. Although this research focused less on learning gains than on possible "enablers" of learning, a case was made for how to improve student attentiveness and attitudes.

When Yarbrough and Price (1981) began to investigate their direct-instructional model in music education, they reported that approximately 81% of students' off-task behaviors were attributable to nonperformance activities and lack of teacher eye contact. Increased teacher approval occurred during performance activities; conversely, increased teacher disapproval occurred during nonperformance activities. In the classes observed, many reinforcement errors occurred as observed teachers approved incorrect student responses. There was a high frequency of teacher feedback regarding students' academic responses, and a low frequency of social reinforcement (i.e., approving or disapproving feedback regarding on-task or off-task behaviors, respectively). The researchers also found that student attention was highest with the teachers who used the most eye contact.

Kostka (1984) investigated rates of reinforcements on student attention in private piano lessons. Elementary students received the most approvals. Secondary students spent more lesson time performing. Adults were most on task during their lessons regardless of teacher approvals and disapprovals. Elementary students were off task 14% of the time. Approvals during the observed lessons were not at the 75% to 80% level recommended by previous research; however, there was no evidence of negative effects on students' attention, with the exception of elementary students. According to Yarbrough and Hendel (1993),

Table 19.3 Coding of Teaching Units (Yarbrough and Price, 1981, pp. 212–213)

Teacher Presentations

1a: Academic task (i.e., telling students how to perform a passage or where to start).

1s: Social task (i.e., telling students how to behave or discussing future activities).

1c: Conducting task (i.e., nonverbal modeling or conducting signals).

1o: Off-task statements (i.e., not related to academic or social tasks).

Student Response

2p: Performance by entire ensemble.

2s: Section performance.

2v: Verbal response.

2nv: Nonverbal response.

Teacher Reinforcement

3va: Verbal academic or social approval (positive statement).

3vd: Verbal academic or social disapproval (negative statement).

3fa: Facial approval of academic or social behavior.

3fd: Facial disapproval of academic or social behavior.

Errors: Encircled 3va, 3fa (approval of inappropriate behavior), encircled 3vd, 3fd (disapproval of appropriate behavior), encircled 3vd/fa or 3va/fd (conflicting feedback).

---

elementary students understand and respond to approving and verbally expressed feedback more positively than to the converse.

Madsen and Duke (1985) maintain that most music teachers do not effectively deliver deserved or contingent reinforcements. Their teacher education students considered disapprovals less effective than approvals that were characterized as "good," "beneficial," and "effective." Teacher education students, however, also perceived approvals as less favorable for older students than for younger students. Additionally, students who were trained in behavior modification techniques indicated that disapprovals were more potent than approvals. Schmidt's (1995) research on students' perceptions of teacher feedback also suggested that approvals associated with performance improvements (contingent feedback) were considered most effective by students. Taylor (1997) extended results of extant research on students' perceptions of teacher feedback by focusing on teachers' uses of praise as reinforcement. Her operational definitions of praise were based on the following premise:

> As students understand it, deserved praise is contingent on student performance or behavior . . . , and instructional praise is more directly controlled by the teacher to [encourage student cooperation]. (p. 537)

She found that students were able to detect when a teacher's praise was deserved and directed toward a good performance, and when praise was used to provide encouragement and gain student cooperation.

Few studies have established a relationship between approving/disapproving feedback and music achievement, or between increased student attention and music achievement. During the past 30 years, there has been some conjecture that increased student attention resulting from contingent reinforcement should produce increased music achievements. This hypothesis has not been verified.

Complete Three-Step Instructional Model

Table 19.3 presents the operational definitions of the components of the three-step instructional model initially proposed and researched by Yarbrough and Price (1981). The researchers accepted a complete teaching unit as a combination of: (1) Teacher Presentation (i.e., 1a, 1s, or 1c); (2) Student Response (i.e., 2p, 2s, 2v, or 2nv), and (3) Teacher Reinforcement (i.e., 3va, 3vd, 3fa, or 3fd). The researchers' operational definitions of teacher and student behaviors have been foundational to a number of research studies in ensemble rehearsals (Arnold, 1995; Goolsby, 1997, 1999; Price, 1983; Yarbrough & Hendel, 1993; Yarbrough & Price, 1989), elementary music classrooms (Hendel, 1995; Yarbrough & Hendel, 1993), instrumental music lessons (Benson, 1989; Duke & Madsen, 1991; Speer, 1994), and teacher training (Bowers, 1997; Jellison & Wolfe, 1987; Maclin, 1993; Price, 1992; Price, Ogawa, & Arizumi, 1997; Price & Yarbrough, 1993/1994; Wolfe & Jellison, 1990; Yarbrough & Price, 1989; Yarbrough, Price, & Bowers, 1991; Yarbrough, Price, & Hendel, 1994). The three steps used to define direct instruction in music have been researched independently more rigorously and often than as complete instructional sequences. Researchers whose efforts should lead to further investigations on complete instructional cycles in music are Yarbrough, Price, and Hendel. Additionally, Duke's (1994, 1999/2000) proposal to examine music instruction in terms of "rehearsal frames" deserves attention as does Colprit's (2000) application of his model to string instruction. The efforts of the latter two researchers are discussed in the section on future methodological challenges.

In their first study of complete cycles of direct instruction, Yarbrough and Price (1981) found that observed lessons contain many incomplete teaching units and reinforcement errors. During observed lessons, there was a high frequency of teacher feedback regarding students' academic responses and a low frequency of social reinforcement (i.e., approving and disapproving feedback regarding on-task and off-task behaviors). Results supported previous research that showed that music and active involvement in music are intrinsically reinforcing.

In 1983, Price extended the 1981 study by investigating the effects of varied complete teaching units on students' attention, attitudes, and performance achievements. Three teaching-unit treatments were administered to a 48-member wind ensemble during five rehearsals for each treatment. The three treatments were: Treatment A—conductor provides directions as to where to begin playing followed by ensemble performance; Treatment B—conductor provides an academic task followed by directions and ensemble performance; and Treatment C—conductor provides an academic task, followed by directions, ensemble performance, and feedback. Because previous research suggested that participation in and performance of music is intrinsically reinforcing, each aforementioned treatment was considered a complete teaching unit. Treatment C was based on the three-step instructional model operationally defined in the 1981 study. One of Price's intents appeared to lie in testing the strength of the reinforcing nature of music with and without specific teacher feedback. As hypothesized, Treatment C produced higher performance scores and more positive attitudes than Treatments A and B. Active student participation, however, increased student attention regardless of the amount of teacher instruction, directions, and feedback.

Yarbrough and Price (1989) extended their earlier research by examining the extent to which results of extant research on effective teaching was being applied in actual music teaching and learning environments. The researchers videotape-recorded and transcribed music classes and rehearsals of freshman and sophomore music education majors, and of experienced band and choral music teachers (N = 79). Prospective and experienced teachers' applications of the three-step instructional model was ascertained by determining if teachers used complete teaching units, referred to as 1–2–3 teaching cycles or units and labeled "sequential patterns of instruction of music" (p. 179). Modifications of the 1981 model were: Teacher Presentations—1d (giving directions), 1dc (giving the "do it" signal), and 1q (asking questions); and Student Response—2p (performance by entire class/ensemble). Additionally, the researchers indicated that errors in a teaching cycle occurred if: (1) a teaching unit contained only directions and no music task information; (2) directions interrupted the flow between task presentation and student response; (3) teacher feedback was not related to the task presented; or (4) reinforcement errors occurred (e.g., providing approving feedback for an incorrect student response).

In the 1989 study, results showed that more time was spent in "incorrect" than in "correct" teaching units. Two common incorrect teaching units were: the teacher gave directions and music information, indicated a "do it" signal (e.g., ready-play), students responded, teacher stopped students, and provided no feedback or disapproving feedback unrelated to information and directions given prior to student responses; and the teacher provided some music information followed by a long list of directions that disrupted students' attentions to the music information and task.

The observed teachers gave directions, and the students performed more than half of the lesson time, and only 7% of the instructional time was devoted to teacher feedback. Experienced band and choral music teachers provided far more disapproving feedback (approximately 70% disapprovals) than did freshman and sophomore music education majors. Almost an equal amount of teacher presentations consisted of giving directions and talking about music. Student responses were characterized as performance-oriented, with minimal verbal and nonverbal responses. Clearly, in music classes and rehearsals, students' performances are considered as on-task responses to a teacher-given challenge.

Yarbrough and Price (1989) found the high rate of observed disapproving feedback among experienced music teachers disturbing, and they emphasized that such disapproving feedback is counterproductive to good instruction. Their three-step direct instructional model emphasizes the importance of providing corrective feedback rather than "punishing" students for incorrect responses. The researchers recommended that in music teacher education programs, time must be devoted to instructing teachers about how to give directions, present music information, allow for student responses, and *provide appropriate feedback* relative to the acquisition of skills and knowledge.

Hendel (1995) extended Yarbrough and Price's operational definitions of correct and complete teaching units; she accepted delays in reinforcement or feedback as part of a correct and complete teaching unit (p. 187). In her view, teacher feedback could be delayed and still be effective. Her extended, complex teaching units included four or more delays of feedback but still ended in a simple 1–2–3 teaching unit. This 1–2–3 pattern was characterized by extended teacher commentary, frequent practice, and time for additional and thorough student responses. Hendel considered some teaching cycles complete because of the intrinsically reinforcing nature of active and fast-paced participation and instruction in music.

In Hendel's study, teachers changed instructional behaviors quickly and noticeably that were classified as high-intensity teaching behaviors. Elementary music teachers gave more verbal approval than nonverbal approval. Additionally, most teachers completed more teaching units during the observed music lessons than had been reported by Yarbrough and Price (1981, 1989). When simple and complex teaching units were combined, the elementary teachers used correct and complete sequential patterns of music instruction 89% of the time. Techniques to facilitate these units were identifying music elements, drill, ear-training, sight-reading, echo clapping and body percussion, vocal modeling, discussing, accompanying, guided experimenting and discovering, and cross-curricular integration.

Hendel cautioned that the modified and extended sequential patterns of instruction used in her study require additional research prior to generalization.

Future Methodological Challenges

Most of the research reviewed in this chapter focused on systematically observing *teacher behaviors* to describe music teaching effectiveness. Embedded in that focus was the identification of teacher-student interactions that characterize particular classroom practice in music. Rarely were those interactions treated as independent variables whose effect on music achievements was determined. To remedy that situation, Duke (1994, 1999/2000) proposed "rehearsal frames" as units of analysis that seem to provide a potentially efficacious observational paradigm. Duke described a paradigm to identify what music teachers do to accomplish positive changes in student behaviors. Duke explained that effective teachers know how to skillfully arrange and manage tasks in a way that facilitates the acquisition of identifiable goals:

> In nearly all examples of excellent music performance instruction are periods of concentrated attention and effort directed toward the skill of music making—periods during which students play or sing and teachers instruct and evaluate, all of which is directed toward the development of students' knowledge and skills. It is this aspect of instruction on which "rehearsal frames" [quotation marks by editor] focus. (1999/2000, p. 19)

Rehearsal frames require time to analyze each element within a frame and to determine the extent to which a particular element and an entire frame contribute to students' accomplishment of a defined target goal. In Duke's paradigm, attention is on student learning. According to Duke, numerous rehearsal frames occur throughout a music lesson or rehearsal. A rehearsal frame begins when the music teacher identifies a skill or concept that needs to be improved or expanded, and ends when the target goal is accomplished, or when work on a new goal is initiated. With the help of *SCRIBE*, a computerized observation program designed by Duke and Farra (1997), frequencies and durations of selected events or behaviors within a frame are recorded. Three types of presentations provide the results: (1) a graphic time line, which is the visual representation of the sequence and durations of the recorded events; (2) a summary table of all frequencies, durations, rates per minute, total durations, and mean episode durations along with their corresponding standard deviations; and (3) a chronology of all recorded events.

Using Duke's proposed model of rehearsal frames and his computerized analysis procedure, Colprit (2000) identified and analyzed the rehearsal frames of 48 violin and cello lessons that were taught by 12 Suzuki string teachers. She selected two students from each studio and recorded three consecutive lessons for each of them. The observed lessons comprised the performance of musical excerpts that had been introduced to the students prior to the observation. Following Duke's model, each lesson was analyzed by rehearsal frames. A frame began when a teacher stated a specific target goal and ended when the teacher indicated either verbally or nonverbally that the target had been achieved or that the student was getting close to achieving the target. Acquisition of a target goal was described by Colprit as follows:

> If a student performance trial was accurate according to the goal defined by the teacher for that trial, or the performance trial was a closer approximation of the goal defined by the teacher than was the preceding performance trial, then it was evaluated as successful. Student performance trials were judged to be unsuccessful if the performance was not accurate according to the goal defined by the teacher for that trial and the performance trial was no closer an approximation of the goal defined by the teacher than was the preceding performance trial. If the target was unclear or the student could not be heard or seen sufficiently for the observer to make a judgment, the performance was labeled "unevaluated." . . . Rehearsal frames were categorized according to teacher-selected performance goals. Goals, or targets, were articulated by the teacher or inferred from teacher modeling. Targets included any aspect of student performance that the teacher sought to improve. . . . Two independent reliability observers analyzed 12 randomly selected lesson excerpts, one of four excerpts from each studio. (2000, p. 211)

With a reported interobserver reliability of .76 and .74, respectively, between the researcher's evaluations and the two expert evaluations, Colprit accepted the obtained observer consistency as the reliability for all data and calculated for each frame, including both consecutive successful and unsuccessful student performance trials. She found that only 42% of the total of identified target goals were achieved or relatively achieved. Additionally, after the achievement of a target goal, if a teacher asked a student to perform the excerpt again, rarely did the student achieve the same target twice. In only 15% of all rehearsal frames did students successfully complete two consecutive performance trials. Nonetheless, 61% of all frames ended with one successful trial, indicating the teachers' desires to move on to new learning goals after some success in the previous one.

From these descriptions, it is clear that a researcher has many decisions to make when determining the presence or absence of rehearsal frames, the completion of successful and unsuccessful performance trial performances, and, as Colprit did, the categorization of target goals according to focus and content. Also, interobserver reliability is just the beginning of establishing trustworthiness of data.

Colprit's efforts are interesting and promising for other researchers to follow. To conduct such multidimensional research, however, music education researchers face methodological challenges in light of the many choices and decisions the researcher must make, each of which require measurement integrity. For example, any researcher who wants to relate observational variables to learning outcomes across different groups of students and across teachers needs to define what constitutes: (1) satisfactory levels of performance improvement, (2) unbiased and analogous levels of teacher standards, and (3) comparable learning outcomes. Each of these areas, however, are independently subject to the same requirements of construct validity and measurement reliability; otherwise, one risks simply quantifying subjective impressions to give the data the appearance of objectivity.

Duke and Prickett (1987) and Yarbrough and Henley (1999) agree that previous systematic observation and evaluation studies of music teacher behaviors have relied on defining, measuring, and evaluating skills that may be only tangentially related to music teaching effectiveness. Research on the evaluation of teaching effectiveness supports that observers' reactions vary greatly and are influenced by several factors, such as the position of the camera used to videotape-record the teaching and learning situations (Duke & Prickett, 1987), and the format and focus of observations (Prickett & Duke, 1992; Standley & Greenfield, 1987). Ten years ago, Duke and Blackman (1991) called for specific methods of describing, summarizing, and rating the performance of music teachers as they relate to effects of music teaching behaviors on students' acquisition of music instructional objectives. Recently, Duke (1999/2000) elaborated on this issues by discussing the results of a review of 25 years (1972–1997) of research on evaluating teaching effectiveness in which only 13 of the 86 studies measured student music learning. Yarbrough and Henley (1999) stress that few, if any, studies have questioned if effective teaching exists in the presence of undesired or "poor" student response. To satisfy the concerns of Duke (1999/2000) and Yarbrough and Henley (1999), research must be designed to determine if observed teacher behaviors are the *cause* of, rather than merely related to, specific students' music learning outcomes.

Perhaps a larger question, however, is how to achieve construct and content validity of the measures described as learning outcomes. The rating of performances, traditionally a standard procedure in music, still is elusive enough that it does not meet standardized criteria of learning gains across different teachers, schools, school settings, school districts, or states. Because of this lack of standardization, measures of music learning outcomes as currently used in observational research are still subjective and lo-calized. By contrast, there also is a case to be made for the value of the subjective nature of measuring and evaluating music learning outcomes. Of considerable controversy across states and disciplines, standardization of learning outcomes is integral and crucial to the construct of direct instruction described in this chapter.

Froehlich (1995) completed a review of measurement traditions in music teaching and learning environment, which illuminated the need of establishing both the validity and reliability of observational tools more rigorously than seems to have been the practice of the past. Most important in this regard is a clear separation between assessing observer agreement/consistency on the one hand and consistency of observed teaching behavior on the other. Froehlich cautioned that valid observations should not only be derived from specific instructional theory but also that they must be reflective of the reality of the classroom or rehearsal as intended and perceived by the teachers as well as by students who participate in the instructional situation (1995, p. 182). Qualitative techniques may complement, extend, and corroborate quantitative approaches for assessing the relative effectiveness of observed teacher-student interactions.

Systematic observation as a tool to determine teaching effectiveness is useful as long as the theories to which a researcher subscribes are clearly delineated and their rigor upheld. This applies to all three dimensions in which theory guides practice: (1) the curriculum theory that informs the development of any teaching effectiveness measures, (2) the pedagogical theory that governs the determination of appropriate and inappropriate teaching behaviors, and (3) the measurement theory that governs how we integrate independent and dependent variables in ways that allow us to yield credible and accurate data and, ultimately, results.

The researchers whose work has been reviewed in this chapter have pursued answers to questions that seem to be elusive in music education. What are characteristics and outcomes of music teaching effectiveness? To what extent can the effects of direct instruction on music learning be measured effectively, reliably, and validly? Answers to these questions have not been derived from the reviewed research. Direct instruction seems appropriate for developing basic music skills and knowledge. Our experiences as teachers and musicians naturally support that over time such skills and knowledge are fundamental to mastering global or complex music skills and knowledge, such as creating, listening, valuing, and performing. Accumulated empirical evidence has yet to confirm this hypothesis as related to precisely what music teachers do to effect desired changes in student behaviors that ultimately may lead to independent musicianship. Continued pursuit of sequential and systematic research on the value of direct instruction in music is needed with the consequential emphasis on analyzing the effects of the instructional model on advancing music skills and knowledge, and on expanding music attitudes.

REFERENCES

Arnold, J. A. (1995). Effects of competency-based methods of instruction and self-observation on ensemble directors' use of sequential patterns. *Journal of Research in Music Education, 43*, 127–138.

Becker, W., & Carnine, D. W. (1981). Direct instruction: A behavior theory model for comprehensive educational intervention with the disadvantaged. In S. W. Bijou & R. Ruiz (Eds.), *Behavior modification: Contributions to education* (pp. 145–210). Mahwah, NJ: Lawrence Erlbaum Associates.

Becker, W. C., Engleman, S., & Thomas, D. R. (1971). *Teaching: A course in applied psychology*. Chicago: Science Research Associates.

Benson, W. L. (1989). The effect of models, self-observation, and evaluation on the modification of specified teaching behaviors of an applied music teacher. *Update: Applications of Research in Music Education, 7*(2), 28–31.

Bereiter, C., & Engelman, S. (1966). *Teaching disadvantaged children in the preschool*. Chicago: Science Research Associates.

Bowers, J. (1997). Sequential patterns and the music teaching effectiveness of elementary education majors. *Journal of Research in Music Education, 45*, 428–443.

Brendel, J. K. (1996). Time use, rehearsal activity, and student off-task behavior during the initial minutes of high school choral rehearsals. *Journal of Research in Music Education, 44*, 6–14.

Byo, J. L. (1990). Recognition of intensity contrasts in gestures of beginning conductors. *Journal of Research in Music Education, 38*, 157–163.

Cassidy, J. W. (1990). Effect of teaching intensity training on preservice teachers' instruction accuracy and delivery effectiveness. *Journal of Research in Music Education, 38*, 164–174.

Cassidy, J. W. (1993). A comparison between students' self-observation and instructor observation of teacher intensity behaviors. *Bulletin of the Council for Research in Music Education, 115*, 15–30.

Coffman, D. D. (1990). Effects of mental practice, physical practice, and knowledge of results on piano performance. *Journal of Research in Music Education, 38*, 187–196.

Colprit, E. J. (2000). Observation and analysis of Suzuki string teaching. *Journal of Research in Music Education, 48*, 206–221.

Dickey, M. R. (1991). A comparison of verbal instruction and nonverbal teacher student modeling in instrumental ensembles. *Journal of Research in Music Education, 39*, 132–142.

Duke, R. A. (1994). Making lasting change in musical performance: The rehearsal frame as a model for prescriptive analysis of music teaching. *Journal of Band Research, 39*, 78–95.

Duke, R. A. (1999/2000). Measures of instructional effectiveness in music research. *Bulletin of the Council for Research in Music Education, 143*, 1–49.

Duke, R. A., & Blackman, M. D. (1991). The relationship between observers' recorded teacher behavior and evaluation of music instruction. *Journal of Research in Music Education, 39*, 290–297.

Duke, R. A., & Farra, Y. (1997). *SCRIBE: Simple computer recording interface for behavior evaluation*. Austin, TX: Learning and Behavior Resources.

Duke, R. A., & Madsen, C. K. (1991). Proactive versus reactive teaching: Focusing observation on specific aspects of instruction. *Bulletin of the Council for Research in Music Education, 108*, 1–14.

Duke, R. A., & Prickett, C. A. (1987). The effect of differentially focused observation on evaluation of instruction. *Journal of Research in Music Education, 35*, 27–37.

Flanders, H. C. (1970). *Analyzing teaching behavior*. Reading, MA: Addison-Wesley.

Forsythe, J. L. (1975). The effect of teacher approval, disapproval, and errors on student attentiveness: Music versus classroom teachers. In C. K. Madsen, R. D. Greer, & C. H. Madsen, Jr. (Eds.), *Research in music behavior* (pp. 49–55). New York: Teachers College Press.

Forsythe, J. L. (1977). Elementary student attending behavior as a function of classroom activities. *Journal of Research in Music Education, 25*, 228–239.

Forsythe, J. L., & Kelly, M. M. (1989). Effects of visual-spatial added cues on fourth-graders' melodic discrimination. *Journal of Research in Music Education, 37*, 372–377.

Froehlich, H. C. (1977). The relationship of selected variables to the teaching of singing. *Journal of Research in Music Education, 25*, 115–130.

Froehlich, H. C. (1979). Replication of a study of teaching singing in the elementary general music classroom. *Journal of Research in Music Education, 27*, 35–45.

Froehlich, H. C. (1995). Measurement dependability in the systematic observation of music instruction: A review, some questions, and possibilities for a (new?) approach. *Psychomusicology, 14*, 182–196.

Froehlich-Rainbow, H. (1984). *Systematische Beobachtung als Methode musikpadagogischer Unterrichtsforschung: Eine Darstellung anhand amerikanischer Materialien* [Systematic observation as a research technique in music education research: A description of American studies.] (Vol. 21 of the series: *Musikpädagogik: Forschung und Lehre*. [Music education: research and teaching.] S. Abel-Struth (Ed). Mainz: Schott.

Goolsby, T. W. (1996). Time use in instrumental rehearsals: A comparison of experienced, novice, and student teachers. *Journal of Research in Music Education, 44*, 286–303.

Goolsby, T. W. (1997). Verbal instruction in instrumental rehearsals: A comparison of three career levels and preservice teachers. *Journal of Research in Music Education, 44*, 286–303.

Goolsby, T. W. (1999). A comparison of expert and novice music teachers' preparing identical band compositions: An operational replication. *Journal of Research in Music Education, 47,* 174–187.

Greer, R. D., Dorow, L. G., & Randall, A. (1974). Music listening preferences of elementary school children. *Journal of Research in Music Education, 22,* 284–291.

Greer, R. D., Dorow, L. G., Wachhaus, G., & White, E. R. (1973). Adult approval and student music selection behavior. *Journal of Research in Music Education, 21,* 345–354.

Greer, R. D., Randall, A., & Timberlake, D. (1971). The discriminative use of music listening as a contingency for improvement in vocal pitch acuity and attending behavior. *Bulletin of the Council for Research in Music Education, 26,* 10–18.

Haack, P. A. (1972). Use of positive and negative examples in teaching the concept of musical style. *Journal of Research in Music Education, 20,* 456–461.

Hargiss, G. (1965). The development of an evaluation of self-instructional materials in basic music theory for elementary teachers. *Bulletin of the Council for Research in Music Education, 4,* 1–6.

Hendel, C. (1995). Behavioral characteristics and instructional patterns of selected music teachers. *Journal of Research in Music Education, 43,* 182–203.

James, W. (1890). *The principles of psychology.* Massachusetts: Harvard University Press. [1981 reprint]

Jellison, J. A., & Wolfe, D. E. (1987). Verbal training effects on teaching units: An exploratory study of music teaching antecedents and consequents. In C. K. Madsen & C. A. Prickett (Eds.), *Applications of research in music behavior* (pp. 135–148). Tuscaloosa: University of Alabama Press.

Jetter, J. T., & Wolff, J. L. (1985). Effect of ratio of positive and negative instances on efficiency of music concept training. *Journal of Research in Music Education, 32,* 31–43.

Kostka, M. J. (1984). An investigation of reinforcements, time use, and student attentiveness. *Journal of Research in Music Education, 32,* 113–122.

Kuhn, T. L. (1975). The effect of teacher approval and disapproval on attentiveness, music achievement, and attitude of fifth-grade students. In C. K. Madsen, R. D. Greer, & C. H. Madsen (Eds.), *Research in music behavior.* New York: Teachers College Press.

Linklater, F. (1997). Effects of audio- and videotape models on performance achievement of beginning clarinets. *Journal of Research in Music Education, 45,* 402–414.

Maclin, J. P. (1993). The effect of task analysis on sequential patterns of music instruction. *Journal of Research in Music Education, 41,* 48–56.

Madsen, C. K. (1990). Teacher intensity in relationship to music education. *Bulletin of the Council for Research in Music Education, 104,* 38–46.

Madsen, C. K., & Alley, J. M. (1979). The effect of reinforcement on attentiveness: A comparison of behaviorally trained music therapists and other professionals with implications for competency-based academic preparation. *Journal of Music Therapy, 16*(2), 70–82.

Madsen, C. K., & Duke, R. A. (1985). Behavioral training in music education: Perception of approval/disapproval in music. *Bulletin of the Council for Research in Music Education, 85,* 119–130.

Madsen, C. K., & Geringer, J. M. (1983). Attending behavior as a function of in-class activity in university music classes. *Journal of Music Therapy, 20,* 30–38.

Madsen, C. K., Greer, R. D., & Madsen, C. H. (Eds.). (1975). *Research in music behavior: Modifying music behavior in the classroom.* New York: Teachers College Press.

Madsen, C. K., & Madsen, C. H. (1972). Selection of music listening or candy as a function of contingent versus noncontingent reinforcement and scale singing. *Journal of Music Therapy, 9,* 190–198.

Madsen, C. K., & Madsen, C. H. (1981). *Teaching/discipline: A positive approach for educational development* (3rd ed.). Boston: Allyn & Bacon. (First published 1970)

Madsen, C. K., Moore, R. S., Wagner, M. J., & Yarbrough, C. A. (1975). A comparison of music as reinforcement for correct mathematical responses versus music as reinforcement for attentiveness. *Journal of Music Therapy, 12,* 84–95.

Madsen, C. K., Standley, J. M., & Cassidy, J. W. (1989). Demonstration and recognition of high and low contrasts in teacher intensity. *Journal of Research in Music Education, 37,* 85–92.

Madsen, C. K., Wolfe, D., and Madsen, C. H. (1969). The effect of reinforcement and directional scalar methodology on intonation improvement. *Bulletin of the Council for Research in Music Education, 18,* 22–23.

Moore, R. S. (1981). Comparative use of teaching time by American and British elementary music specialists. *Bulletin of the Council for Research in Music Education, 67–68,* 62–68.

Murray, K. C. (1975). The effect of teacher approval/disapproval on the performance level, attentiveness, and attitude of high school choruses. In C. K. Madsen, R. D. Greer, & C. H. Madsen (Eds.), *Research in music behavior: Modifying music behavior in the classroom.* New York: Teachers College Press.

Porter, H. B. (1969). An integrated course in music literature, theory, and ensemble performance for talented high school students. *Bulletin of the Council for Research in Music Education, 16,* 47–48.

Price, H. E. (1983). The effect of conductor academic task presentation, conductor reinforcement, and ensemble practice on performers' musical achievement, attentiveness, and attitude. *Journal of Research in Music Education, 31,* 245–258.

Price, H. E. (1992). Sequential patterns of music instruction and learning to use them. *Journal of Research in Music Education, 40,* 14–29.

Price, H. E., Ogawa, Y., & Arizumi, K. (1997). A cross-cultural examination of music instruction analysis and evaluation techniques. *Bulletin of the Council for Research in Music Education, 133,* 121–128.

Price, H. E., & Yarbrough, C. (1993/1994). Effect of scripted sequential patterns of instruction in music rehearsals on teaching evaluations by college nonmusic majors. *Bulletin of the Council for Research in Music Education, 119,* 170–178.

Prickett, C. A., & Duke, R. A. (1992). Evaluation of music instruction by musicians and nonmusicians assigned differential observation tasks. *Bulletin of the Council for Research in Music Education, 113,* 41–50.

Radocy, R. E., & Boyle, J. D. (1997). *Psychological foundations of musical behavior* (3rd ed.). Springfield, IL: Charles C. Thomas.

Rainbow, E. L., & Froehlich, H. C. (1987). *Research in music education: An introduction to systematic inquiry.* New York: Schirmer Books.

Rosenshine, B. V. (1976). Recent research on teaching behaviors and student achievement. *Journal of Teacher Education, 27,* 61–64.

Rosenshine, B., & Furst, N. (1973). The use of direct observation to study teaching. In R. M. W. Travers (Ed.), *Second handbook of research on teaching.* Chicago: Rand McNally.

Rosenthal, R. K. (1984). The relative effects of guided model, model only, guide only, and practice only treatments on the accuracy of advanced instrumentalists' musical performance. *Journal of Research in Music Education, 32,* 265–274.

Rosenthal, R. K., Wilson, M., Evans, M., & Greenwalt, L. (1988). Effects of different practice conditions on advanced instrumentalists' performance accuracy. *Journal of Research in Music Education, 36,* 250–257.

Ross, S. L. (1985). The effectiveness of mental practice in improving the performance of college trombonists (Doctoral dissertation, Northwestern University). *Dissertation Abstracts International, 46,* 921A.

Sang, R. C. (1987). A study of the relationship between instrumental music teachers' modeling skills and pupil performance behaviors. *Bulletin of the Council for Research in Music Education, 91,* 155–159.

Schmidt, C. P. (1995). Attributions of success, grade level, and gender as factors in choral students' perceptions of teacher feedback. *Journal of Research in Music Education, 43,* 313–329.

Sheldon, D. A. (2000). Preservice and inservice teachers' perceptions of band music content and quality using self-report and behavioral measures. *Journal of Research in Music Education, 48,* 10–25.

Sims, W. L. (1986). The effect of high versus low teacher affect and passive versus active student activity during music listening on preschool children's attention, piece preference, time spent listening, and piece recognition. *Journal of Research in Music Education, 34,* 173–191.

Speer, D. (1994). An analysis of sequential patterns of instruction in piano lessons. *Journal of Research in Music Education, 42,* 14–26.

Standley, J. M., & Greenfield, D. G. (1987). The effect of a focused observation task and its transfer on the analysis of a kindergarten music class by pre-senior versus pre-internship music education/music therapy majors. In C. K.

Madsen and C. A. Prickett (Eds.), *Applications of research on music behavior.* Tuscaloosa: University of Alabama Press.

Taylor, O. (1997). Student interpretations of teacher verbal praise in selected seventh- and eighth-grade choral classes. *Journal of Research in Music Education, 45,* 536–546.

von Glaserfeld, E. (1995). A constructivist approach to teaching mathematics. In L. P. Steffe & J. Gale (Eds.), *Constructivism in education.* Mahwah, NJ: Lawrence Erlbaum Associates.

Wagner, M. J., & Strul, E. P. (1979). Comparisons of beginning versus experienced elementary music educators in the use of teaching time. *Journal of Research in Music Education, 27,* 113–125.

Witt, A. C. (1986). Use of class time and student attentiveness in secondary instrumental music rehearsals. *Journal of Research in Music Education, 34,* 34–42.

Wolfe, D. E., & Jellison, J. A. (1990). Music and elementary education students' evaluations of music-teaching scripts. *Journal of Research in Music Education, 38,* 311–321.

Yarbrough, C. (1975). Effect of magnitude of conductor behavior on students in selected mixed choruses. *Journal of Research in Music Education, 23,* 134–146.

Yarbrough, C. (1988). Content and pacing in music teaching. *Current issues in music education, 13,* 9–28.

Yarbrough, C., & Hendel, C. (1993). The effect of sequential patterns on rehearsal of high school and elementary students. *Journal of Research in Music Education, 41,* 246–257.

Yarbrough, C., & Henley, P. (1999). The effect of observation focus on evaluations of choral rehearsal excerpts. *Journal of Research in Music Education, 47,* 308–318.

Yarbrough, C., & Price, H. E. (1981). Prediction of performer attentiveness based on rehearsal activity and teacher behavior. *Journal of Research in Music Education, 29,* 209–217.

Yarbrough, C., & Price, H. E. (1989). Sequential patterns of instruction in music. *Journal of Research in Music Education, 37,* 179–187.

Yarbrough, C., Price, H. E., & Bowers, J. (1991). The effect of knowledge of research on rehearsal skills and teaching values of experienced teachers. *Update: Applications of Research in Music Education, 9*(2), 17–20.

Yarbrough, C., Price, H. E., & Hendel, C. (1994). The effect of sequential patterns and modes of presentation on the evaluation of music teaching. *Bulletin of the Council for Research in Music Education, 120,* 33–45.

Yoder-White, M. G. (1993). Effects of teaching intensity on sixth-grade students' general music achievements and attitudes (Doctoral dissertation, University of North Carolina at Greensboro) *Dissertation Abstracts International, 55*(02A), 237.

Self-Regulation of Musical Learning

20

A Social Cognitive Perspective

GARY E. MCPHERSON
BARRY J. ZIMMERMAN

Over the past decade, researchers have taken various approaches to studying how musicians acquire and refine their skills as performers. Some of the most important research has been undertaken by music psychologists who have studied the quantity and quality of experts' practice (Ericsson, Krampe, & Tesch-Römer, 1993; Sloboda, Davidson, Howe, & Moore, 1996). Evidence across other pursuits such as poetry, painting, mathematics, chess, and sport (Bloom, 1985; Chase & Simon, 1973; Ericsson, 1996; Hayes, 1989; see further Lehmann & Davidson, this volume) confirm findings in music (Ericsson, Krampe, & Tesch-Römer, 1993; Sloboda, Davidson, Howe, & Moore, 1996) that experts undertake vast amounts of practice over a period of more than 10 years to perfect their skills to mastery level (Hayes, 1989; Weisberg, 1999). In music, international level violinists invest more than 10,500 hours of "deliberate practice" on their instrument by the age of 20 (an average of almost 2 hours per day across a 15-year period), in contrast to around 8,000 hours for professional players and 4,000 hours for music teachers (Ericsson, Krampe, & Tesch-Römer, 1993). One could assume from these findings that practice does indeed make perfect.

Although research on prodigies and elite performers provides valuable insight into the nature of expertise in music, more work is needed on "normal" performance before researchers will be in a position to more accurately determine what happens during the many years that it takes to develop instrumental skill, and how different levels of motivation might affect an individual's practice across such a lengthy period. Clearly, in a "Nintendo" age in which children have many distractions and in which only a small percentage of school instrumentalists go on to perform as professionals or amateurs after leaving school (McPherson, 1995), there is a need for more research over the entire range of abilities that can clarify more precisely what teachers can do to improve their students' abilities. This research is more urgent if one compares the advances in other areas of academic and motor learning over recent decades with the less-developed research base that currently exists in music.

In contrast to the expertise-oriented perspective studied by music psychologists, reviewed by Lehmann and Davidson (chap. 30) elsewhere in this volume, an important body of educational research has focused on the processes that students adopt or acquire as they mature into independent learners. *Self-regulated learning,* a field in which some of the most important recent advances in the study of cognitive development have occurred, is a useful paradigm from which to study how learners acquire the tools necessary to take control of their own learning and thereby learn effectively (Bandura, 1991). Like any academic or motor task, learning a musical instrument requires a great deal of self-regulation, which is evident when students become "metacognitively, motivationally, and behaviorally active participants in their own learning process" (Zimmerman, 1986, p. 308).

Researchers describe self-regulation as cyclical because feedback obtained from prior performance helps a learner to adjust their performance and future efforts. Adjustments of this type are necessary because personal, behavioral, and environmental factors are constantly changing during learning and performance. According to Zimmerman (2000a), these factors are observed and monitored using the three self-oriented feedback loops shown in figure 20.1.

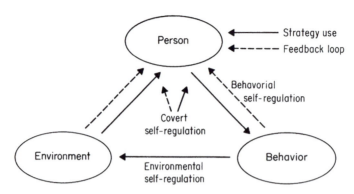

Figure 20.1. Triadic Forms of Self-Regulation. From B. J. Zimmerman, "A Social Cognitive View of Self-regulated Academic Learning," 1989, *Journal of Educational Psychology*, 81, p. 330. Copyright 1989 by the American Psychological Association. Reprinted with permission

Behavioral self-regulation involves self-observation to strategically adjust one's performance processes or method of learning, whereas *environmental self-regulation* refers to observing and adjusting environmental conditions and outcomes (e.g., finding somewhere quiet to practice). *Covert self-regulation* occurs as a result of monitoring and adjusting cognitive and affective states, such as consciously focusing attention on the music instead of the audience, in order to relax and perform better. How productively learners monitor these three sources of self-control influences both the effectiveness of their strategic adjustments and the nature of their beliefs in themselves. According to this perspective, the triadic feedback loops are assumed to be open, because self-regulated learners proactively increase performance discrepancies by raising goals and seeking more challenging tasks. For example, when musicians decide to perform more challenging literature, they make success more difficult to achieve but use the outcome discrepancies to motivate themselves to attain higher level skills. In this way, self-regulation involves triadic processes that are proactively as well as reactively adapted to the attainment of personal goals (Zimmerman, 2000a). This is why researchers need to be sensitive to the influence of variations in context and personal experience (Zimmerman, 1989). Students' personal capacity to self-regulate depends on learning and development, with older and more experienced learners more able to regulate their own learning (Bandura, 1986).

To look at teaching and learning from a perspective of self-regulation holds great potential for research in music education, because efficient learning in music requires at least as much self-regulation as any academic subject or other area of motor learning. Indeed, we would even speculate that learning to play a musical instrument may require more self-regulation than most other domains, particularly in the early stages of development where there are many difficulties to overcome, and when children often experience confusion and failure. Unlike most academic sub-

jects, music involvement is also frequently optional. It relies on a great deal of autonomy, especially in situations where it is up to the child to decide when and where to practice, or whether, or how, to avoid new, difficult, or unlearned repertoire (O'Neill & McPherson, in press).

In contrast to a growing body of literature available in academic and motor domains, only a handful of studies have been undertaken on self-regulation in music. Therefore, many gaps still exist, with many issues remaining to be resolved. One of our prime aims in this chapter is to generate interest on this topic and to provide a framework from which future research might be conducted. Where relevant, we will outline studies that have compared novice players with experts and professionals. It should be noted, however, that our main intention is to focus our discussion on studies with school-aged musicians rather than college or professional performers, in order to differentiate the model proposed here with the strand of research in music psychology that has sought to clarify higher levels of professional and expert performance. This is organized according to two major sections. The first provides a review of existing literature in music according to six key self-regulatory processes, whereas the second discusses practical and theoretical implications for music teaching and learning.

A Framework for Studying Self-Regulated Learning in Music

We do not view self-regulation as a fixed characteristic, such as a personality trait, ability, or stage of development but, rather, as a context-specific set of processes that students draw on as they promote their own learning (Zimmerman, 1998a, 1998b). These processes affect one or more of six dimensions of musical self-regulation as shown in table 20.1. Column 1 identifies the essential scientific question that can be used to underpin research related to

Table 20.1 Dimensions of Musical Self-Regulation

Scientific Question	Psychological Dimensions	Socialization Processes	Self-Regulation Processes
Why?	Motive	Vicarious or direct reinforcement by others	Self-set goals, self-reinforcement, and self-efficacy
How?	Method	Task strategies are modeled or guided socially	Self-initiated covert images and verbal strategies
When?	Time	Time use is socially planned and managed	Time use is self-planned and managed
What?	Behavior	Performance is socially monitored and evaluated	Performance is self-monitored and evaluated
Where?	Physical environment	Environments are structured by others	Environments are structured by self
With whom?	Social factors	Help is provided by others	Help is sought personally

the six psychological dimensions shown in column 2. Column 3 describes the socializing processes that help facilitate the development of the self-regulatory processes listed in column 4. Taken together, these four columns provide the basis for studying key processes involved in efficient musical learning and also for devising strategies that can help optimize music teaching. Extant research will be discussed in the order of the six dimensions of motive, method, time, behavior environment, physical, and social factors.

Motive

To learn a musical instrument, a child must be able to concentrate and move through different tasks in the face of many potential distractions. Environmental factors, such as peer intrusions and a noisy work environment, and personal factors, such as inappropriate practice strategies, confusion, and changing interests and goals, can all too easily distract a young child. Maintaining concentration in the face of these obstacles requires a great deal of volition and personal self-motivation, which researchers (Corno, 1989; Zimmerman, 1998b) believe kick in to control concentration and aid progress when different types of environmental and personal obstacles conflict with learning. Volition and self-motivational processes are an implicit part of explanations concerning how a young child's initial enthusiasm for learning an instrument can, over time, become self-regulating. The motive dimension of our model therefore explains how children come to value their learning, choose to continue learning, and persist with their musical practice (McPherson & Renwick, 2001). As shown in table 20.1, vicarious or direct reinforcement by others provides a foundation from which young learners can develop the types of self-regulatory processes needed for them to develop the self-motivation to persist with their efforts. Although exceptions such as Louis Armstrong and other fa-

mous musicians easily can be found, music psychologists generally agree that parental support is a major ingredient in this process (Gembris & Davidson, in press).

Parental Support. During their early years, children come to learn that they must take responsibility for their own actions. Their earliest experiences are regulated by their parents, who enforce rules of behavior for everyday tasks. These rules provide the context in which to acquire knowledge, attitudes, and skills that will eventually enable a child to cope with more formal aspects of learning after school starts (Corno, 1995; Goodnow & Warton, 1992; Warton, 1997; Warton & Goodnow, 1991). Corno (1989, 1994, 1995) believes that these socialization practices help children acquire an awareness of their own functioning in terms of the cognitive, motivational, and affective resources they will use to guide their subsequent learning.

The parents' role in determining how quickly a child will develop self-regulatory behaviors does not diminish when the child enters school but continues well into adolescence (Warton, 1997). This is because children do not always make a link between remembering to do certain activities and the need to take personal responsibility to do the activities without being reminded. One study from the United States shows that less than 10% of parents of fifth-graders viewed homework as their child's sole responsibility (Chen & Stevenson, 1989). In Australia, Warton (1997) interviewed 98 children about their homework practices. Questions focused on the children's knowledge of the purpose and value of homework, the types of homework activities they were normally asked to complete at home, and their understandings of and feelings toward having to complete homework. An important component of Warton's interview focused on aspects of self-regulation, particularly in terms of reminders. Results show that less than one third of her second-graders viewed homework as their own responsibility and something that they themselves had to remember to complete. Around 76% of the second-grade children reportedly were reminded by their parents to do their homework. A girl said: "It would be a favor to Mum if I remember without her having to tell me" (Warton, 1997, p. 219). By Grade Four, 72% still reported being reminded and by Grade Six, 50% of the children still received parental reminders. Warton's results show that children received constant support in the form of reminders and checking from both parents and teachers to complete homework, and that this was maintained across the entire elementary school grades. These results are consistent with a study of fifth-grade American children (Chen & Stevenson, 1989), where it was found that only 8% of the students viewed homework as their own responsibility.

Families where homework is a priority and where parents are actively involved in facilitating their child's out-of-school work provide a conducive environment for young children to develop the skills that enable them to eventually take charge of their own learning (Warton, 1997). Hoover-Dempsey and Sandler (1995) believe that such parental involvement in homework activities occurs in three ways: modeling, by demonstrating how to work through assignments; reinforcement, through praise, encouragement, and passive involvement; and direct instruction, by drilling and other activities designed to promote factual learning (see further Hoover-Dempsey et al., 2001; Warton, 2001).

These points highlight important similarities as well as some interesting differences between school homework and musical practice. While most parents would feel comfortable engaging in each of these three ways to help their own child's homework, few parents have the requisite knowledge and background in music to assist their child through modeling or direct instruction. For many parents, therefore, reinforcement is the primary means by which they help their child to cope with the continual demands of maintaining a regular practice schedule. This is especially true after the early weeks of instruction, when the novelty of learning an instrument starts to diminish and the reality of maintaining a consistent practice schedule starts to set in (McPherson & Davidson, in press).

In the study of seven cases on the home practice of children who began band instruments in Australian schools (McPherson & Renwick, 2001), the researchers obtained home practice videotapes from 27 of a larger sample of 157 Grade Three and Four children who were involved in a 3-year longitudinal study that sought to clarify the environmental and personal catalysts that shape their musical development. After careful viewing of the videotapes to cull out children who were irregular with their videotaping, or who seemed to be unduly influenced by having a camera on them while they practiced, seven children were selected for more extensive analysis using the software package *The Observer* (Noldus, Trienese, Hendriksen, Jansen, & Jansen, 2000). Using this technique, which allows the researcher to watch and code observed behaviors directly onto a computer for subsequent analysis, the researchers were able to compile a detailed record of each child's practice. Results from this analysis of young beginners show that in the first year of their learning, parents were in close proximity about 65% of the time a child practiced. Eighty percent of this time was spent listening, 10% guiding (e.g., asking what piece the child would play next), and 9% took an active teaching role. By the third year of the study, a higher level of autonomy was observed in the children, with parents present only 23% of the time. Almost all of this time was spent passively listening to the child's practice rather than guiding or actively teaching.

Many children view practicing as a chore or as boring in the same way that they view their school homework (McPherson & Davidson, in press; Pitts, Davidson, & McPherson, 2000). McPherson and Davidson (in press) report that over 80% of the 157 Grade Three and Four beginning band students who were involved in the same longitudinal study needed some sort of reminder from their parents in order to do their practice in the month after taking up their instrument. But by the end of their first 9 months, the mothers' reports of whether they were reminding their child to practice had dropped to 48%. Citing comments obtained from structured interviews with the parents during the period studied, McPherson and Davidson conclude that by this time the mothers had made an assessment of their child's ability to cope with practice, as well as their own capacity to devote energy into regulating their child's practice through continual reminders and encouragement to practice. Some mothers continued to support practice schedules even though the child's interest had decreased markedly. Other mothers started to withdraw their reminders, possibly based on an assessment that their child may not be able to cope emotionally, that if they were really interested then they would do it anyway, or because they were unwilling themselves to invest in the time and effort needed to regulate their child's daily schedule. It is not surprising therefore that, with so much variability in parental involvement and in how their children learn to regulate their own practice, wide differences in performance ability and intrinsic motivation appeared soon after the children started learning their instruments (McPherson & Davidson, in press; Pitts, Davidson, & McPherson, 2000; see also Zdzinski, 1996).

Studies of child prodigies show that most had parents who systematically supervised their practice (Lehmann, 1997; Sosniak, 1985, 1987). The children also became accustomed to performing in front of their family and friends before giving their first recital. Their parents' and teachers' interest in their development helped them to gradually build the confidence, motivation, and persistence that would eventually distinguish them as performers (Sosniak, 1987). Thus, parental encouragement and support were important as the prodigies developed the personal discipline necessary to persist with the many hours of practice needed to develop their skill to an elite level. The parents not only applauded and rewarded their child's initial attempts to perform in front of their family and friends but also supported and encouraged their efforts when interest flagged or skills stalled (Sosniak, 1990). Less than successful efforts were seen as a challenge to be overcome rather than as a debilitating failure (Sosniak, 1990). According to Sosniak (1987):

> Parents kept students practicing an hour a day, for instance, until the students began to work consistently on their own initiative. As the youngsters increased their time at the keyboard parents learned to place higher priority on the practice than on having the child wash the dinner dishes or take out the garbage. They also learned to live with, and enjoy, the noise of music-making at all hours of the day and night. The parents' respect for and appreciation of the child's music-making inspired the child further, and so on. (p. 528)

A recent study of 257 English students (aged 8 to 18) drawn from a variety of musical backgrounds demonstrates that many of the elements cited above for prodigies are also common in the "normal" population (Davidson, Sloboda, & Howe, 1995/1996; Sloboda & Davidson, 1996). In broad terms, this evidence suggests that high-achieving student musicians tended to have parents who actively supported their child's practice, especially during the initial stages where the parents either sat in on lessons or actively sought regular feedback from the child's teacher. The parents also supported their child's practice by verbal reminders to practice, by encouragement, moral support, and, in some cases, direct supervision. Parental involvement was most evident in the early stages of development when a child's ability to self-regulate learning was least evident. Then, as the child's developing self-motivation started to increase and they became more autonomous in lessons and practice, the parents, many of whom did not have a musical background themselves, started to withdraw their direct involvement. However, they still maintained a high level of moral support for their child's high involvement with music. In contrast, low-achieving student musicians tended to receive little parental support during their early years but, during their teenage years, parental pressure to practice and attend lessons increased markedly. The researchers viewed this as a last effort by the parents to keep their child learning (Davidson, Howe, Moore, & Sloboda, 1996; see also Davidson,

Howe, & Sloboda, 1997; Davidson, Sloboda, & Howe, 1995/1996; Sloboda & Davidson, 1996).

Results of these Australian and British investigations run parallel with evidence from Zdzinski (1994, 1996) in the United States. He studied 406 instrumental music students from five band programs in rural New York and Pennsylvania and found that parental involvement was significantly related to the students' performance level, and their affective and cognitive musical outcomes. These effects were more evident at the elementary level than for junior and senior high school. This result is consistent with a study by O'Neill (1997), who studied 6- to 10-year-old instrumentalists. She reports a significant relationship between the parents' involvement in lessons and children's progress. More able students tended to have parents who were more likely to seek information from the child's teacher about how to assist their child, and also talk with the teacher about how their child's home practice was progressing.

Self-motivation.   According to self-regulated learning theory, understanding why some students and not others decide to engage in an activity such as learning an instrument and practicing regularly involves studying the causes of students' self-motivation and a number of key self-motivation beliefs and processes, such as goal-setting, self-efficacy perceptions, intrinsic interest, and attributions.

Hallam (1994, 1997) compared differences between novice and professional performers using interviews and analysis of the novices' practice sessions. Her analyses show that more capable musicians are aware of their own strengths and weaknesses, possess extensive knowledge about the nature of different tasks and what they need to do in order to complete them, and are able to adopt a range of strategies in response to their needs. In this way, professional musicians are able to set short- and long-term goals for themselves, and to mentally note what they want to accomplish during each daily practice session or over the weeks or months leading up to a professional performance. These are exactly the types of characteristics that educational researchers (Zimmerman, 1998a) believe typify self-regulated learners.

Obviously, the highly regulated practice habits of expert musicians result from many years of deliberate practice and are also influenced by a variety of intrinsic and extrinsic motivations, such as wishing to perform well or needing to master new repertoire for an upcoming concert. In contrast, a typical beginning musician will need to be supported as they learn how to define their own practice goals. Barry and McArthur (1994) cite evidence that practice is more effective when it is goal-oriented and directly related to the task being practiced. In their survey of 94 applied music teachers, 66% reported always or almost always asking their students to set specific goals for each of their practice sessions. However, only 14% reported always or almost always requiring their student to keep a written record of their practice objectives (see also Barry, 1992).

According to Lehmann and Ericsson (1997) teachers should use a range of pedagogical and technical devices to encourage student goal setting and subsequent self-monitoring, in order to improve practice. Although much research needs to be undertaken to validate this claim, McPherson (1989) speculates that asking students to evaluate their own and other's performance not only will help to keep them on task but also develop their capacity to internalize goals and to monitor their own progress. After reviewing literature, he concluded that one strategy for achieving this would be for students to use a practice diary in which they set their own goals for practice completion and write in any problems they have encountered between lessons. McPherson advises teachers to review their students' comments at some point during each lesson and also write in comments that help focus the learner's attention on weekly goals, specific instructions that help focus their attention on how they are supposed to play the repertoire being learned, what parts need most practice, practice strategies (e.g., slow vs. fast practice), and other self-reflective strategies that encourage learners to develop the kinds of goal-setting and monitoring strategies needed for them to be able to manage their own learning in ways that eventually will become self- rather than teacher-regulated.

Related to learners' ability to set goals for themselves and to reinforce their own learning is their sense of competence or self-efficacy. Bandura (1997) defines self-efficacy as "the conviction that one can successfully execute the behavior required to produce the outcomes" (p. 79). Self-efficacy is a key component of self-beliefs, because students who believe in their own capacity are more likely to persist despite obstacles, encouragement, and confirmatory feedback (Zimmerman, 2000a). Studies on academic achievement show that perceptions of personal competence "act as determinants of behaviour by influencing the choices that individuals make, the effort they expend, the perseverance they exert in the face of difficulties, and the thought patterns and emotional reactions they experience" (Pajares, 1996a, p. 325; see also Bond & Clark, 1999; Hackett, 1995; Pajares, 1996b). Indeed, research in academic subjects suggests that students with high self-efficacy are more likely to be more confident, choose more challenging tasks, exert more effort, persist longer, and be less likely to experience debilitating anxiety (Bandura, 1986; Pajares, 1996a; Zimmerman, 2000b). Importantly, these studies also show that students avoid tasks and situations in which they feel they are inadequate, and tend to concentrate on tasks and activities in which they feel they can cope (Pintrich & Schunk, 1996).

Examining these findings for music performance, McPherson and McCormick (1999) theorized that music students who display high self-efficacy expectations would be more likely to achieve in a difficult performance area, such as a formal music examination, than their peers who display the same level of skill but lower personal expectations. Completing a questionnaire immediately before entering the performance examination, 190 pianists aged between 9 and 18 responded to items involving self-regulatory learning components (cognitive strategy use, self-regulation) and motivational components (intrinsic value, anxiety/confidence, self-efficacy) of instrumental learning, and self-efficacy, as measured by how well each student thought they would do on their performance examination. Results were consistent with the researchers' predictions. Self-efficacy accounted for the greatest part of the variance of the students' examination result, a finding that highlights the importance for musicians to enter a stressful music examination with a positive belief in their own capacity to succeed (see also McCormick & McPherson, in press). This finding is in accord with educational research showing that students who display high self-efficacy expectations tend to perform at a more advanced level in examinations than their peers who display the same level of skill but lower personal expectations (Pintrich & Schunk, 1996).

According to Zimmerman (1998a), understanding why some learners are more self-motivated than others involves differentiating between the various levels of self-beliefs and values that students bring to their learning. Education research shows that even elementary school children can differentiate levels of intrinsic motivation for different school subjects, but that a general motivational orientation can also be found for each individual that is less domain-specific (Gottfried, 1985).

In McPherson's longitudinal study cited earlier, 157 third- and fourth-grade children were interviewed immediately before they commenced learning a band instrument in eight different school instrumental programs (McPherson, 2000). The questionnaire McPherson devised included a range of dimensions theorized to influence their subsequent learning. As part of the interviews, children were asked open-ended questions concerning how long they thought they would continue playing their new instrument. Later, in the same interview, they were asked to identify whether they thought they would play their instrument "just this year," "all through primary [i.e., elementary] school," "until I'm an adult," or "all of my life." Information obtained from both the open-ended and circled responses was condensed into short-, medium-, and long-term categories of commitment to playing. Results show that even before commencing lessons, 7- and 8-year-old children were able to differentiate between their interest in learning a musical instrument, the importance to them of being good at music, whether they thought their learning would be useful to their short- and long-term goals, and also the cost of their participation, in terms of the effort that they felt would be needed to continue improving. For many of these children, learning an instrument was no different from participating in a team sport, taking up a hobby, or other recreational pursuits. Many were intrinsically interested in learning an instrument but did not see it as important to their long-term future careers. Others were less intrinsically motivated but recognized the utility value of learning in terms of their overall education. For the majority of children, learning an instrument was something useful to do while they were at school but of far less value in later life. Only a handful viewed their involvement as something that could possibly lead to a future career. The children's predictions of how long they expected to play immediately before they commenced learning their instrument were then compared with their results on the *Watkins-Farnum Performance Scalep*, obtained 9 months after they started learning, and their yearly practice, as assessed by averaging out their parents' reports of how much practice they were doing at three evenly spaced periods across their first 9 months of learning. Students who displayed short-term commitment were the lowest achievers, irrespective of whether they were undertaking low, moderate, or high levels of musical practice. Students who expressed medium-term commitment achieved at a higher level according to the amount of their practice during their first 9 months of playing. The highest achieving students were those who displayed long-term commitment to playing coupled with high levels of practice. Similarly O'Neill (1999), who worked with 60 English student musicians, shows that her subjects' perception of the importance of a musical task predicted the amount of practice they undertook, while Hallam (1998), who worked with 109 violin and viola students (aged 6–16), found that her subjects' attitude about practice was a crucial factor for whether they dropped out of instruction.

Method

Summarizing her extensive research, Hallam (1997) suggests that practice will only become purposeful and self-determined when a student acquires a range of *task-oriented strategies* to draw on. Thus, in order to understand the method dimension, it is important to consider the types of skills, knowledge, and understandings that allow children to choose or adapt one particular method over others when engaging with music. As table 20.1 and the discussion that follows indicates, task strategies are often modeled or guided socially, and as a result of increasing experience with the discipline become more and more self-initiated. At the highest level are self-

regulated learners who are methodical in the way they approach their learning and not only plan how they will practice but "spontaneously invent increasingly advanced strategies to improve their performance" (Nielsen, 1999, p. 275). The review of pertinent literature on methods learners use to engage in practice is divided into three sections: (1) developing task-oriented strategies, (2) practicing for yourself compared to practicing for the teacher, and (3) mental strategies and self-instruction.

Developing Task-oriented Strategies. One of the ways to study task-oriented strategies is to map out the different stages of development as skills improve. Studies of this type suggest that distinct changes occur as expertise develops (Barry & Hallam, in press; Gruson, 1988; Hallam, 1994). McPherson and Renwick's (2001) analysis of seven beginning band students' home practice reveals that over 90% of practice time was spent simply playing through a piece from beginning to end, without adopting a specific strategy to improve performance. The analyses, using the computer interface described previously, showed that specific strategies, such as singing, silent fingering, and silent inspection of the music each accounted for less than 2% of the beginners' total practice time. Barry and Hallam (in press), in reviewing literature on this issue, suggest that many beginners are not always aware of where they are going wrong, perhaps because they have not developed an appropriate internal aural schemata to identify and monitor their own mistakes. Slowly, as their skills develop, they begin to identify errors using what Williamon and Valentine (2000) refer to as a musical "stutter," by stumbling over and correcting individual notes. Finally, as students' growing awareness of larger structures develops, they begin to repeat slightly larger units of note patterns until they are able to focus their attention on identifying and improving difficult sections. The tendency for young musicians, therefore, is to focus on getting the notes correct but, as their expertise develops, they start attending more and more to rhythm, other technical aspects of their playing, and, finally, to the expressive dimensions of musical performance (Barry & Hallam, in press).

These results are in accord with Gruson's (1988) pioneering study with 43 pianists, aged between 6 and 46. Separating the players into 11 levels, based on the syllabus of the Toronto Royal Conservatory of Music, Gruson recorded their first practice sessions on previously unlearned repertoire and then analyzed these using an observational scale with 20 categories. As expected, the players made fewer errors as they became more familiar with each piece. However, players in the more proficient levels tended to use more self-guiding speech and verbalizations as well as strategies, such as practicing both hands separately and rehearsing sections longer than a measure. Gruson's interviews with the subjects about their practicing habits confirmed her analysis of the practice session recordings that the frequency and cognitive complexity of strategies reported increased according to musical expertise.

Practicing for Yourself Compared to Practicing for the Teacher. It has been known for some time that one way of fostering positive motivation lies in designing programs for students that take advantage of their own individual goals, interests, and self-perceptions (Eccles-Parsons, 1983). To date, most studies of children's practice have examined repertoire that the student has been assigned by their teacher with almost no effort to determine how choice might affect a student's sense of mastery, confidence, and persistence in learning new material. However, a study that investigated this issue was undertaken by Renwick and McPherson (2000), who used the computer interface described earlier to compare a 12-year-old clarinetist practicing pieces that had been assigned by her teacher with work on a piece that she had asked to learn. In one practice session, the young player spent on average 0.9 seconds practicing per note in the score for her teacher-assigned repertoire. With the piece she wanted to learn, this increased to 9.8 seconds per note: an 11-fold increase. A number of other remarkable differences were also observed. For example, when playing teacher-assigned repertoire, the girl practiced almost exclusively using her "default" play-through approach, by correcting errors on route as she worked her way through the piece. In contrast to her efforts on the teacher-assigned repertoire, the young girl's self-regulatory approach to the work she wished to learn scaffolded her to the types of behaviors that Gruson (1988), Miklaszewski (1989), and Nielsen (1999) suggest typify the deliberate practice strategies employed by experts, such as increasing her use of silent fingering and silent thinking, singing, deliberate alteration of tempo when repeating sections, and practicing longer sections.

Although a great deal more work needs to be done to investigate this more thoroughly, the results are consistent with other disciplines that indicate that allowing students' choice of what to work on and of which method to use can increase their intrinsic motivation and task involvement (see further Pintrich & Schunk, 1996; Stipek, 1998). Although no empirical evidence in music has been found, allowing students the opportunity of choosing the order in which they complete assigned repertoire also might exert a positive effect on their self-regulation (see further McPherson, 1989). If this is true, then music teachers need to offer students real choices between the best possible materials and methods. Students who are always learning pieces that are selected by their teacher may be likely to feel that they are learning these pieces to satisfy their teachers rather than because they themselves want to learn

them. Allowing some choice with regard to the types of pieces a child will learn could be an important dimension of helping to instill a feeling of control of their own learning. This, in turn, makes the learner an active participant in the instructional process (McPherson, 1989).

Mental Strategies and Self-Instruction. Tentative findings in music are consistent with research across academic learning and motor areas of skill development, which suggest that self-regulated learners actively choose to employ learning strategies such as task strategies, imagery, and self-instruction (Zimmerman, 2000b). Working with 101 high school wind players, McPherson (1993, 1997) undertook a content analysis of their reflective comments to describe what they were doing in their mind before they began playing, which he could compare with their scores on measures designed to test their ability to perform by sight, by ear, from memory, and by improvising. For example, on the sight-reading measure, students were scored higher if they mentioned looking to remind themselves of the key or time signature of the music they were about to start playing, analyzed the first section of the music, or scanned the music to identify possible obstacles. Content analysis of the playing by ear and from memory tasks coded responses according to whether the musicians reported strategies that were independent of the instrument or sound of the item; independent of the instrument but involving singing inwardly; or involving kinesthetic recall on an instrument linked with sound. For the improvisation items, student responses were separated into four categories: no plan, the first note or pattern dictating the final shape and course of the improvisation; a vague conception of what might be achieved but with this idea not always adopted once the improvisation had commenced; some idea for shaping the improvisation, such as thinking about the range and style that could be used; or distinct preconceived plan for shaping the response and moving fluently between ideas.

On each of the measures, self-regulated musicians consciously employed more sophisticated and musically appropriate strategies as they prepared their performance. The highest scoring student on the test of playing from memory displayed a mature level of metacognitive ability. First, he chanted the rhythm of the melody to himself to establish an appropriate tempo and feel. He then sang the melody through before mentally rehearsing it a few times from beginning to end. To check that he had memorized the melody correctly, he then looked away for a brief period in order to rehearse the melody in his mind. This was followed by a brief period in which he isolated and practiced a problem section before returning to mentally rehearsing the melody in its entirety. McPherson (1997) reported a significant correlation ($p < .001$) between scores on each of the measures he administered and the learning strategies the students used to prepare for and monitor their performance.

These results are similar to those of Cantwell and Millard (1994), who studied six 14-year-old students selected on the basis of their extreme scores on a learning process questionnaire. The latter was designed to identify whether students tended to adopt a "deep" or "surface" approach to learning. Findings indicated that students who adopted a deep approach defined the problem in musical rather than technical terms, although they knew that they needed to achieve automaticity in technical matters. Students who adopted a surface approach tended to use rote-learning strategies and sought external feedback. The authors suggest that "technically skilled musicians who approach the task of learning new music with surface motivations and strategic behaviours may be less likely to incorporate the high-order attributes associated with competent musicianship" (1994, p. 62).

The Norwegian music educator Siw Nielsen (1997, 1998, 1999, 2000) is one of the first researchers to complete a doctorate on musical performance that is specifically based on principles of self-regulated learning theory. In an English-language article, Nielsen (1999) explored and identified the learning strategies of two organ students as they prepared a complex piece for performance. Her description of how the two organists prepared their performance provides a fascinating account of how they were able to use learning strategies "to select relevant areas, to join parts of the piece as a whole, and to relate auditive 'pictures' beyond the score to the performing of the piece" (Nielsen, 1999, p. 289). Nielsen's detailed analysis enabled her to compile a preliminary scheme for classifying learning strategies in musical practice. She concluded that "students need to reflect on their use of strategies during practice as a prerequisite for being able to use a range of skills systematically" (p. 289).

Gabrielsson's (1999) extensive review of research on the performance of music provides additional support that successful musicians strategically plan how they will control and monitor their playing when practicing and performing. Varied practice, mental rehearsal, motor exercises, memorization techniques, responding to perceptual feedback, and building a mental representation that can be easily translated into sound are some of the many strategies that are integrated into the armory of expert performers. As a supplement to Gabrielsson's survey, Wilson (1997) suggests that stage fright can be controlled when musicians cognitively restructure their own thoughts and feelings about their public performances by anticipating the symptoms of their anxiety and turning them into constructive use. Self-regulated musicians are therefore more likely to "psych" themselves up for a performance by using positive inner talk and other optimistic strategies. In contrast, musicians without these skills tend to be so afraid of failure that they will deliberately think of excuses for a poor result prior to their performance (Wilson, 1997; Wilson & Roland, in press).

Time

According to educational theorists, self-regulated students are able to plan and manage their time more efficiently than unregulated learners (Zimmerman, 1994, 1998a). In relation to music, the time dimension of musical self-regulation (see table 20.1) refers to how a learner's use of time moves from being socially planned and managed to self-planned and managed.

Tentative findings suggest that young musicians' practice becomes increasingly more efficient as they develop their skills on an instrument. McPherson and Renwick (2001) found that 73% (range 57–82%) of their first year students' videotaped home practice, measured from the first to the last note of each practice session, was spent playing their instrument. This rose to 84% (range 76–90%) by Year Three, suggesting that these beginners were beginning to use their time more efficiently. As the ranges in parentheses indicate, however, there also were large differences between students. The majority of the students' playing time was spent on repertoire (Year One: 84%; Year Three: 93%). Technical work (scales and arpeggios) took up the remainder. Interestingly, the rest of these musicians' practice time was spent on nonplaying activities such as looking for printed music, talking or being spoken to, daydreaming, responding to distractions, and expressing frustration. Less than 6% of nonpracticing time was spent resting.

Research in academic subjects shows that many nonself-regulating children actively avoid studying or use less time than allocated (Zimmerman & Weinstein, 1994). This was also true in McPherson and Renwick's analysis of beginners' practice. The least efficient learner spent around 21% of his total practice sessions talking with his mother about his practice tasks and expressing displeasure at his repeated failure to perform correctly, while others were seen to call out to a parent, "Am I allowed to stop yet?"

From a different perspective, Sloboda and Davidson (1996) describe "formal" and "informal" aspects of home practice. In their study of 257 school-aged students, drawn from various levels of music training, high-achieving musicians tended to do significantly greater amounts of "formal" practice, such as scales, pieces, and technical exercises, than their less successful peers. But the high achievers were also likely to report more "informal" practice, such as playing or improvising their favorite pieces by ear. Sloboda and Davidson concluded that these "informal" ways of practicing contribute to musical success, because the highest achieving students are able to find the right balance between freedom and discipline in their practice. Similarly, McPherson and McCormick (1999) administered a self-report questionnaire to 190 pianists (aged 9 to 18) that was designed to explore motivational and self-regulatory components of instrumental performance. The researchers employed factor analysis to categorize three aspects of practice: *informal creative activities* (i.e., playing by ear for enjoyment, improvising music), *repertoire* (i.e., learning new pieces, performing older familiar pieces), and *technical work* (i.e., using a warm-up routine, practicing scales, studies and sight-reading music). The amount of time students reportedly practiced each week in each of these three areas was significantly related to the quality of their cognitive engagement during their musical practice. It also depended on how much the students enjoyed music and their instrument. Pianists who achieved higher levels of practice were more likely to rehearse music in their minds and to make critical ongoing judgments concerning the success of their efforts. These musicians also were more capable of organizing their practice in ways that provided for efficient learning, such as practicing the pieces that needed most work and isolating difficult sections of a piece that needed further refinement. Although further work is needed to validate and clarify these findings, the results suggest that students who are more cognitively engaged while practicing not only tend to do more practice but also enjoy learning their instrument more and are more efficient with their learning.

Musicians also need to be able to pace and manage the use of their time. For example, even young musicians will increase the quantity and quality of the time they spend practicing in the weeks leading up to a significant performance such as a music recital or examination (Hallam, 2000; Sloboda & Davidson, 1996).

Behavior

A distinguishing characteristic of self-regulated learners is that they will notice when they do not understand something or when they are having difficulty learning a particular skill (Thomas, Strage, & Curley, 1988). The ability to react by choosing, modifying, and adapting one's performance based on feedback obtained while performing is therefore central to the process of self-regulation (Zimmerman, 2000a). In terms of the dimensions of self-regulation proposed in table 20.1, students' performance can be socially monitored and evaluated by knowledgeable others (e.g., teachers and parents). But to be truly self-regulating, practice needs to become self-monitored and evaluated.

Metacognition. One of the principal means by which students monitor and control their performance is meta-cognition, which refers to thinking about thinking. It occurs in two ways during learning. The first are the thoughts students have about what they know and do not know, and the second are the thoughts they have about regulating their own learning (Shuell, 1988). As students become more self-regulated, they develop along both dimensions; first, by becoming more aware of their abilities to remember, learn, and solve problems, and, second, by developing more strategic efforts to manage their cognitive activities when learning, thinking, and problem solving (Brunning, Schraw, & Ronning, 1999). For example, as musicians gain experience, they become more aware of the time it will take to learn a new piece as well as different strategies to help them perform correctly (Barry & Hallam, in press). Although this growing awareness of knowledge and skills is important, unless students elect to monitor and control their own cognitive processes they are unlikely to become effective learners (Brunning, Schraw, & Ronning, 1999).

An important component of helping students acquire metacognitive abilities is the teacher's willingness to have the students describe what goes on in their minds as they think. Pogonowski (1989) suggests that a good metacognitive analogy to practicing the piano would involve making yourself aware of how you want a particular phrase to sound, and controlling and monitoring your cognitive resources to make it sound the way that you feel makes most sense musically. By contrast, not using metacognitive awareness would involve thinking about something else either during or at the end of the performance. While the fingers may have had a workout, you would not have been using your metacognitive processes to monitor and control the product.

Hallam's (1997, 2000) studies of string players show that expert musicians have developed extensive metacognitive skills that enable them to make accurate assessments of their own strengths and weaknesses. These skills allow them to respond to different performance situations and to draw on a range of strategies by which they can overcome a variety of technical and expressive problems. The experts' metacognitive abilities seemed to be highly individual, and although there were similarities across some aspects of their practice, there was also considerable variation between individuals. For example, Hallam (2000) reports a number of differences in the regularity of her experts' practice, the way they structured their practice, and the manner in which they approached warming up and refining their technique. They also used a wide variety of ways to prepare for a performance. Some developed their interpretation as their playing became more fluent, others made detailed plans of how they were going to learn a piece in advance, while still others made changes to their interpretation along the way. In contrast, Hallam's school-aged students showed little evidence of specific performance preparation. Although 92% of her sample reportedly undertook more focused and technically oriented practice when it led to a music examination, their practice usually depended on task requirements. In stressful performance situations, such as a recital or music examination, the students employed various self-monitoring and evaluative strategies that included treating the performance as though it was a lesson, consciously avoiding thinking about it, and actively focusing their concentration and attention on the music rather than their feelings about how they were being assessed (Hallam, 2000). They also devoted more time to self-guiding speech as their fluency to perform a work increased (Hallam, 1997).

The studies by Hallam (1997, 2000) provide important data on the individual variation of school-aged string players as they manage and control their own practice. Some completed all task requirements and could quickly identify difficulties as they practiced, concentrate their efforts on the difficult sections, and integrate these into their whole performance. Other students completed task requirements but tended to work on large sections of a work rather than focus on difficulties. The least self-regulating students did not complete task requirements, tended to practice only the first and not subsequent sections of the music, and wasted considerable amounts of time during their practice.

Self-evaluation. In what ways do students respond to feedback, monitor their own progression, and evaluate how effectively they are learning? Although few music studies have been undertaken to determine how musicians evaluate their own progression, available evidence does suggest that successful instrumentalists employ a distinct self-regulatory approach when completing challenging tasks. For example, McPherson (1993, 1994) administered the *Watkins-Farnum Performance Scale* (WFPS) to 101 high school wind players who were asked immediately after they completed the test exactly how they had prepared for their performance of each exercise. A comparison of the highest and lowest scoring students revealed distinct differences in the way these musicians prepared for their performance. Low-scoring students tended not to seek information that might assist their performance, such as checking the key or time signature of the work. Typical of their explanation were comments such as, "I was looking to see what note it started on and singing the rhythm of the first part in my mind." Very few were able to remember the key and time signature of the music when the researcher unexpectedly covered the music immediately before they were asked to perform. Likewise, when the music was covered unexpectedly immediately after they completed the example, only a couple of students were able to remember any of the dynamic markings in the three-line example that had two dynamic indications (i.e., *mp* and *f*) and a crescendo.

In contrast, content analysis of comments on the same tasks by the highest scoring students showed that they made themselves more aware of these important details before commencing their performance. One student had even been taught by his teacher to state aloud the key and time signature of each example before commencing to perform. Another student said: "I first look at the key and time signatures, and then try and run over the harder sections by singing them in my mind as I finger them on my instrument." These comments were typical of the highest-scoring students, all of whom mentioned taking note of the key and time signature as well as scanning the music to find and mentally rehearse difficult obstacles before they started to play. This finding is consistent with comments by Salis (1977), Stebleton (1987), and Wolf (1976), that competent sight-reading depends on the ability to identify familiar patterns and to spend time evaluating the musical material before beginning to perform.

Other evidence of high school musicians' ability to respond to feedback and monitor their own playing is reported by McPherson (1993, 1994). He reports evidence that more self-regulated players were more capable of adjusting and correcting their performance after playing a wrong note that was not in the key of the music. In these cases, aural feedback seemed to act as a cue for the correction of the error, such as a piece in F major, in which a B♭ was sometimes played as a B♮. Self-regulated students monitored their playing to correct errors in subsequent sections of the piece.

Based on his analysis of educational research on this issue, Zimmerman (2000a) proposed four general aspects that people use to evaluate themselves: mastery, previous performance, normative, and collaborative criteria. Mastery involves the use of a graduated sequence from easy to hard, evident in graded music examinations or instrumental method books that are carefully structured and sequenced according to increasing difficulty. The use of such process goal hierarchies predisposes a learner to adopt mastery criteria when self-evaluating because the sequential order of the subgoals provides a ready index of mastery. The learner knows, for example, that repertoire at the front of a book is easier than pieces toward the back of the book, and also that Book 1 is easier than Book 2. Previous performance or self-criteria involves comparing one's current level of achievement with earlier levels. This type of evaluation highlights learning progress that results from repeated practice.

Whereas mastery and previous performance evaluations involve judging changes in your own performance, normative criteria involve comparing your own progression with the progress of others (e.g., other members of an ensemble). The main drawback of this type of self-evaluation is that it focuses learners' attention on social factors, such as how well they are doing in comparison with their peers.

Normative criteria also tend to emphasize negative aspects of functioning, such as when an ensemble loses a music competition despite having improved in comparison with their previous efforts. Finally, collaborative criteria are relevant to group activities. In some ways, the role of a tuba player in an ensemble is distinctly different from that of a clarinetist because each instrument fulfills a different role in the ensemble. The criteria of success for tuba players are different than those used for other sections of an ensemble, and how well a tuba player can work cooperatively with the rest of the ensemble becomes the ultimate criterion of success. Review of research (Zimmerman, 2000a; Covington & Roberts, 1994) on these four evaluative standards suggests that mastery criteria enhance motivation and achievement more than normative criteria.

Motivational Orientations.   Dweck (1986, 2000) believes that children's motivational patterns influence their behavior in predictable ways. For example, *adaptive mastery-oriented* students tend to continue working hard when faced with failure and enjoy putting effort into achieving their goals. These types of learners remain focused on trying to achieve, despite difficulties that might come their way. In contrast, *maladaptive helpless-oriented* students often fail to establish reasonable goals for themselves, or goals that are within their reach. When they feel that the situation is out of their control and that nothing they can do will help, they tend to avoid further challenges, lower their expectations, experience negative emotions, give up, or perform more poorly in the future (Dweck, 1986, 2000; Dweck & Leggett, 1988; Henderson & Dweck, 1990; see also O'Neill & McPherson, in press).

These motivational patterns also have been studied in music by O'Neill (1997). At the outset of investigating the cognitive-emotional-performance patterns of 46 children (aged 6 to 10) during their first year of learning an instrument, the children were administered a problem-solving task and procedure used to assess their motivational patterns (O'Neill & Sloboda, 1997). Eighteen children were defined as maladaptive helpless-oriented. Before they commenced learning, this group was compared to 28 children who were defined as adaptive mastery-oriented. O'Neill believes that studying these two motivational patterns is important, because bright and skilled children can display either orientation. Her results provide convincing evidence of how children who displayed mastery-oriented motivational patterns on a problem-solving task before commencing their instrument progressed to a higher level of achievement at the end of their first year of learning than did children who displayed maladaptive helpless motivational patterns. According to O'Neill (1997):

Helpless children evaluate achievement situations in terms of performance goals where the aim is to display their com-

petence and avoid failure and negative judgements of their performance. In contrast, mastery children tend to choose learning goals which emphasise the need to increase their competence. As a result, mastery children tend to view failure as merely part of the learning process, rather than something to be avoided. (p. 65)

Physical Environment

Self-regulated learners know that the physical environment can affect their learning and will actively seek to structure and control the setting where their learning takes place (Zimmerman, 1998a). In terms of our proposed model (see table 20.1), children come to realize the importance of these skills every time a teacher demonstrates good posture or a parent turns off the television so they won't be distracted from their practice. To date, very little research attention in music has been focused on this issue and on the ways in which some children and not others will structure their environment to ensure more effective learning.

Obviously, some students have little control over the setting where they can practice. For example, placing a piano in a family room close to a television can result in tension between siblings, especially in situations where one child wishes to practice at the same time that another wants to watch television. However, results of the McPherson and Renwick (2001) analysis of practice videotapes provide some tentative clues to how beginning band instrumentalists structure their environment. The instrumentalists chose a wide variety of locations when practicing, ranging from the privacy of a bedroom to a busy family living room. Some even appeared in different rooms on different days, which the researchers suggest might mean that, depending on the family situation for that particular day, the students were consciously choosing an appropriate place to practice. While this action might enable them to obtain help from other family members whenever needed, it also meant that they were more likely to be distracted. Additional data obtained from child and parent interviews led to the conclusion that the physical environment was mostly well equipped with a music stand and an appropriate chair. However, distinct differences between children were noticeable. Some held their instrument correctly while seated or standing with a straight back and appropriate playing position, in contrast to others who were much less consistent with their posture. In one practice video, a young learner even sat cross-legged on his pillow with the bell of his instrument resting on his bed. In this study, the children differed quite markedly in the way they structured their environment, even from the first time they took their instrument home to practice.

Work by Hallam (2000) also provides further tentative evidence concerning how some musicians employ environmental structuring to help them learn. Her interviews with

22 professional musicians and 55 student musicians, aged 8–16, reports various strategies for coping with practice. One very perceptive self-regulating player even commented:

> I get the metronome out. I'm a great believer in the metronome. Well it's a discipline . . . if you're not feeling like practicing . . . the metronome concentrates your mind in a way that nothing else seems able to do, because you've got to concentrate on it. (Hallam, 2000)

In music, the use of an "idealized model," such as CD recordings, is becoming increasingly common to aid students' performance (Barry & McArthur, 1994a). Most band and string methods now incorporate play-along recordings, while Suzuki's talent education program has long employed recordings that children are asked to listen to repeatedly as an aid to learning repertoire on their instrument. Such devices help focus children's attention on what they are doing and also make learning more enjoyable and productive.

Social Factors

When faced with difficulties, socially self-regulated learners rely on and actively seek help from knowledgeable others, in addition to available resources. As our survey below shows, help is often provided by parents and teachers as well as siblings, peers, and other resources, such as books and recordings. Understanding this dimension of table 20.1 involves examining the subtle distinction between help that is provided by others, in contrast to help that is sought personally. As with the other five psychological dimensions of our model, only limited evidence sheds light on this important issue.

Parents. The importance of parental involvement has been mentioned earlier as it applies to supporting and nurturing young children's motivation for homework and musical practice. Taken together, these findings suggest that parents play an important role in facilitating the self-regulatory mechanisms that will eventually allow their children to take control of their own learning.

Recent evidence by Hallam (2000) provides some additional evidence of how novice musicians use social factors to regulate their learning when they prepare to perform in front of an examiner whom they have not met before. Almost 70% of the 55 novice string musicians under investigation adopted some kind of strategy to learn to overcome performance anxiety. In the weeks leading up to their examination, the more self-regulated players asked to play in front of parents or other family members, or arranged to be tested by someone else in a mock examination.

Teachers. Hays, Minichiello, and Wright (2000) suggest that effective music teachers act like mentors to their students, by stimulating and guiding their cognitive and technical skills in a nurturing but rigorous environment. The relationship between student and teacher can be intense, thereby affecting the developing musicians' conceptualization of themselves and their musical goals. Other studies (Davidson, Moore, Sloboda, & Howe, 1998) support these results. Sloboda and Davidson (1996) reported on interviews they completed with 257 young musicians aged from 8 to 18. They used bipolar rating scales to measure the students' perception of their teachers' personal, teaching, and performance characteristics. Findings showed that the students' first teacher was perceived differently across the sample. High-achieving students typically regarded their first teacher as chatty, friendly, and a good player, in contrast to students who ceased playing, who often regarded their first teacher as unfriendly and a bad player. According to these researchers, as students mature and become more competent players, they start to differentiate more and more between the professional and personal qualities of their teachers, such that they may think, for example, that their teacher is condescending and strict but also a brilliant player.

The researchers suggest that the most important qualities of a child's first teacher are to be able to communicate well and to pass on their love of music. Teachers who display these qualities are more likely to increase motivation because their students perceive learning as something that is fun and enjoyable. Later, after the child has started to develop skills on the instrument, the externally reinforced support received from parents and teachers develops into an intrinsic desire to improve performance skills. Self-motivation of this sort means that students perceive learning as something that they can control themselves, with subsequently less need to rely on the external reinforcement provided by either parents or teachers (Sloboda & Davidson, 1996).

Siblings and Peers. To date, the influence of siblings and peers has not received the same attention from researchers as parents and teachers. However, it would be unwise to conclude that their influence is any less significant, given Davidson, Howe, and Sloboda's (1997) comments that older siblings often take on the role of a teacher for their younger brother or sister, although rivalry and personality conflict between siblings also can hinder or stimulate a young child's musical development. Likewise, the influence of peers and older role models a student may strive to emulate has received virtually no attention from systematic research. It is highly likely, however, that in certain instances their influence might be profound. Even asking advice from another player in the ensemble indicates a readiness to seek information that can benefit one's per-

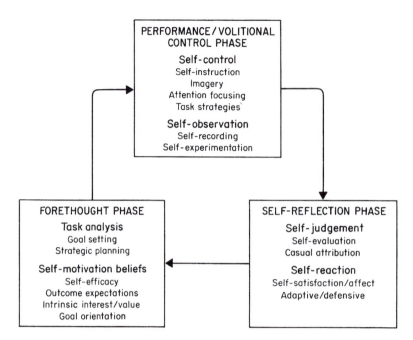

Figure 20.2. Self-Regulated Learning Cycle Phases. Adapted from B. J. Zimmerman and M. Campillo, "Motivating Self-Regulated Problem Solvers," in J. E. Davidson & R. J. Sternberg (eds.), *The Nature of Problem Solving*, 2001, New York: Cambridge University Press. Copyright 2001 by Cambridge University Press. Adapted with permission.

formance. Research in academic disciplines shows that nonself-regulated learners are reluctant to seek advice, either because they are unsure of what to ask, or perhaps afraid of how they might appear (Newman, 1994).

Other Resources. Finally, a self-regulated student musician will actively seek information and help from other sources, such as recordings and books. We could find no specific research that mentions this issue in music, although there are various reports in academic learning (see, for example, Newman, 1994; Zimmerman & Martinez-Pons, 1986, 1988). Anecdotal evidence suggests, however, that self-regulated musicians will listen to recordings or look up information in books in order to clarify aspects of performance technique and expression that they may be working to improve. Such instances of actively seeking help from other sources help to sustain a musician's motivation, particularly during difficult periods in the learning process.

Practical and Theoretical Implications for Music Teaching and Learning

Possessing the self-regulatory skills to get a job done is one thing, but it is an entirely different matter to "apply them persistently in the face of difficulties, stressors, or competing distractions" (Zimmerman, 1995, p. 219). Consequently, studying self-regulatory process also involves try-

ing to understand the cyclical processes whereby students mobilize, direct, and sustain their learning efforts.

Self-regulation as a Cyclic Process

Zimmerman (1998b) views self-regulated learning as an open-ended cyclic process that occurs in three phrases: forethought, performance/volitional control, and self-reflection (see figure 20.2).

Forethought refers to the thought processes and personal beliefs that precede efforts to engage in a task and that therefore influence subsequent learning. *Performance/volitional control* involves processes that occur during learning that affect concentration and performance. After learning has occurred, *self-reflection* influences the learner's reaction and subsequent response to the experience. As shown in figure 20.2, these processes are cyclical, because the learner's *self-reflection* feeds back into forethought to influence future learning efforts (Zimmerman, 2000a).

Forethought. This can occur in two major ways as a student learns a musical instrument (see figure 20.2). Setting both short- and long-term goals enables learners to establish standards for their performance and therefore is an important motivational process. Students who set clear goals for themselves are more likely to gain pleasure and feel confident about their abilities, focus their efforts as they learn, work harder, and persist with instruction, particularly when faced with difficulties (Pintrich & Schunk, 1996). The essence of goal setting is being able to break larger goals into manageable ones, such as spending time learning a new technique on an instrument (e.g., triple-tonguing on flute or trumpet) in order to master more difficult repertoire, which in turn can subsequently expand one's performance opportunities. To facilitate these processes, students are encouraged to plan their learning behavior strategically by devising methods that are appropriate for the task and setting and to focus on what they are doing now in order to work toward their larger goals (Hofer, Yu, & Pintrich, 1998).

As skills develop, their effectiveness often declines such that another strategy becomes necessary. An example would be a novice musician switching from the strategy of performing warm-up material from the printed score to a strategy whereby it is played from memory. Because intrapersonal, interpersonal, and contextual conditions are so diverse and changeable, self-regulated musicians need to continuously adjust their goals and choice of strategies (Zimmerman, 2000a). Students' goal orientations also affect their motivation to self-regulate. For example, Dweck and Leggett (1988) summarized research indicating that mastery goals account for between 10% and 30% in students' use of learning strategies.

These processes are affected by a number of personal beliefs that motivate self-regulated learners using the above-mentioned skills. Self-efficacy is also of critical importance, because it is particularly salient in specific performance activities (Bandura, 1997; Zimmerman, 2000b). Self-efficacy may seem closely tied to theories of self-concept and self-competence in that it does include personal judgments of ability (Pintrich & Schunk, 1996). Where it differs, however, is that self-efficacy also includes being able to organize and execute the actions or skills necessary to demonstrate competent performance. For example, self-efficacy for music performance not only implies a self-recognition of being a good instrumentalist but also explicit judgments for possessing the skills necessary to perform in front of others, such as in a music recital or concert.

Another important distinction is that self-efficacy judgments are made in relation to a specific type of performance (Pintrich & Schunk, 1996; Stipek, 1998). A trumpeter might lower his or her efficacy judgments for playing a high note in a particular piece because of a sore embouchure, while a pianist may display lower self-efficacy when faced with the challenge of learning a difficult piece in what he or she might feel is too short a time frame. These self-efficacy judgments subsequently interact with the learner's outcome expectations. While a student musician might feel confident of obtaining an "A" for the performance requirements of a course, outcome expectations refer to the consequences this grade might have in the future,

such as deciding whether to go on to study music after leaving school (Zimmerman, 2000a). As Zimmerman (2000a) explains, "The more capable people believe themselves to be, the higher the goals they set for themselves and the more firmly committed they remain to those goals" (p. 18). Self-regulated learners also tend to believe in their own ability because they adopt hierarchical process goals that are personally satisfying and see these as milestones in a lifelong mastery process. This is evident when musicians come to value performing not for the external rewards such as parental praise or obtaining a high grade at school but, rather, for the sheer intrinsic pleasure of performing masterfully. In this way, the level of a student's *intrinsic interest* influences whether a learner will continue their efforts to learn, without the need to receive tangible rewards (Zimmerman, 1998a).

Performance/Volitional Control.   In the second phase of a self-regulated learning cycle, researchers focus on two processes that they believe enable learners to optimize their performance, self-control, and self-observation.

Self-control processes help musicians focus on their performance and what they are playing. These processes help musicians optimize their efforts, through such means as self-instruction (overtly or covertly describing how to execute a task), imagery, attention focusing, and task strategies. For example, musicians can instruct themselves through the use of self-talk to reinforce how they should master a difficult passage that needs to be learned during a practice session. *Self-instruction* of this type helps students to monitor and control their concentration during learning (Vygotsky, 1962). On other occasions musicians will use a form of inner self-speech (e.g., "I can do this!") to "psych" themselves up before or during a major performance. This strengthens a musician's ability to focus attention on the performance and can also help alleviate performance anxiety. Mental imagery, according to Kohut (1985), involves creating "mental blueprints" of specific performance goals or tasks. Their application in perceptual-motor activities such as music are particularly important. Musicians, for example, often use mental imagery to plan, enhance, and model what they are learning to perform physically.

Self-regulated learners use a variety of resources to focus their attention, thereby blocking out distractions and concentrating more effectively on what they are doing. Efficient musical practice would seem reliant on how well a musician is able to attend to his or her performance, and also on task strategies that affect the learner's implementation of strategic or other learning methods. For example, young musicians who break a difficult work down into smaller units that can be isolated and practiced separately are likely to be more successful and attentive as they practice than would similar student musicians who perform the same piece from beginning to end without more concentrated efforts to refine the sections in which they are having difficulty.

The second type of performance process, self-observation, helps inform a learner about the presence or lack of progress. Researchers who study this process as it relates to motor skills recommend limiting self-monitoring to key processes or outcomes, as too much monitoring can interfere and disrupt one's performance. Self-monitoring can be complicated even further by the fact that as skills are acquired, less intentional monitoring is required, particularly as skills become automatic.

Carver and Scheier (1981) recommend encouraging students to shift their self-monitoring to a more general level, such as from the action itself to the immediate environment and the outcomes of that action. A good example would involve shifting attention from interpreting the visual symbols used to represent crescendos and diminuendos in music notation, to an inward feel for how the music should and could be expressed. Two critical types of self-observation include self-recording and self-experimentation.

Self-recording, rarely used by musicians, is an effective way to monitor one's progress. For example, musicians who tape-record and then analyze repertoire are able to use this information as a means of assessing which sections of the pieces they need to work on most and how much they have improved since their last recording. Similarly, musicians can experiment with pieces they already know how to play in order to evaluate whether a piece might work better at a faster tempo, whether the dynamic shadings could be further exaggerated, or whether the use of more subtle tonal colors might enhance their performance.

Self-reflection. This third phase of self-regulated learning occurs in four ways: self-evaluation, causal attributions, self-satisfaction/affect, and "adaptivity." Self-evaluation is usually one of the initial self-reflective processes and involves comparing information with some standard or goal, such as judging feedback given by an ensemble director, comparing one's performance with peers, or reacting to an examiner's written assessment after a music performance or recital. Self-regulated learners are often keen to evaluate how well they are doing in comparison with their peers, and when no formal standards are available will often resort to comparing their performance with others. Typical self-regulated musicians will attribute their success to correctable causes that can be improved through more effort, even during long stretches where their practice produces meager results (Zimmerman, 2000a). When students attribute their success or failure to ability rather than effort, they are more likely to give up trying to improve.

Self-judgments are integrally related to the satisfaction or dissatisfaction derived from performing well or poorly,

and the conclusions a person then makes for improving future efforts to learn or perform. Self-satisfaction perceptions are important because learners choose to engage in activities and learning experiences that are satisfying and make them feel good. They avoid activities and learning experiences that they do not find satisfying, that do not make them feel good, and that result in anxiety (Bandura, 1991). According to Zimmerman (2000a):

> When self-satisfaction is made conditional on reaching adopted goals, people give direction to their actions and create self-incentives to persist in their efforts. Thus, a person's motivation does not stem from the goals themselves, but rather from self-evaluative reactions to behavioral outcomes. (p. 23)

When self-regulated learners draw conclusions about their efforts, they make adaptive or defensive inferences that subsequently influence their future efforts. Adaptive inferences can direct learners to new or better forms of performance self-regulation, such as choosing a better or more effective strategy (Zimmerman & Martinez-Pons, 1992). By contrast, defensive inferences tend to limit personal growth, especially in situations where the learner feels helpless, procrastinates, avoids tasks, or ceases active engagement because of apathy (Garcia & Pintrich, 1994).

Self-reactions affect forethought processes and can therefore dramatically impact on future courses of action toward a musician's most important goals (Zimmerman, 2000a). For example, self-satisfaction can strengthen a musician's self-efficacy beliefs for mastering challenging new repertoire, learning goal orientations, and intrinsic interest in the task. When musicians' self-motivational beliefs are enhanced, they are more likely to feel inclined to continue their cyclical self-regulatory efforts in order to attain their goals. The social cognitive model shown in figure 20.2 is useful in helping to explain the cyclical processes across the life span whereby achievers persist and feel fulfilled, as well as the avoidance and self-doubts of nonachievers (Zimmerman, 2000a).

Various recommendations can be drawn from the discussion to this point concerning how future research in music education might draw on the self-regulatory perspective outlined in this chapter. One of the most important needs is studies using the cyclical model defined in figure 20.2 to determine how practice processes become self-enhancing and self-sustaining. In academics and sports, goal setting and strategy choice training have been found to affect not only students' performance effectiveness but also their self-monitoring, attributions, self-satisfaction, self-efficacy, and intrinsic interest. Students who set strategic process goals to monitor those processes tend to make attributions regarding their effectiveness (Zimmerman & Kitsantas, 1997). This increases many self-motivational beliefs (self-satisfaction, self-efficacy, outcome expectations, and intrinsic interest). By contrast, untrained students typically set outcome goals, lack defined strategies, attribute outcomes to a lack of ability, and tend to make defensive self-reactions rather than adaptive ones (Zimmerman & Kitsantas, 1997). In this way, multidimensional research based on a cyclical model of self-regulation has the potential of explaining how self-enhancing as well as self-defeating cycles of musical practice are established.

Development of Self-regulatory Skill

The perspective offered here might be criticized by those who would argue that young children are unable to regulate their own learning. While this view is partially true, many parents can testify that children as young as three will sing songs louder or softer to attract or avoid parental attention, a sign of self-regulation at a basic level. Research on academic subjects shows that developmental changes in self-regulatory behavior occur during the early years of schooling. Although second-graders display some basic forms of self-regulation such as simple strategies, the processes are not fully integrated in self-regulatory cycles until around eighth grade (Bonner, 1998). Current evidence suggests that there is an intermediate level of integration (e.g., goal setting predicting strategy use and self-efficacy judgments) around fifth grade. The available evidence suggests, therefore, that the acquisition of self-regulatory processes starts early, and then becomes integrated into cycles with increasing age and experience.

Several developmental theories of self-regulation regarding young children (between birth and approximately 6 years of age) such as Kopp's (1982) and Vygotsky's (1962) theories, deal with relatively simple motoric acts. However, as shown in table 20.2, the self-regulatory view proposed here to describe complex skills in music assumes that self-regulation has social origins and

emerges in four distinct levels: observation, emulation, self-control, and self-regulation (see Zimmerman, 2000a; Schunk & Zimmerman, 1997). Technically, this is not a developmental model but, rather, a hierarchical learning model based on the proposition that learners who follow the sequence will learn more effectively and in a more self-regulated way. Data to verify this assumption have recently been building in both sport and academic writing (Kitsantas, Zimmerman, & Cleary, 2000; Zimmerman & Kitsantas, 1999).

For music, the four-level model posits that new skills (such as triple-tonguing on a trumpet) should be initially acquired cognitively through observing (including listening to) a model. When the skill has been discriminated, it can more easily be acquired motorically through emulative efforts, especially with social feedback and support from teachers. Modeling and personal feedback enable the player to learn to control their practice efforts. The third level involves self-controlled efforts to practice the skill in solitary but structured contexts, such as working through triple-tonguing examples from a relevant practice book. When the skill becomes automatized, the learner can practice varying it (e.g., for speed and dynamics) according to changing contexts (e.g., a Sousa march vs. the "Trumpeter's Lullaby"). At this point, the learner shifts to personal outcomes as the criterion to modulate the skill, such as one's personal reaction or an audience's reactions (see table 20.2).

Conclusion

This chapter has outlined how theories of self-regulated learning can provide an overarching framework for studying how music students acquire the skills, knowledge, and attitudes to take control of their own learning. We have argued that self-regulation can be viewed as a socially embedded cognitive construct, based on our belief that research using this paradigm would significantly enhance present knowledge on how children acquire the complex range of skills needed for them to persist with their music learning.

Practical and theoretical implications for research in music abound, particularly as very little research currently exists using this framework. For example, expert-novice studies could be conducted to investigate differences in specific self-regulatory processes for different types of musical instruments. Like experts in other disciplines, musicians have highly refined self-regulatory techniques (i.e., goals, strategies, methods of self-monitoring, types of attributions, and adaptive judgments) that need to be identified for each instrument or vocal training. By contrast, novice learners tend to focus unsystematically on performance outcomes rather than specific techniques, and this leads

Table 20.2 Developmental Levels of Regulatory Skill

Level	Name	Description
1	Observation	Vicarious induction of a skill from a proficient model
2	Emulation	Imitative performance of a general pattern or style of a model's skills with social assistance
3	Self-control	Independent display of the model's skill under structured conditions
4	Self-regulation	Adaptive use of skill across changing personal and environmental conditions

Note. From *Handbook of Self-regulation* (p. 29), by M. Boekaerts, P. R. Pintrich, & M. Zeidner (Eds.), 2000, San Diego, CA: Academic Press. Reprinted with permission.

them to make ability attributions and self-defensive reactions.

Research could lead to systematic efforts to train students to focus on self-regulatory processes. For example, beginning brass players could be taught to focus on such sound-enhancing techniques as forming a correct embouchure, abdominal breathing, and sustained air columns, rather than on outcome-driven methods, such as pressing to hit notes. By investigating not only improvements in playing skill but also in students' acquisition of cyclical self-regulatory processes, music teachers will have a much better sense of whether students can practice effectively on their own and whether they are being self-motivated to continue their musical development. Investigation of planned practice episodes and daily self-recording accomplishments may yield benefits in music as it has in academic and sport functioning.

Research that clarifies more precisely how students develop into self-regulated musicians deserves special attention from music education researchers who are capable of drawing on and integrating into their studies some of the major developments in educational research. Adapting and expanding current theories on this issue and drawing on and integrating information from other areas of educational psychology will enable music education researchers to develop more sophisticated theories of musical development that can be used to underpin future teaching and learning in music. Such an emphasis would significantly strengthen music education research because it would help to broaden the paradigms from which the environmental and personal catalysts that shape teaching and learning in music traditionally have been studied.

REFERENCES

Bandura, A. (1986). *Social foundations of thought and action: A social cognitive theory.* Englewood Cliffs, NJ: Prentice Hall.

Bandura, A. (1991). Self-regulation of motivation through anticipatory and self-reactive mechanism. In R. A. Dienstbier (Ed.), *Nebraska Symposium on Motivation*: Vol. 38. *Perspectives on motivation* (pp. 69–164). Lincoln: University of Nebraska Press.

Bandura, A. (1997). *Self-efficacy: The exercise of control.* New York: Freeman.

Barry, N. H. (1992). The effects of practice strategies, individual differences in cognitive style, and gender upon technical accuracy and musicality of student instrumental performance, *Psychology of Music, 20,* 112–123.

Barry, N., & Hallam, S. in press. Practicing. In R. Parncutt & G. E. McPherson (Eds.), *The science and psychology of musical performance: Creative strategies for teaching and learning.* New York: Oxford University Press.

Barry, N. H., & McArthur, V. (1994). Teaching practice strategies in the music studio: A survey of applied music teachers. *Psychology of Music, 22,* 44–55.

Bloom, B. S. (Ed.). (1985). *Developing talent in young people.* New York: Ballantine.

Bond, M., & Clark, R. E. (1999). Comparison between self-concept and self-efficacy in academic motivation research. *Educational Psychologist, 34,* 139–153.

Bonner, S. (1998). *Developmental changes in self-regulated learning during a multi-trial sort-recall task.* Unpublished doctoral dissertation at the City University of New York.

Brunning, R. H., Schraw, G. J., & Ronning, R. R. (1999). *Cognitive psychology and instruction* (3rd ed.). Upper Saddle River, NJ: Prentice Hall.

Cantwell, R. H., & Millard, Y. (1994). The relationship between approach to learning and learning strategies in learning music. *British Journal of Educational Psychology, 64,* 45–63.

Carver, C. S., & Scheier, M. F. (1981). *Attention and self-regulation: A control-theory approach to human behavior.* New York: Springer-Verlag.

Chase, W. G., & Simon, H. A. (1973). Perception in chess. *Cognitive Psychology, 4,* 55–81.

Chen, C., & Stevenson, H. W. (1989). Homework: A cross-cultural examination. *Child Development, 60,* 551–561.

Corno, L. (1989). Self-regulated learning: A volitional analysis. In B. J. Zimmerman & D. H. Schunk (Eds.), *Self-regulated learning and academic achievement: Theory, research, and practice* (pp. 111–141). New York: Springer-Verlag.

Corno, L. (1994). Student volition and education: Outcomes, influences, and practices. In D. H. Schunk & B. J. Zimmerman (Eds.), *Self-regulation of learning and performance* (pp. 229–251). Hillsdale, NJ: Erlbaum.

Corno, L. (1995). Comments on Winne: Analytic and systematic research are both needed. *Educational Psychologist, 30,* 201–206.

Covington, M. V., & Roberts, B. (1994). Self-worth and college students: Motivational and personality correlates. In P. R. Pintrich, D. R. Brown, & C. E. Weinstein (Eds.), *Student motivation, cognition, and learning: Essays in honor of Wilbert J. McKeachie* (pp. 157–187). Hillsdale, NJ: Erlbaum.

Davidson, J. W., Howe, M. J. A., Moore, D. G. & Sloboda, J. A. (1996). The role of parental influences in the development of musical performance, *British Journal of Developmental Psychology, 14,* 399–412.

Davidson, J. W., Howe, M. J. A., & Sloboda, J. A. (1997). Environmental factors in the development of musical performance skill over the life span. In D. J. Hargreaves & A. C. North (Eds.), *The social psychology of music* (pp. 188–206). Oxford: Oxford University Press.

Davidson, J. W., Moore, J. W., Sloboda, J. A., & Howe, M. J. A. (1998). Characteristics of music teachers and the progress of young instrumentalists. *Journal of Research in Music Education, 46,* 141–160.

Davidson, J. W., Sloboda, J. A., & Howe, M. J. A. (1995/1996). The role of parents and teachers in the success and failure of instrumental learners. *Bulletin of the Council for Research in Music Education, 127,* 40–44.

Dweck, C. S. (1986). Motivational processes affecting learning. *American Psychologist, 41,* 1040–1048.

Dweck, C. S. (2000). *Self-theories: Their role in motivation, personality and development.* Philadelphia, PA: Psychology Press.

Dweck, C. S., & Leggett, E. (1988). A social-cognitive approach to motivation and personality. *Psychological Review, 95,* 256–273.

Eccles-Parsons, J. (1983). Children's motivation to study music. In *Motivation and creativity: National symposium on the applications of psychology to the teaching and learning of music* (pp. 31–40). Washington, DC: Music Educators National Conference.

Ericsson, K. A. (Ed.). (1996) *The road to excellence.* Mahwah, NJ: Erlbaum.

Ericsson, K. A., Krampe, R. T., & Tesch-Römer, C. (1993). The role of deliberate practice in the acquisition of expert performance. *Psychological Review, 100,* 363–406.

Gabrielsson, A. (1999). The performance of music. In D. Deutsch (Ed.), *The psychology of music* (2nd ed., pp. 501–602), San Diego, CA: Academic Press.

Garcia, T., & Pintrich, P. R. (1994). Regulating motivation and cognition in the classroom: The role of self-schemas and self-regulatory strategies. In D. H. Schunk & B. J. Zimmerman (Eds.), *Self-regulation of learning and performance: Issues and educational applications* (pp. 127–153). Hillsdale, NJ: Erlbaum.

Gembris, H., & Davidson, J. W. (2002). Environmental influences on development. In R. Parncutt & G. E. McPherson (Eds.), *The science and psychology of musical performance: Creative strategies for music teaching and learning* (17–30). New York: Oxford University Press.

Goodnow, J. J., & Warton, P. M. (1992). Understanding responsibility: Adolescents' views of delegation and follow-through within the family. *Social Development, 1,* 89–106.

Gottfried, A. E. (1985). Academic intrinsic motivation in elementary and junior high school students. *Journal of Educational Psychology, 77,* 631–645.

Gruson, L. M. (1988). Rehearsal skill and musical competence: Does practice make perfect? In J. A. Sloboda (Ed.), *Generative processes in music* (pp. 91–112). Oxford: Clarendon Press.

Hackett, G. (1995). Self-efficacy in career choice and development. In A. Bandura (Ed.), *Self-efficacy in changing societies* (pp. 232–258). New York: Cambridge University Press.

Hallam, S. (1994). Novice musicians' approaches to practice and performance: Learning new music. *Newsletter of the European Society for the Cognitive Sciences of Music, 6,* 2–10.

Hallam, S. (1997). Approaches to instrumental music practice of experts and novices: Implications for education. In H. Jørgensen & A. C. Lehmann (Eds.), *Does practice make perfect? Current theory and research on instrumental music practice* (pp. 89–108). Oslo, Norway: Norges musikkhøgskole.

Hallam, S. (1998). The predictors of achievement and dropouts in instrumental tuition. *Psychology of Music, 26,* 116–132.

Hallam, S. (2000). The development of performance planning strategies in musicians. In C. Woods, G. B. Luck, R. Brochard, S. A. O'Neill, & J. A. Sloboda (Eds.), *Proceedings of the Sixth International Conference on Music Perception & Cognition.* Keele, Staffordshire, England: Keele University Department of Psychology (CD-ROM).

Hayes, J. R. (1989). Cognitive processes in creativity. In J. A. Glover, R. R. Ronning, & C. R. Reynolds (Eds.), *Handbook of creativity* (pp. 135–145). New York: Plenum.

Hays, T., Minichiello, V., & Wright, P. (2000). Mentorship: The meaning of the relationship for musicians. *Research Studies in Music Education, 15,* 3–14.

Henderson, V. L., & Dweck, C. S. (1990). Motivation and achievement. In S. S. Feldman & G. R. Elliott (Eds.), *At the threshold: The developing adolescent* (pp. 308–329). Cambridge, MA: Harvard University Press.

Hofer, B. K., Yu, S. L., & Pintrich, P. R. (1998). Teaching college students to be self-regulated learners. In D. H. Schunk & B. J. Zimmerman (Eds.), *Self-regulated learning: From teaching to self-reflective practice* (pp. 57–85). New York: Guilford Press.

Hoover-Dempsey, K. V., Battiato, A. C., Walker, J. M. T., Reed, R. P., DeJong, J. M., & Jones, K. P. (2001). Parental involvement in homework. *Educational Psychologist, 36*(3), 195–209.

Hoover-Dempsey, K. V., & Sandler, H. M. (1995). Parental involvement in children's education: Why does it make a difference? *Teachers College Record, 97,* 310–331.

Kitsantas, A., Zimmerman, B. J., & Cleary, T. (2000). The role of observation and emulation in the development of athletic self-regulation. *Journal of Educational Psychology, 91,* 241–250.

Kohut, D. L. (1985). *Musical performance: Learning theory and pedagogy.* Englewood Cliffs, NJ: Prentice Hall.

Kopp, C. B. (1982). Antecedents of self-regulation: A developmental perspective. *Developmental Psychology, 18,* 199–214.

Lehmann, A. C. (1997). The acquisition of expertise in music: Efficiency of deliberate practice as a moderating variable in accounting for sub-expert performance. In I. Deliege & J. Sloboda (Eds.), *Perception and cognition of music* (pp. 161–187). Hove, England: Psychology Press.

Lehmann, A. C., & Ericsson, K. A. (1997). Research on expert performance and deliberate practice: Implications for the education of amateur musicians and music students. *Psychomusicology, 16,* 40–58.

McCormick, J., & McPherson, G. E. (in press). The role of self-efficacy in a musical performance examination: An exploratory structural equation analysis. *Psychology of Music.*

McPherson, G. (1989). Cognitive mediational processes and positive motivation: Implications of educational research for music teaching and learning. *Australian Journal of Music Education, 1,* 3–19.

McPherson, G. E. (1993). *Factors and abilities influencing the development of visual, aural and creative performance skills in music and their educational implications.* Unpublished doctoral dissertation, University of Sydney, Australia.

McPherson, G. E. (1994). Factors and abilities influencing sight-reading skill in music. *Journal of Research in Music Education, 42,* 217–231.

McPherson, G. E. (1995). Redefining the teaching of musical performance. *The Quarterly Journal of Music Teaching and Learning, 6,* 56–64.

McPherson, G. E. (1997). Cognitive strategies and skills acquisition in musical performance. *Bulletin of the Council for Research in Music Education, 133,* 64–71.

McPherson, G. E. (2000). Commitment and practice: Key ingredients for achievement during the early stages of learning a musical instrument. In R. Walker (Ed.), *Proceedings of the 18th International Society for Music Education Research Commission, Salt Lake City, USA, July 10–15, 2000,* 245–250. (To be published in a forthcoming issue of *Bulletin of the Council for Research in Music Education*)

McPherson, G. E., & Davidson, J. W. (in press). Musical practice: Mother and child interactions during the first year of learning an instrument. *Music Education Research.*

McPherson, G. E., & McCormick, J. (1999). Motivational and self-regulated learning components of musical practice. *Bulletin of the Council for Research in Music Education, 141,* 98–102.

McPherson, G. E., & Renwick, J. (2001). A longitudinal study of self-regulation in children's musical practice. *Music Education Research, 3*(1), 169–186.

Miklaszewski, K. (1989). A case study of a pianist preparing a musical performance. *Psychology of Music, 63,* 81–97.

Newman, R. S. (1994). Academic help seeking: A strategy of self-regulated learning. In D. H. Schunk & B. J. Zimmerman (Eds.), *Self-regulation of learning and performance: Issues and educational applications* (pp. 283–301). Hillsdale, NJ: Erlbaum.

Nielsen, S. G. (1997). Self-regulation of learning strategies during practice: A case study of a church organ student preparing a musical work for performance. In H. Jørgensen & A. C. Lehmann (Eds.), *Does practice make perfect? Current theory and research on instrumental music practice* (pp. 109–122). Oslo, Norway: Norges musikkhøgskole.

Nielsen, S. G. (1998). *Selvregulering av læringsstrategier under øving: En studie av to utøvende musikkstudenter på høyt nivå.* [Self-regulation of learning strategies during practice: A study of two gifted church organ students possessing a high level of technical skill]. Oslo: The Norwegian Academy of Music. (NMH publications 1998:3)

Nielsen, S. G. (1999). Learning strategies in instrumental music practice. *British Journal of Music Education, 16*(3), 275–291.

Nielsen, S. G. (2000). Self-regulated use of learning strategies in instrumental practice. In C. Woods, G. B. Luck, R. Brochard, S. A. O'Neill, & J. A. Sloboda (Eds.), *Proceedings of the Sixth International Conference on Music Perception & Cognition.* Keele, Staffordshire, UK: Department of Psychology (CD-ROM).

Noldus, L. P. J. J., Trienes, R. J. H., Hendriksen, A. H. M., Jansen, H., & Jansen, R. G. (2000). The Observer Video-Pro: New software for the collection, management, and presentation of time-structured data from videotapes and digital media files. *Behavior Research Methods, Instruments & Computers, 32,* 197–206.

O'Neill, S. A. (1997). The role of practice in children's early performance achievement. In H. Jørgensen & A. C. Lehmann (Eds.), *Does practice make perfect? Current theory and research on instrumental music practice* (pp. 53–70). Oslo, Norway: Norges musikkhøgskole.

O'Neill, S. A. (1999). Achievement-related self-perceptions and subjective task values in the practice behaviour of young musicians. Forthcoming.

O'Neill, S. A., & McPherson, G. E. (2002). Motivation. In R. Parncutt & G. E. McPherson (Eds.), *The science and psychology of musical performance: Creative strategies for teaching and learning* (31–46). New York: Oxford University Press.

O'Neill, S. A., & Sloboda, J. A. (1997). The effects of failure on children's ability to perform a musical test. *Psychology of Music, 25,* 18–34.

Pajares, F. (1996a). Self-efficacy and mathematical problem-solving of gifted students. *Contemporary Educational Psychology, 21,* 325–344.

Pajares, F. (1996b). Self-efficacy beliefs in academic settings. *Review of Educational Research, 66,* 543–578.

Pintrich, P. R., & Schunk, D. H. (1996). *Motivation in education: Theory, research and applications.* Englewood Cliffs, NJ: Prentice Hall.

Pitts, S., Davidson, J., & McPherson, G. E. (2000). Developing effective practise strategies: Case studies of three young instrumentalists. *Music Education Research, 2*(1), 45–56.

Pogonowski, L. (1989). Metacognition: A dimension of musical thinking. In E. Boardman (Ed.), *Dimensions of musical thinking* (pp. 9–19). Reston, VA: Music Educators National Conference.

Renwick, J., & McPherson, G. E. (2000). "I've got to do my scale first!": A case study of a novice's clarinet practice. In C. Woods, G. B. Luck, R. Brochard, S. A. O'Neill, & J. A. Sloboda (Eds.), *Proceedings of the Sixth International Conference on Music Perception & Cognition.* Keele, Staffordshire, England: Keele University Department of Psychology (CD-ROM).

Salis, D. L. (1977). *The identification and assessment of cognitive variables associated with reading of advanced music at the piano.* Unpublished doctoral dissertation, University of Pittsburgh.

Schunk, D. H., & Zimmerman, B. J. (1997). Social origins of self-regulatory competence. *Educational Psychologist, 32,* 195–208.

Shuell, T. J. (1988). The role of transfer in the learning and teaching of music: A cognitive perspective. In C. Fowler (Ed.), *The Crane Symposium: Toward an understanding of the teaching and learning of music performance* (pp. 143–167). Potsdam: Potsdam College of the State University of New York.

Sloboda, J. A., & Davidson, J. W. (1996). The young performing musician. In I. Deliege & J. A. Sloboda (Eds.), *Musical beginnings: Origins and development of musical competence* (pp. 171–190). New York: Oxford University Press.

Sloboda, J. A., Davidson, J. W., Howe, M. J. A., & Moore, D. G. (1996). The role of practice in the development of performing musicians. *British Journal of Psychology, 87,* 287–309.

Sosniak, L. A. (1985). Learning to be a concert pianist. In B. S. Bloom (Ed.), *Developing talent in young people* (pp. 19–67). New York: Ballantine Books.

Sosniak, L. A. (1987). The nature of change in successful learning. *Teachers College Record, 88,* 519–535.

Sosniak, L. A. (1990). The tortoise, the hare, and the development of talent. In M. J. A. Howe (Ed.), *Encouraging the development of exceptional skills and talent* (pp. 477–506). Leicester, England: The British Psychological Society.

Stebleton, E. (1987). Predictors of sight-reading achievement: A review of the literature. *Update, 6,* 11–15.

Stipek, D. (1998). *Motivation to learn* (3rd ed.). Needham Heights, MA: Allyn & Bacon.

Thomas, H. W., Strage, A., & Curley, R. (1988). Improving students' self-directed learning. *The Elementary School Journal, 88,* 313–326.

Vygotsky, E. (1962). *Thought and language.* Cambridge, MA: MIT Press.

Warton, P. M. (1997). Learning about responsibility: Lessons from homework. *British Journal of Educational Psychology, 67,* 213–221.

Warton, P. M. (2001). The forgotten voices in homework: Views of students. *Educational Psychologist, 36*(3), 155–165.

Warton, P. M., & Goodnow, J. J. (1991). The nature of responsibility: Children's understanding of "your job." *Child Development, 62,* 156–165.

Weisberg, R. W. (1999). Creativity and knowledge: A challenge to theories. In R. Sternberg (Ed.), *Handbook of creativity* (pp. 226–250). Cambridge, England: Cambridge University Press.

Williamon, A., & Valentine, E. (2000). Quantity and quality of musical practice as predictors of performance quality. *British Journal of Psychology, 91,* 353–376.

Wilson, G. D. (1997). Performance anxiety. In D. J. Hargreaves & A. C. North (Eds.), *The social psychology of music* (pp. 227–245). New York: Oxford University Press.

Wilson, G. D., & Roland, D. (2002). Performance anxiety. In R. Parncutt & G. E. McPherson (Eds.), *The science and psychology of musical performance: Creative strategies for music teaching and learning* (47–61). New York: Oxford University Press.

Wolf, T. (1976). A cognitive model of musical sight-reading. *Journal of Psycholinguistic Research, 5,* 143–172.

Zdzinski, S. F. (1994). Parental involvement, gender, and learning outcomes among instrumentalists. *Contributions to Music Education, 21,* 73–89.

Zdzinski, S. F. (1996). Parental involvement, selected student attributes, and learning outcomes in instrumental music. *Journal of Research in Music Education, 44,* 34–48.

Zimmerman, B. J. (1986). Becoming a self-regulated learner: Which are the key subprocesses? *Contemporary Educational Psychology, 11,* 307–313.

Zimmerman, B. J. (1989). A social cognitive view of self-regulated academic learning. *Journal of Educational Psychology, 81,* 329–339.

Zimmerman, B. J. (1994). Dimensions of academic self-regulation: A conceptual framework for education. In D. H. Schunk & B. J. Zimmerman (Eds.), *Self-regulation of learning and performance: Issues and educational applications* (pp. 3–21). Hillsdale, NJ: Erlbaum.

Zimmerman, B. J. (1995). Self-efficacy and educational development. In A. Bandura (Ed.), *Self-efficacy in changing societies* (pp. 202–231). Cambridge, England: Cambridge University Press.

Zimmerman, B. J. (1998a). Academic studying and the development of personal skill: A self-regulatory perspective. *Educational Psychologist, 33*(2/3), 73–86.

Zimmerman, B. J. (1998b). Developing self-fulfilling cycles of academic regulation: An analysis of exemplary instructional models. In D. H. Schunk B. J. & Zimmerman (Eds.), *Self-regulated learning: From teaching to self-reflective practice* (pp. 1–19). New York: Guilford Press.

Zimmerman, B. J. (2000a). Attaining self-regulation: A social cognitive perspective. In M. Boekaerts, P. R. Pintrich, & M. Zeidner (Eds.), *Handbook of self-regulation* (pp. 13–39). San Diego, CA: Academic Press.

Zimmerman, B. J. (2000b). Self-efficacy: An essential motive to learn. *Contemporary Educational Psychology, 25,* 82–91.

Zimmerman, B. J., & Kitsantas, A. (1997). Developmental phases in self-regulation: Shifting from process to outcome goals. *Journal of Educational Psychology, 89,* 29–36.

Zimmerman, B. J., & Kitsantas, A. (1999). Acquiring writing revision skill: Shifting from process to outcome self-regulatory goals. *Journal of Educational Psychology, 91,* 1–10.

Zimmerman, B. J., & Martinez-Pons, M. (1986). Development of a structured interview for assessing student use of self-regulated learning strategies. *American Educational Research Journal, 23,* 614–628.

Zimmerman, B. J., & Martinez-Pons, M. (1988). Construct validation of a strategy model of student self-regulated learning. *Journal of Educational Psychology, 80,* 284–290.

Zimmerman, B. J., & Martinez-Pons, M. (1992). Perceptions of efficacy and strategy use in the self-regulation of learning. In D. H. Schunk & J. Meece (Eds.), *Student perceptions in the classroom: Causes and consequences* (pp. 185–207). Hillsdale, NJ: Erlbaum.

Zimmerman, B. J., & Weinstein, C. E. (1994). Self-regulating academic study time: A strategy approach. In D. H. Schunk & B. J. Zimmerman (Eds.), *Self regulation of learning and performance: Issues and educational applications* (pp. 181–199). Hillsdale, NJ: Erlbaum.

21

Motivation and Achievement

MARTIN L. MAEHR

PAUL R. PINTRICH

ELIZABETH A. LINNENBRINK

What Is Motivation and Why Is It Important?

Motivation has been and continues to be of interest to those who are concerned with teaching and learning. Although researchers and theorists differ dramatically in their views on how motivation emerges and is instantiated in academic settings, they tend to agree on certain types of "behavior" as signifiers of motivation. Thus, before reviewing and discussing personal and contextual factors that may influence "motivation," it is necessary, first, to step back and consider the behavior that makes teachers, parents, and researchers conclude that individuals differ in "motivation." Only then will the research, theory, and implications of this large body of literature be evident. Therefore, we begin this chapter by discussing a variety of actions, feelings, and thoughts that both teachers and researchers describe as indicators of "motivation." In doing so, we hope to underline the importance of this topic for educators as well as researchers. A second purpose is to clarify what motivational researchers study when they study motivation, what they observe, how they measure, and ultimately what they are trying to predict and explain.

Behavioral Indicators of Motivation

The study and understanding of motivation is concerned first with observable behaviors that reflect engagement in a particular activity (see table 21.1). More specifically, four action patterns are the focus of motivation research: choice and preference, intensity, persistence, and quality. Variation in the degree to which these patterns are reflected in students' behaviors surrounding a particular activity, such as learning to play the piano, can give music educators an idea about the aspiring pianist's motivation to learn.

Choice and Preference. Even in the most highly controlled situation, students vary in the attention they direct toward the learning activity. Some seem to "choose" to engage in the activity while others are simply "off task"; that is, they are investing their energies elsewhere. Observed differences in the direction of behavior and particularly the presumed choice among alternative courses of action are primary aspects of motivational research (Maehr & Midgley, 1996; Pintrich & Schunk, 2002). Indeed, even a quick review of the literature will reveal that, especially prior to the last decade or so, most of the research was concerned with directional issues (e.g., Atkinson & Feather, 1967; Atkinson & Raynor, 1974; Maehr & Sjogren, 1971). Of course, choices made as well as the direction of action taken are still considered important components of motivated behavior today (e.g., Cordova, 1993).

In the classroom, the importance of choice and preference is often reflected when students are given a variety of options. For instance, when a band director gives students time to practice a particular passage individually, there may be variation in student behavior in this situation. The director may observe that some students "choose" to practice the passage, while others may simply talk to the student sitting next to them. In this instance, the band director could assume that the students who chose to practice instead of talk are more "motivated." In the same manner, an individual's choice to continue to practice the piano at home, even in the absence of a teacher or a parent, would

Table 21.1 Examples of Behavioral Indicators of Motivation

	Academic	Musical
Choice and preference	Choosing to enroll in an advanced science class	Choosing to practice the piano instead of watching television
Intensity	Focusing all of one's attention on solving algebra equations	Focusing all of one's attention on practicing a difficult passage
Persistence	Continuing to work on writing a report for social studies even when it becomes difficult	Continuing to practice the flute after rehearsal ends
Quality of engagement	Monitoring one's understanding of a novel and rereading portions until one understands	Finding aspects of a piece that are difficult to play and working on those passages until they can be played correctly

reflect motivated behavior. In many cases, when students engage in an activity in the absence of others or rewards, they are said to be intrinsically motivated. In addition, choice behavior can refer to behavior over longer time periods such as when students continue to try out for the band in high school or college or decide to major in music in college. However, this is just one aspect of students' motivated behavior that we must consider.

Intensity. Motivation research has not only been concerned with the choices made, but also with the intensity of the action taken. The desultory way in which a child approaches an assigned task, such as practicing scales, sharply contrasts with the involved and focused manner of a student learning a favorite piece of music. So, it is not just whether or not a student chooses to engage in an activity but also the degree to which he or she becomes involved in the activity that reflects motivated behavior. In most cases, effortful action such as trying hard at the task is the best exemplar of intensity.

Persistence. Persistence is a third and commonly employed indicator of motivation. Obviously, educators are not only interested in whether individuals choose to do something but also whether and for how long they persist in this choice. When a music student elects to practice her violin rather than watch television or play with friends, that is interesting choice behavior. It is also interesting how long she remains engaged in the activity, reflecting persistence. Equally, perhaps even more interesting, is the observation that this child repeatedly returns to play the violin each time she is given a chance. This and similar observations have been taken as indicators of "continuing motivation," a motivational observation that is thought to be especially important as it may indicate an extended investment in learning, the kind of extended investment needed if schooling is to have its desired effects (see Hoffman, 1992; Hughes, Sullivan, & Mosley, 1985; Maehr, 1976; Pascarella, Walberg, Junker, & Haertel, 1981).

Quality. Of course, educators are not only interested in whether or not a student chooses to engage in a task and for how long. They are equally, if not even more, interested in the quality of the investment observed (Ames & Ames, 1984). And, increasingly in the last decade or so, quality of engagement has become a major focus of motivational research. Researchers have focused on several types of variables including academic venturesomeness (e.g., Clifford, 1988; Maehr, 1983), strategic approaches to a learning task (e.g., Pintrich & De Groot, 1990; Pintrich & Garcia, 1991, 1994), and thoughtful and critical engagement while investing in an activity (e.g., Pintrich, Cross, Kozma, & McKeachie, 1986; Pintrich & Schrauben, 1992).

Returning to the example of a young musician learning a piece of music, we can see that the quality of engagement is especially important. Although a student may decide to practice his trumpet over playing soccer with his friends (choice), may continue to practice for an extended period of time (persistence), and may exhibit focused engagement throughout (intensity), the benefits of this extended and intense practice may not be realized if an effective practice strategy is not used (see table 21.1). Thus, if the student repeatedly plays the piece he is learning, but does not attend to certain sections that may be more difficult, we would say that he is not self-regulating or engaged in a critical assessment of his playing. In contrast, another student showing similar levels of choice, intensity, and persistence, who attends to those difficult passages by playing them repeatedly and breaking them down into various parts, is displaying a different and arguably higher quality of engagement. This student is regulating his practice and responding critically to areas that need more work. Music educators should find it readily apparent that the quality of the behavior as well as the choice, persistence, and intensity are key for learning and achievement. Moreover, recent motivation research has indicated that such qualitative differences in how individuals carry out a learning activity are influenced by the same or similar antecedents as those that influence the direction and intensity of the action taken.

Affective and Cognitive Indicators of Motivation

As important as action is as an indicator of motivation, it is not the only indicator. At least two other psychological systems figure prominently into any definition of motivation: affect and cognition. How people *feel* and *think* about something is also important in inferring the level and depth of motivation.

Affect.   Psychologists studying motivation have, at one point or another, considered affect (or emotions) as playing an important role in motivational processes (Pintrich & Schunk, 2002). However, the nature of this role differs based on one's theoretical perspective. For instance, the James-Lange theory of emotion suggests that emotions are not important for instigating affect but, rather, occur after the behavior. Others suggest that affect may motivate behavior. For instance, interest or curiosity may instigate engagement in a particular task whereas fear or anxiety may reduce engagement.

In terms of classroom learning, the various emotions that people display when learning can help us to understand their motivation. For instance, when a person experiences intense anxiety or nervousness before and during the playing of a solo, this represents the quality (most likely negative) of the affective or emotional experience for that individual. This anxiety can also relate to behavior in that it may undermine performance immediately and ultimately encourage avoiding the activity altogether. Conversely, when a person expresses enjoyment or pleasure through engaging in an activity, it is clear that they find that particular activity motivating or interesting. In addition to indicating underlying motivation, affect may also play a role in the motivational processes by changing the way that people respond to feedback.

Cognition.   Although at one point in the history of the study of motivation, behavioral mechanisms dominated motivational theories, cognitions have regained their importance in understanding motivational processes (Graham & Weiner, 1996). These cognitive aspects refer not only to how a person's thoughts impact his or her motivation but also to the types of thoughts that result based on various motivational processes. For instance, when a person talks and thinks about certain topics in certain ways, she probably reveals something about what is important to her—and what drives and frames what she does. The dreams we have, our obsessions and fixations, doubtless also indicate something about what choices we will make and how we will pursue these. Certainly clinical psychology, beginning with Freud, has taught us this and our personal experiences have reinforced this idea. Increasingly, motivational researchers have examined the levels and complexity of cognition as phenomena that are closely tied to motivational processes. Thus, it has become increasingly important to understand when and why individuals do and do not exhibit high-level thinking processes, reasoning, creativity—and it has been found that factors that affect action and emotion also influence thought.

So, why study motivation? Clearly engaging students in activities in school is essential for learning. That is, if we can create classroom environments that promote engagement and persistence for all students, we are more likely to see the types of academic outcomes we would like. For instance, if we want students in a band class to learn a difficult piece, we will need them to engage in thoughtful practice, even when it becomes challenging and difficult. An obstacle to this type of thoughtful, engaged practice is a lack of motivation. A student who has no desire or motivation to practice is unlikely to choose to engage in the type of careful practice that is necessary to learn the piece. Thus, understanding how to motivate students is key to reach desired educational outcomes. In addition to motivating students to reach certain academic outcomes, motivation as an end in and of itself may also be of importance to educators. That is, educators may also be interested in shaping students so that they are interested in pursuing various academic areas after leaving school. This may be especially crucial for music educators who may have the development of an appreciation and interest in music as a primary goal for educating students.

The burden of researchers and the challenge for teachers is one of determining the tasks and conditions that elicit the investment of children in learning and the development of an appreciation for and interest in learning itself. Of course, more is needed than just a designation of a basis for inferring variation in motivation. The primary question for researchers and educators alike is what brings it about, what "causes" it. Here the answers become much more complicated. It is impossible to summarize every particular theory that has been proposed; instead, we portray prototypical examples of theorizing that have currency in explaining motivation and achievement patterns.

There are a variety of theoretical models that have been proposed in the last century or so to explain motivation. From a historical perspective, it is important to note that early work in the field of motivation began by focusing on internal factors as motivating behavior such as volition and needs. However, during the behavioral revolution of the early 20th century in the United States, the focus turned away from internal forces to external forces, which could be reliably measured and manipulated. Then, the cognitive revolution in psychology reoriented motivational theorists to again consider internal cognitions as determining behavior. This gave rise to more current social-cognitive theories, which emphasize cognitions as well as reactions to the environment. For the purposes of this review, we will focus on the broad general dichotomy between behavioral and social-cognitive theories.

Within the category of behavioral theories, we include conditioning theories (e.g., Skinner, 1953; Thorndike, 1913) as well as need and drive theories (e.g., Hull, 1943). These behavioral and dynamic conceptions of motivation encompass a range of thinking about motivation, much of which originated from our understanding of animal behaviors. With this view comes a focus on the external environment and how the organism reacts to this external environment behaviorally in terms of choice, intensity, persistence, and quality of behavior. In some cases, such as for "need theorists," this view also considers what the biological needs of the organism are and whether those are met by the environment (Hull, 1943). Individuals should respond positively to environment situations that help to fulfill basic biological needs.

In contrast, social cognitive theories focus more on stimuli originating within the individual, in particular their cognitions and affects. That is, motivation is thought to be derived from expectations, values, interest, one's sense of self, attributions about success or failure, and goals or purposes, all of which originate primarily within the individual. Social cognitive models also concentrate on the four behavioral indicators of motivation, but they give equal or more weight to the cognitive and affective experiences of individuals. A number of social cognitive theories are prominent in the study of motivation today including Expectancy × Value theory (Atkinson, 1957; Eccles, 1983), self-efficacy theory (Bandura, 1982), attribution theory (Weiner, 1986), achievement goal theory (Ames, 1992; Dweck & Leggett, 1988; Nicholls, 1984), and intrinsic motivation theory (Csikszentmihalyi, 1985; Deci, 1980; Deci & Ryan, 1985; Renninger, Hidi, & Krapp, 1992). We focus on these five primary theories in our review of social cognitive models of motivation.

We seek here to describe these various theories and illustrate key aspects in the ways in which these theories differ. Briefly, these differences arise from: (1) the degree to which they concentrate on cognitive or affective motivational variables; and (2) a differential focus on the sources for motivation such as the immediate environment, the person as a thinking and feeling entity, and/or some combination of the two. Finally, it is important to note that these theoretical models have their strengths and weaknesses. No one approach fits all the evidence nor provides the ultimate answer for how to motivate others or ourselves.

Behavioral and Dynamic Conceptions of Motivation

Reinforcement Theories

Perhaps one of the oldest but still commonly applied "theories" of motivation is that rewards encourage, and punishments discourage, continued action. It is the "common-sense" approach for some, sometimes justified by incidental references to previous work by Skinner and others who extensively applied tangible and nontangible rewards to achieve "behavior modification" (Pintrich & Schunk, 2002).

The systematic study of reinforcement was most likely initiated by Thorndike (1932), one of the earliest and most influential educational researchers. More recently, of course, it was the radical behaviorism of B. F. Skinner (e.g., Skinner, 1953) that really served to establish reinforcement as necessary for changing behavior—and learning. Especially with the development of what was called "programmed learning," educators of a generation ago were introduced to his thorough analysis of behavior and to a systematic way of presenting materials, focusing action, reinforcing responses, and thereby leading students systematically through a step-by-step set of responses toward an acquired skill or body of knowledge. The basic ideas behind behavioral analysis and reinforcement are reflected in "behavior modification" programs typically applied in special cases with problem children. As a brief aside, a good deal of social cognitive research focuses on rewards and how they influence motivation. We will, however, focus our discussion here on the basic findings based on behaviorist theories. In the second portion of the chapter, in which we discuss intrinsic motivation theories, we elaborate in greater detail on the various effects of rewards and praise for intrinsic motivation.

For most educators today, the knowledge gained from this era boils down largely to a number of small but not unimportant points. First, positive reward or reinforcement is better than punishment or negative reinforcement (Rachlin, 1991). This emphasis on positive rewards is prevalent largely because positive reward structures are less ambiguous regarding what the student should do. Negative responses generally by themselves only provide information regarding what should not be done but provide no alternatives. As a result, simply saying "no" without providing an alternative does not result in change. Negative responses (or lack of response) also can have unwanted motivational effects such as negative feelings toward the source of reinforcement, to the activity, or toward oneself, especially when the receiver perceives no behavioral alternatives (Rachlin, 1991). So, many educators have come away with the impression that punishment and negative reinforcement should be used sparingly, if at all, but that it is always and everywhere appropriate to use positive reinforcement. But it turns out that it is not quite that simple.

Positive responses, whether stated approval or tangible reward, are often problematic as well. This is especially the case when learning occurs within a social group (as is the case with school). Thus, the approval or reward of one person may also simultaneously imply something not wanted about others in the group. And it also can convey unwanted meanings to the person who receives the reward or approval. The cases are multiple here, but we consider a few to suggest the possibilities. On the one hand slow learners may often receive more than their share of rewards, as the teacher feels they need "special help." But what does this "say" to the rest of the class—and to the receiver of the reward, the student who is granted special recognition? On the other hand, certain recognition is reserved for a unique few: top grades, honors, and scholarships. And, they are virtually unavailable to most regardless of how hard they try. Because most students cannot hope to receive these honors, these rewards are not reinforcing for most of the class. Furthermore, these honors and rewards may not even be reinforcing for those who do receive them. The point is that following reinforcement theory or a commonsense reward and punishment "theory" of motivation is likely to founder on the shoals of meaning: what the students perceive and how they construe the teacher's actions (a focus of social cognitive theories) as well as their peer's reaction to their receiving or not receiving.

Moreover, conveying reward and punishment is often done in terms of the conveyer's biases. Here, the research on teacher expectancy effects is instructive. There is, of course, a long line of research on how expectations lead to action that confirms what was expected. Most educators are aware of an early study by Rosenthal and Jacobson (1968) that indicated that when teachers were informed that (randomly selected) students in their class were diagnosed as having a potential for exhibiting a special spurt in intellectual ability in the course of the year, this "prophecy" was fulfilled. Why? Apparently, because the teachers tended to act differently toward those with the "special growth potential" (Cooper & Good, 1983; Jussim, 1991). It is likely that the action involved not only attention (reinforcing in itself) but also differential attempts to reward or reinforce evidence of growth. That in itself proved to be very disconcerting to many educators. Even more interesting were later studies (e.g., Rubovits & Maehr, 1971, 1973) that indicated that teachers were likely to act differently not only to students of different ability levels but also to students of different ethnic backgrounds. For example, the teacher sample that was white seemed to exhibit a certain wariness and inhibited interaction with gifted African-American students. Doubtless, teachers can be made aware of and change such tendencies, but the point is that in many cases teachers and their students are the unwitting captives of their prejudices and misperceptions as they reward, punish, and reinforce.

The central point here is that reinforcement theory provides only a very limited perspective and limited guidelines for motivating students within the complex world of a classroom. Students are not necessarily motivated by what an external agent, such as the teacher, believes is motivating. They are motivated by their perceptions of acts. Whatever happens in the classroom is mediated through the thoughts and beliefs that the student holds: how they construe what happens and what it means to them. Even if teachers could be sure that they were administering reinforcers according to an acceptable plan, the student may not receive the message they hope to convey. Although rewards and punishments may have their place, that place is clearly limited by the nature of interactions within the booming and buzzing world of the classroom.

So, our conclusion, and generally the conclusion of most researchers on motivation, is that one can hardly rely on reinforcement theory and the systematic administration of rewards alone. Their possible use in certain special one-on-one situations or in across-the-board recognition when the class as a whole may have achieved a goal might have a certain value, but that value is realized only in the degree to which the individuals involved see themselves as involved in the outcome—and the reward or punishment as significant to them. For, as we will soon see in presenting more recent social cognitive research on motivation, it is not the reward (or punishment) given per se, but the *meaning* of the reward and punishment that determines reactions.

Need Theories

Reinforcement theory or notions of how, when, and where rewards and punishments control motivation almost seem to presume that "needs" and "drives" determine behavior. Whereas strict behaviorists such as Skinner did not see any reason to refer to inner states as a determinant of behavior, many considered it quite logical to view reinforcement as effective if it reduced, satisfied, or met a "need" (Hull, 1943). Of course, theories based on this simple notion have taken various forms, but the essential framework of "need theories" is that individuals are driven by certain internal primary needs such as hunger or thirst (Hull, 1943). These "needs" give rise to "drives," or energy directed toward fulfilling the need. Once the need is met, the person (or animal) returns to a somewhat steady state of quiescence— at least as far as pursuing that particular need is concerned.

While this model seems to portray behavioral patterns most often seen in animals lower rather than higher on the phylogenetic scale, it has often been applied to the realm of human behavior. For instance, most teachers and many parents have heard middle school principals explain a broad array of student behavior in terms of hormones (e.g., "middle school children are hard to teach because of their raging adolescent hormones"). While primary drives obviously play a role in the life of humans, they are not in and of themselves determinant of much of the motivation that guides learning and achievement. In construing the nature of motivation in humans, researchers and theorists have found it necessary to suggest that there are certain "secondary needs," which are derivatives perhaps of primary needs in some way (McClelland, 1985). A major hypothesis here is that in the course of satisfying primary needs, animals and humans acquire "secondary drives" such as need of affiliation and need for achievement. These secondary needs work in much the same way as primary needs in that they "motivate" the individual to pursue a particular course of action in order to fulfill an inner need.

McClelland's (1985) seminal research on these secondary needs provided the groundwork, and continues to have a profound influence, for much of the research on achievement in academic settings. In this research, the motive to achievement was central and it was assumed that individuals had a need to achieve, which drove or motivated them to take on and strive to be successful at achievement tasks. Moreover, this need to achieve varied across individuals; with some individuals (e.g., CEOs of large corporations, star athletes, world-famous scientists) having more of this need to achieve and a strong drive to be successful while other individuals did not have such a strong level of the need for achievement. The stress was not on the variable nature of this need but on its persistence as a stable personal trait that differentially characterized individuals across times, places, and situations.

McClelland's (1985) work was founded on the idea that the motivation to achieve is an acquired need, emerging at an early age in response to the way in which the child is reared. Early socialization patterns, such as the relative stress on independence training as well as on the value of pursuing and succeeding at challenging tasks, were thought to influence the development of an achievement motive. Since there was only a modicum of work conducted on this training, it is difficult to elaborate a great deal more on what parents do or could do to develop an achievement-motivated child other than encourage them to seek out and try hard to perform well at worthy and challenging tasks. Consistent with this, parents were encouraged to reinforce independence and attempts at personal betterment.

From McClelland's work, it appears that some individuals are more invested in achievement across multiple settings and over extended time periods than others. That is, these individuals strive to achieve not just in school, but also in play, in work, and even, perhaps, in social and interpersonal settings. This observation has given rise to the notion that motivation for achievement can be an important driving force in our lives, even if it is not a primary need such as hunger. It is this type of observation that has given rise to designating achievement as an enduring, acquired "need." But there are certain reservations that should be noted in reference to conceptualizing motivation for achievement in terms of a "need."

First, there is very little evidence that motivation for achievement operates in a cyclical fashion—as needs are often thought to operate (Pintrich & Schunk, 2002). All we really see is certain people being more invested in achievement than others, sometimes across a wide array of achievement situations, sometimes only in a very limited set of instances. Typically, when individuals succeed at a task or a line of endeavor, they do not rest for long, but show a persistence far greater than those who do not succeed. Moreover, at least as McClelland and his colleagues have measured motivation to succeed, it is not necessarily constant across achievement situations and appears to vary over time and across situations. Thus, an early study (Horner, 1968) indicated that young women showed a drop in achievement motivation as they approached their 20s (in an earlier era, a time of courtship and marriage, rather than career preparation) but an increase in achievement motivation after 40 (when the "nest was emptying" and career options could be pursued). And many teachers and parents have seen a "lazy" child change, when he experiences a new teacher or a new school, has a new set of friends, experiences a series of successes rather than a series of failures. So, insofar as a "need for achievement" represents persistent personal tendencies or a stable trait, caution in using the construct is advised.

The point here is whether "need" is the best metaphor for discussing the varying patterns of actions, thoughts, and feelings directed toward (or away from) achievement. Some of the responses seem to be "role-related," as in the case of gender differences—and therewith a function of social expectations, group membership, and social norms, rather than stable personality traits. Other responses seem to be responses to developmental stations in life and sometimes very context-bound. Increasingly, for these and other reasons, theory has moved to conceptualize motivation in general, and motivation to achieve specifically, in terms of thought processes as in the social cognitive theory. McClelland himself in one of the last publications he authored before his death (McClelland, Koestner, & Weinberg, 1989) suggested that achievement could be conceptualized in terms of "attitudes," as these are conceptualized within the currently dominant social cognitive theories. However, he made a special point of emphasizing the emotive and largely subconscious nature of achievement and other secondary needs, and suggested that they operated as "latent attitudes."

While theorizing has shifted a bit away from the consideration of "needs" as the primary source of human action, there are several other contributions that the need-drive paradigm has made toward the fuller understanding of complex human motivation patterns. First, need theory called specific attention to an affective component that is likely tied to motivation, including motivation for achievement. There is hope and satisfaction associated with succeeding at an achievement task. There is fear and anxiety in anticipating and experiencing failure. Although it seems obvious that emotions would be associated with motivation, it is often the case that their nature and contribution is only incidentally considered. It is especially a danger when social cognitive models of motivation are proposed and employed, as they tend to emphasize cognition. The reasons for this failure to adequately consider emotions are understandable; we simply know all too little about emotions and how they figure into action, thought, learning, and achievement. Need theories, such as McClelland's original formulation, could only go so far in explicating and assessing their role because of the state of our knowledge then. It has improved some today, but still remains a frontier for psychological research. In sum, although "need theories" of achievement are not especially popular at the moment, they present certain important notions related to how we conceptualize motivation. The lessons learned from conceptualizing motivation in need terms can and should figure into more current theories of social cognition and motivation.

Social Cognitive Conceptions of Motivation

Even as behaviorism reigned and the albino rat was the favorite subject for research in many psychological laboratories, Tolman (e.g., 1932, 1949) dared to suggest that "expectancies," thoughts about what might occur if certain action was taken, were critical to decisions made by animals as well as humans. And although theories of unconscious processes were a dominant feature of the motivational literature (e.g., Brill, 1938), there were voices that emphasized the role that conscious processes, thought, beliefs, and attitudes had in motivation (Allport, 1937; Rogers, 1969).

The foundation for today's strong emphasis on social cognitive models of motivation was laid largely by theorist-researchers such as Lewin, who focused attention on everyday problems in the social world such as leadership, attitudes, group processes, goals pursued, and choices made. In a seminal piece of research, Lewin and his colleagues initiated studies on "levels of aspiration" and how this manifestly cognitive variable influenced feelings and behavior. In a now classic motivational study, he and his colleagues (Lewin, Dembo, Festinger, & Sears, 1944) demonstrated how perceptions and feelings of "success" and "failure" were associated with reaching personal goals ("levels of aspirations") rather than with the objective level of performance exhibited. Moreover, they went on to demonstrate that it was not just "success" or "failure" that influenced goals but also social psychological factors such as group membership and norms. This served as the basis for a "social cognitive" revolution in the study of moti-

vation. This social cognitive view of motivation was further clarified by Heider (1944, 1946, 1958), an important member of Lewin's extended group who showed that stimulus events including "success," "failure," "reward," and "punishment" had effects only when certain internal, cognitive attributions were made.

In addition to previous levels of "success" and "failure," Lewin and his group showed that several other important factors affected the goals individuals set (Weiner, 1992). More specifically, their research suggested that, in certain circumstances, individuals set goals to conform to group norms and that the goals they set were not necessarily based on past performance. The "Law of Effect" regarding positive reinforcement certainly was not operating here—at least, not in any simple sense. In short, in these and other studies, Lewin and his colleagues systematically showed how goals, aspirations, and complex thoughts were intervening to vary the meaning of reinforcement, choices made, and the experience of "success" and "failure." They showed that subjectively based perceptions, influenced by personal past experience as well as social context, figured strongly into what course of action was taken. Furthermore, they demonstrated that this subjective reality is only partially, and not all that reliably, correlated with objective reality (reality perceived by others).

While Lewin was probably not self-consciously a "motivational researcher," these early studies and the interpretations that accompanied them are in fact a primary basis of contemporary research on motivation today. Clearly, it led to the notion that motivation could be viewed in terms of choices that individuals made including one-time choices, such as a career decision, and repeated choices, such as choosing to continue working on a task when other attractive alternatives regularly presented themselves. This facet of Lewin's thought was extended by Atkinson, who benefited from both the tutelage of McClelland and the research tradition initiated by Lewin.

Expectancy × Value Theory

Basically, Atkinson (1957) proposed an advanced form of Lewin's (Lewin et al., 1944) "Level of Aspiration" model of motivation. This form consisted of the following components: expectancy, value, fear of failure, and hope for success. First, he built on the notion anticipated by Lewin and elaborated on by economic theorists that choices are a function of expectancy and value. That is, that one chooses to do or keep on doing what one thinks they can do (expectancy) and what they value doing (value). This assertion is reasonably logical and might be defined as "commonsense." However, Atkinson suggested that persons would vary in their decision-making patterns, a possibility not often considered by decision theorists. Building especially on the early efforts in defining the need for achievement of McClelland, his mentor, Atkinson proposed that individuals approached achievement tasks, where the outcome was to a degree uncertain and fully predictable, with both Hope and Fear—with persons with a high "need" for achievement (as McClelland defined it) actually tending to hold more hope for success for achievement in the pursuit of achievement tasks and relatively less fear of failure. Accordingly, the person who has higher hope than fear (High in Achievement Motivation) is more likely to choose and continue to persist at a moderately uncertain outcome task and, hence, "succeed."

Aside from operationalizing complex conceptions of motivation so that they could be systematically studied, Atkinson's work has had a broad influence on the study of motivation. It further pushed the cognitive nature of the origins of motivation, while giving place to affect. In addition, it eventuated in a massive body of literature that had an impact on conceptualizing motivation in achievement settings (Maehr & Sjogren, 1971). The operative focus was on confronting and overcoming challenge—who did it, why, and with what results. But it also reinforced concern with fear of failure or achievement anxiety. These dual orientations continue to be a focus for the field of motivation today (Covington & Roberts, 1994; Pintrich & Schunk, 2002).

However, the primary residue from Atkinson's efforts lies within a slightly different Expectancy × Value model of motivation, which has guided the work of Eccles and her colleagues. Arguably the most prolific current motivational researcher, Eccles has examined a wide array of issues related to motivation and achievement (Eccles, 1983; Eccles & Wigfield, 1995; Eccles, Wigfield, & Schiefele, 1998; Wigfield & Eccles, 1992; Wigfield, Eccles, & Rodriguez, 1998). A considerable portion of this longitudinal research has been conducted in school settings, with a special emphasis given to the motivational patterns exhibited by individuals at various stages of development. In comparison to the laboratory studies testing early versions of expectancy-value theory, this work has been based in the ecologically valid settings of classrooms and schools. The findings from this research can be applied much more easily to education because of the emphasis on real students in real classrooms, confronting real choices. The theory and research have focused on both expectancy and value components of achievement motivation.

The Role of Expectancies and Self-Perceptions of Ability. Eccles and her colleagues have conducted a number of large-scale correlational field studies examining expectancies and ability perceptions across a variety of domains in a variety of age levels. Expectancy refers to students' expectations or beliefs that they will do well in the future on tasks, whereas self-perceptions of ability concern students'

judgments of their competence at these tasks. Two correlational studies examining elementary students' expectancies and perceptions of ability in four domains (English, math, sports, and instrumental music) may be of particular interest to music educators. In particular, Eccles and her colleagues (Eccles, Wigfield, Harold, & Blumenfeld, 1993; Wigfield, Eccles, Yoon, Harold, Arbreton, Freedman-Doan, & Blumenfeld, 1997) showed that elementary students do not distinguish between future expectations and perceptions of ability; that is, they found one factor representing students' expectancies. However, this expectancy variable was distinct for the four domains investigated, suggesting that it is important to measure expectancies for a particular domain of interest when studying the impact of expectancies on achievement and choice behavior. Furthermore, these data show that in all areas except sports, students' expectancies decreased across the elementary school years, and these decreases were the largest in the domain of instrumental music.

Eccles and her colleagues (Eccles, 1983; Eccles, Wigfield, Flanagan, Miller, Reuman, & Yee, 1989; Wigfield, 1994; Wigfield & Eccles, 1992) also have investigated the role of expectancy and ability perception constructs in achievement in a series of large-scale correlational field studies. These studies used both cross-sectional and longitudinal designs where upper elementary and junior high students were given self-report measures of their self-perceptions of ability and expectancy for success in math and English at the beginning of one school year and at the end of that same year. In some of their studies, these same students were then followed for a number of years and given the same self-report measures, again at the beginning and at the end of subsequent school years. At the same time, the researchers also collected data on the students' actual achievement on standardized tests and course grades. They then used path analytic and structural equation modeling techniques that allowed them to examine the relative effects of expectancy and ability perceptions versus grades on subsequent perceptions and grades. These studies have consistently shown that students' self-perceptions of ability and their expectancies for success are the strongest predictors of subsequent grades in math and English, even better predictors of later grades than were previous grades. These studies also found the same relation for self-reported outcome measures of effort and persistence in these domains. These general findings emerged across a number of studies highlighting the importance of students' expectancies and self-perceptions of competence as mediators between the environmental or cultural context and actual achievement behavior and involvement.

In contrast to these relations between competence perceptions and expectancies and achievement, the findings for choice are not as clear-cut. Although earlier research by Atkinson and others showed that expectancy beliefs related to students' choice behavior, more recent research on student academic choices does not show as strong a role for expectancy beliefs (Pintrich & Schunk, 2002). Eccles and Wigfield and their colleagues find in their field studies that the value beliefs concerning the students' perceptions of the importance, utility, and interest in the task were better predictors of their intentions to continue to take math and of their actual enrollment decision (Wigfield, 1994; Wigfield & Eccles, 1992; see also Feather, 1982, 1988). Accordingly, from an expectancy-value perspective, it appears that expectancy beliefs are more closely tied to actual achievement and engagement, but that value beliefs are more closely tied to choice behaviors that would provide the student with the opportunity to achieve in the future.

The Role of Values. In Atkinson's original model, values were defined as the inverse of the probability of success, resulting in little research on incentive value in comparison to the probability of success. However, current expectancy-value models such as the work by Eccles and her colleagues have reinvigorated the study of values in achievement motivation by demonstrating that values have a distinct role to play in achievement dynamics.

In the Eccles model, values are defined in terms of four components: importance, utility, interest value, and cost, although the first three are the most researched. Importance (also called attainment value) refers to the student's own personal beliefs about how important doing well on the task is to her. It also is related to identity, such that doing well on the task is important to one's own identity. For example, if a student identifies herself as a "musician," then doing well at music "tasks," such as a musical performance, has high importance or attainment value. Utility value refers to the perceived usefulness of the task for future goals. Again, if a student has a goal of becoming a musician, then music courses would have higher utility value for this student than other courses such as English or chemistry. Interest refers to the personal intrinsic interest the individual has for the task or domain, often defined in terms of how much they enjoy or like to do activities related to the task or domain. Finally, cost concerns the perceived costs associated with the activity, such as loss of time or high perceived need for effort to do the task. For example, an adolescent might see continuing on in music as a cost in terms of the amount of time that must be devoted to practicing that takes away time for other social or academic activities, or that there may be social costs in terms of having friends in the band rather than friends in athletics. In addition to these values being distinct from each other, they are also distinct within different domains. So, a student may have utility value for music but not sports. As with expectancies, it appears that values de-

cline as students move through the elementary years, except for valuing sports (Eccles et al., 1993; Wigfield et al., 1997).

In their research, Eccles and her colleagues have shown that these components of values are also empirically distinct from the expectancy components (Eccles & Wigfield, 1995). In other words, students distinguish tasks that personally interest them from those tasks or activities that they might see as important or useful to them. In addition, these value components are separate from expectancy components. Eccles and her colleagues, however, show that there is a positive correlation between expectancy and value components and that this relation becomes stronger as children get older (Wigfield et al., 1997). So, we tend to like and value those activities we are good at and vice versa, although it is not clear which develops first. Most likely, there is a reciprocal relation between expectancy and value over the course of development, whereby children become interested in an activity and spend more time doing this activity, thereby developing actual skills and accompanying competence beliefs. In the same manner, as they believe they are competent at the activity, they will come to do it more and develop more interest in the activity, although there is a need for developmental research on this kind of reciprocal relation over time.

More important, the research on values shows that although these beliefs are positively correlated with actual achievement (grades and performance on standardized tests), they are not the best predictors of these achievement outcomes. It appears that expectancies and self-perceptions of ability are much better predictors of actual achievement outcomes. However, in terms of choice to take more courses in a domain, values such as importance, utility, and interest are better predictors of choice behavior than the expectancy components (Eccles, 1983; Wigfield & Eccles, 1992).

Thus, from an educational perspective, enhancing students' expectancies is important for improving achievement while increasing value may result in future choice behavior of taking more courses in a given domain. Both teachers' and parents' perceptions of students' competence have been linked to students' own expectancies (Wigfield et al., 1997). In addition, teachers can help students to increase their expectancies by helping them develop the necessary skills to succeed on a particular task. In the music domain, it may be that a high school orchestra director may want to help students develop adaptive expectancy and competency beliefs for students currently in the orchestra, while an elementary or middle school director may want to work on increasing the values and interest beliefs of younger students in the hope they will choose to continue on with their music education once they are in high school.

Self-efficacy Theory

Self-efficacy theory also is concerned with the role of competence judgments and expectations. In particular, Bandura (1982, 1986, 1989, 1997) has developed a social cognitive model of behavior that includes self-efficacy as a major construct. Bandura and others have applied the model to a variety of domains, including mental health, such as coping with depression and phobias; health behavior, such as recovery from a heart attack and cessation of smoking; decision making and sales performance in business; athletic performance; career choices; and academic achievement. In the educational domain, Schunk (1989a, 1989b, 1991) has been the leading theorist and researcher regarding the role of student self-efficacy in classroom settings.

In this model, self-efficacy is defined as "people's judgments of their capabilities to organize and execute courses of action required to attain designated types of performances" (Bandura, 1986, p. 391). Self-efficacy represents people's judgments of their abilities in the same way as in expectancy-value research (Eccles, 1983) or research on general self-concept (Harter, 1992). There are, however, some important differences. First, the definition of self-efficacy includes "organize and execute courses of action," which represents the theory's more specific and situational view of perceived competence in terms of including the behavioral actions or cognitive skills that are necessary for competent performance. For example, self-efficacy in music would not be merely a self-recognition of being good at playing one's instrument but, rather, explicit judgments of having particular technical or musical skills necessary to perform or learn a specific piece of music.

A second aspect that distinguishes self-efficacy from self-concept and self-competence is that it is used in reference to some type of goal ("attain designated types of performance"). Again, this reflects the more situational perspective of efficacy theory in contrast to the personality and developmental heritage of expectancy-value and perceptions-of-competence research. The goal may be determined by the individual or by the task conditions and environment (or their interaction), but the important point is that judgments of efficacy are in reference to this goal. One implication of the inclusion of a specific goal is that self-efficacy judgments for very similar tasks may vary as a function of intraindividual or environmental differences. For example, skilled and experienced runners may lower their efficacy judgments for maintaining their usual time for a 10-kilometer run because of a nagging muscle pull. In an academic setting, a student's self-efficacy for learning a particular topic in mathematics may be lower because of the difficulty of the material to be learned in contrast to material covered earlier in the course. A musician might not feel as efficacious for a particular performance due to

the difficulty of the program that evening. In colloquial terms, these individuals have lower than usual "self-confidence" in their capabilities to perform a specific task at a certain level of competence.

Efficacy theory also proposes that outcome expectations form a second construct related to motivational behavior and affect. Outcome expectations are judgments or beliefs regarding the contingency between a person's behavior and the anticipated outcome. This notion of contingency between response and outcome is similar to Rotter's (1966) construct of locus of control regarding the contingency between behavior and reinforcement. In addition, in terms of the anticipation of success, it is similar to expectancy for success from expectancy-value theories. As Bandura (1986) puts it, "The belief that one can high jump six feet is an efficacy judgment; the anticipated social recognition, applause, trophies, and self-satisfactions for such a performance constitute the outcome expectations" (p. 391). In the academic domain, students would have efficacy judgments of their capabilities, skills, and knowledge to master school-related tasks, and also have outcome expectations about what grades they might receive on the tasks. A musician might have very high efficacy for playing a solo at a competition, but also realize that he might not win the top prize due to the level of talent at the competition. Although efficacy beliefs and outcome expectations are usually positively correlated, it is possible for a student to have a relatively high efficacy belief for a task, but low outcome expectations. For example, a college student in an organic chemistry class might have relatively high efficacy beliefs about personal capability to master the material, but low outcome expectations about grades on exams because of the very high competition among premed students and the grading curve instituted by faculty to weed out the weaker students from the medical school admission process.

Although Bandura proposes both of these motivational constructs, the theory and subsequent research focus on the role of self-efficacy beliefs. Bandura (1986) suggests that outcome expectations are heavily dependent on efficacy judgments: "If you control for how well people judge they can perform, you account for much of the variance in the kinds of outcomes they expect" (p. 393). Bandura (1986) notes that outcomes are connected to actions; how one behaves largely determines the actual outcome and, in the same way, beliefs about outcome expectations are dependent on self-efficacy judgments. He gives the example that drivers who are not confident in their ability to negotiate a winding mountain road (low efficacy) will conjure up images of wreckage and injuries (one type of outcome expectation), whereas those confident in their ability will anticipate the grand views from the mountains. A musician might not be confident about a particularly difficult passage in a piece and before and during the playing of that passage may be anxious and imagine making mistakes and playing poorly. In contrast, a high efficacy individual would concentrate on playing the passage and enjoy the challenge and difficulty of that passage.

Self-efficacy is related to choice behavior in terms of task choice, but it also has been related to career choices. For example, Betz and Hackett (1981, 1983; Hackett & Betz, 1981) have shown that although there are structural and social influences on career choices, self-efficacy is an important mediator of these external influences and has a direct bearing on career choice. In addition, they suggest that the gender differences that emerge in vocational choices are due to differences in self-efficacy; males feel more efficacious for careers in math and science, whereas females feel more efficacious for careers traditionally held by women.

Besides choice, self-efficacy has been related to the quantity of effort and the willingness to persist at tasks (Bandura & Cervone, 1983, 1986; Schunk, 1991). Individuals with strong efficacy beliefs are more likely to exert effort in the face of difficulty and persist at a task when they have the requisite skills. Individuals who have weaker perceptions of efficacy are likely to be plagued by self-doubts and to give up easily when confronted with difficulties. However, there is some evidence that self-doubt (weak efficacy) may foster learning when students have not previously acquired the skills. As Bandura (1986) notes, "Self-doubt creates the impetus for learning but hinders adept use of previously established skills" (p. 394). Salomon (1984) found that students high in efficacy were more likely to be cognitively engaged in learning from media when the task was perceived as difficult, but they were likely to be less effortful and less cognitively engaged when the media were deemed easy.

Besides the quantity of effort, the quality of effort in terms of the use of deeper processing strategies and general cognitive engagement of learning has been strongly linked to self-efficacy perceptions (Pintrich & Schrauben, 1992). For example, Pintrich and De Groot (1990) found that junior high students high in efficacy were more likely to report using various cognitive and self-regulatory learning strategies. In a series of experimental studies, Schunk (1982, 1983a, 1983b, 1983c, 1983d, 1984, 1987, 1991) found that students who had stronger self-efficacy beliefs were able to master various math and reading tasks better than students with weaker efficacy beliefs. In addition, these studies showed that efficacy was a significant predictor of learning and achievement, even after prior achievement and cognitive skills were taken into consideration. Accordingly, we would expect musicians high in efficacy beliefs to practice more effectively because they would be more likely to self-regulate as they practice. This type of

practicing should then result in increased achievement in music.

Attribution Theory

Attribution theory emphasizes the importance of understanding *why* events occur in the world (Graham & Weiner, 1996). Although this theory was not originally proposed to understand academic achievement, Bernard Weiner (1985, 1986) adapted earlier theories to explain attributions based on success and failure in academic settings. Briefly, Weiner (1986) proposed that individuals analyze the current situation for perceived causes by considering both environmental factors such as social norms as well as personal factors such as prior knowledge and beliefs about one's competence. These perceived causes can be categorized based on three causal dimensions: stability, locus, and control. These categorizations are then linked to specific psychological consequences (future expectancies, self-efficacy, affect), which in turn influence behavioral consequences (choice, persistence, level of effort, achievement).

Thus, according to Weiner (1986), the particular causes for success and failure are not the key motivational factors in attribution theory; rather, it is the causal dimension into which these causes can be classified that predicts psychological and behavioral outcomes. Both theoretical and empirical analyses (Weiner, 1986; Weiner, Frieze, Kukla, Reed, Rest, & Rosenbaum, 1971) suggest that *locus*, whether the cause is internal or external to the individual, *stability*, how stable the perceived cause is, and *controllability*, whether the perceived cause can be controlled or not, are the three most important dimensions to consider. Accordingly, a specific cause can be categorized into one of eight cells (Pintrich & Schunk, 2002). For instance, a student who does well might say it was because of luck (external, unstable, uncontrollable) or long-term effort (internal, stable, controllable). Another student who failed an exam might attribute the failure to instructor bias (external, stable, controllable) or lack of ability (internal, stable, uncontrollable). Motivational dynamics come into play in this process when the individual asks "why" she did well or poorly, or why she succeeded or failed. It is the "answer" to this why question that attributional theory has focused on in research.

The stability dimension seems to be the most important in predicting future expectancies (Weiner, 1986). For any given outcome (either success or failure), a person who attributes outcomes to a stable cause will expect a similar outcome in the future. Accordingly, if a student attributes success to a stable outcome she will expect success for a similar task in the future, thus enhancing the strength of her future expectancy for success. Another important outcome is emotion. Both the locus and the controllability dimensions are related to various emotions people experience in response to success or failure (Weiner, 1986). For instance, esteem-related affects such as pride are related to the locus dimension, while social-related affects such as guilt and shame are related to the controllability dimension. Of course, considering all three dimensions is important for understanding psychological and behavioral consequences.

In general, it is adaptive to see success as a function of stable and internal factors such as ability, skill, or talent, since it is likely that these factors will be present for future tasks. However, attributions for success to unstable, controllable, internal factors such as effort also can be particularly adaptive in that the level of effort can be adjusted to the situation as necessary (whereas ability or talent may not always be sufficient for succeeding at a difficult task). In contrast, it is more adaptive to attribute failure to lack of effort (did not practice the piece enough), or bad luck, or just a difficult task (the selection is an especially difficult piece of music). If those factors can change and are unstable, then failure is not a given the next time the task is undertaken.

Individuals' beliefs about the causes of events can be changed through feedback and other environmental manipulations to facilitate the adoption of positive control and attributional beliefs. For example, there has been research on attributional retraining in achievement situations (e.g., Foersterling, 1985; Perry & Penner, 1990) that suggests that teaching individuals to make appropriate attributions for failure on school tasks (e.g., effort attributions instead of ability attributions) can facilitate future achievement. Attributional patterns can also be altered by the teacher's reactions to success or failure (Graham, 1984). For instance, if a teacher expresses pity following a student's failure, the student is more likely to make attributions to low ability (internal, stable, uncontrollable). Of course, there are a variety of issues to consider in attributional retraining including the specification of which attributional patterns are actually dysfunctional, the relative accuracy of the new attributional pattern, as well as the issue of only attempting to change a motivational component instead of the cognitive skill that also may be important for performance (cf., Blumenfeld, Pintrich, Meece, & Wessels, 1982; Weiner, 1986).

Achievement Goal Theory

There are a number of different goal theories such as Locke and Latham's (1990) model, which concentrates on the specific "objectives" that individuals set for themselves (e.g., sell 10 automobiles this month; get an 85 on the test; play this piano piece all the way through from memory without mistakes or hesitation). Ford (1992) also proposes a goal theory that focuses on the larger goals that individuals might adopt (a goal of happiness; a goal of superiority). In addition, there is research on social goals (Urdan & Maehr, 1995; Wentzel, 1991) but, given space limitations, we focus here on achievement behavior. Within the research on achievement behavior in academic settings, the most active relevant area of current research is achievement goal theory.

There are a number of variants of achievement goal theories for achievement behavior, but the main construct that is involved is goal orientation, which concerns the purposes for engaging in achievement behavior. In contrast to Locke and Latham's (1990) goal-setting theory that focuses on specific objectives (e.g., get 10 problems correct), achievement goal theory is concerned with why individuals want to get 10 problems correct and how they approach this task. Goal orientation represents an integrated pattern of beliefs that leads to "different ways of approaching, engaging in, and responding to achievement situations" (Ames, 1992, p. 261). In addition, goal orientation can reflect a type of standard by which individuals will judge their performance or success, which then has consequences for other motivational beliefs such as attributions and affect as well as actual performance and behavior.

There may be a number of different goal orientations, but the two that are always represented in the different goal orientation theories have been labeled learning and performance goals (Dweck & Leggett, 1988; Elliott & Dweck, 1988), or task-involved and ego-involved goals (Nicholls, 1984), or mastery and performance goals (Ames, 1992; Ames & Archer, 1987, 1988), or task-focused and ability-focused goals (Maehr & Midgley, 1991). There is some disagreement among these researchers about whether all these goal pairs represent the same constructs (see Nicholls, 1990), but there is enough conceptual overlap to treat them in similar ways in a review chapter such as this one. Accordingly, we will use the terms task and ego goals to refer to the two general goal orientations.

The distinction between task and ego goals parallels to some extent the distinction between intrinsic and extrinsic motivation. The focus in achievement goal theories, however, is on a more specific cognitive goal that is more situational and context dependent than the general, more personality-like intrinsic and extrinsic motivation constructs that come from a more organismic, not contextual, perspective. If a student adopts a task goal orientation, then she should be focused on learning, mastering the task according to self-set standards, developing new skills, improving her competence, trying to accomplish something challenging, and trying to gain understanding or insight (Ames, 1992; Dweck & Leggett, 1988; Maehr & Midgley, 1991; Nicholls, 1984; and cf. Harter, 1981).

An ego goal orientation, in contrast to a task orientation, represents a focus on relative ability and how ability will be judged, for example, trying to surpass normative performance standards, attempting to best others' performance (I got a better grade than everyone else in the classroom), and seeking public recognition of this performance level (Ames, 1992). More recently, there have been models that have suggested that ego goals can be divided into two types, an approach ego goal and an avoidance ego goal (Elliot, 1999; Harackiewicz, Barron, & Elliot, 1998; Middleton & Midgley, 1997; Pintrich, 2000a, 2000c). Students who are motivated by an approach ego goal are oriented to being better than others, to appear to be smarter or more talented (the best musician in the band), and to best others in competitions. In contrast, an avoid ego goal seems to orient students to seek to avoid looking dumb or stupid relative to others (i.e., avoid playing a wrong note in orchestra so as not to look dumb).

Dweck and her colleagues (e.g., Dweck, 1999; Dweck & Elliott, 1983; Dweck & Leggett, 1988) suggest that goal orientation is a function of different theories about the nature of intelligence. In this model, theories of intelligence are defined as students' perceptions about how ability and intelligence change over time. Dweck proposes that there are two basic implicit theories of intelligence: incremental and entity theories. Incremental theories of intelligence reflect students' beliefs that their intelligence and ability can change and can increase with time and experience. In contrast, entity theories of intelligence represent the belief that ability is fixed, stable, and unchanging, so students think they will not be able to increase their ability or intelligence over time. In the same manner, musicians with an entity view may believe that musical talent is entity-like with little possibility of change or improvement over time, whereas incremental theorists in music would believe that with experience and learning, musical skill can develop and improve over time.

In Dweck's research, these two beliefs are usually operationalized as opposite sides of a dichotomous variable and students should have one or the other implicit theory. The model, however, suggests that there may be a continuum between entity and incremental beliefs and that individuals may show mixed theories of beliefs about intelligence. These beliefs should be somewhat stable over time once the students are older than 12 or 13 years. Accordingly, these theories of intelligence are more traitlike than many other more contextual models of goals, although theories of ability/intelligence may vary by domain. For example, you may have an entity belief about your ability in mathematics, but you may have an incremental theory of ability for English coursework. This does not just apply to academic domains, however. Individuals may have an entity theory of ability to play basketball because of their

short height, but may be incrementalists in terms of their ability to play tennis or to learn how to do their job. Furthermore, more recent revisions to goal theory suggest that students can adopt multiple goals simultaneously (i.e., both task and ego goals) and that considering the relative levels of both goals is important in predicting academic outcomes (Pintrich, 2000b).

These different patterns of goals have been related to a number of different motivational and behavioral outcomes. First, goal orientation has been associated with patterns of attributions in a number of studies. In general, the research shows that a task goal orientation is linked to a positive, adaptive pattern of attributions, whereas an ego goal orientation is linked to a maladaptive, helpless pattern of attributions (Ames, 1992; Dweck & Leggett, 1988). When operating under a task goal orientation, students are concerned with learning and mastery of a task and increasing their ability. This schema seems to lead students to interpret outcome feedback in different ways than those following an ego goal orientation, where the focus is on maintaining or enhancing their ability and there is a concern with how ability is assessed. In the task goal orientation, students are more likely to see a strong link between their effort and the outcome and make more effort attributions for both success and failure. In addition, students with a task goal orientation see effort linked in a positive manner with ability, that is, that more effort means more ability.

In contrast, an ego goal orientation seems to lead to using ability attributions for both success and failure, and it is well known that ability attributions for failure (when ability is conceived of as stable) are maladaptive and can lead to learned helpless patterns of behavior (Dweck & Leggett, 1988; Weiner, 1986). In addition, students with an ego goal tend to see effort and ability as inversely related as opposed to the positive relation under a task goal. The ego-oriented students tend to think that the harder they try, the less ability they have, and this belief can lead them to be at risk for avoiding effort in order to protect their ability and self-worth (Covington & Omelich, 1979). It is important to note that in Dweck and Leggett's model (1988), this helpless pattern will emerge if students have an ego orientation and low confidence or efficacy in their intelligence. If students have an ego orientation but high confidence in their intelligence, then an ego orientation can lead to a mastery-like pattern of adaptive attributions and adaptive behavior like seeking challenges and persistence.

Besides these attributional patterns, task and ego goals also have been associated with various affective outcomes. Given the attribution-affect link specified in attributional theory, it is not surprising that task goals seem to lead to pride and satisfaction when successful and guilt when not successful (Ames, 1992; Jagacinski & Nicholls, 1984,

1987). These affective outcomes are usually generated by attributions that stress the controllability of behavior (such as effort), and if task goals lead to more effort attributions, then these emotions would be expected to follow by attribution theory (Weiner, 1986). Task goals also have been associated with reports of more intrinsic interest in and positive attitudes toward learning tasks (Ames, 1992; Butler, 1987; Meece, Blumenfeld, & Hoyle, 1988; Stipek & Kowalski, 1989). In general, although many of these studies were correlational, which makes it difficult to infer causality, it appears to be fairly well established empirically that the adoption of a task goal is associated with an adaptive pattern of attributions and positive affect that will help a student try hard, persist, and ultimately do better on academic tasks.

In fact, there have been other studies that have linked task and ego goals to more quantitative academic behaviors like effort and persistence as well as the quality of engagement. Again, task goals are linked to more time spent on learning tasks and more persistence at these tasks in comparison to ego goals (Ames, 1992; Butler, 1987; Elliott & Dweck, 1988). Moreover, there are a number of studies that have shown that task goals, in contrast to ego goals, lead to more cognitive engagement, especially the use of deeper processing strategies and self-regulated learning strategies. For example, Pintrich and De Groot (1990) showed that junior high students, who adopted an intrinsic goal focused on learning, were more likely to report using cognitive strategies such as elaboration (summarizing, paraphrasing) and self-regulatory strategies such as comprehension monitoring. Pintrich and his colleagues also have found this same relation in college students (see Pintrich, 1989; Pintrich & Garcia, 1991, 1993; Pintrich & Schrauben, 1992; Pintrich, Smith, Garcia, & McKeachie, 1993). Ames and Archer (1988) also have found a relation between a classroom focus on task goals and student reports of deeper cognitive engagement. In addition, in more experimental laboratory studies, both Graham and Golan (1991) and Nolen (1988) have found that task goals lead to more cognitive engagement in terms of the use of more cognitive strategies and also better actual performance on learning tasks such as memory for words and text comprehension.

In the context of music education, students with a task orientation would be more likely to engage in adaptive behaviors that should enhance their development of musical skill. These students would be more likely to persist, even on pieces they find challenging and where failure is a possibility. Furthermore, students with a task orientation should engage in more effective practice, monitoring their progress and working on areas that are particularly troublesome. In contrast, students with an ego goal orientation are less likely to persist in the face of difficulty. These stu-

dents also may be less inclined to practice because they may view practicing as a signal that they do not have "musical talent" (i.e., if they have talent, they should not need to practice).

Intrinsic Motivation Theory

All the social cognitive theories we have discussed so far tend to emphasize the cognitive aspects of motivation such as expectations, efficacy judgments, attributions, and goals. Intrinsic motivation theory is social cognitive as well, but the different intrinsic motivation models highlight the importance of more affective aspects of motivation. There are a number of different models that can be considered under intrinsic motivation theories, but we focus on three general perspectives. First, we discuss the views of Deci and Ryan and their self-determination theory, and then we briefly summarize the research of Csikszentmihalyi (1985) on intrinsic motivation and flow. We conclude with the research on personal and situational interest (Renninger et al., 1992).

Self-determination Theory. Deci and Ryan (Deci, 1980; Deci & Ryan, 1985, 1991; Ryan & Deci, 2000) are the most well-known researchers in the area of intrinsic motivation. Their model of intrinsic motivation and self-determination includes both social cognitive constructs as well as needs. Their model assumes that there are three general needs that individuals seek to satisfy: the need for competence, the need for autonomy, and the need for relatedness. The need for competence represents a general drive to master and be effective in interactions with the environment (White, 1959) and the need for relatedness reflects a need to belong or to experience close interpersonal relations with others. The need for autonomy is assumed to reflect an individual's need to experience self-determination and control of their own behavior, in a sense to experience the freedom to make their own choices without external control or constraints. When the environment affords the satisfaction of these needs, individuals are generally more intrinsically motivated and experience greater satisfaction and general well-being. If these needs are frustrated by environmental contingencies (e.g., controlling rewards), then individuals will be less intrinsically motivated (Deci & Ryan, 1985: Ryan & Deci, 2000).

When students are intrinsically motivated, they are more likely to seek out and master challenges, which satisfy their needs to be competent and self-determining (Deci & Porac, 1978). Challenges need to be within students' reach. If challenges are too easy, they will seek ones that are more difficult; if too difficult, they may abandon their efforts. Intrinsic motivation will suffer when individuals cannot exercise self-determination. They want to feel responsible for their actions and free to make choices. Unfortunately, in many classrooms, students have few choices about what to do and when and how to do it. Self-determination theory also predicts that intrinsic motivation will be diminished when individuals believe their actions are extrinsically determined (i.e., they are rewarded for engaging in an activity).

Deci and Ryan (1987) have summarized the research on the contextual features that support or curtail self-determination and intrinsic motivation. These features include the element of providing rewards that are controlling, such as rewards given to merely engage in an activity, which seem to decrease self-determination. Threats and deadlines also can curtail self-determination as they become more controlling and individuals feel compelled by the deadline rather than by interest in the activity. A third negative feature is evaluation and surveillance. Although a common characteristic of classrooms, in experimental studies, evaluation and surveillance have been shown to decrease interest and intrinsic motivation (Deci & Ryan, 1987). Two positive features that support self-determination are the amount of choice allowed and positive feedback regarding competence and efficacy. These five contextual features are all part of everyday life in classrooms, and teachers need to be sensitive to how they can affect students' self-determination and intrinsic motivation, although it is unlikely that teachers can remove them completely.

At times, it is difficult to design classrooms that grant autonomy and self-determination. For instance, there are extrinsic structures, controls, and rewards that may not fit with the child's quest for self-determination but help to produce good behavior and desirable social functioning in school. In some instances, it may be more desirable to keep some structures in place even with the knowledge that self-determination is diminished. Eventually, these extrinsic motivators may become internalized and part of the self-regulation process (Deci & Ryan, 1991; Ryan, Connell, & Deci, 1985). The process involves the movement of these extrinsic values from being external to the individual and experienced as "outside" the self, to being experienced as "internal" or part of the self.

While intrinsic motivation concerns activities that are autotelic—engaged in for their own sake—which by definition are self-determined, extrinsic motivation involves a progression from behaviors that originally were extrinsically motivated but became internalized and now are self-determined. The first level includes what Deci and his colleagues call external regulation. For example, students initially may not want to work on their music but do so to obtain parental or teacher rewards and avoid punishment. There is very little self-determination in this situation. At the next level of extrinsic motivation, students may engage in a task because they think they should and may feel guilty if they do not do the task (e.g., practice the piano). Deci and his colleagues call this introjected regulation because the source of motivation is internal (feelings of "should," "ought," guilt) to the person but not self-determined since these feelings seem to be controlling the person. The third level is called identified regulation and here individuals engage in the activity because it is personally important to them. For example, a student may practice for hours in order to do well in a musical production. This behavior represents the student's own goal, although the goal has more utility value (see Wigfield & Eccles, 1992) than intrinsic value such as learning. The final level of extrinsic motivation is integrated regulation, whereby individuals can integrate various internal and external sources of information into their own self-schema and engage in behavior because of its importance to their sense of self. This final level is still instrumental, rather than autotelic as in intrinsic motivation, but integrated regulation does represent a form of self-determination and autonomy. As such, both intrinsic motivation and integrated regulation will result in more cognitive engagement and learning than external or introjected regulation (Rigby, Deci, Patrick, & Ryan, 1992).

The role of rewards in facilitating or constraining intrinsic motivation and other cognitive, affective, or behavioral outcomes has become controversial again (cf. Cameron & Pierce, 1994; Deci, Koestner, & Ryan, 1999; Eisenberger & Cameron, 1996) and even resulted in a newly edited book on the issue (Sansone & Harackiewicz, 2000). In general, current research has attempted to move beyond too simplistic generalizations such as "rewards are good" (a general reinforcement perspective; see earlier section in this chapter) or "rewards are bad" (a classic intrinsic motivation perspective) to more nuanced views. Of course, all rewards have the potential to control behavior and to inform individuals about their competence and the relative salience or weight of each aspect determines the effect on intrinsic motivation. Rewards control behavior when they are given contingent on individuals accomplishing a given task or performing at a certain level. Thus, teachers tell students they can have free time after they finish their work, supervisors tell employees they will get a pay raise if they boost company profits, parents tell children they can play outside once they have finished practicing the violin. When people view rewards as controlling their behavior (they believe they are acting the way they are in order to earn the reward), they attribute their actions to factors outside of themselves (e.g., the reward) and they lose a sense of self-determination and motivation. Once the reward contingency is no longer in effect, there is nothing compelling them to work at the activity, so their interest declines.

However, rewards may not always be detrimental. Rewards also convey information about one's skills or competence when they are linked to actual performance or progress, such as when teachers praise students for learning new skills or acquiring new knowledge, supervisors give workers merit raises for performing better, and parents give rewards based on improved musical skill. People who derive such performance information from rewards feel efficacious and experience self-determination. Interest is sustained even when the reward contingency is removed because people place the locus of causality of behavior inside themselves (e.g., desire to learn).

Research studies have shown that such factors as task-contingent rewards (rewards given for working on tasks regardless of level of performance), offers to receive good player awards, deadlines, imposed goals, avoidance of unpleasant stimuli, surveillance, and social evaluation can diminish intrinsic motivation (Cameron & Pierce, 1994; Deci & Ryan, 1991; Morgan, 1984). In contrast, intrinsic motivation is maintained or enhanced when people are given choices or allowed to work in an environment perceived as supporting autonomy rather than as controlling (Deci & Ryan, 1991). Positive feedback that enhances perceived competence also raises intrinsic motivation (Deci, Vallerand, Pelletier, & Ryan, 1991).

Flow and Intrinsic Motivation. Perspectives on intrinsic motivation emphasize such qualities as perceived control, the desire for autonomy, and the need to master the environment. A perspective on intrinsic motivation closely aligned with these perspectives has been advanced by Csikszentmihalyi (1975; Csikszentmihalyi & Rathunde, 1993) and is referred to as emergent motivation, which denotes motivation stemming from the discovery of new goals and rewards as a consequence of interacting with the environment. Csikszentmihalyi believes that behavior is governed by intrinsic and extrinsic motivational forces. Extrinsic forces are preprogrammed biologically (e.g., food, sleep) or derived from the reward structure in which the individual is socialized (money, prestige). Intrinsic forces grow out of the individual's belief that it is worthwhile to strive toward a given outcome.

Csikszentmihalyi (1985) studied individuals who engaged in intrinsically motivating activities and found that their experiences reflected complete involvement with the activities. This involvement, or flow, is defined as "the holistic sensation that people feel when they act with total involvement" (Csikszentmihalyi, 1985, p. 36). Individuals experiencing flow are so intensely involved with a task that they may lose awareness of time and space. They also seek a flow experience for itself rather than for anticipated rewards. Although flow can be experienced with any activity, it is more likely to occur with activities that allow for free expression and creativity such as games, play, music, and art. For example, a musician playing a piece who becomes so involved in the music and her playing so that extraneous stimuli from the concert hall, the audience, even distracting thoughts about the self are lost to consciousness is said to be in a flow state.

Flow represents a state of equilibrium between the amount of challenge in activities and an individual's capabilities. People feel bored when their perceived skills exceed their opportunities for using them; they become anxious when they believe that challenges exceed capabilities. Flow can vary in intensity, with the critical variable being the ratio of challenge to skill. Csikszentmihalyi (1982) describes a research study in which the Experience Sampling Method was employed. Adults carried beepers that sounded several times a week, at which time subjects rated themselves on two dependent variables: affect (comprising items "happy," "cheerful," "sociable") and activation (comprising "active," "alert," "strong"). Subjects also judged their situation for challenges present and skills available. The amount of time individuals judged themselves to be in flow (defined as challenges and skills present and equal to one another) was related positively to affect and activation.

These findings have implications for teaching and learning because they highlight the importance of ensuring that challenges and skills are in balance and sufficiently high to counter apathy. Unfortunately, many school activities do not challenge students. Flow will suffer when students have few opportunities to structure their environments in ways that might maximize flow, such as by establishing challenging goals and mastering difficult tasks that build beliefs in their capabilities. From a music educator's perspective, this highlights the importance of choosing a repertoire where challenges and skills are in balance. Although this may be difficult to accomplish for all students playing a variety of instruments in an orchestra or band, music directors should consider how the selection of pieces balances both challenges and skill for the various instruments across the repertoire. That is, one piece may balance challenge and skill for the wind instruments while another piece balances challenge and skills for the strings. If this cannot be done at the group level, selection of solo pieces could be set to balance challenge and skill for individuals.

Personal and Situational Interest. The third perspective on intrinsic motivation is represented by researchers who have focused on personal interest. Researchers who have investigated personal interest have conceptualized it as a personality trait or a personal characteristic of the individual that is a relatively stable, enduring disposition of the individual (Krapp, Hidi, & Renninger, 1992). In addition, this personal interest is usually assumed to be directed toward some specific activity or topic (a particular interest in sports, science, music, dance, computers, etc.) in contrast to curiosity, which is assumed to be a characteristic of the person that is more diffusely directed (e.g., someone who is generally curious about many things). For example, much of the vocational education and career choice literature is based on assessing individuals' interests in different activities and careers. In the previous section, Eccles and Wigfield's concept of intrinsic interest would be conceptually similar to personal interest. Other researchers (see review by Schiefele, Krapp, & Winteler, 1992) have measured personal interest as a preference for certain topics (e.g., I prefer music to science), a general liking for the subject area (e.g., I like music), personal enjoyment (e.g., I enjoy practicing my instrument), and sometimes importance or personal significance of the topic (e.g., music is important to me).

In contrast to the more personality or traitlike characteristic of personal interest, situational interest has been defined by researchers as interest that is generated mainly by environmental conditions (Krapp et al., 1992). The researchers who have studied situational interest have often been reading researchers who have been investigating text-based interest and trying to understand how different aspects of texts can generate and sustain interest on the part of readers. There are many different features of texts that can generate interest, such as novelty, surprise, complexity, ambiguity, and inclusion of certain types of themes (e.g., death, sex). Given this situated perspective, researchers have tended to ignore individual differences and have looked for general principles to describe how the features of the environment (classrooms, media, computers, textbooks) can generate interest. Hidi and Anderson (1992) note, however, that situational interest is different from just arousal or curiosity (cf. Berlyne, 1960) because situational interest may be tied to very specific content (e.g., a story about space travel), not only structural features (novelty, surprise) of the text or environment, and it may last longer than simple arousal and may develop into a personal interest. In a music classroom, playing orchestral arrangements of more popular pieces may help to capitalize on situational interest.

The third construct of interest, interest as a psychological state, reflects an interactive and relational perspective on interest, whereby an individual's personal interest interacts with the interesting environmental features to produce the psychological state of interest in the person (Krapp et al., 1992). For example, a student may have a fairly high level of personal interest in science-related topics and, in her reading class, she occasionally gets to read expository texts about science topics. On these occasions, she experiences a heightened psychological state of interest in contrast to other occasions during reading class when she reads about other topics. There has been less research on this relational construct in comparison to the work on personal and situational interest, although in many studies of the other two constructs, individuals have experienced a psychological state of interest.

Renninger (1990, 1992; Renninger & Wozniak, 1985) has been one of the researchers most involved with developing a research program on interest that reflects this relational construct of interest as a psychological state. She has conceptualized interest not just in terms of a personal preference or liking for an activity or topic, but as occurring only when the individual has both high value for an activity (choosing to do it, thinking it is important) and high stored knowledge about the activity or topic. It is only under these conditions that Renninger would label the state as interest. The argument is that if individuals have very little knowledge of an activity or topic, then it is hard for them to judge their interest in it. In addition, individuals usually have more knowledge about activities that have a high level of interest and value for them. Accordingly, if a person has a high value for an activity but low knowledge of the activity, then Renninger does not consider this interest; she labels this state as attraction. Noninterests are defined by high stored knowledge for an activity but low value for the activity. Renninger (1992) does not label the fourth cell in this two-by-two matrix of knowledge and value, which would represent the low value and low knowledge cell, but the psychological state would be unconcern, indifference, and ignorance about the topic.

Although there are problems in both the theoretical conceptions of interest and in the measurement of interest, the research has revealed fairly consistent results regarding how interest is related to other cognitive and achievement outcomes. First, in terms of cognitive outcomes, interest is generally related positively to measures of memory, attention, comprehension, deeper cognitive engagement, and thinking (Schiefele, 1991; Tobias, 1994), as suggested in most lay or folk psychology theories on the role of interest in learning. For example, Renninger and Wozniak (1985) have shown that preschoolers' interest in different activities predicts their attention, recognition, and recall memory for these objects at a later point in time. Schiefele (1991), using both experimental and correlational designs, has shown that college students' personal interest was positively related to the use of deeper cognitive processing strategies such as elaboration, seeking information when confronted with a problem, engagement in critical thinking, and self-reported time and effort investment. In addition, Schiefele (1991) reported that personal interest was negatively related to the use of a more surface processing strategy, rehearsal. Pintrich and his colleagues (Pintrich, 1989; Pintrich & De Groot, 1990; Pintrich & Garcia, 1991) have shown that personal interest and task value measures are correlated positively with deeper processing strategies such as the use of elaboration and organizational strategies as well as reports of critical thinking and time and effort regulation strategies in both college and junior high samples. The research on situational interest and text-based learning shows basically the same pattern of relations (Alexander,

Kulikowich, & Jetton, 1994; Hidi & Anderson, 1992; Tobias, 1994), although the findings are somewhat more complicated by the type of text involved (narrative vs. expository text, linear vs. nonlinear text) and levels of student prior knowledge.

Motivational Theory and Educational Practice

Thus far, we have reviewed the various theories of student motivation. This review should be helpful in giving music educators an understanding of the complexity of student motivation; however, it is also important to consider how changes to the classroom context may impact students' motivation. Therefore, we now turn to a brief discussion of the relation of the classroom context to student motivation. We focus on social cognitive conceptions of motivation rather than behavioral conceptions as the social cognitive conceptions are more generally accepted.

Of the social cognitive theories of motivation, achievement goal theory is perhaps the most situated theory. Accordingly, researchers studying student motivation have spent a good deal of time considering how differences in classroom context impact students' adoption of achievement goals. This work has been summarized by Ames (1992; see also Maehr & Midgley, 1996). Briefly, she organizes the research findings around three dimensions of classrooms: (1) tasks and learning activities, (2) evaluation practices and use of rewards, and (3) distribution of authority and responsibility. We use this framework here as a way to discuss how the classroom context relates not only to achievement goals but also to students' expectations, values, self-efficacy, interest, and attributions.

Tasks and learning activities are important influences on student motivation and cognition (Blumenfeld, Mergendoller, & Swarthout, 1987; Doyle, 1983). First, the amount of variety and diversity in tasks can help maintain student interest and, by decreasing the amount of public comparability and opportunities for social comparison regarding performance, help students adopt a task-goal orientation (Marshall & Weinstein, 1984; Nicholls, 1989; Rosenholtz & Simpson, 1984). Furthermore, allowing students to choose among a variety of tasks also provides more opportunities for students' needs for autonomy to be met and thus enhances intrinsic motivation. A second feature of tasks concerns how they are introduced and presented to students. If the teacher can help students see the personal relevance and the meaningfulness of the content for their own learning, this can then facilitate an adoption of a task-goal orientation (Brophy, 1987; Meece, 1991) as well as enhance personal value. A third feature concerns the level of difficulty of the task. Achievement goal theory suggests that tasks offering an optimal level of challenge

for students (i.e., tasks that can be mastered with effort but are neither easy enough to produce boredom nor hard enough to produce anxiety) can facilitate a task-goal orientation (Ames, 1992; Lepper & Hodell, 1989; Malone & Lepper, 1987). Furthermore, appropriately challenging tasks may help students develop higher efficacy judgments as they succeed at an activity that is just beyond their current level or understanding. An ideal balance between skill and challenge for the task can also help to facilitate flow. Finally, Ames (1992) notes that tasks that are structured to highlight specific, short-term, or proximal goals can help students marshal their efforts toward these goals and feel efficacious as they accomplish these goals.

Following this line of thought, it is important for music educators to consider the tasks they assign students. For instance, providing students with a diverse selection of solo pieces both in terms of difficulty and variety of musical styles would likely facilitate a task-goal orientation and would help to capitalize on students' interest. Furthermore, by guiding students toward pieces that are challenging but not too difficult and that utilize the musician's strengths, music educators can help to enhance students' efficacy for learning to play their instruments.

In addition to task selection, the evaluation practices and reward systems used in classrooms can have a large impact on students' goal adoption (Ames, 1992) as well as students' interest (e.g., Lepper, Greene, & Nisbett, 1973). In terms of achievement goals, evaluation practices that focus on students' ability relative to others tend to foster the adoption of ego goals, while a focus on each student's individual improvement as a criteria for evaluation relates to an increase in task goals. It is important to note that both informal evaluation and formal evaluation can impact motivation; therefore, educators must carefully consider the messages they send both in everyday, informal evaluations and more formal but less frequent evaluations.

Evaluation systems can also influence the types of attributions that students make. Evaluating students on their overall ability rather than improvement can suggest to students that musical ability is fixed. When students do not succeed under these types of circumstances, they are likely to make maladaptive attributions such as attributing their failure to internal, uncontrollable dimensions. In addition to evaluation practices, reward systems in classrooms must be carefully analyzed before they are implemented. Given the evidence that external rewards may undermine students' intrinsic interest, it is essential for music educators to consider the messages they send to students through reward systems.

The last dimension that Ames (1992) discusses concerns the authority structure of the classroom. The general principle is that students should be given some choice and control in the classroom setting, the same principle that intrinsic motivation theorists (Deci & Ryan, 1985) propose as important for intrinsic motivation. Research from both goal theory and intrinsic motivation theory suggests that the provision of some control and choice for students increases their interest in the task and their cognitive engagement in the task (Ames, 1992). Music education has many opportunities to provide students with choice and autonomy. In terms of the repertoire, students can be allowed to choose from a variety of pieces. Furthermore, there are ample opportunities for students to guide their own learning such as having students work in sectionals where students can set the pace for their learning and determine which areas of a particular piece on which to focus their energies.

At the same time, as Corno and Rohrkemper (1985) point out, students must have the necessary cognitive and self-regulatory skills to be able to cope with the responsibility that comes with increases in autonomy. It may be that very young children or students with learning problems may not have the self-regulatory skills that would enable them to adapt to a classroom situation that allows a great deal of choice. If the students are unable or unwilling to regulate their own behavior in line with classroom opportunities for choice and control, then it is unlikely that these opportunities will have a positive influence on students' motivation and achievement (Ames, 1992).

In summary, music educators must consider a variety of aspects of the classroom environment including the tasks they use, the design of evaluation and reward systems, and their use of authority in the classroom. In considering these features, it is important to keep in mind how various structures may impact students' motivation, thus influencing their engagement in learning.

Conclusion

The last several decades have seen an increased interest in student motivation and the role that motivation plays in achievement and performance. The current focus on social cognitive models has already helped us understand the dynamics of student motivation and achievement in much richer depth and detail than earlier behavioral and needs-based models. Moreover, the focus in social cognitive models on cognitions as well as emotions, values, and interest, make it much easier to integrate and link motivational theories and constructs with cognitive constructs, which are so crucial to learning. In many ways, the current research on motivation and cognition has highlighted the importance of including both "will" and "skill" in our models of achievement and learning. We are finally coming to understand that student learning is always a function of both motivation and cognition and that it makes little theoretical or practical sense to develop models that only emphasize one or the other perspective.

Future Directions

At the same time, there is still much to be done and future theory and research must address a number of different issues. We outline five future directions here, although there are clearly many avenues for the development of theory and research (see Pintrich, 2000a; Zeidner, Boekaerts, & Pintrich, 2000).

Developing a Consistent Nomenclature of Motivational Constructs.   As Zeidner et al. (2000) point out, research on self-regulation employs many different terms, some of which refer to the same processes by different names, some of which have the same names for different processes. Murphy and Alexander (2000) have made a similar claim in reference to the motivation literature. In this chapter, we have discussed a number of different theoretical models and many of them do refer to similar constructs with different names. In fact, a novice to the field of motivation is almost always overwhelmed by the terms and confused by the fact that many of them refer to what seem like very similar constructs. There is a need for motivational theorists to begin to develop a consistent terminology for their constructs. At the same time, as Pintrich (2000a) has pointed out, there are often good metatheoretical, as well as theoretical and empirical, reasons for having different labels for similar constructs. Some of the models discussed in this chapter make quite different metatheoretical assumptions about human nature and, by implication, about motivation. In addition, there are theoretical reasons to have different labels, such as the two terms, self-competence and self-efficacy, to reflect a distinction between a more stable personal schema about competence and a more contextualized and situated judgment of efficacy. Finally, some of the constructs are not empirically related to one another, even if they are similar theoretically (Pintrich, 2000a). Given these issues, it is important to develop a consistent nomenclature, but it is also important to maintain distinctions when warranted by theory or empirical evidence.

Clarifying Motivational Structures and Processes.   The models we have discussed in this chapter have clearly shown the role of motivational constructs, such as self-efficacy, attributions, goals, values, and interest, in facilitating learning and achievement. At the same time, there has been little work on how these different constructs are represented cognitively or structurally. That is, in comparison to the work in cognition that has addressed how various knowledge or cognitive structures are actually stored or represented in the mind, motivational researchers have not really tackled this problem. In addition, there has been very little specification of the psychological processes by which these various motivational constructs have their influence on learning and achievement. In fact, most of the models assume that the motivational constructs have their effects through increasing effort or persistence (two of the observable motivational behaviors mentioned at the very beginning of this chapter). However, there is a need for further delineation and specification of the various cognitive processes that are set in motion by motivational constructs. We have some good evidence about how motivation is linked to self-regulation and strategy use (Pintrich, 2000c), but there is still much more to be done. We have very little evidence about how motivational constructs may help to activate different knowledge structures or how they interact with basic cognitive processes such as attention, perception, and memory. In addition, the links between social cognitive motivational constructs and the learning of fine motor skills, which are applicable to art, music, and athletic domains, are largely unexplored.

Integrating Affective and Emotional Processes More Fully into the Models. The motivational theories and models discussed in this chapter do include various affect and emotions. For example, attributional theory has emotions as outcomes of a rational cognitive process of attributional analysis (Weiner, 1986). Intrinsic motivation and goal theories also include affects as outcomes of various motivational processes. However, in most of these models, affect and emotions are secondary to the basic social cognitive processes. This emphasis has helped motivation theory and research develop in the same way as other general cognitive models of learning (Pintrich & Schunk, 2002). At the same time, there has been a tendency to ignore or downplay the role of affect and emotions as central to motivational processes. There is a need to integrate affective processes more fully into our cognitive models of motivation. In addition, in reaction to the dominating and overwhelming cognitive and rational focus of psychology over the last 30 years or so, there is a trend developing toward the inclusion of implicit or unconscious processes as important precursors of behavior (see Bargh & Ferguson, 2000). In some ways, this trend harkens back to psychology's roots in more dynamic psychology (e.g., Freudian and psychodynamic theories), but it is leavened and balanced with social and cognitive mechanisms based on the research of the past 30 years. In terms of motivation, this trend will lead to the development of more models and research that attempt to integrate implicit motives (McClelland et al., 1989) and other affective and unconscious processes with our standard social cognitive models.

Contextualizing Motivation Theory and Understanding the Interactions Between the Context and Individual Motivational Processes. Given the historical psychological lineage of motivation theory and research, there has been a tendency to focus on the individual and ignore contextual

factors and their role in the activation and development of motivation. Many of the models discussed in this chapter represent traditional psychological perspectives that focus on the individual as well as the cognitive and motivational processes inside the individual's mind. However, currently there is great interest in social constructivist models of learning that focus on the context and attempt to break down the barrier between the individual and the context (Hickey, 1997). There are many different variants of these social constructivist models, some essentially deny the utility of any "inside-the-head" constructs, while other models accept cognitive constructs as long as it is clear that these cognitions are situated or activated in local context (Hickey, 1997; Pintrich & Schunk, 2002). It seems clear that models that completely eschew any cognitive constructs are not viable and do not fit empirical evidence, but how best to integrate contextual and cognitive factors remains an open question for future research and theory. Motivation theory and research has been slow to deal with this issue and has tended to adopt some version of the standard psychological person-context interaction model. Of course, this model has utility and has been and continues to be useful. However, it also seems clear that the traditional person-context interaction model does not capture the dynamics of motivation within and across contexts nor does it address the bidirectionality of the relations between contextual features and the individual. Clearly there is a need for new models of the context that consider how contexts can shape, define, facilitate, and constrain an individual's motivation and, at the same time, consider how the individual changes and regulates the context.

Development of Applications and Interventions to Facilitate Motivation. As we develop better models of motivational processes and come to understand how they are contextualized in the classroom and other real-life situations, we also will be able to develop better interventions to improve motivation. Of course, there have been a number of different types of interventions to develop motivation in school settings (e.g., Maehr & Midgley, 1996; see Pintrich & Schunk 2002, for a review), but there is still a need to refine these applications and determine how they can be adapted to different school and classroom contexts, as well as different disciplinary contexts. In the cognitive literature, there is a growing body of literature on general "design" principles to improve instruction in order to facilitate learning and development (Bransford, Brown, & Cocking, 1999; Brown, 1997). However, the research in this area and the design principles are almost solely based on the cognitive research and have not incorporated motivational research to any great extent (Hickey, 1997). There is a need for the development of motivational design principles that can serve this function and these principles should be integrated with the cognitive design principles. The general framework laid out by Maehr and Midgley (1996) around the different features of the classroom (see the last section of this chapter) serve as an excellent starting place for this type of work. Nevertheless, these general design principles still need to be adapted and molded to fit the disciplinary contexts in which they are used. Although there is certainly research that has applied motivation principles and constructs to music education (e.g., Austin, 1991; Austin & Vispoel, 1998; Vispoel & Austin, 1993), there is much to be done in terms of application of the ideas, models, and constructs summarized in this chapter to understanding and improving music education. We hope that this chapter leads to much more theory and research in this area that will not only deepen our understanding of motivation in general but also improve the motivation of all individuals for music appreciation and education.

REFERENCES

Allport, G. W. (1937). *Personality: A psychological interpretation*. New York: Henry Holt.

Alexander, P., Kulikowich, J., & Jetton, T. (1994). The role of subject-matter knowledge and interest in the processing of linear and nonlinear texts. *Review of Educational Research, 64,* 201–252.

Ames, C. (1992). Classrooms: Goals, structures, and student motivation. *Journal of Educational Psychology, 84,* 261–271.

Ames, R., & Ames, C. (1984). Systems of student and teacher motivation: Toward a qualitative definition. *Journal of Educational Psychology, 76,* 535–556.

Ames, C., & Archer, J. (1987). Mothers' beliefs about the role of ability and effort in school learning. *Journal of Educational Psychology, 79,* 409–414.

Ames, C., & Archer, J. (1988). Achievement goals in the classroom: Students' learning strategies and motivation processes. *Journal of Educational Psychology, 80,* 260–267.

Atkinson, J. (1957). Motivational determinants of risk-taking behavior. *Psychological Review, 64,* 359–372.

Atkinson, J. W., & Feather, N. T. (Eds.) (1967). *A theory of achievement motivation*. New York: John Wiley & Sons.

Atkinson, J. W., & Raynor, J. O. (Eds.) (1974). *Motivation and achievement*. New York: John Wiley & Sons.

Austin, J. R. (1991). Competitive and non-competitive goal structures: An analysis of motivation and achievement among elementary band students. *Psychology of Music, 19,* 142–158.

Austin, J. R., & Vispoel, W. P. (1998). How American adolescents interpret success and failure in classroom music: Relationships among attributional beliefs, self-concept and achievement. *Psychology of Music, 26,* 26–45.

Bandura, A. (1982). Self-efficacy mechanism in human agency. *American Psychologist, 37,* 122–147.

Bandura, A. (1986). *Social foundations of thought and action: A social cognitive theory*. Englewood Cliffs, NJ: Prentice Hall.

Bandura, A. (1989). Social cognitive theory. In R. Vasta (Ed.), *Annals of child development, Vol. 6* (pp. 1–60). Greenwich, CT: JAI Press.

Bandura, A. (1997). *Self-efficacy: The exercise of control*. New York: Freeman.

Bandura, A., & Cervone, D. (1983). Self-evaluative and self-efficacy mechanisms governing the motivational effects of goal systems. *Journal of Personality and Social Psychology, 45,* 1017–1028.

Bandura, A., & Cervone, D. (1986). Differential engagement of self-reactive influences in cognitive motivation. *Organizational Behavior and Human Decision Processes, 38,* 92–133.

Bargh, J. A., & Ferguson, M. J. (2000). Beyond behaviorism: On the automaticity of higher mental processes. *Psychological Bulletin, 126,* 925–945.

Berlyne, D. E. (1960). *Conflict, arousal, and curiosity*. New York: McGraw-Hill.

Betz, N. E., & Hackett, G. (1981). The relationship of career-related self-efficacy expectations to perceived career options in college women and men. *Journal of Counseling Psychology, 28,* 399–410.

Betz, N. E., & Hackett, G. (1983). The relationship of mathematics self-efficacy expectations to the selection of science-based college majors. *Journal of Vocational Behavior, 23,* 329–345.

Blumenfeld, P., Mergendoller, J., & Swarthout, D. (1987). Task as a heuristic for understanding student learning and motivation. *Journal of Curriculum Studies, 19,* 135–148.

Blumenfeld, P., Pintrich, P. R., Meece, J., & Wessels, K. (1982). The formation and role of self-perceptions of ability in the elementary classroom. *Elementary School Journal, 82,* 401–420.

Bransford, J., Brown, A., & Cocking, R. (1999). *How people learn: Brain, mind, experience, and school*. Washington, DC: National Academy Press.

Brill, A. A. (Ed. & Trans.). (1938). *The basic writings of Sigmund Freud*. New York: Random House.

Brown, A. (1997). Transforming schools into communities of thinking and learning about serious matters. *American Psychologist, 52,* 399–413.

Brophy, J. (1987). On motivating students. In D. Berliner & B. Rosenshine (Eds.), *Talks to teachers* (pp. 201–245). New York: Random House.

Butler, R. (1987). Task-involving and ego-involving properties of evaluation: Effects of different feedback conditions on motivational perceptions, interest, and performance. *Journal of Educational Psychology, 79,* 474–482.

Cameron, J., & Pierce, W. D. (1994). Reinforcement, reward, and intrinsic motivation: A meta-analysis. *Review of Educational Research, 64,* 363–423.

Clifford, M. M. (1988). Failure tolerance and academic risk-taking in ten- to twelve-year old students. *British Journal of Educational Psychology, 58,* 15–27.

Cooper, H. M., & Good, T. L. (1983). *Pygmalion grows up: Studies in the expectation communication process*. New York: Longman.

Cordova, D. L. (1993) *The effects of personalization and*

choice on students' intrinsic motivation and learning. Unpublished doctoral dissertation, Stanford University.

Corno, L., & Rohrkemper, M. (1985). The intrinsic motivation to learn in the classroom. In C. Ames & R. Ames (Eds.), *Research on motivation in education* (Vol. 2, pp. 53–90). New York: Academic Press.

Covington, M. V., & Omelich, C. L. (1979). Effort: The double-edged sword in school achievement. *Journal of Educational Psychology, 71,* 169–182.

Covington, M. V., & Roberts, B. (1994). Self-worth and college achievement: Motivational and personality correlates. In P. R. Pintrich, D. R. Brown, & C. E. Weinstein (Eds.), *Student motivation, cognition, and learning: Essays in honor of Wilbert J. McKeachie* (pp. 157–187). Hillsdale, NJ: Erlbaum.

Csikszentmihalyi, M. (1975). *Beyond boredom and anxiety.* San Francisco: Jossey-Bass.

Csikszentmihalyi, M. (1982). Toward a psychology of optimal experience. In L. Wheeler (Ed.), *Review of personality and social psychology* (Vol. 3, pp. 13–36). Beverly Hills, CA: Sage.

Csikszentmihalyi, M. (1985). Emergent motivation and the evolution of the self. In D. A. Kleiber & M. L. Maehr (Eds.), *Advances in motivation and achievement* (Vol. 4, pp. 93–119). Greenwich, CT: JAI Press.

Csikszentmihalyi, M., & Rathunde, K. (1993). The measurement of flow in everyday life: Toward a theory of emergent motivation. In J. E. Jacobs (Ed.), *Nebraska symposium on motivation 1992* (Vol. 40, pp. 57–97). Lincoln: University of Nebraska Press.

Deci, E. L. (1980). *The psychology of self-determination.* Lexington, MA: D. C. Heath.

Deci, E. L., Koestner, R., & Ryan, R. M. (1999). The undermining effect is a reality after all—Extrinsic rewards, task interest, and self-determination: Reply to Eisenberger, Pierce, and Cameron (1999) and Lepper, Henderlong, and Gingras (1999). *Psychological Bulletin, 125,* 692–700.

Deci, E. L., & Porac, J. (1978). Cognitive evaluation theory and the study of human motivation. In M. R. Lepper & D. Greene (Eds.), *The hidden costs of reward: New perspectives on the psychology of human motivation* (pp. 149–176). Hillsdale, NJ: Erlbaum.

Deci, E. L., & Ryan, R. M. (1985). *Intrinsic motivation and self-determination in human behavior.* New York: Plenum.

Deci, E. L., & Ryan, R. M. (1987). The support of autonomy and the control of behavior. *Journal of Personality and Social Psychology, 53,* 1024–1037.

Deci, E. L., & Ryan, R. M. (1991). A motivational approach to self: Integration in personality. In R. A. Dienstbier (Ed.), *Nebraska symposium on motivation 1990* (Vol. 38, pp. 237–288). Lincoln: University of Nebraska Press.

Deci, E. L., Vallerand, R. J., Pelletier, L. G., & Ryan, R. M. (1991). Motivation and education: The self-determination perspective. *Educational Psychologist, 26,* 325–346.

Doyle, W. (1983). Academic work. *Review of Educational Research, 53,* 159–199.

Dweck, C. (1999). *Self-theories: Their role in motivation, personality, and development.* Philadelphia, PA: Psychology Press.

Dweck, C. S., & Elliott, E. S. (1983). Achievement motivation. In P. H. Mussen (Ser. Ed.) & E. M. Heatherington (Vol. Ed.), *Handbook of child psychology: Vol 4. Socialization, personality, and social development* (4th ed., pp. 643–691). New York: Wiley.

Dweck, C., & Leggett, E. (1988). A social-cognitive approach to motivation and personality. *Psychological Review, 95,* 256–273.

Eccles, J. (1983). *Expectancies, values, and academic behaviors.* In J. T. Spence (Ed.), *Achievement and achievement motives* (pp. 75–146). San Francisco: Freeman.

Eccles, J., & Wigfield, A. (1995). In the mind of the actor: The structure of adolescents' achievement task values and expectancy-related beliefs. *Personality and Social Psychology Bulletin, 21,* 215–225.

Eccles, J., Wigfield, A., Flanagan, C., Miller, C., Reuman, D., & Yee, D. (1989). Self-concepts, domain values, and self-esteem: Relations and changes at early adolescence. *Journal of Personality, 57,* 283–310.

Eccles, J., Wigfield, A., Harold, R. D., & Blumenfeld, P. (1993). Age and gender differences in children's self- and task perceptions during elementary school. *Child Development, 64,* 830–847.

Eccles, J., Wigfield, A., & Schiefele, U. (1998). Motivation to succeed. In W. Damon (Series Ed.) & N. Eisenberg (Vol. Ed.). *Handbook of child psychology: Vol. 3. Social, emotional, and personality development* (5th ed., pp. 1017–1095). New York: Wiley.

Eisenberger, R., & Cameron, J. (1996). Detrimental effects of reward: Reality or myth? *American Psychologist, 51,* 1153–1166.

Elliot, A. J. (1999). Approach and avoidance motivation and achievement goals. *Educational Psychologist, 34,* 169–189.

Elliott, E., & Dweck, C. (1988). Goals: An approach to motivation and achievement. *Journal of Personality and Social Psychology, 54,* 5–12.

Feather, N. T. (1982). *Human values and the prediction of action: An expectancy-valence analysis.* Hillsdale, NJ: Erlbaum.

Feather, N. T. (1988). Values, valences, and course enrollment: Testing the role of personal values within an expectancy-valence framework. *Journal of Educational Psychology, 80,* 381–391.

Foersterling, F. (1985). Attributional retraining: A review. *Psychological Bulletin, 98,* 495–512.

Ford, M. (1992). *Motivating humans: Goals, emotions, and personal agency beliefs.* Newbury Park, CA: Sage.

Graham, S. (1984). Communicating sympathy and anger to black and white students: The cognitive (attributional) consequences of affective cues. *Journal of Personality and Social Psychology, 47,* 40–54.

Graham, S., & Golan, S. (1991). Motivational influences on cognition: Task involvement, ego involvement, and depth of information processing. *Journal of Educational Psychology, 83,* 187–194.

Graham, S., & Weiner, B. (1996). Theories and Principles of Motivation. In D. C. Berliner & R. Calfee (Eds.), *Handbook of educational psychology* (pp. 63–84). New York: Macmillan.

Hackett, G., & Betz, N. E. (1981). A self-efficacy approach to the career development of women. *Journal of Vocational Behavior, 18,* 326–339.

Harackiewicz, J. M., Barron, K. E., & Elliot, A. J. (1998). Rethinking achievement goals: When are they adaptive for college students and why? *Educational Psychologist, 33,* 1–21.

Harter, S. (1981). A new self-report scale of intrinsic versus extrinsic orientation in the classroom: Motivational and informational components. *Developmental Psychology, 17,* 300–312.

Harter, S. (1992). The relationship between perceived competence, affect, and motivational orientation within the classroom: Processes and patterns of change. In A. K. Boggiano and T. Pittman (Eds.), *Achievement and motivation: A social-developmental perspective* (pp. 77–114). New York: Cambridge University Press.

Heider, F. (1944). Social perception and phenomenal causality. *Psychology Review, 51,* 358–373.

Heider, F. (1946). Attitudes and cognitive organization. *Journal of Psychology, 21,* 107–112.

Heider, F. (1958). *The psychology of interpersonal relations.* New York: Wiley.

Hickey, D. (1997). Motivation and contemporary socio-constructivist instructional perspectives. *Educational Psychologist, 32,* 175–193.

Hidi, S., & Anderson, V. (1992). Situational interest and its impact on reading and expository writing. In K. A. Renninger, S. Hidi, & A. Krapp (Eds.), *The role of interest in learning and development* (pp. 215–238). Hillsdale, NJ: Erlbaum.

Hoffman, L. M. (1992). *Continuing motivation in elementary school children: A naturalistic case study.* Unpublished doctoral dissertation, Ohio State University, Columbus.

Horner, M. S. (1968). *Sex differences in achievement motivation and performance in competitive and non-competitive situations.* Unpublished doctoral dissertation, University of Michigan, Ann Arbor.

Hughes, B., Sullivan, H. J., & Mosley, M. L. (1985). External evaluation, task difficulty, and continuing motivation. *Journal of Educational Research, 78,* 210–215.

Hull, C. L. (1943). *Principles of behavior: An introduction to behavior theory.* New York: Appleton-Century-Crofts.

Jagacinski, C., & Nicholls, J. (1984). Conceptions of ability and related affects in task involvement and ego involvement. *Journal of Educational Psychology, 76,* 909–919.

Jagacinski, C., & Nicholls, J. (1987). Competence and affect in task involvement and ego involvement: The impact of social comparison information. *Journal of Educational Psychology, 79,* 107–114.

Jussim, L. (1991). Social perception and social reality: A reflection-construction model. *Psychological Review, 98,* 54–73.

Krapp, A., Hidi, S., & Renninger, K. A. (1992). Interest, learning, and development. In K. A. Renninger, S. Hidi, & A. Krapp (Eds.), *The role of interest in learning and development* (pp. 3–25). Hillsdale, NJ: Erlbaum.

Lepper, M. R., Greene, D., & Nisbett, R. E. (1973). Undermining children's intrinsic interest with extrinsic reward: A test of the "overjustification" hypothesis. *Journal of Personality and Social Psychology, 28,* 129–137.

Lepper, M. R., & Hodell, M. (1989). Intrinsic motivation in the classroom. In C. Ames & R. Ames (Eds.), *Research on motivation in education* (Vol. 3, pp. 73–105). San Diego: Academic Press.

Lewin, K., Dembo, T., Festinger, L., & Sears, P. (1944). Level of aspiration. In J. M. Hunt (Ed.), *Personality and the behavioral disorders* (Vol. 1, pp. 333–378). New York: Ronald.

Locke, E. A., & Latham, G. P. (1990). *A theory of goal setting and task performance.* Englewood Cliffs, NJ: Prentice Hall.

Maehr, M. L. (1983). On doing well in science: Why Johnny no longer excels—why Sarah never did. In S. Paris (Ed.) *Learning and motivation in the classroom* (pp. 179–210). Hillsdale, NJ: Lawrence Erlbaum.

Maehr, M. L. (1976). Continuing motivation: An analysis of a seldom considered educational outcome. *Review of Educational Research, 46,* 443–462.

Maehr, M. L., & Midgley, C. (1991). Enhancing student motivation: A schoolwide approach. *Educational Psychologist, 26,* 399–427.

Maehr, M. L., & Midgley, C. (1996). *Transforming school cultures.* Boulder, CO: Westview Press.

Maehr, M. L., & Sjogren, D. (1971). Atkinson's theory of achievement motivation: First step toward a theory of academic motivation? *Review of Educational Research, 41,* 143–161.

Malone, T. W., & Lepper, M. R. (1987). Making learning fun: A taxonomy of intrinsic motivations from learning. In R. E. Snow & M. J. Farr (Eds.), *Aptitude, Learning, and Instruction: Vol 3: Cognitive and Affective Process Analysis* (pp. 223–253). Hillsdale, NJ: Lawrence Erlbaum.

Marshall, H., & Weinstein, R. S. (1984). Classroom factors affecting students' self-evaluations: An interactional model. *Review of Educational Research, 54,* 301–325.

McClelland, D. C. (1985). *Human motivation.* Chicago, IL: Scott Foresman.

McClelland, D. C., Koestner, R., & Weinberger, J. (1989). How do self-attributed and implicit motives differ? *Psychological Review, 96,* 690–702.

Meece, J. (1991). The classroom context and students' motivational goals. In M. L. Maehr & P. R. Pintrich (Eds.), *Advances in motivation and achievement* (Vol. 7, pp. 261–286). Greenwich, CT: JAI Press.

Meece, J. L., Blumenfeld, P., & Hoyle, R. (1988). Students' goal orientations and cognitive engagement in classroom activities. *Journal of Educational Psychology, 80,* 514–523.

Middleton, M., & Midgley, C. (1997). Avoiding the demonstration of lack of ability: An under-explored aspect of goal theory. *Journal of Educational Psychology, 89,* 710–718.

Morgan, M. (1984). Reward-induced decrements and increments in intrinsic motivation. *Review of Educational Research, 54,* 5–30.

Murphy, P. K., & Alexander, P. (2000). A motivated exploration of motivation terminology. *Contemporary Educational Psychology, 25,* 3–53.

Nicholls, J. (1984). Achievement motivation: Conceptions of ability, subjective experience, task choice, and performance. *Psychological Review, 91,* 328–346.

Nicholls, J. (1989). *The competitive ethos and democratic education.* Cambridge, MA: Harvard University Press.

Nicholls, J. (1990). What is ability and why are we mindful of it? A developmental perspective. In R. Sternberg & J. Kolligian (Eds.), *Competence considered* (pp. 11–40). New Haven: Yale University Press.

Nolen, S. B. (1988). Reasons for studying: Motivational orientations and study strategies. *Cognition and Instruction, 5,* 269–287.

Pascarella, E. T., Walberg, H. H., Junker, L. K., & Haertel, G. D. (1981) Continuing motivation in science for early and late adolescents. *American Educational Research Journal, 18,* 439–452.

Perry, R. P., & Penner, K. S. (1990). Enhancing academic achievement in college students through attributional retraining and instruction. *Journal of Educational Psychology, 82,* 262–271.

Pintrich, P. R. (1989). The dynamic interplay of student motivation and cognition in the college classroom. In C. Ames & M. L. Maehr (Eds.), *Advances in motivation and achievement: Motivation enhancing environments* (Vol. 6, pp. 117–160). Greenwich, CT: JAI Press.

Pintrich, P. R. (2000a). An achievement goal theory perspective on issues in motivation terminology, theory, and research. *Contemporary Educational Psychology, 25,* 92–104.

Pintrich, P. R. (2000b). Multiple goals, multiple pathways: The role of goal orientation in learning and achievement. *Journal of Educational Psychology, 92,* 544–555.

Pintrich, P. R. (2000c). The role of goal orientation in self-regulated learning. In M. Boekaerts, P. Pintrich, & M. Zeidner (Eds.), *Handbook of self-regulation* (pp. 451–502). San Diego, CA: Academic Press.

Pintrich, P. R., Cross, D. R., Kozma, R. B., & McKeachie, W. J. (1986). Instructional psychology. *Annual Review of Psychology, 37,* 611–651.

Pintrich, P. R., & De Groot, E. (1990). Motivational and self-regulated learning components of classroom academic performance. *Journal of Educational Psychology, 82,* 33–40.

Pintrich, P. R., & Garcia, T. (1991). Student goal orientation and self-regulation in the college classroom. In M. L. Maehr & P. R. Pintrich (Eds.), *Advances in motivation and achievement* (Vol. 7, pp. 371–402). Greenwich CT: JAI Press.

Pintrich, P. R., & Garcia, T. (1993). Motivation and self-regulation in the college classroom. *Zeitschrift für Pädagogische Psychologie, 7,* 99–107.

Pintrich, P. R., & Garcia, T. (1994). Self-regulated learning in college students: Knowledge, strategies, and motivation. In P. R. Pintrich, D. R. Brown, & C. E. Weinstein (Eds.), *Student motivation, cognition, and learning: Essays in honor of Wilbert J. McKeachie* (pp. 113–133). Hillsdale, NJ: Lawrence Erlbaum Associates.

Pintrich, P. R., & Schrauben, B. (1992). Students' motivational beliefs and their cognitive engagement in the classroom academic tasks. In D. Schunk & J. Meece (Eds.), *Student perceptions in the classroom* (pp. 149–183). Hillsdale, NJ: Lawrence Erlbaum Associates.

Pintrich, P. R., & Schunk, D. (2002). *Motivation in education: theory, research, and applications* (2nd ed.). Upper Saddle River, NJ: Prentice Hall.

Pintrich, P. R., Smith, D. A. F., Garcia, T., & McKeachie, W. J. (1993). Reliability and predictive validity of the Motivated Strategies for Learning Questionnaire (MSLQ). *Educational and Psychological Measurement, 53,* 801–813.

Rachlin, H. (1991). *Introduction to modern behaviorism.* New York: Freeman.

Renninger, K. A. (1990). Children's play interests, representation, and activity. In R. Fivush & J. Hudson (Eds.), *Knowing and remembering in young children* (pp. 127–165). Cambridge: Cambridge University Press.

Renninger, K. A. (1992). Individual interest and development: Implications for theory and practice. In K. A. Renninger, S. Hidi, & A. Krapp (Eds.), *The role of interest in learning and development* (pp. 361–395). Hillsdale, NJ: Erlbaum.

Renninger, K. A., Hidi, S., & Krapp, A. (Eds.). (1992). *The role of interest in learning and development.* Hillsdale, NJ: Erlbaum.

Renninger, K. A., & Wozniak, R. H. (1985). Effect of interest on attentional shift, recognition, and recall in young children. *Developmental Psychology, 21,* 624–632.

Rigby, C. S., Deci, E. L., Patrick, B. C., & Ryan, R. M. (1992). Beyond the intrinsic-extrinsic dichotomy: Self-determination in motivation and learning. *Motivation and Emotion, 16,* 165–185.

Rogers, C. R. (1969). *Freedom to learn.* Columbus, OH: Merrill.

Rosenholtz, S. J., & Simpson, C. (1984). The formation of ability conceptions: Developmental trend or social construction? *Review of Educational Research, 54,* 31–63.

Rosenthal, R., & Jacobson, L. (1968). *Pygmalion in the classroom.* New York: Holt, Rinehart, & Winston.

Rotter, J. (1966). Generalized expectancies for internal versus external control of reinforcement. *Psychological Monographs, 80,* 1–28.

Rubovits, P. C., & Maehr, M. L. (1971). Pygmalion analyzed: Toward an explanation of the Rosenthal-Jacobson findings. *Journal of Personality and Social Psychology, 19,* 197–203.

Rubovits, P. C., & Maehr, M. L. (1973). Pygmalion black and white. *Journal of Personality and Social Psychology, 25,* 210–218.

Ryan, R. M., Connell, J. P., & Deci, E. L. (1985). A motivational analysis of self-determination and self-regulation in education. In C. Ames & R. Ames (Eds.), *Research on motivation in education* (Vol. 2, pp. 13–51). New York: Academic Press.

Ryan, R. M., & Deci, E. L. (2000). Self-determination theory and the facilitation of intrinsic motivation, social development, and well-being. *American Psychologist, 55,* 68–78.

Salomon, G. (1984). Television is "easy" and print is "tough": The differential investment of mental effort in learning as a function of perceptions and attributions. *Journal of Educational Psychology, 76,* 647–658.

Sansone, C., & Harackiewicz, J. M. (Eds). (2000). *Intrinsic and extrinsic motivation: The search for optimal motivation and performance.* San Diego: Academic Press.

Schiefele, U. (1991). Interest, learning, and motivation. *Educational Psychologist, 26,* 299–323.

Schiefele, U., Krapp, A., & Winteler, A. (1992). Interest as a predictor of academic achievement: A meta-analysis of research. In K. A. Renninger, S. Hidi, & A. Krapp (Eds.), *The role of interest in learning and development* (pp. 183–212). Hillsdale, NJ: Erlbaum.

Schunk, D. H. (1982). Effects of effort attributional feedback on children's perceived self-efficacy and achievement. *Journal of Educational Psychology, 74,* 548–556.

Schunk, D. H. (1983a). Ability versus effort attributional feedback: Differential effects on self-efficacy and achievement. *Journal of Educational Psychology, 75,* 848–856.

Schunk, D. H. (1983b). Developing children's self-efficacy and skills: The roles of social comparative information and goal setting. *Contemporary Educational Psychology, 8,* 76–86.

Schunk, D. H. (1983c). Goal difficulty and attainment information: Effects on children's achievement behaviors. *Human Learning, 2,* 107–117.

Schunk, D. H. (1983d). Reward contingencies and the development of children's skills and self-efficacy. *Journal of Educational Psychology, 75,* 511–518.

Schunk, D. H. (1984). Sequential attributional feedback and children's achievement behaviors. *Journal of Educational Psychology, 76,* 1159–1169.

Schunk, D. H. (1987). Peer models and children's behavioral change. *Review of Educational Research, 57,* 149–174.

Schunk, D. H. (1989a). Self-efficacy and achievement behaviors. *Educational Psychology Review, 1,* 173–208.

Schunk, D. H. (1989b). Self-efficacy and cognitive skill learning. In C. Ames & R. Ames (Eds.), *Research on motivation in education* (Vol. 3, pp. 13–44). San Diego: Academic Press.

Schunk, D. H. (1991). Self-efficacy and academic motivation. *Educational Psychologist, 26,* 207–231.

Skinner, B. F. (1953). *Science and human behavior.* New York: Free Press.

Stipek, D., & Kowalski, P. (1989). Learned helplessness in task-orienting versus performance-orienting testing conditions. *Journal of Educational Psychology, 81,* 384–391.

Thorndike, E. L. (1913). *Educational psychology: Vol. 2. The psychology of learning.* New York: Teachers College Press.

Thorndike, E. L. (1932). *The fundamentals of learning.* New York: Teachers College Press.

Tobias, S. (1994). Interest, prior knowledge, and learning. *Review of Educational Research, 64,* 37–54.

Tolman, E. C. (1932). *Purposive behavior in animals and men.* New York: Appleton-Century-Crofts. (Reprinted in 1949, 1951, University of California Press, Berkeley.)

Tolman, E. C. (1949). There is more than one kind of learning. *Psychological Review, 56,* 144–155.

Urdan, T. C., & Maehr, M. L. (1995). Beyond a two-goal theory of motivation and achievement: A case for social goals. *Review of Educational Research, 65,* 213–243.

Vispoel, W. P., & Austin, J. R. (1993). Constructive response to failure in music: The role of attribution feedback and classroom goal structure. *British Journal of Educational Psychology, 63,* 110–129.

Weiner, B. (1985). An attributional theory of achievement motivation and emotion. *Psychological Review, 92,* 548–573.

Weiner, B. (1986). *An attributional theory of motivation and emotion.* New York: Springer-Verlag.

Weiner, B. (1992). *Human motivation: Metaphors, theories, and research.* Newbury Park, CA: Sage.

Weiner, B., Frieze, I., Kukla, A., Reed, L., Rest, S., & Rosenbaum, R. (1971). *Perceiving the causes of success and failure.* Morristown, NJ: General Learning Press.

Wentzel, K. (1991). Social and academic goals at school: Motivation and achievement in context. In M. L. Maehr & P. R. Pintrich (Eds.), *Advances in motivation and achievement: Goals and self-regulatory processes* (Vol. 7, pp. 185–212). Greenwich, CT: JAI Press.

Wigfield, A. (1994). Expectancy-value theory of achievement motivation: A developmental perspective. *Educational Psychology Review, 6,* 49–78.

Wigfield, A., & Eccles, J. (1992). The development of achievement task values: A theoretical analysis. *Developmental Review, 12,* 265–310.

Wigfield, A., Eccles, J. S., & Rodriguez, D. (1998). The development of children's motivation in school contexts. In P. D. Pearson & A. Iran-Nejad (Eds.), *Review of Research in Education* (Vol. 23, pp. 73–118). Washington, DC: American Educational Research Association.

Wigfield, A., Eccles, J. S., Yoon, K. S., Harold, R. D., Arbreton, A. J. A., Freedman-Doan, C., & Blumenfeld, P. C. (1997). Change in children's competence beliefs and subjective task values across the elementary school years: A 3-year study. *Journal of Educational Psychology, 89,* 451–469.

White, R. W. (1959). Motivation reconsidered: The concept of competence. *Psychological Review, 66,* 297–333.

Zeidner, M., Boekaerts, M., & Pintrich, P. R. (2000). Self-regulation: Directions and challenges for future research. In M. Boekaerts, P. R. Pintrich, & M. Zeidner (Eds.), *Handbook of self-regulation* (pp. 749–768). San Diego, CA: Academic Press.

Developmental Characteristics of Music Learners

22

MARIA RUNFOLA

KEITH SWANWICK

Although the title of this chapter differs from that by Hargreaves and Zimmerman (1992) in the first edition of this Handbook, we further develop their themes. As Hargreaves and Zimmerman warned us then, the scope of the topic remains enormous to date. We acknowledge this difficulty and our debt to the previous authors, who made an important contribution in clarifying some issues of musical development. They also have raised many more questions, which we address throughout this chapter. Although we shall take a somewhat different approach, there is a necessary continuity between their work and ours, and we shall refer to their work fairly frequently.

In this endeavor, the authors have been asked to focus on the quality of the research under review, adopting a critically selective stance. They also have been asked to deal substantially with work with which they have been closely associated, namely that of Gordon and Swanwick and Tillman. This inevitably affects the balance of the text and the reader should not therefore expect equal weight placed on each and every researcher.

As a preliminary, we note the gradual shift from the concept of inherited *talents,* for example, Seashore and Kwalwasser (Kwalwasser & Dykema, 1930; Seashore, 1938) and the related notion of musical *intelligence* (Wing, 1961), to the ideas of music *abilities* (Bentley, 1966) and *aptitude* (Gordon, 1997a). The research on specific musical abilities, such as aural discrimination, singing, or instrumental playing, has been summarized and discussed in a number of publications (Boyle, 1992; Deutsch, 1982; Shuter-Dyson & Gabriel, 1968). The basis for much of this research has been discrimination of isolated pitch and rhythm differences, or the ability to distinguish between other submusical sound materials, such as recognition of

the number of notes in a chord or judgments of intensity and timbre. Resisting what he called atomistic measures of this type, Wing (1961) sought to measure generic musical intelligence and to provide the "musical age" of a subject. Wing's work was weakened, however, by its narrowly idiomatic musical material, drawn from a small corner of the classical repertoire, which clearly favors someone versed in this music as performer or listener. Tests such as Wing's could not be applied in a contemporary multicultural community, and therefore cannot be viewed as measures of intelligence in the generic sense that Wing intended.

The tendency to separate and measure different musical functions continues, although tempered by more recent psychological theories. Radocy and Boyle gave a comprehensive overview of descriptive thought regarding development of discrete musical behaviors, and acknowledged the lack of normative data available on this topic (Radocy & Boyle, 1988). Recently, Brophy (2000) reviewed research, beginning with the work of Piaget, pertaining to the nature of cognitive musical growth in children. Brophy concluded that there were "general trends in the musical cognitive development of children ages three through eleven . . . and that the development of musical cognitive ability appears to be linear and favorably encouraged by musical experience" (p. 39). He summarized his conclusions in figure 22.1.

Brophy contended that most studies "support the idea that musical understanding unfolds gradually over time and is not acquired in 'stages.' The importance of sequenced musical experiences to learning music is underscored by these research findings, and new music curricula are reflecting these results" (Brophy, 2000, p. 40). The is-

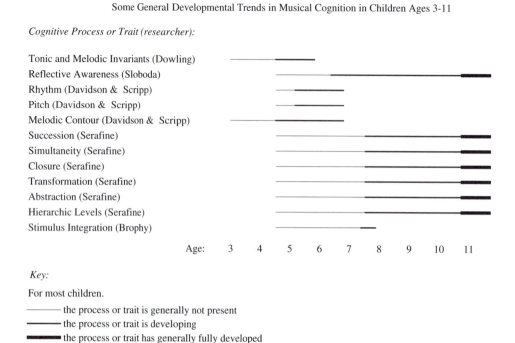

Figure 22.1. Some general developmental trends in musical cognition in children ages 3–11. Adapted from T. S. Brophy, *Assessing the Developing Child Musician*, 2000, Chicago: G.I.A. Publications. Used by permisssion.

sue of "stages" is certainly one that requires attention. To some the word suggests a somewhat rigid progression through a series of developmental benchmarks at specific ages. This we would wish to avoid. Indeed, some researchers (Haines & Gerber, 2000, p. 4; Gordon, 1997a, p. 9) have posited that such developmental profiles only provide useful parameters for teachers and that students may function developmentally at levels that vary from their chronological ages.

Brophy further maintained that "because music consists of melody, rhythm, harmony, timbre, and form, the development of understanding of each of these elements is acquired at different rates for individual students," and referred readers to *Music in Childhood* (Campbell & Scott-Kassner, 1995) for examples of developmental sequences for the elements of music. Although Campbell and Scott-Kassner (1995) summarized children's developmental stages for rhythm, melody, singing, attitudes, movement, instrumental technique, and creating music, they did not present a theory of development as such. Rather, they reviewed existing research to underscore the potential impact of a theoretical framework on music learning and "the link of teacher to the child/learner, as it relates teaching events to learning processes and demonstrated learning outcomes" (p. 16).

Some of this we regard as problematic. Although it may be helpful to be aware of how students handle the various aspects of music, attempts to show that specific musical abilities develop before or after others have been largely confounded by the absence of any theoretical frame of reference. While Hargreaves (1986) has asserted that the development of rhythmic skills are among the first to emerge (p. 61), and Bentley (1966) has argued that the ability to discriminate rhythm develops earlier than an ability to discriminate pitch and to perceive chords, their evidence is culled from dramatically varying instruments of measure. For instance, a measure of rhythm pattern discrimination, such as Bentley gives, cannot be compared with his quite separate measure based on counting the number of notes in chords. The tests are discrete and the results are calibrated differently. It is no more logical to compare the results of these tests than it would be to compare tire pressures on a car with the oil level. There is no connective theory. This problem occurs in Brophy (2000) when he writes of the understanding of musical elements developing at different rates (p. 40). There can be no baseline for comparing say, melodic with rhythmic development, unless we have a persuasive theory of musical development and understanding, a meta-theory that overarches specific measures of individual skills.

Similar problems exist with empirical studies of early musical development, which may produce lists of interesting observations but fall short of theoretical coherence. For example, the earliest musical experiences can be traced to the developing fetus in utero and is most likely provided by the mother's heartbeat. Thus, musical development can be said to begin some time before birth as the human brain and body begins to respond to sound. Some researchers have documented fetal awareness of the presence of music in his or her environment (Vaughn, 1996; Wilkin, 1996; Woodward, 1992), while others have documented infant ability to detect minute differences in melodic contour and rhythmic phrases (Chang & Trehub, 1977; Krumhansl & Jusczuk, 1990; Trehub, Bull, & Thorpe, 1984). Currently, researchers have become interested in the possibility that some forms of music instruction may increase the spatial-temporal reasoning abilities of preschool-aged children (Rauscher et al., 1997), rekindling an interest in the utilitarian or "instrumental" value of music education and in the concept of transfer.

Some researchers have observed the responses of preschool children to sound and music. An early worker in this field was Moog (1976). Although he may be criticized for an unsystematic analysis of data and for the small cultural locus within which his observations were made, his descriptive accounts of the responses and development of 50 children aged between 6 months and 5 1/2 years at each of 10 age levels are of interest.

Moog played the children tapes of children's songs, rhythmically spoken words, nonsense words, and rhythms on percussion instruments, instrumental music, and various nonmusical sounds, such as road traffic noise. He observed that somewhere between 3 and 6 months, babies begin to respond actively to the quality of sounds, and that, by the age of 1 year, children often move rhythmically to music. After the first year, when vocalization has begun, Moog observed a distinction between prespeech babbling and musical babbling, which seemed to involve exploration of pitch variation. During the second year, Moog noted an increase of physical movement in response to his recordings and, thereafter, he observed an increasingly strong relationship between music and play.

Following Moog, other researchers (Davidson, 1983; Dowling, 1982, 1984), seeking more systematically to observe the development of singing, have recorded the spontaneous musical utterances of young children and noted increasing control over melodic contours, interval size, and tonality through the early years. Several researchers have observed the intermingling of spontaneous singing and conventional songs, especially around the age of 3 and after (Hargreaves, 1986, pp. 71–74). While the ideas elucidated by these works are useful, the research generally lacks a robust theoretical frame within which to locate these specific and limited developments. Following Hargreaves and Zimmerman, we shall therefore focus on the relative strengths of major musical development theories and on their implications for our understanding of development and music education.

Theories of Development and Musical Development

Drawing on general theories in developmental psychology (Hargreaves & Zimmerman, 1992), we have identified four specific criteria for evaluating developmental theories in general and for music in particular. Since the concept of development is related to observable change of some kind, we contend that there are a number of criteria that help in the evaluation of work in the field of musical development. These are as follows:

1. Any theories and associated evidence should comprehensively reflect the nature of musical behavior.
2. Theories and underlying assumptions should be valid across a range of musical activities or "modalities": composing (including improvisation), performing, and audience-listening.
3. Evidence should be systematically and reliably produced to support or challenge theoretical assertions.
4. Developmental theories should take into account both the natural developmental inclinations of individuals and the cultural environment in which their development is realized.

Stating this last criterion opens up a crucial issue, which now has to be addressed. There is an old debate about the relative emphasis on what used to be called "nature" or "nurture." Traces of the developmental theory of Rousseau with its implication of maturational unfolding and "ripeness" can be found in Gesell, Freud, Erikson, and Piaget. Alternatively, from the "tabula rasa" of Locke through the behaviorism of Pavlov, Watson, and Skinner, to the social-learning theories of Bandura and Vygotsky, researchers have emphasized the environmental and social shaping of development. Of course, no major maturational theorist has denied the crucial developmental role of environment and no environmentalist discounts the predisposition of a person or other organism to respond to physical or cultural conditions. For example, Piaget never suggested that children could learn in a cultural vacuum. Rather, in his own work, he was not particularly concerned to investigate what educational strategies or social conditions might speed up development and he saw no problem with the idea that each child might have his or her own optimal rate for transition when moving on into various stages.

Vygotsky is often seen as challenging the Piagetian view of development as an "unfolding" of an organism without reference to cultural and physical environment (Hargreaves & Zimmerman, 1992). But there are also strong similarities between Piaget and Vygotsky. The latter saw development as a spiral and thought that children passed through the same point at each new revolution while advancing to a higher level (Vygotsky, 1978, p. 56). Vygotsky, like Piaget, viewed development as a complex dialectical process embodying qualitative transformations. What distinguishes Vygotsky's work from Piaget's is his concern with what he calls "the zone of proximal development," the space between the level of independent problem solving and the level of potential achievement with adult guidance or in interaction with able peers, that is, with the social process. This theory is not a denial of maturation; rather, it extends the range of the theoretical spotlight to cover a certain type of educational transaction.

Another consideration for researchers is the distinction between "quantitative" and "qualitative" changes in the development of children's minds. Although change can be quantitative in the sense that children become more skilled in performing particular tasks, developmental change is usually located within a qualitative frame. According to Bruner's (1973) theory of representational systems, early childhood is characterized by what he called the enactive mode of representation, which is essentially sensory-motor. Put simply, we think with what we are doing. Iconic representation advances on this dependency on actual objects and involves the ability to bring absent objects or events to mind, a qualitative shift. Bruner's third representational mode is that of the symbolic, where flexible combinations of symbols enable an element of freedom in conceptual relationships and permit novel combinations and abstract thought. Bruner echoes Piaget's proposal of qualitative changes in children's development; however, Piaget did not extend this idea to accept that earlier ways of thinking may have their own virtue. According to Crain (1992), Piaget overlooked the possibility that earlier modes of representation may be better adapted to artistic expression, a point supported by Gardner. The implication of this omission could be that artistic work is somehow conceptually regressive, or is at least less intellectually developed than some other forms of "intelligence." In contrast, Gardner posits some kind of equivalence among the "multiple intelligences" (1973).

Like both Piaget and Vygotsky, Koopman (1995) conceived of developmental change as fundamentally qualitative in nature. According to Koopman, if there are qualitative differences in a developmental process, there is always an implication of two or more stages. Koopman argues that development involves a process of change over a period of time in which two or more stages can be observed, each being a precondition for the following stage.

According to Crain, developmental stage theorists, such as Piaget, Erikson, and Kohlberg, took the view that a theory of cognitive stages should meet five quite stringent criteria (Crain, 1992, p. 264).

1. Stages imply qualitatively differentiated patterns of behavior.

2. Stage descriptions deal with general issues rather than specific achievements. (This is very similar to the second criterion above referring to general validity across different activities or modalities.)
3. Stages unfold in an invariant sequence.
4. Stages are cultural universals. (This may be thought highly problematic. We might, however, expect a good theory to have explanatory power beyond a single cultural group, although "widespread" might be a better word than "universal.")
5. Stages are hierarchic, in that early structures are integrated into later ones.

Although some theories do not meet all of these criteria or resist the very idea of stages, we do expect to find patterns, for example, of linguistic or sensory-motor development in growing children. These expectations do not violate respect for individual or cultural differences, for the concept of a stage is not so fixed as to leave no possibility for unique interpretation, cultural difference, or variation. Nor are stages rigidly linked with ages, although there may be strong connections. We shall therefore accept the criteria above as a guide to evaluating existing theories of musical development.

Thus, we wish to see how far the theories under review meet not only our general criteria but also how they match these specific developmental stage criteria. If a theory of cognition claims to address qualitative difference, how much more so should a theory of an art such as music? And where a theory does not deal with general issues but is developed around specific and limited musical skills, to what extent is it then possible to find explicit theoretical connections with other modalities? Can such a theory be applied beyond the isolated skill? The idea of an invariant sequence suggests that we would expect to find some predictive power in any theory of musical development. We ought to be able to determine the next possible development, a step surely important for music educators. A serviceable developmental model should demonstrate some continuity of musical development and this may well imply a hierarchical integration of newly evolving stages. Even if a researcher believes that developmental theories ought to be specific to cultural settings, a robust theory should at least be capable of mapping musical development across a range of musical and cultural settings. Furthermore, in the special case of music, we might suppose that a valid developmental theory reflects the essential nature of musical activity.

In summary, then, we shall consider the extent to which theories of musical development match the following. They should: have musical validity, have relevance across different musical activities, take account of both maturation and cultural setting, identify qualitative, sequential and hierarchical changes, have widespread cultural application, and be supported by systematically gathered data. These criteria have informed our selection from the literature and to a large extent determined where the spotlight of review is placed.

We begin with Serafine, who offers a direct challenge to traditional psychological models and whose approach is concerned with underlying cognitive processes. We then consider symbol system issues that characterize the work of Gardner and colleagues at Project Zero and to some extent the work of Bamberger before discussing the related issue of musical "concepts." Finally, we discuss in some detail the contribution of Gordon, much of which is psychometric in character, and that of Swanwick, which is to some extent Piagetian, although it does not assume the usual cognitive framework.

Serafine and Generic Processes

In her book *Music as Cognition,* Mary Louise Serafine set out to counter what she sees as reductionist work in the psychology-of-music and musical development (1988, pp. 6–7). Serafine was unimpressed by the earlier fascination for codifying music research into measurable parameters, such as time, timbre, pitch, and loudness. Serafine categorized entities such as tones and chords per se as sound materials rather than elements. For Serafine, isolated pitches and scales and chords are not musical entities but analytical devices, the product of thinking about music rather than thinking in music. This is a helpful distinction made some time ago by Susanne Langer and articulated by many others, including Swanwick (1979, pp. 8–10). There is a conceptual relationship between Serafine's "coherent" musical units, which are heard moving in time, and Swanwick's expressive "gestures" or "character," in which sound materials are transformed into musical entities and "tones" are heard as "tunes" (Swanwick, 1999). This paradigm appears also to underlie Gordon's pedagogical focus on vocabulary building within the context of music. It also reflects Gordon's using whole-part-whole sequences, wherein a whole piece of music is presented through listening or singing, followed by work on patterns to develop tonal and rhythm vocabulary, then back to recognizing, improvising with, and performing the patterns learned within the context of the whole piece of music (Gordon, 1997b).

Reflecting this perspective, Serafine (1980) argued that sound materials are premusical, or submusical, and that since they are not construed into musical meaning, the perception and labeling of these materials falls short of musical interpretation. Serafine has been strongly critical of atomistic attempts to measure the perception of changes in these materials, and she has put forward what she claims to be an overarching theory of core cognitive processes. Her project attempted to identify pan-stylistic, generic processes and at the greatest level of generalizability she de-fined music as "thinking in or with sound." A fundamental question informing her work is "what is the nature and source of musical thought?" (Serafine, 1980, p. 1).

In developing the thesis that music is a form of thought, Serafine made several related claims. One is that musical transactions are not to be seen as a linear transaction between composers, performers, and listeners but as connective transactions between any of these and a piece of music. Serafine therefore proposed an explicit theory of mind, or to be more precise, of musical mind. However, she did concede that cognitive processes may be either style-specific or generic; that is to say, while certain musical processes are thought to be universal or widespread, there are others that are identified with idiomatic practices. It is with the last of these that Serafine was concerned.

Serafine established a generic set of cognitive processes, which she viewed as underlying all musical production and musical perception (although for perception we should perhaps substitute musical "conception"). Serafine thus attempted to present a meta-psychological model that stood outside of specific and different musical activities or modalities. The main characteristic of this universal cognitive activity is awareness of movement in time (Serafine, 1980, p. 69). Tones are not heard in isolation nor as pairs of stimuli to be identified or discriminated but are sensory experiences from which the listener constructs musical properties. This constructive temporal process takes place in two ways, first as succession, where basic coherent units are conceived ("idiomatic construction"). These musically meaningful units are transformed into longer configurations through processes of motivic chaining, by patterning through repetition and alternation and by the boundaries between phrase groupings. Second is the dimension of *simultaneity,* when two or more meaningful sound events or units are heard as superimposed, combined into a new integral whole. Finally, Serafine identified four nontemporal processes. These are: closure, stability, or resolution; transformation, similarity, and difference in the same event, for example, in changes of mode, tempo, or ornamentation; abstraction, the relocation of events in a new place, perhaps over a long time period; and hierarchic levels, awareness of the overall formal structure of a piece.

Leaving aside the obvious problem of nomenclature, in that all of these processes are really in some sense "temporal," Serafine's theory meets at least some of the criteria for music developmental theories. First, it claims to comprehensively reflect the essential nature of musical activity. Serafine established a generic meta-theory overlaying different specific musical activities, in this way meeting the criterion of validity across different modalities. However, her empirical work has only been in the audience-listener mode: The children involved are basically doing "tests." The criterion of systematically acquired and reliable evidence is by no means clearly met. It also should be noted that the relationship between Serafine's theory and her observational method is not particularly clear. Several tests were given to children including pitch discrimination, Piagetian number conservation and several tasks requiring "correct" answers to questions involving recognition of relationships between small musical items. For example, the "motivic chaining" task asked whether or not a longer phrase is made up of previously heard smaller phrases. It also seems clear that the influence of cultural (including an educational) environment is not a variable for consideration. Musical development from her standpoint is predominantly ontogenetic in emphasis.

Whether Serafine's theory is able to map musical development across a range of musical and cultural settings is therefore also problematic, although this might be said of many candidates for a theory of musical development. For example, we might notice her reference to "pieces" of music rather than "performances" of music. There is here an implication of certain Western traditions involving the presentation of notated compositions. This may be a limiting aspect of her theory, insofar as many types of musical production relying solely on aural transmission could be excluded. There is no evidence to support the stage theory criterion of observability in different cultural settings.

Serafine did not deal systematically with age-related changes. She implies the existence of qualitatively differentiated developmental layers but there is little systematically gathered evidence for this. Replication and extension of Serafine's empirical observations would be required in order to give sufficient confidence that the criterion of methodological reliability was convincingly met.

Symbol System Theories and Musical Concepts

Project Zero.   The work of Howard Gardner and others remind us that Project Zero has had a considerable impact on arts educators. Gardner's theory of multiple intelligences has done much to give teachers working in these curriculum areas a sense that their activity is important and that the arts are intelligent activities.

Gardner's theory focused on the concept of symbol systems, which he defined as follows: "Symbolization requires appreciation of an object and the capacity to link the object known to a picture, label, or other kind of element that denotes it" (Gardner, 1973, p. 90).

For Gardner, music and the other arts are distinctive modes of symbolic communication. In the case of music, he presumed a relationship between musical patterns and the affective life of the individual, stressing the importance of both ontogenetic and phylogenetic elements:

It appears that the child has various predispositions to handle stimuli in a certain way, but that only gradually are these predispositions modified by the environment and related to other predispositions. (1973, p. 40)

Gardner's concept of multiple intelligences was really an elaboration of the idea of multiple symbolic forms, an older formulation familiar to readers of Langer and others. According to this view, music is a unique symbolic form in the medium of sound, and young children are as able to appreciate these qualities as are adults. Symbol use is seen as central to children's artistic development.

As members of the Project Zero team, Davidson and Scripp also focused on children's use of symbols; however, they extended their argument to conclude that the development of children could be studied through a visual symbolic medium. Davidson and Scripp asked children between 5 and 7 years of age to write down a familiar song so that other children would recognize it. From these data, Davidson and Scripp identified a range of notations from simple marking to approximations of Western staff notation. These data were to some extent age-related. Davidson and Scripp also compared children and adults with or without musical training. They concluded that the use of conventional notation is an indicator of higher levels of music development, surely a problematic assertion in view of the aural/oral basis of much of the world's music. They also are quite prescriptive:

When literacy skills are not developed alongside technical instrumental training, the result is a fragmented knowledge of music and ultimate disintegration of skills. When literacy skills fail to develop, students compensate for the lack of integration in their training by substituting "what they know about music" for what they hear. (Davidson & Scripp, 1989, p. 77)

According to Davidson and Scripp, the interaction of motor and literacy skills enables

the student to link performance, concept and percept. Reflective thinking appears as an important dimension of musical development that arises from the more enactive stages where skills are first manifest, and are later linked to the symbolic literacy skills of the musical culture. The most effective levels of a music education must encompass this perspective. (1989, p. 80)

In their essay "Surveying the Coordinates of Cognitive Skills in Music," Davidson and Scripp (1992) linked musical production directly with the making of musical scores (p. 396). They then annexed the concept of symbols to focus on visual notations. In this respect, they departed from Gardner, who argued that the sounding forms of music define musical intelligence. Gardner identified as savants those who have marked musical performance and aural abilities independent of notational ability. While the savants that Gardner described do not use music notations, they did engage in a symbolic form at a fairly high level. It is therefore questionable whether the study of visual representations of music can, by itself, comprehensively inform us about children's musical development. In terms of our other criteria, it is also problematic as to whether this procedure would hold for non-Western cultures, or indeed for Western people with musical backgrounds when the emphasis is strongly aural/oral, such as pop and rock music. Thus, these studies appear to be strongly biased toward musical traditions involving staff notation, arguing that the closer a student's notations resemble staff conventions, the more musically developed the student may be. As we have seen with Gardner's savants, this is not necessarily so.

According to our research, musical development per se does not depend on translating musical images into notations or words; to argue that would shift the methodological focus from musical development to notational or linguistic development, different domains. Following Gardner and Davidson and Scripp's theories, any development taking place might be explained within the domain of notational representation rather than music. Studies of symbol systems by themselves offer no way of distinguishing these variables.

Despite these theoretical shortcomings, a number of music development researchers have placed significant weight on the analysis of notations (Adachi & Bradshaw, 1995; Bamberger, 1982, 1994; Barrett, 1997; Christensen, 1992; Cohen, 1985; Davidson & Scripp, 1989, 1992; Gromko & Poorman, 1998; Upitis, 1990). This approach was justified in a study by Barrett, who claimed that invented notations of musical experience may be viewed "as indicators of musical thinking" (1999, p. 71). Barrett asserted that the notations children use "to symbolize their experience of the world is representative of their thinking about the world." However, we would argue that music itself is an activity that is in some way representative of our experience of the world; that this is in fact a primary symbolic system. Notations, verbal descriptions, or graphic representations are secondary systems, offering a kind of translation from the original representational domain. In this process, some loss of information is inevitable.

In terms of our criteria for a strong developmental theory, this kind of work does not comprehensively reflect the nature of musical activities and behavior, does not appear valid across a range of musical activities or "modalities," and does not address the relationship between the natural developmental inclinations of individuals and their cultural environment. When evaluated by the stringent criteria of stage theory, the development of notations is not necessarily qualitatively differentiated; rather, it is quantitative, more of the same at a greater level of detail. It is also questionable as to whether the developmental descriptions of Davidson and Scripp effectively address general issues, rather than specific achievements. Finally, there appear to be insufficient data to determine whether there is an invariant developmental sequence or whether these stages can be generalized to non-Western cultures.

Bamberger's Theory of Developmental Cumulation.

Jeanne Bamberger also has studied musical development, focusing on the relationship between children's notations and musical performance, specifically playing Montessori bells. From her observations, she concluded that children's musical development is "multiple" and "cumulative."

> I argue that the changing mental organizing structures that guide hearings, constructions, and descriptions at various ages and stages of musical development do not constitute a unidirectional progression in which earlier mental structures are replaced by later ones. Rather, foci of attention among relevant aspects of musical structure shift but also cumulatively build on one another. I conclude that the goal of musical development is to have access to multiple dimensions of musical structure, to be able to choose selectively among them, to change focus at will. (Bamberger, 1991, pp. 3–4)

Bamberger found that "the use of notations helped to 'shape their users' internalized, active organizing constraints'" (1991, p. 15). She argued that musical symbols (notations) help children's musical understanding in a cognitive process, involving several levels, which she referred to as "multiple hearings." According to Bamberger, as students increase their capacity to make multiple hearings, their musical skills become more developed (1991, p. 124).

Bamberger's systematic methodology explored the relationship between visual apparatus and children's musical development, but it did not involve children experiencing or learning music in other ways. As part of a laboratory procedure, her observations were based on normative values, correct answers in the performance of simple melodies. Bamberger's theories and associated evidence do not comprehensively reflect the nature of musical activities and behavior and are not valid across a range of musical activities or "modalities" such as composing (including improvising), performing, and audience-listening. Furthermore, Bamberger did not consider the interaction between the natural developmental inclinations of individuals and of the cultural environment in which children's musical development is realized.

A close reading of Bamberger's theory of developmental cumulation suggests that there may be stages with qualitatively differentiated patterns of behavior, although Bamberger stressed the interchangeability of "levels" rather than an invariant sequence. While Bamberger did not produce evidence for cultural universality, she has suggested in her work that there may be hierarchical stages in which early structures are integrated into later ones.

Concepts and Conservation.   As we have seen, much of the thinking of the Cambridge (MA) researchers closely identified musical with notations of one kind or another. There is also a related assumption about the cognitive nature of musical development and especially the idea of musical "concepts," which is shared by many who approach music from the cognitive psychological angle. Under the heading concepts and schemata in music, Hargreaves and Zimmerman discussed the influence of Piaget on the psychology of music. From multiple encounters with music, we develop musical concepts that enable us to make comparisons and discriminations, to organize sounds, to generalize, and, finally, to apply the emerging concepts to new musical situations (Hargreaves & Zimmerman, 1992, p. 385).

Hargreaves and Zimmerman distinguished concepts and higher levels of generalization from mental images. Bruner also made this distinction in terms of iconic and symbolic modes of representation, as did Piaget through his notion of internalized mental actions and formal operations. Hargreaves and Zimmerman, however, asserted that conceptual labeling, categorizing, and organizing musical "perceptions" provides "the key for later study and enjoyment of the complexities of music." Musical development thus proceeds from sensory-motor schemata through representation in musical images to "the ability to handle an increasing number of concepts" (Hargreaves & Zimmerman, 1992, p. 386).

Hargreaves and Zimmerman reviewed several studies influenced by Piagetian theory, focusing on musical conservation. Much of the work of Zimmerman and Sechrest has been influenced by Piaget's conservation laws, which were seen to lead to stable operational thinking. In subsequent studies, Hargreaves affirmed that there may be developmental sequences of this type. For example, within the area of rhythmic concepts, Hargreaves observed that there is a progression from beat to pattern to meter. However, it may be that teachers attempt to teach "beat," "pattern," and "meter" in that order, rather than this being a natural development. It seems unlikely that even very young children are unresponsive to different patterns or meters, although to actually describe metric change is certainly more advanced in linguistic terms. However, as noted above, verbal or other forms of conceptual analysis may screen out important musical understanding. Is "swing," for example, a musical concept? It is temptingly easy to replace the study of whole musical behaviors with fragmentary aural tests or the study of evolving isolated musical "concepts." Likewise, researchers should avoid the pitfalls of relying too heavily on conservation, which appears to be a somewhat narrow approach to musical development and, like analysis of notations, may constrict our concept of musical understanding.

In order to gain a broader view, we look to generic psychological characteristics of symbol systems, identified by Piaget as he plotted development from sensory-motor to conceptual intelligence (Piaget, 1951, pp. 238–239). His account is a useful description of what a symbol system includes, whether scientific, mathematical, or artistic. In essence, the onset of internally represented actions allows the generation of relationships between these representations (concrete operations). Through socially shared systems of signs we can communicate with others:

> These interweaving elements characterize thought and production in the arts just as they do in philosophic deliberation, scientific reasoning, or mathematical thinking. Whether painting a picture, improvising music, dancing or refining a poem we translate experience into particular images, bringing these images into new relationships and articulating our thinking within systems of signs. (Swanwick, 1999, p. 8)

These elements may work together to establish a generic concept of musical intelligence. In order to understand what counts as musical development, it seems best to attend not only to sensory discrimination, or look for evidence only in words or notations, or to give normative tests. A very rich source of evidence for language development is to observe children actually using language to generate meaning. If music also is a symbol system, then similar possibilities should exist for exploring musical development. As we have discussed, studying notations and test results may be helpful in developing and to some extent revealing musical cognition, but they do not in themselves lie within the sonorous, symbolic mode of music. Researchers who rely on secondary forms of representation may overlook important features of musical development. Observing actual musical production is likely to be more informative.

Two scholars have developed theories based on such observations of music making by children. Edwin Gordon (1997a) has observed students in instructional contexts and described a possible model for how we learn when we learn music. Keith Swanwick and June Tillman (1986), by contrast, have identified a "spiral" of musical development drawn from observations in educational settings where students are encouraged to explore rather than reproduce music.

Edwin Gordon's Music Learning Theory

Throughout his work, Edwin Gordon provides an analysis of the process through which people of all ages learn music. Gordon's focus is on the concept of audiation, which he defines as the ability to hear and comprehend in the mind, the sound of music that is no longer or may never have been physically present (1976a).

Gordon's initial description of how we learn music was first reported in the monograph *How Children Learn*

When They Learn Music (Gordon, 1967b). In 1971, he presented a more detailed account of the process. Aligned with Gagne's eight general types of learning, the first four types were grouped under the heading of "perception" (in subsequent publications called discrimination) and the final four types were grouped under the heading "conceptualization" (subsequently called inference) (1971a, p. 90). Through interactive classroom observations, Gordon found that the adaptation of Gagne's types of learning was less applicable to music, having more exceptions than agreement with what Gordon observed. As his work progressed, Gordon moved away from the Gagne-based model to a learning sequence grounded in musical skills, that is, the developed or acquired abilities to listen to and perform music (vocally, or kinesthetically, or instrumentally) through audiation. In 1984, he proposed a music learning theory and later defined it as "the analysis and synthesis of the sequential manner in which we learn when we learn music" (1987, p. 19). This theory continues to inform his work and the work of others.

Gordon's theory is one of learning and not teaching. Gordon believes that understanding process provides a theoretical framework on which teachers can plan effective music instruction, explaining what students need to know at a particular level of learning in order to proceed to a more advanced level. Practice relating to the theory is designed to encourage students to audiate, which ideally we begin to do at about 5 years of age (Gordon, 1997c). There are three types and seven stages of preparatory audiation followed by eight types and six stages of audiation. In addition, there are eight levels of skill in two generic categories: discrimination and inference. And there are two separate content learning sequences: tonal and rhythm.

Influenced by the writings of others such as Mainwaring (1933), Ortmann (1937), Bean (1939), Van Nuys and Weaver (1943), and, to a great extent, Smith (1971), Gordon concluded that music, albeit not a language but a literature, is learned in much the same way that we learn language. Taggart and Gouzouasis (1995) presented a description of the language-music acquisition metaphor.

Gordon identified four "vocabularies" of music in hierarchical order—listening, speaking, reading, and writing—and maintained that an individual's musical aptitudes, nurtured by appropriate guidance and instruction, determine the extent to which these vocabularies are acquired. For example, if a student has high tonal aptitude, there is a better chance of developing a high tonal vocabulary. If the same student has a low or average rhythm aptitude, then it follows that the development of the rhythm vocabulary will be low or average. Gordon asserts that unless a good musical environment continually nourishes the level of music aptitude with which a child is born, the child's music aptitude will decrease and, for all intents and purposes, may be lost. Moreover, unless this innate potential is nourished before age 9 (and the sooner the better), environmental influences will no longer affect the innate potential. There are then implications for providing an appropriate musical environment at the earliest possible age.

A basic tenet of music learning theory is interactive music making, dialectic between student and teacher as they engage in a musical language. The use of songs without words offers students musical sound material without the distraction of words that might be more familiar than the musical sounds. The variety of tonalities and meters provides a rich vocabulary with which they may create dialogue and also prepares students for listening to various styles of music. Moreover, the encouragement of natural sounds, that is, music babble, in acculturation provides a basis for natural dialogue, improvisation, and creativity. Through these activities the developmental sequence is activated, beginning with preparatory audiation.

Preparatory Audiation.   Gordon has identified three stages of preparatory audiation: acculturation, imitation, and assimilation. Acculturation begins with an initial stage of absorption, in which children are aware of sounds, and become active participants. This activity consists largely of random responses and any movement and babbling appear to have no relation to the musical sounds the children hear. In the last stage of acculturation, the children relate their movement, breathing, and babble to the music they hear. The second type of preparatory audiation is imitation, wherein a child begins to shed egocentricity by realizing that his or her musical sounds do not match the sounds heard in their musical environment. Next, tonal patterns and rhythm patterns are imitated with some precision. Assimilation then occurs as young children recognize their lack of coordination when singing, chanting, and moving and they begin to perform patterns with greater precision, the final stage of preparatory audiation. Following this stage, young children are prepared for audiation and formal music instruction. They are then able to participate in music activities with an objective sense of tonality and meter.

Hicks (1992) conducted exploratory research to record the responses of young children to music stimuli in order to validate the stages of acculturation. Eight children, in randomly assigned intact classes, were videotaped while receiving music lessons of chanting and singing without texts, and movement activities. The responses, documented by three independent judges, were categorized as looking, nonpulsating, pulsating, miscellaneous, vocal, and anticipatory. Hicks drew several conclusions that generally upheld the stages of acculturation as theorized by Gordon. Moreover, she observed that young children began to make purposeful movement responses to music before they began to make purposeful vocal responses.

Audiation. Almost 10 years after coining the word audiation, Gordon conducted a study "to substantiate objectively the stages of audiation, to determine whether the stages of audiation are common to both tonal audiation and rhythm audiation, and to determine the extent of the relationships among audiation skills and music aptitudes" (1985, p. 37). Twenty-seven kindergarten children served as subjects for the study. Gordon reasoned that the conditioned musical responses of older children and adults would not yield precise information to the extent that might be found by analyzing the natural musical responses of young children. The subjects received instruction in tonal patterns and rhythm patterns by a music specialist 4 days a week and dance by a movement specialist 1 day a week. After a semester's instruction, Gordon measured their aptitude with the *Primary Measures of Music Audiation* (PMMA) and recorded their individual vocal performances of tonal patterns and rhythm patterns. Gordon adjudicated the taped performances using two additive rating scales. Reliability for PMMA and the performance evaluations ranged from .78 to .92 and were considered high enough to provide objective information. Based on a series of intercorrelations and correlations among the parts of the rating scales and also the PMMA subtests and composite scores, Gordon concluded that stages of audiation existed and noted similarities in the processes of tonal audiation and rhythm audiation. Furthermore, he identified interrelationships among the abilities of 5-year-old children to audiate, to perform rhythmically, and their level of developmental rhythm aptitude. However, despite the relationship between 5-year-old children's ability to audiate tonally and their level of developmental tonal aptitude, there was no relationship between the level of developmental tonal aptitude and the tonal performances of 5-year-olds (1985, pp. 49–50).

Taggart (1989) validated the overall hierarchy of the stages of tonal audiation, but noted some exceptions to Gordon's earlier findings that processes of tonal audiation and rhythm audiation are nearly the same (Gordon, 1985).

Learning Sequences: Skills and Content. In Gordon's model, informal guidance through the types and stages of preparatory audiation is followed by formal instruction through application of three interdependent sequences of music learning: skills, tonal content, and rhythm content. Supporters claim the theory is solid and "based on available evidence from research in the psychology of music and related disciplines" (Holahan, 1986, p. 153). Critics argue that supportive research is minimal (Colwell, 1991). Cutietta (1991) noted that some negative criticism of Gordon's work may be the result of Gordon inspiring his students to test different aspects of his theories through their own research (p. 76).

Much of Gordon's early work involved classically designed studies directed toward the nature, description, measurement, and evaluation of music aptitude. Thus music aptitude was of prime importance to his research agenda and that of his students (Fosha, 1964; Foss, 1972; Rainbow, 1963; Schleuter, 1971, 1991; Tarrell, 1964; Thayer, 1971; Volger, 1973; Walters, 1991; Young, 1969). Gordon continues to develop tests, and perhaps his most rigorous research is in test development (Gordon, 1965, 1967a, 1967c, 1969, 1970; 1971a, 1971b, 1975, 1979, 1986a, 1986b, 1986c, 1986d, 1988, 1989, 1990, 1997c, 1998). A number of researchers investigated developmental music aptitude (Bell, 1981; Holahan, 1983; Kane, 1994; Woodruff, 1983), while others continued the study of stabilized aptitude (Bolton, 1995; Geissel, 1985). These classically designed studies, along with observational research, some in the form of participant observation and others as interactive field participation, enabled researchers to study and promote the learning process and provided objective indirect evidence on which the skills learning sequence is based.

For example, the research of Dittemore (1968), De-Yarman (1971), Miller (1972), and MacKnight (1975) "indirectly corroborate the importance of developing an oral vocabulary of tonal patterns and rhythm patterns (especially as opposed to learning theoretical tonal and rhythmic functions of individual notes) prior to reading notation" (Gordon, 1976a, p. 3).

The skills sequence is shown in figure 22.2. There are two generic levels of learning: Discrimination Learning, based on and including perception (Gordon, 1976a, p. 8), in which persons learn by rote; and Inference Learning, in which persons use in unfamiliar order or apply to unfamiliar material what has been learned by rote at the discrimination level. The levels and sublevels of learning are listed separately, beginning with the most elementary levels. However, after each level or sublevel of learning is achieved, it becomes a part of and interacts with the next higher level or sublevel in the skill sequence.

Gordon has become increasingly immersed in observation of and experimentation with young children in an effort to gain further insight into the process of music learning. His doctoral students have continued to study in the more classical tradition questions relevant to the validation of music learning theory. Many of these studies did not yield significant results; those that did confirmed the sequencing for students with low music aptitude. Such findings, and the belief that music aptitude interacts with appropriate sequencing of instruction, encouraged Gordon's reasoning that certain types of sequencing are better for students with below-average music aptitude, while other types of sequencing might be better for students with av-

Levels and Sublevels of Skill Learning Sequence

DISCRIMINATION

AURAL/ORAL

VERBAL ASSOCIATION

PARTIAL SYNTHESIS

SYMBOLIC ASSOCIATION
Reading—Writing

COMPOSITE SYNTHESIS
Reading—Writing

INFERENCE

GENERALIZATION
Aural/Oral—Verbal—Symbolic
Reading—Writing

CREATIVITY/IMPROVISATION
Aural/Oral—Symbolic
Reading—Writing

THEORETICAL UNDERSTANDING
Aural/Oral—Verbal—Symbolic
Reading—Writing

Figure 22.2. Levels and sublevels of the skill learning sequence. Adapted from E. E. Gordon, *Learning Sequences in Music: Skill, Content, and Patterns—A Music Learning Theory,* 1997, Chicago: G.I.A. Publications. Reprinted with permission.

erage, or above-average, music aptitude (Gordon, 1991b, p. 50)

Belmondo (1986) gathered objective information about partial synthesis as a readiness for music reading. The specific problems of his study were to determine (1) the comparative effects of two methods of tonal instruction on high school students' music reading achievement and (2) the effects of music aptitude level on the two methods. After rote learning major and minor tonal patterns with and without solmization, 34 high school choral students were randomly assigned to either the experimental or control group. The experimental group received partial synthesis instruction, while the control group continued instruction with traditional choral activities. A 5-point rating scale was used to evaluate students' performances on the criterion measures, made up of familiar and unfamiliar major and minor patterns. Belmondo concluded that partial synthesis instruction serves as an effective readiness for tonal music reading and sight-reading in major and minor tonalities for low-aptitude students.

Several comparative studies have been completed with the following conclusions: Laban-based movement instruction has a positive effect on rhythm achievement of high school students (Jordan, 1986) and on developmental

rhythm aptitude of elementary children with low aptitude (Cernohorsky, 1991); any type of movement instruction is beneficial for the musical development of preschool children generally (Blesedell, 1991) but, because they respond to music and movement stimuli first through visual and aural absorption, caregivers should provide the best movement and chanting models possible (Reynolds, 1995). College students who are taught to perform and identify rhythm patterns in various meters were found to reach a higher level of rhythmic achievement than students who are taught to read, listen to, and identify various types of meter represented in recorded musical excerpts (Stockton, 1983).

Several investigators have been interested in questions relating to children's singing. Young children, regardless of cultural diversity or amount of music instruction received, demonstrated higher singing achievement when pitch pattern instruction included a combination of diatonic and pentatonic patterns rather than diatonic or pentatonic pitch pattern instruction alone (Jarjisian, 1981, 1983). When difficulty of patterns was investigated, Feierabend (1983) observed significant differences on singing achievement and aural discrimination ability for first-grade children. Results were inconclusive, however, regarding the effects of singing songs with and without words (Levinowitz, 1987). Tonal pattern instruction based on sequential skills combined with a content of arpeggio patterns resulted in superior tonal audiation and performance of notated music (Gamble, 1989). Studies regarding development of tonal and rhythmic capabilities of young children (DiBlassio, 1984; Saunders, 1991) confirmed earlier findings of De-Yarman, Dittemore, and Miller.

When statistical significance was not achieved in some of these studies, the researchers argued that there was evidence to bear on practical significance. Review of these studies revealed some limitations in design, most probably attributable to the typical exigencies of a student's completing doctoral study. For example, experimental treatments were applied for short periods of time or many had small samples but still used parametric techniques. Others included multiple criterion measures but multivariate techniques were not used in the analyses of data. If these studies are replicated with larger samples, longer periods of instruction, and more appropriate statistical techniques, results might yield significant findings and thus confirm, refine, or refute elements of Gordon's theory. In any event, Saunders (1991) concluded that the extant research raises many more questions than it answers: for example, what are the most appropriate music performance tasks to measure the types of audiation; what is the nature of the stages of audiation among persons of different age levels and within different achievement groups; what is the physiology of the brain in relationship to the unique brain functions associated with the different stages of audiation; what objective evidence is there of the existence of the types and stages of audiation; and what is the role and contribution of each of the stages of audiation within each form of music behavior. (p. 136).

The content sequences were based on objective direct evidence gathered from three studies directed toward the experimental development of taxonomies of tonal patterns and rhythm patterns. As a first step toward building the taxonomies (1974), Gordon took advantage of an extant data set collected for the national standardization of the *Iowa Tests of Music Literacy* (ITML) (1970). Each pattern was analyzed, systematically documented, and organized according to its musical content following a system explained in *The Psychology of Music Teaching* (Gordon, 1971a, pp. 69–72, 96–98) and the *ITML Manual* (1970, pp. 9–11). Next, difficulty and discrimination levels based on item analyses for all subjects who participated in the ITML standardization program were noted for each pattern. Growth rates were calculated by comparing the difficulty level of each ITML test item for students in grades four through six and for students in grades 10–12.

Gordon designed the second study (Gordon, 1976b) to address some of the limitations of the first study. Specifically, he included tonalities other than major and minor, meters other than duple and triple, and classified patterns as basic or complex based on relative difficulty level of the patterns as defined in the first study, instead of arbitrarily classifying them based on their frequency of use in traditional anthologies (Gordon, 1976b, p. 5).

Eight hundred sixty-two tonal patterns and 533 rhythm patterns were recorded on 21 individual tapes in the exact order they appeared in the taxonomies developed in the first study. A second set of tapes, with the order of categories within each classification reversed and the patterns in random order, was recorded in order to gather appropriate reliability data. Over 10,000 fourth-, fifth-, and sixth-grade students in 48 school systems in five states listened to the tapes over several months. As they listened to pairs of patterns, they indicated whether the second pattern of each pair was the "same" or "not the same" as the first. If they were unsure, they would select the "?" as their response. Gordon reasoned that the word "different" should not be used because in fact "the second pattern of a pair is never different from the first pattern of a pair (the second pattern of a pair is always a rerecording of the first pattern of a pair)" and the "data would lack precision if indeed, the second pattern of a pair was ever different from the first pattern of a pair" (Gordon, 1976b, p. 67).

Difficulty level of patterns was determined from the mean and standard deviation of the pattern difficulty level distributions, while growth rate of the patterns was obtained by subtracting the difficulty level of a pattern for the fourth-grade combined groups from the difficulty level

of that pattern for the composite group (1976b, p. 72). Again, Gordon acknowledged the limitations of the study:

> In a study of this type, the validity of the sampling techniques is always open to question. While it can be assumed that the students who participated in the study represent a normal range of musical aptitudes and musical achievement (all students in a given class were required to participate) and that they were exposed to a variety of methodological approaches, the sample is not stratified nor is it strictly random (although tapes were assigned to groups at random). (p. 143)

In the final study (Gordon, 1978), a relatively small group of subjects (273 fourth-grade students and 82 eighth-grade students) was used "so that they could be intensively observed" (p. 1). The content of and procedures for administering the tape recordings were similar to those of the two earlier studies. The techniques used to analyze the data also were similar but included factor analyses for greater precision in the interpretation of difficulty levels and growth rates as well as categorization of patterns.

Validity. To what extent, then, does the work of Gordon meet our criteria for a major developmental theory? Does it have broad musical validity across a range of musical activities or "modalities"? Gordon proposes that once students have gained musical understanding through audiation, they will be able "to perform and to respond aesthetically, and to use symbolic representations of their and others' aesthetic feelings to the extent that their music aptitudes will allow" (Gordon, 1989, p. 21). Compositional processes are encouraged but only when sequentially appropriate and as provided for at the inference level of creativity/improvisation. Gordon believes in a continuum relationship between composition and improvisation, with improvisation a higher skill than composition by virtue of the restriction it places on performers. Some might be tempted to interpret Gordon's work as directed primarily toward theoretical understanding of music symbols and structures, thus suggestive of a pedagogical slant that analyzes music in limited ways. However, if one views his work as broadly conceived with regard to literacy, then it is clear that music literacy, the ability to read and write music, becomes a powerful tool, which is in turn critical to development of other ways of being musical such as performance, creativity, and participation.

Does Gordon's work identify qualitative, sequential, and hierarchical change? From the description above, it can be seen that Gordon's music learning theory describes a process in which students move progressively through stages of preparatory audiation, audiation, and achievement of hierarchical skills of listening, performing, improvising, reading and writing music, composing, and, finally, theoretical understanding. Each level of learning embodies the characteristics and qualities of the previous levels, but the levels are associated not with chronological age but with musical age.

Does Gordon's work have widespread cultural application? If we believe that music is important to the quality of human life and that all humankind has the ability to audiate, the question is this: Do we have reason to believe that the types and stages of audiation, including preparatory audiation, would be different for individuals regardless of the style or function of music in their environment? Because an oral tradition is basic to musical transmission, it seems unlikely that the skill sequence, beginning with aural/oral, would be significantly different in its application to music learning of persons from diverse environments. However, the content of the tonal patterns and rhythm patterns used in the research may be ethnocentric to the extent that Gordon's taxonomies were established with patterns characteristic of music from a Western style. Therefore, the patterns may be appropriate only to those whose musical sensibilities were shaped by Western musical traditions.

Reliability. Opinion on whether there has been systematic and reliable gathering of evidence to support or challenge Gordon's assertions seems to be mixed. Colwell and Abrahams (1991) have argued that "there is no research which is sufficiently definitive to indicate the degree of truthfulness or error in the research of Gordon and his writings" (p. 19). Gordon (1991) acknowledged that there is less documentation with regard to music learning theory and related matters than with his work on music aptitude. He suggested, however, that the primary concern to music educators is "whether the hierarchical order of the sequential levels of music learning theory and the stages of audiation are logical" (p. 62). Gordon's music tests have been a major influence on the research of others. Schleuter (1991) provided a complete listing of research relevant to *Musical Aptitude Profile* (MAP) from 1965 to 1991, revealing the considerable examination Gordon's battery of tests has endured, both for its inherent properties and as a control variable for other research. Shuler (1991a) reviewed research either directly or indirectly relevant to music learning theory (MacKnight, 1975; McDonald, 1991; Palmer, 1974, 1976; Shuler, 1987, 1991a; Stockton, 1983). Saunders stated "there has been a great deal of research done by Gordon and others to substantiate the rudimentary concept of audiation" but observed that "there is relatively little research to corroborate Gordon's more detailed speculation identifying and defining the six different stages of audiation or their role in the seven different types of audiation" (1991a, p. 132). Saunders concluded that Gordon has provided a powerful theory in need of further objective investigation. Beall (1991), by contrast, stated that Gordon's work is "inflexible," and that this "limits the positive

influence the extensive research and writing could have in the profession" (1991, p. 88). Others (Shuler, 1991) appear to value the work of Gordon, but caution the profession to maintain traditional practice "until such time as decisive research evidence surfaces either in support of or in contradiction to the fundamental principles of music learning theory" (p. 56).

The Swanwick/Tillman Developmental Spiral

Developmental theories of music education that depend on analysis of secondary symbol systems (notations) or on separated observations of melodic, rhythmic, harmonic, and other behaviors, or rely on testing only aural perception may have attractive scientific possibilities in terms of control and reliability. However, the issue of musical validity is a real one for such methodologies. In an attempt to address this difficulty, Swanwick and Tillman's 1986 study of musical development was based on a generic theory of musical experience and on observations of actual music making under fairly open conditions. The work has been widely cited and extensively reviewed and further research by Swanwick and others have since addressed questions both of validity and reliability.

The Theoretical Context. In *A Basis for Music Education* (Swanwick, 1979), Swanwick set forth categories of hierarchical educational objectives for music. These include skill acquisition (later to become materials), recognizing and producing expressive gesture (later to be referred to as "expression"), identifying and displaying the operation of norms and deviations (later designated as form), and aesthetic response (ultimately to be labeled value). Swanwick further developed this approach and subsequently linked it to Piagetian concepts in *The Arts in Education: Dreaming or Wide Awake?* In that transcript of an earlier professorial lecture, Swanwick argued that mastery, imitation, and imaginative play are essential psychological elements in all artistic engagement (Swanwick, 1983, 1988). In specifically musical terms, these are identified with perceiving and controlling sound materials, projecting and locating expressive character, and awareness of interrelationships between expressive gestures, that is, dynamic structure. This is the theoretical basis of the later detailed developmental theory and it was an attempt to synthesize and "psychologize" major strands of debate in aesthetics. Technique, expression, form, and value are thus not seen as competing but as complementary elements of music experience. The most developed form of the theory is that music is a multilayered human experience, where layers not only interact vertically but also laterally, as minds assimilate and accommodate to musical processes.

In publications cited here, Swanwick attempted to sketch a generic epistemology for music, to answer Sera-

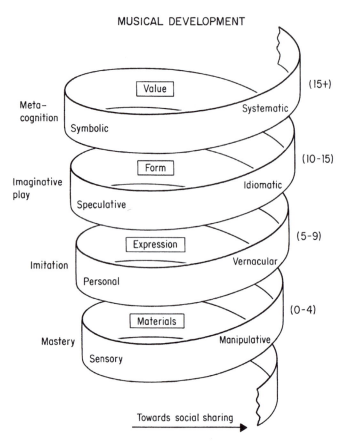

MUSICAL DEVELOPMENT

Figure 22.3 The Swanwick-Tillman spiral model of musical development. Originally published in K. Swanwick and J. Tillman, "The Sequence of Musical Development: A Study of Children's Composition," 1986, *British Journal of Music Education*, 3(3), p. 306. Used by permission.

fine's question: "What is the nature and source of musical thought?" (Serafine, 1980, p. 1). It is this issue that received attention rather than the creation of a developmental model. Initially, there was little engagement with Serafine's other question of how children acquire musical capabilities, although educational implications of the epistemology were explored in some detail (Swanwick, 1979). The link between the epistemological issue and the subsequent developmental model was made explicit, particularly in the article by Swanwick and Tillman (1986) and later in Tillman's thesis (1987). Further empirical and theoretical work has been discussed by Swanwick (1991, 1994) and by Swanwick and França (1999).

The London Study. The data collected by Tillman were crucial to the eventual developmental theory. Unnotated compositions were produced by children, mostly aged 3 to 11, from several ethnic and cultural groups in London schools. These were part of normal classroom activities and the pieces were tape-recorded, an activity that continued over 4 years, nine times each year, yielding 745 com-

positions from 48 children. There was thus a cross-section of music from children of different ages and in some cases a longitudinal spectrum of compositions from individual children. The compositions ranged from brief spontaneous utterances to more sustained and rehearsed musical inventions. Collecting compositions in this way was thought to be both ecologically sensitive and having greater musical validity than giving written tests. The data was grouped into clusters having similar properties and these fitted with Swanwick's original conception of four levels or layers of musical thinking (fig. 22.3): *materials, expression, form,* and *value* (Swanwick & Tillman, 1986).

Further evaluation of the compositions led to seeing that on each of four levels there was a transformation from assimilatory, personal response to music (the left side) to accommodatory "social sharing" (the right side). This dialectical relationship was more fully developed by Swanwick in *Musical Knowledge,* in which he clustered several concepts under the generic headings of "intuition" and "analysis." These pick up the conceptual basis of the left and right side of the spiral model and are associated respectively and broadly with assimilation and accommodation, with musical encounter and musical instruction, the aesthetic and the artistic, personal interpretation and cultural transmission (Swanwick & Tillman, 1986, p. 176). Koopman (1995) rightly saw the left side as a "subjective pole," concerned with self-directedness, while the right side "represents a dialogical relation with the external world" (60).

The developmental spiral thus consists of eight "modes" of musical functioning, two on each layer or level. The terminology for these modes drew on earlier observations by Bunting (1977) of children composing in the classroom. Each of these modes was seen as a qualitative shift. An initial phase of exploring sounds transforms into manipulative control. With this technical ability musical expression becomes possible, at first spontaneous but later more conventional with vernacular commonplaces of phrase and sequence. These conventions are later assimilated into musical form, initially as speculation and then in specific styles or idioms. Beyond this lies the possibility of symbolic value for the individual and systematic musical commitment. The concept of "value" involves more than enjoyment and denotes the phenomenon of people becoming consciously aware of the importance of music, a *meta-cognitive* process. The essence of these developmental elements has been captured in short criterion descriptions:

Materials

Level 1—Sensory: Humans apparently take pleasure in sound itself, particularly in timbre and extremes of loud and soft. They enjoy exploring instruments in a spontaneous, loosely organized way, marked by unsteady pulse and a disregard for the significance of variations in tone color.

Level 2—Manipulative: The handling of instruments shows some control and repetitions are possible. Regular pulse may appear along with technical devices suggested by the physical structure and layout of available instruments; such as *glissandi*, scalic and intervallic patterns, trills and *tremolo*. Compositions tend to be long and repetitive as the composer enjoys the feeling of managing the instrument.

Expression

Level 3—Personal expressiveness: Expressiveness is apparent in changes of speed and loudness levels. There are signs of elementary phrases—musical gestures—which are not always able to be exactly repeated. There is drama, mood, or atmosphere, perhaps with reference to an external "programmatic" idea. There will be little structural control and the impression is of spontaneity without development of ideas.

Level 4—The vernacular: Patterns appear—melodic and rhythmic figures that are able to be repeated. Pieces may be quite short and will work within established general musical conventions. Melodic phrases may fall into standard two-, four-, or eight-bar units. Metrical organization is common along with such devices as syncopation, melodic and rhythmic *ostinati,* and sequences. Compositions will be fairly predictable and show influences of other musical experiences: singing, playing, and listening.

Form

Level 5—The speculative: Compositions go beyond the deliberate repetition of patterns. Deviations and surprises occur, although perhaps not fully integrated into the piece. There is expressive characterization that is subject to experimentation, exploring structural possibilities, seeking to contrast or vary established musical ideas. After establishing certain patterns, a frequent device is to introduce a novel ending.

Level 6—The idiomatic: Structural surprises are integrated into a recognizable style. Contrast and variation take place on the basis of emulated models and clear idiomatic practices, frequently, although not always, drawn from popular musical traditions. Harmonic and instrumental authenticity is important. Answering phrases, call and response, variation by elaboration, and contrasting sections are common. Technical, expressive, and structural control is demonstrated in longer compositions.

Value

Level 7—The symbolic: Technical mastery serves musical communication. Attention is focused on formal relationships and expressive character that are fused together in an impressive, coherent, and original musical statement. Particular groups of timbres, turns of phrase, and harmonic progressions may be developed and given sustained concern. There is a strong sense of personal commitment.

Level 8—The systematic: Beyond the qualities of the previous level, works may be based on sets of newly generated musical materials, such as a scales and note rows, novel systems of harmonic generation, electronically created sounds, or computer technology. The possibilities of musical discourse are systematically expanded.

Adapted from Swanwick and Tillman (1986)

Although social contexts were not explicitly exemplified, they are implicit in the right-hand dimension, in the concept of manipulative control—which makes it possible for people to make music together, in the idea of the vernacular—common shared music processes and in the idiomatic with its implications of social conventions of style and genre. Even the "systematic," with its connotations of creating new musical processes and forms, can be seen as social, in that existing conventions may be challenged. For these reasons, the original spiral diagram had an arrow from left to right captioned "towards social sharing."

Further theoretical and empirical work was reported in subsequent publications (Swanwick, 1988, 1991, 1994). Consequently, it can be argued that the concepts underlying the criteria for composing are good indicators of more general musical development (Swanwick, 1994, p. 85). Swanwick has further clarified the underlying theory of the affective/cognitive processes, especially the parallels with Piaget (Swanwick, 1994, pp. 96–98). From early childhood, he sees a musical interaction of accommodation and assimilation, of imitation and play. Very young children are engrossed in experimenting with sounds, playfully assimilating them to private worlds. As Piaget puts it, they have "a preoccupation with individual satisfaction." As they move toward a degree of mastery they can be seen to be enjoying "the functional pleasure of use" (Piaget, 1951, pp. 87–99), and accommodating to the demands of repetition and control. A characteristic of mastery play is the element of repetition, enjoying what Piaget calls virtuosity.

The level of "materials" corresponds with the concept of sensory-motor intelligence, in which the musical image is embodied in the exploration and eventual management of sounds. Representative imitation is seen to lie at the root of musical expressiveness and this is quickly followed by a tendency to accommodate to vernacular patterns and conventions "out there" in the environment of musical discourse. Representation thus passes quickly from fairly spontaneous or personal assimilative activity to stylization, to the "collective rule." Swanwick (1994) eventually thought it best to drop the term "imaginative play" as a generic term for engagement with musical form and substitute instead "constructional play." The speculative element crucial to musical form is then more clearly seen to have an assimilatory bias, as do the other left-hand modes, while the "idiomatic" mode on the right locates musical form within stylistic conventions, the distinctive constructional "games" that are developed within rule frameworks. This goes some way to meeting Koopman's observation that the connections with Piaget's mastery, imitation, and imaginative play may not be "as compelling as they seem" (Koopman, 1995, p. 58).

Validity.   The first issue of validity concerns the model itself and the extent to which it may be said to give an adequate picture of the elements of musical development. As Hargreaves and Zimmerman (1992) point out, any evaluation of such a theory has to take into account the range of musical phenomena it attempts to explain. This theory can hardly be attacked for limitations of this type. The explicit integration of expressive, formal, and value dimensions is musically more comprehensive than many previous attempts to model musical development in terms of limited functions, for example, measuring discrimination between sound materials (higher and lower, or longer and shorter) or attempting to study conservation of melodic or rhythmic elements. Nor is development assessed through secondary functions, such as ability to handle graphic or notational representation or by verbal description. Swanwick argues that the four layers with their eight modes between them capture the richness of musical understanding (Swanwick, 1994). This may be an ambitious theory but it has yet to be supplanted by an alternative theory of equivalent descriptive and analytic power and educational relevance.

A second validity question concerns the relationship between the layers and age. Here there have been misunderstandings. For example, both Davies (1992) and Marsh (1995) pointed out that a child might work in several developmental layers at the same time. This is certainly true. Swanwick drew attention to the spread of the compositions of individuals at any age and also to the cumulative nature of the developmental sequence. "We do not merely pass through one of these modes but carry them forward with us to the next" (Swanwick, 1988, pp. 63–64). Popular convention asserts (wrongly) that Piaget thought each stage somehow separate from the others. For example, Gardner asserted that for Piaget "the child does not even have access to his earlier forms of understanding. Once he is out of a stage, it is as though the prior stage had never happened" (Gardner, 1993, pp. 26–27). This a curious interpretation of Piaget. For example, when writing of the development of children through what he calls the successive structures (sensory-motor, symbolic, preconceptual, intuitive, and rational), Piaget (1951) told us plainly that "it is essential to understand how each of these behaviors is continued in the one that follows, the direction being from a lower to a higher equilibrium. It is for this reason that in our view a static analysis of discontinuous, stratified levels is unacceptable" (p. 291).

Nor should we assume that the "child" in Piaget's theory somehow stands outside of cultural influence. As Ser-

afine (1980) has pointed out, Piaget was an interactionist, emphasizing "the reciprocal effects of both the external milieu and the internal cognitive structures" (p. 3). Similarly, the Swanwick/Tillman model supposed that musical development is structural, embodying a coherent system, subject to transformations and tending toward equilibrium between assimilation and accommodation, between personal motivation and musical cultural conventions.

Although Swanwick and Tillman proposed an invariant sequence of development in that certain structures of musical thought precede others, there was no suggestion of a rigid age timetable. In general, though, very young children do not usually aspire to idiomatic authenticity but enter the world of music with some excitement over sound materials and enjoy control of them before engaging with vernacular conventions. By the age of 14 years or so, making music in idiomatic ways becomes a strong imperative for many young people. For Swanwick and Tillman the process of musical development was not a once-in-a-lifetime, linear affair. The broken ends of their helix indicate that the layers are recursive: For example, when people encounter new music or a performer begins to work on a new piece, or when a composer engages with a new computer music program, in these situations of challenge they are likely to find themselves once again at the start of the process.

Reliability.   Questions have been raised as to whether the initial assessment or "coding" of the compositions was sufficiently objective (Hargreaves & Zimmerman, 1992). In addition, there are issues concerning the sample of children: For instance, could these findings be repeated in another cultural setting? Furthermore, there was a relative dearth of data from older children to support the "valuing" layer of the spiral, which is not adduced from compositional data. Koopman (1995) drew attention to this conceptual discrepancy between the first three layers and the fourth (p. 57).

Partly to meet such legitimate concerns, a replication of the original study was conducted in a different cultural setting, that of the Greek part of Cyprus (Swanwick, 1991). More than 600 recordings of children's compositions were collected, and from these 28 were selected at random with a single sorting rule—that there should be seven items from each of four age groups: 4/5; 7/8; 10/11; 14/15. Seven primary and secondary music teachers were asked to independently assign each of the compositions to one of the criterion statements on a "best fit" basis. The relationship between the actual ages of the children and the placing of compositions by the spiral criteria was statistically significant. There was a clear ascending relationship between age and the order of the criteria and high levels of interjudge agreement (Swanwick, 1994, p. 111).

The Musical Modalities of Musical Production, Performance, and Perception.   It is not actually correct to say that the Swanwick and Tillman model is based on children's compositions and cannot explain activities in other modalities (Hargreaves & Zimmerman, 1992, p. 388). The specific data of this study are indeed those of children's compositions but, as we indicated earlier, major elements of the theory derive from earlier work by Swanwick on the nature of musical knowledge, on a generic epistemology. There is also some empirical evidence on this issue of the effectiveness of the theory to deal with what Hargreaves and Zimmerman call musical production and musical perception. Similar criteria to those for composition have been employed in the assessment of musical performance and high levels of agreement have been reported between judges on the hierarchical order of these performance statements (Swanwick, 1994, pp. 108–110).

The structure and theoretical concepts of the developmental spiral have also been used by Hentschke (1993) in both England and Brazil to examine children's perception of music as "audience-listeners." Younger children tended to comment on sound materials and expressive character while reference to musical form appeared mostly among the children around and after the age of 10, hardly ever before. It seemed that the development of audience-listening follows the same sequence as composing and that the layers of musical understanding might indeed provide a reasonably robust genetic epistemology for music. França (Silva, 1998) conducted a study using a version of the criteria in Portuguese for the area of audience-listening and found significant judge accordance in sorting the randomized sets of statements into a hierarchy that matches the predicted order (Swanwick & França, 1999).

This study and its associated theory raise an interesting and important issue related to modalities. If it is possible to have a meta-theory of musical development, which applies to production, performance, and perception, might an individual show developmental differences between the modalities? As Koopman (1995) said, the concept of musical understanding overarches composing, interpreting, listening, and judging.

In considering musical development, we thought it important to distinguish between *activities* and *understanding,* between *behavior* and *cognition.* We may characterize cognition or understanding as one of the residues of activity. It is what we take away with us when the activity is over and bring back on subsequent occasions. The same is true of skills. It is not illogical to say that a tennis player is exceptionally good, even at a time when she is not actually playing. In the same way, we may have a high level of understanding even if on specific occasions we are unable to demonstrate it. For example, if we converse for a time with a fairly normal child of 4 or 5 years of age, we

are likely to become aware of a wide vocabulary and a confident use of most grammatical forms. Conversely, the written language of the same child is likely to reveal much less linguistic ability and would not be a good indicator of the child's language (rather than literacy) ability.

The particular activity, the modality of articulation, can to a greater or lesser extent reveal or conceal levels of understanding. For instance, a gifted jazz improviser who may be asked to perform at sight from a difficult notated score by Debussy may be unable to demonstrate a high level of musical development. Similarly, a fluent and sensitive performer of notated Western classical pieces may be quite inarticulate if asked to improvise. Only if we have some confidence in a developmental theory, which overarches diverse activities, is it possible to evaluate levels of musical cognition and make this kind of comparison.

França argued that the theoretical basis of the spiral offers a valid general theory of musical understanding (Silva, 1998; Swanwick, 1999). She worked with 20 Brazilian children between 11 and 13 years of age. Each child made tape recordings of three memorized piano performances, recorded three of their own compositions, and discussed and made written notes on three recorded pieces of music, all of which were heard three times. These "products" in the three modalities of performing, composing, and audience-listening were assessed by judges—experienced teacher-musicians—using criterion statements based on the eight spiral modes. There were high levels of interjudge reliability. An interesting finding is that, while most of the children's work displayed matching levels of musical understanding for composing and audience-listening, their performances were usually less developed. The education relevance of this kind of study may be significant, particularly in terms of the range of activities suggested in or mandated by curriculum guidelines.

In evaluating this work according to our criteria, it seems that the theory and associated evidence is valid in that it comprehensively reflects the nature of music across a range of activities. The various empirical replications and extensions of the project strengthen the claims of reliability. The model is premised on qualitatively differentiated patterns of behavior and early structures are integrated into later ones. There is no evidence to contradict the claim that the musical layers (or stages) unfold in an invariant sequence and there is some evidence that the developmental sequence is culturally widespread.

One outstanding issue is the relationship of the spontaneous natural developmental of individuals and the cultural environment in which this development is realized. The left and right sides of the spiral raise but do not develop this issue and work is needed along Vygotskian lines, exploring musical production and perception in terms of the zone of proximal development, looking particularly at the influence of language and peer-modeling. We remember, though, that Vygotsky saw development as a complex dialectical process with qualitative transformations (Vygotsky, 1978, p. 73). The manipulative, vernacular, idiomatic and systematic modes are essentially social, accommodatory. The theory does not therefore ignore or rule out the social dimension, although much work remains to be done in this area.

Relationships Among the Theories

There are a number of possible connections among some of the theories we have reviewed. For example, Gordon's detailed theory of early childhood development corresponds closely with that part of the Swanwick/Tillman model. From birth to 2–4 years, Gordon specifies the period of "acculturation" and notes that children hear the sounds of music in the environment, then move and babble in response but without relation to the music, although they may attempt to do this. Swanwick calls this the sensory mode. Gordon identified a period of "imitation," in which children focus on the musical environment and are able to copy with some precision tonal and rhythmic patterns. Swanwick labels this the "manipulative" mode, and it lies on the accommodatory or right side of the spiral. There is then, at around the beginning of schooling, a move toward "assimilation," where Gordon observed that thought is focused primarily on the self. According to Gordon, at this time children are to be offered informal structured guidance rather than be instructed.

Although Gordon focused on children performing patterns, songs, and chants, and the Swanwick/Tillman and Swanwick/Stavrides data (Swanwick, 1994) was drawn from more open composing activities, it seems that there may be a connection between them. As Gordon reminded us, children "cannot be taught to assimilate pitch, rhythm and movement. . . . They can only accomplish this by themselves" (1997b, p. 78). Similarly, on the Swanwick/Tillman spiral, personal expressiveness is unique to the individual child.

We have previously noted the conceptual relationship between Serafine's "coherent" musical units, and Swanwick's expressive "gestures" or "character." There also are conceptual connections between the Swanwick and Tillman speculative and idiomatic modes of musical form, where structural relationships are construed between expressive units, and Serafine's categories of succession and simultaneity. The "nontemporal" concepts of closure, transformation, abstraction, and hierarchic levels also identify some of the gestalt processes underlying the speculative and idiomatic modes.

The left and right of the spiral may be compared to Bamberger's *intuitive* and *formal* types of musical knowledge (Bamberger, 1978) and with what Hargreaves calls *empiricism*—a child's "idiosyncratic construction" of experience and *rationalism*—formal, adult ways of thinking (Hargreaves, 1986, p. 78). Similar distinctions are also embodied in Bamberger's *figural* and *metric* features of children's notations, although she resisted equating the representation conventions of metric notation with musical understanding, and warned that, where school music concentrates on reading and writing standard notation, there may be a loss of intuitive musical sensitivity. As Hargreaves pointed out, phrase shapes and various subtleties of articulation are left out of metric notations but may be captured more effectively in figural shapes (Hargreaves, 1986, p. 99). Swanwick also warned against losing opportunities to experience the left-hand elements of the spiral model in the formal transactions of classrooms (Swanwick, 1994).

There are connections also with the work of Gardner. Koopman gave a table showing Gardner's earlier and later model alongside that of Swanwick and Tillman (table 22.1).

We note the relative lack of detail in the Gardner model. From the point of view of teachers of music, it is hard to relate to the absence of developmental concepts for many crucial years of schooling and instruction. It is therefore perhaps not surprising that, when discussing musical development and music education, Koopman did this in terms only of the Swanwick/Tillman theory.

In a similar way, Hargreaves and Galton have constructed, from the literature, a table for several arts domains that drew substantially on Swanwick and Tillman for musical composition and attempted to correlate development in composing, singing, musical representation (notation), and melodic perception alongside five generic headings (table 22.2). This goes some way to identifying likely developmental relationships both within music modalities and across the other arts.

Implications for Teaching and Learning

From this review of developmental theories, a number of implications can be drawn for teaching and learning. There seem to be two main areas in which we see the implications of a comprehensive developmental theory for musical transactions in classrooms and studios.

Curriculum Design

The first implication is in terms of broad curriculum planning in schools and colleges. Curriculum activities may be focused toward specific aspects of musical development at different broadly identified stages, working with the grain

Table 22.1 Development of Musical Understanding

Gardner (1973)	Gardner et al. (1990)	Swanwick and Tillman (1986)
I Free exploration	1 Preconventional	1a Sensory
II Implicit understanding	2 Conventional	1b Manipulative
		2a Personal
		2b Vernacular
		3a Speculative
		3b Idiomatic
III Distanced relationship,		4a Symbolic
reflection	3 Postconventional	4b Systematic

(Koopman, 1995, p. 61)

of development. In the very early years of schooling and at preschool level, sensory exploration and the encouragement of manipulative control would be the main aim. In the first years of schooling, this could be taken further forward and expressive elements of music would come more sharply into focus. Kratus (1993) noted that there are few studies of children's emotional response to music. His study of the responses of children aged 6 to 12 years suggested that his sample interpreted the emotional character of a piece of music (Glenn Gould playing excerpts from Bach's *Goldberg Variations*) with a high degree of consistency. His conclusions included the view that, since 6-year-olds were able to interpret emotion in music to the same extent as those children who were 12, formal music education does not seem to have an effect. Nor should teachers feel they need to teach students the associations of happy/sad, excited/calm, although these might be starting points for analyzing musical elements.

While this may be true, there surely is work for educators to do assisting in the process of refining perception of feeling qualities and in facilitating students' expressive production. This may involve movement, dance, drama, and visual images, all of which might help promote, stimulate, and intensify awareness of expressiveness. By the age of 10 or so, we also would be looking to further the production and recognition of musical speculation, an awareness of the uniquely contextual nature of the contrasts and repetitions essential to musical form. Moreover, depending on each individual's music aptitudes, a number of tonal patterns and rhythm patterns would be part of one's musical vocabulary.

Young people in high schools are often seeking to enter a "grown-up" world of music. The resources of formal education are not always organized to match the musical development of young people. These include appropriate instrumental and performance settings and equipment, along with the expertise of a range of teachers, so that there can be some basis of choice for the student who is becoming idiomatically aware or who has

high music aptitude with commensurate achievement. Drawing on musical agencies outside the school may be one powerful strategy in providing elements of idiomatic authenticity.

Musical Development and the Organization of Teaching and Learning

The second way in which an understanding of musical development might inform music education concerns individual development. Although schools are organized into classes, persons develop as individuals. It is surely helpful for a teacher to be able to relate to developmental change with awareness of subsequent possibilities. For example, that engagement in the vernacular may evolve into the more imaginatively speculative. This may enable the teachers to ask a stimulating question, make a suggestion, or choose material that may have more meaning and developmental consequences for the individual. When beginning to learn a new instrument or to perform a new piece, for example, we may observe and assist student development. It may be necessary from time to time to move to a lower layer in order to move to other layers more musically and securely. For instance, it may be a benefit to take an instrumentalist back to the enjoyment of the exploratory sensory mode. This approach helps counteract habits of listening insensitively to sound quality, a habit that may have been acquired by learning a performance repertoire by rote, imitation, and decoding of notation, rather than through audiation, which encourages understanding of the flow of music, tone quality, chord progressions, form, style, expression, and instrumentation.

Furthermore, if teachers can acquire specific information about the various music aptitudes of each student, they may better be able to provide professional and artistic experiences appropriate to the individual characteristics of music learners. In this regard, a standardized music aptitude test along with sensitive observation may assist in objective evaluation of students' individual musical differ-

Table 22.2 Five Phases of Artistic Development

DOMAIN-SPECIFIC DEVELOPMENTS

Phase	Cognitive Aesthetic Development	Drawing	Writing	Singing	Musical Representation	Melodic Perception	Musical Composition
Metacognitive (15– years)	Independence from cultural styles and context	Freedom from artistic styles	Self-reflection in relation to social roles				Enactive and reflective strategies
Rule systems (8–15 years)	Development of artistic conventions and style sensitivity	"Visual realism," viewer-centred	Story grammar analysis of structural complexity	Intervals, scales	Formal-metric	Analytic recognition of intervals, key stability	"Idiomatic" conventions
Schematic (5–8 years)	Emphasis on realism and subject matter	Baselines, skylines	Standard narrative forms	"First draft" songs	Figural-metric: more than one dimension	"Conservation" of melodic properties	"Vernacular" conventions
Figural (2–5 years)	Concrete, mechanistic	Preschematic "intellectual" realism	"Frame" or outline stories	"Outline" songs: coalescences between spontaneous and cultural songs	Figural: single dimension	Global features: pitch, contour	
Presymbolic (0–2 years)		Scribbling	Scribbling, symbolic play	Babbling, rhythmic dancing	Scribbling, "action equivalents"	Recognition of melodic contours	Sensory, manipulative

From *Aesthetic Learning: Psychological Theory and Educational Practice*, by D. J. Hargreaves and M. Galton. *Yearbook on the Arts in Education.* Eds. B. Reimer and B. A. Smith. Chicago: NSSE, 1992.

ences and provide information so that instruction can be adapted and potential maximized. As we have seen, although comparison between different musical activities requires a robust theory of musical cognition, it is important to look for and assess development in relation to particular achievements. Indeed, such an analysis is essential for effective teaching. Gordon's insistence on objective measurement of music aptitude and achievement is complimented by Swanwick's concern for the quality of musical experience during educational transactions.

The recursive nature of musical development is particularly suggestive for organizing teaching sequences or musical projects. In one sense progression in music may be thought of as linear, quantitative, or horizontal. We may see education in music as proceeding from relatively simple to more complex and technically advanced material. But progression also may be seen as layered, as qualitative, or as vertical. For example, and with reference again specifically to the Swanwick and Tillman model, a curriculum sequence may be viewed as recurring spirals along the horizontal where the level of musical material changes over time, perhaps from high-low or loud-soft distinctions, through pentatonic melodies to other tonal series or harmonic progressions. The "vertical" dimension informs the critical judgment of teachers and students and raises the question of how many layers are involved in musical production or in-audience response. Gordon's skill and content sequences can be used to guide the "horizontal" sequence of the curriculum with long- and short-range objectives, based on the way music skills interact with one another, thus providing a sequential scheme for introducing and extending awareness and control of musical materials and expressive features. Students therefore would be provided with a foundation for developing musical understanding in an organized and coherent way without losing the potential richness of musical experience.

Conclusion

Very broadly, the main implications for music education to be drawn from this discussion are as follows:

- Research has been able to identify patterns of musical development, some of these in specific areas of musical perception and production and having generic theoretical implications.
- These theories have broad musical validity, are relevant across different activities, take account of both "nature" and "nurture," identify qualitative, sequential, and hierarchical changes, have widespread cultural application, and are supported by systematically gathered data.
- Musical development may be generically construed as consisting of cumulative layers.

- Understanding musical development is suggestive for curriculum design and for organizing instructional activities.
- Once students have developed beyond early childhood, they may move freely between all or any of the layers, provided that the activity is rich enough in musical possibilities.
- Developmental sequences are recursive and may be reactivated in new musical contexts.
- Integration of different musical modalities may provide opportunities for the development of musical cognition and response.
- As well as providing musical models and structures, it is important to leave room for assimilatory activity, where the student absorbs and decides for him or herself.

While there is still considerable information we do not have about how individuals develop musically, we do know quite a lot about musical development and how to promote it. There is strong evidence from several sources for a broad developmental sequence during early childhood and that this may be reactivated subsequently with new musical experiences. We also know that education may positively influence this. However, it is not at all clear that formal education (schooling) may not necessarily be the optimum environment. Much work remains to be done on musical learning outside of instructional programs as part of lifelong enculturation and on the effect of different levels of instructional framing, especially less-directive and more loosely sequenced or informal teaching and learning in the early stages of one's development. The future of music education may not depend so much on schools as we know them but on things such as opportunities in local communities and the global communities of the Web. Musical development is likely to become increasingly problematized and pluralized, and we may expect existing models and theories to be further challenged.

REFERENCES

Adachi, M., & Bradshaw, D. H. (1995). *Children's symbolic representations of rhythm patterns across tasks.* Paper presented at the biennial meeting of the Society for Research in Child Development, at Indianapolis, Indiana, USA.

Bamberger, J. (1978). Intuitive and formal musical knowing: Parables of cognitive dissonance. In S. S. Madeja (Ed.), *The arts, cognition and basic skills* (pp. 173–209). St Louis, MO: CEMREL.

Bamberger, J. (1982). Revisiting children's descriptions of simple rhythms: A function for reflection-in-action. In S. Strauss (Ed.), *U-shaped behavioural growth* (pp. 191–226). New York: Academic Press.

Bamberger, J. (1991). *The mind behind the musical ear: How children develop musical intelligence.* Cambridge, MA: Harvard University Press.

Bamberger, J. (1994). Coming to hear in a new way. In R. Aiello (Ed.), *Musical perceptions* (pp. 131–151). Oxford: Oxford University Press.

Barrett, M. (1997). Invented notations: A view of young children's musical thinking. *Research Studies in Music Education, 8*, 2–14.

Barrett, M. S. (1999, September). *Children and music development perspectives.* Paper presented at the International Music Education Symposium, at University of Tasmania, Hobart, Tasmania, Australia.

Beall, G. (1991). Learning sequences and music learning. *The Quarterly Journal of Music Teaching and Learning II* (1 & 2), 87–96.

Bean, K. L. (1939). An experimental approach to the reading of music. *Psychological Monographs 50.*

Bell, W. (1981). *An investigation of the validity of the* Primary Measures of Music Audiation *for use with learning disabled children.* Unpublished doctoral dissertation, Temple University, Philadelphia.

Belmondo, D. J. (1986). *A study of the effectiveness of partial synthesis as a readiness for tonal music reading.* Unpublished doctoral dissertation, Temple University, Philadelphia.

Bentley, A. (1966). *Measures of musical abilities.* London: Harrap.

Blesedell, D. S. (1991). *A study of the effects of two types of movement instruction on the rhythm achievement and developmental rhythm aptitude of preschool children.* Unpublished doctoral dissertation, Temple University, Philadelphia.

Bolton, B. (1995). *An investigation of same and different as manifested in the developmental music aptitudes of students in first, second and third grades.* Unpublished doctoral dissertation, Temple University, Philadelphia.

Boyle, J. D. (1992). Evaluation of music ability. In R. Colwell (Ed.), *Handbook of research on music teaching and learning* (pp. 247–265). New York: Schirmer Books.

Brophy, T. S. (2000). *Assessing the developing child musician.* Chicago: G. I. A. Publications.

Bruner, J. S. (1973). The growth of representational processes in childhood. In J. Anglin (Ed.), *Beyond the information given: Studies in the psychology of knowing* (pp. 313–324) New York: W. W. Norton.

Bunting, R. (1977). The common language of music, music in the secondary school curriculum. *Schools Council Working Paper 6.* York: York University.

Campbell, P. S., & Scott-Kassner, C. (1995). *Music in childhood: From preschool through the elementary grades.* New York: Schirmer.

Cernohorsky, N. C. (1991). *A study of the effects of movement instruction adapted from the theories of Rudolf von Laban upon the rhythm performance and developmental rhythm aptitude of elementary school children.* Unpublished doctoral dissertation, Temple University, Philadelphia.

Chang, H. W., & Trehub, S. E. (1977). Auditory processing of relational information by young infants. *Journal of Experimental Child Psychology, 24,* 324–331.

Christensen, C. (1992). *Music composition, invented notation and reflection: Tools for music learning and assessment.* Unpublished doctoral dissertation, Rutgers University, New Brunswick, NJ.

Cohen, S. R. (1985). The development of constraints on symbol-meaning structure in notation: Evidence from production, interpretation, and forced-choice judgements. *Child Development, 56*(1), 177–195.

Colwell, R., & Abrahams, F. (1991). Edwin Gordon's contribution: An appraisal. *The Quarterly Journal of Music Teaching and Learning II* (1 & 2), 19–36.

Crain, W. (1992). *Theories of development.* Englewood Cliffs, NJ: Prentice Hall.

Cutietta, R. A. (1991). Edwin Gordon's impact on the field of music aptitude. *The Quarterly Journal of Music Teaching and Learning II* (1 & 2), 73–77.

Davidson, L. (1983). Tonal structures of children's early songs. *Bulletin of the British Psychological Society, 36,* A119–A120.

Davidson, L., & Scripp, L. (1989). Education and development in music from a cognitive perspective. In D. J. Hargreaves (Ed.), *Children and the arts: The psychology of creative development* (pp. 59–86). Leichester: Open University Press.

Davidson, L., & Scripp, L. (1992). Surveying the coordinates of cognitive skills in music. In R. Colwell (Ed.), *Handbook of research on music teaching and learning* (pp. 392–413). New York: Schirmer Books.

Davies, C. (1992). Listen to my song: A study of songs invented by children aged 5 to 7 years. *British Journal of Music Education, 9*(1), 19–48.

Deutsch, D. (1982). *The psychology of music.* New York and London: Academic Press.

DeYarman, R. M. (1971). *An experimental analysis of the development of rhythmic and tonal capabilities of kindergarten and first grade children.* Unpublished doctoral dissertation, University of Iowa, Iowa City.

DiBlassio, R. V. (1984). *An experimental study of the development of tonal and rhythmic capabilities of first grade children.* Unpublished doctoral dissertation, Temple University, Philadelphia.

Dittemore, E. E. (1968). *An investigation of some musical capabilities of elementary school students.* Unpublished doctoral dissertation, University of Iowa, Iowa City.

Dowling, W. J. (1982). Melodic information processing and its development. In D. Deutsch (Ed.), *The psychology of music* (pp. 413–429) New York: Academic Press.

Dowling, W. J. (1984). Development of musical schemata in children's spontaneous singing. In W. R. C. Crozier (Ed.), *Cognitive processes in the perception of art* (pp. 145–166) Amsterdam: Elsevier.

Feierabend, J. (1983). *The effects of specific tonal pattern training on singing and aural discrimination abilities of first grade children.* Unpublished doctoral dissertation, Temple University, Philadelphia.

Fosha, R. L. (1964). *A study of the concurrent validity of the Musical Aptitude Profile.* Unpublished doctoral dissertation, University of Iowa, Iowa City.

Foss, R. V. (1972). *An investigation of the effect of the provision of the in doubt response on the validity of the Iowa*

Tests of Music Literacy. Unpublished doctoral dissertation, University of Iowa, Iowa City.

Gamble, D. K. (1989). *A study of the effects of two types of tonal pattern instruction on the audiational and performance skills of first-year clarinet students.* Unpublished doctoral dissertation, Temple University, Philadelphia.

Gardner, H. (1973). *The arts and human development.* New York: Wiley.

Gardner, H. (1993). *The unschooled mind.* London: Fontana. (First published in 1991)

Geissel, L. S. (1985). *An investigation of the comparative effectiveness of the Musical Aptitude Profile, the Intermediate Measures of Music Audiation, and the Primary Measures of Music Audiation with fourth grade students.* Unpublished doctoral dissertation, Temple University, Philadelphia.

Gordon, E. E. (1965). *Musical Aptitude Profile.* Boston: Houghton Mifflin.

Gordon, E. E. (1967a). The contribution of each Music Aptitude Profile subtest to the overall validity of the battery. *Council for Research in Music Education, XII,* 32–36.

Gordon, E. E. (1967b). *How children learn when they learn music.* Iowa City: Author.

Gordon, E. E. (1967c). *A three-year longitudinal predictive validity study of the Musical Aptitude Profile.* Iowa City: University of Iowa Press.

Gordon, E. E. (1969). An investigation of the intercorrelation among Musical Aptitude Profile and Seashore Measures of Musical Talents subtests. *Journal of Research in Music Education, XVII,* 236–271.

Gordon, E. E. (1970). First-year results of a five-year longitudinal study of the musical achievement of culturally disadvantaged students. *Journal of Research in Music Education, 18*(3), 195–221.

Gordon, E. E. (1971a). *The psychology of music teaching.* Englewood Cliffs, NJ: Prentice Hall.

Gordon, E. E. (1971b). Second-year results of a five-year longitudinal study of the musical achievement of culturally disadvantaged students. *Experimental Research in the Psychology of Music: Studies in the Psychology of Music, 7,* 131–143.

Gordon, E. E. (1971c). Third-year results of a five-year longitudinal study of the musical achievement of culturally disadvantaged students. *Experimental Research in the Psychology of Music: Studies in the Psychology of Music, 8,* 45–64.

Gordon, E. E. (1974). Toward the development of a taxonomy of tonal patterns and rhythm patterns: Evidence of difficulty level and growth rate. *Experimental Research in the Psychology of Music: Studies in the Psychology of Music, 9,* 219–232.

Gordon, E. E. (1975). Fourth-year and fifth-year final results of a longitudinal study of the music achievement of culturally disadvantaged students. *Experimental Research in the Psychology of Music: Studies in the Psychology of Music, 10,* 24–52.

Gordon, E. E. (1976a). *Learning sequence and patterns in music.* Buffalo, NY: Tometic Associates.

Gordon, E. E. (1976b). *Tonal and rhythm patterns, an objective analysis: A taxonomy of tonal patterns and rhythm patterns and seminal experimental evidence of their difficulty and growth rate.* Albany: State University of New York Press.

Gordon, E. E. (1978). *A factor analytic description of tonal and rhythm patterns and objective evidence of pattern difficulty level and growth rate.* Chicago: G.I.A. Publications.

Gordon, E. E. (1979). *Primary Measures of Music Audiation: A music aptitude test for kindergarten and primary grade children: Manual.* Chicago: G.I.A. Publications.

Gordon, E. E. (1985). Research studies in audiation: I. *Bulletin of the Council for Research in Music Education, 84,* 34–50.

Gordon, E. E. (1986a). A factor analysis of the Musical Aptitude Profile, the Primary Measures of Music Audiation, and the Intermediate Measures of Music Audiation. *Bulletin of the Council for Research in Music Education, 87,* 17–25.

Gordon, E. E. (1986b). Final results of a two-year longitudinal predictive validity study of the Instrument Timbre Preference Test and Musical Aptitude Profile. *Council for Research in Music Education, 89,* 8–17.

Gordon, E. E. (1986c). *The nature, description, measurement, and evaluation of music aptitudes.* Chicago: G.I.A. Publications.

Gordon, E. E. (1986d). *Primary Measures of Music Audiation and the Intermediate Measures of Music Audiation: A music aptitude test for kindergarten and first, second, third, and fourth grade children. Manual.* Chicago: G.I.A. Publications.

Gordon, E. E. (1987). The nature, description, measurement, and evaluation of music aptitudes. Chicago: G.I.A. Publications.

Gordon, E. E. (1988). The effects of instruction based upon music learning theory on developmental music aptitudes. *Research in Music Education, 2,* 53–57.

Gordon, E. E. (1989). *Advanced Measures of Music Audiation.* Chicago: G.I.A. Publications.

Gordon, E. E. (1990). *Predictive validity studies of Advanced Measures of Music Audiation.* Chicago: G.I.A. Publications.

Gordon, E. E. (1991a). A response to Volume 2, 1 & 2 of *The Quarterly. The Quarterly Journal of Music Teaching and Learning, 2*(4), 62–72.

Gordon, E. E. (1991b). Sequencing music skills and content. *American Music Teacher, 41*(2), 22–51.

Gordon, E. E. (1997a). *Learning sequences in music: Skill, content, and patterns—a music learning theory.* Chicago: G.I.A. Publications.

Gordon, E. E. (1997b). *A music learning theory for newborn and young children.* Chicago: G.I.A. Publications.

Gordon, E. E. (1997c). Taking another look at the established procedure for scoring the Advance Measures of Music Audiation. *GIML Monograph Series, 2,* 75–91.

Gordon, E. E. (1998). *Harmonic Improvisation Readiness Record* and *Rhythm Improvisation Readiness Record.* Chicago: G.I.A. Publications.

Gromko, J. E., & Poorman, A. S. (1998). Developmental trends and relationships in children's aural perception and symbol use. *Journal of Research in Music Education*, 46(1), 16–23.

Haines, B. J., & Gerber, L. L. (2000). *Leading young children to music*. Upper Saddle River, NJ: Pearson Education.

Hargreaves, D. J. (1986). *The developmental psychology of music*. Avon, UK: Cambridge University Press.

Hargreaves, D. J., & Galton, M. (1992). Aesthetic learning: Psychological theory and educational practice. In B. Reimer and R. A. Smith (Eds.), *Yearbook on the Arts in Education* (pp. 124–150). Chicago: NSSE.

Hargreaves, D. J., & Zimmerman, M. (1992). Developmental theories of music learning. In R. Colwell (Ed.), *Handbook of research on music teaching and learning* (pp. 377–391). New York: Macmillan.

Hentschke, L. (1993). *Musical development: testing a model in the audience-listening setting*. Unpublished doctoral dissertation, University of London, Institute of Education, London.

Hicks, W. K. (1992). *An investigation of the initial stages of preparatory audiation*. Unpublished doctoral dissertation, Temple University, Philadelphia.

Holahan, J. (1983). *The effects of four conditions of "same" and "different" instruction on the developmental music aptitudes of kindergarten children receiving tonal pattern training*. Unpublished doctoral dissertation, Temple University, Philadelphia.

Holahan, J. (1986). Teaching music through music learning theory: The contribution of Edwin E. Gordon. In M. L. Mark, *Contemporary music education* (2nd ed., pp. 152–172). New York: Schirmer.

Iowa Tests of Music Literacy. (1970). Iowa City: Bureau of Educational Research and Service.

Jarjisian, C. S. (1981). *The effects of pentatonic and/or diatonic pitch pattern instruction on the rote-singing achievement of young children*. Unpublished doctoral dissertation, Temple University, Philadelphia.

Jarjisian, C. S. (1983). Pitch pattern instruction and the singing achievement of young children. *Psychology of Music*, 11, 19–25.

Jordan, J. M. (1986). *The effects of informal movement instruction derived from the theories of Rudolf von Laban upon the rhythm performance and discrimination of high school students*. Unpublished doctoral dissertation, Temple University, Philadelphia.

Kane, M. J. (1994). *The effects of teacher training upon the developmental music aptitude and music achievement of kindergarten students*. Unpublished doctoral dissertation, Temple University, Philadelphia.

Koopman, C. (1995). Stage theories of musical development. *Journal of Aesthetic Education*, 29(2), 49–66.

Kratus, J. (1993). A developmental study of children's interpretation of emotion in music. *Psychology of Music* 2(1), 3–19.

Kwalwasser, J., & Dykema, P. W. (1930). *Kwalwasser-Dykema music tests*. New York: Fischer.

Krumhansl, C. L., & Jusczyk, P. W. (1990). Infants' perception of phrase structure. *Psychological Science*, 1(1), 70–73.

Levinowitz, L. M. (1987). *An experimental study of the comparative effects of singing songs with words and without words on children in kindergarten and first grade*. Unpublished doctoral dissertation, Temple University, Philadelphia.

MacKnight, C. B. (1975). The effects of tonal pattern training on the performance achievement of beginning wind instrumentalists. *Experimental Research in the Psychology of Music: Studies in the Psychology of Music*, 10, 53–76.

Mainwaring, J. (1933). Kinesthetic factors in the recall of musical experience, *British Journal of Educational Psychology*, 3, 284–307.

Marsh, K. (1995). Children's singing games: Composition in the playground? *Research Studies in Music Education*, 4, 6–8.

McDonald, J. C. (1991) The application of Gordon's empirical model of learning sequence to teaching the recorder. *The Quarterly Journal of Music Teaching and Learning II* (1 & 2), 110–117.

Miller, P. H. (1972). *An experimental analysis of the development of tonal capabilities of first grade children*. Unpublished doctoral dissertation, University of Iowa, Iowa City.

Moog, H. (1976). *The musical experience of the pre-school child*. London: Schott Music.

Ortmann, O. (1937). Span of vision in note reading. *30th Yearbook of the Music Educators National Conference*, 88–99.

Palmer, M. H. (1974). *The relative effectiveness of the Richards and the Gordon approaches to rhythm reading for fourth grade children*. Unpublished doctoral dissertation, University of Illinois, Urbana-Champaign.

Palmer, M. H. (1976). Relative effectiveness of two approaches to rhythm reading for fourth-grade students. *Journal of Research in Music Education*, 24(3), 110–118.

Piaget, J. (1951). *Play, dreams and imitation in childhood*. Norton Library, 1962 ed. New York: Norton.

Radocy R., & Boyle, J. D. (1988). *Psychological foundations of musical behavior*. Springfield, IL: Charles C. Thomas.

Rainbow, E. L. (1963). *A pilot study to investigate constructs of musical aptitude*. Unpublished doctoral dissertation, University of Iowa, School of Music, Iowa City, Iowa.

Rauscher, F. H., Shaw, G. L., Levine, L. J., Wright, E. L., Dennis, W. R., Newcomb, R. L. (1997). Music training causes long-term enhancement of preschool children's spatial-temporal reasoning. *Neurological Research*, 19, 2–8.

Reynolds, A. M. (1995). *An investigation of the movement responses performed by children 18 months to three years of age and their caregivers to rhythm chants in duple and triple meters*. Unpublished doctoral dissertation, Temple University, Philadelphia.

Saunders, T. C. (1991). The stages of music audiation: A survey of research. *The Quarterly Journal of Music Teaching and Learning II* (1 & 2), 131–137.

Schleuter, S. L. (1971). *An investigation of the inter-relation* of personality traits, musical aptitude, and musical achievement. Unpublished doctoral dissertation, University of Iowa, Iowa City.

Schleuter, S. L. (1991). Research studies relevant to the Musical Aptitude Profile: A bibliography. *The Quarterly Journal of Music Teaching and Learning II* (1 & 2), 78–85.

Seashore, C. E. (1938). *The psychology of music.* New York: McGraw-Hill.

Serafine, M. L. (1980). Piagetian research in music. *Bulletin of the Council for Research in Music Education 62*, 1–21.

Serafine, M L. (1988). *Music as cognition: The development of thought in sound.* New York: Columbia University Press.

Shuler, S. C. (1987). *The effects of Gordon's learning sequence activities on music achievement.* Unpublished dissertation, University of Michigan, Ann Arbor.

Shuler, S. C. (1991a). A critical examination of the contributions of Edwin Gordon's music learning theory to the music education profession. *The Quarterly Journal of Music Teaching and Learning II* (1 & 2), 37–58.

Shuler, S. C. (1991b). The effects of Gordon's learning sequence activities on vocal performance achievement of primary music students. *The Quarterly Journal of Music Teaching and Learning II* (1 & 2), 118–129.

Shuter-Dyson, R., & Gabriel, C. (1968). *The psychology of musical ability.* London and New York: Methuen.

Silva, M. C. C. F. (1998). *Composing, performing and audience-listening as symmetrical indicators of musical understanding.* Unpublished doctoral dissertation, University of London, Institute of Education, London.

Smith, F. (1971). *Understanding reading: A psycholinguistic analysis of reading and learning to read.* New York: Holt, Rinehart, & Winston.

Stockton, J. L. (1983). *An experimental study of two approaches to the development of aural meter discrimination among students in a college introductory class.* Unpublished doctoral dissertation, Temple University, Philadelphia.

Swanwick, K. (1979). *A basis for music education.* London: Routledge.

Swanwick, K. (1983). *The arts in education: Dreaming or wide awake?* London: University of London Institute of Education.

Swanwick, K. (1988). *Music, mind and education.* London: Routledge.

Swanwick, K. (1991). Further research on the developmental spiral. *Psychology of Music, 19,* 22–32.

Swanwick, K. (1994). *Musical knowledge: Intuition, analysis and music education.* London and New York: Routledge.

Swanwick, K. (1999). *Teaching music musically.* London and New York: Routledge.

Swanwick, K., & Tillman, J. (1986). The sequence of musical development: a study of children's composition. *British Journal of Music Education, 3*(3), 305–339.

Swanwick, K., & França, C. C. (1999). Composing, performing and audience-listening as indicators of musical understanding. *British Journal of Music Education, 16*(1), 3–17.

Tillman, J. (1987). *Towards a model of the development of*

musical creativity: A study of the compositions of children aged 3–11. Unpublished doctoral dissertation, Institute of Education, University of London, London.

Taggart, C. C. (1989). *An investigation of the hierarchical nature of the stages of audiation.* Unpublished doctoral dissertation, Temple University, Philadelphia.

Taggart, C. C., & Gouzouasis, P. (1995). Music learning and language learning: A metaphor from an organismic perspective. *Update: Applications of Research in Music Education 13*(2), 9–11.

Tarrell, V. V. (1964). *An investigation of the validity of the Gordon Musical Aptitude Profile.* Unpublished doctoral dissertation, University of Iowa, Iowa City.

Thayer, R. W. (1971). *An investigation of the interrelation of personality traits, musical achievement, and different measures of musical aptitude.* Unpublished doctoral dissertation, University of Iowa, Iowa City.

Trehub, S. E., Bull, D., & Thorpe, L. A. (1984). Infants' perception of melodies: The role of melodic contour. *Child Development, 55,* 821–830.

Upitis, R. (1990). Children's invented notations of familiar and unfamiliar melodies. *Psychomusicology, 9,* 89–106.

Van Neuys, K., & Weaver, H. E. (1943). Memory span and visual pauses in reading rhythms and melodies. *Psychological Monographs 55,* 33–50.

Vaughn, C. (1996). *How life begins: The science of life in the womb.* New York: Times Books.

Volger, T. (1973). *An investigation to determine whether learning effects accrue from immediate sequential administration of the six levels of the Iowa Tests of Music Literacy.* Unpublished doctoral dissertation, University of Iowa, Iowa City.

Vygotsky, L. S. (1978). *Mind in society: The development of higher psychological processes.* V. John-Steiner, E. Souberman, M. Cole, & S. Scribner (Eds.) Cambridge, MA: Harvard University Press.

Walters, D. L. (1991). Edwin Gordon's music aptitude work. *The Quarterly Journal of Music Teaching and Learning II* (1 & 2), 65–72.

Wilkin, P. E. (1996). A comparison of fetal and newborn responses to music and sound stimuli with and without daily exposure to a specific piece of music. *Bulletin of the Council for Research in Music Education, 127,* 163–169.

Wing, H. D. (1961). *Standardised Tests of Musical Intelligence.* Windsor, UK: National Foundation for Educational Research. (Originally published in 1939)

Woodruff, L. (1983). *A predictive validity study of the Primary Measures of Music Audiation.* Unpublished doctoral dissertation, Temple University, Philadelphia.

Woodward, S. C. (1992). *The transmission of music into the human uterus and the response to music of the human fetus and neonate.* Cape Town, University of Cape Town, South Africa.

Young, W. T. (1969). *An investigation of the relative and combined power of musical aptitude, general intelligence, and academic achievement tests to predict musical attainment.* Unpublished doctoral dissertation, University of Iowa, Iowa City.

Creativity Research in Music, Visual Art, Theater, and Dance

MAUD HICKEY

Because engagement in the arts generally is assumed to offer opportunities for inherently creative acts, it is easy to presume that research in the arts and research in creativity are naturally intertwined. This is not true and, in fact, although a very large body of literature on "General" creative thinking exists, a much smaller proportion of research focuses exclusively on creativity in the arts. The purpose of this chapter is to review the empirical research of creativity in music, visual art, dance, and theater in order to better understand what is known about creative development, learning, and thinking in these disciplines. One goal is to extend the literature review of creative thinking in music begun by Webster (1992) and to supplement it with examples of empirical studies of creativity in the other arts that have been published in the past 20 years. The chapter concludes with a discussion of the most compelling issues in creativity research and how these might influence a research agenda for the future.

Review Parameters

Next to providing an operational definition of "creativity," additional factors are detailed that guided my choice of studies to be included in this chapter.

Operational Definition of Creativity

A creative product is one that is both novel (to its creator) and is "appropriate" or "valuable" in the context of a domain, and a creative person is one who produces creative products (Mayer, 1999). This definition proves useful in suggesting that creativity involves the act of fashioning an original product and that creative thinking is a cognitive act. This means that creative thinking is a process con-

nected to a tangible, albeit novel, product. Therefore, both the process by which a person works toward the completion of an artistic product and the product itself require attention in any research on artistic creativity. For the purpose of this chapter, only empirical studies were chosen if the explicit focus was on creativity or creative thinking in music, visual art, dance, or theater, and whose subjects ranged from preschool-aged through college level.

Music Composition Research

A growing body of research is that which examines the processes or products of children's music compositions (i.e., Barrett, 1997; Carlin, 1997; van Ernst, 1993; Gromko, 1996; Henry, 1995; Seals, 1990; Wilson & Wales, 1995). While the act of music composition may essentially be creative, the majority of music composition studies focus on the technical characteristics or technical processes of composition rather than on the explicit creative aspects of the compositional process or product. A number of recent studies also pay attention to the use of digital technology in music composition (i.e., Emmons, 1998; Erkunt, 1998; Folkestad, Lindström, & Hargreaves, 1997; Hickey, 1997; Ladányi, 1995; Robinson, 1995; Tsisserev, 1997), but do not explicitly examine the effects of this technology on creativity. An in-depth presentation of the issues involved with digital technology and musical learning can be found elsewhere in this Handbook.

While the study of the compositional processes in children is important for furthering our understanding of children's musical development, they are not included in this review unless the focus of the research was on the processes or products of creative thinking itself. Exceptions are those studies in music composition or visual art that are important because they form a foundation for continued work in creativity research (such as in developmental research). Studies of creativity in the arts that offer theoretical, philosophical, biographical, or autobiographical perspective have been excluded from this review.

Content General or Content Specific?

A long-standing and lively debate in creativity research pertains to the issue of whether creativity is a general "trait" that extends across all domains, or is only content specific. Most recently, Baer (1998) and Plucker (1998) provided a point-counterpoint illustration of that debate. While the fundamental construct of a general creativity trait is presumed in divergent production creativity tests such as the *Torrance Tests of Creative Thinking (TTCT)* (Torrance, 1974), researchers such as Baer (1991, 1993, 1994) and Runco (1989) argue for trait-specific creativity. Runco suggests not only that creativity skills are uncommon across different domains, but they may be specific to media within a domain. Others, such as Conti, Coon, and Amabile (1996), Plucker (1999), and Guastelle and Shissler (1994) propose that a certain level of creativity skill carries across different domains. Results from research that examines the relationship between general creativity skills and creativity in the arts are mixed (reviewed later in this chapter).

Continued effort toward the understanding of domain-versus content-specific creativity is warranted. It is clear that the differences in findings are artifacts of the different techniques used to measure creativity (such as checklists, divergent production tests, and "real-life" assessments). Differences in results may also be accounted for based on the age differences of subjects. The studies reviewed in this chapter assume either, or both, the domain-specific and general creativity view, mostly without acknowledging this unresolved issue.

The remainder of this chapter is organized in four sections: a brief overview of the history of research on creativity in general, and in music, visual art, dance, and theater in particular; a review of recent empirical studies organized according to their theoretical or methodological focus; a discussion of the new research topics in creativity research; and concluding remarks that include ideas for a future research agenda.

Historical Background—A Brief Overview

J. P. Guilford's 1950 presidential address to the American Psychological Association is often marked as the beginning of empirical research on creativity. Guilford, and subsequently Torrance, had an immense influence on the field of psychometric measurement of creative thinking. The *Torrance Tests of Creative Thinking* (TTCT) (Torrance, 1974)

have been the most widely used standardized measures of general creative thinking ability. The TTCT are paper-and-pencil tests that come in both verbal ("Thinking Creatively With Words") and figural ("Thinking Creatively With Pictures") versions. In each of the versions, subjects are asked to guess causes or consequences, or provide ideas for product improvement or unusual uses for a variety of problems. Responses are scored for fluency, flexibility, originality, and elaboration. Fluency is determined by the sheer quantity of responses, flexibility by the number of different categories of responses, originality by the uniqueness of the response (relative to a set of responses), and elaboration is scored by the details given in the response. These factors influenced the psychometric work on creative thinking in music (Webster, 1977, 1987b, 1990, 1994) as well as in visual art (Efland, 1990; Eisner, 1965; Lowenfeld, 1958).

Early Creativity Research in Music and Visual Art

There were three notable and pioneering research projects in children's visual art and music in the 1940s. Research in visual art by Munro, Lark-Horovitz, and Barnhart, (1942), and in children's creative music composition by Doig (1941, 1942a, 1942b) took place at the Cleveland Museum of Art. Doig analyzed the creative aspects of children's music compositions while Munro et al. examined the creativity of children's visual art productions. From 1937 to 1948, Moorhead and Pond (1978) carried out unique qualitative research of children's creative music exploration at the Pillsbury Foundation School in Santa Barbara, California. These studies are exceptional, first of all because of their longitudinal nature, and, second, because there were no equivalent studies of creativity in music again until the late 1960s.

Lowenfeld had tremendous influence directing the agenda of visual art research and education during the decades of the 1950s and 1960s. His seminal text *Creative and Mental Growth* (Lowenfeld, 1947) provided the first in-depth developmental basis for children's artistic education and advocated an educational philosophy that endorsed the development of creativity and aesthetic sensitivity in art classes. Seven subsequent publications of this text were as successful and influential as the first. Lowenfeld created an atmosphere for creativity in art education that opposed the "rules-based" and mechanical drawing present in earlier decades (Efland, 1990). The movement toward more creativity in visual art education was not unlike the movement toward more creative and comprehensive curriculums in music education during the early 1970s.

Creativity research in visual art gained momentum in the 1960s (e.g., Hausman, 1959) because of the initiatory and influential efforts of Lowenfeld (Efland, 1990). Eisner reported in the 1965 *Yearbook for the National Society for the Study of Education* (NSSE) that over 30% of the studies published in *Studies in Art Education* between its inception in 1959 and 1965 were studies dealing with creativity in art. Research on creative thinking in music became prominent in the early 1970s. Greenhoe (1972) and Rhodes (1971) began that decade examining the theoretical and philosophical implications of creative thinking for music education, while Vaughan (1971), Gorder (1976), and Webster (1977a) led the renewal of empirical research studies of creative thinking in music.

The founding of "Harvard Project Zero" in 1967 signifies the beginning of change toward constructivist and cognitive approaches to understanding artistic creativity (Gardner, 1982). In visual art education, this change meant moving from promotion of self-expression and creativity to more curricular and comprehensive approaches (Eisner, 1965). "Discipline-oriented curricula," or the beginning of what is now known as Disciplined Based Arts Education (DBAE), began during that decade with research supported by plentiful government and foundation funds (Efland, 1990; Eisner, 1988). A similar, curricular, and comprehensive approach to music education developed in the 1960s, although it did not seem to have the lasting effect of the DBAE approach. This period of comprehensive and more academic approaches to the design of visual art and music curriculums coincides with a decline in studies of creativity in both music and art for several years.

Theater and Dance Education and Research

Theater and dance education experienced great progress during the 1960s, although they still lag far behind music and visual arts in education and research efforts (Faber, 1997). The modern dance movement in the beginning of the 20th century, led by Isadora Duncan, changed dance both spiritually and pedagogically. Dance as a curricular subject, however, was slow to be recognized for its own merit *outside* of the physical education curriculum. Not until the 1960s did dance earn recognition as a division within performance arts departments rather than as an attachment to physical education (Faber, 1997). This had a positive influence on dance education at the K–12 level. Similarly, theater education did not take hold in public school education until it became more prevalent in the universities and colleges in the 1950s (Colaresi, 1997).

Because of the later starts for dance and theater in education, there is a paucity of empirical studies in these disciplines. Systematic research regarding creativity in dance education is virtually nonexistent (Bonbright, 1999; Faber, 1997; Schwartz, 1993) and research on creativity in theater is equally sparse (Colaressi, 1997; Vitz, 1983).

Recent Empirical Studies

This review of recent empirical studies is organized according to the following theoretical or methodological foci: developmental studies; assessment studies; cognitive studies; and confluence studies.

Developmental Studies

Research on the development of creativity in children or adults in any of the art disciplines is sparse. Among some of the research that exists, one finds that both visual art aesthetic development and general creativity development demonstrate similar and characteristic U-shaped growth. Research on the development of musical creativity in children or adults is nonexistent.

General Creativity.   Research in general creativity indicates a U-shaped development that begins with a period of high creativity in early childhood (marked by play and freedom from conformity), is followed by a slump in the middle years, and then reemerges in a more sophisticated form of creativity for some in adulthood (Albert, 1996; Keegan, 1996; Runco & Charles, 1997). Although there is no consensus as to the exact age that a slump occurs, it seems to be prominent either at the start of school or between the ages of 9 and 12 and there are disagreements as to whether creativity is different in degree or in kind once it reemerges in adulthood (cf. Albert, 1996; Keegan, 1996). Keegan (1996) acknowledges the apparent gap between the creative child and creative adult, but suggests that it is a continuous developmental process with less of a "gap" or slump, as others assert. In contrast, Albert (1996) and others (e.g., Bloom, 1985; Feldman, with Goldsmith, 1991; Gardner, 1993; Winner, 1996) propose that childhood creativity poorly predicts adult, real-world creativity.

Creativity Development in Visual Art.   A U-shaped curve of aesthetic growth in visual art has been proposed by Gardner (1982), and Gardner and Winner (1982). Between the ages of 3 and 7, there occurs a "golden age of drawing" in which children produce not only large quantities of drawings but also ones that are highly creative, which sometimes bear resemblance to those created by adult artists. There is a dramatic change in children's drawings about the age of 7 and the creativity of their output hits a "low" during the middle adolescence years. During this time, children create fewer drawings, and experiment less with colors, shapes, patterns, and ideas; drawings become more representational, less abstract, and less creative than in the previous stage. Only a small percentage of children eventually break from the conformity of the middle school years and strive to become creative adult artists (Gardner, 1982; Winner, 1996).

Findings from studies by Baer (1996), Flannery and Watson (1991), Runco (1989), and Rostan (1997) contradict the hypothesis of U-shaped aesthetic growth in visual art. Baer (1996) proposes that the picture is not as bleak as Gardner and others suggest. He found that the creativity ratings of children's original collages showed a significant increase from kindergarten through fifth grade. Flannery and Watson (1991) studied pencil drawings of 106 third-, fourth-, and fifth-grade children and found that, while perceived confidence in drawing correlated negatively with grade level, there were increases in realism as well as originality of drawings as children got older. Runco (1989) also did not find any curvilinear relationship between age and assessments of creativity, originality, technical skill, and aesthetic appeal of varied artwork from 104 fourth-, fifth-, and sixth-grade children. Rostan (1997) sought to determine the relationships between age and problem finding, ideation, evaluation, and expertise, and to determine the relationship between the problem situation (open or closed) and novelty in art. The subjects were 60 "highly motivated arts students" (those who chose to participate in extracurricular art classes). Rostan found no curvilinear relationship between age and other variables. However, there was a curvilinear relationship between novelty and age when the "expertise variable" was removed.

Gardner (1982), Gardner and Winner (1982), Albert (1996), and others (e.g., Runco & Charles, 1997), acknowledge the contested aspect of the U-shaped developmental theory, which presumes that creativity that is manifest in childhood exploration is as intentional and meaningful as that of the adult artist. Researchers also admit that the influence of school and society may have a greater impact on the U-shaped growth than any natural cognitive growth. Other concerns about the theory of U-shaped artistic development include that it is based on a Western ideal of the "modern" art genre only, and that there is a question of what the bottom of the curve actually represents (i.e., lack of aesthetic quality, creativity, or technique).

Development of Creative Thinking in Music. There is no model of creative development in music, per se, but a model of music development proposed by Swanwick and Tillman (1986; Swanwick, 1991) might be used to examine creative growth in music because it was developed based on analyses of compositions and improvisations. Swanwick and Tillman's model (1986) is based on assessments of 745 various composition and improvisation tasks by 48 children, aged 3 to 11. There were several different tasks, some in which children worked individually and, in others, in small groups. Unlike the U-shaped development proposed in general creativity and in visual art, the Swanwick and Tillman model suggests an invariant and progressive sequence of development as children move from stages of early mastery (ages 0–4), through imitation (ages 4–9), imaginative play (ages 10–15), and, finally, to metacognition (ages 15+). Within each of these stages children move from unusual or personal style to more idiomatic tendencies. By the age of 7 or 8, children are able to create patterns and phrases that fall into two-, four- or eight-bar units (the end of the "Imitation" stage). It is important to point out that Swanwick and Tillman did not study subjects older than the age of 11 and therefore mostly speculated about development beyond this age.

Like Swanwick and Tillman, Kratus (1989) also examined developmental trends in children's musical composition processes. The approach that Kratus took, however, was much more systematic. Independent judges analyzed 10 minute segments of children's composition processes and categorized each 5-second interval as either: "exploration" (music sounds unlike any music played earlier); "development" (music sounds similar but not identical to music played earlier); "repetition" (music sounds the same as music played earlier); or "silence" (no music is heard). Results indicated that significant differences in musical processes existed across the age levels in the use of exploration, development, and silence. As children grow, they use more of the compositional strategies of development and repetition over exploration and silence. Younger children seemed unable to develop complete musical ideas and centered their time more around a process-oriented versus product-oriented thinking. Kratus (1994) also infers that early elementary children are less able to generate and develop complete musical ideas than upper elementary children, and that upper elementary children do this in ways similar to adult composers.

The model by Swanwick and Tillman and hypotheses by Kratus seem to be in direct contrast to a U-shaped development curve suggested in general creativity and in visual art development. Those who suggest a U-shaped development, however, are strictly examining aesthetic and creative ability, while the work by Swanwick and Tillman and Kratus follows children's progression toward the technical mastery of musical composition. As the slump at the bottom of the creativity "U" curve suggests a literal or realistic stage, therefore, the progression toward the ability to compose tonally and rhythmically centered compositions by the age of 9, as suggested by Swanwick and Tillman (1986) and Kratus (1989, 1994) is not as dissimilar to the U-shaped model as first thought. More research is needed in music to see what happens to children's creative development beyond this middle level age.

A few studies in music composition suggest alternatives to the sequence proposed by Swanwick and Tillman

(1986). In studies of the development of 3- to 13-year-old children's "intuitive music-making," Davies (1986, 1992, 1994) explicitly compares her findings to those of Swanwick and Tillman (1986) and to the U-shaped curve of artistic development proposed by Gardner (1982). Davies (1986) speculates that although progress occurs in children's spontaneous song making as they grow older, it is mainly portrayed as an increase of technical skills and greater confidence in handling musical material. Davies suggests that young children have the capacity for very early creative and imaginative facility in song making. Qualitative analyses of 32 5- to 7-year-old children's songs over a period of 18 months showed that children were able to create complete songs beginning at the age of 5 (Davies, 1992). Marsh (1995) also found, like Davies, that very young children were capable of demonstrating abilities outlined in the highest levels of the Swanwick and Tillman (1986) model. Marsh studied children's processes of innovation and composition in relation to text, music, and movement in playground games as well as children's awareness of these processes. Marsh's qualitative analyses of 448 examples of playground songs and clapping games by children aged 5 to 12 years revealed that variants of children's playground songs are produced by deliberate process of innovation: reorganization of formulae; elaboration; and condensation across all ages.

It is difficult to compare the developmental models reviewed thus far, since they focus on the development of different skills. While the art model and general creativity model of U-shaped development seem to measure complexity and originality, results from studies by Swanwick and Tillman and Kratus measure more convergent qualities such as phrase structure, completeness and tonal and metric regularity. There is a need to compare *creative* development in music and the other arts to development in general creativity and to the current developmental trends in music (Swanwick & Tillman, 1986) and music composition (Kratus, 1989; Davies, 1986, 1992, 1994; Marsh, 1995) in order to get a complete picture of the development of artistic creative skills in children. In addition, it would prove fruitful for researchers to compare and discuss similarities and differences in creativity development across the various art forms. This, of course, will require a consensus on the criteria that determine creativity, and the creation of valid measurement tools to track this phenomenon.

Assessment

The assessment literature in general creativity is only recently beginning to grow more diverse.[1] As mentioned previously, the widely used TTCT clearly dominated the field of psychometric research in general creativity. There have been no parallel efforts toward the development of psychometric tools to study creativity in any of the arts except for Webster's *Measurement of Creative Thinking in Music-II* (MCTM-II) (1994). Sparked by the "cognitive science revolution" of the 1960s (Gardner, 1985), more variety in research and assessment methods have influenced a recent "golden age" of research in creative thinking and assessment methodologies (Plucker & Renzulli, 1999). Although the previous decades provided a foundation for psychometric study, recent work is much more complex and comprehensive than its beginnings.

Recent criticism of the TTCT and similar divergent thinking measures has prompted greater variety and more conceptually complex approaches to the measurement of creativity (Amabile, 1996; Brown, 1989; Hocevar & Bachelor, 1989; Michael & Wright, 1989; Plucker & Renzulli, 1999; Plucker & Runco, 1998). The greatest criticism is that the theoretical constructs for the divergent thinking measures came first, then validated using specialized tests such as factor analyses, but not ever validated against any external measure of creative productivity. "The basic problem seems to be that creativity tests had only *apparent* construct validity and certainly not criterion validity" (Brown, 1989, p. 8). Another criticism is that the early tests of divergent thinking are paper-and-pencil tests that cannot possibly capture the greater and more complex instances of "real-life" creative endeavors.

The most commonly used tests or procedures (not counting researcher-designed measures) used to rate creativity in the studies reviewed for this chapter are briefly described in table 23.1.

Webster's MCTM, discussed and fully described elsewhere (e.g., Webster, 1987b, 1990, 1992, 1994), is the most well-known measure of a creative musical potential, and, like the TTCT, measures divergent thinking factors as well as the convergent factor of musical syntax. The MCTM requires subjects to manipulate a round sponge ball on the piano, play on pitched temple blocks with a mallet, and use their voice with a microphone and amplifier to create musical sounds in a gamelike atmosphere. Ten different tasks are divided into the three parts of "Exploration," "Application," and "Synthesis." Each of the 10 tasks are scored for some or all of the factors of musical extensiveness (length of time on task), musical flexibility (manipulation of the parameters of high/low, soft/loud, and fast/slow), musical originality (unique response), and musical syntax (musically logical). These subscore categories are standardized and averaged for a composite MCTM score. Recent research has compared MCTM scores to other kinds of musical tests. Amchin (1996) designed a Measure of Instrumental Creative Musical Response (MICMR) for rating the creativity of melody completion phrases on Orff instruments. Relationships between the MCTM posttest scores and the MICMR scores were slightly negative for both control and treatment groups.

Table 23.1 Tests of Creativity Used in Studies Reviewed in this Chapter

Title, Author	Age	Method	Factors Measured
Torrance Tests of Creative Thinking (Verbal and Figural editions) (Torrance, 1984)	Kindergarten through graduate	Paper/pencil—provide solutions to several kinds of problems	Fluency, flexibility, originality, elaboration
Thinking Creatively in Action and Movement (Torrance, 1981)	3–8 years	Verbal or action responses to produce alternative ways of moving; to improvise alternative solutions to problems	Fluency, originality, imagination
Wallach and Kogan Creativity Measure (1965)	Grade 5	Individualized. Verbal cues to solicit as many uses as possible for items; visual cues to solicit interpretations of abstract designs.	Number of responses; uniqueness of responses
Consequences Form A-I (Guilford & Guilford, 1980)	Grades 9 through adult	Paper/pencil; provide answers to new or unusual situations to problems	Originality, ideational fluency
Creativity attitude survey: Manual (Schaefer, 1971)	Grades 4–6	30 Statements with Yes/No answers. Designed for evaluating effectiveness of programs to enhance creativity	Creativity items
Consensual Assessment Technique (no author)	All ages	Assessment of creative product	Subjective rating of creativity by experts
Measure of Creative Thinking in Music (Webster, 1994)	4–10 years	Musical improvisation tasks using piano, temple blocks and voice manipulations	Extensiveness, flexibility, originality, musical syntax

Both pre- and posttest composite scores of Gordon's *Intermediate Measures of Music Audiation* (IMMA) (1982) were significantly related to MICMR scores, while MCTM scores showed a weak nonsignificant relationship to IMMA scores. Amchim suggests that the MICMR may likely assess convergent forms of creative thinking, while the MCTM assesses more divergent creative thinking skills. Amchin (1996) and Hickey (1995) found very low or negative correlations between holistic creativity ratings of children's improvisations or composition and scores from Webster's MCTM. This suggests that the different approaches are measuring different factors, perhaps all related to creativity, but that still need to be determined.

Consensual Assessment Technique. As an alternative to the divergent factor approach toward creative assessment, Amabile's (1996) development of a "Consensual Assessment Technique" (CAT) has emerged as a tool for measuring the creativity of artistic and business products. Amabile suggested that creative ability is best measured by assessing the creative quality of the products that are a result of creative endeavors. Furthermore, she proposed that subjective assessment of such products by experts in the domain for which the product was created is the most valid way to measure creativity (1996). The consensual assessment technique for rating creativity, then, is to rate the creativity of products using experts' agreed on—consensual—ratings of these products.

Amabile (1996) reports, by author, task/product, subjects, and judges used, the results of approximately 53 different studies that utilized the consensual assessment technique for rating creativity in a variety of artistic domains (visual art, poetry, storytelling). The interjudge reliabilities for the reported studies are consistently high. Several researchers have utilized or tested the CAT in visual art (e.g., Amabile & Gitomer, 1984; Baer, 1996; Barnard, 1993; Baumgarten, 1994; Hennessey, 1994; Koestner, Ryan, Bernieri, & Holt, 1984; Runco, 1989), and in poetry and story writing (Baer, 1994; Hennessey & Amabile, 1988), with consistently strong interjudge reliabilities, supporting the construct validity of this technique. The Consensual Assessment Technique has been modified and used successfully for rating the creativity of musical compositions by Bangs (1992), Hickey (1995), Daignault (1997), and Brinkman (1999), and for rating musical improvisations by Amchin (1996) and Priest (1997).

While the consensual assessment technique assumes that "expert" judges can reliably rate creative products, recent research has examined who the best "experts" might be. Runco, McCarthy, and Svenson (1994) sought to determine which group of judges were most reliable for judging the creativity of visual artwork when using consensual assessment. Forty-seven college-level subjects completed three artworks to be self-rated, rated by peers, and rated by professional artists for creativity. The self-assessment rankings and peer assessments rankings for subjects' artworks were similar, while professional judges also correctly ranked the drawings, but the differences between rankings were not significant and the scores given by the professionals were much lower than those given by the students. Runco et al. (1994) concluded that perhaps the professionals were not as sensitive to differences among products and were overly critical. Hickey (2000) sought to find the best group of judges when using a consensual assessment technique to rate the creativity of children's music compositions. She compared the reliability of creativity ratings of 10-year-old children's original musical compositions among different groups of judges. The interjudge reliabilities for each group's creativity ratings were: .04 for composers; .64 for all music teachers; .65 for instrumental music teachers; .81 for general/choral teachers; .70 for music theorists; .61 for seventh-grade children; and .50 for second-grade children. Similar to Runco's conclusion, Hickey suggested that maybe the best "experts" for judging creativity are not those who are professionals in the field but, rather, those closest to the students who are creating the works (in this case, teachers).

Webster and Hickey (1995) compared the reliability of open-ended ("consensual assessment" type) scales to more closed, criterion-defined scales for rating children's musical compositions and creativity. They discovered that rating scales using consensual assessment as outlined by Amabile were more, or at least as, reliable than scales with more specific criterion items.

Problem Finding.   Another approach to the assessment of creativity has been the quantification of "problem-finding" behavior as a measure of creativity. This concept was defined early by Getzels (1964) and developed later by Getzels and Csikszentmihalyi (1976) in visual art. Getzels and Csikszentmihalyi hypothesized that the first step in creative activity involves the discovery or formulation of the problem itself, or problem finding. They hypothesized that if creativity lies in problem-finding ability, then artists' behaviors of manipulating, exploring, and selecting the elements of the problem should be closely related to the creativity displayed in a finished product. Results of an empirical study with college-age visual artists showed significant relationships between the problem-finding behavior of the artists and the creative quality of their art products (Getzels & Csikszentmihalyi, 1976). Researchers have since used "problem-finding" measures for creativity, or have at least shown clear relationships between problem-finding behaviors and creative abilities in visual art (e.g., Chand & Runco, 1993; Dillon, 1982; Runco, 1994; Sapp, 1997; Wakefield, 1985, 1991, 1994) and in music (Brinkman, 1999; Hickey, 1995).

Assessment of Improvisation.   McPherson (1993) created a tool for assessing the improvisational ability of high school

instrumentalists, which combines ideas from the assessment techniques discussed thus far. A series of improvisation tasks were rated on Instrumental Fluency, Musical Syntax, Creativity, and Musical Quality using 5-point scales. Only the "anchors" of the scales were defined, leaving a relatively subjective approach to rating. Results showed high interjudge reliability for all items, and high internal consistency for a composite score.

In all of the arts, is it clear that there is a need for continued research and development of imaginative and valid measures of creativity. Webster's pioneering and continued effort in the development of the MCTM should be the standard and model from which to work (Webster, 1987b, 1990; Webster, Yale, & Haefner, 1988). The tasks in the MCTM are more realistic than typical paper-and-pencil tests, because they examine real-time and authentic creative musical tasks. There is a need to continue to examine more holistic and realistic assessment tools as an alternative to, or in combination with, the divergent factor approach. Consensual assessment and problem-finding techniques offer alternatives in the arts for rating the artistic creativity of children. More studies need to examine the relationships, differences, and similarities in the various measurement tools and work toward using the best features of each in order to create a valid and reliable measure of creative thinking in art.

Cognitive Studies

Cognitive studies in artistic creativity are those that seek to understand the mental representations, processes, and products underlying creative thought. The methodology is largely quantitative, as most of the studies are interested in examining relationships between and effects on creative thinking. This section begins with a review of studies examining creative processes in music, followed by studies that investigate relationships between creativity and other variables and studies that look at the effects of variables such as task design or instruction on creativity.

Creative Thinking Processes in Music.   A model of the creative thinking process in music has been proposed by Webster (1987a). Webster's model depicts the creative process of composition, performance, and analysis as moving through several stages and being influenced by enabling conditions and enabling skills before converging to a product. Although the creative aspects of music composition have been examined, there are few or no studies that look at the creative aspects of performance and analysis or listening. Dunn (1997) is the only person recently (since Webster's 1992 review) to empirically examine the music listening as a creative process. Dunn analyzed the reflective verbal responses and "listening maps" created by 29 undergraduate college students after they listened to a 1-

minute, 40-second piece of music. The analyses supported Dunn's hypothesis that creative listening is a phenomenon that is a unique, individual process, and can be represented mentally and visually.

Hickey (1995) focused on the creative musical exploration processes of fourth- and fifth-grade subjects who were placed either in "low" or "high" creativity groups (based on CAT assessments of final music compositions). In this study, subjects were recorded while they explored a music composition/learning program using a MIDI synthesizer. Analyses of the exploration process data showed that the high creative group developed musical ideas more often, and experimented and repeated musical ideas more often in their exploration processes than those in the low group. In addition, all of the high group subjects' compositions appeared, in whole or part, at some point during their exploration process, while, among those in the low creativity group, the emergence of subjects' final compositions during their music exploration was very inconsistent. Daignault (1997) followed a similar procedure by examining differences in children's approach to MIDI improvisation and composition tasks based on high or low creativity grouping. Quantitative and qualitative analyses revealed that, whereas the low groups of subjects tended to generate process-oriented improvisations, the high groups improvised product-oriented music (similar to Hickey's finding that subjects' compositions appeared some point during this process). During the development phase of the task, the high groups refined as well as substantially extended their improvisations. In addition, Daignault found differences between subjects in a group rated for high craftsmanship and subjects in a group rated for high creativity: The high craftsmanship group generated much of the musical material found in their finished compositions by manipulating the notation rather than by improvising as did the high creativity group. Both Hickey and Daignault discovered clear differences between process orientation of high and low creativity groups. Further examination of these differences in approaches to improvisation and compositions are warranted in order to better understand the creative thinking styles of children.

Relationships between Creativity and Aptitude or Achievement.

The group of studies that examined relationships between music creativity and music aptitude, as well as with other variables, provide mixed results. Although previous research (Webster, 1992) showed no relationship between musical creativity and musical aptitude, a recent study (Auh, 1997) found significant positive relationships between "compositional creativity" scores of 67 fifth- and sixth-grade subjects and tonal musical aptitude (as measured by the Gordon *Musical Aptitude Profile*, 1965), musical achievement (measured by the Colwell *Music Achievement Tests*, 1968) and academic grades. The mea-

surement for "compositional creativity" rated melodies for "craftsmanship" (which rated tonal center and rhythmic regularity), "musical syntax," "repetition of song," musical originality, and musical sensitivity. It should be noted that three of these five variables ("craftsmanship," "musical syntax," "repetition") are more related to technical ability than to creativity, thereby, perhaps, explaining the positive relationship with the aptitude and achievement scores. Auh also found that among the variables of formal music experiences, informal music experiences, musical self-esteem, musical aptitude, musical achievement, academic grades, IQ, and gender, the best predictor of "compositional creativity" in music was informal musical experiences.

Doxey and Wright (1990) examined the relationships between preschool children's musical aptitude (as measured by Gordon's *Primary Measures of Music Audition* [PMMA], 1979), children's general creativity (as measured by Torrance's *Thinking Creatively in Action and Movement,* 1981), and the physical and social environments of the home and school. The study reported significant relationships between the PMMA scores and the creativity scores. In a multiple regression analysis, the only variable that was a significant predictor of the PMMA composite score, however, was a score of general cognitive ability.

Uszynska (1998) sought to determine which variables— psychological, pedagogic, or social—contributed most to the artistic and verbal creative capacities of 6-year-old children. A group of 643 children were tested for, among other dimensions, intellectual capacity, divergent thinking as measured by Guilford's (1950) "tests of divergent thinking," and verbal and artistic creativity (author-designed tests). The results of correlations between all of the variables showed that factors most related to children's artistic creative capacity were: intellectual ability, competence of the preschool teacher, general creative thinking, and the self-esteem of the child. Uszynska concluded that there is a "great differentiation of creative capacity levels of children" (p. 133), and that the most significant factors may be those influenced by children's preschool teachers.

Effect of Task Design on Artistic/Creative Product.

Studies from the general creativity literature have shown consistently that open-ended and intrinsically motivating tasks are optimal for creativity (Amabile, 1996; Getzels, 1964; Sternberg, 1999). Findings from research in the arts show similar results. Burnard (1995) designed a qualitative study to investigate how task design influences students' composition experience. Eleven 15- and 16-year-old subjects completed four compositions, each involving a different type of task ranging from "prescription" (specific directions) to "freedom" (no directions other than to write for the medium of voice). Through qualitative data analyses of the compositions, subject interviews, and journal entries, Burnard found that the "prescription" task was preferred by students with advanced practical and theoretical backgrounds and the "freedom" task led to the most wide-ranging responses in individual expression. The students who preferred the "freedom" task were characterized by strong interpersonal interest, desire for individuality in expression, and independent working styles. Although Brinkman (1999) found no significant effect for problem finding (open or closed assignment) or creativity style (adaptor or innovator) on the creativity scores of musical melodies composed by 32 high school instrumental subjects, he found that subjects did show a significant preference for the open-style problems.

In visual art, Amabile and Gitomer (1984) discovered that 2- to 6-year-old children engaged in a "choice" condition for creating artistic collages had significantly higher creativity ratings on their collages than children in a "no-choice" condition. Baumgarten (1994) examined 220 children in third, fourth, and fifth grade, and found that they produced more creative art projects when working in a self-directed setting with minimal procedural and time constraints on their choices and behaviors compared to those in more constrained settings.

Bangs (1992) tested the effects of extrinsic and intrinsic motivation on the creativity of musical compositions created on xylophones by 37 third-grade children. Using a Consensual Assessment Technique to rate the creativity of pre- and posttreatment music compositions, she found that extrinsic motivation caused a decline in musical creativity scores and intrinsic motivation treatment caused a significant rise in musical creativity scores. Gerrard, Poteat, and Ironsmith (1996) sought to determine the effects of the immunization of external constraints on creativity and the effect of intrinsic motivation training on self-esteem on third-grade children in a collage-making task. No changes in self-esteem scores were found, but intrinsic motivation training was found to be effective in immunizing children against the negative effect of rewards on creativity. Although it is generally agreed that extrinsic rewards are detrimental to creativity, they show that training against this effect can be productive.

Arts Experiences and Creativity. Does studying the arts make people more artistically or generally creative? And does the type of instruction affect the creativity of the learner? These are questions posed in a number of studies and, again, with mixed results. The first group of studies are correlation studies that examined relationships between arts experiences and creativity. In a meta-analysis of four correlation studies, Moga, Burger, Hetland, and Winner (2000) found a slight positive relationship between studying the arts and general creativity measures. A study by Hamann, Bourassa, and Aderman (1991) examined the

relationships of high school subjects' creativity scores to arts experiences (visual art, drama, theater, dance, music), experiences in music, improvisation and jazz experience, and academic achievement. One hundred forty-four high school students who had experience in either visual art, theater, or music completed the Guilford and Guilford (1980) *Consequences* measure to assess creativity. There were no significant differences in creativity scores based on any of the arts experience variables. When GPA was used as a covariate, however, an analysis of covariance (ANCOVA) did show a significant main effect for musical experience and theater, with high experience in these areas producing higher mean creativity scores. A 1990 study by Hamann, Bourassa, and Aderman sought to determine the relationships between general creativity scores (measured by the *Consequences* test) and number of years of experience in music or other arts of 55 college-level students. The researchers found significantly higher general creativity scores for music majors than nonmusic majors, and for subjects who had more years of experience in the arts (10+ years) than those with less experience with the arts (0–10 years).

Conversely, Howell (1990) found no significant difference among general creativity scores (as measured by the TTCT) of 144 high school subjects with varying arts education experience (music, visual art, theater, dance), and no significant difference among creativity scores of subjects by type of arts experience (music or visual art or other). Brennan (1982) found no positive relationship between creativity in dance (as judged by a "creative movements test") and general creativity factors (verbal, figural, and personality creativity measures) of graduate and undergraduate college dance students.

Correlations between domain-specific and general creativity may be mostly dependent on age. Hong, Milgram, and Gorsky (1995) found that general creativity (as measured by an adaptation of the Wallach and Kogan tests [1965]) was the best predictor of "real-life" artistic creative performance of second-grade children. Hong et al. also found significant intercorrelations among drama and literature, drama and visual art, literature and visual art, and music and visual art. Sports and dance were not significantly related to the other domains. They suggest that, at young ages, children have not yet developed domain-specific skills. This hypothesis coincides with the Howell (1990) and Brennan (1982) studies, who found domain-specific creativity does not relate to general creativity in older students, yet contradicts the findings of Hamann et al. (1990, 1991) and Moga et al. (2000). The differences in measures and the different types of instruction used in each of the studies most likely are the cause of these discrepancies and highlight the need for better and more consistent creativity assessment tools.

Several studies have examined the effect of different kinds of arts training on creativity. Moga et al. (2000) performed two meta-analyses of experimental studies; one that looked at verbal creativity scores as the outcome, and the other that looked at figural creativity scores as the outcome. The meta-analyses showed no causal relationship between arts study and verbal creativity, and found some support for causal relationship between studying the arts and figural creativity tests. Only three studies were examined in each meta-analysis.

Thompson (1991) worked with 39 middle school subjects to determine the creative effectiveness of two different approaches toward visual art education. A treatment group received 9 weeks of interdisciplinary art instruction, including specific instruction for creative thinking, and science instruction to motivate sources of imagery. A control group received lessons in traditional two-dimensional art with emphasis on design and composition. The control group also learned creative thinking skills using brainstorming and synectics techniques. While there were no significant differences between groups on the TTCT (figural version) total score, there were significant gains on the posttest TTCT "originality" subscore for the control group, as well as significant gains in "enthusiasm" for art by the control group. Kim (1998) compared the effects of creative dance instruction versus standard dance instruction on the creative thinking abilities of seventh-grade female students in Korea. The creative dance group made significant gains over the control group on all subscores of the figural form of the TTCT after an 8-week treatment period. Schmidt, Goforth, and Drew (1975) worked with 78 kindergarten students over an 8-week period to observe whether children who engaged in creative dramatics would score higher on creativity tests than children who had not. The randomly assigned treatment group who received creative dramatics instruction scored significantly higher on creativity (as measured by an adaptation of the 1965 Wallach and Kogan tests [Rotter, Langland, & Berger, 1971]) than the control group subjects. Bennett (1982) investigated the effects of creative experience in drama on the creativity (as measured by a "Creativity Attitude Survey"; Schaefer, 1971), self-concept, and achievement of 55 fifth- and sixth-grade students. Utilizing a pretest–posttest control group design, treatment group subjects were involved in a 12-week program involving the writing, preparation, and presentation of an original musical drama. Although Bennett found no statistically significant differences between groups in self-concept or achievement, there were significant posttest creativity score increases in the treatment group, while the control group creativity scores went down. The outcomes in all of these studies are not surprising, as the training/experimental conditions involved creative activities; yet, they also point to the strong con-

clusion that training for creativity in the arts might, in fact, strengthen general creativity skills.

Perrine (1989) found opposite results when considering the effect of musical theater participation on the creativity of 100 sixth-grade subjects. The only significant differences between the treatment and control groups in the posttest was on the elaboration subscores of the figural TTCT. This may be because the treatment in Perrine's study consisted only of rehearsing songs and dialogue from several Broadway musicals in order to perform revue-type shows, rather than explicit creative thinking training or techniques such as those used in the previous studies.

Gibson (1989), Luftig (2000), and Dillard (1982) were interested in the effect of multiple arts experiences on creativity. Gibson (1989) compared the differences in the development of creativity skills between a group of sixth- and seventh-grade students that had only music instruction (music improvisation) and a group that received multiple arts instruction (music, visual art, movement). While Gibson found gains for music creativity (as measured by Webster's "Thinking Creatively with Music"; 1977b) and general creativity (as measured by the TTCT figural) in both groups, the gains were greater and significant for subjects in the multiple-arts group than the music-only group. Luftig (2000) found that after infusion in a multiple arts curriculum program over one school year, subjects in grades 2, 4, and 5 showed significant gains in posttest creative thinking scores (TTCT figural) over subjects who did not experience this curriculum. Dillard (1982) tested the effect of fine arts (music, drama, and visual arts) participation on the creativity (measured by TTCT figural) of gifted children in grades K–3. After participation for 1 hour/week over 7 months, Dillard found significant improvement in creativity scores of subjects in kindergarten and grade 3, and for the combined grade levels.

Hobbs Trapp (1998) examined the effects of art criticism training on the creativity of junior-high level subjects. Utilizing a pretest–posttest control group design, she found that subjects who had art criticism training did not perform significantly higher on the TTCT than those who did not have this training. In an attempt to determine whether copying deters the general creativity of third- and fourth-grade subjects, Munson (1993) worked with third- and fourth-grade subjects over a 24-week period[2] in which groups underwent conditions of copying for a length of time or freestyle drawing for an equivalent length of time. The freestyle group posttest TTCT (figural) scores were significantly higher than the copying groups in elaboration and originality subscores as well as the total score.

Although Webster, in his 1992 review, found that standard music instruction alone does not effect musical creativity, both Priest (1997) and Fung (1997) found positive effects for *creative* musical training on musical creativity scores. Priest (1997) compared the effect of creative and comprehensive teaching lessons on the creative and musical development of fifth-grade band students. The treatment group activities included creating notations, playing by ear, composing variations and original compositions, and improvising, over a 16-week period. Two control groups worked on the basics of performance and played music from method books. Musical creativity for the experimental group ($N = 14$) was assessed by judges who rated a sample of improvisations, variations, and compositions using a researcher-designed "Consensual Musical Creativity Assessment." Results indicated that subjects in the experimental group performed significantly better than the control group on "play by ear" exercises from a "Measure of Extended Instrumental Music Achievement," but not as well on sight-reading exercises. And, as expected, *Musical Aptitude Profile* (Gordon, 1965) scores were not significant predictors of creativity. Priest did not compare creativity differences between the control and experimental groups.

Fung (1997) found that first- and second-grade children who participated in a "sound exploration" program (which consisted of several workshops allowing children to explore, experiment, and improvise with sounds) scored significantly higher on factors of musical flexibility, musical originality, and musical syntax on Webster's MCTM-II (1994) than children who did not participate in the program. Amchin (1996) compared the effects of verbal instruction and feedback (versus no verbal feedback) during improvisation on the musical creativity of 129 fourth- and fifth-grade children in Orff-based classroom activities. He found no significant differences between the experimental and control groups on musical creative thinking scores as measured by the MCTM. There was no significant posttest improvement for either treatment or control group on MCTM scores.

This section on cognitive studies comprises the largest of all sections, with most studies focusing on either the relationship between general creativity and arts training, or the effect of arts training (or type of training) on creativity. While the correlation studies present conflicting results, it seems general creativity can be positively affected when arts instruction focuses on creative techniques. It also appears likely that either the type of task and/or instruction has an effect on the creativity of children in arts-related learning. Intrinsic motivation, open task, or choice are the best conditions for creative activities, and some artistic and creative instruction seems to enhance creative thinking skills. Exceptions were that verbal instruction and feedback (Amchin, 1996), art criticism training (Hobbs Trapp, 1998), and copying (Munson, 1993) did not boost general creativity of subjects compared to subjects without these treatments. Multiple arts experiences rather than music alone seem to be best for general creativity skills (Dillard, 1982; Gibson, 1989; Luftig, 2000), and creative teaching

in music can boost the musical creativity of students (Priest, 1997; Fung, 1997).

Confluence Studies

Perhaps the most promising field to emerge in the study of creativity is that which hypothesizes that several components (such as domain and field characteristics, social/cultural contexts, historical forces, events, and trends) must converge for creativity to occur—that is, a confluence of factors. As Mayer (1999) pointed out: "The narrow focus on cognition epitomized by the psychometric and experimental approaches should be widened to recognize the social, cultural, and evolutionary context of creative cognition" (p. 458). A confluence approach is illustrated in models of creative thinking that involve more than analyses of creative thought processes or products. Examples of such models include those by Amabile (1996), Feldman, Csikszentmihalyi, and Gardner (1994), and Sternberg (1988). Amabile proposes a model that combines intrinsic motivation, domain-relevant knowledge and abilities, and creativity-relevant skills. Feldman et al. propose a three-facet model of creativity that includes the individual, the domain, and the field. Sternberg combines intelligence, style, and personality factors as critical components of creativity.

There are two empirical studies in the arts that fall into the "confluence" category. Claire (1993) illustrated how peer social processes have a great influence on children's creative productivity. In her qualitative study of three fifth-grade classrooms, Claire discovered that when student engagement in work is diverted by teacher-student interactions or other hierarchically oriented factors (as opposed to peer-social interactions), then the creative processes were jeopardized. However, subjects' creativity was enhanced when there were mutual and supportive peer interactions on creative work. This was especially true in music classes. James (1997) studied the sculpture artwork of a college nonart major in the context of a college classroom environment and based her findings on a framework of a "systems" approach to creativity. There is a need for more contextual and confluence approaches to the study of creativity in the arts. Perhaps the best model for this kind of research are the examples of multidimensional studies of exceptional young performing artists by Howe (1999), Sloboda, Davidson, Howe, and Moore (1996), Sloboda and Howe (1991), or prodigies (Bloom, 1985; Feldman, with Goldsmith, 1991). In these studies, multiple collections of data over time provide a rich picture of how and why talented young performers progress. Similar studies of the lives of exceptional *creative* child composers, improvisers, and other artists would contribute to a better understanding of the development of, and influential factors on, creativity in these fields.

Promising Topics of Research

The study of creativity in the arts is a relatively young field. While the groundwork has been laid with research in quantitative assessment and several cognitive studies, there are additional topics worth pursuing further in this field. Two areas of study—children's play and improvisation—are relatively recent and promise potentially rich research from which to deepen our understanding of creativity in the arts.

Children's Play

There is a growing group of studies that examine children's natural "musical play," and make connections between these behaviors in natural or classroom settings and creative or divergent thinking. Studies by Davies (1986, 1992, 1994), Marsh (1995), Campbell (1998), and Tarnowski and Leclerc (1994) observe children's creative musical play in natural settings such as playgrounds, or in different settings in a music classroom. All find that children are capable of complex music making *outside* of the "classroom music" culture, and all find a mixed multitude of social/cultural/family influences on children's generative musical gestures. Tarnowski and Leclerc (1994) found a negative effect of adult observation on children's musical exploration and play activities. Although these studies do not necessarily focus on "musical creativity," they can provide a background and beginning from which to frame a theory of creativity in music.

Improvisation

As improvisation is a kind of "spontaneous music making," we might consider it a helpful tool toward understanding creativity in music. There are far fewer studies related to improvisation in children than composition, and none focused directly on the concept of "creativity" in improvisation. In his survey of research of methods and models of improvisation, Pressing (1988) found the field was "far too meagre to have any definite repercussions for improvisation" (p. 129). Specific studies of creativity related to improvisation were only those early studies by Vaughan (1971), Gorder (1976), and Webster (1977a) that used improvisation tasks in assessing musical creativity (Pressing, 1988). The field of research on improvisation is young, and the recent new studies are beginning, simply and effectively, to help define the term itself in relation to children's music making and play. Burnard (1999) and Kanellopoulus (1999) offer examples of research with qualitative insights into the improvisatory world of children. It would be fruitful if continued research into children's improvisation were combined conceptually with the field of creativity. Excellent commentary by Sawyer (1999a, 1999b), Hargreaves (1999), Baily (1999), and Welch (1999) outlines clear and provocative research needs focused on improvisation.

Recommendations for the Future

Since the review of research of creativity assessment literature in music by Webster (1992), there have been more studies added to this base of knowledge. The group of cognitive studies reviewed in this chapter seem to point, at least in these early stages, to positive effects of creative arts experiences on creativity and to certain conditions for promoting creativity. No certain conclusions can be made yet, however, until more studies confirm these preliminary results.

There still exists a great need for more focused theories and discussion on the concept of creativity in the arts, which would lead to more systematic research. For whatever reasons, the excitement and activity over research on creativity in the arts peaked in the 1970s and then declined, with perhaps only a minor resurgence in the decade of the 1990s. As implied earlier, the period of comprehensive and more academic approaches to the design of visual art and music curriculums may have effected this decline of interest in the study of creativity in both music and art. The more recent research interest in music is in the area of music composition, which is only tangential to the focus of creativity; interest in this topic may have been triggered in the United States by the publication of the *National Standards for Arts Education* (Consortium of National Arts Education Associations, 1994).

There is a need for researchers interested in creativity in the arts to define a conceptual starting point as a basis for study. Once this is established, more imaginative ideas for assessment should be developed. The meaning of the word "creativity" or creative thinking is often assumed or implied in studies that focus on children's musical compositions, but the analyses more often relate to uses of tonal Western harmony and metric systems rather than stemming from a theory of creativity. Most of the visual art studies reviewed did not use assessment tools that specifically measured "artistic creativity" but instead assessed general creativity using the Torrance measures (1974, 1981). The problem-finding and consensual assessment concepts, which have been utilized mostly on college-aged or older subjects, offer alternative starting points toward the development of more valid and reliable assessment tools for measuring artistic creativity in children. There is room for tremendous growth in the creativity assessment field.

There also is a need for more longitudinal and confluence studies of creativity in children. There are no clear connections between the lives of creative artistic children and creative adult artists. What makes a *creatively* artistic child different than a less creative child who, nonetheless, can perform or draw technically well? Answers to this and similar questions through more in-depth qualitative study will aid in the understanding of developmental trends in artistic creativity as well as in educational applications for promoting creativity—a goal worth pursuing.

A final and very important concern is that, among the research studies on creativity in the arts, there are few that make clear connections to applications in the classroom. This need is especially felt in music, where teachers are expected to teach improvisation and composition, but with little guidance for making these lessons develop the creative side of children. Lessons learned from quality research of creativity in music and the other arts need to be passed on to the education community for practical application. When these connections are made, along with the continued study of creativity in music and the arts, there will be exciting possibilities for more creative growth and development of children in our arts classrooms.

NOTES

1. For more comprehensive descriptions of the field of psychometric approaches to creativity, see Plucker and Renzulli (1999) and Hocevar and Bachelor (1989).

2. The issue of the detriments of "copying" on children's artistic abilities and creativity was thoroughly discussed since the time Lowenfeld introduced creativity as an output of artistic education (Effland, 1990; Lowenfeld, 1947).

REFERENCES

Albert, R. S. (1996). Some reasons why childhood creativity often fails to make it past puberty into the real world. In M. A. Runco (Ed.), *Creativity from childhood through adulthood: The developmental issues* (pp. 43–56). San Francisco: Jossey-Bass.

Amabile, T. M. (1996). *Creativity in context: Update to the social psychology of creativity.* Boulder, CO: Westview Press.

Amabile, T. M., & Gitomer, J. (1984). Children's artistic creativity: Effects of choice in task materials. *Personality and Social Psychology Bulletin, 10*(2), 209–215.

Amchin, R. A. (1996). Creative musical response: The effects of teacher-student interaction on the improvisation abilities of fourth- and fifth-grade students. (Doctoral dissertation, University of Michigan, 1995). *Dissertation Abstracts International, 56*(8), 3044A.

Auh, M. (1997). Prediction of musical creativity in composition among selected variables for upper elementary students. *Bulletin of the Council for Research in Music Education, 133,* 1–8.

Baer, J. (1991). Generality of creativity across performance domains. *Creativity Research Journal, 4,* 23–39.

Baer, J. (1993). *Creativity and divergent thinking: A task-specific approach.* Hillsdale, NJ: Lawrence Erlbaum Associates.

Baer, J. (1994). Generality of creativity across performance domains: A replication. *Perceptual and Motor Skills, 79,* 1217–1218.

Baer, J. (1996). Does artistic creativity decline during elementary school? *Psychological Reports, 78,* 927–930.

Baer, J. (1998). The case for domain specificity of creativity. *Creativity Research Journal, 11*(2), 173–177.

Baily, J. (1999). Ethnomusicological perspectives on Sawyer's ideas. *Psychology of Music, 27*(2), 208–210.

Bangs, R. L. (1992). *An application of Amabile's model of creativity to music instruction: A comparison of motivational strategies.* Unpublished doctoral dissertation, University of Miami, Coral Gables, Florida.

Barnard, S. S. (1993). Interior design creativity: The development and testing of a methodology for the consensual assessment of projects. (Doctoral dissertation, Virginia Polytechnic Institute and State University, 1992). *Dissertation Abstracts International, 53*(8), 2780A.

Barrett, M. (1997). Invented notations: A view of young children's musical thinking. *Research Studies in Music Education, 8,* 2–14.

Baumgarten, M. D. (1994). The effects of constraint on creative performance. (Doctoral dissertation, University of California, Los Angeles). *Dissertation Abstracts International, 57*(7), 1997.

Bennett, O. (1982). *An investigation into the effects of a creative experience in drama upon the creativity, self-concept, and achievement of fifth and sixth grade students.* Unpublished doctoral dissertation, Georgia State University, Atlanta, Georgia.

Bloom, B. (1985). *Developing talent in young people.* New York: Ballantine.

Bonbright, J. M. (1999). Dance education 1999: Status, challenges, and recommendations. *Arts Education Policy Review, 101*(1), 33–39.

Brennan, M. A. (1982). Relationship between creative ability in dance and selected creative attributes. *Perceptual and Motor Skills, 55,* 47–56.

Brinkman, D. J. (1999). Problem finding, creativity style and musical compositions of high school students. *Journal of Creative Behavior, 33*(1), 62–68.

Brown, R. T. (1989). Creativity. What are we to measure? In J. A. Glover, R. R. Ronning, & C. R. Reynolds (Eds.), *Handbook of creativity* (pp. 3–32). New York: Plenum Press.

Burnard, P. (1995). Task design and experience in composition. *Research Studies in Music Education, 5,* 32–46.

Burnard, P. (1999). Bodily intention in children's improvisation and composition. *Psychology of Music, 27*(2), 159–174.

Campbell, P. S. (1998). *Songs in their heads: Music and its meaning in children's lives.* New York: Oxford University Press.

Carlin, J. (1997). Music preferences for compositions by selected students aged 9–15 years. *Bulletin of the Council for Research in Music Education, 133*, 9–13.

Chand, I., & Runco, M. (1993). Problem finding skills as components in the creative process. *Personality & Individual Differences 14*(1), 155–162.

Claire, L. (1993). The social psychology of creativity: The importance of peer social processes for students' academic and artistic creative activity in classroom contexts. *Bulletin of the Council for Research in Music Education, 119*, 21–28.

Colaresi, J. M. (1997). *Case study of a high school theatre teacher: planning, teaching and reflecting.* Unpublished doctoral dissertation, University of Maryland, College Park.

Colwell, R. (1968). *Music Achievement Tests.* Chicago: Follett Educational Corporation.

Consortium of National Arts Education Associations. (1994). *National Standards for Arts Education.* Reston, VA: Music Educators National Conference.

Conti, R., Coon, H., & Amabile, T. M. (1996). Evidence to support the componential model of creativity: Secondary analyses of three studies. *Creativity Research Journal, 9*(4), 385–389.

Daignault, L. (1997). Children's creative musical thinking within the context of a computer-supported improvisational approach to composition. (Doctoral dissertation, Northwestern University, 1996). *Dissertation Abstracts International, 57*, 4681A.

Davies, C. D. (1986). Say it till a song comes (reflections on songs invented by children 3–13). *British Journal of Research in Music Education, 3*(3), 279–293.

Davies, C. D. (1992). Listen to my song: a study of songs invented by children aged 5 to 7 years. *British Journal of Music Education, 9*, 19–48.

Davies, C. D. (1994). The listening teacher: an approach to the collection and study of invented songs of children aged 5 to 7. In H. Lees (Ed.), *Musical connections: Tradition and change. Proceedings of the 21st world conference of the International Society of Music Education* (pp. 120–128). Tampa, FL: ISME.

Dillard, G. (1982). *The effect of a fine arts program on the intelligence, achievement, creativity and personality tests scores of young gifted and talented students.* Unpublished doctoral dissertation, East Tennessee State University, Johnson City, Tennessee.

Dillon, J. T. (1982). Problem finding and solving. *Journal of Creative Behavior, 16*(2), 97–111.

Doig, D. (1941). Creative music: I. Music composed for a given text. *Journal of Educational Research, 35*, 262–275.

Doig, D. (1942a). Creative music: II. Music composed on a given subject. *Journal of Educational Research, 35*, 344–355.

Doig, D. (1942b). Creative music: III. Music composed to illustrate given music problems. *Journal of Educational Research, 36*, 241–253.

Doxey, C., & Wright, C. (1990). An exploratory study of children's music ability. *Early Childhood Research Quarterly, 5*, 425–440.

Dunn, R. E. (1997). Creative thinking and music listening. *Research Studies in Music Education, 8*, 42–55.

Efland, A. D. (1990). *A history of art education: intellectual and social currents in teaching the visual arts.* New York: Teachers College Press.

Eisner, E. W. (1965). American education and the future of art education. In W. R. Hastie (Ed.), *Art education. The sixty-fourth yearbook of the National Society for the Study of Education* (pp. 299–325). Chicago: NSSE.

Eisner, E. W. (1988). The Kettering curriculum for elementary art (1968). In S. M. Dobbs (Ed.), *Research readings for discipline-based art education: A journey beyond creating* (pp. 16–29). Reston, VA: National Art Education Association.

Emmons, S. E. (1998). *Analysis of musical creativity in middle school students through composition using computer-assisted-instruction: A multiple case study.* Unpublished doctoral dissertation, University of Rochester, New York.

Erkunt, H. (1998). *Computers as cognitive tools in music composition.* Unpublished doctoral dissertation, Boston University, Boston, Massachusetts.

Ernst, B. V. (1993). A study of the learning and teaching processes of non-naive music students engaged in composition. *Research Studies in Music Education, 1*, 22–39.

Faber, R. (1997). *The pedagogic and philosophic principles of the National Standards for Dance Education.* Unpublished doctoral dissertation, American University, Washington, DC.

Feldman, D. H. (1999). The development of creativity. In R. J. Sternberg (Ed.), *Handbook of creativity* (pp. 169–186). Cambridge, UK: Cambridge University Press.

Feldman, D. H., Csikszentmihalyi, M., & Gardner, H. (1994). *Changing the world: A framework for the study of creativity.* Westport, CT: Praeger.

Feldman, D. H., with Goldsmith, L. T. (1991). *Nature's gambit: Child prodigies and the development of human potential.* New York: Teachers College Press.

Fischer, C. W. (1989). *Effects of a developmental drama-inquiry process on creative and critical thinking skills in early adolescent students.* Unpublished doctoral dissertation, Kansas State University, Manhattan.

Flannery, K. A., & Watson, M. W. (1991). Perceived competence in drawing during the middle childhood years. *Visual Arts Research, 10*(1), 66–71.

Folkestad, G., Lindström, B., & Hargreaves, D. J. (1997). Young people's music in the digital age. *Research Studies in Music Education, 9*, 1–12.

Forseth, S. D. (1980). Art activities, attitudes, and achievement in elementary mathematics. *Studies in Art Education, 21*(2), 22–27.

Fung, C. V. (1997). Effect of a sound exploration program on children's creative thinking in music. *Research Studies in Music Education, 9*, 13–19.

Gardner, H. (1982). *Art, mind and brain: A cognitive approach to creativity.* New York: Basic Books.

Gardner, H. (1985). *The mind's new science. A history of the cognitive revolution.* New York: Basic Books.

Gardner, H. (1993). *Creating minds: An anatomy of creativity seen through the lives of Freud, Einstein, Picasso, Stravinsky, Eliot, Graham, and Gandhi.* New York: Basic Books.

Gardner, H., & Winner, E. (1982). First intimations of artistry. In S. Strauss (ed.), *U-shaped behavioral growth* (pp. 147–168). New York: Academic Press.

Gerrard, L. E., Poteat, G. M., & Ironsmith, M. (1996). Promoting children's creativity: Effects of competition, self-esteem, and immunization. *Creativity Research Journal, 9*(4), 339–346.

Getzels, J. W. (1964). Creative thinking, problem solving, and instruction. In E. R. Hilgard (Ed.), *Theories of learning and instruction* (pp. 240–276). Chicago: University of Chicago Press.

Getzels, J., & Csikszentmihalyi, M. (1976). *The creative vision: A longitudinal study of problem finding in art.* New York: John Wiley.

Gibson, S. M. (1989). A comparison of music and multiple arts experiences in the development of creativity in middle school students. (Doctoral dissertation, Washington University, 1988.) *Dissertation Abstracts International, 49* (12), 3543A.

Gorder, W. (1976). *An investigation of divergent production abilities as constructs of musical creativity.* Unpublished doctoral dissertation, University of Illinois at Urbana-Champaign.

Gordon, E. (1965). *Music aptitude profile.* New York: Houghton Mifflin Company.

Gordon, E. (1979) *Primary measures of music audiation.* Chicago: G.I.A. Publications.

Gordon, E. (1982). *Intermediate measures of music audiation.* Chicago: G.I.A. Publications.

Greenhoe, M. (1972). *Parameters of creativity in music education: An exploratory study.* Unpublished doctoral dissertation, University of Tennessee, Knoxville, Tennessee.

Gromko, J. E. (1996). In a child's voice: An interpretive interaction with young composers. *Bulletin of the Council of Research in Music Education, 128,* 37–51.

Guastelle, S. J., & Shissler, J. E. (1994). A two-factor taxonomy of creative behavior. *Journal of Creative Behavior, 28*(3), 211–221.

Guilford, J. P. (1950). Creativity. *American Psychologist, 14,* 205–208.

Guilford, J. P., & Guilford, J. S. (1980). *Consequences: Manual of instructions and interpretations.* Orange, CA: Sheridan Psychological Services, Inc.

Hamann, D. L., Bourassa, R., & Aderman, M. (1990). Creativity and the arts. *Dialogue in Instrumental Music Education, 14*(2), 59–68.

Hamann, D. L., Bourassa, R., & Aderman, M. (1991). Arts experiences and creativity scores of high school students. *Contributions to music education. 18,* 36–47.

Hargreaves, D. (1999). A psychologist's response to Sawyer. *Psychology of Music, 27*(2), 205–207.

Hausman, J. J. (Ed.). (1959). *Research in art education: 9th Yearbook.* Washington, DC: National Art Education Association.

Hennessey, B. A. (1994). The consensual assessment technique: An examination of the relationship between ratings of product and process creativity. *Creativity Research Journal, 7*(2), 193–208.

Hennessey, B. A., & Amabile, T. M. (1988). Story-telling: A method for assessing children's creativity. *Journal of Creative Behavior, 22*(4), 235–246.

Henry, W. (1995). *The effects of pattern instruction, repeated composing opportunities, and musical aptitudes on the compositional processes and products of fourth-grade students.* Unpublished doctoral dissertation, Michigan State University, East Lansing.

Hickey, M. (1995). *Qualitative and quantitative relationships between children's creative musical thinking processes and products.* Unpublished doctoral dissertation, Northwestern University, Evanston, Illinois.

Hickey, M. (1997). The computer as a tool in creative music. *Research Studies in Music Education, 8,* 56–70.

Hickey, M. (2000). The use of consensual assessment in the evaluation of children's music compositions. In C. Woods, G. Luck, R. Brochard, F. Seddon, and J. A. Sloboda (Eds.), *Proceedings from the Sixth International Conference on Music Perception and Cognition* [CD-ROM], Keele, UK, August, 2000.

Hobbs Trapp, D. D. (1998). An examination of the effects of an art criticism training model on the creative productions of selected junior high students. (Doctoral dissertation, University of Kansas, 1996). *Dissertation Abstracts International, 58*(10), 3807A.

Hocevar, D., & Bachelor, P. (1989). A taxonomy and critique of measurements used in the study of creativity. In J. A. Glover, R. R. Ronning, & C. R. Reynolds (Eds.), *Handbook of creativity* (pp. 53–76). New York: Plenum Press.

Hong, E., Milgram, R. M., & Gorsky, H. (1995). Original thinking as a predictor of creative performance in young children. *Roeper Review, 18*(2), 147–149.

Howe, M. J. A. (1999). Prodigies and creativity. In R. J. Sternberg, (Ed.), *Handbook of creativity* (pp. 431–446). Cambridge, UK: Cambridge University Press.

Howell, C. D. (1990). *The relationship between arts education and creativity among high school students.* Unpublished doctoral dissertation, University of Northern Colorado, Greeley.

James, P. (1997). Learning artistic creativity: A case study. *Studies in Art Education, 39*(1), 74–88.

Kanellopoulus, P. (1999). Children's conception and practice of musical improvisations. *Psychology of Music, 27*(2), 175–191.

Keegan, R. T. (1996). Creativity from childhood to adulthood: A difference of degree and not of kind. In M. A. Runco (Ed.), *Creativity from childhood through adulthood: The developmental issues* (pp. 57–66). San Francisco: Jossey-Bass.

Kim, J. (1998). The effects of creative dance instruction on creative and critical thinking of seventh grade female students in Seoul, Korea. (Doctoral dissertation, New York University, 1988). *Dissertation Abstracts International, 59* (5), 1378A.

Koestner, R., Ryan, R. M., Bernieri, F., & Holt, K. (1984). Setting limits on children's behavior: The differential effects of controlling vs. informational styles on intrinsic motivation and creativity. *Journal of Personality, 52*(3), 233–248.

Korzenik, D. (1995). The changing concept of artistic giftedness. In C. Golom (Ed.), *The development of artistically gifted children* (pp. 1–30). Hillsdale, NJ: Lawrence Erlbaum Associates.

Kratus, J. (1989). A time analysis of the compositional processes used by children ages 7 to 11. *Journal of Research in Music Education, 37*(1), 5–20.

Kratus, J. (1994). The way children compose. In H. Lees (Ed.), *Musical connections: tradition and change. Proceedings of the 21st world conference of the International Society of Music Education* (pp. 128–140). Tampa, FL: ISME.

Ladányi, K. S. (1995). *Processes of musical composition facilitated by digital music equipment.* Unpublished doctoral dissertation, University of Illinois at Urbana-Champaign.

Lowenfeld, V. (1947). *Creative and mental growth; a textbook on art education.* New York: Macmillan.

Lowenfeld, V. (1958). Current research on creativity may revolutionize our teaching methods. *NEA Journal, 47*(8), 538–540.

Luftig, R. L. (2000). An investigation of an arts infusion program on creative thinking, academic achievement, affective functioning, and arts appreciation of children at three grade levels. *Studies in Art Education, 41*(3), 208–227.

Marsh, K. (1995). Children's singing games: Composition in the playground? *Research Studies in Music Education, 4,* 2–11.

Mayer, R. E. (1999). Fifty years of creativity research. In R. J. Sternberg (Ed.), *Handbook of creativity* (pp. 449–460). Cambridge, UK: Cambridge University Press.

McPherson, G. (1993). Evaluating improvisational ability of high school instrumentalists. *Bulletin of the Council for Research in Music Education, 119,* 11–20.

Michael, W. B., & Wright, C. R. (1989). Psychometric issues in the assessment of creativity. In J. A. Glover, R. R. Ronning, & C. R. Reynolds (Eds.), *Handbook of creativity* (pp. 33–52). New York: Plenum Press.

Moga, E., Burger, K., Hetland, L., & Winner, E. (2000). Does studying the arts engender creative thinking? Evidence for near but not far transfer. *Journal of Aesthetic Education, 34*(3–4), 91–104.

Moorhead, G., & Pond, D. (1978). *Music for young children.* Santa Barbara: Pillsbury Foundation for the Advancement of Music Education. (Reprinted from the 1941–1951 editions)

Munro, T., Lark-Horovitz, B., & Barnhart, E. (1942). Children's art abilities: Studies at the Cleveland Museum of Art. *Journal of Experimental Education, 11*(2), 97–129.

Munson, A. E. (1993). The relative effects of freestyle vs. copying on creativity of third and fourth graders. (Doctoral dissertation, Oklahoma State University, 1992). *Dissertation Abstracts International, 53*(8), 2652A.

Paiser, D., & van den Berg, A. (1997). The mind of the beholder: Some provisional doubts about the U-curved aesthetic development thesis. *Studies in Art Education, 38*(3), 158–178.

Perrine, V. B. (1989). *The effect of participation in a musical theatre production on the self-concept, attitude toward music and music class, and creative thinking skills of middle school students.* Unpublished doctoral dissertation, University of Alabama, Tuscaloosa.

Plucker, J. A. (1998). Beware of simple conclusions: The case of content generality of creativity. *Creativity Research Journal, 11*(2), 179–182.

Plucker, J. A. (1999). Reanalyses of student responses to creativity checklists: evidence of content generality. *Journal of Creative Behavior, 33*(2), 126–137.

Plucker, J. A., & Renzulli, J. S. (1999). Psychometric approaches to the study of human creativity. In R. J. Sternberg (Ed.), *Handbook of creativity* (pp. 35–61). Cambridge, UK: Cambridge University Press.

Plucker, J. A., & Runco, M. A. (1998). The death of creativity measurement has been greatly exaggerated: Current issues, recent advances, and future directions in creativity assessment. *Roeper Review, 21*(1), 36–39.

Pressing, J. (1988). Improvisation: Methods and models. In J. A. Sloboda (Ed.), *Generative processes in music: The psychology of performance, improvisation, and composition* (pp. 129–178). New York: Oxford University Press.

Priest, T. L. (1997). *Fostering creative and critical thinking in a beginning instrumental music class.* Unpublished doctoral dissertation, University of Illinois at Urbana-Champaign.

Rhodes, E. (1971). A comparative study of selected contemporary theories of creativity with reference to music education in the secondary schools. (Unpublished doctoral dissertation, Louisiana State University and Agricultural and Mechanical College). *Dissertation Abstracts International, 31*(9), 5610B.

Robinson, N. G. (1995). *An examination of the influence of visual feedback and reflection time on the pitch and duration characteristics of 9-year-olds' musical compositions.* Unpublished doctoral dissertation, Teachers College, Columbia University, New York.

Rostan, S. M. (1997). A study of young artists: The development of talent and creativity. *Creativity Research Journal, 10,* 175–192.

Rotter, D. M., Langland, L., & Berger, D. (1971). The validity of tests of creative thinking in seven-year-old children. *Gifted Child Quarterly, 15,* 273–278.

Runco, M. A. (1989). The creativity of children's art. *Child Study Journal, 19*(3), 177–189.

Runco, M. A. (Ed.) (1994). *Problem finding, problem solving, and creativity.* Norwood, NJ: Ablex.

Runco, M. A. (Ed.) (1996). *Creativity from childhood through adulthood: The developmental issues.* San Francisco: Jossey-Bass Publishers.

Runco, M. A., McCarthy, K. A., & Svenson, E. (1994). Judgments of the creativity of artwork from students and professional artists. *The Journal of Psychology, 128*(1), 23–31.

Runco, M. A., & Charles, R. E. (1997). Developmental trends in creative performance. In M. A. Runco (Ed.), *The creativity research handbook: Vol. I* (pp. 115–152). Cresskill, NJ: Hampton Press.

Sapp, D. P. (1997). Problem parameters and problem finding in art education. *Journal of Creative Behavior, 31*(4), 282–298.

Sawyer, K. (1999a). Improvised conversations: Music, collaboration, and development. *Psychology of Music, 27*(2), 192–204.

Sawyer, K. (1999b). Moving forward: Issues for future research in improvisation and education. *Psychology of Music, 27*(2), 215–216.

Schaefer, C. E. (1971). *Creativity attitude survey: Manual.* Jacksonville, IL: Psychologists and Educators.

Schmidt, T., Goforth, E., & Drew, K. (1975). Creative dramatics and creativity: An experimental study. *Educational Theatre Journal, 27,* 111–114.

Schwartz, P. (1993). Creativity and dance: Implications for pedagogy and policy. *Arts Education Policy Review, 95*(1), 8–16.

Seals, K. A. (1990). A cross-sectional investigation of the melodic composition abilities of elementary and junior high school students. (Doctoral dissertation, University of Kansas, 1989). *Dissertation Abstracts International, 50*(11), 3510A.

Sloboda, J. A., & Howe, M. J. A. (1991). Biographical precursors of musical excellence: An interview study. *Psychology of Music, 19,* 3–21.

Sloboda, J. A., Davidson, J. W., Howe, M. J. A., & Moore, D. G. (1996). The role of practice in the development of performing musicians. *British Journal of Psychology, 87,* 287–309.

Sternberg, R. J. (1988). A three-facet model of creativity. In R. J. Sternberg (Ed.), *The nature of creativity* (pp. 125–147). Cambridge, UK: Cambridge University Press.

Sternberg, R. J. (Ed.). (1999). *Handbook of creativity.* Cambridge, UK: Cambridge University Press.

Swanwick, K. (1991). Further research on the musical development sequence. *Psychology of Music, 19,* 22–32.

Swanwick, K., & Tillman, J. (1986). The sequence of musical development: A study of children's composition. *British Journal of Music Education, 3*(3), 305–339.

Tarnowski, S. M., & Leclerc, J. (1994). Musical play of preschoolers and teacher-child interaction. *Update: Applications of Research in Music Education* (Fall/Winter), 9–16.

Thompson, K. M. C. (1991). *Assessing the creative effectiveness of two approaches to teaching art at the middle school level.* Unpublished doctoral dissertation, University of Georgia, Athens.

Torrance, E. P. (1974). *The Torrance tests of creative thinking: Technical-norms manual.* Bensenville, IL: Scholastic Testing Services.

Torrance, E. P. (1981). *Thinking creatively in action and movement.* Bensenville, IL: Scholastic Testing Service.

Tsisserev, A. (1997). *An ethnography of secondary school student composition in music—a study of personal involvement within the compositional process.* Unpublished doctoral dissertation, University of British Columbia, Canada.

Uszynska, J. (1998). Artistic and verbal creative capacity of 6-year-old children and their psychopedagogic and social conditioning. *International Journal of Early Years Education, 6*(2), 133–141.

Vaughan, M. (1971). Music as model and metaphor in the cultivation and measurement of creative behavior in children. (Doctoral dissertation, University of Georgia). *Dissertation Abstracts International, 32*(10), 5833A.

Vitz, K. (1983). A review of empirical research in drama and language. *Children's Theatre Review, 32*(4), 17–25.

Wakefield, J. F. (1985). Towards creativity: Problem finding in a divergent-thinking exercise. *Children Study Journal, 15,* 265–270.

Wakefield, J. F. (1991). The outlook for creativity tests. *Journal of Creative Behavior, 25*(3), 184–193.

Wakefield, J. F. (1994). Problem finding and empathy in art. In M. A. Runco (Ed.), *Problem finding, problem solving, and creativity* (pp. 99–115). Norwood, NJ: Ablex Publishing.

Wallach, M. A., & Kogan, N. (1965). *Modes of thinking in young children: A study of the creativity-intelligence distinction.* New York: Holt, Rinehart & Winston.

Webster, P. (1977a). *A factor of intellect approach to creative thinking in music.* Unpublished doctoral dissertation, Eastman School of Music, University of Rochester, New York.

Webster, P. (1977b). *Thinking creatively with music.* Unpublished manuscript.

Webster, P. (1987a). Conceptual bases for creative thinking in music. In J. Peery, I. Peery, & T. Draper, (Eds.), *Music and child development* (pp. 158–174). New York: Springer-Verlag.

Webster, P. (1987b). Refinement of a measure of creative thinking in music. In C. Madsen & C. Prickett (Eds.), *Applications of research in music behavior* (pp. 257–271). Tuscaloosa: University of Alabama Press.

Webster, P. (1990, March). Study of internal reliability for the *Measure of Creative Thinking in Music (MCTM).* Paper presented at the General Poster Session of the MENC National Convention, Washington, DC.

Webster, P. (1992). Research on creative thinking in music: The assessment literature. In R. Colwell (Ed.), *Handbook of research on music teaching and learning* (pp. 266–280) New York: Schirmer Books.

Webster, P. (1994). *Measure of creative thinking in Music-II (MCTM-II).* Administrative guidelines. Unpublished manuscript.

Webster, P., & Hickey, M. (1995). Rating scales and their use in assessing children's compositions. *The Quarterly Journal of Music Teaching and Learning, VI* (4), 28–44.

Webster, P., Yale, C., & Haefner, M. (1988, April). *Test-Retest reliability of Measures of Creative Thinking in Music for children with formal music training.* Paper presented at the poster session, MENC National In-Service Meeting, Indianapolis, IN.

Welch, G. F. (1999). Education and musical improvisation: In response to Keith Sawyer. *Psychology of Music, 27*(2), 211–214.

Wilson, S. J., & Wales, R. J. (1995). An exploration of children's musical compositions. *Journal of Research in Music Education, 43*(2), 94–111.

Winner, E. (1996). *Gifted children: Myths and realities.* New York: Basic Books.

Computer-Based Technology and Music Teaching and Learning

24

PETER R. WEBSTER

The computer revolution in music education won't begin until we rethink what we want education to be. Only then can we clarify our goals and bring them into focus. Only then can we know how to use the computer. Only then can we know what we want in educational software. At the very least we must have software that is genuinely interactive and genuinely individualized. There are hundreds of ways to misuse computers in education and only a few ways to use them properly.

P. R. Lehman,
The Class of 2001: Coping with the Computer Bandwagon

In a publication written some 16 years ago designed to warn against the computer "bandwagon" that might affect adults in 2001, Paul Lehman's words continue to warrant consideration. Intelligent use of music technology to assist music teaching and learning is of major concern in the 21st century. If the dollars that will be spent on hardware and software for music education in this decade are to be considered a wise investment, we need the best information possible on how to use these resources for maximum effectiveness.

Most will agree that music technology today is not a passing fad but an established part of the educational scene. Since the publication of the first Handbook in 1992 and the chapter on technology by Higgins (1992), substantial changes have occurred in computer hardware, software, and Internet growth and accessibility. These changes have resulted in more affordable and powerful resources than in any other time in our history. Still, the question remains: What do we really know about the effectiveness of music technology?

This chapter will attempt to provide a perspective on this question by summarizing the major writings published from 1990 to fall 2000. The chapter begins with an introductory section that deals with matters of definition and focus; a summary of forces that shape our current educational climate for music technology is also included. The remainder of the chapter is divided into four parts. The background section does not place emphasis on original, empirical work, but does create perspective for the empirical work. It begins with a summary of research reviews both in and outside of music. A sampling of advocacy positions for music technology follows, with writings on curriculum development and technology standards. This section ends with a profile of writings that are cautious about and critical of technology.

The core studies section includes the bulk of the summarized research. It is organized by sections devoted to music listening, performing, and composition. A special topics section includes brief summaries of the role of the researcher as programmer, use of technology in assessment, and gender and music technology. The conclusion includes recommendations for future research.

Introduction

What is music technology? Most modern dictionaries provide definitions of "technology" that center on the use of applied science for the improvement of a particular domain, such as industry, agriculture, or the arts (Agnes, 1999, p. 1470). Given this and what we know about the nature of music, one possible definition for music technology might be: *inventions that help humans produce, enhance, and better understand the art of sound organized to express feeling.* Such a focus on inventiveness in service

416

to music as art helps to place music technology historically and purposefully. Music technology is more than designing a hardware solution to a music performance problem, more than learning how to use a music notation program. It is more than designing a multimedia presentation for a music history class or using an intelligent accompaniment program to help learn a new work. It is all these things, plus a way of engaging with music in an effort to improve the musical experience while always respecting the integrity of the art.

It is often said that technology is not the point of what musicians do as much as the means to make the musical experience better. This is a useful perspective, particularly in the context of abuses of technology in music making and teaching. It is also true that technology has always played a major role in the development of music of all types and in all cultures. Certainly the importance of technology in framing the musical experience in certain kinds of contemporary concert music inspired by electronic music studios and in the continued development of popular music styles such as the many varieties of rock music (Jones, 1992) must be noted. In these styles, both the inspiration and production of the music is so closely connected to technological resources that the distinction of technology as only "tool" becomes more difficult.

Regardless of one's view of the centrality of technology as part of the music experience, there is no denying that children today do not know a world without computers, electronic keyboards, MP3 files and players, compact discs, the Internet, and other digital music devices and formats. Additionally, they will come to know new music technology that none of us can completely understand today.

Chapter Limitations

As with other chapters in this Handbook, it was not possible to include all studies on this topic discovered during database searches. Over 150 citations in music alone were identified and reviewed carefully, but only 98 appear here. In all categories, I had to make hard decisions about which studies to feature. Judgment about quality was the most important criterion, but this was tempered with a desire to represent interesting designs and new directions of research.

Because of space concerns, I have included no summary of the utilitarian role of technology in the capture of data for general research analysis. It should be clear to all that advances in technology make capture of critical information about music experience especially effective and that such a review might well be valuable in another context. For this Handbook, only work that featured music technology as the point of analysis or as a compelling force in design was included.

Readers of the technology chapter in the first Handbook will note a decision to limit research reported here to computer-based technology, including music software and computer hardware peripherals related to music teaching and learning. There is no mention of instructional television, teaching machines that are not computer-based, stand-alone audiotape, slides, or motion pictures. This decision is based in part on space limitations but, more important, on the climate today in schools, which is dominated by computer-related technology.

Finally, I do not include the many recent developments in distance learning and the many technological developments in internet-based support for instruction and collaboration. This is included in a separate chapter by Fred Rees in part II (chap. 16).

Forces That Shape the Technological Climate in Music Teaching and Learning

In the last 10 years, three major forces have shaped the development of technology in schools and have dramatically affected the variables for research. The first is the rapid technical development of hardware and software, aided by commercial research and a strong economy worldwide. The second is the ubiquity of computer-based technology and changes in expertise among students and those that teach them. A final force are the changes in how we teach, fueled by our understanding of how students learn best.

Technological Development.   A close reading of the writings that are summarized here reveals several aspects of change in computer-based technology. (Comprehensive texts such as the one by Williams and Webster [1999] provide detailed descriptions of these developments, including definitions of terms.) At the start of the new century, personal computers for less than $1000 can record, edit, print, and play back music at a level acceptable for professionals. These machines have unprecedented levels of computing power, as evidenced by processor speed, memory, and connectivity. Stand-alone and internet-based software programs are now commonly available, providing significant music experiences for listening, performance, improvisation, and composition. This software makes liberal use of multimedia such as digital audio and video, graphics, and MIDI. The relative ease of software development for most teachers and researchers without advanced programming skills has aided significantly in the development of content-rich interactive software that can be delivered locally or remotely from the internet. Advances in the digital representation, compression, and delivery of analog sound have resulted in a new and lasting respect for the power of computer-based technology to aid in teaching (Mark, 1994).

Availability and Integration.   A second major force that shapes our educational climate is the dramatic growth in technology availability and integration. In terms of internet access, over 63% of United States public classrooms in 1999 were connected to the internet. This figure is expected to grow dramatically in the coming years as efforts to wire the entire school population continue. Teachers are far more computer savvy than 10 years ago. *Education Week*'s online edition (*Technology Counts: 1999 National Survey of Teachers' Use of Digital Content,* 2000) reported the following based on a return rate of 1,407 questionnaires from a stratified sample of 15,000 classroom teachers at the elementary school level and English, math, science, and social studies teachers at the middle and high school levels:

- Schools have an average of one computer for every 5.7 students, a dramatic rise from 1997 when the ratio was closer to one computer for 27 students
- 97% of teachers surveyed use a computer at home and/ or at school for professional activities
- 53% use software for classroom instruction and 61% use the internet in their teaching
- 77% use software as supplementary work, while 17% use it as a primary focus, a small 6% use it as "quiet" or "bonus" time activity. Similar results were noted for internet use

Although the survey revealed that teachers continue to have difficulty finding appropriate software and internet sites for their work and continue to be frustrated with lack of resources and the monetary expense, these figures show a continual improvement in the presence and use of technology in teachers' professional work when compared to data from past years. As might be expected, the teachers surveyed expressed the wish for more time to develop experience and education themselves in the use of technology—especially the ability to discern what digital content would be best for students and then how best to use it.

Credible data on the availability of technology in music instruction in K–12 settings is beginning to emerge. The most thorough study of any one state's music teachers was completed by Reese and Rimington (2000). A systematic, random-sampling procedure was used to create an accessible sample of 493 schools in Illinois that represented a balance according to size, location, and level of instruction. Three mailings and follow-up telephone calls yielded a total return rate of 65%. Seventy-six percent of respondents indicated using a computer at school and nearly half of the sample indicated that there was a computer in the music area. Surprisingly, only 16% reported that the music area had computers linked to the internet, although nearly half of the music teachers reported that they had personal access to the internet at home. The work also revealed that

one-third of the music teachers and their students use specifically music or multimedia software.

Hess (1999) questioned high school seniors (*n* = 156) as they auditioned for entrance into college to study music. He found that nearly all students felt they were computer literate to some degree and the vast majority reported having a computer at home and had access to the internet. Just under 40% indicated that they had used music software, primarily notation and sequencing titles. Both the work of Hess and Reese and Rimington also demonstrate the need to improve the manner in which we teach music technology on the college level if students are to understand its breadth and potential.

Taylor and Deal completed a pilot survey of music teachers in three states (1999) and extended this work to a national sample (*n* = 991) from all regions of the United States (2000). Over 85% of the teachers reporting in the national survey indicated that computers were within or close to the music area. An equal percentage indicated that computer technology can be used with many or some types of music instruction, but a majority of teachers (61%) have yet to integrate such technology into their teaching. Of those that did not integrate, the vast majority stated that they would like to do so and nearly all said that they would like to learn more about technology.

Such data provide some evidence of the availability and integration of technology in general and of music technology specifically into K–12 teaching. Conclusions from such work demonstrate that more work needs to be done to prepare teachers of music to use technology wisely in schools and that the current teacher population needs more in-service work in order to use the resources already in place. Clearly the availability and integration of music technology is moving forward and is influential in the design and interpretation of research reported here.

Teaching Philosophy.   The final force that underscores much of the more contemporary research on music technology is the interest in constructionism as a basis for learning. Although not really new to educational theory, with roots that can be traced to Piaget and Dewey, constructionistic thinking has been given focus in writings on school reform (Gardner, 1991; Papert, 1993). The basic goal of constructionism is to place emphasis on creativity and to motivate learning through activity. Learning is seen as more effective when approached as *situated in activity* rather than received passively. In their introduction to an edited volume on constructionism in practice, Kafai and Resnick said:

> Constructionism differs from other learning theories along several dimensions. Whereas most theories describe knowledge acquisition in purely cognitive terms, constructionism sees an important role for affect. It argues that learners are

most likely to become intellectually engaged when they are working on *personally meaningful* (authors' italics) activities and projects. (Kafai & Resnick, 1996, p. 2)

At the heart of these ideas is the shift away from thinking about education as being centered solely in the mind of the teacher and more as a partnership between teaching and student, with the teacher as the major architect of learning. Project-centered learning is celebrated with students working to solve problems. Affect is seen as part of and as an aid in the learning experience. It is argued that if children learn this way, facts are learned in a situated context that helps to make clear why the facts are important in the first place. The teacher assumes more the role of a "guide on the side" as opposed to a "sage on the stage." This approach is particularly appropriate for the integration of computer-based technology in music and is the logic behind those studies that use simulation (Magnusson, 1996), hypermedia,[1] and internet-based resources as a focus for investigation.

Background Writings

Reviews

For a complete picture of the historical development of music technology and of the research prior to the studies summarized here, the reviews by Higgins (1992), Peters (1992), Berz and Bowman (1994, 1995), Walls (1997), and Williams and Webster (1999) are recommended. The chapter by Higgins and the 1994 Berz and Bowman monograph chronicle the early work on music technology research. Higgins summarized well the classic problems with research on music technology, including poor design, Hawthorne effects, inadequate treatment, and the confounds that the changing nature of technology bring. More important, he argued for a change from simplistic studies that pit music technology itself against traditional instruction to a more complex design that considers context and individual differences in students (Higgins, 1992, p. 491). The 1994 Berz and Bowman monograph provides a detailed review of selected studies completed before 1994 and summarizes by pointing to the relative neutral to positive findings or experimental work overall. They point to research generally showing positive attitudes toward music technology by students and that technology's support for improving performance skills such as error detection and rhythmic accuracy is promising.

The 1995 Berz and Bowman article and the text by Williams and Webster are good sources for historical developments in hardware and software in terms of computer-aided instruction. Berz and Bowman defined four research cycles, the last of which was called "emerging" technologies, beginning in 1989 (1995, pp. 18–20). Hypermedia tradition is summarized and related to the development of the World Wide Web. Developments in artificial intelligence and virtual reality are included. Throughout the Williams and Webster text, the authors provide historical overviews and timelines for computer-assisted instruction, music notation and sequencing, multimedia, and other topics.

Nonmusic Research Literature

Music education researchers interested in studying music technology cannot afford to ignore the rich data on technology and education in other disciplines. It is impossible to adequately summarize this literature here, but mention of a few recent studies will help place the music literature in perspective and offer clues to how to approach the general literature. The *Journal of Educational Computing Research* has published work since 1985 and is an excellent source for major trends in the literature. Several new journals have emerged in recent years, including the *Journal of Interactive Learning Research, Interactive Learning Environments*, the *Journal of Educational Multimedia and Hypermedia*, and the *Journal of Learning Sciences*. Studies of importance also have appeared in the standard education and psychology literature.

Reviews. Kozma (1991) reviewed research on learning with media in part as a reaction to a pointed article by Clark (1983), which argued that media had no real effect on learning and that we should place a moratorium on such research. Kozma reviewed over a hundred studies dealing with books, television, computers, and multimedia. He concluded:

> The process of learning with computers is influenced by the ability of the medium to dynamically represent formal constructs and instantiate procedural relationships under the learner's control. These are used by some learners to construct, structure, and modify mental models; other students can rely on prior knowledge and processes, and use of computers is unnecessary. (1991, p. 205)

Kozma further concluded that the medium of computers is an excellent way to examine the cognitive processes of learning.

Several meta-analytic studies on the efficacy of traditional computer-assisted instruction (CAI) are reported in the nonmusic literature. Fletcher-Finn and Gravall (1995) completed a meta-analysis of 120 studies selected from 355 published from 1987–1992 and identified through ERIC searches. Studies were selected on the basis of availability, methodological strength, experimental design, and the research setting (must have been in a classroom content).

Course content included mathematics, reading/writing, science/medicine, arts, and education. The results were consistent with other meta-studies, showing a small but positive gain for all course content groupings. The average effect size was .24, which is equivalent to raising students' scores from the 50th to the 60th percentile. Interestingly, the greatest gain was with preschool/kindergarten, with an effect size of .55. The authors suggested that the small, positive effect size might be explained by superior CAI materials and not to the computer usage itself.

A similar meta-study was completed two years later by Christmann and Lucking (1991) examining junior and senior academic achievement. A thousand studies were examined and 27 experimental studies chosen that had at least 20 students in each group. Results showed an average effect size of .21. Music was one of the content disciplines studied (an investigation of seventh-grade music achievement), with an effect size of .23. The authors noted a varying rate of success for CAI among content disciplines, with English being the lowest and science the highest. They also suggested study of CAI embedded in teaching environments that have characteristics shown to have strong effect sizes of their own, such as cooperative learning, instructional time, home support, higher-order questions, and individualized instruction.

This recommendation of expanding the focus of such studies was taken a step further in work by Schacter and Fagnano (1999), which summarized the results of 12 meta-analyses representing different disciplines. The effect sizes reported by these studies ranged from .25 to .57. Their plea, however, was for further research to focus not on traditional CAI that used drill and practice but to examine work using more recent theories of learning (sociocultural theories, constructivist theories, and cognitive science) that use project-based, interactive and internet-based and multimedia strategies. Mayer (1997) is an example of an educational researcher who has done extensive work with multimedia teaching in science. His work and those of his colleagues demonstrate that multimedia-supported activities (animation with text) do increase ability of science students to understand cause and effect and to creatively transfer learning to other settings.

The unbridled enthusiasm that one senses in the general educational literature for the benefits associated with recent hypermedia forms (stand-alone and Web-based) is brought into perspective by an excellent review article by Dillon and Gabbard (1998). This study is highly recommended as a model for researchers interested in writing a review paper. The authors examined research cited in ERIC and PsycLIT from 1990 to 1996, which used measured results from learning outcomes that showed changes in behavior or task performance. Of the 111 studies that made the first cut, only 30 were retained. Studies eliminated were judged to have poor controls for student ability or inadequate descriptions of treatment. The authors divided the studies into three themes: comprehension of presented material, learner control over presentation of material, and individual differences in learning style. Studies in each section were carefully described and summarized. The authors concluded that: (1) hypermedia may be best in tasks that require rapid searching and data comparison, (2) increased learner control over access is useful for students with higher ability and more difficult for those with lower ability, and (3) learner ability and willingness to explore may be a factor in the success of hypermedia software (p. 345). A general observation was that the quality of empirical evidence for hypermedia technology for improving learning is poor and that further theoretical and empirical research is vital.

Study of Thinking. There is interest in the general literature in the link between technology and teaching thinking. Herrington and Oliver (1999) described qualitative work that "investigated students' thinking as they used an interactive multimedia program based on the situated learning approach" (pp. 4–5). The subjects were preservice math teachers and the focus was on assessment. Media employed included video clips of both assessment in action and student and teacher interviews, together with text. A complex task was presented to four groups of two students each, which involved the response to a hypothetical letter of complaint about math assessment from a parent and a follow-up memo from the principal to the teaching teams asking them to fix the problem. The subsequent use of the multimedia program by the four groups of two teachers to solve this problem was videotaped and the discussions and media use was transcribed and coded for analysis. The work provided a useful description of how to code such interchanges in order to verify the presence of higher order thinking. Characteristics are keyed to the external literature on thinking. Types of talk were analyzed and results showed substantial amounts of higher-order thinking.

Two other studies on thinking are worth noting. Clements (1995) reviewed studies that evaluated how computers enhanced creative thinking. He evaluated studies of creative thinking and production in writing and computer programming (Logo computer language), pointing to the general conclusion that thinking in such disciplines is greatly enhanced—especially if the technology use is embedded into constructionist contexts. In a more specific research effort, Liu (1998) examined experimentally whether engaging elementary school students in hypermedia authoring improved creative thinking skills as measured by the figural portion of the *Torrance Tests of Creative Thinking*. One group of fourth-grade students used the multimedia program *HyperStudio* individually to create stacks on plants and oceans. Another group worked in teams of four to create collaborative projects on the same topics.

Results showed that both groups significantly increased their creative thinking scores and that the collaborative group created more creative projects as judged by experts. Students who were evaluated as having low and moderate ability of a scholastic aptitude test showed greatest gains.

Conceptual Positions in Music

We now consider thoughtful writings in music that help form a background for systematic study. There is a lack of meaningful writing in this regard. Indeed, a philosophy of music education that embraces and celebrates music technology is an intriguing idea whose time has yet to come. What we do have are some position papers on the role of computer technology in music education. A few of these are summarized here briefly, as a way to stress the importance of this kind of thinking for researchers and practitioners.

Shifts in How We Conceptualize Teaching.   Several experts have suggested that technology helps us rethink the way we teach music. In addition to assistance with skill development, technology can simulate music experiences in order to broaden the art form for a wide range of people and offers an entirely new medium for performance. For example, Brown (1999) imagined digital media as more than just tools for learning. It is common to think of a computer and its related music peripherals and software as simply convenient tools for support of the musical experience. Brown believed it is more than that. He argued that digital media can become an instrument for music expression and, perhaps surprisingly for some, a medium of musical thought. For Brown, technology and humanity are not a dualism. If digital media are considered only as tools, this dualism is maintained. Instead, he insisted that "coming to a humane conception of technology requires acknowledgment that being technological is a human trait, not an independent force" (1999, p. 11). Brown thought of digital media as an instrumental medium not only because it is capable of transmitting musical ideas but because of the way musicians use it and relate to it. The notion of control, as in computer as tool, "is replaced by one of partnership where computers are conceived as instruments; controlling and utilizing are replaced by a notion of engaging" (p. 12). Such an idea of engagement for students has a fundamental effect on the way to think about teaching with music technology and, in turn, effects our research agenda.

On a more pragmatic level, Lord (1993) wrote about technology's role in rethinking how we teach aural skills. He reminded us of the objectivist model of aural training as fact and skill. Such approaches assume transfer, value rigidity of thought, and isolate musical elements from context. Running counter to this are ideas associated with con-

structivist philosophy (as noted earlier in this chapter). Lord suggested that experiments in intelligent tutors and expert systems in music theory are closer to the constructivist philosophy but have their own inherent problems. Both drill and practice and intelligent tutors work within the same confines of a teacher-directed world; because of this, Lord imagined a need for a paradigm shift in the way we teach aural skills on the college level. He prescribed a focus on the music technology workstation (computer and MIDI keyboard) with music sequencing software as a basic setting for teaching aural skills and musicianship. He said: "What if we thought of a music workstation less as a task manager and more as a phenomenarium—a learning environment in which all aspects of the musical world are available to study, to manipulate, and to use creatively, at least in simulated form?" (1993, p. 112). Lord pointed to this setting as ideal for a constructionist philosophy that encourages music context, musical questioning, focus on sound, and creative thinking as ways to teach aural skills.

Hoffmann (1991), reflecting on his teaching at the New England Conservatory, also commented on the way we teach college music theory. Hoffman presents an argument for technology helping in forming a closer bond between composer, performer, and listener by allowing more people to become familiar with the process of music making. He also described his work with cooperative learning at the conservatory and the role that technology has helped him teach more musically the aspects of harmony that are important to musical understanding. The advantages of cooperative learning are described, as well as the disadvantages.

Music Thinking.   Another theme that emerges in the literature is music thinking. Moore (1989), Webster (1990), and Upitis (1992) have all presented strong cases for using technology to stimulate thinking skills in music and to motivate students to think creatively in sound. MacGregor (1992) went further by suggesting the need for better learning theory to guide design of music composition software for young children. MacGregor pointed to the need for composition software for young children that allowed the user to have control over learning sessions, contain age-appropriate language or symbol systems, stress qualitative rather than quantitative aspects of music, and provide an alternate method for notation. Interestingly, most of these requirements have been met in recent software programs designed to encourage composition for young children (Nelson, 1998).

Other approaches to thinking embrace different starting points. For instance, some work has been done on music and artificial intelligence. Smith and Smith (1993) contributed some preliminary work from a compositional perspective and Schaffer (1990, 1991) has done so from music theory. Such work is complicated and may well bear fruit in future efforts to design more sensitive software for music experiences.

Music Performance.   Although there has been some indication that research on the effectiveness of technology for performance education is continuing in the form of experiments with acoustical analysis and pitch following software, there has not been a large interest in research among the applied faculties in higher education. Tomita and Barber (1996) have speculated on the use of computer-controlled player pianos such as the Yamaha Disklavier and the Bosendorfer SE as an important aid to piano instruction. They report on preliminary experiments at the University of Leeds in the United Kingdom using such technology. In general, such technology has been used more often in cognition research and has been considered more of an oddity in applied work.

Curriculum Contributions.   A number of published works are aimed at offering comment on curriculum integration. All of these writings are anecdotal, placing emphasis on "why," "what," and "how to" and focusing less on empirical evidence for technology's effectiveness. They are included here in the background section of the chapter because they contain clues for the construction of a conceptual base for research. For example, Jaeschke's dissertation (1996) offered strategies for incorporating technology into schools that meet the music portion of National Standards for Arts Education. Inspired by the Manhattanville Music Curriculum Project, he provided creative-based curriculum sequences that he field-tested.

Forest (1995) provided a description of how she integrated technology into an urban elementary school setting where 90% of the children qualify for free-lunch programs. She profiled the role technology played in teaching complex music ideas by describing interactive MIDI software that supports music reading and composition. The author reported an improvement in overall academic test scores, but the link to the technology use specifically awaits more systematic investigation. Similar writings were contributed by Chamberlin, Clark, and Svengalis (1993) for keyboard programs in middle schools, Nelson (1991) for general music curricula in middle schools using Gordon's learning music theory as a base, and Rogers (1997) and Busen-Smith (1999) for secondary schools in the United Kingdom. The Nelson and Busen-Smith articles are especially useful because they have some theoretical grounding, offered quite specific details on content, and provided some data on effectiveness.

Reese (1998) offered an excellent guide to designing curricula in schools by stressing the "systems approach" to hardware and software choice. This approach urges teachers to think of the choice of computer hardware and software as an integrated set of decisions based on teaching philosophy and context. Kassner (2000) provided perspective on the use of music technology in classrooms in which only one computer can be used. The article explained how the computer can become a significant aid for total instruction and not marginalized as an "extra."

Finally, researchers should read carefully the recent development of technology curriculum standards, especially work by Music Educators National Conference (MENC) (*Opportunity-to-learn standards for music technology,* 1999). This document provides technology guidelines for preschool to high school regarding curriculum and scheduling, staffing and equipment, and materials and software. Deal and Taylor (1997) provided a useful standards model for the development of technology for higher education and the Technology Institute for Music Education (TI:ME) (http://www.ti-me.org) provides certification standards for music teachers who use technology in teaching.

Cautions and Criticisms

The majority of the literature that has been described so far has provided strong advocacy positions for music technology in the schools. A solid preparation for conducting research on this topic, however, should include a careful reading of those who offer words of caution and criticism. Both the music and general literatures contain such work.

Music Literature.   Austin (1993) reminded us of the natural continuum that forms between technophobes (often viewed as traditionalists) and technocentrists (often viewed as radicals). He pointed to the problems created by those who fall on either end of the continuum as they either ignore technology completely or imagine technology as a panacea for the ills of education. Austin cited research, similar to the status studies by Reese and Rimington and Taylor and Deal, that demonstrated the gap between available technology in schools and teachers that are prepared to use it. This is not a criticism of the effectiveness of technology, necessarily, but is a concern for planning and may be a good topic for systematic work.

Austin wondered if technology really saves time. Technology does make a number of routine tasks faster, but other tasks rush in and our time is consumed in a way that makes us all work harder. The time problem was also raised as part of an informal survey of independent, private music teachers by Hermanson and Kerfoot (1994). The survey was supportive of the integration of technology experiences into private lessons, but one negative finding was the time needed to set up such experiences and deal with the technical "bugs."

Austin also cited some classic problems with research in music technology that are noted, too, in the nonmusic literature:

The body of research that has examined the effects of technology on student attitudes and achievement is still experiencing growing pains. Not enough effort has been made to rule out rival hypotheses (e.g., Hawthorne effect, experimenter bias), test for long-term vs. short-term outcomes, explore the way in which technology might interact with learner or instructional context characteristics, or interpret any benefits ascribed to technology in terms of system costs. My hunch is that technology does reap rewards, but for whom? In what contexts? For how long? And at what price? (Austin, 1993, pp. 8–9)

Argersinger (1993), writing in the *Jazz Educators Journal,* warned about the "ease" of music notation and sequencing programs leading to abuses of the "cut and paste" feature that creates less than sophisticated music. He also pointed to the problems that digital audio sampling creates in the use of other artist's musical ideas or sounds. This particular concern was reinforced more recently by the legal battles between the Websites designed to facilitate the distribution of music in the form of MP3 files and the Recording Artists Institute of America, which represents the vast majority of recording companies (Reece, 1998). Argersinger also raised a concern about music technology adversely affecting the development of music literacy by instantly rendering a score in a manner such that students are discouraged from developing inner hearing.

Caputo (1993–1994) offered an important view of music technology in the schools from a feminist perspective. She wondered if technology "is neutral, in that it remains outside the bounds of cultural politics, or are there consequences that are intimately linked to gender issues embedded in the application of technologies in the classroom" (p. 86). She takes exception to the idea that all students might profit equally from technology, pointing to the fact that not all students are the same. She feels that the rational, linear kind of thinking that often is celebrated in music technology is not the only way of knowing. The assertion is made that female students are socialized to pursue more relational, analogic ways of knowing and must operate differently when using technology. This sets them up for failure when compared to boys who, presumably, find linear and rational approaches more to their liking. She also warns the reader to be aware of hidden biases in software that might affect gender construction.

Finally, Folkestad (1996) raised a classic problem in the minds of many music educators, spoken and sometimes not: fear and alienation regarding the new technology and also of the young people who have acquired its possibilities (p. 26). He suggested that this is especially true for compositional activities with technology when the traditional role of performer is usurped:

This conflict, involved in the meeting with music technology, and in which some teachers have found it hard to

decide whether it should be regarded as a threat or a possibility, implies that earlier concepts and views of musical phenomena have to be reconsidered and redefined. . . . Accordingly, when some music teachers express misgivings regarding whether children will still learn how to play an instrument properly, this might rather be a defense of their own competence, values and position, all of which are seen as questioned by the new ways of creating and relating to music. (1996, p. 27)

Nonmusic Literature. In the last 10 years, a number of writers have cautioned against the wholesale acceptance of technology in the schools. Postman's writings (1992, 1995) contained strong objections to the role technology has played in defining our culture. Writing from a reasoned, philosophical perspective, he worried about technology's potential to marginalize human and social values. Individuality itself, he maintained, is threatened by widespread use of technology. He wrote:

I am not arguing against using computers in school. I am arguing against our sleepwalking attitudes toward it, against allowing it to distract us from more important things, against making a god of it. (Postman, 1995, p. 44)

This sentiment is present in other writings critical of technology in the schools. Stoll (1999), in his most readable volume *High Tech Heretic,* took a similar position, adding a number of concerns about the use of technology as entertainment as opposed to real learning. His writing is not cynical but skeptical, and offered a number of excellent arguments about technology integration that should be read by all researchers and those developing theory. From a practical perspective, especially interesting are his chapters on the abuses of *PowerPoint* as a presentation aid and the wisdom of donating old, unworkable computers to schools.

Perhaps the most comprehensive description of problems facing technology in the schools comes from the writings of Jane Healy. In her early book, *Endangered Minds* (Healy, 1990), she questioned the role of computers in schools in terms of thinking skills. She raised concerns about what we really know about the brain's improvement through typical computer use. But it was her most recent book, *Failure to Connect* (1998), which presented the most complete treatment of the subject. The volume is rich with personal descriptions of her visits to schools; she blended these descriptions with references to the professional literature. Topics covered in the book include problems with computer cost and adequate planning, disconnections between computer use and curriculum intent, blind acceptance of technology as the savior of educational problems, health concerns, and the inability of educators and researchers to show real evidence of improvement in learning. She also wondered about the concept of including technology in schools in order to better prepare students for the workplace; in this context, she suggested that possibly we have lost touch with what education is about (1998, p. 106).

The book is full of implications for research. Her treatment of what "information" really is about and how it can be used for real student learning is admirable. For example, her distinction between procedural, conceptual, and strategic knowledge in a domain and its relationship to technology support is informative (1998, p. 140). She also profiled the questions surrounding hypermedia and the "bricolage" approach that encourages exploration as opposed to linear teaching (p. 149). Her treatment of the role computers play in the development of creative thinking is also noteworthy:

> The fullest development of human intelligence includes the ability to use one's mind in creative ways. In fact, this particular facet of mind is doubtless the one that will enable our children to stay in charge of their ever-"smarter" digital servants. Whether and how early computer experiences expand or contract creativity is one of the most important issues in today's research agenda. (1998, p. 163)

Healy profiled both horrific and exemplary uses of technology in the schools—offering a reasonable balance between the clear abuses and the real gains that technology can provide. Like most of the general literature that is critical of technology in the schools, Healy's concerns are less about the presence of the technology and its ultimate potential, and more about the application of such research in an educational enterprise that is bereft of philosophy, theory, research, enlightened practice, and just plain common sense.

Core Studies

This section includes summaries of empirical work in music teaching and learning since 1990 that addresses music technology directly. It is organized by type of music experience studied and further divided by appropriate subcategories.

Music Listening/Skills Development: K–12

Eight studies were identified in this category and four are reviewed here; all use experimental designs. McCord (1993) reported on the effects of computer-assisted instruction on development of music fundamentals understanding in middle school instrumental students. She created her own *HyperCard* interactive program with MIDI support in order to teach note name identification, key and time signatures, rhythmic counting, and identification of symbols and scales. All 178 students in the instrumental program from three middle schools participated in individual exposure to the software for 45–50 minutes during class time. Prior to analysis, students were grouped into a low-, middle-, or high-level group according to their instrumental performance ability. Results showed significant gains in each group's ability on written tests of music fundamentals. Direct comparison to a control group with no computer instruction was not part of the design.

Arms (1997) investigated meter and rhythm discrimination with 136 fourth- through sixth-grade children in general music classrooms. Computer experiences in the treatment group consisted of exposure to commercial composition software and some work with drill and practice programs for approximately 20 minutes for 18 days. The control group did not use this software, but did participate in movement, game, and classroom instrument experiences. Both groups were presented the same 10-minute scripted lesson on rhythm and meter discrimination. Results showed no advantage for the experimental classes on a standardized measure of achievement, pretest to posttest. Careful examination of both the nature of dependent variables measured and the kind of experimental treatment brings into some question what was really being studied.

Goodson (1992) documented the development and trial of an interactive hypermedia program for basic music listening. Her study involved 128 sixth-grade students. Using a four-group comparison model that included groups with no contact, traditional instruction, computer instruction in small groups, and computer instruction with one large group, she found interactive hypermedia instruction required less instructional time in order to achieve equal or higher scores on a 22-item music listening test.

In a well designed study of the effect of (1) hypermedia use, (2) cognitive style (field dependence/independence), and (3) gender on both short- and long-term retention of factual information, Bush (2000) investigated 84 sixth- and seventh-grade students after individually completing either a 40-minute session with two specially designed *HyperCard* stacks or a group expository lesson on the same subject. The subject matter was a lesson on the steel bands of Trinidad. Hypermedia content included text, audio, digital photographs, and movies. To form the groups, Bush administered a measure of field dependence/independence (FD/FI) to computer-experienced boys and girls in a "middle income" neighborhood in western Canada. Four groupings were created (Gender × Style) and students from each were randomly assigned to form a balanced experimental and control grouping. Pretest data showed equivalency for content knowledge. The dependent variable was a 20-question, multiple-choice test that was evaluated for validity and reliability. This posttest was given once at the end of the experiment and again after a 6-week time period.

Results indicated statistically significant differences with both posttests for treatment in favor of the control group (expository lecture) and for FI students. There were no differences for gender. The results for cognitive style, which showed FI students doing well in both conditions but FD doing less well in computer-based groups, reinforced past research. The gender result demonstrated that, despite evidence that male/female attitudes may differ for technology (see the special topics section of this chapter), real achievement as measured by the test does not. The result for the main effect of treatment was a surprise in light of other studies on multimedia in music instruction. Bush speculated that the nature of the multiple-choice test might not be a good predictor of what was learned in multimedia work. He also wondered if the expository lecture was better at preparing the students for multiple-choice assessment. Another possibility might be the short time for software use in an unstructured environment has no real effect on factual recall.

In this category, the only study with high school students was reported by Prasso (1997). She investigated the effect of computer-based song writing on student ability to sight-sing. Her theory was that the use of computer composition software to write melodies might provide a level of intrinsic motivation and instant aural/visual feedback that would increase achievement in sight-singing. Sixty high school students from a New York City school formed both the experimental and control groups. Random assignment was not possible, but sight-singing pretests were used to determine some degree of equivalency. Students created three melodies over a 45-day period and sang these melodies as part of choral warm-ups. The control group wrote melodies out with paper and pencil with no computer assistance; experimental students working in a lab wrote melodies with a computer and MIDI technology. Results of a reliable and valid posttest of sight-singing performance assessment showed statistically significant gains for the experimental group.

Music Listening/Skills Development: College

The majority of work in music listening/skills development has occurred with college-age students. Eighteen studies were identified and eight noted here. The studies are divided into work with nonmusic major students, often in the context of courses devoted to music fundamentals or appreciation, and work with music majors.

Nonmajors: Music Fundamentals.

Two studies have focused on elementary education majors' preparation to teach music as part of their future general classroom teaching. Lin (1994) studied the effect of 4 weeks of hypermedia instruction of various kinds on student achievement on an aural music instrument identification task with 45 students. The types of hypermedia tested included computer-controlled laser videodisc, computer-controlled CD audio, and directed versus open-ended styles of content presentation. Results showed no difference in dependent variable testing of instrument identification with all groups doing well. Descriptive data on student attitude compiled showed significant preferences for hypermedia formats as opposed to a control group, with definite preferences for laser-disc technology and the open-ended style of presentation. Additional descriptive data was obtained by observation and posttreatment interviews.

In an extensive two-part investigation, Parrish (1997) investigated the use of computer-aided instruction to teach music fundamentals as part of nonmajor fundamentals classes. Both experiments were designed to evaluate the use of music technology outside of regular class time to teach music fundamentals (basic music notation, metric organization, scales, key signatures, intervals, and musical terms). Both studies used experimental and control groups, used multiple instructors, and were conducted over a 15-week college semester (100–150 minutes per week of class contact). Experiment 1 ($n = 148$) was designed to evaluate the custom software group (treatment) against the use of a commercial drill and practice program (control). Experiment 2 ($n = 95$) evaluated the custom software against a no-computer group that received in-class instruction on music fundamentals. The custom software was developed carefully using content analyses of several textbooks on music fundamentals designed for these types of classes. The software used folk song materials much like that which teachers would eventually use in the classroom in order to define and demonstrate the music theory. Interactive techniques were used that blended drill and practice with context-based examples using the folk songs. Mastery tests were included in the software for students to self-assess their knowledge. The software was made available for outside class use to the treatment groups of both experiments and instructors answered questions in class but did no significant teaching of theory content. Posttest scores in each experiment showed no significant difference between the students' scores on a music fundamentals test, demonstrating that out-of-class work with the custom software was as effective as in class teaching of music fundamentals. Each instructor in experimental treatment groups was able to spend significant time on other, less routine music topics. The work also demonstrated the importance of the instructor because posttest scores varied (significantly in Experiment 1) by class.

Nonmajors: Music Appreciation.

Placek (1992) reported results of a study that evaluated the effect of a custom-designed, interactive computer program that controlled an audio CD. The program provided text and spoken audio information about music history and music style characteristics in different periods of music history (e.g., Baroque, Classical, Romantic). The program provided listening examples from prerecorded excerpts and allowed the student to take a quiz for mastery in identification of music style periods from audio clips. Results were posted after each quiz and students were encouraged to use the program again and again. Three intact classes of college students were used, one designated as control ($n = 12$) and the other two as the experimental groups ($n = 28$) that were given access to the software. The dependent variable was a written test of style identification. Pretest and posttest data were used in a design that used the pretest as a covariate. Results showed significant difference in posttest means in favor of the experimental treatment.

Duitman (1993) designed somewhat similar research, but used commercially available, interactive CD-ROM software that was intended to encourage exploration of masterworks in a nonsequential manner. These resources typically provide a full digital audio recording of a masterwork, such as Beethoven's Ninth Symphony, and include links to portions of the recording for random audition. Supplemental material typically includes text and images that explain the work in detail, including information about the performance ensemble. Historical background information is included and a game is added at the end to test understanding. Buitman formed two groups and randomly assigned students to each. The control group had no contact with the commercial software, but the experimental group was encouraged to use the software to prepare a final essay project. The dependent variable was a multiple-choice test on course content and did not relate directly to material on the commercial CDs. As a result, both groups showed significant gains from pretests but showed no significant difference between groups. Final project essays that might well have shown significant difference between groups because of their direct connection to software use were not considered part of the data analysis. The mismatch between the nature of the linear tasks required by the posttest and the nonlinear nature of the treatment experience is a typical problem in this kind of research.

Finally, a study of learning style[2] and mode of instruction (CD-ROM tutorial and expository teaching methods) and their effects on an achievement test of aural identification of musical properties and cognitive knowledge was completed by Bauer (1994). This well-designed work represented a different slant on music technology integration because it did not investigate one approach versus another but, rather, the effect of one type of instruction on other variables. Bauer was interested in the identification of what learning style characteristics contributed to achievement on the CD-ROM experience and on an expository teaching experience. Learning style was evaluated by the use of the *Productivity Environment Preference Survey* (PEPS) that

yields scores on 20 subscales. The CD-ROM program used was a commercial one similar to the masterworks software described earlier. In this case, the Strauss tone poem *Till Eulenspiegel* was used. Subjects ($n = 120$) were randomly selected from a pool of 775 students across all 4 years in college. Average age was 21.1 years and there were 45 males and 75 females. Students were assigned randomly to four groups, using a classic Solomon design. Results of pretest analysis showed no significant differences between groups and no effects for use of pretesting were found. Groups were then combined into two for resulting analysis. Subjects in each group were pretested, then administered the PEPS, and then either given a 1-hour expository lesson on the Strauss work (group teaching) or were given 1 hour to explore the software (individual sessions). Both groups were given an outline of the major objectives before the 1-hour period. This was done to give focus to both learning experiences. A posttest was administered to each group. Material for the pretests and posttests was drawn directly from the objectives of the teaching and answers to the questions were clearly contained in both the expository group teaching and in the CD-ROM software.

Multiple regression procedures were used by regressing the subscale scores on PEPS against first the achievement scores for the expository group and then for the CD-ROM group. No significant scores were found for the expository group, with only 11% of the variance in the achievement scores found by the PEPS set. Bauer reasoned that this may be the case because students can adapt their learning styles to traditional lectures. They have had a great deal of practice with lecture formats and can learn effectively if the lecture contains a variety of media and presentational styles. Evidence from the multiple regression for the CD-ROM group was strikingly different. The subscales of Late Morning, Evening/Morning, Afternoon, and Tactile Preferences had positive, significant relationships to the achievement scores, and the subscales of Kinesthetic Preferences and Needs Mobility resulted in negative correlation. Over 31% of the variance in achievement scores for the CD-ROM group was explained. Bauer provides logical explanations for these findings, given the nature of the computer learning and its availability at differing times during the day. Bauer's work is important because it moves the nature of research on music technology to empirical issues about individual learning and not about what is best for groups.

Music Majors. As older literature reviews document (Berz & Bowman, 1994; Higgins, 1992), studies on music theory and aural skills dominated college-level music technology research in the 1970s and 1980s. This last decade has seen a shift to a richer blend of topics, including music history and education, as well as general studies and performance. A review of the papers accepted for presentation at the national meeting of the Association for Technology in Music Instruction (ATMI) (http://www.music.org/atmi) over the last 20 years revealed this trend. Hughes (1991), for example, studied the ability of college music history students to aurally identify core repertoire in music with the aid of hypermedia instruction. Students from an undergraduate music literature class were assigned randomly to a control and an experimental group ($n = 17$ in each group) and given a pretreatment questionnaire to determine equivalency of background and knowledge. Control and experimental group students experienced the usual instruction in class, which included repeated listening to works. Experimental subjects were given the additional opportunity outside of class time to use a specially designed *HyperCard* stack with CD-ROM support that contained guided listening for the literature studied in class. Results of posttests on the ability to identify composer, title, and movement or sections of pieces showed significantly higher scores for the experimental group. It is not clear if the significant difference was because of a novelty effect or if the results indicated a real positive influence from the technology.

In a work similar in design to Bauer's with nonmajors, Fortney (1995) examined the effect of music instruction with an interactive audio CD-ROM on the music achievement of music education majors with different learning styles. Fortney used the *Gregorc Style Delineator* (GSD) scale that places subjects into one of four categories of learner and placed 48 music education majors into the four groupings. He found no different in achievement test scores at the end of an individual, 90-minute period of exploration of a commercial CD-ROM program devoted to Stravinsky's *Rite of Spring*. Unlike Bauer, Fortney recorded behavioral data on the way each of the students used the program. Information about the number of times each subject deviated from the program sequence, time spent on individual sections of the program, and the number of supplemental cards (e.g., glossary visits, playing of extra musical examples) was recorded and compared to learning styles. The Abstract and Concrete Random learning styles used significantly more supplemental cards. This idea of a content analysis of how the hypermedia program was used is a good model for further research.

The final research summarized in this category carries on the traditional CAI model in music theory[3] that was so evident in past years. Ozeas (1992) studied the effect of computer-assisted drill and practice on internal identification and sight-singing performance. Students ($n = 58$) in a solfège class were randomly assigned to either a control or experimental group. The control group met for the entire semester, three times per week with an instructor. The experimental group met for 2 days per week, with the 3rd day devoted to work with the drill and practice program. Placement test data at the start of the semester showed no

difference between groups. Ozeas reported midterm grades on a progress test to be significantly different in favor of the control group, but that final test grades showed no significant difference. A separate investigation of those students with low placement test scores demonstrated that they did much better when they were able to meet three times per week with an instructor. Continued analysis of how different types of students react to and achieve with this kind of teaching support is needed.

Performance: K–College

The second major division of core studies in music pertains to music performance. Twenty-nine studies were identified since 1990, a major increase in this category from previous years. Thirteen of these works are noted here, divided into subcategories by performance medium.

Instrumental Performance. Orman (1998) reported results of a project to evaluate the effect of a multimedia program on beginning saxophonists' achievement and attitude. Experimental and control groups were formed from sixth-grade students ($n = 44$) in four middle schools. She developed an interactive computer program of 11 chapters covering topics such as instrument history, care, assembly, posture, hand position, and tonguing. Each chapter had an introduction and a summary section that highlighted the main concepts and was narrated by a cartoon character consistently in each chapter. Content was based on a number of topics in beginning saxophone books and verified by experts. Students were encouraged to interact with the program by using the computer mouse to solve problems and use their own saxophone for certain tasks. The program was designed to keep track of student progress and allow reentry at the point of departure if a student decided to stop after a short time. Orman designed her work to support short periods of instruction by having students in the experimental group complete sections of 8–15 minutes with the computer in a nearby room, then return to regular band class. Students completed the program in 15–17 days. Results on posttests of both written knowledge and video-recorded ability to apply understanding favored the experimental group significantly. Data also demonstrated strong, positive attitudes for the computer-assisted instruction.

Malave (1990) experimented with young instrumentalists as well but with beginning clarinetist tone quality. He used computer equipment to render a graphic representation of a model tone quality in terms of spectrum, intensity of partials, wave form, and envelope. Students were encouraged to emulate the model tone using the visual prompts as aids. Students who had reached a defined level of performance ability were assigned randomly to control and experimental groups of 15 junior high students each. Experimental subjects received exposure to the graphic system during a 30-minute private lesson. Control students received similar lessons but had no computer exposure. The time period lasted for 10 weeks, after which independent judges rated the students' tone quality. Pretests were administered as well and gain scores between pretest and posttest data showed no significant difference in ratings; however, ninth-grade students showed the most gain and an acoustical analysis of their resultant tone quality showed close matches to the model.

This use of technology in the studio is likely to gain more acceptance as studio instructors become more aware of technology and the equipment becomes more available. One current example of a studio teacher well known for his use of graphic analysis of music performers is Richard Miller at the Oberlin Conservatory. More information can be found at Miller's Website (http://www.oberlin.edu/con/divinfo/voice/obsvac) and his work is published in various journals of singing (e.g., Miller & Franco, 1994).

Surprisingly, only one major study was identified in the domain of jazz that used technology as a major focus. Fern (1995) completed descriptive work that evaluated the effectiveness of an interactive computer program focused on jazz improvisation. The program combined basic aural and theoretical elements of jazz improvisation and used CD-ROM and MIDI technologies. Transcription skill was stressed along with approaches to individual practice. Students who used the program were college student volunteers with varying levels of jazz experience. Results, expressed in questionnaire and interview data, demonstrated positive attitudes toward the program and suggested improved attention to human feedback.

Two qualitative studies in instrumental performance are worth mention. Simms (1997) studied the effect of a computer game on the motivation of four beginning piano students. She supplied a rich description of the use of an interactive music computer game designed to help the user with note identification and note-playing. Simms collected data from personal observations and interviews with students, parents, and teachers. The period of observation was 5 weeks with the game and 4 weeks following. Using a theory of personal investment designed by Maehr and Braskamp, she provided profiles of each student's background, use of the game, and results after the game was used. She reported that students enjoyed the game if they were successful but found they avoided more difficult levels. Some indicators of motivation continued after the game's use, but the effect was not uniform. This research is noteworthy for its use of quantitative data to explore the complex dynamic between teacher and student needs with technology as part of the mix.

Kim (1996) completed an interesting case study of three intermediate violin students and their use of computer-based, historical, and theoretical information about music

they were studying in their lessons. She determined that the computer work motivated students to seek more information about music studied in lessons and that there was evidence that the students used the supplementary information effectively in their applied study. This work is important because it is philosophically grounded in the spirit of comprehensive music instruction and the emerging national emphasis on this that is demonstrated by the National Standards in the Arts.

Vocal Performance. Simpson (1996) investigated pitch accuracy among high school choral students and its possible improvement with technology-assisted visual and aural feedback. The subjects were 69 students in an urban, multiethnic high school, divided evenly into three groups. The first group received teacher-guided instruction in a small group in addition to the regular choral rehearsal. The second group received visual/aural feedback on pitch as part of the choral rehearsal. The third group received both the small-group instruction and the technology help. Comparison between posttests demonstrated showed no significant difference, but the second group, which received just the technology treatment, did improve from posttest scores.

Interested in the effect of hypermedia instruction on the understanding of vocal anatomy, Ester has completed a number of studies using his custom-designed *HyperCard* stacks with graphics and animation. The work reviewed here (Ester, 1997) used 52 undergraduate music majors, divided evenly by gender. Students were divided into three groups, one with no technology but with a lecture, a second with exposure to just the special stacks, and the third with both the lecture and the stacks. Each group received a study sheet. Students using the hypermedia were allowed to explore the software freely. Subsequent analysis of use data showed no difference in overall time spent by all three groups. Results showed that, when controlling for academic achievement and pretest results, students in the hypermedia groups did significantly better on a test of vocal anatomy. Interestingly, Ester reports that the group that had only the hypermedia scored the highest. If vocal anatomy is deemed important in the education of singers and teachers do not have significant time to spend on class or studio instruction on this topic, this research indicates that a hypermedia instruction module might work well.

In a descriptive investigation using quasi-qualitative techniques, Repp (1999) wondered how students and teacher might adapt to the use of three different technologies as part of applied voice instruction: autoaccompaniment software in rehearsal and performance; internet as a tool for augmenting lesson material and communication; and the measurement of acoustic phenomena as part of the lesson instruction. Data were drawn from six students who received eight 45-minute voice lessons and included weekly logs, observations, and survey questions. What is interesting about this study was the inclusion of the teacher's perspective of the technology's effectiveness as well as the students.

Repp reported that the internet materials as part of the lesson yielded mixed results. Inclusion of the computer's display of internet information was awkward to use as part of a live lesson. Better results were noted as an outside resource, but pages were not accessed extensively. As a communication tool, the internet worked well when all parties used it routinely. The spectral analysis technology allowed students to see wave patterns of their own voice, but Repp concluded that the results were questionable in terms of real effect on improving singing. Three features of the automatic accompaniment software (*Smartmusic*) were used: the accompaniment capabilities, the tuner, and the warm-up feature. Instructor reaction to all three parts was quite favorable. Student reaction was positive toward the accompaniment software and less enthusiastic toward the spectral work; however, the range of opinion was on the positive side for all. In general, students enjoyed having access to the technology outside of the lesson time more than inside. This preference for out-of-class access is worth investigating further.

Accompaniment Support.   Repp's work with accompaniment is a good introduction to this next subcategory. *Smartmusic* (originally known as *Vivace*) personal computer software is designed to evaluate a solo performer's acoustic signal, judge quickly where the performer is in the score, and produce the accompaniment for MIDI software interpretation in fast enough time to be sensitive to the soloist's tempo changes. Three studies are worth noting in addition to Repp's descriptive work.

Tseng (1996) described its use with flute students using a cross-participant, case study approach. Her results supported the notion that the software helps music learning, intonation, and performance preparation. Ouren (1998) also used this software, but with middle school wind performers. Using pre- and postinterviews and independent assessments of performance achievement, he studied eight students' progress over a 6-week period. No control group was employed. Performance evaluations showed improvement for seven of the eight students, especially in rhythm and interpretation/musicianship. Interview data indicated positive reactions to the technology.

Sheldon and her colleagues (1999) have contributed the most controlled work to date with this technology. They examined differences

in performance quality ratings between instrumentalists who prepared solo music selections in three different conditions (with no accompaniment, with live accompaniment, and with intelligent digital accompaniment) and gave subsequent performances in two different conditions (without accompaniment and within the prescribed accompaniment mode). (1999, p. 253)

Instrumental undergraduate music education majors (volunteers) were subjects. They were asked to play a secondary instrument that: (1) they did not normally use in a performance ensemble, (2) was not part of the family of instruments that constituted their major, and (3) they had studied only for a semester in a methods course. The researchers reasoned that the participants would be able to conform to random assignment needs (balancing for instrument type and solo music) while still having playing ability similar to a target population that might benefit the most from this type of software. Three groups of 15 were created and students were asked to prepare a solo comparable to a typical level found in junior high school. Groups were limited to a 6-week preparation period, similar to the time frame often found in school conditions. Those in the no accompaniment group (NA) were asked to practice the solo with no accompaniment for 1.5 hours per week; those in the live accompaniment group (LA) were asked to work for the same time with a live accompanist; and the digital group with technology (DA) was asked to do the same thing but with the computer simulation. Knowledge of how to use the equipment by the DA group was ensured (including the many options possible with the software) and practice time was assumed to have been completed as requested. At the end of the practice period, soloists performed the solo without accompaniment and then again with the prescribed accompaniment mode. Performances were tape-recorded in a high-quality sound studio.

Five impartial and experienced judges rated the performances according to established procedures. Six performance subscales were used: tone quality, intonation, rhythm, technique, interpretation, and articulation. Inter-judge reliability ranged from .75 to .81. Main effects for group difference and performance difference were not found; however, there was a main effect for subscales with the highest ratings achieved for rhythm and articulation. Interesting interaction effects between subscales, groups, and performance conditions are worth evaluating carefully for clues to further research. For example, the subscales for the second performance generally paralleled the first performance except for the NA group for subscales of tone quality, intonation and interpretation. Certain individual means were of interest, including the low score for interpretation in the DA group during the second performance and the very high rating for rhythm in the DA group in the same performance. The researchers discuss implications extensively in the article.

Error Detection and Score Study.   Three dissertations are noted here. Two have addressed error detection and a third studied score knowledge. All systems were developed to be used as supplements to college conducting courses.

Jones (1991) developed a computer-assisted error detection system that used random-access audio and printed music score examples. The system allowed errors to be embedded in the score and the task for 11 subjects was to detect the errors. Statistical analyses showed significant growth during the teaching period with the largest gains occurring by the fifth session. Gruner (1993) used an experimental design with 24 students. He designed a computer-assisted instruction program that taught error detection skills in synthesized, multivoiced experts from traditional school band music. Each group studied conducting, but the experimental group used the computer program. Gains from pretest to posttest results on a measure of error detection based on taped examples of real band music demonstrated a significant difference in favor of the experimental group.

Hudson (1996) tested the effectiveness of a computer-assisted program designed to teach score study skills using model work from the music literature. Conducting students at four universities were used, creating two groups of 22 students in both an experimental and control group. A pretest was given to all students that evaluated their previous knowledge of a work for band. The experimental group experienced the computer program for six sessions over a 3-week period in addition to classroom conducting experience. The control group experienced no computer-assisted instruction. Posttests showed significant gains for the experimental group.

Composition: K–12

The last category of core studies is the newest, emerging largely in the last 10 years. All of the nine works cited in this category have a common theme: the investigation of composition using music technology as a major component not only for data capture or as a medium but also as a focus of the research itself. Studies in this category include work on compositional strategy and creative thinking in which the technology is central to the research questions and design.

Strategy.   Some of the most extensive and rich work done on computer-based, compositional thinking was reported by Folkestad and his associates (Folkestad, Hargreaves, & Lindström, 1998). This study is also available as a published dissertation (Folkestad, 1996). The purpose was to document the process of creation for 129 pieces by 14-, 15-, and 16-year-olds over a 3-year period in Sweden. MIDI files (887 in all) were collected during the process of

composition and interviews and observations of participants were recorded. Students with no previous compositional experience worked after school, once a week. Interviews with the students were conducted after the completion of a composition in order to understand how each student worked and what the thought processes were. The interviews were done at the computer workstation (computer with standard sequencing software and keyboard synthesizer) and access to previous versions of the compositions was possible. Unit of analysis was the group of compositions and not the 14 students, so many strategies were noted across subjects.

From the data, a typology for compositional strategies emerged. Two principal types were labeled "horizontal" and "vertical." Horizontal composers worked at the start with a conception of the piece from beginning to end. Further divisions of this approach included how the composer used the keyboard or the computer. Horizontal composers tended to complete one line at a time. Some composers worked exclusively on the computer and others would opt to use an acoustic instrument, such as a guitar, to work out ideas first before entering them into the computer. Vertical composers worked on bits of the whole at a time with one part completed before moving on the next vertical space. Some vertical composers had an idea of the whole "orchestra" ahead of time and defined each line of the vertical space from the start. Others worked this out as they composed bits of the work. This research is useful because it resulted in a model that other researchers can use to investigate different-aged children, differences caused by past experience, or with different media. Folkestad's dissertation is published with a CD recording of sample compositions so that others can hear the subtleties of the typology.

Where Folkestad examined several students and their many compositions using a traditional sequencing program and a MIDI keyboard, Stauffer (in press) reported work with one child on a limited number of projects and used a graphics-based program with a drawing metaphor. The *Making Music* software allows users to create musical gestures using the mouse as a drawing device. Tools are provided that allow the user to manipulate the graphic representations musically, including alterations in all the usual ways a composer works. After describing her role as a consultant in the development of the software, Stauffer described the composition processes of one 8-year-old child, Meg, as she manipulated the software to compose. The description tells a rich story of how Meg developed a musical style by exploring and developing fluency with sound over time. Different types of exploring and developing are described. In telling the story, Stauffer integrates previous research in composition and creative thinking as examples of Meg's behavior. Several passages of the descriptions of

Meg's work relate to the emerging typology of Folkestad. Stauffer concluded her qualitative investigation by noting:

the media with which children compose, such as the software program used in this project, may further enable their composing by allowing children to both see and hear their work as they create it as well by extending their options (e.g., via "tools" available in the software) for composing. (p. 26 in draft)

Younker (1997) used technology in an imaginative way to offer a platform for composition that allowed for the analysis of thought processes and strategies of different-aged children. Nine students, ranging in age from 8 to 14, were asked to compose using a standard software sequencer with a computer and MIDI keyboard much like the one used by Folkestad. Younker asked children to work with the software for seven, 1-hour sessions. The first two sessions were done in groups during which time the technology was learned and aspects of music discussed. This was followed by five sessions done individually with the researcher to capture data and a final session where compositions were shared with the group. Students were asked to think aloud while composing at the computer and respond to questions in an unstructured fashion. Data revealed differences in thought processes and strategies that could serve as the basis for a developmental model. The technology allowed for a standard environment to judge compositional behavior.

MacInnis (1996) contributed a qualitative study of three high school students, working in an autoethnographic approach that used composing with computers and journaling. Rather than organizing her results by traditional concepts of music elements, MacInnis allowed the student's interaction with the technology to define 38 different exemplars of music experience. The MIDI data that emerged from the traditional sequencer allowed students to openly perform, create, and listen without reference to traditional music theory. Personal constructions of musical experience were stressed.

Ladányi (1995) also used a qualitative case study approach to examine the compositional thought processes of four high school students from a suburban high school. Observations and intensive interviews formed the basis for the study. A computer and MIDI keyboard was used, together with a music notation program. Audio from the keyboard was routed into the video camera to allow the researcher to evaluate the video and audio more clearly. Evaluation of both open- and close-ended tasks revealed very different compositional styles. One of her major findings was that there may well be four classifications of novice composers at this level: archetypal—possessing the "gift" of imaginative ideas, but without much experience

and knowledge; style emulator—strongly influenced by popular genres with few original ideas of their own; technician—students who seem to concentrate on surface details without connecting to deeper musical meaning; and super composer—students with the "gift" and with past training and experience to achieve a high level of attainment. Ladányi observed that the technology allowed a balance between structure and freedom and allowed each student to construct their own effective learning with only modest teacher/researcher intervention.

On the other end of the age scale, Phillips and Pierson (1997) described the compositional explorations of two students, one 5-year-old and another severely handicapped 12-year-old with limited communication skills. The authors described observations of compositional tasks using a computer program with iconic representation of sound[4] rather than traditional notation. They argued that software of any type can be "powerful" or "empowering." Powerful software can do lower-level thinking skills quite quickly and accurately, but empowering software can visually represent patterns and relationships in clear ways, allowing higher-level thinking.[5] The icon-based software used in this work allowed the students to move small pictures that represented fragments of sound around on the screen to create melodies. This environment solves the problem of high memory loads for specific patterns that younger students must maintain in order to compose longer works. The two descriptions provided in this article are actually taken from a longer account of 21 subjects who used this program effectively (Pierson, 1996). Phillips and Pierson reported that a typical strategy in composing using this interface was: trial and error, listening, making value judgments, and editing. This was similar to one of the approaches noted by Folkestad. The authors concluded their work by pointing to scaffolding approaches in teaching that allow students to master a higher-level task if the lower-level obstacles are removed initially.

Creative Thinking Approaches. Much of the work summarized above is more naturalistic in nature, not beginning with a defined theoretical structure but letting the strategies define theory. Other research using technology to examine composition begins with the intent to compositional behavior using the creativity literature (and other literatures) as a foundation. Hickey has completed studies evaluating creative thinking ability. Process and product data were compared from a creative thinking perspective with 21 fourth- and fifth-grade subjects (Hickey, 1995). MIDI data were unobtrusively captured from a custom *HyperCard* stack that controlled a keyboard synthesizer and was designed to encourage compositional thinking. The program guided the subjects through a variety of possibilities organized around five musical elements: melody, rhythm, texture, timbre, and dynamics. The MIDI data created by the custom program was cleverly collected for both the process and product data analysis. Final compositions were evaluated by a panel of judges using consensual assessment techniques. Compositions rated in the high third and low third were then evaluated descriptively and quantitatively.

Hickey used this same custom program to explore two subjects in detail (Hickey, 1997). In this work, she was interested in the subjects' moments of most creative output in relation to a theory of interaction between reward and task conditions. Because the technology records experimentation with musical materials unobtrusively, Hickey was able to capture and compare compositional thinking products when the subjects were exploring and developing ideas (presumably not under pressure for a final, evaluated product) and under more demanding conditions for a final product. She provided background information on both students, placing the resulting data in context. The comparison of musical content under both conditions revealed qualitatively different descriptions, with the less pressured situation resulting in far more creative content based on the established notions of divergence and convergence. The relationships between these conditions of task structure and creative music making await much more systematic work, but the use of technology to reveal these subtleties is worth mentioning.

Daignault (1996) examined children's computer-mediated strategies in relation to craftsmanship and creative thinking. Twenty-five subjects ranging in age from 10 to 11 were asked to (1) record three to eight improvisations into a typical sequencer program; (2) select the one they preferred; and (3) develop the selection further using graphic, "piano-roll" notation. The main data came by observing carefully the development process using a video camera trained on the computer screen. Interestingly, this use of a video camera for data collection was greatly improved by Seddon and O'Neill (Seddon & O'Neill, 2000), who reported use of a special video card in a computer that recorded student behavior directly to videotape.

Using techniques similar to Hickey, Daignault asked judges to consensually assess the final developed compositions for craftsmanship and creativity and the top- and bottom-rated compositions served as an indicator of which process data to evaluate carefully. Analyses of process data for high and low craftsmanship and creativity led to conclusions about compositional thinking.

Emmons (1998) used a qualitative case study approach to observe six seventh-grade students' work with a traditional music sequencer in the development of compositions within a general music class situation. This work is unique because of its situated context. Results suggested a nonlinear process that embraced concept formation, preservation, and revision.

Special Topics

This final section briefly summarizes selected work that falls outside of the core studies of traditional music experience. Each topic represents an important trend in the literature.

Researcher as Programmer

There is a clear trend for researchers in music to rely less on technical expertise from outside the discipline and to develop more of their own software technology. Much of this is the result of better authoring tools as was noted in the Background section of this chapter. Many of the studies described in the Core Studies section feature custom-built software for the capture of data. A few other published accounts of software development are worth noting.

Lipscomb has documented the development of multimedia course materials (1994) and noted certain problems in developing cross-platform software in music (1998). Wood (1998) reported on the development of two interactive composition programs development for children's compositional thinking similar to studies reported by Phillips and Pierson (1997). Kozzin and Jacobson, two music theory professors, have developed interactive guides for music history to accompany the Norton masterworks series (Wittlick, 1996).

Readers interested in the trend toward the development of software by music educators also should note the work summarized in the chapter on internet developments by Fred Rees in part II of this Handbook. Briefly noted here is the excellent work done by Reese and Hickey on the development of internet-based resources for the exchange of compositions created by students (Reese & Hickey, 1999). The sites described encourage communication between students, teacher education candidates, composers, and music education professors. The potential for systematic research on music composition and its assessment using these tools is an exciting prospect.

Computers and Music Assessment

Technology-assisted assessment continues to be of interest to music educators and researchers. Venn (1990) developed and evaluated a computer-based interactive measure of common objectives in elementary general music using a personal computer and audio CD-ROM. After reviews of published music tests, state music curricula guides, and basal textbooks, he chose four musical elements for content inclusion: melody, rhythm, texture, and tonality. Tasks were devised that evaluated the child's ability to indicate a change in the element, identify compositional devices related to the element, and identify a place in a musical selection where a change in an element occurred. The software recorded the results. Test-retest reliability for 30 students was .79 for the total measure.

In a much larger project, Peters (1993) reported on the results of an investigation sponsored by the National Endowment of the Arts and the U.S. Department of Education. The project was aimed at the development of hardware and software that could evaluate pitch matching ability and tonal memory of students using acoustical signals and without the use of MIDI keyboard technology as the method for evaluation. Goals of the work included: (1) the creation of a computer-testing station to judge performance of pitch and rhythm, (2) the collection of data for testing purposes, (3) the profiling of student performance, and (4) the creation of tutorial software. All goals were achieved using commercial products and custom software. The technology was successfully field-tested in six public school sites of different types.

Pearlman (1993) summarized efforts to computerize the Graduate Record Exam (GRE) in music using commercial multimedia authoring software. It was field-tested twice in 1992 and the results indicated that more work was necessary before it could be adopted commercially by the Educational Testing Service. The report did indicate that the scoring algorithm was workable but that further funded research was necessary to make it acceptable. Since that time, the general ability portion of the GRE has been developed for computer-based administration.

Meeuwsen and his colleagues have developed a computerized assessment of rhythm performance (Meeuwsen, Flohr, & Fink, 1998). The *Rhythmic Performance Test— Revised* (RPT-R) is computer-generated and is in two parts. The first part asked children to tap along using a computer key with five different versions of a folk tune, synchronizing their tapping with the basic pulse. Tempi for the five versions ranged from 110 beats per minute to 150. The computer recorded the deviations of the tapping in milliseconds. Part II provided 20 varying rhythm patterns that were to be auditioned, remembered, and played back by tapping a computer key. Pilot testing of the measure was promising, with good reliability and factor-analytic verification of the two-part division of skill.

Finally, Webster and Hickey (in press) reported on the computerization and first trial of Webster's Measures of Creative Thinking in Music-II. The measure was designed to evaluate the creative thinking of children aged 6 to 10 using quasi-improvisatory tasks with informal instruments. A version of the measure was adapted (Hickey as programmer) to be self-administered by a computer using a set of MIDI drum pads, a MIDI keyboard, and foot pedal. MIDI data representing creative responses were recorded by the computer for subsequent analysis by judges.

Music Technology and Gender

Questions surrounding music technology and gender in school-aged children are not well studied. There is a predominate view that computers, especially computer gaming, is significantly favored by males (Healy, 1998, p. 161). There is evidence that shows that high school males use computers more often for class work than females (Schofield, 1995) and that, by the time students reach college, attitudes toward computers and instructional technology is much more favorable for males then females (Collis et al., 1996, p. 108). Interestingly, I could find no studies that specifically address gender issues in music technology in the United States.

There are two significant studies in the United Kingdom and one related investigation in Sweden that are worth careful reading. Comber, Hargreaves, and Colley (1993) and Colley, Comber, and Hargreaves (1997) reported the results of a two-stage, funded project to investigate gender and educational computing in the humanities. Surveys from students and teachers in schools surrounding the Leicestershire district in England were summarized in the first study. Students ranged in age from 11 to 18 with the total number of students being at least 280, although the exact number is not clear from the report. The survey revealed that older males were more confident than females in their use of music technology but that younger males and females were more balanced. The data also suggested that, for both males and females, there is the attitude that males are more able in music technology, even though the reality may well be different. The sample data did show that attitudes toward simpler forms of music technology such as electronic keyboards were balanced between genders and that all felt that music technology helped them do better in music achievement. Older girls did show some drop in interest in music technology. The qualitative data that emerged from both the interviews with students and teachers indicated a belief that males naturally gravitated toward music technology. Interviews with teachers indicated no conscious effort to encourage female students to participate more actively in music technology activities. Most teachers agree that there is nothing to indicate any innate advantages for males over females and that differences in attitudes and behavior are likely to be cultural and likely changeable with proper school experiences.

The second study used the same assessment techniques and added a focus on the effects of school type. The sample was much larger ($n = 1115$) and was drawn from 11 schools in Leicestershire, Birmingham, and Coventry. Many of the same findings were noted. One new finding was that younger students in single-sex schools were more positively disposed to music technology than older students; however, the difference was less pronounced in coeducational schools. One conclusion of the researchers is that a single-sex school might be a more nurturing environment for females as they gain more confidence in music technology usage.

The Swedish work (Folkestad, Lindström, Hargreaves, Colley, & Comber, 1996) used similar methodology but sampled two Swedish schools, one urban and one rural. A younger age group, ages 12–13 ($n = 92$) and an older age group, ages 15–16 ($n = 141$) were used. The results showed that females use computers less than males except for music making. Creative use of the computer was seen by the Swedish students as more like a *music* activity and less like a *computer* activity. This suggested that further research in the context of how computers are used in music technology might be useful. Clearly, more focused research—especially in the United States—on gender and music technology is needed.

Conclusion

There is much to be excited about in the work described above. There is also much work to do. In studying the background of music technology research, it is clear that we have continuing growth in the availability of powerful resources, but we also need to help in-service teachers find the time to learn about these resources and to offer effective models of integration. Teacher education programs need to continue to be redesigned to include ample experiences with music technology. Clearly, older types of drill and practice CAI are now being blended with exploratory, hypermedia experiences. The data shows that when traditional CAI is matched with lower-level assessment techniques, a small and positive gain in learning is achieved.

The data also show that we have not yet learned how to evaluate the exploratory experiences, nor really know how to integrate these approaches conceptually into our music teaching. This is true not only for general instruction but also certainly for music as well. The articles by Brown and Lord are thoughtful writings that speak to how we might engineer the power of the technology.

There is much reason to move cautiously with our claims about music technology. The writings of Healy and Stoll need to be widely read and debated, as should the results of reviews such as those of Dillon and Gabbard. Not all of the cautions and concerns raised by these writers apply to music, but many do. Perhaps the most important concern is that both our research and practice integrate technology with a strong theory of instruction behind the reasons for doing so. That, together with a plan for thoughtful reflection on the results and how they will be assessed for individual students, will take us a long way.

Specific Directions

In music listening and skills development, there is continued evidence that traditional CAI works relatively well when students have a clear idea of the tasks. But teachers and researchers should also look for ways to integrate and assess the hypermedia content that Bush writes about. The evaluation of this type of exploratory software needs to be done carefully and with an eye toward variables such as cognitive style and gender. These two variable sets seem most valuable to pursue in new research efforts. It also seems evident that we need more sensitive and thoughtful dependent variables to really assess this kind of software. The possibility that existed in the work by Duitman to review the essay assignment as a measure of technology success is an example of what might be done.

The point made by Parrish about technology instruction effectively teaching knowledge and skills in such a way as to free the teacher to concentrate on other kinds of instruction is a very compelling concept for future research. The difficult challenge is in finding the balance between what can be done effectively by technology and what can be reinforced and explored by a live teacher. This probably varies from context to context.

In much of the research reported here, student attitude toward the use of hypermedia software was nearly always positive. The importance of this cannot be overlooked, for it goes beyond an explanation based on just the novelty effect. It makes sense that students naturally enjoy exploring ideas, solving interesting tasks, and applying lower-level skills to solve problems, but an important question is whether this enjoyment is directly connected to music experience. We need to find ways to more systematically evaluate this by watching specifically how students use the technology. A combination of qualitative and quantitative study is necessary to do this well. The work by Bauer and Fortney is important in this regard.

It was most gratifying to see the growth in technology studies in performance. Nevertheless, more work needs to be done by applied faculty around the country who teach in university settings and in private studios. Orman's research design, which integrated small amounts of focused exploration in the context of a band rehearsal, was a nice model for additional research. Part of the success of this work and that of Bauer was that students understood what was to be learned through the use of technology and also were encouraged to explore in the ways they wished.

Work on the effectiveness of intelligent accompaniment software seems promising. Sheldon and her colleagues designed a complex and clever investigation of this software that revealed a number of clues for further work. More research, such as that reported by Repp, is needed by studio teachers who might use this technology in their classroom. Similarly, research on error detection with technology in conducting settings is compelling. Here is a clear example of the way in which research can inform practice.

The qualitative work by Simms and Kim are good models for performance research. I was especially intrigued by Kim's evaluation of how historical and theoretical knowledge was integrated into the studio by way of technology and how this appeared to enrich performance study. This is an excellent line of inquiry that has a firm conceptual base in today's educational climate.

Work in composition with technology has clearly captured the imaginations of many. Folkestad's work is critical for developing a theoretical framework for understanding how students tend to naturally approach composition tasks. Such work provides a solid foundation for continued work but also presents wonderful models for new researchers. Hickey's work with evaluating creativity in composition is equally impressive and should continue to inspire studies about music learning. Stauffer's qualitative evidence raises a number of fascinating questions about how children make decisions.

In all of this work, the computer serves not only as a convenient recording medium but also as a powerful tool for allowing children to show evidence of their cognitive processing. The distinction made by Phillips and Pierson between "powerful" and "empowering" speaks to the fascinating debate about lower versus higher levels of thinking and about how to teach competence in a discipline in an age of such powerful technology. As Turkle reminded us:

> Children use the computer in their process of world and identity construction. They use it for the development of fundamental conceptual categories, as a medium for practice of mastery, and as a malleable material for helping forge their sense of themselves. The computer is a particularly rich and varied tool for servicing so wide a range of purposes. It enters into children's process of becoming and into the development of their personalities and ways of looking at the world. It finds many points of attachment with the process of growing up. Children in a computer culture are touched by technology in ways that set them apart from the generations that have come before. (Turkle, 1984, p. 165)

The Bottom Line

So, is music technology effective and is it worth the trouble? On balance and on a very basic level, the answer to this question is yes. Does music technology hold the key for solving all our music teaching problems? Of course not. Are there abuses in its use? Absolutely. Does it always improve learning? No, much depends on the context—especially the teacher and its use instructionally. Is it worth the trouble to keep studying its role in music teaching and learning? Unconditionally, yes.

Perhaps the question about music technology's effectiveness is posed too simplistically. Because of the definition of music technology stated here, because of the ubiquity of technology in today's culture and in the entire history of music as art, because of the basic human nature of teachers as seekers of new ways to explain difficult ideas, the question is not *if* technology is effective as much as *how* can we make technology *more* effective. Stated in another way, asking if technology is really effective is somewhat like asking if a pencil or a pen is really effective in teaching music. The answer depends in large part on other variables. Certainly music technology costs more than pencils or pens and, because of this, its use must be studied carefully. But apart from the money, the development and study of technology as a means of teaching music helps make our theories, research, curricula, teaching strategies, and our entire professional development much stronger. To take full advantage of technology in teaching, we are invited to go to the core of what music is and determine best how to teach what we find. At the end of the day, that is the point of it all.

NOTES

Note: I would like to offer a special word of thanks to Sam Reese, William Bauer, and David B. Williams, who offered significant help in the preparation of this chapter.

1. "Hypermedia" is a term referring to software that chunks information of all media types into nodes that can be selected dynamically (McKnight, Dillon, & Richardson, 1991).

2. "Learning style" is not generally considered synonymous with "cognitive style," which was used in the Bush study. Learning style is thought to be a broader construct that includes cognitive style, affective and physiological phenomena, whereas cognitive style refers to modes of perceiving, remembering, and thinking.

3. Additional efforts to evaluate the integration of music technology into traditional music theory and aural skills curricula in higher education continues at campuses like the University of Delaware (Arenson, 1995), University of Kentucky (Lord, 1993), Indiana University, and the New England Conservatory. Published studies of effectiveness at these institutions await completion.

4. This use of movable icons that represent sound is similar in nature to the "Tune Blocks" first used by Bamberger in the 1970s to explore musical thinking. A modern version (Bamberger, 2000) has recently been published in the form of a textbook with accompanying software. Research with this new resource is highly recommended as a way to extend this line of inquiry.

5. This approach is celebrated in the work of Papert (1993) and is not without controversy. The argument centers on whether the teaching of the lower-level knowledge is ultimately necessary for real success. This is a rich area for research in music.

REFERENCES

Agnes, M. (Ed.). (1999). *Webster's new world college dictionary* (4th ed.). New York: Macmillan.

Arenson, M. A. (1995). *Computer lessons for written harmony.* Newark, DE: University of Delaware. (ERIC Document Reproduction Service No. ED416824)

Argersinger, C. (1993). Side-effects of technology on music and musicians. *Jazz Educators Journal, 26*(1), 33.

Arms, L. (1997). *The effects of computer-assisted keyboard instruction on meter discrimination and rhythm discrimination of general music education students in the elementary school.* Unpublished doctoral dissertation, Tennessee State University, Memphis.

Austin, J. (1993). Technocentrism and technophobia: Finding a middleground for music educators in the next millennium. In D. Sebald (Ed.), *Technological directions in music education* (pp. 1–10). San Antonio, TX: IMR Press.

Bamberger, J. (2000). *Developing musical intuitions: A project-based introduction to making and understanding music.* New York: Oxford University Press.

Bauer, W. (1994). *The relationships among elements of learning style, mode of instruction, and achievement of college music appreciation students.* Unpublished doctoral dissertation, Kent State University, Kent, Ohio.

Berz, W. L., & Bowman, J. (1994). *Applications of research in music technology.* Reston, VA: Music Educators National Conference.

Berz, W. L., & Bowman, J. (1995). An historical perspective on research cycles in music computer-based technology. *Bulletin of the Council for Research in Music Education, 126,* 15–28.

Brown, A. (1999). Music, media and making: humanizing digital media in music education. *International Journal of Music Education, 33,* 10–17.

Busen-Smith, M. (1999). Developing strategies for delivering music technology in secondary PGCE courses. *British Journal of Music Education, 16*(2), 197–213.

Bush, J. E. (2000). The effects of a hypermedia program, cognitive style, and gender on middle school students' music achievement. *Contributions to Music Education, 27*(1), 9–26.

Caputo, V. (1993–94). Add technology and stir: Music, gender, and technology in today's music classrooms. *Quarterly Journal of Music Teaching and Learning, 4–5*(4–1), 85–90.

Chamberlin, L. L., Clark, R. W., & Svengalis, J. N. (1993). Success with keyboards in middle school. *Music Educators Journal, 79*(9), 31–36.

Christmann, E., & Lucking, R. (1991). Microcomputer-based computer-assisted instruction within differing subject areas: A statistical deduction. *Journal of Educational Computing Research, 16*(3), 281–296.

Clark, R. (1983). Reconsidering research on learning from media. *Review of Educational Research, 53,* 445–459.

Clements, D. (1995). Teaching creativity with computers. *Educational Psychology Review, 7*(2), 141–161.

Colley, A., Comber, C., & Hargreaves, D. (1997). IT and music education: What happens to boys and girls in coeducational and single sex schools. *British Journal of Music Education, 14*(2), 119–127.

Collis, B., Knezek, G., Lai, K., Miyashita, J., Pelgrum, W., Plomp, T., & Sakamoto, T. (1996). Reflections. In G. Knezek (Ed.), *Children and computers in school* (pp. 105–130). Mahwah, NJ: Lawrence Erlbaum.

Comber, C., Hargreaves, D. J., & Colley, A. (1993). Girls, boys and technology in music education. *British Journal of Music Education, 10*(2), 123–134.

Daignault, L. (1996). *A study of children's creative musical thinking within the context of a computer-supported improvisational approach to composition.* Unpublished doctoral dissertation, Northwestern University, Evanston, Illinois.

Deal, J. J., & Taylor, J. A. (1997). Technology standards for college music degrees. *Music Educators Journal, 84*(July), 17–23.

Dillon, A., & Gabbard, R. (1998). Hypermedia as an educational technology: A review of the quantitative research literature on learner comprehension, control, and style. *Review of Educational Research, 68*(3), 322–349.

Duitman, H. E. (1993). *Using hypermedia to enrich the learning experience of college students in a music appreciation course.* Unpublished doctoral dissertation, Ohio State University, Columbus.

Emmons, S. (1998). *Analysis of musical creativity in middle school students through composition using computer-assisted instruction: A multiple case study.* Unpublished doctoral dissertation, University of Rochester, Eastman School of Music, New York.

Ester, D. P. (1997). Teaching vocal anatomy and function via HyperCard Technology. *Contributions to Music Education, 24*(1), 91–99.

Fern, J. L. (1995). *The effectiveness of a computer-based courseware program for teaching jazz improvisation.* Unpublished doctoral dissertation, University of Southern California, Los Angeles.

Fletcher-Flinn, C., & Gravall, B. (1995). The efficacy of computer assisted instruction (CAI): A meta-analysis. *Journal of Educational Computing Research, 12*(3), 219–242.

Folkestad, G. (1996). *Computer based creative music making: Young people's music in the digital age.* Göteborg, Sweden: Acta Universitatis Gothoburgensis.

Folkestad, G., Hargreaves, D., & Lindström, B. (1998). Compositional strategies in computer-based music-making. *British Journal of Music Education, 15*(1), 83–97.

Folkestad, G., Lindström, B., Hargreaves, D., Colley, A., & Comber, C. (1996). *Gender, computers and music technology experience and attitudes.* Goteborg: Department of Education and Educational Research, Goteborg University.

Forest, J. (1995). Music technology helps students succeed. *Music Educators Journal, 81*(5), 35–48.

Fortney, P. M. (1995). Learning style and music instruction via an interactive audio CD-ROM: An exploratory study. *Contributions to Music Education, 22,* 77–97.

Gardner, H. (1991). *The unschooled mind: How children think and how schools should teach.* New York: Basic Books.

Goodson, C. A. (1992). *Intelligent music listening: An interactive hypermedia program for basic music listening skills.* Unpublished doctoral dissertation, University of Utah, Salt Lake City.

Gruner, G. L. (1993). *The design and evaluation of a computer-assisted error detection skills development program for beginning conductors utilizing synethetic sound sources.* Unpublished doctoral dissertation, Ball State University, Muncie, Indiana.

Healy, J. (1990). *Endangered minds: Why our children don't think.* New York: Simon & Schuster.

Healy, J. M. (1998). *Failure to connect: How computers affect our children's minds, for better or worse.* New York: Simon & Schuster.

Hermanson, C. D., & Kerfoot, J. (1994). Technology assisted teaching: Is it getting results? *American Music Teacher, 43*(6), 20–23.

Herrington, J., & Oliver, R. (1999). Using situated learning and multimedia to investigate higher-order thinking. *Journal of Interactive Learning Research, 10*(1), 3–24.

Hess, G. (1999). The computer literacy of prospective music students: A survey. In S. Lipscomb (Ed.), *Sixth International Conference on Technological Directions in Music Learning* (pp. 96–99). San Antonio, TX: IMR Press.

Hickey, M. (1995). *Qualitative and quantitative relationships between children's creative musical thinking processes and products.* Unpublished doctoral dissertation, Northwestern University, Evanston, Illinois.

Hickey, M. (1997). The computer as a tool in creative music making. *Research Studies in Music Education, 8*(July), 56–70.

Higgins, W. (1992). Technology. In R. Colwell (Ed.), *Handbook of research on music teaching and learning* (pp. 480–497). New York: Schirmer Books.

Hoffmann, J. A. (1991). Computer-aided collaborative music instruction. *Harvard Educational Review, 31*(3), 270–278.

Hudson, M. E. (1996). *The development and evaluation of a computer-assisted music instruction program as an aid to score study for the undergraduate wind band conducting student.* Unpublished doctoral dissertation, University of Florida, Gainesville.

Hughes, T. H. (1991). *A hypermedia listening station for the college music literature class.* Unpublished doctoral dissertation, University of Arizona, Tucson.

Jaeschke, F. G. (1996). *Creating music using electronic music technology: Curriculum materials and strategies for educators.* Unpublished doctoral dissertation, Columbia University Teachers College, New York.

Jones, D. L. (1991). *Design and trial of a computer-assisted system supplying practice in error detection for preservice instrumental music educators.* Unpublished doctoral dissertation, University of Georgia, Athens.

Jones, S. (1992). *Rock formation: Music, technology, and mass communication.* Newbury Park, CA: Sage Publications.

Kafai, Y., & Resnick, M. (Eds.). (1996). *Constructionism in pracice: designing, thinking, and learning in a digital world.* Mahwah, NJ: Lawrence Erlbaum.

Kassner, K. (2000). One computer can deliver whole-class instruction. *Music Educators Journal, 86*(6), 34–40.

Kim, S. (1996). *An exploratory study to incorporate supplementary computer-assisted historical and theoretical studies into applied music instruction.* Unpublished doctoral dissertation, Columbia University Teachers College, New York.

Kozma, R. (1991). Learning with media. *Review of Educational Research, 61*(2), 179–211.

Lehman, P. R. (1985). *The class of 2001: Coping with the computer bandwagon.* Reston, VA: Music Educators National Conference.

Ladányi, K. (1995). *Processes of musical composition facilitated by digital music equipment.* Unpublished doctoral dissertation, University of Illinois at Urbana-Champaign.

Lin, S. (1994). *Investigation of the effect of teacher-developed computer-based music instruction on elementary education majors.* Unpublished doctoral dissertation, University of Illinois at Urbana-Champaign.

Lipscomb, S. (1994). Advances in music technology: The effect of multimedia on musical learning and musicological investigation. In D. Sebald (Ed.), *Technological directions in music education* (pp. 77–96). San Antonio, TX: IMR Press.

Lipscomb, S. (1998). The trials and tribulations of developing cross-platform multimedia applications in music education. In S. Lipscomb (Ed.), *Fifth International Conference on Technological Directions in Music Education* (pp. 45–49). San Antonio, TX: IMR Press.

Liu, M. (1998). The effect of hypermedia authoring on elementary school students' creative thinking. *Journal of Educational Computing and Research, 19*(1), 27–51.

Lord, C. H. (1993). Harnessing technology to open the mind: Beyond drill and practice for aural skills. *Journal of Music Theory Pedagogy, 7,* 105–117.

MacGregor, R. C. (1992). Learning theories and the design of music compositional software for the young learner. *International Journal of Music Education, 20,* 18–26.

MacInnis, P. (1996). *Experiencing and understanding a computer-based music curriculum: A teacher's story.* Unpublished doctoral dissertation, University of Toronto, Canada.

Magnusson, S. J. (1996). Complexities of learning with computer-based tools: a case of inquiry about sound and music in elementary school. *Journal of Science Education and Technology, 5*(4), 297–309.

Malave, J. E. (1990). *A computer-assisted aural-visual approach to improve beginning students' clarinet tone quality.* Unpublished doctoral dissertation, University of Texas at Austin.

Mark, D. (1994). Digital revolution as a challenge to music education. *ISME Yearbook, 75–83.*

Mayer, R. (1997). Multimedia learning: Are we asking the right questions? *Educational Psychologist, 32*(1), 1–19.

McCord, K. (1993). Teaching music fundamentals through technology in middle school music classes. In K. Walls (Ed.), *Third International Conference on Technological Directions in Music Education* (pp. 68–71). San Antonio, TX: IMR Press.

McKnight, C., Dillon, A., & Richardson, J. (1991). *Hypertext in context.* Cambridge, UK: Cambridge University Press.

Meeuwsen, H., Flohr, J., & Fink, R. (1998). Computerized assessment of synchronization and the imitation and timing of rhythm patterns. In S. Lipscomb (Ed.), *Fifth International Conference on Technological Directions in Music Education* (pp. 93–95). San Antonio, TX: IMR Press.

Miller, R., & Franco, C. (1994). Spectral components of five cardinal vowels in the soprano singing voice considered by means of the sequential vowel diagonal. *The NATS Journal, 50,* 5–7.

Moore, B. (1989). Musical thinking and technology. In E. Boardman (Ed.), *Dimensions of musical thinking* (pp. 111–117). Reston, VA: Music Educators National Conference.

Nelson, B. J. (1991). The development of a middle school general music curriculum: A synthesis of computer-assisted instruction and music learning theory. *Southeastern Journal of Music Education, 3,* 141–148.

Nelson, G. (1998). Who can be a composer: New paradigms for teaching creative process in music. In S. Lipscomb (Ed.), *Fifth International Conference on Technological Directions in Music Learning* (pp. 61–66). San Antonio, TX: IMR Press.

Opportunity-to-learn standards for music technology. (1999). Reston, VA: MENC, The National Association for Music Education.

Orman, E. K. (1998). Effect of interactive multimedia computing on young saxophonists' achievement. *Journal of Research in Music Education, 46*(1), 62–74.

Ouren, R. W. (1998). *The influence of the Vivace accompaniment technology on selected middle school instrumental students.* Unpublished doctoral dissertation, University of Minnesota, Minneapolis.

Ozeas, N. L. (1992). *The effect of the use of a computer assisted drill program on the aural skill development of students in beginning solfège.* Unpublished doctoral dissertation, University of Pittsburgh, Pennsylvania.

Papert, S. (1993). *The children's machine: Rethinking school in the age of the computer.* New York: Basic Books.

Parrish, R. T. (1997). Development and testing of a computer-assisted instructional program to teach music to adult non-musicians. *Journal of Research in Music Education, 45*(1), 90–102.

Pearlman, M. (1993). *An application of multimedia software to standardized testing in music.* (Report No. ET-RR-93-36). Princeton, NJ: Educational Testing Service. (ERIC Document Reproduction Service No. ED385601)

Peters, G. D. (1992). Music software and emerging technology. *Music Educators Journal, 79*(3), 22–25, 63.

Peters, G. D. (1993). Computer-based music skills assessment project: A portal to artistic innovation. *Bulletin of the Council for Research in Music Education, 117,* 38–45.

Phillips, R., & Pierson, A. (1997). Cognitive loads and the empowering effect of music composition software. *Journal of Computer Assisted Learning, 13*(2), 74–84.

Pierson, A. (1996). *The development of the use of micro-electonics in music education in schools.* Unpublished doctoral thesis, University of Nottingham, England.

Placek, R. W. (1992). Design and trial of a computer-controlled programme of music appreciation. In H. Lees (Ed.), *Music education: Sharing musics of the world, proceedings of the 20th World Conference of the International Society for Music Education* (pp. 145–152). Seoul, Korea.

Postman, N. (1992). *Technopoly: The surrender of culture to technology.* New York: Knopf.

Postman, N. (1995). *The end of education.* New York: Knopf.

Prasso, N. M. (1997). *An examination of the effect of writing melodies, using a computer-based song-writing program, on high school students' individual learning of sight-singing skills.* Unpublished doctoral dissertation, Columbia University Teachers College, New York.

Reece, D. (1998). The Billboard report: Industry grapples with MP3 dilemma. *Billboard, 110,* 1.

Reese, S., & Hickey, M. (1999). Internet-based music composition and music teacher education. *Journal of Music Teacher Education,* 25–32.

Reese, S., & Rimington, J. (2000). Music technology in Illinois public schools. *Update, 18*(2), 27–32.

Repp, R. (1999). The feasibility of technology saturation for intermediate students of applied voice. In S. Lipscomb (Ed.), *Sixth International Conference on Technological Directions in Music Education* (pp. 16–21). San Antonio, TX: IMR Press.

Rogers, K. (1997). Resourcing music technology in secondary schools. *British Journal of Music Education, 36*(2), 129–136.

Schacter, J., & Fagnano, C. (1999). Does computer technology improve student learning and achievement? How, when, and under what conditions? *Journal of Educational Computing and Research, 20*(4), 329–343.

Schaffer, J. W. (1990). Intelligent tutoring systems: New Realms in CAI? *Music Theory Spectrum, 12*(2), 224–235.

Schaffer, J. W. (1991). A harmony-based heuristic model for use in an intelligent tutoring system. *Journal of music theory pedagogy, 5*(1), 25–46.

Schofield, J. (1995). *Computers and classroom culture.* Cambridge, UK: Cambridge University Press.

Seddon, F., & O'Neill, S. (2000). Influence of formal instrumental music tuition (FIMT) on adolescent self-confidence and engagement in computer-based composition. In C. Woods, G. Luck, R. Brochard, F. Seddon, & J. Sloboda (Eds.), *Sixth International Conference on Music Perception and Cognition* (CD-ROM). Keele, UK: Keele University.

Sheldon, D., Reese, S., & Grashel, J. (1999). The effects of live accompaniment, intelligent digital accompaniment, and no accompaniment on musician's performance quality. *Journal of Research in Music Education, 47*(3), 251–265.

Simms, B. (1997). *The effects of an educational computer game on motivation to learn basic musical skills: A qualitative study.* Unpublished doctoral dissertation, University of Northern Colorado, Greeley.

Simpson, E. H. (1996). *The effects of technology-assisted visual/aural feedback upon pitch accuracy of senior high school choral singing.* Unpublished doctoral dissertation, University of Hartford, Connecticut.

Smith, B., & Smith, W. (1993). Uncovering cognitive processes in music composition: Educational and computational approaches. In M. Smith, A. Smaill, & G. A. Wiggins (Eds.), *Music education: An artificial intelligence approach conference* (pp. 56–76). Edinburgh, Scotland: Springer-Verlag.

Stauffer, S. (in press). Composing with computers: Meg makes music. *Bulletin of the Council for Research in Music Education.*

Stoll, C. (1999). *High tech heretic: Why computers don't belong in the classroom and other reflections by a computer contrarian.* New York: Doubleday.

Taylor, J., & Deal, J. (1999). Integrating technology into the K–12 music curriculum: A pilot survey of music teachers. In S. Lipscomb (Ed.), *Sixth International Technological Conference on Directions in Music Learning* (pp. 23–27). San Antonio, TX: IMR Press.

Taylor, J., & Deal, J. (2000). *Integrating technology into the K–12 music curriculum: A national survey of music teachers.* Retrieved from http://otto.cmr.fsu.edu/~deal_j/Survey _files/v3_document.htm

Technology Counts: 1999 national survey of teachers' use of digital content. (2000). Retrieved from http://www.edweek.org/sreports/tc/99/articles/survey.htm

Tomita, Y., & Barber, G. (1996). New technology and piano study in hgher education: Getting the most out of computer-controlled player pianos. *British Journal of Music Education, 13*(2), 135–141.

Tseng, S. (1996). *Solo accompaniments in instrumental music education: The impact of the computer-controlled Vivance on flute student practice.* Unpublished doctoral dissertation, University of Illinois at Urbana-Champaign.

Turkle, S. (1984). *The second self.* New York: Simon & Schuster.

Upitis, R. (1992). Motivating through technology: Lasting effect or passing fancy? *American Music Teacher, 41*(6), 30–33.

Venn, M. (1990). *An investigation of the applicability of recent advances in computer technology to the development of a computer-based, random-access audio test of common criterion-referenced objectives in elementary music.* Unpublished doctoral dissertation, University of Illinois at Urbana-Champaign.

Walls, K. (1997). Music performance and learning: The impact of digital technology. *Psychomusicology, 16*(1–2), 68–76.

Webster, P., & Hickey, M. (in press). MIDI-Based Adaptation and Continued Validation of the *Measures of Creative Thinking in Music* (MCTM). In M. Campbell (Ed.), *Conference in Honor of Marilyn Zimmerman.* Urbana: University of Illinois.

Webster, P. R. (1990). Creative thinking, technology, and music education. *Design for Arts in Education, 91*(5), 35–41.

Williams, D., & Webster, P. (1999). *Experiencing music technology* (2nd ed.). New York: Schirmer Books.

Wittlick, G. (1996). Review of *The Norton CD-ROM masterworks: Interactive music guides for history, analysis, and appreciation, Vol 1. Journal of Music Theory Pedagogy, 10,* 189–206.

Wood, R. (1998). Using authoring software to observe children's musical compositions. In S. Lipscomb (Ed.), *Fifth International Conference on Technological Directions in Music Education* (pp. 72–76). San Antonio, TX: IMR Press.

Younker, B. (1997). *Thought processes and strategies of eight, eleven, and fourteen year old students while engaged in music composition.* Unpublished doctoral dissertation, Northwestern University, Evanston, Illinois.

Part IV
MUSICAL COGNITION AND DEVELOPMENT

Andreas Lehmann
Editor

Introduction: Music Perception and Cognition

ANDREAS C. LEHMANN

Research in perception and cognition in music has seen tremendous growth over the last two decades (see Levitin, 1999). The reason for this expansion is not that music research has emerged only recently as a new discipline; instead, it appears that whoever had been interested in music years ago but did not dare to do music research can now freely admit to his or her "vice." As a result, the field has become extremely diversified and includes psychologists, sociologists, and anthropologists as well as AI researchers, physiologists, and acousticians. Many of them are active musicians with varying degrees of firsthand experience, while other scientists simply think that music is a convenient domain for their purposes. Common to all is the desire to find out more about how our brain processes the auditory input we then experience as music. Unfortunately, the issues that entice researchers are not always identical to those that appeal to music educators, who, after successful mastery of the scientific jargon, are often disappointed to discover how difficult it is to apply the findings to the classroom. Admittedly, some research done today might only prove its usefulness many years from now.

In the wake of recent advances in neurobiology, trying to separate perception and cognition has become less appropriate and practicable. Where, for example, does music cognition actually begin? Does it start in the cochlea or right after the cochlea, or does it emerge out of the simultaneous firing of neurons in different cortical areas? And how does our individual genetic makeup influence music perception and cognition? Where do our memories and feelings enter into the perception and cognition game? As a result, and in order to be of maximal use for music educators, in this part of the book we did not adhere to a strong division of perception and cognition but rather understood cognition in its broader sense, namely, how it applies in the context of experience, training, development, and culture.

This part with its six chapters does not purport to cover the whole range of topics relevant to music perception and cognition. We have tried to capitalize on emergent issues and research done since the publication of the first Handbook. In our experience, music educators as a group are likely to look at the research presented in the following six chapters. We should keep in mind, however, there is probably not *the* music educator, as there is not *the* music psychologist. Any choice of issues discussed, references cited, or references omitted (due to space limitations) will have to be the result of subjective decisions. A review of the literature is never objective, because the writer has an agenda, which is to introduce a personal view on a topic. With the help of the many reviewers who made thoughtful suggestions to improve the draft chapters, the chapters should now match the needs of aspiring or in-service music educators and music education researchers.

The chapters follow a certain logic in that the first four chapters proceed from the basic neurological and cognitive processes to a panoramic view of musical development and the theories behind research on learning. The last two chapters concentrate on music performance skills, musical expression, and the audience. Wilfried Gruhn and Frances Rauscher introduce neuropsychological and neurophysiological research as it relates to learning. They also introduce some learning theories that essentially can be viewed as theories of cognition, and they clarify one hotly debated topic in music education, namely, the question of transfer of learning, which sometimes serves as a justification for music education in schools. William Forde Thompson and E. Glenn Schellenberg are experts in basic music cognition with all its developmental and cultural implications. Their chapter abounds with pointers to current research methodology and brings to our attention the processes in music perception we often take for granted (e.g., melody perception, timbre, rhythm). Heiner Gembris gives a more global survey of topics and issues in developmental psychology. While emphasizing cognitive aspects, he also incorporates sociological and cultural aspects. This chapter is closely tailored to the questions frequently asked by music educators. Bruce Torff comes from the general area of educational psychology. His chapter places research on music perception and cognition into the larger context of research on music learning and development with its changing epistemological facets. The contextualist perspective presented by Torff is today an accepted and important position for music education. Reinhard Kopiez reviews the area of performance research in which great progress has been made internationally. Most interestingly, researchers are no longer interested solely in motor programming and internal clocks (although these topics are still under scrutiny) but also interested in knowing how we communicate and understand musical expression. As a trained musicologist, the author is able to bring modern research into contact with its historical roots. Jane W. Davidson and I sum up some of the research in skill acquisition, which stresses the environmental aspects of music learning, especially in learning to play an instrument. In some ways, this chapter acts as a counterweight to the chapter by Gruhn and Rauscher, which emphasizes the "hardware" aspects of musical learning.

For those readers looking for an update in one of the areas mentioned earlier, each chapter should provide a suitable point of entry. For the novice reader the chapters offer a thorough introduction into the topics of music psychology that are relevant to music educators.

REFERENCE

Levitin, D. (1999). [Review of the book *The psychology of music* (2nd ed.), edited by Diana Deutsch]. *Music Perception, 16,* 495–505.

The Neurobiology of Music Cognition and Learning

25

WILFRIED GRUHN

FRANCES RAUSCHER

Music Learning and Cognition

The last century has provided a wealth of important data about cognition and learning. However, with the cognitive revolution in developmental psychology and the rise of Piaget's theory within developmental psychology, the emphasis shifted from learning to thinking. Consequently, we now know quite a bit about children's thinking at different ages, but we know little about how they learn. The movement away from studying children's learning reflected more than a shift in interest; it also reflected an assumption that development and learning are fundamentally different processes. However, learning and cognition are two sides of the same coin. What one knows is largely based upon what one has learned, and learning, of course, generates knowledge. Therefore, any theory of development that has little to say about how children learn is a seriously limited theory of development.

Over the past decade, the emergence of the interdisciplinary field of cognitive neuroscience has led to the realization that the neural basis of cognition and learning can be empirically studied. Such investigations commonly lead to fresh insights and theories about a variety of developmental processes. This chapter reviews current research on the neural basis of music learning and cognition with the view that neuroscientific research is as relevant to musical processes as knowledge and concepts gained from the study of, for example, perception, emotion, and motor function. Where possible, we refer the reader to relevant chapters elsewhere in this Handbook for a greater degree of technical detail.

A brief survey of the literature on learning (and cognition) will provide the framework for our particular neu-

robiological perspective. Four different approaches to investigating learning are reviewed: behaviorism (Watson, 1913), cognitive psychology (Piaget, 1947, 1959), sociohistorical theory (Vygotsky, 1934/1962), and connectionism (see McClelland, 1995).

Behaviorism

The behaviorists viewed developmental changes in behavior as relying on several basic principles of learning, particularly classical conditioning (Pavlov, 1927) and operant conditioning (Skinner, 1953), as initially demonstrated by animal experiments. For example, Ivan Pavlov's experiments with dogs revealed that a neutral stimulus (a bell) begins to elicit a response (salivation) after being repeatedly paired with another stimulus (food) that already elicits that response. A stimulus–response chain (S → R) can be strengthened by repetition and reinforcement, and the response will gradually generalize. Learning, according to the behaviorists, occurs when a behavioral change can be linked to a stimulus presumed to have caused that change and can thus be objectively measured. However, the behaviorists failed to do justice to the organization of human behavior and the complex inner processes that are responsible for generating it. For example, although the neuronal activity of learning in the human brain cannot be observed directly, it clearly plays a major role in behavior. From a behaviorist point of view, however, the mind remains a "black box" about which one can only speculate and which therefore cannot contribute very much to the scientific study of behavior. Any introspection into the processes of learning was seen by the behaviorists as neither reliable nor relevant to the understanding of behavioral processes. This limitation in the behaviorist view, along with the emergence of computer science, encouraged investigators to attempt to describe the cognitive processes that are necessary to generate and control complex human behavior. This event became known as the "cognitive revolution."

Cognitive Psychology

The cognitive revolution represented a qualitative shift from an emphasis on behavior toward an emphasis on understanding the inner processes involved in cognition and intellectual growth. The *constructivist* perspective emphasizes the active role of the child in constructing advanced forms of cognition that transcend less adequate earlier forms (Baldwin, 1894/1968). Constructivists believe that one should begin the study of children's cognitive development by exploring the foundational concepts with which children come equipped at birth and then go on to document any change that may take place in these concepts with age. Jean Piaget was perhaps the most influential developmental psychologist to carefully observe children's development. Based on his own observations of his three young children, Piaget built a cognitive theory of the awakening of intelligence in children. According to Piaget, children progress through a series of five universal stages of development, which are characterized by "sensori-motor intelligence," "preoperational and symbolic thinking," "intuitive thought," "concrete operations," and "formal operations" (1947, 1959). As they progress through these stages, children develop cognitive schemas through interaction with the environment and other persons. The forms of these schemas are different at different stages of their development, and it is this difference that gives the thought of young children its unique character. Piaget hypothesized that the progression of humans through the four developmental stages is biologically determined. In any given stage, new experiences are "assimilated" to the existing set of schemata. Transition from one form of thought to the next is driven by "accommodation," a process by which existing schemata are broken down and then reorganized into new and more adaptive patterns, in turn leading to a highly differentiated cognitive structure. This model was expanded, elaborated, and modified by others (Aebli, 1980/1981; Case, 1972; Pascual-Leone & Smith, 1969). Thus the term *mental representation* became a key signature of the cognitive revolution. Piaget's theory was applied to musical development by Pflederer Zimmerman (1984; Pflederer Zimmerman & Webster, 1983) and to music learning (slightly modified) by Bamberger (1991).

Piaget and successors to his theory have expanded our understanding of development by revealing substantial domain-specific cognitive capabilities that children possess from early in life. These theorists emphasize that learning at all ages involves an active interchange between structures in the mind and information from the environment. Mental structures are joined with processes, such as assimilation and accommodation, to actively contribute to cognitive development.

Sociohistorical Theory

Contextual models, sometimes called systems views, emphasize that the transformation from infant to adult takes place via a complex, multidirectional system of influences (Gottlieb, 1991). These theorists are concerned with understanding how the broad range of biological, physical, and sociocultural settings affect learning and development. For example, Lev S. Vygotsky's sociohistorical theory from the 1930s stresses the importance of cultural tools, symbols, and ways of thinking that the child acquires from more knowledgeable members of the community (1934/1962). Development is viewed as a dynamic, never-ending transaction that involves continuing, reciprocal exchanges: People and settings transform the child, who in turn affects the people and settings that surround him or her, which further reshape the child, in an endless progression. According to the sociohistorical view, knowledge does not originate in the environment alone (as the behaviorists claimed) or in the interaction between the individual and the environment (as the constructivists maintained). Rather, knowledge originates in the social, linguistic, and material history of the individual's culture and its tools, concepts, and symbol systems. Children's participation in cultural activities with the guidance of others allows them to "internalize" their community's tools for thinking. Thus efforts to understand individual cognitive development and learning must consider the social roots of both the tools for thinking that children are learning to use and the social interactions that guide children in use of these tools. Vygotsky's concept of the zone of proximal development posits that development proceeds through children's participation in activities slightly beyond their competence with the assistance of adults or more skilled children. These ideas were expanded by other Soviet researchers, most notably Luria (1961) and Leont'ev (1981). The translation of Vygotsky's work into English marked the beginning of widespread use of Vygotskian ideas in the United States and Western Europe.

Connectionism

Connectionism offers a fresh perspective to the understanding of learning by focusing research on the microstructure of cognition. Connectionist theory is extremely rich in terms of its implications for brain development.

Highly sophisticated brain-imaging techniques, such as electro- and magneto-encephalography (EEG and EMG), event-related potential (ERP), magnetic resonance imaging (MRI), computer tomography (CT), and positron emission tomography (PET), permit a new view of the active brain. The topography of brain areas involved in aural perception and learning has been elaborated and transcribed into brain maps. The study of highly complex network structures and interconnections has laid the foundation for a connectionist model of "parallel distributed processing (PDP)" (Rumelhart & McClelland, 1986). The theory behind PDP is bound to the hypothesis of the modularity of mind (Fodor, 1983). Here the input systems refer to different brain areas that are highly specialized in processing particular properties of the incoming auditory stimulation, such as pitch, loudness, location of the sound source, melodic contour, and so forth. The possibility of exactly measuring the neural activation, the intensity and distribution of activation patterns, and the localization and lateralization of domain-specific processing tasks across the cortex have enabled new avenues for the investigation of the physiological foundations of music cognition and music learning (Hodges, 1996).

Along with the development and implementation of the imaging techniques, computer models of artificial "neural" networks have been developed to investigate strategies in problem-solving and decision-making processes (Fiske, 1993; Griffith & Todd, 1999; Todd & Loy, 1991). The connectionist approach can be seen as a neurally inspired model of information processing, in which groupings of neurons are interconnected in input layers (by which signals enter the system), output layers (which represent the outcome of the network), and hidden layers (which compute the more complex nonlinear relationships within the network). (For a more detailed introduction to connectionist ideas, see Bechtel & Abrahamsen, 1991.) Thus connectionist modeling can provide a functional understanding of the sequential structure of decision-making processes that are performed by an activation of units ("nodes") at an input layer, their gradual selection from a hidden layer, which corresponds to their semantic or syntactic weight, and finally their progression to an output layer. Cognition here is the result of a process of propagation and back-propagation within different layers of selection. Learning describes the tracing of paths and connections in that neural network.

In light of the neurobiological exploration of brain activities involved in music cognition and learning, mental representation has become a crucial component of learning. If neural networks function as the neural correlate for musical representations, then learning must be related to physiological conditions in the brain, that is, to the *activity* of neurons, to the *connectivity* among neurons, cell assemblies, and brain areas, and to the *neuronal plasticity* of the brain—especially the establishment, growth, and progressive differentiation of genuine musical representations with respect to their strength, localization, and extension in both hemispheres.

Neurobiological Foundations of Cognition and Learning

Cognition can be seen as the result of a pattern-matching process by which mental representations are activated through perceived stimuli. The term *mental representation* covers a broad array of meanings and is often used synonymously with *mental models* (Johnson-Laird, 1983), *scripts* (Schank & Abelson, 1977), *frames* (Minsky, 1980), *schemas* (Aebli, 1980/1981; Piaget, 1959) or *neural networks* (Todd & Loy, 1991). In addition to the debate on the meaning of mental representations, there is also a debate on the nature of mental representations. In one view, representations are seen as veridical images that are stored in the mind and can be retrieved from it; that is, they are *depictive* in nature (Kosslyn, 1994), whereas another perspective holds that representations result from formal processes and accumulated experiences that are *propositional* in nature (Pylyshyn, 1973). In music, depictive representation of a chord shows, for example, the real image of the position of fingers on a keyboard or the picture of the notation, whereas propositional representation results from knowledge in terms of statements about that chord as a sum of many experiences.

In this section, we will only refer to the neural cortical substrates for sensory representations. We ask the following questions: How are musical (sound) representations characterized, and how, if possible, can we begin to understand the developmental processes of neural connections? Methodologically, four strategies are commonly employed to investigate the learning brain: (1) the observation of persons with brain lesions that cause particular deficits; (2) animal experiments that study neuronal brain reactions; (3) the measurement of infants' information processing, especially sensory and auditory temporal processing; and (4) the implementation of brain-imaging techniques for a clear and precise identification and localization of changes in brain activation.

Neurons are highly specialized to respond to particular qualities of stimuli, for example, to a section of a band of frequencies (pitch), to a movement of sounds up and down (direction), to the intensity of sound (loudness), and so forth. Neurons of a particular brain area represent different features. Unfortunately, little research exists on the auditory sensory mapping of the associative cortex. In cognition, distributed processing of sensory information must be coordinated for the creation of what is eventually perceived by the conscious mind. As M. E. Martinez (1999) has put it:

> The human mind is not a video camera. We do not process and store countless sensory bits; rather, we construct our inner and outer worlds according to the organizing principle of meaning. The fact that knowledge can be represented in different ways implies that knowledge is not a sensory transcription of the external world into the inner world of the mind. (p. 21)

Single cortical neurons with similar "interests" tend to be vertically arrayed in cortical columns like thin cylinders (Calvin, 1996). The best-known columns are the visual cortex's orientation columns, but little is known about aural orientation columns and representations. The data available, however, suggest the existence of complex musical structures that are processed in distributed areas and are connected in coherent networks or cell assemblies. What we perceive as music originates from distributed processing but combines into one conscious feature that forms a robust mental representation.

Experimental programs have demonstrated that formal training and informal experience in varied environmental situations cause measurable changes in the neurochemistry and even in the neuroanatomy of the brain (Black & Greenough, 1998). Even the cortical maps of adult primates can be radically altered through environmental input (Kempermann et al., 1997). This neuronal plasticity is crucial for the neurobiology of learning. As Ramon y Cajal stressed at the end of the 19th century, learning is deeply involved in, if not biologically based upon, the formation of new synaptic connections. Since Donald O. Hebb (1949) theorized that chemical changes in a cell's dendrites increase the likelihood that it will activate neighboring cells, remarkable empirical progress has been made in the investigation of synaptic connectivity and its impact on the electrochemical transmission between neurons. "This basic concept of a cooperative set of modifiable connections as the basis of learning and memory, along with the Hebb synapse, continues to have substantial influence on neural network theory" (Black & Greenough, 1998, p. 56).

If learning is associated with synaptic growth, the investigation of the formation of synaptic contacts in the human cerebral cortex becomes enormously important. It has been documented for animal and human brains that the synaptic density—the number of synapses per neuron or per unit volume of cortical tissue—changes over life spans and defines the limits of the processing capacity (Huttenlocher, 1979, 1984). In human beings, synaptogenesis takes place prenatally and in early infancy. By the age of 1 year it reaches a plateau stage, followed by a progressive synapse decline, which happens most rapidly dur-

ing preschool years (Huttenlocher, 1984). However, there are regional differences in synaptogenesis in human brains. Huttenlocher (Huttenlocher & Dabholkar, 1997) compared the development in two cortical areas: the auditory and prefrontal cortex. He found that synaptic density increases more rapidly in the auditory cortex (maximum at age 3 months) than in middle frontal gyrus (peak after age 15 months). Here synaptic growth occurs concurrently with growth of dendrites and axons and with myelination of the subcortical white matter. The following phase of synapse elimination also starts earlier in the auditory cortex, where it reaches a mature level by age 12 years, than in the prefrontal cortex (Huttenlocher & Dabholkar, 1997). The exuberant overproduction of neuronal connections during infancy may be seen as an anatomical substrate for neural plasticity (Huttenlocher, 1990) that has a tremendous impact on the unique structure of early learning. The discovery of an inverted u-shaped structure in brain development is confirmed by the development of glucose metabolism. Cerebral glucose consumption rises from birth until about 4 years of age, maintains from 4 to about 9–10 years, and then gradually declines (Chugani, 1998). These findings have important implications for our understanding of brain plasticity and critical periods for learning.

Recently neuroscientists at Geneva University (Müller, Toni, & Buchs, 2000) have investigated the chemical changes that influence synaptic strength. The researchers stimulated rat brain slices to produce long-term potentiation (LTP). If a receiving neuron has been activated, the incoming neurotransmitter induces LTP by flooding calcium ions into the spine. An hour after treatment, 20% of the synapses had developed double spines, forming a second spine adjacent to the active one. Müller concludes that LTP triggers "a duplication of the active synapse" (Baringa, 1999, p. 1661). Presumably this causes an increase in synaptic strength.

The neurobiological foundations for learning are derived from studies that suggest that experience or learning induces changes in the brain that relate to cortical thickness (Diamond et al., 1964), the size of cell bodies (Diamond, 1967), the size of synaptic contact areas (West & Greenough, 1972), an increase in dendritic spines (Globus et al., 1973), a parallel increase in the number of synapses per neuron (Turner & Greenough, 1985), the thickness of the corpus callosum (Schlaug, Jäncke, Huang, Stalger, & Steinmetz, 1995), an increase in hippocampal neurons (Kempermann et al., 1997), the size of the left planum temporale (Pantev et al., 1998), and the doubling of spines through LTP (Müller et al., 2000). These research findings relate either to the growth of number or size of new synaptic connections by formal training or enriched environmental experience or to the growth of stronger and bigger already-existing synapses. In any case, the evidence of neurochemical and neuroanatomical plasticity is basic for the neurobiology of learning, that is, for the formation and modification of mental representations. In particular for young children, it is evident—despite Bruer's reluctance (see "Discussions and Conclusions")—that early music training leads to an expansion of the representation of sound in the auditory cortex (Rauschecker, 1999).

For cognition and learning experiments, the localization of task-specific cortical areas has been empirically investigated (see "Brain Research on Music Cognition and Learning"). Even the specialization within the auditory cortex has been clarified by its subdivision into four distinct territories (Gaschler-Markefski, Baumgart, Tempelmann, Woldorff, & Scheich, 1998). The contribution of different cortical areas to music processing still remains a major focus of research in neuroscience. From patients with surgical lesions we know about different strategies of musical-information processing. They demonstrate, for example, that a right temporal cortectomy impairs the use of both contour and interval information, whereas a left temporal cortectomy interferes with interval information only (Liegeois-Chauvel, Peretz, Babai, Leguitton, & Chauvel, 1998). In general, the acquisition of implicit knowledge through neuronal self-organization that results from mere exposure to music (Peretz, Gaudreau, & Bonnel, 1998) should not be underestimated, as Tillmann, Bharucha, and Bigand have shown by experiments that dealt with tone, chord, and key relationships, including memory judgments, and expectancies (2000). Furthermore, the learning context plays an important role in memory retrieval, especially for infants who displayed a 7-day retention only when the music played during the retention test matched the training music (Fagen et al., 1997). However, all that knowledge about functional cortical areas cannot suffice as the only explanation for the neurobiological processes involved in music learning. In this section, learning is, therefore, exclusively defined as the process of incrementally developing and altering the structure of mental representations.

Following the experimental brain studies on learning primarily conducted with animals, researchers have recently conducted EEG studies on music learning of children (aged 12–14) and adults (aged 17–39) (Altenmüller & Gruhn, 1997; Altenmüller, Gruhn, Parlitz, & Liebert, 2000; Gruhn, 1997; Gruhn, Altenmüller, & Babler, 1997; Liebert et al., 1999). These studies reveal that significant changes in auditory activation patterns are induced by different types of learning that correspond to formal instruction and informal musical exposure. Subjects who received informal instruction by singing and playing supported the efficiency of the phonological loop at the aural-oral level and, by this, developed procedural knowledge. This learning strategy evidenced increased activation patterns at the

right frontal and bilateral parieto-occipital lobes, which may be ascribed to a global way of processing through the integration of visuo-spatial associations). However, music processing of subjects who received formal verbal instruction evidenced an increased activation of left fronto-temporal brain regions, which might refer to a more local strategy (Altenmüller & Gruhn, 1997).

In another long-term learning experiment, subjects displayed different activation patterns depending upon how successfully they performed a task. Those who succeeded in the task, regardless of the type of learning (declarative versus procedural), demonstrated a shift to the *right* fronto-temporal lobes, whereas brain activation in those subjects who did not succeed focused in the *left* fronto-temporal regions. Therefore, it appears that a simple right-left dichotomy with music in the right hemisphere is an oversimplification. Any music processing involves both hemispheres equally but in an asymmetric specialization that depends upon many intra- and interpersonal factors. Perhaps different types of processing (global versus local processing; Peretz, 1990; see "Brain Research on Music Cognition and Learning") produce a lateralization effect because different cognitive strategies are applied individually.

Brain activation patterns can also differentiate long-term from short-term learning. In a short-term ear-training experiment (Liebert et al., 1999), researchers found an overall increase of brain activation, whereas experiments with long-term learning demonstrated a general decrease of brain activation. These findings seem to support that long-term learning causes a structural change within mental representation, which may be called formal (Bamberger, 1991; Gruhn, 1998). Formal representations produce a more distributed, widely spread neuronal network and may therefore need only a reduced cortical brain potential, presumably due to the involvement of subcortical regions in the representation of genuine musical qualities. (This must be shown by functional fMRI studies.) There is good reason to assume that, biologically, learning is accomplished by a move from one type of cortical representation (which might be called figural, according to Bamberger, 1991) to a different type of cortical representation that involves subcortical layers. The essence of this model is based upon different encodings of the processing and storing of musical information and knowledge. Learning, therefore, effects the transformation from cortical to integral cortical-subcortical representations.

In instrumental training, motor skills and auditory skills collaborate. The activation of representation in one area is linked to that of a corresponding area that is not directly stimulated. This process has been described as coactivation. Bangert, Parlitz, et al. (1999) demonstrated that subjects exhibit a slight coactivation of the sensorimotor cortex in a passive auditory task even 20 minutes after a keyboard-training session. Likewise, fronto-temporal regions were activated in pianists during a mute motor task. This clearly suggests that cortical activation patterns, even during a strictly limited task, display a widely distributed network far beyond a simple image of the involved activity. Learning, in a neurobiological sense, is due to the establishment of those networks.

Neurobiological Research on Music and Learning

Overview

A comprehensive review of brain development is beyond the scope of this chapter. However, M. H. Johnson (1998) has identified four factors that we believe are important to any understanding of the neurobiology of music learning and cognition.

First, there are neural structures in the brain that are common to both humans and other mammals, both primate and nonprimate. Differences between humans and other animals primarily concern the extent of the cerebral cortex. Subcortical structures, such as the hippocampus and cerebellum, are structurally similar across mammalian species.

Second, the cerebral cortex, hippocampus, and cerebellum continue to develop throughout childhood. Although the vast majority of neurons are present at birth (Rakic, 1995), synapses, dendrites, and fiber bundles continue to develop postnatally, perhaps as a function of experience. Myelin, the fatty sheath that surrounds neuronal pathways (and is thought to increase the efficiency of information transmission), also increases dramatically after birth. The immaturity of the human brain at birth may explain some of the limitations on learning and cognition present in infants and children. Similarly, the dynamic postnatal development of the cortex allows more intentional, purposeful behavior.

Third, different areas of the cerebral cortex develop at different rates. For example, Conel's (1939/1967) study of cortical development in the human infant led him to conclude that the cortex develops in an "inside-out" fashion, with outer brain layers developing in advance of inner layers. Differential development *between* cortical regions (i.e., visual cortex and frontal cortex) has also been documented (Huttenlocher, 1990). These patterns of development may influence information processing.

Finally, studies on cortical plasticity suggest that cortical specialization is heavily influenced by experience. Although primary cortices are genetically predetermined, there is a high degree of modulation with respect to the extension and connectivity of functional brain areas according to experience and learning. Therefore, brain plasticity can be seen as fundamental for the development of mental representations.

Empirical Methods

The recent explosion of knowledge of brain development makes the task of relating it to cognitive changes considerably more viable. Consequently, efforts to correlate neural changes to cognitive changes have increased dramatically over the past two decades. However, because a multitude of neuroanatomical variables change over the first decade of life, it is unwise to make causal inferences that regard the relationship between changes in specific brain areas to specific cognitive changes. Evidence of temporal correlation can, however, be supported by empirical methods. A variety of techniques are now available to developmentalists interested in the biological basis of cognitive development. Some of these methods, such as PET, require the injection of a radioactive dye and are therefore of limited use for studying the cognitive functioning of healthy children and adults. Others, such as EEG, ERP, and functional MRI (fMRI), are currently being employed. These imaging techniques are described by Hodges and Flohr in this volume (chap. 52).

While the new functional brain-imaging techniques promise to provide researchers with important information that regards the relationship of brain structure and function to learning and cognition, somewhat similar questions can be explored through the use of animals as subjects. Research on animals (mostly rodents) has contributed a great deal to our understanding of the relation between brain and behavior. The field of molecular genetics, for example, has opened up new possibilities for investigating this relationship. In particular, mice that undergo lesions in the alpha-calcium-calmodulin kinase II gene are unable to perform certain learning tasks in adulthood (Silva, Paylor, Wehner, & Tonegawa, 1992). These types of techniques, in which certain genes from the genome of an animal are either removed or lesioned, permit the investigator to answer questions that regard genetic contributions to learning and behavior and are particularly well suited when applied to established animal models of development.

Further insight into the relations between brain and behavior can be found in studies in which the brain is removed in order to examine it at the cellular level. For example, studies that used this technique suggest that rats reared in an "enriched" environment after weaning show a wealth of enduring neurobiological and behavioral changes. Rats raised with stimulus objects such as running wheels, rubber tubes, nibble bars, and such in their cages show morphological and biochemical alterations in cortical and hippocampal formation and perform better on learning and memory-dependent tasks than animals raised in normal laboratory conditions (see Renner & Rosenzweig, 1987, for review). Similar effects have been found for rats raised in socially enriched conditions, in which animals are housed with several siblings rather than in pairs or isolation (Pacteau, Einon, & Sindon, 1989). Furthermore, recent research has demonstrated that rats exposed to complex music learned a spatial maze faster and with fewer errors than rats exposed to minimalist music, white noise, or silence (Rauscher, Robinson, & Jens, 1998), results that appear to be a function of increased hippocampal dendritic density in the animals exposed to the complex music (Rauscher & Koch, 2000). Taken together, these studies strongly suggest a morphological change in mammalian cortex as a function of environmental stimulation.

Marker tasks, behavioral tasks that have been linked to particular brain regions by neuroimaging studies, provide another useful approach to understanding brain development and learning. By testing individuals of varying ages with different versions of these tasks researchers can relate levels of task performance to the functional development of different brain regions. A number of marker tasks have recently been developed for the functioning of structures involved in oculomotor control and visual attention shifts (M. H. Johnson, 1998).

Brain Research on Music Cognition and Learning

There may be no other area of music psychology that has seen as much recent advancement as research on music-induced plasticity of the brain. For example, Gottfried Schlaug and his colleagues found that a small neural structure in the cerebral cortex that processes sound signals, the planum temporale, was larger in the left hemisphere and smaller in the right in the brains of musicians than of non-musicians (Schlaug, Jäncke, Huang, & Steinmetz, 1994), an effect that was later found to be due to musicians who possessed perfect pitch and who began their musical training before the age of 7 (Schlaug et al., 1995). Schlaug and his colleagues also reported that musicians, particularly those who had begun their training before age 7, had thicker corpus callosi (the band of nerve tissue that connects the left and right hemispheres) than nonmusicians (Schlaug et al., 1994).

Other correlational studies also suggest that instrumental instruction affects brain development. Elbert, Pantev, Wienbruch, Rockstroh, and Taub (1995) asked string players and nonmusicians to move the fingers of their left hands while magnetoencephalography (MEG) measurements were taken. The researchers found that magnetic response from the right primary somatosensory cortex—a brain region that controls the left-hand fingers—was larger for the string players than it was for the nonmusicians. Furthermore, the magnitude of the response was related to

the age at which the string players began instruction, with those who began lessons earlier evidencing the largest response. Finally, a recent paper by Pantev and his colleagues reported that auditory cortical representation was 25% larger in musicians than in nonmusicians, regardless of the instrument played and the presence of perfect pitch (Pantev et al., 1998). The younger the instrumental training began, the larger the cortical reorganization. Effects were found for subjects who began to practice before age 9.

Many studies have compared cortical processing of aural imagery tasks with perception tasks (Reisberg, 1992; Zatorre & Halpern, 1993; Zatorre, Halpern, et al., 1996). Zatorre and Halpern (1993) hypothesized that similar neuronal mechanisms may underlie both imaginal and perceptual processing. A PET study demonstrated that although many of the same regions appear to be involved in imagined and perceived tonal-pattern processing, two inferior frontopolar regions showed significant increase of blood flow only for the imagery task (Zatorre et al., 1996). This may refer to different aspects of the generation of auditory information from memory. However, in an experiment on the effects of unilateral temporal-lobe excision on perception and imagery Zatorre and Halpern (1993) found that patients with right temporal-lobe excision showed a significant decrease in both perceptual and imagery tasks. The interaction of aural imagery and music perception plays an important role in music learning because aural imagery depends on already-established mental representations that are a prerequisite for any type of discrimination learning.

Correspondingly, different processing strategies influence lateralization effects and particular musical properties call for different activation areas. In a study with unilateral brain-damaged patients, Peretz (1990) found two types of musical-information processing that she called local and global processing. If, on the one hand, the processing is interval-based, focusing on local properties as single tones and distances, the left hemisphere is dominant; if, on the other hand, the processing is contour-based, focusing on the more global aspects of a tune, then the right hemisphere is dominant. Similar results support these findings. In an EEG study, Breitling, Guenther, and Rondot (1987) found different bilateral involvement for different stimulus conditions (single tone, scale, melody). Only in the melody condition (global processing) was the right hemisphere more activated.

In general, it can be stated that lateralization effects mirror the asymmetric specialization of brain functions, depending on acoustic aspects of stimuli as well as individual cognitive processing strategies.

Discussion and Conclusions

Until recently, the majority of the research on the neurobiology of learning in general and music learning in par-

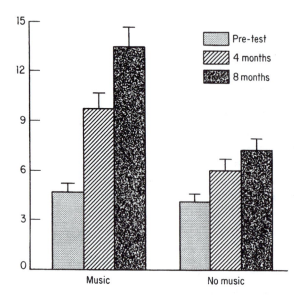

Figure 25.1. Spatial-temporal scores of kindergarten children (School District of Kettle Moraine) before and after music or no training: correct joins/minute.

ticular was descriptive and focused mainly on cerebral localization of function. (See Hodges and Flohr in this Handbook, chap. 52, for a review of these studies.) However, neuropsychologists are now beginning to approach music learning from a more "cognitive" or "information-processing" position. Simply knowing that left unilateral neglect follows posterior right hemisphere lesions does not tell us anything about the specific mechanism(s) responsible, nor how these mechanisms operate to produce the symptom. Thus the goal today is to identify the particular *processes* that are enhanced, maintained, or disrupted after intervention or cerebral damage and determine how these processes relate to specific neural substrates or neural systems.

The purpose of the research cited earlier was to discover how developmental processes affect brain and cognition, particularly in the early years. These studies suggest that early instrumental instruction may actually physically shape and mold the young brain. However, Bruer (1999) cautions us against drawing excessive conclusions from these data. Although there may indeed exist a relationship between music cognition and brain development, our knowledge of this relationship is far from complete, and alternative explanations for the data should be considered. For example, Elbert et al.'s (1995) research with string players measured the brain's response to an overlearned skill—fingering a keyboard. It stands to reason that any overlearned motor activity, for example, typing, would produce similar brain reorganization. This study, therefore, was not directly about music. Furthermore, although Schlaug, Jäncke, Huang, and Steinmetz (1994, 1995) and

Pantey, Oostenveld, Engellen, Ross, Roberts, and Hoke's (1998) findings suggest that early music engagement affects the brain's pitch/auditory processing regions, it is not clear that the age at which subjects began instruction, rather than how long they had been playing, produced the effects. In other words, the larger brain response may be the result of longer time on task, rather than age of task onset.

It is also not clear in these studies whether the morphological effects were caused by the music instruction. Studies that compare musicians to nonmusicians are correlational, not causal. They therefore do not address whether differences in brain structure between these two groups of subjects are a function of the music exposure or of inborn atypicalities in the brains of musicians that may attract them to music making in the first place. Clearly, longitudinal causal studies are needed to investigate the maturation of cognitive abilities and brain regions before and during early versus later onset music instruction. It is important to note that no scientific studies have directly investigated the effects of music instruction on the adult brain. We must be careful not to ignore the fact that brain development continues until death.

Transfer Effects

According to conventional opinion, music has an effect on cognitive achievement. Therefore, experimental findings that actually confirm transfer effects would have an important impact on educational policies with respect to school music curriculum. Consequently, there is an increasing interest in inquiries on whether music can really improve the mind (Overy, 1998). Thus several longitudinal observations of schoolchildren who received extra music lessons within their regular school curriculum were performed in Europe (Bastian, 2000; Spychiger, 1995). Here effects of music on social behavior and school achievement appeared.

In an experimental memory study, Chan, Ho, and Cheung (1998) found that music training improved verbal memory because verbal memory is mediated mainly by the left temporal lobe, which is larger in musicians than in nonmusicians. Although Chan used subjects from Hong Kong whose native language was tonal (a language in which verbal memory includes pitch memory), the greater effect on verbal than on visual memory tasks in musicians possibly indicates a general transfer effect.

Just recently, a meta-analysis of studies on the relationship between music and academic achievement (Winner & Hetland, 2000) has examined the outcome of studies on music and reading skills, music and mathematics, and music and spatial-temporal reasoning. Twenty-four correlational studies and six experimental studies on the impact of music on the development of reading skills were examined (Butzlaff, 2000). Whereas correlational studies showed that students who studied music scored significantly higher on standardized reading tests, there was no reliable effect supported by the experimental studies. With respect to an impact of music instruction on mathematics, a total of 25 correlational and experimental studies were examined. The analysis revealed a small but evident association between music and mathematics achievement: Individuals who voluntarily chose to study music privately and those who were exposed to a music curriculum in school produced higher mathematical scores than those who did not (Vaughn, 2000). However, a positive relationship is not sufficient to establish a causal link. Furthermore, listening to background music had no notable effect.

The explosion of studies that explore the transfer of musical processing to spatial processing compels us to examine these data from a neurophysiological perspective. Two lines of behavioral research have been pursued: the effects of *listening* to music on *adult* spatial abilities and the effects of *instrumental instruction* on *children's* spatial abilities. Two recent meta-analyses (Hetland, 2000a, 2000b) have examined the studies relevant to these inquiries. The first analysis explored the so-called Mozart effect, the finding that college students who listened to 10 minutes of Mozart's piano sonata K. 448 scored higher on spatial-temporal tasks than students who listened to taped relaxation instructions or silence (Rauscher, Shaw, & Ky, 1993). Hetland's (2000b) meta-analysis of 36 studies that involved approximately 2,500 subjects revealed a moderate, robust effect that "is limited, however, to a specific type of spatial task that requires mental rotation in the absence of a physical model" (p. 33). Despite Hetland's conclusion, it must be noted that attempts to reproduce Rauscher, Shaw, and Ky's (1993) findings have been inconsistent. For example, in a series of experiments designed to replicate the Mozart effect through use of the same musical composition as well as similar control conditions and dependent measures, Steele and his colleagues achieved negative results (e.g., Steele et al., 1999).

The second meta-analytic review, also undertaken by Hetland (2000a), examined studies on the effects of instrumental instruction on children's spatial abilities (see, for example, Rauscher et al., 1997). Figure 25.1 portrays the effect for kindergarten children. The results of this analysis revealed an overall effect size of $r = .37$, an effect that was deemed "remarkably consistent" and could be "generalized to similar populations of preschool- and elementary-school-aged children, while they are engaged in similar kinds of active music programs, with or without keyboard instruments, taught in groups or individual lessons. The effect cannot be explained away by a Hawthorne effect, nonequivalence of experimental groups, experimenter bias, or study quality. It is a solid finding" (Hetland, 2000a, pp. 41–42).

We will not attempt to undertake a critical analysis of these studies, but instead, as per the focus of this chapter, we will comment on their possible neurophysiological implications. The motivation for research on the transfer of music listening or instruction to spatial task performance came from a neural connectionist model of the mammalian brain proposed by Xiaodan Leng and Gordon Shaw (Leng & Shaw, 1991). Based on Mountcastle's columnar principle of cortex, the model proposed that families of neural networks respond to and compare spatial features of objects. By mathematically deriving their firing probabilities the researchers determined that the networks evolved according to symmetries modified by Hebb learning rules. These neural network patterns (lasting tens of seconds over large cortical areas) corresponded to spatial-temporal task performance (requiring the transformation of mental images over time). Leng and Shaw therefore predicted that certain musical forms and instruction might stimulate these firing patterns, thereby enhancing spatial-temporal performance.

Although it is impossible to "prove" a neural model of brain function, Leng and Shaw's (1991) hypothesis is supported by data. For example, Alzheimer patients who listened to the Mozart sonata or silence demonstrated improved spatial-temporal performance following Mozart (J. K. Johnson, Cotman, Tasaki, & Shaw, 1998; J. K. Johnson, Shaw, Vuong, Vuong, & Cotman, 1999). Neuroscientists have investigated the effect through the use of EEG and fMRI. EEGs of subjects who performed a spatial-temporal task after listening to the Mozart sonata revealed a carryover effect in parietal and frontal cortex; no carryover was found when reading a story was substituted for the task (Sarnthein et al., 1997). EEGs of epilepsy patients, some comatose, showed decreased seizure activity during exposure to the sonata rather than silence or control music (Hughes, Daaboul, Fino, & Shaw, 1998; Hughes, Fino, & Melyn, 1999). The compositions differentially activated the prefrontal, occipital, and cerebellar regions—all regions associated with spatial-temporal reasoning. These findings, although specific to music listening, may also have neurophysiological implications for the effects of music instruction on certain spatial abilities.

Parsons, Hodges, and Fox (1998) have proposed an alternative theory. These researchers suggest that the rhythmic elements of music, processed in the cerebellum, are responsible for the enhancement of spatial tasks (such as mental rotation tasks) that also require cerebellar function. A recent experiment by Parsons and his colleagues (cited in Hetland, 2000a) supports this hypothesis. Subjects performed two spatial-temporal tasks following one of five conditions: auditory exposure to rhythm without melody (a popular song bass line), auditory exposure to melody without rhythm (a melody presented in a steady beat), visual exposure to rhythm (a pulsating square on a computer screen), auditory exposure to a continuous tone, or silence. Enhanced performance of the spatial-temporal tasks was found following only the auditory and visual rhythmic conditions. This suggests that the enhancement of spatial-temporal tasks is due to rhythm, regardless of the modality of presentation.

Other explanations for these transfer effects can be found in the cognitive literature. For example, Rauscher (1999) has proposed that several of the elements of music cognition described by Serafine (1988)—temporal succession and simultaneity, nontemporal closure, transformation, and abstraction—may be musically analogous to the cognitive processes required to solve certain visuo-spatial tasks. Perhaps some of the skills involved in learning music transfer to the performance of particular spatial skills.

The importance of studying the transfer of musical learning to spatial learning becomes evident when one considers the overall significance of spatial abilities to cognitive function. High levels of spatial ability have frequently been linked to creativity, not only in the arts but in science and mathematics as well (Shepard, 1978; West, 1991). Physicists (Albert Einstein, James Clerk Maxwell, Michael Faraday, and Hermann von Helmholtz), inventors (such as Nikola Tesla and James Watt), and other scientists displayed high levels of spatial abilities and reported that these abilities played an important role in their most creative accomplishments. In psychology, Shepard (1978) has given particularly lucid accounts of the role of spatial imagery in his own thinking. Involuntary dream images were the source of many of his most creative and influential contributions, including the idea for his research on mental rotation, the first method of nonmetric multidimensional scaling, and the computer algorithm that underlies additive nonhierarchical cluster analysis. Given the prominent role of spatial abilities both in models of human abilities and in models of cognition, studies that demonstrate that music instruction may influence spatial reasoning have important educational implications. However, due to the fact that there is as yet no commonly accepted theoretical approach that adequately accounts for these transfer effects, we recommend discretion in both the interpretation of research results and their application.

Music Learning by Individuals with Brain Disorders

Patients with Mental Disorders

The study of brain-damaged populations has always been a major area of research for investigating cognitive functioning of the human brain. Unfortunately, results of studies of brain-damaged patients are neither consistent nor easy to interpret, because the loss of a particular ability may not necessarily be attributed to a damaged brain area or specific module of information processing. Rather, loss of ability may instead be due to an interruption of important connections between collaborating cell assemblies. However, the effect on musical skills can be observed in musicians with brain injuries who suffer from music alexia and agraphia (Brust, 1980). Namely, developmental musical dyslexia in children who have difficulties reading music has been studied (N. Gordon, 2000), just as general dyslexia, which has significant effects on children's musical abilities to recognize musical tone sequences and differentiate tone colors and sound intensities, has been (Kurth & Heinrichs, 1976). Therefore, investigations of the development of musical abilities in populations with brain disorders, as well as those with genetic abnormalities, offer valuable research. In particular, individuals with Williams syndrome, Down's syndrome, Alzheimer's and Huntington's disease, and musicogenic epilepsy are rather informative with respect to particular musical abilities.

There is an extended body of research that investigated Alzheimer's disease and its impact on musical abilities. It is well documented that previously acquired musical skills (e.g., singing and playing an instrument) remain accessible despite otherwise severe cognitive impairment. A case study of an 82-year-old musician reports relatively spared anterograde and retrograde procedural memory for music making (Crystal, Grober, & Masur, 1989). Similarly, J. Johnson and Ulatowska (1995) studied the progression of deterioration of Alzheimer's patients in music and language. They found that song texts in connection with the tunes persisted while speech was profoundly disturbed. This supports Gardner's (1983/1985) theory of unique multiple intelligences, that is, that music as a manifestation of intelligence constitutes a faculty per se and is to a large degree uncorrelated with other cognitive abilities.

A notable affinity for music is documented for children with Down's and Williams syndromes. Quantitative studies of brain morphology demonstrate a distinctive dysmorphology unlike that of other forms of mental retardation (Lenhoff et al., 1997). A highly selective effect of brain development appears to accompany Williams syndrome: Patients demonstrate a reduced cerebral size and a significant increase of neocerebellar vermal lobules, whereas individuals with Down's syndrome evidence a reduction in both cerebellar components (Jernigan & Bellugi, 1990; Levitin & Bellugi, 1998). These individuals often possess relatively intact verbal working memory but are more impaired in spatial working memory (Levitin & Bellugi, 1995, p. 375). Therefore, they demonstrate deficient spatial coordination on the motoric level but perform general musical tasks sufficiently. Moreover, subjects with Williams syndrome have a striking independence of rhythmic abilities and show a propensity for creative rhythmic productions. The obvious evidence for this quality is called rhythmicity or rhythmic musicality by Levitin and Bellugi

(1998). Although children with Williams syndrome fail in Piagetian conservation tasks, they demonstrate a clear conservation of musical time and rhythm. This may be linked with a general predominance of local over global processing strategies, especially in the processing of visual stimuli (Bellugi, Lai, & Wang, 1997). In a rhythm repetition task, children with Williams syndrome often do not repeat correctly the global structure but use local variations for creative completions (Levitin & Bellugi, 1998). A similar affinity for music and musical rhythm is reported for children with Down's syndrome. In a comparative study with other mentally challenged and normal children, children with Down's syndrome exhibited the same level of rhythm discrimination as normal children but did differ from other mentally challenged children (Stratford & Ching, 1983).

These findings with subjects with Down's and Williams syndrome suggest that musical abilities and other cognitive functioning may develop independently, perhaps due to neuroanatomical differences in the brain disorders of these patients. This suggests that music may not only serve a therapeutic goal, especially in Alzheimer's patients (Aldridge, 1994; Glynn, 1992; Lord & Garner, 1993), but it may also serve as a special tool for learning due to the evident interaction between *rhythmicity* and brain function (Thaut, Kenyon, et al., 1999) as well as movement and vocal sound production (Gruhn, 2001). This explanation also relates to the striking effect of music on the motor control of patients with Parkinson's disease. Also, researchers have shown that patients with Huntington's disease could significantly modulate their gait velocity during self-paced and rhythmic metronome cueing, but velocity adaptations did not fit with an exact synchronization of steps and metric impulses (Thaut, Miltner, et al., 1999). Effects are also reported from patients with epilepsy where brainwave abnormalities occur during music-induced seizures (Critchley, 1977). Just recently, fewer clinical seizures and fewer generalized bilateral spike and wave complexes were reported from a patient with Lennox-Gastaut syndrome after regular exposure to Mozart's piano sonata K. 448 (Hughes et al., 1999).

Deaf Children with Cochlear Implants

During the last two decades, advanced technology has been applied to the treatment of deaf (or severely hearing-impaired) children who still have an active hearing nerve. An artificial cochlea can be implanted to stimulate the hair cells of the cochlea by electrodes that are activated through electric impulses from an outside microphone. Cochlear implant (CI) surgeries have become routine in Europe, Australia, and the United States since the 1980s, and younger and younger prelingually deaf children can now be treated. The most appropriate time window for an ef-

ficient surgery is between age 2 and 4, that is, before the development of prosody has already been stabilized. Although there is only limited access to music transmitted by the available technology of today (Fujita & Ito, 1999), further generations of speech processors (such as Nucleus, Clarion, and Med-el) will expand the range of formats by developing different strategies through use of either time resolution (CIS = continuous interleaved sampling strategy), spectral peak resolution (SPEAK strategy), or a combined strategy (ACE = advanced combined encoder).

There is an enormous amount of research on speech development and aural processing in CI patients and an increasing interest in music perception as well (Gfeller et al., 1997; Ito et al., 1995; Pijl, 1997). Here we discuss the neurobiological development of primary and secondary auditory cortices of deaf patients. Up to now, very little has been known about the cortical development of CI patients after they recover auditory cortex areas. These areas, like the visual cortices of children born blind, are underdeveloped and utilized by other sensory representations. Perception of different sounds evoked through electrical stimulation must be learned with respect to sound discrimination and the gradual attribution of meaning to discernible sounds. A clear understanding of the neurobiological development of mental representation can facilitate this learning process, the goal of which relates to speech acquisition. As we know from neurolinguistics, even the semantics of a language are carried out through sequential structures in time. Therefore, music, especially rhythm patterns, may function as a cortex trainer for CI patients to gain or regain perceptive and expressive competence. Only EEG measurements (because MEG and MRI cannot be applied to the highly sensitive cochlear electrodes) can demonstrate whether sound stimulation actually arrives at the brain stem and how auditory and associative cortices develop during listening training and sound exposure. The aforementioned interaction of movement and brain function (Thaut, Kenyon, et al., 1999) plays an important role in the learning process here, because the motor system responds so sensitively to the auditory priming and, vice versa, rhythmic auditory stimulation corresponds with motor activation.

Applications to Music Education

Results from brain research and neurobiological findings alone can hardly lead to immediate applications and recommendations for music education. These data cannot be directly transferred to educational practice because scientific descriptions are essentially different from educational prescriptions. Empirical data are based upon objective facts and verifiable procedures; scientific research is committed to objectivity, reliability, and validity. Judgments in education, however, are value judgments to a large degree. Normative decisions on values can never be deduced objectively from empirical descriptions. As Gardner (1999) puts it: "We could know what every neuron does and we would not be one step closer to knowing how to educate our children," because "the chasm between 'is' and 'ought' is unbridgeable" (pp. 60, 79).

Mental representation has become the key notion of the cognitive revolution during the decade of the brain (Gardner, 1999). Therefore, one possible application to music education may involve the fostering of mental representations (see chap. 30, by Andreas C. Lehmann and Jane W. Davidson in this volume). As already mentioned, education is based on decisions that are grounded in value judgments that deal with the "what" and "why" of teaching, but findings in neurobiology may indicate new ways of "how" to teach. Teaching interacts with the disposition and potential of each individual. Although neurobiological findings cannot tell us why to teach music of a particular culture and what to select from the broad variety of musical traditions, empirical findings can advise us on how and when to teach so that mind, memory, perception, and cognition can be developed most effectively. From that perspective, the neurobiology of cognition and learning allows us to draw the following tentative conclusions:

1. Learning is the process by which one develops and incrementally differentiates mental representations. Therefore, music learning focuses on the development of genuine musical representations that are characterized by different forms of encoding.
2. Procedural knowledge (knowing how) is more appropriate in music cognition than formal declarative knowledge (knowing about). Immanent musical properties (pulse, meter, tonality, intervals, motifs, contours, etc.) are represented by neuronal connections that can only be recognized when activated through aural stimulation. Conversely, these musical entities can only be articulated in singing or playing if developed as mental representations. Conscious activation may be called audiation (E. E. Gordon, 1980/1997). It takes place when neuronal representations are activated in thinking, listening, or music making.
3. This calls for the idea of teaching music *musically* (Gruhn, 1997; Swanwick, 1999), that is, advancing those teaching strategies and learning modes that promote the development of genuine musical representations by priming an aural-oral loop.
4. There is increasing evidence that music learning may transfer to other areas of learning (e.g., spatial learning). The possible mechanisms of this transfer, either cognitive or neurophysiological, are still unknown. Much more work is needed before applications to educational practice can be derived from these studies.
5. The same caution should also be applied to studies on the lateralization effects in music. Music is processed in both hemispheres, but there exists an asymmetric predominance that depends on the applied cognitive strategy (global versus local; verbal versus procedural). Therefore, music teaching and learning should take into consideration that different strategies engage different brain areas. The more interconnected these areas are, the more stable the developed representations will become.
6. Research on individuals with mental disorders has clearly demonstrated that musical abilities develop independently of other domains of cognition. Therefore, these studies suggest that each person forms his or her individual intelligence profile. Music education should take advantage of the individual's potential within the musical domain rather than hoping for possible extramusical transfer effects. Music education must develop the individual's unique musical aptitude to its highest possible level.

Further research questions that regard the development of appropriate methods for teaching and learning remain, such as:

- How do motor, aural, and visual representations interact?
- What role does memory play in "formal" representation?
- How is global versus local processing in music localized?
- What is the neuronal substrate of different types of representation (figural versus formal)?
- What kinds of subcortical representations are engaged in music processing?
- How do cortical and subcortical representations interact in music learning?
- Are there culture-specific types of brain processing and formation of mental representation and, if so, what are the optimal ways of teaching music within and between cultures?

The ongoing dramatic progress in brain research has spawned the investigation of many aspects of music learning in a more sophisticated way than was ever thought possible. This research may in the long run open new insights into the learning and understanding of music, with far-reaching applications for music education.

REFERENCES

Aebli, H. (1980/81). *Denken—das Ordnen des Tuns*, 2 vols. Stuttgart, Germany: Klett-Cotta.

Aldridge, D. (1994). Alzheimer's disease: Rhythm, timing and music as therapy. *Biomedicine and Pharmacotherapy, 48*(7), 275–281.

Altenmüller, E., & Gruhn, W. (1997). *Music, the brain, and music learning. Mental representation and changing activation patterns through learning* (GIML series vol. 2). Chicago: G.I.A.

Altenmüller, E., Gruhn, W., Parlitz, D., & Liebert, G. (2000). The impact of music education on brain networks. Evidence from EEG studies. *International Journal for Music Education, 35*, 47–53.

Baldwin, J. M. (1968). *The development of the child and of the race.* New York: Augustus M. Kelly. (Original work published 1894)

Bamberger, J. (1991). *The mind behind the musical ear: How children develop musical intelligence.* Cambridge, MA: Harvard University Press.

Bangert M. W., Parlitz, D., & Altenmüller, E. (1999). Neuronal correlates of the pianists' "inner ear." *International Conference on Musical Imagery,* Oslo, Norway.

Barinaga, M. (1999). Learning visualized, on the double. *Science 286,* 1661.

Bastian, H. G. (2000). *Musik(erziehung) und ihre Wirkung: Eine Langzeitstudie an Berliner Grundschulen* [Music education and its effects]. Mainz, Germany: Schott.

Bechtel, W., & Abrahamsen, A. (1991). *Connectionism and the mind: An introduction to parallel processing networks.* Cambridge, MA: Blackwell.

Bellugi, U., Lai, Z., & Wang, P. (1997). Language, communication and neural systems in Williams syndrome [Special issue: *Communication processes in children with developmental disabilities*]. *Mental Retardation and Developmental Disabilities Research Review, 3,* 334–342.

Black, J. E., & Greenough, W. T. (1998). Developmental approaches to the memory process. In J. Martinez & R. Kesner (Eds.), *Neurobiology of learning and memory* (pp. 55–88). San Diego, CA: Academic Press.

Breitling, D., Guenther, W., & Rondot, P. (1987). Auditory perception of music measured by brain electrical activity mapping. *Neurophysiologia, 25,* 765–774.

Bruer, J. T. (1999). *The myth of the first three years.* New York: Free Press.

Brust, J. C. (1980). Music and language: Musical alexia and agraphia. *Brain, 103*(2), 357–392.

Butzlaff, R. (2000). Can music be used to teach reading? *Journal of Aesthetic Education, 34*(3–4), 167–178.

Calvin, W. H. (1996). *How brains think.* New York: Basic Books.

Case, R. (1972). Learning and development: A neo-Piagetian interpretation. *Human Development, 15,* 339–358.

Chan, A. S., Ho, Y. C., & Cheung, M. C. (1998). Music training improves verbal memory. *Nature, 396,* 128.

Chugani, H. T. (1998). A critical period of brain development: Studies of cerebral glucose utilization with PET. *Preventive Medicine, 27*(2), 184–188.

Conel, J. L. (1967). *The postnatal development of the human cerebral cortex* (Vols. 1–8). Cambridge, MA: Harvard University Press. (Original work published 1939)

Critchley, M. (1977). Musicogenic epilepsy. In M. Critchley & R. Hensen (Eds.), *Music and the brain* (pp. 344–353). Springfield, IL: Charles C. Thomas.

Crystal, H. A., Grober, E., & Masur, D. (1989). Preservation of musical memory in Alzheimer's disease. *Journal of Neurology, Neurosurgery, and Psychiatry, 52*(12), 1415–1416.

Diamond, M. C. (1967). Extensive cortical depth measurements and neuron size increases in the cortex of environmentally enriched rats. *Journal of Comparative Neurology, 131,* 357–364.

Diamond, M. C., Krech, D., & Rosenzweig, M. R. (1964). The effects of an enriched environment on the histology of the rat cerebral cortex. *Journal of Comparative Neurology, 123,* 111–119.

Elbert, T., Pantev, C., Wienbruch, C., Rockstrub, B., & Taub, E. (1995). Increased cortical representation of the fingers of the left hand in string players. *Science, 270,* 305–307.

Fagen, J., Prigot, J., Carroll, M., Pioli, M., Stein, A., & Franco, A. (1997). Auditory context and memory retrieval in young infants. *Child Development, 68*(6), 1057–1066.

Fiske, H. E. (1993). *Music cognition and aesthetic attitudes.* Lewiston: Edwin Mellen.

Fodor, J. A. (1983). *The modularity of mind.* Cambridge, MA: MIT Press.

Fujita, S., & Ito, J. (1999). Ability of nucleus cochlear implantees to recognize music. *Annals of Otology, Rhinology, and Laryngology, 108,* 634–640.

Gardner, H. (1985). *Frames of mind: The theory of multiple intelligences.* New York: Basic Books. (Original work published 1983)

Gardner, H. (1999). *The disciplined mind.* New York: Simon & Schuster.

Gaschler-Markefski, B., Baumgart, F., Tempelmann, C., Woldorff, M. G., & Scheich, H. (1998). Activation of human auditory cortex in retrieval experiments: An fMRI study. *Neural Plasticity, 6*(3), 69–75.

Gfeller, K., Woodworth, G., Rubin, D., Wih, S., & Knutson, J. (1997). Perception of rhythmic and sequential pitch patterns by normally hearing adults and adult cochlear implant users. *Ear and Hearing, 18*(3), 252–260.

Globus, A., Rosenzweig, M. R., Bennett, E. L., & Diamond, M. C. (1973). Effects of differential experience on dendritic spine counts in rat cerebral cortex. *Journal of Comparative and Physiological Psychology, 82,* 175–181.

Glynn, N. J. (1992). The music therapy assessment tool in Alzheimer's patients. *Journal of Gerontological Nursing, 18*(1), 3–9.

Gordon, E. E. (1997). *Learning sequences in music. A music learning theory* (5th ed.). Chicago: G.I.A. (Originally published 1980).

Gordon, N. (2000). Developmental dysmusia (developmental musical dyslexia). *Developmental Medicine and Child Neurology, 42*(3), 214–215.

Gottlieb, G. (1991). Experimental canalization of behavioral development: Theory. *Developmental Psychology, 27,* 4–13.

Griffith, N., & Todd, P. M. (Eds.). (1999). *Musical networks: Parallel distributed perception and performance.* Cambridge, MA: MIT Press.

Gruhn, W. (1997). Music learning: Neurobiological foundations and educational implications. *Research Studies in Music Education, 9,* 36–47.

Gruhn, W., Altenmüller, E., & Babler, R. (1997). The influence of learning on cortical activation patterns. *Bulletin of the Council for Research in Music Education, 133,* 25–30.

Gruhn, W. (1998). *Der Musikverstand: Neurobiologische Grundlagen des musikalischen Denkens, Hörens und Ler-*

nens [The music brain: neurobiological basis of musical thinking, listening, and learning]. Hildesheim, Germany: Olms.

Gruhn, W. (2001). Musikalische Lernstadien und Entwicklungsphasen beim Kleinkind. Eine Langzeituntersuchung zum Aufbau musikalischer Respräsentationen bei Kindern bis zum 4. Lebensjahr. *Diskussion Musikpädagogik, 9,* 4–33.

Hebb, D. O. (1949). *Organization of behavior.* New York: Wiley.

Hetland, L. (2000a). Learning to make music enhances spatial reasoning. *Journal of Aesthetic Education, 34,* 179–238.

Hetland, L. (2000b). Listening to music enhances spatial-temporal reasoning: Evidence for the "Mozart effect." *Journal of Aesthetic Education, 34,* 105–148.

Hodges, D. A. (Ed.). (1996). *Handbook of music psychology* (2nd ed.). San Antonio, TX: IMR Press.

Hughes, J. R., Daaboul, Y., Fino, J. J., & Shaw, G. L. (1998). The "Mozart effect" in epileptiform activity. *Clinical Electroencephalography, 29,* 109–119.

Hughes, J. R., Fino, J. J., & Melyn, M. A. (1999). Is there a chronic change of the "Mozart effect" on epileptiform activity? A case study. *Clinical Electroencephalography, 30*(2), 44–45.

Huttenlocher, P. R. (1979). Synaptic density in human frontal cortex—Developmental changes and effects of aging. *Brain Research, 163*(2), 195–205.

Huttenlocher, P. R. (1984). Synapose elimination and plasticity in developing human cerebral cortex. *American Journal of Mental Deficiency, 88*(5), 488–496.

Huttenlocher, P. R. (1990). Morphometric study of human cerebral cortex development. *Neuropsychologia, 28,* 517–527.

Huttenlocher, P. R., & Dabholkar, A. S. (1997). Regional differences in synaptogenesis in human cerebral cortex. *Journal of Comparative Neurology, 387*(2), 167–178.

Ito, J., Takagi, A., Kauno, M., & Honjo, I. (1995). Results with the currently used cochlear implant. *Annals of Otology, Rhinology, and Laryngology Supplement, 166,* 298–300.

Jernigan, T. L., & Bellugi, U. (1990). Anomalous brain morphology on magnetic resonance images in Williams syndrome and Down syndrome. *Archives of Neurology, 47*(5), 529–533.

Johnson, J. K., Cotman, C. W., Tasaki, C. S., & Shaw, G. L. (1998). Enhancement in spatial-temporal reasoning after a Mozart listening condition in Alzheimer's disease: A case study. *Neurological Research, 20,* 666–672.

Johnson, J. K., Shaw, G. L., Vuong, M., Vuong, S., & Cotman, C. W. (1999). *Spatial-temporal reasoning in Alzheimer's disease: A group study.* Unpublished manuscript submitted for publication.

Johnson, J., & Ulatowska, H. (1995). The nature of the tune and text in the production of songs. *Music Medicine 2.* St. Louis: MMB Music.

Johnson, M. H. (1998). The neural basis of cognitive development. In W. Damon (Ed.), *Handbook of child psychology: Vol. 2. Cognition, perception, and language* (5th ed.) (pp. 1–49). New York: Wiley.

Johnson-Laird, P. N. (1983). *Mental models: Toward a cognitive science of language, inference, and consciousness.* Cambridge, MA: Harvard University Press.

Kempermann, G., Kuhn, H., & Gage, F. (1997). More hippocampal neurons in adult mice living in an enriched environment. *Nature, 386,* 493–495.

Kosslyn, S. M. (1994). *Image and brain: The resolution of the imagery debate.* Cambridge, MA: MIT Press.

Kurth, E., & Heinrichs, M. (1976). Musical-rhythmic discrimination ability and recall in children with reading and spelling disorders. *Psychiatrie, Neurologie und Medizinische Psychologie (Leipzig), 28,* 559–564.

Leng, X., & Shaw, G. L. (1991). Toward a neural theory of higher brain function using music as a window. *Concepts in Neuroscience, 2,* 229–258.

Lenhoff, H. M., Wang, P. P., & Greenberg, F. (1997). Williams syndrome and the brain. *Scientific American, 277*(6), 68–73.

Leont'ev, A. N. (1981). The problem of activity in psychology. In J. V. Wertsch (Ed.), *The concept of activity in Soviet psychology* (pp. 37–71). Armonk, NY: Sharpe.

Levitin, D., & Bellugi, U. (1998). Musical abilities in individuals with Williams syndrome. *Music Perception, 15*(4), 357–389.

Liebert, G., Gruhn, W., Parlitz, D., Trappe, W., Bangert, M., & Altenmüller, E. (1999). Kurzzeit-Lerneffekte musikalischer Gehörbildung spiegeln sich in kortikalen Aktivierungsmustern wider. In *Proceedings of the 1999 Annual Meeting of the German Society for Music Psychology* (pp. 32–33). Karlsruhe, Germany.

Liegeois-Chauvel, C., Peretz, I., Babai, M., Laguitton, V., & Chauvel, P. (1998). Contribution of different cortical areas in the temporal lobes to music processing. *Brain, 121*(10), 1853–1867.

Lord, T. R., & Garner, J. E. (1993). Effects of music on Alzheimer patients. *Perception and Motor Skills, 76*(2), 451–455.

Luria, A. R. (1961). *The role of speech in the regulation of normal and abnormal behavior.* New York: Liveright.

Martinez, M. E. (1999). Cognitive representations: Distinctions, implications, and elaborations. In I. E. Sigel (Ed.), *Development of mental representation* (pp. 13–31). Mahwah, NJ.: Erlbaum.

McClelland, J. L. (1995). A connectionist perspective on knowledge and development. In T. J. Simon & G. S. Halford (Eds.), *Developing cognitive competence: New approaches to process modeling* (pp. 157–204). Hillsdale, NJ: Erlbaum.

Minsky, M. (1980). K-lines: A theory of memory. *Cognitive Science, 4,* 117–133.

Muller, D., Toni, N., & Buchs, P. A. (2000). Spine changes associated with long-term potentiation. *Hippocampus, 10*(5), 595–604.

Overy, K. (1998). Discussion note: Can music really "improve" the mind? *Psychology of Music 26*(1), 97–99. [See also responses to Overy's paper, next issue, 26(2), 197–210.]

Pacteau, C., Einon, D., & Sinden, J. (1989). Early rearing environment and dorsal hippocampal ibotenic acid lesions:

Long-term influences on spatial learning and alternation in the rat. *Behavioural Brain Research, 34,* 79–96.

Pantev, C., Oostenveld, R., Engellen, A., Ross, B., Roberts, L. E., & Hoke, M. (1998). Increased auditory cortical representation in musicians. *Nature, 392,* 811–814.

Parkinson, A. J., & Parkinson, W. S. (1998). Speech perception performance in experienced cochlear-implant patients receiving the SPEAK processing strategy in the Nucleus Spectra-22 cochlear implant. *Journal of Speech, Language, and Hearing Research, 41*(5), 1073–1087.

Parsons, L., Hodges, D., & Fox, P. T. (1998). Neural basis of the comprehension of musical harmony, melody, and rhythm. *Proceedings of the Cognitive Neuroscience Society Meeting,* San Francisco.

Pascual-Leone, J., & Smith, J. (1969). The encoding and decoding of symbols by children. A new experimental paradigm and a neo-Piagetian theory. *Journal of Experimental Child Psychology, 8,* 328–355.

Pavlov, I. P. (1927). *Conditioned reflexes* (G. V. Anrep, Trans.). New York: Oxford University Press.

Peretz, I. (1990). Processing of local and global musical information by unilateral brain damaged patients. *Brain, 113,* 1185–1205.

Peretz, I., Gaudreau, D., & Bonnel, A. M. (1998). Exposure effects on music preference and recognition. *Memory and Cognition, 26*(5), 884–902.

Pflederer Zimmerman, M. (1984). The relevance of Piagetian theory for music education. *International Journal of Music Education, 3,* 31–34.

Pflederer Zimmerman, M., & Webster, P. (1983). Conservation of rhythmic and tonal patterns of second through six grade children. *Bulletin of the Council for Research in Music Education, 73,* 28–49.

Piaget, J. (1947). *La psychologie de l'intelligence.* Paris: Librairie Armand Colin.

Piaget, J. (1959). *La naissance de l'intelligence chez l'enfant.* Neuchâtel: Delachaux & Niestlé.

Pijl, S. (1997). Labeling of musical interval size by cochlear implant patients and normally hearing subjects. *Ear and Hearing, 18*(5), 364–372.

Pylyshyn, Z. W. (1973). What the mind's eye tells the mind's brain: A critique of mental imagery. *Psychological Bulletin, 80,* 314–329.

Rakic, P. (1995). Corticogenesis in human and nonhuman primates. In M. S. Gazzaniga (Ed.), *The cognitive neurosciences* (pp. 127–145). Cambridge, MA: MIT Press.

Rauschecker, J. P. (1999). Auditory cortical plasticity: A comparison with other sensory systems. *Trends in Neurosciences, 22*(2), 74–80.

Rauscher, F. H. (1999). Music exposure and the development of spatial intelligence in children. *Bulletin of the Council for Research in Music Education, 142,* 35–47.

Rauscher, F. H., & Koch, J. E. (2000). *The effects of exposure to music on spatial processing sites.* Unpublished raw data.

Rauscher, F. H., Robinson, K. D., & Jens, J. J. (1998). Improved maze learning through early music exposure in rats. *Neurological Research, 20,* 427–432.

Rauscher, F. H., Shaw, G. L., & Ky, K. N. (1993). Music and spatial task performance. *Nature, 365,* 611.

Rauscher, F. H., Shaw, G. L., Levine, L. J., Wright, E. L., Dennis, W. R., & Newcomb, R. L. (1997). Music training causes long-term enhancement of preschool children's spatial-temporal reasoning. *Neurological Research, 19,* 1–8.

Reisberg, D. (Ed.). (1992). *Auditory imagery.* Hillsdale, NJ: Erlbaum.

Renner, M. J., & Rosenzweig, M. R. (1987). *Enrichment and impoverished environments: Effects on brain and behavior.* New York: Springer.

Rumelhart, D. E., & McClelland, J. L. (1986). *Parallel distributed processing: Explorations in the microstructure of cognition.* Cambridge, MA: MIT Press.

Sarnthein, J., von Stein, A., Rappelsberger, P., Petsche, H., Rauscher, F. H., & Shaw, G. L. (1997). Persistent patterns of brain activity: An EEG coherence study of the positive effect of music on spatial-temporal reasoning. *Neurological Research, 19,* 107–116.

Schank, R. C., & Abelson, R. P. (1977). *Scripts, plans, goals, and understanding: An inquiry into human knowledge structure.* New York: Wiley.

Schlaug, G., Jäncke, L., Huang, Y., & Steinmetz, H. (1994). In vivo morphometry of interhemispheric asymmetry and connectivity in musicians. In I. Deliège (Ed.), *Proceedings of the 3d International Conference for Music Perception and Cognition* (pp. 417–418). Liège, Belgium: ESOM (Centre de Recherches et de Formation Musicales de Walbnie).

Schlaug, G., Jäncke, L., Huang, Y., Staiger, J. F., & Steinmetz, H. (1995). Increased corpus callosum size in musicians. *Neuropsychologia, 33*(8), 1047–1055.

Serafine, M. L. (1988). *Music as cognition: The development of thought in sound.* New York: Columbia University Press.

Shepard, R. N. (1978). The mental image. *American Psychologist, 33,* 125–137.

Silva, A. J., Paylor, R., Wehner, J. M., & Tonegawa, S. (1992). Impaired spatial learning in a-calcium-calmodulin kinase II mutant mice. *Science, 257,* 206–211.

Skinner, B. F. (1953). *Science and human behavior.* New York: Macmillan.

Spychiger, M. (1995). *Mehr Musikunterricht an den öffentlichen Schulen?* Hamburg, Germany: Kovac.

Steele, K. M., Dalla Bella, S., Peretz, I., Dunlop, T., Dawe, L. A., Humphrey, G. K., Shannon, R. Z., Kirby, J. L., & Olmstead, C. G. (1999). Prelude or requiem for the Mozart effect? *Nature, 400,* 827.

Stratford, B., & Ching, E. Y. (1983). Rhythm and time in the perception of Down's syndrome children. *Journal of Mental Deficiency Research, 27,* 23–38.

Swanwick, K. (1999). *Teaching music musically.* London: Routledge & Kegan Paul.

Thaut, M. H., Kenyon, G. P., Schauer, M., & McIntosh, G. (1999). The connection between rhythmicity and brain function. *IEEE Engineering in Medicine and Biology Magazine, 18*(2), 101–108.

Thaut, M. H., Miltner, R. Lange, H. W., Hurt, C., & Hoemberg, V. (1999). Velocity modulation and rhythmic synchronization of gait in Huntington's disease. *Movement Disorders, 14*(5), 808–819.

Tillmann, B., Bharucha, J. J., & Bigand, E. (2000). Implicit learning of tonality: A self-organizing approach. *Psychological Review, 107*(4), 885–913.

Todd, P. M., & Loy, D. G. (Eds.). (1991). *Music and connectionism.* Cambridge, MA: MIT Press.

Turner, A. M., & Greenough, W. T. (1985). Differential rearing effects on rats' visual cortex synapses. 1. Synaptic and neuronal density and synapses per neuron. *Brain Research, 329,* 195–203.

Vaughn, K. (2000). Music and mathematics: Modest support for the oft-claimed relationship. *Journal of Aesthetic Education, 34*(3/4), 149–166.

Vygotsky, L. S. (1962). *Thought and language* (E. Hanfmann & G. Vaker, Trans.). Cambridge, MA: MIT Press. (Original work published 1934)

Watson, J. B. (1913). Psychology as the behaviorist views it. *Psychological Review, 20,* 158–177.

West, T. (1991). *In the mind's eye: Visual thinkers, gifted people with learning difficulties, computer images, and the ironies of creativity.* Amhurst, NY: Prometheus Books.

West, R. W., & Greenough, W. T. (1972). Effect of environmental complexity on cortical synapses of rats: Preliminary results. *Behavioral Biology, 7,* 278–284.

Winner, E., & Hetland, L. (2000). The arts in education: Evaluating the evidence for a causal link. *Journal of Aesthetic Education, 34*(3/4), 3–10.

Zatorre, R., & Halpern, A. (1993). Effect of unilateral temporal-lobe excision on perception and imagery of songs. *Neuropsychologia, 31*(3), 221–232.

Zatorre, R., Halpern, A., Perry, D., Meyer, E., & Evans, A. (1996). Hearing in the mind's ear: A PET investigation of musical imagery and perception. *Journal of Cognitive Neuroscience, 8,* 29–46.

Cognitive Constraints on Music Listening

26

WILLIAM FORDE THOMPSON

E. GLENN SCHELLENBERG

Studies of music perception and cognition adopt a variety of theoretical viewpoints and use a diverse range of methods and analytic approaches. A survey of recent articles reveals a richly interdisciplinary field, comprising studies that range from psychophysical investigations of isolated tones to examinations of long musical segments in tonal, atonal, and non-Western styles. Although *cognition* is often distinguished from *perception*, we will not delimit our discussion in this manner. Some perceptual phenomena, such as visual illusions, are relatively impervious to learning (e.g., knowledge of the illusion does not make it disappear), but most perceptual tasks elicit knowledge structures to some extent. The terms *perception* and *cognition* represent different points on a continuum of research on mental processing, which ranges from studies of automatic processes that depend little on experience to studies of processes that depend critically on learning and knowledge.

Research measures also vary widely. They include results of neuroimaging techniques, responses to music by special populations (e.g., brain-damaged patients, individuals with Williams's syndrome), aesthetic judgments, measurements taken from music performances, infants' responses to musical stimuli, and subjective ratings of musical stimuli obtained from musically trained or untrained adults and children. Consequently, a vast and confusing body of data has been accumulated that has yet to be embedded within a widely accepted framework for understanding music cognition. The development of such a framework has been hampered by differences in opinion on at least three issues of substance: the relative contributions of innate structures and exposure to music, the most appropriate level at which to investigate and explain

music cognition, and the kinds of stimuli and methods that are most appropriate for studying relevant cognitive processes and mechanisms.

Perhaps the most contentious issue in the psychology of music concerns the relative role of innate structures and learning in musical experience. Some educators and researchers take a dim view of nativist constructs such as musical *talent* (Howe, Davidson, & Sloboda, 1998) and assume a prominent role for learning, education, and enculturation. To support their position, they point to patterns of within-group similarities and between-group dissimilarities across different musical cultures and historic periods (e.g., Walker, 1996). By contrast, nativists argue that although such instances of learning are conspicuous, they are nevertheless constrained by underlying cognitive principles. Three classes of evidence point to the importance of innate cognitive endowments. First, competence in many domains is achieved early and rapidly, despite large differences in experience. Second, competence is often domain-specific, implicating specialized cognitive modules (Fodor, 1983). Third, there is often a marked disparity between models of environmental influences and the mental representations acquired by learners, which implies that information processing is constrained by cognitive biases and perceptual predispositions and assimilated into preexisting knowledge structures.

A second issue concerns the most appropriate level at which to investigate and explain psychological phenomena related to music. Are listening, performing, and composing music best understood in terms of neurons and networks or in terms of mental schemata and prototypes? Studies directed at different analytic levels often pose different questions, use different methods, and promote different theories. Reductionism holds that explanations based on psychological constructs such as schemata and prototypes are reducible—with the help of yet-to-be-discovered bridging laws—to neurological events in the brain. In this view, theories of cognition should be reducible to neural models. The opposing position, argued by Fodor (1983), is that psychological explanations are not always reducible to neural states or that they may be realized in multiple configurations. It would therefore be impossible to identify systematic bridging laws that connect psychological states (e.g., beliefs, desires) to specific brain states. Rather, psychology would need to construct its own autonomous generalizations through use of a specialized "language of thought." In this view, theories of music cognition can be developed somewhat independently of advances in neuroscience. One danger with this strategy is that when psychological principles are not linked to plausible physiological mechanisms it can be difficult to evaluate their validity.

A third area of disagreement involves balancing concerns for experimental control with concerns for ecological validity. Can studies that use stimuli comprising a few pure tones tell us about the cognitive processes that are activated when one listens to a symphony played by an orchestra? Can the responses of Western listeners to Western music provide insight into cognitive mechanisms that operate independently of cultural knowledge? Concerns about the use of artificial (nonmusical) stimuli raise questions about whether a psychological process, mechanism, or neural resource generalizes to a wider range of stimuli than those used in a particular experiment. In cases where general auditory or cognitive mechanisms are at issue, concerns about ecological or cross-cultural validity may be unnecessary. For example, the neural resources involved in segregating multiple auditory sources (i.e., in *auditory stream segregation*) are almost certainly the same when listening to nonmusical tone sequences, Western music, non-Western music, speech signals, and environmental sounds (Bregman, 1990).

It is also likely that the mechanisms engaged to process pitch contour (upward, downward, or lateral pitch movement) for short sequences of pure tones are the same as those engaged for long musical phrases. Such mechanisms are also likely to be involved in the processing of speech intonation. Dissanayake (2000) argues that music and speech intonation share a common ancestry in temporal-spatial patterns of emotional communication, which are particularly adaptive for promoting attachment between mothers and infants. If so, then the same neural resources may be responsible for processing contour in music and in speech (Patel, Peretz, Tramo, & Labreque, 1998).

Some auditory processes are automatically invoked for all possible acoustic stimuli, including music, and therefore operate regardless of the style of the music or the cultural context in which music is heard. Many researchers, especially those with a strong background in cognition, are interested in precisely these basic processes. Because research on general auditory mechanisms and their connection to musical experience requires careful experimental control, the use of naturalized music-listening conditions is not always advantageous. Naturalized conditions introduce uncontrolled influences (and, consequently, variance in the data) related to personal, social, cultural, or historical knowledge, which can mask or distort the cognitive processes under investigation.

In other cases—when cognitive processes depend on musical context—it is necessary to use more naturalized conditions. For example, the expressive use of timing and loudness in music performance depends not only on local features (intervallic patterns, phrasing) but also on knowledge of harmony and key (Thompson & Cuddy, 1997), on composer-specific aspects of expression (Thompson, 1989), and on goals related to adjudication criteria (Thompson, Diamond, & Balkwill, 1998). Furthering our understanding of such issues *requires* an examination of actual music performances. Thus, despite thoughtful critiques of studies that involve artificial stimuli and simple tone patterns (e.g., Serafine, 1988), a complete understanding of music cognition requires the convergence of data obtained using varying approaches and methods. Attempts to restrict the field to particular types of stimuli or experimental approaches will only delay progress in this regard.

In this chapter, we describe a sample of current discussions, debates, and empirical evidence in music cognition. Issues are not resolved quickly, and many that were raised by pioneers in the field continue to dominate. Certain shifts in focus have occurred over the past decade, however. First, there is a renewed interest in studies of brain function, following developments in neuroimaging techniques, advances in neural network modeling, and insights gained from studies of brain-damaged patients (see also chap. 25, by Gruhn and Rauscher, in this volume). A second shift has been to studying listeners' perception of *emotions* expressed by music (see also chap. 29, by Reinhard Kopiez, in this volume), mirroring attempts by researchers in cognition and neuroscience to understand the role of emotion in memory, reasoning, and problem solving. Third, there has been widespread effort to evaluate the psychological validity of influential theories that attempt to unify music and psychology within a single framework (e.g., Generative Theory of Tonal Music, Implication-Realization Model). Fourth, following a neo-Darwinian movement across a number of fields, there has been a renewed interest in evolutionary perspectives on music (e.g., Wallin, Merker, & Brown, 2000). Examination of all of these issues would require considerably more than a single chapter, so we have limited our discussion to a sample of the issues that currently motivate the field.

Fundamentals of Pitch Perception and Cognition

Studies of pitch have dominated the field of music cognition over the past 20 years, paralleling a similar emphasis in music theory and education. Pitch studies have been a fruitful area of investigation because people are remarkably accurate at discriminating between pitches (Burns, 1999). Moreover, mental representations of pitch are richly structured. This structure partly reflects culture-specific conventions in music. Through passive or active exposure, listeners internalize regularities in the music of their own culture, forming long-term knowledge schemata into which novel music stimuli are assimilated. Nonetheless, processing limits and biases also constrain mental representations of pitch. For example, the limits of working memory constrain our ability to encode brief but unfamiliar melodies with accurate detail. Because of such limits, unfamiliar melodies are represented largely in terms of pitch contour (Dowling & Harwood, 1986).

Physical Acoustics: Sensory Consonance and Dissonance

Any naturally occurring sound, such as a cough or a piano tone, can be described as a complex of pure tones (i.e., sine waves) or *partials,* each with its own frequency, amplitude, and phase. *Fourier analysis* is the mathematical technique that allows us to analyze a complex sound in terms of its pure-tone components. We do not normally perceive the individual partials of a complex sound because cognitive mechanisms operate to fuse them together, leading us to experience a unitary sound. According to *Ohm's acoustical law,* however, under certain listening conditions we have a limited ability to hear some of the individual partials of a complex sound.

Any sound with a discernible pitch has a *periodic waveform,* in that the waveform continuously repeats itself over time. The *period* is the time taken for one complete cycle of the waveform and is the reciprocal of the repetition rate. The repetition rate usually determines the perceived pitch (exceptions include *circular tones,* discussed later) and is measured in cycles per second, or hertz (1 Hz = 1 cycle/sec). In general, when the repetition rate of a periodic sound is increased, the perceived pitch increases. The partials of any periodic waveform fall along the *harmonic series* and are called harmonics. If the lowest frequency component of the sound is n, then the other harmonics—called overtones—are members of the set $2n, 3n, 4n, 5n,$ and so on. That is, each overtone has a frequency that is an integer multiple of the lowest or *fundamental* frequency of the complex. An important property of the harmonic series is that additional overtones do not alter the overall repetition rate of the waveform (which is determined by the fundamental frequency) and therefore do not change the perceived pitch of the complex.

Helmholtz (1863/1954) observed that several aspects of music, such as scale structure and harmony, have compelling parallels in physical acoustics. He noted that music from several cultures involves important scale notes that map onto the harmonics of complex tones. In the major scale, the fifth scale degree (*sol*) is equivalent (i.e., in note name, or tone *chroma*) to the third harmonic of a complex periodic tone built on the first note of the scale (*doh*) and the third scale degree (*mi*) is equivalent to the fifth harmonic. The most important musical intervals used in Western music are also found in the harmonic series. The first and second harmonics are separated by an octave, the second and third harmonics are separated by a perfect fifth, the third and fourth harmonics are separated by a perfect fourth, the fourth and fifth harmonics are separated by a major third, and the fifth and six harmonics are separated by a minor third.

Harmonic overtones are not perceived as individual pitches. When one is presented with a periodic complex tone, only one pitch is usually perceived. Other mechanisms, however, are sensitive to harmonic spectra. For example, complex tones with different spectral contents are perceived as having different sound qualities, tone colors, or *timbres.* Harmonic overtones also affect the degree of *sensory consonance* and *dissonance* of tone combinations presented simultaneously. Tone combinations with fundamental frequencies that are related to one another by small-integer ratios, such as the octave (2:1) and the perfect fifth (3:2), have several harmonics in common and lead to sensory consonance. In contrast, tone combinations with fundamental frequencies that are not related to one another other by small-integer ratios, such as the minor second (16:15), lead to sensory dissonance. Such combinations contain harmonic frequencies that are not identical but that fall within a *critical band* (a range of frequencies within which sensory interactions occur), which results in rapid amplitude fluctuations that give rise to perceived *roughness and beating.* Sensitivity to sensory consonance and dissonance is thought to be independent of knowledge and enculturation. Long-term knowledge of music also affects judgments of consonance, and this aspect of music experience is referred to as musical consonance.

If sensitivity to sensory consonance and dissonance is independent of knowledge and enculturation, then young infants might be expected to exhibit a natural preference for consonance. Researchers have examined infants' preference for one type of music over another type by letting them "choose" which type of music they hear. Such experiments typically place an infant between two loudspeakers. When the infant looks toward the speaker on his or her left, he or she hears one type of music, but he or she hears a different type of music when he or she looks toward the speaker on his or her right. Hence, the infant is "controlling" what he or she hears by the direction of his or her gaze. Because infants tend to have a bias to look rightward, it is important to *counterbalance* the stimuli presentations. That is, half of the infants hear Piece A from the speaker on their left and Piece B from the speaker on their right, whereas the other half hear Piece B from the left and Piece A from the right.

Results based on this "infant preference" method reveal that infants look longer toward a speaker that is playing a consonant version of a musical piece than they do toward a speaker that is playing a dissonant version of the same piece. These findings suggest that listeners have an innate preference for sensory consonance and/or an innate dislike of sensory dissonance. As infants develop, these basic preferences are overlaid with effects of learning and enculturation, which contribute to the experience of *musical* consonance and dissonance. These effects of learning may run counter to initial predispositions: Indeed, insofar as the aesthetic quality of chords can be judged outside of a musical context, the most beautiful may involve considerable dissonance.

Zentner and Kagan (1996) presented 4-month-old infants with a melody accompanied by a single "harmony" line. The melody and accompaniment were separated by minor seconds in the dissonant condition but by major and minor thirds in the consonant condition. Infants preferred the consonant versions. Trainor and Heinmuller (1998) extended these findings by considering the influence of harmonics in pairs of complex tones, which can interact with each other and give rise to sensory dissonance. They found that 6-month-old infants preferred to listen to perfect fifths and octaves rather than tritones and minor ninths (which give rise to greater sensory interference between harmonics). The findings illustrate that infants are sensitive to sensory consonance and dissonance and exhibit a preference for consonant over dissonant tone combinations.

Studies of discrimination provide further evidence that sensitivity to sensory consonance and dissonance is innate. Specifically, it comes naturally for listeners to discriminate combinations of tones on the basis of their consonance or dissonance. Schellenberg and Trainor (1996) presented 7-month-old infants and adults with a background pattern of simultaneous fifths (7 semitones) presented at varying pitch levels. Listeners were tested on their ability to discriminate the intervals in the background pattern from a new interval, which was either a tritone (6 semitones) or a fourth (5 semitones). Fifths and fourths are consonant intervals, whereas tritones are dissonant. Both age groups used the consonance and dissonance to discriminate these intervals. Although the fifth and fourth differ more from each other in terms of interval size, the fifth and tritone were better discriminated. Presumably, the dissonance of

the tritone made it stand out from the perfect fifth, whereas the relative consonance of the perfect fourth made it sound similar to the fifth. In short, sensitivity to sensory consonance and dissonance is evident very early in development. Listeners can learn to appreciate dissonance, but they begin life with an initial preference for consonance.

If sensitivity to sensory consonance is a basic property of the auditory system, one might ask how this property affects scale structures and tuning systems. In most scales from around the world, consonant intervals (e.g., octaves, perfect fifths and fourths) are structurally important. For example, tones separated by octaves are considered to be similar in virtually all musical cultures. In North Indian scales, tones separated by a fifth (the *sa* and *pa*) are structurally important and are typically sounded continuously throughout a piece. The most common pentatonic scale (exemplified by the black notes on the piano), which is found in Chinese and Celtic music, can be formed by choosing any pitch as an arbitrary starting tone and adding a second tone a fifth higher, another tone a fifth higher than the second tone, and so on, until a collection of five pitches is obtained. The scale is formed by octave-transposing the collection of tones so that they fall within a single octave.

In Western music, two similarly "natural" tuning systems for the chromatic scale have been used historically (for a review see Burns, 1999). One, called Pythagorean tuning, extends the pentatonic scale described earlier with additional tones that continue the "cycle of fifths." In the other, called just intonation, the scale is formed by tuning notes so that their fundamental frequencies form small-integer ratios with the fundamental frequency of the first note of the scale (*doh*). Both of these scales limit the possibility of transpositions between keys, because some instances of particular intervals (e.g., the perfect fifth between C and G) are tuned differently from other instances (e.g., C♯ and G♯).

Equal temperament represents a compromise solution. It guarantees that all intervals (i.e., all perfect fifths or all major thirds) are tuned identically and that important intervals do not deviate greatly from small-integer frequency ratios (fifths and fourths deviate from exact small-integer ratios by 2% of a semitone; major and minor thirds are slightly more mistuned). These minor deviations, although discriminable in some cases, are no greater than the typical tuning deviations observed in the performances of singers or stringed-instrument players. Moreover, such small departures from exact small-integer ratios have little effect on the perceived consonance of these intervals, which may explain why equal temperament has endured for many years.

Models of Pitch Perception

Pitch height is the most basic dimension along which pitches are perceived to vary; it refers to the continuum that extends from low to high pitches (which corresponds to a logarithmic function of frequency, or cycles per second). The psychological relevance of this continuum is evident in similarity judgments for pairs of pitches: Tones closer in pitch are considered more similar than tones separated by greater pitch distance. The pitch-height continuum is also evident in neural activity in the cochlea. High frequencies stimulate the basal portions of the basilar membrane, low frequencies stimulate the apical portions, and intermediate frequencies affect intermediate portions.

In constructing a model of pitch perception, one may start with the basic dimension of pitch height and then consider additional dimensions along which pitch seems to vary. Most models of pitch perception consider the special status of the octave among intervals. As noted, tones with fundamental frequencies separated by an octave are perceived to be similar in virtually all musical cultures. *Pitch chroma* refers to the quality of pitch that is independent of the octave register in which it occurs. In Western music, tones separated by an octave are given the same name (e.g., A, B, C), implicating their equivalence in some sense. Further evidence for this view comes from listeners with musical training, who perceive similarities between tones that are separated by an octave (Allen, 1967; Kallman, 1982).

If pitch chroma and pitch height are *basic* dimensions of pitch perception, one should expect to find similar evidence among naive listeners. When musically untrained adults or children judge the similarity between pure tones, however, they tend to focus exclusively on the dimension of pitch height (Allen, 1967; Kallman, 1982; Sergeant, 1983). For example, C_4 and $C\#_4$ (notes separated by a semitone) are perceived to be highly similar, but C_4 and C_5 (notes separated by an octave) are perceived to be no more similar than C_4 and B_4 (notes separated by a major seventh). These findings do not rule out the possibility that sensitivity to the chroma dimension could be uncovered with tasks that measure *implicit* rather than *explicit* knowledge of musical associations. However, the findings make it clear that music educators should not assume that octave equivalence is explicitly understood by naive listeners.

An early psychological model of pitch perception incorporated the two dimensions of pitch height and pitch chroma. As shown in figure 26.1, these two dimensions are depicted as orthogonal dimensions of a geometrically regular helix—a monotonic dimension of pitch height and a circular dimension of pitch chroma. Shepard (1964) reported evidence that these dimensions are psychologically relevant and orthogonal. He created tones with well-defined chroma but ambiguous height. Such *circular tones* were constructed by combining 10 pure-tone components spaced at octave intervals and imposing a fixed amplitude

envelope over the frequency range such that components at the low and high ends of the range approach the hearing threshold.

Although the overall pitch height of any circular tone is somewhat indeterminate, listeners experience certain circular tones as "higher" or "lower" than others. In particular, listeners tend to perceive the relative height of these tones so as to maximize their pitch proximity. For example, when presented the circular tones C followed by D, one can perceive the second tone as either "higher" or "lower" than the first tone (C up to D or C down to D). Both interpretations are possible because their individual pitch heights are ambiguous. Nonetheless, listeners typically perceive the second tone (D) as higher than the first tone (C), because this interpretation implicates a pitch distance of only 2 semitones. Listeners almost never perceive the second tone as lower than the first tone, because that

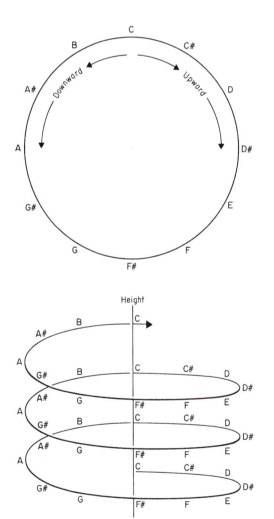

Figure 26.1. The chroma circle and the helical model of pitch. The helical model combines two dimensions of pitch: height and chroma.

interpretation would implicate a pitch distance of 10 semitones.

Shepard created fascinating patterns of circular tones in which chroma varied continuously around a "chroma circle" (see figure 26.1). For ascending patterns, he shifted all of the octave-spaced components up in frequency (adding new components at the low end of the amplitude envelope) until the complex returned to the initial configuration. When chroma was shifted continuously in a clockwise direction around the chroma circle (C, C♯, D, D♯, etc.), the pattern was perceived as ascending endlessly. When chroma was shifted continuously in a counterclockwise direction (C, B, A♯, A, etc.), the pattern was perceived as descending endlessly. That is, listeners perceived changes in pitch chroma but not in overall pitch height. Most important, these effects were perceived by musically trained and untrained listeners alike. By making pitch height indeterminate, Shepard demonstrated that pitch chroma has perceptual significance, even for untrained listeners. Thus, although untrained listeners may lack explicit knowledge of the similarity between tones with the same chroma, they nonetheless demonstrate sensitivity to chroma.

If pitch class and pitch height are orthogonal, then the relative height of circular tones that are directly opposite on the circle, such as C and F♯, should be ambiguous or indeterminate. Deutsch addressed this prediction in a series of experiments (for a review, see Deutsch, 1999b). She reported that, for a given individual, certain circular tones (i.e., chromas) are reliably and consistently judged as being "higher" than the circular tone that is opposite on the circle, suggesting that the perceived height of a tone is systematically related to its pitch chroma. For example, some listeners reliably perceive a successive presentation of two particular circular tones separated by a tritone (e.g., C and F♯) as upward pitch movement, whereas others perceive the same two tones as downward pitch movement. This so-called tritone paradox and related findings imply that pitch chroma and pitch height are not entirely independent.

Shepard (1982, 1999) and others have proposed more elaborate models of pitch perception with additional dimensions besides those based on height and chroma. These models account for affinities between tones separated by perfect fifths and fourths, which are said to be relevant for musically trained listeners tested with harmonically rich tones presented in musical contexts. Even more elaborate models have been proposed to account for affinities between tones separated by thirds. The establishment of a musical key also shapes pitch judgments. For example, in the context of the key of C major C and G are more strongly associated with each other than E and B, even though both tone pairs represent a perfect fifth interval (Krumhansl, 1979).

The effects of musical context on judgments of pitch were examined in a series of investigations conducted by Krumhansl and her colleagues (see Krumhansl, 1990). They used the "probe-tone" technique in a variety of musical contexts (Krumhansl & Kessler, 1982; Krumhansl & Shepard, 1979). The method involves presentation of a musical stimulus that clearly defines a musical key (e.g., scale, cadence, chord sequence) followed by a "probe" tone. Listeners rate how well each probe tone in the chromatic scale fits with the established key.

When musically trained listeners are tested with this method, probe-tone ratings are quite consistent across listeners. As one might expect, their ratings mirror predictions from music theory. When a major key is established, a probe tone that corresponds to the tonic of the key has the highest rating, followed by the dominant and mediant, then the other tones in the key (diatonic tones), and finally the nondiatonic tones. This *tonal hierarchy* is more easily uncovered with musically trained than untrained participants, illustrating the influence of learning. School-age children's implicit knowledge of the hierarchy improves dramatically from 6 to 11 years of age (Krumhansl & Keil, 1982), although 6-year-olds know that different tones vary in goodness once a musical context is established (Cuddy & Badertscher, 1987). Thus, although sensory dissonance is perceived by infants and musically untrained adults, judgments of pitch relations are also influenced by musical training, which suggests that our perceptions of pitch and pitch relations result from a combination of innate and learned factors.

Evidence of sensitivity to the tonal hierarchy early in development can be explained—in part—by psychoacoustic influences (Schellenberg & Trehub, 1994): Probe tones with high stability values (*doh, mi, sol, fa*) have the largest degree of sensory consonance with the established tonic. Alternatively, because the frequency of occurrence of tones in real pieces of music closely mirrors the tonal hierarchy, children may learn implicitly that tones heard more often in a musical piece are particularly stable. Indeed, we know that listeners are highly sensitive to pitch distributional information in music. Oram and Cuddy (1995) presented listeners with atonal sequences in which 1 tone occurred eight times, another tone occurred four times, and 4 other tones occurred once each. Following each sequence, listeners rated the extent to which various probe tones fit with the sequence in a musical sense. Ratings reflected the frequency with which each pitch occurred in the context. Thus, when listening to unfamiliar music, listeners readily construct a hierarchy of pitch importance using frequency-of-occurrence information.

Absolute Pitch

It is often asserted that most listeners are sensitive to *relative* pitch but not to *absolute* pitch. *Relative pitch* refers to the ability to produce, recognize, or identify pitch relations, such as those that define a musical interval or a melody. To illustrate, "Twinkle, Twinkle, Little Star" can be sung in a high or a low voice or performed on a piccolo or a tuba. As long as the pitch relations conform to those of the melody, it is usually recognizable. *Absolute pitch* refers to the ability to produce, recognize, or identify an individual pitch (e.g., middle C) without reference to any other pitch. Whereas relative pitch is the norm among trained and untrained listeners, absolute pitch is rare, occurring in about 1 in 10,000 people (Takeuchi & Hulse, 1993). Absolute pitch can be a valuable skill for musicians, but it can also interfere with the ability to perceive pitch relations (Miyazaki, 1993). Because melodies are defined by pitch and duration relations rather than with reference to any absolute pitch, relative pitch is arguably a more musical mode of pitch processing.

Nonetheless, absolute-pitch processing may be more relevant to musical experience than common wisdom dictates. First of all, everyone has the ability to retain absolute pitch briefly in working memory. Otherwise, discriminating between one pitch and a subsequently presented pitch would be impossible. But some forms of long-term memory for absolute pitch also may be quite common. Halpern (1989) asked participants to sing familiar tunes (e.g., "Happy Birthday") on different occasions. Repeated performances of a tune remained in the same key more often than one would expect to occur by chance. In other words, listeners may encode some absolute-pitch information along with the relative-pitch information that defines the tunes they hear.

In studies of memory for pure tones and familiar recordings, absolute-pitch information again appears to be retained in long-term memory, even by listeners with no training in music. In one study, Levitin (1999) asked musically untrained listeners to carry a tuning fork with them for a week and to listen repeatedly to the tone it produced. Listeners were subsequently tested on their memory for the pitch of the tone. In another study (Levitin, 1994), untrained listeners were asked to sing the first few words of their favorite rock song. In both studies, listeners showed remarkable pitch accuracy, with the most common response being virtually *perfect* memory for the absolute pitch of the tuning fork or recording. In the latter study, listeners also exhibited nearly perfect memory for tempo (Levitin & Cook, 1996). These results confirm that absolute memory for pitch and tempo is more prevalent than previously assumed (see also Terhardt & Seewann, 1983).

In sum, although relative pitch is easily encoded and accessed from long-term memory, sensitivity to absolute pitch also plays a role in musical experience. In particular, memory for absolute pitch is likely to be evident for brief periods of time and for stimuli that are heard repeatedly at an identical pitch.

Melody

We now turn to a discussion of the perception and cognition of *melodies,* or tones presented sequentially. We begin with a focus on what listeners remember when they hear a melody. Which features of the melody are likely to be remembered, and which are likely to be forgotten? Melodies can be considered at different levels of analysis, including local structure (intervals, contours), higher order structure (phrases, movements), and abstract structure (scales, keys).

Melodic Intervals

Can infants remember melodic intervals? The answer is an unequivocal *yes,* but not all intervals are processed and remembered equally well. Rather, infants, as well as children and adults, have processing biases and preferences for consonant (pleasant-sounding) intervals, which may account for the predominance of such intervals across musical cultures.

Experiments that test listeners' perception of intervals are similar to those that test their perception of contour. Listeners are typically asked to discriminate one interval from another. Because an interval change always involves a change in absolute pitch, the intervals are typically presented in transposition so that listeners must attend to interval size (i.e., pitch relations). Otherwise, they could perform the task merely by detecting shifts in absolute pitch. This type of "same/different" discrimination task allows researchers to determine which intervals are easy to process and remember and which are difficult. If an interval is easily processed, then memory for it will be relatively stable and permanent and listeners should find it easy to detect slight alterations to that interval. By contrast, if an interval is difficult to process, listeners will be unable to form a stable and lasting representation of the interval, making it less likely that a slight alteration would be detected.

In one series of experiments (Schellenberg & Trehub, 1996a), adults and 6-year-old children were required to detect 1-semitone changes in interval size. They were asked to discriminate two different intervals presented one after the other: fifths (7 semitones) from tritones (6 semitones), tritones from fourths (5 semitones), minor ninths (13 semitones) from octaves (12 semitones), and octaves from major sevenths (11 semitones). Each pair was presented in both orders. Such a discrimination task requires listeners to compare a memory representation for the standard interval (presented first) with a currently available comparison interval (presented second). Thus if the standard interval is stable in memory, then it should be easily discriminated from the comparison interval. As predicted,

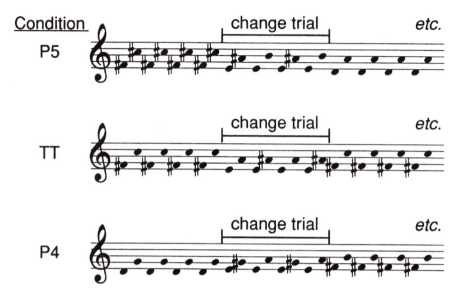

Figure 26.2. Stimuli from Schellenberg and Trehub (1996b). Sequences consisted of two alternating tones, transposed after the two tones were presented four times. The alternating tones were separated by a perfect fifth (P5, top panel), a tritone (TT, middle panel), or a perfect fourth (P4, lower panel). Infants 6 months of age were tested on their ability to detect displacements of the top tone during change trials.

performance was asymmetric in all instances. When the standard interval was relatively consonant and the comparison interval was dissonant, both children and adults could discriminate the intervals. When the standard was dissonant and the comparison was consonant, however, performance fell to chance levels. These findings suggest that listeners form relatively stable memory representations for octaves, fifths, and fourths.

Why do listeners form stable memories for these melodic intervals? One possibility is that they occur frequently in Western melodies and are therefore well recognized. A related interpretation is that familiarity with octaves, fifths, and fourths within *simultaneous* combinations of tones (many chords contain these intervals) influences judgments of the same intervals presented melodically. Both "learning" hypotheses imply rather high-level abstraction and generalization of musical relations, however, and would not predict similar effects in young infants, who have very little exposure to music.

In a study with 6-month-old infants (Schellenberg & Trehub, 1996b), a similar processing advantage was identified for fifths and fourths over tritones. Infants heard a repeating pattern of alternating pure tones separated by one of three intervals, as shown in figure 26.2. After 8 tones (4 low-pitched and 4 high-pitched), the pattern was shifted upward or downward in pitch (figure 26.2). On "no-change" trials, the shift was an exact transposition, such that the interval associated with the first 8 tones was repeated at a new pitch register. On "change" trials, every other high-pitched tone was displaced downward by a

semitone, creating intervals that were different from that associated with the first 8 tones (figure 26.2). Infants were capable of detecting these differences in interval size when the initial interval was a fifth or fourth but not when it was a tritone. In other words, they demonstrated a clear processing advantage for consonant over dissonant intervals, even for pure tones presented sequentially in non-musical contexts. Similar findings have been obtained from infants tested with simultaneously presented pairs of tones (i.e., harmonic intervals; Schellenberg & Trehub, 1996b; Trainor, 1997). The results suggest that there is a basic processing advantage for consonant intervals.

Melodic Contour

The *contour* of a melody refers to its pattern of upward and downward changes in pitch over time, irrespective of the absolute pitches involved or the specific size of the intervals between pairs of adjacent tones. Figures 26.3a and 26.3b display melodies with a different contour, a different interval structure, and different absolute pitches. By contrast, figures 26.3a and 26.3c illustrate melodies with the same contour but different intervals and absolute pitches. Figures 26.3a and 26.3d display melodies with the same interval structure yet different absolute pitches (one is an *exact transposition* of the other). Finally, figures 26.3a and 26.3e illustrate melodies that are identical in all respects: absolute pitch, intervallic structure, and contour.

How would these melodies be retained, or *mentally represented,* in memory? One possibility is that our mental

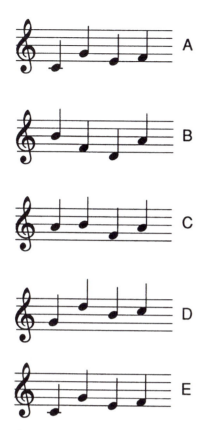

Figure 26.3. The "standard" melody in panel A has an up–down contour. The melody in panel B has a different contour, different intervals, and different pitches. The melody in panel C has the same contour as the standard but different intervals and pitches. The melody in panel D has the same contour and intervals as the standard, but different pitches; it is an exact transposition. Finally, the melody in panel E has the same contour, intervals, and pitches as those in the standard.

representations are more-or-less veridical and include absolute pitches, precise intervals between tones, and melodic contour. In that case, only the melodies displayed in figures 26.3a and 26.3e would be represented equivalently in memory. Although absolute pitches play a role in musical experience, as noted earlier, explicit memory for melodies is more often based on pitch relations.

A second possibility is that listeners' mental representations are determined by abstracting a sequence of intervals and discarding information about absolute pitch. If so, then the melodies shown in figures 26.3a, 26.3d, and 26.3e would be represented equivalently in memory, while the other two melodies would have different representations. For novel melodies, however, listeners often have difficulty retaining the exact pattern of intervals, which suggests that unfamiliar melodies are seldom represented with this level of precision.

A third possibility is that listeners' mental representations are relatively crude, determined simply by the direc-

tion of the upward and downward shifts in pitch (i.e., melodic contour). Fine-grained information about intervals and absolute pitch might not be perceived and encoded accurately during listening. In that case, the melody in figure 26.3a would be represented merely by its contour of up–down–up. In that case, the mental representations of four of the five melodies would be equivalent (a, c, d, e).

Note that these melodic features (contour, intervals, and absolute pitch) are embedded hierarchically. If listeners remember the absolute pitch of each of the tones in a melody, they can reconstruct the intervals between tones and the melodic contour. If listeners remember the sequence of intervals (but not the absolute pitches), then they can reconstruct the melodic contour. Conversely, melodies that differ in contour necessarily differ in interval size and absolute pitch. Melodies that differ in one or more intervals may or may not differ in contour, but at least 1 tone must differ in absolute pitch.

Research indicates that listeners' mental representations of novel melodies contain contour information but relatively little information about absolute pitch or exact interval size. Memory for the absolute pitches of novel melodies tends to be poor, and memory for the exact intervals between notes also tends to be poorer than memory for contour. Findings from studies of infants are particularly compelling in this regard (for a review, see Trehub, Schellenberg, & Hill, 1997). Moreover, the findings for adults' memories for novel melodies converge nicely with those from infants (for a review, see Dowling, 1994).

Studies with adults often adopt the same-different experimental method described in "Melodic Intervals." On each experimental trial, listeners hear a "standard" (original) and "comparison" melody and judge whether they are the same or different. By systematically varying the ways in which the comparison differs from the standard (as in figure 26.3) and assessing the effects of such changes on judgment accuracy, one can determine which features are represented in memory. Listeners make errors about the interval and absolute-pitch information of novel melodies relatively soon after they are presented. By contrast, listeners retain contour information for longer periods of time.

The experimental method is necessarily altered for studies with infants. Infant listeners are trained to turn their head toward a loudspeaker when they hear a change in an auditory stimulus presented repeatedly (e.g., a melody), a process that occurs naturally anyway. When this response is reinforced with illuminated and activated toys, infants maintain their interest in the task. If they reliably turn their head toward the speaker for certain melodic changes but not for others, we can conclude that the former changes are relatively detectable for infants, whereas the latter changes are relatively undetectable. Several studies have confirmed that contour changes are very noticeable for infants, whereas changes that maintain contour but alter absolute pitch or interval size are far less noticeable (Trehub et al., 1997). In short, infants perceive and remember the contour of melodies.

Why is melodic contour so easy to remember? Many have speculated that our sensitivity to contour in music stems from the adaptive importance of contour in speech. Studies of speech perception in infancy reveal that infant-directed speech (i.e., *motherese*) differs from adult-directed speech in a number of systematic ways (Fernald, 1991) and that infants prefer to listen to infant-directed rather than adult-directed speech (Cooper & Aslin, 1990; Fernald, 1985). One of the distinctive aspects of infant-directed speech is its exaggerated use of pitch contour. Different pitch contours are used to express different messages to infants (e.g., approval, arousal, etc.), and the alterations that adults make in their speech to infants are remarkably similar across cultures (Fernald et al., 1989). Hence, sensitivity to contour patterns in speech could facilitate bonding between infants and their caregivers and the language-acquisition process. Such sensitivity has obvious adaptive value and could account for infants' sensitivity to contour in music.

Researchers have identified a number of implications of this heightened sensitivity to melodic contour. First, melodies with fewer changes in contour are perceived as "simpler" than melodies with more contour changes (Boltz & Jones, 1986). Second, listeners attend more to notes at points of contour change than they do to notes that are embedded within an ongoing contour (Dyson & Watkins, 1984). For example, when listeners are presented with a 5-tone sequence with an up–up–down–down contour (see figure 26.4), their attention is drawn more to the middle (third) tone—the point of contour change—than it is to the second or fourth tone. In other words, tones at *contour points* (at contour changes or at the beginning or end of melodies) are more likely to be represented in memory than are other tones. It follows, then, that melodies with a relative abundance of contour points contain a relative abundance of salient bits of information and should be relatively challenging to process and remember.

Scale Structure and Enculturation

A survey of the scales of various musical cultures suggests rather strongly that music is constrained by basic psychological processes. For example, virtually all scales have five

Figure 26.4. The melody has an up–up–down contour. The first, middle, and last tones can be considered contour points.

to seven notes per octave. There is a consensus in the literature that the limited number of notes in these scales stems from limitations in the capacity of working memory. Several decades ago, Miller (1956) demonstrated that for any continuous dimension (e.g., brightness, loudness) adults can reliably categorize instances into a maximum of seven categories, give or take about two categories. Because this limitation of working-memory capacity extends across domains and modalities, one would expect that pitch categories would be similarly limited. Hence, music composed with scales that have more than 7 tones is likely to exceed the cognitive capacities of many listeners. This constraint may explain why many people find it challenging to listen to 12-tone (serialized) music.

A second characteristic of scales that may stem from basic psychological constraints is the structural importance of intervals that closely approximate perfect consonances, such as octaves, perfect fifths, and perfect fourths. These structural features may reflect an innate preference for consonance, as well as an innate processing advantage for consonant over dissonant intervals (as noted earlier).

A third property of scales is that most have differently sized steps between consecutive tones in the scale. For example, the major scale has intervals of 1 and 2 semitones in size between adjacent scale notes. The most common pentatonic scale has steps of 2 and 3 semitones. In fact, scales from around the world (except for the whole-tone and 12-tone scales) have this property of unequal steps. One often-noted exception is a scale from Thailand, although there is doubt about its proposed equal-step structure in musical practice (Morton, 1976). Why would scales exhibit this "unequal-step" property?

One explanation is that unequal steps arise because consonant intervals (fifth, fourth, major third) are formed from a small number of scale notes. Balzano (1980), however, argued that unequal steps also confer a psychological benefit, because they allow tones to have different functions within the scale. In the major scale, each note has a unique set of intervals that it forms with the other notes from the scale. In C major, for example, F and B are related to each other by the interval of an augmented fourth, but C is not related to any scale note by that particular interval. This distinctive property allows listeners to differentiate scale tones from one another and to isolate a focal or tonic tone (*doh*). A focal or tonic tone functions as a mental referent to which other tones can be compared. The ability to determine a focal tone and differentiate scale tones may make unequal-step scales advantageous from a psychological standpoint.

In a test of whether the use of unequal steps confers a basic processing advantage to listeners, Trehub, Schellenberg, and Kamenetsky (1999) tested adults and 9-month-old infants on their ability to process and remember three scales (see figure 26.5). One was the unequal-step major scale, another was an unfamiliar scale formed by dividing the octave into 7 equal steps (Shepard & Jordan, 1984), and a third was a completely unfamiliar unequal-step scale. This third scale was formed by dividing the octave into 11 equal steps and then constructing a 7-tone scale that had four 2-step intervals and three 1-step intervals.

Both age groups were tested on their ability to detect when the 6th scale step was displaced upward slightly. Infants showed relatively good performance for the familiar (major) and the unfamiliar unequal-step scales but poor performance for the unfamiliar equal-step scale. These results provide evidence that scales with unequal steps are inherently easier for infants to process and represent than equal-step scales. For infants, music composed with equal-step scales, such as whole-tone (e.g., music by Debussy) or 12-tone (e.g., music by Schönberg) scales, may be more difficult to perceive and remember than music composed with unequal-step scales.

Adults showed a different pattern of responding. For the familiar major scale, they could detect the upward displacement of the 6th scale step. By contrast, for both unfamiliar scales (equal- or unequal-step), adults had difficulty detecting when the 6th scale step was displaced upward. This finding suggests that with years of exposure to the scale (or scales) from one's musical culture, the initial processing advantage for unequal-step scales is eliminated. When the listener is fully enculturated, he or she is familiar and comfortable with conventional scales, whereas unconventional scales of all types (including unfamiliar unequal-step scales) sound foreign and are difficult to perceive and remember.

A related study reveals a similar pattern of findings, in which another basic predisposition is gradually overwhelmed by culture-specific knowledge. It is safe to assume that melodies with an abundance of repeated tones are "simple" and therefore easier to perceive and remember than less repetitive melodies. In other words, tone repetition is a basic feature of melodic simplicity. In support of this idea, Schellenberg and Trehub (1999) reported that infants 9 months of age found it easier to process and remember 5-tone sequences with 2 repeated tones than similar sequences with only 1 repeated tone. This finding held whether the sequences were conventional (based on a major triad) or relatively unconventional (based on a diminished triad).

Interestingly, this effect of tone repetition varied as a function of age and exposure to music. For 5-year-old children, processing advantages for tone repetition were also apparent, but the effect was greater for conventional than for unconventional melodies. For adults, however, such advantages were observed only for conventional melodies. Presumably, adult listeners had difficulty assimilating unconventional melodies into their existing schemata and this difficulty overwhelmed any potential advantage of tone repetition. More generally, it appears that basic cognitive processes (such as processing advantages for tone repetition or for unequal-step scales) can be strongly affected by age and experience.

Large Melodic Structures

How do listeners know when one musical phrase ends and another begins? Do composers capitalize on perceptual predispositions? Are musical phrases structurally similar in any ways to linguistic utterances? Can infants use cues in the music to segment music properly?

Krumhansl and Jusczyk (1990) tested infants' preferences for Mozart pieces that were "correctly" or "incorrectly" segmented. Correctly segmented pieces had pauses inserted *between* phrases. Incorrectly segmented pieces had pauses inserted *within* phrases. To an adult listener, both versions sound somewhat strange, although the former version seems more musical because the pauses occur at "natural" breaks in the music. Looking times indicated that infants preferred the correctly segmented pieces, in which segments tended to end with relatively long notes and downward pitch contours. Interestingly, spoken utter-

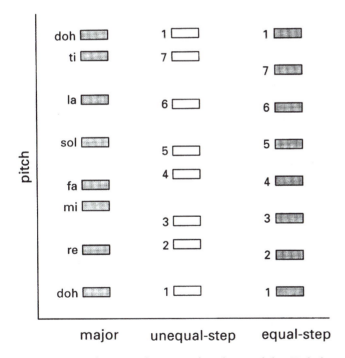

Figure 26.5. Schematic diagram of scales used by Trehub, Schellenberg, and Kamenetsky (1999). Each scale has seven tones per octave. One was the familiar scale (left). The other was completely artificial. The unequal step scale (middle) was formed by dividing the octave into eleven equal steps and selecting a subset of seven tones. The equal-step scale (right) was formed by dividing the octave into seven equal steps.

ances also tend to end with words of relatively long duration and downward pitch contour. This correspondence between spoken utterances and musical phrases leads to two related interpretations of the results: (1) Infants might prefer the "correctly" segmented pieces because they bear structural similarities to spoken utterances, which infants have learned from being exposed to speech, or (2) downward contours and extended durations naturally mark the end of all auditory signals. Either way, the findings indicate that listeners implicitly understand at a very early age that melodic phrases tend to end with downward pitch motion and notes of relatively long duration. Such cues allow listeners to segment melodies into melodic groups such as phrases and motifs and to identify boundaries between larger forms such as movements and sections.

In addition to phrase boundaries, the perception of melodic groups is influenced by other auditory cues such as pitch proximity and timbral similarity of notes (for a review, see Deutsch, 1999a). Such cues not only influence perceived connections between *adjacent* notes in a melody, but they can also induce perceived connections between salient or significant notes across several melodic groups, leading to the perception of *higher level* melodic structures. That is, melodic groups are perceived at multiple hierarchic levels, and excerpts with the same higher level structure are perceived as similar despite differences in surface structure (Serafine, Glassman, & Overbeeke, 1989).

Lerdahl and Jackendoff (1983) proposed a comprehensive and influential theory of melody that emphasized its hierarchic structure. They first noted that Western tonal melodies can be analyzed into essential notes and ornamental notes. Ornamental notes are notes in the melody that can be removed without altering the essential character of the melody. After ornamental notes are removed, what is left is a simplified version of that melody. With this idea as a starting point, Lerdahl and Jackendoff (1983) used the term *reductional structure* to describe how large-scale melodic structures can be analyzed into simpler and simpler skeletons. They proposed two ways in which melodies can be simplified.

In time-span reduction, certain beats and groups in a melody are designated as ornaments on other groups and beats. This simplification process is continued in an interactive manner, which results in a tree diagram that specifies the relative dominance of each event. In prolongation reduction, primary points of tension and relaxation are differentiated from subordinate points of tension and relaxation, which again results in a tree diagram. Both types of tree diagrams illustrate how smaller melodic units combine to form large-scale melodic structure. Palmer and Krumhansl (1987a, 1987b) found that time-span reduction was able to predict listeners' judgments of phrase endings in music by Mozart and Bach. Other research supports the psychological validity of prolongation reduction (Bigand, 1990; Dibben, 1994).

Melodic Expectancies

As listeners hear a melody, they continuously form expectancies about upcoming notes they will hear. Sometimes we expect a particular note, but usually our expectations are not so specific. Rather, some notes seem relatively likely, whereas other notes seem less likely. Learning and exposure to musical styles exert a large influence on such expectancies. Is there a role for basic cognitive processes in the formation of melodic expectancies?

According to Narmour (1990), the answer is yes. His theory of melodic expectancy, called the Implication-Realization Model, posits that listeners' expectancies are formed from a combination of bottom-up and top-down factors (see Krumhansl, 1995, or Thompson, 1996, for a review). In Narmour's use of these terms, *bottom-up* refers to innate or hardwired cognitive and perceptual tendencies; *top-down* refers to expectancies that result from experience, either with music in general or with a particular musical piece. As examples, pitch proximity (expecting notes that are proximate in pitch) is considered to be an innate influence on melodic expectancy, whereas tonality (expecting notes in proportion to their importance in the scale) is thought to be based on long-term knowledge of Western music.

Two experimental methods have been used to test expectancies. In one method, listeners hear a fragment of a melody followed by a test tone. Their task is to rate how well the test tone continues the fragment. The assumption is that tones that conform to listeners' expectancies will be rated as relatively good continuations. The other method is a production task, in which participants play or sing a continuation to a stimulus provided by the experimenter. The main finding from all of the relevant studies is that *proximity* explains the lion's share of the variation in listeners' responses, regardless of experimental method, musical style, and participants' music training or cultural background (e.g., Cuddy & Lunney, 1995; Schellenberg, 1996, 1997; Thompson, Cuddy, & Plaus, 1997). In general, tones that are proximate in pitch to the last tone heard are the most expected (see von Hippel, 2000). This association is more-or-less linear, such that tones further and further away from the last tone heard receive lower and lower ratings or are less likely to be sung or played.

Narmour (1990) proposed several bottom-up principles of melodic expectancy. In an examination of Narmour's theory, however, Schellenberg (1997) observed that bottom-up expectancies can be largely explained by just two basic principles. The first principle is *pitch proximity*, described earlier. The second principle is *pitch reversal*. Pitch reversal describes expectancies for an upcoming tone to be proximate to the penultimate tone heard, as well as expectancies for a change in pitch contour after a large melodic leap (von Hippel & Huron, 2000). This simple model has proven to be equal or superior to Narmour's original model across listeners who vary in musical training or cultural background, across stimulus contexts (real melodies or 2-tone stimuli), with both production and perceptual-rating methods, and with melodies from Western tonal, atonal, and non-Western repertoires (Schellenberg, 1997; see Thompson & Stainton, 1998, for another simplified model). Schellenberg's model has also equaled the success of the original model in studies conducted with children (Schellenberg & Purdy, 2000).

In short, there is strong evidence that proximity is an innate cognitive principle that influences the formation of melodic expectancies. The role of proximity in melodic expectancy represents perhaps one of the clearest examples of a basic psychological process influencing music perception and cognition. Proximity is known to be a robust predictor of perceptual grouping in vision. Consider the illustration in figure 26.6. The average perceiver visually groups the elements on the basis of proximity: Items that are close together are perceived as a group. The same holds true for audition in general (see the section on auditory stream segregation) and for music in particular. Tones that are proximate in pitch tend to be grouped together. Hence, a melody that contains many large leaps in pitch is difficult to perceive as a unified whole, whereas a melody with mostly stepwise motion (rather than leaps) tends to be perceived as a unified group of tones.

Implicit Memory for Melody

The effects of learning that result from exposure to music are often subtle. Moreover, as the following section illus-

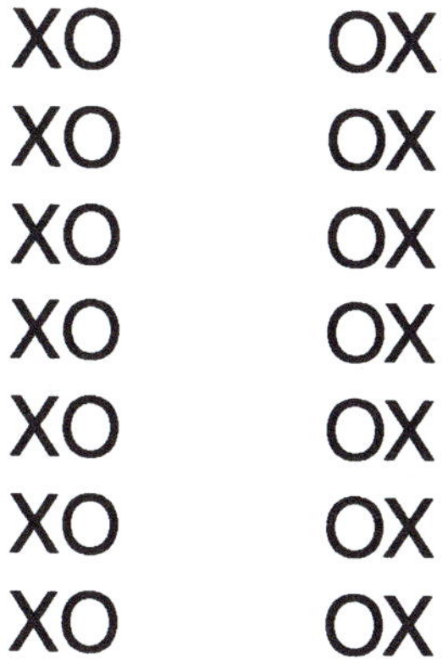

Figure 26.6. The figure illustrates how proximity influences perceptual grouping in vision. The viewer sees four columns of letters. Note the similarity in shape between the second and third columns, and between the third and fourth columns, because of proximity.

trates, they often occur without conscious awareness. It is widely acknowledged that experiences frequently affect our behavior in the absence of conscious awareness. Such effects are thought to reflect an *implicit* memory system that operates independently of conscious or *explicit* memory (Schacter, 1987). Recent advances in the understanding of implicit memory systems suggest an exciting direction for future studies of music cognition.

Implicit memory for music may explain how listeners develop an appreciation for the music of their culture. Indeed, most musical experiences are probably influenced by implicit memory. As Crowder (1993) argues, "The re-entry of a fugue theme, the occurrence of a leitmotif, or the development section of a remembered sonata-movement subject may all be examples of implicit music memory" (p. 134). Empirical studies support Crowder's suggestion. Passive exposure to music leads to implicit knowledge of tonal relations (Tillman, Bharucha, & Bigand, 2000), musical preferences (Peretz, Gaudreau, & Bonnel, 1998), and expectancies for melodic continuations (Thompson, Balkwill, & Vernescu, 2000).

Thompson, Balkwill, and Vernescu (2000) presented listeners with atonal melodies (target melodies) as they performed a counting task or a visual task. The latter tasks reduced the *depth of processing* of the melodies, making it difficult for listeners to remember them explicitly. In a subsequent task, listeners heard the same melodies, as well as novel melodies that were constructed similarly. For each melody, listeners rated the extent to which they expected the final note, on a scale from 1 (unexpected) to 7 (expected). Ratings were higher for the melodies that were heard previously than for novel melodies, which illustrates that mere exposure to music affects melodic expectancy. Most notably, this effect could not be explained by explicit memory for the melodies. In other words, mere exposure to melodies led to implicit memory for those melodies in the form of melodic expectancies. The results provide insight into how listeners internalize the music of their own culture and how they learn to appreciate unconventional music. Repeated exposure to music composed in a consistent manner leads to the development of stable expectancies for typical melodic patterns. Eventually, the music becomes somewhat predictable and "makes sense" to the listener.

Harmony and Key

Implied Harmony

Because melodies are so often heard with a harmonic accompaniment, listeners gradually learn to associate isolated melodies with plausible harmonic accompaniments, even when none is present. Consider the melody illustrated in figure 26.7 (from Trainor & Trehub, 1992, 1994). The melody implies a shift from a tonic harmony in the first measure to a dominant harmony in the second measure. Musically trained listeners are highly sensitive to this implied harmony and consistently identify the implied harmonic change. Are untrained listeners also sensitive to these shifts in implied harmony? If so, how does sensitivity to implied harmony change over development?

In one experiment (Trainor & Trehub, 1992), adults and 8-months-olds were tested on their ability to discriminate alterations to the melody shown in figure 26.7, which was presented repeatedly in varying transpositions. In each case, the alteration consisted of an upward displacement to the sixth tone in the melody. For some listeners, the displacement was a shift upward by 1 semitone (e.g., from G to G#), which is a small alteration in terms of interval size but inconsistent with the implied harmony. For other listeners, the displacement was a shift upward by 4 semitones (e.g., from G to B), which is a much larger change in interval size but consistent with the implied dominant harmony. Adult listeners found the former change—which violated the implied harmony—easier to detect than the latter change, which was consistent with the implied harmony. Infant listeners performed equally well in both conditions. Interestingly, infant listeners actually outperformed adults at detecting the larger but harmonically consistent shift in pitch. In other words, adult listeners appear to have a very well developed sense of implied harmony that they acquired through years of exposure to music, such that changes in a melody that are consistent with the implied harmony are relatively unnoticeable. By contrast, infants appear to be less sensitive to implied harmony.

When does sensitivity to implied harmony develop? A follow-up experiment (Trainor & Trehub, 1994) addressed this question by testing listeners 5 and 7 years of age. The children were asked to detect the 1-semitone harmony-violating change, the 4-semitone harmony-consistent

change, and an intermediate 2-semitone shift (e.g., from G to A) that was consistent with the underlying key signature (C major) but violated the implied harmony. The 5-year-olds found the 1-semitone change easier to detect than the other changes. In other words, the shift that violated both the implied harmony and the underlying key signature was more noticeable than the other shifts. For the 7-year-olds, the 2-semitone shift that violated the implied harmony but not the key was easier to detect than the 4-semitone harmonically consistent shift. These data, considered in conjunction with those from the previous study, indicate a systematic developmental progression. Infant listeners have a relatively poor sense of key. By 5 years of age, children are sensitive to key membership but not to implied harmony. By 7 years of age, children are sensitive to implied harmony.

Implied Key

Tonal melodies are those that suggest a musical key (C major, F minor, etc.). Such melodies are characterized by a number of properties: (1) They are mainly composed of scale notes, (2) tones that are stable in the key (e.g., *doh, mi, sol, fa*) tend to be sounded for relatively long durations, and (3) they often begin and end with the tonic (*doh*) or with another note from the tonic triad (*mi* or *sol*). Listeners rely on these types of regularities to derive the key for a particular melody.

The frequency distribution of tones in a melody and their relative durations are usually strongly and positively associated with the "tonal hierarchy" of the melody's key (Krumhansl, 1990). Krumhansl (1990, 2000b) suggests that listeners match the accumulated durations of the notes they hear to mental representations of the tonal hierarchies for all possible keys. The key with the strongest association is perceived as the key. Other theories of key perception are reviewed by Vos (2000) and by Auhagen and Vos (2000). For example, listeners may rely on the presence of relatively rare intervals (e.g., the tritone) that are associated with particular keys (Browne, 1981) or conduct a relatively low-level acoustical analysis of the musical stimuli (Leman, 2000).

With music that contains simultaneously sounded notes, listeners readily derive a sense of key from isolated voices or from the harmonies that are created by combining those voices (Cuddy & Thompson, 1992; Thompson & Cuddy, 1992). Interestingly, the key implications in a harmonic progression (i.e., a sequence of chords) are somewhat independent of the key implications carried by the individual voices, which, in turn, may be somewhat different from one another (Thompson, 1993). For example, attending to a sequence of chords might suggest an abrupt change from one key to a psychologically distant key. By contrast, attending to an individual voice (e.g., the melody line) in the

Figure 26.7. Stimulus melody used by Trainor and Trehub (1992, 1994). The melody implies a tonic-dominant shift in harmony from the first to the second measure. The melody was presented continuously in transposition. Listeners were tested on their ability to detect when the circled tone was displaced upward. Such displacements violated the key and the implied harmony (1 semitone up, to G#), the harmony but not the implied key (2 semitones up, to A), or neither (4 semitones up, to B).

same polyphonic texture might suggest a smoother transition between more related keys. The use of timing and loudness in expressive performance can further influence perceived movement from one key to another (Thompson & Cuddy, 1997). These findings suggest that melody, harmony, and key are not mentally represented in a strictly hierarchic manner. Rather, melodic features may implicate key and key movement somewhat independently of the harmony.

Perceiving Voices in Harmony

The interdependence of melody and harmony has been a focal point in theoretical discussions of Western music (e.g., Lerdahl & Jackendoff, 1983; Meyer, 1973; Narmour, 1990, 1992). Although mutually intertwined, these two aspects of music often work in different ways. For example, different levels of tension or dissonance in melodies and their harmonic accompaniments may be a source of aesthetic interest. This is often true in the music of Brahms, where intense dissonances outlined in the melodic line may be offset by warm supporting harmonies. Other evidence, described earlier, illustrates that melodies and their harmonic accompaniments may also differ in how they implicate key and key change. In short, melodies have psychological effects that are somewhat different from the harmonies in which they are embedded.

The composition of polyphonic music must therefore achieve a balance between melodic and harmonic goals. This balance is partially guided by established conventions of Western tonal composition, which are often formalized as "rules" of harmonic progression and voice leading. Although these rules may be "broken" by composers for aesthetic purposes, a close examination of them reveals important insights into their cognitive origins. In particular, several rules of voice leading are related to more general principles of auditory scene analysis (Bregman, 1990; for a detailed discussion, see Huron, 2001). *Auditory scene analysis* refers to the set of general processes that allow perceivers to organize acoustic information that arrives at the ear as distinct sound events or sources. These basic auditory processes allow listeners to hear an individual speaker in a crowded room or to track individual voices in polyphonic music.

Music students are often taught skills of voice leading with no reference to principles of auditory scene analysis. Instead, educators explain voice-leading practices in terms of cultural and historical factors or imply that voice-leading conventions cannot be understood outside of a particular cultural and historical context. This explanation provides an incomplete picture, and students would benefit from a basic understanding of auditory scene analysis. Furthermore, advances in computer technology and sound synthesis now allow composers to explore timbres, melo-

dies, and harmonies that are unconstrained by the acoustical properties of natural instruments. An understanding of the nature of auditory stream segregation is especially important for such compositions.

Huron (2001) identified several general principles of auditory scene analysis that play a critical role in voice-leading practices. These principles were established through over 20 years of research that used both musical and nonmusical stimuli. This body of research is summarized by Bregman (1990) and will not be reviewed here. Rather, we will describe how the most well established of these principles are instantiated in our perceptions of individual tones and voices in polyphonic music and culturally encoded as rules of voice leading.

Beginning with the perception of individual tones, the conditions that lead to a clear sense of pitch are linked to the pitch range conventionally used in harmonic writing. Pitch clarity varies with the fundamental frequency of tones. Pitch perception tends to be clearest in a region that corresponds roughly to the center of a piano keyboard (extending from F_2 to G_5 and centered at 300 Hz, which is approximately 2 semitones higher than middle C). By contrast, listeners' sense of pitch is much poorer for the lowest and highest notes on the piano. The distribution of pitches in both Western and non-Western music corresponds precisely with the region associated with high pitch clarity. This correspondence suggests that harmonic writing reflects a tacit goal of using tones with a clear sense of pitch.

Mechanisms of auditory scene analysis also operate to link acoustic events over time. Pitch proximity represents one of the most important cues for such temporal grouping. To reiterate an idea discussed earlier, a sequence of tones is most readily perceived as a group or "stream" when the pitch distance between temporally adjacent tones is small. Tones with pitches that are distant from one another tend to be perceptually segregated into separate streams. In music, this effect is exploited in pseudopolyphony or compound melodies, where a single sequence of notes may be written so as to evoke the impression of two distinct melodic lines. As the pitch distance between successive tones is increased, creating alternating high- and low-pitched tones, listeners become more and more likely to perceive two streams (two separate melodies). This effect of pitch separation is known to depend on tempo. As tempo is decreased, a larger pitch separation is needed to evoke an impression of two auditory streams (van Noorden, 1975).

Thus the coherence of an individual voice is enhanced if temporally adjacent tones are proximate in pitch. When leaps in pitch are introduced in a voice, coherence can be maintained by reducing tempo. Consistent with these findings, rules of voice leading restrict the use of large leaps in part writing. When wide leaps are unavoidable, composers tend to use long durations for the notes that form the leap (the first note, the second note, or both notes), a convention called *leap lengthening*. The convention of avoiding large leaps maps directly onto listeners' sensitivity to the effects of pitch proximity on auditory stream segregation. The convention of leap lengthening mirrors an additional sensitivity to the interactive effects of proximity and tempo.

Yet another convention in voice leading is also relevant to pitch proximity. To ensure perceptual independence of voices, the pitches of temporally adjacent tones within each voice should be more proximate than the pitches of temporally adjacent tones in different voices; otherwise, confusions in voice attribution may occur. Such confusions are especially probable if voices "cross" in pitch register, in which case streaming mechanisms may group part of one voice with a continuation of the other voice. Not surprisingly, part crossing is avoided in voice leading, especially for music with three or more voices (Huron, 1991a).

Independence of voices is also affected by "harmonicity." This principle describes the mechanism by which the partials of periodic sounds are grouped into unified auditory events. Specifically, frequencies that fall along the harmonic series tend to be fused (DeWitt & Crowder, 1987), giving rise to a single pitch sensation and a timbre associated with the entire spectrum. In harmonic writing, the same mechanism may partially fuse tones from different voices, which works in opposition to the more general goal of creating independent voices. Such fusion among different tones helps to account for our perception of chords as higher order musical units. In voice-leading practice, however, it is often desirable to avoid strong fusion effects in the interest of emphasizing the melodic component of individual voices.

The pitch intervals that most promote tonal fusion are the unison, octave, and perfect fifth (perfect consonances). For music that is composed to emphasize independence of voices, composers appear to avoid tonally fused intervals. Huron (1991b) showed that in the polyphonic writing of J. S. Bach tonally fused intervals are avoided in direct proportion to the strength with which each interval promotes tonal fusion. Unisons occur less often than octaves, which occur less often than perfect fifths, which occur less often than other intervals. This observation implies a tacit understanding of how tonal fusion can undermine the musical goal of separation of voices.

Like harmonicity, pitch comodulation (i.e., different voices or pure-tone components that vary similarly in contour and interval size) is used as a cue for unifying the harmonics of individual sound events. Here tonal fusion is promoted between sounds that have positively correlated pitch motions. The mechanism described by this principle is especially important for unifying the components of sounds that involve inharmonic overtones, which would not be fused by mechanisms attuned merely to harmonicity. Tonal fusion is strongest if pitch motion is precise with respect to log frequency (i.e., exactly the same shifts in interval size), although any positively correlated pitch motion contributes to tonal fusion.

Again, voice-leading conventions reflect this cognitive principle. Similar pitch motion between two voices is avoided, especially when voices are separated by an interval that promotes tonal fusion (unison, octave, fifth). Although identical or "parallel" pitch motion is particularly eschewed, all cases of similar motion are avoided as a general principle. This general psychological principle is formalized in rules that discourage parallel unisons, octaves, and fifths and in rules that encourage contrary melodic motion among voices.

The spacing of tones within chords reflects another acoustic principle, namely, the association between sensory dissonance and pitch register. Briefly, there is less potential for sensory dissonance between voices in the upper pitch register than between voices in the lower pitch register. Although we often think of certain intervals as consonant (e.g., the perfect fifth) and others as dissonant (e.g., the tritone), sensory dissonance is influenced by pitch register as well as interval size. A more direct measure of sensory dissonance considers the occurrence of interactions among partials, which is related to the concept of a critical band.

A critical band is defined as the range of frequencies within which *masking effects* (in which the presence of one tone affects the audibility of another tone), *loudness summation* (in which overall loudness corresponds to the sum of the amplitude of 2 tones), and other interactions among frequencies occur. Such interactions are the basis for sensory dissonance. Importantly, critical bandwidth decreases (as measured in log frequency) as pitch register increases. The result is that a given musical interval (e.g., a major third) yields fewer interactive effects and is therefore associated with less sensory dissonance when that interval is played in a higher pitch register than when it is played in a lower pitch register. This effect is manifested in the spelling of chords; the pitch separation between lower voices is much larger on average than the pitch separation between upper voices (Plomp & Levelt, 1965). This aspect of polyphonic writing may function to maintain a balance of relative consonance and dissonance across pitch regions.

Interestingly, when dissonance between two voices occurs, it is possible to reduce its salience by emphasizing the melodic structure within which the dissonant tones occur. This may be accomplished by adhering more assiduously to the principles that enhance auditory stream segregation. When stream segregation is enhanced, tonal fusion and dissonance are inhibited (Wright & Bregman, 1987).

To summarize, the connection between voice-leading conventions and auditory scene analysis exemplifies multiple ways in which musical practice and basic cognitive mechanisms intersect. The connection also helps to explain how listeners perceive melodies within a harmonic context. Mechanisms of auditory stream segregation allow listeners to track individual melodies and voices, whereas tonal fusion emphasizes harmonic structure and the combining of individual voices into a unitary event (a chord). Other perceptual principles and their relation to rules of voice leading are outlined by Huron (2001). Cognitive principles other than those related to auditory scene analysis (e.g., short-term memory limitations) are also relevant to voice-leading practices but are beyond the scope of this review.

Rhythm

Investigations of the perception and cognition of musical time include examinations of the limits of temporal discrimination, studies of temporal expectancies (e.g., *when* the next musical event will occur), and experiments that test listeners' experience of time in long musical passages. Most studies, however, focus on the perception of rhythm. Rhythm perception is strongly influenced by the interonset interval (IOI), which is the time between the onset of one tone and the onset of the next tone.

Experiences of rhythm, like experiences of pitch, are partly shaped by cognitive constraints. For example, listeners perceive temporal organization most readily when IOIs fall within a limited range. If IOIs are much less than 100 ms, listeners tend to hear the sequence as one continuous event; if they are greater than 1,500 ms, listeners tend to hear a sequence of disconnected events. For temporal patterns that involve IOIs between 100 and 1,500 ms, listeners tend to perceive rhythmic patterns of up to 5 seconds in duration, which is the approximate limit of auditory sensory memory (Darwin, Turvey, & Crowder, 1972). Thus cognitive constraints limit the range of IOIs within rhythmic patterns as well as the duration of rhythmic patterns.

Lerdahl and Jackendoff (1983) made a useful distinction between meter and grouping, which can be viewed as distinct aspects of rhythm. *Meter* refers to regular cycles of strong and weak accents. Listeners are highly sensitive to meter and associate strong accents with phrase boundaries (Palmer & Krumhansl, 1987a, 1987b). Accent strength is determined by changes in intensity, note density, and musical structure (e.g., pitch contour, tonality). Listeners show a bias to hear metrical interpretations (alternations of strong and weak beats) as binary, even when sequences are ternary (Vos, 1978). More generally, small-integer ratios of durations (e.g., sequences that contain only quarter notes and eighth notes) are easier to process than more complex rhythms. Meter is hierarchically organized, with cycles at one level (e.g., groups of two beats) nested within cycles at higher levels (e.g., groups of four

beats). Listeners tend to perceive one level of the metric hierarchy as more salient than others. Some models of meter identify this level as the *tactus*, or the level at which it is most natural to tap one's foot.

Metrical patterns are recognized and reproduced more accurately than nonmetrical patterns (e.g., Bharucha & Pryor, 1986; Essens, 1995). Moreover, perceptual asymmetries, similar to those noted earlier for pitch, are evident for rhythm. When listeners are asked to discriminate two patterns—one metrical and one nonmetrical—performance is better when the metrical pattern is presented first and the nonmetrical pattern second than when the identical patterns are presented in the reverse order (Bharucha & Pryor, 1986). This response pattern implies that metrical frameworks facilitate the efficiency with which auditory temporal patterns are processed and represented. It is relatively easy to detect alterations to metrical patterns because they have relatively stable representations. Metrical patterns also place less demand on attentional resources than nonmetrical patterns do, because they provide a frame of reference within which rhythmic structure can be processed and represented.

Grouping refers to perceived associations between events. As with metrical structure, temporal grouping structure is hierarchically organized, with small groups of two or three notes nested within larger groups, such as phrases. At the highest level of the hierarchy are groups that correspond to sections and movements of music. Empirical studies generally support the psychological reality of grouping structure in music (Deliège, 1987). The grouping mechanisms associated with music perception appear to be general cognitive mechanisms that are also implicated in the processing of speech and other auditory stimuli (Patel et al., 1998).

Although both meter and grouping are hierarchically structured, they need not coincide with each other. Rhythm is defined as the interaction between meter and grouping. Remarkably, there is little psychological work on this interaction; instead, researchers have examined these aspects of rhythm separately. Empirical studies have confirmed that listeners are sensitive to both metrical and grouping structure.

One issue examined in studies of rhythm is the concept of the musical pulse, which is related to meter and can be measured in cycles per minute. Fraisse (1982) noted that three distinct temporal phenomena (walking pace, heart rate, sucking rate in newborns) tend to have a rate of between 60 and 120 events per minute, a range that also includes the tempi of most pieces of music. The implication is that music may be linked to physiological motion. This link is manifested explicitly when listeners dance or tap to music. Early evidence for the link was provided by Gabrielsson (1973a, 1973b), who reported that judgments of the similarity between rhythmic patterns are strongly affected by a perceptual dimension related to movement. Other support for a link between music and physiological motion was provided by Kronman and Sundberg (1987), who showed that ritards in music have a close correspondence with deceleration when walking or running (see also chapter 29 by Kopiez in this volume).

Several models of rhythm have been proposed, each designed to capture a particular aspect of rhythm perception. Some existing models consider only temporal cues to meter, such as onset times and durations, ignoring influences of pitch, phrasing, and harmony on the perception of rhythm. Parncutt's (1994) model assumes cognitive biases for certain metrical experiences. In particular, certain levels in the metrical hierarchy are assumed to be more salient than others, with a bias toward the metrical level that approximates the *tactus*.

Another question concerns the kinds of neural units that might be involved in tracking the meter of complex music. In Large and Jones's (1999) model, meter is tracked through use of a small set of oscillatory neural units that vary from one another in their natural resonance. Because the oscillators are able to adjust their phase and period to external periodicities, units with natural resonances closest to existing periodicities lock on and track the tempo. Related to this issue is the question of how simple patterns (i.e., small-integer ratios of duration) are represented in memory when the durations and periodicities of actual performances are highly variable. In order to account for this *quantization problem*, Desain's (1992) connectionist model assumes that rhythmic experiences are biased toward temporal patterns defined by small-integer ratios.

Some researchers have examined the extent to which pitch and rhythm interact in perception and memory. This question may be relevant to music educators because pitch and rhythmic skills are often assessed separately in traditional pedagogical exercises, implying distinct cognitive mechanisms for processing these dimensions. Music theory also suggests a separation between rhythm and pitch. For example, the Schenkerian reduction technique for analyzing tonal works assumes that surface temporal relations operate independently of pitch structure.

Results on this issue suggest that pitch and rhythm interact at some levels of processing but operate independently at other levels. Jones, Boltz, and Kidd (1982) reported that rhythmically accented tones in a melody are better recognized than unaccented tones. Similarly, if pitch and rhythm patterns imply different metrical groupings, memory for melodic sequences is generally poor (Boltz & Jones, 1986; Deutsch, 1980). Such findings suggest that pitch and rhythm are integrated in memory for music. Additional evidence for nonindependence of pitch and rhythm processing comes from a study that required listeners to rate the emotionality (i.e., happiness, sadness, scariness) of melodies (Schellenberg, Krysciak, & Campbell, 2001). The melodies' pitch and rhythmic properties proved to be interactive in their influence on listeners' ratings.

Other researchers contend, however, that pitch and rhythm are processed independently. In some experiments, pitch and rhythm have made statistically independent contributions to judgments of melodic similarity (Monahan & Carterette, 1985) and to ratings of phrase completion (Palmer & Krumhansl, 1987a, 1987b). Moreover, memory for the pitch and rhythm patterns of a short melody is far better than memory for how those features are combined. Thompson (1994) presented listeners with two test melodies followed by two comparison melodies. The task was to indicate if the two comparison melodies were identical to the two test melodies, disregarding the order in which the melodies occurred. In one condition, participants performed a distractor task as the melodies were presented. In another condition, participants listened attentively to the melodies. When the comparison melodies involved a novel pitch pattern or a rhythm that was not present in the test melodies, performance was highly accurate for participants in both conditions. When the comparison melodies were constructed by combining the pitch pattern of one test melody with the rhythm of the other test melody (or vice versa), however, distracted participants performed poorly. That is, distracted participants were relatively insensitive to the manner in which pitch and rhythm were combined.

Neuropsychological studies provide converging evidence that pitch and rhythm are processed separately. Whereas some brain-damaged patients exhibit normal pitch perception but impaired rhythm perception, other patients show the opposite pattern. One patient who sustained a lesion in the left temporal lobe was unable to discriminate between sequences that differed in temporal structure, but he had no difficulty in discriminating between sequences that differed in pitch structure. By contrast, another patient with damage to the right temporal lobe showed the opposite pattern of discrimination skills. Such impairments suggest that some areas of the brain are responsible for processing pitch, whereas other neuronally distinct areas are responsible for processing rhythm (Peretz, 1996; Peretz & Kolinsky, 1993; Peretz & Morais, 1989). (For more extensive discussions of rhythm, see Clarke, 1999, or Krumhansl, 2000a.)

Timbre

Timbre is notoriously difficult to define. It is often described as the attribute that distinguishes sounds that are equivalent in pitch, duration, and loudness. Timbre is influenced by the pattern of partials that are present in complex waveforms and how those partials change over time (i.e., *transient* or *dynamic* attributes). A sawtooth waveform, which contains all harmonics, has a timbre that is distinct from that of a square waveform, which contains only odd-numbered harmonics. The sound of a plucked instrument such as a harp has a relatively rapid amplitude onset, whereas the sound of a bowed instrument such as a violin has a more gradual onset. In naturally occurring sounds, inharmonic partials (i.e., partials with a frequency equal to a noninteger multiple of the fundamental) also affect timbre. When inharmonic partials are removed from a piano note, for example, the note sounds artificial and unfamiliar.

For many instruments, the fundamental frequency has the greatest intensity of all harmonics in the frequency spectrum. Intensity typically decreases for higher frequency components. An inverse relationship between harmonic number and intensity (called spectral rolloff) does not hold for all instruments, however. For some instruments, certain harmonics may be disproportionately intense, giving that instrument its unique timbral character. A "bright"-sounding tone, such as that produced by a clarinet, typically contains high-frequency harmonics sounded at relatively high amplitudes.

When other aspects of a tone are held constant, differences in the frequency spectrum are associated with differences in timbre. We know, however, that the frequency spectrum is not entirely responsible for timbre, because tones with very different spectra can be perceived as having the same timbre. For example, examination of the frequency spectrum for a note played very softly on a trumpet reveals that most of the partials associated with trumpet sounds are absent. Nonetheless, the note is still perceived as emanating from a trumpet. More generally, the frequency spectrum associated with a given instrument may be quite different for soft and loud sounds despite their perceptual invariance.

Figure 26.8 provides an illustration of the dimensions of a musical instrument associated with its perceived timbre. The figure shows the partials that are present, their relative intensity, and how their intensity changes over time. For this particular instrument—a clarinet—the constituent frequency components vary in intensity at approximately the same rate. For other instruments, such as a piano, different partials change intensity at different rates. In many instances, onset or "attack" cues (i.e., transient cues during the initial portion of the spectrum) are important for perceiving timbre.

Formants are also thought to influence the perception of timbre. A formant is a range of frequencies with high amplitude relative to other frequencies, which is a consequence of the resonant properties of the sound source (e.g.,

the body of an acoustic guitar). Formants correspond to local peaks in a frequency spectrum. Fixed-frequency formants are particularly interesting because they remain relatively constant across the tessitura of an instrument. Whereas individual partials of a sound provide information about timbre by their relation to one another and to the fundamental frequency, fixed-frequency formants are resonant frequencies that do not change in proportion with changes in overall pitch. The harmonics that fall within the formant region resonate louder than other frequencies, giving the sound (e.g., a musical instrument) its particular timbral character.

Hajda, Kendall, Carterette, and Harshberger (1997) describe various methods that have been used to identify the acoustic properties that influence the perception of timbre. These include identification tasks (*name that timbre*), grouping and classification tasks (*match similar-sounding timbres*), semantic rating scales (*rate how bright or dull a timbre sounds*), discrimination tasks (*are two timbres the same or different?*), and similarity ratings (*rate how similar two timbres sound*). In a classic experiment, Grey (1977) asked musically trained listeners to provide similarity ratings for pairs of notes, which came from a set of nine different instrumental timbres. Notes were presented with the same fundamental frequency, intensity, and duration so that they varied only in timbre. His analysis revealed that three distinct dimensions could account for a good portion of the variance in similarity ratings.

Various follow-up studies have yielded different results regarding the underlying dimensions that influence the perception of timbre. In almost all cases, "brightness" appears to be a significant perceptual dimension. Instruments with a wide range of spectral energy (e.g., the oboe) are perceived as having a brighter timbral character than instruments with a more restricted range of spectral energy (e.g., the French horn). The influence of onsets (attacks) and other temporal properties—important in some studies but not in others—depends on the specific timbres used in the stimulus set and the duration of the stimuli (see Hajda et al., 1997).

Another way to identify acoustic attributes that are essential to instrument identification is to simplify the waveforms of instrumental notes without fundamentally changing the perceived timbre. Grey and Moorer (1977) showed that removing certain acoustic properties does not significantly affect judgments of instrument timbre. For example, removing amplitude and frequency modulations of individual partials resulted in subtle changes to timbre, but these manipulations did not alter the perceived instrument associated with the sound.

Yet another approach is to examine how readily tone sequences that involve different timbres form separate auditory streams. Iverson (1995) presented listeners with se-

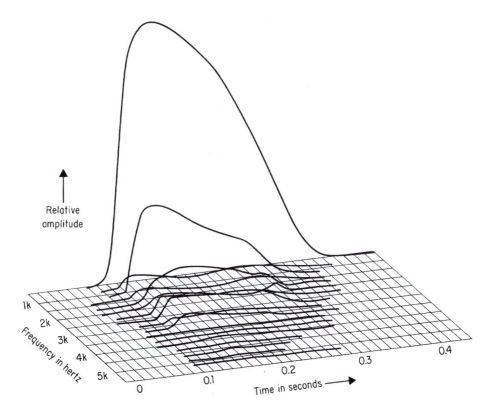

Figure 26.8. Transient attributes of sound. Frequency is displayed as a function of time and intensity.

quences that consisted of two different orchestral tones and asked them to rate the extent to which one or two sequences were being played. Auditory stream segregation was influenced by differences in both static spectra (the pattern of partials present) and dynamic attributes. Moreover, the results converged with similarity judgments obtained by Iverson and Krumhansl (1993) on the same tones. That is, similarity judgments predicted the extent to which timbres segregated into separate auditory streams, with similar timbres less likely than dissimilar timbres to split into separate streams.

How rapidly do listeners register timbre? Robinson and Patterson (1995) tested the limits of listeners' ability to identify the timbre and pitch of tones that varied in duration. Whereas identification of pitch proved to be a function of duration, identification of timbre was independent of duration. Listeners required several complete cycles of a periodic signal to identify pitch accurately but only one or two cycles (i.e., milliseconds) to identify timbre. These results make intuitive sense when one considers that pitch is determined by frequency (number of cycles per second). Therefore, a listener needs to hear several cycles in order to determine how rapidly a cycle repeats. By contrast, one or two cycles of a tone contain information about the components present in the frequency spectrum, which allow for identification of timbre.

In a related investigation, researchers tested the limits of listeners' ability to identify recordings (Schellenberg, Iverson, & McKinnon, 1999). In an experimental version of *Name That Tune* (the song-identification game played on television and radio), listeners matched extremely brief excerpts (100 or 200 milliseconds) from recordings of popular songs with the song titles and artists. Listeners' performance was better than chance with excerpts of 1/5 of a second. Performance deteriorated with shorter excerpts (1/10 of a second) but was still better than chance. Other manipulations involved low-pass and high-pass filtering and playing the excerpts backward. Performance fell to chance levels for the low-pass-filtered and backward excerpts but was unaffected by high-pass filtering. In short, successful identification of the recordings required the presence of dynamic, high-frequency spectral information. Note that the excerpts were too brief to convey any relational information (re pitch and duration) and that the absolute pitch of the excerpts would be identical whether they were played backward or forward. Thus successful performance presumably stemmed from accurate and detailed memory of the recordings' timbres, which consisted of many complex tones from many different instruments.

By definition, timbre and pitch are different. Nonetheless, some studies suggest that timbre and pitch are not perceived independently. For example, it is easier to judge whether 2 tones (Crowder, 1989), 2 chords (Beal, 1985), or 2 melodies (Radvansky, Fleming, & Simmons, 1995) are the same when standard and comparison stimuli are played on identical rather than different musical instruments. This finding suggests that—despite our experience of pitch and timbre as distinct musical qualities—they interact with each other in music processing.

Krumhansl and Iverson (1992) used another approach to study interactions between pitch and timbre. Participants were asked to classify stimulus items into two groups as quickly as possible based on a specified "target" attribute (e.g., pitch). Not only did the target attribute vary; an irrelevant attribute (e.g., timbre) also varied from trial to trial. Performance on the categorization task was relatively good when variation in the irrelevant attribute was correlated with variation in the target attribute but relatively poor when variation in the irrelevant attribute was uncorrelated with variation in the target attribute. That is, subjects were unable to attend to the pitch of a tone without being affected by its timbre, and vice versa. This finding provides converging evidence that pitch and timbre are not perceptually separable from each other.

Although pitch and timbre may be integrated successfully at some points in the information-processing system, listeners can also become confused about the ways in which pitches and timbres are combined. In one experiment, participants listened for particular combinations of pitch and timbre in arrays of tones that were presented simultaneously but emanated from different locations in the auditory field (Hall, Pastore, Acker, & Huang, 2000). An examination of errors indicated that participants often perceived an *illusory conjunction* of pitch and timbre. That is, participants often heard the timbre of one tone combined with the pitch of another tone. Estimates of the illusory conjunction rate ranged from 23 to 40%. The findings provide evidence that after an initial stage in which individual features of musical tones are registered (e.g., pitch, timbre) there is a stage in which these separately registered features are integrated (feature integration). Illusory conjunctions arise when errors occur at the *feature-integration* stage of processing.

What is the relation between timbre and harmony? The principle of harmonicity, outlined by Bregman (1990), suggests that partials that fall along the harmonic series of a single note are fused together, such that listeners perceive the distinct timbral qualities of each note holistically. When two instruments play the same note, or two different notes with many harmonics in common, there may be some confusion in this process. Such fusion effects actually contribute to our perception of harmony. For example, if one plays two piano notes separated by a fifth, those two notes have several partials in common. Perceptual mechanisms will tend to fuse or "confuse" some of the components of the two different notes, giving rise to emergent timbral ef-

fects. Compositions by Debussy exemplify the varied timbral effects of combining tones.

Although pitch and rhythmic relations are usually considered to define musical structure, some contemporary composers and theorists (e.g., Lerdahl, 1987; Slawson, 1985) have considered the possibility that timbre might be used compositionally in a way that is analogous to the use of pitch. One challenge with this compositional approach is that timbre has a powerful influence on auditory stream segregation. Thus any large shift in timbre is likely to signal a separate auditory stream, which would conflict with the goal of creating a coherent sequence analogous to a melody. Nonetheless, changes in timbre that correspond to reductions in sensory dissonance (i.e., fewer harmonics falling within a critical band)—and increases in fusion—may be perceived as a change from *tension* to *release,* which commonly occurs at points of musical closure (Pressnitzer, McAdams, Winsberg, & Fineberg, 2000). In other words, changes from relatively dissonant to relatively consonant timbres have some of the resolving properties of a perfect cadence.

It is also clear that timbre has a profound influence on our appreciation of music. For example, imagine a piano piece composed by Chopin performed by a horn section or a song by U2 played on an accordion. Such changes in instrumentation would undoubtedly affect our experience of the music.

Conclusion

At the outset, we identified the nature–nurture controversy as one of the most contentious issues in the psychology of music, as it is in the field of psychology as a whole. We argued that experiences of music are shaped by a combination of enculturation and cognitive constraints. We cited numerous sources of evidence for psychological constraints on music experience. Such constraints include working-memory limitations, sensitivity to sensory consonance and dissonance, the perceptual salience of pitch contours, perceptual grouping as a function of proximity, predispositions that favor simple meters and rhythms, processing biases for intervals with small-integer ratios, and reliable memories for the absolute pitch and timbre of frequently encountered auditory stimuli. Even rules of counterpoint and voice leading are strongly linked to cognitive constraints.

Influences of enculturation were also implicated throughout our review. Listeners learn about their native musical system through formal training or from simple exposure. This knowledge then influences music cognition in several ways, acting in conjunction with unlearned factors. Examples of learning include the development of sensitivity to the hierarchy of various scale steps in music and to the harmonies that are implied when listening to melodies. Even our expectations of what will happen next in a melody are shaped by implicit memory for music to which we have been passively exposed. In some cases, enculturation may actually overwhelm or reduce initial predispositions.

Distinguishing innate from learned factors in music perception and cognition is challenging because cognitive predispositions not only affect listeners' perceptions of music, but they also affect music composition and hence musical structure. Exposure to musical structure, in turn, shapes listeners' perceptions, in that listeners internalize persistent regularities in music. What results is a bootstrapping process that entangles innate and learned influences on music perception. As an example, if pitch proximity is a basic principle of perceptual grouping, then most melodies should have a predominance of proximate tones (Dowling & Harwood, 1986). But if listeners are exposed repeatedly to melodies with an abundance of pitch proximity, a general expectancy for proximate tones could result from learning. Infant studies have provided a valuable technique for disentangling innate and learned influences on music perception.

Although extreme versions of cultural determinism have been proposed (Walker, 1996), the enormous body of evidence for cognitive constraints on music processing is far too compelling to dismiss. In this regard, it should be emphasized that the existence of innate processing abilities and biases need not limit our ability to appreciate or perceive music, because effects of learning and enculturation allow us to develop preferences and schemata that extend beyond our initial predispositions. Conversely, natural processing abilities allow our appreciation of music to extend beyond the limits of individual enculturation. For example, by attending to basic perceptual cues Western listeners are able to appreciate emotional meaning in Hindustani ragas, even if they have never been exposed to such music and have no knowledge of the *raga-rasa* system (Balkwill & Thompson, 1999).

Although listeners are able to appreciate music from other cultures, existing evidence on innate processing abilities cannot account for the enormous diversity and complexity of musical styles both within and across cultures. No list of processing biases can readily account for the innovation and complexity of Bach fugues, serialized music, or Hindustani ragas. This complexity can only be explained in terms of a uniquely human mode of enculturation in which modifications of cultural traditions are accumulated over time (Tomasello, 1999). The music of Bach and Mozart was not invented in its entirety at a single point in time. Rather, other composers invented related versions of these styles, and these versions were then modified. This process of *cumulative cultural evolution* requires not only creative invention but also accurate trans-

mission (i.e., learning) of existing innovations. Accurate transmission of a musical composition or style—whether through demonstration or recorded in notation—allows individuals to build upon existing levels of complexity. What results within each culture is an accumulation of modifications, which lead to a diverse range of musical styles within and between cultures. Underlying all of these unique styles, however, are the processing biases and predispositions that have fascinated scholars for over a hundred years.

REFERENCES

Allen, D. (1967). Octave discriminability of musical and nonmusical subjects. *Psychonomic Science, 7,* 421–422.

Auhagen, W., & Vos, P. G. (2000). Experimental methods in tonality induction research: A review. *Music Perception, 17*(4), 417–436.

Balkwill, L. L., & Thompson, W. F. (1999). A cross-cultural investigation of the perception of emotion in music: Psychophysical and cultural cues. *Music Perception, 17*(1), 43–64.

Balzano, G. J. (1980). The group-theoretic description of 12-fold and microtonal pitch systems. *Computer Music Journal, 4,* 66–84.

Beal, A. L. (1985). The skill of recognizing musical structures. *Memory and Cognition, 13,* 405–412.

Bharucha, J. J., & Pryor, J. H. (1986). Disrupting the isochrony underlying rhythm: An asymmetry in discrimination. *Perception and Psychophysics, 40*(3), 137–141.

Bigand, E. (1990). Abstraction of two forms of underlying structure in a tonal melody. *Psychology of Music, 18*(1), 45–59.

Boltz, M., & Jones, M. R. (1986). Does rule recursion make melodies easier to reproduce? If not, what does? *Cognitive Psychology, 18,* 389–431.

Bregman, A. S. (1990). *Auditory scene analysis: The perceptual organization of sound.* Cambridge, MA: MIT Press.

Browne, R. (1981). Tonal implications of the diatonic set. *In Theory Only, 5,* 3–21.

Burns, E. M. (1999). Intervals, scales, and tuning. In D. Deutsch (Ed.), *The psychology of music* (2nd ed., pp. 215–264). San Diego, CA: Academic Press.

Clarke, E. F. (1999). Rhythm and timing in music. In D. Deutsch (Ed.), *The psychology of music* (2nd ed., pp. 473–500). San Diego: Academic Press.

Cooper, R. P., & Aslin, R. N. (1990). Preference for infant-directed speech in the first month after birth. *Child Development, 61,* 1584–1595.

Crowder, R. G. (1989). Imagery for musical timbre. *Journal of Experimental Psychology: Human Perception and Performance, 15,* 472–478.

Crowder, R. G. (1993). Auditory memory. In S. McAdams & E. Bigand (Eds.), *Thinking in sound: The cognitive psychology of human audition* (pp. 113–145). Oxford: Clarendon Press.

Cuddy, L. L., & Badertscher, B. (1987). Recovery of the tonal hierarchy: Some comparisons across age and levels of musical experience. *Perception and Psychophysics, 41,* 609–620.

Cuddy, L. L., & Lunney, C. A. (1995). Expectancies generated by melodic intervals: Perceptual judgments of melodic continuity. *Perception and Psychophysics, 57,* 451–462.

Cuddy, L. L., & Thompson, W. F. (1992). Asymmetry of perceived key movement in chorale sequences: Converging evidence from a probe-tone investigation. *Psychological Research, 54,* 51–59.

Darwin, C. J., Turvey, M. T., & Crowder, R. G. (1972). An auditory analogue of the Sperling partial report procedure: Evidence for brief auditory storage. *Cognitive Psychology, 3,* 255–267.

Deliège, I. (1987). Grouping conditions in listening to music: An approach to Lerdahl & Jackendoff's grouping preference rules. *Music Perception, 4*(4), 325–360.

Desain, P. (1992). A (de)composable theory of rhythm perception. *Music Perception, 9*(4), 439–454.

Deutsch, D. (1999a). Grouping mechanisms in music. In D. Deutsch (Ed.), *The psychology of music* (2nd ed., pp. 299–348). San Diego, CA: Academic Press.

Deutsch, D. (1999b). The processing of pitch combinations. In D. Deutsch (Ed.), *The psychology of music* (2nd ed., pp. 349–412). San Diego, CA: Academic Press.

Deutch, D. (1980). The processing of structured and unstructured tone sequences. *Perception and Psychophysics, 28,* 381–389.

DeWitt, L. A., & Crowder, R. G. (1987). Tonal fusion of consonant musical intervals: The oomph in Stumpf. *Perception and Psychophysics, 41,* 73–84.

Dibben, N. (1994). The cognitive reality of hierarchic structure in tonal and atonal music. *Music Perception, 12*(1), 1–25.

Dissanayake, E. (2000). Antecedents of the temporal arts in early mother–infant interactions. In N. L. Wallin, B. Merker, & S. Brown (Eds.), *The origins of music* (pp. 388–410). Cambridge, MA: MIT Press.

Dowling, W. J. (1994). Melodic contour in hearing and remembering melodies. In R. Aiello & J. A. Sloboda (Eds.), *Musical perceptions* (pp. 173–190). New York: Oxford University Press.

Dowling, W. J., & Harwood, D. L. (1986). *Music cognition.* Orlando, FL: Academic Press.

Dyson, M. C., & Watkins, A. J. (1984). A figural approach to the role of melodic contour in melody recognition. *Perception and Psychophysics, 35,* 477–488.

Essens, P. J. (1995). Structuring temporal sequences: Comparison of models and factors of complexity. *Perception and Psychophysics, 57*(4), 519–532.

Fernald, A. (1985). Four-month-olds prefer to listen to motherese. *Infant Behavior and Development, 8,* 181–195.

Fernald, A. (1991). Prosody in speech to children: Prelinguistic and linguistic functions. *Annals of Child Development, 8,* 43–80.

Fernald, A., Taeschner, T., Dunn, J., Papousek, M., de Boysson-Bardies, B., & Fukui, I. (1989). A cross-language study of prosodic modifications in mothers' and fathers' speech to preverbal infants. *Journal of Child Language, 16,* 477–501.

Fodor, J. A. (1983). *The modularity of mind.* Cambridge, MA: MIT Press.

Fraisse, P. (1982). *Rhythm and tempo.* In D. Deutsch (Ed.), *The psychology of music* (pp. 149–180). New York: Academic Press.

Gabrielsson, A. (1973a). Similarity ratings and dimension analyses of auditory rhythm pattern. *Scandinavian Journal of Psychology, 14,* 161–176.

Gabrielsson, A. (1973b). Adjective ratings and dimension analyses of auditory rhythm patterns. *Scandinavian Journal of Psychology, 14,* 244–260.

Grey, J. M. (1977). Multidimensional perceptual scaling of musical timbres. *Journal of the Acoustical Society of America, 61,* 1270–1277.

Grey, J. M., & Moorer, J. A. (1977). Perceptual evaluations of synthesized musical instrument tones. *Journal of the Acoustical Society of America, 62,* 454–462.

Hajda, J. M., Kendall, R. A., Carterette, E. C., & Harshberger, M. L. (1997). Methodological issues in timbre research. In I. Deliège & J. Sloboda (Eds.), *Perception and cognition of music* (pp. 253–306). Hove, East Sussex, UK: Psychology Press.

Hall, M. D., Pastore, R. E., Acker, B. E., & Huang, W. (2000). Evidence for auditory feature integration with spatially distributed items. *Perception and Psychophysics, 62,* 1243–1257.

Halpern, A. R. (1989). Memory for the absolute pitch of familiar songs. *Memory and Cognition, 17,* 572–581.

Helmholtz, L. F. von (1954). *On the sensations of tone as a physiological basis for the theory of music* (A. J. Ellis, Ed. & Trans.). New York: Dover. (Original work published 1863)

Howe, M. J. A., Davidson, J. W., & Sloboda, J. A. (1998). Innate talents: Reality or myth? *Behavioral and Brain Sciences, 21,* 399–442.

Huron, D. (1991a). The avoidance of part-crossing in polyphonic music: Perceptual evidence and musical practice. *Music Perception, 9*(1), 93–104.

Huron, D. (1991b). Tonal consonance versus tonal fusion in polyphonic sonorities. *Music Perception, 9*(2), 135–154.

Huron, D. (2001). Tone and voice: A derivation of the rules of voice leading from perceptual principles. *Music Perception, 19*(1), 1–64.

Iverson, P., & Krumhansl, C. L. (1993). Isolating the dynamic attributes of musical timbre. *Journal of the Acoustical Society of America, 94,* 2595–2603.

Iverson, P. (1995). Auditory stream segregation by musical timbre: Effects of static and dynamic acoustic attributes. *Journal of Experimental Psychology: Human Perception and Performance, 21,* 751–763.

Jones, M. R., Boltz, M., & Kidd, G. (1982). Controlled attending as a function of melodic and temporal context. *Perception & Psychophysics, 32,* 211–218.

Kallman, H. J. (1982). Octave equivalence as measured by similarity ratings. *Perception and Psychophysics, 32,* 37–49.

Kronman, U., & Sundberg, J. (1987). Is the musical ritard an allusion to physical motion? In A. Gabrielsson (Ed.), *Action and perception in rhythm and music*. (Publications issued by the Royal Swedish Academy of Music. No. 55) (pp. 57–68). Stockholm: Adebe Reklam.

Krumhansl, C. L. (1979). The psychological representation of musical pitch in a tonal context. *Cognitive Psychology, 11*, 346–374.

Krumhansl, C. L. (1990). *Cognitive foundations of musical pitch*. Oxford: Oxford University Press.

Krumhansl, C. L. (1995). Music psychology and music theory: Problems and prospects. *Music Theory Spectrum, 17*(4), 53–80.

Krumhansl, C. L. (2000a). Rhythm and pitch in music cognition. *Psychological Bulletin, 126*, 159–179.

Krumhansl, C. L. (2000b). Tonality induction: A statistical approach applied cross-culturally. *Music Perception, 17*(4), 461–480.

Krumhansl, C. L., & Iverson, P. (1992). Perceptual interactions between musical pitch and timbre. *Journal of Experimental Psychology: Human Perception and Performance, 18*, 739–751.

Krumhansl, C. L., & Jusczyk, P. W. (1990). Infants' perception of phrase structure in music. *Psychological Science, 1*, 70–73.

Krumhansl, C. L., & Keil, F. C. (1982). Acquisition of the hierarchy of tonal functions in music. *Memory and Cognition, 10*, 243–251.

Krumhansl, C. L., & Kessler, E. (1982). Tracing the dynamic changes in perceived tonal organization in a spatial representation of musical keys. *Psychological Review, 89*, 334–368.

Krumhansl, C. L., & Shepard, R. N. (1979). Quantification of the hierarchy of tonal functions within a diatonic context. *Journal of Experimental Psychology: Human Perception and Performance, 5*, 579–594.

Large, E. W., & Jones, M. R. (1999). The dynamics of attending: How we track time-varying events. *Psychological Review, 106*, 119–159.

Leman, M. (2000). An auditory model of the role of short-term memory in probe-tone ratings. *Music Perception, 17*(4), 481–510.

Lerdahl, F., & Jackendoff, R. (1983). *A generative theory of tonal music*. Cambridge, MA: MIT Press.

Levitin, D. J. (1994). Absolute memory for musical pitch: Evidence from the production of learned melodies. *Perception and Psychophysics, 56*, 414–423.

Levitin, D. J. (1999). Memory for musical attributes. In P. R. Cook (Ed.), *Music, cognition, and computerized sound* (pp. 209–227). Cambridge, MA: MIT Press.

Levitin, D. J., & Cook, P. R. (1996). Memory for musical tempo: Additional evidence that auditory memory is absolute. *Perception and Psychophysics, 58*, 927–935.

Meyer, L. (1973). *Explaining music: Essays and explorations*. Chicago: University of Chicago Press.

Miller, G. A. (1956). The magical number seven, plus or minus two: Some limits on our capacity for processing information. *Psychological Review, 63*, 81–97.

Miyazaki, K. (1993). Absolute pitch as an inability: Identification of musical intervals in a tonal context. *Music Perception, 11*(1), 55–72.

Monahan, C. B., & Carterette, E. C. (1985). Pitch and duration as determinants of musical space. *Music Perception, 3*(1), 1–32.

Morton, D. (1976). *The traditional music of Thailand*. Los Angeles: University of California Press.

Narmour, E. (1990). *The analysis and cognition of basic melodic structures*. Chicago: University of Chicago Press.

Narmour, E. (1992). *The analysis and cognition of melodic complexity*. Chicago: University of Chicago Press.

Oram, N., & Cuddy, L. L. (1995). Responsiveness of Western adults to pitch-distributional information in melodic sequences. *Psychological Research, 57*, 103–118.

Palmer, C., & Krumhansl, C. L. (1987a). Independent temporal and pitch structures in determination of musical phrases. *Journal of Experimental Psychology: Human Perception and Performance, 13*, 116–126.

Palmer, C., & Krumhansl, C. L. (1987b). Pitch and temporal contributions to musical phrase perception. *Perception and Psychophysics, 41*, 116–126.

Parncutt, R. (1994). A perceptual model of pulse salience and metrical accent in musical rhythms. *Music Perception, 11*(4), 409–464.

Patel, A. D., Peretz, I., Tramo, M., & Labreque, R. (1998). Processing prosodic and music patterns: A neuropsychological investigation. *Brain and Language, 61*, 123–144.

Peretz, I. (1996). Can we lose memories for music? The case of music agnosia in a nonmusician. *Journal of Cognitive Neuroscience, 8*, 481–496.

Peretz, I., Gaudreau, D., & Bonnel, A. M. (1998). Exposure effects on music preference and recognition. *Memory and Cognition, 26* (5), 884–902.

Peretz, I., & Kolinsky, R. (1993). Boundaries of separability between melody and rhythm in music discrimination: A neuropsychological perspective. *Quarterly Journal of Experimental Psychology, 46A*, 301–325.

Peretz, I., & Morais, J. (1989). Music and modularity. *Contemporary Music Review, 4*, 279–293.

Plomp, R., & Levelt, W. J. M. (1965). Tonal consonance and critical bandwidth. *Journal of the Acoustical Society of America, 37*, 548–560.

Pressnitzer, D., McAdams, S., Winsberg, S., & Fineberg, J. (2000). Perception of musical tension for nontonal orchestral timbres and its relation to psychoacoustic roughness. *Perception and Psychophysics, 62*, 66–80.

Radvansky, G. A., Fleming, K. J., & Simmons, J. A. (1995). Timbre reliance in nonmusicians' and musicians' memory for melodies. *Music Perception, 13*(2), 127–140.

Robinson, K., & Patterson, R. D. (1995). The duration required to identify an instrument, the octave, or the pitch chroma of a musical note. *Music Perception, 13*(1), 1–15.

Schacter, D. L. (1987). Implicit memory: History and current status. *Journal of Experimental Psychology: Learning, Memory, and Cognition, 13*(1), 501–518.

Schellenberg, E. G. (1996). Expectancy in melody: Tests of the implication-realization model. *Cognition, 58*, 75–125.

Schellenberg, E. G. (1997). Simplifying the implication-realization model of melodic expectancy. *Music Perception, 14*(3), 295–318.

Schellenberg, E. G., & Trehub, S. E. (1994). Frequency ratios and the perception of tone patterns. *Psychonomic Bulletin & Review, 1,* 191–201.

Schellenberg, E. G., & Purdy, K. T. (2000, August). *Melodic expectancies in 7- and 8-year-olds.* Paper presented at the 6th International Conference on Music Perception and Cognition, Keele, UK.

Schellenberg, E. G., Krysciak, A., & Campbell, R. J. (2000). Perceiving emotion in melody: Interactive effects of pitch and rhythm. *Music Perception, 18*(2), 155–171.

Schellenberg, E. G., Iverson, P., & McKinnon, M. C. (1999). Name that tune: Identifying popular recordings from brief excerpts. *Psychonomic Bulletin & Review, 6,* 641–646.

Schellenberg, E. G., & Trainor, L. J. (1996). Sensory consonance and the perceptual similarity of complex-tone harmonic intervals: Tests of adult and infant listeners. *Journal of the Acoustical Society of America, 100,* 3321–3328.

Schellenberg, E. G., & Trehub, S. E. (1996a). Children's discrimination of melodic intervals. *Developmental Psychology, 32,* 1039–1050.

Schellenberg, E. G., & Trehub, S. E. (1996b). Natural intervals in music: A perspective from infant listeners. *Psychological Science, 7,* 272–277.

Schellenberg, E. G., & Trehub, S. E. (1999). Culture-general and culture-specific factors in the discrimination of melodies. *Journal of Experimental Child Psychology, 74,* 107–127.

Serafine, M. L. (1988). *Music as cognition: The development of thought in sound.* New York: Columbia University Press.

Serafine, M. L., Glassman, N., & Overbeeke, C. (1989). The cognitive reality of hierarchic structure in music. *Music Perception, 6*(4), 397–430.

Sergeant, D. (1983). The octave: Percept or concept? *Psychology of Music, 11,* 3–18.

Shepard, R. N. (1964). Circularity in judgments of relative pitch. *Journal of the Acoustical Society of America, 36,* 2345–2353.

Shepard, R. N. (1982). Structural representations of musical pitch. In D. Deutsch (Ed.), *The psychology of music* (pp. 343–390). New York: Academic Press.

Shepard, R. N. (1999). Pitch perception and measurement. In P. R. Cook (Ed.), *Music, cognition, and computerized sound* (pp. 149–165). Cambridge, MA: MIT Press.

Shepard, R. N., & Jordan, D. C. (1984). Auditory illusions demonstrating that tones are assimilated to an internalized scale. *Science, 226,* 1333–1334.

Slawson, W. (1985). *Sound color.* Berkeley: University of California Press.

Takeuchi, A. H., & Hulse, S. H. (1993). Absolute pitch. *Psychological Bulletin, 113,* 345–361.

Terhardt, E., & Seewann, M. (1983). Aural key identification and its relationship to absolute pitch. *Music Perception, 1*(1), 63–83.

Thompson, W. F. (1989). Composer-specific aspects of musical performance: An evaluation of Clynes' theory of "pulse" for performances of Mozart and Beethoven. *Music Perception, 7*(1), 15–42.

Thompson, W. F. (1993). Modeling perceived relationships between melody, harmony, and key. *Perception and Psychophysics, 53,* 13–24.

Thompson, W. F. (1994). Sensitivity to combinations of musical parameters: Pitch with duration, and pitch pattern with durational pattern. *Perception and Psychophysics, 56*(3), 363–374.

Thompson, W. F. (1996). A review and empirical assessment of Eugene Narmour's *The Analysis and Cognition of Basic Melodic Structures* (1990) and *The Analysis and Cognition of Melodic Complexity* (1992). *Journal of the American Musicological Society, 1009* (1), 127–145.

Thompson, W. F., Balkwill, L. L., & Vernescu, R. (2000). Expectancies generated by recent exposure to melodic sequences. *Memory and Cognition, 28,* 547–555.

Thompson, W. F., & Cuddy, L. L. (1992). Perceived key movement in four-voice harmony and single voices. *Music Perception, 9*(4), 427–438.

Thompson, W. F., Cuddy, L. L. (1997). Music performance and the perception of key. *Journal of Experimental Psychology: Human Perception and Performance, 23,* 116–135.

Thompson, W. F., Cuddy, L. L., & Plaus, C. (1997). Expectancies generated by melodic intervals: Evaluation of principles of melodic implication in a melody completion task. *Perception and Psychophysics, 59,* 1069–1076.

Thompson, W. F., Diamond, C. T. P., & Balkwill, L. (1998). The adjudication of six performances of a Chopin etude: A study of expert knowledge. *Psychology of Music, 26,* 154–174.

Thompson, W. F., & Stainton, M. (1998). Expectancy in Bohemian folksong melodies: Evaluation of implicative principles for implicative and closural intervals. *Music Perception, 15*(3), 231–252.

Tillman, B, Bharucha, J. J., & Bigand, E. (2000). Implicit learning of tonality: A self-organizing approach. *Psychological Review, 107*(4), 885–913.

Tomasello, M. (1999). *The cultural origins of human cognition.* Cambridge, MA: Harvard University Press.

Trainor, L. J. (1997). The effect of frequency ratio on infants' and adults' discrimination of simultaneous intervals. *Journal of Experimental Psychology: Human Perception and Performance, 23,* 1427–1438.

Trainor, L. J., & Heinmiller, B. M. (1998). The development of evaluative responses to music: Infants prefer to listen to consonance over dissonance. *Infant Behavior and Development, 21,* 77–88.

Trainor, L. J., & Trehub, S. E. (1992). A comparison of infants' and adults' sensitivity to Western musical structure. *Journal of Experimental Psychology: Human Perception and Performance, 18,* 394–402.

Trainor, L. J., & Trehub, S. E. (1994). Key membership and implied harmony in Western tonal music: Developmental perspectives. *Perception and Psychophysics, 56,* 125–132.

Trehub, S. E., Schellenberg, E. G., & Hill, D. S. (1997). The origins of music perception and cognition: A developmental perspective. In I. Deliège & J. Sloboda (Eds.), *Perception and cognition of music* (pp. 103–128). Hove, East Sussex, UK: Psychology Press.

Trehub, S. E., Schellenberg, E. G., & Kamenetsky, S. B. (1999). Infants' and adults' perception of scale structure. *Journal of Experimental Psychology: Human Perception and Performance, 25,* 965–975.

van Noorden, L. P. A. S. (1975). *Temporal coherence in the perception of tone sequences* (Doctoral dissertation, Technisch Hogeschool Eindhoven). Eindhoven, The Netherlands: Druk vam Voorschoten.

von Hippel, P. (2000). Redefining pitch proximity: Tessitura and mobility as constraints on melodic intervals. *Music Perception, 17*(3), 315–327.

von Hippel, P., & Huron, D. (2000). Why do skips precede reversals? The effect of tessitura on melodic structure. *Music Perception, 18*(1), 59–85.

Vos, P. G. (1978). *Identification of meter in music* (Internal Report 78 ON 06). Nijmegen, The Netherlands: University of Nijmegen.

Vos, P. G. (2000). Tonality induction: Theoretical problems and dilemmas. *Music Perception, 17*(4), 403–416.

Walker, R. (1996). Can we understand the music of another culture? *Psychology of Music, 24,* 103–114.

Wallin, N. L., Merker, B., & Brown, S. (Eds.). (2000). *The origins of music.* Cambridge, MA: MIT Press.

Wright, J. K., & Bregman, A. S. (1987). Auditory stream segregation and the control of dissonance in polyphonic music. *Contemporary Music Review, 2,* 63–92.

Zentner, M. R., & Kagan, J. (1996). Perception of music by infants. *Nature, 383,* 29.

The Development of Musical Abilities

27

HEINER GEMBRIS

A considerable amount of research on musical development has been published in recent years. This particular survey addresses the following questions: Which results of developmental psychology should parents and teachers be aware of? What should they know about the development of musical abilities? There are obviously no simple answers to these questions since they depend on individual interests of the reader. However, there are a lot of general aspects of musical development that can be of general interest to parents and educators.

A central aspect of this chapter will be the description of typical age-related characteristics and the different influencing factors of development. In addition, we will establish connections to developmental theories, to pedagogical considerations, and to the state of research in relevant areas. A detailed outline of developmental theories is not intended since it can be found in other chapters of this book. Since research in the area of development and cognition is often incomplete and controversial, our account will inevitably resemble a puzzle with some pieces missing rather than a painting with straight lines.

Areas of Research

The current developmental psychology of musical abilities may be in one of its most productive stages in history. We can distinguish at least five areas of research that have opened up new perspectives on musical abilities of humans in the last 10 to 15 years: the examination of fetal learning before and infant learning after birth, neurobiological research, expertise research, life-span development of musical abilities, and the emergence of developmental theories. Brief characterizations of these key aspects are presented in the following sections.

The Examination of Fetal Learning Before and Infant Learning After Birth

New research methods in infant studies (e.g., video and computer technology, habituation paradigm) have enabled reliable investigations of children's perceptual and cognitive abilities even at preverbal stages of development. The results show a surprising degree of competence not only in general development but also in the area of musical perception and communication. Moreover, research has clearly shown that the perceptions of sounds and music not only emerge after birth but already have started weeks and even months before birth (for reviews see Lecanuet, 1996; Trevarthen, 1999–2000).

This leads to the question of whether and, if so, how musical abilities should be fostered by educational activities with infants and perhaps even during prenatal stages of development. One consequence might be that music education in the future will start even earlier than today. In addition, research on infants has shown to be relevant beyond the developmental psychology of music, because it refers back to the anthropological and psychological basis of music, hence to the question of musical universals and basics of musical expression.

Neurobiological Research

In neurobiological research, the development of visual image-mapping procedures (e.g., magnetic resonance imaging [MRI], positron emission tomography [PET]) provided new evidence for neurobiological correlates of musical activities (see also chap. 25, by Gruhn and Rauscher, in this volume). Schlaug, Jäncke, Huang, Staiger, and Steinmetz (1995) showed that the planum temporale, a brain area in the left temple region, is anatomically more developed in musicians, especially those with absolute pitch, than in nonmusicians. It has also been shown that the corpus callosum, which connects the two hemispheres of the brain, is morphologically more highly developed in musicians than nonmusicians. Another study group found that the specific area of the motor cortex that coordinates the movements of the left hand is more anatomically extended in string players than in nonmusicians (Elbert, Pantev, Wienbruch, Rockstroh, & Taub, 1995). This enlargement, correlated with the age at which the persons started to play their instruments, suggests that the anatomical or neurological/neurobiological differences between musicians and nonmusicians are a result of musical training and development and that these differences may, in turn, be a factor in any variations in musical development.

In a longitudinal study, Hassler (1991, 1992) found that biological parameters correlated with musical development. She observed female and male adolescents over a period of 8 years and examined the relationship between the level of the male sex hormone testosterone, which changes during puberty, and the development of spatial and musical abilities. Among other things, musical talent for composing was clearly related to a tendency toward androgyny (cf. Kemp, 1996, p. 109). Music education and research on musical development should direct more attention to the phase of puberty.

Expertise Research

Expertise research focuses on the crucial role of deliberate practice for the development of musical abilities (see chap. 30, by Andreas C. Lehmann and Jane W. Davidson, in this volume). From this point of view, expert performance can be seen as a result of the accumulated hours of training and deliberate practice over a lifetime. After the acquisition of expert performance in a number of areas like sports and chess was addressed, the expertise approach was successfully adapted to the domain of music (e.g., Ericsson, Krampe, & Tesch-Römer, 1993; Krampe, 1994; Jørgensen & Lehmann, 1997). Recently the expertise paradigm has also become a helpful approach to study other levels of instrumental performance (Sloboda & Davidson, 1996; Sloboda, Davidson, Moore, & Howe, 1994). Expertise research, with its focus on environmental variables, and behavioral genetics and neurobiological research, with its emphasis on innate capacities, together have stimulated the old nature–nurture debate.

Life-Span Development of Musical Abilities

Investigating the development of musical abilities of adults was another force that led to new perspectives in developmental psychology. Until recently, music education and the psychology of music focused primarily on childhood and adolescence. However, the fact that the proportion of older people is increasing in our societies and more adults are looking for meaningful leisure activities resulted in a greater need for research on the development and influence of musical abilities in an aging population. The establishment of the life-span perspective for developmental psychology was an important premise for the awareness that the development of musical abilities was a lifelong process. Biographical studies on musicians were rediscovered and their relevance increased (e.g., Gembris, 1997; Manturzewska, 1990, 1995).

The Emergence of Developmental Theories

In the last 10 to 15 years, a remarkable change has also occurred in the area of theory development. For a long time, a number of general theories, for the most part not specific to music like the theory of Piaget or the earlier idea of the biogenetic and psychogenetic law, determined theories of musical development. In recent years, a number of theories specifically related to music or at least to particular areas of musical development were established, for example, for the usage of musical symbols (Davidson & Scripp, 1992), singing (e.g., Davidson, 1994); the learning of newborns and infants (Gordon, 1990), composition (Swanwick, 1994), the development of musical and artistic competence (Hargreaves, 1996), or the professional careers of instrumentalists (Manturzewska, 1995) (see chapter 28 on theories, in this volume). These theories do not always agree whether or not the acquisition of musical abilities can be considered domain-specific processes of development. Hargreaves (1996, p. 153) concludes that domain-specific processes are likely to play a role especially in the acquisition of high levels of musical abilities. However, there are stages of development for cognitive abilities that appear at certain ages, and those can be observed in various domains. A future task for theory development will be to draw a clear distinction between domain-specific and general processes of development.

"Research findings often are not readily or obviously applicable to practices" (Haack, 1992, p. 461). What Haack says about research on the acquisition of music-listening skills is true of most developmental psychology of music. On the one hand, research should thus be more concerned with particular problems of music education. On the other hand, processes of musical development will also benefit from theory development and basic research, which cannot be easily adopted to practice but offer important explanations and orientations.

General Assumptions

Musical abilities have to be understood in inclusive fashion as an amalgamate of many factors, including instrumental and vocal abilities, music-specific cognitive processes, emotional experiences, musical experiences, motivation, musical preferences, attitudes, and interests.

The Universality of Musical Abilities

An important starting point for looking at the development of musical abilities is the assumption that every human being is musical and that it is possible and promising to develop this musicality. It is usually assumed that musical abilities are normally distributed, which means that most people are of average musicality in much the same way as most people are of average intelligence. Assuming that musicality is normally distributed means that 68% of people are of average musicality, while 14% are less musical and 14% are more musical than the average. Approximately 2% are highly gifted and a further 2% have a low musical talent. Therefore, there are no completely unmusical people, just as there are no totally unintelligent people. Since everybody possesses at least some degree of musical aptitude, everybody can also benefit from musical instruction despite individual difference in innate capacities (Gordon, 1987).

Musical Development as a Lifelong Process

It is another premise that musical development is a lifelong process. Musical development occurs as part of the general development of an individual over the life span. It does not end—as is often assumed—by the end of adolescence. Also, it is difficult to say exactly when musical development begins. Since children are able to perceive acoustic stimuli like voices and music in the last weeks before birth and recognize them in their first days of life, we may assume that musical experiences and musical learning start before birth. From a theoretical point of view, musical development does not end until the end of life. Unfortunately, for a lot of people the development seems to have ceased a long time before the end of their lives. Yet music therapy with older people is being undertaken and only makes sense if we assume that there is potential for development at this age.

Development as Changing Dynamics of Growth, Maintenance, and Loss

Development is understood here not just as positive changes like improvement and growth but as an interplay of benefits, maintenance, and loss of abilities (e.g., Baltes, Lindenberger, & Staudinger, 1998). This interaction changes over the life span, for example, due to specialization. Whereas benefits are prevalent during childhood and adolescence, the proportion of loss increases with age.

If we consider musical development part of the general development that includes cognitive, emotional, sensorimotor, and social components, it is also affected by the interplay of benefit and loss. For instance, while sensorimotor abilities decrease throughout adulthood and can influence instrumental playing, musical experiences and musical knowledge can increase at the same time. Thus even though some loss of abilities may occur over the life span, teaching and learning music during adulthood may still be beneficial for musical development.

Individual Differences

It is well documented that large developmental differences in music abilities already exist at an early age and in adolescence. They are caused by differences in giftedness and talent and the sociocultural background as well as by lessons, motivation, and practice (e.g., Kelly & Sutton-Smith, 1987). During adulthood, these individual differences, for example, among professionals, amateurs, and people untrained in music, become even more pronounced due to commitment and practice in the case of professionals and lack of use in nonmusicians. Therefore, research on musical development, especially development in adulthood, requires a strong differential perspective. One approach distinguishes between "normative" and "specialist" development (Hargreaves, 1996, p. 150). Normative development is "that which naturally happens to children as they grow up in a given culture regardless of any specialized attention or guidance," while specialist development and specialist education "is consciously devoted to the development of high levels of musical skill or expertise" (Hargreaves, 1996, p. 150). Even though Hargreaves advises against the strict separation of these two aspects, further distinctions seem to be necessary. Different aspects also become obvious if the careers and the development of musicians in jazz, rock, and popular music are compared with those in classical music. In such nontraditional domains there is a lack of theoretical concepts to describe the musical development.

Cross-Generational Differences

Since musical development is culturally and historically embedded, it is affected by the changing historical and cultural surroundings, especially the changes in musical culture. Children's musical development depends much on the current musical culture, which can differ largely from their parents' culture. This becomes obvious when one compares the musical development of the generation that grew up with rock and popular music as a main influence to that of the generation before. Hence, contemporary history can affect musical development (Gembris, 1997). The rise of new media technology (e.g., computers and the internet) and the emergence of new musical styles contribute to an increasing variety of musical development in the fields of composition, performance, listening, and preferences. Therefore, parents and teachers should be aware that the children's and student's musical development may differ considerably from their own. Correspondingly, research on musical development should broaden its focus on traditional Western art music to include all styles (e.g., Hemming & Kleinen, 1999).

Musical Development: 0 to 10 Years

The basic musical abilities that are required for participation in one's own musical culture are developed in the first 10 years of life. This process of enculturation takes place automatically and subconsciously, without the need of formal instruction. Musical stimulations that arise from the individual social and cultural environment seem to be most important. A musically rich social environment can lead to certain musical abilities' being acquired earlier than in a social environment with less musical activity (Kelly & Sutton-Smith, 1987). But the development of basic musical abilities can also be positively influenced through teaching. Morrongiello (1992) observed that musical practice leads to more precise perception of melodies, better musical memory, and an earlier sensitivity for keys. Other studies confirm that the acquisition of certain musical abilities can be accelerated through teaching; however, students without lessons do catch up after a while (e.g., Behne, 1974). The possibility to accelerate the development of basic musical abilities through lessons may be constrained by their connection with general mental, emotional, and sensorimotor developmental processes (Gembris & Davidson, in press). Note that since large individual differences can occur in both general and musical development, the age-related details that follow are points of reference, and divergent ages cannot easily be interpreted as indicating unusual talent or developmental retardation.

Prenatal Development

The onset of musical learning and musical memory lies before birth. The nerve cells of the inner ear start to work in the fifth or sixth month of pregnancy and respond to midrange frequencies. Approximately in the seventh month of gestation, the fetus perceives extrauterine acoustic stimuli. When children are born, they have already had some acoustic experiences. An experiment by Feijoo (1981) showed that babies stopped crying when they listened to short melodies that had been presented to them over a period of 4 weeks during the sixth to eighth month of

pregnancy. Satt (1984) provided evidence for the ability of 16 newborns to recognize a lullaby that they had heard every day during the last 2 months of pregnancy. Hepper (1991) demonstrated the ability of infants just a few days old to recognize the main tune of a television series that they already heard before birth. Another study showed that newborns seemed to remember single words from a story read out loud by their mothers during the last 6 weeks of pregnancy (DeCaspar & Spence, 1986). These results demonstrate that reactions to music must already occur during prenatal development. However, the methods used in these experiments still offer no reliable distinction between direct reactions of the child and indirect reactions influenced by the mother's reaction.

The fact that unborn children can react to music has been taken up by the music industry, which offers a number of CDs especially designed for pregnant women. These products supposedly have a positive influence on the health of the mother and the unborn child. Experiments with animals have demonstrated that prenatal auditory deprivation leads to a retarded development, while careful acoustic enrichment seemed to improve the structure and function of auditory tracts in the fetus (Lecanuet, 1996, p. 18).

Development of Musical Perception

Pitch.   Infants can show performance superior to adults in the ability to perceive small pitch differences. A study with American infants and adults demonstrated the ability of 6-month-old infants to recognize single tones that were played out of tune in Western (major/minor) and non-Western scales (Javanese *pelog* scale) (Lynch, Eilers, Oller, & Urbano, 1990). Adults who grew up in a Western music culture did recognize tones out of tune in major and minor scales but not those out of tune of the *pelog* scale. The authors concluded that children are born with a potential to perceive the scales of different cultures equally well. However, in the process of enculturation scale-related perception schemes develop regardless of formal musical instruction for scales in one's own culture, while other perceptual abilities for non-culture-specific scales decrease (Lynch & Eilers, 1991). Similar findings exist for speech perception.

A number of experiments with infants and adults investigate the possible existence of innate dispositions or perceptual capacities that would favor specific intervals or scales. The results are ambiguous and inconsistent; in general, there is some evidence for the special position of the octave and perfect fifth in interval perception. Demany and Armand (1984) found out that higher and lower octaves were perceived as equivalent by 3-month-old infants.

Obviously, infants were already sensitive to pitch and timbre at that age, although there was only little influence of musical experience. Other experiments indicated that the perfect fifth could be an interval whose perception and brain processing were supported by some universal, prototypical-cognitive representation (Lynch, 1993).

Melody Perception.   Growing research over the last 20 years supports the idea that infants' sensations are not just vague and mellow; instead, their reactions can be interpreted as recognizing behavior (see Fassbender, 1996, for a review). By the age of 6 months, infants are capable of distinguishing several short melodies with the melodic contour as the most important distinguishing feature. At this age they cannot yet recognize absolute pitch or specific intervals (Dowling, 1988, 1999). Most of the present studies indicate that melodic perception in its early stages aligns itself with the melodic contour and moves on to more specific details with increasing age (Dowling, 1999). Lamont's (1998) experiments demonstrate that informal musical experience is more important for general musical enculturation than playing an instrument, at least for children aged 6 to 11. However, during adolescence (11 to 16 years) the accuracy of melodic perception only improves if someone is musically active (e.g., plays an instrument). She concludes: "Enculturation (and school music) alone is insufficient for continued development after the age of 11" (p. 23).

Schwarzer's (1997) results run contrary to those mentioned before. She observed a tendency toward analytic perception for children (ages 5 to 7), whereas adults perceived the presented melodies in a holistic fashion. The children's perception was based on melody-unspecific features like loudness and timbre and not on melodic contour, whereas adults were oriented toward melody-specific contour. These inconsistent results can possibly be explained by the different task settings.

Another important concept for the development of musical perception is the distinction between equal and different stimuli (Deliège, Mélen, & Bertrand, 1995; Gordon, 1981, p. 41). Structuring and processing of perception already take place at infant age according to the principles of Gestalt psychology: namely, grouping of stimuli according to similarity, closeness, and conciseness (Fassbender, 1996). These are also the basis for auditory grouping or auditory stream segregation and can be regarded as universal principles. They contribute to the transformation of temporal relationships of note sequences into a meaningful, rhythmical "Gestalt," just as pitch relations and pitch sequences are transformed into a melodic contour.

Cross-modal Perception.   Essential for the development of musical perception of infants is their ability to recognize connections among auditory stimuli, visual stimuli, and touch. This specific ability is called cross-modal perception and was demonstrated in different experiments (e.g., Meltzoff, Kuhl, & Moore, 1991; Papoušek, 1996). The infant perceives the acoustical characteristics of the maternal voice (melody, contour, tempo, rhythmical structure, timbre) as synchronous with and analogous to his or her own sensory perception, to visual experiences, and to the movements of the mother. The development of such cross-modal perceptual schemata is likely to play an important role for the perception of musical expression.

Rhythmic Abilities.   There are different indicators and approaches to examine the development of rhythmic abilities, that is:

- the ability to distinguish between identical and different rhythms,
- the preference for simple or complex rhythms,
- the reproduction of rhythms through clapping,
- the ability to move to presented rhythms, and
- the investigation of rhythmical structure in children's songs.

Early studies in the 1960s already demonstrated that newborns are able to distinguish between regular and irregular heartbeat or click sounds (Spiegler, 1967). Other researchers found that 5-month-old infants could recognize changes of simple rhythms (long–short vs. short–long) (Shuter-Dyson & Gabriel, 1981, p. 107). Even though children already seem to have some rhythmic awareness and are able to distinguish between simple rhythms, a more precise perception of rhythms develops only gradually. Regular meter in singing first becomes noticeable during the 2nd year of life, first in very short then in increasingly longer segments (Dowling & Harwood, 1986, p., 194). These abilities are clearly age-related, and considerable individual differences exist.

The results from investigations about rhythm perception during preschool age are quite divergent. The children Rainbow (1980) observed over a period of 3 years took 2 years before a marked increase of rhythmic abilities was noted. Conversely, Ramsey (1983) identified a developmental jump in the perception and (sung) performance of rhythms in a melody between the third and fourth year of life. He also found corresponding progress in the perception of melodic intervals between the fourth and fifth year of life. The author concludes that the perception of rhythm precedes the perception of melody.

Between the third and fourth year of life, children start to distinguish roughly between slow and fast. Four-year-olds seem to be able to identify slow and fast tempi and use appropriate terms and can demonstrate their understanding with concomitant body movements. For children at this age, fast and slow seems to be the central aspect of music (Young, 1982). Yet most of them are not capable of making comparative judgments (e.g., slow and slower). Furthermore, these children start to prefer rhythms in which they can identify regular structures (Zenatti, 1993). To show this preference, 4-year-olds need simple rhythms without sixteenth and eighth notes or dotted eighths, while 5-year-olds seem to have no problem even with more complex rhythmic structures. This may be related to the fact that children age 5 and up have a more sophisticated notion of time in general (Pouthas, 1996, p. 136; also Dowling, 1999).

Synchronization of Rhythm with Movement. The beginnings of synchronization between music and movements can be first observed with children aged 18 months to 2 years (Moog, 1976). Starting with the age of 2 1/2 years, children seem to be able to match their movements to the music for a short period of time. Still, imitating someone's clapping, synchronized clapping, and marching to the beat of the music are tasks that 3- to 4-year-olds can hardly accomplish (Rainbow, 1980). However, it is possible that children at this age are able to perceive rhythms that they cannot reproduce themselves through movement. They can clap a given rhythm more easily if they speak it before clapping it. Also, it is easier for them to repeat a spoken rhythm than a regular meter (Rainbow & Owen, 1979). Generally, children have fewer difficulties representing or realizing rhythms through use of their voice. Therefore, the voice is the most appropriate educational medium to teach rhythms to 3- and 4-year-olds (Rainbow, 1980). At the age of 5, children seem to be able to synchronize their movements (taps) to rhythms with somewhat less than adult accuracy (Gerard & Auxiette, 1992).

While studies from the 1970s concluded that the concept of meter did not develop until the age of 7 and stabilized by the age of 9, more recent studies show that 5-year-old children can already maintain a given meter. An increase of rhythmic abilities could possibly be explained by a stronger and earlier influence of the mass media, which may accelerate the general musical enculturation. Alternatively, research methods and measurements may have simply become more sophisticated and sensitive.

Harmony and Tonality. Even though findings about the development of tonal sensitivity are not consistent throughout, a clear tendency can be observed: More recent studies record younger ages than did previous studies for harmonic perception and the preference for consonance over dissonance. Based on experiments from 1913, Valentine (1962) found that children were able to distinguish between major and minor at the age of 9 and those with

intensive musical training between the ages of 5 and 7. Imberty (1969) first noticed this ability in children at the age of 7, while it can be observed at the age of 5 and younger today. Again, the increased influence of the mass media could account for the fact that children become accustomed to the Western major-minor tonal system at an earlier age, which in turn may lead to an acceleration in the identification of harmonies (Zenatti, 1993, p. 192). With the use of refined research methods, these effects could possibly be observed at even younger ages.

In a number of experiments with 5- to 10-year-olds, Zenatti (1993) examined the musical preference for tonality versus atonality and consonance versus dissonance. The children listened to pairs of musical stimuli (e.g., a tonal and an atonal melody) presented from tape and were asked which melody, rhythm, or chords of the two versions they preferred. Children younger than 5 were still at chance level; that is, they had no clear preference. However, at the age of 6 the preference for consonant harmonization increased as rapidly as the dislike for atonal melodies and dissonance. By the age of 9 or 10 the preference for tonality and consonance was between 90 and 95% (cf. Zenatti, 1993, p. 182; also Minkenberg, 1991, for supporting results). This suggests that enculturation into the Western tonal system is virtually concluded at that age. As a result, the openness to contemporary music or music from non-Western cultures constantly decreases after the age of 5 or 6. An educational countermeasure could be presentation more of nontonal music to preschool children and indicating to them that it can be enjoyed just the same as familiar music.

Timbre. A question of interest to music educators is whether preschool and primary school children are able to recognize and distinguish different instruments by their sound. In a number of experiments with preschool children, Schellberg (1998) found an enormous increase in the ability to distinguish timbres by 4- to 6-year-olds. Most of the 5- and 6-year-olds were able to distinguish and recognize conventional musical instruments—which they knew from their music lessons—even in combination with other instruments from the orchestra.

Recognition of Emotional Expressions in Music. The ability to perceive and distinguish basic acoustic-musical parameters is the premise for the understanding of musical expression and its emotional meaning. Recognizing emotional expressions in music requires a general emotional ability of perception and differentiation.

Even though infants are not able to distinguish between different face expressions in the first 6 weeks of their life, they are able to recognize familiar voices (cf. Rauh, 1995, p. 230). At an early age, they distinguish and express various emotions via the acoustic channel. With different types of crying they communicate their current feelings (Wolff, 1969). Based on their long-term efforts, M. and H. Papoušek demonstrated the infant's ability to understand the emotional-communicative meaning of different melodic-rhythmic contours in nonverbal vocalization in parent–child interactions (e.g., H. Papoušek, 1996; M. Papoušek, 1996; Papoušek & Papoušek, 1986). Infants seem to attribute the same meanings to the same melody contours, independent of the culture they grow into.

Between the ages of 6 weeks and 4 months, infants begin to distinguish happy, sad, and neutral facial expressions, first in actual faces and later in schematic pictures. Another important aspect for the perception of expression can be identified between the fourth and the ninth month of life: By that age, infants are able to perceive cross-modal relationships between vocal and gestural qualities of facial expressions. Next infants start to recognize the reason for a person's happy or angry reaction; that is, they establish the connection between certain events and the corresponding facial expression of familiar adults (Rauh, 1995, p. 230).

There is currently very little work on the recognition of emotional expression in music for infants and children younger than 3, and we do not know to what extent infants or toddlers actually perceive expressions, say, in the music their parents play to them with the goal of improving the child's well-being.

Various studies focus on the understanding of musical expression at preschool age and at school age. For example, children had to match schematic pictures of face expressions to a number of musical excerpts. Some researchers also included verbal statements, and the children were asked to either indicate which emotions they identified or give free descriptions of what they felt (Cunningham & Sterling, 1988; Minkenberg, 1991; Trehub, 1993). Most of the studies are limited to fundamental emotions ("happy-sad," "angry-frightened," or "calm-excited"), although exceptions exist where more emotions are considered. One of the most important results is that children 3 to 4 years old matched a surprisingly large number of pictures correctly to the music (Cunningham & Sterling, 1988; Dolgin & Adelson, 1990; Kastner & Crowder, 1990).

The examples presented in these experiments usually consisted of short pieces or excerpts from classical instrumental music. It should be noticed that, despite its wide distribution and generally easier musical structure, none of the studies included rock or pop music as stimuli. Correctly matching the pictures to the music largely depended on the kinds of emotions expressed as well as on the kinds of musical stimuli; some emotions were recognized more easily than others. Children seemed to better recognize the emotions "happy" and "sad" than "angry-frightened" and

"calm-excited" (Cunningham & Sterling, 1988; Dolgin & Adelson, 1990; Kratus, 1993; Terwogt & van Grinsven, 1988). In addition, emotions were not recognized equally well on different instruments. For example, Dolgin and Adelson (1990) found that 4-year-olds identified the intended musical expression of a melody more accurately in a sung presentation than in an instrumental presentation on the violin. Studies with adults showed a better understanding for "sadness" if the emotion was presented vocally or on a violin and a better understanding for "anger" when the emotion was presented on drums (Behrens & Green, 1993).

It appears that the ability to recognize musical expression is dependent both on the importance of music in the home and on the influence of music education. Some studies suggest that the ability to recognize musical expression improves through music education; however, the effect is rather weak (Behrens & Green, 1993; Kratus, 1993). There is hardly any evidence for gender-related effects, as boys and girls do not differ in the ability to recognize musical expression (Giomo, 1993).

Mechanisms for the Recognition of Expressions

Which musical characteristics contribute to the recognition of expressions of children? What role do the fundamental categories of major and minor play? Research results that concern the emotional perception of major and minor are ambivalent. Whereas adults clearly relate major to happy and minor to sad, 4- to 8-year-olds are quite inconsistent and uncertain in assigning expressions to certain modes (Trehub, 1993; see also chap. 26, by Thompson and Schellenberg, in this volume).

If 3- or 4-year old children are already capable of recognizing emotional expression in music although the feeling for tonality only stabilizes at primary school age, there must be other characteristics of expression than major and minor for the children's identification of emotional expression. Terwogt and van Grinsven (1991) found that adults as well as 5-year-olds seem to be oriented toward a rhythm and melody. In another experiment, Dolgin and Adelson (1990) copied the melodic gesture of melodies from emotional speech. Four-year-olds and adults correctly recognize the emotional expressions of most melodies. In an experiment with 4- to 8-year-olds, Trehub detected that fast notes and ascending melodies were perceived as happy. However, slow and low notes and descending melodies were perceived as sad. Similar effects can be found through use of prosody in language (Trehub, Trainor, & Unyk, 1993) or the nonverbal interactions between infants and their parents (see earlier). It can be concluded that there must exist some prototypical gestures or movements of acoustic expression that are independent from tonality and common to both language and music. Interestingly, the Italian composer Claudio Monteverdi (1567–1643) used the prosody of the language as a basis for his *stile concitato* compositions to increase the affective power of his music.

Perception of Further Nonmusical Meanings

Children are not only able to perceive emotional expressions in music, but they are also able to recognize metaphoric representations of extramusical content. Some informative experiments were carried out by Trainor and Trehub (1992) in which children between the ages of 3 and 6 were asked to match parts of Prokofiev's composition *Peter and the Wolf* to a number of pictures (wolf, bird, cat, duck, etc.). The results showed that 3-year-old children were already capable of identifying extramusical characters within music and this ability improved with age. Another study was carried out by Graml, Kraemer, and Gembris (1988) with children of primary and secondary schools. Starting with the first grade, children were already able to match—with relative accuracy—excerpts from Stravinsky's *Firebird* and other compositions with pictures of the characters described in the music. Starting with grade level 4, the children were capable of solving all items correctly.

Again we could ask ourselves which musical characteristics enable the children to assign the right pictures to the music. According to Trainor and Trehub (1992), imitative and metaphoric characteristics of the music give rise to the expression: For instance, musical tension and relaxation serves as an analogue to emotional tension and relaxation, and high and low pitches convey spatial aspects; musical movement is mapped onto nonmusical movement, musical onto nonmusical power and mass (e.g., the elephant in the *Carnival of the Animals* by Camille Saint-Saëns). Thus cross-modal perceptual schemata may play an important role (see earlier).

As soon as the children's linguistic development is sufficiently advanced, which commonly happens around the ages of 7 to 10, they can be interviewed about their musical experiences. In a longitudinal study, one author discovered three kinds of thoughts and feelings in children. The first kind included thoughts and moods directly related to the music, such as thoughts about the composer or the performer. The second kind included associations caused by the music, such as thoughts about the morning light or sad things. The third kind included thoughts about actual situations experienced by the children while listening to or performing music, such as listening to music at school or while going to bed (cf. Minkenberg, 1991, p. 267).

In summary, we can state that a basic understanding of musical expression already exists at the ages of 3 to 4 and becomes more differentiated as the children grow older. The current studies do not separate whether the emotions expressed by the music were just recognized or experienced concurrently. Other variables, such as musical home environment, music lessons, and gender had little or no effect on the children's recognition of musical expression.

Graphic Representation of Music

Research on musical development has recently been influenced by the symbol-system approach (Davidson & Scripp, 1992). This resulted in an increased interest in graphic and symbolic representations of melodies and rhythms, which allow interesting insights into the development of musical thinking (e.g., Gromko, 1994; Smith, Cuddy & Upitis, 1994). To study the ability to create graphic representations, children (or adults) are first asked to repeat a given rhythm, melody, or song by clapping or singing. Then they are instructed to generate a "notation" for the music that is supposed to enable a third person to reproduce the music without having heard it before. A number of researchers have offered typologies for the development of graphic representation of music and the underlying musical thinking. (e.g., Bamberger, 1991; Upitis, 1987).

The children's representations led the authors to postulate two different kinds of underlying processing strategies. A first strategy resulted in the production of a sequentially ordered series of symbols. For instance, children under the age of 5 tended to simply jot down the rhythmic impulses of the melody. Older children reproduced a single dimension of the melody, either its rhythmic structure or its melodic contour. All of this changes between the ages of 6 and 8: Then rhythmic impulses are grouped together and pitch representation becomes dominant. Hereafter, both aspects can be integrated from 7 years on.

Coordination of Different Aspects of Perception ("Conservation")

Although it is currently unclear if Piaget's theory of cognitive development can be adequately transferred to the domain of music (cf. Case, 1998; Haith & Benson, 1998; Gardner, 1991; Hargreaves, 1986), research based on this theory has undoubtedly produced central insights into musical development. According to Piaget's theory, children start to develop the ability to coordinate several different aspects of perception (*conservation*) around the age of 7 years during the *concrete-operational stage*. For the development of musical abilities this implies that, for instance, children have to reach at least 7 years before they can pay attention to and coordinate rhythm and melody simultaneously. Older work had already demonstrated that 8-year-old children identified different melodies as variations of the *same* melody when rhythmic, melodic, or tonal changes had been made (Pflederer, 1964; Pflederer & Sechrest, 1968). This ability to coordinate different aspects of music, that is, to *conserve,* increases with age, although, as Nelson (1987, p. 26) found, it does not necessarily develop at the same time in different domains. Other studies provided evidence for an intermediate stage, where children can perceive but not coordinate more than one dimension at a time (Flammer, 1996, p. 129). For example, children at this age are mostly able to identify transposed melodies, but they have difficulties describing pitch relations with the right words, like *high* and *low* (Flowers & Costa-Giomi, 1991; also Shuter-Dyson, 1982, p. 75). As a consequence, these abstract notions should not be used for pre-school-age music education and rather be replaced by metaphorical pictures.

The Development of Singing.   The common roots of singing and speaking are the nonverbal vocalizations of the infant, which are an immediate expression of its basic feelings. Parents intuitively tune in to the child's noises to establish communication with the infant. These child-directed vocalizations are called motherese and can be seen as a *prelinguistic alphabet* (M. Papoušek, 1996). It is likely that children during preverbal development experience and process musical impressions in the same way as the prosody of the language (Trehub et al., 1993). These nonverbal vocalizations represent at the same time prelinguistic and premusical means of expressions.

A number of authors agree on the fact that most of these melodic contours consist of descending glissando figures after the first 3 or 4 months of life (e.g., Fox, 1990). M. Papoušek (1994) describes four different types of melodic contours of vocalization in early childhood (descending, ascending-descending, ascending and complex, and repeated ascending and descending), the frequency of which depends on the age of the infant and the situational context. Descending contours prevail in the first months of life, but later the melodic contours become more varied and the proportion of other contours increases. The large range of observed interindividual variability could be caused by developmental differences as well as by problems of research methodology.

By the end of the first year of life, it becomes possible to separate singing and speaking in the preverbal vocalizations of most children. Children themselves experiment with the voice and seem to try out its range and possibilities in "vocal play" (Stadler, 2000). It is possible to understand vocal play in Piagetian terminology as a kind of sensorimotor play. This kind of behavior typically appears between the 12th and the 18th month of life. The two fundamental cognitive processes that underlie vocal play and imitation are assimilation and accommodation (cf. Stadler, 2000, p. 55). Accommodation takes place when children are trying to adapt their imagination and vocal expression to a given model such as the phrase of a song. Assimilation occurs when children receive new information (e.g., a new melody) and integrate it into an already-existing schema.

Another kind of singing was characterized by Dowling (1999) as an articulation of syllables with vowels that are slightly prolonged and appear on stable pitches. The author also observed a sequential organization of the *song,* referring to more or less stabilized tonal patterns. According to Dowling, the first actual singing can be observed between the 6th and the 18th month of life. At first, these glissando-like improvisations on single syllables occupy only a narrow pitch range. Later they turn into recognizable songs, often with a sequential organization of the sounds. Thus a typical song of an 18-month-old-child consists of an often-repeated phrase with a steady melodic contour at a continuously changing level of pitch. The song is quite often interrupted by breathing; however, the rhythmical contour remains within the phrase and sometimes even stretches over several phrases. These songs are often derived from the rhythm of language.

In their second year of life, children are able to sing single short phrases of a song, frequently turning them into spontaneous improvisations and repeating them quite often. Microtonal figures in spontaneous singing slowly make way for more accurate intervals, resulting in an overall impression that is clearly related to the diatonic system (cf. Moog, 1976). Between the ages of 3 and 4, children combine different songs and song fragments into something like a medley. They can repeat songs they hear and increase phrase contour of the presented song by trial and error. Other researchers observed that children could reproduce all of the lyrics, the main rhythms, and also the formal segments of a song starting at the age of 4 (cf. Shuter-Dyson & Gabriel, 1981, p. 117).

Children will have acquired the singing range of an octave with all its steps once they are 6 or 7 years old (Davidson, 1994; Minkenberg, 1991). Although they still might miss certain pitches, this does not mean they are unable to recognize the pitches (Goetze, Cooper, & Brown, 1990). The development of the ability to sing comes to an end around the age of 8 years. Generally, by this time children are able to sing a song correctly. This ability remains at this level unless music instruction and practice follow. As always, however, a broad range of interindividual differences are observable. The singing abilities of untrained adults are not much different from those of 8- to 10-year-old children (see Davidson, 1994; Davidson & Scripp, 1990, p. 66; Minkenberg, 1991; Stadler, 2000, for further details).

Theories on the Development of Singing.   According to Stadler (2000, for summary) the different concurrent theoretical approaches to the development of singing can be categorized into three groups. The first group comprises the speech-dominated *theories of sequence*. The principal argument here is that songs are learned in a certain order, namely, lyrics, rhythm, melody contour/phrases, precise intervals (e.g., Hargreaves, 1986; Moog, 1976; Welch & White, 1994). A second group consists of explanations that implicate the *order of intervals*. Here intervals or successions of notes appear developmentally in a specific and unreversible succession, namely, first the fifth, followed by the third and fourth and then the sixth. This theory assumes innate structures that are supposedly based on the acoustical properties of the harmonic series (e.g., Metzler, 1962; Werner, 1917). The third group could be labeled *contour theories*. Proponents of this approach advance the notion that the learning process begins with the melodic contour and that pitch and tonality follow. Learning to sing is thus assumed to proceed from global to more local features. According to Davidson's (1994) theory of contour schemata, the development of a contour schema starts with a falling third into which the other intervals are placed. The contour schema will then expand with the child's age: at first to a fourth and up to a sixth, which is mastered by the age of around 6 or 7. One author, however, raises a number of critical arguments against all of these theories and suggests the following course of development (Stadler, 2000):

1st step: Early beginnings; vocalizations as the expression of an infant's basic feelings

2nd step: Shifted imitations; development of rituals and extended vocal play

3rd step: Imitation without understanding of rules and inventing of arbitrary rules

4th step: Generalization of examples; ability to sing larger units

5th step: Implicit integration of conventional rules into actions; increasing control of one's own singing

6th step: Beginning reflecting on one's own actions, means, symbols and terms; use of notation for the production and reproduction of music. (p. 144)

Musical Development: 10 to 20 Years

Preferences, Aesthetic Values, and Cultural Identity

Whereas the first 8 to 10 years of life are characterized by musical enculturation with a concomitant adoption of the culture's principles and conventions, the ensuing 10 years are dominated by the search for and the establishment of one's own place within a musical culture. This own posi-

tion is reached with the development of individual musical preferences and tastes. Generally, the term *preference* is used to describe the

affective reactions to a piece of music or a certain style of music that reflect the degree of liking or disliking for that music, and is not necessarily based on cognitive analysis or aesthetic reflection regarding the music in question. (Finnäs, 1989, p. 2)

In contrast, *musical taste* refers to long-term preferences for certain musical styles.

The development of preferences is mainly influenced by one's socialization into a given sociocultural environment, including parents, school, social class, peers, and mass media (see Zillmann & Gan, 1997, for an overview). It is difficult to determine the degree of relevance of each of the factors, since their importance changes over the lifetime and may even vary depending on the context. In general, the influence of parents and school decreases during adolescence, at the same time when the importance of peers and media increases. Furthermore, the degree of certain influences is determined by a person's social class.

We should also realize that adolescents not only are passively influenced by their sociocultural environment in the development of their musical preferences but also are rather actively choosing and shaping their own environment. This view of self-socialization is a relatively recent one and has been adapted to music by Müller (1999). Musical self-socialization takes place in an unhampered fashion far away from the influences of formal education, preferably within the youth culture.

"Open-earedness" During Childhood

For children younger than 8, 9, or 10, musical preferences are less important and less stable than those of teenagers. Therefore, children are more open toward and tolerant of unfamiliar or unconventional types of music (LeBlanc, 1991, for an overview). This musical openness (*open-earedness*; Hargreaves, 1982) of children of preschool and primary school age stems from the less strong internalization of musical conventions and rules than that of adolescents and adults. In addition, the links between preferences on the one hand and cultural values, different ways of hearing, and functions of music on the other hand are less tight at that age. Open-earedness is an opportunity for music education to introduce children to all kinds of unfamiliar music, be it avant-garde or non-Western, against which adults or adolescents might already have established prejudices.

Current research provides evidence for a decrease of "open-earedness" with the beginning of adolescence (LeBlanc, 1991). At the same time, a preference for the music of one's peers starts to emerge. This process is closely related to the construction of a personal and social identity. Furthermore, LeBlanc (1991) observed a rebound effect at the end of adolescence, when listeners tended to return to the music that played a role in late childhood before the beginning of adolescence. This hypothesis awaits further investigation.

Significance of Music Listening for Teenagers

With the beginning of adolescence, sometimes even earlier, listening to music, the orientation toward music, and knowledge about musicians and stars become more and more important. On average, musical preferences and attitudes dramatically change between the 10th and 20th year of life. Around this time, musical preferences separate from the taste of parents and teachers. The close connections to the adult musical world that exist during childhood are replaced by the desire to establish one's own musical taste and world. In this context, the taste of peers plays an important role and also the music industry's current products and the identification with specific musical styles, groups, idols, and stars.

It is typical for teenagers to change their preferences quickly and to experience music with strong accompanying emotions (Behne, 1986). This becomes manifest in the strong enthusiasm for their currently preferred music and a correspondingly strong rejection of other musical styles. Because their preferences mirror the strong emotional impact of the music, adolescents are often quite adamant when it comes to defending *their* current preferences (Behne, 1997, p. 149). This close emotional relationship does not exist during childhood or adulthood to nearly the same degree.

As adolescence is relatively short compared to the entire life span, it is the time in which the greatest changes of musical preferences occur. This period is most important for the musical development not only because of the dramatic changes in preferences but also because the behavioral patterns of listening acquired by the end of adolescence will remain prevalent for adulthood (Behne, 1986, p. 56; Dollase, Rüsenberg, & Stollenwerk, 1986, p. 183; Holbrook & Schindler, 1989; Lehmann, 1994). A distinctive preference for the music of one's youth can be quite frequently observed at a much older age (e.g., Jonas, 1991). A study of Holbrook and Schindler (1989) demonstrated that preferences of adults from different generational cohorts were clearly related to the music that was popular when they were about 24 years old.

Emergence of Preferences for Popular Music

Musical preferences start to develop at primary school age but remain subject to change for a long time. Typically, the preference for popular music gradually increases while other music is getting less popular (e.g., Montgomery, 1996). Between the ages of 8 and 10, children begin to orient themselves toward popular music and lose interest in other, for example, classical, music.

A methodological remark is in order here. The fact that verbal and behavioral preferences do not match is quite well known (e.g., Behne, 1986, 1997; Finnäs, 1989; Lehmann, 1994). It is a peculiarity of preference research that evaluative statements about music that are based on verbal labels will be more negative than preferences reported after listening to an actual example. The reason is that verbal preferences seem to be influenced by socialization to a greater extent than behavioral preferences. Verbal preferences therefore represent the publicly expressed musical taste of a peer group, while behavioral preferences represent a more *private* taste (compare Behne, 1997, and Finnäs, 1989). Thus it is entirely possible for a student to generally dislike a genre like opera but, when confronted with a recording of, say, "Che gelida manina" from Puccini's *La Boheme,* be quite touched.

K.-E. Behne (1986) carried out an investigation into the verbal and listening (behavioral) preferences of over 1,000 students aged 10 to 22. He observed that different classical music styles, when presented verbally (word labels), were viewed as a homogenous complex by the majority of the adolescents. However, when actual examples of classical music styles were presented (listening preferences), classical music was not rejected as a whole.

Among the various youth subcultures there are those in which classical music is rated highest on preference scale (e.g., Bastian, 1989, p. 236). Naturally, this group represents a minority. Still, some music-listening studies have demonstrated a surprising tolerance for different classical music genres among younger and older people as well as openness to the "oldies but goldies" of popular music among older people (Gembris, 1995).

Increasing Consumption of Music and Use of Mass Media

The development of musical preferences is accompanied by an expanding music consumption, which can already be observed around the age of 10 and remains at a high level during adolescence. Different researchers found out that the amount of time watching television increases rapidly between childhood and early adolescence and decreases slowly thereafter (Huston & Wright, 1998, p. 1001). Current studies also provide evidence for an increase of the time spent listening to music from childhood to adolescence. For better or worse, the growing availability of music videos, compact discs, minidiscs, the internet, and mp3 players is likely to contribute to the ubiquity of music consumption. Children and adolescents who play an instrument seem to use the mass media less and in a more re-flective manner than those who do not (e.g., Scheuer, 1988, p. 206). Taken together, the time allotted to music in for-mal settings (school) contributes only a small fraction to the overall amount of music to which young people listen. This does not necessarily mean that education has no in-fluence at all upon the development of musical preferences.

Based on his own and other researchers' work, Dollase (1997) proposed a 3-stage model to explain the develop-ment of interest in music and of individual preferences: First, there is a rise, starting with the age of 10; interests plateau starting with the age of 13 during the second stage; finally, speed of development declines after the age of 25. As always, age details only serve as points of reference, while individual differences may be large.

Gender Differences

In general, there seem to exist hardly any differences be-tween girls and boys regarding musical instruments or mu-sical styles during childhood (Maidlow & Bruce, 1999). However, the increase in preference for popular music dur-ing adolescence seems to be more pronounced for boys than for girls; that is, girls' dislikes of nonpopular music are less strong than those of the boys. Also, girls seem to like a broader range of classical music (Hargreaves, Comber, & Colley, 1996). The authors explain this with the fact that girls generally take more instrumental lessons and are thus ahead in music education, resulting in a wider acceptance of different musical styles. Some researchers do find gender differences. Martin, Clarke, and Pearce (1993), for instance, found that boys prefer rock and heavy metal music while girls had a preference for popular music. These differences are obviously related to the gender stereotyping of certain musical styles (see Green, 1997; and Maidlow & Bruce, 1999, for detail on gender differences with regard to preferences).

Functions of Music, Listening Styles, and Preferences

The functions that music can assume in an individual's life can be considered the essential influencing factors in the development of musical preferences (Behne, 1986; Dollase, 1997; Lehmann, 1994). Music already serves specific func-tions during infancy and childhood, yet this functionality is largely imposed on the child (e.g., lullabies, children's songs, etc.) rather than self-chosen. However, the wide dis-tribution of tape recorders, compact disc players, and other technical media makes it possible even for small children to listen to music whenever they choose. The functional use of music expands in adolescence in parallel with the increase in amount of listening. Music is used consciously

or unconsciously for various reasons in everyday life. For example, Baacke (1993) presents the following possible list of functions:

- Specific musical preferences act as a sign of identification for specific youth cultures which distinguishes them from one another
- Source of information on new lifestyles, fashion and hab-its
- Separation from adults who reject youth-specific music
- Stimulation for dreams and wishes
- Establishing of own physical identity by discovering movement through dancing
- Summons to be active and protest
- Escape from everyday life
- Possibility to identify with idols like rock music stars
- Expression of protest and opposition against everyday culture
- A means of stimulation and mood control (p. 232)

It is obvious from a number of further studies that mu-sical preferences develop in response to functional aspects of music (e.g., Lehmann, 1994; Mende, 1991). The use of music as a coping strategy, for compensating for problems, or for mood management plays an important role. De-pending on an actual situation, different styles of listening are used to invoke various functional aspects. Pronounced gender differences are found, and according to Behne (1997) boys gravitate toward a more stimulative listening style, whereas girls tend to adhere to a more sentimental listening style:

Results show surprisingly clearly how strongly individual listening styles are connected with the experience of indi-vidual problems, depression appearing to be the most im-portant experience in this context. In most cases, plausible explanations for the interrelations between problem ex-perience and listening style are possible. (p. 157)

Musical Preferences and Music Education

Musical preferences must be reckoned with in music edu-cation. On the one hand, they may provide the impulse for music instruction; on the other hand, they may also be a result of teaching. Music education usually strives for a pluralistic and tolerant musical taste. However, there are diverging opinions about whether or not teachers should try to influence the musical tastes of their students (cf. Finnäs, 1989, p. 43). Current knowledge makes it appear un-likely that music education can have a lasting effect on young people's musical preferences, especially during the first stage in the development of preferences and during puberty. At this time, the open-earedness is limited and the emotions run high. A survey of research into the possibil-ities of influencing musical preferences (cf. Finnäs, 1989) finds that students will generally not prefer music that is slow or rhythmically, melodically, and harmonically complex or vocal music. However, the preference for music increases once it becomes more familiar. In light of this, it may be advisable to repeat the presentation of unknown music in more than one lesson. Also, information about composers or musicians as well as live concerts can positively influence an interest in unfamiliar music.

Puberty as a Critical Phase in Musical Development

Puberty is a time of significant change, not only with respect to the development of musical preferences. During this time, decisions are made about instrumental music education with far-reaching consequences. Even in the biographies of professional musicians, turning points and setbacks can be observed at the onset of puberty (Manturzewska, 1990). A study among violinists provided evidence for a critical stage between the ages of 12 and 16. The best musicians were able to increase their amount of practice more than the average during this period (e.g. Ericsson et al., 1993; Krampe, 1994; see chap. 30, by Andreas C. Lehmann and Jane W. Davidson, in this volume). Making music and practicing an instrument thus becomes an important part of one's personal identity. Many other students drop out of instrumental lessons during this time. The reason is that young people's longing for autonomy and their search for personal identity now require more freedom and less rigid guidance (see Grimmer, 1991). Unfortunately, many teachers' abilities to cope with these changed desires in instrumental music lessons are quite limited.

Parents and teachers know very well that puberty is a critical stage for musical development. It is surprising that research has not yet adequately addressed the influences of changes in personality, motivation, interests, and sociopsychological conditions typical for this developmental stage on music instruction.

Developmental Processes Throughout Adulthood

The development of basic musical abilities, musical preferences, and aesthetic values takes place in the first two decades of life even in the absence of music education. However, more refined musical development requires deliberate activities and instruction. The range of individual differences with regard to music in adulthood encompasses the results of impressive specialization of the professional musician as well as the stagnation and decrease of musical abilities due to a lack of interest and motivation. This sec-

tion offers a survey of research on musical development in adulthood, which is still in its infancy. I will first present some general comments on biological and cultural aspects of general conditions of aging during adulthood (cf. Baltes et al., 1998).

General Conditions of Aging: Biological Aspects

A number of age-related cognitive, sensory, and physiological changes occur in adulthood that can impact musical activities. Although these changes also affect younger adults, their influence increase at older ages (see Birren & Schaie, 1996, for relevant chapters). Starting around the age of 30, human physiological functions lose about 1% of their efficiency every year. In addition, the speed of cognitive processing and the discrimination of stimuli already start to decrease in early adulthood (e.g. Baltes et al., 1998; Jennen & Gembris, 2000; Park, 1999; Swartz et al., 1994). Another generally accepted effect of aging is the continuous decline of hearing. However, the body's great capacity for compensation can hide this slow process of reduction for a long time. Only when a critical limit is reached do these changes in physiological processes start to become a problem (Maier, Ambühl-Caesar, & Schandry, 1994, p. 167). For example, at older ages the decrease of sensorimotor speed and dexterity along with a reduction of the sense of touch and other micromotor impasses can lead to difficulties in instrumental playing.

A severe problem for singers is the change of the voice with age. This change is not directly related to chronological but to biological age, and it can be accompanied by effects like the loss of the chest voice, the fast change of pitch and timbre of the voice, the loss of intensity and resonance, and the reduced ability to control the many parameters involved in singing. Fortunately, these characteristics do not emerge all at the same time (Habermann, 1986, p. 148; Moore, Staum, & Brotons, 1992; Sataloff, 1992; Seidner & Wendler, 1997, p. 180).

The beginning of age-induced decline of physiological functioning is subject to individual differences and cannot be linked to a specific age. In addition, the amount of age-related changes and their significance for musical activities differ widely and depend also on other factors such as the level of musical training. For example, due to their maintenance practice, professional piano players are less affected by the decline of manual abilities than untrained amateurs of similar ages (Krampe, 1994; Krampe & Ericsson, 1996).

General Conditions of Aging: Cultural Aspects

Whereas the influence of biological aspects in the changes of function increases with age, the opposite is true for cultural influences. Even though the direct influence of culture on development lessens as an individual matures, existing differences in musical development, which stem from the time of childhood and adolescence, give rise to continuously increasing differences in the course of adulthood. This becomes obvious when professional musicians are compared to amateurs and people who are untrained in music. Musicians broaden the gap between themselves and less trained individuals through constant work and further development, while nonmusicians suffer a continuous decline because of their different professions and other activities. This means that developmental courses of professional musicians and amateurs point in opposite directions.

Creative Productivity of Composers Over Their Lifetimes

One of the first studies on the life-span development of creative work was carried out by Charlotte Bühler (1933/ 1959). Depending on the domain, different trajectories and peaks of creativity were found. An early study by Lehman and Ingerham (1939) showed that the peak of creativity for composers of classical music was reached between the ages 35 and 45. However, the age with the highest productivity seemed to depend on the specific musical genre. For instance, the peak for instrumental music occurred between the ages of 25 and 29, while most of the operas were composed between the ages of 35 and 40. Similar differences were encountered that concerned other musical forms, like symphonic music, chamber music, and sacred music. Using a different methodology, Dennis (1966) obtained converging results. For example, composers of chamber music reached their creative peaks between the ages of 30 and 39, whereas composers of operas had their highest productivity between the ages of 40 and 49. A remaining methodological problem of these studies is how to define and measure musical creativity if one does not only want to consider the number of compositions but also quality and other aspects (cf. Gembris, 1998, p. 383).

More recently, a barrage of studies by Simonton have investigated the possible influences of culture, society, history, and biographical situation on creative productivity (e.g., Simonton, 1997, for a review). Based on his work, the author put forth a mathematical model that suggests that the lifetime trajectory of musical productivity (composition) could be represented by a tilted J-shaped function. Hence, the creative process rises quickly up to a peak that falls around the age of 40 (give or take a few years depending on the musical genre), after which there is a steady decrease. Of course, these kinds of statistical and graphic representations of creative productivity over the life span are idealized and based on averages. Given that individual differences of adults increase with age (see earlier), actual composers can differ from one another to a large extent.

Developmental Trajectories of Professional Instrumentalists

The social and individual preconditions for musical careers have been addressed in a number of studies by Manturzewska (1990, 1995). She examined the careers of 165 successful Polish musicians of different generations. The data collected consisted mainly of biographical interviews supplemented by archival material and quantitative data. Sosniak's (1985) studies of the careers of pianists were also based on biographical interviews.

Manturzewska (1995) identified six stages in the careers of professional instrumentalists in Western art music and characterized those according to the activities undertaken by the instrumentalists during those phases. The final phase after skill acquisition and a life of concertizing was marked by the fact that professional musicians turned to teaching as their main activity (see also chap. 30 in this volume for a broader discussion of skill acquisition). In another study among retired members of a first-class American orchestra, D. W. E. Smith (1988) observed that most of the musicians stopped playing completely. Due to a lack of motivation, they gave up regular practice and their performance no longer met their expectations. Furthermore, health problems may have resulted from giving up musical activities (cf. Darrough & Boswell, 1992, for a review).

The developmental stages that Manturzewska (1995) observed for outstanding musicians and that Sosniak (1985) described for concert pianists cannot be generalized to all professional musicians. The data are based on exceptional and successful musicians. Nowadays musicians' careers change structurally because many instrumentalists or singers do not hold steady jobs anymore. Instead, they earn a living with multiple and frequently changing jobs that may include nonmusical ones. In addition, becoming a professional musician through a conservatory degree does not necessarily mean that one will be working as a musician throughout the whole professional life. Both tendencies are supported by empirical data (Gembris, in prep.; HEFCE), and the consequences for the musicians' personal and professional identity as well as for the development of musical abilities have yet to be explored.

Maintaining High Performance in Old Age Through Practicing

A study among younger (average age: 24) and older (average age: 60) amateur and professional pianists was carried out by Krampe (1994; see also Krampe & Ericsson, 1996), who provided evidence that continuous musical activity counteracted the decline of musical performance in old age. Famous piano players like Artur Rubinstein (1887–1982) and Vladimir Horowitz (1903–1989), who still played concerts and produced records when they were more than 80 years old, illustrate that even very old persons can produce outstanding instrumental achievements. However, the examples mentioned are rare exceptions, and normally age-related declines cannot be prevented. It is possible to ameliorate the situation through the use of deliberate strategies like optimization, selection, and compensation (cf. Baltes & Baltes, 1989). Baltes, Lindenberger, and Staudinger (1998) offer the following interpretation of a television interview given by the 80-year-old Rubinstein:

> First, Rubinstein said that he played fewer pieces (selection); second, he indicated that he now practices these pieces more often (optimization); and third, he said that to counteract his loss in mechanical speed he now used a kind of impression management such as introducing slower play before fast segments, so to make the latter appear faster (compensation). (p. 1055)

However, it is likely that only pianists and conductors can maintain these kinds of outstanding results at old age, while it might be impossible for woodwind, brass, or string players. Those will be affected earlier by the decrease of sensorimotor functions as a result of aging. Additional problems for violin players that would lead to weaknesses in intonation and bowing could be the decline of the sense of touch along with the reduction of the skin's sensibility and reduced agility and speed.

Even though biological changes of the voice are also unavoidable, singers can work against them to a certain degree. Sataloff (1992, p. 20) suggests that in order to maintain a good physical condition it is necessary to exercise. Also, regular technical practice eliminates undesirable tremolo and improves the smoothness, exactness, and stamina of the voice for old as well as for young singers. According to Sataloff, many functions of the voice could be maintained at higher levels much longer than it is generally believed. Thus a singing career could possibly be extended beyond the age of 60 and into the seventh decade of life.

Musical Learning of Adult Amateurs and Nonmusicians: Cognitive Aspects

Findings on the development of musical abilities and interests of adult amateurs and nonmusicians are still inconclusive. Some authors have examined musical learning in areas including instrumental playing, sight-reading or sight-singing, rhythmic-melodic imitation, and aural training (Gibbons, 1983). The hypothesis that performance generally decreases with age is not supported by these studies (e.g., Klüppelholz, 1993). Even though learning might be more difficult in middle-aged and old-age groups, the overall achievements remained the same. In general, musical learning seems to be possible at every age.

Low self-confidence with regard to one's own musical performance and learning capabilities due to age may be more detrimental to a positive musical development than the actual decline of learning abilities. A fresh evaluation of one's own expectations, along with the idea that making music is enjoyable and requires neither high-level performance skills nor great talent, may provide a suitable basis for successful learning. Optimistically speaking, most of the older people have a considerable potential quite comparable to that of younger people and this can be activated by learning, practice, and deliberate training (Baltes & Baltes, 1989, p. 90; Staudinger, Cornelius, & Baltes, 1989). At the same time, these capacities do have limitations that cannot be altered even by intensive training (Baltes & Kliegl, 1992). There is no reason to assume that these capacities do not exist for musical abilities. On the contrary, current studies with adult nonmusicians demonstrate the possibility of learning new musical abilities with appropriate training. According to Gordon (1987), only very few people make use of all their existing capacities for musical abilities.

A number of studies clearly point to the fact that limitations to musical achievement are likely to increase with age (as far as psychomotor skills go). Older people need more time and more repetitions than younger individuals to attain the same level of performance (Mack, 1982). Also, a poorer musical long-term memory was observed by Bartlett and Snelus (1980). Finally, D. S. Smith (1991) examined the short-term memory of older people. Depending on their health status and social living conditions, memory capacities turned out to vary greatly. On the whole, these and other studies demonstrate that the decline of short-term memory of old people also applies to music, while significant interindividual differences can occur.

Although adults do not seem to be at a larger disadvantage in the cognitive domain than children and adolescents, their learning potential for instrumental technique is clearly limited (Klüppelholz, 1993). It would be possible to detail the difference between children's and adults' instrumental achievements by applying a "testing-the-limits" paradigm, an approach already applied to cognitive abilities (Baltes et al., 1998, p. 1066). However, no such studies in music have yet been carried out.

Adults who want to learn music have different motivations, learning styles, and learning difficulties from those of children. They tend to address their learning tasks primarily cognitively. It is common for adults to start to learn an instrument because they want to play in an ensemble or because they want to create new social contacts. Indeed, making music increases well-being and contributes to a balanced personality (Klüppelholz, 1993). The actual level of achievement and the desire to perform as a soloist are less important. Taking into account what we know about adult cognition and motivation is important for designing appropriate educational goals and methods.

Preferences During Adulthood

Most studies on musical preferences focus on the time of adolescence. The few existing studies on old people's preferences have emerged from the context of music therapy. Their results have been used for developing music programs in retirement homes and musicotherapeutic interventions. It became obvious from these studies that musical preferences primarily depended on the age and also on the social class. The effect of the chronological age on a person's musical preferences is mixed as well with the effects of the present point of time and with the effects of belonging to a specific generation (cohort). Therefore, age effects on musical preferences of adults should be viewed as a result of a combination of these three factors.

Musical preferences primarily depend on the individual and social functions of music. Thus the developmental perspective has to take into account age-related functions of music and age-related changes of functions (cf. Dollase et al., 1986; Mende, 1991). Lehmann (1994) showed convincingly that not only preferences changed with age but also the reasons for listening to music and the approaches to music. For example, with increasing age physiological and motor aspects relinquished their importance to the need for relaxation and empathy (Lehmann, 1994, p. 176).

A number of studies have demonstrated that older people, depending on their educational level and social environment, disliked current popular music and instead preferred other musical styles like country music, classical music, or traditional jazz. Quite often, older people's favorite music was the popular music of their youth (e.g. Gibbons, 1977; Holbrook & Schindler, 1989; Jonas, 1991; Moore et al., 1992). They also tended to prefer lower sound volumes and slower musical tempi (Moore et al., 1992).

Affective processes also undergo a lifelong development, as does the ability to recognize emotional expression in music. Current findings based on psychological data suggest that older persons experience fundamental emotions at a generally lower level of intensity than younger persons and that, in the case of geriatric patients, they show a decline in recognition of facial expression (Brosgole et al., 1983; Brosgole, Kurucz, Plahovinsak, Sprotte, & Havelihwala, 1983; Filipp, 1996). Complex emotions like those that arise from a musical experience have not yet been examined.

Even though experimental studies on the recognition of musical expression and on the ability to experience music in adulthood and old age are lacking, we can still derive some hypotheses for future research. The recognition of musical expression and the ability to experience music ought to depend on general factors (e.g. health status, social environment, etc.). Also, the development of recognition of musical expression is likely to be influenced by how much time a person devotes to music, if he or she is listening to music or actively making music, and if music in general holds a special status in that person's life. Just as existing abilities in other areas disappear as a result of lack of use and training, it is likely that musical abilities will decrease (disengagement or disuse hypothesis). This explanation could serve as a good reason for a lifelong active contact with music, especially since research on emotion has shown that even the most brilliant intelligence is hampered by the lack of emotional abilities (e.g., Damasio, 1997). Thus music seems to be an agreeable way to create and to maintain rich emotional experiences over the lifetime.

Conclusion

Considering the large individual differences in the musical development, the future psychology of life-span development of musical abilities will have to be a differential psychology. There is no such thing as a "normal" or average musical biography. For adult age in particular, it would appear to be more promising to focus on the existing diversity instead of trying to establish an "average."

Developmental psychology of music should not focus only on those cognitive or instrumental abilities that are readily measured. Instead, the ability to experience music, musical skills, and attitudes are also part of the musical development. Furthermore, changes of musical desires, interests, and motivations take place throughout life. Thus what we mean by *musical development* may be entirely different at different stages of life. While the first 10 years of life consist of the acquisition of basic musical abilities, musical development during adulthood possibly includes an expansion of musical preferences and the growth of musical understanding. Therefore, the notion of musical development as a continuum will in itself have to be reconsidered and subsequently expanded.

The idea of optimization through selection and compensation (see Baltes et al., 1998) and the concept of plasticity should provide new starting points for research on musical development. During adulthood or old age, musical activities are not merely leisure activities but rather play an important role in an individual's life as they help form identities, establish and maintain social contacts, and activate cognitive and emotional functions. Thereby musical activities contribute to a person's quality of life and well-being. Studies in the context of music therapy showed that the use of music in nursing homes and in geriatrics had a positive effect on cognitive functioning such as memory, mobilization, and social behavior (e.g., Clair & Bernstein, 1990; Pollack & Namazi, 1992; Prickett & Moore, 1991; Whitcomb, 1994). Although more research is badly needed, these facts illustrate the great importance of musical activities, especially during late adulthood and old age. As the number of older people in our society increases, the research results mentioned earlier will gain political importance, because if musical activities increase the quality of life and have positive effects on health, then they are extremely useful to society.

Encouraging musical learning in childhood and adolescence is an investment sure to produce long-term benefits at more mature ages. Even if no explicit support of the musical development has taken place during the early part of life, musical learning, musical activities, and some musical development are still possible during adulthood. Thus we can agree with the composer Robert Schumann who, in his musical rules for home and life ("Musikalische Haus- und Lebensregeln"), stated that "there is no end to learning."

NOTE

I am grateful to Mirjam Schlemmer and Jan Hemming for their indefatigable help with the English manuscript and the reviewers for their insightful comments.

REFERENCES

Baacke, D. (1993). Jugendkulturen und Musik. In H. Bruhn, R. Oerter, & H. Rösing, (Eds.), *Musikpsychologie: Ein Handbuch* (pp. 228–237). Reinbek, Germany: Rororo.

Baltes, P. B., & Baltes, M. M. (1989). Optimierung durch Selektion und Kompensation: Ein psychologisches Modell erfolgreichen Alterns. *Zeitschrift für Pädagogik, 35,* 85–105.

Baltes, P. B., & Kliegl, R. (1992). Further testing of limits of cognitive plasticity: Negative age differences in a mnemonic skill are robust. *Developmental Psychology, 28,* 121–125.

Baltes, P. B., Lindenberger, U., & Staudinger, U. M. (1998). Life-span theory in developmental psychology. In W. Damon & R. M. Lerner (Eds.), *Handbook of child psychology: Vol. 1. Theoretical models of human development* (5th ed.) (pp. 1029–1143). New York: Wiley.

Bamberger, J. (1991). *The mind behind the musical ear: How children develop musical intelligence.* Cambridge, MA: Harvard University Press.

Bartlett, J. C., & Snelus, P. (1980). Lifespan memory for popular songs. *American Journal of Psychology, 93,* 551–560.

Bastian, H. G. (1989). *Leben für Musik. Eine Biographie-Studie über musikalische (Hoch-) Begabungen.* [A life for music: A biographical study on high ability in music]. Mainz, Genmany: Schott.

Behne, K.-E. (1974). Psychologische Aspekte der Musikalität. In *Forschung in der Musikerziehung* (pp. 74–94) Mainz, Germany: Schott.

Behne, K.-E. (1986). *Hörertypologien: Zur Psychologie des jugendlichen Musikgeschmacks.* Regensburg, Germany: Bosse.

Behne, K.-E. (1997). The development of "Musikerleben" in adolescence: How and why young people listen to music. In I. Deliège & J. Sloboda (Eds.), *Perception and cognition of music* (pp. 143–159) Hove, UK: Psychology Press.

Behrens, G. A., & Green, S. B. (1993). The ability to identify emotional content of solo improvisations performed vocally and on three different instruments. *Psychology of Music, 21,* 20–33.

Birren, J. E., & Schaie, K. W. (Eds.). (1996). *Handbook of the psychology of aging* (4th ed.). San Diego, CA: Academic Press.

Brosgole, L., Kurucz, J., Plahovinsak, T. J., Boettcher, P., Sprotte, C., & Haveliwala, Y. A. (1983). Facial-affect recognition in normal pre-school children and in elderly persons. *International Journal of Neuroscience, 20*(1–2), 91–102.

Brosgole, L., Kurucz, J., Plahovinsak, T. J., Sprotte, C., & Haveliwala, Y. A. (1983). Facial and postural-affect recognition in senile elderly persons. *International Journal of Neuroscience, 22*(1–2), 37–46.

Bühler, C. (1959). *Der menschliche Lebenslauf als psychologisches Problem* (2nd. ed.). Göttingen, Germany: Hogrefe. (Original work published 1933)

Case, R. (1998). The development of conceptual structures. In W. Damon, D. Kuhn, & R. Siegler (Eds.), *Handbook of child psychology: Vol. 2. Cognition, perception and language* (5th ed., pp. 745–800). New York: Wiley.

Clair, A., & Bernstein, B. (1990). A comparison of singing, vibrotactile, and nonvibrotactile instrumental playing responses in severely regressed persons with dementia of the Alzheimer's type. *Journal of Music Therapy, 27,*(3), 119–125.

Cunningham, J. G., & Sterling, R. S. (1988). Developmental change in the understanding of affective meaning in music. *Motivation and Emotion, 12,*(4), 399–413.

Damasio, A. R. (1997). *Denken, Fühlen und das menschliche Gehirn.* Munich, Germany: dtv.

Darrough, G. P., & Boswell, J. (1992). Older adult participants in music: A review of related literature. *Council for Research in Music Education, Bull. no. 111,* 1–24.

Davidson, L. (1994). Songsinging by young and old: A developmental approach to music. In R. Aiello (Ed.), *Musical perceptions* (pp. 99–130). New York: Oxford University Press.

Davidson, L., & Scripp, L. (1990). Education and development in music from a cognitive perspective. In D. J. Hargreaves (Ed.), *Children and the arts* (pp. 59–86). Philadelphia: Open University Press.

Davidson, L., & Scripp, L. (1992). Surveying the coordinates of cognitive skills in music. In R. J. Colwell, (Ed.), *Handbook of research on music teaching and learning: A project of the Music Educators National Conference* (pp. 392–413). New York: Schirmer Books.

Davidson, L., & Welsh, P. (1988). From collection to structure. The developmental path of tonal thinking. In J. A. Sloboda (Ed.), *Generative processes in music: The psychology of performance, improvisation, and composition* (pp. 260–285). Oxford: Clarendon Press.

DeCasper, A. J., & Spence, M. J. (1986). Prematernal speech influences newborn's perception of speech sounds. *Infant Behavior and Development 9*, 133–150.

Deliège, I., Mélen, M., & Bertrand, D. (1995). *Development of music perception: An integrative view.* Paper presented at the Seventh European Conference on Developmental Psychology (pp. 23–27). Kraków, Poland.

Demany, L., & Armand, F. (1984). The perceptual reality of tone chroma in early infancy. *Journal of the Acoustical Society of America, 76* (1), 57–66.

Dennis, W. (1966). Creative productivity between the ages of 20 and 80 years. *Journal of Gerontology, 21*, 1–8.

Dolgin, K., & Adelson, E. (1990). Age changes in the ability to interpret affect in sung and instrumentally-presented melodies. *Psychology of Music, 18*, 87–98.

Dollase, R. (1997). Musikpräferenzen und Musikgeschmack Jugendlicher. In D. Baacke, (Ed.), *Handbuch Jugend und Musik* (pp. 341–368). Opladen, Germany: Leske + Burich.

Dollase, R., Rüsenberg, M., & Stollenwerk, H. J. (1986). *Demoskopie im Konzertsaal.* Mainz, Germany: Schott.

Dowling, W. J., & Harwood, D. L. (1986). *Musical cognition.* Orlando, FL: Academic Press.

Dowling, W. J. (1988). Tonal structure and children's early learning of music. In J. A. Sloboda (Ed.), *Generative processes in music: The psychology of performance, improvisation, and composition* (pp. 113–128). Oxford: Clarendon Press.

Dowling, W. J. (1999). The development of music perception and cognition. In D. Deutsch (Ed.), *The psychology of music* (2nd ed., pp. 603–627). San Diego, CA: Academic Press.

Elbert, T., Pantev, C., Wienbruch, C., Rockstroh, B., & Taub, E. (1995). Increased cortical representation of the fingers of the left hand in string players. *Science, 270*, 305–307.

Ericsson, K. A., Krampe, R. T, & Tesch-Römer, C. (1993). The role of deliberate practice in the acquisition of expert performance. *Psychological Review, 100*(3), 363–406.

Fassbender, C. (1996). Infants' auditory sensitivity towards acoustic parameters of speech and music. In I. Deliège & J. A. Sloboda, (Eds.), *Musical beginnings: Origins and development of musical competence* (pp. 56–87). Oxford: Oxford University Press.

Feijoo, J. (1981). Le foetus Pierre et le loup: Ou une approche originale de l'audition prenatale humaine. In E. Herbinet & M. C. Busnel (Eds.), *L'aube des Sens* (pp. 192–209). Paris: Stock.

Filipp, S. H. (1996). Motivation and emotion. In J.-E. Birren & K. W. Schaie (Eds.), *Handbook of the psychology of aging* (4th ed., pp. 218–235) San Diego, CA: Academic Press.

Finnäs, L. (1989, Fall). How can musical preferences be modified? *Council for Research in Music Education, Bull. no. 102*, 1–58.

Flammer, A. (1996) *Entwicklungstheorien: Psychologische Theorien der menschlichen Entwicklung* (2nd ed.). Bern, Switzerland: Huber.

Flowers, P. J., & Costa-Giomi, E. (1991). Verbal and nonverbal identification of pitch changes in a familiar song by English- and Spanish-speaking preschool children. *Council for Research in Music Education, Bull. no. 107* 1–12.

Fox, D. B. (1990). An analysis of the pitch characteristics of infant vocalizations. *Psychomusicology, 9*, 21–30.

Gardner, H. (1991). *The unschooled mind.* New York: Basic Books.

Gembris, H. (1995). Musikpräferenzen, Generationswandel und Medienalltag. [Music preferences, change of generation and everyday life with media]. In G. Maas (Ed.), *Musiklernen und Neue (Unterrichts-) Technologien*, Musikpädagogische Forschung, Vol. 16 (pp. 124–145). Essen, Germany: Die blaue Eule.

Gembris, H. (1997). Time specific and cohort specific influences on musical development. *Polish Quarterly of Developmental Psychology, 3*(1), 77–89.

Gembris, H. (1998). *Grundlagen musikalischer Begabung und Entwicklung* [Foundations of musical talent and development]. Augsburg, Germany: Wissner.

Gembris, H. (in prep.). The Alumni Project: The professional development of recent graduates from German music academies. In J. Davidson & H. Eiholzer (Eds.), *The music practioneer: Exploring practices and research in the development of the expert music performer, teacher and listener.*

Gembris, H., & Davidson, J. (2002). The role of the environment in musical development. In R. Parncutt & G. E. McPherson (Eds.), *The science and psychology of musical performance* (17–30). New York: Oxford University Press.

Gerard, C., & Auxiette, C. (1992). The processing of musical prosody by musical and non-musical children. *Music Perception, 10*, 93–126.

Gibbons, A. C. (1977). Popular music preferences of elderly people. *Journal of Music Therapy, 14*(4), 180–189.

Gibbons, A. C. (1983). Primary measures of music audiation scores in an institutionalized elderly population. *Journal of Music Therapy, 20*(1), 21–29.

Giomo, C. J. (1993). An experimental study of children's sensitivity to mood in music. *Psychology of Music, 21*, 141–162.

Goetze, M., Cooper, N., & Brown, C. J. (1990). Recent research on singing in the general music classroom. *Council for Research in Music Education, Bull. no. 104*, 16–37.

Gordon, E. E. (1981). Wie Kinder Klänge als Musik wahrnehmen. Eine Längsschnittuntersuchung zur musikalischen Begabung. In K.-E. Behne (Ed.), *Musikalische Sozialisation: Musikpädagogische Forschung*, (Vol. 2, pp. 30–63). Laaber, Germany: Laaber Verlag.

Gordon, E. E. (1987). *The nature, description, measurement, and evaluation of music aptitudes.* Chicago: GIA.

Gordon, E. E. (1990). *A music learning theory for newborn and young children.* Chicago: GIA.

Graml, K., Kraemer, R. D., & Gembris, H. (1988). Filmdokumentation Musikpädagogische Forschung "Der Feuervogeltest": Studien zum musikalischen Gedächtnis. In C.

Nauck-Börner (Ed., Arbeitskreis Musikpädagogische Forschung), *Musikpädagogische Forschung* (Vol. 9, pp. 163–178). Laaber, Germany: Laaber Verlag.

Green, L. (1997). *Music, gender, education.* Cambridge, UK: Cambridge University Press.

Grimmer, F. (1991). *Wege und Umwege zur Musik: Klavierausbildung und Lebensgeschichte.* Kassel, Germany: Bärenreiter.

Gromko, J. E. (1994). Children's invented notations as measures of musical understanding. *Psychology of Music, 22,* 136–147.

Haack, P. (1992). The aquisition of listening skills. In R. J. Colwell (Ed.), *Handbook of research on music teaching and learning: A project of the Music Educators National Conference* (pp. 451–465). New York: Schirmer Books.

Habermann, G. (1986). *Stimme und Sprache: Eine Einführung in ihre Physiologie und Hygiene* (2nd ed.). Stuttgart, Germany: Thieme.

Haith, M. M., & Benson, J. B. (1998). Infant cognition. In D. Kuhn & R. S. Siegler (Eds.), *Handbook of child psychology: Vol. 2. Cognition, perception, and language* (5th ed., pp. 199–254). New York: Wiley.

Hargreaves, D. J. (1982). The development of aesthetic reaction to music [Special issue], *Psychology of Music, 51–54.*

Hargreaves, D. J. (1986). *The developmental psychology of music.* Cambridge: Cambridge University Press.

Hargreaves, D. J. (1996). The development of artistic and musical development. In I. Deliège & J. A. Sloboda, (Eds.), *Musical beginnings: Origins and development of musical competence* (pp. 145–170). Oxford: Oxford University Press.

Hargreaves, D. J., Comber, C., & Colley, A. (1996). Effects of age, gender, and training on musical preferences of British secondary school students. *Journal of Research in Music Education, 44*(3), 242–250.

Hassler, M. (1991). Maturation rate and spatial, verbal, and musical abilities: A seven-year longitudinal study. *International Journal of Neuroscience, 58,* 183–198.

Hassler, M. (1992). The critical teens: Musical capacities change in adolescence. *European Journal of High Ability, 3,* 89–98.

Hemming, J., & Kleinen, G. (1999). The beginning of musical careers in jazz, rock & pop: A practice diary study among school bands. In N. Jeanneret & K. Marsch (Eds.), *Opening the umbrella: An encompassing view of music education: Proceedings of the 12th National Conference of the Australian Society for Music Education (ASME)* (pp. 69–75). Baulkham Hills, Australia: Margret McMurtry.

Hepper, P. G. (1991). An examination of foetal learning before and after birth. *Irish Journal of Psychology, 12,* 95–107.

HEFCE [Higher Education Funding Council for England]. (1998). Report 98/11. Retrieved January 15, 2001, from http://www.hefce.ac.uk/pubs/hefce/1998/98_11.htm

Holbrook, M. B., & Schindler, R. M. (1989, June). Some exploratory findings on the development of musical tastes. *Journal of Consumer Research, 16,* 119–124.

Huston, A. C., & Wright, J. C. (1998). Contributions of television toward meeting the informational and educational needs of children. *The Annals of the American Academy of Political and Social Science, 557,* 9–23.

Imberty, M. (1969). *L'acquisition des structures tonales chez l'enfant.* Paris: Klincksieck.

Jennen, M., & Gembris, H. (2000). Veränderungen des musikalischen Tempos bei Dirigenten: Eine empirische Untersuchung anhand von Schallplattenaufnahmen von Mozarts "Don Giovanni" und "Die Zauberflöte." In K.-E. Behne, G. Kleinen, & H. de la Motte-Haber, (Eds.), *Musikpsychologie: Bd. 15. Die Musikerpersönlichkeit* (pp. 29–46). Göttingen, Germany: Hogrefe.

Jonas, J. L. (1991). Preferences of elderly music listeners residing in nursing homes for art music, traditional jazz, popular music of today, and country music. *Journal of Music Therapy, 28*(3), 149–160.

Jørgensen, H., & Lehmann, A. C. (Eds.). (1997). *Does practice make perfect? Current theory and research on instrumental music practice.* Oslo: Norwegian State Academy of Music.

Kastner, M., & Crowder, R. G. (1990). Perception of the major/minor distinction. IV. Emotional connotation in young children. *Music Perception, 8*(2), 189–202.

Kelley, L., & Sutton-Smith, B. (1987). A study of infant musical productivity. In J. C. Peery, I. Weiss Peery, & T. W. Draper (Eds.), *Music and child development* (pp. 35–53). New York: Springer.

Kemp, A. (1996). *The musical temperament: Psychology and personality of musicians.* Oxford: Oxford University Press.

Klüppelholz, W. (1993). *Projekt Musikalische Erwachsenenbildung an Musikschulen, 1990–1992: Abschlussbericht der wissenschaftlichen Begleitung.* Bonn, Germany: Verband Deutscher Musikschulen.

Krampe, R. T. (1994). *Studien und Berichte des Max-Planck-Instituts für Bildungsforschung: Vol. 58. Maintaining excellence: Cognitive-motor performance in pianists differing in age and skill level.* Berlin, Germany: Vertries edition sigma.

Krampe, R. T., & Ericsson, K. A. (1996). Maintaining excellence: Deliberate practice and elite performance in young and older pianists. *Journal of Experimental Psychology: General 125,* 331–359.

Kratus, J. (1993). A developmental study of children's interpretation of emotion in music. *Psychology of Music, 21,* 3–19.

Lamont, A. (1998). Music, education, and the development of pitch perception: The role of context, age and musical experience. *Psychology of Music, 26,* 7–25.

LeBlanc, A. (1991). *Effect of maturation/age on music listening preference: A review of literature.* Paper presented at the Ninth National Symposium on Research in Music Behavior, Cannon Beach, OR.

Lecanuet, J.-P. (1996). Prenatal auditory experience. In I. Deliège & J. A. Sloboda (Eds.), *Musical beginnings: Origins and development of musical competence* (pp 3–34). Oxford: Oxford University Press.

Lehmann, A. C. (1994). *Habituelle und situative Rezeptionsweisen beim Musikhören: Eine einstellungstheoretische Untersuchung* [Habitual and situational music listening patterns]. Frankfurt, Germany: Peter Lang.

Lehman, H. C., & Ingerham, D. W. (1939). Man's creative years in music. *Scientific Monthly, 48,* 431–443.

Lynch, M. P. (1993). Prototypical representations of musical structure in infancy: Theoretical exploration and a pilot study. *Psychomusicology, 12,* 31–40.

Lynch, M. P., & Eilers, R. E. (1991). Children's perception of native and nonnative musical scales. *Music Perception, 9*(1), 121–132.

Lynch, M. P., Eilers, R. E., Oller, D. K., & Urbano, R. C. (1990). Innateness, experience, and music perception. *Psychological Science, 1*(4), 272–276.

Mack, L. S. (1982). *Self-concept and musical achievement in the adult learner.* Unpublished dissertation, University of Illinois at Urbana-Champaign.

Maidlow, S., & Bruce, R. (1999). The role of psychology research in understanding the sex-gender paradox in music—Plus ça change. *Psychology of music 27*(2), 147–158.

Maier, K., Ambühl-Caesar, G., & Schandry R. (1994). *Entwicklungspsychophysiologie: Körperliche Indikatoren psychischer Entwicklung.* Munich, Germany: Beltz Psychologie Verlags Union.

Manturzewska, M. (1990). A biographical study of the lifespan development of professional musicians. *Psychology of Music, 18,* 112–138.

Manturzewska, M. (1995). A biographical study of the lifespan development of professional musicians. In M. Manturzewska, K. Miklaszewski, & A. Bialkowski (Eds.), *Psychology of music today (Proceedings of the International Seminar of Researchers and Lecturers in the Psychology of Music)* (pp. 311–337). Radziejowice, Poland: Warsaw Fryderyk Chopin Academy of Music.

Martin, G., Clarke, M., & Pearse, C. (1993). Adolescent suicide: Music preference as an indicator of vulnerability. *Journal of the Academy of Child and Adolescent Psychiatry, 32*(2), 530–535.

Meltzoff, A. N., Kuhl, P., & Moore, M. K. (1991). Perception, representation, and the control of action in newborn and young infants towards a new synthesis. In M. J. S. Weiss & P. R. Zelazo (Eds.), *Newborn attention: Biological constraints and the influence of experience* (pp. 377–411). Norwood, NJ: Ablex.

Mende, A. (1991). Musik und Alter: Ergebnisse zum Stellenwert von Musik im biographischen Lebensverlauf. *Rundfunk und Fernsehen, 39*(3), 381–392.

Metzler, F. (1962). Strukturen kindlicher Melodik. *Psychologische Beiträge, 7,* 218–284.

Minkenberg, H. (1991). *Das Musikerleben von Kindern im Alter von fünf bis zehn Jahren.* Frankfurt, Germany: Peter Lang.

Montgomery, A. P. (1996). Effect of tempo on music preferences of children in elementary and middle school. *Journal of Research in Music Education, 44*(2), 134–146.

Moog, H. (1976). *The musical experience of the pre-school child* (C. Clarke, Trans.). London: Schott.

Moore, R. S., Staum, M. J., & Brotons, M. (1992). Music preferences of the elderly: Repertoire, vocal ranges, tempos, and accompaniments for singing. *Journal of Music Therapy, 29*(4), 236–252.

Morrongiello, B. A. (1992). Effects of training on children's perception of music: A review. *Psychology of Music, 20,* 29–41.

Müler, R. (1999). Musikalische Selbstsozialisation. In J. Fromme, S. Kommer, J. Mansel, & K.-P. Treumann (Ed.), *Selbstsozialisation, Kinderkultur und Mediennutzung* (pp. 113–125). Opladen, Germany: Leske + Budrich.

Nelson, D. (1987). An interpretation of the Piagetian model in light of the theories of Case. *Council for Research in Music Education, Bull. no. 92,* 23–34.

Papoušek, H. (1996). Musicality in infancy research: Biological and cultural origins of early musicality. In I. Deliège & J. A. Sloboda (Eds.), *Musical beginnings: Origins and development of musical competence* (pp. 37–55). Oxford: Oxford University Press.

Papoušek, M. (1994). *Vom ersten Schrei zum ersten Wort. Anfänge der Sprachentwicklung in der vorsprachlichen Kommunikation* [From the first cry to the first word. Beginnings of language development in the pre-verbal communication]. Bern, Switzerland: Huber.

Papoušek, M. (1996). Intuitive parenting: A hidden source of musical stimulation in infancy. In I. Deliège & J. A. Sloboda (Eds.), *Musical beginnings: Origins and development of musical competence* (pp. 88–112). Oxford: Oxford University Press.

Papoušek, M., & Papoušek, H. (1986). *Structure and dynamics of human communication at the beginning of life.* European Archives of Psychiatry and Neurological Science, vol. 236, no. 1, 21–25.

Park, D., & Schwarz, N. (Eds.). (1999). *Cognitive aging. A primer.* London: Psychology Press.

Pflederer, M. (1964). The responses of children to musical tasks embodying Piaget's principle of conservation. *Journal of Research in Music Education, 12,* 251–268.

Pflederer, M., & Sechrest, L. (1968). Conservation-type responses of children to musical stimuli. *Council for Research in Music Education, Bull. no. 13,* 19–36.

Pollack, N. J., & Namazi, K. H. (1992). The effect of music participation on the social behavior of Alzheimer's disease patients. *Journal of Music Therapy, 29*(1), 54–67.

Pouthas, V. (1996). The development of perception of time and temporal regulation of action in infants and children. In I. Deliège & J. Sloboda (Eds.), *Musical beginnings: Origins and development of musical competence* (pp. 115–141). Oxford: Oxford University Press.

Prickett, C. M., & Moore, R. S. (1991). The use of music to aid memory of Alzheimer's patients. *Journal of Music Therapy, 28*(2), 101–110.

Rainbow, E. (1980). A final report on a three-year investigation of the rhythmic abilities of preschool aged children. *Council for Research in Music Education, Bull. no. 62,* 69–73.

Rainbow, E., & Owen, D. (1979). A progress report on a three-year investigation of the rhythmic ability of preschool aged children. *Council for Research in Music Education, Bull. no. 59,* 84–86.

Ramsey, J. H. (1983). The effects of age, singing ability, and instrumental experiences on preschool children's melodic perception. *Journal of Research in Music Education, 31*, 133–145.

Rauh, H. (1995). Frühe Kindheit. In R. Oerter & L. Montada (Eds.), *Entwicklungspsychologie*, (3rd ed.) (pp. 167–309). Weinheim, Germany: Psychologie Verlags Union.

Sataloff, R. T. (1992). Vocal aging medical considerations in professional voice users. *Medical Problems of Performing Artists, 7*(1), 17–21.

Satt, B. J. (1984). *An investigation into the acoustical induction of intrauterine learning.* Unpublished dissertation, University of California at Los Angeles.

Schellberg, G. (1998). *Zur Entwicklung der Klangfarbenwahrnehmung von Vorschulkindern.* Münster, Germany: Lit Verlag.

Scheuer, W. (1988). *Zwischen Tradition und Trend: Die Einstellung Jugendlicher zum Instrumentalspiel* [Between tradition and trend: Adolescents' attitudes toward playing a musical instrument]. Mainz, Germany: Schott.

Schlaug, G., Jäncke, L., Huang, Y., Staiger, J. F., & Steinmetz, H. (1995). Increased corpus callosum size in musicians. *Neuropsychologia, 33*(8), 1047–1055.

Schwarzer, G. (1997). Analytic and holistic modes in the development of melody perception. *Psychology of Music, 25*, 35–56.

Seidner, W., & Wendler, J. (1997). *Die Sängerstimme: Phoniatrische Grundlagen der Gesangsausbildung* (3rd ed.). Berlin: Henschel.

Shuter-Dyson, R. (1982). Musical ability. In D. Deutsch (Ed.), *The psychology of music* (pp. 391–412). New York: Academic Press.

Shuter-Dyson, R., & Gabriel, C. (1981). *The psychology of musical ability.* London: Methuen.

Simonton, D. K. (1997). Products, persons, and periods: Historiometric analyses of compositional creativity. In D. Hargreaves & A. North (Eds.), *The social psychology of music* (pp. 107–122). Oxford: Oxford University Press.

Sloboda, J., & Davidson, J. (1996). The young performing musician. In I. Deliége & J. Sloboda (Eds.), *Musical beginnings: Origins and development of musical competence* (pp. 171–190). Oxford: Oxford University Press.

Sloboda, J. A., Davidson, F. W., Moore, D., & Howe, M. (1994). Formal practice as a predictor of success and failure in instrumental learning. In I. Deliège (Ed.), *Proceedings of the 3rd International Conference for Music Perception and Cognition* (pp. 124–128). Liège, Belgium: ESCOM (Centre de Recherches et de Formation Musicales de Wallonie).

Smith, D. S. (1991). A comparison of group performance and song familiarity on cued recall tasks with older adults. *Journal of Music Therapy, 28* (1), 2–13.

Smith, D. W. E. (1988). The great symphony orchestra—A relatively good place to grow old. *International Journal of Aging and Human Development, 27*(4), 233–247.

Smith, K. C., Cuddy, L. L., & Upitis, R. (1994). Figural and metric understanding of rhythm. *Psychology of Music, 22*, 117–135.

Sosniak, L. A. (1985). Learning to be a concert pianist. In B. S. Bloom (Ed.), *Developing talent in young people* (pp. 19–67). New York: Ballantine Books.

Spiegler, D. M. (1967). *Factors involved in the development of prenatal rhythmic sensivity.* Unpublished dissertation, West Virginia University.

Stadler, S. (2000). *Spiel und Nachahmung: Über die Entwicklung der elementaren musikalischen Aktivitäten* [Play and imitation: About the development of basic musical activities]. Aarau, Switzerland: Nepomuk.

Staudinger, U. M., Cornelius, S. W., & Baltes, P. B. (1989). The aging of intelligence: Potential and limits. *Annals AAPSS, 503*, 44–58.

Swanwick, K. (1994). *Musical knowledge: Intuition, analysis and music education.* London: Routledge & Kegan Paul.

Swartz, K. P., Walton, J. P., Hantz, E. C., & Goldhammer E. (1994). P3 event-related potentials and performance of young and old subjects for music perception tasks. *International Journal of Neuroscience, 78*, 223–239.

Terwogt, M. M., & van Grinsven, F. (1988). Recognition of emotions in music by children and adults. *Perceptual and Motor Skills, 67*(3), 697–698.

Terwogt, M. M., & van Grinsven, F. (1991). Musical expression of moodstates. *Psychology of Music, 19*, 99–109.

Trainor, L. J., & Trehub, S. E. (1992). The development of referential meaning in music. *Music Perception, 9*(4), 455–470.

Trehub, S. E. (1993). The music listening skills of infants and young children. In T. J. Tighe & W. J. Dowling (Eds.), *Psychology and music: The understanding of melody and rhythm* (pp. 161–176). Hillsdale, NJ: Erlbaum.

Trehub, S. E., Bull, D., & Thorpe, L. A. (1984). Infant's perception of melodies: The role of melodic contour. *Child Development, 55*, 821–830.

Trehub, S., Trainor, L., & Unyk, A. (1993). Music and speech processing in the first year of life. In H. W. Reese (Ed.), *Advances in child development and behavior* (Vol. 24, pp. 1–35). New York: Academic Press.

Trevarthen, C. (1999–2000). Musicality and the intrinsic motive pulse evidence from human psychobiology and infant communication [Special issue], *Musicae Scientiae*, 155–199.

Upitis, R. (1987). Children's understanding of rhythm: The relationship between musical development and music training. *Psychomusicology, 7*(1), 41–60.

Valentine, C. W. (1962). *The experimental psychology of the beauty.* London: Methuen.

Welch, G. F., & White, P. (1994). The developing voice Education and vocal efficiency—A physical perspective. *Council for Research in Music Education, Bull. no. 119*, 146–156.

Werner, H. (1917). Die melodische Erfindung im frühen Kindesalter: Eine entwicklungspsychologische Untersuchung. In *Sitzungsberichte der Kaiserlichen Akademie der Wissenschaften in Wien, Philosophisch-historische Klasse* (Vol. 182, pp. 1–100). Vienna: Tempsky.

Whitcomb, J. B. (1994). "I would weave a song for you." Therapeutic music and milieu for dementia residents. *Activities, Adaptation and Aging, 18*(2), 57–74.

Wolff, P. H. (1969). The natural history of crying and other vocalizations in early infancy. In B. Foss (Ed.), *Determi-*

nants of infant behavior (Vol. 4) (pp. 81–109). London: Methuen.

Young, L. P. (1982). *An investigation of young children's music concept development using nonverbal and manipulative techniques.* Unpublished dissertation, Ohio State University.

Zenatti, A. (1993). Children's musical cognition and taste. In T. J. Tighe & W. J. Dowling (Eds.), *Psychology and music: The understanding of melody and rhythm* (pp. 177–196). Hillsdale, NJ: Erlbaum.

Zillman, D., & Gan, S.-L. (1997). Musical taste in adolescence. In D. Hargreaves & A. North (Eds.), *The social psychology of music* (pp. 161–187). Oxford: Oxford University Press.

A Comparative Review of Human Ability Theory

Context, Structure, and Development

28

BRUCE TORFF

A quick look around the world yields abundant examples of impressive human accomplishments. People are able to set new records in athletics, publish groundbreaking scientific works, and produce beautiful and challenging new music and art. Examples such as these raise old and vexing questions about the human abilities involved in complex performances like those in athletics, science, music, and art. To what extent do complex performances require abilities unique to particular domains and disciplines (e.g., language, mathematics)? To what extent are complex performances dependent upon general abilities that cut across domains and disciplines? How and why did abilities take this form, over the aeons? How do abilities change with age and experience? How can they be fostered?

These questions have been tackled over the centuries by a diverse group of psychologists, philosophers, sociologists, anthropologists, educators, and others focused on cognition, learning, development, and education. Historically, complex performances have posed a daunting challenge for these researchers. Accordingly, psychological work in the last century has made more headway with simpler performances that are easily measured, especially ones in laboratory settings that allow researchers to control the context in which tasks and instruments are implemented. Complex performances are far harder to study, and the psychological literature reflects this fact. As a result, practitioners and educators in many disciplines find the psychological literature too remote to be of much value (Egan, 1992).

But in recent decades, new theory and research have offered fresh perspectives on the development and nurturance of human abilities. Since the "cognitive revolution" that began in the late 1950s, attention has focused on the intellectual aspects of performances previously thought to be outside the realm of the cognitive. Traditionally, abilities in disciplines such as athletics, music, and art have been cast as "talents" that are conceptually distinct from "cognitive" abilities such as language and mathematics. The new perspective encompasses the cognitive underpinnings of all human abilities, even in matters athletic and aesthetic. Across the vast range of domains and disciplines, cognitive aspects of performance are coming under scrutiny, with human abilities cast increasingly as developing intellectual competences rather than fixed and innately specified aptitudes. It should be noted that this new body of cognitive work accompanies related investigations by researchers interested in other aspects of human experience, including philosophical, social, affective, moral, and practical ones.

The wealth of new ideas makes it a propitious time for a review of the literature in recent decades, with the goal of addressing anew some old questions about human abilities, especially as they are used in complex performances. It turns out that new theory and research dispute some widely held assumptions about human abilities and their development. In this chapter I review recent trends in theoretical conceptions of human abilities and explore their educational implications.

It may seem strange for this chapter to appear in a handbook on music education, since I make no effort here to examine musical ability specifically. This chapter takes a more general perspective on the abilities that underlie complex performances, for two reasons: to provide a review of theory in the psychological literature that may prove of interest to musical practitioners and educators and to stimulate discussion about the larger framework of which musical abilities are part, especially concerning the extent to which musical ability is unique to the domain of music or linked to other, extramusical abilities.

Psychology of Abilities: Past and Present

No discipline has a longer and more contentious history than studies of the human mind. Beginning perhaps with Plato's *Meno,* two millennia of scholarly attention have focused on the mind's structure, development, and nurturance. For most of this history, the workings of the mind have been viewed as issues of interest largely in the discipline of philosophy. But the industrial revolution brought forth a great flurry of activity in the sciences, and scholars interested in the mind sought "scientific" methods for studying their quarry. Psychology diverged from philosophy in the late 19th century, armed with newly crafted research methods modeled on the hard sciences. The new science of the mind put forward three theoretical models of human abilities.

First, the new focus on instrumentation and research methods led to a particular theoretical/methodological perspective of the mind, one that focused exclusively on observable behavior. This perspective is known variously as *behaviorism* and *learning theory* (e.g., Skinner, 1954; Thorndike, 1932; Watson, 1924). Eschewing constructs that can only be inferred to exist and cannot be observed directly (e.g., cognitive structure, knowledge), behaviorists explain human behavior in terms of the rewards and punishments associated with it. As such, behavior is under the control of externally imposed contingencies of reinforcement, and studying how these contingencies affect behavior is the goal of psychology. From the behaviorist perspective, abilities are patterns in behavior forged by a reinforcement history.

A second theory of human intellect became prominent in the 20th century—the "genetic epistemology" of Piaget, Inhelder, and associates (Piaget, 1983; see Gruber & Voneche, 1977). What is commonly known as *Piagetian theory* posits the mind as a general computational device that develops in predictable stages of development given the right kind of environmental interaction. Terms such as *equilibration, assimilation,* and *accommodation* were coined to describe the psychological processes involved in interaction and stage change. According to Piaget, abilities are outward manifestations of underlying cognitive structures that are innately specified but triggered through action on the environment.

The third theory of the psychology of human abilities is the notion of *general intelligence* (e.g., Eysenck, 1986; Thurstone, 1938). From this viewpoint, the human mind is structured with a single overarching cognitive ability called general intelligence, or *g.* The theory of general intelligence aims to predict individual differences in performance on intelligence tests and tests of other abilities. The high correlations among these various tests, the argument goes, support the claim that a general processing capacity constrains all intelligent action.

For decades, proponents of behaviorism, Piagetian theory, and general intelligence showed little regard for one another's perspective, underscoring the preparadigmatic character of psychological research. No widely accepted paradigm organizes modern psychology, as in physics, for example.

But disparate as these historically important models may be, they have in common a set of three related assumptions about human abilities. First, the three theories focus on the action of individual people. Each assumes that environmental elements such as language and culture have little impact on underlying cognitive structures and processes. Since abilities are viewed as fundamentally context-independent, it follows that the individual mind is the unproblematic unit of analysis for psychological research. Second, the three theories focus on domain-general universals of human development—structures and processes that are common to all individuals and that function similarly in different domains and disciplines. The three theories seek the basic laws of psychology, akin to the basic laws of physics. Third, the three theories assume that cognitive growth and learning occur along a smooth and unimpeded developmental path, given the right care and experiences. This trio of assumptions has done much to frame the debate about the structure and development of human abilities, outline the methods by which abilities have been studied, and establish the pedagogies by which abilities have been nurtured at home and in school.

These assumptions have come under fire in the decades since the cognitive revolution, as the traditional models have waned in influence. In what follows I examine each assumption in turn in light of recent theory and research in human abilities.

Contexualization of Psychological Theory and Research

Surrounding the individual learner is an environment filled with social, physical, and symbolic elements (e.g., languages, tools, notations). These environmental elements form the *context* in which abilities are developed and used. At issue in this section is the role of contextual factors in the structure and development of abilities—and the related methodological point that concerns the appropriate unit of analysis in psychological research.

Behaviorists, Piagetians, and *g* researchers have in common the pursuit of universals of learning and development that operate in all unimpaired individuals in a similar manner across domains and disciplines. Environmental elements are thought to provide the content used by human abilities but not to influence underlying patterns of thought, which are presumed to stem from domain-general structures or processes. It follows from this view that the individual person is the appropriate unit of analysis in psychological research.

Role of Context and Culture in Cognition.   Recent theory and research do not dispute the biological basis of abilities but make a persuasive case for sociocultural factors. There is now a substantial literature that demonstrates striking cultural differences in patterns of thought (see Bakhtin, 1981; Cole, 1996; Hutchins, 1990; Kaiping & Nisbett, 1999; Rogoff, 1990; Torff, 1999a). For example, Asians and Westerners give consistently dissimilar interpretations of a visual display, interpreting the figure-ground relationship in fundamentally different ways (Kaiping & Nisbett, 1999).

A host of similar findings have yielded the broad consensus that abilities are far more context-dependent than previously thought. Environmental elements such as languages and notations influence underlying patterns of thought. Thus the range of factors relevant to studies of human abilities must be expanded to include contextual ones, and the pursuit of universals ought to be viewed in new and less expansive light. After a century of largely ignored calls for a "second psychology" based on culture and context (Cahan & White, 1992), a new view emerged: In the course of development in a culture, the individual is exposed to (and becomes dependent upon) a variety of contextual elements that guide the way the individual mind develops. These contextual elements are products of culture. For a comprehensive understanding of abilities to be crafted, theory and research must take into account the culture in which abilities are created and given meaning.

The emergence of contextualism has coincided with a surge of interest in a sociocultural theory of cognitive development put forth by Vygotsky and independently by Mead in the 1930s (Mead, 1934/1956; Vygotsky, 1978; see also Cole, 1996; Wertsch, 1985). The essence of sociocultural theory is the claim that the mind is socially formed—that is, the structure and function of cognitive abilities are *constituted* by culture as the individual interacts with the sociocultural environment. The individual's performance is supported by a variety of culturally created *mediators,* which include physical tools, social conventions, and symbolic media. Learning (*internalization*) occurs as individuals construct mental representations and habituate actions as guided by mediational elements. According to sociocultural theory, cultural concepts form the foundation of the way individuals make sense of the world, and the individual's thought processes are thus imprinted through interaction with the cultural environment. In recent decades, four new lines of sociocultural theory and research

have appeared, under the headings "Everyday Cognition," "Socially Shared Cognition," "Distributed Cognition," and "Situated Cognition."

Everyday cognition: With the rise of sociocultural theory came a spate of studies of thinking and learning in nonacademic contexts, much of it under the banner of *everyday cognition* (Lave, 1988; Lave & Wenger, 1993; Rogoff & Lave, 1984). Researchers who looked outside the classroom at instances of everyday activity—on the job and at home—found examples of ingenious strategies that people devised to exploit environmental affordances and overcome situational constraints. For example, truck drivers were found to stack milk crates through use of a context-embedded method of counting that is remarkably effective, if remote from the school-oriented approach of making a formal count (Scribner, 1984). Studies of everyday cognition reveal how seldom the strategies people use in life and on the job resemble the formal knowledge taught in schools. Sociocultural theory points up the learning inherent in everyday settings—visiting a restaurant, completing a tax form, programming a VCR. Focusing on the ubiquity of mediators in the world around us, sociocultural theory underscores that learning occurs everywhere, all the time—even when there is no intent to teach or learn. From this perspective, the terms *education, socialization,* and *enculturation* are closely related notions, if not outright synonyms.

Socially shared cognition: Sociocultural theory pays particular attention to one form of cultural mediation—the efforts made and encouragement given by other people. The growing interest in *socially shared cognition* refers to the study of how people come to engage in shared belief (Resnick, Levine, & Teasley, 1991). Apart from knowledge people hold through direct observation, all knowledge is the result of entering into a shared belief with a group of like-minded others called a *community of practice.* According to researchers focused on socially shared cognition, learning occurs when the learner comes to agreement with other people with whom the learner interacts in a community of practice. People in the United States share the belief that John Wilkes Booth assassinated Lincoln because we participate in a community of practice—the one that concerns the historical beliefs of American culture as taught in secondary schools. Of course, such beliefs may later be rethought and changed; as with any other cultural product, beliefs about history are dynamic and evolve as the culture does.

Bruner (1990, 1996) uses the term *intersubjectivity* to describe interactional processes through which individuals come to share beliefs with others. Through intersubjective exchange, Bruner suggests, people fail to arrive at the exact same construal of events but come to enough of a shared understanding to make sense of what's going on and continue the interaction. Intersubjectivity is at the heart of sociocultural theory, because it is shared belief in communities of practice that orients the individual and gives the world meaning.

Distributed cognition: If cognitive activities are shared between person and context, it follows that part of the resources (the "intelligence") required to get something done is handled by the environment, like a sort of prosthetic (Perkins, 1995). In communities of practice, people are assisted by the *intelligences of the cultural environment*—the physical, social, and symbolic elements that do part of the job. Abilities are thus said to be *distributed*—spread between person and environmental elements. For example, lawyers have at their disposal thick books that detail laws and precedents; we expect a lawyer not to memorize everything but to also know how to look things up. From the perspective of distributed-cognition researchers, the abilities needed in law are in part in the practitioners' heads but in part distributed among the various intelligences of the cultural environment.

Situated cognition: A strong form of sociocultural theory has come forward under the headings "situated" and "situative" cognition (Greeno, 1998; Lave & Wenger, 1993; Seely Brown, Collins, & Duguid, 1989). From this perspective, individuals and situations cocreate activity and thus cannot be studied separately. Abilities are seen as outgrowths of particular situational affordances and constraints, and only in context do they make sense. People develop strategies for doing things that depend on a certain context, and only in this context are they able to work without difficulty.

Dependence on situational affordances and constraints means that it is very difficult for individuals to transfer knowledge across contexts, even isomorphic ones. (Every teacher has had the experience of teaching something only to find that the lesson did not transfer as needed to a nearby context.) According to situated-cognition researchers, transfer occurs through generalization of knowledge, but this process can be fraught with difficulty. As a result, people often find it hard to work unless the environmental support is just right. Consider, for example, that there are places to which you are able to drive but to which you are unable to give another person adequate directions. You know the route, but only well enough to get yourself there, as if by "feel." Embedded in the environment are memory cues—environmental objects that, when presented to your senses and intermingled with your memories of the terrain, help you to make all the necessary turns. Memory and learning, it turns out, are not simply mental achievements—they are collaborations between the individual and a particular set of environmental circumstances.

The situative perspective underscores that all learning is a product not only of the person's intellectual efforts but also of whatever situational elements are present when the learning occurs. All learning is thus linked to its situation of origin, and it is of utmost importance for educators and researchers to explore how situational affordances and constraints influence learning.

Abilities as Situated Knowledge and Skill.   Abilities, according to sociocultural theory, are culturally established but individually internalized patterns of knowledge and skill crafted to fit situational affordances and constraints. Some of these constraints and affordances cohere into specific disciplines, (e.g., bowling, psychology), while others are everyday shared ways of doing things (e.g., restaurant scripts). From this perspective, abilities are patterns in socially shared and physically distributed knowledge in a community of practice. As a result, to see all the elements of the working psychological system that supports complex performances, one must look at the larger system, the person and cultural context.

Methodological Implications.   Sociocultural theory also raises new issues, ones that challenge key methodological assumptions in psychology. Years ago it was observed that animals in zoos behave differently from their counterparts in the wild; it follows that human behavior might well be as artificial in typical laboratory experiments in psychology. A concern for "ecological validity" prompts sociocultural psychologists to question the extent to which the bulk of laboratory work in psychology provides an accurate indication of the way people act in the real world (Cole, 1971, 1996). The experimental laboratory is by no means a context-neutral environment; rather, it has a set of procedures, expectations, and scripts all its own. From this perspective, a truer measure of human behavior comes from studies in real-world settings, despite the methodological difficulties involved.

Hence, the unit of analysis in research changes from individual person to *person-in-cultural context.* As a result, many research initiatives have shifted from laboratory settings, where variables can be controlled, to the larger world, where the full range of factors can be addressed. Sociocultural theory has as its burden the need to study processes that are supremely difficult (and often impossible) to operationalize and control. As difficult as it is to do good psychology and sociocultural theory at the same time, this has the benefit of reflecting the full range of influences on human cognition and learning (Olson & Bruner, 1996).

Taking Stock: Contextualization of Theory and Research. Sociocultural theory yields some novel views of how cognition is structured, how it develops, what learning is, and how psychological research ought to proceed. This work rebuts the assumption that abilities are context-independent "talents" undergirded by mental structures that can be teased out for isolated analysis. Sociocultural theory emphasizes that abilities are stitched together by situational elements—products of culture. The view of abilities as situated actions calls into question the assertion that psychological work ought to focus on the functioning of the individual person. Analysis of the person–in–social context is a significant methodological complication but one that promises to provide psychological studies that seem more meaningful to practitioners interested in the abilities used in complex performances.

Human Abilities: Multiple and Interconnected

The second set of recently questioned assumptions about human abilities concerns the *range* of cognitive processes involved in abilities. The three traditional theories have in common a pursuit of overarching domain-general processes, structures, or principles that apply to all areas of human cognition (e.g., spatial cognition, language). Behaviorists posit a single law of learning in which abilities are shaped by contingencies of reinforcement. Piaget's theory views abilities as evidence of domain-general thought processes linked to predictable stagelike developmental changes in underlying cognitive structure. Finally, general-intelligence theorists posit a general cognitive capacity (*g*) that underlies all abilities. The question is, in a nutshell: To what extent are abilities domain-general or domain-specific?

In contrast to the traditional theories, recent theories offer a profusion of "pluralistic" (domain-specific) views. As the following review indicates, this literature is remarkably diverse but with a common thread. Widespread is the view that abilities are supported by a range of cognitive skills, some typically hidden, and these multiple abilities include ones that are particular to a domain (e.g., pitch and rhythm are essential elements of music) as well as cross-domain capacities (e.g., language figures in countless domains). In what follows I describe four bodies of such work: evolutionary psychology, cognitive-developmental psychology, pluralistic models of intelligence, and expertise.

Evolutionary Psychology.   Applying Darwin's work to the evolution of the human mind, evolutionary psychologists examine the adaptive pressures that have caused the mind to develop the way it has over time (see Barkow, Cosmides, & Tooby, 1992). This line of theory and research has included an explicit claim that the human mind is configured with a variety of *modules*—separate, task-specific cognitive abilities that evolved in response to the environmental challenges faced by the human species (Cosmides & Tooby, 1987; Tooby & Cosmides, 1990). Here the mind is considered to be something like a Swiss Army knife, designed with mechanisms specialized to meet the challenges that have arisen in particular environments. According to evo-

lutionary psychologists, these modules are numerous and include innately specified capacities for facial recognition, spatial relations, rigid objects mechanics, tool use, social exchange, motion perception, and a great many others. These modules are thought to be content-rich; that is, modules provide not only sets of procedures for solving problems but also much of the information needed to do so.

According to evolutionary psychologists, culture is involved in phylogenetic change but not ontogenetic change (as posited in sociocultural theory). Modules are seen as forms of innate hardwiring that are largely unaffected by environmental influences such as social norms or educational practices and thus are not thought to undergo significant developmental changes as the individual ages. As a result of this adevelopmental view, cultural contexts are not thought to initiate change of any kind in the cognitive activities of individuals.

It is through culture, however, that people have responded to most, if not all, of the adaptive pressures that face them; for example, the need to communicate has given rise to language, a cultural product that serves the needs of individuals and guides the evolution of the species through natural selection. Evolutionary psychologists find it useful to study cultures to see how they respond to different environmental challenges. Hence, evolutionists, like sociocultural theorists, take the person-in-context as the relevant unit of analysis in psychological research. According to evolutionary psychologists, cultures do not change individual minds, but culturally manifested responses to adaptive pressures direct the evolution of the human species.

From the perspective of evolutionary psychology, abilities comprise patterns in behavior that draw upon combinations of multiple but independent cognitive capacities that have evolved over time. Abilities are the product of a long history of evolution, and therefore the close scrutiny of complex performances offers a glimpse of how cultures exploit such abilities, effectively guiding the development of the species. (Although Darwin pondered why music is so prevalent across cultures despite an apparent lack of adaptive advantages, it remains unclear a century later how natural selection has resulted in musical ability.)

Cognitive-Developmental Psychology.   With the three traditional models of human abilities in decline in recent decades, researchers have been emboldened to investigate entities that these influential theories explicitly proscribed—innately specified cognitive mechanisms that emerge early in life without interaction with the environment. Recent cognitive-developmental theory and research are rooted in the work of Chomsky (1968), whose nativist account of language acquisition dealt a devastating blow to its behaviorist and Piagetian rivals, and Fodor (1983), whose theory that posited a modular set of hardwired input systems ushered in a new era of skepticism about domain-general constructs and a new focus on domain-specific processes. Cognitive-developmentalists have presented a variety of nativist constructs under such monikers as first principals, p-prims, constraints, and early-developing modules (S. Carey & Gelman, 1991; Gelman & Au, 1996). These innately specified structures are seen as guiding frameworks for specific types of cognitive activity, and they need not be called into conscious awareness in order to work (Torff & Sternberg, 2001b).

From this perspective, human cognition is to a significant extent domain-specific rather than domain-general (Gelman & Au, 1996; Hirschfeld & Gelman, 1994). Domains are thought to be modular components of an innately specified cognitive system and are thus not equivalent to culturally specified "disciplines" described by socioculturists and evolutionists, among others. Detailed studies of human performances rooted in innately specified structures have been reported in several domains, including language (Pinker, 1994, 1998); psychology or "theory of mind" (Astington, 1993; Wellman, 1990); quantitative reasoning (Gelman & Brenneman, 1994); spatial cognition (Kellman, 1996; Spelke, 1994; Spelke & Hermer, 1996); and biology (Atran, 1994; C. Carey, 1985; S. Carey & Smith, 1993; Keil, 1989, 1994).

The extent to which these intuitive constructs "develop" in any meaningful sense of the word is a contentious issue among psychologists. Some see these innately specified constructs as guiding all subsequent cognition, throughout the life span, without evincing significant developmental changes (Spelke, 1994; Spelke & Hermer, 1996). This is Mother Nature's programming for thought, and it grows but does not significantly change, much as infants have 10 fingers that grow larger and more dexterous but not fundamentally different in structure.

Other psychologists argue that profound developmental changes are evident in innately specified structures. Perhaps the leading proponent of the development of cognitive abilities is Susan Carey, whose "conceptual change" model has proven influential (S. Carey, 1985; S. Carey & Smith, 1993). Conceptual judgments change significantly as the child develops, the argument goes, as a new set of beliefs replaces an old set with which the new one is qualitatively different and inconsistent (in Carey's term, incommensurable). Educational interventions, Carey argues, have the power to usher along developmental changes that individuals need to make if they are to develop accurate representations of the physical, mathematical, psychological, and biological worlds, and perhaps others as well.

The adevelopmental view also has been criticized by Karmiloff-Smith (1993), who puts forth a general theory of developmental changes in psychological structure and function called representational redescription. Karmiloff-Smith describes cognitive development in terms of three phases of representational character of knowledge in a domain: (1) implicit (unavailable to conscious awareness; (2) explicit level 1 (conscious but unavailable to verbal report), and (3) explicit level 2 (available to verbal report). Moreover, as this developmental progression occurs, knowledge from one domain becomes increasingly available to other modules, and thus knowledge that begins as domain-specific becomes increasingly generalized. Developmental change therefore involves a process of increasing connections ("mapping") across domains, as knowledge becomes increasingly available to conscious awareness.

From the perspective of cognitive-developmental theory and research, human abilities are deployments of domain-specific cognitive structures and processes. Moreover, complex performances require the interconnection of multiple sets of modules. This view is similar to that of the evolutionary psychologists. Where the majority of cognitive-developmentalists depart from the evolutionists is in the extent of ontogenetic development of the cognitive structures that underlie human abilities. According to cognitive-developmentalists, as individuals gain experience in the world, developmental changes occur in the structure and function of abilities.

Pluralistic Models of Intelligence.   Psychologists interested in human intelligence also have a long and disputatious history about the generality or specificity of abilities (Anderson, 1992). General-intelligence theories have been offset by pluralistic models in the antiquity from Plato and more recently with Guilford's multifactorial model (1967). This debate has changed considerably of late as a new set of pluralistic views has appeared (Torff & Warburton, in press). As noted, these views tend to blur the line between talent and intelligence, gathering them together in a unified but multifaceted model of human abilities.

The most influential among these new pluralistic models is the theory of multiple intelligences, or MI (Gardner, 1983/1993, 1999; Torff & Gardner, 1999). MI theory holds that human abilities can be understood as combinations of eight underlying sets of neurobiological potentials or intelligences: logical-mathematical, linguistic, spatial, bodily-kinesthetic, musical, naturalistic, interpersonal, and intrapersonal. According to MI theorists, these intelligences are combined as needed in real-world disciplines. For example, cello performance requires, at a minimum, logical-mathematical (dealing with mathematical aspects of notation), linguistic (working with terms such as *legato*), musical (information processing of pitch, rhythm, and timbre, among other things), interpersonal (working collaboratively with conductor, orchestra, and audience), and intrapersonal (expression, self-regulation). In accordance with the cognitive developmentalists, MI theory calls for ontogenetic change, making the suggestion that abilities change as combinations of intelligences are elaborated. According to Gardner and colleagues, the individual's abilities are shaped by the way a domain uses and blends the various intelligences.

Sternberg's "triarchic" theory parses human intelligence differently from MI but continues the latter's emphasis on ontogenetic development (Sternberg, 1988). Sternberg's theory holds that human abilities comprise three related cognitive processes—analytic (capacity to render critical judgments), creative (capacity to generate novel responses), and practical (capacity to adapt to the situation at hand). Like MI theorists, Sternberg suggests that individuals pull together these three sets of abilities as needed to accomplish objectives in real-world disciplines and domains. Hence, successful performances result from using these three abilities as disciplines require them. At the same time, there is a tendency in educational settings to overemphasize analytical ability and underplay creative and practical abilities. Educational benefits follow from an educational regimen that restores balance to the three sets of abilities (Sternberg, Torff, & Grigorenko, 1998).

Expertise.   The final set of pluralistic views of human abilities is put forth by researchers interested in expertise (see Bereiter & Scardamalia, 1993). Here the emphasis is on the development of discipline-specific expertise—the capacity to engage successfully in the tasks required in a real-world discipline (e.g., chess, auto mechanics). In this view, what is important about abilities is structured not by underlying modules of cognitive functioning (a domain-specific view) but by the external world of disciplines and canons of knowledge and skill they contain (a discipline-specific view). Researchers have investigated the discipline-specific abilities in disciplines as diverse as chess (Chase & Simon, 1973), physics (Chi, Glaser, & Farr, 1988), and teaching (Shulman, 1990). The functionalist tack taken by expertise researchers concentrates on the disciplinary organization of thought; placing less emphasis on underlying structural changes such participation might cause. From this perspective, abilities are a direct response to the requirements of the task, discipline, and culture at hand. Expertise researchers see abilities as forms of developing expertise, and this development is structured by the way the discipline does things. The literature on expertise is akin to the sociocultural theory in that it examines culturally crafted knowledge; however, only the socioculturalists focus on changes in cognitive structure that result from real-world activities.

Taking Stock: Multiple and Interconnected Human Abilities.
A brief review of several theoretical models that posit multiple forms of human abilities has revealed diverse ways of parsing these abilities. It may seem a chaotic picture, but these models converge to support a new view of the structure of human abilities with a pair of important insights.

First, these models predicate themselves on the idea that abilities are multiple, not singular. No domain-general or discipline-general laws, structures, or principles underlie abilities, according to the new views. Second, complex performances are supported by vital combinations of skills. Some of these skills operate primarily within a particular domain or discipline, but many abilities are used across domains. With complex performances supported by multiple abilities, it is unsurprising but significant that important abilities are sometimes hidden from view.

Developmental Challenges in Integration of Abilities

The third broad shift in the psychology of abilities involves a new view of the extent of (and character of) developmental changes in abilities as individuals gain age and expertise. The traditional models of human abilities—behaviorism, Piaget, and general intelligence—share an optimistic view of the trajectory of human development. Behaviorists assume that abilities gradually accrue as reinforcement is administered. Piagetians assume that stage changes in cognitive functioning occur as the individual is afforded appropriate opportunities to act on the environment. General-intelligence researchers assume that people gain knowledge and skill given individual differences in general processing capacity.

These optimistic stances are called into question by a burgeoning body of theory and research in the psychology of human abilities. The assumption that "natural" human development is a smooth and unfettered process has been undermined by evidence that development can be hindered when the abilities needed in a domain or discipline are not integrated.

Most teachers have had the experience of teaching something to a group of students, only to find that the students' previously existing ideas have interfered with the lesson. These experiences have been corroborated by some troubling research. For example, studies in the domain of physics show that students hold fast to misconceived notions about force and agency (notions derivative of "Aristotelian" dynamics), even after successfully passing a course that features the prevailing "scientific" view of the physical world ("Newtonian" dynamics) (diSessa, 1993; Larkin, 1983; McCloskey, Camarazza, & Green, 1980). Even students who perform in an exemplary manner in the course revert to intuitive but inaccurate ideas about physics when tested outside the classroom.

In this example, educational outcomes are influenced by *intuitive conceptions*—knowledge or knowledge structures that need not be available to conscious reflection but act to facilitate or constrain task performance (see Torff & Sternberg, 2001a, 2001b). The domain of physics has provided the "smoking gun" that shows that learning can be impeded, sometimes severely, by intuitive conceptions. Similar phenomena have been noted in a variety of other domains, which include biology (e.g., Keil, 1989, 1994), numerical reasoning (e.g., Gelman, 1991; Gelman & Brenneman, 1994), and psychology (or "theory of mind") (e.g., Astington, 1993; Leslie, 1987; Wellman, 1990).

A set of three themes emerges from these bodies of work. First, as illustrated in the physics example, individuals employ a variety of intuitive conceptions that exert a powerful force on the kind of thinking they do in all sorts of situations, inside and outside the classroom. Seldom brought to conscious awareness, intuitive conceptions are typically hidden from view and often take the form of assumptions on which patterns of thought and action are predicated. One need not, for example, have conscious awareness of one's thinking to successfully recognize faces or add small quantities. Abilities, in this view, are constituted in part by knowledge and skill of which people have conscious access and also by intuitive forms of knowledge and skill.

Second, powerful as intuitive conceptions are for making commonsense judgments, at times they are oversimplified, misleading, or inaccurate. In some instances, intuitive conceptions may be consistently and unambiguously helpful; for example, innately specified facial recognition capacities that operate nonconsciously have little in the way of a downside. However, intuitive conceptions have the power to assist or detract from learning, depending on the context at hand. For example, intuitive conceptions about number and quantity make it seem sensible to people that larger numbers correspond to greater quantities. This intuitive conception makes decimals a breeze and fractions a nightmare, since the latter counterintuitively decrease in quantity as the denominator grows larger. Gardner (1991) classifies these difficulties into three categories: simplifications (e.g., analysis of political debates as bifurcated between the good guy and bad guy), misconceptions (e.g., naive beliefs about the physical world), and rigidly applied algorithms (e.g., inflexibility in quantitative reasoning that underlies difficulties with fractions).

The third theme emergent in the intuitive-conceptions literature is the most vexing for educators. Substantial evidence supports the claim that intuitive conceptions often persist despite efforts to improve or replace them. For example, S. Carey and Smith (1993) report little success that results from efforts to initiate conceptual change from misconceived intuitive notions to accurate scientific ones (in the domain of epistemological beliefs). Gardner (1991) and Gardner, Torff, and Hatch (1996) review research that yields similar results. Intuitive conceptions are often difficult to dislodge, even by the best of teachers.

Taken together, the three themes point to a complex trajectory for the development of abilities. Complex performances require the intermingling of various forms of ability, intuitive and otherwise, and these multiple abilities may fail to integrate as needed. Or they may conflict outright. The abilities required in complex performances are not only numerous; they also are in danger of discordance, resulting in difficulties in gaining needed knowledge and skill.

Theoretical Models of Disjunctures Between Abilities. The question arises why such a situation should emerge. What conditions or characteristics produce such disjunctures? Answers to this question come from both sides of the nature–nurture aisle.

Evolutionary psychologists put forth an explanation that centers on the suggestion that not all of our genetic inheritance (of evolved, innately specified modules) serves the modern human well. Evolutionary pressures work slowly, but in the last two millennia human cultures have moved at a breakneck pace. In that time, the genetic makeup of the human mind has not evolved significantly, but cultures have changed human life in countless ways. So, while modern humans are adapted to the life of the Pleistocene-era hunter-gatherer, most people live in a different and more complex sort of world—society in the information age. The modern human is, in this view, fundamentally maladapted to the current environment. It follows, then, that modern humans should evince ways in which their behavior seems ill suited to contemporary challenges, intellectual and otherwise. Evolutionary psychologists suggest that not always does the adaptive legacy we have from our forebears support our performance in the modern world.

A similar view can be seen among cognitive-developmental psychologists. Part of Piaget's legacy was his demonstration that young children often exhibit distinctive conceptions of the world. More recent theory attributes these conceptions to a combination of innate constraints on learning and early experience (S. Carey & Gelman, 1991). Together with the evolutionists, cognitive-developmentalists press the case that the human genetic endowment is a root cause of the challenges of integration of abilities. But cognitive-developmentalists place additional emphasis on ontogenetic changes in the development of abilities. At the heart of these disjunctures lie the problems inherent in the developmental interplay of endogenous factors (nature) and exogenous ones (nurture).

Sociocultural theorists have little quarrel with evolutionist and cognitive-developmental theory, but they locate the primary causes for disjunctures elsewhere, at least in part: in interactions between the individuals and the ambient culture. Consider, for example, the concept of *folk psychology*—a set of socially shared ideas about how the mind works and what learning and knowledge are (Bruner,

1990, 1996; Olson & Bruner, 1996). A culture's folk psychology is a shared conception of how people think, how they should act, and how they learn, among other things. But not always do the precepts of a culture's folk psychology prove to be a boon to educators. Rather, folk beliefs can come into conflict with the formal concepts created and taught by experts in a discipline, leading to the disjunctures between abilities noted earlier.

Beliefs about teaching and learning called *folk pedagogy* help to make the point. In Western culture, especially in the United States, a popular folk belief holds that learning occurs when students absorb information from the environment and thus the best teaching occurs when the environment is made rich with information transmitted to students from teachers, books, and other sources. Studies of teachers' beliefs show that prospective teachers often hold fast to a "transmission model" of teaching, despite the "constructivist" view (taught in most teacher-education programs) that knowledge is constructed individually by each learner, based on environmental input and individual reflection (e.g., Brookhart & Freeman, 1992; Bruner, 1996; Doyle & Carter, 1996; Hollingsworth, 1989; Kagan, 1992; McLaughlin, 1991; Morine-Dershimer, 1993; Shulman, 1990; Strauss, 1993; 1996; Strauss & Shilony, 1994; Torff, 1999b; Torff & Sternberg, 2001a, 2001b); Woolfolk Hoy, 1996; Zeichner & Gore, 1990). Of course, the constructivist pedagogy might ultimately be found wanting. But it seems clear that people who are trained in education hold powerful intuitive conceptions about teaching and learning and these intuitive conceptions exert a great deal of influence on the way people think and act in classroom settings.

Folk pedagogy predisposes individuals to think and teach in particular ways, some of which are inconsistent with the concepts and practices characteristic of expert teaching. As with intuitive conceptions in other domains, folk pedagogy may tend to persist despite successful participation in preservice training programs. Becoming an expert teacher, then, is not simply a matter of gaining new knowledge or of replacing inadequate preconceptions in a straightforward manner. Rather, explicit efforts by teachers of educational psychology are needed to counter these uncritically held beliefs, principally by encouraging prospective teachers to engage in activities that facilitate relevant forms of cognitive change.

This example makes clear that intuitive conceptions held by teachers—as well as those held by students—influence educational outcomes, and not always for the better. The example also illustrates how sociocultural theory, as well as the cognitive-developmental and evolutionary theory, accounts for disjunctures between abilities. The shared beliefs in a community of practice may ill fit the time-honored procedures and practices created by disciplinary experts, resulting in disjunctures between abilities.

Taking Stock: Developmental Challenges in Integration of Abilities.   The traditional models portray development as a smooth process of acquisition of knowledge and skill in a discipline, but the psychological literature tells a more disquieting tale. Disjunctures between abilities exert a hidden and problematic force on the development of abilities. The literature on intuitive conceptions supports the view that the development of complex performances entails the intermingling of various forms of ability, intuitive and otherwise, and these multiple abilities may fail to integrate as needed, or they may come into conflict. The abilities required in complex performances are not only numerous; they also are in danger of discordance, resulting in difficulties in gaining the knowledge and skill needed in complex performances.

Educational Implications

Complex performances, it turns out, are supported by multiple context-dependent abilities that integrate with development but sometimes require specific educational interventions to integrate adequately. The next sections explore the educational implications of this viewpoint. Following the three shifts discussed earlier, the call here is for pedagogy that is contextualized, pluralistic, and integrative.

Education in Context

If knowledge and skill are shaped through context and only in context do tasks make sense, then any pedagogy begins with a detailed analysis of the abilities the domain or discipline requires, with the goal of crafting educational practices to foster the needed abilities. Chess masters, for example, ought to analyze their craft to determine its constituent abilities. Such an analysis focuses on a set of reflective questions. What abilities are needed in the discipline, and in what contexts are they used? To what extent does schooling help people to develop the full range of culturally situated skills needed for success in a career? To what extent does schooling give people the skills needed to be knowledgeable participants in lay discourse outside one's career area? These questions probe the ecological validity (in education the notion is typically called authenticity) of educational interventions. At issue is *contextualization*—the extent to which vehicles for curriculum and assessment appropriately reflect (and prepare students for) the challenges of adult life in the real world (Gardner, 1999). Contextualization prompts educators to ground their work more soundly in the disciplines, for example by making science teaching less like school (typically emphasizing memorizing of scientific facts) and more like professional science (e.g., designing and executing studies) and avocational science activities (e.g., reading and discussing a science article in a newsweekly).

But to say that contextualization of curriculum and assessment is a laudable aim is not to say that each and every lesson should consist of real-world activities. After all, scales are not played at musical recitals, but they have a rich purpose in the practice room. Decontextualized activities can be a means to an end; the key, however, is the connection ultimately made with the authentic activity in the discipline.

Contextualization of assessment has long been a vexing concern in education. High-stakes testing remains a key component in educational decision making in many countries, including the United States. At the same time, the strands of theory and research reviewed earlier support *assessment in context*: assessment procedures that are performance-based (allowing students to participate in assessment as they have in the classroom) and ongoing (as opposed to single-administration testing).

The Full Range and Interconnection of Abilities

A key component of contextualized educational practices concerns teaching for the full range of abilities needed in a domain or discipline. Detailed analysis of a domain inevitably yields a broad range of intradomain and interdomain abilities. As noted, no general laws explain all in a domain, so a domain-specific view is vital to understanding human abilities. At the same time, domain-specific work can lead to fragmented, insular pockets of theory and research. This in turn obfuscates vital interdomain connections of abilities, narrowing the scope of theory and research. Clearly, a key objective is to teach for abilities that are unique or specific to a domain or discipline (e.g., timbre in music). But the second, more overlooked abilities are the interdomain (interdiscipline) ones.

Contextualized learning of the diversity of skills needed in a domain or discipline has led many investigators to analysis and expansion of *apprenticeship* models of learning and teaching. Viewing teaching as multiple forms of assisted performance, not just instruction, apprenticeships feature three qualities in accord with the modern psychology of abilities. First, apprenticeships allow students access to useful forms of expert models. Models range from distal (watching golf on television) to proximal (watching your golf teacher) (Torff, 1997). Instructor modeling provides proximal encounters with expert performance, as well as opportunities for coparticipation and successive approximation. Rudimentary as this point is, many a golf and music lesson includes little performance by the mentor. Second, apprenticeship-type learning can be extended in fruitful ways, leading to the term *cognitive apprenticeship* (Collins, Brown, & Newman, 1989). The idea here is to make often-hidden expert thinking available to students.

The goal is to make expert thinking visible and audible, encompassing not just how the expert works but also how he or she thinks when working—how the expert identifies, defines, operationalizes, and solves problems. *Cognitive apprenticeship* refers to the practice of engaging students in all the aspects of expert performance, not just the public ones. Third, apprenticeships have the virtue of stressing distributed knowledge. The sociocultural theory discussed earlier makes persuasive the claim that only a portion of the wherewithal of a performance resides in the head; the remainder is distributed in symbolic media, physical tools, and social conventions. Apprenticeships focus on combinations of person and context, a distributed approach to learning and teaching.

Integration of Abilities

The research reviewed earlier supports the conclusion that not always is the path to expertise in a domain or discipline a smooth one. The specter of conflicts between abilities calls for diagnostics that identify the difficulties that obtain in a particular domain or discipline. This is seldom done, as in the physics example discussed earlier. The finding about intuitive physics came as a surprise to many in the world of science teaching. Similar surprises may await educators in other disciplines.

Psychologists and educators are working to counter these difficulties, and the emerging consensus among them is that learners must confront naive views, to think about them and question them, not work around them. Learning about Newton did not dislodge the flawed intuitive physics. What's needed is pedagogy that requires students to critically analyze their intuitive responses and to consider ways in which they might be improved. In what is in essence a constructivist response to the problem, the focus falls on teaching for integration between abilities, with the aim of strengthening the relationships among abilities required in a discipline.

Promising initiatives that aim to enhance this integration fall under the various headings *reflective thinking* (Gardner, 1991; Paris & Ayres, 1994), *reflective teaching* (Liston & Zeichner, 1996), and *teaching for understanding* (Wiske, 1993). These programs in reflective thinking engage learners in their own assessment by requiring them to answer questions about their work, the way it was made, and ways in which it could be improved. Reflective thinking takes place formally in critique sheets attached to student work but also less formally in conversations between and among students and teachers. Teachers have much to gain by asking questions that encourage students' involvement in their own assessment. These practices help students to build their own understandings of the discipline but also to examine the extent to which their naive views require revision. Telling students how their intuitions are inadequate holds little hope; a better approach is to encourage students to engage in the kind of reflective thinking that critically analyzes intuitive views.

The foregoing educational suggestions are hardly new, and they are not presented as such. Traditional educational methods have much to offer educators interested in fostering human abilities. But they also are lacking in some respects, namely, in terms of contextualization of learning and assessment, range of abilities covered, and integration of the abilities required in a domain or discipline. The bottom line for educators interested in abilities: Look closely at the domain and contextualize your practices in it, pay attention to the numerous and diverse abilities the domain requires, and take care that students can integrate these abilities as needed in complex performances.

Conclusion

In the psychology of abilities since the cognitive revolution, no paradigm has been secured, but it has been a fertile period. A set of hoary assumptions has come under fire as new theory and research have appeared. The emerging view highlights that abilities are context-dependent and thus culturally situated, multiple with important interconnections between different abilities, and sometimes difficult to draw together as needed even by the best of teachers.

The science of human abilities is still not a coherent picture, so practitioners and educators interested in complex performances still have much to wonder about in terms of the psychology and nurturance of the abilities that underlie tasks in their disciplines. But the new view portends well for future theory, research, and practice in the psychology of abilities, as the emerging views are explored across a broad range of domains and disciplines.

REFERENCES

Anderson, M. (1992). *Intelligence and development: A cognitive theory.* Oxford: Blackwell.

Astington, J. (1993). *The child's discovery of the mind.* Cambridge, MA: Harvard University Press.

Atran, S. (1994). Core domains versus scientific theories. In L. Hirschfeld & S. Gelman, (Eds.), *Mapping the mind: Domain-specificity in cognition and culture* (pp. 316–340). Cambridge: Cambridge University Press.

Bakhtin, M. (1981). *The dialogic imagination.* Austin: University of Texas.

Barkow, J., Cosmides, L., & Tooby, J. (Eds.). (1992). *The adaptive mind: Evolutionary psychology and generation of culture.* New York: Oxford University Press.

Bereiter, C., & Scardamalia, M. (1993). *Surpassing ourselves: An inquiry into the nature and implications of expertise.* New York: Open Court.

Brookhart, S., & Freeman, D. (1992). Characteristics of entering teacher candidates. *Review of Educational Research, 62,* 37–60.

Bruner, J. S. (1990). *Acts of meaning.* Cambridge, MA: Harvard University Press.

Bruner, J. (1996). *The culture of education.* Cambridge, MA: Harvard University Press.

Cahan, E., & White, S. (1992). Proposals for a second psychology. *American Psychologist, 47*(2), 224–235.

Carey, C. (1985). *Conceptual change in childhood.* Cambridge: Bradford/MIT.

Carey, S., & Gelman, R. (Eds.). (1991). *The epigenesis of mind.* Hillsdale, NJ: Erlbaum.

Carey, S., & Smith, C. (1993). On understanding the nature of scientific knowledge. *Educational Psychologist, 28*(3), 235–251.

Chase, W., & Simon, H. (1973). Perception in chess. *Cognitive Psychology, 4,* 55–81.

Chi, M., Glaser, R., & Farr, M. (Eds.). (1988). *The nature of expertise.* Hillsdale, NJ: Erlbaum.

Chomsky, N. (1968). *Language and mind.* New York: Harcourt Brace Jovanovich.

Cole, M. (1971). *The cultural context of learning and thinking.* New York: Basic Books.

Cole, M. (1996). *Cultural psychology: A once and future discipline.* Cambridge, MA: Harvard University Press.

Collins, A., Brown, J., & Newman, S. (1989). Cognitive apprenticeship: Teaching the crafts of reading, writing, and mathematics. In C. Resnick (Ed.), *Knowing, learning, and instruction: Essays in honor of Robert Glaser* (pp. 453–494). Hillsdale, NJ: Erlbaum.

Cosmides, L., & Tooby, J. (1987). From evolution to behavior: Evolutionary psychology as the missing link. In J. Dupre (Ed.), *The latest and the best: Essays on evolution and optimality* (pp. 227–306). Cambridge, MA: MIT Press.

diSessa, A. (1993). Toward an epistemology of physics. *Cognition and Instruction, 10,* 105–225.

Doyle, W., & Carter, K. (1996). Educational psychology and the education of teachers: A reaction. *Educational Psychologist, 31*(1) 51–62.

Egan, K. (1992). Review of "The Unschooled Mind" (by Howard Gardner). *Teachers College Record, 94,* 2, 397–406.

Eysenk, H. (1986). The theory of intelligence and the psychopsysiology of cognition. In R. J. Sternberg & D. R. Detterman (Eds.), *What is intelligence: Contemporary viewpoints on its nature and definition* (pp. 1–34). Norwood, NJ: Ablex.

Fodor, J. A. (1983). *The modularity of mind.* Cambridge, MA: MIT Press.

Gardner, H. (1991). *The unschooled mind.* New York: Basic Books.

Gardner, H. (1993). *Frames of mind:* The theory of multiple intelligences. New York: Basic Books. (Original work published 1983)

Gardner, H. (1999). *Intelligence reframed.* New York: Basic Books.

Gardner, H., Torff, B., & Hatch, T. (1996). The age of innocence reconsidered: Preserving the best of the progressive tradition in psychology and education. In D. Olson & N. Torrance (Eds.), *Handbook of psychology in education* (pp. 28–55). Cambridge, MA: Blackwell.

Gelman, R. (1991). First principles organize attention to and learning about relevant data: Number and animate–inanimate distinction as examples. *Cognitive Science, 14,* 79–106.

Gelman, R., & Au, T. (Eds.). (1996). *Perceptual and cognitive development.* New York: Academic Press.

Gelman, R., & Brenneman, K. (1994). First principles can support both universal and culture-specific learning about number and music. In E. Hirschfeld & S. Gelman (Eds.), *Mapping the mind: Domain-specificity in cognition and culture* (pp. 369–390). New York: Cambridge University Press.

Greeno, J. (1998). The situativity of knowing, learning, and research. *American Psychologist, 53*(1), 5–26.

Gruber, H., & Voneche, P. (1977). *The essential Piaget.* New York: Basic Books.

Guilford, J. (1967). *The nature of human intelligence.* New York: McGraw-Hill.

Hirschfeld, L., & Gelman, S. (Eds.). (1994). *Mapping the mind: Domain-specificity in cognition and culture.* Cambridge: Cambridge University Press.

Hollingsworth, S. (1989). Prior beliefs and cognitive change in learning to teach. *American Educational Research Journal, 26,* 160–189.

Hutchins, E. (1990). *Culture and inference.* Cambridge, MA: Harvard University Press.

Kagan, D. (1992). Implications of research on teacher belief. *Educational Psychologist, 27,* 65–90.

Kaiping, P., & Nisbett, R. (1999). Culture, dialectics, and reasoning about contradiction. *American Psychologist, 54*(9), 741–754.

Karmiloff-Smith, A. (1993). *Beyond modularity.* Cambridge, MA: MIT Press.

Keil, F. (1989). *Concepts, kinds, and cognitive development.* Cambridge: MIT Press.

Keil, F. (1994). The birth and nurturance of concepts by domains: The origins of living things. In E. Hirschfeld & S. Gelman (Eds.), *Mapping the mind: Domain-specificity in cognition and culture* (pp. 234–254). New York: Cambridge University Press.

Kellman, P. (1996). The origins of object perception. In R. Gelman & T. Au (Eds.), *Perceptual and cognitive development* (pp. 3–48). New York: Academic Press.

Kuhn, D. (1989). Children and adults as intuitive scientists. *Psychological Review, 96*(4), 674–689.

Lave, J. (1988). *Cognition in practice.* Cambridge, MA: Cambridge University Press.

Lave, J., & Wenger, E. (1993). *Situated learning.* Cambridge, MA: Cambridge University Press.

Leslie, A. (1987). Pretense and representation: The origins of "theory of mind." *Psychological Review, 94,* 412–426.

Liston, P., & Zeichner, K. (1996). *Reflective teaching.* Mahwah, NJ: Erlbaum.

McCloskey, M., Camarazza, A., & Green, B. (1980). Curvilinear motion in absence of external forces: Folk beliefs about the motion of objects. *Science, 210,* 1141–49.

McLaughlin, J. (1991). Reconciling care and control: Authority in classroom relationships. *Journal of Teacher Education, 40*(3), 182–195.

Mead, G. (1956). *The social psychology of George Herbert Mead.* A. Strauss (Ed.). Chicago: University of Chicago Press. (Original work published 1934)

Morine Dershimer, G. (1993). Tracing conceptual change in preservice teachers. *Teaching and Teacher Education, 9,* 15–26.

Olson, D., & Bruner, J. (1996). Folk psychology and folk pedagogy. In D. Olson & N. Torrance (Eds.), *Handbook of education in human development* (pp. 9–27). Oxford: Blackwell.

Paris, S., & Ayres, L. (1994). Promoting students' reflections through classroom activities. In *Becoming reflective students and teachers with portfolios and authentic assessments.* Washington, DC: American Psychological Association Books.

Perkins, D. (1995). *Outsmarting I.Q.: The emerging science of learnable intelligence.* New York: Free Press.

Piaget, J. (1983). Piaget's theory. In P. Mussen (Ed.), *Handbook of child psychology* (Vol. 1, pp. 103–128). New York: Wiley.

Pinker, S. (1994). *The language instinct.* New York: Morrow.

Pinker, S. (1998). *How the mind works.* New York: Morrow.

Resnick, L., Levine, J., & Teasley, S. (Eds.). (1991). *Perspectives on socially shared cognition.* Washington, DC: American Psychological Association Books.

Rogoff, B. (1990). *Apprenticeship in thinking.* Cambridge, MA: Harvard University Press.

Rogoff, B., & Lave, J. (Eds.). (1984). *Everyday cognition.* Cambridge, MA: Harvard University Press.

Scribner, S. (1984). Studying working intelligence. In B. Rogoff & J. Lave (Eds.). (1984), *Everyday cognition* (pp. 9–40). Cambridge, MA: Harvard University Press.

Seely Brown, J., Collins, A., & Duguid, P. (1989). Situated cognition and the culture of learning. *Educational Researcher, 18*(1), 32–42.

Shulman, L. (1990). Reconnecting foundations to the substance of teacher education. *Teachers College Record, 91*(3), 300–310.

Skinner, B. (1954). The science of learning and the art of teaching. *Harvard Educational Review, 24,* 86–97.

Spelke, E. (1994). Initial knowledge: Six suggestions. *The Cognition, 50,* 431–445.

Spelke, E., & Hermer, L. (1996). Early cognitive development: Objects and space. In R. Gelman, & T. Au (Eds.), *Perceptual and cognitive development* (pp. 72–107). New York: Academic Press.

Sternberg, R. (1988). *The triarchic mind: A new theory of human intelligence.* New York: Viking.

Sternberg, R. (1998). Abilties are forms of developing expertise. *Educational Researcher, 27,* 11–20.

Sternberg, R., Torff, B., & Grigorenko, E. (1998, September). Teaching triarchically improves school achievement. *Journal of Educational Psychology, 90*(3), 374–384.

Strauss, S. (1993). Teachers' pedagogical content knowledge about children's minds and learning: Implications for teacher education. *Educational Psychologist, 28*(3), 279–290.

Strauss, S. (1996). Confessions of a born-again constructivist. *Educational Psychologist, 31*(1), 15–22.

Strauss, S., & Shilony, T. (1994). Teachers' models of children's minds and learning. In L. Hirschfeld & S. Gelman (Eds.), *Mapping the mind: Domain-specificity in cognition and culture* (pp. 455–473). Cambridge: Cambridge University Press.

Thorndike, E. (1932). *The fundamentals of learning*. Englewood Cliffs, NJ: Merrill/Prentice Hall.

Thurstone, L. L. (1938). *Primary mental abilities*. Chicago: University of Chicago Press.

Tooby, J., & Cosmides, L. (1990). On the universality of human nature and the uniqueness of the individual: The role of genetics and adaptation. *Journal of Personality, 58,* 375–424.

Torff, B. (1997). Into the wordless world: Implicit learning and instructor modeling in music. In V. Brummet (Ed.), *Music as intelligence* (pp. 77–92). Ithaca, NY: Ithaca College Press.

Torff, B. (1999a). Beyond information processing: Cultural influences on cognition and learning. In S. Ulibarri (Ed.), *Maria Montessori explicit and implicit in the 20th century* (pp. 8–39). Mexico City: Association Montessori Internationale.

Torff, B. (1999b). Tacit knowledge in teaching: Folk pedagogy and teacher education. In R. Sternberg & J. Horvath (Eds.), *Tacit knowledge in professional practice* (pp. 195–214). Mahwah, NJ: Erlbaum.

Torff, B., & Gardner, H. (1999). The vertical mind: The case for multiple intelligences. In M. Anderson (Ed.), *The development of intelligence* (pp. 139–160). London: University College Press.

Torff, B., & Sternberg, R. (2001a). Intuitive conceptions among learners and teachers. In B. Torff & R. Sternberg (Eds.), *Understanding and teaching the intuitive mind: Student and teacher learning* (pp. 3–26). Mahwah, NJ: Erlbaum.

Torff, B., & Sternberg, R. (Eds.). (2001b). *Understanding and teaching the intuitive mind: Student and teacher learning.* Mahwah, NJ: Erlbaum.

Torff, B. & Warburton, E. (in press). Old and new models of intelligence: The assessment conundrum. In M. Pearn (Ed.), *Individual deveopment in organisations.* London: Wiley.

Vygotsky, L. (1978). *Mind in society.* Cambridge, MA: Harvard University Press.

Watson, J. (1924). *Behaviorism.* New York: Norton.

Wellman, H. (1990). *The child's theory of mind.* Cambridge, MA: Bradford/MIT.

Wertsch, J. (1985). *Vygotsky and the social formation of mind.* Cambridge, MA: Harvard University Press.

Wiske, M. (Ed.). (1993). *Teaching for understanding.* San Francisco: Jossey-Bass.

Woolfolk Hoy, A. (1996). Teaching educational psychology: Texts in context. *Educational Psychologist, 31*(1), 35–40.

Zeichner, K., & Gore, J. (1990). Teacher socialization. In W. Houston (Ed.), *Handbook of research on teacher education* (pp. 329–349). New York: Macmillian.

29

Making Music and Making Sense Through Music

Expressive Performance and Communication

REINHARD KOPIEZ

Music and Meaning

Music itself seems to be an ideal medium to communicate meaning, perhaps much more effective than language. This may apply even if the meaning is not directly related to the musical structure itself but rather to associations evoked from listening to it. As Cook (1998, p. 3f.) demonstrates in his functional analysis of television commercials, "advertisers use music to communicate meanings that would take too long to put into words, or that would carry no conviction in them . . . Rock stands for youth, freedom, being true to yourself. . . ." Seen from this point of view, we participate daily in a continual experiment in which meaning is attributed to music by watching commercials. This is true regardless of the situation in which we encounter music. Generalizing more broadly: whatever stimuli human beings encounter or whichever activities they take part in, there is a constant wish to seek meaning.

Already by 1894 Bolton and Meumann had published two remarkable studies. Meumann's review investigated the impressions formed by 17 subjects upon listening to an isochronous sequence of clicks, that is, a series of events with equal temporal distance. Similarly, the 28 subjects in Bolton's study listened to isochronous clicks and were then "invited to say anything that suggested itself to them, whatever the character" (p. 184). When asked to count the clicks, the subjects—even those with no musical appreciation at all—used counting systems that grouped the clicks into units of 2 or 4. Both authors termed the effect tic-toc effect, which has today become known as subjective rhythmization. (Some subjects in Bolton's study reported a rhythmic grouping but also in larger groups that depended on the rate of the isochronous sequence; see p. 215.) Although these findings were concerned with little more than

fundamental levels of perception, it would seem that the input of isochronous clicks is enough to stimulate our tendency to attribute meaning to rhythmic events. The same phenomenon can be experienced when listening to the metronomically exact version of a composition from a MIDI file, where all notes have been set to the same intensity and nominal duration—a so-called deadpan rendition. If you do not listen to this artificial product for too long, this extreme realization sounds surprisingly better than one would suppose, and although it may not be aesthetically pleasing, it is not completely "dead" in the sense of being meaningless (see also Thompson & Robitaille, 1992).

This simple experiment sheds light on the importance of the composed structure for the perception of meaning in music: Despite the absence of expressive shaping, the musical structure itself conveys meaning and can communicate sense—at least to some degree. Even in an unexpressive realization it is possible to perceive sections, modulations, and so on. At the same time, it would seem that musical communication consists of at least two layers: First, there is a structural layer (given by the composer's score); and second, there is an expressive layer (added by the performer's realization of the score). Bear in mind that musical communication is not complete until these two layers are related, implemented, and communicated to the listener. It is important to note that as of this day, music psychologists have not yet fully understood the complex processes of musical communication.

The Meaning of Music

In the history of music aesthetics and music psychology, three possible answers have been proposed to the question of what meaning music might possess:

Answer 1. Music does not have any meaning at all. Although there are no authors of musical aesthetics who assume that music has no meaning at all and is little more than "a tickle in the ear," there are indications in the writings of Kant (1790/1987, sect. 16, p. 2) that assume that music without text does not express a specific statement and can be described as "amusement of the senses" (*Spiel der Empfindungen*). This does not mean, however, that purely instrumental music (e.g., a free fantasy) can be described within the category of pleasant only and not of beautiful. As far as I can see, Burke (1852, part 3, sect. 25) comes closest to a sensually "objective" aesthetic. In his treatise, he argues that the initial impact of a musical performance causes a spontaneous emotional impression, which is subsequently followed by a rational aesthetic judgment (cf. Allesch, 1987, p. 148).

Meaning, of course, does not exist in the sense that it does in spoken language, but from the "no meaning at all" point of view it would be hard to explain why, even in the case of purely instrumental compositions, listeners attribute emotions such as happiness and sadness to a piece of music. Behne (1982, p. 128) offers a different theoretical explanation that suggests it would be naive to assume that a composer's intention was to communicate in a one-way fashion what he himself felt while composing a specific piece. On the contrary, the fascination of music is caused by the listener's impression of a two-way "quasi communication." Music not only offers perceived expression but also requires the listener to tune into a "simulation of communication." This point of view is also shared by Kraut (1992, p. 21) in his reflections on musical indeterminacy and how it relates to the understanding of music. In his view, the fact that music is not a spoken language does not represent any deficit. Rather, he indicates that the ambiguous characteristics of all music can be considered a strength of this communication medium.

Answer 2. The meaning of music is its musical form. There are two sources that support the idea that the meaning of music can be found in cognitive acts only, such as the perception of musical form. The first of these is the 19th-century position adopted by music aesthetics and succinctly summarized by the music critic Eduard Hanslick (1891/1986, p. 29). His opinion that music comprises only "tonally moving forms" (*tönend bewegte Formen*) is confirmed in the title of the second chapter of his book, which states that "the representation of feeling is not the content of music" (p. 8). Despite the fact that Hanslick's ideas and assertions are often considered to be extremely formalist, they may still contain a fair amount of accuracy. Suggesting that music is not free of feelings, although not necessarily represented directly but instead dynamically, he asks:

What, then, from the feelings, can music present if not their content? Only that same dynamic mentioned above. It can

reproduce the motion of a physical process according to the prevailing momentum: fast, slow, strong, weak, rising, falling. Motion is just one attribute, however, one moment of feeling, not feeling itself. (p. 11)

A secondary source dates from the late 1950s, a time when psychology was largely dominated by cognitive psychology, which had deliberately excluded emotions and feelings from their discussions (see, e.g., Gardner, 1985). The influence of this tendency upon music psychology can be seen in the second edition of Deutsch's *Psychology of Music* (1999), with its surprising lack of a chapter on music and emotion. Fortunately, this trend is changing and emotion is now viewed as a very important topic in both psychology and music psychology.

Answer 3. The meaning of music is the expression of emotion. The extreme opposite of purely formal aesthetics is Hausegger's (1885) aesthetics of expression (*Ausdrucks-ästhetik*). In his evolutionary approach, influenced by Darwin's 1872 treatise *The Expression of the Emotions in Animal and Man* (Darwin, 1872/1965), Hausegger developed a theory of "listening to and understanding music" based on an intuitive and universal understanding of emotional expression (*Mitempfindung*). In his view, musical expression is a strong force that guarantees emotional understanding without prerequisites. Today Hausegger's position is supported by the fact that for most people, namely, those without professional involvement, music does not satisfy a cognitive function, such as the understanding of musical form, but an emotional function. A supporting position is maintained by Cooke (1959, p. 12), who writes: "And those who have found music expressive of anything at all (the majority of mankind) have found it expressive of emotions."

While the educational importance of this last point offers potential for discussing not only musical knowledge but also emotional musical experiences in the classroom, there is still a long way to go before a unifying theory of musical meaning or a theory of emotion in music can be posited. The three possible answers to our opening question provided in this section are only representative of the wide range of possibilities of meaning in music. Important related topics such as programmatic music, metaphysical phenomena, and music as an expression of motion are outside the scope of this chapter.

Focus of This Chapter

As outlined earlier, musical communication is a complex, multifaceted subject and still lacks a comprehensive definition. Therefore, in this chapter I will focus primarily on the following questions:

1. Is a performance the result of an intentional process that tries to communicate the performer's view of a

piece with a minimum amount of ambiguity, or is it the result of ad hoc decisions, generated in the course of performance?

2. Does a composition have only one meaning, thus limiting the various interpretations of a piece, or is there unlimited freedom of individuality in performance?

3. Are there any rules for the expressive shaping of performance that would facilitate the communication of meaning?

4. How reliable are the performer's so-called expressive acoustical cues decoded by the listener, and how do they serve as a basis of emotional communication?

5. Finally, is music a "universal language" understood by everybody without prerequisites?

In this chapter I will discuss musical communication from three points of view: the performer's and the listener's standpoints and the side of the music itself (i.e., what is communicated by the structural elements of the music?). Without an understanding of these three perspectives it may not be possible to fully understand the concept of musical communication.

Excluded from this chapter, however, are basic cognitive processes such as stream segregation and models of tonal relations and developmental aspects that could be relevant to the understanding of music by children (see chap. 26 by Thompson and Schellenberg in this volume). In addition, only limited space has been afforded to the area of skill acquisition (see chap. 30, by Lehmann and Davidson, this volume). Furthermore, this chapter does not intend to be a review of literature on performance research (this means research on a musician's performing activities and acoustical results). The interested reader can obtain such an overview in the three existing extensive publications by Gabrielsson (1999), Kopiez (1996), and Palmer (1997).

The Development of Performance Plans

If we suppose that all performing musicians have a "message" for their audience and use the expressive and technical means to communicate their personal view of a composition, the question still remains: How does this message develop within the preparatory phase of a performance? Two different answers can be considered that are located at opposite ends of a continuum: First, we could assume that the complete concept of the performance of a composition is present from the initial contact with the music and stays invariant throughout the entire preparation; second, it could be that the development of a performance plan is characterized by an interactive process that affects the whole preparation phase. In the latter case, aspects such as expressive performance plans, fingering, coping with difficult passages, analytical insight into the structure

of the piece, and listening to recordings of other musicians would all interact. Thus the performance plan would emerge over the entire preparation phase, making the performer's message increasingly clear, strong, and coherent. For a scientific explanation of these performance plans, we need analytical tools to describe the sounding results. We will refer to the tempo variations of a performance in the form of a curve as "timing profile" and to the time span within which expressive shaping occurs as the "time frame." Timing has been chosen as the dominant parameter since it is the most widely investigated one in performance research. This does not, however, imply that other parameters such as dynamics are less important for the understanding of expressive intentions.

Results of Performance Research

Performance as Imaginary Narration.   A performance plan does not simply consist of the formal representation of music only but also includes noncognitive components that encompass, among other things, images, moods, and imaginative musical characters (Gabrielsson, 1999, p. 502). In this respect, the reduction of meaning to musical structure would be an oversimplification of the complex situation of musical communication. Yet as Shaffer (1992) points out, musical meaning also includes so-called narrative elements such as "imaginary protagonists." Seen in this light, "the performer's interpretation can be viewed as helping to define the character of the protagonist" (p. 265). The theoretical foundations of this narrative performance theory can be found in E. Tarasti's (1994) *Theory of Musical Semiotics,* the strength of which is demonstrated through a comparative and phenomenological analysis of 22 recordings of the *Mélodie française* "Après un rêve" and a sample analysis (by writing a so-called modal grammar) of Chopin's G-Minor Ballad. Tarasti's theory can be applied easily to the analysis of performance or can be used by music critics. Such a perspective of performance planning suggests that a performer uses a top-down strategy in developing an overall performance plan as well as a bottom-up strategy with more relevance to local events. In addition, expression marks in the score play an important role in the development of these local and global strategies. Experimental support for this view was obtained by Shaffer (1992) by removing expression marks from the edited score and comparing the resulting performances to renditions performed from the original score (1995). He also found that playing from an unedited score induced less consistent timing across repeated renditions. This observation encourages the idea that expression markings clarify the musical character and thereby contribute to the communication of musical meaning. Similarly, these findings are supported by a listening study carried out by Watt and Ash (1998), which used unfamiliar pieces of music to investigate the attribution of personal traits such as "gender" (male/female) and "age" (young/old). Due to the high consistency between evaluators involved in this experiment, the authors concluded that "music is perceived as if it were a person making a disclosure" (p. 47) and went on to suggest that because of the similarity between psychological reactions to both real people and music, "music creates a virtual person" (p. 49). One consequence for further investigations in musical communication is that it would be more effective to ask subjects to refer to elements relevant to the narrative structure of music as indices for successful communication, instead of free associations or nonmusical entities.

Strategies for the Development of Performance Plans. To obtain greater insight into the strategies employed during the creation of an interpretation, Hallam (1995) interviewed 22 pianists about their study techniques for learning an unknown composition. Only a minority of the subjects (9%) were purely holistic learners who would initially play through the piece and attempt to acquire an idea of the overall conception of the work before starting their detailed practice. Thirty-two percent of the players employed an intuitive/serialistic strategy (playing of small sections) and developed their interpretation as the music was learned (p. 120). The majority of the players were so-called versatile learners (45%), who used a holistic as well as a serial strategy—a learning style that can be classified as a combined top-down and bottom-up strategy. It follows, then, that a balanced relationship between integration (global perspective) and differentiation (local perspective) is a feature of every outstanding work of art and a fundamental issue in musical aesthetics. As an educational consequence Hallam argues for the use of either holistic or versatile strategies after analyzing the piece or listening to different recordings, yet it is also possible that learning styles may depend on the musical style of a composition. As Childs (1992) demonstrated in a self-report study with professional musicians, the practice of contemporary music was characterized by a certain sequence of phases: The rhythmic structure, which is often highly complex, is practiced in the first phase; the "correct notes" are practiced in the second; and details of expression become part of the performance plan in the third phase.

A methodological flaw in many studies is the unwanted effects of "rationalization" that result from retrospective interviews. Consequently, researchers are sometimes better advised to directly observe musicians' practice. Such a method of direct observation with tape recording was used by Gruson (1988) for her analyses of piano practice behavior among advanced and novice pianists and by Mik-

laszewski (1989) who video-recorded a single case study of a pianist.

Representation of Performance Plans. We now know that musicians use elaborate strategies to develop a performance plan that guarantees a high degree of reproducibility, but how are these performance plans represented in memory and controlled during execution? Already Skinner (1932; also Seashore, 1936) has shown in her groundbreaking studies on timing that musical interpretation is not accidental, but that note durations can be repeated consistently across several renditions. This observation is supported by the findings of Repp (1992a), who demonstrated that the correlation between the repetition of the first section in 28 recordings of Schumann's *"Träumerei"* varied, in most cases, between $r = .80$ and $r = .90$. Likewise, Skinner made the interesting observation that even if a player tries to play inexpressively and metronomically (in a so-called deadpan version), he or she will produce measurable tempo deviations, for example, with ritardandi corresponding to phrase endings. From this it is possible to conclude that, on the one hand, musical knowledge seems to be organized in phrases and that, on the other hand, a player is unable to ignore the perceived phrase units.

As Palmer (1989) explains in her "parameter theory" of performance, an interpretation is stored in memory as a basic performance pattern, the timing profile of which is modified when the player intends to give a different interpretation of a piece (instead of generating a completely new profile or program). We have to keep in mind that Palmer's timing analyses as well as those of most other authors are based on note-to-note interonset durations where the term *interonset interval* refers to the time span between the onset of two consecutive events. As long as we use analytical methods that concern timing within only a specific time frame (represented by means of a timing curve), we cannot conclude that only this time layer is affected by parameter changes. Therefore, we ought to compare the simultaneous shaping of time in time frames of various sizes (for a new theoretical approach see Langner, 2000, in press; Langner, Kopiez, & Feiten, 1998).

The Coding/Decoding Process of Musical Expression

The Relation Between Structure and Expression

Musical expression can be investigated from two perspectives. On the one hand, there is the "emotional expression" of music (such as the communication of different moods), and on the other hand there is "structural expression," which is strongly related to the structural features of music. These structural features, such as cadences that indicate segment boundaries to the listener, help the listener to separate the stream of music into sections such as motifs or phrases. Although both perspectives are relevant for the explanation of the communicative processes in music, the structural expression is relevant for the communication on different hierarchical levels.

The Assumption of "Isomorphism." The dominant structure-expression theory of expressive communication of meaning assumes that there is a strong relationship between compositional structure and musical expression. The theoretical foundation for this concept was provided by S. Langer (1953) with the assumption of isomorphism, that is, a close relationship between the structural features of a composition—such as hierarchical organization—and the expression intended by the composer. This assumption has been influential in this field of study (e.g., Palmer, 1997, who assumes that structure constrains expression). As early as 1936, Henderson was able to show that performers obviously use a hierarchical categorization of the compositional structure to modify with different weightings the nominal values in the score; for example, more important events on higher levels such as phrase boundaries would be emphasized through use of a dynamic accent, lengthening of the duration, or asynchronization. Following this theory, it would seem to be the performer's priority to uncover the musical structure encoded in the score and to communicate these insights to the audience—a view that has received wide support in empirical research.

Presenting melodies in different metrical contexts, Sloboda (1985) observed that pianists changed certain note parameters, namely, articulation and note length, in accordance with the different metrical positions on which a note fell. In a subsequent listening experiment, listeners could clearly identify the performer's intention. The importance of structural expression was also shown in a study by Repp (1997b) where the timing curves of a Debussy prelude played by 10 famous pianists were compared to the timing profiles of 10 graduate students, recorded nearly unrehearsed. Despite large interindividual differences in preparation and experience, timing curves were found to be extremely similar. A further experiment, based on the theoretical predictions of Lerdahl and Jackendoff's (1983) *Generative Theory of Tonal Music*, was carried out by Todd (1985). He discovered that the extent of a ritardando was proportional to the importance of the affected phrase boundary: More important phrase boundaries received more slowing than less important ones.

Clarke (1987, 1988, 1993) also showed that this close relationship between expression and musical structure is a necessary (but not wholly sufficient) prerequisite for adequate understanding of the performer's interpretive intention. In a series of experiments, he found that listeners gave a more qualified evaluation of a performance when the expressive modifications were congruent with the musical structure. Thus it would seem that expressive phrasing is determined by structural features, descriptions, and "mental representations of musical structure" (Palmer, 1992, p. 249). While the performer may use expressive cues to communicate his intention and understanding to the listener, we have to keep in mind that the listener not only perceives the musical structure but also evaluates whether or not the performer has understood the music.

Beyond Structural Constraints: Irrational Components of Expressive Performance. The question remains open as to whether a performance is simply the result of structural constraints and can be described by the process of "rational composition of performance," meaning that the performer synthesizes a performance by analytically weighting structural features (see Mazzola & Beran, 1998). While there has been very little research aimed at investigating the extent to which performances are influenced by factors that include structure, gesture, and mood, Clarke (1993; also Clarke & Baker-Short, 1987) has indicated a need to modify the strict rationalistic model of performance generation.

Clarke set up manipulated performances that required players to imitate a rubato passage, the timing profile of which had been inverted or shifted by one eighth note or one measure. Such a transformation resulted in a contradiction between musical structure and expressive intention. When the subjects (skilled pianists) tried to imitate these versions, it could be seen that timing was more accurate and stable in the original than in the manipulated version. Consequently, it appears that the relationship between structural and expressive features is a necessary but not sufficient condition for the explanation of expressive performance. As of now, little is known about the impact of the performer's emotions or sense of movement on the shaping of a performance. It may therefore come as no surprise that completely synthesized performances of complete pieces based on complex mathematical transformations of pitch, harmony, and time parameters (e.g., Mazzola & Beran, 1998) sound musically plausible, albeit artistically unspectacular.

The recordings of Glenn Gould, whose performances have been evaluated by music critics as intentionally unconventional, bear witness to the claim that there has to be artistic individuality in addition to some rule-governed performance. Although experience of musical performance suggests strong evidence for the importance of an additional "human factor," current research cannot provide any explanations as to the nature of such an irrational component (see Shaffer, 1989). Consequently, more analysis of unconventional performances is necessary in order to gain a deeper insight into the scope of artistic individuality beyond the limits of the accepted "rules."

Rule-Based Performance Grammar

The Analysis-by-Synthesis Approach.   In everyday life, rules facilitate communication and help to avoid ambiguity. If this is the case, could it not then be possible that a similar mechanism also operates in the communication of musical expression? The observation that alike musical structures cause parallel expressive features has already been pointed out by Lussy (1873/1882). In his treatise on the application of musical expression to performance, Lussy analyzed expression marks in the scores of several different composers and identified 17 rules for the application of accelerando (e.g., through the course of repeated notes, at harmonic changes, or at rising melodic lines) and 32 rules for the application of ritardando (e.g., at falling melodic lines, at phrase endings, or at groups of lower notes that follow a series of high notes). Each of these rules, he argued, was illustrated by a vast number of notated examples for pupils to practice. It is this work that provides the backdrop to the scientific investigation of rule-based systems of musical expression developed by Scandinavian researchers (e.g., Friberg, 1995; Gabrielsson, 1999; Sundberg, Frydén, & Askenfelt, 1983; for a review). In the early studies, Sundberg, Frydén, and Askenfelt used an analysis-by-synthesis approach to test the adequacy of the output of their generative system. The approach outlined earlier has been labeled generative in view of the fact that performances are generated by the application of expressive grammars and rule-based systems. In simple terms, the procedure is the following: First rules of expression are formulated by listening to recordings of outstanding artists. (It is interesting to note that most of the rules were suggested by an experienced violinist, Lars Frydén!). Then these rules are implemented in a computer program that generates artificial interpretations. Finally, the synthesized and original versions are compared and the rule system subsequently improved. Recent progress of the performance synthesis project is documented in Friberg (1999), and models are implemented in software such as *Melodia* by Roberto Bresin and *Director Musices* by Anders Friberg. Thompson, Sundberg, Friberg, and Frydén (1989, p. 63) assert that "the musical quality of performances is improved by applying rules." However, the same authors remark that the simple addition of rules generated only "unmusical" results, due to the overemphasis on detail. In most cases, the application of no more than five rules was sufficient to produce an acceptable result.

Critical Assessment of the Rule-Based Approach.   Oosten (1993) seriously criticizes the generative approach, arguing that rules are a necessary but not entirely sufficient condition for the generation and communication of musically accepted performance synthesis. This is due in part to the primarily local effect of a rule (instead of being concerned with elements of greater structural importance; see experiment by Todd [1985] described earlier) and to the intuitive nature of the generative approach. Moreover, the simple application of a rule set seems to be a "hit the wall" strategy for the most part, which considers neither the style-specific application of an expression rule nor the fact that rules are not always applied consistently by a performer within a composition. Current performance research still has no theoretical framework for the shaping of expressive parameters within larger time frames. The experience of outstanding live performances, however, confirms that there must be an expressive layer responsible for the communication of, for instance, tension and resolution, which cannot be analyzed by any of the existing scientific methods. Langner and Kopiez (1995) showed that large-scale oscillations, triggered by the timing profile of a performance with a time frame of 60 seconds or more, can be important features of professional performances. In the same way, existing analyses support the assumption that the depth of a performer's musical thought influences the communication of expressive tension and perhaps of a performance's overall musical quality, yet such a hypothesis still awaits confirmation. In summary, it can be argued that the rule-based approach only partially explains the phenomenon of expressive interpretation and cannot account entirely for its complexity. In other words, the rule-based approach can *simulate* but not *imitate* a real performance.

Are Interpretations Uniform or Individual?

Music cannot be performed using just any method, and performance variability seems to be limited by a criterion of "correctness." The national anthem, for example, can be jazzed up only so much before it ceases to be the national anthem. Similarly, with regard to the parameter tempo, it is impossible to double or triple the tempo of music and have it remain the same piece of music or communicate the same message. Being too fast or too slow makes some music unmusical and changes its character completely. What does this mean for the performance of pieces from the classical repertoire?

Historical Background of Performance Individuality.   The limited standard repertoire of our musical culture relies on individuality to distinguish one performer from another. Although it is usual for listeners to prefer specific artists, it remains unclear how this individuality can be identified in the acoustical data of a particular interpretation. In order to produce the unmistakable characteristics that identify a particular performer, the performer has to reproduce his or her personal rendition of a composition with great consistency, thereby practically minimizing the intraindividual variability. The historical situation of performance expectations has not always been that of the present day. On the contrary, Czerny's (1839/1991) treatise on musical performance (Czerny was Beethoven's piano teacher and one of the foremost piano teachers of his time) advocated the idea that performances should be variable from one time to another instead of being uniform. He demanded from competent performers an "always different" performance ("jedesmal eine andere Vortragsweise anzuwenden," p. 25), especially when repeating a passage several times within a composition. From this we can assume that, at least in the 19th century, performers gave a wider variety of performances than today and different artistic aspects of a composition could be communicated—as long as the character of the work was not compromised.

Performance Individuality in Schumann's "Träumerei." The current state of performance research points to a different situation in recent times. Repp (1992a) analyzed the timing of 28 recordings of Schumann's "Träumerei," played by 24 different pianists. Analysis of interonset intervals in the first eight measures showed that players could be grouped, by means of a principal component analysis, into four categories: Group 1 was dominated by the recordings of Horowitz, Group 2 by those of Cortot, Group 3 represented the mainstream, and Group 4 contained the remaining performers. The author concluded that a tendency toward uniformity could be observed due to timing constraints at phrase boundaries that allowed only a small degree of freedom. In a subsequent study, Repp (1992b) concentrated on the principle melodic gesture of "Träumerei" (which consists of six notes) and found instances of additional constraints that could limit artistic individuality. Subsequent experiments revealed that when the timing profile of this motif was shifted only those timing profiles whose shapes were parabolic were judged positively by the listeners. This result was explained by "classes of optimal temporal shapes for melodic gestures . . . that musically acculturated listeners know and expect . . . within which artistic freedom and individual preference can manifest themselves" (p. 221). Similar experiments that concern the variability of performance still continue to the present day, as shown in a recent study by Repp (1998) in which the author analyzes 115 recordings of Chopin's Etude in E major, op. 10, no. 3, by 108 artists. Using a principal component analysis, the first five bars of the Etude could be described by four factors, accounting for most of the timing variance (76%).

Do Timing Curves Represent Individuality in Performance? At this point, some criticism should be made concerning the validity of Repp's (1992a) results: By including the tim-

ing data of the whole piece, he obtained only one general factor with no differentiation among the 28 recordings and found also that a reduction in the number of included notes increased the number of factors. In addition, the timing clusters for the first melodic gesture did not correspond to the three main factors found in the principal component analysis of the first eight measures. Also, the perceptual experience when listening to the recordings does not correspond to such an undifferentiated statistical grouping. Where does this mismatch arise? We could assume that such a method of analyzing timing (or other variables) on a note-to-note level offers only a very limited insight into the nature of musical interpretation and the ideas communicated by the player. Consequently, we suggest that future methods of timing analysis include the possibility of *simultaneous* timing analysis of layers with different time-frame sizes (on a bar-to-bar level or a phrase-to-phrase level) of the same performance. Only such an approach would be commensurate with the complexity of musical thought observed in outstanding performers.

The considerations outlined earlier raise a further question: Is the performer's ability to shape time and intensity limited by the listeners' expectancies? Inspired by research into the attractiveness of human faces, Repp (1997a) carried out a so-called average performance experiment, in which listeners were asked to rate 11 performances of "Träumerei" in terms of quality and originality. One of the listening examples had been generated from the average timing and intensity data of the 10 other MIDI recordings. The pedaling sequence remained constant throughout all 11 versions. Repp found that the "average version" was ranked second-highest in terms of performance quality but second-lowest in terms of individuality. A plausible interpretation of the results offered by the author assumes that listeners develop a performance prototype that guides their expectancies; the average version could fulfill this expectancy and provide an ideal interpretation due to the compensation of extremes through the averaging. Despite the absence of a convincing theoretical explanation for this effect, the same preferential tendency for "averaged versions" can be observed in the evaluation of rhythmic performances. In a cross-cultural study on the perception of rhythm, Kopiez, Langner, and Steinhagen (1999) found a consistently high evaluation of the average performance of rhythm samples.

Different Perspectives of Analysis: Local and Global Expressive Shaping. One of the priorities for performance analysis in the future should be to develop methods and theories that allow for the analysis to take place within time frames of varying levels. Only the consideration of local as well as global levels of expressive shaping in the same performance will enable adequate analysis of the complex phenomenon of musical interpretation and communication. One example of how such a theoretical framework could function is given by Mazzola (1995) in his "inverse performance theory," which uses analytical data (so-called analytical weights) from a score analysis by a special software (Rubato[1]). These weights are used as predictor variables for the individual timing curves in multiple regression analysis. As demonstrated in Beran and Mazzola (2000), this decomposition of a complete performance (the authors call it analytical semantics) into analytical weights for the melodic, metric, and harmonic structure explained between 65 and 85% of the microstructure timing of a performance. This finding strongly supports the assumption that a close relationship exists between expressive intentions and compositional features, where the first can be explained with reference to the second. Such an approach goes far beyond the surface analysis of a small section by Repp (1992a) and gives detailed insight into the complexity of musical thought. Although Beran and Mazzola (2000) were able to confirm the fundamental structure of Repp's principal component analysis, large individual differences were shown to exist in relation to the relative importance of single structural parameters (harmony, melody, metric). In the case of Horowitz's three performances of "Träumerei," the performer's view of the piece obviously changed over time: After his first recording of the piece, in 1947—which was dominated by a very localized melodic and metrical thinking (a kind of "performance nearsight")—Horowitz's interpretation became more coherent in his 1963 and 1965 recordings. The different time perspectives in the studies by Repp (1992a) and Beran and Mazzola (2000) also go some way toward explaining the seemingly contradictory results achieved. As a result, it could be argued that although the timing of the first eight bars and the single melodic gestures remain unchanged over decades, more global timing concepts reveal changes when the piece is analyzed as a whole.

In light of these considerations, it is evident that inverse performance theory is also of great practical importance since it offers the transformation of the metaphorical language of musical criticism into an exactly defined parametric space. At the same time, however, it must be pointed out that research that concerns the relationship between performance features and the structural properties of the score is still new and expanding.

Decoding Expression: The Role of Acoustical Cues

In his famous treatise on flute playing from the 18th century, Quantz (1752/1966, p. 164) writes: "Hence in playing you must regulate yourself in accordance with the prevailing sentiment, so that you do not play a very melancholy Adagio too quickly or a cantabile Adagio too slowly." Clearly, in terms of the Adagio mentioned here by

Quantz, tempo is a global cue that supports the dominant character and affect of a piece, yet nowadays there are other factors, such as original instrumentation and tuning, that should be kept in mind. In addition, Quantz's statement sheds light on the relationship between the structural features of a composition and the expressive intentions of a performer. As Meyer (1956, p. 199) notes, the score gives more or less specific indications as to the composer's intention, but it depends on the performer to intensify or integrate these structural cues into a form that can be communicated to the listener. Thus a useful contribution for music theory is elaboration of the basic principles of emotive importance, such as expectancy or gestalt continuation. As the famous "Tristan chord" from the prelude to Wagner's *Tristan and Isolde* paradigmatically shows, emotional meaning will always be contextually dependent on structural features, which prevents the simple categorization of structural elements into a "catalog of emotions."

We assume that musical performance contains numerous so-called acoustical cues, such as timbre, tempo, and articulation, which help to facilitate the communication of the performer's intentions. A necessary condition for the communicative function, however, is the reliable decoding of such cues from the auditory stream. Research of the last decades into music performance as well as research into cross-modal perception of expressive qualities of object (see Beldoch, 1961, for less recent research) has given us some insight into the basic mechanisms of this cue extraction process: When measuring the degree of identification of 10 feelings, including anger, joy, and love, in different media (vocal, visual arts, and music), Beldoch found expressive qualities to be relatively consistent, yet the total congruence did not exceed 40% of correct identifications.

The Interdependence of Expressive Cues.   Our next question concerns the parameters of musical expression, their hierarchy, and their interrelation. Concerning the hierarchy of expressive parameters, Kamenetzky, Hill, and Trehub (1997) presented short, 30-second-long musical examples played in four versions: one with no variations in tempo and dynamics, another with variations in tempo and dynamics, another with variations in tempo only, and another with variations in dynamics only. The results showed that variation in tempo only caused a significantly lower evaluation on the "expressive" scale than variations in dynamics only or in tempo and dynamics. Although caution must be exercised regarding generalizations because of the very limited duration of the examples, a possible hierarchy of expressive parameters seems to exist.

In the same manner, two further studies produced more evidence of the interactive nature of expressive parameters. Dudek (1992), for example, carried out a recognition experiment of piano performances with interchanged velocity and timing data, holding one parameter constant in each version. In total, timing and intensity were used equally frequently for the identification of performances, but substantial individual differences were noted within the sample of 16 compositions played in different styles. Rather than provide a simple hierarchy of expressive factors, these findings emphasize the importance of the interaction between structural features of the composition and the listener's preferences for expressive parameters.

The second study, carried out by Dougherty in 1993, used the method of cross-synthesis of four emotions (i.e., the transfer of spectral features from one item to the other) from spoken language (anger, fear, joy, and sadness) to a short sequence of notes played on the violin with three specific expressive parameters (timbre, pitch contour, and speech tempo). The fact that the emotional state of "non-cross-synthesized" violin tones was identified as accurately as that of unmanipulated speech led the author to conclude that there was no single-feature mechanism for cue detection. Since the reliability of identification improved with the increasing number of expressive parameters involved in cross-synthesis, it is possible to conclude that the interaction between expressive parameters plays a decisive role in the correct identification of emotional intentions in performance.

Communicating Expressive Intentions to the Audience.

An early study that concerned the communication of the more complex aspects of a player's ideas to the audience was undertaken by Senju and Ohgushi (1987). Subjects who rated 10 performances of the opening of Mendelssohn's Violin Concerto through use of a semantic differential most commonly identified the intention of a "powerful" performance. Having subjects verbalize performance impressions, however, did not result in effective identification of the relevant aspects of expressive performance. Concerning the communication of dynamics, Patterson (1974) found that most woodwind players had a dynamic range too small to cover the six different degrees of intensity (from *pianissimo* to *fortissimo*) that require a range of roughly 30 decibels. Oboists, for example, often produced a span of only two dynamic levels. Since greater dynamic contrasts make music more exciting, the author suggests the use of exercises to enlarge the dynamic range. However, we have to remember that the perception of dynamics is also influenced by instrument-specific expectations of the listener. Perception can differ from reality.

Nakamura's 1987 study focuses on the fundamental role of dynamics (and not timing!) in the communication of expressive intentions. In his experiment, subjects heard musical excerpts and identified instances of crescendo much more reliably than instances of decrescendo in the corresponding score. It is possible, however, that such an effect is both instrument- and context-specific. Here the perceptual basis could form a template for the recognition

of increases in intensity. This last assumption is supported by the results of Huron (1991), who, in his analysis of the frequency of crescendo and decrescendo markings in 435 piano works by 14 composers, found a significantly greater number of crescendos than decrescendos. This bias in dynamic markings is termed ramp archetype and is based on a neural mechanism that facilitates detection of increasing rather than decreasing intensities.

A categorization of three levels of expression (no expression, appropriate, exaggerated) across different instruments was observed in a study by Kendall and Carterette (1990), which revealed that both musicians and nonmusicians were able to distinguish, to a certain and not totally reliable degree, between performances of a short melody on different instruments with different levels of expression. Besides the fact that the subjects appeared to use timing as an expressive cue, the authors stress that there was no support for the idea of an all-encompassing grammar that mediates the communication between performer and listener (p. 160). Of course, the perceived expression of a performance is influenced not only by acoustical cues but also by visual ones (see chap. 30 in this volume).

Conditions of Successful Recognition of Expressed Emotions.

Is formal music education a necessary condition for the successful recognition of expressive cues, or can an expressive intention be communicated by a performer even to "uneducated" listeners or children? In a perception experiment with 4- to 9-year-old children, Rodriguez (1998) conducted a "same-or-different" discrimination test that used mechanical and expressive versions of a tune. He found that subjects answered with 66% overall accuracy, but that the degree of correct answers increased with age, starting from 46% among kindergarten children and ending with 70% accuracy among fourth graders. Giomo (1992) investigated whether mood in music, as a holistic impression, was correctly recognized by 5- to 9-year-old children. Using a pictorial, nonverbal response paradigm, she was able to show that age played no role in the effective categorization of classical music examples into three mood dimensions (softness, pleasantness, solemnity). While no positive influence could be attributed to taking instrumental lessons, the author discovered an effect of sociocultural background that pointed to the influence of both the subjects' home music environment and musical experience.

These findings provide evidence for the idea that the perception of expressive features in music is perhaps an ability that must be nurtured and developed through education and listening experience. On the background of other studies that relate to age-dependent recognition of emotional expression in music, a more complex picture emerges. In a labeling task devised by Cunningham and Sterling (1989), for example, it was noted that preschoolers were already astonishingly consistent in associating certain attributes (happiness, sadness, anger, and fear) with musical excerpts presented to them. Dolgin and Adelson (1990) also found age differences in the recognition of emotional expression between 4- and 9-year-olds. Similarly, Terwogt and Grinsven (1991) noted that the agreement in recognition of happiness, anger, and sadness in music excerpts increased between the ages 5 and 7 years; conversely, Kratus (1993) found no developmentally based effect in the recognition of emotional states in 30 musical excerpts among 6- to 22-year-old subjects. Bear in mind that there is, as yet, no standardized mood-recognition task in music that uses a fixed repertoire of music examples from clearly defined selection criteria. As long as each study uses different stimuli, the varying results can be attributed not only to this incomparability but also to other relevant factors such as age and gender. Unfortunately, this is a serious methodological difficulty for all studies in the field.

Physical Correlates of Emotional Characters. A Swedish research group led by Alf Gabrielsson has recently started to focus on the coding/decoding process of acoustical cues in the communication of expressive intentions. They are interested in knowing "what . . . a performer[s] do to generate the intended emotional character of the music"? (Gabrielsson, 1995, p. 35; for further information on the running project "Expressive Performance in Music, Dance, Speech, and Body Movement" see also http://www.psyk.uu.se/hemsidor/alf.gabrielsson). In their opinion, musical expression includes both, structure and performance. The principal method employed is experimental in the sense that a performer is instructed to play a given passage with different emotional characters (happy, sad, solemn, angry, soft, and indifferent). Upon completion of this task, the acoustical parameters of the performance are analyzed. An important result that arose out of the analysis of the recordings was that performers used a wide variety of durational modifications, especially concerning the proportional relationships between different note lengths. However, dynamics, articulation, and timbre also played an instrument-dependent role and were modified in correspondence with the intended expression. For example, "angry" and "happy" versions were played faster than those excerpts meant to illustrate other characters, and in happy versions the durational proportions were softened.

There are obvious reasons to investigate the connection between motion and musical expression. For example, Clynes's "theory of sentics" (1977) assumes that for each basic emotion there exists a specific dynamic form. Although Clynes's theory is not uncontroversial (see Edgewater, 1999, p. 167; Repp, 1989, 1990 for critiques), Gabrielsson used Clynes's Sentograph device to assess the correspondence between the expressive parameters and the expressive finger movements of an imagined performance for the same musical excerpt. The results indicated a close relationship between emotion and motion, which supports the central hypothesis that "we may consider emotion, motion, and music as being isomorphic" (Gabrielsson, 1995, p. 37).

An early experimental investigation into communicative processes was undertaken by Gabrielsson and Juslin (1996). In this study, musicians were asked to perform melodies from different styles of music (folk songs, classical tunes) on different instruments (violin, electric guitar, voice) with different emotional characters (happy, sad, angry, fearful, tender, solemn). Listeners then rated the performances regarding how clearly they perceived the intended character, a task that represents a basic paradigm for all research in expressive communication. Results showed that listeners were in general agreement and that a wide range of expression among instruments, styles, and players was observed. Analysis of the acoustical data showed an astonishingly flexible handling of the musical structure: One of the melodies was played on a flute with a "sad" character at 50 beats per minute and another by a violinist with a "happy" character at 250 beats per minute. Although the authors compiled a provisional "feature-catalogue" of musical characters, the results raise an important issue, namely, that of the constraints of musical material. If the same melody can be played five times faster, achieving a different expressive character, the question of the existence of a "natural character" determined by the compositional structure remains open to discussion! Therefore, we suggest that the term *character* should be used to denote a unique "fingerprint" of a piece that gives it its unifying impression. Beethoven's *Pastoral* Symphony (Kirby, 1970) and the powerful atmospheric spell of the "Wolfsschluchtszene" (Wolf's glen scene) in Weber's *Freischütz* (Ruiter, 1989) might serve as famous examples of such characters. In this sense, the term *character* has two connotations: It is connected first to the specific expressive individuality of a piece and second to the unmistakable emotions presented in a performance.

The Cue-Utilization Paradigm. The most recent research in the analysis of acoustical cues generated by the performer and their relevance for musical communication is best represented by Juslin (1997, 2000, 2001; Juslin & Madison, 1999). This approach can be characterized as a cue-utilization paradigm where performers are instructed to play a short popular tune with different fundamental emotions, such as happiness, sadness, anger, and fear. The players may use all expressive parameters in free variation. In a subsequent "labeling task," listeners decode and rate the intensity of the communicated emotions. In principle, Juslin adopted the research paradigm that Scherer and Oshinsky (1977) used in their research on the perception of expression in synthesized 8-tone sequences. They also produced a catalog of expressive code. Juslin's theoretical framework was taken from functionalistic emotional psychology and Brunswik's functionalistic and probabilistic approach to perception: It assumes that "basic" emotions are perceived much more clearly than "other" emotions due to their importance for the phylogenetic development—a basic mechanism that could also be important in musical communication. Such an assumption is supported by Juslin, who showed that the decoding of expressive intentions reaches an overall stability of nearly 80%.

At this point, some critical points that concern research on the communication of emotion and the validity of results should be made:

- *Impact of structural features.* At present, the cue-utilization paradigm offers no predictions that regard the impact of the composition's structural features, such as tone system, scale, or orchestration. In order to develop a clearer understanding of such features, research would have to consider the interaction between a "happy" tune played with "sad" intentions in a very slow tempo and vice versa. As long as little is known about structural constraints, the validity of any results should be considered preliminary. A more complex picture emerges in the most recent reports on "inherent expression" (see Lindström, 2000; Madison, 2000): Emotional expression is determined by the musical structure itself, an adequate performance, and the interaction between performance variability and structure. While the intensity of emotional expression can be both reinforced as well as reduced by performance variability, some emotional characters are not influenced at all when performance variability is experimentally removed.
- *Relationship between global and local cues.* There is currently no theory to explain the relationship between local and global expressive elements. Listening experience produces strong evidence for the complex and hierarchical nature of the influence of single emotional features; we do not simply extract emotional cues locally. The 200-year-long debate in musical aesthetics about the term *musical character* underscores the importance of a unifying mechanism called character, which "rules" a whole composition (see Ruiter, 1989). Nevertheless, as long as samples with durations of only a few seconds are used (such as in the study by Gabrielsson and Juslin, 1996), we cannot reach an adequate understanding of this emotional hierarchy. At the same time, we should not forget the results of other researchers (e.g., Karno & Konecni, 1992; Tillman & Bigand, 1996) that showed that listeners are "embarrassingly" insensitive to global structural properties when judging the emotional expression of manipulated (so-called scrambled) versions of a piece of music.
- *"Subjective" induction of emotions versus "objective" labeling.* Listeners in Juslin's study were given a labeling task, but there was no control over whether they could objectively label the perceived expressive code and keep this decision uninfluenced by the emotions induced by the music. Quite simply, it is uncertain exactly what was judged—expression or impression. This problem of separating impression from expression is a fundamental problem in all "music and emotion" research. A further problem is the immediate induction of emotions. As Nyklicek and Doornen (1997) were able to show, heartbeat as well as breathing patterns were strongly influenced by selected structural parameters of the music such as tempo. Despite the fact that the authors chose only very extreme and basic emotions for their examples, this effect was intensified when subjects were initially introduced to the expected emotions. From an evolutionary perspective, it follows that there is a basic mechanism for the immediate detection of certain emotional states; Juslin is right with regard to this point. And his view is supported by the findings of Peretz, Gagnon, and Bouchard (1998) in a judgment study with brain-injured listeners. The subjects' emotional judgment was quite consistent, immediate, and seemingly uninfluenced by their condition regardless of whether presented musical excerpts were "happy" or "sad": The judgment was mostly influenced by musical structure (mode and tempo). In addition, we do not know how an individual's "emotional quotient" influences the perceived emotional intensity. At the same time, it should be remembered that most musical states are not based on clear, fundamental emotions. For example, music may well result in "boredom"—a feeling/emotion that can surely not be classified as a fundamental emotion.
- *Model of emotion and consciousness.* The theoretical model used in the explanation is an "umbrella" model in which all emotions are assembled under one "hat." Criticizing the use of this model, LeDoux (1996) argues that each emotion should be considered as a complex and autonomous system that works along with psycho-physiological reactions. As long as our understanding of just one of those systems is incomplete, it is impossible to reach any conclusion as to the nature of the whole emotional system. If we believe that listening to music can activate memorable musical experiences, it follows that the only way to investigate the complex phenomenon of musical communication is to adopt a systemic approach. This approach would cover the ongoing (conscious or unconscious) process of evaluation and interpretation while listening to music.
- *Ambiguity.* If musical communication aspires to being unambiguous, would a functionalistic approach be adequate for the explanation of emotional communication? Aesthetic experience appears to be characterized only by the paradoxical mechanism of ambiguous input (musical message) that results in unambiguous output (listening experience). If certainty in identification of expression were a genuine priority of music, we could be sure that human evolution would have created a form of music less ambiguous (maybe with fewer possible emotions)—

in a communicative sense—than that already observed. We may conclude that in spite of its importance, cue utilization is only a secondary phenomenon of the listening process and that the functionalistic perspective remains limited to a few basic emotions.

Can We Understand Music Without Prerequisites?: The Myth of Music as a "Universal Language"

The idea that music might be a universal language that can be understood without prerequisites and independently from the individual's cultural background is a widely held conviction. Although this belief is asserted with great persistence in both politics and everyday life, this issue is not simple, judged from the standpoint of music psychology. It is already clear that the study of musical universals and the biological foundations of music have contributed a new perspective characterized by comparative research methodologies (see Carterette & Kendall, 1999). While this has resulted in the creation of new research disciplines such as biomusicology (Wallin, Merker, & Brown, 2000), aimed at providing us with a fascinating insight into the auditory perception among animals (see Fay, 1988, for an extensive data collection), it is still very difficult to draw conclusions from the literature relevant to the human music perception. Very often, the studies of comparative music psychology, based on studies of animal behavior, are obtained with simple stimuli that have little resemblance to real music. Although interesting in themselves, the results that concern "virtual pitch in cats" (Hefner & Whitfield, 1976), "octave stretching" (Carterette & Kendall, 1999, p. 739), or "octave identity" (surely not a universal; see Hulse & Page, 1988; Hulse, Takeuchi, & Braaten, 1992) have little immediate bearing on the human listening experience.

Having said this, it is important to recognize the contribution of researchers who investigate auditory perception in animals and newborn infants, which allow great insight into the importance of the basic processes in music listening and have shown that such processes appear on a "hardware" basis in all vertebrates regardless of cultural influences. For instance, studies by Porter and Neuringer (1984) revealed that pigeons can first learn to distinguish between musical styles (e.g., Bach and Stravinsky) and then successfully transfer their acquired stylistic knowledge to unfamiliar examples in a discrimination test. Hulse and Cynx (1986) found that auditory stream segregation already works in starlings, while Fassbender's (1996) study of auditory capacity in early infancy concluded that most musically relevant perceptual mechanisms, such as contour perception, are probably developed at a very early age. It is essential here to realize that music is not considered a

spoken language and, as Sloboda (1985, p. 12) points out, it would indeed "be foolish to claim that music is simply another natural language." It should, however, be kept in mind that music shares certain structural similarities with spoken language, such as its hierarchical organization. Temporal proximity alone does not rule the perception of music; in fact, we as listeners construct hierarchical relationships while listening to music in real time.

The Cultural Dependency of Expressive Decoding. A review I have written (in press) argues that unfortunately most of the research concerned with so-called perceptual invariants is a long way away from explaining relevant aspects of musical experience. This can be seen in a study by Hulse, Takeuchi, and Braaten (1992), who demonstrated that the ability to recognize the transposition of a melody—a musically relevant universal—was lacking in young children (3-year-olds and younger) and animals. Similarly, investigations into the communication of meaning and emotion in music show disappointing results. In their study of the cross-cultural understanding of Indian raga modes in excerpts of Hindustani music, Balkwill and Thompson (1999) asked Western listeners to rate the degree of joy, sadness, anger, and peace displayed in 12 excerpts. Their results showed that listeners were sensitive to the intended emotions of "joy" and "anger" in the music, but that the impressions of "peace" and "sadness" could not often be so clearly distinguished. (Incidentally, impressions of peace and sadness are not always easily distinguished in Western music, either.) In addition, the researchers noticed that an association between emotional and structural features could be observed: impressions of "joy" were associated with fast tempi and low melodic complexity while "sadness" was linked to slow tempi and high melodic complexity. Despite the importance of the findings outlined earlier, it would seem that assigning emotional labels to music still does not reach far beyond the surface of the complex interaction between humans and music. As a result, we are encouraged to further question whether or not the emotional responses reported may in fact be influenced by musical features as well as by cultural factors.

In a series of studies designed to investigate the cross-cultural understanding of emotional content in music, examples were chosen from Western classical music, new age genres, and traditional Asian Indian music (Gregory & Varney, 1996). These were then rated for their emotional content by both Western listeners and listeners with also an Indian background (bicultural). The fact that these were unable to demonstrate clear consistency in their identification of, for example, the various seasons in Antonio Vivaldi's *Four Seasons* led the authors to conclude that "the affective response to music is determined more by cultural tradition than by the inherent qualities of the music" (p. 47). The most recent and extensive of these cross-cultural studies on emotional response (Bhatti & Gregory, 2000) used samples of religious music from both Asian Indian and Western cultures with durations of between 2 and 15 minutes. These excerpts were then rated by Western and Pakistani listeners in order to establish similarities and differences in the affective ratings. Western listeners gave lower ratings than Pakistanis to the spiritual content of religious Qawwali music, while Christian rock music was only considered to be "arousing" and "uplifting" by those Western listeners familiar with Christian practices. From this short review of cross-cultural research in music, it is clear that the search for universals in musical experience results in an inconsistent and contradictory pattern of results.

The most obvious conclusion to be drawn from the aforementioned findings is that music experience is heavily constrained by the listener's individual background and that it would require *tremendous* efforts to adapt to an unfamiliar cultural system. Those cultural experiences come into play especially in the affective response to unknown music. Despite a current lack of sound factual evidence, the issues of musical universals and music as a universal language are touted persistently. This suggests a need for explanation and research, and if we do not want to reject this appealing claim, we will have to seek alternative answers.

Proposal for Culturally Independent Universals in Music

It could be that an alternative approach is needed. Guided by the hypothesis that there are at least three factors that could be commonly associated with musical perception in all cultures, we would suggest that the potential oversimplification that results from the focus on premusical variables be avoided by focusing on the variables of synchronization, expectancy, and musical tension and movement.

Synchronization. When people listen to music, reactions in the form of synchronized tapping or clapping can often be observed—a form of behavior that, according to Merker (2000a, 2000b), is not limited to humans but has also been observed in the glowing of fireflies and the chirping of crickets. This entrainment of living beings into an existing rhythmic pulse raises the issue of the possible existence of an evolutionary fundamental for this specific behavior. In attempting to provide a rationale for this idea, Merker (2000a) refers to a primarily sociobiological function, reminding us that synchronized chorusing increases the signal range, thereby increasing the probability of attracting potential mates. Furthermore, as observed in chimpanzees, synchronized calling at the site of a recently dis-

covered food source indicates cooperation with external individuals, also attractive for possible mating partners. This capacity to synchronize to an external trigger pulse is indeed an astonishing phenomenon, and, as Fraisse (1982) indicates, it is a form of behavior that is strongest in humans at an interonset interval of 500 to 600 milliseconds. Nevertheless, there is a substantial difference between the synchronous calling of monkeys and the performance of music by humans in the sense that chimpanzees cannot keep time independently (e.g., continue a given pulse). This leads us to conclude that the ability to synchronize seems to be an indispensable condition for most kinds of human musical activities: Neither drumming ensembles, groups of dancers, nor a string quartet would be able to perform together without this fundamental capacity. Although synchronization can also be observed for visual stimuli (yet it is superior for auditory stimuli), this capacity would appear to be a musically relevant universal that can be found in the cross-cultural ubiquity of metric music that exists in present-day cultures. Furthermore, it is clear that the capability to desynchronize is equally important since only the variation between exact synchronization and intentional desynchronization produced the "human touch" in musical performance.

Expectancy. Expectancy is a general cognitive mechanism that makes assumptions that concern the further processing of an event. While it can be applied to whatever phenomena we meet, it is also relevant to the concept of music perception. In the case of musical rhythm, for example, we can observe that all listeners create hypotheses as to how a given pattern will be continued or what the metrical position of the next beat will be (e.g., Desain, 1992). Yet expectancy also influences the perception of harmony and other musical parameters, and even when one is listening to unfamiliar (e.g., non-Western) music there is still a tendency to build expectancies. Using a probe tone paradigm, Castellano, Bharucha, and Krumhansl (1984) demonstrated that when Western listeners were able to perceive tonic (first) and dominant (fifth) degrees in an Indian raga, they did not assimilate the modal system to the Western diatonic system. The importance of culturally specific knowledge was also identified in a study by Krumhansl and Keil (1982), in which Western listeners were asked to complete a melody based on the Indonesian equidistant 5-tone *sléndro* scale. The findings suggest that although the cross-cultural familiarity of perception was limited to processing strategies, further culturally specific knowledge was needed to achieve a deeper understanding of the genre.

In relation to melodic perception, the theory of musical expectancy has been developed to a more advanced degree in the writings of Meyer (1956) and Narmour (1990). According to Meyer, listening to music can best be described using a "smoker" metaphor:

If, for example, a habitual smoker wants a cigarette and, reaching into his pocket, finds one, there will be no affective response. . . . If, however, the man finds no cigarette . . . and then remembers that the stores are closed . . . he will very likely begin to respond in an emotional way. (p. 13).

Meyer (p. 5) regards the idea of universalism as one error of music psychology, besides hedonism and atomism, and claims that "music in a style with which we are totally unfamiliar is meaningless" (p. 35). However, I propose that the general tendency to build up expectancies while listening to music (regardless of the specific cultural experience) is worthy of consideration as a potential musical universal. In Narmour's theory of expectancy, his "implication-realization model" (which is similar to Meyer's ideas yet more formalized), we find a universally applicable perceptual model for melody. Broadly speaking, the first component, namely, implication, derives from the similarity/dissimilarity of melodic elements and causes us to hypothesize about a likely continuation of the melody. Subsequently, the "realization" part confirms or rejects any hypotheses and leads to aesthetic interest. The two characteristics of this model are: that top-down processes (such as acquired style-specific knowledge) work together with bottom-up processes (mainly innate gestalt laws) and that small intervals imply the continuation of a melody with similar intervals and in the same direction, while large intervals imply following smaller intervals, a change in direction, and closure. Although verification is still needed for Narmour's model and some criticisms have been voiced (e.g., the model's bias for tonal Western music; see Krumhansl et al., 2000), we can assume that expectancy may play an important role in the debate that surrounds musical universals.

In their recent cross-cultural study on melodic expectancy among North Sami *yoiks*, Krumhansl, Toivanen, Eerola, Toiviainen, and Louhivuori (2000) found evidence to support the claim that "listeners are sensitive to statistical information in novel styles which gives important information about basic underlying structures" (p. 14). Moreover, despite general similarities among the responses given by Western, Finnish, and Sami subjects in the probe tone experiment, the authors concluded that style knowledge strongly influenced melodic expectancy and that the judgments of the Sami subjects familiar with the *yoik* style were least influenced by schematic Western tonal knowledge.

Musical Tension and Movement. Another fundamental experience in musical perception that may be relevant to other factors besides rhythm is that of movement. When talking about movement, we are not so much concerned with the tapping of one's foot to a piece of music, but we are referring to the sensation of psychoenergetic forces—an inner phenomenon that manifests itself physically through observable body movements. Although Gabrielsson (1995, p. 37) has claimed that "we may consider emotion, motion, and music as being isomorphic," there is to the present day no theoretical framework that can explain these processes. The fact is that the degrees of belief in psychoenergetic effects varies among authors.

A strong belief in the psychoenergetic effects of music is apparent in the writings of Jaques-Dalcroze (1921, chap. 12). He posits that the main function of rhythmic education is to enable the student to play or symbolize the rhythms he or she experiences. Interestingly, the author does not refer to any explanation of the inner processes but chooses to concentrate exclusively on the expression of inner sensations through bodily movement, culminating in the exclamation that "rhythm is movement" (Moore, 1992). Due to a lack of research into the relationship between expressed and perceived movement, we cannot speak to the relation between strength of musical feelings and strength of physical sensation. The very sophisticated theoretical framework of the Swiss musicologist Kurth (1931) seems to come closest to the musical experience. In his view, analysis of the sensation of psychic movement is the key to the understanding of musical communication. Although terms such as *power, space,* and *matter* seem to refer to a physicalist approach, Kurth identifies more differences than similarities between physical and psychic processes. His writings contain a complete research program for future music psychology—centered around the term of *movement*—which has not yet been widely recognized.[2] However, difficulties with the implementation of this program may result because modern experimental methods may not necessarily be compatible with the type of predictions that Kurth made.

Researchers have also presented evidence for the importance of perceived movement. Repp (1992b), for example, found that the optimal temporal shaping for the principal melodic gesture of "Träumerei" could best be described by a parabolic timing function, referring to a motion metaphor. As Sloboda (1998, p. 24) points out, musical experience involves sensations such as tension and resolution: "The structural description does not in itself incorporate . . . [these] feeling[s]." This implies that the feeling of being moved must have an internal, psychoenergetic basis and that therefore any kinematic model (models that try to explain an experience of motion that is caused by music, e.g., an ascending scale), such as those reviewed in Palmer (1997), can only account very superficially for this phenomenon. It is also difficult to describe the relationship between perceived tension or movement and aesthetic experience. Fredrickson (1995) found that the resulting curve for the "perceived tension" when listening to a Haydn symphony (measured in real time with a Continuous Response Digital Interface [CRDI]) showed more variability and local changes than continuous ratings of the "aesthetic experience" (see Krumhansl, 1997, for a review of tension research). The variable "aesthetic experience" could be interpreted as the result of an integration of several other psychoenergetic aspects. As long as we do not have a theoretical framework or a definition of what musical tension is and how it is perceived, we cannot be certain what exactly the CRDI measures. Gjerdingen (1988) attempted to map the changes in pitch and intensity of the human singing voice onto a two-dimensional so-called Gjerdingen melogram in the form of a moving line. This way the author hoped to communicate the microstructure of vocal lines in Indian music, in which the microstructure of a single note is at the same time relevant to the impression of a lively character of singing but also hard to transcribe into our staff notation. Gjerdingen (1994) also investigated the related phenomenon of "apparent motion" induced by music. To summarize, support has been found for the assumption that musical movement and tension are, together, a further culturally independent fundamental.

Implications for Music Education

This chapter set out to show that the process of musical communication was dependent on the existence of relevant knowledge and experience on the part of the listener. As I have argued elsewhere (Kopiez, in press), there is some convincing evidence that suggests that listeners always listen to music with "their own ears" and that music appreciation is based on culturally specific knowledge and education. The multicultural makeup of today's classroom, with its accompanying disparity of cultural knowledge and experience, does not allow for a simple, unified way to nurture communication skills. One suggestion seems tenable, however: The listening (and music-making) experience should take precedence over normative rules; this means that teachers should avoid oversimplified "labeling" of musical expression to explain the contents of music. Rodriguez (1998, p. 57) claims that "learning experiences in the music classroom should be designed to nurture sensitivity to musical expression," but how can this be realized under such difficult conditions? We would like to propose a few simple methods as starting points for the teacher who is trying to impart to his or her students the peculiarities of musical communication:

- *Spoken language.* It is relatively easy to read and record a short poem with and without different states of expression. Listeners' attention can be focused on parameters such as accents, accelerations, and dynamic shaping. With more technically advanced means, it would be interesting to extract parameters such as speech melody as cues for specific emotional states in language by using appropriate software (e.g., Boersma, 1999). Students can also be confronted with the impact of different speech melodies that correspond to different intended expressions.

- *Mechanical versus expressive performance in music.* As Burnsed (1998) has shown, a significant preference for folk songs played with expressive dynamics over those played without expression already exists in elementary school students from Grades 1 to 5, and even in musically less educated students expressive shaping increases aesthetic attractiveness. The basic experience of expression in music can be imparted on any instrument and by using any simple melody with the following setting. The required technical equipment amounts only to a simple MIDI sequencer for the generation of the unexpressive version and editing of the expressive deviations in the editor window. In order to demonstrate the difficulty of consistent expressive shaping, nominal note values can also be manipulated by the use of a graphic MIDI editor.

- *Synthesis of emotions.* Another approach, which would allow pupils to gain more insight into the communication of musical meaning, involves the use of software such as Director Musices (see Friberg, 1999) or the simple program referred to by Rodriguez (1998) for the synthesis of emotions in a given piece of music. These files or other synthesized versions of MIDI files can be evaluated by means of a semantic differential (scale with polar adjectives) regarding the intended emotion. Moreover, to demonstrate the importance of different expressive parameters in music, the expressive deviations in melodies can be "deconstructed" by setting the timing and intensity deviations to their nominal value.

- *Improving expressive communication.* As a result of the insight that expressive performance is based on a rule system that has to be learned by player and listener, Woody (1999) showed that successful imitation of expressive dynamics in a short piano composition by a student correlated with the correct verbal identification of the expressive features used in the aural model before attempting an imitative performance. To improve communication between teacher and student on the one hand and performer and listener on the other, the author suggests that verbal instructions about the intended aural model are given to the student before trying an imitative performance. Finally, only a conscious and clear performance plan can guarantee easy perception of expressive intentions by the listener. Such an imitative exercise (accompanied by verbal reports of the perceived expressive intentions) could easily be realized through the use of simple melodies played with different expressive features. In a recent investigation by Juslin and Laukka (2000), performers were instructed to communicate different emotions to the subjects. After cognitive feedback about intended and perceived acoustical cues was given, accuracy of expressive communication increased by about 50%. These findings suggest that cognitive feedback is a useful tool in improving communication between player and audience. Actually, both of these approaches might be adapted to group situations.

Although some myths and illusions in the field of musical communication may have been shaken in this chapter, I would like to close with an optimistic perspective: Music psychology is still far from fully explaining the mechanisms of musical communication. It is certain, however, that this form of communication functions reliably in everyday life, in spite of its vague character. Much research remains to be undertaken if we are to gain deeper insight into the nature of musical communication. Although spoken language offers a much greater degree of communicative clarity, some commonalities between language and music exist. The famous physicist Niels Bohr used a metaphor to explain the general problem of communication in language; his words can easily be applied to the situation of musical communication:

Washing dishes is just like language. Both the water and the tea towels are dirty, but we can still succeed in cleaning the plates and glasses. Similarly, language involves unclear concepts and a logic that is limited—in ways that we do not directly understand—to specific areas of application. In spite of this, we can develop a clear understanding of the natural world. (cited in Heisenberg, 1986, p. 190)

NOTES

I would like to thank the following people for stimulating discussions and invaluable comments on earlier drafts of this article: Alf Gabrielsson, Patrik Juslin, Gunter Kreutz, Jörg Langner, Guerino Mazzola, Richard Parncutt, Ulrich Pothast, and four anonymous reviewers.

1. For the software see http://www.ifi.unizh.ch/groups/mml/musicmedia/rubato/rubato.html

2. Although there are certain similarities between the ideas of Kurth and those of the German pianist Truslit (1938; partially translated by Repp [1993]), there is no evidence of any personal contact. The writings of Kurth have partially been translated into English (see Rothfarb, 1988, 1989; and Rehding, 1995).

REFERENCES

Allesch, C. G. (1987). *Geschichte der psychologischen Ästhetik* [History of psychological aesthetics]. Göttingen, Germany: Hogrefe.

Balkwill, L.-L., & Thompson, W. F. (1999). A cross-cultural investigation of the perception of emotion in music: Psychophysical and cultural cues. *Music Perception, 17*(1), 43–64.

Behne, K.-E. (1982). Musik—Kommunikation oder Geste? [Music—Communication or gesture?] *Musikpädagogische Forschung, 3,* 125–143.

Beldoch, M. (1961). *The ability to identify expressions of feelings in vocal, graphic, and musical communication.* Unpublished doctoral dissertation, Columbia University, New York.

Beran, J., & Mazzola, G. (2000). Timing microstructure in Schumann's "Träumerei" as an expression of harmony, rhythm, and motivic structure. *Computers and Mathematics with Applications, 39,* 99–130.

Bhatti, S., & Gregory, A. (2000). Cross-cultural study of affective responses to Qawwali. In C. Woods, G. Luck, R. Brochard, F. Seddon, & J. A. Sloboda (Eds.), *Proceedings of the 6th International Conference on Music Perception and Cognition,* (pp. 1321–1328). Keele, UK: Keele University.

Boersma, P. (1999). Praat [Computer software] Retrieved October 22, 1999, from http://www.fon.hum.uva.nl/praat

Bolton, T. L. (1894). Rhythm. *American Journal of Psychology, 6,* 145–238.

Burke, E. (1852). *The works and correspondences: Vol. 8. A philosophical inquiry into the origin of our ideas of the sublime and beautiful.* London: Rivington. (Original work published 1756/57)

Burnsed, V. (1998). The effect of expressive variation in dynamics on the musical preference of elementary school students. *Journal of Research in Music Education, 46,* 396–404.

Carterette, E. C., & Kendall, R. A. (1999). Comparative music perception and cognition. In D. Deutsch (Ed.), *The psychology of music* (2nd ed., pp. 725–791). San Diego, CA: Academic Press.

Castellano, M. A., Bharucha, J. J., & Krumhansl, C. L. (1984). Tonal hierarchies in the music of North India. *Journal of Experimental Psychology: General, 113,* 394–412.

Childs, C. (1992, February). The identification of style-specific performance practices in contemporary music. *Abstracts of the 2nd International Conference on Music Perception and Cognition,* 95–96.

Clarke, E. F. (1987). Levels of structure in the organization of musical time. *Contemporary Music Review, 2,* 211–238.

Clarke, E. F. (1988). Generative principles in music performance. In J. A. Sloboda (Ed.), *Generative processes in music: The psychology of performance, improvisation, and composition* (pp. 1–26). Oxford: Clarendon Press.

Clarke, E. F. (1993). Imitating and evaluating real and transformed musical performances. *Music Perception, 10*(3), 317–341.

Clarke, E. F., & Baker-Short, C. (1987). The imitation of perceived rubato: A preliminary study. *Psychology of Music, 15*(1), 58–75.

Clynes, M. (1977). *Sentics: The touch of emotions.* New York: Anchor Press.

Cook, N. (1998). *Music: A very short introduction.* Oxford: Oxford University Press.

Cooke, D. (1959). *The language of music.* London: Oxford University Press.

Cunningham, J. G., & Sterling, R. S. (1988). Developmental change in the understanding of affective meaning in music. *Motivation and Emotion, 12,* 399–413.

Czerny, C. (1991). *Von dem Vortrage* [On performance] (Third part of the piano textbook, Op. 500) (U. Mahlert,

Ed.). Wiesbaden, Germany: Breitkopf. (Original work published 1839)

Darwin, C. (1965). *The expression of the emotions in animal and man.* Chicago: University of Chicago Press, 1965. (Original work published 1872)

Desain, P. (1992). A (de)composable theory of rhythm perception. *Music Perception, 9*(4), 439–454.

Deutsch, D. (Ed.). (1999). *The psychology of music* (2nd ed.). San Diego, CA.: Academic Press.

Dolgin, K. G., & Adelson, E. H. (1990). Age changes in the ability to interpret affect in sung and instrumentally-presented melodies. *Psychology of Music, 18*(1), 87–98.

Dougherty, T. J. (1993). *The perception of emotional content in non-speech audio.* (Doctoral dissertation, Claremont Graduate School, California, 1993). *Dissertation Abstracts International 54*(1), 524–525B.

Dudek, J. A. (1992). Listener's choice of timing or intensity information as prominent in piano performance style recognition (Doctoral dissertation, Ohio State University, 1992). *Dissertation Abstracts International, 53*(5), 1315A.

Edgewater, I. D. (1999). Music hath charms . . . : Fragments toward constructionist biocultural theory, with attention to the relationship of "music" and "emotion." In A. L. Hinton (Ed.), *Biocultural approaches to the emotions* (pp. 153–181). Cambridge: Cambridge University Press.

Fassbender, C. (1996). Infants' auditory sensitivity towards acoustic parameters of speech and music. In I. Deliège & J. Sloboda (Eds.), *Musical beginnings: Origins and development of musical competence* (pp. 56–87). Oxford: Oxford University Press.

Fay, R. R. (1988). *Hearing in vertebrates: A psychophysics databook.* Winnetka, IL: Hill-Fay.

Fraisse, P. (1982). Rhythm and tempo. In D. Deutsch (Ed.), *The psychology of music* (pp. 149–180). San Diego, CA: Academic Press.

Fredrickson, W. (1995). A comparison of perceived musical tension and aesthetic response. *Psychology of Music, 23*(1), 81–87.

Friberg, A. (1995). *A quantitative rule system for musical performance.* Unpublished dissertation, Royal Institution of Technology, Stockholm.

Friberg, A. (1999). Director Musices [Computer software] retrieved May 1999 from http://www.speech.kth.se/music/performance

Gabrielsson, A. (1995). Expressive intention and performance. In R. Steinberg (Ed.), *Music and the mind machine* (pp. 35–47). Berlin, Germany: Springer.

Gabrielsson, A. (1999). Music performance. In D. Deutsch (Ed.), *The psychology of music* (2nd ed., pp. 501–602). San Diego, CA: Academic Press.

Gabrielsson, A., & Juslin, P. N. (1996). Emotional expression in music performance: Between the performer's intention and the listener's experience. *Psychology of Music, 24*(1), 68–91.

Gardner, H. (1985). *The mind's new science: A history of the cognitive revolution.* New York: Basic Books.

Giomo, C. J. (1992). The development of children's esthetic sensitivity to mood in music: An experimental study comparing five- and nine-year-olds using a non-verbal mode of response. (Doctoral dissertation, University of Colorado, Boulder, 1992). *Dissertations Abstracts International 53*(6), 1715-A.

Gjerdingen, R. O. (1988). Shape and motion in the microstructure of song. *Music Perception, 6*(1), 35–64.

Gjerdingen, R. O. (1994). Apparent motion in music? *Music Perception, 11*(1), 335–370.

Gregory, A. H., & Varney, N. (1996). Cross-cultural comparisons in the affective response to music. *Psychology of Music, 24*(1), 47–52.

Gruson, L. M. (1988). Rehearsal skill and musical competence: Does practice make perfect? In J. A. Sloboda (Ed.), *Generative processes in music: The psychology of performance, improvisation, and composition* (pp. 91–112). Oxford: Clarendon Press.

Hallam, S. (1995). Professional musicians' approaches to the learning and interpretation of music. *Psychology of Music, 23*(2), 111–128.

Hanslick, E. (1986). *On the musically beautiful: A contribution towards the revision of the aesthetics of music* (G. Payzant, Trans. and Ed.). Indianapolis: Hackett. (Original work published 1891 as *Vom musikalisch Schönen: Ein Beitrag zur Revision der Ästhetik der Tonkunst*)

Hausegger, F. von (1885). *Die Musik als Ausdruck* [Music as expression]. Vienna: Konegen.

Hefner, H., & Whitfield, I. C. (1976). Perception of the missing fundamental in cats. *Journal of the Acoustical Society of America, 59,* 915–919.

Heisenberg, W. (1986). *Der Teil und das Ganze: Gespräche im Umkreis der Atomphysik* [Physics and beyond: Encounters and conversations] (6th ed.). Munich, Germany: Piper.

Henderson, M. T. (1936). Rhythmic organization in artistic piano performance. In C. E. Seashore, (Ed.), *Studies in the psychology of music: Vol. 4. Objective analysis of musical performance* (pp. 281–305). Iowa City, IA: University of Iowa Press.

Hulse, S. H., & Cynx, J. (1986). Interval and contour in serial pitch perception by a passerine bird, the European starling (*Sturnus vulgaris*). *Journal of Comparative Psychology, 100,* 215–228.

Hulse, S. H., & Page, S. C. (1988). Toward a comparative psychology of music perception. *Music Perception, 5*(4), 427–452.

Hulse, S. H., Takeuchi, A. H., & Braaten, R. F. (1992). Perceptual invariances in the comparative psychology of music. *Music Perception, 10*(2), 151–184.

Huron, D. (1991). The ramp archetype: A score-based study of musical dynamics in 14 piano composers. *Psychology of Music, 19*(1), 33–45.

Jaques-Dalcroze, E. (1921). *Rhythm, music, and education* (H. Rubinstein, Trans.). New York: Putnam.

Juslin, P. N. (1997). Perceived emotional expression in synthesized performances of a short melody: Capturing the listener's judgment policy. *Musicae Scientiae, 2*(1), 225–256.

Juslin, P. N. (2000). Cue utilization in communication of emotion in music performance: Relating performance to perception. *Journal of Experimental Psychology: Human Perception and Performance, 26*, 1797–1813.

Juslin, P. N. (2001). Communicating emotion in music performance: A review and a theoretical framework. In P. N. Juslin & J. A. Sloboda (Eds.), *Music and emotion: Theory and research* (pp. 309–337). New York: Oxford University Press.

Juslin, P. N., & Laukka, P. (2000). Improving emotional communication in music performance through cognitive feedback. *Musicae Scientiae, 4*(4), 151–183.

Juslin, P. N., & Madison, G. (1999). The role of timing patterns in recognition of emotional expression from musical performance. *Music Perception, 17*(2), 197–221.

Kamenetzky, S. B., Hill, D. S., & Trehub, S. E. (1997). Effect of tempo and dynamics on the perception of emotion in music. *Psychology of Music, 25*(2), 149–160.

Kant, I. (1987). *Critique of judgment* (W. S. Pluhar, Trans. and Ed.). Indianapolis: Hackett. (Original work published 1790 as *Kritik der Urteilskraft*)

Karno, M., & Konecni, V. J. (1992). The effects of structural interventions in the first movement of Mozart's symphony in G-Minor, K. 550, on aesthetic preference. *Music Perception, 10*(1), 63–72.

Kendall, R. A., & Carterette, E. C. (1990). The communication of musical expression. *Music Perception, 8*(2), 129–164.

Kirby, F. E. (1970). Beethoven's Pastoral Symphony as a "sinfonia caracteristica." *Musical Quarterly, 56*, 605–623.

Kopiez, R. (1996). Aspekte der Performanceforschung [Aspects of performance research]. In H. de la Motte-Haber, *Handbuch der Musikpsychologie* [Handbook of music psychology], (2nd ed., pp. 505–587). Laaber, Germany: Laaber Verlag.

Kopiez, R. (in press). Der Mythos der Musik als universell verständliche Sprache [The myth of music as a universal language]. In C. Bullerjahn & W. Löfler (Eds.), *Musikermythen: Alltagstheorien, Legenden und Medieninszenierungen*. Hildesheim, Germany: Olms.

Kopiez, R., Langner, J., & Steinhagen, P. (1999). Afrikanische Trommler (Ghana) bewerten und spielen europäische Rythmen [Cross-cultural study of the evaluation and performance of rhythm]. *Musicae Scientiae, 3*(2), 139–160.

Kratus, J. (1993). A developmental study of children's interpretation of emotion in music. *Psychology of Music, 21*(1), 3–19.

Kraut, R. (1992). On the possibility of a determinate semantics for music. In M. Riess-Jones & S. Holleran (Eds.), *Cognitive bases of musical communication* (pp. 11–22). Washington, DC: American Psychological Association Books.

Krumhansl, C. L. (1997). Musical tension: Cognitive, motional, and emotional aspects. In A. Gabrielsson (Ed.), *Proceedings of the Third Triennial ESCOM Conference Uppsala* (pp. 3–12). Uppsala, Sweden: Uppsala University.

Krumhansl, C. L., & Keil, F. C. (1982). Acquisition of the hierarchy of tonal functions of music. *Memory and Cognition, 10*, 243–251.

Krumhansl, C. L., Toivanen, P., Eerola, T., Toiviainen, P., Järvinen, T., & Louhivuori, J. (2000). Cross-cultural music cognition: Cognitive methodology applied to North Sami yoiks. *Cognition, 76*, 13–58.

Kurth, E. (1931). *Musikpsychologie* [Music psychology]. Berlin, Germany: Hesse.

Langer, S. (1942). *Philosophy in a new key.* Cambridge, MA: Harvard University Press.

Langer, S. (1953). *Feeling and form.* London: Routledge & Kegan Paul.

Langner, J. (2000). Rhythm, periodicity and oscillation. In C. Woods, G. Luck, R. Brochard, F. Seddon, & J. A. Sloboda (Eds.), *Proceedings of the 6th International Conference on Music Perception and Cognition* (pp. 574–578). Keele, UK: Keele University.

Langner, J. (in press). *Musikalischer Rhythmus und Oszillation: Eine theoretische und empirische Erkundung* [Musical rhythm and oscillation: A theoretical and empirical investigation] Frankfurt, Germany: Peter Lang.

Langner, J., & Kopiez, R. (1995). Oscillations triggered by Schumann's "Träumerei": Towards a new method of performance analysis based on a "Theory of oscillating systems" (TOS). In A. Friberg & J. Sundberg (Eds.), *Proceedings of the KTH symposium on grammars for music performance* (pp. 45–58), Stockholm.

Langner, J., Kopiez, R., & Feiten, B. (1998). Perception and representation of multiple tempo hierarchies in musical performance and composition: Perspectives from a new theoretical approach. In R. Kopiez & W. Auhagen (Eds.), *Controlling creative processes in music* (pp. 13–36). Frankfurt, Germany: Peter Lang.

LeDoux, J. E. (1996). *The emotional brain: The mysterious underpinnings of emotional life.* New York: Simon & Schuster.

Lerdahl, F., & Jackendoff, R. (1983). *A generative theory of tonal music.* Cambridge, MA: MIT Press.

Lindström, E. (2000). Interplay and effects of melodic structure and performance on emotional expression. In C. Woods, G. Luck, R. Brochard, F. Seddon, & J. A. Sloboda (Eds.), *Proceedings of the 6th International Conference on Music Perception and Cognition*, (p. 825). Keele, UK: Keele University.

Lussy, M. (1882). *Musical expression: Accents, nuances, and tempo in vocal and instrumental music.* London: Novello. (Original work published 1873 as *Traité de l'expression musicale: Accents, nuances et mouvements dans la musique vocale et instrumentale* [Paris: Heugel])

Madison, G. (2000). Interaction between melodic structure and performance variability on the expressive dimensions perceived by listeners. In C. Woods, G. Luck, R. Brochard, F. Seddon, & J. A. Sloboda (Eds.), *Proceedings of the 6th International Conference on Music Perception and Cognition* (pp. 817–824). Keele, UK: Keele University.

Mazzola, G., & Beran, J. (1998). Rational composition of performance. In R. Kopiez & W. Auhagen (Eds.), *Controlling creative processes in music* (pp. 37–67). Frankfurt, Germany: Peter Lang.

Mazzola, G. (1995). Inverse performance theory. In *Proceedings of the International Computer Music Conference* (pp. 533–540). San Francisco: International Computer Music Association.

Merker, B. (2000a). Synchronous chorusing and human origins. In N. L. Wallin, B. Merker, & S. Brown (Eds.), *The origins of music* (pp. 315–327). Cambridge, MA: MIT Press.

Merker, B. (2000b). Synchronous chorusing and the origins of music [Special issue]. *Musicae Scientiae*, 59–74.

Meumann, E. (1894). Untersuchungen zur Psychologie und Aesthetik des Rhythmus [Investigations into the psychology and aesthetic of rhythm]. *Philosophische Studien, 10*, 249–322, 393–430.

Meyer, L. B. (1956). *Emotion and meaning in music.* Chicago: University of Chicago Press.

Miklaszewski, K. (1989). A case study of a pianist preparing a musical performance. *Psychology of Music, 17*(2), 95–109.

Moore, S. F. (1992). *The writings of Emile Jaques-Dalcroze: Toward a theory for the performance of musical rhythm.* Unpublished doctoral dissertation, School of Music, Indiana University, Bloomington.

Nakamura, T. (1987). The communication of dynamics between musicians and listeners through musical performance. *Perception and Psychophysics, 41*, 525–533.

Narmour, E. (1990). *The analysis and cognition of basic melodic structures: The implication-realization model.* Chicago: University of Chicago Press.

Nyklicek, T., & Doornen, V. (1997). Cardiorespiratory differentiation of musically-induced emotions. *Journal of Psychophysiology, 11*, 304–321.

Oosten, P. van (1993). Critical study of Sundberg's rules for expression in the performance of melodies. *Contemporary Music Review, 9*, 267–274.

Palmer, C. (1992). The role of interpretive preferences in music performance. In M. Riess Jones & S. Holleran (Eds.), *Cognitive bases of musical communication* (pp. 249–262). Washington, DC: American Psychological Association Books.

Palmer, C. (1989). Mapping musical thought to musical performance. *Journal of Experimental Psychology: Human Perception and Performance, 15*, 301–315.

Palmer, C. (1997). Music performance. *Annual Review of Psychology, 48*, 115–138.

Patterson, B. (1974). Musical dynamics. *Scientific American, 231*(5), 78–95.

Peretz, I., Gagnon, L., & Bouchard, B. (1998). Music and emotion: Perceptual determinants, immediacy, and isolation after brain damage. *Cognition, 68*, 111–141.

Porter, D., & Neuringer, A. (1984). Music discrimination by pigeons. *Journal of Experimental Psychology: Animal Behavior Process, 10*, 138–148.

Quantz, J. J. (1966). *On playing the flute* (E. R. Reilly, Trans. and Ed.). London: Faber. (Original work published 1752 as *Versuch einer Anweisung die Flöte traversiere zu spielen*)

Rehding, A. (1995). *(Mis)Interpreting Ernst Kurth.* Unpublished master's thesis, University of Cambridge, 1995.

Repp, B. H. (1989). Further tests on composers' pulses in computer performance of piano music from the Classical period. *Journal of the Acoustical Society of America, 85*, 66.

Repp, B. H. (1990). Patterns of expressive timing in performances of a Beethoven minuet by 19 famous pianists. *Journal of the Acoustical Society of America, 88*, 622–641.

Repp, B. H. (1992a). Diversity and commonality in music performance: An analysis of timing microstructure in Schumann's "Träumerei." *Journal of the Acoustical Society of America, 92*, 2546–2568.

Repp, B. H. (1992b). A constraint on the expressive timing of a melodic gesture: Evidence from performance and aesthetic judgment. *Music Perception, 10*(2), 221–242.

Repp, B. H. (1993). Music as motion: A synopsis of Alexander Truslit's (1938) "Gestaltung und Bewegung in der Musik." *Psychology of Music, 21*(1), 48–72.

Repp, B. H. (1997a). The aesthetic quality of a quantitatively average music performance: Two preliminary experiments. *Music Perception, 14*(4), 419–444.

Repp, B. H. (1997b). Expressive timing in a Debussy prelude: A comparison of student and expert pianists. *Musicae Scientiae, 1*(2), 257–268.

Repp, B. H. (1998). Individual differences in shaping a musical phrase: The opening of Chopin's Etude in E Major. In S. W. Yi (Ed.), *Proceedings of the 5th International Conference on Music Perception and Cognition* (pp. 27–34). Seoul, Korea: Seoul National University.

Rodriguez, C. X. (1998). Children's perception, production, and description of musical expression. *Journal of Research in Music Education, 46*(1), 48–61.

Rothfarb, L. A. (1988). *Ernst Kurth as theorist and analyst.* Philadelphia: University of Pennsylvania Press.

Rothfarb, L. A. (1989). Ernst Kurth's *Die Voraussetzungen der theoretischen Harmonik* and the beginnings of music psychology. *Theoria: Historical Aspects of Music Theory, 4*, 10–33.

Ruiter, J. de (1989). *Der Charakterbegriff in der Musik: Studien zur deutschen Ästhetik der Instrumentalmusik, 1740–1850* [The idea of character in music: German studies on the aesthetics of instrumental music, 1740–1850]. Stuttgart, Germany: F. Steiner.

Scherer, K. R., & Oshinsky, J. S. (1977). Cue utilization in emotion attribution from auditory stimuli. *Motivation and Emotion, 1*, 331–346.

Seashore, C. E. (Ed.) (1936) *Studies in the psychology of music: Vol. 4. Objective analysis of musical performance.* Iowa City, IA: University of Iowa Press.

Senju, M., & Ohgushi, K. (1987). How are the player's ideas conveyed to the audience? *Music Perception, 4*(4), 311–324.

Shaffer, L. H. (1989). Cognition and affect in musical performance. *Contemporary Music Review, 4*, 381–389.

Shaffer, L. H. (1992). How to interpret music. In M. Riess-Jones & S. Holleran (Eds.), *Cognitive bases of musical communication* (pp. 263–278). Washington, DC: American Psychological Association Books.

Shaffer, L. H. (1995). Musical performance as interpretation. *Psychology of Music, 23*(1), 17–38.

Skinner, K. (1932). *Some temporal aspects of piano playing.* Unpublished doctoral dissertation, University of Iowa, Iowa City.

Sloboda, J. A. (1985). *The musical mind: The cognitive psychology of music.* Oxford: Oxford University Press.

Sloboda, J. A. (1998). Does music mean anything? *Musicae Scientiae, 2*(1), 21–31.

Sundberg, J., Frydén, L., & Askenfelt, A. (1983). What tells you the player is musical? An analysis-by-synthesis study of music performance. In J. Sundberg (Ed.), *Studies of music performance* (Publications issued by the Royal Swedish Academy of Music, No. 39) (pp. 61–75). Stockholm: Adebe Reklam.

Tarasti, E. (1994). *A theory of musical semiotics.* Bloomington: Indiana University Press.

Terwogt, M. M., & Grinsven, F. van (1991). Musical expression of moodstates. *Psychology of Music, 19*(2), 99–109.

Thompson, W. F., & Robitaille, B. (1992). Can composers express emotions through music? *Empirical Studies of the Arts, 10*(1), 79–89.

Thompson, W. F., Sundberg, J., Friberg, A., & Frydén, L. (1989). The use of rules for expression in the performance of melodies. *Psychology of Music, 17*(1), 63–82.

Tillman, B., & Bigand, E. (1996). Does formal musical structure affect perception of musical expressiveness? *Psychology of Music, 24*(1), 3–17.

Todd, N. P. M. (1985). A model of expressive timing in tonal music. *Music Perception, 3*(1), 33–58.

Truslit, A. (1938). *Gestaltung und Bewegung in der Musik.* Berlin, Germany: Vieweg.

Wallin, N. L., Merker, B., & Brown, S. (Eds.). (2000). *The origins of music.* Cambridge: MIT Press.

Watt, R. J., & Ash, R. L. (1998). A psychological investigation of meaning in music. *Musicae Scientiae, 2*, 33–54.

Woody, R. H. (1999). The relationship between advanced musicians' explicit planning and their expressive performance of dynamic variations in an aural modeling task. *Journal of Research in Music Education, 47*, 331–342.

30 Taking an Acquired Skills Perspective on Music Performance

ANDREAS C. LEHMANN

JANE W. DAVIDSON

Psychologists seem to agree that musical skills share many common features with skill-related phenomena in other areas outside of music, such as language, games, sports, science, and other domains. Music making entails perceptual skills (e.g., apprehending structural information as well as social information, including nonverbal cues exchanged between performer and audience), cognitive skills (e.g., memory, decision making, pattern recognition), and of course motor skills. These skills function, interact, and evolve in complex ways that we are slowly starting to understand. However, since each performer, be it the professional orchestra musician who earns his or her living playing an instrument or the amateur who plays solely for enjoyment, is a unique individual with his or her individual biography, there is no such thing as "the musical skill." Instead, the ways in which the skill was developed as well as the final skill structure will necessarily differ from person to person as a result of individual learning histories. Each performer has artistic intentions, that is, a message to be conveyed. Some of these intentions are related to communicating information about the musical structure and expressive embellishments to it for aesthetically driven goals. For instance, slowing at a cadence point has become recognized generally in Western music as sounding "better" than not slowing. Other intentions are more emotionally directed, such as playing a piece "sorrowfully" or "happily." Of course, music making does not happen in a vacuum; it most always involves other people, be they co-performers or members of the audience with whom the performer communicates. As a socially and culturally grounded skill, music making is one of the most important activities in all cultures. Attempting to understand musical skill is one way of paying tribute to the tremendous achievements of past and present musicians. At the same time, we may be able ultimately to derive suggestions for the improvement of music teaching and learning.

The integrative metaphor for this chapter—which will connect the different aspects that regard musical skills and their acquisition—is the image of a Western classical performer who has just stepped onto the stage to perform in front of an audience. We will first consider the performer's current skills that are about to be displayed in some form; we will then discuss the "hidden" side of these skills, namely, their acquisition in the course of the musician's biography; and finally, we will address issues that surround the display of skills, more specifically the interaction between audience and performer and the interaction among performers. This section addresses issues that pertain to socially situated cognition and sociocultural influences on cognitive processing. A brief concluding section will address educational consequences of research discussed in this chapter. Throughout the chapter, we will address the qualitative and quantitative aspects that may distinguish different levels of performance and comment on research methodologies that are employed to assess these issues. We will attempt to answer the following questions: What does the performer bring to the task of performing; what does skill acquisition entail; and finally, what happens during performance? When we talk about performers, we do not refer to expert or elite performers only but rather to any person who steps out on stage with the intention to perform in front of other people.

What the Performer Brings to the Task: Skills and Skill Components

General Introduction to Skill Research

Research into skill and skill acquisition has been conducted since the late 1800s, but we have seen a dramatic upsurge in recent years in many areas of human endeavor (see Proctor & Dutta, 1995, for an introduction to human skill and performance). There is hardly any area (domain) of human performance that has not been investigated: reading and writing, flying airplanes, reading X rays, almost every athletic skill, typing, stockbroking, music making, and, foremost, chess playing (Ericsson & Charness, 1994; Ericsson & Lehmann, 1996; also, see Palmer, 1997, for a review of research on music performance). The common denominator of all these activities is the requirement for "coordinated processes of perception, cognition, and action" (Proctor & Dutta, 1995, p. 1). However, there are many methodological venues for the study of human performance.

The complexity of the skill under investigation varies widely: While some researchers are more interested in basic processes, restricting themselves to the study of relatively simple skills in well-controlled laboratory situations (e.g., reaching motions, tapping, solving simple logic problems), other researchers try to tackle more complex skills in realistic settings inside and outside of the laboratory (e.g., memorizing a song, acquiring a new piece of music, judging music performance). The sophistication or expertise of the participant is also a factor to consider: We can expose participants to tasks they have never seen before and track their learning curves, or we can study established experts who are performing tasks that are highly familiar to them. Furthermore, tasks can be performed in different types of environments, which require various degrees of flexibility or transfer. Some so-called closed environments offer stable conditions under which to perform the task (e.g., chess), while other environments are open, forcing the participant to operate under unpredictable conditions (e.g., mountain climbing). In music, we could maybe classify the performance of rehearsed solo repertoire as a closed skill while improvisation (especially in an ensemble) could be classified as an open one.

What emerges as a finding from the literature is that "a skill is a skill is a skill," meaning that the findings are consistent across domains regardless of the stimulus onto which we direct our perception, cognition, or action. Skill researchers assume that human beings by and large cope with the problems they are facing in any domain by applying roughly similar perceptual, cognitive, and psychomotor solutions. Thus by studying one area of skill, such as musical skill acquisition and expertise, we learn some things about other domains and vice versa. The ultimate goal is to apply the results to education and benefit future generations of learners and their teachers.

Obviously, acquiring one skill does not allow us to perform all skills but only those with similar task characteristics; in other words, the transfer of skills from one domain to another is rather limited (see Tunks, 1992, for a more detailed discussion of transfer of learning). For example, the transfer of knowledge and skills (if we want to

make this distinction and not assume that knowledge is an essential part of the skill) from one musical instrument to another depends on how similar the two instruments are. Pianists can easily adapt to playing on a harpsichord and saxophone players may experience few difficulties learning the flute, but switching to a string instrument would be difficult for them. As obvious as this would seem, this fact is not trivial, because it demonstrates a touchstone in skill research: namely, the domain-specificity of skills. This finding suggests that even high-level experts may experience problems if the stimulus material does not completely match typical requirements. For example, if an outstanding trumpet player with extensive experience in playing band music attempts to sight-read or memorize atonal music, he or she might be confronted with unexpected limitations. In the worst case, our brave trumpeter may not outperform a good band student. This finding is sometimes called the structure-by-skill (or expertise) interaction, because it means that skilled individuals only perform at superior levels when the stimuli are representative for the structural properties for which the cognitive mechanisms were developed. Furthermore, transfer may vary from one skill level to the next as Palmer and Meyer (2000) showed. In their experiment, beginning and advanced pianists learned melodies and later were asked to perform them with a different hand, a different clef, or different notes (retaining the original fingering). The results showed virtually no transfer for the novices while the experts demonstrated reasonable transfer in expected ways, and the authors suggest that "as skill increases, mental representations for performance become dissociated from the movements required to produce a musical sequence" (pp. 66–67).

The issue of specificity leads us to a related characteristic of skilled or expert performance, namely, that skilled performers become maximally adapted to the task demands under which they usually operate. For this, performers undergo extensive adaptations with regard to physiological, psychomotor, and cognitive factors that allow them to be suited optimally for the task at hand. For example, athletes show a number of physiological adaptations, such as enlarged hearts or altered angles of rotation of their limbs or even neurophysiological changes that distinguish them from nonexperts. For example, the angle of forearm rotation of pianists is altered in comparison to violinists, and both differ from the normal population (Wagner, 1988). These changes reflect habitual usage and movement demands of different instrumentalists. Also, the coordination of sensory input and motor responses is enhanced: Tennis players, for instance, can respond to advance visual cues of their opponents in lieu of having to react merely to the quickly approaching ball, which would leave no time to select a response and perform a suitable movement. In music sight-reading, better readers perform very different eye movements from less skilled readers, allowing the better readers to make "intelligent" use of the limited viewing time by looking ahead (Goolsby, 1994). Probably the most pronounced changes occur at the cognitive level that involves problem-solving and memory skills that are tailored to the experts' needs. Over time, experts have built up what are referred to as retrieval structures, which allow them to encode quickly and meaningfully what they see or hear and manipulate the information in desirable ways (Ericsson & Kintsch, 1995). This enables fast access to information stored in long-term memory, whereas novices often have problems storing and subsequently retrieving the information. For example, chess experts have stored large numbers of chess positions in long-term memory and are able to plan several moves in advance. Concert pianists have to memorize copious amounts of material and do so by practicing cues or prompt points at which they could continue should they have memory lapses (Chaffin & Imreh, 1997, 2000), and actors work hard at understanding the character they are portraying and his or her motives (Noice & Noice, 1997).

Why Study High-Level Performers?

The term *expert* is frequently used in the context of skill research, and many studies have investigated proficient performers rather than so-called novices, that is, beginners or amateurs. But why bother talking about experts when we may be interested in studying how school-age children learn to perform music? There are several answers to this question:

1. Experts already show those cognitive and psychomotor adaptations that nonexperts are still trying to acquire, and therefore looking at experts might lead us to better understand where the novice's development is heading.

2. Experts are usually more able to verbalize and explain what happened in the course of performance, while novices can be quite surprised that they could do a given task at all; often they cannot report anything about their performance (e.g., Hargreaves, Cork, & Setton 1991). This is possibly the reason why many musicians like reading biographies of and books by famous musicians: These books usually contain deep and informative (and sometimes controversial) insights into musical processes not readily available to the lesser expert.

3. The performance of experts has been demonstrated to be less variable and less affected by extraneous conditions than that of novices, which is an important methodological consideration for laboratory studies (Ericsson & Smith, 1991). Several researchers have demonstrated that pianists can reproduce their own performance with extreme accuracy, which allows us to study reliable timing mechanisms in performance (see chap. 29, by Kopiez, in this volume). Conversely, trying to study the same timing mechanisms in another group of musicians, such as band students, would be more difficult since it is known that mood, motivation, and variability in skill can create large amounts of variance in the performance data (Proctor & Dutta, 1995).

Therefore, while studying experts has its merits, it also has its drawbacks, in that we do not know exactly how well our results generalize from one population to the other. It is necessary to undertake studies that involve various levels of performance (e.g., Drake & Palmer, 2000; Palmer & Meyer, 2000) and even study people who drop out of music studies (e.g., Sloboda, Davidson, Howe, & Moore, 1996) to ensure the validity and applicability of research findings.

What Is a Musical Skill and Are Different Musical Skills Related?

Having taken a more general survey of skill research, we can now apply some of these terms and principles to musical skills. What constitutes a skill in music depends on the cultural settings and historical time under consideration (see Gembris, 1997, for a similar argument that concerns musicality). For example, the musical skills required for the performance of music in the Western European art music tradition are different from those of gamelan performance in Bali or from the skills required to produce computer music or any form of popular music. Focusing on the Western classical tradition, we shall consider performances with or without a score of rehearsed music and the activities of sight-reading and improvisation. Of course, a marching band member, a musical actor, or an opera singer will have to perform other tasks concurrently with his or her main musical task.

In general, a skill can only be characterized by the task constraints or requirements that it imposes. For example, sight-reading requires the on-line matching of visual input to patterns in long-term memory, with subsequent programming and execution of a motor program. When the matching does not occur fluently due to real-time demands, the reader has to engage in problem solving and internally reconstruct the score by guessing, omitting, and improvising note sequences. Finally, sight-reading entails the strategic use of head and eye movements when it comes to coordinating the reading of the score with the playing of the instrument, especially when displacement of the limbs is required that would ordinarily warrant visual monitoring (e.g., on the piano, harp, double bass). Hence, sight-reading will consist of various subcomponents that together make up a culturally useful skill. A similar analysis could be done for any other musical activity. In sum, a (musical) skill defines itself by the task demands it imposes (Ericsson & Lehmann, 1996) and hence by a specific constellation of accompanying cognition, perception, and actions (L. Davidson & Scripp, 1992; see also chapter by Gruhn and Rauscher for how some of this constellation is neurophysiologically implemented).

A significant question for educators is whether all musical skills, such as reading, memorizing, and playing by ear, have a common mediating cognitive mechanism or are all isolated subskills. The domain of music has borrowed these ideas from research in intelligence, where researchers long assumed that a general factor (g) influenced many cognitive skills. Not only would such a unified musical mechanism facilitate learning different musical skills because training one skill would suffice to training them all, but it would also show up in studies as a positive correlation between different musical performance measures. A major study that involved several musical skills was undertaken by McPherson (1995), who designed some new performance measures and investigated 101 children of two different age groups with regard to a variety of musical skills, including playing by ear, playing from memory, sight-reading, performing rehearsed music, and improvising. The published results of the entire sample of trumpet and clarinet players showed strong positive correlations among all subskills. For example, the better you play by ear, the better you will play rehearsed music.

It is difficult to say if McPherson's results would be the same for other instrument categories, but if we assume some similarities, the correlations suggest a very close association of different musical skills. This flies in the face of everyday experience, for many of us "know" that good performers of rehearsed music are often poor or just passable improvisers. How then can we explain McPherson's results? The answer lies in McPherson's combining of two groups with unequal skill levels (school years 7 to 9 [younger group] and 10 to 12 [older group]). The intercorrelations for the musical skills are significantly lower for individual groups. Indeed, the correlation between improvisation and performance of rehearsed music drops for both groups to a level closer to what we would expect. However, the correlation remained surprisingly high for the older children. This high correlation in the older group could be caused by large skill differences within the group. Or it may be that better performers are more likely to seek out improvisational activities and try to learn to improvise. Whatever the reason, despite some seemingly contradictory findings, the association of individual musical subskills is rather moderate. Two alternative accounts are possible for the remaining correlation: It is possible that some skills transfer such that learning to play an instrument might foster musical reading as well as memory and musical imagery as a by-product, or there is indeed some underlying common factor or mechanism consistent with the idea of a musical intelligence (Gardner, 1983). The decision for or against one account (or a combined version) remains speculative until further empirical evidence is available.

However, the educational consequences of the view that musical skills are rather specific is clear, namely, that each requires its own specialized training. For example, if you want your students to be able to improvise, you have to offer activities that would promote this skill, such as creating melodies, copying improvisations by ear, and listening to other people improvise. Unfortunately, at this point we do not know much about expressive skills and their acquisition, but it is likely that also here imitation of idiomatic patterns and listening experience plays an important role.

Key Component of Musical Skills: Mental Representation

Mental representations form a central concept in skill and expertise research, as they do in other areas of cognitive psychology, where they basically denote the "memory of an object or event, which is used to gauge whether a perception is a representation of the object or event in question" (Stuart-Hamilton, 1996, p. 74). It is the internal representation in memory that the performer produces while trying to encode or manipulate a relevant stimulus in a given situation. A common everyday term is *mental image* (e.g., Trusheim, 1991), although this description unduly favors only one form of representation, namely, the visual one, which may not be the only and most appropriate one. It is more consistent with contemporary psychological theory to argue that different phenomenological experiences of memory content (aural, visual, kinesthetic, etc.) are simply different modes of representation of the same thing, which can be demonstrated by asking people to switch between modes (from visual to aural). However, it is also apparent from research in learning styles that individuals prefer one mode to the other, which can become a problem in teaching if this preference differs between student and teacher.

The ability to generate and use mental representations efficiently is presumably one of the hallmarks of expert performers, and some music teachers even postulate that music making happens in your head, with the motor execution being of secondary importance only. L. Davidson and Scripp (1992, p. 405) report an anecdote that involves the cellist Pablo Casals and demonstrates the incredible flexibility afforded to performers by efficient mental representation. The master, after teaching a piece of music to a student with one set of fingerings and bowings, completely changed both a few weeks later, to the great astonishment of the student. Obviously, the mental representation will depend on the musical task at hand (e.g., improvisation, rehearsed performance, memorization) and vary from performer to performer. Also, a study by Palmer and Meyer (2000) was mentioned earlier in the context of transfer of skills as an example of how representations may change from one skill level to the next. The following example will make this claim more tangible: A beginning trumpet student's mental representation of a piece of music might consist of simply a sequence of valve combinations, while a more advanced student might also represent the underlying chord progression along with some expressive information, some aural image of the sounds, and maybe a visual representation of how the score looks.

Performance can emerge with or without appropriate underlying representations, and music educators know that intuitively, if not explicitly. We generally presume that the goal of music education is to enable the student to form the mental representations necessary to enjoy and produce meaningful musical material. Yet most educators would agree that it is also possible to learn a given piece by mindless drilling and be able to produce it even when no understanding of the task and the material is present. A nonmusical example for this distinction would be the learning of a few useful phrases in a foreign language just prior to taking a trip to a different country. We might be able to say "good morning" or "thank you," but we would be unable to converse in the language or change the memorized phrases. The simplest musical example that comes to mind is playing "Chopsticks" (or the German equivalent, "Flohwalzer"), a piece that many people can play on the piano even without training. It requires mere visual orientation and hitting black or white keys and counting up to six. Useful mental representations are involved when musicians can learn new pieces based on what was learned previously and when the learned musical material can be manipulated in various ways (e.g., transposition, changing of speed or dynamics, adapting to a different performance style, changing fingerings to accommodate speed).

In an experiment on musical memory, Lehmann and Ericsson (1997a) asked pianists to memorize short pieces of music by repeatedly presenting them with the score and then having them perform the piece from memory. Once the piece was learned, the pianists were asked to perform it under changed conditions, such as performing with only one hand or transposing the piece to a nearby key. Those pianists who had memorized the piece the fastest were more accurate in reproducing it under changed performance conditions. In the transposition task, for instance, faster memorizers immediately chose a new fingering that differed from that previously employed during memorization. Also, the results suggested that there was a common mediating mechanism to encoding (memorizing) and problem solving during recall. It is somewhat counterintuitive that faster memorization would actually enable better performance on subsequent performance under changed task demands. We believe, though, that better memorizers are likely to construct and use mental representations of the music, which would facilitate memorization as well as the subsequent manipulation of the memorized music. This ac-

count would substantiate the anecdote mentioned earlier about Pablo Casals.

The fact that music performance is mediated by mental representation does not preclude some degree of automaticity. The performer cannot at all times be aware of every performance aspect—this would overload human information-processing capacity. However, the mental representation of the piece should be such that the performer can switch between levels of consciousness, going from an unfocused and quasi-automatic "letting the music flow" to a conscious attention to specific expression or note sequences. Being able to step back but also zoom in on detail if necessary is a desired state of mastery that differs from the novice's possibilities.

In sum, experts have been shown to possess sophisticated mental representations for information in their respective domains (see Ericsson, 1996; Ericsson & Lehmann, 1996, for reviews). For example, chess players seem to have some kind of generic mental template in which chess pieces are placed; the input can be either written, aurally presented, or visually presented positions. Some musicians may develop similar templates that allow them a more flexible performance. The next section elaborates on this point by looking at two cognitive models of musical skill that implicate those mental representations.

Matrix of Cognitive Skills. In their excellent chapter on the coordinates of cognitive skills in music, L. Davidson and Scripp (1992) describe their own model for cognitive music processing, the Matrix of Cognitive Skills in Music (p. 395). The purpose of our brief review of Davidson and Scripp's model (see figure 30.1) is to show how cognitive processes can be classified and mapped to a given task (in this case, making music) and how plausible models are derived despite the fact that the exact functioning and structural nature of the model's component is hidden from the observer. In principle, each aspect of the model would be amenable to empirical testing and validation that used appropriate experimental methods. This model draws heavily on the insights gained from Harvard's famous Project Zero (in which the authors were involved) and provides a tool for a comprehensive and integrative understanding of how musicians think. *Thinking* in this context is interpreted as creating a *network of understanding,* an idea that the authors borrow from Perkins (1989). The whole of cognitive musical skills is divided into six categories, labeled ways of knowing, which can be traced in musical production, perception, and reflection on music. Those processes may be situated outside the musical performance situation or during performance, thus constituting different *conditions of knowledge.* The musician's ways of knowing outside the performance situation exist in fixed or declarative form (knowing what), while the ways of knowing during performance are of a more dynamic or procedural nature

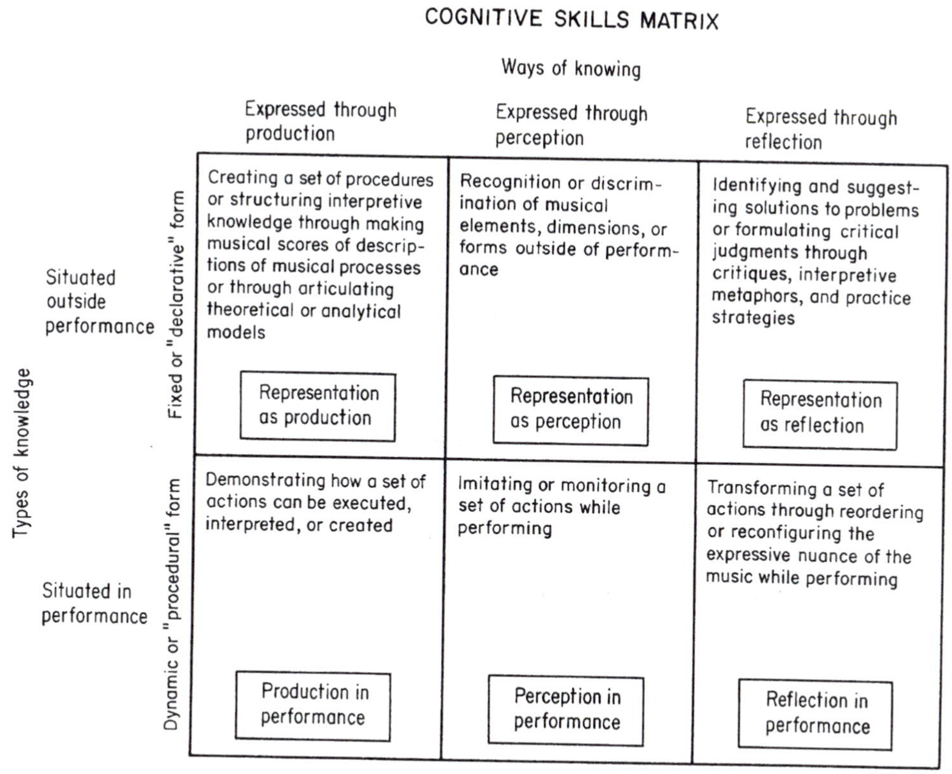

COGNITIVE SKILLS MATRIX

Ways of knowing

	Expressed through production	Expressed through perception	Expressed through reflection
Situated outside performance (Fixed or "declarative" form)	Creating a set of procedures or structuring interpretive knowledge through making musical scores of descriptions of musical processes or through articulating theoretical or analytical models — Representation as production	Recognition or discrimination of musical elements, dimensions, or forms outside of performance — Representation as perception	Identifying and suggesting solutions to problems or formulating critical judgments through critiques, interpretive metaphors, and practice strategies — Representation as reflection
Situated in performance (Dynamic or "procedural" form)	Demonstrating how a set of actions can be executed, interpreted, or created — Production in performance	Imitating or monitoring a set of actions while performing — Perception in performance	Transforming a set of actions through reordering or reconfiguring the expressive nuance of the music while performing — Reflection in performance

Types of knowledge

Figure 30.1. Davidson and Scripp's (1992) Matrix of Cognitive Skills in Music: Two conditions of knowledge crossed with three ways of knowing.

(knowing how). Each way of knowing captures a necessary and distinctly different set of cognitive skills. Thus *production* encompasses composing as well as interpretive performance (and presumably also sight-reading and improvisation); *perception* covers those aspects of thinking that support discrimination and judgment; *reflection* acknowledges the importance of reenvisioning, reconceptualizing, and reviewing a performance. These three ways of knowing are crossed with the two conditions of knowledge.

The authors present evidence for the development of some of these representations of knowledge and posit that the different parts of their matrix are sometimes formed in the individual musician independently from one another. For example, a musician might be a star performer but unable to notate a simple tune correctly (L. Davidson & Scripp, 1992, p. 401). This last point is most interesting for music educators, since it documents a common classroom observation. At the same time, it reinforces the educator's goal to promote not only individual skills but also the interaction and interconnectedness among them.

The model itself does not make any claims about underlying processes and the exact nature of the representations involved. The authors clearly state that the different ways of knowing are learned and trained and that they can be practiced through use of "cognitive tools" (p. 404), better known to educators as teaching methods, such as mod-

eling and the utilization of metaphors. Accordingly, we can analyze teaching situations, as do L. Davidson and Scripp (pp. 404–406), with regard to the types of representations they are likely to produce. The idea that teaching results in representation is shared with the next model to be described, in which certain representations are seen as central to music making and hence the goal of teaching and practice.

Triangular Model of Mental Representation in Music Performance. The claim for the model described in the following is that instruction could be tailored to result in the postulated representations (Ericsson, 1997; Lehmann & Ericsson, 1997b). Whereas the Davidson and Scripp model was rather descriptive in nature, relying on the translation of a general psychological model of skills to musical skills in declarative and procedural instances, the following model aims at providing musicians with a framework for their work. The triangular model of musical performance skills assumes that musicians need at least three different types of mental representations. Those representations correspond to (1) a goal representation, (2) a production representation, and (3) a representation of the current performance. (Woody, 1999a renames those representations goal imaging, motor production, and self-monitoring.) It is appropriate to conceive of these representations as answers to questions that teacher and student can ask, namely, "what should the music sound like?" "how is the sound achieved?" and "what is coming out right now?" Consequently, the goal representation captures whatever the performer does internally to represent the desired auditory outcome (including decisions about how to interpret the piece); the production representation entails the procedural knowledge of the performer of how to execute the music on the instrument; the representation of the current performance is the internal description of what is being produced at the moment (see figure 30.2).

There is empirical and everyday evidence for the existence of the proposed mental representations. Although they are not directly observable, indicators for their existence and functioning can be found in task performance and through the use of verbal reports (think-aloud protocols). Task performance under changed or stressful conditions often reveals flaws in the functioning of our representations and deficient interactions among the three components. The following are examples of flawed representations: The player knows that a crescendo is coming up and thinks he or she is playing it, but the teacher or audience does not hear anything. The singer is out of tune with the piano but is satisfied with the performance (problem with motor and current performance representation but correct goal imaging). A player is not sure how a piece continues, yet the right notes still come out of his or her musical instrument (motor representation and memory function, but the goal representation is deficient). The performer knows how it should sound but realizes that what is being produced is not correct (problem with establishing a motor representation but correct goal imaging and monitoring of ongoing performance). Some researchers have analyzed performance errors in experiments with the explicit aim to uncover underlying representations (e.g., Palmer, 1992; Repp, 1996). Another useful research method is for participants to report their thoughts retrospectively, so that performance errors can be matched to cognitive processes. These reports can follow a fixed scientific method (e.g., Ericsson & Simon, 1993), and they can be used as teaching tools (Woody, 1999a).

The following example stems from a controlled study that shows that representations play a role in musical expression. Woody (1999b) investigated pianists' ability to imitate short expressive model performances played to them from a computer. In between hearing the model and playing their imitations, subjects verbalized their thoughts about the expressive features they had heard in the aural model. Interestingly, those features that were explicitly identified were performed differently from those not reported. Regarding musical features that were not familiar, participants who were able to identify them performed them more accurately; the performances of the other participants generally excluded these types of unusual features! Musically appropriate (idiomatic) features of models were reproduced by almost all participants, but those who explicitly identified them performed at more pronounced overall levels (e.g., louder crescendos, softer descrescendos). This is somewhat surprising, because contrary to the results described earlier, musicians tend to think that expressive performance emerges "by intuition" or from the quasi-automatic (subconscious) imitation of expressive performances heard during the lesson or on a recording.

Experts have tried at all times to construct certain representations (even though they do not use this term) by employing or teaching specific practice strategies. For example, playing a memorized piece while watching television (probable effect: forces motor representation to act independently from goal representation), thinking through the piece note by note or playing on a muted instrument (probable effect: goal imaging independent of motor representation), playing louder than necessary or audio-taping performance (probable effect: strengthens representation of current performance, "listening to oneself").

As with sports, methods to improve training in music are becoming more sophisticated. For example, Edlund (2000) presented a method by which musicians were able to listen to themselves from a distance, similar to how the audience would hear them in a larger room. This was done by recording the music through use of a microphone positioned some distance away from the sound source and immediately transmitting the sound back to the player into a special headphone. First testing suggested that this method was greatly appreciated by musicians because it gave them otherwise unavailable and richer feedback on their current performance.

In short, mental representations form the core of any skill and the result of practice (see next section), and musicians require specific types of representations that allow them to cope successfully with the performance demands. Functional problems with the representations and their enactment during performance may lead to errors and break-

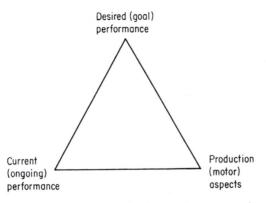

Figure 30.2. Triangular model of mental representations in music performance.

downs in performance. Such problems can be remedied by designing practice activities that carefully isolate aspects of performance and make them accessible to conscious cognitive processing, which, in turn, gives rise to a smooth, flexible performance.

Hidden From the Audience: Skill Acquisition and Development

It is fair to say that nobody is born with the skills necessary to go onstage to perform and that skills do not accrue overnight but take a long time to develop. Granted, there are individual differences in personality, speed of development, and motivation, but even the most "gifted" individuals require large amounts of training and practice to develop noteworthy levels of performance. This development or skill acquisition phase is especially of interest once the level of performance exceeds the average adult level prevalent in the population, a level that is almost passively acquired through acculturation. For example, most people can sing the national anthem or whistle popular tunes; however, in Western classical music, we are concerned with levels of performance that come about as a result of deliberate and time-consuming instruction and training (which could include expert singers and whistlers). In this part of the chapter, we will discuss the development of expertise in music, introduce the concept of deliberate practice, and address issues that surround practice, such as the preparation of a specific piece and practice efficiency (see J. W. Davidson, Howe, & Sloboda, 1997; Lehmann, 1997b, for reviews).

Life-Span View on Skill Development

Skills develop over long periods of time, and most researchers divide this time into distinct phases with more or less clear boundaries (Bloom, 1985; Ericsson, Krampe, & Tesch-Röumer, 1993; Manturzewska, 1990). During the initial, preinstruction phase, the individual comes in contact with the domain through the immediate home environment. Playful interactions with music seem to be the rule rather than guided instruction, which sets in during the second phase. This early instruction continues until the student makes a full-time commitment to the domain, thereby entering a third phase. Most music students never make this transition unless they want to become musicians. A later phase is reached when the by-now-professional musician has risen to the peak of his or her career and is trying to make a lasting contribution to the field. One could postulate yet another phase, namely, that of maintaining the skill against a decline due to age with a possible shift of occupation from stage performance to teaching, as is the

case in many musicians' lives (Krampe & Ericsson, 1996; Manturzewska, 1990).

As we can imagine, the people and circumstances that contribute to the individual's skill acquisition as he or she progresses vary from one phase to the next. While the first teacher is often a warmhearted and friendly person who knows the child well, later teachers may be far more demanding and less amiable or pedagogically able. Not only the teachers but also the home environment play a role in the development of expertise. Being supportive parents does not simply mean allowing children to take lessons and paying for them. A truly supportive environment encompasses parents who go to the lessons, who monitor practice at home by making sure the students practice regularly or even assist and supervise practice more closely, and who create a generally positive value system concerning music learning (Bloom, 1985; J. W. Davidson, Howe, Moore, & Sloboda, 1996; Lehmann, 1997b; Manturzewska, 1995; Persson, 1996; Sloboda & Howe, 1991; Zdzinski, 1996).

Individual Differences in Musical Skills as a Result of One's Biography

The level of performance reached after years of training and practice is an amalgam of different subskills developed over time and influenced by the individual's biography. This biography also entails a cultural and even historical dimension. For example, piano teaching and training in the 1900s not only promoted the playing of rehearsed material but also fostered the acquisition of improvisational skills (Gellrich & Sundin, 1993). Also, teaching methods and materials became available and evolved over time, as was the case for jazz music. But also at the level of the individual, skill acquisition is a unique experience that results in a unique set of skills. Take, for example, an average music student who starts playing a musical instrument in school and practices very little at home and contrast this situation with that of a musical prodigy who has been privately tutored since early childhood. This ensures not only unique musical biographies (and hence skill trajectories) but also a distinctive artistic voice. Given that practice is the most common activity musicians engage in during skill acquisition, we will look at it more closely now (see Hallam, 1997, for extensive references that regard practice).

Scientific Approach to Practice: Deliberate (Formal) Practice

In 1993, a seminal article by Ericsson, Krampe, and Tesch-Römer appeared titled "The Role of Deliberate Practice in the Acquisition of Expert Performance," which has since spawned a wide variety of research in music. The authors propose the concept of deliberate practice (other authors employ the term *formal practice*), which basically posits that the amount of goal-directed (not always enjoyable), deliberate, and effortful training activities, that is, practice, is positively correlated with the attained level of performance. More deliberate practice thus leads to higher levels of performance. This idea was inspired by two complementing facts:

1. A claim was made earlier by Simon and Chase (1973) that even high-level experts need around 10 years of preparation to attain an international level of skills; this finding has been corroborated by results from other domains, among them music (Bloom, 1985) and sports (Starkes, Deakin, Allard, Hodges, Hayes, 1996). Obviously, time spent is only one indicator of effort invested in meaningful training activities during this time.

2. Before Simon and Chase, Fitts and Posner (1967) had made their "monotonic benefits assumption," stating that repetition leads to increased speed—on simple motor tasks! This Power-Law-of-Practice (it might be exponential; see Heathcote, Brown, & Mewhort, 2000) has been applied successfully also to music (Drake and Palmer, 2000) and offers a simple argument in favor of a "do a lot of the same thing" approach to music learning. Ericsson et al. (1993) argue to the contrary, namely, that just a lot of the same is unproductive (a view supported by many musicians, e.g., Wynton Marsalis, 1995). Instead, there are certain constraints on practice that determine its success.

The stated constraints of practice are resources, effort, and motivation. First of all, teachers, exercises, instruments, and practice environments need to be available to the learner. Second, deliberate practice requires attentional resources, that is, mental effort, and it can therefore only be sustained over many months and years without symptoms of physical and psychological burnout when applied in moderation. Around 4 or 5 hours a day seems to be the optimal amount for adults—less, of course, for children. Finally, the person needs to be motivated. Although Ericsson et al. make no assumption about how this motivation comes about or how it is maintained, other authors view motivation as a direct result of talent (e.g., Winner, 1996, especially for prodigious children) or as a by-product of expert teaching (e.g., Gholson, 1998, for a detailed analysis of Dorothy DeLay's teaching). Motivational differences, which may be personality-related, seem to play a decisive role in being successful at the beginning of instruction (Duke, 1999; O'Neill & Sloboda, 1997).

In Ericsson et al.'s original studies, three groups of violinists were compared with regard to the amount of time they had spent practicing over their life span. Two groups were made up of the "best" and "good" students as rated by their academy teachers, and the last group consisted of aspiring instrumental music teachers. To ascertain whether the "best" students were comparable to current professionals, the authors also surveyed members of a professional orchestra. Results showed that experts had practiced more, even at younger ages (see figure 30.3a). Adversely, even at advanced ages, amateurs only accumulated a fraction of the time that full-timers accrued. The results are generally consistent with a later study by Sloboda, Davidson, Howe, and Moore (1996), who investigated a large sample of music students at five different levels of achievement: from the highest level of achievement (Group One in figure 30.3b) to students who had abandoned playing altogether (reported as Group Five in the figure). The better students had practiced more, even in the beginning stages of learning.

Since correlations do not necessarily show causation, it cannot be ruled out that other variables might have caused better performers to practice more. For example, one could argue that more talented people tend to be more motivated and therefore practice more and thus the difference between the groups was really due to differences in innate dispositions (for an extensive coverage of this and other aspects of the nature–nurture debate see Howe, Davidson & Sloboda, 1998, and some 30 commentaries published with the target article).

Assessing deliberate practice is usually done by interviewing the subjects and obtaining retrospective estimates of practice for every year since the start of practice. Critics have suggested that these estimates may be unreliable and that time practicing alone may not be a good indicator for deliberate practice. Although this criticism is viable, there are also arguments in favor of this method of assessing practice. First, errors in estimates will likely affect all subjects of a given study similarly and therefore not influence the pattern of results, only the absolute magnitude of the estimates. This magnitude varies considerably among instruments anyway, with string and keyboard players topping the list of instrumentalists (Jorgensen, 1997). Second, if we find significant effects such as those described earlier, we are probably underestimating the real effect size, since the estimates will include amounts of time with nonoptimized practice. Third, the type of training activity assessed with estimates depends on the goal of the study: Time at the instrument may be a suitable indicator for classical music training but not so for skill acquisition in jazz (although good jazz musicians practice by themselves, too). To use the retrospective estimates method in chess you might need to assess the time spent studying published games (Charness, Krampe, & Mayr, 1996), in sight-reading you might need to assess time spent accompanying (Lehmann & Ericsson, 1996), and in wrestling you might need to assess the time on the mat (Starkes et al., 1996).

What we learn from these studies is that the amount of optimized practice is related to the attained performance. Contrary to some criticisms of the expertise view, this approach does not rule out possible individual differences in aptitude; it merely focuses our view on those aspects of

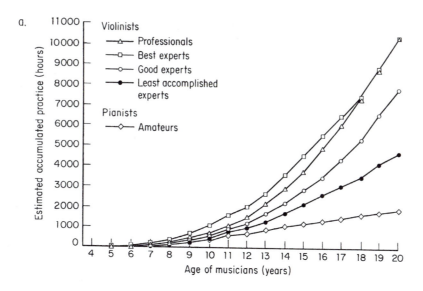

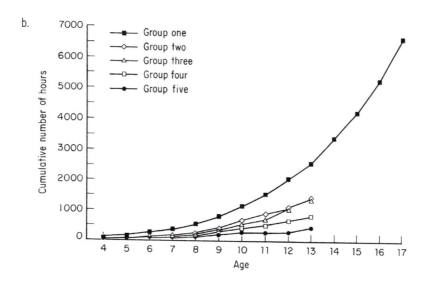

Figure 30.3. Relation between accumulated life-time deliberate/formal practice and attainment in instrumental music performance. Figure 3a: Study with experts by Ericsson, Krampe, & Tesch-Römer, 1993. Figure 3b: Study with novices by Sloboda, Davidson, Howe, & Moore, 1996.

skill acquisition that we can influence as educators. The criticism that this approach neglects the quality of practice has already been alluded to and will be discussed in the next section.

Aspects That Surround Practice

Practice Efficiency. Practice is a fickle thing. Despite our best intentions to work effectively (whatever this means at a given time), our goals escape us, we fail to listen to our results, we simply do not know how to practice a certain trouble spot, or we are simply too tired to muster up the necessary attention. A number of factors influence the ef-fectiveness of practice, including person-related aspects and task-related aspects. Among the person-related aspects we can list age and maturational factors, motivation, so-cioeconomic background and education, current psycho-physiological states (e.g., tired, hungry, unhappy, having mental presets), and musical self-concepts. Other aspects pertain more to the practice activity itself, such as length of practice time, distribution of practice across time (es-pecially over longer periods of time), practice strategies, and supervision (Barry, 1992; Hallam, 1992; Harnisch-macher, 1997; Lehmann, 1997b; Rideout, 1992). When conditions are unfavorable, we are not actually engaging in deliberate practice anymore but simply wasting time.

Therefore, a student's apparent lack of progress in spite of reported adequate amounts of practice might actually be related to suboptimal conditions during practice.

Practicing as a Skill.   In light of the many factors that play a role in making practice efficient, it comes as no surprise that experts and novices differ in the way they practice. What emerges as a consistent finding from studies that looked at the preparation of a specific piece or performance (Chaffin & Imreh, 2000; Gruson, 1988; Hallam, 1992, 1995; Jorgensen, 1997; Lehmann & Ericsson, 1998; Miklaszewski, 1989; Nielsen, 1997; Palmer, 1997; Williamon & Valentine, 2000); is that deliberate practice is allocated in response to encountered problems. Since this requires metacognitive or monitoring skills on the part of the musician, learning to practice is in itself a skill that needs to be acquired. Therefore, teachers should take great care to teach their students how to practice correctly (Barry & McArthur, 1994).

The Performance, the Performer, Audience, and Co-performers

In the Course of a Performance

A multitude of subskills acquired and the concert piece rehearsed, the performer comes to the stage with a mental representation of the music that will allow smooth execution and some degree of flexibility to cope with problems. As mentioned earlier, once the piece is well practiced, multiple performances demonstrate great consistency, even when long time intervals between performances occur (Clynes & Walker, 1982). The consistency does not only apply to factors like reproducing similar overall timing profiles, but many very particular moments within a piece can be systematically reproduced as well. For example, it is well known that slowing will always occur at certain structural moments in a piece, like phrase boundaries, and an individual performer will tend to give proportionally similar amounts of slowing at a given musical feature (Todd, 1985; see chap. 29 in this volume for a review). Gabrielsson and Juslin (1996) demonstrated that when musicians have an explicit emotional intention their interpretations of a particular musical feature will be consistently produced. For instance, playing in a happy manner encourages performances that are up-tempo and played in a detached or bouncy style. Sad interpretations are slower and much more legato (also Juslin, 2001). It can be assumed that though there may be some error variability from one performance to the next, the emotional intention along with the musical structure will create a specific set of constraints on how the music is performed. Through practice, the interpretative aspects have become an inte-grated part of the motor programming in the mental representation of the piece and enable an accurate, fluent, and highly automatized interpretation of the music.

It would be naive, of course, to say that once a representation of a piece has been established through rehearsal it will not be subject to *some* variability or manipulation in the performance process. Performers can and want to remain flexible. A detailed example clarifies this point. Clarke and Davidson (1998) studied two performances of Chopin's Prelude op. 28, no. 4, given by a professional pianist who was asked to vary his interpretations of the piece. After each rendition he was encouraged to disclose his interpretative intentions. Although there were similarities between the performances (timing extensions occurring at similar locations in both performances, for instance), there were also some striking differences, with the first rendition beginning much louder than the second. A structural analysis of this Chopin prelude reveals that it can be viewed either in a binary AA' structure or in a more unified manner. The researchers concluded that the pianist varied the two interpretations by highlighting each of the two possible structural frameworks. The pianist offered little precise knowledge of what he did to create differences between the two performances, other than saying that in the first interpretation he was preoccupied with knowing whether or not one of the researchers had children and so saw a scene with children and claiming that in the second interpretation he imagined the piece within a rugged moorland landscape. This use of visual imagery is commonly reported by many creative and performing artists as a means of focusing their expressive intentions. Experts often lack declarative knowledge about how they achieve certain moment-by-moment changes, and our example illustrates that performers often do not have a full awareness of what they do during a performance. Instead, they monitor and influence the lower level processes from higher and more abstract levels—such as a guiding idea or atmosphere.

From the general psychology literature it is known that arousal, with all its associated physiological traits (increased heart rate and thus heightened oxygen supply), can facilitate mental operations and can often result in performance task improvements in many domains (Gleitman, 1991). Musical performance is no different, for when circumstances produce optimal arousal, highly focused, energized, and inspired performances are often reported (Evans, 1994). M. Cziksentmihalyi (1990) has referred to the intense experience of optimal performance as "flow." Given the overwhelmingly positive reports of the enhanced quality of "flow-driven" or "inspired-feeling" performances, it seems important that the performer should aim to optimize his or her arousal level to become focused on the task. This implies arousal management, which, in turn, is also a characteristic of high-level performers (Wilson, 1997). The key point is, of course, that one cannot produce an "inspired" performance without having extensive and easily operationalized knowledge. The relevant task-related physical and mental skills are achieved in often arduous and time-consuming rehearsal and practice sessions.

Obviously, excessive arousal is undesirable, as it leads to performance anxiety (see Wilson, 1997, for a concise coverage), and thus the potential for being creative moment by moment is reduced. If, for example, the anxiety leads to an increase in heart rate that causes palpitations, the performance may be impaired. Indeed, violinists often report the dire consequences of palpitations on their ability to control their bowing arm, with the racing heart leading to an arm tremor.

So far, we have looked at individual performance. But musical performance is a social act, and whether it is real or virtual (in the recording studio, for example), the audience is critical in shaping the actual performance event. Also, coperformers influence how the performance is negotiated and presented to an audience (J. W. Davidson, 1997).

Social Facilitation Effects

Social facilitation has been reported in psychological research since the 19th century. For example, Triplett noted in 1897 that racing cyclists achieved faster times when they were racing against one another rather than the clock (cited in Zajonc, 1965). Subsequently, many experiments have shown the facilitating effects of coaction on human performance. In part this effect is accounted for by the *mere presence* of another person eliciting an arousal response (Zajonc, 1965), but it is Cottrell's (1972) *learned evaluation hypothesis* that provides an account representative of current belief. It suggests that facilitation depends upon a positive cognitive appraisal and concomitant physiological features, such as increased heart rate and visual acuity. In Western art music performance situations, it is typically an evaluative audience that is perceived as being most highly "threatening," but appraisal can vary depending on the performer's mood state at a given point in time and on the perceived trustworthiness of the coperformers. Indeed, the adage "a trouble shared is a trouble halved" is of salience here.

Social Display and the Cueing of Codes: Etiquette and Context

Like any social interaction, coperformer and performer-audience behaviors are dependent on the communication of information. Of course, the music itself is usually the primary medium to be communicated, and performers and audience need to be able to "share" in the musical code. A strong corpus of research now indicates this to be the

case, with coperformers adapting to one another's musical intentions to create a coordinated musical whole (Williamon & Davidson, 2000), audiences being able to detect even small expressive changes to the music (e.g., Sloboda, 1992), and both performers and audience having similar ideas about what the musical material is communicating (e.g., Sundberg, Frydén, & Friberg, 1995). But the music itself is not the only communicative force, for rules of social etiquette determine other standards, from how the performers and audiences should dress to how they behave toward each other. For example, pop musicians are far more obviously interactive with their audiences than classical musicians and often engage in activities to involve the audience directly—singing the chorus and dancing to an instrumental interlude (J. W. Davidson, 1997). Due to these sociocultural influences on cognitive processing, it seems necessary to explore the ways in which the moment-by-moment cues between performer and audience are perceived and processed in the performance context.

Nonverbal Communication

It is well known that vision is the dominant perceptual sense, with at least 75% of all information being communicated through this channel; hearing only covers 13% and touch 6% (Long, 1997). Also, an increasing amount of research reports the critical role that body movements have in the communication of musical performance information. For example, J. W. Davidson (1993, 1994) found that audiences detect finely grained information about musical expression and intention from musicians' body movements as well as their sounds. This is not surprising, of course, since the body produces the musical sounds and is driven by and itself cues the mental representations of the music. But in a climate where different and contradictory teaching philosophies about how to train musicians to play their instruments abound, it is worth critically evaluating the role of nonverbal aspects of performance communication in detail.

The first major point is that nonmusicians tend to be more reliant on the visual cues than the musical cues to discern whether a performer is playing with or without expression (J. W. Davidson, 1995). The visual cues that differentiate between performances range from varying quantities of movement (varying from stillness to rapid actions like cyclical body swaying) to the use of specific gestures that seem to form a movement repertoire (Davidson, in press). In terms of musical expression, it has been reported that the varying degrees of movement and the employment of gestural cues are inevitable and largely desirable performance actions. Indeed, J. W. Davidson and Dawson (1995) showed that when performers were only able to make restricted movements in the music-learning process both sound and movement aspects of their final performances were much more constrained and less aesthetically appealing than when musicians were encouraged to use their bodies in a natural manner. The more obviously culturally determined gestures, such as an illustrative lifting of the saxophone bell to highlight the effort involved in playing while also creating an impression of playing with more intensity, are also reported as being desirable but need to be presented at an optimal level: Too many and the performance seems overly exaggerated; too few and the performance seems stilted (Clarke & Davidson, 1998).

The second point of emphasis is that many performance movements have clear roles:

- to communicate the expressive intention (for instance, a sudden surge forward to facilitate the execution of a loud musical passage or a high curving hand gesture to link sections of the music during a pause);
- to communicate directly with the audience or coperformers about issues of coordination or participation (for example, nodding the head to indicate "now" for the audience to join in a chorus of a song or exchanging glances for the coperformer to take over a solo in a jazz piece);
- to draw attention or signal virtuosity (for example, a singer's outstretched arm gesture as he or she sings a high sustained note in order to demonstrate this achievement);
- to signal extramusical concerns (for example, gesturing to the audience to remain quiet);
- to present information about the performer's personality, with his or her individualized characteristics providing important cues (muted contained gestures or large extravagant gestures, for example).

Other performance movements offer no specific value to the audience as interpretative cues but are the by-products of psychophysical or educational practices that surround performance. For example, singers often stand characteristically "rooted" on both feet in order to facilitate breath support. Although the audience may not read such cues in their assessment of the performance, such movements add to the overall style and content of the performance.

Taken together, the facts about performance movement suggest that it is necessary for musicians to be able to use the full potentiality of their movements in their preparation and performance to make their music optimally communicable. Of course, performance traditions have roles to play, with some types of movement being inappropriate to some contexts (for instance, gesturing for audience participation in a classical concert) or meaningless for the uninitiated onlooker (for example, some emblematic movements in non-Western dance traditions). Observations by musicologists and psychologists indicate that for a truly effective visual communication with audience and coperformers a balance in the articulation of musical expression, coordination, and virtuosic display within the social convention needs to be attained (Cook, 1998; J. W. Davidson, 1997).

Coordination

Performers in ensembles have been found to share characteristics in timing, which indicate that the entire group has to be considered as one body with different parts to it and with some sort of unifying performance plan (Gabrielsson, 1999; chap. 29 in this volume). For example, in Baroque music performance the melody instruments lead, while in jazz music the rhythm sections lead. By *leading*, we mean that the onsets of new notes or harmonic changes came earlier for some instruments than for others. Whether instrumentalists are aware of this or not at any given time is a secondary concern. More important is the notion that asynchronies must be coordinated by having specific ideas about how the end result should sound and by being able to time individual performance within the time frame of the other musicians. If it were the case that the melody instruments tried to get ahead all the time, we should observe a steady increase in tempo (which we do not, at least not in professional performances). Thus performance in an ensemble requires a common idea of what the piece should sound like. Unfortunately, in most classrooms only one person, namely, the band or choral director, knows what the result should be. Therefore, successful ensemble performance has to rely partly on a shared mental representation, which has to be communicated to one another either via the conductor or through congruent body movements of the different members of the ensemble. This is demonstrated in figure 30.4.

Williamon and Davidson (2000) suggest that the balance between individual and shared representation emerges during rehearsal and by the time of performance coperformers are far more focused on shared rather than individual musical goals. For instance, in a case study (which obviously has only limited generalizability) the researchers traced two pianists who worked on and then presented piano duo and duet repertoire in a concert. Initially, issues such as when to place a chord and who should lead at a certain point were central to their preparation concerns, but as a joint plan emerged, two interesting phenomena occurred: (1) both began to move in a similar manner (a rhythmic swaying that demonstrated some link to the musical pulse) to facilitate the coordination of the music; (2) by the performance, they were looking at each other constantly to negotiate subtle and more creative timing variations than those structured in the rehearsals. Thus there was a critical shift to a joint plan and action. Given the limited scope of the study, it is unclear at this point how these coordinative and communicative skills emerge and what types of training would facilitate their development,

Figure 30.4. Two panels showing at the top a group of musicians with individual mental representations (desired performance or goal images) and at the bottom a group with a shared mental representation.

but it is evident that teachers should note these kinds of changes in behavior and attempt to find strategies to promote their development.

The Audience's Account

Appeal and Gender.   As noted when considering the critical role of nonverbal behavior in music performances, audiences are generally sensitive to musical cues of various types; however, there are all kinds of factors that influence observer judgment. For instance, Wapnick, Darrow, Kovacs, and Dalrymple (1997) carried out a brief study of university entrance auditions for singers and discovered that those who were more animated, smiled more often, and established more eye contact with their audience were rated more highly and thought to be more attractive. In addition, J. W. Davidson and Coimbra (2001) found that musical quality was only one of a number of audience concerns with singers. Critical additional factors included whether or not the performer looked tense and how verbal introductions were delivered. Indeed, the "display" that surrounded the music was of equal salience. Like Wapnick et al., Davidson and Coimbra discovered that first written comments by the audience tended to be about attractiveness, with phrases like "odd-looking chap" and "pretty girl, pretty voice."

In a series of experiments that used video recordings of female or male performers playing either a jazz or a classical piece of music, subjects were asked to rate the performances and the performers (Behne, 1994, chaps. 1–4). The subjects were not aware that the sound tracks for a given piece were always identical, only the performers had been substituted. The results revealed a strong influence of the visual attributes on the evaluation of the performance, and gender stereotypes, such as female: expressive/dramatic and male: technical/precise, emerged. Consistent with results by J. W. Davidson (see earlier), musicians tended to extract more information from the visual display about the underlying musical interpretation than did non-musicians.

Gender stereotypes also exist at the level of choice of instrument. O'Neill and Boulton (1996) and Scheuer (1988) reported peer pressure for children to learn only instruments appropriate to their gender: Flutes were deemed most appropriate for girls, drums for boys! An interview by Johnsen (1992) with Rebecca Bower (an American trombonist and one of the first successful female section leaders in a professional orchestra in the United States) showed that gender biases are rife in music. Bower said that at auditions she was refused jobs on grounds of being a woman in a man's world (trombonists are male, after all!) and that audiences tended to be shocked to see that someone "so frail and feminine" could play such a loud "male instrument." Not surprisingly, the switch to "blind" auditions, that is, auditions that use a screen, has led to a considerable increase of women in professional orchestras since the 1970s (Goldin & Rouse, 1997).

Race and Gender. Of course, men and women behave and dress differently, and so audiences react to performers differently, too. Indeed, anyone who has attended various religious services will attest that African-American gospel singers and their audiences are far less inhibited than their Anglo-Saxon counterparts. Racial issues, like those having to do with gender or any other kind of social bias, are complicated and mostly undesirable. In Europe at least, there is not an established tradition of black classical musicians. When J. W. Davidson (2001) asked audiences to evaluate men and women musicians of black and white origin, they discovered that both black and white male and female audience members preferred the performances by black women. Objectively, the women were no better than the other performers (indeed, the video sound track they were apparently performing was made by another performer and was the same as that used for the other performers). The researchers interpreted this result as an illustration of positive discrimination in favor of black women, who are not usually associated with classical music. Elliott (1995), however, found many more typical and negative race and gender biases when black and white flute and trumpet students were viewed and evaluated: Whites were rated higher than blacks, and black women were rated much worse than black men on their abilities to play a stereotypical male instrument—the trumpet.

To summarize, the display of skill takes place in a social setting and is therefore influenced (biased) in much the same way by social perceptions as are all nonmusical social situations. More important, musicians have to acquire nonverbal means of underlining their musical "messages,"

and they have to learn how to coordinate their performances with other musicians—musically and physically.

The Acquired Skills Perspective in Music Education

Research in the acquisition of complex everyday skills has favored expert performance as an object of study—if we disregard the laboratory research on basic cognitive functioning for a moment. Although a number of reasons outlined earlier certainly justify this bias, many results are not immediately applicable to the classroom. Similarly, the focus on extremely gifted children and musical prodigies is less interesting to educators who are not commonly confronted with these special children. However, experts as well as prodigious children are interesting in that they are living proof that education can facilitate the attainment of high levels of performance. If we assume that experts and prodigies operate on the same physiological mechanisms and constraints as do ordinary people, we can try to adapt insights from this research to teaching methods for individual and group instruction (Lehmann & Ericsson, 1997b). In this respect, skill research offers a promising perspective for music educators.

Other educationally important aspects of skill acquisition and display that await further investigation are musical creativity (improvisation, composition) and performance (body movements and communication among performers). It is particularly disturbing that these aspects have not been investigated thoroughly, since they are essentials for our aesthetic experience, which sets musical activities apart from other human behaviors. We sometimes tend to think that creative skills (e.g., improvisation) and highly adaptive skills (e.g., sight-reading) are difficult to teach because their goals are to produce something new or react to something unfamiliar. However, this is not necessarily the case. For example, over the years jazz teachers have already prepared the grounds for skill research in their area by developing ample methods and materials for teaching an art that appeared difficult, if not impossible, to teach before.

Mainly because music also relates to emotion and expression, musicians consider their field something special compared to other areas of human performance—and in many ways it certainly is. Yet people outside music, such as biology teachers, actors, and athletes, would probably object to this view and claim that their fields also relate to emotions, their communication, or their management. It is correct that music encompasses mental, physical, affective, and social cognitions or actions, while other activities focus on a single aspect (e.g., cognition in chess). Music is becoming an increasingly popular playing field for many empirical researchers most likely because it involves the whole person. This research, undertaken by large numbers of researchers outside music education in an attempt to understand human behavior, is likely to benefit music education and its quest for understanding musical cognition and action specifically. So, rather than viewing ourselves as endowed with a unique, unexplainable skill, we should allow others to show us how our abilities fit into the bigger picture.

The perspective on musical behavior outlined in this chapter may suggest to some readers an oddly strong emphasis on the environment (nurture) at a time when neurophysiology and behavioral genetics are showing convincingly how strong the influences of nature can be. Although leading researchers, including Maccoby (2000), do agree that behavioral genetics has solidly documented the influence of genetics on behavior, she argues on the basis of her review that "when genetic factors are strong, this does not mean that environmental ones, including parenting, must be weak. The relation between the two is not a zero-sum game, and the additive assumption [i.e., that heritability indices are subtracted from 100 to yield the variance explained by the environment] is untenable" (p. 22). What applies to parenting could easily be said for other social learning situations, such as those provided by music education.

Many research methodologies employed in skill research—which by definition is research in teaching, learning, and performance—could be turned into educational tools by clever practitioners. Take, for instance, the verbal protocol methodology mentioned earlier. If researchers can ask their subjects to think aloud in order to find out what cognitive processes play a role during performance, why should teachers not use similar strategies to get into their students' heads (Woody, 1999a)? Such attempts would also serve to bridge the gap between research and teaching, which is sometimes regrettably large.

The most important characteristic of research in skill acquisition and human performance is that this research opens up an optimistic view for educators because it does not focus on innate abilities (see Howe, 1999, for supporting arguments). A common misconception is that skill researchers deny or ignore individual differences that arise from factors beyond training and practice; this is certainly not the case. But if we can explain some individual differences in performance by taking recourse to acquired cognitive mechanisms, such as mental representations or aspects of practice, rather than by attributing individual differences to (almost) immutable genetic or dispositional factors, educators have a chance to consider those explanations in designing future education. High performance is certainly not the be-all and end-all of music education, but the need to achieve satisfactory levels of performance

(however one defines them) will always be part of successful music teaching and learning.

REFERENCES

Barry, N. (1992). The effects of practice strategies, individual differences in cognitive style, and gender upon technical accuracy and musicality of student instrumental performance. *Psychology of Music, 20,* 112–123.

Barry, N. H., & McArthur, V. H. (1994). Teaching practice strategies in the music studio: A survey of applied music teachers. *Psychology of Music, 22,* 44–55.

Behne, K. E. (1994). *Gehört, gedacht, gesehen: Zehn Aufsätze zum visuellen, kreativen und theoretischen Umgang mit Musik* [Ten papers on the visual, creative and theoretical approach to the musical experience]. Regensburg, Germany: Con Brio.

Bloom, B. S. (Ed.). (1985). *Developing talent in young people.* New York: Ballantine.

Chaffin, R., & Imreh, G. (1997). "Pulling teeth and torture": Musical memory and problem solving. *Thinking and Reasoning, 3,* 315–336.

Chaffin, R., & Imreh, G. (2000). Practicing perfection: A case study of a concert pianist. In C. Woods, G. B. Luck, R. Brochard, S. A. O'Neill, and J. A. Sloboda (Eds.). *Proceedings of the Sixth International Conference on Music Perception and Cognition* [CD-ROM]. Keele, UK: Department of Psychology, Keele University.

Charness, N., Krampe, R. T., & Mayr, U. (1996). The role of practice and coaching in entrepreneurial skill domains. In K. A. Ericsson (Ed.), *The road to excellence* (pp. 51–80). Mahwah, NJ: Erlbaum.

Clarke, E. F., & Davidson, J. W. (1998). The body in performance. In W. Thomas (Ed.), *Composition-performance-reception* (pp. 74–92). Aldershot, UK: Ashgate.

Clynes, M., & Walker, J. (1982). Neurobiological functions of rhythm, time and pulse in music. In M. Clynes (Ed.), *Music, mind, and brain* (pp. 171–216). New York: Plenum.

Cook, N. (1998) *Analysing musical multimedia.* Oxford: Clarendon Press.

Cottrell, N. B. (1972). Social facilitation. In C. G. McClintock (Ed.), *Experimental social psychology* (pp. 131–169). New York: Holt, Rinehart & Winston.

Cziksentmihalyi, M. (1990). *Flow: The psychology of optimal experience.* New York: Harper & Row.

Davidson, J. W. (1993). Visual perception of performance manner in the movements of solo musicians. *Psychology of Music, 21,* 103–113.

Davidson, J. W. (1994). What type of information is conveyed in the body movements of solo musician performers? *Journal of Human Movement Studies, 6,* 279–301.

Davidson, J. W. (1995). What does the visual information contained in music performances offer the observer? Some preliminary thoughts. In R. Steinberg (Ed.), *The music machine: Psychophysiology and psychopathology of the sense of music* (pp. 105–113). Heidelberg, Germany: Springer.

Davidson, J. W. (1997). The social in music performance. In D. Hargreaves & A. North (Eds.), *The social psychology of music* (pp. 209–248). Oxford: Oxford University Press.

Davidson, J. W. (2001). Gender and race bias in the judgement of Western art music performance. Manuscript submitted for publication.

Davidson, J. W. (in press). Understanding the expressive movements of a solo pianist. *Musikpsychologie, 16*.

Davidson, J. W., & Coimbra, D. C. (2001). Investigating performance evaluation by assessors of singers in a music college setting. *Musicae Scientiae, 5*, 33–54.

Davidson, J. W., & Dawson, J. C. (1995). The development of expression in body movement during learning in piano performance. *Conference Proceedings of Music Perception and Cognition Conference* (p. 31). Berkeley: University of California.

Davidson, J. W., Howe, M. J. A., Moore, D. M., & Sloboda, J. A. (1996). The role of parental influences in the development of musical ability. *British Journal of Developmental Psychology, 14*, 399–412.

Davidson, J. W., Howe, M. J. A., & Sloboda, J. A. (1997). Environmental factors in the development of musical performance skill in the first twenty years of life. In D. J. Hargreaves & A. C. North (Eds.), *The social psychology of music* (pp. 188–203). Oxford: Oxford University Press.

Davidson, L., & Scripp, L. (1992). Surveying the coordinates of cognitive skills in music. In R. Colwell (Ed.), *Handbook of research on music teaching and learning* (pp. 392–413). New York: Schirmer Books.

Drake, C., & Palmer, C. (2000). Skill acquisition in music performance: Relations between planning and temporal control. *Cognition, 74*, 1–32.

Duke, R. A. (1999). Teacher and student behavior in Suzuki string lessons: Results from the international research symposium on talent education. *Journal of Research in Music Education, 47*, 293–307.

Edlund, B. (2000). Listening to oneself at a distance. In C. Woods, G. B. Luck, R. Brochard, S. A. O'Neill, & J. A. Sloboda (Eds.), *Proceedings of the Sixth International Conference on Music Perception and Cognition* [CD-ROM]. Keele, UK: Department of Psychology, Keele University.

Elliott, D. C. A. (1995). Race and gender as factors in the judgement of musical performance. *Bulletin of the Council for Research in Music Education, 127*, 50–56.

Ericsson, K. A. (1996). The acquisition of expert performance: An introduction to some of the issues. In K. A. Ericsson (Ed.), *The road to excellence* (pp. 1–50). Mahwah, NJ: Erlbaum.

Ericsson, K. A. (1997). Deliberate practice and the acquisition of expert performance: An overview. In H. Jorgensen & A. C. Lehmann (Eds.), *Does practice make perfect? Current theory and research on instrumental music practice* (pp. 9–51). Oslo, Norway: Norges musikkhogskole.

Ericsson, K. A., & Charness, N. (1994). Expert performance: Its structure and acquisition. *American Psychologist, 49*, 725–747.

Ericsson, K. A., & Kintsch, W. (1995). Long-term working memory. *Psychological Review, 102*, 211–245.

Ericsson, K. A., Krampe, R. T., & Tesch-Römer, C. (1993). The role of deliberate practice in the acquisition of expert performance. *Psychological Review, 100*, 363–406.

Ericsson, K. A., & Lehmann, A. C. (1996). Expert and exceptional performance: Evidence for maximal adaptations to task constraints. *Annual Review of Psychology, 47*, 273–305.

Ericsson, K. A., & Simon, H. (1993). *Protocol analysis: Verbal reports as data.* Cambridge: MIT Press.

Ericsson, K. A., & Smith, J. (1991). Prospects and limits in the empirical study of expertise. In K. A. Ericsson & J. Smith (Eds.), *Toward a general theory of expertise: Prospects and limits* (pp. 1–38). Cambridge: Cambridge University Press.

Evans, A. (1994). *The secrets of musical confidence.* London: Thornsons.

Fitts, P., & Posner, M. I. (1967). *Human performance,* Belmont, CA: Brooks & Cole.

Gabrielsson, A. (1999). The performance of music. In D. Deutsch (Ed.), *The psychology of music* (2nd ed., pp. 501–602). San Diego, CA: Academic Press.

Gabrielsson, A., & Juslin, P. N. (1996). Emotional expression in music performance: Between the performer's intention and the listener's experience. *Psychology of Music, 24*, 68–91.

Gardner, H. (1983). *Frames of mind: The theory of multiple intelligences.* New York: Basic Books.

Gellrich, M., & Sundin, B. (1993). Instrumental practice in the 18th and 19th centuries. *Bulletin of Council for Research in Music Education, 119*, 137–145.

Gembris, H. (1997). Historical phases in the definition of musicality. *Psychomusicology, 16*, 40–58.

Gholson, S. A. (1998). Proximal positioning: A strategy of practice in violin pedagogy. *Journal of Research in Music Education, 46*, 535–545.

Gleitman, H. (1991). *Psychology,* New York: W. W. Norton.

Goldin, C., & Rouse, C. (1997). *Orchestrating impartiality: The impact of "blind" auditions on female musicians.* (Working Papers, No. 5903). Cambridge: National Bureau of Economic Research (NBER).

Goolsby, T. W. (1994). Profiles of processing: Eye movements during sightreading. *Music Perception, 12*, 97–123.

Gruson, L. M. (1988). Rehearsal skill and musical competence: Does practice make perfect? In J. A. Sloboda (Ed.), *Generative processes in music: The psychology of performance, improvisation and composition* (pp. 91–112). London: Oxford University Press.

Hallam, S. (1992). *Approaches to learning and performance of expert and novice musicians.* Unpublished doctoral thesis, University of London.

Hallam, S. (1995). Professional musicians' approaches to the learning and interpretation of music. *Psychology of Music, 23*, 111–128.

Hallam, S. (1997). What do we know about practicing? Toward a model synthesizing the research literature. In H. Jorgensen & A. C. Lehmann (Eds.), *Does practice make perfect? Current theory and research on instrumental music practice* (pp. 179–231). Oslo, Norway: Norges musikkhogskole.

Hargreaves, D., Cork, C. A., & Setton, T. (1991). Cognitive strategies in jazz improvisation: An exploratory study. *Canadian Journal of Research in Music Education, 33*, 47–54.

Harnischmacher, C. (1997). The effects of individual differences in motivation, volition, and maturational processes on practice behavior of young instrumentalists. In H. Jorgensen & A. C. Lehmann (Eds.), *Does practice make perfect? Current theory and research on instrumental music practice* (pp. 71–88). Oslo, Norway: Norges musikkhogskole.

Heathcote, A., Brown, S., & Mewhort, D. J. K. (2000). The power law repealed: The case for an exponential law of practice. *Psychonomic Bulletin and Review, 7*, 185–207.

Howe, M. J. A. (1999). *The psychology of high abilities*. New York: New York University Press.

Howe, M. J. A., Davidson, J., & Sloboda, J. A. (1998). Innate talent: Reality or myth? *Behavioral and Brain Sciences, 21*(3), 419–421.

Johnsen, G. (1992). An interview with Rebecca Bower. *Music Educator's Journal, 78*(7), 39–41.

Jorgensen, H. (1997). Time for practicing? Higher level music students' use of time for instrumental practicing. In H. Jorgensen & A. C. Lehmann (Eds.), *Does practice make perfect? Current theory and research on instrumental music practice* (pp. 123–140). Oslo, Norway: Norges musikkhogskole.

Juslin, P. N. (2001). Communication of emotion in music performance: A review and a theoretical framework. In P. N. Juslin & J. A. Sloboda (Eds.), *Music and emotion: Theory and research* (pp. 309–337). Oxford: Oxford University Press.

Krampe, R. T., & Ericsson, K. A. (1996). Maintaining excellence: Deliberate practice and elite performance in young and older pianists. *Journal of Experimental Psychology: General, 125*, 331–359.

Lehmann, A. C. (1997a). Acquired mental representations in music performance: Anecdotal and preliminary empirical evidence. In H. Jorgensen & A. C. Lehmann (Eds.), *Does practice make perfect? Current theory and research on instrumental music practice* (pp. 141–164). Oslo, Norway: Norges musikkhogskole.

Lehmann, A. C. (1997b). Acquisition of expertise in music: Efficiency of deliberate practice as a moderating variable in accounting for sub-expert performance. In I. Deliege & J. Sloboda (Eds.), *Perception and cognition of music* (pp. 165–191). London: Erlbaum, Taylor & Francis.

Lehmann, A. C., & Ericsson, K. A. (1993). Sight-reading ability of expert pianists in the context of piano accompanying. *Psychomusicology, 12*, 182–195.

Lehmann, A. C., & Ericsson, K. A. (1996). Structure and acquisition of expert accompanying and sight-reading performance. *Psychomusicology, 15*, 1–29.

Lehmann, A. C., & Ericsson, K. A. (1997a). Expert pianists' mental representations: Evidence from successful adaptation to unexpected performance demands. In A. Gabrielsson (Ed.), *Proceedings of the Third Triennial ESCOM Conference* (pp. 165–169). Uppsala, Sweden: Uppsala University.

Lehmann, A. C., & Ericsson, K. A. (1997b). Research on expert performance and deliberate practice: Implications for the education of amateur musicians and music students. *Psychomusicology, 16*, 40–58.

Lehmann, A. C., & Ericsson, K. A. (1998). Preparation of a public piano performance: The relation between practice and performance. *Musicae Scientiae, 2*, 69–94.

Long, K. (1997). Visual-aids and learning. Retrieved September 2000, from University of Portsmouth, Department of Mechanical and Manufacturing Engineering. Web site: http://www.mech.port.ac.uk/av/AVALearn.htm.

Maccoby, E. E. (2000). Parenting and its effects on children: On reading and misreading behavior genetics. *Annual Review of Psychology, 51*, 1–28.

Manturzewska, M. (1990). A biographical study of the life-span development of professional musicians. *Psychology of Music, 18*, 112–139.

Manturzewska, M. (1995). Das elterliche Umfeld herausragender Musiker. In H. Gembris, R. D. Kraemer, & G. Maas (Eds.), *Musikpädagogische Forschungsberichte 1994* (pp. 11–22). Augsburg, Germany: Wissner.

Marsalis, W. (1995). *Tackling the monster: Marsalis on practice* [VHS tape 66312]. New York: Sony Classical Film and Video.

McPherson, G. (1995). The assessment of musical performance: Development and validation of five new measures. *Psychology of Music, 23*, 142–161.

Miklaszewski, K. (1989). A case study of a pianist preparing a musical performance. *Psychology of Music, 17*, 95–109.

Nielsen, S. G. (1997). Self-regulation of learning strategies during practice: A case study of a church organ student preparing a musical work for performance. In H. Jorgensen & A. C. Lehmann (Eds.), *Does practice make perfect? Current theory and research on instrumental music practice* (pp. 109–122). Oslo, Norway: Norges musikkhogskole.

Noice, T., & Noice, H. (1997). *The nature of expertise in professional acting: A cognitive view*. Mahwah, NJ: Erlbaum.

O'Neill, S. A., & Boulton, M. J. (1996). Boys' and girls' preferences for musical instruments: A function of gender. *Psychology of Music, 24*, 171–183.

O'Neill, S., & Sloboda, J. (1997). Effects of failure on children's ability to perform a musical test. *Psychology of Music, 25*, 18–34.

Palmer, C. (1992). The role of interpretive preferences in music performance. In M. Riess-Jones & S. Holleran (Eds.), *Cognitive bases of musical communication* (pp. 249–262). Washington, DC: American Psychological Association.

Palmer, C. (1997). Music performance. *Annual Review of Psychology, 48*, 115–138.

Palmer, C., & Meyer, R. (2000). Conceptual and motor learning in music performance. *Psychological Science, 11*, 63–68.

Perkins, D. (1989). Art as understanding. In H. Gardner & D. Perkins (Eds.), *Art, mind, and education: Research from Project Zero* (pp. 111–131). Urbana: University of Illinois Press.

Persson, R. S. (1996). Brilliant performers as teachers: A case study of commonsense teaching in a conservatory setting. *International Journal of Music Education, 28,* 25–36.

Proctor, R. W., & Dutta, A. (1995). *Skill acquisition and human performance.* Thousand Oaks, CA: Sage.

Repp, B. H. (1996). The art of inaccuracy: Why pianists' errors are difficult to hear. *Music Perception, 14,* 161–184.

Rideout, R. R. (1992). The role of mental presets in skill acquisition. In R. Colwell (Ed.), *Handbook of research on music teaching and learning* (pp. 472–479). New York: Schirmer Books.

Scheuer, W. (1988). *Zwischen Tradition und Trend: Die Einstellung Jugendlicher zum Instrumentalspiel.* Mainz, Germany: Schott.

Simon, H. A., & Chase, W. G. (1973). Skill in chess. *American Scientist, 61,* 394–403.

Sloboda, J. A. (1992) Empirical studies of emotional response to music. In M. Riess-Jones & S. Holleran (Eds.), *Cognitive bases of musical communication* (pp. 33–46). Washington, DC: American Psychological Association.

Sloboda, J. A., Davidson, J. W., Howe, M. J. A., & Moore, D. M. (1996). The role of practice in the development of expert musical performance. *British Journal of Psychology, 87,* 287–309.

Sloboda, J. A., & Howe, M. J. A. (1991). Biographical precursors of musical excellence: An interview study. *Psychology of Music, 19,* 3–21.

Starkes, J. L., Deakin, J., Allard, F., Hodges, N. J., & Hayes, A. (1996). Deliberate practice in sports: What is it anyway? In K. A. Ericsson (Ed.), *The road to excellence* (pp. 81–106). Mahwah, NJ: Erlbaum.

Stuart-Hamilton, I. (1996). *Dictionary of cognitive psychology.* London: Jessica Kingsley.

Sundberg, J., Frydén, L., & Friberg, A. (1995). Expressive aspects of instrumental and vocal performance. In R. Steinberg (Ed.), *Music and the mind machine: The psychophysiology and psychopathology of the sense of music* (pp. 49–62). New York: Springer.

Todd, N. P. M. (1985). A model of expressive timing in tonal music. *Music Perception, 3,* 33–58.

Trusheim, W. H. (1991). Audiation and mental imagery: Implications for artistic performance. *Quarterly Journal of Music Teaching and Learning, 2,* 138–147.

Tunks, T. W. (1992). The transfer of music learning. In R. Colwell (Ed.), *Handbook of research on music teaching and learning* (pp. 437–447). New York: Schirmer Books.

Wagner, C. (1988). The pianist's hand: Anthropometry and biomechanics. *Ergonomics, 31,* 97–131.

Wapnick, J., Darrow, A. A., Kovacs, J., & Dalrymple, L. (1997). Effects of physical attractiveness on evaluation of vocal performance. *Journal of Research in Music Education 45,* 470–479.

Williamon, A., & Davidson, J. W. (2000). Coordinating duo piano performance. In C. Woods, G. B. Luck, R. Brochard, S. A. O'Neill, & J. A. Sloboda (Eds.), *Proceedings of the Sixth International Conference on Music Perception and Cognition,* [CD-ROM]. Keele, UK: Department of Psychology, Keele University.

Williamon, A., & Valentine, E. (2000). Quantity and quality of musical practice as predictors of performance quality. *British Journal of Psychology, 91,* 353–376.

Wilson, G. D. (1997). Performance anxiety. In D. Hargreaves & A. North (Eds.), *The social psychology of music* (pp. 229–248). Oxford: Oxford University Press.

Winner, E. (1996). The rage to master: The decisive role of talent in the visual arts. In K. A. Ericsson (Ed.), *The road to excellence* (pp. 271–302). Mahwah, NJ: Erlbaum.

Woody, R. H. (1999a). Getting into their heads. *American Music Teacher, 49*(3), 24–27.

Woody, R. H. (1999b). The relationship between advanced musicians' explicit planning and their expressive performance of dynamic variations in an aural modeling task. *Journal of Research in Music Education, 47,* 331–342.

Zajonc, R. B. (1965). Social facilitation. *Science, 149,* 269–274.

Zdzinski, S. F. (1996). Parental involvement, selected student attributes, and learning outcomes in instrumental music. *Journal of Research in Music Education, 44,* 34–48.

Part V
SOCIAL AND CULTURAL CONTEXTS

Marie McCarthy
Editor

Social and Cultural Contexts of Music Teaching and Learning: An Introduction

MARIE MCCARTHY

Consideration of social and cultural influences has always been important to understanding the music teaching and learning process. During the first half of the 20th century, education scholars John Dewey and Lev Vygotsky and music educators James Mursell, Paul Farnsworth, and Charles Seeger brought distinctive social and cultural perspectives to bear on this complex phenomenon. Paradigm shifts in the mid- and late-20th century have further expanded awareness of the interdependence of social, cultural, and cognitive factors in human development and, thus, in music teaching and learning. This broadening of horizons is now beginning to penetrate the philosophies and theories that underlie practices of music education, and it is quite evident in the diversity of topics included in this part of the Handbook.

A complex array of factors has historically diminished the importance of sociology as a conceptual lens for understanding music education, giving it less prominence than philosophy, history, and psychology. Thus, a research tradition with a clearly delineated sociological focus is underdeveloped in the profession, although studies investigating the role of motivation in music learning and the development of musical preferences stand as notable exceptions. Certain developments in the last 10 to 15 years, however, have nurtured and facilitated the completion and dissemination of research focused on music education as a social and cultural phenomenon. First and foremost has been the move toward a more democratic curriculum and pedagogy that embodies the diversity of students' social, cultural, and musical values. Second, music education philosophers are increasingly coming to view music as social action and to consider music teaching and learning as a process that is embedded in social and cultural values and meanings. Third, theoretical perspectives originating in so-

cial constructivism, social transmission and transformation theories, critical theory, and situated cognition, among others, are providing new lenses to investigate life in classrooms and other music education settings.

Fourth, a growing tolerance for diversity and a need for incorporating different perspectives into analyzing and interpreting behaviors and events have motivated music education researchers to reach beyond traditional disciplinary boundaries in conceptualizing and designing research studies. As a subset of this movement, research methodologies in music education have become more diversified, and this is particularly relevant to the advancement of knowledge about music education as a social and cultural phenomenon. Research questions that attempt to probe the most human paradox of identity formation, to explore the complex political and cultural conditions that shaped music education in another era or in another culture, or to compare the dynamics of music transmission in different cultural contexts demand a range of research methodologies to achieve such ends. An overview of current research methodologies in education, ethnomusicology, sociology, anthropology, and cultural studies, for example, reveals a rich array of research designs and tools. Taking advantage of these developments in research design will require interdisciplinary dialogue, interdisciplinary team research, and intense evaluation of studies that utilize innovative approaches to research methodology.

Finally, developments internal to the music education research community have also advanced a sociocultural agenda. Research groups such as the Social Sciences SRIG (Special Research Interest Group of the Music Educators National Conference [MENC]), the Gender Research in Music Education SRIG and the History SRIG, and GRIME International have highlighted the importance of expanding the parameters of research questions and methodologies in order to acknowledge and access the meaning of music education as a sociocultural process. In a similar manner, certain commissions of the International Society for Music Education (ISME) provide a forum for discussing issues and sharing research studies pertaining to social and cultural contexts of music education—in particular, the commissions on Community Music Activity and on Music in Cultural, Educational, and Mass Media Policies. Other forums include the Education Committee within the Society for Ethnomusicology and the two sociology of music education conferences held at the University of Oklahoma in 1995 and 1999.

One of the hallmarks of scholarship dealing with social and cultural dimensions of music education is its interdisciplinarity. Chapters in this part draw on theoretical perspectives and research findings from a number of disciplines, ranging from social psychology to cultural studies, feminism to ethnomusicology. The title of this part, "Social and Cultural Contexts," highlights the importance of context in accessing and understanding the meanings and values embedded in the teaching-learning process. According to the ethnomusicologists Herndon & McLeod (1979, 1990), a context is "an interweaving of factors" (p. 49) that provides "a framework of explanation" (p. 26). The unraveling and interpretation of those elements or factors are primary aims of research that seeks to provide a social and cultural explanation of the music transmission process. Such research is not limited to certain topics; rather, it permeates all contexts of music education, formal to informal, public school to community music settings, teacher education to the very research process itself. In a sense, this part has a dual thrust, addressing the relationship of music education to schooling and to education as a broad cultural concept. A basic assumption is that individuals learn and are influenced by the values and practices of multiple subcultures and that such influences are central to understanding and researching music in formal education. This all-embracing approach to music education is reflected clearly in the chapters presented in this part. As editor of this part, I found it a challenge to bring together chapters that would represent the multiple sites of social and cultural influence in music education and at the same time draw together unifying threads of continuity. What emerged is revealing in terms of the types of questions music education researchers are investigating and the paradigms that frame their research. Of equal importance, the point made by Richard Colwell that "the Handbook is valuable for articulating what we don't know as much as for reporting what we do know and believe" (1992, p. xi) is well illustrated in this part.

In that context, it is important to acknowledge the status of research in the various topics chosen for presentation. Many of these topics were not included in the first *Handbook of Research on Music Teaching and Learning* (Colwell, 1992). In fact, only three of the nine chapter topics addressed here—sociology and music education, multicultural music education, and historiography—were included in discrete chapters in the first Handbook. In this publication, the topic of sociology and music education is divided into two chapters, one by Stephen Paul and Jeanne Ballantine that focuses on the sociology of education and connections to music education research and one by Renate Mueller that identifies perspectives from the sociology of music relevant to music education. Music educators in the past have used theories and ideas from both of these subdisciplines differently, and thus they warrant separate chapters to highlight their unique relationship with and contributions to music education.

Although the phrase "multicultural music education" does not appear in any chapter title, Barbara Reeder Lundquist reviews literature that investigates the values, challenges, and practices of "culturally expanded music education." In the first Handbook, George Heller and Bruce Wilson provided a foundational chapter on historical research; the subject is revisited here by Gordon Cox, who focuses on a range of social and cultural approaches to historiography that provide expanded lenses for studying and interpreting the past.

Developments of the last two decades in related fields of inquiry such as social psychology, ethnomusicology, feminism, cultural studies, and critical theory have resulted in a considerable body of research literature with direct implications for theory and practice in music education. Literature from these fields is acknowledged in several chapters in this part. Adrian North, David Hargreaves, and Mark Tarrant identify research studies that highlight the influence of various social and cultural processes on musical behavior and values. Addressing the topic of music transmission and learning beyond the formal classroom setting, C. K. Szego provides a conspectus of ethnographic research drawn primarily from ethnomusicology and music education, also including studies from folklore and anthropology.

The impact of various critical theories on music education is prominent in at least two chapters: Paul Woodford's contribution on the social construction of music teacher identity in undergraduate music education majors and Roberta Lamb, Sondra Howe, and Lori Dolloff's review of research on feminism, feminist research, and gender research relating to and within music education. It could be argued that the chapter on music teacher education belongs in the teacher education section. As Woodford points out, however, the topic is an extremely complicated one and requires examination of literature in several related areas, including sociology and social psychology. The status of feminist and gender research in music education is unique. Lamb, Howe, and Dolloff explain that feminist and gender perspectives (as well as research on these perspectives) have assumed a minor role in music education when compared to other educational areas. This chapter serves to initiate serious consideration of the issues that surround feminist and gender studies in music education and to outline a future research agenda for music educators. In a similar way, Kari Veblen and Bengt Olsson's chapter on community music is at the forefront of efforts to document an emerging field of research for music education communities worldwide. This chapter is related in content to Don Coffman's chapter on lifelong learning in music (chap. 13) and chapters 47–51, on connections between school-based programs and those of community arts and cultural organizations.

The scope of each chapter in this part is broad and varied, but a closer look will show the presence of certain recurring issues. These include identity formation as it pertains to gendered musical roles of the young child, sociomusical roles of the adolescent, the emerging professional role of the undergraduate music education major, and the musical identity of the elderly in community music settings. The challenges of accommodating multiple perspectives of music, of culture, and of gender are brought to the surface by several authors. The role of mass-mediated culture in the music transmission process and the related issue of how music educators might improve instruction by knowing how students learn and interact with music in other parts of their lives (media, community, popular culture) is a dominant theme. Finally, it is clear that a future research agenda addressing the social and cultural dimensions of music teaching and learning depends heavily on interdisciplinarity both in expanding theoretical assumptions and enriching the research process.

It seems noteworthy that other issues grounded in social contexts did not appear consistently throughout the chapters, and they are highlighted here as areas for future consideration. Socioeconomic status is a strong element in articulating the relationship between musical participation and society and providing insights into both access to and participation and achievement in music education; yet its effects were generally not included in the reports of research or not articulated as dominant in the music transmission process. A second area is that of institutional contexts and their impact on the culture of music education. As noted by Paul and Ballantine, sociology of education includes both the processes involved in education *and* the structures of education settings. Sociocultural and musical values are reproduced or transformed in such institutions, and investigating these sites, using both quantitative and qualitative research methodologies, will illuminate the practices of music education therein.

It seems possible that in subsequent handbooks of research in music education, one may not find a section on social and cultural contexts per se. If this is the case, the absence will not be attributable to a diminishing concern with their value and importance later in the 21st century but rather to their embeddedness in all research studies pertaining to music education. These chapters represent a beginning effort to bring together studies that seek to unravel the complex relationships between individuals who participate in music education and the sociocultural and social-psychological contexts that interact to give meaning and value to their participation.

REFERENCES

Colwell, R. (Ed.). (1992). *Handbook of research on music teaching and learning.* New York: Schirmer Books.

Herndon, M., & McLeod, N. (1990). *Music as culture* (2nd ed.). Richmond, CA: MRI Press. (Original work published 1979)

The Sociology of Education and Connections to Music Education Research

31

STEPHEN J. PAUL

JEANNE H. BALLANTINE

From popular culture to "high" culture and throughout history, much can be learned from how music functions within cultural contexts and how individuals in culture are taught and learn about music. Although sociologists have long recognized that music is an important part of any culture (Etzkorn, 1989, p. xiii), the sociology of music and the sociology of music education have become recognized fields in their own right only recently (Rideout, 1997a). Likewise, musicologists increasingly tap into the sociological literature for insight into the historical, social, and political contexts of music. The emerging links portend an exciting collaboration among sociologists, musicologists, and music educators (Hilliard, 2000).

The subfield of the sociology of education provides a direct link to music education through discussions of theory and research methods. In the pages that follow we address several important topics: (1) the nature and scope of the sociology of education, (2) the historical background of the sociology of education, (3) key topics in the sociology of education, (4) theoretical streams in the sociology of education, (5) method and methodology in the sociology of education and music education, (6) the development of the sociology of music education, and (7) suggestions for a future research agenda in the sociology of music education.

What Is the Sociology of Education?

The field of the sociology of education considers both the structure of educational settings and the processes involved in education. For instance, through the process of sociali-

zation, people learn roles expected of them, including musical roles as listeners, learners, performers, or teachers. The process of stratification determines where people fit into the social structure and their resultant lifestyles, including the types of music that reflect the lifestyle or group with which they identify. In addition, innovations in musical traditions and tastes challenge group norms and can be harbingers of social change.

Education can be both formal and informal. Children take formal music lessons and learn about music in school. As important as the formal lessons are, however, the informal experiences one gains from listening to various types of music, relating to the subcultures they represent, including dress and behaviors, and receiving messages from the lyrics, can be equally influential. Much of an individual's music education is, in fact, informal in nature, learned from peers and the often-dominant media culture. This illustrates the point that music experiences are closely related not only to education but also to group affiliations, family and socialization, religious upbringing, and socioeconomic and even sociopolitical status. For instance, individuals from upper-class backgrounds are more likely to have experiences with classical music traditions (Barnes, 1986; DiMaggio, Useem, & Brown, 1978; Mueller, 1951, 1956).

Music education issues with sociological implications are ever-present for students, parents, members of communities, and casual observers of society. Consider the following questions of interest to sociologists of education and music education. When should early childhood education begin, including music education? What impact does popular culture have on children and adults, including trends in music? How do race, class, and gender impact on music learning and appreciation? How does music affect people's identity as members of particular interest groups? Are members of deviant subcultures influenced by the music they listen to? How can educators take advantage of music in their teaching? In what social contexts does music occur, and how does music affect social contexts? The list of questions for research stimulates the imagination and encourages us to delve more deeply into the interconnections between the sociology of education and music education.

Historical Background

The field of sociology of music is in its infancy, although the foundations have existed for much of sociology's history. Similarly, the sociology of education as a field of study is young. One of the first recognized sociologists, Emile Durkheim (1858–1917), taught pedagogy at the Sorbonne in Paris before sociology was recognized as a major field; he is generally considered the first person to recommend that education be approached from a systematic, objective, sociological perspective.

In their historical overview of the field of the sociology of education, Karabel and Halsey write that "except for the brilliant exposition by Durkheim and inspiration by Weber and Marx, the contributions in the first half of the [20th] century were meager" (1977, p. 2). The contributions of George Herbert Mead (1934, 1938) have in recent years also become classical underpinnings in one of today's most important strands of the sociology of education, interaction theory.

In the years prior to World War II, the study of education was coming into its own, and sociology had a primary role to play. The American publication *Journal of Educational Sociology* was founded in 1927; its articles were written primarily by educational researchers rather than academic sociologists. The field of "educational sociology" was growing but still struggling for respectability. Educational sociologists were employed primarily in schools of education rather than departments of sociology because of their marginal status in the early days of the field. Today sociologists of education reside in both departments of sociology and of education.

The founding of the journal *Sociology of Education* in 1963 may be seen as an attempt both to integrate the subject within the larger concerns of sociology and to benefit from the growing prestige of the parent discipline (Karabel & Halsey, 1977, p. 3). The journal is now housed in the premier professional organization, the American Sociological Association (ASA), which also includes a large number of members in its Section on Sociology of Education. Two other major organizations are dedicated to the sociology

of education—the American Educational Research Association (AERA) Sociology of Education Special Interest Group (SIG), and the International Sociological Association (ISA) Research Committee on Sociology of Education. The maturation of the field has also been marked by publication of the *Handbook of Theory and Research for the Sociology of Education* (Richardson, 1986) and the *Handbook of the Sociology of Education* (Hallinan, 2000).

Key Topics

Sociologists of education studying the dynamics of educational settings have a broad range of interests. A summary follows of some of the areas of research that have attracted the greatest attention. Many of the functions of education discussed by functional theorists are controversial among researchers, teachers, policy-makers, and community members. For example, sociologists raise questions related to the role of the media both in and out of educational institutions in educating and socializing children. (Smith, 1993). This has led to research on such controversial topics as Channel 1 television, which includes advertising in classrooms. Another topic of research on functions of education focuses on what culture should be passed on to children. This is particularly relevant in multicultural classrooms and communities in which competing interest groups wish to have their concerns be part of the curriculum (Jackson, Boostrom, & Hansen, 1993).

Disaffected, alienated youth in schools often cause discipline problems, and with these problems come gangs, violence, drugs, and alcohol in schools; the function of social control and how to carry it out is another major topic in school research (McEvoy & Welker, 2000). Should disruptive students be suspended or expelled, increasing the likelihood of their becoming dropouts? An important and controversial function centers on the selection and allocation of students into classes, tracks, and future jobs or higher education (Gamoran, 1995). This important topic looks at school and community practices and behaviors of students that impact their postschool placements. These and other questions surrounding the functions of education guide the research agendas of many sociologists of education.

The topic of stratification is also the subject of much research in all major theoretical perspectives (Coleman, 1990; Turner, 1960), from issues of sex role socialization to integration of schools to the experience of various minority groups in schools. Specific topics involve the experiences and success rates of students in public versus private schools (Cookson & Persell, 1985); alternative school plans such as magnet schools, choice options, voucher programs, and charter schools (Chubb & Moe, 1990); ability grouping or tracking of students (Oakes, 1985, 1986); the role of home life and family in school achievement (Schneider & Coleman, 1993); and "at-risk" and underclass students (Kozol, 1991).

As mentioned, sociologists are interested in structure and process in groups and organizations. Sociologists of education are no exception. Studies of how students learn their roles (Gracey, 1967), classroom and school organization, the school as a bureaucracy, and centralized versus decentralized decision-making are among the topics that make up the research agenda on school organization (Meyer, Scott, & Strang, 1986).

Many factors external to the school affect the educational system and learning of children. These "environmental factors" provide many topics of research. What role do families play in the achievement of children and their musical training? How does religion interact with education in the United States and in other countries? What are methods of financing schools, and can an equitable method be found to give all students an equal chance for education? In fact, what role does funding play in quality education? What are legal and political opportunities and limitations faced by educational institutions? These are only a few of the "environmental factors" facing school systems.

Comparative education as a field considers educational systems around the world. Major studies comparing achievement in different countries are one example of comparative studies (Organization for Economic Cooperation and Development, 1995). Another example is the study of trends in developing countries that follow the models of developed countries in their curricula development (Benavot, 1992; Meyer, Ramirez, & Soysal, 1992).

Educational movements and change in educational systems provide yet another area of research for sociologists of education (Carnoy & Levin, 1986; McLaren, 1997). The preceding examples give a brief overview of some of the concerns of sociologists in general. The following section traces the development of major ideas in the sociology of education.

Theoretical Streams

The sociological theories utilized in the sociology of education are closely related to the main theoretical streams in the larger body of sociological research. In fact, sociologists of education have contributed several new branches to the main theoretical streams of sociology and are now seen as making vital contributions to the larger field. Many of these theoretical streams are useful in understanding music education, as we shall illustrate later in these pages.

Functional Theory

By the 1950s the prevailing sociological theory was functionalism, or functional theory, known also as structural-functionalism. The theory has roots in the field of anthropology and other social sciences. Durkheim was one of the primary proponents of application of functionalist theory in sociology, and he applied the theory to his studies of educational systems. Among his classic works in education are *Education and Sociology* (1956), *Moral Education* (1961), and *The Evolution of Educational Thought* (1977). Functional theorists hold the view that social systems such as educational systems are normally in balance, meaning that all the parts of the system work together to create a "functional" system. For instance, the educational system in most societies works together with the family, political, economic, and religious systems to create a whole working society. When one of the parts of the system is out of balance or is not working properly, the whole system is under strain (Parsons, 1959). Stresses and strains in one part push borders and influence changes in other social arenas. The goal is to return the system to equilibrium.

Educational research based on functional theory views the education system or school as a mechanism for students' induction into social classes (Coleman et al., 1966). If the system is in equilibrium, or balance, the school will prepare students for their roles in the larger society and a smooth transition will take place. However, if that transition is not smooth, disequilibrium occurs. For example, disruptive students or dropouts do not fit the model of a balanced system, and their presence can cause disequilibrium as the educational system tries to cope with the disruption to its otherwise smooth functioning. Often social policy and evaluation of social programs have been based on functional theory, assuming an equilibrium model; they have put little emphasis on problem areas that exist in the system, such as disruptive students. These assumptions of maintaining equilibrium have meant that policies affecting curriculum decisions, school policies on tracking, and offerings of "frill classes" such as the arts do not always address underlying problems in the educational system.

How does functional theory apply to the sociology of music education? There is little research in music education that can be traced specifically to this theory. Perhaps this is true in part because the bulk of research in music education has been carried out since functionalist theories were in vogue. There has been functionalist research on audience preferences and musical taste (Geigor, 1950; Schuessler, 1948). Most do not focus, however, on educational issues, but rather simply report the social makeup of audiences.

Conflict Theory

In the 1960s, the United States and many other countries were experiencing political turmoil. Change was rapid and stemmed from protests by disenfranchised groups. Functional theory, based on the value of equilibrium and bringing disruptions under control, was seen by many sociologists as unable to explain the disruptions in society based on inequalities. Therefore, many social scientists, including sociologists, turned to conflict theory to find help in explaining the disruptions and rapid change. Conflict theorists started examining such subjects as the "counterculture" in America, the problems caused as ethnic groups began to pursue and gain political power, and issues related to gender power relations. They studied political power as a force in curriculum development and gender and ethnic issues as they apply to school culture and curriculum development. For instance, should cross-cultural or non-Western, as well as youth-oriented "pop" and "rock," musical traditions, be a part of classroom learning in the United States?

In general, conflict theory stems from the classic writings of Karl Marx and Friedrich Engels (1947), and Max Weber (1958). Though each provided a different slant on the theory, the basic idea is that society is composed of competing economic and interest groups. The "haves" (bourgeoisie) and the "have-nots" (proletariat) are in a constant state of tension as each group struggles to maintain and improve its position. The "haves" control power, wealth, influence, privilege, and access to the best education, while the "have-nots" struggle to gain more of the valued resources. This in turn leads to the possibility of conflict between competing groups. The struggle for power influences the structure and functioning of organizations such as schools and the hierarchy that evolves as a result of power relations. The "haves," according to Marx, often use their power to protect and perpetuate their privileged positions. However, the resulting tensions can lead to conflict and eventual overthrow of the existing power structure.

Many noted educational critics and sociological theorists have contributed directly and indirectly to conflict theory in the sociology of education (Apple, 1993; Bowles & Gintis, 1976; Hurn, 1993; Jencks et al., 1979; Kozol, 1991; Young, 1971). In the second half of the 20th century, several conflict theorists presented schools as agents of reproduction and students as resisting their status ascription (Kozol, 1991; Willis, 1979). Reproduction theorists argue that schools reproduce the social class statuses of their students; schools often serve fairly homogeneous neighborhoods, thus helping to solidify existing class boundaries. In addition, in most schools students are tracked into groupings that represent social class lines. Studies of schools in different neighborhoods illustrate that social class differences affect the curriculum, methods of teaching and discipline, and other aspects of schooling (Lubeck, 1985; Kozol, 1991). Because some students feel they have no chance to get ahead and schooling is a waste of time, they resist school authority. These ideas are directly applicable to music and music education: students' musical

choices can be an indication of this resistance (Walcott, 1997). The classic rock song by Pink Floyd, "We don't want no education, we don't want no thought control," is a literal illustration of resistance theory.

In music education, conflict theories are the underpinning for much research into issues of gender in music and into multicultural and popular music. Feminist perspectives and the role of women in music-making and music teaching have produced recent scholarship in music education, including a complete issue of the *Quarterly Journal of Music Teaching and Learning* (vol. 4, no. 4, 1993). Other significant writings include Green (1993, 1994, 1996); Lamb (1990, 1993, 1994, 1996); McCarthy (1996), and O'Toole (1997). Answering the challenges brought by the introduction of musics from many cultures, including popular culture, scholars in music education have examined issues facing teachers and schools (Burton, 1997; Elliott, 1995; Palmer, 1996; Volk, 1998; Vulliamy & Shepherd, 1983; Walcott, 1997).

A main criticism of functional and conflict theory is that both approaches focus on the macro level of society. While they are useful perspectives for studying large-scale social phenomena, they are hardly suitable for approaching small-group issues related to classroom, peer group, or student-teacher interactions. Thus, interaction theories started to garner attention and support (Becker, 1952, 1953, 1963; Becker, Greer, Hughes, & Strauss, 1961).

Interaction Theory

By the 1950s and into the 1960s, some sociologists were moving away from attempts to explain large-scale macro-level phenomena and focusing instead on social-psychological questions: individuals in interaction with each other; small group interactions; formation of student and teacher attitudes, values, and self-concept; and influences on student achievement, including socioeconomic status (Ballantine, 2001, pp. 14–16). The underlying themes of this approach are that individuals who share a culture are most likely to interpret and define social situations in similar ways because of their similar socialization and cultural experiences. This results in common "definitions of the situation" and norms to guide social behaviors.

Two branches of interaction theory, labeling theory and exchange theory, further refine the interactionist approach. Labeling theory is useful in understanding how students perceive themselves and how this affects their decisions, behaviors, and interactions. For instance, if a student is constantly told that he or she has real musical talent or that he or she should forget the idea of learning an instrument because he or she is tone deaf, the student may accept the definitions and act accordingly. In other words, students incorporate the labels given by others—parents, teachers, peers—into their self-concept and act to some extent as they are expected to according to the label. Exchange theory assumes that there are costs and rewards for our actions and interactions. Reciprocal interactions create bonds between individuals. Thus, if a student wants the reward of belonging to a particular group, adopting the musical likes and dislikes of that group is likely to enhance the student's status and security in the group.

Contemporary Theoretical Approaches in the Sociology of Education

A current trend in sociological theory is to combine micro-level and macro-level analysis. For instance, Bernstein (1975, 1990) argues that structure and interaction reflect each other and must be viewed together to understand educational systems. His goal over the past 35 years has been to "prevent the wastage of working-class educational potential" (Bernstein, 1961, p. 308). Bernstein combines societal and institutional analysis with interaction analysis, linking language and educational processes and outcomes (Bernstein, 1975, 1990). According to Sadovnik (2001), Bernstein "has examined how speech patterns reflect students' social class backgrounds and how students from working class backgrounds are at a disadvantage in the school setting because schools are essentially middle class organizations" (p. 23).

Works of George Herbert Mead such as *Mind, Self and Society* (1934) and *The Philosophy of the Act* (1938) became the backdrop for the work of those who followed in the interactionist tradition. Mead was a colleague of John Dewey at the University of Chicago, and his ideas on the central role of society in affecting individuals' perceptions and concept formation appear in Dewey's writings. Mead carefully delineated the process that was later to be called, by others, symbolic interactionism. He called it "social behaviorism," noting that there exists a social influence on behavior that intercedes between stimulus and response, thus allowing individuals to mediate or make their own meanings from the symbolic acts (including language) of others. In their similarity to Dewey's ideas, Mead's concepts may be considered foundational not only for the interactionist stream in sociology but also the constructivist concept in education.

Berger and Luckmann's *Social Construction of Reality* (1963) was a later contribution. The "new" sociology of education, which developed in Britain in the 1960s, falls in part into the tradition of interaction theories. Primarily a micro-level approach, it focuses on sociological influences on individuals. It inspired educational research studies on labeling of students (Rosenthal & Jacobson, 1968), on interaction between teachers and students (Bernstein, 1996), and on social influences on individuals' acquisition of knowledge (Epstein, 1995; Corsaro & Eder, 1990; and Hallinan & Williams, 1990). In music education, Rum-

below's work entitled *Music and Social Groups: An Interactionist Approach of the Sociology of Music* (1969), was at the forefront of this movement. He used the symbolic interaction theories of Mead to develop concepts of the "musical gesture" as a social phenomenon and discussed student-teacher interactions and the role of the musician in music education.

Bernstein's work on individuals' systems of creating meaning is called "code theory" because it considers how people understand their worlds and how this affects reproduction of social class. Because he draws on the works of Durkheim, Weber, Marx, and interaction theorists, some feel his work provides a synthesis among these traditions. By looking at the language patterns of children in schools, Bernstein brought to the fore issues of the relationship of individual differences among students, family background, schools, and the social class placement of students. Children from working-class and middle-class families bring different language patterns, or codes, to school, and these in turn affect their educational experiences. For instance, working-class children do not have the "elaborated code," or language patterns, needed for success in school and are therefore at a disadvantage in school performance. In music education, similar issues arise because students' music uses a different musical gesture and vocabulary than the "classical music" typically taught in the schools.

In his later work, Bernstein considered the pedagogical practices used by teachers to produce, distribute, and reproduce "official knowledge" taught in schools. Official knowledge, he argues, reflects the power relations in society. "Bernstein's project seeks to link microprocesses (language, transmission, and pedagogy) to macroforms to show how cultural and educational codes and the content and process of education are related to social class and power relations" (Sadovnik, 2001, pp. 24–25). In music education, the "official music" has been, as was mentioned earlier, the music of the elite, so-called classical music. There is, however, a movement toward a wider repertoire in published school music texts, which often now include various ethnic, world, and popular music selections.

Another theorist who attempts to synthesize the work of Durkheim, Marx, and others is Pierre Bourdieu, a leading contemporary French sociologist of education and thinker who is having a major influence on discussions of the role of education in the class struggle (Bourdieu, 1977). Bourdieu sees status in society as the prize, with "economic capital" (financial assets), "social capital" (networks of connections), and "cultural capital" (specialized skills and knowledge, including educational credentials) being major contributors to one's position (Bourdieu, 1984). For instance, "cultural capital" refers to the background the child brings to school in the form of parents' educational levels, reading materials in the home, and cultural experiences—visits to museums, theaters, and concerts and access to things money can buy. Education and culture "are hugely important in the affirmation of differences between groups and social classes and in the reproduction of those differences" (Eakin, 2001, p. B9).

Bourdieu argues that everyone reaches adulthood with "habitus," a predisposition to succeed or fail. People internalize class distinctions through their early experiences, with school being a major factor. Cultural socialization gives children the cultural capital to achieve (or not) in school. In his work *Distinction,* he argues that "if you own certain pieces of difficult modern art or enjoy difficult pieces of Bach, you have developed the cultural apparatus to enjoy these things. You have to study HOW people consume rather than WHAT they consume" (quoted in Eakin, 2001, p. B11). His recent work *On Television* (Bourdieu, 1998) points out that television commentators substitute "cultural fast food" for substantive argument, providing the masses with less cultural capital than is available.

Another central concept in Bourdieu's work is "symbolic violence," power that manages to impose meanings as legitimate by concealing the power relations that are the basis of its force. This type of power is found in schooling, child-rearing, museums, musical and artistic venues, and other aspects of socialization. Although schools may appear to be neutral, they in fact privilege upper- and middle-class children through their symbolic representations and cultural domination, using language, ideas, and knowledge of art, music, and literature (Sadovnik, 2001).

Randall Collins began to synthesize macro power relations and micro social/interaction processes into a conflict theory of society (1971). In an influential book, *The Credential Society* (1978), he argues that competition between groups and social classes has stimulated the increase in credentials needed for jobs. This increase is a result of middle-class professionals attempting to raise their status.

Postmodern theory refers in part to "a world that transcends the economic and social relations of the industrial world." (Sadovnik, 2001, p. 28). Several common strands characterize postmodern theory. For instance, these theorists reject the idea that there can be one all-encompassing theory of the world; rather they argue for theories that are localized and specific to individual cases. Second, in reaction to modernist theorists who separate theory and practice, postmodernists see a connection between theory and practice. Postmodernists also stress democratic responses rather than authoritarian or totalitarian ones. Schools are seen as sites to instill the values of democracy. Postmodernists seek to move away from racist, sexist ideologies and address interests of all groups of people. They see interactions between individuals and groups as based on power and domination and they argue for exploring, understanding, and accepting differences (McLaren, 1991).

Postmodern theory is closely related to conflict and *critical educational theory.* A writer who influenced the early postmodern movement in the United States and the Americas was Paulo Freire (1972), with his work on the Brazilian underclass. Today many postmodern theorists consider schools and classrooms as political settings and teachers as agents of change. Postmodernism has evolved into a constellation of related theories, and there is much overlap within and between these theories.

Henry Giroux (1981, 1991) links past branches of conflict theory, modernism, postmodernism, and feminism into a theory of *critical pedagogy.* His argument includes the following elements: education produces knowledge *and* political subjects, students need to be aware that their voices can make a difference, and differences between students need to be recognized and respected. Underrepresented students' voices need to be heard along with representatives of their groups.

Constructivism can trace its roots back to the writings of Dewey, Piaget, Bruner, and Vygotsky. It has evolved from the field of education (Brooks & Brooks, 1993) rather than from sociology but retains strong roots in and connections to the sociology of education. Basically, constructivism is a "meaning-making" theory; individuals create new meanings based on the interaction between what they know from past experience and what they learn in their present environment (Richardson, 1997). It is a descriptive (how people learn) rather than a prescriptive (how people *should* learn) theory.

While this definition is generally agreed on, there is considerable disagreement found between the two primary constructivist approaches—the psychological Piagetan approach and the situated social constructivist approach. The first approach regards meaning-making as an individual process. Learning is facilitated by the teacher by creating "cognitive dissonance" in order to give opportunities for the learners to reorganize their cognitive maps. Richardson (1997) points out that, in this approach, "issues of power, authority and the place of formal learning are seldom addressed" (p. 6).

Social constructivism centers meaning-making on social rather than individual factors. Within this rubric, two forms emerge. The first is that of situated cognition, which is developed by interaction between the individual and the environment, with both changing as a result. Action is required for learning. The second form, emerging from Vygotskian theory, focuses meaning-making on social interactions. These interactions create challenges in a "zone of proximal development" that foster increasingly complex learning. Vygotsky's theory is remarkably similar in its basic tenets to Mead's symbolic interactionism (Valsiner & Van der Veer, 1988). Although Vygotsky emphasizes the developmental aspects of interaction and Mead focuses on the overall interactive process, social constructivism and symbolic interactionism "share intellectual roots" (Valsiner & Van der Veer, 1988, p. 117).

Method and Methodology

We make a distinction, following Bogdan and Biklin (1998), between *method* and *methodology*. They define a *method* as a strategy that is utilized in carrying out a research project, such as setting up control groups in an experimental study, using surveys for descriptive research, or doing interviews. *Methodology* is the underlying theoretical and philosophical *stance* a researcher takes. If the two basic methodological paradigms are quantitative and qualitative, then various methods can be used in either or both paradigms. As Bogdan and Biklin point out (1998, p. 32), the same or similar methods can be used with radically different methodological assumptions.

Having noted this essential difference, we can look at sociology, the sociology of education, and the sociology of music education in terms of both method and methodology. Starting with methodology, sociologists in the functionalist and conflict theory streams historically have used a quantitative approach toward research. They primarily were doing macro-scale research, looking for trends in and aspects of social behavior in large populations. Methods used in quantitative research in education include experiments, surveys (interviews and questionnaires), analysis of large data banks, observations using various instruments and scales, and computer programs.

Interactionist sociologists found that quantitative methodology was not always adequate to their task of analyzing interactions on a micro scale. They needed to be able to analyze personal, especially one-to-one, interactions. Interactionists, along with anthropologists, were on the forefront of developing qualitative methodology. Methods typically utilized in qualitative research include participant observation (observations where the researcher becomes part of the group being studied in order to understand the group as an "insider" would understand it); open-ended questionnaires; various case study methods (historical, biographical, reflective); analysis of subjects' documents (diaries, journals, photographs); and combinations of all of these. Often researchers will use multiple data collection procedures in order to triangulate (or validate) their information.

Studies in the sociology of education and music education have made use of all of these methods and more, using both quantitative and qualitative methodologies. A number of studies also combine methods and methodologies; it is not uncommon, for instance, for a quantitative survey on a fairly large sample to be followed with qualitative interviews of some subjects in order to gain more depth of understanding into the topic being studied.

Developments

From the early days of music education research, a psychological foundation was primarily utilized (McCarthy, 1997; Rideout, 1997a). Only in the last decade of the twentieth century did a sociological paradigm become common (Paul, 2000). As a means of "linking" the theory to the research, we give a brief exposition of key studies in music education that use sociology or the sociology of education either as a theoretical basis or as a research perspective.

Music education as an organized profession gained cohesiveness around the turn of the 20th century. The Music Supervisors National Conference (later the Music Educators National Conference, MENC) was founded in 1907. McCarthy relates that the agenda of the group, in the early years of its existence, was largely a social one, advocating social values for music in the schools and supporting community music programs like literally united school music and music of the citizenry (1997, p. 75). This trend continued, and these social values were articulated by educational sociologist David Snedden in the 1920s and 1930s in several books (Snedden, 1920, 1924, 1931). He engaged in an animated debate with Charles Farnsworth, music education professor at Columbia University, the essence of which can be summarized as follows: Snedden advocated social value for music in schools; Farnsworth believed the value of music to lie in the immediate joy the individual derived from it, regardless of any later social value that might be achieved (Lee, 1983). James Mursell, in the 1930s, also advocated a social agenda for music education. McCarthy observes:

One might then ask: If music in education in the early decades of this century was so driven by a social agenda, and if a sociological philosophy of music education, albeit an elementary one, was disseminated publicly by 1935, why are we not [at the time of her writing in 1995] more advanced in our efforts to define a sociology of music education? (1997, p. 79)

McCarthy gives three reasons for the lapse in the sociological perspective in music education: educational sociology itself declined in the 1930s and 1940s, psychology dominated sociology in early music education research, and "the old values surrounding 'art for art's sake' lingered on in music education thought and practice" (McCarthy, 1997, p. 79).

Into this vacuum stepped Max Kaplan. He was a music educator who, in the late 1940s, studied with a sociologist, Florian Znaniecki, at the University of Illinois. His dissertation, *The Musician in America: A Study of His Social Roles* (Kaplan, 1951), was an early milestone in the serious theoretical study of music education issues from a sociological view. His books *Music Education in a Changing World* (1958) and *Foundations and Frontiers of Music Education* (1966) furthered these ideas and gave a broad readership to them. He used a combination of all three theoretical streams (functionalist, conflict, and interactionist theories) to describe his subjects. His research is functionalist in that he dwells on institutions as they exist in society at large and within the musical hierarchy. He is a conflict theorist when he asserts that the musician must be studied as a *deviant* from society. He spends a great deal of his study in the interactionist frame in discussing and researching the "social role" of musicians. While Kaplan's work throughout his lifetime centered largely in the field of leisure studies, he returned to his music education roots in 1988 (Kaplan, 1988) and again in 1997 (Kaplan, 1997).

John Mueller (1958) contributed a sociology chapter to *Basic Concepts of Music Education* (1958), a yearbook published by the National Society for the Study of Education. Mueller's chapter, entitled "Music and Education: A Sociological Approach," primarily explored the nature of musical taste as a social phenomenon. He did not explicitly draw from sociological theory but primarily cited references from aesthetics and from his own earlier works (Mueller, 1951, 1956). His book *The American Symphony Orchestra: A Social History of Musical Taste* was published in 1951, the same year that Max Kaplan's dissertation was finished, and although claiming a "social perspective," Mueller's interest in sociology seems to be limited to this one concept of social influences on musical taste. He does not share Kaplan's wider ranging interest in and coverage of sociological issues across the spectrum of problems in education and music education.

Howard White (1964) wrote *The Professional Role and Status of the School Music Teacher in American Society*, a dissertation that was a survey of over 1,000 music teachers and 100 ex–music teachers, followed by interviews of selected participants. His analysis utilized a number of sociological theories and perspectives. Among the theorists he consulted were Kaplan (1958), Merrill (1957), Merton (1957), Parsons (1949), Riesman (1950), Waller (1932), and Znaniecki (1934). White, in his introduction, writes:

> Paralleling the written history of the development of music as an art there is a story yet to be told of the historical and contemporary individuals who, in their own manner, teach and significantly help perpetuate the practice of music. If one accepts the thesis that music is a cultural pattern—a learned pattern of behavioral responses—then it becomes necessary to be greatly concerned with the forces that tend to aid or inhibit the teachers of music. What value does society place on a music teacher's work? Is he given any prestige specifically for the work he does? Furthermore, if music is a cultural pattern, the study of it as a cultural force interacting with and affecting human be-

> ings must lean heavily on the disciplines of sociology—the study of people and societies in interaction, and psychology—the study of an individual's behavioral responses interacting with given stimuli. (1964, p. 3)

This description frames many of the studies in the sociology of music education that were to follow. He mentions: music as a cultural pattern and education as perpetuation of culture, the value of music in society, the role and status of music teachers, and the study of music and education being based primarily in the two disciplines of psychology and sociology.

In his study, White concluded that music teachers have a definite and strong social role and that the teacher's role is seen with respect by society and his or her immediate circle of friends. He wrote that the social role of the music teacher is congruent with typical American cultural values (as opposed to the social role of the musician, which he labels as "deviant") and that the primary reason for persons leaving the music teaching profession was a desire for a higher salary.

White presented the following as one of his "additional conclusions." This strong call for sociological research in the field of music education foreshadowed the emphasis that came some 30 years later, in the 1990s, on music as a cultural phenomenon:

> Any thorough study of music must necessarily include a study of those people who practice and perpetuate the art and the social role that they play. A study of music, of and by itself, isolated from the culture in which it resides, elicits a myopic interpretation that fails to account for music's being a social art of interaction where all its elements interact with all other cultural elements. (1964, p. 430)

Also in 1964, Johannes Riedel published an article in the *Journal of Research for Music Education* entitled "The Function of Sociability in the Sociology of Music and Music Education." This article succinctly described "sociability" as follows:

> (a) that which embraces the feeling of belonging to a group—a family, a community, or a nation; (b) that which embraces the feeling of togetherness through the performance of music, be it religious, classical, popular, or folk; and (c) that which promotes the formation of interest groups, of organizations, and of societies. (Riedel, 1964, p. 149)

Riedel described the various forms of "sociability" that occur in musical practices and then applied the concept to music education. His theory echoed sentiments that recently have become more prominent in the literature: "the major objective of music education must be the satisfaction of the intellectual and emotional needs of the general student in the primary and secondary school, the college, and the university" (p. 152). This statement is a call for an emphasis on general music for all students, as opposed to the teaching of the talented. Furthermore, "since sociability is one of the major objectives of music education, music education itself should be examined from a musico-sociological point of view" (p. 153).

Riedel outlined the sociology of music from a historical perspective, and then lamented that the sociology of music education was yet to be formally launched:

> Music educators . . . have taken advantage of the writings of the American sociologists, Max Kaplan and John H. Mueller, to expand their own capabilities in the field of music education. A proper literature of the sociology of music education, however, does not presently exist. (p. 154)

Riedel traced the role of "music educator" over the ages and ended with a plea for mutual respect and cooperation among the academic disciplines of the music academy: "By becoming aware of the fact that sociability is the bond which unites music, music education, and musicology, this day of co-operative understanding in both fields has arrived" (p. 158).

Allen Stuart Rumbelow's dissertation *Music and Social Groups: An Interactionist Approach to the Sociology of Music* (1969) was an important work for the sociology of music education. It was clearly based in interactionist theory, specifically the work of G. H. Mead, and presented a wide-ranging exposition on topics of music and music teaching. Rumbelow discussed music as a communicative form, developing an interactionist definition of the "musical gesture" akin to Mead's concept of the "gesture" as the kernel of interaction and communication between people. He further explored this idea of "musical gesture" with a detailed discussion of the common chord as an initial gesture in what he refers to as "occidental" music (Western art music). He conjectured on a system of musical aesthetics that could be developed from the basis of the social acceptance of music. He studied music and social control—situations where music is used to accentuate and highlight social group connections and values. Military and church music are two such examples.

More important for music education, Rumbelow wrote about the role and status of musicians. He also discussed pupil-teacher interaction. His work more specifically detailed the interaction processes in the development of the musician, teacher, and music pupil role than did that of White. Though the dissertation was written in the major field of sociology, his work must be counted as an important influence in the sociology of music education, as a number of later interactionist studies have cited him (Broyles, 1996; Clinton, 1991; Cox, 1994; Gray, 1998; L'Roy, 1983; Paul, 1988; Wolfgang, 1990).

Through the 1970s several reports and articles dealing with sociological topics appeared in the *Yearbooks* of the International Society for Music Education (Benner, 1974, Jankowski, 1981; Linder, 1976; McKeller, 1973; Ringuette, 1981; Tapper, 1976; Tomasek, 1979) but sociology was largely ignored in American music education research journals. McKeller and Linder emphasized issues more related to the sociology of music per se, while Benner, Tapper, Tomasek, Jankowski, and Ringuette were interested in sociological perspectives on the future of music education.

In the 1970s and 1980s John Shepherd and Graham Vulliamy published a number of articles, both separately and together (Shepherd, 1982, 1983; Vulliamy, 1975, 1984; Vulliamy & Shepherd, 1983, 1984a, 1984b); one of their major concerns was the inclusion of popular music in school curricula. They addressed both the sociology of music and the sociology of music education, outlining reasons, based in Marxist theory, why the music of students, as opposed to the music of the establishment, holds a legitimate place in schooling (Vulliamy & Shepherd, 1984a, 1984b). These writings present perhaps the first in-depth sociological analysis of the issue of what kinds of music should be taught in schools, and why. They enter into a point-counterpoint discussion (reminiscent of the Snedden-Farnsworth debate) with Swanwick (1984), which centers on the difference between a sociological (Vulliamy and Shepherd) and a psychological/aesthetic (Swanwick) rationale for music in the schools. Fox and Wince (1975) also contributed thoughts on a similar subject in their article in *Youth and Society* entitled "Music Taste Cultures and Taste Publics."

Also in the 1970s and 1980s there were several studies on "teacher role perception" or "self-concept" of music teachers (Barnes, 1972; Baxter, 1977; Dick, 1977; Moller, 1981; Williams, 1972) appeared. These studies utilized various role perception inventory instruments but did not approach the depth of analysis or breadth of sociological perspective in White (1964). An article authored by Foster (1976) detailed sociological forces at play in instrumental music groups. He used a quite interesting collection of theorists (Kurt Back, Theodore Mills, and Josephine Klein) to make his points about students' motivation to perform well in ensembles.

In 1977, Christopher Small published the book *Music, Society, Education*, which marked his entry into the field of the sociology of music and music education. With this and his later publications, *Music of the Common Tongue* (1987) and *Musicking* (1998), Small raised a significant voice in advocating a social and sociological perspective on music and music education. He is generally credited with bringing into common use the word "musicking," a contraction of "music-making," which emphasizes the fact that music is an activity performed by people in social settings.

Barnes (1980) reviewed the background and conceptual foundations of the sociology of music education. This was another attempt, perhaps the first since Riedel (1964), to synthesize and summarize the field of the sociology of music education, as opposed to the sociology of music.

In 1983 DiAnn L'Roy completed a dissertation entitled *A Study of Teacher Role Development Among Undergraduate Music Education Majors*. L'Roy's work follows directly from Rumbelow; she cites him extensively. Following Carper (1970), she studied the role development of undergraduate music education majors and found that students in her sample had a relatively weak "teacher" role compared to their "musician" role. The factors that students cited in strengthening their role as teacher were participation with children in teaching activities and developing job-specific skills of music teaching (such as writing marching band drills for band directors). L'Roy's dissertation was advised by Hildegard Froehlich at the University of North Texas, who later advised other studies in the sociology of music education (Clinton, 1991; Cox, 1994; Paul, 1988).

Barbara Lundquist (1986) conjectured on a "sociomusical research agenda for music in higher education." This work is certainly a landmark for bringing together a number of theories to formulate a research perspective:

> Where the development and refinement of a pancultural theory of music is the goal, the focus of sociomusical research becomes the identification of common structures and processes underlying the relationships between human beings and music phenomena and identifying the principles by means of which they interact. (p. 53)

Lundquist set forth the areas of intelligence, auditory perception, music preference, music analysis, mass media, tradition and change, social stratification, social and cultural reproduction, acculturation, sociomusical behavior, interaction, and politics as "issues for further sociomusical research." While it is beyond the scope of this outline to detail studies in all of these areas, it is noteworthy that the issue of "cultural reproduction" had been studied by Haughton just 2 years before in Ontario schools (Haughton, 1984).

Also in the 1980s, Schoen (1981) studied sociological factors in the music education of Mexican-American children. Williams (1987) raised the question of whether current models for music education research and teaching reflected the social nature of human beings. Paul (1988) employed a philosophical-sociological methodology to study the problem of the effectiveness of justifications for school music programs. Drawing from interactionist theory, he argued that the norms and values of the clientele social groups of the public schools should be considered when presenting arguments attempting to justify the place of music in the schools. His thesis embodied a criticism of the "aesthetic education" justification that was prominent in the 1960s and 1970s. Early field experience was the focus of an interactionist study by Wolfgang (1990) that examined the effects of various elements of school-based activity on the professional teacher role development of music education majors.

In the decade of the 1990s the sociology of music education as a research area began to flourish and to expand as a mature field in its own right. It is notable that there were too many studies extant in this last decade of the 20th century for review in this chapter. We therefore outline major trends, highlight important studies, and describe major events.

Brian Roberts began writing about the roles of musicians and educators in the early part of this decade (Roberts, 1991a, 1991b). He published two books that present sociological analyses of the world of the university music school, *A Place to Play: The Social World of University Schools of Music* (Roberts, 1991a), and *I, Musician* (Roberts, 1993). He primarily draws on interactionist tradition in his analyses and presents a comprehensive look into the social intercourse that comprises musical and educational activities in the institution.

Thomas Regelski, following the theoretical stream of critical theory, critiqued various aspects of music education practice (Regelski, 1996, 1997). His essay in *Critical Reflections on Music Education,* entitled "Taking the 'Art' of Music for Granted: A Critical Sociology of the Aesthetic Philosophy of Music" (Regelski, 1996), uses a sociological analysis to critique the "aesthetic education" movement. In this and later writings he explicitly derives his work from the phenomenology of Berger and Luckmann, as well as Habermas and other critical theorists, in arguing that the practice of music as an art is situated, social, and political.

Wayne Bowman, although primarily writing as a philosopher in music education, also contributed to the discussion of music education as a social universe (Bowman, 1994a, 1994b, 1994c). His article in the *Quarterly Journal of Music Teaching and Learning* in 1994(a) asked music educators to consider the following questions (p. 55):

- What kind of sociality is reflected and legitimated in this music? How?
- Whom does this music empower and whom does it marginalize?
- What counts as music in this setting?
- How do those whose music this is express themselves about it or use it?
- Who controls its production and dissemination? How?

These questions embody a number of the theoretical streams outlined earlier in this chapter. Bowman touches on legitimation theory, gender theory, reproduction theory, and the idea of cultural capital. He goes on to say: "If music is truly central to human sociality, the domain of educationally relevant musical inquiry cannot be arbitrarily defined to exclude its social, moral, and political implications" (p. 55). Bowman, among other theorists of the 1990s, continues to pile evidence on Snedden's side of the Snedden-Farnsworth debate, which was that social aspects of music education were at least as important as psychological aspects.

In the spirit of the same debate, David Elliott published *Music Matters* in 1995. As a "new philosophy of music education" he presented another counterargument to the "aesthetic education" rationale and used Csikszentmihalyi's "flow" theory as a means to explain the psychological phenomenon of "peak experience" in music. More fundamentally, however, Elliott based his philosophy on the notion that music is first and foremost a cultural phenomenon. For him, music is (1) situated in musical practices, which are expressed as social groups of musicians who perform, listen, and create in a socially determined musical style; (2) primarily an action, or "something that people do"; and (3) something that must be understood in the context of its social reality (Elliott, 1995).

McCarthy (2000, p. 4) writes that *Music Matters* is advocating primarily social values: "social learning, active participation (musicing), human interaction, actual reality, shared knowledge, and communal values." Paul (2000) connects Elliott's philosophy with G. H. Mead's concept of "the act" as the kernel of human interaction (Mead, 1938) and shows how Elliott's praxial philosophy is congruent with symbolic interactionism in this sense: "it is interesting that the word *act* that Mead chose is also at the root of the words *action, activity, actual, practice, practical, and praxial.*" (Paul, 2000, p. 13). In these fundamental ways and more, Elliott's philosophy contains at its foundation a sociological perspective.

Developing theories through the early years of the 1990s, researchers Lucy Green (1993, 1994, 1996, 1999) and Roberta Lamb (1990, 1993, 1994) have brought attention to sociological issues in music and music education, especially as they pertain to "the . . . well-researched groups of social class, ethnicity and gender . . . but other groups abound, including those of age, religion, nationality, sub-culture and many more." (Green, 1999). Their research follows from the general stream of conflict theory but draws primarily from critical pedagogy and feminist theory.

In 1995, a milestone event was held in Norman, Oklahoma: "Symposium '95: The Sociology of Music Education," the first research conference entirely dedicated to the field of sociology of music education (Rideout 1997b). Four years later, "Symposium '99: The Sociology of Music

Education II," also resulted in a publication (Rideout & Paul, 2000).

Topics researched in the 1990s included cultural and multicultural contexts of music education (Andrews, 1993; Brändström & Wilkund, 1996; Destreri, 1990; Rose, 1990; Stewart, 1991; Veblen, McCoy, & Barrett, 1995), socialization, role development, and identity formation of musicians and music teachers (Broyles, 1996; Claire, 1993; Gray, 1998; Holmquist, 1995; Keating, 1998; Paul, 1998; Prescesky, 1996; Schmidt, 1994); and social theories of music education (Ash, 1995; Bontinck, 1991; Humphreys, 1997; Jorgensen, 1993; Mojola, 1997).

Research groups exist within the MENC that have influenced the study of the sociology of music education. The Social Science SRIG was founded in the late 1970s under the name "Sociology, Social Psychology, and Anthropology SRIG" (Barnes, 1980). Its original charter from the Music Education Research Council was to study

folkways, mores, laws, institutions; status, position, roles; actor, significant others; expectations, norms, role performance, stereotypes, sanctions, conformity; consensus, role conflict; culture, race, rituals, social structure, ethnicity; group dynamics, group interaction, sociometry, class, power, authority, community, religion, alienation, deviation; professional organizations, government, legislation, public policy; comparative music education, demographics, economics, values and value systems. (Barnes, 1980, p. 93)

Other SRIGs have evolved which have focused on some of the topics originally in the Social Science SRIG's charter, most notably the Community and Adult Music SRIG and the Gender Research in Music Education SRIG (GRIME). In addition, the *Quarterly Journal of Music Teaching and Learning* published a complete issue, "Sex Equity in Music Education," in 1993, as well as two issues entitled "Research in Social Psychology of Music, 1 and 2" in 1994 and 1995.

The connection between the Philosophy and Social Science SRIGs is strong. The papers presented at Philosophy SRIG sessions and symposia and articles in the *Philosophy of Music Education Review (PMER)* have often contained sociological perspectives and foundational concepts. A perusal of the bibliographies of these papers confirms the presence of sociologists and sociological theory as well as a wide range of philosophical perspectives.

The sociological view has begun to be shared more and more in the writings of music education researchers on a variety of topics. It may or may not be too soon to talk of a "paradigm shift" in music education theory and thinking toward social perspectives on music teaching and learning, but it is undeniable that the sociological view of music education issues is much clearer than it was in 1990. The reigning research paradigm of the early history of music education research, that of experimental psychology, has now been joined by a sociological paradigm. Perhaps in the long term a balance is to be found.

Research Agenda for the Future: Some Suggestions for Scholars

The sociology of education is a 20th-century phenomenon, with most of its ideas and research being published since 1900. The sociology of *music* education began to develop as a field in its own right after 1950. In the 1990s, the sociology of music education grew exponentially, with a wider range of topics and methodologies being considered and with scholarly publications increasing dramatically. This chapter's exposition of a multitude of possible theoretical approaches is presented as a stimulus for music educators to look at their field from ever-broadening perspectives.

We have outlined basic theoretical approaches to the sociology of education, including the three traditional streams of functional, conflict, and interaction theory. Recent theorists such as Bernstein, Bourdieu, Collins, Freire, and Giroux have refined and synthesized these theories in developing more contemporary approaches to the sociology of education. A review of the literature shows that music educators using a sociological approach have followed many of these streams in developing their research and lines of argumentation. Our purpose here is to encourage music educators to continue following these streams, as well as to branch out and even create new sociological perspectives that follow directly from the interactions among music, musicians, audiences, music teachers, and other clientele groups surrounding musicking and schooling. In this section we suggest some possible avenues for this work.

Before outlining a future research agenda, however, we should note the range of sociological inquiry that was reported in the first edition of this Handbook (Colwell, 1992). There was a section entitled "Social and Institutional Contexts," which included the chapters "Professional Organizations," "Multicultural Music Education in a Pluralistic Society," "Trends and Issues in Policy-Making for Arts Education," "The Nature of Policy and Music Education," and "Research Methods in International and Comparative Music Education." The lead chapter in this section, "Sociology and Music Education," by Charles Hoffer, primarily covered research into the social and cultural factors affecting musical taste and choice. In this context he discussed social, economic, and age-level stratifi-

cation, as well as conformity, role expectation, and self-image as agents of musical choice.

Sociological topics in music education reviewed in the first Handbook (Colwell, 1992) are still pertinent 10 years later; indeed, the list has grown. An expanding number of areas within music education can bear analysis and study by sociological methods. As a means of organizing topics, we shall take a look back at the charter of the original Social Science SRIG (Barnes, 1980), which still today provides a fruitful starting point for continued and future research efforts. The charter suggests study of *"status, position, roles; expectations, norms, role performance, stereotypes, sanctions, [and] conformity."*

Perhaps one priority might be determining more accurately just "who we are" as a music education profession. Studies would be welcomed essentially replicating the study of White (1964), which looked rather broadly at the role of music teachers, asking them about their own self-image and social status. With music teacher shortages seemingly on the increase in many parts of the United States, this kind of information could be valuable to music educators and administrators interested in recruitment and retention of teachers. Further study of teacher roles, job descriptions and satisfaction, and demographics such as salary and benefits may shed light on and help improve music educators' efforts to improve their lot as one of the clientele groups in school systems.

The socialization of musicians is a subject that music educators are beginning to study (Roberts, 1991a, 1993). If we consider music teaching and learning as a socialization process, many music education issues need study in terms of their impact on individuals and groups. These issues include ideology, induction, retention, justification, pedagogy, and strategic and tactical issues of instructional design.

Further, an important research topic is the function of significant persons in the teaching and learning of music, in other words, the *"actor [and] significant others."* The sociological significance of the relationship between teachers and students is an important area for the study of teaching and learning effectiveness. The relationships between "actors" in social roles are common sociological subjects, and music educators can focus on teacher-student, student-student, teacher-teacher, teacher-administrator, teacher-parent, and other interactions that occur within and among the clientele groups of the schools.

A related issue needing further study is teacher education in music. In order to understand and improve the process of bringing neophytes into the profession as "music educators," we need to gain a greater understanding of factors that influence preservice teachers as they are attracted to, enter, move through, and graduate from teacher education programs. The concept of "significant other" is certainly pertinent here, as young teachers need relationships of significance in order to develop their membership in the reference group "teachers" and find mentors who can guide them in their growth and development.

In addition, the multicultural nature of contemporary society demands study of *"consensus, role conflict; culture, race, rituals, social structure, [and] ethnicity."* Music educators must continue to improve their knowledge of the processes of musical understanding, especially in the teaching and learning of music in classrooms. The transmission of music from diverse cultures presents enormous new challenges for many classically trained music educators. Issues of authenticity versus breadth of coverage are difficult and tenacious. How many different ethnic musical traditions should we teach in schools? Should we teach the cultural music of the particular students in our class (e.g., *mariachi* music in a Hispanic school), or should we strive to explore with them music of other cultures? How can one teacher become expert in many different musical cultures, when it takes 4 to 5 years to develop a modicum of expertise in the Western European tradition taught in university music schools? What about popular music as a subject for academic attention in schools? Since Shepherd and Vulliamy began seriously exploring this topic more than 20 years ago, have schools adopted curricula that include youth music and popular and rock music? What roadblocks still bar this path?

We should add "gender" to the original list of topics in the SRIG charter. Gender issues, including those facing teachers and students in schools, can highlight role conflicts and political and personal power differentials. How do we help teachers and students to develop healthy perspectives on authoritarian versus empowering teaching styles? Is it important to explore teaching metaphors such as "school as factory" or "learning as production" versus "school as garden" or "learning as growth"? Selection of music for the classroom needs to be carefully considered; "gendered" music, as scholars like McClary (1991) have pointed out, holds an influence on music education, as exemplified in curricula and textbooks.

Related political and power issues include *"group dynamics, group interaction, sociometry, class, power, authority, community, religion, alienation, [and] deviation."* These topics bear upon the previous discussion, in terms of the degree to which music of the elite is still the music of the schools. Some would argue that much school music is not in fact of the elite tradition but is a "watered-down" or popularized version of "semiserious" music. How do social class and community play into these issues? How do expectations of schools toward performing groups affect repertoire? How do expectations of parents and administrators affect curricula? Can curricula be flexible enough to include more than large ensembles at the high school level? Are all students at all grade levels deserving of opportunities to study and perform music of a wide range of cultures and social and economic classes?

There exist many subcultures in schools, where issues of authority, alienation, class, power, and deviation are powerful determinants of musical experience and musical choice. These groups exhibit musical gestures that have much to say about their lives, beliefs, and cultures. Can music education adapt to the needs of these students? It can be argued that "mainstream" music education (that form of music education expressed by typical curricula and courses taught in typical public schools) has largely ignored musical subcultures and thus left many students out of the formal music education process.

Among the least-studied areas in music education have been *"professional organizations, government, legislation, public policy, folkways, mores, laws, [and] institutions."* These functions of musical society have been largely ignored in research yet have great impact on the profession and on musical life in general. The MENC claims a large membership; yet it has been the subject of very little research into its actual influence among the clientele in music. Governmental and legislative policy also has been largely ignored in terms of impact on music education. Legal issues facing music teachers are little understood and seldom discussed or researched.

There is little research extant on other institutions within the music education profession, including groups such as the Orff (Orff-Schulwerk Association) and Kodály (Organization of American Kodály Educators) associations; various band and orchestra organizations such as the American School Band Directors Association (ASBDA), American Bandmasters Association (ABA), National Band Association (NBA), National String Orchestra Association (NSOA), American String Teachers Association (ASTA), and College Band Directors National Association (CBDNA); the International Association of Jazz Educators (IAJE); choral organizations such as the American Choral Directors Association (ACDA); and industry groups such as the Music Industry Conference.

A broader survey, as well as in-depth analysis, of the entire profession of music education across international lines is needed, including *"comparative music education, demographics, economics, [and] values and value systems."* Comparative studies of music education in America and other countries can give music educators valuable information and insight into many of the issues listed in previous categories. International practices vary widely, yet little is published that directly compares and contrasts systems. Demographic and economic information on music education—programs, students, teachers, client groups of the schools, the schools themselves—would be valuable for advocacy efforts. The discussion of values and value systems for music education has been extensive and recently has begun to take on a sociological perspective. This trend is encouraging and should continue.

As called for by Riedel in 1964, a "sociomusicological" mind-set can be appropriate for addressing a wide variety of issues and concerns in music education; we applaud and encourage that approach and look for continued growth in research in the sociology of music education.

REFERENCES

Andrews, B. W. (1993). Music instruction in a multicultural context: Conflict in patterns of socialization. *Canadian Music Educator, 34*(5), 9–16.

Apple, M. W. (1993). *Official knowledge.* New York: Routledge.

Ash, S. (1995). Equality of opportunity in music education: A sociological analysis. *Canadian Music Educator, 37*(1), 23–25.

Ballantine, J. H. (2001). *The sociology of education: A systematic analysis* (5th ed). Upper Saddle River, NJ: Prentice-Hall.

Barnes, S. H. (1972). *The high school instrumental teacher role: An exploration of interposition consensus.* Unpublished doctoral dissertation, Ohio State University, Columbus.

Barnes, S. H. (1980). The sociology of music education: Conceptual foundations and historical referents. *Contributions to Music Education, 8,* 93–95.

Barnes, S. H. (1986). Social composition of performing arts audiences in America as one measure of the efficacy of the program in music education. *Bulletin of the Council for Research in Music Education, 88,* 32–50.

Baxter, S. G. (1977). *The relationship of self-concept and career choice among university music students.* Unpublished doctoral dissertation, University of Kentucky, Lexington.

Becker, H. S. (1952). Social-class variations in the teacher-pupil relationship. *Journal of Educational Sociology, 25,* 451–465.

Becker, H. S. (1953). The teacher in the authority system of the public school. *Journal of Educational Sociology, 26,* 128–141.

Becker, H. S. (1963). *Outsiders: Studies in the sociology of deviance.* Glencoe, IL: Free Press.

Becker, H. S., Greer, B., Hughes, E. C., & Strauss, A. (1961). *Boys in white: Student culture in medical school.* Chicago: University of Chicago Press.

Benavot, A. (1992). Curricular content, educational expansion, and economic growth. *Comparative Education Review, 36*(2).

Benner, C. H. (1974). Implications of social change for music education. *ISME Yearbook, 11,* 34.

Berger, P., & Luckmann, T. (1963). *The social construction of reality.* Garden City, NY: Doubleday.

Bernstein, B. (1961). Social class and linguistic development: A theory of social learning. In A. H. Halsey, J. Floud, & C. A. Anderson (Eds.), *Education, economy and society* (pp. 288–314). New York: Free Press.

Bernstein, B. (1975). *Class, codes and control: Vol. 3.* London: Routledge.

Bernstein, B. (1990). *The structuring of pedagogic discourse: Class, codes and control: Vol. 4.* London: Routledge.

Bernstein, B. (1996). *Pedagogy, symbolic control and identity theory, research, critique.* London: Taylor and Francis.

Bogdan, R. C., & Biklin, S. K. (1998). *Qualitative research for education: An introduction to theory and methods.* Boston: Allyn and Bacon.

Bontinck, I. (1991). The changing media landscape and its consequences for music education policies. *International Journal of Music Education, 17,* 5–13.

Bourdieu, P. (1977). Cultural reproduction and social reproduction. In J. Karabel & A. H. Halsey (Eds.), *Power and ideology in education* (pp. 487–511). New York: Oxford University Press.

Bourdieu, P. (1984). *Distinction: A social critique of the judgment of taste.* Cambridge: Harvard University Press.

Bourdieu, P. (1998). *On television* (P. P. Ferguson, Trans.). New York: New Press.

Bowles, S., & Gintis, H. (1976). *Schooling in capitalist America: Education and the contradictions of economic life.* New York: Basic Books.

Bowman, W. D. (1994a). Sound, sociality, and music: Part 1. *Quarterly Journal of Music Teaching and Learning, 5*(3), 50–59.

Bowman, W. D. (1994b). Sound, sociality, and music: Part 2. *Quarterly Journal of Music Teaching and Learning, 5*(3), 60–67.

Bowman, W. D. (1994c). Sound, society, and music proper. *Philosophy of Music Education Review, 2*(1), 14–24.

Brändström, S., & Wilkund, C. (1996). The social use of music and music education. *Canadian Music Educator, 37*(3), 33–37.

Brooks, J. G., & Brooks, M. G. (1993). *In search of understanding: The case for constructivist classrooms.* Alexandria, VA: Association for Supervision and Curriculum Development.

Broyles, J. (1996). *The effects of videotape analysis on teacher role development in music student teachers.* Unpublished doctoral dissertation, University of Oklahoma, Norman.

Burton, B. (1997). The role of multicultural music education in a multicultural society. In R. R. Rideout (Ed.), *On the sociology of music education* (pp. 81–84). Norman: University of Oklahoma School of Music.

Carnoy, M. & Levin, H. (1986). Educational reform and class conflict. *Journal of Education, 168*(1), 35–46.

Carper, J. (1970). The elements of identification with an occupation. In H. S. Becker (Ed.), *Sociological work* (pp. 189–201). Chicago: Aldine.

Chubb, J. E., & Moe, T. M. (1990). *Politics, markets and America's schools.* Washington, DC: Brookings Institution.

Claire, L. (1993). Social psychology of creativity: The importance of peer social processes for students' academic and artistic creative activity in classroom contexts. *Bulletin of the Council for Research in Music Education, 119,* 21–28.

Clinton, J. (1991). *An investigation of the self-perceptions certified fine arts teachers have toward their roles as artist and instructional staff members in selected public high schools of Oklahoma.* Unpublished doctoral dissertation, University of North Texas, Denton.

Coleman, J. S., et al. (1990). *Equality and achievement in education.* Boulder, CO: Westview Press.

Coleman, J. S., (1966). *Equality of educational opportunity.* Washington, DC: U.S. Department of Education.

Collins, R. (1971). Functional and conflict theories of educational stratification. *American Sociological Review, 36*(6), 1002–1019.

Collins, R. (1978). *The credential society.* New York: Academic Press.

Colwell, R. (Ed.). (1992). *Handbook of research on music teaching and learning.* New York: Schirmer Books.

Cookson, P. W., Jr., and Persell, C. H. (1985). *Preparing for power: America's elite boarding schools.* New York: Basic Books.

Corsaro, W. A., & Eder, D. (1990). Children's peer cultures. *Annual Review of Sociology, 16,* 197–220.

Cox, P. H. (1994). *The professional socialization of Arkansas music teachers as musicians and educators.* Unpublished doctoral dissertation, University of North Texas, Denton.

Destreri, L. D. G. (1990). Do musics need sociology tout court, a sociology of professions or a sociology of technological communication? *International Journal of Music Education, 15,* 19–21.

Dick, R. L. (1977). *Teacher role perception of music student teachers before and after student teaching at the University of Northern Colorado.* Unpublished doctoral dissertation, University of Northern Colorado, Greeley.

DiMaggio, P., Useem, M., & Brown, P. (1978, November). *Audience studies of the performing arts and museums: A critical review* (Research Report 9). Washington DC: National Endowment for the Arts.

Durkheim, E. (1956). *Education and sociology* (S. D. Fox, Trans.). Glencoe, IL: Free Press.

Durkheim, E. (1961). *Moral education* (E. K. Wilson & H. Schnurer, Trans.). Glencoe, IL: Free Press.

Durkheim, E. (1977). *The evolution of educational thought.* (P. Collins, Trans.). London: Routledge.

Eakin, E. (2001, January 6). The intellectual class struggle. *New York Times,* pp. B9–B11.

Elliott, D. J. (1995). *Music matters: A new philosophy of music education.* New York: Oxford.

Epstein, J. L. (1995, May). School/family/community partnerships. *Phi Delta Kappan,* 701–712.

Etzkorn, K. P. (1989). (Ed.). Preface. In P. Honigsheim, *Sociologists and music: An introduction to the study of music and society through the later works of Paul Honigsheim* (pp. xiii–xvi). New Brunswick, NJ: Transaction.

Foster, D. L. (1976). The ensemble as a sociological group. *Instrumentalist, 31*(2), 40.

Fox, W. S., & Wince, M. H. (1975). Music taste cultures and taste publics. *Youth and Society, 7,* 198–224.

Freire, P. (1972). *Pedagogy of the oppressed.* New York: Herder and Herder.

Gamoran, A., (1995). An organizational analysis of the effects of ability grouping. *American Educational Research Journal, 32*(4), 687–715.

Geigor, T. (1950). A radio test of musical taste. *Public Opinion Quarterly, 14,* 453–460.

Giroux, H. (1981). *Ideology, culture and the process of schooling.* Philadelphia: Temple University Press.

Giroux, H. (1991). *Postmodernism, feminism, and cultural politics: Redrawing educational boundaries.* Albany: State University of New York Press.

Gracey, H. L. (1967). Learning the student role: Kindergarten as academic boot camp. In D. Wrong & H. L. Gracey (Eds.), *Readings in introductory sociology.* New York: Macmillan.

Gray, M. E. (1998). *Teacher or performer: Role identification among piano majors.* Unpublished doctoral dissertation, University of Oklahoma, Norman.

Green, L. (1993). Music, gender and education: A report on some exploratory research. *British Journal of Music Education, 10*(3), 219–254.

Green, L. (1994). Gender, musical meaning, and education. *Philosophy of Music Education Review, 2*(2), 99–105.

Green, L. (1996). Gender, musical meaning and education. In L. R. Bartel & D. J. Elliott (Eds.), *Critical reflections on music education: Proceedings of the second international symposium on the philosophy of music education* (pp. 229–236). Toronto: Canadian Music Education Research Centre, University of Toronto.

Green, L. (1999). Research in the sociology of music education: Some introductory comments. *Music Education Research, 1*(2), 159–170.

Hallinan, M. T. (Ed.). (2000). *Handbook of the sociology of education.* New York: Kluwer Academic.

Hallinan, M. T., & Williams, R. A. (1990). Students' characteristics and the peer-influence process. *Sociology of Education, 63*(2), 122–132.

Haughton, H. (1984). Music as social and cultural reproduction: A sociological analysis of educational processes in Ontario schools. *Canadian University Music Review, 5,* 38–59.

Hilliard, D. C. (2000). *Personal observations on the sociology of music.* Unpublished manuscript.

Holmquist, S. P. (1995). *A study of community choir members' school experiences.* Unpublished doctoral dissertation, University of Oregon, Eugene.

Humphreys, J. T. (1997). Expanding the horizons of music education history and sociology. *Quarterly Journal of Music Teaching and Learning, 7*(2–4), 5–19.

Hurn, C. J. (1993). *The limits and possibilities of schooling* (3rd ed.). Boston: Allyn and Bacon.

Jackson, P. W., Boostrom, R. E., & Hansen, D. T. (1993). *The moral life of schools.* San Francisco: Jossey-Bass.

Jankowski, W. (1981). Social and cultural roles of the music schools system in Poland [Abstract]. *ISME Yearbook, 8,* 90–91.

Jencks, C., et al. (1979). *Inequality: A reassessment of the effects of family and schooling in America.* New York: Basic Books.

Jorgensen, E. R. (1993). On building social theories of music education. *Bulletin of the Council for Research in Music Education, 116,* 33–50.

Kaplan, M. (1951). *The musician in America: A study of his social roles (introduction to a sociology of music)*. Unpublished doctoral dissertation, University of Illinois, Urbana.

Kaplan, M. (1958). *Music education in a changing world*. Washington, DC: Music Educators National Conference.

Kaplan, M. (1966). *Foundations and frontiers of music education*. New York: Holt, Rinehart and Winston.

Kaplan, M. (1988). Society, sociology, and music education. In J. T. Gates (Ed.), *Music education in the United States: Contemporary issues* (pp. 3–32). Tuscaloosa: University of Alabama Press.

Kaplan, M. (1997). Sociology and music education: Issues and connections. In R. R. Rideout (Ed.), *On the sociology of music education* (pp. 55–64). Norman: University of Oklahoma School of Music.

Karabel, J., & Halsey, A. H. (1977). *Power and ideology in education*. New York: Oxford University Press.

Keating, J. (1998). Identity formation in music education: A conversation with fourth year music education students. *Canadian Music Educator, 40*(1), 61–64.

Kozol, J. (1991). *Savage inequalities: Children in America's schools*. New York: Crown.

Lamb, R. (1990). Are there gender issues in school music? *Canadian Music Educator. 31*(6), 9–14.

Lamb, R. (1993). Possibilities of/for feminist music criticism in music education. *British Journal of Music Education, 10*(3), 169–180.

Lamb, R. (1994). Feminism as critique in philosophy of music education. *Philosophy of Music Education Review, 2*(2), 59–74.

Lamb, R. (1996). Feminism as critique in philosophy of music education. In L. R. Bartel & D. J. Elliott (Eds.), *Critical reflections on music education: Proceedings of the second international symposium on the philosophy of music education* (pp. 237–263). Toronto: Canadian Music Education Research Centre, University of Toronto.

Lee, W. R. (1983). The Snedden-Farnsworth exchanges of 1917 and 1918 on the value of music and art in education. *Journal of Research in Music Education, 31*(3), 203–213.

Linder, K. (1976). The place and function of music in contemporary society. *ISME Yearbook, 3,* 30–32.

L'Roy, D. (1983). *The development of occupational identity in undergraduate music education majors*. Unpublished doctoral dissertation, University of North Texas, Denton.

Lubeck, S. (1985). *Sandbox society: Early education in black and white America*. London: Falmer.

Lundquist, B. R. (1986). Sociomusical research agenda for music in higher education. *Bulletin of the Council for Research in Music Education, 86,* 53–70.

Marx, K., & Engels, F. (1947). *The German ideology*. New York: International.

McCarthy, M. (1996). Wheels within wheels: Feminism, gender, and multicultural music education, a response to Green and Lamb. In L. R. Bartel & D. J. Elliott (Eds.), *Critical reflections on music education: Proceedings of the second international symposium on the philosophy of music education* (pp. 264–272). Toronto: Canadian Music Education Research Centre, University of Toronto.

McCarthy, M. (1997). The foundations of sociology in American music education (1900–1935). In R. R. Rideout (Ed.), *On the sociology of music education* (pp. 71–80). Norman: University of Oklahoma School of Music.

McCarthy, M. (2000). "Music Matters": A philosophical foundation for a sociology of music education. *Bulletin of the Council for Research in Music Education, 144,* 3–10.

McClary, S. (1991). *Feminine endings: Music, gender, and sexuality*. Minneapolis: University of Minnesota Press.

McEvoy, A., & Welker, R. (2000). Antisocial behavior, academic failure, and school climate: A critical review. *Journal of Emotional and Behavioral Disorders, 8*(3), 130–140.

McKeller, D. A. (1973). Sociomusicology: The next horizon for music education. *ISME Yearbook, 1,* 73–79.

McLaren, P. (1991). Schooling the postmodern body: Critical pedagogy and the politics of enfleshment. In H. Giroux (Ed.), *Postmodernism, feminism, and cultural politics: Redrawing educational boundaries* (pp. 195–203). Albany: State University of New York Press.

McLaren, P. L. (1997). Decentering whiteness: In search of a revolutionary multiculturalism. *Multicultural Education, 5*(1), 4–11.

Mead, G. H. (1934). *Mind, self and society: From the standpoint of a social behaviorist*. Chicago: University of Chicago Press.

Mead, G. H. (1938). *The philosophy of the act*. Chicago: University of Chicago Press.

Merrill, F. E. (1957). *Society and culture*. Englewood Cliffs, NJ: Prentice-Hall.

Merton, R. K. (1957). *Social theory and social structure*. Glencoe, IL: Free Press.

Meyer, J. W., Ramirez, F., & Soysal, Y. N. (1992). World expansion of mass education: 1870–1980. *Sociology of Education, 65,* 128–149.

Meyer, J. W., Scott, W. R., & Strang, D. (1986). *Centralization, fragmentation, and school district complexity*. Stanford, CA: Stanford Policy Institute, Stanford University.

Mojola, C. (1993). Process of music education from a systematic approach and its implications in providing an improved relationship between contemporary musical production and society. *Bulletin of the Council for Research in Music Education, 119,* 37–40.

Moller, L. E. (1981). *The relationship of role perceptions of the secondary school music educator and the resultant effect on job satisfaction*. Unpublished doctoral dissertation, University of Kansas, Lawrence.

Mueller, J. H. (1951). *The American symphony orchestra: A social history of musical taste*. Bloomington: Indiana University Press.

Mueller, J. H. (1956). The social nature of musical taste. *Journal of Research in Music Education, 4*(2), 113–22.

Mueller, J. H. (1958). Music and education: A sociological approach. in N. B. Henry (Ed.), *Basic concepts in music education: The fifty-seventh yearbook of the National Society for the Study of Education* (pp. 88–122). Chicago: University of Chicago Press.

Oakes, J. (1985). *Keeping track: How schools structure inequality*. New Haven: Yale University Press.

Oakes, J. (1986). Tracking, inequality, and the rhetoric of reform: Why schools don't change. *Journal of Education, 168*(1), 60–80.

Organization for Economic Cooperation and Development. (1995). Indicators of education's systems. In *Digest of International Education Statistics*. Washington, DC: U.S. Department of Education.

O'Toole, P. (1997). Escaping the tradition: Tensions between the production of values and pleasures in the choral setting. In R. R. Rideout (Ed.), *On the sociology of music education* (pp. 130–137). Norman: University of Oklahoma School of Music.

Palmer, A. J. (1996). On a philosophy of world musics in music education. In L. R. Bartel & D. J. Elliott (Eds.), *Critical reflections on music education: Proceedings of the second international symposium on the philosophy of music education* (pp. 127–145). Toronto: Canadian Music Education Research Centre, University of Toronto.

Parsons, T. (1949). *Essays in sociological theory pure and applied.* Glencoe, IL: Free Press.

Parsons, T. (1959). The school class as a social system: Some of its functions in American society. *Harvard Educational Review, 29,* 297–318.

Paul, S. J. (1988). *Aesthetic justifications for music education: A theoretical study of their usefulness.* Unpublished doctoral dissertation, University of North Texas, Denton.

Paul, S. J. (1998). The effects of peer teaching experiences on the professional teacher role development of undergraduate instrumental music education majors. *Bulletin of the Council for Research in Music Education, 137,* 73–92.

Paul, S. J. (2000). The sociological foundations of David Elliott's "Music Matters" philosophy. *Bulletin of the Council for Research in Music Education, 144,* 11–20.

Prescesky, R. (1996). *A study of preservice music education students: Their struggle to establish a professional identity.* Unpublished doctoral dissertation, McGill University, Montreal.

Regelski, T. A. (1996). Taking the "art" of music for granted: A critical sociology of the aesthetic philosophy of music. In L. R. Bartel & D. J. Elliott (Eds.), *Critical reflections on music education: Proceedings of the second international symposium on the philosophy of music education* (pp. 23–58). Toronto: Canadian Music Education Research Centre, University of Toronto.

Regelski, T. A. (1997). Musicians, teachers, and the social construction of reality. In R. R. Rideout (Ed.), *On the sociology of music education* (pp. 95–111). Norman: University of Oklahoma School of Music.

Richardson, J. G. (Ed.). (1986). *Handbook of theory and research for the sociology of education.* New York: Greenwood Press.

Richardson, V. (1997). *Constructivist teacher education: Building a world of new understandings.* Bristol, PA: Falmer Press.

Rideout, R. R. (1997a). Antecedents to a sociology of music education. In R. R. Rideout (Ed.), *On the sociology of music education* (pp. 65–70). Norman: University of Oklahoma School of Music.

Rideout, R. R. (Ed). (1997b). *On the sociology of music education.* Norman: University of Oklahoma School of Music.

Rideout, R. R., & Paul, S. J. (Eds.). (2000). *On the sociology of music education II: Papers from the music education symposium at the University of Oklahoma.* Amherst: University of Massachusetts Press.

Riedel, J. (1964). The function of sociability in the sociology of music and music education. *Journal of Research in Music Education, 12*(2), 149–58.

Riesman, D. (1950). *The lonely crowd.* New Haven: Yale University Press.

Ringuette, R. (1981). Music education and new techniques in social sciences. *ISME Yearbook, 8,* 124.

Roberts, B. A. (1991a). *A place to play: The social world of university schools of music.* St. John's: Memorial University of Newfoundland.

Roberts, B. A. (1991b). Sociological reflections on methods in school music. *Canadian Music Educator, 32*(5), 20–25.

Roberts, B. A. (1993). *I, musician.* St. John's: Memorial University of Newfoundland.

Rose, A. M. (1990). *Music education in culture: A critical analysis of reproduction, production, and hegemony.* Unpublished doctoral dissertation, University of Wisconsin, Madison.

Rosenthal, R., & Jacobson, L. (1968). *Pygmalion in the classroom.* New York: Holt, Rinehart and Winston.

Rumbelow, A. S. (1969). *Music and social groups: An interactionist approach to the sociology of music.* Unpublished doctoral dissertation, University of Minnesota, Minneapolis.

Sadovnik, A. R. (2001). Theories in the sociology of education. In J. Ballantine & J. Z. Spade (Eds.), *Schools and society* (pp. 15–31). Belmont, CA: Wadsworth.

Schmidt, M. E. (1994). *Learning from experience: Influences on student teachers' perceptions and practices.* Unpublished doctoral dissertation, University of Michigan, Ann Arbor.

Schneider, B., & Coleman, J. S. (1993). *Parents, their children and schools.* Boulder, CO: Westview Press.

Schoen, D. E. (1981). Study of selected cultural, sociological and psychological factors in the music education of Mexican-American children [Abstract]. *Missouri Journal of Research in Music Education, 4*(5), 94–95.

Schuessler, K. F. (1948). Social backgrounds and musical taste. *American Sociological Review, 13,* 330–335.

Shepherd, J. (1982). A theoretical model for the sociomusicological analysis of popular musics. *Popular Music, 2,* 145–177.

Shepherd, J. (1983). Conflict in patterns of socialization: The role of the classroom music teacher. *Canadian Review of Sociology and Anthropology, 20*(1), 22–43.

Small, C. (1977). *Music, society, education.* London: Calder.

Small, C. (1987). *Music of the common tongue: Survival and celebration in Afro-American music.* London: Calder.

Small, C. (1998). *Musicking: The meanings of performing and listening.* Hanover, NH: University Press of New England.

Smith, M. E. (1993). *Television violence and behavior: A research summary.* Washington, DC: Office of Educational Research and Improvement.

Snedden, D. (1920). *A digest of educational sociology*. New York: Teachers College Press, Columbia University.

Snedden, D. (1924). *Educational applications of sociology*. New York: Century.

Snedden, D. (1931). *Cultural educations and common sense*. New York: Macmillan.

Stewart, C. (1991). *Who makes music? Investigating access to high school music as a function of social and school factors*. Unpublished doctoral dissertation, University of Michigan, Ann Arbor.

Swanwick, K. (1984). Problems of a sociological approach to pop music in schools. *British Journal of Sociology of Education, 5*(1), 49–56.

Tapper, K. H. (1976). Music, man, society: Music education for the future: A Swedish report. *ISME Yearbook, 3*, 96–104.

Tomasek, A. (1979). Music education: Factor of humanisation of man (Social, cultural and historical aspects). *ISME Yearbook, 6*, 115–122.

Turner, R. (1960). Sponsored and contest mobility. *American Sociological Review, 25*, 855–867.

Valsiner, J., & Van der Veer, R. (1988). On the social nature of human cognition: An analysis of the shared intellectual roots of George Herbert Mead and Lev Vygotsky. *Journal for the Theory of Social Behavior, 18*(1), 117–136.

Veblen, K. K., McCoy, C. W., & Barrett, J. R. (1995). Where did you come from? Where do you go? Searching for context in the music curriculum. *Quarterly Journal of Music Teaching and Learning, 6*(3), 46–56.

Volk, T. M. (1998). *Music, education, and multiculturalism: Foundations and principles*. New York: Oxford University Press.

Vulliamy, G. (1975). Music education: Some critical comments. *Journal of Curriculum Studies, 7*(1), 18–25.

Vulliamy, G. (1984). Sociological view of music education: An essay in the sociology of knowledge. *Canadian University Music Review, 5*, 17–37.

Vulliamy, G., & Shepherd, J. (1983). Sociological approach to pop music in teaching: A response to Swanwick. *ISME Yearbook, 10*, 189–197.

Vulliamy, G., & Shepherd, J. (1984a). The application of a critical sociology to music education. *British Journal of Music Education, 1*(3), 247–266.

Vulliamy, G., & Shepherd, J. (1984b). Sociology and music education: A response to Swanwick. *British Journal of Sociology of Education. 5*(1), 57–78.

Walcott, R. (1997). Post modern sociology: Music education and the pedagogy of rap. In R. R. Rideout (Ed.), *On the sociology of music education* (pp. 180–190). Norman: University of Oklahoma School of Music.

Waller, W. (1932). *The sociology of teaching*. New York: Wiley.

Weber, M. (1958). The Chinese literati. In H. H. Gerth & C. W. Mills (Eds. and Trans.), *Max Weber: Essays in sociology* (pp. 422–433). New York: Oxford University Press.

White, H. G. (1964). *The professional role and status of the school music teacher in American society*. Unpublished doctoral dissertation, University of Kansas, Lawrence.

Williams, D. B. (1987). Do our models for music research and teaching reflect our human social nature? *Bulletin of the Council for Research in Music Education, 90*, 65–72.

Williams, R. O. (1972). Effects of musical aptitude, instruction and social status on attitudes toward music. *Journal of Research in Music Education, 20*(3), 362–69.

Willis, P. (1979). *Learning to labor: How working class kids get working class jobs*. Aldershot, England: Saxon House.

Wolfgang, R. E. (1990). *Early field experience in music education: A study of teacher role socialization*. Unpublished doctoral dissertation, University of Oregon, Eugene.

Young, M. F. D. (Ed). (1971). *Knowledge and control: New directions of the sociology of education*. London: Collier-Macmillan.

Znaniecki, F. (1934). *The method of sociology*. New York: Farrar and Rinehart.

32

Perspectives from the Sociology of Music

RENATE MUELLER

Sociology of music is the application and development of sociological theories and methodologies to investigate musical behavior and attitudes as social action in dialogue with disciplines such as musicology and music education. This chapter focuses on sociological perspectives of music that are relevant to music education. The first step will be to shed some light on contemporary sociological debates and their implications for sociology of music. Second, historical sociological perspectives on musical behavior are presented in relation to the aforementioned debates. Third, contemporary perspectives on culture and media are briefly discussed. Fourth, contemporary perspectives from sociology of music are covered theoretically and accompanied by examples of research studies. Appropriate research methods to investigate musical decisions and interactions in sociocultural contexts are also discussed. Finally, some aspects of a sociological orientation of music education are addressed.

This chapter does not aim to provide a complete overview of the sociology of music, since the field is still characterized by confusion and lack of agreement on such basic questions as subject matter and methodology, as described by Blomster (1976) 25 years ago. The interrelationship of youth, music, and culture is thought to be most relevant to music education, especially since young people's music and the ways they interact with music are to a great extent still ignored and devalued in music education. The sociology of music is the study of the role of music in various cultures, and in today's societies many cultures exist side by side. Therefore, the general theoretical perspectives presented in this chapter are applicable to other important issues in the field, such as the cultures of the elderly, of professional musicians, and of music educators.

Contemporary Sociological Debates

Contemporary sociological debates about modern societies address the maintenance versus the dissolving of traditional social boundaries. The relevance of the debate and the equality of both views are revealed in the title of the third joint conference of the sociological associations from Germany, Switzerland, and Austria in 1998: "Boundless Society." One focus of the conference, among others, was the role of culture in times of social change during which social constraints dissolve (Honegger, Hradil, & Traxler, 1999). The same issue has been addressed in sociological debate in the United States (Alexander & Seidman, 1990).

As a result of such debate, music as a cultural activity in social contexts appears in a new light: Is music just a means of reproducing social inequality in a "class society"? Or is music a means to overstep social boundaries in an "individualized society" where individuals make their choice between sociocultural contexts to which they want to belong or from which they wish to be set apart? Assuming that in modern societies individuals can shape their own biographies, the use of mass media and music serves to constitute personal, social, and cultural identities and is no longer viewed as merely leisure time activity, although that function still exists. Paradigm shifts both in mass media and in music research replaced the massification perspective with the taste cultures hypothesis. The massification perspective suggests that modern societies are increasingly homogenized by mass media while the taste cultures hypothesis says that aesthetic values are heterogeneous. This strengthens the view that, for example, music audiences actively interacting with music include a variety of musical attitudes and behaviors. In their interaction with music and mass media, young people acquire audiovisual competencies and symbolic knowledge that help them to localize themselves consistently in highly differentiated youth cultures.

On the other hand, cultural activities such as fandom can be interpreted as searching for new forms of social orientation and social order (Fiske 1992).[1] The question remains whether and how individual choices underlying musical activities and musical preferences are socially influenced and help to maintain social stratification or to build new taste publics. There is empirical evidence that music is more distinctive than other forms of cultural practice. Due to theoretical and empirical issues in contemporary sociology, the sociology of music is very closely connected to the sociology of culture, especially the sociology of popular culture and the sociology of mass media. Traditionally, it is also strongly related to the sociology of art.

Since the end of the 1970s the study of culture has been revitalized after decades of being viewed as sociologically insignificant. This involved a revival in sociology of culture studies. For example, in the 1980s the American and German sociology associations founded sections on the sociology of culture. Today American as well as European sociologists again ascribe social influence to culture (Alexander & Seidman, 1990; Featherstone, 1995; H-P. Mueller, 1994). Lifestyle, everyday consumption, and everyday aesthetics are understood as expressions of culture. Relations between lifestyle patterns and social inequality are under sociological investigation. Sources of social inequality such as gender, ethnicity, homosexuality, and social class are addressed in culture and media debates (Dines & Humez, 1995).

Historical Perspectives

Pioneers of a Sociology of Music

The pioneer work in the sociology of music presented here even today offers insights into interesting aspects of musical behavior and of music sociological theory and methodology. The rediscovery and publication of Paul F. Lazarsfeld's survey of 110,312 radio listeners of the RAVAG, the Austrian broadcasting company, in 1932 is an impressive example of research in the sociology of music. Neurath (1996) rediscovered Lazarsfeld's manuscript, and Mark (1996b) published it originally as part of the "Music and Society" series, edited by the Vienna Institute of the Sociology of Music. Neurath (1996), Mark (1996a, 1996b), and Poettker (1996) appreciated the methodological significance of the RAVAG study. Lazarsfeld was one of the fathers of empirical social research, of market and opinion research, and of sociological mass media research, which developed in distinct contrast with the more psychologically oriented survey methods in the United States.

Methodologically as well as theoretically, the RAVAG study is of great sociological significance. It addresses the everyday problems of a broadcasting company, and it is a differentiated pioneer study investigating radio audience requests and musical preferences on a large scale. Sociologically remarkable is the fact that Lazarsfeld treated radio listening as social action and differentiated the audience into age, gender, and occupation groups and into rural and urban audiences. In addition, the particular importance of music to the listeners as well as to the radio company—more than 50% of its broadcast time was spent on music—shows its music sociological relevance. Moreover, broadcasting stations define their profile by the means of their "music color," audience studies are main issues of the sociology of music, and radio still is one of the contexts of music socialization (Mark, 1996a, p. 9). Furthermore, the study's practical aspects were strongly concerned with cultural policy questions pertaining to the goals "to educate the masses" and to take into consideration the listeners' requests. The study deals with the radio audience's limited appreciation of "serious," that is, classical, music genres, which received the highest rejection of all items, whereas light music genres received the highest attachment of all items. Listeners of all occupations wanted the radio company to reduce the portion of "serious" music genres, though workers said this more than intellectuals. "Popular symphonic concerts" were least rejected among other "serious" music genres, including "symphonic concerts." Lazarsfeld suggested that this is an effect of the term "popular" (1932, p. 9). Thus another important issue of music sociological interest is addressed in Lazarsfeld's study, the problem of the social construction of musical barriers, which seems to be related with verbal terms of musical genres.

Geiger (1950) successfully tested the hypothesis "that public aversion was directed more against the term 'classical' than against classical music itself" (p. 454). Geiger suggests "some kind of public prejudice . . . to the effect that 'classical music is not for us, the plain people' . . . without ever having given it a fair trial" (pp. 454–455). A radio experiment in Denmark was undertaken with the same pieces by Haydn, Schubert, Mozart, Beethoven, and Mendelssohn-Bartholdy being announced as "popular grammophone music" (p. 456) and played without a break one Saturday, then repeated the following Saturday, announced as "classical music" with musical terms given in detail, such as opus number, key, and specifying the measure in Italian. The latter experimental condition, presenting classical music as "classical," reduced the audience by half (p. 460). Geiger interprets his result as indicating "the prevalence of a 'snobbism in reverse': the public has a more refined musical taste than it likes to admit" (p. 460). Both studies raise the methodological problem of investigating musical taste by valuating verbal terms and not musical pieces. (The Vienna School, located at the Vienna Institute of the Sociology of Music, is systematically tracing its roots back to empirical sociology of music [Blaukopf, 1995; Bontinck, 1996; Mark 1985, 1996b], one example of which is Lazarsfeld's radio research.)

Another pioneer of empirical sociology of music is John H. Mueller (Mark, 1985). Mueller investigated, among other matters, the social nature of musical taste, and its trends, and the aesthetic systems of societies, which are understood as systems of social norms, "aesthetic folkways," and which are documented, for example, in the repertoires of the American symphony orchestra. In Mueller's view, beauty is not in the music itself but is subject to valuations and controversies among different social groups. Mueller (1951) was the first to apply statistical methods to the history of orchestral repertoires. Thus he was able to compare taste structures of different towns and influences of conductors and of political events on the development of taste (see also Mueller, 1961). According to Mark (1985), Mueller's empirical sociological research was not appreciated among those sociologists of music or musicologists who sought the essence of musical taste as a private rather than a social phenomenon and were opposed to the idea that art music should and can be viewed from the market analytical perspective of audience expectations.

Principles of methodology and philosophy of science implicated in an empirical sociology of music have been elaborated in a project that investigates traces of the methods and ways of thinking of a "Vienna School of Music Sociology." These are: (1) the preference for empirical investigation as opposed to speculation, (2) the idea of the unity of natural science and the humanities, (3) the striving for the presentation of scientific findings in a language within everybody's grasp, and (4) the intention to apply scientific findings to social practice within education, art, and cultural policy (Blaukopf, 1995, p. 20). On the other hand, theoretically, the Vienna School remains committed to Weber's (1921/1972) sociology of music approach, without taking up adequately any of the aforementioned challenging debates in contemporary sociology.

Bourdieu's View of Culture

Bourdieu (1968, 1979; Bourdieu et al., 1965) views cultural practice as the reflection and reproduction of social inequality. The social background presupposes the social use of culture that perpetuates features of socioeconomic status such as income, occupation, and educational level. The cultural transmission of social status is explained by the appropriation of not only economic capital but especially cultural and social capital, including the mastery of culture codes. Social and cultural capital are understood in terms of titles and cultural properties, cultural and social

competencies, knowledge, and behavior patterns. Symbolic capital implies the social legitimacy of a person's social and cultural capital. Through socialization a person acquires dispositions for cultural and social practice, the habitus, which include patterns of thought, perception, and action.

The concept of culture codes is the central part of Bourdieu's theory of art perception. Cultural artifacts have symbolic codes embedded in them. They make sense only to those socialized in these symbolic codes. If the relevant code is not mastered, confusion of interpretation occurs and a work cannot be appropriated. The roots of Bourdieu's sociological critique of the judgment of taste are as follows: The aesthetic judgment of taste denies that in fact it is a social judgment and ignores that dominant culture artifacts are coded at all and that some people are inducted into dominant culture codes from birth. Thus aesthetics serves as the ideology legitimating the social differentiation between "high" and "low" culture and between those who master high and dominant culture codes and those who do not. Families and schools transmit socially conditioned inequalities of cultural competence, pretending that culture is a gift "bestowed on certain people by Nature" (Bourdieu, 1968, p. 212). Bourdieu writes: "To enable culture to fulfill its primary function of class cooptation . . . it is necessary . . . that the link between culture and education . . . be forgotten, disguised, and denied" (Bourdieu, 1968, p. 212). In this context, Bourdieu argues, educated people are consequently "carried towards that kind of ethnocentrism which may be called class-centrism and which consists in considering as natural . . . a way of perceiving which is but one among other possible ways and which is acquired through education" (Bourdieu, 1968, p. 206).

In this chapter the idea of aesthetics criticized by Bourdieu will be referred to as the "aesthetic paradigm." The aesthetic paradigm goes back to Kant's concept of aesthetics (Kant, 1790/1963, p. 70). It combines the indifferent and unconcerned aesthetic attitude with the idea of the purity of the unvarnished view of the aesthetic object. In Bourdieu's words, this is "the myth of the 'fresh eye' " (Bourdieu, 1968, p. 205), which is necessary to dismiss because "there is no perception which does not involve an unconscious code" (p. 205). Kant's disinterested contemplation, the aesthetic attitude, viewed as the only adequate way to perceive art, is an aristocratic privilege; it is accompanied by "natural" disgust for trivial, barbarian culture, with entertainment looked on as the appropriate way to consume trivial culture. This is called the "popular aesthetic" in contrast to the "aesthetic attitude" in Bourdieu's theory.

The popular aesthetic pleads for a strong connection between life and art and therefore appreciates the content of art works rather than their form. Bourdieu takes the dichotomy of these two ways of perceiving and consuming art works for granted; his lack of awareness of the diversity of popular culture and its audiences prompts Bourdieu to dismiss the aesthetic paradigm completely. Traces of the aesthetic paradigm as "relics of an aristocratic past" (Bourdieu, 1968, p. 215) still remain in music educational and musicological thinking, often combined with the ethnocentric cultural imperialism of defining any cultural artifact as aesthetically correct or not (Lewis, 1978, p. 18).

The Sociology of Art Music

The superiority of art music to other kinds of music is presupposed if the sociology of music is not perceived to be anything other than the sociology of art music. This is often the case in sociology as well as in musicology. It corresponds to the idea that the only music worthy of scientific attention is Western art music; "musicology is, almost by definition, concerned with Western classical music, while other musics, including even Western popular music, are dealt with under the rubric of ethnomusicology" (Small, 1998, p. 3). The sociological and musicological restriction to art music also implicates another aspect of the aesthetic paradigm that has been sharply criticized by Small: the superiority of the autonomous musical work to processes of creating, performing, perceiving music, and responding to music. This aspect of the aesthetic paradigm ignores the meaning of musical practice, of "musicking," in human life (pp. 4–18). Similarly, Silbermann writes that the sociological study of music is not a means to explain "the nature and the essence of music itself. . . . It is thus the first aim of the sociology of music to demonstrate the dynamic character of the social practice 'music' " (Silbermann, 1957, pp. 64–65). The efforts of Small and Silbermann clearly strive for conceptualizing sociology of music as a sociological rather than a musicological discipline.

The sociology of music is not well established as a discipline of sociology. For example, the sociology associations of Germany, Great Britain, Switzerland, and the United States do not have music or art sociology sections and research committees; only since 1995 has the sociology association of Austria had a section on the sociology of art and music. Considerations about the discipline's lack of music sociologists assume a lack of scholarship in art music (H-P. Mueller, 1994, p. 57). A conference on the occasion of the 25th anniversary of the Vienna Institute of the Sociology of Music confirmed the idea that the sociology of music above all needs scholars with competencies in art music and musicology (Bontinck, 1992; Institut für Musiksoziologie, 1991; Kapner, 1992).

The dismissal of the aesthetic paradigm (Etzkorn, 1996, p. 154) and of the equation of music with art music is overdue in a sociology of music that claims to be relevant to music education and thus aims to investigate, to understand, and to explain musical interactions of young people in social and cultural contexts. Competencies typically ac-

quired through training in art music may enable sociologists to describe and explain musical behavior of a tiny minority, the art music audience, composers, and musicians. Such competencies would provide the researcher with the wrong key for deciphering and analyzing popular music and music videos. To focus on the sociological aspects of music cultures and tastes of the majority of people, musical and audiovisual competencies are necessary. An example is the ability to distinguish musically between different styles of hip-hop and their particular musical roots. These styles and roots correspond with social demarcations by which young people identify or set themselves apart from others, for example, the way they take a stance toward issues such as sexism, racism, and violence (Berry, 1994; Dufresne, 1991; Fiske, 1994; Perry, 1995; Toop, 1991).

The Sociology of Popular Culture

The sociology of popular culture took a long time to develop as an established area of study. Lewis (1978) discussed the difficulties and problems that sociology faced in dealing with popular culture; many of these remain in sociological thinking, especially in musicological and pedagogical thinking. From an aesthetic and moral standpoint, popular culture—even if it is no longer called "brutal culture" or "mass culture"—is avoided by many social scientists. In addition, the ongoing and often strongly ideological debate about the function of popular culture in society prevents researchers from investigating seriously the impact of popular culture on audiences and on cultural and social development. In sociology, musicology, and pedagogy, the devaluation of popular culture is sometimes still connected with the questioning of the scientific value of investigating popular culture.

Major themes in the critique of popular culture have been the negative, profit-minded character of its creation, the negative, debasing, and exploitive effects it has on high culture, and the negative effects it has on the audience and on society, since it is assumed to reduce society's level of civilization and encourage totalitarianism by creating passive audiences (Lewis, 1978, p. 9). This pessimistic view of culture, the massification perspective and the taste publics hypothesis, provided the main perspective in British and American sociology of music during the 1970s and 1980s (Bradley, 1981, pp. 205, 214; Denisoff & Bridges, 1983, p. 52; Lewis, 1977, p. 39; Robinson & Fink, 1986).

The Massification Perspective

The massification perspective is based on the concept of a mass society that is increasingly homogenized by mass media. The culture industry (Adorno, 1975/1990a) and mass media are seen as responsible for the growing standardization of art and culture and the decay of art and culture into mass consumer goods of undemanding quality. This view is taken, among others, by the Frankfurt School (critical theory) of Horkheimer and Adorno. Both the standardization of cultural objects and the uniformity of consumers are addressed. In addition to that, the ways of consumption are characterized by affirmation and the desire to maintain the society's status quo. Adorno clarifies these points when he writes: "The autonomy of works of art . . . is tendentially eliminated by the culture industry" (1975/1990a, p. 276) and "The power of the culture industry's ideology is such that conformity has replaced consciousness" (p. 289). Popular music helps garble consciousness (Adorno, 1962/1976, p. 53). This position is seen as the apocalyptic view of modernity, highlighting its dehumanizing features (Seidman, 1990, p. 220). Huyssen (1984/1990) argues that the massification perspective should be related to its origin as a defensive strategy meant to protect high culture against the threat of totalitarianism in the age of Stalin and Hitler (p. 369).

The Taste Cultures Hypothesis

The taste cultures hypothesis developed in opposition to the massification perspective. It assumes heterogeneous aesthetic values instead of homogenous tastes and musical preferences. This early version of this hypothesis suggests that social positioning by factors such as age, gender, ethnicity, and social class distinguish between different taste publics (Denisoff & Bridges, 1983, p. 52; Lewis, 1977, p. 39).

The sociology of popular culture addresses the implications of the term "popular culture," as opposed to "folk culture," on the one hand and "high culture" on the other. Different hypotheses about linkages between the social structure of a society and its dominant cultural pattern exist (Lewis, 1978, p. 16). Gans (1974) developed the idea of the "industrial pattern," assuming that the cultural strata consisting of taste cultures parallel class strata. In industrial societies taste cultures develop, strongly correlated to social class lines, from high culture, upper middle, lower middle, and lower to quasi-folk low culture. Taste publics are defined as aggregates of people whose cultural choices underlie the same tastes and aesthetic standards. Eleven years later Gans (1985) observed "a new taste culture that seems to cut across and blend upper and lower-middle culture" (p. 26). The postindustrial pattern, as opposed to the industrial pattern, would imply that in postindustrial societies taste cultures no longer are correlated with social class (Lewis, 1978, p. 18). This turns out to be the later version of the taste cultures hypothesis. But Gans only views one single taste culture blending cultures. Different taste cultures exist and differ in their ways of deciphering cultural symbols and ascribing meaning to lyrics, music, and visual images. The question remains whether people who constitute taste publics live in different social settings and whether they live under conditions of social inequality. Research that tests the massification hypothesis against the early version of the taste cultures hypothesis will be reported briefly here in connection with Adorno's sociology of music.

Aspects of Adorno's Sociology of Music

Adorno's (1962/1989) sociology of music is presented here because of its continuing significance in music education, music sociology, and musicology. On the basis of two chapters of Adorno's *Introduction to the Sociology of Music* (1962/1989) it will be shown how the massification perspective is implicated in Adorno's sociology of music. The first is Adorno's typology of listeners ("Types of Musical Conduct") and the second is Adorno's view of popular music ("Popular Music"). The basic concept of Adorno's sociology of music is the presupposition that the structural features of works of music determine the listener's reaction to it (Adorno, 1941/1990b, 1962/1989).

Adorno's theory regarding types of music listeners (Adorno, 1962/1989, pp. 14–34) consists of a hierarchy of "appropriate" listening behaviors corresponding to a presupposed hierarchy of musical genres. On top of the scale we find "great" music, for example, musical works of the late Bach or of Schönberg. The appropriate reaction to music is "structural" listening, unaffected by matters of performance and of arrangement. "Great" music and structural listening are argued to be superior to other music as well as to other musical behavior. Etzkorn writes that "Adorno abhors sociological and musical pluralism: 'If the zither player and Bach have the same right, if individual taste is the only criterion, great music is deprived of the only thing that makes it great and valid' " (Adorno, 1962/1976, p. 120, quoted by Etzkorn, 1978, p. 1037).

The devaluation of music genres such as pop songs or jazz is very closely related to that of listening reactions, expressed in words like the following: "unconnected listening," "substitute listening," "mass listening," "vulgar snobbism" (Adorno, 1962/1989, pp. 14–34). According to Adorno (1941/1990b), the main difference between "great" music and popular music is standardization, with standard reactions the primary aim of popular music. In his opinion, popular music creates listening habits, distraction, and inattention (p. 302).

It is imputed to the listeners of popular music that they are easily manipulated, anti-intellectual, politically conforming to any government, and resistant to structurally analyzing music (Adorno, 1941/1990b, 1962/1989). According to Adorno, those who listen to popular music do not want to hear anything else (1962/1989, p. 44). This approach reveals a dehumanizing attitude itself, which culminates with the following sentences:

It is the banality of present-day popular music—a banality relentlessly controlled in order to make it salable—which brands that music with its crucial trait. The trait is vulgarity. We might almost suspect that this is the most avid concern of the audience that the maxim of their musical mentality is indeed Brecht's line: "But I don't want to be human." (Adorno, 1962/1989, p. 27)

Adorno's sociology of music does not consist of empirical statements; it rather posits unquestioned beliefs and essentialist definitions for what "great" and popular music are, what their essence is and what therefore would be appropriate musical conduct. It supports the aesthetic paradigm presented earlier. In addition, it reveals the ethnocentrism of those having access to higher education (Etzkorn, 1978). While Adorno's unempirical and subjective approach dominates German musicological and music educational thinking and research (Mueller, 1990, pp. 21–46), it has been fiercely attacked in British and American sociology of music for its elitist, snobbish, and authoritarian assumptions, which exclude many musical activities from music sociological study (Blomster, 1976, p. 109; Bradley, 1981, p. 214; Etzkorn, 1978, 1982, p. 556). Karbusicky (1974, p. 387) criticizes the unsystematic nature of Adorno's types of musical conduct. Blaukopf (1982) and Etzkorn (1978) point out its subjectivity, but Blaukopf appreciates Adorno as a pioneer of popular music research (p. 302).

There has been empirical research pursuing "crucial tests" of the massification perspective and Adorno's music sociological position of homogeneity of musical taste, according to the "sameness" of popular music, as opposed to the early version of the taste cultures hypothesis. Surveys on musical taste were undertaken after 1958 and heterogeneous taste cultures were found that mainly differed according to race categories, but age and social class were also associated with aesthetic preferences (Denisoff & Levine, 1972; Lewis, 1977, p. 41). Denisoff and Levine, who drew on an earlier study of Gans's taste cultures hypothesis, surveyed 919 students and found that social inequality differentiates between musical taste cultures (p. 252). No one musical genre found the support of the majority of the students. In Adorno's view—and that is the reason for criticizing Adorno's approach as "unempirical"—these studies would not be interpreted as falsifying the standardization hypothesis. Instead, the differences between musical styles and examples under investigation in the studies mentioned, such as folk, Motown, jazz, country and western, and rock, would be argued as being restricted to the "surface" behind which an "eternal sameness" lurks (Adorno, 1962/1989, pp. 42, 44). The decay of modernism is an idea that is not meant to be falsifiable, and it is rather an assumption than a hypothesis that popular music is an indicator for the decay of modernism (p. 36).

Considering the broad critique of Adorno's sociology of music, it is surprising that in 1993 a new theoretical approach to music education was established by Thomas Regelski (1998) and Terry Gates, the MayDay Group (2001a), which draws on the thinking of the Frankfurt School. One of the two main purposes of the MayDay Group is "to apply critical theory and critical thinking to the purposes and practices of music education" (MayDay Group, 2001b). In a position paper (Regelski, 1998), Regelski argues that "the hegemony of 'classical music' that has resulted from aesthetic ideology concerning music and music value is widely under attack by postmodern multiculturalism for its ethnocentric bias" (p. 2). Nevertheless, it is not taken into consideration that the thinking of the school of sociology on which the MayDay Group bases itself, and of one of that school's scholars, Adorno, is partly responsible for the persistence of the aesthetic ideology and of the massification perspective in music sociological and music education thinking.

Contemporary Sociological Perspectives on Culture

The New Consumer Society

From the 1960s on, social movements such as the women's, black, Hispanic, Asian, and gay and lesbian movements discredited the Frankfurt School view that genuine opposition had disappeared in mass society (Seidman, 1990, p. 230). Social movements are caused by marginal social groups' demand for social inclusion and empowerment and for legitimacy of their cultural products. This is interpreted as the social base of those changes in art and culture that are termed postmodernism. There was a "shift away from the high cultural stance of distanced moral indignation and condemnation of the impoverished mass culture towards embracing and celebrating the popular and mass culture aesthetic" (Featherstone, 1995, p. 76). The hierarchical distinction between high art and popular culture collapsed. The eclectic mixing of aesthetic codes, paired with playfulness and irony, occurred together with the acceptance of the differentiation within the arts and the heterogeneity of lifestyles, the constant flow of images and signs, found for example in MTV, destabilizing long-held symbol systems (Featherstone, 1995, pp. 43, 75; Huyssen, 1984/1990; Kaplan, 1990, p. 140; Seidmann, 1990, p. 231). "The *high* and the *low* . . . exist side by side, each aesthetically contributing to the other, and oftimes enjoyed by the same persons" (Kaplan, 1990, p. 147). Consequently aesthetic contemplation as one pleasurable way to "consume" cultural artifacts no longer is restricted to the consumption of "high" culture, and it has become obvious that art consumption in contemporary culture is not restricted to aesthetic contemplation as it was conceived by Kant.

Cultural change in the late 20th century culminated with the idea of "the aestheticization of everyday life" (Featherstone, 1995, p. 44; Schulze, 1992). This idea refers to the other side of the sociological debate just exposed. Lifestyle patterns are looked on as being able to dissolve traditional social structure (Schulze, 1992). While Gans (1985) saw one taste culture blending several cultures, in the 1990s the postindustrial pattern is viewed as a new type of linkage between social structure and culture. Cultural practice crystallizes around new horizontal social strata that replace social class. In this view, individuals still form groups, but the criteria of grouping are specific to lifestyle rather than to social class. Schulze (1992) provided empirical evidence for this view in a survey of 1,000 people.

Postmodernism is viewed as produced by globalization, which "refers to the process whereby the world increasingly becomes seen as 'one place' " (Featherstone, 1995, p. 114). A global culture is conceptualized as "sets of practices, bodies of knowledge, conventions of life-styles that have developed in ways which have become increasingly independent of nation-states" (p. 114). Featherstone writes that globalization would be misunderstood if it is seen as producing a unified and integrated common culture (p. 115). It rather leads to "heightened attempts to draw the boundaries between the self and others" and to focus on rediscovering "particularity, localism, and difference" (p. 114). In contrast to Schulze's idea of an aesthetization of everyday life that dissolves social constraints, the idea of a global culture leading to identity constructions that emphasize particularity still awaits empirical research. In recent mass media research, especially in music video research, we find the first steps in this research direction.

The Sociology of Mass Media

Paradigm shifts from the massification perspective to the taste cultures perspective, and from the aesthetic paradigm to the aestheticization of everyday life, occurred both in the study of popular culture and in mass media research (Gans, 1985; Featherstone, 1995; Lewis, 1977, 1978; Schwichtenberg, 1993b, 1993c; Winter & Eckert, 1990). They involved changing concepts of society, from homogenous to culturally highly differentiated. New concepts of audiences, of aesthetic commodities, and of aesthetic consumption induced methodological shifts. These shifts are documented, for example, in the development of music video research (Behne & Mueller, 1996; R. Mueller, 1994) because MTV can be interpreted as a document of the aestheticization of everyday life. In the early days of television, music video research started with negative journalistic valuation of music videos and with content-analytical work rushing to conclusions about effects. Surveys of viewers rather than listeners and experimental approaches to music video effects on students in laboratory situations followed. From the 1990s on, music video research describes and explains music video consumption as a social process, especially as a process of musical self-socialization and identity construction, in which different social meanings are ascribed to sounds and images. For example, young people are found to define a wide range of diverse gender role definitions according to the specific life situations they have to cope with (Brown & Schulze, 1990; Kalof, 1993; Petersen, 1987; Thompson, Pingree, Hawkins, & Draves, 1991).

Research questions turned from "What do the media do with the people?" to "What do the people do with the media?" Openness has become one of the main features of aesthetic and media texts, which are viewed, to some extent, as polysemic (Moores, 1990). Cultural objects such as pieces of music and music videos have the capacity to initiate cultural struggle over meaning. For example, Madonna videos provoked multiple and contradictory meanings in public as well as in cultural and media theory (Brown & Schulze, 1990). The last-mentioned kind of cultural struggle focuses on a question which always has been attributed to youth cultures and popular cultures in general and especially to mass culture disseminated by media: Are music videos vehicles for dominant ideologies or do they have any revolutionary impact? (Brown & Schulze, 1990, p. 89; Schulze, White, & Brown, 1993; Schwichtenberg, 1992, 1993c). Madonna videos offer material for the construction of different cultural identities and for multiple identities (Schwichtenberg, 1993b), and since they offer subcultural (multiracial, homosexual, feminist) images and symbols within mainstream media (Schwichtenberg, 1993a, p. 319) and thus represent subcultures, they cannot simply be looked on as adjusted to the society's status quo. Audiences are conceptualized building their own interpretations; they ascribe meaning to cultural objects and define identities by using images and symbols. Audiences are not constrained to the use of collective patterns of meaning construction such as gender roles; they use them to different degrees (Fiske, 1995). Accordingly, it is said: "Thus, when we ask 'what does this text mean?' we also must ask 'for whom?' " (Brown & Schulze, 1990, p. 89).

Contemporary Sociological Perspectives on Musical Interaction

Contemporary sociological debates about the social meaning of culture in modern societies raise many music sociology research questions. These address, first, musical self-

socialization and identity construction and, second, the role of social constraints, social inequality, and social differentiation in interaction with music. Musical socialization and self-socialization deal with issues of appropriation of music and media worlds. Related to the role of social constraints in interaction with music, questions are raised concerning young people's choices between aesthetic options and whether these are biased by age, gender, social class, education, and ethnicity. An overview of the cultural studies approach and the sociology of popular music is a prerequisite to understanding issues of musical self-socialization and identity construction and the role of social constraints, social inequality, and social differentiation in interaction with music. Before these sociological perspectives on musical behavior are presented, some light will be shed on appropriate research methods in this field.

Research Methods in Sociology of Music

Research on musical interaction requires music-oriented methods and methodological experience with which sociology is unfamiliar. Music education and the psychology of music provide research methods for investigating musical behavior in social contexts and the construction of social meanings of music. This seems to be particularly important for sociological thinking and research, because there is empirical evidence that music is more distinctive than other forms of cultural practice. For example, the studies of Bourdieu (1979), Schulze (1992), Lazarsfeld (1932), and Eichner (1996) have shown that music plays a prominent role among other aesthetic commodities.

According to Bourdieu, nothing helps to present one's own class more impressively, and nothing documents one's own class affiliation as accurately, as musical taste. No other cultural practice is as revealing as visiting a concert or playing a noble instrument. Music is considered to be absolutely the "pure" art (Bourdieu, 1979, pp. 41–42).

In his investigation of the new consumer society, Schulze (1992) distinguishes between three everyday aesthetic patterns of culture consumption: a high-culture pattern, a trivial pattern, and a sensation-seeking pattern (pp. 125–153). Musical preference items load higher on factors of everyday aesthetic patterns than most other such cultural preferences as television programs, literature, and newspapers (pp. 628–629). In addition, musical items measure affiliation to the trivial and sensation-seeking pattern much more consistently than other items (pp. 620–621).

To the respondents on the Austrian broadcasting program in Lazarsfeld's RAVAG study in 1932, music also was obviously much more impressive than other radio programs (Lazarsfeld, 1932): "Statements about music . . . documented more arousal than those about literature" (Lazarsfeld, 1932, p. 10; my translation). Statements related to the music program revealed stronger differences due to education and social class than statements concerned with other radio programs (Lazarsfeld, 1932, p. 18).

Similarly, in a study drawing on Schulze's theory, Eichner (1996) found that whereas Schulze's taste cultures could be distinguished with respect to their judgment of the music pieces in the questionnaire, they did not differ with respect to their judgment of pieces of art in the questionnaire. In contrast to the other studies, Eichner used audio ("sounding") and visual questionnaires that presented music and pictures by means of the multimedia computer.

The leading theoretical concept in the sociology of music, as it has been developed here, is young people's interaction with music as a matter of individual decisions in social and cultural contexts. Research methods are required that allow close empirical contact with young people's musical and audiovisual choices. Research designs cannot be restricted to discursive methods but need to include methods presenting the musical as well as the audiovisual material itself. "Classical" methods of social research, such as survey methods (e.g., Bourdieu, 1979; Lazarsfeld, 1932; Schulze, 1992), experiments, observation, and content analysis, apply to the field of sociology of music but should be combined with research methods presenting pieces of music, music videos, and pictures to the respondents. Methods presenting sounds and images overcome the limitations of verbal investigations of musical interaction.

The investigation of people's interaction with music aims to study their aesthetic judgments and musical preferences, their musical perception, their musical experiences and attitudes, the ascription of meaning and attractiveness to sounds and music videos, and their real aesthetic choices. This can be either studied by observation of the "real" musical interactions (e.g., Berry, 1990; Schaeffer, 1996) or with the help of audio questionnaires (e.g., Finnäes, 1987, 1989; Mueller, 1990), audiovisual questionnaires, and experimental designs. Three methods to investigate musical taste are presented here: verbal, audio, and revealed preferences; the semantic differential, continuous response methods; and computer-aided interviewing (e.g., Eichner, 1996; Rhein, 2000).

Today we are more frequently surrounded by music than by verbal expressions of music. Thus we cannot presume that the young people under music sociological investigation have knowledge about the verbal expressions of music used in paper-and-pencil questionnaires. Even pioneer studies in the field, such as Lazarsfeld's (1932) and Geiger's (1950), found the investigation of musical behavior biased if respondents judge musical terms and not the music itself. However, most of the research in the field does

not make use of sounding pieces of music, and the methodological problem of a lack of clear understanding of genre terms plays a minor role (e.g., Bryson, 1996, pp. 895–896; Robinson & Fink, 1986, p. 229). On the other hand, one might argue, any investigation about musical exclusion, such as Bryson's (1996), depends on music. Karbusicky (1974, p. 253) and Blaukopf (1974, p. 232) therefore claimed that the "sounding" questionnaire should be the primary method of the sociology of music and that it avoids misunderstanding when using verbal expressions for music. These two traditional methods of research on musical preferences are called "sounding preferences" and "verbal preferences." Both of them consist of verbal responses about musical experiences.

In contrast, experimental designs are created that provoke musical behavior itself, such as aesthetic-choice behavior (Konecni, 1979; Konecni & Sargent-Pollock, 1976). Preferences are revealed as respondents decide within the experimental situation to which type of music they want to listen. Subjects make their aesthetic choice, for example, by pressing one of two buttons connected with a two-channel tape. Another type of aesthetic behavior is investigated in the study of Holbrook and Gardner (1993). Respondents decided how long they wished to expose themselves voluntarily to musical excerpts that were presented on cassettes. Thus verbal, sounding, and revealed preferences are viewed as indicators for "musical taste" or "musical preference" and are investigated by different methods.

During the presentation of aesthetic objects, semantic differentials permit the researcher to measure attitudes, meanings, and images related to music or music videos immediately and rather independently from respondents' verbal capacities. Respondents are able to visualize their attitudes toward pieces of music without verbalizing their emotions and perceptions themselves, and their attitudes can be quantified and compared. The semantic differential is one of the traditional methods within music sociology research (e.g., Miller, 1990).

Continuous response measurement (CRM) offers another opportunity to quantify musical and audiovisual experiences as the interviewees provide feedback simultaneously with their experiences of a music video. Continuous response measurement plays a role in communication research, where Lazarsfeld again was a pioneer studying radio audiences with his program analyzer (Hollonquist & Suchman, 1979), and in music education research (e.g., Brittin, 1996). The continuous response method allows the researcher to view changes of judgment in the course of a piece of music or a music video, while verbal and sounding preferences view the whole piece at once.

The costs of studies with audiovisual questionnaires using the aforementioned features of musical research were and are much higher than those of paper-and-pencil questionnaires, thus less frequently undertaken. For example, a sounding questionnaire requires that musical excerpts be selected, recorded, and randomly presented to the subjects for evaluation. Costs can be reduced considerably if audiovisual questionnaires are presented by the computer and if questionnaire-authoring systems are used. This means a democratization of research methodologies that otherwise would be available only to big companies.

For example, within the system FrAuMuMe, the presentation of questionnaires, of musical events, of pictures, and of music videos, and the gathering of data, as well as the preparation of data analysis, are carried through and controlled by the computer system (Mueller, 1995a, 1996a, 1999). This system includes all of the conventional types of questions used in social research connected with audiovisual presentations. Beyond that, the system integrates observations, such as response-time measurement. Different audiovisual presentations can be used as treatments within classical experimental designs. The interactivity of the system allows the respondents to make their choices between musical pieces and music videos.

Audiovisual questionnaires can facilitate the research of young people's interaction with music, as this type of research presents the actual musical and the audiovisual material to a generation whose world is saturated with symbols, sounds, and images. Beyond that, the instrument respects adolescents of different educational, cultural, and ethnic backgrounds, not requiring that they talk about their musical interaction in elaborated speech.

The Cultural Studies Approach: Youth Cultures as Aesthetic Production

The cultural studies approach has been developed since the end of the 1950s by the Center for Contemporary Cultural Studies (CCCS) in Birmingham, England. There are many focuses within cultural studies emphasizing the aesthetic aspect of youth cultures and the idea that young people are not just consumers but producers of culture: youth cultures, their relation within society and their aesthetic styles (Hall, Clarke, Jefferson, & Roberts, 1976; Hebdige, 1979; Willis, 1990), rock music as the most important form of youth style (Frith, 1978), girl cultures and fan cultures (McRobbie, 1990; Nava, 1984), and mass media consumption and policies (Fiske, 1989). The following review of the cultural studies approach acknowledges the heterogeneity and multidisciplinarity of music, youth, and media sociologists and draws mainly from those publications that focus on youth cultures and youth cultural style (Hall et al., 1976; Hebdige, 1979; Willis, 1990).

The cultural studies approach, based on Marxism, holds that youth cultures are class specific, thus opposing the myth of a universal youth culture and contradicting the notion of the late 1950s and early 1960s that class no

longer had an impact on people's experiences. The cultural studies approach was the first to see youth cultures in a more differentiated way than simply as cultures that oppose their parents' generation. Youth cultures are viewed in their twofold function, to serve as a distinction first from the adult generation and, second, from the dominant culture, as it is represented in the educational institutions, and, at the same time, from the specific youth culture of the dominant culture. This means that youth cultures draw from their parents' cultures because they share the social class conditions of their parents.

The cultural studies approach radically dismisses the aesthetic paradigm. Musically oriented proletarian youth cultures are viewed unreservedly as innovative and creative aesthetes of young proletarians' everyday life; subcultures of youth are seen as a whole way of life and as a bundle of "rituals of resistance" against the dominant culture. With this approach, students are investigated interacting, while other scholars on youth culture have developed their theories about youth sitting at their desks.

As an example of the CCCS work in the 1970s, skinhead culture was explored (Clarke, 1976a, 1976b; Hebdige, 1979). The first skinheads appeared in the early 1970s in London as protesters against the loss of their territories in London's traditional laborers' residential quarters, thus expressing a sense of alienation in their home country. They shared this feeling with London's West Indian immigrants through a music genre called ska, characterized by its pulsing liveliness and its great difference from the music of the mods and hippies, to which group skinheads did not want to belong. Ska developed into reggae, which meant that it slowed down and started to express political ideas of black immigrants. Thus, part of the skinhead culture separated from the West Indians both musically and politically. Skinhead culture means the symbolic recovery of community in an environment of collapsing traditional territorial and social structures. One feels as though one is in a big family, constituting a sense of collective solidarity against oppression by those who want to order one about. Subcultural symbolism indicates shared knowledge and shared meanings. Violence is a symbol within proletarian male youth cultures. Male lower class cultures are body-oriented cultures. Body orientation is usually expressed in violent defense of territories. The skinhead outfit at that time was styled to be proletarian, consisting of bald heads, working clothes, boots, and suspenders, all of which symbolize a proletarian culture. In addition, bald heads mean a demarcation from longhaired intellectuals like hippies.

The broad effect that cultural studies has had is particularly remarkable. Blake (1995), a representative of cultural studies, although critical of the approach, argues that

the work of Hebdige, Frith, and Chambers in particular has escaped the boundaries of the academy and become mainstream. . . . [T]he project of cultural studies has allowed for the revaluation of cultural value . . . [and made] the critical but positive examination of aspects of popular culture acceptable. [p. 221] In addition, it has been specific to this approach that music is viewed as an important part of specific cultures within which people express their experiences of society and their cultural identities. (p. 219)

According to Blake, more recently, within cultural studies a recent debate can be observed that is comparable to the debate described above, questioning the relationship between culture and society. Thus, it is discussed whether the notion of class as one of the most important organizing principles of people's experiences should be discarded in the face of new cultural developments. Consequently, McRobbie (1993) emphasizes the importance of gender and Fiske that of gender and age (1992, 1995) and that of ethnicity (1994) as sources of social discrimination. Fiske (1992) uses Bourdieu's theory, especially the concept of cultural capital, but he criticizes it for the restriction on class as the major dimension of social discrimination, and he adds gender, race, and age as axes of discrimination (p. 32).

In Blake's opinion, one of the most important contributions of cultural studies is the feminist work of McRobbie and others. While in the 1960s and 1970s "youth" tended to mean young men, from the 1980s on, youth cultural experiences and practices of girls, such as girls' reading materials, their responses to television, and, most important, their experience of fandom, "the ways in which young girls as consumers of popular music express their collective power" (Blake, 1995, p. 223), have been explored. McRobbie (1993) questions whether rave culture does provide any cultural policy for its participants besides asking them to "shut up and dance."[2] In what ways does rave enable aesthetic production? McRobbie argues that there is cultural production in graphics, fashion design, fan magazines, retail, music production, and other forms of audiovisual image-making and that there is a strong aesthetic dimension in these kinds of productivity. This is interpreted as a strong preference for the cultural sphere to find an occupation in and to earn a living within the aestheticization of everyday life. This indicates that living the rave subculture creates a whole way of life and provides the opportunity for learning and sharing skills by practicing them. This provides an opportunity to make a choice of how to live, and it opens pathways for future life skills and alternatives to higher education. McRobbie revisits her former argument (McRobbie & Garber, 1976) about the passive role girls played in youth cultures and emphasizes particular female creativity and activity in rave culture. She argues that today more options for flexibility in female role definitions are available than in male roles. In arguing this way McRobbie explicitly takes over positions that are aware of the aforementioned cultural changes and, consequently, dismisses some of the old either–or dichotomies in cultural studies theory, such as commercial–authentic and resistance–adjustment.

The Sociology of Popular Music

From the 1980s onward, the sociology of popular music developed in the United States as an established area of study. Scholarship in the sociology of popular music emerged from an attachment to the cultural studies approach represented mainly in two journals, *Popular Music* and *Society and Popular Music*. Rock music was not considered "as a matter of serious sociological interest" (Cookson, 1994, p. x) until 1994 when *Adolescents and Their Music* (Epstein, 1994) was published as the first volume in a series devoted to "New Directions in Sociology." Accordingly, and confirming the notion of the sociology of popular music as "sociology's forgotten stepchild" (Groce & Epstein, 1994, p. 329), the attitude of the articles was partly defensive (e.g., Berry, 1994). According to Groce and Epstein (1994), the study of popular music has become an interdisciplinary endeavor of fields such as communications, journalism, broadcasting, and ethnomusicology (p. 330). Issues that are addressed in research in the sociology of popular music (Groce & Epstein, 1994, p. 331) range from theoretical and methodological comments (e.g., Foret, 1991) to historical and critical analyses (e.g., Weinstein, 1991), and from the production of popular music, its performers and performances (e.g., Finnegan, 1989) and other industrial roles to the consumption of popular music and its audiences (e.g., Berry, 1990), from women in popular music (e.g., Bayton, 1988/1990) to the content of popular music and of music videos (e.g., Brown & Campbell, 1986). In the opinion of Groce and Epstein, four areas of study within the sociology of popular music have experienced significant growth since 1980. These are women in popular music; "small-time" or "local-level" performers, in addition and contrast to those who have attained commercial success; roles other than that of performer or producer, such as sound engineers and mixers; and the content and impact of music videos (p. 330). Surprisingly, research on audiences of music videos is excluded from Groce and Epstein's annotated bibliography. Since content analyses of music videos do not allow any inference about their impact on young people watching and listening to them, the question "What do young people do with music videos?" is excluded. There are a lot of research studies in this field, some of which are discussed in chapter 33.

One example of audience studies is presented here to give an idea of research on young people interacting with popular music in the youth cultural context and using it

in the construction of their identities. Berry's study (1990) focuses on the relationship between self-esteem and the use of rap music. Using interviews, observation, and questionnaires, Berry studied 115 low-income black youths, ages 13 to 18, participating in an Upward Bound program. For the majority of the interviewees, rap music was the favorite music. Berry observed that rap music was attracting young people and inspiring them to participate in different activities such as moving, dancing, rapping along, beat-boxing in sync (i.e., using the mouth and throat to produce rhythms), writing their own raps, and sometimes even performing them. Likewise, Berry conceived a local rap concert as a "definitely participatory gathering" (p. 92). Rap is an important element within the interviewees' everyday life, and they relate it to their own experiences. Rappers tell them stories about the urban street life and about shared experiences in their own language. Berry concludes as a result of her 2-year investigation of musical experiences among low-income black adolescents that hip-hop culture helps her interviewees cope with their reality. Rap music "has shortened the distance between low-income status and achievement, creating a more positive self-concept among these youths" (p. 106). Berry explains her findings against the backdrop of theories and studies relating self-esteem of minorities with their visibility on television: low visibility of minorities on television denies their existence and confirms their low self-esteem. Rap music represents their cultural identity on television, legitimizes their daily existence, and makes them feel in control of their lives because they own or are able to appropriate the talents to be rappers themselves.

In his study of the Los Angeles uprisings, Fiske (1994) also addressed the demand of social inclusion and empowerment of the racially oppressed. He argues, like Berry, that "black frustration with white refusal to listen (to 'the injustices that go on in the ghetto', Ice-T) is what Whites miss when they understand the anger in rap as merely incitement to violence" (p. 483). Fiske points out that rap artists represented the black voice during the Los Angeles uprisings. They were allowed to speak, not only on MTV. Because the uprisings made white America listen to the voices of the racially oppressed, the uprisings are understood as "in part, loud public speech by those whose voices are normally silenced or confined to their own media" (p. 484). Thus, racial inequality and discrimination are some of the social contexts within which the social use of music has been investigated.

Another social context of inequality and disrespect is related to gender issues. Berry (1990) remarks that males are more strongly connected with rap music and that rap music mostly takes over male perspectives. On the contrary, female rap does exist (Dufresne, 1991; Toop, 1991). Women's rap expresses sexual subjectivity and being in control as a means to empower self; this is seen as similar to the way that women's blues spoke against women's subordination (Perry, 1995; Roberts, 1991). The gender issue is very closely connected with the issue of sex, addressing the sexually explicit nature of the lyrics of, for example, 2 Live Crew, or taking up the problem of degrading portrayals of women in music videos and in lyrics. Female rappers—as well as the audience—hold various positions concerning this issue, ranging from "if men can do it we can too" (Hoes with Attitude) to creating the Intelligent Black Women's Coalition and trying to improve black female teenagers' self-esteem (Yo Yo) (Berry, 1994, p. 174; Dufresne, 1991; Toop, 1991).

Other researchers (Brown & Campbell, 1986; Sun & Lull, 1986) conclude that adolescents are seeking information about their social life and their future adult life. They do so to different extents and use music and media with different amounts of exposure. In addition, their reliance on rock music as a source of information, as evidenced by the effort put into listening, the importance of rock music in their lives, the reading of lyrics, differ too. In her survey using self-reporting questionnaires, Rouner (1990) asked 175 15- to 18-year-olds about their use of music and media. She found that (1) reliance on rock music as a source of information and (2) involvement with rock music had stronger effects on achieving knowledge about rock music than mere exposure to rock music.

Musical Self-Socialization

As individualization and aestheticization are the main features of modern societies, identity and biography become matters of individual choice. Particularly because of the destandardization and individualization of biographies, musical taste and cultural practices serve to define people's social and cultural identities and their distinction from other social groups. Cultural consumption is viewed as a result of individuals' aesthetic choices of membership in a range of musical cultures and of corresponding lifestyles. "The crucial component . . . is choice of the life-style by the individuals free even from one's family" (Kaplan, 1990, p. 147). Socialization is viewed as self-socialization, and the development of identity is seen as the social construction of identity.

Globalization and postmodernism induce "a decentring of the subject, whose sense of identity and biographical continuity give way to fragmentation and superficial play with images, sensations" (Featherstone, 1995, p. 44). This is seen as "the breakdown of individuals' sense of identity through the bombardment of fragmented signs and images" (p. 44). According to Featherstone, the solution would be to discard "the old essentialist self" (p. 45) and to conceive the individual no longer as something unified and consistent but "as a bundle of conflicting 'quasiselves,'

a random and contingent assemblage of experiences" (p. 45) and to discard the belief "that life is a meaningful project" (p. 44). In contrast to this point of view, it can be shown that sociological theories offer a notion of the self between "the old essentialist self" and "a random assemblage of experiences." The concept of "the old essentialist self"—if it ever has been a serious sociological identity concept—does not offer a realistic perspective for individuals bound to interact in a variety of social contexts and roles, and "a random assemblage of experiences" consequently means that individuals are not identical with themselves. That life has become a somewhat random assemblage of experiences may be the case; this, however, challenges the individuals to do "identity work," that is, to make sense of their lives.

Sociological theories offer a range of ways to conceptualize the relationship between the individual and society. These concepts range from individuals who seem under social coercion to individuals looked on as shaping their identities over a lifetime. The latter concept draws on the symbolic interactionist concept of the self (Goffman, 1959, 1961, 1963; Mead, 1934). In symbolic interaction, individuals are forced to maintain identity in interactions with contradictory, inconsistent, conflicting, and indefinite expectations. Both shared meanings and individual particularity are presumed for the maintenance of identity and interaction. Audiovisual and verbal symbol systems are used to present identity in such a way as to ensure individual particularity and, at the same time, shared meanings. From the standpoint of symbolic interactionism, identity means the lifelong balancing between being like everybody else and being like nobody. In this view, identity construction is a challenging, lifelong task in societies that do not predetermine biographies by birth. "The presentation of self in everyday life" may become even more complicated within postmodernism and globalization because of the increasing number of options to use images and symbols to present the self and, consequently, the increasing number of possible identities. But the sociological view of identity as it is provided by Goffman already takes into account challenges like this.

Young people draw on their experiences in music and media when they construct their lives as meaningful projects. Adolescents' aesthetic choices, such as becoming a member in a youth culture (e.g., Mueller 1996b), becoming a fan of a music star or group (e.g., Rhein, 2000), or becoming a member of a band or an orchestra (e.g., Schaeffer, 1996), are conceptualized as processes of musical self-socialization (Mueller, 1995b). Young people choose socializing environments and cultural codes that ascribe social meaning to aesthetic objects such as music videos; they socialize themselves by their choice of membership in cultures, by their efforts to become familiar with the chosen cultural codes, and by shaping these cultures and contributing to their cultural production (see Berry, 1990, and McRobbie, 1993).

Youth cultures are viewed as centers of musical self-socialization where young people autodidactically appropriate cultural capital by means of which they both gain social appreciation and definitions of boundaries that separate them from others (Fiske, 1992). Fiske criticizes Bourdieu's underestimation of the creativity of popular culture and its role in distinguishing between different social formations within the lower classes, which Bourdieu sees as homogeneous (p. 32). In terms of the significance of popular culture, Fiske adds to Bourdieu's notion of cultural capital that of popular cultural capital.

The aestheticization of everyday life implicates "an emphasis upon images over words" (Featherstone, 1995, p. 76). This coincides with the individuals' appropriation of audiovisual, perceptive, and productive competencies as popular cultural capital, for example, to identify those musical symbols that are symbolically excluded by the peer group. In so doing, they gain knowledge of music life and media events that can be viewed as expert knowledge, patterns of behavior and style, and competencies of musical and visual production.

In his review of fandom research, Fiske (1992) concludes: "Fans are among the most discriminating and selective of all formations of the people and the cultural capital they produce is the most highly developed and visible of all" (p. 48). Rhein (2000), in a survey of 217 adolescents between 11 and 15 years of age, investigated musical activities of teenie-fans and nonfans. Teenie-fans are those young people who report being a fan of a music group/music star or being a fan of a type of music. Rhein found that 57.2% of the girls and 42.8% of the boys in this particular sample reported being a fan, a surprising outcome that questions the stereotypical perception of fandom being a female phenomenon. Rhein presented an audiovisual questionnaire to her respondents, including sound and visual images; the interviewees were not questioned by an interviewer but by the computer program. Rhein found that fans using the range of popular music were more intensive than nonfans in their appropriation and presentation of popular cultural capital. For example, fans strive to own new compact discs as well as fan commodities such as T-shirts of their favorite music, they appropriate knowledge about their favorite music, and they are proud if they are looked on as experts by their peers. According to the significance the adolescents ascribed to fandom in their lives, they were differentiated into several levels of intensity of fandom. Another result showed that in song-, fan-, and music-related activities, the diversity of activities practiced varied according to fandom intensity. Song-related activities, for example, are singing along, playing the song on a musical instrument, and memorizing the lyrics. Fan-related activities, for example, are writing letters, paintings, and lyrics to the star or to a fan magazine and doing "fan-talk." Music-related activities, for example, are going to a concert, watching music television, and reading music magazines. In addition to the reported results of differences between adolescent fans and nonfans it was evident that all of the young people under investigation participated in popular music culture and devoted themselves, even if not to the same extent as fans, to the appropriation of popular culture. Rhein's study suggests that young people's self-socialization during music and media experiences is not a phenomenon of particularly engaged young people, such as fans, but is a social and cultural reality of today's societies.

An example of young people making sense of their lives interacting with music, specifically being a member of a band, can be found in Schaeffer (1996). He observed six youth bands made up of low-educated young men as they began professional apprenticeships. The respondents perceived this specific passage in terms of a life crisis. Schaeffer defined the band's successful style development (stylistic integration) as the appropriation of a habitus that included the bands' reflection on their own aesthetics. It developed in three steps: the experimental phase, the self-reflection phase, and, finally, the phase of the stylistic integration. This affirms the band's particular style, and a strong communication among the band's members is presumed. Stylistic disintegration occurs if the band remains in the first, experimental, phase. Schaeffer found musical and stylistic integration processes coinciding with a development of group solidarity within the peer group that went far beyond the band's sharing ecstatic musical experiences on the one hand and experiences of performance in public on the other hand. Furthermore, they shared the social experiences of making sense of their lives. Schaeffer observed a correspondence between musical-stylistic integration on the one hand and coping with life situations on the other. Those bands remaining in stylistic disintegration showed features of retreat and escapism, did not seem to solve their adolescent crises, and felt marginalized and socially excluded by the educational system.

Symbolic Exclusion: Social Constraints and "Social Glue"

Within processes of social discrimination based on social inequality, music is a symbolic means of social exclusion. For example, those who claim that rap music causes delinquency use music as a means for social exclusion, whereas those who promote rap music's popularity use it as a means of social inclusion. Individuals use musical taste to reinforce symbolic boundaries between themselves and categories of people they dislike (Bryson, 1996) and, in addition, to reinforce a sense of belonging, community, and solidarity (Bernstein, 1981; Bourdieu et al., 1965). The role of music in this case is that of a "social glue." Social exclusion is a "process of social selection that is based on a previously determined set of cultural criteria . . . [and] symbolic exclusion is the source of those 'previously determined cultural criteria' " (Bryson, 1996, p. 885). Musical exclusion is a type of symbolic exclusion, and it is defined as the dislike for various musics.

Nearly all approaches mentioned in this chapter include the idea of individuals' need to belong to cultural contexts and to be set apart from others in order to define their identity. Thus identity work implies boundary work that continuously re-creates the positive, negative, and neutral attitudes toward cultural cues like music (Bryson, 1996). In Bourdieu's theory (1968, 1979; Bourdieu et al., 1965) the concept of symbolic exclusion or distinction has various aspects: to "the plain people" symbolic exclusion occurs on the part of opera houses and museums and to intellectuals on the part of laborers' bars. The message of social exclusion is "Do not enter." Mental reservations are made, thresholds are perceived and not passed, the message is "This is not for us." Societies and social settings differ with respect to the extent of social constraint they impose on their members. In restrictive settings, members are limited to only one culture code; members who appreciate excluded symbolisms are at risk of being socially excluded. That means the role of music as a social glue is predominant. The peer group message is "You are not one of us if you like Mozart." The message for "the plain people" under restrictive social conditions may sound like "You want to be better than us by appreciating Mozart," including the message "You will no longer be one of us" or "You will be different." This offers a sociological explanation of Geiger's concept of "snobbism in reverse" and of music educators' concept of "adolescents' barriers of musical interaction" (Mueller, 1990), and it explains the reproduction of social inequality. In the specific case of Geiger's study, exclusive symbolism is implicated in musical terms like opus number, key, and specification of tempo in Italian. Exclusive symbols elicit the attitude that " 'classical music is not for us, the plain people' " (Geiger, 1950, p. 454) with the result of "never having given it a fair trial" (p. 454). By omitting the exclusive symbols, the audience was given the opportunity to give classical music a fair trial. This has enormous consequences for music education, if one of its goals is musical tolerance.

Nonrestrictive settings encourage the expression of personal uniqueness and the autonomous use of musical symbols, that is, the use of more than one cultural code. Symbolic exclusiveness occurs less frequently than in restrictive settings. The use of exclusive symbolism—if there is any—does not bring the threat of social exclusion or social depreciation. These aspects of Bourdieu's theory of cultural codes are very similar to Bernstein's theory of linguistic codes (see chapter 31), and they are highly applicable to Goffman's aforementioned concept of identity construction. People share definitions of excluded symbolism within those social settings to which they desire to belong. Their conformity differs with respect to how restrictive the particular social setting acts and how low their self-esteem is. Thus, nonrestrictive social settings and high self-esteem are requisite social conditions for musical tolerance. Musical tolerance and symbolic exclusion both are applicable within both positions of the aforementioned sociological controversy, presuming that a minimum of social bonds—more or less coercive—is seen as essential to social life. Whether social boundaries such as social classes are looked on as collapsing, as loosening, or as remaining, music exclusion occurs, with various consequences to individuals and social settings and with various levels of restriction and self-esteem.

Empirical evidence is contributed by several studies (Bryson, 1996; Finnäes, 1987, 1989; Mueller, 1990; Peterson & Kern, 1996). Renate Mueller (1990) focused on ways to investigate the social conditions within which adolescents' musical experiences take place and especially the social context within which adolescents show musical flexibility: musical tolerance, the openness to and acceptance of different styles of music. Musical tolerance is defined as one aspect of musical flexibility, whereas musical flexibility is seen as the level on which a person is able to appreciate, to be familiar with, or at least to accept more than one musical code.

Using five fictitious social situations, Mueller tested the hypothesis that musical tolerance varies with the degree to which peer pressure is prevalent. The situations compared were: listening to music, listening to the radio or watching television, participating in classroom music instruction, dancing, and being with friends. The respondents, 360 students (fourth to tenth grade, elementary and junior high school), repeatedly listened to five musical excerpts of different styles, including a very popular song from the Top Ten, one example of unfamiliar popular music (zydeco), an aria from an opera, a "classical" pop song (reggae), and classical music. Respondents were asked whether they would accept interacting with each of these five pieces of music within each of these five situations. The social condition of being with friends elicited the least degree of tolerance; the social condition of listening to music allowed for the greatest level of tolerance. The following situations lie in between these two, in the following order with decreasing tolerance: listening to the radio or watching TV, participating in classroom music instruction, and dancing.

Musical tolerance varies with different social contexts and grows with decreasing social constraint, in this case fictitious peer pressure. It can be concluded that adolescents' musical behavior is misjudged as being generally intolerant and prejudiced. The social context of musical interaction should be taken into consideration.

Finnäes (1987) addressed the question of the adequacy of perceived peer preferences for music. He asked 359 seventh- and eighth-graders to mark their own preferences and to estimate their peers' preferences for five descriptions of music ("classical music," "music which sounds peaceful and relaxing," "rock," "music which sounds tough and hard," "music which is harsh and provocative") and of four pieces of music (Schubert, Telemann, Iron Maiden, Sex Pistols). The results showed consistent overestimation of peers' preferences for "tough/protesting/rock-oriented" music and underestimation of peers' preferences for quiet and traditional kinds of music. Finnäes concluded that misperception of peers' preferences "may cause the individual to conform to partly fictitious norms" (p. 164). A practical implication of this study, among others, for music education is "facilitating pupils' communication of their genuine musical experiences to each other" (p. 164). Another educational application suggests discussing results like these with young people. In a second study of adolescents ages 12 to 14, using the same method, Finnäes (1989) found that the respondents had a tendency to give lower preference ratings for classical music and folk music when the ratings were given in front of their classmates than when they were given privately. Finnäes's presumption that private preference ratings for rock music would be lower than publicly given ratings could not be confirmed. Using Geiger's terminology (1950, p. 592), this study provides further empirical evidence that young people have a more refined musical taste than they like to admit in front of their classmates.

Bryson's (1996) results provided empirical evidence for the concept of restrictive versus nonrestrictive conditions related to musical exclusiveness versus musical tolerance. Bryson analyzed data from the 1993 General Social Survey and found that musical exclusiveness, measured as the dislike of musical genres, decreases with level of education. Political tolerance was found to be associated with musical tolerance, defined as the absence of dislike for a music genre or the indifference to music (p. 885). Racism toward nonwhites increases dislike of those musical genres whose fans are nonwhite. Furthermore, Bryson observed a specific pattern of musical exclusiveness associated with musical tolerance: the musically tolerant, defined as disliking only a few music genres, dislike those musical genres whose fans have the least education, such as gospel, country, rap, and heavy metal.

This partly contradicts results of Peterson and Kern (1996), who found that the musically tolerant prefer lowbrow music to middlebrow music. This result is explained in terms of snobbism that prefers music created by socially marginal groups ("lowbrow" music) to commercial forms of music ("middlebrow" music) (p. 901). Peterson and Kern use a different notion of musical tolerance, that of "musical omnivorousness." This is a concept specifically meant to distinguish between snobs (highbrows) and other people. Snobbism is operationally defined as liking classical music and opera best of all musical genres. Omnivorousness is the degree to which people like lowbrow music (country music, bluegrass, gospel, rock, and blues) and middlebrow music (mood/easy-listening music, Broadway musicals, and big band music). In comparing two national surveys conducted in the United States in 1982 and 1992, Peterson and Kern (1996) found a shift in the basis for marking elite status, from snobbish exclusion to omnivorous appropriation. In 1992 highbrows reported liking more kinds of nonelite (lowbrow and middlebrow) music than highbrows did a decade earlier, and in 1992 highbrows were more omnivorous than nonhighbrows (p. 904). The authors interpreted their results as a shift from highbrows' ethnocentrism to cultural relativism, focusing on means of consumption rather than on what is consumed. In addition, they say that while snobbish exclusion was an effective marker of status in a relatively homogeneous society, omnivorous inclusion is better adapted to an increasingly global society (p. 906). Since Peterson and Kern viewed respect for other cultures as aesthetic understanding, appreciation, and knowledge, Bryson's notion of multicultural capital (p. 888), emphasizing breadth and tolerance of taste, is applicable to the concept of omnivorous inclusion.

These two studies are located within the contemporary sociological debates about social inequality and culture, specifically the social use of music. They relate Bourdieu's approach to recent social and cultural changes. Open questions remain that require further research on the operational definitions and social conditions of musical tolerance and musical exclusion.

Music Education and the Sociology of Music

Music sociologists investigate social contexts of young people's musical experiences, and music educators should follow their lead. Around young people's interactions with music a lot of teaching and learning might be initiated. Adorno's position is that, on the contrary, the music that young people prefer and their musical activities are depreciated; thus their cultural identities are disrespected. They are stereotyped with respect to their listening and visual habits, which are presupposed to be standardized, passive, and intolerant toward any other type of music.

Small (1998, pp. 207–221) argues that if music education labels the students' music as unaesthetic and if their musical preferences, abilities, and activities by definition are excluded from school, the consequence is demusicalization, a process during which many students are successfully taught to think that they are unmusical. According to Small, schools contribute to this process because of a hidden logical chain underlying school music practice: Some musics (e.g., classical music and marching band music) are claimed to be the only real music, and students not interested in this "real" music are labeled as unmusical. Beyond that, students are discouraged from singing at school, labeled as tone-deaf, silenced, and thus intimidated. The result is that students' social, cultural, and personal identities are ignored, devalued, and violated in institutions of education. Small argues that all musicking is serious musicking and, second, that everyone is capable of musicking well, in the areas of performing and listening. Virtuosity as a question of musical quality has to be related to the capabilities of the performers.

Music educators should be aware of the "symbolic exclusion-thresholds" and "adolescents' barriers of musical interaction" mentioned earlier and avoid interpreting them as "unwillingness." Instead, opportunities might be considered to enable young people to give excluded musics "a fair trial." What is labeled as "unwillingness" rather should be accepted as young people's fear of losing membership in the particular cultural group to which they want to belong. Ignoring this fear of being socially excluded means to threaten young people's identity.

As has been shown in this chapter, acceptance of young people's cultures by media or by educational institutions will improve their self-esteem and their musical tolerance. Ignorance of these relations leaves schools themselves symbolically exclusive and continues their production of "snobbism in reverse." Thus, Geiger's 50-year-old explanation of "snobbism in reverse" still holds: Social pressures may lower the appeal of classical music.

> In our schools, in popular lectures, in educational periodicals and in connection with so-called instructive concerts, it is frequently emphasized that classical music can be properly understood and fully enjoyed only by those who have acquired some musical training. . . . By over-stressing the desirability of previous training . . . the musically untrained may be discouraged . . . from listening to serious music. (Geiger, 1950, pp. 453–454)

Popular culture capital in opposition to "high" culture capital usually does not provide social recognition in educational institutions like schools. On the other hand, in societies with increasing options of lifestyle definitions, educational culture loses its claim to be superior to other cultures; dominant culture looses its claim to being dominant. Educational institutions can take the opportunity to solve their legitimating crisis by respecting not only adolescents' different cultures but also their autodidactically appropriated musical and audiovisual competencies. If educational institutions deny adolescents interaction with music and media, they ignore a powerful reservoir of

teaching and learning: musical instruction from youth to youth, from young experts to young nonexperts.

NOTES

1. Fandom is a cultural activity that selects from the repertoire of mass media entertainment a performer, a narrative, or a genre that is particularly enjoyed and appreciated. Fandom means participation in a fan culture and productive appropriation of fan-specific knowledge, competencies, and behavior patterns (Fiske, 1992; Brown & Schulze, 1990).

2. Rave culture or techno culture is a youth culture musically oriented around techno music. Rave is focused on dancing. The opportunity for the display of style is the "party" (McRobbie, 1993, p. 25).

REFERENCES

Adorno, T. W. (1976). *Introduction to the sociology of music.* New York: Seabury Press. (Original work published 1962)

Adorno, T. W. (1989). *Einleitung in die musiksoziologie: Zwoelf theoretische vorlesungen* [Introduction to the sociology of music]. Frankfurt: Suhrkamp. (Original work published 1962)

Adorno, T. W. (1990a). Culture industry reconsidered. In J. C. Alexander & S. Seidman (Eds.), *Culture and society* (pp. 275–282). Cambridge, England: Cambridge University Press.

Adorno, T. W. (1990b). On popular music. In S. Frith & A. Goodwin (Eds.), *On record: Rock, pop and the written word* (pp. 301–314). London: Routledge.

Alexander, J. C., & Seidman, S. (Eds.). (1990). *Culture and society.* Cambridge, England: Cambridge University Press.

Bayton, M. (1990). How women become musicians. In S. Frith & A. Goodwin (Eds.), *On record: Rock, pop and the written word* (pp. 238–257). London: Routledge. (Original work published 1988)

Behne, K. E., & Mueller, R. (1996). *Rezeption von Videoclips—Musikrezeption: Eine vergleichende Pilotstudie zur musikalischen Sozialisation* [Perception of music videos—perception of music. A comparative pilot study on musical socialization]. *Rundfunk und Fernsehen, 44,* 365–380.

Bernstein, B. (1981). *Studien zur sprachlichen Sozialisation* [Studies on language socialization]. Frankfurt: Ullstein.

Berry, V. T. (1990). Rap music, self-concept and low-income black adolescents. *Popular Music and Society, 14,* 89–107.

Berry, V. T. (1994). Redeeming the rap music experience. In Epstein, 1994, 165–187.

Blake, A. (1995). British youth culture: Does it still exist? In N. Bailer & R. Horak (Eds.), *Jugendkultur* [Youth culture] (pp. 206–238). Vienna: WUV-Universitätsverlag.

Blaukopf, K. (1974). Postscript: Towards a new type of research. In I. Bontinck (Ed.), *New patterns of musical behavior of the young generation in industrial societies* (pp. 231–234). Vienna: Universal Edition.

Blaukopf, K. (1982). *Musik im Wandel der Gesellschaft: Grundzuege der Musiksoziologie* [Music in changing society: Foundations of the sociology of music]. Munich: Piper.

Blaukopf, K. (1995). *Pioniere empiristischer Musikforschung: Oesterreich und Boehmen als wiege der modernen kunstsoziologie* [Pioneers of empirical music research. Austria and Bohemia as the cradle of the modern sociology of art]. Vienna: Hoelder-Pichler-Tempsky.

Blomster, W. V. (1976). Sociology of music: Adorno and beyond. *Telos, 28,* 81–112.

Bontinck, I. (Ed.). (1992). *Kulturpolitik, kunst, musik: Fragen an die soziologie* [Culture policy, art, music: Questions to sociology]. Vienna: Verlag des Verbandes der wissenschaftlichen Gesellschaften Oesterrichs.

Bontinck, I. (Ed.). (1996): *Wege zu einer Wiener Schule der Musiksoziologie: Konvergenz der disziplinen und empiristische tradition* [Toward a Vienna School of music sociology: Convergence of disciplines and empirical tradition]. Vienna: Guthmann-Peterson.

Bourdieu, P. (1968). Artistic taste and cultural capital. In Alexander & Seidman, 1990, 205–215.

Bourdieu, P. (1979). *Distinction: A social critique of the judgement of taste.* Cambridge, MA: Harvard University Press.

Bourdieu, P., Boltanski, L., Castel, R., Chamboredon, J-C., Lagneau, G., & Schnapper, D. (1965). *Photography: A middle-brow art.* Stanford, CA: Stanford University Press.

Bradley, D. (1981). Music and social science: A Survey. *Media, Culture and Society, 3,* 205–218.

Brittin, R. V. (1996). Listeners' preference for music of other cultures: Comparing response modes. *Journal of Research in Music Education, 44,* 328–340.

Brown, J. D., & Campbell, K. (1986). Race and gender in music videos: The same beat but a different drummer. *Journal of Communication, 36,* 94–106.

Brown, J. D., & Schulze, L. (1990). The effects of race, gender, and fandom on audience interpretations of Madonna's music videos. *Journal of Communication, 40,* 88–102.

Bryson, B. (1996). "Anything but heavy metal": Symbolic exclusion and musical dislikes. *American Sociological Review, 61,* 884–889.

Clarke, J. (1976a). The skinheads and the magical recovery of working class community. In S. Hall, J. Clarke, T. Jefferson, & B. Roberts (Eds.), *Resistance through rituals: Youth subcultures in post-war Britain* (pp. 9–74). London: Hutchinson.

Clarke, J. (1976b). Style. In S. Hall, J. Clarke, T. Jefferson, & B. Roberts (Eds.), *Resistance through rituals: Youth subcultures in post-war Britain.* London: Hutchinson.

Cookson, P. W. (1994). Series preface. In J. S. Epstein, (Ed.). *Adolescents and their music: If it's too loud you're too old* (pp. ix–x). New York: Garland.

Denisoff, R. S., & Levine, M. H. (1972). Youth and popular music: A test of the taste culture hypothesis. *Youth and Society, 4,* 237–255.

Denisoff, S. R., & Bridges, J. (1983). The sociology of popular music: A review. *Popular Music and Society, 9,* 51–62.

Dines, G., & Humez, J. M. (1995). (Eds.). *Gender, race and class in media: A text-reader.* Thousand Oaks, CA: Sage.

Dufresne, D. (1991): *Yo! Rap revolution.* Neustadt, Germany: Schwinn, 1992.

Eichner, K. (1996). *Multimedia-Befragung: Auswertung eines computergestuetzten Multimedia-Interviews ueber den Zusammenhang zwischen sozialen Milieus und Technikakzeptanz* [Evaluation of a computer-assisted multimedia survey about the relationship between social milieus and acceptance of technique]. Hamburg: Institute of Sociology, University of Hamburg.

Epstein, J. S. (Ed.) (1994). *Adolescents and their music: If it's too loud you're too old.* New York: Garland.

Etzkorn, K. P. (1978). Introduction to *The Sociology of Music,* by Theodor W. Adorno. *American Journal of Sociology, 83,* 1036–1037.

Etzkorn, K. P. (1982). On the sociology of musical practice and social groups. *International Social Science Journal, 34,* 555–569.

Etzkorn, K. P. (1996). Aspekte der Rezeption Max Webers. Musiksoziologie in den Vereinigten Staaten [Aspects of the reception of Max Weber's sociology of music in the United States]. In I. Bontinck (Ed.), *New patterns of musical behavior of the young generation in industrial societies* (pp. 149–158). Vienna: Universal Edition.

Featherstone, M. (1995). *Undoing culture.* London: Sage.

Finnäes, L. (1987). Do young people misjudge each others' musical taste? *Psychology of Music, 15,* 152–166.

Finnäes, L. (1989). A comparison between young people's privately and publicly expressed musical preferences. *Psychology of Music, 17,* 132–145.

Finnegan, R. (1989). *The hidden musicians: Music-making in an English town.* Cambridge, England: Cambridge University Press.

Fiske, J. (1989). *Reading the popular.* Boston: Unwin Hyman.

Fiske, J. (1992). The cultural economy of fandom. In L. A. Lewis (Ed.), *The adoring audience: Fan culture and popular media* (pp. 30–49). London: Routledge.

Fiske, J. (1994). Radical shopping in Los Angeles: Race, media and the shere of consumption. *Media, Culture and Society, 16,* 469–486.

Fiske, J. (1995). Gendered television: Femininity. In G. Dines, & J. M. Humez (Eds.). *Gender, race and class in media: A text-reader* (pp. 340–347). Thousand Oaks, CA: Sage.

Foret, M. (1991). Some theoretical-methodological problems of the research on popular music. *Popular Music and Society, 15,* 1–10.

Frith, S. (1978). *The sociology of rock.* London: Constable.

Gans, H. J. (1974). *Popular culture and high culture: An analysis and evaluation of taste.* New York: Basic Books.

Gans, H. J. (1985). American popular culture and high culture in a changing class structure. *Prospects, 10,* 17–37.

Geiger, T. (1950). A radio test of musical taste. *Public Opinion Quarterly, 14,* 3, 453–460.

Goffman, E. (1959). *The presentation of self in everyday life.* New York: Anchor Books.

Goffman, E. (1961). Role distance. In E. Goffman (Ed.), *Encounters: Two studies in the sociology of interaction* (pp. 83–152). Indianapolis: Bobbs-Merrill.

Goffman, E. (1963). *Stigma*. Englewood Cliffs, NJ: Prentice-Hall.

Groce, S. B., & Epstein, J. S. (1994). Recent theory and research in the sociology of popular music: A selected and annotated bibliography. In J. S. Epstein (Ed.), *Adolescents and their music: If it's too loud you're too old* (pp. 329–388). New York: Garland.

Hall, S., Clarke, J., Jefferson, T., & Roberts, B. (Eds.). (1976). *Resistance through rituals: Youth subcultures in post-war Britain*. London: Hutchinson.

Hebdige, D. (1979). *Subculture: The meaning of style*. London: Methuen.

Holbrook, M. B., & Gardner, M. P. (1993). An approach to investigating the emotional determinants of consumption durations: Why do people consume what they consume for as long as they consume it? *Journal of Consumer Psychology, 2*, 123–142.

Hollonquist, T., & Suchman, E. A. (1979). Listening to the listener: Experiences with the Lazarsfeld-Stanton program analyser. In P. F. Lazarsfeld & F. N. Stanton (Eds.), *Radio research 1942–43* (pp. 265–334). New York: Arno Press.

Honegger, C., Hradil, S., & Traxler, F. (Eds.). (1999). *Grenzenlose Gesellschaft?* [Boundless society?]. Opladen, Germany: Leske and Budrich.

Huyssen, A. (1990). Mapping the postmodern. In J. C. Alexander & S. Seidman (Eds), *Culture and Society* (pp. 355–375). Cambridge UK: Cambridge University Press. (Original work published 1984)

Institut fuer Musiksoziologie. (1991). *Berichte und Informationen* [Reports and information] (No. 15). Vienna: Hochschule für Musik und Darstellende Kunst in Wien.

Kalof, L. (1993). Dilemmas of feminity: Gender and the social construction of sexual imagery. *Sociological Quarterly, 34*, 639–651.

Kant, I. (1963). *Kritik der urteilskraft* (Gerhard Lehmann, Ed.). Stuttgart: Reclam. (Originally published 1790)

Kaplan, M. (1990). *The Arts: A social perspective*. London: Associated Universities Presses.

Kapner, G. (1992). Nachdenkliches zur kunstsoziologie [Reflections on the sociology of art]. In I. Bontinck (Ed.), *New patterns of musical behavior of the young generation in industrial societies* (pp. 45–59). Vienna: Universal Edition.

Karbusicky, V. (1974). Zur empirisch-soziologischen Musikforschung [Toward an empirical-sociological musicology]. In Kneif, 1975, 253–267.

Kneif, T. (Ed.). (1975). *Texte zur musiksoziologie* (2nd ed.). Laaber, Germany: Laaber, 1983.

Konecni, V. (1979). Determinants of aesthetic preference and effects of exposure to aesthetic stimuli: Social, emotional, and cognitive factors. In B. A. Maher (Ed.), *Progress in experimental personality research*: Vol. 9 (pp. 149–197). New York: Academy Press.

Konecni, V. J., & Sargent-Pollock, D. (1976). Choice between melodies differing in complexity under divided-attention conditions. *Journal of Experimental Psychology, 2*(3), 347–356.

Lazarsfeld, P. F. (1932): Hoererbefragung der RAVAG [Radio listeners survey]. In Mark, 1996b, 27–40.

Lewis, G. H. (1977). Taste cultures and culture classes in mass society: Shifting patterns in American popular music. *International Review of the Aesthetics and Sociology of Music, 8*, 39–48.

Lewis, G. H. (1978). The sociology of popular culture. *Current Sociology, 26*(3), 1–160.

Lull, J. (Ed.). (1992). *Popular music and communication* (2nd ed.). Newbury Park, CA: Sage.

Mark, D. (1985). *John H. Mueller: Ein pionier der musiksoziologie*. [John H. Mueller: A pioneer of the sociology of music]. Vienna: Verlag des Verbandes der wissenschaftlichen Gesellschaften Oesterreichs.

Mark, D. (1996a). Entstehungsgeschichte, kulturelles Umfeld und Rezeption der RAVAG-Studie von 1932. In D. Mark (Ed.), *Paul Lazarsfelds Wiener RAVAG-Studie 1932* [History, cultural context and reception of the RAVAG-study of 1932] (pp. 75–104). Muehlheim, Germany: Guthmann-Peterson.

Mark, D. (Ed.). (1996b). *Paul Lazarsfelds Wiener RAVAG-Studie 1932*. Muehlheim, Germany: Guthmann-Peterson.

Mark, D. (1996c). Vorwort [Preface]. In D. Mark (Ed.), *Paul Lazarsfelds Wiener RAVAG-Studie 1932* (pp. 7–10). Muehlheim, Germany: Guthmann-Peterson.

MayDay Group. (2001a). [On-line]. Available: http:members.aol.com/jtgates/maydaygroup/.

MayDay Group. (2001b). [On-line]. Available: http:members.aol.com/jtgates/maydaygroup/history.html.

McRobbie, A. (1990). *Feminism and youth culture: From Jackie to just seventeen*. London: MacMillan.

McRobbie, A. (1993). Shut up and dance: Youth culture and changing modes of femininity. *Young, 1*(2), 13–31.

McRobbie, A., & Garber, J. (1976). In S. Hall, J. Clarke, T. Jefferson, & B. Roberts (Eds.), *Resistance through rituals: Youth subcultures in post-war Britain* (pp. 217–237). London: Hutchinson.

Mead, G. H. (1934): *Mind, self, and society*. Chicago: University of Chicago Press.

Miller, R. F. (1990). The semantic differential in the study of music perception: A theoretical overview. *Quarterly Journal of Music Teaching and Learning, 1*, 63–73.

Moores, S. (1990). Texts, readers and contexts of reading: Developments in the study of media audiences. *Media, Culture and Society, 12*, 9–29.

Mueller, H-P. (1994). Kultur und soziale ungleichheit: Von der klassischen zur neueren kultursoziologie [Culture and social inequality: From classical to modern sociology of culture]. In I. Moerth & G. Froehlich (Eds.), *Das symbolische kapital der lebensstile: Zur kultursoziologie der moderne nach Bourdieu* [The symbolical capital of lifestyle: Toward a sociology of culture of modernity after Bourdieu] (pp. 55–74). Frankfurt: Campus.

Mueller, J. H. (1951). *The American symphony orchestra: A social history of musical taste*. Bloomington: Indiana University Press.

Mueller, J. H. (1961). *Statistical reasoning in sociology*. New York: Houghton Mifflin.

Mueller, R. (1990). *Soziale bedingungen der umgehensweisen jugendlicher mit musik: Theoretische und empirisch-statistische untersuchung zur musikpaedagogik* [The social conditions of young people interacting with music: A theoretical and empirical-statistical investigation in music education]. Essen, Germany: Die Blaue Eule.

Mueller, R. (1994). Music video in social context. In I. Deliège (Ed.), *Proceedings of the Third International Conference for Music Perception and Cognition* (pp. 361–362). Liège, Belgium: University of Liège.

Mueller, R. (1995a). Neue Forschungstechnologien: Der multimedia-fragebogen in der musiksoziologischen und musikpaedagogischen forschung [New research technologies: The multimedia-questionnaire in music sociological and music pedagogical research]. *Rundfunk und Fernsehen, 43*(2), 205–216.

Mueller, R. (1995b). Selbstsozialisation: Eine theorie lebenslangen musikalischen lernens [Self-socialization: A theory of lifelong musical learning]. In K-E. Behne, G. Kleinen, & H. de la Motte-Haber (Eds.), *Musikpsychologie: Jahrbuch der Deutschen Gesellschaft fuer Musikpsychologie: Vol. 11* [Music psychology: Yearbook of the German Association of the Psychology of Music] (pp. 63–65). Wilhelmshaven, Germany: Noetzel.

Mueller, R. (1996a). Computer assisted empirical investigation of music listening in social and cultural context: The sounding questionnaire on the multimedia computer. In K. P. Etzkorn & S. Helms (Eds.), *Policy Concerns with Media Influences on Music Listening* (pp. 63–65). Koln: International Society for Music Education.

Mueller, R. (1996b). Skinheads and violence: Blame it on oi!—music? In R. R. Pratt & R. Spintge (Eds.), *MusicMedicine: Vol. 2* (pp. 117–128). Saint Louis: MMB Music.

Mueller, R. (1999). MultiMedia in der empirischen musikrezeptionsforschung [MultiMedia in empirical musicological research]. In K-E. Behne, G. Kleinen, & H. dela Motte-Habe (Eds.), *Musikpsychologie: Jahrbuch der Deutschen Gesellschaft fuer Musikpsychologie: Vol 14* (pp. 163–176). Goettingen, Germany: Hogrefe.

Nava, M. (1984). *Gender and generation.* London: Sage.

Neurath, P. (1996). Die methodische bedeutung der RAVAG-Studie von Paul F. Lazarsfeld: Der Wiener bericht von 1932 und seine rolle fuer die entwicklung in Amerika [The methodological significance of the RAVAG-study of Paul F. Lazarsfeld: The Vienna report and its role in developments in the United States]. In D. Mark (Ed.), *Paul Lazarsfelds Wiener RAVAG-Studie 1932* (pp. 11–26). Muehlheim, Germany: Guthmann-Peterson.

Perry, I. (1995). It's my thang and I'll swing it the way that I feel! Sexuality and black women rappers. In G. Dines & J. M. Humez (Eds.), *Gender, race and class in media: A text-reader* (pp. 524–530). Thousand Oaks, CA: Sage.

Peterson, E. E. (1987, March). Media consumption and girls who want to have fun. *Critical Studies in Mass Communication, 4,* 37–50.

Peterson, R. A., & Kern, R. M. (1996). Changing highbrow taste: From snob to omnivore. *American Sociological Review, 61,* 900–907.

Poettker, H. (1996). E-Musik und ihr Publikum: Fruehe quantitative untersuchungen von Paul F. Lazarsfeld und Theodor Geiger [Serious music and its audience: Early quantative studies of Paul F. Lazarsfeld and Theodor Geiger]. In I. Bontinck (Ed.), *New patterns of musical behavior of the young generation in industrial societies* (pp. 103–117). Vienna: Universal Edition.

Regelski, T. A. (1998). *Critical theory and praxis: Implications for professionalizing music education: Part 4. Curriculum: Ideology versus phronesis of "good results."* [On-line]. Available: http:members.aol.com/jtgates/maydaygroup/crittheory4.html.

Rhein, S. (2000). Being a fan is more than that: Fan-specific involvement with music. *The World of Music, 42,* 95–109.

Roberts, R. (1991). Music videos, performance and resistance: Feminist rappers. *Journal of Popular Culture, 25*(2), 141–152.

Robinson, J. P., & Fink, E. L. (1986). Beyond mass culture and class culture: Subcultural differences in the structure of music preferences. In S. J. Ball-Rokeach & M. G. Cantor (Eds.), *Media, audience and social structure* (pp. 226–239). Beverly Hills, CA: Sage.

Rouner, D. (1990). Rock music's use as a socializing function. *Popular Music and Society, 14,* 97–107.

Schaeffer, B. (1996). *Die band: Stil und aesthetische praxis im jugendalter* [The band: Style and aesthetic practice among youth]. Opladen, Germany: Leske and Budrich.

Schulze, G. (1992). *Die erlebnisgesellschaft: Kultursoziologie der gegenwart* [Constructing the new consumer society]. Frankfurt: Campus.

Schulze, L., White, A. B., & Brown, J. D. (1993). "A sacred monster in her prime": Audience construction of Madonna as low-other. In C. Schwichtenberg (Ed.), *The Madonna connection: Representational politics, subcultural identities, and cultural theory* (pp. 15–37). Boulder, CO: Westview Press.

Schwichtenberg, C. (1992). The popular pleasures of visual music. In J. Lull (Ed.), *Popular music and communication* (2nd ed., pp. 116–133). Newbury Park, CA: Sage.

Schwichtenberg, C. (1993a). About the book and editor. In C. Schwichtenberg (Ed.), *The Madonna connection: Representational politics, subcultural identities, and cultural theory* (p. 319). Boulder, CO: Westview Press.

Schwichtenberg, C. (1993b). Introduction: Connections/intersections. In C. Schwichtenberg (Ed.), *The Madonna connection: Representational politics, subcultural identities, and cultural theory* (pp. 1–11). Boulder, CO: Westview Press.

Schwichtenberg, C. (Ed.). (1993c). *The Madonna connection: Representational politics, subcultural identities, and cultural theory.* Boulder, CO: Westview Press.

Seidman, S. (1990). Substantive debates: Moral order and social crisis—perspectives on modern culture. In J. C. Alexander & S. Seidman (Eds.), *Culture and society* (pp. 217–235). Cambridge, England: Cambridge University Press.

Silbermann, A. (1957). *The sociology of music.* Westport, CT: Greenwood Press.

Silbermann, A. (1979). Soziologie der kuenste [Sociology of art]. In R. Koenig (Ed.), *Handbuch der empirischen so-*

zialforschung: Vol. 13 [Handbook of empirical social research] (pp. 117–345). Stuttgart: Deutscher Taschenbuch Verlag.

Small, C. (1998). *Musicking: The meanings of performing and listening.* Hanover, NH: University Press of New England.

Sun, S-W., & Lull, J. (1986). The adolescent audience for music videos and why they watch. *Journal of Communication, 36,* 115–125.

Thompson, M., Pingree, S., Hawkins, R. P., & Draves, C. (1991). Long-term norms and cognitive structures as shapers of television viewer activity. *Journal of Broadcasting and Electronic Media, 35,* 319–334.

Toop, D. (1991). *Rap attack.* London: Serpent's Tail.

Weber, M. (1972). *Die rationalen und soziologischen grundlagen der musik* [Rational and sociological foundation of music]. Tübingen: Mohr. (Original work published 1921)

Weinstein, D. (1991). *Heavy metal: A cultural sociology.* New York: Lexington.

Willis, P. (1990). *Common culture.* London: Open University Press.

Winter, R., & Eckert, R. (1990). *Mediengeschichte und kulturelle Differenzierung* [Media history and cultural differentiation]. Opladen, Germany: Leske and Budrich.

33 Social Psychology and Music Education

ADRIAN C. NORTH

DAVID J. HARGREAVES

MARK TARRANT

Music is an inherently social phenomenon: the patterns and regularities that exist in physical sounds only take on musical meaning when they are interpreted as such by groups of people. This is not a particularly surprising or radical view, of course: Many authors have pointed out that music and other artistic stimuli do not exist in a "social vacuum" (e.g., Arnheim, 1952; Konecni, 1982; Munro, 1963) and that this social and cultural context must be addressed by research. Indeed, Farnsworth's (1969) textbook attempted to explicitly address social and cultural influences on musical behavior. The research literature in music psychology and music education has nevertheless continued to neglect the social dimension to a surprising degree, and this encouraged us to explore the contemporary implications of this view in *The Social Psychology of Music* (Hargreaves & North, 1997).

Individuals' musical development and learning is a central part of this, of course, so that its explanation must inevitably involve a detailed account of the "musical environment." This environment varies considerably in different countries around the world, each of which has its own historical background, cultural traditions, educational systems, and curricula. We have explored the ways these influences shape the nature of pupils' musical development and learning in our book *Musical Development and Learning: The International Perspective* (Hargreaves and North, 2001a), which brings together expert authorities from all around the world.

Many of the chapters in this Handbook focus on the teaching and learning of music in schools and in other educational institutions: a primary emphasis is on *formal* music education. In this chapter we take a broader view of

"musical learning and development" that includes what happens in *informal* as well as in formal settings. Children in the 21st century learn from a bewildering and ever-expanding variety of sources, including the media, the internet, MIDI equipment, personal hi-fi and recording equipment, and so on. Formal music education forms only one part of a much broader picture, and our chapter is conceived in this light.

We review research that deals with broader social and cultural influences on musical behavior, which takes us well beyond the bounds of what might conventionally be regarded as "music education" into the fields of developmental, social, and cognitive psychology, communications research, ethnomusicology, sociology, and education. This is an ambitious undertaking, and it is important to ground our analysis in a consistent conceptual framework in order to maintain a sense of coherence and perspective. We do so by drawing on Doise's (1986) distinction between four levels of influence that can be identified in explanations of social behavior. These range from explanations that focus on the individual to those that place much more emphasis on the social systems and cultures in which an individual acts.

Doise's four levels are the *intraindividual*, the *interindividual/situational*, the *social-positional*, and the *ideological*, and the chapter uses this as its central organizing principle. We begin on the *intraindividual* level by considering the social psychological effects of music listening on the individual. We review research concerning the potentially deleterious effects of pop music on young people; consumer behavior; task performance; and medical applications of music. Next we consider the social psychology of musical performance, concentrating in particular on performance anxiety: the latter can be seen to exist on Doise's *interindividual/situational* level, since it considers the effects of small groups and situations on behavior. We move next to the *social-positional* level, considering the roles that individuals play in the social groups to which they belong. In this section we review research from the perspective of experimental social psychology on how and why musical taste might play a role in the membership of social groups. Finally, we move to the broadest cultural (*ideological*) level, where we discuss large-scale social and cultural influences on musical behavior. Here we discuss the evolution of musical fashions over time and ethnomusicological approaches to music.

The clear implication of this wide-ranging review is that "music education" and indeed music psychology need to be redefined in terms of a much wider agenda than has hitherto been adopted, and we conclude the chapter by summarizing the main features of such an agenda.

Effects of Music Listening on Behavior: The Intraindividual Level

The vast majority of studies in music psychology have considered the effects of external factors on musical behavior: They focus on how changes in some aspect of individuals or their circumstances can affect musical listening, musical performance, or more general musical competence. However, recent years have given rise to research on the effects of music on other aspects of behavior; studies have dealt with how varying musical properties can produce changes in the behavior of individuals. This research is particularly exciting because studies of external influences have implications for only music, whereas the effects of music have implications for a much broader community. For example, research on the effects of music on consumer behavior (see hereafter) is of interest to people concerned with music *as well as* people concerned with marketing, economics, copyright law, and so on. Similarly, research concerning the effects of music on the immune system (see hereafter) is of interest to people concerned with music and also those interested in health care.

This research has typically investigated the short-term effects of background music that is experienced incidentally during the course of other tasks. Some authors (e.g., Chabris et al., 1999) have explored the potential link between music listening and aspects of intelligence. This debate is ongoing and includes four main lines of research: on the effects of music on young people's beliefs and values; on consumer behavior; on concurrent task performance; and on the outcome of health care procedures.

Pop Music and Young People

One particular feature of pop music is the hero worship of performers by fans (see, e.g., Olson & Crase, 1990). A consequence of this has been concern about the potentially deleterious effects that pop music may have on its (primarily young and therefore supposedly more impressionable) listeners. In 1985, Tipper Gore (the wife of the former vice president, Al Gore), founded the Parents' Music Resource Center (PMRC). The PMRC was concerned with pop music lyrics, arguing that "hidden messages and backward masking" were corrupting "virgin minds." The PMRC appeared before the Senate Committee on Commerce, Science and Transportation on September 19, 1985, stressing that they would not be satisfied until

1. "Questionable" lyrics were printed and provided with their respective recordings
2. "Objectionable" album covers were sold in plain brown wrappers (or sold in areas segregated from other albums)
3. Rock concerts were rated in terms of their suitability for younger age groups
4. MTV segregated "questionable" video recordings into specific late-night viewing slots

This was perhaps the culmination of decades of debate concerning the moral effects on young people of listening to pop music and more recently watching pop music videos. Pop music styles such as rock-and-roll, psychedelic rock, punk, heavy metal, and rap have all been criticized for their antiestablishment, liberal stance. However, this is not something unique to pop music or even music as a whole. Picasso's *Guernica* is perhaps the best-known protest painting, and countless writers have been imprisoned for their views. In the musical domain, Shostakovich was reprimanded by the Russian government for his unpatriotic music; and Charlie Parker's use of drugs was widely known, as was Miles Davis's outspoken support for the civil rights movement. Nevertheless, pop music and particularly pop music television have been the focus of most recent studies on the putative "immoral" effects of the arts on perceivers. There is already a sizable discursive literature on the subject (e.g., Pettegrew et al., 1995; Schwichtenberg, 1992; Sherman & Etling, 1991). However, data-driven research is coming more to the fore and may be grouped under the following subheadings.

Prevalence, Status of the Fans, and Content. The first group of studies considers the prevalence of exposure to "problem" music and the demographic status of its fans. Larson, Kubey, & Colletti (1989; see also Kubey and Larson, 1990) report that adolescence represents a shift in preference toward music videos away from television and music listening, particularly among males. Greeson (1991) found that music videos were evaluated more positively by working-class participants and those who seldom or never attended church. Wass, Miller, and Stevenson (1988) studied 994 ninth to twelfth graders: 17.5% were fans of rock music with lyrics that promoted homicide, suicide, or satanic practices. These fans were more likely to have parents who never married or remarried and to be white, male, and enrolled in urban schools.

Similarly, Wass, Raup, Cerullo, & Martel (1988) found that 24% of urban high school students were fans of music with themes of homicide, satanism, and suicide. Of these, three-quarters were males and nearly all were white. Interestingly, they also had a liberal attitude regarding the music: As compared with fans of other styles, they were more likely to believe that young children should be allowed to listen to music with destructive themes, and fewer of them believed that adolescents might commit murder or suicide as a result of having listened to such songs (see also Wass, Miller, & Redditt, 1991).

Several authors have considered similarities between the goals of music television and those of commercial music radio, such as attracting specific audiences for advertising purposes and keeping these viewers watching until the next advertising break (see, e.g., Denisoff, 1985; Levy, 1983; Sherman & Etling, 1991; A. S. Wolfe, 1983). Content analyses of pop music videos suggest that they are produced to achieve these aims. Sherman and Dominick's (1986) content analysis of 166 videos reported violence in 56.6% of them; sexual imagery in more than 75%; and that 81% of the videos containing violence also included sexual imagery. Baxter, de Riemer, Landini, and Leslie (1985) carried out a content analysis of 62 videos: sex, violence, and crime were again found to occur frequently, although the sexual and violent content was characterized by suggestiveness and innuendo rather than explicit portrayal. Pardun and McKee (1995) found that religious imagery was twice as likely to occur in videos that also used sexual imagery than in videos that had no sexual imagery: The combination of sex and religion was found in over 25% of the videos.

There is direct evidence that these typical features might enhance viewers' enjoyment of the videos. Hansen and Hansen's (1990a) experimental study found that the musical and visual appeal of pop videos was positively influenced by the degree of their sexual (although not violent) content. Similarly, Zillmann and Mundorf (1987) found that both sexual and violent images in isolation intensified participants' appreciation of a music video, although the combination of the two did not enhance appreciation.

Delinquency.   Other studies have considered the relationship between adolescent musical tastes and delinquency. For example, Hansen and Hansen's (1991) questionnaire study found that heavy metal fans were higher on measures

of "Machiavellianism" and "machismo" and lower on measures of "need for cognition" than were nonfans: Similarly, punk fans were less accepting of authority than nonfans. Robinson, Weaver, and Zillmann (1996) found that undergraduates who scored highly on measures of psychoticism and reactive rebelliousness enjoyed rebellious videos more than did participants who scored low on these factors. Similarly, Bleich, Zillmann, and Weaver (1991) assessed 16- to 19-year-old participants' trait rebelliousness and enjoyment of three nondefiant rock music videos. Highly rebellious participants enjoyed the nondefiant videos less than did nonrebellious participants, and the former group also consumed less nondefiant rock music. Finally, Hansen and Hansen (1990b) found that experimental exposure to antisocial music videos increased participants' tolerance of antisocial behavior (i.e., an obscene hand gesture) as compared with exposure to nonantisocial videos.

However, the evidence for a relationship between taste for rebellious music and delinquency may not be straightforward. Took and Weiss (1994) compared 12- to 18-year-old participants who preferred rap and heavy metal with those who preferred other musical styles. As one might expect, the former group had a higher incidence of several problem behaviors (e.g., drug and alcohol use and arrests). However, when gender was controlled, only the incidence of below average school grades and a history of counseling remained significantly different between the groups. Although delinquent behaviors might be more prevalent among the fans of particular styles, this could be simply because such styles tend to attract more male followers and not because of the music itself. Indeed, Roe (1995) argued that pop music should not be considered in isolation from other factors when discussing adolescent delinquency. Similarly, Rosenbaum and Prinsky (1991) argue that young people may not become delinquent *because* of their musical taste: Instead, labeling people as "delinquent" on the basis of their dress and musical taste may push them into a deviant role in the eyes of the criminal justice system. We return to this issue of causality later.

Sexual Attitudes.   Three studies have shown a link between exposure to music videos and permissive sexual attitudes, particularly in females. Strouse and Buerkel-Rothfuss (1987) found that consumption of music television was positively associated with permissiveness in females and that this was positively associated with self-esteem. Strouse, Buerkel-Rothfuss, and Long (1995) and Toney and Weaver (1994) found the same effect, arguing that it was stronger in females from "unsatisfactory" family environments.

Attitudes Toward Violence.   Although Wann and Wilson (1996) suggested that there may be no link between attitudes toward violence and pop music, four remaining studies suggest that this is not the case. Rawlings, Hodge, Sherr, and Dempsey (1995) reported that preference for aggressive styles of popular music was related to psychoticism. Johnson, Gatto, and Jackson (1995) found that participants exposed to violent videos (rather than nonviolent or no-music videos) expressed a higher probability that they would engage in violence and greater acceptance of violence against a woman described in a vignette (see also Johnson, Gatto, & Jackson, 1995). Johnson, Adams, Ashburn, and Reed (1995) found that females exposed to videos featuring women in sexually subordinate roles showed greater acceptance of teen-dating violence than did females not exposed to these videos (although, interestingly, the same effect was not found in male participants). Finally, Peterson and Pfost (1989) asked male high school undergraduates to view rock videos varying in their erotic and violent content. Participants exposed to nonerotic violent videos were again generally more accepting of aggression toward women.

Discrimination.   Zillmann et al. (1995) asked African-American and white high school students to watch videos featuring popular rock, nonpolitical rap, or radical political rap. The participants then took part in a mock student government election in which African-American and white candidates presented ethnically liberal, neutral, or radical platforms. After exposure to radical political rap videos, white participants gave more support to a liberal African-American candidate and less support to a white radical candidate: radical political rap may motivate whites to support efforts toward greater racial harmony.

Studies on sexual discrimination are less encouraging, however. Hansen and Hansen (1988) asked participants to watch a stereotypical (woman as sex object) or neutral music video before then watching a man and woman interact in a job interview. Participants who saw the stereotypical videos regarded the female job applicant as nonthreatening, competent, and sensitive when she reciprocated a sexual advance, whereas the effect was absent when participants saw the neutral video (see also Hansen, 1989). It should perhaps therefore be of some concern that two studies demonstrate the pervasion of the sex stereotyping of women in pop videos. Sommers-Flanagan, Sommers-Flanagan, and Davis's (1993) content analysis of 40 videos found that the women depicted engaged in more sexual and subservient behavior than did the males and that the women were more often the object of sexual advances. Similarly, Seidman (1992) found that sexual stereotyping was prevalent in the occupational roles fulfilled by men and women in videos: Males were more adventurous, domineering, and aggressive, whereas females were more affectionate, dependent, and nurturing. Furthermore, over one-third of females wore revealing clothing, as compared with

just 4% of males. These findings mirror journalistic/sociological work that has described the women in videos as "vampiric dominatrixes" (McKenna, 1983) and as "the comic book fantasies of adolescent males" (Gehr, 1983, p. 40).

Effects on Females.   In conjunction with those studies just described concerning attitudes toward sexual permissiveness and acceptance of violence, two other studies show that the effects of pop videos may be particularly detrimental for females. Strouse, Roscoe, and Goodwin (1994) found that involvement with pop music was associated with females' acceptance of sexual harassment, particularly among those from "unsatisfactory" or "nonintact" families. Second, Tiggemann, and Pickering's (1996) study of female adolescents found a positive correlation between the amount of music videos watched and scores on a Drive for Thinness subscale of the Eating Disorders Inventory.

Suicide.   Heavy metal vocalist Ozzy Osbourne sang in "Suicide Solution" that "Suicide is the only way out / Don't you know what it's really all about," and several studies have considered the role of such lyrics in promoting youth suicide. Plopper and Ness's (1993) analysis of American pop music sales charts indicated that death songs enjoy disproportionate popularity. Martin, Clarke, and Pearce (1993) found significant associations between a preference for rock/metal and suicidal thoughts, acts of deliberate self-harm, depression, delinquency, illegal drug use, and family dysfunction. Similarly, Sun and Lull (1986) studied 587 high school students and found that weekday MTV viewing was related to two factors predictive of suicide, namely unhappiness at school and low socioeconomic status. However, weekday viewing was also associated with something that would be expected to ameliorate suicidal tendencies, namely the amount of time spent with friends.

Perhaps the best-known evidence in this area, however, is provided by Stack and Gundlach's (1992) study of country music. They found that the frequency with which country music is played on the radio was positively related to the suicide rate among metropolitan white adult males, even when potentially contaminating variables such as gun ownership, poverty, and divorce were taken into account. The authors argued that this is because the popular themes of country lyrics dwell on factors that may predispose suicide (e.g., marital discord, alienation from work, etc.). While the music may not directly cause suicide, Stack and Gundlach seem to argue that it may well be a predisposing factor that, combined with other life difficulties, is sufficient to push somebody over the edge. Following a similar methodology, Stack, Gundlach, and Reeves (1994) also found evidence of a positive relationship between American heavy metal magazine subscriptions and youth suicide.

Perhaps less well known are two studies that follow up Stack and Gundlach's (1992) study, questioning its conclusions. Maguire and Snipes's (1994) attempt to replicate the finding indicated "a *negative, though insignificant* effect on white urban suicide rates" (p. 1239, our emphasis; see also Stack & Gundlach, 1994). Mauk, Taylor, White, and Allen (1994) argue that the original Stack and Gundlach (1992) data taken from the population as a whole may not predict individuals' behavior: For example, none of the individuals who committed suicide may have actually listened to country music radio. Mauk et al. also argue that we still know nothing about the direction of causality: Maybe people who were going to kill themselves anyway listen to country music, such that the music reflects their feelings. Note also that although some intervening variables were controlled by Stack and Gundlach (e.g., gun ownership), their correlational design means that there may be other relevant factors that were not considered (e.g., number of friends). We will never know whether these arguments held true for the unfortunate participants of Stack and Gundlach's study: However, the criticisms are sufficient if not to refute then at least to cast doubt on their conclusions. Indeed, it is worth noting that although these correlational questionnaire studies provide only limited evidence of a relationship between music and suicide, the single experimental study of the phenomenon has yielded negative results: Ballard and Coates (1995) found no effects of musical style (rap or heavy metal) or lyrical content (nonviolent, homicidal, suicidal) on participants' suicidal ideation, anxiety, or self-esteem.

A Case for Censorship?   It would seem that the empirical evidence concerning the relationship between music and suicide is at worst inconclusive and at best negative (which corresponds with the judgment of the American courts; see, e.g., Litman & Farberow, 1994). Indeed, the evidence concerning music and suicide leads to many arguments that also apply to the research on music and problem adolescent behaviors discussed earlier. First, although the sentiments of the Ozzy Osbourne lyric quoted earlier are not too difficult to discern, research shows that listeners are generally very poor at understanding lyrics, correctly interpreting them at only chance level (Greenfield & Koyamatsu et al., 1987; Konecni, 1984). Furthermore, Walls, Taylor, and Falzone (1992) found that subliminal messages in recordings did not influence participants' perception of musical tempo. If these findings are correct, then it is difficult to see how pop music lyrics *could* directly incite problem behaviors.

The existing research is also limited methodologically. At the risk of overgeneralizing, it can be said that researchers have tended to carry out two types of study. The first type are correlational studies relating the frequency of exposure to music to measures of various problem behaviors.

The advantage of this approach is that it reflects any effects that might be attributable to prolonged naturalistic exposure to "problem" music. However, one limitation of this correlational method concerns its inability to attribute any effects to one specific cause: A correlational approach means that it is impossible to determine whether any deleterious effects on behavior are attributable to the hypothesized visual/musical components or to some other factor. Furthermore, correlational studies do not allow determination of the direction of causality: Is exposure to videos the cause of problem behavior, or does a tendency toward problem behavior lead to people enjoying "rebellious" music?

Other research has presented experimental participants with a small number of videos and then asked them to provide mood ratings either directly or by responding to a vignette describing, for example, violent behavior. These studies do allow precise stimulus control and the determination of cause and effect and are limited by their artificiality. In particular, they tell us nothing about the *long-term* effects of pop music and music video in the real world. Furthermore, they often fail to control for variations in participants' degree of previous exposure to pop music or videos or preexisting levels of tolerance for problem behaviors/attitudes. This "baggage," which participants bring into the lab with them, may well distort or swamp whatever effects are induced by the experimental manipulation.

There are two more general methodological problems with the existing literature. First, there is a very strong North American bias, which means that the results may not be generalizable to other countries. For example, one of us spent several hours watching a Turkish music television station (KRAL TV) on a recent holiday and found that women were portrayed as much more subservient than in typical American/West European videos. For example, one video featured an attractive young man leaving his new wife because she was overweight!

In addition to being culturally biased, the findings discussed here are also potentially dated. The ephemeral nature of pop music means that new styles of music and video come and go rapidly. For example, a style of music called gangsta rap was prominent in the early to mid-1990s that frequently glamorized delinquent/criminal behaviors. However, more recent rap songs have stressed reconciliation and education. Arguments based on gangsta rap might not apply to more recent rap songs.

There are also several theoretical issues that remain unresolved. For example, although some encouraging recent work has considered the role of music and music video in priming adolescents' schema, particularly regarding gender stereotypes (see, e.g., Hansen, 1989, 1995; Hansen & Hansen, 1988; Johnson, Gatto, & Jackson, 1995; Zillmann, Aust, Hoffman, & Love, 1995), much of the existing research has tested rather vague theoretical premises. Another potentially useful theoretical approach that deserves further attention concerns social modeling processes of the type most commonly associated with Bandura (e.g., 1977). Similarly, it is probable that much of the existing research on television violence in general is of direct relevance to the issue of "problem" musical styles.

We therefore return to the issue with which this section began: Should pop music be censored? In addition to well-known liberal arguments concerning freedom of speech, we would advocate three further points. First, the evidence is as yet inconclusive. While there are studies that suggest a *relationship* between pop music and undesirable attitudes/behaviors, the methodological problems described earlier mean that we are still some way from being able to make an unequivocal assessment concerning *causality*. Furthermore, there is some evidence that music videos might actually have positive effects by, for example, promoting racial tolerance (Zillmann et al., 1995) or religious symbolism (Pardun & McKee, 1995). In addition, as we will show in more detail later, there is clear evidence that pop music can assist in identity development during adolescence. Even if research were to eventually establish reliably that pop music and video could *cause* deleterious effects, it seems that a case-by-case approach might be preferable to blanket censorship. Indeed, Tapper and John's (1994) content analysis concluded that the visual elements of music videos vary so much that it is inappropriate to consider them as homogenous.

A second group of arguments against censorship center around the idea that pop music and music videos are not necessary and sufficient for the elicitation of problem behavior/attitudes. First, while some music videos do contain elements that may be socially undesirable, they contain no elements that could not be seen on any newsstand, mainstream television station, or networked personal computer. Second, delinquency, racism, sexism, and violence are all social problems that existed before the founding of modern pop music and so cannot have been created by it. Many young people listen to thousands of hours of pop music without ever becoming suicidal, violent, sexist, or delinquent: In spite of several decades of research, we still just don't understand the putative relationship between pop music and socially undesirable behavior.

Consumer Behavior

The use of music in shops, bars, and the like has long been the source of considerable lighthearted derision. The playwright J. B. Priestley once bragged of having "had it turned off in the best of places," and the comedian Lily Tomlin once expressed fears that the guy who invented Muzak might be inventing something else! Lanza (1994) has provided a fascinating history of commercial music. This per-

haps reached its zenith (or some would say its nadir) with the invention of piped music in the 1920s by Brigadier General George Owen Squier, a graduate of the prestigious United States Military Academy at West Point.

However, it is a popular misconception that background music is a recent phenomenon (Lanza, 1994). For example, Greek mythology tells that Orpheus played his lyre to inspire Jason and the Argonauts' quest for the Golden Fleece and that Hermes charmed the 100-eyed Argus with a reed flute lullaby. The third-century Roman grammarian Censorinus wrote that "music serves to make toil as bearable as may be, as when it is used by the steersman in a moving galley"; and a flute orchestra purportedly accompanied the erection of Rome's Messina. During the Middle Ages, Christian soldiers of the early Crusades hired battlefield musicians to play the same Arabic military music that the Saracens had used to defeat them in previous battles; and Gregorian monks would perform plainsong outside their monastery to uplift agricultural workers. More recently, musicians are often appalled to learn that many pieces from the standard classical repertoire were composed specifically as background music: Bach's *Goldberg Variations* were written to cure the insomnia of the man who commissioned them, Count Kaiserling; and Mozart and Telemann both took account of the fact that their compositions would serve as background music for the court.

Music in modern commercial practice is a hi-tech, multibillion-dollar industry that employs the latest satellite and computer technology. Large corporations commission research of their own (see Hodges & Haack, 1996). While the impressive findings of this work must be treated with some scepticism, independent researchers have also become interested in the field: North and Hargreaves (1997d) have reviewed this work in detail, and we present here a brief overview of the empirical literature.

The role of music in television advertisements has given rise to the most investigations in the field. Gorn's (1982) classic study presented pictures of either light blue or beige pens in conjunction with music that participants either would like (from the film *Grease*) or would not like (classical Indian music). Afterward participants were allowed to take one of the two types of pen, supposedly as a reward for participation; 79% chose the pen associated with liked music (see also Bierley, McSweeney, & Vannieuwkerk, 1985; Tom, 1995). This classical conditioning approach has been criticized, however, since several studies have failed to produce similar effects (Allen & Madden, 1985; Alpert & Alpert, 1989; Pitt & Abratt, 1988). Others have demonstrated that classical conditioning effects may be due to demand characteristics: Kellaris and Cox (1989) found that pen selection choices could be influenced by merely *imagining* liked or disliked music being played in the background.

Finally, Park and Young (1986) and Gorn (1982) found that liked music can condition product preferences only when viewers have no motivation to consider information presented in the advertisement. This research is consistent with the elaboration likelihood model (or ELM; Petty & Cacioppo, 1981; Petty, Cacioppo, & Schumann, 1983). This says that persuasion should be aided by liked music when consumers do not have the motivation, opportunity, and ability to process product-relevant information. However, if consumers do have the motivation, opportunity, and ability to process product-relevant information, then liked music will be ineffective; in this case music can only improve viewers' purchase intentions if it enhances their ability to process the product information or guides them toward considering it in a particular way. Indeed, MacInnis and Park (1991) found that purchase intentions resulting from a shampoo advertisement were improved by music that "fitted" the product (i.e., the pop lyric "You make me feel like a natural woman"). The authors argued that the music activated certain types of information about the product, causing viewers to consider it as, for example, feminine and natural (see also Kellaris, Cox, & Cox, 1993).

In addition to research concerning telephone on-hold waiting time (see, e.g., Kellaris & Mantel, 1994; North, Hargreaves, & McKendrick, 1999), other studies have considered the role of music in commercial premises. Perhaps the one consistent finding to have emerged is that fast music makes customers act more quickly. For example, Milliman (1986) found that fast music in a restaurant led to diners eating more quickly than did slow music (see also McElrea & Standing, 1992; Milliman, 1982; Roballey et al., 1985; Smith & Curnow, 1966). Other studies have considered the effect of music on the atmosphere of such places. North and Hargreaves (1996) found that liking for the music in a cafeteria led to liking for the cafeteria; greater willingness to return; a greater propensity to visit the source of the music (namely, a small welfare advice stall); and a greater degree of openness toward others. Several more recent studies in the same cafeteria, a bar, and a city center bank (North & Hargreaves, 1998; North, Hargreaves, & McKendrick, in press) found that different types of music can produce different types of atmosphere and that these effects can be explained in terms of three dimensions, namely, dynamic/upbeat, aggressive, and cerebral: Variations in these "atmospheres" mediated the amount that customers were prepared to spend.

However, customer spending has been addressed most directly by research on musical "fit." This has concerned whether music can encourage customers to consider products in a particular way, favoring one choice alternative. North, Hargreaves, and McKendrick (1997) played French accordion music and German oompah band music next to a supermarket display of French and German wines. Consistent with the notion of "fit," when the French music was played, French wine outsold German wine, whereas when the German music was played, German wine outsold French (see also Areni & Kim, 1993). While discussing the effects of music on sales, we should also mention a study by Zullow (1991). He obtained lyrics for the top 40 songs in the United States for each year between 1955 and 1989. These were analyzed in terms of their degree of depressive content. Fluctuations in this could predict the U.S. government's principal measure of consumer optimism, which in turn predicted gross national product with a 1- to 2-year time lead. It is tempting to conclude that pop lyrics can cause recession! A similar study of our own is currently testing this notion (North, Hargreaves, & Gillet, 2000).

Task Performance

Music is often experienced in the course of other activities such as driving or homework. Perhaps the most theoretically coherent explanation of how music might affect performance on these tasks is provided by Konecni's (e.g., 1982) cognitive processing approach. One of the classic findings of experimental psychology is that people have a finite cognitive processing resource, which can be devoted to any particular task or instead divided between two or more tasks. Humans working on two tasks at once do so at a lower level of efficiency than could be achieved if carrying out the tasks in isolation. So listening to music while doing some other task (e.g., homework) takes up some of the processing resource that would otherwise have been devoted to the task: Performance on the task will be hampered. Furthermore, music requires more cognitive resource as it becomes more complex, louder, and faster or as it is less familiar, and so these types of music ought to cause more disruption to the performance of a concurrent task.

Given this clear-cut theoretical framework, it is unfortunate that empirical support is so mixed. A small number of studies may be seen as providing indirect support. Kiger (1989) investigated the effects of music of "low information load," "high information load," and silence on performance on a text comprehension task. Comprehension was best in the first condition and worst in the second. These results were explained in terms of high-information load music competing for attentional space and interfering with the information-processing task. Similarly, North and Hargreaves (1999b) asked participants to play a computer motor racing game while listening to either a loud, fast (i.e., demanding) or slow, quiet (i.e., relatively undemanding) version of the same piece. Participants in the former condition produced worse lap times.

However, several other studies have reported that the processing demands of music have *no* effect on task performance. D. E. Wolfe (1983) found that variations in musical volume had no effect on participants' ability to solve mathematical problems. Sogin (1988) found that jazz, classical, and pop music (which could each reasonably be expected to impose different processing demands) failed to produce differing effects on an eye-hand coordination task (see also Madsen, 1987). Finally, Mayfield and Moss (1989) found that calculations were carried out more quickly in the presence of fast (i.e., demanding) rather than slow (i.e., relatively undemanding) music, in direct contradiction of the theory just outlined.

This inconsistent pattern of results is almost certainly attributable to variations between the studies in terms of the processing demands of the music; task difficulty; nature of the task (e.g., verbal/numerical versus visual/spatial); participants' degree of attention to the music and the task; and their motivation to complete the latter successfully. As such, the cognitive processing theory is a clear candidate for theoretical and applied research: Loud, fast music might affect driver safety in cars fitted with music systems, and listening to music while completing homework might decrease students' grades.

Health Care

There is an extensive literature on music therapy that, despite occasional methodological shortcomings, provides some initial indication that music can have a positive impact on clinical psychological/psychiatric disorders (by fostering communication skills and emotional expressiveness in clients with learning difficulties, for example). This literature has been reviewed extensively elsewhere, and we will not duplicate these reviews here. However, Bunt (1997) points to a second and much more recent strand of research that is of interest here: This has investigated the health benefits of (usually background) music in patients suffering nonpsychological disorders. In these cases music is employed as an adjunct to other forms of (usually medical) therapy in an attempt to address illnesses with a direct physical cause.

Standley (1995) carried out a meta-analysis on research concerning music in therapy. These studies have investigated seven basic techniques, namely, passive music listening, active music participation, music and counseling, music and developmental or educational objectives, music and stimulation, music and biofeedback, and music and group activity. Standley's meta-analysis shows the extent to which music can influence medical outcomes; and the larger the resulting "effect size" for any one procedure, the greater the effect that music had. Standley found that music could have a positive impact on 125 of the 129 dependent vari-

ables she investigated. Some of these variables and their associated effect sizes are shown in table 33.1 (see Ammon, 1968; Bob, 1962; Bonny, 1983; Budzynski, Soyva, & Adler, 1970; Chetta, 1981; Cofranesco, 1985; Curtis, 1986; Frank, 1985; Gfeller, Logan, & Walker, 1988; Goloff, 1981; Locsin, 1981; Monsey, 1960; Oyama et al., 1983; Scartelli, 1982; Schuster, 1985; Shapiro & Cohen, 1983; Staum, 1983; Tanioka et al., 1985). Standley also noticed some interesting trends within these general effects. Music was generally more effective for females than males and for children and adolescents rather than adults. In addition, behavioral and physiological measures indicated more of an impact than did patient self-reports.

These studies have been supplemented in recent years by a number of findings indicating that music may also improve the efficiency of the immune system. Although typically carried out on small samples in laboratory settings, such findings are extremely provocative, since they

Table 33.1 Examples of Medical/Dental Factors Influenced by Music

Variable	Effect Size
Podiatric pain	>3.28
Pediatric respiration	3.15
Pulse (dental patients)	3.00
Use of analgesia (dental patients)	2.49
EMG	2.38
Blood pressure (dental patients)	2.25
Distraction (hemodialysis)	2.08
Observed pediatric anxiety	1.97
Grasp strength (stroke patients)	1.94
Cortisol (surgical recovery)	1.80
Perceived anxiety (cardiac patients)	1.77
Headache pain intensity	1.76
Pain (debridement of burns)	1.52
Post-operative pain	1.49
Obstetrical relaxation	1.32
Intracranial pressure	1.21
Length of labor (childbirth)	0.99
Perceived satisfaction	0.98
Pain (abortion)	0.96
Helplessness (dental patients)	0.94
Walking speed (stroke patients)	0.94
Relaxation (open heart surgery)	0.88
EMG (spasticity)	0.85
Exhalation strength	0.83
Blood pressure (surgery)	0.82
Crying (neonates)	0.72
Weight gain (neonates)	0.71
Contentment (cancer patients)	0.67
Cervical dilation time	0.52
Physical comfort	0.51
Emesis intensity (chemotherapy)	0.47
Sleep (open heart surgery)	0.42

Adapted from Standley, 1995, and Bunt, 1997.

suggest that music might help maintain good health. For example, Rider et al. (1990; see also Rider & Weldin, 1990) had one group listen to 17 minutes of specially composed background music, while another did not. Those who heard music showed a significantly greater increase in secretory immunoglobulin A (IgA) production than did the group without music. IgA has been used as a general indicator of the strength of the immune system and is the first line of defense against upper respiratory infection. The music group also had a significantly lower level of symptomatology both 3 and 6 weeks later than did the group without music. In a study funded by the Muzak Corporation, Charnetski, Brennan, and Harrison (1997) had undergraduates listen to 30 minutes of either Muzak, a radio station playing the same style of music, an alternating tone/click stimulus, or silence. Levels of IgA increased by 14.1% in the Muzak group and 7.2% in the radio group, whereas they decreased in the two remaining groups.

In a similar vein, Bartlett, Kaufman, and Smeltekop (1993) found that music could increase levels of interleukin-1 (which is released when the immune system is to attack an invading microorganism) and decrease levels of cortisol (a stress-related hormone) (see also Muller et al., 1994; Rider & Achterberg, 1989). There is a clear need for further research to determine whether music can really influence the immune system; how this effect operates; and the length of time for which the potential benefits endure.

Musical Performance: The Interindividual/Situational Level

Performance Anxiety

We now move to Doise's interindividual/situational level of explanation of musical behavior in considering the effects of small groups and situations on individuals. So far, this chapter has focused primarily on music listening. However, musical performance (even among eminent artists like Rachmaninoff) is also subject to a major social psychological influence, namely, performance anxiety (or "stage fright"). This field has been reviewed recently by Wilson (1994, 1997; Wills & Cooper, 1988), and our coverage here draws heavily on this.

The symptoms of stage fright are similar to those associated with other fear responses, namely, major activation of the sympathetic nervous system, which deals with the "fight or flight" response to danger. The physiological symptoms reflect this readiness for emergency action, including, for example, quickened pulse (causing palpitations); release of stored energy from the liver (causing edginess); the cessation of digestion, which diverts energy to the muscles (causing "butterflies" and nausea), and diversion of bodily fluids (e.g., saliva) into the bloodstream

(causing a dry mouth and difficulties swallowing). Wesner, Noyes, and Davis (1990) found that 61% of their 302 musicians reported either "marked" or "moderate" distress at performance, and 47% reported "marked" or "moderate" impairment of their performance skills as a result of anxiety. Similarly high prevalence levels are reported by several other studies (e.g., Fishbein, Middlestadt, Ottati, Strauss, & Ellis, 1988; Liden & Gottfries, 1974; Marchant-Haycox & Wilson, 1992; Steptoe & Fidler, 1987; van Kemenade, van Son, & van Heesch, 1995).

Clearly, with symptoms such as those just outlined, musicians' level of physiological arousal might well be a crucial concept in explaining the effect of stage fright on performance. It is widely acknowledged that there is an inverted-U relationship between arousal and performance on a range of tasks, such that performance is worse under conditions of either very low or very high arousal (i.e., extreme boredom or nervousness). Wilson (1997) integrates much of this evidence in arguing that three factors should be taken into account when applying this inverted-U theory to a given individual performance, namely, a performer's trait anxiety: Some people have higher baseline arousal than others, predisposing them toward performance anxiety; task mastery: Arousal/anxiety will be lower when the performer knows his/her piece well, mitigating against performance anxiety; and prevailing situational stress: People experience more arousal/anxiety when their performance is to be evaluated (Abel & Larkin, 1990; Brotons, 1994). We might add a fourth factor, namely, those life stress factors that musicians bring with them to any performance, such as work overload or underload or negative interpersonal relationships (e.g., Cooper & Wills, 1989; Steptoe, 1989; Wills & Cooper, 1988).

These factors interact in determining the performer's level of arousal: For example, performers prone to anxiety should deliberately attempt to relax before examinations. These considerations may be more important than first seems, since Hardy and Parfitt's (1991) catastrophe theory says that once performers' arousal becomes superoptimal, the decline in performance is rapid rather than gradual, as implied by the inverted U: In effect, performers may simply panic, and any degree of superoptimal arousal may prove catastrophic.

Treatments of stage fright, unsurprisingly, operate by reducing anxiety. Popular drugs such as alcohol and cannabis have anxiety-reducing properties and induce mild euphoria as well. The latter effect is both a blessing and a curse, since musicians feels better about their performance but also as a result of this are disposed to take the drug again, potentially leading to dependence. Behavior therapy treats performance anxiety as a social phobia: It aims, for example, to gradually desensitize the performer to the arousal-inducing properties of performance. Other behavioral therapies aim to reduce the incidence of self-destructive thoughts produced by the musician; and Clark and Agras (1991) found that such techniques may be more effective than drug-based approaches. The Alexander Technique (Valentine, Fitzgerald, Gorton, Hudson, & Symonds, 1995) and hypnotherapy (Stanton, 1994) may also alleviate performance anxiety.

Social Processes During Performance

Davidson (1997) noted her surprise that the social psychology of music performance has been neglected when there has been so much social psychological research on listening. Her basic argument is simple yet powerful, pointing out that sociocultural rules dictate and give value to musical performance such that there is constant interaction within and between the audience and the performers. Four of Davidson's examples illustrate the point.

First, historical factors exert a strong influence on contemporary performance. In 1782 the Italian violin teacher Viotti moved to Paris and began a dynasty in which great teachers taught pupils who became great teachers themselves (e.g., Baillot, Alard, and Sarasate). In effect, Viotti's ideas on performance were passed down through several generations of violinists. Second, concert etiquette is also subject to strong sociocultural norms. For example, while it is permissible to wave banners and sing along at a rock concert, such behavior at a classical concert might result in ejection. However, this would not be the case if you were attending the *Last Night of the Proms,* a famous annual British concert involving patriotic singing and clapping, in which people would think it strange if you did *not* respond similarly to the works of Elgar. Third, orchestras, rock bands, and the like are groups of individuals, and the ability to produce good music may depend on group processes. Murningham and Conlon (1991) showed that successful string quartets had directive but democratic leaders and were able to recognize and resolve differences of opinion using previously agreed-on procedures (see also, e.g., Atik, 1994; Faulkner, 1973). Finally, performers' nonverbal signals indicate their musical intentions to both colleagues and audience members. Clayton (1985) found that the timing and dynamics of groups of musicians were less coordinated when the performers could not see one another: similarly, Davidson (1995) found that nonmusician listeners may rely almost entirely on visual information from the performer in judging his or her expressive intentions (e.g., to play in an exaggerated, understated, or normal manner).

It is possible to speculate on many other such effects that might influence musical performances and audience members' interpretations of these. This is an area in which research potential far outweighs the amount of empirical work that has been carried out, and we look forward to more research in this field. For example, it may be that performers' clothing, age, or ethnic background may be a cue employed by pop music listeners in classifying the precise genre of particular songs: the distinction between punk and heavy metal may have as much to do with the length of the performers' hair as with the characteristics of the music itself. Similarly, North and Hargreaves (1997a) found that performers' physical attractiveness could influence listeners' responses to both performers and their music.

Prestige, Conformity, and Intergroup Effects: The Sociopositional Level

We now consider another of Doise's hierarchy of levels of influence to address sociopositional effects on musical behavior: As noted in the introduction, these consider musical behavior in terms of an individual's membership of different social groups. A number of experimental studies have indicated generally that music is evaluated more positively if it is of a higher level of prestige than other music or if it is valued positively by significant others such that the individual feels pressured to conform in his or her own judgment. These studies have been reviewed extensively elsewhere (Hargreaves, 1986; see Rigg, 1948, for one particular example).

Why should such effects occur, however? The notion of taste publics and the potential demographic basis of musical taste have been the subject of considerable investigation and speculation from sociologists (see Russell, 1997). Researchers within this tradition would argue that certain social groups favor certain musical styles (and other leisure options) because of factors such as their sex, income, and so on. However, theories derived from experimental social psychology might also be able to explain why particular groups of people are attracted to particular musical styles.

This social psychological research has targeted adolescents because of their high involvement with music (see Zillmann & Gan, 1997). One of the principal conclusions of the research has been that adolescents' statements about musical preference convey much more to others than information about music alone. Rather, they activate stereotypical perceptions of people's qualities, including the degree to which they are considered attractive, sophisticated, intelligent, or fun (North & Hargreaves, 1999a; Zillmann & Bhatia, 1989). It is significant that adolescents report taking particular account of others' musical interest in their decisions concerning friendship formation (Tarrant, 1999). As with similarities in other important domains (e.g., Argyle & Henderson, 1985; Byrne, 1971; Eiser, Morgan, Gammage, Brooks, & Kirby, 1991), sharing similar musical interests may be a crucial factor affecting the decision whether or not to become someone's friend: A friend with very different musical interests may not be a very useful reference point for the validation of one's own musical preferences (see van Wel, 1994).

Statements about music are therefore important because they enable adolescents to convey to others the appropriateness of their own values. By affiliating with certain musical styles, adolescents might be able to form positive self-evaluations, particularly if this affiliation is approved by peers (see Brown & O'Leary, 1971). Through this process, adolescents might also be able to enhance their self-image. For example, Tarrant (1999) asked participants to compare their own musical preference with that of their reference groups. Participants chose to associate themselves to a greater extent than their reference groups with positively valued music and associated themselves to a lesser extent than their reference groups with negatively valued music: This suggests that musical preference is one means by which adolescents attempt to make positive social comparisons between themselves and others in their social network. Participants also reported a *degree* of correspondence between their own and others' preferences, indicating that the desire to enhance the self does not necessarily depend on the devaluation of the comparison other: This is consistent with the nonmusical literature on social comparisons (e.g., Affleck & Tennen, 1991; Codol, 1975; Dunning, Meyerowitz, & Holsberg, 1989).

Predictions derived from social identity theory (SIT) (Tajfel, 1978; Tajfel & Turner, 1986; Turner, 1975) also might explain intergroup factors in people's musical behavior; SIT begins from the assumption that a substantial portion of an individual's self-concept is defined in terms of group memberships. Categorization of the self as a member of a particular group, the ingroup, automatically excludes a certain number of other people, the outgroup. As soon as such a categorization becomes salient, group members act in terms of it and seek to distinguish the ingroup from the outgroup by engaging in intergroup discrimination. The extent of this discrimination is hypothetically mediated by self-esteem: Depleted or threatened self-esteem motivates increased discrimination, and successful discrimination enhances or restores self-esteem (Abrams & Hogg, 1988).

The basic consequences of social categorization are well documented. In a series of laboratory studies Tajfel and his colleagues (e.g., Billig & Tajfel, 1973; Tajfel, Flament, Billig, & Bundy, 1971) showed that participants' allocation of monetary rewards to the ingroup and the outgroup followed a clear differentiation strategy: Rather than allocating the maximum possible amount of money to the ingroup (irrespective of the outgroup allocation), participants consistently chose to assign the greatest amount of money to the ingroup while *at the same time* assigning the *least* amount of money to the outgroup. The act of merely categorizing people into groups (no matter how arbitrarily these are defined) was sufficient to initiate this process.

Similar results have also been found in preexisting social groups when using comparative dimensions other than monetary allocation. Hunter, Platow, Howard, and Stringer (1996) investigated adolescents from Catholic and Protestant schools in Northern Ireland: Participants employed ingroup-favoring biases when asked to evaluate other pupils from their own school (ingroup) and pupils attending a school of the other religious denomination (outgroup). Perhaps more interesting, these evaluations also led to increases in participants' self-esteem (see also Hunter, Brien, & Grocott, 1999). Similarly, Branscombe and Wann (1994) demonstrated that participants who were highly identified with their national group (American) and whose self-esteem had been lowered through a threat to this identity showed increased derogation of a Russian outgroup compared to those participants who were not highly identified with their national group. As in Hunter, Platow, Howard, & Stringer's (1996) study, the participants also exhibited increased self-esteem following the intergroup task.

It seems intuitively plausible that social identity might also mediate musical behavior, although empirical research is lacking. The consequences of musical affiliation may be particularly marked in (although need not necessarily be restricted to) adolescence. As has been noted elsewhere (e.g., Zillmann & Gan, 1997), adolescents go to great lengths to demonstrate their affiliation with particular subcultures through, for example, specific clothing and hairstyles. Such behavior undoubtedly serves as a badge of identification with a perceived musical "elite" and facilitates intergroup differentiation (Larson, 1995; see also Cohen, 1972; Frith, 1983).

A recent series of studies directly explored the relationship between musical preference and social identity in adolescence. In one study (Tarrant, 1999), participants were categorized randomly into one of two groups on the basis of a supposed preference for paintings. Following this, they were required to estimate the preferences of the ingroup and outgroup for excerpts of *rock and pop* and *classical* music. It was expected that the ingroup would be associated to a greater extent than the outgroup with rock and pop music and to a lesser extent than the outgroup with classical music. The study failed to reproduce the effects of categorization that had been so convincingly demonstrated by Tajfel et al. (1971). However, when the study was repeated in a more naturalistic context, using preexisting social groups and styles of music nominated by adolescents themselves, the effects of social categorization were clear (Tarrant, Hargreaves, & North, 2001). The participants reported significant differences between the ingroup and outgroup for several styles of music. Dance, indie, and pop music had been categorized in a pilot study as "liked music," and fans of such music had been associated with positive characteristics (e.g., being popular). Accordingly, the ingroup was perceived to like these styles *more* than the outgroup. In contrast, classical and jazz music were categorized in the pilot study as "disliked music," and their fans were associated with negative characteristics (e.g., being boring). The ingroup was perceived to like these styles of music *less* than the outgroup.

By responding as they did, it is likely that the adolescents were by implication also associating the ingroup with the positive characteristics of fans of liked music to a greater extent than they were the outgroup. At the same time they can be seen as associating the ingroup with the negative characteristics of disliked music to a lesser extent than they were the outgroup. Importantly, the participants' discriminatory behavior was related to their self-esteem: Lower self-esteem was associated with subsequent increased intergroup differentiation and outgroup derogation along the musical preference measures. More generally, this study highlights that such categorization effects perhaps only occur when people are presented with musical categories that are relevant to their identity (see Hunter et al., 1996; Turner, 1975). It also makes clear the crucial role that social identity and group affiliation play in adolescents' daily interactions (see Gavin & Furman, 1989; Heaven, 1994), illustrating how music might contribute to this process.

Research along these lines can also explain the importance attached by particular ethnic and minority groups to their musical culture. For example, the city of Leicester in England (where two of us work) has a community of Indian/Pakistani ethnic origin that comprises over 25% of the total city population. This community is served by a proliferation of specialist radio stations (e.g., Sabras), cinemas, and music festivals and even a local free-access terrestrial television channel (MATV), the latter being extremely rare, if not unique, in Britain's heavily regulated television industry. A similar situation has arisen in other areas (e.g., Miami, in the United States, with its large Cuban community; Quebec in Canada, with its large French-speaking community), and it seems clear that the maintenance of group identity may explain why. This is a clear candidate for future research within SIT.

Cultural Influences: The Ideological Level

Musical Fashions

From considering social psychological influences on music in a particular place and time, we now move to another of Doise's levels to consider broader cultural (or what Doise called "ideological") influences. In this section we consider how musical taste evolves over time. While some

of these studies have employed human participants, others have used very different methodologies, such as computerized analyses of archival data sources, such as music encyclopedias.

Farnsworth's (1969) research on fashions in classical music is deservedly well known in the United Kingdom and North America. He used a variety of archival information sources (e.g. contents of orchestral programs, radio programs, and reference books) in conjunction with people's rankings of the composers. For example, one study looked at the frequencies with which 92 composers were listed in the programs of the Boston Symphony Orchestra over each of the 5 decades from 1915 to 1965. The most striking finding was the degree of similarity between the top names on these five lists: Beethoven, Brahms, Mozart, and Wagner figured most prominently. This accords with Mueller and Hevner's (1942) analysis of the programs of seven leading U.S. orchestras over the period 1936–41. Similar consistency was found in Farnsworth's analysis of the "serious music" programs broadcast by the Pacific Gas and Electric Company over the period 1941–43.

Farnsworth's data also provides direct evidence of variation in composers' eminence over time. Table 33.2 shows the mean rankings of composers elicited by Farnsworth from musicologists in 1938, 1944, 1951, and 1964. Although the general pattern is one of consistency and stability, slow changes nevertheless do occur. Palestrina's positions were 5, 6.5, 10, and 12, for example, while those of Haydn were 6, 5, 4, and 4. If we look at the positions of Brahms in the table, we can discern something like an inverted-U curve, which peaks in 1951, and a similar pattern holds for Schubert, a few places lower. Farnsworth's calculation of the correlations between these sets of rankings shows that there are indeed significant changes in ranking patterns over time. The 1964 rankings correlate 0.95 with the 1951 rankings, but only 0.78 with the 1938 rankings, for example. Similarly, Mueller and Hevner's (1942) analysis of concert programs from several American orchestras between 1876 and 1941 showed that the resemblances between programs were greatest in contiguous decades. The correlation between the decades starting in 1915 and 1925 (1915/1925) was 0.98, for example, whereas the equivalent figures for 1915/1935, 1915/1945, and 1915/1955 were 0.90, 0.90, and 0.89. In short, the "great" composers are always regarded as such, but the extent of this varies over time.

More recently, Simonton (see, e.g., 1984, 1994, 1997) has used computerized content analysis techniques in order to code large numbers of themes from the classical repertoire. For example, Simonton (1980) employed a database of 15,618 themes by 479 classical composers. For all practical purposes, this could be taken as the entire thematic repertoire of classical music, and the advantages of this over conventional experimental approaches, which are

Table 33.2 Eminence Rankings by Musicologists in Four Different Years

Rank	1938	Rank	1944	Rank	1951	Rank	1964
1	Bach	1	Bach	1	Beethoven	1	Bach
2	Beethoven	2	Beethoven	2	Bach	2	Beethoven
3	Wagner	3	Mozart	3	Brahms	3	Mozart
4	Mozart	4	Wagner	4	Haydn	4	Haydn
5	Palestrina	5	Haydn	5	Mozart	5	Brahms
6	Haydn	6.5	Brahms	6.5	Schubert	6	Handel
7	Brahms	6.5	Palestrina	6.5	Debussy	7	Debussy
8	Monteverdi	8	Schubert	8	Handel	8	Schubert
9	Debussy	9	Handel	9	Wagner	9	Wagner
10	Schubert	10	Debussy	10	Palestrina	10	Chopin
11	Handel	11	Chopin	11	Chopin	11	Monteverdi
12	Chopin	25	Monteverdi	15	Monteverdi	12	Palestrina

Adapted from Farnsworth, 1969.

based on samples of themes, are obvious. The "esthetic" qualities of the themes were assessed according to two variables, namely, "thematic fame" (rated on the basis of music appreciation textbooks, record-buying guides, thematic dictionaries, etc.) and "repertoire melodic originality," which was defined as the uncommonness, or statistical infrequency, of the first five two-note transitions in a theme, relative to the entire repertoire. Simonton found that the most famous themes over time were those of intermediate repertoire melodic originality. There was also a general increase in repertoire melodic originality over time, with cycles superimposed over this broad tendency.

An explanation for the results of both Simonton and Farnsworth might lie in Martindale's notion of the *Clockwork Muse* (1990). This argues that at any one time, melodies of *intermediate* arousal-evoking properties are preferred (see also Berlyne, 1971). This is because moderately arousing melodies are processed more efficiently, leading to the activation of pleasure responses from the brain. This can explain Simonton's finding that the most famous themes at the time of his research were those of *intermediate* repertoire melodic originality. Martindale goes on to argue that over time, melodies have to become increasingly arousing in order to maintain listeners' attention. This accounts for the general increase in originality over time found by Simonton.

However, melodies become arousing through properties such as their volume or tempo (see, e.g., Berlyne, 1971); they can only become, for example, so fast or loud, before they cease to be recognizable as "music" or cause hearing impairment! Therefore, from time to time composers make their work arousing by developing a new style. The music composed within this style need not be particular (e.g.) loud or fast, because the novelty of the style is itself arousing. However, over time the impact of the style itself lessens, and composers again need to produce work that is

(e.g.) louder and faster to maintain listeners' attention. Eventually, this again leads to composers employing a new style. This process of stylistic revolutions can account for the cycles in originality described by Simonton: Melodic originality is low when a new style has recently been introduced and increases as the style itself becomes less novel. This process also bears marked similarities with the preference-feedback hypothesis proposed by Sluckin, Hargreaves, and Colman (1982, 1983; North & Hargreaves, 1997c).

Would the same principles apply for pop music, the popularity of which is heavily influenced by record companies and radio stations (see, e.g., Rothenbuhler & McCourt, 1992)? Some studies indicate that the pop music charts are subject to regularities and rules (see, e.g., Dixon, 1982; North & Hargreaves, 1995) and that record buying can be predicted to a certain extent (Lacher & Mizerski, 1994; Meenaghan & Turnbull, 1981). However, there is a real lack of research, and findings are far from clear-cut.

The Ethnomusicological Perspective

We move now to the broadest level on which social psychological influences can be investigated. Psychologists and researchers within other disciplines often fall into the trap of cultural specificity: to forget that their findings were elicited at a particular point in history and from within a particular culture. It is thus often sobering to consider any set of findings within the context of ethnomusicology (see Blumenfeld, 1993; May, 1980; Merriam, 1964; Nettl, 1980) that investigates the music of different societies. As Gregory (1997) points out, ethnomusicology is a hybrid such that at one extreme are musicologists whose interests lie in the structure of the music and the instruments while at the other extreme are anthropologists whose primary concern is with the roles music plays in culture.

That music cannot be researched as something belonging exclusively to the modern Western world is indicated most dramatically by Hodges and Haack's (1996) time line of artistic behaviors. For example, bows have been found dating from 70,000 years ago that are thought to have been as much musical instruments as weapons. Ceremonies may have been accompanied by music up to 60,000 years ago, and music of artistic significance was probably being produced about 30,000 years ago. Furthermore, the evidence for findings such as these comes from all around the world (e.g., France, Russia, the United States, Egypt, Tanzania, China, etc.).

Rather than attempting any kind of comprehensive review, we offer instead a few simple examples of the functions of music in other societies and draw two general conclusions. First, they indicate that musical behavior is clearly rooted in particular cultures, with respect to both listening and "performing." Second, following from this, conventional laboratory studies as carried out by music psychologists are *extremely* limited in their ability to explain such phenomena. It is debatable whether an ethnomusicologist would ever approve of experimental research on music, but from a psychological viewpoint there is a clear case for investigating whether cross-cultural differences might exist regarding the particular phenomenon in question (see, e.g., Arom, Léothaud, & Voisin, 1997). Such studies may highlight the extent to which findings are culture bound, possibly even to the extent that the research topic itself is only of interest in the Western world.

Merriam (1964) stresses that ethnomusicology is an approach to all types of music and not just non-Western varieties. Nevertheless, since the majority of this chapter has concerned the functions of music in the industrialized world, we concentrate here on the functions of music in other cultures. These have been reviewed recently by Gregory (1997), who identified 16 basic functions of music that are found in many different cultures. These are:

1. Lullabies. These are found in virtually all cultures and share similar musical properties, for example, smooth descending contours, repetition, and a slow tempo.
2. Games. Songs are related to skipping, dancing, or other rhythmic activity that may be part of preparation for adult life.
3. Work music. Music is still used to these ends in some traditional African societies. For example, while cutting grass, the Frafra people of Ghana swing their cutlasses in time with accompaniment provided by musicians (Nkeita, 1988).
4. Dancing. Dancing to music is found in almost all cultures, and the associations between the two is often complex.
5. Storytelling. The medieval wandering minstrel has parallels in several cultures, particularly in southwest

Asia. Similarly, West African griots sing stories about the past and present, often spreading gossip and slander. Independent griots will sing in praise of people who pay them and slander those who refuse.

6. Ceremonies and festivals. Music is fundamental to marriage, initiation, and funerals in most cultures. However, the qualities of the music used in these ceremonies varies enormously. For example, some types of Javanese funeral music could sound uplifting to Western listeners.
7. Battle. Music was used for inspiration and communication by the armies of Egypt, Greece, and Rome, and the Ottoman and British empires.
8. Communication. Some languages (e.g., in central Africa) feature pitch, intensity, and duration differences for different syllables, and the specific values of these vary depending on those for neighboring syllables (Bebey, 1975). In effect, music cannot always be distinguished from speech.
9. Personal symbol. The Saami people of Scandinavia each have their own personal song, which is given to them by parents or lovers. This effectively becomes a personal acoustic symbol.
10. Ethnic or group identity. Australian aborigines have songs that may only be sung by members of a particular clan or related clans. Similarly, Unionists and Republicans in Northern Ireland have quite distinct songs that convey political affiliation.
11. Salesmanship. We described the effects of music on consumer behavior earlier, but the use of music by market stallholders to publicize their wares has a tradition stretching from the East End of London to Africa.
12. Healing. Music therapy is practiced in a range of cultures. Harp-lute players of West Africa act as healers or soothsayers. Some forms of music in Mali are believed to have a sacred healing role for both the individual and society by facilitating communication with the spirits and the Creator. The Navaho of North America use music for a similar function, believing the power will weaken if it is used too frequently.
13. Trance. Music is used to induce trance states during special ceremonies. This can be found in, for example, the Americas, Mali, Bali, Siberia, South Africa, and Sumatra. Rouget (1985) distinguishes different types of trance relating to voluntary shamanism and involuntary possession, with different uses of music for each.
14. Personal enjoyment. Music serves this function in many cultures, often as part of community social events.
15. Court music. This is developed specifically for the ruling class: Commoners may have only a vague awareness of its existence. Examples of countries where this has been the case include Japan, China, India, and many Islamic countries.
16. Religious music. Music has been used as a means of attracting people to and teaching them about particu-

lar religions (e.g., the Jesuit conversion of Brazil). Some religious communities have maintained the same musical tradition for several hundred years (e.g., the chanting of Tibetan monks).

Of course, any classification of this type is partly arbitrary. Different classifications abound (e.g., Hodges & Haack, 1996), although they all necessarily overlap in many ways. Ultimately, of course, music has as many different functions as there are listeners and musicians: Virtually all musical behavior is related to the culture in which it takes place.

A New Agenda for Research

There can be little doubt from our review that many diverse social and cultural factors influence the musical learning and development of individuals and that many of these occur outside formal music education. The implication, as we pointed out earlier, is that the agenda for research in music education as well as music psychology needs to be drawn much more widely. We conclude by outlining five broad issues that should form part of the new agenda.

Recognizing the Interdisciplinary Context

Most music psychologists regard themselves as social scientists, and as such use empirical methods (whether quantitative, qualitative, or both) in order to obtain evidence, which they use in developing rational explanations of musical behavior. Two issues immediately arise: that musical activities are inherently *social* and that scientific methods are being used in the explanation of artistic behavior. These considerations mean that research must necessarily be interdisciplinary in nature. In order to provide accurate and ecologically appropriate descriptions and explanations of the events in question researchers must draw on the theories and perspectives of other social science and humanities disciplines, such as anthropology, sociology, and ethnomusicology, as well as music itself.

Musical behavior does not occur under "sterile" laboratory conditions, divorced from the external social world, and researchers need to adopt different aims, objectives, and methodologies from the different disciplines on which they draw. The task of music education researchers is to apply the insights that are gained from these interdisciplinary endeavors to the real-life problems facing pupils, teachers, and other professionals involved in the teaching and learning of music. This necessarily involves even wider interdisciplinary thinking within education in tackling issues such as curriculum design, pupil assessment, multicultural education, or classroom management.

Implications of the Democratization of Music

The definition of music itself raises various philosophical, cultural, and even political questions; we have already seen that music can serve many different functions, such as maintaining one's position in the social world, establishing a personal identity, or serving as the backdrop to various other activities. What qualifies as "music," and the reasons for listening to it, varies from context to context and from person to person, and our social psychological approach implies that all musical forms are equally worthy of consideration. As one of us wrote some years ago, "music psychology [and education] must consider its subject-matter in all its forms, 'classical' or 'popular,' ethnic or Western, old or new, good or bad, if it is to possess scientific validity" (Hargreaves, 1986, p. 29). Judgments of the quality or "seriousness" of particular pieces, composers, or styles can only be made according to the aesthetic standards appropriate to the particular sociocultural context in which that music is experienced (see Frith, 1996; Walker, 1996).

These issues have immediate practical implications in the promotion of multicultural music education. To understand how and why an American child listens to classical music may tell us almost nothing about how and why an Estonian child listens to runic melodies, or indeed Western pop music, and music teachers must bear their pupils' backgrounds and cultural expectations in mind when introducing world musics in the classroom.

Research and Practice Should Be Theory Driven

The indispensability of theory in determining successful practice, as well as in guiding research, has been argued before (e.g., Swanwick, 1977; Hargreaves, 1986). Recognizing the importance of social psychological factors in musical behavior requires us to make three more specific points, however. First, as noted earlier, a social psychological approach sometimes reveals that theories are situation specific. Second, if research is to draw on social psychological factors, it is unnecessary to "reinvent the wheel" by attempting to determine from scratch the processes by which sociocultural factors mediate musical behavior. A body of mainstream social psychological theory already exists, and research on music in intergroup contexts is already drawing on this. Finally, it is important to recognize that sociocultural factors influence the type of theories that researchers produce. There is a clear contrast between the "top-down" macroscopic theories adopted by many East European music psychologists, for example, and the more "bottom-up" microscopic approaches favored by those working within the Anglo-American tradition (see, e.g., Manturszewska, Miklaszewski, & Biatkowski, 1995).

Recognizing the Interdependence of Theory and Practice

Theories and research evidence are of questionable utility unless they ultimately lead to some change in practice. Music educators, along with practitioners in areas such as marketing, broadcasting, and therapy, need theories in order to make sense of the problems they face in working life. If this is to occur, researchers must explain how their findings can be applied to everyday situations. In short, we need an applied psychology of music that devises theories and then explains their relevance to music practitioners. Although this issue and the possible ways around it have been debated for decades in music education, our own recent international review reveals that disappointingly little progress has been made (Hargreaves & North, in press). Although the study of musical learning and development has made some important strides forward in recent years, there is depressingly little evidence of its impact on practical decision-making in music education the world over.

Increasing the Diversity of Research Methodology

Most research in music psychology has employed a quantitative approach, and this has obvious limitations in explaining musical behavior, which is embedded in complex cultural and educational contexts. Qualitative research may well make a valuable contribution (see, e.g., Richardson, 1996) since music psychology has a great deal to gain by investigating the "real world" of music in a manner that reflects people's conscious experience of it (Persson & Robson, 1995). Music education research needs not only to draw on the wide variety of quantitative and qualitative techniques that are available to psychologists but also to draw on action research, participant observation, and other techniques that are more widely employed in other disciplines.

In conclusion, musical behavior and experience are intrinsically social phenomena, and musical learning and teaching need to be viewed as such. Music education, in the broad sense in which we have defined it here, interacts with the extramusical world on a variety of different levels: It reflects the intrapersonal, interpersonal, immediate situational, and cultural and historical contexts in which music is experienced and produced. Explaining the interaction between music and the social world has far-reaching implications for theory, practice, and research methodology in music psychology and music education; five aspects of this have been outlined here and constitute our "new agenda" for research. This agenda is necessarily quite general in nature; the rapid changes that are taking place in society, technology, and everyday musical experience mean that future research must put it into practice at a more detailed level.

REFERENCES

Abel, J. L., & Larkin, K. T. (1990). Anticipation of performance among musicians: Physiological arousal, confidence, and state anxiety. *Psychology of Music, 18,* 171–182.

Abrams, D., & Hogg, M. A. (1988). Comments on the motivational status of self-esteem in social identity and intergroup discrimination. *European Journal of Social Psychology, 18,* 317–334.

Affleck, G., & Tennen, H. (1991). Social comparison and coping with major medical problems. In J. Suls & T. A. Wills (Eds.), *Social comparison: Contemporary theory and research.* Hillsdale, NJ: Erlbaum.

Allen, C. T., & Madden, T. J. (1985). A closer look at classical conditioning. *Journal of Consumer Research, 12,* 301–315.

Alpert, J. I., & Alpert, M. I. (1989). Background music as an influence in consumer mood and advertising responses. *Advances in Consumer Research, 16,* 485–491.

Ammon, K. (1968). *The effects of music on respiratory distress.* American Nurses Association Clinical Session.

Areni, C. S., & Kim, D. (1993). The influence of background music on shopping behavior: Classical versus top-forty music in a wine store. *Advances in Consumer Research, 20,* 336–340.

Argyle, M., & Henderson, M. (1985). *The anatomy of relationships: And the rules and skills needed to manage them successfully.* London: Heinemann.

Arnheim, R. (1952). Agenda for the psychology of art. *Journal of Aesthetics and Art Criticism, 10,* 310–314.

Arom, S., Léothaud, G., & Voisin, F. (1997). Experimental ethnomusicology: An interactive approach to the study of musical scales. In I. Deliège & J. Sloboda (Eds.), *Perception and cognition of music.* Hove, England: Psychology Press.

Atik, Y. (1994). The conductor and the orchestra: Interactive aspects of the leadership process. *Leadership and Organization Development Journal, 13,* 22–28.

Ballard, M. E., & Coates, S. (1995). The immediate effect of homicidal, suicidal, and nonviolent heavy metal and rap songs on the moods of college students. *Youth and Society, 27,* 148–168.

Bandura, A. (1977). *Social learning theory.* Englewood Cliffs, NJ: Prentice-Hall.

Bartlett, D., Kaufman, D., & Smeltekop, R. (1993). The effects of music listening and perceived sensory experiences on the immune system as measured by interleukin-1 and cortisol. *Journal of Music Therapy, 30,* 194–209.

Baxter, R. L., de Riemer, C., Landini, A., & Leslie, L. (1985). A content analysis of music videos. *Journal of Broadcasting and Electronic Media, 29,* 333–340.

Bebey, F. (1975). *African music: A people's art.* Westport, CA: Lawrence Hill.

Berlyne, D. E. (1971). *Aesthetics and psychobiology.* New York: Appleton-Century-Crofts.

Bierley, C., McSweeney, F. K., & Vannieuwkerk, R. (1985). Classical conditioning of preferences for stimuli. *Journal of Consumer Research, 12*, 316–323.

Billig, M., & Tajfel, H. (1973). Social categorization and similarity of intergroup behaviour. *European Journal of Social Psychology, 3*, 27–52.

Bleich, S., Zillmann, D., & Weaver, J. B. (1991). Enjoyment and consumption of defiant rock music as a function of adolescent rebelliousness. *Journal of Electronic and Broadcasting Media, 35*, 351–366.

Blumenfeld, L. (1993). *Voices of forgotten worlds: Traditional music of indigenous people.* Roslyn, NY: Ellipsis Arts.

Bob, S. R. (1962). Audioanalgesia in paediatric practice: A preliminary study. *Journal of the American Podiatry Association, 52*, 503–504.

Bonny, H. L. (1983). Music listening for intensive coronary care units: A pilot project. *Music Therapy, 3*, 4–16.

Branscombe, N. R., & Wann, D. L. (1994). Collective self-esteem consequences of outgroup derogation when a valued social identity is on trial. *European Journal of Social Psychology, 24*, 641–657.

Brotons, M. (1994). Effect of performing conditions on music performance, anxiety, and performance quality. *Journal of Music Therapy, 31*, 63–81.

Brown, R. L., & O'Leary, M. (1971). Pop music in an English secondary school system. *American Behavioral Scientists, 14*, 400–413.

Budzynski, T., Soyva, J., & Adler, C. (1970). Feedback-induced muscle relaxation: Application to tension headache. *Behaviour Therapy and Experimental Psychiatry, 1*, 205–211.

Bunt, L. (1997). Clinical and therapeutic uses of music. In D. J. Hargreaves & A. C. North (Eds.), *The social psychology of music* (pp. 249–267). Oxford: Oxford University Press.

Byrne, D. (1971). *The attraction paradigm.* New York: Academic Press.

Chabris, C. F., Steele, K. M., Bella, S. D., Peretz, I., Dunlop, T., Dawe, L., Humphrey, G., Shannon, R., Kirby, J., Olmstead, C., & Rauscher, F. (1999). Prelude or requiem for the "Mozart effect"? *Nature, 400*, 826–828.

Charnetski, C., Brennan, F. X., & Harrison, J. F. (1997). *The effect of music on secretory immunoglobulin A (IgA).* Paper presented at the Eastern Psychological Association Convention.

Chetta, H. D. (1981). The effect of music and desensitization on pre-operative anxiety in children. *Journal of Music Therapy, 18*, 74–87.

Clark, D. B., & Agras, W. S. (1991). The assessment and treatment of performance anxiety in musicians. *American Journal of Psychiatry, 148*, 598–605.

Clayton, A. M. H. (1985). *Coordination between players in musical performance.* Unpublished doctoral dissertation, University of Edinburgh.

Codol, J.-P. (1975). On the so-called "superior conformity of the self" behavior: Twenty experimental investigations. *European Journal of Social Psychology, 5*, 457–501.

Confranesco, E. M. (1985). The effect of music therapy on hand grasp strength and functional task performance in stroke patients. *Journal of Music Therapy, 22*, 125–149.

Cohen, S. (1972). *Folk devils and moral panics: The creation of the Mods and Rockers.* London: MacGibbon and Kee.

Cooper, C., & Wills, G. I. (1989). Popular musicians under pressure. *Psychology of Music, 17*, 22–36.

Curtis, S. L. (1986). The effect of music on pain relief and relaxation of the terminally ill. *Journal of Music Therapy, 23*, 10–24.

Davidson, J. W. (1995). What does the visual information contained in music performances offer the observer? Some preliminary thoughts. In R. Steinberg (Ed.), *The music machine: Psychophysiology and psychopathology of the sense of music.* Berlin: Springer Verlag.

Davidson, J. W. (1997). The social in musical performance. In D. J. Hargreaves & A. C. North (Eds.), *The social psychology of music.* Oxford: Oxford University Press.

Denisoff, R. S. (1985). Music videos and the rock press. *Popular Music and Society, 10*, 59–61.

Dixon, R. D. (1982). LP chart careers: Indices and predictors of ascent and descent in popularity. *Popular Music and Society, 8*, 19–43.

Doise, W. (1986). *Levels of explanation in social psychology.* Cambridge, England: Cambridge University Press.

Dunning, D., Meyerowitz, J. A., & Holzberg, A. D. (1989). Ambiguity and self-evaluation: the role of idiosyncratic trait definitions in self-serving assessments of ability. *Journal of Personality and Social Psychology, 57*, 1082–1090.

Eiser, J. R., Morgan, M., Gammage, P., Brooks, N., & Kirby, R. (1991). Adolescent health behaviour and similarity-attraction: Friends share smoking habits (really), but much else besides. *British Journal of Social Psychology, 30*, 339–348.

Farnsworth, P. R. (1969). *The social psychology of music* (2nd ed). Ames: Iowa State University Press.

Faulkner, R. R. (1973). Orchestra interaction: Some features of communication and authority in an artistic organization. *Sociological Quarterly, 14*, 147–157.

Fishbein, M., Middlestadt, S. E., Ottati, V., Strauss, S., & Ellis, A. (1988). Medical problems among ISCOM musicians: Overview of a national survey. *Medical Problems of Performing Artists, 3*, 1–8.

Frank, J. (1985). The effects of music therapy and guided visual imagery on chemotherapy induced nausea and vomiting. *Oncology Nursing Forum, 12*, 47–52.

Frith, S. (1983). *Sound effects: Youth, leisure, and the politics of rock.* London: Constable.

Frith, S. (1996). *Performing rites.* Oxford: Oxford University Press.

Gavin, L. A., & Furman, W. (1989). Age differences in adolescents' perceptions of their peer groups. *Developmental Psychology, 25*, 827–834.

Gehr, R. (1983). The MTV aesthetic. *Film Comment, 19*, 37, 39, 40.

Gfeller, K., Logan, H., & Walker, J. (1988). The effect of auditory distraction and suggestion on tolerance for dental restorations in adolescents and young adults. *Journal of Music Therapy, 27*, 13–23.

Goloff, M. S. (1981). The responses of hospitalized medical patients to music therapy. *Music Therapy, 1*, 51–56.

Gorn, G. J. (1982). The effect of music in advertising on choice behavior: A classical conditioning approach. *Journal of Marketing, 46,* 94–101.

Greenfield, P. M., Bruzzone, L., Koyamatsu, K., & Satuloff, W. (1987). What is rock music doing to the minds of our youth? A first experimental look at the effects of rock music lyrics and music videos. *Journal of Early Adolescence, 7,* 315–329.

Greeson, L. E. (1991). Recognition and ratings of television music videos: Age, gender, and sociocultural effects. *Journal of Applied Social Psychology, 21,* 1908–1920.

Gregory, A. H. (1997). The roles of music in society: The ethnomusicological perspective. In D. J. Hargreaves & A. C. North (Eds.), *The social psychology of music* (pp. 123–140). Oxford: Oxford University Press.

Hansen, C. H. (1989). Priming sex-role stereotypic event schemas with rock music videos: Effects on impression favorability, trait inferences, and recall of a subsequent male-female interaction. *Basic and Applied Social Psychology, 10,* 371–391.

Hansen, C. H. (1995). Predicting cognitive and behavioral effects of gangsta rap. *Basic and Applied Social Psychology, 16,* 43–52.

Hansen, C. H., & Hansen, R. D. (1988). How rock music videos can change what is seen when boy meets girl: Priming stereotypic appraisal of social interactions. *Sex Roles, 19,* 287–316.

Hansen, C. H., & Hansen, R. D. (1990a). The influence of sex and violence on the appeal of rock music videos. *Communication Research, 17,* 212–234.

Hansen, C. H., & Hansen, R. D. (1990b). Rock music videos and antisocial behavior. *Basic and Applied Social Psychology, 11,* 357–369.

Hansen, C. H., & Hansen, R. D. (1991). Constructing personality and social reality through music: Individual differences among fans of punk and heavy metal music. *Journal of Broadcasting and Electronic Media, 35,* 335–350.

Hardy, L., & Parfitt, G. (1991). A catastrophe model of anxiety and performance. *British Journal of Psychology, 82,* 163–178.

Hargreaves, D. J. (1986). *The developmental psychology of music.* Cambridge, England: Cambridge University Press.

Hargreaves, D. J., & North, A. C. (Eds.). (1997). *The social psychology of music.* Oxford: Oxford University Press.

Hargreaves, D. J., & North, A. C. (Eds.). (2001a). *Musical development and learning: The international perspective.* London: Continuum.

Hargreaves, D. J., & North, A. C. (2001b). Conclusions: The international perspective. In D. J. Hargreaves & A. C. North (Eds.), *Musical development and learning: The international perspective* (pp. 220–234). London: Continuum.

Hargreaves, D. J., & North, A. C. (in press). *The developmental psychology of music* (2nd ed.). Cambridge, England: Cambridge University Press.

Heaven, P. C. L. (1994). *Contemporary adolescence: A social psychological approach.* Melbourne: Macmillan.

Hodges, D. A., & Haack, P. A. (1996). The influence of music on human behavior. In D. A. Hodges (Ed.), *Handbook of music psychology* (pp. 469–555). San Antonio, TX: IMR Press.

Hunter, J. A., O'Brien, K. S., & Grocott, A. C. (1999). Social identity, domain specific self-esteem and intergroup evaluation. *Current Research in Social Psychology, 4,* 160–177. (http://www.uiowa.edu/~grpproc)

Hunter, J. A., Platow, M. J., Howard, M. L., & Stringer, M. (1996). Social identity and intergroup evaluative bias: Realistic categories and domain specific self-esteem in a conflict setting. *European Journal of Social Psychology, 26,* 631–647.

Johnson, J. D., Adams, M. S., Ashburn, L., & Reed, W. (1995). Differential gender effects of exposure to rap music on African American adolescents' acceptance of teen dating violence. *Sex Roles, 33,* 597–605.

Johnson, J. D., Gatto, L., & Jackson, L. A. (1995). Violent attitudes and deferred academic aspirations: Deleterious effects of exposure to rap music. *Basic and Applied Social Psychology, 16,* 27–41.

Kellaris, J. J., & Cox, A. D. (1989). The effects of background music in advertising: A reassessment. *Journal of Consumer Research, 16,* 113–118.

Kellaris, J. J., Cox, A. D., & Cox, D. (1993). The effect of background music on ad processing: A contingency explanation. *Journal of Marketing, 57,* 114–125.

Kellaris, J. J., & Mantel, S. P. (1994). The influence of mood and gender on consumers' time perceptions. *Advances in Consumer Research, 21,* 514–518.

Kiger, D. M. (1989). Effects of music information load on a reading-comprehension task. *Perceptual and Motor Skills, 69,* 531–534.

Konecni, V. J. (1982). Social interaction and musical preference. In D. Deutsch (Ed.), *The psychology of music.* New York: Academic Press.

Konecni, V. J. (1984). Elusive effects of artists' "messages." In W. R. Crozier & A. J. Chapman (Eds.), *Cognitive processes in the perception of art* (pp. 71–93). Amsterdam: Elsevier.

Kubey, R., & Larson, R. (1990). The use and experience of the new video media among children and young adolescents. *Communication Research, 17,* 107–130.

Lacher, K. T., & Mizerski, R. (1994). An exploratory study of the responses and relationships involved in the evaluation of, and in the intention to purchase new rock music. *Journal of Consumer Research, 21,* 366–380.

Lanza, J. (1994). *Elevator music.* London: Quartet Books.

Larson, R., Kubey, R. W., & Coletti, J. (1989). Changing channels: Early adolescent media choices and shifting investments in family and friends. *Journal of Youth and Adolescence, 18,* 583–599.

Larson, R. W. (1995). Secrets in the bedroom: Adolescents' private use of media. *Journal of Youth and Adolescence, 24,* 535–550.

Levy, S. (1983, December). How MTV sells out rock and roll. *Rolling Stone, 30,* 33, 34, 37, 74, 76, 78, 79.

Liden, S., & Gottfries, C. (1974). Beta-blocking agents in the treatment of catecholamine-induced symptoms in musicians. *Lancet, 2,* 529.

Litman, R. E., & Farberow, N. L. (1994). Pop-rock music as

precipitating cause in youth suicide. *Journal of Forensic Sciences, 39,* 494–499.

Locsin, R. (1981). The effect of music on the pain of selected post-operative patients. *Journal of Advanced Nursing, 6,* 19–25.

MacInnis, D. J., & Park, C. W. (1991). The differential role of characteristics of music on high- and low-involvement consumers' processing of ads. *Journal of Consumer Research, 18,* 161–173.

Madsen, C. K. (1987). Background music: Competition for focus of attention. In C. Madsen & P. Prickett (Eds.), *Applications of research in music behavior* (pp. 315–325). Tuscaloosa: University of Alabama Press.

Maguire, E. R., & Snipes, J. B. (1994). Reassessing the link between country music and suicide. *Social Forces, 72,* 1239–1243.

Manturszewska, M., Miklaszewski, K., & Biatkowski, A. (Eds.). (1995). *Psychology of music today.* Warsaw, Poland: Fryderyk Chopin Academy of Music.

Marchant-Haycox, S. E., & Wilson, G. D. (1992). Personality and stress in performing artists. *Personality and Individual Differences, 13,* 1061–1068.

Martin, G., Clarke, M., & Pearce, C. (1993). Adolescent suicide: Music preference as an indicator of vulnerability. *Journal of the American Academy of Child and Adolescent Psychiatry, 32,* 530–535.

Martindale, C. (1990). *The clockwork muse: The predictability of artistic styles.* New York: Basic Books.

Mauk, G. W., Taylor, M. J., White, K. R., & Allen, T. S. (1994). Comments on Stack and Gundlach's "The effect of country music on suicide": An "achy breaky heart" may not kill you. *Social Forces, 72,* 1249–1255.

May, E. (Ed.). (1980). *Musics of many cultures.* Berkeley: University of California Press.

Mayfield, C., & Moss, S. (1989). Effect of music tempo on task performance. *Psychological Reports, 65,* 1283–1290.

McElrea, H., & Standing, L. (1992). Fast music causes fast drinking. *Perceptual and Motor Skills, 75,* 362.

McKenna, K. (1983, August). Videos—low in art, high in sex and sell. *Los Angeles Times Calendar,* 66.

Meenaghan, A., & Turnbull, P. W. (1981). The application of product life cycle theory to popular record marketing. *European Journal of Marketing, 15,* 1–50.

Merriam, A. P. (1964). *The anthropology of music.* Evanston, IL: Northwestern University Press.

Milliman, R. E. (1982). Using background music to affect the behavior of supermarket shoppers. *Journal of Marketing, 46,* 86–91.

Milliman, R. E. (1986). The influence of background music on the behavior of restaurant patrons. *Journal of Consumer Research, 13,* 286–289.

Monsey, H. L. (1960). Preliminary report of the clinical efficacy of audioanalgesia. *Journal of the California State Dental Association, 36,* 432–437.

Mueller, J. H., & Hevner, K. (1942). *Trends in musical taste.* Bloomington: Indiana University Press.

Muller, A., Horhold, M., Bosel, R., Kage, A. (1994). Einflusse aktiver Musiktherapie auf Stimmungen und Immunkom-

petenz psychosomatischer Patienten. *Psychologische Beitrage, 36,* 198–204.

Munro, T. (1963). The psychology of art: Past, present, and future. *Journal of Aesthetics and Art Criticism, 21,* 264–282.

Murningham, J. K., & Conlon, D. E. (1991, June). The dynamics of intense work groups: A study of British string quartets. *Administrative Science Quarterly,* 165–186.

Nettl, B. (1980). Ethnomusicology: Definitions, directions, and problems. In E. May (Ed.), *Musics of many cultures* (pp. 1–9). Berkeley: University of California Press.

Nkeita, J. H. K. (1988). *The music of Africa.* London: Gollancz.

North, A. C., & Hargreaves, D. J. (1995). Eminence in pop music. *Popular Music and Society, 19,* 41–66.

North, A. C., & Hargreaves, D. J. (1996). The effects of music on responses to a dining area. *Journal of Environmental Psychology, 16,* 55–64.

North, A. C., & Hargreaves, D. J. (1997a). The effect of physical attractiveness on responses to pop music performers and their music. *Empirical Studies of the Arts, 15,* 75–89.

North, A. C., & Hargreaves, D. J. (1997b). Experimental aesthetics in everyday life. In D. J. Hargreaves & A. C. North (Eds.), *The social psychology of music* (pp. 84–103). Oxford: Oxford University Press.

North, A. C., & Hargreaves, D. J. (1997c). Liking for musical styles. *Musicae Scientiae, 1,* 109–128.

North, A. C., & Hargreaves, D. J. (1997d). Music and consumer behavior. In D. J. Hargreaves & A. C. North (Eds.), *The social psychology of music* (pp. 268–289). Oxford: Oxford University Press.

North, A. C., & Hargreaves, D. J. (1998). The effects of music on atmosphere and purchase intentions in a cafeteria. *Journal of Applied Social Psychology, 28,* 2254–2273.

North, A. C., & Hargreaves, D. J. (1999a). Music and adolescent identity. *Music Education Research, 1,* 75–92.

North, A. C., & Hargreaves, D. J. (1999b). Music and driving game performance. *Scandinavian Journal of Psychology, 40,* 285–292.

North, A. C., Hargreaves, D. J., & Gillett, R. T. (2000). Pop music lyrics 1960–1998 and the sociocultural zeitgeist. Manuscript in preparation.

North, A. C., Hargreaves, D. J., & McKendrick, J. (1997). In-store music affects product choice. *Nature, 390,* 132.

North, A. C., Hargreaves, D. J., & McKendrick, J. (1999). Music and on-hold waiting time. *British Journal of Psychology, 90,* 161–164.

North, A. C., Hargreaves, D. J., & McKendrick, J. (in press). The effects of music on atmosphere and purchase intentions in a bank and a bar. *Journal of Applied Social Psychology.*

Olson, M., & Crase, D. (1990). Presleymania: The Elvis factor. *Death Studies, 14,* 277–282.

Oyama, T., Hatano, K., Sato, Y., Kudo, M., Spintge, R., & Droh, R. (1983). Endocrine effect of anxiolytic music in dental patients. In R. Droh & R. Spintge (Eds.), *Angst, schmerz, musik in der anasthesie.* Basel: Editiones Roche.

Pardun, C. J., & McKee, K. B. (1995). Strange bedfellows:

Symbols of religion and sexuality on MTV. *Youth and Society, 26,* 438–449.

Park, C. W., & Young, S. M. (1986). Consumer response to television commercials: The impact of involvement and background music on brand attitude formation. *Journal of Marketing Research, 23,* 11–24.

Persson, R., & Robson, C. (1995). The limits of experimentation: On researching music and musical settings. *Psychology of Music, 23,* 39–47.

Peterson, D. L., & Pfost, K. S. (1989). Influence of rock videos on attitudes of violence against women. *Psychological Reports, 64,* 319–322.

Pettegrew, J., Lewis, L. A., Brown, J. D., Schulze, L., Zook, K. B., Perry, I., Rose, T., & Ledbetter, J. (1995). Music videos and rap music: Cultural conflict and control in the age of the image. In G. Dines & J. M. Humez (Eds.), *Gender, race, and class in media.* Thousand Oaks, CA: Sage.

Petty, R. E., & Cacioppo, J. T. (1981). *Attitudes and persuasion: Classic and contemporary approaches.* Dubuque, IA: Brown.

Petty, R. E., Cacioppo, J. T., & Schumann, D. T. (1983). Central and peripheral routes to advertising effectiveness: The moderating effect of involvement. *Journal of Consumer Research, 10,* 135–146.

Pitt, L. F., & Abratt, R. (1988). Music in advertisements for unmentionable products: A classical conditioning experiment. *International Journal of Advertising, 7,* 130–137.

Plopper, B. L., & Ness. M. E. (1993). Death as portrayed to adolescents through top 40 rock and roll music. *Adolescence, 28,* 793–807.

Rawlings, D., Hodge, M., Sherr, D., & Dempsey, A. (1995). Toughmindedness and preference for musical excerpts, categories, and triads. *Psychology of Music, 23,* 63–80.

Richardson, J. T. E. (Ed.). (1996). *Handbook of qualitative research methods in the social sciences.* London: British Psychological Society.

Rider, M. S., & Achterberg, J. (1989). Effect of music assisted imagery on neutrophils and lymphocytes. *Biofeedback and Self Regulation, 14,* 247–257.

Rider, M. S., Achterberg, J., Lawlis, G. F., Goven, A., Toledo, R., & Butler, J. R. (1990). Effect of immune system imagery on secretory IgA. *Biofeedback and Self-Regulation, 15,* 317–333.

Rider, M. S., & Weldin, C. (1990). Imagery, improvisation, and immunity. *Arts in Psychotherapy, 17,* 211–216.

Rigg, M. G. (1948). Favorable versus unfavorable propaganda in the enjoyment of music. *Journal of Experimental Psychology, 38,* 78–81.

Roballey, T. C., McGreevy, C., Rongo, R. R., Schwantes, M. L., Steger, P. J., Wininger, M. A., & Gardner, E. B. (1985). The effect of music on eating behavior. *Bulletin of the Psychonomic Society, 23,* 221–222.

Robinson, T. O., Weaver, J. B., & Zillmann, D. (1996). Exploring the relation between personality and the appreciation of rock music. *Psychological Reports, 78,* 259–269.

Roe, K. (1995). Adolescents' use of the socially disvalued media: Towards a theory of media delinquency. *Journal of Youth and Adolescence, 24,* 617–631.

Rosenbaum, J. L., & Prinsky, L. (1991). The presumption of influence: Recent responses to popular music subcultures. *Crime and Delinquency, 37,* 528–535.

Rothenbuhler, E. W., & McCourt, T. (1992). Commercial radio and popular music: Processes of selection and factors of influence. In J. Lull (Ed.), *Popular music and communication* (2nd ed.). London: Sage.

Rouget, G. (1985). *Music and trance: A theory of the relations between music and possession.* Chicago: University of Chicago Press.

Russell, P. A. (1997). Musical tastes and society. In D. J. Hargreaves & A. C. North (Eds.), *The social psychology of music.* Oxford: Oxford University Press.

Scartelli, J. P. (1982). The effect of sedative music on electromyographic biofeedback assisted relaxation training of spastic cerebral palsied adults. *Journal of Music Therapy, 19,* 210–218.

Schuster, B. L. (1985). The effect of music on blood pressure fluctuations in adult hemodialysis patients. *Journal of Music Therapy, 22,* 146–153.

Schwichtenberg, C. (1992). Music video: The popular pleasures of visual music. In J. Lull (Ed.), *Popular music and communication* (2nd ed.). Newbury Park, CA: Sage.

Seidman, S. A. (1992). An investigation of sex role stereotyping in music videos. *Journal of Electronic and Broadcasting Media, 36,* 209–216.

Shapiro, A. G., & Cohen, H. (1983). Auxiliary pain relief during suction curettage. In R. Droh & R. Spintge (Eds.), *Angst, schmerz, musik in der anasthesie* Basel: Editiones Roche.

Sherman, B. L., & Dominick, J. R. (1986). Violence and sex in music videos: TV and rock 'n' roll. *Journal of Communication, 36,* 79–93.

Sherman, B. L., & Etling, L. W. (1991). Perceiving and processing music television. In J. Bryant & D. Zillmann (Eds.), *Responding to the screen: Reception and reaction processes.* Hillsdale, NJ: Erlbaum.

Simonton, D. K. (1980). Thematic fame, melodic originality, and musical zeitgeist: A biographical and transhistorical content analysis. *Journal of Personality and Social Psychology, 39,* 972–983.

Simonton, D. K. (1984). *Genius, creativity, and leadership.* Cambridge, MA: Harvard University Press.

Simonton, D. K. (1994). *Greatness: Who makes history and why.* New York: Guilford Press.

Simonton, D. K. (1997). Products, persons, and periods: Historiometric analyses of compositional creativity. In D. J. Hargreaves & A. C. North (Eds.), *The social psychology of music.* Oxford: Oxford University Press.

Sluckin, W., Hargreaves, D. J., & Colman, A. M. (1982). Some experimental studies of familiarity and liking. *Bulletin of the British Psychological Society, 35,* 189–194.

Sluckin, W., Hargreaves, D. J., & Colman, A. M. (1983). Novelty and human aesthetic preferences. In J. Archer & L. Birke (Eds.), *Exploration in animals and humans.* London: Van Nostrand Reinhold.

Smith, P. C., & Curnow, R. (1966). "Arousal hypothesis" and

the effects of music on purchasing behavior. *Journal of Applied Psychology, 50,* 255–256.

Sogin, D. W. (1988). Effect of three different musical styles of background music on coding by college-age students. *Perceptual and Motor Skills, 67,* 275–280.

Sommers-Flanagan, R., Sommers-Flanagan, J., & Davis, B. (1993). What's happening on music television? A gender role content analysis. *Sex Roles, 28,* 745–753.

Stack, S., & Gundlach, J. H. (1992). The effect of country music on suicide. *Social Forces, 71,* 211–218.

Stack, S., & Gundlach, J. H. (1994). Country music and suicide: A reply to Maguire and Snipes. *Social Forces, 72,* 1245–1248.

Stack, S., Gundlach, J., & Reeves, J. L. (1994). The heavy metal subculture and suicide. *Suicide and Life Threatening Behavior, 24,* 15–23.

Standley, J. (1995). Music as a therapeutic intervention in medical and dental treatment: Research and clinical applications. In T. Wigram, B. Saperston, & R. West (Eds.), *The art and science of music therapy.* Langhorne: Harwood Academic.

Stanton, H. E. (1994). Reduction of performance anxiety in music students. *Australian Psychologist, 29,* 124–127.

Staum, M. J. (1983). Music and rhythmic stimuli in the rehabilitation of gait disorders. *Journal of Music Therapy, 20,* 69–87.

Steptoe, A. (1989). Stress, coping, and stage fright in professional musicians. *Psychology of Music, 17,* 3–11.

Steptoe, A., & Fidler, H. (1987). Stage fright in orchestral musicians: A study of cognitive and behavioural strategies in performance anxiety. *British Journal of Psychology, 78,* 241–249.

Strouse, J. S., & Buerkel-Rothfuss, N. L. (1987). Media exposure and the sexual attitudes and behaviors of college students. *Journal of Sex Education and Therapy, 13,* 43–51.

Strouse, J. S., Buerkel-Rothfuss, N., & Long, E. C. J. (1995). Gender and family as moderators of the relationship between music video exposure and adolescent sexual permissiveness. *Adolescence, 30,* 505–521.

Strouse, J. S., Roscoe, B., & Goodwin, M. P. (1994). Correlates of attitudes toward sexual harassment among early adolescents. *Sex Roles, 31,* 559–577.

Sun, S-W., & Lull, J. (1986). The adolescent audience for music videos and why they watch. *Journal of Communication, 36,* 115–125.

Swanwick, K. (1977). Belief and action in music education. In M. Burnett (Ed.), *Music education review: Vol. 1.* London: Chappell.

Tajfel, H. (1978). *Differentiation between social groups: Studies in the social psychology of intergroup relations.* London: Academic Press.

Tajfel, H., Flament, C., Billig, M. G., & Bundy, R. P. (1971). Social categorization and intergroup behavior. *European Journal of Social Psychology, 1,* 149–178.

Tajfel, H., & Turner, J. C. (1986). The social identity theory of intergroup behavior. In S. Worschel & W. G. Austin (Eds.), *Psychology of intergroup relations* (2nd ed.) (pp. 7–24). Chicago: Nelson-Hall.

Tanioka, F., Takazawa, T., Kamata, S., Kudo, M., Matsuki, A., & Oyama, T. (1985). Hormonal effect of anxiolytic music in patients during surgical operations under epidural anaesthesia. In R. Spintge & R. Droh (Eds.), *Music in medicine.* Basel: Editiones Roche.

Tarrant, M. (1999). *Music and social development in adolescence.* Doctoral dissertation, University of Leicester.

Tarrant, M., Hargreaves, D. J., & North, A. C. (2001). *Social categorization, self-esteem, and the estimated musical preferences of adolescents. Journal of Social Psychology, 141,* 565–581.

Tiggemann, M., & Pickering, A. S. (1996). Role of television in adolescent women's body dissatisfaction and drive for thinness. *International Journal of Eating Disorders, 20,* 199–203.

Tom, G. (1995). Classical conditioning of unattended stimuli. *Psychology and Marketing, 12,* 79–87.

Toney, G. T., & Weaver, J. B. (1994). Effects of gender and gender role self-perceptions on affective reactions to rock music videos. *Sex Roles, 30,* 567–583.

Took, K. J., & Weiss, D. S. (1994). The relationship between heavy metal and rap music and adolescent turmoil: Real or abstract? *Adolescence, 29,* 613–623.

Turner, J. C. (1975). Social comparison and social identity: Some prospects for intergroup behavior. *European Journal of Social Psychology, 5,* 149–178.

Valentine, E. R., Fitzgerald, D. F. P., Gorton, T. L., Hudson, J. A., & Symonds, E. R. C. (1995). The effect of lessons in the Alexander Technique on music performance in high and low stress situations. *Psychology of Music, 23,* 129–141.

van Kemenade, J. F. L. M., van Son, M. J. M., & van Heesch, N. C. A. (1995). Performance anxiety among professional musicians in symphonic orchestras: A self-report study. *Psychological Reports, 77,* 555–562.

van Wel, F. (1994). A culture gap between the generations? Social influences on youth cultural style. *International Journal of Adolescence and Youth, 4,* 211–228.

Walker, R. (1996). Can we understand the music of another culture? *Psychology of Music, 24,* 103–114.

Walls, K., Taylor, J., & Falzone, J. (1992). The effects of subliminal suggestions and music experience on the perception of tempo in music. *Journal of Music Therapy, 29,* 186–197.

Wann, D. L., & Wilson, A. M. (1996). Associations among rock music videos, locus of control, and aggression. *Psychological Reports, 79,* 642.

Wass, H., Miller, M., & Redditt, C. A. (1991). Adolescents and destructive themes in rock music: A follow-up. *Omega Journal of Death and Dying, 23,* 199–206.

Wass, H., Miller, M. D., & Stevenson, R. G. (1989). Factors affecting adolescents' behavior and attitudes towards destructive rock lyrics. *Death Studies, 13,* 287–303.

Wass, H., Raup, J. L., Cerullo, K., & Martel, L. S. (1988). Adolescents' interest in and views of destructive themes in rock music. *Omega Journal of Death and Dying, 19,* 177–186.

Wesner, R. B., Noyes, R., & Davis, T. L. (1990). The occurrence of performance anxiety among musicians. *Journal of Affective Disorders, 18,* 177–185.

Wills, G., & Cooper, C. L. (1988). *Pressure sensitive: Popular musicians under stress.* London: Sage.

Wilson, G. D. (1994). *Psychology for performing artists: Butterflies and bouquets.* London: Kingsley.

Wilson, G. D. (1997). Performance anxiety. In D. J. Hargreaves & A. C. North (Eds.), *The social psychology of music* (pp. 229–245). Oxford: Oxford University Press.

Wolfe, A. S. (1983). Rock on cable: On MTV: Music television, the first video music channel. *Popular Music and Society, 9,* 41–50.

Wolfe, D. E. (1983). Effects of music loudness on task performance and self-report of college-aged students. *Journal of Research in Music Education, 31,* 191–201.

Zillmann, D., Aust, C. F., Hoffman, K. D., Love, C. C. (1995). Radical rap: Does it further ethnic division? *Basic and Applied Social Psychology, 16,* 1–25.

Zillmann, D., & Bhatia, A. (1989). Effects of associating with musical genres on heterosexual attraction. *Communication Research, 16,* 263–288.

Zillmann, D., & Gan, S. (1997). Musical taste in adolescence. In D.J. Hargreaves & A.C. North (Eds.), *The social psychology of music.* Oxford: Oxford University Press.

Zillmann, D., & Mundorf, N. (1987). Image effects in the appreciation of video rock. *Communication Research, 14,* 316–334.

Zullow, H. M. (1991). Pessimistic rumination in popular songs and newsmagazines predict economic recession via decreased consumer optimism and spending. *Journal of Economic Psychology, 12,* 501–526.

Music, Culture, Curriculum, and Instruction

BARBARA REEDER LUNDQUIST

A musicologist described an experience at the New York World's Fair where a Hopi man seemed to be dancing spontaneously. Two other Hopi men appeared and the three of them did the same dance in absolute synchrony of rhythm and gesture. The limitations of her initial perception became apparent to her. Such cultural revelations permeate academic literature, reflecting increasingly "open 'conversations' between different understandings, different vocabularies, different cultural paradigms" (Tarnas, 1991, p. 402), affecting thinking and educational practice (Jordan, 1992; Volk, 1998).

Global forces also influence music education. People, ideas, goods, and cultural practices are on the move to quite dissimilar cultural areas (Rosenau, 1997). As people move, so do their musics. Music, and other performing arts, have become sites for reestablishing and maintaining cultural identities threatened by contact and conflicts in new communities. Awareness of connections between school and community cultures has escalated, as has acknowledgment of student cultures.

In this complex context, music educators consider questions of culture, curriculum, and instruction. Sensitivity to the relation of culture and schooling supports attempts to forge culturally diverse educational practices. Research in music education examines issues surrounding these practices.

Overview of Research

This overview of research in music education dealing with cultural diversity begins with a discussion of the problematic term "multicultural," and rationales for cultural diversity in music education. Subsequent sections address culturally expanded music education from the following perspectives: curriculum, instruction, teacher preparation and professional development, selected contextual issues pertaining to curriculum and instruction, and exemplary programs. The chapter closes with a discussion of the context and status of research and identifies topics that merit further research.

There are reviews of research dealing with teaching and learning of a broad range of musics in music classrooms in the United States (e.g., Campbell, 1991b; Jordan, 1992; Quesada & Volk, 1997), as well as the institutional history of these practices (Volk, 1998). This review attempts to identify issues being examined in recent research. It focuses on studies in the United States and in English, despite the fact that "multicultural music education exists today in a global context" and "its development in the United States is only one piece of the picture" (Lees, 1992; Lepherd, 1995; Volk, 1998, p. 126). It is beyond the scope of this chapter to deal with international conceptualizations and practices of culturally expanded music education.

Multicultural Music Education: A Problematic Term

Approaches to educational acknowledgment of cultural diversity in the United States reflect educational and political agendas. Multicultural education is a construction of the late 20th century. It forms an umbrella under which various curricular agendas gather (Norman, 1999, p. 39), from concern for educational equity (Green, 1983) to expanding musical content. Hollinger (1995) criticizes "multiculturalism" as a movement that has drawn energy from a variety of constituencies and tries to address wide-ranging questions, but with underlying principles and vocabulary that remain too vague to allow closely reasoned discourse (p. 2).

Moodley (1995) identifies "cross-cutting themes" in multicultural education, including "education for cultural pluralism, education about cultural difference, education of the culturally different, education for cultural preservation, and education for multicultural adaptation" (p. 808; Sleeter & Grant, 1987). "Multicultural" education often describes effects of coexistence of diverse groups in a shared social system. But it also refers to a social ideal: "a policy of support for exchange among different groups of people to enrich all while respecting and preserving the integrity of each" (Elliott, 1990, p. 151, citing Pratte, 1979, p. 141), a kind of cultural pluralism. Ravitch (1990) has used "cultural democracy" to express recognition that understanding culture in the United States requires paying attention to a diversity of contributors (pp. 339–340). "Multiculturalism" is used to criticize as well as generate educational change (Lemann, 2000; Ravitch, 2000; Kearns & Harvey, 2000; Schlesinger, 1991).

Because of its extensive use in the research literature of this period, the term "multicultural" appears in this review. However, the multiplicity of perspectives and objectives observable in "multicultural" music education (Norman, 1994, 1999; Okun, 1998), the lack of clarity of goals, and the differences among its adherents indicate that it is problematic.

Rationales for Acknowledging Cultural Diversity in Music Education

Volk (1998) identifies three ideas supporting cultural diversity in music education: recognition of a culturally diverse U.S. population (Seeger, 1996); development of global understanding (p. 3, citing Montalto, 1982; Anderson & Campbell, 1989, 1996; Banks, 1988; Dewey, 1916; Reimer, 1993); and "concern for balance, tolerance, the wise use of resources, and respect for other inhabitants of the earth" (p. 5). Jordan (1992) adds that

the advancement of cultural pluralism allows many different groups to maintain their cultural heritage or to assimilate other cultural traits, as they will. Such is the basis of a democracy. Differences among groups become a national resource and the emerging common culture a mosaic of subsidiary cultures. (p. 737)

Seeger (1996) thinks of exposure to a variety of musical traditions as central to education in the 21st century, which is "certain to be filled with complex cultural choices and increasing international and intercultural interdependence" (p. x). Gardner (2000) agrees, perceiving "virtue in a pluralistic canon, one that deliberately draws on different historical, cultural, and ideological sources. Indeed, in a nation whose population is itself diverse, such eclecticism is

both needed and desirable" (pp. 57–58; Banks, 1993; Gay, 1995).

There are a variety of policy statements by professional organizations in education and in music that provide similar support for incorporating musics of the world's cultures in music instruction in the schools (Campbell, 1994; Damm, 2000; Volk, 1998). There is international support, including the "Policy on Musics of the World's Cultures" of the International Society for Music Education (ISME) (1994; Lundquist & Szego, 1998, pp. 17–19).

In support of ISME's policy recommendation, Nettl (1998) speaks of the global task "to facilitate the study and teaching of the music of the world" in contemporary music classrooms around the world. He argues that urgency is generated by such factors as musics of the world's cultures combining "to produce new kinds of music appealing to a large, multicultural audience" (p. 23).

Social science research indicates that cultural differences are not expected to diminish, despite globalization of media. Roosens (1989) notes that researchers examining culture change in the early 1960s thought that "direct and continuous contact between groups of different cultures would lead to a decrease in the differences among them." However, he has found that where aspects of a culture have been lost, ethnic groups are introducing new cultural markers to affirm their identity (p. 9).

Theoretically, students are able to form a more realistic perspective on the cultures of diverse groups in the United States by studying their musics and, since music is a pan-human phenomenon, to form a more authentic global perspective on music as a result of studying selected musics across the world's cultures (Jorgenson, 1990).

Curriculum

Nettl (1997) identifies broad goals for culturally expanded music curricula as, first, "to present the varieties of the world's musics" and, second, "to present ways of looking at music" (p. 3; Davis, Harrison, Johnson, Smith, & Crawford, 1995).

In addition to models (Elliott, 1989; Pratte, 1979), Jordan (1992) identified two approaches to developing curriculum in the studies she reviewed. One approach uses Western musical concepts and elements as a framework to organize instruction (p. 740; Anderson & Campbell, 1989; Campbell & Scott-Kassner, 1995; Volk, 1998, p. 6). Just as the sonic dimensions of music cultures differ, conceptualizations of music also vary among cultures (Feld, 1982; Keil, 1979; Sakata, 1983). However, this approach assumes that even when these concepts do not appear by name in the musics of the areas studied (Burton, 1996, pp. 11–39), these musical concepts supply a point of entry for the ear and provide structure for instruction and channels for comparisons across music cultures.

It is not clear how often music educators use non-Western, culture-specific categories (e.g., Keil, 1979), employing indigenous terms (with necessary translations or transliteration) to represent the musical thought of a culture. No specific data were found regarding effects of the use of terms indigenous to the culture studied, although students can handle clear instructional presentations of unfamiliar cultural categories (Edwards, 1994).

The second approach identified by Jordan (1992, p. 740) centers on performance (Bloom, 1985; Elliott, 1995, pp. 173–176; Lundquist, 1998, p. 44; Nettl, 1997; Small, 1980). Goldberg's (1993) interviews with North American and Australian traditional performing musicians indicate the importance of performance in learning music. Volk and Holmes (in press; Bieber, 1997) are interested in broadening instrumental performance skills through the use of musical materials from a variety of cultures. Jordan (1992, p. 741) notes that learning and positive student attitudes result from students' active participation in music-making. She didn't find evidence of problems resulting from performance limitations related to the study of world musics, including lack of skills, appropriate music instruments, or other technology.

Another approach concentrates on the study of representative musics of the world's cultures and aspects of their context (e.g., Palmer, 1975). Surveys of geographical and regional musics, sometimes with a topical approach (Fowler, Gerber, & Lawrence, 1994; Volk, 1998, p. 112), are also used.

Edwards (1998) is convinced of the effectiveness of a limited, in-depth experience with a music culture, supported by emphasis on the music's cultural context. Experience with a respected musician from the music culture is preferred.

Curriculum Content

There are choices about which musics will be studied and in which settings (Volk, 1998, p. 16); between a single music culture, topics, or broader surveys. Whatever the curricular details, Nketia (1996) urges that emphasis be placed on musical understanding, not just a "musical supermarket" featuring "a touch of this and a taste of that" (in Volk, 1998, p. 194).

Anderson and Campbell (1996) suggest "organizing study units around cultural groups highlighted in the social studies curricula at each grade level," assisted by colleagues in social studies, language arts, art, and dance for sociocultural depth (p. 6). Edwards (1994) notes that "relevance to the child's world is critical for a depth of learning to take place" (p. 130).

Cultural demographics are suggested as a basis for selection (Moore, 1993). The percentage of teachers using music of ethnic groups in their geographical area, and those who do not appear to use student demographics to affect their choice, does not seem to vary much across regions of the country (Damm 2000; Roberts, 1982). Amount of time spent in lessons dealing with the musics of particular ethnic groups is limited; in terms of American Indian music, the percentage of instructional time spent seems very low (Damm, 2000; Moore, 1993; Yudkin, 1990).

Anderson (1992) writes that curricula need to reflect the expertise of the teacher as well as demographics (p. 54). Campbell (1996a) prefers a repertoire that is "musically in balance with the teacher and her musical life in a multicultural and global society" (p. 26). Effects of parents' expectations on music curricula are a potential area for research (e.g., McCarthy, 1999; Musgrove, 1982, in Moodley, 1995, p. 817).

Rubrics for selection of music cultures studied include: (1) music as a pan-human phenomenon (Jorgenson, 1990; Nettl, 1998; Waterman, cited in Okun, 1998, p. 99); (2) music in liberal arts education (e.g., Davis et al., 1995, p. iii); (3) music and instructional objectives (e.g., Waterman, cited in Okun, 1998, p. 100; Music Educators National Conference, 1994); (4) endangered music cultures (Chaudhuri, 1992; Curtis, 1907/1996, p. 1; Palmer, 1975, p. 22; Malm, 1992; Malm & Wallis, 1992), and languages (Crystal, 2000; Nettle & Romaine, 2000); and (5) encouragement from representatives of local or regional cultural groups. A Siçangu elder of the Lakota Sioux (1996) said: "Music is my history. It tells me who I am. If I do not look at songs and say 'This is *me*,' I have lost myself."

Nettl (1998) writes that knowledge of social and cultural context is necessary to understand and appreciate a music (p. 23; Volk, 1998, p. 188). Although this seems to be widely accepted, Yudkin (1990), McCarthy and Stellacio (1994a), and Robinson (1996) found that many teachers in the United States are not convinced. Klinger (1996b) asks how contextualization influences instruction and whose responsibility it is: music educator, classroom teacher, or culture-bearer. She asks: "Is music to be used to teach culture and ethnicity, or is cultural and ethnic contextualization used to teach music?" (p. 11).

Contextual concerns also apply to music learning. McCarthy (1999) points out that "as a cultural practice, music functions in highly complex and powerful ways to advance ideologies and to form and transform the identity of communities" (p. 13). She says that "the transmission of music process . . . is not a neutral, innocent activity but one underpinned by a strong motivation to define the parameters of human identity for an individual or group of individuals within a community" (p. 13). Trimillos (1989) observes that each system of musical transmission "concentrates upon those elements of musical idiom most critical to its identity as a discrete music. Musical distinctiveness becomes important when a society recognises the political as well as the aesthetic dimension of its musical expression" (p. 33; Szego, 1999).

McAllester (in Campbell, 1996b, p. 10) notes that much of our education is not functionally contextualized; that is, we teach potentially useful knowledge and experience in most Western classrooms, regardless of subject, and appropriate cultural orientation is necessary, but not at the expense of the sonic dimension of the music.

Instruction

In a review of literature in multicultural music education, Campbell (1991b) identifies good teaching as an ingredient that ensures exemplary results in accomplishment of instructional goals, regardless of the musical tradition being taught (in Duke, 1999; Quesada & Volk, 1997, p. 60).

Ethnomusicological studies inform instruction (see chapter 38; Lundquist, 1998; McCarthy, 1999) by suggesting instructional processes that are either culture-specific or applicable across cultural settings (e.g., Feld, 1984). Booth (1986) compared the process of traditional instruction in the North Indian tabla that emphasizes literacy and memorization with contemporary oral instruction involving improvisation, noting that the "context in which the music occurs is important to the teaching method employed" (Quesada & Volk, 1997, p. 51). By examining instructional approaches used in the transmission of music in other cultures, Campbell (1991a) attempted to add to our knowledge of instructional possibilities. Although characteristics of instruction vary across cultures, there may be similarities from a communication perspective (Wulff, 1988, 1993). Observation of the effects of a range of culturally diverse instructional agents and strategies is needed.

Addo's (1992) study responded to Amoaku's (1982) suggestion of observable parallels between traditional African instructional methods and those of Orff Schulwerk. Amoaku suggested an adaptation of Orff Schulwerk for African use in music education (in Addo, 1992, p. 267). Addo examined Orff Schulwerk and Kodály pedagogy, together with Ghanaian traditional methods, finding that it was feasible to combine these "complementary" (p. 271) approaches. The prevalence of Orff Schulwerk and its instrumentarium also suggests research on the use of global instrument-types (e.g., dulcimers, flutes, double reeds, and percussion) to perform music from a variety of cultures, noting similarities and differences in use, including tuning (e.g., Jessup, 1983).

Booth (1986), Trimillos (1989), Lundquist (1998), and McCarthy (1999) note that transmission depends on aspects of music the tradition emphasizes, the variety of roles teachers play (Adachi, 1992), and patterns of social interaction (Vygotsky, 1976; Wertsch, 1985). Oral and written means for transmitting music culture have been examined (e.g., Holmes, 1990; Nettl, 1983). However, Finnegan (1988) points out that mixed media seem to occur naturally in instruction (p. 141), perhaps supported by expanded perspectives on notation (Bennett, 1983).

Instruction and Achievement

Gay (1995) claims that pedagogy using culturally sensitive instructional strategies results in high levels of achievement (p. 28). Increased student interest and involvement could be expected where there is cultural familiarity and experience-near (Geertz, 1984/1986) connections. However, further research is needed to examine these claims and to investigate instructional strategies said to be particularly effective with specific groups of students (e.g., Damm, 2000; Grant & Secada, 1990; Ladson-Billings, 1994).

In one important study, Edwards (1994) examined the "nature of musical or non-musical achievement acquired from each of four instructional approaches in American Indian music" (p. 63). The four approaches to instruction included

> large-group lessons with authentic instruments, an American Indian guest artist, use of authentic (native) instruments in small-group learning centers, and the use of nonauthentic instruments in small-group learning centers. Five intact classes were randomly assigned to one of the treatment groups or a control group using traditional music curriculum with no Indian music taught by the regular music teacher at a school near Phoenix, Arizona. The investigator observed the classes and trained the teacher. (p. iii)

Fourth-grade students' attitudes toward and perceptions of American Indian music and culture were also examined since "an integrated interdisciplinary" perspective was utilized across the instructional approaches so that students were exposed to "varied aspects of American Indian cultures" (p. 64). Results of her study indicate that fourth-grade students "are capable of four levels of responses from multicultural music instruction: knowledge/skills/attitudes, cultural awareness, sensitivity, and valuing" (1998, p. 62) and "can achieve a depth of understanding about another culture previously undocumented, to [her] knowledge" (p. 79; Klinger, 1996a; Teicher, 1996). Edwards's work refines questions about instructional goals and strategies, use of interdisciplinary materials in music instruction, and attributes of student achievement in culturally expanded music education classes.

Teacher Attitudes

Teicher (1997) notes the positive effects of multicultural music lesson planning and implementation on attitudes of preservice elementary teachers. But Teicher found no difference in attitudes regarding "preparedness for multicultural music teaching, nor attitudes of willingness to teach in culturally diverse environments" (p. 415; McInerny, 1987). Robinson (1996) observes that teachers appear to have little commitment to meeting needs of children from diverse backgrounds through alternative styles of teaching (p. 73). Allan and Hill (1995) identify a tendency for educators to believe that if ethnic diversity is not characteristic of a specific region, culturally expanded education is not necessary.

Damm (2000) finds that "teachers who have had exposure to American Indian music through college course work are more likely to focus a higher percentage of yearly instructional time on American Indian music in the curriculum" (p. 92). He also finds that attendance at a powwow positively affects teaching of American Indian music (p. 93). Quesada (1992) provides teachers' reports of increased instructional effectiveness resulting from a workshop accompanying instructional materials. Damm (2000) also reports that "workshops are found to be a significant factor influencing the inclusion of American Indian music in elementary school programs" (p. 92), especially such contextual features as dance and games.

Robinson (1996) notes that school districts are responsible for providing evidence of their commitment not only to hire teachers with multicultural preparation but also teachers of color (p. 213). Offers of continuing in-service training, a multicultural resource facility, and a comprehensive plan for multicultural music education (Banks, 1993; Gay, 1995; Robinson, 1996) are within the purview of school districts. Teachers may need to become more assertive in requests to school districts for in-service education, including opportunities to observe master music teachers and local musicians from one or another music culture and assistance with grants for guest artists' residencies.

Moodley (1995) identifies the problematic nature of biased, insensitive, or naive teachers working with multiethnic educational materials (pp. 816–817). Volk (1991) assessed the attitude of instrumental music teachers toward multicultural music in schools. She suggests that the ambivalence of instrumental music teachers toward musics of world cultures in their instruction is related to a lack of training and a lack of materials (1991, p. 54; Volk & Holmes, in press).

Some teachers report that they do not want to teach the music of a specific ethnic group because of a fear of offending members of that ethnic group (Damm, 2000, p. 90). This may also reflect concerns regarding issues of mu-

sical ownership, authenticity of instruction, and appropriateness for specific age levels or school settings.

Teachers may report a positive attitude toward musics of the world's cultures in instruction, but this may not be reflected in practice (e.g., Volk, 1991). Moore (1993) also finds little correlation between attitudes toward world musics and instructional practice (in Quesada & Volk, 1997, p. 49). In fact, Navarro (1989) found that music educators tend to teach only the content that they have internalized.

Student Attitudes

Volk (1998) writes that research "since 1985 has shown that multicultural education has a positive impact on students' attitudes toward, and knowledge about, other cultures" (p. 92). Jordan (1992) writes that more research is needed on "the emotional-attitudinal mind-set of the student, necessary not only for the motivation to master a foreign musical system but also to foster responsiveness at beginning levels of understanding" (p. 738). Jordan cited Rokeach's (1960) study that seemed "to reinforce the proposition that conceptual and perceptual processes have strong correlations" and that "the willingness of a subject to be open or closed to new ideas may be related to personality development in early childhood," calling for additional research in this area (Jordan, 1992, p. 738). Additional studies were not found.

In a review of studies regarding changes of students' attitudes affected by the study of musics from a variety of cultures, Quesada and Volk (1997) cited McNeill (1975), Mumford (1984), and Stephens (1984). In England, Boyce-Tillman (1996) used the work of Mumford and Stephens, among others, in the development of her framework for intercultural dialogue in music, so there is international research collaboration in this area. Jordan (1992, p. 741) noted positive attitudes resulting from students' active participation in culturally diverse music-making.

Guest Artists

Guest artists appear in schools on occasional visits, workshops, performances, or in time-limited residencies (e.g., Edwards, 1994). Extended collaboration with a guest artist yields amazing benefits, including valued friendships. Where funds are available, cooperative teaching strategies can be explored. It is both a privilege to have musicians from another culture in music classrooms and an essential contribution to teachers' and students' learning. Mutually respectful interaction with artists in a musical style or from a specific area transforms multicultural music education. Reports speak to the meaning this kind of classroom experience can have for all involved. There are factors to consider beyond awareness of the artist's background and status, congruent expectations, helping students to understand when heavy accents, soft voices, lack of intensity in instructional leadership, or different teaching tempo are observed (Klinger, 1996a, 1996b; Kushner, 1991). Most often, students are able to handle the experience with grace, especially when the length of the session is congruent with their ability to concentrate. Lack of accessibility of musicians from specific cultures, along with lack of funds, is problematic (Damm, 2000).

Instructional Materials and Technology

Teaching materials discuss music and instruments, introduce cultural performances, guide listening lessons, assist with procuring instruments and instrument-making, provide discographies of contemporary as well as traditional music, list and provide locations of additional resources, and identify supplemental instructional aids, including books, song collections, ethnographic information, and source books (Burton, cited in Damm, 2000).

Palmer's (1975) invitation to members of the profession to develop teaching materials (in Jordan, 1992, p. 740) has been accepted. Many more materials can be found for music-making, most with accompanying cassettes and CDs. Palmer also called for source books (e.g., Jessup, 1992; Lundquist & Szego, 1998) and reference works (e.g., Broughton & Ellingham, 2000; Broughton, Ellingham, Muddyman, & Trillo, 1994; Broughton, Ellingham, & Trillo, 1999; Diagram Group, 1997; *Garland Encyclopedia of World Music*, 1998; Myers, 1992, 1993). Materials either with videos or in video format for supplementary instructional assistance in music or integrated arts of a variety of cultures are also available (e.g., Opala & Schmidt, 1998), although more are needed. Volk (1998) notes that "method books are available for learning to play instruments from around the world, but they are culture-specific and do not yet have translations" (p. 187). She also points to the lack of materials that deal with teaching culturally expanded content in settings with a diverse student population.

Palmer (1975) suggested the creation of "an extensive data bank cross-referenced for various kinds of information and materials for music specialists" (in Jordan, 1992, p. 740). Ease of retrieval, expandability, lack of expense, and indicators of appropriateness for particular age and stage levels are among those attributes for which Palmer expressed the need. There are a variety of encyclopedias on CD-ROM that feature geography, history, aspects of culture, and musical examples and arts from specific areas of the world. Anku's (1998) work demonstrates the possibility of musician-teachers from specific cultures creating materials, using a variety of media, that come to grips with salient structural features of a musical style or genre.

The textbook continues to define instructional aims, content, and sequence as well as to influence some teach-

ers' perspectives (Eisner, 1990, pp. 32–33). In Damm's (2000) study, "nearly all respondents (92.9%) who included American Indian music checked textbooks as their source for repertoire" (p. 94). Contemporary music texts have resource lists and accompanying CDs and videos. According to Diaz (1980), increase in the cultural diversity of repertoire found in U.S. music textbooks can be credited to teachers' demand. Series music texts have been analyzed but may need to be reexamined periodically "for representativeness, cultural context, various issues of authenticity, and inclusion of pronunciation guides" (Robinson, 1996, p. 218).

Increasing numbers of instructional resources feature music educators working with musicians from a specific culture (e.g., Burton, 1993; Burton & Kreiter, 1998; Jones & Hawes, 1972; Nguyen & Campbell, 1990; Sam & Campbell, 1991; Wilson, Wilson, & Burton, 1994), with ethnomusicologists (e.g., Campbell, 1996b), or with collections of resources by experts in the music of particular areas (e.g., Anderson & Campbell, 1989, 1996). Collections of songs from members of a music culture (e.g., Paredes, 1995; Peña, 1985; Serwadda, 1974) or reports of knowledge and skills learned from members of a tradition have been collected (e.g., Campbell, McCullough-Brabson, & Tucker, 1994; Han & Campbell, 1992; Harpole & Fogelquist, 1991; Sorrell, 1990; Tenzer, 1991). Information about music in culture from specific areas of the world is also forthcoming, written by musician-scholars from those geographical areas (e.g., Santos, 1995), musicologists (e.g., Downing, 1997), or music educators (e.g., Mans, 1997). Materials are available that, in addition to those already mentioned, assist with multicultural music instruction (e.g., Steinmetz, with Garfias, Jameson, & Jameson in press; George, 1987).

Quality materials for school vocal ensembles (e.g., Conlon, 1992) and instrumental groups (Bieber, 1997; Schmid, 1992; Volk, 1992, 1998, pp. 176–177; Volk & Holmes, in press; Volk, Spector & Scott, 1996) are more available, but multicultural music for instrumental performance ensembles remains difficult to locate.

Studies continue to be needed to evaluate the use of different categories of instructional materials and to help teachers become aware of the materials that are available (e.g., Carter, 1996).

Damm (2000) speaks of the lack of accessibility of musicians and information on the music from specific cultures, as well as a lack of funds for instructional materials, including audiovisual materials. An online data base providing a resource for teachers would be very useful, including websites that provide instructional assistance. Cable available to each contracted music educator could allow access to musical examples from musics of the world's cultures for use in the classroom, addressing a longstanding problem of lack of access to the materials of music study. Music has always been allied with technology. Palmer (1975) expressed the need for technology that would allow such features as pitch systems from other areas of the world to be duplicated in the classroom. Jessup (1983) presented a practical solution with her methods for altering tuning of marimbas to lend authenticity to the performance of her transcriptions of Mandinka balafon music from Gambia. Electronic samplers provide access to the sound of non-Western instruments, but funds remain problematic.

Contextual Issues

Among issues that have received little research in music education are ethnicity and ethnic identity, bimusicality and multimusicality, authenticity, cultural boundary-crossing, and ethnic representation in music class enrollment.

Ethnicity and Ethnic Identity

Nettl (1998) points to "the increased significance of ethnicity, the desire of ethnic groups throughout the globe to maintain some cultural independence, and the realization that one of the principal markers of ethnicity is the group's distinctive music" (p. 23). Banks's (1988) typology of stages of ethnicity theorizes that ethnicity can be dynamic. The stages of his typology begin with complete absorption in one way of perceiving the world, moving through ethnocentrism, with its awareness of difference and value on separation, to adjustments in ethnicity affected by personal observation and experience, to biethnicity, in which an individual is competent in more than one cultural setting, and to transcultural and global competence.

Phinney (1990) also observes that "ethnic identity is a dynamic concept" (p. 508); changes can occur in situations in which there is contact with other groups. Roosens (1989) supports the perception of ethnic identity as dynamic. In fact, he observes that individuals have preferences for certain aspects of their ethnic identity and may creatively adjust those or other aspects as they move through sociocultural situations.

These observations reflect findings of cross-cultural psychology, especially transitional perspectives (e.g., Adler, 1975) on cultural boundary-crossing (Szego, 1999). Research in cross-cultural psychology indicates that cross-cultural competence is not only achievable but is a raison d'être for cultural studies (e.g., Taft, 1980).

Phinney's (1990) review of literature reveals that an individual's positive sociocultural identity, or self-identity, is one function of ethnicity. "A far less studied aspect of diversity has been the psychological relationship of ethnic and racial minority group members with their own group,

a topic dealt with under the broad term *ethnic identity*" (p. 499; McCarthy, 1997). She found that "ethnic identity is central to the psychological functioning" (p. 499) of people in racial and ethnic groups.

Some multiethnic or multicultural education programs suggest positive effects of such a program on students' self-identity or self-esteem. Phinney observes that questions remain about "the role of ethnic identity in self-esteem, its relationship to acculturation, and its place in the development of personal identity" (p. 511). Smelser (1989) also cautions that, while self-esteem is a central sociopsychological variable, it is conceptually complicated, making an effective research design problematic.

Reflecting on particularist programs, Jordan (1992) warns that "there is an inherent danger in advocating an ethnocentric curriculum to replace established curricula in an effort to raise the self-esteem and academic achievement of children from ethnic or minority backgrounds . . . [implying] that the only way to reach self-determination is through one's own heritage" (p. 742) and with teachers representing one's own ethnicity.

Bimusicality and Multimusicality

Widely quoted when topics of bilingual ability are discussed is Goethe, who said, "Who does not know another language does not know his own" (Evans, 1968). Nettl (1997) points out that "some individuals and some entire communities are bilingual; this is true of many North American Native American peoples today. Similarly, many Native American communities are 'bimusical,' using traditional Native American music and Western music equally but for different purposes" (p. 5; see also 1983, pp. 50–51).

In his examination of bimusicality, Hood (1960; May, 1967; May & Hood, 1962) focused on developing musicianship in specific musical traditions, especially such attributes as aural and tonal memory and rhythmic competence, as well as performance skills, including improvisation. Jordan (1992) indicates that "the primary problems related to the learner involve musical capacity" (p. 738) and cites Palmer (1975), who points to early research tending to affirm that " 'restraints on the musicality of peoples are culture bound rather than intrinsic limitations of the human intellect and musical capacity' " (p. 142, in Jordan, 1992, p. 738; Teicher, 1996).

Buckner (1974)

focused on the history of music education in the African-American community of Kansas City, Kansas from 1905 to 1954. This study showed that the musics of African-Americans were being taught concurrently with the musics of the Western European tradition in these schools, offering perhaps the first documented example of music teaching for bimusicality in the public schools. (in Quesada & Volk, 1997, p. 48)

For some, the term "bimusical" does not denote varying degrees of competence but refers to someone like Wynton Marsalis, who is judged to be equally expressive in two music cultures. To an educator this suggests a need for research. Many music educators are bimusical in terms of degrees of cross-style performance competence in both Western classical music repertory and in jazz. Since these musical traditions both have Western cultural roots, does cross-style performance count as bimusicality? What about the African roots of jazz? Too little is known about bimusicality, about bimusical music educators, about kinds and degrees of bimusicality, and the implications of cross-cultural competence for musical life.

Authenticity

Authenticity is a concern from the earliest discussions of cultural diversity in music repertoire (Edwards, 1994; Elliott, 1989; Jordan, 1992; Klinger, 1996a, 1996b; Palisca, 1964; Palmer, 1975, 1992). Appropriate performance practice has always been a critical dimension of music-making and materials (Edwards, 1994, pp. 129–130; criteria in Tucker, 1992; Damm, 2000).

Volk (1998) describes egregious musical examples whose authenticity lies only in their titles, melodies appearing with different texts in inappropriate musical settings, incongruous incorporation of elements of the melodies and rhythms of another culture, and awkward arrangements (pp. 178–179). Some teachers report that they use chordal accompaniment for repertoire without harmony (Damm, 2000, p. 91) and culturally incongruent vocal practices. Gardner (2000) thinks that "multicultural curricula and approaches are beneficent" if attention is given to issues of "standards and accuracy" (p. 58). Klinger (1996a) warns, however, that "some amount of compromise and adaptation" may be necessary for some musical performances to be appropriate for specific levels of schooling (p. 156).

Early on, music educators' apparent lack of concern for authenticity (e.g., Volk, 1998, p. 27) may be traceable to the perspective and methods of folk song collectors and composers who collected and then arranged melodies for piano solos, duets, and other small ensembles. Providing a culturally attractive, performable musical example of "folk" music was a value for earlier collectors and composers, such as Grieg, rather than providing an "authentic" musical record, as attempted by Bartok and Kodály. That was the practice; that was the expectation. "Ethnomusicology and its acceptance of music in, and as, culture, raised the consciousness of music education in that regard" (Volk, 1998, p. 177).

From a traditional perspective, the Zimbabwean mbira virtuoso and teacher Ephat Mujuru (personal communication, Spring 1973) pointed to the lack of physical and psychological endurance, as well as knowledge of culturally congruent musical ideas sufficient to sustain hours of performance, that would keep his most advanced American educator-students from performing effectively in Shona ceremonies in Zimbabwe (e.g., naming ceremonies). However, he rejoiced that his mbira teacher-students and their students would at least be more qualified listeners, able to recognize and respect the abilities of Shona musicians.

Trotter (personal communication, Winter 1991) described a qualified listener as one who has internalized the sonic probabilities of a musical style or genre. One can listen to a musical example and imitate it, with assistance and performance evaluation by a member of the culture, but too often music educators have not had access to contextualized performances. Performance experience is as important to qualified listening (Hood, 1971/1982; Geringer & Madsen, 1995; Kjelland & Kerchner, 1998) as it is to understanding musical ideas or concepts.

Volk (1998) points out that the voice "is standard the world over" although "replicating vocal timbres from various vocal styles may take time, careful listening, and practice" (1998, p. 179). There are questions concerned with effects on the physiology of the voice. No studies were found that addressed this point in terms of specific vocal practices or age levels.

Pembrook (1997) found that "using authentic instruments may be the most effective way of introducing music from another culture" (in Volk, 1998, p. 256), but the range of substitution is wide (Damm, 2000, p. 90). Instrumental timbres may be easier to replicate than some vocal ones, either by purchasing the instrument, using electronic techniques, performance techniques (e.g., bending pitches), or culturally valued principles of instrument construction (e.g., Jessup, 1983), as illustrated in Craig Woodson's workshops in the 1980s. This is a problematic area for teachers.

Klinger (1996b) wonders "who determines what is the most authentic musical and cultural representation" (p. 11). The answer from the profession appears to be: any culture member (e.g., Campbell, 1994). However, Klinger realizes that "two individuals from the same ethnic group may interpret the same piece of music quite differently" (1996b, p. 156). In fact, she argues that "multiple 'authenticities,' equally legitimate, yet different from each other, can and do exist" (p. 197). Klinger cites Waterman's suggestion that teachers examine cultures to identify sacrosanct traditions and values placed on ideas of authenticity (p. 158) and criteria for judgment.

Borroff (personal communication, June 16, 1991) views the six style periods in Western concert music as six different cultures. For her, implications for authentic performance of music from these periods do not reside only in performance on accurate copies of instruments of the periods but also on the need for performers to aim for the same reaction in listeners that the musicians of those periods sought in theirs: exhilaration. Music that is performed properly provides a context that "frames and legitimates ritualized interactions" and serves as an "affective valence" for a successful event (Waterman, 1990, p. 214). Stokes (1997) notes that music "provides means by which people recognise identities and places, and the boundaries which separate them" so "musical performance, as well as the acts of listening, dancing, arguing, discussing, thinking and writing about music, provide the means by which ethnicities and identities are constructed and mobilised" (p. 5; Feld & Basso, 1996).

Santos points out that "while authenticity is indeed a legitimate concern in the context of preserving tradition, its very concept is founded on the idea of cultural stasis, a belief that has been refuted by modern scholarship and the very dynamic nature of living traditions" (cited in Klinger, 1996b, p. 157; Moodley, 1995, p. 816; Santos, 1995). The range of variability in each music culture and musical performance is especially affected when people are traveling all over the world and their cultures with them (Clifford, 1992). Authenticity is a complicated issue.

Cultural Boundary-Crossing

Cultural boundary-crossing (Malinowski, 1945; Savaglio, 1992; Solbu, 1997, p. 74; Szego, 1999) and developing cross-cultural competence (Banks, 1991, p. 9) are almost ubiquitous in this age of mediated musical globalization. Palmer (1975) suggested that teachers might consider functioning musically in at least one music culture other than their own. Students come to school with different, but quite specific, musical backgrounds. Assisting teachers and students to cross-cultural boundaries in the course of music study would seem to be a primary objective, even where Western concert music is the only focus. Szego (1999) examines cultural boundary-crossing in a school setting in Hawaii.

There is a lack of clear evidence "regarding the effects of cross-cultural exposure on musical perception, the developmental readiness of various ages for the study of world musics, the effectiveness of various approaches, and the question of bimusical and multimusical capacity" (Jordan, 1992, p. 744). Yet a host of musicians report the need for musical boundary-crossing in their lives as performers, especially in urban areas where continued economic viability is connected with musicians' ability to develop a cross-style and cross-cultural repertoire, employing appropriate performance techniques, whether in local or regional folk and traditional musics, in popular styles, jazz, or re-

ligious music. Further examination of the formal educational implications of this phenomenon is needed.

Ethnic Representation in Music Class Enrollment

Research examining enrollment patterns in terms of proportionality of diverse students in music classes continues (Floyd, 1988). Casper (1989) observed low minority participation in high school vocal jazz ensembles in the Pacific Northwest. Factors contributing to this were unknown. She theorized that proportionate minority participation in vocal jazz ensembles depends on a high degree of cultural convergence between school and community. Where the community and school are both highly integrated (e.g., on a military base) and other contextual variables do not appear to obtain, there is proportionate representation of minority population in the vocal jazz class. Campbell (1993) referred to theories of Casper (1989) and Gates (1991) in her observation of low participation of newly arriving Indochinese in music electives.

Lind (1997) examined the classroom environment in choral music programs with proportionate and low Hispanic enrollment to investigate aspects of the classroom environment that encouraged Hispanic participation, to document cultural differences in assessment of choral classroom environments, and to compare assessments of the choral classroom environment with a normative sample of high school classes. Her analyses revealed differences in students' assessments of classroom environments between choral classroom environments with proportionate Hispanic enrollment and programs with low Hispanic enrollment. Her study supports the observation that not all students in a classroom have the same experiences.

Walker and Hamann (1995) found that students of all ethnicities ranked teacher effectiveness as the most influential dimension in the decision to continue to participate in a music group. Lind suggests the need for a number of additional studies, including a longitudinal study of continued participation patterns and examination of the cultural differences that influence classroom practices, such as choral repertoire selection.

Teacher Preparation and Professional Development

Student teachers are being asked to operate effectively in a social, historical, and aesthetic context, which is not at all the same—and is vastly more complex—than the cultural context for which they have been prepared in typical higher education. Any experience they have with the variety of music cultures that exist in the United States, and in their classrooms, is probably based on happenstance and is not likely to be authenticated by higher education.

Grant and Secada (1990) studied teachers' preparation for diversity. They looked at the demographics of teacher and student populations, finding cultural homogeneity in the teaching force facing increasing diversity in the student population. Demographics and biographies of university professoriate were not examined. They asked why a diverse population of teachers is needed. They looked for such evidence as the positive impact of teachers of color on achievement of students of color, positive effects on students from diverse backgrounds from working with teachers reflecting the same diversity, and positive implications of offering experience with people from different backgrounds working together and sharing authority (p. 406) as well as cultural knowledge and skills. They identified a need for information about diverse students' reaction to teacher education programs, including the degree to which special skills are noticed and developed, or if students are encouraged to sublimate cultural strengths, for which they are sought, in order to fit into the expectations of a traditional teacher education program. Financial costs of teacher preparation programs may also be an issue for underrepresented segments of the population. Data concerning these issues in music education were not found.

Evidence regarding behavioral commitment (Elliott, 1989) to multicultural music instruction suggests a higher-than-expected chasm between teachers' beliefs, as reported by them, and their instructional practice. Although teachers speak supportively of incorporating the musics of other cultures in their classrooms, many either do not get to it because of lack of time or lack of preparation or do so superficially (McCarthy & Stellacio, 1994a; Robinson, 1996; Yudkin, 1990). McCarthy and Stellacio (1994b) also report that teachers are concerned with musical authenticity, request workshops or course work with teachers native to the culture, seek knowledge of local venues where the music can be heard, need descriptions of the cultural context of musics and appropriate audiovideo resources with pronunciation guides for assistance with a range of native languages, and want resource recommendations with reviews. However, Robinson (1996) found that where efforts were made to meet these concerns, teachers didn't take advantage of them. She observed that teachers used English translations even when the original language was present in song texts with pronunciation guides. Where lack of preparation was cited, Robinson found that few teachers took advantage of in-service educational opportunities available to them.

Although half of the teachers reported that they had been exposed to some "multicultural content," Robinson found that that exposure appeared to "be of little value" (p. 207) to them. She uncovered the widespread perception among elementary music teachers that "multicultural education is for 'others' and thus the standard Eurocentric education of public schools in this country already meets their needs" (p. 206). In elementary general music practices, Robinson observed pervasiveness of "qualities known to be in opposition to multicultural education such as rigidity, task orientation, narrow minded conceptions and ethnocentrism" (p. 206).

Higher Education

Institutions of higher education share in the responsibility to prepare music teachers for teaching in multicultural and multiethnic classrooms (Lundquist, 1991; Nyberg, 1975). Yet Contreras (cited in Grant & Secada, 1990) observes that teacher preparation programs

> assume that teacher education students will pick up the necessary knowledge, skills and attitudes that will help them teach classes of socioculturally diverse students without any direct instruction and planned experience. Moreover, teacher educators assume that most of the schools will continue to be monocultural and monosocial, therefore, there is no obligation to commit time and resources to preparing teachers to teach children who are at risk of being miseducated and undereducated. (p. 412)

So whose responsibility is it?

Most of the studies Quesada and Volk (1997) reviewed that dealt with the preparation of music teachers examined the presence of musics of the world's cultures in music education curricula in higher education or developed "course materials for preservice or inservice teachers" (p. 58). Quesada's (1992) study was the only one cited that included the "actual training of inservice teachers" (p. 58).

Chin (1996) analyzed college catalogs and bulletins to determine what multicultural music courses are being offered at institutions accredited by the National Association of Schools of Music (1995). Chin's study indicates that over half of the institutions did not list music courses with multicultural content or listed only one, with public and private institutions differing slightly, minimal effects of geographic location, and a slight variation among them related to levels of music degrees offered. A fairly small percentage of existing multicultural music courses are required for music degrees, the largest number are offered at the undergraduate level, and most were designed for students other than music majors meeting general education requirements. Chin also looked at course content, finding only a few designed for music education majors and more dealing with music from a specific area of the world, as well as interdisciplinary and ethnomusicological courses, some of which involved performance. Chin examined two institutions of different sizes that were among those offering the most multicultural music courses in an attempt to identify how their programs developed. Like Montague

(1988), Moore (1993), and Norman (1994), Chin found that faculty members in higher education who had training or experience with music of cultures different from their own were more likely to implement a multicultural program in music (1996, p. 87).

Lack of adequate teacher education for cultural diversity or uneven incorporation of multicultural concerns in in-service teacher education exists globally (Allan & Hill, 1995; Figueroa, 1995; McCarthy & Stellacio, 1994a, 1994b; Moodley, 1995; Volk, 1998; Yudkin, 1990). Jordan (1992) wrote that "both preservice and inservice training for teachers have been inadequate" (p. 744). They appear to remain so, even though instructional materials have increased and improved in both quality and quantity. But they alone cannot "solve the problems of teacher competency" (p. 744). In fact, "teacher preparation for a multicultural society tends to be 'contested, fragmented and in large measure theoretical' " (Moodley, 1995, p. 804). Investigations of effects of workshops, courses, cultural events, and guest artists need to continue, as do investigations of biography and professional experiences of effective multicultural music educators. This is also indicated for the professoriate.

Alternative undergraduate courses are also suggested. The preservice music education courses described in Montague's (1988) study included mandated multicultural music education courses, "methods courses with a multicultural component," and elective courses, all taught by music educators, and both elective and required ethnomusicology courses. Montague found that

> many of the music educators interviewed believed that multicultural education could not be accomplished without first being addressed in higher education at the pre-service level of instruction. The ethnomusicologists agreed, but in general saw competence as the most essential need, stating that without the proper experience with varied musics, essential listening and/or performance skills, and knowledge of musical terms in contexts beyond western traditions, students would be reluctant to introduce music of other cultures in public school settings, which is born out in the literature. In addition, ethnomusicologists felt that collaboration between departments must be initiated before advancement in multicultural education could be fully realized on a scale broad enough to make a difference. (in Jordan, 1992, p. 740)

Volk (1998) writes that "a consistent pronunciation guide for all languages does not yet exist" (p. 187, citing Burton, 1996). However, a phonetic system does exist that is used globally. Most voice majors take a course in phonetics in order to pronounce words accurately in performance. It may be critical for music educators to take phonetics; it could increase their effectiveness in dealing with pronunciation of unfamiliar languages.

Volk (1998) points out that "ensembles providing performance opportunities in the music of another culture are relatively scarce in academia, although they abound in the community" (p. 187), especially in urban areas. Some methods of liaison between them and programs for teacher education might be created and examined. Volk (1998), Anderson, (1992), and Sands (1993) suggest an independent study project, at either the undergraduate or graduate level, undertaken in cooperation with a musician from a music culture. This project could involve lessons as well as ensemble performance, with reports and audio/video documentation and evaluation to be undertaken cooperatively. Volk (1998) and Sands (1993) speak to the importance of a multicultural music methods course, which some music education departments are already offering (Okun, 1998).

Among those who have examined requirements of graduate programs for doctoral students who will prepare music educators, Lundquist (1991) suggests a combination of course work in ethnomusicology and music education, with selected emphases to include experience with alternative approaches to instruction. Henderson (1993) simply says that schools of music should be able to demonstrate competence in multicultural music education as they do in Western music studies.

The degree of diversity within communities across the United States, to say nothing of the differences that occur internationally, suggests a need for teachers and students to be able to deal with a broad palette of musics, each of which is undergoing continuous change. Research is needed to better understand ways for teachers to cope with perpetually changing, unfamiliar musical styles.

Personal experience as well as professional preparation and experience can contribute to teachers' effectiveness (Lanier & Little, 1986). Teachers may have to be responsible for preparing themselves to have some degree of expertise in musics of the world's cultures (Boyer-White, 1988). From that perspective, some dissertations probably document music educators' preparation in this area (e.g., Mans, 1997). Lundquist (2000) observes that a teacher's continuing research is a source of energy for practice. She suggests that expectation and rewards for experimental research in higher education may have the unintended effect of cooling research energy connected with preparation for teaching. Teachers observed to be effective in multicultural settings seem to be, among other things, proactive students of specific music cultures (e.g., Ellis, 1985). This needs examination.

There is another dimension of this research challenge to music educators. Existing studies examine aspects of transmission of a specific music culture, amplifying understanding (Campbell, 1991a; Trimillos, 1989). Studies have focused on music transmission in a geographical area

(Veblen, 1991, 1994, 1996; McCarthy, 1990, 1999). One study looked at music transmission in a church setting (Mbanugo, 1986, reviewed in Klinger & Goolsby, 1996). These studies contribute to the point raised by Allen Britton (cited in McCarthy, 1990, p. viii; McCarthy, 1999, p. 9) that when educational monographs in music are large enough in number and can be related to each other along some dimension, historical examination of music education and its impact on cultural life from a global perspective can be undertaken. While the issue of ethnographic research is beyond the scope of this chapter (see chap. 38), it may be critical to an examination of the effects of expanding music repertoire in schools.

Musical Preference

Volk (1998) quotes Hood's (1971/1982) statement that "the intrinsic value of a piece of music, regardless of its tradition, may be appreciated by an individual, regardless of his background or prior lack of exposure to The Tradition, through the unconscious application of critical method" (p. 351). Blacking (1971, 1973) adds that there is a level beyond which an "outsider" cannot reach without deeper exposure to the music culture. Nonetheless, Volk (1998) cites the general agreement "that the greater the knowledge one has about the culture, and the expectations or rules of its music, the greater the understanding, or perception of meaning, of that music will be" (p. 6; Lee, 1988, in Jordan, 1992; Nakazawa, 1988).

Darrow, Haack, and Kuribayashi (1987) examined the consistency of terminology used by Japanese and American college students to describe musics of both cultures to test the supposition that listeners drawn from roughly the same subculture will use synonymous words to describe the character of much of Western music (p. 245; Farnsworth, 1969, p. 80). The authors credited acculturation effects of Western musics and instruments on Japanese subjects for the similarities in words chosen to characterize the Western examples and the unfamiliarity of Western listeners with Eastern examples to account for the disparate responses between groups in regard to Japanese examples. They also investigated the students' preferences related to the musics of the two cultures, trying to tease out possible "relationships between musical experience and preferences" (p. 237; Shehan, 1984). In general, there was a preference for instrumental over vocal music and for Western music, with American subjects preferring jazz and the Japanese subjects Mozart, whether or not they had supplemental musical experiences. Supplementary experience positively affected the range of preference, although questions remain about the role of schooling and sociopolitical circumstances in the broadening of tastes.

Fung is among researchers who are systematically pursuing studies to increase understanding of music preference and other issues related to a global perspective of music. As an example, Fung (1994) examined the relationship between undergraduates' preferences for world musics and their attitudes following their exposure to multicultural educational values. Many researchers had suggested that changes in musical preference and taste might result from multicultural music education.

> This supported the thesis of Koizume Fumio (cited in Nakazawa, 1988, p. 80) that "children who are educated in two different cultural systems are able to take on the musical culture of both with little difficulty; these 'bimusical' children can also easily accept a third and fourth musical culture." Therefore, preference for musical styles from a culture other than one's own may involve broader social, political, and cultural experiences and attitudes. (p. 46)

Fung also wanted to examine the relation "between the attitude toward the world's people and the preferences for world musics" (p. 46). Foreign language training and age were additional independent variables. Fung found a "significant correlation between world music preference and multicultural attitudes," supporting the view that "social/cultural attitudes play a role in world music preference" (p. 54; Edwards, 1994).

Comparing response modes, Brittin (1996) reports that "assessing and understanding listeners' musical preferences is important to those wishing to cultivate tolerance, appreciation, or fondness for musical practices of many cultures" (p. 329). Musical experience is a factor affecting music preference, including experience with world musics, and so is familiarity with the musical example, depending on the space of time between repetitions and the initial attitude of the listener toward the example (other factors in LeBlanc, 1982, 1987). Brittin investigated undergraduate music and nonmusic majors' and junior high musicians' static and continuous responses indicating preferences for music of other cultures using a 10-point Likert scale and continuous ratings during the musical excerpts using a continuous response digital interface. The continuous responses were higher than the Likert scales, where the less experienced listeners or those less comfortable with the musical example seemed to have made their judgment or remembered and reported their experience at the point when they least liked the example, with some possible implications for instruction. Brittin believes that "continuing to explore factors that lead to acceptance of unfamiliar musical practices is certainly warranted. By learning more about ways to maximize students' positive reactions to new musics, music educators can increase the probability of students enjoying a rich and varied musical environment" (p. 338).

Exemplary Programs

A variety of multicultural music education programs reporting varying levels of success (Holmes, personal communication, November 2000) appear among case studies in Lundquist and Szego (1998). Berry and Singh (1998) report on a workshop and recital of classical music of North India presented by the Indian Music Group of Manchester, England, in area classrooms. Goodkin describes his foundational multicultural music education program at the San Francisco School, utilizing Orff Schulwerk pedagogy. Senanes (1998) reports on in-service training in Argentina modeled on the pedagogical strategies and publications of Professor Maria del Carmen Aguilar of the National University of Buenos Aires, who attempts not only to extend students' knowledge of and experience with the folklore of Argentina but also to reflect the composer's focus on creative music-making. Del Valle (1998) relates developments in multicultural music education in the Philippines to the culturally diverse presence in music education at the University of Philippines' College of Music, influenced by the work of ethnomusicologist-composers from Jose Maceda to Ramon P. Santos, and its effects on instructional programs.

Skyllstad (1998) reports on a Norwegian school project in multicultural music education intended to promote interracial understanding. This 3-year program cooperated with Rikskonsertene, the Ministry of Culture's organization promoting access to live music for people of all ages. Skyllstad writes that "in Oslo schools, one out of every four students is of foreign descent. This presents a great challenge to school authorities and educators" (p. 95). In 1989, Rikskonsertene introduced a 3-year project, "The Resonant Community," with the objective of contributing to racial harmony in Norwegian elementary schools through an educational program rooted in the immigrants' own cultural heritage, emphasizing music and dance. Among the findings of this careful study, Skyllstad identified a significant increase in reports of freedom from harrassment from students in the first test group. Students also reported retention of positive attitudes toward immigration and immigrants, and continued to have a relatively high degree of openness to music played, drawing attention to a discrepancy between adhering to group norms in musical taste and the effects of active involvement with unfamiliar musics. Skyllstad invites more research.

Lundström, Olsson, Saether, and Svensson (1998) studied whether one experience could provide a meaningful intercultural encounter for preservice teachers. A 2-week course was instituted in which groups of preservice teachers worked with musicians representing unfamiliar music cultures or musical styles. These groups prepared a concert with the visiting musicians, created an instructional program, and completed a written report on their work. A second component of the project was the availability of 3 weeks of study abroad for additional "in-depth performance studies" (p. 106), as, for example, in Gambia for intensive study of the Mandinka *kora,* Wolof drumming, and Fula singing. Since the project's completion, this component has been part of the curriculum and is financed by the normal institutional budget.

As a result of this work and Saether's (1993), Campbell (2001) has developed a weeklong cultural immersion experience for undergraduate music education students in the "big river" country of the Yakama Indians in central Washington. The experience, buttressed theoretically by Titon's (1997) ethnomusicological model, emphasizes the lived experience of people making music and students attempting to develop more accurate, culturally sensitive perceptions of people from unfamiliar cultures by being with them. Students' awareness of the need for alternative instructional strategies and of differences in responses to instruction is facilitated by undergraduate groups teaching lessons developed across 6 weeks of focused research on a specific music of the world's cultures, providing experiences with world musics for the Yakama students.

Ethnomusicologist Charles Keil is the director of Musicians United for Superior Education (MUSE). Keil's theory is that any traditional way of drumming, dancing, and singing has the power of generations behind it and children can feel that power, absorb or acquire the skills of that tradition, fuse it with other traditions, and innovate and create new styles. Keil has also been effectively teaching teachers.

David Ward-Steinman has been director of the Comprehensive Musicianship (CM) program of San Diego State University's School of Music and Dance for a number of years. The 4-year program features consistent modularization of content into three areas each semester: CM core (theory, composition, aural skills); CM history (world music, jazz, and a systematic survey of the six main periods of Western music history); and CM lab activity (performance in several different world music ensembles, early music or new music ensembles, jazz improvisation, and traditional performance groups and computer applications in music). The CM activities of conducting, composing, improvising, and performing appear in each module.

Although many of these programs have addressed issues of assessment, this information is not readily available. Gay (1995) reminds us that assessment studies of exemplary multiethnic-multicultural programs are in short supply and are greatly needed to inform practice. Studies in the 1990s began to evaluate various aspects of multicultural music programs (e.g., Edwards, 1994, 1998), but assessment is an area ripe for studies related to cultural diversity in music education.

Reflections on Research

Attention to larger contexts within which research problems are nested is critical to examination of issues that cross cultural and disciplinary boundaries. Discovery of larger connections through awareness of features of the constellation within which issues are located could increase the power of the research. As an example, Wong (1992) points out that the West has "embraced diversity as an essential condition of the search for truth." Concerns about destructive effects of cultural diversity fail to understand that "intellectual diversity is the paradigm for multicultural diversity" (p. 5).

Some researchers examine and express their perspectives on culture (e.g., McCarthy, 1990, 1999). Some remain unaware of the complexity of the idea of culture and changes in the concept of culture in which the transmission of music across the generations has been located (Dworkin, 1992; Eagleton, 2000; Moodley, 1995, p. 816; Volk, 1998, p. 7; Williams, 1953/1993, 1958). Some seem unaware of changes in the vectors of power that have prepared the way for culturally plural music instruction (Kammen, 1999). Multiple perceptions of reality are increasingly unavoidable. Eagleton (2000) points out that "culture as sign, image, meaning, value, identity, solidarity and self-expression is the very currency of political combat, not its Olympian alternative. In Bosnia or Belfast, culture is not just what you put on the cassette player; it is what you kill for" (p. 38).

Researchers' perspective on music and music culture also deserves thought and explication. McCarthy (1999) chose four perspectives on music to structure her discussion of music transmission: music as culture, canon, community, and communication. "Musical culture is created within community; efforts by communities to pass on their traditions create canons of practice, of repertoire, and of pedagogy; the transmission of music is facilitated by a broad range of communication media and technologies" (p. 9).

There are a number of models of music cultures (e.g., Slobin, 1993; Titon & Slobin, 1996). Nettl (1998) points to the use of Merriam's (1964) three-part model of a guide for study of

> a) music sound (or the "music itself"); b) behavior (e.g., events, lessons, audience behavior, relationship of musicians to each other); and c) concept (i.e., the ideas and beliefs about music). This model has helped researchers; it is also sufficiently simple to be helpful even to young students." (p. 25)

Because all elements of culture are constantly being reaffirmed or renegotiated, music cultures are dynamic systems (e.g., Nettl, 1997, pp. 5–6). This is not often accounted for in the literature.

An ethnomusicological perspective on music and music cultures supports music educators who are threading their way through the musics of the United States, the Americas, and other musics of the world's cultures (Lundquist, 1998; Nettl, 1998). Nettl (1998) points out that

> it is people who work in ethnomusicology who have made the world's musics available to academics and educators and musicians. And it is ethnomusicologists who have grappled most with the difficulties inherent in looking at and listening to musics outside one's own background, with the problems of studying music both in its own cultural context and also from a comparative perspective, and with ways of seeing what it is that music does in culture. (pp. 23, 28)

This perspective, and its potential effect on commitment to cultural diversity in music education, is worth examining.

Culture, music cultures, and tastes in the United States also need thought to place music education research in context. Garfias (1983) lists major ethnic traditions and style complexes that flourish in the United States (pp. 30–31). Kammen (1999) reflects that with the democratization of cultural authority in the United States has come the increasing importance of cultural power, not only of ethnic groups but also of corporate capital, with links to the media, technological developments, and the rise of mass cultural production (p. 151; Nettl, 1985).

Kammen (1999) notes that change in the degree of recognition of plurality in culture and in tastes in the United States "has not been neatly linear but more nearly cyclical" (p. 9). This is also the case with music and music culture in the United States, where cycles seem to obtain (Merriam, 1955). Olneck (1990) observes cyclic movements in education that acknowledge cultural diversity. Olneck believes these movements have attracted "the power of constraints and mediating mechanisms that determine curricular and pedagogical form," suggesting "that the tolerable and attainable limits of pluralism in American public education remain narrow" (p. 147). Cyclic processes may also relate to the dynamics of culture in the United States. For example, Kammen (1999) argues that "the single most important lesson to be learned from the history of cultural stratification in the United States is that distinct taste levels have indeed existed, yet they have been permeable and increasingly subject to being shared across lines of class, race, and degrees of education" (p. 73). Researchers' awareness of the context of issues examined seems to be increasingly important.

In the context of music education, some general issues are especially pressing. The degree of sufficiency in terms of commitment, preparation, and experience for teachers who are judged to be effective multicultural music educators is not understood. Edwards (1994) and Lundquist (1998) observe that even when a culture-bearer is not present, an effective musician-teacher who is interested in the tradition, is knowledgeable about it, and continues study of it can positively affect students' musical achievement (p. 44). Closer examination of this observation is needed.

Edwards (1994, 1998) claims that an in-depth experience, even a limited one, supported by emphasis on the cultural environment within which the music is nested, is effective for students in terms of gains in knowledge, skills, and attitudes, and observable growth in cultural awareness, sensitivity, and valuing (p. 62) A similar participatory experience is reported in teacher education (Campbell, 2001; Lundstrom, Olsson, Saether, & Svensson, 1998; Saether, 1993; see also, e.g., Lanier & Little, 1986; Navarro, 1989; Quesada, 1992; Skyllstad, 1998). This work is important. Musicians understand and accept the long-term commitment and discipline needed to become expressive in any musical tradition. The idea that short-term, in-depth experiences can facilitate teachers' and students' understanding of the richness of global music-making is a promising development. More needs to be known.

Effective partnerships with musicians from a variety of music cultures have become more common, although in some places access to culture-bearers is limited by geography and economics (Damm, 2000), as is access to authentic audio and video materials documenting their musics. Some music cultures limit access of "outsiders" to sustain cultural identity; some do so on the basis of function and some because of issues of ownership. Limited access to audio materials is also connected with economics and the music industry (e.g., Malm, 1992). Perhaps audio and video materials could focus on a specific, sharable musical example, with a teaching segment by a member of the culture and presentation of the example in its context. Musical styles can also be the subject of such materials (e.g., *Education of a Singer at the Beijing Opera*, 1995).

Problems related to cultural accuracy and effective instructional materials continue in all parts of the world. When a musical example uses inappropriate pitches, inaccurate rhythms, unsuitable harmonies, or incongruous timbres, it is not only inauthentic but also decontextualized and decultured. This is applicable to music from any tradition, in any style. The problem with culturally inappropriate musical transcriptions or performances is the lack of qualification traceable to the minimal self-doubt of a culturally inexperienced or disrespectful listener. This is an ongoing problem that may be linked with ethnocentrism and racism (e.g., Allport, 1954/1988). These perspectives may also affect the disparity between teachers' reports of their beliefs and attitudes and their limited instructional commitment. Some teachers report little reason to incorporate musics of the world's cultures, because there are few

local "ethnic" residents. This syndrome is observed in many areas of the world, "across the curriculum for all pupils" (Allan & Hill, 1995; Figueroa, 1995, p. 750; Hoff, 1995; Moodley, 1995), especially in areas where ethnic minorities are few in number. Such perceptions are worth examining, to reveal their source in preservice experience and formal music education and to note their effects on music instruction and learning. It may be necessary to reemphasize that all of us are ethnic and all musical examples are ethnic. There is the old joke about Balinese gamelan performers listening to Beethoven to hear some ethnic music. Informed, culturally expanded education depends on how it "is located in the broader economic, political, and social structures" (Moodley, 1995, p. 817).

The speed of technology-supported change in music cultures requires ongoing attention to musical developments (Volk, 1998, p. 186). Media-supported student culture has become a large issue in many parts of the world. Influences of Western culture and technology are ubiquitous. In many areas of the world, "jazz, rock, and popular musics have been included in most curricula . . . and are taught in many classrooms. These musics are often preferred by all the students, regardless of their homelands." (Hoff, 1995, p. 147). Banks (1995) reminds teachers that students need to understand how knowledge construction works, specifically "how [knowledge] reflects human interests, ideology, and the experiences of people who create it." The students also need a chance to create and document their own perspective to see how this works. All involved can come "to understand why it is essential to look at the nation's experience from diverse ethnic and cultural perspectives to comprehend fully its past and present" (p. 19).

Issues of continuing concern in more than one area of the world include achieving public consent necessary to support culturally diverse educational programs (Hoff, 1995, p. 835; Volk, 1998). Expectations of some school programs have expanded to include international offerings (e.g., international baccalaureate programs), and many more school music programs include units of study on global music-making, as well as musics of the United States and the Americas. Those critical of this direction in education continue to provide important perspectives (e.g., Ravitch, 1990, 2000; Schlesinger, 1991).

Globally there is continuing interest in musics of the world's cultures in education (Floyd, 1996; Massey, 1996; Volk, 1998, pp. 130–131). There also appears to be a global current of interest among educators in "respect for persons," or "mutuality" (Lynch, 1983, in Figueroa, 1995, p. 789). Common interests exist also in "antiracism, cultural studies, and strategies designed to create greater equality of educational opportunity" (Allan & Hill, 1995, p. 763).

The crucial need is for thorough consideration of basic assumptions, observations, and recommendations for educational policy regarding musics of the world's cultures in music education. Consideration of these issues could be based on the ISME Policy on Music of the World's Cultures (1994). Solid ground is needed for clarification and support of this important area of music education and as foundation for future research. Even if music educators have diverse perspectives, clarity is critical about: why musics of the world's cultures are taught, what perspectives on music and culture support this practice, for whom the instruction is designed, what music cultures and what aspects of these cultures as well as levels of competence are attempted and assessed, and who is doing the teaching and what background they must have to be effective.

REFERENCES

Adachi, M. (1992). *The role of the adult in the child's early musical socialization* (Systematic Musicology Technical Report Series, No. 9206). Seattle: University of Washington School of Music.

Addo, A. O. (1992). A survey of music teaching strategies in Ghanaian elementary schools as a basis for curriculum development. In H. Lees (Ed.), *Music education: Sharing musics of the world* (pp. 267–273). Christchurch, New Zealand: The Printery, University of Canterbury.

Adler, P. S. (1975). The transitional experience: An alternative view of culture shock. *Journal of Humanistic Psychology, 15*(4), 13–23.

Allan, R., & Hill, B. (1995). Multicultural education in Australia: Historical development and current status. In J. A. Banks & C. A. M. Banks (Eds.), *Handbook of research on multicultural education* (pp. 763–777). New York: Macmillan.

Allport, G. W. (1988). *The nature of prejudice.* Cambridge, MA: Addison-Wesley. (Original work published 1954)

Amoaku, W. K. (1982). Parallelisms in the traditional African system of music education and Orff-Schulwerk. *Journal of the International Library of African Music, 6*(2), 116–119.

Anderson, W. M. (1992). Rethinking teacher education: The multicultural imperative. *Music Educators Journal, 78*(9), 52–55.

Anderson, W. M., & Campbell, P. S. (Eds.). (1989). *Multicultural perspectives in music education.* Reston, VA: Music Educators National Conference.

Anderson, W. M., & Campbell, P. S. (Eds.). (1996). *Multicultural perspectives in music education* (2nd ed.). Reston, VA: Music Educators National Conference.

Anku, W. (1998). Teaching creative dynamics of African drumming: A cross-cultural teaching approach. In B. R. Lundquist & C. K. Szego, with B. Nettl, R. Santos, & E. Solbu (Eds.), *Musics of the world's cultures. A source book for music educators* (pp. 75–84). Nedlands, Western Australia: Callaway International Resource Centre for Music Education.

Banks, J. A. (1988). *Multiethnic education: Theory and practice* (2nd ed.). Boston: Allyn and Bacon.

Banks, J. A. (1991). *Teaching strategies for ethnic studies* (5th ed.). Boston: Allyn and Bacon.

Banks, J. A. (1993). Education and cultural diversity in the United States. In A. Fyfe & P. Figueroa (Eds.), *Education for cultural diversity: The challenge for a new era* (pp. 49–68). New York: Routledge.

Banks, J. A. (1995). Multicultural education: Historical development, dimensions, and practice. In J. A. Banks & C. A. M. Banks (Eds.), *Handbook of research on multicultural education* (pp. 3–24). New York: Macmillan.

Bennett, H. S. (1983). Notation and identity in contemporary popular music. *Popular Music, 3,* 215–234.

Berry, S., & Singh, H. (1998). North Indian classical music in the classroom. In B. R. Lundquist & C. K. Szego, with B. Nettl, R. Santos, & E. Solbu (Eds.), *Musics of the World's cultures: A source book for music educators* (pp. 49–55). Nedlands, Western Australia: Callaway International Resource Centre for Music Education.

Bieber, A. B. (1997). *Adapting, transcribing and arranging world music for western instrumental performance.* Unpublished doctoral dissertation, Columbia University, New York.

Blacking, J. (1971). Toward a theory of musical competence. In D. DeJager (Ed.), *Man: Anthropological essays in honour of O.F. Raum* (pp. 19–34). Cape Town, South Africa: Struik.

Blacking, J. (1973). *How musical is man?* Seattle: University of Washington Press.

Bloom, B. S. (Ed.). (1985). *Developing talent in young people.* New York: Ballantine Books.

Booth, G. (1986). *The oral tradition in transition: Implications for music education from a study of North Indian tabla transmission.* Unpublished doctoral dissertation, Kent State University, Kent, OH.

Boyce-Tillman, J. (1996). A framework for intercultural dialogue in music. In M. Floyd (Ed.), *World musics in education* (pp. 43–94). Hants, UK: Scolar Press.

Boyer-White, R. (1988). Reflecting cultural diversity in the music classroom. *Music Educators Journal, 75*(4), 50–54.

Brittin, R. V. (1996). Listeners' preference for music of other cultures: Comparing response modes. *Journal of Research in Music Education, 44*(4), 328–340.

Broughton, S., & Ellingham, M. (Eds.). (2000). *World music: The rough guide: Vol. 2. Latin and North America, Caribbean, India, Asia and the Pacific.* London: Rough Guides.

Broughton, S., Ellingham, M., Muddyman, D., & Trillo, R. (Eds.). (1994). *World music: The rough guide.* London: Rough Guides.

Broughton, S., Ellingham, M., & Trillo, R. (Eds.). (1999). *World music: The rough guide: Vol. 1. Africa, Europe, and the Middle East.* London: Rough Guides.

Buckner, R. T. (1974). *A history of music education in the Black community of Kansas City, Kansas, 1905–1954.* Unpublished doctoral dissertation, University of Minnesota, Minneapolis.

Burton, B. (1993). *Moving within the circle: Contemporary Native American music and dance.* Danbury, CT: World Music Press.

Burton, J. B. (1996). Native peoples of North America. In W.

M. Anderson & P. S. Campbell (Eds.), *Multicultural perspectives in music education* (2nd ed., pp. 11–39). Reston, VA: Music Educators National Conference.

Burton, J. B., & Kreiter, M. (1998). *Voices of the wind.* Danbury, CT: World Music Press.

Campbell, P. S. (1991a). *Lessons from the world: A cross-cultural guide to music teaching and learning.* New York: Schirmer Books.

Campbell, P. S. (1991b, November). *What's wrong with this picture? Cries for research in multicultural music education.* Paper presented at the American Orff-Schulwerk Association Conference, San Diego, CA.

Campbell, P. S. (1993). Cultural issues and school music participation: The new Asians in American schools. *Quarterly Journal of Music Teaching and Learning, 4*(2), 45–56.

Campbell, P. S. (1994). *Musica exotica:* Multiculturalism and school music. *Quarterly Journal of Music Teaching and Learning, 5*(2), 65–75.

Campbell, P. S. (1996a). Music, education, and community in multicultural societies. In M. McCarthy (Ed.), *Crosscurrents: Setting an agenda for music education in community culture* (pp. 4–33). College Park, MD: University of Maryland.

Campbell, P. S. (1996b). *Music in cultural context: Eight views on world music education.* Reston, VA: Music Educators National Conference.

Campbell, P. S. (2001). Lessons from the Yakama. *Mountain Lake Reader.* Cincinnati: University of Cincinnati.

Campbell, P. S., McCullough-Brabson, E., & Tucker, J. C. (1994). *Roots and branches.* Danbury, CT: World Music Press.

Campbell, P. S., & Scott-Kassner, C. (1995). *Music in childhood: From preschool through the elementary grades.* New York: Schirmer Books.

Carter, L. R. D. (1996). *The world is welcome here: A survey of multicultural music teaching materials with annotated bibliography designed to assist the elementary classroom teachers.* Unpublished doctoral dissertation, Claremont Graduate School, Claremont, CA.

Casper, J. S. L. (1989). *Contextual variables in the maintenance of proportionate minority participation in high school vocal jazz ensembles.* Unpublished doctoral dissertation, University of Washington, Seattle.

Chaudhuri, S. (1992). Preservation of the world's music. In H. Myers (Ed.), *Ethnomusicology: An introduction* (pp. 365–374). New York: Norton.

Chin, L. (1996). *Multicultural music in higher education: Two case studies.* Unpublished doctoral dissertation, University of Oregon, Eugene.

Clifford, J. (1992). Travelling cultures. In L. Grossberg, C. Nelson, & P. A. Treichler (Eds.), *Cultural studies* (pp. 96–116). New York: Routledge.

Conlon, J. C. (1992). Explore the world in song. *Music Educators Journal, 78*(9), 46–51.

Crystal, D. (2000). *Language death.* Cambridge, England: Cambridge University Press.

Curtis, N. (Coll., Ed., Arr.). (1996). *The Indians' book: An offering by the American Indians of Indian lore, musical and narrative, to form a record of the songs and legends of their race.* Avenel, NJ: Portland House. (Original work published 1907)

Damm, R. J. (2000). *Repertoire, authenticity, and instruction: The presentation of American Indian music in Oklahoma's elementary schools.* New York: Garland.

Darrow, A. A., Haack, P., & Kuribayashi, F. (1987). Descriptors and preferences for Eastern and Western musics by Japanese and American nonmusic majors. *Journal of Research in Music Education, 35*(4), 237–248.

Davis, P., Harrison, G., Johnson, D. M., Smith, P. C., & Crawford, J. F. (1995). *Teaching Western literature in a world context.* New York: St. Martin's Press.

Del Valle, L. G. (1998). Multiculturalism: An evolving concept in the teaching of music in the Philippines. In B. R. Lundquist & C. K. Szego, with B. Nettl, R. Santos, & E. Solbu (Eds.), *Musics of the world's cultures: A source book for music educators* (pp. 89–93). Nedlands, Western Australia: Callaway International Resource Centre for Music Education.

Dewey, J. (1916). Nationalizing education. *Journal of Proceedings and Addresses of the National Education Association, 54,* 185–186.

Diagram Group. (1997). *Musical instruments of the world: An illustrated encyclopedia.* New York: Sterling.

Diaz, M. C. (1980). *An analysis of the elementary school music series published in the United States from 1926 to 1976.* Unpublished doctoral dissertation, University of Illinois, Urbana.

Downing, A. A. (1997). *Let 'er buck: Music in cowboy culture of the Powder River Basin, Wyoming.* Unpublished doctoral dissertation, University of Colorado, Boulder.

Duke, R. A. (1999). Measures of instructional effectiveness in music research. *Bulletin of the Council for Research in Music Education, 143* 1–48.

Dworkin, D. L. (1992). *Views beyond the border country: Raymond Williams and cultural politics.* London: Routledge.

Eagleton, T. (2000). *The idea of culture.* Oxford: Blackwell.

Education of a singer at the Beijing Opera. (1995). FFH 4346. Princeton, NJ: Films for the Humanities and Sciences.

Edwards, K. L. (1994). *North American Indian music instruction: Influences upon attitudes, cultural perceptions, and achievement.* Unpublished doctoral dissertation, Arizona State University, Tempe.

Edwards, K. L. (1998). Multicultural music instruction in the elementary school: What can be achieved? *Bulletin of the Council for Research in Music Education, 138,* 62–82.

Eisner, E. W. (1990). *Qualitative inquiry in education.* New York: Teachers College Press.

Elliott, D. J. (1989). Key concepts in multicultural music education. *International Journal of Music Education, 13,* 11–18.

Elliott, D. J. (1990). Music as culture: Toward a multicultural concept of arts education. *Journal of Aesthetic Education, 24*(1), 147–166.

Elliott, D. J. (1995). *Music matters: A new philosophy of music education.* New York: Oxford University Press.

Ellis, C. J. (1985). *Aboriginal music: Education for living.* St. Lucia, Australia: University of Queensland Press.

Evans, B. (Comp., Arr.). (1968). *Dictionary of quotations.* New York: Delacorte Press.

Farnsworth, P. R. (1969). *The social psychology of music.* Ames: Iowa State University Press.

Feld, S. (1982). *Sound and sentiment: Birds, weeping, poetics, and song in Kaluli expression.* Philadelphia: University of Pennsylvania Press.

Feld, S. (1984) Communication, music, and speech about music. *Yearbook for Traditional Music, 16,* 1–18.

Feld, S., & Basso, K. H. (1996). *Senses of place.* Santa Fe, NM: School of American Research Press.

Figueroa, P. (1995). Multicultural education in the United Kingdom: Historical development and current status. In J. A. Banks & C. A. M. Banks (Eds.), *Handbook of research on multicultural education* (pp. 778–800). New York: Macmillan.

Finnegan, R. (1988). Transmission in oral and written traditions: Some general comments and postcript. In *Literacy and orality: Studies in the technology of communication* (pp. 139–179). Oxford: Blackwell.

Floyd, M. (1996). Approaching the musics of the world. In M. Floyd (Ed.), *World musics in education* (pp. 24–42). Hants, England: Scolar Press.

Fowler, C. (1966). The misrepresentation of music: A view of elementary and junior high school music materials. In B. Kowell (Ed.), *New perspectives in music education: source book* (pp. 289–295). Washington, DC: Music Educators National Conference.

Fowler, C., with Gerber, T., & Lawrence, V. (1994). *Music! Its role and importance in our lives.* New York: Glencoe.

Fung, C. V. (1994). Undergraduate nonmusic majors' world music preference and multicultural attitudes. *Journal of Research in Music Education, 42*(1), 45–57.

Gardner, H. (1986). The development of competence in culturally defined domains: A preliminary framework. In R. A. Shweder & R. A. Le Vine (Eds.), *Culture theory: Essays on mind, self, and emotion* (pp. 257–275). Cambridge, England: Cambridge University Press. (Original work published 1984)

Gardner, H. (2000). *The disciplined mind.* New York: Penguin Books.

Garfias, R. (1983). Music in the United States: Community of cultures. *Music Educators Journal, 69*(9), 35–36.

The Garland encyclopedia of world music. (1998–). Vols. 1–10. New York: Garland.

Gates, J. T. (1991). Music participation: Theory, research, and practice. *Bulletin of the Council for Research in Music Education, 109,* 1–36.

Gay, G. (1995). Curriculum theory and multicultural education. In J. A. Banks & C. A. M. Banks (Eds.), *Handbook of research in multicultural education* (pp. 25–43). New York: Macmillan.

Geertz, C. (1986). "From the native's point of view": On the nature of anthropological understanding. In R. A. Shweder, & R. A. LeVine (Eds.), *Culture theory: Essays on mind, self, and emotion* (pp. 123–136). Cambridge, England: Cambridge University Press. (Originally published 1984)

George, L. (1987). *Teaching the music of six different cultures.* Danbury, CT: World Music Press.

Geringer, J. M., & Madsen, C. K. (1995). Focus of attention to elements: Listening patterns of musicians and nonmusicians. *Bulletin of the Council for Research in Music Education, 127,* 80–87.

Goldberg, M. R. (1993). *The complexities of musical performance: A multicultural perspective.* Unpublished doctoral dissertation, Harvard University, Cambridge, MA.

Goodkin, D. (1998). Polycentric music education. In B. R. Lundquist & C. K. Szego, with B. Nettl, R. Santos, & E. Solbu (Eds.), *Musics of the world's cultures: A source book for music educators* (pp. 56–74). Nedlands, Western Australia: Callaway International Resource Centre for Music Education.

Grant, C. A., & Secada, W. G. (1990). Preparing teachers for diversity. In W. R. Houston (Ed.), *Handbook of research on teacher education* (pp. 403–422). New York: Macmillan.

Green, T. F. (1983). Excellence, equity, and equality. In L. S. Shulman & G. Sykes (Eds.), *Handbook of teaching and policy* (pp. 318–341). New York: Longmans.

Han, K. H., & Campbell, P. S. (1992). *The lion's roar: Chinese lou-gu music.* Danbury, CT: World Music Press.

Harpole, P. W., & Fogelquist, M. (1991). *Los mariachis! An introduction to Mexican mariachi music.* Danbury, CT: World Music Press.

Henderson, C. (1993). Preparing future music teachers for dealing with minority students: A profession at risk. *Quarterly Journal of Music Teaching and Learning, 4*(2), 35–44.

Hoff, G. R. (1995). Multicultural education in Germany: Historical development and current status. In J. A. Banks & C. A. M. Banks (Eds.), *Handbook of research on multicultural education* (pp. 821–838). New York: Macmillan.

Hollinger, D. A. (1995). *Postethnic America: Beyond multiculturalism.* New York: Basic Books.

Holmes, R. A. (1990). *A model of aural instruction examined in a case of fiddle teaching.* Unpublished doctoral dissertation, University of Washington, Seattle.

Hood, M. (1960, May). The challenge of bi-musicality. *Ethnomusicology, 4* 55–59.

Hood, M. (1982). *The ethnomusicologist.* Kent, OH: Kent State University Press. (Original work published 1971)

International Baccalaureate Organization. (2001). *International Baccalaureate Program.* [On-line]. Available: info@ibo.org.

International Society for Music Education. (1994). Policy on music of the world's cultures. In B. R. Lundquist & C. K. Szego, with B. Nettl, R. Santos, & E. Solbu (Eds.), *Musics of the world's cultures: A source book for music educators* (pp. 17–19). Nedlands, Western Australia: Callaway International Resource Centre for Music Education.

Jessup, L. (1983). *The mandinka balafon: An introduction with notation for teaching.* La Mesa, CA: Xylo.

Jessup, L. (1992). *World music: A source book for teaching.* Danbury, CT: World Music Press.

Jones, B., & Hawes, B. L. (1972). *Step it down: Games, plays, songs, and stories from the Afro-American heritage.* New York: Harper and Row.

Jordan, J. (1992). Multicultural music education in a pluralistic society. In R. Colwell (Ed.), *Handbook of research on music teaching and learning* (pp. 735–748). New York: Schirmer Books.

Jorgenson, E. R. (1990). Music and international relations. In J. Choy (Ed.), *Culture and international relations* (pp. 56–71). New York: Praeger.

Kammen, M. (1999). *American culture, American tastes: Social change and the twentieth century.* New York: Knopf.

Kearns, D. T., & Harvey, J. (2000). *A legacy of learning: Your stake in standards and new kinds of public schools.* Washington, DC: Brookings Institution.

Keil, C. (1979). *Tiv song.* Chicago: University of Chicago Press.

Kjelland, J. M., & Kerchner, J. L. (1998). The effects of music performance participation on the music listening experience: A review of literature. *Bulletin of the Council for Research in Music Education, 136,* 1–55.

Klinger, R. (1996a). From glockenspiel to mbira: An ethnography of multicultural practice in music education. *Bulletin of the Council for Research in Music Education, 129,* 29–36.

Klinger, R. (1996b). *Matters of compromise: An ethnographic study of culture-bearers in elementary music education.* Unpublished doctoral dissertation, University of Washington, Seattle.

Klinger, R., & Goolsby, T. (1996). Review. *Bulletin of the Council for Research in Music Education, 129,* 57–61.

Kushner, S. (1991). Musicians go to school: A case of knowledge, control, and cross-professional action. *American Educational Research Journal, 28*(2), 275–296.

Ladson-Billings, G. (1994). *The dreamkeepers: Successful teachers of African American children.* San Francisco: Jossey-Bass.

Lanier, J. E., & Little, J. W. (1986). In M. C. Wittrock (Ed.), *Handbook of research on teaching* (3rd ed., pp. 527–569). New York: Macmillan.

LeBlanc, A. (1982). An interactive theory of music preference. *Journal of Music Therapy, 19,* 28–45.

LeBlanc, A. (1987). The development of music preference in children. In J. C. Peery, I. W. Peery, & T. W. Draper (Eds.), *Music and child development* (pp. 137–157). New York: Springer-Verlag.

Lee, H. (1988). *The development and trial of resource materials focusing on traditional Korean music idioms for a senior high school general music course in Korea.* Unpublished doctoral dissertation, University of Michigan, Ann Arbor.

Lees, H. (Ed.). (1992). *Music education: Sharing musics of the world.* Christchurch, New Zealand: The Printery, University of Canterbury.

Lemann, N. (2000, September 25). Dumbing down: Did progressivism ruin our public schools? *New Yorker,* 89–91.

Lepherd, L. (Ed.). (1995). *Music education in international perspective: National systems.* Toowoomba, Australia: University of Queensland Press.

Lind, V. R. (1997). *The relationship between Hispanic enrollment and the classroom environment in secondary choral music programs.* Unpublished doctoral dissertation, University of Arizona, Tucson.

Lundquist, B. R. (1991). Doctoral education of multiethnic-multicultural music teacher educators. *Design for arts in education, 92*(5), 21–38.

Lundquist, B. R. (1998). A music education perspective. In B. R. Lundquist & C. K. Szego, with B. Nettl, R. Santos, & E. Solbu (Eds.), *Musics of the world's cultures: A source book for music educators* (pp. 38–46). Nedlands, Western Australia: Callaway International Resource Centre for Music Education.

Lundquist, B. R. (2000). The teaching researcher: A sense of place. In R. R. Rideout & S. J. Paul (Eds.), *On the sociology of music education II: Papers from the Music Education Symposium at the University of Oklahoma* (pp. 1–18). Amherst, MA: University of Massachusetts.

Lundquist, B. R., & Szego, C. K., with Nettl, B., Santos, R., & Solbu, E. (Eds.). (1998). *Musics of the world's cultures: A source book for music educators.* Nedlands, Western Australia: Callaway International Resource Centre for Music Education.

Lundström, H., Olsson, B. O., Saether, E., & Svensson, S. (1998). Higher music education in a multicultural society. In B. R. Lundquist & C. K. Szego, with B. Nettl, R. Santos, & E. Solbu (Eds.), *Musics of the world's cultures: A source book for music educators* (pp. 102–109). Nedlands, Western Australia: Callaway International Resource Centre for Music Education.

Lynch, J. (1983). *The multicultural curriculum.* London: Batsford Academic and Educational.

Malinowski, B. (1945). *The dynamics of culture change.* New Haven: Yale University Press.

Malm, K. (1992). The music industry. In H. Myers (Ed.), *Ethnomusicology: An introduction.* (pp. 349–364). New York: Norton.

Malm, K., & Wallis, R. (1992). *Media policy and music activity.* London: Routledge.

Mans, M. S. (1997). *Namibian music and dance as ngoma in arts education.* Unpublished doctoral dissertation, University of Natal, Durban, South Africa.

Massey, I. (1996). Getting in tune: Education, diversity and music. In M. Floyd (Ed.), *World musics in education* (pp. 7–23). Hants, England: Scolar Press.

May, E. (1967, December). An experiment with Australian aboriginal music. *Music Educators Journal, 54,* 47–50.

May, E., & Hood, M. (1962, April–May). Javanese music for American children. *Music Educators Journal, 48,* 38–41.

Mbanugo, C. E. (1986). *Music transmission processes among children in an Afro-American church.* Unpublished doctoral dissertation, State University of New York, Buffalo.

McCarthy, M. (1997). Irish music education and Irish identity: A concept revisited. *Oidas, 45,* 5–22.

McCarthy, M. (1999). *Passing it on: The transmission of music in Irish culture.* Cork: Cork University Press.

McCarthy, M., & Stellaccio, C. (1994a April 6). Maryland's multicultural practices in general music. Presentation at the Social Science SRIG meeting, Music Educators National Conference biennial convention, Cincinnati, OH.

McCarthy, M., & Stellaccio, C. (1994b). The value of a multicultural music curriculum: Survey of Maryland general music teachers. *Maryland Music Educator, 40*(3), 25–27.

McCarthy, M. F. (1990). *Music education and the quest for cultural identity in Ireland, 1831–1989.* Unpublished doctoral dissertation, University of Michigan, Ann Arbor.

McInerny, D. M. (1987). Teacher attitudes to multicultural curriculum development. *Australian Journal of Education, 31*(2), 129–144.

McNeill, W., Jr. (1975). *Verbal and creative responses by fifth grade children to three types of Black American folk music.* Unpublished doctoral dissertation, Pennsylvania State University, University Park.

Merriam, A. P. (1955). Music in American culture. *American Anthropologist, 57,* 1173–1181.

Merriam, A. P. (1964). *The anthropology of music.* Evanston, IL: Northwestern University Press.

Montague, M. J. (1988). *An investigation of teacher training in multicultural music education in selected universities and colleges.* Unpublished doctoral dissertation, University of Michigan, Ann Arbor.

Montalto, N. V. (1982). *A history of the intercultural education movement—1924–41.* New York: Garland.

Moodley, K. A. (1995). Multicultural education in Canada: Historical development and current status. In J. A. Banks & C. A. M. Banks (Eds.), *Handbook of research on multicultural education* (pp. 801–820). New York: Macmillan.

Moore, J. A. (1993). *An assessment of attitude and practice of general music teachers regarding global awareness and the teaching of music from a multicultural perspective in American schools.* Unpublished doctoral dissertation, Kent State University, Kent, OH.

Mumford, J. E. (1984). *The effect on the attitudes of music education majors of direct experiences with Afro-American popular music ensembles: A case study.* Unpublished doctoral dissertation, Indiana University, Bloomington.

Musgrove, F. (1982). *Education and anthropology: Other cultures and the teacher.* Toronto: Wiley.

Music Educators National Conference. (1994). *National standards for arts education.* Reston, VA: MENC.

Nakazawa, N. (1988). *School music, environment, and music preferences: A comparison of Japanese students living in Japan and Japanese students living in the United States.* Unpublished doctoral dissertation, Columbia University Teachers College, New York.

National Association of Schools of Music (NASM). (1995). *National Association of Schools of Music 1995–1996 handbook.* Reston, VA: National Association of Schools of Music.

Navarro, M. (1989). *The relationship between culture, society, and music teacher education.* Unpublished doctoral dissertation, Kent State University, Kent, OH.

Nettl, B. (1983). *The study of ethnomusicology: Twenty-nine issues and concepts.* Urbana: University of Illinois Press.

Nettl, B. (1985). *The Western impact on world music: Change, adaptation, and survival.* New York: Schirmer Books.

Nettl, B. (1997). Introduction: Studying musics of the world's cultures. In B. Nettl, C. Capwell, P. V. Bohlman, I. K. F. Wong, & T. Turino, *Excursions in World Music.* (2nd ed., pp. 1–13). Upper Saddle River, NJ: Prentice-Hall.

Nettl, B. (1998). An ethnomusicological perspective. In B. R. Lundquist & C. K. Szego, with B. Nettl, R. P. Santos, & E. Solbu (Eds.), *Musics of the world's cultures: A source book for music educators* (pp. 23–28). Nedlands, Western Australia: Callaway International Resource Centre for Music Education.

Nettle, D., & Romaine, R. (2000). *Vanishing voices: The extinction of the world's languages.* Oxford: Oxford University Press.

Nguyen, P., & Campbell, P. S. (1990). *From rice paddies and temple yards: Traditional music of Vietnam.* Danbury, CT: World Music Press.

Nketia, J. H. K. (1996, July). Plenary speech. Conference of the International Society for Music Education, Amsterdam.

Norman, K. (1999). Music faculty perceptions of multicultural music education. *Bulletin of the Council for Research in Music Education, 139,* 37–49.

Norman, K. N. (1994). *Multicultural music education: Perceptions of current and prospective music education faculty music supervisors, and music teachers.* Unpublished doctoral dissertation, University of Michigan, Ann Arbor.

Nyberg, R. (1975). *The development, implementation and evaluation of an introductory course in ethnic music for use in the secondary school.* Unpublished doctoral dissertation, University of Miami.

Okun, M. J. (1998). *Multicultural perspectives in undergraduate music teacher education programs.* Unpublished doctoral dissertation, University of New Mexico, Albuquerque.

Olneck, M. R. (1990, February). The recurring dream: Symbolism and ideology in intercultural and multicultural education. *American Journal of Education,* 147–174.

Opala, J., & Schmidt, C. (1998). *The language you cry in.* California Newsreel [On-line]. Available: www.newsreel.org.

Palisca, C. V. (1964). *Music in our schools: A search for improvement* (Bulletin No. 28, U.S. Department of Health, Education, and Welfare). Washington, DC: U.S. Government Printing Office.

Palmer, A. J. (1975). *World musics in elementary and secondary music education: A critical analysis.* Unpublished doctoral dissertation, University of California, Los Angeles.

Palmer, A. J. (1992). World musics in music education: The matter of authenticity. *International Journal of Music Education, 19,* 32–40.

Paredes, A. (1995). *A Texas-Mexican cancionero: Folksongs of the lower border.* Austin: University of Texas Press.

Pembrook, R. G. (1997). The effect of mode of instruction and instrument authenticity on children's attitudes, information recall and performance skill for music from Ghana. *Bulletin of the Council for Research in Music Education, 133,* 115–120.

Peña, M. (1985). *The Texas-Mexican conjunto: History of a working-class music.* Austin: University of Texas Press.

Phinney, J. (1990). Ethnic identity in adolescents and adults: Review of research. *Psychological Bulletin, 108*(3), 499–514.

Pratte, R. (1979). *Pluralism in education: Conflict, clarity, and commitment.* Springfield, IL: Thomas.

Quesada, M. A. (1992). *The effects of an in-service workshop concerning Puerto Rican music on music teachers' self-efficacy and willingness to teach Puerto Rican music.* Unpublished doctoral dissertation, Kent State University, Kent, OH.

Quesada, M. A., & Volk, T. M. (1997). World musics and music education: A review of research, 1973–1993. *Bulletin of the Council for Research in Music Education, 131,* 44–66.

Ravitch, D. (1990, Winter). Multiculturalism: E pluribus plures. *American Scholar,* 337–354.

Ravitch, D. (2000). *Left back: A century of failed school reforms.* New York: Simon and Schuster.

Reimer, B. (1993). Music education in our multimusical culture. *Music Educators Journal, 79*(7), 22.

Roberts, M. (1982). *A comparison of elementary music educator practices and rationale for the inclusion of musical variety in aesthetic education toward broadening musical taste.* Unpublished doctoral dissertation, Washington University, St. Louis.

Robinson, K. M. (1996). *Multicultural general music education: An investigation and analysis in Michigan's elementary schools, K–6.* Unpublished doctoral dissertation, University of Michigan, Ann Arbor.

Rokeach, M. (1960). *The open and closed mind.* New York: Basic Books.

Roosens, E. E. (1989). *Creating ethnicity: The process of ethnogenesis.* Newbury Park, CA: Sage.

Rosenau, J. N. (1997, November). The complexities and contradictions of globalization. *Current History,* 360–364.

Saether, E. (1993). Training Swedish music teachers in Gambia: In search of a model for multicultural music education. In M. Phillip-Leitman (Ed.), *Teaching world music* (pp. 103–108). Basel: Basel Conservatory Press.

Sakata, H. L. (1983). *Music in the mind: The concepts of music and musician in Afghanistan.* Kent, OH: Kent State University Press.

Sam, A.-S., & Campbell, P. S. (1991). *Silent temples, songful hearts: Traditional music of Cambodia.* Danbury, CT: World Music Press.

Sands, R. M. (1993). Multicultural music teacher education. *Journal of Music Teacher Education, 2*(2), 17–24.

Santos, R. P. (Ed.). (1995). *The musics of ASEAN.* Manila: Committee on Culture and Information.

Savaglio, P. C. (1992). *Polish-American music in Detroit: Negotiating ethnic boundaries.* Unpublished doctoral dissertation, University of Illinois, Urbana.

Schlesinger, Jr., A. M. (1991, July 8). The cult of ethnicity, good and bad. *Time,* 21.

Schmid, W. (1992). World music in the instrumental program. *Music Educators Journal, 78*(9), 41–44.

Seeger, A. (1996). Foreword. In W. M. Anderson & P. S. Campbell (Eds.), *Multicultural perspectives in music education* (2nd ed., pp. x–xi). Reston, VA: Music Educators National Conference.

Senanes, G. (1998). Folklore para armar: Recreation and use of folk music in the classroom. In B. R. Lundquist & C. K. Szego, with B. Nettl, R. Santos, & E. Solbu (Eds.), *Musics of the world's cultures: A source book for music ed-*

ucators (pp. 85–88). Nedlands, Western Australia: Callaway International Resource Centre for Music Education.

Serwadda, W. M., with Pantaleoni, H. (1974). *Songs and stories from Uganda.* New York: Crowell.

Shehan, P. K. (1984). The effect of instruction method on preference, achievement and attentiveness for Indonesian gamelan music. *Psychology of Music, 12*(1), 34–42.

Siçangu Elder of the Lakota Nation of the Sioux. (1996, February 7). Ethnomusicology in the schools. Presentation at School of Music, University of Washington, Seattle. (Name withheld by request)

Skyllstad, K. (1998) The resonant community: A school project to promote interracial understanding. In B. R. Lundquist & C. K. Szego, with B. Nettl, R. Santos, & E. Solbu (Eds.), *Musics of the world's cultures: A source book for music educators* (pp. 94–101). Nedlands, Western Australia: Callaway International Resource Centre for Music Education.

Sleeter, C. E., & Grant, C. A. (1987). An analysis of multicultural education in the United States. *Harvard Educational Review, 57*(4), 421–444.

Slobin, M. (1993). *Subcultural sounds: Micromusics of the West.* Hanover, NH: Wesleyan University Press.

Small, C. (1980). *Music, society, and education* (rev. ed.). London: Calder.

Smelser, N. J. (1989). Self-esteem and social problems: An introduction. In A. M. Mecca, N. J. Smelser, & J. Vasconcellos (Eds.), *The social importance of self-esteem* (pp. 1–23). Berkeley: University of California Press.

Solbu, E. (1997). The multitude of cultures and their musics: Reflections on music education based on an ISME developing project. In *Report of world musics forum—Hamamatsu—1996* (pp. 74–79). Tokyo: Foundation for the Promotion of Music Education and Culture.

Sorrell, N. (1990). *A guide to the gamelan.* London: Faber and Faber.

Steinmetz, J., with Garfias, R., Jameson, B., & Jameson, P. (In press). *Music for Kids.* (Musical activities for elementary school children, book with projects and 10 CDs of songs, dances, and musics from the world's cultures, intended for children in the U.S.). Naxos Records.

Stephens, R. W. (1984). *The effects of a course of study on Afro-American popular music in the undergraduate curriculum.* Unpublished doctoral dissertation, Indiana University, Bloomington.

Stokes, M. (1997). Introduction: Ethnicity, identity and music. In M. Stokes (Ed.), *Ethnicity, identity and music: The musical construction of place* (pp. 1–27). Oxford: Berg.

Szego, C. K. (1999). *Musical meaning-making in an intercultural environment: The case of Kamehameha Schools.* Unpublished doctoral dissertation, University of Washington,

Taft, R. (1980). Coping with unfamiliar cultures. In N. Warren (Ed.), *Studies in cross-cultural psychology* (pp. 121–153). New York: Academic Press.

Tarnas, R. (1991). *The passion of the Western mind: Understanding the ideas that have shaped our world view.* New York: Ballantine Books.

Teicher, J. M. (1996). The children of the Thygaraja festival:

A study in bimusicality and cultural identity. *Quarterly Journal of Music Teaching and Learning, 6*(3), 76–89.

Teicher, J. M. (1997). Effect of multicultural music experience on preservice elementary teachers' attitudes. *Journal of Research in Music Education, 45*(3), 415–427.

Tenzer, M. (1991). *Balinese music.* Berkeley, CA: Periplus Editions.

Titon, J. T. (1997). Knowing fieldwork. In G. F. Barz & T. J. Cooley (Eds.), *Shadows in the field: New perspectives for fieldwork in ethnomusicology* (pp. 87–100). New York: Oxford University Press.

Titon, J. T., & Slobin, M. (1996). The music-culture as a world of music. In J. T. Titon (Ed.), *Worlds of music: An introduction to the music of the world's peoples* (3rd ed., pp. 1–16). New York: Schirmer Books.

Trimillos, R. D. (1989). Hálau, Hochschule, Maystro, and Ryú: Cultural approaches to music learning and teaching. *International Journal for Music Education, 14,* 32–43.

Tucker, J. C. (1992). Circling the globe: Multicultural resources. *Music Educators Journal, 78*(1), 37–40.

Veblen, K. K. (1991). *Perceptions of change and stability in the transmission of Irish traditional music: An examination of the music teacher's role.* Unpublished doctoral dissertation, University of Wisconsin, Madison.

Veblen, K. K. (1994). The teacher's role in transmission of Irish traditional music. *International Journal of Music Education, 24,* 21–30.

Veblen, K. K. (1996). Truth, perceptions, and cultural constructs in ethnographic research: Music teaching and learning in Ireland. *Bulletin of the Council for Research in Music Education, 129,* 37–52.

Volk, T. M. (1991). Attitudes of instrumental music teachers toward multicultural music in the instructional program. *Contributions to Music Education,* (18), 48–56.

Volk, T. M. (1992). Multicultural selections for band and orchestra. *Music Educators Journal, 78*(9), 44–45.

Volk, T. M. (1998). *Music, education, and multiculturalism: Foundations and principles.* New York: Oxford University Press.

Volk, T. M., & Holmes, R. A. (in press). *World on a string.* Van Nuys, CA: Alfred.

Volk, T. M., Spector, J., & Scott, W. G. (1996). Recent compositions with a multicultural perspective. *School Music News, 59*(6), 26–27.

Vygotsky, L. (1976). Play and its role in the mental development of the child. In J. S. Bruner, D. Jolly, & K. Sylva (Eds.), *Play—Its role in development and evolution* (pp. 537–554). New York: Basic Books.

Walker, L. M., & Hamann, D. L. (1995). Minority recruitment: The relationships between high school students' perceptions about music participation and recruitment strategies. *Bulletin of the Council for Research in Music Education, 124,* 24–38.

Waterman, C. A. (1990). *Jújù: A social history and ethnography of an African popular music.* Chicago: University of Chicago Press.

Wertsch, J. V. (1985). *Culture, communication, and cognition: Vygotskian perspectives.* New York: Cambridge University Press.

Williams, R. (1993). The idea of culture. In J. McIlroy & S. Westwood (Eds.), *Border country: Raymond Williams in adult education.* Leicester, England: National Institute of Adult Contemporary Education. (Original work published 1953)

Williams, R. (1958). *Culture and society, 1780–1950.* London: Chatto and Windus.

Wilson, C. G., Wilson, R. L. H., & Burton, J. B. (1994). *When the Earth was like new: Western Apache songs and stories.* Danbury, CT: World Music Press.

Wong, F. F. (1992, October). Diversity and our discontents. *AAHE Bulletin, 45*(2), 3–5.

Wulff, D. H. (1988, November 5). *Case studies of the communication of effective university instructors.* Paper presented at the seventy-fourth Annual Meeting of the Speech Communication Association, New Orleans.

Wulff, D. H. (1993, October). Tales of transformation: Applying a teaching effectiveness perspective to stories about teaching. *Communication Education, 42,* 377–397.

Yudkin, J. J. (1990). *An investigation and analysis of world music education in California's public schools, K–6.* Unpublished doctoral dissertation, University of California, Los Angeles.

Feminism, Feminist Research, and Gender Research in Music Education

35

A Selective Review

ROBERTA LAMB

LORI-ANNE DOLLOFF

SONDRA WIELAND HOWE

Music studies on the whole and music education in particular are behind other disciplines in taking advantage of the theories and approaches to research that have been established by feminism, feminist research, and gender research. This disadvantages the profession because there is now so much to come to terms with. Yet at the same time it is advantageous in that it enables us to make use of important groundwork laid in other disciplines. This chapter marks an important first step for music education.

Feminism as a political movement and an intellectual theory; feminism, women's studies, and gender studies in education; and feminism, women's studies, and gender studies in music provide direct links to feminism, feminist research, and gender research in music education. Thus, this chapter addresses several important topics:

- A brief summary of feminism, with its connections to women's studies and gender studies
- A brief summary of the development of educational feminism and gender studies in education
- A brief review of feminism, women's studies, and gender studies in music

The chapter also provides:

- A three-part model for reviewing feminism and gender research in music education today
- A review of the history of women in music education according to this model

- A review of feminist theory and gender studies in music education curriculum and practice according to this model
- Some feminist challenges to music education

This chapter marks the first recognition by the music education profession of feminism and gender as a research field. The priority was set to define a basic framework for the research field and identify important resources rather than to analyze the issues presented in the research within the field of feminism and gender in music education. Since chapter 33 reviews much gender-related literature in psychology, that research is not considered within this chapter. The enormity of the task means that this chapter presents the topic inadequately. Any researcher who plans to pursue feminist or gender-based research in music education must become familiar with the interdisciplinary feminist and gender-based literature in women's studies, education, and music, as well as the literature in music education. To do less would be irresponsible.

Background to Feminism and Feminist, and Gender Research in Music and Education

Feminism and Women's Studies

"What is feminism?" is primarily a question of ontology, asking about the nature and properties of feminism. Just as no one would expect "What is music?" to be definitively answered in one essay or one book or one lifetime (see

Alperson, 1987; Adorno, 1973, 1984; Bowman, 1998; Langer, 1942, 1953), it would be folly to expect "What is feminism?" to be sufficiently defined in one presentation. This review chapter provides an introduction to feminist and gender research and directs readers to some of the diverse sources addressing feminism and gender. Because women's studies and gender studies are such interdisciplinary, rich, and rapidly growing academic fields, the references provided herein are offered as examples only of the extensive source materials available. (Rather than list a plethora of significant articles, anthologies on a topic have been cited; therefore, the publication date indicated is later than when the essays were written.)

Three Waves of Feminism. While research indicates an extensive history of feminism,[1] contemporary thought generally classifies three different "waves" of feminism. The first wave is frequently identified as beginning in the mid–19th century (Americans cite the 1848 Seneca Falls conference) and extending through the suffrage movements to the post–World War II era. Intellectually, the first wave included Virginia Woolf (1929) and Simone de Beauvoir (1949/1953) among its authors. The second wave began in the mid-1960s. The third wave appeared in the 1990s.

Feminism matured as a grassroots political movement and an intellectual endeavor during the second wave. Women worked to improve their status through education, legal reform (particularly legal equity and reproductive rights), social policy, and political action. Women of color challenged sexism and racism, both within feminism[2] and outside it, insisting that

> [f]eminism is a struggle to end sexist oppression. Its aim is not to benefit solely any specific group of women, any particular race or class of women. It does not privilege women over men. It has the power to transform in a meaningful way all our lives. Most importantly, feminism is neither a lifestyle nor a ready-made identity one can step into. (hooks, 2000/1984, p. 28)

Representative source readings on second wave feminism can be found in Humm (1992) and Nicholson (1997). Women's studies, beginning as single courses in other departments, became the academic base for feminist research. Women's studies is characterized by interdisciplinarity, so the following references need to be seen as crossing those disciplinary boundaries. Major feminist texts that became the foundation for women's studies were published in: literature, history, psychology, sociology, science, and education; however, feminist literary criticism and women's history provided the initial model for the first feminist scholarship in music. Thus, the publication of Kate Millett's *Sexual Politics* (1970), which marked the beginning of feminist literary criticism in the second wave, and Gerda

Lerner's book *The Majority Finds Its Past* (1979)[3] became significant precursors for the development of feminist scholarship in music.

A hallmark of second wave feminism, including academic feminist work, has been the integration of political action and intellectual thought (Bowles & Klein, 1980; de Lauretis, 1986). During the 1980s feminist theory blossomed as a mode of analysis and critique, with a strong emphasis on maintaining links between feminist theories and feminist practices (e.g., hooks, 2000; Malson, O'Barr, Westphal-Will, & Wyer, 1986; Weed, 1989). Some feminist theories grew from particular disciplines, and others were original to feminism: liberal, Marxist, socialist, radical, psychoanalytical, existentialist, postmodernist (Tong, 1989). The term "gender" came into use to identify the social and cultural processes that assign people to categories of maleness and femaleness, while "sex" was reserved for biology. The term "sex-gender system" acknowledged a complex relationship between social, cultural, and biological characteristics. Yet even as these terms were established, they were contested in a way that symbolizes the constant shifting ground of feminist scholarship. Feminist methodology developed with close links to theory (e.g., Harding, 1987; Reinharz, 1992; Stanley & Wise, 1983). Simultaneously, feminist theories reconsidered epistemological questions (e.g., Code, 1991; Collins, 2000/1991; Harding, 1986; Harding & Hintikka, 1983; Hartsock, 1983; Stanley, 1990), the relationship between mind and body (e.g., Jaggar & Bordo, 1989), and the construction of the category "woman" (e.g., Fuss, 1989; Riley, 1988; Spelman, 1988). These arguments contemplated what is socially constructed and what is essential. This constant linking of theory and practice led to vigorous debates within feminist circles as issues of process and exclusion were considered (e.g., Hirsch & Keller, 1990). Women of color, lesbians, disabled women, older women, women of different political and religious backgrounds, sex trade workers, working-class and poor women, immigrant women—all had reason to challenge feminism to address their issues as women and feminists.

> There has been no other movement for social justice in our society that has been as self-critical as feminist movement. Feminist willingness to change direction when needed has been a major source of strength and vitality in feminist struggle. That internal critique is essential to any politics of transformation. Just as our lives are not fixed or static but always changing, our theory must remain fluid, open, responsive to new transformation. (hooks, 2000, p. xiii)

These difficult debates continue into current feminist thought and practice; however, most feminists see the debates themselves as a strength of feminism.

By the late 1980s feminism and many other modes of thought were borrowing and sharing principles, then integrating them into expanded theories. These exchanges involved, particularly, postmodernism, poststructuralism, and critical theory, and, by the 1990s, cultural studies (Grossberg, Nelson, & Treichler, 1992) and queer theory (Fuss, 1991; Pinar, 1998). A highly influential construct, introduced by Butler (1990), suggested that gender is performative, that is, not stable but a repeated practice appearing to be natural. Thus, postmodern performativity presents multiple genders rather than a male–female dichotomy. During the mid-1990s, the media proclaimed a postfeminist era,[4] but when feminism did not go away they termed it a third wave of feminism. Young women, often daughters of second wave feminists, comprise this third wave (e.g., Heywood & Drake, 1997), but third wave is also where the changing roles of men and male participation become explicit. The role of men in feminism (e.g., Digby, 1998), masculinities (Kimmel, 1995, 2000; Smith, 1996), queer politics (e.g., Abelove, Barale, & Halperin, 1993; de Lauretis, 1991), including transgender issues (Blasius, 1998; MacDonald, 1998), and popular culture become important areas of study in the academic third wave. This change of focus is often called gender studies. Of particular interest to music scholars is the burgeoning "youth music as cultural activism" within the third wave, although its documentation is more often found in cultural studies than in music studies (e.g., Swiss, Sloop, & Herman, 1998; Whiteley, 1997). Communication between generations is also seen as a project of the third wave (Looser & Kaplan, 1997). The third wave speaks of feminisms and feminist movements that take up antiracism, antipoverty, sexual orientations, ecological issues, and global issues, although concern with these issues began in the second wave. The intersections of antiracist, critical feminisms in the context of globalization and development continue to be at the forefront of feminist struggles (Ackerly, 2000; Dua & Robertson, 1999; Ng, Staton, & Scane, 1995).

On the other hand, feminists express wariness (e.g., Modleski, 1991) that the gender studies that developed in this third wave has the potential, if it disconnects from liberation politics, to lose sight of the central emancipatory project and that women will disappear from the picture yet again. At the same time, gender studies would not have come into existence without feminist analysis of the construction "woman," which then made a place for the study of "man" as a social construction and the meanings of "masculinity" in political, social, and creative life.

It could be said that where second wave feminism was concerned primarily with equal rights for women and women's issues (including the constructivist-essentialist debates), the third wave is concerned with the differences among women, and among women and men, in a postmodern world. In reality, current feminisms defy the neat packages of second wave and third wave. Haraway's

(1991) endeavor to contextualize feminisms, where such markers as race, ethnicity, class, sexual orientation, age, and ability are not separated from gender, is indicative of current feminist thinking:

> I am arguing for politics and epistemologies of location, positioning, and situating, where partiality and not universality is the condition of being heard to make rational knowledge claims. These are claims on people's lives; the view from a body, always a complex, contradictory, structuring and structured body, versus the view from above, from nowhere, from simplicity. (p. 195)

Contemporary feminisms do not so much propose a single truth as aim to encourage communities that accommodate critique, questioning, dissent, and disagreement (Crow & Gotell, 2000). These communities include all kinds of people and demand constant challenge of the status quo.

Feminism, Women's Studies, and Gender Studies in Education

Feminism, women's studies, and gender studies in education followed paths similar to those just described for the three waves of feminism. First wave will not be discussed. The second wave added women to the curriculum and worked to achieve equity in education. The third wave emphasizes differences, postmodernity, and contextualizing gender and feminism so that race, ethnicity, social class, and sexuality are not separated.

Feminism and Women's Studies in Education—Second Wave. Early education feminism anthologies (e.g., Rich & Phillips, 1985) indicate that education researchers were concerned with women's issues found in the feminist movement itself. Feminist research and practice in education included: uncovering sexism in historical perspectives of education; identifying women leaders in education; justifying equal opportunities and affirmative educational programs; creating nonsexist curricula; studying the status of women in education as a profession; and identifying how boys' and girls' experiences in school and school achievements differed. Two women philosophers contributed greatly to the theorizing to support these major changes in education. Maxine Greene, who has been called "a 'mother' of education feminism" (Stone, 1994, p. 9), began to write during the mid-1970s about the value of female experience, a "lived world" demonstrated through literature[5] and history, and sexism in the schools (Greene, 1978). Jane Roland Martin examined the status of women in educational philosophy (Martin, 1982). She followed this with the classic *Reclaiming a Conversation: The Ideal of the Educated woman* (Martin, 1985), which provided a place for women to begin participating in philosophy.

Many U.S. equity projects were spurred by Title IX of the 1972 Education Amendments, the Women's Educational Equity Act of 1974, Title IV of the Civil Rights Act of 1964, and the Vocational Education Amendments of 1976 (Klein, 1985, p.xii). One project produced the *Handbook for Achieving Sex Equity through Education* (Klein, 1985), which focuses on practical administrative and pedagogical practices and strategies, although it begins with an examination of the assumptions of equity. Maxine Greene contributes a philosophical argument for educational equity that is grounded in history, psychology, and human rights (Greene, 1985). Equity projects in North America often promoted the inclusion of women in the curriculum, such as in history, literature, and art (Hedges & Wendt, 1980) courses, as well as investigating ways to encourage girls to study the higher levels of math, science (e.g., Mura, Kimball, & Cloutier, 1987), and technology (e.g., Collis, 1987) and participate in sports (e.g., Dewar, 1987). They were often quite practical in focus and, in addition to providing the means toward instructional materials, resources, and appropriate classroom interaction, examined men as victims of sexism and the economic costs of limiting girls' opportunities (Sadker & Sadker, 1982).[6]

The exploration and valorization of an ethics of caring (Noddings, 1984), or connectedness, and women's ways of knowing (Belenky, Clinchy, Goldberger, & Tarule, 1986), growing from Gilligan's (1982) work in psychology and moral development, were other aspects of feminism and women's studies in education during the second wave. Gilligan suggested that females experience different stages of moral development than males and that these stages are more relational than rule bound. Belenky et al. conducted research to examine these theories, concluding that women did have five unique epistemological perspectives on knowing, although the researchers would not call these perspectives "stages." As with the expansion of feminism to include gender (already mentioned), there were feminists who were concerned that reclaiming caring, intuition, and other "feminine" qualities could manage to reinforce and reinstate the male/female hierarchy. In addition, other scholars have raised many legitimate challenges regarding the systemic racism and class bias to be found in the work of Gilligan (1982), Noddings (1984), and Belenky et al. (1986); however, space does not permit further discussion in this chapter.

It seemed that a great deal of educational change and improvement had been made during the second wave, yet the American Association of University Women (AAUW) commissioned a report on girls in education because the organization was concerned that girls were disappearing from equity discussions. This was confirmed for the AAUW when none of the U.S. Department of Education's America 2000 National Educational Goals was gender specific. The report reviewed 1,300 research studies, found that progress toward equity did not meet public perception of having achieved equity, and contributed 40 recommendations to bring gender equity to every aspect of schooling in order to provide excellence and equity for all students (American Association of University Women Educational Foundation, 1995).

Feminism and Women's Studies in Education—Third Wave. Maxine Greene's influence continues today, as she integrates the concepts of social, racial, and feminist difference within her writing. Her influence is acknowledged by many of the most original feminist educational thinkers: Sari Biklen (1995), Deborah Britzman (1991), Mary Bryson and Suzanne de Castell (1997), and Carmen Luke and Jennifer Gore (1992). Greene sees imagination as "what makes empathy possible" (1995, p. 3). Throughout her work she refers to women writers. She talks about the "realization that the individual does not precede community," the significance of "visions of possibility" (p. 195), and opening the "ground of critical community" in order to find ways "to make the ground palpable and visible to our students, to make possible the interplay of multiple voices, of 'not quite commensurable visions' " (p. 198). These ideas prove critical to arts educators. The second edition of *Women and Education* (Gaskell & McLaren, 1991) moves into the postmodern, thus becoming a very different book from the first edition (Gaskell & McLaren, 1987). It emphasizes difference, problematizing "the female experience," asking "whose knowledge?" and addressing racism directly. In one of five chapters addressing "whose knowledge?" and the only chapter about an arts discipline, Lamb (1991b) presents a postmodern dialogue on curriculum theory, pointing to the intimacy, trust, and contextual understanding required among those who speak, in order for that dialogue to lead to knowledge. She develops the postmodern dialogue further in Lamb (1994). In other work, Biklen's (1995) longitudinal analysis of the gendered work of school teaching compares the perspectives of contemporary teachers and historical teachers, and examines how meanings about teachers circulate through many cultural forms. Britzman (1991) contributes her critical, poststructuralist study of practice teaching as professional preparation. Lather (1991) connects feminist research with feminist pedagogy through postmodern analysis of the many relations of power in process. Lewis (1993), Ellsworth (1997), and Ropers-Huilman (1998) are among those feminist scholars who examine power relations in teaching. Lewis interrogates the voice and silence, examining both as resistance and as communication. Ellsworth challenges the workings of power in pedagogy, the "mode of address" that "is one of those intimate relations of social and cultural power that shapes and misshapes who teachers think students are, and who students come to think themselves to be" (Ellsworth, 1997, p. 6). The difficulty of claiming a place for social justice and democracy through feminist teaching in the face of neoconservatism becomes fundamental to Ropers-Huilman (1998) in her study of feminist teaching. Armatage (1999) challenges the "trend towards idealizing diversity in our universities as a marketing tool," presenting an anthology that contests current thinking about equity, even as it is "at least in part bathed in the light of consciousness and knowledge of current questioning of the discursive field of diversity/equity" (p. 13). Within this anthology, Lamb (1999) questions mentoring as an equity strategy in the context of patriarchal relations. Feminist debates about racism, heterosexism, privilege, and power do erupt in education, as described by Gaskell and Willinksy in the "Introduction" and Henry in the "Introduction Revisited" to *Gender in/forms curriculum: From Enrichment to Transformation* (Henry, 1995). Both essays address the difficult "nonconference" that produced the book of 14 subject-based chapters, including one on art education (Collins, 1995) and one on music education (Lamb, 1995). The editors commented:

> We do learn from conflict, if only slowly. In this reframing power is central to how the issues are taken up. Power cannot be ignored in pedagogy. . . . Power cannot be ignored in the political struggles to create institutional change. We have to learn to work constructively across differences in power, as well as differences in experience. (Gaskell & Willinksy, 1995, p. 13)

Gender Studies in Education. Gender studies in education evolved out of education feminism. There appear to be three strands developing in gender studies: gender theory; studies of masculinity or masculinities as social construction; and lesbian/gay studies, or queer theory. Curriculum projects formerly called "sex equity" are now labeled "gender equity." Gender theory is applied in contexts that are more conservative because it avoids the emancipatory politics or lesbian presence within feminism. Yet gender theory can be important in critical approaches to education when it takes the idea of genders in relation very seriously. For example, Gabriel and Smithson (1990) use gender theory to examine power relations in pedagogy. Blair and Holland (1995) consider gender as one kind of difference that is mixed up with many kinds of difference (e.g., race, ability, sexuality, class) and then pursue this gender mix through autobiography, marginalization, history, psychology, and political theory.

This difference leads very well into the second major strand developing in gender studies: the social construction of masculinities. While Kimmel is the most prolific author in this field (1987, 1990, 1996, 1998), many scholars are engaging in critical studies of masculinities. Digby (1998) suggests that "[S]urveying the possibilities for men's feminist theorizing, teaching, and living from a variety of per-

spectives" makes it possible to "mark places for men in feminism" as well as "put up warning signs, map difficult terrain, and point to uncharted territories" (pp. 5–6). Stecopoulos and Uebel (1997) ask: "How do men inhabit simultaneously their color and their gender?" (p. 2) and what is "the dialectic between racial and gender differences"? (p. 5). These scholars address sexuality and sexual orientations in masculinity as well.

Although there are several texts dealing with masculinity in education, two are especially worth noting. Mac an Ghaill (1994) presents a 5-year study of "schooling as a masculinizing agency." He describes his major concern as a "critical examination of the way in which dominant definitions of masculinity are affirmed within schools, where ideologies, discourses, representations and material practices systematically privilege boys and men" (p. 4). Gilbert and Gilbert's (1998) study of masculinity in schools includes popular culture, behavior, violence, and literacy.

Lesbian and gay studies, or queer theory,[7] is the third stream of gender studies. As Pinar (1998) suggests, "[h]omophobia (not to mention heterosexism) is especially intense in the field of education, a highly conservative and often reactionary field" (p. 2). He summons education to

> come to its senses regarding the presence of gay and lesbian youth in the schools, not a few of whose teachers are also gay and lesbian. It is past time to correct the repression of queers in the curriculum, especially in history and literature and the arts. . . . Queer pedagogy displaces and decenters; queer curriculum is noncanonical, for starters. (p. 3)

Sears (1987) was one of the first to encourage educators to address the issues facing gay and lesbian students in high schools and continues to present important work challenging heterosexism. Britzman's (1995) call to "stop reading straight" became a very influential essay in education queer theory. Similarly, Bryson and de Castell (1993) articulated theories of queer pedagogy. Pinar's anthology presents a significant collection of education queer theorists. In one of these essays, Walcott (1998) looks at the intersections of black literature, community, and sexuality with rap music, with a concern for interconnectedness rather than dichotomy.

Feminism, Women's Studies, and Gender Studies in Music

Feminism, women's studies, and gender studies in music follow the three waves of feminism[8] but in a more compressed chronology than education. First wave will not be discussed. The second wave uncovered women composers and performers, added women and music courses to the curriculum, and examined the status of women in music. Currently, second wave research continues in music while third wave feminist/gender/queer music scholars emphasize difference, postmodernity, and contextualizing gender/feminism to be inclusive of race, ethnicity, social class, and sexuality.

Feminism and Women's Studies in Music—Second Wave. Feminist research in music began as a search to recover women composers and musicians who had been lost to traditional music history. This was a needed compensatory history, growing from the work of Lerner (1979) and others. Questions regarding the periodization of music history and the differential values placed on particular kinds of music, for example, the symphony as exemplar rather than the parlor song, were raised as more information regarding historically gendered practices was discovered. Feminist scholars turned to literary criticism, particularly "gynocriticism," a term referring to the sociohistorical and materialist study of literature written by women (Showalter, 1985), and to feminist aesthetics (e.g., Ecker, 1985; Korsmeyer & Hein, 1993) for models that might be adapted to understanding music from a feminist perspective. Battersby's (1989) analysis of genius, virtuosity, creativity, and aesthetic philosophy has been particularly useful for feminist criticism of music. These two streams of writing a compensatory women's music history and considering the possibilities of feminist music criticism were the primary scholarly focus during the second wave in music. Many music and/or women's studies departments offered some form of a "women and music" course. The College Music Society carried out two studies of the status of women in music in colleges and universities (Reich, 1988). Jane Bowers assessed the effect of feminist scholarship in music (1989) and proposed directions for the new scholarship (1990).

Many biographies and critical studies of individual women composers and musicians were undertaken at this time and will not be mentioned here.[9] Five books are essential to a basic understanding of feminism and women's studies in music: Bowers and Tick (1986), Koskoff (1989), McClary (1991), Citron (1993), and Cook and Tsou (1994). Bowers and Tick (1986) was the first anthology of feminist musicological research and focused on retrieving biographies and music but also set these women within historical and social context. Its focus is limited to Western art music and historical musicology; yet nearly every chapter mentions education in some way. Those that feature education are cited later in this chapter. Koskoff (1989) edited the first anthology of ethnomusicological studies that "focus on women's cultural identity and musical activity" (p. x). Since a major focus in ethnomusicology is transmission, many of these essays have relevance for music education. The most important contribution of this book, one that continues to be as relevant in 2001 as it was when first written, is Koskoff's introduction, where

she first formulated a three-part model of music-gender-power. She developed these ideas further (Koskoff, 1991), but the initial questions remain: "First, to what degree does a society's gender ideology and resulting gender-related behaviors affect its musical thought and practice? And second, how does music function in society to reflect or affect inter-gender relations?" (Koskoff, 1989, p.1) McClary (1991) applied principles of feminist criticism to canonic instrumental and dramatic music, contemporary art music, and popular music; however, it was her analysis of gendered meanings in "absolute" music that caused a tidal wave in musicology. McClary's groundbreaking work provided a means for others to extend and build on her initial explorations. Using feminist theory, Citron (1993) explored the musical canon in creativity, professionalism, gendered discourse, and reception, concluding with a critique of canonicity in the university music curriculum. Cook and Tsou (1994) crossed the border between ethnomusicology and historical musicology, presenting feminist perspectives on topics in both disciplines within the same book, encouraging greater discussion across the music profession. Many of these essays include references to pedagogical practice or education as a socializing agent.

Feminism and Women's Studies in Music—Third Wave. Feminism and women's studies in music today have moved from the compensatory (although such work is still important) to a more critical and self-reflexive scholarship, which emphasizes interdisciplinarity, not only with literature, history, sociology, and psychology but also (and perhaps more important) within music itself. Music theory and composition, ethnomusicology, and historical musicology have become closely entwined. Methodologies are borrowed. Disciplinary lines are crossed and blurred. Performers present music by historic and contemporary women composers. They might even comment on gender through performance. Ruth Solie proposes that

> feminism in music scholarship is a critical theory of music and of music history that engages broad questions of social context, representation, and meaning. . . . Feminist scholars share the postmodern conviction that all knowledge is situated and that "objectivity" is a phantom; they conceive both personal and scholarly life in terms of responsibility and (often) activism; and they find, experientially, that political and scholarly commitments have inevitably been commingled even—perhaps especially—among those who disclaim or repudiate any such entanglement. (Solie, 1997, p. 7)

Feminist scholarship in music today examines music and musicians situated within a lived world. Issues of racism and class privilege are still very difficult ones for feminist scholars in music to address. The history of music as an academic discipline may make it more difficult to address racism and class privilege than it has been in education or women's studies, and the arguments remain more polite. Culture, ideology, representation, and difference—all terms requiring much discussion and definition—are now central to feminist music scholarship, particularly within criticism or interpretation. Ruth Solie's "Introduction: On 'Difference' " (Solie, 1993) is a good introduction to "difference" as a category for interrogation in music scholarship. The 15 essays included in *Musicology and Difference* (Solie, 1993) examine duality, fluidity, power, gender ideology, identity, class, lesbian and gay signification in the music, and anthropological analysis of music.

Feminist music scholarship in musicology features pedagogy prominently. As women and music courses were created, scholars realized that conventional pedagogical approaches to music history were inappropriate because they failed to challenge assumptions of historiography and socialization. This interest in pedagogy was expressed by music theorists, ethnomusicologists, and composition professors, as well as musicologists. While some of this work is cited later in this chapter, other examples bear mentioning here. Panels on pedagogy in university music classrooms appear at professional conferences, most often sponsored by the organization's status of women committee or student concerns committee. Citron (1990) was one of the first to examine the education of women in university music schools and to ponder the effects on their socialization as musicologists or composers. Further, Citron (1993) devotes the last chapter of her book to pedagogical questions as a function of "the canon in practice." Strategies for introducing feminist concepts to students who might be offended by the word "feminism" are the topic for Burkett (1996). Diamond struggles with the ethics of teaching in searching for "a systematic pedagogy for counterpointing the voices of speakers from radically different positions and working to understand what frames their discourse" (Diamond, 1996, p. 29). Parenti (1996) proposes a feminist music composition curriculum.

In the "women in music" article in *The New Grove Dictionary,* Tick, Ericson, and Koskoff (2001) indicate the broad context of feminism and women's studies in music today. This definition later states that women in music includes the collective experience of women within Western and non-Western musical traditions. Moisala and Diamond (2000) provide a significant new anthology that serves as a model for such inclusive scholarship. Although the research presented in this anthology is framed by ethnomusicology, it includes a wide range of disciplinary methods: education, ethnomusicology, feminist studies, historical musicology, popular music studies, music technology, and sociology. The introduction, known among the authors as "the conversation" because it was written collectively via e-mail, and the pedagogical content found in some of the essays, particularly Pegley's (2000) and Mc-

Cartney's (2000), demonstrate a means of communicating across differences that could very well become a pedagogical model for educators. In another context, Sarkissian (1999) presents a theoretical and practical model for teaching about gender, women, and diverse cultures.

Gender Studies.   As already noted, the chronology of feminism and gender studies is compressed in music. Music scholars took advantage of the work already done in other disciplines, so that gender theory, studies of masculinities, and lesbian and gay studies, or queer theory, are contiguous and very much a part of feminism in music. Kahlberg (2001), writing the definition of "gender" for *The New Grove Dictionary* (Sadie, 2001), emphasizes the relational and semiotic nuances of gender as applicable in music. The theoretical underpinnings can be traced through postmodernism and the concept of gender as performative, that is, altered over time and context. The concern expressed by feminists in women's studies and education that women will disappear again through gender studies is a concern for some feminist scholars in music, because aspects of this work are not connected to an emancipatory project.

It may be that lesbian and gay studies, or queer theory, developed in music before gender studies. The Gay and Lesbian Study Group of the American Musicological Society (AMS) was founded in 1989. The following year a Composers and Sexuality panel was on the AMS conference program, and then several papers based in queer theory were presented at the 1991 Feminist Theory and Music conference. Brett and Wood (2001) provide an extensive entry for *The New Grove Dictionary* (Sadie, 2001) on gay and lesbian music. The most important book to lesbian and gay studies in music is *Queering the Pitch* (Brett, Wood, & Thomas, 1994). The editors note that the book is concerned

> less with identities than with representations, performances and roles. Its emphasis is on throwing into question old labels and their meanings so as to reassociate music with lived experience and the broader patterns of discourse and culture that music both mirrors and actively produces. (pp. viii–ix)

As in ethnomusicology, transmission of and socialization into musical practice are crucial. Consequently, the third section of this book, "Consorts," has the greatest relevance for music education. Rycenga (1994) outlines lesbian compositional processes that she sees as collaborative and in-relation, a part of a community of musicians. Attinello (1994) presents a preliminary sociological study of gay choir structure. Pegley and Caputo (1994) present a dialogue on music in the lives of two adolescent girls, specifically discussing what was learned through music. Pegley and Caputo attempt to re-create the performance of the original presentation, one that involved voices in conversation and overlapping and recorded excerpts of musical examples, in the way that the dialogue is laid out as text, using different columns and texts to convey this performance. Similarly, Lamb (1997) explores representations of sexual identity and its construction through music and music education in a linear re-presentation of a multimedia performance/paper that included costume, poetry, photographs, and musical scores.

Feminism, Women's Studies, and Gender Studies in Music Education

Feminism, women's studies, and gender studies in music education do not follow the three waves of feminism evident in education and in music. Consideration of feminist issues in music education is so recent that the three waves are compressed into one. Music education did not demonstrate concern with issues addressed in second wave educational feminism: uncovering sexism in historical perspectives of music education; justifying equal opportunities and affirmative educational programs; and creating nonsexist curricula in music. The second wave issue that interested music education researchers was identifying how boys' and girls' experiences in musical achievements differ (as is noted later in this chapter); however, that exploration was limited to identifying sex stereotyping of musical instruments. Interest in other second wave issues, such as identifying women leaders in music education and studying the status of women in education as a profession (as is noted later in this chapter), is much too recent to be considered second wave. Music education has not yet been influenced by third wave feminism, gender studies, studies of masculinity, or queer theory, although third wave kinds of research are beginning to be published, particularly outside of traditional music education venues. There is not space in this chapter to present an analysis as to why music education has been so isolated from these theories while the same theories have had an impact on education as a discipline and music as a discipline. This is an important topic that deserves critical exploration and thorough analysis.

In order to complete this review, it became necessary to turn to the music education literature itself to devise an appropriate model to analyze feminist and gender-based research within music education. A review of recent research suggests three categories where feminism, feminist research, and gender research have had some influence:

- Research bearing the unacknowledged influences of feminist research, women's studies, and gender studies
- Research that is primarily compensatory in nature

- Research that challenges disciplinarity through its examination of gender, difference, and power

These three categories, then, provide the foundation for a three-part model for examining research in music education

Unacknowledged Influences of Feminist Research, Women's Studies, and Gender Studies

Unacknowledged influences are those where awareness of concerns about gender equality or gender differences or feminist theory are acknowledged but not identified as feminist in contemporary social organization. One example might be the substitution of the word "gender" for "sex" in quantitative studies, which has been the practice in music education research for several years. Another example might be the way the theoretical constructs developed in the 1980s by feminist historians have become a part of some music history survey courses, even when the instructor does not teach from a feminist perspective. Unacknowledged influences, particularly in education, could be summarized in the refrain "I'm not a feminist, but . . ." (e.g., I believe women should be paid the same as men for the same work, boys and girls should have equal opportunities in schools, etc.).

Compensatory Research in Feminist Research, Women's Studies, and Gender Studies

Compensatory research seeks to uncover facts about women and girls or to make knowledge more accurate by representing gender as meaningful in situations where the facts were not known or the meaning not recognized. Compensatory research adds women composers and musicians or feminist content to the curriculum, or it entertains aspects of gender issues or feminist thought without disturbing disciplinary boundaries or the political balance of power. Thus, compensatory research is often called the add-women-and-stir phenomenon. Compensatory research is central to the liberal tradition of equal opportunities; however, the liberal tradition envelops both the unacknowledged feminist influences and the compensatory applications of feminist theory in music education. Research into the effects of sex-role or gender-role stereotyping of musical activities, such as instruments (particularly as it concerns girls) and choral singing (particularly as it concerns boys) are examples of compensatory projects. This research would be considered second wave, if it had coincided chronologically.

Gender, Difference, Power: Challenges to Disciplinarity

This third category includes research that through its examination of the relationships among gender, power, and difference calls into question the very structure of knowledge and of music and the means we use to transmit knowledge and music through social structures, such as those found in composition, performance, and education. These challenges to the music education discipline can take ideas from the unacknowledged influences and compensatory research and stretch them past their limits. This research speculates and wonders, or it engages in empirical study where gender(s) is (are) fundamental. Such research not only acknowledges the political but also embraces it. This research could be considered third wave and postmodern.

All three categories of research influenced by feminist theories and gender theories are important and valuable to music and music education. In practice, not one of these categories is completely distinct from the others, because they are all apparent in current research in music education. One of the most fascinating and stimulating aspects of today's feminist theories in practice is the layered complexity that proposes new questions and contradictions—presenting a "yes, but" situation—such that easy answers and clean categories do not exist. These three categories function as tools to assist a reader to organize thinking about and understanding recent research. They have not been proposed as a new orthodoxy. These three categories do not exist in a historic progression, for example, while the compensatory add-women-and-stir approach has been around music for 2 decades, much research still desperately needs to be done in order to add all of the facts that could be discovered about women in music and music education. Rather, it behooves music educators to embrace the unacknowledged influences, the compensatory, and the challenges to the discipline and to welcome the contributions each category of gender and feminist research brings toward greater understanding of gender and music. Separately, each category is diminished. If research on gender-difference-power were not challenging the definitions, the compensatory would not appear so reasonable and rational. If the compensatory research were not increasing the knowledge base, none of these new facts or rediscovered women musicians or modified ways of knowing would enter society to the point of becoming an unacknowledged influence. A complex and contradictory set of influences is no more a progression than history itself.

The next two parts of this chapter demonstrate how this model might be used. The emphasis is on compensatory research and challenging disciplinarity, because these are the two categories where gender is important to the research. Because of space constraints the studies in the unacknowledged influences category, which are numerous and do not consider gender directly, are not included. Sondra Wieland Howe presents an analysis of the history of women in music education. Lori-Anne Dolloff examines

feminist theory and gender studies in curriculum and practice.

History of Women in Music Education

Status of Historical Research

The roles of women and gender issues have been neglected in the available accounts of the history of music education.

> It is time to use a broader definition of the history of music education, telling the story of the education of students of all age groups, in music of all types, and in diverse community settings. . . . Various methodologies should be used including oral history, sociology, and ethnomusicology. As these new methods are used and different perspectives taken, a more comprehensive, richer, fuller historical account will emerge. (Howe, 1998)

The history of music education has been a chronological account of the teaching of Western music in public schools with an emphasis on major male leaders, the history of institutions, and the development of organizations. Livingston (1997) and Humphreys (1997) found an inequitable representation of women in the basic histories of music education in the United States. Authors of historical accounts have been men, and they have mainly used secondary sources that neglected women. This history needs to be reconstructed, using many primary sources, a variety of methodologies, and available research from other fields (musicology, ethnomusicology, sociology). Scholars need to look at the implications of race, class, and gender as they describe the past in its cultural context. As scholars investigate the roles of women in the history of music education and study the effect of gender on the development of music education, a new history will emerge that will enlighten us about the roles of both men and women and will have the potential to transform understandings of music and music education.

There is a large body of historical knowledge about women in music education, and this knowledge base is expanding. Women from various cultures and different countries have been involved in leadership roles in schools, teacher training, publishing, and performing in the public spheres of society. In the private spheres they have worked as independent teachers and served as patrons of the arts. Most of the historical work on women in music education is not written with a feminist agenda. Since the task of the authors is to recover invisible women, this research is compensatory. Authors have uncovered facts about women's roles to reconstruct history without disturbing the boundaries of the discipline.

Compensatory Research

Because of limited space, most of the historical literature reviewed here is about music education in the United States, but the issues and questions raised can be applied to constructing a history for other countries. The whole area of music in convents since the Middle Ages and the development of parochial school music education has not been covered. Historical research from feminist perspectives on leadership, teacher training and conservatories, women's roles in publishing, performing ensembles, piano teachers and patrons, black women music educators, and international perspectives are all under the compensatory research category.

Leadership in Public Schools and Professional Organizations

Women have served as leaders in the development of public school music education in the United States. Women have taught choral and instrumental music in public schools since the 19th century and have been active in the Music Education Division of the National Education Association (NEA), the Music Supervisors National Conference (MSNC), and the Music Educators National Conference (MENC). Eleven women, from Frances Clark to June Hinckley, have served as president of MSNC/MENC (Howe, 1999).

Since the 1960s, dissertations have been written about American public school leaders: Mabelle Glenn (Holgate, 1962), director of music in Kansas City and textbook editor; Lilla Belle Pitts (Blanchard, 1966), president of the MENC during World War II and faculty at Columbia Teachers College; Frances Elliott Clark (Stoddard, 1968), first president of MSNC and educator at RCA Victor; and Vanett Lawler (Izdebski, 1983), who was active in the International Society for Music Education (ISME). The dissertations from the 1960s were written before the development of feminist scholarship, but they contribute to the body of basic knowledge about women needed for feminist research. Research is needed on Marguerite Hood (1903–92), MENC president, editor, and faculty at the University of Michigan; Frances Andrews (1908–76), faculty at Pennsylvania State University and president of MENC during tumultuous times in the early 1970s; and Mary Hoffman (1926–97), textbook editor and faculty at the University of Illinois. A forthcoming encyclopedia, *Women and Music in America Since 1900* (Burns, in press), will include many articles on individual women and other topics related to gender issues.

Women have been involved in various movements that have been incorporated into public school teaching. Satis Coleman developed programs of "creative music" at Teachers College, Columbia University (Boston, 1993; Southcott, 1990; Volk, 1996). Grace Nash (Cole, 2000; Orrell, 1995) was a pioneer of the Orff method in the United States. Work needs to be done on the many women involved in developing and promoting the Orff, Kodály, Suzuki, and Dalcroze methods and the introduction of these methods in public schools. There is probably a wealth of information in the archives of these organizations.

At state and local levels, women are leaders in organizations that promote school music, provide contests and performing opportunities for children, and establish concert series. Laudon (2000) describes the activities of independent music teachers in the Minnesota Music Teachers Association, and Cooper (1992) describes the projects of the Thursday Musical of St. Paul, Minnesota, during the 20th century. Parker (1982, 1987) describes female music teachers in St. Paul schools and community. Historical societies, archives of music organizations, and published local histories contain a wealth of material on women in music organizations. Women in the late 19th century and throughout the 20th century have worked in their communities to both support public school music and create music opportunities for children outside of the school systems.

Teacher Training and Conservatories.
Research should compare the educational opportunities for women and men during various periods of history. For centuries, men have had opportunities to develop musical skills in military organizations and have brought their skills in band music into schools and communities. In the 18th and 19th centuries, men were self-taught and worked as itinerant musicians. Since the late 19th century, they have been educated in teacher-training institutions, colleges, and universities, often taking leadership roles as professors and administrators.

Women have had different educational experiences since they were not trained in the military (until the second half of the 20th century) and women have not been free to learn as respectable itinerant musicians. For centuries women received private music instruction and training in convents and girls' schools. Since the 19th century, women as well as men have been trained in teacher-training institutions and conservatories.

Women have established music schools and conservatories. Julia Crane established the Crane School of Music in Potsdam, New York (Claudson, 1969). Research is needed on women founders of conservatories: Clara Bauer, Cincinnati Conservatory; Jeannette Thurber, the National Conservatory of Music in New York; Janet Daniels Schenck, the Manhattan School of Music; and Mary Louise Curtis Bok, the Curtis Institute of Music in Philadelphia (see Ammer, 1980, pp. 226–228; Whitesitt, 1991, p. 309).

Women have been students in American and European conservatories since the 19th century. At the New England Conservatory of Music (Miller, 1933; McPherson & Klein, 1995), they prepared for careers as teachers and performers since the 1860s. It is disappointing that two recent books on the Juilliard School and the Indiana University School of Music ignore women and women's contributions. Olmstead (1999) describes the reign of the male administrators, politics, and finances at Juilliard but only briefly describes the outstanding faculty, many of whom were women. Logan's (2000) book is a history of administration, buildings, and fund-raising at Indiana, completely ignoring students and faculty.

Women's Roles in Publishing.   In the 19th century, public-school music textbook authors were men, but women anonymously helped in translating and editing. Women were very active in textbook publishing in the 20th century. There is a need for more research on music textbooks, by both female and male authors. Scholars can study the relationship between the published texts and the actual music activities in the classroom, gender implications of songs, and the relationship between music and pictorial images.

There are many areas of publishing where women have been involved. Women were successful in writing and publishing hymns in the 19th century as they used their musical skills in churches and temperance organizations and promoted positive social values (Claghorn, 1984; Rothenbusch, 1989). Women have written choral and instrumental music for schools and churches. Tick's (1997) excellent biography of Ruth Crawford Seeger tells how Seeger transcribed, arranged, and published American folk song collections for children. Brubaker (1996) analyzed piano methods in the United States from 1796 to 1995, and many of these methods were published by women.

Performing Ensembles.   Women have always performed vocal and instrumental music, but they have experienced prejudice in professional performing careers. When classical and jazz women musicians found their opportunities limited, they formed their own ensembles. Neuls-Bates (1986; 1996, pp. 192–205) and Ammer (1980, pp. 99–115, 200–223) describe women's orchestras in the United States. McCord (in press) discusses women in the International Association of Jazz Educators (IAJE) and women in jazz education at the college level.

While women have found success as performers in symphony orchestras today, they have experienced more limited opportunities in conducting (Lawson, 1984, 1991). Gould (1988, 1996) examines gender issues in the careers of women band directors. Feather (1987) discusses female band directors in American higher education and the difficulties women face building conducting careers. These authors go beyond a description of the situation to examine issues; they seek ways of making changes in the male-dominated areas of the performing profession.

Piano Teachers and Patrons.   Women have been encouraged to stay in the private domestic sphere, performing at home, teaching piano and voice, volunteering in church, and serving as patrons of the arts in their local communities. Although the 19th-century "piano girl," cultivating amateur feminine music skills to make herself more marriageable, has disappeared in the United States (Tick, 1986), the field of independent teaching and piano pedagogy is still dominated by women. The Music Teachers National Association (MTNA), founded in 1876, has contributed to the professionalism of independent music teaching through certification programs, conferences, and contests, as teachers teach in homes, commercial studios, colleges, and universities. While independent (or private) teaching has been a feminine field, the MTNA did not have a female president until Celia Mae Bryant, 1970–73 (Ulrich, 1976, pp. 188–189).

The area of piano teaching has only recently been covered in historical accounts. Allen (1987) describes piano teachers who founded music schools or taught at conservatories. She discusses method books published by women and the development of modern pedagogy. Sturm, James, Jackson, and Burns (2000) briefly summarize a century of piano teaching, covering methods, teacher training, journals, the MTNA, and the National Conference on Piano Pedagogy.

Whitesitt (1991) shows how women have supported the arts since the Renaissance. In the 20th century they have raised money for educational institutions, symphony orchestras, foundations, and festivals. Patrons can stay in the domestic sphere, working "behind the scenes" to support the arts while maintaining a traditional role in the family. Locke (1994) discusses the paradoxes of the woman music patron, raising interesting issues. Women patrons are underreported, and they are accused of being elitist and ignoring women composers and performers, but they still perform valuable services today. These issues are explored further in Locke and Barr (1997).

Black Women Music Educators.   Black women have been active in all these areas: teaching, leading organizations, establishing schools of music, publishing and composing, and performing. There is a rich body of research on the black experience that all educators should study. Southern (1997), in her history of the music of black Americans, generously acknowledges the contributions of women as they promoted music in their communities. They transmitted their musical heritage on plantations in antebellum America, performed and conducted groups in black urban churches, taught in schools and studios, and were active in African-American organizations. Walker-Hill (1992) describes the nurturing musical scene in Chicago as women composers had opportunities in black churches and the Chicago Women's Orchestra. They studied at the Chicago University of Music, the American Conservatory, and Chicago Musical College.

Handy (1998a) describes black women in bands and orchestras. The International Sweethearts of Rhythm (Handy, 1998b) performed throughout the United States and Europe, and many of these women had long, successful careers in public schools. Karpf (1999) describes Emma Azalia Hackley's experiences in teaching community music, teaching music reading and appreciation, and promoting African-American music. Schmalenberger is writing a dissertation about Harriett Gibbs Marshall, who founded the Washington Conservatory of Music. Good sources for material on black music are the Center for Black Music Research at Columbia College in Chicago and the Schomburg Center for Research in Black Culture in New York City.

International Perspectives. Scholars in the United States need to look at the growing body of research in other countries, written in English and other languages. Feminist research is needed on the history of music education in many countries and the transmission of teaching materials and methodologies across cultures. Some publications in Spanish include Frega's (1994) account of women musicians in Argentina and Torres's (1995) collection of articles on women in Spanish-speaking countries. Ostleitner and Simek (1991) analyze the perceptions of women in Austrian textbooks from the 1980s. They analyze instrument choices and social roles of women as portrayed in words and pictures, study the inclusion of female composers and poets, and observe the views of women in song tests. The authors sharply criticize underrepresentation and negative views of women in Austrian music textbooks. Myers (1993) gives a historical account of women's orchestras in Sweden, 1870–1950, showing their entrance into the public sphere and opportunities at Stockholm Music Conservatory in the 19th century and the founding of ensembles and work opportunities for women in the 20th century.

In Japan, women participated in the introduction of Western music during the Meiji period as teachers, translators, and performers (Howe, 1993, 1995). Nobu Koda studied music in the United States and Japan, returning to Japan to teach and compose in the early 20th century (Kobayashi, 1999). The Australian educator Emily Patton introduced tonic sol-fa to Japan in the early 20th century (Stevens, 2000). Hyde (1998) describes the development of the tonic sol-fa method in England by Sarah Glover. This is a short list of intriguing sources on women music educators in many lands. There is a need for comprehensive accounts of the history of music education in many individual countries, including the contributions of both women and men.

Challenging the Discipline

There is an impressive body of scholarship that was published in the 1990s, describing activities of women in dissertations, articles, and book chapters. More historical accounts of compensatory research are needed to recover the female music educators of the past. Scholars should be publishing comprehensive books on women music educators similar to the books published on women composers by musicologists in the 1980s. Tick, Ericson, and Koskoff's (2001) article "Women in Music" surveys women's contributions to Western classical traditions and world music and includes an extensive bibliography that will help music educators.

Currently there are fewer articles "challenging the discipline" than reporting compensatory research. Feminist scholars need to challenge the music education discipline, raising issues and defining music education to include a broader scope than public school music, using many types of primary sources, and incorporating scholarship from other disciplines like musicology and ethnomusicology. Howe (1998) suggests challenging the canon of past historical research by using new perspectives: American music from a black (or black female) perspective; a view of women's contributions throughout history, back to the Middle Ages; an analysis of both private and public spheres of music-making; and a study of oral traditions, including Native American singers. McCarthy (1999) describes three phases of gender research: an additive phase, in which women are identified and assimilated into the curriculum; a deconstructive phase, in which women's contributions are analyzed to determine why they have not been recognized; and a reconstruction phase, as issues of music and gender are examined from various perspectives. These three phases should also identify issues of gender as they intersect with issues of race, class, and ethnicity. Gould (1992b) traces the role of music teaching from the feminization of music teaching in the late 19th and early 20th century to the hierarchical stratification in the 20th century with women teaching younger students and men teaching older students, college music, and supervising female teachers.

Koza's (1988) research goes beyond history as an account of great individuals as she analyzes music instruction as viewed in *Godey's Lady's Book,* 1830–77. Koza (1990) studies the goals of instruction for both girls and boys; the value of instruction for moral character, health, and marriage prospects; and the types of music taught in this 19th-century culture. In a 1991 article she examines women's private and public musical spheres in texts and pictures, suggesting that contemporary thought about women is still influenced by Victorian ideology.

Further research of this kind is needed as feminists challenge the discipline. A feminist perspective of the history of music education will incorporate feminist scholarship from other disciplines as it analyzes gender relationships, investigates the interaction of music in public and private spheres, and looks at the impact of social context in describing music of the past.

Feminist Theory and Gender Studies in Curriculum and Practice

Grumet and Stone (2000) characterize the construction of curriculum as "a decision about what matters" (p. 183). The development of feminist theory and gender research has resulted in an expansion in our conceptions of what "matters" in school and university classrooms. What matters is not only the musical content of our programs but our pedagogy—how we interact musically and personally with our students, the way we design our musical environments to be inclusive of and to provide opportunities for all students. Lamb (1990) poses a series of questions that identify important areas for inquiry in feminist and gender-related studies in music. The questions raised by Lamb are echoed in those that emerged from the music, gender, and education conference in Bristol, England (Glover, 1993). The conference addressed issues of inclusion of women's music, sex stereotyping of instruments and musical roles, the vocabulary of our pedagogy, and the differences in participation and experience of males and females as learners and teachers. These themes appear in many of the studies reviewed hereafter. The music education research community has generally been slow in investigating issues of feminist theory and gender issues in relation to school and university music. The studies reviewed indicate that scholars are beginning in greater numbers to explore issues from a gendered perspective. Researchers are engaging in systematic inquiry into what matters in the music curriculum.

The areas of research reviewed in this section include both compensatory and challenging research agenda. Those studies that fall under the compensatory umbrella include: the gender stereotypes of musical instruments and performance; composition and improvisation; technology; gender-specific role models; and textbook analyses. Studies that fall into the category of challenging the politics of music education deal with issues of feminist pedagogy; gender studies that focus on both the "silent" females and the "missing" males; and the notion of music education and music teaching as feminized areas.

The Feminization of Music Teaching and Learning

Scholars in the field of education have explored the cultural constructions of teachers and teaching practice (see especially Biklen, 1995; Grumet, 1988; Weber & Mitchell, 1995). At the heart of these constructions is the perception that teaching is a feminized domain. Morton (1994a, 1997) attributes the marginalized place of music in schools to the feminization of music education. Music teaching is doubly feminized, because of both the status of teaching as women's work and the feminine gender associations of music. The feminine association of music, Morton contends, is a result of the historical representation of "intellectualism" that has valued "intellectual" pursuits over those perceived as "emotional." Thus music and education are considered "soft" subjects. This is a concern for students, teachers, and scholars, as there is a sense that their educational pursuits are not recognized as valuable (1994a, p. 114). As an examination of the politics of knowledge and power in music, Morton's research is an example of research that challenges the practice of music education. She holds that music education should explore feminist theory as a resource "to challenge the socio-cultural constructions of the gendered rendering of 'hard' and 'soft' subjects in the knowledge industry" (1994, p. 118). According to Morton, factors contributing to the exploitation of

> music as emotional sustenance, the ritual of music as spectacle, the selfless musical service to enhance other subject areas, and even the habitual burden of justification are all symptoms of and prescriptions for the feminized location of school music as well as the internalization of intimations of inferiority. (p. 118)

Morton maintains that music educators may acknowledge the feminized location of music but do not acknowledge the significance of that location, leading to a false consciousness (p. 120). In order to improve this trivialized location within schools, Morton insists that music educators "must reinforce their gender-sensitive frame of action with a critical appreciation for the numerous socio-cultural hierarchies framing curricular studies and practice" (p. 164).

Lamb (1997) explores the hierarchy of male/female musical behaviors:

> [M]usic proper is a feminine discipline within the academic hierarchy. Musical genius as personified in the composer or virtuoso is masculine, although his muse is feminine. The music teacher of children is feminine while the master teacher of great musicians masculine. The piano teacher, choral conductor, school music teacher may be feminine, but the symphonic maestro is most assuredly

masculine. The adequate teacher, the amateur musician is feminine, but the great master, the professional is masculine. (p. 93)

Similarly, Gould (1992a) addresses the existence of female and male gendered behaviors in music education. She follows legitimation theories to suggest that leadership or "implemental" behaviors are legitimate for males, while expressive actions are legitimate for females (p. 10). In Gould's view this is reflected in women choosing elementary music teaching "because it allows them to assume an expressive role" and in men choosing band directing "because it allows them to assume an implemental role" (p. 10).

In a later study, Gould (1994) portrays the practice of music education as being simultaneously gendered male and female (p. 95). On the one hand, feminization of the teaching profession leads to "other" status being accorded to education in general and music education in particular. She quotes Susan B. Anthony to highlight the issue of status relative to other professions:

> Do you not see that so long as society says a woman is incompetent to be a lawyer, minister, or doctor, but has ample ability to be a teacher, that every man of you who chooses this profession tacitly acknowledges that he has no more brains than a woman? (p. 94)

Gould holds, however, that in relationship to their students, women teachers are in positions of power and therefore are gendered male. The experience of simultaneous female/male gendering leads to contradictions and a bifurcated consciousness (p. 95). Gould recommends a transformation of the concept of music educator, rooted in the everyday lives of music educators. She insists that the transformation extend beyond the implementation of feminist pedagogies and the study of music by women and persons of color to include viewing the landscape from "marginalized positionalities." She includes women, people of color, lesbians and gay men, differently abled individuals, and young and/or untenured faculty (p. 96).

Feminist Pedagogy Challenges the Music Curriculum

In articles and book chapters that challenge the conceptual framework of how we practice music education, feminist scholars are working to adapt the vast amount of scholarship in feminist pedagogy undertaken in other areas to the field of music education. Coeyman (1996) reiterates that content and process in teaching cannot exist independently of each other. She recommends a feminist pedagogy as a way of addressing the challenges of curriculum reform. These changes in the undergraduate music curriculum include teaching new subject areas, such as world music,

popular music, and women's studies, and encountering a more diverse student population. While acknowledging that many of the principles are practiced without being labeled "feminist pedagogy," Coeyman seeks to articulate a feminist pedagogy in music. Feminist pedagogy:

- Addresses subject matters, teaching methods, and personal dynamics in and out of the classroom which are particularly conducive to studying women and gender issues by using vocabularies which address aspects of gender and sexuality as integral components of this subject matter.
- promotes an understanding of how gender and sexuality shape teaching, learning, and awareness of knowledge.
- is rooted in a socially-based, student-centered orientation to teaching, which considers learning as encompassing not only mastery of a specific body of knowledge but also the process of becoming, a personal assimilation of culture for each of us individually.
- permits faculty and students alike to speak with their own voice, on their own terms. (pp. 76–77)

Four principles are proposed by Coeyman as the foundation of developing a feminist pedagogy for both women's studies in music, and the general music major curriculum: diversity, opportunities for all voices, shared responsibility, and orientation to action.

Lamb (1995) maintains that it is the prevalence of the master-apprentice mode of education in music that continues to silence women's musical voices. Lamb (1996) provides an exploration of the contradiction between feminist pedagogy and the hegemonic structure of music and music education. One of the tenets of feminist education is the legitimacy of life experience as a subject of analysis. Lamb maintains that life experience is not valued in music study (p. 125). Another area of discord is the contrast between the interdisciplinary nature of feminist education and music education as a discipline-based field. Lamb identifies the continuing struggle between commitment to creating and practicing a feminist pedagogy and accommodating professional standards of pedagogy and musicianship (p. 129).

O'Toole (1997b) provides an examination of feminist theory in the context of three other pedagogical models: progressive education, humanist education, and critical pedagogy. This study pinpoints similarities between the models, as well as setting forth the suggestion that feminist pedagogy is not exclusively for women. O'Toole proposes that feminist pedagogy provides:

> new ways to theorize power relations based in the diversity of women's experiences and ways of interacting. These experiences have provided new grounds for critique and for pedagogical innovations, and offer both girls and boys opportunities for developing values different from those promoted by capitalism and patriarchy. (pp. 138–139)

It is important, according to O'Toole, to maintain a separate identity for feminist pedagogies in order to ensure "that the work and experience of women does not become assimilated or erased, once again, by those promoting more traditional forms of pedagogy" (p. 139).

Gender Studies: Examining and Challenging the Gendered Context of Practice

Green (1993, 1997) has made substantial inquiry into the gendered nature of the musical experience in schools. Green (1993) explores secondary school music teachers' perceptions about students' musical achievement. Gathering data by means of a questionnaire, Green elicited teacher's "common-sense notions" and assumptions about gendered musical relationships and compared them to students' results on the General Certificate of Secondary Education (GCSE) in music. Participants were asked to make judgments on achievement in specific musical behaviors, indicating whether they thought "girls," "boys," or "both equally" were more likely to be successful at musical behaviors such as: playing an instrument, singing, composing, listening, and notation-reading and -writing. Another component of the questionnaire examined perceptions of musical participation, asking respondents to indicate whether "girls," "boys," or "both equally" preferred to engage in classical music, popular music, or other world music. Respondents were asked to give reasons for their answers and to offer "any further comments about gender and music which are of general interest and/or relevance to your answers" (p. 222). Green offers large transcriptions of representative comments to support the emergent themes. Results indicated that most teachers perceived girls to have greater success and interest in singing and playing; that teachers perceive a clear distinction between "feminine" and "masculine" style; that boys have greater confidence in compositional and improvisational activities, that boys show more affinity to technology and pop/rock music; and, that girls' interaction with music can be characterized as more "passive," while that of boys is more "active" in involvement. Another issue that emerged was the importance of role models and the media in the development of patterns of musical involvement. The underlying contention is that "despite appearances . . . which suggest that girls have a high level of musical autonomy and success in schools, girls in fact fulfill musical roles which are ultimately circumscribed by deeper historical definitions of femininity as musically inferior" (p. 250).

Hanley (1998) replicates Green's study in a Canadian context. Revising Green's questionnaire, Hanley compared teachers' perceptions of gender issues with Grade 12 examination results. Her results concurred in a large part with Green's. Many teachers said that they thought that the sexes are "equal but different" (p. 54). Answers indicated that girls were perceived as being "considerably more successful than boys at singing, and somewhat more successful at playing, listening, and notation" (p. 54). As with Green's study, girls were seen to prefer classical music. Ratings from a study of adolescents by Hargreaves, Comber, and Colley (1995) show a similar result, that girls generally like a wider range of styles than boys do. Heavy metal and rock showed a significant main effect for gender in boys, while girls gave higher ratings for reggae, chart pop, jazz, classical, folk, and opera. In Hanley's study, boys were perceived by teachers to be more successful at composition. The teacher assumptions and conclusions that emerged were:

- Teachers assumed that equal access was sufficient to rectify any gender problems beyond getting more boys to sing
- They accepted the way girls and boys were in music class as perhaps unfortunate but not reversible
- There is reason for music teachers to reexamine their expectations of both girls and boys
- Teachers tended to perpetuate certain negative gender stereotypes in spite of their stated attempts to be fair
- Evidence of provincial grades contradicted teachers' perceptions of success in composition
- The possible negative impact of technology on girls' interest in composition has not been widely acknowledged. Linking composition exclusively with technology could discourage many girls from trying, thus reinforcing the stereotype of composition as a male preserve. (pp. 67–68)

Musical Instruments: Equal Access as Compensatory Practice

One of the most-studied gender issues in music education is that of sex stereotyping or gender association of musical instruments. This research seeks to describe the gendered perception of musical instruments and women's access to a range of musical opportunities. The studies are predominantly compensatory in nature. Researchers frequently express the goal of improving the equality of access to instrumental experiences and improving awareness of gender issues in instrumental programs.

Abeles and Porter (1978) examined the perception of musical instrument gender associations. In a series of studies, they elicited responses from parents, university students, elementary-aged children, and preschoolers. All ages associated flute and clarinet with "feminine" and drums and trumpet with "masculine." There was evidence, however, that the method of introduction of the instruments at the preschool level affected the sex stereotyping. Similar studies were carried out by Griswold and Chroback

(1981), Delzell and Leppla (1992), Fortney, Boyle, and DeCarbo (1993), and Zervoudakes and Tanur (1994), with similar results. In a related study, Porter and Abeles (1979) examine sex roles that operate in school music programs. The authors report on their earlier research and argue for greater freedom of choice, based on statistics that show a difference in the number of music-related career options for women versus those for men.

Girls and Women in Music Education: "Silent Participants"

In an analysis of music education research as reported in the *Music Supervisors' Journal*, 1914–24, Koza (1993) examined the prevalence and nature of gender-related studies in music education. She found that explicitly gender-related studies tended to focus on issues pertaining to males, particularly "missing males" in music programs. Pedagogical issues pertaining to females were overlooked. References to females took the form of remarks about "women's responsibilities" (p. 224), generally in the sense of nurturing their children's musical growth and advocating for school music programs. A second category discussed women's contributions to musical life (p. 226). Faced with the overwhelming emphasis on issues of male participation in music programs, historically and currently, Koza asks, "do current practices designed to solve the missing males problem work to the detriment of girls, and if so, how?" (p. 228). The same issue has guided the work of O'Toole (1998, 1997a, 1997b, 1997c, 1994, 1995). O'Toole (1998) maintains that while some choral textbooks may address issues of vocal range and repertoire for female voices, they do not address many other issues. She identifies some of the important issues as:

> identity issues that accompany puberty for girls, the subtle lessons learned from studying a mostly male-centered curriculum in all school subjects, the loss of opportunities they will experience as they outnumber boys in their choral programs by as much as 3:1, and the consequences of subjecting themselves to an activity where the societal and professional beliefs are that boys who sing are special, while girls who sing are ordinary. (p. 9)

O'Toole considers evidence that boys have advantages over girls as a result of teachers' stereotypic perceptions of gender roles and their subsequent interactions with students. Situating her study within the larger framework of evidence from studies in general education, O'Toole identifies several areas in the policy and practice of choral music education that affect the education of girls in choirs: gender expectations in choirs; the choral hierarchy of valuing mixed voice choirs over all others, and men or boy choirs

over women; repertoire that reproduces gender stereotypes; vocal range issues; different treatment of boys and girls in the classroom; and the perception that the quality of a choral ensemble is dependent on the number of males singing in it (pp. 15–23). She concludes that "ironically, although singing in a choir is considered a feminine activity, it is the male singers who are privileged." This study includes three extensive appendices of resources to increase awareness of the issues and provide further reading.

Repertoire issues are the focus of Morton (1994b). Morton examines the gender messages in children's song materials in two music textbooks and two music resource books, finding an abundance of male-dominated songs in the folk repertoire. She concludes, however, that even the use of nonsexist lyrics in song materials in textbooks may not result in musical experiences that are nonsexist in nature: "although textbooks may change, teachers' presentations may not" (p. 214).

In her earlier studies, O'Toole (1993, 1995) examines the ways that pedagogy in choral rehearsals perpetuates the male hegemonic structure and devalues girls' participation in choirs. O'Toole (1994) maintains that choral pedagogy is rooted in discourse that gives the director power, making the position of the singers subject to the discipline of the director (p. 69). Drawing on the work of Foucault, she examines rehearsal techniques, the architecture of choral rooms and seating of choir members, and reliance on the director's musical judgment to construct the performance as ways of contributing to the docility of singers. She suggests that there needs to be a rethinking of choral practices, including the way we think about the choral body and the product orientation to practice. O'Toole (1995) is a study of three curriculum projects in which the traditional choral pedagogy is intentionally challenged. Through experimental pedagogy, the ways rehearsal techniques tightly control knowledge acquisition were "broken open" (p. 383). Students planned curriculum, conducted, coached, and critiqued the choir, generally roles assigned to the all-knowing conductor. Students reported feeling compelled to change their role as a passive singer. A second way in which pedagogy was challenged was in reconfiguring the architecture of the physical space of the rehearsal. Students changed the way they used the rehearsal room and rehearsed in a variety of less traditional venues. In addition to changing the use of space, there were frequently a variety of activities taking place beyond a directed rehearsal (p. 387). O'Toole's research broke open the politics of choral pedagogy in two specific ways. First, the repertoire was not presented as if it were "a series of culturally pre-determined facts. The meanings and performances of musical motifs were negotiated by a cacophony of voices. Students and teachers created meanings that were culturally and politically sensitive to the moment" (p. 388).

Compensatory Research in Curriculum Content: Composition and Improvisation

Cousens (1997) takes the choral experience of female students as a starting point for her research. Her work focuses on beliefs about the role of women composers and their inclusion in the curriculum and the encouragement of young women to see composition as a viable career option. Cousens surveyed female students in 10 secondary schools in Ontario to collect their views of the choral repertoire, career aspirations, and role models in the choral setting and their experiences composing music. A survey of their vocal teachers elicited views about the criteria used in repertoire selection, inclusion of compositional components in the curriculum, and the inclusion of the works of Canadian women composers. She concludes that gender is not a criterion in repertoire selection in these high schools and that studying the work of women composers may inspire female students to pursue careers in composition.

Improvisation is another area in which participation seems to be affected by gender. McCord (1996) maintains that women do not feel as comfortable playing improvised solos as men. She cites the pianist, composer, and jazz educator Ellen Rowe, who finds that girls and women "are reluctant to play improvised solos because they fear they will be viewed as too masculine" (p. 30). Another jazz educator, Robin Connell, sees it as an issue of the social politics of the performance environment. She finds that it is a matter of encouraging the females in the ensemble to balance the opportunities for all "voices" to be heard.

> I give tons of encouragement to all of my students, but try to be especially sensitive to situations where a boy may be assertive and in effect be continually blocking an opportunity for the girl next to him (i.e. to improvise). This does not mean the boy should be penalized, rather the girl should be prompted to speak up if she is interested. (p. 30)

Challenging Traditional Curriculum Content: Girls and Technology

Another area in which there has been a perception of male association is technology. Caputo (1994) examines the evolving role of technology in the music classroom. She maintains that the digital knowledge of computer technology devalues knowledge that cannot be communicated in a digital format, particularly experiential knowledge. Caputo posits that this is a gendered issue because of the socialization of modes of thought.

> Girls are socialized to pursue, for the most part, relational, analogic ways of knowing, but they must unlearn these ways in order to be successful with technology. Thus, girls are set up for failure on some level as they confront technology and are measured by a male norm. (p. 89)

She cautions that the use of music technology should be informed by an examination of the social consequences of its use, so that music technology does not become a barrier to developing musical potential (p. 90). This echoes Hanley's (1998) concern that linking composition to technology may discourage many girls from trying, thus reinforcing the stereotype of composition as a male preserve. Pegley (1995) also addresses the "non-neutrality" of music technology. She is particularly concerned with the impact of technology on the physical space of a music room and the students' sense of place within it (see O'Toole, 1994, and the notion of architecture). Her initial questionnaire rated the choices of various technology centers by girls and boys. The results seemed to indicate that girls preferred centers involving less computer manipulation and more personal interaction while boys tended to choose more individualized, technologically based centers (p. 56). Pegley followed the questionnaire with in-depth observations of two students, one boy and one girl, to test these results. She concludes that despite some individual unique strategies, the two students were not unlike the other students in the class. Pegley makes the argument for recognizing the gender-determined responses to technology and the sense of place in the classroom (p. 58).

Role Models: Compensatory Research in Gender-specific Role Association

Gould (1996) explored the experience of women in college band directing, a field traditionally assigned to men. She interviewed women band directors to create a "reflexive tale" of their experiences, from initial involvement through their continuing career. Of particular interest was the influence and availability of role models in their decision to become college band directors. None of the participants identified a woman band director as being "influential" in their decision-making process, but each did report the presence of someone who encouraged or enabled them. Grant (2000) studied mentoring and the impact of gender-specific role models on the career aspirations and success of women conductors. She interviewed women college band directors at four career stages. The students who were interviewed struggle with issues of professional identity. One of the young women believed that "women seem to have difficulty standing on the podium and demanding anything of the musicians" (p. 99). Grant holds that the model for the profession has been determined by men. It is difficult for women to fit themselves into a style of conducting and rehearsing that may not be "natural" to them. She reminds us that children's image of a conductor is still the white-haired older male presented in many textbooks. While the women in Grant's study said working with a good musician was more important than seeking a same-sex mentor, there was agreement that seeing successful women on the podium and working with a same-sex mentor would be an asset in their development.

The lack of women role models is also of concern in the area of jazz education. McCord (1996) reports on two women who have addressed this dearth. Through the International Association of Jazz Educators program called "Sisters in Jazz," jazz vocalist Sunny Wilkinson finds mentors for young women who are interested in jazz (p. 31). Another jazz performer, Ann Patterson, has found that young women seek her out after concerts to tell her that they never knew girls could play the saxophone (p. 31).

Gender Studies Comes to Music Education: Boys and Men, the "Missing Males"

Research into the male experience of music education has largely focused on lack of participation by males in music programs or on men in those areas traditionally viewed as "feminine." Many scholars (including Acker, 1994; Gates, 1989; Green, 1997, 1993; Hanley, 1998; Koza, 1994; Mizener, 1993) have reported a perception or portrayal of singing as belonging to girls or being unmasculine. One of the recurring themes in much of the literature is the lack of participation by boys in choirs and other singing activities. Koza (1994, 1993) refers to this as the "missing male" problem (p. 51). She questions, however, the standard claims given in choral textbooks. Sherban (1996) conducted observations of Grade 1 and Grade 5 classes to examine boys' participation in and attitudes toward singing. She interviewed both male and female students, the teacher, and the administrator. Issues of gender, particularly the genderization of choral music, emerge.

Adler (1999) holds that part of the problem is the tendency in music education to provide strategies designed to manipulate "the students' attitudes through motivating strategies, rather than exposing teachers' and society's underlying attitudes and expectations" (p. 29). Following Koza (1994), he examines the stigma of being a male with a high voice. Adler proposes that teachers contribute to the stigmatization of the unchanged male voice in several ways. First, teachers often surround the issues with an air of "unmentionability." Second, some teachers mislabel unchanged voices with changed-voice labels to establish a "masculine ideal." Singing with a "high voice" is then considered a feminine thing (p. 30). The problem does not stop with the changed voice, however. Boys are often not taught to properly retune their ears and bodies for the new sounds that they are making, leading to dropping out of programs (p. 31). For Adler, the solution comes through educating boys in the proper use of their voices and honest dialogue about the vocal mechanism.

Based on the definitions of Morton (1997), Roulston and Mills (2000) investigated male teachers' experience in the feminized environment of music education. The study focuses on two teachers' accounts of practices adopted specifically to work with boys and the role of the male music teacher. Analysis of the interviews suggests that these teachers' gendered interpretations of their work "both serve to reinscribe and reinforce dominant constructions of masculinity, and existing gendered relations of power" (p. 234). There is evidence that in appealing to boys through the use of music they like (heavy metal) and the use of competitive sport analogies, such male teachers may legitimize the homophobic and misogynist attitudes that they seek to avoid. The authors argue for balance in the call for more male teachers in typically female roles with an informed awareness of the masculinity that they bring to their work.

Applications of Theory to Curriculum Content

A Compensatory School Music Curriculum.   The applications of feminist theory and gender studies to curriculum content have been mostly in the category of compensatory research. Researchers seek to establish models and develop curriculum materials for the inclusion of the music of women composers, artists, and conductors in the classroom. The earliest application of feminist musicology and theory to curriculum in music education was the work of Lamb (1988). In her study, Lamb seeks to set out a feminist perspective in music education and to develop a model for including the works of women composers in the elementary general music class in order to provide a gender-balanced curriculum. She suggests several strategies for moving toward a balanced presentation of music in the classroom. In addition to approaches that emphasize the contributions of women in the curriculum, Lamb also suggests teaching individual "great works," composed by both women and men, instead of the traditional "great composers" approach. In a later study she explains her focus on composition.

> Performing is a visible aspect of music. Composing, on the other hand is not an activity of which the average student is directly conscious, especially since it is a solitary activity. Therefore, introducing students to the music and background of women composers from various historical eras and providing experiences in composition offer many possibilities as pedagogical tools for developing nonsexist processes of music education. (Lamb, 1991a, p. 683)

The 1992 special issue of *Music Educators Journal* (MEJ), "Women in Music" (Blakeslee, 1992), provides a compendium of articles focusing on making an "awareness of women's accomplishments in music available to all students" (Atterbury, 1992, p. 27). This journal issue addresses women's issues in music education through articles on curriculum resources and awareness of issues of sex equity and through interviews with three successful women musicians. Three articles focus on specific curriculum content. Allen and Keenan-Takagi (1992) provide an annotated bibliography of choral repertoire by women composers. Palmquist and Payne (1992) offer resources for expanding the band and orchestral repertoire to include works by women. Lindeman (1992) explores strategies for including the contributions of women composers, conductors, and performers into the elementary classroom. This issue of *MEJ* is also an excellent resource for providing images of contemporary women in music. Among the articles that seek to address awareness of gender issues, Richardson's (1992) study of women's experience in music education offers insights into constructing a musical life, in the voices of 18 professional music educators. Interviews with trombonist and music educator Rebecca Bower (Johnsen, 1992), conductor Catherine Comet (Scanlan, 1992), and composer Ellen Taaffe Zwilich (DeLorenzo, 1992) offer perspectives from three women in musical roles generally considered "male." The women's stories serve as opportunities for young women to see role models and to expand all students' notions of musical roles.

Textbooks: Compensation or Reaction? Music textbooks are often treated as a bellwether to the sensitivities of society. Koza (1992, 1994), Lamb (1988), Morton (1994b), and O'Toole (1995, 1998), among others, all mention the role of textbooks in influencing people's perceptions of appropriate and inappropriate musical activities and behaviors. Koza (1992) holds that feminist scholars have taken particular interest in textbook content because of the perception that textbooks contain knowledge that is authoritative (p. 29). She provides an important list for the analysis of sexism in music materials:

- Evidence of a belief that musical activities in general are unmasculine
- A distinction between amateur and professional musicians that translates into the absence or underrepresentation of professional women musicians
- A greater likelihood of anonymity among females than among males, especially among females who are professional musicians
- Exclusion, underrepresentation, or stereotyping in representations of players of specific musical instruments
- Exclusion, underrepresentation, or stereotyping in representations of specific musical activities (p. 30)

Koza (1994) and O'Toole (1998) find that choral methods textbooks tend to ignore issues that pertain to women. When gender is acknowledged, it is usually male. Moreover, Koza finds that the masculine/male identity depicted in methods textbooks reinforces compulsory heterosexuality. She analyzes the ways that textbooks suggest redress-

ing the lack of boys and men in choral programs and maintains that the proposed solutions draw on and reinforce "discourses that socialist feminists find problematic" (p. 59). O'Toole (1998) offers a historical analysis of representation of boys in choral method books. She finds that while the language has grown "more subtle" over the years, the message remains the same: "choral directors will successfully recruit male singers only if they acknowledge the young males need to be manly" (p. 29).

Moving Beyond Compensation: Challenging University and College Curriculum Practice. Much of the early feminist research in music took place within the area of musicology. This research led to resources for the so-called add-women-and-stir compensatory approaches to curriculum reform. Scholarship on works by women composers and a feminist aesthetic led to efforts to create equality of access and opportunity and the creation of courses in "women's studies in music." While this has been an important step in creating a more inclusive music curriculum in the academy, there is much work to be done in the realms of "how" the curriculum is delivered (Lamb, 1997; Simpson, 1993). The discussion of feminist pedagogies and issues surrounding radical restructuring in areas of postsecondary education has been slower to appear in scholarly discourse. Lamb (1995) outlines the features in music education informed by feminist music criticism:

> There would be an emphasis on critical participation and empowerment. In pragmatic terms this results in an integration of women into music and a specialized scholarship of women in/and music. It means giving attention to the meanings of the ways we teach and learn. It means finding alternatives to the master-apprentice model. It means changing the definitions of music and theorizing about music education as we know them. It means we listen to feminist music criticism, hear, and respond, in ways that open up the score rather than close it down. (p. 129)

Challenging the traditional model of music education in the academy is often an isolating experience, as explored by Lamb (1996). She offers insights from her own struggles to integrate a feminist perspective with education at a school of music. Lamb found that her efforts were often met with resistance as students experienced a "dissonance" between their expectations of education in music and an emancipatory pedagogy (p. 128).

Weber and Mitchell (1995) affirm the early socialization of teachers into the feminized status of teaching. Girls begin early in life to "play" school (p. 42). Boys, they suggest, may in fact see "teacher" as "what they are not, something against which they can identify their maleness" (p. 43). They make the case for examining educators' childhood images of what constitutes "teacher" as a component of teacher education. One of the ways that Weber and Mitchell access these images is through drawing. They hold that drawings express deep issues about professional identity. Dolloff (1999) adapts the idea of using pictures in music teacher education. Students are asked to draw both their ideal teacher and themselves as teacher in an effort to compare their images and their realities. The complexity of the images expressed is fertile ground for the development of individual-centered teacher education. As students interact with their own drawings, describing them for peers and reflecting on them in their journals, they are led to an awareness of their own assumptions, biases, and beliefs. Dolloff holds that it is through this creation of opportunities for reflection that teachers are able to create their own "teacher voice" instead of simply replicating the teaching styles of their own educational history.

Conclusion

There are other areas where currently there is sufficient literature available to warrant reviewing feminist and gender-based music education literature using the three-part model of research. We identified these areas as philosophy, popular music studies, technology, music composition, social psychology of music education, sociology of music education, and ethnomusicology.

The membership of Gender Research in Music Education[10] has developed an extensive list of topics within music education that require further study from feminist and gender-based perspectives. So much feminist and gender-based research is needed that research on any topic would be worth pursuing.

While gender has been a component of music education research for decades, especially as an unacknowledged influence, studies relating feminism and feminist theory to music education are lagging behind progress made by scholarship in other educational areas. Compensatory studies, as noted earlier, are providing the materials to improve the visibility of women and women's music in the practice of music education. There is a continuing need for studies such as these to help teachers find curriculum resources and to heighten sensitivity to the gendered nature of our practice. As well, compensatory studies assist us in obtaining more complete knowledge of music education as a discipline. There continues to be a need for compensatory research in all areas of music education.

Scholars are also challenging the way we practice music education for all students in the light of feminist theory. Much work remains to be done in challenging the discourse of music education, particularly as already noted in the areas of pedagogy, university music studies, and music teacher education. The next generation of music teachers needs to encounter university and college programs that allow students to confront the issues of power, unequal

opportunity, and the gendered nature of the musical canon. Scholars need to design models that embody the principles that they claim to espouse. Continued dialogue and philosophical debate are needed to help articulate the foundation for such work. As recommended earlier, music education research needs to incorporate feminist scholarship from other disciplines, especially musicology, ethnomusicology, sociology, and education, as it analyzes gender relationships, investigates the interaction of music in public and private spheres, and looks at the impact of social context. Feminist perspectives of music education history need to challenge the discipline by incorporating black, Hispanic, and Asian musicians and music educators, oral traditions, and women (musicians, composers, and teachers) from many centuries. These diverse perspectives need to be considered in all areas of music education research. One way to proceed is for music education to open its borders and increase communication with other areas of music studies and other disciplines outside of music. It would be particularly useful for music education scholars to interact with others who are interested in pedagogical issues in these areas of study and disciplines by participating in such groups as the Society for Ethnomusicology Music Education Section, the women or gender committees of other music professional organizations, the International Alliance for Women in Music, or Gender Research in Music Education.

If feminism, feminist research, and gender research are to have the kind of impact on music education that they have had on education and on music, then music education scholars will need to challenge disciplinarity in music education. Such a challenge involves looking at these issues with imagination, seeking "visions of possibility" (Greene, 1995, p. 195) in order to build the "ground of critical community" (p. 198) where empathy is possible, where we consider all of this in relation. If, when examining music education, we use Greene's concept of imagination in conjunction with Koskoff's (1989) two principles of gender ideology in music and society—"First, to what degree does a society's gender ideology and resulting gender-related behaviors affect its musical thought and practice? And second, how does music function in society to reflect or affect inter-gender relations?" (p. 1)—then we could problematize "the canon," "the female experience," "knowledge," and "race" in the musical thoughts and practices that are music education, for starters. Further, Pinar (1998) acknowledges the homophobic, highly conservative and often reactionary qualities of education, pointing especially to the arts. Surely, music education as a subdiscipline of that field is implicated in its practices, and needs to "stop reading straight" (Britzman, 1995) as well. While we examine and question, we cannot ignore the role that power plays in research as well as in pedagogy and institutional change.

In challenging disciplinarity, we need to examine power relations in teaching and how meanings about teaching, learning, and teachers circulate through many cultural forms. Such examination is difficult because it calls into question the very structures of knowledge and of music and the means we use to transmit knowledge and music through social structures of education. It may be some time before we could build on Solie's (1997) definition of feminism in music scholarship (cited earlier) to create a description of feminism in music education, but when we can, that description might look something like this: Feminism in music education scholarship might some day be a critical theory of music and of music education that engages broad questions of social context, representation, and meaning. Sharing the postmodern conviction that all knowledge is situated and that "objectivity" is a phantom and conceiving personal, pedagogical, and scholarly life in terms of responsibility and activism, music educators would recognize that political and scholarly commitments commingle, even perhaps especially among those who disclaim or repudiate any such entanglement. Such an understanding of feminism in music education scholarship challenges much of what is most cherished by the music education profession.

NOTES

1. For example, Joan Kelly (Kelly-Gadol) analyzed the *Querelle des Femmes* (1400–1789) (Kelly, 1982) during the French Revolution. In England. Mary Wollstonecraft published *Vindication of the Rights of Women* (1792/1967).

2. Ena Dua presents a first wave–second wave–third wave model of the history of antiracist feminist thought in Canada (Dua, 1999).

3. For many years women's history dealt with finding the "lost" women in white European and North American history.

4. Although not the first to do so, the most recent example is a cover of *Time* magazine that proclaimed feminism dead (June 1998).

5. During the 1980s, Maxine Greene introduced me to a great deal of philosophy and poetry, including one particular Muriel Rukeyser poem (1973) that continues to inspire my work, "Kathe Kollwitz": "What would happen if one woman told the truth about her life? The world would split open" (Chester & S. Barba, p. 73).

6. For a thorough discussion of curriculum inclusion projects, instructional materials, and nonsexist classroom interaction before 1987, see Lamb (1988).

7. de Lauretis (1991) coined the term to include a list of nonnormative, nonheterosexual orientations.

8. See Koskoff's definition of three waves of feminist music scholarship (Koskoff, 2000, p. x).

9. Consult the *Norton/Grove Dictionary of Women Composers* (1995) and the *New Grove Dictionary of Music and Musicians* (2001) for more references to individuals.

10. Gender Research in Music Education (GRIME) is a professional organization founded in 1991 at the first Feminist Theory and Music Conference. It now consists of two sections: GRIME-International (founded 1991) and GRIME-MENC (founded 1998). An e-mail list was established in 1996 and a webpage, http://qsilver.queensu.ca/~grime/index. html, in 1998. GRIME meets annually, alternating between Feminist Theory and Music (odd years) and MENC (even years). Several other music professional organizations provide resources for feminist scholars and a means of locating others working in similar areas. These can be located via the GRIME webpage.

REFERENCES

Abeles, H., & Porter, S. (1978). Sex-stereotyping of musical instruments. *Journal of Research in Music Education, 26*(2), 65–75.

Abelove, H., Barale, M. A., & Halperin, D. M. (Eds.). (1993). *The lesbian and gay studies reader.* New York: Routledge.

Acker, S. (1994). *Gendered education.* Toronto: OISE Press.

Ackerly, B. A. (2000). *Political theory and feminist social criticism.* Cambridge, England: Cambridge University Press.

Adler, A. (1999). A survey of teacher practices in working with male singers before and during the voice change. *Canadian Journal of Research in Music Education, 40*(4), 29–33.

Adorno, T. (1973). *Philosophy of modern music* (A. G. Mitchell & W. V. Blomster, Trans.). New York: Seabury Press.

Adorno, T. (1984). *Aesthetic theory* (C. Lenhardt, Trans.). London: Routledge and Kegan Paul.

Allen, S. F., & Keenan-Takagi, K. (1992). Sing the songs of women composers. *Music Educators Journal, 78*(7), 48–51.

Allen, D. (1987). Women's contributions to modern piano pedagogy. In J. L. Zaimont (Ed.), *The musical woman: An international perspective: Vol. 2* (pp. 411–44). Westport, CT: Greenwood Press.

Alperson, P. (Ed.). (1987). *What is music? An introduction to the philosophy of music.* University Park: Pennsylvania State University Press.

American Association of University Women Educational Foundation. (1995). *How schools shortchange girls—The AAUW report: A study of major findings on girls and education.* New York: Marlowe.

Ammer, C. (1980). *Unsung: A history of women in American music.* Westport, CT: Greenwood Press.

Armatage, K. (Ed.). (1999). *Equity and how to get it: Rescuing graduate studies.* Toronto: Inanna.

Atterbury, B. W. (1992). Old prejudices, new perceptions. *Music Educators Journal, 78*(7), 25–27.

Attinello, P. (1994). Authority and freedom: Toward a sociology of the gay choruses. In P. Brett, E. Wood, & G. C. Thomas (Eds.), *Queering the pitch: The new gay and lesbian musicology* (pp. 315–346). New York: Routledge.

Battersby, C. (1989). *Gender and genius: Towards a feminist aesthetics.* Bloomington: Indiana University Press.

Belenky, M. F., Clinchy, B. M., Goldberger, N. R., & Tarule, J. M. (1986). *Women's ways of knowing: The development of self, voice, and mind.* New York: Basic Books.

Biklen, S. K. (1995). *School work: Gender and the cultural construction of teaching.* New York: Teachers College Press.

Blair, M., & Holland, J., with Sheldon, S. (Eds.). (1995). *Identity and diversity: Gender and the experience of education.* Philadelphia: Multilingual Matters, The Open University.

Blakeslee, M. (Ed.). (1992, March). Special focus on women in music [Special issue]. *Music Educators Journal 78* (7).

Blanchard, G. L. (1966). *Lilla Belle Pitts: Her life and contributions to music education.* Unpublished doctoral dissertation, Brigham Young University, Provo, UT.

Blasius, M. (1998, April). Contemporary lesbian, gay, bisexual, transgender, queer theories, and their politics. *Journal of the History of Sexuality 8*(4), 642–674.

Boston, S. C. (1993). *Satis N. Coleman (1878–1961): Her career in music education.* Unpublished doctoral dissertation, University of Maryland, College Park.

Bowers, J. (1989). Feminist scholarship and the field of musicology: 1. *College Music Symposium 29,* 81–92.

Bowers, J. (1990). Feminist scholarship and the field of musicology: 2. *College Music Symposium, 30,* 1–13.

Bowers, J., & Tick, J. (Eds.). (1986). *Women making music: The Western art tradition, 1150–1950.* Urbana: University of Illinois Press.

Bowles, G., & Klein, D. (1980). *Theories of women's studies.* London: Routledge and Kegan Paul.

Bowman, W. D. (1998). *Philosophical perspectives on music.* New York: Oxford University Press.

Brett, P., & Wood, E. (2001). Gay and lesbian music. In S. Sadie (Ed.), *The New Grove Dictionary of Music and Musicians: Vol. 9* (2nd ed., pp. 597–608). London: Macmillan.

Brett, P., Wood, E., & Thomas, G. C. (Eds.). (1994). *Queering the pitch: The new gay and lesbian musicology.* New York: Routledge.

Britzman, D. (1991). *Practice makes practice: A critical study of learning to teach.* Albany: State University of New York Press.

Britzman, D. (1995). Is there a queer pedagogy? Or, stop reading straight. *Educational Theory, 45*(2), 151–165.

Brubaker, D. (1996). *A history and critical analysis of piano methods published in the United States from 1796 to 1995.* Unpublished doctoral dissertation, University of Minnesota, Minneapolis.

Bryson, M., & de Castell, S. (1993). Queer pedagogy: Praxis makes imperfect. *Canadian Journal of Education, 18*(3), 285–305.

Bryson, M., & de Castell, S. (1997). *Radical in(ter)ventions: Identity, politics, and difference/s in educational praxis.* Albany: State University of New York Press.

Burkett, L. (1996). Feminist music scholarship: An informal guide to "getting it." *Indiana Theory Review, 17*(1), 67–76.

Burns, K. H. (Ed.) (in press). *Women and music in America since 1900: An encyclopedia.* Westport, CT: Oryx Press.

Butler, J. (1990). *Gender trouble: Feminism and the subversion of identity.* New York: Routledge.

Caputo, V. (1994). Add technology and stir: Music, gender, and technology in today's music classrooms. *Quarterly Journal of Teaching and Learning, 4, 5*(4, 1), 85–90.

Citron, M. (1990). Gender, professionalism and the musical canon. *Journal of Musicology, 8*(1), 102–117.

Citron, M. (1993). *Gender and the musical canon.* Cambridge, England: Cambridge University Press.

Claghorn, G. (1984). *Women composers and hymnists.* Lanham, MD: Scarecrow Press.

Claudson, W. D. (1969). The philosophy of Julia E. Crane and the origin of music teacher training. *Journal of Research in Music Education, 17*(4), 399–404.

Code, L. (1991). *What can she know?: Feminist theory and the construction of knowledge.* Ithaca, NY: Cornell University Press.

Coeyman, B. (1996). Applications of feminist pedagogy to the college music major curriculum: An introduction to the issues. *College Music Symposium, 36,* 73–90.

Cole, J. (2000). Grace Nash: Nine decades of graceful teaching. *Teaching Music, 7*(6), 44–48.

Collins, G. P. (1995). Art education as a negative example of gender-enriching curriculum. In J. Gaskell & John Willinsky (Eds.), *Gender in/forms curriculum* (pp. 43–58). New York: Teachers College Press.

Collins, P. (2000). *Black feminist thought: Knowledge, consciousness, and the politics of empowerment* (2nd ed). London: Routledge.

Collis, B. (1987). Adolescent females and computers: Real and perceived barriers. In J. Gaskell & A. McLaren (Eds.), *Women and education: A Canadian perspective* (pp. 117–131). Calgary: Detselig.

Cook, S., & Tsou, J. (Eds.). (1994). *Cecelia reclaimed: Feminist perspectives on gender and music.* Urbana: University of Illinois Press.

Cooper, L. (1992). *Thursday Musical: The first century, 1892–1992.* Minneapolis: Thursday Musical.

Cousens, M. (1997). *The influence of choral works by Canadian women on senior secondary students in Ontario.* Unpublished master's thesis, Ontario Institute for Studies in Education, University of Toronto.

Crow, B., & Gotell, L. (Eds.). (2000). *Open boundaries: A Canadian women's studies reader.* Toronto: Prentice-Hall.

de Beauvoir, S. (1953). *The second sex.* New York: Knopf. (Originally published in France by Librairie Gallimard, 1949)

de Lauretis, T. (Ed.). (1986). *Feminist studies/Critical studies.* Bloomington: Indiana University Press.

de Lauretis, T. (Ed.). (1991). Queer theory [Special issue]. *differences, 3*(2).

DeLorenzo, L. C. (1992). Three interviews: Ellen Taaffe Zwilich. *Music Educators Journal, 78*(7), 46–47.

Delzell, J., & Leppla, D. A. (1992). Gender association of musical instruments and preferences of fourth-grade students for selected instruments. *Journal of Research in Music Education, 40,* 93–103.

Dewar, A. (1987). Knowledge and gender in physical education. In J. Gaskell & A. McLaren (Eds.), *Women and ed-*

ucation: A Canadian perspective (pp. 265–288). Calgary: Detselig.

Diamond, B. (1996). Strategies for confronting patriarchy in the music school. In *Compendium International Conference on Music, Gender and Pedagogies, 26–28 April 1996*, 26–36. Göteborg, Sweden: School of Music and Musicology at the University of Göteborg.

Digby, T. (Ed.). (1998). *Men doing feminism.* New York: Routledge.

Dolloff, L. (1999). Imagining ourselves as teachers: The development of teacher identity in music teacher education. *Music Education Research, 1*(2), 191–207.

Dua, E. (1999). Canadian anti-racist feminist thought: Scratching the surface of racism. In E. Dua & A. Robertson (Eds.) *Scratching the surface: Canadian anti-racist feminist thought* (pp. 7–31). Toronto: Women's Press.

Dua, E., & Roberston, A. (Eds.) (1999). *Scratching the surface: Canadian anti-racist feminist thought.* Toronto: Women's Press.

Ecker, G. (Ed.). (1985). *Feminist aesthetics.* London: Women's Press.

Ellsworth, E. (1997). *Teaching positions: Difference, pedagogy, and the power of address.* New York: Teachers College Press.

Feather, C. A. (1987). Women band directors in American higher education. In J. L. Zaimont (Ed.), *The musical woman: An international perspective: Vol. 2* (pp. 388–410). Westport, CT: Greenwood Press.

Fortney, P. M., Boyle, J. D., & DeCarbo, N. J. (1993). A study of middle school band students' instrument choices. *Journal of Research in Music Education, 41*(1), 28–39.

Frega, A. L. (1994). *Mujeres de la música* [Women in music]. Buenos Aires: Planeta.

Fuss, D. (1989). *Essentially speaking: Feminism, nature and difference.* New York: Routledge.

Fuss, D. (Ed.). (1991). *Inside/Out: Lesbian theories, gay theories.* New York: Routledge.

Gabriel, S. L., & Smithson, I. (Eds.). (1990). *Gender in the classroom: Power and pedagogy.* Urbana: University of Illinois Press.

Gaskell, J., & McLaren, A. (1987). *Women and education: A Canadian perspective.* Calgary: Detselig.

Gaskell, J., & McLaren, A. (1991). *Women and education* (2nd ed.). Calgary: Detselig.

Gaskell, J., & Willinsky, J. (1995). Introduction: The politics of the project. In J. Gaskell & J. Willinsky (Eds.), *Gender in/forms curriculum* (pp. 1–14). New York: Teachers College Press.

Gates, J. T. (1989). A historical comparison of public singing by American men and women. *Journal of Research in Music Education, 37*(1), 32–47.

Gilbert, R., & Gilbert, P. (1998). *Masculinity goes to school.* New York: Routledge.

Gilligan, C. (1982). *In a different voice.* Cambridge: Harvard University Press.

Glover, J. (1993). Music, gender and education conference, Bristol University, March 1993. *British Journal of Music Education, 10*(3), 151–152.

Gould, E. S. (1988). *Occupational sex segregation: Wyoming high school band directors, 1973–1988.* Unpublished master's thesis, University of Wyoming, Laramie.

Gould, E. (1992a). Gender-specific occupational role models: Implications for music educators. *Update: Applications of Research in Music Education, 11*(1), 8–12.

Gould, E. S. (1992b). Music education in historical perspective: Status, non-musicians, and the role of women, *College Music Symposium, 32*, 10–18.

Gould, E. (1994). Getting the whole picture: The view from here. *Philosophy of Music Education Review, 2*(2), 92–98.

Gould, E. S. (1996). Initial involvements and continuity of women band directors: The presence of gender-specific occupational models. *Dissertation Abstracts International-A, 57* (4), 1533.

Grant, D. E. (2000). The impact of mentoring and gender-specific role models on women college band directors at four different career stage. *Dissertation Abstracts International-A, 61* (3), 926. (University Microfilms No. AAT 9966225)

Green, L. (1993). Music, gender and education: A report of some exploratory research. *British Journal of Music Education, 10*, 219–253.

Green, L. (1997). *Music, gender, education.* Cambridge, England: Cambridge University Press.

Greene, M. (1978). *Landscapes of learning.* New York: Teachers College Press.

Greene, M. (1985). Sex equity as a philosophical problem. In S. S. Klein (Ed.), *Handbook for achieving sex equity through education* (pp. 29–43). Baltimore: Johns Hopkins University Press.

Greene, M. (1995). *Releasing the imagination: Essays on education, the arts, and social change.* San Francisco: Jossey-Bass.

Griswold, P. A., & Chroback, D. A. (1981). Sex-role associations of music instruments and occupations by gender and major. *Journal of Research in Music Education, 29*(1), 57–62.

Grossberg, L., Nelson, C., & Treichler, P., with L. Baughman & J. M. Wise (Eds.). (1992). *Cultural studies.* New York: Routledge.

Grumet, M. (1988). *Bitter milk: Women and teaching.* Amherst: University of Massachussetts Press.

Grumet, M., & Stone, L. (2000). Feminism and curriculum: Getting our act together. *Journal of Curriculum Studies, 32*(2), 183–197.

Handy, D. A. (1998a). *Black women in American bands and orchestras* (2nd ed.). Lanham, MD: Scarecrow Press.

Handy, D. A. (1998b). *The International Sweethearts of Rhythm* (rev. ed.). Lanham, MD: Scarecrow Press.

Hanley, B. (1998). Gender in secondary music education in British Columbia. *British Journal of Music Education, 15* (1), 51–69.

Haraway, D. (1991). *Simians, cyborgs, and women: The reinvention of nature.* New York: Routledge.

Harding, S. (1986). *The science question in feminism.* Ithaca, NY: Cornell University Press.

Harding, S. (Ed.). (1987). *Feminism and methodology: Social science issues.* Bloomington: Indiana University Press.

Harding, S., & Hintikka, M. B. (1983). *Discovering reality: Feminist perspectives on epistemology, metaphysics, methodology, and philosophy of science.* Dordrecht, Holland: Kluwer.

Hargreaves, D. J., Comber, C., & Colley, A. (1995). Effects of age, gender, and training on musical preferences of British secondary school students. *Journal of Research in Music Education, 43*(3), 242–250.

Hartsock, N. (1983). *Money, sex, and power: Toward a feminist historical materialism.* New York: Longman.

Hedges, E., & Wendt, I. (1980). *In her own image: Women working in the arts.* Old Westbury, NY: Feminist Press.

Henry, A. (1995). Introduction revisited: Better a maroon than a mammy. In J. Gaskell & J. Willinsky (Eds.), *Gender in/forms curriculum* (pp. 15–19). New York: Teachers College Press.

Heywood, L., & Drake, J. (Eds.). (1997). *Third wave agenda: Being feminist, doing feminism.* Minneapolis: University of Minnesota Press.

Hirsch, M., & Keller, E. F. (Eds.). (1990). *Conflicts in feminism.* New York: Routledge.

Holgate, G. (1962). *Mabelle Glenn: Her life and contributions to music education.* Unpublished doctoral dissertation, University of Southern California, Los Angeles.

hooks, b. (2000). *Feminist theory: From margin to center* (2nd ed.). Cambridge, MA: South End Press.

Howe, S. W. (1993). Women music educators in Japan during the Meiji period. *Bulletin of the Council for Research in Music Education, 119,* 101–109.

Howe, S. W. (1995). The role of women in the introduction of western music in Japan. *Bulletin of Historical Research in Music Education, 16*(2), 81–97.

Howe, S. W. (1998). Reconstructing the history of music education from a feminist perspective. *Philosophy of Music Education Review, 6*(2), 96–106.

Howe, S. W. (1999). Leadership in MENC: The female tradition. *Bulletin of the Council for Research in Music Education, 141,* 59–65.

Humm, M. (Ed.). (1992). *Modern feminisms: Political, literary, cultural.* New York: Columbia University Press.

Humphreys, J. T. (1997). Sex and geographic representation in two music education history books. *Bulletin of the Council for Research in Music Education, 131,* 67–86.

Hyde, D. (1998). *New-found voices: Women in nineteenth-century English music* (3rd ed.). Aldershot, England: Ashgate.

Izdebski, C. (1983). *Vanett Lawler (1902–1972): Her life and contributions to music education.* Unpublished doctoral dissertation, Catholic University of America, Washington, DC.

Jaggar, A. M., & Bordo, S. R. (Eds.). (1989). *Gender/body/knowledge: Feminist reconstructions of being and knowing.* New Brunswick, NJ: Rutgers University Press.

Johnsen, G. (1992). Three interviews: Rebecca Bower. *Music Educators Journal, 78*(7), 39–41.

Kahlberg, J. (2001). Gender. In S. Sadie (Ed.), *The New Grove Dictionary of Music and Musicians:* Vol. 9 (2nd ed., pp. 645–647). London: Macmillan.

Karpf, J. (1999). The vocal teacher of ten thousand: E. Azalia Hackley as community music educator, 1910–22. *Journal of Research in Music Education, 47*(4), 319–30.

Kelly, J. (1982). Early feminist theory and the *Querelle des Femmes,* 1400–1789. *Signs, 8*(1) 4–28.

Kimmel, M. S. (Ed.). (1987). *Changing men: New directions in research on men and masculinity.* Beverly Hills, CA: Sage.

Kimmel, M. S. (Ed). (1990). *Men confront pornography.* New York: Crown.

Kimmel, M. S. (Ed.). (1995). *The politics of manhood: Profeminist men respond to the mythopoetic men's movement (and mythopoetic leaders answer).* Philadelphia: Temple University Press.

Kimmel, M. S. (1996). *Manhood in America: A cultural history.* New York: Free Press.

Kimmel, M. S. (Comp.). (1998). *Men's lives.* Boston: Allyn and Bacon.

Kimmel, M. S. (2000). *The gendered society.* New York: Oxford University Press.

Klein, S. S. (Ed.). (1985). *Handbook for achieving sex equity through education.* Baltimore: Johns Hopkins University Press.

Kobayashi, M. (1999). *Josei sakkyoku-ka retsuden* [Portraits of women composers]. Tokyo: Heibonsha.

Korsmeyer, C., & Hein, H. (Eds.). (1993). *Aesthetics in feminist perspective.* Bloomington: Indiana University Press.

Koskoff, E. (Ed.). (1989). *Women and music in cross-cultural perspective.* Urbana: University of Illinois Press.

Koskoff, E. (1991). Gender, power, and music. In J. L. Zaimont (Ed.), *The Musical Woman: An International Perspective: Vol. 3. 1986–1990* (pp. 769–788). Westport, CT: Greenwood Press.

Koskoff, E. (2000). Foreword. In P. Moisala & B. Diamond (Eds.), *Music and gender* (pp. ix–xiii). Urbana: University of Illinois Press.

Koza, J. E. (1988). *Music and references to music in "Godey's Lady's Book," 1830–77.* Unpublished doctoral dissertation, University of Minnesota, Minneapolis.

Koza, J. E. (1990). Music instruction in the nineteenth century: Views from *Godey's Lady's Book,* 1830–77. *Journal of Research in Music Education, 38*(4), 245–257.

Koza, J. E. (1991). Music and the feminine sphere: Images of women as musicians in *Godey's Lady's Book,* 1830–1877. *Musical Quarterly, 75* (2), 103–129.

Koza, J. E. (1992). Picture this: Sex equity in textbook illustrations. *Music Educators Journal, 78*(7), 28–33.

Koza, J. E. (1993). The "missing males" and other gender issues in music education: Evidence from the *Music Supervisors' Journal,* 1914–1924. *Journal of Research in Music Education, 41*(3), 212–232.

Koza, J. E. (1994). Big boys don't cry (or sing): Gender, misogyny, and homophobia in college choral methods texts. *Quarterly Journal of Music Teaching and Learning, 4,* 5(4,1), 48–64.

Lamb, R. (1988). Including women composers in music curricula: Development of creative strategies for the general music class, grades 5–8. (Doctoral dissertation, Teachers College, Columbia University, 1987). *Dissertation Abstracts International-A 48* (10), 2568.

Lamb, R. (1990). "Are there gender issues in school music?" *Canadian Music Educator, 31*(6), 9–13.

Lamb, R. (1991a). Including women composers in school music curricula, grades 5–8: A feminist perspective. In J. L. Zaimont (Ed.), *The musical woman: An international perspective: Vol. 3. 1986–1990* (pp. 682–713). Westport, CT: Greenwood Press.

Lamb, R. (1991b). Medusa's aria: Feminist theories and music education, a curriculum theory paper designed as readers theatre. In J. Gaskell & A. McLaren (Eds.), *Women and education* (pp. 299–319). Calgary: Detselig.

Lamb, R. (1994). Aria senza accompagnamento: A woman behind the theory. *Quarterly Journal of Teaching and Learning, 4,5*(4,1), 5–20.

Lamb, R. (1995). Tone deaf/symphonies singing: Sketches for a musicale. In J. Gaskell & J. Willinsky (Eds.), *Gender in/forms curriculum* (pp. 109–135). New York: Teachers College Press.

Lamb, R. (1996). Discords: Feminist pedagogy in music education. *Theory into Practice, 35*(2), 124–131.

Lamb, R. (1997). Music trouble: Desire, discourse, education. *Canadian University Music Review, 18*(1), 85–98.

Lamb, R. (1999). "I never really thought about it": Master/apprentice as pedagogy in music. In K. Arnatage (Ed.), *Equity and how to get it: Rescuing graduate studies* (pp. 213–238). Toronto: Inanna.

Langer, S. K. (1942). *Philosophy in a new key: A study in the symbolism of reason, rite, and art.* Cambridge: Harvard University Press.

Langer, S. K. (1953). *Feeling and form: A theory of art developed from philosophy in a new key.* New York: Scribner's.

Lather, P. (1991). *Getting smart: Feminist research and pedagogy with/in the postmodern.* New York: Routledge.

Laudon, R. T. (2000). *Minnesota Music Teachers Association: The profession and the community, 1901–2000.* Eden Prairie, MN: Minnesota Music Teachers Association.

Lawson, K. (1984). A woman's place is at the podium. *Music Educators Journal, 70*(9), 46–49.

Lawson, K. (1991). Women conductors: Credibility in a male-dominated profession. In J. L. Zaimont (Ed.), *The musical woman: An international perspective: Vol. 3* (pp. 197–219). Westport, CT: Greenwood Press.

Lerner, G. (1979). *The majority finds its past: Placing women in history.* New York: Oxford University Press.

Lewis, M. G. (1993). *Without a word: Teaching beyond women's silence.* New York: Routledge.

Lindeman, C. A. (1992). Teaching about women musicians: Elementary classroom strategies. *Music Educators Journal, 78*(7), 56–59.

Livingston, C. (1997). Women in music education in the United States: Names mentioned in history books. *Journal of Research in Music Education, 45*(1), 130–144.

Locke, R. P. (1994). Paradoxes of the woman music patron in America. *Musical Quarterly 78*(4), 798–825.

Locke, R. P., & Barr, C. (Eds.) (1997). *Cultivating music in*

America: Women patrons and activists since 1860. Berkeley: University of California Press.

Logan, G. M. (2000). *The Indiana University School of Music: A history.* Bloomington: Indiana University Press.

Looser, D., & Kaplan, E. A. (Eds.). (1997). *Generations: Academic feminists in dialogue.* Minneapolis: University of Minnesota Press.

Luke, C., & Gore, J. (Eds.). (1992). *Feminisms and critical pedagogy.* New York: Routledge.

Mac an Ghaill, M. (1994). *The making of men: Masculinities, sexualities and schooling.* Philadelphia: Open University Press.

MacDonald, E. (1998, Fall). Critical identities: Rethinking feminism through transgender politics. Sexualities and feminisms issue. *Atlantis, 23*(1), 3–12.

Malson, M. R., O'Barr, J. F., Westphal-Wihl, S., & Wyer, M. (Eds.). (1986). *Feminist theory in practice and process.* Chicago: University of Chicago Press.

Martin, J. R. (1982, May). Excluding women from the educational realm. *Harvard Educational Review, 52*(2), 133–142.

Martin, J. R. (1985). *Reclaiming a conversation: The ideal of the educated woman.* New Haven: Yale University Press.

McCarthy, M. (1999). Gendered discourse and the construction of identify: Toward a liberated pedagogy in music education. *Journal of Aesthetic Education, 33*(4), 109–125.

McCartney, A. (2000). Cyborg experiences: Contradictions and tensions of technology, nature, and the body in Hiledgard Westerkamp's "Breathing Room." In P. Moisala & B. Diamond (Eds.), *Music and gender* (pp. 317–335). Urbana: University of Illinois Press.

McClary, S. (1991). *Feminine endings: Music, gender, sexuality.* Minneapolis: University of Minnesota Press.

McCord, K. (1996). The state of the art today. In *Sung and unsung: Jazz women: Symposium and concerts, October 19 and 20, 1996* (pp. 28–33). N.P.: Smithsonian Institution.

McCord, K. (in press). Jazz education. In K. H. Burns (Ed.), *Women and music in America since 1900: An encyclopedia.* Westport, CT: Oryx Press.

McPherson, B., & Klein, J. (1995). *Measure by measure: A history of New England Conservatory from 1867.* Boston: Trustees of New England Conservatory of Music.

Miller, E. (1933). *The history and development of the New England Conservatory of Music.* Unpublished B.M. thesis, New England Conservatory of Music, Boston.

Millett, K. (1970). *Sexual politics: Feminist literary theory.* New York: Routledge.

Mizener, C. P. (1993). Attitudes of children toward singing and choir participation and assessed singing skill. *Journal of Research in Music Education, 41*(3), 233–245.

Modleski, T. (1991). *Feminism without women.* New York: Routledge.

Moisala, P., & Diamond, B. (Eds.). (2000). *Music and gender.* Urbana: University of Illinois Press.

Morton, C. A. (1994a). Feminist theory and the displaced music curriculum: Beyond the add and stir projects. *Philosophy of Music Education Review, 2*(2), 106–121.

Morton, C. A. (1994b). "Whistle, daughter, whistle, and you shall have a man": Sexism in children's song materials. In P. Bourne, P. Masters, N. Amin, M. Gonick, & L. Gribowski (Eds.), *Feminism and education: A Canadian perspective: Vol. 2* (pp. 203–220). Toronto: Centre for Women's Studies in Education, Ontario Institute for Studies in Education.

Morton, C. A. (1997). The "status problem": The feminized location of school music and burden of justification. *Dissertation Abstracts International-A, 58*(6), 2130. (University Microfilms No. AAT NN18953)

Mura, R., Kimball, M., & Cloutier, R. (1987). Girls and science programs: Two steps forward, one step back. In J. Gaskell & A. McLaren (Eds.), *Women and education: A Canadian perspective* (pp. 133–149). Calgary: Detselig.

Myers, M. (1993). *Blowing her own trumpet: European ladies' orchestras and other women musicians 1870–1950 in Sweden.* Göteborg, Sweden: University of Göteborg.

Neuls-Bates, C. (1986). Women's orchestras in the United States, 1925–45. In J. Bowers & J. Tick (Eds.), *Women making music: The Western art tradition, 1150–1950* (pp. 349–369). Urbana: University of Illinois Press.

Neuls-Bates, C. (1996). *Women in music: An anthology of source readings from the Middle Ages to the present* (rev. ed.). Boston: Northeastern University Press.

Ng, R., Staton, P., & Scane, J. (Eds.). (1995). *Anti-racism, feminism, and critical approaches to education.* Toronto: Ontario Institute for Studies in Education Press.

Nicholson, L. (Ed.). (1997). *The Second Wave: A reader in feminist theory.* New York: Routledge.

Noddings, N. (1984). *Caring: A feminine perspective on ethics and moral education.* Berkeley: University of California Press.

Olmstead, A. (1999). *Juilliard: A history.* Urbana: University of Illinois Press.

Orrell, S. (1995). *The work of Grace C. Nash in music education in the United States.* Unpublished doctoral dissertation, University of Houston.

Ostleitner, E., & Simek, U. (1991). *Ist die musik männlich? Die darstellung der frau in den österreichischen lehrbüchern für musikerziehung* [Is music manly? The representation of women in Austrian textbooks for music education]. Vienna: Universitäts Verlag.

O'Toole, P. (1994). I sing in a choir but I have "no voice!" *Quarterly Journal of Music Teaching and Learning, 4, 5*(4, 1), 65–77.

O'Toole, P. (1995). Re-directing the choral rehearsal: A feminist, post structural analysis of power relations in three choral settings (Doctoral dissertation, University of Wisconsin, Madison, 1994). *Dissertation Abstracts International-A 55*(7), 1864.

O'Toole, P. (1997a). Escaping the tradition: Tensions between the production of values and pleasures in the choral setting. In R. Rideout (Ed.), *On the sociology of music education* (pp. 130–148). Norman: University of Oklahoma.

O'Toole, P. (1997b). Examining the political projects of four pedagogies: Progressive humanistic, critical, and feminist. *Dialogue in Instrumental Music Education, 21*(2), 126–141.

O'Toole, P. (1997c). What have you taught your female singers lately? *Choral Cues, 27*(2), 12–14.

O'Toole, P. (1998). A missing chapter from choral methods books: How choirs neglect girls. *Choral Journal, 39*(5), 9–32.

Palmquist, J.E., & Payne, B. (1992). The inclusive instrumental library. *Music Educators Journal, 78*(7), 34–38.

Parenti, S. (1996). Composing the music school: Proposals for a feminist composition curriculum. *Perspectives of New Music, 34,* 66–72.

Parker, L. F. (1982). *Women in music in St. Paul from 1898 to 1957 with emphasis on the St. Paul public schools.* Unpublished doctoral dissertation, University of Minnesota, Minneapolis.

Parker, L. F. (1987). Women in music education in St. Paul, Minnesota from 1898 to 1957. *Bulletin of Historical Research in Music Education, 8*(2), 83–90.

Pegley, K. (1995). Places, everyone: Gender and the non-neutrality of music technology. *The Recorder, 37*(2), 55–59.

Pegley, K. (2000). Gender, voice, and place: Issues of negotiation in a "Technology in Music Program." In P. Moisala & B. Diamond (Eds.), *Music and gender* (pp. 306–316). Urbana: University of Illinois Press.

Pegley, K., & Caputo, V. (1994). Growing up female(s): Retrospective thoughts on musical preferences and meanings. In P. Brett, E. Wood, & G. C. Thomas (Eds.), *Queering the pitch: The new gay and lesbian musicology* (pp. 297–314). New York: Routledge.

Pinar, W. F. (Ed.). (1998). *Queer theory in education.* Mahwah, NJ: Erlbaum.

Porter, S., & Abeles, H. A. (1979, January). So your daughter wants to be a drummer? *Music Educators Journal,* 46–49.

Reich, N. (Ed.). (1988). *Women's studies/Women's status* (CMS Report No. 5). Boulder, CO: College Music Society.

Reinharz, S. with Davidman, L. (1992). *Feminist methods in social research.* New York: Oxford University Press.

Rich, S. L., & Phillips, A. (1985). *Women's Experience and Education* (Harvard Educational Review Reprint Series No. 17). Cambridge: Harvard Educational Review.

Richardson, C. P. (1992). The improvised lives of women in music education. *Music Educators Journal, 78*(7), 34–38.

Riley, D. (1988). *Am I that name? Feminism and the category of "woman" in history.* New York: Macmillan.

Ropers-Huilman, B. (1998). *Feminist teaching in theory and practice: Situating power and knowledge in poststructural classrooms.* New York: Teachers College Press.

Rothenbusch, E. (1989). The joyful sound: Women in the nineteenth-century United States hymnody tradition. In E. Koskoff (Ed.), *Women and music in cross-cultural perspective* (pp. 177–94). Urbana: University of Illinois Press.

Roulston, K., & Mills, M. (2000). Male teachers in feminised teaching areas: Marching to the beat of the men's movement drums? *Oxford Review of Education, 26*(2), 221–237.

Rukeyser, M. (1973). Kathe Kollwitz. In L. Chester & S. Barba (Eds.), *Rising tides: Twentieth century American women poets* (pp. 70–75). New York: Washington Square Press.

Rycenga, J. (1994). Lesbian compositional process: One lover-composer's perspective. In P. Brett, E. Wood, & G. C. Thomas (Eds.), *Queering the pitch: The new gay and lesbian musicology* (pp. 275–296). New York: Routledge.

Sadie, J. A., & Samuel, R. (1995). *The Norton/Grove dictionary of women composers*. New York: Norton.

Sadie, S. (Ed.) (2001). *The new Grove dictionary of music and musicians* (2nd ed.). London: Macmillan.

Sadker, M., & Sadker, D. (1982). *Sex equity handbook for schools*. New York: Longman.

Sarkissian, M. (1999). Thoughts on the study of gender in ethnomusicology: A pedagogical perspective. *Women and Music 3*, 17–27.

Scanlan, M. (1992). Three interviews: Catherine Comet. *Music Educators Journal, 78*(7), 42–4.

Schmalenberger, S. (2001). The Washington Conservatory of Music and African-American experience. Doctoral dissertation in progress, University of Minnesota, Minneapolis.

Sears, J. (1987). Peering into the well of loneliness: The responsibility of educators to gay and lesbian youth. In A. Molnar (Ed.), *Social issues and education* (pp. 79–100). Alexandria, VA: Association for Supervision and Curriculum Development.

Sherban, R. A. (1996). *Peering through the transparencies of singing, gender and the music classroom* (Master's thesis, University of Calgary, 1995). (University Microfilms No. AAT MM03157)

Showalter, E. (Ed.). (1985). *The new feminist criticism: Essays on women literature and theory*. New York: Pantheon Books.

Simpson, H. (1993). Seeking the female, through the holistic study of music. *British Journal of Music Education, 10*, 163–167.

Smith, P. (Ed.). (1996). *Boys: Masculinities in contemporary culture*. Boulder, CO: Westview Press.

Solie, R. (1993). Introduction: On "difference." In R. Solie (Ed.), *Musicology and difference: Gender and sexuality in music scholarship*. Berkeley: University of California Press.

Solie, R. (1997). Defining feminism: Conundrums, contexts, communities. *Women and Music 1*, 1–11.

Southcott, J. (1990). A music education pioneer: Dr. Satis Naronna Barton Coleman. *British Journal of Music Education, 7*(2), 123–132.

Southern, E. (1997). *The music of black Americans: A history* (3rd ed.). New York, Norton.

Spelman, E. V. (1988). *Inessential woman: Problems of exclusion in feminist thought*. Boston: Beacon Press.

Stanley, L. (1990). *Feminist praxis: Research, theory and epistemology in feminist sociology*. New York: Routledge.

Stanley, L., & Wise, S. (1983). *Breaking out: Feminist consciousness and feminist research*. London: Routledge and Kegan Paul.

Stecopoulos, H., & Uebel, M. (Eds.). (1997). *Race and the subject of masculinities*. Durham, NC: Duke University Press.

Stevens, R. (2000). Emily Patton: An Australian pioneer of tonic sol-fa in Japan. *Research Studies in Music Education, 14*, 40–49.

Stoddard, E. M. (1968). *Frances Elliott Clark: Her life and contributions to music education*. Unpublished doctoral dissertation, Brigham Young University, Provo.

Stone, L., with Boldt, G. M. (Eds.). (1994). *The education feminism reader*. New York: Routledge.

Sturm, C. A., James, M., Jackson, A., & Burns, D. B. (2000). Celebrating 100 years of progress in American piano teaching: Part 1. 1900–1950. Part 2. 1950–2000. *American Music Teacher, 50*(2, 3), 24–32.

Swiss, T., Sloop, J., & Herman, A. (Eds.). (1998). *Mapping the beat: Popular music and contemporary theory*. Oxford: Blackwell.

Tick, J. (1986). Passed away is the piano girl: Changes in American musical life, 1870–1900. In J. Bowers & J. Tick (Eds.), *Women making music: The Western art tradition, 1150–1950* (pp. 325–348). Urbana: University of Illinois Press.

Tick, J. (1997). *Ruth Crawford Seeger: A composer's search for American music*. New York: Oxford University Press.

Tick, J., with Ericson, M., & Koskoff, E. (2001). Women in music. In S. Sadie (Ed.), *The New Grove Dictionary of Music and Musicians: Vol. 27*. (2nd ed., pp. 519–542). London: Macmillan.

Tong, R. (1989). *Feminist thought: A comprehensive introduction*. Boulder, CO: Westview Press.

Torres, M. M. (Ed.) (1995). *Música y mujeres: Género y poder:* [Music and women: Gender and ability]. N.p.: Hinrichsen.

Ulrich, H. (1976). *A centennial history of the Music Teachers National Association*. Cincinnati: Music Teachers National Association.

Volk, T. M. (1996). Satis Coleman's "Creative Music." *Music Educators Journal, 82*(6), 31–34, 47.

Walcott, R. (1998). Queer texts and performativity: Zora, rap, and community. In W. F. Pinar (Ed.), *Queer theory in education* (pp. 157–171). Mahwah, NJ: Erlbaum.

Walker-Hill, H. (1992). Black women composers in Chicago: Then and now. *Black Music Research Journal, 12*(1), 1–23.

Weber, S., & Mitchell, C. (1995). *"That's funny, you don't look like a teacher": Interrogating images and identity in popular culture*. London: Falmer Press.

Weed, E. (Ed.). (1989). *Coming to terms: Feminism, theory, politics*. New York: Routledge.

Whiteley, S. (1997). *Sexing the groove: Popular music and gender*. New York: Routledge.

Whitesitt, L. (1991). Women's support and encouragement of music and musicians. In K. Pendle (Ed.), *Women and music: A history* (pp. 301–313). Bloomington: Indiana University Press.

Wollstonecraft, M. (1967). *Vindication of the rights of women* (Charles Hagleman, Jr., Ed.). New York: Norton. (Original work published 1792).

Woolf, V. (1929). *A room of one's own*. New York: Harcourt, Brace and World.

Zervoudakes, J., & Tanur, J. (1994). Gender and musical instruments: Winds of change? *Journal of Research in Music Education, 42*(1), 58–67.

The Social Construction of Music Teacher Identity in Undergraduate Music Education Majors

36

PAUL G. WOODFORD

Sociology is the systematic study of society and its institutions and the ways individuals and groups interact. Sociologists examine the nature and structure of, and relations among, various groups with a view to obtaining a more comprehensive understanding of social life (Wallace & Wolf, 1999, p. 3). Of particular interest to many sociologists is how individuals and groups evolve in their thinking and social practices over time yet manage to develop and sustain a sense of personal and collective identity (Green, 1999, p. 160). Social constructivists go even further, asserting that our perceptions and understandings of the world and everyday reality are socially mediated and constructed, meaning that they are built up through social experience and interaction (Green, 1997, p. 192). As Small (1998) explains,

> What each of us holds to be reality is not objective or absolute but is, to use the sociologists' term, socially constructed. It is composed of learned sets of assumptions about the relationships of the world, and it is those, overlapping and varying, that constitute the pattern of meanings that holds together groups of human beings, whether large or small, from empires and nations to associations, clubs, families, and bonded pairs. How we acquire that sense of what is reality is a dialectical process between, on the one hand, the experience and the inborn temperament of each individual and, on the other, the perceptions of the various social groups to which he or she belongs. (p. 131)

Identity, too, is socially constructed in the sense that knowledge of self and others and of appropriate behavior within particular social roles and contexts is acquired through prior experience (Dolloff, 1999b; Roberts, 1991b). But if everything is socially constructed—if knowledge is contingent upon social relations—then it is also amenable to contestation and change. Social construction,

as a philosophical and epistemological outlook on the nature of knowledge, thus has distinct political overtones (Frazer, 1995, p. 829).

The pursuit of identity, defined as the imaginative view or role that individuals project for themselves in particular social positions, occupations, or situations (Dolloff, 1999b, p. 192; McCall & Simmons, 1978, p. 65; Roberts, 1991b, p. 32), is central to social construction educational models. The aim of those models is usually to empower students to construct their own identities free from societal and institutional norms and conventions that are deemed limiting (Kincheloe & McLaren, 2000, p. 282). Self-determination is the goal (Rose, 1998, p. 30). Not all social constructivists in education are overtly political, and they vary in degree of commitment. Nevertheless, there is a consensus among them that educational institutions tend to stifle individual and collective initiative, thereby inhibiting the search for personal and professional identity among students (Apple, 1982; Apple & Beane, 1995; Bourdieu, 1977; Gramsci, 1971; Greene, 1993; Hlebowitsh, 1992).

Although, ironically, now the norm in North American teacher education institutions and programs (Torff, chap. 28), social construction is still relatively new to the field of music teacher education, having only made significant inroads into music teacher education programs as part of the recent resurgence of interest among the profession in social philosophy (e.g., Bowman, 1994; Elliott, 1995; McCarthy, 1997; Regelski, 1997, 1998; Roberts, 1997; Rose, 1990; Woodford, 1995, 1996b). The social construction of music teacher identity in undergraduate music education majors is an extremely complicated topic requiring examination of several related literatures, including sociology, teacher education, psychology, social psychology, philosophy, and music education. Music teacher education usually encompasses study in all of those disciplines.

Major questions addressed in this chapter include: (1) What is the nature of the socialization process whereby undergraduate music education majors are inducted into music education practice and traditional notions of music teacher role-identity? (2) What are some of the social, developmental, pedagogical, or other impediments frustrating the construction of an appropriate professional role-identity in undergraduates? and (3) What research-based theoretical and pedagogical models exist to guide music teacher educators in the development of curricula intended to promote the self-conscious construction of professional identity in music education majors?

As is briefly discussed in the conclusion of this chapter, the research examined herein suggests that social construction in music teacher education remains more of a philosophical and political ideal than a social reality. Despite the increasing prevalence of social construction models in music teacher education, undergraduates appear to be not so much constructing an identity for themselves as replicating past practices, including traditional notions of music teacher identity (Beynon, 1998; Harwood, 1993; L'Roy, 1983; Prescesky, 1997; Roberts, 1991a, 1991b, 1991c, 1993, 2000b). Criticisms of social construction notwithstanding, were it possible to develop an understanding of how undergraduate music education majors are socialized to music education practice and professional role-identity, music teacher educators might be better positioned to propose needed educational reforms to counteract societal and institutional impediments to the self-conscious construction of professional identity. The chapter should accordingly be of interest to music teacher educators and graduate and undergraduate music education majors.

The Socialization of Music Education Majors to Music Teacher Identity

In order to explain why and how undergraduate music education majors may be impeded in constructing their professional identities as music teachers, it is necessary to examine how school and university students are socialized to preexisting notions of music teacher identity. Wright's (1991) study of the influence of belief systems on musical experience sheds light on the socialization of students to professional practice and identity by explaining how social belief and knowledge systems both inform and restrain our thinking. Although less concerned with the problem of identity per se, his study clearly revolves around that issue. He takes a phenomenological approach in explaining that belief and knowledge are reciprocal elements in the relativistic social process whereby identity and social reality are mediated, modified, or transformed as individuals and groups interact using symbols and symbol systems (p. 170). Phenomenological sociologists are interested in how

people's perceptions and interpretations of everyday reality are shaped by their previously acquired, but tacit, beliefs (Wallace & Wolf, 1999, p. 253).

Referring to the classic texts *The Social Construction of Reality* by Berger and Luckmann (1966) and *A Sociology of Belief* by Borhek and Curtis (1975), Wright (1991) explains that this sociological process takes the form of a dialectic between objectivity and subjectivity within a culture, wherein social belief and knowledge are internalized by individuals as subjective reality (p. 111). By this means, the existing social order, as represented by society's institutions, is continually reconstructed, maintained, and legitimated. Problems occur, though, when people treat human products, including beliefs and knowledge, as sacrosanct and thus immutable. Berger and Luckmann (1966) employ the construct of reification to explain how people sometimes forget their authorship or role as creative agents in the shaping of the human world. The problem of reification also applies to social roles and institutions, as, for example, happens when music teachers and institutions fail to critically examine particular methodologies or traditions (Elliott, 1995; O'Toole, 1993; Regelski, 1997, 1998). Reification is socially undesirable because it impedes the dialectical process, thereby rendering individuals and institutions passive rather than active agents in the reconstruction of social reality (Ashley & Orenstein, 2001, p. 45; Wallace & Wolf, 1999, p. 283).

Socialization is an intersubjective, face-to-face interaction among individuals and can take either of three related forms, labeled primary and secondary socialization and ascriptive recruitment. All three function to impart knowledge and belief to individuals and to provide them with a worldview and sense of identity. As such, they are important to understanding problems in the construction of professional identity in undergraduate music educator majors.

Primary socialization takes place in childhood and is effected through significant others, such as family members, teachers, or others with whom individuals identify emotionally. "The child takes on the significant others' roles and attitudes, that is, internalizes them and makes them his own" (Berger & Luckmann, 1966, pp. 121–122). Secondary socialization takes place after childhood as a result of career and lifestyle choices and involves the acquisition of specialized institutional knowledge, such as occurs when music students commence university studies (Wallace & Wolf, 1999; Wright, 1991). Ascriptive recruitment refers to beliefs and knowledge that are made available or denied to individuals on the basis of age, gender, culture, socioeconomic status, or other factors (Duster, 1997; Wright, 1991). Ascriptive recruitment probably figures prominently in the socialization of undergraduate music education majors during childhood. For this reason, and because problems with ascriptive factors such as gender and ethnicity are broached in the research literature addressing the primary socialization of music education majors, ascriptive recruitment is treated in the following pages after primary and before secondary socialization processes.

Primary Socialization of Music Education Majors

Most peoples' understandings of the teaching profession and of teacher identity are probably initially acquired through primary socialization. As Beynon (1998) notes, applicants to undergraduate teacher education programs "have already spent about 15,000 hours observing teaching and learning and may be already socialized (perhaps subconsciously) to the norms and expectations of the profession" (p. 83; see also Dolloff, 1999a, 1999b; L'Roy, 1983). Music education majors may be more acculturated than most undergraduates to professional norms through primary socialization, since many of them attribute their interest in music teaching to the positive impact of family and former school or private music teachers (Beynon, 1998; Cox, 1997; Duling, 2000; L'Roy, 1983; Roberts, 2000a). The decision to pursue a music education career is typically made in high school, and many undergraduate music education majors report having already identified with particular music teacher roles before commencing music teacher education degree programs (Beynon, 1998; Cox, 1997; Duling, 2000; Gillespie & Hamann, 1999; L'Roy, 1983; Mark, 1998; Prescesky, 1997; Roberts, 1991a, 1991b, 1991c).

Several survey studies indicate that many undergraduate music education majors and experienced music teachers are products of musical homes. The implication is that they model themselves after, or receive encouragement from, musical parents or other family members with respect to career choice. Cox (1997), in a survey of 310 experienced Arkansas music teachers, found that 50% of those surveyed had at least one parent who was a musician, while 20% also had at least one parent who was a teacher or educator (p. 114). Mark (1998) reported a similar finding among more than 200 active Austrian music educators, 90% of whom had at least one musician-parent (p. 9). Surveys, though, while helpful in obtaining categorical information about respondents' histories, can provide little insight into the nature and quality of relationships, including the extent to which children are influenced in their career decisions and selection of appropriate professional role-identities by parents, family, and others. The research for the most part remains vague and inclusive, suggesting little more than that family, including parents and grandparents (Cox, 1997, p. 115), play a role in encouraging individuals to pursue music teaching careers and that there may be some differences therein according to gender and

applied instrument. The nature of that role remains unexamined and unexplained.

String majors may be more subject to parental influence than are other music education majors. In a seminal study of the development of occupational identity in undergraduate music education majors, L'Roy (1983) used questionnaires and interview techniques to collect data from 165 undergraduate music education majors at North Texas State University about their professional backgrounds. More than 50% of string music education majors ($N = 20$) reported that they came from musical homes (p. 179). They were also more influenced by musical parents than were other music education majors, although how or to what extent was neither reported nor explained in her dissertation. Unlike other music education majors, it was the string majors' parents, and not their former school music teachers, who served as significant others and professional role models (p. 179). As is discussed shortly in reference to the secondary socialization processes of undergraduate music education majors, this may account somewhat for certain problems that string majors experience in the construction of their identities as music teachers. Despite their stated music education major, L'Roy's string majors were at best ambivalent about music teaching (p. 74).

Quite possibly, though, and because her sample of string music education majors was small, L'Roy's (1983) findings with respect to parental influence on the socialization of string majors were anomalous compared to other institutions. Her findings might only have reflected the particular professional program and institutional climate at North Texas State University during the early 1980s (p. 79). In a more recent survey of 153 string majors at 17 American universities, Gillespie and Hamann (1999) found that only a very small percentage of string majors (1.1%) credited their families with influencing their choice of teaching career (p. 275). Obviously more research is needed before any conclusions can be reached about the influence of parents on the career choice and professional identity of undergraduate music education string majors.

As expected, the majority of undergraduate music education majors appear to be socialized to professional practice and identity by school and private music teachers. The better adjusted students in L'Roy's (1983) study, that is, those who identified themselves as music educators, reported positive school experiences coupled with encouragement from their school music teachers as motivating their career choices (p. 168). Band majors experienced a stronger sense of loyalty and connection with their former high school band teachers than did other music education majors. Even in university they continued to model themselves and their sense of music teacher identity after their former band directors (p. 173). This, L'Roy proposed, accounted for the band majors' more clearly defined sense of professional identity and levels of confidence with respect to career plans relative to other music education majors, and particularly string majors (p. 165).

Revealingly, with respect to the combined influence of family and former school music teachers on career choices and professional roles, Cox (1997) reported that prospective music education majors were far more likely to receive advice and encouragement to pursue a career as a musician than a teacher. "Subjects recalled more persons who had influenced them as musicians than . . . as future teachers and educators" (p. 114). This included influential former school music teachers whose encouragement was most often given in the form of praise for musical performance skill and not for verbal skills or potential talent as a teacher (p. 117). This helps explain findings reviewed later in this chapter with reference to secondary socialization processes that many undergraduate music education majors conceive of themselves as performers or general musicians and not as music educators. Music education majors appear to be socialized in school as performers or general musicians and not as future music teachers (Cox, 1997; L'Roy, 1983; Roberts, 1991a, 1991b, 1991c).

The problem of lack of appropriate encouragement may be worse for high school string students. String teachers may actually ignore students interested in pursuing teaching careers. Frink (1997), in a survey of 187 undergraduate string majors at the Big Ten American universities, found that while two-thirds of respondents did not consider their former teachers as professional role models, 60% of respondents reported receiving no encouragement from them at all with respect to pursuing teaching careers (as cited in Gillespie & Hamann, 1999, p. 268). Gillespie and Hamann (1999) noted a similar perceived lack of personal interest on the part of high school orchestra teachers in students expressing an interest in teaching (p. 276). Undergraduate music education string majors viewed their former music teachers as role models, but the relationship was relatively weak and possibly negative. No doubt these are contributing factors to professional identity problems among undergraduate string majors and to the continued shortage of string teachers in American schools. Studies show that enrollment in school string programs is on the rise in the United States, while the number of string teachers remains stable (Gillespie & Hamann, 1998, p. 82). Much recruitment work needs to be done if sufficient numbers of string teachers are to be obtained to meet the future needs of American schools.

An especially interesting finding arising from Cox's (1997) study is that there may be differences in the manner in which men and women are socialized to the music teaching profession. There is also some evidence suggesting that these socialization patterns may be changing and evolving with time. Cox's male subjects ($N = 133$) were more influenced in their choice of university major by former school music teachers or ensemble directors (72% of male

subjects were instrumentalists), a finding that is consistent with White's (1967) study in which men, and particularly band directors, reported being more oriented to a particular professional role while tending to socialize with other directors. Women ($N = 177$), of whom 69% were vocalists, were more indebted to former classroom teachers (Cox, 1997, p. 113). Cox's female subjects were also influenced in their choice of major by former school music teachers and directors but, more than the men, indicated that private music teachers were also influential. Female vocalists in particular indicated that they were indebted to their mothers, although how and to what extent remains unanswered (p. 114).

Finally, with respect to gender differences in the primary socialization of music teachers, Cox's (1997) experienced female music teachers reported more frequently than did the males that they had been encouraged during adolescence to pursue teaching roles, although "not to the same extent that musical involvement was encouraged" (pp. 116–117). Other research shows that high-achieving male students enrolled in school music programs receive more encouragement from parents and music teachers with respect to the development of musical skills than do female students (Davidson, Howe, & Sloboda, 1997, p. 202; Davidson, Moore, Sloboda, & Howe, 1998, p. 143; Trollinger, 1993, p. 35). These findings might help account for the fact that males, although outnumbered by females in school and university undergraduate music programs, continue to dominate the professional musical world and are generally more successful in their careers (Eaklor, 1993; Green, 1997; Lamb, 1993, p. 9; O'Neill, 1997, p. 49; Payne, 1996; Trollinger, 1993). Male dominance of the profession may be attributable in part to socially constructed and perceived gender role-identities, a problem that, despite its obvious relevance to the construction of music teacher identity, is largely ignored in the research literature reviewed in this chapter. Possibly, female students' successes in school and university are tempered by their "perceptions of women in the 'real' world as inferior to men" (O'Neill, 1997, p. 58; see also Atterbury, 1993; Belenky, Clinchy, Goldberger, & Tarule, 1986; Green, 1993). If such is the case then this and other gender problems, including ones of sexual orientation (Attinello, 1994), ought perhaps be taken into account by researchers and music teacher educators when devising social construction pedagogical models and curricula (Barkin & Hamessley, 1999; Hargreaves & North, 1999).

Much the same complaint can be made about the lack of acknowledgment in the research literature of problems of ethnicity and, to a lesser extent, socioeconomic status in the construction of music teacher identity. The overwhelming majority of public school teachers in the United States and Canada are from white, middle-class backgrounds (McIntyre & Byrd, 1996), a fact that is mirrored in much of the music education research and pedagogical literature on the social construction of music teacher identity. Only two studies reviewed for this chapter addressed the issue of providing appropriate non-Caucasian role models in culturally diverse music classrooms (Hamann & Cutietta, 1996; Walker & Hamann, 1993). None of the research-based theoretical or pedagogical models reviewed herein directly addresses issues of race or ethnicity.

Ascriptive Recruitment

The problem of lack of adequate gender and minority representation in the music teaching profession is one of ascriptive recruitment. Children from different socioeconomic and cultural backgrounds are likely to be exposed to different social and musical beliefs and knowledge. Musical preferences and other aspects of identity may thus be a reflection to some extent of social stratification and other ascriptive characteristics (Bartel, 1995; Crozier, 1997; Hargreaves & North, 1999; Kingsbury, 1988; Stokes, 1994). These differences can determine which career paths and lifestyles are available to individuals, as, for example, happens when students possessing abundant knowledge of alternative musics but lacking knowledge of the Western classical tradition are barred from pursuing careers as music teachers (Abeles, Hoffer, & Klotman, 1994; Kingsbury, 1988; Roberts, 2000a; Rose, 1990, 1995; Small, 1996, 1998; Vulliamy, 1977; Vulliamy & Shepherd, 1984). School evaluation policies are usually representative of middle-class norms and values. These policies may effectively deny access to higher education to students from other social backgrounds (Apple, 1982; Apple & Beane, 1995; Beynon, 1998; Duster, 1997; Rose, 1990). Even if students from less privileged backgrounds are successful in gaining admittance to music teacher programs, they may be "impeded in their understanding of what is important and may not be able to achieve the desired results" (Beynon, 1998, p. 86; see also Green, 1994, 1999; Hargreaves & North, 1997; Olsson, 1997; Russell, 1997).

Middle-class university students are more likely to be admitted to and succeed in music teacher education programs by virtue of possessing superior knowledge of the Western musical canon and of appropriate behavior in those social contexts (Beynon, 1998; Kingsbury, 1984, 1988). Several researchers, however, have recently asked whether undergraduate music education majors possess the requisite knowledge of popular and other alternative musical idioms needed to be successful school music teachers in a diverse musical society (Bowman, 1994; Roberts, 1998, 2000c; Rose, 1990). This begs the question of how, upon entering the music teaching profession, those students are to incorporate into their curricula, and be genuinely enthusiastic about, popular and other "musics with

which they have little if any identification and practically no experience" (Reimer, 1998, p. 76).

University schools of music and teacher education institutes must bear at least some of the blame for the lack of adequate musical representation in the schools and in their own programs, since it is they who set the criteria for admission to music teacher education programs and through whose "narrow portals" undergraduates must pass before gaining entrance to the teaching profession (Roberts, 1998, p. 2). The problem is one of musical and pedagogical conservatism and thus also social relevance in a changing, postmodern educational world (Green, 1999; O'Toole, 1993; Roberts, 2000c; Rose, 1990; Woodford, 1998). There may also be personality factors involved in the construction of music teacher identity, since experienced music teachers are said to possess conservative tendencies that may have been instilled in them in their own schooling (e.g., Kemp, 1982, 1996; Roberts, 1991b; Small, 1996; White, 1967; Witkin, 1974). This raises the intriguing possibility that certain aspects of personality, too, may be socially constructed. Before considering that possibility, it is first necessary to examine the secondary socialization processes of undergraduate music education majors within the university context.

Secondary Socialization of Music Education Majors

One would think that secondary socialization would figure most prominently in the construction of music teacher identity in undergraduate music education majors. Undergraduates are thought to be inducted within the university into a new social order with adult ways of thought, belief, and knowledge. In time, and as they become accommodated to the new social environment, there ought to be a corresponding shift in their worldviews and sense of identity (Woodford, 1996b; Wright, 1991, p. 212). Clearly, though, if the research cited is any indication, the most salient factors in the construction of music teacher identity occur through primary and not secondary socialization processes (Cox, 1997). This is a serious problem warranting careful examination. Before reviewing the appropriate literature, and because the research studies in question assume more explicit theoretical orientations, it is necessary to say a few brief words about sociological theory in general. This will help the reader understand both the intent and limitations of those studies.

Sociologists have traditionally approached theorizing and analysis of subject matter from one of two basic orientations or emphases, labeled micrological and macrological. The former refers to fine-grained analyses of person-to-person interactions and individual behaviors, whereas the latter approach is characterized as a more global perspective. The interest is in identifying broad social trends and developing general explanatory propositions and theories with high predictive power. The assumption is that human behavior is more or less determined or explicable (e.g., Marx's theory of social evolution). Microsociological analyses, on the other hand, tend to emphasize human creativity and individual action (Wallace & Wolf, 1999, pp. 6–8). As such, they make fewer general assumptions about human behavior. The two orientations are not exclusive, but they reflect underlying and differing assumptions about the nature of human behavior that ought to be kept in mind when examining the music education literature. Increasingly, however, sociologists are beginning to take a more eclectic and expansive approach to examining social phenomena, "one that incorporates the macrostructural, microinteractional, and interpretive levels of analysis" (Wallace & Wolf, 1999, p. 404; see also Chambers, 2000, p. 858). As I will show shortly, this approach characterizes some of the more recent sociological research in music education (e.g., Beynon, 1998; Rose, 1998).

The music education research reviewed in this chapter is representative of both micrological and macrological orientations. Phenomenological studies such as Wright's (1991) and the so-called symbolic interactionist studies by L'Roy (1983) and Roberts (1991a, 1991b, 1991c, 1993, 1997, 1998, 2000c) are best described as micrological, although Roberts's studies are also concerned with macrological issues. Symbolic interactionists examine how identity is built up, or constructed, through social interaction within a community using symbols and symbol systems (Wallace & Wolf, 1999, p. 191). Symbolic interactionism has been the most pervasive sociological model in music education research in the past (Roberts, 2000c, p. 55; Paul, 1998; Wolfgang, 1990).

L'Roy's (1983) study is probably more accurately described as symbolic interactionist than Roberts's (1991c), as there were fewer assumptions made and no attempt to generalize beyond the particular institutional culture examined (L'Roy, 1983, p. 166). Roberts's (1991c) purpose was to develop a general model of the professional socialization of music education majors. Other studies by Rose (1990, 1998) and Beynon (1998) using critical-conflict theory, reviewed later in this chapter, take a more macrological approach, in that music teacher education is assumed to be riddled with class and other struggles. Conflict theorists emphasize "purposive individuals and groups acting to secure their ends" (Wallace & Wolf, 1999, p. 7). To that extent they are less deterministic, but they still assume that human behavior is potentially fully explicable (Ashley & Orenstein, 2001, p. 40).

Roberts's (1991c) ethnographic study of the construction of professional identity in undergraduate music education majors begins with a micrological analysis of un-

dergraduate music education majors' professional beliefs and understandings and the ways they are shaped by various social forces within the university setting. His is a seminal and important study in that it was the first attempt to make explicit undergraduate music education majors' perceptions of their everyday social reality in their own words.

L'Roy's (1983) study of the development of occupational identity in undergraduate music education majors at North Texas State University addressed many of the same problems as Roberts (1991a, 1991b, 1991c). But while claiming to use a qualitative methodology and occasionally incorporating into her text anecdotal reports from subjects obtained by means of focused interviews, she essentially only reported on quantitative data obtained by means of a questionnaire (L'Roy, 1983, pp. 80–82). The reader is informed of how many or what percentage of undergraduates subscribed to a particular opinion or understanding of role-identity but is left with little sense of how those opinions or understandings were shaped by social forces (Roberts, 1991c, p. 19). The same observation applies to Cox's (1997) study of the professional socialization of Arkansas music teachers. Both L'Roy's and Cox's studies are essentially descriptive in nature.

Roberts's (1991c) work is less overtly political and ideological in nature than that of some of the researchers examined later in this chapter, particularly the critical-conflict theorists Rose (1998) and Beynon (1998). Nevertheless, he is clearly critical of the musical and educational establishments and the ways undergraduates' self-perceptions are shaped by societal and institutional norms and conventions.

Although Roberts's (1991c) study was micrological in approach, in that undergraduates' social interactions were examined within the context of five Canadian university schools of music, his study was deliberately a nomothetic one. The intention was to generalize beyond the particular institutions examined (Roberts, 2000b, p. 64). His aim was to build grounded theory. Participant observation and unstructured interviews were used to gather data from 116 undergraduate music education majors (1991c, pp. 26–27). As theoretical propositions emerged from observation of undergraduates in their natural environments, analysis of data was used to inform, guide, and refine further data collection, leading to the development of ever more sophisticated theoretical postulates (p. 25). The advantage of this "constructive" methodological approach is that it can reveal previously unknown and unanticipated factors while serving to place more empirically based research, such as L'Roy's (1983), in context (Charmaz, 2000, p. 510; Verrastro & Leglar, 1992, p. 691). Because the two studies are complementary, sharing a common theoretical framework and research agenda, and because the researchers obtained similar findings, their results are conflated and examined together hereafter. Several other related studies, including most notably Cox's (1997) study of the professional socialization of music teachers, are also occasionally referred to for purposes of corroboration.

Roberts (1991b) examines how the meaning of labels such as "musician" and "music teacher" is constructed and contested by music education students through social interaction as part of their search for professional identity (p. 30). These labels and their meanings are significant because they are indicative of undergraduates' self-perceptions, professional beliefs, and understandings of professional roles relative to experienced music teachers and university music teacher educators (Froehlich & Paul, 1997).

Music teachers are described by Roberts (1991b) as being intensely conservative, while university schools of music are characterized by a "precise hierarchy" of musical types and social roles (p. 30). Not surprisingly, given the institutional emphasis usually placed on performance in North American schools of music, the role of performer-musician is often ranked by students as being of primary importance and higher social status within the university musical community (Cox, 1997; L'Roy, 1983, p. 146; Roberts, 1991c). School music teachers and music education majors apparently agree that music teaching is a function of musicianship (Roberts, 1991b, p. 32). This effectively means that music education majors must continually compete with performance and other majors for recognition and social status (1991c, p. 57). Surprisingly, Roberts (1991b) found that undergraduate music education majors lacked any sense of teacher identity at all, "except in the form of 'musician' as 'teacher' " (p. 34). Although many of the undergraduates recognized that they could not realistically compete as performers, they nevertheless continued to see themselves in that light, or as "well-rounded musicians" (p. 37).

Similar observations had previously been made by L'Roy (1983) with reference to her North Texas State University music education majors, more than half of whom (N = 165) identified themselves as performers (p. 157). Particular concern was expressed for string music education majors, who for reasons outlined earlier, "as a group did not view themselves as educators" and whose "training seemed to have little impact on the development of a self-concept as a music educator" (p. 179). This increased the probability of them experiencing future role conflicts and job dissatisfaction.

According to Roberts (1991b), the construction of students' identities as performers or musicians during the undergraduate years involves an interaction between their own idealized self-perceptions and their public reputations within the university musical community (p. 35). Problems in identity occur when idealized self-perceptions and role-identities are not reconciled with social reality, as happens, for example, when music education students naively idealize themselves as performers even in the face of more realistic self-perceptions and role-identities (p. 35; L'Roy, 1983, p. 47). The difficulty for music education students in idealizing themselves as performers, aside from constantly having to compete with performance majors for social status, is that the pursuit of a performance reputation can detract from other endeavors that might be equally important to music teacher practice and identity (Roberts, 1991c, p. 124). Further, those who have been marginalized on the basis of perceived lack of performance skill may experience a reduction in motivation and commitment to their academic program and profession. If music education majors invest too much of themselves in performance at the expense of other aspects of their professional preparation and identity, and if they fail to achieve the level of performance desired or expected, they may be needlessly setting themselves up for role conflict and failure (L'Roy, 1983, p. 47).

Prescesky (1997) found as much in her ethnographic study of 4 undergraduate music education majors at McGill University. Analysis of undergraduates' personal biographies and autobiographical and journal writings revealed that those who primarily conceived of themselves as performers felt conflicted in their professional identities. Students who invested less of themselves in their identities as performers while seeking a more balanced view of their professional roles appeared better adjusted to music teaching.

There are several reasons why many music education majors perceive themselves as performers or musicians despite the fact that it is not always in their best interests with respect to the construction of professional self-esteem and identity. As has already been suggested, one reason is that music education majors have been socialized to be performers first and teachers second (Beynon, 1998; Froehlich & L'Roy, 1985, p. 67; L'Roy, 1983, pp. 144, 184; Roberts, 1991c). The fact that the American and Canadian undergraduate music education majors continued to identify themselves as performers or musicians suggests that there may be serious problems in the professional socialization of undergraduate music education majors. But then, as Cox (1997) counters, because music education majors have been socialized as performers, they can only respond as musicians and cannot assume an appropriate professional role until such time as they actually begin teaching.

This begs the question of how undergraduates can be expected to construct an appropriate professional music teacher identity during their university edication. The problem may be more serious than first appears since research by L'Roy (1983) and Roberts (1991c), and Cox (1997) shows that even experienced music educators "view themselves more as musicians than as teachers" (p. 117). This ought to be cause for concern among music teacher educators, for it suggests that university music education programs may be ineffective in instilling in undergraduate music education majors, and particularly string music education majors, an appropriate sense of music teacher identity (L'Roy, 1983, p. 179).

Supporting evidence for this supposition is found in the observation that many music education majors fail to recognize their academic music education courses as preparatory to actual teaching (Beynon, 1998, p. 92; L'Roy, 1983, p. 184; Roberts, 1991b, p. 36). L'Roy (1983) attributes this gap between theory and practice to reliance on inappropriate reference groups and role models (p. 168). L'Roy (1983), Roberts (1991c), Beynon (1998), and Prescesky (1997) all found that while undergraduate music education majors look to several reference groups for professional guidance, including applied instructors and former school teachers, music education faculty are not usually among them. On those rare occasions that undergraduates do look to music education faculty for guidance and as role models, it is in their capacities as applied instructors or ensemble directors (L'Roy, 1983). This is cause for concern, says L'Roy, as at this point in their careers undergraduates ought to be modeling themselves after their university music education instructors and not just their parents, secondary school teachers, or applied instructors (p. 168). As was said previously, students enter university with lay conceptions of music teacher identity and professional roles acquired through years of experience with school music teachers (Beynon, 1998). Many of those conceptions are probably myopic and stereotypical and possibly even incorrect, as students' experiences and perceptions are necessarily limited (Duling, 2000; L'Roy, 1983, p. 87).

The proper aim of music teacher education, according to L'Roy (1983) and Roberts (2000b), is to replace those lay images of their chosen occupation with a more appropriate professional identity, one based on education and not performance. The same admonition was made previously in the final report of the Music Educators National Conference (MENC) Commission on Teacher Education in Music (1972), in which the commissioners stated that music education majors should internalize the role of the teacher and not the performer (p. 48). Besides, as White (1967) concluded from his own interactionist survey study of the professional role and status of school music teachers ($N = 1000$), despite their own belief in the centrality of performance in music education, experienced music educators share more social characteristics in common with teachers than with professional musicians (p. 8; see also L'Roy, 1983, p. 58). In the end, some kind of balance between and integration of the two role-identities is probably desirable (Roberts, 2000b; Rose, 1998; Stubley, 1998, p. 163). Possibly, that balance may shift and change according to changing occupational demands (Roberts, 2000b, p. 73).

Another reason why music education majors and even experienced teachers conceive of themselves as performers or musicians is that the field of music education is loosely defined, involving knowledge and skills from a number of overlapping fields of study (L'Roy, 1983). A well-structured field like performance, with a more clearly defined knowledge base coupled with specific tasks and work-related skills, can be expected to promote a stronger sense of professional identity than one that is less well defined, such as music education (p. 9). A strong sense of professional identity is important to professional success, as it gives direction and purpose to action, whereas a weak one leads to indirection, confusion, and inaction (p. 8). This makes the development of a strong professional music teacher identity in undergraduate music education majors all the more vital, for without it, and in addition to experiencing identity conflicts and loss of professional interest, they may be confused in their professional and curricular goals. Perhaps music education majors are drawn to performance for its clarity of purpose and more clearly delineated body of knowledge, at least within the Western classical music tradition that usually prevails within the university setting (Kingsbury, 1984, 1988; McClary, 1991; Roberts, 2000a; Small, 1996). The performer label and role are probably more easily conceptualized and understood by music education majors and teachers (L'Roy, 1983, p. 162).

Social status is yet another reason why music education majors in the studies examined placed a higher premium on performance (L'Roy, 1983; Roberts, 1991a, 1991b, 1991c). For music education majors, social status is afforded them on the basis of perceived level of musicianship and not teacher expertise. Roberts's music education majors perceived performance to be held in higher regard within the university school of music, with most of the opportunities for status rewards and progression tied to it (1991c, pp. 92, 98). Their sense of professional identity evolved with, and in relation to, their perceived social status as musicians on their respective major instruments and not with reference to the field of music education and its problems (1991b, p. 36; 1991c, p. 71; L'Roy, 1983). If anything, they felt stigmatized by being labeled music educators (L'Roy, 1983; Roberts, 1991c, p. 94).

This emphasis on performance as the major criterion and determinant of self-worth and social status within the university school of music, though, may only be a reflection of current North American cultural and educational values. The situation may be different in other parts of the world, where less institutional emphasis may be placed on the performance ability of music education students (e.g., Mark, 1998, p. 9; Roberts, 2000b, p. 65). In a recent publication, though, and referring to a study by Swedish researcher Bouij (1998), Roberts notes that there may be a parallel in the socialization processes of Canadian music education majors and Swedish "music-teacher-students"

(Roberts, 2000b, p. 67). Because Roberts acknowledges that Bouij's work advances his own project, it is reviewed here in some detail.

Bouij's (1998) model of the socialization of Swedish "music-teacher-students" to professional practice and identity is based on a longitudinal and ethnographic study of 169 individuals as they progressed through a 4-year music teacher education program and into professional life. As in Roberts's (1991c) study, the intention was to build grounded theory. Data obtained from "informants" by means of interviews and questionnaires were analyzed and led to the proposition that "music-teacher-students" and novice teachers exhibit one of two basic and anticipatory orientations, or salient role identities, toward music teaching that are extensions of personality.

As Bouij (1998) explains, students entering the field may be predisposed to be pupil-centered or content-centered in their approaches to teaching, with the musicianly correlates being "all-round musician" and "performer." These salient role-identities (see fig. 36.1) are linked to personality, inasmuch as the former implies an emphasis on interpersonal relationships—education of the whole child through music—while the latter implies a more intrapersonal and objective approach to musical subject matter (p. 25). Both are reflections of the individual's perception or understanding of educational content and goals. The educational institution and program of studies provide an arena in which students struggle to legitimize their self-perceptions along the lines proposed by Roberts (1991b, 1991c).

This struggle for social recognition and status may lead to changes in role-identity, such as occurred with Roberts's Canadian students when they experienced an identity defeat in pursuit of performance aspirations. Failing to sustain their identities as performers, they became *only* teachers or all-around musicians. This is hardly a solid foundation for the development of a music teacher identity and successful teaching career. As Bouij (1998) comments, "A failed musician cannot easily assert to be a pupil-centered teacher with his credibility intact" (p. 30). In some individuals, however, a crisis in faith such as that experienced by Roberts's Canadian students may prompt them to contemplate new, and perhaps more realistic, self-perceptions and role-identities. For these music education majors, the music education program may function as a "cooling out" period during which they gradually adjust to their new sense of identity as a teacher. Performance majors, in the face of identity defeat, do not always have that option (Prescesky, 1997; Roberts, 1993, p. 192). In Bouij's (1998) experience with Swedish students, the more dramatic shift in role-identity from pure performer to pupil-centered teacher was unusual (p. 31). Performers were able to make the horizontal transition to conservatory-style teaching but were less apt, or able, to make the vertical transition to public school teaching. It was this observation that prompted Bouij to propose that the form of teaching praxis that individuals pursued—the public school or conservatory—was more a reflection of personality than conscious intelligent choice (p. 31).

It is this separation of Swedish students into conservatory and public school streams that Roberts (2000b) thinks is paralleled in Canada. Unlike Sweden, Canada has no state-supported and -operated conservatory system, so music education majors opt instead for either secondary or elementary school music teaching. Undergraduates identifying themselves with the label "performer" may be more likely to "drift" into high school teaching, while those identifying themselves as "general musicians" may end up teaching primary and elementary music (p. 67). The implication is that there may be differences in personality or temperament between these two groups. At the moment, however, this observation remains at the level of impression or supposition, as Roberts's original (1991b, 1991c) study was only concerned with the preservice preparation of music teachers. The only basis for his observation of undergraduates drifting into particular teacher roles was anecdotal evidence collected from interviews with only 8 experienced Newfoundland music teachers. The interviews were conducted by an undergraduate student (Roberts, 2000b, p. 68).

Personality Factors

There is some empirical evidence supporting the notion that performers and secondary and elementary school music teachers differ temperamentally (Kemp, 1996, 1997; Wubbenhorst, 1994). Whether or to what degree those differences are attributable to inborn personality dimensions

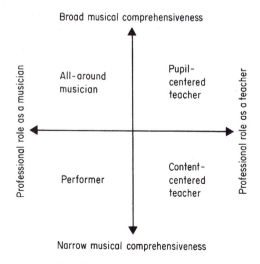

Figure 36.1. Bouij's (1998) salient role-identities.

or differences in professional roles and expectations, however, remains a subject for future research. Kemp (1996), in his book *The Musical Temperament: Psychology and Personality of Musicians,* attributes at least some differences in personality and temperament among performers and secondary and elementary music teachers to the latter (p. 217).

While sharing many traits in common with professional musicians, music teachers on the whole are reported to be more extroverted and conservative (Kemp, 1982, 1996, 1997; Roberts, 1991c; Wubbenhorst, 1994). For obvious reasons it is more important for music teachers than for performers to be able to relate to others. Further, there is more social pressure placed on music teachers to "appear 'normal' and conventional" (Kemp, 1996, pp. 220, 222; see also Beynon, 1998; Paul, 1998; Wolfgang, 1990). One interpretation of the foregoing is that the profession attracts or selects conservative individuals while simultaneously reinforcing their conformist tendencies (White, 1967). As was noted earlier in this chapter, less conventional individuals are probably discouraged from pursuing public school music teaching careers.

Research by Kemp (1982) and Wubbenhorst (1994) also reveals that experienced secondary school music teachers may be more tough-minded, logical, and analytical in their decision-making and more dedicated to performance than their elementary school counterparts. This would appear to support the hypothesis that there may be "inborn" personality differences between secondary and elementary music teachers. These differences, however, might only be reflections to some extent of differing institutional and occupational realities. Secondary school music teachers are probably "required to develop a more tough-minded and logical attitude to their work" while elementary teachers are said to "discount" their musician's intuition in order to attend to the more immediate social and other needs of young children (Kemp, 1996, p. 226). It is in this sense that personality or temperament may be said to be socially constructed.

One confounding factor in the research into the personalities of musicians and music teachers is that any findings might only be artifacts of the particular cultures and educational systems in which the research was conducted. Much of the research available was undertaken in the United States and Great Britain, countries with different cultural and educational systems and, possibly, different expectations with respect to appropriate music teacher roles and behavior. Moreover, participants in the studies reviewed by Kemp (1996) varied considerably in their ages and levels of experience, thus making it difficult to compare them with much confidence (p. 225), while the research tools employed (e.g., *Myers-Briggs Type Indicator, Cattell's Sixteen Personality Factor Questionnaire,* and the *Eysenck Personality Inventory*) rely on a bewildering array

of theoretical and psychological constructs and traits that are somewhat nebulous. Finally, the majority of the studies define the term "musician" very narrowly, equating it with classical or orchestral musicians. The observations made herein about the personalities of music teachers and musicians probably only apply to those trained in the classical musical tradition. At best they should be considered only tentative generalizations.

Technical Rationality in Music Teacher Education

If temperament can be shaped by individuals' learned perceptions and understandings of occupational roles and appropriate behavior therein, then it can also be influenced through schooling. Students have their own learned perceptions and understandings of their roles and places within educational institutions that are shaped by educational norms, conventions, and expectations, including epistemological and pedagogical ones.

Many social constructivists attribute the conservatism of music education majors and their failure to connect theory with practice to the continued prevalence of technical rationality in music teacher education (Beynon, 1998; Elliott, 1995; Kincheloe & McLaren, 2000; Regelski, 1997, 1998; Rose, 1998; Schön, 1987; Woodford, 1996a; Woodford & Dunn, 1998). The term "technical rationality" refers to a positivistic epistemology of knowledge and practice according to which practitioners are conceived as instrumental problem-solvers trained to select the appropriate technical means for solving well-formed problems (Schön, 1987, pp. 3–4). As Regelski (1998) explains, this approach to education breeds intellectual passivity and an overreliance on methods and technique, as if using good methods and sophisticated techniques will "automatically bring about good results" (p. 6). Students are required to develop their technical expertise using various performance and teaching methodologies but are not encouraged to critically examine them or to consider the moral, social, and political implications of their actions. The role for music education and performance students is that of a sophisticated technician charged with reproducing rather than producing culture and not a moral agent of change empowered to breathe new life into performance or teaching practices (Kincheloe & McLaren, 2000; Rose, 1990; Small, 1996, pp. 191–192; Taruskin, 1995). As a result, novice teachers "teach the way they were taught" (e.g., Beynon, 1998; Elliott, 1995; Kemp, 1996; Paul, 1998; Regelski, 1998; Schön, 1987).

Evidence of the continued prevalence of technical rationality in music education is readily obtainable. Several researchers and writers describe preservice music teachers as being perceived and treated by educational institutions "as merely passive receptacles" of expert and traditional knowledge (Beynon, 1998, p. 90; Elliott, 1995; O'Toole, 1993; Regelski, 1997, 1998; Small, 1987; Woodford, 1996a, 1996b, 1998). Others describe them as being obsessed with technique at the expense of musicality and interpretation (Kingsbury, 1984; Roberts, 1991c). The concern has also been expressed that music teachers may be too dependent on particular methodologies and pedagogical practices (O'Toole, 1993; Regelski, 1998; Reimer, 1989; Woodford, 1998). The authority of traditional musical and teaching canons is seldom questioned or challenged. As a result, many music teacher education programs continue to rely on transmission educational models and the teaching of pedagogy over inquiry (Dolloff, 1999a, p. 35.)

Kingsbury (1984), in his account of the social structure and process in an American conservatory, provides one possible explanation of how technical rationality in education renders students passive. Referring to Sennett and Cobb's book *The Hidden Injuries of Class* (1972), Kingsbury argues that talent is a social construct and symbol of inequality in the sense that it implies a social hierarchy and class structure that perpetuates itself through the recruitment of an elite. An attribution of talent is a badge of authority that legitimates a particular class—Sennett and Cobb argue that the distinction between talented individuals and the undistinguished masses is one of class—while relegating others to inferior social status (as cited in Kingsbury, 1984, p. 80). Intellectual and musical passivity might be attributable to what Sennett and Cobb refer to as "hidden injuries." These are injuries to the individual's psyche and self-confidence attributed to sustained occupational and educational adversity and resulting in feelings of inferiority and powerlessness and a loss of dignity that are assimilated into personal and professional identity (p. 79). Classical music is implicated in this hierarchical social structure. As Kingsbury writes, "what we informally call 'classical' music is music of the talented, by the talented, and . . . for the talented as well" (p. 84).

Kingsbury does not specifically address music education majors and their problems, but the implication is obvious. So long as undergraduate music education majors base their sense of professional identity primarily on their performance status, that is, on their perceived level of musical talent with respect to performance of the Western musical canon, they will probably continue to be rendered passive by their feelings of inferiority and low professional self-esteem. Indeed, Roberts found that his university music students typically associated classical music, particularly technically demanding varieties, with higher social status. Affiliation with contemporary, jazz, and other music resulted in a reduction in status (1991c, pp. 134, 141). This, of course, comes as no surprise. Throughout much of the 20th century, music teachers blithely assumed that their role was to develop in children "musical taste along the lines of Western art music . . . to propagate and socialize the musical tastes of the socially elite class among all classes" (McCarthy, 1997, p. 74; see also Britton, 1966, p. 18; Regelski, 1998, p. 5; Vulliamy & Shepherd, 1984, p. 262; White, 1967, p. 9; Witkin, 1974, p. 120). Many music teachers probably still think this way today (Choksy, 1999; Reimer, 1998; Roberts, 1991a, 1991b, 1991c, 2000a).

In sum, music teacher education programs, because they tend to reify tradition, including the beliefs that music educators are primarily performance and methods teachers and gatekeepers to the "masterworks," breed intellectual passivity and conservatism in music education majors (Small, 1987, 1996, pp. 185–198; Roberts, 2000a; Woodford, 1998). They are socialized to be followers and not intellectual and visionary leaders in the sense described by the MENC (1972, 1987), emphasizing that new teachers ought to model intellectual curiosity and various personal and leadership qualities so that they can envision and initiate needed changes.

Critical Ethnography: Integrating Theory, Research, and Practice

Social constructivists in education are also interested in developing leadership qualities in their students, but the leadership desired is usually of a particular kind that acknowledges and takes into account the moral and political dimensions of schooling and that, further, is attentive to social power dynamics (Kincheloe & McLaren, 2000, p. 284). Drawing on critical theorists of the Frankfurt School and writers such as Gramsci (1971), Bourdieu (1977), Giroux (1983), and Freire (1985), music teacher educators Rose (1990, 1998) and Beynon (1998) view the construction of music teacher identity as a social and political process whereby individual music education majors and teachers learn to challenge and resist the hegemony of the musical education establishment and tradition. Their research explores, while simultaneously attempting to redress, problems in the construction of music teacher identity. Ultimately, their purpose is to develop a critical pedagogy that empowers undergraduates to construct their own professional identities.

As Beynon (1998) writes, critical theory "is a subversive way of investigating current power structures in our society, of uncovering areas of injustice to individuals, and of seeking solutions to repress the powerful and emancipate those without power" (p. 84). Music teachers are viewed as intellectuals, social activists, and cultural workers charged with transforming education and, ultimately, society (Beynon, 1998, p. 99; Rose, 1998, p. 25). Both researchers describe the secondary socialization process for prospective music teachers as involving the development of a critical consciousness and a period of adjustment in professional identity as undergraduates negotiate the gap between student and teacher. Critical theory is applied both as a lens and general framework for examining and interpreting music education problems and as a guide to their own ethnographic research and developing pedagogy. Their approaches to research are decidedly more macrological and more overtly political than those of other researchers examined previously in this chapter.

Rose's (1998) ethnographic study is part of a long-term, collaborative, and interdisciplinary action-research project at the Memorial University of Newfoundland dedicated to investigating and understanding teachers' professional thinking and development, particularly during the internship or teaching practicum experience (p. 24). The Reflective and Critical Internship Program (RCIP) model was developed both to provide a theoretical framework for the project and to outline a critical pedagogy for developing a critical consciousness in prospective music and other teachers. This critical consciousness is thought to be instrumental in providing an intellectual basis for the autonomous formation of teacher identity. There are five interactive and interdependent pedagogical categories, or forms of action, to the RCIP model (see figure 36.2). They are describing/contextualizing, bringing and recognizing cultural capital, engaging in communication, problematizing dominant practices and discourses, and functioning as intellectuals and cultural workers. These categories act as lenses for guiding supervisors' and student-teachers' analyses of internship experiences while also functioning as conceptual tools for provoking further teacher development. Information about students' perceptions of their internship experiences was collected by means of interviews, group discussions, interactive journals, and participant observation. Unfortunately, nowhere is it reported how many music education majors were actually involved in the study. The reader is only provided a narrative summary with occasional anecdotes illustrating student progression through the RCIP model (see fig. 36.2).

The first pedagogical form of action, describing/contextualizing, refers to the beginning of a process of self-exploration in which interns examine their own beliefs and actions in light of institutional social realities. The second step in the construction of music teacher identity, bringing and recognizing cultural capital, involves raising students' consciousness with respect to ideological and cultural differences while encouraging them to begin viewing themselves "as critical agents in the production of their own culture" (Rose, 1998, p. 32). The third category of pedagogical action, engaging in communication, implies communication and the sharing of ideas, beliefs, and knowledge as part of the dialectical process whereby meaning is socially constructed. Communication allows for the development of new personal relationships and possibilities with

THE RCIP (REFLECTIVE AND CRITICAL INTERNSHIP PROGRAM)
A MODEL FOR TEACHER EDUCATION
A. Singh, C. Doyle, A. Rose, W. Kennedy
Faculty of Education, Memorial University of Newfoundland
St. John's, Newfoundland, Canada A1B 3X8

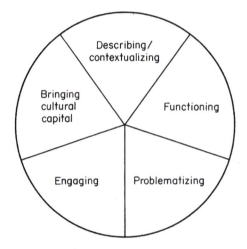

- Describing/contextualizing
- Bringing cultural capital
- Engaging in communication
- Problematizing dominant practices and discourses
- Functioning as intellectuals and cultural workers

Figure 36.2. The RCIP model.

respect to curricular innovations and professional identity (p. 34).

The fourth category of pedagogical action, problematizing dominant practices and discourses, is highly politicized and refers to the process of critically examining dominant beliefs and practices that are often taken for granted (Rose, 1998, p. 35). Interns typically struggle with questions of classroom management, policy, and identity relative to tradition and the status quo. The question of identity is particularly problematical for music interns, most of whom wish to be identified and labeled as "good musicians over all else" (p. 37). Referring to research by Roberts (1991a, 1991b, 1991c; 1993), Rose notes that for many interns feelings of self-worth and success are dependent on performance ability and need to be continually validated by others. Some interns, though, admitted feeling torn between their identities as musicians and educators, while still others expressed awareness of a period of transition as they negotiated the gap between musician and prospective music educator. In the end, most music interns managed to reconcile the two identities by acknowledging that some healthy balance was desirable (p. 38).

The fifth and last category of pedagogical action, functioning as intellectuals and cultural workers, refers to the socialization of music education interns to the role of social activist. Linking education to wider social movements and political power struggles, Rose (1998) views teachers as social activists empowered to struggle individually and "collectively to transform schools into democratic public spheres" (p. 38). The distinction is made between education and training, with interns encouraged to view pedagogy as a form of cultural practice that ought to be subjected to criticism and revision and not just as the transmission of traditional knowledge and skills.

Beynon's (1998) study at the University of Western Ontario was also part of a larger interdisciplinary one, although the time frame was more circumscribed, lasting only one full preservice year and a few months beyond (p. 91). Interviews, journal entries, and participant observation both in class and during student teaching were used to gather data about 6 music education students' perceptions of their experiences and evolving sense of professional identity. Analysis of the data revealed that there may be at least four stages to the development of this critical consciousness and sense of professional identity in prospective music teachers. Like the previous studies by Roberts (1991c) and Rose (1998), Beynon's results are conveyed in narrative form, albeit with more frequent use of student anecdotes.

As in many Canadian faculties of education, student teachers at the University of Western Ontario already possess an undergraduate degree and alternate during the preservice year between academic courses and teaching practica. Beynon's (1998) interns began the first practicum experience with an initial and unproblematical conception of teaching practice and professional identity. Already socialized to the music teaching profession and its traditional beliefs and practices through prior experience as pupils, interns assumed a naively anti-intellectual stance toward music teaching while simultaneously emulating and attempting to replicate their cooperating teachers' practices (p. 89).

The second stage in student-teachers' development was prompted by an introduction to principles of critical theory (Beynon, 1998, p. 98). Consistent with other studies showing that preservice teachers experience shock when required to contemplate alternate conceptions of teacher identity and practice (e.g., Britzman, 1991), Beynon's (1998) students initially resisted the new learning while expressing feelings of disappointment, anger, frustration, or apathy. The third stage in development was entered when students grudgingly acknowledged the potential merits of critical theory and began to critically examine and then relinquish their earlier ideologies and concepts of professional identity (p. 98). This marked the beginning of the development of a critical consciousness leading to consideration of an alternate understanding of music teacher practice and identity. The final stage in this developmental scheme was reached only after preservice music teachers were able to conceptualize themselves as social activists.

This only happened, however, after the conclusion of the academic year and teaching practica. Further, Beynon acknowledged that it remained to be seen whether graduates of her program actually applied theory to practice in their own teaching (p. 99). She remained pessimistic that more than a few new music teachers, even those completing a program such as hers, would challenge the status quo.

Perhaps the most significant observations Beynon (1998) makes are that the conscious construction of music teacher identity is perhaps born out of contradiction and paradox and that preservice music teachers require assistance in bridging the gap between university and school, theory and practice. Beynon's interns reported experiencing a number of frustrating contradictions, paradoxes, and power struggles in their preservice program as they negotiated differing values between school and university. Their sense of professional identity emerged as they attempted to intellectually come to grips with those problems (p. 92). This would not have occurred at all, however, without Beynon's assistance in the form of dialogic interviews with interns. As she writes, "without . . . ongoing dialogic discussion, these student teachers were unable to see the relationships between school and university" (p. 95). Without her active and sustained involvement in engaging students to intellectualize about their own practice, these students, too, would have failed to appreciate that music teaching entails a unity of theory and practice.

The conscious construction of music teacher identity evidently requires sustained intellectual prompting from university instructors if novices are to question and challenge the currently prevailing educational system. Challenging the educational establishment, though, may be viewed by some as a form of countercultural and subversive activity. This may be dangerous for new music teachers to undertake. Accordingly, Beynon (1998) concludes, new music teachers choosing to follow a critical path "must become teacher-leaders" (p. 101). Unfortunately, she does not explain what this means.

Conclusion

Current research into the social construction of music teacher identity in undergraduate music education majors, while helpful in understanding the social and intellectual development of undergraduate music education majors, remains far from adequate. Given that undergraduates were the focus of this chapter, proportionately more consideration was given to examining secondary than primary socialization processes or ascriptive factors. Several of the more important studies examined in this chapter were qualitative in nature. The researchers were interested in investigating the socialization of undergraduates to professional practice and identity within particular institutional settings, as described in their own words. Institutional cultures are influenced and shaped by the broader educational and cultural contexts in which they are located. Thus it is only to be expected that institutions and music teacher programs located in different parts of the United States or Canada, or in the United Kingdom or Sweden, might differ in important respects. This makes generalization somewhat hazardous. Nevertheless, and because "qualitative researchers are not devoid of interest in generalization" (Bresler & Stake, 1992, p. 79), certain general observations were made throughout this chapter about the professional socialization of undergraduate music education majors. Those general observations should not be interpreted as final, definitive answers to the problem of music teacher identity construction but as potentially useful insights that can inform music teacher education practice.

The total number of music teacher education programs examined in the literature was small, as was the total number of undergraduate music education majors interviewed and observed. Further, the results of the qualitative studies examined were reported only anecdotally. This can be a problem when using larger groups of informants, and particularly when the researcher intends to generalize beyond the purely local event, as did Roberts (1991c). The problem is perhaps less with recognizing the researchers' own biases than with ensuring that informants' viewpoints, taken both individually and collectively, are accurately represented (Fontana & Frey, 2000, p. 659). Increasingly, as social scientists "resituate the local within the larger contexts of regional, national, and even global events," they are resorting to both qualitative and quantitative methods (Chambers, 2000, p. 858). Roberts (1991c) and Bouij (1998) each interviewed more than 100 informants. Had descriptive graphics and statistics been used to indicate levels of agreement among music education majors with respect to their professional self-perceptions, their studies would have been considerably strengthened.

Many more and better studies are needed using both qualitative and quantitative methods, and further comparisons need to be made among institutions representing different regional, national, and cultural settings, before a better understanding of music teacher identity construction can be obtained. More longitudinal studies such as those of Rose (1998) and Beynon (1998), albeit using greater numbers of informants, would provide much-needed information about how music education majors negotiate the various gaps and stages in their undergraduate education. Regrettably, Rose neglected to state the number of informants employed in her study, while Beynon's study, like that of Prescesky (1997), employed so few that it is best described as only a pilot study (see also Paul, 1998). In consequence, and although both Rose and Beynon clearly intended that the results of their studies be gener-

alized (Rose was developing a general pedagogical model of preservice teacher education based on critical theoretic principles, while Beynon called for changes in the educational system based on results obtained from only six interns), the reader ought to be especially cautious before reaching any conclusions.

It would help were future researchers to include in their models and analyses more explicit information about the ways undergraduates differ in their socialization to professional identity according to applied major, gender, race, and socioeconomic class. L'Roy (1983) concluded that band, choral, and string music education majors differed so much with respect to choice of role label (i.e., performer versus educator) and commitment to music education as to be deserving of separate study in the future (p. 187). Her study provides useful descriptive information about those students and the persons most influential on their choices of careers but has little say about the nature or intensity of the relationships (p. 172). Quite possibly, too, some of the differences in personality that Kemp (1996) noted among brass, woodwind, percussion, and choral musicians and between male and female musicians may be attributable to some extent to differences in socialization (Green, 1997). Given that many music education majors define themselves as musicians first and teachers second and that there are obvious gender inequities in the music education profession (Trollinger, 1993; O'Neill, 1997), this information would seem relevant to the construction of music teacher identity.

As was recommended in the report by the MENC Task Force on Music Teacher Education for the Nineties (MENC, 1987), music teacher educators need to take a longer view with respect to the socialization of future music teachers, "a process that begins prior to the college program of preparation and extends throughout an active career" (p. 13). It would obviously be profitable for researchers to examine more closely that process beginning in childhood and continuing through university and beyond. This would provide a much broader picture of the changes and maturation, or lack thereof, in undergraduates' and novice teachers' thinking with education and experience. It could also provide new insight into problems in identity construction among children, undergraduates, and new teachers. Currently, the research into music teacher identity construction among school children, most of which was carried out by means of surveys of undergraduates' and experienced music teachers' childhood recollections, remains superficial.

Despite flaws in the research, several interesting observations emerge from the literature. These tentative findings can be used to guide future research. Clearly, many high school students contemplating a music education career model themselves and their sense of professional identity after their school music teachers and performance instructors (Beynon, 1998; Dolloff, 1999b; L'Roy, 1983; Paul, 1998; Prescesky, 1997; Roberts, 1991c; Wolfgang, 1990). Although probably a necessary starting point for the self-conscious construction of music teacher identity, once formed, these naive and nascent role-identities appear to be resistant to change in university. In fact, none of the researchers whose work was reviewed in this chapter reported clear evidence of undergraduates self-consciously constructing a professional identity for themselves. Although some undergraduates experienced a shift in identity from "musician" to "music teacher" (Hargreaves & North, 1999, p. 79), this was only after much prodding from their professor/researchers. Beynon (1998) was in the end pessimistic that her undergraduates would challenge the status quo. "These new teachers," she said, "will not be ones to implement reform or question current practice" (p. 101).

This presents a serious challenge for social construction music education models, for it suggests that many, and perhaps a majority of, undergraduate music education majors have not so much begun constructing a professional identity for themselves as emulated their former teachers. It was just this kind of observation that led Hacking (1999) in his critique of social construction to conclude that the *self* is more social product than construct (p. 15). To the extent that identity is sculpted through experience, education, and personal choice with respect to the pursuit of preexisting and narrowly conceived roles, it is a social product. Reflective and critical pedagogies actually assume as much; that people, including undergraduates, tend to be intellectually passive or subject to a false consciousness (e.g., Kincheloe & McLaren, 2000; Regelski, 1998; Woodford, 1995).

Although differing in important ways, reflective and critical models of music teacher education share a common purpose or intent, which is to prompt and stimulate intellectual growth and maturation in undergraduates such that they can transcend tradition and the status quo and thereby transform society (Beynon, 1998; Dewey, 1900/1990; Regelski, 1998; Rose, 1998; Woodford, in press). Both reflective and critical pedagogical models are properly understood as aspects of larger moral and political projects (Woodford & Dunn, 1998; Kincheloe & McLaren, 2000, p. 291). At present, and particularly given the state of research and lack of clear evidence of the efficacy of those models, social construction in music education remains at the level of a philosophical and social ideal and not a social reality. But then, reflective and critical pedagogies are relatively new to music teacher education, having only begun to make inroads into the literature during the past decade (e.g., Rose, 1990). The studies by L'Roy (1983) and Roberts (1991b) were completed before reflective and critical pedagogies became more the norm in music teacher education. It is therefore too soon to dismiss them as ineffective in accomplishing their goal of self-determination for undergraduates. At the same time, researchers should realize that self-determination is an existential goal that cannot be assessed in any meaningful way except personally. This makes it all the more difficult to assess the extent to which those pedagogies are successful in accomplishing their ends.

Many of the researchers whose work was reviewed in this chapter attribute undergraduate music education majors' intransigence with respect to the self-conscious construction of professional identity to the continued prevalence of technical rationality and transmission models in school and university (Beynon, 1998; Dolloff, 1999a, 1999b; Regelski, 1997, 1998; Woodford, 1996a). The research and pedagogical models presented here by Rose (1998) and Beynon (1998), based on principles of critical theory, help locate music education problems within wider social and cultural contexts while also counteracting some of the more insidious effects of traditional educational models. Noticeably absent in the music education research literature, though, are similar research studies based on Deweyan principles and models. Dewey was one of the "forerunners of and direct contributors to the symbolic interactionist perspective" (Wallace & Wolf, 1999, p. 191). Inasmuch as Dewey made fewer assumptions about the actual content of education—he was wary of overprescribing to students and teachers—his approach to educational matters is more micrological than macrological (Dewey, 1900/1990, 1916; Westbrook, 1991; Woodford, in press; Woodford & Dunn, 1998). North American music educators have long had an affinity for Dewey and his educational philosophy (Elliott, 1995; McCarthy, 1997; Mursell, 1956; Reimer, 1989). Quite probably it is his moderation that appeals to them (Hlebowitsh, 1992, p. 81). Music teacher education research studies based on Deweyan educational models, were they to be carried out in the future, might thus be seen as more relevant and appropriate within the American philosophical and music education communities.

Music teacher educators are limited with respect to their direct influence on the public schools, but they can begin to address the problems of conservatism and intellectual passivity in music education majors by integrating reflective and critical educational practices throughout their own curricula, and not, as is all too often the case, in a seminar during the last year of the music teacher education program. An important aim of constructivist music teacher education models is to progressively challenge undergraduates to explore a wide variety of teacher roles and literature as means of prompting them to rethink their own limited understandings.

One of the first steps in any reflective or critical model of music teacher education is to make students' beliefs explicit so that they can be subjected to critical scrutiny; otherwise, "there can be no hope of integrating personal experience and professional knowledge" (Dolloff, 1999a, p. 35; Regelski, 1998; Woodford, 1995). Given that many music education majors idealize themselves as musicians or performance teachers-in-training, probably the first thing that music teacher educators should do in the freshman year is to challenge students' beliefs with respect to performance being the primary determinant of their social status and professional identity. Various researchers and writers describe music teachers as having multiple roles and responsibilities, including but not limited to performer, composer, conductor, critic, musicologist, mentor, facilitator, social activist, politician, music listener, music theorist, public intellectual, diplomat, travel agent, administrator, confidante, instructor, public speaker, moral agent, and visionary and democratic leader (Beynon, 1998; Kaplan, 1966; Morton, 1998; Olsson, 1997; Richardson, 1998; Rose, 1998; Woodford, 1996b). Taken together, these roles constitute a social framework for music education thought and practice and thus also for the personal and professional exploration and growth of music education majors.

Few, if any, people can be equally adept in all of those areas, but it is important that undergraduates realize the full compass of music teacher practice available to them while progressively trying to explore, develop, and broaden their expertise. For to the extent that they are limited in their understanding of music teacher practice and role-identities, music education majors are also limited in realizing their potentialities as music teachers. By exploring, understanding, and appreciating the multiplicity and complexity of music teacher practice, music education majors can develop their intelligences, forms of expertise, and personalities—in short, their identities as music teachers—to the fullest extent possible (for a similar argument see Reimer, manuscript in preparation; see also Richardson, 1998).

Music teacher educators ought not be too concerned if undergraduates immediately fail to recognize them as potential professional role models (L'Roy, 1983; Roberts, 1991a). One probable explanation for their oversight is that undergraduates might not be sufficiently mature or experienced to judge who is or is not an appropriate professional role model. Perry (1968), in his own research into stages of intellectual and ethical development of undergraduate students, found that many undergraduates are simply not ready to make the conscious commitment to a particular belief system, worldview, and corresponding sense of professional identity that characterizes more mature kinds of thinking (Brand, 1988; Harwood, 1993;

Woodford, 1996b). The university may actually exacerbate this problem of professional immaturity by isolating undergraduates from the real world of public school teaching. Further, although they are introduced in the university to adult and professional ways of thinking and knowledge, undergraduates have little power and influence and only marginal social status therein (Vulliamy & Shepherd, 1984, p. 251). For many music education majors, and particularly given the continued prevalence of transmission models in undergraduate education, university may seem just a continuation of high school. As already mentioned, constructing a professional identity takes considerable time, as it entails a process of personal growth and maturity that probably cannot be fully realized in any one degree program.

Music teacher educators ought not become too discouraged, then, if undergraduates continue to cling to, and model themselves after, their former school teachers. Possibly, and given sufficient breadth and depth of educational experience, coupled with appropriate and sustained prompting from music teacher educators, music education majors may begin to see the validity of alternate music teacher models and role-identities. If nothing else, once they begin teaching, their "college mentors may still serve as useful models in memory" (Harwood, 1993, p. 15).

REFERENCES

Abeles, H. F., Hoffer, C. R., & Klotman, R. H. (1994). *Foundations of music education* (2nd ed.). New York: Schirmer Books.

Apple, M. (Ed.). (1982). *Cultural and economic reproduction in education: Essays on class, ideology, and the state*. London: Routledge and Kegan Paul.

Apple, M. W., & Beane, J. A. (Eds.). (1995). *Democratic schools*. Alexandria, VA: Association for Supervision and Curriculum Development.

Ashley, D., & Orenstein, D. M. (2001). *Sociological theory: Classical statements* (5th ed.). Boston: Allyn and Bacon.

Atterbury, B. (1993). What do women want? *Quarterly Journal of Music Teaching and Learning, 4, 5*(4,1), 100–104.

Attinello, P. (1994). Authority and freedom: Toward a sociology of the gay choruses. In P. Brett, E. Wood, & G. C. Thomas (Eds.), *Queering the pitch: The new gay and lesbian musicology* (pp. 315–346). New York: Routledge.

Bartel, L. R. (1995). Cultural equity in music education. *The Recorder, 37*(2), 51–54.

Barkin, E., & Hamessley, L. (Eds.). (1999). *Audible traces: Gender, identity, and music*. Zurich: Carciofoli Verlagshaus.

Belenky, M. F., Clinchy, B. M., Goldberger, N. R., & Tarule, J. M. (1986). *Women's ways of knowing: The development of self, voice, and mind*. New York: Basic Books.

Berger, P. L., & Luckmann, T. (1966). *The social construction of reality: A treatise in the sociology of knowledge.* Garden City, NY: Doubleday.

Beynon, C. (1998). From music student to music teacher: Negotiating an identity. In P. Woodford (Ed.), Critical thinking in music: Theory and practice [Monograph]. *Studies in Music from the University of Western Ontario,* 17 (pp. 83–105).

Borhek, J. T., & Curtis, R. F. (1975). *A sociology of belief.* New York: Wiley.

Bouij, C. (1998). Swedish music teachers in training and professional life. *International Journal of Music Education, 32,* 24–31.

Bourdieu, P. (1977). *Outline of a theory of practice.* Cambridge, England: Cambridge University Press.

Bowman, W. (1994). Sound, sociality and music. *Quarterly Journal of Music Teaching and Learning, 5*(3), 50–67.

Brand, M. (1988). Toward a better understanding of undergraduate music education majors: Perry's perspective. *Bulletin of the Council for Research in Music Education, 98,* 22–31.

Bresler, L., & Stake, R. E. (1992). Qualitative research methodology in music education. In R. Colwell (Ed.), *Handbook of research on music teaching and learning* (pp. 75–90). New York: Schirmer Books.

Britton, A. (1966). Music education: An American specialty. In B. C. Kowal (Ed.), *Perspectives in music education* (pp. 15–28). Washington, DC: Music Educators National Conference.

Britzman, D. P. (1991). *Practice makes practice: A critical study.* Albany: State University of New York Press.

Chambers, E. (2000). Applied ethnography. In N. K. Denzin & Y. S. Lincoln (Eds.), *Handbook of qualitative research* (2nd ed., pp. 851–869). London: Sage.

Charmaz, K. (2000). Grounded theory: Objectivist and constructivist methods. In N. K. Denzin & Y. S. Lincoln (Eds.), *Handbook of qualitative research* (2d ed., pp. 509–535). London: Sage.

Choksy, L. (1999). *The Kodály method II: Folksong to masterwork.* Upper Saddle River, NJ: Prentice-Hall.

Cox, P. (1997). The professional socialization of music teachers as musicians and educators. In R. Rideout (Ed.), *On the sociology of music education* (pp. 112–120). Norman: University of Oklahoma.

Crozier, W. R. (1997). Music and social influence. In D. J. Hargreaves & A. C. North (Eds.), *The social psychology of music* (pp. 67–83). Oxford: Oxford University Press.

Davidson, J. W., Howe, M. J. A., & Sloboda, J. A. (1997). Environmental factors in the development of musical performance skill over the life span. In D. J. Hargreaves & A. C. North (Eds.), *The social psychology of music* (pp. 188–206). Oxford: Oxford University Press.

Davidson, J. W., Moore, D. G., Sloboda, J. A., & Howe, M. J. A. (1998). Characteristics of music teachers and the progress of young instrumentalists. *Journal of Research in Music Education, 46*(1), 141–160.

Dewey, J. (1916). *Democracy and education: An introduction to the philosophy of education.* New York: Macmillan.

Dewey, J. (1990). *The school and society.* Chicago: University of Chicago Press. (Original work published 1900)

Dolloff, L. A. (1999a). Building professional identity: The role of personal story in music teacher education. *Canadian Journal of Research in Music Education, 40*(4), 35–37.

Dolloff, L. A. (1999b). Imagining ourselves as teachers: The development of teacher identity in music teacher education. *Music Education Research, 1*(2), 191–207.

Duling, E. (2000). Student teachers' descriptions and perceptions of their mentors. *Update: Applications of Research in Music Education, 19*(1), 17–21.

Duster, T. (1997). The stratification of cultures as the barrier to democratic pluralism. In R. Orrill (Ed.), *Education and democracy: Re-imagining liberal learning in America* (pp. 263–286). New York: College Entrance Examination Board.

Eaklor, V. L. (1993). The gendered origins of the American musician. *Quarterly Journal of Music Teaching and Learning, 4,5*(4,1), 40–46.

Elliott, D. J. (1995). *Music matters: A new philosophy of music education.* New York: Oxford University Press.

Fontana, A., & Frey, J. H. (2000). The interview: From structured questions to negotiated text. In N. K. Denzin & Y. S. Lincoln (Eds.), *Handbook of qualitative research* (2nd ed., pp. 645–672). London: Sage.

Frazer, E. (1995). Social constructionism. In T. Honderich (Ed.), *The Oxford companion to philosophy* (p. 829). Oxford: Oxford University Press.

Freire, P. (1985). *The politics of education.* South Hadley, MA: Bergin and Garvey.

Frink, K. L. (1997). *Undergraduate string majors' attitudes toward high school orchestra experiences, high school orchestra instructors, and string teaching.* Unpublished master's thesis, University of Colorado, Boulder

Froehlich, H., & L'Roy, D. (1985). An investigation of occupancy identity in undergraduate music education majors. *Bulletin of the Council for Research in Music Education, 85,* 65–75.

Froehlich, H., & Paul, S. (1997). Introduction. In R. Rideout (Ed.), *On the sociology of music education* (pp. v–vi). Norman: University of Oklahoma.

Gillespie, R., & Hamann, D. L. (1998). The status of orchestra programs in the public schools. *Journal of Research in Music Education, 46*(1), 75–86.

Gillespie, R., & Hamann, D. L. (1999). Career choice among string music education students in American colleges and universities. *Journal of Research in Music Education, 47*(3), 266–278.

Giroux, H. (1983). *Theory and resistance in education.* London: Heinemann.

Gramsci, A. (1971). *Selections from prison notebooks.* (Q. Hoare & G. Smith, Trans. & Eds.). New York: International.

Green, L. (1993). Music, gender and education: A report on some exploratory research. *British Journal of Music Education, 10*(3), 219–253.

Green, L. (1994). Gender, musical meaning, and education. *Philosophy of Music Education Review, 2*(2), 99–105.

Green, L. (1997). *Music, gender, education.* Cambridge, England: Cambridge University Press.

Green, L. (1999). Research in the sociology of music education: Some introductory concepts. *Music Education Research, 1*(2), 159–169.

Greene, M. (1993). Imagination, community and the school. *Review of Education, 15,* 223–231.

Hacking, I. (1999). *The social construction of what?* Cambridge: Harvard University Press.

Hamann, D. L., & Cutietta, R. A. (1996). Music teachers as role models for Hispanic American students. *Quarterly Journal of Music Teaching and Learning, 7*(2–4), 102–111.

Hargreaves, D. J., & North, A. C. (1997). *The social psychology of music.* Oxford: Oxford University Press.

Hargreaves, D. J., & North, A. C. (1999). The functions of music in everyday life: Redefining the social in music psychology. *Psychology of Music, 27,* 71–83.

Harwood, E. (1993). Learning characteristics of college students: Implications for the elementary music education methods class. *Quarterly Journal of Music Teaching and Learning, 4*(1), 13–19.

Hlebowitsh (1992). Critical theory versus curriculum theory: Reconsidering the dialogue on Dewey. *Educational Theory, 42*(1), 69–82.

Kaplan, M. (1966). *Foundations and frontiers of music education.* New York: Holt, Rinehart and Winston.

Kemp, A. E. (1982). Personality traits of successful music teachers. *Psychology of Music* [Special issue]. *Proceedings of the Ninth International Seminar on Research in Music Education,* 72–75.

Kemp, A. E. (1996). *The musical temperament: Psychology and personality of musicians.* Oxford: Oxford University Press.

Kemp, A. E. (1997). Individual differences in musical behaviour. In D. J. Hargreaves & A. C. North (Eds.), *The social psychology of music* (pp. 25–45). Oxford: Oxford University Press.

Kincheloe, J. L., & McLaren, P. (2000). Rethinking critical theory and qualitative research. In N. K. Denzin & Y. S. Lincoln (Eds.), *Handbook of qualitative research* (2nd ed., pp. 279–313). London: Sage.

Kingsbury, H. O. (1984). *Music as a cultural system: Structure and process in an American conservatory.* Unpublished doctoral dissertation, Indiana University, Bloomington.

Kingsbury, H. O. (1988). *Music, talent, and performance: A conservatory cultural system.* Philadelphia: Temple University Press.

Lamb, R. (1993/1994). Aria senza accompagnamento: A woman behind the theory. *Quarterly Journal of Music Teaching and Learning, 4,5*(4,1), 5–20.

L'Roy, D. (1983). *The development of occupational identity in undergraduate music education majors.* Unpublished doctoral dissertation, North Texas State University, Denton.

Mark, D. (1998). The music teacher's dilemma: Musician or teacher? *International Journal of Music Education, 32,* 3–22.

McCall, G., & Simmons, J. L. (1978). *Identities and interactions.* New York: Free Press.

McCarthy, M. (1997). The foundations of sociology in American music education (1900–1935). In R. Rideout (Ed.), *On the sociology of music education* (pp. 71–80). Norman: University of Oklahoma.

McClary, S. (1991). *Feminine endings: Music, gender, and sexuality.* Minneapolis: University of Minnesota Press.

McIntyre, D. J., & Byrd, D. M. (Eds.). (1996). *Preparing tomorrow's teachers: The field experience.* Thousand Oaks, CA: Corwin Press.

Morton, C. (1998). Critical thinking and music education: Nondiscursive experience and discursive rationality as musical friends. In P. Woodford (Ed.), Critical thinking in music: Theory and practice [Monograph]. *Studies in Music from the University of Western Ontario, 17* (pp. 63–81).

Mursell, J. (1956). *Music education principles and programs.* Morristown, NJ: Silver Burdett.

Music Educators National Conference. (1972). *Final report of the Commission on Teacher Education in Music.* Reston, VA: Author.

Music Educators National Conference. (1987). *Music teacher education: Partnership and process.* Reston, VA: Author.

Olsson, B. (1997). The social psychology of music education. In D. J. Hargreaves & A. C. North (Eds.), *The social psychology of music* (pp. 290–305). Oxford: Oxford University Press.

O'Neill, S. A. (1997). Gender and music. In D. J. Hargreaves & A. C. North (Eds.), *The social psychology of music* (pp. 46–63). Oxford: Oxford University Press.

O'Toole, P. (1993). I sing in a choir but I have "no voice"! *Quarterly Journal of Music Teaching and Learning, 4*(4), 65–76.

Paul, S. J. (1998). The effects of peer teaching experiences on the professional teacher role development of undergraduate instrumental music education majors. *Bulletin of the Council for Research in Music Education, 137,* 73–92.

Payne, B. (1996). The gender gap: Women on music faculties in American colleges and universities, 1993–1994. *College Music Symposium, 36,* 91–102.

Perry, W. (1968). *Forms of intellectual and ethical development in the college years.* New York: Holt, Rinehart and Winston.

Prescesky, R. E. (1997). *A study of preservice music education students: Their struggle to establish a professional identity* (Doctoral dissertation, McGill University, 1997). *Dissertation Abstracts International, 59*(08A), 2898.

Regelski, T. A. (1997). Musicians, teachers, and the social construction of reality. In R. Rideout (Ed.), *On the sociology of music education* (pp. 95–111). Norman: University of Oklahoma.

Regelski, T. A. (1998). Critical theory as a foundation for critical thinking in music. In P. Woodford (Ed.), Critical thinking in music: Theory and practice [Monograph]. *Studies in Music from the University of Western Ontario, 17* (pp. 1–21).

Reimer, B. (1989). *A philosophy of music education* (2nd ed.). Englewood Cliffs, NJ: Prentice-Hall.

Reimer, B. (1998). Viewing music education in the United States through Irish eyes. *College Music Symposium, 38,* 74–79.

Reimer, B. (1999). Musical roles and musical minds: Beyond

the theory of multiple intelligences. Manuscript in preparation.

Richardson, C. P. (1998). The roles of the critical thinker in the music classroom. In P. Woodford (Ed.), Critical thinking in music: Theory and practice [Monograph]. *Studies in Music from the University of Western Ontario, 17* (pp. 107–120).

Roberts, B. A. (1991a). *Musician: A process of labelling.* St. John's: Memorial University of Newfoundland.

Roberts, B. A. (1991b). Music teacher education as identity construction. *International Journal of Music Education, 18,* 30–39.

Roberts, B. A. (1991c). *A place to play: The social world of university schools of music.* St. John's: Memorial University of Newfoundland.

Roberts, B. A. (1993). *I, musician: Towards a model of identity construction and maintenance by music education students as musicians.* St. John's: Memorial University of Newfoundland.

Roberts, B. A. (1997). The sociological grid to curriculum inquiry in music education. In R. Rideout (Ed.), *On the sociology of music education* (pp. 143–153). Norman: University of Oklahoma.

Roberts, B. A. (1998). Editorial. *International Journal of Music Education, 32,* 1–2.

Roberts, B. A. (2000a). Gatekeepers and the reproduction of institutional realities: The case of music education in Canadian universities. *Musical Performance, 2*(3), 63–80.

Roberts, B. A. (2000b). A North American response to Bouij: Music education student identity construction revisited in Sweden. In R. R. Rideout & S. J. Paul (Eds.), *On the sociology of music education II* (pp. 63–74). Amherst: University of Massachusetts.

Roberts, B. A. (2000c). The sociologist's snare: Identity construction and socialization in music. *International Journal of Music Education, 35,* 54–58.

Rose, A. M. (1990). *Music education in culture: A critical analysis of reproduction, production, and hegemony.* Unpublished doctoral dissertation, University of Wisconsin, Madison.

Rose, A. M. (1995). A place for indigenous music in formal music education. *International Journal of Music Education, 26,* 39–54.

Rose, A. M. (1998). Exploring music teacher thinking: A reflective and critical model. In P. Woodford (Ed.), Critical thinking in music: Theory and practice [Monograph]. *Studies in Music from the University of Western Ontario, 17* (pp. 23–44).

Russell, P. A. (1997). Musical tastes and society. In D. J. Hargreaves & A. C. North (Eds.), *The social psychology of music* (pp. 141–158). Oxford: Oxford University Press.

Schön, D. A. (1987). *Educating the reflective practitioner.* San Francisco: Jossey-Bass.

Sennett, R., & Cobb, J. (1972). *The hidden injuries of class.* New York: Knopf.

Small, C. (1987). *Music of the common tongue: Survival and celebration in Afro-American music.* London: Calder.

Small, C. (1996). *Music, society, education* (3rd ed.). Hanover, NH: Wesleyan University Press

Small, C. (1998). *Musicking: The meanings of performing and listening.* Hanover, NH: Wesleyan University Press.

Stokes, M. (1994). *Ethnicity, identity and music: The musical construction of place.* Oxford: Berg.

Stubley, E. (1998). Thinking critically or thinking musically: Defining musical performance as subject matter. In P. Woodford (Ed.), Critical thinking in music: Theory and practice [Monograph]. *Studies in Music from the University of Western Ontario, 17* (pp. 157–172).

Taruskin, R. (1995). *Text and act: Essays on music and performance.* New York: Oxford University Press.

Trollinger, L. M. (1993). Sex/gender research in music education: A review. *Quarterly Journal of Music Teaching and Learning, 4,5*(4,1), 22–38.

Verrastro, R. E., & Leglar, M. (1992). Music teacher education. In R. Colwell (Ed.), *Handbook of research on music teaching and learning* (pp. 676–696). New York: Schirmer Books.

Vulliamy, G. (1977). Music as a case study in the "new sociology of education." In J. Shepherd, P. Virden, G. Vulliamy, & T. Wishart (Eds.), *Whose music? A sociology of musical languages* (pp. 201–232). London: Latimer.

Vulliamy, G., & Shepherd, J. (1984). The application of a critical sociology to music education. *British Journal of Music Education, 1*(3), 247–266.

Walker, L. M., & Hamann, D. L. (1993). The importance of African-American role models in music education. *Quarterly Journal of Music Teaching and Learning, 4*(2), 64–69.

Wallace, R. A., & Wolf, A. (1999). *Contemporary sociological theory: Expanding the classical tradition* (5th ed.). Upper Saddle River, NJ: Prentice-Hall.

Westbrook, R. (1991). *John Dewey and American democracy.* Ithaca, NY: Cornell University Press.

White, H. G. (1967). The professional role and status of music educators in the United States. *Journal of Research in Music Education, 15*(1), 3–10.

Witkin, R. (1974). *The intelligence of feeling.* London: Heinemann.

Wolfgang, R. E. (1990). Early field experience in music education: A study of teacher role socialization (preservice teachers) (Doctoral dissertation, University of Oregon, 1990). *Dissertation Abstracts International, 52*(01), 137.

Woodford, P. (1995). Critical thinking in music: What is it? *Canadian Music Educator, 37*(1), 36–40.

Woodford, P. (1996a). Evaluating Edwin Gordon's music learning theory from a critical thinking perspective. *Philosophy of Music Education Review, 4*(2), 83–95.

Woodford, P. (1996b). Musical intelligence in the world: Negotiating the social world of music. *Quarterly Journal of Music Teaching and Learning, 7*(2–4), 49–63.

Woodford, P. (1998). A critique of fundamentalism in singing: Musical authenticity, authority, and practice. In B. Roberts (Ed.), *Sharing the voices: The phenomenon of singing* (pp. 269–278). St. John's: Memorial University of Newfoundland.

Woodford, P., & Dunn, R. (1998). Beyond objectivism and relativism in music: Critical thinking as a foundation for musical democracy. In P. Woodford (Ed.), Critical thinking in music: Theory and practice [Monograph]. *Studies in Music from the University of Western Ontario, 17* (pp. 45–62).

Woodford, P. (in press). Democracy and music education: A prolegomenon. *Studies in Music from the University of Western Ontario.*

Wright, J. E. (1991). *Belief systems and their influence on musical experience.* Unpublished doctoral dissertation, Northwestern University, Evanston.

Wubbenhorst, T. (1994). Personality characteristics of music educators and performers. *Psychology of Music, 22,* 63–74.

Transforming Research in Music Education History

37

GORDON COX

The question "What is history?" is the subject of fierce debate: History is a science that discovers; it is an art that creates; historical narratives are constructions governed by the same rules and constraints as literature; "history with purpose" can realize some grand metaphysical theme; history has ended. Historians today are being forced to rethink, in the light of postmodernist criticism, the categories and assumptions that have underpinned their work (see Evans, 1997; Munslow, 2000).

Research in music education history cannot remain immune from this debate. Indeed, I base this chapter on the premise that music education history is, like the history of education, "a contested and changing terrain" (Aldrich, 2000, p. 63). The challenge of facing up to contest and change was acknowledged by Heller and Wilson (1992) in their chapter in the first edition of this Handbook. They called for "new interpretations of old subjects" (p. 102). More specifically, they detailed the following research needs: revision of existing studies, application of new techniques, and cooperation with fields outside music education. Heller and Wilson's suggestions comprise the kernel of this chapter. However, while they focused on the detail of researching music education history in the American context, I shall present a critical review of historical accounts with a general emphasis on Anglo-American literature, but including an international dimension.

The purposes of this chapter are fourfold: to offer a critique of the classic approaches to music education history; to generate suggestions for transforming the scope of music education history; to explore selected areas of study that illustrate possibilities for this broadening of horizons; to suggest ideas for research, based on the notion of "a usable past" (Hansot & Tyack, 1982).

Classic Approaches to Historical Research in Music Education

Judged by the quantity of dissertations, articles, and books on the subject, there is evidence of a continuing interest in music education history. In American universities, there has been a steady stream of dissertations on the history of music education (see Humphreys, Bess, & Bergee, 1996–97). For 20 years, researchers have been nurtured by the pioneering efforts of George Heller, the founding editor of *The Bulletin of Historical Research in Music Education* (see McCarthy, 1999b). In 2000, the *Bulletin* was renamed the *Journal of Historical Research in Music Education,* and it is edited by Jere Humphreys. Outside the United States, moreover, a number of significant books have been published since 1990 that have sought to uncover and reconstruct the history of music teaching and learning in different countries, including Canada (Green & Vogan, 1991), Germany (Gruhn, 1993), Great Britain (Cox, 1993; Pitts, 2000) and Ireland (McCarthy, 1999a).

This recent research activity has its roots in a substantial corpus of classic histories of music education published during the 20th century in the United Kingdom (see Scholes, 1947; Simpson, 1976; Rainbow, 1967, 1989, 1990), and in the United States (see Birge, 1928; Britton, 1950, 1989; Sunderman, 1971; Tellstrom, 1971; Mark, 1978; Keene, 1982; Mark & Gary, 1992). In spite of such achievements, however, the work has tended to be marginalized by education historians both in the United Kingdom (see Cox, 1999, p. 449) and the United States (see Heller & Wilson, 1992, p. 105).

What are the broad characteristics of this research? I shall focus critically on the work of Rainbow in the United

Kingdom, and on the critiques by American music education historians of the classic histories of American music education. My purpose is to deal with the assessment of previous work in the light of new insights and perspectives, bearing in mind that all historians are restricted by the sources available to them, and are influenced by their own worldview and value system.

In the United Kingdom, Bernarr Rainbow (1914–1998) almost single-handedly kept the flame of historical research in music education alight, from the publication of *The Land Without Music* (1967) to *Music in Educational Thought and Practice* (1989). *The Land Without Music* is a landmark study in its detailed and scholarly investigation of musical education in England between 1800 and 1860, and its continental antecedents. Rainbow wrote out of pedagogical concerns: He wanted to find out why English achievements in the teaching of singing at sight came to be supplanted by continental methods until the arrival of John Curwen, who synthesized the different strands.

On closer examination it can be argued that the book was a justification for Rainbow's aesthetic, political, and educational outlook. It was essentially whiggish, it emphasized the heroes (notably John Curwen), and praised successful revolutions (specifically the tonic sol-fa movement). However, Rainbow looked back to a golden age of sight-singing and hand signs that in reality probably never existed. In effect, he treated sight-singing texts like master plans: It was taken for granted that the development of an effective method would reap untold benefits on popular music education. Furthermore, there is little detail from Rainbow's account of the teachers or pupils who used these instructional texts. Moreover, the indigenous vernacular musical culture is portrayed as deprived in some way, and problematic for formal instructional methods.

In the United States, the classic histories of music education represent major contributions to music education scholarship. Livingston (1997) has highlighted their achievements: Birge's (1928) remarkable detail and attention to the political aspects of music education; Tellstrom's (1971) investigation of the relationship of music education to the development of major educational movements; Keene's (1982) breadth of interest in dealing with various historical and philosophical tendencies; Mark's (1978) thorough treatment of the contemporary period; Mark and Gary's (1992) comprehensive account that attempts to include contributions to music education in the United States from traditions other than European.

The critique of such work focuses on the issues of the relative coverage of men and women (Livingston, 1997), geographic representation (Humphreys, 1997), and the concentration on white Eurocentric traditions (Volk, 1993). Humphreys (1998) helpfully compares and contrasts the contributions of Birge and Allen Britton. He views Birge as a talented amateur who tended not to validate his sources and who skewed his research to his own region of residence. Britton's (1950, 1989) work, by contrast, was rigorous and document driven with at least some emphasis placed on validation. He became the most prominent and influential American historian of music education, and trained several dozen historians who still constitute the nucleus of the cadre of American music education historians. Nevertheless, Humphreys critically observes that Britton's students exhibit a certain homogeneity in their approach to music education history, with an emphasis on leading individuals, programs, and institutions at the expense of rank-and-file music education, formal and institutionalized music education at the expense of other types, and a bias toward certain regions, men, and European-style musical practices.

Howe (1998) sums up the position succinctly:

> The extant scholarly publications on the history of music education, written by white male authors, are chronological with an emphasis on white male educators in public school music. They also have emphasized the music teaching of white educators teaching the music of North European countries. New approaches, different primary sources, and different research methods could produce a comprehensive history of music education. (pp. 97–98)

More specifically, Howe argues that alternative perspectives of the history of music education in the United States could include those of African Americans and women in music education. Research methodology might draw on techniques derived from oral history, sociology, and ethnomusicology. The purpose of all this would be to assemble a more comprehensive, richer, and fuller history of music education. Howe's mention of new approaches, different primary sources, and different research methods helpfully prompts us to consider the wider dimensions of the history of education.

Broadening Horizons

The history of education as a field of enquiry has had its ups and downs, but it has long moved away from a concentration on "the great educators," the history of institutions and administration (acts and facts), and a celebration of state-sponsored education since the 19th century (see McCulloch & Richardson, 2000, pp. 40–51; Richardson, 1999). From the late 1960s, it has achieved much in its embrace of a whole raft of approaches that Cohen (1999) has detailed, including social control and social conflict, urban history, family history, history of women, history of people of color, history of religious minorities, and history "from the bottom up." Even this is not an exhaustive list, however. Other significant influences have included functionalism, Marxism, and poststructuralism.

Lee (1991) takes up some of these issues in his discussion of research in music education history. He argues that in order to professionalize the field, we need to know and be aware of what the specialized content is. His definition of music education is encouragingly inclusive: It comprises all deliberate efforts to pass music from one generation to another. This means investigating both formal and informal instruction, state-sponsored music education, and music education outside the aegis of the state, the learning and teaching of music by ordinary people in unstructured settings, as well as that undertaken by specialists in structured settings. Essentially, the focus is on the act of learning or teaching some aspect of music.

Lee's list of areas to be explored is illuminating, and includes: a wider contextual consideration; an intensified interest in the philosophy of history and of historiography; an exploration of the implications of the newer historical research (outlined by Cohen above); an engagement with international and comparative perspectives; an exploration of newer techniques (including statistics, demography); and oral history.

All of this has considerable potential for researchers in the field, which Cohen (1999) expands on in his discussion of the new cultural history of education. He argues that they should: attempt to cross disciplinary boundaries; read history into any cultural artifact, whether "elite" or popular; regard any cultural artifact as text in history. Such attempts may bring researchers to postmodernist history, which in Evans's (1997) judgment has encouraged historians to look more closely at the documents, to think about texts and narratives in fresh ways, and has opened up many new areas and subjects for research.

I argue in the rest of this chapter that historians of music education should focus on the following concerns: research should be responsive to the social, historical, ideological, and cultural contexts in which the teaching and learning of music take place; due attention should be paid to the actual teaching and learning of music; and that music education is a broad area encompassing both formal and informal settings. To illustrate something of the potential riches of the interactions between these concerns I turn to three areas of interest: first, the relationship between music education, national, and cultural identity; second, curriculum change and conflict; and third, historical perspectives of music educators working in public schools and studios.

Music Education, and National and Cultural Identity

The relationships and interactions between music and the formation of national and cultural identity through formal and informal instruction contain fruitful possibilities for music education historians. I shall focus on three examples

of research that deal with the very different contexts of music education in Ireland, Barbados, and India. These three distinct countries are, however, linked through their relationship as former colonized territories of Great Britain. Finally, in this section, I shall indicate briefly the potential of a related field, that of missionary endeavor.

McCarthy's (1999a) study of music education in 19th- and 20th-century Ireland explores the relationship between musical and cultural development through an investigation of the music transmission process. Underlying it is the notion of national identity, supported by a view of music as the embodiment of a set of values and beliefs that are inextricably linked to power structures and ideologies. Ireland provides a valuable site for such an investigation, shaped as it has been by the two political ideologies of colonialism and nationalism. The institutions and communities, which contributed to the sense of statehood, were frequently associated with musical participation, and this participation in McCarthy's eyes served as both a maker and marker of identity.

The central conflict between traditional Irish musical culture and the conventions of the Western Classical style in the mid-19th century found its most extreme manifestation within formal schooling, in particular the normal schools (teachers colleges), in which the musical diet was based on the Hullah Method of singing at sight. McCarthy views this practice as culturally discontinuous with the experience of the majority of young people the system sought to educate. In contrast were the informal flowerings of Irish musical culture, including temperance bands, the Irish Ballad associated with the Young Ireland movement, and traditional music and dance activity.

It becomes clear, as McCarthy concludes, that the strongest and most successful traditions in the transmission of music in Irish culture have developed outside of the formal systems. She identifies three causes of the primary weakness of music education in formal institutions in Ireland: cultural fragmentation produced by colonialism; dependence on a weak economy; and the dominant role of competing political ideologies in providing the raison d'être for music as a subject in the curriculum. In comparison, the hope for the future is for an agenda based on democracy, diversity, and inclusiveness.

McCarthy's work, through its engagement with the wider horizons of colonialism and nationalism, resonates with experiences in different parts of the world. I have selected two tightly focused studies of aspects of music education in Barbados and India in order to pursue this notion of musical colonialism.

The Barbados educational system provides the backdrop for Cameron McCarthy's (1999) research on the British influence on the school song genre of Barbadian public schools. These songs emerged in the late 19th century; they are "part of the lineaments . . . of a borrowed or imposed tradition of English school ritual that thrives in Barbadian schools today in the postcolonial era" (1999, p. 156). On one level, the songs serve the purpose of fostering school solidarity, consensus, and group identity, but they also contain complex symbolic messages.

According to McCarthy's analysis of songs from 24 Barbadian high schools, the elite, middle-class grammar school songs situate the Barbadian child as an autonomous agent of empire with the promise of a better social future. They help reflect the tradition that education in Barbados was committed to producing a black intellectual elite, a middle-class that was positioned with the British and the empire, and between the lower classes and the national white planter-mercantile elites. The songs fabricate the class divide, which has underpinned the Barbadian education system (derived from British imperialism).

This divide is evident in the school songs of the Barbadian primary and comprehensive schools, which, according to McCarthy, are regarded as inferior to the grammar schools. Their songs "have a different ring to them" (1999, p. 166); they emphasize industry and hard work for the black working-class youth. The school songs of Barbadian high schools thus draw lines between manual and mental labor, desire for "cultivation," and the desire for doing the "tasks at hand." McCarthy's conclusion is that the songs embody paradoxes that go beyond a constructed loyalty to empire, and develop ideas of ownership of knowledge, ownership of fate, and emancipation through learning.

The complexity of cultural dualism is taken up by Farrell (1997) in his exploration of the place of Indian music within the context of colonialism. One of Farrell's investigations concerns the promulgation of staff notation as an aid to musical literacy. The Bengali musicologist Tagore (1840–1914) was a tireless music educator who had an intense interest in the creation of a national music and a belief in the purity of Hindu music as handed down in Sanskrit sources. He wanted to find the most appropriate notations for Indian music, and to establish institutionalized music education. The question of how Indian music should be written down for educational purposes became the center of a fierce debate in the 1870s between Tagore and Charles Baron Clark, inspector of schools in Bengal. Clark believed staff notation would be the best medium for instruction. Intriguingly, Tagore and the nationalists fought the British on their own ground, and tried to match with a Hindu version of staff notation. As Farrell observes, the parameters of the struggle were always defined by the colonizer rather than the colonized. Staff notation in this context became ideological: It was "the musical tool par excellence for spreading the structures and paradigms of Western musical systems" (1997, p. 67).

Farrell's study, however, hints at the paradoxes contained within the colonial context. For example, S. W. Fallon, a British Raj official, was inspector of schools in Bihar,

North India, and wrote a report to the Bengal government in 1873, requesting funds for the introduction of song materials he had collected into the music education system of Indian schools. Fallon wanted to relay back to Indians in schools authentic aspects of their own culture, rather than imposing an artificial idea of Indian classical music derived from classical sources. His plans were wide-ranging and based on an in-depth knowledge of local culture. Although it is not known whether or not his populist scheme came to fruition, it was one of several initiatives to institutionalize music education in India. Farrell points out that the forms these institutions took functioned paradoxically as symbols of both Indian nationalism and loyalty to the British authorities.

Finally, in this discussion of music education and national and cultural identity, there is one related area of research, inextricably linked with colonialism, which contains rich possibilities as a further field of investigation: the relationship between missionary endeavors, native peoples, and music education. A selection of extant work hints at the cultural and historical potential of such an approach: the musical instruction of Native Americans by the Jesuits in Latin America (De Couve, Dal Pino, & Frega, 1997), the musical influences of the Moravians on the Labrador Coast Inuit (Lutz, 1982), the educational impact of British missionaries on music in the schools of Kenya (Agak, 1998), the development of *The Cherokee Song Book* by the dedicated New England evangelicals Lowell Mason and Samuel A. Worcester (Lee, 1997), and the role of brass bands in the hands of British missionaries as a replacement/antidote for "uncivilized" native practices (see Herbert & Sarkissian, 1997).

The studies that I have reviewed in this section demonstrate some of the potential that is to be found in locating music education within the wider parameters of power structures, including those of colonialism and nationalism. More specifically, postcolonial theory has the potential to generate new and ongoing debates among historians of education concerning the ethical issues involved in reclaiming the past from the privileged position of "whiteness," and increasing our curiosity about racial, cultural, and gender divisions (Goodman & Martin, 2000).

We need more research that will illuminate our understanding of music education's function in fostering a sense of identities that have to be constantly invented, transformed, and recovered. The result of such investigation should serve to encourage music educators to question aspects of their own music education tradition that they may take for granted.

The Music Curriculum: Change and Conflict

If music is so bound up with social and cultural identity, it is hardly surprising that its place in the school curriculum should be fiercely contested and surrounded by controversy. We require some historical compass in order to make sense of it all.

It is the argument of Goodson and Marsh (1996) that curriculum theorists have developed amnesia concerning the historical past. But the recovery of a historical perspective could make all the difference to our understanding of the school curriculum and the positioning of subjects within it. The problem is that the curriculum generally is regarded as a given by the majority of teachers, children, and parents, something natural and immutable. But Goodson and Marsh maintain that it is a social artifact, an archetype of "the division and fragmentation of knowledge within our societies" (1996, p. 150). By studying the history of school subjects, we come to realize that they are "the most quintessential of social and political constructions" (1996, p. 1). In the discussion that follows, I focus on three pieces of research that examine the music curriculum as a heavily contested area in the United States, Australia, and the United Kingdom.

The entrance of music into the American public schools, according to Eaklor (1985), highlighted the uniquely American ambivalence between musical and extramusical considerations. She places early public school music within the context of New England psalmody and contemporary social thought, and notes the conflict between music's function as a moral or social art, and its cultivation as art. This tension was to be exemplified in the later history of the singing schools, which had originally been founded in 18th-century America to improve music in public worship. On the one hand, the urban singing school was transformed into an institute for training singers, while, on the other hand, the country singing school retained its social and religious functions.

In the postrevolution era, there was a repudiation of traditional American hymnody, fuguing tunes, and shape notes in favor of new European techniques concentrating on correctness and simplicity. But Eaklor also notes the tussle at the heart of the public school system itself: It was regarded both as an agent of change and as a conservative sanctuary of rural and traditional values. The musical dilemma was that the rejection of the indigenous shape notes had been achieved in favor of European methods: A method of educating the masses was overturned through using methods for teaching the few. Eaklor's conclusion is that the adoption of European notation and Pestalozzianism was inconsistent with the ostensibly nationalist goals of the school system.

In 19th-century Australia, according to Weiss (1995), the arts entered the public schools at worst by default, through an uneasy alliance of the aesthetic and the moral in justifying music's place on the curriculum. The multiplicity of intentions ascribed to singing were later developed by Inspector W. J. McBride in 1906 into six justifications: Pleasure, Ethical Reasons, Discipline, Patriotism, the Physical, and the Intellectual. Attempting to serve these multifarious purposes might result in satisfying none of them.

Weiss warns against thinking that educational progress is inevitable, or indeed uniform across all subjects in the curriculum. Three examples illustrate the gist of her argument. First, the humble and quite cheap private venture schools that existed before state schools offered more choice in the curriculum—including music. Second, although progressive education (child-centered rather than teacher- and subject-centered) established itself between the 1910s and 1930s, it did not have an automatic impact on music. It might have been thought that the arts lent themselves quite obviously to the aims of progressive education, but music expanded less than the visual arts during this period. The new educational discourse might stress individual expression, but opportunities for "free expression" in music were still hedged about by teacher direction. Moreover, the ideas of progressive educationists had virtually no impact on communal musical events such as the popular demonstrations of massed singing by children at the annual Decoration Concerts. Weiss warns that we should not be misled into believing that the discourse of the time represents totally the practice. In other words, the rhetorical curriculum might well be different from the enacted curriculum; there was a gulf between theory and practice. Third, the variety of educational contexts adds to the complexity of the music education historian's task. For example, music in Australian private and Catholic schools inhabited different musical worlds from the public schools, and from each other.

Weiss's conclusion is that the process of change never ceases. Two factors, she argues, may affect future attitudes to music in schools: The arts are still "fads and frills"; and the growing importance of the federal government in educational policy will increasingly determine the purpose and direction of public education, with a stress on the basics, and a view of the arts as being of secondary importance. The significance of Weiss's article is that it does not regard the history of music education in schools as a story of continuing improvement but is, rather, a vessel buffeted in different directions by political and educational pressures.

Finally, the pressures of more recent political concerns and pressures on the music curriculum are best exemplified in the United Kingdom by the work of Shepherd and Vulliamy (1994) in their ostensibly sociological study of the introduction of a national music curriculum. They frame their analysis by a historical discussion of the rise of the "new sociology of education," which in Britain had its roots in cultural relativism. Central to their argument was that the alienation of children from school music, apparent both in the United Kingdom and Canada, was caused by the music curriculum being based on criteria abstracted from the tradition of the established Western canon. Shepherd and Vulliamy believed that popular music should be introduced according to the criteria associated with those who created and appreciated the music. This sociohistorical context provided the basis of their fundamental disagreement with the Conservative government's proposals for a curriculum based on the Western canon. These proposals were countered by the more radical ideas put forward by the Music National Curriculum Working Party, which reflected the musically pluralist nature of contemporary society. Such notions, however, did not represent the monocultural image of England that Margaret Thatcher's Conservatives had in mind. The ensuing battle was appropriately described by Shepherd and Vulliamy as "The Struggle for Culture."

All this research concerning change and conflict in the music curriculum emphasizes the importance for historians of analyzing the preactive definitions of music before it enters the classrooms, because such definitions come to be seen as natural and unquestioned, and result in the curriculum tensions that have been explored in this section: in the United States, the ambivalence between the musical and the extramusical; in Australia, the uneasy alliance between the moral and the aesthetic; and, in the United Kingdom, the assumption that the music curriculum should be based on the established Western canon.

One of the problematic areas for music education historians researching the curriculum is tackling the historical context of genres that are unfamiliar to them because of their training but are central to the lives of young people, such as popular music, jazz, and the music of different cultures. A start has been made with Elliott's (1985) study of the origins and development of jazz education in Canada, Brehony's (1998) sociohistorical study of representations of schooling in rock and pop music, Livingston's (2000) examination of the historical labels of country music, and Volk's (1998) substantial historical perspective concerning multiculturalism in American music education. Investigating the history of these crucially significant musics in educational contexts is a priority because they encapsulate many of the conflicts and contestations concerning music's rightful place as a curriculum subject.

Music Educators

Music teachers are central to the effective implementation of the school curriculum, yet, as we observed in the opening discussion of classic approaches to music education history, we know little about them. Because of this neglect, I shall focus on mainstream research, which has investigated the contributions of leading figures in public school music education rather than grassroots teachers. I shall do this,

however, within a framework that will hopefully suggest new possibilities for greater inclusiveness. I shall follow my discussion of public school music educators with a consideration of studio music educators.

Public School Music Educators. In her insightful discussion of the uses of biography in the study of educational history, Finkelstein (1998) makes a comparison:

> Biography is to history what the telescope is to the stars . . . biography provides a unique lens through which one can assess the relative power of political, economic, cultural, social and generational processes on the life chances of individuals, and the general revelatory power of historical sense-making. (p. 45)

Finkelstein asserts that biography provides four indispensable entrées into the study of history through its relationship with the origin of new ideas, as a window on social possibility, as an aperture through which to view the relationship between educational practice and social change, and as a form of mythic overhaul.

Many of the traditional biographies of great music educators focus on Finkelstein's first entrée, the origin of new ideas. Howe's (1997) biography of the American music educator, Luther Whiting Mason (1818–1896) lies in this category. We might describe Mason's big idea as the promulgation of an internationalist view of music education. He worked toward this first through synthesizing ideas from many places into the *National Music Course* (1870), which was the first school music textbook series in America. Howe traces the international network of connections Mason later developed through his endeavors, particularly in Germany and Japan. Mason's purpose was ambitious: to construct a worldwide system of music education. His activities were prodigious: He headed the committee in Germany that published his *Neue Gesangschule* based on his *National Music Course;* he was employed in Japan in the Meiji period to teach young pupils, to participate in teacher training, to perform and to create music materials; he exerted strong influence on the official Japanese three-volume song collection for schools. Moreover, Mason had ideas for developing an international textbook, although this remained a dream. Howe provides, through her judicious handling of a rich variety of primary sources, a highly detailed picture of music education innovations in the United States, Germany, and Japan during the 19th century. It helps us escape something of the parochialism that can bedevil research in this field.

The discovery of social possibility, the second of Finkelstein's suggested relationships between history and biography, is characterized in the story of Charles Faulkner Bryan (1911–1955), particularly in relation to his career in the Works Progress Administration (WPA) (Livingston, 1999). The WPA had been introduced by President Roosevelt to provide jobs in the 1930s, and to help the country recover from the Great Depression. Music education programs were introduced that were innovative, daring, and often successful.

In his role as supervisor of the Tennessee WPA program, Bryan, who was a Roosevelt supporter, wanted to widen music education access by providing model concert bands and by enabling children to receive free instrumental lessons. He organized a statewide training institute for WPA teachers in Tennessee based on topics such as class piano, folk music, and music education. Lessons were provided in a multiplicity of settings: settlement houses, government housing projects, and churches. The program was extended to all races. Bryan's booklet on the class piano was one way he envisaged of fulfilling the project's democratic aims: He advised teachers to employ an informal, nonthreatening manner with their students, and to be sure to make room for students with lesser abilities. Bryan insisted on a new egalitarianism and the integration of music into everyday life. One of his priorities was to establish new music organizations in the growing towns and cities located near army camps and munitions factories. In Livingston's account we are provided with an inclusive vision of music education through the work of an influential music educator, who possessed a deep sense of conviction about the social possibilities contained within music during a period of intensive educational reconstruction.

Finkelstein's third entrée for biographical studies into the study of history enables researchers to view relationships between educational processes and social change. In this respect, there has been a historical silence concerning the contributions and achievements of female music educators. There are encouraging signs that this silence is starting to be addressed (see Howe, 1993, 1994, 1998, 1999; Stevens, 2000), but the work is fragmentary, and generally unrelated to the concerns of feminist scholarship.

However, the biography of Ruth Crawford Seeger (1901–1953) by Judith Tick (1997) does provide a possible model for such work. The account focuses on the multiple and divided selves of Crawford Seeger. She is remembered as a composer for her modernist works written between 1930 and 1932. Around 1932 she lost her psychic equilibrium, according to Tick, and burned her score of the Sonata for Violin and Piano. After that, she virtually ceased composing. Tick alludes to "a terrible inner crisis about which no further information survives" (1997, p. 200).

For the rest of her life, Crawford Seeger became identified as a tireless worker for the urban folk revival movement, as well as the "matriarch" of one of its best-known families. She also made a substantial contribution to music education. As a female musician, she was clearly affected by the changing political and social upheavals of the Depression years, as well as by her marriage to the radical musicologist Charles Seeger. In her move toward the left, she became "a politically committed artist" (Tick, 1997, p. 190). The couple moved to Washington, DC, in 1935, in order for Charles to take up a full-time post with the Resettlement Administration, which involved training and placing professional musicians in communities of displaced and homeless people. Crawford Seeger hurled herself thereafter into motherhood, teaching, and folk music. Her work in a Washington cooperative nursery school between 1941 and 1943 launched her career as a music consultant in early education, which culminated in the publication of the highly influential collection of *American Folk Songs for Children* (1948). Tick describes how Crawford Seeger meshed the values of progressive education with those of the urban folk revival movement. She shifted the emphasis in the classroom away from individual creativity toward group participation, and through the "folk movement" of mothers' cooperatives "she centered the revival into the world of women and women's work" (1997, p. 290). Ruth Crawford Seeger may have been the "liver of too many lives at once" (1997, p. x), but her achievement was that she acted out the inevitable tensions and paradoxes within herself. The importance of this biography for music education historians is that it demonstrates the possibilities of developing links between gender, music, politics, and the experience of education within an exploration of the life of a significant female music educator in 20th-century America.

Finally in the consideration of Finkelstein's categories, we come to "mythic overhaul," what we might call the challenging of stereotypes. Sang (1991) investigated the status of Lowell Mason as "the father of music education in America," by examining in some detail the relative contributions of William Woodbridge, who had been impressed by the musical work of Nageli and Pfeiffer and introduced their musical adaptations of Pestalozzian ideas to music educators in America, and Elam Ives, Jr., who translated their work and was probably the first American singing teacher to employ their principles into his singing teaching. While Sang argues for a greater recognition of Ives's contribution, he nevertheless concludes that Mason should still retain his role as one of the leading figures in introducing music into the American public school curriculum. The significance of Sang's article lies in its reassessment of the accounts provided by some of the classic histories, and in its detailed catalogue of misunderstandings regarding the contributions of this trio of American music educators.

In her content analysis of the first 20 volumes of the *Bulletin of Historical Research in Music Education*, McCarthy (1999b) notes that biographical studies comprise the largest single category of papers, with a clear emphasis on men. There is little work that attempts to define, analyze, and interpret the typical activities of music teachers and their students in schools. The research tradition is still dominated by the great music educators.

The Studio Teacher. A second strand of research focusing on music educators is concerned with the studio, or private music teacher. We move away here from the narrowly biographical approach, and encounter a wider range of sources and methods. Of particular significance is the innovative work on music teachers in 18th-century England by Richard Leppert, who in *Music and Image* (1988) devotes a chapter to "Music Education as Praxis." As evidence, he uses images of the teaching of music to upperclass amateurs in England during the period found in paintings, drawings, and prints.

In England, foreigners, particularly Italians, were prized as music teachers. As a result of his analysis of the visual portrayal of music teachers, Leppert concludes that they were ambivalent creatures, proud yet deferential, both servants and entrepreneurs, tradesmen and professionals. An abiding concern on behalf of the parents, which arises through Leppert's reading of his visual evidence, was the effect of the music teacher on the female student. The ideal music teacher was a male gender version of the girl's mother: good-tempered, genteel, no vulgarity, no physical constraints, softness of voice.

In an earlier related study, Leppert (1985) concerned himself with the lives of music masters who ministered to the children of the upper class. He wanted to indicate the kinds of social conventions at play, and to illuminate the general relation between musical life in 18th-century England and the social forces that in part controlled it. Through exploring the lives and financial conditions of well-known music teachers, including Burney and Herschel, Leppert observes that metropolitan teachers were able to live "a genteel but restricted life" (1985, pp. 157–158), but the job was not easy with its long hours and stiff competition for students. In the provinces, such teachers remained poor all their lives, and had to put up with satire, cope with mediocrity for much of the time, and deal with pupils who were proud dabblers expecting to receive compliments.

Leppert's work is innovative in using visual representation as evidence, and in its focus on the teacher within a historical treatment of an ideology of music anchored in practice. An exploration of 20th-century images of music teachers in schools and studios as featured in the movies is a fertile area for future investigation (see Brand & Hunt, 1997).

In contrast to this is work that considers the problematic history of the profession of studio music teaching. Roske (1987) focused on the growth of private music teaching in 19th-century Germany. For his methodology, he utilized social statistics. Roske located a systematic index of private music teachers in the directories of the North German town Altona (now part of Hamburg), and was thus able to trace the professionalization of music instruction through a period of 50 years. In 1802, the town had only two music teachers but, by 1845, 45 music teachers were listed. The picture of employment, however, was somewhat complex. Roske delineated three work situations for such teachers: full-time music teachers, music teachers with additional music-related employment, and music teachers with additional employment in nonmusic fields. This complexity was compounded by a good deal of mobility within the profession. Nearly one third of Roske's sample were not engaged in private music teaching in the town for longer than 5 years.

Another key theme in the study was the place of female studio teachers. There was a steady rate of growth in their numbers: by 1849 they comprised 35.9% of the town's studio music teachers. In particular, piano teaching became the domain of (mostly married) women. Roske draws attention to a trend in his study toward a gradual feminization of the entire music teaching profession. However, females had a less steady status within the profession than males.

Studio music teachers are characterized in this selection of research as being somewhat marginal figures. The contrasting research techniques based on visual images and social statistics illustrate something of the methodological possibilities that are available. A key area for future research is understanding and perhaps countering this marginality by investigating attempts to gain professional status for this group of music educators (see Ehrlich, 1985).

Toward a Usable Past for Music Educators

Within the current educational climate in the United Kingdom, there are constant pleas for research to improve the quality of educational practice in schools, and to solve practical problems (see McCulloch, 2000, pp. 5–6). In the United States some years ago, Heller and Wilson (1982) insisted that historical research in music education "must treat questions that contemporary practitioners are concerned about" (1982, p. 14).

How can this be done? How can researchers move away from Rainbow's rose-tinted view of the educational past, into an engagement with the present? McCulloch (1994) is helpful in his argument that establishing the dynamic connections between past, present, and future implies an educational history that is present-minded, seeking to provide an understanding of the problems and possibilities of the present. Through such an approach, it is possible to construct "a usable past" (Hansot & Tyack, 1982), in which the problems and limitations of past traditions can be delineated, with the intention of evaluating current educational policies (for a fiercely opposed view, however, see Cohen, 1999, pp. 24–29).

I will suggest five possibilities for the development of "a usable past" for music educators. As examples, I shall select research that predominantly relates to the United Kingdom context, but that nevertheless has much wider implications.

First, an engagement with contemporary policy: Historical studies that confront policy making decisions create a dialogue between research and practice. Gammon (1999), for example, treats the cultural politics of the English National Music Curriculum between 1991 and 1992 as just one aspect of government policy that involved:

> disregarding and "distressing" professionals, the destruction of institutions and the centralisation of power whilst at the same time the denial of such centralisation through the rhetoric of increased choice and the improvement of standards. (Gammon, 1999, p. 131)

Such research serves as a salutary reminder to music educators of Reese's (1986) observation that the power to influence the curriculum, to select textbooks, to inaugurate innovative programs depends ultimately on political strength.

Second, the development of a curriculum history that disentangles the complexities, constraints, and disappointments of curriculum reform. In my own research (Cox, in press) on the influence of two major curriculum development projects in music sponsored by the Schools Council in the 1970s, I point to the deep division they came to represent between those educators who believed that children's music should comprise children creating their own music, and others who were more concerned with children recreating other people's music. The point of such work is that it enables curriculum developers in music to visit "a whole storehouse of old solutions that are regularly and often unwittingly recycled to meet familiar problems" (Hansot & Tyack, 1982, p. 16).

Third, addressing what Rousmaniere (1997) refers to as "the historical silence on teachers' work" (p. 5). By not attending to teachers' accounts of their experience, historians have misread the actual conditions of teachers' work, and have underestimated their ability to shape schooling in many different ways (see Altenbaugh, 1997; Finkelstein, 1989). Life history research provides a method of rescuing this silent history, and illuminating present-day concerns. For example, Morgan's (1998) study of the life histories of instrumental teachers focuses upon upbringing, perspectives, and beliefs about music education, learning experiences, and critical events. In particular, Morgan confronts the feelings of marginalization that many of these instrumental teachers reported. Research in this tradition articulates the voices of teachers and brings them out of the shadows (see Sparkes, 1994). It has implications for the training, recruitment, retention, and the continuing professional development of music teachers.

Fourth, to encourage and enable music teachers to engage with a range of ideas from the past and the present and so begin to construct a philosophical basis for classroom practice, with the intention of helping them gain a depth of understanding that could enhance their teaching. In *A Century of Change in Music Education* (2000), Stephanie Pitts identifies a body of key texts in music education with the intention that, through reading them, music educators will be prompted to ask fundamental questions about the music curriculum, and then to generate their own answers. Through this process, Pitts envisages that music teachers might capture or recapture an enthusiasm for music education.

Finally, to establish international connections across and between cultures, which will eventually result in historically grounded comparative work (for example, an international study of the history of formal schooling in music, which might act as a counterpoint to Campbell's [1991] cross-cultural guide to music teaching and learning with its emphasis on traditional music learning). As a result, music educators working in a variety of countries and cultures can be encouraged to question what they take for granted in their practice.

Conclusion

I have attempted to uncover some of the ideas and assumptions that have underpinned the orthodoxy of research in the history of music education and then to survey some rather scattered pieces of research, which have suggested fresh approaches and methods. In this review of the classic histories of music education I was anxious to counter tendencies, which, with the benefit of hindsight, might be regarded as myopic and narrow. One way of countering such tendencies, I have suggested, is for music education historians to learn from the insights of social scientists, while at the same time remaining rooted in pedagogical concerns (what might be regarded in the case of education history and social history as "two parallel strands of research overlapping at many points" [Cunningham, 1989, p. 79]). It is in facing up to the tension between the social and the pedagogical traditions that the future of historical research in music education lies.

In pursuing this idea, and in the subsequent process of rethinking the categories and assumptions of music education history, I have found the notion of "the enlarging vision" (McCulloch & Richardson, 2000, pp. 68–78) helpful. It relates to the major impact of the social sciences on historical research in education since the 1980s. Historians of education are increasingly drawing on aspects of sociology, cultural studies, and anthropology in their research. This, in turn, influences the scope of their interpretative perspectives to encompass such crucial areas of concern as gender, race, and social class. In order to glimpse the possibilities of an "enlarging vision," researchers are being encouraged to incorporate the following key processes into their work: engagement in a critical and skeptical dialogue with theory; exploration of the potential of methodological pluralism (also see Humphreys, 1996, 1997) and the new technologies as research tools (see Crook, 2000).

The development of an "enlarging vision" by music education historians could well be strengthened by a commitment to the three central concerns that have formed the nub of this chapter: Research should be responsive to the social, historical, ideological, and cultural contexts in which the learning and teaching of music take place; due attention should be paid to the actual teaching and learning of music; and music education should be viewed as an essentially broad area of activity, encompassing both formal and informal settings. Furthermore, this commitment could be underpinned by a deeper involvement on the part of researchers with the history of education as a field of study, and with the varieties of historical traditions in the teaching and learning of music across different cultures. All this could transform research in music education history and thus offer a greatly extended understanding of the historical richness of music teaching and learning in all its diversity. As a result of such rethinking, music education historians might not only be able to imagine the past but also might play a powerful role in the crucial debates about the present and the future of music education.

REFERENCES

Agak, H. O. (1998). Gender in school music in the Kenyan history of music education. In C. v. Niekerk (Ed.), *ISME '98 Proceedings* (pp. 1–21). Pretoria: ISME.

Aldrich, R. (2000). A contested and changing terrain: History of education in the twenty-first century. In D. Crook & R. Aldrich (Eds.), *History of education for the twenty-first century* (pp. 63–79). London: University of London Institute of Education. Bedford Way Papers.

Birge, E. B. (1928). *A history of public school music in the United States*. Philadelphia: Oliver Ditson. (Reprinted 1966 Reston, VA: MENC).

Brand, M., & K. Hunt (1997). The celluloid music teacher: An examination of cinematic portrayals of music teaching and music education in films. In R. Rideout (Ed.), *On the sociology of music education* (pp. 138–142). Norman: University of Oklahoma School of Music.

Brehony, K. J. (1998). "I used to get mad at my school": Representations of schooling in rock and pop music.

British Journal of Sociology of Education, 19(1), 113–134.

Britton, A. (1950). *Theoretical introductions in American tune-books to 1800*. Unpublished doctoral dissertation, University of Michigan, Ann Arbor.

Britton, A. (1989). The how and why of teaching singing schools in eighteenth-century America. *Bulletin of the Council of Research in Music Education, 99*, 23–41.

Campbell, P. S. (1991). *Lessons from the world: A cross-cultural guide to music teaching and learning*. New York: Schirmer.

Cohen, S. (1999). *Challenging orthodoxies: Toward a new cultural history of education*. New York: Peter Lang.

Cox, G. (1993). *A history of music education in England 1872–1928*. Aldershot: Scolar.

Cox, G. (1999). Towards a usable past for music educators. *History of Education, 28*(4), 449–458.

Cox, G. (in press). A house divided? The Schools Council and music education in the UK in the 1970s. *Journal of Historical Research in Music Education.*

Crook, D., & R. Aldrich. (2000). *History of education for the twenty-first century*. London: University of London Institute of Education. Bedford Way Papers.

Crook, D. (2000). Net gains? The Internet as a research tool for historians of education. In D. Crook & R. Aldrich (Eds.), *History of education for the twenty-first century* (pp. 36–49). London: University of London Institute of Education. Bedford Way Papers.

Cunningham, P. (1989). Educational history and educational change: The past decade of English historiography. *History of Education Quarterly, 29*(1), 77–94.

De Couve, A. C., Dal Pino, C., & Frega, A. L. (1997). An approach to the history of music education in Latin America. *Bulletin of Historical Research in Music Education, 19*(1), 10–39.

Eaklor, V. L. (1985). The roots of an ambivalent culture: Music, education, and music education in antebellum America. *Journal of Research in Music Education, 33*(2), 87–99.

Ehrlich, C. (1985). *The music profession in Britain since the eighteenth century: A social history*. Oxford: Clarendon Press.

Elliott, D. (1985). Jazz education in Canada: Origins and development. *Bulletin of Historical Research in Music Education, 6*, 17–28.

Evans, R. J. (1997) *In defence of history*. London: Granta Books.

Farrell, G. (1997). *Indian music and the West*. Oxford: Clarendon Press.

Finkelstein, B. (1989). *Governing the young: Teacher behavior in popular primary schools in nineteenth-century United States*. London: Falmer.

Finkelstein, B. (1998). Revealing human agency: The uses of biography in the study of educational history. In C. Kirdell (Ed.), *Writing educational biography: Explorations in qualitative research* (pp. 45–49). New York: Garland.

Gammon, V. (1999). Cultural politics of the English national curriculum for music, 1991–1992. *Journal of Educational Administration and History, 31*(2), 130–147.

Goodman, J., & Martin, J. (2000). Breaking boundaries: Gender, politics, and the experience of education. *History of Education, 29*(5), 383–388.

Goodson, I. F., & Marsh, C. J. (1996). *Studying school subjects: A guide.* London: Falmer.

Green, J. P., & Vogan, N. (1991). *Music education in Canada: A historical account.* Toronto: University of Toronto.

Gruhn, W. (1993). *Geschichte der Musikerziehung.* Hofheim: Wolke Verlag.

Hansot, E., & Tyack, D. (1982). A usable past: Using history in educational policy. In A. Lieberman & M. W. McLaughlin (Eds.), *Policy making in education: Eighty-first yearbook of the National Society for the Study of Education, Part One* (pp. 1–22). Chicago: NSSE.

Heller, G. N., & Wilson, B. D. (1982). Historical research in music education: A prolegomenon. *Bulletin of the Council for Research in Music Education, 69,* 1–20.

Heller, G. N., & Wilson, B. D. (1992). Historical research. In R. Colwell (Ed.), *Handbook of research on music teaching and learning.* New York: Schirmer.

Herbert, T., & Sarkissian, M. (1997). Victorian bands and their dissemination in the colonies. *Popular Music, 16*(2), 165–179.

Howe, S. (1997). *Luther Whiting Mason: International music educator.* Warren, MI: Harmonie Park Press.

Howe, S. (1998). Reconstructing the history of music education from a feminist perspective. *Philosophy of Music Education Review, 6*(2), 96–106.

Howe, S. (1999). Leadership in MENC: The female tradition. *Bulletin of the Council of Research in Music Education, 141,* 59–65.

Howe, S. W. (1993/4). Women music educators in Japan during the Meiji period. *Bulletin of the Council for Research in Music Education, 119,* 101–109.

Humphreys, J. T. (1996/7). Expanding the horizons of music education history and sociology. *Quarterly Journal of Music Teaching and Learning, 7,* 5–19.

Humphreys, J. T. (1997). Sex and geographic representation in two music education history books. *Bulletin of the Council for Research in Music Education, 131,* 67–86.

Humphreys, J. T. (1998). The content of music education history? It's a philosophical question, really. *Philosophy of Music Education Review, 6*(2), 90–95.

Humphreys, J. T., Bess, D. M., & Bergee, M. J. (1996–7). Doctoral dissertations on the history of music education and music therapy. *Quarterly Journal of Music Teaching and Learning, 7,* 112–124.

Keene, J. A. (1982). *A history of music education in the United States.* Hanover, NH: University Press of New England.

Lee, W. (1991). Toward the Morphological Dimensions of Research in the History of Music Education. In M. McCarthy & B. D. Wilson (Eds.), *Music in American schools 1838–1988* (pp. 114–117). College Park: University of Maryland.

Lee, W. (1997). Lowell Mason, Samuel A. Worcester, and *The Cherokee singing book. Chronicles of Oklahoma, 75*(1), 32–51.

Leppert, R. D. (1985). Music teachers of upper-class amateur musicians in eighteenth-century England. In A. W. Atlas (Ed.), *Music in the classic period: Essays in honor of Barry S. Brook* (pp. 133–158). New York: Pendragon.

Leppert, R. D. (1988). *Music and image: Domesticity, ideology and socio-cultural formation in eighteenth-century England.* Cambridge: Cambridge University Press.

Livingston, C. (1997). Women in music education in the United States: Names mentioned in history books. *Journal of Research in Music Education, 45*(1), 130–144.

Livingston, C. (1999). The WPA music program as exemplified in the career of Charles Faulkner Bryan. *Journal of Historical Research in Music Education, 21*(1), 3–20.

Livingston, C. (2000, June). *Naming country music: An historian looks at meanings behind the labels.* Paper presented to the Philosophy of Music Education International Symposium, Aston University, UK.

Lutz, M. M. (1982). *Musical traditions of the Labrador Coast Inuit.* Ottawa: National Museums of Canada. (Canadian Ethnology Service Paper No. 79)

Mark, M. L. (1978). *Contemporary music education.* New York: Schirmer.

Mark, M. L., & Gary, C. L. (1992). *A history of American music education.* New York: Schirmer. (Second edition 1999 Reston, VA: MENC)

Mason, L. W. (1870). *The national music course.* Boston: Ginn.

McCarthy, C. (1999). Narrating imperialism: The British influence in Barbadian public school song. In C. McCarthy, G. Hudak, S. Miklaucic, & P. Saukko (Eds.), *Sound identities: Popular music and the cultural politics of education* (pp. 153–173). New York: Peter Lang.

McCarthy, M. (1999a). *Passing it on: The transmission of music in Irish culture.* Cork, Ireland: Cork University Press.

McCarthy, M. (1999b). *The Bulletin of Historical Research* in music education: A content analysis of articles in the first twenty volumes. *Bulletin of Historical Research in Music Education, 20*(3), 181–202.

McCarthy, M., & Wilson, B. D. (Eds.). (1991). *Music in American schools 1838–1988.* College Park: University of Maryland.

McCulloch, G. (1994). *Educational reconstruction: The 1944 education act and the twenty-first century.* London: Woburn Press.

McCulloch, G. (2000). Publicizing the educational past. In D. Crook & R. Aldrich (Eds.), *History of education for the twenty-first century* (pp. 1–16). London: University of London Institute of Education. Bedford Way Papers.

McCulloch, G., & Richardson, W. (2000). *Historical research in educational settings.* Buckingham, UK: Open University.

Morgan, C. (1998). *Instrumental music teaching and learning: A life history approach.* Unpublished doctoral thesis, University of Exeter, UK.

Munslow, A. (2000). *The Routledge companion to historical studies.* London: Routledge.

Pitts. S. (2000). *A century of change in music education: Historical perspectives on contemporary practice in*

British secondary school music. Aldershot, England: Ashgate.

Rainbow, B. (1967). *The land without music: Musical education in England 1800–1860 and its continental antecedents.* London: Novello.

Rainbow, B. (1989). *Music in educational thought and practice: A survey from 800 BC.* Aberystwyth, Wales: Boethius Press.

Rainbow, B. (1990). *Music and the English public school.* Aberystwyth: Boethius.

Richardson, W. (1999). Historians and educationists: The history of education as a field of study in post-war England—Part 1: 1945–72. *History of Education, 28*(1), 1–30.

Roske, M. (1987). The professionalism of private music teaching in the 19th century: A study with social statistics. *Bulletin of the Council for Research in Music Education, 91,* 143–148.

Rousmaniere, K. (1997). *City teachers: Teaching and school reform in historical perspective.* New York: Teachers College Press, Columbia University.

Sang, R. C. (1991). Woodbridge, Mason, Ives, and Pestalozzianism: A perspective on misunderstanding and controversy. In M. McCarthy & B. D. Wilson (Eds.), *Music in American schools 1838–1988* (pp. 66–70). College Park: University of Maryland.

Scholes, P. (1947). *The mirror of music 1844–1944: A century of musical life in Britain as reflected in the pages of the* Musical Times. London: Novello and Oxford University Press.

Seeger, R. C. (1948). *American folk songs for children.* Garden City, NY: Doubleday.

Shepherd, J. & Vulliamy, G. (1994). The struggle for culture: A sociological case study of the development of a national music curriculum. *British Journal of Sociology of Education, 15*(1), 27–40.

Simpson, K. (Ed.). (1976). *Some great music educators: A collection of essays.* London: Novello.

Stevens, R. (2000). Emily Patton: An Australian pioneer of tonic sol-fa in Japan. *Research Studies in Music Education, 14,* 40–49.

Sunderman, L. F. (1971). *Historical foundations of music education in the United States.* Metuchen, NJ: Scarecrow Press.

Tellstrom, A. T. (1971). *Music in American education, past and present.* New York: Holt, Rinehart & Winston.

Tick, J. (1997). *Ruth Crawford Seeger: A composer's search for American music.* New York: Oxford University Press.

Volk, T. (1993). The history and development of multicultural music education as evidenced in the *Music Educators Journal 1967–1992. Journal of Research in Music Education, 41*(2), 137–155.

Volk, T. M. (1998). *Music, education, and multiculturalism: Foundations and principles.* New York: Oxford University Press.

Weiss, S. (1995). Fundamental or frill? Music education in Australian schools since the 1880s. *Research Studies in Music Education, 5,* 55–65.

Music Transmission and Learning

38

A Conspectus of Ethnographic Research in Ethnomusicology and Music Education

C. K. SZEGO

Music transmission and learning are fundamentally social achievements; even music makers who claim to be self-taught engage in cognitive, kinetic, and affective operations that are informed by their participation in broader spheres of human culture. This chapter turns its attention to those spheres by surveying musical ethnographies representing social groups in many different parts of the world. Ethnography's contribution to understanding learning and transmission lies not only in its sensitivity to the culturally specific and socially constituted nature of these processes and the phenomena that attend them but also the ways in which they are individually realized.

The central body of this chapter is devoted to thematic summaries of the music transmission and learning literature in ethnomusicology and in music education, with brief mention given to other disciplines. It begins, however, with a cursory outline of the ethnographic enterprise, as viewed by ethnomusicologists, and concludes with suggested directions for research.

Ethnography: A Brief Overview

Researchers studying music transmission and learning must select an appropriate research paradigm—one that helps answer their questions and that suits their epistemological convictions. Some of the most powerful tools for collecting data on cultural practice and experience fall under the methodological rubric of ethnography, the primary mode of inquiry in ethnomusicology, anthropology, and folklore. The objectives of ethnography are to apprehend the way that people construct, operate in, experience, and make sense of their world; to do so in situ; and to do so in a way that affects people's normative conduct as little as possible. To uphold the two principles at work here—holism and naturalism—ethnographic researchers engage the people they study as consultants,[1] speaking with them and observing them in a chosen spectrum of activities.

If ethnography is commonplace and largely unquestioned in disciplines such as ethnomusicology, such has not been the case in music education, where ethnography has been a feature of research for a span of less than 20 years (Kreuger, 1987). Becker (1983) contends that for educators generally, this is largely because ethnographic data are not easily translated into applied practice. Concerns about the research paradigm itself, for example, the reliability and validity of data, are also linked to its perceived utility. There is now a large literature that speaks to such concerns generally (e.g., LeCompte & Goetz, 1982), and in music education specifically (e.g., *Bulletin of the Council for Research in Music Education, 122* and *130*);[2] addressing them here, however, is beyond the scope of this overview.

Ethnomusicology and its sister disciplines continue to discuss the means of carrying out ethnographic research, its ethical implications, limitations, and outcomes. Outlined briefly here are some common perspectives and suggested sources on these topics.

Approaching the Field: Anthropological Perspectives

Flexibility is a key characteristic (and requirement) of ethnography. Theories and research questions that serve as entry into the field may be broadly or narrowly drawn but, regardless of how they are formulated, the focus of one's work necessarily will be adjusted during the course of fieldwork in response to changing conditions or to data already collected. For example, one may discover that students of a particular teacher pay twice as much for lessons as other students; that in turn might suggest an investigation into tuition structures or the principles of exchange in that society generally. Expanding the horizons of a study in this manner is largely dependent on researchers and their aspirations toward holism.[3]

Although ethnographers may do their best to apprehend the ways in which a group or individual transmits and learns music, it is important to acknowledge that one person's ability to share in another's world of experience is always partial (Geertz, 1983). This is true for people in the same society who share the "same" culture as it is for people who cross-recognized cultural boundaries in their work. Indeed, "insiders" have as much to learn as "outsiders." Ethnographers' adoption of a culturally relativistic attitude and their avoidance of ethnocentrism, therefore, are only attempts to preclude inappropriate judgment, not a denial of bias, which can never be eliminated completely.

Ethnographer bias has a number of sources: One is a function of the researcher's own socialization or enculturation; another is a function of preparation for the field, which requires grounding in the literature. Ethnographers enter the field, consciously or not, with theories or narratives that guide their observation and understanding of events (Bruner, 1986). Reaching new understandings, which is the goal of ethnography, is therefore often a matter of throwing off old ones—a process that requires a reflective posture (Rice, 1988).

Conducting Fieldwork

Myers (1992a) discusses field preparations for musical ethnographers whose research site lies far from their "own backyard." Beyond such disciplinary specifics, however, the essential tools of fieldwork practice are shared across disciplines: participant-observation and interviewing—Ives (1980), Jackson (1987), Hammersley and Atkinson (1995); note-taking—Sanjek (1990); audio-recording—Society for Ethnomusicology (1994); and video-recording—Collier and Collier (1986), Zemp (1988). Ethnography, however, is not defined simply in terms of one's direct or mediated interactions with others or with things in the present; musical practices have history, and the past is rarely absent from the words our consultants speak. Thus, the fieldworker is often an ethnohistorian, too, collecting aural or documented history (see Barber & Berdan, 1998), and the fieldworker's final account frequently reflects this duality of time-space and research expertise by merging synchronic and diachronic perspectives.

Whereas the principles of conducting fieldwork remain constant, fieldwork practices change. Recent interest in

phenomenology, for example, descriptions of perceptual experience,[4] has led to increasing use of feedback interviews and colistening activities, for example, Berger (1999). And although there is much ambivalence toward surveys and questionnaires in anthropology and ethnomusicology, some researchers are giving more consideration to written (as opposed to aural) data that their consultants can supply, as for example Szego (1999).

As in all research, ethical issues are paramount. Every ethnographer, if he or she is socially sensitive, is likely to encounter an ethical challenge in the course of conducting or disseminating research (see, for example, Bresler, 1995). Issues of ownership, legal copyright, permission, acknowledgment, and remuneration are particularly salient for those documenting music in any way (Seeger, 1992). Slobin (1992) provides cases for deliberation, and the Society for Ethnomusicology Ethics Committee (1999) has issued general guidelines for conduct in the field, in the realm of publication, and in educational settings. Still, the issues can be extraordinarily complex. Pillay (1994), for example, comments on the ethical challenge presented by his insider status. As a teacher and Indian studying Indian school music in apartheid South Africa, he was privy to information that outsiders were not. Unable to record interviews for fear of alienating or endangering his consultants, he relied on memory to rewrite each conversation on completion, and withheld publication until his consultants could no longer be hurt by their disclosures.[5]

Although most music educators will not be faced with Pillay's dilemma, they will be aware of the challenges presented by studying educational settings like schools, as well as working with children and youth. Because of the social and legal responsibilities teachers and administrators hold toward their young charges, as well as their answerability to parents, schools are sensitive research environments. Permitting access to students often requires a significant investment of trust (and time) on the part of an institution; permission, therefore, is not always forthcoming and access can be delimited in unexpected ways. Whereas it should be noted that working with children is profoundly different from working with adults and may require adjustment of role and methodology (Caputo, 1995; Fine, 1995; Kushner, 1995), it is not inherently more problematic than the other fieldwork relationships ethnographers must constantly negotiate.

Analytic Processes

In ethnography, unlike in other research paradigms, analysis is not a stage that is entirely separate from data gathering. The ethnographer will have many different types of qualitative data to analyze, such as field notes, observations, and interviews, and the task of finding patterns in the data and making sense of them is both science and art (see, for example, Goetz & LeCompte, 1981; Strauss, 1987; Strauss & Corbin, 1998). Depending on the type of data collected, textual, narrative, or discourse analyses also may be in order (see, for example, Cortazzi, 1993; Finnegan, 1992).

Specific to music researchers is analysis of musical sound, which may be aided by transcription. Ethnomusicologists have given much thought to issues of transcription and thus a brief introduction to the literature is warranted. Seeger (1977) distinguishes between two kinds of transcription: prescriptive transcription is "a blueprint of how a specific piece of music shall be made to sound," and descriptive transcription is "a report of how a specific performance of any music actually did sound" (p. 68). Although the stated purpose of prescriptive transcription is clear, in practice there are some thorny issues. Most important is the issue of representation. What kinds of signs are best suited to communicating actual or intended sounds? Even with significant adaptations, Western notation in the service of non-Western music often leads to "misconceptions, violations of musical logic and distortions of objective and acoustic fact" (Ellingson, 1992a, p. 139).

Another distinction between types of transcription borrows from linguistics. Theoretically, "etic" transcriptions are indiscriminately detailed (if that is possible), whereas "emic" transcriptions record only those details significant to members of the culture whose music is being portrayed. However, the same issues of representation haunt either approach. In a classic article, Ellingson (1992a) enumerates transcriptional alternatives (e.g., graphs, number notations, conceptual transcriptions) that ethnomusicologists have invented to depict the sounds of Western and non-Western musics. As for technique, no single approach prevails. Widdess (1994), for example, advocates transcription in consultation with the performers themselves.

Transcription often is a means to analyze musical style, a handy (and sometimes deceptive) tool for individuals attempting to learn the music of another culture (see Rice, 1994). Blum's (1992) historical review of ethnomusicological approaches to musical analysis is by far the most comprehensive.

"Writing Culture"

Ethnography refers both to a research approach and an account of the individuals or groups that have been studied. Representing people, their practices, ideas, and music, is a necessarily delicate task. Because "the ethnographer does not . . . perceive what his informants perceive" (Geertz, 1983, p. 58), the goal of ethnographic writing is to balance "experience-near" and "experience-distant" perspectives on cultural experience, that is, to mediate local concepts and globalize them, too.

Clifford (1986) emphasizes that ethnographic accounts are interpretive constructions rather than objective windows on truth. Therefore, it is incumbent on the ethnographer to reveal his or her biases where possible. Given that researchers cannot help but affect the environment in which they work (reactivity), Myerhoff and Ruby (1982) not only encourage researchers to disclose and evaluate the assumptions/theories/narratives that have guided their research but also to document all methods of research and relationships with consultants. These recommendations are a corrective to much anthropological and ethnomusicological scholarship that, even into the 1980s, revealed few details about ethnographic practice or experience.[6] This is vital if we understand that personal associations developed in the course of research invariably invoke power relations. Power is used here, not in the sense of one person forcing another to do something (although that is also a concern), but in the sense of access and control over cultural objects and images. Through writing—but also through audio-recordings and documentary film[7]—the ethnographer controls images of the people she or he has studied and makes them available for public consumption. The asymmetrical relationship between observer and observed can be mitigated to some extent through judicious disclosure.

Finally, ethnography is always a work-in-progress. Feld (1987), for example, discusses insights gained from having the Kaluli (in Papua New Guinea) read his book about their music. The practice of sharing the final product with those who have contributed to and are portrayed by the ethnographic project is not only a gesture of respect but also a statement of accountability representing another phase in the dialectic of understanding.

Conspectus of Research

The literature on music transmission and learning to be surveyed here also reveals an ethnomusicological perspective and focuses on exemplars drawn from two primary disciplines—ethnomusicology and music education. These two bodies of literature are treated separately, largely because there has been so little dialogue between them and because the objectives that guide them are so divergent. Ethnomusicologists generally strive for "thick description" (Geertz, 1973) of cultural practices with the sole objective of understanding those practices, while music educators customarily seek ethnographic data with a view to rethinking and perhaps changing instructional practice.

Although the conspectus is selective in terms of disciplinary reach, it does acknowledge relevant work in the fields of folklore, psychology, and education, too. Of course, researchers who carry out ethnographic research in music transmission and learning often bridge disciplinary distinctions; where possible, those instances have been marked in the narrative.

The conspectus is also selective in terms of the bibliographic record. Indeed, the literature has been delimited in a number of ways: (1) it is almost exclusively in English; (2) it does not encompass historical issues associated with "transmission," for example, stability and change in repertoire over significant spans of time or geography; and (3) it does not specifically address notation systems used in different societies, although notational style can help shed light on the culturally specific operations of any method of transmission (see Ellingson, 1992b).

Status of Research on Music Transmission and Learning in Ethnomusicology

The ethnographic study of music transmission and learning in ethnomusicology predates that of music education. Still, ethnomusicologists[8] and folklorists have spent proportionately little time studying these processes or the ways they are shaped by culture. Because of the holistic nature of ethnography, ethnomusicological accounts do frequently contain references to music transmission and learning; but these references, embedded in larger discussions of sociomusical phenomena, often are very brief or very general. For example, Waterman's (1955) and Yamada's (1983) treatments of skill and repertoire acquisition among the Yirkalla (Australia) and Iatmul (Papua New Guinea), respectively, are auxiliary to their central objective, which is the portrayal of music as an enculturative mechanism. In some societies, transmission and learning are so closely coupled to other processes that they are subsumed by discussions of them. Song acquisition in traditional male Blackfoot (North America) culture, for example, was (and is) tied integrally to composition: A song could be learned from another human being, but more often it was imparted by a supernatural power who appeared to the recipient in a vision (Nettl, 1989). Among Blackfoot, the vision experience conflates the learning of a song with its creation. Therefore, while the ethnomusicological literature often lacks tightly focused descriptions of music transmission and learning, there is considerable breadth of reference and approach to the topic. The ethnomusicological literature also has given fairly equal consideration to what are commonly referred to as "formal" and "informal" contexts of transmission and learning.

The relative paucity of studies devoted exclusively to music transmission and learning within ethnomusicology and within folklore arises from divergent disciplinary trends. Ethnomusicology itself presents a bit of a paradox.

The publication of *The Anthropology of Music* by Merriam (1964) signaled many ethnomusicologists' new commitment to anthropology—its theories, methodologies, and even its intellectual biases. The generous apportionment given to music learning in that landmark publication, coupled with the theoretical currency of functionalism, inspired others to include discussion of musical socialization in their ethnomusical accounts. Yet, educational processes and the most commonly identified recipients of education—children and youth—have received sporadic attention by ethnomusicologists generally. Caputo (1995) argues that in anthropology the study of children and youth cultures has been devalued, largely because of the way they have been regarded as "passive receptors" of adult-driven processes of socialization. Likewise, the study of school culture has been ghettoized, because of the strong feminine presence in the teaching profession; in other words, teaching has been tied conceptually to women and children and not to spheres of masculine dominance such as political economy (Caputo, 1995). Extending these arguments to ethnomusicology, inconsistent attention to transmission and learning seems to stem ultimately from perceptions about the status and power of its primary subjects.

Since the 1980s, increasing emphasis on interdisciplinarity has broadened interest in music transmission and learning among ethnomusicologists. Much of the interest has been aroused by European sociology, as well as women's studies. Summarizing briefly, the sociologist Pierre Bourdieu (1973) was one of the first to tie learning to political economy by studying the role that early familial socialization and subsequent schooling had on individuals' accumulation of "cultural capital" and, ultimately, their socioeconomic status. The growth of women's/gender studies and rising numbers of female scholars in the disciplines of ethnomusicology and folklore have helped endorse the study of women's musical roles (e.g., Herndon & Ziegler, 1990; Koskoff, 1989), including their roles as teachers, and opened the door for observation of females' gender-segregated transmission/learning activities.

Studies of Music Transmission and Learning in Ethnomusicology

As mentioned, Merriam's 1964 publication marks an important turning point in ethnomusicology and in scholars' attention to music transmission and learning. Merriam devotes an entire chapter to "Learning," suggesting new directions for research and summarizing the literature.[9] Many of the studies he cites, as well as his own work, are characterized by structural-functionalism (or functionalism), a theoretical perspective borrowed from anthropology and current in ethnomusicology in the 1960s and

1970s[10] that envisioned "culture" as an organic entity with a number of structural components, each of which worked to maintain the smooth, integrated functioning of the whole (see Radcliffe-Brown, 1952). Music was regarded as one of those components. Merriam's agenda for the study of music learning can be regarded as a logical extension of this way of thinking: The way a society successfully produces new generations of music-makers is one of the mechanisms that allows a cultural system to be self-perpetuating.

Studies following Merriam's anthropological model, especially those dealing with sub-Saharan Africa and using a functionalist perspective, usually allotted a portion of the narrative to the discussion of musical competence and its acquisition. Ethnomusicologists focused their gaze on both shared and specialized musical competences.

Shared Musical Competence

Pursuing an essentialist objective, Wachsmann's (1966) article on the sources of pan-African musicality simultaneously promotes and upholds the notion that in African societies there is a basic musical competence shared by all. He argues for unconscious motor learning that takes place when an African child, placed on its mother's back, senses the acoustic vibrations and rhythms generated by her work and dance movements. He also notes the generous approval children receive for their attempts to dance, even at the prewalking stage. Later, the viscerality of musical experience is consciously reproduced by drummers who tap rhythms on the shoulders of novice players when they are off stroke. Although Wachsmann's data are presented anecdotally, culture-specific studies represented by Zemp (1971), Nketia (1973), and Blacking (1973) confirm his observations about infant socialization. Adding support to the hypothesis that fundamental music skills are distributed equally, these studies also mention the collective instruction in song and dance that all young males and females commonly receive during initiation, in what are often referred to as "bush schools."[11,12]

Blacking (1967) outlines some of the conditions for creating shared musical competence among the Venda (southern Africa). An anomaly in the ethnomusicological literature because of its focus on children's music, Blacking claims that if basic musical competence is not universal among the Venda, then it is very close: "*Most* [italics added] Venda children are competent musicians: they can sing and dance to traditional melodies, and many can play at least one musical instrument" (1967, p. 29). In time, Blacking extended his observations on the musical capabilities of the Venda to the human species as a whole, borrowing from linguistic theory to suggest that all people are biologically predisposed to making music (Blacking, 1971).

This theory has made Blacking the most cited ethnomusicologist in the music education literature.

Selection and Training of Music Specialists

Many, if not most, treatments of transmission and learning in the Africanist literature of the 1960s and 1970s actually were directed toward the cultivation of musical specialists in an aural apprenticeship system. Although there is little unity in approach (some identify agents of transmission, others learning progression), even the sparsest descriptions typically identify selective factors in becoming a musician, that is, the variables that put individuals on the path to realizing (or denying) their musical capacities. One of the subtexts guiding these narratives is Merriam's distinction, borrowed from anthropology, between ascription and achievement (Merriam, 1964, pp. 130–133). Merriam argued that the role of musician was more often ascribed, that is, inherited or assigned at birth, than achieved.

According to Blacking (1971, 1973), the Venda say that exceptional musical ability is congenital, although they credit the social environment as most important for the support and encouragement it can provide. Sons of male musicians are in a favored position to acquire necessary skills, although only a few born to musicians actually emerge as such. Social position also can be a selective factor: A boy of noble birth who demonstrates musical prowess is expected to turn his back on music as a potential vocation in favor of governance. No restrictions apply to female nobility, who are free to actualize their full musical potential.[13]

The Bala (central Africa) believe that musicians are born, not made, but that musical talent, while usually inherited patrilineally, is also divinely arranged (Merriam, 1973). Thus, nonmusical parents can give birth to musical offspring, and musical parents can have offspring of varying musical ability. In any case, learning certain core instruments is a process of informal observation of or apprenticeship to a master musician over a period of many months, and both processes are marked by imitation. On reaching an appropriate level of proficiency, teachers give their students permission to perform in public and reap the profits of their early performance earnings. Merriam's learning profiles of four musicians highlight the variability of pedagogical approach and the uniform importance of practice in achieving mastery.

Mandinka (Gambia) verbal artists and instrumentalists known as *jalolu* (sing. *jali*) are hereditary musicians. Knight (1973) briefly outlines the apprenticeship process that young males, from as early as age 5, undergo to learn the instrument played by their fathers. Training is administered by a nonfamily member and consists largely of observation and imitation. Novices hone visual and kinetic skills before aural skill so that players of the 21-string *kora* learn ostinato patterns first and tuning last. And although *kora* players accompany their own singing, it is not considered necessary to teach them how to vocalize, too.

Goody (1982) summarizes selective factors for Dagomba (Ghana) drummers and fiddlers, based on anthropologist Oppong's (1973) work.[14] Male children of drummers are obligated to learn their father's occupation under threat of death or madness. Furthermore, when a woman from a drumming family marries, "the men of her [paternal kin group] have a right to claim one of her [male] children to be taught drumming" (Oppong, 1973, p. 114). The reason is that drummers' ritualized singing is essential for legitimating high chiefs' position; here role heredity is linked less to belief in genetic predisposition than it is to the buttressing of political power. Male fiddlers, too, are likely to follow their fathers' occupational roles, but the same obligations do not apply to them.

Berliner's (1978) chapter on learning *mbira* among the Shona (Zimbabwe) provides an extended treatment of the process of transmission. *Mbira* is a struck idiophone, played with right and left thumbs and right index finger. Because the societal role of the male *mbira* player is a specialized one, learning is not open to everyone. Mastery is attributed to two sources, spirits and teachers. As Berliner notes,

> The first manifest interest a person shows in the mbira and the person's early manifest skill in mbira playing are often interpreted as the reappearance of the long-dormant talent of an ancestor who was himself a skilled player. In contemporary Zimbabwe, as new and old ideologies mix young musicians express a slightly modified view of this role of the spirits. A person could conceivably learn to play the mbira without the help of an ancestor, but he would most likely have to struggle harder to learn, and he would have less chance of becoming a really great mbira player. (1978, p. 137)

Although the notion of hereditary talent is germane here, functionally spirits appear to players in dreams either to encourage or to demonstrate specific pieces.

Mbira playing is also achieved through indirect and direct learning from teachers. Novices observe advanced *mbira* players in action, memorizing the patterns of one digit at a time and practicing later on borrowed instruments. When direct learning from a teacher takes place, it is acknowledged through remuneration, unless teacher and student are related. While no single pedagogical approach prevails—the teacher can break a piece into its component parts or teach each digit separately—developing strength and technique takes priority over expanding repertoire. In time, *mbira* players also learn to play without looking at the instrument, to rely on motor memory, and to embellish melody. The Shona recognize five levels of musicianship on

the basis of repertoire mastery and acquired skill, namely, the ability to play leading and contrasting, interlocking parts, and to improvise variations.

While Merriam's ascription-achievement distinction clearly informs Berliner's and other scholars' discussions of selective factors, the fact that the terms are often not used or heavily qualified suggests they do not match reality closely enough. Not only do elements of ascription and achievement blend together, straining the dichotomy, but also cultural beliefs change; Berliner, for example, suggests that postcolonial experience has modified the Shona's traditional beliefs in ascription.

If, unlike Berliner, most ethnomusicological treatments of transmission and learning during the 1960s and 1970s are short on detail, it is usually because they are part of an ethnographic project that takes a very broad approach to documenting the musical culture of an ethnic or occupational group. Only by recently escalated ethnomusicological standards might some of these studies be faulted for silencing consultants' voices; of particular note is the general lack of children's voices in all cases, even Blacking's study. A more general criticism is that in all but a few studies, the functionalist perspective prevents authors from registering variability of consultants' opinions or observed practices.

Student-Teacher Relationships

Another theme in the ethnomusicological literature is student-teacher relationships. Perhaps because of the exalted position of teachers in Asian societies, Asian music cultures emerged as an important locus for the study of music transmission and learning in the 1980s and 1990s. This literature documents the nature of student-teacher relationships, the institutions that grow around them, and the pedagogies they enact. Centered on indigenous classical music traditions,[15] this literature leaves behind the theme of shared musical competence. Moving away from functionalist interpretations, which tend to assume cultural stasis, these studies also mark changes in transmission as a response to modernity. Research on India, Thailand, and Japan offers numerous examples.

India.   Selection to the role of professional musician and to a particular musical specialization in the North Indian classical tradition depends on a number of social considerations, including one's caste, familial occupation, gender, and religion (Neuman, 1980). Once committed to a particular musical path, however, three elements are required to become a performer: will or discipline, a teacher or guide, and spiritual grounding or divine intercession. Discipline manifests itself in practice (*riaz*), which is conceptually elaborated in terms of length, continuity, quality, and sacrifice. Thus, *riaz* carries with it a moral connotation, and a student or teacher's ability to persevere in practice is a prime indicator of his (or her) spiritual status.

Success in the acquisition of musical technique, repertoire, and style also is dependent on the teacher-student (*guru-shishya*) relationship, which is characterized by the same affinities and responsibilities that obtain between father and son.[16] A devoted disciple, who typically lives with his *guru* and carries out household duties, is obedient to and holds deep affection for his teacher. In this way, a disciple learns the ways of a musician's life, and if his *guru* feels lovingly toward him, he will be the privileged recipient of esoteric knowledge associated with the *guru*'s stylistic "school" or *gharana*. Transmission of that knowledge is entirely aural, as notation is considered an inappropriate expedient.

Neuman traces the origins of the *gharana* to the mid-19th century, when India was modernizing. *Gharana*s were formed largely by Muslim musicians whose rules for intermarriage and transmission of musical knowledge created "a relatively small circle of [hereditary] specialists" and select disciples (1980, p. 204). *Gharana*s distinguished musicians and their students through shared pedigree. Since 1947, however, recruitment of nonhereditary musicians has increased dramatically and, even prior to that, musical education was available through music schools, although the intensity and level of training they provided did not produce professionals.

Post's (1989) largely historical study chronicles changes to women's musical roles with the rise of 19th-century *gharana*s. Previously, female musician/dancers belonged to a stigmatized courtesan class, but as court and temple patronage of these professionals diminished, they became associated with a *gharana*. The quality of training they received from a *guru* and the repertoire they acquired helped them achieve "a new level of respect . . . which was equal to that of the male performers" (1989, p. 104).

Setting aside social considerations, Booth (1987, 1996) documents teachers' methods and materials of transmission in the North Indian drumming (*tabla*) tradition, one that stresses improvisational creativity. *Qaida*s are rhythmic phrases committed to memory through kinetic repetition and verbal recitation of drum syllables; variations on these phrases "offer stereotypical models of the creative process" and can produce competent, if not expert, improvisers as early as age 6 (Booth, 1987). *Qaida*s are transmitted aurally and notation is limited to occasional use for mnemonic purposes only, making the student-teacher relationship paramount. Modern, group-based instruction offered to music hobbyists, however, depends heavily on notation.

Thailand. Both Wong (1991) and Myers-Moro (1993) examine classical music transmission in Bangkok. Noting that "the Southeast Asian paradigm of the all-knowing teacher and the submissive disciple originated in classical India" (Wong, 1991, p. 18), Wong contrasts the social organization of Thai musicians and the nature of traditional student-teacher relationships with that described by Neuman (1980). There are similarities, such as the bestowal of special pieces, representing the teacher's stylistic school and lineage, on favored disciples. Social ties, however, are more fluid, and it is not unusual for students to study with more than one teacher in a lifetime. Wong also describes the interdependence of student and teacher (or *khru*, from Sanskrit *guru*) in broader social terms, as a manifestation of Thai patron-client relations.

According to Myers-Moro, students in the 1980s were engaged with a range of pedagogies along a continuum, each representing adaptations to contemporary contexts. In the 19th century, aural transfer of repertoire from teacher to student was predicated on repetition and memorization, carried out in a live-in, domestic arrangement. This model exists today on a far lesser scale and often in modified form, for example, abbreviated lessons at a university. More common is the deintensified, one-on-one lesson supplemented by notation and even tape recorder. At the extreme end of the continuum is classroom instruction aided by computer technology. There is a reciprocal relationship between level of commitment and where a student is on the continuum; and the extent to which a student learns to play and improvise idiomatically is also implicated by his or her place on the continuum. Wong notes that, since the development of university music departments, women play instruments once relegated exclusively to men, but that attaining the status of a primary disciple and, thus, a professional musician is still largely limited to men.

Traditionally trained students pass through a series of rites acknowledging their expanding technique and musical understanding; each of five levels is marked by sacred repertoire, demanding ever-increasing amounts of spiritual strength. The rites occur in conjunction with the *wai khru* ritual that honors teachers. Here, the cosmological significance of teachers comes into play. Thai Buddhism regards deities as teachers, and deities of music are directly invoked in *wai khru* in order to transfer "the spiritual power of the first, primordial teacher to present day performers" (Wong, 1991). Before musicians and dancers can perform the sacred repertoire for *wai khru*, they must be initiated by a male master teacher possessing secret, divine knowledge, thus giving them the means to actualize the sacred in the ritual. Through the lens of performance theory, Wong examines the social and ritual power invested in these male officiants by virtue of their esoteric knowledge.

Japan. Read and Locke's (1983) study of the Yamada "school" of *koto* performance describes the hierarchical *iemoto* system of transmission that has dominated Japanese arts since the 17th century. The autocratic head of this system is the hereditary *iemoto*. Charged with preservation of a style, she[17] teaches by rote, demanding strict imitation. In addition, she licenses teachers, grants membership to her "school," bestows performance names, and awards certificates of achievement. If her musical prowess is great, she can expect lifelong loyalty and demand high fees from her students; in fact, students are expected to study under only one *iemoto* in their lifetime. Variables determining rank below the *iemoto* are detailed, as are horizontal relationships, for example, student-student. The authors defend criticisms brought against the system by other Japanese, for example, repression of artistic freedom and high fees.[18]

Whereas Pecore (2000) touches on the delicate cultural semantics surrounding teacher fees, the focus of this article is the introduction of traditional Japanese music into the school system by one of its primary agents, Chihara Yoshio, in the 1960s. Bemoaning the narrow focus of Japanese public schools on Western music, Chihara took up *koto* study under an *iemoto*, then arranged and taught the materials he had acquired to public school students, creating an alternative to the *iemoto* system. In fact, the *iemoto* system's association with Japan's feudal era is one of the reasons for curricular exclusion of traditional music prior to the 1960s. Still secondary to Western music instruction, traditional Japanese music was sanctioned by a national government that saw it as a contribution to the national identity project of the 1970s and the internationalization movement in the 1990s.

Motegi (1984) contrasts traditional with modern teaching methods for singers and instrumentalists in Japanese puppet theater, a domain that remains outside the *iemoto* system. Traditionally, a musician acquired competence by joining his teacher's household at age 6/7 and frequenting public spaces shared by artists. Individual lessons relied on aural instruction with minimal dependence on notation. When puppet theater was threatened by a postwar decline in patronage, new methods were adopted. Traditionalists claim that group lessons, standardized scores, and audiotapes have changed performance practice, narrowing singers' emotional range and treatment of melody.

Classical music transmission systems, as illustrated by North Indian, Thai, and Japanese examples, are hierarchically organized and characterized by prescribed, often ceremonially recognized student-teacher relationships; connection to a particular teacher/lineage and their associated style forms the nucleus of a musician's sociomusical identity. Despite the existence of written notation, teachers historically have relied on aural instruction; both the means of transmission and the nature of the student-teacher relationship, however, have been altered by the presence of modern institutions, for example, universities, as well as new economies and technologies.

Unlike the largely functionalist, African studies cited earlier, the studies cited in this section tend to center on a particular pedagogical phenomenon or institution, providing richer, more focused descriptions. There is another departure from functionalist studies, which, by assuming the homogeneity of cultural practices and their efficacy in maintaining social cohesion, often failed to register tensions or contradictory pieces of evidence. Neuman, for example, exposes a gap between musicians' folkloric constructions of *gharana* antiquity and its actual historical depth, which only emphasizes the importance of the *gharana* to musicians' sociomusical identity.

With the exception of Myers-Moro and Wong, most studies fail to acknowledge the cultural ethos that drives student devotion to teacher, and few address directly the issue of reliance on teacher through rote learning when written notation is available.[19] One wonders, for example, if this "restricted literacy" (Goody, 1968) is a recognition of the prescriptive limitations of notation. Finally, studies such as Pecore's demonstrate one of the strengths of ethnography, that is, its potential for relating microcosmic (individual) practices to macrocosmic (historical and national) forces.

Emergent Directions for Ethnomusicological Research in Music Transmission and Learning

Cross-Cultural Comparison of Transmission Systems

As illustrated in the previous section, generalizations about transmission systems within a geocultural area tend to be rather limited, because not all ethnographers investigate the same phenomena. For that reason (and others), contemporary ethnomusicologists have generally avoided cross-cultural comparison. However, some ethnographers are in a position to compare two or more transmission systems through direct experience. Booth's (1996) discussion of *qaida*s, for example, draws comparisons with Euro-American transmission practices. He notes, for example, that the distinction between pedagogical and performance materials made in the Western pianistic tradition is clearer than in the North Indian *tabla* tradition.

Based on the observation that transmission and learning reflect the relative importance of musical and extramusical properties in each culture, Trimillos (1983) has developed a model for comparing cultural priorities embedded in systems of transmission. He recommends identifying those properties considered *essential* to a particular transmission system, those that are *desirable*, and those that are only *incidental*. The model is tested comparing transmission of ancient Hawaiian chant, South Indian drumming, vocal improvisation among the Tausug (Philippines), and Japanese court music. In another study, Trimillos (1989) contrasts means of transmission and content transmitted in four "formal" educational systems, noting, for example, that in the German *Musikhochschule*, "entitlement to repertory is determined in the first instance by the voice type, not by a particular teacher and the repertory he 'owns,' " as is the case in Hawaiian *halau*. The strength of Trimillos's model lies in the fact that categories for comparison are not imposed a priori but are suggested by the cultural groups in question.

Integrating Cognitive and Social Perspectives in the Study of Musical Competence

Brinner (1995) suggests a more general typology for studying transmission and learning across cultures: progression/pace, processes/methods, and agents/contexts/means of acquisition. Beyond the surface comparison of music cultures that Brinner presents using this typology, his book is a watershed, both for its sustained and particularized discussion of transmission and learning in the Javanese *gamelan* tradition, and for its delineation of taxonomic categories of learning strategy.

Music learning in Javanese culture is portrayed as the development of a *variety* of competences by each individual but not all shared equally by them. In characterizing competences, Brinner reconsiders a number of categories used in cognitive psychology and education: active versus passive; intuitive versus explicit; conscious versus automatic; and procedural versus declarative knowledge. Not only does he operationalize these vis-à-vis Javanese music making, but also he questions their characterization as dichotomous polarities and their discreteness in actual practice.

Javanese obtain competences primarily through participation in performing ensembles. This is made possible by a "loosely hierarchical order of instruments" (144) within the *gamelan* ensemble, requiring varying types and levels of competence. Thus, a novice can be absorbed into an ensemble with relative ease, allowing passive knowledge to be converted into active knowledge. Once engaged, repetition, feedback, imitation, inference, and interpretation are the primary processes of acquiring competences. Brinner distinguishes between different types of imitation: (1) simultaneous, consecutive, and delayed imitation differentiate the time elapsed between presentation of the musical model and its reproduction (pp. 136–137); and (2) deductive imitation, selective imitation, and emulation differentiate the conditions and quality of the learner's perception and his reproduction of the musical model (p. 138).

The strength of Brinner's work lies in the scrupulous attention he brings to commonly used terms such as "im-

itation," and his revelation of the logic underlying "informal" transmission processes. His integration of cultural and cognitive perspectives, furthermore, demonstrates how specific musicocognitive competences are invoked by particular cultural practices and contexts.

Music Transmission and Learning That Crosses Cultural Boundaries

Music transmission and learning that crosses cultural boundaries is implicated in the ethnomusicological enterprise itself: Ethnographers sometimes attempt to acquire proficiency in the musical traditions they study. Indeed, several studies document the ethnomusicologist's or the accomplished adult musician's expansion of skill.

Sudnow (1978), a classically trained pianist, provides a phenomenological account of his mastery of jazz improvisation, cataloguing each development in the dialectic between his conscious understanding of pianistic knowledge and his hands' enactment of it.[20] Chernoff (1979) narrates his attempts to learn West African drumming styles. Whereas Sudnow and Chernoff seem to follow relatively normative paths within the systems of learning they adopted as adults, Rice (1994) claims that his learning of the Bulgarian bagpipe followed a trajectory quite opposite that of Bulgarians: Western musical training facilitated his grasp of melodic and rhythmic phrases but hindered his ability to acquire the instrument's idiomatic ornamental style. Rice also notes the tension between his own motivations for learning and his teacher's motivations for instructing him: "As an outsider, I wanted to produce a single sound . . . out of context and for its own sake. He, however, wanted me to be able to function as a musician who could play for dancing" (p. 81). Another Westerner, Ziporyn (in Bamberger & Ziporyn, 1992), describes his strategy of "getting it wrong" for the sake of acquiring rules of improvisation in Balinese *gamelan*, a tradition in which there are no explanatory models, in which formal understanding is tacit, and in which etiquette precludes overt criticism. In a reversal of the typical pattern of cultural crossover, Szego (1999) discusses the difficulty that contemporary young Hawaiians, trained in Western techniques of vocal production, experience when they try to reproduce a Hawaiian vocal aesthetic.

Hood's (1960) notion of "bimusicality" is implicated in all these instances. However, not all cross-cultural learning aspires to the level of proficiency suggested by this term. Kurokawa (2000), for example, notes that older Japanese women in the 1980s who studied Hawaiian *hula* were motivated more by a desire for physical fitness and nostalgia for pre- and postwar Hawaiian hit songs than for mastery of another cultural form. In the 1990s, a younger group was attracted to *hula* because "it did not require uncomfortable narrow shoes, too much stamina, or a . . . male partner" (p. 63). This group, however, pursued indigenous musical and movement models more devotedly by inviting *hula* masters to Japan and by traveling to Hawaii to study with them. Japanese *hula* schools, furthermore, took on features of the *iemoto* system (see Read & Locke, 1983).

The Role of Gender in Transmission and Learning of Musical Genres

The gender-specific activity described by Kurokawa (2000) indicates ethnomusicologists' increasing interest in and access to women's musical activity. Related to this and reflecting trends in the humanities and social sciences in general, ethnomusicologists have begun considering the ways that gender constrains and enables the learning of music.

Spearritt (1995) reveals that instrumental practice among newly initiated Iatmul men takes place late at night, a regulation governed by considerations of gender. Among Iatmul, flutes are an exclusively male domain, and women and children have to be shielded from them and their sounds. Drums, by contrast, signal the voices of ancestors, which women and children should be exposed to. It is important, however, that they hear credible renditions of ancestral voices, requiring novice male drummers to practice when women and children are thought to be asleep.

Baily and Doubleday (1990) compare acquisition of cognitive and motor skills among male and female children from both musician and nonmusician families in Islamic Afghanistan, a society marked by gender segregation.[21] Although the musical environment of musician families was considerably richer, all children received exposure to women's domestic music and taught themselves through imitation and participation, without benefit of explanation. Whereas girls and boys from musician families reached a considerable level of professional skill by puberty, girls from nonmusician families, limited to singing and playing the frame drum, were discouraged from music making as they entered their teens. Only boys in the same group could expect to acquire more musical skill, and then only by persevering against family resistance.

Rice (1996) details gender-specific musical roles and learning processes in Bulgaria. Traditionally, learning to sing was a female activity, acquired in the process of performing manual labor. Daughters joined in with or "followed" the singing of older females, who also provided explicit models and feedback. Sons learned instruments entirely through self-instruction as they passed time herding, usually without adult encouragement. Learning to sing, however, was more important to young women than learning an instrument was to young men: The severity of their domestic labors and the abuses they suffered made singing a psychological necessity, and its teaching more pertinent.

Bulgaria's communist era saw the introduction of didactic methods for instrumentalists. Already skilled instru-mentalists (and singers) were organized into professional folk ensembles, and promising youth streamed into high schools designed expressly for training musicians. Both groups were taught how to read music by classically trained musicians. As music making became lucrative, parents encouraged their sons to learn music, thus giving rise to the male instrumental teacher. In this case, the development of a new, gender-specific role is tied to the development of a new social ideology.

In the traditional Bulgarian and Afghani examples, gender intersects with occupational role to determine which instrument(s) can be learned and the relative ease with which they can be learned. Speaking more generally, transmission and learning can vary as a function of gender in several ways: genre(s) or instrument(s) learned; access to models; method of transmission; timing of learning experiences (in the life cycle, diurnally, seasonally); possible levels of mastery; and degree of social support. Clearly, the social and religious ideologies on which constructions of gender are predicated can result in uneven or unequal access to musical resources; thus, gender-focused studies are linked to another group of studies that examine music transmission and learning in terms of power.

Power Relations and Politics in "Formal" Educational Settings

Wherever control of musical resources is at issue, power relations are invoked. Musical institutions, especially Western-style schools and the control they wield, have served as profitable sites for study in the last two decades. And it is to this realm of transmission and learning that ethnomusicologists have applied social theory quite consistently.

Colonial education that privileges the learning of a foreign music over indigenous music is an obvious site for exploring power relations. Szego (1999) documents this historical phenomenon as it transpired in a missionary-type school in Hawaii. Using Bourdieu (1973), Szego argues that Hawaiian women who studied at the school in the late 19th and early 20th centuries accumulated cultural capital or prestige by learning to play piano, thus standing a greater chance of improving their socioeconomic condition. By the middle of the 20th century, the school had come to be known for its curricular emphasis on Western-style singing; regular public displays of student singing, however, came to reinforce the social stereotype of Hawaiians as entertainers, a stereotype that helped stall their socioeconomic advancement.

Learning indigenous music in a foreign context also can be politically charged. Pillay (1994) documents the ways that Indians ("Asians") in South Africa interpreted musical instruction in that country's persistent but failing apartheid system. Many students, parents, and teachers in separate

Indian public schools questioned the motives of a government that insisted on teaching students Indian, Afrikaner, and English, but not African, musics. Many regarded the appeal to their own cultural heritage as insidious: In addition to creating a falsely homogenous Indian identity and attempting to keep Indians out of the black struggle, "Indian music [was] used . . . for 'Indianizing' the image of the Indian school, thereby strengthening the government's case for the retention of its apartheid policies" (1994, p. 287). Here, Pillay contests the functionalist notion of music as an integrative force in society.

Not only the type of music but also the pedagogical approach to it has political ramifications. Shepherd and Vulliamy (1983), a transoceanic sociomusicologist-educator team, conducted research in British and Canadian classrooms. Whereas British schools taught only Western European art music, Canadian high school students played big band, Broadway, and light classical pieces. These latter styles were sufficiently like the music of the students' culture to appease them. Therefore, no apparent clash between school music and student culture existed, as it did in Britain. The authors argue that where aurally based popular music was presented, it was devalued, not by explicitly denigrating it, but by relying on notation, thus eliminating crucial aspects of the music, such as timbre, from the discussion. Drawing on McLuhan's (1962) and Goody and Watt's (1968) theory that "the medium of communication in any group . . . plays a pervasive role in the structuring of that group['s] . . . reality" (Shepherd, 1979, p. 3), the authors conclude that school music based on notation misrepresents the music that articulates students' social realities and identities.

Kingsbury (1988) is one of the first ethnomusicologists to examine a Western institution, and his study in an American conservatory focuses on the relationship of highly developed learners to their esteemed master teachers and to each other: (1) The teacher's role as an interpreter, whose authority could override even that of the score, not only put him or her in a position of power but also marked the process of transmission as an aural one; (2) Because teachers' distinctive artistic qualities were highly valued, pedagogies perceived as a threat to individualism were resisted, for example, Suzuki; (3) Teachers' reputations were enhanced by their students' successes, and vice versa, in a pattern of "reciprocal prestige-lending" (1988, p. 41); and (4) In the company of similarly accomplished musicians, students constantly measured and had others measure the amount of "talent" they had. However, attributions of talent had to be weighed against their source: "The validity of a given person's musical talent is a direct function of the relative esteem of the persons who have attributed the talent to the person" (1988, p. 68). Finally, Kingsbury observed that, in master classes, praise was usually given to already accomplished performers, which only served to in-

crease regard for them, while criticism further inhibited those with less skill, leading to the conclusion that "musical performance skill could . . . be seen to be both product and producer of social power" (p. 103). Here Kingsbury draws on Giddens's (1984) structuration theory, which posits a dialectical relationship between structure (sociocultural constraints imposed on human beings) and agency (the ways that human beings actualize or transform those constraints).

The merits of structuration theory and other social theories notwithstanding, these four studies illustrate the nature of power differentials in institutional processes of transmission and learning: Musical resources may be controlled through access to (or denial of) repertoire, through interpretation and relative mastery of repertoire, and through the contexts in which mastery was displayed. The degree of authority that learners exerted over their musical education can vary as a function of their age, ethnicity, gender, or performance prowess.

Structural inequalities exposed by the application of social theories, and the critiques that may be implied by them, do not invalidate the notion of cultural relativism; to the contrary, social theories tested against culturally specific data can lead to their further refinement. Nonetheless, these four studies do raise the issue of the relationship between observer and observed: In the case of Kingsbury, Shepherd and Vulliamy, and Pillay, each ethnographer was experientially or historically connected to the transmission systems investigated, that is, Western contemporary or colonial institutions, giving them the status of insiders and thus bringing them closer to much of the work and historical objectives of researchers in music education.

Status of Research on Music Transmission and Learning in Music Education

While ethnomusicologists have only recently forayed into the study of Western or Western-style institutions, these educational settings have been the special domain of researchers in music education. Research in music education is frequently carried out within the researcher's own community (or a community that is very accessible and within the researcher's own cultural milieu), situations that provide greater license for criticism. Indeed, one of the explicit objectives of research in music education, guided historically by the experimental paradigm, is to improve educational practice, which may or may not entail critique of existing practice. Thus, the implications section in music educators' ethnographic accounts often are shaped by a disciplinary imperative to evaluate and to effect change.

Studying music transmission and learning using ethnographic research techniques is, however, a relatively recent trend in music education, and represents a significant departure for a discipline rooted in the experimental paradigm. Like the field of education generally, some studies fall into the category of what Ogbu (1981) calls "microethnography." That is, they are based on brief, scheduled visits with the group or individual under study (often by necessity), and do not attempt to "show how education is linked with the economy, the political system, local social structure, [or] the belief system of the people" (p. 6).

Music education studies now tend toward greater holism, even if they are carefully bounded, and influence of the experimental paradigm is often subtly evident. Speaking in relative terms, it is not unusual for music educators to begin their investigations with specific hypotheses and/ or narrowly focused questions, while ethnomusicologists typically begin research with only a general theoretical perspective (e.g., functionalism, structuration theory) or broadly formulated questions. Methodologically, there is greater reliance on questionnaires and structured interviews, and it is quite common for observations of videotaped data to be validated by independent researchers. Observation may be guided by protocols, making certain qualitative data quantifiable, thus giving descriptors like "many" and "fewer"—so common in the ethnomusicological literature—greater precision. These things taken together tend to make the narrative structure and texture of an ethnographic account in music education explicitly hypothesis- or question-driven, unlike the historical structures that so frequently shape ethnomusicological accounts. Although there are exceptions, music educators' ethnographies also tend to be characterized by enumerative rigor and an economy of cultural contextualization.

Whereas researchers in music education have focused, historically, on the study of "formal" contexts of teaching and learning, acceptance of the ethnographic research paradigm coincides with a greater consideration of more "informal" contexts. Research in music education also has embraced demographic groups almost completely ignored by ethnomusicologists, that is, children and youth.

Studies of Music Transmission and Learning in Music Education

Discontinuities Between Transmission and Learning in "Formal" Educational Settings and Students' Musical Experiences

As ethnographic technique gains currency in music education, observational studies of the Western classroom proliferate. Studies focus on teachers, students, or both, as well as the way these actors interact with institutional forces (e.g., Stake, Bresler, & Mabry, 1991). Common themes such as multicultural education (e.g., Klinger, 1996;

Stellaccio, 1995) and acquiring compositional or improvisational skill (e.g., Della Pietra & Campbell, 1995; Marsh, 1995; Wiggins, 1994) unite the literature. Because it is beyond the scope of this chapter to survey any significant portion of these studies, and because many are cited in other chapters, selection has been stringent. This discussion is limited to studies that expose discontinuities between "formal" music study and students' independent musical experiences.

Campbell's (1998) study of children at play and in school is one of the most insightful ethnographic studies in music education to date. Broadly focused on the meaning of music in children's lives, Campbell's interviews with children reveal them to be highly articulate and musically engaged in an extraordinary variety of modes outside school. An example is the 8-year-old who learned to reproduce, from her grandmother's videotapes, the repertoire and singing style of 1930s starlet Jeanette MacDonald. The teacher considered her popular music tastes inappropriate for school music instruction and characterized her adult, MacDonaldesque vibrato as "premature," despite its stunning accuracy.

Kushner's (1991a, 1991b) close observation of schoolchildren in British schools reveals them to be active interpreters and managers of their instructional world. In one case, Muslim children had to negotiate conflicting messages from home and school cultures. At home, students were taught that singing English songs and playing instruments was morally suspect, whereas their teachers encouraged musical creation. Although children acted out this conflict among themselves, they were adept at concealing it from their teachers. Kushner also documented distinct modes of talk in the learning environment; students engaged in regulated, civil "frontstage" (Goffman, 1973) talk in the presence of teachers and in pointed "backstage" talk among their colearners.

Bresler's (1993) observations and interviews with teacher and students in an American university theory class reveal the tensions between paper- versus aural-based approaches to music theory. The teacher presented theory as an inflexible rule-based system with little recourse to musical sound, and objective measures were used to test students' music-writing ability. Coupled with a teacher-centered mode of delivery, the curriculum, as operationalized, did not match formally stated course objectives. Interviews with students representing all levels of achievement in the course reveal their perceptions of the advantages and inadequacies of their teacher's approach, as well as their adaptive and nonadaptive strategies. For example, some students with little musical background excelled in the course because they could adhere to the rules without having to curb their musical instincts. Others were frustrated by working only with notated symbols, because it either failed to satisfy their aural curiosity or did not allow them to exercise their aural judgment. Bresler's inclusion of student perceptions exposes a vulnerability of Shepherd and Vulliamy's (1983) study, discussed earlier. In their analysis, which addresses a similar theme, it is difficult to know whether the instructional problem identified by the authors is felt by students at all. In Bresler's case there is no question; she is, however, equally critical of the teacher's failure to connect theory with students' musical experience.

All three studies are notable for the attention they give student perspectives, and Kushner's richly descriptive portrayal of styles of communication exploits the advantages of ethnography well. Pursuing student opinion and listening closely to student discourse not only reveals their occasional wrestle with the pedagogical environment but also the nature and depth of their subjective musical experiences and the meanings they attach to them.

Transmission and Learning in Community

Community-based contexts have also attracted the attention of music education scholars. Mbanugo's (1986) description of aural procedures of transmission in the junior and youth church choirs of an African-American church is supported by thick description of church culture. Aurality characterizes every step of the transmission procedure: The choir director-pianist "lifts" songs from recordings, which are then taught by rote to choristers with aid of mnemonic devices, for example, tapes for home practice. Mbanugo notes that both "formal" and "informal" instruction characterize church transmission practices: The former designates choir rehearsals, while the latter refers to the slow absorption of musical know-how through exposure to adult singers in church.

Investigations of change in community-based transmission systems resulting from national or ethnic revival parallels ethnomusicologists' descriptions of Asian traditions transformed by modern conditions. Garrison (1985) explores Scottish Gaelic fiddling on Cape Breton Island (Canada), where, in the 1970s, as family- and community-based contexts for transmission declined, fiddling classes were instituted as a way of revitalizing the tradition. Garrison's study reveals systematic relationships between teaching contexts, agents of transmission, and the pedagogical methods they use. Generally speaking, teachers in class contexts use note literacy to supplement aural transmission of tunes, the result being fiddlers' diminished ability to learn tunes well by ear. Contexts for developing public performance expertise also have changed; community dances and kitchen parties have been supplanted by the concert stage, while demographically, the ranks of female fiddlers have swelled to outnumber males.

Veblen (1991, 1996) also examines changes in teaching as a function of cultural revival. Transmitting traditional folk tunes in Ireland is still largely a two-person enterprise, with a large onus on students to pick tunes up from their teachers' aural models. And teachers still become teachers because of their demonstrated ability to play, rather than their pedagogical expertise. Nonetheless, transmission is more consciously planned and the teacher has become a professional in the efficient delivery of instruction: Transmission may take place in a classroom setting; the teacher may be someone other than a relative or neighbor and will thus be remunerated; and teacher-student contact is more regular. Proliferation of national and community-based cultural organizations means that repertoire is no longer limited to local practice and more people have an opportunity to develop musical skill. Technology, for example, taped recording of lessons, and the media's ability to reproduce and disseminate a single performance of a tune, has led to both standardization of transmitted repertoire and accessibility.

While music educators have largely applied ethnographic techniques to the study of music transmission and learning in their "own backyards," some have applied their methodological skill to cultures other than their own.[22] Kreutzer's (1997) long-term fieldstay in a Shona (Zimbabwe) community comes closest to the ideals of traditional anthropological ethnography. Focusing on the outcomes rather than processes of learning, Kreutzer measures the development of melodic competence among children, ranging in age from birth to 7.5 years.

The data reveal a sequence in the development of song acquisition, for example, intentional sound patterning at 6 months of age and discrete pitches in the last half of the 2nd year. At age 5.5, the average child can match adults' pitch precision and tonal consistency, and, by 6, they can produce harmony. Comparing the Shona data with that of American children, Kreutzer concludes that while the two develop in similar sequence, vocal productions of the former are more accurate. Setting the issue of data comparability aside, Kreutzer's "hard" data provide a different measure of support for theories of shared musical competence found in the Africanist literature of the 1960s and 1970s. The integration of music into Shona quotidian life, both "informally" and "formally,"[23] as well as children's pitch sensitivity, exercised by speaking a tonal language, are forwarded as possible explanations for their superior level of competence.

Mans's (1997) discussion of rural, community-based transmission and learning and its urban counterpart in contemporary Namibia points to the delinking of "informal" and "formal" systems. Although elements of aural apprenticeship are still practiced in rural parts, it is on the decline. In towns and cities, private tuition in Western music and dance is in great demand; however, high fees and the cost of Western instruments put them beyond the reach of the average Namibian. Mans also notes that the time required to play with a degree of satisfaction is greater than most young people are willing to invest. Thus, many neophyte musicians terminate their studies before they have developed any significant degree of mastery.

The quantifiable nature of Garrison's and Veblen's interview and questionnaire data and Kreutzer's videotape data give their results numerical precision, whereas attention to cultural context, especially in Mbanugo and Veblen, bring these studies closer to ethnomusicological and folklore scholarship. Interpretation is sometimes wanting: One wonders why females in Garrison's study have risen to the forefront of the revival and what their experiences mean to them. Indeed, the opportunity to explore consultants' subjectivity, which ethnography generously affords, is not fully utilized. It should be noted that Garrison's work represents the earliest example of ethnographic study in music education in this chapter. Researchers should find her checklist of topics for data collection, which foreshadows Brinner's more general typology, quite useful.

Transmission and Learning in Youth Cultures: In the Garage

A movement in the sociology of education in the 1970s prompted new discussion of the Western music curriculum and its content. Educators such as Vulliamy (1977) examined the styles of music considered worthy of being taught, that is, that counted as legitimate school knowledge. Excluded from the British curriculum was popular music. The debate that ensued over popular music, coupled with developments in cultural studies, brought increasing attention to youth's musical cultures. Although much work remains to be done, Campbell (1995b) follows the lead of the sociologist Bennett (1980) and others by examining one of the most important milieus for music making among American male youth—the garage band.[24] Most of the white, early teenage personnel in the two bands observed by Campbell had acquired a basic level of music literacy through school instruction and instrumental study. Learning rock music, however, was a process of independent, repeated listening to a recorded song (usually with instrument in hand) and replicating it, then discussing and practicing partially learned songs collectively. Rehearsals were led by one of the more expert players, who determined the order of play, "counted-off," called out chord names, and functioned as a performance model. Not a "teacher," per se, his role was to "draw the others toward greater musical accuracy" (1980, p. 18). Band members also listened to a taped recording of the first run-through of a song, analyzing and critiquing it against the authoritative original.

Transmission and Learning in Children's Cultures: On the Playground

A particular subset of child-centered musical ethnography in music education has its roots in the folklore tradition of collecting children's musical games, for example, Newell (1963 [1883, 1903]), Gomme (1964 [1894, 1898]), Fowke (1969), Knapp and Knapp (1976), and Opie and Opie (1985). The primary interest of these folklorists was song texts, rather than their performers or the cultural contexts in which they were performed. An exception is Jones and Hawes (1972), in which Hawes provides descriptions of Jones's transmission of games to her peers. This scholarly tradition continues, spilling over its original disciplinary boundaries into music education and, to a lesser extent, ethnomusicology. A growing literature now exists on girls' handclapping games in North America in which scholars are giving due consideration to processes of transmission and learning, for example, Merrill-Mirsky (1988), Riddell (1990), Harwood (1992), Addo (1997), Gaunt (1997), and Marsh (2001).

Riddell (1990) identifies peers and slightly older children as transmitters of singing games among fifth graders in Los Angeles. Although school recess and lunch periods provided key opportunities for transmission, children regarded musical games as gratifying alternatives to school music and the skill set it developed. Riddell argues that the children's democratically distributed knowledge of games had an equalizing function that school transmission practices breached. The kinds of limitations imposed by and on researchers working with children are illustrated by this study; videotaping of singing games took place in a television studio, and school policy limited contact with singers, with the result that interviews were conducted with children from the same area but not the same school.

Harwood (1992) characterizes aural transmission of handclapping games among midwestern African-American girls as holistic. Accomplished players did not have the patience to slow down or isolate elements of melody, text, or movement so that novice players could assimilate them more easily. Novices therefore had to extract data from a complete model, singing under their breath and marking the actions of more expert handclappers as they observed them. Furthermore, when errors were made in the performance of games, either by accomplished or novice players, the players always resumed play at the beginning of the game.

Harwood's data calls into question the notion of nonhierarchical learning advanced by Riddell. Not only were there distinct levels of skill, but expert players monitored the movements of others within game circles and, within the parameters of the game, removed players whose lack of manual dexterity caused the game to break down. This had the effect, however, of identifying mistakes, and the desire to hold out longer in subsequent games provided further motivation for practice. Harwood also notes the temporal flexibility involved in learning games. Unlike the directed learning they experienced in music class, girls worked for varying lengths of time on games according to personal predilection and the social occasions that presented themselves.

Ethnomusicologists Merrill-Mirsky (1988) and Gaunt (1997) confirm aural processes of transmission. Both examine the role of handclapping games in constructing social identities, namely gender and ethnicity; Gaunt, for example, refers to African-American game-songs as "oral-kinetic etudes" that prepare girls for later participation in black adult musical contexts.

Singing games are present in many different children's cultures and commonalties in the teaching/learning process are significant. Marsh (2001) discusses the teaching and learning of musical playground games among multiethnic elementary school children in Australia. The primary, but not exclusive, pattern of transmission was from Anglo-Australians to children of other ethnic groups. Marsh hypothesizes that the use of vocables (nonsemantic word sounds) facilitated the learning of song-games by children with minimal or developing English competence. Vocables also were highly adaptive: Not only could players indigenize them, but also they encouraged the inclusion of non-English words into song-game texts. Interethnic transmission also was helped by the perceived novelty of immigrant children's games, by the self-assurance and popularity of the individuals attempting to teach new games to others, and appropriate social conditions, for example, secure friendships. Like Riddell, Harwood, and Merrill-Mirsky, Marsh found that playground transmission was facilitated by various media, including television; unlike other studies, she found that it also was reinforced by classroom instruction.

The holistic method of teaching observed by Harwood and Marsh also was found among schoolgirls in Ghana (Addo, 1997). Children were, however, able to break songs into sections and sequence them for the purposes of teaching an adult, in this way demonstrating a didactic method associated with adult Ghanaian performance. Addo also notes that repetition of a song game's opening motif signaled the start of a peer teaching/learning episode, thus marking it as an event; learning also was facilitated through the semantic and nonsemantic verbalizations of onlookers, a type of encouragement and reinforcement of learning that Addo likens to midwifery.

In addition to style of peer encouragement, which could serve as a fruitful point of comparison with other studies, Addo's recognition that Ghanaian girls *can* parse games for instructional purposes, but that they eschew such methods for themselves, is extremely valuable. The strength of these studies as well as a number of other studies in the music education literature, for example, Kushner (1991a, 1991b) and Campbell (1998), lies in their revelation of children and youth as active agents in the construction of their own culture, who make considered pedagogical choices in the transmission of their chosen repertoire and in their own learning.

Other Ethnographic Studies of Music Transmission and Learning

Although the preponderance of ethnographic studies on music transmission and learning is situated in the ethnomusicology and music education literatures, it is not delimited by discipline or even mode of representation.

With regard to academic discipline, folklorists' robust interest in children's musical games has been duly noted. Folklorists have, historically, also treated children and youth cultures as appendages to the adult world, and for a long time were largely concerned with collecting, categorizing, and analyzing musical texts, rather than studying the behavior of tradition bearers themselves.[25] Finnegan's (1989) exploration of a single community's music in Britain is a departure from this model and reveals two principal didactic processes. Classical music training focused on note literacy and marked musicians' progress through examinations. Relying on aural sources, players of rock, jazz, folk, and country music escaped the pressure of examinations but also were denied their social validation. To the classically trained "this mode looked . . . easy, undisciplined and 'low level' " (1989, p. 137). Some community ensembles, like brass bands, contained players who learned in both ways, that is, "informally," from fellow band members or family; and "formally," at school or in half-hour weekly lessons.

In the field of cognitive psychology and music cognition, the literature is expanding. Many of these studies seek qualitative data that stretch the notion of ethnography by breaching the principle of naturalism, for example, they train subjects to do things they might not ordinarily do. However, naturalism is upheld in many studies. Kelley and Sutton-Smith[26] (1987) observed infants in their first 2 years in a variety of everyday settings. They compare the demonstrated abilities of children from homes with professional musicians as parents, musically oriented but not professionally trained parents, and nonmusically oriented parents. The data suggest that the number of musical agents in the home environment and the musical stimulation, as well as the attention and reinforcement they provide, are positively correlated with the rate of children's musical development. Adachi (1994) examines the way that an adult can function as a young learner's practice partner, and how the same learner takes on an adult role when transmitting musical signs to others.

In education, Sosniak's (1985) study of 16 pianists, each a finalist in an international piano competition, is notable. Interviews with the pianists and their parents revealed three phases of learning, marked by increasing investment in practice, in competition, and in an identity as a professional pianist; decreasing parental supervision; and progression toward more expert pedagogical support.

With regard to modes of representation, alternative media for presenting ethnographic data are autobiography and film. Quiquemelle (1994), for example, visually documents the educational process of a singer at the Beijing opera. And there are two autobiographies of note: Sitarist Ravi Shankar (1968) personalizes the *guru-shishya* relationship described by Neuman (1980); and Frank Mitchell (1978) reflects on his protracted training as a Navajo Blessingway singer. Mitchell began serious study with his father-in-law as an adult, receiving particularly sacred songs only after he could demonstrate his ability to conduct the Blessingway ceremony correctly and sincerely. Mitchell's father also taught him but refused to transmit his Corn Bundle songs: "He asked me to learn them from someone else. He said that if I took everything from him, he would not be able to survive on earth. That is the same reason we hesitate to tell about our ceremonies to strangers who come from some place outside the reservation" (Mitchell, 1978, p. 237). Despite criticism from others, Mitchell did ask ethnographers to tape sacred songs for posterity, and credited his aptitude for learning and retaining such a large corpus not only to his own ability but also to spiritual assistance. The trust that Mitchell placed in researchers highlights one of the most rewarding features of ethnography and is a poignant reminder of the kinds of responsibility inherent in conducting this kind of research.

Directions for Future Research

Those willing to assume such responsibility have a rich field to explore. At this juncture, it would be appropriate to suggest some directions for research and even some specific research questions that might profit from a methodology that examines subjective experience and behavior and their relation to social values and organization, to political and socioeconomic structure, and even to material culture.

Synthesis and Comparison of Ethnographic Studies

Readers of this review will note that there has been very little synthesis of findings. There are a number of reasons for this. First, ethnographic studies rarely build on one another. That is, one ethnographer rarely seeks to replicate another's study or to refine or dispute a theory advanced by another study. This is largely a function of the geographic and group-boundedness of ethnographic research: scholars working contemporaneously (and even at a historical distance from one another) do not often overlap in the territory they cover or the specific groups they study.

Second, general conclusions about musical transmission and learning as a panhuman phenomenon are premature, because so much of the world has yet to be covered, and where it has, it has been covered in different ways. There is, in fact, considerable resistance to cross-cultural comparison within the disciplines of ethnomusicology and anthropology generally. One of the prime arguments against comparison is that it requires universal categories, that is, one needs to compare like things. However, ethnographic data often undermine the notion of universality: Musical and other cultural phenomena may look or sound the same across cultures, but they may be conceptualized or perceived very differently. Nonetheless, Brinner (1995) has suggested some potential categories, for example, types of imitation, that would be extremely useful for refining contextual descriptions if not for actual cross-cultural comparison. And Trimillos (1983) has offered a culturally sensitive model for comparison that could be helpful in exploring a number of themes, for example, the role of the supernatural in transmission and learning. Even following some very general rubrics for research offered by Garrison (1985) would be helpful for moving the ethnographic study of music transmission and learning out of its presently fragmented state.

Who Are Our Consultants?

As ethnomusicologists in the era of functionalism did not reveal much about their methods or the individuals with whom they worked, it is often difficult to get an accurate reading of their consultants' ages. What we know of ethnomusicological accounts from the 1960s and 1970s, however, is that they were usually based on long-term fieldwork in a community that allowed for observation of people at all ages. By reading between the lines and listening for consultants' voices, one can surmise that ethnomusicologists worked most closely with adults, somewhat less with adolescents, and with children hardly at all. Although there are important exceptions to this generalization, the most apparent gap in the ethnomusicologically oriented literature is the study of children's musical transmission and learning. Studies by music educators on girls' playground singing games provide some compensation for this deficit.

This directive for child-centered ethnographic studies is not tied simply to the need for understanding a critical window in human musical development. Ethnomusicological investigations of musical transmission and learning in non-Western societies have been based, historically, on work with adults who speak to the learning process retrospectively. Furthermore, many of these consultants are master musicians who possess rather esoteric knowledge; thus, theories derived from these interactions may be imbued with greater representational authority than is warranted. Music educators and ethnomusicologists might take some cues from folklorists and engage consultants who, in terms of expertise, represent a broader population of music learners.

There are other potentially useful foci: Traditionally, the people that ethnomusicologists studied were defined by their membership in an ethnic group, and ethnographers of music education studied people defined by their role (e.g., teacher) or their membership in an age group, learning group, or institution. As music educators and ethnomusicologists transgress those traditional boundaries and categories, they may consider not only groups of people whose transmission and learning of music has been neglected—for example composers—but also those who fail to or choose not to develop their musical potential.

The teaching/learning experience of our consultants changes over time and learning can take place over a lifetime. Although there are a few who can claim even half a lifetime of observation of a teaching/learning phenomenon (see Nettl, 1995), speaking more practically, longitudinal studies could be made feasible through the formation of collaborative, intergenerational teams of researchers. Indeed, it would be valuable to understand shifts in the subjective experience of learning that individuals encounter between childhood and maturity, and to understand how those shifts might be correlated with structural and cultural changes.

Communication Styles

How actors in the business of music transmission and learning organize their communication has received more attention from music educators, for example, Kushner (1995), than ethnomusicologists. Beyond the Western classroom, we know little about how students and teachers speak to each other—for example, what forms and levels of address, what kinds of talk and participant structures (see Pelissier, 1991) characterize each learning scenario? How do nonverbal channels of communication such as gesture and proxemics figure into instructional interactions? Portraits of transmission and learning that pay attention to these forms of discourse will enlighten us to the extramusical communicative competence that acquiring music demands of learners. The content of discourse, of course, is as important as its form or style. One of the insights gained from Kingsbury's (1988) close listening to conservatory talk is the extent to which transmission and learning are guided by metaphors, such as "talent," which take on different meanings in different contexts. Ethnog-

raphers might profitably ask, "What are the metaphors that organize instructional communication, when are they used, and how do they affect musical practice?"

Rethinking "Formal" and "Informal" Education

Transmission and learning do not always fall into the neat compartments that academic labels like "formal" and "informal" suggest. Nor are such labels value-free. In the field of education, "the paradigm of formal education is the style of schooling developed in the industralized West. It has been defined as deliberate, carried on 'out of context' in a special setting outside of the routines of daily life, and made the responsibility of the larger social group. 'Informal education' refers to education that takes place 'in context' as children participate in everyday adult activities. It is the predominant form in many nonindustrialized societies" (Strauss, 1984, p. 195). As Strauss notes, the dichotomy is inherently ethnocentric and tied too closely to institutional contexts (p. 198). As an alternative, she suggests "intentional" and "incidental" learning processes, distinguished by intent to remember; the former is further classified by how well or loosely defined its procedures are.

For the sake of clearly delineating the boundaries of studies, it may indeed be helpful to make distinctions between "intentional" and "incidental" modes of education, but even these separately conceptualized systems may not be so separate in practice or in the lives of our consultants. Understanding how the "intentional" and "incidental" are bridged and linked or even obviated in practice is something that could best be discovered through the ethnographic study of, say, a single individual's transmission and learning experience.

Expanding the Ethnographic Toolkit: Phenomenology

Even if we accept the categories "formal" and "informal" and treat formality as a continuum, the "informal" region of the continuum could profitably be explored using phenomenology. For example:

(1) How do listeners learn songs from the radio? Is there a hierarchy of attention to different parameters of a song that listeners invoke to facilitate their own learning? Where and how do they "practice," and how do they craft their own understandings of song learning? These kinds of questions are ideally suited to phenomenology or the close observation that living in situ facilitates.

(2) Several studies in this chapter cited self-instruction as the method for learning popular music. The way that self-learners use and interpret instructional "how-to" guides, for example, could be understood through the

application of feedback techniques, such as those used by Wineburg (1991).

(3) Nettl (1983) recommends that ethnomusicologists take the time to find out how people practice—"what activities they are actually engaging [in] when they are teaching themselves, [and] when they are carrying out the instructions of a teacher" (p. 324). If practice is "mindful," how is it so? What does the learner experience in the course of "mindless" practice? Again, a phenomenological approach, illustrated by Sudnow's (1978) self-study, could add much richness to the standard observational approach of ethnographic fieldwork.

Multidimensional Studies: Linking Research Paradigms

Although ethnographers make claims to holism, perhaps it is time to stretch the definition of this word. A multidimensional study of music transmission and learning in a particular culture might embrace both ethnographic and experimental research paradigms by following a path from external stimulus to cognitive processing to meaning-making. One possible reading of "external stimulus" could be the process of transmission and its multiple cultural variables. This would best be discovered through ethnographic technique and represented through "thick description." How individuals process particular bits of information conveyed in the course of transmission could be assessed through a controlled, culturally sensitive, experimental procedure. To round out the study, the actual meanings that individuals construct and the perceptions they achieve could be subject to phenomenological study and description.

Conclusion

The emphasis on phenomenology, on selection of consultants, and on the individual in these closing paragraphs is in some respect a preventive measure against overstating the importance of culture in music transmission and learning. Transmission and learning are socially constituted and culturally specific, but they are not determined by culture in any absolute way. Individuals working within the structure of transmission systems are certainly guided by those structures, but learners also exercise agency by manipulating them to their own ends and needs.

Finally, what is striking about the ethnomusicological and music education literatures on music transmission and learning is the degree to which they are disconnected. Music educators have generally paid much more attention to the ethnomusicological literature than ethnomusicology has to music education (see Smith, 1987). Music education's historically deep attachment to experimental meth-

ods may have contributed to this scenario. There is, however, much to be gained from an exchange of ideas and a broadening of theoretical bases. Some common ground has already been established with the use of critical theory, but the social theories that ethnomusicologists borrow from anthropology, political science, and sociology still have much to offer music educators. Likewise, ethnomusicologists would be wise to acquaint themselves with the precise analytic tools of music education, its attention to interpersonal dynamics, and theories of cognition and socialization. Movement in these directions would be a promising start for a new era of disciplinary cross-fertilization.

NOTES

1. "Consultant" is now a preferred alternative to "informant."

2. The use of qualitative research methodology, of which ethnography is a subset, was the theme of two conferences hosted by the University of Illinois in the mid-1990s. The conferences were reflective of and instrumental in the growing legitimization of an alternative research paradigm in music education. "Whereas the 1994 conference served as an 'introduction' for the music education research community to the qualitative paradigm, the 1996 event attempted to extend the agenda of the previous symposium to consider issues concerning qualitative research design, criteria for judging the process and products of qualitative investigation, the ethics of qualitative inquiry, and narrative style and voice" (Grashel, 1996, p. 1).

3. Jackson (1987) notes that, while folklorists engage in fieldwork, their aims are often different from that of anthropologists, and, by extension, ethnomusicologists. Whereas anthropologists are often long-term residents of a community outside their own, folklorists "rarely attempt to understand whole communities, and rarely do they attempt to discover and analyze a set of symbolic forms by which whole communities function. . . . The kinds of questions folklorists attempt to answer do not usually demand the total immersion required by many anthropological inquiries. Folklorists can do fieldwork evenings or on weekends; they can also do it full time for a week or month or year. They are more flexible in options than anthropologists" (p. 65).

4. The fundamental goal of phenomenology as elucidated by Edmund Husserl is description—not of things, but of one's experience of things or phenomena (Hammond, Howarth, & Keat, 1991, p. 1). Experience may be constituted in many different ways; in addition to remembering, dreaming, anticipating, and so on, an important class of experience is perception. Experience, furthermore, is intentional, which is to say that it is intended toward or is directed toward some object of perception, remembrance, and so on. As such, experience "always refers to something beyond itself and therefore cannot be characterized independently of this" (pp. 2–3). Husserl's and other phenomenologists' understanding of experience and acts of perception, however, do not require the object to exist empirically. Therefore, the thing (the phenom-

enon) to be studied in a phenomenological exploration of music is not the music itself, but the perception or experience of it. Likewise, a phenomenological exploration of music learning is not an exploration of learning behavior or pedagogical methods, but the perceptual experience of learning music. Thus, in its attempt to describe experiences of things and things as they are experienced, phenomenology stands in opposition to the positivist position: It shifts emphasis from questions about the reality of the world to questions about the contents of consciousness. In other words, meaning does not reside in an object/phenomenon but is a process of construction or interpretation; in fact, acts of perception and interpretation help to construct their objects.

5. Of his own motives and responsibilities, Pillay asks, "Does one avoid such research in the hope of steering unnecessary governmental pressure away from family, friends, and community members? Or is silence an acceptance of the given political situation? As an inside researcher with vested interests in dismantling apartheid it made sense for me to make known my findings in a forum outside the country during the state of emergency, but not to have the article printed, since many government-subsidized universities have access to [journals] there, until I was certain that the process of [political] reform was irreversible" (Pillay, 1994, p. 292).

6. In music education, ascendancy of the experimental research paradigm has made full documentation of research methodology a given. There has been, however, a distinct hierarchy of expectations for revealing details of fieldwork experience within ethnomusicology: Complete methodological documentation has been a customary requirement for dissertations, with fewer details found in book-length treatments of a subject, and almost none at all in peer-reviewed journals. Having said this, the general trend is toward greater revelation, where revelation does not compromise the safety or integrity of consultants.

7. It is important to recognize that cultural representation can take many forms. Nichols (1991) identifies different styles of documentary film and the ethical implications of each.

8. There are quite a few ethnomusicologists who have one or more degrees in anthropology, and thus refer to themselves as both anthropologists and ethnomusicologists.

9. His summary draws numerous examples from Africa primarily, and also from Native American cultures, Bali, and various parts of Oceania. That literature is not cited in this review.

10. Theoretical trends in ethnomusicology sometimes lag behind anthropology by a decade or more.

11. The inference to be drawn from these descriptions is that there are no individuals who do not participate in the musical activities of the group. All are capable of acquiring the song and dance repertoire taught them in initiation schools, although some are certainly better than others.

12. Note the use of the present tense, referred to as the "ethnographic present." Readers should not assume that the conditions that existed at the time of research and publication exist today.

13. Regarding the progress of learning, Blacking deals only with children's songs that are shared by all. The orga-

nization of social activity determines the order in which the two child song genres are acquired. For example, *ngano* are learned first, because seasonally structured social life brings children (and adults) together in late autumn and winter evenings, where such material can be learned. Contradicting the commonly held notion that music learning involves increasingly more complex cognitive tasks, Blacking claims that "children's songs are not always easier than adult songs, and children do not necessarily learn the simple songs first" (1967, p. 29).

14. Oppong (1973), published in Ghana, does not have wide circulation and is difficult to find; hence, the decision to work from Goody's summary.

15. Classical music traditions are generally identified by the presence of a professional class of musicians patronized by an elite group, for example, a court or government. Usually urban-based, musicians typically are trained in a literate tradition that stresses virtuosity.

16. *Guru*s or *ustad*s are always male, or were at the time of Neuman's research.

17. *Koto* is an instrument largely played by women.

18. For a Western-biased critique of Japanese teaching and learning methods, see Malm (1959).

19. Shehan's (1987) review of literature and Davidson's (1989) own musings do offer insight into the question of cultural ethos.

20. Another important study that addresses the learning of improvisatory jazz skills is Berliner (1994).

21. Because of rapidly changing conditions in Afghanistan, Baily and Doubleday purposely avoid use of the ethnographic present. This description follows their lead.

22. Interest in the "other" is also indicated by the work of Campbell, who has culled the ethnomusicological literature to write on song acquisition among Native Americans (1989) and the cultivation of classical musicianship in Thailand (1995a).

23. Shona daily life provides continuous exposure to traditional and syncretic genres and styles, which all children can acquire through casual aural transmission. Schoolchildren also learn British didactic songs through rote instruction and solfège.

24. Bennett's work coincides with interest in youth cultures that has its genesis in cultural studies. Hebdige's (1979) seminal work on British working-class subculture is representative of research carried out in this discipline: Short on ethnographic fieldwork, cultural studies has nonetheless focused on youth cultures and the ways that youths actively transform the meanings of cultural artifacts, including music, that circulate in the adult world. Closely aligned with the development of cultural studies is the study of popular music, and in a similar way, contemporary popular music's focus on youth cultures has given added legitimacy to studying the musical practices of this demographic group.

25. As always, there are important exceptions to this generalization. Botkin (1963 [1937]) provides rich and insightful, if somewhat brief, social contextualization for his collection of American youths' play-party songs. Regrettably, he does not address their transmission or learning.

26. Sutton-Smith is a folklorist.

REFERENCES

Adachi, M. (1994). The role of the adult in the child's early musical socialization: A Vygotskian perspective. *The Quarterly Journal of Music Teaching and Learning, 5*(3), 26–35.

Addo, A. O. (1997). Children's idiomatic expressions of cultural knowledge. *International Journal of Music Education, 30,* 15–25.

Baily, J., & Doubleday, V. (1990). Patterns of musical enculturation in Afghanistan. In F. R. Wilson and F. L. Roehmann (Eds.), *Music and child development: Proceedings of the 1987 Denver conference* (pp. 88–99). St. Louis, MO: MMB Music Inc.

Barber, R. J., & Berdan, F. F. (1998). *The emperor's mirror: Understanding cultures through primary sources.* Tucson: University of Arizona Press.

Bamberger, J., & Ziporyn, E. (1992). Getting it wrong. *The World of Music, 34*(3), 22–56.

Becker, H. S. (1983). Studying urban schools. *Anthropology and Education Quarterly, 14*(2), 99–108.

Bennett, H. S. (1980). *On becoming a rock musician.* Amherst, MA: University of Massachusetts Press.

Berger, H. M. (1999). *Metal, rock, and jazz: Perception and the phenomenology of musical experience.* Hanover, NH: Wesleyan University Press.

Berliner, P. (1978). *The soul of mbira.* Berkeley: University of California Press.

Berliner, P. (1994). *Thinking in jazz: The infinite art of improvisation.* Chicago: University of Chicago Press.

Blacking, J. (1967). *Venda children's songs: A study in ethnomusicological analysis.* Johannesburg: Witwatersrand University Press.

Blacking, J. (1971). Towards a theory of musical competence. In E. J. de Jager (Ed.), *Man: Anthropological essays presented to O. F. Raum* (pp. 19–34). Cape Town: C. Struik.

Blacking, J. (1973). *How musical is man?* Seattle: University of Washington Press.

Blum, S. (1992). Analysis of Musical Style. In H. Myers (Ed.), *Ethnomusicology: An introduction* (pp. 165–218). New York: W. W. Norton.

Booth, G. (1987). The North Indian oral tradition: Lessons for music education. *International Journal of Music Education, 9,* 7–9.

Booth, G. (1996). The transmission of a classical improvisatory performance practice. *International Journal of Music Education, 26,* 14–26.

Botkin, B. A. (1963). *The American play-party song.* New York: Frederick Ungar. (Original work published in 1937).

Bourdieu, P. (1973). Cultural reproduction and social reproduction. In R. Brown (Ed.), *Knowledge, education and cultural change* (pp. 71–112). London: Tavistock.

Bresler, L. (1993). The social organization of achievement: A case-study of a music theory class. *Curriculum Journal, 4*(1), 37–58.

Bresler, L. (1995). Ethical issues in qualitative research methodology. *Bulletin of the Council of Research in Music Education, 123,* 33–41.

Brinner, B. (1995). *Knowing music, making music: Javanese gamelan and the study of musical competence and interaction.* Berkeley: University of California Press.

Bruner, E. M. (1986). Ethnography as narrative. In V. Turner & E. Bruner (Eds.), *The anthropology of experience* (pp. 139–155). Urbana: University of Illinois Press.

Bulletin of the Council of Research in Music Education, 122 (1994). Special Issue: Qualitative Methodologies in Music Education Research Conference.

Bulletin of the Council of Research in Music Education, 130 (1996). Special Issue: Qualitative Methodologies in Music Education Research Conference II.

Campbell, P. (1989). Music learning and song acquisition among Native Americans. *International Journal of Music Education, 14,* 24–31.

Campbell, P. (1995a). The making of musicians and musical audiences in Thailand. *International Journal of Music Education, 25,* 20–28.

Campbell, P. (1995b). Of garage bands and song-getting: The musical development of young rock musicians. *Research Studies in Music Education, 4,* 12–20.

Campbell, P. (1998). *Songs in their heads: Music and its meaning in children's lives.* New York: Oxford University Press.

Caputo, V. (1995). Anthropology's silent 'others': A consideration of some conceptual and methodological issues for the study of youth and children's cultures. In V. Amit-Talai & H. Wulff (Eds.), *Youth cultures: A cross-cultural perspective* (pp. 19–42). London: Routledge.

Chernoff, J. M. (1979). *African rhythm and African sensibility: Aesthetics and social action in African musical idioms.* Chicago: University of Chicago Press.

Clifford, J. (1986). Introduction; Partial truths. In J. Clifford & G. E. Marcus (Eds.), *Writing culture: The poetics and politics of ethnography* (pp. 1–26). Berkeley: University of California Press.

Collier, J., & Collier, M. (1986). *Visual anthropology: Photography as a research method.* Rev. and exp. ed. Albuquerque: University of New Mexico Press.

Cortazzi, M. (1993). *Narrative analysis.* London: Falmer Press.

Davidson, L. (1989). Observing a yang ch'in lesson: Learning by modeling and metaphor. *Journal of Aesthetic Education, 23*(1), 85–99.

Della Pietra, C. J., & Campbell, P. S. (1995). An ethnography of improvisation training in a music methods course. *Journal of Research in Music Education, 43*(2), 112–126.

Ellingson, T. (1992a). Transcription. In H. Myers (Ed.), *Ethnomusicology: An introduction* (pp. 110–152). New York: W. W. Norton.

Ellingson, T. (1992b). Notation. In H. Myers (Ed.), *Ethnomusicology: An introduction* (pp. 153–164). New York: W. W. Norton.

Feld, S. (1987). Dialogic editing: Interpreting how Kaluli read sound and sentiment. *Cultural Anthropology, 2*(2), 190–210.

Fine, G. A. (1995). Methodological problems of collecting folklore from children. In B. Sutton-Smith, J. Mechling, T. W. Johnson, & F. R. McMahon (Eds.), *Children's folklore: A source book* (pp. 121–139). New York: Garland.

Finnegan, R. (1989). *The hidden musicians: Music-making in an English town.* Cambridge: Cambridge University Press.

Finnegan, R. (1992). *Oral traditions and the verbal arts: A guide to research practices.* London: Routledge.

Fowke, Edith. (1969). *Sally go round the sun: 300 songs, rhymes and games of Canadian children.* Toronto: McClelland and Stewart.

Garrison, V. (1985). *Traditional and non-traditional teaching and learning practices in folk music: An ethnographic field study of Cape Breton fiddling.* Unpublished dissertation, University of Wisconsin, Madison.

Gaunt, K. D. (1997). *The games Black girls play: Music, body, and "soul."* Unpublished dissertation, University of Michigan, Ann Arbor.

Geertz, C. (1973). *The interpretation of cultures: Selected essays.* New York: Basic Books.

Geertz, C. (1983). "From the native's point of view": On the nature of anthropological understanding. In *Local knowledge: Further essays in interpretive anthropology* (pp. 55–69). New York: Basic Books.

Giddens, A. (1984). *The constitution of society: Outline of the theory of structuration.* Cambridge, MA: Polity Press.

Goetz, J. P., & LeCompte, M. D. (1981). Ethnographic research and the problem of data reduction. *Anthropology and Education Quarterly, 12*(1), 51–70.

Goffman, E. (1973). *The presentation of self in everyday life.* Woodstock, NY: Overlook Press.

Gomme, A. B. (1964). *The traditional games of England, Scotland and Ireland.* Repr. New York: Dover. (Original work published 1894)

Goody, E. N. (1982). Traditional states: Responses to hierarchy and differentiation. In *Parenthood and social reproduction: Fostering and occupational roles in West Africa* (pp. 110–142). Cambridge: Cambridge University Press.

Goody, J. (1968). Introduction. In J. Goody (Ed.), *Literacy in traditional societies* (pp. 1–26). Cambridge: Cambridge University Press.

Goody, J., & Watt, I. (1968). The consequences of literacy. In J. Goody (Ed.), *Literacy in traditional societies* (pp. 27–84). Cambridge: Cambridge University Press.

Grashel, J. (1996). Introduction. *Bulletin of the Council for Research in Music Education, 130,* 1.

Hammersley M., & Atkinson, P. (1995). *Ethnography: Principles in practice.* New York: Routledge.

Hammond, M., Howarth, J., & Keat, R. (1991). *Understanding phenomenology.* Cambridge, MA: Basil Blackwell.

Harwood, E. (1992). Girls' handclapping games: A study in oral transmission. *Bulletin of the International Kodály Society, 17*(1), 19–25.

Hebdige, D. (1979.) *Subculture: The meaning of style.* London: Methuen.

Herndon, M., & Ziegler, S. (Eds.). (1990). *Music, gender, and culture.* Wilhelmshaven, Germany: Florian Noetzel Verlag.

Hood, M. (1960). The challenge of bi-musicality. *Ethnomusicology 4,* 55–59.

Ives, E. D. (1980). *The tape-recorded interview: A manual for field workers in folklore and oral history.* Knoxville: University of Tennessee Press.

Jackson, B. (1987). *Fieldwork.* Urbana: University of Illinois Press.

Jones, B., & Hawes, B. L. (1972). *Step it down: Games, plays, songs, and stories from the Afro-American heritage.* New York: Harper & Row.

Kelley, M., & Sutton-Smith, B. (1987). A study of infant musical productivity. In J. C. Peery, I. W. Peery, & W. Thomas (Eds.), *Music and child development* (pp. 35–53). New York: Springer-Verlag.

Kingsbury, H. (1988). *Music, talent, and performance: A conservatory cultural system.* Philadelphia: Temple University Press.

Klinger, R. (1996). From glockenspiel to mbira: An ethnography of multicultural practice in music education. *Bulletin of the Council for Research in Music Education, 129,* 29–36.

Knapp, M., & Knapp, H. (1976). *One potato, two potato: The secret education of American children.* New York: W. W. Norton.

Knight, R. C. (1973). *Mandinka jaliya: Professional music of the Gambia.* Unpublished dissertation, University of California, Los Angeles.

Koskoff, E. (Ed.). (1989). *Women and music in cross-cultural perspective.* Urbana/Chicago: University of Illinois Press.

Kreuger, P. J. (1987). Ethnographic research methodology in music education. *Journal of Research in Music Education, 35*(2), 69–77.

Kreutzer, N. J. (1997). *The nature of music acquisition among selected Shona-speaking people of rural Zimbabwe as reflected in the vocal productions of children from birth to seven years.* Unpublished dissertation, Indiana University, Bloomington.

Kurokawa, Y. (2000). Hula halau in Tokyo—A case study of hula schools. *Perfect Beat, 4*(4), 61–72.

Kushner, S. (1991a). Musicians go to school: A case of knowledge, control, and cross-professional action. *American Educational Research Journal, 28*(2), 275–296.

Kushner, S. (1991b). *The children's music book: Performing musicians in school.* London: Calouste Gulbenkian Foundation.

Kushner, S. (1995). Learning from experience: The construction of naturalistic methodology for evaluating music education. *Bulletin of the Council for Research in Music Education, 123,* 97–111.

LeCompte, M. D., & Goetz, J. P. (1982). Problems of reliability and validity in ethnographic research. *Review of Educational Research, 52*(1), 31–60.

Malm, W. P. (1959). *Japanese music and musical instruments.* Rutland, VT: Charles E. Tuttle.

Mans, M. E. (1997). *Namibian music and dance as ngoma in arts education.* Unpublished doctoral dissertation, University of Natal, Durban, South Africa.

Marsh, K. (2001). It's not all black or white: The influence of the media, the classroom and immigrant groups on children's playground singing games. In J. C. Bishop & M.

Curtis (Eds.), *Play today in the primary school playground: Life, learning and creativity* (pp. 80–97). Buckingham, UK: Open University Press.

Marsh, K. (1995). Children's singing games: Composition in the playground. *Research Studies in Music Education,* (4), 2–11.

Mbanugo, C. E. (1986). *Music transmission processes among children in an Afro-American church.* Unpublished doctoral dissertation, State University of New York at Buffalo.

McLuhan, M. (1962). *The Gutenberg galaxy; The making of typographic man.* Toronto: University of Toronto Press.

Merriam, A. P. (1964). Learning. In *The anthropology of music* (pp. 145–164). Evanston, IL: Northwestern University Press.

Merriam, A. P. (1973). The Bala musician. In Warren L. d'Azevedo (Ed.), *The traditional artist in African societies* (pp. 250–281). Bloomington: Indiana University Press.

Merriam, A. P. (1982). *African music in perspective.* New York: Garland.

Merrill-Mirsky, C. (1988). *Eeny meeny pepsadeeny: Ethnicity and gender in children's musical play.* Unpublished doctoral dissertation, University of California, Los Angeles.

Myerhoff, B., & Ruby, J. (1982). Introduction. In J. Ruby (Ed.), *A crack in the mirror: Reflexive perspectives in anthropology* (pp. 1–35). Philadelphia: University of Pennsylvania Press.

Mitchell, F. (1978). *Navajo Blessingway singer: The autobiography of Frank Mitchell, 1881–1967.* C. J. Frisbie & D. P. McAllester (Eds.), Tucson: University of Arizona Press.

Motegi, K. (1984). Aural learning in *gidayu-bushi*: Music of the Japanese puppet theatre. *Yearbook for Traditional Music, 16,* 97–108.

Myers, H. (1992a). Fieldwork. In H. Myers (Ed.), *Ethnomusicology: An introduction* (pp. 21–49). New York: W. W. Norton.

Myers-Moro, P. (1993). *Thai music and musicians in contemporary Bangkok.* Berkeley: Centers for South and Southeast Asia Studies, University of California at Berkeley.

Nettl, B. (1983). How do you get to Carnegie Hall? In *The study of ethnomusicology; Twenty-nine issues and concepts* (pp. 323–332). Urbana: University of Illinois Press.

Nettl, B. (1989). *Blackfoot musical thought: Comparative perspectives.* Kent, OH: Kent State University Press.

Nettl, B. (1995). *Heartland excursions: Ethnomusicological reflections on schools of music.* Urbana: University of Illinois Press.

Neuman, D. M. (1980). Becoming a musician. In *The life of music in North India: The organization of an artistic tradition* (pp. 30–58). Detroit, MI: Wayne State University Press.

Newell, W. W. (1963). *Games and songs of American children.* Repr. New York: Dover. (Original work published 1883)

Nichols, B. (1991). *Representing reality: Issues and concepts in documentary.* Bloomington: Indiana University Press.

Nketia, J. H. K. (1973). The musician in Akan society. In W. L. d'Azevedo (Ed.), *The traditional artist in African societies* (pp. 79–100). Bloomington: Indiana University Press.

Ogbu, J. U. (1981). School ethnography: A multilevel approach. *Anthropology and Education Quarterly, 12*(1), 3–29.

Opie, I., & Opie, P. (1985). *The singing game.* Oxford: Oxford University Press.

Oppong, C. (1973). *Growing up in Dagbon.* Accra: n.p.

Pecore, J. T. (2000). Bridging contexts, transforming music: The case of elementary school teacher Chihara Yoshio. *Ethnomusicology, 44*(1), 120–136.

Pelissier, C. (1991). The anthropology of teaching and learning. *Annual Review of Anthropology, 20,* 75–95.

Pillay, J. (1994). Indian music in the Indian school in South Africa: The use of cultural forms as a political tool. *Ethnomusicology, 38*(2), 281–301.

Post, J. (1989). Professional women in Indian music: The death of the courtesan tradition. In E. Koskoff (Ed.), *Women and music in cross-cultural perspective* (pp. 97–109). Urbana: University of Illinois Press.

Quiquemelle, M-C. (1994). *The education of a singer at the Beijing Opera.* VHS, 26 mins. Princeton: Films for the Humanities and Sciences.

Radcliffe-Brown, A. R. (1952). *Structure and function in primitive society: Essays and addresses.* London: Routledge & Kegan Paul.

Read, C., & Locke, D. (1983). An analysis of the Yamada-ryu Sokyoku iemoto system. *Hogaku, 1*(1), 20–52.

Rice, T. (1988). Understanding three-part singing in Bulgaria: The interplay of theory and experience. *Selected Reports in Ethnomusicology, 7,* 43–57.

Rice, T. (1994). *May it fill your soul: Experiencing Bulgarian music.* Chicago: University of Chicago Press.

Rice, T. (1996). Traditional and modern methods of learning and teaching music in Bulgaria. *Research Studies in Music Education, 7,* 1–12.

Riddell, C. (1990). *Traditional singing games of elementary school children in Los Angeles.* Unpublished doctoral dissertation, University of California, Berkeley.

Sanjek, R. (Ed.). (1990). *Fieldnotes: The makings of anthropology.* Ithaca, NY: Cornell University Press.

Seeger, A. (1992). Ethnomusicology and music law. *Ethnomusicology, 36*(3), 345–359.

Seeger, C. (1977). Prescriptive and descriptive music writing. In *Studies in musicology, 1935–1975* (pp. 168–181). Berkeley: University of California Press.

Shankar, R. (1968). *My music, my life.* n.p.: Vikas Publications.

Shehan, P. (1987). The oral transmission of music in selected Asian cultures. *Bulletin of the Council for Research in Music Education, 92,* 1–14.

Shepherd, J. C. (1979). Music and social control: An essay on the sociology of musical knowledge. *Catalyst, 13,* 1–54.

Shepherd, J., & Vulliamy, G. (1983). A comparative sociology of school knowledge. *British Journal of Sociology of Education, 4*(1), 3–18.

Slobin, M. (1992). Ethical Issues. In H. Myers (Ed.), *Ethnomusicology: An introduction* (pp. 329–336). New York: W. W. Norton.

Smith, B. B. (1987). Variability, change, and the learning of music. *Ethnomusicology, 31*(2), 201–220.

Society for Ethnomusicology. (1994). *A manual for documentation: Fieldwork & preservation for ethnomusicologists.* n.p.: Society for Ethnomusicology.

Society for Ethnomusicology Ethics Committee. (1999). Ethical considerations. *SEM Newsletter, 33*(1), 10.

Sosniak, L. A. (1985). Phases in learning. In B.S. Bloom (Ed.), *Developing talent in young people* (pp. 409–438). New York: Ballantine Books.

Spearritt, G. D. (1995). No practising in public: The training of musicians in a Middle Sepik society. In F. Callaway (Ed.), *Essays in honour of David Evatt Tunley* (pp. 177–190). Nedlands, Australia: CIRCME.

Stake, R., Bresler, L., & Mabry, L. (1991). *Custom and cherishing: The arts in elementary schools.* Champaign: National Arts Education Research Center, University of Illinois.

Stellaccio, C. K. (1995). *Theory to practice: An ethnographic analysis of multicultural curriculum and pedagogy in elementary general music.* Unpublished doctoral dissertation, University of Maryland, College Park.

Strauss, A. (1987). *Qualitative analysis for social scientists.* New York: Cambridge University Press.

Strauss, A., & Corbin, J. (1998). *Basics of qualitative research: Techniques and procedures for developing grounded theory.* 2nd ed. Thousand Oaks, CA: Sage Publications.

Strauss, C. (1984). Beyond "formal" versus "informal" education: Uses of psychological theory in anthropological research. *Ethos, 12*(3), 195–222.

Sudnow, D. (1978). *Ways of the hand: The organization of improvised conduct.* Cambridge, MA: MIT Press.

Szego, C. (1999). *Musical meaning-making in an intercultural environment: The case of Kamehameha Schools.* Unpublished doctoral dissertation, University of Washington, Seattle.

Trimillos, R. D. (1983). The formalized transmission of culture: Selectivity in traditional teaching/learning systems in four high skill music traditions. *East-West Culture Learning Institute, 9*(1/2), 1–9.

Trimillos, R. D. (1989). Hālau, Hochschule, Maystro,
and Ryū: Cultural approaches to music learning and teaching. *International Journal of Music Education, 14,* 32–43.

Veblen, K. K. (1991). *Perceptions of change and stability in the transmission of Irish traditional music: An examination of the music teacher's role.* Unpublished doctoral dissertation, University of Wisconsin, Madison.

Veblen, K. K. (1996). Truth, perceptions, and cultural construct in ethnographic research: Music teaching and learning in Ireland. *Bulletin of the Council for Research in Music Education, 129,* 37–52.

Vulliamy, G. (1977). Music as a case study in the 'new sociology of education.' In J. Shepherd, et al. (Eds.), *Whose music? A sociology of musical languages* (pp. 201–232). New Brunswick, NJ: Transaction Books.

Wachsmann, K. P. (1966). Negritude in music. *Composer, 19,* 12–15.

Waterman, R. A. (1955). Music in Australian aboriginal culture—Some sociological and psychological implications. *Journal of Music Therapy, 5,* 40–50.

Widdess, R. (1994). Involving the performers in transcription and analysis: A collaborative approach to *dhrupad. Ethnomusicology, 38*(1), 59–80.

Wiggins, J. H. (1994). Children's strategies for solving compositional problems with peers. *Journal of Research in Music Education, 42*(3), 232–252.

Wineburg, S. S. (1991). On the reading of historical texts: Notes on the breach between school and academy. *American Educational Research Journal, 28*(3), 495–519.

Wong, D. (1991). *The empowered teacher: Ritual, performance, and epistemology in contemporary Bangkok.* Unpublished doctoral dissertation, University of Michigan, Ann Arbor.

Yamada, Y. (1983). Musical performance as a means of socialization among the Iatmoi. *Bikmaus, 4*(3), 2–16.

Zemp, H. (1971). Éducation musicale. In *Musique Dan; La musique dans la pensée et la vie social d'une société Africaine.* Paris: Mouton & Co.

Zemp, H. (1988). Filming music and looking at music films. *Ethnomusicology, 23*(3), 393–427.

Community Music

Toward an International Overview

39

KARI VEBLEN

BENGT OLSSON

Music teaching and learning takes place in many different contexts, from formal to informal. There often is affiliation, reciprocity, overlap, or cross-fertilization between more structured and less structured settings. This chapter examines various facets of music in the community, as distinct from music education in K–12, or higher education frameworks. Because of its inclusive nature, this subject naturally overlaps with chapters 10, 11, and 16 (early childhood and adult education, technology); chapters 44 and 45 (teaching in urban and rural environments, in community settings); and chapter 47 (initiatives of community music and cultural organizations with schools). We focus on the contexts of community music in an international perspective and seek to provide complementary research to these other, more specific treatments.

Community music is pervasive and an integral part of cultures worldwide. Limitations of our literature search such as language barriers and uneven or inaccessible documentation constrain us, however, to emphasize those settings in which community music is formally named, described, and documented.

What Is Community Music?

What is community music? How is the term "community music" defined worldwide? What are common characteristics? Are there representative activities and settings?

Although defined differently internationally, all definitions concur that community music concerns people making music. For music educators, this term implies opportunities for participation and education through a wide range of mediums, musics, and musical experiences. Community music (CM) activities and programs often are based on the premise that everyone has the right and ability to make and create music.

Consider the following possible scenarios for CM activities: church choirs; brass bands; local orchestras; music programs for the young; Elderhostel; singalongs at the seniors' center; ethnic celebrations; parades; fêtes; festivals; Internet users; fan clubs; chat rooms; youth bands (rock, garage, punk, and the latest thing); adult barbershop quartets; doo-whop singing; nonprofit coffeehouses with local performers; barn dances, contra dances and square dances with live musicians; the local jazz "scene"; recorder ensembles; bell ringers; local music schools; private piano studios; and voice lessons in the home. This can only be a partial list of music-making possibilities.

Perhaps music making is the sole purpose of the gathering, or perhaps it is one of several purposes. Common characteristics may be traced through these different settings. CM should be viewed more as a dynamic and vital force, however, rather than limited to any fixed set of factors.

Characteristics of Community Music

Community Music involves active participation in music making of all kinds (performing, improvising, and creating).[1] The kinds of music employed encompass a wide range and diversity of musics, as seen from the list of scenarios here. Music may occur with cultural events, folkways, and other arts. The music may reflect the cultural life of a geographical community, re-created community, or imagined community.

Musical communities take many forms. While music-making groups may crystallize into unique structures, there are certain characteristics that facilitate positive group dynamics. Procedures and structures don't seem to be fixed determinants. There may be a conductor, people may take turns leading and following, or there may be a collective.

In many musical groups, membership is voluntary and self-selected. The individual has freedom within the group to explore new roles. One reoccurring theme in musical communities concerns the fluidity of knowledge, expertise, and available roles. The individual has the ability to move through a variety of roles, from observer, to participant, to shaper and creator, finding different ways to participate. There is a sense of individual responsibility to the group and a reciprocal sense of group responsibility to the individual. Identity and self-expression are potent factors within the collective; belonging, coding, immigration, assimilation, and globalization are all played out through musical communities.

Similarly, community music activities may involve a wide range of participants—from early childhood through older adulthood, and may be intergenerational in some instances. There is frequently an awareness of the need to include disenfranchised and disadvantaged individuals or groups. Sometimes the efforts are part of the mission of a community center, settlement house, or church. Music making may be part of an outreach effort in social work situations, including youth intervention programs, prisons, hospitals, institutions, and care facilities. Implicit in these programs is the recognition that participants' social and personal growth is as important as their musical growth. Often there is a belief in the value and use of music to foster intercultural and interpersonal acceptance and understanding. Many programs stress the acknowledgment of both individual and group ownership of musics and respect for the cultural property of a given community.

The development of active musical knowing (including verbal musical knowledge, where appropriate) is stressed. Typically, CM fosters multiple learner/teacher relationships and processes including models of apprenticeship and partnership. Within musical systems, learner and instructor may collaborate; interaction may take place within a group setting, but there is room for unique expression and individual instruction. There may be flexible teaching, utilizing a variety of learning and facilitation modes such as oral, notational, holistic, experiential, and analytic. Processes may be emphasized over products of music making. See table 39.1 for a summary of CM characteristics.

Because this aspect of music education is both heavily documented in some instances and scantily researched, if at all, in others, this chapter will explore community music activity through three complementary lenses:

- Ethnomusicological and sociological research on music teaching and learning practices outside formal schooling

Table 39.1 Characteristics of community music activities

- Emphasis on a variety and diversity of musics that reflect and enrich the cultural life of the community and of the participants
- Active participation in music making of all kinds (performing, improvising, and creating)
- Development of active musical knowing (including verbal musical knowledge, where appropriate)
- Multiple learner/teacher relationships and processes
- Commitment to lifelong musical learning and access for all members of the community
- Awareness of the need to include disenfranchised and disadvantaged individuals or groups
- Recognition that participants' social and personal growth are as important as their musical growth
- Belief in the value and use of music to foster intercultural acceptance and understanding
- Respect for the cultural property of a given community and acknowledgment of both individual and group ownership of musics
- Ongoing commitment to accountability through regular and diverse assessment and evaluation procedures
- Fostering of personal delight and confidence in individual creativity
- Flexible teaching, learning, and facilitation modes (oral, notational, holistic, experiential, analytic)
- Excellence/quality in both the processes and products of music making relative to individual goals of participants
- Honoring of origins and intents of specific musical practices

- Emerging field of professional music education/service
- International trends: networks and services

Music Teaching and Learning Practices Inside and Outside Formal Schooling

This section focuses on ethnographies and sociological studies with implications for music education. Because of the volume and variety of information available to us, we make a distinction between research (in-depth inquiry: for example, a doctoral dissertation) and research-based studies (interpretive articles that use data from other sources). This section presents geographically diverse research, which is organized thematically.

Ethnomusicological and Sociological Studies of Community Music

The fields of ethnomusicology and sociology offer significant models for research in CM as well as for music education.[2] There are many ethnographies of music making in different localities conducted over the past 300 years;[3] however, recent interest in issues of affinity groups, identity, changing media of transmission, globalization, and other determinants expressed through musical communities have prompted a new wave of studies. Sociological macro perspectives exploring connections between sounds and society (Martin, 1995) are reformulated in micro studies within community music through themes such as local musical values within institutions and communities, identity as musician or teacher, formal/informal teaching and learning, and authenticity in performances.[4]

Musical Worlds, Associations, and Scenes. A number of scholars are interested in concepts of cultural alliances and associations. The anthropologist Arjun Appadurai proposes new ways to think about everyday life and mass-mediated public culture.[5] Appadurai (1990)[6] suggests that culture can be experienced as concurrent technoscapes, finanscapes, mediascapes, ethnoscapes, and ideoscapes. In his formulation, the global movements of technology, resources, images and words, peoples, and ideas allow individuals to inhabit many different spheres simultaneously.[7]

Finnegan's (1989) *Hidden Musicians: Music-making in an English Town* explores the parallel musical worlds existing within a single English town. Finnegan also notes the relationships between local and outside musical institutions. She considers and discards the terms "community" and "network" as too closed and geographically bound in favor of "musical pathways" to describe the fluid, complex, and dynamic relationships she found. Similarly, in popular music studies, Cohen (1991, 1999) and others use the term "scene" to describe and negotiate differences between locally grounded and more fluid and mobile music connections.[8]

Affinity Groups and Identity

Slobin (1993) examines the rich interplay of musical-cultural identities within pluralistic societies and suggests why being a part of a music-making group may be all-absorbing for some individuals:

> The central fact is that today music is at the heart of individual, group, and national identity, from the personal to the political, from the refugee mother's lullaby to the "Star-Spangled Banner" at the baseball game. (p.11)

Competing cultural dynamics are revealed through "small musics in big systems." Slobin describes "micromusics" or "subcultural sounds" as the smaller units, which affirm cultural identity within a dominant musical superculture. Groups include communities linked by performers or instructors and personal webs of contact. He suggests that: "Their nature—personal, dynamic, and interactive—may ensure their continuing existence."[9]

Slobin discusses three overlapping spheres of cultural activity: "choice," "belonging," and "affinity groups." He characterizes affinity groups as "a jointly imagined world that arises from a set of separate strivings temporarily fused at a moment of common musical purpose" (p. 60).

Hast (1994) uses Slobin's model of affinity groups as she illustrates how community is formed around the expressive culture in New England contra dance. She notes factors that attract musicians and callers as well as dancers into this community. Herman (1997) considered the attraction of sacred harp singing to modern secular groups in California. This American genre of hymn singing has spread beyond its southern religious contexts to become widespread in the United States over the past 20 years.[10]

Transmission in affinity groups may rely on sharing between enthusiasts, neighbors, and family. Burton (in press) documented intergenerational group playing and learning in fiddle music of central Texas communities. Tunnell and Groce (1998) observed that family and community were very influential in formative identity of semiprofessional bluegrass musicians.

Other recent studies investigate affinity groups centered around jazz, heavy metal, rock, and other popular genres.[11] In addition to communities that perform music together, there are musical affinity groups that may never meet face-to-face. Research is just emerging concerning virtual music communities and new modes of interacting using the latest media.[12]

A number of studies explore how individuals express identities through the medium/community of a musical genre. Pierson (1998) uses ethnographic case studies to chronicle how Estonian people protested Soviet repression in the "Singing Revolution." Estonians customarily congregate every 5 years for song festivals at which church, youth, and traditional musics are sung. A gathering in 1988 became the focal point for peaceful protest. By 1991, the Estonians regained their independence. Other examples of political action through music include poignant studies of communities past and present.[13] Ake (1998) explores the musics and related identities generated through various jazz genres through the 20th century. The communities, historical contexts, influential performers, images, and commodifications of jazz are examined, as well as the influences of programs in jazz education at the college level. The relationship between performer and community is the subject of Beisswenger's 1997 dissertation on Melvin Wine. Beisswenger analyzes how this West Virginian fiddler draws on his Appalachian community and family traditions, simultaneously reinforcing community and satisfying personal musical goals.

A number of recent ethnographies link music making, identity, and immigrant or diasporic communities.[14] Burdette (1997) analyzes a German American singing society in Indiana. He found that the participants shared common ethnic heritage, but not much knowledge about German culture or language. Consequently, as the singers seek to create "gemutlichkeit" or social harmony through song and attending rites, they create complex identities combining old and new elements. Moloney (1992) documents continuity and change in Irish music in America. He notes many factors that contribute to the vibrancy of this music, including the nature of transmission and multiplicity of social contexts. Diehl's (1998) work addresses Tibetan refugees in north India, with a focus on new music being made by the Tibetan youth. The young musicians seek their own voice using music from their homeland and a complex palate of new sounds.

Nebesh (1998) investigated the Ukrainian diaspora through music and dance. She finds that Ukrainians remaining in their homeland preserve and continue their music as part of their identity. The immigrant community she researched in Pennsylvania, however, seeks to construct a Ukrainian-American identity. Cherwick (1999) investigated Ukrainian polka bands performing in the Canadian prairie provinces, noting influences of commercial recordings, hybridization with country and western music in the 1960s, increased ethnic awareness, and rising popularity. Zhang's (1994) study of Chinese-American communities in the San Francisco Bay area notes that the first immigrants use music to assimilate, while the second- and third-generation Chinese Americans use music to find and assert new identity. Zhang concludes that musical communities in the Bay area preserve older styles and also help develop new Asian-American musical genres.

The concept identity is also discussed within teacher training in terms of a tension between a musician code and a teacher code (Bouij, 1998a, 1998b; Roberts, 1990, 1993). In his 1990 study of Canadian teacher training, Roberts discusses how students construct identities such as "performer" or "musician" during their studies at the university. Roberts notes that there is a continual tension between official teachers' models within the institution "for who they are and who they are to become."

Bouij (1998) emphasizes the concept "role-identity," which embraces the students "imaginative view" of themselves as they like to think of themselves being and acting during their teacher training. During the process of socialization within the teacher-training departments, Bouij distinguishes different role identities from the point of view of the professional roles that students see ahead of them (teacher or musician) and what degree of musical comprehensiveness they see as being adequate for this professional role. Bouij refers to broad and narrow comprehensiveness and shows that the institutionalized teacher training tends to focus only on the roles of a narrow mainstream performer and strong teacher, and thereby neglects other possible role identities more closely linked to the heterogeneous musical life of the communities.

Formal/Informal Settings and Authenticity

A Swedish study concluded that music teaching and learning occurs differently in informal settings (such as youth clubs and teenagers' homes), and formal institutions (such as music schools) (Gullberg, 1999). Other research in various geographic settings (Cohen, 1991; Finnegan, 1989; Heiling, 2000; Sernhede, 1995; Stålhammar, 1995; Thornton, 1995) investigated learning through peer group spontaneous activities. Such unplanned group activities were described as voluntary, informal, and open, as opposed to the enforcement, institutionalization, and target orientation of schooling. Fornäs et al. (1995) considered the learning processes in three different teenage rock bands in three Swedish cities. They found different learning "worlds" typical of the bands: the objective world or external learning directed toward the material world (practical competence and cognitive knowledge); the shared world or the intersubjective learning (cultural and relational skills); and the subjective world or learning of the inner world (self-knowledge, identity, and expression). The authors stress that these learning processes qualify the individual for both the fields of music and life in general. Sernhede (1995) further emphasizes these new learning processes in relation to creativity during adolescence. He found that teenagers form their identity through musical experiences and activities outside school, rather than within the narrower framework of the target-oriented school world.[15]

Stålhammar (1995) takes a similar approach in his investigation of a music project in a Swedish public or compulsory school involving instrumental tutors from the community music school. Different aspects of the concept "musical experience" are developed in order to explain why different obstacles in education are salient. The musical expectations of the participants—mainly the pupils—played a crucial role and, when their subjective experiences were considered to be important, both interaction and creativity were driven forward.

Studies within ethnomusicology, anthropology, and sociology have in many ways challenged traditional forms of music education and tuition within different institutions. Music teaching and learning in outreach settings of a variety of communities has been emphasized as an alternative to music education in schools and universities. The issue of formal/informal training has its starting point in these alternatively based research perspectives. Furthermore, methodological models and techniques borrowed from ethnomusicology and related fields have influenced research within music education and teacher training as well.

From the perspective of traditional music education, this tension between formal/informal training has much in common with the classic dichotomy of theory/practice. The distinction between theories of socially shared learning and theories of cognitive development is treated as a contradiction, instead of using productively their differing foci, methodologies, and empirical work.[16] Many of the people involved in community music projects lack economic support from local, regional, or national funding sources. By contrast, universities and local music schools have become aware of the need for educating musicians and music teachers for community outreach.

A different approach to the same discussion about the relationship between teacher training and community music has prompted Olsson (1993, 1997) to investigate how "new musical styles and genres"—rock, jazz, folk music—were implemented within Swedish music teacher training. Two concepts are emphasized—context-dependent and context-independent instrumental tuition—in order to bring the relationship between context and transfer of knowledge and teaching into focus. Context-dependent or content-based instrumental tuition is closely connected to musical values and views of knowledge integrated in certain contexts, that is, the ways musicians in a certain context perform, value, and transfer the core aspects of a certain style are directly transformed into the tuition process. The dependence aspect implies an adaptation of learning processes to musical practices typical for the local community. The context-independent transfer of knowledge, by contrast, is more related to institutional rules independent of local musical values and qualities.

Cohen (1991) presents empirically the attitudes of rehearsing and composing within two different bands from the perspective of context-dependence. Lilliestam (1995) focuses on "oral traditions" and principles of learning in terms of imitation from records and "playing by ear." Finnegan (1991) treats the formal-informal aspect as the contrast between the classical mode of professional and formalized teaching by recognized specialists and the self-taught or apprentice-type process of the more popular music traditions.[17]

Another salient concept emerging from many sociological studies about formal and informal teaching and learning is "authenticity" and "authentic learning environments" (Farrell, 1991, 1997; Hemphill-Peoples, 1992; Johnson, 2000; Norfleet, 1997; Olsson, 2001; Palmer, 1992; Ruud, 1996, 1997; Stokes, 1994), emphasizing social aspects of musical learning. "Authenticity" as a concept is considered frequently in world musics literature (Johnson, 2000). Factors seen as crucial to authenticity are context and purpose. Palmer (1992) asks "to what degree compromise is acceptable before the essence of music is lost and no longer representative of the tradition under study" (p. 32).

The principles behind authentic learning environments predominantly are linked to theories of socially shared learning: They emphasize collective, contextual, and informal learning settings. The outside world is portrayed as more efficient at teaching than formal frameworks. The concept of "authentic culture" plays an essential role in this construct, because it highlights the dichotomy between cultural core values and artificial or theoretical models.

The concept authenticity itself is theoretically oriented toward discussions about individuals and identity (Cohen, 1991; Olsson, 2001; Ruud, 1996, 1997; Stokes, 1994; Thornton, 1995). A musical discourse is developed of what is really significant for music out of the conception that an inner dialogue is the basis for artistic expression (Berkaak & Ruud, 1994; Ruud, 1997). Thornton (1995) emphasizes that music is perceived as authentic when it "rings true" or "feels real," when it has "credibility" and comes across as "genuine."[18] Thus, authenticity is connected to the idea that some musics are more "natural" than other musics, related to the current debate about the extent to which styles such as rock music are "more from the heart" and more "real" than comparatively "artificial such as the mainstream pop music" (Olsson, 2001). In their study of a Norwegian rock group, Berkaak and Ruud (1994) demonstrate that the commercial aspects of the music market are negotiated in relation to the band's own aesthetic values: Authenticity is crucial to the members in the band. Cohen (1991) focuses on the attitudes among two band members to music and music making in relation to record companies as a conceptual pattern based on a dichotomy between "creativity–commerce," "musical content/quality–image/superficiality," and "artist/integrity–selling out" (1991, p. 134).[19] Within anthropology and folklore, the issue of authenticity concerns research in folk traditions and their transmission.[20]

Transmission in Communities

A number of recent studies in music education use models and techniques borrowed from ethnomusicology and anthropology. Enculturation, continuity, and change are explored through ethnographies of musical community. For example, Addo (1995) examines enculturation and learning patterns in children's games on playgrounds in Ghana, West Africa. She notes the ways in which children play together, creating and recreating their culture. Veblen (1991), studying Irish traditional music in Ireland, documents the changing contexts of transmission and the development of community structures to reconstitute or replace older contexts. McEntire (1990) explores the unique musical fabric of the Orkney Islands (Northern Scotland), influenced by Scandinavia, the Isles, the Hudson Bay area of Canada, and parts of the United States. During 4 years of fieldwork in the Orkneys, McEntire discovered that traditional ballads, as well as contemporary songs, are part of that island's rich continuing fabric of local musics. Through Seoul-based case studies, Paek (1999) describes social institutions that revitalized Korean traditional music transmission.

Mbanugo (1986) chose an African-American church in Buffalo, New York, as a site to study music teaching and learning as a cultural process. Although the subjects were mostly schoolaged children, parents, choir supervisors, and other adults became part of the study. Mbanugo found that religious beliefs brought individuals together to become a community, and that music was an integral part of that ideology. A decade later, Townsend (1996) found corresponding processes while exploring transmission in an African-American church, in this case a Baptist church in Aurora, Illinois. Townsend's research led him to conclude that the music and music-teaching processes found in an African-American church context could be transferred to a school setting.

Intergenerational Aspects of Community Music

Heiling (2000) studied an intergenerational amateur brass band within a Free Church in Sweden. He found that the joy of playing together and a strong goal orientation are interdependent on group coherence. Goal-acceptance and goal-fulfillment are limited by the degree of group coherence in the band. By contrast, social community and group coherence are limited by differences in the goal-acceptance of the members. Thus, the quest for artistic perfection is not only a matter of competence of the conductor and the band members but also of the individual member being engaged in a continuous social activity.[21]

Lifelong amateur music making is the subject of several music education doctoral dissertations using ethnographic research tools. Belz (1994) examined the German Gesangvereine (or Singing Clubs) in Germany over 1.5 years, as both an interviewer and participant/observer. Her study concludes that singers in Gesangvereine feel their involvement is constructive personally, as a way to continue music education and experience. Singers perceive that they are members of a community, both relating to others and preserving common cultural and historical heritage. Danforth (1995) used his 17-year association with a Native American community in Madison, Wisconsin, to investigate singing and socializing on a Woodland Indian "Drum." A Drum is a group of Indian people, mostly men, who make music during practice sessions, community events, and intertribal powwows. Danforth found that these activities were a meaningful way for individuals to connect with each other, tribal elders, and Woodland Indian traditions.

Clearly, then, there is a rich and revealing body of international research on music teaching and learning inside and outside formal schooling. Accordingly, we see many connections between CM programs and traditional music education, as well as implications for each. For example, workers in CM advocate lifelong learning perspectives and a broader definition of "teaching contexts." CM offers a broader way of looking at how music is used in a variety of settings, for expanded ranges of participants, to a wider

means than previously studied. In this emerging field, music making may be a means to a therapeutic or social end. The next section of our discussion briefly surveys professional organizations that currently are promoting aspects of CM.

The Emerging Field of Professional Music Education

The International Society for Music Education (ISME) has established seven commissions to investigate, report on, and develop particular areas of importance.[22] Established in 1984, the Commission for Community Music Activity is the youngest of these. The influence of this group as a catalyst and an international forum for research, however, cannot be underestimated.

Biennial seminars hosted by the ISME Commission for Community Music Activity have met since 1988 in different countries; these events offer participants opportunities to share in the host country's CM activities, and to be involved in an exchange of research and views. Seminars have focused on themes such as the community musician and new professional, CM in multicultural societies, training musicians and music educators to meet community needs, interaction between professionals and amateurs, the role of CM in a changing world, CM as lived and shared music making, and CM in the new millennium. This group generates publications and sponsors a Web page to link CM workers internationally.[23] Further information on this group may be obtained through ISME publications and the ISME website.[24]

Several private websites and e-mail lists connect CM workers worldwide.[25]

National Professional Organizations

In Australia, the Community Arts Network (CAN) provides advisory services, networking information, training, a professional journal, and four websites for CM workers. Incorporated in 1980, CAN receives funding from the Australian Council (the federal arts funding body) and Arts SA (the state arts funding body). CAN consults with and advocates to the government regarding funding and policy for community cultural development.[26]

The Nordic countries (Denmark, Finland, Norway, and Sweden, coupled with Iceland, Greenland, and the Faroe Islands) have developed a comprehensive CM organizational network under the umbrella of the Nordic Music Committee (NOMUS). NOMUS is the subcommittee of the Nordic Council of Ministers, dedicated to music cooperation among the affiliated countries. The committee initiates, oversees, and finances joint projects, such as commissioned works, musical performances, seminars, conferences, and educational courses.[27]

The United Kingdom–based Sound Sense is a national development agency for participatory music making in the community. Sound Sense advocates and lobbies for CM groups to the government, funding bodies, and media. This agency provides networking and contacts, professional development, disability advice, publications, and a journal.[28]

The Music Network in the Republic of Ireland seeks to make live music accessible to all, regardless of geographic location or circumstance, through partnerships with locally based groups. This network, established in 1986 by the Irish Arts Council, promotes educational partnerships, compiles publications, promotes projects and concerts, and maintains a website.[29] Another Irish organization that promotes community arts more broadly is Creative Activity for Everyone (CAFE).[30]

Over the past century, in the United States, the Music Educators National Conference (MENC) has supported partnerships and initiatives between schools and communities. Publications have been generated.[31] MENC promotes research in focused areas through Special Research Interest Groups (SRIGs). Membership in the SRIGs is voluntary. In 1998, the MENC Adult and Community Music Special Research Interest Group (SRIG) was established. Thus far, the new group has sponsored a national panel, a series of papers, an emerging website, and a newsletter. Further information on this group may be obtained through MENC channels.[32]

International Trends: Networks and Services

This section examines national trends using a combination of research, research-based, and personal observations. We rely on a combination of research and research-based materials (Australia and New Zealand); the in-depth work of one scholar (Europe: Austria); research-based materials linked with personal observations (United Kingdom and Ireland); research linked with personal observations (Scandinavian and Nordic countries); and research material (North America). Our reporting is confined to those geographic areas accessible to us and is, therefore, incomplete.

CM is defined variously in different countries. The term varies according to social conditions in each setting and may serve as a marker to describe the relationship between school music and other transmission processes or networks in the community. Often the term "Community Music" signifies codified and funded networks and services, with matching training programs. CM workers may be licensed, operate through government networks, apply for grants, and so forth.

In some places, music instruction may be available to schoolaged students and other citizens through extraschool schemes. Countries with notable community music systems include the United Kingdom, Australia and New Zealand, Austria, Scandinavia, and North America.

Emerging Programs: South Africa

Although the notion of CM as a structured experience is more documented in the English-speaking world, there are emerging programs in other parts of the world as well. Key themes in emerging programs are issues of access, participation, and equity. Comprehensive research of social conditions, political factors, and funding sources are limited at this time (Thorsén, 2000).[33] Studies range from extensive treatments of associations that promote music in a region[34] to many minor reports of ongoing action research projects. Although there is a major lack of research and written reports of CM activities, it is our impression that the emphasis of need for support is discussed in many countries around the world. In societies with social tensions and unstable political systems, the role of CM activities appears to be underlined by the authorities. South Africa is cited here as an example of emerging trends elsewhere.

South African music education carries a heritage from missionaries who implanted church music, and from the British education system that focused on European musical values (Thorsén, 2000). Music seldom existed as an examined subject in "black" schools. The policy of giving equal education to all members of society is therefore a core aim in postapartheid South Africa.

Soodyall and Goodall (in press) focused on the inservice training of music teachers, together with community workers, within a participatory action research project. The aim of the project was to "upgrade the quality of music teaching" and "to develop a model of sustainable development" for all teachers involved. As the use of African music in the classroom is emphasized, music teachers and community musicians participate with different musical backgrounds. Music teachers are encouraged to get involved in traditional African music performances. Community musicians, by contrast, are invited to redefine their position and role as "untrained community musicians." The distinction of "trained" and "untrained" is avoided consciously by labeling all participants "teachers" and "facilitators," "blurring the boundaries" between formal and informal training.

Higgins (in press) emphasizes issues of facilitation in community music programs such as the logistics of structuring workshops, and implementing effective arts development programs. In particular, he records difficulties he experienced with South African community musicians reluctant to participate in school-oriented group performances. Higgins stresses the need for educating "facilitators" or "animateurs" in community outreach.

Thorsén (2000) discusses music teaching and learning in South Africa in a broad perspective. He notes interrelated and overlapping paths of development and musical training that an individual musician may follow. Thorsén distinguishes between four pedagogical systems (traditional, informal, semiformal, and formal) that highlight differences between formal school music and community music. These four systems are governed by divergent principles: a national curriculum *or* local purposes; formal *or* informal music contexts; and a focus on music education *or* music socialization.

Australia and New Zealand.   Over the past 20 years, a conscious CM movement has grown in Australia. In 1978, the federal government's arts funding authority, the Music Board of Australia Council, began funding for CM coordinators. The initial handful of CM coordinators quickly organized centers (15 centers by 1985), and solidified a national coalition with networks of educator/musicians and established conferences on CM (Harrison, 1996, pp. 41–42). Platts (1991) describes the initiative of a postgraduate diploma in CM at the University of Western Australia, with reference to four other community arts programs.

Recent research in Australia has been directed toward providing CM models. Of community music in Australia, Harrison comments, "Our music comes from so many different places and consists of so many different styles which continually cross the lines of amateur and professional practice. The issues, for people working in CM, are the context and the principles of community development, as much as the styles and forms of the music itself" (1996, p. 40).

Cahill (1998), in a handbook published in association with the Music Council of Australia, defines CM in Australia as "cultural synergy." She offers guidelines for setting up programs and describes three large-scale development projects.[35]

Breen (1994) undertakes a topology of interest continuums sponsored by public funding in Australia. Breen asserts that CM is extremely mobile, comfortable with simple means or with the latest in digital technology. He identifies communities of music interest, not listed in any particular order in table 39.2. Furthermore, Breen identifies a corresponding typology of seven purposes for CM in Australia: utilitarian, industrial, oppositional, pluralist, normative, consensus, welfare.[36]

Mumford (in press) describes the university/community collaboration at the University of Tasmania. This program began in 1985 with several goals, including to enhance formal music education opportunities for instrumentalists

Table 39.2 Communities of music interest

Geography
Precinct—Local—Regional—National—Global
Users
Children—youth—ethnic—adult—senior citizens—disabled—unemployed—"ordinary garden variety"
Genres
Acoustic—folk—rock—pop—experimental—world music—women—choir—acapella—orchestra—brass bands—theater
Industry
Personal—subcultural/specialist—recording—print—radio—television

(Breen, 1994, p. 317)

and to encourage local community participation. Mumford describes the successes of this program and offers it as a model that may be applicable for other communities.

Nazareth (1999, in press) offers an expanded framework for music education that acknowledges links between schools and communities. She comments, "A coherent and coordinated approach to education through music, one that acknowledges the inter-relatedness and complementary nature of early childhood, school, tertiary, post-school and third age music education, can encourage the enduring effects of education to be realized" (in press).

Community music in New Zealand, according to Moore (1998), consists of "a multitude of largely unconnected institutions including performance ensembles, training operations and a smattering of social intervention work" (p. 52). Moore's study of CM funding in the United Kingdom, Scandinavia, and New Zealand reveals how much is done with the comparatively limited resources allotted in New Zealand.

Moore notes that social intervention criteria (which provide impetus for much UK funding) are not significant in New Zealand. Drummond (1989) and Croxon (1996), however, describe ways in which CM projects can promote cultural awareness and access within this pluralistic society.

CM programs in New Zealand may extend or link with formal educational systems. Buckton (1995) describes a survey of music educators in Auckland who perceive the CM worker as a music teacher who works outside the classroom in any of a number of venues. Richie and Wallis (1989) and Wallis (in press) describe a successful CM school in Christchurch that partners with area music programs. Wilberg and Sharman (1989) document CHIMES, a cooperative in Wellington that began as an early childhood enrichment, but has expanded to all ages and many forms of music making.

Europe: Austria.   In Austria, issues concerning CM focus mainly on regional cultural policy and problems connected with a federalist structure (Mark, 1990, 1992, 1998). Since cultural affairs are, generally speaking, within the domain of Austrian provinces, the structural setup for community music shows a considerable degree of variation in the different provinces. Music schools, for example, vary from a detailed regulation in one province to total independence in another. Mark (1990, 1992, 1998) emphasizes different obstacles and problems in training qualified instrumental teachers for an expanding labor market.

One problem is the need for a sufficient number of trained music teachers; another is the relationship between teacher training departments and the local musical life. The number of pupils has increased continually during the last 3 decades, but teacher training has been unable to deliver trained teachers to meet these demands. Consequently, there is a lack of music teachers with appropriate training in many of the music schools. The shortage of university trained music teachers is not the only problem.

Mark (1998) also emphasizes favoring students with a classical musical training in the entrance examinations to higher music education. Furthermore, these students have a narrow and traditional aesthetic view of music in the communities. Mark proposes a review of the curriculum in teacher training, putting a stronger emphasis on "music education in the age of media explosion," "music education for the global village," and "music education in a multicultural society," in order to meet the challenges of new social and cultural demands. He emphasizes principles such as:

1. emphasis on the musical behavior of people rather than exclusively on music as a work of art;
2. acceptance of the existence of a variety of equally valid musics;
3. conveyance of attitudes such as tolerance, empathy, respect for differing tastes;
4. stressing the emotional meaning of music . . . rather than merely the rational, structural, analytical and related aspects;
5. emphasis on the processes of musical socialization and the reception of music;
6. regarding teaching not as a one-way street but as a mutual learning process between teachers and pupils;
7. consideration of the multifunctionality of music in our society. (Mark, 1992, p. 23)

By focusing on these principles, Mark delineates the characteristics of present teacher training in Austria.

Europe: Scandinavia/Nordic Countries. "Scandinavia" is a collective term for Denmark, Finland, Norway, and Sweden. The term "Nordic countries" is used to designate an even wider region: Scandinavia, Iceland, Greenland, and the Faroe Islands. As a political designation, "Nordic" implies the pursuit of similar aims and collaborative projects.

The first CM schools in Scandinavia (in Denmark and Sweden, primarily) were established during the early 1930s. After World War II, CM schools began to increase rapidly. In the early 1980s, most Scandinavian communities supported their own music schools through public funding or cooperative efforts with private institutions (Gustavsson, 2000; Vinther, 1997). Indeed, Scandinavia tends to employ a top-down approach to funding CM projects, in which national governments enable local communities to strengthen local musical initiatives.

For example, policies established in the 1970s and 1980s enabled local communities to develop institutional orchestras and bands of their own and to make musical cultures more accessible to many more people by facilitating participation in local jazz, rock, popular, and folk music programs. In some cases, these community music schools developed amid the tension between compulsory public school curricula and local musical life[37] (Gustavsson, 2000). In Denmark, the Rhythmic Music Movement (a movement for tuition in jazz, rock, and other kinds of African-American based musics) led to a distinct school system and teacher training approach (Nielsen, 1998; Olsson, 2001). In Norway and Sweden, national agencies were constituted to distribute all kinds of music around these nations.

The trend toward more active public participation in music led to the need for alternative forms of music teaching and learning. Consequently, teacher-training students were obliged to take part in practical musical projects in communities, with the goal of learning how to involve new groups of participants who had little previous experience with music making (Brändström & Wiklund, 1995; Nielsen, 1998; Olsson, 1993, 2001; Stålhammar, 1996; Vinther, 1997).

Brändström and Wiklund (1995) studied issues of selection, choice, and gender in CM schools and music teacher training. Brändström and Wiklund note that students tend to be recruited from certain socioeconomic backgrounds and that this social bias increases with advancing age. How children understand and use the local community music school depends to a large extent on their social and musical backgrounds. Furthermore, the authors argue, there are distinct differences in the way children view their futures: Higher musical goals are set for pupils at the music schools in terms of their immediate studies and their future occupation as compared to children not involved in music schools. This group of musically devoted children forms the recruitment pool for music teacher-training programs within universities. So, community music schools are not only important for recruitment but also for influencing musical values as well.

It is not always evident what the means of CM development are at the local community level. Persson (1998) found that the success of the local music schools depended on the relationship between these schools and important bands and orchestras in their relevant communities. In other words, an important local musical life is the best guarantee for the funding of CM schools.

Notwithstanding these points, it is important to emphasize that in Scandinavia there are many amateur and professional choirs (Henningsson, 1996), ensembles (Heiling, 2000), teenage "garage rock bands," and immigrant bands outside the formal system (Ronström, 1990) who either pay their own costs, or secure support from private sources. When communities give support, it is mostly with a strong emphasis on social intervention, lifelong learning, and the needs of disadvantaged groups in the community. The gap between these bands, ensembles, and choirs and the institutionally based musical life is, however, sometimes enormous.

In summary, community music in Scandinavia is not an explicitly formulated concept. It is characterized by a strong national or regional support for organizations that collaborate with public schools or music schools. Other groups embracing nonmainstream music (avant-garde music, jazz, heavy metal, or ethnic musics) are rarely supported with public funds. Research in Scandinavian CM focuses on educational issues such as teacher training or instrumental tuition in music schools, or is found in ethnomusicological literature.

Europe: United Kingdom. Cole (1999) traces the term "Community Music" in the United Kingdom back to the 1960s and 1970s and the radical artist's movement. Its aim of developing a more accessible and participatory approach to music emphasized the interaction between people, the process rather than the product. One driving force in the early British CM movement was the then radical notion of cultural democracy and opening public access to the arts. Early CM workers questioned what they perceived as the hegemony of "high art" over other musics such as traditional and popular genres.

Cole (1999) stresses, however, that the discussion about CM has not always been politically formulated. For example, much CM work in the early 1970s focused on education, creative group work, and participation. New musical ideas developed by composers such as John Paynter and collaboration with professional musicians challenged formal music education. Furthermore, a view of art as welfare proposed that people are fulfilled by cultural experiences when they take the form of recreational activities (i.e., singing in choirs, playing in bands and ensembles).

Higgins (in press) discusses the formalization of the CM movement in the United Kingdom with the formation of Sound Sense in the early 1990s. This agency devoted to CM workers continues to evolve methodologies and philosophy as yet to be analyzed in research. Higgins quotes from agency material for his definition of community music: "improves quality of life," "contributes to lifelong learning and personal development," and "helps to develop community and social cohesion." The core intention of CM, according to Higgins, is the "conscious intention to enable access" to music and musical participation. The distinction between participatory music practices in general and CM is the conscious intention to work on an "equal opportunities policy" (Higgins, in press).

Cole (1999) further emphasizes this ideology by drawing attention to the focus on geographical areas or groups that are in some way disadvantaged. Community music is a vehicle for breaking down barriers between people and music in terms of "access," "participation," and "partnership."[38]

One outstanding feature of CM and education in the United Kingdom has been the work by professional orchestras in schools and other contexts in order to attract new and more diverse audiences. The success of orchestras such as the London Sinfonietta during the 1980s has been apparent to many other art organizations.[39]

Winterston (1999) observes the "model approach," the practice most frequently adopted by education teams working with orchestras in schools. In the "model approach," students create and perform, basing their works on specific compositions. The creative music workshop involving professional musicians was intended to support music in the classroom. Today, there is a shift in emphasis from teachers and pupils to the artistic and personal development of the orchestras' own members. "Who benefits?" Winterston asks, and formulates a strong critique against many projects:

> The marketing imperative has meant that shortcomings in educational programs have sometimes been overlooked and therefore not been addressed: music organizations are tied to their funders, therefore it is not in their interest to be critical of their own activities. (p. 152)

The aim to increase the audience will not be achieved. An inability to focus on the true obstacles, Winterston says, makes the rationale for the projects seem naive. It is not a matter of different aesthetic values that prevent people from visiting concert halls. The true barriers are cultural rather than musical and are a "reflection of the elitist position that art music holds."

In light of this debate, new expectations have been raised in higher music education concerning expanded roles for musicians. The changed focus on new audiences and different music projects has made evident the lack of social skills in a musician's training. Ritterman (1999) labels this as the "transferable skills debate," in order to include all the new demands for the appropriate training of musicians. In one sense, the problem is how a performer trained in one tradition is able to learn and perform music from another tradition. Educational concepts such as "project-based learning" and "contextual learning" have been introduced in order to overcome these obstacles. At the same time, a new labor market outside the traditional orchestra has emerged.[40]

In summary, community music in the United Kingdom is based on intentions such as "access," "participation," and "partnership," with an ambition to focus on disadvantaged groups in British society.[41] Within higher music education, courses in training professional community musicians have been developed to broaden musicians' social and musical skills and expand the labor market for musicians.

North America: Canada and the United States. The organization of CM in North America resembles an organic configuration with a number of ecosystems developing simultaneously. Because information is both profuse and diffuse, this section can only offer a hint of the CM mosaic that exists in Canada and the United States.[42]

The term "Community Music" has been in use in music education circles in North America for much of the 20th century, although its meaning has been used variously and often vaguely.[43] Foy (1988) describes the Community Song Movement, initiated by the Music Supervisors' National Conference in 1913, which persisted into the 1930s. During World War I, massed community sings such as those conducted by Mabelle Glenn in Bloomington, Illinois, were an important patriotic manifestation of CM.[44] Mark and Gary (1992) note that CM as a social movement became important again during World War II; it was to remain important throughout the 1950s.

Although a comprehensive history of CM in North America is yet to be written, a number of studies document a seminal community musician/educator,[45] an institution or association,[46] a region,[47] a particular segment of society,[48] or a musical group.[49]

In a general survey of CM activities in the United States, Leglar and Smith (1996) describe what they find as "compatible pockets of diversity" (p. 95). They categorize CM groups in the United States by: (1) community music schools; (2) community performance organizations; or (3) ethnic/preservation groups. In addition to Leglar and Smith's categories, the following groups also are found:[50] (4) religious; (5) associative organizations with schools; (6) outreach initiatives of universities and colleges; and (7) informal, affinity groups.

Community music schools. Community music schools consist of both individual, isolated freestanding academies and members of the National Guild of Community Schools. The network of schools that make up the National Guild of Community Schools of the Arts originated as settlement houses for immigrants. The movement to establish settlement houses came directly from England at the end of the 19th century as part of progressive efforts in community action.[51] The guild includes 283 member schools throughout the United States at the time of this writing. Two of the oldest and best known of these are the Hull House in Chicago, founded in 1889, and the Third Street Music School Settlement, founded in New York in 1894. The newest schools in the guild are only a few months old.

The National Guild's mission is "Arts for All." The guild itself is an advocate for the arts; it sponsors research, distributes publications, serves as a conduit for funding and seeks to connect like-minded organizations. The guild's website (http://www.natguild.org/) describes many programs, events, and resources. Member schools offer music instruction to more than 300,000 students on a regular basis and reach hundreds of thousands of people in their special events.[52]

The National Guild and other CM schools provide instruction in a variety of music systems, as well as expanded services.[53] Training in Orff, Kodály, Dalcroze, Suzuki, and various early childhood methodologies may be a featured part of the school's offerings (Buescher, 1993; Nardo, 1996). Blaker (1995) investigated Suzuki method violin instruction programs in CM schools in the United States. She noted that the Suzuki method (or Talent Education) and CM schools were two areas of music education that expanded substantially in the last part of the 20th century. Adelson (2000) describes the range of programs available through the inner-city MERIT (Music Education Reaching Instrumental Talents) music programs.

Graessle (1998) surveyed adult music programming in guild schools to find that private instruction was the most frequently offered program for adults. Enrollment information indicated that adults were about 15% of the student population. Pflieger (1985) found that guild schools more frequently offer music than other arts (dance, drama, or visuals arts). A majority of schools have outreach programs in adult education, performance, public and private school programs, early childhood, and day care. Pflieger notes that while most schools offer partial scholarships, few offer special scholarships of financial assistance for the handicapped.

Community performance organizations. Community performance organizations include orchestras, bands, choirs, and many other nonprofit groups. Numerous small-scale studies document specific musical organizations. Coffman (in press) describes his community band, a member of the New Horizons bands for older adults initiated by Roy Ernst from the Eastman School of Music in Rochester, New York. The program has expanded since its inception in 1991 to some 50 bands throughout North America. Coffman organizes the reasons that seniors give for joining a band into three categories: social, personal well-being, and musical.[54] Carson (1992) recounts the first

30 years of the Northshore Concert Band (NCB) of Wilmette, Illinois, from 1956 to 1986. Carson asserts that the NCB is the most influential amateur adult band since its founding and that it may serve as a model for other bands.

Other studies of performing groups have examined demographics, educational levels, musical experiences, and motivation for participation (Tipps, 1992; Spell, 1989; Spencer, 1996). Bowen (1995) identifies current adult CM band activity in the three southern states of Georgia, Alabama, and Florida. In his profiles of band members, Bowen found that two thirds of band members were male, most were white, more than half held a college degree, and half had majored in music during their college career. Vincent (1997) examined mixed-voice adult community choruses in the state of Kentucky. She determined that Kentucky community chorus singers were generally white, well educated, with average or above average salaries. Choirs were composed of two-thirds women, most of whom had previous positive musical experiences. Holmquist (1995) surveyed community choir members from three Oregon cities. All amateur singers in Holmquist's study shared certain traits, among which were an insider language, a sense of community, memory of a "peak experience," and past involvement in high school performances. Hosler (1992) surveyed the brass band movement in the United States and Canada, and found that membership included individuals with a wide variety of educational backgrounds and musical experiences. Most of the bands surveyed were amateur organizations existing for individual musical enjoyment and contributing to the community. Other current studies of groups include an examination of the Phoenix Boys Choir (Schaffer, 1992); a survey of Massachusetts CM bands (Thaller, 1999); a study of literacy in a volunteer chorus (Green, 1998); and an ethnography of amateur orchestra musicians (Park, 1995).

Ethnic/preservation groups. Ethnic/preservation groups include multiple immigrant communities as well as First Peoples groups[55] and recreated traditions groups. (See the section on ethnomusicological and sociological studies in this chapter for more on immigrant circles.) Gatherings often serve as a way to celebrate or build community. Mathews (2000) looks at contemporary Native American powwows, gathering places for intergenerational and intercultural dancing, singing, and storytelling. Mathews notes that these events are flourishing as traditions revitalize and attract younger participants.

In addition to preserving traditions, CM groups in North America also may recreate, improvise, invent, or adopt traditions. Bealle (1989) considers an old-time music and dance community united by its interests. The concept of tradition in this instant serves to unite the group not to its own past but to the past of a remote cultural other. In a similar vein, Lausevic (1998) examines past and present International and Balkan dance and music groups in the

United States. Contemporary participants or "Balkanites" are mostly urban/suburban, highly educated Americans of various European origins.

Ethnic/preservation CM groups often offer alternative methods of teaching and learning music to participants. Dabczynski (1994) documented a recontextualized setting for traditional fiddling at a fiddle and dance summer camp held in upstate New York. He notes that in addition to recreating traditional transmission, the camp successfully created a responsive and warm community. Veblen (1995) described a constellation of recurring factors in teaching and learning in her comparative study of Irish-American and Norwegian-American musicians in the midwestern United States.

Religious capacities. Some CM musicians participate in religious capacities as organists, soloists, and cantors, or as members of church choirs, processional bands, and many other kinds of ensembles. Although many religious groups perform publicly, members may feel that they are not really performing for an audience; they are worshiping or fulfilling a role in a liturgical service. Sometimes the music and rituals are part of an immigrant or displaced community, thus serving to preserve heritage as well as worship.

Allen (1987) examined gospel performance in New York City's African-American churches. He finds that in addition to extending the Sunday morning workshop service, gospel performances help maintain southern rural identity, religion, and values, while integrating new urban performance styles. Gallo (1998) undertook a study of the dynamics of the Ethiopian Orthodox Church in Toronto. Immigrants to this church have adapted what was a strict and written Ethopian musical tradition to a flexible oral musical practice, resulting in many changes in performance, aesthetics, symbolism, instrumentation, and transmission.

Buis (1996) and David (1994) both examined regional variations of the African-American ring-shout tradition, which combines movement and music in ritual. Buis documents what he describes as the only remaining community in the United States that practices the ring-shout as handed down by former slaves. David's research looks at the Singing and Praying Bands in Maryland and Delaware that are derived from the ring-shout tradition. Meetings of Singing and Praying Bands culminate in a march that symbolizes the spiritual solidarity that members refer to as "being on one accord." Hall (1998) traces the origins of New Orleans jazz funerals to African roots, first performed in 1795 by the dissident slave community in that city. Hall asserts that jazz funerals serve to link the dead and living and to articulate the community's identity.

Robertson's (1996) study of the role of singing in the Christian Science Church revealed not only the importance of music in worship but also its emphasis on nontheatrical simplicity. Views of the church's founder, Mary Baker Eddy, had lasting influence on the character of music in these services. Ihm (1994) investigated current music practices of 535 congregations of the Independent Christian Churches in the United States. Roughly 80% of the congregations in this research have adult choirs, 60% have children's choirs, and about one quarter have teen choirs. Most choir members have had little private music instruction.

Associative organizations with schools. In North America, CM frequently has a relationship to school music making, as CM advocates feel that a strong fabric of CM life complements opportunities in schools.[56] A number of collaborations and partnerships in the United States are explored in a recent MENC publication (Draper, 1999). Babineau (2000) explores a number of initiatives in Canada that extend or enrich curriculum.[57]

Many orchestras, opera companies, and other professional organizations partner with school systems, as well as with other branches of the community. Patterson (1991) investigates school outreach programs organized by professional opera companies to find that over 1 million students experienced live opera presentations. Himes (1992) focuses on the Fairfax Symphony Orchestra's educational programs, noting the positive influence they have on community and teacher perceptions of the arts. Lamb (in press) describes a decade of partnership between symphony, schools, and university in Kingston, Ontario, Canada. (See chap. 47 for more on outreach and artist in the school programs.)

Outreach initiatives of universities and colleges. Many universities and colleges undertake outreach programs in their communities. These programs may include choirs, bands, orchestras, and other ensembles, as well as outreach efforts into schools, early childhood or senior centers as well as sponsorship of local arts and music events. Werner (1996) surveyed 700 community colleges in the United States to find that community college music programs are expanding at a rapid rate. Werner's study also identified many linkages between college and community in these music programs. Baily (1997) details a case study of the University Musical Society of the University of Michigan. The Musical Society, a nonprofit arts organization as well as a member of the university "family" has successfully promoted music and other arts in the communities and in the university over a period of time.

Several researchers sought to design outreach models, based on observations of one or more programs. Alexander (1997) surveyed the 46 divisional schools of the National Guild of Community Schools of the Arts for relationships in areas of administration, budget, faculty, and curriculum. Divisional schools are member institutions of the National Guild that were developed by music conservatories or college and university programs. Noting the

characteristics of exemplary programs, Alexander suggests guidelines for CM school administrators. Single (1991) designed a program at Ohio State University based on demographic information. Robinson (1999) proposes a theory of collaboration he calls "tensegrity," or tensional integrity, based on observations of the first 2 years of partnership between a university school of music and an urban public school district. Robinson's theory acknowledges that people, not structures, make partnerships work, and that these groups draw energy from differences, rather than from consensus and uniformity. Other studies (Shellhouse, 1990; Hardin, 1997) reported CM activities as part of an analysis of community college music programs.

Informal affinity groups. Slobin (1993) defines affinity groups as "charmed circles of like-minded music-makers drawn magnetically to a certain genre that creates strong expressive bonding"[58] (p. 98). One example of an affinity group might be musicians attending an early music summer school who meet to play, learn, dance, buy, and sell music from another time. Because there are no recordings of what early music sounds like, however, this genre offers performers the chance to reinvent (or reinterpret)—and to gather with others of like mind.

Conclusion

This chapter is an initial attempt to document and articulate an emerging awareness and professionalization of Community Music. CM is not new—we have always known rich fabrics of participatory music making. Moreover, music educators, both individually and collectively, have always worked in many settings. What *is* new is the flourishing of scholarly interest in this area, as well as recent international initiatives. As official networks promote and deliver services in Australia, Europe, and North America, various organizations and individuals are attempting to define CM, locally and internationally. This broadening of vision for music educators promises many opportunities for research, such as:

- investigating the variety of successful teaching and learning strategies found in CM settings
- exploring political, socioeconomic, and other implications of existing CM frameworks
- charting the diversity and attributes of music educators in nontraditional frameworks and mediums
- researching interactions and fluidity of roles in group context
- documenting individual case studies of CM, as well as channels, pathways, and other possible configurations
- investigating funding principles of CM in order to mirror issues of cultural policy in practice
- chronicling individuals, collaborations, and structures
- expanding the scope of international documentation

- encouraging reporting of research from Asia, South America, the Middle East, Africa, and other sites
- promoting interdisciplinary approaches to CM research, including group ethnography, collaborations between practitioner and researcher, longitudinal studies, and comparative studies
- building on insights gained through ethnomusicological, sociological, and other related studies.

NOTES

1. This section offers the authors' synthesis of principles and theories behind Community Music. Our synthesis is informed by research and draws on the conclusions of the International Society for Music Education's Community Music Activity Commission seminars 1990–2000.

2. Boundaries between research in sociology and ethnomusicology are, however, often vague and not always easy to demarcate (Stokes, 1994).

3. See Livingston et al. (1993) for a collection of mini-ethnographies based in Champaign-Urbana, Illinois. Although a listing of all significant ethnographies is beyond the scope of this footnote, some recent studies of musical communities include the following: Bahamas (Wood, 1995); Bali (Bakan, 1993); Bolivia (Solomon, 1997); Brazil (Albrecht, 1991); Central African Republic (Kisliuk, 1991); China (Witzleben, 1987); Dominican Republic (Pacini, 1989); Japan (Condry, 1999); Madagascar (Edkvist, 1997); Nigeria (Anagah, 1988); Romania (Nixon, 1993); Thailand (Myers-Moro, 1988); South India (Kassebaun, 1994); and the United States (Russell, 1999; Washburne, 1999).

4. Blacking (1991) is reflecting on a major shift of emphasis in scholarly thinking about music and music-making: "anthropology provides the best reasons for developing an essential musical theory that is not ethnocentric" (1991, p. 63). Horner and Swiss (1999) approach the boundaries between sociology and anthropology/ethnomusicology in terms of "locating popular music in culture" through examining the ways popular music can be understood in relation to key terms like ideology, discourse history, and so on, or "locating culture in popular music," focusing on how different meanings of the vocabulary of popular music "help shape the music and our experience of it" (1999, p. 2). Finnegan (1989) stresses the fact that, in musicology, one powerful definition of music embraces musical works, not performance in music.

5. Ingrid Monson (2000) summarizes Appadurai and his frequent collaborator Breckenridge's work.

6. Lipsitz (1993, p. 5) takes Appadurai's theory as a starting point for his exploration of radical and recontextualized modern musical fusions.

7. Grandien (1991) makes the distinction between "mediation," in which music becomes mediated when transmitted by media, "mediaization," which covers the accommodation of media-transformed music in its sound-structure, and "mediaization," which covers both the processes of adaptation to media and the outcomes of the processes as apparent in practice (p. 321).

8. Kruse (1993) describes the musical subcultures at American colleges as "musical scenes."

9. There is a related notion that each individual constructs his or her own musical world. See Crafts, Cavicchi, and Keil (1993) and Campbell (1998).

10. *The Sacred Harp*, primary tune book of sacred harp singers, was compiled in 1844 and uses a four-shape musical notation popular at that time in America. Sacred harp singing has continued as a practice but only recently has become adopted outside of its religious contexts.

11. These recent studies of musical affinity groups include Japanese jazz (Atkins, 1997); a continuum of metal, rock, and jazz communities in Ohio (Berger, 1995); Reggae bands in Rhode Island (Chabot, 1992); a Hungarian counterculture community (Szemere, 1998); Salsa music in pan-Latin settings (Berrios-Miranda, 2000); Heavy Metal fans (Gencarelli, 1993; Walser, 1993); and popular music among Old Order Amish youth in Pennsylvania (McNamara, 1997).

12. See Bryant (1995), Neff (1996), and Kibby (2000) for more on virtual communities.

13. Horowitz (1994) explores ethnic affinity groups of Israeli Mediterranean music. Flam (1988) studies Jewish songs of the Holocaust from a Polish ghetto, while Koehler (2000) examines the sociopolitical implications of the German Workers' Choral Association (comprising nearly 500,000 Germans) in light of the Nazis' rise to power.

14. Recent studies of immigrant or diasporic communities include examinations of Chinese-American groups in New York City (Zheng, 1993); Louisiana Cajun and zydeco musicians in Northern California (DeWitt, 1998); Albanian wedding music makers in Yugoslavia and North American sites (Sugarman, 1993); Polish-American immigrants in Detroit (Savaglio, 1992); Ukrainian groups in Alberta, Canada (Koszarycz, 1999); and Puerto Rican communities in New York (Glasser, 1991).

15. Finnegan (1989) emphasizes that music and music making have many nonmusic implications as well, in which patterns such as sociability and socially recognized positions in the group or community are prominent.

16. For theories of socially shared learning, see Lave and Wenger (1991) and Chaiklin and Lave (1993).

17. "On the one hand there was the hierarchical and highly literate classical music training with its externally validated system of grades and progress, entered upon primarily by children and strongly supported by parents, schools and the local network of paid teachers, with the aim of socializing children into the traditions of classical music theory and compositions through instruction in instrumental skills via written forms. Against this was the other mode: embarked on as a self-chosen mission primarily by adults and teenagers; not necessarily approved or encouraged by parents or schoolteachers; lacking external official validation, central bureaucratic organization or any 'career' through progressive grades; resting on individual aspiration and achievement in a group music-making and 'oral' context rather than a hierarchically organized examination system" (Finnegan, 1989, p. 140).

18. "In an age of endless representations and global mediation, the experience of musical authenticity is perceived as a cure both for alienation (because it offers feelings of com-

munity) and dissimulation (because it extends a sense of the really 'real')" (Thornton, 1995, p. 26).

19. Kruse (1993) emphasizes the concept "alternative music" as something similar to authenticity; a certain set of social practices—"practices of consumption, of production, of interaction—a sense of community."

20. See Johnson (2000) for an exposition of the concept of authenticity in folklore and anthropology literature.

21. See Patterson (1985) for a discussion of motivational factors in community bands in Massachusetts.

22. The ISME commissions are: Music in Schools and Teacher Education; Research; Education of the Professional Musician; Music in Educational, Cultural and Mass Media Policies; Music in Special Education, Music Therapy and Music Medicine; Early Music Education; and Community Music Activity.

23. The ISME commissions and other useful links may be located through the ISME website: http://www.isme.org/

24. Contact ISME through their website http://www.isme.org/ and also by e-mail: isme@iinet.au or fax : ++61-(0) 8-9386-2658.

25. See http://www.boerger.org/c-m/ to locate CM groups and join an orchestra/band e-mail list.

26. A current handbook giving an overview and contact information for Australian arts organizations may be found at http://www.ozco.gov.au/resources/publication/corporate/handbook. There are four Community Arts Network (CAN) websites: In Adelaide, SA: http://www.cansa.on.net; in Perth, WA: http://www.canwa.com.au; in Casula, NSW: www.communityarts.org.au; in New Farm, QLD: http://www.qldcan.org.au

27. *Nordic Sounds,* an English-speaking magazine published quarterly, is devoted to Nordic musical life. The e-mail address for *Nordic Sounds* is: nordic.sounds@nomus.org and their home address is *Nordic Sounds,* 14 Christian Winthers vej, DK-1860 Fredriksberg C, Denmark.

The NOMUS Catalogue, an address and telephone register of music institutions in Nordic and Baltic countries, may be ordered by contacting the NOMUS general secretariat via e-mail: gen.secr@nomus.org

28. Sound Sense may be contacted through e-mail: info@soundsense.org/ or website: www.soundsense.org/

29. Music Network Ireland's website is http://www.musicnetwork.ie

30. The email address for CAFE is cafe@connect.ie, and their home address is CAFE, 10–11 South Earl Street, Dublin 8, Ireland.

31. The MENC publication *Music for Everybody* (copyright 1950) notes that "CM is not a kind of music; rather it is all kinds of music. . . . A broad CM program may include not only those activities that provide for music participation, but also related activities" (n.p.). This publication provides a kind of scrapbook with guidelines, reports, and pictures of many different CM activities in the United States, such as the PTA Mothers' Singing Group in San Diego, California, playing flutophones. Mark and Gary (1982) provide an overview of MENC CM activities. Draper (1999) presents portraits of current CM programs in the United States.

32. The MENC SRIGs may be accessed through the MENC website: http://www.menc.org

33. Reporting of developing programs tends to articulate ideals and multicultural goals (Mannergren, 2000).

34. Rosse (1995) traces the role of local clubs and large societies in Northern India in promoting "Hindu" music during 1860–1930. Stuempfle (1990) describes the steel band movement in Trinidad and Tobago from its inception in the 1930s as a street music to its current status based both in grassroots groups and also in national structures. Three studies explore African musical associations: Ngige-Nguo (1990) examines Gi kuky society and educational structures in Kenya; Gunderson (1999) looks at farmer-musician guilds and porter associations in Tanzania; and Nicholls (1992) probes the relationship of rural development projects to the music and dance associations of the Igede of Nigeria.

35. The three comprehensive Australian CM projects mentioned are Community Music Victoria, Dandenong Ranges Music Council, and Orange Music Association.

36. Breen (1994) gives seven kinds of CM formations in Australia. Utilitarian projects are the least developed situations: Here, a CM worker contributes minimal opportunities for community participation. Industrial projects link performance or product with media and possibly commercial enterprises. Oppositional situations refer to using CM to express political or minority views. Pluralistic formations set forth access and tolerance as priorities in music making. Normative formations indicate that music happens within defined affinity groups such as ethnic migrant circles. Consensus structures denote programs targeted at specific groups, often with aims of social uplift. Welfare programs exist to bring musical participation to disadvantaged social groups.

37. According to Gustavsson (2000), CM schools in Scandinavia developed in part because of tensions between compulsory school and musical life and between progressive and traditional ideals of schooling. Traditionalists advocate views and values closely connected to the cultural heritage with its aesthetic-based didactics. Advocates of progressivism favor a broader aesthetic, wider choices of music and preferences for performance, and experiences that promote musical creativity. The community music schools belonged in the start to the latter pole but over the course of the past 50 years have become more closely linked to the aesthetic pole.

38. One good example of this ideology was the "Tower Hamlet" project during the 1980s, in which all children in schools in certain areas of London were involved in string tuition with no regard to social background or traditional connection to the instrument within families. A key person in the project was the well-known British string pedagogue Sheila Nelson.

39. London Sinfonietta's work can be followed through an Internet facility: www.soundintermedia.co.uk/treeline-online/

40. A pioneer within British Higher Music Education was Professor Peter Renshaw at the Guildhall School of Music and Drama in London, whose ideas about new roles for musicians has been most influential.

41. Moore (1998) presents a system of funding providers crucial to the community music movement. The national

agency "Sound Sense" is a key actor in this process of seeking arts funding.

42. This section compresses and combines programs in Canada and the United States, although funding systems, history, and philosophies may differ.

43. Peter Dykema was a driving force and commentator of the CM movement, which he defined as "all types of music which may exist in a community." Frank Beach and Edgar Gordon also were influential. See Mark and Gary (1992, pp. 238–243) and McCarthy (1995). The slogan "Music for Everybody" is often attached to the term Community Music, beginning in the 1920s. Bartholomew and Lawrence's book on training song leaders entitled *Music for Everybody: Organization and Leadership of Community Music Activities,* copyrighted 1920, gives instructions for song leading and wonderful pictures of massed factory sings, and boys in Niagara Falls at a moving picture theater who sing "between reels under trained leadership."

44. *Community Music: A Practical Guild for the Conduct of Community Music Activities,* copyright 1926, talks about the democratization of music: "(Before and during World War I) . . . the value of music as a force in citizenship building and community morale began to interest those who formerly had no musical interest as such and the movement for music for all received the support of public-spirited citizens, business men and community groups" (p. 4). In her study of purpose statements in community songbooks from 1916 to 1996, Hair (1999) concludes that the basic argument given for promoting community singing in the United States is for transmitting heritage.

45. Comprehensive studies of community music leaders include profiles of Anne Grace O'Callaghan from Atlanta, Georgia (Tolbert, 1997); George Oscar Bowen of Flint, Michigan (Spurgeon, 1990); gospel musician Dorothy Love Coates of Birmingham, Alabama (McAllister, 1995); bandmaster R. B. Hall of Maine (Bowie, 1993); folk dance and music specialist Jane Farwell of Dodgeville, Wisconsin (Christensen, 1999); Lena Milam of Beaumont, Texas (Babin, 1987); Mennonite musician Joseph W. Yoder of Mifflin County, Pennsylvania (Kasdorf, 1997); Edgar B. "Pop" Gordon, known for his pioneering radio music education in Wisconsin (Angevine, 1985); Amos Sutton Hayden, music and religious leader in Ohio (Fletcher, 1988); Hugh Hodgson of Georgia (McDade, 1988); Bernard Jacob Pfohl, who influenced Moravian bands in North Carolina (Rothrock, 1991); and Hattie Rhue Hatchett from Ontario, Canada (Stewardson, 1994).

46. Histories of settlement schools include a profile of the Third Street Music School Settlement in New York City, 1891–1984 (Pagano, 1997); the Hull House in Chicago (Green, 1998); and a general history (Egan, 1989). For a history of the John C. Campbell Folk School in Brasstown, North Carolina, see Culbertson (1985). Spurgeon (1994) chronicles the Community Music Association in Flint, Michigan.

47. Regional studies include examination of influences of industrial bands in the southern United States (LeCroy, 1998); rural reform 1900–1925 (Lee, 1997); Italian wind bands in Pennsylvania milltowns between 1890 and 1986 (Rocco, 1986); progressive reform and music making in Chicago from

1869 to 1930 (Vaillant, 1999); music in the utopian community of New Harmony, Indiana from 1825 to 1864 (Sluder, 1987); and the piano in a coal mining area of West Virginia, 1890 to 1960 (Perkins, 1994). Studies of musical life in cities include Annapolis, Maryland from 1649 to 1776 (Hildebrand, 1992); Kitchener, Ontario, Canada, from 1911 to 1939 (Pieper, 1996); and in Cinncinati from 1865 to 1991 (Cahall, 1991).

48. Studies of a particular segment of society include music of pioneer Mormon women in Utah (Fife, 1994); music in the Shaker societies in the United States (Klein, 1990); religious songs in Maine (Davenport, 1991); and immigrant musics as showcased through an Exposition in New York in 1921 (Abramovitch, 1996). Puerto Rican music and community in New York City from World War I to World War II was traced by Glasser (1991). Norris (1994) chronicled music of black and white communities in Petersburg, Virginia, 1865–1900 and Parker (1983) studied the influences of women in music in St. Paul from 1898 to 1957.

49. Histories of musical groups include brass bands in the Mid-Willamette Valley, Oregon (Weddle, 1989); Welsh choral music in the 19th century (Pohly, 1989); the Northshore Concert Band of Wilmette, Illinois (Carson, 1992); the Maennerchor tradition (Snyder, 1991); the Baltimore Symphony Orchestra (Spencer, 1994); the Society for the Preservation and Encouragement of Barber Shop Quartet Singing in America (Ayling, 2000); the Dalesburg Cornet Band (Olson, 1997); and early choral music in Charlotte, North Carolina (Engelson, 1994, 1996). Contemporary case studies of musical groups include the Wild Rose Old Fiddler's Association in Edmonton, Alberta (Stormer, 1997); the New Jersey Ridgewood Concert Band, which is dedicated to lifelong learning (Wilhjelm, 1998); seven CM childrens' choirs in Florida (Howle, 1999); and the Salvation Army Chicago Staff Band (Rowden, 1996).

50. Note the correlations between these categories and Breen's typology of Australian CM formations.

51. Jane Addams and Ellen Gates Starr were inspired by their visit to Toynbee Hall settlement houses in London to establish Hull House in Chicago in 1889.

52. Herman (2000) announced a large grant to a program entitled Partners in Excellence, which will identify and nurture exemplary public school and arts organization partnerships.

53. See Fabregas (1992) for a description of an electronic music program in a CM school in New York City.

54. For other examples of CM programs for seniors, see Darrough (1990), Robertson (1992), Chiodo (1997), and Tatum (1985).

55. In Canada, native groups such as the Inuit may be referred to as First Peoples or First Nations. In the United States, these groups may be termed Native Americans, American Indians, or by specific tribal names such as Apache.

56. Michael Mark writes, "Today there is a rich variety of community music opportunities throughout the country. These opportunities continue to complement music opportunities in schools. In the best situations, school and community music leaders work together to maintain a strong community music life. There is a question, however, of the proper relationship between school and community music" (Mark, 1992,

quoted in Leglar and Smith, 1996, p. 106). Kim (2000) describes the interplay between local community support and schools in Seattle, Washington, between 1960 and 1976.

57. These include programs such as Learning Through the Arts, launched by The Royal Conservatory of Music in Toronto; ArtsSmarts in Montreal; ArtStarts in Schools in British Columbia, a world music program initiated by Valerie Dare in Vancouver schools; Changing Arts Programs linked to Canadian orchestras; Composer in Electronic Residence through York University in Toronto; and three programs in Nova Scotia—Music in Medicine through Dalhousei University Halifax, Arts inFusion, and the Scotia Festival of Music in Halifax.

58. See ethnomusicological studies for more on Slobin and affinity groups.

REFERENCES

Abramovitch, I. (1996). *America's making exposition and festival (New York, 1921): Immigrant gifts on the altar of America.* Unpublished doctoral dissertation, New York University, New York.

Adelson, D. (2000). The MERIT music program. *International Journal of Music Education, 35,* 8–11.

Addo, A. O. (1995). *Ghanaian children's music cultures: A video ethnography of selected singing games.* Unpublished doctoral dissertation, University of British Columbia, Vancouver, BC, Canada.

Ake, D. A. (1998). *Being jazz: Identities and images.* Unpublished doctoral dissertation, University of California, Los Angeles.

Albrecht, R. J. (1991). *The technologizing of the song : An ethnography and oral history of musical change in a small Brazilian town.* Unpublished doctoral dissertation, New York University, New York.

Alexander, C. R. (1997). *Relationships between community music programs and their affiliated collegiate music schools.* Unpublished doctoral dissertation, Peabody College for Teachers of Vanderbilt University, Nashville.

Allen, R. R. (1987). *Singing in the spirit: An ethnography of gospel performance in New York City's African-American Church community.* Unpublished doctoral dissertation, University of Pennsylvania, Philadelphia.

Anagah, I. N. M. (1988). *North-eastern Igbo music: A case study of Efvu Odabara/Itutara music and its social function among the Izhiangbo people of Nigeria.* Unpublished doctoral dissertation, Queen's University of Belfast.

Angevine, B. G. (1985). *"Dear Pop," A biography of Edgar B. Gordon.* Unpublished doctoral dissertation, University of Kansas, Lawrence.

Appadurai, A. (1990). Disjuncture and difference in the global cultural economy. *Public Culture, 2*(2), 1–24.

Atkins, E. (1997). *This is our music: Authenticating Japanese jazz, 1920–1980.* Unpublished doctoral dissertation, University of Illinois, Urbana-Champaign.

Ayling, B. C. (2000). *An historical perspective of international champion quartets of the Society for the Preservation and Encouragement of Barber Shop Quartet Singing in America, 1939–1963.* Unpublished doctoral dissertation, Ohio State University, Columbus.

Babin, L. R. (1987). *Lena Milam, 1884–1984: Music educator and pioneer in the development of community music in Beaumont, Texas.* Unpublished doctoral dissertation, Louisiana State University, Baton Rouge.

Babineau, N. (2000). Enriching the curriculum—enriching the community: Canadian partnerships for arts education. In M. Taylor & B. Gregory (Eds.), *Music of the spheres: ISME conference proceedings* (pp. 12–28). Regina: Impact Printers.

Baily, I. E. (1997). *The place of higher education in the arts: The example of the University Musical Society of the University of Michigan.* Unpublished doctoral dissertation, University of Michigan, Ann Arbor.

Bakan, M. B. (1993). *Balinese Kreasi Baleganjur: An ethnography of musical experience.* Unpublished doctoral dissertation, University of California, Los Angeles.

Bealle, J. R. (1989). *American folklore revival: A study of an old-time music and dance community.* Unpublished doctoral dissertation, Indiana University, Bloomington.

Beisswenger, D. A. (1997). *Fiddling way out yonder: Community and style in the fiddle music of Melvin Wine.* Unpublished doctoral dissertation, University of Memphis, Tennessee.

Belz, M. J. D. (1994). *The German Gesangverein as a model of life-long participation in music.* Unpublished doctoral dissertation, University of Minnesota, Minneapolis.

Berger, H. M. (1995). *Perception in the moral continuum of history: An ethnography of metal, rock and jazz in Northeast Ohio.* Unpublished doctoral dissertation, Indiana University, Bloomington.

Berkaak, O. A., & Ruud, E. (1994). *Sunwheels, fortellinger om et rockeband* [Sunwheels, stories about a rock band]. Oslo: Universitetsforlaget.

Berrios-Miranda, M. (2000). *The significance of salsa music to national and pan-Latino identity.* Unpublished doctoral dissertation, University of California, Berkeley.

Blacking, J. (1991). Towards a reintegration of musicology. In A. Buckley, K. O. Edström, & P. Nixon (Eds.), *Proceedings of the Second British-Swedish Conference on Musicology: Ethnomusicology. Cambridge, 5–10 August 1989.* Göteborg: Göteborgs universitet, skrifter från den musikvetenskapliga institutionen, 26: 61–69.

Blaker, S. L. (1995). *A survey of Suzuki violin programs in community music schools in the United States.* Unpublished doctoral dissertation, Ohio State University, Columbus.

Bouij, C. (1998a). *Musik—mitt liv och kommande levebröd: En studie I musiklärares yrkessocialisation* [Musik—My life and future profession: A study in the professional socialization of music teachers]. Doctoral dissertation, Göteborg: Göteborgs universitet, skrifter från institutionen för musikvetenskap No 56.

Bouij, C. (1998b). Swedish music teacher in training and professional life. *International Journal of Music Education, 32,* 24–32.

Bowen, C. K. (1995). *Adult community bands in the Southeastern United States: An investigation of current activity and background profiles of the participants.* Unpublished doctoral dissertation, Florida State University, Tallahassee.

Bowie, G. W. (1993). *R. B. Hall and the community bands of Maine.* Unpublished doctoral dissertation, University of Maine.

Brändström, S., & Wiklund, C. (1995). *Två musikpedagogiska fält: En studie om kommunal musikskola och musiklärarutbildning* [Two music-pedagogy fields: A study of municipal music schools and music teacher education]. Unpublished doctoral dissertation, Umeå University.

Breen, M. (1994). Constructing the popular from public funding of community music. *Popular Music, 13*(3), 313–326.

Bryant, W. (1995). *Virtual music communities: The Folk-Music Internet Discussion Group as a cultural system.* Unpublished doctoral dissertation, University of California, Los Angeles.

Buckton, R. (1995). Community music. In N. Bruce, J. Hanfling, & D. Downer (Eds.), *Music '95 Music on the move: Puoru Nekehia* (pp. 20–27). Wellington, NZ: New Zealand Society for Music Education.

Buescher, R. J. E. (1993). *A description of community music programs for preschool children sponsored by selected colleges and universities in the United States.* Unpublished doctoral dissertation, University of South Carolina, Columbia.

Buis, J. (1996). African slave descendants in an American community: The ring-shout tradition of the Georgia Sea Islands. In M. A. Leglar (Ed.), *The role of community music in a changing world: Proceedings of the International Society for Music Education 1994 Seminar of the Commission on Community Music Activity* (pp. 62–70). Athens: University of Georgia.

Burdette, A. R. (1997). *Celebrating localities: Performance and community in a German American singing society.* Unpublished doctoral dissertation, Indiana University, Bloomington.

Burton, B. (in press). Passing it on: Teaching fiddle styles in the fiddle music of Central Texas communities. *Studies in Music.*

Cahall, M. C. (1991). *Jewels in the queen's crown: The fine and performing arts in Cincinnati, Ohio, 1865–1919.* Unpublished doctoral dissertation, University of Illinois, Urbana-Champaign.

Cahill, A. (1998). *The community music handbook: A practical guide to developing music projects and organizations.* Neutral Bay, NSW: The Music Council of Australia.

Campbell, P. S. (1998). *Songs in their heads: Music and its meaning in children's lives.* New York: Oxford University Press.

Carson, W. S. (1992). *A history of the Northshore Concert Band, Wilmette, Illinois, 1956–1986: The first thirty years.* Unpublished doctoral dissertation, Arizona State University, Tempe.

Chabot, R. R. (1992). *Local version(s): Rhode Island reggae bands as "projects."* Unpublished doctoral dissertation, State University of New York at Buffalo.

Chaiklin, S., & Lave, L. (Eds.). (1993). *Understanding practice: Perspectives on activity and context.* Cambridge: Cambridge University Press.

Cherwick, B. A. (1999). *Polkas on the prairies: Ukrainian music and the construction of identity.* Unpublished doctoral dissertation, University of Alberta, Edmonton, AB, Canada.

Chiodo, P. A. (1997). *The development of lifelong commitment: A qualitative study of adult instrumental music participation.* Unpublished doctoral dissertation, State University of New York at Buffalo.

Christensen, P. E. (1999). *Jane Farwell: Adult educator and social recreation leadership trainer.* Unpublished doctoral dissertation, University of Wisconsin, Madison.

Coffman, D. (in press). Older adult community bands: New horizons for instrumental music. *Studies in Music.*

Cohen, S. (1999). Scenes. In B. Horner & T. Swiss (Eds.), *Key terms in popular music and culture* (pp. 239–250). Malden, MA: Blackwell.

Cohen, S. (1991). *Rock culture in Liverpool: Popular music in the making.* Oxford: Clarendon Press.

Cole, B. (1999). Community music and higher education: A marriage of convenience. In *Making music work. Fostering professional skills among those studying music in higher education* (pp. 139–150). Professional integration project. London: Royal College of Music.

Condry, I. (1999). *Japanese rap music: An ethnography of globalization in popular cultures.* Unpublished doctoral dissertation, Yale University, New Haven.

Crafts, S. D., Cavicchi, D., & Keil, C. (1993). *My music.* Hanover, NH: Wesleyan University Press.

Croxon, M. (1996). Through legends to cultural learning: A bicultural perspective to the use of music-drama. In M. A. Leglar (Ed.), *The role of community music in a changing world: Proceedings of the International Society for Music Education 1994 Seminar of the Commission on Community Music Activity* (pp. 119–126). Athens: University of Georgia.

Culbertson, A. E. (1985). *Music and dance at the John C. Campbell Folk School in Brasstown, North Carolina, 1925–1985.* Unpublished doctoral dissertation, Indiana University, Bloomington.

Dabczynski, A. H. (1994). *Northern week at Ashokan, 1991: Fiddle tunes, motivation and community at a fiddle and dance camp.* Unpublished doctoral dissertation, University of Michigan, Ann Arbor.

Danforth, R. J. (1995). *The Madtown Singers: An ethnography of leisure and learning on a Woodland Indian Social Drum.* Unpublished doctoral dissertation, University of Wisconsin, Madison.

Darrough, G. P. (1990). *Older adult participants in selected retirement community choruses.* Unpublished doctoral dissertation, Arizona State University, Tempe.

Davenport, L. G. (1991). *Maine's sacred tunebooks, 1800–1830: Divine song on the Northeast Frontier.* Unpublished doctoral dissertation, University of Colorado at Boulder.

David, J. C. (1994). *On one accord: Community, musicality, and spirit among the singing and praying bands of Tide-*

water Maryland and Delaware. Unpublished doctoral dissertation, University of Pennsylvania, Philadelphia.

DeWitt, M. F. (1998). *The Cajun and Zydeco music and dance scene in Northern California: Ethnicity, authenticity, and leisure.* Unpublished doctoral dissertation, University of California, Berkeley.

Diehl, K. M. (1998). *Echoes from Dharamsala: Music in the lives of Tibetan refugees in north India.* Unpublished doctoral dissertation, University of Texas, Austin.

Draper, A. (Ed.). (1999). *Music makes the difference: Programs and partnerships.* Reston, VA: MENC.

Drummond, J. (1989). The multicultural dimension. In J. Drummond & D. Sell (Eds.), *Contact, Interactions, Symbiosis: Amateur and Professional Music makers in the Community: Proceedings of the International Society for Music Education 1988 Seminar of the Commission on Community Music* (pp. 105–107). Wellington, NZ: University of Canterbury.

Edkvist, I. B. (1997). *The performance of tradition: An ethnography of Hira Gasy popular theatre in Madagascar.* Doctoral dissertation, Uppsala University, Uppsala.

Egan, R F. (1989). *Music and the arts in the community: The Community Music School in America.* Metuchen, NJ: Scarecrow Press.

Engelson, R. A. (1994). *A history of adult community choirs in Charlotte, North Carolina: 1865–1918.* Unpublished doctoral dissertation, Arizona State University, Tempe.

Fabregas, E. (1992). *Designing and implementing an electronic music program in a community music school in New York City.* Unpublished doctoral dissertation, Columbia University Teachers College, New York.

Farrell, G. (1991). Musical crossovers: Questions and observations on Indian music education. *Proceedings of the Second British-Swedish Conference on Musicology: Ethnomusicology. Cambridge, 5–10 August, 1989.* Göteborg: Skrifter från den musikvetenskapliga institutionen, Göteborgs universitet, 26: 113–120.

Farrell, G. (1997). Thinking, saying, playing: Children learning to play the tabla. *Bulletin of the Council for Research in Music Education, 133,* 14–19.

Fife, J. L. (1994). *Pioneer harmonies: Mormon women and music in Utah, 1847–1900.* Unpublished master's thesis, Utah State University, Salt Lake City.

Finnegan, R. (1989). *Hidden musicians: Music-making in an English town.* Cambridge: Cambridge University Press.

Flam, G. (1988). *Singing for survival: Songs of the Lodz ghetto, 1940–1945.* Unpublished doctoral dissertation, University of California, Los Angeles.

Fletcher, W. H. (1988). *Amos Sutton Hayden: Symbol of a movement.* Unpublished doctoral dissertation, University of Oklahoma, Norman.

Fornäs, J., Lindberg, U., & Sernhede O. (1995). In garageland: rock, youth, and modernity (J. Teeland, Trans.). London: Routledge.

Foy, P. S. (1988). *The creation of a standardized body of song suitable for American school children: A history of the Community Song Movement and suggested entries for a contemporary songlist.* Unpublished doctoral dissertation, University of South Carolina, Columbia.

Gallo, A. (1998). *A lone sacred space, an old musical tradition: The dynamics of the Ethiopian Orthodox Church in Toronto through its music.* Unpublished doctoral dissertation, University of Montreal, Canada.

Gencarelli, T. F. (1993). *Reading "Heavy Metal" music: An interpretive communities approach to popular music as communication.* Unpublished doctoral dissertation, New York University, New York.

Glasser, R. (1991). *"Que vivio tiene la gente aqui en Nueva York": Music and community in Puerto Rican New York, 1915–1940.* Unpublished doctoral dissertation, Yale University, New Haven.

Graessle, R. K. (1998). *Adult music programming in member schools of The National Guild of Community Schools of the Arts.* Unpublished doctoral dissertation, University of Oklahoma, Norman.

Grandien, B. (1991). Medialization and music practice in Nepal. *Proceedings of the Second British-Swedish Conference on Musicology: Ethnomusicology. Cambridge, 5–10 August 1989.* Göteborg: Göteborgs universitet, skrifter från den musikveten skapliga institutionen, 26: 319–329.

Green, V. B. (1998). *Enhanced musical literacy through participation in the adult amateur/volunteer chorus: A descriptive study.* Unpublished doctoral dissertation, Columbia University Teachers College, New York.

Green, S. L. (1998). *"Art for life's sake": Music schools and activities in United States social settlements, 1892–1942.* Unpublished doctoral dissertation, University of Wisconsin, Madison.

Gullberg, A-K. (1999). *Form språk och spelregler: En studie i rock musicerande inom och utan för musikhögskolan* [Form, discourse and rules of performance: A study of playing rock music inside and outside a state college of music]. Licentiatuppsats. Piteå: Musikhögskolan i Piteå, avdelningen för musikpedagogik.

Gunderson, F. D. (1999). *Musical labor associations in Sukumaland, Tanzania: History and practice.* Unpublished doctoral dissertation, Wesleyan University, Middletown.

Gustavsson, J. (2000). *Så ska det låta. Studier av det musik-pedagogiska fältets fram växt* [Studies of the evolution of the music education field in Sweden 1900–1965]. Unpublished doctoral dissertation, Uppsala: Acta Universitatis Upsaliensis, Uppsala studies in education, No 91.

Hair, H. I. (1999). Purpose statements and song categories of selected community songbooks. *Bulletin of the Council for Research in Music Education, 141,* 54–58.

Hall, A. (1998). *New Orleans jazz funerals: Transition to the ancestors.* Unpublished doctoral dissertation, New York University, New York.

Hardin, L. E. (1997). *A descriptive analysis of Alabama public community and junior college music programs.* Unpublished doctoral dissertation, University of Alabama, Tuscaloosa.

Harrison, G. (1996). Community music in Australia. In M. A. Leglar (Ed.), *The role of community music in a changing world: Proceedings of the International Society for Music Education 1994 Seminar of the Commission on Community Music Activity* (pp. 39–45). Athens: University of Georgia.

Hast, D. (1994). *Music, dance and community: Contra Dance in New England.* Unpublished doctoral dissertation, Wesleyan University, Middletown.

Heiling, G. (2000). *Spela snyggt och ha kul: Gemenskap, sammanhållning och musikalisk utveckling i en amatörorkester* [Play well and have fun: Community, group-coherence, and musical development in an amateur brass band]. Doctoral dissertation, Malmö: Malmö Academy of Music: Studies in music and music education No 1.

Hemphill-Peoples, J. M. (1992). *An investigation of factors that have influenced the styles of black religious music in selected black churches of Buffalo, New York.* Unpublished doctoral dissertation, State University of New York at Buffalo.

Henningsson, I. (1996). *Kör i cirkel—ett forum för individuell och kollektiv utveckling* [Choir singing in a study circle—A forum for individual and collective development]. Rapp.ort av ett FoU-projekt inom Frikyrkliga Studieförbundet, KFUK_KFUMs studieförbund, Sveriges Kyrkliga Studieförbund och Musikhögskolan i Göteborg, Göteborgs universitet.

Herman, J. (2000). A public schools/ community schools project in the USA. *International Journal of Music Education, 35,* 18.

Herman, J. L. (1997). *Sacred harp singing in California: Genre, performance, feeling.* Unpublished doctoral dissertation, University of California, Los Angeles.

Higgins, L. (in press). Collaborations over distance. *Studies in Music.*

Hildebrand, D. K. (1992). *Musical life in and around Annapolis, Maryland (1649–1776).* Unpublished doctoral dissertation, Catholic University of America, Washington, DC.

Himes, J. L. (1992). *Symphonic educational programs: A study of the Fairfax Symphony Orchestra.* Unpublished master's thesis, American University, Washington, DC.

Holmquist, S. P. (1995). *A study of community choir members' school experiences.* Unpublished doctoral dissertation, University of Oregon, Eugene.

Horner, B., & Swiss, T. (Eds.) *Key terms in popular music and culture* (pp. 239–250). Malden, MA: Blackwell.

Horowitz, A. (1994). *Musika yam tikhonit Yisraelit: Cultural boundaries and disputed territories.* Unpublished doctoral dissertation, University of Pennsylvania, Philadelphia.

Hosler, N. (1992). *The brass band movement in North America: A survey of brass bands in the United States and Canada.* Unpublished doctoral dissertation, Ohio State University, Columbus.

Howle, M. J. M. (1999). *Seven community children's choirs in Florida: Function in the community, organizational patterns, and conductors' theories and practices.* Unpublished doctoral dissertation, University of Florida, Gainesville.

Ihm, D. E. (1994). *Current music practices of the Independent Christian Churches in the United States.* Unpublished doctoral dissertation, University of South Carolina, Columbia.

Johnson, S. (2000). Authenticity: Who needs it? *British Journal of Music Education, 17* (3), 277–287.

Kasdorf, J. M. (1997). *Fixing tradition: The cultural work of Joseph W. Yoder and his relationship with the Amish community of Mifflin County, Pennsylvania.* Unpublished doctoral dissertation, New York University, New York.

Kassebaun, G. R. (1994). *Katha: Six performance traditions and the preservation of group identity in Karnataka, South India.* Unpublished doctoral dissertation, University of Washington, Seattle.

Kibby, M. D. (2000). Home on the page: A virtual place of music community. *Popular Music, 19* (1), 91–100.

Kim, P. C. (2000). *Making music their own: School music, community, and standards of excellence in Seattle, 1960–1975.* Unpublished doctoral dissertation, University of Washington, Seattle.

Kisliuk, M. R. (1991). *Confronting the quintessential: Singing, dancing, and everyday life among Biaka pygmies.* Unpublished doctoral dissertation, New York University, New York.

Klein, N. K. (1990). Music and music education in the Shaker Societies of America. *Bulletin of Historical Research in Music Education, 11* (1), 33–47.

Koehler, W. S. (2000). *"The politics of songs": The German Workers' Choral Association as a cultural and sociopolitical entity in comparative perspective, 1918–1933.* Unpublished doctoral dissertation, Brandeis University, Waltham.

Koszarycz, A-M. (1999). *Collection and documentation of Ukrainian folk songs in Kalyna Country, Edmonton, Alberta, Canada (1997).* Unpublished master's thesis, University of Calgary, Canada.

Kruse, H. (1993). Subcultural identity in alternative music culture. *Popular Music, 12* (1), 33–41.

Lamb, R. (in press). Symphony education: The story of a successful community arts partnership. *Studies in Music.*

Lausevic, M. (1998). *A different village: International folk dance and Balkan music and dance in the United States.* Unpublished doctoral dissertation, Wesleyan University, Middletown.

Lave, K., & Wenger, E. (1991). *Situated learning: Legitimate peripheral participation.* Cambridge, England: Cambridge University Press.

LeCroy, H. F. (1998). Community-based music education: Influences of industrial bands in the American South. *Journal of Research in Music Education, 46*(2), 248–264.

Lee, W. R. (1997). Music education and rural reform, 1900–1925. *Journal of Research in Music Education, 45*(2), 306–326.

Leglar, M. A., & Smith, D. S. (1996). Community music in the United States: An overview of origins and evolution. In M. A. Leglar (Ed.), *The role of community music in a changing world: Proceedings of the International Society for Music Education 1994 Seminar of the Commission on Community Music Activity* (pp. 95–108). Athens: University of Georgia.

Lilliestam L. (1995). *Gehörsmusik. Blues, rock och muntlig tradering* [Playing by ear: Blues, rock and oral tradition]. Göteborg: Akademiförlaget.

Lipsitz, G. (1994). *Dangerous crossroads: Popular music, postmodernism and the poetics of place.* London: Verso.

Livingston, T. E., Russell, M., Ward, L. F., & Nettl, B. (Eds.). (1993). *Community of music: An ethnographic seminar in Champaign-Urbana.* Champaign, IL: Elephant and Cat.

Mannergren, J. (2000). *Musik, makt and mångfald—möten med Sydafrika* [Music, power and pluralism—Meetings with South Africa]. Göteborg: Musikhögskolan, Göteborgs universitet.

Mark, D. (1990). *Musikschule 2000: Der Bedarf an Musikschullehrern.* Schriftenreihe Musik und Gesellschaft, Heft 21. Vienna: Verlag der Wissenschaftlichen Gesellschaften Österreichs.

Mark, D. (1992). Music teacher training in the year 2000: A perspective from Vienna. In *Music teacher training in the year 2000—Three European perspectives.* International conference in research on music education, September 15–17, 1992. Göteborg: Skrifter från musikvetenskap, No 32, pp. 5–24.

Mark, D. (1998). The music teacher's dilemma—musician or teacher? *International Journal of Music Education, 32,* 3–23.

Mark, M. L., & Gary, C. L. (1992). *A history of American music education.* New York: Schirmer Books.

Martin, P. J. (1995). *Sounds and society: Themes in the sociology of music.* Manchester, UK: Manchester University Press.

Mathews, L. (2000). *The Native American Powwow: A contemporary authentication of a cultural artifact.* Unpublished doctoral dissertation, University of New Mexico, Albuquerque.

Mbanugo, C. E. (1986). *Music transmission processes among children in an Afro-American Church.* Unpublished doctoral dissertation, State University of New York at Buffalo.

McAllister, A. B. (1995). *The musical legacy of Dorothy Love Coates: African American female gospel singer, with implications for education and theater education.* Unpublished doctoral dissertation, Kansas State University, Manhattan.

McCarthy, M. (1995). The foundations of sociology in American music education (1900–1935). In R. Rideout (Ed.), *On the sociology of music education* (pp. 71–80). Norman: University of Oklahoma.

McDade, M. B. (1988). *Hugh Hodgson: The fostering of music in Georgia (1928–1960).* Unpublished doctoral dissertation, University of Georgia, Athens.

McEntire, N. C. (1990). *Sitting out the winter in the Orkney Islands: Folksong acquisition in Northern Scotland.* Unpublished doctoral dissertation, Indiana University, Bloomington.

McNamara, R. T. (1997). *Uses of popular music by Old Order Amish youth in Lancaster County, Pennsylvania.* Unpublished doctoral dissertation, Temple University, Philadelphia.

Moloney, M. (1992). *Irish Music in America: Continuity and change.* Unpublished doctoral dissertation, University of Pennsylvania, Philadelphia.

Monson, I. (2000). The Charles Seeger Lecture 2000. *SEM Newsletter, 34*(4), 1–3.

Moore, E. (1998). *Who pays the piper? Community music education funding.* Dunedin, NZ: Winston Churchill Fellowship Trust.

Mumford, M. (in press). An exploration of social capital as it is evidenced in successful community/institutional collaboration. *Studies in Music.*

Music Educators National Conference. (1950). *Music for everybody.* Chicago: MENC.

Myers-Moro, P. A. (1988). *Thai music and musicians in contemporary Bangkok: An ethnography.* Unpublished doctoral dissertation, University of California, Berkeley.

Nardo, R. L. (1996). *California survey of music in early childhood: Teacher preparation and the role of the community college.* Unpublished doctoral dissertation, University of Southern California, Los Angeles.

Nazareth, T. C. (1999). *Lifelong learning: Music education for adult beginners.* Unpublished doctoral dissertation, University of Western Australia, Nedlands.

Nazareth, T. C. (in press). Making connections: Advancing the music agenda for the new millennium. *Studies in Music.*

Nebesh, D. L. (1998). *"Because it's ours": Constructing identity in the Ukrainian Diaspora through Hutsul music and dance.* Unpublished doctoral dissertation, University of Maryland Baltimore County.

Neff, M. L. (1996). *Media usage among folk music communities.* Unpublished doctoral dissertation, University of Florida, Gainesville.

Ngige-Nguo, J. E. (1990). *The role of music amongst the Gikuyu of the central province of Kenya.* Unpublished doctoral dissertation, Queen's University of Belfast, Northern Ireland.

Nicholls, R. W. (1992). *Music and dance associations of the Igede of Nigeria: The relevance of indigenous communication learning systems to rural development projects.* Unpublished doctoral dissertation, Howard University, Washington, DC.

Nielsen F.V. (1998). *Almen musikdidaktik* [The general didactics of music]. Copenhagen: Akademisk Forlag, 2. Reviderade och bearbejdede udgave.

Nixon, P. J. (1993). *Transylvanian nexus: Human interdependencies and music making in the Gurghiu Valley.* Unpublished doctoral dissertation, American Baptist Seminary of the West, Berkeley, CA.

Norfleet, D. M. (1997). *"Hip-hop culture" in New York City: The role of verbal musical performance in defining a community.* Unpublished doctoral dissertation, Columbia University, New York.

Norris, E. M. (1994). *Music in the black and white communities in Petersburg, Virginia, 1865–1900.* Unpublished doctoral dissertation, Ohio State University, Columbus.

Olson, R. S. (1997). *The history and development of the Dalesburg Cornet Band.* Unpublished doctoral dissertation, University of Northern Colorado, Greeley.

Olsson, B. (1993). *Sämus—en musikutbildning i kulturpolitikens tjänst? En studie om en musikutbildning under 70-talet* [Sämus—music education in the service of cultural policy? A study of a music education during the 1970s]. Doctoral dissertation, Göteborg: Skrifter från musikvetenskap, nr 33, musikhögskolan i Göteborg.

Olsson, B. (1997). The social psychology of music education. In D. J. Hargreaves & A. C. North (Eds.), *The social psychology of music.* Oxford: Oxford University Press.

Olsson, B. (2001). Scandinavia. In D. J. Hargreaves & A. C. North (Eds.), *Musical development and learning: The intenational perspective*. London: Cassell.

Pacini, H. D. (1989). *Music of marginality: Social identity and class in Dominican Bachata*. Unpublished doctoral dissertation, Cornell University, Ithaca.

Paek, I. (1999). *Transmission processes in Korean traditional music: Contemporary musical practice and national identity*. Unpublished doctoral dissertation, Queen's University of Belfast, Northern Ireland.

Pagano, M. J. (1997). *The history of the Third Street Music School Settlement, 1891–1984. Music school and social settlement: The dual identity of the original music school settlement*. Unpublished doctoral dissertation, Manhattan School of Music, New York.

Palmer, A. J. (1992). World musics in education: The matter of authenticity. *International Journal of Music Education, 19*, 32–40.

Park, J. H. (1995). *On the margin between "high" culture and "ordinary" everyday life: Social organization of the amateur orchestra and its musicians*. Unpublished doctoral dissertation, Syracuse University, New York.

Parker, L. F. (1983). *Women in music in St. Paul from 1898 to 1957 with emphasis on the St. Paul public schools*. Unpublished doctoral dissertation, University of Minnesota, Minneapolis.

Patterson, F. C. (1985). *Motivational factors contributing to participation in community bands of the Montachusett region of North Central Massachusetts*. Unpublished doctoral dissertation, University of Connecticut, Storrs.

Patterson, M. R. (1991). *A survey of educational outreach programs for children by professional opera companies*. Unpublished doctoral dissertation, University of Oklahoma, Norman.

Perkins, C. C. (1994). *The piano in an American society: The coalfield area of Bluefield, West Virginia, 1890–1960*. Unpublished doctoral dissertation, University of South Carolina, Columbia.

Persson, T. (1998). *Det låg i luften . . . Den kommunala musikskolans framväxt: En studie av musikskolorna i Mörbylånga, Tranås, Kiruna och Borås* [The growth of community music schools: A study of music schools in four Swedish communities]. Licentiatuppsats. Gothenburg: Gothenburg University.

Pflieger, D. B. (1985). *Community schools of the arts: Outreach, scholarship, and financial assistance programs*. Unpublished doctoral dissertation, Louisiana State University and Agricultural and Mechanical College, Baton Rouge.

Pieper, L. E. (1996). *Culture and community, Kitchener, 1911–1939: Music, radio, film, and theatre*. Unpublished master's thesis, University of Guelph, Canada.

Pierson, S. J. (1998). *We sang ourselves free: Developmental uses of music among Estonian Christians from repression to independence*. Unpublished doctoral dissertation, Trinity Evangelical Divinity School.

Platts, A. (1991). A postgraduate diploma in community music in Western Australia. In J. Drummond (Ed.), *The community musician: Training a new professional*. Report of the Oslo Seminar of the ISME Commission on Community Music Activity 1990 (pp. 73–77). Oslo: The Norwegian Affiliation of International Society for Music Education.

Pohly, L. L. (1989). *Welsh choral music in America in the nineteenth century*. Unpublished doctoral dissertation, Ohio State University, Columbus.

Ritchie, J., & Wallis, G. (1989). A profile of music in Christchurch. In J. Drummond & D. Sell (Eds.), *Contact, interactions, symbiosis: Amateur and professional music makers in the community: Proceedings of the International Society for Music Education 1988 Seminar of the Commission on Community Music* (pp. 63–75). Wellington, NZ: University of Canterbury.

Roberts, B. A. (1990). *The social construction of "musician" identity in music education students in Canadian universities*. Unpublished doctoral dissertation, University of Stirling, Scotland.

Roberts, B. A. (1993). *I, musician: Towards a model of identity construction and maintenance by music education students as musicians*. St. John's, NF: Memorial University of Newfoundland.

Robertson, P. L. (1996). *The role of singing in the Christian Science Church: The forming of a tradition*. Unpublished doctoral dissertation, New York University, New York.

Robertson, W. D. (1992). *A survey of music education programs for senior citizens in Mecklenburg County, North Carolina*. Unpublished doctoral dissertation, University of North Carolina, Greensboro.

Robinson, M. (1999). *A theory of collaborative music education between higher education and urban public schools*. Unpublished doctoral dissertation, University of Rochester, Eastman School of Music.

Rocco, E. S. (1986). *Italian wind bands: A surviving tradition in the milltowns of Lawrence and Beaver Counties of Pennsylvania*. Unpublished doctoral dissertation, University of Pittsburgh.

Ronström, O. (Ed.). (1990). *Musik och kultur* (Music and culture). Lund: Studentlitteratur.

Rosse, M. D. (1995). *The movement for the revitalization of "Hindu" music in Northern India, 1860–1930: The role of associations and institutions*. Unpublished doctoral dissertation, University of Pennsylvania, Philadelphia.

Rothrock, D. K. (1991). *The perpetuation of the Moravian instrumental music tradition: Bernard Jacob Pfohl and the Salem, North Carolina, Bands (1879–1960)*. Unpublished doctoral dissertation, University of North Carolina, Greensboro.

Rowden, M. L. (1996). *A history of The Salvation Army Chicago Staff Band, 1954–1994*. Unpublished doctoral dissertation, University of Illinois, Urbana-Champaign.

Ruud, E. (1996). *Musikk og verdier* [Music and values]. Oslo: Universitetsforlaget.

Ruud, E. (1997). *Musikk og identitet* [Music and identity]. Oslo: Universitetsforlaget.

Russell, M. A. (1999). *Listening to Decatur: Musical ethnography in an Illinois city, 1992–1997*. Unpublished doctoral dissertation, University of Illinois, Urbana-Champaign.

Savaglio, P. C. (1992). *Polish-American music in Detroit: Negotiating ethnic boundaries*. Unpublished doctoral dissertation, University of Illinois, Urbana-Champaign.

Schaffer, R. E. (1992). *History of the Phoenix Boys Choir: From 1947 through 1989.* Unpublished doctoral dissertation, Arizona State University, Tempe.

Sernhede, O. (1995). *Modernitet, adolescens and kulturella uttryck* [Modernity, adolescents and cultural expression]. Unpublished doctoral dissertation, Göteborg, Göteborgs universitet, institutionen för socialt arbete.

Shellhouse, B. C. (1990). *An analysis of community college music departments in the state of Illinois.* Unpublished doctoral dissertation, Columbia University Teachers College, New York.

Single, N. A. (1991). *An arts outreach/audience development program for schools of music in higher education.* Unpublished doctoral dissertation, Ohio State University, Columbus.

Slobin, M. (1993). *Subcultural sounds: Micromusics of the west.* Hanover, NH: Wesleyan University Press.

Sluder, C. K. (1987). *Music in New Harmony, Indiana, 1825–1865: A Study of the music and musical activities of Robert Owen's Community of Equality.* Unpublished doctoral dissertation, Indiana University, Bloomington.

Snyder, S. G. (1991). *The "Maennerchor" tradition in the United States: A historical analysis of its contribution to American musical culture.* Unpublished doctoral dissertation, University of Iowa, Iowa City.

Solomon, T. J. (1997). *Mountains of song: Musical constructions of ecology, place, and identity in the Bolivian Andes.* Unpublished doctoral dissertation, University of Texas, Austin.

Soodyall, M., & Goodall, S. (in press). Action research in music education: Beyond the classroom and community. *Studies in Music.*

Spell, G. M. (1989). *Motivational factors and selected sociodemographic characteristics of Georgia community chorus participants as measured by the education participation scale, the community chorus participation scale, and the personal inventory form.* Unpublished doctoral dissertation, University of Georgia, Athens.

Spencer, W. D. (1996). *An attitude assessment of amateur musicians in adult community bands.* Unpublished doctoral dissertation, University of North Texas.

Spencer, W. B. (1994). *The Baltimore Symphony Orchestra, 1965–1982: The Meyerhoff years.* Unpublished doctoral dissertation, Peabody Institute of the Johns Hopkins University, Baltimore.

Spurgeon, A. L. (1990). *George Oscar Bowen: His career and contributions to music education.* Unpublished doctoral dissertation, University of Oklahoma, Norman.

Spurgeon, A. L. (1994). The Community Music Association in Flint, Michigan, 1917–1920. *Bulletin of Historical Research in Music Education, 16* (1), 29–42.

Stålhammar, B. (1995). *Samspel. Grundskola—musikskola i samverkan: En studie av den pedagogiska och musikaliska interaktionen i en klassrumssituation* [Interplay—school and music school in collaboration: A study of pedagogic and musical interaction in a classroom situation]. Doctoral dissertation, Göteborg: Göteborgs universitet, skrifter från den musikvetenskapliga avdelningen, nr 41, musikhögskolan i Göteborg.

Stewardson, R. G. (1994). *Hattie Rhue Hatchett (1863–1958): An interdisciplinary study of her life and music in North Buxton, Ontario.* Unpublished master's thesis, York University, Toronto, ON, Canada.

Stokes, M. (Ed.). (1994). *Ethnicity, identity and music: The musical construction of place.* Providence, RI: Berg Publishers.

Stormer, L. A. (1997). *The study of an old tyme fiddling club: Re-creation of rural community.* Unpublished master's thesis, University of Alberta, Edmonton, AB, Canada.

Stuempfle, S. (1990). *The steelband movement in Trinidad and Tobago: Music, politics and national identity in a new world society.* Unpublished doctoral dissertation, University of Pennsylvania, Philadelphia.

Sugarman, J. C. (1993). *Engendering song: Singing and the social order at Prespa Albanian weddings.* Unpublished doctoral dissertation, University of California, Los Angeles.

Szemere, A. (1998). *Pop culture, politics, and social transition.* Unpublished doctoral dissertation, University of California, San Diego.

Tatum, M. E. (1985). *A descriptive analysis of the status of music programs in selected retirement residences and senior citizens' centers in the Southeastern United States.* Unpublished doctoral dissertation, Indiana University, Bloomington.

Thaller, G. P. (1999). *The community contributions, recruitment, and retention practices of select adult community bands in eastern Massachusetts.* Unpublished doctoral dissertation, University of Cincinnati.

Thornton, S. (1995). *Club cultures: Music, media and subcultural capital.* London: Polity Press.

Thorsén, S-M. (1997). Music education in South Africa—striving for unity and diversity. *Svensk Tidskrift för Musikforskning, 79,* 91–109.

Thorsén, S-M. (2000, October). *The second liberation struggle—Cultural identities in South African music education.* Paper presented at the Nordic Africa Institute's Conference: Playing with identities in contemporary music in Africa. Åbo/Turku, Finland.

Tipps, J. W. (1992). *Profile characteristics and musical backgrounds of community chorus participants in the Southeastern United States.* Unpublished doctoral dissertation, Florida State University, Tallahassee.

Tolbert, P. M. (1997). *Anne Grace O'Callaghan: Music educator, community arts advocate and professional leader.* Unpublished doctoral dissertation, University of Georgia, Athens.

Townsend, R. T. (1996). *The music teaching and learning process in an African-American Baptist Church.* Unpublished doctoral dissertation, University of Illinois, Urbana-Champaign.

Tunnell, K. D., & Groce, S. B. (1998). The social world of semiprofessional bluegrass musicians. *Popular Music and Society, 22*(4), 55–77.

Vaillant, D. W. (1999). *Musical publics: Progressive reform and music making in Chicago, 1869–1930.* Unpublished doctoral dissertation, University of Chicago.

Veblen, K. K. (1991). *Perceptions of change and stability in the transmission of Irish traditional music: A study of the music teacher's role.* Unpublished doctoral dissertation, University of Wisconsin, Madison.

Veblen, K. K. (1995). *Sociology of music education: Remembered homelands, chosen destinations and the construction of musical identity.* In R. Rideout (Ed.), *On the sociology of music education* (pp. 22–42). Norman: University of Oklahoma.

Veblen, K. K., & Elliott, D. J. (in press). Community music: Foundations and practices. *Studies in Music.*

Vincent, P. M. (1997*). A study of community choruses in Kentucky and implications for music education.* Unpublished doctoral dissertation, University of Kentucky, Lexington.

Vinther, O. (1997). *Musikkonservatorierne og musikskolerne. En relationsanalyse. Med teoretisk perspektivering af Frede V. Nielsen* [Conservatories and community music schools. An analysis of relationship]. Aarhus: Det jydske musikkonservatorium.

Wallis, G. (in press). The burgeoning growth of a community school. *Studies in Music.*

Walser, R. (1993). *Running with the devil: Power, gender, and madness in heavy metal music.* Hanover, NH: Wesleyan University Press.

Washburne, C. J. (1999). *Salsa in New York: A musical ethnography.* Unpublished doctoral dissertation, Columbia University, New York.

Weddle, J. W. (1989). *Early bands of the Mid-Willamette Valley, 1850–1920.* Unpublished doctoral dissertation, University of Oregon, Eugene.

Werner, O. (1996). *Music programs in the community college.* Unpublished doctoral dissertation, Colorado State University.

Wilberg, H., & Sharman, E. (1989). Who does the modeling? Parents as teachers. In J. Drummond & D. Sell (Eds.), *Contact, interactions, symbiosis: Amateur and professional music maker s in the community: Proceedings o f the International Society for Music Education 1988 Seminar of the Commission on Community Music* (pp. 88–93). Wellington, NZ: University of Canterbury.

Wilhjelm, C. C. (1998). *A case study of the Ridgewood Concert Band, a New Jersey community band dedicated to lifelong learning.* Unpublished doctoral dissertation, Columbia University Teachers College, New York.

Winterston, J. (1999). The community work of orchestras and opera companies: The experiment is over. In *Making music work: Fostering professional skills among those studying music in higher education.* Professional integration project. London: Royal College of Music.

Witzleben, J. L. (1987). *Silk and bamboo: Jiangnan Sizhu instrumental ensemble music in Shanghai.* Unpublished doctoral dissertation, University of Pittsburgh.

Wood, V. N. M. (1995). *Rushin' hard and runnin' hot: Experiencing the music of the Junanoo parade in Nassau, Bahamas.* Unpublished doctoral dissertation, Indiana University, Bloomington.

Zhang, W. H. (1994). *The musical activities of the Chinese American communities in the San Francisco Bay area: A social and cultural study.* Unpublished doctoral dissertation, University of California, Berkeley.

Zheng, S. (1993). *Immigrant music and transnational discourse: Chinese American music culture in New York City.* Unpublished doctoral dissertation, Wesleyan University, Middletown.

Part VI
MUSIC TEACHER EDUCATION

Liz Wing
Janet R. Barrett
Editors

Introduction: Fuzzy Teacher Education

JAMES RATHS

This part of the Handbook includes some of the finest essays I have ever read in one collection dealing with research on teacher education. The chapters here are concerned with the major issues of the day, from teacher education curriculum, student teaching, teacher research, to professional development. The authors are primarily music educators and their interests are essentially focused on teacher education in the field of music. However, almost every chapter author agreed to address the assigned topics by reviewing the research in music teacher education more broadly conceived and then interpolating the meaning of that research for music teacher education. As a whole, they have performed their tasks admirably.

One characteristic of a review, perhaps in any field, is a feeling at the close that what we know is dwarfed by what we don't know. This outcome is perhaps more prominent in teacher education than in most fields. The reader will note here by simply scanning the final pages of each selection how modest and how tentative the authors are about their respective topics. Why such tentativeness? It is important to grasp the nature of the authors' challenge by considering at least two perspectives on the field.

The first has to do with the "fuzziness" of teacher education. Brule (1985) recounts the efforts to capture the complexities of the real world in fuzzy systems where the traditional Aristotelian logic encompassing true or false as the only values worthy of consideration was rejected for three-value and four-value systems. The fuzzy axioms attempted to accommodate real-world situations found in the study of "expert systems" in which the meaning of "true" and "false" was less than clear and less than useful. Fuzzy systems provide researchers with a broader, richer field of data and with procedures for manipulating the evidence that are more promising and more isomorphic with the complexities of the real world. The complexity of

teacher education, its fuzziness, often will not yield to traditional research procedures whether they are qualitative or quantitative. Perhaps dramatic breakthroughs in teacher education await new, non-Aristotelian research procedures to accommodate its fuzziness.

The second context is developmental; teacher education can be conceived as being in a very immature state. This view draws from the history of medical education so nicely documented in Lewis Thomas's essays collected under the title *The Youngest Science*. Thomas (1983) describes the field of medicine at the turn of the century as follows:

> The medical literature of those years makes horrifying reading today; paper after learned paper recounts the benefits of bleeding, cupping, violent purging, the raising of blisters by vesicant ointments, the immersion of the body in either ice water or intolerably hot water, endless lists of botanical extracts, cooked up and mixed together under the influence of nothing more than pure whim, and all these things were drilled into the heads of medical students—most of whom learned their trade as apprentices in the offices of older, established doctors. (pp. 19–20)

Based on Lewis's description, imagine a *Handbook on Medical Education* written in 1911. It would commission authors to review the literature and summarize the results. Those authors would have a task similar to those facing the authors of the chapters in this section. Looking back on the literature of the day, Thomas was horrified. Perhaps as teacher educators in the year 2100 review these chapters, they will be equally horrified by the ignorance and dogmatism they find in the literature reviewed in this section (I am confident they will still value the scholarly way in which literature was reviewed). Of course, it is my guess that this will only happen if, in the intervening 100 years, new procedures for determining what is more likely to help

757

others learn and what is less likely to help others learn can be determined by procedures that are not yet available to scholars. In sum, we must hope that teacher education as a field of research will develop and mature over the next 100 years as did medicine in the 20th century.

In all practical fields, researchers have at one time or another depended on trial-and-error approaches to solve problems. Trial and error is useful when the researcher knows that an error is made. Conant (1961) described how Edison was seeking to find an element that would incandesce in a partial vacuum. He tried whatever he could get his hands on and was successful when tungsten worked. He knew it worked because he could see it. How does a teacher know that cooperative learning works? Or that requiring student teachers to keep reflective logs works? In these latter cases, there is no clear and sharp indication of "it works."

Given the fuzziness of the field, its relative immaturity, and the lack of clear-cut criterion variables, there is a view of research and its purposes that may serve us well at this time. Lewis's horror on viewing the early research work in medicine was that it was false. Modern perspectives suggest strongly that what medical researchers were reporting early in the century was rooted in superstition and igno-rance. But is it reasonable to believe that research in any field at any time reports immutable truths that will stand the test of time?

Perhaps it is more reasonable to see research less as providing road maps for practice and more as suggesting alternative views that serve to make our conceptions more complex and complicated and to prompt our reconsideration of our own current views and practices. Scholars who read this collection of essays in this manner will not be looking for the resolution of enduring problems in teacher education, but instead will be seeking insights into the issues or even some solace as practitioners in finding that some of the efforts they have been making have been studied by others with interesting results.

REFERENCES

Brule, J. F. (1985). *Fuzzy systems—a tutorial.* Retrieved from http://www.austinlinks.com/Fuzzy/tutorial.html

Conant, J. B. (1961). *Trial and error in the improvement of education.* Alexandria, VA: Association for Supervision and Curriculum Development.

Thomas, L. (1983). *The youngest science.* New York: Bantam.

Reform-Minded Music Teachers

A More Comprehensive Image of Teaching for Music Teacher Education

DENNIS THIESSEN

JANET R. BARRETT

Teachers stand at the center of an insistent and polyphonic conversation about educational change. Teaching, by its very nature, is characterized by periods of stasis and flux, but teachers find that expectations for the rate, degree, and effects of educational change have intensified during this current era of school reform. Voices within elementary and secondary schools, as well as the voices of those who stand outside of schools altogether, have joined the chorus to call for changes in teaching practices, in the ways schools are organized, and in the relationship of teachers to the students and communities they serve. This complex and shifting landscape of reform poses a particular challenge to teacher educators who must prepare beginning teachers to take their places alongside their more experienced colleagues who are concurrently transforming their practices within continually evolving school structures. Inclusive and comprehensive notions of what teachers do in those contexts—how they initiate and respond to change—can inform the restructuring of teacher education programs.

In this chapter, we suggest that recent initiatives to reform teacher education are founded on restricted images of teachers and teaching that are rooted in preservice teachers' biographies, expressed in descriptions of teachers' work and knowledge, and implied in pedagogical strategies for learning to teach. In place of these narrow conceptions, we describe an expanded image—that of the reform-minded teacher—to portray expanded realms of a teacher's influence in and beyond the classroom. This view will be related to the current literature on educational change and the dilemmas and paradoxes of change that shape and influence teachers' work in schools. Recent models, networks, and studies of school reform also will

be described in order to prod thinking, to provide alternative frameworks, and to prompt comparisons among various initiatives. We do not intend, however, to provide a music teacher's handy guide to school reform models, nor to advocate specific features of these models to follow or adopt. Instead, these comprehensive school reform (CSR) models provide a concrete way to highlight recent emphases on change and to elaborate the changing role of teachers in reform, both platforms for a renewed, revitalized, and expanded place for teachers in improving our schools.

Insights from the change literature and CSR models also suggest that traditional conceptions of subject matter and the roles of teachers who teach those subjects will change as connections between people and ideas become increasingly interdependent. This ecological view has profound implications for the scope and character of music teachers' work and for the students they serve, and lends deep credence to the value of music programs in the ongoing transformation of schools. The capacity of music teachers to act as savvy, informed change agents is another focal point of this chapter, as is the need to instill and encourage these capacities for change in beginning teachers. To these ambitious ends, we will synthesize principles and practices derived from the emerging literature on teachers within the most promising and successful schools. We will illustrate these key ideas using a narrative device, a letter from a reform-minded music teacher participating in school reform initiatives. In the letter, the music teacher explores the counterpoint of possibility and reality as she transforms her practice in the classroom, and moves beyond the classroom to engage in collaborative work with teachers

759

in the school and other individuals in the community. This will lead to an expanded definition of the role of the music teacher as a specialist, and implications of reform-mindedness for teacher education programs.

Although many of the avenues and ideas for change discussed in this chapter bear significant ramifications for the work of teachers already in the field, we have chosen to illustrate these themes of change within the context of preservice music teacher education. Music teacher education has traditionally focused on the development of musical and pedagogical skills in preparing future teachers for the general music, choral, or instrumental classroom. Heightened expectations and increased requirements for musical study and teacher licensure, however, have led to overpacked and unfocused curricula through accretion rather than design. Music teacher educators face the substantial task of developing comprehensive and crosscutting, yet concentrated, programs. Preservice music teachers, in the formative stages of developing their identities and practices, base their views of teaching at least in part on the prominent images of learning to teach and program pedagogy that are embedded in these programs. A curriculum that promotes an attitude of reform-mindedness and develops preservice teachers' capacities to implement change will move teacher education closer to realizing Eisner's (1998) challenge that "universities ought to provide prospective teachers with cutting-edge visions of educational possibilities; they ought to help them imagine what is not now, but what might be" (p. 212). We will return to Eisner's call at the close of this chapter as we incorporate three forces for change and five broad themes into a view of a reform-minded curriculum for music teacher education.

Teacher Education Reform

Recent efforts to improve the initial preparation of teachers have been dominated by the need to define and to elaborate three interrelated and often reciprocal images: the image of teaching that beginning teachers should learn (Fullan, 1993b; Smylie, Bay, & Tozer, 1999; Thiessen & Pike, 1992); the image of learning to teach that should inform and guide how beginning teachers learn (Borko & Putnam, 1996; Feiman-Nemser & Remillard, 1996; Wideen, Mayer-Smith, & Moon, 1998); and the image of pedagogy that should govern what beginning teachers do in their program (Carter & Anders, 1996). Although changes can begin with any of the three images, the image of teaching is the compass and catalyst for the most significant reforms. For example, the prior assumptions and beliefs of beginning teachers (image of learning to teach) are important to understand and examine because these biographical forces may affect the extent to which begin-

ning teachers seriously consider or eventually embrace the ideas and practices represented in the program (image of teaching). A new program strategy such as requiring beginning teachers to complete an action research project (image of pedagogy) provides experiences that enact certain principles about teacher learning (e.g., school-based, experiential image of learning to teach), an approach defined in the end by a change in the capacities of and disposition toward teaching (e.g., here favoring an inquiry-oriented image of teaching). The dynamic connections among these three images then is ultimately framed and guided by an underlying image of what teaching involves.

Image of Teaching

As part of the growing emphasis on accountability (Murphy & Adams, 1998), the more standardized notions of teaching have become an especially important cornerstone in teacher education reform. One of the more influential initiatives has been the development of a set of standards developed by the Interstate New Teacher Assessment and Support Consortium (INTASC) which define what newly licensed teachers should know and be able to do (Interstate New Teacher Assessment and Support Consortium, 1992). These standards are described in the following 10 principles:

Principle 1: The teacher understands the central concepts, tools of inquiry, and structures of the discipline(s) he or she teaches and can create learning experiences that make these aspects of subject matter meaningful to students.

Principle 2: The teacher understands how children learn and develop and can provide learning opportunities that support their intellectual, social, and personal development.

Principle 3: The teacher understands how students differ in their approach to learning and creates instructional opportunities that are adapted to diverse learners.

Principle 4: The teacher understands and uses a variety of instructional strategies to encourage students' development of critical thinking, problem solving, and performance skills.

Principle 5: The teacher uses an understanding of individual and group motivation and behavior to create a learning environment that encourages positive social interaction, active engagement in learning, and self-motivation.

Principle 6: The teacher uses knowledge of effective verbal, nonverbal, and media communication techniques to foster active inquiry, collaboration, and supportive interaction in the classroom.

Principle 7: The teacher plans instruction based on knowledge of subject matter, students, the community, and curriculum goals.

Principle 8: The teacher understands and uses formal and informal assessment strategies to evaluate and ensure the continuous intellectual, social, and physical development of the learner.

Principle 9: The teacher is a reflective practitioner who continually evaluates the effects of his/her choices and actions on others (students, parents, and other professionals in the learning community) and who actively seeks out opportunities to grow professionally.

Principle 10: The teacher fosters relationships with school colleagues, parents, and agencies in the larger community to support students' learning and well-being.

The first eight principles focus almost exclusively on the desired teaching knowledge, dispositions, and performances of beginning teachers' work with students in classrooms, with principles 1 and 7 addressing discipline-specific knowledge directly. While principles 9 and 10 focus on their work outside the classroom (with some reference in principle 7 to collegial planning and knowledge about the local community), these areas are comparatively less prominent and more general. The message is clear. Teaching as embodied in the INTASC standards is mainly about classroom work. Beginning teachers need to concentrate on those capacities (e.g., make subject matter meaningful, adapt instruction to the diversity of the learners, motivate students to learn, etc.) that are critical to their effectiveness in classrooms.

We do not question the importance of preparing teachers for their responsibilities in the classroom. This emphasis on the classroom work of teachers, in our view however, fails to adequately acknowledge the work of teachers in other contexts and, consequently, underplays the interdependence of what teachers do inside and outside the classroom. Numerous accounts and reviews of teachers' lives and careers (Bullough Jr., 1997; Goodson, 1997; Hatch, 1999; Lacey, 1977; Lieberman & Miller, 1999; Rallis & Rossman, 1995; Zeichner & Gore, 1990) demonstrate that, right from the outset of and continuing throughout their careers, the professional work of teachers encompasses an intricate web of responsibilities that extend beyond yet remain connected to their commitments to students. Some of these observers have represented this wider agenda by portraying teachers as reflective (Schön, 1983) or contemplative (Miller, 1994) practitioners, curriculum (Clandinin & Connelly, 1992) or decision makers (Smith, 1989), innovators (Doyle, 1990; Randi & Corno, 1997), and moral stewards (Goodlad, 1990). Such images recognize the time teachers spend away from the classroom with colleagues, administrators, and resource personnel in the school to plan, organize, and coordinate what they do on behalf of their students. Others have argued that the sphere of influence and engagement of teachers have expanded even further. Such images as pragmatic visionaries

(Day, 1999), reformers (Thiessen 1993; Thiessen & Kilcher, 1992) or change agents (Fullan, 1993b; Glatthorn, 1993; Smylie, Bay, & Tozer, 1999), community (Liston & Zeichner, 1990) or political (Cochran-Smith & Lytle, 1999; Smyth, 1997) activists, or social theorists and transformative intellectuals (Giroux, 1988) convey a professional world in which teachers, in concert with other stakeholders, are deeply involved in forums and bodies where they evaluate and, when warranted, improve those structures, conditions, and policies that frame what they do in the school. Clearly teachers work both in and on behalf of their classrooms. Accordingly, we argue that improving the preparation of beginning teachers needs to be based on an expanded image of what teachers do.

Figure 40.1 conceptualizes what teachers do in terms of three overlapping realms of work: in the classroom, in the corridors, and as part of other communities. Thiessen and Anderson (1999) describe these three realms as follows:

In the classroom is where students learn on their own, with other students, and through their interactions with teachers. It includes student learning inside the school (e.g., formal classrooms, halls, library, playground) and outside the school (e.g., neighborhood, parks and woodlands, museums). *In the corridors* is where teachers work with other adults, primarily inside the school, to organize, facilitate the operation of, and make decisions about the school and its development. This can involve a wide range of relationships and forums: teachers with other teachers (e.g., committees, departments, action research teams); teachers with parents (e.g., parent-teacher groups); teachers with resource personnel (e.g., in study groups or work teams with special education teachers, English-as-a-Second-Language teachers, consultants, psychologists, social workers); and teachers with administrators and other stakeholders (e.g., steering committees, school councils). *As part of other communities* is where teachers, students, administrators, and other school personnel interact with groups and organizations outside the school to improve and extend the capacity of the school. These linkages can be with local associations, (e.g., business, social agencies), other professional groups (e.g., networks of schools, universities), and government (e.g., district, state). (pp. 2–3)

The nested configuration of figure 40.1 conveys the embedded relationship among the three realms of teachers' work. What teachers do in one realm inevitably implicates what they do in one or both of the other realms. Notwithstanding the primary emphasis on what they do in the classroom, by including the other two realms in the preparation of beginning teachers, they learn the more inclusive and comprehensive image of teaching, a focus that includes but extends beyond the classroom.

In this reconceptualization, beginning teachers learn about the three embedded realms of their future work through pedagogical approaches that provide for experi-

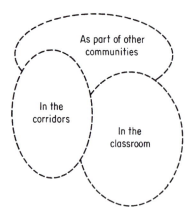

Figure 40.1. Realms of teachers' work.

ences within and across these realms and are guided by insights into those forces that affect their development in these three contexts. The overarching intent is to help beginning teachers ready themselves for a career where they can both facilitate the development of their students through productive and responsive approaches in the classroom and enhance these classroom-based practices through their efforts on behalf of their students in their work with colleagues and other stakeholders within (in the corridors) or associated with the school (as part of other communities).

Comprehensive School Reform

A common characteristic of many of the images of teachers noted in the previous section is the disposition to explore and, where justified, to make changes in what they do in one or more of their realms of work.[1] This deeply ingrained and habitual dedication to improvement on the part of teachers—what we call their *reform-mindedness*—is prominent in much of the literature in educational change (A. Hargreaves, Lieberman, Fullan, & Hopkins, 1998), especially in the current emphasis on and study of comprehensive school reform. Before we turn to the place of teachers in schoolwide reform, we provide a brief glimpse into the state of change in education.

Paradoxes and Dilemmas in Educational Change

The landscape of forces and counterforces to reform continue to shift. Murphy and Adams (1998) trace the attempts to enhance the quality of American schooling through three eras of *excellence* since 1980, from intensification to restructuring to reformation. Across these rapidly shifting eras, the role of government changed from tightening regulations to building capacity throughout the

system to developing accountability mechanisms; the expectations of teachers evolved from complying to mandates to affecting decisions about the improvement of their schools to assisting in the creation of professional standards to govern their development and practice; the more distant and outside voices from the community, especially parents, were heard more often inside the school (with the emergence of site-based management) and as they exerted their rights to determine what kind of schools their children should attend; and market strategies steadily became part of the landscape through more school choice (e.g., charter schools) and eventually in the form of privatization (rising incidence of vouchers, deregulation, home schooling). Amid and prodded by the push and pull of these various political, structural, and social agendas, teachers have had to carve their own path of reform.

In his characterization of our postmodern age, A. Hargreaves (1995) describes the following five paradoxes:

- Many parents have given up responsibility for the very things they want the school to address.
- Business often fails to use the skills that it demands schools produce.
- More globalism produces more tribalism.
- More diversity and integration is accompanied by more emphasis on common standards and specialization.
- Stronger orientation to the future creates greater nostalgia for the past. (pp. 14–15)

For teachers, this age of paradox augurs in a work life dominated by the seemingly contradictory pulls between: embracing change and protecting continuity; responding to local needs and pursuing global priorities; adhering to standards and supporting variability; making autonomous decisions and increasing their accountability to others; and engaging in more integrated and differentiated (specialized) practices. Clearly the presumed certainty of past reform efforts and strategies has given way to a period of constantly searching for ways to cope with the more chaotic and unpredictable conditions of recent times (A. Hargreaves, 1994).

In a similar vein, Fullan (1999) offers a counterintuitive series of lessons for thinking about the change process, a series that helps us "to develop the mindset and instincts to take more effective action" (p. 13). Undeterred by the enduring dilemmas that baffle and confound reform (Ogawa, Crowson, & Goldring, 1999), Fullan (1993a) recognizes that it is in "one's ability to work with polar opposites" (p. 40) where the forces of change are harnessed and transformed. The lessons then call on teachers to find ways to address both of the following poles: individualism (diversity) and collaboration (and some degree of consensus); top-down and bottom-up governance; compliance, mutual adaptation, and invention; personal/professional discretion and social/organizational goals; and guided paths to follow and uncharted territory to discover. These core dilemmas then provide the catalysts for change, not as problems to solve or issues to resolve, but as the tensions to probe, engage, and even provoke in the course and the service of school reform.

Such paradoxes and dilemmas add another level of uncertainty, chaos, and complexity to an already complicated professional life. Teachers have to balance changes from those that come from external mandates, those that arise from problems they want to solve, and those that emerge from the naturally occurring or unanticipated events in any school year (Louis, Toole, & Hargreaves, 1999). The plot and plight of teachers in reform is an ever-changing saga of adjustment, invention, or reconstruction.

> Teachers learn to cope with changes that frequently do not unfold in any predictable or sequential manner despite attempts to bring some kind of order to how things develop. Occasionally, the process seems circular as teachers revisit, modify or extend, or add to what they do in ways that eventually include more colleagues and other stakeholders. The story often involves starts and stops, obstacles, confrontations, and crises. At some points, the changes seem more intense, frenetic, and visible; and at other moments, the changes are less evident, appear inert, or are even undetectable. Some changes have a limited shelf life, while others become part of the metamorphic story of the many incidental, accidental, and judicious actions that ultimately become chapters in the biography of reform in the school. It is in the daily habit of teachers tinkering in and around the edges of practice—wondering about new possibilities, puzzling through new alternative ideas, and experimenting with innovative approaches—that the roots of school reform take hold, are nurtured, and grow. (adapted from Thiessen & Anderson, 1999, pp. 6–7)

Models, Networks, and Studies of School Reform

Despite considerable variation in priorities and approaches, comprehensive school reform initiatives tend to stress the following: high standards for all children; a consensus about fundamental goals and how to achieve these goals; a focus on both the distinct and the interrelated elements of all subjects and grade levels; continuous involvement in professional and organizational learning; a capacity to inquire into and evaluate the development of students, teachers, and the school; the involvement of parents and community; linkages with other professional and policy-based groups; procedures and forums for making joint decisions; and a synergy among what the people intend, the strategies encourage, and the structures support. Stated with reference to figure 40.1, CSR targets or implicates all three realms of teachers' work. Many of the CSR

initiatives occur in a network of schools committed to a particular model of school reform that they faithfully implement and help to sustain and refine through the creative applications and critique of the principles and practices that define the model.

Network-Based School Reform Models. While numerous school reform networks began prior to 1990 (e.g., the School Development Program, Association for Direct Instruction, and the Coalition of Essential Schools), the last decade of the 20th century saw a rapid increase in the development of both school reform models and networks. Schoolwide reform steadily gained in prominence, in part because of the strategic moves by the federal government. The creation of the New American Schools Development Corporation (now known as the New American Schools or NAS) in 1991, initially funded the development of 11 "break the mold" designs and, by 1995, supported the "scaling up" of 7 of the original 11 designs in an effort to expand the application to other schools within and outside the districts in which these models were first tried. In 1998, the Comprehensive School Reform Demonstration legislation enabled over 2,500 schools to receive funds for the implementation of "research-based, whole-school" models. Seventeen models were cited in this initiative, seven of which were the NAS designs assisted in 1995. There are a number of guides now available that describe the various models, review the available evidence on the impact and implementation of each model, and offer advice to those in schools and school districts about how best to choose a model best suited to their situation and needs.

Table 40.1 lists those CSR models that appear in two or more of five guides.[2] The five guides—*The Catalog of School Reform Models* (Northwest Regional Educational Laboratory, 1999), the *Obey-Porter* list from the Comprehensive School Reform Demonstration Program (McChesney & Hertling, 2000),[3] *An Educators' Guide to Schoolwide Reform* produced by the American Institutes of Research (Herman et al., 1999), *Show Me the Evidence! Proven and Promising Programs for America's Schools* from the Center for Research on the Education of Students Placed At Risk (Slavin & Fashola, 1998) and *What We Know: Widely Implemented School Improvement Programs* from the Laboratory for Student Success (Wang, Haertel, & Walberg, 1997a, 1997b)—provide information that permits some rating and ranking of the models. For example, the American Institutes of Research (Herman et al., 1999) rates the models in terms of the evidence of positive affects on school achievement and the support provided to schools by the developer. Success For All and High Schools That Work fare the best when both student achievement and developer's support are considered; Community for Learning, Different Ways of Knowing, Direct Instruction, and Expeditionary Learning Outward Bound

Table 40.1 Comprehensive School Reform Models

	Grade Level[a]	Number of Schools[a]	Laboratory for Student Success	Northwest Regional Educational Laboratory	Center for Research on the Education of Students Placed at Risk	Comprehensive School Reform Demonstration Program	American Institutes of Research
Accelerated Schools	K-8	1000	●	●	●	●	●
America's Choice	K-12	300		●	●	●	●
ATLAS Communities	Pre K-12	57		●	●	●	●
Audrey Cohen College	K-12	16		●	●	●	●
Coalition of Essential Schools	K-12	251	●	●	●	●	●
Community for Learning	K-12	53	●	●		●	●
Co-NECT	K-12	58		●	●	●	●
Core Knowledge	K-8	700	CURR	●	●		●
Different Ways of Knowing	K-7	300	CURR	●			●
Direct Instruction	K-6	150		●	●	●	●
Edison Project	K-12	25		●	●		
Expeditionary Learning Outward Bound	K-12	47		●	●	●	●
Foxfire Fund	K-12	N/A	CURR	●			●
High Schools that Work	9-12	700		●		●	●
High/Scope	K-3	100		●			●
League of Professional Schools	K-12	175		●			●
Modern Red Schoolhouse	K-12	43		●	●	●	●
Onward to Excellence	K-12	1000		●			●
Paideia	K-12	80	CURR	●	●	●	●
Roots and Wings	Pre K-6	200		●	●	●	●
School Development Program	K-12	721	●	●	●	●	●
Success for All	Pre K-6	747	CURR	●	●	●	●
Talent Development High School	9-12	7		●		●	●
Urban Learning Centers	Pre K-12	19		●		●	●

[a]The grade level designations and number of schools are from the *Catalogue of School Reform Models*. (Northwest Regional Educational Laboratory, 1999).

follow next based on the strength or promise shown in the studies reviewed. The Northwest Regional Educational Laboratory (1999) creates a matrix of the models using a 3 point rubric to estimate the degree to which each model addresses eight of the nine components defined by the Comprehensive School Reform Demonstration program to determine eligibility for funding. The Accelerated Schools, America's Choice, Different Ways of Knowing, Roots and Wings, and Success For All consistently attend to these components. The Center for Research on the Education of Students Placed At Risk reviews programs based on the evidence available on effectiveness and replicability. Success For All, Roots and Wings, and Direct Instruction meet the criteria for student achievement and are widely replicable. The Laboratory for Student Success at the Mid-Atlantic Regional Educational Laboratory (Wang, Haertel, & Walberg, 1997a) first differentiates between comprehensive reform and curriculum reform programs (the abbreviation CURR in table 40.1 represents those models the authors categorize as primarily curriculum reform programs) and then describes the models in terms of program practices and program implementation requirements.

Those models that combine the greatest number of research-based curriculum and organizational practices are Community for Learning, Accelerated Schools, Coalition of Essential Schools, the School Development Program, and Success For All.

The CSR models vary considerably in their beliefs about why change is necessary, what needs to change, how to make desired changes, and what matters when determining if the changes are successful (Hatch, 1998; Traub, 1999). The impetus for change ranges from a desire to improve the education of impoverished inner-city children (e.g., Success For All, Community for Learning) to a commitment to overcome the intellectually barren record of elementary and secondary classrooms (e.g., Core Knowledge, Paideia) to the drive to transform the insipid, socially limiting, and structurally flawed world of schools (e.g., Coalition of Essential Schools, League of Professional Schools). The models differ on where to focus their change efforts with some that concentrate on school culture (e.g., School Development Program), some on the improvement of instruction (e.g., Direct Instruction, Different Ways of Knowing), and some on the alignment of changes in curriculum and assessment, organization, and governance (e.g., Accelerated Schools, Edison Project). In their efforts to stimulate change, the models vary in the extent to which they explicitly direct how the school develops. Some require relatively close adherence to prescribed practices especially in the use of materials and teaching approaches in the classroom (e.g., Success For All, Paideia). Others provide limited or general guidance in classroom practices but are more specific about the way the school organizes itself to promote its reforms (e.g., Modern Red Schoolhouse, School Development Program). Still others work within a set of principles that encourages the school to devise its own translation of these principles into classroom and organizational practices (e.g., Coalition of Essential Schools). And when it comes to determining the success, the models concentrate on one or more of the following four criteria: student outcomes (*model as effected*); level of implementation in terms of recommended support structures and strategies (*model as implemented*); the quality of the experience especially for students and teachers (*model as experienced*); and the defensibility of the underlying assumptions and values (*model as framed*) (Werner, 1982). While all models recognize the importance of all four criteria, some judge their impact primarily on student achievement (e.g., Roots and Wings) and use the level of implementation, the reported experiences with the program, and the analysis of core assumptions and values to explain how and why the results occured. Others see student outcomes as simply one manifestation of how the underlying assumptions and values of the model are both practiced and lived by all those who have a stake in the school (e.g., Coalition of Essential Schools). In this context, the four criteria become interrelated benchmarks of what the model represents and strives to enact. Regardless of their variations, the CSR models reach deeply into and across all three realms of teachers' work lives.

Studies of School Reform.   Arguably the most comprehensive review of the research on CSR models is *An Educator's Guide to Schoolwide Reform* from the American Institutes of Research (Herman et al., 1999; see also New American Schools, 1999; Slavin & Fashola, 1998). Sometimes conducted by the developers themselves, sometimes by the developers in conjunction either with school participants in the network or with independent researchers, and sometimes by independent researchers or even in teams of independent researchers and school participants (e.g., Paideia: Sekayi, Peterman, Stakich, Caputo, & Sawchik, 1999; Accelerated Schools: Poetter, Gay, Elifritz, & Hofacker, 1999), the studies not only capture the range in school practices and impact of these models but also display diversity in research design and rigor. Notwithstanding the many promising findings, we are still in the midst of a growth spurt in research on CSR models with all the

associated inconsistencies, surprises, debates (Pogrow, 2000), and developments of an area of study that is barely a decade long. As Stringfield (2000) observes, these guides reveal a story of "a badly fractured research community, and the effects of a decade of methodological pluralism" (pp. 207–208) and the need for better designed, more long-term, and contextually sensitive studies.

The study of reform-oriented schools has a longer and wider history than CSR research. From earlier studies on attempts to introduce experimental schools (Doyle, 1978), to support such school improvement models as Individually Guided Education (Klausmeier & Wisconsin Associates, 1990), or to enhance innovative practice (Emrick & Peterson, 1978; Crandall & Associates, 1982) to more recent studies on school effectiveness and school improvement (Gray et al., 1999; Reynolds, Creemers, Hopkins, Stoll, & Bollen, 1996; Teddle & Reynolds, 2000), successive generations of researchers have tried to unlock the mysteries of sustained and comprehensive school reform. The comparatively recent examinations have frequently embraced such images as the moving school (Rosenholtz, 1989; Stoll & Fink, 1996), the self-managing (Caldwell & Spinks, 1988) or empowered school (D. H. Hargreaves & Hopkins, 1991), the evolutionary school (Joyce, Calhoun, & Hopkins, 1999), or the high reliability (Stringfield, 1995) or learning (Leithwood & Louis, 1998) organization to describe the kind of schools that are capable of systemic change. Like the network-based research cited earlier, these studies usually explore the changes in the classroom, in the corridors, or as part of other communities though only some dwell on the implications of such changes on these three realms of work of teachers (Elmore, Peterson, & McCarthey, 1996; Newmann & Wehlage, 1995; Thiessen & Anderson, 1999).

Role of Teachers in School Reform

We find it puzzling that we have to remake the case for the central prominence of teachers in school reform. Yet, amid the growing pressure to change the entire system (Education Commission of the States, 1999; National Commission on Teaching and America's Future, 1996) and to return to large-scale reform (Fullan, 2000; Murphy & Adams, 1998), teachers seem more in the background bolstered, enabled, or prodded by the more powerful organizational and political forces that frame and govern their work. Even the architects of the CSR models, despite frequent reference to the importance of teachers in the change process, are more likely to describe the core principles and practices of the models in terms of the school. For example, in the 10 principles of the Coalition of Essential Schools, teachers are the agent (subject) of reform only once: The principal and teachers should perceive themselves as generalists first and specialists second. In Onward to Excellence, like numerous other models, it is the school that takes action, here in terms of 10 steps to implement the model. Certainly teachers are either presumed or implicated in most of the actions or guiding principles, but by personifying the school and leaving teachers unnamed and between the lines, it is not always clear whether teachers are the educational reformers or the educationally reformed (Thiessen, 1992).

In contrast to the more obscure or uneven characterization in much of the current accounts of reform, the reform-mindedness of teachers in the snapshots and case studies of the more promising and successful schools both inside and outside networks is more prominent.[4] These up-close portrayals find teachers immersed in reforms in all three realms of their work. They are the protagonists of change mindful of and responsive to the needs of their students and those conditions that create the best opportunities for the development of their students, classrooms, and school. As reforms evolve, their voices are heard, their choices recognized, their knowledge sought and interrogated, and their changes engaged and extended. As the lens widens to encompass still broader vistas in the name of systemic and large-scale reform, the role of the teacher becomes even more crucial to understand and foreground. The next section delves further into this changing and reform-minded role and the many manifestations of this role for music teachers.

Reform-Minded Music Teachers

In this section, we recast what we know about the principles and practices of some of the most promising and successful schools within and outside of networks so that we can directly portray and critically examine the role of teachers in school reform. We focus on what teachers in these productive learning environments do in the classroom, in the corridors, and as part of other communities, highlighting those domains of practice that most teachers address. In the following sections on each realm, we present the work of teachers in three interrelated segments. In the first segment, we begin with a review of those features of the CSR models that directly describe or implicate teachers in order to provide a sense of how the work of teachers in each realm is changing. We then combine the main trends represented in the models, the more embedded accounts of teachers in some of the more insightful case studies (see note 4), and our knowledge of the lives and careers of music teachers to create a fictional letter written by a middle school general music teacher. In the letter, the music teacher reflects on the implications of her involvement in a school committed to comprehensive reform. Although the insights and reflections could have arisen from a music teacher's work in an elementary or high school

setting, or in a band, chorus, or orchestra program, shifting reconfigurations of teachers' roles and responsibilities within a changing middle school environment seemed especially appropriate for portraying a reform-minded teacher's beliefs and practices. We also wanted to mirror the demographic composition of the teaching force by making the author of the letter female. In the absence of systematic studies on the role of music teachers in comprehensive school reform efforts, this narrative device offers an alternate lens by examining teachers' experiences not as generalizations but "in their integrity and particularity instead" (Greene, 1995, p. 10). The final segment turns to the related studies of school reform and to the wider literature on educational change to corroborate and elaborate the image of the reform-minded music teacher developed in the first two segments. In so doing, we provide a cornerstone for our recommendations in the final section about reforming music teacher education.

In the Classroom

The CSR models present a wide of array of classroom practices for teachers to consider.[5] In its summary of the curriculum and instructional dimensions, the North Central Regional Laboratory (2000) notes the following variations:

> All of the comprehensive reform models propose fundamental changes in curriculum and instruction, but their approaches differ. Some models provide developed curriculum and prescribed methods of instruction; others have partially developed materials that lend themselves to further development and adaptation on site; yet others require on-site development with a student-centered focus. In many of the programs, instructional processes often call for changes in student groupings. Most of the programs include performance-based assessments aligned with the curriculum and instruction. (p. 2)

Teachers are faced with either the need to adopt and adapt practices advocated by the model or the challenge to invent their own practices based on one or more principles inherent in the philosophy of the model.

At the more prescribed end of the spectrum, teachers can choose from such structured alternatives as the scripted and interactive lessons of Direct Instruction, the subject-based and year-by-year content sequence outlined by Core Knowledge, the individualized instructional strategies available through the training in the Adaptive Learning Environments Model provided by Community for Learning, or the multidimensional reading program (e.g., including features such as phonics, whole language, cooperative learning, continuous assessment) of Success For All. Other models propose classroom practices that, although relatively specific in their orientation, are open to greater variations in their application. These include such directions as the learning expeditions (e.g., combining authentic projects, fieldwork, and service) in Expeditionary Learning Outward Bound, the thematic and purpose-centered framework in Audrey Cohen College (e.g., in grade 5, the two purposes studied are captured in the statements, "We improve the environment" and "We use technology to meet human needs"), collaborative inquiry and higher order analytical skills in Accelerated Schools, or teaching for understanding (e.g., attention to basic skills and their link to problem solving, developmentally appropriate practices, goal-oriented, in-depth study) in ATLAS Communities. Still other models recommend few if any particular classroom practices but instead encourage teachers to develop their own approaches based on a small number of guiding principles. The common principles of the Coalition of Essential Schools stress personalized, concentrated study ("less is more"), mastery of central skills and knowledge (e.g., demonstrated through projects or exhibitions), and a "teacher-as-coach and student-as-worker" relationship in the classroom. In the Foxfire Fund, the core practices involve students in active, creative, and cooperative learning in both the classroom and the community ("community as a learning laboratory"). Students collaborate with their teacher in the design and development of what they do.

Despite these differences, the reform-minded teachers in these schools nonetheless share a common agenda in how they seek to improve their classrooms. Reform-minded teachers strive to work with their students in ways that:

- Provide more focused, sustained, and in-depth opportunities to learn;
- Vary the structure, form, and context of their learning experiences;
- Interrelate different modes of assessment with ongoing decisions about curriculum and instruction; and
- Engage students in making sense of why, what, how, where, and under what circumstances they should learn.

The following passage is the first part of a letter from a reform-minded music teacher who teaches general music in a middle school setting. She reflects on what it is like to be in a school immersed in a long-term comprehensive reform process and, in this excerpt, on the special challenges of the above classroom-based reform agenda.

Dear Music Educators:

My life in school is very different now that my school has agreed to participate in a school reform network. The nature of my work includes more time with colleagues, more involvement in school-level decisions, more contact, and even partnerships with more people outside the school . . . all of which enrich and extend the professional role I play. This involvement matters to the extent that it inter-

sects with and supports what I do in the classroom. The most significant aspect of my job is the ongoing pursuit of how best to work with my students.

In this pursuit, I both establish routines and routinely adjust and modify what I do as circumstances shift, relationships evolve, and different needs and demands emerge. Sometimes this occurs as part of the natural rhythm of the year, sometimes as a response to unanticipated events, and sometimes as a result of a conscious effort to alter what I usually do. Consequently, when changes come from either outside or through personal invention, they are tested in a classroom that is perpetually changing. It inevitably takes some time for me to find the best way to incorporate these changes into my own practice. I am always mindful of the fit between these changes and both the goals I have and the expectation my students have for the music classroom. I have to work through some or all of the following questions:

- Do I want to do this?
- Is it worth doing?
- Can I do it?
- Will I be able to adapt it to my situation?
- How do I know if I am doing it effectively?
- How do I determine if it works and is an improvement on what I did before?
- When, and under what conditions, can I stop doing it and replace it with something I find or create that is better?

As I address these changes, I am conscious of the degree to which any change alters the pedagogical norms of the classroom, especially those that frame the routines and habits that surround my relationship with my students. Many of the things I have changed focus either on the kind of work my students do or on the strategies or roles I adopt to stimulate or support their work, and over time, inevitably on both.

The most significant change in my classroom has come as a result of reflecting on the quality of the students' experience in my previous activities-based curriculum. Up until now, students in my classroom willingly participated in lessons that I designed and taught, but I made most of the musical decisions. I have changed the focus of my work to incorporate more projects in which the students solve musical problems, compose and improvise music, and learn to interpret and evaluate their musical efforts. Another change relates to the development of my understanding of the goals and scope of the entire middle school curriculum, so that I am more open to opportunities for students to make stronger, informed connections between what happens in music class to their interests and understandings in other disciplines. The overall atmosphere in my classroom demonstrates these shifts. Students work more regularly to assist, guide, or critique other students, have a greater involvement in the assessment and design of their learning, and assume a greater investment in acquiring skills they can use to make music outside of class. They have more responsibility for and control over more decisions about their work and a greater voice in how we improve what happens in the classroom.

As the work of my students changes, so does the nature of what I do. I design fewer daily lessons but more extended and intensive units of study. I spend more time on helping students perform and understand fewer works than before, and I am more selective about the works we choose to study. As a consequence, I feel more satisfied about the lasting impact of our work. I find that I make greater use of technological resources in the school as I investigate new works, and I bring in a greater variety of poems, art works, and extramusical examples to complement our discussions about music. I have also invited musicians from the community to work with the students, and have made better use of field trips to concerts and performances in the community. As the range of musical experiences in the classroom has become more diverse, so have my assessment practices. I assess more often and through a broader range of authentic performance tasks. Though I am inclined to devote more time to creating opportunities for my students to make sense and take charge of their own learning (e.g., cooperative learning, inductive and inquiry-oriented teaching, problem solving), my facilitation still includes moments of guidance, intervention, or direction with particular students, for the development of certain skills or proficiencies, or at specific points in a unit of study. Facilitating learning and empowering students thus can take many forms in the warp and woof of classroom life.

As has been the case for some time, I can pursue many of these changes with my students on my own. Yet what matters in the classroom is frequently connected to what I do on behalf of the classroom with colleagues and other relevant parties inside and outside the school. It is in these other arenas where we build the norms and conditions which make it possible for all of us to elaborate and extend why, what, how, where, and under what circumstances our students learn.

Reform-minded music teachers, like their colleagues in other classrooms or disciplines, enthusiastically yet critically continue in their search for how to improve the classroom experience of all students. While some embrace a relatively specific set of classroom practices or a particular pedagogical orientation (e.g., prescribed as part of the condition of membership in a CSR network), most become judicious and discriminating inventors and users of an increasingly diverse repertoire of teaching models and strategies. They implicitly endorse a kind of methodological ecumenism, recognizing that authentic learning can occur through various means and modalities (Newmann & Associates, 1996).[6] Their pragmatic challenge (Day, 2000; Soltis, 1994) involves making defensible choices among existing innovations or constructing something new when relevant approaches are neither available nor immediately applicable. This is a process of invention and adaptation more than of implementation (Murphy, 1995; Randi & Corno, 1997). Reform-minded music teachers function in the same way as good musical arrangers, extracting the prominent themes and motives of the reform initiative to create a new setting of the ideas, one that fits the available resources of the school and the particularities of the students and teachers involved in the change.

In the Corridors

In recent years, the work of teachers in the most promising and successful schools has arguably changed the most in the corridors. Many teachers no longer feel they are living in isolation from one another in the independent world of their own classrooms. They increasingly work under conditions and within structures that bring them together to compare perspectives and practices, to develop or adapt new approaches, and to share in those decisions that directly and indirectly affect what they do in their classrooms and throughout the school. Although the focus of such work appears targeted at either their own development or the organizational development of the school, teachers value, persist with, and build on these changes only if their efforts clearly benefit what happens in their classrooms.

In comparison to the continuum of prescribed to guided to principled practices available to classroom-level reforms (see previous section), the changes proposed by the CSR models for the corridors are less differentiated and less developed. Nonetheless two broad categories of reforms are evident: one with required or strongly recommended structures and procedures where teachers work within particular organizational arrangements or processes designed to support the implementation of prescribed classroom practices; and the other with orientations or principles that teachers need to embrace in order to create the kind of working environment that is conducive to and resonant with the changes sought in their classrooms. Again, teachers are faced with a choice between developing relationships and norms defined by a model or building their own school culture based on a model's belief system.

In the more structured and directed CSR models, teachers can become agents of a designated change system, play an instrumental and strategically significant part in a complex infrastructure of the school, or adopt a greater range of roles and responsibilities. Onward to Excellence, for example, outlines 10 steps teachers need to follow over the first 2 years to enhance their collective capacity:

- conduct an initial assessment to determine the school's areas of need;
- develop a "school performance profile" that shows trends in student achievement;
- establish one or two broad goals for school improvement related to increased student performance;

- study research on best practices related to their school goals;
- review their current instructional practices in relationship to the research;
- determine how to improve student learning in areas of these goals;
- develop an implementation plan;
- carry out the implementation plan (identifying resources, organizing training, and changing practices);
- monitor progress toward meeting the goal(s); and
- review the school's progress toward meeting the goal(s) and setting new goals after the first goals have been met (Herman et al., 1999).

A School Leadership Team (consisting of the principal, teachers, community members, and, in secondary schools, students) manages the reform process, while an External Study Team (consisting of representatives from such organizations as educational service centers, local universities, the district central office, or other Onward to Excellence schools) evaluates, monitors, and provides feedback about the school's progress in meeting its goals.

Teacher participation on teams, councils, or committees is expected in most of the more structured CSR models. In most schools, teachers work with the principal, other teachers, parents, community members and, sometimes, students to guide, evaluate, and maintain the integrity of how the school enacts the model (e.g., Advisory Committee in Success For All; School Leadership Team in ATLAS Communities; School Advisory Council in High Schools That Work). Frequently, some of the work devolves to a series of committees. For example, the priority on standards-based reform in the Modern Red Schoolhouse is dependent on the interconnected work of six committees (community involvement, curriculum, organization and finance, standards and assessment, technology, and professional development) whose chairs in turn sit on the Leadership Team (with the principal, other faculty members, parents, and community representatives). Some of these network schools use instructional or academic teams (e.g., America's Choice, Expeditionary Learning Outward Bound, Talent Development High School) to reorganize and reconceptualize curriculum delivery, sometimes in configurations that combine disciplines or grade levels. Other schools have instructional teams to support their colleagues in the application of preferred teaching approaches (e.g., Community For Learning). Outside the classroom, then, teachers find themselves with a greater say in the business of the school, albeit among a greater number of voices that are now part of decisions that affect the direction their school takes.

In addition to this structural involvement in the implementation of the model, teachers also can exercise some leadership through the various differentiated staffing strategies available. Some teachers become either full- or part-time facilitators (e.g., Community For Learning, Success For All, Paideia), coaches (e.g., Accelerated Schools), or instructional coordinators (e.g., America's Choice, Talent Development High School). These roles simply formalize in one or more positions the expanding responsibilities that most teachers have added to their world in the corridors. Their routines now encompass organizational arrangements (e.g., schedules, staffing configurations), professional support for colleagues (e.g., peer coaching, arranging professional learning opportunities), and schoolwide decision making.

Some of these CSR models, despite their structural precision, do have some features that recognize the principle of collaborative autonomy for teachers. The ATLAS Community schools rely on whole-faculty study groups to stimulate professional development and classroom reform. Similarly, the architects of the Modern Red Schoolhouse believe that teachers, in cooperation with the principal, should have considerable latitude in making decisions about curriculum, staffing, and the allocation of resources, especially time and budget. The Coalition of Essential Schools and the League of Professional Schools, however, create an image of the desired workplace through a set of principles that teachers then translate into the corridor realities appropriate to their own context.

The 10 common principles of the Coalition of Essential Schools[7] are based on an image of a school that asks teachers to create a fair, responsive, and equitable learning community for all students and colleagues. The League of Professional Schools strives to democratize education through a three-part framework that involves teachers in the development of a teaching and learning covenant in association with those who have a stake in the school; in a shared governance with staff, school administrators, parents, students, and community members; and an action research cycle that continuously examines current practices and informs decisions about how best to improve the student experience with and success in the school. Interestingly, teachers in the schools of both of these models may in fact adopt structures (e.g., leadership teams, block scheduling) and strategies (e.g., collegial forms of professional development, inquiry-based decision making) similar to those described above for more prescribed and directive models. With the Coalition of Essential Schools and the League of Professional Schools, the difference is that teachers devise their own manifestations of the guiding principles of their respective models based on a view of the kind of school they hope to construct in the process.

The reform-minded teachers across these schools, although varying in the focus and form of their corridor practices, do come together in their devotion to making the changes in their own work lives that simultaneously improve their experiences with students in the classroom.

They work with colleagues and other stakeholders in the school in ways that:

- Build their capacity for joint work;
- Focus on school-based, collaborative, and inquiry-oriented professional learning;
- Create a balance and connection between disciplinary and interdisciplinary curriculum practices; and
- Expand their involvement in and commitment to making shared decisions about classroom and school improvement.

The following excerpt continues the letter from the reform-minded music teacher started in the last section. In this segment of the letter, the teacher reflects on her changing life in the corridors and how she interrelates her professional development with improvements in her classroom and across the school.

I am busier than ever these days outside the classroom. It seems I am constantly working with colleagues and other associates (principal, resource personnel, parents, community members) in one forum or another. We do not always have the time to meet or, when we do, the time never seems to be enough to get done what we need to accomplish, to delve into and learn from the expertise around the table, or to find some level of consensus among those who can bring quite different perspectives to our deliberations. Collaboration can be difficult, frustrating, even inefficient—with endless hours spent on what feels like relatively minor decisions. Sometimes, especially when we are mired in debate or indecision, I long for the days when I was more an island unto myself comfortably living in the splendid isolation in my own classroom. But I cannot achieve alone what we are capable of doing together. This interdependence is crucial to the success in my classroom and indeed across all classrooms.

Much of the collaborative work occurs around instructional matters. I work with three different interdisciplinary teams, each responsible for a cohort of students. Since the students are with one or more teachers from the team most days, we can rearrange the schedule to suit our needs. Frequently the students come to the music room to participate in activities that depend upon ready access to musical equipment and materials. Sometimes I travel to the various wings where the cohort groups are housed for planning meetings and coteaching lessons. Only a few years ago, I was almost always isolated from the rest of the school in the arts wing. I now spend much more time working with students and teachers in many locations within the school including the music room.

Although the transition to different forms of scheduling was a difficult one, we now have longer periods to enable collaboration and special projects. Entire days may be devoted to a project or field trip. In addition to my individual planning period each day, I meet with the teams on a rotating schedule so we can figure out how to best make these changing patterns of time allocation, space usage, and social configuration serve the needs of the range of students in our charge. As teams, we can overcome what used to be organizational barriers to many good ideas each of us used to have but could not put into practice. Now we are free to explore learning experiences we would not have thought possible before. Students can now engage in more in-depth (e.g., projects), interactive (e.g., small groups), and experiential (e.g., laboratory practice) learning under conditions that best support their development.

Initially, I worried that music would get lost in the interdisciplinary maze created by serving on teams. In fact, I now have more opportunities to pursue how music can influence or interact with student learning in many areas. In addition to the usual time I have with students in my music class, the Visual Arts teacher and I have developed a series of interarts lessons in which we explore with students ways to perceive and respond to works of art and music. Students in the cohort groups are required to do capstone projects twice a year; we act as consultants and mentors for students who choose to integrate art or music into their project work. I frequently coordinate with the teams to explore historical or cultural studies that rely heavily on music and art as key components of social history. These interdisciplinary alliances have enhanced the integrity and impact of our yearly exploration of a large theme or issue. In each of these interdisciplinary initiatives, we sort through where our respective disciplines do and do not intersect and, in the process, both reaffirm the distinct contribution of, in my case, music, and discover how we can mutually enhance each other's aspirations for the students we share. The result is a more prominent albeit more differentiated place for music across the curriculum.

All of this takes time and considerable relearning for all of us. We are, in effect, asking of ourselves what we are requiring of our students. We want our students to share ideas; illustrate, give advice about, or critique the application of a new approach; and use their ongoing dialogue as a reference point and catalyst for further advancement. When I live by these same principles, my students have not only a more interactive classroom (with teachers in various cooperative arrangements and students in small groups and cohorts) and more interrelated work patterns, but also an example (in the collegial acts of teachers) of how they should relate to one another in this reconfigured environment. How I teach students to learn is how I have to learn to work with my colleagues—a critical element in my professional learning. Fortunately, we recognize this need to help each other learn how to work differently in the classroom and with each other.

In addition to the naturally occurring development that comes from working in close quarters with colleagues on teams, I have participated in such peer teaching and support strategies as: (1) peer coaching by meeting periodically with three other music teachers to share and support each other's efforts to try out new practices in the classroom; (2) demonstrations, training, and mentoring through visiting classrooms in many disciplines to observe the application of different teaching approaches. I also attend a workshop by, or work in my classroom with, a colleague whose assigned role is to facilitate the implementation of instructional methods or models many of us have agreed to try in our classrooms; and (3) induction by serving as a buddy to two teachers new to the school, one who is an experienced physical and health teacher transferred from another school and another who is a first-year music teacher. We meet formally and informally to discuss their transition in a new school and visit each other's classrooms to get a sense of and compare each other's practices. By situating my professional learning in the workplace, I can negotiate with my colleagues how best to take advantage of one another's expertise so that the shared experience simultaneously serves my own and the school's development.

Probably the most powerful and sustained learning happens when these school-based and collaborative strategies are framed within an ongoing deliberation about and inquiry into our changing practices. I have gathered data about my own practice (e.g., as part of study groups, critical friends groups, research-in-action teams), the school's programs (e.g., curriculum review process, alignment/backward mapping), and key problems (e.g., underachievement)—a process that inevitably invites comparison and critique and challenges us to consider yet another cycle of collegial development.

My shared learning and work does not stop here. From more semiautonomous teams (where we have considerable latitude to determine schedules, student groupings, curriculum structure and delivery, classroom management norms and incentives) to school improvement committees, I have an influence on the goals, infrastructure, and general running of the school, along with others who also have more access to the places where decisions are made (e.g., parents, students). I also "follow the decision out the door" and thus become part of ensuring that the decisions reach everyone implicated by and responsible for translating these directions into practice (including me). In this way, those who decide what to do are also many of same people who do what is decided. Much dialogue and debate still ensues because most of us have a greater investment in all phases of the decision-making cycle and a need to forge a consensus on what is best for the school. Sometimes we have to learn how to disagree, to address diversity, and to work with conflict as a force for change.

I confess that I do not like conflict; I often wish it would go away or get resolved instantly any time it arises. At the same time, I do admit that it is often when I am confronted with an entirely different point of view, that I learn the most about the changes that matter to me. Furthermore, it is in the interchange with those who least agree with me where deeper understandings most emerge—issues I never fully appreciated; implications I was too quick to dismiss; and even solutions I did not expect to come from the clash of ideas yet now see as better than where I first began. . . . Although I still have an aversion to conflict, I also recognize that conflict is inevitable and necessary for a community to grow and change. Once in a while, I even provoke conflict when agreement seems too quick, without

sufficient debate to make sure the path we appear to want without question was the one we still want after a thorough interrogation. It is only through such perseverance that we can sort out our disagreements and find a common ground on which to build the kind of school we seek for our students and ourselves.[8]

Reform-minded music teachers recognize that the success of their increasingly intense work in the corridors depends on their capacity to maintain a close link to what matters most to the improvement of their classrooms (Elmore, Peterson, & McCarthey, 1996; Smylie & Perry, 1998). Their efforts need to construct and nurture a professional community with characteristics similar to those outlined by Louis, Kruse, & Associates (1995): (1) a collective focus on student learning; (2) a shared image of the kind of professional community desired and a common understanding of how the values underlying their notion of professional community also inform the kind of classroom community they should develop with their students in the classroom; (3) an ongoing consideration of and discourse about classroom and school issues and directions; (4) the persistent commitment to collaborative acts with colleagues and other stakeholders in and connected to the school; and (5) an openness to examining, comparing, and building on the diverse strengths of each other's practices (pp. 232–234). Their orientation is also consistent with recent calls for teachers to adopt a more open (Organization of Economic Cooperation and Development, 1990), interactive (Fullan & Hargreaves, 1991), radical (Fielding, 1999), or even postmodern (A. Hargreaves, 2000) sense of professionalism. It is also related to the continued urgings from various quarters to root teacher education programs in the image of teachers as change agents or reformers (Clandinin & Connelly, 1998; Cochran-Smith & Lytle, 1999; Fullan, 1993a, 1993b; Murphy, 1995; Rallis & Rossman, 1995; Smylie, Bay, & Tozer, 1999; Thiessen, 1997). The renewed and expanded lives of reform-minded music teachers in the corridors—as colleagues, inquirers, learners, and decision makers—has its greatest and most enduring impact only when their work is done on behalf of the classroom.

As Part of Other Communities

The work of teachers outside the classroom is not just confined to the corridors. In a growing number of CSR models, teachers are also involved with a wide range of individuals and organizations outside the school. Such connections with those *out there* (A. Hargreaves & Fullan, 1998) often occur *in here*. For example, the previous section on the work of teachers in the corridors notes the increased participation of parents and other community members on school councils or committees. In some cases, teachers in partnership with community groups or organizations are *out there* in ways that expand the horizons of learning to the streets and neighborhoods in the region. Regardless of the locale, the work of teachers recognizes both a shared responsibility with and an accountability to the many constituencies who have a stake in the success of the school.

Not all CSR models include strategies or principles designed to foster and guide the activities of teachers outside the school. Most models, however, do address the importance of bringing key stakeholders, especially parents, into the school more frequently and with more prominent and influential roles. In addition to their advisory and, in some cases, decision-making responsibilities within the school governance structure, parents find themselves working alongside teachers in such tasks as teaching (e.g., homework that involves parents in partnership with their children in Talent Development High School; in support of learning expeditions in Expeditionary Learning Outward Bound) or gathering data to review and inform the development of the school (e.g., Accelerated Schools and AT-LAS Communities). The School Development Program recommends a nine-part process (three mechanisms, three operations, three guiding principles) to coordinate the efforts of all of the communities' caregivers:

Mechanisms
- School Planning and Management Team: develops and monitors a Comprehensive School Plan; includes administrators, teachers, support staff, parents, and others.
- Student and Staff Support Team: helps improve the social climate of the school; includes social workers, counselors, special education teachers, and other staff with child development and mental health backgrounds.
- Parent Team: promotes parent involvement in all areas of school life.

Operations
- Comprehensive School Plan: gives direction to the school improvement process; covers academics, school climate, staff development, public relations, and other areas.
- Staff Development Plan: focuses teacher training on needs related to the goals and priorities specified in the comprehensive plan.
- Monitoring and Assessment: generates data on implementation and results; allows teams to modify the school's approach where necessary.

Guiding Principles
- No-Fault Approach to Problem-Solving: lets teams solve and analyze problems without recrimination.
- Consensus Decision Making: promotes dialogue and common understanding.
- Collaboration: enables both the principal and the teams to have a say in the management of the school. (North-

west Regional Educational Laboratory, 1999, pp. 117–118)

Other models extend these inclusive practices to strategies and structures that take the school to the home. The Family Support Team in Success For All, the Parent Center in the Modern Red Schoolhouse, and the Family and Community Center in the Urban Learning Centers engage teachers in concert with service providers (e.g., counselors, attendance officers, social workers) in actions that both facilitate greater involvement of parents in their children's learning and help families to obtain assistance from whichever social agencies or community groups can best provide for their needs. These approaches are based on the belief that the development of at-risk students, in particular, depends on a coordinated and intensive system of support that simultaneously responds to their learning needs in the classroom and to the factors and conditions of their life that affect their chances of success in school (e.g., nutrition, shelter, security, clothing).

When CSR models require more integration with organizations in the region or within the school district, teachers assume the role of linking agents (e.g., members on vocation-based advisory councils with local business members to advise on how best to combine college preparatory and vocational studies in High Schools That Work; school-to-career coaches to connect the high school to business, industry, and postsecondary institutions in America's Choice). With those models that recommend either the development of local affiliations (e.g., Onward to Excellence encourages clusters of four to five schools to work together) or more coordinated programs across elementary, middle, and high schools (e.g., ATLAS Communities, High Schools That Work), teachers usually facilitate or coordinate how the changes in their school are part of a more systemic reform process. In either linkage, teachers help their colleagues to establish programmatic partnerships with those with a vested interest in the prior or future learning of students in their schools.

Three of the CSR models explicitly stress a community-based learning component: learning expeditions in Expeditionary Learning Outward Bound; work-based learning or cooperative education in High Schools That Work; and the "community as a learning laboratory" orientation embodied in the 11 core practices of the Foxfire Fund (e.g., connections between class work and the community are clear; there is an audience beyond the teacher for student work; the work is characterized by active learning). Although not always framed in activities outside the school, many of the project-centered and interdisciplinary initiatives advocated by a number of the models require connections to or time in the community (e.g., ATLAS Communities, Audrey Cohen College, Coalition of Essential Schools, Co-NECT, Urban Learning Centers). When such community-based experiences become sustained and integral elements of student learning, the kind of interdependent lives emerging for teachers in the corridors extends to those in the many communities to which the school belongs.

The reform-minded teachers in the most promising and successful schools are increasingly redefining the borders of their learning community. They work with parents, community members, and other educational and social groups with an affiliation to or interest in the school in ways that:

• Involve students in numerous learning milieus outside the school;
• Build effective teaching and learning partnerships; and
• Mutually inform, guide, and respect their respective priorities and practices.

The following excerpt completes the letter from the reform-minded music teacher. In this concluding section, the teacher describes and comments on the greater interaction with and demands of many sectors of society and on the possibilities that these enhanced connections create for improving classroom and school experiences.

My time is not only devoted to learning how to work more collaboratively with colleagues in the corridors. My work also encompasses quite a number of connections with the many others who have a stake in what schools do and become—especially parents, other educators, individuals (e.g., musicians), or other organizational representatives in the community. Although I have always had contact with many parents through their attendance at concerts and music department events, I interact with parents more often and in a wider range of circumstances: (1) about the progress of their children through "homework hotlines" and electronic communication and during student-led parent/teacher conferences; (2) while teaching them about instructional innovations at parent seminars or workshops/demonstrations; (3) in the course of in-class projects (e.g., parents evaluating projects, working as tutors) or at-home tutoring (e.g., training and resources for parents to assist them in working with their children in ways consistent with innovative practices in the school); (4) on school committees and councils; and (5) in formal and informal coalitions to submit proposals, copresent at conferences, or lobby for support for the school's reforms.

I have many occasions where I work with other educators—from other schools, a regional professional development center, or a nearby university. Often these are long-term relationships in which these "critical friends" get to know our school and adapt what they provide to the unique circumstances under which I teach. I have served as the cooperating teacher for several student teachers from the university, and find that I am frequently called to speak to student teaching seminars or to consult with my university colleagues as they make changes to the teacher education program.

Then there are the activities that come from our involvement in a national school reform network. With this affiliation comes contact with like-minded schools and various forms of training and support from the network so that we can become more proficient at and consistent with those practices we feel best embody the values and principles that bring these schools together in the first place. For many years now, I have worked with musicians both in the classroom and in various performance settings outside the school. Often these ventures away from the school have been part of our commitment to serve the community. As these links to parents, guest artists, and community groups become more ongoing and programmatic, they take on more the character of partnerships. I have access to a wide range of musical mentors for my students, who bring an eclectic mix of musical styles and areas of musicianship for them to consider. In these more partnered situations, I am a teaching educator providing access to and counsel for approaches I previously did mainly on my own. We mutually design learning experiences so that what my students do in the classroom informs and is informed by what they do outside school. As a result, my students see how adults in the community combine their musical participation with their vocational and avocational interests.

Expanding the horizons of learning (by working with those outside the school) then also expands the team of those involved in what and how students learn—a welcomed albeit complicated widening of my work especially when this already includes an in-school team with their own collaborative dispositions! We have to somehow interrelate the collective ideas of my school-based team with those of one or more partners outside the school such that the learning experiences we co-construct make sense to and are stimulating for our students—a hectic, complicated, bold, and exciting venture to say the least! We are faced with the challenge of sorting out the extent to which music is a primary feature of the experiences (or one of many elements in an interdisciplinary unit) and the role of each of the in-school and out-of-school teaching partners in providing and coordinating these experiences.

In addition to these pedagogical partnerships, we have more and more links with agencies which support the welfare of children and their families. The socioeconomic circumstances of so many of our students make it difficult for them to sustain their effort, to take advantage of what is available to them, or succeed as they can and should in school. In our attempts to forge these links, the boundaries between school, family, and community can become blurred or even unclear. Yet, for these students, their risk of not succeeding in school is too great for us to worry about where the borders of school begin or end.

At the same time these partnerships have become more influential in my work, I have strengthened my resolve to exercise my professional judgment as I commit my energies and resources to the projects that will have the greatest impact on my students' learning. I continue to weigh potential opportunities against what I feel is in the best interest of the music program and the overall quality of the students' experience. I have found, however, that although I try to be discriminating as we explore possible avenues for collaboration within and outside the school, I cannot always predict or control what my students learn from these encounters. Many times, I feel that the lessons they learn transcend the difficulties we face in organizing the experiences, particularly as they learn about the diverse needs and characteristics of our surrounding community.

To what extent and in what way should either collegial or "outside" sources influence or determine the decisions I ultimately have to make each day in the classroom? Sorting out my moral accountability to students and parents; my professional accountability to colleagues, the field of music, the profession, and myself; my contractual accountability to the district and the state department of education; and my social accountability to various segments in society is a constant struggle of moral and ethical obligation.

Such challenges are only outnumbered by the possibilities generated when our work as teachers changes. We have a deep commitment to improving what happens in and on behalf of classrooms within an environment where connections among people, ideas and practices matter. As reform-minded music teachers, we can make good on these possibilities of improving our classrooms by redefining how we work with students in the classroom, by creating organizational conditions that support innovation and collaborative endeavors, by engaging in more collective and school-based forms of professional learning, by extending the scope of shared responsibility for student learning and school reform, and by expanding beyond traditional boundaries of learning through interdisciplinary and community-based learning experiences.

Musically Yours,
A reform-minded music teacher

Reform-minded music teachers appreciate that what they do with students is part of and not apart from the many communities (e.g., parent, business, education) connected to the school. Their actions are inevitably and reciprocally linked in a kind of ecological bond between educational and social development (Fullan, 1999). Working with those *out there* begins in the classroom and the corridors where parents and others share in both the instructional duties previously reserved for teachers alone and the decisions that affect how the school supports the improvement of classroom practice. In this transition, teachers often act as mentors and coaches in support of their teaching and decision-making partners. Such closer ties with those from outside initially improve communication with parents and other stakeholders and increase the number of ideas, resources, or people considered and included in the school reform effort. Over time, and especially when such ties lead to long-term, school-community partnerships, reform-minded music teachers—in concert with colleagues and outside partners—can boldly redefine and redirect the scope and context of student learning.

Implications of Reform-Mindedness for Music Teacher Education

Before we create a portrayal of a music teacher education curriculum based on this image of the reform-minded teacher, we need to take stock of those forces that may complicate the path toward such a program. Certain traditions, issues, and tensions—such as the view of music teaching as a specialized form of practice, the balance of identity between musician and teacher, the prominence of performance in music programs, and the pressing advocacy needs of music programs in schools—are part of the underlying assumptions and structures of music education. These themes are deeply ingrained in the music education community, forming part of the ethos that shapes the professional identity of most music teachers (Tyack & Cuban, 1995). There are also tensions that arise from the way music teacher educators have responded to conflicting and competing demands for programmatic change.

In music teacher education, these traditions, issues, and tensions manifest themselves in the preservice teachers' experience at the university. On campus, the structure of the music teacher education curriculum is closely and necessarily intertwined with disciplinary requirements for the development of musicianship. In order to attain high standards of performance and achievement upheld by the music faculty, preservice music teachers devote considerable time and energy to their musical studies and the advancement of their performing abilities. The knowledge they construct about music often closely mirrors long-standing traditions and assumptions about music as a means of highly refined artistic, aesthetic, personal, and cultural expression. Close contact with faculty members in schools of music and their influence as musical mentors strengthens preservice teachers' resolve to uphold these standards and traditions of musical practice in their own developing work and performance. The preservice teachers' affiliation with music as a discipline is solidified and deepened throughout the university program, corresponding to the emergence of their developing identities and capabilities as musicians. At times these identities come into conflict with the demands of time and effort for education courses and field experiences. Within music methods courses, preservice teachers also strengthen their views of teaching, the standards that teachers hold for their work, and the distinguishing traditions and characteristic practices of various subspecializations within music education (as instrumental, vocal, or general music teachers).

In schools, preservice teachers are likely to work with cooperating teachers who strengthen these robust images of specialization. The socialization of student teachers along these lines continues as the specialist identity is engraved more deeply in school settings, in part because of differences in the ways specialist and generalist teachers are assigned students for required and elective classes, in the ways music classes are scheduled, in the placement of music facilities within the school, and in the interactions of formal and informal networks of specialist and generalist teachers within schools. To the extent that this orientation prepares preservice music teachers to forge a strong place for music within the overall curriculum of the school, and to create rigorous, vibrant music classrooms for students, the disciplinary stance is healthy and warranted. More constrained and entrenched images of music teachers as specialists may impair preservice teachers' abilities to serve as future change agents in schools, however. Periodic struggles to establish and maintain the status of music within elementary and secondary schools have resulted in narrowly construed and sometimes defensive positions taken by music educators as they understandably attempt to protect and maintain music programs in schools. At the extreme, these defensive stances lead to the balkanization of music teachers (A. Hargreaves, 1994) and the isolation of music programs. Current calls for advocacy within the profession and also from outside the profession (perhaps springing from media portrayals of music teachers at risk of losing their programs) also may result in less positive and enduring images of music teachers' work by exacerbating preservice teachers' fears of the tenuous presence of and vacillating support for music programs. Unwittingly, overly forceful advocacy efforts may also foster a distrust of administrators, other teachers within the school, and political forces within the community, or they may amplify a general resistance to change. These persistent portrayals may lead to further isolation of the newly licensed specialist from the ongoing mission and interactions of the school community.

Other factors might complicate a shift toward a new, more reform-minded tradition. Programs have suffered from an additive approach, in which often worthy ideas have been incorporated into programs without deleting old requirements, or reconceptualizing programs anew. General calls for the reform of music teacher education have recommended many avenues for improving the structure and content of the curriculum (Boardman, 1990; Colwell, 2000; Leonhard, 1985; Meske, 1985), reconfiguring concepts of teacher knowledge (Bresler, 1995b; Elliott, 1992; Reimer, 1993; Wing, 1993), forming partnerships between university programs and schools (Music Educators National Conference, 1987), and invigorating efforts to evaluate music teachers and music teacher education programs (Collins, 1996; Colwell, 1985; Shuler, 1996). Other themes for music teacher education reform have focused on the incorporation of the National Standards (Abrahams, 2000;

Byo, 1999; Shuler, 1995), multicultural perspectives (Campbell, 1994; Volk, 1998), contemporary assessment practices (Colwell, 1998), and constructivist models of learning (Webster, 1998).

Another source of tension comes from forces outside the music teacher education community who hold a stake in the preparation of music teachers. These forces can exert pressure on musical components of the curriculum (often related to National Association of Schools of Music [NASM] accreditation requirements, state licensing requirements for music teachers, or standards of professional associations), or requirements related to teaching in general (including the National Council for the Accreditation of Teacher Education [NCATE], licensing requirements for all teachers, and generic teaching skills, dispositions, and capabilities emphasized by colleges of education). There are perennial tensions between these perspectives, most often expressed in criticisms of the proportion of time and degree of emphasis spent in classes devoted to musicianship or classes devoted to teaching.

Music teacher educators, caught in the crossroads and sometimes the crossfire of initiatives from teacher education reforms, licensing requirements, accreditation guidelines, personal beliefs, prior experience, and research findings from comprehensive school reform movements in elementary and secondary schools, seek a coherence of principle and practice in constructing a curriculum for reform-minded music educators. The risks of running aground are considerable, particularly without a compass of clear purpose. Music teacher education programs too narrowly focused may lead to insularity and reproduction of constrained roles for music teachers within schools. Programs that are diffused and disintegrated may fail to prepare music teachers for their roles at all. The knowledge base for preservice music teachers must be recast to embrace a more inclusive description of what music teachers should know and be able to do as effective change agents in school environments. Smylie, Bay, and Tozer (1999) observe that "it is often assumed that teacher educators know what capacities teachers need to be effective agents of change and can help them to develop these capacities. The research on preservice and inservice teacher education indicates, however, that these assumptions are not necessarily valid. . . . If the expectation that teachers should be agents of change is taken seriously, the capacities this work requires of them must be considered more closely" (p. 29). Our image of the reform-minded music teacher is one response to this concern.

We call for an examination and a reframing of the predominant image of music teacher as specialist within music teacher education. A reform-minded image of teaching can both build on the core traditions and strengths of music teachers while at the same time provide a foundation to address some of the enduring issues and tensions in ways that would eventually recast their role and significance in educational reform. Three overarching principles might guide this restructuring. First, the expanded realms of music teachers' work portrayed in this chapter suggest that music teacher educators need to situate the formation of a strong disciplinary expertise and identity within a wider geography of influence and action for music teachers. Any changes in how student teachers learn to teach or in the pedagogical strategies developed for the teacher education program then would be based on and ultimately interconnected with this three-tiered image of the reform-minded music teacher. Program standards, course content, and field experiences would be examined to determine the extent to which they incorporate and integrate these expanded realms of the classroom, corridors, and community.

A second principle is focused on this embedded image of teaching in an ecological view of schooling in which teachers look for justified ways to take advantage of reciprocal and mutual connections between people and ideas. Themes of collaboration and community will likely become more visible components of teacher education programs and more common attributes of developing professional identity. As practices and programs evolve, so will the reciprocal interests of teachers for the overall improvement of students' and teachers' lives in schools. This principle of reciprocality and mutuality also animates thinking about the disciplinary character of music as a subject with clearly delineated boundaries of schedule, location, and pedagogical practices. A more organic and ecological stance toward disciplinary knowledge is rooted in the notion that music is influenced by and, in turn, influences other realms of human experience. This suggests a more comprehensive approach to music learning that is infused with valid concepts, examples, and insights from other disciplines. In turn, music often serves as a catalyst for a more comprehensive examination of complementary subjects in other classrooms within the school, ensuring that music learning is not confined exclusively to the music room. This ecological view also calls for music teachers to develop their "latitudinal knowledge" (Noddings, 1999, p. 215) of related subjects and learn to make crucial distinctions between subservient and synergistic approaches to connecting the curriculum (Bresler, 1995a). These reciprocal meanings are continually evolving and transforming through collaborative invention and social interaction for students and teachers. Understanding this interdependence makes valid interdisciplinary work both possible and imperative.

A third principle emphasizes the development of teachers' change agentry—their commitment to and skill in improving what happens in and on behalf of classrooms. The portrayal of broader dimensions of the social and intellectual work of teachers—leading to self-renewal and school renewal—lends credence to a reconceptualization of program pedagogy in music teacher education. This reconcep-

tualization converges around *change* as a thematic axis for organizing preprofessional experience. It implies new ways of thinking about how preservice teachers learn, with whom, and about what central topics. We suggest that the study of music teachers as change agents, using inquiry-based methods in collaborative contexts, holds particular promise for preparing beginning teachers for their future lives in schools. Innovative teachers who continually renew their practice by engaging in cycles of inquiry, action, and reflection can serve both as subjects and models of study and as mentors and partners with university music educators in helping preservice teachers realize their potential as agents of change. Through participating in inquiry with music teachers in reform-oriented environments, preservice teachers can more readily perceive how educational innovations and initiatives oscillate in cycles of change and continuity, standardization and variation, autonomy and accountability, and integration and differentiation. They can see how teachers move forward in the midst of these pulls and tensions, looking at their work critically and creatively in changing school contexts.

Creating a Reform-Minded Program

The last section of this chapter portrays how these three overarching forces—the expanded realms of work, mutual and reciprocal relationships of people and ideas, and change agentry—would guide the creation of a reform-minded program for music teachers. Our "future perfect portrayal" is based on this expanded image of music teachers' work, and features a combined description of various images/practices of learning to teach and pedagogy. Admittedly, some of the elements and components of this proposed view are already in place in some teacher education programs. By taking such artistic license, however, we strive to open up an imaginative space for readers to envision what teacher educators infused with such a reform-minded orientation "will have done." The closing paragraph of the reform-minded music teacher's letter provides five themes we will take up as organizers for examining these implications of reform-mindedness for music teacher education, as she calls for music teachers to improve classrooms by 1) redefining how we work with students in the classroom, 2) creating organizational conditions that support innovation and collaborative endeavors, 3) engaging in more collective and school-based forms of professional learning, 4) extending the scope of shared responsibility for student learning and school reform, and 5) expanding beyond traditional boundaries of learning through interdisciplinary and community-based learning experiences.

Redefining How Music Teachers Work with Students in the Classroom. Music teacher educators will cultivate attitudes of pedagogical reform-mindedness by moving preservice teachers toward expanded views of what transpires within the music classroom. They will encourage beginning teachers to confront and reshape deeply ingrained images of music classrooms formed through prior personal experience, to expand the range of possibilities for music learning by studying, experiencing, inventing, and evaluating innovative practices, and to implement and adapt these approaches in field settings that are conducive to change. Much in the same way that the author of the letter describes the challenges of teaching in a perpetually evolving classroom in which changes in expectations for student learning are mirrored in the teacher's own shifts of understanding, music teacher educators will attend to the ways that the intellectual environment of the university classroom and their own practices serve as exemplary models of change as well.

Preservice teachers' intellectual histories as learners will provide them with implicit theories about music learning and teaching. Music teacher educators will employ a variety of narrative and observational strategies to help preservice teachers articulate these assumptions and beliefs that often enable or inhibit perceptive thinking about the complex array of actions and interactions within classrooms. Thoughtful examination of prior experience and current practice in music teaching will lay the groundwork for preserving worthy traditions and inspiring the creation of new initiatives. Subtle and profound shifts in the underlying assumptions will fuel changes in teachers' beliefs and intentions for the classroom. The principles identified through this examination will become the framework on which preservice teachers can form revised theories of curriculum, instruction, and assessment in music.

A preservice teacher's ability to design a student-centered music curriculum that draws from an eclectic variety of musical styles and sources will be of paramount importance for engaging and sustaining student involvement. Preservice teachers will introduce their students to an expanded range of musical styles, performance practices, and genres. Expanded access to a panoramic array of musical scores, materials, recordings, and performers will provide a breadth of choices for students and teachers, and a heightened responsibility for preservice teachers to articulate how they will select music for study, and how they will bring student's prior musical experiences and interests to bear on this selection. Instructional capabilities will also expand as preservice teachers benefit from technological developments in generating and manipulating original music, and providing avenues for students to explore and develop their compositional ideas using various media. The temptation to sample indiscriminately and superficially from this rich menu of musical examples and styles will be overcome by recommending that preservice teachers concentrate on fewer musical works or styles in greater depth. An intense focus on fewer works will also

enable preservice teachers to focus on the artistry of curriculum design, experimenting with the rhythms of introducing, developing, and pulling together episodes of learning into cohesive and satisfying learning experiences. In the midst of this wealth of curricular ideas, preservice teachers will develop their abilities to design sound, imaginative curricula "from scratch" and also will adapt and revise curricular ideas that have been developed by others. This orientation to curriculum making will give them the necessary latitude for making contextually sensitive decisions that fit the characteristics and attributes of their students and school settings.

Reform-minded preservice music teachers will diversify the instructional landscape of the curriculum by opening up avenues for a greater number of students to participate in music and by expanding the menu of choices for students who typically seek out musical study. This diversification will include both types of musical experience (from a traditional performance emphasis to the incorporation of more improvisation, composition, analysis, interpretation, and evaluation), instructional settings (from teacher-directed whole class settings to more student-directed projects, small ensembles, use of music technology labs, and mentoring of student-directed independent work), and variety of offerings (from traditional instrumental and vocal ensembles to guitar, percussion, keyboard, electronic classes, or ethnic ensembles). Many of these avenues for diversification will also lead to increased student independence and responsibility for selecting, creating, analyzing, conducting, interpreting, and presenting their own music while concurrently directing, monitoring, and critiquing their own work. As students exercise greater control over their own learning, the function of the teacher will shift accordingly to that of coach, resource broker, mentor, or guide.

Redefinitions of curriculum and instruction will also involve corresponding revisions of assessment practices in the classroom. Preservice teachers will employ a variety of methods and strategies for evaluating what and how well students learn. Music learning will be evaluated along several dimensions, such as the developmental trajectory of an individual student's growth, the overall progress of groups of students, and the musical achievements of the entire program. The experiential character of music learning will offer many opportunities for the kind of authentic, performance-based assessments that vividly reveal the developing sophistication of students' musical thinking and depth of understanding. Again, the preservice teacher will adapt and invent means to evaluate students' learning that offer representative and valid samples of what students know and are able to do. Reform-minded preservice teachers will also realize that the responsibility for assessment must be shared with students if they are to develop as independent musicians, and so they will offer opportunities for student input in evaluating the products and processes of learning in a musical classroom. Communicating the results of assessment clearly to students, parents, administrators and other stakeholders will require preservice teachers to develop skills in collecting, interpreting, representing, and reporting information. The insights derived from formative and summative assessments will fold back into the design of subsequent learning opportunities for students, thereby integrating curriculum, instruction, and assessment into a spiraling cycle of improvement.

Creating Organizational Conditions That Support Innovation and Collaborative Endeavors. Teacher education will empower beginning teachers to contribute to substantive school reform efforts by building their capacities for joint work and encouraging imaginative thinking about perennial issues in teaching and learning. An emphasis on personal and collaborative initiatives for enhancing school experience will equip beginning teachers to take their place in schools with the assurance that, in spite of their relative inexperience, they have valuable ideas to contribute and the fortitude to cope with the demands of changing and sometimes ambiguous environments. In their prior experience, preservice teachers have witnessed how their own music teachers have taken disparate assortments of students and blended them into cohesive organizations and ensembles, so they will have some familiarity with the kind of clear purpose and focus that collaborative work requires in order to be effective. Participation in joint projects and school leadership teams will be expected of music teachers in school reform efforts, so a reform-minded curriculum will provide opportunities for preservice teachers to acquire and develop the needed skills and dispositions for these forms of participation within the school.

The organizational conditions we refer to in this context are those that music teacher educators will create within the university setting of the music methods block and the school settings used for the placement of student teachers. Although university classrooms can scarcely recreate the conditions practicing teachers face in elementary and secondary schools, their use as fertile hatcheries for ideas, closely interfaced with field experiences, will lead to the development of preservice teachers' capacities for innovative and collaborative endeavors. We further acknowledge that these collaborative expectations will significantly enlarge the scope of what has traditionally been included within music teacher education programs. Music teacher educators will need to consider carefully how the three realms of teachers' work that are essential to the redefined role of the music specialist will be emphasized and incorporated into the overall program. A graduated approach will still stress the development of preservice music teachers' competence and skills within the classroom as the initial focus of the music methods block and the field expe-

riences. As beginning teachers demonstrate growing confidence in their work with students, assignments and experiences will be added progressively to the methods block to provide collaborative experience with peers and other teachers and, finally, experience with individuals and groups outside of the school setting. Preservice teachers will also be directed to consider the elements of school environments that encourage innovative thinking, including adequate time for study and contemplation, the use of rich resources and materials to inform the process, available research on best practices, and space for informal and formal discussions. They will solicit the help of peers and mentors to offer friendly critique for emerging ideas. The considerable resources of the university, along with greater flexibility in scheduling than many teachers experience in elementary and secondary schools, will give preservice teachers a rich, congenial, and contemplative environment for considering innovative practices.

Learning to collaborate will be a central feature of the curriculum. Preservice teachers engaged in group work within the methods classroom will focus on developing collaborative skills before branching out to work with others outside the music methods setting. Preservice music teachers will be expected to collaborate with education majors on substantive interdisciplinary projects, for example, learning how to relate music to other subjects in meaningful ways, and also to convey the essential character of musical experience to their peers who live outside of the music building. A capstone experience within the music methods block will involve group collaborations with arts groups or ensembles within the university, or the development of outreach programs for school children. During the student teaching semester or year, student teachers will experience a similarly tiered progression, concentrating first on establishing a firm footing in the music classroom before working with other teachers in the school on collaborative ventures. Student teachers will also concentrate on the communities in which their cooperating schools are located, and will establish networks and productive relationships among students, teachers, community musicians, parent groups, arts organizations, and agencies for the welfare of students.

Engaging in More Collective and School-Based Forms of Professional Learning. Preservice teachers who experience teaching as a form of inquiry within their university programs will be well prepared to participate in inquiry-based forums for professional learning within the landscape of school reform. In moving from technical conceptions of teaching to more constructivist and reflective orientations, music teacher educators will seek to develop deeply thoughtful and inquisitive practitioners who can interrogate their own knowledge and raise provocative questions about music and the cultural, social, and political context of schools. Collective inquiry will encourage preservice teachers to consider multiple perspectives and solutions to perennial problems, and to respect the processes of lively discussion and debate in group settings. Preservice teachers' abilities to build consensus and to garner support for new ideas will be fostered in these settings, leading to clearer and more cogent rationales for change.

Just as teachers in reform-based schools engage in the study of their own practices, proposed changes in the school's programs, or key problems of shared concern in the school and community, preservice teachers will investigate similarly varied and salient topics. Study groups will examine such perennial problems of practice as the construction of fair, manageable, and musically meaningful systems for grading students' work in music and reporting their progress to others. They will focus on programmatic goals, such as the development of new offerings to attract the substantial population of students in secondary schools who do not elect to participate in school music programs. The subject of inquiry will also address the effects of schoolwide initiatives on music instruction, such as the impact of block scheduling or the assignment of students to cohort groups.

Resources for portraying and studying the expanded realms of teachers' work in changing environments will be developed as materials for inquiry within music teacher education classrooms. Although field experiences give tangible access to the unfolding drama of classroom life in real time, the quantity and pace of the events are often too much for beginning teachers to absorb. Case materials—in written, videotaped, or digitized formats—will be especially useful in teacher education classrooms in that they allow preservice teachers to stop and reflect on classroom events, reread or replay them to confirm their observations, and, especially, to enhance their abilities to notice and reflect on the complexities and subtleties that are part of any teaching and learning setting. Compelling descriptions or documentaries of innovative programs that feature music teachers collaborating with other teachers within the school or with guest artists, community musicians, or arts organizations will stretch preservice teachers' imaginations toward wider realms of influence. They will study forms of collaboration and the conditions that enable teachers to collaborate most productively. Rich ethnographies of classroom life and interviews with teachers who see themselves as catalysts for change will be developed.

Extending the Scope of Shared Responsibility for Student Learning and School Reform.

The credibility and integrity of a reform-minded view of teacher education rests on the abilities of preservice teachers to recognize how shared aims for student learning are expressed in the actions and intentions of teachers, parents, administrators, support personnel, and school board and community members.

Cooperating teachers will narrate and translate for beginning teachers the rather complex and intricate web of relationships undergirding the mission of the school. Preservice teachers will realize how their initial contributions to the school community align with the varied goals of the school's stakeholders. Clearly, the social dimensions of a teacher's work will be essential components of the teacher education curriculum, enabling the development of preservice teachers' intrapersonal and interpersonal skills as they take their places alongside others in schools. Their reform-minded inclinations and views of the possible will be shaped in the midst of this fluctuating interplay of people and ideas.

Throughout the methods block and student teaching experience, preservice teachers will realize how themes of change are manifest across the realms of teachers' work within the school. In addition to participating in the transformation of learning within the music classroom described earlier in this chapter, preservice teachers will observe and assist the work of select committees, school leadership teams, and study groups. They will be assigned responsibilities to consult with resource personnel who provide specialized services and to gather information about particular students' academic or social progress. Opportunities for interaction with parents will be explored, including assisting with parent-teacher conferences, planning presentations for parents, or working with music support groups sponsored by parents.

Expanded realms of shared decision making will be incorporated into the structure of the curriculum as music teacher educators will first invite preservice teachers to participate in making joint decisions within the methods classroom (both with the professor and with other students). Shared decision making among preservice teachers, university professors, and cooperating teachers will be a natural outgrowth of this commitment. Cooperating teachers and methods teachers will model collegial, critical inquiry as they involve beginning teachers in exploring options for innovative practice and choosing the best route among those options. They will foster risk-taking and innovation by giving preservice teachers the necessary latitude within the classroom to develop their own ideas, rather than remaining in the shadow of their own pedagogical approaches. The three-way interactions of the cooperating teacher, music teacher educator as supervisor, and student teacher will further capacities along these lines through more democratic, interactive, and participatory forms of supervision. The customary focus of supervisory visits on events within the classroom will be augmented to evaluate how the student teacher participates in collaborative efforts and shared decision making within the corridors and in other communities beyond the classroom that forward the overall educational aims of the school.

Music teacher educators will seek partnerships with cooperating teachers who display a strong sense of efficacy and a penchant for positive change. Together, they will construct meaningful formative experiences for preservice teachers that place the goals of the school and the university in complementary balance. Music teacher educators will also support the ongoing inquiry-based efforts of the cooperating teacher by providing resources or expertise, and by enlisting the preservice teachers' help in gathering information about students' learning. The cooperating teacher's skill and enthusiasm for collaborative work, as well as the collegial climate for joint work within the school, will be important criteria for the selection of field sites. Practicing teachers as partners in music teacher education will also serve as advisors and consultants in the transformation of university curricula to promote expanded views of teachers' work. Teachers who have shown leadership in school reform efforts will offer valuable expertise in restructuring teacher education programs.

Expanding Beyond Traditional Boundaries of Learning Through Interdisciplinary and Community-Based Learning Experiences.
Reform-minded music teachers will expand traditional boundaries of learning and expand their roles as music specialists by creating a balance and connection between disciplinary and interdisciplinary curriculum practices, by involving students in numerous learning milieus outside the school, and by forging teaching and learning partnerships with stakeholders in the community. Music teachers will continue to assume primary responsibility for orchestrating and carrying out a comprehensive, sequential curriculum for music learning, but the scope of that curriculum and the settings in which it transpires will be expanded.

Music teacher educators will provide metaphors, models, and examples that will help preservice teachers with little biographical experience to engage in substantive interdisciplinary work. Imaginative metaphors will be used to convey an alternate representation of music's integrative possibilities to preservice teachers suggesting, for example, that the nucleus of musical study certainly involves extensive engagement with essential elements, works, performance practices, and processes, but the permeable walls of the cell allow meanings that are expressed in history, culture, art, literature, and other forms of experience to flow into the classroom for the purpose of enriching musical understanding. Rich experiences will demonstrate how insights from other disciplines enhance the performance, creation, and interpretation of musical works. Field experiences will provide models for the collaborative work of classroom generalists and specialists as they forge strong connections for students. Beginning teachers will also explore how models of instruction can increase students' abilities to discover meaningful relationships themselves. Through collaborative interdisciplinary work, music teach-

ers will develop their knowledge of the general curriculum, building a repertoire of topics, examples, representations, and analogies to enliven and engage students' interests. Preservice teachers will learn to distinguish when it makes sense for students to engage in musical activities that are unmediated by references to other disciplines and when it makes sense to draw insights for music making from a broad and eclectic range of sources and stances. By distinguishing between subservient and synergistic approaches to connecting the curriculum, preservice teachers will learn to use these critical powers to elevate the overall quality of collaborative curricular work in schools.

Music teacher educators will also experience heightened responsibilities for directing beginning teachers toward greater community involvement. Although it is typical for music teacher educators to be involved directly in the identification and selection of cooperating teachers and school sites for preservice teachers' placement, the *field* in field placements has traditionally been interpreted as the world of the elementary or secondary school. Teacher educators will be challenged to identify new community alliances for the mutual benefit of preservice teachers and participants in music activities outside of schools. Redesigned programs will promote partnerships with community agencies and organizations that offer arts education to the very youngest members of the community (in preschool, day care, or parent education courses) as well as to adult learners (through community choirs, bands, orchestras, and adult continuing education programs, for example). Additional avenues will underscore preservice teachers' commitment to students at risk (in after-school, weekend, or summer programs) or students with special needs (such as Very Special Arts programs). Preservice teachers will also be encouraged to become active in community arts organizations. Curricula for school outreach initiatives will be designed for universities and schools to work in tandem with orchestras, dance companies, theater groups, and other arts organizations. Artist-in-residence programs will represent another fertile avenue for cultivating partnerships. Relationships with performers, composers, and music critics in the community will be fostered, perhaps with the resultant effect of disintegrating some of the perceived distinctions students and teachers maintain between music in schools as separate from "real music" in the outside world.

From Vision to Practice

In this chapter, we have described an expanded image of the work of music teachers who contribute to school reform initiatives by examining and reshaping their classroom practice, collaborating with others within the school, and establishing partnerships with various communities outside the school. We have also portrayed the ecological, collaborative, and interdisciplinary nature of this work, and the reform-minded dispositions teachers need to make substantive changes in classrooms, schools, and communities. We argue that these overarching notions, drawn from the literature on change and from principles and practices of teachers working within school reform networks, should be integrated more closely with teacher education programs. In the absence of a body of research on music teachers' participation in school reform initiatives, we have synthesized salient themes and ideas for program pedagogy centered around this reform-minded view for music teacher education.

The research community in music teacher education clearly needs to turn its attention to the changing roles of music educators within the landscape of educational reform. If music teachers are to function as change agents in general initiatives to reform schools, in the ongoing transformation of music education as a discipline, and in the developmental formation of their own beliefs and practices, we will need broad and ambitiously conceived agendas for inquiry. Such studies could focus on the experience of individual teachers engaged in reform, on the interactions of teachers within communities, on the effects of reform initiatives on music programs and students' music learning, or on the conceptual foundations that form the basis of teacher knowledge and praxis. Case studies of music teachers engaged in school reform could be juxtaposed with case studies of preservice teachers enrolled in music teacher education programs, for example, to provide a context for examining assumptions about learning to teach and program pedagogy that bridge the worlds of the university and school setting. Comprehensive evaluations of music programs in elementary and secondary schools participating in CSR initiatives would provide valuable insights about the effects of these reform efforts on music teaching and learning that, in turn, could strengthen the rationale for transforming current teacher education programs. Studies that address the conditions that enable teachers to collaborate productively and to engage in substantive interdisciplinary work also hold particular importance for the music teacher education curriculum. Studies such as these will guide our efforts to prepare reform-minded music teachers, moving from an imagined view to practice and policies informed by inquiry. As expectations for school reform heighten, so does the need to conduct research that situates music education and music teachers as integral elements in the "change story" of schools.

NOTES

1. In contrast to those who sometimes equate reform with imposing regulations and policies from outside (e.g., Goodlad, 2000; A. Hargreaves, 1995), we associate the term "reform" with the capacity of individuals and organizations to imagine anew, to see new possibilities, and to improve those conditions that most affect the development of students, educators, and the school (e.g., Jacobs, 1995).

2. Some comprehensive school reform models appeared in only one of the guides and, consequently, are not included in table 40.1. For example, the Northwestern Regional Educational Laboratory (1999) also listed the Center for Effective Schools, the Child Development Project, *MicroSociety,* Montessori, The Learning Network, and the Ventures Initiative and Focus System. The American Institutes of Research (Herman et al., 1999) also included the Basic Schools Network. The Laboratory For School Success (Wang, Haertel, & Walberg, 1997a) also described Higher Order Thinking Skills, the National Writing Project, and Reading Recovery. The Center for Research on the Education of Students Placed At Risk (Slavin & Fashola, 1998) also reviewed Consistency Management and Cooperative Discipline.

3. Although 17 models appeared on the *Obey-Porter* list, districts can choose from other models or programs not on this list or develop their own approach. The Comprehensive School Reform Demonstration Program requires that the selected or designed model or program address the following nine components: effective, research-based methods and strategies; comprehensive design with aligned components; professional development; measurable goals and benchmarks; support within the school; parental and community involvement; external technical support and assistance; evaluation strategies; and coordination of resources (Northwest Regional Educational Laboratory, 1999).

4. Snapshots are quick and more focused glimpses on particular practices of teachers engaged in the process of school reform. Traub (1999) in *A Consumer's Guide to Schoolwide Reform* provides snapshots of 10 models in action based on visits to schools nominated by the CSR designers. Outside the networks, useful snapshots of teachers at work are available in such volumes as Lieberman and Miller (1999). Case studies offer more extended accounts (usually in chapters, articles, or books) of the interconnected lives of teachers across all three realms of their work. In schools from CSR networks, Bottoms and Mikos (1995), Knight and Stallings (1995), Miles and Darling-Hammond (1998) offer some illuminating portrayals. Beyond the networks, valuable insights into the widening and productive worlds of teachers are found in: Elmore, Peterson, and McCarthey (1996; see the analysis of Northeastern Elementary School); Maehr and Midgley, 1996; Newmann and Associates (1996; see the discussion of Cibola High School, Red Lake Middle, Careen Elementary, and Lamar Elementary); or Louis, Kruse, and Associates (1995; see the review of the Metro Academy and Thomas Paine High School).

5. Much of the information about the models in these sections (in the classroom, in the corridors, as part of other communities) comes from the summaries in *The Catalog of School Reform* (Northwest Regional Educational Laboratory, 1999) and *An Educator's Guide to Schoolwide Reform* (Herman et al., 1999).

6. Newmann and Associates (1996) developed and applied a set of standards for authentic achievement and pedagogy. The standards include three criteria significant to intellectual

accomplishment: construction of knowledge (organization of information, consideration of alternatives); disciplined inquiry (prior knowledge based, in-depth understanding, elaborated communication); and value beyond school (problem connected to the world beyond the classroom, audience beyond school).

7. Ten principles that guide school reform in the Coalition of Essential Schools: The school should focus on helping children learn to use their minds well; the school's goal should be simple: that each student master a limited number of essential skills and areas of knowledge; the school's goal should apply to all students; teaching and learning should be personalized to the maximum feasible extent; the governing practical metaphor of the school should be student-as-worker, teacher-as-coach; the diploma should be awarded on demonstration of mastery of the central skills and knowledge of the school's program; the tone of the school should stress unanxious expectation, trust, and decency; the principal and teachers should perceive themselves as generalists first and specialists second; teacher loads should be 80 or fewer pupils, and per-pupil cost should not exceed traditional costs by more than 10%; the school should demonstrate nondiscriminatory and inclusive policies, practices, and pedagogies.

8. Portions of this segment of the letter are adapted from Thiessen and Anderson (1999, chap. 4).

REFERENCES

Abrahams, F. (2000). National standards for music education and college preservice music teacher education: A new balance. *Arts Education Policy Review, 102*(1), 27–31.

Boardman, E. (1990). Music teacher education. In W. R. Houston (Ed.), *Handbook of research on teacher education* (pp. 730–745). New York: Macmillan.

Borko, H., & Putnam, R. (1996). Learning to teach. In D. Berliner & R. Calfee (Eds.), *Handbook of educational psychology* (pp. 673–708). New York: Macmillan.

Bottoms, G., & Mikos, P. (1995). *Seven most improved high schools that work: Sites raising achievement in reading and science.* Atlanta, GA: Southern Regional Education Board.

Bresler, L. (1995a). The subservient, co-equal, affective, and social integration styles and their implications for the arts. *Arts Education Policy Review, 96*(5), 31–37.

Bresler, L. (1995b). Teacher knowledge: A framework and discussion. *Bulletin of the Council for Research in Music Education, 123*, 26–30.

Bullough, R., Jr. (1997). Becoming a teacher: Self and the social location of teacher education. In B. Biddle, T. Good, & I. Goodson (Eds.), *International handbook of teachers and teaching: Volume I* (pp. 79–134). London: Kluwer Academic Publishers.

Byo, S. J. (1999). Classroom teachers' and music specialists' perceived ability to implement the national standards for music education. *Journal of Research in Music Education, 47*, 111–123.

Caldwell, B., & Spinks, J. (1988). *The self managing school.* Lewes, Sussex: Falmer Press.

Campbell, P. S. (1994). Multiculturalism and the raising of music teachers for the twenty-first century. *Journal of Music Teacher Education, 3*(2), 21–29.

Carter, K., & Anders, D. (1996). Program pedagogy. In F. B. Murray (Ed.), *The teacher educator's handbook: Building a knowledge base for the preparation of teachers* (pp. 526–557). San Francisco: Jossey-Bass.

Clandinin, D. J., & Connelly, F. M. (1992). Teacher as curriculum maker. In P. Jackson (Ed.), *Handbook of research on curriculum* (pp. 363–401). New York: Macmillan Publishing Company.

Clandinin, D. J., & Connelly, F. M. (1998). Stories to live by: Narrative understandings of school reform. *Curriculum Inquiry, 28*(2), 149–164.

Cochran-Smith, M., & Lytle, S. (1999). Relationship of knowledge and practice: Teacher learning in communities. In A. Iran-Nejad & P. Pearson (Eds.), *Review of research in education: Volume 24* (pp. 249–306). Washington, DC: American Educational Research Association.

Collins, I. H. (1996). Assessment and evaluation in music teacher education. *Arts Education Policy Review, 98*(1), 17–21.

Colwell, R. (1985). Program evaluation in music teacher education. *Bulletin of the Council for Research in Music Education, 81*, 18–62.

Colwell, R. (1998). Preparing student teachers in assessment. *Arts Education Policy Review, 99*(4), 29–36.

Colwell, R. (2000). The music education/arts education path. *Arts Education Policy Review, 101*(3), 19–20.

Crandall, D., & Associates. (1982). *People, policies, and practices: Examining the chain of school improvement* (Vols. 1–10). Andover, MA: The Network.

Day, C. (1999). *Developing teachers. The challenges of life-long learning.* London: Falmer Press.

Day, C. (2000). Teachers in the twenty-first century: Time to renew the vision. *Teachers and teaching: Theory and practice, 6*(1), 101–115.

Doyle, W. (1978). Paradigms for research on teacher effectiveness. In L. Shulman (Ed.), *Review of research in education: Volume 5* (pp. 163–198). Itasca, IL: F.E. Peacock.

Doyle, W. (1990). Themes in teacher education research. In W. Huston, M. Haberman, & J. Sikula (Eds.), *Handbook of research on teacher education: Volume 1* (pp. 3–24). New York: Macmillan.

Education Commission of the States. (1999). *Comprehensive school reform: Five lessons from the field.* Denver, CO: Education Commission of the States.

Eisner, E. W. (1998). *The kind of schools we need: Personal essays.* Portsmouth, NH: Heinemann.

Elliott, D. J. (1992). Rethinking music teacher education. *Journal of Music Teacher Education, 2*(1), 6–15.

Elmore, R., Peterson, P., & McCarthey, S. (1996). *Restructuring in the classroom: Teaching, learning, and school organization.* San Francisco: Jossey-Bass.

Emrick, J., & Peterson, S. (1978). *A synthesis of findings across five recent studies in educational dissemination and change.* San Francisco: Far West Laboratory.

Feiman-Nemser, S., & Remillard, J. (1996). Perspectives on

learning to teach. In F. Murray (Ed.), *The teacher educator's handbook: Building a knowledge base for the preparation of teachers* (pp. 63–91). San Francisco: Jossey-Bass.

Fielding, M. (1999). Radical collegiality: Affirming teaching as an inclusive professional practice. *Australian Educational Researcher, 26*(2), 1–34.

Fullan, M. (1993a). *Change forces: Probing the depths of educational reform.* London: Falmer Press.

Fullan, M. (1993b). Why teachers must become change agents. *Educational Leadership, 50*(6), 12–17.

Fullan, M. (1999). *Change forces: The sequel.* London: Falmer Press.

Fullan, M. (2000). The return of large-scale reform. *Journal of Educational Change, 1*(1), 5–28.

Fullan, M., & Hargreaves, A. (1991). *What's worth fighting for in your school?* Toronto: Ontario Public School Teachers' Federation.

Giroux, H. (1988). *Teachers as intellectuals: Toward a critical pedagogy of learning.* Granby, MA: Bergin & Garvey.

Glatthorn, A. (1993). *Teachers as agents of change: A new look at school improvement.* Washington, DC: National Education Association.

Goodlad, J. (1990). *Teachers for our nation's schools.* San Francisco: Jossey-Bass.

Goodlad, J. (2000). Educational renewal and the arts. *Arts Education Policy Review, 101*(4), 11–14.

Goodson, I. (1997). Patterns of curriculum change. In A. Hargreaves, A. Lieberman, M. Fullan, & D. Hopkins (Eds.), *International handbook of educational change* (pp. 231–241). Boston: Kluwer Academic Publishers.

Gray, J., Hopkins, D., Reynolds, D., Wilcox, B., Farrell, S., & Jesson, D. (1999). *Improving schools: Performance and potential.* Buckingham: Open University Press.

Greene, M. (1995). *Releasing the imagination: Essays on education, the arts, and social change.* San Francisco: Jossey-Bass.

Hargreaves, A. (1994). *Changing teachers, changing times: Teachers' work and culture in the postmodern age.* New York: Teachers College Press.

Hargreaves, A. (1995). Renewal in the age of paradox. *Educational Leadership, 52*(7), 14–19.

Hargreaves, A. (2000). Four ages of professionalism and professional learning. *Teachers and Teaching: History and Practice, 6*(2), 151–182.

Hargreaves, A., & Fullan, M. (1998). *What's worth fighting for out there?* New York: Teachers College Press.

Hargreaves, A., Lieberman, A., Fullan, M., & Hopkins, D. (1998). *International handbook of educational change: Volume 5.* London: Kluwer Academic Publishers.

Hargreaves, D. H. (1995). School culture, school effectiveness and school improvement. *School Effectiveness and School Improvement, 6*(1), 23–46.

Hargreaves, D. H., & Hopkins, D. (1991). *The empowered school.* London: Cassell.

Hatch, J. (1998). The differences in theory that matter in the practice of school improvement. *American Educational Research Journal, 35*(1), 3–81.

Hatch, A. (1999). What preservice teachers can learn from studies of teachers' work. *Teaching and Teacher Education, 15*, 229–242.

Herman, R., Aladjem, D., McMahon, P., Masem, E., Mulligan, I., O'Malley, A., Quinones, S., Reeve, A., & Woodruff, D. (1999). *An educator's guide to schoolwide reform.* Arlington, VA: Educational Research Service.

Interstate New Teacher Assessment and Support Consortium (INTASC). (1992). *Model standards for beginning teachers licensing and development: A resource for state dialogue.* Washington, DC: Council of Chief State School Officers.

Jacobs, R. M. (1995). Communicating and teaching: Applied communication theory for teacher educators. In M. O'Hair & S. Odell (Eds.), *Educating teachers for leadership and change: Teacher education yearbook III* (pp. 163–186). Thousand Oaks, CA: Corwin Press.

Joyce, B., Calhoun, E., & Hopkins, D. (1999). *The new structure of school improvement: Inquiring schools and achieving students.* Buckingham: Open University Press.

Klausmeier, H., & Wisconsin Associates. (1990). *The Wisconsin Center for Education Research.* Madison, WI: Wisconsin Center for Education Research.

Knight, S., & Stallings, J. (1995). The implementation of an Accelerated School model in an urban elementary school. In R. Allington & P. Walmsley (Eds.), *No quick fix: Rethinking literacy programs in America's elementary schools* (pp. 236–251). New York: Teachers College Press.

Lacey, C. (1977). *The socialization of teachers.* London: Methuen.

Leithwood, K., & Louis, K. S. (1998). *Organizational learning in schools.* Lisse, Netherlands: Zeitlinger Publishers.

Leonhard, C. (1985). Toward reform in music teacher education. *Bulletin of the Council for Research in Music Education, 81*, 10–17.

Lieberman, A., & Miller, L. (1999). *Teachers—Transforming their world and their work.* New York: Teachers College Press.

Liston, D., & Zeichner, K. (1990). *Teacher education and the social conditions of schooling.* New York: Routledge.

Louis, K. S., Kruse, S. D., & Associates. (1995). *Professionalism and community: Perspectives on reforming urban schools.* Thousand Oaks, CA: Corwin Press.

Louis, K. S., Toole, J., & Hargreaves, A. (1999). Rethinking school improvement. In J. Murphy & K. S. Louis (Eds.), *Handbook of research in educational administration* (2nd ed., pp. 251–276). San Francisco: Jossey-Bass.

Maehr, M., & Midgley, C. (1996). *Transforming school cultures.* Boulder, CO: Westview Press.

McChesney, J., & Hertling, E. (2000). The path to comprehensive school reform. *Educational Leadership, 57*(7), 10–15.

Meske, E. B. (1985). Teacher education: A wedding of theory and practice. *Bulletin of the Council for Research in Music Education, 81*, 65–73.

Miles, K., & Darling-Hammond, L. (1998). Rethinking the allocation of teaching resources: Some lessons from high-performance schools. *Educational Evaluation and Policy Analysis, 20*(1), 9–29.

Miller, J. (1994). *The contemplative practitioner: Meditation in education and the professions.* Westport, CT: Bergin & Garvey.

Music Educators National Conference. (1987). *Music teacher education: Partnership and process.* Reston, VA: Author.

Murphy, J. (1995). Changing the role of teachers. In M. O'Hair & S. Odell (Eds.), *Educating teachers for leadership and change: Teacher education yearbook III* (pp. 311–323). Thousand Oaks, CA: Corwin Press.

Murphy, J., & Adams, J. (1998). Reforming America's schools: 1980–2000. *Journal of Educational Administration, 36*(5), 426–444.

National Commission on Teaching & America's Future. (1996). *What matters most: Teaching for America's future.* New York: Teachers College Press.

New American Schools. (1999). *Working toward excellence: Examining the effectiveness of New American School designs.* Washington: Author.

Newmann, F., & Wehlage, G. (1995). *Successful school restructuring.* Madison, WI: Center on Organization and Restructuring of Schools.

Newmann, F., & Associates. (1996). *Authentic achievement: Restructuring schools for intellectual quality.* San Francisco: Jossey-Bass.

Noddings, N. (1999). Caring and competence. In G. A. Griffin (Ed.), *The education of teachers (Ninety-eighth yearbook of the National Society for the Study of Education)* (pp. 205–220). Chicago: University of Chicago Press.

North Central Regional Educational Laboratory. (2000). *Comprehensive school reform: Making good choices for your school.* Oak Brook, IL: Author.

Northwest Regional Educational Laboratory. (1999). *Catalog of school reform models.* Portland: Author.

Ogawa, R., Crowson, R., & Goldring, E. (1999). Enduring dilemmas of school organization. In J. Murphy & K. S. Louis (Eds.), *Handbook of research on educational administration* (2nd ed., pp. 277–295). San Francisco: Jossey-Bass.

Organization of Economic Cooperation and Development (OECD). (1990). *The teacher today.* Paris: Author.

Poetter, T., Gay, J., Elifritz, K., & Hofacker, L. (1999). *Mapping school change in an Accelerated School.* Columbus, OH: Ohio Department of Education.

Pogrow, S. (2000). Success For All does not produce success for students. *Phi Delta Kappan, 82*(1), 67–80.

Rallis, S., & Rossman, B. (1995). *Dynamic teachers: Leaders of change.* Thousand Oaks, CA: Corwin Press.

Randi, J., & Corno, L. (1997). Teachers as innovators. In B. Biddle, T. Good, & I. Goodson (Eds.), *International handbook of teachers and teaching* (pp. 1163–1221). Boston: Kluwer Academic Publishers.

Reimer, B. (1993). Avoiding extremes of theory and practice in music teacher education. *Journal of Music Teacher Education, 3*(1), 12–22.

Reynolds, D., Creemers, B., Hopkins, D., Stoll, L., & Bollen, R. (1996). *Making good schools: Linking school effectiveness and school improvement.* London: Routledge.

Rosenholtz, S. J. (1989). *Teachers' workplace: The social organization of schools.* New York: Teachers College Press.

Schön, D. (1983). *The reflective practitioner: How professionals think in action.* New York: Basic Books.

Sekayi, D., Peterman, F., Stakich, K., Caputo, D., & Sawchik, C. (1999). *A patchwork quilt of change.* Columbus, OH: Ohio Department of Education.

Shuler, S. C. (1995). The impact of National Standards on the preparation, inservice professional development, and assessment of music teachers. *Arts Education Policy Review, 96*(3), 2–14.

Shuler, S. C. (1996). Assessing teacher competence in the arts: Should Mr. Holland have gotten the gig? *Arts Education Policy Review, 98*(1), 11–15.

Slavin, R., & Fashola, O. (1998). *Show me the evidence! Proven and promising programs for America's schools.* Baltimore, MD: Center for Research on the Education of Students Placed At Risk.

Smith, C. (1989). *Teacher as decision-maker.* Bloomington, IN: Grayson Bernard.

Smylie, M., & Perry, G. (1998). Restructuring schools for improving teaching. In A. Hargreaves, A. Lieberman, M. Fullan, & D. Hopkins (Eds.), *International handbook of educational change* (pp. 976–1005). Boston: Kluwer Academic Publishers.

Smylie, M., Bay, M., & Tozer, S. (1999). Preparing teachers as agents of change. In G. Griffith (Ed.), *The education of teachers (Ninety-eighth Yearbook of the National Society for the Study of Education, Part I, pp. 18–62).* Chicago: University of Chicago Press.

Smyth, J. (1997). Teaching and social policy: Images of teaching for democratic change. In B. Biddle, T. Good, & I. Goodson (Eds.), *International handbook of teachers and teaching: Volume II* (pp. 1081–1144). London: Kluwer Academic Publishers.

Soltis, J. (1994). The new teacher. In S. Hollingsworth & H. Sockett (Eds.), *Teacher research and educational reform (Ninety-third Yearbook of the National Society for the Study of Education, Part I* (pp. 245–260). Chicago: University of Chicago Press.

Stoll, L., & Fink, D. (1996). *Changing our schools.* Buckingham: Open University Press.

Stringfield, S. (1995). Attempting to enhance students learning through innovative programs: The case for schools evolving into high reliability organizations. *School Effectiveness and School Improvement, 6*(1), 67–96.

Stringfield, S. (2000). A synthesis and critique of four recent reviews of whole-school reform in the United States. *School Effectiveness and School Improvement, 11*(2), 259–269.

Teddle, C., & Reynolds, D. (2000). *The international handbook of school effectiveness research.* London: Falmer Press.

Thiessen, D. (1992). Canada. In P. Cookson Jr., A. Sadovnik, & S. Semel (Eds.), *International handbook of educational reform* (pp. 69–96). New York: Greenwood.

Thiessen, D. (1993). In the classroom, in the corridors and in the boardroom—The professional place of Canada's teachers in future policy making. *Journal of Education Policy, 8*(3), 283–304.

Thiessen, D. (1997). Transforming how teachers learn. *Orbit, 29*(2), 18–21.

Thiessen, D., & Anderson, A. (1999). *Getting into the habit of change in Ohio Schools: The cross-case study of 12 transforming learning communities.* Columbus, OH: Ohio Department of Education.

Thiessen, D., & Kilcher, A. (1992). *A review of recent literature on innovations in teacher education.* Toronto: Centre for Teacher Education.

Thiessen, D., & Pike, R. (1992). *Project 95+: Image of the future teacher.* Toronto: Teacher Education Council, Ontario.

Traub, J. (1999). *Better by design?: A consumer's guide to schoolwide reform.* Washington, DC: Thomas B. Fordham Foundation.

Tyack, D., & Cuban, L. (1995). *Tinkering toward Utopia: A century of public school reform.* Cambridge, MA: Harvard University Press.

Volk, T. M. (1998). *Music, education, and multiculturalism: Foundations and principles.* New York: Oxford University Press.

Wang, M., Haertel, G., & Walberg, H. (1997a). *What we know: Widely implemented school improvement programs.* Philadelphia: Laboratory for Student Success.

Wang, M., Haertel, G., & Walberg, H. (1997b). *Characteristics of twelve widely implemented educational reforms.* Philadelphia: Laboratory for Student Success.

Webster, P. R. (1998). The new music educator. *Arts Education Policy Review, 100*(2), 2–6.

Werner, W. (1982). *Evaluating program implementation.* Vancouver: Centre for the Study of Curriculum and Instruction, University of British Columbia.

Wideen, M., Mayer-Smith, J., & Moon, B. (1998). A critical analysis of the research on learning to teach: Making the case for an ecological perspective on inquiry. *Review of Educational Research, 68*(2), 130–178.

Wing, L. (1993). Music teacher education: Coming to our senses. *Bulletin of the Council for Research in Music Education, 117,* 51–65.

Zeichner, K., & Gore, J. (1990). Teacher socialization. In R. Houston, M. Haberman, & J. Sikula (Eds.), *Handbook of research in teacher education* (pp. 329–348). New York: Macmillan.

41

Teaching as a Profession

Two Variations on a Theme

RANDALL PEMBROOK

CHERYL CRAIG

This chapter centers on a topic around which a seeming overabundance of research has developed. Much of this literature is of a conventional bent: lists of attributes, characteristics, statistics, tables, and graphs describing who teachers are, how they are educated, how long they stay in the profession, the qualities that make teachers "professionals," and so on. This literature has evolved largely from an outsider perspective in which teachers have been examined as a group of professionals. More recently, a new approach has evolved that inquires into the personal, experiential, narratively constructed world of professional educators. In contrast to the first approach, research in this second vein is written from an insider perspective and situates teachers' identities and their knowledge in their professional contexts.

Two Variations

In this chapter, teaching as a profession, approached from these vastly different outlooks, will be presented as "two variations on a theme." Following a general introduction to the profession called teaching, Variation I focuses on an insider, personal, narrative, experiential account of teaching as a profession, while Variation II centers on an outsider account of teachers as a group of professionals. These very different accounts form the source of much of the dissonance and many of the incongruities that mark the field of education. A discussion of these tensions and discrepancies concludes this chapter.

What Is the Profession Called Teaching?

The question of what constitutes a profession and how a professional practice becomes lived lies at the heart of

teaching. In his work in the area of moral philosophy, MacIntyre (1984) framed the idea of a professional practice. Working from the belief that artists practice their arts, MacIntyre described a professional practice as follows:

> A practice involves standards of excellence and obedience to rules as well as the achievement of goods. To enter into a practice is to accept the authority of those standards and the inadequacy of [one's] own performance as judged by them. It is subject to [one's] own attitudes, choices, preferences and tastes which currently partially define the practice. Practices . . . have a history: games, sciences, and arts have histories. Thus, the standards are not themselves immune from criticism, but nonetheless [one] cannot be initiated into a practice without accepting the authority of the best standards realized so far. (p. 190)

MacIntyre's research, which connects the personal and the communal to the professional, sketches the complexity of what it means to be an educator. Schön's inquiries (1983, 1987, 1991) shed additional light on the matter.

Schön situates his longitudinal studies in his personal puzzles and wonders about the differences in the kinds of knowledge honored in academia and the kinds of competence valued in professional practices. He characterizes the struggle as being between the "high ground of theory" and the "swampy lowland" he calls practice. He names the dilemma as one of rigor versus relevance:

> In the varied topography of professional practice, there is a high hard place where practitioners can make effective use of research-based theory and technique, and there is swampy lowland where situations are confusing "messes" incapable of technical solution. The difficulty is that the

problems of the high ground, however great their technical interest, are often relatively unencumbered by clients of the larger society while in the swamp are the problems of the greatest human concern. Shall the practitioner stay on the high, hard ground where he can practice rigorously, as he understands rigor, where he is constrained to deal with problems of relatively little social importance? Or shall he descend to the swamp where he can engage in the important and challenge problems if he is willing to forsake technical rigor? (1983, p. 42)

Taken together, MacIntyre's and Schön's accounts provide a backdrop for studying teaching as a profession: MacIntyre, through sharing ideas relating to self and the sharing of ideals; Schön, through situating teaching and other professions in relation to theory and practice. How research by MacIntyre and Schön, along with the contributions of key figures like Schwab (1971) on a theory of "the eclectic," is interpreted in the field of education lays the backdrop for the two variations on the "teaching as a profession" theme offered in this work.

Variation I: Teaching as a Profession

To those who study teaching from an insider perspective, MacIntyre's and Schön's research leads to the formulation of similar questions: the question of what knowledge teachers as professionals hold and express in their practices and the question of how knowledge is developed and shared in community. These research interests are ones to which Connelly and Clandinin (2000) and others (i.e., Bach, 1997; Beattie, 1995; Conle, 1996; Craig, 1995a; Davies, 1995; DeCarion, 1998; Dickson, 1998; Elbaz, 1981; He, 1998; Huber, 1999; Olson, 1995; Phillion, 1999; Rose, 1997; Whelan, 1999) have devoted their inquiries. Connelly and Clandinin's human experience strand, according to Fenstermacher (1994), represents one of the three most respected approaches to research on the study of teaching approaches in the world. Tom Russell and Hugh Munby represent a second highly respected approach, while the research of Marilyn Cochran-Smith and Susan Lytle forms the third approach that Fenstermacher recognized. A fourth body of research, not considered in Fenstermacher's review, is Shulman's (1986a, 1986b) pedagogical content knowledge research. In the background sits the Carnegie Foundation's unfailing commitment to the professionalization of teaching through the development of a knowledge base for teaching.

Even though the terms employed by researchers who write in the human experience approach to teacher thinking are similar to those used in other works, the approach differs in fundamental ways from more conventional research on teacher professionalism. The emphasis on a particular understanding of teacher knowledge solidly anchors

the discussion of teaching as a profession in the notion of experience. Clandinin and Connelly (1998) explain:

> From our point of view what is missing is an understanding of knowledge, not so much as something given to people, but as something narratively embodied in how a person stands in the world. Knowledge as attribute can be given; knowledge as narrative cannot. The latter needs to be experienced in context. (p. 157)

Teaching: A Profession Grounded in Experience

John Dewey stressed the importance of "experience" to the educational enterprise and outlined its fundamental qualities. Dewey (1938) viewed experience as individually continuous and socially interactive. To him, "the two principles of continuity and interaction are not separate from one another. They intercept and unite. They are, so to speak, the longitudinal and lateral aspects of experience" (p. 43). In Dewey's view, educational experience not only unfolds on an individual continuum, but the shape of that continuum is "socially funded" by the continuity of experience of other persons and embedded in particular sociocultural, historical contexts shaped over time. Consequently,

> Experience is more than a simple given of life. It is not only an event; it is also an achievement. The qualities of the world are there for those who have the skills to take them. It is one of our culture's most significant tasks, one for which our schools have a special responsibility, to provide the tools and to develop the skills through which the child can create his or her own experience. (Eisner, 1988, p. 15)

Dewey's relentless emphasis on educational experience, together with his unshaken belief in teachers as minded professionals, form the building blocks for Clandinin and Connelly's conceptualization that teachers hold and express a special kind of knowledge, a knowledge that they term *personal practical knowledge*.

Teachers' Personal Practical Knowledge

"When we see practice," Clandinin and Connelly (1995) explain, "we see personal practical knowledge at work" (p. 7). To the authors, the term *personal practical knowledge* denotes the knowledge of individual teachers. It offers a way to understand teachers as knowers: of themselves, of their situations, of children, of subject matter, of teaching, of learning (Connelly & Clandinin, 1999). Where music teachers are concerned, the notion of appreciating music, knowing how to perform, and the ability to make sense of and judge the qualities of aesthetic experiences would naturally be included in the definition. Deweyan in origin,

[Personal practical knowledge] is a term designed to capture the idea of experience in a way that allows us to talk
about teachers as knowledgeable and knowing persons.
Personal practical knowledge is in the teacher's past experience, in the teacher's present mind and body, and in
future plans and actions. Personal practical knowledge is
found in the teacher's practice. It is, for any teacher, a particular way of constructing the past and the intentions of
the future to deal with the exigencies of a present situation.
(Connelly & Clandinin, 1988, p. 25)

Not only is personal practical knowledge a practically oriented term, it is, as suggested earlier, a narratively oriented
concept. As Clandinin (1992) makes apparent, "[It] is a
kind of knowledge, carved out of, and shaped by situations; knowledge that is constructed and reconstructed as
we live our stories and re-tell and re-live them through the
process of reflection" (p. 125).

Research to date has conceptualized the personal practical knowledge of preservice teachers and in-service educators in terms of images (i.e., Applebaum & Du, 1999;
Clandinin, 1986; Craig, 1992, 1999), metaphors (i.e.,
Craig, 2001; He, 1995; Samson, 1999; Whelan, 1999),
rules and principles (i.e., Elbaz, 1981), personal philosophy
(i.e., Kroma, 1983; Marland, 1995), rhythms and cycles
(i.e., Clandinin, 1986; Connelly & Clandinin, 1993; Stevenson, 1989), and culture (i.e., Craig, 2001; He, 1998;
Phillion, 1999). Further studies have inquired into the narrative authority of teachers (Olson, 1993, 1995) and the
notion of narrative resonance (Conle, 1996, 1999).

The narrative authority research extends the complexity
of personal practical knowledge into a "social, public, and
self-reflective realm" (Olson & Craig, 2001) and raises the
question of whose teacher stories get listened to and which
stories are given authoritative status. Olson (1995) explains,

Because the narrative version of knowledge construction is
transactional, authority comes from experience and is integral as each person both shapes his or her own knowledge and is shaped by the knowledge of others. Thus, narrative authority becomes the expression and enactment of
a person's personal practical knowledge that develops as
individuals learn to authorize meaning in relationship with
others. (p. 123)

She continues:

By both telling and living stories of practice, narrative authority involves both voice and action. However, because
teachers' and preservice teachers' lives are not lived in isolation, each person becomes simultaneously an author of
their own stories as well as an actor in stories authored by
others. Thus, the narrative authority of each educator is
both enhanced and constrained by the narrative authority
of others. (Olson & Craig, 2001, p. 670)

Here Olson makes visible the method through which
meaning becomes public and shared among professionals.
Here the "standards of excellence" introduced earlier by
MacIntyre arise from negotiations in community as opposed to statements written on paper.

The narrative resonance work (Conle, 1999) also takes
the research strand in a new direction. It provides a way
to bring theory and story together to better understand
practice. The research on narrative resonance helps to transcend the theory-practice split that Schön described as an
enduring dilemma of the professions. As Conle points out,
"It is possible to pull theory into an ongoing experiential
narrative and expand a story into another spiral of telling,
this time by incorporating theory as it is transformed by
experience" (p. 22). These and other offshoots of the personal practical knowledge research represent productive
research agendas in their own right.

Teachers' Professional Knowledge Landscapes

The personal practical knowledge focus allowed Clandinin
and Connelly to center on the life, work, and lived and
storied, relived and restoried, compositions of individual
teachers. Increasingly, however, questions concerning the
shaping effects of context on teachers' knowing appeared
and reappeared. Maintaining their interest in teacher
knowledge, Clandinin and Connelly (1995) turned their
attention to how knowledge becomes both formed and expressed as teachers engage in their daily work. They developed the professional knowledge landscape metaphor to
help situate a teacher's practice within a professional backdrop.

Situated at the intersection where teachers' personal
practical knowledge and professional knowledge meet, the
professional knowledge landscape metaphor bridges the
personal and the professional in a unique way. In Clandinin and Connelly's (1995) words,

A landscape metaphor is particularly well suited to our
purposes. It allows us to talk about space, place and time.
Furthermore, it has a sense of expansiveness and the possibility of being filled with diverse people, things, and
events in different relationships. Understanding professional knowledge as comprising a landscape calls for a notion of professional knowledge as composed of a wide variety of components and influenced by a wide variety of
people, places, and things. Because we see the professional
knowledge landscape as composed of relationships among
people, places, and things, we see it as both an intellectual
and moral landscape. (p. 5)

Conceptualizing the contexts of teaching as multiple scenes
on a professional landscape deeply roots teachers' personal
practical knowledge in context over time. Such studies pay
attention to a teacher's knowledge on its own terms, and

landscape situations in their own terms (Craig, 1998). What results are grainy accounts richly grounded in experience and the particularities of place. Where music teachers are concerned, these accounts would include practice scenes in the classroom as well as performance scenes in in-school and out-of-school places on the landscape.

Most teachers' experiences occur in in-classroom places (Clandinin & Connelly, 1995; Craig, 1995b; Huber & Whelan, 1995), places where teachers are in relationship with students. In Clandinin and Connelly's (1996) opinion,

Classrooms are, for the most part, safe places, generally free from scrutiny where teachers are free to live stories of practice. These lived stories are essentially secret ones. Furthermore, when these secret lived stories are told, they are, for the most part, told to other teachers in other secret places. (p. 25)

However, other parts of teachers' work take shape in out-of-classroom places (Clandinin & Connelly, 1995; Craig, 1995b), communal places where teachers meet all the other people and ideas connected to the educational enterprise. The out-of-classroom place is described as:

a place filled with knowledge funneled into the school system for the purpose of altering teachers' and children's classroom lives. Teachers talk about this knowledge all the time. We make reference to "what's coming down the pipe"; "what's coming down now"; "what will they throw down on us next." In these metaphorical expressions ... teachers express their knowledge of their out-of-classroom place as a place littered with imposed prescriptions. It is a place filled with other people's visions of what is right for children. Researchers, policy makers, senior administrators and others, using various implementation strategies, push research findings, policy statements, plans, improvement schemes and so on down ... the conduit into this out-of-classroom place on the professional knowledge landscape. (Clandinin & Connelly, 1996, p. 26)

These two different places on the landscape offer distinct vantage points from which to consider teachers' experiences in the educational enterprise and, in fact, comprise some of the differences between the two variations on the theme of teaching as a profession featured in this work. Tensions arising from these vastly different places create "dilemmas that gnaw at [teachers'] souls" (Craig, 1995c, p. 24). For music educators, these tensions may come in the form of packaged programs that discount teacher knowledge or an emphasis on performance, as opposed to music education, in reduced instructional time (Colwell, 2000). They also might appear as fund-raising dilemmas or tensions between students or even parents regarding who is selected to perform solo parts. These are only a few examples of the multitude of dilemmas that music teachers face daily on the professional knowledge landscape of schools.

Stories shape the contours of the educational landscape and form the horizons of their knowing. Sacred stories (Crites, 1971) are pervasive, communal stories that have a canonical, taken-for-granted quality to them. They are the stories that tend to be accepted unquestionably. The second type of stories, cover stories (Crites, 1979), are the stories that teachers tell in out-of-classroom places when their lived classroom experiences run contrary to the plot lines that have been authorized to be told. "Cover stories," explain Clandinin and Connelly (1996), "enable teachers whose teacher stories are marginalized by whatever the current story of school is to continue to practice and to sustain their teacher stories" (p. 25). Common cover stories told by music educators, for example, tend to "cover up" the disenfranchisement of their subject area within school programs and their marginalization as teachers of noncore areas of study.

An explanation of these two kinds of stories leads to a discussion of a related matrix of stories: teacher stories—stories of teachers—school stories—stories of school. Each of the stories in the matrix is narrated from a slightly different perspective; each casts a revealing light on a different set of particulars. As the narrative terms suggest, *teacher stories* are the stories that teachers tell, while *stories of teachers* are stories that are told about teachers. Following that line of thinking, *stories of school* are stories given to schools and *school stories* are the stories that people are expected to tell that fit with the school's plot line. As can be seen, each of the narratives in this thumbnail sketch is interconnected and brings different aspects of the professional knowledge landscape into view.

Craig added further narratives to the matrix to serve her research purposes: *stories of community* and *community stories, stories of parents* and *parent stories* (2000), and *stories of reform* and *reform stories* (in press). These narratives reveal further complexities marking the professional knowledge landscape of schools. They bring to the surface additional forces that shape teachers' personal practical knowing.

Two pieces form useful examples. The first work (Craig, 2000) is of special interest to music educators because it is written in the form of a two-part musical invention with codas that link the story of a teacher and a teacher's story with the story of the school and school stories. The second study adds stories of reform and reform stories to the matrix to create a story constellation (Craig, 2001), and features the personal practical knowledge of four teachers as opposed to one. In the latter work, the teachers turn to the British short story *The Monkey's Paw* (Jacobs, 1912) and other monkey metaphors to help them make sense of their experiences of a state-directed, national reform initiative. In both these examples, the moral, emotional, and aesthetic qualities, along with the intellectual dimensions, of teachers' personal practical knowledge come sharply into view.

Teachers' Knowledge Communities

The "knowledge communities" conceptualization is a "key idea" that captures how teachers develop their knowledge on the professional knowledge landscape (Soltis, 1995). To Soltis, they are "safe havens in which genuine community provides shelter for real dialogue and the sharing of stories, human stories of relation and reflection" (p. vii). Lodged in different places on and off school landscapes, "communities of knowing" are composed of:

> the individuals and groups of people with whom educators make sense of their practices. Whereas relationships in the conduit are imposed by the hierarchy of position and the hierarchy of knowledge, relationships in knowledge communities are naturally formed around "commonplaces of human experience" (Lane, 1988). Outside the influence of the conduit, knowledge communities are secure places where educators share their knowledge. (Craig, 1999, pp. 163–164)

Music educators, for example, would have individuals and groups of musicians, family members, and teachers who would form their knowledge communities. Among these might be a trusted instructor or a fellow student from the past.

The promise of knowledge communities is that they are places where "educators are vibrantly present, where their voices are unconditionally heard, where their relationships are authentic and secure" (Craig, 1995c, p. 140). In such places, the dialectic between the individual teacher and the community of educators is nurtured. Knowledge communities recognize and value the personal practical knowledge of teachers while connecting teachers to communal ways of knowing their profession.

Teacher Identity

As Connelly and Clandinin pursued questions of teacher knowledge in their professional knowledge landscape inquiries, they discovered that teachers responded to the questions they posed from what appeared to be more of an identity than a knowledge perspective. In short, the teachers gave the questions an unexpected, epistemological turn. This was how Connelly and Clandinin (1999) described what happened over time:

> We developed the notions of personal practical knowledge and professional knowledge landscape, both narrative educational concepts, as a way of understanding teacher knowledge. Teachers and others who work in schools resonated with this language. . . . By their responses we were

encouraged to continue framing our questions in terms of knowledge. However, we began to sense subtle differences. We noticed that teachers seemed to be trying to answer different questions. Their questions were ones of identity. They were questions of "Who am I in my story of teaching?" "Who am I in my place in the school?" "Who am I in children's stories?" "Who am I in parents' stories?" and so on. . . . In graduate student writing, in teacher inquiry groups, and in research meetings, teachers were more inclined to ask questions along the lines of "Who am I in this situation?" than "What do I know in this situation?" Teachers seemed more concerned to ask questions of who they are than of what they know. (1999, p. 3)

Interestingly, as ideas concerning knowledge, context, and identity came together in the research studies, the embodied nature of knowing (Johnson, 1987, 1991)—as opposed to the idea of knowledge as an attribute outside persons—became increasingly prominent. In the field of music, for example, it is evident that teachers, when left to their own devices, are more inclined to ask questions concerning their complex identities as educators and musicians as opposed to listing the considerable knowledge they have come to know (Mark, 1998).

Connelly and Clandinin introduced the phrase, *stories to live by,* to help make critical connections between and among phenomena relating to knowledge, context, and identity. The narrative term helped to uncover important differences between the stories that teachers and administrators live by. While teacher stories were found to be rich in identity, principal stories were distinguished by how they were positioned in relation to the conduit and its hierarchy of power and position. This led Clandinin and Connelly (1999) to wonder how social reconstruction and inquiry might be reimagined so that educators could look to one another "for sources of ideas, sources of authority, and sources of action" as opposed to looking up and down the conventional hierarchy in ways that constrain how all lives are lived on the professional knowledge landscape of schools (p. 175).

Generative Professional Development and the Development of Teaching Practices

Most recently, Olson and Craig (2001) have paid special attention to how conventional approaches to teacher professional development might shed the "teacher training" metaphor that dominates educational history and current practices, a topic that Collay and Leglar also touch on in chapter 44 and that Hookey takes up more extensively in chapter 46. Working from the notion that teachers filter all their experiences, including their professional development experiences, through their personal practical knowledge, Olson and Craig make the case that their ideas relating to narrative authority and knowledge community development are integral to understanding how generative approaches to professional development might be practiced. Through featuring longitudinal research with a preservice teacher and an in-service teacher, Olson and Craig illustrate how teachers articulate their narrative authority in knowledge communities and show why knowledge communities are critical to sustained development of narrative authority. They argue that attending to these critical matters creates opportunities to engage teachers and prospective teachers in generative professional development experiences. When these important considerations are not taken into account, teachers may disregard the substance of professional development offerings and focus instead on the extent to which the professional development experiences lacked meaning and relevance to their own and their students' ways of being (Craig, 2001). Given the dismal record of how unproductive and futile this approach can be, Olson and Craig call for "a critical shift in the theory-practice relationship to one of creating spaces for the sharing of narrative authority in knowledge communities. . . . Without this fundamental repositioning," they maintain, "the confirmation of, refinement in, or transformation of, teachers' or prospective teachers' practices will be greatly diminished."

In Variation I of "teaching as profession," teaching has been discussed from the personal, experiential, narrative perspective of a well-established research strand on the study of teaching. Following a general discussion of teaching as a profession and key observations concerning teacher professionalism, a summary of the early personal practical knowledge work was offered. Variation I then featured a discussion of the professional knowledge landscape research, and considered a number of promising related studies concerning narrative authority, narrative resonance, and teachers' knowledge communities. The relationship of teacher knowledge to teacher identity, as well as an insightful discussion concerning how productive teacher professional development might be lived, were further topics that were considered. Metaphors and conceptual underpinnings were additionally introduced that situate and illuminate how music teachers' lives are lived on the professional knowledge landscape of schools. The centrality of experience, so vital to professional practice in general and to music education in particular, was threaded throughout.

In the remainder of this chapter, attention will turn to Variation II and the shifting nature of teachers' professional knowledge landscapes, the facts and figures that describe its composition and conditions that have developed over time. As Variation II unfolds, readers are asked, in the spirit of Variation I, to consider the idea of "anticipated [teaching] lives" in relation to lives that are actually lived (Connelly & Clandinin, 1999, p. 116). Attempting to blend the Variation I, personal, experiential approach with the Variation II, conventional, "teachers as a group" approach will awaken readers to the enormous social, economic, and educational entailments and changes that shape teachers' contextual experiences, influence what they come to know, and form the horizons of who they can be and become on the professional knowledge landscapes of schools.

Variation II: Teaching as a Profession

As with Variation I, Variation II also finds its roots in MacIntyre's discussion of a professional practice and Schön's theory-practice discussion. To a large extent, Variation II centers on the history of educational practice described by MacIntyre and the high ground of quantifiable theory to which Schön referred.

The Composition and Conditions of the Professional Knowledge Landscape of Schools: An In-depth Look

In the early 1970s, a *Phi Delta Kappan* survey indicated that the public worried about the teaching force, listing it as one of their primary concerns when considering the quality of schools (Gallup, 1970). Today, the public appears to have more confidence in educators, as teacher quality no longer appears near the top of that list (Rose & Gallup, 2000). In spite of the fact that today's teachers have a great deal more training in subject matter and teaching techniques compared to the general public, 60% of Americans think that they (parents/guardians) are the primary determinant as to whether their children learn.

Individuals choose to enter the teaching profession for a variety of reasons. Most (68%) have a strong desire to work with young people. Between one quarter and one half value education in society (42%), love their discipline (37%), or had a teacher function as a positive role model (31%). Fewer appear to make their choice based on extrinsic perquisites such as summer vacations (20%) or job security (18%) (National Education Association [NEA], 1997). In a similar fashion, music educators choose to enter the teaching profession because of intrinsic motivations. "Music teachers . . . overwhelmingly believe that their work is significant" (Hoffer, 1982, p. 59). However, during the 1980s, nearly half (46%) of the music teachers surveyed said that if they had it to do again, they would *not* choose teaching as a profession or were not planning on staying in teaching their entire working career (Hoffer, 1982; Phelps, 1983). Since that time, the level of job satisfaction that teachers experience appears to have risen. Data from the 1980s and 90s (National Center for Educational Statistics [NCES], 1991, 1992, 1993, 1997, 2000) indicate that the percentage of teachers who said that they *certainly* would be willing to become teachers again if they had that choice to make rose from about 33% to 40% for the years described and an additional 26% said they *probably* would go into the profession again.

Demographics

The P–12 teaching profession witnessed tremendous growth in the last half of the 20th century as a result of the baby boom in the 1950s and 1960s and the second generation "echo" (baby boomers' children going to school) in the 1980s and 1990s. Data indicate that the number of P–12 teachers in the United States grew from slightly under 1 million in 1950 to slightly over 3 million presently (NCES, 1997; Schlechty & Vance, 1983). By 2008, NCES projects a teaching force of nearly 3.5 million. The decade of the 1950s witnessed a 48% growth in the teaching force and the 1960s saw even greater expansion of the work force (52%). Although the rate of growth slowed in the 1970s, the echo effect caused another expansion cycle with 41% growth in the teaching profession between 1979 and 1996.

Economic and industrial changes and the resulting demographic shifts have had a major impact on the educational landscape and may continue to do so. Recent data projections from the NCES website (http://www.ncei.com) indicate that, between the years 1996 and 2006, total P–12 public and private enrollments will increase from 51.4 million to 54.5 million. The largest growth percentages are expected to be for schools in the West (16%) and South (7%) with the Northeast remaining stable and the Midwest dropping slightly. States expecting the biggest P–12 enrollment increases include California (20%), Hawaii (18%), and New Mexico (16%). Between 1996 and 2008, the number of high school graduates is projected to grow by 20% nationally, with Nevada (97%), Florida (45%), and Hawaii (34%) showing the largest increases. This growth will result in the need for more high school teachers with the number projected to reach 2.08 million (+19%) in 2008. If these figures are correct, over half the P–12 teaching force soon will be at the high school level, compared to slightly over one quarter (28%) at the present time according to NEA data. Presently, 48% of teachers practice at the elementary level, while 23% teach junior high or middle school students (NEA, 1997).

In looking at the ethnic distribution for those recently entering the P–12 teaching profession (3 years of experience or less) and comparing it to the teachers with 20 or more years experience, the percentage of black teachers has decreased by 2 points, while the percentage of Hispanic teachers increased nearly 4 points (NCES, 1997; NEA, 1997). "As student populations become more diverse, the teacher population is becoming less so" (Futrell, 1999, p. 30). At various points in the 1990s, the teaching work force was somewhere between 88–90% white, 6–9% black, 3–4% Hispanic, and 1% Asian, while the student body consisted of 16% blacks and 12% Hispanics (NCES, 1997; NEA, 1996; Statistical Abstract of the U.S. [SAUS], 1999).

Although one quarter to one third of the population of teachers is over 50 years old (Futrell, 1999; NCES, 1997), the overall population of the traditional teaching force is not aging very quickly (the grand mean increased from 40 to 43 years of age between the late 1980s and the mid-1990s). However, a trend of individuals entering the teaching profession later in life creates the possibility of a dramatically heightened mean in future years (Basinger, 1999; Cornett, 1990). Baker and Smith (1997) suggest that retirement of present teachers will be an important factor affecting the demand for teachers during the next 20 years.

As one might expect, almost all P–12 public school teachers (99%) have at least a bachelor's degree (NCES, 1997). Also, more than half (55%) of all P–12 public school teachers have a master's degree or 6-year diploma with 2% possessing doctorates, a dramatic increase from 1961 when only 23% held advanced degrees (NEA, 1997). As a result of these educational experiences, teachers consider themselves well prepared to teach (Darling-Hammond, 2001; Gray et al., 1993; Howey & Zimpher, 1993; Kentucky Institute for Education Research, 1997).

Differing datasets appear very similar in describing the average work week of a P–12 educator (NCES, 1997; NEA, 1997). They indicate a cumulative total of 45–49 hours on average with 33–36 hours at school, 9–11 hours outside (e.g., homework and lesson preparation), and 3–6 hours outside school with student interactions (e.g., coaching, field trips, etc.). Respondents for the NCES data pool indicated that they typically worked 45 weeks per year.

Many researchers have investigated the concept of P–12 teacher longevity. Before exploring this, however, it is worth noting that 7 of 10 education majors never enter the teaching workforce (Kirkpatrick, 1992; Marso & Pigge, 1997). Consequently, 70% of the *potential* workforce has no longevity whatsoever. According to NEA and NCES data, the percentage of educators staying 20 years or longer in the profession is somewhere between 35% and 46% of those who begin a career in P–12 education. They suggest that the profession is relatively stable each year, with 86% of its members retaining the same position in the ensuing fall term, 7% moving to another P–12 teaching assignment, and only 7% leaving teaching to retire, seek other employment, or deal with family responsibilities (Baker & Smith, 1997). These figures closely parallel those reported by the National Association of State Directors of Special Education (1990). Other studies suggest that a percentage of the 7% who leave will return to teach at a later time in their lives (NCES, 1997). The NEA (1997) reports that the overall average experience level for full-time teachers is 16 years with slightly under one fifth of the teaching profession (17%) possessing 5 years or less of experience.

In contrast to the current picture of stability outlined by NCES, NEA, and others, nearly 2 decades ago Schlechty and Vance (1983) provided a much more alarming picture of longevity in the profession. They reported that between 40–50% of teachers stayed 7 years or less. Of that group of leavers, 66–75% left within 4 years and 15% left after only 1 year. Some of those data were verified by others (e.g., Villeme & Hall, 1983–1984). More recent research indicates that, for teachers who do choose to leave, there are several reasons including unsupportive environments (Rosenholtz, 1989), insufficient certification/preparation (Miller, Brownell, & Smith, 1999), high stress (Billingsley & Cross, 1992), lack of administrator or parental support (Billingsley & Cross, 1992; NCES, 1997), lack of resources (Billingsley & Cross, 1992; NCES, 1997), and lack of respect for teachers (NCES, 1997).

There appears to be a difference in longevity between those teaching at P–12 public and private schools. Public school teachers are more experienced, with 35% having 20 or more years teaching experience compared with 22% at private schools (NCES, 1997). However, only one third to one half of these public school teachers plan to continue teaching until retirement (Moracco, D'Arienzo, & Danford, 1983; NCES, 1997). In contrast, over one half of the private school teachers reported they were planning on teaching until retirement age (NCES, 1997). This may be explained by the fact that teachers at private schools experience more of the crucial positive elements of teaching such as administrative support, faculty cooperation, parental support, student respect for teachers, and rule enforcement (NCES, 1997). Interestingly, those leaving the profession appear to be younger (Grissmer & Kirby, 1987; NCES, 1991), more likely to be in 4-year than 5-year training programs (Andrew & Schwab, 1995; Baker, 1993; Denton & Peters, 1988; National Commission on Teaching and America's Future, 1996; Shin, 1994), Caucasian (Singer, 1993), and of higher intelligence (Pavalko, 1970) as measured by the Scholastic Achievement Test (SAT).

The P–12 workforce is largely populated by women, who occupy almost three quarters of the P–12 teaching positions in this country including 83% at the elementary level and 51% at the secondary level (NCES, 1997; NEA, 1997; SAUS, 1999). Apple (1987) and Darling-Hammond (2001) suggest that, because the teaching profession historically has consisted of females, salaries have been adversely affected. Teacher salaries became less competitive compared to other professions in the late 1970s and early 1980s that, along with the anticipation of rising school enrollments as a function of the baby boom echo, led to predictions of severe teacher shortages for the late 1980s

and early 1990s (NCES, 1997). Thereafter, the idea of alternative certification began to receive strong support. Fortunately, the salary trend of the late 1970s has reversed. "In constant 1995 dollars, the average public school teacher's annual salary has recovered from the decline of the 1970's" (NCES, 1997, p. vi).

The data appear to support that claim. In 1997, reports indicated that teachers averaged $35,549 with over half earning additional income of $3,636, thus totaling an annual figure of around $40,000. Although this total is above the national average by between $4,000 and $5,000, it is below the salaries of other professions requiring similar educational backgrounds (NEA, 1997). Slightly newer data from the American Federation of Teachers (2000) listed the 1998 salary for a public school teacher as $39,347 with the beginning teacher averaging $25,735. Indexed to 1999 dollars, this figure is almost $2,000 higher than the average for government workers but falls considerably below figures for attorneys ($71,500), engineers ($64,489), and accountants ($45,919). Beginning salaries also lagged behind other professions such as engineering ($42,682), computer science ($40,920), and business administration ($34,831). In general, public school teachers' salaries are between one-fourth and one-fifth of those of physicians, about one-third of lawyers, and about half of private sector managers and educational administrators (NCES, 1997). Compared to private school teachers, however, public school educators earn between 40–50% more.

Interestingly, most teachers initially do not seek a career in education because of salary (Perie & Baker, 1997). Teachers "do not choose to teach with the goal of earning a high income, rather, they are attracted to the profession because they like working with children, they want to help improve the lives of young people or contribute to the community or they want to work in a given subject area" (NCES, 1997, p. 85). Perhaps surprisingly, nearly half reported that they were satisfied or somewhat satisfied (13% satisfied, 32% somewhat satisfied) with their salaries with the remainder expressing dissatisfaction at some level (25% somewhat dissatisfied, 31% strongly dissatisfied) (NCES, 1997). These figures representing teacher salary perceptions are slightly better than they were in the 1980s. It is also worth noting that, of those who prepared to teach but did not, only 3% said they chose not to because of low pay (NCES, 1997).

In spite of these positive data, some have recognized problems associated with teachers' salaries. Teacher salaries are front-loaded especially for those entering with a master's degree. Teachers reach the maximum pay scale within the first half of their careers. After that, "teachers have relatively little incentive to remain in the profession over the long term when they can earn higher incomes in other occupations" (NCES, 1997, p. 2). NCES suggests that if teachers want serious salary increases they must leave teaching. In spite of this front-loading, salary levels still do not appear to be an overriding issue regarding longevity in the profession. "Although some have suggested that teachers leave teaching for better pay or other career opportunities, this belief is not strongly supported by . . . data" (NCES, 1997, p. 108). Only 7% of leavers reported abandoning the teaching profession to obtain better pay or benefits. In relation to improving the teaching force by raising salaries, some suggest that salary increases would tend to increase the longevity of present teachers rather than attracting new applicants (Ballon & Podgursky, 1995).

Using the general education figures as a backdrop, the profession of P–12 music teaching can be compared and contrasted. According to the Market Data Retrieval database used by the Music Educators National Conference (MENC), there are 119,064 P–12 music teachers, with 62,453 identifying their job as primarily elementary (52%), 24,350 self-identifying as middle school or junior high teachers (20%), 24,975 as high school educators (21%), 6,635 stating that they serve in multilevel positions (6%), and 651 (1%) serving in special or vocational education (MENC, 2000). These figures are very close to the overall distributions for P–12 teachers in general with a slightly larger percentage of the music education workforce occurring at the elementary level and slightly smaller percentage at high schools. Between 1998 and 2000, the number of jobs was remarkably stable with a change of only 0.3%. There were 32,520 choral directors (27% of the population), 31,589 general music teachers (27%), 31,247 band directors (26%), and 7,070 orchestra directors (6%). The remainder used generic or more encompassing titles such as music teacher or instrumental music teacher. This database indicated that 15,704 of the teachers were teaching in a new position in 1999–2000, which is approximately double the number of position changes one might expect based on NCES (1997) data regarding movement within the teaching profession.

Overall, the music education workforce consists of 60% females and 40% males. At the elementary level, the percentage of females is even higher (73%), although this figure drops to 53% at the middle school/junior high level and to 37% at the high school level. Only 19% of high school band directors are female compared to 54% of high school choir directors.

More demographics specific to secondary music education teachers were recently compiled by MENC (National Survey of Music Educators in Public Secondary Schools: Summary Report, August, 2000). Figures for this group closely parallel overall general education data. For example, 98% of the music teachers held bachelor's degrees, 55% held master's degrees and 2% held doctorates. That over half of the secondary music educators and four fifths of orchestra directors held a master's degree (Gillespie & Hamann, 1998) may be important in light of Bea-

ver's (1972/1973) results suggesting master's graduates are more successful.

The overwhelming majority of secondary music teachers are white (94%) with blacks representing 3% of the teaching force and Hispanics around 1%. Some consolation regarding diversity in the workplace may be taken, however, from the fact that even though the percentages are small, those individuals who are currently receiving doctorates in music education at universities and will serve as models for the next generation of college music education majors are slightly more diversified with blacks constituting 8% of the population, Asians 7%, and Hispanics 3%. Percentages have increased slightly during the past decade (National Association of Schools of Music, 1990, 1995, 1999). However, these data along with information from others indicate that, like other disciplines in education, music teachers are still overwhelmingly white (Gillespie & Hamann, 1998, 1999; MENC, 2000).

Over half (52%) of secondary music teachers have taught more than 16 years with only about one quarter (23%) reporting less than 5 years of teaching experience. With regard to age, 31% of secondary music educators are below 35 years of age, one quarter (26.7%) are between 36 and 45, one third (33.9%) are between 46 and 55, and the remainder over 55. Similar to the general education data, almost half of the music teachers (44%) were planning on leaving teaching within 10 years, even though only 7% of respondents were within 10 years of retirement age. MENC figures regarding those wishing to leave the profession approximate the data of Gillespie and Hamman (1998). Unfortunately, it appears that the attrition rate for arts educators is higher than for the teaching profession in general (Hamann & Gordon, 2000). Crucial factors causing people to leave the music education profession include: isolation from experienced faculty members, unmotivated students, lack of assistance in developing teaching skills, the misconception that they would be fully prepared to teach as a result of college methods classes, unrealistic teaching assignments, and vague rules (DeLorenzo, 1992).

According to the MENC secondary survey, in contrast to the general education figures, secondary music is largely populated with male teachers (61%). However, exceptions to this may be found at other levels or teaching areas. For example, more women than men are teaching orchestra classes in the schools (Gillespie & Hamann, 1998). Unlike many general education positions, music teachers are itinerant with slightly more than half of the high school educators teaching at least one middle school class and a third of the population also teaching in elementary settings (MENC, 2000). These figures are considerably higher than the data from the Market Data Retrieval set, where only 6% labeled their position as "combined."

The concept of the emerging/prospective music education workforce and how its numbers compare to slightly

Table 41.1. Students in Music Education (ME) and Music Programs in the 1990s

	1990	1995	1999
Institutions with ME programs	433	432	435
ME majors (Fall semester)	22,488	25,461 (+13%)[a]	28,907 (+14%)
ME degrees awarded (July–June)	2,903	2,995 (+3%)	3,567 (+19%)
Total music major enrollment	78,340	82,074 (+5%)	93,419 (+14%)
Total number of music degrees awarded	12,356	12,827 (+4%)	14,985 (+17%)

[a]Parenthetical figures represent the percentage increase from the previous year indicated.

Source: NASM HEADS data reports 1990, 1995, and 1999.

older figures can be found in table 41.1. In examining the table, which indicates the number of music education students at National Association of Schools of Music (NASM) institutions at 3 points during the last decade, it is interesting to note that, between 1990 and 1995, the rate of growth in music education programs surpassed the growth of music enrollments overall. However, since 1995, the growth rate in music education has remained even with overall figures. Growth in the number of music education majors in the 1990s contrasts with a general education trend occurring from 1971 to the mid-1990s, where the percentage of university education majors dropped from 21% to 9% (Futrell, 1998). It is also worth noting that while the number of music education degrees awarded increased 3% between 1990 and 1995, the most recent NASM figures show a dramatic increase in degrees conferred.

Personalities

Because selected characteristics, behaviors, and skills (e.g., communication patterns and organizational models) of effective teachers are addressed in other chapters within this Handbook, the present section is limited primarily to a discussion of the personality traits of effective teachers. Additional reading by authors including Odden (1983), Beach and Reinhartz (1984), Fant, Hill, Lee, and Landes (1985), Hosler and Schmid (1985), Brophy and Good (1986), Westerman (1989), and Lowman (1996) in general education and Doane (1981), Farmilo (1981), Todd and Roberts (1981), Baker (1982), Kvet and Watkins (1993), and Hamann (1995) in music education are recommended pertaining to general characteristics of good teachers.

However, because one particular characteristic, teacher intelligence, has become such a dominant factor in teacher

recruiting, admission decisions, and even retention, a brief discussion of it here appears warranted. During the period from 1975 to 1979, freshmen who were planning to major in education ranked 17th out of 19 groups of college majors in math skills and 14th in English skills (Schlechty & Vance, 1983). This situation created a concern that the teaching profession was not attracting the "best and the brightest" to educate and inspire the next generation of Americans, which, in turn, led to a wave of educational reform by groups such as the National Council for the Accreditation of Teacher Education (NCATE). One fairly uniform standard they advocated was the establishing of a 2.5 minimum grade point average (GPA) for entrance into education programs. During the 1990s, GPAs of teacher education graduates rose to a point where they were higher than the overall university average, with a median of 3.25 (Gray et al., 1993; NCES, 1997).

The personalities of successful educators have fascinated researchers over an extended period of time in the 20th century. Thirty years ago, Wink (1970) said that "[e]vidence is accumulating to support the belief that personality is an important function in a teacher's achievement" (p. 234). Since then, many have argued that personality is the *most* important factor in determining teacher success (Mamchur & Nelson, 1984; Schechtman, 1989; Young, 1990). Hamann, Lineburgh, and Paul (1998) found that emotional expressivity (nonverbal sending), emotional sensitivity (receiving and decoding nonverbal messages), and social control (directing communication) explained 25% of the variance in teaching effectiveness evaluations for music teachers in training. As interest in teacher personality grew, Riggio and Zimmerman (Riggio, 1986) developed a Social Skills Inventory, which they claimed gave some indication of a teacher's future success.

Authors such as Wubbenhorst (1991) and DeNovellis and Lawrence (1983) have underscored the importance of a teacher's personality, because it is indelibly linked with the manner in which the individual behaves in the classroom. Krueger (1976) suggests assertiveness training as a recommended activity for success. He also states that personality variables are "related to music teaching success in fairly powerful ways" (p. 24).

Many have suggested that there is a weak link between personality variables and success (Davidson, Moore, Sloboda, & Howe, 1998; Goodstein, 1987; Mann, 1980; Wubbenhorst, 1994). However, several studies indicate that educators are more effective when they possess or reflect the personality traits appearing in table 41.2. Traits listed in this table can be manifested in isolation (e.g., neat, responsible, self-controlled) or during interactions with students (e.g., encouraging, friendly, interested in students), especially in group management situations (e.g., authoritative, flexible, persistent). Kemp (1982) and Schmidt (1989) suggest that a teacher must be extroverted to succeed to the fullest, and, perhaps not surprisingly, Gordon and Yocke (1999) found that a majority of teachers were. However, Kemp points out the seeming contradiction that music teachers precede their professional teaching lives, which emphasize interaction and extroversion, with many years of prolonged practice in isolation. Another interesting observation can be found in the work of Lutz (1964), who noted that successful teachers are happy. Whether this was a preexisting personality trait or evidence that the individuals had selected the appropriate profession and were experiencing satisfaction because of it was not fully explored.

The presence of certain personality traits may be more important at certain times and in selected settings than others. For example, traits such as leadership and self-control initially are thought to be much more important in achieving success than music skills such as piano and singing ability (Teachout, 1997). However, for more advanced students, the teacher's performance skills displace personality variables as students progress in their own skill level (Davidson, et al., 1998). This evolution may partly explain why music education undergraduates, certainly sophisticated performers themselves, tend to focus on performance skills and think of themselves more as performers than teachers during the early years of their collegiate training (Wolfgang, 1990). On a slightly different tangent, Davidson, et al. (1998) suggest that the perceived personality of a teacher may depend on the level of the student. While a successful student may view an action as encouraging (e.g., suggesting that a student should take a solo to contest), that same action may be viewed as pushy by a less confident student.

Farmilo (1980) reports that there is no relationship between a teacher's creativity and effectiveness but that there is a strong correlation between a teaching style and the teacher's effectiveness *ratings*. Perhaps that is why studies have indicated that personality traits are somewhat similar between good and bad music teachers (Davidson et al., 1998; Goodstein, 1987) as well as teachers and performers (Wubbenhorst, 1994). It would appear that, if individuals can adopt the behaviors associated with positive teaching, they may be successful even if those behaviors or traits are not "natural."

The previous list in table 41.2 is quite positive. However, Slack (1977) documented some negative personality traits common to music teachers including high anxiety, hysteria, and paranoia. According to the author, these often are caused by the extremely high standards music teachers set for themselves. Slack and other authors cited in table 41.2 also list traits in seeming opposition (e.g., restrained and gregarious, or sober vs. humorous). This may imply the need for teachers to exhibit different temperaments in different situations.

Table 41.2. Personality Attributes in Successful Teachers

Trait	Author
Internal qualities	
Broad interests	Lutz (1963)
Confident/Secure/Strong ego strength/Tough minded	Lutz (1963)
	Farmilo (1981)
	Bullock (1974)
	Kemp (1982)
Conscientious/Responsible	Slack (1977)
	Ervin (1949)
Creative/Imaginative	Bullock (1974)
	Slack (1977)
Emotionally stable/Not neurotic	Lutz (1963)
	Slack (1977)
Energetic/Enthusiastic/Enthusiastic toward music	Brand (1985)
	Baker (1982)
	Coats & Smidchens (1966)
	Ervin (1949)
Happy/Optimistic	Lutz (1963)
	Maxwell (1970)
Independent/Self-sufficient	Slack (1977)
	Bullock (1974)
Neat	Ervin (1949)
Not compulsive	Lutz (1963)
Restrained/Reserved	Bullock (1974)
	Slack (1977)
Self-control/Self-disciplined	Teachout (1997)
	Slack (1977)
Relating to Others	
Caring/Empathetic	Brand (1985)
	Ervin (1949)
	Goleman (1995)
Chatty	Davidson et al. (1998)
Emotional sensitivity (i.e., decoding student non-verbal signals)	Hamann et al. (1998)
Encouraging	Davidson et al. (1998)
Extroverted	Kemp (1982)
	Schmidt (1989)
Friendly/Gregarious/People-oriented	Davidson et al. (1998)
	Lutz (1963)
Gentle	Slack (1977)
Humble	Bullock (1974)
Humorous/Sense of humor	Ervin (1949)
	Baker (1982)
Interested in students	Baker (1992)
Relaxed	Davidson et al. (1998)
Sober	Bullock (1974)
Trusting	Slack (1977)
Social control/Group management	
Authoritative	Maxwell (1970)
Cooperative	Slack (1977)
Dramatic	Ervin (1949)
Expressive (i.e., capable of non-verbal sending)	Hamann et al. (1998)
Fair (as per discipline)	Baker (1992)
Flexible	Kurtz & Kremer (1982)
	Lutz (1963)

Trait	Author
Exhibiting leadership/Proactive	Teachout (1997)
	Goodstein (1987)
	Kvet & Watkins (1993)
Patient	Ervin (1949)
Persistent	Bullock (1974)
Realistic	Kemp (1982)
	Bullock (1974)
Strong (as per discipline)	Baker (1982)

Job Satisfaction

It would appear that many teachers are happy or some-what happy to be in the profession but the level of happiness is not consistent throughout various levels and disciplines. Elementary teachers are more satisfied than secondary instructors with their jobs, females more so than their male colleagues, and teachers at large schools more than those at smaller institutions (Ma & MacMillan, 1999; NCES, 1997; Parker, 1993; Pembrook & Fredrickson, in press; Qualls, 1987). Private school teachers appear more satisfied than those in public school settings and teachers, in general, are more satisfied than individuals in other professions such as industrial work (NCES, 1997; Qualls, 1987). The level of anxiety experienced by individual teachers may explain much of the variance in their satisfaction levels (Parker, 1993).

Teachers, in general, seem to experience job satisfaction as a result of support from principals (NCES, 1997; Perie & Baker, 1997) and music educators take particular pleasure in student success, student valuing of music, and parental support (Heston, Dedrick, Raschke, & Whitehead, 1996; MENC, 2000). Perhaps one of the reasons private school teachers plan on staying in the teaching profession longer is because almost three times as many feel that parents they encounter are supportive (NCES, 1997). Parker (1993) found that the level of agreement between teachers and school administrators regarding roles and workload significantly predicted teachers' job satisfaction. Collaboration/positive interactions with co-workers were reported as an important element for satisfaction by DeLorenzo (1992), Ponce (1995), and Pembrook and Fredrickson (in press), particularly for those with less than 15 years of experience. However, DeLorenzo (1992) and Ponce (1995) reported that this valuing of collaboration was less pronounced in individuals teaching for longer periods of time who took more satisfaction from pay raises. These authors also reported that working with ensembles was a major source of satisfaction for music teachers.

Job Dissatisfaction

Although many aspects of teaching appeal to those in the profession, there are also a considerable number of factors that contribute to teachers' dissatisfaction in the workplace. These include:

1. Inappropriate student behavior and attitudes (Heston et al., 1996).
2. Taxing teaching loads and the ensuing physical exhaustion (Bramhall & Ezell, 1981; DeLorenzo, 1992; Hamann & Daugherty, 1984; Hamann, Daugherty, & Mills, 1987; Hamann, Daugherty, & Sherbon, 1988; Heston et al., 1996; Hodge, Jupp, & Taylor, 1994; Stubblefield, 1984).
3. Stress/anxiety (Holt, Fine, & Tollefson, 1987; Slack, 1977).
4. Unclear goals (Hamann et al., 1987).
5. Paperwork such as developing budgets and equipment requests (Ponce, 1995).
6. Low salaries (Schlechty & Vance, 1983).
7. Lack of recognition (Hamann et al., 1987).
8. Common aspects of the teaching environment such as interruptions, high standards, out-of-date material, poor resources, poor discipline, and vague rules (DeLorenzo, 1992; Friedman, 1991; Hamann et al. 1987; Hodge et al., 1994; Ponce, 1995; Qualls, 1987; Sandene, 1995).
9. Lack of variety in the teaching situation (Schlechty & Vance, 1983).

Of these factors, one that seems to be particularly dangerous is stress. "Teacher work stress has intensified over the past 30 years" (Hodge et al., 1994, p. 66). Results from research by Holt et al. (1987) indicated that 67% of teachers described their work environment as always or usually stressful. The authors attribute this to teachers' feelings of increased responsibility for students' academic, social, and moral lives. Unfortunately for music educators, music teachers are one of the most stressed groups (Hodge et al., 1994; Malik, 1970). Stubblefield (1984) reported no difference in stress for music educators of various grade levels but did report that there was a difference in perceived stress levels of men and women.

According to Wilder and Plutchik (1982), music teachers are particularly susceptible to burnout. Although many aspects contributing to teacher dissatisfaction are common across the teaching profession regardless of subject matter, several have been identified as particularly burdensome for music educators. These include time requirements, student apathy, lack of student motivation, inadequate salary, class scheduling, class size, lack of pedagogical knowledge and planning, program budgets, extended hours, and lack of administrative support (Gordon, 1997; Haack & Smith,

2000; Hodge et al., 1994). The MENC survey of secondary music teachers indicated that music teachers typically deal with class sizes of 40 or more students (compared to a general national average of 17 as reported by Grissmer and Kirby [1997]). This discrepancy, in turn, complicates the task of maintaining discipline. Pembrook and Fredrickson (in press) found that teachers were significantly less satisfied with a day's events when the worst aspect of that day was perceived to be poor student behavior. To complicate things further, with an average music educator staff size of two per district (MENC, 2000 survey), music teachers appear frustrated about where they can turn for advice on handling these discipline problems (DeLorenzo, 1992; Hodge et al., 1994). Additionally, the MENC secondary survey indicated that between 26 and 44% of music teachers (depending on school type and location) reported inadequate resources to do the job. It is no wonder then, that practically no music teachers perceive their discipline as the easiest to teach while over half consider it the most difficult (Hodge et al., 1994). Haack and Smith (2000) agree, calling music education "the most challenging job in the teaching profession" (p. 24), especially for new music teachers.

"Teacher trainers report that burnout is often the highest-rated subject on needs-assessment measures designed to identify major teacher concerns" (Farber, 1991, p. 4). Bramhall and Ezell (1981) and Hall, Villeme, and Phillippy (1988) suggest that burnout is emotional overstimulation, not fatigue or boredom or depression. It is a loss of idealism, energy, purpose, and concern. Burnout frequently results in a teacher losing sympathy for students and developing negative attitudes toward work. Burnout can be caused by constant nonresolution, lack of closure, or overcommitment. Those suffering from burnout lose the ability to laugh, are angered easily, and are more prone to sickness, absenteeism, and early retirement (Hodge et al., 1994).

Burnout is not an isolated factor that only affects the weak. In fact, Hamann et al. (1987) suggest that those affected are "often the most productive, dedicated, and committed in their fields" (pp. 128–129). As Bramhall and Ezell (1981) point out, "you have to have been on fire to burn out" (p. 24). Interestingly, one of the early indicators of burnout is overenthusiasm for the job. Although the seeds of burnout are planted during the early phases of a teacher's career in times of overwhelming stress (McDonald & Eliam, 1980), the results can affect individuals immediately *or* after they have been in the field for many years (Wilder & Plutchik, 1982).

Dissatisfaction with employment, whether it manifests itself in teachers being generally disillusioned or escalates to a level classified as burnout, may, in part, explain high attrition rates in the field of teaching. According to Dwor-

kin (1987), teachers are three times as likely to want to resign their jobs as compared to those in similar professions of equal training. Some attribute this to the fact that teaching is a helping profession (Bramhall & Ezell, 1981).

According to the literature, certain segments of the profession are at greater risk of burnout. For example, secondary teachers and those unprepared through methods classes to deal with discipline problems are very vulnerable (Farber, 1991). Ayalon (1989) reported that those who did not perceive appropriate recognition from administrators or colleagues and those less inclined to value student progress predictably suffered higher levels of burnout at the end of the school year. Rosenman and Friedman (1983) believe that burnout is more likely associated with individuals reflecting Type A behaviors. These include individuals who are ambitious, aggressive, and competitive. Frequently these educators show an inability to relax away from work, are oriented toward achievement, and consistently deny failure. They almost always engage in multiple activities and are overly conscious of time. Many of these behaviors and their relation to burnout are underscored by research of Hamann, Daugherty, and Mills (1987) and Hamann, Daugherty, and Sherbon (1988). These authors suggest that one of the reliable predictors of burnout in public school music teachers is a feeling that there is too much work and not enough time to complete tasks. Those who overplan, need to win, desire recognition, cannot relax without feeling guilty, and overschedule with multiple projects involving deadlines are particularly vulnerable. The authors identified two other groups vulnerable to burnout. These include single or divorced teachers and those who have been teaching music between 4 and 12 years. Hamann et al. (1988) and Gordon (1997) have reported differences in burnout rates as a function of gender with males suffering from the problem at significantly higher rates than females. Gordon also reported that urban teachers experience greater stress regarding student discipline and motivation than colleagues at suburban or rural schools.

Because burnout is perceived to be a severe problem for teachers in P–12 settings, a large body of research attempting to document possible solutions has emerged. Research studies by Brown (1987) and Hodge et al. (1994) approach the problem by suggesting activities that the individual teacher can control. Many authors advocate the use of coping mechanisms such as religion, reading, diet, sports, muscle tension relaxation techniques, peer networks, and additional classroom management training to prevent burnout, while others suggest that administrators can help teachers deal with burnout by encouraging changes in their living and working patterns (Evers, Gerrichhauzen, & Tomic, 2000; Sandene, 1995). Examples include (1) giving staff control over decision making (i.e., site-based autonomy), (2) providing evaluation of teachers with meaningful feedback, (3) helping overloaded faculty scale back on the scope, scale, or difficulty of tasks (this may include encouraging faculty to restrict their summer teaching activities), and (4) advocating extraduty pay for activities such as basketball pep bands. Other solutions requiring administrative support have been outlined by Ayalon (1989) who concluded that recognition, planning time, and smaller class sizes may reduce attrition caused by burnout. Perhaps the solution for burnout should begin with a change in administrators' perceptions. These are not bad or weak people burning out but rather people in bad situations (Bramhall & Ezell, 1981).

According to Sandene (1995), readers should be careful in evaluating burnout research and the prescribed solutions because of the small samples and lack of longitudinal methodology. Interestingly, Cooper (1986), employing a true experimental design incorporating a control group, found that the use of relaxation and self-esteem tapes did *not* significantly lower the stress levels of music teachers.

Teacher Recruitment

"Despite brief periods of surplus, there has always been a shortage of willing and qualified teachers" (Sedlak & Schlossman, 1986, p. vii). Many authors anticipated severe teacher shortages in the 1980s. These predictions apparently were accurate, albeit premature with larger shortages occurring in the late 1990s (Archer, 1996; Hendrie, 1996; NCES, 1997; Riley, 1996; White, 1996). "Although the teacher shortage that was predicted for the early 1990s did not materialize then, schools in many communities are now bursting at the seams as the baby boom 'echo' reaches school age" (NCES, 1997, p. 1). According to the Scholastic Inc./CCSSO Teachers' Voice 2000 survey, almost 50% of schools reported a shortage of qualified teachers. Wilcox (2000) indicates that "teacher demand is up nationwide" (p. 26) and, according to figures from the United States Department of Education (2000), 2 million new teachers will be hired by 2010.

In contrast, Feistritzer (1993) suggested that "the demand for more and better teachers is being met" (p. 118). The apparent shortage of teachers is not attributable to actual low numbers but, rather, because of teacher turnover, with individuals moving from school to school (Murnane & Vegas, 1997). Feistritzer and also Schlechty and Vance (1983) put forward the argument that two factors prevent acute teacher shortages: alternative certification—which allows people with bachelor's degrees in majors other than education to enter the teaching force—and a pool of teachers who have left teaching but are available to reenter in times of shortage. In 1993–1994, this reserve pool represented 2% of those holding teaching credentials

(NCES, 1997). In the future, this group, predominantly women, could be called on in greater numbers. Interestingly, some think that the size of this group is shrinking (Baker & Smith, 1997).

Schlechty and Vance (1983) suggest that the predictions for teacher shortages that occurred in the late 1970s and 1980s were based on expected growth of P–12 student population (which occurred); rising attrition rates (which did not occur, partially because salaries and morale of teachers increased during the 1980s and 90s [Baker & Smith, 1997]); and static numbers of teachers wanting to enter the profession (which also did not occur as alternative certification made entry into the profession more accessible to groups previously excluded).

The concept of raising the bar by establishing standards for entry into the profession is also an important issue in recruiting. Because state legislators control standards and because there is a financial advantage in having a large workforce (i.e., high supply) in order to keep salaries low and the budgets of school districts balanced, standards will never be raised to the point where they cause severe problems in recruiting, admitting, or certifying teachers (Goodlad, 1990). Even if standards are raised, alternative certification can act as a safety valve such that teachers can be found even if they have nontraditional credentials. Ironically, when traditional methods of recruiting teachers fail to produce certified individuals for positions in school districts, the district can petition the state for alternative, provisional, or temporary certification for potential candidates who under other conditions could not be certified (Pembrook & Vasconcellos, 2001). Therefore, if a shortage of certified teachers can be used as a justification to hire someone not typically recognized as a teacher, the only way a genuine shortage can occur in the profession is if the total demand exceeds the number of people *wishing* to teach. Such policies may explain why "on average, less than 1% of teaching positions were vacant or temporarily filled by a substitute" (NCES, 1997, p. 100).

Ironically, more than 15 years ago, Schlechty and Vance (1983) suggested that the higher admission standards might cause shortages of traditionally certified teachers in the classroom not primarily because of the seemingly obvious notion that it would eliminate potential teachers at the entry point to the process but, rather, because teachers with lower entrance scores (e.g., ACT results) in the past had stayed longer in the teaching profession. They suggested that efforts to raise entrance requirements to eliminate the bottom 20% of those entering university teacher education programs would cause not only short-term effects on the front end of the process but also long-term effects on the number of teachers still working 15–20 years after graduation. These authors speculated that eliminating the bottom quintile of entering students at schools of education would eventually result in a reduction of the teaching force by half, assuming all other things remained equal (e.g., attrition rates, salaries, etc.).

Darling-Hammond (2001) indicates that "today, there is no absolute shortage of teachers, but a shortage in particular fields and locations" (p. 71). Some of these fields and locations include schools serving large proportions of low-income students; special education; mathematics; science; bilingual education; music education, particularly string music education; elementary education; and English (Gillespie, 1997; NCES, 1997). The severity of the shortage of music teachers was underscored by the inclusion of a statement in the Housewright Declaration acknowledging the need for recruiting (Hinckley, 2000). This shortage appears particularly severe in states experiencing rapid growth. For example, in 1999, Florida reported that 12% of its new hires in music did not have traditional music certification (Florida Department of Education, 1999). The teacher shortage may be most dramatic in inner-city schools, with two thirds of those districts hiring noncertified teachers (Foster, 2000).

Many administrators find that in selected areas it is so difficult to initially recruit teachers they are forced to offer cash bonuses. Interestingly, NCES (1997) reported that the percentage of districts using such bonuses to attract teachers moved from 1% in 1987–88 to 2% in 1993–1994. Shortages appear especially severe in special education with 7.4% of total positions unfilled or filled by people not certified (United States Department of Education, 1996).

Authors such as Winslow (1949), Brand (1987), Madsen, Smith, and Feeman, (1988), Gillespie and Hamann (1998, 1999), O'Laughlin (1999), and Wilcox (2000) have suggested effective ways to generate interest in music teaching careers. They include: (1) collaborations between college and high school faculty to identify future music teachers, perhaps as early as their junior year; (2) daily activities or peer tutoring led by other students in P–12 music programs; (3) performances in quality music ensembles and private lessons that generate excitement among music students; (4) videotapes and brochures from national offices of organizations such as MENC or the American String Teachers Association; (5) technology-based approaches incorporating Internet advertising and online applications; and (6) discussions with students regarding the rewards of P–12 teaching. Unfortunately, music teachers apparently are often more negative than positive in their comments to students about entering the profession (Bergee, 1992; Frink, 1997).

In addition to these activities, it is important to know *when* to recruit music teachers and who these potential teachers are consulting in making career decisions. A majority of music teachers decide to enter music as a profession before age 14 and music education, specifically, around the time of high school graduation (Froehlich &

L'Roy, 1985). Apparently, former or current music teachers are very important in this career decision, particularly high school ensemble directors and private music teachers. Family members also provide valuable input (Bergee, 1992; Burgstahler, 1966; Jones, 1964; L'Roy, 1983; Ploumis-Devick, 1983). Most prospective teachers at some point have served as student conductors or teachers' aides. College music students' first choices in music tend toward performing, then private teaching, followed by university teaching, directing secondary ensembles, elementary teaching, and, finally, church music. Unfortunately, as Shellahamer (1984) notes, too often (in over 50% of the universities surveyed), college music majors are advised into music education simply because they are not performing well enough to become performance majors.

The process for successfully recruiting minorities into the profession of teaching has received considerable attention in recent years. According to research by Astin (1992) and Darling-Hammond (1984), "the defection of highly able students from teaching [in the 1980s] was most pronounced for women and minority college students" (Darling-Hammond, 2001). Darling-Hammond, Dilworth, and Bullmaster (1996) indicate that as teaching salaries increased once again, along with standards in the late 1980s and early 1990s, the numbers of minority entrants to teaching began to rebound.

The Teacher Education Policy (TEP) profile (1997) listed the activities of states specifically pertaining to their efforts in minority recruiting. More than two thirds reported processes for recruiting minorities into teaching. Examples included: High School Future Teacher Clubs (e.g., Hawaii), state-mandated minority recruiting plans for every district (Illinois), Ford Foundation grant money to identify and recruit minorities interested in teaching (Georgia), and short-term salaried sabbaticals for paraprofessionals while they receive teacher training (Connecticut). Alaska forgives educational loans after teachers have served for 5 years in a district that nominates them, and states such as Arkansas and Colorado have had governor's funds or state incentive funds specifically for minorities. Unfortunately, according to TEP, many of the initiatives begun in the 1980s have not continued, often because of a lack of funding. College costs prohibit many minorities from enrolling in traditional teacher training programs, but this may be offset with mentor programs to recruit individuals of color and help them complete their college training (Futrell, 1999).

Traditional Standards in Recruiting/Certifying

Traditionally, there have been two primary points of review for those seeking to become teachers. The first is the initial screening for admission to teacher education programs in college and the second is the state licensing or certification process that occurs immediately after graduation for most prospective teachers. Many of the entrance requirements for teacher education programs are specifically linked to the concept of teacher intelligence. Individual state-mandated entrance criteria as outlined by TEP (1997) include high school and college grade point average (typically 2.5), Pre-Professional Skills Test (PPST) minimum scores (see table 41.3, based on TEP, 1997; Feistritzer & Chester, 2000; NASDTEC, 2000; Pembrook & Vasconcellos, 2001), writing samples, and SAT scores (e.g., 840 in Florida). Some states such as Delaware and New Hampshire allow higher education institutions to establish their own minimum standards. Interestingly, a study by Williford (1993) in North Carolina indicated that mandated, statewide increases in admission criteria for teacher training programs led to higher passing rates by prospective teachers on the National Teacher Examination, even though most schools saw the new standards as burdensome.

Authors during the past 2 decades have documented the rising level of minimum scores required for admission to teacher education programs (Brand, 1987; Erbes, 1982, 1985, 1987, 1992; Guyton & Farokhi, 1987; Peterson & Speaker, 1996; TEP, 1997). These are summarized in table 41.3. In addition to these criteria, those seeking to become music teachers also often must demonstrate music skills through applied auditions, juries, music placement exams, and interviews with music education personnel (Shellahamer, 1984). Colwell (2000) and Mark (1998) point out the ongoing dilemma faced by those preparing music teachers regarding whether they function more as musicians, thus making music skills paramount during evaluation for admission, or as educators, implying the importance of pedagogical abilities. Interestingly, Shellahamer indicated that only 12% of schools validated these selection criteria. From this limited review, only academic achievement and jury grades were considered valid selection criteria for future teachers. Pembrook, Fuelberth, and Harden (in press) reported that applied skills and college GPA did not correlate with music education students' teaching success in methods class demonstrations. Some question current admission criteria and suggest that more qualitative measures should be incorporated in the model (Petersen & Speaker, 1996).

As previously described, Goodlad (1990) has proposed that there is a financial advantage for universities to keep standards low, thus attracting large numbers of education majors (i.e., credit hour production) and ensuring sufficient numbers of teachers. In contrast, Sedlak and Schlossman (1986) suggest that "it has proved possible, time and again, to raise standards during periods of protracted shortage. Not only has the raising of standards not exacerbated teacher shortages, it may even—at least *where accompanied by significant increases in teachers' salaries* [italics added]—have helped to alleviate them and, at the same time, enhanced popular respect for teaching as a profession" (p. 39).

Teacher certification by a state agency has been traditionally tied to students completing a minimum number of hours or courses at designated higher education institutions within a state. These experiences typically have led to a degree in education with certification for teaching a specific discipline or age group (e.g., music education or elementary education). According to Kirkpatrick (1992), the original intent of state certification was to protect the public from frauds as well as minimal teacher standards established by local school boards.

Erbes (1983, 1986) reported that the certification process was fairly stable in the period of the 1970s and early 1980s but began to change around 1983. At that point, many states began to require prospective teachers to pass tests such as the National Teacher Examination (NTE) and Pre-Professional Skills Test (PPST) before becoming certified. Since the early 1980s, nearly all states have introduced tests for initial licensing (Darling-Hammond & Barnett, 1988; Howey & Zimpher, 1993). Other models in lieu of the traditional 4-year college degree leading to automatic lifetime certification have appeared in the past 15 years. Reports from the Holmes Group (1986) and Carnegie Forum on Education and the Economy (1986) called for alternatives including levels of certification (e.g., instructor, teacher, advanced teacher) and 5-year programs featuring a 4-year bachelor of arts or science degree in a discipline (e.g., mathematics) followed by a 1-year master's program in education. Some states have used this, at least in part, as a model in establishing state certification standards.

One of the preeminent researchers in certification, Darling-Hammond (2001), suggests that "systems of licensing and certification that directly assess what teachers know and can do are gradually replacing the traditional methods of requiring graduation from an approved program or tallying specific courses as the basis for granting program approval, a license, or credit for professional growth." In the October 1990 issue of the *Music Educators Journal*, MENC outlined such a system that could lead to recognition as a "nationally certified master music educator." The designation was based on a combination of accomplishments such as artistry, professional development, and peer/administrator review. Many states now are requiring a mentoring program during beginning teachers' first years of work. This is followed by peer or administrative review and evaluation before an extended professional license is issued (Pembrook & Vasconcellos, 2001).

Darling-Hammond (2001) cites an impressive number of studies documenting that fully licensed/certified teachers are more effective in their fields (Ashton & Crocker, 1986, 1987; Begle, 1979; Begle & Geeslin, 1972; Bledsoe, Cox & Burnham, 1967; Darling-Hammond, 1990; Druva &

Table 41.3 Teacher Education Entrance, Exit, and Continuing Education Requirements

State	Entrance Requirements	Certificate Requirements	Continuing Education Requirements	Phone/Website
AL	2.5 GPA 300 SBST	2.5 GPA	6 semester hours	334-242-9977 alsde.edu
AK	IHE	IHE Praxis I Reading Writing Math Courses in multicultural & Alaskan studies	6 semester hours in 5 years	907-465-2831 eed.state.ak.us/teachercertification
AZ	IHE	IHE SBST SSMT AZ Constitution Test	District determines	602-542-2029 ade.state.az.us/certification
AR	2.5 GPA Praxis I Reading 170 Writing 171 Math 169	2.5 GPA NTE 642 Praxis II 111 PS = 145 Praxis II 112 PS = 150 Praxis II 113 PS = 150	6 semester hours in 6 years	501-682-4345 N/A
CA	Take SBST	SBST-123 Praxis I SSMT	150 hours PD every 5 years	888-921-2682 ctc.ca.gov
CO	Take SBST	Pass SBST SSMT Praxis I	6 semester hours in 5 years	303-866-6628 cde.state.co.us
CT	Interview Writing Sample Praxis I or SAT 1000 or ACT-Comp 24	Pass Praxis I or SBST or Praxis II 111 PS = 150 and Praxis II 113 PS = 153	90 hours PD every 5 years	860-566-5201 state.ct.us/sde
DE	IHE	Pass Praxis I Reading 175/322[a] Math 174/319 Writing 173/319	6 semester hours in 5 years	800-273-9500 doe.state.de.us
FL	40% SAT (840) ACT (20) or 2.5 GPA GenEd	2.5 GPA Pass SBST	120 hours PD or 6 semester hours every 5 years	850-487-1785 flrn.edu/doe
GA	Take SBST 2.5 GPA	Pass SBST Exceptional Child Course Praxis II 111 PS = 150 Praxis II 113 PS = 154 2.5 GPA	6 semester hours or 10 staff hours every 5 years	404-656-2446 mail@gapsc.com
HI	IHE	Pass Praxis I Praxis II 111 PS = 145 Praxis II 113 PS = 139	N/A	800-305-5104 k12.doe.hi.us
ID	2.5 GPA	IHE	N/A	208-332-6800 sde.state.ide.us/certification
IL	IHE	Pass SBST	District determines	800-845-8749 isbe.state.il.us
IN	2.5 GPA	NTE Comm. 653 GenKn 647 ProfKn 646 NTE Specialty Pass SBST	6 semester hours every 5 years	317-232-9010 state.in.us/psb
IA	Praxis I	IHE	8 renewable units every 5 years	225-342-4411 state.ia.us/educate/programs/boee

State	Entrance Requirements	Certificate Requirements	Continuing Education Requirements	Phone/Website
KS	2.75 GPA GenEd	2.5 GPA NTE ProfKn 642 PPST Read 173 Math 174 Writing 172 PLT 161	6–8 semester hours every 5 years or 120 in-service points	785-296-2288 ksbe.state.ks.us
KY	ACT 19 or ACT 21 enhanced 2.5 GPA Review of basic skills Ability to work with children Praxis I	NTE CommSk 646 GenKn 643 ProfKn 644 Praxis I Praxis II 111 PS = 146 Praxis II 113 PS = 150	6 semester hours every 3 years	502-573-4606 kde.state.ky.us
LA	NTE GenKn 644 CommSk 645 2.2 GPA	Praxis I Praxis II 110 PS = 530 2.5 GPA	6 semester hours every 5 years	225-342-4411 louisianaschools.net
ME	IHE	Praxis I	6 hours of approved credit every 5 years	207-287-5944 N/A
MD	IHE	Praxis I Praxis II 112 PS = 147 Praxis II 113 PS = 154	6 semester hours every 5–7 years	410-767-0100 dsd.state.md.us
MA	IHE	SBST SSMT	*N/A*	781-338-6600 doe.mass.edu
MI	IHE	Pass SBST Speciality Area Test	6 semester hours or 18 CE units every 5 years	517-335-0508 state.mi.us/mde/off/ppc
MN	Take PPST	Pass PPST Reading 173 Writing 172 Math 169 Human Relations Course	125 hours of CE units every 5 years	651-582-8200 http://cfl.state.mn.us
MS	2.5 GPA NTE CommSk 651 GenKn 646	NTE ProfKn 649 Praxis II 113 PS = 139	80 SD credits or 3 semester hours or 4 CE units every 5 years plus 16 in-service hours annually	601-359-3483 mde.k12.ms.us
MO	Pass IHE ACT/SAT requirement Pass SBST	2.5 GPA Praxis II 113 PS = 151	12 semester hours of academic credit every 7 years	573-751-4369 dese.state.mo.us
MT	IHE	NTE ProfKn 648 GenKn 644 CommSk 648 or SBST 2.0 GPA	60 PD units every 5 years	406-444-3150 metnet.state.mt.us
NE	PPST Reading 170 Math 171 Writing 172 2.5 GPA	IHE 2.5 GPA Praxis I	6 semester hours every 6 years	402-471-2295 nde.state.ne.us
NV	PPST Reading 172 Math 170 Writing 172	PPST 3 parts Praxis II 111 and Praxis II 113 PS = 150 NV Constitution Test	6 credits of PD every 5 years	702-486-6455 nsn.k12.nv.us/nvdoe

(continued)

State	Entrance Requirements	Certificate Requirements	Continuing Education Requirements	Phone/Website
NH	IHE	IHE	50 hours of in-service every 3 years	603-271-2407 state.nh.us
NJ	2.5 GPA Field experience	2.5 GPA NTE GenKn 649 (Elementary teachers) Praxis II 113 PS = 143	Lifetime certificate Districts must offer in-service	609-292-0877 N/A
NM	IHE	NTE GenKn 645 ProfKn 630 CommSk 644 SBST	Personal Development Plan reviewed every 9 years	505-827-6587 sde.state.nm.us
NY	IHE	SBST Child Abuse Orientation	Lifetime certificate with masters	518-474-3901 highered.nysed.gov/tcert/
NC	2.5 GPA Praxis I Reading 176 Writing 174 Math 173	NTE ProfKn 649 NTE Specialty Test Praxis II 111 and 113 PS = 299 (total requirement)	10 semester hours every 5 years	919-807-3310 ncpublicschools.org
ND	2.5 GPA SBST	2.5 GPA 2 hours of credits in Native American Studies	4 semester hours every 5 years	701-328-1439 state.nd.us/espb
OH	IHE reviews basic skills	Praxis II 522 = 168 or 523 = 168 or 524 = 165 and 113 = 154	Master's plus 12 semester hours = lifetime certificate	614-466-3593 ode.state.oh.us/cp/ctp
OK	2.5 GPA PPST general proficiency	SBST (general, teaching, and subject area)	5 semester hours every 5 years	405-521-3337 N/A
OR	NTE Core CommSk 659 GenKn 654 or PPST Math 175 Writing 171 Reading 174	NTE Specialty NTE Core ProfKn 661	9 quarter hours every 5 years	503-378-3586 N/A
PA	IHE	NTE ProfKn 643 GenKn 644 CommSk 646 3.0 GPA Praxis II 113 PS = 158	State mandated CE experiences as outlined by district	717-787-2967 pde.psu.edu
RI	Interview Basic Skills assessed	GPA quarter pt higher than IHE required minimum	6 credits every 5 years	401-222-4600 ridoe.net
SC	2.5 GPA SBST	NTE ProfKn 642 Praxis II 110 PS = 480	6 credits every 5 years or comparable in-service	803-734-8466 scteachers.org
SD	2.5 GPA Basic Skills competence	IHE	6 semester hours every 5 years	605-773-3553 state.sd.us/decaaccount/counting.htm

State	Entrance Requirements	Certificate Requirements	Continuing Education Requirements	Phone/Website
TN	2.5 GPA PPST Math 169/314[a] Reading 169/315 Writing 172/318 Interview Field experiences	NTE CommSk 651 GenKn 647 ProfKn 643 Praxis II 111 (no PS requirement) Praxis II 113 PS = 150	90 PD credits every 10 years	615-532-4885 state.tn.us/education
TX	70th percentile SBST	SBST (pedagogy) SSMT	Lifetime certificate Use staff development centers	512-469-3000 sbec.state.tx.us
UT	IHE	IHE	100 PD credits every 5 years	801-538-7793 usoe.k12.ut.us
VT	Basic skills competence	Portfolio Praxis I	Minimum teaching experience every 7 years	802-828-2445 N/A
VA	2.5 GPA	NTE CommSk 649 GenKn 639 ProfKn 639 Praxis II 113 PS = 160	180 points every 5 years based on courses, publications, travel, etc.	804-371-2522 pen.k12.va.us
WA	2.5 GPA Basic skills competence 50th percentile on SAT/GRE	IHE	150 CE units every 5 years	360-753-6773 k12.wa.us/cert
WV	IHE	PPST Reading 172/319[a] Math 172/317 Writing 171/316 Computer Literacy Praxis II 113 PS = 155 2.5 GPA	6 semester hours every 5 years	304-558-7010 http://wvde.state.wv.us/
WI	2.5 GPA PPST Reading 175 Writing 174 Math 173 50 hours of human relations work with minorities, disabled, or low-income	IHE 2.75 GPA Praxis I	6 semester hours every 5 years	608-266-1879 dpi.state.wi.us
WY	IHE	IHE	5 semester hours every 5 years	307-777-6261 k12.wy.us

All website addresses are preceded with http://www., except for MN and WV.
[a]First score is pencil version; second score is computer verison.
Note: SBST = State Basic Skills Test; IHE = Determined by each institution of higher education; SSMT = State Subject Matter Test; PD = Professional development; Praxis II 110 = Music education; Praxis II 111 = Music concepts and processes; Praxis II 112 = Music analysis; Praxis II 113 = Music content knowledge; PS = Passing score; N/A = No available information.

Anderson, 1983; Erekson & Barr, 1985; Evertson, Hawley, & Zlotnick, 1985; Gomez & Grobe, 1990; Greenberg, 1983; Grossman, 1989; Guyton & Farokhi, 1987; Haberman, 1984; Hawk, Coble, & Swanson, 1985; Hice, 1970; LuPone, 1961; Olsen, 1985; Perkes, 1967–1968). However, others (e.g., Kirkpatrick, 1992) suggest that data show little difference in quality and effectiveness between certified and noncertified teachers. Kirkpatrick called for a 10-year moratorium on certification during which all college graduates would be allowed to teach in their discipline concentration. It would appear that, in certain disciplines, such drastic measures may be needed. NCES (1997) reported that over one-third of English, foreign language, mathematics, science, and social studies classes were taught by teachers with neither an undergraduate major or minor in the field. In schools where over 40% of the students were on reduced-lunch programs, the figure approached nearly half of the teachers (47%). Kirkpatrick also has called for a national certification test to establish a uniform standard and allow for portability of credentials.

Despite such proposals, licensing of teachers presently is still accomplished at the state level. "Variances between states exist [pertaining to minimum criteria for teacher education programs] but much commonality on major factors appears as different state minimum teacher education standards are reviewed" (Westerman, 1989, p. 25). One group that has undertaken the task of quality control for teacher education and helped create this commonality is NCATE. Darling-Hammond (2001) reports that the number of states establishing partnerships with NCATE for approval of teacher education institutions has risen to over 80% with about two-thirds of the nation's teachers being trained at NCATE-approved colleges and universities. As part of a project called NCATE 2000, universities wishing to retain their NCATE accreditation must begin providing evidence that graduates know their subject matter and use it effectively in teaching.

Most states now require a passing score on a state-mandated exam before individuals can be certified to teach (TEP, 1997). Gallup polling, as reported in the *Phi Delta Kappan* from 1984 to 1989, indicated that over 80% of the general public supported this concept, whereas about 60% of those in teaching did. One popular test is the Praxis II Examination. However, states differ on whether teachers should be required to pass the general portion (e.g., Maine) or both the general and the discipline specific portion before receiving certification (e.g., Arkansas, Louisiana, Mississippi).

Other requirements for traditional licensure include a bachelor's degree in teacher education, additional tests (e.g., a test on the constitution in California), specialty courses such as mainstreaming, computers, and Native American studies, or minimum scores on the Praxis exams. Whereas master's degrees usually lead to a more advanced title or longer period of certification, at least one state (Arizona), perhaps as a reaction to the Holmes and Carnegie recommendations, by law forbids the requirement of a master's degree for initial teacher certification (TEP, 1997). To retain certification, many states require professional development hours or college courses.

In the early 1990s, music educators seeking certification were generally required to take some sort of general skills/knowledge test with 80% of states requiring such activity. In addition, about 40% were requiring subject matter tests (Erbes, 1992). While the percentage of states requiring some type of test using state or nationally normal results has remained close to 80%, the percentage requiring demonstrations of subject matter knowledge has increased to nearly 60%. States appear equally divided between granting P–12 music as an all encompassing certification versus a targeted licensure for choral, instrumental, and general

music teachers at elementary and secondary levels (Pembrook & Vasconcellos, 2001).

Depending on the source and the time frame, different pictures are presented regarding the certification areas and actual teaching duties of the workforce. NEA (1962, 1997) reported that, in 1961, 68.6% of teachers were teaching in their field of college preparation, but, by 1996, the percentage had increased to 82.6. In contrast, Darling-Hammond (2001) reported that, in the 1990s, the percentage of unlicensed teachers or those with substandard credentials varied from less than 1% in some states to nearly half in others. Nationally, in 1994, over one quarter (27%) of those who were new entrants into public school teaching held no license or a substandard license in their main teaching field (Darling-Hammond, 2001; Darling-Hammond, 1997). According to the MENC Secondary Report, 97% of teachers held standard teaching certificates in music education with only 1% reporting probationary certificates and none reporting provisional certificates. In rapidly expanding states, however, the percentage may be much higher.

Correlations between Selected Standards and Teaching Effectiveness

There is an inherent implication that the standards established increase the likelihood of, or at least correlate significantly with, effective teaching behaviors. Much of the literature does not support this assumption. Heller and Clay (1993) suggest that the best approach for establishing the validity of entrance criteria would be to grant everyone admission (including those who fall below the criteria) and track the results for all. Obviously, there are ethical and political problems in following this course. Similarly, Conklin (1985) has suggested that, although high scores on the SAT, ACT, Praxis I/II, or PPST may not guarantee that teachers will succeed, low scores on those same exams seem likely to indicate that a person will not do well in teaching.

Another challenging part of the correlation process in evaluating teaching success is determining the measure of success. Studies have suggested principals' ratings, student learning, and behaviors taught in the teacher training program as logical correlates. This latter approach is frequently the dependent measure when evaluating student teachers and may produce vastly different results than using other teaching ratings. According to Wing (1993), "Music teaching effectiveness can be predicted on the basis of GPA, faculty ratings, and perhaps personality characteristics if the criterion of effectiveness is observer judgment. The picture clouds when student achievement is the criterion" (p. 56).

A review of the literature discussing significant correlations between teaching effectiveness and selected factors suggests several possible indicators of eventual success. These include:

1. The number of college methods classes (including music methods) and the student's GPA in those classes (Chadwick, Michael, & Hanshumaker, 1972; Ellsworth, 1985; Nelson & Woods, 1985; Westerman, 1989).
2. Upper-level college GPAs, especially in education courses (Guyton & Farokhi, 1987; Moore, 1991).
3. Praxis scores, particularly if the correlate is principals' ratings of teachers or first-time teaching demonstrations (Ayers & Qualls, 1979; Heller & Clay, 1993; Pembrook, Fuelberth, & Harden, in press).
4. Personality attributes (e.g., composite rating regarding self-confidence, reliability, adaptability/flexibility, and self-reliance). (See table 41.2.)
5. Subject matter knowledge (Schmidt & Hicken, 1986).

The evidence regarding correlations between methods classes and teaching success is particularly informative in light of reports that suggest that teacher education courses are considered unhelpful by veteran teachers (Kagan, 1992; Leslie & Lewis, 1990). Also, "it is interesting to note that the Professional Knowledge portion of the NTE was one of the better predictors of teacher effectiveness" (Heller & Clay, 1993, p. 8).

Despite the previously cited evidence, an even larger body of evidence questions the relationships between standard measures and teacher effectiveness. According to Schalock (1988), "we are essentially without any reliable predictors of who will or will not be good teachers" (p. 8). In measuring the relationship between SAT, GPA, and NTE results and teacher effectiveness, research indicates that those variables are not good predictors (Ayers & Qualls, 1979; Barr, 1987; Conklin, 1985; Colwell, 1985; DeRee, Reynolds, & Martin-Reynolds, 1986; Dobry, Murphy, & Schmidt, 1985; Evertson et al., 1985; Heller & Clay, 1993; Mamchur & Nelson, 1984; Marso & Pigge, 1997; Murray, 1986; Nelson & Wood, 1985; Olstad, 1987; Pratt, 1986; Riggs & Riggs, 1991; Schalock, 1988; Schechtman, 1989; Schmidt & Hicken, 1986; Young, 1990). Darling-Hammond has reviewed much of the literature and has suggested that it is very difficult to predict teaching success based on state certification test scores (see Andrews, Blackmon & Mackey, 1980; Ayers & Qualls, 1979; Darling-Hammond, Wise, & Klein, 1995; Quirk, Witten, & Weinberg, 1973). The reliability of grades in predicting teacher effectiveness also has been questioned by many (Dobry, et al., 1985; Flaitz, 1987; Pembrook, et al., in press; Schmidt & Hicken, 1986; Stedman, 1984; Westerman, 1989). In a bit of irony, some older studies have documented significant *negative* correlations between standard admission criteria for teacher education and success in teaching. These include Pugach and Raths's study (1983) regarding the NTE and Shim's (1965) study on GPA. In the Shim study, students learned more when working with teachers whose college GPA was below 2.5. Given today's teacher GPA standards, this study would be nearly impossible to replicate. Specifically, in music, in addition to the aforementioned studies, ability on an applied instrument or the number of years in private lessons did not correlate with teaching success nor did gender or age (Chadwick et al., 1972; Pembrook, et al., in press).

To resolve the apparent contradictions of the previous paragraphs, the work of Quirk et al. (1973) should be considered. They suggest that when tests and ratings do not correlate, it is difficult to know whether the results occur because the study used an invalid or unreliable test, an inaccurate teacher effectiveness rating system, or actually documented a situation in which no correlation existed between the two concepts being investigated. If almost all teachers are rated highly by their evaluators, as Quirk indicates, it becomes difficult to establish strong correlations. Quirk suggests that principals' 1st- and 3rd-year ratings do not correlate highly on the same individuals and are notoriously unreliable.

Alternative Certification

Various justifications for alternative certification have been proposed. One is based on the concept that individuals who possess a great deal of subject matter expertise (e.g., Bill Gates in computing/business, Henry Bloch in accounting, or Zubin Mehta in orchestral conducting) should be allowed to teach that discipline in P–12 settings. In most states, if the individual has a bachelor's degree and is willing to enroll in selected continuing education experiences, alternative certification can be granted (Feistritzer, 1993). In addition, alternative, provisional, or temporary certification also is often granted to people *while* they are completing coursework toward traditional certification even though this action probably would not be considered in fields with equivalent educational requirements such as medicine, law, or engineering. As former MENC president Carolynn Lindeman asks, "Would you really want to be operated on by a doctor who has not met high standards in medical training?" (Wilcox, 2000, p. 28).

Another approach to alternative certification deals with those teaching "out-of-field." This is based on a philosophy that those who know how to teach can be effective in any discipline regardless of specific subject matter expertise. Although NCES reports a very small percentage (8%) teaching with no certification or major in their discipline, Baker and Smith (1997) reported that in the mid-1990s, 16% of English classes, 22% of math courses, and 30%

of physics classes were being taught by those without a background in the discipline.

Although some oppose alternative certification, Feistritzer (1990, 1993, 1994), Klagholz (2000), Shen (1999), and Basinger (1999) acknowledge benefits of attracting teachers through this procedure. In particular, they suggest that those seeking alternative certification are more willing to work in inner-city schools and are more likely to be members of a minority. Shen reports that over 15% of those receiving alternative certification are minorities versus 12% of those completing traditional certification programs. In states such as New Jersey and Texas, the discrepancies are even higher, with 20 to 43% of alternative certificates being awarded to minorities (Feistritzer, 1993). Overall, those receiving alternative certificates produce higher scores on teacher certification tests and have lower attrition rates.

Virginia and New Jersey were the first states to promote alternative certification with Old Dominion providing initial leadership in the movement (Cornett, 1990; Klagholz, 2000). A review of the TEP (1997) alternate certification procedures indicates that over 90% of the states had alternative routes to certification with interesting prerequisites such as Peace Corps experience or positive peer evaluation. Some states limit alternative certification to the secondary level only.

In 1992, Erbes reported that alternative certification of music teachers did not appear to be a common practice. A more recent survey indicates that alternative certification has become much more popular in the past 9 years, with over 80% of the states reporting alternative certification or licensing for music teachers. In fact, several states reported multiple options for receiving alternative certification (Pembrook & Vasconcellos, 2001). However, it appears that most states are concerned in balancing obvious needs for music teachers with the integrity of maintaining standards. As such, compared with traditional certification procedures, most alternative certification programs require identical test results and nearly identical course requirements either initially before temporary certification is granted or eventually before a final professional license is awarded. Education plans outlining required coursework typically are developed with the aid of faculty in recognized teacher education programs or administrators in school districts. Most states also establish time frames in which this coursework must be completed to retain the temporary teaching certificate.

The concept of alternative certification is supported strongly by various populations (NCES, 1997). These include school board presidents (85%), superintendents (82%), public school principals (77%), private school principals (88%), private school teachers (68%), and, interestingly, public school teachers (56%). MENC, the largest music education organization, with over 90,000 members, recently endorsed the concept of alternative licensing in the Housewright Declaration (Hinckley, 2000).

One important question that arises from the alternative certification movement is whether there is any difference in learning as a result of being taught by a traditionally trained teacher versus one with alternative certification. Darling-Hammond's literature in this area was cited earlier. However, Gomez and Grobe (1990) and Kirkpatrick (1992) argue that it is difficult to find convincing evidence for the greater effectiveness of traditionally trained teachers, primarily because 90% of *all* teacher ratings fall into the top categories, thus making it nearly impossible to determine differences based on any sorting variables such as educational training. Perhaps because of such data, Colwell (2000) states that "more than a few colleges [have] examined the possibility that the uncertified applied music major might be as successful as the traditionally educated music teacher at accomplishing the goals of instruction" (p. 20).

Who Should Be Recruited?

As a way of summarizing previous information pertaining to teacher characteristics, personalities, and potential success, the question of who should be recruited to teach can be answered in a number of ways depending on the recruiting mission. If the goal is to reduce teacher shortages in disciplines where they are most severe, the answer would be that those with bachelor's degrees in math, science, special education, English, foreign languages (especially Spanish), and music (especially strings) should be recruited. If the focus is to recruit individuals who will be the most effective in the classroom, then the answer might be those who have the characteristics listed in table 41.2, especially those who exhibit confidence, flexibility and self-reliance. Also, those with a master's degree; large numbers of methods classes, especially in educational techniques; good upper-level GPAs, again, especially in educational methods classes; and a firm grasp of their subject matter, particularly as evidenced by the major area portion of the NTE, may be expected to do well based on research literature. If the task is to recruit individuals who will stay in the classroom longer, then recruiters should consider those who are older than the traditional beginning teacher, those from 5-year programs, non-Caucasians, and those of average intelligence. If the perspective is to create a situation in which the teaching profession mirrors the student population according to ethnicity, recruiters must attract blacks and Hispanics who are willing to teach. The data indicate that those entering the workforce with alternative certification are more likely to be of color and willing to work in urban settings. Authors have suggested mentoring programs, loan forgiveness policies, and early contacts by university representatives in high school settings as possible ways to accomplish this. Pertaining to music education, the answer regarding who should be recruited is probably best summarized by the work of Gillespie and Hamann (1999), who reported that the most successful music teachers are those who love teaching, music, children, playing, and being a role model.

Revisiting the Two Variations on the Theme of Teaching as a Profession

The numerous considerations described in the more substantial Variation II of this chapter portray the many historical and quantifiable conditions and entailments that comprise teachers' professional knowledge landscapes as outlined in Variation I and speak volumes to its enormities and complexities. As can be seen, teachers' professional knowledge landscapes are complicated places where much is known about its attributes, the Variation II theme, and little is known about how the multiplicity of attributes—both known and unknown—come together to shape teachers' experiences and sense of themselves as professionals over time, the Variation I theme. Lesser yet has been discovered about how teachers facilitate the creation of knowledge communities in their classrooms with students and how this leads to productive student learning. The personal practical knowledge and professional knowledge landscape research, the Variation I theme, asks these different sets of questions and attempts to show, as Geertz (1995) says,

> how particular events and unique occasions, an encounter here, a development there, can be woven together with a variety of facts and a battery of interpretations to produce a sense of how things go, have been going, and are likely to go. (p. 3)

A perspective such as the one described above is needed to balance the proliferation of research in the Variation II teaching as a profession theme that has accumulated over the years.

In this chapter, a sketch of a major line of inquiry on the study of teaching has been shared as one variation on the theme of teaching as a profession. It offers a conceptual framework that situates the profession of teaching within the complexities of school contexts. That overview was interfaced with "a variety of facts and a battery of interpretations" presented in Variation II. The second variation on a theme encouraged readers to question why things are the way they are within the teaching profession and how they got to be that way. Before that, readers were asked to

keep in mind anticipated teaching lives and lives actually lived on the professional knowledge landscape of schools. It is to this point that we return as we conclude this chapter, for it is here where the tensions and discrepancies between Variation I and Variation II of the teaching as a profession themes are most felt.

The facts and figures in Variation II point to trends—some hopeful, others devastating, and still others inconsequential—which shape the contours of the professional knowledge landscape of schools. While these entailments and conditions are highly instructive, they do not—and, by their very design, cannot—tell us how these matters come together in teachers' lives through the experiences that teacher live and relive, and the stories they tell and retell as professional educators. It is at the critical intersection between the two variations on the teaching as a profession theme where the stuff of commensurate or incommensurate professional lives is made. At this crucial juncture where theory and practice meet and desires and realities converge, more consonant music needs to be made.

REFERENCES

American Federation of Teachers Website. (2000). *Survey and analysis of salary trends, 1998.* Retrieved from www.aft.org/research/survey99/

Andrew, M., & Schwab, R. L. (1995). Has reform in teacher education influenced teacher performance? An outcome assessment of graduates of eleven teacher education programs. *Action in Teacher Education, 17,* 43–53.

Andrews, J. W., Blackmon, C. R., & Mackey, A. (1980). Preservice performance and the National Teacher Examinations. *Phi Delta Kappan, 6*(5), 358–359.

Apple, M. W. (1987). The de-skilling of teaching. In F. S. Bolin & J. M. Falk (Eds.), *Teacher renewal* (pp. 59–75). New York: Teachers College Press.

Applebaum, S. D., & Du, J. (1995). Learning to dance in administration: A two-step in professional development. In D. J. Clandinin & F. M. Connelly (Eds.), *Teachers' professional knowledge landscapes.* Toronto: Teachers College Press.

Archer, J. (1996). Today, private schools span diverse range. *Education Week, 16*(9), 1, 12–15.

Ashton, P., & Crocker, L. (1986). Does teacher certification make a difference? *Florida Journal of Teacher Education, 3,* 73–83.

Ashton, P., & Crocker, L. (1987). Systematic study of planned variations: The essential focus of teacher education reform. *Journal of Teacher Education 38,* 2–8.

Astin, A. W. (1992). *What matters in college? Four critical years revisited.* San Francisco: Jossey-Bass.

Ayalon, A. (1989). *Predictors of beginning teacher burnout.* (ERIC Document Reproduction Service No. ED 308 145)

Ayers, J. B., & Qualls, G. S. (1979). Concurrent and predictive validity of the National Teacher Examinations. *Journal of Educational Research, 73*(2), 86–92.

Bach, H. (1997). *A visual narrative concerning curriculum, girls, photography, etc.* Unpublished doctoral dissertation, University of Alberta, Edmonton, Alberta, Canada.

Baker, P. B. (1981). The development of a music teacher checklist for use by administrators, music supervisors, and teachers in evaluating music teaching effectiveness. *Dissertation Abstracts International, 42,* 3489A. (UMI No. 820 1803)

Baker, T. (1993). A survey of four-year and five-year program graduates and their principals. *Journal of the Southeastern Regional Association of Teacher Educators, 2*(2), 28–33.

Baker, D., & Smith, T. (1997). Teacher turnover and teacher quality: Refocusing the issue. *Teacher College Record, 99*(1), 29–35.

Ballon, D., & Podgursky, M. (1995). Recruiting smarter teachers. *Journal of Human Resources, 30*(2), 326–338.

Barr, R. (1987). Reform of teacher education and the problem of quality assurance. *Journal of Teacher Education, 38*(5), 45–51.

Barth, G. W. (1960). Some personality and temperament characteristics of selected school music teachers. (Doctoral dissertation, University of Southern California, Los Angeles). *Dissertation Abstracts International, 22*(01), 0149A.

Basinger, J. (1999, January 14). Colleges widen alternate routes to teacher education. *Chronicle of Higher Education,* A18–A19.

Beach, D. M., & Reinhartz, J. (1984). What is good teaching? Using criteria of effective teaching to judge teacher performance. *NASSP Bulletin, 68*(475), 31–37.

Beattie, M. (1995). *Constructing professional knowledge in teaching: A narrative of change and development.* New York: Teachers College Press.

Beaver, M. E. (1972/1973). An investigation of personality and value characteristics of successful high school band directors in North Carolina. *Dissertation Abstracts International, 34*(05), 2674A (UMI No. 67–11).

Begle, E. G. (1979). *Critical variables in mathematics education.* Washington, DC: Mathematical Association of America and National Council of Teachers of Mathematics.

Begle, E. G., & Geeslin, W. (1972). *Teacher effectiveness in mathematics instruction: National Longitudinal Study of Mathematical Abilities Reports No. 28.* Washington, DC: Mathematical Association of America and National Council of Teachers of Mathematics.

Bergee, M. J. (1992). Certain attitudes toward occupational status held by music education majors. *Journal of Research in Music Education, 40,* 104–113.

Billingsley, B. S., & Cross, L. H. (1992). Predictors of commitment, job satisfaction, and intent to stay in teaching: A comparison of general and special educators. *Journal of Special Education, 25,* 453–471.

Bledsoe, J. C., Cox, J. V., & Burnham, R. (1967). *Comparison between selected characteristics and performance of provisionally and professionally certified beginning teachers in Georgia.* Washington, DC: U.S. Department of Health, Education, and Welfare.

Bramhall, M., & Ezell, S. (1981). How burned out are you? *Public Welfare, 39*(1), 23–27.

Brand, M. (1985). Research in music teacher effectiveness. *Update, 3*(2), 13–16.

Brand, M. (1987). The best and the brightest: Screening prospective music teachers. *Music Educators Journal, 73*(6), 32–36.

Brophy, J., & Good, T. L. (1986). Teacher behavior and student achievement. In M. C. Wittrock (Ed.), *Handbook of research on teaching* (3rd ed., pp. 328–375). New York: Macmillan.

Brown, P. A. (1987). An investigation of problems which cause stress among music teachers in Tennessee. *Dissertation Abstracts International, 48*(03), 0521A.

Bullock, J. A. (1974). An investigation of the personality traits, job satisfaction attitudes, training and experience histories of superior teachers of junior high school instrumental music in New York State. (Doctoral dissertation, University of Miami, Coral Gables, 1973). *Dissertation Abstracts International, 35*(04), 2029A.

Burgstahler, E. E. (1966). Factors influencing the choice and pursuance of a career in music education: A survey and case study approach. (Doctoral dissertation, Florida State University, 1966). *Dissertation Abstracts International, 27,* 2552A.

Carnegie Forum on Education and the Economy. (1986). *A nation prepared: Teachers for the 21st century.* Hyattsville, MD: Carnegie Foundation.

Chadwick, C., Michael, W., & Hanshumaker, J. (1972). Correlates of success in practice teaching in music at the University of Southern California. *Educational and Psychological Measurement, 32,* 1073–1078.

Clandinin, D. J. (1986). *Classroom practice: Teacher images in action.* London: Falmer Press.

Clandinin, D. J. (1992). Narrative and story in teacher education. In T. Russell & H. Munby (Eds.), *Teachers and teaching: From classroom to reflection.* Philadelphia: The Falmer Press.

Clandinin, D. J., & Connelly, F. M. (1995). *Teachers' professional knowledge landscapes.* New York: Teachers College Press.

Clandinin, D. J., & Connelly, F. M. (1996). Teachers' professional knowledge landscapes: Teacher stories—stories of teachers—school stories—stories of school. *Educational Researcher, 25*(3), 24–30.

Clandinin, D. J., & Connelly, F. M. (1998). Stories to live by: Narrative understandings of school reform. *Curriculum Inquiry, 28*(2), 149–164.

Clandinin, D. J., & Connelly, F. M. (2000). *Narrative inquiry: Experience and story in qualitative research.* San Francisco: Jossey-Bass.

Coats, W. D., & Smidchens, U. (1966). Audience recall as a function of speaker dynamism. *Journal of Education Psychology, 57,* 189–191.

Colwell, R. (1985). Program evaluation in music teacher training. *Bulletin of the Council for Research in Music Education, 81,* 18–62.

Colwell, R. (2000). The music education/arts education path. *Arts Education Policy Review, 101*(3), 19–20.

Conklin, R. (1985). Teacher competency testing: The present situation and some concerns on how some teachers are tested. *Education Canada, 25*(1), 12–15.

Conle, C. (1996). Resonance in preservice teacher inquiry. *American Educational Research Journal, 33*(2), 297–325.

Conle, C. (1999). Why narrative? Which narrative? Struggling with time and place in life and research. *Curriculum Inquiry, 29*(1), 7–32.

Connelly, F. M., & Clandinin, D. J. (1988). *Teachers as curriculum planners: Narratives of experience.* New York: Teachers College Press.

Connelly, F. M., & Clandinin, D. J. (1993). Cycles, rhythms, and the meaning of school time. In L. W. Anderson & H. J. Walberg (Eds.), *Timepiece: Extending and enhancing learning time.* Reston, VA: National Association of Secondary School Principals.

Connelly, F. M. & Clandinin, D. J. (1999). *Shaping a professional identity: Stories of educational practice.* New York: Teachers College Press.

Cooper, G. H. (1986). Self-esteem enhancement of public school music teachers: An experiment in positive self-reinforcement. (Doctoral dissertation, University of Northern Colorado, 1986). *Dissertation Abstracts International, 47*(6), 2069–2070A.

Cornett, L. M. (1990). Alternate certification: State policies in the SREB states. *Peabody Journal of Education, 67*(3), 55–83.

Craig, C. (1992). *Coming to know in the professional context: Beginning teachers experience.* Unpublished doctoral dissertation, University of Alberta, Edmonton, Alberta, Canada.

Craig, C. J. (1995a). Knowledge communities: A way of making sense of how beginning teachers come to know. *Curriculum Inquiry, 25*(2), 151–175.

Craig, C. J. (1995b). Dilemmas in crossing the boundaries on the professional knowledge landscape. In D. J. Clandinin & F. M. Connelly (Eds.), *Teachers' professional knowledge landscapes.* New York: Teachers College Press.

Craig, C. J. (1995c). Safe places on the professional knowledge landscape: Knowledge communities. In D. J. Clandinin & F. M. Connelly (Eds.), *Teachers' professional knowledge landscapes.* New York: Teachers College Press.

Craig, C. J. (1998). The influence of context on one teacher's interpretive knowledge of team teaching. *Teaching and Teacher Education, 18*(8), 371–383.

Craig, C. J. (1999). Life on the professional knowledge landscape: Living the image of "principal as rebel." In F. M. Connelly & D. J. Clandinin (Eds.), *Shaping a professional identity: Stories of educational practice.* New York: Teachers College Press.

Craig, C. J. (2000). Stories of school/teacher stories: A two-part invention on the walls theme. *Curriculum Inquiry, 30*(1), 11–41.

Craig, C. J. (2001). The relationship between and among teacher narrative knowledge, communities of knowing, and school reform: A case of 'The Monkey's Paw.' *Curriculum Inquiry, 31*, 303–331.

Crites, S. (1971). The narrative quality of experience. *Journal of the American Academy of Religion, 399*(3), 291–311.

Crites, S. (1979). The aesthetics of self-deception. *Soundings, 62,* 107–129.

Darling-Hammond, L. (1984). *Beyond the commission reports: The coming crisis in teaching.* Santa Monica, CA: RAND Corporation.

Darling-Hammond, L. (1990). Teaching and knowledge: Policy issues posed by alternative certification for teachers. *Peabody Journal of Education, 67*(3), 123–154.

Darling-Hammond, L. (1997). *Doing what matters most: Investing in quality teaching.* New York: National Commission on Teaching.

Darling-Hammond, L. (2001). Standard-setting in teaching changes in licensing, certification, and assessment. In V. Richardson (Ed.), *Handbook of research on teaching* (4th ed.). Washington, DC: American Educational Research Association.

Darling-Hammond, L., & Barnett, B. (1988). *The evolution of teacher policy.* Santa Monica, CA: The RAND Corporation.

Darling-Hammond, L., Dilworth, M., & Bullmaster, M. (1996, January). *Educators of color.* Paper presented at the Conference of Recruiting, Preparing and Retaining Persons of Color in the Teaching Profession, Washington, DC.

Darling-Hammond, L., Wise, A., & Klein, S. (1995). *A license to teach: Building a profession for 21st century schools.* Boulder, CO: Westview Press.

Davidson, J. W., Moore, D. G., Sloboda, J. A., & Howe, M. J. (1998). Characteristics of music teachers and the progress of young instrumentalists. *Journal of Research in Music Education, 46*(1), 141–160.

Davies, A. (1995). Learning to live a competing story of teacher education. In D. J. Clandinin & F. M. Connelly (Eds.), *Teachers' professional knowledge landscapes.* New York: Teachers College Press.

DeCarion, D. (1998). *A narrative inquiry into home: A space called 'anywhere.'* Unpublished doctoral dissertation, University of Toronto, Toronto, Ontario, Canada.

DeLorenzo, L. C. (1992). The perceived problems of beginning music teachers. *Bulletin of the Council for Research in Music Education, 113,* 9–25.

DeNovellis, R., & Lawrence, G. (1983). Correlations of teacher personality variables (Myers-Briggs) and classroom observation data. *Research in Psychological Type, 6,* 37–46.

Denton, J. J., & Peters, W. H. (1988). *Program assessment report: Curriculum evaluation of a non-traditional program for certifying teachers.* College Station, TX: Texas A&M University.

DeRee, G., Reynolds, B., & Martin-Reynolds, J. (1986). Grade point average and high school background as correlates of teacher effectiveness in rural settings. *Journal of Rural and Small Schools, 1*(1), 15–16.

Dewey, J. (1938). *Experience and education.* New York: Collier Books.

Dickson, M. (1998). *Slipping the bonds: A narrative inquiry of elementary women educators in leadership roles.* Unpublished doctoral dissertation, University of Toronto, Toronto, Ontario, Canada.

Doane, C. P. (1981). The development and evaluation of a test to assess selected characteristics of prospective music educators. (Doctoral dissertation, Ohio State University, 1980). *Dissertation Abstracts International, 42*(10), 4346A.

Dobry, A. M., Murphy, P. D., & Schmidt, D. M. (1985). Predicting teacher competence. *Action in Teacher Education, 7*(1,2), 69–74.

Druva, C. A., & Anderson, R. D. (1983). Science teacher characteristics by teacher behavior and by student outcome: A meta-analysis of research. *Journal of Research in Science Teaching, 20*(5), 467–479.

Dworkin, A. G. (1987). *Teacher burnout in public schools.* Albany, NY: State University of New York Press.

Eisner, E. W. (1988). The primacy of experience and the politics of method. *Educational Researcher (June/July),* 15–20.

Elbaz, F. (1981). The teacher's 'practical knowledge': Report of a case study. *Curriculum Inquiry, 11*(1), 43–71.

Ellsworth, E. V. (1985). A descriptive analysis of the characteristics of effective high school orchestra directors including a study of selected rehearsal characteristics. (Doctoral dissertation, University of Wisconsin, 1984). *Dissertation Abstracts International, 47*(6), 2070A.

Erbes, R. L. (1982). Music teacher education: Toward the twenty-first century. In R. Colwell (Ed.), *Symposium in music education.* Urbana, IL: University of Illinois.

Erbes, R. L. (1983). *Certification practices and trends in music teacher education.* Reston, VA: MENC.

Erbes, R. (1985). The revolution in teacher certification. *Music Educators Journal, 71*(3), 34–39.

Erbes, R. (1986). *Certification practices and trends in music teacher education.* Reston, VA: MENC.

Erbes, R. (1987). A new era in teacher certification. *Music Educators Journal, 73*(6), 42–46.

Erbes, R. (1992). *Certification practices and trends in music teacher education.* Reston, VA: MENC.

Erekson, T. L., & Barr, L. (1985). Alternative credentialing: Lessons from vocational education. *Journal of Teacher Education, 36*(3), 16–19.

Ervin, M. T. (1949). How is your teaching personality? *Music Educators Journal, 36*(2), 18–19.

Evers, W., Gerrichhauzen, J., & Tomic, W. (2000). *The prevention and mending of burnout among secondary school teachers: A technical report.* (ERIC Document Reproduction Service No. ED 439091).

Evertson, C., Hawley, W., & Zlotnick, M. (1985). Making a difference in educational quality through teacher education. *Journal of Teacher Education, 36*(3), 2–12.

Fant, H. E., Hill, C., Lee, A. M., & Landes, R. (1985). Evaluating student teachers: The national scene. *The Teacher Educator, 21*(2), 2–8.

Farber, B. A. (1991). *Crisis in education: Stress and the American teacher.* San Francisco: Jossey-Bass.

Farmilo, N. R. (1981). The creativity, teaching style, and personality characteristics of the effective elementary music teacher (Doctoral dissertation, Wayne State University). *Dissertation Abstracts International, 42*(02), 591A.

Feistritzer, D. E. (1990). *Alternative teacher certification: A state-by-state analysis.* Washington, DC: National Center for Education Information.

Feistritzer, C. E. (1993). National overview of alternative teacher certification. *Education and Urban Society, 26*(1), 18–28.

Feistritzer, C. E. (1994). The evolution of alternative teacher certification. *Educational Forum, 58,* 132–138.

Feistritzer, C. E., & Chester, D. (2000). *Alternative teacher certification: A state-by-state analysis 2000.* Washington, DC: National Center for Education Information.

Fenstermacher, G. (1994). The knower and the known. The nature of knowledge in research in teaching. In L. Darling-Hammond (Ed.), *Review of Research in Education, 20,* 3–56.

Flaitz, J. (1987, November). *Non-academic indicators of teacher effectiveness—A review of the literature.* Paper presented at the Mid-South Educational Research Association, Mobile, AL.

Florida Department of Education. (1999, March). *Information on teacher supply and demand for use in determining 1999–2000 critical teacher shortage areas.*

Foster, E. (2000). *The urban teacher challenge.* Belmont, MA: Recruiting New Teachers, Inc.

Friedman, I. A. (1991). High- and low-burnout schools: School culture aspects of teacher burnout. *Journal of Educational Research, 84*(6), 325–33.

Frink, K. L. (1997). *Undergraduate string majors' attitudes toward high school orchestra experiences, high school orchestra instructors and string teaching.* Unpublished master's thesis, University of Colorado, Boulder.

Froehlich, H., & L'Roy, D. (1985). An investigation of occupancy identity in undergraduate music education majors. *Bulletin of the Council for Research in Music Education, 85,* 65–75.

Futrell, M. (1999). Recruiting minority teachers. *Educational Leadership, 56*(8), 30–33.

Futrell, M. (1999). *The essential profession: A national survey of public attitudes toward teaching, educational opportunity, and school reform.* Belmont, MA: Recruiting New Teachers, Inc.

Gallup, G. H. (1970). The second annual Gallup survey of the public's attitudes toward the public schools. *Phi Delta Kappan, 52*(2), 97–112.

Gallup, G. H. (1980). The twelfth annual Gallup poll of the public's attitudes toward the public schools. *Phi Delta Kappan, 62*(1), 33–46.

Gallup, A. M. (1984). The sixteenth annual Gallup poll of the public's attitudes toward the public schools. *Phi Delta Kappan, 66*(1), 23–38.

Gallup, A. M. (1985). The seventeenth annual Gallup poll of the public's attitudes toward the public schools. *Phi Delta Kappan, 67*(1), 35–47.

Gallup, A. M. (1986). The eighteenth annual Gallup poll of the public's attitudes toward the public schools. *Phi Delta Kappan, 68*(1), 43–59.

Gallup, A. M., & Elam, S. M. (1988). The twentieth annual Gallup poll of the public's attitudes toward the public schools. *Phi Delta Kappan, 70*(1), 33–46.

Gallup, A. M., & Elam, S. M. (1989). The twenty-first annual Gallup poll of the public's attitudes toward the public schools. *Phi Delta Kappan, 71*(1), 41–56.

Geertz, C. (1995). *After the fact: Two countries, four decades, one anthropologist.* Cambridge, MA: Harvard University Press.

Gillespie, R. A. (1997). String teacher training: Using history to guide the future. *American String Teacher, 47*(4), 62–66.

Gillespie, R., & Hamann, D. L. (1998). The status of orchestra programs in the public schools. *Journal of Research in Music Education, 46*(1), 75–86.

Gillespie, R., & Hamann, D. L. (1999). Career choice among string music education students in American colleges and universities. *Journal of Research in Music Education, 47*(3), 266–278.

Goleman, D. (1995). *Emotional intelligence.* New York: Bantam Books.

Gomez, D. L., & Grobe, R. (1990, April). *Three years of alternative certification in Dallas: Where are we?* Paper presented at the Annual Meeting of the American Educational Research Association, Boston, MA.

Goodlad, J. I. (1990). *Teachers for our nation's schools.* San Francisco: Jossey-Bass.

Goodstein, R. E. (1987). An investigation into leadership behaviors and descriptive characteristics of high school band directors in the United States. *Journal of Research in Music Education, 35,* 13–25.

Gordon, D. (1997). An investigation and analysis of environmental stress factors experienced by P–12 music teachers (Doctoral dissertation, University of Northern Iowa, 1996). *Dissertation Abstracts International, 58*(11), 4171A.

Gordon, H., & Yocke, R. (1999). Relationship between personality characteristics and observable teaching effectiveness of selected beginning career and technical education teachers. *Journal of Vocational and Technical Education, 16*(1), 47–66.

Gray, L., Cahalan, M., Hein, S., Litman, C., Severynse, J., Warren, S., Wisan, G., & Stowe, P. (1993). *New teachers in the job market: 1991 update.* Washington, DC: U.S. Department of Education, OERI.

Greenberg, J. D. (1983). The case for teacher education: Open and shut. *Journal of Teacher Education, 34*(4), 2–5.

Grissmer, D. W., & Kirby S. N. (1987). *Teaching attrition: The uphill climb to staff the nation's schools* (Report No. 0-8330-0869-2). Santa Monica, CA: The RAND Corporation. (ERIC Document Reproduction Service No. ED 291 735)

Grissmer, D. W., & Kirby S. N. (1997). Teacher turnover and teacher quality. *Teachers College Record, 99*(1), 45–55.

Grossman, P. L. (1989). Learning to teach without teacher education. *Teachers College Record, 91*(2), 191–208.

Guyton, E., & Farokhi, E. (1987). Relationships among academic performance, basic skills, subject matter knowledge and teaching skills of teacher education graduates. *Journal of Teacher Education, 38*(5), 37–42.

Haack, P., & Smith, M. V. (2000). Mentoring new music teachers. *Music Educators Journal, 87*(3), 23–27.

Haberman, M. (1984, September). *An evaluation of the rationale for required teacher education: Beginning teachers with or without teacher preparation.* Paper presented at the National Commission on Excellence in Teacher Education, University of Wisconsin-Milwaukee.

Hall, B. W., Villeme, M. G., & Phillippy, S. W. (1988). Predisposition for burnout among first-year teachers. *Teacher Educator, 24*(2), 13–21.

Hamann, D. L. (1995). Preservice teachers' teaching effectiveness and social skill development. *Southeastern Journal of Music Education, 7,* 1–12.

Hamann, D. L., & Daugherty, E. D. (1984). Teacher burnout: The cost of caring. *Update, 2*(3), 7–10.

Hamann, D. L., Daugherty, E. D., & Mills, C. R. (1987). An investigation of burnout assessment and potential job related variables among public school music educators. *Psychology of Music, 15*(2), 128–140.

Hamann, D. L., Daugherty, E. D., & Sherbon, J. (1988). Burnout and the college music professor: An investigation of possible indicators of burnout among college music faculty members. *Bulletin of the Council for Research in Music Education, 98,* 1–21.

Hamann, D. L., & Gordon, D. G. (2000). Burnout: An occupational hazard. *Music Educators Journal, 87*(3), 34–39.

Hamann, D. L., Lineburgh, N., & Paul, S. (1998). Teaching effectiveness and social skill development. *Journal of Research in Music Education, 46*(1), 87–101.

Hawk, P., Coble, C., & Swanson, M. (1985). Certification: It does matter. *Journal of Teacher Education, 36*(3), 13–15.

He, M. F. (1995). *A cross-cultural perspective on the impact of metaphors on teachers' thinking.* Paper presented at the meeting of the International Association of Teachers' Thinking, Ontario, Canada.

He, M. F. (1999). *Professional knowledge landscapes: Three Chinese women teachers' enculturation and acculturation processes in China and Canada.* Unpublished doctoral dissertation, University of Toronto, Toronto, Ontario, Canada.

Heller, H. W., & Clay, R. J. (1993). Predictors of teaching effectiveness: The efficacy of various standards to predict the success of graduates from a teacher education program. *ERS Spectrum, 11*(1), 7–11.

Hendrie, C. (1996). Enrollment crunch stretches the bounds of the possible. *Education Week, 16*(2), 1, 12–15.

Heston, M. L., Dedrick, C., Raschke, D., & Whitehead, J. (1996). Job satisfaction and stress among band directors. *Journal of Research in Music Education, 44*(4), 319–327.

Hice, J. (1970). The relationship between teacher characteristics and first-grade achievement. (Doctoral dissertation, University of Georgia, 1970). *Dissertation Abstracts International, 31*(08), 4036.

Hinckley, J. (2000). Why vision 2020? *Music Educators Journal, 86*(5), 21–24, 66.

Hodge, G., Jupp, J., & Taylor, A. (1994). Work stress, distress, and burnout in music and mathematics teachers. *British Journal of Educational Psychology, 64*(1), 65–76.

Hoffer, C. (1982). Work related attitudes and problems of Indiana music teachers. *Psychology of Music, 10* (Special Issue), 59–62.

Holmes Group. (1986). *Tomorrow's teachers: A report of the Holmes Group.* East Lansing, MI: Holmes Group.

Holt, P., Fine, M. J., & Tollefson, N. (1987). Mediating stress: Survival of the hardy. *Psychology in the schools, 24,* 51–58.

Hosler, A. M., & Schmid, J. (1985). Relating factor traits of elementary, secondary, and college teachers. *Journal of Experimental Education, 53*(4), 211–215.

Howey, K. R., & Zimpher, N. L. (1993). *Pattern in prospective teachers: Guides for designing preservice programs.* Columbus: Ohio State University.

Huber, J. (1999). *Negotiating the interface of embodied knowledge within the professional knowledge landscape.* Unpublished doctoral dissertation, University of Alberta, Edmonton, Alberta, Canada.

Huber, J., & Whelan, K. (1995). Knowledge communities in the classroom. In D. J. Clandinin & F. M. Connelly (Eds.), *Teachers' professional knowledge landscapes.* New York: Teachers College Press.

Jacobs, W. W. (1912). The monkey's paw. *The lady of the barge.* New York: Harper and Brothers.

Johnson, M. (1987). *The body in the mind: The bodily basis of meaning, imagination, and reason.* Chicago: University of Chicago Press.

Johnson, M. (1991). Embodied knowledge. *Curriculum Inquiry, 19*(4), 361–377.

Jones, M. O. (1964/1965). Factors influencing students in the choice of music as a career. (Doctoral dissertation, Florida State University). *Dissertation Abstracts International, 25,* 5152.

Kagan, D. (1992). Professional growth among preservice and beginning teachers. *Review of Educational Research, 62*(2), 129–169.

Kemp, A. (1982). Personality traits of successful student music teachers [Special Issue]. *Psychology of Music,* 72–75.

Kentucky Institute for Education Research. (1997). *The preparation of teachers for Kentucky Schools: A survey of new teachers.* Frankfort, KY: Author.

Kirkpatrick, D. (1992). *Rethinking teacher certification.* (ERIC Document Reproduction Service No. ED 399 254)

Klagholz, L. (2000). *Growing better teachers in the Garden State: New Jersey's "alternate route" to teacher certification.* (ERIC Document Reproduction Service No. ED 435 135)

Kroma, S. (1983). *Personal practical knowledge of language in teaching.* Unpublished doctoral dissertation, University of Toronto, Toronto, Ontario, Canada.

Krueger, R. J. (1976). An investigation of personality and music teaching success. *Bulletin of the Council for Research in Music Education, 47,* 16–25.

Kurtz, C., & Kremer, L. (1982). Personality characteristics and teaching behavior. *Education, 102*(4), 359–365.

Kvet, E. J., & Watkins, R. C. (1993). Success attributes in teaching music as perceived by elementary education majors. *Journal of Research in Music Education, 41*(1), 70–80.

Lane, B. (1988). *Landscapes of the sacred: Geography and narrative in American spirituality.* New York: Paulist Press.

Leslie, C., & Lewis, S. (1990, October 1). The failure of teacher education. *Newsweek,* 58–60.

L'Roy, D. (1983). The development of occupational identity in undergraduate music education majors (Doctoral dissertation, University of North Texas, 1983). *Dissertation Abstracts International, 44,* 2401A.

Lowman, J. (1996). Characteristics of exemplary teachers. *New Directions for Teaching and Learning, 65,* 33–40.

LuPone, L. (1961). A comparison of provisionally certified and permanently certified elementary school teachers in selected school districts in New York State. *Journal of Educational Research, 55,* 53–63.

Lutz, W. W. (1964). The personality characteristics and experiential background of successful high school instrumental music teachers. *Dissertation Abstracts International, 24*(09), 3781A (UMI No. 64-12920)

Ma, X. & MacMillan, R. (1999). Influences of workplace conditions on teachers' job satisfaction. *Journal of Educational Research, 93*(1), 39–47.

MacIntyre, A. (1984). *After virtue: A study in moral theory.* Notre Dame, IN: University of Notre Dame Press.

Madsen, C. K., Smith, D. S., & Feeman, C. (1988). The use of music in cross-age tutoring within special education settings. *Journal of Music Therapy, 25*(3), 135–144.

Malik, J. A. (1970). *Causes of withdrawal from public school music teaching of baccalaureate recipients from Colorado State College between 1960 and 1969.* Unpublished doctoral dissertation, University of Northern Colorado, Greeley.

Mamchur, C., & Nelson, D. (1984). *Predicting teacher effectiveness: A final report on a proper linear regression approach to selection for teacher education in British Columbia.* (Report No. 85:03). Vancouver, British Columbia: Educational Research Institute of British Columbia. (ERIC Document Reproduction Service No. Ed 261 092)

Mann, P. L. (1980). Personality and success characteristics of high school band directors in Mississippi (Doctoral dissertation, University of Southern Mississippi, 1979). *Dissertation Abstracts International, 40*(10), 5356A.

Mark, D. (1998). The music teacher's dilemma—Musician or teacher? *International Journal of Music Education, 32,* 3–23.

Marland, P. W. (1995). Implicit theories of teaching. In L. W. Anderson (Ed.), *International encyclopedia of teaching and teacher education* (2nd ed., pp. 131–136). Cambridge, UK: Pergamon.

Marso, R., & Pigge, F. (1997). Entering personal and academic characteristics of a longitudinal sample of persisting and nonpersisting teachers seven years after commencement of teacher preparation. *Journal of Experimental Education, 65*(3), 243–54.

Maxwell, E. B. (1970). Personal traits and professional competencies of band directors achieving success as measured by contest ratings. (Doctoral dissertation, Texas Tech University, 1970). *Dissertation Abstracts International, 31*(10), 5273A.

McDonald, F. J., & Eliam, P. (1980). *The problems of beginning teachers: A crisis in training.* Princeton, NJ: Educational Testing Service.

Miller, M., Brownell, M. T., & Smith, S. (1999). Factors that predict teachers staying in, leaving, or transferring from the special education classroom. *Exceptional Children, 65*(2), 201–218.

Moore, D. (1991). Correlations of National Teacher Examination core battery scores and college grade point average with teaching effectiveness of first-year teachers. *Educational and Psychological Measurement, 51*(4), 1023–1028.

Moracco, J. C., D'Arienzo, R. V., & Danford, D. (1983). Comparison of perceived occupational stress between teachers who are contented and discontented in their career choice. *The Vocational Guidance Quarterly, 38*(2), 44–51.

Murnane, R., & Vegas, E. (1997). The nation's teaching force. *Teachers College Record, 99*(1), 36–44.

Murray, F. (1986). Teacher education. *Change, 18*(6), 19–25.

Music Educators National Conference. (2000). *National survey of music educators in public secondary schools: Summary report.* Unpublished manuscript.

National Association of Schools of Music. (1990). *Data summaries: Higher education arts data services.* Reston, VA: Author.

National Association of Schools of Music. (1995). *Data summaries: Higher education arts data services.* Reston, VA: Author.

National Association of Schools of Music. (1999). *Data summaries: Higher education arts data services.* Reston, VA: Author.

National Association of State Directors of Special Education. (1990, May). Special education faces a mounting crisis: How to recruit, train, and hold on to qualified teachers and related services personnel. *Liaison Bulletin.* Washington DC: Author.

National Association of State Directors of Teacher Education and Certification. (2000). *The NASDTEC manual: Manual on preparation and certification of educational personnel.* Kendall-Hunt.

National Center for Education Statistics. (1991). *Careers in Teaching: Following members of the high school class of 1972 in and out of teaching.* Washington DC: U.S. Department of Education.

National Center for Education Statistics. (1992). *Public elementary and secondary schools and agencies in the United States and outlying areas: School year 1990–91.* Washington, DC: U.S. Department of Education.

National Center for Education Statistics. (1993). *America's teachers: Profile of a profession.* Washington, DC: U.S. Department of Education.

National Center for Education Statistics. (1997). *America's teachers: Profile of a profession.* Washington, DC: U.S. Department of Education.

National Center for Education Statistics. (2000). *Projections of education statistics to 2008.* Washington, DC: U.S. Department of Education.

National Commission on Teaching and America's Future. (1996). *What matters most: Teaching for America's future.* New York: National Commission on Teaching and America's Future, Teachers College.

National Education Association. (1962). *Music and art in the public schools.* West Haven, CT: Research Division.

National Education Association (1997). *Status of the American public school teacher, 1995–1996.* West Haven, CT: Research Division.

Nelson, B., & Wood, L. (1985). The competency dilemma. *Action in Teacher Education, 7*(1, 2), 45–57.

Odden, A. (1983). *Research findings on effective teaching and schools.* Denver, CO: Education Commission of the States.

O'Laughlin, J. (1999). Recruiting and hiring high-quality teachers. *ERS Spectrum, 17*(4), 31–39.

Olsen, D. (1985). The quality of prospective teachers: Education vs. noneducation graduates. *Journal of Teacher Education, 36*(5), 56–59.

Olson, M. R. (1993). *Conceptualizing narrative inquiry in (teacher) education.* Unpublished doctoral dissertation, University of Alberta, Edmonton, Alberta, Canada.

Olson, M. R. (1995). Conceptualizing narrative authority: Implications for teaching and teacher education. *Teaching and Teacher Education, 1*(2), 119–125.

Olson, M. R., & Craig, C. J. (2001). Opportunities and challenges in the development of teachers' knowledge: The development of narrative authority through knowledge communities. *Teaching and Teacher Education, 17*(6), 667–684.

Olstad, R. G. (1987). *Predictive validity of GPA, CAT, and NTE science specialty tests on scores of a performance based student teaching evaluation instrument.* (Research Report No. 871). Seattle: University of Washington, Teacher Education Research Center. (ERIC Document Reproduction Service No. ED 282 761).

Parker, L. J. (1993). The relationship between personality factors and job satisfaction in public school band directors. (Doctoral dissertation, University of Kansas, 1991). *Dissertation Abstracts International, 53*(11–A), 3838.

Pavalko, R. M. (1970). Recruitment to teaching: Patterns of selection and retention. *Sociology of Education, 43,* 340–355.

Pembrook, R., & Vasconcellos, H. (2001, January). *Traditional and alternative music certification practices in the United States.* Poster session presented at the annual meeting of the Missouri Music Educators Association, Osage Beach, MO.

Pembrook, R., & Fredrickson, W. (in press). "Prepared yet flexible:" Insights from daily logs of music teachers. *Bulletin of the Council for Research in Music Education.*

Pembrook, R., Fuelberth, R., & Harden, M. (in press). First impressions: Correlations between initial teaching demonstrations and selected factors. *Southeastern Journal of Music Education.*

Perie, M., & Baker, D. (1997). *Job satisfaction among America's teachers: Effects of workplace conditions, background characteristics, and teacher compensation: Statistical analysis report.* (ERIC Document Reproduction Service No. ED 412 181).

Perkes, V. (1967–1968). Junior high school science teacher preparation, teaching behavior, and student achievement. *Journal of Research in Science Teaching, 6*(4), 121–126.

Petersen, G. J., & Speaker, K. M. (1996). *An examination of admission criteria to programs of teacher education.* (ERIC Document Reproduction Service No. ED 401 278)

Phelps, T. K. (1983). A survey of factors affecting job satisfaction and dissatisfaction of music educators in high schools and junior high schools in Idaho. (Doctoral dissertation, University of Utah, 1982). *Dissertation Abstracts International, 43*(07), 2271A.

Phillion, J. (1999). *Narrative inquiry in a multicultural landscape: Multicultural teaching and learning.* Unpublished doctoral dissertation, University of Toronto, Toronto, Ontario, Canada.

Ploumis-Devick, E. (1983). Career development patterns of male and female music education majors at the Florida State University. (Doctoral dissertation, Florida State University, 1983). *Dissertation Abstracts International, 44,* 2080A.

Ponce, F. K., (1995). Job satisfaction among high school choral music teachers in the state of Ohio. (Doctoral dissertation, Ohio State University, 1994). *Dissertation Abstracts International, 55*(07A), 1864A.

Pratt, D. (1986). Predicting career success in teaching. *Action in Teacher Education, 8*(4), 25–34.

Pugach, M. C., & Raths, J. D. (1983). Testing teachers: Analysis and recommendations. *Journal of Teacher Education, 34*(1), 37–43.

Qualls, B. A. (1987). A study of the factors influencing job satisfaction among Texas high school band directors. (Doctoral dissertation, University of North Texas, 1986). *Dissertation Abstracts International, 47*(11), 4048A.

Quirk, T. J., Witten, B. J., & Weinberg, S. (1973). Review of studies of the concurrent and predictive validity of the National Teacher Examinations. *Review of Educational Research, 43*(1), 89–114.

Riggio, R. E. (1986). Assessment of basic social skills. *Journal of Personality and Social Psychology, 51,* 649–660.

Riggs, I., & Riggs, M. (1991). Predictors of student success in a teacher education program: What is valid, what is not. *Action in Teacher Education, 12*(4), 41–46.

Riley, R. (1996). *A back to school special report: The baby boom echo.* Washington, DC: U.S. Department of Education.

Rose, C. P. (1997). *Stories of teacher practice: Exploring the professional knowledge landscape.* Unpublished doctoral dissertation, University of Alberta, Edmonton, Alberta, Canada.

Rose, L. C., & Gallup, A. M. (2000). The thirty-second annual Phi Delta Kappa/Gallup poll of the public's attitudes toward the public schools. *Phi Delta Kappan, 82*(1), 41–66.

Rosenholtz, S. J. (1989). *Teacher's workplace: The social organization of schools.* New York: Longman.

Rosenman, R. H., & Friedman, M. (1983). Relationship of Type A behavior pattern to coronary heart disease. In H. Selye (Ed.), *Selye's guide to stress research.* New York: Scientific and Academic Editions.

Samson, F. (1999). A first year vice-principal's position on the landscape: In and out-of-classroom splits. In F. M. Connelly & D. J. Clandinin (Eds.), *Shaping a professional identity: Stories of educational practice* (pp. 135–140). New York: Teachers College Press.

Sandene, B. (1995). Determinants and implications of stress,

burnout, and job dissatisfaction among music teachers. *Update, 13,* 25–31.

Schalock, J. D. (1988). Teacher selection: A problem of admission criteria, certification criteria, or prediction of job performance? In W. J. Gephart & J. Ayers (Eds.), *Teacher education evaluation* (pp. 1–22). Boston: Kluwer Academic Publishers.

Schechtman, Z. (1989). The contribution of interpersonal behavior evaluation to the prediction of initial teaching success: A research note. *Teaching and Teacher Education, 5*(3), 243–248.

Schlechty, P. C., & Vance, V. S. (1983). Recruitment, selection and retention: The shape of the teaching force. *Elementary School Journal, 83*(4), 469–487.

Schmidt, C. P. (1989). Applied music teacher behavior as a function of selected personality variables. *Journal of Research in Music Education, 37,* 258–271.

Schmidt, C. P., & Hicken, L. (1986). An investigation of selected variables as predictors of achievement in music student teaching. *Contributions to Music Education, 13,* 39–47.

Scholastic Inc./CCSO Teachers' Voice 2000 Survey. (2000). Scholastic and the Council of Chief State School Officers.

Schön, D. A. (1983). *The reflective practitioner: How professionals think in action.* New York: Basic Books.

Schön, D. A. (1987). *Educating the reflective practitioner.* San Francisco: Jossey Bass.

Schön, D. A. (1991). *The reflective turn: Case studies in and on educational practice.* New York: Teachers College Press.

Schwab, J. (1971). The practical: Arts of eclectic. *School Review, 81,* 469–489.

Sedlak, M., & Schlossman, S. (1986, November). *Who will teach? Historical perspectives on the changing appeal of teaching as a profession.* Santa Monica, CA: The RAND Corporation.

Shellahamer, B. R. (1984). Selection and retention criteria in undergraduate music teacher education programs: Survey, analysis, and implications. (Doctoral dissertation, Ohio State University, 1983). *Dissertation Abstracts International, 45*(06), 1679A.

Shen, J. (1999). Alternative certification: Math and science teachers. *Educational Horizons, 78*(1), 44–48.

Shim, C. P. (1965). A study of the cumulative effect of four teacher characteristics on the achievement of elementary school pupils. *Journal of Educational Research, 59*(1), 33–34.

Shin, H. S. (1994, April). *Estimating future teacher supply: An application of survival analysis.* Paper presented at the annual meeting of the American Educational Research Association, New Orleans, LA.

Shulman, L. (1986a). Those who understand: Knowledge growth in teaching. *Educational Researcher, 15*(2), 4–14.

Shulman, L. (1986b). Paradigms and research programs for the study of teaching. In M. C. Wittrock (Ed.), *Handbook of research on teaching* (3rd ed.). New York: Macmillan.

Singer, J. D. (1993). Once is not enough: Former special educators who return to teaching. *Exceptional Children, 60,* 58–72.

Slack, J. (1977). Values and personalities of selected high

school choral music educators. *Journal of Research in Music Education, 25,* 243–255.

Soltis, J. F. (1995). Foreword. In D. J. Clandinin & F. M. Connelly (Eds.), *Teachers' professional knowledge landscapes.* New York: Teachers College Press.

Statistical Abstract of the United States: 119th Edition. (1999). Washington DC: Treasury Department, Bureau of Statistics.

Stedman, C. H. (1984). Testing for competency: A pyrrhic victory? *Journal of Teacher Education, 35*(2), 2–5.

Stevenson, S. (1989). *Learning to live new rhythms of teaching.* Unpublished master's project, University of Calgary, Calgary, Alberta, Canada.

Stubblefield, P. (1984). The relationship between stress, job satisfaction, and teaching assignments among music educators in the state of Michigan (Doctoral dissertation, Michigan State University, 1983). *Dissertation Abstracts International, 45*(03), 0782A.

Teacher education policy in the states: A 50-state survey of legislative and administrative actions (1997). (ERIC Document Reproduction Service No. ED 410 224)

Teachout, D. (1997). The relationship between personality and the teaching effectiveness of music student teachers (Doctoral dissertation, Kent State University, Kent, OH, 1996). *Dissertation Abstracts International, 58*(07), 2581A.

Todd, M., & Roberts, D. (1981). A comparative study of Jungian psychological traits of art and music education majors. *Research in Psychological Type, 3,* 73–77.

United States Department of Education. (1996). *Eighteenth annual report to congress on the implementation of the individuals with disabilities education act.* Washington, DC: U. S. Government Printing Office.

United States Department of Education. (June, 2000). Statistics division.

Villeme, M. G., & Hall, B. W. (1983–1984). Higher ability education graduates: Do they enter and stay in teaching? *The Teacher Educator, 19*(3), 11–15.

Westerman, J. E. (1989). Minimum state teacher certification standards and their relationship to effective teaching: Im-

plications for teacher education. *Action in Teacher Education, 11*(2), 25–32.

Whelan, K. (1999). *Toward places of community: Border crossing of possibility on the professional knowledge landscape.* Unpublished doctoral dissertation, University of Alberta, Edmonton, Alberta, Canada.

White, K. A. (1996). Crowded, dilapidated schools lack welcome mat for students. *Education Week, 16*(5), 1, 12–13.

Wilcox, E. (2000). Recruiting for the profession. *Teaching Music, 8*(2), 25–31.

Wilder, J. F. & Plutchik, R. (1982). Preparing the professional: Building prevention into training. In W. S. Pain (Ed.), *Job stress and burnout: Research theory and intervention perspectives* (pp. 113–132). Beverly Hills, CA: Sage Publications.

Williford, L. E. (1993). *Perceived impact of state rules and regulations on teacher education programs.* (ERIC Document Reproduction Service No. ED 372 067)

Wing, L. (1993). Music teacher education: Coming to our senses. *Bulletin of the Council for Research in Music Education, 117,* 51–65.

Wink, R. L. (1970). The relationship of self-concept and selected personality variables to achievement in music student teaching. *Journal of Research in Music Education, 18*(3), 234–241.

Winslow, R. W. (1949, November–December). Recruiting music teachers is the job of all. *Music Educators Journal, 36,* 13, 43–45.

Wolfgang, R. (1990). Early field experience in music education: A study of teacher role socialization (Doctoral dissertation, University of Oregon, Eugene, 1990). *Dissertation Abstracts International, 52*(01), 0137A.

Wubbenhorst, T. M. (1991). Music educators' personality types as measured by the Myers-Briggs Type Indicator. *Contributions to Music Education, 18,* 7–19.

Wubbenhorst, T. M. (1994). Personality characteristics of music educators and performers. *Psychology of Music, 22*(1), 63–74.

Young, M. (1990). Characteristics of high potential and at risk teachers. *Action in Teacher Education, 11*(4), 33–40.

42

Changing Concepts of Teacher Education

GLENN E. NIERMAN

KEN ZEICHNER

NIKOLA HOBBEL

This chapter will discuss preservice teacher education in the United States today, both from a general perspective and in relationship to the particular situation of music education. Following a discussion of the nature of students, faculty, and programs in U.S. preservice programs, we will examine a few issues that are currently of major concern in debates and discussions about teacher education reform. Finally, we will examine the nature of teacher education programs in music education, and several current problems in the practice of music education in today's standards-based reform environment.

Preservice Teacher Education in the United States: Participants and Programs

Over 1,300 colleges and universities in the United States offer teacher education programs. Additionally, many alternative programs sponsored by others (e.g., school districts, state education departments, and private providers) have been created in the last 2 decades in response to shortages of teachers in particular subject areas and locations. This section will provide a description of the students, faculty, and the variety of programs in the general teacher education landscape. Later in the chapter, the specific nature of teacher education programs in music education will be discussed.

Teacher Education Students and Faculty

The demographic profile of those who go into teaching is in sharp contrast to the increasingly diverse student pop-

ulation in the public schools. Teaching continues to be a largely white and female profession. Approximately 81% of prospective teachers are women (Darling-Hammond & Sclan, 1996) and all but about 15% of these are white (American Association of Colleges for Teacher Education [AACTE], 1999). Most prospective teachers are also monolingual English speaking and have very little direct experience other than through the media with those who have ethnic, racial, social class, and linguistic backgrounds different from their own (Zimpher, 1989). The implications of this cultural encapsulation of most preservice teachers will be discussed later in this chapter. Alternative routes to teaching tend to attract more males and teachers of color than do traditional college and university-based programs (Stoddart & Floden, 1996), but generally the percentage of students of color in teacher education programs has been declining for a variety of reasons, including increased opportunities for higher paying jobs in other fields and the increased focus on teacher testing that has had discriminatory effects on minorities (Gitomer & Latham, 1999).

Despite perceptions from the outside that teacher education students are academically less capable than those with other majors, recent studies show that this perception is an oversimplification of a much more complex reality. Following the external criticisms of standards in teacher education programs in the 1970s and 1980s, most institutions have required higher grade point averages and test scores for admission to their teacher education programs (Darling-Hammond & Berry, 1988; SRI International, 1999). As a result, the academic qualifications of prospective teachers are now as strong as or stronger than those of the average college graduate (Darling-Hammond & Sclan, 1996). For example, a recent survey of adult literacy compared the literacy level of teachers with others and shows that, on average, teachers perform as well as other college-educated adults on all dimensions of literacy tested (Bruschi & Coley, 1999). Also, in contrast to previous claims that teachers lack the academic ability of other college-educated professionals, the data in a recent Educational Testing Service study of SAT and ACT scores suggest that teachers in academic subject areas have academic skills that are equal to or higher than those of the average college graduate (Gitomer & Latham, 1999). However, in this same study, elementary education majors who passed the ETS Praxis II content examinations had lower ACT and SAT scores than those for all college graduates. In reality, the academic competence of elementary education majors varies by institution. In some programs, elementary education students complete a major in an academic discipline and, even when they do not, they sometimes perform as well or better than noneducation majors in arts and sciences courses. On some campuses, limited enrollment teacher education programs are among the most difficult programs to enter, and in postbaccalaureate programs, more stringent graduate school criteria affect the admissions process (e.g., Andrew, 1983; Olsen, 1985).

Zimpher and Sherrill (1996), drawing on a series of studies of teacher education in the United States conducted by the American Association of Colleges for Teacher Education (AACTE) from 1987 to 1995, provide a demographic picture of school, department, and college of education faculty who work in teacher education programs. As is the case for prospective teachers, most education school faculty are Anglos, although there is some variation depending on program location. In all of the AACTE demographic studies, the percentage of Anglo faculty ranged from 91 to 93%, results that are consistent with the findings in Goodlad's (1990) national study of teacher education programs. There are some exceptions to this general picture. For example, a 15% minority population was found among urban teacher educators in one of the AACTE studies (AACTE, 1994). Despite the overall scarcity of minorities among faculty in education units, the racial and ethnic diversity in these units is somewhat higher than that in other areas such as the arts and sciences, fine arts, engineering, and so on (AACTE, 1993).

The cultural insularity of the education professoriate presents a serious obstacle to the goal of preparing teachers who are able to be successful with the full range of pupils who attend U.S. public schools. Although contrary to outside perceptions, over 80% of education faculty have had an average of 10 years of teaching experience in elementary and secondary schools (Zimpher & Sherrill, 1996), but they have not had this experience in settings similar to those where new teachers are desperately needed: urban and rural districts serving students of color and others living in poverty. The lack of ethnic/racial diversity and cross-cultural teaching experience among teacher education faculty in both education and arts and science units suggests that teacher education programs need to employ clinical and adjunct faculty and even community members without professional certification, who have the relevant cultural and teaching knowledge needed by prospective teachers. Research clearly shows the effectiveness of employing teacher educators who have been successful teachers in the settings for which students are being prepared, and of utilizing community members as instructors (Zeichner & Hoeft, 1996).

Program Models

Despite the existence of multiple entry routes into teaching and an increase in requirements from state education departments, the 4-year undergraduate program continues to be the most popular way in which teachers enter the profession. The 5-year integrated program model is the second most used pathway into teaching and has grown in recent years as a result of teacher educators having to fit many new professional education requirements into their programs (Scannell, 1999). Typically, students in these two types of programs receive a degree in education, with some completing joint majors in education and a subject discipline. The courses that prospective teachers take in these programs usually include a general education component, a major or minor in an academic content area, social and psychological foundations of education, methods courses in the teaching of particular subjects or generic methods courses, and a variety of supervised field experiences culminating in a full-time student teaching experience or internship (Goodlad, 1990). These components will be discussed in more detail in relation to music education later in this chapter.

Another model is the 5th-year add-on certification program in which students usually complete 1, but sometimes 2, years of professional education course work and supervised field experiences in addition to an undergraduate degree in a discipline. Some of these graduate programs offer a master's degree on completion. Although most teacher education students continue to be young high school graduates who attend college full time, approximately one third of those who enter teacher education programs do so after having received a bachelor's degree, and about two thirds of the institutions that offer teacher education programs offer at least one program at the postbaccalaureate level (Feistritzer, 1999). Finally, a growing number of alternative routes into teaching of varying lengths and content are often aimed at specific populations such as paraprofessionals, career changers, former Peace Corps volunteers, and retired military personnel (Feistritzer, 1994).

Although some claims have been made about the superiority of particular structural models of teacher education such as the 5-year extended program (e.g., National Commission on Teaching and America's Future [NCTAF], 1996), the empirical evidence about the effects of different models is scarce. For example, many of the claims about the value of the 5-year extended program are based on the studies of the 5-year program at the University of New Hampshire (e.g., Andrew, 1983) and cannot necessarily be generalized to other areas of the country. Even in programs that are structured as 5-year programs, many of the students transfer in after 2 years or, in areas of teacher shortage, leave to begin teaching before program completion. In the end, it is sometimes the case in areas of high community college attendance or teacher shortage that a very low percentage of students actually completes all 5 years of a 5-year teacher education program in a single institution (Liston & Zeichner, 1991).

The research on graduate teacher education programs shows mixed results as to the efficacy of postbaccalaureate preparation models. Here, as in the case of alternative certification models generally, the research that has evaluated particular models in comparison with other models is too flawed to enable any firm conclusions (Hawley, 1990). For example, many of the studies that evaluated the effectiveness of graduate teacher education programs did not take into account the particular characteristics of the programs and lumped together programs with very different characteristics. They also did not distinguish the particular contexts in which graduates of the different kinds of programs taught. For example, although Master of Arts in Teaching (MAT) programs drew many academically talented individuals into teaching who would not have entered teaching through a traditional program (Coley & Thorpe, 1985), very few of these teachers taught in low-income schools in urban or rural areas where they were most needed (Zeichner, 1989). Because of the weaknesses in the design of program evaluations, recommendations about the superiority of particular program models are on very shaky ground empirically.

In part, as a result of increased requirements by state education departments and the voluntary national accrediting body, National Council for Accreditation of Teacher Education (NCATE), for programs to articulate a coherent conceptual framework, a number of specific conceptual models for teacher education programs have emerged. These models have existed throughout the 20th century (Liston & Zeichner, 1991), but it is only recently that they have been explicitly articulated by teacher educators. There are a number of different views of the variety of conceptual orientations to teacher education (e.g., Feiman-Nemser,

1990). One of us has made sense of different conceptual approaches to educating teachers in terms of different traditions of practice in teacher education programs (Zeichner, 1993).

Four traditions have influenced the curriculum of U.S. teacher education programs over the last 100 years and are present in different ways in all preservice programs. They are: an academic tradition that emphasizes the subject matter preparation of teachers; a developmentalist tradition that stresses the study of one's pupils as a basis for classroom action; a social efficiency tradition that focuses on the mastery of teaching skills and standards based on educational research; and a social reconstructionist tradition that seeks to prepare teachers who consciously address the social and political implications of their teaching and teaching contexts and actively work to build a more just and humane society. Studies of teacher education programs in a variety of institutions have indicated that individual programs always embrace multiple commitments and, within this multiplicity, they develop certain priorities and unique identities. Even programs that have clear ties to particular teacher education traditions such as UCLA's Center X (social reconstructionist) and UC-Berkeley's Developmental Teacher Education Program (developmentalist) address all of the traditions in their curricula. The particular ways in which programs define the traditions and emphasize them give preservice teacher education programs their unique conceptual identities.

Over the last decade, most teacher education programs have embraced the notion of teachers as reflective practitioners and have developed program identities with a focus on preparing reflective teachers (e.g., Valli, 1993). This movement in teaching and teacher education that has developed under the banner of reflection can be seen as a reaction to the view of teachers as technicians who narrowly construe the nature of the problems confronting them and merely carry out what others, who are removed from the classroom, want them to do. Underlying the apparent similarity among those who have embraced the concept of reflective teaching are vast differences in views of schooling, teaching, learning, and the social order. In fact, it has come to the point now where the whole range of beliefs about these things has been incorporated into the discourse about reflective teaching and the term of reflection, without further elaboration, has lost its meaning (Zeichner & Liston, 1996). Teacher education programs using reflection as a descriptor for their conceptual approach often emphasize very different things in practice, some of which are purely technical and instrumental and contrary to the lofty rhetoric that is associated with these programs in the abstract (Calderhead, 1989). The label of reflective teacher education is thus inadequate by itself as a descriptor for an approach to teacher education.

Current Developments in U.S. Teacher Education

This section will discuss a few of the major issues that currently dominate the field of teacher education in the United States at the beginning of the 21st century. These are: the struggle between those who seek to upgrade the professional status of teaching through a standards-based reform and those who seek to deregulate teacher education; the attempt to have teacher education viewed as a college- or university-wide responsibility rather than as a task of only an education unit; the development of new partnership arrangements between schools, colleges, and departments of education and schools for the initial and continuing preparation of teachers; and the increased effort to prepare teachers for cultural diversity.

The Struggle Between Advocates of Professionalization and Deregulation

As we write this chapter, teacher education is at the center of a national debate on educational quality. Two conflicting views of the desirable future for teacher education are framing much of what is happening in the United States. On the one hand, advocates of the professionalization agenda, building on the recommendations of the 1996 report of the National Commission on Teaching and America's Future (NCTAF) (Darling-Hammond, 1997), are calling for an end to emergency teaching licenses, higher standards for entry to and exit from teacher education programs including performance-based assessments, external examinations of teacher content knowledge, mandatory national program accreditation, professional development schools, national board certification for teachers, and autonomous professional standards boards in each state. On the other hand, advocates of deregulating teacher education such as those associated with the Fordham Foundation (e.g., Ballou & Podgursky, 1999; Kanstoroom & Finn, 1999) have proposed greater ease of entry into teaching through alternative routes, a greater emphasis on school-based experiences and content knowledge and teacher testing, and less emphasis on methods and educational foundations courses in preservice teacher education, as well as an end to what they see as a higher education monopoly on the preparation of teachers.

As a result of these debates, two kinds of reforms are occurring simultaneously in U.S. preservice teacher education. First, on the professionalization side, and as a result of either state education department mandates or of the new performance-based voluntary national accreditation mechanism (NCATE, 2000), most teacher education programs are being transformed into a performance-based mode with explicit sets of teaching and content standards that graduates are required to meet prior to receiving an initial teaching license. These standards are usually assessed by examining evidence accumulated in teaching portfolios and often are supplemented by external examinations of teachers' content knowledge administered by the states (Darling-Hammond & Snyder, 2000; Zeichner & Wray, 2001). Over the last decade, most teacher education institutions in response to external critics of teacher quality have made it more difficult to enter and complete a teacher education program by raising academic and nonacademic entrance and exit criteria, and have increased the amount of field experience in programs.

Second, to meet severe shortages of teachers in certain fields such as special education and in certain geographical areas such as most high-poverty rural and large urban districts, new alternative routes to teaching have been opened in most states that enable individuals to enter teaching with varying amounts of preparation in educational methods and foundations apart from a supervised intership experience. In some situations in which the shortages are the greatest, such as in California, preservice preparation through an alternative program sometimes takes place while teachers are already in the classroom full time. Alternative routes vary greatly in the amount of professional education coursework that they include and in the amount of involvement with a college or university. Some of these programs are run by school districts, others by states, some by private providers, and still others by universities in collaboration with school districts (Dill, 1996). Although claims have been made about the benefits or lack of effectiveness of alternative routes to prepare teachers for underserved areas (e.g., California Commission on Teacher Credentialing, 1996; Darling-Hammond, 1994; Shen, 1998; Stoddart & Floden, 1996), these programs are so varied in their structure and curricula that it is not very useful to attempt to draw conclusions about this general category of programs apart from attention to their particular characteristics (e.g., amount of content and professional preparation, ways of mentoring candidates, etc.).

The most recent entries into the alternative teacher education field are for-profit providers such as Edison, Sylvan Learning, and the University of Phoenix (Morey, 1999), and distance teacher education programs such as CAL STATE TEACH in California that enable candidates to complete a substantial amount of their initial education for teaching, other than a supervised internship, at home on their computers (e.g., Nielson, 1997). It is very clear from all of this activity that, despite the fact that colleges and universities continue to prepare the majority of new teachers in traditional preservice programs, they no longer have a monopoly. The number of teachers being prepared in alternative certification programs continues to rise each year, and most large urban school districts have come to rely increasingly on teachers prepared through alternative programs.

Teacher Education as an Institutional Responsibility

Despite the location of some teacher education programs in arts and science units of colleges and universities and the existence of some programs that are run jointly by education and arts and science units, most teacher education programs in the United States have been housed in schools, colleges, and departments of education with little involvement in programmatic issues of other faculty outside of these units. The isolation of teacher education from the mainstream of university life has been associated with low status and a less than fair share of institutional resources in comparison with other high-status programs that are seen to contribute more to departmental and institutional prestige (Monk & Brent, 1996).

Over the last decade, a variety of efforts have been underway to encourage stronger connections between education and arts and science faculty with regard to the preparation of teachers. One of the best known of these is the Project 30 Alliance (Murray & Fallon, 1989). This program has stimulated collaborative initiatives in teacher education between education and arts and sciences faculty in a variety of institutions related to five themes: subject matter understanding; general and liberal education; pedagogical content knowledge; international, cultural, and other human perspectives; and increasing the representation of underrepresented groups in teaching. The National Science Foundation has also funded the Collaboratives for Excellence in Teacher Education program for a number of years, which has supported the joint development of new courses for the preparation of mathematics and science teachers by education and arts and science faculty (National Science Foundation [NSF], 1997). Another example, along these lines, is the Council of Basic Education and AACTE's Standards-based Teacher Education Project (STEP), which focuses on aligning entrance and exit criteria, content and pedagogical preparation, and candidate assessment in selected teacher education programs in Georgia, Maryland, Kentucky, and Indiana with these states' P–12 content and performance standards (AACTE, 2000).

Recently, three major higher education organizations (The Association of American Universities, The American Council on Education, and the American Association of State Colleges and Universities) have issued reports on teacher education directed at institutional presidents, chancellors, and provosts, that emphasize the importance of placing teacher education at the center of the institutional agendas of colleges and universities (Association of American Universities [AAU], 1999; American Council on Education [ACE], 1999; American Association of State Colleges and Universities [AASCU] 1999). These reports argue, in part on the basis of research (Scannell, 1999), that one of the characteristics of successful teacher education programs is that arts and sciences and education faculty have found effective ways to work together. They also argue that more attention needs to be paid to the important contribution to the education of teachers that is made by subject matter faculty in the arts and sciences. Research has convincingly shown that prospective teachers, including those who complete full academic majors, frequently do not understand academic content well enough to explain things clearly to their pupils (McDiarmid, 1994). These reports call for a greater value to be placed on good work in teacher education in the faculty reward systems of colleges and universities.

New School and University Partnerships

Traditionally, the main role that P–12 teachers and administrators have played in preservice teacher education is to provide placement sites for student teachers during the one or more supervised clinical experiences that are completed as part of preparation for initial certification. School-based teacher educators have typically had little or no role in program development and instruction. Recently, in response to continuing dissatisfaction with traditional models, most teacher education programs throughout the United States have attempted to develop new and more productive ways to relate to their school partners in the education of new teachers and in the continuing professional development of teachers. The professional development school (PDS) is currently the most popular of these new forms of school-university partnerships in teacher education. The PDS model was stimulated in the 1980s by the Holmes Group, a consortium of research universities involved in teacher education reform (Holmes Group, 1990), and by the efforts of Goodlad and his National Network for Educational Renewal (Sirotnik & Goodlad, 1988). Professional development schools or professional practice schools as they are sometimes called, focus on four areas: support of student learning; the education of new teachers; the continuing professional development of school and university faculty; and research and development directed at the improvement of teaching and learning (Whitford & Metcalf-Turner, 1999).

In terms of preservice teacher education, these partnerships have attempted to address some of the enduring problems of clinical teacher education that have interfered with teacher learning during practicums, student teaching, and internships. These problems include the lack of a planned and purposeful curriculum for clinical experiences, poor articulation between campus and field program components, and wide variation in the quality of teacher mentoring and supervision (Zeichner, 1992). Although there is much variation in how these partnerships have developed across the country (e.g., Levine & Trachtman, 1996), professional development schools generally have involved a number of common elements, such as more time spent in schools for clinical experiences, greater access to university supervisors and to the knowledge of practicing teachers, greater preparation in mentoring for cooperating teachers, and a greater role for P–12 teachers in program development, evaluation, and instruction.

Although professional development schools have in some cases resulted in a number of improvements in clinical teacher education, they also have been criticized for their lack of attention to issues of equity and diversity (Valli, Cooper, & Frankes, 1997), and for their failure to include communities as members of their partnerships (Murrell, 1998). These partnerships also have failed to alter the low status of clinical teacher education in colleges and universities and have not been able to generate much hard money support from their institutional partners (Howey, Arenos, Galluzzo, Yarger, & Zimpher, 1995). Consequently, professional development schools have remained marginal entities in both higher education and the schools.

Preparing Teachers for Cultural Diversity

Almost every publication on the state of teacher education in the United States today includes a discussion of the growing disparity between the candidates who are seeking an initial teaching license and the pupils who populate our public schools. The increasing diversity and economic poverty of public school pupils in the United States are very clear. Today, one out of every three pupils enrolled in our public elementary and secondary schools is a racial or ethnic minority, and, by the year 2035, this group is expected to become a numerical majority of P–12 public school students in the United States. More than one in seven of children between the ages of 5 and 17 speaks a language other than English at home and over one third of these homes are of limited English proficiency. More than one in five children under 18 lives in poverty and in many urban and rural districts most of the pupils served live in families with incomes below the poverty level (e.g., Dilworth, 1992; Villegas & Lucas, in press; Zeichner & Hoeft, 1996). Additionally, despite some progress in selected areas, there continues to be an achievement gap between the poor students of color in public schools and middle-class students (Villegas & Lucas, in press). The failure of American public

schools to enable all children to receive a high-quality education regardless of their race, ethnic background, and social class background represents a major crisis in our society.

Recent analyses of research on the preparation of teachers for cultural diversity (e.g., Grant & Secada, 1990; Irvine, 1992; Ladson-Billings, 1995; Villegas & Lucas, in press; Zeichner & Hoeft, 1996) have reached several conclusions about what needs to be done to prepare all teachers to work successfully with today's economically, racially, and linguistically diverse pupil population. First, there is a growing consensus that the currently dominant method of admitting students to teacher education programs based only on academic criteria (e.g., grades and test scores) needs to change. Research has shown that many teacher education students come to their preparation programs viewing student diversity as a problem rather than as a resource, that their conceptions of diversity are highly individualistic (e.g., focusing on personality factors and ignoring contextual factors such as ethnicity), and that their ability to talk about student differences is very limited. These students generally have very little knowledge about the history and contributions of the different cultural groups in the United States, and they often have negative attitudes about cultural groups other than their own. They also frequently express discomfort about interacting with adults from backgrounds different than their own (Zeichner & Hoeft, 1996; Zimpher & Ashburn, 1992).

It is becoming increasingly clear that the selection process for teacher education programs needs to screen candidates for their commitment and potential ability to work with the economically and culturally diverse students who are in the public schools. New screening devices like the urban teacher interview (Haberman, 1993) are being utilized in many places to assess candidates' cultural competence in addition to their academic competence. A number of teacher education programs across the country, both traditional and alternative, deliberately seek to attract candidates who have potential to work with a diverse pupil population and emphasize the development of intercultural teaching competence and the ability to enact culturally responsive teaching (e.g., Oakes, 1996; Zeichner, 1998). Other programs have emphasized the recruitment of more diverse candidates into teaching and have demonstrated success under certain conditions in attracting, preparing, and retaining more teachers of color (Villegas & Clewell, 1998).

In addition to the issue of admission into teacher education programs, we now have a greater understanding of the kind of instructional experiences within programs that foster the intercultural teaching competence of novice teachers. These strategies involve increasing both self-knowledge and knowledge about others, the development of high expectations for the learning of all students, and the development of skills and dispositions to learn about the families and communities of their pupils, and to teach in a way that builds on the cultural resources that pupils bring to school (e.g., Delpit, 1995; Ladson-Billings, 1990; Villegas, 1991).

There is a consensus in the literature that the development of one's own cultural identity is a necessary precursor to cross-cultural understanding (Banks, 1991). The use of life history, narrative, and immersion experiences has been shown, under particular conditions, to be effective in helping prospective teachers reexamine their worldviews and to develop greater cultural sensitivity (e.g., Cochran-Smith, 1995; Gomez & Tabachnick, 1991; Zeichner & Melnick, 1996). A next step, according to many scholars, is to help prospective teachers learn more about cultural perspectives different than their own, and about how culture and language influence the learning process (Cazden & Mehan, 1990). Here, teacher educators have done a variety of things, including exposing prospective teachers to course content on perspectives and ethnic groups that have not been made available to them in their prior education, using case studies that portray the complexities of teaching in diverse schools and communities (e.g., Kleinfeld, 1998), and providing carefully structured and supported cultural immersion experiences in which teachers learn firsthand from community members about the cultural resources and traditions in the communities in which pupils live (e.g., Stachowski & Mahan, 1998).

Simply having more knowledge about the cultures and communities of pupils is inadequate. Teachers need to learn how to translate this knowledge into culturally responsive teaching practices in the classroom. For example, because teaching builds upon and modifies pupils' prior knowledge, culturally responsive teachers select and use instructional materials that are relevant to pupils' experiences outside of school (Ladson-Billings, 1994), design instructional activities that engage students in personally and culturally appropriate ways (Irvine, 1992), make use of pertinent examples or analogies drawn from pupils' daily lives to introduce or clarify new concepts (Villegas, 1991), organize instruction to build on rules of discourse from the home and community cultures (Garcia, 1993), manage the classroom in a way that takes into consideration different interaction styles (Tikunoff, 1985), and use a variety of evaluation strategies that maximize students' opportunities to display what they actually know in ways that are familiar to them (Moll, 1988). A variety of strategies have been used to attempt to develop prospective teachers' capabilities to teach, including carefully supervised field experiences in culturally diverse schools, action research to learn about pupils' families and communities, and methods courses taught with the involvement of experienced teachers who have been successful in culturally diverse schools.

The literature makes it very clear that more than conventional university classes are necessary to enable the kind of personal transformations that need to occur in prospective teachers. It is also clear that no experience by itself, such as a field experience in a diverse school, will necessarily contribute to this transformation under all conditions. In some cases, well-intentioned experiences designed to challenge the stereotypes and prejudices that novice teachers bring to their programs may serve to strengthen and reinforce these stereotypes (Haberman & Post, 1992).

Although most teacher educators acknowledge, in principle, the importance of preparing teachers for cultural diversity, much work still needs to be done to translate these beliefs into reality. In many places, some prospective teachers still complete their teacher education programs without having supervised field experiences in schools and communities where they are exposed to pupils and adults from backgrounds different from their own. In many places, one course in multicultural education is the extent of the effort to prepare teachers for diversity, while the rest of the program maintains a monocultural perspective (Zeichner & Hoeft, 1996), and many novice teachers are still reluctant to seek teaching positions in high-poverty schools where the need is greatest. In addition to the program-level factors that have been alluded to earlier, the literature also makes it clear that the success of teacher education programs in developing the intercultural sensitivity and teaching competence that are needed depends on the support that the institution as a whole gives to affirming a commitment to diversity (Price & Valli, 1998; Villegas & Lucas, in press). Efforts of teacher educators within their programs to implement the kind of strategies discussed above will not be sufficient without this broader institutional support. A lot of important work remains to be done in this area, which is probably the single most important issue facing teacher educators at the beginning of this new century.

Although we have described a few of the critical issues that dominate current efforts at teacher education reform in the United States, there are certainly other issues that have been significant. The next part of this chapter, which takes up the specific case of music teacher education, will address a few of these other issues, such as the internationalization and technologicalization of education.

The Structure of Traditional Models of Music Teacher Education

The literature on models of preservice music teacher education may be organized by the framework or structure of the programs. In order to understand the changing conceptual nature of the discipline, it is first necessary to comprehend the structure of its traditional models. This section of the chapter will identify trends in music teacher education by first reviewing the structure of traditional music teacher education models imposed by various kinds of institutional settings, then describing structure as directed by approach to content, and concluding with a discussion of the emerging trends in traditional curriculum content categories.

The Structure of Institutional Settings

Colwell (1985) reports that music teacher education "has a long history from its formal inclusion as a performance option in Emma Willard's School for Girls in 1814 through the conventions, institutes, and one-, two-, three-, and four-year nondegree programs of the late 19th century" (p. 20). Music education historians usually identify the teacher conventions that began about the same time as systematic programs in teacher training, the late 1820s, as the beginning of music teacher education. These conventions were courses offered in cities for a short time. With this limited training, music teachers were subjected to examinations to determine their fitness to teach. Conservatories, such as the New England Conservatory and conservatories at Chicago, also played a role in music teacher education in the mid-19th century, with their programs of education for music supervisors. "By the beginning of the 20th century, the common practice for certification of music teachers was to accept successful completion of a training program in lieu of an examination or, in some states and cities, to require the completion of a 'normal' program and the passing of the examination" (Colwell, 1985, p. 21). The early 1920s provided the stage for the beginning of the band contest movement and the 4-year music education degree.

At the beginning of the 21st century, nearly all music teacher preparation programs are found within institutions of postsecondary education. Types of institutions of higher education offering music teacher preparation programs range from teachers' colleges, whose primary purpose is teacher preparation, to research institutions in which teacher education in general may be a small part of the overall research and doctoral-granting mission. In addition, liberal arts colleges and comprehensive universities (multipurpose institutions which offer primarily the baccalaureate degree and are distinguished from teachers' colleges and liberal arts colleges in that "they award a significant portion of their degrees in two or more professional or occupational disciplines such as engineering, business administration" [Gimmestad & Hall, 1994, p. 5996]) have programs aimed at the preparation of music education specialists. A review of music teacher education curricula from these various kinds of institutions shows what might be expected: Liberal arts programs tend to emphasize a broad, general preparation outside of the music discipline, whereas programs in schools of music (in comprehensive or doctoral-granting universities) tend to emphasize performance. Other than Colwell's (2000) historical account of music teacher preparation in the United States in this century, descriptive research about distinctions, location, and effectiveness of programs at these different institutions is limited.

As with other teacher education programs, music teacher education programs are located in arts and sciences units of colleges/universities; in colleges of fine and performing arts; in schools, colleges, or departments of education; or are administered jointly by education and arts and sciences/fine arts units. Because of the nature of skill development involved in preparing music educators, it is speculated that more music teacher preparation programs are located outside of education units than is the case with other subject matter certification programs.

Many traditional music teacher preparation programs have experienced increases in the total number of hours needed for graduation. Some of these additions come as a result of the "professionalization agenda" mentioned earlier in the chapter. Requirements have been added, typically within the professional education and music education components, making it difficult for students to actually complete a program in 4 years. By contrast, the number of hours in some music teacher education programs has actually been reduced by state statutes limiting the number of hours that can be required for baccalaureate degrees, as is the case in Florida.

Whether a program takes 4 or 5 years to complete seems to be a function of its approach to curriculum content. Some institutions offer programs that are intentionally designed to take 5 full academic years to complete and culminate with the granting of a baccalaureate degree. Others, such as the University of Kansas (George Duerksen, personal communication, January 2001), confer a baccalaureate degree at the completion of the first 4 years and then require additional graduate hours for certification. Students at the University of Miami holding a B.M. degree in Music "may work toward certification in music education concurrently with the M.M. degree in Music Education" (*Graduate Studies at the University of Miami School of Music*, n.d., ¶ 5). Tina Scott of Oregon State University (personal communication, January 2001) reports that music teacher education programs in Oregon "are required by the Oregon Department of Education to be 5-year, 'add-on' programs." Students at the University of Oregon complete a Bachelor of Music in Music Education degree and then "move into both our 'Fifth-Year Program for Music Teacher Licensure' and the Master of Music in Music Education degree program." At the University of Oregon, the 5th year is five terms (summer through summer) and includes three terms of student teaching. Then the master's degree is finished with an additional summer's term after the student is teaching in the field (*UO School of Music: Academic Studies,* 2000, ¶3). David Elliot, at the University of Toronto (personal communication, 2001), indicates that "[M]ost Canadian provinces have always used the five-year, 'add-on' certification concept (programs in which students complete usually one, but sometimes two, years of professional education coursework and supervised field experiences in addition to an undergraduate degree in music)."

The Structure of Music Teacher Education Curricula

Within the structure of a 4- or 5-year degree program, music teacher education programs have traditionally been organized and structured according to a sequence of courses and the balancing of on-campus and in-school field experiences. In the United States, the National Council for Accreditation of Teacher Education (NCATE) (2000) has suggested that teacher education programs be designed according to an established knowledge base, that is, various skills and knowledge that teachers need to be successful. In most traditional music teacher education programs, four general domains of knowledge are typically addressed: general education; content knowledge; pedagogical knowledge; and pedagogical content knowledge, a concept proposed by Shulman (1987) as a result of studies of novice and expert teachers. This division, without the distinction between pedagogical knowledge and pedagogical content knowledge, is reflected in the curricular structure for baccalaureate degrees in music education of the National Association of Schools of Music (NASM) (2001, p. 93). Dust (1995) found that this curricular framework was also prevalent in most Canadian music teacher education programs.

General Education. Music education students, like students with other majors, are expected to acquire a body of knowledge and skills that all college graduates should possess as educated citizens. These include the ability to communicate in written and oral language; basic computational and mathematical skill; the uses of technology; and a general knowledge of history, literature, the arts, and the sciences. As a result of the "professionalization agenda," these components of general education are receiving more emphasis in many music teacher education programs.

Content Knowledge. Of the four traditions influencing the nature of teacher education programs over the past century, the academic tradition, that is, an emphasis on the subject matter, seems to be the predominant focus for many music teacher education programs. The following

music competencies are typically addressed in music teacher education programs: performance, aural skills, analysis, composition, arranging, improvisation, repertory, literature, history, and conducting. There are those both in the United States and abroad (Binkowski, 1977; Colwell, 2000; Marks, 1994) who feel that perhaps there has been too much emphasis on the development of musical content knowledge and not enough emphasis on the pedagogical domains. This conjecture seems to be reinforced by survey studies such as that of Jennings (1988), who found that student teaching and methods (pedagogical content knowledge courses) were ranked higher than content knowledge courses such as conducting, applied lessons, music theory, and music history by practicing college and high school band directors in terms of their own teaching effectiveness. Teacher education in music, with its emphasis on content knowledge, seems to be substantially different from teacher preparation programs in other disciplines, in which methods, curriculum, psychology, and philosophy courses are the core of preprofessional preparation.

Pedagogical Knowledge. Pedagogical knowledge includes areas such as assessment strategies, lesson planning, classroom management, learning theories, philosophical frameworks, use of technology, and knowledge of multicultural issues. It is beyond the scope of this section to discuss each of these areas in detail, but mention of a relatively new focus in research in the area and several representative research studies is in order.

Bresler (1995) has been concerned about the "monopoly of university-based research on the production of formal knowledge" (p. 2). She believes that what is missing in the pedagogical knowledge literature are "the voices of teachers, their questions, and concerns, and the interpretive frames they use to understand and improve their own classroom practices" (p. 27), which she and others have termed "teacher knowledge." She cites the Berkshire Study (Berkshire Local Education Authority, 1989), conducted by teachers in their music classrooms in England, as a major contribution to pedagogical knowledge of curriculum in general, and to a better understanding of the debate on assessment in the arts in particular. The teachers/researchers in the Berkshire project voiced concern about the use of graded tests in music that were based on external, empirical criteria (and also the aesthetic theory on which these are based). Among the findings of the study were that teachers need to be knowledgeable about aesthetic theories, as well as sensitive to their own preferences and predictions, when selecting assessment techniques for use in their classrooms.

Lesson planning and classroom management are also considered to be pedagogical knowledge. A qualitative study by Richards and Killen (1996) conducted with music education students in Australia found that preservice teachers draw from two sources of knowledge in lesson planning: the written agenda, which is influenced by the university pedagogical program, and the unwritten agenda, influenced by the preservice teachers' own beliefs about teaching. Snyder (1996), in studying classroom management and the music student teacher, found that cooperating teachers were a primary influence on student teachers, both with respect to specific classroom management techniques and the classroom environment created for them. Furthermore, he found that experience in front of the class in combination with the student teachers' particular level of readiness were the main contributors to change and improvement in the observed classroom management approaches. Smith (1994) concluded that a mentoring program for beginning teachers, such as that in operation in Minnesota, has much to offer in terms of assisting with classroom management, daily class planning, and knowledge of political structure, among other topics. In all three of these studies, teacher knowledge—either through personal experience or from the voices of experience—was found to be influential in acquiring pedagogical knowledge.

There are those who argue that for too long music teacher preparation programs have dwelt on the mechanics of teaching and ignored the philosophical dimensions. Palmer (1995), for example, believes that college music educators should take into account the nature of music and teaching as spiritual, and infuse the preparation of music educators with all the dimensions of spirituality. Parr (1996), in applying the ideas of Bruner, Greene and Howard to music teacher preparation, proposes a reconceptualization that focuses on creating self, symbolic mediation, practice, philosophical reflection, and political advocacy. Kahrs (1992) argues that the undergraduate level is the appropriate level for teaching aesthetics by integrating it within the curriculum.

Pedagogical Content Knowledge. Pedagogical content knowledge (PCK) is that domain that enables students to construct knowledge of subject matter for use in teaching as a result of experiences in music methods classes and related field experiences. PCK represents more than a simple combination of general knowledge, content knowledge, and pedagogical knowledge. Although it is an amalgamation of these, it is also a representation of additional knowledge and skills that excellent teachers possess. For example, it includes knowledge of typical misconceptions that students will have when learning a particular concept. It involves having the knowledge and ability to call on analogies, illustrations, examples, and demonstrations that will facilitate learning for specific students. It also includes knowledge of the learner's back-

ground, of experiences and culture brought to the classroom and how these may influence learning specific subject matter content.

In the last two decades, many traditional music teacher education programs have prided themselves on incorporating more and earlier field experiences into their programs in order to help students acquire pedagogical content knowledge as previously described. This apprenticeship model to teacher training is certainly highly valued by those who complete the program. Yet, few researchers have attempted to examine the results of programmatic changes to increase pedagogical content knowledge in a systematic way. Wing (1993) asserts that music teacher educators have identified a number of competencies that can be acquired through college programs but feels that there are "few clues regarding the relationship of these teacher competencies to student learning or the degree to which learnings in college transfer to teacher behaviors in the school classroom or rehearsal setting" (p. 56). Bisset (1993) used qualitative research techniques to study the effect of peer coaching, observation, and actual teaching in developing insights into real-life classroom teaching for five preservice music educators in an elementary setting. Findings of this study suggest that the idea of the novice being inducted into the profession through direct encounters and through modeling has much to offer in terms of helping the beginning teacher construct the kinds of synthesized knowledge (PCK) necessary to be successful in the music classroom. Studies such as this, although providing some insight into learning to teach, are difficult to generalize beyond the specific situation examined. This is an area that deserves further study.

Current Challenges in the Practice of Preservice Music Teacher Education

Colwell (1985), in his exhaustive review of program evaluation in music teacher education, argued at that time that "[T]he literature on program evaluation in music education is sparse" (p. 19), and it appears that little has changed in the last 15 years. There are a few studies (Marks, 1994; Moore, 1995; Shires, 1990) that have attempted to assess the effectiveness of music teacher preservice training through survey methods, but such studies fall somewhat short in raising probing questions about current goals, practices, and outcomes.

Traditional preservice music teacher programs in the United States are currently being confronted with challenges in several major areas: (1) music and the "core curriculum"; (2) redefinition in light of the National Arts Standards; (3) directives from professional accrediting agencies; (4) internationalization and technologicalization;

and (5) the "hidden curriculum" and the "null curriculum." It is the purpose of this section of the chapter to summarize the research literature through which these challenges have been identified and present potential solutions.

Music and the "Core Curriculum"

Except in magnet or satellite schools specializing in the arts, music as a subject area in many schools in the United States in practice does not form part of the "core curriculum," that is subject areas in which all students should demonstrate skills and knowledge before graduation. This is clearly demonstrated by the fact that in many secondary schools, credits in the visual and performing arts are not required for graduation; or if there is such a requirement, it is six to eight times less than the number credits required in "core" subjects such as English, science, math, or social studies. This situation has made it difficult to recruit and retain music educators who are worried about security in a profession that is seemingly viewed as expendable in times of financial crisis.

Several recent research studies regarding music's effect on spatial-temporal reasoning and the so-called Mozart Effect (Rauscher, Shaw, & Ky, 1995; Rauscher, Shaw, Levine, Wright, Dennis, & Newcomb, 1997) and a commissioned review of the literature regarding research that shows music study supporting growth in other curricular areas (Cutietta, Hamann, & Walker, 1995) have somewhat offset the effect of the reform movement *Goals 2000,* which has been interpreted to stress the "core curriculum" at the expense of the arts. Extolling the virtues of the so-called extramusical values of music education, that is, claiming that the study of music is important because it enhances growth in other areas rather than being important for its own sake, would have enormous implications for change in music teacher preparation programs. While the debate about this philosophical shift continues, little response to the debate has manifested itself in music teacher education programs.

In some states (Nebraska, for example), legislatures have not included the arts in the definition of the core curriculum, and, therefore, standards have not been written for music and the arts. In an attempt to attach music and the arts to the core curriculum, some educators in these states have advocated "crosswalking" objectives in music and the arts to objectives in the other core subjects in which standards have been written. The concept of "crosswalking" refers to finding ways in which various learning activities can be used simultaneously (or crosswalked) to achieve objectives in two or more disciplines, for example, understanding form in music and form in geometry (Nierman, 2000). If crosswalking is to be promoted as part of a curricular framework for the teaching and learning of music, it would seem that careful scrutiny regarding how crosswalking affects student learning is warranted. Such studies have yet to be conducted.

Redefining Music Education in Light of the National Arts Standards

The drive to make music a part of the core curriculum also resulted in the formation of the *National Standards for Arts Education* (Consortium of National Arts Education Associations, 1994). Since at least the beginning of the 20th century, with the rise of instrumental music in the public schools, performance training and providing entertainment for the community have been a part of the philosophical justification for including music in the school curriculum. In the past, the profession has called for a more comprehensive approach to music education curriculum in the form of Comprehensive Musicianship (Evaluative Criteria for Music in Education, 1968); but, in practice, music for many P–12 students involves learning to perform music for the next public appearance or contest. With the passage of Goals 2000 Educate America Act and the acceptance of the *National Standards for Arts Education* by then Secretary of Education Richard Riley, music educators in the United States are not only being asked to teach P–12 students to sing and play an instrument but also to compose, improvise, make connections with events and knowledge in other disciplines, and meet other important content standards.

As was the case with systematic studies of the overall effectiveness of the traditional music teacher education curricula, only descriptive studies were found that have examined the impact of the National Music Standards on music teacher preparation. Adderley (1996) completed a survey of college faculty and P–12 music educators in South Carolina to determine whether teachers are prepared to help students meet the voluntary national standards for music education. The findings revealed that college faculty believed that they are relatively effective in preparing teachers to help students achieve the standards, but the teachers did not believe that they were adequately prepared to implement the standards by their undergraduate education. Interestingly, faculty and teachers alike gave themselves the lowest ratings for three standards—improvising; composing; and understanding relationships between music, the other arts, and disciplines outside the arts. Kirkland (1996) also surveyed South Carolina teachers and concluded that according to the teachers' self-reports, only the performance-oriented standards (standards 1 and 2) were being met at the highest proficiency levels.

In California, Byo (1997) surveyed general education classroom teachers and music specialists to examine their perceptions about pertinent factors affecting the successful teaching of the National Music Standards. Among her findings were that music teachers believed they were most effective implementing the evaluating, listening and analyzing, and singing standards. Generalists, by contrast, believed they were most effective implementing the history and culture, other subjects, and singing standards. Both groups indicated an overall lack of time and resources to effectively teach most standards.

The National Music Standards have been adopted by MENC—The National Association for Music Education—as the framework for P–12 music curricula in the United States, and, as such, it would seem that music teacher education curricula would reflect changes to prepare teachers to teach accordingly. Shuler (1995) contends, however, that, whereas the standards are not very radical from a philosophical perspective they do pose major challenges for programs in the traditional university music department. Based on program descriptions available via the Internet, it appears that Duquesne University has actually redesigned its undergraduate (Mary Pappert School of Music: Undergraduate program of study, 2000) and graduate (Mary Pappert School of Music: Graduate program of study, 2001) music education programs based on the conceptual framework provided by the standards. However, Colwell (1995) points out that without empirical research and assessment, the voluntary National Music Standards will plummet to the rank of "educational fad." It is likely that a greater influence of the National Music Standards will be seen in the future as state licensing criteria enfold the preservice teacher's knowledge of the P–12 standards into the requirements for licensure. As we write this chapter, MENC is in the process of compiling and verifying the extent to which the National Music Standards have been incorporated into state standards.

Directives from National Accrediting Agencies

Just as music teacher education programs are influenced by guidelines directly from the profession itself in the form of the National Music Standards promoted by the MENC, so there are also influences from outside music education in the form of standards from accrediting agencies. Two of the most influential such agencies are the National Council for Accreditation of Teacher Education (NCATE) and the National Association of Schools of Music (NASM).

Previous NCATE standards required institutions to design programs based on an established knowledge base, that is, various skills and knowledge that teachers need to be successful. Now it is no longer sufficient just to be able to articulate the knowledge base that provides the framework for a program. Today's NCATE (2001) is interested in outcomes. Questions such as What are students learning? How can this learning be documented? and What evidence can be used to document that curricular decisions have been based on student learning? become relevant.

Perhaps in response to and certainly concomitant with NCATE's emphasis on assessment, some states are developing a performance-based approach to teacher licensing. The Indiana Professional Standards Board (IPSB), for example, has developed extensive standards for each licensing area (*Indiana Professional Standards Board*, 2000). These standards are related to the INTASC standards (*INTASC Core Standards*, n.d.). All teacher-training institutions in Indiana must submit Unit Assessment Plans to the IPSB by June of 2002.

NCATE has certainly caused the faculty of many music teacher training programs to rethink their approach to documenting student learning, and the NASM also has precipitated change in the areas of multicultural music, composition, improvisation, and technology.

The need for knowledge of musics outside the Western European tradition and of technological developments applicable to various teaching areas will be discussed in the next section, but it should be noted that these areas have been the focus for many music administrators interested in bringing their institutions in line with NASM accrediting guidelines in these areas. In NASM's 2001–2002 Handbook (2001), it appears that the association is softening somewhat its stance on the study of multicultural music. In the 1999–2000 Handbook, NASM (1999) directed that "[S]tudents *must* [italics added] have opportunities through performance and academic studies to work with music of diverse cultural sources, historical periods, and media" (p. 79). However, in the same section of the 2000–2001 Handbook, the following statement is made concerning history and repertory:

> With regard to specific content, music has a long history, many repertoires, and multiple connections with cultures. Content in and study of these areas are vast and growing. Each institution is responsible for choosing from among this material when establishing basic requirements. (p. 83)

Likewise, in the section of the 2000–2001 Handbook applying to baccalaureate degrees in music education, the language regarding multicultural music study is not very commanding: "Teachers should be prepared to relate their understanding of musical styles, the literature of diverse cultural sources, and the music of various historical periods" (p. 94).

In the area of technology, NASM standards also have undergone a similar degree of increased flexibility. The 1999–2000 Handbook calls for students to "... be made familiar with the capabilities of technology as they relate to composition, performance, analysis, teaching, and research" (p. 79). The 2000–2001 Handbook is much less specific: "Students must acquire: . . . Working knowledge of the technological developments *applicable to their area of specialization* [italics added]" (p. 83).

On the one hand, institutions will have more flexibility in meeting program requirements for multicultural music study and technology in these times of shrinking budgets. On the other, it will be less compelling for many institutions to make changes toward a more diverse, contemporary curriculum in music repertory and technology without more prescriptive standards.

Internationalization and Technologicalization

Change does not take place in a vacuum. Just as the cry for accountability led to national standards in many curriculum areas, so multicultural developments and the tendency toward internationalization in contemporary society are signaling enormous changes for music and music teacher education. There is a more rapid change in and blending of musical styles. Furthermore, there is simply a larger number of musical styles available to the listening public simultaneously. A marked increase in the development of music-related media and technologies challenges and excites music teachers and performers.

Both Schwadron (1985) and, 15 years later, Spearman, in her presentation to the Housewright Symposium on the Future of Music Education, consider societal changes, including internationalization and technological forces, to be "two of the most influential phenomena of life in the United States and the world" (Spearman, 2000, p. 155). Indeed, both topics have generated considerable research interest within the context of music teacher education programs.

As a result of the changing demographics of our American society and the increased contact with people from around the world brought about by rapid changes in the communication and commerce sectors, many states are requiring coursework in the form of multicultural education or human relations training be a part of teacher education programs. In some instances, preservice field experiences in multicultural settings are also required. Volk's (1993) study of articles in the *Music Educators Journal* from 1967 to 1992 revealed the growth of multicultural music education. Furthermore, Quesada and Volk's (1997) review of doctoral studies that concerned teaching of world musics in the United States listed in *Dissertation Abstracts International* from 1973 to 1993 showed that research topics included philosophical and historical questions, studies of students' attitudes and achievements, teachers' attitudes and training, and a compilation and evaluation of teaching materials.

Surveys and case studies have been used to examine the multicultural component of music teacher education programs. Montague (1988) studied teacher training in multicultural music education in selected universities and colleges using interview techniques and found that while many exemplary courses existed, the general nature of state laws resulted in many inconsistencies within states as to the quality and quantity of the multicultural music component. Dunbar (1995) examined changes in music teacher education policies in Wisconsin. Using the University of Washington Music Teacher Education Program as the focus of a case study, Okun (1998) investigated how undergraduate music teacher education programs can respond to recent laws and regulations stressing pluralistic values. Employing more traditional descriptive survey techniques, Norman (1994) and Lacy (1985) questioned music educators, music supervisors, and music education faculty about the multicultural component of music teacher education programs. Fiese and DeCarbo (1995) surveyed selected music educators from large urban areas in the United States where multicultural theories are put into practice every day. The general consensus of these studies seems to be that although there is a wide range of positive and negative attitudes present toward multicultural music education, most P–16 educators recognize the need to reflect the changing cultural demographics of the United States in music teacher education programs. Many would like to have multicultural content infused into the entire curriculum, rather than focused in one or two courses.

Several studies outside the area of music teacher preparation merit attention. In studying preservice teachers taking music education courses as part of an elementary education program, Teicher (1997) found a significant relationship between exposure to multicultural music and expressed willingness to teach it. However, no effect was observed on attitudes toward teaching in culturally diverse environments, a finding that coincides with concerns raised in the "Preparing Teachers for Cultural Diversity" section found earlier in this chapter. Delpit's (1984) ethnographically based evaluation of a mother tongue medium instructional program in the North Solomons Province of Papua New Guinea moves beyond the study of strictly educational issues to include linguistic, psychological, socioeconomic, political, religiocultural, historic, demographic, and geographic factors. Considering educational issues and reforms more broadly, such as captured in the Delpit study, has much to suggest for those educational researchers in this country who conduct studies that can more fully inform practice.

Just as music teacher education programs have undergone changes in content to accommodate policy changes regarding multicultural education, so the use of technology in these programs has undergone adjustments. A look back at the first edition of the *Handbook of Research on Music Teaching and Learning* (Colwell, 1992) reveals just how rapid the changes have been, both in terms of use of technology in music teacher education classrooms and in training preservice educators to use technology in P–12 classrooms. For example, there is no mention of the Internet or digital video cameras in Verrastro and Leglar's (1992) chapter on music teacher education. Only research supporting the theory that videotapes are an effective way to provide feedback is reviewed. In fact, Higgins (1992), in his chapter on technology, comments, "Research utilizing MIDI is just beginning" (p. 488). The terms *interactive multimedia* and *hypermedia* were listed under the heading "Emerging Technologies in Music Research" (pp. 488–489). It is beyond the scope of this chapter to review extensively technological changes that have found their way into music teacher education programs. That will be done elsewhere in this Handbook. However, a brief mention of research dealing with changes in the technological content of music teacher education programs is in order. Evidently, change in this area is not occurring at a rapid pace. Marks (1994) concluded that less than 50% of California's preservice music teacher training programs require a course in music technology. Mager (1997) found that few programs require MIDI courses as part of their curriculum. There are some innovative uses of technology to be found, however, such as Ester's (1997) use of hypercard technology to teach vocal anatomy and function. Based on a survey of members of the Florida Music Educators Association, Tredway (1994) proposed a course of instruction for undergraduate music education majors by which fundamental knowledge and skills concerning audio, video, and computer devices could be taught.

The "Hidden Curriculum" and the "Null Curriculum"

In contrast to the technological area with its overt curricular objectives, not all knowledge, skills, and attitudinal "residue" are part of the intended outcome of the curriculum. Ginsburg and Clift (1990) describe the "hidden curriculum" of teacher education as the messages transmitted to students through institutional contexts as well as the structure and processes of the programs themselves. They suggest that these messages relate to several themes: (1) teaching is a low-status profession; (2) teachers as a professional group lack power; and (3) teacher education coursework and practica tend to communicate an inaccurate view about knowledge as an absolute body of facts created by informed persons. Music teacher education graduates, like preservice teachers in other areas, may experience these misconceptions as a result of their schooling. Perhaps another message of the hidden curriculum is that

college music educators are "out of step" with the reality of the real purpose of music in the schools—to provide entertainment for the community—as experienced by students in various practicum settings.

Music teacher education programs can also be characterized by their "null curricula," that is, what is not included in the curriculum (Flinders, Noddings, & Thornton, 1986). They suggest that the ethics of teaching and the biological roots of human behavior are examples of the null curriculum in teacher education. Katz and Raths (1985) further suggest that the development of professional character is not typically included as a goal of teacher education programs. Other examples of the null curriculum in music teacher education programs include practice in error diagnosis from the podium (VanOyen & Nierman, 1998) and modeling of techniques for teaching aesthetic understanding in rehearsal settings (Schnoor, 1999).

What hidden beliefs about music education in schools do preservice teachers bring with them to their work as a result of their preprofessional education? What is not a part of music teacher education curricula that is needed? It would seem that it is in our best interest to research the answers to these questions.

Nontraditional Concepts of Music Teacher Education

Among the current developments in teacher education reported earlier in the chapter, advocates of the deregulation agenda and the development of new partnerships appear to have had the most influence on music teacher education programs. This section of the chapter will focus on partnership models in music teacher education and alternative paths to music teaching.

Partnership Models in Music Teacher Education

As has been the case in teacher education programs in general, the traditional role that P–12 music educators and building administrators have played in preservice music teacher education is to provide placement sites for field experiences. In response to continuing dissatisfaction with traditional models, some preservice music teacher education program designers have found alternatives that purport that the most appropriate way to train teachers is to do so in a collaborative manner with one or more of the "stakeholders" (school boards, schools, universities, departments of education, professional organizations) working together collaboratively to meet the challenges of induction into the profession. Robinson (1999), for example, proposed a theory of collaborative music education between higher education and urban public schools that could assist in meeting the challenge of preparing music educators for multicultural settings.

School-university cooperative efforts in preservice music teacher education were studied by Gregory (1995). His research revealed that more than 90% of the colleges and universities in his study cooperated with P–12 schools. However, this "cooperation," in the form of assigning students for field experiences and simply keeping communication channels open, is far less substantial than the collaboration recommended by the Holmes Group (1990) philosophy, which call for P–12 music educators to be equal partners with university professors in preservice education decision making. Furthermore, Gregory found that college professors were not rewarded for P–12 collaborative efforts in the form of credit toward tenure or remuneration. Perhaps Warren's (1989) observation, based on a survey of in-service music teachers in New York and New Jersey, which indicated that very few music teachers have participated in true school-university collaborations, gives a more accurate view of the status of actual partnerships between college and P–12 music educators.

Nevertheless, there are some college/university music teacher preparation programs that utilize a collaborative, partnership model that holds promise for meeting challenges in music teacher preparation. The "professional development school" (PDS) model (Holmes Group, 1990) is one of the most common P–12/higher education music partnerships. Professionals from these institutions work together in areas such as teacher selection, curriculum development, and practica design. As of this writing, there are PDS sites involving music in Rochester, New York (Conkling & Henry, 1999), Muncie, Indiana (Ester, personal communication, January 2001), and Lincoln, Nebraska (Nierman, 1986).

If the Holmes model is to gain more acceptance, however, there will need to be a closer correlation between the perceptions of P–12 music educators and college professors regarding just what are effective activities for maintaining a good working knowledge of trends in P–12 schools. In a 1995 survey by Hamann and Lawrence, college music professors believed that the most effective strategies for keeping current were: conducting research on problems affecting schools; guest-conducting at music festivals; and presenting at conferences and in-service workshops. In contrast, the P–12 teachers surveyed listed the following as activities most effective for keeping their college colleagues up-to-date: guest teaching; serving on joint committees with public school teachers; and working for a semester as a full-time music teacher in the schools. Woody (1998) notes that "the perceptions of the public school teachers, compared to those of the college professors, more closely resemble the Holmes Group's recommendations for improving partnerships" (p. 32).

Other examples of promising partnerships grounded in tenets other than those of the Holmes group include the University of Arizona's Institute for Innovation in String Music Teaching. With the help of a grant from the American String Teachers Association (*Grants for String Projects—Call for Applications,* 1999), students from the public schools are brought to the campus and provided with bowed string instruction in a heterogeneous class setting. The teachers in the institute are primarily undergraduate string education students, although high school students are also given the opportunity to teach. The teachers observe class lessons taught by a master teacher and are encouraged to develop skills based on this model.

Alternative Paths to Music Teaching

Whether collaboratively or unilaterally planned, music teacher education programs that lead to initial licensure of music teachers have traditionally been based almost exclusively on the successful completion of a state-approved distribution of college coursework. In 1995, Shuler noted, however, that more and more states are moving toward content area tests, such as the National Teacher Examination in Music, to determine readiness to enter the field. In some states, teachers already certified in a subject area need only pass the National Teacher Exam in an additional subject area to have an added endorsement. These tests are becoming increasingly more performance-based, says Shuler, and "[T]he ETS's new Praxis series is a significant step toward standardized, performance-based assessment . . . in music and art" (1995, p. 12). As states move toward standardized, performance-based assessments, music teacher education programs will need to undergo change to prepare their graduates to demonstrate a certain body of skills and knowledge in real music classrooms rather than merely to show that they have completed a body of coursework. Changes such as these in teacher assessment are signaling changes for music teacher education programs.

From a review of the literature on music teacher education, it seems evident, however, that overall few large-scale, programmatic changes have taken place to date. There does seem to be less confidence in traditional music teacher education programs as music teachers shortages become a reality. Colwell (2000) notes that some universities have responded by instituting graduate programs in which musicians can obtain teacher certification in about a year or three summers (p. 20). Two such "fast-track" programs, Alternate Route to Teacher Certification I (ARCI) and Alternate Route to Teacher Certification II (ARCII), have been in place in Connecticut for about 10 years (Alternate Route to Teacher Certification, n.d.). Planning is currently underway to modify the original 8-week program to include 27 weeks of academic training and 12 weeks of student teaching. The Arizona State University has also begun an expedited postbaccalaureate program (Jeff Bush, personal communication, January 2001), in which instrumental skills classes are compacted into a 10-week period, and methods and general education courses are similarly compressed.

There is also a movement underway to "out-source" music and art in some districts (Hagen, personal communication, January 2001). In other words, music and art teachers who are state-certified in their subjects are being replaced by individuals from private companies and persons who are deemed qualified to teach in schools, simply because they play in a band or orchestra. This was one of the issues involved in a recent teachers strike in Buffalo, New York.

Toward Solving the Dilemmas of Research on Preservice Music Teacher Education

This final section of the chapter is an overview of the preservice music teacher education research literature for the purpose of identifying what is known about traditional and nontraditional music teacher education models and which topics in the area need further investigation. The structure selected for this discussion is based on Yarger and Galluzzo's (1983) "Matrix for Exploring Research in Inservice Teacher Education" (pp. 169–189), which was adapted to examine research on preservice music teacher education. Conceptually, research types are the rows of the matrix, and questions about the research are the columns as shown in figure 42.1. The questions themselves will serve as the organizers for the section, and will illuminate areas of need in research on preservice music teacher education.

What Exists?

Turning to the research literature to answer the question "What exists in preservice music teacher education programs?" is perplexing. Program descriptions, such as those found on various websites, are the most available information. Although many scholars would not include descriptions of programs as "research," they are a source, in the absence of comprehensive surveys, of the most accessible picture of what is happening in preservice music teacher education. Program descriptions can present difficulties, however, in that they are typically less than objective because they are often constructed in order to promote the success of a program.

Case studies describing music teacher education programs, such as that of Okun (1998), are more limited in number than program descriptions but also are more tenable accounts of the problems encountered and the pro-

cesses employed in educating future music teachers. Encouraging results showing change in preservice music educator's teaching behaviors and attitudes are evident in some case studies; but, unfortunately, there are few case studies of program activities such as that of Delpit (1984). There is a need for more case studies describing the "how to" of music teacher education from a broad perspective. Examining the Duquesne University Website (http://www.duq.edu/music/music.html) provides useful information, but a case-study approach to examining such programs could provide data and questions that would serve to inform subsequent research.

As the result of survey data, some information exists about the types of problems that music teachers view as important and the types of programs they have encountered in comparison with those programs they would like to have received. A limitation of this kind of survey data is that they suggest what exists in terms of perceptions of experience, beliefs, and desires for the future.

What is appropriate in preservice music teacher education has been almost exclusively in the research literature from a client perspective, that is, teachers. While this is not entirely inappropriate, perceptions of education professionals other than practitioners—school administrators, policy makers, professors—also must be considered. The question of appropriateness, often referred to as "needs," is typically addressed by well-executed surveys, such as that of Jennings (1988).

Several gaps are evident in the literature on appropriateness. A considerable amount has been written on the development and implementation of policy in music teacher education, but there is little *research* in this area. Second, there seems to be no shortage of ideas about how to improve programs, but there is little research on the effectiveness of these ideas and if they are appropriate. Do changes in programs more appropriately address students' needs? For example, where is the evidence that shows more and earlier field experiences result in improved teaching and learning in music? Finally, there is little research to show that undergraduate music program content was derived from substantive needs.

What Is Feasible?

The question of feasibility is certainly related to the question of appropriateness (content), but it is more generally related to the political, economic, and motivational arenas. Yarger and Galluzzo (1983) paraphrase the feasibility question this way: "Given the worst of all worlds, the best of all worlds, and the world we live in, what factors operate that will either inhibit or facilitate program developers and clients from doing exactly what they might want to do in terms of inservice [preservice] education?" (p. 172). Examples of feasibility questions include: What is

Questions	What Exists?	What Is Appropriate?	What Is Feasible?	What Is Effective?
Research Types				
Program Descriptions				
Case Studies				
Surveys				
Correlational Studies				
Experiments				

Figure 42.1. A Matrix for Exploring Research on Preservice Music Teacher Education.

possible for institutions in charge of music teacher preparation to deliver? What will state departments authorize? What will accrediting agencies approve? What federal and state laws must be considered? Who will pay for the activity? It is commonly known that documentation of cost effectiveness in teacher education in general (and music teacher education in particular) is challenging. When good programmatic ideas are put into practice, professionals often "fill in the gaps" when cost becomes a factor. Teacher educators seem to have a history of dealing with inadequate resources, but research based on questions of cost effectiveness must not continue to be ignored. Perhaps correlational studies, which are currently almost nonexistent in the field, could provide a positive first step.

What Is Effective?

Finally, the question of effectiveness addresses outcomes of preservice music teacher education programs—attitudinal, cognitive, behavioral outcomes. Such questions can best be addressed through experimental studies; but in the real world of music teacher education, precise controls necessary for valid and reliable designs are not always possible. Therefore, experimental studies in preservice music teacher education will almost always necessitate quasi-experimental designs; or, again, perhaps correlational studies and qualitative studies will have to provide a starting point.

In the area of effectiveness, shortcomings appear in the literature. There seems to be a lack of coordinated, longitudinal research on program effectiveness. The majority of the literature focuses on short-term events such as the effect of a particular instructional strategy in a semester class. Perhaps MENC's Instructional Strategies or Measurement and Evaluation SRIGs can be exhorted to address this weakness. What we need is program evaluation of the highest caliber—systematic gathering of data over an extended period of time. Such research would focus on what music educators entering the profession know and are able to do in promoting P–12 students' musical learning from a broad perspective, which can then be generalized to a number of different institutional settings.

REFERENCES

Adderley, C. L., III. (1996). Music teacher preparation in South Carolina colleges and universities relative to the national standards: Goals 2000. *Dissertation Abstracts International, 57* 4680. (UMI No. AAI97-11655)

Alternate route to teacher certification. (n.d.). Hartford, CT: Department of Higher Education. Retrieved February 21, 2001, from http://www.ctdhe.org/dheweb/ARC/ALT.htm

American Association of Colleges for Teacher Education. (1993). *Briefing book.* Washington, DC: Author.

American Association of Colleges for Teacher Education. (1994). *RATE IV: Teaching teachers, facts and figures.* Washington, DC: Author.

American Association of Colleges for Teacher Education. (1999). *Teacher education pipeline IV.* Washington, DC: Author.

American Association of Colleges for Teacher Education. (2000). *Standards-based teacher education project.* Washington, DC: Author.

American Association of State Colleges and Universities. (1999). *A call for teacher education reform.* Washington, DC: Author.

American Council on Education. (1999). *To touch the future: Transforming the way teachers are taught.* Washington, DC: Author.

Andrew, M. (1983). The characteristics of students in a five-year teacher education program. *Journal of Teacher Education, 34*(1), 20–23.

Association of American Universities. (1999). *Resolution on teacher education.* Washington, DC: Author.

Ballou, D., & Podgursky, M. (1999). Reforming teacher preparation and licensing: What is the evidence? *Teachers College Record, 102*(1), 5–27.

Banks, J. (1991). Teaching multicultural literacy to teachers. *Theory into Practice, 4*(1), 135–144.

Berkshire Local Education Authority. (1989). *Classroom issues in assessment and evaluation in the arts.* Reading, UK: Author.

Binkowski, B. (1977). The education of the music teacher. *International Society for Music Education Yearbook, 4,* 69–74.

Bisset, W. M. (1993). The apprenticeship approach to teacher training: A case study in music education. *Master's Ab-*

stract International, 32-02, 0406. (UMI No. AAGMM 83100)

Bresler, L. (1993). Teacher knowledge in music education. *Bulletin of the Council for Research in Music Education, 118*, 1–20.

Bresler, L. (1995). Teacher knowledge: A framework and discussion. *Bulletin of the Council for Research in Music Education, 123*, 26–30.

Bruschi, B., & Coley, R. (1999). *How teachers compare: The prose, document, and quantitative skills of America's teachers.* Princeton: Educational Testing Service.

Byo, S. J. (1997). General education classroom teachers' and music specialists' perceived ability to implement the national standards for music education. *Dissertation Abstracts International, 58*(02A), 0409. (UMI No. AAG 9722351)

Calderhead, J. (1989). Reflective teaching and teacher education. *Teaching and Teacher Education, 5*(1), 43–51.

California Commission on Teacher Credentialing. (1996, December). *The effectiveness of district intern programs of alternative certification in California.* Sacramento: Author.

Cazden, C., & Mehan, H. (1990). Principles from sociology and anthropology: Context, code, classroom, and culture. In M. Reynolds (Ed.), *Knowledge base for the beginning teacher* (pp. 47–57). Washington, DC: American Association of Colleges for Teacher Education.

Cochran-Smith, M. (1995). Color blindness and basket making are not the answers: Confronting the dilemmas of race, culture, and language diversity in teacher education. *Harvard Educational Review, 32*(3), 493–522.

Coley, R. J., & Thorpe, M. E. (1985). *A look at the MAT model of teacher education and its graduates: Lessons for today.* Princeton, NJ: Educational Testing Service.

Colwell, R. (1985). Program evaluation in music teacher education. *Bulletin of the Council for Research in Music Education, 81*, 18–64.

Colwell, R. (Ed.) (1992). *Handbook of research on music teaching and learning.* New York: Schirmer Books.

Colwell, R. (1995). Will voluntary national standards fix the potholes of arts education? *Arts Education Policy Review, 96*(5), 2–11.

Colwell, R. (2000). The music education/arts education path. *Arts Education Policy Review, 101*(3), 19–20.

Conkling, S. W., & Henry, W. (1999). Professional development partnerships: A new model for music teacher preparation. *Arts Education Policy Review, 100*(4): 19–23.

Consortium of National Arts Education Associations. (1994). *National standards for arts education.* Reston, VA: Music Educators National Conference.

Cutietta, R., Hamann, D., & Walker, L. (1995). *Spin-Offs.* Elkhart, IN: United Musical Instruments.

Darling-Hammond, L. (1994). Who will speak for the children? How Teach for America hurts urban schools and children. *Phi Delta Kappan, 76*(1), 21–34.

Darling-Hammond, L. (1997). *Doing what matters most: Investing in quality teaching.* New York: National Commission on Teaching and America's Future.

Darling-Hammond, L., & Berry, B. (1988). *The evolution of teacher policy.* Santa Monica, CA: The Rand Corporation.

Darling-Hammond, L., & Sclan, E. (1996). Selecting and preparing culturally competent teachers for urban schools. In J. Sikula (Ed.), *Handbook of research on teacher education* (2nd ed., pp. 67–99). New York: Macmillan.

Darling-Hammond, L., & Snyder, J. (2000). Authentic assessment of teaching in context. *Teaching and Teacher Education, 16*(5–6), 523–545.

Delpit, L. D. (1984). Language, culture, and self-determination: An ethnographically based evaluation of an experiment in schooling in Papua New Guinea. *Dissertation Abstracts International, 45*(06A), 1624. (UMI No. AAG8421180)

Delpit, L. (1995). *Other people's children: Culture and conflict in the classroom.* New York: The New Press.

Dill, V. (1996). Alternative teacher certification. In J. Sikula (Ed.), *Handbook of research on teacher education* (2nd ed., pp. 932–960). New York: Macmillan.

Dilworth M. (1992). *Diversity in teacher education.* San Francisco: Jossey-Bass.

Dunbar, J. C. (1995). Music teacher education governance in Wisconsin: An historical and grounded case study viewed through a multicultural education lens. *Dissertation Abstracts International, 56*(08A), 3044. (UMI No. DA9536155)

Dust, T. J. (1995). Curricular structure and the music and music education components of secondary music education programs at Canadian institutions of higher education. *Dissertation Abstracts International 57*(04A), 1533. (UMI No. DA9626980)

Ester, D. P. (1997). Teaching vocal anatomy and function via hypercard technology. *Contributions to Music Education, 24*(1), 91–99.

Evaluative Criteria for Music in Education. (1968, March). *Music Educators Journal, 54*, 66–67.

Feiman-Nemser, S. (1990). Teacher preparation: Structural and conceptual alternatives. In W. R. Houston (Ed.), *Handbook of research on teacher education* (pp. 212–233). New York: Macmillan.

Feistritzer, E. (1994). The evolution of alternative teacher certification. *The Educational Forum, 58*(2), 132–138.

Feistritzer, E. (1999). *The making of a teacher: A report on teacher preparation in the U.S.* Washington, DC: Center for Education Information.

Fiese, R. K., & DeCarbo, N. J. (1995). Urban music education: The teachers' perspective. *Music Educators Journal, 81*(6), 27–31.

Flinders, D. G., Noddings, N., & Thornton, S. J. (1986). The null curriculum: Its theoretical basis and practical implications. *Curriculum Inquiry, 16*(1), 33–42.

Garcia, E. (1993). Language, culture, and education. *Review of Research in Education, 19*, 51–100.

Gimmestad, M. J., & Hall, G. E. (1994). Teacher education programs: Structure. In T. Husen and T. N. Postlethwaite (Eds.), *International encyclopedia of education* (2nd ed., Vol. 11, pp. 5995–5999). New York: Pergamon.

Ginsburg, M. B., & Clift, R. T. (1990). The hidden curriculum of pre-service teacher education. In W. R. Houston, M. Haberman, & Sikula, G. (Eds.), *Handbook of re-*

search on teacher education (pp. 450–468). New York: Macmillan.

Gitomer, D., & Latham, A. (1999). *The academic quality of prospective teachers.* Princeton, NJ: Educational Testing Service.

Gomez, M. L., & Tabachnick, B. R. (1991). Telling teaching stories. *Teaching Education, 4*(2), 129–138.

Goodlad, J. (1990). *Teachers for our nation's schools.* San Francisco: Jossey-Bass.

Graduate Studies at the University of Miami School of Music. (n.d.). Miami, FL: University of Miami. Retrieved February 21, 2001, from http://www.music.miami.edu:591/grad-Studies/

Grant, C., & Secada, W. (1990). Preparing teachers for diversity. In W. R. Houston (Ed.), *Handbook of research on teacher education* (pp. 403–422). New York: Macmillan.

Grants for String Projects—Call for Applications. (1999). Reston, VA: American String Teachers Association. Retrieved February 21, 2001, from http://www.astaweb.com/grant_projects.html

Gregory, M. K. (1995). Collaboration for music teacher education between higher education institutions and K–12 schools. *Journal of Resarch in Music Education, 43,* 47–59.

Haberman, M. (1993). Teaching in multicultural schools: Implications for selection and training. In L. Hayon, H. Vonk, & R. Fessler (Eds.), *Teacher professional development: A multiple perspective approach* (pp. 267–294). Amsterdam: Swets & Zeitliger.

Haberman, M., & Post, L. (1992). Does direct experience change preservice teachers' perception of low income minority children? *Midwestern Educational Researcher, 5*(2), 29–31.

Hamann, D. L., & Lawrence, J. E. (1995). University music educators' perceptions of the importance of public-school-related off-campus activities. *Journal of Research in Music Education, 43,* 330–341.

Hawley, W. (1990). The theory and practice of alternative teacher certification: Implications for the improvement of teaching. *Peabody Journal of Education, 67*(3), 3–34.

Higgins, W. (1992). Technology. In R. Colwell (Ed.), *Handbook of research on music teaching and learning* (pp. 480–497). New York: Schirmer Books.

Holmes Group. (1990). *Tomorrow's schools: Principles for the design of professional development schools.* East Lansing, MI: Michigan State University College of Education.

Howey, K., Arends, R., Galluzzo, G., Yarger, S., & Zimpher, N. (1995). *Teaching teachers—Relationships with the world of practice.* Washington, DC: American Association of Colleges for Teacher Education.

Indiana Professional Standards Board. (2000). Indianapolis, IN: Indiana Professional Standards Board. Retrieved February 21, 2001, from http://www.state.in.us/psb/

INTASC Core Standards. (n.d.). Washington, DC: The Council of Chief State School Officers. Retrieved February 21, 2001, from http://www.ccsso.org/intascst.html

Irvine, J. J. (1992). Making teacher education programs culturally responsive. In M. Dilworth (Ed.), *Diversity in teacher education* (pp. 79–92). San Francisco: Jossey-Bass.

Jennings, D. L. (1988). The effectiveness of instrumental music teacher preservice training experiences as perceived by college and high school band directors. *Dissertation Abstracts International, 50*(04A), 0825. (UMI No. AAG 8910137)

Kahrs, S. (1992). The aesthetic dimension in the preparation of music education majors at the undergraduate level. *Dissertation Abstract International, 53*(07A) 2226. (UMI No. AAG9235429)

Kanstoroom, M., & Finn, C. E. (Eds.). (1999). *Better teachers, better schools.* Washington, DC: Fordham Foundation.

Katz, L. G., & Raths, J. D. (1985). Dispositions as goals for teacher education. *Teaching and Teacher Education, 1*(4), 301–307.

Kirkland, N. J. (1996). South Carolina schools and Goals 2000: National Standards in Music (Doctoral dissertation, University of South Carolina, 1996). *Dissertation Abstracts International, 57*(03A), 1069. (UMI No. AAI 9623096)

Kleinfeld, J. (1998). The use of case studies in preparing teachers for cultural diversity. *Theory into Practice, 37*(2), 140–147.

Lacy, L. C. (1985). A survey and evaluation of music teacher education programs in selected, accredited black private colleges and universities in the United States. *Dissertation Abstracts International, 46*(09A), 2610. (UMI No. AAG8526204)

Ladson-Billings, G. (1990). Culturally relevant teaching. *The College Board Review, 155,* 20–25.

Ladson-Billings, G. (1994). *The dreamkeepers: Successful teachers of African American children.* San Francisco: Jossey-Bass.

Ladson-Billings, G. (1995). Multicultural teacher education: Research, practice, and policy. In J. Banks (Ed.), *Handbook of research on multicultural education* (pp. 747–759). New York: Macmillan.

Levine, M., & Trachtman, R. (Eds.). (1996) *Making professional development schools work: Politics, practice, and policy.* New York: Teachers College Press.

Liston, D., & Zeichner, K. (1991). *Teacher education and the social conditions of schooling.* New York: Routledge.

Mager, G. E. (1997). The status of MIDI in the curricula of higher education institutions offering degree programs in music. *Dissertation Abstracts International, 58*(06A), 2126. (UMI No. AAG9737469)

Marks, L. L. (1994). The effectiveness of music teacher preservice training in California's colleges and universities: Professional preparation and teacher retention. *Dissertation Abstracts International, 56* 3494. (UMI No. AAI9601026)

Mary Pappert School of Music: Graduate program of study. (2001, January 4). Pittsburgh, Pennsylvania: Duquesne University. Retrieved February 19, 2001, from http://www.duq.edu/music/gradprogstudy.html

Mary Pappert School of Music: Undergraduate program of study. (2001, January 4). Pittsburgh, Pennsylvania: Duquesne University. Retrieved February 19, 2001, from http://www.duq.edu/music/uggradprogstudy.html

McDiarmid, G. W. (1994). The arts and sciences as preparation for teaching. In K. Howey & N. Zimpher (Eds.), *Informing faculty development for teacher educators* (pp. 99–137). Norwood, NJ: Ablex.

Moll, L. (1988). Some key issues in the teaching of Latino students. *Language Arts, 65,* 102–108.

Monk, D., & Brent, B. (1996). Financing teacher education and professional development. In J. Sikula (Ed.), *Handbook of research on teacher education* (2nd ed., pp. 227–241). New York: Macmillan.

Montague, M. J. (1988). An investigation of teacher training in multicultural music education in selected universities and colleges. *Dissertation Abstracts International, 49–08A,* 2142. (UMI No. AAG8821622)

Moore, P. S. (1995). Beginning teachers' perceptions of their preprofessional preparation program and their need for follow-up assistance. *Dissertation Abstracts International, 56–06A,* 2205. (UMI No. AAI9535886)

Morey, A. (1999, October). *The growth of for-profit higher education in the U.S.: Implications for teacher education.* Paper presented at the annual meeting of the Teacher Education Council of State Colleges and Universities, Denver, CO.

Murray, F., & Fallon, D. (1989). *The reform of teacher education for the 21st century: Project 30 year one report.* Newark, DE: University of Delaware.

Murrell, P. (1998). *Like stone soup: The role of the professional development school in the renewal of urban schools.* Washington, DC: American Association of Colleges of Teacher Education.

National Association of Schools of Music. (1999). *National Association of Schools of Music handbook 1999–2000.* Reston, VA: Author.

National Association of Schools of Music. (2001). *National Association of Schools of Music handbook 2001–2002.* Reston, VA: Author.

National Commission on Teaching and America's Future. (1996). *What matters most: Teaching for America's future.* New York: Author.

National Commission on Teaching and America's Future (1997). *Doing what matters most: Investing in quality teaching.* New York: Author.

National Council for Accreditation of Teacher Education. (2000, January). NCATE 2000: Continuing accreditation and beyond. Workshop presented at the Wyndham City Center Hotel, Washington, DC.

National Council for Accreditation of Teacher Education. (2001). *Professional standards for the accreditation of schools, colleges and departments of education.* Washington, DC: Author.

National Science Foundation. (1997). *Collaboratives for excellence in teacher preparation.* Washington, DC: Author.

Nielson, H. D. (1997). Quality assessment and quality assurance in distance teacher education. *Distance Education, 18*(2), 284–317.

Nierman, G. E. (1986, July). *The university and the K–12 school system: Partners in preparing future music educators.* Paper presentation at the XVII World Congress of the International Society of Music Education, Innsbruck, Austria.

Nierman, G. E. (2000). The Nebraska Music Education Ac-

cord & LB 1441: Toward standards for the visual and performing arts. *Nebraska Music Educator, 58*(3), 34–35.

Norman, K. N. (1994). Multicultural music education: Perceptions of current and prospective music education faculty, music supervisors, and music teachers. *Dissertation Abstracts International, 56*(01A), 0131. (UMI No. AAI9513446)

Oakes, J. (1996). Making the rhetoric real. *Multicultural Education.* (1996, Winter), 4–10.

Okun, M. J. (1998). Multicultural perspectives in undergraduate music teacher education programs. *Dissertation Abstracts International, 59*(03A), 0766. (UMI No. AAG 9826648)

Olsen, D. (1985). The quality of prospective teachers: Education vs. noneducation graduates. *Journal of Teacher Education, 36*(5), 56–59.

Palmer, A. J. (1995). Music education and spirituality: A philosophical exploration. *Philosophy of Music Education Review, 3*(2), 91–106.

Parr, N. (1996). Towards a philosophy of music teacher education: Applications of the ideas of Jerome Bruner, Maxine Greene, and Vernon A. Howard. *Dissertation Abstracts International, 57-09A,* 3867. (UMI No. AAG 9701030)

Price, J., & Valli, L. (1998). Institutional support for diversity in preservice teacher education. *Theory into Practice, 37*(2), 114–120.

Quesada, M. A., & Volk, T. M. (1997). World musics and music education: A review of research, 1973–1993. *Bulletin of the Council for Research in Music Education, 131,* 44–66.

Rauscher, F. H., Shaw, G. L., & Ky, K. N. (1995). Listening to Mozart enhances spatial-temporal reasoning: Towards a neurophysiological basis. *Neuroscience Letters, 185,* 44–47.

Rauscher, F. H., Shaw, G. L., Levine, L. J., Wright, E. L., Dennis, W. R., & Newcomb, R. L. (1997). Music training causes long-term enhancement of preschool children's spatial-temporal reasoning. *Neurological Research, 19*(2), 2–8.

Richards, C., & Killen, R. (1996). Preservice music teachers: Influences on lesson planning. *British Journal of Music Education, 13*(1), 31–47.

Robinson, M. (1999). A theory of collaborative music education between higher education and urban public schools. *Dissertation Abstracts International, 60*(04A), 1059. (UMI No. AAG9926394).

Scannell, D. (1999). *Models of teacher education.* Paper prepared for the American Council on Education Task Force on Teacher Education. Unpublished manuscript.

Schnoor, N. (1999). Collegiate wind band conductors' beliefs and attitudes toward aesthetic aims and their incorporation of strategies designed to develop aesthetic sensitivity into the rehearsal setting. *Dissertation Abstracts International, 60*(05A), 1495. (UMI No. AAG9929227)

Schwadron, A. (1985). Aspects of an emerging challenge in music education. *Journal of the Indian Musicological Society, 16*(1), 17–20.

Shen, J. (1998). Alternative certification, minority teachers, and urban education. *Education and Urban Society, 31*(1), 30–41.

Shires, L., Jr. (1990). Teacher preparation needs of music education graduates from Northern Arizona University. *Dissertation Abstracts International, 51*(05A), 1543. (UMI No. AAG902)

Shuler, S. C. (1995). The impact of National Standards on the preparation, in-service professional development, and assessment of music teachers. *Arts Education Policy Review, 96*(3), 2–14.

Shulman, L. S. (1987). Knowledge and teaching: Foundations of the new reform. *Harvard Educational Review, 57*(1), 1–22.

Sirotnik, K., & Goodlad, J. (1988). *School-university partnerships in action.* New York: Teachers College Press.

Smith, M. V. (1994). The mentoring and professional development of new music educators: A descriptive study of a pilot program. *Dissertation Abstracts International, 55* (09A), 2759. (University Microfilms No. AAG9718257)

Snyder, D. W. (1996). Classroom management and the music student teacher (music teacher). *Dissertation Abstracts International, 58* (01A), 0117. (University Microfilms No. AAG9501133)

Spearman, C. (2000). How will societal and technological changes affect the teaching of music? In C. Madsen (Ed.), *Vision 2020: The Housewright symposium on the future of music education* (pp. 155–184). Reston, VA: MENC—The National Association for Music Education.

SRI International. (1999). *Teacher development: A literature review.* Washington, DC: U.S. Department of Education.

Stachowski, L., & Mahan, J. (1998). Cross-cultural field placements: Student teachers learning from schools and communities. *Theory into Practice, 37*(2), 155–162.

Stoddart, T., & Floden, R. (1996). Traditional and alternative routes to teacher certification: Issues, assumptions, and misconceptions. In K. Zeichner, S. Melnick, & M. L. Gomez (Eds.), *Currents of reform in preservice teacher education* (pp. 80–108). New York: Teachers College Press.

Teicher, J. M. (1997). Effect of multicultural music experience on preservice elementary teachers' attitudes. *Journal of Research in Music Education, 45*, 415–27.

Tikunoff, W. (1985) *Applying significant bilingual instructional features in the classroom.* Rosslyn, VA: National Clearinghouse for Bilingual Education.

Tredway, C. (1994). A curriculum for the study of audio, video, computer, and electronic music technology for undergraduate music education majors based on a survey among members of the Florida Music Educators Association. *Dissertation Abstracts International, 55*(11A), 3483. (UMI No. AAI9509007)

UO School of Music: Academic studies. (2000). Eugene, OR: University of Oregon. Retrieved February 21, 2001, from http://music1.uoregon.edu/AcademicStudies/Departments/education.html

Valli, L. (Ed.). (1993). *Reflective teacher education programs: Cases and critiques.* Albany: State University of New York Press.

Valli, L., Cooper, D., & Frankes, L. (1997) Professional development schools and equity: A critical analysis of the rhetoric and research. *Review of Research in Education, 22*, 251–304.

VanOyen, L., & Nierman, G. E. (1998). The effects of two instrumental score preparation approaches on the error detection ability of student conductors. *Contributions to Music Education, 25*(2), 85–97.

Verrastro, R. E., & Leglar, M. (1992). Music teacher education. In R. Colwell (Ed.), *Handbook of research on music teaching and learning* (pp. 480–497). New York: Schirmer Books.

Villegas, A. M. (1991). *Culturally responsive teaching for the 1990's and beyond.* Washington, DC: American Association of Colleges for Teacher Education.

Villegas, A. M., & Clewell, B. C. (1998). Increasing the number of teachers of color for urban schools. *Education & Urban Society, 31*(1), 42–61.

Villegas, A. M., & Lucas, T. (in press). *Educating culturally responsive teachers: A conceptually coherent and structurally integrated approach.* Albany: State University of New York Press.

Volk, T. M. (1993). The history and development of multicultural music education as evidenced in the *Music Educators Journal*, 1967–1992. *Journal of Research in Music Education, 41*, 137–155.

Warren, M. D. L. (1989). The development of models for inservice music teachers' education based on selected school-university collaborations. *Dissertation Abstracts International, 50*(08A), 2420. (UMI No. AAG9002606)

Whitford, B. L., & Metcalf-Turner, P. (1999). Of promises and unsolved puzzles: Reforming teacher education through professional development schools. In G. Griffin (Ed.), *The education of teachers* (pp. 257–278). Chicago: University of Chicago Press.

Wing, L. (1993). Music teacher education: Coming to our senses. *Bulletin of the Council for Research in Music Education, 117*, 51–65.

Woody, R. H., III. (1998). Music teacher education and the Holmes Group. *Contributions to Music Education 25*(2), 27–37.

Yarger, S. J., & Galluzzo, G. R. (1983). Toward solving the dilemmas of research on inservice teacher education. In K. R. Howey & W. E. Gardner (Eds.), *The education of teachers: A look ahead* (pp. 163–191). New York: Longman.

Zeichner, K. (1989). Learning from experience in graduate teacher education. In A. Woolfolk (Ed.), *Research perspectives on the graduate preparation of teachers* (pp. 12–29). Englewood Cliffs, NJ: Prentice Hall.

Zeichner, K. (1992). Rethinking the practicum in the professional development school partnership. *Journal of Teacher Education, 43*(4), 296–307.

Zeichner, K. (1993). Traditions of practice in U.S. teacher education programs. *Teaching and Teacher Education, 9*(1), 1–13.

Zeichner, K. (Ed.). (1998). Preparing teachers for cultural diversity. (Special issue) *Theory into Practice, 37*(2).

Zeichner, K., & Hoeft, K. (1996). Teacher socialization for

cultural diversity. In J. Sikula (Ed.), *Handbook of research on teacher education* (2nd ed., pp. 525–547). New York: Macmillan.

Zeichner, K., & Liston, D. (1996). *Reflective teaching.* Mahwah, NJ: Erlbaum.

Zeichner, K., & Melnick, S. (1996). The role of community field experiences in preparing teachers for cultural diversity. In K. Zeichner, S. Melnick, and M. L. Gomez (Eds.), *Currents of reform in preservice teacher education* (pp. 176–196). New York: Teachers College Press.

Zeichner, K., & Wray, S. (2001). The teaching portfolio in U.S. teacher education programs: What we know and what we need to know. *Teaching and Teacher Education, 17*(5), 613–621.

Zimpher, N. (1989). The RATE project: A profile of teacher education students. *Journal of Teacher Education, 40*(6), 27–31.

Zimpher, N., & Ashburn, E. (1992). Countering parochialism in teacher candidates. In M. Dilworth (Ed.), *Diversity in teacher education* (pp. 40–62). San Francisco: Jossey-Bass.

Zimpher, N. & Sherrill, J. (1996). Professors, teachers, and leaders in SCDEs. In J. Sikula (Ed.), *Handbook of research on teacher education* (2nd ed., pp. 279–305). New York: Macmillan.

Strengthening the Teaching of Music Educators in Higher Education

43

SUSAN WILCOX

RENA UPITIS

Teaching in higher education brings unique challenges to music education, as it involves the bridging of the higher education cultures of universities and colleges with the complexities of contemporary music education. Consequently, this chapter focuses on the research on teaching in higher education in general as well as on specific issues that arise in the domain of music education. It is presented in three sections that discuss, respectively: the challenges of teaching in music education as influenced by the nature of university and college programs and the background experience of music educators; the development of faculty members' expertise in teaching, including the preparation of graduate teaching assistants; and strategies for fostering the teaching of university and college music educators.

The Challenges of Teaching in Music Education in Higher Education

Unique issues in the development of university music educators arise out of the interaction between the general issues regarding university teaching and the specific features of music and music education. These issues include but are not limited to the evolution of music in higher education and the background preparation of university music educators, differences between elementary and secondary music teaching and preparation in the United States and other countries, and current trends in music education and the music industry.

J. P. Green and Vogan (1991) have documented the complexity of the roots of music in higher education across jurisdictions. This complexity is due, in part, to the many academic purposes that music has served, most notably, "the professional training of musicians, including specialized programs for music teachers; academic courses within the arts and humanities curricula; [and] music methods as a function of teacher training for generalists or elementary classroom teachers" (p. 400). Further, there are clear differences between British and French traditions, university and conservatory approaches, European and American practices, and academic and professional concerns (Bartle, 1996; Brookhart, 1988; J. P. Green & Vogan, 1991). As Green and Vogan claim, "An unraveling of these strands is central to an understanding of the evolution of music in higher education" (p. 400).

One central strand identified by Green and Vogan (1991) and others is that a generalist approach to teacher education typically has been employed in the preparation of elementary classroom teachers in many countries, including the United States and Canada (Bresler, 1993; J. P. Green & Vogan, 1991), with an emphasis on integrated and multi-arts approaches to music education (Andrews, 2000; Lehman & Sinatra, 1988). However, a more specialized approach continues to apply in the preparation of teachers for secondary schools, where the focus is on providing comprehensive, discipline-based programs with an emphasis on ensemble performance. However, even at the secondary level of teacher preparation there is considerable variation across jurisdictions, with undergraduate preparation that ranges from 1 to 4 years and with some jurisdictions requiring master-level degrees for secondary teaching (J. P. Green & Vogan, 1991; Lehman & Sinatra, 1988). In particular, the typical pattern in Canada is for music teachers to be prepared in 1- or 2-year programs in faculties of education, after earning an undergraduate degree in music performance or composition at a school or department of music. However, many U.S. music teachers receive their university training in 4-year undergraduate music education programs that are often housed in schools of music, rather than in faculties of education.

The preparation of secondary school music teachers was one of the factors that contributed to the growth of music faculties and music education faculties across North America in the 1960s, when secondary school instrumental music programs enjoyed a similar expansion. Graduates of university music programs, which included performance ensembles that had parallels in the secondary system, returned to secondary schools as teachers, and this interaction between secondary and tertiary levels of education contributed to the continuing importance of performance and performance-related emphases in music education programs (J. P. Green & Vogan, 1991). However, this phenomenon also made it possible for universities to hire musicologists, theorists, composers, and performers so that new university specializations emerged in theory and composition, music history, and so on. At the same time, music began to play a greater role in the academic and cultural life of the university (J. P. Green & Vogan, 1991). As a result of the nature of growth in music and music education, most university music educators associated with secondary school music programs received the bulk of their training in programs and private lessons that featured performance on a single instrument or family of instruments, with an emphasis on Western music (J. P. Green & Vogan, 1991; Leong, 1997; Leonhard, 1991; Stake, Bresler, & Mabry, 1991), and these faculty members were in some sense "separate" from the musicologists, composers, and theorists. Indeed, some have suggested that there has been an undue emphasis on music performance (Leonhard and House, cited in Elliott, 1995) as a result, pointing out that a performance emphasis is in stark contrast to the training of, for example, composers or musicologists. Further, while performance experience and preparation are certainly germane to university teaching, the claim has been made that it only addresses a limited number of issues and skills that university music educators must possess for the coming decades. That is, the current music curriculum in elementary, middle, and secondary schools, in Canada and the United States and in other countries, is often broader than that which university music educators have themselves experienced (Errington, 1993).

One of the emerging trends in music in higher education arises out of the growing interactions among musicologists, music theorists, psychologists, and music educators (Fiske, 2000) and the consequent questions that have been directed toward the traditional music education curriculum based on performance and conservatory traditions. Some might claim that these interactions have been long overdue,

for the schism between the performance faculty and those who teach other aspects of music education in higher education has, at times, been great (Fiske, 2000; J. P. Green & Vogan, 1991). These interactions have led to serious and lively debate on such issues as multiple intelligences (Gardner, 1983), music across cultures (Campbell, 1991; Reimer, 1994), critical thinking (Brophy, 2000; Music Educators National Conference [MENC], 1994), gender issues (L. Green, 1997), and postmodernism and poststructuralism (Fiske, 2000; Hanley, 2000). As a result, the so-called masterpieces that constitute the Western musical canon are undergoing scrutiny and will continue to be scrutinized as educators call into question the "elite" notion of masterpieces, while at the same time rediscovering "lost composers and music" (Fiske, 2000, p. 294). Further, the new millennium promises a new era of contemporary music (Fiske, 2000). These trends in higher education will serve to further define music education in higher education over the coming decades. As a result, there will be a need for continued professional development of higher education music education faculty, along with the need for an increase in meaningful interactions among faculty members with differing expertise.

Yet another trend that promises to have an enormous effect on music education in higher education is the growing prevalence of technology. Simply put, the students teachers face in schools today are not the students they taught a decade or two ago (Tapscott, 1997). Technology is pervasive in students' lives; television, electronic games, and recorded music have altered the ways in which students process information and learn. Technology will play an exceedingly important and very specific role in the learning and performing of music as well (Research Studies in Music Education [RSME], 1994; Stevens, 1994), even though the preparation of future music teachers often still lacks this dimension, partly because university faculty lack the expertise to provide such preparation (Deal & Taylor, 1997; Roberts, 2000; Williams & Webster, 1996; Yip, 2000). And there are further complications. As Roberts (2000) recently noted:

> Computers make it possible for people who have little or no knowledge of traditional theory to compose music . . . music programs must now provide training in technology . . . or . . . face extinction. [But] "embracing" technology . . . has its costs. The time required to deliver technology courses leaves less time for more traditional courses. Technology eats a big hole in the music budget. (pp. 17–18)

Roberts's observation brings into focus the role of industry in the support of technology in music education, for many schools and faculties have found it necessary to turn to the industry for financial support and equipment.

Swanwick raises the sobering possibility that music education might be colonized by multinational companies (1996, cited in Hanley, 2000). Further, Gouzouasis (2000) has argued that

> mass media have the most prevalent impact on the music preferences of people living in Western-influenced societies. Our music cultures are directed by huge multinational corporations . . . it is the music tastes and whims of musically illiterate executive producers and lawyers that dominate what we hear, how much we hear it, when we hear it, and where we hear it—not just in North America, but on much of our planet. And with the convergence of various technology platforms and the convergence of Internet and "content providers" (i.e., music companies such as Warner, Columbia, and Atlantic Records) our music choices and tastes will become even more defined by mass media. (pp. 236–237)

Another effect of music technology is described by Hanley (1999, 2000), who argues that the use of technology has replaced one type of myth—that most people can't compose music—with another, namely, that anyone can compose music through use of the appropriate computer tools. Gouzouasis (2000) took this observation one step further by claiming that "music may be the only profession that has simultaneously been most positively and negatively affected by technological developments" (p. 249). He concluded that the trend will continue unless the profession "makes a serious effort to put innovation ahead of preservation," emphasizing the creative aspects of music making over more traditional performance- and notation-based approaches (p. 249).

There is a further argument for closer attention to the creative aspects of music making and, consequently, the need for professional development in higher education to address this issue. Scholars, ethnographers, and philosophers have argued that "music, like language and possibly religion, is a species-specific trait of [humankind]" (Blacking, 1973, p. 7). Further, the very existence of music-specific neurons in the brain indicates that music is a fundamental and essential aspect of being human (Nelson & Bloom, 1997; Weinberger & McKenna, 1988). Others who are keen observers of children's musical behavior have claimed that "all children, to a greater or lesser degree, are musical" (Campbell, 1998, p. 169). What is inherent in these views, however, is that musicality is not expressed in the same way by all people. Further, school music has exposed and enhanced some forms of musicality, such as performance, over others—namely, creative expression and composition. In fact, many scholars and practitioners claim that composition is a specific musical ability everyone possesses (c.f., Hargreaves, 1986; Kratus, 1989; Reimer, 1997; Upitis, 1990, 1992), and that the challenge for schooling is to make composition a central feature of music educa-

tion (Campbell, 1998; Tsisserev, 1997; Upitis, 1992). As Tsisserev (1997) has argued, there is a need for adolescent students in particular to express their creative impulses through the arts and secondary schools would do well to institutionalize more composition courses to address the creative impulse in ways that are not possible through performance courses alone. This view is shared by others and is not new (e.g., Schafer, 1976, cited in Kennedy, 2000), but the importance of moving in this direction at this time is significant, as we are also witnessing a proliferation of technologically advanced composing tools in the popular culture. If the arguments of Tsisserev and others are taken seriously, then there will be a need for specific professional development in higher education to accommodate these new directions in teacher education.

The training of music educators in higher education also colors what graduates of undergraduate and graduate music education programs view as important; not surprisingly, the most valued aspects of the music curriculum, as identified by classroom teachers, reflect the training that the classroom teachers themselves received (Bates, Frederickson, & Lamb, 2000; J. P. Green & Vogan, 1991; Roberts, 1993). Thus learning concepts such as melody, rhythm, and form is more highly valued than gaining knowledge of world musics, electroacoustic music, or composition (Bates et al., 2000). Those aspects of the curriculum that are less highly valued are also taught less well, if they are taught at all. For example, although music curricula throughout North America and other parts of the world now feature the teaching of world musics, the type and extent of this teaching depend a great deal on teachers' exposure to different musics both before and during their university training, on their experience with broad-based high school music programs, and on their comfort with world musics (Johnson, 1997; K. Marsh, 2000). Communication with colleagues, research on world musics, and preparation in bachelor-of-music and bachelor-of-music-education or bachelor-of-education degrees tend to be less often used as sources for teaching world musics (Johnson, 1997), a situation that is perpetuated by those teaching in higher education as a result of their own prior experiences, which, on the whole, did not include world musics or some of the other areas that are now evolving. Interestingly, the lack of published teaching resources appears not to be an issue; rather, the crux of the problem is that "teachers lack confidence to implement multicultural music programs [reflecting] the fact that, in their preservice training, many teachers have not acquired a conceptual framework for, or positive disposition towards, the implementation of such programs" (K. Marsh, 2000, p. 243). Similar arguments can be made for other neglected aspects of the music curriculum that were simply not an issue only a decade ago.

The Development of Faculty Expertise

A substantial number of Ph.D. graduates start jobs in colleges and universities "never having taught before and never having any formal instruction in how to teach" (Weimer, 1990, p. 9). Although "courses or clinical experiences concerning the research and skills of teaching are seldom part of the formal education" (Fife, 1995, p. xi) of future teachers in higher education, when a faculty member is hired it is assumed the individual already possesses the necessary skills of teaching. The underlying assumption about university teaching is that good teachers are born, not made. Another powerful assumption that shapes current practices is "if you know it, you can teach it" (Weimer, 1990, p. 4). Historically, faculty members' content and disciplinary expertise has been accepted as equivalent to instructional expertise. Faculty preparation in graduate school thus offers very little or no instruction in *how* to teach, focusing instead on preparing faculty members who are *content* experts. Many contemporary teaching practices reflect an old idea of higher education as a realm of learned persons who share their knowledge with novices in the field. Most teachers "hope by virtue of an association with an academic discipline, students will learn how people in the field solve problems, generate theories, raise questions, and test answers" (Weimer, 1990, p xiii).

There is a long history of student complaints about the quality of university teaching (Bok, 1991). Calls for reform became especially prominent in the 1960s, and serious attention was finally given to the nature of preparation for teaching that professors had received. The most common remedy for inadequate preparation was engagement of faculty members in collegial activities to improve the quality of their teaching. The field of faculty development was born at that time (see Gaff & Simpson, 1994, for a history of faculty development in the United States) and has since become a field of study and practice with its own literature and conventions of practice (Brew, 1995; Paulsen & Feldman, 1995; Webb, 1996), with attention growing in the past decade. The changing profile of undergraduate students and expanded purposes of undergraduate education, declining resources, and increasing enrollments, plus a deeper appreciation for the complexity of student learning processes, have fueled recent efforts to bring about change. There is a wide range of approaches to the development of teaching, reflecting the complexity of faculty roles; faculty members typically control the content of teaching (in their roles as curriculum/course planners) and the institutional environment for teaching (in their roles as administrators) as well as the methods of teaching (in their roles as classroom teachers). The literature is concerned with the development of faculty members' instructional expertise over the course of their careers as teachers and is not restricted to preparatory education for university and college teaching.

The Preparation of Graduate Assistants and the Induction of New Faculty Members

The career-long development of faculty expertise in teaching should begin with the training of graduate students who play a teaching role at the university level and also include induction programs for new faculty members. The seeds for a developmental approach to improvement are best planted at an early stage in university teaching. In the case of music education, we might argue that preparation for teaching should extend to undergraduate programs and include curricular requirements in pedagogy for all music majors, given that almost all music professionals will teach in some capacity at some point in their careers.

The preparation of graduate teaching assistants deserves special mention since for many future faculty members, the teaching assistantship is their first experience of university teaching. The employment of teaching assistants (TAs) serves several functions: helping universities meet the need for undergraduate instructors, providing funding for graduate students, and preparing the faculty of the future to teach. "TA activities are quite complex and require specific skills which are not developed through normal course work" (Saroyan & Amundsen, 1995, p. 6). Nonetheless, it is only in the past few years that "increasing pressure to assure quality instruction for undergraduates being taught by TAs has resulted in the implementation of some type of teacher training programs for TAs at most universities" (Richlin, 1995, p. 260). Since the explosion of interest in graduate students as teachers, entire issues of publications (J. D. W. Andrews, 1985) and books (Nyquist, Abbott, & Wulff, 1989) have been dedicated to the training of TAs, guides to programs have been produced (Lambert & Tice, 1993), and conferences and professional gatherings have taken place (Chism, 1987; Lewis, 1993). Currently there is tremendous variation in the teaching development experiences of graduate students. Many TAs receive absolutely no preparation for their duties and minimal support and others participate in specialized TA training programs offered by the university's instructional/faculty development unit, while some graduate students enroll in credit courses and/or certificate programs designed to prepare them for their immediate TA duties and their future life as university or college professors.

To train TAs, both formal and informal apprenticeship experiences are deemed suitable. Accumulated empirical evidence suggests that TA training has a positive, though limited, impact on both TAs and the students with whom they interact and that "it is possible to improve the teaching of TAs by means of certain kinds of direct and indirect interventions" (Saroyan & Amundsen, 1995, p. 3). Abbott,

Wulff, and Szego (1989) reviewed 13 research studies that investigated the impact of TA training programs and found that every study reported significant effects of some component of the training provided. Richlin's (1995) review of the literature demonstrates that some methods of working with assistants are more effective than others. Angelo and Cross (1989) have categorized TA training programs into four general approaches:

- inspiration/information (through written materials, lectures, and demonstrations by experts);
- specific skills training (through workshops, seminars, and short courses);
- clinical/technical consultations (through observation, videotaping, and one-to-one consultation with instructional expert); and
- coaching/mentorship (observation and informal and structured interviews with faculty mentor from the same discipline).

In addition, Angelo and Cross propose the use of a fifth approach: classroom research, where the primary focus is to improve student learning and TAs are required to take responsibility for educational development by raising questions about teaching, devising projects to explore questions, and interpreting data on student learning.

Although there is a need for future academics who are effective teachers, a national survey in the United States reported that the development of future faculty remains a relatively unimportant objective of teaching assistant programs (Sell, 1987, cited in Richlin, 1995, p. 257). "There is continuing tension between the views that a TAship is an apprenticeship to a lifelong career and that it is strictly financial aid" (Richlin, 1995, p. 259). Saroyan and Amundsen (1995) recommend that the training of TAs should be considered to be both a short-term and a long-term investment. In the short term, training can have a direct impact on the quality of the course to which a TA is assigned; in the long term, it can serve as an apprenticeship for a lifelong career (Boehrer & Sarkisian, 1985) that yields academics who have training, expertise, and experience both in their subject area and in general and discipline-specific pedagogy. Faculty are acculturated to the norms and values of academic life during their graduate student years, and "the process of becoming a TA influences the thoughts and feelings one has about the academy, as well as the types of activities one pursues as a professor" (Staton & Darling, 1989, p. 21). Teaching preparation must be an integral part of the graduate education process, not separate from it (Schuster, 1990), and the teaching assistantship offers the perfect opportunity to begin preparation for teaching.

Sprague and Nyquist (1989) posit three phases of TA development: TA as senior learner, TA as colleague-in-training, and TA as junior colleague, and capture the transitory nature of the TA role as well as the sense of progression that occurs during an apprenticeship. K. S. Smith and Kalivoda (1998) studied the process by which graduate students used a positive TA experience (including participation in a well-established TA mentoring program) to make a successful transition into faculty roles. The researchers found that disciplinary, departmental, and institutional forces, in combination with individual characteristics of the TAs, shaped a set of professional values. These values helped the TAs to form strategies for success in securing a first faculty position and in balancing professional roles during the first year as a faculty member. For recommendations that concern how graduate education should address the issue of adequately preparing professors for their roles, especially through the improvement of TA training for teaching, see Richlin (1995).

Looking specifically at the experiences of new and junior faculty, Tierney and Bensimon (1996) report that "faculty are socialized about teaching in the most haphazard way" (p. 64). New and junior faculty often begin their academic careers "under serious pressures and in dysfunctional academic communities," noted Cox (1995), and "the resulting stress and lack of preparation for teaching leads to 'survival teaching' unless there are thoughtful interventions" (p. 286). Menges (1999) describes the situation of new and junior faculty who participated in the New Faculty (research) Project:

> Despite their strong scholarly preparation, new faculty experience problems and dilemmas in managing competing responsibilities, in establishing fruitful relationships with others, and in getting sufficient feedback in order to celebrate what is going well and remedy what must be changed. (p. xvii)

The well-being of faculty actually declined over the first 3 years in their new jobs. Two significant dilemmas that affect the teaching of new faculty are, first, the well-known problem of how to allocate work time to meet competing responsibilities and, second, the question of how to profit from performance reviews as a means for development when reviews are designed to serve institutional needs more than faculty needs (Menges, 1999).

All new faculty must master three complex activities: teaching, scholarship, and collegiality. Boice (1992) observed that success at any one of the three areas rarely comes in isolation from success in the other two. His study (Boice, 1991) of the experiences of new faculty showed a surprisingly slow pattern of establishing comfort and student approval in the classroom; findings depict new faculty as badly in peril of establishing poor habits of teaching that will persist. Boice found that new faculty as teachers tend to teach as they were taught, equate good teaching with content, teach defensively, blame external factors for poor student ratings, be passive about change and improvement, and allow narrow, short-term goals to dominate their actions. Boice also found that a small subgroup of new faculty ("quick-starters") teach with obvious comfort (presentations are unhurried and encourage active student involvement), are optimistic about students, seek advice from colleagues, and quickly establish a balance of time spent on teaching preparation, on collegiality, and on scholarship. The keys to their success include moderation (especially in terms of time spent on class preparation) and involvement (immersion in the campus community).

Walker and Hale (1999, p. 230) report that "the well-being of new faculty is heartiest when the institution in which they work supports, promotes and rewards teaching." They explain that great teaching requires enormous human energy. Thus

> it is not enough for new instructors to be merely *satisfied* with their work. Throughout a long career, to maintain even moderate levels of energy, faculty must constantly renew themselves or, if they are fortunate, teach at institutions that have environments and programs that support faculty *vitality*. (p. 234)

Although programs to better prepare faculty for teaching have tended to focus on graduate TAs, recent efforts to provide more comprehensive and systematic support for new faculty during the crucial induction period have been described in the literature. Austin (1992) described the success of the Lilly Teaching Fellows Program, which has involved more than 750 teachers at 43 major American universities, in terms of its ability to significantly assist new faculty in dealing with their most challenging professional concerns. The goals of the award-winning Teaching Scholars Program for junior faculty at Miami University, Ohio (Cox, 1995) are to provide faculty with opportunities to obtain information on teaching and learning, observe successful teaching and practice using new skills and knowledge, investigate teaching problems and projects, share ideas and advice with senior faculty mentors, experience the scholarship of teaching and establish colleagueship across disciplines, and share, via outreach, their enthusiasm and experiences with other new faculty. All full-time faculty in tenurable positions are eligible to participate in the 2nd through 5th years of their teaching; a subgroup is chosen to participate each year.

For comprehensive detailed summaries of research findings and strategies for improving the lives and careers of new and junior faculty, see Boice (1992), Menges and Associates (1999), and Sorcinelli and Austin (1992). We are not aware of any empirical studies of teaching development programs designed specifically for new or junior music faculty. Note that the initial training of university teach-

ers has developed in a different direction in the United Kingdom than in the United States (Gibbs, 1998). A national certification scheme for university teaching programs in the United Kingdom concentrates on new tenure-track faculty rather than TAs and on course design rather than on classroom practice, tends to be much more intensive, and is more closely linked to personnel decisions than in the United States.

Teaching Development Processes

Some of the theoretical and conceptual foundations for practice and research in teaching development draw on existing theory in other areas. For example, faculty development has been linked theoretically with models of career development (Brookes & German, 1983) and of organizational development (Keller, 1983). R. Smith (1983) and R. Smith and Schwartz (1985), drawing on Argyris and Schön's (1974) action theory, devised strategies for helping faculty identify their assumptions about teaching. Other researchers have used cognitive theory as a means of understanding faculty members' knowledge of their subject matter and of their instruction (Resnick, 1981; Shulman, 1986, 1998).

Others have tried to construct the beginnings of a general theory of educational development. Zuber-Skerritt (1992) has described the process of professional development as one in which the academic "as a self-directed learner and problem-solver" engages in "a process of learning and knowing" (p. 146). To develop means "to learn and to change for the better, to move from one stage to the next; it means to change one's personal constructs (consisting of both thought and feeling), attitudes, and the values underlying one's strategies and actions" (p. 177). Weimer (1990) prescribes a five-step process as one means faculty might use to "guide their pursuit of better teaching": develop instructional awareness; gather information from students and peers; change and make choices; implement alterations; and assess effectiveness. Zuber-Skerritt and Weimer both convey an image of active and self-directed engagement by the faculty member in a step-by-step development process. Kozma (1985) noted, however, that change in teaching is not necessarily a systematically planned or even intentional process. His theory of instructional innovation is grounded in data from the analysis of four institutional projects. He found that new teaching behaviors evolved from past practices and usually represented alternative expressions of attitudes, values, preferences, and philosophies embedded in previously used techniques; new teaching practices are generally not considered and adopted (or rejected) deliberately and systematically but, rather, are adopted based on their closeness to previous practice. Ramsden (1992) also hinted at an evolutionary aspect to change when he described the process of development in teaching as "a shift from a simple way of understanding teaching to a complex, relativistic, and dynamic one" (p. 250), which involves a "change from simple to complex, from absolute to relative, from the unquestioning acceptance of authority to a search for personal meaning, from discrete techniques to the expression of skills within an ordered, yet ultimately provisional system" (p. 267).

There is a body of work focused on professors' personal theories or metaphors for teaching and how they make meaning of teaching (Fox, 1983; Kugel, 1993; Pratt, 1992; Tiberius, 1986). One theoretical framework that takes teachers' theories of teaching into account depicts the process of teaching improvement as a four-level developmental process, each stage characterized by distinctive perceptions of teaching and learning and associated teaching practices. At the first and least developed stage, the instructor views teaching as presenting information. By the fourth stage, the instructor views teaching as a "complex interaction of students, content and teacher actions" (Sherman, Armistad, Powler, Barksdale, & Reif, 1987, pp. 78–79). Ramsden (1992) has described three generic ways of understanding the role of the teacher (i.e., three theories of teaching) in higher education: teaching as telling or transmission, teaching as organizing student activity, and teaching as making learning possible. Clearly influenced by stage theories of development, Ramsden posited that these theories of teaching have a progressive, or hierarchical, structure: The third theory is the most sophisticated and therefore most desirable. A study designed to test the validity of Ramsden's framework supported the descriptions of the three theories but did not support the notion of a hierarchical relationship between them; development in thinking about teaching was recursive—individuals fluctuate back and forth between levels—rather than unidirectional (Amundsen & Saroyan, 1993). It appears that movement between the stages of development is encouraged by an opportunity for structured reflection, sufficient time to make shifts in thinking and action, considerable involvement, moderate levels of challenge, and peer support and encouragement (Amundsen, Gryspeerdt, & Moxness, 1993). Kember (1997) has recently connected faculty members' conceptions of and approaches to teaching with students' conceptions of and approaches to learning. He shows that studying teaching conceptions is important because they are related to measures of the quality of student learning. Kember depicts teaching conceptions as influencing teaching approaches, which in turn affect student learning approaches and subsequently learning outcomes. This model implies that real changes in teaching and learning quality are only likely to be brought about by changes in faculty beliefs about teaching.

Models of Intervention to Foster Teaching Development

Early reviewers of the research literature that concerns the effectiveness of faculty development programs and activities (Centra, 1976; Gaff, 1975; Hoyt & Howard, 1978) found that while evaluation of interventions was rare, the literature reported consistent participant satisfaction with the services provided. Levinson-Rose and Menges (1981) reviewed the research that evaluated the impact of more than a decade's worth of faculty and instructional development activities. Although research quantity and quality were lower than they had hoped, most of the studies supported the intervention in question. They were able to make some specific recommendations to practitioners that concerned the probable effectiveness of certain improvement strategies: (1) workshops and seminars are useful to motivate and raise consciousness but unlikely to produce lasting changes unless there is follow-up; (2) end-of-course student evaluations can positively affect subsequent teaching, particularly if ratings are accompanied by consultation; and (3) concept-based training (for example, films that illustrate six basic concepts in questioning) may be less costly, disruptive, and intimidating than the practice-based training required by microteaching and minicourses. In 1991 Weimer and Lenze updated the Levinson-Rose and Menges study, reviewing the literature published in the 1980s on five interventions to improve instruction (workshops, consultation, instructional improvement grants, distribution of resource material, and colleagues helping colleagues). Research reviewed offered some inconclusive support for current interventions. Weimer and Lenze concluded (similarly to Levinson-Rose and Menges a decade earlier) that there is a need for more and better research and that the study of instructional interventions needs to derive from theoretical and conceptual bases.

R. Smith (1995), in a critical analysis of efforts to improve the quality of teaching and learning, contends that it is not clear that teaching well really matters in higher education, despite the numerous programs to support and encourage the improvement of teaching that have been developed over the last 25 years. He suggests that what is required is "nothing short of a radical transformation of the culture of the academy, including our fundamental conceptions of teaching and scholarship" (p. 20). Many recent teaching interventions, especially those that focus the scholarship of teaching, are designed to directly address this problem of taking teaching seriously by recognizing and rewarding teaching contributions.

While research and debate continue into both the nature of the teaching developmental process and the characteristics of effective teaching improvement programs, there is an immediate and ongoing requirement to encourage faculty members to change and grow in a positive direction. Two recent compilations (Seldin & Assoc., 1995; Wright & Assoc., 1995) of research-based teaching improvement practices provide links between the theoretical/research literature and the prescriptive literature that promote particular developmental practices and serve as useful introductions to teaching improvement in higher education for people new to the field. This section reviews a range of approaches to fostering teaching development by identifying five different generic models of intervention in the developmental process. Although our review of the literature suggests that each one of the models has the potential to improve teaching and foster educator development, we are unaware of research that tests these models of intervention, especially in the context of music education.

1. *Research (development as using research on teaching and learning to inform teaching).* An important step in improving teaching is conducting research on teaching (see Dunkin & Barnes, 1986; McKeachie, 1990; McKeachie, Pintrich, Lin, & Smith, 1986). One way to use research to intervene in development is to disseminate research-based knowledge of teaching among university teachers so that they can use it to improve their practice (see Menges, Weimer et al., 1996). More recently, research in higher education has focused more and more on the quality and characteristics of student learning (Barr & Tagg, 1995; Brookfield, 1991), and there is an increasing emphasis on informal classroom research or action research conducted by practitioners (Cross, 1990; Schratz, 1990; Zuber-Skerritt, 1992). Boyer's (1990) reconceptualization of teaching as scholarship calls upon all faculty members to approach their teaching as a form of serious intellectual work, the implication being that such scholarship will foster the development of teaching and learning (Taylor, 1993).

2. *Evaluation (development as using evaluative feedback to make improvements).* The evaluation of teaching in higher education was originally introduced as an instrument for enhancing teaching quality. There is an extensive literature on evaluating teaching (d'Appolonia & Abrami, 1997; H. M. Marsh, 1984; McKeachie, 1997a); the focus here is on the impact of summative teaching evaluations on the development of teaching and on the value of formative feedback for teaching development purposes (Centra, 1993; Murray, 1997; Ryan, 2000). Trends (Ory, 2000) of particular interest include a drive to assess learning outcomes rather than teaching processes (Angelo & Cross, 1993) and a greater emphasis on faculty members evaluating their own teaching including a movement to encourage the use of teaching portfolios as a means of developing and documenting teaching effectiveness (Edgerton, Hutchings, & Quinlan, 1991; Seldin, 1996; Shore, et al., 1986) and a call to take collegial responsibility for the assessment and development of teaching through the peer review process (Hutchings, 1995, 1996).

3. *Education/training (development as an adult learning process).* In one way, the professional development of university teachers has always been seen as a process of adult learning, in which faculty members learn to teach through the experience of teaching. Recognizing the shortcomings of such a laissez-faire model of development has led some to promote more formal preparatory training for beginning teachers (as described earlier) and others to emphasize the requirement for critical reflection if teachers are indeed to learn from their ongoing experiences in the classroom (Brookfield, 1995; Schön, 1983). The traditional sabbatical may be seen as an opportunity for reflection on previous classroom experiences. If development means learning and changing for the better and faculty members are viewed as self-directed learners and problem solvers engaged in a personal process of growth, then adult learning theory (Candy, 1991; Mezirow, 1991) is particularly relevant in understanding and promoting professional development. Cranton (1994, 1996) has argued that adult education can provide a much-needed theoretical framework for teaching development, a framework that brings with it some important implications for effective development practice.

4. *Conversation/consultation/mentorship (development through relationships with colleagues).* One long-standing model of intervention (Boud & McDonald, 1981; Knapper & Piccinin, 1999) is based on the idea that teachers may experience problems that are not easily resolved and may block the process of development. Through consultation with an experienced and knowledgeable colleague, the roots of the problem may be discovered and a path to resolution cleared. The clinical-therapeutic tradition influenced early versions of this model; more recently, peer consultation (Boud, 1999) and mentoring programs (Boyle & Boice, 1998) are the norm, reflecting an understanding that all faculty members can benefit from collegial teaching partnerships throughout their careers. Recent trends include efforts to expand the conversational circle by making teaching "community property" (Palmer, 1993, 1998).

5. *Curricular/disciplinary (development through attention to what is being taught).* In higher education there is little understanding of the link between being a subject matter expert and being a teacher (Amundsen, Saroyan, & Gryspeerdt, 1999) and too little discussion about how faculty members become effective teachers in their disciplines. Shulman's (1986) discussion of content knowledge, pedagogical content knowledge, and curricular knowledge has made a significant contribution here, capturing the idea that how one teaches is related to what one teaches and is thus shaped by disciplinary/interdisciplinary concerns. Curriculum development may have been undervalued in traditional efforts to improve university teaching; recent

calls for wholesale curricular reform demand that faculty members connect content with method (Conrad & Haworth, 1995). Another significant trend is the move to discipline-based professional development (Diamond & Adam, 1996; Jenkins, 1996; Morss & Donagy, 1998). This trend is of particular relevance in the teaching of music, where subject mastery is of paramount importance, as indicated in a recent Canadian study (Beynon, 2000), where cooperating or host teachers who worked with student teachers indicated that "subject matter knowledge was an essential qualification to be a music teacher" (p. 112). Further, the cooperating teachers in the study "assumed that they would only ever work with student teachers who were already accomplished musicians with the requisite baccalaureate background in musicianship, performance, and conducting" (pp. 112–113). This view, namely, that "novice teachers cannot be successful as music teachers unless they have the prerequisites" (p. 113), is of direct relevance to higher music education, particularly where student teachers lack the requisite skills or where the requisite skills are beyond those taught in the baccalaureate or those that music professors themselves possess (e.g., skills in technology, improvisation, and composition).

Themes

Some common threads run through the different models of teaching development described here. Themes that dominate the most recent literature, which are likely to shape future practices, include discipline- or department-based development, increasingly intentional and systematic approaches to development, an emphasis on community building and collegial relationships, and attention to the ultimate goal of improved student learning. The focus, overall, is on faculty members as members of a community of teachers who take responsibility for their own development by reflecting critically on the ways their personal practices are promoting valued learning outcomes in their students.

Strategies for Fostering the Teaching of University and College Music Educators

It is clear that music educators must prepare future teachers to "adapt to the complexity of their circumstances . . . to deal with a wide range of musics . . . and to deal with many students encompassing wide age ranges, cultural/socioeconomic backgrounds, and abilities" (Bates et al., 2000, p. 36). While there is widespread endorsement of the need for professional development for music educators at all levels of education (Andrews, 2000; Morin, 1994),

there is considerably less agreement on the "knowledge and instructional skills required of elementary and secondary teachers . . . nor agreement on the most appropriate approaches to . . . teacher education and professional development" (Andrews, 2000, p. 456). For this reason, the strategies for intervention that might be proposed to develop the teaching of university music educators must necessarily be broad and varied.

Because of the emphasis on performance that marks the preparation of many music professors involved in higher education, the claim has been made that university music educators must learn to adapt their teaching strategies to involve a broad range of prior abilities and experiences, as well as approaches to music education that they themselves might not have encountered in their music training. For example, elementary music teachers must be prepared to teach large groups of children with no prior music background, and this form of teaching may be unfamiliar to many university music educators—yet they are expected to prepare teachers for just such a situation. Also, it is not surprising that the teaching of improvisation and composition is not featured in many elementary music programs, for many university music educators themselves have not learned to improvise and compose. Leonhard (1991) reports that only 16% of American public elementary school music programs feature improvisation and music is most often taught in the American elementary schools by music specialists (approximately 88%). In Canada, where there are fewer music specialists, improvisation and composition may be featured even less often (Bartel & Elliott, 1994). Consequently, one of the challenges in higher education is to help university music educators develop their own learning and teaching beyond performance, conducting, appreciation, and theory—areas in which they themselves were schooled. The importance of featuring improvisation and composition in the curriculum is underscored by the arguments made by Gouzouasis (2000) in the earlier section: If teachers of music are unable to attend to the very real current issues that intertwine technology, music, and composition through a healthy balance of both heritage and innovation, then music programs at elementary, secondary, and tertiary levels of education are bound to suffer. Despite the limits of performance-based training, however, the performance perspective can provide the basis for further learning. That is, performance is often characterized by ensemble (indeed, many elementary and secondary programs are rooted in the ensemble traditions of bands, orchestras, and choirs); ensemble performances rely on strong relationships with peers and, as indicated earlier in the chapter, it is through peer learning that much professional development in higher education can take place (Boud, 1999).

Against this background, what specific forms of professional development hold most promise for music education? First, university and college music faculty—like their colleagues in other disciplines—must initially receive better preparation for teaching than they've had in the past. Professional development should begin early with teacher training for graduate students and should include attention to new faculty induction. A collegial approach to the training of graduate teaching assistants and junior faculty may inject new life into the teaching of more senior faculty. Being more intentional about preparing future and beginning teachers can involve all faculty members, at all stages of development, in thoughtful and productive conversations about university teaching and can stimulate change in the culture of a department. This is highly desirable given that effective professional development must continue throughout the career span of faculty, with serious attention given to the quality of teaching over the duration of faculty careers as music educators. In addition to preparatory education for teaching, we propose three key strategies for professional development to consider.

1. *Talking about teaching with our colleagues.* One clear conclusion, reached through reference to decades of accumulated faculty development experience and research, is the value of making teaching community property (Palmer, 1993). When faculty open the classroom door—actually and/or metaphorically—to colleagues and talk thoughtfully about their teaching, good things happen. Accordingly, we recommend that university music educators contribute to their own teaching community by initiating collegial teaching conversations. Initiatives may be formal (teaching circles, seminars, brown-bag lunches, guest speakers, etc.) or informal ("you'll never believe what happened in my class today"), but they need to be reflective, honest, and curious. Useful teaching conversations can begin with the particulars of specific classroom situations or be prompted by attention to contemporary curricular concerns or technology issues in music, for example. What is important for the development of teaching is that discussions about issues become conversations among colleagues who have a variety of music abilities and experiences with real implications for classroom practice. In other words, faculty need to talk about what to teach *and* how to teach it, addressing educational concerns at a personal and practical level.

2. *Preparing and assessing teaching portfolios.* A teaching portfolio documents an individual's development and accomplishments as a teacher (Edgerton, Hutchings, & Quinlan, 1991; Seldin, 1996). In the portfolio, teachers articulate their philosophy of teaching, describe their teaching responsibilities and activities, and present evidence of their effectiveness. Preparing a portfolio is a reflective process that demands that teachers critically reconsider their teaching and then present an argument for their approach that will make sense to their colleagues. Teaching is treated

as a form of scholarship worthy of peer review (Hutchings, 1995, 1996). The expectation of collegial assessment of the portfolios means that members of the music community must set explicit standards for themselves as university music educators, standards that reflect the varied roles of today's music faculty. A wider range of activities that demonstrates scholarship, including creative works, is documented in the portfolio, and judgments that concern the teacher's effectiveness are collected from a variety of sources that include but are not limited to students.

Portfolios promote critical reflection and encourage faculty to be explicit about what's involved in teaching, and their use has the net effect of changing the criteria upon which faculty performance is judged. When tenure and promotion decisions are based on portfolio assessment, an overt and significant link is made between teaching excellence and the rewards of tenure and promotion. Portfolios allow and encourage faculty to place as much emphasis on teaching as is currently placed on other forms of scholarship in the university setting and can have a considerable impact on promotion through the ranks. Finally, preparing and evaluating teaching portfolios makes teaching public property, which brings with it real benefits for the overall development of university and college teaching (Hutchings, 1995, 1996).

3. *Developing subject mastery.* Subject expertise is not typically considered to be problematic among university and college faculty in most disciplines—in fact, they have been hired on the basis of their expertise. However, we have seen that university music educators face unique problems of expertise in meeting the demands of the contemporary music curriculum. For many of them, developing new areas of subject mastery is key to developing instructional expertise. Fortunately, resources have been developed that university music educators can use to learn about those areas of music instruction that are unfamiliar to them (e.g., Williams & Webster, 1996, on music technology), but it is apparent that new kinds of learning and subsequent teaching often involve an experiential component as well (e.g., Elliott, 1995; Smithrim, 1997; Upitis, Smithrim, & Soren, 1999). Such professional development also requires university music educators to imagine themselves as—for example—composers. Just as the culture at large treats "music as talent," university educators themselves may treat composition and creation as something that is attainable by only an elite few. But as Elliott (1995) argues, "Knowing how to make music well . . . is neither a gift nor a talent in the sense of an innate ability that some infants are born with and others are not . . . Musicianship is not an accident of birth" (pp. 234–235). Learning a new subject can remind a teacher of what is involved in learning and thus help teachers focus on student learning in the university and college classroom. While academic

leaves are typically granted for the purposes of scholarship, extending personal mastery in subjects that range from performance and conducting to world musics, composition, and technology is an ideal sabbatical activity for university faculty.

All three of these proposed strategies for fostering music teaching require further research, particularly in terms of developing designs for specific interventions and assessing the impact of specific programs. Taking a cue from Boyer's (1990) call to all faculty members to attend to the scholarship of teaching, we recommend that music faculty not wait for others to do their research for them (or *on* them) but step forward and take responsibility for conducting research into their own professional development initiatives. Individual music teachers and those with whom they collaborate must learn to reflect critically and deliberately on approaches used in particular contexts and make the effort to conscientiously report findings in the music education literature, if the goal is to better our collective understanding of teaching development.

Goodlad (2000) reminds us that the most promising renewal efforts are likely to occur under what might be termed an ecological model of educational change, that is, where the context is of paramount consideration. The identification of strategies that might lead to positive changes in higher music education is not enough: The cultural context (Sarason, 1982, cited in Goodlad, 2000) is of critical importance if the change is to be effective. This means that the local circumstances in any given music education department are at least as important as the interventions that might be undertaken. And as Goodlad suggests, renewal and the arts themselves mesh with a "natural attraction . . . ; renewal . . . and the arts anticipate a symbiotic relationship [that involves] creativity and innovation [in the] disciplined learning that gives the team, the faculty, the orchestra command of the components that inescapably constitute performance [where] . . . the essence is in the doing" (p. 13). We would do well to contemplate higher music education renewal with such symbiotic goals in mind.

REFERENCES

Abbott, R. D., Wulff, D. H., & Szego, C. K. (1989). Review of research on TA training. In J. D. Nyquist, R. D. Abbott, & D. H. Wulff (Eds.), *New directions for teaching and learning: No. 39. Teaching assistant training in the 1990s* (pp. 111–124). San Francisco: Jossey-Bass.

Amundsen, C., Gryspeerdt D., & Moxness, K. (1993). Practice-centered inquiry: Developing more effective teaching. *Review of Higher Education, 16*(3), 329–353.

Amundsen, C. L., & Saroyan, A. (1993, April). *Toward more effective teaching in higher education: A case study.* Paper presented at the annual meeting of the American Educational Research Association, Atlanta, GA.

Amundsen, C., Saroyan, A., & Frankman, M. (1996). Changing methods and metaphors: A case study of growth in university teaching. *Journal on Excellence in College Teaching, 7*(3), 3–42.

Amundsen, C., Saroyan, A., & Gryspeerdt, D. (1999, April). *Learning to teach in higher education: A situation of missing models.* Paper presented at the annual meeting of the American Educational Research Association, Montreal, Quebec, Canada.

Andrews, B. (2000). Curricular reference points for changing teacher education practices in arts education. In M. Taylor & B. Gregory (Eds.), *Proceedings of the International Society for Music Education 24th World Conference* (pp. 456–462). Edmonton, Alberta: University of Alberta.

Andrews, J. D. W. (Ed.). (1985). *New directions for teaching and learning: No. 22, Strengthening the teaching assistant faculty.* San Francisco: Jossey-Bass.

Angelo, T., & Cross, K. P. (1989). Classroom research for teaching assistants. In J. D. Nyquist, R. D. Abbott, & D. H. Wulff (Eds.), *New directions for teaching and learning: No. 39. Teaching assistant training in the 1990s* (pp. 99–108). San Francisco: Jossey-Bass.

Angelo, T., & Cross, K. P. (1993). *Classroom assessment techniques: A handbook for college teachers* (2nd ed.). San Francisco: Jossey-Bass.

Argyris, C., & Schön, D. (1974). *Theory in practice.* San Francisco: Jossey-Bass.

Austin, A. E. (1992). Supporting the professor as teacher: The Lilly teaching fellows program. *Review of Higher Education, 16*(1), 85–106.

Baldwin, R. G. (1990). Faculty career stages and implications for professional development. In J. H. Schuster, D. W. Wheeler, & Assoc., *Enhancing faculty careers: Strategies for development and renewal* (pp. 20–40). San Francisco: Jossey-Bass.

Barr, R., & Tagg, J. (1995, November/December). From teaching to learning—a new paradigm for undergraduate education. *Change,* 13–25.

Bartel, L., & Elliott, D. (1994). *Proceedings of the Second International Symposium on the Philosophy of Music Education: Critical reflections on music education.* Toronto: University of Toronto.

Bartle, G. (1996). *International directory of music education: Details of institutions and music education qualifications.* Nedlands: Callaway International Resource Centre for Music Education, University of Western Australia.

Bates, D., Frederickson, K., & Lamb, R. (2000). Chaos3: The next generation. In M. Taylor & B. Gregory (Eds.), *Proceedings of the International Society for Music Education 24th World Conference* (pp. 29–37). Edmonton: University of Alberta.

Beynon, C. (2000). Who is teaching the next generation of teachers? Implications for music education in the new millennium. In B. Hanley & B. A. Roberts (Eds.), *Looking forward: Challenges to Canadian music education* (pp. 103–125). Toronto: Canadian Music Educators Association.

Blacking, J. (1973). *How musical is man?* Seattle: University of Washington Press.

Boehrer, J., & Sarkisian, E. (1985). The teaching assistant's point of view. In J. D. W. Andrews (Ed.), *New directions for teaching and learning: No. 22. Strengthening the teaching assistant faculty.* San Francisco: Jossey-Bass.

Boice, R. (1991). New faculty as teachers. *Journal of Higher Education, 62,* 150–173.

Boice, R. (1992). *The new faculty member: Supporting and fostering professional development.* San Francisco: Jossey-Bass.

Bok, D. (1991). The improvement of teaching. *Teachers College Record, 93*(2), 236–251.

Boud, D. (1999). Situating academic development in professional work: Using peer learning. *International Journal for Academic Development, 4*(1), 3–10.

Boud, D., & McDonald, R. (1981). *Educational development through consultancy.* Guildford, UK: Society for Research into Higher Education.

Boyer, E. L. (1990). *Scholarship reconsidered: Priorities of the professoriate.* Princeton, NJ: Carnegie Foundation for the Advancement of Teaching.

Boyle, P., & Boice, R. (1998). Systematic mentoring for new faculty teachers and graduate teaching assistants. *Innovative Higher Education, 22*(3), 157–179.

Bresler, L. (1993). Music in a double-bind: Instruction by non-specialists in elementary schools. *Bulletin of the Council for Research in Music Education, 115,* 1–13.

Brew, A. (Ed.). (1995). *Directions in staff development.* Buckingham, UK: Open University Press and the Society for Research into Higher Education.

Brookes, M., & German, K. (1983). *Meeting the challenges: Developing faculty careers* (ASHE-ERIC Higher Education Research Report No. 3). Washington, DC: Association for the Study of Higher Education.

Brookfield, S. (1991). Grounding teaching in learning. In M. Galbraith (Ed.), *Facilitating adult learning: A transactional process* (pp. 33–56). Malabar, FL: Krieger.

Brookfield, S. (1995). *Becoming a critically reflective teacher.* San Francisco: Jossey-Bass.

Brookhart, E. (1988). *Music in American higher education: An annotated bibliography.* Warren, MI: Harmonie Park Press.

Brophy, T. S. (2000). What is the question? Developing critical thinking in the elementary classroom. In M. Taylor & B. Gregory (Eds.), *Proceedings of the International Society for Music Education 24th World Conference* (pp. 67–75). Edmonton: University of Alberta.

Campbell, P. S. (1991). *Lessons for the world: A cross-cultural guide to music teaching and learning.* New York: Schirmer Books.

Campbell, P. S. (1998). *Songs in their heads.* New York: Oxford University Press.

Candy, P. (1991). *Self-direction for lifelong learning.* San Francisco: Jossey-Bass.

Centra, J. (1976). *Faculty development practices in U.S. colleges and universities* (Project Report 76-30). Princeton, NJ: Educational Testing Service.

Centra, J. (1993). *Reflective faculty evaluation.* San Francisco: Jossey-Bass.

Chism, N. (Ed.). (1987). *Institutional responsibilities and responses in the employment and education of TAs: Readings from a national conference.* Columbus: Center for Teaching Excellence, Ohio State University.

Conrad, C. F., & Haworth, J. G. (Eds.). (1995). *Revisioning curriculum in higher education.* Needham Heights, MA: Simon & Schuster.

Cox, M. (1995). The development of new and junior faculty. In A. Wright & Assoc., *Teaching improvement practices: Successful strategies for higher education* (pp. 283–310). Bolton, MA: Anker.

Cranton, P. (1994). Self-directed and transformative instructional development. *Journal of Higher Education, 65*(6), 726–744.

Cranton, P. (1996). *Professional development as transformative learning.* San Francisco: Jossey-Bass.

Cross, K. P. (1990). Teaching to improve learning. *Journal on Excellence in College Teaching, 1,* 2–22.

d'Appolonia, S., & Abrami, P. (1997). Navigating student ratings of instruction. *American Psychologist, 52*(11), 1198–1208.

Deal, J. J., & Taylor, J. A. (1997). Technology standards for college music degrees. *Music Educators Journal, 54,* 17–23.

Diamond, R., & Adam, B. (1996). *The disciplines speak: Rewarding the scholarly, professional and creative work of faculty.* Washington, DC: American Association for Higher Education.

Dunkin, M. J., & Barnes, J. (1986). Research on teaching in higher education. In M. C. Wittrock (Ed.), *Handbook of research on teaching* (3rd ed., pp. 754–777). New York: Macmillan.

Edgerton, R., Hutchings, P., & Quinlan, K. (1991). *The teaching portfolio: Capturing the scholarship of teaching.* Washington, DC: American Association for Higher Education.

Elliott, D. (1995). *Music matters: A new philosophy of music education.* New York: Oxford University Press.

Errington, E. P. (1993). *Arts education: Beliefs, practices and possibilities.* Geelong, Victoria, Australia: Deakin University Press.

Fife, J. D. (1995). Foreword. In M. B. Paulsen & K. A. Feldman, *Taking teaching seriously: Meeting the challenge of instructional improvement* (ASHE-ERIC Higher Education Report No. 2) (pp. xi–xiii). Washington, DC: George Washington University, Graduate School of Education and Human Development.

Fiske, H. (2000). A 2020 vision of music education. In B. Hanley & B. A. Roberts (Eds.), *Looking forward: Challenges to Canadian music education* (pp. 273–299). Toronto, Ontario: Canadian Music Educators Association.

Fox, D. (1983). Personal theories of teaching. *Studies in Higher Education, 8*(2), 151–163.

Gaff, J. (1975). *Toward faculty renewal: Advances in faculty, instructional, and organizational development.* San Francisco: Jossey-Bass.

Gaff, J. G., & Simpson, R. D. (1994). Faculty development in the United States. *Innovative Higher Education, 18*(3), 167–176.

Gardner, H. (1983). *Frames of mind: The theory of multiple intelligences.* New York: Basic Books.

Gibbs, G. (1998). Developments in initial training and certification of university teachers in the UK: Implications for the U.S. *To Improve the Academy, 17,* 69–84.

Goodlad, J. I. (2000). Educational renewal and the arts. *Arts Education Policy Review 101*(4), 11–14.

Gouzouasis, P. (2000). Understanding music media: Digital (re)genesis or cultural meltdown in the 21st century. In B. Hanley & B. A. Roberts (Eds.), *Looking forward: Challenges to Canadian music education* (pp. 225–250). Toronto, Ontario: Canadian Music Educators Association.

Green, J. P., & Vogan, N. F. (1991). *Music education in Canada: A historical account.* Toronto, Ontario, Canada: University of Toronto Press.

Green, L. (1997). *Music, gender, education.* Cambridge, UK: Cambridge University Press.

Hanley, B. (1999). Challenges to Canadian teacher education in the arts. In B. Roberts (Ed.), *Connect, combine, communicate: Revitalizing the arts in Canadian schools* (pp. 163–184). Sydney, Nova Scotia, Canada: University College of Cape Breton Press.

Hanley, B. (2000). What's ahead? Challenges for music education in Canadian schools. In B. Hanley & B. A. Roberts (Eds.), *Looking forward: Challenges to Canadian music education* (pp. 11–40). Toronto, Ontario: Canadian Music Educators Association.

Hargreaves, D. J. (1986). *The developmental psychology of music.* Cambridge, UK: Cambridge University Press.

Hoyt, D. P., & Howard, G. S. (1978). The evaluation of faculty development programs. *Research in Higher Education, 8*(1), 25–38.

Hutchings, P. (1995). *From idea to prototype: The peer review of teaching: A project workbook.* Washington, DC: American Association for Higher Education.

Hutchings, P. (1996). *Making teaching community property: A menu for peer collaboration and peer review.* Washington, DC: American Association for Higher Education.

Jenkins, A. (1996). Discipline-based educational development. *International Journal for Academic Development, 1*(1), 50–62.

Johnson, S. (1997). *High-school music teachers' meanings of teaching world musics.* Unpublished master's thesis, Faculty of Education, Queen's University, Kingston, Ontario, Canada.

Keller, G. (1983). *Academic strategy: The management revolution in American higher education.* Baltimore, MD: Johns Hopkins University Press.

Kember, D. (1997). A reconceptualization of the research into university academics' conceptions of teaching. *Learning and Instruction, 7*(3), 255–275.

Kennedy, M. (2000). Music for *all* Canadians: Dreams or reality at the high school level. In B. Hanley & B. A. Roberts (Eds.), *Looking forward: Challenges to Canadian music education* (pp. 139–156). Toronto, Ontario: Canadian Music Educators Association.

Knapper, C., & Piccinin, S. (Eds.). (1999). *New directions for teaching and learning: No. 79. Using consultants to improve teaching.* San Francisco: Jossey-Bass.

Kozma, R. (1985). A grounded theory of instructional innovation in higher education. *Journal of Higher Education, 56*(3), 300–319.

Kratus, J. (1989). A time study of the compositional processes used by children ages 7–11. *Journal of Research in Music Education, 37*(1), 5–20.

Kugel, P. (1993). How professors develop as teachers. *Studies in Higher Education, 18*(3), 315–328.

Lambert, L. M., & Tice, S. L. (1993). *Preparing graduate students to teach: A guide to programs that improve undergraduate teaching and develop tomorrow's faculty.* Washington, DC: American Association for Higher Education.

Lehman, P., & Sinatra, R. (1988). Assessing arts curricula in the schools: Their role, content, and purpose. In J. T. McLaughlin (Ed.), *Toward a new era in arts education* (pp. 53–79). New York: American Council for the Arts.

Leong, S. (1997). *Music in schools and teacher education: A global perspective.* Nedlands: Callaway International Resource Centre for Music Education and ISME Commission for Music in School and Teacher Education, University of Western Australia.

Leonhard, C. (1991). *The status of arts education in American public schools.* Urbana: Council for Research in Music Education, School of Music, University of Illinois at Urbana-Champaign.

Levinson-Rose, J., & Menges, R. (1981). Improving college teaching: A critical review of research. *Review of Educational Research, 51,* 403–434.

Lewis, K. G. (1993). *The TA experience: Preparing for multiple roles.* Stillwater, OK: New Forums Press.

Marsh, H. M. (1984). Students' evaluation of university teaching: Dimensionality, reliability, validity, potential biases, and utility. *Journal of Educational Psychology, 76,* 707–754.

Marsh, K. (2000). Making the connection: Changing attitudes to multicultural and indigenous music in pre-service music education in Australia. In M. Taylor & B. Gregory (Eds.), *Proceedings of the International Society for Music Education 24th World Conference* (pp. 242–255). Edmonton: University of Alberta.

McKeachie, W. J. (1990). Research on college teaching: The historical background. *Journal of Educational Psychology, 82*(2), 189–200.

McKeachie, W. J. (1997a). Critical elements in training university teachers. *International Journal for Academic Development, 2*(1), 67–74.

McKeachie, W. (1997b). Student ratings. *American Psychologist, 52*(11), 1187–1197.

McKeachie, W. J., Pintrich, P. R., Lin, Y. G., & Smith, D. A. F. (1986). *Teaching and learning in the college classroom: A review of the research literature.* Ann Arbor: National Center for Research on Improving Postsecondary Teaching and Learning, University of Michigan.

Menges, R. (1999). Preface. In R. Menges & Assoc., *Faculty in new jobs* (pp. xvii–xxi). San Francisco: Jossey-Bass.

Menges, R., & Associates. (1999). *Faculty in new jobs.* San Francisco: Jossey-Bass.

Menges, R. J., Weimer, M., & Assoc. (1996). *Teaching on solid ground: Using scholarship to improve practice.* San Francisco: Jossey-Bass.

Mezirow, J. (1991). *Transformative dimensions of adult learning*. San Francisco: Jossey-Bass.

Montgomery, A. (2000). Elementary school music: Reflections for the future. In B. Hanley & B. A. Roberts (Eds.), *Looking forward: Challenges to Canadian music education* (pp. 127–138). Toronto, Ontario: Canadian Music Educators Association.

Morin, F. L. (1994). A professional development model for planned change in arts education. *Canadian Journal of Research in Music Education, 35*(7), 17–28.

Morss, K., & Donagy, M. E. (1998). Discipline-based academic development through a tripartite relationship. *International Journal for Academic Development, 3*(2), 136–145.

Murray, H. G. (1997). Does evaluation of teaching lead to improvement of teaching? *International Journal for Academic Development, 2*(1), 8–23.

Music Educators National Conference. (1994). *What every young American should know and be able to do in the arts: National standards for arts education*. Reston, VA: Author.

Nelson, C., & Bloom, F. (1997). Child development and neuroscience. *Child Development, 68*(5), 970–987.

NyQuist, J. D., Abbott, R. D., & Wulff, D. H. (Eds.). (1989). *New directions for teaching and learning: No. 39. Teaching assistant training in the 1990s*. San Francisco: Jossey-Bass.

Ory, J. C. (2000). Teaching evaluation: Past, present and future. In K. Ryan (Ed.), *New directions for teaching and learning: No. 83. Evaluating teaching in higher education: A vision for the future* (pp. 13–18). San Francisco: Jossey-Bass.

Palmer, P. (1993, November/December). Good talk about good teaching: Improving teaching through conversation and community. *Change*, pp. 8–13.

Palmer, P. (1998). *The courage to teach: Exploring the inner landscape of a teacher's life*. San Francisco: Jossey-Bass.

Paulsen, M. B., & Feldman, K. A. (1995). *Taking teaching seriously: Meeting the challenge of instructional improvement* (ASHE-ERIC Higher Education Report No. 2). Washington, DC: George Washington University, Graduate School of Education and Human Development.

Pratt, D. D. (1992). Conceptions of teaching. *Adult Education Quarterly, 42*(4), 203–220.

Ramsden, P. (1992). *Learning to teach in higher education*. London: Routledge & Kegan Paul.

Reimer, B. (1994). Can we understand music of foreign cultures? In H. Lees (Ed.), *Musical connections: Tradition and change* (pp. 227–245). Auckland, New Zealand: University of Auckland.

Reimer, B. (1997). Music education and the twenty-first century. *Music Educators Journal, 84*(3), 33–38.

Research Studies in Music Education (1994). *Special focus issue: Technology in music education*. Queensland, Australia: University of Southern Queensland Press.

Resnick, L. (1981). Instructional psychology. *Annual Review of Psychology, 32*, 659–704.

Richlin, L. (1995). Preparing the faculty of the future to teach. In A. Wright & Assoc., *Teaching improvement practices:*

Successful strategies for higher education (pp. 255–282). Bolton, MA: Anker.

Roberts, B. A. (1993). *I, musician: Towards a model of identity construction and maintenance by music education students as musicians*. St. John's, Canada: Memorial University of Newfoundland.

Roberts, B. A. (2000). Editorial. In B. Hanley & B. A. Roberts (Eds.), *Looking forward: Challenges to Canadian music education* (pp. 5–10). Toronto, Ontario: Canadian Music Educators Association.

Robertson, D. L. (1999). Professors' perspectives on their teaching: A new construct and developmental model. *Innovative Higher Education, 23*(4), 271–294.

Ryan, K. (Ed.). (2000). *New directions for teaching and learning: No. 83. Evaluating teaching in higher education: A vision for the future*. San Francisco: Jossey-Bass.

Saroyan, A., & Amundsen, C. (1995). The systematic design and implementation of a training program for teaching assistants. *Canadian Journal of Higher Education, 25*(1), 1–18.

Schön, D. (1983). *The reflective practitioner*. New York: Basic Books.

Schratz, M. (1990). Researching while teaching: A collaborative action research model to improve college teaching. *Journal on Excellence in College Teaching, 1*, 98–108.

Schuster, J. H. (1990). Strengthening career preparation for prospective professors. In J. H. Schuster, D. W. Wheeler, & Assoc., *Enhancing faculty careers: Strategies for development and renewal* (pp. 65–83). San Francisco: Jossey-Bass.

Schuster, J. H., Wheeler, D. W., & Assoc. (1990). *Enhancing faculty careers: Strategies for development and renewal*. San Francisco: Jossey-Bass.

Seldin, P. (1996). *The teaching portfolio: A practical guide to improved performance and performance/tenure decisions* (2nd ed.). Bolton, MA: Anker.

Seldin, P., & Assoc. (1995). *Improving college teaching*. Bolton, MA: Anker.

Sherman, T. M., Armistad, L. P., Powler, F., Barksdale, M. A., & Reif, G. (1987). The quest for excellence in university teaching. *Journal of Higher Education, 48*(1), 66–84.

Shore, B. M., Foster, S. F., Knapper, C. K., Nadeau, G. G., Neil, N., & Sim, V. (1986). *Guide to the teaching dossier: Its preparation and use* (Rev. ed.). Ottawa, Ontario: Canadian Association of University Teachers.

Shulman, L. (1986). Knowledge and teaching: Foundations of the new reform. *Harvard Educational Review, 57*, 1–22.

Shulman, L. (1998). Course anatomy: The dissection and analysis of knowledge through teaching. In P. Hutchings (Ed.), *The course portfolio* (pp. 5–12). Washington, DC: American Association for Higher Education.

Smith, K. S., & Kalivoda, P. L. (1998). Academic morphing: Teaching assistant to faculty member. *To Improve the Academy, 17*, 85–102.

Smith, R. (1983). A theory of action perspective on faculty development. *To Improve the Academy, 2*, 47–58.

Smith, R. (1995). Reflecting critically on our efforts to improve teaching and learning. *To Improve the Academy, 14*, 5–25.

Smith, R., & Schwartz, F. (1985). A theory of effectiveness: Faculty development case studies. *To Improve the Academy, 4,* 63–74.

Smithrim, K. (1997). Free musical play in early childhood. *Canadian Music Educator, 38*(4), 17–24.

Sorcinelli, M., & Austin, A. (Eds.). (1992). *New directions for teaching and learning: No. 50. Developing new and junior faculty.* San Francisco: Jossey-Bass.

Sprague, J., & Nyquist, J. D. (1989). TA supervision. In J. D. NyQuist, R. D. Abbott, & D. H. Wulff (Eds.), *New directions for teaching and learning: No. 39. Teaching assistant training in the 1990s* (pp. 37–53). San Francisco: Jossey-Bass.

Stake, R., Bresler, L., & Mabry, L. (1991). *Custom and cherishing: The arts in elementary schools.* Urbana: Council for Research in Music Education, School of Music, University of Illinois at Urbana-Champaign.

Staton, A., & Darling, A. (1989). Socialization of teaching assistants. In J. D. NyQuist, R. D. Abbott, & D. H. Wulff (Eds.), *New directions for teaching and learning: No. 39. Teaching assistant training in the 1990s* (pp. 15–22). San Francisco: Jossey-Bass.

Stevens, R. (1994). *Technology and music teaching and learning.* Geelong, Victoria, Australia: Deakin University Press.

Tapscott, D. (1997). *Growing up digital: The rise of the Net-generation.* New York: McGraw-Hill Ryerson.

Taylor, K. L. (1993). The role of scholarship in university teaching. *Canadian Journal of Higher Education, 23*(3), 64–79.

Tiberius, R. G. (1986). Metaphors underlying the improvement of teaching and learning. *British Journal of Educational Technology, 2*(17), 144–156.

Tierney, W. G., & Bensimon, E. M. (1996). *Promotion and tenure: Community and socialization in academe.* Albany: State University of New York Press.

Tsisserev, A. (1997). *An ethnography of secondary school student composition in music: A study of personal involvement within the compositional process.* Unpublished doctoral dissertation, Faculty of Education, University of British Columbia, Vancouver, Canada.

Upitis, R. (1990). *This too is music.* Portsmouth, NH: Heinemann.

Upitis, R. (1992). *Can I play you my song? The compositions and invented notations of children.* Portsmouth, NH: Heinemann.

Upitis, R. (2000). Teaching in the 21st century. In M. Uszler (Ed.), *The well-tempered keyboard teacher* (2nd ed., pp. 197–223). New York: Schirmer Books.

Upitis, R., Smithrim, K., & Soren, B. (1999). When teachers become artists: Teacher transformation and professional development. *Music Education Research, 1*(1), 23–35.

Walker, C. J., & Hale, N. M. (1999). Faculty well-being and vitality. In R. Menges & Assoc., *Faculty in new jobs* (pp. 216–239). San Francisco: Jossey-Bass.

Webb, G. (1996). *Understanding staff development.* Buckingham, UK: Open University Press.

Weimer, M. (1990). *Improving college teaching: Strategies for developing instructional effectiveness.* San Francisco: Jossey-Bass.

Weimer, M., & Lenze, L. F. (1991). Instructional interventions: A review of the literature on efforts to improve instruction. In J. C. Smart (Ed.), *Higher education: Handbook of theory and research* (Vol. 7, pp. 294–333). New York: Agathon Press.

Weinberger, N., & McKenna, T. (1988). Sensitivity of single neurons in auditory cortex to contour: Toward a neurophysiology of music perception. *Music Perception, 5,* 355–390.

Williams, D. B., & Webster, P. R. (1996). *Experiencing music technology: Software, data, and hardware.* New York: Schirmer Books.

Wright, A., & Assoc. (1995). *Teaching improvement practices: Successful strategies for higher education.* Bolton, MA: Anker.

Yip, L. C. R. (2000). A comparison of the information technology music curricula in teacher education programs: Implications for curriculum development. In M. Taylor & B. Gregory (Eds.), *Proceedings of the International Society for Music Education 24th World Conference* (pp. 433–443). Edmonton: University of Alberta.

Zuber-Skerritt, O. (1992). *Professional development in higher education: A theoretical framework for action research.* London: Kogan Page.

Research by Teachers on Teacher Education

44

MARY LEGLAR

MICHELLE COLLAY

To speak of craft is to presume a knowledge of a certain range of skills and proficiencies. It is to imagine an educated capacity to attain a desired end-in-view or to bring about a desired result. Where teachers are concerned, the end-in-view has to do with student learning; the desired result has to do with the "match" between what students have learned and what their teachers believe they have taught.

Maxine Greene, "How Do We Think About Our Craft?"

How do teacher educators think about their craft? Historically, teacher education has been shaped by theoreticians rather than by practitioners. During the past two decades, teachers and teacher educators have begun to study their own work more closely, to apply research in the classroom, and to assume primary responsibility for expanding the knowledge of their craft. By examining and analyzing their craft, teachers and teacher educators create both new knowledge and new interpretations, and the long-cherished distinctions between practitioner and researcher begin to blur. In the view of contemporary scholars, knowing about and doing are inextricably linked. Cole and Knowles (2000) emphasize this important point: "First and foremost, we see teaching as inquiry. In other words, teaching is researching" (p. 1). Teachers theorize rather than just apply theory, and they do this from their earliest days of preservice study.

This chapter focuses on research by teachers and teacher educators that has implications for preservice music teacher education, defined here as undergraduate music education course work and field experiences that precede formal student teaching. The discussion opens with a brief consideration of developments that served as a prelude to teacher research. The literature review is then presented in three sections. The first section surveys literature that de-

scribes who good teachers are, what they do, and what they know. The second focuses on literature that has recently emerged from research being conducted by teacher educators and teachers on the ways in which professionals learn and develop. In the third and final section, trends in contemporary literature are identified, and recommendations are made about future study of the central questions of this chapter: How can teacher inquiry improve teacher preparation, and how can teacher preparation foster teacher inquiry?

Research on Teaching: Formative Influences

Challenges to the professional status of teachers and teacher educators originated in the late 19th century with the divergent views of constructivist philosophers such as John Dewey and objectivist psychologists such as Edward L. Thorndike (Lucas, 1997; Wing, 1991). Between the objectivist and constructivist viewpoints lay significant differences in basic assumptions about knowledge, knowers, and learning: whether knowledge is objective or relative, inert or active, received or constructed; whether knowers discover or create knowledge; and whether learning is authority-directed or learner-directed (Schwandt, 1994). Thorndike's approach prevailed, dominating education during much of the 20th century. The reasons for this were complex, including a perceived need to standardize schooling for increasingly diverse urban populations, a movement away from local control of schooling, and the influence of industrial practices. Schools became more like factories, and teachers became more like line workers who required supervision (Cuban, 1984; Herbst, 1989; Mattingly, 1975).

Although attempts were made to professionalize teaching by the "scientific" study of curriculum, teaching, and supervision, one effect of these studies, paradoxically, was to justify greater control of teachers (Doyle, 1990; R. Ducharme & M. Ducharme, 1996). For example, tests developed by Thorndike and his colleagues to measure academic learning were used by school leaders to exert pressure on individual teachers to raise scores (Beatty, 1996). Thus, these early efforts did not create autonomy and authority for teachers but, rather, standardized a hierarchical work structure with teachers at the bottom (Perrenoud, 1996). Teaching was relegated to the level of a "semi-profession" (Etzioni, 1969). Compared to medicine and law, which have been successfully professionalized, teaching was and still is perceived to lack "a core of specialized, technical knowledge" (Doyle, 1990, p. 8).

Just as teachers have been regarded as semiprofessionals, teacher educators have been described as the stepchildren of higher education (Lucas, 1997) and teacher education research as a "poor relation" of educational research (Zeichner, 1999). Teacher education remained marginalized even as programs became more extensive and standardized. By the late 1930s, normal schools, the main source of trained teachers since the mid-19th century, had been absorbed or converted into state colleges and many research universities had established departments of education. These, however, often had affiliations with more established departments, such as philosophy and psychology—disciplines that continue to be privileged over teacher education, which was not and is not considered a discipline in its own right (Colwell, 2000; Zeichner, 1999). Even within colleges of education, the traditional professoriate avoided direct involvement with the practical aspects of teacher education. From this divergence of theory and practice emerged two types of faculty: researchers, who analyzed curriculum, instruction, and policy; and teacher educators. Teacher educators, many of whom had public school experience, knew firsthand the challenges of applying decontextualized theory to the classroom (Cole & Knowles, 2000). The traditional culture of research that prevailed in the academy, however, pressured them to undertake "objective" research agendas, thus perpetuating the theory–practice divide.

The triumph of the objectivist, scientific paradigm during the first part of the 20th century had far-reaching implications for almost every aspect of research on teaching. The disregard for nonquantifiable practitioner knowledge not only constrained knowledge about teacher knowing; it also severely limited the potential of teachers to legitimize their profession. Missing from the knowledge base for teaching were the voices of teachers themselves, the questions teachers ask, the ways teachers use writing and intentional talk in their work lives, and the interpretive frames teachers use to understand and improve their own classroom practices. Limiting the official knowledge base to what academics have chosen to study and publish has

contributed to a number of problems, including discontinuity between what is taught in universities and what is practiced in classrooms, practitioners' ambivalence about the claims of academic research, and a general lack of information about classroom life from an insider's perspective (Cochran-Smith & Lytle, 1992; Cohn & Kottkamp, 1993).

A movement to recognize teachers as authorities in their own right rather than as passive recipients of university-generated knowledge emerged in the 1970s (Doyle, 1990; Shulman, 1987). Cochran-Smith and Lytle (1999) described a confluence of several traditions of teacher research, each of which "constructs the role of teacher as knower and as agent in the classroom and in larger education contexts" (p. 16). Some of these traditions implied a distinct criticism of existing modes of educational research and of the power relations that result from dependence on university-based findings. By the mid-1980s, researchers and practitioners alike were urging a return to Dewey's cooperative, constructivist concept. Issues of power and voice, autonomy and authority, were brought to the forefront (Clandinin & Connolly, 1995; Lee & Yarger, 1996; Perrone, 1989). Critics questioned the usefulness of research guided by an agenda set outside the classroom and argued that classroom teachers' lack of autonomy in creating new knowledge was contributing to their status as semiprofessionals (Cuban, 1984; Erickson, 1986; Herbst, 1989). In the words of Cochran-Smith and Lytle (1999), "The teacher research movement is frontally about altering relations of knowledge and power and about the important connections of teaching and research" (p. 21).

Review of the Literature

Research on Teacher Knowing: From Description to Inquiry

The quest to map the territory called teacher knowing requires ongoing, systematic inquiry that includes critique of conventional research and continued efforts to broaden perspectives for new research. This section presents a brief chronicle of the research that formed conceptions of good teaching throughout the 20th century. The discussion proceeds from the early efforts to describe the characteristics of good teachers, to observations of what teachers do in the classroom, to explorations of what they know about what they do, to the genesis of the currently emerging view of teachers as independent inquirers.

Two caveats are in order. First, much more research has been conducted in general education than in music education, and the general education research base is therefore stronger and more coherent. Second, although the movement away from research conducted by "outsiders" toward inquiry conducted by teachers is one of the prominent themes in recent research on teaching, no research approach, including those rooted in the objectivist paradigm, can be dismissed as unproductive. All in some measure have contributed and may yet contribute to what is known about how teachers learn to teach.

Characteristics of Good Teachers.   One of the earliest topics of interest to researchers was the existence of a supposed "teaching personality" and its relationship to teacher effectiveness. By 1960 more than 10,000 studies had been conducted on teacher effectiveness (Good, 1996), many of them preoccupied with identifying the personal qualities that good teachers possessed. These characteristics ran the gamut from superior intellectual abilities, to experience in caring for children, to strong interests in reading, music, painting, and community affairs. In other words, the ideal teacher was the ideal citizen: intelligent, well educated, and well adjusted (Arends, Winitzky, & Tannenbaum, 2001). The prevailing methodology of the early teacher personality studies was descriptive, and most were poorly designed and reported only weak relationships between particular characteristics and good teaching.

Although by the mid-1960s scholars in general education had already begun to doubt that there was such a thing as an ideal teacher personality—or at least that such a personality could be defined or easily identified (Getzels & Jackson, 1963)—music teacher educators continued to show interest in personality research well into the 1980s (Verrastro & Leglar, 1992). Relationships were reported between teacher effectiveness and enthusiasm for teaching, caring for students, and self-confidence, among other traits. Among the social skills found to be linked to effectiveness were skill in nonverbal communication, skill in receiving and interpreting the nonverbal communication of others, and ability to engage others in social discourse (Hamann, Lineburgh, & Paul, 1998). On the whole, however, music education researchers have been no more successful than their general education counterparts in identifying specific personality traits that contribute to teaching effectiveness, especially as measured by student achievement. Taebel (1992) reviewed an impressive array of studies that reported "practically no relationship between personality measures and student outcomes" (p. 313). In fact, four researchers cited by Taebel found that independent context variables such as school size and students' socioeconomic status were stronger predictors of teaching success than were teacher characteristics. As Lehman (1986) has observed, lists of teacher skills and characteristics

often seem to be merely vast compilations of all the desirable qualities anyone can think of. These qualities are always good to have, but very long lists are useless because some traits are clearly more important than others, because strengths in some can compensate for weakness in others, and because no one has all of them anyway. (p. 8)

What Good Teachers Do.   One of the central concerns of the 1960s, in both the academic and the political arenas, was equity. Researchers in the social sciences as well as education turned their attention to the relationship between equality of opportunity and success in school. Until then it had been simply assumed that good schools produce better students than poor schools do. The mammoth report *Equality of Educational Opportunity,* commonly known as the Coleman Report (Coleman et al., 1966), suggested that student achievement is not greatly influenced either by schools or by teachers; differences in learning, according to Coleman and his colleagues, are more closely linked to such extraeducational variables as intellectual ability and the social class of the parents. These findings supplied powerful ammunition for critics of public education. In response, teacher educators opened the gates to release a flood of research that flowed in a very different direction from the older personality studies. It became crucial to refute critics by showing that teachers, like other professionals, possess particular knowledge and specific skills and that this kind of knowing and doing makes a demonstrable difference in student learning. This was, directly or indirectly, the aim of much of the teacher effectiveness research for the next two decades.

Spurred on by the need to identify specific teacher skills that contribute to student learning, researchers attempted to assemble lists of observable competencies considered essential for effective teaching. Primed by the recognition that music performance is based on a well-defined set of skills, music teacher educators embraced competency research enthusiastically. While it is hard to argue with the need to attain basic skills, the lists produced by competency research were so extensive and so unfocused that they proved difficult to organize into a manageable curriculum. Ultimately, it was not clear how music teacher educators could best support preservice teachers' development in so many areas. Further, many, if not most, competency studies were based on teacher opinion questionnaires, which failed to show which teacher behaviors actually contributed to student learning. Partly for these reasons, the research vein of teacher competencies, a central focus of studies during the 1980s, has received less attention since then. Yet the seemingly endless lists of competencies did serve to call attention to the scope and complexity of the professional's knowledge. Further, the common method of relying on the opinions of teachers to establish or rank competencies represented a tacit acknowledgment on the part of researchers that practitioners possess a unique understanding of what they do, why they do it, and how it ought ideally to be done.

Much of the research conducted in the wake of the

Coleman Report, including competency studies, was limited by the failure to observe classroom processes systematically (Dunkin & Biddle, 1974). In response, researchers turned to a process–product approach, attempting to forge a firm link between what took place in the classroom and student learning outcomes. Process–product research is rooted in functionalist psychology, a pragmatic approach that is concerned with the interaction of people and their environment. Process–product research in teacher effectiveness tends to focus on the ways in which teachers adapt to their classroom environments: planning, teachers' interactive thoughts and decisions, and teachers' beliefs and attributions (Berliner, 1990). A characteristic of process–product research is its focus on teacher behaviors and characteristics; student behaviors are considered chiefly as a measure of the teacher's success in adapting to a particular environment. It should be noted that process–product research, unlike personality studies, deals with teacher characteristics that can be altered and thus are amenable to training. Grant and Drafall (1991) provided a 10-year summary of teacher effectiveness studies in music education as well as an excellent discussion of the strengths and weaknesses of process–product research.

In the early 1980s, a series of reform initiatives prompted by reports such as *A Nation at Risk* provoked a new generation of teacher evaluation protocols, which included the Praxis series developed by the Educational Testing Service. These follow closely the tradition of earlier process–product studies and seek to isolate specific teaching skills and correlate their relationship to student achievement. In addition, the Interstate New Teacher Assessment and Support Consortium (INTASC) standards for preservice teachers and the National Board for Professional Teaching Standards (NBPTS) for experienced teachers are now used as a framework for more comprehensive teacher evaluation. By the end of the 1990s, some states had established similar evaluation procedures for conferring advanced licensure.

Some of the more coherent groups of studies in music teacher education have been conducted within the process–product tradition. This research has succeeded in establishing that certain teacher behaviors do have an effect on student attitudes and perhaps on student achievement. Over a 20-year period, Yarbrough and associates have produced a cluster of well-designed studies on the effect of teacher behaviors on student attitude and on-task behavior (Price & Yarbrough, 1993; Yarbrough, 1975; Yarbrough & Hendel, 1993; Yarbrough & Price, 1981, 1989; Yarbrough, Price, & Hendel, 1994). Findings indicated that teacher magnitude (for example, eye contact, voice volume, and facial expressions) had an effect on student attentiveness but not on achievement. Another important cluster of studies centers on Madsen's (1990) investigations of teacher intensity, defined as "(1) sustained control of the

student/teacher interaction with (2) efficient, accurate presentation of subject matter combined with enthusiastic affect and pacing" (p. 38). The work of Madsen and his associates suggests that there is a statistically significant relationship between teacher intensity and effectiveness; that the concept of intensity can be easily defined, measured, taught, demonstrated, and recognized; and that training can enhance the ability to maintain intensity (Madsen & Geringer, 1989).

Music education researchers working in the process–product tradition also focused considerable attention on another teacher behavior: the modeling of musical skills. Concerned with the amount of time spent in teacher talk (at least 40% in most studies) and aware of the literature suggesting that student attentiveness is at a low point during teacher talk, investigators sought to show that modeling is a more effective technique than verbal communication. Dickey (1992) reviewed the findings of modeling research through about 1991 and found strong support for the hypothesis that modeling promotes student achievement.

Although process–product research is valuable for its insistence that teaching processes are worthy of careful observation, a narrow focus on what teachers do excludes consideration of what they know, and knowledge is the basis of action. Overemphasis on teachers' observable actions had unfortunate results on classroom instruction, the most egregious example being the development of "teacher-proof" materials (Reimer, 1993). In sum, according to Reimer, "Both the practical results of such research, and the assumptions that it was founded on, were fundamentally flawed" (p. 15).

What Good Teachers Know.   Critics of process–product research found an influential voice in 1985 when Lee S. Shulman, in his presidential address to the American Educational Research Association, charged that the behavioral view of teaching as an observable skill was insufficient. Just as important as what the teacher *did* was what the teacher *knew,* which Shulman (1986) called pedagogical content knowledge. He took issue with the "cookbook" approach of the previous two decades, arguing that the distinguishing characteristic of a profession is "the indeterminacy of rules when applied to particular cases" (p. 20). For Shulman, theory and practice were inextricably interrelated, and any research that focused exclusively on either theory or practice would provide a distorted picture of the complexities of teaching.

Self-described "old-fashioned behaviorists" like David C. Berliner (1986, p. 8) were also coming to the conclusion that it was important to understand "what knowledge domains are required for successful classroom performance" (p. 9). Following the work of researchers who attempted to establish what it means to be an expert in any field, from chess to physics, Berliner and his colleagues compared the thought processes of expert teachers with those of novices (e.g., Berliner, 1986; Sabers, Cushing, & Berliner, 1991). Summarizing the accumulated results of expert/novice research, Berliner (1995) proposed a set of "descriptive propositions about pedagogical expertise":

1. Experts excel mainly in their own domain and in particular contexts.
2. Experts often develop automaticity for the repetitive operations needed to accomplish their goals.
3. Experts are more sensitive to the task demands and social situation when solving problems.
4. Experts are more opportunistic and flexible in their teaching than are novices.
5. Experts represent problems in qualitatively different ways than do novices.
6. Experts have fast and accurate pattern recognition capabilities. Novices cannot always make sense of what they experience.
7. Experts perceive meaningful patterns in the domain in which they are experienced.
8. Although experts may begin to solve problems more slowly, they bring richer and more personal sources of information to bear on the problem that they are trying to solve. (pp. 48–51)

With its emphasis on teacher knowledge, research on expert teaching can be seen as a bridge between empirical process–product research on one side of an imaginary gorge and teacher-driven inquiry on the other. As Berliner insists, process–product studies contributed a great deal to the body of knowledge about effective teaching. Most important, behaviorally oriented research did succeed in establishing, beyond a reasonable doubt, that what the teacher does makes a difference in student learning. Yet the recognition that "ordinary" teachers can be experts in a complex field helped to accelerate the trend away from process–product studies.

The change in emphasis from what teachers do to what teachers know produced changes in methodology as well. Since thoughts are not observable phenomena, they cannot serve as the subject of empirical research. Ideally, quantitative studies strive for a large, representative population from which the researcher can generalize. Qualitative studies, however, make no pretense of generalizability. They are situated, or rooted, in context—and no two contexts are alike. The two methodologies are not mutually exclusive, any more than thinking and doing are mutually exclusive. Qualitative results can be used to reinforce and interpret quantitative data, and vice versa.

Music education researchers have been slow to adopt qualitative methods and even slower to turn these methods to the study of their own practice. In the early 1990s, Bresler (1992, 1993, 1994) elucidated qualitative paradigms in

a series of articles published in two widely circulated music education research journals. Shortly thereafter, Hendel (1995) reported the results of a study that employed both quantitative and qualitative methodologies to explore what effective music teachers know and do. The purpose of the research was to

> (a) identify factors that contribute to effective music teaching; (b) examine the relationship of teacher-defined traits, which emerge qualitatively, to operationally defined characteristics of effective instruction resulting from quantitative research; and (c) explore the complementary nature of qualitative and quantitative research. (p. 183)

Hendel's discussion exemplifies the role of qualitative research in situating and interpreting quantitative data. For example, she noted that discrepancies among the teachers in the use of time, which were identified with quantitative methods, could be attributed to qualitatively identified factors in the teaching environment: availability of equipment, for example. The qualitative and quantitative data aligned in confirming some earlier findings—for example, that expert teachers use more complete sequences of instruction, that high magnitude is associated with effectiveness, and that good teachers have clear objectives, established procedures, high expectations, and a love of the subject and of teaching.

Teacher Inquiry: Contemporary Practice

The concept of the teacher as knower, articulated most influentially by Shulman, has not only encouraged the use of broader methodological approaches to teacher education research; it has also prompted a reexamination of the concept of preservice teacher education. The traditional compartmental model of the curriculum—foundations, psychology, methods, field experiences—is giving way to the view that learning to teach should be a seamless experience (V. Richardson & Placier, 2001). Recent evidence suggests that teacher educators are experimenting with critical and inquiry-centered approaches to preservice education (Cochran-Smith & Lytle, 1999). Attention to reflective inquiry is becoming a central feature in the contemporary teacher education curriculum, preparing preservice teachers to conduct valid, even publishable, research (Cole & Knowles, 2000; Feiman-Nemser, in press).

Teacher-generated research is distinguished by the nature of the research questions, the methods of inquiry, and the cogency of the findings. Teacher researchers explore problems that are important to teachers. They recognize that the classroom is not a laboratory where experiments can be conducted under controlled conditions. They often work in collaborative teams, discussing methodology along with the topic of study. In fact, the changing conditions of the teaching/learning setting require innovative and boundary-blurring methodologies for anyone who chooses to study learning, whether teachers or outsiders. Finally, much teacher research is highly context-dependent, and the teacher researcher does not necessarily intend to produce findings that can be generalized to other contexts.

Action research may be the most familiar term for classroom research by teachers (Schmuck, 1997; Sprinthall, Reiman, & Thies-Sprinthall, 1996). Clandinin and Connelly (1995) referred to the processes of teacher researchers as "personal experience methods," and S. Hollingsworth (1992) and colleagues participated in "collaborative conversations." More recently, the term *inquiry* has been used, often with a qualifying adjective: *practical inquiry* (Cochran-Smith & Lytle, 1999; Newell, 1996; V. Richardson, 1994), *collaborative inquiry* (Wasley, King, & Louth, 1995), or *reflexive inquiry* (Cole & Knowles, 2000).

Schmuck (1997) described a three-stage cycle of action research that begins with reflecting on past experiences, reading literature, and brainstorming with colleagues (the "initiation" phase); moves to reflection on current activities, which leads to modification of practice (the "detection" phase), and ends in collecting data to determine results over time (the "judgment" phase). For preservice teachers, the initiation phase includes writing in learning journals, developing portfolios, using case studies, and modeling. Detection takes place in simulations and authentic experiences such as tutoring and microteaching. More extensive field experiences, especially student teaching, furnish the context for judgment. In this section the literature is organized according to these three phases, with the proviso that the formal student-teaching experience is outside the scope of this chapter.

The published literature in music education on the approaches commonly recommended for encouraging reflective inquiry in preservice teachers is not extensive and is uneven in coverage and quality. While reports of success in using reflective strategies abound and are useful in terms of description, few rigorous studies have been conducted. The use of qualitative methodology in particular is relatively new in music education, and researchers are less familiar with its rigors than with those of the quantitative paradigm. The primary criteria for inclusion in the discussion that follows were not methodological but topical; further, many of the studies cited are context-bound, and the researchers made no claims to generalizability. In sum, it cannot be said at this point that sufficient empirical evidence exists to support the superiority of any of these approaches over traditional strategies. However, there are enough studies that suggest the efficacy of these approaches and enough experienced music teacher educators who advocate them to justify the hypothesis that the instructional strategies described later may well encourage the development of reflective practitioners.

Initiation: Early Experiences with Inquiry. Reflection is central to the concept of teacher as inquirer. Developing habits of reflection in novice teachers is therefore an important task of teacher educators (Killion & Todnem, 1991). Dewey (1933) defined reflection as "active, persistent and careful consideration of any belief or supposed form of knowledge in light of the grounds that support it and further conclusions to which it tends" (p. 9). Schön (1983) extended Dewey's ideas into the concept of the reflective practitioner, a term that has been discussed and variously defined by many in the education community during the last decade. Structured reflection addresses preservice teachers' struggle to link theory and practice (Boyd, 1998). Reflection

> involves a cycle of thought and action in which educators explore their values, attitudes, thoughts, and experiences, as well as underlying issues of practice; identify and analyze critical incidents in their personal and professional lives; develop new realizations and appreciations as means to reconstruct their knowledge and worlds; and engage in behaviors that are congruent with their construction of reality. (Black, Sileo, & Prater, 2000, p. 71)

A compelling reason to encourage reflection within systematic inquiry is that preservice teachers' beliefs and attitudes about teaching and learning are deeply embedded and play a large role in determining what they learn and how they learn it (Resnick, 1989). Students enter the teacher preparation program with firm ideas of "good" and "poor" teaching, founded on their observations of their own teachers and parents (Knowles, 1992; Lortie, 1975). Experience-based understandings supplement, interfere with, or negate theoretical information and teaching practices presented in the university or in the student-teaching situation (Feiman-Nemser & Buchmann, 1987; Holt-Reynolds, 1994; Zeichner & Tabachnick, 1981). These preexisting beliefs, whether productive or problematic, are difficult to challenge in the few short years of teacher education (Feiman-Nemser, in press; Krueger, 1985; Tabachnick & Zeichner, 1984). Pajares (1992) suggests that students will alter or discard beliefs only if teachers are perceived as viable authorities and are able to introduce new ideas to explain their experiences. Others contend that beliefs and attitudes can be altered if they are identified and examined during the teacher education program (V. Richardson, 1996).

The literature in music education, though less extensive, also indicates the need to encourage preservice teachers to examine the effects of their past experiences on their beliefs about teaching (Gohlke, 1994; Richards & Killen, 1993). Schmidt (1998), using qualitative methods, explored the definitions of good teaching held by four music student teachers. Like preservice teachers in other fields, the prospective music teachers entered the program with notions about teaching that often proved more robust than—and in fact probably determined—the ideas and information they acquired during the program. Particularly informative is Schmidt's comment about the student teachers she observed: "Had I been alert, they gave ample indication, even in the junior-year instrumental methods course, of the depth of the difference among their definitions of 'good' teaching—hence, of their personal goals for their preservice education" (p. 39). Postulating that the identification and evaluation of students' personal beliefs enlighten the process of preservice education, Schmidt recommended techniques for expanding the range of students' experiential understandings: autobiographical writing, journal keeping, studying case histories, guided observation of actual or videotaped classrooms, and discussion with preservice and in-service teachers about their beliefs and practices.

Students do not automatically engage in reflective thinking or systematic inquiry; it is a learned process for some, if not all. In the initiation phase of preservice teacher development, several approaches show promise in encouraging reflective thinking. The commonality among these approaches—which include learning journals, portfolios, case studies, and modeling—is that all require preservice teachers to share with the methods instructor the responsibility for constructing their own knowing.

Learning journals: Learning journals are reflective logs or diaries that document personal learning over time. The primary purpose of journal keeping is to encourage preservice teachers to thoughtfully and deliberately record their reactions to course content, methodology, and teaching experiences and to examine the values and assumptions on which these reactions are founded. Thus journal writing is considered a powerful tool for encouraging reflective thinking (LaBoskey, 1994). Journal writing is a dialogue with self, a means of exploring contextual meanings and gaining perspective (Hedlund, Furst, & Foley, 1989). Several related objectives have been articulated: to build confidence by placing value on student thought, to make held values and assumptions clear and therefore more easily examined, to provide an outlet for anxiety about classroom experiences, to promote autonomy by bringing students' responsibility for learning into focus, and to facilitate problem solving by identifying and defining problems (Calderhead, 1993). Journals can also provide students with an opportunity to communicate confidentially with their instructors and receive personalized feedback (Tama & Peterson, 1991). And finally, analysis of journal entries can guide improvement in teaching practice and curriculum.

Learning journals can be extremely informal recordings of events or focused narratives that detail personal perceptions of facts, themes, concepts, or events encountered in the learning environment. Focused or guided journals are used most often in education settings. Sileo, Prater, Luckner, Rhine, and Rude (in press) outline various types of entries and the functions they serve in learning journals: diary entries, used as an outlet for students' reactions or to record events; notebook entries, used to foster critical and reflective thought about course content; dialogue entries, which allow students to engage the instructor in written conversation; integrative entries, which focus on student ability to synthesize personal knowledge to support or contradict ideas or concepts; and evaluative entries, which involve self-assessment and analysis of shifts in attitude or ideas.

According to Rozmajzl (1992), 70% of music teacher educators have incorporated journal writing into methods courses and field experiences. The reported benefits include offering teacher educators a different kind of access to preservice teachers' thinking; providing preservice teachers with a concrete way to practice reflective thinking; providing direction for individualized instruction; encouraging preservice teachers to focus on their own problems and come to their own realization about needed change in their instructional practices; motivating them, through the process of self-dialogue, to improve practice, independent of teacher prodding; fostering autonomous thinking; and providing a basis for topic selection in methods classes (Fallin & Goetze, 1999). Addressing the perennial theory/practice conundrum, Tarnowski (1997) analyzed the journals of 67 practicum students and found that they offered clues about which aspects of their instruction students were able to transfer from methods class to a practicum situation. They were most able to apply information about lesson planning. Lesson implementation was found to be more difficult. Journal comments revealed that the preservice teachers felt inadequate to understand the learning levels of the students, deliver adequate explanations and directions, form appropriate questions, manage the classroom, anticipate the responses of the children, and select/design valid evaluation techniques.

The usefulness of journal writing, predictably, seems to depend in part on the care with which the approach is implemented. Students have reported a lack of time to complete reflections in a thoughtful manner, and their journals have shown lack of understanding about levels of reflection and a tendency to be preoccupied with the practical, technical aspects of teaching (Black et al., 2000). Barry (1996) explored the opinions of preservice music teachers in regard to the usefulness of six selected strategies to promote reflective practice. While students ranked all strategies high, journal writing was ranked last for usefulness and next to last for requiring thought and reflection.

Although considerable anecdotal evidence favors the well-planned inclusion of journal keeping in teacher education, important questions remain, suggesting several directions that future research might take. For example, what do prospective teachers gain from journal writing? Do all students gain equally from the experience? If not, what are the factors—such as inadequate guidance or lack of writing skills—that limit its usefulness? Most important, are the effects of journal writing seen in teaching? (Black et al., 2000; E. R. Ducharme & M. K. Ducharme, 1996).

Portfolios: Portfolios have entered the mainstream of educational practice in the last decade. The word *portfolio* can be applied to almost any collection of student work, from a file of drafts and works in progress to a carefully chosen collection of "best work." Dietz (1995) describes three types of portfolios for teachers: the presentation portfolio (résumé or album), the learning portfolio (envelope of the mind), and the working portfolio (evidence of the fulfillment of required competencies, standards, or outcomes) (pp. 40–41). The content and use of a portfolio parallel teacher development: Students often begin to collect documentation before they gain the sophistication to use such documentation to judge their work or meet a performance standard. Experienced teachers gather and analyze data to document expertise. As state certification officials implement standards-based assessments, portfolios that contain evidence of competence will become more standard practice in preservice programs as well as becoming a requirement for practicing teachers.

In general, educators use portfolios as a form of alternative assessment or as a strategy for enhancing reflective thinking. Wade and Yarbrough (1996) suggest that portfolios (1) represent student growth over a long period of time; (2) allow students to document their own learning and provide educators with a means to evaluate growth and achievement; (3) give students opportunities for input: what materials to include, how to organize the materials, how the materials might be evaluated; (4) go beyond what tests can reveal about learning by showing authentic student work; and (5) encourage student self-reflection about their own change and growth.

Although the literature in general education indicates considerable enthusiasm for the use of portfolios in teacher education, problems have been identified (Wade & Yarbrough, 1996). Not all students demonstrate reflective thinking, and many do not perceive the assignment as being useful. Some find assembling a portfolio a frustrating and disturbing task. Frustration generally occurs because students understand neither the purpose nor the process of the assignment and therefore do not invest adequate time or effort. Also, students who have not developed habits of reflective and independent thinking find the open-ended, choice-oriented nature of the assignment threatening. Consequently, they do not enjoy it or make a personal investment in the final product. As a result, meaningful connections are not made between student learning (por-trayed by the portfolio contents) and their personal-professional lives in the "real" world of teaching.

In spite of these limitations, the consensus of published opinion favors portfolios. Recommendations in the literature in general education include several steps teacher educators can take to promote the effectiveness of portfolio assignments. The following suggestions are culled from multiple sources: Make clear the purpose of the portfolio; encourage individual expression and ownership of the project; articulate connections between assignments (portfolio content) and "real-world" living; provide some structure by giving a few required assignments, establishing due dates, and setting aside definite times for in-class sharing and feedback from instructor and peers; and constantly evaluate the process and how the students are using the portfolios.

The few published articles that deal with the use of portfolios in music teacher education are reports of the implementation of a portfolio requirement at a single university. Kerchner (1997) describes the use of portfolios in an undergraduate choral methods class. Central to the success of the project were teacher/student sharing of responsibility for learning and assessment; freedom of students to focus on individual goals related to pedagogical, philosophical, musical, and personality issues; and firsthand experience with an assessment procedure that could be implemented in the future. Mitchell (1997) reported that a major recommendation made by students who assembled portfolios as senior music education majors was that the process of gathering materials for the portfolio be instituted earlier in the program. In response, the department developed a 4-year portfolio sequence in which students compiled a body of material for use in the senior portfolio. C. P. Richardson (1995), reporting on the implementation of portfolios at the master's level, identified two main benefits: students learn to "take ownership of their own learning," and "portfolio assessment . . . offers students firsthand experience with a holistic, student-centered method of evaluation that they may come to value" (p. 21).

Case studies: Renewed interest in the use of case methods in teacher education dates to the mid-1980s. Factors that contribute to this interest include the prestige of business and legal education, where case studies have long been important; the widespread influence of Shulman's (1986) concept of pedagogical content knowledge; and the insistence by proponents of craft knowledge that teaching is highly contextualized (McAninch, 1995). According to Richert (1991), "Cases provide the potential for connecting the act of teaching with the cognitions and feelings that motivate and explain that act. They offer a vehicle for making the tacit explicit" (p. 117).

Cases may be used as an instructional strategy, or they may be constructed with a research problem in mind.

Teacher educators use cases as exemplars, as opportunities to practice analysis and contemplate action, and as stimulants to personal reflection (Merseth, 1996). Cases can also encourage the development of problem-solving skills and foster decision making and can be used to introduce methods students to the professional thinking of teachers—that is, to the process of identifying the important and overriding features of a complex situation, analyzing these in terms of their effect in the teaching/learning context, determining possible actions, and making choices. Employed for this purpose, cases do not present solutions but merely real situation problems for students to analyze and respond to (Wasserman, 1994).

Cases used in instruction can be fictional or constructed through careful research. Traditional materials for case study include textbook, teacher-constructed, and researcher-constructed cases. Cases are now included in many methods textbooks, and entire volumes of cases are available for use in preservice course work (e.g., in music education, Abrahams & Head, 1998). It is also becoming more common to use cases written by preservice teachers enrolled in methods classes. Some have criticized this practice, claiming that emphasis is unduly placed on the construction of the report rather than on reflective discussion. Others have argued that the process of writing—what to write, how to write, and what to emphasize in the story—develops habits of reflection (Richert, 1991).

Several descriptions of the use of cases in music teacher education have been published during the last decade. C. P. Richardson (1997) reported success in using cases based on the authors' classroom experiences in elementary and secondary methods classes for promoting cooperative thinking and problem solving. Conway (1999) described the process of developing teaching cases for instrumental music methods courses through cooperative analysis of teachers' practices. Assessing the results of a project using videotaped cases in a music methods class, Barrett and Rasmussen (1996) articulated some of the perceived advantages:

> Video cases framed in a process of inquiry provide opportunities for preservice educators to engage in discourse regarding the nature of music, to articulate personal understandings of musical content, teaching, learning, and school contexts, and to raise significant questions about the nature and purposes of music education. (p. 87)

Wing (1994) presented a lucid discussion of the process of constructing researched cases for use as a text in preparing teachers. Describing an ambitious project then in its third year, Wing commented: "Most of what we . . . have accomplished to date I would place in chapter 1 of the story as *only a beginning*" (p. 9). Wing's assessment underscores the complexity involved in the construction and use of cases in teacher education. Concluding that "all the effort involved in these constructions is well spent" (p. 9), Wing nevertheless sounded several cautionary notes, including the difficulty of situating the cases in context and the need to avoid a prescriptive or evaluative stance. The literature in general education offers several further caveats: Cases are an inefficient teaching approach, they are episodic and thus difficult to organize into a coherent whole in students' minds, and teaching by the case method requires special expertise and effort on the part of the teacher educator. Some scholars contend that support for the use of cases in teacher education is largely anecdotal, "more a matter of conjecture and faith than of evidence" (McAninch, 1995, p. 587).

Although studies report positive findings about the opportunity to teach content and the processes of professional thinking through cases, there is limited research on the relationship between the use of case-based instruction in the teacher education program and the performance of program graduates in the classroom. In one of the few systematic studies undertaken to examine the use of cases in the preparation of music teachers, Bailey (2000) employed videotaped and narrative cases along with student-written cases with his students in their methods class and during student teaching. Focus of the cases was on classroom management, student learning, and the goals and objectives of the music education curriculum. Using King and Kitchener's (1994) Reflective Judgment Model to analyze students' engagement with the cases, Bailey concluded that case-based instruction can be effective in fostering deeper levels of reflection but that its effectiveness in so doing depends upon the individual student, the quality of the case, and the current circumstances of the student:

> Some students simply did not want to think deeply about the materials presented in the cases. (Often, students were looking for easy, quick answers to the problems they encountered.) When the students had reason to interact with the themes of the cases (attempting to solve problems in their teaching situations or resolving a dilemma contained in the case which they believed applied to their development as teachers), they would think more deeply about the materials presented in the cases. In this study, cases that (1) were based on real classroom situations, (2) presented a certain dissonance with the students' previous experience, and (3) required resolution were the most effective. (p. 331)

Modeling: For teacher educators, modeling the processes of reflective thinking is an essential first step toward encouraging preservice teachers to develop habits of reflective thought. The success of all other approaches used to foster reflective thinking about teaching depends, to a great extent, on the initial impact made by teacher modeling.

Modeling reflective thinking requires the methods teacher to demonstrate the process by thinking aloud. For example, Atterbury (1994) suggested an out-loud critical review by the music methods teacher of the planning, presentation, and outcome of the class just presented. Pautz (1989) suggested that methods teachers "talk through" the thought processes involved in planning a lesson as they demonstrate the procedure. Students are thus introduced to the essence of reflective thought by listening to the monologue of the teacher and then trying to imitate the verbalized cognitive steps in their own thinking. This suggests that the monologue should not be haphazard but that it should demonstrate the essentials of critical thinking: consideration of what is known, what is felt, and what is acted upon (Brockbank & McGill, 1998).

Prospective secondary music teachers are particularly in need of such models for performance classes. There is evidence that the focus of director instruction changes with increased classroom experience, moving from the correction of lower level problems such as wrong notes to explanations of style and interpretation (Goolsby, 1997). Modeling of reflective thinking by university ensemble directors may help novice teachers make this transition sooner. For example, conductors can think out loud about why certain decisions were made, pieces selected, rehearsals structured a certain way, or instrumentation modified to improve the quality of the performance.

While being able to engage in reflective thinking as a solitary activity is a necessary first step, it is not sufficient. If one accepts that knowledge is contextually constructed and that meaning is created in relation to others, reflection and the creation of meaning is undeniably a social process—one based on dialogue between teachers and learners (and learners together) about the issues and material before them. For reflective dialogue to happen, the teacher must also play a specific role—namely, that of facilitator. The focus becomes the students' learning, and the student learners become the center and focus of the dialogue. The teacher, as facilitator, takes responsibility for creating the conditions conducive to reflective dialogue until student learners are familiar with the process. The importance of prompting critical dialogue and helping students become comfortable with it cannot be underestimated. It is an essential component of all cooperative learning projects initiated in the methods classroom, of all exercises that center on the critique of peer teaching, of all discussions of lessons observed either in the school or via videotape, and of all conversations between student and supervisor in field experiences.

Finally, the ability to engage in reflective dialogue with other teachers in the teacher/learning community is central to the growth of teacher professionalism at all levels (Cady, Distad, & Germundsen, 1998; Collay, 1998; Halliday, 1998). As Hookey (1999) pointed out, "One may think of professional conversation as a form of collaborative action research. For practitioners, conversation is a critical element in the creation of new knowledge. . . . Scholarship proceeds through documentation of sustained talk, analysis, and the evolution of understanding" (p. 40).

Detection: Inquiry Within Authentic Experiences. All participants in the education of teachers agree that there is no substitute for well-designed field experiences. Until the late 1960s and early 1970s, laboratory schools on the campuses of colleges and universities played a large role in the preparation of teachers, providing an abundance of authentic experiences. The demise of such laboratories was brought about chiefly by budgetary restraints and the felt need for "real schools and real students," because the students who attended these laboratory schools often did not represent the school population at large. The attempt to fill the gap resulted in the integration of "laboratory experiences" into the pre-student-teaching curriculum. These activities are thought to construct a bridge between campus and field experiences by providing a controlled atmosphere for preservice teachers to practice specific instructional behaviors and skills. The activities include but are not limited to tutoring, leading small groups or sectionals, microteaching, and virtual experiences via video technology. Mentor teachers often use tutoring and small group work as a preamble to working with larger groups, but the profession has not acknowledged or studied this common transitional phase of teacher development. There is, however, a substantial amount of research on microteaching, and in the last decade, technology-enhanced instruction has become a topic of interest to researchers.

Microteaching: The commonly articulated purpose of microteaching is to give the student an opportunity to practice specific skills or strategies until a level of "competency" has been reached (Cruickshank & Metcalf, 1990). The essential constant in microteaching is that it provides practice in a "scaled-down" situation. The experience typically involves four phases: The teaching skill to be practiced is introduced, often via videotaped model; the student practices the modeled skill in a 5- to-20-minute "microteach"; a videotape of the session is reviewed and critiqued by the student and the instructor; and the student repractices the skill in light of the critique (MacLeod, 1995, p. 573).

One of the older strategies for providing authentic experiences, microteaching is still widely used in methods classes, perhaps because it can be carried on without sophisticated venues, materials, or technological support. Microteaching can be supplemented and enriched by the use of technology-dependent strategies such as videotapes for self-, peer, and supervisor analysis. Observational and evaluation systems, ranging from traditional paper-pencil observation report forms to sophisticated computer programs such as SCRIBE (Duke, Buckner, Cavitt, & Colprit, 1997), have been designed to facilitate such analyses.

As a research topic, microteaching peaked in the early 1970s, though it continued to attract attention into the 1990s. As with other teaching strategies, research findings on its effectiveness are mixed. McIntyre, Byrd, and Foxx (1996) summarized several positive results, among them better questioning skills, better classroom climate, and more meaningful lessons during student teaching. Other studies found no differences between students who had participated in microteaching and those who had not (Copeland & Doyle, 1973). It seems that behaviors practiced in microteaching are more likely to be used in student teaching if they are used by the cooperating teacher (Copeland, 1977). In today's climate of accountability, however, MacLeod's (1995) observation is very much to the point: It would be "difficult to conceive of any satisfactory test of the effectiveness of microteaching that made use of student performance criteria" (p. 576).

Technology-enhanced instruction: In the 1990s, virtually every major theory of learning was used as a guide for the development of technology-supported instruction. Video, the oldest of the commonly used technologies, has been used extensively since the 1980s to support instruction in teacher education. Thousands of multimedia and hypermedia programs based on CD-ROM or DVD technology are in development or already on the market. Among newer approaches, distance education combines many facets of pedagogy and often encompasses the spectrum of available technology.

The emphasis of video and interactive multimedia is not so much to provide answers as to create environments that prompt problem solving and reflection. Video cases are being produced in increasing numbers; and while most researchers hesitate to recommend them over actual field observation, they do offer some advantages. Video cases demonstrate a broad range of teaching styles and situations for analysis and reflective discussion. They can stimulate preservice teachers to reflect on expert teacher thinking, background information on students shown in video episodes, alternative solutions to problems presented in the episodes, and/or the contrasts between expert and novice professionals (Tomlinson, 1999). Witte (1998) recommends using interactive video cases prior to and in conjunction with school experiences. Even more authentic access to schools can be provided through the use of interactive video conferencing systems, which allow preservice teachers to observe actual classroom teaching as it occurs (McCloud & Rose, 1995).

The extent to which technology actually contributes to preservice teacher learning is unclear. In particular, empirical research that verifies the effectiveness of using technology in methods classes is very sparse. Leglar and Smith (1997) conducted a study of the effect of an interactive multimedia instructional unit on lesson planning. Although the experimental group enjoyed the unit and felt that they had profited from it, their posttreatment lesson plans were only somewhat better than those written by the control group, with the difference not reaching statistical significance. Parrish (1997) reported similarly inconclusive results in a study of a computer program designed to help preservice elementary teachers learn music fundamentals. Multimedia technology has been used successfully to teach simple skills such as instrument care and hand position (e.g., Orman, 1998). Long-term studies are needed to assess the effects of technology on complex skills such as lesson planning, but to date little has been attempted in music education.

Despite the paucity of supporting research, the extent to which technology can support music teacher education seems, at this point, to be almost limitless. In addition to video-based technology, music teacher educators are designing and utilizing technology in numerous ways (Walls, 2000). The greatest activity is taking place in instrumental music education, where interest has been shown in such topics as the use of digital accompaniment. For example, Sheldon, Reese, and Grashel (1999) conducted an empirical study that compared the effects of practicing with no accompaniment, live accompaniment, and intelligent digital accompaniment on the performances of 45 undergraduate instrumental music education majors. They found no differences among the groups in performance quality across two performances, and in fact only the group that practiced with no accompaniment improved from the first to the second performance. The study, though well designed, was limited to a small group of subjects at a single university; as the authors point out, studies that use a larger sample and allow longer practice times may produce different results.

Some technologies are as yet inadequately explored in music teacher education. Examples include distance learning, which can be expected to effect drastic changes in higher education (Evans & Nation, 2000) and ultimately in the way teachers are educated. Although distance learning can be highly structured and directive, new models are more often learner-centered (Olgren, 2001). Distance learning offers possibilities that represent a paradigm change in higher education, "from a dominant theory of expository teaching and reception learning to a dominant system of learning by working out" (Peters, 2000, p. 16). Particularly appealing to teacher educators who are attempting to encourage reflective conversation is the potential of distance learning to engender social interactions among widely dispersed learners (Jegede, 2000).

Reese and Hickey (1999) described two Internet-based projects that paired preservice music teachers with middle and high school students who were composing original music. The university students served as one-on-one mentors, analyzing, commenting, and offering suggestions about the younger students' work. All communication took place on the Internet. At the end of both projects, the preservice teachers felt that their confidence and their ability to give feedback had improved and the middle and high school students were pleased with the interchange. However, it was not evident that the young composers had actually made any changes in their work in response to their mentors' feedback.

At this stage in the development of technology, the rapidity with which technology is developing seems, paradoxically, to limit the quality and quantity of traditional research on technology-assisted instruction. It is significant that, among the studies conducted so far that are applicable to music teacher education, most are limited in scope. To design, implement, evaluate, and publish the results of a comprehensive long-term study would take several years, by which time the technology used in the study could very well be outmoded. Therefore, most researchers seem reluctant to undertake the kind of lengthy, complex research that would be required to establish that technology-assisted instruction actually helps preservice music education students become better teachers.

Judgment: Inquiry Within Field Experiences. Field experiences have proven to be one of the most highly valued and most problematic areas of teacher education (Verrastro & Leglar, 1992). While a spectrum of field experience offers preservice teachers the opportunity to refine practice and make judgments about effectiveness, the assumption that theory will be automatically implemented in practice is flawed and has not been borne out by research. One reason for this is the lack of integration between what is presented in formal coursework and what is experienced in the field. For example, preservice programs that focus on the development of reflective teachers must provide field experiences where preservice teachers can see reflective practices being modeled and can receive encouragement to develop their own reflective practice. Reflective teaching can also be facilitated in practicum situations through specific reflective activities assigned by the methods teacher (Feiman-Nemser, in press). The development of reflection in pre-student-teaching field experiences therefore necessitates a close collaboration between university and school personnel.

Moving toward a synthesis between teacher education programs and school programs calls for some deliberate restructuring of field experiences in terms of time, length, format, and personnel. R. Bullough (1989) suggested that field experiences should begin during the first term of preservice education and continue throughout the program—extending and reinforcing the reflective simulated experiences encountered in the college classroom. Introducing students to multiple sites in the course of their preservice

program has certain advantages. Because context changes practice, students would gain a certain amount of flexibility in their thinking, decision making, and practice if they had the opportunity to work with various grade levels and in several socioeconomically and culturally diverse communities. This type of field program configuration would also dilute the impact of any one context—a weakness frequently cited regarding lengthy single-site student teaching and field experiences (Cinnamond & Zimpher, 1990; Zeichner, 1987). Further, multiple settings would provide a larger experiential base for students to draw from in making a successful transition from college life to professional employment. Bullough and Gitlin (1991) propose grouping students into cohorts that proceed through coursework and field experiences as a unit. This shared experience would give the students more opportunities to explore meanings and develop their identities as professionals. All of the preceding suggestions for transforming the practicum experience dramatically emphasize the need for closer relationships with schools.

In 1987 the Music Educators National Conference (MENC) Task Force on Teacher Education called for partnerships between schools and universities for the purpose of improving the education of music teachers. Partnership models could provide preservice teachers with an integrated model for learning, promote the reciprocal exchange of knowledge between the schools and universities, facilitate conversation and collaboration between veteran and novice teachers, provide incentives for veteran teachers to remain current with pedagogical methods, and provide opportunity for methods teachers to model teaching practice in an authentic setting—giving credence to what is taught in the methods class. A similar call came in 1990 from the Holmes Group, an association of 100 research universities with teacher preparation programs, which suggested the establishment of professional development schools with P–12 partners. Such institutions would provide clinical experiences for the development of prospective teachers, as well as opportunities for the continued professional development of experienced teachers. They were also to be sites for research and development activities conducted collaboratively by teachers and university professors.

Both of these "partnership" calls have motivated music educators to look for new ways to provide reflective authentic experiences for preservice teachers. Kerchner (1998) reported success in designing and implementing a collaborative relationship between the Oberlin Conservatory of Music and the North Ridgeville (Ohio) Middle School. Members of the collaboration offered music experiences to middle school students based on requirements of the National Standards for Music Education and provided apprenticeships for preservice teachers supported by university-based instruction. Results of the project were positive. The participating preservice teachers identified what was effective about their teaching and what needed improvement. They were also able to suggest specific strategies for improving their lesson planning, presentation, and evaluation procedures. Their evaluations of the experience were overwhelmingly positive.

Creating a Culture of Inquiry

Creating a culture of inquiry throughout the profession is essential to the improvement of practice. Traditionally, the responsibility for creating and expanding knowledge about teaching has rested almost exclusively with university-based researchers. When and if practitioners are involved in the process, it is usually as a source for data and as consumers of the university's research product. As data sources, practitioners have served the profession well by allowing researchers to examine their practice. As consumers, however, they have been considerably less enthusiastic. Even when concerted efforts are made to disseminate research-generated knowledge, teachers tend to regard research as irrelevant. There is little evidence that teachers look to research for guidance in their practice—a fact that has occasioned much hand-wringing in the research establishment.

Why is it that teachers are so willing to cooperate with researchers and so reluctant to apply—or even read—what researchers have learned? The most common answer has been that practitioners do not have ready access to research results and that studies are written in such impenetrable prose that teachers do not have the time or the expertise or the inclination to decipher them. The research establishment, spearheaded in music education by MENC, has attempted to bridge the chasm between scholarship and the classroom. Reader-friendly research reports have appeared in publications that reach a more general audience, such as the *Music Educators Journal;* publications such as *Update* have focused on application-oriented studies; and practitioners have continually been exhorted to pay attention to research. None of this has had any noticeable effect.

In recent years, an increasing number of researchers, first in general education and then in music education, have come to think that these efforts have failed to hit the target because they are aimed in the wrong direction. Bennett Reimer (1992) suggested that the basic problem is not dissemination but ownership:

> When school teachers and administrators are enculturated to regard research as a natural and ongoing function for which they hold major responsibility, and when what gets researched and how research is carried on are determined by the very people who will benefit most from it, research

is likely to become the essential source for educational improvement it deserves to be. (p. 10)

Regelski (1994) contended that the positivist research paradigm "has had little success in professionalizing educationists," partly because researchers, working in isolation, are pursuing their own narrow agendas and because research based on these agendas has not produced much useful information. Researchers' distance from the school context—their status as "outsiders"—has prevented them from identifying and exploring issues that are important to practitioners. Regelski, writing from the viewpoint of critical theory, argued that "the major reason for the irrelevance of this research for teachers is its 'elsewhereness' " (p. 65). "Most research done in music education," he went on to say, "fails to have any impact simply because the problems selected are not seen as problems by those who presumably would benefit from their solution" (p. 79).

Teacher Ownership of Inquiry. Teacher educators now view it as important to involve practitioners not merely as consumers but also as producers of research. Music teacher educators now write about "action research" and "collaborative research." Teacher-generated research results in greater ownership of the questions and findings and challenges the existing imbalance in knowledge creation. Erickson (1994) described this power continuum as follows: At one extreme, the university-based researcher sets the question and the practitioner helps find the answer; at the other, the practitioner sets the question and the university researcher helps answer it. In the former pattern, as Erickson pointed out, "University ways of knowing predominate" (p. 11); the latter pattern thus holds more promise as a bridge over the theory–practice divide.

Miller (1996), who undertook an extensive collaborative action research study as an elementary general music teacher, noted that the practitioner properly sets the agenda for action studies:

> Although most research is undertaken for the purpose of ultimately improving practice or knowledge, action research is generated from a felt need at the critical level of the practicing teacher, so the main goal is an immediate and personal solution. (p. 100)

Several characteristics of action research make it especially appropriate as a central feature of a culture of inquiry: "(1) It is collaborative, (2) it addresses practical classroom problems, (3) it bolsters professional development, and (4) it requires a specialized structure to ensure both time and support for the research initiative" (Sprinthall, Reiman, & Thies-Sprinthall, 1996, p. 694). Action research, as Adelman (1994) noted, is inherently democratic in outlook, with all participants having access to the data and sharing ownership.

Music educators, though they have clung to traditional paradigms and methodologies until fairly recently, began in the 1990s to show considerable interest in action and collaborative research. Because the methodology is quite complex, practitioners often undertake their first action research projects to fulfill the requirements for a graduate degree. Several general music teachers have reported that conducting research had a profound effect on their practice—which is the primary goal of action research (Miller, 1994; Wiggins, 1994). A central theme is a movement away from the model of teacher as authority to that of teacher as facilitator. For example:

> I have learned to teach from the "side" of the classroom rather than from the "front." I have developed a far greater respect for what children can accomplish on their own and for the processes they choose for finding solutions to problems. I have learned to follow their leads . . . to stay out of the way when my ideas are not needed and to encourage students to develop their own ideas whenever possible. (Wiggins, 1994, pp. 34–35)

Similar effects on practice were reported by Hookey (1994) and Wiggins and Bodoin (1998).

There have been few studies of student-led inquiry in preservice music teacher education. Conway (1999) described a study in which undergraduates were introduced to action research but did not demonstrate thoughtful reflection. Conway's work, though limited, should serve to prompt a much-needed discussion of the implications of the teacher research movement for preservice teacher education. It is clear that the development of reflective, knowing, inquiring music teachers requires deep, systemic changes in undergraduate teacher preparation programs. So far, progress has been glacial. Reimer's observations, made a decade ago (1992), still largely hold true:

> At present it is almost unheard of for undergraduate music education majors to be given any sustained instruction in methods of research. At the master's level a single course is the rule, and that course is generally designed primarily for consumers rather than producers of research, reflecting the widespread assumption that consumership is the proper role of school teachers. . . . So we will have to engage in an almost complete reconceptualization of when, how, and what kinds of research training need to be offered to prepare school teachers to be effective researchers. (p. 11)

The Future of Teacher Inquiry.   Three important themes are evident in this review. First, the processes, perspectives, and practice of inquiry challenge the one-directional "theory into practice" rubric imposed and perpetuated by tra-

ditional research methods. Second, teacher educators perform a critical role in catalyzing teacher inquiry to bridge the gap between theory and practice. Third, teacher inquiry is central to the evolution of teaching from a semi-profession to a true profession.

Substantial difficulties lie in the path of those who are attempting to create a culture of teacher inquiry. Most serious among these is the failure of the education system at all levels to reward or even allow for teacher research. At the P–12 level, demands on practitioners' time and resources are already so heavy that it is unlikely that many teachers will conduct research unless they are enrolled in a degree program where they are expected to do so. It is noteworthy that the majority of published teacher research in music education was initiated as a degree program requirement. Change will require a radical restructuring of the workload expectations and the reward systems that prevail in the nation's public school systems. Matters are scarcely better at the university level, where traditional research approaches are sanctioned and action research is still poorly understood. In current circumstances, many teacher educators may hesitate to invest time and resources in training preservice teachers to carry out action research.

Nonetheless, teachers and teacher educators who have developed habits of reflective inquiry will inevitably be drawn to an examination of their own practice. It is the cumulative knowledge attained as a result of shared deliberations that can effect change. The professional conversation among music teacher educators can be expected to center on three unanswered questions:

What kinds of systematic teacher inquiry can most improve student learning? Positivistic research methods have achieved little toward comprehensively assessing student learning, and constructivist, qualitative approaches—while theoretically better suited to the complexities of the music classroom—may be no more fruitful if researchers continue to ask unimportant questions or employ shallow methodology. Before qualifying or quantifying the outcomes of inquiry-based curriculum, music teacher educators must first capture and come to an understanding of the practices and products created by such a curriculum. This is also true for teacher education evaluators who seek to judge the quality of preservice programs (Kennedy, 1996).

Is the formation of "professional" teachers outside the scope of university programs? Music teacher educators, following the lead of their colleagues in general education, need to increase their efforts to create and use program designs based on inquiry, to articulate the advantages of collaborative efforts in conducting and disseminating research, to demonstrate how an inquiry-centered curriculum supports the development of professionals, and to include teacher research across the spectrum of publications. A thorough commitment to teacher inquiry would necessitate not only a radical restructuring of the teacher education curriculum but also a rethinking of the academic publication process. This would involve, on the part of teacher educators, a willingness to defy the traditional culture of the academy and the premium it places on "pure" research.

When P–12 and university-based researcher/practitioners collaborate, who will set the agenda? University researchers now have a near-monopoly on research activities, and the questions they ask are not the same as those that interest P–12 practitioners. If the theory–practice chasm is to be bridged, practitioners' questions need to be fully addressed within a culture of inquiry that permeates the profession.

Coda

A century ago, Dewey developed a concept of the school in which teacher educators, teachers, and students formed a creative community of scholars. In the current teacher research movement, an important impetus is the voluntary invention of "new configurations of collaboration and partnership among teachers and university-based faculty" (Cochran-Smith & Lytle, 1999, p. 16). Important to the encouragement of partnership is the creation of new opportunities for exchange. By participating in lively conversations as members of a diverse and inclusive community, music teacher educators expand and enrich the way they think about their craft. They collaborate with P–12 practitioners to establish the music education community's professional identity and to guide the initiation of new professionals. By adopting a stance as reflective inquirers, they create their own craft knowledge and stamp their professional performance with their own interpretive creativity. In so doing, they become at once craftspeople and artists:

> Thinking about educating teachers as a craft, an art, and a profession, thinking about what it might mean to release the newcomers to learn how to learn, teacher educators can think of themselves as empowering. And the desired end-in-view? To enable persons to reach beyond, to seek in distinctiveness and membership for what is not yet. (Greene, 1984, p. 66)

REFERENCES

Abrahams, F., & Head, P. (1998). *Case studies in music education.* Chicago: GIA.

Adelman, C. (1994). To the meeting of like minds: The issue of collaboration. *Bulletin of the Council for Research in Music Education, 122,* 70–82.

Arends, R. I., Winitzky, N. E., & Tannenbaum, M. D. (2001). *Exploring teaching: An introduction to education* (2nd ed.). New York: McGraw-Hill.

Atterbury, B. W. (1994). Developing reflective music educators. *Journal of Music Teacher Education, 4*(1), 6–12.

Bailey, R. M. (2000). *Visiting the music classroom through the use of the case method in the preparation of senior-level music teacher education students: A study of reflective judgment.* Unpublished doctoral dissertation, University of Cincinnati, Ohio.

Barrett, J. R., & Rasmussen, N. S. (1996). What observation reveals: Videotaped cases as windows to preservice teachers' beliefs about music teaching and learning. *Bulletin of the Council for Research in Music Education, 130,* 75–88.

Barry, N. H. (1996). Promoting reflective practice in an elementary music methods course. *Journal of Music Teacher Education, 5*(2), 6–13.

Beatty, B. (1996). Rethinking the historical role of psychology in educational reform. In R. Olson & N. Torrance (Eds.), *The handbook of education and human development.* Cambridge, MA: Blackwell.

Berliner, D. C. (1986). In pursuit of the expert pedagogue. *Educational Researcher, 15*(7), 5–13.

Berliner, D. C. (1990). The place of process–product research in developing the agenda for research on teacher thinking. *Educational Psychologist, 24*(4), 325–344.

Berliner, D. C. (1995). Teacher expertise. In L. W. Anderson (Ed.), *International encyclopedia of teaching and teacher education* (2nd ed., pp. 46–57). Tarrytown, NY: Pergamon/Elsevier Science.

Black, R. S., Sileo, T. W., & Prater, M. A. (2000). Learning journals, self-reflection, and university students' changing perceptions. *Action in Teacher Education, 21*(4), 71–89.

Boyd, P. (1998). Becoming reflective professionals: An exploration of preservice teachers' struggles as they translate language and literacy theory into practice. *Action in Teacher Education, 19*(4), 61–78.

Bresler, L. (1992). Qualitative paradigms in music education research. *Quarterly Journal of Music Teaching and Learning, 3*(1), 64–79.

Bresler, L. (1993). Teacher knowledge in music education research. *Bulletin of the Council of Research for Music Education, 118,* 1–20.

Bresler, L. (1994). Qualitative methodology in music education. *Bulletin of the Council for Research in Music Education, 122,* 9–14.

Brockbank, A., & McGill, I. (1998). *Facilitating reflective learning in higher education.* Philadelphia: Society for Research in Higher Education and Open University Press.

Bullough, R. (1989). Teacher education and teacher reflectivity. *Journal of Teacher Education, 40*(2), 15–21.

Bullough, R., & Gitlin, A. (1991). Educative communities and the development of the reflective practitioner. In R. Tabachnick & K. Zeichner (Eds.), *Issues and practices in inquiry-oriented teacher education* (pp. 33–55). London: Falmer Press.

Cady, J., Distad, L., & Germundsen, R. (1998). Reflective practice groups in teacher induction: Building professional community via experiential knowledge. *Education, 119*(3), 459–470.

Calderhead, J. (1993). The contribution of research on teachers' thinking to the professional development of teachers.

In C. Day, J. Calderhead, & P. Denicolo (Eds.), *Research on teacher thinking: Understanding professional development* (pp. 11–18). Washington, DC: Falmer Press.

Cinnamond, J., & Zimpher, N. (1990). Reflectivity as a function of community. In R. Clift, W. R. Houston, & M. Pugach (Eds.), *Encouraging reflective practice in education: An analysis of issues and programs* (pp. 57–72). New York: Teachers College Press.

Clandinin, D. J., & Connolly, F. M. (1995). *Teachers' professional knowledge landscapes.* New York: Teachers College Press.

Cochran-Smith, M., & Lytle, S. L. (1992). Communities for teacher research: Fringe or forefront? *American Journal of Education, 100,* 298–324.

Cochran-Smith, M., & Lytle, S. L. (1999). The teacher research movement: A decade later. *Educational Researcher, 28*(7), 15–25.

Cohn, M., & Kottkamp, R. (1993). *Teachers: The missing voice in education.* Albany: State University of New York Press.

Cole, A., & Knowles, G. (2000). *Researching teaching: Exploring teacher development through reflexive inquiry.* Boston: Allyn & Bacon.

Coleman, J. S., Campbell, E. Q., Hobson, C. J., McPartland, J. J., Mood, A. M., Weinfield, F. D., & York, R. L. (1966). *Equality of educational opportunity.* Washington, DC: U.S. Government Printing Office.

Collay, M. (1998). Recherche: Teaching our life histories. *Teaching and Teacher Education, 14*(3), 245–255.

Colwell, R. (2000). The music education/arts education path. *Arts Education Policy Review, 101*(3), 19–20.

Conway, C. M. (1999). The development of teaching cases for instrumental music methods courses. *Journal of Research in Music Education, 47*(4), 343–356.

Copeland, W. (1977). Some factors related to student teacher classroom performance following microteaching training. *American Educational Research Journal, 14*(1), 147–157.

Copeland, W., & Doyle, W. (1973). Laboratory skill training and student teacher classroom performance. *Journal of Experimental Education, 42*(1), 16–21.

Cruickshank, D. R., & Metcalf, K. K. (1990). Training within teacher preparation. In W. R. Houston (Ed.), *Handbook of research on teacher education* (pp. 469–497). New York: Macmillan.

Cuban, L. (1984). *How teachers taught.* New York: Longman.

Dewey, J. (1933). *How we think.* New York: Prometheus.

Dickey, M. R. (1992). A review of research on modeling in music teaching and learning. *Bulletin of the Council of Research in Music Education, 113,* 27–40.

Dietz, M. (1995). Using portfolios as a framework for professional development. *Journal of Staff Development, 16*(2), 40–43.

Doyle, W. (1990). Themes in teacher education research. In W. R. Houston, M. Haberman, & J. Sikula (Eds.), *Handbook of research on teacher education* (pp. 3–24). New York: Macmillan.

Ducharme, E. R., & Ducharme, M. K. (1996). Needed research in teacher education. In J. Sikula, T. J. Buttery, &

E. Guyton (Eds.), *Handbook of research on teacher education* (2nd ed., pp. 1030–1046). New York: Macmillan.

Ducharme, R., & Ducharme, M. (1996). Development of the teacher education professoriate. In F. Murray (Ed.), *The teacher educator's handbook: Building a knowledge base for the preparation of teachers* (pp. 691–714). San Francisco: Jossey-Bass.

Duke, R. A., Buckner, J. J., Cavitt, M. E., & Colprit, E. (1997). Applications of SCRIBE: Systematic observation and analysis of teacher–student interactions in music. In K. C. Walls (Ed.), *Proceedings of the fourth international technological directions in music education conference* (pp. 1–2). San Antonio, TX: IMR Press.

Dunkin, M., & Biddle, B. (1974). *The study of teaching.* New York: Holt, Rinehart & Winston.

Erickson, F. (1986). Qualitative methods in research on teaching. In M. Wittrock (Ed.), *Handbook of research on teaching* (3rd ed., pp. 119–161). New York: Macmillan.

Erickson, F. (1994). Where the action is: On collaborative action research in education. *Bulletin of the Council for Research in Music Education, 123,* 10–25.

Etzioni, A. (Ed.) (1969). *The semi-professions and their organization: Teachers, nurses, social workers.* New York: Free Press.

Evans, T., & Nation, D. (2000). Introduction. In T. Evans & D. Nation (Eds.), *Changing university teaching: Reflections on creating educational technologies* (pp. 1–9). London: Kogan Page.

Fallin, J., & Goetze, M. (1999). Footprints. *Mountain Lake Reader, 1,* 74–76.

Feiman-Nemser, S. (in press). From preparation to practice: Designing a continuum to strengthen and sustain teaching. *Teachers College Record.*

Feiman-Nemser, S., & Buchmann, M. (1987). When is student teaching teacher education? *Teaching and Teacher Education, 3*(4), 255–273.

Getzels, J., & Jackson, P. (1963). The teacher's personality and characteristics. In N. Gage (Ed.), *Handbook of research on teaching* (pp. 506–582). Chicago: Rand McNally.

Gohlke, L. J. (1994). *The music methods class: Acquisition of pedagogical content knowledge by preservice music teachers.* Unpublished doctoral dissertation, University of Washington, Seattle.

Good, T. L. (1996). Teaching effects and teacher evaluation. In J. Sikula, T. J. Buttery, & E. Guyton (Eds.), *Handbook of research on teacher education* (2nd ed., pp. 617–665). New York: Macmillan.

Goolsby, T. W. (1997). Verbal instruction in instrumental rehearsals: A comparison of three career levels and preservice teachers. *Journal of Research in Music Education, 45*(1), 21–40.

Grant, J. W., & Drafall, L. E. (1991). Teacher effectiveness research: A review and comparison. *Bulletin for the Council of Research in Music Education, 108,* 31–48.

Greene, M. (1984). How do we think about our craft? *Teachers College Record, 86*(1), 55–67.

Halliday, J. (1998). Technicism, reflective practice and authenticity in teacher education. *Teaching and Teacher Education, 14*(6), 597–605.

Hamann, D. L., Lineburgh, N., & Paul, S. (1998). Teaching effectiveness and social skill development. *Journal of Research in Music Education, 46*(1), 87–101.

Hedlund, D. E., Furst, T. C., & Foley, K. T. (1989). A dialogue with self: The journal as an educational tool. *Journal of Humanistic Education and Development, 27,* 105–113.

Hendel, C. (1995). Behavioral characteristics and instructional patterns of selected music teachers. *Journal of Research in Music Education, 43*(3), 182–203.

Herbst, J. (1989). *And sadly teach: Teacher education and professionalization in American culture.* Madison: University of Wisconsin Press.

Hollingsworth, S. (1992). Learning to teach through collaborative conversation: A feminist approach. *American Educational Research Journal, 29*(2), 373–404.

Holt-Reynolds, D. (1994). When agreeing with the professor is bad news for preservice teacher educators: Jeneane, her personal history, and coursework. *Teacher Education Quarterly, 21*(1), 13–35.

Hookey, M. (1994). Music education as a collaborative project: Insights from teacher research. *Bulletin of the Council for Research in Music Education, 123,* 39–46.

Hookey, M. (1999). Charting the conceptual terrain in music teacher education: Roles for maps and models, metaphors and mirrors. *Mountain Lake Reader, 1,* 40–49.

Jegede, O. (2000). The wedlock between technology and open and distance education. In T. Evans & D. Nation (Eds.), *Changing university teaching: Reflections on creating educational technologies* (pp. 45–55). London: Kegan Page.

Kennedy, M. (1996). Research genres in teacher education. In F. Murray (Ed.), *The teacher educator's handbook: Building a knowledge base for the preparation of teachers* (pp. 120–152). San Francisco: Jossey-Bass.

Kerchner, J. L. (1997). Portfolio assessment: Tracking development. *Journal of Music Teacher Education, 6*(2), 19–22.

Kerchner, J. L. (1998). A model for educational partnerships. *Journal of Teacher Education, 8*(1), 7–14.

Killion, J. P., & Todnem, G. R. (1991). A process for personal theory building. *Educational Leadership, 48*(6), 14–16.

King, P., & Kitchener, K. (1994). *Developing reflective judgment: Understanding and promoting intellectual growth in adolescents and adults.* San Francisco: Jossey-Bass.

Knowles, J. G. (1992). Models for understanding pre-service and beginning teachers' biographies: Illustrations from case studies. In I. F. Goodson (Ed.), *Studying teachers' lives* (pp. 99–152). London: Routledge & Kegan Paul.

Krueger, P. J. (1985). *Influences of the hidden curriculum upon the perspectives of music student teachers: An ethnography.* Unpublished doctoral dissertation, University of Wisconsin–Madison.

LaBoskey, V. K. (1994). *Development of reflective practice: A study of preservice teachers.* New York: Teachers College Press.

Lee, O., & Yarger, S. J. (1996). Modes of inquiry in research on teacher education. In J. Sikula, T. J. Buttery, & E. Guyton (Eds.), *Handbook of research on teacher education* (2nd ed., pp. 14–37). New York: Macmillan.

Leglar, M. A., & Smith, D. S. (1997, March). *Evaluating interactive videodisc instruction in a music teacher education program.* Paper presented at the Southern Division MENC Conference, Nashville, TN.

Lehman, P. R. (1986). Teaching music in the 1990's. *Dialogue in Instrumental Music Education, 10*(1), 3–18.

Lortie, D. (1975). *Schoolteacher.* Chicago: University of Chicago Press.

Lucas, C. J. (1997). *Teacher education in America: Reform agendas for the twenty-first century.* New York: St. Martin's Press.

MacLeod, G. R. (1995). Microteaching in teacher education. In L. W. Anderson (Ed.), *International encyclopedia of teaching and teacher education* (2nd ed., pp. 573–577). Tarrytown, NY: Pergamon/Elsevier Science.

Madsen, C. K. (1990). Teacher intensity in relationship to music education. *Bulletin of the Council for Research in Music Education, 104,* 38–46.

Madsen, C. K., & Geringer, J. M. (1989). The relationship of teacher "on-task" to intensity and effective music teaching. *Canadian Journal of Research in Music Education, 30,* 87–94.

Mattingly, P. (1975). *The classless profession: American schoolmen in the nineteenth century.* New York: New York University Press.

McAninch, A. R. (1995). Case methods in teacher education. In L. W. Anderson (Ed.), *International encyclopedia of teaching and teacher education* (2nd ed., pp. 583–588). Tarrytown, NY: Pergamon/Elsevier Science.

McCloud, B., & Rose, E. (1995). Impact NC: Impact on education: Impact on life. In K. C. Walls (Ed.), *Proceedings of the second international technological directions in music education conference* (pp. 38–40). San Antonio, TX: IMR Press.

McIntyre, C. J., Byrd, D. M., & Foxx, S. M. (1996). Field and laboratory experiences. In J. Sikula, T. J. Buttery, & E. Guyton (Eds.), *Handbook of research on teacher education* (2nd ed., pp. 171–193). New York: Macmillan.

Merseth, K. K. (1996). Cases and case methods in teacher education. In J. Sikula, T. J. Buttery, & E Guyton (Eds.), *Handbook of research on teacher education* (2nd ed., pp. 722–744). New York: Macmillan.

Miller, B. A. (1994). Integrating elementary music instruction with a whole language first-grade classroom. *Bulletin of the Council for Research in Music Education, 123,* 36–39.

Miller, B. A. (1996). Integrating elementary general music: A collaborative action research study. *Bulletin of the Council for Research in Music Education, 130,* 100–115.

Mitchell, B. (1997). Using portfolios in undergraduate music education. *Journal of Music Teacher Education, 7*(1), 23–27.

Newell, S. (1996). Practical inquiry: Collaboration and reflection in teacher education reform. *Teaching and Teacher Education, 12*(6), 567–576.

Olgren, C. H. (2001). Distance learning in higher education. In K. Mantyla (Ed.), *The 2000/2001 ASTD distance learning yearbook.* New York: McGraw-Hill.

Orman, E. K. (1998). Effect of interactive multimedia computing on young saxophonists' achievement and attitude. *Journal of Research in Music Education, 46,* 62–74.

Pajares, M. (1992). Teachers' beliefs and educational research: Cleaning up a messy construct. *Review of Educational Research, 62*(3), 307–332.

Parrish, R. (1997). Development and testing of a computer-assisted instructional program to teach music to adult non-musicians. *Journal of Research in Music Education, 45,* 90–102.

Pautz, M. P. (1989). Musical thinking in the general music classroom. In E. Boardman (Ed.), *Dimensions of musical thinking* (pp. 65–72). Reston, VA: Music Educators National Conference.

Perrenoud, P. (1996). The teaching profession between proletarization and professionalization: Two models of change. *Prospects, 26*(3), 509–529.

Perrone, V. (1989). *Working papers: Reflections on teachers, schools, and communities.* New York: Teachers College Press, Columbia University.

Peters, O. (2000). The transformation of the university into an institution of independent learning. In T. Evans & D. Nation (Eds.), *Changing university teaching: Reflections on creating educational technologies* (pp. 10–23). London: Kegan Page.

Price, H. E., & Yarbrough, C. (1993, January). *Effect of scripted sequential patterns of instruction in music rehearsals on teaching evaluations by college nonmusic majors.* Paper presented to the Southern Division of the Music Educators National Conference, Savannah, GA.

Reese, S., & Hickey, M. (1999). Internet-based music composition and music teacher education. *Journal of Music Teacher Education, 9*(1), 25–32.

Regelski, T. A. (1994). Action research and critical theory: Empowering music teachers to professionalize praxis. *Bulletin of the Council for Research in Music Education, 123,* 63–89.

Reimer, B. (1992). An agenda for music teacher education, part II. *Journal of Music Teacher Education, 1*(2), 5–11.

Reimer, B. (1993). Avoiding extremes of theory and practice in music teacher education. *Journal of Music Teacher Education, 2*(1), 12–22.

Resnick, L. (1989). Introduction. In L. Resnick (Ed.), *Knowing, learning, and instruction: Essays in honor of Robert Glaser* (pp. 1–24). Hillsdale, NJ: Erlbaum.

Richards, C., & Killen, R. (1993). Problems of beginning teachers: Perceptions of pre-service music teachers. *Research Studies in Music Education, 1,* 40–51.

Richardson, C. P. (1995). Portfolio assessment at the master's level. *Journal of Music Teacher Education, 4*(2), 14–21.

Richardson, C. P. (1997). Using case studies in the methods classroom. *Music Educators Journal, 84,* 17–21.

Richardson, V. (1994). Conducting research on practice. *Educational Researcher, 23*(5), 5–10.

Richardson, V. (1996). The role of attitudes and beliefs in learning to teach. In J. Sikula, T. J. Buttery, & E. Guyton (Eds.), *Handbook of research on teacher education* (2nd ed., pp. 102–119). New York: Macmillan.

Richardson, V., & Placier, P. (2001). Teacher change. In V. Richardson (Ed.), *Handbook of research on teaching* (4th ed.). Washington, DC: American Educational Research Association.

Richert, A. D. (1991). Using teacher cases for reflection and enhanced understanding. In A. Lieberman & L. Miller (Eds.), *Staff development for education in the 90's* (pp. 113–132). New York: Teachers College Press.

Rozmajzl, M. (1992). Preparatory field experiences for elementary music education majors. *Update: Applications of Research to Teaching, 11*(1), 19–24.

Sabers, D. S., Cushing, K. S., & Berliner, D. C. (1991). Differences among teachers in a task characterized by simultaneity, multidimensionality, and immediacy. *American Education Research Journal, 28,* 63–88.

Schmidt, M. (1998). Defining "good" music teaching: Four student teachers' beliefs and practices. *Bulletin for the Council of Research, 138,* 19–46.

Schmuck, R. (1997). *Practical action research for change.* Arlington Heights, IL: IRI/SkyLight.

Schön, D. A. (1983). *The reflective practitioner: How professionals think in action.* New York: Basic Books.

Schwandt, T. A. (1994). Constructivist, interpretivist approaches to human inquiry. In N. K. Denzin & Y. S. Lincoln (Eds.), *Handbook of qualitative research* (pp. 118–137). Thousand Oaks, CA: Sage.

Sheldon, D. A., Reese, S., & Grashel, J. (1999). The effects of live accompaniment, intelligent digital accompaniment, and no accompaniment on musicians' performance quality. *Journal of Research in Music Education, 47,* 251–265.

Shulman, L. (1986). Those who understand: Knowledge growth in teaching. *Educational Researcher, 15*(2), 6.

Shulman, L. (1987). Knowledge and teaching: Foundations of the new reform. *Harvard Educational Review, 57*(1), 1–22.

Sileo, T. W., Prater, M. A., Luckner, J. L., Rhine, B., & Rude, H. A. (in press). Strategies to facilitate preservice teachers' active involvement in learning. *Teacher Education and Special Education.*

Sprinthall, N. A., Reiman, A. J., & Thies-Sprinthall, L. (1996). Teacher professional development. In J. Sikula, T. J. Buttery, & E. Guyton (Eds.), *Handbook of research on teacher education* (2nd ed., pp. 666–703). New York: Macmillan.

Tabachnick, B., & Zeichner, K. (1984). The impact of the student teaching experience on the development of teacher perspectives. *Journal of Teacher Education, 35*(6), 28–36.

Taebel, D. K. (1992). The evaluation of music teachers and teaching. In R. Colwell (Ed.), *Handbook of research on music teaching and learning* (pp. 310–329). New York: Macmillan.

Tama, M. C., & Peterson, K. (1991). Achieving reflectivity through literature. *Educational Leadership, 48*(6), 22–24.

Tarnowski, S. M. (1997). Transfer of elementary music methods and materials into an early practicum experience as seen through preservice teacher journals. *Bulletin for the Council of Research in Music Education, 131,* 42–43.

Tomlinson, P. (1999). Conscious reflection and implicit learning in teacher preparation. Part II: Implications for a balanced approach. *Oxford Review of Education, 25*(4), 533–534.

Verrastro, R. E., & Leglar, M. (1992). Music teacher education. In R. Colwell (Ed.), *Handbook of research on music teaching and learning* (pp. 676–696). New York: Schirmer.

Wade, R. C., & Yarbrough, D. B. (1996). Portfolios: A tool for reflective thinking in teacher education? *Teachers and Teacher Education, 12*(1), 63–79.

Walls, K. C. (2000). Technology for future music educators. *Journal of Music Teacher Education, 9*(2), 14–21.

Wasley, P., King, S., & Louth, C. (1995). Creating coalition schools through collaborative inquiry. In J. Oakes & K. Quartz (Eds.), *Creating new educational communities* (pp. 203–223). Chicago: University of Chicago Press.

Wasserman, S. (1994). Using cases to study teaching. *Phi Delta Kappan, 75*(8), 602–611.

Wiggins, J. H. (1994). Teacher-research in a general music classroom: Effects on the teacher. *Bulletin of the Council for Research in Music Education, 123*, 31–35.

Wiggins, J., & Bodoin, K. (1998). Painting a big soup: Teaching and learning in a second-grade general music classroom. *Journal of Research in Music Education, 46*(2), 281–302.

Wing, L. (1991). The music teacher educator curriculum: Crisis and deliberation. *Design for Arts in Education, 92*(5), 11–16.

Wing, L. (1994). Beyond the how-to manual in music teacher education. *Southeastern Journal of Music Education, 6*, 1–16.

Witte, R. H. (1998). Use of an interactive case study to examine school learning problems. *Teaching of Psychology, 25*(3), 224–226.

Yarbrough, C. (1975). Effect of magnitude of conductor behavior on students in selected mixed choruses. *Journal of Research in Music Education, 23*, 134–146.

Yarbrough, C., & Hendel, C. (1993). The effect of sequential patterns on rehearsal evaluations of high school and elementary students. *Journal of Research in Music Education, 41*, 246–257.

Yarbrough, C., & Price, H. E. (1981). Prediction of performer attentiveness based on rehearsal activity and teacher behavior. *Journal of Research in Music Education, 29*, 209–217.

Yarbrough, C., & Price, H. E. (1989). Sequential patterns of instruction in music. *Journal of Research in Music Education, 37*, 179–187.

Yarbrough, C., Price, H. E., & Hendel, C. (1994). The effect of sequential patterns and modes of presentation on the evaluation of music teaching. *Bulletin of the Council for Research in Music Education, 120*, 33–45.

Zeichner, K. (1987). Preparing reflective teachers: An overview of instructional strategies which have been employed in preservice teacher education. *International Journal of Educational Research, 11*(5), 565–575.

Zeichner, K. (1999). The new scholarship in teacher education. *Educational Researcher, 28*(9), 4–15.

Zeichner, K., & Tabachnick, B. R. (1981). Are the effects of university teacher education "washed out" by school experience? *Journal of Teacher Education, 32*(3), 7–11.

45

Research in Music Student Teaching

ROGER RIDEOUT

ALLAN FELDMAN

The term *student teaching* refers to a specified time period when music education students are placed in an elementary or secondary school setting to work with a music teacher who helps them create and implement lesson plans, assess student learning, and master the administrative tasks that accompany being a music teacher. The time period usually falls in the senior year of undergraduate study after all professional course work and mandatory early field experiences are completed. Each state sets the length of time that student teachers must work in school settings. According to Arends (1991), a single student-teaching placement averages 480 clock hours and most students are assigned to a specific site for 12 weeks. Yet these numbers are not supported by other surveys. Andrews (1999) notes that only four states specify hours of work and the range is from 150 to 300 clock hours. Other states define placements as full-time weeks of direct student contact that range from 1 to 18. Patrick and Schleuter (1999) determined that music placements last anywhere from 10 to 34 weeks, with no mention of clock hours. McClellan (1995), in surveying Missouri college and university music departments, found the range from 1 to 18 weeks. Patrick and Schleuter along with McClellan report that most music students are placed in two different settings in order to meet K–12 instructional demands mandated by state laws.

Once students are assigned to sites, they complete formal observations and teaching under the guidance of a cooperating teacher who serves as a role model and provides strategies for developing their professional skills (Gallant, 1992, 1994). Because teaching duties vary at different grade levels, music student teachers may work with elementary students on pitch-matching and music-reading skills, conduct music ensembles in rehearsal and concert at the middle and high school level, and lecture in music theory, literature, and interdisciplinary arts topics. In some school districts, student teachers work in computer labs or other technology centers and teach keyboard or guitar classes as well as improvisation and jazz performance techniques.

Student teaching serves as an apprenticeship, a time to learn how to teach through close supervision by an experienced master teacher. When viewed in this way, student teaching is an example of what Lave and Wegner (1991) call legitimate peripheral participation. Student teachers have a legitimate role as teachers in the classroom, including limited power and responsibilities of that role, but begin on the edge of the educational situation and move toward the center until they have reached a position of full participation as teachers. Preservice teachers put into action the educational theories learned in collegiate study and try out specific methods of instruction and assessment. They develop expertise through immersion in the "laboratory" of real-life schooling.

While most discussions refer to student teaching as either a time to learn from a master teacher or a time to try out what was learned in professional education courses, one conclusion seems clear: Student teaching is the single most important event in the undergraduate preparation for teaching (Rogers, 1995). The reason is simple. Student teaching demands that participants integrate their life experiences, formal educational activities, field observations of master teachers, music content knowledge, and pedagogical methods in the service of coherent instructional presentations that help students learn.

Music researchers in the last decade have employed various models in their efforts to understand the meaning that students, cooperating teachers, and university supervisors derive from the student-teaching experience. In this chapter, we examine selected examples of their work as well as some earlier studies that serve as the theoretical foundation of their research.

The Research on Music Student Teaching

Researchers have attended to the elements of the student teaching "triad" in order to identify the influence of the college supervisor, the cooperating teacher, and the school setting on students' teaching success.

The Student

A number of techniques have been employed to help music student teachers explore their development as teachers. Coleman (1999) used Fuller and Brown's stages of concern (1975) and Van Manen's levels of reflection (1988) as theoretical frames to interpret the data generated from student journal writing, videotape analysis, and specific questions that concern teaching objectives and activities at their common teaching site. Coleman concluded that his three female student teachers made few connections to their undergraduate teacher education curriculum because they could not move beyond Fuller's (1969) initial "survival stage." He believed his efforts at helping them develop beyond that stage were ineffective because the process of reflection had not been developed systematically as part of their undergraduate teacher education curriculum. Without a foundation in reflective processes, his demands on their thinking were a complicating factor in their student-teaching experience.

Likewise, Broyles (1997) used participant questionnaires, teacher observation instruments, journals, and videotape analysis to help 12 student teachers move through Fuller's (1969) stages. She used these techniques to measure their development and self-realization of occupational identity as a music teacher. By the conclusion of her study, she believed her students moved successfully through Fuller's stages and ended their student-teaching experience with positive identities as teachers.

Schmidt (1994) explored student self-perceptions and the effects of student teaching on those perceptions. Using "learning from experience" as a unifying theme, she developed a process of constructing meaning about music and music student teaching from prior individual experiences. Schmidt observed that her students "lacked developed schema for the concepts and theories underlying school routines as well as clear positive internal models from which to generate alternative practices" (p. 423). She concluded that the family was powerful in shaping student teachers' values, priorities, and ways of interacting with people. She found that "the strength and clarity of each one's underlying sense of 'myself' was a stronger influence

on the outcome of the student teaching experience than the sense of 'self as teacher.' " Also, she noted that the students seem to learn "those ideas and practices that fit with their already existing perceptions and did not appear to hear others that were presented" (p. 419). Interestingly, Schmidt said that her subjects who deemed the student-teaching experience positive were those whose cooperating teacher accepted them as they were. In other words, their preexisting concepts of themselves had to be accepted and validated by the cooperating teacher before the students saw their interaction with that cooperating teacher as credible and potent.

Schmidt (1998) extended her research to explore definitions of "good teaching" held by instrumental music student teachers. After analyzing participant observation data and interviews, she concluded that her subjects derived the majority of their teaching practices from their own experience as students, meaning their definitions of what constituted good teaching were based not on pedagogical principles but on their own memories of teachers. Schmidt calls for an expanded range of experiences in preservice education in order to increase exposure to a variety of teaching styles and responsibilities.

Snyder (1996) used content analysis techniques to develop themes about student beliefs that concerned music teaching, the music curriculum, and the student-teaching experience as they related to classroom management. Basing his argument on Hollingsworth (1989), Brand (1982), and Schmidt (1994), Snyder used nonparticipant observation, interviews, videotapes, journals, and an author-constructed on/off task frequency instrument to help his students become aware of their predilections toward classroom management. He concluded that "personal histories seemed to have more effect on these students' developing classroom management approaches than the methods classes encountered at the university. Prior experience with school-aged children in particular related to better classroom control" (p. 202). His findings are consistent with those of Schmidt (1994) in that "prior history"—the varying life experiences one brings to the study of teaching—is stronger than theories studied. Individuals seem to process information and adapt methodological principles according to preexisting attitudes, perspectives, and values developed in the home, the community, and precollege educational activities. Snyder also noted that the two student teachers who served as subjects in the pilot study for his dissertation had fewer classroom control problems than the two subjects in the study itself. He attributed this to the fact that both pilot subjects were placed with cooperating teachers who shared their perspectives on classroom management, meaning they were "in sync" with their cooperating teachers immediately and felt very comfortable with the management style they had in place. Finally, Snyder's data clarified three stages of development for student teachers according to Fuller's (1969) classifications. Snyder redefined these as self, subject matter, and students. Early in student teaching, his subjects were more concerned with their performance and missed aspects of student behavior and slips in content presentation. As the semester progressed, the student teachers focused on presenting the content accurately and appropriately to the students. As the semester ended, the student teachers seemed more aware of the behavior of the students in their classes. Clearly, experience in the classroom allowed his subjects to be more at ease as the semester progressed. Once comfortable with themselves in this setting, the subjects could address other matters. Only at the end of the student teaching period were they sufficiently confident to lose themselves in the act of teaching and focus solely on student behavior. Snyder concluded that the university supervisor, the methods courses, and the music curriculum, generally, had far less effect on developing effective classroom management methods than the cooperating teacher and the students' own personal history. While that may come as no surprise to most teacher educators, Snyder's contribution to our understanding of student readiness is that students filter their undergraduate teacher preparation activities through preexisting mind-sets formed from personality traits, concepts, and values developed prior to beginning collegiate study.

Realizing that research supports the argument that individual prior histories affect attitude, role identity adoption, perception of teaching tasks, and so forth, Drafall (1991) engaged all of her participants in forming student-teaching assessment criteria. She utilized reflective journals, interviews, and conferences among herself as supervisor, the cooperating teachers, and the student teachers. The continual exchange of information and intercommunication were intended to develop more positive teacher behaviors. The processes of participation and assessment were based on the belief that student teachers possess the power to become whatever they want and that conscious and continual self-reference is the best mode of improving oneself and making students conscious of and responsible for professional activity. Drafall's democratic approach to student-teaching assessment and the formative evaluation goals on which it is based remove student achievement from the evaluation equation. The student-teaching process is enveloped in establishing explicit theoretical models and practical teaching goals. Participants are colleagues, and the student teacher is merely less experienced. Drafall subsumes variables such as personality, training, commitment, professional identity, and confidence under the premise that the novice can and will achieve the desired goals through an explicit supervision process. Drafall's dissertation is the fullest explication of the image of the student teacher as a dynamic, integrated person capable of

consciously altering behavior to improve learning. She contends that student teachers inherently possess the power to develop to Fuller's (1969) third level through explicit processes and that a democratic supervisory model can facilitate growth.

In a further refinement of Drafall's assessment measures, Grant and Drafall (1996) compared student teachers' open-ended narratives used for reporting weekly activities to more closed forms in which students responded to specific questions about their teaching. They concluded that while the closed forms encouraged brief, precise responses and the open-ended narratives more wide-ranging ones, the requirement "to think on paper" was important for all students and all the responses indicated serious efforts at reflection.

In these studies, the authors used existing theoretical models borrowed from general education, most notably Fuller's model of teacher development (1969) and Schön's theory of knowledge- and reflection-in-action (1987). Their assessment focused on language-based techniques such as journal writing, questionnaire responses, written analyses of videotaped teaching sessions, and such, as ways of making self-reflection and teacher development more explicit. (This is consistent with work by Grimmett [1990], Schulman [1986], Tabachnick [1980], and Zeichner & Liston [1987].) Except for Broyles, all authors had one or more students whose development peaked at an early stage (according to Fuller's model) or could not overcome the differences between their expectations and the realities they confronted in the student-teaching process. Also, students had criteria in place that allowed them to examine their own performance in context. Finally, students completed the student teaching experience aware of issues that impeded their success or left them feeling unrealized as teachers. They engaged in processes that attempted to empower them as equal participants and to recognize their power to effect change.

Research studies on occupational identity or professional commitment to teaching are based on earlier research by L'Roy (1983) and Hearson (1983). Using a symbolic interactionist theoretical framework, L'Roy interviewed 165 undergraduate music education majors at the University of North Texas. She asked them to select terms that defined their perceived occupational roles, such as performer, music educator, band director, choral director, elementary music teacher, and so on. Her students fell, generally, into two groups: those who saw themselves as performers and for whom a career in music education was an "insurance policy" and those who saw themselves as educators. She notes that "students who conceived of themselves as educators expressed more commitment to a career in the field of music education in comparison to those who viewed themselves as performers" (p. 165) and when students were interviewed they could rarely think of or articulate broad goals for music education. They had a difficult time expressing what they thought they would be accomplishing as individuals as well as what their profession should have as objectives. (p. 148)

L'Roy observed that her subjects had little commitment to the norms and values of music teachers. They viewed themselves as performers instead. Only the students who had spent some time teaching, whether in summer camp or high school or as undergraduates, seemed to identify with teaching as a career. L'Roy concluded that because undergraduates had limited opportunities to teach themselves or to analyze teaching through observation, they had no sense of what it meant to be a music teacher.

Hearson (1983) used case study methodology to examine "specific dimensions of previous experiences working with youth and leadership activities to the consequent development of self-confidence and leadership abilities during the course of music student teaching" (p. 372). He worked with 16 student teachers for the first 8 weeks of a student-teaching semester. Using a battery of self-evaluative instruments and interviews, he compiled a pre-student-teaching experience profile for each subject. By having students complete the instruments prior to student teaching and then again after 8 weeks of student teaching, Hearson was able to assess development on a number of criteria. He concluded that while prior teaching experiences seemed to foster feelings of self confidence before students began student-teaching, the experience itself resulted in a slight loss of self confidence. Yet this loss was balanced by a marked increase in leadership abilities. His final observation that the effect of student teaching was "greatly dependent upon specific situational factors of the student teaching setting" (p. 369) introduced the student-teaching setting as a mitigating factor in the student's development as a music teacher.

Wolfgang (1990) attempted to ameliorate the problem of role identity as a music teacher by a concerted effort to structure early field experiences. He created observation instruments designed to guide students in the analysis of classroom activities and teacher behavior. Twenty-one students enrolled in early field experience coursework used the instruments and completed interviews, questionnaires, and daily journal writing. After a semester's work, Wolfgang concluded that his students had a greater understanding of the teacher's role and returned to their undergraduate studies with renewed vigor.

The research of the last decade indicates that prior history or life experiences prior to student teaching greatly affect perception of individual potential, occupational roles, and curricular expectations. This begs the question "What are the experiences common to music study at the high school and college that influence the formation of these perceptions?" Most students choose music education as a major because of their positive experiences in high school and a vague identity association with their high school teachers. By the time students enter a teacher preparation program, they have worked with any number of music teachers whose modeling is far more powerful than the formal education they receive in their undergraduate curricula. Cox (1997) examined this issue when she tried to identify the "significant others" who inspired music teachers. Cox sent questionnaires to and conducted follow-up interviews with 310 music teachers in Arkansas, asking them who first inspired them and supported their decision to become teachers. While a family member was cited most, subjects then identified an ensemble director in church or school who encouraged them to continue in music. Cox's subjects "identified more persons who had influenced them as musicians than they could recall persons who had influenced them as future teachers" (p. 116). Her findings are consistent with findings of the researchers mentioned earlier. The role of teacher and the role of musician intertwine and overlap in the minds of students.

Student teaching may be the first time music education majors make decisions, independently, about what knowledge is needed to solve a problem, direct information outward to another, assess another's performance, or focus on improving someone other than themselves. For some, these demands are unexpected and overpowering and seem only to rip them from the comfortable world in which they have succeeded as students and musicians. Performance technique and successful participation in musical activities, measured by seating position and accolades from instructors, constitute success in the pecking order of high school and undergraduate education. Yet such standards are of limited value as a teacher, and the disconnection between academic preparation and the real world of teaching is never more acute than in the initial weeks of student teaching.

The College Supervisor

The role of the supervisor has not received the same attention as that of the student teacher. Yet the supervisory role has appeared in nearly all of the research in music student teaching of the last decade. The authors of most of the dissertations and published research are supervisors themselves. Drafall, Snyder, Schmidt, and Broyles designed studies in which their supervisory role is embedded in the student-teaching process. Their research may have focused on student attitude, student performance, student development, and so forth, but in designing and conducting the research they exert a supervisory influence on the contexts in which the subjects work. For example, Drafall's democratic process has the supervisor as an equal partner in the assessment of student teacher performance. Raiman's (1975) effort to determine the priority of skills needed to be successful as a music teacher was meant to provide supervisors with the criteria by which to assess student teacher performance. Koozer (1987) attempted to create an evaluation instrument for choral student teachers. Questionnaires completed by experts and teachers yielded 29 criteria that were adapted to an evaluation instrument for supervisors and students.

In their review of research on field experiences, Verrastro and Leglar (1992) concluded that a crucial problem "is lack of involvement on the part of university faculty, both before and during the experience" (p. 686). Such a conclusion challenges the profession. Why are university supervisors seen as uninvolved or ineffective? Koehler-Richardson (1988) has suggested several reasons. First, supervisors have a relatively limited impact on classroom practices because observation and feedback sessions are few compared to those of the cooperating teacher. Andrews (1999) indicates that all states require a college-level supervisor to evaluate the student, although he provides no indication of the number of observations these supervisors must complete. Arends (1991) indicates that supervisors average one visit every 2 weeks. Patrick and Schleuter (1999) indicate the range for music supervisors is between five and seven observations per placement, while McClellan's (1995) subjects reported a range of two to eight. Yet the supervisor's contact and interaction with the student teacher is less than that of the cooperating teacher. Competing time commitments and teaching duties at their teaching positions prevent supervisors from becoming equal and full participants in the daily activities student teachers confront. Second, Koehler-Richardson (1988) notes that efforts by the supervisor to call practice into question can be interpreted as criticism of the cooperating teacher or of the policies of the school. Daily contact between the cooperating teacher and the student teacher often creates a bond in which the supervisor is seen as an interloper. Third, supervisors find it extremely difficult to "raise the level of discourse" (p. 28) about teaching. The cooperating teacher is most concerned with practice in the context of his or her school and classroom and may not use the teaching models discussed at the university level. This places the student teacher in a position where innovative teaching is discouraged or not allowed. In such a situation, the student teacher may use the supervisor's visit to plead an excuse for not implementing new practices. This means that the supervisor may be powerless to assist the student teacher or may develop an adversarial relationship with either the cooperating teacher or the student teacher.

Glass (1997) undertook a holistic description of the role of the university supervisor and the ways in which that role can influence music student teacher development. She concluded that the central issues that faced the supervisor were communication among triad members and supervisory style. In the evidence compiled from participant and nonparticipant observations, interviews, and videotape analysis, Glass confirmed Koehler-Richardson's observation that the "supervisor engaged in instructional strategies and theoretical connections to practice [while] the cooperating teacher emphasized delivery issues, classroom management, and focused on individual children" (p. 247).

These problems have led supervisors to reconsider their role. The supervisor remains the individual who assigns grades for the course work but is seen by the cooperating teacher and student teacher as a facilitator, enabler, and guide. The supervisor monitors a process, adjusts the contexts in which the participants work, and promotes the reflective dialogues that develop the student teacher. Schmidt (1994) hints at this in her observation that effective supervision is, in essence, "the ability to help preservice teachers frame their experiences in educative ways and to frame themselves in a positive light" (p. 444). This model implies that the supervisor and, by implication, the teacher preparation curriculum influence student teaching by establishing learning contexts and by explicating the procedures for assessment and evaluation. Yet this model also recognizes that the supervisor, by dint of limited appearance in the school setting, may not have full understanding of the day-to-day pressures the student teacher confronts.

The Cooperating Teacher

Only a few music researchers have studied the role of the cooperating teacher. Brand (1982) found no difference in classroom management beliefs between 47 student teachers and their cooperating teachers before or after the student-teaching experience. Schleuter (1988) analyzed data from student teacher journals, participant observation sessions, structured and informal interviews, and audiotapes to determine the level and type of preactive and postactive thinking about curriculum. She concluded that the cooperating teacher exerted the most influence on curricular thinking, yet not always in a positive way. One cooperating teacher provided a list of yearly curricular goals and encouraged her student teacher to create lesson plans to meet those goals without demanding that the student teacher follow her model. The other cooperating teachers did not address goals but expected student teachers to follow the instructional model they employed in their classrooms. Schleuter's study illustrates a paradox: Many teachers integrate curricular goals so completely into their personal teaching style that they assume student teachers can identify these goals through observation. These teachers have forgotten that goals need to be made explicit in order to help young teachers focus on aspects of instructional delivery.

As in the case of the supervisor, the cooperating teacher's role and influence are embedded in much of the music student-teaching research. As Schmidt and Snyder noted earlier, students identify with the cooperating teacher most effectively when that teacher shares common values and validates the student's beliefs about teaching. Less formal evidence in the studies indicates that the student teacher may "bond" with the cooperating teacher, thereby creating a relationship that affects the objectivity the student needs to develop teaching skills. This bond can also undercut the supervisor's ability to work with the student and validate teaching practices at that site. The supervisor's efforts to question practice can be seen as challenges made from the "outside," from someone who doesn't understand the contexts of instruction at that site. Towell's (1998) research supports this. He scripted lessons for two student teachers in an effort to introduce improvisatory teaching principles into band rehearsal routines. He found that "there was lack of adequate support and communication for employing the interventions in the field . . . [and my] analysis became problematic as it wasn't included as part of the contextual processes and routines of the cooperating teachers" (p. 300). While Drafall asked her cooperating teachers to complete some training in the assessment model she formed, most authors have treated the cooperating teacher as an independent variable, someone whose instructional setting and learning context are independent of the conditions of the research study.

The School Setting

As the research discussed earlier indicates, students base their expectations on their own experiences and, to a lesser degree, on the theoretical models presented in methods courses. This condition may make it difficult for student teachers to adapt to the realities they confront in a given educational setting. Just as the cooperating teacher "fit" is essential for a positive experience, so, too, is the school setting. Krueger (1985) was the first to examine this issue in music education. Basing her work on Berlak and Berlak (1981), Lacey (1977), and Zeichner and Tabachnick (1981), Krueger closely followed the development of two student teachers and their emerging commitment to teaching as an occupational identity. Her conclusions were that the context of teaching determined the teacher's development of positive role identity. By that she means that several variables combined to determine student teachers' success at developing a positive sense of themselves as music teachers. These included issues related to the site itself, such as the conditions of the facilities, the makeup of the student constituency, the established curricular goals of the specific cooperating teacher, the student teacher's ability to

alter these goals, difficulty with conforming to methodologies, expectations developed while a student, and the student's ability to adapt basic personality predispositions to the demands these conditions created. In combination, these variables affected the students' decision whether to consider teaching as a career. One student in Krueger's study found the experiences too overwhelming and lost ground in developing a teacher commitment, while these experiences only confirmed the second student's strong desire to teach.

Krueger (1987) is one of the few music education researchers to address the "hidden curriculum," which she defines as "embedded structures of schools, maintaining technical controls which inhibit free exploration of music and arts" (p. 49). She means that the established goals of the school site, those aspects of daily instruction that are unexamined and assumed to be correct academically and musically, actually affect the student teachers' ability to pursue what they were taught is proper instruction. In her first study, Krueger (1985) noted specifically that two students found the demands of performance deadlines prevented them from developing instructional units in music theory and aesthetic value.

The academic preparation of teachers generally exposes students to curricular models that are ideal and represent the potential for music learning. But schools develop curricula according to mandates from various educational constituencies such as legislatures, departments of education, school boards, parents, administrators, community culture, and such, and the reality of the classroom differs greatly from those models. Krueger observed that student teachers find it hard to compromise their imagined world of music teaching with the reality of public school classrooms.

Some Interpretations

How can we frame the research of the last decade? To answer this question, we turned to Zeichner and Gore (1990), whose work in early field experience provides three models for such analysis. In their Functionalism Model, student-teaching success is measured through personality development, behavioral adjustment, and teacher modeling. The intent is to determine whether student teachers can adapt successfully to the existing school conditions. The world "is" and successful individuals adapt. The work of Coy (1976), Panhorst (1968), and Turrentine (1962) can be classified in this model. By isolating those variables that affect music student teachers' success at adapting to teaching tasks, such authors are devising ways to ease the student's adaptive struggle. Zeichner and Gore's Interpretive Model argues that while the world "is," the individual is an agent of his or her own adapting. Teacher education research within this model tries to engage students in understanding the issues and processes they confront in adapting. Clearly, the studies by Schmidt, Drafall, Snyder, Broyles, and Krueger fit this model. Zeichner and Gore's third model, Critical Approaches, sees the world as existing in an eternal dialectic with the individual for whom a constant "power conflict" exists. Teacher education research within this tradition has interpreted the world as potentially coercive and restrictive on issues of curriculum, gender, race, knowledge, and the act of teaching. Only Hearson's observations and Krueger's discussion of the hidden curriculum could fall within this third category. Generally, issues of gender, race, ethnicity, social class, generational theory, and such have been ignored by music researchers.

In his most recent examination, Zeichner (1999) classifies teacher preparation research into five major categories: survey research, case studies of teacher education programs, conceptual and historical research, studies of learning to teach, and examinations of the nature and impact of teacher education activities that include self-study research. Research in music student teaching is almost entirely contained within Zeichner's fourth category. The studies reviewed here contribute to understanding

> the impact of teacher education programs on prospective teachers through . . . the use of particular strategies such as portfolio development, service learning, case studies and narrative that help prospective teachers reexamine the beliefs and attitudes they bring to teacher education programs. (p. 11)

Some Observations

In light of the research reviewed in this chapter, what challenges appear for the next decade? First, it seems to us, is the question of student learning. Assessing preservice teachers' success by measuring their students' learning is noticeably absent from the literature. Holding novice teachers accountable for student learning poses problems because they rarely are able to change the instructional environment at their site. But isn't student mastery of musical concepts and skills the intent of music teaching? Certainly researchers need to assure that the preservice teaching process is flexible and responsive to preservice teachers' development, that assessment and evaluation are constructive, and that preservice teachers' personal integrity is upheld. Yet researchers must examine preservice teacher effort in light of improved student learning.

Second, we could find no research that examined music preservice teacher interaction with special/exceptional or gifted children. Nearly two decades after mainstreaming and gifted programs have become commonplace in all schools, music research has not attended to the special nature of instruction for these student groups or to the preparation that preservice teachers receive.

Third, no one has followed up on Krueger's implications that student-teaching placement is held hostage by curricular demands that prohibit full involvement. Any of us who have been supervisors know of teachers who are reluctant to give student teachers free rein in a classroom or to relinquish the podium sufficiently to allow preservice teachers the time to develop their fledgling skills. Perhaps no other area of student teaching is more repressed or ignored than that related to issues of classroom and rehearsal access. Too many preservice teachers are mere student assistants, completing attendance records, supervising sectionals, filling in while the cooperating teacher answers the phone. The extent to which cooperating teachers actually provide appropriate and meaningful time *as teachers* is not discussed in the literature. Perhaps that is so because college and university personnel feel powerless to control such classroom activity. But if that is the case, then research is needed that identifies model programs and develops certification criteria that will assure all student teachers have supportive and sharing cooperating teachers.

Fourth, research in music student teaching must question current practice (Colwell, 2000). While several authors noted their subjects' disappointment at being unable to implement particular methodologies or curricular objectives, none of the studies we reviewed was designed to question the current practices of music education. This is understandable, although regrettable. If teacher educators want the preservice teaching experience to be positive and developmental, then they cannot prepare students to teach differently than current practice allows. Yet without a critique of current practice, without a serious rethinking of what it means to be musically educated in the 21st century, the music education profession cannot embrace the reform agendas that dominate educational thinking in America today. Music education must be willing to accept the deeper challenges before schools, such as efficiency and effectiveness of instruction and student mastery of prescribed concepts and skills.

Fifth, we want to think that student teachers come from preparation curricula that challenge them to have new ideas, experiment with new methods, and design instruction wherein all parties work together as partners in the discovery process (Wing, 1993). The reality is that most teacher preparation curricula are quite narrow and based on the instructional/ensemble practices at college-level music departments. Rarely do they accommodate special music students such as guitarists or jazz pianists, and most curricula fail to prepare students for general music study at the middle and high school levels. Music students rarely experience the entire pre-K–12 curriculum in the course of their undergraduate study. We could find no research that addressed the student-teaching problems and successes that preservice teachers face when they are placed at sites that do not reflect their academic interests or music preparation.

Sixth, few school music curricula welcome reform. Music traditions, public relations agendas in the schools, and sociocultural expectations about music affect the ability of music educators to address reform issues. Finding a means of challenging current practice while preparing a new generation of music teachers should be at the forefront of research in music student teaching.

Seventh, music education programs must prepare a new and more diverse teacher force. In their review of teacher education research, Wideen, Mayer-Smith, and Moon (1998) note that "the typical candidate for teacher education in the United States and Canada is white Anglo-Saxon, lower or middle-class female who has grown up in a suburban or rural area. She is monolingual in English" (p. 141). As Gomez (1994) observed earlier, this poses fundamental problems for teacher preparation. "An increasingly homogeneous population of teachers [is] instructing an increasingly heterogeneous population of students" (p. 320). Music teacher education programs must actively recruit in minority communities. Yet one can question whether these minority communities find themselves represented in the current practices of music education. We have no research on minority presence in our public school music programs or in our music teacher preparation programs. Equally, we have no research that assesses the extent to which teacher preparation programs prepare student teachers to instruct in Native American music, world music, or popular and vernacular genres from varying subcultures. Research in music student teaching must address the problems minority individuals have in finding their own voice and their own place in the music education curriculum as well as the preparation/implementation of varied musical cultures in P–12 practice.

Eighth, nearly all of the research in student teaching of the last decade has embraced reflection as a method of improving teaching, but not always according to Schön's original design. Zeichner and Liston (1996) liken this interest to a "bandwagon of reflective teaching." While any historical review of reflection in teacher education could begin with Dewey's (1933) work on thinking, learning, and decision making through reflection on experience, there is almost universal agreement that the current movement began after Donald Schön's (1983) publication of *The Reflective Practitioner*. Since then the idea of reflective teaching has become so ubiquitous that in many ways the term has lost its meaning. To a large extent, this has occurred because it is common for educators to confuse reflection with "thinking about." Zeichner and Liston respond to this confusion by distinguishing between reflective teaching and technical teaching and by providing readers with a list of key features of reflective teaching. Technical teaching is

a search for solutions to problems without examining and questioning the goals, values, and assumptions that constitute the educational situation in which the teacher's practice is immersed. In contrast, when teachers think about, examine, and question these aspects of teaching, they are engaged in reflection. They make this more explicit in their list of key features. Reflective teachers: (1) examine, frame, and attempt to solve the dilemmas of classroom practice; (2) are aware of and question the assumptions and values they bring to teaching; (3) are attentive to the institutional and cultural contexts in which they teach; (4) take part in curriculum development and are involved in school change efforts; and (5) take responsibility for their own professional development (Zeichner & Liston, 1996, p. 6).

Others, including Grimmett and Erikson (1988), Rearick and Feldman (1999), Valli (1997), and Van Manen (1991), have similarly distinguished reflective thinking from simply thinking about. These authors have made clear that one can distinguish among different forms of reflection, such as technical, practical, and emancipatory (Van Manen, 1991) and autobiographical, collaborative, and communal (Rearick & Feldman, 1999). However, these authors often fail to make explicit the point that reflection is more than teacher thinking that involves the key features that Zeichner and Liston identify. That is because most of the descriptions of reflection in the literature are normative (Pedevillano & Feldman, n.d.). There is an expectation that when teachers "correctly" reflect on their practice there is a tendency toward more democracy, equity, care, or constructivist practice, to name just a few of possible teleological goals. In short, this normative aspect of reflection requires that questions of the purpose, content, or quality of reflective activities should remain central in order for reflection to become a tool that will eventually empower teachers and improve schools and educational policy (Valli, 1997).

Several studies promote limited reflective practice in preservice music teachers. For example, Barry (1994) looked at (1) teaching experiences, (2) journal writing, (3) peer observations, (4) receiving notes/feedback from peer observations, (5) self-assessment, and (6) consultation/conversation with the university supervisor. Barry and Shannon (1997) asked students to produce portfolios and reflect on their teaching experiences. Grant and Drafall (1996) used reflective journals, as noted earlier, while Richards (1999) used case studies to promote reflection. In addition, Parr (1996) examined the philosophical roots of reflective practice while Schmidt (1994) and Stegman (1996) asked their student teachers to reflect on their teaching through guided questions that influenced instructional judgments, decisions, and teaching actions.

Action research (Cochran-Smith & Lytle, 1993) can be thought of as an extension of the reflective practitioner movement. It, too, has become a common part of teacher education programs. For the purposes of this discussion, we define action research as systematic inquiry by practitioners to improve teaching and learning (Cochran-Smith & Lytle, 1993; McKernan, 1988; Noffke, 1997; Rearick & Feldman, 1999). Therefore, when student teachers engage in action research they seek to improve their own teaching while improving their teaching situation. Our search of music student-teaching research did not locate references on action research in preservice music teacher education. Clearly, action research has had little impact on research in music education and music student teaching even though its potential contributions were expounded 30 years ago (Colwell, 1972) and were reiterated in 1995 (Erickson, 1995; Ross, 1995).

As a final comment, the normative aspect of reflection in teacher education leads us to one additional perspective, that of the democratic classroom. During much of the last century there has been an undercurrent, sometimes quite strong, of a critique of American schooling based on principles of democracy. This critique began with the work of Dewey (1916) and argues, basically, that while the United States claims to be a democracy and that public schools are the way that the American democracy educates children to be citizens in a democracy (Cuban, 1984; Tyack, 1974), U.S. schools themselves are undemocratic institutions (e.g., Apple, 1982; Beyer, 1996; Bowles & Gintis, 1976). In response to this criticism, educators have called for the democratization of schools, in terms both of its structures and the ways teachers teach (Goodlad, 1990).

The proponents of democratic classrooms (e.g., Beyer, 1996; Cunat, 1996; Vavrus, Walton, Kido, Diffendal, & King, 1999; Wraga, 1998) contrast "business as usual" in American schools—knowledge delivery, task completion, and classroom management through "point systems" of assessment (Feldman, Kropf, & Alibrandi, 1998)—with classrooms in which teachers trust students to assume responsibility for their own learning and rely on "the power of pooled and cooperative experience" (Dewey, 1991, p. 2). Democratic educators reject schools as reproducers of inequities in society and instead see the overall purpose of education as engaging students "to develop the skills and attitudes necessary to become people who can and will contribute to the making of a vital, equitable, and humane society" (Cunat, 1996, p. 130).

Cunat has made explicit what some of the components of a democratic classroom would be in response to her own question, "What is democratic education?" She provides her readers with an operational definition in which democratic education is evidenced by: a learning community that "recognizes and validates the individuality and responsibility of each participant"; a learning community that "works cooperatively and reflectively to engage in ex-

periences that are determined by aims and objectives set at the local level"; a curriculum that integrates education with social development and social conscience; and teachers and students who have a sense they have a responsibility to effect social and political change and do so (Cunat, 1996, p. 130).

Democratic school environments are those that are learner-centered and collaborative and in which decision making includes all stakeholders (Vavrus et al., 1999). Teachers can help to create these environments in their classrooms through the use of "democratic teaching practices" (Mullins, 1997). These include teachers' exhibiting trust in their students to take responsibility for their learning, the use of collaborative learning strategies in which students are made responsible for their learning, the use of classroom management techniques that rely on authentic learning experiences rather than "busywork," and the clear communication of high expectations (Mullins, 1997). Democratic classrooms are also ones that are based on constructivist learning principles (e.g., Brooks & Brooks, 1993; National Research Council, 1999), in which student learning begins with students' own knowledge, understanding, and experiences. Classroom activities build on these in the assimilation and accommodation of new knowledge and understanding. Democratic classrooms are also based on the notion of connected learning (Belenkey, Clinchy, Goldberger, & Tarule, 1986). They are ones in which it is accepted that knowledge is a social construction and that "all knowledge reflects the power and social relationships within society, and that an important purpose of knowledge construction is to help people improve society" (Vavrus et al., 1999, p. 125).

Clearly, the question for teacher educators is "How can teacher education programs be shaped to produce teachers who can create educational situations that can be recognized as democratic?" Vavrus et al. (1999) describe such a program that they developed at Evergreen State College. Their program is one that models what teachers ought to do by incorporating the components described earlier. Preservice teachers are engaged in classroom activities in which they question their own beliefs about teaching, schools, and students. These activities are based on an interdisciplinary approach that weaves together three themes: democracy and schooling, a multicultural and antibias perspective, and developmentally appropriate teaching and learning. These themes also shape the students' prepracticum and practicum experiences. For example, the field handbook developed by Vavrus and his colleagues guides the students through observations and experiences that focus the students' attention on school environments, student–student interactions, student–teacher interactions, management styles, and "implied theories of learning, management policies, curricular choices, and equity issues" (p. 124). When students engage in student teaching, they are evaluated on their performance through use of a performance assessment instrument that looks for evidence of the enactment of democratic principles. A major difficulty that arises in this portion of the teacher education program is the availability of cooperating teachers who share the democratic classroom philosophy and teach in schools that support this approach.

What would democratic teaching and teacher education look like in music education? Unfortunately, there is little in the literature that helps answer this question. Drafall's (1991) model of student-teaching supervision is the only effort to address directly democratic processes in student teaching. By establishing procedures that assured all parties shared an equal voice in the assessment and evaluation process, Drafall attempted to establish a democratic student-teaching environment. While some researchers have focused on the implementation of democratic practices within the classroom (e.g., Ames, 1993; Nimmo, 1997), others have questioned what it would mean for music education to be democratic. For example, Fuller (1994) and May, Lantz, and Rohr (1990) have questioned the content of the school music curriculum in relation to the ethnic and racial diversity of American schools.

Another type of critique can be found in two recent doctoral dissertations in which basic tenets of music education are questioned. For example, Goble (1999) challenges the status quo with this question: "What is the societal purpose of public school music education in the United States as an emerging post-modern society?" He answers this through a pragmatic and historical analysis of music in the United States and other societies. He concludes that music education in the United States should move away from its focus on producing musicians to the goal of introducing students to diverse cultural forms of music activity in order to raise the public's awareness of the significance of music in people's lives. Goble suggests that this will allow music education to have a role in maintaining the democratic aspects of society. Parr (1996) takes a philosophical approach to the issue of democracy in music education through her consideration of the work of Jerome Bruner, Maxine Greene, and Vernon Howard. Parr concludes that music education students need to understand themselves in their cultures and that music teacher preparation programs should be reconceptualized to focus on the process of creating self, philosophical reflection, and political advocacy.

In conclusion, it is clear that researchers in music student teaching over the last decade have appropriated modes of inquiry from general education and adapted them to the unique instructional settings that constitute music teaching. They have explicated the role of student teaching in forming students' professional identity and appropriate teaching behaviors as well as in revealing some of the effects that preservice teacher curricula, teaching sites, cooperating teachers, and supervisors have on the growth and professional development of student teachers. Their research confirms two perennial issues: that student teaching remains a transitional time when students' lives and academic experiences meld with the professional demands of music teaching, and that no single model can ameliorate the disparity that occasionally exists between the students' own values, university-level teacher preparation goals, and the realities of teaching in today's schools. What emerges from our reading of the research is that while issues of personal/professional development and identity have been examined from varying theoretical perspectives, larger issues of student achievement, professional practice, and the teacher workforce remain unexplored.

REFERENCES

Ames, R. (1993). Collaborating to build an opera ensemble. *Music Educators Journal, 79*(6), 31–34.

Andrews, T. E. (Ed.). (1999). *The NASTEC manual 1998–1999: Manual on the preparation and certification of educational personnel.* Dubuque, IA: Kendall/Hunt.

Apple, M. (1982). *Cultural and economic reproduction in education.* Boston: Routledge & Kegan Paul.

Arends, R. (1991). Special focus: Laboratory, clinical, early field, and student teaching experiences. In *Research about teacher education project: Rate IV teaching teachers* (pp. 10–18). Washington, DC: American Association of Colleges for Teacher Education.

Barry, N. H. (1994, November). *Promoting reflective practice among undergraduate education majors in an elementary music methods course.* Paper presented at the Annual Meeting of the Mid-South Educational Research Association, Nashville, TN.

Barry, N. H., & Shannon, D. M. (1997). Portfolios in teacher education: A matter of perspective. *Educational Forum, 61*(4), 320–328.

Belenkey, M. F., Clinchy, B. M., Goldberger, N. R., & Tarule, J. M. (1986). *Women's ways of knowing: The development of self, voice, and mind.* New York: Basic Books.

Berlak, H., & Berlak, H. (1981). *Dilemmas of schooling: Teaching and social change.* New York: Methuen.

Beyer, L. (1996). *Creating democratic classrooms: The struggle to integrate theory and practice.* New York: Teachers College Press.

Bowles, S., & Gintis, H. (1976). *Schooling in capitalist America.* New York: Basic Books.

Brand, M. (1982). Effects of student teaching on the classroom management beliefs and skills of music teachers. *Journal of Research in Music Education, 30*(4), 255–265.

Brooks, J., & Brooks, M. (1993). *In search of understanding: The case for constructivist classrooms.* Alexandria, VA: Association for Supervision and Curriculum Development.

Broyles, J. (1997). Effects of videotape analysis on role development of student teachers in music (Doctoral dissertation, University of Oklahoma, 1997). *Dissertation Abstracts International, 58*(03A), 823.

Cochran-Smith, M., & Lytle, S. (1993). *Inside/outside: Teacher research and knowledge.* New York: Teachers College Press.

Coleman, T. R. (1999). *The music student teaching experience: Making connections.* Unpublished doctoral dissertation, University of Cincinnati, Ohio.

Colwell, R. (1972). *A critique of research studies in music education. Final report.* USOE Research Project 5-9-230306.

Colwell, R. (2000). The music education/arts education path. *Arts Educational Policy Review, 191*(3), 19–20.

Cox, P. (1997). The professional socialization of music teachers as musicians and educators. In R. R. Rideout (Ed.), *On the sociology of music education* (pp. 112–120). Norman, OK: School of Music.

Coy, K. F. (1976). A study of the student teaching programs in music of selected institutions of higher education (Doctoral dissertation, University of Maryland, 1976). *Dissertation Abstracts International, 37*(06A), 3559.

Cuban, L. (1984). *How teachers taught: Constancy and change in American classrooms 1890–1980.* New York: Longman.

Cunat, M. (1996). Vision, vitality, and values: Advocating the democratic classroom. In L. E. Beyer (Ed.), *Creating democratic classrooms: The struggle to integrate theory and practice* (pp. 127–149). New York: Teachers College Press.

D'Arca, L. (1985). A comparative survey of the qualifications training and function of supervisors of student teachers in music at selected midwestern colleges and universities (Doctoral dissertation, University of Missouri, 1988). *Dissertation Abstracts International, 47*(02A), 458.

Dewey, J. (1916). *Democracy in education.* New York: Macmillan

Dewey, J. (1933). *How we think.* Lexington, MA: Heath.

Dewey, J. (1991). Democracy and educational administration. In J. Boydston (Ed.), *The later works* (Vol. 11, pp. 217–225). Carbondale: Southern Illinois Press.

Drafall, L. (1991). The use of developmental clinical supervision with student teachers in secondary choral music: Two case studies (Doctoral dissertation, University of Illinois, 1991). *Dissertation Abstracts International, 52*(11A), 3852.

Erickson, F. (1995). Where the action is: On collaborative action research in education. *Bulletin of the Council for Research in Music Education, 123*, 10–25.

Feldman, A., Kropf, A., & Alibrandi, M. (1998). Grading with points: The determination of report card grades by high school science teachers. *School Science and Mathematics, 98*(3), 40–48.

Fuller, F. F. (1969). Concerns of teachers: A developmental conceptualization. *American Educational Research Journal, 6*(2), 207–266.

Fuller, F. F. (1994). The arts for whose children? A challenge to educators. *NASSP Bulletin, 78*, 1–6.

Fuller, F. F., & Brown, O. H. (1975). Becoming a teacher. In K. Ryan (Ed.), *The seventy-fourth yearbook of the National Society for the Study of Education: Part II* (pp. 25–52). Chicago: University of Chicago Press.

Gallant, M. W. (1992). An overview of issues in music student teaching, related research, and a sample study of the effects of classroom characteristics on evaluation of student teaching (Doctoral dissertation, Ohio State University, 1992). *Dissertation Abstracts International, 53*(05A), 1439.

Gallant, M. W. (1994). Helping the music student teacher. *Music Educators Journal, 80*(6), 21–23.

Glass, S. B. (1997). The role of the university supervisor and its influence on the development of the music student teacher: Two case studies (Doctoral dissertation, Columbia University, 1997). *Dissertation Abstracts International, 58*(05A), 1631.

Goble, J. S. (1999). Ideologies of music education: A pragmatic, historical analysis of the concept "music" in music education in the United States (Doctoral dissertation, University of Michigan, 1999). *Dissertation Abstracts International, 60*(05A), 1493.

Gomez, M. L. (1994). Teacher education reform and prospective teachers' perspectives on teaching "other people's" children. *Teaching and Teacher Education, 10*(3), 319–334.

Goodlad, J. I. (1990). Studying the education of educators: From conception to findings. *Phi Delta Kappan, 71*(9), 698–701.

Grant, J. W., & Drafall, L. E. (1996). *Developmental thinking in student teaching experience.* Unpublished paper, American Educational Research Association, New York City. (ERIC Document Reproduction Service No. ED 397031)

Grimmett, P., & Erickson, G. (Eds.). (1988). *Reflection in teacher education.* New York: Teachers College Press.

Grimmett, P. C. (1990). *Reflections on reflection: The student teaching seminar.* Paper presented at the annual conference of the Eastern Educational Research Association, Clearwater, FL. (ERIC Document Reproduction Service No. ED 322087)

Hearson, R. H. (1983). Leadership and self-confidence: A case study investigation of the relationship of prior experiences to self-confidence, leadership, and student teaching activities (Doctoral dissertation, University of Illinois, 1983). *Dissertation Abstracts International, 45*(01A), 111.

Hollingsworth, S. (1989). Prior beliefs and cognitive change in learning to teach. *American Educational Research Journal, 26*(2), 160–189.

Koehler-Richardson, V. (1988). Barriers to the effective supervision of student teaching: A field study. *Journal of Teacher Education, 39*(2), 28–34.

Koozer, R. R. (1987). A comparison of the evaluative criteria for the choral music student teacher (Doctoral dissertation, Arizona State University, 1987). *Dissertation Abstracts International, 48*(12A), 3068.

Krueger, P. J. (1985). Influences of the hidden curriculum upon the perspectives of music student teachers: An ethnography. (Doctoral dissertation, University of Wisconsin–Madison, 1985). *Dissertation Abstracts International, 46*(05A), 1223.

Krueger, P. J. (1987). The hidden curriculum: An ethnography. *Dialogue in Instrumental Music Education, 11*(1), 37–53.

Lacy, C. (1977). *The socialization of teachers.* London: Methuen.

Lave, J., and Wegner, E. (1991). *Situated learning: Legitimate peripheral participation.* Cambridge: Cambridge University Press.

L'Roy, D. (1983). The development of occupational identity in undergraduate music education majors (Doctoral dissertation, University of North Texas). *Dissertation Abstracts International, 44*(08A), 2401.

May, W., Lantz, T., & Rohr, S. (1990, April). *"Whose" content, context, and culture in elementary art and music textbooks?* Paper presented at the Annual Meeting of the American Educational Research Association, Boston.

McClellan, N. (1995). Student teaching programs in music education at Missouri institutions of higher learning. *Missouri Journal of Research in Music Education, 32,* 24–29.

McKernan, J. (1988). The countenance of curriculum action research: Traditional, collaborative, and emancipatory-critical conceptions. *Journal of Curriculum and Supervision, 3*(3), 173–200.

Mullins, S. L. (1997). *Images of democratic educators.* Paper presented at the Annual Meeting of the National Council for the Social Studies, Cincinnati, OH.

National Research Council. (1999). *How people learn: Brain, mind, experience and schools.* Washington, DC: National Academy Press.

Nimmo, D. (1997). Judicious discipline in the music classroom. *Music Educators Journal, 83*(4), 27–32.

Noffke, S. (1997). Professional, personal, and political dimensions of action research. *Review of Research in Education, 22,* 305–343.

Panhorst, D. L. (1968). *Evaluation procedures for student teachers in music.* Unpublished doctoral dissertation, University of Rochester, NY.

Parr, N. C. (1996). Toward a philosophy of music teacher education: Applications of the ideas of Jerome Bruner, Maxine Greene, and Vernon A. Howard (Doctoral dissertation, Indiana University, 1996). *Dissertation Abstracts International, 57*(09A), 3867.

Patrick, L., & Schleuter, L. (1999). *Student teaching questionnaire: Results.* Unpublished report of the Mountain Lake Colloquium for General Music Methods.

Pedevillano, E., & Feldman, A. (n.d.). *Existential reflection in teacher education.* Xerox.

Raiman, M. L. (1975). The identification and hierarchical classification of competencies and objectives of student teaching in music through a partial delphi survey (Doctoral dissertation, University of Connecticut, 1975). *Dissertation Abstracts International, 35*(11A), 710.

Rearick, M., & Feldman, A. (1999). Orientations, product, reflections: A framework for understanding action research. *Teaching and Teacher Education, 15*(4), 333–350.

Richards, C. (1999). Can preservice teachers be prepared for student teaching? *Mountain Lake Reader,* Spring, 33–38.

Rogers, G. L. (1995). The student teaching portfolio. *Music Educators Journal, 82*(2), 29–31.

Ross, J. (1995). Research in music education: From a national perspective. *Bulletin of the Council for Research in Music Education, 123,* 123–135.

Schleuter, L. J. (1988). An analysis of elementary general music student teachers' pre-active and post-active thinking about curricula (Doctoral dissertation, Kent State University, 1988). *Dissertation Abstracts International, 49*(11A), 3256.

Schmidt, M. (1994). Learning from experience: Influences on music student teachers' perceptions and practices (experiential learning) (Doctoral dissertation, University of Michigan). *Dissertation Abstracts International, 55*(04A), 936.

Schmidt, M. (1998). Defining "good" music teaching: Four student teachers' beliefs and practices. *Bulletin of the Council for Research in Music Education, 138,* 19–46.

Schön, D. (1983). *The reflective practicner: How professionals think in practice.* New York: Basic Books.

Schön, D. (1987). *Educating the reflective practitioner.* San Francisco: Jossey-Bass.

Schulman, L. S. (1986). Paradigms and research programs in the study of teaching: A contemporary perspective. In M. C. Wittrock (Ed.), *Handbook of research on teaching* (3rd ed., pp. 3–36). New York: Macmillan.

Snyder, D. W. (1996). Classroom management and the music student teacher (Doctoral dissertation, University of Cincinnati, 1996). *Dissertation Abstracts International, 58*(01A), 117.

Stegman, S. F. (1996). An investigation of secondary choral music student teachers' perceptions of instructional successes and problems as they reflect on their music teaching (Doctoral dissertation, University of Michigan, 1996). *Dissertation Abstracts International, 57*(03A), 1070.

Tabachnick, B. (1980). Intern-teacher roles: Illusion, disillusion, and reality. *Journal of Education, 162*(1), 122–137.

Towell, G. L. (1998). Improvisation in teaching: An analogy from jazz performance (Doctoral dissertation, University of Cincinnati, 1998). *Dissertation Abstracts International, 59*(09A), 3412.

Turrentine, E. M. (1962). Predicting success in practice teaching in music (Doctoral dissertation, University of Iowa, 1962). *Dissertation Abstracts International, 23*(08A), 2814.

Tyack, D. (1974). *The one best system: A history of American urban education.* Cambridge, MA: Harvard University Press.

Valli, L. (1997). Listening to other voices: A description of teacher reflection in the United States. *Peabody Journal of Education, 72*(1), 67–88.

Van Manen, J. (1988). *Tales of the field: On writing ethnography.* Chicago: University of Chicago Press.

Van Manen, J. (1991). Reflectivity and the pedagogical moment: The normativity of pedagogical thinking and acting. *Journal of Curriculum Studies, 23*(6), 507–536.

Vavrus, M., Walton, S., Kido, J., Diffendal, E., & King, P. (1999). Weaving the web of democracy: Confronting conflicting expectations for teachers and schools. *Journal of Teacher Education, 50*(2), 119–130.

Verrastro, R. E., & Leglar, M. (1992). Music teacher education. In R. Colwell (Ed.), *Handbook of research on music teaching and learning* (pp. 676–696). New York: Schirmer.

Wideen, M., Mayer-Smith, J., & Moon, B. (1998). A critical analysis of the research on learning to teach: Making the case for an ecological perspective on inquiry. *Review of Educational Research, 68*(2), 130–178.

Wing, L. (1993). Music teacher education: Coming to our senses. *Bulletin of the Council for Research in Music Education, 117,* 51–65.

Wolfgang, R. (1990). Early field experience in music education: A study of teacher role socialization (Doctoral dissertation, University of Oregon, 1990). *Dissertation Abstracts International 52*(01A), 137.

Wraga, W. (1998). *Democratic leadership in the classroom:* *Theory into practice.* Paper presented at the Czech National Civic Education Conference, Olomouc, Czech Republic.

Zeichner, K. M. (1999). The new scholarship in teacher education. *Educational Researcher, 28*(9), 4–15.

Zeichner, K. M., & Gore, J. M. (1990). Teacher socialization. In W. R. Houston (Ed.), *Handbook of research on teacher education* (pp. 329–348). New York: Macmillan.

Zeichner, K. M., & Liston, D. P. (1987). Teaching student teachers to reflect. *Harvard Educational Review, 57,* 23–48.

Zeichner, K. M., & Liston, D. P. (1996). *Reflective teaching: An introduction.* Mahwah, NJ: Erlbaum.

Zeichner, K. M., & Tabachnick, B. R. (1981). Are the effects of university teacher education washed out by school experience? *Journal of Teacher Education, 32*(3), 7–11.

Professional Development

46

MARY ROSS HOOKEY

The professional development of inservice educators is a major concern for many educational stakeholders. The importance of professional development has been highlighted through a national award that recognizes the quality and results of professional development activities (Killion, 1999). In addition to this public recognition of the impact of professional development, a large body of research and scholarship in the general education literature has explored the nature of educators' knowledge, the ways in which educators learn to understand and maneuver their way through educational settings, and the support that different contexts offer for learning and changing educational practice. While the volume of this research has generated several literature reviews, researchers have only begun to explore some of the issues related to the professional learning of inservice music educators. This review highlights what researchers can tell us now about the professional development of inservice music educators, the nature of the issues they faced or uncovered, and the questions that they have left for others to answer. Since the questions we ask and the ways in which we attempt to answer them are influenced by how we conceptualize professional development, this chapter begins by presenting alternate definitions of professional development, reviewing some of the factors that influence the development and use of teachers' professional knowledge, and exploring the assumptions that underlie alternative definitions of professional growth.

The focus of this chapter is on the professional development of experienced music educators, novice music educators in their first years of teaching, and classroom teachers of music. In addition, this chapter is limited to research on teachers and teaching, rather than research by teachers or other music educators. As Richardson (1990) defines this: "Studies conducted by researchers on teaching examine the nature of teachers' knowledge, beliefs, percep-

tions, and other such constructs in relation to learning to teach, teachers' classroom actions, and changes in practice" (p. 5).

Inquiry into one's own practice is, however, a major mode of achieving professional development, so a link is made between this type of inquiry and its impact on personal professional growth. The categories developed by Thiessen and Kilcher (1993) for professional development provide one basis for presenting the research, since they help to highlight the wide range of professional development opportunities available for music educators and consequently for music education research. The chapter closes by considering what we have learned through this review and by drawing on related research in general education to highlight issues and areas for further study on professional development in music education.

Music educators can find compelling reasons for research on professional development in the current set of political, professional, and supply and demand issues. Historically, we are in the midst of educational reform efforts that include professional development as a basic program component to achieve change (Northwest Regional Educational Laboratory, 2000). A large cadre of new teachers will need to be inducted into the profession and supported in the first years of teaching. Participation in professional development activities either is required for induction and sustained licensure (Council of Chief State School Officers, 1998) or is under consideration (Ontario College of Teachers, 2000). Music educators will be forced to deal with these changes, but we have little research on the implications for the professional development of music educators.

There is also a stronger emphasis on professional development from both professional and personal perspectives. Constructivist theories challenge the assumptions we have held about what it means to know and learn. Researchers in fields such as mathematics and science (e.g., Lampert, 1990) have shifted their focus from research on instruction to research on how teachers can help students construct and apply their knowledge. Recently MENC (1998) reaffirmed the need for lifelong learning and published specific research questions related to professional development. At the same time as institutions have been increasing professional development requirements, a growing number of teachers have been actively pursuing their own desire to understand their practice. The literature on teacher research and collaborative action research contains reports by teachers on the motivating influence of professional development (e.g., Black, 1998).

All of these circumstances suggest that it is time to reconsider the strength of research efforts on the inservice professional development of music educators. Despite the current flurry of professional development activity, the music education profession has not given the continuing professional learning of its inservice members the same attention it has given to the learning of preservice students. Verrastro and Leglar (1992) pointed out almost a decade ago that the literature base on the professional development of music educators is small. This still holds true.

This chapter highlights what we now know about professional development in music education, mainly since 1992. As a basis for analyzing the research, I begin by exploring the questions that are raised by conflicting definitions of professional development and differing images of practitioner knowledge and how it develops.

Defining Professional Development

The term *professional development* has multiple meanings. Four that have an impact on how we design and interpret research are:

- professional development as a process of personal professional change,
- professional development as the set of activities designed to promote personal professional change,
- professional development as a lifelong project, and
- professional development as an overarching framework for professional change.

At a fundamental level, *professional development* refers to the change in a teacher's knowledge base and actions. Richardson and Placier (2001) use *professional development* as only one of the terms to describe teacher change. These authors also include a set of experiences designed to promote professional development among their terms, namely, "implementing something new or different" and the research activity of "self study." These experiences stand for the knowledge that they are expected to develop.

Professional development may also be viewed as a professional life "trajectory" (Huberman, 1989). In this view, professional development is "the sum total of formal and informal learning experiences throughout one's career from preservice teacher education to retirement" (Fullan, 1991, p. 326). Stage theories of teacher development that project movement through increasingly complex and more advanced categories contrast to the ebb and flow and alternative paths of teacher change found by Huberman (1989). Teacher education is recognized as only one of many potential sites for professional growth.

When we use the term *professional development* to stand for a framework for professional learning, it sharpens distinctions between types of professional learning opportunities and contexts for professional development research. These distinctions often rest on issues of professionalism and power. The perspective taken on these issues defines who has the right and responsibility to make or take opportunities for professional development, as well as when these rights and responsibilities apply. Sergiovanni and Starratt (1998) use the concept of responsibility to differentiate the professional development framework from the *inservice framework*. The implementation efforts of the 1960s and 1970s put "well-intentioned supervisors . . . in the driver's seat, taking responsibility for the whats, hows, and whens of improvement as they plan and provide inservice and staff development programs they think will be best for teachers" (p. 274). Inservice training was also the responsibility of teacher education institutions, professional educational organizations, and, in some cases, licensing bodies. With its emphasis on research-based instructional models that emanated from process–product studies, inservice served as a form of quality control (Doyle, 1990). Research into these implementation and training efforts, however, indicated that in-service training was not translating into classroom practice (Fullan, 1991). In response, organizational support was intensified. Various tools were developed for use by change agents with inservice teachers. For example, the Concerns Based Adoption Model (Hall & Loucks, 1978) provided supervisors and program implementers with research-based approaches to assess teachers' concerns about implementing a particular program, to determine the levels of use of various program features in the classroom, and to select various interventions to stimulate teacher change. Supervision approaches included strategies that a supervisor could use to assess and respond to a teacher's level of cognitive development (Costa & Garmston, 1985; Glickman, 1985, 1992) or stage of adult development (Oja & Reiman, 1998). These strategies are based on the assumption that it is the responsibility of *someone other than the teacher* to promote teacher growth. Although conflicting conceptions of teacher responsibility for their own learning continued to coexist (Garman, Glickman, Hunter, & Haggerson, 1987), the prevailing image of the teacher began to shift from a person in need of external interventions to a partner in the process. In this view, teachers played "key roles in deciding the direction and nature of their professional development" (Sergiovanni & Starratt, 1998, p. 274).

The balance between institutional and personal professional responsibility is the defining feature of the *professional development framework*. The involvement of teachers in peer coaching (Joyce & Showers, 1980) and a variety of related working arrangements focused research on professional development issues that surround teacher collaboration (e.g., Kohler & Crilley, 1997). The findings provided educators with a set of conditions that promoted professional learning. From one perspective, more collegial work and deliberation represented a move to greater teacher professionalization. From another, administrative efforts to achieve more effective teaching by institutionalizing joint work could lead to control through "contrived collegiality" (Hargreaves & Dawe, 1990). Doyle (1990) summarizes this potential disparity between research intent and administrative application:

> Indeed, some process–product researchers have expressed dismay at some of the ways in which findings from these studies have been applied. . . . These investigators saw research as a tool to enrich the teacher education curriculum, to sensitize teachers to dimensions of teaching that needed to be considered in planning effective strategies, and to help teachers make decisions. But precisely the opposite has frequently happened. Findings from process–product research are being used by administrators, legislators, and government officials to narrow the content of the curriculum, reduce the amount of time needed to complete teacher preparation, and impose inflexible structures and formats on teachers. (p. 13)

Richardson (1994) notes that issues of power

> shifted somewhat to considerations of who creates, constructs, or reconstructs knowledge about teaching practice, whether such knowledge can move beyond the local to the general, and the degree to which local or general knowledge can be used in the improvement of practice. (p. 5)

Under the *renewal framework*, teachers and their fellow educators pursue their commitment to their profession and their students by reflecting on and reevaluating their practice (Sergiovanni & Starratt, 1998). The themes that underlie this framework are knowledge and empowerment, the same themes that Doyle (1990) identifies as "a reaction to the quality control perspective" (p. 13). Research shifts from an emphasis on method to an emphasis on "how a practice works and what meaning it has to teachers and students in a particular context" (p. 20). This meaning may be conveyed through biographical and autobiographical accounts of professional development that illustrate how "teachers patch together a lifelong curriculum in odd and assorted ways" (S. M. Wilson & Berne, 1999, p. 197). Such accounts have the potential to counter the tendency to treat "educational change, leadership, and teacher development in rational, calculative, managerial, and stereotypical masculine ways" (Hargreaves, 1997, p. 13).

The links between teacher knowledge and the experiences designed or chosen to facilitate the development of that knowledge are often acknowledged as complex (e.g., Doyle, 1990; Richardson & Placier, 2001). Little (1982) and others have found that norms of experimentation and collegiality facilitate teacher learning. Lord (cited in S. M. Wilson & Berne, 1999) stresses the importance of a critical collegiality that incorporates "disequilibrium through self reflection" and "empathetic understanding" (p. 203). Despite this support for collegiality, researchers have documented the challenges of achieving these conditions (e.g., DiPardo, 1999; Little, 1985; Thomas, Wineburg, Grossman, Myhre, & Woolworth, 1998). Even when the conditions are met, S. M. Wilson and Berne (1999) argue that "few of these projects had yet completed analyses of what professional knowledge was acquired in those communities of learners" (p. 204).

Within these perspectives, researchers have used a wide range of constructs to investigate and describe teacher knowledge such as practical knowledge, subject matter knowledge, pedagogical content knowledge, aesthetic knowing, and spiritual knowing (Eisner, 1985). Shulman's (1985) seven knowledge categories have stimulated research and can be found among analyses of teacher knowledge in music education (e.g., Eshelman, 1995). Bruner's (1985) distinction between paradigmatic knowledge that is expressed in propositions and experiential knowledge of teaching that is expressed through narrative has been used by a number of scholars and researchers. Munby, Russell, and Martin (2001) conclude that it is problematic to make definitive statements about the links between propositional and experiential knowledge or about the transfer of propositional knowledge to teaching actions. From the perspective of professional development as teacher education, we still do not have a theory "that addresses both how teachers learn about teaching and how knowledge about teaching is used to interpret and solve teaching dilemmas" (Doyle, 1990, p. 17).

Approaches such as reflexive practice (Cole & Knowles, 2000) offer one way to address this issue.

> Reflexive practice comes about by . . . considering elements of general theories in the context of one's own particular theories. As such, teachers are both theory generators and theory users. The integration of elements or principles of both kinds of theories is the essence of reflexive or inquiring practice. (p. 11)

Reports of this work have the potential to provide us with stories of the development of personal professional knowledge. This approach to research on practice contrasts sharply with studies of the knowledge of experts and novices. Studies that compare these two groups do not let us know how experts *become* experts (Bereiter & Scardemalia, 1993). Bereiter and Scardemalia have explored how expertise can be defined differently. Instead of viewing expertise as a state, they define it as a process of "reinvestment" that includes "reinvestment in learning," "seeking out more difficult problems," and "tackling more complex representations of current problems" (pp. 93–94). This concept of reinvestment provides us with new criteria for studying professional development and a new set of lenses for reflecting on the themes and processes reported in case studies.

Richardson (1990) suggests another approach that speaks to how teachers learn about teaching and use that knowledge. Based on her research in light of the literature on teacher change and learning to teach, she proposes an approach for introducing research-based knowledge into schools. She uses Fenstermacher's definition of research-based information as "warranted practice." Change in the direction of using research-based practices involves more than understanding the parameters of an activity. According to Richardson, it involves "taking control of one's justifications" (p. 16). She argues that "empowerment is threatened when teachers are asked to make changes in activities without being asked to examine their theoretical frameworks. In fact, teacher empowerment does not occur without reflection and the development of the means to express justifications" (p. 16).

While professional development is often characterized as a solitary activity, Cochran-Smith and Lytle (1999) are among those who challenge this perspective. As an alternative, they argue for the development of inquiry communities that "exist to make consequential changes in the lives of teachers, and, as important, in the lives of students and in the social and intellectual climate of schools and schooling" (p. 295).

These authors also argue for an understanding of teacher knowledge as *knowledge-of-practice* rather than being experiential, that is, *knowledge-in-practice*, or formal, that is, *knowledge-for-practice*. They return us to issues of power and responsibility by stating

> that knowing more and teaching better are inextricably linked to larger questions about the ends of teacher learning. What is or should be its purposes or consequences? Who makes decisions about these purposes and consequences? In what ways do particular initiatives for teacher learning challenge and/or sustain the status quo? . . . The most significant questions about the purposes and consequences of teacher learning are connected to teacher agency and ownership. (p. 293)

The preceding discussion indicates the complexity of categorizing the research on the professional development of music educators. It provides a brief illustration of issues that surround how professional development is defined, as well as the nature of teacher knowledge and how it grows. Based on the issues outlined earlier, the following questions appear relevant to this review:

1. What do teachers and other music education practitioners know, how do they learn it, and how does this knowledge guide their practice?
2. What are the purposes or consequences of professional development experiences, and in what ways are the teachers individually or collectively implicated in their professional development?

As stated earlier, this review focuses on *research on teachers*. It is appropriate to reaffirm that research on the professional development of teachers is only one approach to understanding the growth of professional knowledge and the impact of differing opportunities to learn. Research carried out *by teachers or other practitioners* represents a significant opportunity for professional development. This could include various individual strategies and approaches such as action research or self-study, self-evaluation or writing, working in mentoring or coaching pairs, and diverse group strategies (Thiessen & Kilcher, 1993). Research by music educators such as Black (1998) provides us with accounts of questions, research strategies, and reports that illustrate how teacher knowledge and practice change. Black's action research enabled her to improve her ability to motivate and develop the self-esteem of her high school vocal music class so that they will be able to take a more active role in their own learning (p. 3). Arnold (1991) used *self-evaluation* to examine his own teaching in relation to the three-step model of direct instruction. The content of videotapes of his teaching and the student participation in his instrumental music class shocked him into confronting his everyday interpretation of events to reinterpret his actions and to change his practice. These teacher researcher accounts illustrate a confrontation between what Argyris (1982) calls theories-in-use and theories-in-action.

Thiessen and Kilcher (1993) argue that *writing* "helps teachers to reflect on the themes, rhythms, and regularities of classroom life" (p. 35). A host of types of writing—logs, diaries, journals, written analyses of curriculum-related materials, stories, biographies, and autobiographies—are all tools for reflection. So are research reports and the writing of curriculum materials, even if research on these areas is nonexistent or difficult to locate. Two books by R. Upitis (1990, 1992), *This Too Is Music* and *Can I Play You My Song?* document the development of the compositional capabilities of elementary students. Authenticity is one criterion for assessing the validity of autobiographical work (Cole & Knowles, 2000). The writing by Upitis rings with the authenticity of the author's experiences. Each book illustrates explorations into important educational questions and the ways in which the author made sense of puzzles, surprises, and problems as the work progressed.

We now turn to the work of *researchers on the professional development* of music educators. Some of the categories identified in an analysis of professional development by Thiessen and Kilcher (1993) have been useful in this review because they recognize differences in professional development *by teachers* versus *for teachers*. This difference highlights the opportunities for research that may be undertaken by teachers as compared to that conducted by external researchers. This will be reviewed under the following headings:

- Research on the Professional Development of Music Educators Within/Across Organizations,
- Research on the Professional Development of Music Educators in Schools,
- Research on the Personal Professional Lives of Music Educators,
- Research on Professional Development Requirements for Licensure and Recertification of Inservice Music Educators, and
- Research on Classroom Teachers as Music Educators.

Research on the Professional Development of Music Educators Within/Across Organizations

The research within and across organizations has two sections. The first set of organizational support systems for professional development includes artist-educators as consultants, teacher leaders, cooperating music teachers as mentors, music supervisors or music resource teachers, and graduate faculty consultants.

Artist-educators as consultants were an integral part of the Professional Development Residency Program (Colwell, 1996–1997), which provided individual on-site support to an arts educator. This assistance was to be ongoing, to be supported by both individual arts educators and the school system, and to involve inquiry, input, reflection, and feedback. The program received funding from the Iowa Arts Council for one year. Although the program might take various directions, representative activities "may introduce new teaching techniques and resources, improve teaching practices, improve schedules and support, or provide greater visibility to the arts programs in the schools" (p. 88). Concerns about the program generally related to a lack of awareness of the program, the visibility of the residency work, and an administrative understanding of

potential opportunities for extending the benefits of the program. In addition to collecting data on the nature of the residency work and teachers' perceptions of its success, the external reviewers collected indicators of the program's impact and comparisons of the residency to college-based teacher education courses. This program evaluation reveals a high level of support for its objectives. This article is one of the few program evaluations widely available. There are both ethical and political issues involved in this type of research. The question remains whether the music education research community can address these tensions successfully to make this type of work more public.

Music *teacher leadership* positions are also designed to offer support for professional development. These "semi-detached teachers" (Biott, 1991) are in positions of personal authority, not administrative power. To date, there has been limited exploration of the role of the music teacher as a teacher leader and advocate for his or her subject matter within the school setting. The role of the *cooperating music teacher as mentor* is another school-based music educator role for which there is some research. This work is discussed in the Handbook in the chapter on student teaching. Only a few studies have examined the role of *music supervisors* or *music resource teachers* (e.g., Jorgensen, 1979, 1980). Part of the difficulty of working in this role lies in the lack of understanding that others have of the work (Rust, Astuto, Driscoll, Blakeney, & Ross, 1998). There is a clear distinction among familiar forms of supervision, consultation, and counseling interactions among supervisors, consultants, resource teachers, and school-based teacher leaders (Knoff, 1988). The essential difference in these interactions is underlined by the following question: Who has the right to set the agenda and direct the interactions in the relationship?

Fallin and Royse (1994) served as *graduate faculty consultants* when they provided seven of their recent music education graduates with advice on how to improve the teaching in some of their most challenging classes. These graduates taught in various grades and programs, and none had the opportunity to receive ongoing support from a music consultant or supervisor. In the process of preparing to do this, the university instructors undertook to widen their own basis for generating suggestions by making comparisons of the novice teaching with videotaped lessons by experienced teachers. The article is titled "Common Problems of the New Music Teacher," but it uses these problems only as the introduction to some systematic work to *address* the problems. Although this article does not discuss the project in these terms, the new teachers and the teacher educators were involved in searching out contexts for their own professional development. The work made a difference to the practice of both groups. An examination of this study brings to mind the discussion around the writing of case studies and narratives as a research-reporting genre. When we are told that the beginning teachers "were able to think about their problems more creatively," inclusion of quotes would make the findings of this study more compelling.

The second set of organizational support systems for professional development includes short courses, graduate courses and programs, centers, professional associations, partnerships and networks.

Short courses have provided researchers with opportunities to address the paucity of studies built on research findings cited by Price (1993). The ongoing work of Yarbrough, of Price, and of Madsen has provided models of extensive research programs based on reference to prevailing theories of learning and instruction. Questions about these studies stem from shifting perspectives of what it means to learn and teach.

Yarbrough, Price, and Bowers (1991) were curious to know if "experienced teachers would choose research-based rehearsal skills if they knew about and valued them" (p. 17). The research is based on Price's finding that "band directors who were using a sequential pattern with a task presentation, student performance, and immediate, related feedback were effective in producing good performance while maintaining high student attentiveness and positive student attitude" (p. 17). The researchers established the values held by their participants through their ratings of various transcripts of excerpts from music rehearsals. The researchers tested their question in a 2-week workshop for 12 experienced teachers on conducting skills. While three of the teachers displayed the "correct or most effective" teaching patterning in the pretest, all did in the posttest videotape. The researchers observed that while the conducting behaviors that the conductors valued did not necessarily match their values-in-use for the act of conducting at the beginning of the study, this changed by the end.

> After research results were presented to them in an understandable way, and after they had opportunities for practicing research-based techniques in a positive environment, these teachers were not only able to value that research, but were able to translate those values into observable behaviors. (p. 19)

Arnold (1995) took this finding as evidence that teachers were unaware of the research findings, not rejecting them. He conducted an experimental study to understand the "effects of competency-based methods of instruction and self-observation on ensemble directors' use of sequential patterns" (p. 127). The study involved members of the experimental group in focused observation of their videotapes that used an operational definition of complete sequential patterns. Arnold found that "the act of recognizing and identifying complete teaching cycles and transferring this knowledge to their respective teaching

styles demonstrated the effectiveness of research-based techniques in modifying teaching behaviors" (p. 134). He concluded that this competency-based process of videotaping and reviewing according to specific guidelines illustrates that "practicing music educators do not need external feedback, evaluation, or instruction to improve their teaching skills" (p. 135).

The nature of professional knowledge that is developed in these studies is made quite clear. Some questions are raised by this study: What kinds of contextual influences might affect the choice of the "correct" sequential instructional pattern? What professional values underpin the choice to use this teaching methodology? How do the students make sense of themselves as musicians under this model of teaching?

Madsen (1990) and his colleagues also carried out an extensive research program related to the concept of teacher intensity. The definition of intensity is "(1) sustained control of the student/teacher interaction with (2) efficient, accurate presentation of subject matter combined with (3) enthusiastic affect and pacing" (p. 38). One experiment involved five afternoon workshops on classroom management for practicing music educators. Participants had time to experiment with the techniques in their classrooms between sessions. The aim was to "ascertain whether effects of teacher intensity could be behaviorally defined and measured within a short, inservice workshop" (p. 39). Teacher intensity has been linked in many studies with effective implementation of direct instruction as a teaching/learning model (Madsen, 1990). With new models of learner-centered instruction and images of constructivist teaching practices, classroom management may require redefinition and "take on a new set of meanings for all participants" (Randolph & Evertson, 1994, p. 55). This raises the question of whether different images of classroom management are applicable to various instructional contexts in music education and, if so, whether they suggest alternative models of learner-centered instruction in performance classes.

Graduate courses and programs constitute another area that is underresearched. Junda's (1994) graduate research project combined self-study with external evaluation. The course director, the instructor, and an independent consultant were all involved in aspects of the research or instruction. The program included two features that have been shown to be effective in other inservice projects, namely, the introduction of new ideas and skills and the opportunity for classroom implementation with coaching and feedback from a knowledgeable teacher. Both teacher participants and their students improved in sight-singing skills and planning, although improvement was reportedly slow to develop. The use of research-based inservice practices for skill development such as in-class coaching and peer support was found to contribute to the success of the course. This is one of the few studies that linked course-work and classroom practice with student gains.

Centers can provide both inservice training and research into the professional development of music educators. In some cases, music may be examined as a component of arts education and relegated to a minor role in reports (e.g., Lincoln Center Institute for the Arts, 2000; Shook-hoff, 1996; Wilson, 1997). In contrast, May (1990, 1993) examined professional development in music education under the auspices of the Center for the Learning and Teaching of Elementary Subjects. May (1990) studied the work of one small support group of three music teachers who met on their own time to engage in curriculum deliberations. Each teacher met over 1,100 students once a week in a 30-minute lesson. The focus of their deliberations was a one-page lesson plan. Her report provides us with a sense of the general categories of music teacher knowledge. She notes their attention to "horizontal planning" by grade and across teachers, "vertical planning" of what should be presented and when, "links and transitions" among prior learning and repertoire, "teaching each other" the way to present a new concept or refine a skill, and "contextual dilemmas" such as "being ousted out of one's music room so that . . . voting booths can be temporarily installed" (p. 34–35). May also provides a description of how the learning proceeded. Each week, the teachers built on one another's expertise to create the next set of plans and reflect on what was or was not accomplished. She concludes that by creating their own conversational space "they have at least six legs to stand on, and they have made public to themselves and to others what learning means in music" (p. 36). This case study provides us with an alternative image of support for music educators who are the only music professionals in their school.

Professional associations may aim to foster long-term professional growth, but there are few reports of the on-going assessment of these courses. Robbins's (1994/1995) article was based on a work in progress. Teachers enrolled in one section of Orff Schulwerk Teacher Training Courses were educated in the process of teacher research. The establishment of a research group provided continuing support for reflective practice over the 2-year project. At the point that the article was written, Robbins was raising questions about the reciprocal influence on the course based on teachers' classroom work. An emerging question fo her was: "How can the interpretive work practiced by the Orff SPIEL teachers 'outside' the course become situated within them as well?"

From Price and Orman's (1999) analysis of MENC conferences, we gain an understanding of the sometimes arbitrary development of conference sessions and how they have changed over the years. The findings related to research show that research occupied 7% of the total number of conference sessions in 1984 and 4.6% in 1998, al-

though these figures represent the same number of research sessions. The authors reflect on an apparent discrepancy between a proportional decline in research sessions with increased interest in research as evidenced by new research journals and the more specific attention to research found in the latest MENC document on music teacher education (1998). While Barry (1998) provides a model study of an arts integration workshop, there has been little or no attention on how music conferences offered either by commercial interests or by music associations, including those offered by MENC, have made a difference to teacher knowledge or practice.

A range of school system and university *partnerships* foster unique opportunities for professional development (Warren, 1989). Froseth (n.d.) reports the results of on-going research into the effects of teacher self-assessment combined with analysis of videotaped instruction. Froseth concludes that "the value of teachers' own interpretations of their work has transcended that of traditional external interpretations. The stark—and sometimes harsh—realities of the videotape were undeniable." As in Black (1988) and Arnold (1991), this is another case of theories-in-action being challenged by theories-in-use (Argyris, 1982).

The North York Choral Development Project (Dolloff, 1994, 1996) was an attempt to counteract the decontextualization of in-service education by placing both teachers and their students into a music-learning context with an expert university-based choral director. Dolloff characterizes this attempt at increasing teacher expertise as a form of cognitive apprenticeship. This is "a model of education that immerses the learner in situations of practice, providing an authentic context in which to develop skills" (1996, p. 5). Teachers were nominated to take part in the project, and they then selected 20 choir members from their schools as participants in choral workshops. The philosophy that underpins this work is praxial (Elliott, 1995). The modeling of the choral expert in the context of seminars, demonstration/rehearsals, and concerts provides multiple models of "expertise-in-use" (Dolloff, 1994, p. 27).

According to their own perceptions, the teachers increased their personal expertise in choral music education as they engaged in seminars, discussions, and music making, all focused on the music literature. This project addressed the issue of building a professional community of choral music educators at the elementary school level, where often there is one music teacher in the school responsible for choral music. Dolloff found that "the teachers' perception of what they had gained was closely related to what they thought their students had gained—increased self-confidence, self-esteem, increased skills which led to more successful performance (teaching or singing)" (p. 7). While we gain a clear image of the workshop process, narratives or other evidence of classroom activity that evolve from this professional development experience might contribute to the reader's understanding of what teachers were learning. This study also raises the issue of evidence in music education research. What alternative forms of representation can music education researchers use that will give us a broader and richer sense of the study?

In other research based on a school-district-university partnership, Robinson (1999) focused on the dynamics of collaboration among people in organizations with vastly different goals and structures. Drawing on artistic principles from the field of architecture, he proposed a theory of collaboration in music education based on principles of tensegrity, or tensional integrity:

> The constructs associated with tensegretic theory allow for an explanation of the complexity of the partnership. Tensegrity structures are systems that stabilize themselves by balancing counteracting forces of compression and tension; stress is balanced and distributed by tension, not just by the strengths of individual structural members. (p. 172)

This image of collaboration is useful to a wide range of educators, as it offers an alternative to the usual hierarchical organizations and is not dependent on music for its subject matter. As Robinson argues, the answer to "how we reconcile the tensions that seem to be an integral part of these relationships . . . may be in how we view these differences" (pp. 271–272). For Robinson, "looking at differences as potentially productive sources of energy is key to functioning in a climate of tension" (p. 272). Both this dissertation and his article in the *Arts Education Policy Review* (1998) provide models of communication through highly descriptive narrative accounts.

Networks have proven highly effective for professional development in connecting people with like interests, either geographically or electronically (Firestone & Pennell, 1997; Huberman, 1995; Lieberman, 2000; Lieberman & Grolnick, 1997). Research into the use of technology in inservice music education is in its infancy. Bush (in press) reports on a project that links graduate music education students with three or four teachers in the field as part of their ongoing course experience. In one activity, teachers pose questions to the class and responses are posted back to the schools. While there are some issues related to using this type of asynchronous communication, Bush concludes that this type of professional interaction can provide a powerful form of mentoring.

Research on the Professional Development of Music Educators in Schools

There is limited research into coaching, mentoring, and group strategies for the professional development of music educators in schools. In some cases, the researcher is also the inservice educator, investigating how the teacher uses a teaching strategy or particular skill and sharing the necessary information about the strategy or skill before the study. Wing (1977) collected data on what her study participant came to know about evaluation in several ways. Wing planned with her, observed her, read the evaluation assignments of the students, and assessed the results jointly. She adjusted her working relationship with the teacher to cross an imagined divide between her role as participant and observer. Wing reports that she did not observe any use of the suggested evaluation techniques as she continued to observe in the teacher's classroom until the posttest was administered at the end of the next unit. Among her conclusions, she writes that "the variable of 'ownership' in an innovation is probably a big factor in the successful implementation and survival of that implementation" (p. 190). Wing reached these conclusions at a time when major implementation studies were trying to understand the same phenomenon. She questions how appropriately the teacher was implicated in her own professional development. Although scholars like S. M. Wilson and Berne (1999) are encouraging us to move beyond an understanding of the process of professional development to what was learned through the experience, this study, through detailed reporting and analysis, provides the reader with "some real insights into human working processes which are integral parts of instruction" (Landon, 1981, p. 136). Two decades after its completion, the study continues to offer evidence that implementation issues in the classroom are as much personal, affective, and intentional as logical. It also illustrates how introducing new ideas into a classroom for a study requires extended negotiation of meaning between the researcher and the participant, with the continuing potential for shifting roles and research purposes.

Support groups, collaborative action research, and various school improvement initiatives are group strategies for professional development in schools. These categories highlight how music occupies a mutual space with many other subject areas. The work of Upitis, Soren, and Smithrim (1998), which is discussed later, and my work (Hookey, 1997) provide school-based examples, where group strategies are applied to make the arts a focus of school change. In both cases, individual arts as well as integrated arts are part of the school improvement initiatives. There is little research on the issue of balance between instruction in distinct art forms and integrated arts instruction.

Research on the Personal Professional Lives of Music Educators

Research on the personal professional lives of music educators has been focused on identifying differences in the nature of music teaching in terms of teacher expertise and experience, on descriptions of exemplary teachers, and on the emergence of personal, professional expertise. Biographies provide images of the significant events across a professional life (Huberman, 1989). The chronology of three professional lives is captured in Baker's (1992) study of three influential music educators. King's (1998) study paints a portrait of an educator whose personal and professional life is marked by themes that organize and justify his personal life and professional work.

Research that focuses on differences among music educators of varying experience and expertise provides us with images of more or less effective practices (e.g., Goolsby, 1996). One of the issues in conducting this type of research is the level of writing skill that one brings to the task. Through detailed accounts set in vivid language there is the potential for a deeper understanding of the issues that music educators have faced and the development of alternative perspectives on perennial issues in music education.

Another issue related to this research focus is how an expert or exemplary teacher is defined. Futhermore, expertise is not automatically linked with experience (Standley & Madsen, 1991). The criteria for defining the exemplary teacher appears closely aligned to the goals of a music education practice. The experienced teachers in Goolsby's study (1996) were selected for their expertise in developing performing ensembles. While they may be experts in this aspect of music education, Goolsby questioned the fact that these teachers did not ask questions of their students. These experienced teachers would appear to be exemplars of instrumental music instruction using consistent sequential patterns, but not exemplars of a comprehensive approach to music performance that stresses critical and creative thinking.

Duling's (1992) case study of two general music educators is based on the assumption that teacher educators need to understand "what the teacher thinks, why he or she has come to think that way, what actions result from the thoughts" (p. 9). His analysis is directed at describing and building a model of the pedagogical content knowledge of the teachers. He also describes the process of professional change and growth of his participants, drawing on observation, stimulated recall, reflective interviewing, and the comparison of concept maps made by the participants. Duling's three categories of pedagogical-content knowledge are derived from participants' explanations of influential relationships with people, contexts, and ideas on their development. A major finding is that the exemplary teachers in this study seek out opportunities for learning and establish both short- and long-term mentoring relationships in the process.

Research on Professional Development Requirements for Licensure and Recertification of Inservice Music Educators

The practice of requiring professional development for renewal of a teaching or administrative certificate is approaching universality in the United States (SRI Associates, 2000). In light of this situation, there is ample potential for research. According to a recent survey (Council of Chief State School Officers, 1998), 47 states had policies that set out professional development activity requirements for recertification. The more than 20 states that had established induction programs also included mentoring. SRI Associates (2000) provides a comprehensive overview of the elements of different induction programs, including their history, annual funding, name, and primary components. While most programs have an evaluation component, research that spans the induction phase is only just beginning. A cursory glance across several state department of education Web sites illustrates the wide variation in limitations imposed on or discretion given to teachers to define what professional growth means. The differences reflect the underlying tensions among perspectives on power and responsibility. When choice is available to teachers, the conception of what counts as a professional development activity is wide. The following activities are suggested as suitable for professional learning by a self-regulatory body for teachers, the Ontario College of Teachers (2000):

- taking academic courses,
- engaging in research activities,
- taking part in professional networks,
- engaging in a variety of individual professional activities,
- mentoring and networking,
- writing and leading professional activities,
- learning through curriculum development or other collaborative work,
- investigating new uses of technology, and
- devising another activity designed to support their professional learning.

The variation appears to be just as wide for "how much" counts as enough professional development. The reported norm in 1998 was six semester credits every 5 years (Council of Chief State School Officers, 1998). Other states used clock hours, while a minority used continuing education units or choices among credits, units, or contact hours.

It is difficult to assess the range of current research into the area of licensure or recertification for practicing teachers, even though a number of states are making their work public (e.g., Olebe, 1999). Connecticut has been selected for this review as an example of a state with a program for inductees that has a research program designed around its program requirements (Connecticut State Department of Education, Division of Evaluation and Research, 2000). The program documentation is accessible, a research program is outlined, and there is an identifiable focus on music educators (Connecticut State Department of Education, Bureau of Program and Teacher Evaluation, 2000b). Connecticut's teacher induction program takes an integrated approach to professional development and teacher evaluation. The Beginning Educator Support and Training (BEST) program (Connecticut State Department of Education, Bureau of Program and Teacher Evaluation, 2000a) is a 2- or 3-year process of support, culminating in the production and evaluation of a teaching portfolio. An indication of the size of the program is that 1,817 portfolios were completed in the spring of 2000. There are 20 research projects related to this program listed for 2000–2001 (Connecticut State Department of Education, Bureau of Program and Teacher Evaluation, 2000b). Some of this research focuses on the relationship of the portfolio to current teacher-evaluation activities, student achievement, criterion validity, opinions of the professional development process by content experts and supervisors, and endorsement by educational stakeholders. The general requirements for the portfolio include organizing and planning instruction, implementing and videotaping instruction, submitting and assessing student work, and analyzing teaching and learning.

The development of a music-teaching portfolio (Connecticut State Department of Education, Division of Evaluation and Research, 2000c) focuses professional support on the three artistic processes that are identified in the Arts Curriculum: creating, performing, and responding with understanding (Connecticut State Department of Education, Division of Teaching and Learning, Bureau of Curriculum and Instruction, 2001). The BEST (Beginning Educator Support and Training) program provides ongoing professional mentoring for classroom work and supports the new teacher in the development of the portfolio. The BEST handbook (Connecticut State Department of Education, Bureau of Program and Teacher Evaluation, 2000a) identifies the parties that should be involved, the minimum time commitment for each party, and a person for new teachers to contact if the mentoring relationship is either not occurring or not helpful. New teachers meet with peers as well as mentors, and new teachers along with the people involved as mentors, classroom observers, and portfolio analysts receive professional development. The case studies that result from this research should reveal additional areas for detailed study. The breadth of methodologies and participants involved have the potential to provide multiple lenses on professional development phenomena.

Research on Classroom Teachers as Music Educators

The use of classroom teachers as music educators at the elementary school level is a political, economic, and teacher-supply issue (Beauchamp, 1997). When classroom teachers provide music instruction, researchers describe how singing songs for fun and substituting new lyrics in familiar tunes are the main fare in the elementary classroom (Stake, Bresler, & Mabry, 1991). The emphasis is mainly on nonmusical ends such as classroom management (Boardman, 1992) or "to illustrate a subject matter, to change pace, and to provide a musical activity as enrichment" (Bresler, 1993). This contrasts with instruction by the music specialist, who is more likely to have a broader vision of music education, stressing aesthetic sensitivity, creative development, and musical expression (Boardman, 1992). These findings suggest that inservice music education is necessary for classroom teachers. Although one can find an extensive literature on their preservice training (Heller, 1999) and research on integrated arts programs, there is a dearth of research on music inservice for classroom teachers.

An example of a longitudinal study on the transformation of classroom teachers as artists (including musicians) and as educators is being carried out by Upitis, Smithrim, and colleagues. They report on two different professional development projects. One is located in a large urban center at an external institution. The other is a school-based model in which all staff members "take part in workshops, interact with artists-in-residence, and pursue individual learning projects over the course of a school year" (Upitis, Soren, & Smithrim, 1998, p. 5). The two models were used as a basis for comparing perceptions of personal and professional growth, changes in teacher knowledge and experience in the arts, effects on teachers' personal theories about the arts, and the effects on children and the community (1998, p. 6). Upitis and colleagues developed a matrix of teacher transformation from preliminary research data and applied it to the two sites. It includes three levels: necessary conditions for teacher transformation in the arts, potential for sustained transformation, and operationalized long-term transformation. The necessary conditions include having a feeling of community, taking personal risks, creating public artifacts, and connecting with prior experiences. Long-term transformation would be shown through "sustained pursuit of new art forms, teacher-designed changes to curriculum, altered life practices, and altered perceptions" (p. 25). This matrix provides the authors with a basis for comparing how teachers' involvement in and commitment to the arts differ. The second paper in the series describes how teachers engage in learning to be an "artist," such as taking up the study of guitar. The researchers conclude that transformation is much more difficult to achieve than their literature review would have led them to predict (Smithrim, Upitis, & LeClair, 1998), but that significant growth is possible for some participants in these programs.

Moving Forward

The research reviewed in this chapter has been stimulated by the press by policy makers for professional development and the driving curiosity of individuals and groups of music education researchers. However, these professional development mandates and questions about practice raise a number of issues and create problems for which there is often no current research.

While the literature base is small, music education researchers are examining large-scale partnerships and change efforts (e.g., Robinson, 1999) as well as undertaking small-scale research (e.g., Black, 1998; Duling, 1992; Wing, 1977). Research methods also vary considerably from experiments (e.g., Arnold, 1996) to case studies (e.g., Dolloff, 1994). Some studies cited in this chapter were founded on behavioristic principles, and some were founded on constructivist principles. This suggests that music education research is moving beyond what has been described as a limited epistemological and methodological stance (Bresler, 1998).

Throughout this review, several issues surfaced. These issues surround notions of power, empowerment, and agency; conceptions of professional development and related theories of learning; contexts that support professional development; and the ethics of research and professional development practices.

Some studies gave us insights into what teachers know and how they learn it. Duling (1992) provided us with a thorough case study of two educators. There is similarity between the way his teacher-participants provide for their own professional growth and Bereiter and Scardemalia's (1993) definition of the learning patterns of experts as *reinvestment*. The search for mentors described by Duling's participants fits the description of a professional who is *reinvesting* in his or her own learning. They are oriented toward achieving growth through mentorship relationships. They do not expect to know all they will need to know in their careers, but they are empowered by an understanding of how to find out. This case study gives us a sense of professional development as a lifelong project.

Some music educators have been shown to value what can be accomplished through competency-based inservice. The meaning of these new skills within a more holistic view of music education practice needs further explanation. What might we learn if we studied the development of teacher knowledge and instructional skill from the per-

spective of apprenticeship, rather than direct instruction? Would this approach support a stronger interpretive discussion (Bresler, 1998)?

When Robinson (1999) used Buckminster Fuller's concept of tensegretic organization to explain the nature of the nonhierarchical educational partnership, he advanced our understanding of the context of professional development. Bush (2000) and May (1990) analyzed two contexts that support the growth of individual music educators. Although whole-school change projects are the norm, researchers have argued that there is also a need for school-based projects and partnerships at the departmental level (Clark & LaLonde, 1992; Hudson-Ross, 1998). Several factors support this approach: differences in complexity and specialization between elementary and secondary schools, differences that exist between the agendas within the whole school or within a department, and different kinds of teaching/learning contexts for music education. Two researchable questions come to mind: Do whole-school initiatives involve music educators and, if so, why and how? How might a community of music educators in one department influence the agenda of the whole school?

In spite of the prevalence of mentoring programs for both experienced and novice teachers and the high number of mentors and cooperating teachers serving as school-based educators, the professional development of these educators has largely been unstudied. Some mentoring relationships develop around programs that stress direct instruction in practical routines (Evertson & Smithey, 2000), while others stress the encouragement of self-reflection and analysis in conjunction with feedback (Veenman, De Laat, & Staring, 1998). This suggests that any professional development program for mentors should articulate the theory of learning that underpins it because this theory affects the choice of learning activities for mentors and the forms of expertise that mentors and, ultimately, their protégés may develop

Mentoring and other collegial relationships are not panaceas for professional development. Studies based on discourse analysis illustrate the major impacts, both positive and negative, that interpersonal interaction has in collegial situations (e.g. Lemma, 1993). Waite (1994) concludes from his research that positional power can be undermined and teacher empowerment gained through certain types of interpersonal interaction. In light of the high level of mentoring activity now occurring, careful documentation, analysis, publication, and critique of the work are needed.

The ultimate assessment of professional development rests on the influence that teacher learning has on the students in the classroom. The life histories of music educators teach us that experiences both inside and outside the formal teacher education setting affect a teacher's practice in the classroom. The provision of formal professional development activities can make a difference to student achievement. It has been found, based on a broad snapshot of the funding of professional development activities, that those states with greater investments in professional development achieve better student results than contiguous states with similar populations (Darling-Hammond, 2000). Findings from several studies in this review based evidence of student learning in relation to professional development activities on observations, student scores, and other performance assessments. Others bring us within sight of the classroom or performing ensemble but never take the opportunity to find links between students' learning and the professional development of their teachers. While some influences may not be known for years, researchers who analyze the linkages between professional development and student learning take us closer to understanding the impact of professional development.

One issue that we have not widely addressed is how to *portray* research findings with examples that are musical as well as verbal. Practice captured on videotape or CD-ROM is a useful resource for research as well as for professional development. Several studies in this review made use of videotapes, but we have not yet made wide use of the available technology for sharing these images.

We do not know what the impact of standards for music education will be on professional development (Colwell, 1995). The potential for professional development exists alongside the potential for abuse of power and disempowerment. Dialogue focused on the ethics of research on professional development practices and the dissemination of the results has only begun (e.g., Bresler, 1996).

Colwell's (1996–1997) program evaluation provides insights into a new form of professional development. There is, however, no widely accessible literature of program evaluation that focuses on music education. Politically, program evaluations can affect continued funding if some results are inconclusive or uncomfortably honest. Researchers face two issues: how to negotiate a contract that allows for the publication of a trustworthy review and how to conduct and report an evaluation in an ethical manner. Public reports must deal with issues of confidentiality and anonymity as they produce honest work. In one brief paragraph in their report, Stake, Bresler, and Mabry (1991) explain how they handle these issues.

> Some readers may find our accounts of arts teaching embarrassing. In those situations in which the teachers or others might be embarrassed or jeopardized by what we saw or wrote, we anonymized the accounts. Our purpose was not to belittle or to arouse the indignations that fuel reform. Our purpose was to improve our collective understanding of what is happening in American elementary schools. (p. 6)

The guiding questions used for the review have only begun to be answered by music education researchers. Because they have been useful for identifying a variety of descriptions, questions, and issues, it is still relevant to ask:

1. What do teachers and other music education practitioners know, how do they learn it, and how does this knowledge guide their practice?
2. What are the purposes and consequences of professional development experiences, and in what ways are the teachers individually or collectively implicated in their professional development?

Both music educators and music education researchers are implicated in attempts to answer these questions. Rhine (1998) argues that it is futile to try to teach educators everything that they need to know. He argues that it is more effective to use research as a tool for informing practitioners of the value of certain practices and orienting them toward ways of thinking and planning. From one perspective, practitioners and researchers occupy worlds with conflicting norms and demands. An important question to ask is, "What might make a difference in their relationship and the use of the research?" Huberman (1990) studied this "chronic two communities problem" (p. 364) across several research sites. He concluded that the linkages between researchers and practitioners before, during, and after a study influenced the impact of the research on practitioners. These linkages also established relationships that went well beyond a single study. Rhine (1998) specifically notes the importance of "consistent discourse between the research community and teacher leaders—the typical providers of continuing education for teachers. . . . Each has something critical to offer the conversation concerning how to ensure the effectiveness of professional development" (p. 30).

Both Huberman's and Rhine's recommendations require active negotiation of research purposes and processes between practitioners and researchers, which in itself is a focus for both professional development and research. In light of the challenges of policy and the number of professionals who seek to understand their context and practice more deeply, there are many opportunities for music educators to develop linkages that will influence the impact of research on professional development.

NOTE

Sincere appreciation goes to Tom Russell, Queens University, Kingston, for his ongoing support, to Lillian Ross for her editorial assistance, to Nipissing University for a faculty research leave, to the editors and reviewers whose feedback on earlier drafts contributed to the development of this chapter, and to authors of theses and papers who provided personal copies of their work.

REFERENCES

Argyris, C. (1982). *Reasoning, learning, and action: Individual and organizational.* San Francisco: Jossey-Bass.

Arnold, J. A. (1991). Using videotape self-analysis to improve teaching during rehearsals. *Update: Applications of Research in Music Education, 19*(1), 10–14.

Arnold, J. A. (1995). Effects of competency-cased methods of instruction and self-observation on ensemble directors' use of sequential patterns. *Journal of Research in Music Education, 43*(2), 127–138.

Baker, K. M. (1992). *Significant experiences, influences and relationships in the educational and professional development of three music educators: Gretchen Hieronymus Beall, Eunice Louise Boardman, and Mary Henderson Palmer.* Unpublished doctoral dissertation, University of Illinois at Urbana-Champaign.

Barry, N. H. (1998). Arts integration in the elementary classroom: Conference development and evaluation. *Update: Applications of Research in Music Education, 17*(1), 3–8.

Beauchamp, G. (1997). Initial training + INSET = confident teachers: A formula for success? *British Journal of Music Education, 14*(1), 69–86.

Bereiter, C., & Scardemalia, M. (1993). *Surpassing ourselves: An inquiry into the nature and implications of expertise.* Chicago: Open Court.

Biott, C. (Ed.). (1991). *Semi-detached teachers: Building support and advisory relationships in classrooms.* London: Falmer Press.

Black, C. (1998). Improving group dynamics and student motivation in a Grade 9 music class. *Ontario Action Researcher, 1,* 11. Retrieved October 31, 2001, from http://www.unipissing.ca/oar/index.htm

Boardman, E. (1992, April). *Music experiences in the early childhood classroom: Conflict between stated goals and classroom practice.* Paper presented at the annual meeting of the American Educational Research Association, San Francisco.

Bresler, L. (1993). Music in a double-bind: Instruction by non-specialists in elementary schools. *Bulletin of the Council for Research in Music Education, 115,* 1–13.

Bresler, L. (1996). Towards the creation of a new ethical code in qualitative research. *Bulletin of the Council for Research in Music Education, 131,* 17–29.

Bresler, L. (1998). Research, policy, and practice in arts education: Meeting points for conversation. *Arts Education Policy Review, 99*(5), 9–15.

Bruner, J. (1985). Narrative and paradigmatic modes of thought. In E. Eisner (Ed.), *Learning and teaching the ways of knowing* [84th yearbook of the National Society for the Study of Education, part 2] (pp. 97–115). Chicago: University of Chicago Press.

Bush, J. (2000). Introducing the practitioner's voice through electronic mentoring. *Journal of Technology in Music Education, 1*(1), 4–9.

Clark, R. J., & LaLonde, D. E. (1992). A case for department-based professional development sites for secondary teacher education. *Journal of Teacher Education, 43*(1) 35–41. (ERIC Document Reproduction Service No. EJ446601)

Cochran-Smith, M., & Lytle, S. (1999). Relationships of knowledge and practice: Teachers learning in communities. In A. Iran-Nejad & D. Pearson (Eds.), *Review of research in education* (Vol. 24, pp. 249–305). Washington, DC: American Educational Research Association.

Cole, A., & Knowles, J. G. (2000). *Researching teaching: Exploring teaching through reflexive inquiry.* Boston: Allyn & Bacon.

Colwell, R. (1995). Voluntary national standards and teacher education. *Bulletin of the Council for Research in Music Education, 125,* 20–31.

Colwell, R. (1996/1997). Professional development residency program. *Quarterly Journal of Music Teaching and Learning, 7*(2–4), 76–90.

Connecticut State Department of Education. (2000a). *Beginning Educator Support and Training (BEST) program.* Retrieved November 10, 2000, from http://www.state.ct.us./sde/dtl/cert/index.htm

Connecticut State Department of Education, Bureau of Program and Teacher Evaluation. (2000b). *Summary of BEST reliability and validity studies for 2000–2001.* Hartford, CT: Author.

Connecticut State Department of Education, Division of Evaluation and Research. (2000c). *BEST Portfolio Forms: Music.* Retrieved November 10, 2000, from http://www.state.ct.us/sde/der/publications/teacher_assessment/index.htm

Connecticut State Department of Education, Division of Teaching and Learning, Bureau of Curriculum and Instruction. (2001). *Arts.* Retrieved February 6, 2001, from http://www.state.ct.us/sde/dtl/curriculum/index.htm

Costa, A., & Garmston, R. (1985). Supervision for intelligent teaching. *Educational Leadership, 42*(5), 70, 72–80.

Council of Chief State School Officers. (1998). *Key state education policies on K–12 education: Standards, graduation, assessment, teacher licensure, time and attendance.* Washington, DC: State Education Assessment Center.

Darling-Hammond, L. (2000). Teacher quality and student achievement: A review of state policy evidence. *Education Policy Analysis, 8*(1), 1–44. Retrieved February 9, 2001, from http://epaa.asu.edu/epaa/v8n1

DiPardo, A. (1999). *Teaching in common: Challenges to joint work in classrooms and schools.* New York: Teachers College Press.

Dolloff, L. (1994). *Expertise in choral music education: Implications for teacher education.* Unpublished doctoral dissertation, University of Toronto, Ontario, Canada.

Dolloff, L. (1996). The North York choral development project: A commitment to professional growth in music education. *Canadian Journal of Research in Music Education, 37*(4), 3–9.

Doyle, W. (1990). Themes in teacher education research. In W. R. Houston (Ed.), *Handbook of research on teacher education* (pp. 3–24). New York: Macmillan.

Duling, E. B. (1992). *The development of pedagogical content knowledge: Two case studies of exemplary general music teachers.* Unpublished doctoral dissertation, Ohio State University, Columbus.

Eisner, E. (Ed.). (1985). *Learning and teaching the ways of knowing* [84th yearbook of the National Society for the Study of Education, part 2]. Chicago: University of Chicago Press.

Elliott, D. J. (1995). *Music matters.* New York: Oxford University Press.

Eshelman, D. A. (1995). *The instructional knowledge of exemplary elementary general music teachers: Commonalities based on David J. Elliott's model of the professional music educator.* Unpublished doctoral dissertation, University of Oklahoma, Norman.

Evertson, C. M., & Smithey, M. W. (2000). Mentoring effects on protégés' classroom practice: An experimental field study. *Journal of Educational Research, 9*(5), 294–304.

Fallin, J., & Royse, D. (1994). Common problems of the new music teacher. *Journal of Music Teacher Education, 4*(1), 13–18.

Firestone, W. A., & Pennell, J. R. (1997). Designing state-sponsored teacher networks: A comparison of two cases. *American Educational Research Journal, 34*(2), 237–266.

Froseth, J. O. (n.d.). *Staff development through teacher video self-assessment: A review of the implications of the National Music Education Research Project in the Flint (MI) community schools.* Retrieved October 20, 2000, from http://music.utsa.edu/tdml/conf-I/I-Froseth.html

Fullan, M. G. (1991). *The new meaning of educational change.* New York: Teachers College Press.

Garman, N. B., Glickman, C. D., Hunter, M., & Haggerson, N. L. (1987). Conflicting conceptions of clinical supervision and the enhancement of professional growth and renewal: Point and counterpoint. *Journal of Curriculum and Supervision, 2*(2), 152–177.

Glickman, C. D. (1985). *Supervision and instruction: A developmental approach.* Boston: Allyn & Bacon.

Glickman, C. D. (Ed.). (1992). *Supervision in transition.* Alexandria, VA: Association for Supervision and Curriculum Development.

Goolsby, T. W. (1996). Time use in instrumental rehearsals: A comparison of experienced, novice, and student teachers. *Journal of Research in Music Education, 44*(4), 286–303.

Hall, G. E., & Loucks, S. F. (1978). Teacher concerns as a basis for facilitating staff development. *Teachers College Record, 80*(1), 36–53.

Hargreaves, A. (1997). Rethinking educational change: Going deeper and wider in the quest for success. In A. Hargreaves (Ed.), *Rethinking educational change with heart and mind: 1997 ASCD yearbook* (pp. 1–26). Alexandria, VA: Association for Supervision and Curriculum Development.

Hargreaves, A., & Dawe, R. (1990). Paths of professional development, contrived collegiality, collaborative culture, and the case of peer coaching. *Teaching and Teacher Education, 6*(3), 227–241.

Heller, G. N. (Ed.). (1999). *Literature on elementary classroom teacher education in music. Professional literature project.* Society for Music Teacher Education, Music Ed-

ucators National Conference. Retrieved June 5, 2000, from http://www.menc.org/publications/books/smte/

Hookey, M. R. (1997). Explaining the arts-based elementary school curriculum in the neighbourhood school. In S. Leong (Ed.), *Music in schools and teacher education: A global perspective* (pp. 104–114). Nedlands, WA: International Society for Music Education (ISME) & Callaway International Resource Center for Music Education (CIRCME).

Huberman, M. (1989). The professional life cycle of teachers. *Teachers College Record, 91*(1), 31–57.

Huberman, M. (1990). Linkage between researchers and practitioners: A qualitative study. *American Educational Research Journal, 27*(2), 363–391.

Huberman, M. (1995). Networks that alter teaching: Conceptualizations, exchanges, and experiments. *Teachers and Teaching: Theory and Practice, 1*(2), 193–211.

Hudson-Ross, S. A. (1998). Discipline-based professional development faculty: A case for multiple-site collaborative reform in the disciplines. *Journal of Teacher Education, 49*(4), 266–275.

Jorgensen, E. R. (1979). Academic and professional preparation of school music supervisors in Canada. *Canadian Music Educator, 21*(1), 52–56.

Jorgensen, E. R. (1980). Preparation of school music supervisors in Canada. *Canadian Music Educator, 21*(3), 10–13.

Joyce, B., & Showers, B. (1980). Improving inservice training: The messages of research. *Educational Leadership, 37*(5), 379–385.

Junda, M. E. (1994). A model in-service music teacher education program. *Journal of Music Teacher Education, 3*(2), 6–19.

Killion, J. (1999). *Islands of hope in a sea of dreams: A research report on the eight schools that received the National Award for Model Professional Development.* Retrieved June 29, 2000, from http://www.wested.org/wested/pubs/online/Pdawards

King, G. (1998). Exemplary music educator: A case study. *Bulletin of the Council for Research in Music Education, 137,* 57–72.

Knoff, H. (1988). Clinical supervision, consultation, and counseling: A comparative analysis for supervisors and other educational leaders. *Journal of Curriculum and Supervision, 3*(3), 240–252.

Kohler, F. W., & Crilley, K. M. (1997). Effects of peer coaching on teacher and student outcomes. *Journal of Educational Research, 90*(4), 240–249. Retrieved October 31, 2000, from Ebscohost database.

Lampert, M. (1990). When the problem is not the question and the solution is not the answer: Mathematical knowing and teaching. *American Educational Research Journal, 27*(1), 29–63.

Landon, J. W. (1981). Review of Lizabeth Ann Wing (1977). *Formative evaluation in the general music classroom.* Unpublished doctoral dissertation. University of Illinois at Urbana-Champaign. *Bulletin of the Council for Research in Music Education, 66–67,* 130–138.

Lemma, P. (1993). The cooperating teacher as supervisor: A

case study. *Journal of Curriculum and Supervision, 8*(4), 329–342.

Lieberman, A. (2000). Networks as learning communities: Shaping the future of teacher development. *Journal of Teacher Education, 51*(3), 221–227.

Lieberman, A., & Grolnick, M. (1997). Networks, reform, and the professional development of teachers. In A. Hargreaves (Ed.), *Rethinking educational change with heart and mind: 1997 ASCD yearbook* (pp. 192–215). Alexandria, VA: Association for Supervision and Curriculum Development.

Lincoln Center Institute for the Arts. (2000). *Reflections.* New York: Author.

Little, J. W. (1982). Norms of collegiality and experimentation: Workplace conditions of school success. *American Educational Research Journal, 19*(3), 325–340.

Little, J. W. (1985). Teachers as teacher advisors: The delicacy of collegial leadership. *Educational Leadership, 43*(3), 34–36.

Madsen, C. K. (1990). Teacher intensity in relationship to music education. *Bulletin of the Council for Research in Music Education, 104,* 38–46.

May, W. T. (1990). *Art/music teachers' curriculum deliberations.* East Lansing, MI: Center for the Learning and Teaching of Elementary Subjects. (ERIC Document Reproduction Service No. ED 328512)

May, W. T. (1993). *A summary of the findings in art and music: Research traditions and implications for teacher education.* (Elementary Subjects Center Series No. 88). East Lansing, MI: Center for the Learning and Teaching of Elementary Subjects. (ERIC Document Reproduction Service No. ED 360247)

MENC (The National Association for Music Education). (1998). *A research agenda for music education.* Retrieved November 1, 2000, from http://www.menc.org/index2.html

Munby, H., Russell, T., & Martin, A. K. (2001). Teachers' knowledge and how it develops. In V. Richardson (Ed.), *Handbook of research on teaching* (4th ed.). Washington, DC: American Educational Research Association.

Northwest Regional Educational Laboratory. (2000). *The catalog of school reform models.* Retrieved November 1, 2000, from http://www.nwrel.org/scpd/natspec/catalog/index.html

Oja, S., & Reiman, A. J. (1998). Supervision for teacher development across the career span. In G. R. Firth & E. F. Pajak (Eds.), *Handbook of research on school supervision* (pp. 463–487). New York: Macmillan Library Reference USA.

Olebe, M. (1999) California Formative Assessment and Support System for Teachers (CFASST): Investing in teachers' professional development. *Teaching and Change, 6*(3), 258–271.

Ontario College of Teachers. (2000). *Professional learning framework for the teaching profession.* Retrieved November 1, 2000, from http://www.oct.on.ca/english/professional_affairs/plf_final.htm

Price, H. E. (1993). Applications of research to music teacher education. *Quarterly Journal of Music Teaching and Learning, 4,* 36–44.

Price, H. E., & Orman, E. K. (1999). MENC national conferences 1984–1998: A content analysis. *Update: Applications of Research in Music Education, 18*(1), 26–32.

Randolph, C., & Evertson, C. (1994). Images of management for learner-centered classrooms. *Action in Teacher Education, 14*(1), 55–63.

Rhine, S. (1998). The role of research and teachers' knowledge base in professional development. *Educational Researcher, 27*(5) 27–31.

Richardson, V. (1990). Significant and worthwhile change in teaching practice. *Educational Researcher, 19*(7), 10–18.

Richardson, V. (1994). Conducting research on practice. *Educational Researcher, 23*(5), 5–10.

Richardson, V., & Placier, P. (2001). Teacher change. In V. Richardson (Ed.), *Handbook of research on teaching* (4th ed.). Washington, DC: American Educational Research Association.

Robbins, J. (1994/1995). Levels of learning in Orff SPIEL. *Bulletin of the Council for Research in Music Education, 123,* 47–53.

Robinson, M. (1998). A collaboration model for school and community music education. *Arts Education Policy Review, 100*(2), 32–39.

Robinson, M. (1999). *A theory of collaborative music education between higher education and urban public schools.* Unpublished doctoral dissertation, University of Rochester, New York.

Rust, F., Astuto, T. A., Driscoll, M. E., Blakeney, M. W., & Ross, J. (1998). Supervision in the fine and performing arts. In G. R. Firth & E. F. Pajak (Eds.), *Handbook of research on school supervision* (pp. 506–517). New York: Macmillan Library Reference USA.

Sergiovanni, T. J., & Starratt, R. J. (1998). *Supervision: A redefinition* (6th ed.). Boston: McGraw-Hill.

Shookhoff, C. (1996). *Aesthetic education at Lincoln Center: Ongoing inquiry.* New York: Lincoln Center Institute for the Arts.

Shulman, L. S. (1985). Knowledge and teaching: Foundations of the new reform. *Harvard Educational Review, 57*(1), 1–22.

Smithrim, K., Upitis, R., & LeClair, J. (1998). *When teachers become musicians and artists.* Queen's University, Kingston, Ontario, Canada. Paper presented at the National Arts, Symposium, Victoria, BC. Retrieved August 15, 1999, from http://educ.queensu.ca/~arts/papers.html

SRI Associates. (2000). *Preparing and supporting new teachers: A literature review.* Washington, DC: U.S. Department of Education.

Stake, R., Bresler, L., & Mabry, L. (1991). *Custom and cherishing: The arts in elementary schools.* Urbana: Council for Research in Music Education, University of Illinois.

Standley, J. M., & Madsen, C. K. (1991). An observation procedure to differentiate teaching experience and expertise in music education. *Journal of Research in Music Education, 39*(1), 5–11.

Thiessen, D., & Kilcher, A. (1993). *Innovations in teacher education: A review of recent literature.* Ontario, Canada: Ministry of Education and Training.

Thomas, G., Wineburg, S., Grossman, P., Myhre, O., &

Woolworth, S. (1998). In the company of colleagues: An interim report on the development of a community of teacher learners. *Teaching and Teacher Education, 14*(1), 21–32.

Upitis, R. (1990). *This too is music.* Portsmouth, NH: Heinemann.

Upitis, R. (1992). *Can I play you my song?: The compositions and invented notations of children.* Portsmouth, NH: Heinemann.

Upitis, R., Soren, B. J., & Smithrim, K. (1998, April). *Teacher transformation through the arts.* Paper presented at the annual meeting of the American Educational Research Association, San Diego, CA. Retrieved August 15, 1999, from http://educ.queensu.ca/~arts/papers.html

Veenman, S., De Laat, H., & Staring, C. (1998). Evaluation of a coaching programme for mentors of beginning teachers. *Journal of In-Service Education, 24*(3), 411–427.

Verrastro, R. E., & Leglar, M. (1992). Music teacher education. In R. Colwell (Ed.), *Handbook of research on music teaching and learning* (pp. 676–696). New York: Schirmer Books.

Waite, D. (1994). Teacher resistance in a supervision conference. In D. Corson (Ed.), *Discourse and power in educational organizations* (pp. 71–86). Cresskill, NJ: Hampton Press.

Warren, M. D. L. (1989). *The development of models of inservice music teachers' education based on selected school-university partnerships.* Unpublished doctoral dissertation, Columbia University Teachers College, New York.

Wilson, B. (1997). *The quiet evolution: Changing the face of arts education.* Los Angeles: Getty Education Institute for the Arts.

Wilson, S. M., & Berne, J. (1999). Teacher learning and the acquisition of professional knowledge: An examination of research on contemporary professional development In A. Iran-Nejad & D. Pearson (Eds.), *Review of Research in Education* (Vol. 24) (pp. 173–209). Washington, DC: American Educational Association.

Wing, L. A. (1977). *Formative evaluation in the general music classroom.* Unpublished doctoral dissertation, University of Illinois at Urbana-Champaign.

Yarbrough, C., Price, H. E., & Bowers, J. (1991). The effect of knowledge of research on rehearsal skills and teaching values of experienced teachers. *Update, 9*(2), 17–20.

Part VII
MUSIC EDUCATION CONNECTIONS

David Myers
Editor

Introduction: The Growing Impact of Partnerships
A Reason for Research

RICHARD J. DEASY

Jane Remer, in *Beyond Enrichment: Building Effective Arts Partnerships with Schools and Your Community* (1996), sketches both a history and a six-stage continuum to describe the maturation of arts education partnerships. More than events of short duration offered by an arts organization at a school or cultural site, strong partnerships involve "full-fledged institutional partners" that are engaged in joint planning; instructional designs integrated with school goals and programs; sustained engagement with students; professional development for artists and teachers; and evaluation and assessment for continuous improvement (pp. 113–115).

While all the types of partnerships on Remer's continuum are practiced with varying effects, the strongest form is particularly worthy of the attention of researchers. It results from and reflects political, educational, and cultural forces that have shaped public education and cultural institutions over recent decades. For schools, economic pressures that tightened school budgets in the early 1970s were an important factor. Many school boards and administrators responded to fiscal constraints by cutting staffing and programming in the arts.

Why are the arts too often perceived as marginal to the primary purposes of schooling and, therefore, vulnerable when money is tight? The British academic and consultant Ken Robinson (2000) suggests two fundamental reasons, based on his analysis across industrialized nations. The first is that learning in the arts is not considered a cognitive activity that yields knowledge and intellectual skills. The second is that learning in the arts is not seen as relevant to the skills needed in the workplace—the primary functional test of curriculum decisions in every industrialized nation. However, Robinson sees hope and joins other analysts in arguing that the transformation of world economies and societies produced by demographic change and new systems of communication, transportation, finance, and governance demand new conceptions of schooling in which learning in the arts plays a central role.

Many advocates of arts education have embraced the viewpoint that the economy drives curricular decisions. They have sought to enlist influential leaders from the world of business and commerce as partners in pressing school authorities to see the economic value and importance of the skills learned in the arts. These efforts appear to be modestly successful, particularly in regions of the country where the economies are clearly dependent on the arts. The Arts Education Partnership has argued that a national labor market study is needed to buttress this argument. But the argument also must be strengthened by richer understandings and descriptions of what students learn when they learn the arts. This is the fundamental research effort that we need. The teaching and learning that take place in the strongest partnerships should be a focus of such studies.

When school arts staffs and programs were cut in the early 1970s, cultural institutions began to expand their education function. Moving beyond their supplementary role in school programs, they sometimes became a primary source of arts experiences. This new role stimulated significant growth, not only in the breadth and scope of educational offerings but also in the attempt to understand the culture and structures of schools, as well as the learning needs and styles of students. Partnerships with schools provided both a context and a cause for this development.

In *Learning Partnerships: Improving Learning in Schools With Arts Partners in the Community* (Dreeszen, Aprill, & Deasy, 1999), an examination of partnerships published by the Arts Education Partnership, as well as in the Arts Survive (Seidel, Eppel, & Martiniello, 2001) study by Steve Seidel and his colleagues at Harvard's Project Zero, a central finding emerged: The strongest and most enduring partnerships are those where the essential feature is an authentic engagement in arts learning and practice by students, teachers, and artists. It is through the persistent and reflective refinement of the practices of the partnership—the design and implementation of the instructional program—that the partners find common ground for their work and the insights that stimulate their personal growth and development. Moreover, Seidel's study of the work of Shakespeare and Company with schools in Massachusetts, Dennie Palmer Wolf's analysis of the Creating Original Opera program of the Metropolitan Opera Guild, and James Catterall's review of the impact of the Chicago Arts Partnership in Education (CAPE) suggest that students in these programs develop rich and complex comprehension and skills in the art forms as well as habits of mind applicable to other academic learning. These and other findings are included in *Champions of Change: The Impact of the Arts on Learning* (Fiske, 1999), a report of seven studies supported by the GE Fund and the John D. and Catherine T. MacArthur Foundation.

What is the nature of the teaching and learning that occur in these kinds of programs? What organizational principles and practices are at work? Exploring these questions through study of the strongest partnerships will yield valuable knowledge for the formulation of education policy and practice. Such research will help to clarify and deepen our understanding of and discourse about what students learn in and through the arts. Equipped with fuller descriptions of the cognitive and affective impact of arts learning, we can more powerfully counter the primary reason the arts are marginal in the school curriculum: They are not thought to embody or give access to important knowledge. We can then make the relevance of that learning to social needs and goals more compelling. The intrinsic value of arts learning is enhanced by that relevance.

A major advance in our understanding of arts education arises from the *practice* of arts teaching and learning that occurs when schools and cultural organizations partner and when teachers and artists join forces to engage students in authentic arts experiences. These practices and student learning should be the major focus of research. However, there are complementary issues worthy of study. Often the strongest partnerships have been instigated or nurtured by financial support from a third party, for instance, by the National Endowment for the Arts or by other foundations and grant makers. Joseph McDonald (Corcoran, McLaughlin, & McDonald, 2000) has analyzed the evaluations of the Annenberg Challenge grants, including the three grants that focus on the role of arts education in transforming whole schools. He argues that "mediating entities"—external

players with authoritative status—are essential for bringing about institutional change. Grant makers may play this role. They have done so in many of the strongest arts education partnerships. Research on the most effective strategies for doing so would give useful guidance to the philanthropic community.

Finally, it would be instructive to compare the growth and maturation of partnerships with the other dominant educational movement of recent decades: standards-based school reform. At present, it is not clear that the standards movement has improved the practices of teaching and learning, either in the arts or in other school subjects. Resources in states and school districts have been largely devoted to improving reading and mathematics. The related state accountability assessments have been the dominant force that shaped teaching practices. The primary contribution of the standards movement, certainly the arts standards effort, to date has been conceptual, itself a substantial achievement. The four arts disciplines have concurred that learning in each of the arts involves comparable processes—called responding, performing, and creating in the *Arts Education Assessment Framework* (National Assessment of Educational Progress, 1997). They have also agreed that arts learning must involve historical, cultural, and aesthetic understanding and judgments as well as technically competent performance. This articulation of arts education has enabled the field as a whole to work more comfortably together and has also made it easier for arts and cultural organizations to join the national arts education conversation. Whether this policy-driven approach to improving teaching and learning will be as fruitful as the complex practices that have emerged from strong partnerships working to implement innovative programs remains to be seen. One would hope for convergence. It is a story researchers should be following.

REFERENCES

Corcoran, T., McLaughlin, M. W., & McDonald, J. (2000, April). *The role of intermediary organization in school reform.* Paper presented at the 81st annual meeting of the American Educational Research Association, New Orleans.

Dreeszen, D., Aprill, A., & Deasy, R. (1999). *Learning partnerships: Improving learning in schools with arts partners in the community.* Washington, DC: Arts Education Partnership.

Fiske, E. (Ed.). (1999). *Champions of change: The impact of the arts on learning.* Washington, DC: Arts Education Partnership and the President's Committee on the Arts and the Humanities.

National Assessment of Educational Progress (1997). *Arts education assessment framework.* Washington, DC: U.S. Department of Education, National Assessment Governing Board.

Remer, J. (1996). *Beyond enrichment: Building effective arts partnerships with schools and your community.* New York: American Council for the Arts.

Robinson, K. (2000, January). *Learning and the arts: Crossing boundaries.* Paper presented at the Invitational Meeting for Education, Arts, and Youth Funders, Los Angeles.

Seidel, S., Eppel, M., & Martiniello, M. (2001). *Arts survive: A study of sustainability in arts education partnerships.* Cambridge, MA: Project Zero, Harvard University Graduate School of Education.

Policy Issues in Connecting Music Education with Arts Education

DAVID E. MYERS

ARTHUR C. BROOKS

47

In 1976 Charles Fowler wrote in the *College Music Symposium* of several national trends in arts education. Indicative of what Fowler called a new arts education, the trends included increased cooperation among arts disciplines, infusion of the arts into academic subjects, and broader representation of all the arts in the curriculum. His thesis was that changes in the field of arts education properly challenged music educators to "broaden our bases, to burst our narrow specialties, to seek a multi-dimensional focus." In support, he identified two specific programs funded by the National Endowment for the Arts (NEA) and the United States Office of Education (USOE): the Artists-in-Schools (AIS) Program, and Interdisciplinary Model Programs in the Arts for Children and Teachers (IMPACT). Characterizing these efforts as a "developing phenomenon," Fowler suggested that the policy direction they represented would require of music educators "a new process of transaction—with the other arts, with artists, . . . and with the entire community" (p. 24). The purpose of this chapter is to review arts education policy developments over the past 35 years, including the trends Fowler identified, and to consider issues that have affected the relationship between music education and the larger policy arena of arts education.

Arts and Humanities Program of the U.S. Office of Education (1965–1974)

Federal support for arts education found its first home in the Cultural Affairs Branch of the Division of Library Services and Continuing Education of the USOE. The Cultural Affairs Branch, established in 1962, was later renamed the Arts and Humanities Branch. In 1965 it became the Arts and Humanities Program (AHP). Until its demise in 1974, AHP served as the primary administrative venue for federal support of arts education. Kathryn Bloom, AHP's director until 1968, also functioned as special adviser on the arts and humanities for the commissioner of education, Francis Keppel.

With strong support from Commissioner Keppel, AHP focused on arts curricula, on developing education programming and school partnerships among community arts organizations, and on supporting research in arts education. According to Murphy and Jones (1976), the AHP's primary function was the administration of research and development funds that became available under the Elementary and Secondary Education Act (ESEA) of 1965. In 1966 an estimated $100 million was devoted to projects that related in some way to arts education, compared to about $20 million in 1965. Title IV of ESEA provided funds specifically for research, with a total allotment of about $11 million over a 5-year period. AHP interpreted its research mandate broadly and, "as the only cohesive arts group within the Federal educational establishment, became a communications center among Government agencies, between Government and arts educators, and . . . between these groups and the arts and education world generally" (p. 5).

The nearly 200 projects supported by USOE/AHP, mostly between 1965 and 1970, included studies in aesthetic education (with defined synonyms of *interdisciplinary, integrated,* and *related arts*); projects that spurred Artists-in-Schools; music education efforts such as the

Manhattanville Project, research on Kodály, research on Suzuki, and the Juilliard Repertory Project; programs that introduced theater and dance in school curriculums; Harvard's Project Zero; and efforts to strengthen the arts in general education (Murphy & Jones, 1976, pp. 5–10). Music education researchers who received grants included, among others, Bennett Reimer, Robert Petzold, Paul Rolland, Marilyn Zimmerman, Marguerite Hood, and Richard Colwell. Though AHP supported projects both within and across arts disciplines (architecture, visual arts, dance, the humanities, media, and theater education, in addition to those mentioned earlier), music education garnered the most money. Murphy and Jones attributed this to two facts: that music education had a longer, if "less sophisticated," history than visual art research and that "the first and for some time the only professional, in the AHP and its forerunners [Harold Arberg] was a music man himself" (p. 9).

During the mid-1960s, the AHP sponsored 32 arts education conferences. Focused on specific disciplines, 12 of these were in art, 6 in music, and the remainder spread across other art forms. Analysts generally concluded that the conferences, though intended to spur research proposals, were better at generating discussion and curriculum projects than at encouraging research. The first conference, which served as a structural model for others, was the Yale Seminar on Music Education in 1963, directed by musicologist Claude Palisca. Most of the participants were composers, performers, conductors, musicologists, music critics, and college faculty. The professional music education community, including the Music Educators National Conference (MENC), had almost no voice in the conference, serving largely in an observer capacity.

The Yale Seminar criticized existing practice in the field of music education and proposed an expanded repertoire, including popular and world music, as well as the inclusion of composition and graded listening activities in music education. Its recommendations inspired a number of curriculum projects, among them the Manhattanville Music Curriculum Program, which incorporated composition, improvisation, contemporary music, and nontraditional instruments. One of the seminar's proposals was *the collaboration of community musicians with schools, "relaxing certification requirements if necessary"* [italics added] (Murphy & Jones, 1976, p. 28). Murphy and Jones considered the Yale Seminar to have been instrumental in fostering such "developments as greater attention to music as literature, musicians in residence, and expanded, upgraded, and modernized school repertoires. Above all, the seminar served to rouse to concerted action at least some segments of the divided realms of music" (p. 29). Four years after the Yale Seminar, MENC mounted its own conference, the Tanglewood Symposium, which engaged leaders from a variety of fields in consideration of the topic Music in American Society. This conference extended a number of topics from the Yale Seminar, linking them with social and technological changes in the society at large.

In 1968 Kathryn Bloom resigned from the AHP in order to administer the John D. Rockefeller 3rd (JDR 3rd) Fund's Arts-in-Education program, a private-sector initiative in arts education that she headed until its termination in 1979. Her departure from the AHP coincided with a shift in federal priorities away from the social concerns of the Kennedy and Johnson eras and toward an emphasis on state and local community support of education. In addition, federal arts support was no longer targeted toward education interests but was increasingly used to support artists and arts organizations.

By 1970 substantial dollars were being transferred from the AHP to the NEA (see "National Endowment for the Arts"). The staff of the AHP was reduced, and the program's influence on arts education was diminished. According to Murphy and Jones (1976), no new research projects were begun and "a battery of changes—some primarily bureaucratic, others broadly social and political—overtook the arts presence within the Federal Government" (p. 65). Between 1970 and 1976, AHP funds were used to support IMPACT, the Artists-in-Schools Program, and the Kennedy Center's Alliance for Arts Education. Support for preexisting research, such as the Aesthetic Education Program of the Central Midwestern Regional Education Laboratory (CEMREL) and Harvard's Project Zero, occurred under the auspices of the newly established National Institute of Education. However, arts education research assumed a low priority within the context of an emphasis on basic skills such as reading and arithmetic. In 1974 the AHP was deactivated, and in 1975 it became simply the Arts and Humanities Staff.

In 1973 the USOE joined with the Kennedy Center to form the Alliance for Arts Education (AAE). The AAE was conceived as a national network of arts educators, with state and local chapters united under the aegis of the Kennedy Center for the purpose of advocating a common agenda for the arts in the curriculum. Kathryn Bloom and other staff from the JDR 3rd Fund consulted on the design and operation of the AAE (Remer, 1990). Killeen (1999a, 1999b) has documented the alliance's evolution, its uneasy relationship with arts educator organizations, the tension that stemmed from the Kennedy Center's efforts to control activities, and the findings of a major study (Wolf & Wolf, 1991) that indicated that, after 18 years of funding, the AAE "had little impact on arts education in the nation's schools" (1999a, p. 14). Though the four major arts education professional organizations in theater, dance, visual arts, and music had cooperated, along with the AHP, in the founding of the AAE, declining fiscal support for the

AHP and the failure of the arts education groups to find common ground resulted in their loss of influence. The AAE became "a vehicle to promote the narrower interests of the Kennedy Center and its performing arts mission" (Killeen, 1999b, p. 17). Efforts have been made to reshape the AAE in the 1990s; however, it is not clear that the organization any longer fulfills a perceived need or that its strong affiliation with the Kennedy Center will permit pursuit of a larger national agenda.

The demise of the AHP marked a loss of federal support for arts education research at a level that has never been recovered. Glidden (1985) remarked that "no agency at the federal level has assumed responsibility for sponsoring or fostering research in arts education on a continuing basis" (p. 15). According to Hoffa (1985), the transition of federal arts education interests from the AHP to the NEA was done with "no visible commitment to either arts education in general or educational research in particular" (p. 33).

National Endowment for the Arts

In 1965 Congress passed the National Foundation on the Arts and Humanities Act, which created the NEA and the National Endowment for the Humanities (NEH). Though arts education was not a legislatively defined purpose of the NEA, the Act emphasized understanding of the arts for "amateur, student, or other nonprofessional groups" (National Foundation on the Arts and Humanities Act of 1965, p. 1064). The act also indicated that programs of the NEA should correlate with other existing federal programs and those undertaken by public agencies or private groups and that institutes should be held to strengthen the teaching of the arts and humanities.

While the NEH has played a relatively modest role in arts education, the NEA has had a relationship with arts education since its inception, most consistently through its artist residency program in schools. The education community had been active in gaining congressional support for the NEA, and linking the arts agency with education prompted a policy connection between the arts and arts education. This connection played out initially through a relationship between the NEA and the AHP (Biddle, 1988; Wyszomirski, 1982). The first cooperative venture was Poets-in-the-Schools, funded with ESEA Title III monies, which were intended to encourage innovative educational programs. The artist residency concept subsequently expanded to other art forms and became known as the NEA's Artists-in-Schools (AIS) Program. In 1969–1970, the USOE transferred a million dollars to the NEA to support AIS (changed to Artists-in-Education in 1980), the largest federally funded program for arts education in U.S. schools. By 1972, at a cost of approximately $1.5 million,

the NEA was placing hundreds of artists who represented all arts categories in the nation's schools. In 1974 the expenditure for AIS was over $3 million (Bumgarner, 1993; Netzer, 1978; Pankratz, 1986).

The first three chairmen of the NEA—Roger Stevens, Nancy Hanks, and Livingston Biddle—included education only broadly in their goals, emphasizing participation, awareness, and artist support. In 1982, however, NEA chairman Frank Hodsoll told Congress he considered arts education a high priority, including comprehensive arts education for all children, more emphasis on education within cultural institutions, and improved arts education through collaborations and partnerships. Despite budget restrictions that limited the NEA's ability to play a direct role in funding arts education apart from artist residencies, as well as a federal priority on educational decision making at state and local levels, Hodsoll spoke widely on learning *in* the arts, learning *about* the arts, and learning *through* the arts, including the integration of art into other subjects. Fraser Barron, an adviser to Hodsoll, declared that though residencies would continue as a mainstay, "the presence of qualified and inspired specialist teachers will be of utmost importance.... Without professional arts educators, . . . arts education won't go far" (1985, p. 28).

Hodsoll's commitment to arts education, along with criticism from arts educator groups that the NEA's education programs amounted to exposure rather than sequential instruction, led to a shift of emphasis for the agency's education efforts. Following the agency's reauthorization in 1985, its pronouncements on arts education increasingly incorporated terms such as *sequential, comprehensive,* and *basic.* According to a briefing paper, "The New NEA Arts-in-Education Program" (1986), prepared for the four major arts education organizations and the higher education organizations in music, art and design, dance, and theater, the NEA's broadened approach to arts education was intended to build collaboration among the arts and education communities for developing more rigorous programs. To this end, the new program encouraged promotion among the public of the need for sequential instruction in the various art forms, consultation of state arts agencies with state education agencies, development of data that regarded arts education in each state, and a high level of consultation with and support for arts education specialists and higher education arts faculties in the development of programs (p. 26).

The revised NEA program found expression through three categories of grants: state Arts-in-Education grants; Arts-in-Schools Basic Education Grants (AISBEG); and Special Projects. The first category continued funding of state arts agencies for artist residencies but encouraged broader programming such as in-service programs, sequential instruction, and institutional collaborations. AISBEG, the "centerpiece" of the new approach, focused on consultation and cooperation between state arts councils and the education community for the purpose of "developing a strong commitment to making the arts a basic part of K–12 education—through comprehensive planning and implementation of excellent sequential arts education" (New NEA Arts-in-Education Program, 1986, p. 27). Special Projects grants were available to education agencies and school districts, as well as arts organizations, to support "high quality arts education projects of regional or national significance" (p. 29).

In 1988 the NEA officially renamed its Artists-in-Education program the Arts in Education program, changing the implied focus from artists to arts education. In the same year, the agency produced *Toward Civilization: A Report on Arts Education,* which acknowledged the importance of trained arts educators in achieving success for arts education. However, *Toward Civilization* also indicated that making arts education a priority would require the support of "governance, education, arts, and business-producer sectors" and suggested that "initiatives from outside the education sector need to be coordinated with state and locally mandated school programs" (National Endowment for the Arts, 1988, pp. 14–15).

In 1991 the NEA moved to incorporate education into all of its program areas by encouraging arts agencies in the area of education, supporting professional artists and the increasing role of arts organizations in arts education, and fostering cooperative programs in support of making the arts a basic component of education. A growing emphasis on arts education partnerships became evident in the agency's funding of two programs: one with the Kennedy Center's Alliance for Arts Education and another with the National Assembly of Local Arts Agencies. Funds were allotted to conduct institutes with representatives from the arts, education, corporate, legislative, and social-service sectors that considered the role of partnerships in arts education. The resulting report, titled *Intersections: Community Arts and Education Collaborations* (Dreeszen, 1992) summarized principles of successful arts education partnerships that were derived from the meetings.

These directions were not without controversy, particularly among arts educators. Chapman (1992) asserted that NEA education programs continued to reflect the interests of artists and arts patrons rather than the needs of schools, and R. A. Smith (1992) decried an underreliance of the NEA on arts educators, asserting that "the Endowment's mission . . . is too important to be left to cultural administrators" (p. 137). Gee (1999a, 1999b) notes that in 1991 AISBEG was subsumed within a category called the Arts Education Partnership Grant, under which artist residencies were retained while consultation with state departments of education and curriculum references were di-

minished. She also details evidence that the NEA and the corporate/philanthropic complex have endorsed an agenda that promotes educational arts programs as a medium of learning across the curriculum, that supports the role of artists and arts organizations in schools, and that promotes the arts as an agent of social change and competitive economic productivity.

In 1997, under an education rubric widely expanded over the original Artists-in-Schools program, the NEA and its state affiliates spent $37 million on 7,400 education projects in over 2,600 communities. Current NEA materials bridge the sequential instruction versus exposure divide by maintaining that the agency "advocates a sequential education . . . that is linked to content standards, taught by qualified teachers, and regularly engages artists." Among specific citations of the kinds of work supported are "integration of the arts with math, science, history and other school subjects," "artist–teacher collaborations," "in-school opera, music theater and dance performances," and "in-school residencies of writers, sculptors, filmmakers, and other artists" (NEA 2000b, p. 1). The NEA "maintains that education in the arts should begin in the pre-school years, be cultivated by families and schools, and continue throughout one's life." The agency partners with state arts agencies to "make the arts basic to pre-K through 12 education" (p. 1). During the 1990s, the NEA cooperated with the U.S. Department of Education (USDOE) in funding the development of the National Standards for Arts Education, the inclusion of the arts in the National Assessment of Educational Progress, the formulation of the Goals 2000 Arts Education Partnership (now the Arts Education Partnership), and national surveys of arts education in the nation's schools.

Federal/Philanthropic Policy Agendas and the Response of Arts Educators

When Kathryn Bloom became head of the JDR 3rd Fund's Arts-in-Education program in 1968, she established priorities that continued her work at the AHP: integration of arts with academics and the use of community arts organization resources for school programs. According to Gee (1999b), the JDR 3rd Fund's "commitment to include 'all the arts' . . . and the belief that the arts should be 'infused' into the entire school curriculum . . . had a lasting impact on governmental and philanthropic funding policies" (p. 6). The fact that Bloom and other JDR 3rd Fund staff consulted on the formation of the AAE (see earlier section on the AHP), thus influencing its programs, is one indicator of the increasing acceptance of these priorities in the federal arts education agenda.

As Gee suggests, however, not only were the themes evident in the work of the AHP and the NEA, but they also influenced privately funded ventures. One example was *Coming to Our Senses: The Significance of the Arts for American Education,* a report on arts education by the Arts, Education, and Americans Panel (1977), funded by the American Council for the Arts and chaired by David Rockefeller. The panel asserted that in a period of economic downturn that caused job losses among arts educators artists should be more widely used in schools, selected for their potential as teachers, and fairly compensated for their education work. Given the fiscal constraints faced by local school systems at the time, funding would had to have come from government arts agencies and private sources. The report recommended that "community-based cultural organizations be maximally used by arts educators" (p. 255), and emphasized the importance of learning in, about, and through the arts. In defining arts education the panel said: "We mean making art, knowing artists, and using art as a general tool of learning" (p. 8). Rockefeller's introduction to the report specifically thanked two individuals who were advocates and advisers: Kathryn Bloom and Nancy Hanks, chair of the NEA.

This long-standing overlap between federal and philanthropic interests and personnel is also exemplified in the recent *Champions of Change* project (Fiske, 1999) and a report, *Young Children and the Arts: Making Creative Connections,* produced by the Task Force on Children's Learning and the Arts: Birth to Age Eight (1998). For *Champions of Change,* seven arts education research studies were funded by the G. E. Fund and the John D. and Catherine T. MacArthur Foundation, in cooperation with the Arts Education Partnership (AEP, formerly the Goals 2000 Arts Education Partnership) and the President's Committee on the Arts and the Humanities. The AEP is itself a partnership of arts, education, business, philanthropic, and government organizations. The preface to *Champions of Change* was written by Richard Riley, U.S. secretary of education in the Clinton administration, and the projects focus on arts organization partnerships with schools and on academic and social outcomes associated with the arts. One of the report's policy recommendations is that arts education partnerships be established to enhance the academic performance of urban students.

Young Children and the Arts, also published by the AEP and funded by Coca-Cola and the American Federation of Teachers, promotes principles that include learning *in, through,* and *about* the arts; connecting arts experiences to early childhood curriculum and literacy development; and engaging arts specialists, practicing artists, and early childhood educators, parents, and caregivers, along with other community resources, in the development of early childhood arts programs. The principles also indicate that

quality arts experiences, which follow a scope and sequence, are important aspects of program development (Task Force on Children's Learning, 1998, p. 2).

Over the years, arts education organizations such as MENC have taken a cooperative, if wary, stance relative to these kinds of shared federal and philanthropic agendas. However, arts educators have not opposed federal support of arts education or collaborations with artists and arts organizations per se. As early as 1977, under the leadership of major music groups, a "loosely organized" Assembly of National Arts Education Organizations proposed a federally sponsored National Institute for Arts Education. This first-time cooperative effort among organizations that represented various arts disciplines resulted in a proposal for federal categorical aid to arts education that would be administered by the institute. The assembly recommended the active engagement of arts teachers in policy making and the development of a program of research, something that had been lost with the demise of the AHP. In addition, the assembly advocated a federal Department of Education, in which arts education would be housed. The assembly preferred a clear functional difference between the Department of Education and the NEA, given the endowment's focus on supporting artists and arts organizations. A statement from the assembly was entered into the Hearing Record of the U.S. Senate Committee on Human Resources, Subcommittee on Education, Arts, and Humanities, on October 5, 1977 (Glidden, 1978).

As evidenced in the earlier example of the Yale Seminar, the rub for arts education organizations has been that they frequently have felt excluded from the development of federal and philanthropic policy agendas. Mahlmann (1985) declared that "arts education professionals who are indeed responsible for the field have no current strategic role in developing arts education plans" (p. 39). In a 1986 report titled *K–12 Arts Education in the United States: Present Context, Future Needs,* arts education organizations, including MENC, charged that "during the last decade, there has been no evidence that the corporate or foundation communities have particular interest in considering the traditional arts education community as a full partner in the national arts enterprise" (p. 10). This report placed the NEA, foundations, and the government generally in the role of promoting advocacy rather than developing sequential arts education programs and suggested that the arts education community was being bypassed in policy initiatives. Among the concerns were policies that promoted reliance on general classroom teachers as arts educators and an emphasis on the arts as a means to learning other subjects. The report also exhorted the arts education community to establish its primacy in arts education policy.

Not surprisingly, arts education organizations endorsed

the NEA's revised arts education program as proposed under Chairman Frank Hodsoll in 1986. Their briefing paper said:

> Arts teachers and their organizations must do their parts to ensure that this tremendous effort of will at the federal level is not vitiated by neglect; cynicism; petty arguments; or failure to link study and practice, the world of art, and civilization in state and local promotions of arts education. (New NEA, 1986, pp. 25–26)

Stressing the collaborative roles of arts agencies, education agencies, and arts educators, the report indicated that the primary goal for arts educators was "to contribute ideas, expertise, and professional skills to any work that state arts agencies undertake to support curriculum-based arts education" (p. 27). The arts organizations apparently believed that the NEA's new approach would help relieve tension with arts education organizations over two aspects of the federal/philanthropic agenda: compromising sequential knowledge building in discrete arts disciplines by emphasizing the collective arts and the use of the arts in support of academics, and diminishing the role of arts specialists by using artists, arts organizations, and classroom teachers to deliver arts instruction.

From 1982 until 1992, the J. Paul Getty Trust funded the Getty Education Institute for the Arts (originally the Getty Center for Education in the Arts), which supported an approach to visual art education called Discipline-Based Art Education (DBAE). DBAE derived from a conceptual evolution that extended the standard practices of creating and producing to include history, criticism, and aesthetics. Though some efforts have been made to link DBAE with music education, the profession in general has not adopted the terminology or the approach, in part because music education had promoted a more comprehensive, conceptually based music curriculum as early as the 1960s. Leilani Lattin Duke (1999), however, who was director of the Getty Education Institute from 1991 until its termination in 1998, believes that Getty influence on arts education policy is evident in the inclusion of the arts in the National Education Goals, the development of national standards in arts education, the development of teacher preparation initiatives, the development of coalitions and partnerships for arts advocacy, and the leveraging of new funds for arts education, including federal and philanthropic initiatives. One of the challenges she believes arts education continues to face is the tension between essentialist and instrumentalist rationales. Her position is clear: "Other subjects stake their claim to a piece of the instructional day because of what they uniquely teach students: the ways of thinking, the lenses with which to see and understand the world. So should the arts" (p. 6).

Perhaps the most cooperative endeavor in recent history

among arts educator organizations such as MENC and government arts and education agencies, including the NEA, the USDOE, and the NEH, was the development of national standards for education in each arts discipline. According to Gee (1999b):

> This was the first, and only, occasion—since the Arts and Humanities Program's support of arts education research in the mid-1960s—that professional arts educators have had a strategic role in arts education policy development at the federal level. (p. 15)

When the NEA promotes itself as an education-oriented agency, however, it must also balance this agenda with its support of arts organizations and the assumptions of arts organizations regarding that support. Gee avers that arts organizations are not completely pleased with having to use education as an avenue for funding, asserting that they "are clearly ambivalent about the entire education enterprise" (p. 13).

Facing congressional calls for defunding, the NEA through the 1990s increasingly chose to emphasize its educational role as a rationale for survival. In 1997, when the Senate Labor and Human Resources Committee introduced a bill to reauthorize the NEA, education played a prominent role. Gee (1999a) argues, in fact, that had the bill passed, "the National Endowment for the Arts would have become, in essence, the National Endowment for Arts Education" (p. 11). Based on claims presented by the NEA, the Consortium of National Arts Education Associations was concerned that Congress and the public might construe the NEA's supplementary function in arts education as a primary instructional role and that arts education might be justified on the basis of extra-arts academic and social outcomes. The consortium united with the National Association of Music Merchants to force a definition of arts education that would specifically call for sequential instruction by qualified teachers, with artists and arts organizations in a supportive role. Throughout an extended and heated debate over the definition and jurisdiction of arts education, the consortium nevertheless reiterated its support for funding the NEA. Ultimately, the parties found agreement around this definition:

> Sequential instruction taught by qualified teachers that is designed to provide students of all ages with the skills and knowledge in the arts in accordance with high national, state, and local standards which may be supported by artists and arts organizations. (Morrison, 1997)

The issues and historical precedents that underlie this watershed attempt to articulate a definition of arts education encompass an array of policy concerns that directly or indirectly affect music education. In the following sections, attention is given to the interwoven issues of public and private funding, the relationship of the arts to academic learning, artist residencies, and education partnerships with arts organizations, all of which impinge on policy connections between music education and arts education.

Government Funding of the Arts

Economic Arguments for Government Arts Funding

Arguments for government support of the arts generally focus on certain "failures" in private markets. Because private markets do not generally consider the arts' intellectual spillover to producers and cultural spillover to society, the private market demand would be below the "true" demand of society for the arts. Due to characteristics of the arts that make them benefit the public at large, the private market, if left alone, would generate too little art.

These external, societal benefits of the arts have been described by a number of writers (e.g., Peacock, 1969), who generally represented one or more of five basic views:

1. The arts have an educational function on a societywide level: The more art there is, the more "cultured" the population will be. Thus arts subsidies can help optimize the amount of available arts education. This view assumes that public subsidies of art are an effective way to undertake an education function and that government involvement in the arts creates the desired impact on the kind and amount of art produced.
2. Production and preservation of the arts not only affect the current generation but presumably benefit future generations as well (Baumol & Bowen, 1966).
3. The arts can be a source of national pride, and their production in this way benefits many people who don't directly participate in their consumption.
4. The arts can stimulate business and growth in a particular region. A concert hall can be stimulus for urban renewal, for example, as businesses are attracted to an area that draws potential customers.
5. The government, by subsidizing either production or consumption, can help to provide equality of opportunity for enjoyment of the arts. This equality generates an external benefit (Feld, O'Hare, & Davidson Schuster, 1983) because, in a private market, the arts would be priced out of the range of most consumers.

Economic Arguments Against Government Arts Funding

First, while the possible failure of private markets is the most common rationale in support of government arts funding, it is also perhaps the most common rationale against such funding. This argument points to the fact that there may be negative spillovers inherent in the production of the arts. If certain art is considered offensive by society, for example, a cost is present that the producer and consumer do not bear. The cost to the larger society is thus greater than the cost incurred by the creators and consumers. If supported by government funding, production of offensive art will not be limited in response to this cost. As a result, producers will market too much and the wrong sort of art.

Second, other sources of external cost may proceed from the government subsidies themselves. For example, subsidies may harm an arts firm's incentives to respond to the desires of consumers. If a growing gap between costs and earned revenues—the so-called income gap in the arts policy literature (Baumol & Bowen, 1965)—is routinely dealt with by way of cost-defraying public subsidies, then arts firms might have little impetus to improve their financial situation through increased demand for their product. This may lead to suboptimal decision making in areas such as repertoire, scheduling, and performance venues.

Third, it is possible that the government's involvement in an arts firm's product may result in inappropriate or wasteful production decisions (C. Wolf, 1979, 1993). Involvement of the government in the market for arts may lead to inefficiencies that increase the cost and change the character of the arts. Thus the benefit imagined from the correction of an original market failure might not occur.

Fourth, arts subsidies raise the issue of distributional costs. Subsidies may disproportionately benefit the wealthiest members of society, because they are more likely to consume the most subsidized art relative to the amount they pay in taxes. In addition, the capacity of arts subsidies to redistribute resources might lead to active attempts by the relatively well-off to distribute resources in their own favor, thus exacerbating the first problem.

Maximizing Benefits and Minimizing Costs Through Arts Education

Cognizant of the external benefits and costs associated with government subsidies, the relevant policy question is how to design funding through the arts and humanities endowments that maximizes benefits while minimizing costs to the public. First, subsidies can concentrate on potential arts consumers rather than arts producers. As noted earlier, producer-oriented subsidies have a tendency to insulate arts firms from the purchasing signals created by consumers. Subsidizing consumption can help to reduce this insulation, provided it is not overly restrictive. In addition, grants to arts organizations are very blunt with respect to the consumers that benefit: lowering a museum's costs will help to push down prices for all consumers and hence may be enjoyed disproportionately by the most well-off. Subsidies to consumers, however, can be targeted to those most "in need" of access to the product. What are examples of consumer-side arts subsidies? The best understood and most widely practiced programs fall in the area of outreach or what is frequently labeled as education: those programs that expose audiences such as schoolchildren to the arts. Funding arts education programs may produce new consumers and hence more art demanded without directly creating potentially deleterious effects in the production of the arts. This may lead not only to positive spillover in the present but also a more stable arts sector in the future (Brooks, 1997).

Second, arts education in the schools can be neatly targeted to specific socioeconomic groups. It cannot be plausibly argued, for example, that government funding for an inner-city school music program is actually appropriated by the wealthiest people in society.

Government Money for Arts Education

Despite the widely reported figure of 36 cents per capita spent annually by the federal government on the arts, this amount in reality is only the government's *direct* support of the NEA. The true level of federal subsidies to the arts is more than three times higher than this (Feld et al., 1983; Schuster, 1987) when both direct and indirect subsidies are considered. Under section 501 of the U.S. Internal Revenue Code, contributions to nonprofit 501(c) organizations are tax-deductible. This covers the majority of fine arts organizations. These deductions lead to tax revenues foregone in the amount of the contribution multiplied by the contributor's tax rate.

The specific expenditures that represent indirect subsidies include: (1) federal, state, and local taxes foregone from deductions to individual and corporate income taxes and (2) federal, state, and local taxes foregone from deductions to capital gains taxes (property gifts). This arrangement forms the basis for arts policy in the United States that can best be described as a "public-private partnership" (Schuster, 1985). While private philanthropic giving represents most "unearned" revenue for the arts, it is automatically accompanied by federal, state, and local government funds. This public money is directed to recipients not at the discretion of any bureaucrat but rather according to the private giving wishes of individual donors. This raises two policy issues:

1. Under this system, at least two-thirds of total government funding to the arts (direct and indirect) is distributed by private individuals, not the government itself. Some may see this as highly democratic: Those who choose to pay most have the greatest influence in funding decisions. Others may see it as just the opposite: Public money is being distributed by relatively few—usually very rich—

individuals. This last criticism has limited the appeal of this system in other countries (Schuster, 1999).

2. Incentives for limited funding of public goods, especially in arts education, may plague this system. Private donors may tend to fund organizations whose activities benefit them directly the most, and thus the indirect public subsidies go to these places as well. Assuming that school arts education rarely has the most direct impact on those who contribute philanthropically to the arts, education may receive less than an optimal level of support.

Though tax revenues foregone on deductible contributions are the most obvious sources of indirect government funding to the arts, other indirect funding streams exist as well. The same principles and policy issues apply to them: (1) tax revenues foregone on income earned by nonprofit organizations (germane only in the case that these revenues would have been earned in the absence of tax-exempt status), (2) import duties foregone on works of art purchased by nonprofits, (3) estate taxes foregone on bequests to nonprofits, and (4) local property taxes foregone.

Effect of Government Subsidies on Private Giving

Thinking is mixed as to how government support affects private giving to nonprofit arts organizations. On the one hand, private funds may be displaced, or "crowded out," by government support. Public support of a social cause may be diminished if the government takes responsibility for its funding. An arts organization may begin to look like a quasi-public agency when a large portion of its revenue comes from government sources (Friedman & Friedman, 1980), to which few people contribute voluntarily. In addition, subsidies to arts firms may make them appear "nonmainstream" in the minds of private donors and hence in need of nonmarket support. Because many donors, particularly corporate donors, are attracted to organizations that appear strong and independent, such a perception may discourage them from giving (Laurie, 1994). Another issue is that private donors may continue a financial relationship with an organization only as long as they can maintain control over the organization (Odendahl, 1990). Government intervention may compromise this control. And finally, because government support is tax-based, greater public support might lead to lower individual disposable income, discouraging private giving (Lingle, 1992).

On the other hand, government support may lead to leveraging or "crowding in" of private monies, especially when the government provides seed money to arts nonprofits. Some government support occurs in the context of matching funds campaigns and consequently is unavailable without matching private dollars. When the government provides a subsidy equal to the private match, the gift generates more benefits to both giver and receiver. Government subsidies are also viewed as proof of quality or reputability, especially for organizations that are not well known. Being worthy of government backing could stimulate the attention of private donors, who would otherwise have ignored the organization. Government involvement might also be seen as a guarantee of "due diligence" on the part of the nonprofit. Public funding is generally granted in return for a promise of a certain level of fiduciary responsibility, thus reassuring donors. All of these arguments are evident in the literature of the NEA (http://www.arts.gov), which indicates that NEA support offers an imprimatur that conveys excellence and prestige and helps leverage private support and generate dollars from other organizations and individuals.

Studies in both the arts and education offer data that can assist in understanding public-private funding issues. Hughes and Luksetich (1999) found that while the link between federal dollars and private donations to art museums was not significant, a dollar in state funds crowded out about 40 cents in private funds. In contrast, they found 48 cents crowded in at the federal level for history museums. Brooks (1999) found no significant relationship for symphony orchestras. In the case of public radio, Kingma (1989) found 14 cents of private funds crowded out on each dollar. The papers on this aspect of education finance are scarcer. Two relevant studies present mixed results. K. M. Day and Devlin (1996) found that volunteer time to educational institutions is crowded out by government funding in Canada. In a study that is harder to interpret, Connolly (1997) found that there is a complementary relationship between internal and external research funding to universities. To the extent that external funding is governmental while internal funding comes from privately do-

nated university funds, this might be thought of as weak evidence of crowding in. The broader literature on crowding out to nonprofits presents a reasonably consistent picture of government funding tending to displace private giving at a rate of somewhere between 20 and 50 cents on the dollar (Brooks, 2000; Steinberg, 1993) a pattern that may be replicated in arts education organizations.

Federal Versus State and Local Funding

Government arts funding occurs at all levels of government, including federal, state, county, and municipal. As might be expected, the total appropriations tend to decrease with the level of government. However, the effective arts subsidy per capita does not. As an example, figure 47.1 compares funding for the arts for the NEA, the Georgia Council for the Arts, and the Atlanta Bureau of Cultural Affairs. While the budget of the NEA is nearly 100 times that of the Atlanta agency, the arts funding per capita is 10 times higher for the latter than it is for the former. Local government funding may have greater significance than federal funding.

In the arts in general and arts education in particular, the question often arises as to the proper level of government funding. Should the federal government oversee arts funding, or should it be left to the states and municipalities? If the latter, what is the proper mechanism to provide the funds? Should the federal government provide grants to local governments to distribute as they see fit (devolution) or provide the funds with instructions for their use (delegation)? Or should localities use their own taxing authority to raise the funds?

Decentralization of government funding is known in the economics literature as "fiscal federalism." There are several instruments for carrying out policy in this area, in-

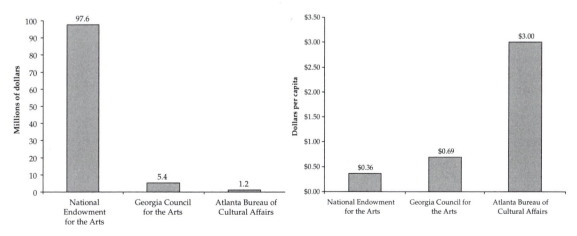

Figure 47.1 Fiscal Year 2000 budgets and appropriations per capita for arts agencies at three levels of government

cluding taxes, debt instruments (e.g., bonds), and intergovernmental grants (Oates, 1999). This last category includes an especially controversial topic in public finance: block grants. Block grants authorize federal aid within a broadly defined range of activities in which recipients—usually states—have substantial discretion over allocation (Posner & Wrightson, 1996). At present, block grants comprise approximately 40% of the total annual federal funding to the states (*Catalogue of Federal Domestic Assistance*, 1995).

Block-granting the NEA's funds has traditionally represented a "middle way" between defunding the controversial agency and maintaining the status quo. This alternative has typically been proposed by moderate Republicans (DiMaggio, 1991). The primary argument against block-granting in the arts is that central funding and spending mandates ensure quality control over programs. Because state arts agencies make approximately six times the number of grants made by the federal government, the implication is that the NEA is focusing its energies on fewer high-caliber projects, whereas the states give out smaller dollops of money to recipients across a wider quality range. The rationale usually involves supposed freedom from local voter anomalies (Dixit & Londregan, 1998), which is a euphemistic way of suggesting that local arts agencies might be persuaded by uncultured voters to fund a locally popular event with little redeeming cultural content. Those who seek funds for arts education will almost certainly balk at this argument, because education programs are less concerned with artistic virtuosity than with access to quality programs in the context of local needs. Thus the state funding pattern may appear to be more favorable to education programs.

This perspective is consistent with the most common argument in favor of block-granting that local agencies understand local needs and tastes better than central agencies (Tiebout, 1956). In the arts, this means recognition of local variation in receptiveness to particular art forms and messages.

Soft- Versus Hard-Money Initiatives in Public Arts Policy

Historically, public arts education policy has tended to focus more on artists than on students and arts educators (Chapman, 1992; Gee, 1999b). The focus on artists means carrying out policy in a soft-money setting: hiring professionals for onetime performances in schools, for example, or having artists conduct professional development workshops for nonarts classroom teachers. In contrast, a hard-money focus means an ongoing, budgeted commitment to education, in which an arts curriculum is not presented as a special event but as part of a continuing commitment to learning.

Three potential weaknesses of the soft-money approach are problematic. First, there is the question of continuity. Soft-money-based arts education does not lend itself to curricular continuity. It is difficult to cobble together a series of single performances that is pedagogically coherent. Second, there is the question of the degree to which soft-money education integrates with the broader school curriculum. If we assume that arts education forms part of a greater educational whole, particularly in settings where thematic curricula have been adopted, isolated arts experiences designed by noneducators may not connect with ongoing learning. Even when efforts are made to connect soft-money initiatives with the curriculum, the imperative for results often associated with short-term funding defies the complexity of teacher–artist relationships and levels of understanding necessary to ensure quality learning experiences. Third, inability to sustain programs because of the time-limited availability of funds means that frequently promised systemic change through the arts is never realized.

Arts Learning and the Academic Curriculum

Assumptions that the arts, whether interdisciplinary or discrete, enhance academic performance has been a long-standing and pervasive force in the federal arts education agenda. One of AHP's sponsored projects in the 1960s was an effort to research transfer from music to academic learning in junior high school students. The results were nonsignificant across a range of academic outcomes, and the study itself was compromised by the fact that only 42 of the original 100 subjects remained by the end (Murphy & Jones, 1976).

A persistent problem in understanding the roles of the arts in schools stems from semantic differences and interpretations of terms. Policy literature frequently tends to reference the arts collectively in arguments for academic impact, even though supporting evidence derives from discrete disciplines. As suggested earlier, the tendency toward speaking about "the arts" has its roots in federal/philanthropic program development that occurred during the 1970s, notably the JDR 3rd Fund's Arts-in-Education program.

Arts in General Education (AGE) was a term that originated with the JDR 3rd Fund's Arts-in-Education program. AGE was implemented in six urban school systems known as the League of Cities for the Arts in Education. Remer (1990), who worked with the program, described AGE as "a concept, a philosophy, a way of looking at schooling and the arts that alters the standard patterns for teaching and learning. . . . It combines the notion of all the arts for everyone with the conviction that the arts have value for their own sake as well as for reaching other desirable ends" (pp. 11–12). Fowler and McMullan (1991) said that AGE programs "made the arts the instructional fabric of the schools for all children" (p. 6). Remer indicated that AGE had also gone by other names, "such as Arts for Learning, Arts in the Basic Curriculum and Arts in Basic Education" (p. 11).

Another program, IMPACT (Interdisciplinary Model Programs in the Arts for Children and Teachers), based on ideas similar to AGE, existed from 1970 to 1972 in five locations that ranged from inner-city to suburban to rural: Philadelphia; Columbus, Ohio; Eugene, Oregon; Glendale, California; and Troy, Alabama. IMPACT attempted to achieve parity of the arts with other subjects, provide programs of high artistic quality, infuse the arts across the curriculum, and incorporate artists and performers from outside the school setting. Funded by the USOE, IMPACT also had support from the NEA, the JDR 3rd Fund, and professional arts education organizations. Though the Arts IMPACT Evaluation Team (1973) declared that "it would be hard to conceive of a plan within which there were more potential seeds for disaster than Project IMPACT" (p. 8), the team found a number of positive outcomes. Among these were greater parity of the arts with other subjects, more favorable student attitudes toward school, and broadened, more child-oriented approaches on the part of classroom teachers.

Comprehensive arts education is another term that has frequently appeared in policy literature since the 1970s. According to Fowler (1988), comprehensive programs involve all the arts for all students, the integration of arts with other subjects, the incorporation of community arts resources, and arts services for special needs students. Pankratz (1986), however, argued that the emphasized theme in comprehensive arts education was extra-arts outcomes, along with creativity and use of community arts resources.

On the matter of addressing the arts collectively, some writers caution that each arts discipline entails unique ways of learning and a distinct body of knowledge. Samuel Hope (1995), executive director of the National Association of Schools of Music, contends that there is no such discipline as "the arts" (p. 27), and that differences in ways of knowing associated with arts disciplines argue for substantive understanding of each art form. Rush (1997) questions whether there are "enough commonalities . . . to speak easily of arts education" (p. 8).

On the issue of arts and academic performance, government agencies and foundations have continued to promote this link, despite the lack of rigorous evaluation studies, the failure of most research to isolate the arts from other factors that influence academic performance, and the lack of convincing evidence of causal relationships (Eisner, 1998; Gee, 1999a; Smith, 1995). Fowler and McMullan (1991) were commissioned by the NEA to research arts

programs relative to academic performance. They found the research evidence so lacking that they were forced to reconceptualize their study and simply document ways in which the arts seemed to contribute to educational excellence. Eisner (1998) concluded that there is limited evidence to support effects of the arts on academic achievement and that justifying arts education on this basis may "undermine the value of art's unique contributions to the education of the young" (p. 15). The Reviewing Education and the Arts Project (REAP) of Harvard University looked at 188 studies amenable to meta-analysis that investigated a relationship between the arts and academic areas. Researchers found insufficient evidence to build justifications for the arts on the basis of contributions to learning in other fields (Winner & Cooper, 2000). From a policy perspective, arguments that link the arts to academic achievement frequently hinge on using every available avenue to achieve a place of permanence for the arts in education. Eisner (1998) has characterized this approach as becoming "whatever people want us to be" (p. 15).

Irwin and Reynolds (1995) argued for teachers to be versed in a discipline-centered approach yet contended that integrated or interdisciplinary approaches between the arts and academics need to be explored. They documented a loss of artistic learning in programs that integrate arts and academics without a clear concept of what integration means, reaching a conclusion that echoes the concerns of arts educator groups with regard to federal policy—that "there is no consensus about the meaning of integration" (p. 15) or its implementation. Hope (1995) suggests that combinations of subjects may be process- or content-focused and that terms such as *disciplinary, multidisciplinary, plurdisciplinary, cross-disciplinary, interdisciplinary,* and *transdisciplinary* carry meanings that can clarify integrative approaches.

Representing the federal policy perspective, Doug Herbert, director of the NEA's Arts Education program, addressed this issue at the May 2000 Model Arts Program Conference. Herbert called the idea of arts as an instructional tool for other subjects "disturbing" (2000, p. 2) and emphasized the importance of maintaining the integrity of individual subjects within programs that integrate the arts with academics. Despite Herbert's use of vocabulary that would probably be pleasing to music and other arts educators, controversy still abounds at the instructional level regarding those approaches that in fact maintain disciplinary integrity while helping students understand relationships across subjects. The policy implications may be most significant at the level of funded projects, which in too many cases do not meet the standards of arts educator organizations for sequential learning within discrete arts disciplines.

As indicated earlier in this chapter, evidence that arts educators have had some impact on policy is apparent in the NEA's 1986 revision of its education programs, the 1997 definition of arts education, and the agency's current statements and literature. Review criteria for all NEA education proposals, regardless of the category or arts discipline under which application is made, for example, music, include the following: (1) "potential to advance the arts as a basic component of the curriculum and to address the National Standards for Arts Education, and/or the relevant state standards for arts education," (2) "potential impact on learning across the curriculum through the arts," and (3) "plans for evaluation" (NEA, 2000a, p. 8). Conscious effort by the federal/philanthropic policy complex to ensure that arts education is promoted as both discipline-specific and cross-curricular is also evident in *Champions of Change* (Fiske, 1999). Here it is argued that "the arts no longer need to be characterized solely by either their ability to promote learning in specific arts disciplines or their ability to promote learning in other disciplines" (p. viii).

Despite the professional arts community's verbal endorsement of sequential and curricular programs, arts educators' ongoing policy concerns have influenced the Consortium of National Arts Education Associations to solicit support from powerful education groups. These groups include the National Education Association, the National School Boards Association, and the National Parent-Teacher Association. At present, however, it is not evident whether their endorsement of arts educators' priorities in fact represents a substantive policy commitment to arts education.

Artists in Schools and Arts Education Partnerships

Artists in Schools

Though artist residencies have existed for over three decades, the function of artists in schools relative to the curriculum has never been entirely clear. Arguments have arisen over whether artists are in schools primarily to practice art or to serve as arts teachers. Moreover, as early as 1975 state coordinators of the NEA's AIS Program indicated a lack of consensus about whether AIS was primarily a way to offer artists employment or a way to enhance student learning (Munley, 1999). Chapman (1982) surmised that federal agencies were promoting an agenda that would allow schools to delegate arts education to artists or social service agencies and hire artists and other noncertified individuals to deliver programs (p. 114). Barron (1985) contended on behalf of the NEA that "we know that in many school districts in sparsely populated states AIE artist residencies have been (and remain) virtually the *only* way to acquaint students with the arts" (p. 26). Un-

derstandably, arts education organizations were concerned that AIS was giving the impression, intentionally or not, that noncertified artists could take the place of certified arts specialists. Arts educators' two-pronged fear was that artists might supplant arts specialists and that exposure would suffice in lieu of ongoing and sequential instructional programs.

The growing assumption that artists and arts organizations could play crucial roles in school arts programs is evident in the increasing number of publications on this topic during the 1980s and 1990s. In 1983 the New England Foundation for the Arts and the American Council for the Arts published *The Arts Go to School: An Arts-in-Education Handbook*. In the introduction, project director Thomas Wolf pointed out that "outside artists and performers can support and enrich a school arts program but they cannot replace art and music teachers who give young people ongoing exposure and training in the arts" (New England Foundation for the Arts & American Council for the Arts, p. 10). In 1988 the National Assembly of State Arts Agencies published *Arts and Education Handbook: A Guide to Productive Collaborations* (Katz, 1988). In chapter 1, Fowler indicated that artists often need help in developing appropriate curricula, adopting teaching strategies, relating to other subjects, and exercising evaluation. From the perspective of arts educator organizations, these needs verified the fact that artists were not qualified to assume teaching roles and that those who were qualified, that is, arts specialists, were not sufficiently involved. Lehman (1986), who served as president of MENC, suggested that

the record . . . shows that the Artists in Education project does not lead to the establishment or significant improvement of sequential arts programs. It has often served to provide minimal arts experiences where school arts programs are weak or nonexistent, but this effort is counterproductive. (p. 14)

Arts educators have never denied a supportive role among artists and arts organizations for purposes of curricular and instructional enrichment. MENC, in fact, had prior experience with artist residencies through the composer residency program funded by the Ford Foundation as part of the Contemporary Music Project. In 1979, the year when music educator Joe Prince became head of the AIS Program, music educators "called AIS an important supplement to curricular education programs in the arts" (Munley, 1999, p. 141). According to Fowler (1984), Prince asserted that AIS/AIE was never intended to replace established arts education programs or to replace arts specialists with practicing artists. In the same article, Fowler also took Chapman (1982) to task for her assertion that arts agencies were conspiring against arts education. Calling Chapman's position territorial, he argued that arts agencies wanted to work collaboratively with arts educators and contended that arts educators' fear of losing their influence, jobs, and authority to artists was "an exaggerated, highly distorted, totally paranoid and unrealistic view" (p. 5).

Representing its constituent body of music educators, MENC historically has been a leader in building bridges among arts education organizations, the arts community, and evolving federal arts education policy (Laws, 1993). In 1986 MENC collaborated with the American Council for the Arts (ACA) to bring leaders from arts and arts education together to consider common concerns in arts education. This body drafted the "Philadelphia Resolution," a document that called for sequential arts programs "strengthened by artists and arts organizations" and "local, state and national policies that result in more effective support for arts education and the professional teachers and artists who provide it" (Pankratz & Mulcahy, 1989, p. 88). A subsequent collaborative symposium at the Interlochen Arts Center resulted in "The Interlochen Proposal," in which representatives of education, arts, and arts education urged that "the content of instructional programs in the arts be developed by the specialist teachers in consultation with artists, administrators, and other knowledgeable persons in the community" (p. 87).

However, even as it worked toward cooperation, MENC joined with other arts education groups to raise cautions about the role of professional artists and arts organizations. In *K–12 Arts Education in the United States: Present Context, Future Needs* (1986), these associations asserted that government arts agencies and organizations of nonprofessionals were promoting a policy agenda that used artists and classroom teachers as instruments of advocacy. Among the related issues was the use of artists selected by organizations outside the school. The report emphasized that *"arts councils were not established to deal with arts education, but with the creation and presentation of art"* (p. 11).

In 1988 Fowler again challenged arts education organizations' assertions that artists were usurping specialists' jobs or that it was the intention of the NEA to set a national agenda for arts education with its AIS/AIE programs. Apparently in direct response to *K–12 Arts Education in the United States,* he reacted to government and foundation interests' being labeled an advocacy movement and suggested that it was arts educators' own defensiveness that had led to their being bypassed in national arts education conversations.

Despite continuing dialogue on these matters, as well as the 1997 definition of arts education, the role of artists in schools continues to be a contentious policy issue. Arts organizations sometimes assume that benefits accrue from the presence of artists in schools regardless of whether their roles have been operationally defined, whether there are arts specialists present, and whether the artists have been trained for classroom work. Richard Deasy, director of the Arts Education Partnership, allows in *American Canvas* (Larson, 1997) that flourishing arts programs in schools depend in part on "well-trained and skilled teachers *and/ or* teaching artists" (p. 103, emphasis added). For some time to come, policy questions that surround whether and how artists ought to be involved in school programs will generate discussion of issues such as preservice education and professional development of artists and teachers; the roles of artists, classroom teachers, and certified arts specialists; curriculum development and instruction in the arts, as well as in programs that integrate arts with academics; and the financial responsibilities of schools versus arts organizations for support of school programs.

Arts Education Partnerships

The early concerns of Chapman (1982) and Eisner (1978) notwithstanding, arts education partnerships grew dramatically from the late 1980s forward. Though the trend has not been analyzed systematically, influential factors included the contemporary education reform movement's emphasis on school–community partnerships, a growing governmental emphasis on public–private partnerships, the desire of foundations and corporate funders to support projects that affected education, and the need for arts institutions to evidence stronger connections with their increasingly diverse communities. Citing the NEA's 1986 *Education Program Guidelines,* Jensen (1992) indicated that collaborations were a primary goal of federal arts education policy (p. 4).

As the NEA continued to move toward education funding that included partnership components, private foundations such as GE, Annenberg, and Texaco began soliciting proposals for projects that involved partnerships between arts organizations and schools. Frequently the requests involved not only partnerships but also projects designed to improve learning in other projects through the arts, to enhance social outcomes, or to contribute to school improvement—all consistent with federal initiatives. While some acknowledged the importance of the arts as discrete disciplines, few Requests for Proposals (RFPs) demonstrated specific interest in strengthening arts curricula for intrinsic outcomes of arts education. Both nationally and locally, *partnership* became a key word in the effort to reinstate abandoned arts programs or to develop expanded arts education opportunities.

Gordon and Stoner (1995), both associated with the Kennedy Center, observed "that the arts have been taught as discrete, compartmentalized disciplines for decades" and extolled the theme of arts education partnerships as they were being promoted through policy at the federal level. Asserting that "artists and arts institutions have traditionally been assigned . . . only a supporting role in the K–12 education of U.S. youth," they argued for "arts specialists . . . and community artists and arts institution/organization staff to work as a team in order to revolutionize arts education practice in this era of education reform." They also asserted that "the Kennedy Center, as the national performing arts center, has committed staff and resources to meet this challenge" (p. 39). In terms of impact on policy, it is important to note that during the 1994 reauthorization of the Elementary and Secondary Education Act (ESEA), a new section was added to support arts education. From 1995 through 1999, all of these funds were allocated to the Kennedy Center and to Very Special Arts, which is closely linked with the Kennedy Center (Gee, 1999a).

By the early 1990s, opera companies, Young Audience chapters, local arts councils, museums, and other institutions had begun framing their education initiatives within partnership contexts, a trend which has not abated at the time of this writing. Numerous orchestras, which included the Boston Symphony, the New York Philharmonic, the Pittsburgh Symphony, the Chicago Symphony, the Milwaukee Symphony, and others, were attempting to move beyond exposure programs to connect with curricular programs in and beyond music. In Boston the partnership was named the Boston Music Education Collaborative and functioned with the intention of helping to rebuild music programs and spur the hiring of additional music specialists. In New York the partnership resulted in employment of music specialists in schools that had not had music teachers since the 1970s. In Milwaukee and Pittsburgh the orchestras worked directly with music specialists in the schools (Myers, 1996).

Partnership initiatives frequently arise from within arts organizations and emphasize programmatic elements consistent with federal policy, which include artist residencies and the relationship of the arts to learning across the curriculum. The NEA's Fiscal Year 2000 music grants, for example, included a large percentage of partnership-type programs, many of them involving orchestras, that incorporated curriculum materials, artist residencies, and educational enrichment for schoolchildren. Recently both government and private funders have also urged the inclusion of professional development for classroom teachers and artists, curriculum materials that are consistent with national and local standards, and assessment of student learning. In addition, many partnerships link their goals to systemic school reform. Some partnerships emphasize a particular arts discipline, while others adopt an "arts" approach.

The challenges of establishing partnerships are not lost on those who attempt them. Gee (1997) documented one effort to establish a partnership out of a grassroots collaboration among public schools, arts organizations, and a university. Despite common interest in the RFP, differing assumptions and expectations among the organizations generated tensions among the partners and absorbed large amounts of time and energy. The tendency to view collaborative effort as service delivery from arts organizations to schools became a major stumbling block, as did issues of leadership, the balance between self-interest and partnership agendas, and the need to fulfill sometimes unclear and lofty expectations of the funder.

Undercofler (1997) concurred with one of Gee's documented concerns in arguing that community-based arts education partnerships too frequently continue a focus on exposure/experiential learning rather than sequential curricula. Echoing the 1977 recommendations of the Assembly of National Arts Education Organizations, Undercofler proposed the engagement of higher education in long-term partnerships, with music teachers being empowered to draw on community resources, provide curriculum leadership, and communicate with diverse audiences.

Evidence of policy that promotes partnerships is apparent in the Arts Education Partnership (AEP), formerly the Goals 2000 Arts Education Partnership, which is administered by the Council of Chief State School Officers and the National Assembly of State Arts Agencies through a cooperative agreement with the National Endowment for the Arts and the USDOE. The partnership meets regularly for forums and produces publications on arts education. A joint publication of the partnership with the President's Committee on the Arts and Humanities, *Gaining the Arts Advantage: Lessons from School Districts That Value Arts Education* (President's Committee on the Arts and Humanities and the Arts Education Partnership, 1999), provides a review of school districts that "have made competence in the arts as well as literacy one of the fundamental purposes of schooling" (p. 4). Supported by the GE Fund, the John D. and Catherine T. MacArthur Foundation, Binney & Smith, the NEA, the USDOE, and the White House Millennium Council, the report lists the first critical success factor for arts education as the active involvement of the community, which includes artists and arts organizations "in the arts politics and instructional programs of the district" (p. 11). A second recent publication, *Learning Partnerships: Improving Learning in Schools with Arts Partners in the Community* (Dreeszen, Aprill, & Deasy, 1999), offers an overview of guidelines for partnership planning and implementation, which include the improvement of learning in the arts as well as in overall academic performance.

In many arts partnership programs, music education is subsumed within a larger arts education context, with limited accountability for the quality of instruction. Goals may tend to emphasize hope for systemic change, improved academic learning, or a better social climate, without specific attention to the quality of teaching and learning within the arts disciplines. A music-teaching demonstration from a widely recognized partnership presented as an exemplar at a recent national meeting indicated not only a low level of music learning but also a vague and poorly conceived effort to connect music with academic learning. Unfortunately, evaluators who look at lofty program goals may find evidence of positive change that could be more of an "epiphenomenon" (Winner & Cooper, 2000) than an indicator of quality arts education. In the words of Barzun (1978), this tendency to attribute a wide array of debatable outcomes to the arts "inflates the plausible or possible into the miraculous" (1978, p. 5) and may, in the long term, diminish not only the effort to ensure quality arts education but also the public's confidence in the role of the arts in schooling.

At its June 2000 meeting in Durham, North Carolina, Arts Education Partnership focused on the topic of the arts and school reform. Featured partnerships included the Arts in the Basic Curriculum Project from South Carolina, the Center for Arts Education in New York City (Annenberg Challenge), the North Carolina A+ Program, the Perpich Center for Arts Education (Annenberg Challenge), and Transforming Education Through the Arts Challenge, known as TETAC.

The notion of arts education partnerships as related to educational reform is exemplifed on a national scale in the TETAC initiative. Growing out of Wilson's (1997) evaluation of DBAE, TETAC is funded by the J. P. Getty Trust and the Annenberg Challenge for Arts Education. It is guided by the National Consortium for Arts Education, which consists of a coalition of regional institutes previously associated with implementation of DBAE (now called comprehensive art education). The 5-year project seeks to connect arts education, primarily visual art education, with whole-school reform. Among its principles are collaboration between teachers and experts in particular subject areas, the use of community cultural institutions, and the teaching of several school subjects simultaneously (Hutchens & Pankratz, 2000). TETAC's national evaluation efforts are based on five goals: (1) institutionalizing support for comprehensive arts education as part of the basic core of learning; (2) demonstrating how comprehensive arts education when integrated with other elements of school reform transforms a school's culture and the lives of its students and teachers; (3) supporting the active engagement and involvement of parents, communities, arts organizations, school reform networks and resources, funders, the broader public, and education professionals in the reform effort; (4) creating an effective combination of documentation, assessment, and evaluation strategies that will ensure rich and reliable ways of knowing what has been accomplished; and (5) creating a means to disseminate in-

formation and successful practices (National Consortium for Arts Education, 2000).

According to Wilson (2000), "Partnerships with arts institutions characterize vital district arts programs" (p. 19). He considers a large number of relationships with community arts institutions and organizations to be one of the central features of an outstanding district arts education program.

Research Issues

Arts Education Policy

From a policy perspective, systematic research on the issues raised in this chapter is relatively slim. This may be because, as Hope (1989) asserts: "Arts education research and scholarship are primarily oriented to scientific experimentalism. . . . Policy-oriented efforts are most often focused on . . . pressure to keep the idea of arts education alive" (p. 75). Attempting to understand the evolution of "arts education" and its implications for music leads to documents that are tied closely with the advocacy environment identified in *K–12 Arts Education in the United States: Present Context, Future Needs*. One must interpolate from records of testimony, position statements, and articles that provide information that often has not been subjected to the rigor of analysis and research-based verification.

Udell (1990), Jensen (1992), Laws (1993), and Munley (1999) are four researchers who explored arts education policy in doctoral dissertations. Investigating specifically the role of the Wisconsin Arts Board in arts education through a historical/descriptive study, Udell found a trend toward declining numbers of artist residencies, along with a growing emphasis on making the arts basic in K–12 education. Such developments would tend to indicate that arts educator organizations' concerns may be having an influence, though it is not clear to what extent the arts board is connecting with ongoing school programs.

A music educator, Jensen (1992) derived seven issues from *Toward Civilization* that served as a basis for a modified Delphi study of the implementation of federal arts education policy at the state level. She found that state education personnel and state arts agency personnel had differing perceptions of the influence of federal policy, no doubt because the agencies have different functions and structures relative to arts and education at the federal level. She also found that while state-level personnel considered collaborations to be the area in which federal policy was most effective, they viewed professional development and teacher recruitment, preparation, and certification as the most important issues.

Using cross-case analysis, Laws (1993) compared policy

development in three professional education associations. In comparing MENC to professional education organizations in mathematics and social studies, Laws concluded that MENC's goal of music for all children is somewhat at odds with current practice and that slow resolution of this issue could undermine efforts to influence broader education policy. She also documented MENC's strong efforts to build consensus among its constituents and to forge coalitions with the arts, arts education, and music industry communities. Laws's findings raise the question of whether music education's emphasis on performance programs helps sustain the assertion by some arts organizations that a select number of talented students have been better served by music programs than has the population of schoolchildren at large. If so, the door inadvertently may be open for arts organizations to claim that their programs serve broad arts, academic, and social goals for all children better than traditional music education programs.

Munley (1999) conducted a case-study analysis of the formulation of arts education policy in the NEA from 1965 to 1993, based on a content analysis of documentary evidence. Among her conclusions were that NEA education decisions are subject more to political than philosophical factors; that NEA policy is primarily symbolic, given the lack of committed resources for a significant impact on arts education; and that a lack of consistent education policy in the NEA is in part a function of lack of clarity about jurisdiction over arts education. Her findings suggest that the NEA is appropriately equipped to be supportive of arts education programs but not to claim a major role in shaping or influencing them.

Instrumental Outcomes and Arts Advocacy

From an advocacy perspective that attempts to convince power brokers of the importance of arts education, the claims for research-based indicators of the instrumental outcomes of arts education are widespread. *Eloquent Evidence: Arts at the Core of Learning* (Murfee, 1995), *Schools, Communities, and the Arts: A Research Compendium* (Welch & Greene, 1995), and *Champions of Change: The Impact of the Arts on Learning* (Fiske, 1999) are examples of publications that present studies to advocate the role of the arts in achieving an array of extra-arts outcomes. The underlying assumption of such publications is evident in the preface to *Champions of Change,* which asserts that "evidence could be collected that would help answer the questions of why positive changes [when young people are involved with the arts] occur and what might be done to replicate them" (p. iv). Of the existing compilations of studies, *Champions of Change* represents a higher overall standard than others in terms of researchers and methodologies. Divided into two portions—"Why the

Arts Change the Learning Experience" and "How the Arts Change the Learning Experience"—the Executive Summary of this report indicates that the arts engage disengaged students, offer a bridge to learning and success in other areas of learning, help develop learning communities, break down walls between classrooms and disciplines, challenge successful students, and connect learning to the world of work. In addition, it is said that the projects researched enable direct involvement with the arts and artists, require staff development for teachers, provide ongoing learning opportunities, encourage self-directed learning, promote complexity in learning, allow management of risk by learners, and engage community leaders and resources (pp. ix–xi). While one study contends that "intensive involvement in a single discipline should probably be thought to be even more important developmentally than high levels of more diverse involvement in the arts" (Catterall, Chapleau, & Iwanaga, 1999), none of the studies systematically evaluates the quality of teaching process or levels of learning within relevant arts disciplines.

Wilson (2000) has said: "There are many crucial factors that lead to the implementation of districtwide arts education programs. Entrepreneurship and linking the arts to nearly every educational reform initiative and opportunity that comes down the pike are crucial" (p. 19). If Wilson is correct, perhaps it should be acknowledged that making a lasting place for arts education in schools requires all the forces that can be mustered, regardless of philosophical differences or the lack of rational support for various claims.

However, commitment to schools and learning suggests that beliefs and questions about music and arts education policy must be subjected to critical analysis and scrutiny, which may lead to disagreements about the role of the arts in schools and the relationships between school arts programs and community arts. Hope (1989) maintains that the emphasis on unity that has arisen from advocacy efforts over the past several decades is not necessarily advantageous to understanding or forging arts education policy. In fact, intense disagreement may engender greater attention to policy, both within and beyond arts education. According to Hope, "The problems are simply too complex for advocacy technique to create solutions" (p. 79).

Artists in Schools

In 1974 Elliot Eisner challenged the apparent assumptions on which the Artists-in-Schools Program of the NEA was based and called for a careful evaluation. In 1975 the NEA contracted with the Western States Arts Foundation (1976) to conduct a research study that surveyed students, artists, teachers, and school administrators. As with many such studies, the bias toward assumed positive outcomes compromised its integrity. While the report offered strong positive perceptions and support from all constituents for the artist residency program, M. Day (1978) found that only a small percentage of teachers reported increases in students' arts interests and most teachers did not indicate perceived increases in verbal performance. According to Day, this study did not fulfill standard parameters of objectivity associated with respectable research. In 1978 Eisner again chastised the NEA for its failure to provide objective evaluation of AIS, citing the program "as an example of the tendency to seek image over reality, public relations over significant improvement, approbation over critical appraisal" (p. 20).

The AIS/AIE programs have received scrutiny in several doctoral dissertations. Among the more recent of these are Mok's (1983), Bumgarner's (1993), and Foster's (1995). Mok reviewed several earlier studies from the 1970s and found that the studies concurred in their recommendations for better planning among participants and active local involvement in the planning process. Mok's qualitative methodology used Eisner's educational criticism and Shuchat-Shaw's method of congruence to analyze programs in Texas and New York in light of the 1980 AIS/AIE goals as stated by the NEA. She concluded that the programs lacked philosophical grounding; however, she also concluded that the programs never purported to be and did not operate as replacements for school arts education programs. Finding little evidence of conflict between artists and teachers in the classroom, she argued that "what hampered . . . acceptance of the programs nationwide was its entanglement with political concerns" (p. 300). She also believed that the lack of arts educators' involvement in the selection of artists and program supervision was the source of many of the challenges raised about the program. Finally, she emphasized that the role of artists is to share their artistry, not to function as educators.

Bumgarner (1993) focused on residency programs in Pennsylvania, along with a contexual comparison based on the programs of six other states, as a basis for her analysis. She used a qualitative approach based on multiple data sources in order to determine the extent to which the residencies advanced basic arts education as part of the core curriculum, benefited a majority of elementary and secondary students, and provided students with substantial arts education experiences. She found that residencies typically focused on basic elements of art forms and not on the NEA-espoused DBAE-style approach, thus leading her to conclude "that the artist residency program is not an effective means of making the arts a more central component of the K–12 curriculum" (p. 463). This finding suggests a philosophical disparity between the NEA's apparent commitment and the implementation of the residency program. Echoing Lehman (1986), Bumgarner also came to believe that the most effective residencies were those that enhanced already-strong arts education programs. Consistent with Mok's findings 10 years earlier, she recommended that the NEA "formulate a more consistent overall education policy" (p. 487).

Foster's history (1995) of the AIE program of the state arts council of Oklahoma documented the evolution from experience/exposure to expectations that artists would "understand how their particular art forms could benefit Oklahoma's educational environment" (p. 227). The study does not offer a critical appraisal of the program or its effectiveness.

Several studies have been conducted on the effectiveness of visiting artists for early childhood education, including those of Moses (1994), Bolanis (1996), Eustis (1998), and T. A. Smith (2000). Moses studied the Wolf Trap Institute for Early Learning Through the Arts, which uses a teaching artist approach with disadvantaged children to improve their readiness for school. Using qualitative methodology, she determined that improving communication between classroom teachers and artists resulted in greater teacher leadership in implementing arts activities. She also concluded that artists needed considerably more training, particularly in the area of early childhood music education, in order to achieve effective integration of the arts into the curriculum.

Bolanis (1996) examined the responses of first- and sixth-grade children to live performances by a woodwind quintet, both before and after the quintet had received training designed to increase the developmental appropriateness of the programs. She found that students' verbal responses were focused more on musical than on nonmusical aspects after the quintet's revised performances.

Eustis's (1998) research focused on developing guidelines for "best practices" of educational programs of regional opera companies. She found that an emphasis on entertainment tended to compromise artistic and educational value, that teachers should be involved in the preparation of educational materials to ensure relevance to the classroom, and that opportunities for close association with artists could make experiences more meaningful.

Smith's (2000) study analyzed existing programs to develop a model for developmentally appropriate chamber music programs for early childhood. Emphasizing "education" over "appreciation," Smith advised quality repertoire, interactive experiences, effective questioning, and excerpt lengths consistent with children's attention spans.

None of the four studies addressed the issue of visiting artists within a context of federal policy, which suggests that, at the classroom level, educators may be more concerned with ensuring the quality of learning experiences than with arguments about who is responsible for what.

Arts Education Partnerships

Like assumptions that artists in schools constitute an automatic avenue of improved arts education, assumptions that partnerships are good for arts education are based more on political expedience and the obvious logic of broadening constituencies than on evidence that school–community cooperation enhances teaching and learning. Whether partnerships can be isolated as a variable in effecting change in teaching and learning is a major question. However, given the fact that arts organizations are not likely to abandon the footholds they are establishing with schools, along with the fact that partnerships afford arts educators an opportunity to enrich learning for their students, it is logical to pursue research to help establish what enhances the educational worth of partnerships.

Dreeszen's (1992) research, a synthesis of findings from NEA-supported institutes on arts education, indicated nine success factors of partnerships: leadership and vision, effective planning, broad-based community representation, teacher participation, artist participation, public awareness and communication, awareness of program catalyst, site-specific program design, and ongoing assessment of the partnership. Myers (1996) derived 6 principles of partnership effectiveness from his case studies of orchestra–school partnerships: the valuing of education within the orchestra, ongoing and adaptive planning among partners, a commitment to sustained programs, implementation of high-quality teaching and learning, shared resources and funding, and evaluation that establishes an accurate profile for continued planning.

The evaluation of the Boston Music Education Collaborative (D. P. Wolf, 1997) looked at student outcomes within the partnership schools and the effectiveness of the partnership itself. Based on the research findings, the report recommended that the partnership work only in schools with a music specialist or with an investment in building a musical culture, that highly skilled curriculum developers be retained, that musicians be more connected with the curriculum, that the partners be more intentional about their commitment of resources to the partnership, and that curriculum links be made out of the inherent skills and understandings associated with music learning, for example, listening and responding. These findings appear to confirm the recommendations of Lehman (1986) and Bumgarner (1993) with regard to linking programs with schools that are committed to music education programs.

Based on his case-study analysis of the partnership between the Eastman School of Music and the Rochester City School District, Robinson (1999) derived a theory of educational collaboration to help explain the ways in which differing agendas, organizational structures, and attributes of personnel within partnering organizations may affect the problem-solving process required to attain the collaborative stature that will impact educational programs. According to Robinson, "Experienced collaborators also know that the ability to function well in a climate of ambiguity, frustration, and tension is part of the job requirement for membership in a partnership" (p. 267).

An arts education partnership evaluation currently under way is attempting to assess the work of the Annenberg-funded New York City Arts Partnership program, administered by the Center for Arts Education. The program consists of 81 site-based partnerships. Using a combination of approaches that include site visits, classroom observations, interviews, surveys, and analysis of school test data, the evaluation will strive to "create a synthesis of project results for reporting back to Annenberg, other funders, and the field at large" (Baker, 2000, p. 2). The evaluation will conduct its research "as close to practitioners as possible" (p. 2). Though a preliminary report suggests that "the successes of local projects are already wide and deep" (p. 4), this same report notes concerns relative to curriculum depth, time for implementing partnerships, uneven professional development, lack of data on the impact on students, and the need for leadership to effect school change through the arts.

A report on the evaluation of the A+ Schools Program in North Carolina sought to document the implementation of A+ in the original pilot group of schools, describe how this implementation interacted with and influenced the schools' cultures, communities, and contexts, and identify the ongoing effects of the reform on administrators, teachers, students, and parents (Thomas S. Kenan Institute for the Arts, 2000). Initiated in 1993, A+ program schools use interdisciplinary units of study that incorporate arts integration as well as daily arts instruction by arts teachers. Partnerships with parents, cultural resources, and higher education are an important component of programs. Early results focused on improvement in student attendance, parent involvement, and student engagement in the classroom. Methods for the systematic assessment begun in 1996 included field observations in schools, observation of professional development, surveys of teachers, students, and parents, profiles of schools, test score analysis, and tracking of the development of the project. As with many evaluations of funded arts education projects, the reported results tended toward the positive, with only limited critical analysis of the project or its outcomes and very limited indicators of the quality of implementation. Selected findings specific to the arts include the following: artistic performances often became "informances," most schools integrated arts-based instruction with the standard program, and schools implemented the program in a manner that works for them. Such findings confirm that the project implemented a program but tell little about the quality or the educational impact. The report indicated that collaborations have been difficult to accomplish, due to lack of time, and that participation in professional development has been inconsistent.

In 1994 the NEA and the USDOE published an arts education research agenda (NEA & USDOE, 1994), and in 1997 the Goals 2000 Arts Education Partnership published a series of priorities for arts education research (Cawelti & Goldberg, 1997). Consistent with long-standing federal/philanthropic agendas, these documents recommend research on the "potential impact of partnerships on arts learning, students, and communities" (NEA & USDOE, 1994, p. 11), studies of the effect of arts education on learning in the arts and other academic areas, and investigations that relate to arts education policy development.

Conclusion

The growing emphasis on partnerships among schools and arts organizations as a delivery model for arts education is not likely to abate in the near future. How arts educator organizations and the federal/philanthropic arts education complex come to terms over the issue of respective roles and responsibilities for arts education is mostly a matter of degree. Each side must be willing to recognize honestly its capacities and limitations and to acknowledge the extent to which individual agendas may need to be modified on behalf of excellent arts education for children. Collaborative programs that assist arts educators in enriching programs through community resources are recognized universally as being beneficial. To ensure the effectiveness of such programs, research must go beyond attempting to demonstrate how arts partnerships, simply because they exist, improve school climates or affect academic performance. It must begin with the question of what constitutes quality teaching and learning in the arts and then investigate factors of quality in partnerships that support arts learning. Among the pressing issues are the respective roles of teachers and artists, the preservice and in-service education of teachers and artists, and the development of high-quality classroom models. Given the organizational complexity of partnerships, it is also important that models be developed for productive institutional relationships that exploit the appropriate and respective roles of schools and arts organizations while building unity within a community for arts education programs. The expectation of funders that arts organizations be actively involved in education portends important changes in the operations of institutions such as symphony orchestras and opera companies, as well as in the preparation of professional musicians.

In an earlier publication (Pankratz & Mulcahy, 1989), Pankratz declared: "To expect arts education research solely to serve current or popular ideas of reform is to destroy the purpose of research in the field" (p. 6). Later, citing the importance of analyzing and evaluating funding policies, he said: "Objectivity is often difficult in the face of legitimation and support from external funders" (p. 17). In the same work, Hope suggested that arts education lacked sufficient policy analysis to overcome the tendency toward "highly promoted arts education panaceas left dying in the forum of ideas" (p. 80). Until arts education policy research can be separated from self-conscious advocacy of arts in the schools and the need to justify arts education on the basis of academic, social, and economic outcomes, the field will continue to lack an objectively derived knowledge base that builds a foundation for policy out of the inherent and distinctive contributions that quality arts learning makes to the educational process.

REFERENCES

Arts, Education, and Americans Panel. (1977). *Coming to our senses: The significance of the arts for American education.* New York: McGraw-Hill.

Arts IMPACT Evaluation Team. (1973). *Arts IMPACT: Curriculum for change—A summary report.* University Park: Pennsylvania State University. (ERIC Document Reproduction Service No. ED084186)

Baker, T. (2000, June). *Template for evaluation description.* Paper presented at the meeting of the Arts Education Partnership, Durham, NC.

Barron, F. (1985). National Endowment for the Arts: Advocate and catalyst. *Design for Arts in Education, 86*(3), 26–30.

Barzun, J. (1978). Art and educational inflation. *Art Education, 31*(6), 4–10.

Baumol, W. J., & Bowen, W. G. (1965). On the performing arts: The anatomy of their economic problems. *American Economic Review, 55,* 495–502.

Baumol, W. J., & Bowen, W. G. (1966). *Performing arts: The economic dilemma.* New York: Twentieth Century Fund, 1966.

Biddle, L. (1988). *Our government and the arts: A perspective from the inside.* New York: American Council for the Arts.

Bolanis, L. S. (1996). *Children's responses to live musical performance by an ensemble without, and then with, pedagogical training.* Unpublished doctoral dissertation, Northwestern University, Evanston, Illinois.

Brooks, A. C. (1997). Toward a demand-side cure for cost disease in the performing arts. *Journal of Economic Issues, 31*(1), 197–207.

Brooks, A. C. (1999). Do public subsidies leverage private philanthropy for the arts? Empirical evidence on symphony orchestras. *Nonprofit and Voluntary Sector Quarterly, 28*(1), 32–45.

Brooks, A. C. (2000). Is there a dark side to government support for nonprofits? *Public Administration Review, 60*(3), 211–218.

Bumgarner, C. (1993). *An analysis of the arts in education program of the National Endowment for the Arts.* Unpublished doctoral dissertation, Pennsylvania State University, University Park.

Catalogue of federal domestic assistance. (1995). Washington, DC: Office of Management and Budget.

Catterrall, J., Chapleau, R., & Iwanaga, J. (1999). Involvement in the arts and human development: General involvement and intensive involvement in music and theater arts. In E. Fiske (Ed.), *Champions of change: The impact of the arts on learning* (pp. 1–13). Washington, DC: Arts Education Partnership and the President's Committee on the Arts and the Humanities.

Cawelti, G., & Goldberg, M. (1997). Priorities for arts education research. Washington, DC: Goals 2000 Arts Education Partnership.

Chapman, L. H. (1982). *Instant art, instant culture: The unspoken policy for American schools.* New York: Teachers College Press.

Chapman, L. (1992). Arts education as a political issue: The federal legacy. In R. Smith & R. Berman (Eds.), *Public policy and the aesthetic interest: Critical essays on defining cultural and educational relations* (pp. 119–136). Urbana: University of Illinois Press.

Connolly, L. S. (1997). Does external funding of academic research crowd out institutional support? *Journal of Public Economics, 64,* 389–406.

Day, K. M., & Devlin, R. A. (1996). Volunteerism and crowding out: Canadian econometric evidence. *Canadian Journal of Economics, 29*(1), 37–53.

Day, M. (1978). Point with pride or view with alarm. In R. A. Smith, (Ed.), *Artists-in-Schools: Analysis and criticism* (pp. 12–19). Urbana: Bureau of Educational Research, University of Illinois at Urbana-Champaign.

DiMaggio, Paul J. (1991). Decentralization of arts funding from the federal government to the states. In S. Benedict (Ed.), *Public money and the muse: Essays on government funding for the arts* (pp. 216–252). New York: W. W. Norton.

Dixit, A., & Londregan, J. (1996). Fiscal federalism and redistributive politics. *Journal of Public Economics, 68,* 153–180.

Dreeszen, C. (1992). *Intersections: Community arts and education collaborations.* Washington, DC: U.S. Department of Education.

Dreeszen, C., Aprill, A., & Deasy, R. (1999). *Learning partnerships: Improving learning in schools with arts partners in the community.* Washington, DC: Arts Education Partnership.

Duke, L. (1999). Looking back, looking forward. *Arts Education Policy Review, 101*(1), 3–7.

Eisner, E. (1974). Is the artist in the schools program effective? *Art Education, 27*(2), 19–23.

Eisner, E. (1978). The state of arts education today and some potential remedies: A report to the National Endowment for the Arts. *Art Education, 31*(8), 14–18, 20–23.

Eisner, E. (1998). Does experience in the arts boost academic achievement? *Art Education, 51*(1), 7–15.

Eustis, L. E. (1998). *Educational outreach programs at regional opera companies: Guidelines for effectiveness.* Unpublished doctoral treatise, Florida State University, Tallahassee.

Feld, A., O'Hare, M., & Davidson Schuster, J. M. (1983). *Patrons despite themselves: Taxpayers and arts policy.* New York: NYU Press.

Fiske, E. (Ed.). (1999). *Champions of change: The impact of the arts on learning.* Washington, DC: Arts Education Partnership and the President's Committee on the Arts and the Humanities.

Foster, G. C. (1995). *The history of the artist-in-residence program of the state arts council of Oklahoma.* Unpublished doctoral dissertation, University of Oklahoma, Norman.

Fowler, C. (1976). The new arts education. *College Music Symposium, 16,* 19–24.

Fowler, C. (1984). Who own arts education? *Design for Arts in Education, 86*(2), 4–7.

Fowler, C. (1988). *Can we rescue the arts for America's children?* New York: American Council for the Arts.

Fowler, C., & McMullan, B. (1991). *Understanding how the arts contribute to excellent education* (Contract DCA 90-50). Washington, DC: National Endowment for the Arts.

Friedman, M., & Friedman, R. (1980). *Free to choose.* New York: Harcourt Brace Jovanovich.

Gee, C. B. (1997). Somewhere over the rainbow: Dreaming an arts and education community partnership. *Arts Education Policy Review, 98*(5), 13–32.

Gee, C. B. (1999a). For you dear—anything!: Part 1. Omnipotence, omnipresence, and servitude "through the arts." *Arts Education Policy Review, 100*(4), 3–18.

Gee, C. B. (1999b). For you dear—anything!: Part 2. Remembering and returning to first principles. *Arts Education Policy Review, 100*(5), 3–22.

Glidden, R. (1978). Report of the CMS committee on government relations, November 1977. *College Music Symposium, 18*(1), 197–199.

Glidden, R. (1985). A research agenda for arts education: The federal responsibility. *Design for Arts in Education, 86*(3), 15–18.

Gordon, D., & Stoner, S. (1995). Beyond enhancement: The Kennedy Center's commitment to education. *Arts Education Policy Review, 96*(4), 38–47.

Herbert, D. (2000, May). *Arts education: From the director.* [Adapted from *Building vision and stability,* paper presented at the Model Arts Program Conference, Los Angeles.] Washington, DC: National Endowment for the Arts. Retrieved November 15, 2000, from http://www.arts.gov.artforms.Artsed/Artsed2.html

Hoffa, H. (1985). The past as precedent. *Design for Arts in Education, 86*(3), 32–39.

Hope, S. (1989). The need for policy studies in arts education. In D. B. Pankratz & K. V. Mulcahy (Eds.), *The challenge to reform arts education: What role can research play?* (pp. 73–83). New York: American Council on the Arts.

Hope, S. (1995). Making disciplinary connections. *Arts Education Policy Review, 96*(5), 26–30.

Hughes, P. N., & Luksetich, W. (1999). The relationship among funding sources for art and history museums. *Nonprofit Management and Leadership, 1,* 21–37.

Hutchens, J., & Pankratz, D. (2000). Change in arts education: Transforming Education Through the Arts Challenge (TETAC). *Arts Education Policy Review, 101*(4), 5–9.

Irwin, R. L., & Reynolds, J. K. (1995). Integration as a strategy for teaching the arts as disciplines. *Arts Education Policy Review, 96*(4), 13–19.

Jensen, J. (1992). *An analysis of federal arts education policy and its implementation at the state level: A modified Delphi study of collaborations as ends and means of the policy process in arts education.* Unpublished doctoral dissertation, University of Texas at Austin.

Katz, J. (Ed.). (1988). *Arts and education handbook: A guide to productive collaborations.* Washington, DC: National Assembly of State Arts Agencies.

K–12 arts education in the United States: Present context, future needs. (1986). Reston, VA: Music Educators National Conference, National Art Education Association, National Dance Association, National Association of Schools of Music, National Association of Schools of Art and Design, National Association of Schools of Theatre, National Association of Schools of Dance.

Killeen, D. (1999a). Can we learn from the past? A history of the Kennedy Center Alliance for Arts Education, part 1: Defining the agenda. *Arts Education Policy Review, 101*(1), 14–23.

Killeen, D. (1999b). Can we learn from the past? A history of the Kennedy Center Alliance for Arts Education, part 2: Controlling the agenda. *Arts Education Policy Review, 101*(2), 7–20.

Kingma, B. R. (1989). An accurate measure of the crowd-out effect, income effect, and price effect for charitable contributions. *Journal of Political Economy, 97,* 1197–1207.

Larson, G. (1997). *American canvas.* Washington, DC: National Endowment for the Arts.

Laurie, M. (1994). Corporate funding for the arts. In O. Robinson, R. Freeman, & C. Riley II (Eds.), *The arts in the world economy* (pp. 67–76). Hanover, NH: Salzburg Seminar (University Press of New England).

Laws, B. B. (1993). *Policy development in professional education associations.* Unpublished doctoral dissertation, George Washington University, Washington, D.C.

Lehman, P. L. (1986). Vantage point no. 8: The professional connection. *Horizon, 29*(4), 12–15.

Lingle, C. (1992). Public choice and public funding of the arts. In Ruth Towse & Abdul Khakee (Eds.), *Cultural economics* (pp. 21–30). Berlin: Springer.

Mahlmann, J. (1985). The federal government and professional arts education associations. *Design for Arts in Education, 86*(3), 37–39.

Mok, J. L. (1983). *Artists-in-Education Program of the National Endowment for the Arts using educational criticism and congruence.* Unpublished doctoral dissertation, New York University, New York.

Morrison, R. (1997, October 17). *Music-News.* American Music Conference.

Moses, M. (1994). *A case study analysis of the impact of the Wolf Trap Institute for Early Learning Through the Arts on select classroom teachers' abilities to integrate the performing arts into their educational curriculums.* Unpublished doctoral dissertation, Union Institute, Washington, D.C.

Munley, S. (1999). *The factors that affect policy formation processes in the arts: Education policies of the National Endowment for the Arts, 1965–1993.* Unpublished doctoral dissertation, Florida State University, Tallahassee.

Murfee, E. (1995). *Eloquent evidence: Arts at the core of learning.* Washington, DC: President's Committee on the Arts and the Humanities, National Assembly of State Arts Agencies, and the National Endowment for the Arts.

Murphy, J., & Jones, L. (1976). *Research in arts education: A federal chapter.* Washington, DC: U.S. Department of Health, Education and Welfare.

Myers, D. E. (1996). *Beyond tradition: Partnerships among orchestras, schools, and communities* (Cooperative Agreement DCA 95-12). Washington, DC: National Endowment for the Arts.

National Consortium for Arts Education. (2000, June). TE-TAC: *National goals and expectations.* Paper presented at the meeting of the Arts Education Partnership, Durham, NC.

National Endowment for the Arts. (1988). *Toward civilization: A report on arts education.* Washington, DC: U.S. Government Printing Office.

National Endowment for the Arts. (2000a). *Grants to organizations: Application guidelines, FY 2001.* Washington, DC: Author.

National Endowment for the Arts. (2000b, September 12). *NEA fact sheet: Arts education.* Washington, DC: Author. Retrieved November 15, 2000, from http://arts.endow.gov/learn/Facts/Artsed.html

National Endowment for the Arts & U.S. Department of Education. (1994). *Arts education research agenda for the future.* Washington, DC: U.S. Government Printing Office.

National Foundation on the Arts and Humanities Act of 1965, 20 U.S.C.A. § 954a et seq. (West 1968).

Netzer, D. (1978). *The subsidized muse.* New York: Cambridge University Press.

New England Foundation for the Arts & American Council for the Arts. (1983). *The arts go to school: An arts-in-education handbook.* New York: American Council for the Arts.

New NEA Arts-in-Education Program, The. (1986). *Arts Education Policy Review, 88*(2), 25–33.

Oates, W. E. (1999). An essay on fiscal federalism. *Journal of Economic Literature, 37,* 1120–1149.

Odendahl, T. J. (1990). *Charity begins at home: Generosity and self-interest among the philanthropic elite.* New York: Basic Books.

Pankratz, D. (1986). Aesthetic welfare, government, and educational policy. *Design for Arts in Education, 87*(6), 12–24.

Pankratz, D. B., & Mulcahy, K. V. (Eds.). (1989). *The challenge to reform arts education: What role can research play?* New York: American Council on the Arts.

Peacock, A. T. (1969). Welfare economics and public subsidies to the arts. *Manchester School of Economics and Social Studies, 37*(4), 323–335.

Posner, P. L., & Wrightson, M. T. (1996). Block grants: A perennial, but unstable, tool of government. *Publius, 26*(3), 87–108.

President's Committee on the Arts and Humanities and the Arts Education Partnership. (1999). *Gaining the arts advantage: Lessons from school districts that value arts education.* Washington, DC: Author.

Remer, J. (1990). *Changing schools through the arts.* New York: American Council for the Arts.

Robinson, M. (1999). *A theory of collaborative music education between higher education and urban public schools.* Unpublished doctoral dissertation, University of Rochester, New York.

Rush, J. C. (1997). The arts and education reform: Where is the model for teaching the arts? *Arts Education Policy Review, 98*(3), 2–9.

Schuster, J. M. (1985). The interrelationships between public and private funding of the arts in the United States. *Journal of Arts Management and Law, 14*(4), 77–105.

Schuster, J. M. (1987). Issues in supporting the arts through tax incentives. *Journal of Arts Management and Law, 16*(4), 31–50.

Schuster, J. M. (1999). The other side of the subsidized muse: Indirect aid revisited. *Journal of Cultural Economics, 23,* 51–70.

Smith, R. A. (1992). Policy for arts education: Whither the schools, whither the public and private sectors. In R. A. Smith & R. Berman (Eds.), *Public policy and the aesthetic interest: Critical essays on defining cultural and educational relations* (pp. 137–152). Urbana: University of Illinois Press.

Smith, R. A. (1995). The limits and costs of integration in arts education. *Arts Education Policy Review, 96*(5), 21–25.

Smith, T. A. (2000). *Chamber music presentations for early childhood audiences: Creating a developmentally appropriate model.* Doctoral dissertation, Eastman School of Music, University of Rochester, New York.

Steinberg, R. (1993). Does government spending crowd out donations? Interpreting the evidence. In A. Ben-Ner & B. Gui (Eds.), *The nonprofit sector in the mixed economy* (pp. 99–125). Ann Arbor: University of Michigan Press.

Task Force on Children's Learning and the Arts: Birth to Age Eight. (1998). *Young Children and the Arts: Making Creative Connections.* Washington, DC: Arts Education Partnership.

Thomas S. Kenan Institute for the Arts. (2000, June). *North Carolina A+ schools program.* Paper presented at the meeting of the Arts Education Partnership, Durham, NC.

Tiebout, C. (1956). A pure theory of local expenditures. *Journal of Political Economy, 64,* 416–424.

Udell, S. S. (1990). *An historical/descriptive study of the Wisconsin Arts Board and its involvement in arts education.* Unpublished doctoral dissertation, University of Wisconsin–Madison.

Undercofler, J. (1997). Music in America's schools: A plan for action. *Arts Education Policy Review, 98*(6), 15–19.

Welch, N., & Greene, A. (1995). *Schools, communities, and the arts: A research compendium* (Cooperative Agreement DCA 94-62). Washington, DC: National Endowment for the Arts.

Western States Arts Foundation. (1976). *A study of the poetry and visual arts components of the AIS Program.* Denver, CO: Author.

Wilson, B. (1997). *The quiet evolution: Changing the face of arts education.* Los Angeles: Getty Education Institute for the Arts.

Wilson, B. (2000). Achieving reform in local school districts: The systematic arts education project. *Arts Education Policy Review, 101*(4), 15–19.

Winner, E., & Cooper, M. (2000). Mute those claims: No evidence (yet) for a causal link between arts study and academic achievement. *Journal of Aesthetic Education, 34*(3–4), 11–76.

Wolf, C. (1979). A theory of nonmarket failure: Framework for implementation analysis. *Journal of Law and Economics, 22*(1), 107–139.

Wolf, C. (1993). *Markets or governments: Choosing between imperfect alternatives.* Cambridge, MA: MIT Press.

Wolf, D. P. (1997). *Scaling up: An evaluation of the Boston Music Education Collaborative and a plan for future development.* Cambridge, MA: Harvard Graduate School of Education, Performance Assessment Collaboratives for Education.

Wolf, T., & Wolf, D. P. (1991). *An evaluation and plan for education at the Kennedy Center: Final report.* Cambridge, MA: Wolf Organization.

Wyszomirski, M. J. (1982). Controversies in arts policymaking. In K. V. Mulcahy & C. R. Swaim (Eds.), *Public policy and the arts* (pp. 11–31). Boulder, CO: Westview.

The Evaluation of Arts Partnerships and Learning in and Through the Arts

48

HAL ABELES

MARY HAFELI

ROBERT HOROWITZ

JUDITH BURTON

Arts Partnerships

This chapter focuses on arts partnerships, that is, ways in which community-based arts organizations such as orchestras, museums, and other arts groups become involved with schools. Some arts partnerships provide enrichment opportunities that offer students a onetime experience with a community-based group, such as a trip to a museum or string quartet performance in the school auditorium. Our focus, however, is on comprehensive partnerships that may include a written curriculum, teacher development workshops, periodic visits to the school by "presenters" from the organization, resource materials provided to each teacher (e.g., compact discs, world instruments, photographs), and culminating activities such as attending a performance of an orchestra at the symphony hall. Specifically, this chapter focuses on partnerships in which arts instruction provided by a community-based arts group is used as a means to promote learning in the arts as well as in subject areas outside of the arts.

This chapter addresses four areas. First, it provides a background for arts partnerships that focus on learning through the arts. Second, the theoretical literature on transfer is presented, along with research on links between arts learning and learning in other subject areas. In this section, issues of establishing causal relationships and building confidence in the findings of research and evaluations are addressed. The third section of the chapter discusses these research design issues as they apply to exam-

ining student learning outcomes in the evaluation of arts partnership programs. The fourth section of the chapter presents practical issues related to evaluating these partnerships.

In this chapter, arts partnership instructional experiences are differentiated from school-based arts instruction that is led solely by a school-based arts specialist. School-based arts education tends to be systematic weekly (or more frequent) instructional activities focused primarily on helping students achieve the varied competencies articulated by a school or district arts curriculum or state or national arts standards. While not necessarily designed to be sequential in terms of curricular activities, some arts partnership programs provide as much or more instructional time than an arts specialist might provide in a school-based arts curriculum.

The number of partnerships between arts groups and schools has increased over the last 30 years or so. Some of these programs began soon after the establishment of the National Endowment for the Arts (NEA) and state arts agencies, which have historically provided funds for community-based arts activities in schools. At times, arts partnerships have been the sole providers of arts experiences for students in schools. For instance, during a period of approximately 25 years most elementary schools in New York City were without arts specialists. During this time, there was a rapid growth of arts organizations that provided outreach to schools in the form of visual and performing arts experiences for children. Likewise, in other parts of the country when budget circumstances eliminated music and other arts specialist positions, community-based arts groups sometimes stepped in as arts education providers. Today, in some schools, arts partnerships function in isolation from arts specialists, so that the arts instruction provided by the community arts groups is parallel, rather than complementary, to the ongoing arts curriculum. However, in an increasing number of schools arts partnerships work collaboratively with arts specialists. In these schools arts specialists may coordinate their curricula so that activities provided by community-based groups extend and deepen student learning in the arts.

The specific goals that arts organizations may adopt for their work with schools are multiple and varied. Some programs seem mainly to be aimed at increasing the visibility of the arts organization in the community, while for others the primary purpose may be to provide additional work opportunities for local artists. In some instances, arts groups have specific long-range audience development as a goal. However, many arts partnerships focus directly on learner-centered outcomes. These student-learning focuses include aesthetic education (e.g., the Lincoln Center Institute), developing arts understandings and skills (e.g., the Hartford Symphony Orchestra's Symphony in the Schools Program), and, in some cases, using the arts as a means to help students acquire knowledge and skills in other academic subjects (e.g., the Baltimore Symphony Orchestra's Arts Excel Program, the Cleveland Orchestra's Learning Through Music Program, and the Chicago Arts Partnerships in Education).

For programs that focus on student learning, program goals are usually directly related to the content focus of the arts group. Orchestras, for example, are often interested in teaching students about the instruments of the orchestra, and museums aim for students to learn about different artists, art mediums, and styles. During the 1990s, as schools faced increased pressure to improve student performance on general achievement measures, most aspects of the school curriculum and many external programs (e.g., after-school tutoring by community volunteers) focused on improving test scores. Community arts groups, through their partnerships with schools, participated in this trend, and many made efforts to design programs that use the arts as a means to help students acquire skills in nonarts areas, sometimes in an effort to influence students' performance on state mastery tests.

This focus on using the arts as a vehicle for learning in other subjects came at a time not only when schools were under pressure to improve test scores but also when research appeared to support a relationship between arts learning and learning in other subject areas. The results of several of these research studies (e.g., Gromko & Poorman, 1998; Hamblen, 1993; Rauscher, Shaw, & Ky, 1993)

became well known as the news media and arts-industry-related groups reported these results. As a consequence, many in the arts community as well as the general public seemed to accept without question this relationship between arts learning and learning in other subject areas. This broad acceptance is illustrated by a 1995 report by the President's Committee on the Arts and Humanities, which asserts, "Teaching the arts has a significant effect on overall success in school" (p. 5). The popularization of research that suggests connections between arts learning and learning in other areas encouraged arts organizations to develop arts partnerships around these instrumental outcomes. This new "learning through the arts" focus, which seemed to promise an improvement in students' academic performance, not surprisingly provided arts organizations with additional funding from agencies and foundations interested in supporting student achievement beyond the arts.

Learning in and Through the Arts

While some arts partnerships began to develop programs to meet the expanded goal of learning through the arts, there was little direction to be found from the research about how to design an arts-based curriculum that would promote such learning. The psychological literature on the theory of transfer also would appear to be useful for curriculum planners involved in these partnerships. However, this literature does not provide clear guidelines on how to develop curriculum that enables transfer. Many arts partnerships that have instrumental goals for student learning appear to be aimed at producing what might be considered the "direct transfer" of learning in an arts area, like music, to learning in another subject, such as science.

Theory of Specific Transfer

The study of transfer has a particular history within the educational psychology tradition, and efforts to sustain a consistent theory of "transfer of learning" or "transfer of training" have had mixed success. Transfer theory is often thought to have begun with Thorndike (Thorndike & Woodworth, 1901), who developed his theory of identical elements at the beginning of the 20th century. Before this, the doctrine of formal discipline held that the learning of challenging subjects like Latin or mathematics focused and disciplined the mind and that these mental skills could then be applied generally to other domains of learning. Thorndike articulated a more specific approach, focusing on the mastery of performance tasks that contained elements applicable to other learning situations. He proposed that a person trained in a task is more likely to be successful in a second task if the two activities shared very similar or common elements. Thorndike found that as tasks differed more widely, as they had fewer elements in common, there was less of a relationship in performance. Thus it might be plausible to assume transfer between reading and spelling, for instance, but not so likely from mathematics to Latin.

A dichotomy between a general approach to transfer theory, as represented by the doctrine of formal discipline, and the specific approach of Thorndike has held to this day. This can be observed when arts partnership programs aim for discipline-specific outcomes (such as improving students' writing skills) or general cognitive outcomes (such as developing creativity). For the past 30 years, the research on transfer has continued to produce other dichotomous models, including "vertical" and "lateral" transfer (Gagne, 1970), "near" and "far" transfer (Gick & Holyoak, 1987), and "high-road" and "low-road" transfer (Salomon & Perkins, 1989).

Theory of General Transfer

Though some arts partnerships seek to develop specific transfer of learning, others have oriented their programs to promote more general ways of thinking that are not discipline-specific but are instead shared among and across disciplines. Often, these general dispositions and characteristics seem to be both cognitive and social, or personal, dimensions of the learner. For example, in a program designed to develop artistic talent, Arts Connection, a partnership based in New York City, identified four general student outcomes:

- *flow:* a state of total absorption in which students are so completely involved in an activity that they lose track of time;
- *self-regulation:* when students are aware of their own learning process and select useful strategies to complete a task;
- *identity:* students beginning to see themselves as professional artists; and
- *resilience:* the ability to bounce back from adverse experiences. (Oreck, Baum, & McCartney, 1999, p. 69)

Such general outcomes are thought to be important characteristics of success both within and outside of the arts.

Eisner (1998) suggests that these kinds of general outcomes, seemingly cultivated through arts programs, are particularly important and that they are also especially difficult to assess or measure. He specifically identifies three dispositional outcomes:

- a willingness to imagine possibilities that are not now but might become,

- a desire to explore ambiguity, to be willing to forestall premature closure in pursuing resolutions, and
- the ability to recognize and accept the multiple perspectives and resolutions that work in the arts celebrates. (p. 15)

In a way similar to the preceding models, Burton, Horowitz, and Abeles (1999, 2000) also identified general outcomes of school-based arts education and arts partnership programs. Based on classroom observations, conversations with teachers, and a review of previous research and theoretical literature, they placed the potential outcomes of arts experiences into three broad categories—Cognitive Capacities, Socio-cultural Capacities, and Personal Learning Capacities (see table 48.1).

Under "Cognitive Capacities," the researchers identified eight general indicators of potential impact from arts learning. The first, "expression of ideas and feelings," is thought to be central to the artistic experience and widely applicable within other domains of learning. "Focused perception" refers to children's ability to attend to subject matter and thereby perceive subtleties, nuances, and distinctions. When a child learns to "make connections," he or she makes unspecified associations among diverse, prior, or ongoing learning experiences. This can develop into the ability to create "layered relationships," thereby constructing new and different relationships through a sense of flow of ideas and through making connections and associations among diverse forms of knowledge to create new unities. Other cognitive indicators identified by the researchers include "construction and organizing of meaning," the way in which children are able to distill new meaning from existing forms or relate new experiences to previous under-

Table 48.1 Potential Outcomes of Arts Experiences

Cognitive Capacities	Socio-Cultural Capacities	Personal Learning Capacities
Expression of ideas and feelings	Cooperative learning	Risk-taking
Focused perception	Compassion and empathy	Confidence
Make connections		Competence
Layered relationships		
Construction and organizing of meaning		
Multiple or alternative vantage points		
Imagining new possibilities		
Sensory learning		

Source: Burton, Horowitz, & Abeles, 1999.

standings, and the ability to take "multiple or alternative vantage points." This is defined as the means by which children perceive and understand various points of view or generate multiple meanings and interpretations. Additional cognitive indicators identified by the researchers were "imagining new possibilities" and "sensory learning."

In the area of "Socio-Cultural Capacities," Burton, Horowitz, and Abeles identified "cooperative learning" and the development of "compassion and empathy." The researchers also identified "Personal Learning Capacities" of impact from arts learning, including "risk-taking," "confidence," and a sense of "competence." As reported in the study, young people deeply engaged in the arts sometimes demonstrated ownership of learning. As they took charge of the learning process, students exhibited pride in the construction and presentation of their work. Finally, through the development of task persistence, they learned to focus, stick with, and succeed in challenging activities.

The theories and models of transfer presented earlier, including the contrasting specific and general views, have implications for arts partnership program developers who are working toward instrumental learning outcomes. It is important for those who design curricula to be clear about the model(s) of transfer on which they are basing their programs and instructional activities. If, on the one hand, a partnership seeks to develop a curriculum based on the "specifics" approach to transfer as described by Thorndike, then tasks or activities in an arts area (e.g., music) would have to share similar or common elements with tasks in another discipline (e.g., science). If, on the other hand, an arts partnership bases a curriculum within the "general" tradition of transfer theory, it is essential that students have ongoing opportunities to develop and practice those general "ways of thinking" and "habits of mind" identified as intended outcomes. For instance, if a curriculum is intended to develop students' awareness of multiple or alternative vantage points, instructional activities must be designed to provide sustained opportunities for students to perceive and understand various points of view and to generate multiple meanings and interpretations about works of art or music.

Studies That Explore the Impact of Arts Learning

Instrumental outcomes of arts learning in partnerships have been examined through program evaluations and research studies. Some of these have tried to approximate traditional experimental research designs through use of quantitative measures. Others have used qualitative research strategies, such as narrative description of teaching and learning activities and interviews with program participants. Some studies have used both quantitative and qual-

itative approaches. There is disagreement among researchers about the evidence necessary to establish a "link" or relationship, particularly a causal relationship, between arts activities and instrumental outcomes. For example, Eisner (1998) and Winner and Hetland (2000a) critique correlational studies that claim causality (see Winner & Hetland, 2000a, pp. 4–5). They point to the need for more traditional causal research designs that employ appropriate comparison groups.

Nevertheless, over the last decade a number of reports have suggested causal links between study in the arts and instrumental outcomes. In 1995 the NEA published *Schools, Communities, and the Arts: A Research Compendium*, which is an annotated bibliography of selected research on the effects of arts teaching and learning. Several of the reports are evaluations of arts partnership programs. Redfield (1990), for example, found that students perceived improvements in higher order thinking, communication, and socialization skills after participation in an artist-in-residence program. The study used a pre-/postprogram evaluation design that compared data collected at the end of artist residencies to a variety of baseline data. The study also used several qualitative techniques, such as classroom observations and focus group interviews. The researchers collected report card grades from preresidency and postresidency marking periods. While grades following the residencies were "significantly" higher than those from the previous grading period, the researchers appropriately cautioned against attributing these gains directly to the residency program. As is typical with evaluation projects, the study did not use a comparison group, as recommended by Eisner and Winner and Hetland. The researchers in Redfield's study's caution in interpreting their findings illustrates both the importance and the difficulty of ruling out rival explanations when a traditional causal research design is not used.

Some researchers advocate building a case for causality by combining both empirical findings and theoretical explanations. Catterall, Chapleau, and Iwanaga (1999) state that causation can be claimed if research is supported by "sound theory, supportive evidence, and ruling out rival explanations" (p. 16). Where researchers are likely to disagree is on the strength or plausibility of a particular theory and on the strategies used to gather and analyze "supportive evidence." Catterall, Chapleau, and Iwanaga used the National Educational Longitudinal Survey (NELS: 88) to track over 25,000 students in American schools for 10 years. They reported that students with high arts involvement outperformed low-arts students on various academic measures and that high arts involvement has a greater sustained impact on these measures for students from low-income backgrounds. The researchers also reported significant relationships between achievement in music and achievement in mathematics and between involvement in theater and gains in reading proficiency, motivation, self-concept, and empathy for others. Though researchers who believe causation is demonstrated only through "true" experimental designs would not place confidence in these correlation findings, Catterall et al. maintain that the three-stage approach establishes causation and provides confidence in their findings.

Burton, Horowitz, and Abeles (1999, 2000) found that arts-rich environments support learning through the development of cognitive, social, and personal capacities discussed earlier in this chapter. This study also did not use a traditional causal research design. To build confidence in the findings from the quantitative portion of the study, the researchers used theory to guide both the design and analysis. Qualitative strategies were employed as a means both to support the quantitative findings and to better understand the results. Using both qualitative and correlational strategies, the researchers compared the experience and performance of students in "high-arts" and "low-arts" groups. They reported that students in the high-arts group were more likely to excel in measures of creativity, expression, risk taking, imagination, and academic self-concept.

In a preliminary field study, the researchers interviewed classroom and arts teachers in 29 schools to understand their perceptions of arts learning and its impact. An analysis of interview data revealed that teachers most often described the impact of arts learning on general capacities, such as creativity, expression, self-esteem, and risk taking, rather than on improvement in specific academic skills. Quantitative measures were selected or developed based on constructs described by the teachers and supported by previous research or theory.

The main study involved 12 schools with 2,400 fourth-, fifth-, seventh-, and eighth-grade students. The students were asked to reconstruct their arts education history. The children were then assigned to quartiles, which represented high arts-exposure, low arts-exposure, and average-exposure groups. The same children were tested in creative thinking abilities and self-concept, and their teachers rated their perceptions of the students' capacity for expression, risk taking, imagination, and cooperative learning. Subsequent analysis revealed that the high-arts group outscored the low-arts group in every measure.

Burton, Horowitz, and Abeles also used qualitative methods to elaborate on the findings of the quantitative component of study. They interviewed administrators, arts teachers, teaching artists, and classroom teachers and observed classes, examined artwork, and watched student performances. Through systematic analysis of this qualitative data, they identified and defined various cognitive, social, and personal learning dimensions that were considered potential indicators of transfer from arts learning.

One quantitative measure, the *Torrance Test of Creativity* (TTCT), yielded scores in fluency, originality, resistance to closure, and elaboration.[1] The high-arts group had 37% of the top scorers in overall creativity, as opposed to 12% in the low-arts group.[2] The largest differences in TTCT results were in the creative dimensions of resistance to closure (35% for the high-arts group compared to 16% for the low-arts group) and elaboration (41% compared to 11%). These findings were consistent with results from the qualitative inquiry. In interviews, teachers described children engaged in the arts as having learned to focus longer and more intently on tasks, acquired "discipline," and applied more detail in their arts and academic work.

The high-arts children also outscored the low-arts group in measures of expression, risk taking, and imagination.[3] Again, the qualitative data supported these results, particularly in the areas of "expression" and "risk-taking." In a measure of academic self-concept,[4] the high-arts group outperformed the low-arts group (41% compared to 18%). Similar results were obtained on individual reading, mathematics, and general school self-concept scores.[5]

Each of the studies presented here looked at the impact of students' arts experiences on general capacities or dispositions, such as risk taking. This places them in the "general" tradition of transfer research. However, Catterall et al.'s study also examined the impact of students' arts experiences on learning in specific disciplines. This study can be placed in the "specifics" tradition of transfer research as well. None of the studies reported here used traditional causal research designs. School-based research does not typically provide the necessary conditions for experimental research designs. Because evaluations of arts partnership programs take place in naturalistic school settings, they are likely to have the same research design limitations as the studies reviewed earlier.

Evaluating Arts Partnership Programs— Strategies That Examine Learning in and Through the Arts

Given the limitations of school-based research in establishing causation and considering the zeal with which arts partnerships attempt to improve students' academic performance through the arts, evaluators of arts partnership programs face several challenges. The first role for evaluators is, as a team that works with the arts organization, to clarify goals for the program and for the evaluation. When an arts partnership focuses on learning in and through the arts, identifying the model of transfer on which to base the project should be an essential component of establishing and refining goals. Goals should focus on the anticipated outcomes for the participants in the program, such as students, as well as on the outcomes for classroom and specialist teachers and teaching artists and performers.

Clarifying Program Goals

Initially some arts partnerships may have broadly stated instrumental goals, for example, "to improve learning throughout the curriculum." These broadly stated goals are of minimal use for evaluation purposes. In many cases, the persuasive language used in program funding proposals and other development documents needs to be refined and clarified to implement and evaluate the program. In initial discussions with an arts organization, evaluators need to help the group to focus goals so that they can be used for curriculum development and evaluation. It is important that the articulated goals are both meaningful to the members of the partnership and useful for the evaluation.

Other arts partnerships may identify very specific instrumental goals, such as "to improve scores on state mastery tests." Goals like these seem particularly attractive to arts partnerships for at least two reasons. First, schools are under considerable pressure to improve mastery test scores, so an arts partnership that intends to improve test scores is appealing to principals and teachers. Second, the quantitative nature of the tests and the increased importance given to these measures by local and national politicians suggest visible and external value. In order to achieve such specific goals, a curriculum must be designed to teach very specific concepts and skills. This suggests that the curriculum would be based on a theory of specifics or direct transfer. One of the challenges in designing such a curriculum is to ensure that it provides authentic and relevant arts learning experiences that will support or lead to learning in other disciplines. It is possible that attempts to design a specifics-based curriculum may instead lead arts partnership programs, in the words of Winner and Hetland, to "teach the arts in ways that will enhance academic (rather than artistic) learning" (2000b, p. 6). Winner and Hetland caution that "teaching the physics of sound in music class rather than the aesthetics of sound" is not an instructional activity that gets at the "heart of the arts." Close examination of the curricula of arts partnerships that focus on specific transfer goals in an effort to improve students' test scores provides examples of lessons that illustrate the problem Winner and Hetland describe.

Some arts partnerships focus on developing more general capacities in students, for example, creativity or "higher order thinking." Perspectives like Gardner's (1983) theory of multiple intelligence, which provides a view of the mind actively creating connections and associations across distinct ways of thinking, have served as an impetus for many of these programs. Further support for this more general approach to transfer is found in the writings of

Burton (1995), Gardner (1983), Greene (1995), and Perkins (1987). They suggest that

> capacities usually identified as "engendered in arts learning" such as creativity, imagination, and critical and divergent thinking are also dimensions that are widely held to characterize thinking in other subject domains. In other words, perceptions of transfer may well be, in part, a function of the degree to which different disciplines share certain cognitive elements, dispositions, or ways of thinking. (Burton, Horowitz, & Abeles, 1999, p. 1)

In helping an arts partnership to clarify goals such as developing imagination or creativity, the evaluator has to ensure that the constructs are defined in a way such that the participants feel comfortable, a curriculum can be developed around the stated goals, and the intended outcomes can be examined in the evaluation. Constructs that are not well defined pose challenges to developing a curriculum and designing instructional approaches and strategies that will lead to such outcomes. Specifying "workable" goals can be problematic, as some involved in the program may want to hold onto a broad conceptualization of a construct such as creativity, while evaluators may feel the need to identify specific student characteristics, dispositions, or behaviors that may indicate the construct's presence in student learning.

The expectations of the arts partnership staff for demonstrating the impact of the program are often different from what may be possible. Some program developers may feel the need to "prove" that their efforts are successful by using some criterion that approximates their long-term goal (e.g., to improve student learning throughout the curriculum of the school). This need to prove or document success may be driven by the organization's perceived mandate to "show" that donors' funds are being used effectively. There is a natural pressure to demonstrate success, so that funding for the project will be continued. It is important for evaluators to help program planners understand that a variety of ways can be used to document the outcomes related to program goals and that direct "causation" may be difficult or impossible to establish.

Program Evaluation Design Issues

The evaluation of a program in which instruction provided by an arts group is used as a means to promote instrumental outcomes must consider the research design issues discussed earlier in this chapter. In programs that seek to improve students' scores on state-mandated mastery tests, the skills and understandings required on these tests often seem distant or remote from the actual activities of the program. In these cases, it may not be clear how the different activities associated with the partnership will facilitate this "transfer" of skills or understandings. Goals like this may appear to make the evaluators' task simple (i.e., monitoring test scores). However, providing evidence of a link between arts experiences offered by an arts partnership program and scores on a mastery test that measures achievement in areas such as language arts and mathematics is often not possible, at least with the limitations of traditional causal research design typically encountered in school-based evaluation projects.

The school-based context in which evaluation projects take place presents at least two significant hurdles when determining how to describe student impact in programs that aim to improve students' scores on statewide tests. First, in a traditional causal research approach to evaluating program impact a comparison group is required to help rule out rival explanations for any results observed. In school settings, such comparison groups are difficult, if not impossible, to find. Often programs involve entire schools, so nonparticipating classrooms within schools are not available for comparisons. Some researchers use cross-school comparison with similar schools in the community or employ a pooled or average performance of all the other schools in the community or larger geographical area. Though such comparisons, often combined with a trend analysis of the scores of the comparative group over several years, have been reported (e.g., Catterall & Waldorf, 1999), neither of these approaches fully satisfies the causal research criterion of a comparison group of randomly assigned students. In addition, it is difficult to find principals of nonparticipating schools who are willing to sacrifice instructional time to facilitate evaluators' need for a comparison group.

The second hurdle presented by school-based contexts is that there are often rival explanations for possible changes in mastery test scores. For instance, schools devote considerable resources to initiatives designed to improve students' scores on these mastery tests. These initiatives often include targeted curricula (in some states, the companies responsible for the development of the tests are now producing textbooks to teach for the test), after-school tutoring, and community-based programs that are designed to improve test scores. These initiatives provide compelling and competing explanations for any improvement observed in the scores. In such settings, it is impossible to attribute change in test scores to any one factor. These design issues, present in most arts partnership settings, limit the use of traditional causal research approaches for program evaluations. Consequently, it is very difficult, if not impossible, for evaluators to demonstrate a direct connection between arts partnership program activities and students' scores on state mastery tests.

Because of the school-based, real-world nature of arts partnership programs, traditional causal research and evaluation designs may have limited feasibility and, therefore,

value. Consequently, evaluators must consider alternative approaches when examining whether or not "logical links" exist between program activities and learning in other disciplines. Such methods would use multiple perspectives and data sources to provide evidence. Evaluators may generate both quantitative and qualitative information to help construct a complete case. Winner and Hetland (2000a) seem to support alternative research strategies when they suggest that with qualitative measures, researchers and evaluators can develop an understanding of "whether the arts lead to deepened understanding of—and engagement in—non-arts areas" (p. 6).

Approaches to evaluation such as the Responsive Evaluation Model described by Stake (1975) and by Guba and Lincoln (1981), provide strategies grounded in qualitative methods that should be considered when evaluating arts partnerships with goals that focus on "learning through the arts." Previously in this chapter, issues of establishing confidence in quantitative findings were reviewed. Researchers who advocate qualitative approaches to evaluation also must consider how to design evaluation projects that build confidence in findings. For instance, Guba and Lincoln (1981, p. 103) describe strategies for establishing "scientific rigor" in qualitative evaluations. They underscore the importance of establishing trustworthiness in the information provided and in the interpretations drawn from it. Guba and Lincoln identify four criteria for establishing scientific "rigor" in naturalistic research: *truth value*: establishing confidence in the findings; *applicability*: generalizing the findings to other contexts; *consistency*: generating the same findings through replication; and *neutrality*: eliminating biases and motives.

When one is undertaking a qualitative evaluation of an arts partnership program, the essential characteristic of the work should be to provide multiple perspectives of the program. Presenting multiple perspectives involves obtaining information about the program by using different information-gathering strategies, such as classroom observations and the review of student work, as well as interviews of different individuals involved in the project, like students, teachers, teaching artists, and program staff. It is only through the use of a number of sources and perspectives that a complete picture of the program will begin to appear. Multiple perspectives can also mean the use of an evaluation team rather than an individual evaluator. A team of evaluators can help address some of the demands of qualitative methods, an issue that is discussed at length by Guba and Lincoln (1981).

Practical Issues in the Evaluation of Arts Partnership Programs

Evaluation is an increasingly important concern for arts partnership programming in schools. Nevertheless, it is often the last factor that arts organizations consider when developing programs. Many arts partnerships initially focus on organizing and managing the delivery of services to schools. As arts partnerships mature, these services can be complex and multidimensional, including curriculum development, artist preparation, and teacher workshops. Because evaluation is often the last factor to be considered, it is also often underfunded and is at times not well integrated into the original program design. While evaluators are often initially selected because they present the image of the outside objective expert, evaluators should be seen as part of the program team, working with program planners and participants to help improve the program and negotiating strategies that will be useful in illustrating the impact of the program on participants.

We mentioned earlier that, for program evaluators, clarifying goals and defining constructs is a necessary first step in the process of designing an evaluation. It is also important for the evaluation team to help the arts partnership staff members negotiate among constituents and stakeholders the modification, clarification, and refinement of program goals, as the evaluation must address multiple audiences.[6]

The process of clarifying goals should also help focus the curriculum development process in an arts partnership program. The curriculum development and the evaluation process must be closely tied. If the arts-based curriculum expects to affect other disciplines directly (specific transfer), does it have a particular theory, model, approach, or guideline in which it is grounded? What strategies does the curriculum use to affect the acquisition of skills and knowledge in other disciplines? Does the partnership have a means of ensuring that a well-designed curriculum will be delivered by fully prepared artists and/or teachers? These questions focus on the quality of the arts partnership instructional experiences, and they are critical if the partnership is expected to have an impact on student learning and achievement.

One means of formalizing communication around the goals is an evaluation proposal. After some initial discussion, a draft proposal for the program evaluation can provide a vehicle both for the evaluators to concretize their understanding of the goals of the program and for the arts group to respond. Because evaluation is seldom part of the planning process, one of the start-up challenges for the evaluation team is to help the program planners refine and target goals while simultaneously initiating the evaluation.

When programs are implemented, one immediate task for the program staff is refining the operation of the program. This should help to address the question of the quality of the teaching and learning experiences provided by the program. King, Morris, and Fitz-Gibbon (1987) point out that one objective of implementation studies is to describe, or document, the program. They suggest that the evaluation report may be the only document that provides an adequate description of the program for those who may wish to replicate it.

Evaluators of arts partnerships must develop strategies for organizing the documentation and reporting of the program outcomes. The organization an evaluator decides to use needs to reflect the concerns of the different audiences for the evaluation, for example, funders, participants, sponsoring arts organization, and principals. Another challenge is to provide information for different audiences that will be viewed as authentic and that will instill confidence, so that the evaluators' interpretations are seen as credible. This is best done by providing multiple perspectives of the program.

One approach to organizing and reporting outcomes is to describe the program's impact on each of the participant groups, including teachers, students, schools, school systems, arts organizations, and teaching artists. The evaluation might look at several dimensions of the impact on each of these groups. Do teachers, for example, develop new instructional strategies and new interest in music? While determining the effect of the program on each of the participating groups should be part of a comprehensive evaluation, students are the primary participants in these programs. Student impact is often *the* factor that audiences for the evaluation use in judging the success of the program.

Identifying student outcomes that should be examined requires a careful review of program planning documents, multiple conversations with program planners and participants, and observation of the program in action. Initially, classroom observations may serve as a key to understanding what student outcomes are possible through the program. By observing teaching artists' presentations and teachers' lessons in classrooms, evaluators can begin to identify possible student outcomes related to the program's curriculum materials and goals. Observation reports that describe what was presented and resulting student activities can provide audiences with an understanding of avenues for potential student learning. Observation and interview protocols, as well as training for evaluators in the use of these instruments, will increase the reliability of the information gathered.

Information regarding the impact of the program on participant groups, such as students and teachers, should be gathered from multiple sources. Classroom teachers, for example, are an important source of information about student learning. Arts partnerships often rely on teachers to help students make connections between arts learning and learning in other disciplines. Teachers can provide evaluators with descriptions of the kinds of student learning they believe may be taking place as a result of the lessons they teach through the program, what connections they see being made. Teachers and evaluators can collaborate to develop ways of gathering data that describe what students are learning as a consequence of the lessons provided by the program, both in the arts and in other subject areas.

Students are also an important source of information and may provide evaluators with clues as to where to look for learning across disciplines. Students may be able to describe connections they have made between disciplines. For example, they may be able to relate how a visiting musician talked about patterning in music and may be able to connect that presentation to learning about patterns in math. Along with teachers and students, principals and parents may also provide information about the impact of the program on students. Ultimately, the goal of the evaluation team is to piece together a picture of student learning that results from the program, from as many perspectives and sources as are available.

Implications

The interest of arts partnerships in focusing on issues of transfer or learning through the arts comes at a time when educators, particularly at the elementary school level, are emphasizing learning across disciplines. When an arts organization develops a curriculum that focuses on interdisciplinary learning, it increases the likelihood that classroom teachers will value the resources and use them in their classrooms.

In the classroom, teachers who use interdisciplinary materials may be attempting to teach for transfer. Evaluators of programs in which teachers teach for transfer are obligated to describe the process in detail and to speculate, along with teachers and program developers, about outcomes that students may be able to demonstrate as a result of these experiences.

As indicated earlier, researchers and evaluators do not agree regarding strategies for establishing confidence in the findings of research or evaluations in the area of learning in and through the arts. Winner and Hetland (2000a) advocate the need for more "theory-driven, quasi-experimental research with better-conceived comparison groups" (p. 7). They, as well as other researchers, call for the use of qualitative methods as a means to better understand learning in and through the arts. Recognizing that evaluations take place in natural school settings, we believe that a combination of strategies is most useful. These should include quantitative methods designed to approximate accepted research designs and to rule out rival explanations for findings. Qualitative methods should also be used, to document and describe the teaching and learning process. These qualitative descriptions will enhance understanding of student learning in and through the arts.

It is important for evaluators to discourage arts partnerships from focusing on goals like improving scores on state mastery tests, as it is difficult to establish with confidence links between partnership activities and such scores. Evaluators should consider documenting more general ways of thinking and learning that may be developed as a result of arts partnership experiences. These could include cognitive dimensions such as *focused perception* and *construction and organization of meaning,* sociocultural dimensions such as *cooperative learning,* and personal learning dimensions such as *risk taking* or those presented by other researchers and theorists. We suspect that these ways of thinking and learning are good places to look for and understand the student outcomes of arts partnerships.

NOTES

1. *Fluency* represents the number of ideas or solutions that a person generates when exposed to a stimulus or problem. *Originality* refers to the unusual quality of responses, while *elaboration* refers to the imagination and exposition of detail. *Resistance to closure* represents the ability to keep open to new possibilities long enough to make the mental leap that makes original ideas possible (Torrance, Ball, & Safter, 1992).

2. The researchers identified the upper 25% of top scorers within each measure and then determined the percentage of those top scorers within both the high- and low-arts groups. A similar analysis was performed for the other quantitative measures.

3. The high-arts group had 36% of the top "expression" scores, compared to 9% in the low-arts group. The high group had 37% of the top "risk-taking" scores, compared to 11% in the low group. In "imagination," the high group had 41% of top scores, while the low group had 14%.

4. The Self-Description Questionnaire.

5. Reading self-concept results indicated 40% of top scorers in the high-arts group compared to 20% in the low group; and in math, 30% compared to 15%. In the general school self-concept scale, 36% were in the high group and 19% in the low group.

6. See Stecher and Davis (1988), *How to Focus an Evaluation.*

REFERENCES

Burton, J. M. (1995, March). *On adolescent thinking in the arts.* Paper presented at the meeting of the National Art Education Association, Houston, TX.

Burton, J., Horowitz, R., & Abeles, H. (1999). Learning in and through the arts. In E. Fiske (Ed.), *Champions of change: The impact of the arts on learning: Curriculum implications* (pp. 35–46). Washington, DC: Arts Education Partnership and the President's Committee on the Arts and the Humanities.

Burton, J., Horowitz, R., & Abeles, H. (2000). Learning in and through the arts: The question of transfer. *Studies in Art Education, 41*(3), 228–257.

Catterall, J. S., Chapleau, R., & Iwanaga, J. (1999). Involvement in the arts and human development: General involvement and intensive involvement in music and theater arts. In E. Fiske (Ed.), *Champions of change: The impact of the arts on learning* (pp. 1–18). Washington, DC: Arts Education Partnership and the President's Committee on the Arts and the Humanities.

Catterall, J., & Waldorf, L. (1999). Chicago arts partnerships in education: Summary evaluation. In E. Fiske (Ed.), *Champions of change: The impact of the arts on learning* (pp. 47–62). Washington, DC: Arts Education Partnership and the President's Committee on the Arts and the Humanities.

Eisner, E. (1998) Does experience in the arts boost academic achievement? *Art Education, 51*(1), 7–15.

Gagne, R. M. (1970). *The conditions of learning.* New York: Holt.

Gardner, H. (1983). *Frames of mind: The theory of multiple intelligences.* New York: Basic Books.

Gick, M. L., & Holyoak, K. J. (1987). The cognitive basis for knowledge transfer. In S. M. Cormier & J. D. Hagman (Eds.), *Transfer of learning* (pp. 239–260). New York: Academic Press.

Greene, M. (1995). *Releasing the imagination: Essays on education, the arts, and social change.* San Francisco: Jossey-Bass.

Gromko, J. E., & Poorman, A. S. (1998). The effect of music training on preschoolers' spatial-temporal task performance. *Journal of Research in Music Education, 46*(2), 173–181.

Guba, E. G., & Lincoln, Y. S. (1981). *Effective evaluation: Improving the usefulness of evaluation results through responsive and naturalistic approaches.* San Francisco: Jossey-Bass.

Hamblen, K. A. (1993). Theories and research that support art instruction for instrumental objectives. *Theory Into Practice, 32*(4), 191–198.

King, J. A., Morris, L. L., & Fitz-Gibbon, C. T. (1987). *How to assess program implementation.* Newbury Park, CA: Sage.

Oreck, B., Baum, S., & McCartney, H. Artistic talent development for urban youth: The promise and the challenge. (1999). In E. Fiske (Ed.), *Champions of change: The impact of the arts on learning: Curriculum implications.* Washington, DC: Arts Education Partnership and the President's Committee on the Arts and the Humanities.

Perkins, D. (1987). The arts as occasions of intelligence. *Educational Researcher, 45*(4), 36–43.

President's Committee on the Arts and the Humanities. (1995). *Eloquent evidence: Arts at the core of learning.* Washington, DC: National Endowment for the Arts.

Rauscher, F. H., Shaw, G. L., & Ky, K. N. (1993). Music and spatial task performance. *Nature, 365*(6447), 611.

Redfield, D. L. (1990). *Evaluating the broad educational impact of an arts education program: The case of the Music Center of Los Angeles County's Artists-in-Residence Program Center for the Study of Evaluation.* Los Angeles: UCLA Graduate School of Education.

Salomon, G., & Perkins, D. N. (1989). Rocky roads to transfer: Rethinking mechanisms of a neglected phenomenon. *Educational Psychologist, 24*(2), 113–142.

Stake, R. E. (1975). *Evaluating the arts in education: A responsive approach.* Columbus, OH: Merrill.

Stecher, B., & Davis, W. A. (1988). *How to focus an evaluation.* Newbury Park, CA: Sage.

Thorndike, E. L., & Woodworth, R. S. (1901). The influence of improvement in our mental functions upon the efficiency of another function. *Psychological Review, 9*, 374–382.

Torrance, E. P., Ball, O. E., & Safter, H. T. (1992). *Torrance tests of creative thinking: Streamlined scoring guide to figural A and B.* Bensenville, IL: Scholastic Testing Service.

Winner, E., & Hetland, L. (2000a). The arts in education: Evaluating the evidence for a causal link. *Journal of Aesthetic Education, 34*(3–4), 3–9.

Winner, E., & Hetland, L. (2000b, November). Does studying the arts enhance academic achievement? *Education Week, 6.*

The "Use and Abuse" of Arts Advocacy and Its Consequences for Music Education

49

CONSTANCE BUMGARNER GEE

In 1973 Jacques Barzun, professor of history at Columbia University, gave a series of six lectures at the National Gallery of Art titled "The Use and Abuse of Art." He explained the origin of the series title in his first lecture, "Why Art Must Be Challenged." Barzun had paraphrased the title of an essay written by Nietzsche, "The Use and Abuse of History," which translated more accurately would mean "The Advantages and Disadvantages or 'Worth' and 'Un-worth' of history in relation to life." Nietzsche, Barzun noted, "came to the conclusion that the historical sense under certain conditions weakens the sense of life." Barzun (1974) informed his audience that throughout the lecture series:

> we shall be asking ourselves whether there may not be un-suspected disadvantages in both our formal and our casual absorption of art—even in our habitual modes of talk about it—all this in order to reach a conclusion about its value and its drawbacks *for life* at the present time. (pp. 3–4)

The primary question I will address in this essay is: In what ways might arts advocacy—what we proclaim art will do for the individual and society in return for investments of time, love, and money—weaken our sense and valuing of art in relation to life and of arts education in relation to learning? To paraphrase Barzun paraphrasing Nietzsche: Might there not be unsuspected disadvantages in our casual absorption, acceptance, and reiteration of promulgated "truths" about the public uses, purposes, and benefits of art? All this in order to reach a conclusion about the value and drawbacks of arts advocacy *for music education* at the present time!

Why Arts Advocacy Must Be Challenged

Advocacy is to many arts activists what art theory was to the cultural intelligentsia of much of the 20th century. Tom Wolfe once wrote of being "jerked alert" from the "warm bath" of the Sunday *New York Times* when he read the following passage by art critic Hilton Kramer:

> Realism does not lack its partisans, but it does rather con-spicuously lack a persuasive theory. And given the nature of our intellectual commerce with works of art, to lack a persuasive theory is to lack something crucial—the means by which our experience of individual works is joined to our understanding of the values they signify. (Wolfe, 1975, p. 4)

Kramer, you see, had given the game away. He had said, in more words than less: "Frankly, these days, without a theory to go with it, I can't *see* a painting" (p. 6). The Word had finally superseded the visual art object. Nowadays it is the Advocated Word that provides the "persua-sive theory" for the support of the arts within the public domain—that is, the means by which to comprehend and measure the general significance and specific uses of art for various public purposes. Organized advocacy initiatives in-form us how to talk and think about art in relation to "quality of life," "community cohesion," "economic im-pact," and "education reform."

Of course all of those commonly cited public-minded purposes are interwoven, multilayered, and, more often than not, interdependent. Certainly for many Americans a good quality of life means having a nice home in a safe, attractive neighborhood. It means living in a place where there are a variety of experiences to enjoy and having the money and time to take advantage of those experiences. Most of us still believe that someone who is willing to work hard has a chance of attaining that American Dream. Yet we are also convinced that someone who has a good education has a tremendous advantage over someone who has a poor education. Obviously, a community with good schools is more desirable than one with poor schools—the economics are better; the quality of life is better; people feel better about themselves, their children, and their neighbors. Over the past few decades, however, the importance of good schools in the United States has come to mean much more than the quality of life available to an individual or found within a given community. Good schools, according to our political and industry leaders, have become a matter of national security, as it is through the education of our citizenry that we are to maintain our "global competitiveness." Being economically superior (or at least competitive) means being able to hold onto a valued way of life in a chaotic, uncertain world. It means being able to perpetuate the American Dream for ourselves, our children, and our children's children, that is, securing ourselves as a nation for the present and future. The various domains of public policy perpetually engage and influence one another from issues that pertain to quality of life and community cohesion, to education, to local, national, and global economies. It is clearly advantageous, perhaps even essential, to be able to associate one's cause with high-stake public concerns. No less is true for the advocate who seeks to elevate the status and funding of the arts.

Most of us who have been educated about and have experience in one or more art forms would readily agree that the arts (fine, "high," popular, and in-between) contribute to some extent to the preceding concerns. Those who have not had much education about or experience with the arts might, at worst, simply not care very much about the subject. Consequently, it is "access" to the arts through repeated exposure, direct experience, and formal schooling that arts advocates believe is key to the civic-minded arts enlightenment of and fiscal support from the general public.

Some of us might also hold another premise: that nationwide accessibility to a quality arts education throughout the elementary and secondary grades is the single most effective, efficient, and democratic way to make it possible for everyone to derive the private and public benefits of the arts. Whether one's primary advocacy incentive is that better and more school and community arts programming is to improve education or to build happier, more stable communities or that better and more arts education is to improve the status and support of the arts, the "improvement" of arts education is central. Politicians may or may

not think of arts education in any of those terms. Yet one thing is certain: As far as arts funding goes, funding for education-oriented ventures (especially where children and the "underserved" are concerned) is viewed by Republicans and Democrats alike as a reasonable and largely uncontroversial expenditure of small amounts of public monies and larger amounts of political endorsement. For all those reasons, references to "education reform" and "school improvement" through in-school and after-school arts education and arts in education programming are highly visible, loudly audible parts of the arts activist's lexicon.

The motivations for prominently including education reform in the arts advocacy litany of public purposes are easy to understand. Exactly how various types of arts education programming advance broader public purposes through more specific promises of higher SAT scores and graduation rates; lower truancy rates; increased self-esteem and multicultural understanding; better workplace, math, reading, and writing skills; and greater self-discipline is less understood. Even so, many arts educators and arts advocates believe sincerely that those frequently cited outcomes and attributes are desirable and deliverable parts of the arts education package. What is hardly understood at all, however, is changes in the content and practice of arts education that may need to occur if those specific goals for education reform and student achievement are to be realized. What are the meanings, manifestations, and consequences of the Advocated Word for K–12 arts education in general and for music education specifically? If we are sincere in our conviction that arts education can and should promote those outcomes, then we need to consider the commitments that will need to be made to move more deliberately toward those ends.

I will address the following questions:

- What do the messages and methods of organized arts advocacy campaigns tell us about the character and worth of arts education in general, and music education specifically?
- What types of K–12 music education programs need to be developed and implemented to ensure delivery of promised outcomes?
- Do those programs provide what is most important for students to learn about music? Are those types of programs ones with which music educators want to be identified?
- What are the benefits and what are the drawbacks of the arts education community's reliance on and reiteration of the Advocated Word?

The questions will be explored by first reviewing the advocacy statements of a cross-section of arts and arts education organizations about the purposes and payoffs of K–12 arts education, with particular attention to music education. Assuming that those claims are largely desirable, it will be instructive to imagine what types of elementary and secondary music programs would most effectively manifest promised outcomes. At the same time, possible discrepancies need to be considered between highly publicized characteristics, purposes, and outcomes of music education and the more private values and priorities of music educators.

The Advocated Word

In a two-part article published in the March/April and May/June 1999 issues of *Arts Education Policy Review,* I reviewed and analyzed the advocacy statements and strategies of arts service and funding organizations such as Americans for the Arts, the National Endowment for the Arts (NEA), the President's Committee on the Arts and the Humanities, the Arts Education Partnership, the National Assembly of State Arts Agencies, the Kennedy Center's Alliance for Arts Education, and the Getty Education Institute for the Arts. The title "For You Dear—Anything!" characterized my findings and conclusions. I found that all manner of social welfare, academic, and economic outcomes were promised in return for fiscal support of various types of out-of-school ("community-based"), in-school, and after-school arts programs. For reasons of economic and political survival, increasing numbers of arts organizations and groups were offering "education services" to K–12 students and "professional development opportunities" to teachers. Moreover, in order to garner greater political clout and fiscal support, most of the organizations named here purposefully confused learning outcomes associated with years of regular arts study with intermittent arts "experiences" and exposure. The arts advocacy literature reviewed was replete with the following claims:

- K–12 education can be "transformed through the arts."
- The resources and services of arts organizations and professional artists (made available through "state and local arts education partnerships") are the key factors in ensuring the success of that transformation.
- Artists and arts institutions have an essential and central position in all aspects of K–12 arts education.
- Every school must hire music, dance, theater, and visual arts teachers as well as musicians, dancers, actors, and artists in order to transform/reform general education and to provide all students with the quality of arts education they ought to receive.
- Youth participation in community arts programs results in much of the same types of academic achievement and positive dispositions toward learning that have been correlated with students' steady enrollment in elementary and secondary school arts courses. (Gee, 1999b)

This section explores whether or not the promotional messages and tactics of the arts advocacy leadership have changed over the past two years. I will also consider the ways in which the advocacy priorities of several prominent music and music education organizations are similar to and differ from the priorities reflected in the messages cited earlier.

Many of the sources used for this summary and analysis can be accessed easily over the Internet through arts and arts education organization home pages and through the hundreds of Web site links that connect a vast network of arts-, arts education–, and arts therapy–oriented groups, programs, and projects. Printed reports and other arts organization–generated advocacy materials are advertised regularly in professional newsletters and journals, at conferences, and through the Internet. Some must be purchased; others are sent by request free-of-charge. Additional materials and information (on-line, faxed, and posted) are available to members of Americans for the Arts, the American Symphony Orchestra League (ASOL), the American Association of Museums, MENC (Music Educators National Conference): the National Association for Music Education, and the National Art Education Association. The Americans for the Arts' legislative updates and the American Symphony Orchestra League's Government Affairs Report are particularly informative.

Although I use the terms *arts education* and *music education* in this chapter, it should be noted that not-for-profit arts organizations and public arts agencies increasingly use the terms *arts participation, arts learning experiences,* and *involvement in the arts* when referring to the realm of arts education. They continued to use interchangeably the terms *arts education* and *arts in education* although the two terms generally connote two different types of programming.[1]

Current Reasons Why Arts and Music Programs Ought to Be Supported

When one is perusing the printed and electronic materials of Americans for the Arts, the Arts Education Partnership, the NEA, the President's Committee on the Arts and the Humanities, the U.S. Department of Education (USDOE), and the National Assembly of State Arts Agencies, the following justifications for the support of after-school, in-school, and community arts programming figure prominently:

- Arts learning improves overall academic performance. Students with high levels of arts participation outperform "arts-poor" students on virtually every measure.
- Students who study or participate in the arts score higher on standardized tests. Music study improves math scores

and spatial skills; reading skills are enhanced by arts learning, particularly through theater and the visual arts.

- "At-risk" students from low-income families benefit most from arts participation.
- Arts learning experiences help students to better know themselves and to better relate to those around them.
- Arts learning develops problem-solving skills, improves reasoning and communication abilities, expands creativity, teaches discipline, promotes teamwork, enhances self-esteem, and provides creative outlets for self-expression.
- Arts programming improves the school culture as a whole by breaking down barriers between disciplines, energizing teachers, motivating students, and improving the physical appearance of school buildings.
- "Nonschool" arts programming reaches many "problem" students not engaged within the school setting. Such programs improve self-esteem, curb delinquent behavior, and help students to perform better academically.[2]

Arts organizations and agencies seem to note more frequently the "intrinsic value" of the arts in their recent advocacy and self-promotional materials than occurred in their mid-1990s publications. In a speech made at the 1999 National Art Education Association convention, NEA chairman Bill Ivey spoke of the arts being "critical to our democracy" because the values of "tolerance, freedom of expression, openness, equality, justice, dignity, and compassion are inherently embedded in our artistic traditions." He added that "the arts are intrinsically important to what it means to be an educated person . . . instruct[ing] us in ways of 'knowing' and 'understanding' our world. Yet he also pointed to the "unfolding story" of the arts and brain development and reiterated many of the same justifications for arts support bulleted earlier, including the ubiquitously cited College Board report that students who study the arts "outperform other students on both the verbal and math portions of the SAT." After advocating for more case-building research that connects arts involvement with improved academic performance, Ivey (1999) then cautioned:

> But as we pursue such insights, we must never forget why we educate our children: to make them productive and contributing members of our society and our democratic nation. Not just to give them a livelihood, but to give them a life. Not just to prepare them for commerce but to prepare them for citizenship.

Ramon Cortines, executive director of the Pew Network for Standards-Based Reform and former chancellor of the New York City Public Schools, wrote the introduction to *Gaining the Arts Advantage* (President's Committee on the Arts and the Humanities & Arts Education Partnership, 1999). He said: "In my experience, the case for the arts is built upon either (1) the intrinsic value of the arts or (2) the value of an arts education's consequences." Cortines

described the two perspectives speaking of humanness and beauty, inspiration and self-discipline, capacities for problem posing and solving, the gross national product, technology, interpersonal skills, and spatial, mathematical-logical, and physical abilities. Tempering his earnest and far-ranging acclaim of the arts and arts education, he noted: "We know, of course, that arts education is not the magic pill that will simultaneously reform schools and boost student achievement" (pp. 5–6).

There have been two significant shifts over the past 2 years in the tone and tenor of the national arts advocacy movement spearheaded most visibly and aggressively by the Arts Education Partnership, the NEA, the President's Committee on the Arts and the Humanities, and Americans for the Arts. Ivey's and Cortines's careful attempts to balance their promotion of instrumental uses of the arts with variously described "intrinsic" benefits of the arts highlights the first shift. Boldfaced, bulleted pronouncements of the arts' ability to raise test scores, improve race relations, reduce crime, and lower teenage pregnancy rates are moderated more frequently by descriptions of inner growth and personal satisfaction derived through arts participation and learning. According to most arts advocacy literature, the improvement of the workforce to ensure economic global competitiveness remains the overarching justification for and ultimate goal of arts education. Increasingly, however, the development of the well-rounded, engaged citizen shares copy space. Of course, happier, better socialized, smarter citizens make happier, better socialized, smarter workers, so the reasoning dovetails nicely.

The second shift in the arts advocacy message is the deliberate avoidance of the phrase *arts education* in favor of *arts participation, arts learning experiences,* and *involvement in the arts.* Linked to all the purposes and benefits of the arts described earlier, *arts learning* is much less site-specific than *arts education.* Arts learning experiences and arts involvement happen everywhere; arts education more frequently connotes school-based or school-associated programming.

The total interchangeability of the advocacy messages among the Arts Education Partnership, Americans for the Arts, the NEA, the President's Committee on the Arts and the Humanities, the National Assembly of State Arts Agencies, and the USDOE is striking at first glance but unsurprising on second thought. The Arts Education Partnership was formed in 1995 by the NEA, USDOE, the National Assembly of State Arts Agencies, and the Council of Chief State School Officers. In 1996 the President's Committee on the Arts and the Humanities and the National Assembly of Local Arts Agencies (NALAA) produced *Coming Up Taller: Arts and Humanities Programs for Children and Youth at Risk.* NALAA merged with the American Council for the Arts in January 1997 to form Americans for the

Arts. The Arts Education Partnership and President's Committee on the Arts and the Humanities copublished *Champions of Change* and *Gaining the Arts Advantage* in 1999. *Learning Partnerships: Improving Learning in Schools with Arts Partners in the Community* was also published in 1999 by the Arts Education Partnership at the request of the USDOE and the NEA. Agency heads and senior staff from all of these organizations, including the Institute of Museum Services and the John F. Kennedy Center for the Performing Arts, sit on one another's advisory boards. The NEA senior deputy chairman (former executive director of the South Carolina Arts Commission), under whose auspices the NEA's education program falls, is married to the counselor to the secretary of the USDOE. USDOE secretary Richard Riley was formerly the governor of South Carolina. The NEA funds the National Assembly of State Arts Agencies, which funds local arts agencies, which constitute the primary membership of Americans for the Arts, which advocates and politicks for and is in turn funded by the NEA and USDOE. Such Washingtonian entwinement is not unusual. I note it only to underscore the mutuality of interests and influences with regard to national and federal arts advocacy and, ultimately, all levels of arts education policy making.

The "Why" of Music Education According to Music and Music Education Organizations

To what extent do the advocacy language and messages of professional music associations resonate with the campaigns of the arts agencies and groups described earlier? In what ways do the publicized perspectives and priorities of MENC: the National Association for Music Education align with or diverge from the perspectives and priorities of national-level music organizations as regards the purposes of music education?

Perhaps the most straightforward way to begin to answer those questions is to look at the formal relationships of and partnerships among several prominent national music organizations, arts advocacy groups, and funding agencies. The ASOL, OPERA America, and MENC are on the Steering Committee of the Arts Education Partnership. With the exception of block grants to state arts councils, music organizations have historically received the greatest share of NEA funding, with the American Symphony Orchestra League and its members heading the list. OPERA America, Chamber Music America, and their member organizations are also regular recipients of NEA funding. The advocacy group National Coalition for Music Education comprises MENC, the National Academy of Recording Arts & Sciences, and NAMM (National Association of Music Merchants) International Music Products Association along with its public relations arm, the Amer-

ican Music Conference. The National Coalition for Music Education was instrumental in advocating successfully for the inclusion of music and the other arts as core subjects listed in the Goals 2000 Educate America Act.

As one might expect, the justifications for music programming offered by these organizations are very similar to the justifications for general arts programming cited earlier. Of all the arts disciplines, however, music has been most directly associated with improved mathematical and spatial-temporal reasoning abilities. Exposure to music is reported to increase brain activity; making music is said to expand the actual size of the brain; studying music is reported to dramatically increase students' reading and math performance; listening to Mozart's Piano Sonata K. 448 temporarily increases spatial scores (i.e., the "Mozart effect") (see Gardiner, Fox, Knowles, & Jeffery, 1996; Grandin, Peterson, & Shaw, 1998; Pantev & Oostenveld, 1998; Rauscher, Shaw, & Ky, 1993). Brain research is the great hope for many music advocates; related findings headline the publications and Web site pages of the American Symphony Orchestra League, OPERA America, Chamber Music America, the American Music Conference, the National Coalition for Music Education, and MENC. The research conclusions of Frances Rauscher and Gordon Shaw on enhanced higher brain functions and improved spatial-temporal abilities are quoted and paraphrased repeatedly.

The Music Education Advocacy Kit was developed and published in 1999 by NAMM and VH-1 Save the Music Foundation. MENC, the American Music Conference, and the National Academy of Recording Arts & Sciences served as consultants for the project. A drawing of Albert Einstein playing the violin covers the outside of the kit and all the materials found inside, including a video, a CD-ROM, an advocacy guidebook, posters, and pamphlets. The key message is "Music makes you smarter!"; the entire focus of the kit is on brain development and academic achievement. The distribution pamphlet makes six points:

Second Graders Do Sixth Grade Math

Music Makes the Brain Grow

Rhythm Students Learn Fractions Better

Music Students Score Higher SATs

Piano Raises Conceptual Math Scores

Substance Abuse Lowest in Music Students

The advocacy kit video, *Music and the Mind*, begins with a girl saying, "If you teach me music, I'll be in a band, not a gang." A boy follows with, "If you teach me music, I'll be better at math, reading, and my SATs." An ABC newscaster reports on the research of Professors Rauscher and Shaw, noting that "the researchers believe the music stimulates early brain development, actually forming new and permanent connections." In a close-up, Shaw reasons, "You can't teach your kids higher mathematics at two or three, but you can teach them music." And VH-1 president Bill Sykes declares:

> There's a perception out there that music education is a luxury, a perk—and it's quite the contrary. Music education really builds the foundation to math and science skills. *It's been proven!* It's been on the cover of magazines; it's been on the evening news.

Available for downloading off the CD-ROM advocate's tool kit are tailored press releases, form letters to parents, and ready-made presentations to school board members that state:

> There's a mountain of scientific evidence that music instruction improves brain development and increases test scores among school children.
> Now there is powerful scientific evidence of a cause and effect link between music instruction and intelligence.

Keeping the "music for music's sake" argument within the advocacy focus appears to be a challenge. Reflecting the same sort of push-pull (and at times, confusion) between the benefits of arts and nonarts learning found in Ivey's speech and Cortines's introduction, the ASOL advises its members:

> In recent years, the "music makes you smarter" argument has been the most obvious route for those seeking to influence policy—but it's advisable to tread very carefully here. . . . In developing your strategy, it's best not to overstate the IQ impact of listening to classical music. Instead, success with policy makers will depend on what we all know orchestras can provide: lifelong music education and participation opportunities, resources that strengthen in-school music instruction . . . , and high-quality performances of symphonic music. (Watts, 2000, p. 56)[3]

The following "facts" upon which the ASOL charges its members to make their local argument for music education seems pale and meandrous in comparison to the driving tone of the NAMM/Save the Music advocacy kit:

> Students do not have sufficient opportunities to learn the arts.
> Students who have access to arts education improve learning across socioeconomic lines.
> In school districts that have made a commitment to arts education, community partnerships are often the most important factor for success. (p. 56)

The ambivalence of the music and music education communities over various intrinsic and extrinsic support arguments is seen most clearly and explored most compre-hensively in MENC literature. MENC publications, advocacy materials, and website links run the gamut of purposes and outcomes of music education. Bold-type sound bites that proclaim increased SAT and IQ scores share journal space with in-depth articles that describe and analyze a broad range of musical and nonmusical research findings and caution against reliance on and uncritical acceptance of sound-bite justifications for music education. One can spend hours on the MENC website linking to and downloading all manner and persuasions of bulleted listings, articles, and advocacy-assistance materials that cite reasons to support music education. One website page beseeches members to "thank Parade Magazine for the exposure it has brought to our profession" and provides a reprint of the magazine article that touts the "evidence that music courses may actually help kids improve reading and math skills." Another website page provides a table of SAT verbal and math mean scores that compares the performance of students who had course work in music both with students who had course work in the other arts and with those who had no arts course work. ("Music: Study or Appreciation" won out over "Music Performance" by 8 points in verbal and 3 points in math. "Acting/Play Production" came in first place in the verbal category with 5 points over "Music: Study or Appreciation"; the two types of coursework were neck and neck in math. Dance came in dead last in both verbal and math.)

In the introduction to the June 1999 issue of *Teaching Music*, MENC president June Hinckley advises music advocates to "use the language of our listeners"—that is, to focus on the justifications for music education that are most likely to impress the person to whom one is making her or his case. If correlations between music and improved reading and math scores, dropout prevention, and school safety are required to gain the person's attention, then speak to those extramusical concerns first and "talk later about the need for rigorous, sequential music instruction" (pp. 6–7). Another article in the same issue of *Teaching Music*[4] provides an overview of music and brain research on young children, carefully noting the inconclusive albeit promising nature of several highly publicized studies (Flohr, Miller, & Persellin, 1999). In the July 1999 issue of *Music Educators Journal*, Bennett Reimer argues that the integrity of music education must be protected from non-music agendas, describing the spatial-temporal argument for the value of music study as "potentially destructive" and "perhaps the most extreme that the music education field has ever faced." Tucked into the August 1999 issue of *Teaching Music* was the glossy insert, "Discover the Power of Music Education." The self-styled "Advocacy Report" begins: "Study after study has proven that music education dramatically increases early brain development and improves students' overall academic performance." The Mozart effect is cited prominently under the subheading "Raises IQ Scores" (Yamaha Band & Orchestral Division, 1999). Another compilation of music and brain research is offered in the December 1999 issue of *Teaching Music* (Wilcox, pp. 29–35). Spatial-temporal and cognitive development, positive attitudes toward a wide range of music, structural changes in and physical expansion of the brain, greater self-confidence and sensitivity, better leadership skills, and higher SAT and IQ scores all mix and mingle as reasons to support music education. Large multicolored sidebars from the MENC website punctuate the article, reiterating the same research findings. Joan Schmidt of the National School Boards Association is quoted as saying:

> They have clearly demonstrated that piano instruction in the early grades significantly improves the spatial-temporal reasoning of children in the primary grades. And that's reason enough to build a better music program. But even more compelling is the news that disadvantaged children show the same kinds of improvement. (p. 34)

The 2000 MENC publication *Music Makes the Difference: Music, Brain Development, and Learning* (with the subsections "Advocacy," "Music and Young Children," "Academic Achievement," and "The Intrinsic Value of Music Education") presents the gamut of justifications under one cover.

MENC represents and advocates for the concerns and interests of its 81,000 members, including 48,000 pre-K–12 music teachers, 6,000 university faculty, 2,800 music administrators, and 8,000 private instructors. The scope and variance of justifications for music education expressed through MENC would appear to reflect the priorities and beliefs of its broad membership. The intensity and specificity of the debate reflect the fact that music education is the primary concern of the MENC membership.

As a service to the profession, MENC is responsible for much of the publication and dissemination of scholarly work within the music education field. The nature and purpose of advocacy and the nature and purpose of scholarly research are very different; in fact, it is not unusual to find them in opposition.[5] Therein, I believe, lies the key distinction between the justifications for music education published by MENC and the advocacy messages publicized by Americans for the Arts and other organizations cited earlier. Many of the same sorts of disparities also appear to exist between MENC and the American Music Conference, NAMM, professional music organizations such as OPERA America and Chamber Music America, and even the National Coalition for Music Education, which is comprised in part by MENC. Scholars and serious practitioners of music education must question and test assumptions made about their profession—and they do so within the public domain. The organization that represents music ed-

ucation professionals and whose mission is to advance music education must make room for dissenting opinions and encourage analytical depth and subtlety. Effective advocacy (even MENC-generated advocacy) has little room for dissent—the more unified the perspective, the easier the Word is to understand and embrace, the better. One might then reasonably wonder to what extent the advocated pedagogical interests and goals of MENC members differ from their private interests and goals for music education. I suspect they vary significantly.

Making Good on the Advocacy Promise

Professor Bennett Reimer creates a K–12 music education scenario built on the following recommendation made by Temple Grandin, Matthew Peterson, and Gordon Shaw (1998):

> We strongly suggest that music education be present in our schools, preferably starting in preschool, to develop "hardware" for ST [spatial-temporal] reasoning in the child's brain. The absolutely crucial (but now neglected) role of ST reasoning in learning difficult math and science concepts must be explored and exploited. (p. 13)

If the development of spatial-temporal reasoning is to be "the point and purpose of music teaching in the schools," then "what, exactly, would this mean for music education?" queries Reimer. The picture Reimer paints of a music education devoted to spatial-temporal reasoning development is devoid of singing, group participation, music that is not symmetrical and sequentially patterned in the Western classical style, creative interpretation, and the study of any instruments other than keyboard. Improvisation and composition would be deferred until their effects on spatial-temporal functioning could be determined. Notation study based on exercises that exploit patterns and symmetries used in Mozart's K. 448 sonata would be intensified. (The study of actual pieces of music might prove to be less effective for spatial-temporal reasoning development and, therefore, unnecessary to notation study.) It would be important to have students listen frequently to that same type of music or auditory stimuli "especially immediately preceding math and science instruction." The evaluation of music and music performance and development of understandings about relationships between music and other disciplines and music in relation to history and culture would be of much less importance, perhaps none at all (Reimer, 1999). Reimer's sardonic portrayal of a music education that has ceased to be about music may be exaggerated, but he makes his point.

Elliot W. Eisner provides a parallel perspective in his 1998 article "Does Experience in the Arts Boost Academic

Achievement?" Pricking the advocacy balloon of unproven assumptions, questionable motives, and other expanding gases, Eisner admonishes arts educators for their ready willingness to deliver the arts up to the SAT cause. He warns that "to use the arts *primarily* to teach what is not truly distinctive about the arts is to undermine, in the long run, the justifying conditions for the arts in our schools." Arts educators must instead "give pride of place to those unique contributions that only the arts make possible" (p. 13). Both Eisner (1998) and Reimer (1999) acknowledge the probable, though difficult to assess, extra-arts learning outcomes of arts study. However, the acceptable use of various extra-arts foci appears to be more a matter of degree for Reimer than for Eisner. Reimer advises:

> Music educators can recognize and even call attention to the many diverse benefits that music study offers without giving the impression, by their arguments or educational practices, that such benefits should ever threaten to replace their fundamental mission. . . . The key factor in maintaining an acceptable balance is the degree to which the program of musical learning is altered in order to serve other purposes. (p. 43)

Acceptable balances, like "intrinsic values," mean different things to different people, depending primarily on wherever one already stands on the arts education purpose–content continuum.[6] Arts educators are all too familiar with the "making and doing" versus "studying about" debates stirred up by various "discipline-based" or "comprehensive" approaches to teaching the arts. We now rock to and fro between scores of likely and unlikely promised outcomes and between ever expanding and contracting definitions of what is more and less essential to the very nature of the making, performing, understanding, and experiencing of the various arts. While Reimer delivers a bleak scenario of music education subsumed by spatial-temporal reasoning development, it is not difficult to imagine other less extreme but ungainly mutations of theater education qua reading programs, dance education qua delinquency-deterrence programs, and visual arts education qua self-help programs.[7] The notion of acceptable balances is pragmatic politically, economically, and intellectually. But how does one tell when the scales are tipped irrevocably?

Imagine if you will: Arts Education as Arts Advocacy Workshop. Imagine a K–12 arts curriculum based on the following topics for study:

- the role of the arts and artists in my community today,
- cultural tourism and other ways that the arts are important to a community's economy,
- arts attendance, participation, and patronage,
- ways the arts bring business and resources to the community,
- advertising and promotion,
- advertising and marketing, and
- support for and participation in the arts.

Imagine a K–12 arts curriculum that recommends the following related activities:

- Identify and discuss particular contributions or roles that musicians, painters, sculptors, actors, and other artists play in your community.
- Contact your municipal government and ask if there is an organization or person responsible for the arts.
- Design a travel poster for your town, city, or country that highlights its characteristics and amenities in the arts.
- Visit your local arts council or commission to determine what artists and arts organizations can be contacted for help and involvement in your project.
- Meet with your mayor or other local government leaders to talk about what is important in a community and share the ideas and priorities you have developed.
- Find out how the arts are supported in your town or state. Compare it to other towns and states.
- Ask the mayor if you can display your project at the town hall, and have students speak to the city or county council about what they learned.

Imagine that such a course of study is a federally funded, highly publicized and lauded "education" project delivered to schools across the nation by the USDOE and the NEA. Naturally, every step of the project is "aligned with the National Standards," dutifully marked in easy to read charts from standard 1 through 9 in dance, music, theater, and visual arts.[8] Perhaps it is that type of program that foreshadows more accurately the future content, purpose, and practice of arts education. Children as li'l advocates and sales reps have well served the commercial sector for years. High-profile, short-term, fanciful theme(park), edutainment projects that spotlight individual artists and the services of arts organizations à la children meeting with the mayor are far more newsworthy than the arduous, day-to-day implementation of sequentially taught school arts programs focused on the study and mastery of an art form.

So what does it take for arts education to deliver various promised benefits and outcomes? Obviously, many arts and arts education advocates are unconcerned. When desired outcomes are shifting continually, when "proof" of those outcomes is regularly unsubstantiated and exaggerated, when promised results are largely undeterminable, the goal is not to make good on promises; it is to keep yourself in the game and the game in play. It matters little whether or not the marketed program offers substantial content in music, visual arts, dance, or theater. Staying in the game is what is important, and these days that cannot be done without a perceived attachment to a popularized public purpose. Staying in the game is the primary benefit of arts advocacy.

The "Single Most Critical Factor" for Success

The preceding discussion has thus far described the justifications used by arts advocates to garner support for arts and arts education programming. There is more, however, to the advocacy message than the "why." Certainly of equal importance and of substantially greater difficulty is the "how"—that is, the posited means by which promised benefits and outcomes are to be realized in return for political and fiscal support of advocates and their cause. While campaign slogans and promised benefits are a dime a dozen, program implementation comes down to whose ideas are selected for development, who leads, who follows, who gets funded, and who gets credit. In the advocacy game, "who" always runs hand in hand with "how."

For arts education researchers and practitioners and arts organization and agency staff there are no areas more divisive than program funding and implementation. Disagreements between the arts education community and the arts community over fiscal and public relations emphases on in-school rather than out-of-school arts programs and over the extent of recognition and support afforded certified K–12 arts teachers as opposed to visiting artists have continued unabated for over three decades (see, for example, Ball, 1986; Bumgarner [Gee], 1994; Chapman, 1982; Eisner, 1974; Lehmann, 1992; Pankratz, 1986; Smith, 1979). That troublesome history is relevant to this analysis for it provides a context for and better understanding of the current vigor of arts advocacy groups in promoting the contributions of the NEA, state arts agencies, arts organizations, and artists to arts education. Again, such unabashed self- and mutual promotion within the arts bureaucracy is not new, but its recent amplification is remarkable.

According to arts advocacy literature and testimonials, in order to attain any and all of the various benefits of arts education recounted earlier, the services of arts organizations and artists are required—period. Directed by the President's Committee on the Arts and the Humanities and the Arts Education Partnership, a study of "successful" school district arts programs is summarized, acclaimed, and marketed in *Gaining the Arts Advantage*. The study's much quoted and reprinted "central finding" asserts that "the single most critical factor in sustaining arts education in their schools is the active involvement of influential segments of the community in shaping and implementing the policies and programs of the district" (p. 9). "Influential segments of the community" is translated loosely to mean "individuals and groups from the broader community actively engage[d] with one another in arts and arts education activities inside and outside of the schools." The number-one "critical success factor" is: "The Community— broadly defined as parents and families, artists, arts organizations, businesses, local civic and cultural leaders and institutions" (p. 11).

Such statements per se are hardly controversial. Certainly broad community support is important for any public program; certainly arts and cultural organizations' services and productions are important resources for schools. Perhaps if the "how" of the advocacy message promulgated by arts agencies and organizations were not focused so overwhelmingly on their own essentiality in arts education and general education, their "single most critical factor" for the success of school arts programming would not bear mention. Perhaps if not for the ever-increasing emphasis on "arts learning experiences" and after-school programs run by arts organization staff such factors for success would be viewed as being completely benign, motivated solely by a genuine desire to improve the education and socialization of millions of school-age children. Indeed, perhaps that is the case. Yet when one has studied other publications of the President's Committee on the Arts and the Humanities and the Arts Education Partnership it is difficult to view unskeptically those prominently reported conclusions.

Champions of Change was published in 1999, shortly before *Gaining the Arts Advantage*. *Coming Up Taller* and *Creative America* were published by the President's Committee on the Arts and the Humanities in 1996 and 1997, respectively. *Coming Up Taller* reports on and advocates for arts and humanities youth development programs for at-risk children outside the schoolhouse and school day. *Creative America* articulates contributions of the arts and humanities to society, reports on trends in private and federal support of cultural organizations and arts and humanities programming, and makes recommendations for strengthening those public and private support systems. Since *Creative America* focuses on support for cultural institutions, perhaps it should be expected that the small section dedicated to arts education would do the same.[9] And it does, but unfortunately, at the expense of schools. The main finding of *Creative America* with regard to "arts education today" is that school-based arts instruction is underfunded, understaffed, and undertaught. The main solution to that problem, according to *Creative America,* is the partnering of schools with cultural organizations. While schools are largely failing students and society, cultural institutions (with the moral leadership and fiscal support of federal cultural agencies) are apparently making great strides forward in arts and humanities education.

As reported in *Creative America, Coming Up Taller* "reveals the often heroic work that many arts, humanities and community organizations perform to serve at-risk youth." Accordingly, more public and private investment should be made in such programs not only as a means to curb antisocial behavior but also because "evidence indicates that important learning through the arts occurs in programs outside the schools" (President's Committee on the Arts and the Humanities, p. 11). *Coming Up Taller* never ceases in comparing out-of-school programs with school programs. Of course, out-of-school programs are much more fun *and effective*. The voluntary aspect of out-of-school programs is "an important part of 'not being like school.' " One of the principles of effective out-of-school programs is to "provide quality staff and quality programming." That means "com[ing] into contact with adults who are experts . . . [and] in frequent, direct contact with artists and scholars themselves." Robert Capanna, executive director of the Settlement Music School in Philadelphia, explains that

> artists process their environment differently. When you put an artist in a teaching environment, they stay an artist. When you put a teacher in that environment and give them some art skills, they are a teacher with some art skills. And the kids know the difference. (President's Committee, 1997, p. 35)

The President's Committee on the Arts and the Humanities points to the need for greater technical assistance for community organizations, most of which "operate with limited staff and small budgets." The committee advocates for increased resources "to expand the effectiveness of programs and enhance staff opportunities." Such staff opportunities would include learning from and training at other centers, travel grants, paid sabbaticals, staff mentorship programs, and performance exchanges (p. 38). If K–12 arts education programs (also operating with limited staff and small budgets) were afforded those same resources, maybe arts teachers might be a bit more heroic, too. Then maybe many of them might be viewed as something more than "teacher[s] with some art skills"—but then again, maybe not.

Champions of Change summarizes and promotes the findings of seven arts intervention research projects. Some of the studies focus on in-school learning experiences; some focus on "nonschool" learning. All of the studies, however, focus on the work and contributions of "outside providers" of arts education—that is, local artists and arts groups that provide services within or outside of the school setting, during or after school hours. With the exception of one study, there is no use of the term *arts* (or *music*) *teacher* throughout the entire report. That same study uses the term *specialist teachers,* as in

> The arts can be taught by three different kinds of instructors, each of whom brings divergent goals, practices, and conceptions of arts learning. These are specialist teachers, general classroom teachers, and external arts providers such as artists and performers from cultural institutions. (Burton, Horwitz, & Abeles, 1999, p. 37)

Otherwise, throughout *Champions of Change* the arts teacher seems curiously invisible; the word *teacher* seems to refer most often, if not always, to the classroom teacher. Perhaps it works out well that way; classroom teachers offer up testimonies such as:

> You must have a professional artist coming into the school. What they bring is their commitment to the art, their own gifts, their drive to create good art, their immersion in the art world, their commitment to excellence. That gets translated to the students and to the teachers who are observing. So an artist brings something into a school that a teacher just can't maintain for six hours a day. (p. 74)

The arts advocacy buzz over the reauthorization of the Elementary and Secondary Education Act (ESEA) and FY2001 appropriations for the USDOE draws attention to the primary interests of the NEA, Arts Education Partnership, and other national-level arts organizations with regards to arts education. "After-school arts learning opportunities" and arts education partnerships between schools and community arts organizations claim front and center stage. Americans for the Arts reports enthusiastically on the pending "improvement" of the Arts in Education section of the ESEA:

> Arts education advocates should be pleased with recent action (5/10/00) taken by the House and Senate Subcommittees on Labor, Health and Education Appropriations for allocating first-time funding for arts in education grants through the U.S. Department of Education. Historically, the Kennedy Center for the Performing Arts and Very Special Arts had solely been funded in this area for their valuable arts education programs. These new, additional funds would further broaden the delivery of arts education programs (both in-school and after-school) to communities nationwide. Grant programs would support a variety of arts education, youth violence prevention, community arts partnerships and model professional development programs, etc. Special recognition was included for the growing research data on the effectiveness of youth arts programs in curbing juvenile delinquency as evidenced in the national YouthARTS study. (Americans for the Arts, 2000)

It is true that since the addition of the Arts in Education section to the ESEA in 1994 all of the funds provided through that legislation have been allocated directly to the Kennedy Center and Very Special Arts (with the exception of $1 million that found its way to the NEA's media arts and literature programs in FY2000).[10] An additional $10 million has been requested for ESEA Arts in Education programming for FY2001 and is proposed to be administered jointly between the NEA and USDOE. Eligible recipients for the grants "would include groups ranging from local and state arts councils to museums and local education agencies" (Americans for the Arts, 2000).

The YouthARTS study was directed by Americans for the Arts with funding from and in collaboration with the NEA and the U.S. Department of Justice. The study was heralded as offering a statistical data-based, rigorous evaluation of community arts programs for at-risk youth and juvenile offenders. When the study was released on January 28, 1999, Americans for the Arts announced that it

> proves what we already believe to be true: arts programs have a demonstrated effect on young people, who are less likely to get involved in delinquent behavior and more likely to succeed in school as a result of participating in such a program. (p. 1)

The YouthArts Tool Kit sells for $75 and includes a 12-minute "Inspirational" videotape and a 28-minute "Instructional Video." The instructional video does not provide a demonstration of teaching but rather an overview of the merits of the YouthARTS project itself. As was noted in a review of the YouthARTS Tool Kit in the autumn issue of *Grantmakers in the Arts*:

> The Tool Kit's introductory brochure announces: "Now we have proof. The results are in," but the proof is not enclosed in the expensive box. . . . Brief, condensed "results" are scattered throughout aspects of the box, but presented without any details or analysis. The project collaborators were right that arts programs for at risk youth are solely in need of rigorous evaluation. . . . The Tool Kit does a fine job of discussing how to develop and manage a program but withholds the substantive information when it comes to explaining why. (Phillips, 1999, p. 43)

Americans for the Arts promotes YouthARTS as central to its professed mission "to advance its goal of ensuring every child access to a high quality arts education." Americans for the Arts (1999) has disseminated "1,000 YouthARTS Toolkits nationwide" as a way to better "support arts education as part of the core curriculum in schools and in the community" (p. 4). In July 1999 the Governing Board of Americans for the Arts adopted a National Agenda for Arts Education that focused primarily on advocacy and public relations. Three agenda initiatives have been established: (1) the YouthARTS USA Public Awareness Campaign, (2) the Mobilizing Local Arts Education Project, and (3) the YouthARTS Development Project (Americans for the Arts, 1999, p. 1).[11]

Two other federal programs garnering considerable interest and support from arts advocacy groups are the after-school 21st Century Community Learning Centers (CCLC [or CLC]) Program and the NEA's "Challenge America" initiative. The USDOE has been very busy advocating for

increased funding for its 21st CCLC Program as a "key component of the Administration's efforts to keep children safe, provide academic enrichment, and other recreational and enrichment opportunities, such as band, drama, arts, and other cultural events for children." Up from $40 million in FY1998 and $200 million in FY1999 to $453 million in FY2000, the 21st CCLC Program was awarded $846 million for FY2001. CCLC is likely to gain $1 billion for FY2002. President Clinton had requested $1 billion for CCLC for FY2001. Campaigning for increased overall US-DOE funding and for specific support for the 21st CCLC Program, Riley warns constituents that because the funding level set by Congress is significantly lower than the amount the president requested, "the Department may not be able to support needed after-school programs in communities across the country" (U.S. Department of Education, 2000, p. 2). The NEA, Americans for the Arts, the American Arts Alliance, the Arts Education Partnership, and the ASOL have been quick to rally behind Riley for the after-school cause and impressively vigilant in pointing out the present and possible benefits of such funding avenues to their members.[12] Organized by the Afterschool Alliance (of which the USDOE is a key partner) and promoted by Americans for the Arts, a "National Day of After-School Programs Awareness" was held on October 12, 2000.

Challenge America served successfully as the NEA's latest stratagem to gain a budget increase from Congress. According to Ivey, "The purpose of Challenge America is to strengthen families, communities and our nation through the arts." The focus will be on "arts education; after-school programs for youth-at-risk; preservation of cultural heritage; broadening access to the arts; and building community partnerships" (1999). Chairman Ivey campaigned hard for congressional approval of a FY2001 presidential request of $150 million for the NEA, $50 million of which was proposed to support Challenge America. Although Congress did not increase the NEA's base budget of $98 million, it did award the Endowment an additional $7 million tagged specifically as the Challenge America Arts Fund. Many arts supporters have noted the significance of the gesture in that it was the first NEA budget increase since 1992.

At the 1999 National Art Education Association convention, Ivey rallied pre-K–university visual arts educators to:

> join us ("your arts endowment") in spreading our message about the importance of the visual arts, music, dance, and theatre to our children and their futures. Tell your congressmen and senators, your state legislators, your city officials, how important quality sequential art programs, taught by qualified teachers, are to your schools, your families, and your communities. And tell them . . . how a

strong Arts Endowment, and our proposed Challenge America initiative, can help improve arts education in your schools and in your communities.

Although school districts will be able to apply for a Challenge America grant, so will arts organizations and other community groups, including social service agencies, chambers of commerce, and tourism and convention bureaus. Forty percent of Challenge America funding is slated to go directly to the state arts agencies in the form of block grants. The priority of school–arts organization partnerships is the integration of artists and community arts resources into pre-K–12 instructional programs. (American Symphony Orchestra League, 1999b, p. 2).[13] It is decidedly unclear as to how Challenge America will significantly advance "quality sequential art programs, taught by qualified teachers." It is unclear as to how that would happen with $7 million or even with $50 million. It is very clear, however, that the NEA, along with its national support network of state and local arts agencies, arts advocacy organizations, and arts institutions, will continue to employ the Challenge America stratagem (or some similar initiative) for future Interior Appropriations budget debates.

"We're the right agency to take the lead [in arts education] even though we can't foot the bill," Bill Ivey announced during the NEA Forum held at Harvard University on February 17, 2000. Leafing through the past decade of NEA public relations materials, one might perceive Ivey's statement to be old news. For many years now and for approximately $10 million annually (most of which funded artist residencies and arts organization outreach programs), the NEA has claimed to "lead the way in arts education reform" and to "put the arts in our children's classrooms" (National Endowment for the Arts, 1996, p. 9). The Arts Endowment avers to play "a unique leadership role" in pre-K–12 education "that encompasses policy development, grantmaking, technical assistance, and research and development" (National Endowment for the Arts, 1998a). Thanks to NEA-supported initiatives, "thousands of artists work in America's schools [offering] residencies, outreach programs, teacher training, special performances, and master classes" (National Endowment for the Arts, 1998b).

While the "why" of the arts advocacy message continues to be uncertain, confused, and diffused, the "how" and, most certainly, the "who" (according to the NEA et al.) are crystal clear. Whatever justification for arts education one chooses to offer, its realization will occur if and only if the services of arts organizations and artists are procured. The message is undeniable: Artists, arts agencies, and arts organizations should be funded to offer "professional development opportunities" for classroom teachers and arts specialists and assist in the design and development of K–12 arts curricula.[14] They should be funded to

teach children within the arts and general classroom and outside of the school setting in venues throughout the community. They should receive support to provide after-school counseling and socializing diversions for at-risk and disadvantaged youth as well as a myriad of "arts access" opportunities for community members young and old. Artists and arts organization staff should be supported in the enhancement of their own teaching and mentoring skills and should receive various other professional development opportunities to ready and renew themselves for the responsibilities mentioned earlier.

However "arts education" is defined, the arts advocacy message is the same. If one defines arts education as being regularly taught, sequentially designed courses of study conducted primarily within the parameters of the classroom, the services of arts organizations and artists are avowed to make a nonexistent program spring to life, a poor program good, and a good program superior. When arts education is spoken of in terms of omnifarious arts activities "placing creative expression at the center of community life" (Ivey, 1999), the services of arts organizations and artists are portrayed as being absolutely essential. The much sought-after golden snitch, "consensus," appears to have been captured by the arts bureaucracy in the final year of the 20th century. It is not the content or purpose of arts education that shimmers in their hands but a fervent belief in their own importance and a unified interest in funding, public relations, and audience development possibilities.

Concerns, Conquests, and Consequences: The Advocacy Movement, the Word, and Arts Education

Three topics remain for discussion within the parameters of this chapter: the use and abuse of research; the ascendancy of—and the arts and arts education communities' dependency on—advosearch; and the triumph of the national arts advocacy movement over the professional arts education community. It is time to attend to the original question: In what ways might arts advocacy—what we proclaim art will do for the individual and society in return for investments of time, love, and money—weaken our sense and valuing of art in relation to life and of arts education in relation to learning?

Concerns of Arts Educators and Other Academicians Over the Use (and Abuse) of Research

For decades, scholars within the arts education field have questioned the motivations of the arts bureaucracy's interest in K–12 arts education. Concerns have been expressed repeatedly about hyperbolic claims made about and on behalf of arts education. Concerns have been expressed over the increasing aggressiveness and momentum of the arts advocacy movement and its deleterious influence on arts education policy formulation. Concerns have been expressed over the entrepreneurial character of arts education "research" dominated by the interests and political agendas of public arts agencies and not-for-profit arts organizations.[15] Most of those concerns have been systematically suppressed and ignored.

More recently, the arena of discussion that questions the veracity and use of various studies that report both causal and corollary associations between arts learning and non-arts outcomes (e.g., improved math and reading skills; transfers of creative thinking and problem-solving abilities from an art form to other academic disciplines, etc.) is expanding beyond the professional arts education field. The Reviewing Education and the Arts Project (REAP), headed by Harvard Project Zero psychologists Ellen Winner and Lois Hetland, offers the most comprehensive analysis and evaluation of such studies to date.[16] While several types of near transfer (or "potentially casual relationships") were substantiated between studying an art form and an area of nonarts achievement, the overarching conclusion of the study is headlined by the title of the lead report: "Mute Those Claims: No Evidence (Yet) for a Causal Link between Arts Study and Academic Achievement." The original title of the report was "Mute Those Claims: The Association Between Arts Education and Academic Achievement Is Due to Self-Selection." Self-selection was indeed found to be the primary factor that correlated arts study with academic achievement in that students who choose to take an arts course are often already doing well academically.[17] In addition, since most studies lacked a control group, any positive effect of the arts could have been attributed to the Hawthorn effect, whereby improved performance by a group of persons taking part in an experiment is due to their perception of being singled out for special consideration.

Winner's and Hetland's conclusions about the "policy implications" of their study—and of other studies that seek to connect arts study with nonarts learning—are most interesting. In effect, the authors state there should be no implications drawn from such research findings for policymaking that pertains to the support or nonsupport of school arts programming. Echoing Eisner, Reimer, and many, many other arts educators, Winner and Hetland (2000) advise:

The arts deserve a justification on their own grounds, and advocates should refrain from making utilitarian arguments in favor of the arts. Such arguments betray a misunderstanding of the inherent value of the arts. As soon as we justify arts by their power to affect learning in an academic area, we make the arts vulnerable. . . . Any evaluation of the educational outcomes of arts education should be based on learning in the arts. . . . We should evaluate the outcomes of the study of the arts by determining the most important kinds of arts understanding that we wish to instill. (pp. 66–67)

Furthermore, most of the evidence for causal and correlational connections between arts study and academic achievement (and other claims of transference between arts study/exposure and higher levels of motivation and socialization) is not evidence at all—it is anecdote and assumption, hype and hope. In the introduction to the REAP report, Winner and Hetland write: "Arts education has been argued to have social, motivational, and academic repercussions. But are such claims rooted in empirical evidence, or are they unsupported advocacy?" Unsupported but not ineffectual advocacy is the answer to their question. To base education policy and publicly supported arts programming on such flawed and faddish findings is foolish and irresponsible. And yet, it is done all the time, reinforcing Bennett Reimer's axiom that "in education policymaking, facts play a minor role in comparison to credulity."

Do the content and purposes of music education, as portrayed by advocacy groups, represent accurately what is most important to know about music education? Or in Winner and Hetland's words, can we discern from arts education advocacy "the most important kinds of arts understanding that we wish to instill"? Do we wish to build our programs upon such knowledge and understandings? Are those the types of programs with which music educators want to be identified? Clearly there is genuine distress among arts educators about these issues.[18] Clearly there are many differences of opinion. Seldom is anything all good or all bad. Various advocacy claims are grounded in more or less truth; some claims and campaigns are more wisely conceived and more thoughtfully presented than others. Yet even advocacy that strives for honest representation of an issue should be distanced from the determination of research agendas and from policy formulation. Professional education organizations such as MENC walk a tightwire between scholarly interests and political activism. Nevertheless, they must be vigilant in their use of and reliance on the Advocated Word. While product promotion is as basic a survival tactic in today's knowledge industry as it has forever been in the commercial sector, there is simply no getting around the antithetical relationship of advocacy and education in that "advocacy seeks believers not questioners" (*K–12 Arts Education in the United States*, 1986, p. 12). *K–12 Arts Education in the United States: Present Context, Future Needs*, published in part by MENC itself, articulates precisely the dangers of mixing advocacy and education:

The primary danger of the advocacy movement is that it aggressively promotes its own solutions not as a basis for policy discussion and negotiation, but as the only rational solution. The advocacy movement assumes that the wisest people have already agreed on a solution; it produces the appearance that a broad range of people have been involved in the decision when, in fact, those indicated as being involved may have been only minimally consulted or consulted under such terms that they participated only in an illusionary sense. Testimony is not debate. The danger is that the advocacy approach assumes no need for debate, and it is in this sense that it is the most elitist approach of all, even though in its operational proposals it suggests that its value is in reaching a broader spectrum of the population. (p. 18)

What do the messages and methods of organized arts advocacy campaigns tell us about the character and worth of arts education in general and music education specifically? All too often they tell us both are commodities and that neither is very important unless it provides a direct means for the buying of favor and funding and for the selling of services. They imply that not only is math more important than music (a postulation with which most parents would agree) but also that music should serve math. They encourage research, program development, and policymaking driven by the scramble of self-promotion and quick fixes. And perhaps most damaging of all, they persuade us to believe that it is acceptable to participate in the promotion of an education-related cause based on unproven assumptions driven forward by political and economic interests.

The line between research and advocacy vanishes when the interests and political agendas of public arts agencies and not-for-profit arts organizations drive arts education policymaking. Research funded and published by an organization, company, or government agency that stands to gain from the "proof" of a specific claim could be called advosearch. When independent research findings are co-opted by marketers and advocates, even the most objective and carefully reported findings are quickly spun into advosearch. There is so much advosearch masquerading as legitimate arts education research these days that many people in the field itself no longer appear to be able to distinguish between them. Policymakers looking for informed perspectives on how to best support K–12 arts education (or, perhaps more realistically, to best advance their own predetermined agendas) have allowed themselves to be duped for decades. The average citizen is lost.[19]

Advosearch: How the Word Is Created, Marketed, and Credentialed

This is how it is done: Co-opt or create a research finding that is useful for the promotion of your cause and, ideally,

for your own role in championing the cause and righting the wrong. It is better to use the previously released research of an academic from a renowned university. If such research is unavailable, you may fund your own study—preferably by someone sympathetic to your cause. (Should the study findings not be to your liking, you always have the option of burying them.) Praise the overall research effort, but do not get bogged down in the subtleties and nuances of the research. Overlook any qualifications the researcher has made about her or his research findings; ignore null and inconclusive effects. Incessantly quote the finding in speeches, printed matter, direct mail campaigns, and testimonies at congressional hearings. (Directly quoting the finding will quickly become cumbersome and unnecessary; begin to experiment with paraphrasing, simplification, and spin.) Connect your cause more securely to the finding with generalized conclusions and appealing overstatements. At this point everyone with interests similar to your own will be applying the same techniques to the same piece of research. The research finding (regardless of its accuracy) is validated by its use as a campaign slogan; the campaign is authorized by the research.

NEA chairman Bill Ivey, Arts Education Partnership director Dick Deasy, and many other arts spokepersons call openly for research to prove various advocacy claims, particularly ones that relate arts experiences to improved test scores and academic performance. The question for serious researchers is: If research proves the opposite, will those findings be published, disseminated, and heeded? If past is precedent, then the answer to that question is "no." At the same time undesired research findings are being buried, new studies that seek to prove the same claims are being called for and funded.[20] In the advocacy world, an assertion that is unproved or disproved is described as being inconclusive, while an assertion that garners a minimal positive effect or most any type of correlation is called fact.[21] Inconclusive research needs further study (generally additional similar research); positive research findings are thrust immediately into the policy mix.

The ways in which research is used in an intensely entrepreneurial, hypermarketed country such as ours ought to be of concern to all scholars and policymakers. Ultimately it is the burden of individual researchers to keep a watchful eye on publicized interpretations and uses of their own and their colleagues' research. It is widely known in academic circles that null and negative findings are rarely published, while positive findings are published, reprinted, and promulgated. Therefore, published research (especially on an effect that many people would like to see substantiated) is often subject to a "positivity bias" that influences disproportionately policymaking, public perception, and further research. For instance, the highly temporary (10- to 15-minute) nature of the Mozart effect frequently either went unmentioned by the media or was noted only in passing. It will be interesting to see how much play is received by psychologist John Harland's finding that British students who study the arts are *less successful* academically (Harlan et al., 2000) and by University of Amsterdam professor Folkert Haanstra's (1999) finding that there is no measurable difference in academic achievement between Dutch students who do and do not study the arts. There has long been and, I hope, always will be an uneasy relationship between academia and the popular press; that uneasiness should extend to advocacy organizations and government agencies as well. The politician interested in reelection, the bureaucrat looking to expand her or his support base and influence, and the gung-ho advocate pushing a perspective (even a perspective the academician favors) are persons to be treated cautiously. Concern, even apprehension, over the interpretation and use of one's own and one's colleagues' research by reporters, politicians, industry leaders, and advocates is smart. All too often subtleties, qualifications, and ambiguities are ignored as the clamor of the sales pitch rings louder and louder.[22] Yet while hype, oversimplification, and assumption rule in the media world, academia is not guileless. Carried along by external acclaim of their work, competent researchers can seem to forget the less than universal applicability of their research findings, adopting an advocacy lexicon devoid of nuance and uncertainty. As the media momentum builds, they can forget to reiterate moderating questions and conclusions that provide a larger, more meaningful context for consideration of research findings.[23] Such behavior among academicians authorizes the transformation of legitimate research into advosearch.

Bully Pulpits and the Bypass Technique

The shadow of a classic iron triangle[24] looms large across the face of arts education when one connects the dots among the NEA and state and local arts councils; the arts advocacy community; and federal and state networks of influential and influenceable legislators and aides.[24] Mutual support and promotion among interested parties is a highly effective means to run the show. The arts bureaucracy is impressively adept at self- and interagency promotion. The NEA applauds itself and applauds and makes grants to state and local arts agencies, arts institutions, and arts advocacy organizations. Everyone else in turn applauds the NEA, one another, and of course themselves. Arts advocacy groups lobby on behalf of the NEA and state and local arts agencies. Everyone joins in the feting of supportive legislators. A feted legislator is often a reelected legislator. And the band plays on.

Iron triangle politics are especially effective if you can co-opt the language and ideas of people who disagree with you. Iron triangle arts players glibly use all the right arts education terminology, speaking glowingly of their own

and one another's work in "making the arts an integral part of the core curriculum," helping to develop "comprehensive, sequentially-instructed K–12 arts curricula," championing the need for "school arts courses to be taught by qualified teachers," and "promoting the national standards," "authentic assessment of student learning," and "ongoing, rigorous program evaluation." They speak piously of initiating "partnerships" between themselves and the education community.[25] In her critique of the NEA's and National Assembly of State Arts Agencies' 1999 publication, *Arts Education in Action: The State Arts Agency Commitment,* arts education consultant Laura Chapman provides an excellent example of the arts bureaucracy's practice of the co-opt technique:

> The preface and introduction have one purpose: to position the NEA and SAAs as the *originators* of key ideas they have long resisted and to delete from historical memory the sources of those ideas in the professional literature of arts educators since the 1960s, including positions taken by national associations of arts educators since the 1980s. . . . The entire report portrays NEA, NASAA, and SAAs as major policy leaders, with an equally major role in managing and implementing a variety of programs that are, in fact, within the normal range of responsibility and expertise of state and local personnel in arts education who are well versed in matters such as curriculum, professional development, and assessment. (p. 37)

The Siamese twin of the co-opt technique is the bypass technique. A passage in *K–12 Arts Education in the United States: Present Context, Future Needs* (1986) explains the arts advocacy movement's use of the bypass technique around the professional arts education community:

> The bypass technique consists of ignoring the work, personalities, and organizations that contributed to the development of music, arts, dance, and theatre education by organizing projects, programs, and public relations approaches that appeal to those in policy levels above those who provide the substantive work in the field. This has been a common technique for all advocacy movement efforts in arts education at the elementary and secondary levels for the past two decades. Professionals and professional organizations representing those who actually teach art are bypassed in favor of their administrative and political superiors who do not have the expertise to make informed evaluations of proposals presented by advocates. . . . Their participation is rewarded by public relations benefits such as being seen in the company of famous individuals, attending national conferences with extensive press coverage, etc.
> The objective of those using the bypass technique is to readjust perceptions about the source of expertise in arts education in the minds of those with policy roles. There is plenty of evidence that the bypass technique has worked: professional arts educators and their organizations find

themselves ignored for the most part by those speaking and acting nationally on behalf of the arts. (16)

It should be noted that this passage was written 15 years ago. The situation for the arts education community clearly has not improved—nor will it. The arts bureaucracy and its supporting advocacy movement have no reason to change their course of action. To do so would undermine decades of successful advancement on the arts education field. They do not need the approval or support of arts educators; in fact, engaging the arts education community at this point would destroy their advantage.

A handful of arts educators have doggedly "fought the good fight," won a few battles, and perhaps in doing so retarded the encroachment. It is my belief, however, that the war is already lost. Decades from now the movement to find a more secure and central position for the in-school study of music, art, dance, and theater will be viewed as an aberration in the history of public elementary and secondary education. Some schools will continue to offer a smattering of arts courses as electives; a few schools will have excellent programs in one or more of the arts. But increasingly, substantive study of an art form will be available only for the very talented at professional arts schools and conservatories or for the merely interested whose parents can afford it, by way of after-school piano, ballet, and painting lessons. In effect, the study and practice of an art form will settle comfortably back into the margins of life experience for all but a privileged and talented few. The "arts advantage" has been gained but not by the arts education community and not by the public school population.

There are reasons that this prediction will come to pass other than the victory of the arts advocacy movement over the interests of the arts education community. The failure of the university arts education community to establish and sustain a critical mass of high quality preservice and in-service teacher education programs will play a major role in the demise of the field. But it is technology and the saturation of our daily lives with popular culture and electronic images that will lead most swiftly to "deschooling" the arts. Jeffrey Kimpton, director of the school of music at the University of Minnesota–Minneapolis, observes (2000): "The more prevalent the arts and media become in our society, the tougher it will be to justify the study of the arts in our schools" (p. 35). Nevertheless, the arts advocacy movement has been a substantial force in the undermining of K–12 arts education.

I do not pretend that the idea of a quality arts education for all students ever came close to being realized. Yet there has been hope, a proud and honorable vision, and a real beginning of forward movement. It was a fragile, perhaps fantastic, dream to begin with and will not withstand such fierce competitiveness from those who were seen originally as allies but have in truth turned out to be predators.

A Weakened Sense of It All

What *is* the difference between "arts education," "arts in education," "arts participation," "arts exposure," "arts learning experiences," and "involvement in the arts"? Which flavor best delivers which taste and learning sensation? Which sensation is more or less important to the individual, to society, to the workforce, to the gross national product, to our security as a nation and propagation as the species *Homo North Americana?* Is it more musical knowledge and technical expertise; a broader understanding of culture and history and the relationships between the two; better math or spatial-temporal skills; better problem-solving abilities; higher SAT scores; improved self-esteem; or better behavior among at-risk youth? It has become almost impossible to discern among the confusion of various genres of arts educationish programming or to think clearly amid the cacophony of desperately promised deliverances. If thus and so is promised by an after-school arts-oriented program for at-risk youth, then shouldn't that be the purpose and product of school arts programming? If it is reasonable to expect such and such an outcome from taking a high school general music course, is it just as reasonable to expect a similar outcome from attending a series of performances by the local chamber music ensemble? If one type of music program is said to have a certain desirable effect, then why should not all music programs be designed to deliver the same effect?

We have reached the point where all our justifications, public purposes, outcomes, goals, effects, and objectives, all the congressional testimonies, Arts Advocacy Days, "Arts Education Month" resolutions, conference speeches, letters to the editor, public relations pamphlets, and advosearch reports, have rendered the already-feeble concepts of "the arts" and "arts education" impotent and meaningless.[26] In his essay "Lilies That Fester," C. S. Lewis (1984) suggests that those who talk most of "refinement," "religion," and "culture" are those most bereft of such attributes. He writes:

Where it is most named it is most absent.... Almost by definition, a religious man, or a man when he is being religious, is not thinking about *religion;* he hasn't the time. *Religion* is what we (or he himself at a later moment) call his activity from the outside.... *Culture,* like religion, is a name given from outside to activities which are not themselves interested in *culture* at all, and would be ruined the moment they were. I do not mean that we are never to talk of things from the outside. But when the things are of high value and very easily destroyed, we must talk with great care, and perhaps the less we talk the better. . . . Many modern exponents of *culture* seem to me to . . . have no shyness where men ought to be shy. They handle the most precious and fragile things with the roughness of an auctioneer and talk of our most intensely solitary and fugitive experiences as if they were selling us a Hoover.

Let us substitute "art" for "culture" in this passage and consider how our intemperate proclamations about what art will do for all people and nations—for "quality of life," "community cohesion," "economic impact," and "education reform"—ultimately weaken our sense and valuing of art as a part of life to be experienced, practiced, and enjoyed. Let us reflect on how our incessant hawking of arts education makes the study of an art form seem so very far removed from the experience and pleasure of learning.

Regaining Our Souls and Credibility

Music educators do not teach to improve learning in math, raise SAT scores, or improve spatial-temporal skills. Music educators teach because they love music and they want others to love it. They teach because they believe that making music alone or with others is an immensely satisfying experience; and they believe that knowing about musical forms and traditions imbues the making and the listening with more intellectual and emotional grist. They teach because they believe that music study provides knowledge and skills that no other study provides. They teach to make a living within a domain of interest they enjoy and that has a powerful influence on people throughout the world. Young people make and study music for precisely the same reasons. Those truths are the basis of responsible advocacy. We must ask for the support of others based on that which we know we want to provide and are able to deliver.

As professionals responsible for the field of arts education, why then do we allow our "most precious" artistic and intellectual pleasures to be presented to others in a package that is unrecognizable to ourselves and largely beside the point to anyone who knows and loves music, theater, dance, or the visual arts? Why do we join in the raucous auction? To whom are we trying to sell this improved-spatial-temporal-higher-SAT-bigger-brain-global-competitiveness Hoover—and why would they buy it? Perhaps it is that we are afraid to do otherwise because we have been convinced that in order to remain in the allocation game—to "survive"—we must persuade politicians, business leaders, school boards, and school administrators that the arts and arts education have "real-world," high-stakes public purpose application. But what if they are buying it as we are selling it, with eyes averted sheepishly

from the truth, with postures submissive and stooped by the crushing pressure to pretend to be all things to all people, to be perceived as serving multiple purposes, to get three for the price of one? Perhaps we allow the charade to march on as we shuffle halfheartedly from bandwagon to bandwagon because we believe ourselves to be ineffectual and that it matters not what choices we make. If that is the truth of it, then the time has come to toss this soul-sucking vacuum into the junk heap. For what is our worth if we have betrayed our own best instincts by seeking to mislead others?

University researchers: It is up to you and me to pay attention to how our research is used and to denounce abuses and misrepresentations publicly and audibly. We must distance research agendas from advocacy demands, and we must advise policymakers to distance policy formulation from advosearch. It is not acceptable for educators to participate in the promotion of an education-related cause based on unproven assumptions regardless of the political, economic, or self-interests involved. It is not acceptable for researchers to ignore sloppy research and unsubstantiated claims within their realm of expertise. It is not acceptable for researchers to stand by passively when such "findings" are used to influence policymaking and program funding and development.

So let us speak up against the hyperbole, against the advosearch, and against self-interest masquerading as public service. But let us speak softly and with great care of those things that are of high value to us personally and professionally. It is then that our survival will be ensured with souls regained and credibility intact.

NOTES

1. The term *arts in education* is used most accurately to describe programs through which artists are brought into schools, arts and community centers, and a variety of other venues to perform and teach. The services of arts organization staff have also become a primary ingredient of arts in education programming. According to the Consortium of National Arts Education Associations (comprising the American Alliance for Theatre and Education, MENC: the National Association for Music Education, National Art Education Association, and the National Dance Association, the consortium represents a membership of over 100,000 music, visual arts, dance, and theater educators), the term *arts education* refers to sequential, comprehensive *school-based* arts instruction. The Philadelphia Resolution (1986) and the National Standards for Arts Education (1994) reinforce the legitimacy of the consortium's position that arts education be a sequenced and comprehensive enterprise at all grade levels, the primary responsibility of which resides with qualified arts teachers, schools, and school boards. The Philadelphia Resolution was devised by representatives from 25 national arts

and arts education organizations; the National Standards for Arts Education was formally endorsed or supported by over 60 national arts associations and organizations. Nevertheless, the terms *arts in education* and *arts education* are often used interchangeably within the arts community. The consortium argues that arts in education does not equal arts education. While arts in education programming may be a component of K–12 arts education, it is only a *part* of or supplement to the larger teaching and learning efforts that comprise and sustain the study of the arts in elementary and secondary schools. (For a more detailed explanation of the issues that surrounded the definitions and use of the term *arts education* see Gee, 1999a, pp. 11–14.)

2. The reasons cited for funding arts programming were taken from a cross-section of materials electronically posted, published, and distributed by the Arts Education Partnership, Americans for the Arts, American Arts Alliance (comprising the Association of Art Museum Directors, Association of Performing Arts Presenters, Dance/USA, OPERA America, and the Theatre Communications Group), NEA, President's Committee on the Arts and the Humanities, U.S. Department of Education and National Assembly of State Arts Agencies. See for instance, American Arts Alliance (2000), p. 2; Americans for the Arts (1999) (which reported on the findings of Americans for the Arts' YouthARTS study and advertised the *YouthARTS Tool Kit* and *YouthARTS Handbook*), p. 1; Fiske (1999), pp. viii–ix; National Assembly of State Arts Agencies & National Endowment for the Arts (1999), p. 5; President's Committee on the Arts and the Humanities & Arts Education Partnership (1999) (justifications for arts support reiterated throughout the section "School District Case Studies and Profiles"); U.S. Department of Education (2000a).

3. Watts makes a sincere attempt to reconcile the advocacy goals of the ASOL with support for school music programs. A refreshingly thoughtful section titled "Speak Up for Specialists" features the New York Philharmonic's education program directed by Thomas Cabaniss, a former music teacher. Cabaniss cautions fellow ASOL members to be very clear when speaking with school administrators "about how important it is that the music teachers be [in the schools] on a permanent and full-time basis." He explains it is crucial that administrators do not view orchestras' education offerings "as a substitute for sequential instruction by in-school music specialists" (62).

4. This article provides a helpful overview of the research findings and methodology of Frances Rauscher, Joyce Eastland Gromko and Allison Smith, Eugenia Costa-Giomi, and the article authors themselves.

5. For a thorough analysis of advocacy technique and its implications for arts education, see Hope (1985), pp. 14–22.

6. Ideas of acceptable balances and intrinsic values vie with "authentic" and "inauthentic" arts encounters and "content-anemic" versus "substantive" arts programming in their ambiguity. Professor emeritus Nancy Smith Fichter (2000) warns that when we forget the

> central characteristics of the arts experience itself [i.e., the individual "art act" of making or doing] . . . we let ourselves be beguiled by programs that purport to give art to

everyone but do so in ways that result in superficial, content-anemic exposure. Those programs offer inauthentic, surrogate, second-hand arts education. (pp. 13–14)

Such a pronouncement would seem to be a straightforward, largely noncontroversial assessment of the importance of physical engagement with the art form in arts education programming. Yet exact meaning is difficult both to convey and to grasp in the current intensely political, advocacy-bloated environment. Descriptive terms that have signaled a particular philosophical orientation within the profession are now recycled so rapidly and applied so indiscriminately that they quickly drag us deeper into the morass rather than help us to see above it. On one hand, Fichter's statement could be read as an indictment of education programming with a significant focus on the historical, philosophical, and theoretical dimensions of art (i.e., "discipline-based arts education"). On the other hand, it may be understood as a stand against the "all the arts for all the children" artist residency programming brought to schools and community centers by state and local arts councils. Certainly any type of program can be superficial, even one that focuses on "doing and making." How one interprets her statement depends largely on where one's biases lie in the muddled mess of arts in education verbiage.

7. The concept of arts activities as behavior modification devices has taken on new meaning at Eastern Connecticut State University, where forced opera attendance is used to punish unruly undergrads ("A New Culture War on Campus," 2000, p. 2). Urban planners already use recorded classical music to discourage teenage loitering in public places. Variations on such programs across the arts might be explored via U.S. Department of Justice–National Endowment for the Arts collaboration. Such tactics also might be employed as part of the Partnership for Conflict Resolution Education in the Arts cosponsored by the NEA and National Center for Conflict Resolution (*Americans for the Arts Monthly Wire*, May 2000). I for one would behave better if threatened with having to again sit through Benjamin Britten's *Death in Venice*.

8. See U.S. Department of Education et al. (1999), pp. 36–47. One can only hope that like the Mars mission itself, the Mars Millennium Project will be canceled to allow time for revision (2000, A1).

9. In *Creative America,* the President's Committee on the Arts and the Humanities notes: "Arts education is one of the strongest predictors of later audience participation. Without providing meaningful arts education, . . . our cultural institutions will face huge challenges in developing the audiences, volunteers, and donors of tomorrow" (pp. 9–10).

10. See Gee (1999a), pp. 9–10, for a more detailed report on annual allocations for ESEA Arts in Education (subpart 1, part D) legislation.

11. The Mobilizing Local Arts Education Project will "research and disseminate information on arts education issues and best practices." The prospect of Americans for the Arts heading up such an initiative is disconcerting. Although the organization obviously excels in dissemination, research of arts education issues and evaluation of best practices is not its forte.

12. For example: The ASOL emphasizes that *an unlimited amount of a* [21st CCLC Program] *award may be used to contract services from community organizations*." (See American Symphony Orchestra League, 1999, pp. 4, 11). The American Arts Alliance focuses the attention of its constituency on CCLC funding with the headline "Arts Education: Federal Money for What You Already Do" (2000, p. 3).

13. Chairman Ivey announced to the National Art Education Association audience that a NEA grant for $65,000 was going "directly to you—our art educators" to enable design professionals to assist educators in the development and implementation of a design education curriculum in Wisconsin.

14. "Teacher training" has become an especially popular activity among public arts agencies and not-for profit arts organizations. OPERA America, the ASOL, the Association of Performing Arts Presenters, Chamber Music America, Chorus America, Dance/USA, and the Theatre Communications Group cohosted a "performing arts educators" forum in July 1999. Training classroom teachers how to use the arts to teach multiple subjects was one of two advertised breakout sessions ("Education Cross-Talk," *OPERA America Newsline*, April 1999). The Arts Education Partnership held a meeting in January 2000 on "professional preparation and continued professional development of teachers and teaching artists" (Arts Education Partnership, 1999). Americans for the Arts reports that "American museums are providing more K–12 educational programs than ever before" along with "learning activities, such as teacher training" (1999, p. 3). But perhaps the most ambitious stride into the realm of teacher education came with the recent acquisition of the Louisiana Institute for Education in the Arts by the Louisiana Alliance for Arts Education, an affiliate of the Kennedy Center Alliance for Arts Education (2000).

15. Scores of scholarly papers have been written over the past three decades that addressed one or more of those concerns. Published in 1986 by the professional arts education associations and national associations of schools of music, art and design, theater and dance, *K–12 Arts Education in the United States: Present Context, Future Needs* (1986), is a particularly important document in this regard. It is worth reading in its entirety, but pages 9–18 are especially germane to issues that surround the effects of the arts advocacy movement on arts education policymaking. Also see Bresler, 1998; Brewer, 1998; Chapman, 2000a; Colwell, 1998; and Pankratz, 1998.

16. The entire Fall/Winter 2000 issue of the *Journal of Aesthetic Education, 34*(3–4), is dedicated to the REAP report "The Arts and Academic Achievement: What the Evidence Shows."

17. The finding that students who self-select into the arts are high academic achievers (thus nullifying claims of causal links between arts study and academic achievement) appears to hold true only in U.S. studies. A Dutch study found no difference in academic achievement between students who did and did not study the arts. A British study showed that studying the arts predicted *poorer* academic performance. Researchers suggest the discrepancies in such findings might be explained by cultural differences in the perceived relationship between arts study and academic ability and attainment (Winner & Hetland, 2000, pp. 51, 57).

18. The National Art Education Association has resorted to an antiadvocacy advocacy campaign. For several years now the NAEA has faxed and posted 1-page missives with 48-point bold-type headlines that read: "Art Is Not Made Basic Through Advocacy. Art Is Basic, Because It's the Way the Human Mind Works" and "If the national arts standards, state arts frameworks, and local art curricula are recognized as core areas of learning for U.S. students, why do arts advocates focus so strongly on the impact of the arts on learning in and across other disciplines?"

19. Evidence that points to erroneous assumptions and interpretations was encapsulated in a letter to the editor of the *Providence Journal* written by Philip Martorella, a Juilliard School of Music master's degree holder. Mr. Martorella (1999) wrote to "refute" a researcher's opinion that "listening to Mozart may have no appreciable impact on the intelligence." He stated that

> other researchers, who strongly believe in the "Mozart effect," have claimed that there are certain musical selections, whether composed by Mozart, or by Baroque composers such as Bach, Vivaldi and Pachelbel, that apparently have caused the activation of both sides of the brain to optimum effect.

Mr. Martorella concluded his refutation with the assumedly rhetorical questions: "Why is it that, after performing and listening to classical music, test scores have skyrocketed in SATs, in science, math and other subjects . . . ? Why is it that retention of data and attention spans have improved dramatically?" The public hoopla over the Mozart effect, on view in letters to the editor across the country, would be laughable if it were not so pernicious. If a highly trained Juilliard graduate so eagerly swallows the bait, the interested public has downed it hook, line, and sinker. Perhaps then it is not they who are lost but music education.

20. Almost everyone opines that the arts are "important in their own right" and that justification for arts education should focus on the unique and important kinds of learning that arise from the study of the arts. There is, however, strong incentive to continue funding and conducting research to find causality between arts study and improved academic performance. The REAP report "The Arts and Academic Achievement" (2000) recommends "there is a clear need for more rigorous research on [the transfer effects of the arts to other disciplines]." The importance of further study is explained from an educational perspective (i.e., "any transfer effects that do exist can be put to effective use by teachers") and from a scientific one (i.e., it can help us better understand "how the mind works and how skills are or are not related to the brain") (p. 7). I do not doubt that those are important and fascinating research areas. Yet I hope that we will not allow arts education research to be dominated by those quests. Many other areas need our attention that affect more directly and immediately the quality of teaching and learning in music, dance, theater, and the visual arts.

21. For months an all too readily accessible example was found on the "Learn About the NEA" webpage at http://arts.endow.gov/learn, where the "NEA Fact" popped up stating: "Recent academic research studies show arts education improves cognitive ability—students exposed to the arts perform better in tests including the SAT." Note the technique of melding the obvious and innocuous (i.e., arts education improves cognitive ability) with a generalized interpretation of statistical corelation (i.e., students exposed to the arts perform better on tests, including the SAT). Also note the word "exposed."

22. University of California at Los Angeles professor James Catterall offered a formal response to Elliot Eisner's critique of his widely publicized research finding that arts study results in improved academic performance. Deflecting the criticism, Catterall (1998) maintained that "arguments touting academic instrumentality are whipped along by advocates of the arts" (p. 6). During a recent panel discussion, Catterall expressed dismay at the overtly advocatory thrust of the 1999 publication *Champions of Change*, in which two of his studies were featured. He stated that neither he nor the other researchers whose work *Champions of Change* championed saw the preface or executive summary before publication. If Catterall was already aware of the proclivity of advocates to "whip along" any and all arguments that might help bolster their cause, why would he express surprise at the tenor and thrust of *Champions of Change?* If advocate proclivity to whip things along disturbed him, why would he allow *Champions of Change* to go to press without having scrutinized the summarization of his own research? Perhaps he was unaware that advocacy is the primary function of the Arts Education Partnership and the President's Committee on the Arts and the Humanities.

23. Although Frances Rauscher made a point of telling her 1998 MENC conference audience that "it would be a terrible shame for music education to have to be justified on the basis of the kind of research I do and the kinds of findings I'm reporting," this sentiment is absent from her published articles (Reimer, 1999, p. 39). When testifying on behalf of NAMM (a funder of her research) before a U.S. House of Representatives appropriations committee, she said: "You may be surprised to learn that recent scientific studies have consistently demonstrated the powerful and positive impact of music instruction on a child's ability to reach his or her full potential in math and science." Rather than express any misgivings about the math/science justification for music instruction, Rauscher recommended that Congress and the administration "use their respective bully pulpits" to encourage dialogue about such findings, dialogue that might "cause school boards across the county to re-evaluate" their elimination of music programs.

24. An "iron triangle" is a closed circle of mutual support between a government agency, its clients (or in this case grant recipients), and supporting legislators.

25. Laura Chapman observes: "The language of partnership and collaboration has two effects. It announces some form of alliance and accord, but it also suppresses hierarchies of significant expertise, effort, commitment, and authority for arts education in schools" (2000, p. 38).

26. The ubiquitous use of the terms *the arts* and *arts education* is an unfortunate linguistic development and an embarrassment to the profession. Both are marketing shorthand that serves to muddle, rather than clarify, our thinking and policymaking. There is art; there is dance, music, theater, visual art, and literature; there is the *study of* dance, the study of music, etc.

REFERENCES

American Arts Alliance. (2000). *Advocacy materials for arts supporters.* Retrieved from http://www.artswire.org/~aaa/material.html

American Arts Alliance. *Dispelling myths about national support of the arts and culture.* Retrieved from http://www.artswire.org/~aaa/myth.html

American Arts Alliance. (2000). Arts education: Federal money for what you already do. *Legislative Update, 5*(5).

American Symphony Orchestra League. (1999a, Spring). Federal funding for after-school learning on the rise. *Government Affairs Report,* Washington, DC.

American Symphony Orchestra League. (1999b, Spring). NEA rolls out new initiative. *Government Affairs Report,* Washington, DC.

Americans for the Arts. (1999, February/March). Beyond the anecdotes: Effects of youth arts programs. *Artslink.*

Americans for the Arts. (1999, November/December). *Artslink.*

Americans for the Arts. (1999, October). *Artslink.*

Americans for the Arts. (2000). *Legislative update on federal arts education legislation.* Retrieved May 11, 2000, from AFTAADV-1@artswire.org

Arts Education Partnership. (1999, November 30). Meeting announcement.

Ball, C. H. (1986). Mutual assistance or mutual debasement? *Design for Arts Education, 87*(6), 2–4.

Barzun, J. (1974). *The use and abuse of art.* Princeton, NJ: Princeton University Press.

Bresler, L. (1998). Research policy and practice in arts education meeting points for conversation. *Arts Education Policy Review, 99*(5), 9–15.

Brewer, T. (1998). Arts education advocacy and research: To what end? *Arts Education Policy Review, 99*(5), 16–20.

Bumgarner, C. M. (1994). Artist in the classroom: The impact and consequences of the National Endowment for the Arts' Artist Residency Program on the K–12 arts education. *Arts Education Policy Review, 95*(3), 14–29, (4), 8–31.

Burton, J., Horowitz, R., & Abeles, H. (1999). Learning and thought. In E. Fiske (Ed.), *Champions of change: The impact of the arts on learning* (pp. 35–46). Washington, DC: Arts Education Partnership and the President's Committee on the Arts and the Humanities.

Catterall, J. (1998). Rebuttal to Elliot Eisner. *Art Education, 51*(4), 6.

Chapman, L. H. (1982). *Instant art, instant culture: The unspoken policy for American schools.* New York: Teachers College Press.

Chapman, L. (2000a). A century of distancing art from the public. *Arts Education Policy Review, 101*(3), 27–28.

Chapman, L. (2000b). Questioning arts education in action: The state arts agency commitment. *Arts Education Policy Review, 101*(3),

Colwell, R. (1998). A long trail awinding: Issues, interests, and priorities in arts education research. *Arts Education Policy Review, 99*(5), 21–29.

Eisner, E. (1974). Is the artist in the schools program effective? *Art Education, 27*(2), 19–23.

Eisner, E. (1998). Does experience in the arts boost academic achievement? *Art Education, 51*(1), 7–15.

Fichter, N. S. (2000). Babel: A reminder. *Arts Education Policy Review, 101*(3), 13–14.

Flohr, J. W., Miller, D., & Persellin, D. (1999). Recent brain research on young children. *Teaching Music, 6*(6), 41–43, 54.

Gardiner, M., Fox, A., Knowles, F., & Jeffery, D. (1996). Learning improved by arts training. *Nature, 381,* 284.

Gee, C. B. (1999a). For you dear—anything!: Part 1. Omnipotence, omnipresence, and servitude "through the arts." *Arts Education Policy Review, 100*(4), 3–18.

Gee, C. B. (1999b). For you dear—anything!: Part 2. Remembering and returning to first principles. *Arts Education Policy Review, 100*(5), 3–22.

Grandin, T., Peterson, M., & Shaw, G. (1998). Spatial-temporal versus language-analytic reasoning: The role of music education. *Arts Education Policy Review, 99*(6), 11–14.

Haanstra, F. (1999). *Arts education and the educational careers of Dutch students.* Unpublished document, University of Amsterdam.

Harland, J., Kinder, K., Lord, P., Stoff, A. Schagen I., & Haynes, J. (with Cusworth, L., White, R. Q., & Paola, R. (2000). *Arts education in secondary schools: Effects and effectiveness.* Slough, UK: National Foundation for Educational Research.

Hinckley, J. (1999). Introduction. *Teaching Music, 6*(6), 6–7.

Hope, S. (1985). Promotion: Past failures, present urgencies. *Design for Arts Education,* 14–22.

Ivey, W. (1999, March). Remarks made by NEA chairman at the National Art Education convention, Washington, DC.

Kimpton, J. (2000). Looking ahead from past experience. *Arts Education Policy Review, 101*(3).

Lehman, P. R. (1992). Winning and losing in the struggle to reform education. *Design for Arts in Education, 93*(5), 2–12.

Lewis, C. S. (1984). Lilies that fester. In *The world's last night and other essays.* New York: Harcourt Brace.

Louisiana Alliance for Arts Education. (2000, November 28). Press release.

Martorella, P. (1999, September 10). "Mozart effect" is real. *Providence Journal,* p. 8.

Music Educators National Conference, National Art Education Association, National Dance Association, National Association of Schools of Music, National Association of Schools of Art and Design, National Association of Schools of Theatre, National Association of Schools of

Dance. (1986). *K–12 arts education in the United States: Present context, future needs.* Reston, VA: Author.

National Assembly of State Arts Agencies & National Endowment for the Arts. (1999, April). *Arts education in action: The state arts agency commitment* (executive summary).

National Endowment for the Arts. (1996). *America in the making.* Washington, DC: Author.

National Endowment for the Arts. (1998a). *Bringing the arts to life for children and adults since 1965.* Washington, DC: Author.

National Endowment for the Arts. (1998b). *Did you know . . . ?* Retrieved April 1998 from http://arts.endow.gov/NEAText/Guide/Facts/DidYa2.html

Pankratz, D. (1986). Aesthetic welfare, government, and educational policy. *Design for Arts Education, 87*(6), 12–24.

Pankratz, D. (1988, May/June). *Arts Education Policy Review, 99*(5), 3–8.

Pantev, & Oostenveld, R. (1998, April 23). Increased auditory cortical representation in musicians. *Nature,* 811–814.

Phillips, F. (1999, Autumn). *Grantsmakers in the Arts, 10*(2), 43.

President's Committee on the Arts and the Humanities. (1996). *Coming up taller.*

President's Committee on the Arts and the Humanities. (1997). *Creative America.*

President's Committee on the Arts and the Humanities & the Arts Education Partnership. (1999). *Gaining the arts advantage: Lessons from school districts that value arts education.* Washington, DC: Author.

Rauscher, F., Shaw, G., & Ky, K. (1993). Music and spatial task performance. *Nature, 365,* 365–611.

Reimer, B. (1999, July). Facing the risks of the "Mozart effect." *Music Educators Journal,* 37–43.

Smith, R. A. (1978). A policy analysis and criticism of the Artists-in-Schools Program of the National Endowment for the Arts. In R. A. Smith (Ed.), *Artist-in-Schools: Analysis and criticism* (pp. 21–41). Urbana: Bureau of Educational Research, University of Illinois at Urbana-Champaign.

U.S. Department of Education (2000, February). *Community Update,* p. 5.

U.S. Department of Education. (2000, August). Federal budget affects local schools. *Community Update,* no. 79.

U.S. Department of Education. (1999). *The Mars Millennium Project handbook.*

Watts, H. (2000, July/August). Be true to your schools. *Symphony,* p. 56.

Wilcox, E. (1999). Straight talk about music and brain research. *Teaching Music, 7*(3), 29–35.

Winner, E., & Cooper, M. (2000, Fall/Winter). Mute those claims. *Journal of Aesthetic Education,* pp. 51, 57.

Wolfe, Tom. (1975). *The painted word.* New York: Farrar, Straus & Giroux.

Yamaha Band and Orchestral Division. (1999, Spring). *Discover the power of music education.* Grand Rapids, MI: Author.

50

Research in Visual Art Education: Implications for Music

LYNN GALBRAITH

There is a rich heritage of visual art education research, which inquires into how visual art enriches and gives aesthetic meaning to peoples' private and public lives and experiences. Researchers explore the studio art-making process; examine how people teach and learn within the related disciplines of aesthetics, art criticism, and art history; and grapple with a variety of theoretical and practical issues that are related, for example, to child development, visual perception, diversity, culture, multiculturalism, social perspectives, gender (including sexual orientation), controversial issues, and technology. They conduct their research using philosophical, quantitative, and qualitative forms of inquiry that are often derived from related disciplines such as sociology, history, anthropology, psychology, and curriculum theory. Essentially, researchers in visual art education confront the exciting challenges—new and old—that visual art provides artists, teachers, and learners within a postmodern world.

The content for this chapter is based on an analysis of research findings in visual art education. Research was examined from the following sources: important research published in journals during the last 20 years (for example, *Journal of Aesthetic Education; Journal of Multicultural and Cross-Cultural Studies in Art Education; Studies in Art Education; Visual Arts Research*); the *Dissertation Abstracts* database; selected doctoral dissertations; existing research analyses (Allison, 1986; Burton, 1991, 1998; Davis, 1977; Hamblen, 1989; Jones & McPhee, 1986; La Pierre & Zimmerman, 1997; La Pierre, Stokrocki, & Zimmerman, 2000); and significant monographs, books, and reports (for example, Smith, 2000). Other sources included the various publications of the National Art Education Association's (NAEA) Research Commission (National Arts Education Association [NAEA], 1994, 1996, 1998). In addition, international journals were examined (for example,

Canadian Review of Art Education; and the United Kingdom's *Journal of Art and Design Education*), given that visual art education research has a long history in other parts of the world.

A series of headings frame this chapter. Interspersed within the text are various research possibilities, questions, links, and topics. The brevity of the chapter permits discussion of selected research themes only; thus, the chapter provides only a *flavor* of what visual art educators actually research, and much of this inquiry is focused on contemporary research issues. I concur with Wilson (1994) that researchers ideally interweave their interests, values, and assumptions about life and human purpose within their research activities. Music and visual art education researchers share similar goals as they inquire into how teaching and learning within music and visual art affect the lives of others, and ultimately themselves. It is hoped that once they breathe in the *flavor* they will develop healthy *appetites* for exploring visual art education research even further.

A Brief Overview of Research in Visual Art Education

Visual art education research comprises a broad range of diverse theories and beliefs, as well as traditional and alternative research methodologies and interpretations that provide a variety of intellectual challenges and perspectives within the field, and that reflect social and ideological change within contemporary society. There is a long tradition of visual art education research (Chalmers, 1999; Jones & McPhee, 1986; Zimmerman, 1997a)—one that has thrived on curiosity and doubt (Chapman, 1982).

Early inquiries in visual art education focused primarily on the studio art experience and tended to be descriptive or philosophical in design (Chapman, 1982), although researchers addressed broader topics such as visual perception, how students respond to art works, and crosscultural differences in learning (see MacGregor, 1972; McFee, 1961; Wilson, 1969). In the 1960s, large-scale studies were funded through the U.S. Office of Education. In the 1970s, the National Endowment for the Arts (NEA) and the J.D. Rockefeller III Fund's Arts in Education Program, acting in concert, sponsored a series of multidisciplinary and community-centered school visual art education programs. Yet, as Chapman (1982) pointed out, research was mixed, in that projects mostly addressed broader educational questions rather than questions specific to teaching and learning in visual art (and music). One NEA project, the "artists-in-the schools" program, still maintains a presence in many states (Bumgarner Gee, 1994). A literature search suggested that research on this topic has been conveyed in the form of published reports rather than as articles in peer-reviewed journals. Thus, there is a dearth of knowledge about how these artists fare, what they teach, and, importantly, *how* they teach. Research on this topic is long overdue, and possibilities exist for further research and collaborative inquiry with music educators.

The Kettering Project at Stanford University (Eisner, 1968), directed by Elliot Eisner from 1968 to 1970, launched an experimental elementary art program that was one of the first to introduce students to studio art, art criticism, and art history. It also employed a written art curriculum and specific evaluation measures, along with the use of art reproductions and museum visits. Other federally funded educational research and development initiatives were the Aesthetic Education Curriculum Program at the Central Midwestern Regional Educational Laboratory (CEMREL) near St. Louis, Missouri, and the Elementary Art Program at the Southwest Regional Laboratory (SWRL) in Los Angeles. Within these programs, curricular materials were developed as a means of promoting critical and historical concepts in art.

Over the last 3 decades, the decline in federal or state sources for large-scale research projects in visual art has limited opportunities for conducting large-scale studies or replicating previous inquiries within the United States (Chapman, 1982; MacGregor, 1998). Researchers have sought funding from philanthropic and private organizations, such as the Spencer Foundation and the Jacob Javits Gifted and Talented Discretionary Grant Program (see Clark & Zimmerman, 1997). Harvard Project Zero is the leading, continuously funded, well-staffed research project that addresses visual art education.

Other researchers (and the field as a whole) benefited from an association with the Getty Institute for Education in the Arts (formerly known as the Getty Center for Education in the Arts) from the mid-1980s to 1998. The Getty Institute sponsored a series of curricular and research projects related to discipline-based art education (DBAE) in which the disciplined knowledge of making studio art is studied comprehensively alongside historical, critical, and aesthetic perspectives (Eisner, 1988; Smith, 2000). The Getty's grants for its regional institutes in various states leveraged more than $24 million for arts-based research over 15 years (Duke, 1999). Some of this funding was supplemented by funds from the U.S. Department of Education, the NEA, and national foundations such as the Annenberg Institute for School Reform.

Most researchers, however, have relied on funds from higher education institutions, state organizations, or the innovative grants programs sponsored by the NAEA and its sister organization, the National Art Education Foundation. The Foundation allocates 10 grants of $3,000 annually for research. These grants are available for both researchers and practitioners. Across the border, Canadian art educators are fortunate in that the Social Sciences and Humanities Research Council of Canada has supported a number of excellent projects over the years (see Irwin, Rogers, & Wan, 1998; MacGregor, 1994).

A Sampling of Research Methodologies

On the whole, however, this general dearth of funding has not deterred researchers. Indeed, there are perhaps positive outcomes in that researchers have embraced theoretical or qualitative methodologies as alternatives to statistical methods and large-scale empirical studies (Hamblen, 1989).

How have visual art education researchers incorporated these diverse methods into their work? A number of researchers have conducted ethnographic studies of teachers and students within a diversity of classroom settings. Hawke (1980) researched the life-world of a visual art education teacher. Stokrocki (1995) has conducted a number of ethnographies on visual art teachers and students from various cultural groups, including a long-term study of a Navajo teacher. Stokrocki employed various forms of in-depth data collection, including participant observation, interviews, and video and audio taping, and alerted us to the complexities inherent within classroom settings and teacher-student interactions, as well as to the cultural perspectives and artistic philosophy of the teacher. Sevigny's (1977) classic study examined the multiple perspectives of student and professor in a university studio art class.

Other researchers have chosen methods that stem from anthropology. Classic examples include Degge's (1975) study of a junior high school class, which was the first visual art education study to use largely ethnographic techniques, and Pohland's (1972) landmark paper, which was instrumental in informing the field about participant observation research. In a recent example, a 3-year case study, Kellman (1997) employed anthropological methods as she sensitively described the role of art in the life of Peter, an 8-year old boy, and his family. Abandoning traditional stereotypes of the handicapped child, Kellman views Peter as an artist who is able to develop a visual vocabulary that allows him to create and express meaning. Kellman's methodology and analysis of Peter's artwork provided insight into Peter's personal world.

Teaching visual art and music requires teachers who are able to pursue instructional and evaluative approaches that strive to relate learning in art and music to the diverse backgrounds, needs, and interests of the students. As Cole and Knowles (2000) suggested, "the act of teaching is informed by multiple forms of knowledge and is representative of a variety of ways of personal, professional, and contextual knowing" (p. 7). Thus, it is not surprising that researchers are actively conducting case studies (Bresler, 1992; Bullock & Galbraith, 1992; Day, 1973; May, 1985; Wolfe, 1997; Zimmerman, 1991) and action research and teacher-as-researcher projects (Anderson, 1997; Donnelly, 1990). Researchers are developing a variety of ways to gain a better understanding of what visual art teachers know and of how teaching and learning take place in classrooms.

As Wilson (1994) noted, experimental research has fallen into disfavor recently. Yet there have been a large number of descriptive and quantitative studies over the years (see Brewer 1999; Chalmers, 1999). Specific examples include the correlation study of Rush, Weckesser, and Sabers (1980) that examined the effects on instruction on teaching contour drawing to children and the work of Koroscik, Short, Stavropolos, and Fortrin, (1992) that employed experimental methods to understand how selected art viewing situations or interventions may help or hinder the interpretation of art meanings held by undergraduate nonmajors. In a national survey of instruction in secondary visual art education, Burton (2001) identified the instructional strategies that secondary teachers prefer to use.

Important sources related to the development of aesthetics within visual art education include the work of Geahigan (1998), Lankford (1992), Parsons and Blocker (1993), Smith (1989), and Smith and Simpson (1992). The influence of sociology has steadily increased over the years (see Lanier, 1969; Nadaner, 1984) and today's researchers are reexamining the place of visual art education from social and democratic perspectives (see Blandy & Congdon, 1987; Duncum, 1990; Freedman, 2000). There is also the influence of psychology (Gardner, 1990; Parsons, 1987), curriculum theory (see Bresler, 1994; Sullivan, 1989), and history (see Bolin, 1995; Stankiewicz, 1997) on contemporary visual art education research.

Visual art education researchers also draw on research methodologies as models for enhancing art education classroom practices and discourse. For example, Chalmers (1981) made a case for the study of art as cultural artifact. He proposed that the cultural anthropologist serve as a model for teachers and students as they work together as ethnographers and explore, research, and discuss art by makers who represent diverse crosscultural perspectives. Further, this work, influenced by McFee (1961), seems particularly relevant for music education in that students and teachers are presented with opportunities to learn about the broad themes and functions of art and music within and across cultures.

Addiss and Erickson (1993) and Korzenik (1985) provided detailed methods and procedures for conducting historical research within and about educational settings. Erickson (1983) advocated for the use of art history inquiry for its pedagogical benefits. In this article, she used the study of sheet music illustrations to indicate how the various aspects of the art-historical process (reconstruction, description, attribution, interpretation, explanation), though sequential in orientation, are often interconnected. Oral histories are also useful for recording the voices of local visual art (or music) educators or for developing stories of how ordinary people learned about visual art (and music) (Stankiewicz, 1997).

Collaborative research is becoming more evident. May (1993) has provided an excellent framework on which to build a case for collaborative action research in visual art education that is easily applicable to music education. One example of this type of collaboration is Anderson's (1997) case study of an artist as teacher who utilized video as both a research method and as a means of undertaking collaborative research along with her students. In another example, Lachapelle (1994) utilized "informant-made videos" in his study of aesthetic learning in adults. Asking participants to record their own art-viewing experiences, he found that the videographic accounts were equal to researcher-conducted audiotaped interviews as a means of collecting verbal statements about works of art. Possibilities exist for developing similar research that includes students in music education classroom research as well as for collecting verbal statements about their responses to music.

Irwin and Rogers (1997), as part of a large-scale collaborative research project, brought together Australia Aborigines with their First Nation counterparts in Canada using videoconferencing facilities. The research examined topics such as the effects of European settlement on Aboriginal art and the cultural conflicts facing contemporary Aboriginal artists. Other forms of alternative reporting have included a parable (Mason, 1980), a translation of research results by researchers in the form of a three-person dialogue (Stuhr, Krug, & Scott, 1995), and personal cultural histories (Zurmuehlen, 1990).

Artistic Inquiry as a Basis for Conducting Research

The work of Eisner (1991) promoted the development of artistic inquiry as a means for conducting research. Eisner's writings on art criticism, educational criticism, and connoisseurship have influenced the field and that of education in general (Coles & Knowles, 2000). Selected research examples include Alexander's (1980) case study of a high school history class using educational criticism and Barone's (1989) use of critical analysis in a case study of a fine arts program in a black elementary school. Lightfoot and Davis (1997) have advocated the use of portraiture as a methodology for conducting research in classrooms and educational institutions.

Who Conducts Research in Visual Art Education?

Most visual art education researchers are higher education faculty, graduate students, and independent scholars (Burton, 1998; Zimmerman, 1997a), although practitioner-based research has been encouraged (Galbraith, 1988; NAEA, 1996; Zimmerman, 1996). Burton's (1998) survey of 332 visual art education educators in higher education institutions ascertained that faculty and doctoral students primarily conduct research in theoretical and conceptual areas, whereas master's level graduate students concentrate on practical matters related to curricular and instructional concerns. Anderson, Eisner, and McRorie (1998) surveyed 124 visual art education graduate programs in the United States and Canada to determine their location, scope, and nature. Their findings indicated that teacher education is central to graduate study at the master's level. In the leading doctoral programs, however, research requirements reflected broad research orientations, ranging from ethnography to statistics to historical research. The authors reported that humanistic rather than scientific methods are preferred, although quantitative and qualitative methods are important components of most degree programs. Given this assessment, the future of visual art education research may reflect an increasing commitment to qualitative concerns and methodologies.

One of the benchmarks of quality research is whether the research is refereed by peers and appears in well-known scholarly journals. A review of the types of research questions, studies, and methodologies undertaken in *Studies in Art Education* over the past 40 years by three distinguished researchers (Brewer, 1999; Chalmers, 1999; Collins, 1999) may be of interest. These authors have presented thoughtful reviews and analyses, all of which provide useful reading.

Contemporary Visual Art Education Research Priorities and Topics

What then are some research topics that might have possible relevance for music education, and in particular, relevance for teaching and learning in music education? The list is not inclusive and is not framed in any particular order of preference.

Child Development and Student Learning

The graphic development of children has been a constant research theme within visual art education. Harvard's Project Zero has produced a substantial body of work about how children develop cognitively and emotionally in relation to making and responding to art, about the use of symbols in children's art, and about how culture influences children's artistic expression (Gardner, 1989). Recently there has been a shift from looking at the child in isolation and as someone whose art-making develops in a definitive progression and stages (Lowenfeld & Britain, 1987) to viewing the child as someone who is capable of constructing art in a range of styles, no matter what "stage" he or she is in (Golomb, 1992; Kindler, 1999; Wilson & Wilson, 1976; Wolf, 1994).

Kindler's (1999) research may be of specific interest to the music educator. She examined the relationship between culture and the development of children's artistic abilities, attitudes, and art-related skills from a crosscultural perspective. Contesting the traditional linear developmental approach to children's graphic development, she suggested instead that visual art educators pay attention to the multiple pictorial repertoires that are very much part of children's artistic development (Kindler, 1999; Kindler & Darras, 1998), including those multiple modalities of expression that allow children to construct meaning through connections across symbol systems within their own specific cultures. She argued further that children develop diverse ways to examine the world pictorially. Children must be exposed to curricula and pedagogy that allow them to use a broader range of pictorial signs and symbols—and, logically, this would seem to apply to music education as well.

Other researchers have explored the relationship between culture and children's graphic development (Wilson & Wilson, 1985). Wilson (1997b) analyzed two sets of Japanese children's artworks; one was in the graphic narrative style, the other was school art in the "high," or fine, art tradition. His research suggested that art derived from popular cultural models allows children to investigate the world in ways that are significant for them and to experiment with life's major themes, dimensions of meaning that are frequently absent from children's life in schools.

Curriculum- and Discipline-Based Art Education

The 1965 Penn State Seminar (see Beittel & Mattil, 1966) served as a landmark in art education research on curriculum, as was the publication *Guidelines: Curriculum Development in Aesthetic Education* (Barkan, Chapman, & Kern, 1970). These guidelines suggested that visual art education was emerging as a structured discipline in its own right and should integrate the teaching of art history and art criticism as well as the content and inquiry processes of the professional artist, art critic, and art historian. Manual Barkan (1962) had argued 3 years earlier that art education reform was also dependent on nurturing the aesthetic lives of teachers and students. In 1978 Clark and Zimmerman proposed that aesthetics be added to the art history, art criticism, and art studio triad. A decade later, through the writings of researchers in the field, the leadership and resources of the emerging Getty Center for Education in the Arts (1985), and the advocacy of the NAEA (National Art Education Association, 1986), visual art educators were encouraged to integrate concepts from the four disciplines—studio production, art criticism, art history, and aesthetics—within all levels of school curricula. Consequently, by the mid-1980s the notion of "discipline-based art education" (Greer, 1984; Clark, Day, & Greer, 1987) had made its imprint on the field. The development of discipline-based art education was not without its critics, and over the years prominent researchers have debated issues related to its growth (see for example, Hamblen, 1987a).

This shift toward a more *comprehensive* (a term later adopted by the Getty Education Institute in the Arts) visual art curriculum was outlined in a series of research papers, books, and curricular materials from the mid-1980s to the late 1990s. Smith's (2000) *Readings in Discipline-Based Art Education: A Literature of Educational Reform* has provided a substantial and significant overview of research developments in discipline-based art education. The Getty Institute sponsored a series of monographs written by significant researchers, including Rudolph Arnheim (1996), Graeme Chalmers (1996), Elliot Eisner (1988), and Howard Gardner (1990), and promoted an internet website (www.artsednet.getty.edu) that is (as of this writing) still in existence. The website features a series of curricular and research projects, including Mary Erickson's historical inquiry entitled *Art in Our World* and Ralph Smith's annotated DBAE bibliography of over 600 research items on the four visual art disciplines and related topics.

Historical Inquiry and Aesthetic Understanding

Music educators may be interested in understanding how children understand history as they learn through historical inquiry and respond to and understand art (see Addis & Erickson, 1993; Erickson, 1995, 1997; Parsons, 1987). In an empirical study on second-grade students, Erickson (1995) found that the students were able to incorporate knowledge of individual artists and develop a limited historical perspective as they look at artworks. In another study, Erickson (1998) examined the effects of instruction in art history information and inquiry on fourth- and eighth-grade students' abilities to interpret an unfamiliar artwork contextually. Before and after instruction art teachers asked their students to interpret an unfamiliar artwork from three differing perspectives: historical artist, viewer, and culture. The results verify that eighth-grade students were more successful in interpreting artworks contextually than fourth-grade students. Yet both fourth- and eighth-grade students were most successful using the historical artist perspective. Furthermore, the findings indicated that art history instruction at both grade levels was able to increase students' ability to interpret artworks contextually. Instruction helped the younger students to understand more fully the historical artist perspective and allowed older students to understand historical perspectives of the viewer, culture, and artist in their contextual interpretation.

A developmental interpretation of some of the differences in students' cognitive responses to art came from Parsons (1987). Using data from interviews with persons of different ages over a 10-year period, he outlined a five-stage theory of aesthetic development. At the first stage, "favoritism," persons are intuitively attracted to artworks' color and subject matter. They rarely judge the artworks. During the second stage, "beauty and realism," concepts are organized around the idea of representation. The third stage is concerned with "expressiveness" and responding to the feeling or thought expressed by the artist. The fourth stage is based on "style and form." Here art-making is viewed as social: works of art exist in public space and are part of a tradition of historical and stylistic relationships. In "autonomy," the fifth stage, the person can evaluate the concepts and values with which the tradition constructs the meanings and values of artworks. The five stages follow one another sequentially and produce progressively better understanding.

Parsons and Blocker (1993) advocated that familiarizing students with basic aesthetic questions allows them to form their own opinions, including opinions about contemporary postmodernist and multicultural thinking. Mason and Rawdling (1993) discussed how the area of aesthetics is a source of curriculum content that facilitates the development of general thinking habits. Russell (1988) found that fifth- and sixth-grade students have the intellectual potential to improve significantly in their verbal reasoning about defining visual art, in that they were able to articulate logically sound thinking related to conceptual issues. The children had received 4 years of discipline-based visual art instruction prior to the study, and Russell pointed out that the findings suggest that it is feasible that students, given an appropriate and sequenced curriculum, may develop the potential for discussing the conceptual tensions inherent in contemporary visual art.

Questioning Strategies, Talking about Art, and Conversations in the Classroom

Research on questioning strategies has significance for music education. Visual art education researchers examine how teachers ask questions and how students respond to visual images and their own art-making. Armstrong and Armstrong's (1977) "Art Teacher Questioning Strategy" provided a guiding framework for asking questions and reflective practice within the classroom. In a later experimental study, Armstrong (1986) examined the effect of teacher training in a visual art production questioning method on teacher questioning and student responses. Hamblen's (1984) questioning typology, based on Bloom's taxonomy of educational objectives (knowledge, comprehension, application, analysis, synthesis, and evaluation), addressed the need for properly formulated questions for classroom discourse about artistic practices. It formed a synthesis between questioning strategies, higher order thinking, and art criticism instruction.

Barrett's (1994) art criticism strategies for talking about and interpreting visual artworks are relevant for music educators, who help students describe, interpret, and evaluate pieces of music or various musical objects and artifacts. Barrett has argued that students should be taught to use such procedures as description, interpretation, and evaluation and should be encouraged to ask certain basic questions, such as, what is here? what is it about? how good is it? is it visual art? (Or is it music?)

Hafeli's (2000) qualitative case study uncovered the ways in which students and a teacher interpreted lesson guidelines, and through an analysis of their conversations, using a "stimulated recall" method, illustrates acts of resistance and negotiation as student ideas, preferences, judgments, and meanings about the art they produced interfaced with the instructional goals and aesthetic views of the teacher. Kakas (1991) also studied the nature of classroom conversations, and a crosscultural study by Makin,

White, and Owen (1996) investigated how Anglo-Australian and Asian-Australian teachers responded differently to children's visual art–making.

Special Populations

Unfortunately, only a handful of researchers have investigated the theoretical and practical issues related to teaching persons with disabilities or who are at risk or are gifted and talented. It is an area in need of research and attention. Nonetheless, Guay's (1993) cross-site analysis presented a thorough and important case study that documented how university student teachers deal with students who experience disabilities. Nyman and Jenkins's (2000) edited volume is informative reading on visual art education with children with special needs, although it is not research specific. Pariser (1981) and Kellman (1997) have studied children with autism, and Blandy (1993), a strong advocate for persons with disabilities, examined community-based lifelong learning in art for adults with mental disabilities. Zimmerman (1985) outlined a theory for labeling artistically talented students in visual art. In a collaborative project (Project ARTS: Arts for Rural Teachers and Students) between Indiana University, New Mexico State University, Converse College in South Carolina, and seven rural elementary schools, Clark and Zimmerman (1997) identified appropriate educational services to underrepresented and underserved artistically talented students in rural schools.

There is little research on the elderly in visual art education, yet the increasing numbers of older and retired adults suggest that music and visual art education researchers must pay greater attention to this population. Jones (1993), using survey and case study methods, examined the influence of age on self-directed learning in university and community adult art students. La Porte's (1998) ethnographic study reported on intergenerational interactions between Hispanic and African American teenagers and homebound older adults during an art program in Harlem, New York. The program included social service, oral history, and art-making and provided a natural setting for the emergence of community. Eschedor's (2000) action-research case study described how a group of older adults successfully used art-making and storytelling as a means of reviewing selected moments in their lives. Smith-Shank's and Schwiebert's (2000) qualitative study using participant self-selected focus group methodologies examined the importance of elderly women's reminiscence of life events through the use of visual memories. Similar studies on how music (both classical and popular) has affected and transformed the lives of the elderly over the years seem particularly applicable and relevant within music education.

Teacher Education and Teacher Beliefs

Teacher education in visual art is an emerging area of research (Davis, 1990; Galbraith, 1995; Zimmerman, 1994, 1997c). Recent changes in teacher education today require that preservice students acquire more knowledge and a variety of pedagogical skills. These changes involve developing a better understanding of how pre- and inservice teachers think about visual art education. Day's (1997) edited volume, *Preparing Teachers of Art,* includes important chapters that identify significant teacher education research and issues. Zimmerman's (1994) comprehensive review of research and practices within preservice visual art education may also be helpful to music educators.

Galbraith (1997) examined the curricular components of visual art preparation programs in the United States. Her findings show that some form of visual art teacher education is taught in over 600 teacher certification programs, yet each program is essentially an autonomous unit that has little contact with other programs, even those that operate within the same state. In later work, Galbraith (2001) examined the working lives of visual art education faculty who work in some of these institutions. She found that many faculty members involved in teacher preparation, particularly in smaller institutions, maintained heavy teaching loads and were responsible for teaching studio, art history, and general education courses as well as those that served visual art education majors. This predilection for teaching has hindered faculty-initiated scholarship on teacher education issues within the field. Moreover, research is sorely missing on the qualifications, beliefs, and practices of faculty members who teach and prepare beginning visual art teachers (Galbraith, 1997; Hutchens, 1997). Despite its sensitivity and complexity, scholarship is much needed on faculty members and their roles within and their impact on visual art and music teacher education.

Chapman (1982) argued that visual art education research has been "child-centered" and has focused on students, especially young children, far more than it has been directed toward the study of teachers, the curriculum, and educational settings. She noted that

> research on the teachers' own artistic and educational philosophy is of special importance in visual art precisely because the art teacher is relatively free to invent the art curriculum—to determine the objectives, content, and activities made available to children. (p. 107)

Fortunately, there are contemporary researchers who are addressing these concerns.

Grauer's (1998) case study research categorized the beliefs toward visual art education that prospective teachers bring to teacher certification programs and examined how or whether their beliefs change during the course of their program. Using the Eisner Art Education Belief Index (Eisner, 1973), she surveyed all of the candidates in a 1-year, postbaccalaureate visual art teacher certification program and conducted in-depth interviews and observations with a sample of four elementary generalist and four secondary visual art specialist preservice teachers. She found that beliefs about education, particularly those regarding the subject matter, were powerful sources of influence on teachers. Beginning teachers' knowledge about visual art, for example, was not as strong an indicator of a willingness to learn about art education as were teachers' beliefs about what visual art education entails.

Kowalchuk's case study (1999) inquired into the beliefs of 37 preservice student teachers. Other than anecdotal accounts, little is known about patterns of successes, challenges, and difficulties encountered by visual art education student teachers. The student teachers wrote guided reflective statements seven times over the course of their student teaching practicum. The findings indicated that the student teachers were challenged both by their lack of ease with the technical aspects of teaching visual art, especially in terms of classroom management and the use of pedagogical strategies, and their lack of ease with subject matter content. The results raised questions about the ways novices articulate subject knowledge in teaching and how teacher education faculty can better assist them to balance instructional and subject matter demands. Richmond (1993) suggested that preservice programs must acknowledge the importance of discussion and critical reflection so that student teachers are invited to enter into pedagogical conversations that will continue throughout their professional lives.

Teacher Leadership

Research on teacher leadership is applicable within music education. Irwin's (1995) ethnographic study of a fine arts supervisor examined the daily, weekly, and monthly "rhythms" of the supervisor over a 4-month period. She studied how the supervisor's practical and experiential knowledge related to curriculum implementation within the political structure of her school district. Irwin found that the supervisor used a series of "images" to construct and make sense of her role as she served as the interface between the student-teacher world of teaching and the school system-world of administrative policies and regulations. Important research findings stem from Zimmerman's (1997b) focus group research with inservice teachers in the Artistically Talented Program at Indiana University. The findings suggested that teachers who know their subject matter content have a heightened understanding of pedagogy, are able to build self-esteem in others, are able to provide choices for students and themselves, and are more likely to become caring leaders in their professional and private lives.

Using feminist methodology that incorporated autobiographical case study techniques, Cera (1998) examined the skills of a visual art educator/teacher leader. Reflective writing, observation, and member checking were used to construct the data. The data were represented in narrative form as partial tales. The results indicated that leadership skills included an understanding of group process dynamics, the ability to facilitate group decision-making, the ability to reflect, an understanding of school change theory, and understanding of what it means to be a professional.

Assessment

Assessment is an issue for both visual art and music educators. Standardized tests have been used in visual art education over the years (see Clark, Day, & Greer, 1987; Clark, Zimmerman, & Zurmuehlen, 1987), although there has been disagreement as to whether and how assessment should occur (Hamblen, 1987b). Portfolio assessment has its roots in visual art, as well as other alternative assessment forms, such as educational criticism and connoisseurship (Eisner, 1985, 1991). However, research on assessment is still needed within the field, especially in terms of examining the National Standards and the standards that have been adopted for the evaluation of students and teachers within the various states. Likewise, assessment issues and research are an international concern. Research examples include a large-scale cross-Canadian study (MacGregor, 1994) on the assessment practices of visual art educators and an edited volume (Boughton, Eisner, & Ligtvolt, 1996) that comprises a series of research studies in the global arena.

Two large-scale studies close to home need mention. First, Sabol (1998) examined the format and content of state visual art achievement tests from all state departments of education within the United States. His findings revealed that the tests varied widely in format and content and that only partial agreement existed among state fine arts coordinators about these assessment concerns. He argued that more study of format and content is required and that the use of achievement tests together with alternative and authentic assessments may result in more accurate profiles of student achievement within visual art.

Wilson's (1997a) report *The Quiet Evolution: Changing the Face of Arts Education* has documented how the Getty Education Institute for the Arts served as a model for educational change. The report reflected one of the largest

evaluation studies ever conducted within visual art education. Using a form of evaluation characterized as "negotiation" (as identified by Guba & Lincoln, 1989), Wilson and his evaluation team evaluated how participants fared within the Getty's Regional Institutes in California, Florida, Minnesota, Nebraska, Ohio, Tennessee, and Texas. The values of the various stakeholders from the Institutes—teachers, administrators, consultants, faculty, and museum educators—were "brought to the fore, examined, and if not always resolved, at least understood by all parties" (Wilson, 1997a, p. 33). Wilson argued that the evaluative reports themselves resembled Eisner's (1991) "educational criticism" in that each of the Institute's programs were akin to texts that were interpreted and evaluated. His conclusions showed that the Institutes were successful in that they allowed for the systematic collaboration of many individuals—teachers, administrators, consultants, researchers—who worked together to change the face of visual art education within their individual states and across the United States as a whole.

Teaching at the College Level

A large number of visual art education faculty members are involved in teaching large visual art "appreciation" or criticism courses to undergraduate nonmajors. Stout (1995) has conducted a series of significant research studies on teaching this student population. This work is of interest to music educators who teach music appreciation courses, world music, and other courses for general education students. For example, in one study, Stout (1995) examined the critical conversations that students generated as they discussed visual artworks. In another study (Stout 1999), a survey of the instructional approaches of college visual art appreciation instructors revealed an emphasis on breadth of coverage, reading from secondary sources, and an interpretation through formal properties rather than an emphasis on constructivist learning theory and actual teaching practice. Stout reflected on her own pedagogical explorations in a large class of approximately 200 non–art majors as she sought to make changes in the course. Fox's (1999) analysis of survey responses from 449 non–art majors enrolled in general education visual art courses indicated that students were more engaged in visual art general education courses if the course content emphasized contemporary issues and if instructors used teaching approaches that helped connect course issues to students' lives.

There is little research on teaching large undergraduate courses for nonmajors, and it is an area that needs study, especially with respect to course content (breadth versus depth), pedagogical issues (lectures versus more interactive strategies), the use of technology, and the employment of graduate teaching assistants.

Gender and Multicultural Studies

The role of gender has a significant place within music and visual art education. For example, how do women artists, composers, and musicians identify themselves? How can one teach using feminist pedagogical principles within music and visual art classrooms? How are females (and males) perceived and taught within music education settings? Feminist researchers within visual art have used a variety of research methodologies as a means of answering their questions (Collins & Sandell, 1994). The influence of women visual art educators, women's art, and feminism has strengthened over the last two decades. The Women's Caucus is a vibrant and active force within the NAEA. An edited volume, *Gender Issues in Art Education*, by Collins and Sandell (1994), a series of histories of women visual art educators (Congdon & Zimmerman, 1993), a variety of feminist-oriented articles (see Garber, 1990; McRorie, 1996) and two special issues of *Studies in Art Education* that featured gender studies, published in 1977 and 1990, have made significant contributions to research in visual art education. The *Journal of Gender Issues in Art Education* is a recent addition to the field and is sponsored by the Women's Caucus of the NAEA.

Garber (1990) recommended that feminist visual art criticism be used as a means of presenting art criticism in that it pays special attention to the worldviews of people of different genders, classes, and races. She described feminist criticism as comprising three components—analytic, activist, and woman-centered. McRorie (1996) and Hicks (1992) have addressed similar concerns within the teaching of art criticism and aesthetics. Sandell (1992) researched the notion of a feminist pedagogy within visual art education. Chanda (1993) presented a theoretical basis for instructing students in non-Western art history. Mullen (1999) studied the pedagogical dimensions of an arts-based educational program inside a Florida female correctional facility. She argued for curricular innovations that enhance knowledge of incarcerated females' creative journeys in the visual and musical arts.

Multicultural concerns have been part of the visual art research agenda for a number of decades. Wasson, Stuhr, and Petrovich-Mwanki (1990) developed six position statements that promote a socioanthropological approach to the study of cultures. Anderson (1995) examined art criticism from a multicultural perspective and argued for critical representation from all cultural groups. Garber (1995), in her study of visual art in the borderlands (the American Southwest), advocated an in-depth approach to the study of cultures. Irwin, Rogers and Wan (1999) ad-

dressed the need for making connections between cultures, especially among Aboriginal and dominant cultures. They focused on three themes: cultural memory, cultural performance, and cultural translation between three Aboriginal cultures on three continents—South Australia, Canada, and Taiwan. In addition, Chalmers (1996) and Mason (1988) have contributed considerably to this area and represent alternative perspectives on this important topic.

Other issues researchers grapple with that have relevance for music education include the challenges that face lesbians and gays in visual art education (Lampela, 1995, 2001), issues of sexual identity in the visual art classroom (Honeychurch, 1995), the historical and theoretical origins of racism and cultural diversity in the public school curricula (Chalmers, 1992), and the aesthetic assumptions and stereotypes that influence the production of visual metaphors and works of art about illness and health (especially AIDS) in society (Garoian, 1997).

Issues in Contemporary Society

Visual art education researchers pay great attention to issues in contemporary society. Much of this work is grounded in concerns for social perspectives, gender, and multiculturalism, as well as revised definitions of what visual art entails in a postmodern society (Efland, Freedman, & Stuhr, 1996; Neperud, 1995). These concerns have been often outlined within philosophical essays, rather than being pursued in terms of empirical or qualitative research.

Duncum (1990) made a case for expanding the notion of visual culture by examining the signs and images of everyday life as opposed to those of "high art." His suggested paradigms encompassed shopping malls, theme parks, advertising, tourism, the internet, and television. This type of study suggested that visual art education in schools should be concerned with popular culture and social concerns (see Freedman & Wood, 1999; Lanier, 1969). Parallels exist in music education, for example, in which the culture of popular music (including radio shows, videos, the cable music channels, and music downloadable from the internet) is compared to that of classical music. Two examples from visual art education research include Smith-Shank's (1998) microethnography of a Grateful Dead concert and Taylor's (1999) 2-year case study of high school students who created computer hypertext websites related to their interpretations of a music video by pop singer Madonna. In the latter study, the students not only connected the music and video to other works of music and visual art, but they also recognized the societal, political, and cultural challenges posed by examining the video.

New Directions in Visual Art Education Research: The NAEA as a Model

During the past decade, the NAEA has been proactive in initiating and supporting research efforts to advance research at all instructional levels and contexts. In 1994, the NAEA Commission on Research in Art Education issued a report, *Art Education: Creating a Visual Arts Research Agenda Toward the Twenty-First Century,* that presented an agenda for research in art education and 10 recommendations for research efforts in the twenty-first century. In an accompanying booklet, *Blueprint for Implementing a Visual Arts Education Research Agenda* (NAEA, 1994), the NAEA Research Commission set about bridging the theory-practice gap by implementing a shared infrastructure that promotes individual and collaborative art education research. Eight research task forces—on demographics, conceptual, curriculum, instruction, contexts, student learning, evaluation, and teacher education—were eventually formed, as well as a plan for how the task forces might develop their research agendas. Under an assigned chair, each task force produced a briefing paper (NAEA, 1996) that outlined the task force's research agenda and intended questions for study. An open invitation was sent to all NAEA members to participate in the research initiative, as researchers, research study participants, or "research consumers." Participation has been significant. For example, the task force on contexts collectively published an edited volume, *Remembering Others: Making Invisible Histories Visible* (Bolin, Blandy, & Congdon, 2000), and because over 200 articles were submitted during the original call for manuscripts, a second collection is under way.

The NAEA has also produced indexes of dates, titles of articles, and authors published in the NAEA journal *Art Education* between 1947 and 1996 and in the NAEA's research quarterly journal *Studies in Art Education* from 1958 to 1997 (both are downloadable from the NAEA website: www.naea-reston.org). Two NAEA initiatives that stand out are the series of monographs that ask invited scholars to reflect on their research (see Lanier, 1991), and the NAEA Archival Series, in which classic texts, such as Elliot Eisner's *Educating Artistic Vision* (1972, 1997), have been reprinted.

The NAEA has also promoted two research indexes, *ARIAD 2* and *ARIAD Australia,* both of which are available on CD-ROM. The databases feature research projects, institutions, and resources in the United Kingdom and Australia. The ARIAD Australia database also includes educational research in music, dance, and drama. One-page digests of recent thinking and research in visual art education (*NAEA Advisories*) and a 3- to 4-page review of research on a given topic (*Translations: Theory into Practice*) are disseminated to all NAEA members at various times over the year. Furthermore, the NAEA Research Commission initiated a new 6-year research plan (2000–2006) that has allocated funds of up to $40,000 annually for targeted research on secondary learning, technology, and professional development in visual art, respectively.

Conclusion

Research in both music and visual art should develop understandings of how persons' lives are forever enriched and even changed by teaching and learning in visual art and music. Researchers in visual art are embracing inquiry into the aesthetic, critical, and historical domains of visual art, as well as production; are exploring the beliefs of teachers and learners; and are meeting head-on the challenges presented by issues of gender and multiculturalism and our very ways of being within contemporary society.

What takes place within classrooms and other educational venues is at the very heart of teaching and learning within music and visual art education. Arguably, one cannot generalize from the case studies of the teaching and learning that take place in these settings; however, these studies, especially when assembled collectively, allow us to contemplate the curricular and instructional beliefs and practices of teachers and to understand more fully how persons learn in different settings with different teachers, and over time. Visual art education research is making major contributions to this area, although more studies must be completed, especially, for example, in relation to assessment, national and state standards, early childhood issues, visual art and the elderly, elementary specialist teaching, teaching at the college level, and visual art teacher preparation.

Visual art education research is exciting, provocative at times, far-reaching, and certainly flavorful. It is hoped that this delineation of some of the various methodologies and studies in visual art education research will help music educators to discover connections and clarify their own visions about what constitutes research in their field.

REFERENCES

Addis, S., & Erickson, M. (1993). *Art history and education.* Urbana: University of Illinois Press.

Alexander, R. (1980). Mr. Jewel as a model: An educational criticism of a high school art history class. *Studies in Art Education, 21*(3), 20–30.

Allison, B. (1986). *Index of British studies in art and design education.* Aldershot, England: Gower.

Anderson, R. (1997). A case study of the artist as teacher through the video work of Martha Davis. *Studies in Art Education, 39*(1), 37–56.

Anderson, T. (1995). Toward a cross-cultural approach to art criticism. *Studies in Art Education, 36*(40), 198–209.

Anderson, T., Eisner, E. W., & McRorie, S. (1998). A survey of graduate study in art education. *Studies in Art Education, 40*(1), 8–25.

ARIAD 2 (n.d.). CD-ROM database. Reston, VA: National Art Education Association.

ARIAD Australia. (n.d.). CD-ROM database. Reston, VA: National Art Education Association.

Armstrong, C. (1986). Stages in inquiry in producing art: Model, rationale, and application to a teacher questioning strategy. *Studies in Art Education, 28*(1), 37–48.

Armstrong, C., & Armstrong, N. A. (1977). Art teacher questioning strategy. *Studies in Art Education, 18*(3), 53–64.

Arnheim, R. (1996). *Thoughts on art education* (Occasional paper 2). Los Angeles: Getty Center for Education in the Arts.

Art education: Creating a visual arts research agenda for the twenty-first century. (1994). Reston: VA: National Art Education Association.

Barkan, M. (1962). Transition in art education: Changing conceptions of curriculum and theory. *Art Education, 15*(7), 27.

Barkan, M., Chapman, L., & Kern, E. (1970). *Guidelines: Curriculum development for aesthetic education.* St. Louis, MO: Central Midwestern Regional Educational Laboratory.

Barone, T. (1989). On equality, visibility, and the fine arts program in a black elementary school: An example of educational criticism. *Curriculum Inquiry, 17*(4), 421–446.

Barrett, T. (1994). Principles for interpreting art. *Art Education, 47*(50), 8–13.

Beittel, K. R., & Mattil, E. L. (Eds.). (1966). A seminar in art education for research and curriculum development (Cooperative Research Project V-002. Final Report). University Park: Pennsylvania State University.

Blandy, D. (1993). Community-based lifelong learning in art for adults with mental retardation: A rationale, conceptual foundation, and supportive environments. *Studies in Art Education, 34*(3), 167–175.

Blandy, D., & Congdon, K. (Eds.). (1987). *Art in a democracy.* New York: Teachers College Press.

Blueprint for implementing a visual arts education research agenda. (1994). Reston, VA: National Art Education Association.

Bolin, P. (1995). Matters of choice: Historical inquiry in art education. In P. Smith (Ed.), *Art education historical methodology: An insider's guide to doing and using* (pp. 44–52). Pasadena, CA: Open Door.

Bolin, P., Blandy, D., & Congdon, K. (Eds.). (2000). *Remembering others: Making invisible histories visible.* Reston, VA: National Art Education Association.

Boughton, D., Eisner, E. W., & Ligtvolt, J. (Eds.). (1993). *Evaluating and assessing the visual arts in education: International perspectives.* New York: Teachers College Press.

Bresler, L. (1992). Visual art in primary grades: A portrait and analysis. *Early Childhood Research Quarterly, 7*(3), 397–414.

Bresler, L. (1994). Imitative, complementary, and expansive: Three roles for visual arts curricula. *Studies in Art Education, 35*(2), 90–104.

Brewer, T. (1999). Forty years of *Studies in Art Education*: 1979–1989. *Visual Arts Research, 25*(1), 14–18.

Bullock, A., & Galbraith, L. (1992). Images of art teaching: Comparing the beliefs and practices of two secondary art teachers. *Studies in Art Education, 33*(2), 86–97.

Bumgarner Gee, C. (1994). Artists in the classroom: The impact and consequences of the National Endowment for the Arts' Artist Residency Program on K–12 arts education. *Arts Education Policy Review, 95*,(3), 14–29.

Burton, D. (1991). *A survey of research interests among art education researchers.* National Art Education Association Seminar for Research in Art Education, Reston, VA.

Burton, D. (1998). Survey of current research in art education. *Studies in Art Education, 39*(2), 183–186.

Burton, D. (2001). How do we teach? Results of a national survey of instruction in secondary art education. *Studies in Art Education, 42*(2), 131–145.

Cera, J. (1998). *Understanding the development of teacher leadership: An autobiographical case study of an art educator.* Unpublished doctoral dissertation, Ohio State University, Columbus.

Chalmers, F. G. (1981). Art education as ethnology. *Studies in Art Education, (23)*2, 6–14.

Chalmers, F. G. (1992). The origins of racism in the public school art curriculum. *Studies in Art Education, 33*(3), 134–143.

Chalmers, F. G. (1996). *Celebrating pluralism: Art, education, and cultural diversity* (Occasional Paper 5). Los Angeles: Getty Education Institute for the Arts.

Chalmers, F. G. (1999). *Studies in Art Education*: The first 10 of 40 years. *Visual Arts Research, 25*(49), 2.

Chanda, J. (1993). A theoretical basis for non-Western art history instruction. *Journal of Aesthetic Education, 27*(1), 73–84.

Chapman, L. (1982). *Instant art, instant culture: The unspoken policy for American schools.* New York: Teachers College Press.

Clark, G., Day, M., & Greer, W. D. (1987). Discipline-based art education: Becoming students of art. *Journal of Aesthetic Education, 21*(2), 130–93.

Clark, G. A., & Zimmerman, E. (1978). A walk in the right direction: A model for visual arts education, *Studies in Art Education, 19*(2), 34–49.

Clark, G., & Zimmerman, E. (1985). A framework for educating artistically talented students based on Feldman's and Clark and Zimmerman's models. *Studies in Art Education, 27*(3), 115–122.

Clark, G., & Zimmerman, E. (1997). *Project ARTS: Programs for ethnically diverse, economically disadvantaged, high ability, visual arts students in rural communities: Identification, curriculum, evaluation.* ED 419765.

Clark, G., Zimmerman, E., & Zurmuehlen, M. (1987). *Understanding art testing: Past influences, Norman C. Meier's contributions, present concerns, and future possibilities.* Reston, VA: National Art Education Association.

Cole, A., & Knowles, J. G. (2000). *Researching teaching: Exploring teacher development through reflexive development*. Boston: Allyn and Bacon.

Collins, G. (1999). *Studies in Art Education: 1989–1998. Visual Arts Research, 25*(1), 19–26.

Collins, G., & Sandell, R. (1994). *Women, art, and education*. Reston, VA: National Art Education Association.

Collins, G., & Sandell, R. (Eds.). (1996). *Gender issues in art education*. Reston, VA: National Art Education Association.

Congdon, K. (1989). Multi-cultural approaches to art criticism. *Studies in Art Education, 30*(3), 176–184.

Congdon, K., & Zimmerman, E. (1993). *Women art educators III*. Bloomington, IN: Women's Caucus of the National Art Education Association.

Davis, D. J. (1977). Research trends in art and art education: 1883–72. In S. S. Madeja (Ed.), *Arts and aesthetics: An agenda for the future* (pp. 109–147). St. Louis, MO: Central Midwestern Regional Education Laboratory.

Davis, D. J. (1990). Teacher education in the visual arts. In R. Houston (Ed.), *Handbook of research on teacher education* (pp. 746–757). New York: Macmillan.

Day, M. (1969). The compatibility of art history and studio art activity in the junior high school art program: A comparison of two methods of teaching art history. *Studies in Art Education, 10*(2), 57–65.

Day, M. (1973). Effects of instruction on high school students' art preferences and art judgments. *Studies in Art Education, 18*, 25–39.

Day, M. (Ed.). (1997). *Preparing teachers of art*. Reston, VA: National Art Education Association.

Degge, R. (1975). A descriptive study of community art teachers with implications for teacher preparation and cultural policy. *Studies in Art Education, 2*(8), 164–175.

Donnelly, N. (1990). Stumbling on aesthetic experience: A factual account of the accidental discovery of aesthetic education in an Irish context. *Studies in Art Education, 31*(3), 141–148.

Duke, L. L. (1999). Looking back, looking forward. *Arts Education Policy Review, 101*(1), 3–7.

Duncum, P. (1990). Clearing the decks for dominant culture: Some first principles for contemporary art education. *Studies in Art Education, 31*(4), 207–215.

Efland, A., Freedman, K., & Stuhr, P. (1996). *Postmodern art education: An approach to curriculum*. Reston, VA: National Art Education Association.

Eisner, E. W. (1968). Curriculum making for the wee folk: Stanford University's Kettering project. *Studies in Art Education, 9*(3), 45–56.

Eisner, E. W. (1972). *Educating artistic vision*. New York: Macmillan.

Eisner, E. W. (1973). *The Eisner belief index*. Unpublished manuscript, Stanford University.

Eisner, E. W. (1985). *The educational imagination: On the design and evaluation of school programs*. New York: Macmillan.

Eisner, E. W. (1988). *The role of discipline-based art education in America's schools*. Los Angeles: J. Paul Getty Trust.

Eisner, E. W. (1991). *The enlightened eye: Qualitative inquiry and the enhancement of educational practice*. New York: Macmillan.

Eisner, E. W. (1997). *Educating artistic vision*. Reston, VA: National Art Education Association.

Erickson, M. (1983). Teaching art history as an inquiry process. *Art Education, 36*(5), 28–31.

Erickson, M. (1995). Second and sixth grade students' art historical interpretation abilities: A one-year study. *Studies in Art Education, 37*(1), 19–28.

Erickson, M. (1997). Transfer within and beyond DBAE: A cognitive exploration of research issues. *Visual Arts Research, 23*, 43–51.

Erickson, M. (1998). Effects of art history instruction on fourth and eighth grade students' abilities to interpret artworks contextually. *Studies in Art Education, 39*(4), 309–320.

Eschedor, J. (2000). *The memory collage project: Art education with older adults*. Unpublished master's thesis, University of Arizona, Tucson.

Fox, J. D. (1999). *Student-perceived enrollment motivation and valuing of three types of visual arts courses selected to fulfill university general education requirements (social reconstruction, art education)*. Unpublished doctoral dissertation, Texas Tech University, Lubbock, TX.

Freedman, K. (2000). Social perspectives on art education in the U.S.: Teaching visual culture in a democracy. *Studies in Art Education, 41*(4), 314–339.

Freedman, K., & Wood, J. (1999). Reconsidering critical response: Student judgments of purpose, interpretation, and relationships in visual culture. *Studies in Art Education, 40*(2), 128–142.

Galbraith, L. (1988). Research-oriented teachers: Implications for art teaching. *Art Education, 41*(5), 50–53.

Galbraith, L. (1995). The preservice art education classroom: A look through the window. In L. Galbraith (Ed.), *Preservice art education: Issues and practice* (pp. 1–30). Reston, VA: National Art Education Association.

Galbraith, L. (1997). What are art teachers taught? An analysis of curriculum components for art teacher preparation programs. In M. D. Day (Ed.)., *Preparing teachers of art* (pp. 45–72). Reston, VA: National Art Education Association.

Galbraith, L. (2001). Teachers of teachers: Faculty working lives and art teacher education in the United States. *Studies in Art Education, 42*(2), 163–181.

Garber, E. (1990). Implications of feminist art criticism for art education. *Studies in Art Education, 32*(1), 17–26.

Garber, E. (1995). Teaching art in the context of culture: A study of the borderlands. *Studies in Art Education, 36*(4), 218–232.

Gardner, H. (1989). Zero-based arts education: An introduction to ARTS PROPEL. *Studies in Art Education, 30*(21), 71–83.

Gardner, H. (1990). *Art Education and human development*. Los Angeles: Getty Center for Education in the Arts.

Garoian, C. (1997). Art education and the aesthetics of health in the age of AIDS. *Studies in Art Education, 391*(1), 6–23.

Geahigan, G. (1998). From procedures to principles, and beyond: Implementing critical inquiry in the classroom. *Studies in Art Education, 39*(4), 293–308.

Getty Center for Education in the Arts. (1985). *Beyond creating: The place for art in America's schools.* Los Angeles: Getty Center for Education in the Arts.

Golomb, C. (1992). *The child's creation of a pictorial world.* Berkeley: University of California Press.

Grauer, K. M. (1998). Beliefs of preservice teachers toward art education. *Studies in Art Education, 39*(4), 350–370.

Greer, W. D. (1984). A discipline-based art education: Approaching art as a subject of study. *Studies in Art Education, 25,* 212–218.

Guay, D. (1993). Cross-site analysis of teaching practices: Visual art education with students experiencing disabilities. *Studies in Art Education, 34*(4), 222–232.

Guba, E., & Lincoln, Y. (1989). *Fourth generation evaluation.* Newbury Park, CA: Sage.

Hafeli, M. (2000). Negotiating "fit" in student art work: Classroom conversations. *Studies in Art Education, 41*(2), 130–139.

Hamblen, K. (1984). An art criticism questioning strategy within the framework of Bloom's taxonomy. *Studies in Art Education,* (26), 141–150.

Hamblen, K. (1987a). An examination of discipline-based art education issues. *Studies in Art Education, 28*(2), 68–78.

Hamblen, K. (1987b). What general education can tell us about evaluation in art. *Studies in Art Education, 4*(28), 246–250.

Hamblen, K. (1989). Research in art education as a form of educational consumer protection. *Studies in Art Education, 24*(3), 169–176.

Hawke, D. (1980). *The life-world of a beginning teacher of art.* Unpublished doctoral dissertation, University of Alberta, Edmonton, Alberta, Canada.

Hicks, L. (1992). The construction of meaning: Feminist criticism. *Art Education, 45*(2), 23–32.

Honeychurch, K. G. (1995). Extending the dialogue of diversity: Sexual subjectivities and education in the visual arts. *Studies in Art Education, 36*(4), 210–217.

Hutchens, J. (1997). Accomplishing change in the university: Strategies for improving art teacher preparation. In M. D. Day (Ed.), *Preparing art teachers* (pp 139–154). Reston, VA: National Art Education Association.

Irwin, R. (1995). *A circle of empowerment: women, education, and leadership.* Albany: State University of New York Press.

Irwin, R., & Rogers, T. (1997). Video-conferencing for collaborative educational inquiry. *Art Education, 50*(5), 57–62.

Irwin, R., Rogers, T., & Wan, Y. (1998). Reclamation, reconciliation, and reconstruction: Art practices of contemporary aboriginal artists from Canada, Australia, and Taiwan. *Journal of Multicultural and Cross-cultural Research in Art Education, 16*(1), 61–72.

Irwin, R., Rogers, T., & Wan, Y. (1999). Making connections through cultural memory, cultural performance, and cultural translation. *Studies in Art Education, 40*(30), 198–212.

Jones, B. J., & McPhee, J. K. (1986). Research on teaching arts and aesthetics. In M. C. Wittrock (Ed.), *Handbook of research on teaching* (3rd ed., pp. 906–916). New York: Macmillan.

Jones, J. E. (1993). The influence of age on self-directed learning in university and community adult art students. *Studies in Art Education, 34*(3), 158–166.

Kakas, K. (1991). Classroom communication during fifth grade students' drawing lesson: Student-student and student-teacher conversations. *Studies in Art Education, 33*(10), 21–35.

Kellman, J. (1999). Drawing with Peter: Autobiography, narrative, and the art of a child with autism. *Studies in Art Education, 40*(3), 258–274.

Kindler, A. (Ed.). (1997). *Child development in art.* Reston, VA: National Art Education Association.

Kindler, A. (1999). From endpoints to repertoires: A challenge to art education. *Studies in Art Education, 40*(4), 330–349.

Kindler, A., & Darras, B. (1998). Culture and the development of pictorial repertoires. *Studies in Art Education, 39*(2), 147–167.

Koroscik, J. S., Short, G., Stavropolous, C., & Fortin, S. (1992). Frameworks for understanding art: The function of comparative art contexts and verbal cues. *Studies in Art Education, 33*(3), 154–164.

Korzenik, D. (1985). Doing historical research. *Studies in Art Education, 36*(5), 18–21.

Kowalchuk, E. (1999). Perceptions of practice: What art student teachers say they learn and need to know. *Studies in Art Education, 41*(1), 71–90.

Lachapelle, R. (1994). *Aesthetic understanding as informed experience: Ten informant-made videographic accounts about the process of aesthetic learning.* Unpublished doctoral dissertation, Concordia University, Montreal.

Lampela, L. (1995). A challenge for art education: Including lesbians and gays. *Studies in Art Education, 36*(4), 242–248.

Lampela, L. (2001). Lesbian and gay artists in the curriculum: A survey of art teachers' knowledge and attitudes. *Studies in Art Education, 42*(1), 146–162.

Lanier, V. (1969). Teaching art as social revolution. *Phi Delta Kappan, 50*(5), 16–23.

Lanier, V. (1991). *The world of art education.* Reston, VA: National Art Education Association.

Lankford, L. (1992). *Aesthetics: Issues and inquiry.* Reston, VA: National Art Education Association.

La Pierre, S. D., Stokrocki, M., & Zimmerman, E. (Eds). (2000, January). Research methods and methodologies for multicultural and cross-cultural issues in art education: Crossing cultural, artistic, and cyber borders: Issues and examples in Art Education Conference, Tempe, Arizona, ED438224.

La Pierre, S. D., & Zimmerman, E. (Eds). (1997). *Research methods and methodologies for art education.* Reston, VA: National Art Education Association.

La Porte, A. (1998). *An ethnographic study of an intergen-*

erational community art program in Harlem, New York City (Hispanic, African-Americans, oral history). Unpublished doctoral dissertation, University of Pennsylvania, Philadelphia.

Lightfoot, S. L., & Davis, J. H. (1997). *The art and science of portraiture.* San Francisco: Jossey-Bass.

Lowenfeld, V., & Britain, L. (1987). *Creative and mental growth.* New York: Macmillan.

MacGregor, R. N. (1972). The development and validation of a perceptual index for utilization in the teaching of art. *Studies in Art Education, 13*(2), 11–18.

MacGregor, R. N. (1990). Reflections on art assessment practices. *Journal of Art and Design Education, 9*(3), 315–327.

MacGregor, R. N. (1994). *Assessment in the arts: A cross-Canada study.* Vancouver, British Columbia, Canada. ED 382560.

MacGregor, R. N. (1998). Two sides of an orange: The conduct of research. *Studies in Art Education, 39*(3), 271–280.

McFee, J. K. (1961). *Preparation for art.* Belmont, CA: Wadsworth.

McRorie, S. (1996). On teaching and learning aesthetics: Gender and related issues. In G. Collins & R. Sandell (Eds.), *Gender issues in art education.* Reston, VA: National Art Education Association.

Makin, L., White, M., & Owen, M. (1996). Creation or constraint: Anglo-Australian and Asian-Australian teacher responses to children's art making. *Studies in Art Education, 37*(4), 226–244.

Mason, R. (1980). *Interpretation and understanding.* Unpublished doctoral dissertation, Pennsylvania State University, University Park, PA.

Mason, R. (1988). *Art education and multiculturalism.* New York: Methuen.

Mason, R., & Rawdling, M. (1993). Aesthetics in DBAE: Its relevance to critical studies. *Journal of Art and Design Education, 12*(3), 357–370.

May, W. (1985). *What art means to third and fourth graders: A two-year case study.* Unpublished doctoral dissertation, Ohio State University, Columbus.

May, W. (1993). "Teachers-as-researchers" or action research: What is it, and what good is it for art education? *Studies in Art Education, 34*(2), 114–126.

Mullen, C. (1999). Reaching inside out: Arts-based programming for incarcerated women. *Studies in Art Education, 40*(2), 143–161.

Nadaner, D. (1984). Critique and intervention: Implications for a social theory of art. *Studies in Art Education, 26*(1), 20–26.

National Art Education Association. (1986). *NAEA quality art education: An interpretation.* Reston, VA: National Art Education Association.

National Art Education Association. (1994). *Blueprint for implementing a visual arts education research agenda.* Reston, VA: National Art Education Association.

National Art Education Association. (1996). *Briefing papers: Creating a visual arts research agenda toward the twenty-first century.* Reston, VA: National Art Education Association.

National Art Education Association. (1998). *NAEA research task force status reports.* Reston, VA: National Art Education Association.

Neperud, R. (Ed.). (1995). *Context, content, and community in art education: Beyond postmodernism.* New York: Teachers College Press.

Nyman, A., & Jenkins, A. (2000). *Issues and approaches to art for students with special needs.* Reston, VA: National Art Education Association.

Pariser, D. (1981). Nadia's drawings: Theorizing about an autistic child's phenomenal ability. *Studies in Art Education, 22*(2), 20–31.

Parsons, M. (1987). *How we understand art: A cognitive developmental account of aesthetic experience.* New York: Cambridge University Press.

Parsons, M., & Blocker, G. (1993). *Aesthetics and education.* Urbana: University of Illinois Press.

Pohland, P. (1972). Participant observation as research methodology. *Studies in Art Education, 13*(3), 4–24.

Richmond, S. (1993). Art, imagination, and teaching: Researching the high school classroom. *Canadian Journal of Education, 18*(4), 366–380.

Rush, J. C., Weckesser, J. K., & Sabers, D. L. (1980). A comparison of instructional methods for teaching contour drawing to children. *Studies in Art Education, 21*(2), 6–12.

Russell, R. L. (1988). Children's philosophical inquiry into defining art: A quasi-experimental study of aesthetics in the elementary school. *Studies in Art Education, 29*(3), 282–291.

Sabol, R. (1998). What are we testing? Content analysis of state visual arts achievement tests. *Visual Arts Research, 24*(1), 1–12.

Sandell, R. (1992). The liberating relevance of feminist pedagogy. *Studies in Art Education, 32*(3), 178–187.

Sevigny, M. J. (1977). *A descriptive study of instructional interaction and performance appraisal in a university studio art setting: A multiple perspective.* Unpublished doctoral dissertation, Ohio State University, Columbus.

Smith, R. A. (1989). *The sense of art: A study in aesthetic education.* New York: Routledge.

Smith, R. A. (Ed.). (2000). *Readings in discipline-based art education: A literature of educational reform.* Reston, VA: National Art Education Association.

Smith, R., & Simpson, A. (1992). *Aesthetics and arts education.* Urbana: University of Illinois Press.

Smith-Shank, D. (1998). Microethnography of a Grateful Dead concert: American subculture aesthetics. *Journal of Multicultural and Cross-cultural Research in Art Education, 14,* 80–91.

Smith-Shank, D., & Schwiebert, V. (2000). Old wives' tales: Questing to understand visual memories. *Studies in Art Education, 41*(2), 178–190.

Stankiewicz, M. (1997). Research methods and methodologies for art education. In S. D. La Pierre & E. Zimmerman (Eds.), *Research methods and methodologies for art education* (pp. 57–73). Reston: VA: National Art Education Association.

Stokrocki, M. (1995). An exploratory microethnographic study of art teaching in one Navajo public school system: The Anglo view of running water. In H. Kauppinen & R. Diket (Eds.), *Trends in art education from diverse cultures* (pp. 181–191). Reston, VA: National Art Education Association.

Stout, C. J. (1995). Critical conversations about art: A description of higher-order thinking generated through the study of art criticism. *Studies in Art Education, 36*(3), 170–188.

Stout, C. J. (1999). Artists as writers: Enriching perspectives in art appreciation. *Studies in Art Education, 40*(3), 226–241.

Stuhr, P., Krug, D., & Scott, A. (1995). Partial tales of three translators: An essay. *Studies in Art Education, 37*(1), 29–46.

Sullivan, G. (1989). Curriculum in art education: The uncertainty principle. *Studies in Art Education, 30*(4), 225–236.

Taylor, P. (1999). *Hypertext-based art education: Implications for liberatory learning in high school.* Unpublished doctoral dissertation, University of Pennsylvania, Philadelphia.

Wasson, R., Stuhr, P., & Petrovich-Mwanki, L. (1990). Teaching art in the multicultural classroom: Six position statements. *Studies in Art Education, 31*(4), 234–246.

Welch, N. (Ed.). (1995). *Schools, communities, and the arts: A research compendium.* Washington, DC: Arts in Education Program, National Endowment for the Arts.

Wilson, B. (1966). An experimental study designed to alter fifth and sixth grade students' perceptions of paintings. *Studies in Art Education, 8*(1), 33–42.

Wilson, B. (1994). Reflections on the relationship among art, life, and research. *Studies in Art Education, 35*(4), 197–208.

Wilson, B. (1997a). *The quiet evolution: Changing the face of arts education.* Los Angeles: Getty Education Institute for the Arts.

Wilson, B. (1997b). Types of child art and alternative developmental accounts: Interpreting the interpreters. *Human Development, 40*(3), 155–168.

Wilson, B., & Wilson, M. (1976). Visual narrative and the artistically gifted. *Gifted Child Quarterly, 20*(4), 432–447.

Wilson, B., & Wilson, M. (1985). The artistic tower of Babel: Inextricable links between culture and graphic development. *Visual Arts Research, 11*(1), 90–104.

Wolf, D. P. (1994). Development as the growth of repertoires. In M. B. Franklin & B. Kaplan (Eds.), *Development and the arts* (pp. 59–78). Hillside, NJ: Erlbaum.

Wolfe, P. (1997). A really good art teacher would be like you, Mrs. C.: A qualitative study of a teacher and her artistically gifted middle school students. *Studies in Art Education, 3*(3), 232–45.

Zimmerman, E. (1985). Toward a theory of labeling artistically talented students. *Studies in Art Education, 27*(1), 31–42.

Zimmerman, E. (1991). Rembrandt to Rembrandt: A case study of a memorable painting teacher of artistically talented 13 to 16 year-old students. *Roeper Review, 13*(2), 76–81.

Zimmerman, E. (1994). Current research and practice about preservice art specialist teacher education. *Studies in Art Education, 35*(2), 79–89.

Zimmerman, E. (1997a). Foreword: Research methods and methodologies for art education. In *Research methods and methodologies for art education* (pp. v–ix). Reston, VA: National Art Education Association.

Zimmerman, E. (1997b). I don't want to sit in the corner cutting out valentines: Leadership roles for teachers of talented art students. *Gifted Child Quarterly, 41*(1), 33–41.

Zimmerman, E. (1997c). Whence come we? Whither go we? Demographic analysis of art teacher education programs in the United States. In M. D. Day (Ed.), *Preparing teachers of art* (pp. 27–44). Reston, VA: National Art Education Association.

A Review of Research in Theater, Dance, and Other Performing Arts Education

Implications for Music

51

KENT SEIDEL

This chapter and its counterpart on visual art education research (see chapter 50) represent an effort to bridge the research on the several arts disciplines within our schools. Traditionally, theater (I will use the term "theater" to refer generally to dramatic endeavor in schools) and dance have existed as largely extracurricular activities or as a small portion of the broader language arts and physical education curricula. Research is still developing in these fields, in comparison to the more established body of literature that exists for both music and visual art education.

What can those in music education learn from the research being pursued in the other performing arts disciplines? The performing arts share many elements—aspects of visual representation, sound, language, movement, and feeling. Recently, the disciplines have come to some agreement regarding what should form the arts learning experience. The *National Standards for Arts Education* (Consortium of National Arts Education Associations, 1994) were written together, an approach that has helped to clarify many ways that the arts disciplines connect. Students should have the opportunity to create as well as to perform; to explore and improvise; to experience a variety of exemplary art; to work with artists; to study the historical and social contexts that lend meaning to works of art; and to reflect on and critique their own and others' artistic work.

Large-scale evaluation and research efforts, such as the 1997 *National Assessment of Educational Progress* (U.S. Department of Education, 1998) and the *Fast-Response Surveys* of the National Center for Education Statistics (U.S. Department of Education, 1995), are providing important baseline data for the four arts education disciplines. Groups such as the Arts Education Partnership have

brought arts, policy, and business leaders together to support research and have outlined national goals in *Priorities for Arts Education Research* (Arts Education Partnership, 1997). In addition, an emphasis on accountability has resulted in a number of evaluations of multiarts and integrated arts programs. More often than not, these evaluative efforts emphasize ways the arts contribute to students' education beyond the (often unmentioned) intrinsic value of learning art for its own sake. All of this—the connections among the arts, accountability pressures, concerns for the role of the arts in student achievement in areas such as math and reading—puts the arts disciplines in a new place with regard to research. These contexts require strengthened communication among the disciplines, more unity where connections will strengthen our work with students and the field, and careful clarification of differences among the arts disciplines and the educational experiences each discipline provides.

Learning from Each Other: Four Areas of Connection

Literature related to theater, dance, and other performance suggests four specific areas worthy of attention from music education researchers and music educators in general. The first is research to *explore the potential of the arts in a changing educational landscape*. This includes exploration of educational goals and pedagogical contexts. The aforementioned aspects of pre-K–12 education—standards-based reform, accountability, "back to basics" concerns about math and reading—challenge each of our disciplines to rethink our historical traditions and evaluate current and future options within the curriculum.

A second area is the *potential of the performing arts to transform school climate and teaching.* While much of the research on music and multiarts programs has explored the effect of the arts on the community and curriculum, the theater literature in particular offers a connection between teaching, performance, and reflective practice that is informative to all arts disciplines.

Third, this chapter looks at research related to theater and dance in the context of *ways of making meaning, thinking, and learning.* It is here that the differences among the arts disciplines are perhaps most distinct.

The fourth area is research that explores *music in the context of theater and dance,* as the three disciplines often come together in performance and in the classroom.

The Literature Reviewed

Sources reviewed for this chapter include numerous journals, books, and unpublished research documents; ERIC clearinghouse materials; U.S. Department of Education resources, including education labs and (Office of Educational Research and Improvement/National Center for Education Statistics) abstracts; online resources, where sources could be identified as reliable; and nearly 200 doctoral dissertations. Dissertations were included because they often offer the newest approaches and address topics that are important but perhaps less attractive to professional researchers. Few ERIC and Department of Education resources are singled out, as many do not contain the "behind the scenes" detail into theory, method, or analysis that this Handbook tries to reference.

Because of space limitations, only the most relevant and recent examples of research are discussed. Special effort is made to note seminal works that will help music colleagues with a specific interest better understand the area of theater or dance in question.

A review of research in the four major arts disciplines I conducted in 1996 revealed slightly more than 300 qualitative and quantitative studies since 1985 that drew well-founded conclusions about the effects of arts education on students in pre-school through 12th grade. A Delphi study (an open-ended, multistage survey of experts) conducted recently with theater education researchers and practitioners (Seidel, 2000) revealed that most respondents knew of only a few studies conducted in each research area of interest.

The literature is dominated by descriptive studies of specific programs—programs often involving the researcher. The result is a collection of disparate ideas for curriculum and instruction techniques but only a few solid findings as

to how those techniques broadly affect students, teachers, schools, and communities. Further, the research often does not adequately discuss results in relation to specific contexts, and studies are not typically replicated in a variety of settings. These issues make generalization and the development of a broad base of knowledge more difficult.

The pressures for greater accountability and the focus on basic academic achievement have resulted in an increasing number of studies utilizing quantitative measures, particularly standardized tests. Unfortunately, these usually focus more on "nonarts" outcomes (such as learning to read) than on arts-related pedagogy and learning outcomes. Still, while the field of performing arts education research may be relatively unmined, there are a few lines of inquiry that are fairly well established and possibly worthy of further exploration by music colleagues.

The Role of the Performing Arts in an Evolving Educational Landscape

The standards movement has posed important new questions to arts educators. What is important for *every* student (not just the gifted, talented, or interested) to know and be able to do in the arts? What is the "essential work" of arts learning in pre-K–12 education? When students and teachers create, perform, and experience the performing arts, what happens that is relevant to their development, to important learning, and to education *as a whole?* How should schools and communities support the best artistic and learning experiences for students? Education reform and the standards movement have brought issues like these to the doorstep of every curriculum content area.

Several recent research efforts have looked at arts learning in the context of the broader curriculum. Catterall's (1995) longitudinal study report on the *Different Ways of Knowing* program includes all four arts and should be familiar to music researchers. The recent *Champions of Change: The Impact of the Arts on Learning* report (Fiske, 1999) offers numerous studies of interest. In particular, Wolf's section, "Why the Arts Matter in Education, or Just What Do Children Learn When They Create an Opera," is a good example of a well-designed field study of some of the questions about "the arts education experience" posed earlier in this chapter. On a broader scale, Frechtling (1999) offers some useful thoughts on capturing the results of arts experiences for students, teachers, and schools in her discussion of the evaluation of the Transforming Education Through the Arts Challenge (TETAC) program. Her advice on managing variables and multiple sources of data and the methodology provided in the semiannual report of the TETAC evaluation (Westat, 2000) should be valuable for both researchers and evaluators attempting to design studies that adequately capture the context, content, and outcomes of the arts experience.

In addition to exploration of why the arts should be in the curriculum, there is an increasing need to research the "how." What should be the relationship among the arts disciplines and between arts disciplines and nonarts subjects?

A growing body of research—largely evaluative in nature—looks at multiple arts programs, where students are participating in programming involving any mix of arts disciplines. However, teasing out the specific contributions of each individual discipline has not been a focus. Although careful attention to specific arts disciplines adds complexity to a study design, it is important if researchers wish to strengthen the value of site-specific findings and explore the interrelationships of the arts with each other and within the school curriculum. In reviewing numerous "integrated arts curriculum" studies, I located no research that paid sufficient attention to the nuances of specific disciplines, curriculum and instruction activities, and contextual detail to allow general conclusions to be drawn about integrating the arts or the dynamics among the arts and other curriculum content areas. The variables are simply too myriad and are not adequately addressed.

Better studies are needed regarding teaching and learning in both arts-integrated and survey-style fine arts curriculum designs. With increasing frequency, a desire to include the arts within pressures of time limitations is resulting in students' receiving either integrated arts (primarily in elementary grades) or "introduction to arts" or "aesthetic education" courses, where all the arts are taught together (generally in secondary and early college level grades).

What are the benefits and disadvantages of these models? Does the interdisciplinary study result in a greater or lesser understanding of the arts? Is there a difference in effect with different types of students? How do teacher roles vary? How do arts specialists see their roles? Do educators from the different arts disciplines hold different beliefs and expectations about the goals of arts instruction for students, and if so, what are the implications for interdisciplinary and multiarts settings in schools, curricula, and research? I located no studies that adequately investigated these difficult and important issues, although a recent dissertation offers a descriptive view of how several educators wrestled with the role of theater in the elementary curriculum. Murray (1998) examines the following research questions:

> How do classroom teachers and a school drama specialist negotiate and interpret the evolving status and function of drama as a potentially generative, artistic teaching and learning tool over the course of two years?

> What is the influence of other individual voices and institutional forces invested in shaping the extent to which drama becomes part of the school's and each individual classroom's culture? (p. 80)

The study provides perspective from the point of view of an on-site researcher, and it may be informative to researchers exploring the role and relationship of other arts and the classroom. However, the action-research approach, even when carefully conducted, begs replication in other sites and with other art forms in order to move toward a better understanding of the relationship between the arts and other subjects.

Researchers wishing to find substantive connection points related to curriculum and instruction among the arts disciplines and between the arts and other curriculum areas may wish to consider two important resources. Recent work by the several associations developing national standards and the National Study of School Evaluation (NSSE) has resulted in the identification of a number of "school-wide goals for student learning" that are addressed by every national standards content area (National Study of School Evaluation [NSSE], 1997). In addition, NSSE's guide to program evaluation in the visual and performing arts (National Study of School Evaluation [NSSE], 1998) offers a number of standards-based constructs for looking at the organizational and instructional capacity of a school. A survey of research related to arts pedagogical methods included in the *Handbook of Research on Improving Student Achievement* (Colwell, 1999) also offers researchers food for thought in developing common conceptual frameworks for design of research related to more than one art form. The *Handbook* summarizes pedagogical approaches that research has shown have a positive impact on student achievement in the various arts disciplines.

A Lesson from Theater: Focusing on "Instrumental Outcomes"

With regard to the "use" of the arts in teaching, it would seem that all areas of arts education are struggling to set an appropriate research agenda. A focus on advocacy to "prove" the value of the arts to education has strongly influenced the direction of research thus far. This defensive posture has resulted in a proliferation of writing about the value of the arts in education but only a limited research base in support of the claims, opinions, and expert reasoning. Two recent discussions of the issue include *Mute Those Claims: No Evidence (Yet) for a Causal Link Between Arts Study and Academic Achievement* (Winner & Cooper, 2000) and *Does Experience in the Arts Boost Academic Achievement?* (Eisner, 1998). According to Eisner, "What instrumental justifications . . . do is to legitimate the marginal position assigned to the arts by those looking for such justifications" (p. 12).

The metaanalysis of studies of the arts and academic achievement recently conducted by Harvard researchers (Winner & Hetland, 2000) found that evidence thus far supports causal links between the arts and "instrumental outcomes" in only a few areas. One of the strongest findings was that work with theater improves students' verbal and other language-related skills. It is worth noting that there is a larger body of research on the relationship between theater and language learning than for other arts and academic links. For most of their areas of inquiry, Winner and Hetland found that sufficient research simply does not exist.

The theater/language connection offers two lessons to consider. First, the findings are a good example of instrumental academic outcomes being in close alignment with the essential work of the art form.

The second lesson is less pleasant. Though research has shown a causal link between arts education and top-priority instrumental outcomes, that is, language skills, the current education system is ill equipped to turn to theater education to help address the language learning needs of our students. Unfortunately, the research has paid little attention to the broader systemic issues that would accompany the changes necessary to address language learning for all students through theater education.

The Potential of the Performing Arts to Transform Schools and Teaching

Do the arts make better schools, or do good schools value the arts? Winner and Cooper (2000) suggest that the correlations between the arts and positive academic outcomes—correlations often incorrectly represented as evidence of causal links—may be indicative of an epiphenomenon. As they put it, "[i]t is possible that schools that decide to grant the arts a central role in the curriculum also make other kinds of reforms in the way that academic subjects are taught" (p. 3). Connections of this sort may be better understood through a growing body of research that explores how the arts help change school climate, engage students, and help teachers and students become more reflective in their educational endeavors.

Learning in and Through the Arts: Curriculum Implications (Burton et al., 1999), for example, includes discussions of arts involvement, school climate, and student engagement. The authors found that "[a]dministrators and teachers in high-arts schools attributed many positive features of their in-school climate to the arts" (p. 40). Catterall, Chapleau, and Iwanaga (1999) also found striking correlations between involvement in the arts and student interest and achievement.

The research is still unclear as to just how arts programs affect school climate and teacher and student performance. Consider a recent study of school climate and the arts (Meoli, 1999) that found little relationship between organizational factors of "school openness" and "school health" and the strength of the arts program within the school. Perhaps echoing Burton et al. (1999), the author concludes that successful school arts programs may be related more to support from the principal and the community. This study also raises questions of the role of the arts in schools. Do the arts transform schools, as many teachers and students will testify, or do they tend to be an epiphenomenon of the creation of a positive school climate? Or perhaps the relationship is still more complex. Each scenario has important implications for arts education researchers.

Quality Teaching, Effective Learning, Good Performance

The investigation of teaching as performance and of teaching and learning as reflective improvisation should be of particular interest to music educators. There is a growing body of literature relating the work of the performing artist and active audience with the work of effective teaching and active learning. As the field of education learns more about teachers and students as reflective practitioners, closer connections are being drawn with performance theory and artist-audience interaction.

An excellent recent discussion of the theoretical framework connecting the two subject areas is *Teaching as a Performing Art* (Sarason, 1999). For practical ideas on the subject, see *Teaching and Performing: Ideas for Energizing Your Classes* (Timpson, Burgoyne, Jones, & Jones, 1997). This work is not research per se but research based, and the authors link the literature on dramatic performance and play with best classroom practice. For a take on the policy issues behind teacher preparation and teacher as performing-artist, see Klein's commentary "To Oz: Changing Theatre Teacher Education" (1993).

Baker-Sennett and Matusov offer a clear summary of the concept of improvisation in schools in "School 'Performance': Improvisational Processes in Development and Education" (1997). They conclude that "not only does improvisational performance provide children with opportunities to engage in sophisticated, collaborative problem-solving processes, it also serves as a tool that revitalizes the way we think about the relationships between teaching, learning, and development" (p. 210).

Several researchers have explored the relationship between teaching and performance. These include Friedman (1988), *Characteristics of Effective Theatre Acting Perfor-*

mance as Incorporated into Effective Teaching Performance; Bellizia (1985), *Drama in Teaching: Using Theatrical Techniques to Influence Teaching Strategies;* and Johnson (1985), *Teaching as a Performing Art: An Analysis of the Performance Skills of Prominent Mathematics Teachers.* Each of these studies provides examples of ways to approach operationalizing the many variables of teaching performance. The literature on self-reflection and reflective practice in teaching and learning also connects well with performing arts education. For a theater-specific example, see Creery (1991), *Being, Knowing, Acting: An Exploration of Reflection in Educational Drama.*

In his study of a professional theater company's work in schools, Steve Seidel (1999) points out that "the Company's approach to teaching Shakespeare is also an elegant exemplar of teaching for deep understanding" (p. 83). Seidel goes on to discuss aspects of "artmaking" that exemplify good teaching. He connects artistic processes with students' learning processes, offering a conceptual framework of project-based learning and "learning in four realms at once" through workshops, rehearsals, and performances. Similar grounded theory approaches in different arts education sites would be very valuable to the field—especially where those studies can work within schools, as opposed to a cocurricular program run by an outside agency.

The Performing Arts as Ways of Thinking and Learning

Research and theory are developing around the performing arts as a new literacy for students to master if they are to be effective in a global information age. Two sources stand out as exemplary for music education researchers interested in views from the theater, dance, and visual arts disciplines: *The Languages of Learning: How Children Talk, Write, Dance, Draw, and Sing their Understanding of the World* (Gallas, 1994) and the *Handbook of Research on Teaching Literacy through the Communicative and Visual Arts* (Flood, Health, & Lapp, 1997).

Critical thinking and creative thinking are difficult concepts to frame and measure, but a number of studies have been conducted to explore various facets of each of these, borrowing heavily from methodology and measurement in the field of psychology. One of the most ambitious investigations of the arts and creativity is Luftig's (1994) research on the SPECTRA+ program, which found positive effects of the arts on students' creativity and appreciation measures. In their metaanalysis of creative thinking studies, Moga, Burger, Hetland, and Winner (2000) conclude that there is some evidence for a connection between arts study and improved creativity, but that the research is still lacking in several respects: (1) few studies exist; (2) in many

studies, students were exposed to the arts for only a short time; and (3) there is great variation in experimental designs and definitions of creativity measures.

Several dance and theater studies related to creativity are worth consideration, for study design as well as to build on the research findings. These include Bennett (1982), *An Investigation into the Effects of Creative Experience in Drama upon the Creativity, Self-concept, and Achievement of Fifth and Sixth Grade Students;* Fischer (1989), *Effects of a Developmental Drama-Inquiry Process on Creative and Critical Thinking Skills in Early Adolescent Students;* Howell (1990), *The Relationship Between Arts Education and Creativity Among High School Students;* and Kim (1998), *The Effects of Creative Dance Instruction on Creative and Critical Thinking of Seventh-Grade Female Students in Seoul, Korea.* While each of these studies offers a careful approach to the creativity research, taken together they point out the need for performing arts researchers to develop a more effective array of methods and measurement techniques. The research is still in the early stages of development and often seems to be starting anew in each circumstance rather than working toward a growing body of literature.

Research also has been conducted on the relationship of dance and theater to critical thinking skills, problem-solving behavior, verbal and visual recall, and other cognitive skills. These have generally drawn less striking conclusions than the creativity studies, possibly because of the wide range of skills involved and the extreme variance in study design, measurement variables, and conceptual frameworks underlying the research. Many studies are exploratory in nature, describing and comparing specific programs, such as Barnard, *A Theoretical and a Practical Construct to Teach Thinking in the Context of Drama-in-Education* (1992), and Myers and Cantino's "Drama Teaching Strategies that Encourage Problem Solving Behavior in Children" (1993).

A seminal work in the theater literature is Helane Rosenberg's *Creative Drama and Imagination: Transforming Ideas into Action* (1987). Rosenberg connects creative drama with child development theories and explores various approaches to cognition, creativity, and use of imaging and imagination in the context of creative drama activities. Researchers interested in better understanding the connection of creative drama, theater, and cognition and child development are also encouraged to review *Creative Drama in a Developmental Context* (Kase-Polisini, 1985).

Dance, Music, and Visual-Spatial Learning

Although more studies are needed, working with dance has been found to lead to improved visual-spatial skills. See, for example, Keinanen, Hetland, and Winner (2000), "Teaching Cognitive Skill through Dance: Evidence for

Near but Not Far Transfer," Disanto-Rose (1986), *Effect of Creative Dance Classes on the Learning of Spatial Concepts;* and Chin (1984), *The Effects of Dance Movement Instruction on Spatial Awareness in Elementary Visually Impaired Students.*

Two studies directly relate dance and movement and related spatial abilities to learning mathematics. *An Analysis of Kinesthetic Learners' Responses: Teaching Mathematics Through Dance* (Westreich, 2000) describes the effectiveness of a dance program in teaching mathematics to at-risk learners, and "The Role of Spatial Ability in Physical Education and Mathematics" (Nilges, 2000) links six physical spatial abilities with mathematics learning. Further exploration of the connection of music, dance, visual-spatial abilities, and mathematics and related learning may be warranted.

Connections Among the Performing Arts Disciplines: Supporting Each Other

Both theater and dance regularly rely on music as an essential element of artistic performance, so it makes sense to study the interrelationship of music and dance and music and theater in educational settings. What is surprising is the lack of research in these areas. Perhaps this is because of the need for multiple areas of expertise among the researchers, as research of this nature involves rather complex aesthetic issues. In any case, all of the performing arts can benefit from research that explores the teaching and learning of music with theater and dance, and the related artistic and educational elements that are involved. The connection, interaction, and mutual support of music with dance and music with theater in educational settings is a wide open field for careful and creative researchers with expertise in music and another discipline.

Some studies exist that examine the role of musical theater in schools—three varied examples are *The Use of Musical Plays in Teaching Basic Skills to Developmentally Disabled Individuals* (Rubino, 1990); *The Narrative Impulse in Absolute Music: Drama as Used by Performer and Teacher* (Boe, 1994), and *High School Musical Theatre and the Meaning Students Give to their Involvement* (Van Houten, 1999). Each of these studies takes a very different focus on the interrelationships of music and theater, while giving both disciplines careful consideration.

Dance researchers have shown an interest in how physical movement can improve music teaching and learning. This, too, is an emerging area of inquiry, as evidenced by the lack of research, except in dissertation form. Some interesting examples are *The Effect of Movement-Based Instruction on the Melodic Perception of Primary-Age General Music Students* (Mueller, 1993); *The Effect of Movement Instruction on Sixth-Grade Beginning Instru-*

mental Music Students' Perception, Synchronization, and Performance with a Steady Beat (Rohwer, 1997); and *Effects of Locomotor Rhythm Training Activities on the Ability of Kindergarten Students to Synchronize Non-locomotor Movements to Music* (Croom, 1998). Each of these studies explored the use of various types of creative movement activities to improve music learning. In a similar vein, the role of dramatic expression, emotion, and acting methods in effective musical performance may be an interesting pursuit. In the context of pre-K–12 education, I found no studies exploring these connections.

Finally, all of the performing arts share elements of social interaction, interpersonal development, and collaborative work that are considered important in education. The question is whether there are unique and important aspects of working with the performing arts that result in key positive educational effects for students. The theater literature in particular has delved into these areas of educational growth, with studies examining the role of theater in developing communication and interpersonal skills, students' ability to work in teams, appreciation for diversity, self-discipline, self-confidence and self-esteem, and moral and character education.

The evaluation of the *Arts Partners* program (Ficklen, 1993), which included multiple art forms, found that the programs were successful in motivating elementary students and giving them alternative ways to succeed and noted student gains in self-confidence and verbal ability. My study of the development of leadership skills among high school theater students (Seidel, 1996) offers a theoretical framework about working in an artistic community within the school that may resonate with many music programs—especially those that include performance, production, and collaborative work as key elements of the educational/artistic process. For an excellent overview of the research related to theater and "attitudes, behavior, and moral reasoning," see *Building Moral Communities Through Educational Drama* (Wagner, 1999, ch. 6).

Improving the Quality and Quantity of Performing Arts Education Research

Reviewing the last 20 years of research in performing arts education has prompted some final recommendations to the field. More effort needs to be invested in the development of appropriate and rigorous qualitative and quantitative methodologies. The complicated human aspects of the arts and education require very robust means of data collection and extraordinary care in supporting findings and conclusions. It is important to develop and adapt replicable measurement methods, shared conceptual frameworks, and common vocabulary to describe arts learning and interventions, so that studies can be replicated, expanded on, and compared in varied settings. The research is currently too reliant on "nonarts" measures, such as academic standardized tests—tests that are often criticized even by the practitioners of the academic areas for which they were designed. Much of the current literature does not allow one to compare findings easily across studies.

The field must also invest in longer term studies that follow a larger number of students through more expansive arts experiences. It is sometimes a surprise that research documents *any* effects of arts education with students, when the arts treatment is often of very short duration—sometimes only a few hours, rarely more than a couple of hours a week for 1 or 2 years, even in the most arts-intensive curriculum efforts. Many researchers have, by necessity or choice, taken a too-convenient approach to the work. Careful attention to a variety of contextual information is important if we are to grasp the big picture of how the performing arts relate to each other and what important benefits they offer students and others in schools. Recent attempts at metaanalysis offer a summary of research that is needed in more areas of inquiry.

Given the exploratory nature of much of the performing arts education research, the field would be well served by more careful attention to improving teacher research methods (a recommended resource is *Inside/Outside: Teacher Research and Knowledge* [Cochran-Smith & Lytle, 1993]). With the limited resources available, it is unlikely that the quality research needed to help answer questions about how to improve arts education for all students will thrive until K–12 educators have the preparation and support to be capable research partners.

The arts disciplines are sufficiently similar to warrant complementary and joint research efforts yet sufficiently distinct to require a great deal of planning, communication, cooperation, and expertise for such research to be done well. Advances in understanding of any of the arts disciplines in education will surely enlighten practitioners and researchers in each of the other disciplines.

REFERENCES

Arts Education Partnership. (1997). *Priorities for arts education research*. Washington, DC: Arts Education Partnership/Council of Chief State School Officers.

Baker-Sennett, J., & Matusov, E. (1997). School "performance": Improvisational processes in development and education. In R. K. Sawyer (Ed.), *Creativity in performance* (pp. 197–212). Greenwich, CT: Ablex.

Barnard, J. B. (1992). *A theoretical and a practical construct to teach thinking in the context of drama-in-education*. Unpublished doctoral dissertation, Brigham Young University, Provo, UT.

Bellizia, F. E. (1985). *Drama in teaching: Using theatrical techniques to influence teaching strategies*. Unpublished doctoral dissertation, Boston University.

Bennett, O. G. (1982). *An investigation into the effects of creative experience in drama upon the creativity, self-concept, and achievement of fifth and sixth grade students*. Unpublished doctoral dissertation, Georgia State University, Atlanta.

Boe, K. M. (1994). *The narrative impulse in absolute music: Drama as used by performer and teacher*. Unpublished doctoral dissertation, University of Wisconsin, Madison.

Burton, J., Horowitz, R., & Abeles, H. (1999). Learning in and through the arts: Curriculum implications. In E. Fiske (Ed.), *Champions of change: The impact of the arts on learning* (pp. 35–46). Washington, DC: Arts Education Partnership.

Catterall, J. S. (1995). *Different ways of knowing: 1991–94 national longitudinal study final report*. Los Angeles: Galef Institute.

Catterall, J. S., Chapleau, R., & Iwanaga, J. (1999). Involvement in the arts and human development: General involvement and intensive involvement in music and theatre arts. In E. Fiske (Ed.), *Champions of change: The impact of arts on learning* (pp. 1–18). Washington, DC: Arts Education Partnership.

Chin, D. L. (1984). *The effects of dance movement instruction on spatial awareness in elementary visually impaired students*. Unpublished doctoral dissertation, University of Northern Colorado, Greeley.

Cochran-Smith, M., & Lytle, S. L. (Eds.). (1993). *Inside/Outside: Teacher research and knowledge*. New York: Teachers College Press.

Colwell, R. (1999). The arts. In G. Cawelti (Ed.), *Handbook of research on improving student achievement* (2nd ed., pp. 22–49). Arlington, VA: Educational Research Service.

Consortium of National Arts Education Associations. (1994). *National standards for arts education*. Reston, VA: Music Educators National Conference.

Creery, K. (1991). *Being, knowing, acting: An exploration of reflection in educational drama*. Unpublished master's thesis, University of Alberta, Edmonton, Alberta, Canada.

Croom, P. L. (1998). *Effects of locomotor rhythm training activities on the ability of kindergarten students to synchronize non-locomotor movements to music*. Unpublished doctoral dissertation, Temple University, Philadelphia.

Disanto-Rose, M. (1986). *Effect of creative dance classes on the learning of spatial concepts and the ability to analyze spatial pathways in dance video by third and fourth grade students*. Unpublished doctoral dissertation, Temple University, Philadelphia.

Eisner, E. W. (1998). Does experience in the arts boost academic achievement? *Art Education, 51*(1), 7–15.

Ficklen, F. (1994). *Arts Partners program report, 1992–93*. Brooklyn: New York City Board of Education, Office of Educational Research.

Fineberg, C. L. (1992). *The arts and cognition: A study of the relationship between Arts Partners programs and the development of higher level thinking processes in elementary and junior high school students.* New York: C. F. Associates.

Fischer, C. W. (1989). *Effects of a developmental drama-inquiry process on creative and critical thinking skills in early adolescent students.* Unpublished doctoral dissertation, Kansas State University, Manhattan.

Fiske, E. (Ed.). (1999). *Champions of change: The impact of the arts on learning.* Washington, DC: Arts Education Partnership.

Flood, J., Heath, S. B., & Lapp, D. (Eds.). (1997). *Handbook of research on teaching literacy through the communicative and visual arts.* New York: Simon and Schuster.

Frechtling, J. (1999, April). *Evaluating arts reform: The evaluator's point of view.* Paper presented at the annual conference of the American Educational Research Association, Montreal.

Friedman, A. C. (1988). *Characteristics of effective theatre acting performance as incorporated into effective teaching performance.* Unpublished doctoral dissertation, Saint Louis University.

Gallas, K. (1994). *The languages of learning: How children talk, write, dance, draw, and sing their understanding of the world.* New York: Teachers College Press.

Howell, C. D. (1990). *The relationship between arts education and creativity among high school students.* Unpublished doctoral dissertation, University of Northern Colorado, Greeley.

Johnson, C. F. (1985). *Teaching as a performing art: An analysis of the performance skills of prominent mathematics teachers.* Unpublished doctoral dissertation, Columbia University, New York.

Kase-Polisini, J. (Ed.). (1985). *Creative drama in a developmental context.* Lanham, MD: University Press of America.

Keinanen, M., Hetland, L., & Winner, E. (2000). Teaching cognitive skill through dance: Evidence for near but not far transfer. *Journal of Aesthetic Education, 34*(3–4), 295–306.

Kim, J. (1998). *The effects of creative dance instruction on creative and critical thinking of seventh-grade female students in Seoul, Korea.* Unpublished doctoral dissertation, New York University.

Klein, J. (1993). To Oz: Changing theatre teacher education. *Bulletin of the Council for Research in Music Education, 117,* 76–91.

Luftig, R. L. (1994). *The schooled mind: Do the arts make a difference? An empirical evaluation of the Hamilton Fairfield SPECTRA+ Program, 1992–93.* Oxford, OH: Miami University.

Meoli, D. C. (1999). *The relationship between school climate and the arts.* Unpublished doctoral dissertation, St. John's University, New York.

Moga, E., Burger, K., Hetland, L., & Winner, E. (2000). Does studying the arts engender creative thinking? Evidence for near but not far transfer. *Journal of Aesthetic Education, 34*(3–4), 91–104.

Mueller, A. K. (1993). *The effect of movement-based instruction on the melodic perception of primary-age general mu-*

sic students. Unpublished doctoral dissertation, Arizona State University, Tempe.

Murray, E. (1998). *Nowhere to hide but together: A narrative case study of three classroom teachers, a drama specialist, and their supporters negotiating toward an artistic vision of teaching through drama in an urban elementary school.* Unpublished doctoral dissertation, Ohio State University, Columbus.

Myers, J. S., & Cantino, H. B. (1993). Drama teaching strategies that encourage problem solving behavior in children. *Youth Theatre Journal, 8*(1), 11–17.

National Study of School Evaluation. (1997). *Indicators of schools of quality: Vol. 10 Schoolwide indicators of quality.* Schaumburg, IL: Author.

National Study of School Evaluation. (1998). *Program evaluation: Visual and performing arts.* Schaumburg, IL: Author.

Nilges, L. (2000). The role of spatial ability in physical education and mathematics. *Journal of Physical Education, Recreation, and Dance, 71*(6), 29–33, 52–53.

Rohwer, D. A. (1997). *The effect of movement instruction on sixth-grade beginning instrumental music students' perception, synchronization, and performance with a steady beat.* Unpublished doctoral dissertation, Ohio State University, Columbus.

Rosenberg, H. (1987). *Creative drama and imagination: Transforming ideas into action.* New York: CBS College.

Rubino, M. A. (1990). *The use of musical plays in teaching basic skills to developmentally disabled individuals.* Unpublished master's thesis, California State University, Long Beach.

Sarason, S. B. (1999). *Teaching as a performing art.* New York: Teachers College Press.

Seidel, K. (1996). *Leaders' theatre: A case study of how high school students develop leadership skills through participation in theatre.* Unpublished doctoral dissertation, University of Cincinnati.

Seidel, K. (2000). What's important: A new study indicates K–12 research priorities. *Teaching Theatre, 11*(4), 12–14.

Seidel, S. (1999). "Stand and unfold yourself": A monograph on the Shakespeare & Company research study. In E. Fiske (Ed.), *Champions of change: The impact of the arts on learning* (pp. 79–90). Washington, DC: Arts Education Partnership.

Timpson, W. M., Burgoyne, S., Jones, C. S., & Jones, W. (1997). *Teaching and performing: Ideas for energizing your classes.* Madison, WI: Magna.

U.S. Department of Education, National Center for Education Statistics. (1995). *Arts education in public elementary and secondary schools: Fast response survey system statistical analysis report.* (NCES 95-082). Rockville, MD: Westat.

U.S. Department of Education, National Center for Education Statistics. (1998). *The NAEP 1997 arts report card* (NCES 1999-486). Washington, DC: Author.

Van Houten, K. E. (1999). *High school musical theater and the meaning students give to their involvement.* Unpublished doctoral dissertation, New York University.

Wagner, B. J. (Ed.). (1999). *Building moral communities through educational drama.* Stamford, CT: Ablex.

Westat. (2000). *Semi-annual report of the evaluation of the transforming education through the arts challenge: October 2000.* Rockville, MD: Author.

Westreich, G. B. (2000). *An analysis of kinesthetic learners' responses: Teaching mathematics through dance.* Unpublished doctoral dissertation, American University, Washington, DC.

Winner, E., & Cooper, M. (2000). Mute those claims: No evidence (yet) for a causal link between arts study and academic achievement. *Journal of Aesthetic Education,* 34(3–4), 11–76.

Winner, E., & Hetland, L. (Eds.). (2000). The arts and academic achievement: What the evidence shows. *The Journal of Aesthetic Education,* 34(3–4) (special issue).

Wolf, D. P. (1999). Why the arts matter in education, or just what do children learn when they create an opera. In E. Fiske (Ed.), *Champions of change: The impact of the arts on learning* (pp. 91–98). Washington, DC: Arts Education Partnership.

Part VIII
NEUROSCIENCE, MEDICINE, AND MUSIC

John W. Flohr
Editor

Introduction

JOHN W. FLOHR

This part is devoted to three related areas: music and neuroscience, performing arts medicine, and musician health. Since the last Handbook there have been many developments in these areas that are of interest to music educators. The purpose of this part is to critically review developments in all three areas and provide recommendations for future research. Health issues relating to keyboard and string music education will be primarily found in chapter 53. Health issues relating to brass and woodwind music education will be primarily found in chapter 54.

Two major related areas, music therapy and vocal musician health, have been omitted from this part. Music therapy is a field of major interest to music educators, and there are several excellent resources available to those who are interested. (The reader is directed to the music therapy association website and others located at the ERIC website, http://ericir.syr.edu.)

The area of vocal function and health in singing has many valuable references. For example, see Sataloff (1998), Andrews (1995), and Miller (1996).

REFERENCES

Andrews, M. (1995). *Manual of voice treatment: Pediatrics through geriatrics.* San Diego: Singular.

Miller, R. (1996). *The structure of singing: System and art in vocal technique.* New York: Schirmer Books.

Sataloff, R. (1998). *Vocal health and pedagogy.* San Diego: Singular.

Music and Neuroscience

52

JOHN W. FLOHR

DONALD A. HODGES

Relationships among the brain, music, and musical abilities are of interest to musicians, psychologists, and neuroscientists. The purpose of this chapter is to provide a detailed and critical overview of the neuroscientific research dealing with music and music education. Unfortunately, a direct translation from neuroscience research into music education at this time is very problematic. Although our understanding of brain and behavior has increased at an exponential rate over the past 10 years, theories of brain functioning and our understanding of the neurobiological forces that shape musical behavior are still in their infancy. The focus will be on ideas helpful to music education from what is known about music and the brain. The chapter is organized into three sections.

1. *Strategies for conducting neuromusical research*. A review of the methodological approaches to conducting neuroscientific research in music. The neuroscience tools reviewed in this section have in many ways revolutionized our ability to examine both the function and structure of the brain. (For a more complete review, see Hodges, 1996b.)
2. *Overall development*. A review of findings relating to overall development, selected topics, and theories and theoretical areas.
3. *Future directions*. A generalized summary of findings and recommendations and considerations for future research directions.

Strategies for Conducting Neuromusical Research

How does one go about studying the phenomenon of music in the brain? The brain's immense complexity, in com-bination with the subtleties and intricacies of human musical behavior, means that conducting neuromusical research is difficult at best. Although there have been tremendous advancements in research tools, no single strategy is able to provide comprehensive answers. Rather, information from every approach possible must be combined to create a more complete understanding. The purpose of this section is to review current strategies, giving for each a rationale for its appropriateness and a critique of its strengths and weaknesses. Only minimal attention is paid to results, as that information is covered more thoroughly in the section on findings.

Throughout this chapter the reader should keep in mind two points. First, the brain is only part of a much larger system that includes the central nervous system (brain and spinal cord) and peripheral nerves (afferent nerve fibers and their receptors, which send messages to the brain, and efferent nerve fibers and their muscles and glands, which take messages from the brain). In addition, the brain regulates the release of hormones into the bloodstream, so that, in effect, the brain extends throughout the body. The second point has to do with mind-brain disagreements. Are the mind and brain one and the same, or are mind and brain separate entities? Untangling such a Gordian knot is beyond the scope of this chapter. Some researchers work from a more purely neurological viewpoint, concerned mainly with physiological processes. Others work from a more cognitive or mental approach. The reader should be aware that modern cognitive neuroscience is beginning to bridge this gap. The concept of psychoneuroimmunology is one that recognizes interconnections among the mind, brain, and body. Music, of course, is a phenomenon that arises out of interactions among all three.

This section is based on six categories: animal research,

fetal and infant research, research on brain-damaged individuals, hemispheric asymmetry research, brain imaging research, neuromotor research, and affective research. These categories are based on a combination of methodologies and subject groupings. They appear to fit most closely with the way the literature is organized and reported. From animals we can learn about antecedents to human musical behavior. From infants we can learn about the brain's wiring for music, relatively independent of the influence of experience. Studying brain-damaged individuals provides the opportunity to isolate areas of the brain involved in musical processing. Hemispheric asymmetry research seeks to reveal how the brain is organized. Brain imaging research provides a window into the working brain. Neuromotor research is concerned with how the brain monitors both expressive (i.e., musical performance) and receptive (i.e., music listening) experiences. Finally, affective research looks into the brain's involvement in emotional responses to music.

Animal Research

Although studying animals may seem like an unusual place to begin, this has been a standard approach in psychology (e.g., Pavlov's dog) and continues in cognitive neuroscience. Investigating the ways animals process sounds gives neuroscientists useful information about human sound processing. Most animals have devices for detecting, analyzing, and responding to sounds. Once a sound has been detected, the animal analyzes it for "meaning," and this meaning shapes behavior. A housecat demonstrates this when it comes running into the kitchen at the sound of the can opener. When humans listen to music, the process is similar in that we analyze the sound for meaning and that meaning shapes our responses.

Significant insights into human musicality can be gained particularly by investigating sound-making and responding behaviors in such species as birds, whales, dolphins, monkeys, and apes (D'Amato, 1988; Geissman, 2000; Marler, 2000; Payne, 2000; Warren, 1993; Whaling, 2000). Sight (e.g., seen in displays of aggression or mating behavior) or smell (e.g., marking territory) are ways animals can communicate. But sound has certain advantages in that it can travel long distances rapidly, operate during day or night, and encode complex and changing messages (Slater, 2000). Therefore, many species have developed sophisticated sound-making behaviors (not only vocalizations but also other noises, such as chest-thumping among gorillas). To assume that animal sounds have nothing to do with human music would be to ignore a significant amount of information and would be counter to linkages found in other types of behavior (e.g., language and social organization).

The opposite is equally true; one cannot automatically assume that there is a direct correlation between animal sounds and human music. Thus, one of the first issues to be dealt with is whether or not animals actually create music. This is a difficult question and one that may elude a definitive answer. It is tempting to anthropomorphize animal sounds; after all, we call it bird*song* because that is what it sounds like to us. But is it music to the animals? Certainly most animal sounds have to do with territoriality, courtship and mating rituals, and signaling (e.g., alarm calls) (Brody, 1991). Slater (2000) remarks that with more than 4,000 species of songbirds alone, and all the varied forms and patterns of their songs, it would not be difficult to find many seemingly musical characteristics embedded in their songs, but that this would most likely be coincidental. Even where birdsongs are more complex, varied, or elaborate than is strictly necessary for biological function, they may be so to achieve distinctiveness. If the point of sound-making is to communicate, it will do no good if the message is lost in a sonic environment rife with many voices. In a cacophonous habitat where many sounds are competing for "airspace," distinctiveness is an advantage. Krause's (1987) niche hypothesis is that each species produces sounds that occupy a particular bandwidth in the overall acoustic spectrum, along with unique rhythm patterns, tonal qualities, and so on. This ensures that the message will not get lost among all the other sounds. Having said that, however, does not preclude an animal deriving pleasure from the act of making sounds. Until we can gain access to their inner worlds, the most we can do is speculate.

In the meantime, this research strategy informs two concerns of music psychologists: What are the evolutionary antecedents of human musicality? What "extra" cognitive structures and processes do humans possess beyond those of other animals that allow for the degree of musicality expressed in all cultures? In the first instance, the sounds of nature (what Krause [1987] terms "biophony") most likely exerted strong influences on early hominid sound-making. It would be quite natural for us to mimic the sounds around us. Of course, with our sophisticated brains, it would not take long for us to move beyond mere mimicry to elaboration, extension, synthesis, and eventually the creation of novel sounds. In time, we would develop our own niche in the biophony. This line of research is important in developing a theory of an evolutionary basis for music (Hodges 1989, 1996a, 2000; Wallin, Merker, & Brown, 2000).

The second concern feeds more directly into the larger question of neuromusicology. For example, animals rely on absolute frequency analysis (D'Amato, 1988) rather than on relative pitch as we do (Trehub, Bull, & Thorpe, 1984). Thus, while various animals can be trained to choose between two songs, they fail miserably if those songs are transposed. By contrast, our adult musicality is possible, in large part, because we deal with pitch relationships. "Yankee Doodle," for instance, is recognizable to us at any pitch center.

There are other cognitive limitations among animals as well. For example, musical forms ranging from simple verse-chorus alternations to lengthy symphonic movements are possible because of our ability to retain musical information for long periods of time. Yet dolphins represent the best animals can do, and they can only recognize the second A section of a simple ABA form if each section is no more than 2 seconds long (Warren, 1993). Once again, however, it must be recognized that testing animals on their capacity for processing human music seems patently unfair. Nevertheless, this line of research does provide evidence of some of the neural mechanisms humans possess that allow for our musicality.

Fetal and Infant Research

In order to understand how the brain is predisposed to music, it would be ideal to look at the brain in a "pure" state, that is, without the influence of the environment. Since this is impossible, studying fetal and infant responses to music allows us to approach a "pure" state with minimal environmental influence. The limitations and difficulties of using babies as subjects seem apparent, but there is much useful information to be gained from this approach. A growing body of literature is focusing on fetal responses to music because in the last trimester before birth, the fetus is capable of responding to sounds in the womb. Researchers can gauge fetal responses by monitoring heart rate and through bodily movements (Abrams & Gerhardt, 1997; Deliège & Sloboda, 1996).

Almost immediately after birth, babies can orient toward sounds and soon after that can pick out the sounds of the mother's voice (Trehub, Schellenberg, & Hill, 1997; Trehub & Trainor, 1993). A significant amount of the interactions between a newborn and its caretakers is based on two-way sound manipulations. The caretakers sing lullabies and talk "baby talk," and there are musical crib mobiles and toys. "Motherese," a term psychologists have coined to refer to the type of baby talk typically spoken to infants, emphasizes pitch, timbre, dynamic inflections, and rhythm patterns in order to convey meaning (Dissayanake, 2000). Clearly, the baby cannot interpret the meaning of words but does learn to interpret the emotional content. Likewise, the baby learns early on to communicate by manipulating the same sonic elements to express mood states such as hunger, pain, fear, happiness, love, and so on. From this line of research, it is clear that infant musical behaviors are exhibited primarily because of inherited mechanisms (Imberty, 2000; Trehub, 2000). While learning takes place from the outset, babies do not need systematic, formal instruction in order to respond to music, speech, and other sounds.

Research on Brain-Damaged Individuals

Another approach that has a long history in neuroscience is to look at individuals who suffer from some form of brain damage, either from trauma, genetic defect, or aging. Studying persons who have suffered a tumor, stroke, or lesion indicates that some individuals suffer from aphasia (loss of language) but not amusia (loss of music) or vice versa. This lends support to the notion that music and language are dissociated; that is, that music and language are represented, at least to a large degree, by separate neural systems (Hodges, 1996b; Marin & Perry, 1999). Both are umbrella terms, in that there are many different forms of aphasia (e.g., loss of speech, comprehension, or the ability to read or write) and amusia (e.g., loss of ability to track pitch, or rhythm, or timbre or loss of familiar tune recognition). Because of the complexity and modularity of both systems, it is also possible that many brain regions are implicated in both language and music (Falk, 2000). (For more details on modularity see hereafter.)

A common research paradigm is to ask brain-damaged subjects to do a variety of music-related tasks. Their inability to do a task successfully (when compared to a person with an undamaged brain) is then linked to anatomical lesion sites. Several notes of caution must be inserted. First, a damaged brain is different from a normal brain, and the assumption that it is operating like the normal brain with the exception of the damaged portion is not necessarily warranted. Second, for older studies in the literature, anatomical lesion sites are not given very precisely; sometimes reports are as vague as "damage on the left side." Third, the case with music is somewhat different from the case with language. While one can reasonably assume that an adult has language competency, adult musical skills may vary all the way from minimal (even including "tone deafness") to highly professional. Thus, if, for example, a brain-damaged person cannot do a given musical task—such as match pitches, recognize familiar tunes, or read music—care must be taken to determine whether he or she had such skills prior to the trauma. (For a detailed review of the effects of brain damage on musical behaviors, see Hodges [1996b, pp. 212–216].)

A second class of subjects is those with inherited cognitive limitations. Musical savants are cognitively impaired but capable of amazing musical feats (Miller, 1989). Individuals with Williams syndrome often have cognitive "peaks" and "valleys," and music appears to be something many of them can do quite well (Levitin & Bellugi, 1998). Musical behaviors are only possible in such individuals because of the presence of specific neural structures. Williams syndrome, in particular, is a fertile area for research in that it may ultimately be possible to link research on genetics (Williams syndrome results from a microdeletion on chromosome 7) with neuroscientific and behavioral data.

A third class of subjects involves those suffering from cognitive dementias due to aging (especially Alzheimer's). Individuals with prior musical backgrounds may retain procedural skills (e.g., singing or playing an instrument) in spite of declining linguistic fluency (Crystal, Grober, & Masur, 1989). In at least one case, an Alzheimer's patient was able to sing the words to familiar songs even though she could no longer communicate via language (Johnson & Ulatowska, 1995). Interestingly, music (among other things) is being recommended to elders as a means of staving off the ravages of Alzheimer's (Golden, 1994). The presence of musical skills, in the absence of linguistic and other skills, once again denotes neural structures devoted to musical processing.

Hemispheric Asymmetry Research

Hemispheric asymmetry, sometimes referred to as cerebral dominance, is concerned with possible differences between the two hemispheres, both in type of processing (e.g., sequential versus holistic) or in responsibility (i.e., which side is more responsible for particular tasks). Although a variety of strategies can be employed—most notably studying brain damaged individuals (discussed previously) and brain imaging (discussed subsequently)—the focus of this brief discussion will be on dichotic listening tasks.

Dichotic listening tasks have been widely used as a means of comparing one side of the brain's performance with the other. Basically, the technique is to present conflicting signals to the right and left ears via headphones. Approximately 70% of the fibers in the auditory pathway are contralateral, meaning that they go from the inner ear to the auditory cortex in the opposite hemisphere. Thus, although both sides receive all the information from each ear, signals from the right ear are more strongly represented in the left hemisphere, and vice versa (Kimura, 1961; Robinson & Solomon, 1974). Contralateral response times are faster than ipsilateral (from one inner ear to the auditory cortex on the same side) (Majkowski, Bochenek, Bochenek, Knapik-Fijalkowska, & Kopec, 1971) and can occlude impulses arriving along ipsilateral pathways (Kimura, 1967). In a typical experiment, subjects might hear a nonsense syllable such as "bleh" in the right ear and "teh" in the left ear (stimuli must be nonsensical, as real words would be immediately recognized). They are then presented with four foils and asked to identify the one they heard. Over a number of trials, consistency in picking out the right ear signal would indicate processing dominance by the left hemisphere and vice versa.

A major limitation of this technique for music research is that the stimuli can be no longer than 2 seconds. If they are longer, the brain can go back and forth, picking up enough information from each ear to make recognition of both stimuli possible. Obviously, only limited musical meaning can be found in 2-second fragments. Also, stimulus variables (the type of sound/music being used), task variables (whether subjects are asked to make global or local decisions), and subject variables (amount of training, gender, handedness, etc.) can make dramatic differences in the results. Sergent was highly critical of this line of research and felt that all such data could be discarded (Sergent, 1993; for an extended review of this literature and discussion, see Hodges [1996b, pp. 222–232]).

For a period of time, primarily during the 1970s, much was made of music being in the right side of the brain. This oversimplification has since been modified. Music is *not* in the right side of the brain alone; both sides are involved. In fact, sophisticated musical processing most likely involves the front-back, top-bottom, and left and right sides of the brain in widely distributed but locally specialized neural networks. Furthermore, selectively changing the focus of attention radically alters brain activation patterns (Platel et al., 1997). Further implications of this line of research are discussed subsequently.

Brain Imaging Research

Modern neuroscientists have a broad range of highly sophisticated research tools at their disposal. These include electroencephalography (EEG), event-related potentials (ERP) derived from EEG, magnetoencephalography (MEG), superconducting quantum interference device (SQUID), magnetic resonance imaging (MRI), functional magnetic resonance imaging (fMRI), positron emission tomography (PET), and transcranial magnetic stimulation (TMS, discussed in the section on neuromotor responses). Space does not allow for much more than a brief description of each of these technologies (see figure 52.1). Because of limited access to equipment, costs involved, and related issues, typical neuroimaging experiments are conducted with a very small number of subjects.

EEG and ERP. Due to neural activity, the brain constantly produces a small amount of electrical current that can be measured; EEG measures the summed activity of millions of brain cells under electrodes placed in various places around the skull (Gur & Gur, 1994). Data are interpreted in terms of frequency (Hz), amplitude (microvolts), form, and distribution (sometimes converted into a brain map). Most often reported are frequency components, including delta (0.5–4.0 Hz), theta (4.5–8.0 Hz), alpha (8.5–12.0 Hz), and beta waves (12.5–32.0 Hz). Electroencephalography has been used for some time to study different levels of arousal and is now being employed to study cognitive processes in general and music processing specifically (Altenmüller, 1993; Barber, 1999; Faita & Besson, 1994).

While EEG tracks the brain's electrical activity over time, ERP examines the brain's immediate response to a

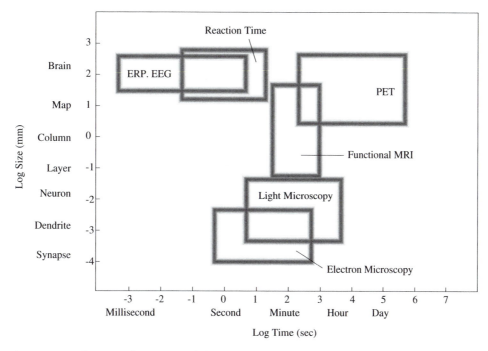

Figure 52.1. Schematic illustration of the spatial (vertical axis) and temporal (horizontal axis) resolution of techniques used to study brain function in humans. The hazy edges of each box suggest that these are approximations and that these techniques may not be limited to these boundaries in the future. This figure emphasizes the different spatial and temporal characteristics of methods used to study the neurobiology of behaviors, none of which alone is sufficient to understand the neural basis of a behavior or its development. (From Janowsky & Carper in Sameroff & Haith, eds., 1996).

stimulus in millisecond (ms) intervals. A computer averages EEG readings following multiple presentations of a stimulus. This allows extraneous aspects of the EEG to be canceled out, while electrical activity occurring in time-locked response to the stimulus is revealed (Brown, Marsh, & Ponsford, 1985). Data are evaluated for directional changes in the wave pattern (either positive or negative), intensity level (amplitude), and latency (time lapse). A P300 wave indicates a positive wave whose maximum amplitude occurred approximately 300 ms after the stimulus, while a N400 wave is a negative wave form occurring approximately 400 ms after the stimulus. The P300 has been more frequently studied in relation to music. It is hypothesized to be an indicator of "working" memory, comparing incoming stimuli to stored memories, and has been linked to the detection of musical events (Cohen & Erez, 1991; Frisina, Walton, & Crummer, 1988; Hantz & Crummer, 1988; Paller, McCarthy, & Wood, 1992; Paulus, 1988; Schwent, Snyder, & Hillyard, 1976).

MEG and SQUID. The brain's electrical activity produces a magnetic field that can be measured just outside the skull through MEG, giving location information about neural activity. SQUID provides refined spatial information, in millimeters, and precise temporal resolution, in milliseconds (Hari, 1990). This approach has been used in only a few studies related to music (Kaufmann, Curtis, Wang, & Williamson, 1991; Williamson & Kaufmann, 1988).

MRI and fMRI. MRI provides very precise information about anatomical structures under the skin but does not provide information about function (Ackerman, 1992). It has been used to show structural features of musician's brains (Amunts et al., 1997; Pantev et al., 1998; Schlaug, Jancke, Huang, & Steinmetz, 1994, 1995). A newer development, fMRI does provide data about both location and function. Currently, there is considerable interest in finding a way to use fMRI to study music. The difficulty is that both MRI and fMRI are very noisy environments for the subjects. The camera's motion within the scanner generates rhythmical noise that competes with musical perception. While it is possible to extract speech or other nonmusical sounds from the ambient noise, it is not so easily done with music. Regular headphones cannot be used, because of the strong magnet. Researchers are attempting to deliver musical stimuli through pneumatic tubes or to develop better antinoise cancellation devices. If these problems are solved, fMRI should prove to be a very valuable approach for studying music cognition.

PET.   In PET, radioactively tagged oxygen, water, or glucose is inhaled or injected into the bloodstream; PET scans then detect brain metabolism or regional cerebral blood flow (rCBF) while the subject engages in an assigned task (Raichle, 1994). By means of paired-image subtraction (subtracting the activations of one task from another), areas of the brain most active during a specific task are identified (Posner & Raichle, 1994). Areas of deactivation (i.e., less active than during rest) also provide useful information. Because PET provides information about function but not location, it is mapped onto MRI data. The combination of the two tells neuroscientists "what" is going on "where." PET is a powerful technique that is revealing important information about music processing (Fox et al., 1995; Parsons, Fox, & Hodges, 1998; Zatorre, 1994; Zatorre, Evans, & Myer, 1994).

Taken collectively, these various brain imaging techniques are opening up new understandings about the brain in general and about music cognition specifically. The most rapid advancements are being made in this field, and music psychologists, music educators, and music therapists should be aware of new findings as they are reported (see Zatorre & Peretz, 2001, for a new compilation).

Neuromotor Research

Musical responses are both expressive (i.e., performing) and receptive (i.e., listening). Musical performance activates motor control areas in the brain to such a high degree that musicians may be considered small-muscle athletes (Wilson, 1986). A PET study of eight professional pianists confirmed this as motor systems in the brain were strongly activated during performance (Fox et al., 1995; Parsons, 2001). Transcranial magnetic stimulation (TMS), a technique for mapping neuromotor pathways, was used with 15 subjects to show that the motor cortex controlling the fingers increased in response to piano exercises, both actual and imagined (Pascual-Leone et al., 1995). Researchers used magnetic source imaging to compare 9 string players with 6 nonmusicians; the main finding was that the string players had greater neuronal activity and a larger area in the right primary somatosensory cortex that controls the fingers of the left hand than controls (Elbert, Pantev, Wienbruch, Rockstrub, & Taub, 1995). These effects were greater for those who started playing at a young age.

Highly precise and rhythmically coordinated movements are critical for musical performance, and investiga-

tors are beginning to identify timing mechanisms in the brain (Freund & Hefter, 1990; Miller, Thaut, & Aunon, 1995; Moore, 1992; Wilson, 1991, 1998). A related issue is focal dystonia, a neuromotor problem in which the brain and hands (or other body parts) fail to communicate properly (Wilson, 1988, 1992; Wilson & Roehmann, 1992). Several concert pianists have had major careers curtailed by a focal dystonia in one hand. Highly practiced movements seem to be most affected, while other uses of the hand remain functional.

In the receptive mode, Thaut and colleagues have produced an impressive body of work on how Parkinsonian and stroke patients can regain motor function (e.g., walking or grasping) through rhythmic entrainment (McIntosh, Thaut, & Rice, 1996; Thaut, Brown, Benjamin, & Cooke, 1995; Thaut, McIntosh, Prassas, & Rice, 1993). Rhythmic timing embedded in music serves as a cue to motor system timing mechanisms in the brain.

Affective Research

Data-gathering techniques for studying affective responses to music fall into three categories: verbal reports, behavioral observations, and physiological responses (Abeles & Chung, 1996). In terms of finding out the brain's role in emotional responses to music, current strategies are quite limited. Recently, PET scans of 10 amateur musicians indicated that different brain regions were activated in response to positive and negative music listening experiences (Blood, Zatorre, Bermudez, & Evans, 1999). Another avenue of approach is found in biochemical analyses of blood samples (for a review see Bartlett, 1996). Music can elicit changes in such biochemicals as endorphins, cortisol, adrenocorticotropic hormone (ACTH), interleukin-1, and secretory immunoglobin A. The brain-music-biochemical relationship is not yet well understood but does hold some promise. In particular, studies in psychoneuroimmunology are being used in music medicine to document the physiological effects (e.g., changes in blood chemistry) that music has on the body (Pratt & Spingte, 1996; Reilly, 1999; Spingte & Droh, 1992). Fear and anxiety can be reduced in many clinical situations through the use of music.

Each of these research strategies has advantages and disadvantages. It is important to integrate findings from the various approaches into a more coherent whole. Where data from different techniques are in disagreement, efforts must be undertaken to resolve discrepancies. Wherever possible, it would be helpful to attack the same problem with more than one strategy. Particularly in the area of neuroimaging, it is important to keep up with new technologies and possibilities (e.g., with development of better sound delivery systems in fMRI).

Overall Development

To what extent do genes specify the intricate working of the human brain? To what extent are the intricate workings of the brain acquired as a result of experiences? New advances in neuroscience have addressed the ancient "nature versus nurture" debate. In general, neuroscience research has shown that neither nature nor nurture alone determines brain development. Human brains at the prenatal stages are already interacting with the environment (Standley, 1998). The brain appears to be more plastic and malleable during the first decade of life than in adulthood. According to Thatcher studies have shown that 40% of short-term and 70% of long-term connections in the brain are influenced by heredity. Therefore, 30% to 60% of the brain's connections come from environmental influences or an interaction of heredity and environmental influences (Thatcher, 1998). Nelson and Bloom (1997) cite numerous demonstrations that show how positive or negative early experiences can alter both the structure and function of the brain. It is also important to remember that a child's brain is not the same as an adult brain. There is agreement that during the first decade of life a child typically has up to twice as much neural activity and connections as an adult (Bates, Thal, & Janowsky, 1992; Chugani, 1998; Chugani, Phelps, & Mazziotta, 1987). The brain makes connections during the prenatal period and throughout life (Gopnik, Meltzoff, & Kuhl, 1999; Janowsky & Carper, 1996). Some connections are found to be predetermined genetically, and others develop from environmental influences (Cossu, Faienza, & Capone, 1994; Ibatoullina, Vardaris, & Thompson, 1994; van Baal, de Geus, & Boomsma, 1998).

Children as young as 1 day old are able to make cognitive choices about their environment (Atkins & Flohr, 2000; Flohr, Atkins, Bower, & Aldridge, 2000; Woodward, Fresen, Harrison, & Coley, 1996). There are clear additive and regressive events in brain development. As shown in figure 52.2, a child at birth may have the largest number of neurons that she or he will ever have. After the age of 2 years, the number of neurons remains nearly the same until 65 years of age. Synapses, the connection between neurons, form in the brain and change as the child develops. (For an explanation directed to educators see Sylwester, 1995.) During early childhood the percent of adult cortical levels of myelin and glial are increasing and may be influenced by the environment. Myelination of the nerve axons increases the efficiency of neural transmission. The glial cell is a major cell type in the brain that nourishes neurons. Interestingly, a study of Einstein's brain showed his brain had significantly more glial cells than the brain of the average human (Diamond, Scheibel, Murphy, &

Harvey, 1985). There are several glial subtypes, but there is not yet enough information to consider an active role for the glial cells in behavioral development (Janowsky & Carper, 1996). Note also that figure 52.2 illustrates a decrease in the level of synapses between the approximate ages of 2 and 8 years. This decrease, theorized to be a type of "synaptic pruning," may occur because networks atrophy over time because of unused or less used connections. Brains do not make more connections and stop. It appears the brain makes more connections than it needs and then deletes unused or less used connections by the process of synaptic pruning. Although there is much growth and activity during the young years, there is evidence that there is room for change in the later years, and recent research indicates that the adult brain is able to produce new cells (e.g., in the hippocampus of adult humans) (Eriksson et al., 1998; Gibbs, 1998; Nelson & Bloom, 1997). The complex interaction of innate abilities and environment will continue to be a viable mode of research. The complexity of the interaction between innate abilities and environment may also depend on the variability inherent in individual differences (Barber, McKenzie, & Helme, 1997). Possible individual differences include emotional traits, temperament, and cognitive and intellectual propensities.

Four concepts central to brain development are addressed in this section: critical periods, optimal periods, windows of opportunity, and plasticity. Critical period refers to the idea that there are time frames in which there will be no development or stunted development if certain stimulation is not present. The brain may be open to experience of a particular kind only during narrow periods of time. Missing a critical period in learning would be as if you were playing the solo triangle part in a symphony and didn't play your quarter note after the 30 measures rest. You missed your chance and the triangle is no longer needed or useful. There are many examples from animals in which experience must be timed very precisely to have an impact. A classic research example investigated the vision of 23 kittens (Hubel & Wiesel, 1970). Nobel Prize–winners Hubel and Wiesel covered one eye of newborn kittens. The kittens grew up with only one eye in use. A few months later the covered eye was opened, but it was in effect not connected to the brain. What makes this a "critical" period is the finding that if the cats are later given visual stimulation, they are unable to use the stimulation to see. When deprived of visual stimulation in the covered eye until after the critical period, the part of their brain dealing with optical sensory data does not develop. One way of looking at critical periods is to imagine a sort of biological clock that only works during a certain period of development. An alternate view may be that experience has changed the brain so that the animal or person perceives and interprets the world in a different way. The ex-

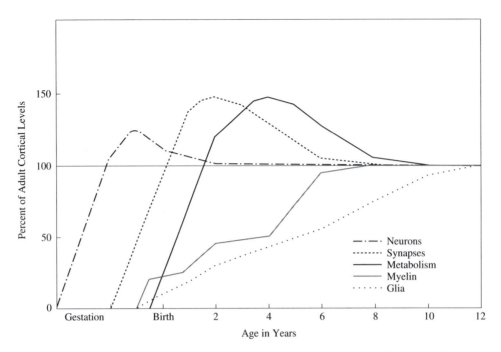

Figure 52.2. Approximation of the time course of additive and regressive events in brain development. (From Janowsky & Carper in Sameroff & Haith, eds., 1996).

periences influence neural wiring, and the neural wiring has an effect on recognition or interpretation of new sensory data. It is presently unknown if the critical period is due to biological clock mechanisms, the brain structures that have developed, or an interaction of the two. There may be critical periods in musical development, and the search for these periods provides a fertile ground for research.

Authors often write about optimal periods as if they were critical periods, although presently there are no identified critical periods in musical development. An optimal period is used to refer to those periods in which development will be faster or easier. For example, it is easier to learn to sing in tune during the ages of 3–6 years than at 25–28 years of age. It may also be easier or more efficient to learn the language of classical, jazz, or any style of music before the age of 6. The period in all these cases is optimal rather than critical. There is no evidence to support the notion that a child cannot learn to sing if she or he does not have music experiences before, for example, 6 years of age.

There are indications of possible critical periods in music. For example, the music educator Gordon advanced the idea of developmental music aptitude (Gordon, 1979, 1990). He has found that children's scores on measures of musical aptitude do not change significantly after the age of approximately 9 years. A few studies indicate optimal

periods and point toward possible critical periods for music training. A group of adults with a history of violin training and a group of adults without violin training had their brains mapped using MEG (Elbert et al., 1995). The area of the somatosensory cortex representing the fingers of the left fingering hand was larger than that in the contralateral hemisphere representing the right bow hand and also larger than the corresponding area in nonmusicians. This finding was consistent with reports of adult human amputees (Nelson & Bloom, 1997). A possible critical period was indicated by a trend for the effect to be larger for individuals who had begun music training before the age of 10. Another optimal period and possible critical period was seen in a study of violin training, where in a sample of 60 musicians and nonmusicians, those who started training before the age of 7 years exhibited increased corpus callosum size (Schlaug, Jänke, Huang, Steiger, & Steinmetz, 1995).

"Windows of opportunity" refers to the idea that there are general time frames in which optimal or critical development will take place. The fact that writers often do not specify the window of opportunity as critical or optimal leads to much confusion. It is important to underline the difference between optimal and critical periods when talking about windows of opportunity for brain development. For example, it is an overstatement of neuroscientific research to say that there is a window of opportunity for music during the ages of 3–7 years and if a parent does not give the child a chance during those ages, the child will not be musical. Bruer writes: "For most learning, particularly learning culturally transmitted skills and knowledge such as reading, mathematics, and music, the windows of experience-dependent opportunity never close" (1999, p. 187). On the other hand, there are indications of how early experience changes the way the brain works. Language research demonstrates how the 6-month to 12-month window of development is important and is an optimal period for sound organization (Gopnik et al., 1999, p. 108). One study of 18 very young babies showed no brain activity differences while listening to native language and foreign language sounds. After a few months native and foreign language stimuli produced a difference in left hemisphere activity (Cheour et al., 1998). The finding may mean that changes in the way a baby hears the sound produce changes in the brain. Are music sounds in general and music sounds of the culture processed in the same way as language sounds during the second 6 months of life? If so, that period in an infant's life would be an optimal window of opportunity that may help children learn music faster or more efficiently than music education later in life.

Work with older populations has shown that there are further chances for the brain to adapt or rewire itself. It is prudent to question the simplistic view that the brain becomes increasingly difficult to modify beyond early childhood. Much brain development occurs in early childhood, but the brain is far from completed even at the end of adolescence. After accidental brain damage, for example, the brain may reassign function from the damaged part of the brain to an uninjured area (Thulborn, Carpenter, & Just, 1999). This idea of how the physical structure of the brain changes as a result of experience is referred to as brain plasticity (Caine & Caine, 1994). "Plasticity" refers to the notion that the brain is very adaptable, fluid, or plastic in the way in which it can adapt. Involvement in music may help keep the brain fluid, or more fluid, as opposed to no musical involvement throughout the human lifespan. A study of 678 nuns has indicated that rich experiences, including music, in older age will help keep the brain pliable and adaptable (Snowdon, 1997, 2001). The study with nuns suggests that the adult brain can reorganize in response to positive experiences in the environment as well as negative experiences in the case of injury.

Theories and Theoretical Frameworks

A theory, or at least a conjecture of what may happen when an idea is applied to a situation, usually drives research. Neuroscience research is not different in this sense, although neuroscientists are not at a stage of precisely unified theories of music and the brain. There are several current theories that warrant attention. Students and scientists are able to use the experimental theories in their own research by testing a theory in new situations or previously studied situations. Various models of brain function and architecture have been proposed over the past century (For an educator's view of several theories see Sylwester [1995, pp. 14–24, 39–46]. For models of brain functioning see Hodges [1996b, pp. 201–205].) An examination of current theories and studies that support them reveals that while some emphasize brain structure, others emphasize function. Many of these theories will undoubtedly be proven incorrect with time, some may be combined with others or new theories, many will be modified, and a few may even stand the test of time. The following theories have been selected from among many in the field because each has possible application to music education. (The theories and theoretical areas are presented in alphabetical order of key-word.)

Developmental Shifts

The theory concerning development shift refers to the idea that at certain times of significant changes, shifts, or "brain spurts," occur in brain development (Epstein, 1978, 1986). These changes are thought to be part of the human biological development program. The shifts can be modified by the environment but are part of a normal developmental sequence. The notion finds its roots in cognitive theory (e.g., Piaget, 1950), and the neurological basis for at least one developmental shift from the ages of 5 to 7 has been related to cognitive theory. Sameroff and Haith compiled several articles that point to the efficacy of the idea that a child's brain chemistry and electrical activity inherently change in significant ways between the ages of 5 and 7 (Janowsky & Carper, 1996). Flohr and Miller (1993, 1995) lend support to this idea in relation to music with a series of EEG studies with 13 young children. One finding was that children at age 7 exhibited significant EEG brain alpha activity differences in response to contrasting styles of music that were not present when the same children were 5 years of age. Music by Vivaldi stimulated different brain responses from the children from Irish folk song music while the children listened to the music and tapped rhythm sticks. These differences occurred in the motor strip and the temporal areas. The differences lend support to the idea of a developmental shift in music processing. Barber et al. (1997) also found brain activity differences in response to different styles of music. Subjects in their study were 21 adult musicians and 25 nonmusicians.

Future research investigating the theory of developmental shift will probably have much to say to music educators and educators in general. For example, when are the neurological attributes of a child best able to process sounds from music or language? Are most 7-year-old children ready (in the neurological sense) for abstract symbols in music, or is it more appropriate at an earlier or later age? Developmental research since Zimmerman's pioneering cognitive research (1971) has affected music education. Developmental "shift" and development research are fertile fields for music education and neurological researchers to collaborate in.

Expert or Habituation

Another theory, "expert" or "habituation" (or even "efficiency") theory, seeks to explain observed decreases in brain activity during certain tasks. One might expect to observe an increase in "thinking" brain activity of a subject during a cognitive task. The opposite phenomenon has been found; experts and students after training show decreases in brain activity as opposed to novices engaged in the same cognitive task. Some studies have supported the idea that less energy or brain electrical activity may be used to perform a task in an expert's brain than in a novice's brain (Languis & Miller, 1992; Miller & Flohr, 1995). The idea is that the brain of a novice learner is less efficient and expends more energy when confronted with a challenging task than the brain of an expert learner (Jensen, 1998). Thus, music instruction should enable children to expend less energy during musical tasks.

There is, however, an alternative idea of why the decreases in activity are observed. Petsche and colleagues suggested that the reduced temporal lobe activity in the beta frequency bands of 75 healthy college students was related to habituation from listening to music (Petsche, Lindner, Rappelsberger, & Gruber, 1988). It can be posited that the subjects developed a habituated type of cortical activity in their listening to music after they were involved in a period of music training. Habituation in an expert musician can also be thought of as the musician going on "automatic pilot" while performing the music. She or he has learned the piece so well that the motor systems and cerebellum take over the performance, and other areas in the cerebral cortex are deactivated, thereby producing less electrical or chemical activity. Parsons and colleagues have found a similar result in their PET scan studies with musicians (Parsons, 2000, 2001; Parsons et al., 1998). Cerebral blood flow in a musician's frontal cortex decreased as the musician performed music on a keyboard as opposed to rest. The reduction in PET scan activity may lend support to the idea that the expert (or a person with training) uses less energy in a well-learned task. However, the expert performer also exhibits greater activation in other areas during performance, and the current data do not show if there is less energy expended in the motor cortex among expert performers, which is what the expert theory would predict. The identified decreases in the research are clearly linked to expert musicians and students involved in music instruc-

tion. Future research will help determine the mechanisms involved.

Emotion or Affective Response

Research combining affective response and music may provide theories and research findings that explain aspects of cognition. Emotions in general (or, more broadly, affective responses) are difficult to study, and much less emotion research has been done than cognition research. Nevertheless, progress is being made in the understanding of relationships between emotion and musical behavior (Juslin & Sloboda, 2001). The emotional import of music experience is a strong component of music and music instruction (Leonard & House, 1972). Reimer reminds us that "[t]eaching and learning music, then, have been understood to be valuable because they improve people's abilities to gain meaningful, gratifying musical experiences" (1999, p. 37).

Neuroscientists today have learned much about the organizing and structuring processes of neural connections and emotional response systems that influence higher thought processes. The way in which cognition is affected may occur through a complex web of bidirectional processing between cortical and subcortical brain structures, neurochemicals and hormones, and through communication between central nervous system processing (including the brain and spinal cord) and the peripheral systems (including the autonomic nervous system and the somatic system) (Atkins, 2000). A significant area of progress is in the brain's effect on the body and emotions through the release of hormones, the area of neurochemistry (Panksepp, 1998; see also the discussion of affective research earlier).

Investigators used PET to examine cerebral blood flow (CBF) changes related to affective responses to music (Blood et al., 1999). Ten participants were scanned while listening to six versions of a novel musical passage varying systematically in degree of dissonance; CBF was observed in paralimbic and neocortical regions as a function of dissonance and of perceived pleasantness/unpleasantness of the music. The authors suggest that music may recruit neural mechanisms similar to those previously associated with pleasant/unpleasant emotional states but different from those underlying other components of music perception and emotions such as fear.

Modularity and Connectionism

Many theories have elements of modularity or connectionism. The theory of "modules" in neuropsychological research refers to the idea that processes relating to music or language, for example, are carried out in distinct brain structures. Extreme modular theory would argue that these regions or modules are largely autonomous. On the other hand, connectionism is a theoretical approach that takes a holistic view of the brain, arguing that the brain functions as a whole and that a part of the brain can be recruited for multiple tasks. Either viewpoint in its extreme form may fail to explain research results, and these two theories may not be mutually exclusive.

Current neuroimaging data suggest that the neural mechanisms supporting music are distributed throughout the brain (Parsons, 2000; Parsons & Fox, 1997). The modular idea is combined with a "connection" idea of interplay among modules. A module of music engages several different brain areas in a coordinated activity and is composed of submodules (e.g., musical syntax operators, timbre operators, and rhythm operators). (For further explanation of modular theory see Restak [1994] and Sylwester [1995].) The submodules are distributed in various regions throughout the brain. At this point of the theory, each submodule appears to be a specialized piece of neural machinery. For a music task, such as playing a C major scale on the piano, the musical brain would have to integrate several submodules in a coordinated activity. There may be modules or supermodules or mechanisms that coordinate among different modules.

Research findings about hemispheric differences and localization can be explained with modular theory in the sense that modular theory regards different submodules each to be a specialized piece of neural machinery. For example, there is a neural network for language and another for music; in each case the neural networks link together locally specialized modules. These modules are largely autonomous, each doing its own work, although it is possible that some modules may be recruited for differing tasks (e.g., prosody for language and certain musical functions may be subserved by the same systems). Increasing evidence is pointing to modularity in music processing, and the data support what is already known about language (Parsons et al., 1998). In addition, anatomical variances are a consideration in modular theory. Perhaps music training affects the actual size of brain areas that are important modules in music-making. For example, the left planum temporale is larger among musicians with absolute pitch, musicians who started serious study before the age of 7, and those with Williams syndrome (Levitin & Bellugi, 1998; Schlaug et al., 1995).

In his work on the effect of music on spatial reasoning, Parsons found that the cerebellum is activated in a coordinated effort with areas of the cortex in music activity (Parsons & Fox, 1997). Hetland (2000b) has used the term "rhythm theory" to describe Parsons's module theory of music and spatial tasks. The rhythmic elements of music (hence rhythm theory) operating in the cerebellum coordinated with areas in the cortex may be responsible for increasing ability to perform spatial-temporal mental rotation tasks. The rhythm theory is a module theory in the way that it explains how different areas of the brain work together.

Altenmüller and others attempted to demonstrate changes in cortical activity patterns with 9 participants (average age 13.8 years) after a 5-week period of music training (Altenmüller, Gruhn, Parlitz, & Kahrs, 1996). The results suggested that musical training produced certain cortical brain activity patterns in different areas of the brain and that these activity patterns may depend on the applied teaching strategies. Flohr, Persellin, and Miller (1996) also reported EEG activity changes in different areas of the brain after a 7-week period with 22 preschool children (average age 5.25 years) receiving music instruction versus children receiving regular classroom instruction. The module theory supports the results of both studies in that different areas of the brain containing submodules operate in a coordinated activity. However, in the second study by Flohr and others, results showed an increase in some areas of the brain in contrast to a decrease in other areas. The module theory does not specify whether the submodules produce increased or decreased electrical activity. In addition, an increase in one module along with a decrease in another part of the brain may represent the way the brain relegates processing resources.

The term "coherence" may be viewed within the modular theory, although coherence has been used to support connectionism. Connectionist models postulate that "cognition occurs through a network of linked nodes. The nodes integrate activation through their excitatory and inhibitory links" (Carpenter, Akira, & Just, 1995, p. 92). Coherence reflects the number and strength of coordination between different brain locations. Some authors believe that coherence demonstrates evidence of anatomical connections and information exchange between two brain locations (Fein, Raz, & Merrin, 1988). Brain imaging studies have shown a relationship between music listening or music instruction and increased coherence activities in children (deBeus, 1999; Malyarenko et al., 1996; Sarnthein et al., 1997).

Coherence studies lend support to the idea that music instruction for children at an early age will promote more profuse and efficient connections. For example, Malyrenko et al. (1996) found that an exposure to music of 1 hour per day over a 6 month period had an effect on the brain electrical activity in a sample of 43 4-year-old preschool children. Brain bioelectric activity parameters indicated that listening to music resulted in an enhancement of the coherence function. DeBeus (1999) ran a coherence analysis on 20 preschool children's EEG data. In a baseline, resting condition and while listening to music, deBeus found increased connectivity for a music-training group versus a no-music-training group. Coherence patterns differentiated children with and without music training during a resting condition, and showed patterns similar to those identified by other researchers comparing trained to untrained musicians. The listening-to-music condition identified connections that included a topographical pattern of auditory analysis, increased working memory activity, increased activity among musically sensitive areas, and increased activity between hemispheres. Two limiting points about coherence are important to note. First, coherence values are not well accepted by all neuroscientists; second, skilled performers in comparison with low-level performers in other fields (e.g., a high-level chess player with a non–chess player, a high-level mathematician with a mathematically unskilled person) would presumably show differences.

Multiple Intelligences

In *Frames of Mind* (1985) and later in *Intelligence Reframed* (1999), Gardner describes the concept of multiple intelligences. Performing, listening to music, improvising, or composing music may require the use of at least eight intelligences. The eight types of intelligence used in music activities may include: music; visual-spatial (in the sense that instruments, e.g., cello, percussion, or piano, have a visual-spatial element); bodily kinesthetic (the way in which fine and gross movement functions in the perception of musical motion and is used in performing music); interpersonal (e.g., conductor and orchestral member); intrapersonal (e.g., expression of feelings through music); language, as in singing; spiritual (e.g., in performance of sacred music, deriving spiritual meaning and interpretation in music); and logical-mathematical (e.g., rhythm durations). Neurological research has indicated that many parts of the brain are utilized as children are engaged in music-making activities. The multiple intelligences idea may help explain why other types of intelligence are apparently affected by music instruction. The theory that several kinds of thinking are required to learn and make music has been called a "near" transfer theory (Hetland, 2000a). The quality of music instruction (Elliott, 1995) or combination of activities used in music instruction could help facilitate the transfer. One should not expect transfer from music to other skills unless significant learning has occurred in music. The idea of multiple intelligences and "near" transfer may help explain the ways brain activity is affected by music instruction (Flohr, Miller, & deBeus, 2000).

Trion Theory

Shaw (2000) proposed a "trion" cortical model for the "coding of certain aspects of musical structure and perception" and defines the trion model as "a highly structured mathematical realization of the Mountcastle organization principle in which the cortical column is the basic neural network of the cortex and is comprised of sub-unit minicolumns, our idealized trions" (p. 229; for more information on this theory see Leng & Shaw, 1991, 2000). The cortex is to a large extent organized into a vertical column of neurons. Shaw proposed that when the brain patterns predicted by his theoretical model were mapped onto pitches and instruments, recognizable human styles of music were found. Shaw's trion model provided a theoretical background for the much-publicized and controversial "Mozart effect" studies (Rauscher, Shaw, & Ky, 1993; Rauscher, Shaw, Ky, & Wright, 1994). This trion theory suggests that the musical and spatial processing areas of the brain are in some way shared, proximal, or overlapping. Thus, the relationship of music and spatial processing are linked by neurological connections in the cortex. Shaw and others write that a prewired neural connection is suggested because of the short-term effect of music instruction on spatial abilities (Graziano, Peterson, & Shaw, 1999).

Any theory including the trion theory is difficult to test with current brain imaging techniques. However, an EEG study and a study outlining a new method of analysis for EEG data have been used to empirically test the trion theory (Sarnthein et al., 1997; Bodner et al., 1999). In the EEG study a carry over of brain activity from listening to music to a spatial test was observed in 3 of 7 subjects. The lack of effect in the other 4 subjects was perhaps due to individual differences, problems in application of the theory, the lack of a general effect, or other unknown causes. Comparing and combining trion theory with other theories will be an interesting area for future research.

Neural Networks and Wiring

The concept of neural networks and wiring of the brain has appeared in our recent popular press, and there is a notion or theory that music (or other environmental experiences) "rewires" the neural networks of the brain. The idea is that babies are born with a basic "wiring" of neural networks. As the child interacts with the environment, the brain builds new connections between existing networks. The number of connections increase, and the way the data are transferred is also changed. As a child grows, connections are made and changed (see figure 52.2). One notion is that music and music instruction may affect the way, number, and quality of connections that are being made during development. The idea that the environment—and music can be part of the environment—interacts with heredity and influences the amount and quality of neural connections is not controversial. One research problem is that our knowledge does not include the extent to which music affects the connections.

Theories taken as a whole are not necessarily mutually

exclusive and may in combination explain many of the effects of music on brain activity, musical development, and general development. One or two theories (e.g., modular and affective response) may prove to be useful in combination with another theory or prove the other theory to be incorrect.

General Findings

1. Human development hinges on the interplay between nature and nurture. Recent brain research challenges old assumptions about talent and innate ability—that the genes humans are born with determine how the brain develops. In general, neuroscience research has shown that nature or nurture alone do not determine brain development. The complex interaction among innate abilities, environment, and the variability inherent in individual differences influences brain development. Although there is much growth and activity during the young years, there is evidence that there is room for change in the brain during the later years.

2. Early care and nurture have a decisive, long-lasting impact on how people develop, their ability to learn, and their capacity to regulate their own emotions (Flohr, Miller, & Persellin, 1999). Children as young as 1 day old are able to make cognitive choices about their environment, including musical choices.

3. Experience changes the physiological structure and operation of our brains. Music and music instruction have an effect on brain activity. Studies using various brain imaging techniques have documented some of these changes as well as differences between trained and untrained musicians.

4. There is fertile ground for research in the several theories of brain function and structure. These theories need to be tested, modified, and combined with research and new techniques of imaging the human brain. Students and scientists may use brain theories in their research by testing a theory in new situations or previously studied situations.

5. The human brain has a remarkable capacity to change, but timing is often important and at some points crucial. Windows of opportunity are either optimal windows or critical windows. Extant research has not yet determined critical windows of opportunity for music education.

6. Improved technology will permit further investigation of the influence of music on the brain. A clearer understanding of how music and music-related tasks are manifested in the activity of the brain is an initial step in developing better instructional strategies for music education.

7. For a period of time, beginning in the 1970s, much has been made of music being in the right side of the brain. This oversimplification has been modified. Music is *not* in the right side of the brain alone; both sides are in-

volved. In fact, sophisticated musical processing most likely involves the front-back, top-bottom, and left and right sides of the brain in widely distributed but locally specialized neural networks.

8. It is important to keep results of recent brain research in perspective. Neuroscience findings can be overstated (Bruer, 1999). On the other hand, it is easy to discount neuroscience findings because of problems with the use of new technology, difficulties interpreting data, and unproven brain theory. The neuroscience technologies are complicated and in evolution. Researchers and consumers of research need familiarity with the limits of each technique to properly assess validity of research.

9. It is important not to overstate and emphasize the nonmusical outcomes of the influence of music on brain development. For example, if a small number of studies are used to emphasize a possible link between music study and mathematical skill, it becomes easy to interpret the goal of music study as the production of good mathematicians. There are clear and meaningful musical outcomes of music education (Leonhard & House, 1972). The expressive import of music does not need a nonmusical outcome to justify music education.

Future Directions

Future directions for neuroscience and music research probably will and should include the following:

1. Development and validation of theories of music learning and brain development supported by neuroscientific research; for example, one research problem is that our knowledge does not include the extent to which music affects the brain connections.

2. Increased infant research; studying fetal and infant responses to music allows us to study the human brain with the least possible effect of prior environmental influence.

3. Music and neuroscience research may reveal activities that will help children develop musical skills more efficiently and effectively. Families and parents will be given information on specific enjoyable, interactive music strategies.

4. More projects dealing with the relation of music to emotion and temperament.

5. Continuing focus on music cognition. How does the human brain organize musical sounds into meaningful experiences? What are the developmental sequences in music cognition? Is music cognition completely autonomous, or are there relationships among various intelligences?

6. Increased use of more than one type of brain imaging to test theories through improvements in brain imaging technology and neurochemistry (Nakamura et al., 1999).

7. Increased collaboration between cognitive neuroscien-

tists, neurobiologists, philosophers, and musicians; there is an increasing interest among neuroscientists in the study of music and the brain. Neuroscientists are interested in using music as a way in which other brain activity may be studied as well as examining music by itself. For example, music is different from language and can be used as a contrast in experiments designed to investigate brain activity and language (Besson, 2000).

8. Continued movement toward research with greater external validity; for example, focus on musical stimuli and musically valid tasks.

9. Better education of the general public and music education profession so that patience is developed for basic research and sophisticated findings are not reduced to promotional "sound bites."

10. Music educators and philosophers may bring to future neuroscience research the appreciation for the fluidity, creative constructs, and context-specificity of music. Music is more than sonorous stimuli; it is connected to cognitive, affective, kinesthetic, and social processes of each individual.

REFERENCES

Abeles, H., & Chung, J. (1996). Responses to music. In D. Hodges (Ed.), *Handbook of music psychology* (2nd ed., pp. 285–342). San Antonio, TX: IMR Press.

Abrams, R., & Gerhardt, K. (1997). Some aspects of the fetal sound environment. In I. Deliège & J. Sloboda (Eds.), *Perception and cognition of music* (pp. 83–101). East Sussex, England: Psychology Press.

Ackerman, S. (1992). *Discovering the brain.* Washington, DC: National Academy Press.

Altenmüller, E. (1993). Psychophysiology and EEG. In E. Niedermeyer & F. L. da Silva (Eds.), *Electroencephalography* (pp. 597–614). Baltimore: Williams and Wilkins.

Altenmüller, E., Gruhn, W., Parlitz, D., & Kahrs, J. (1996). Music learning produces changes in brain activation patterns: A longitudinal DC-EEG study. *International Journal of Applied Music, I,* 28–33.

Amunts, K., Schlaug, G., Jancke, L., Steinmetz, H., Schleicher, A., Dabringhaus, A., & Zilles, K. (1997). Motor cortex and hand motor skills: Structural compliance in the human brain. *Human Brain Mapping, 5,* 206–215.

Atkins, D. H. (2000). The neurochemistry of emotion. In *The brain and mind-body connection.* Denton, TX: Success for Life Early Learning Systems Curriculum, University of North Texas.

Atkins, D., & Flohr, J. W. (2000, June). *Music style ratings in relation to emotional tone of the music and individual variation in emotionality.* Paper presented at the twelfth annual American Psychological Society Conference, Miami.

Barber, B. (1999). *An investigation of neural processes in music cognition using quantitative electroencephalography.* Unpublished doctoral dissertation, University of Melbourne.

Barber, B., McKenzie, S., & Helme, R. (1997). A study of brain electrical responses to music using quantitative electroencephalography (QEEG). *International Journal of Arts Medicine, 5*(2), 12–21.

Bartlett, D. (1996). Physiological responses to music and sound stimuli. In D. Hodges (Ed.), *Handbook of music psychology* (2nd ed., pp. 343–385). San Antonio, TX: IMR Press.

Bates, E., Thal, D., & Janowsky, J. S. (1992). Early language development and its neural correlates. In F. Boller, J. Grafman, S. J. Segalowitz, & I. Rapin (Eds.), *Handbook of neuropsychology* (pp. 69–110). Amsterdam: Elsevier.

Besson, M. (2000, June). *Comparisons between language and music.* Paper presented at Mapping Music in the Brain, a satellite symposium of the annual conference for Human Brain Mapping. San Antonio, Texas.

Blood, A. J., Zatorre, R. J., Bermudez, P., & Evans, A. C. (1999). Emotional responses to pleasant and unpleasant music correlate with activity in paralimbic brain regions. *Nature Neuroscience, 2*(4), 382–387.

Bodner, M., Shaw, G. L., Gabriel, R., Johnson, J., Murias, M., & Swanson, J. (1999). Detecting symmetric patterns in EEG data: A new method of analysis. *Clinical Electroencephalography, 30*(4), 143–148.

Brody, J. (1991, April 9). Not just music, bird song is a means of courtship and defense. *New York Times,* pp. C1, C9.

Brown, W., Marsh, J., & Ponsford, R. (1985). Hemispheric differences in event-related potentials. In D. Benson & E. Zaidel (Eds.), *The dual brain: Hemispheric specialization in humans* (pp. 163–180). New York: Guildford Press.

Bruer, J. T. (1999). *The myth of the first three years.* New York: Free Press.

Caine, R. N., & Caine, G. (1994). *Making connections: Teaching the human brain.* New York: Addison-Wesley.

Carpenter, P. A., Akira, M., & Just, M. A. (1995). Language comprehension: Sentence and discourse processing. *Annual Review of Psychology, 46,* 92.

Cheour, M., Ceponiene, R., Lentokoski, A., Luuk, A., Allik, J., Alho, K., & Näätänen, R. (1998). Development of language-specific phoneme representations in the infant brain. *Nature Neuroscience, 12,* 351–353.

Chugani, H. T. (1998). A critical period of brain development: Studies of cerebral glucose utilization with PET. *Preventive Medicine, 27*(2), 184–188.

Chugani, H. T., Phelps, M. F., & Mazziotta, J. C. (1987). Positron emission tomography study of human brain functional development. *Annals of Neurology, 22*(4), 487–497.

Cohen, D., & Erez, A. (1991). Event-related potential measurements of cognitive components in response to pitch patterns. *Music Perception, 8*(4), 405–430.

Cossu, G., Faienza, C., & Capone, C. (1994). Infants' hemispheric computation of music and speech. In C. Faienza (Ed.), *Music, speech and the developing brain.* Italy: Edizioni Angelo Guerini.

Crystal, H., Grober, E., & Masur, D. (1989). Preservation of musical memory in Alzheimer's disease. *Journal of Neurology, Neurosurgery, and Psychiatry, 52,* 1415–1416.

D'Amato, M. (1988). A search for tonal pattern perception

in cebus monkeys: Why monkeys can't hum a tune. *Music Perception, 5*(4), 453–480.

deBeus, R. (1999). The effects of music training on electro-encephalographic coherence of preschool children. *Dissertation Abstracts International, 60*(09B), 4952.

Deliège, I., & Sloboda, J. (1996). *Musical beginnings: Origins and development of music competence.* Oxford: Oxford University Press.

Diamond, M., Scheibel, A., Murphy, G., & Harvey, T. (1985). On the brain of a scientist: Albert Einstein. *Experimental Neurology, 88,* 198–204.

Dissanayake, E. (2000). Antecedents of the temporal arts. In N. Wallin, B. Merker, & S. Brown (Eds.), *The origins of music* (pp. 387–410). Cambridge, MA: MIT Press.

Elbert, T., Pantev, C., Wienbruch, C., Rockstrub, B., & Taub, E. (1995). Increased cortical representation of the fingers of the left hand in string players. *Science, 270*(5234), 305–307.

Elliot, D. J. (1995). *Music matters: A new philosophy of music education.* New York: Oxford University Press.

Epstein, H. (1978). Growth spurts during brain development: Implications for educational policy and practice. In J. Chall & A. Mirsky (Eds.), *Education and the brain: seventy seventh National Society for the Study of Education.* Chicago: University of Chicago Press.

Epstein, H. (1986). Stages in human brain development. *Developmental brain research, 30,* 114–119.

Eriksson, P. S., Perfilieva, E., Björk-Eriksson, T., Alborn, A., Nordborg, C., Peterson, D. A., & Gage, F. H. (1998). Neurogenesis in the adult human hippocampus. *Nature Medicine, 4,* 1313–1317.

Faita, F., & Besson, M. (1994). Electrophysiological index of musical expectancy: Is there a repetition effect on the event-related potentials associated with musical incongruities? In I. Deliege (Ed.), *Proceedings of the third international conference for music perception and cognition* (pp. 433–435).

Falk, D. (2000). Hominid brain evolution and the origins of music. In N. Wallin, B. Merker, & S. Brown (Eds.), *The origins of music* (pp. 197–216). Cambridge, MA: MIT Press.

Fein, G., Raz, F. F., & Merrin, E. L. (1988). Common reference coherence data are confounded by power and phase effects. *Electroencephalography and Clinical Neurophysiology, 69,* 581–584.

Flohr, J. W., Atkins, D., Bower, T. G. R., & Aldridge, M. A. (2000). *Infant music preferences: Implications for child development and music education* (Music Education Research Report). Austin, TX: Texas Music Educators Association.

Flohr, J. W., & Miller, D. C. (1993). Quantitative EEG differences between baseline and psychomotor response to music. *Texas Music Education Research,* 1–7.

Flohr, J. W., & Miller, D. C. (1995, February). *Developmental quantitative EEG differences during psychomotor response to music.* Paper presented at the Texas Music Educators Convention, San Antonio, Texas. (ERIC Document PS025653)

Flohr, J. W., Miller, D. C., & deBeus, R. (2000). EEG studies with young children. *Music Educators Journal 87*(2), 28–32, 54.

Flohr, J. W., Miller, D. C., & Persellin, D. C. (1999, June). *Recent brain research on young children: Teaching music.* Reston, VA: Music Educators National Conference, pp. 41–43, 54.

Flohr, J. W., Persellin, D. C., & Miller, D. C. (1996, July). *Children's electrophysical responses to music.* Paper presented at the twenty-second International Society for Music Education world conference, Amsterdam. (ERIC Document PS025654)

Fox, P., Sergent, J., Hodges, D., Martin, C., Jerabek, T., Glass, T., Downs, H., & Lancaster, J. (1995, June). *Piano performance from memory: A PET study.* Paper presented at the Human Brain Mapping Conference, Paris.

Freund, H., & Hefter, H. (1990). Timing mechanisms in skilled hand movements. In F. Wilson & F. Roehmann (Eds.), *Music and child development* (pp. 179–190). St. Louis, MO: MMB Music.

Frisina, R., Walton, J., & Crummer, C. (1988). Neural basis for music cognition: Neurophysiological foundations. *Psychomusicology, 7*(2), 99–107.

Gardner, H. (1985). *Frames of mind: The theory of multiple intelligences.* New York: Basic Books.

Gardner, H. (1999). *Intelligence reframed: Multiple intelligences for the twenty-first century.* New York: Basic Books.

Geissmann, T. (2000). Gibbon songs and human music from an evolutionary perspective. In N. Wallin, B. Merker, & S. Brown (Eds.), *The origins of music* (pp. 103–124). Cambridge, MA: MIT Press.

Gibbs, W. W. (1998, November). Dogma overturned: Upending a long-held theory, a study finds that humans can grow new brain neurons throughout life—even into old age. *Scientific American,* 19–20.

Golden, D. (1994, July). Building a better brain. *Life,* 62–70.

Gopnik, A., Meltzoff, A., & Kuhl, P. (1999). *The scientist in the crib.* New York: Morrow.

Gordon, E. (1979). *Primary measures of music audiation.* Chicago: GIA.

Gordon, E. (1990). The nature and description of developmental and stabilized music aptitudes: Implications for music learning. In F. Wilson (Ed.), *Child development.* St. Louis, MO: MMB Music.

Graziano, A. B., Peterson, M., & Shaw, G. (1999). Enhanced learning of proportional math through music training and spatial-temporal training. *Neurological Research, 21,* 139–152.

Gur, R., & Gur, R. (1994). Methods for the study of brain-behavior relationships. In A. Frazer, P. Malinoff, & A. Winokur (Eds.), *Biological bases of brain function and disease* (pp. 261–280). New York: Raven Press.

Hantz, E., & Crummer, C. (1988). Neural basis for music cognition: Psychophysical foundations. *Psychomusicology, 7*(2), 109–115.

Hari, R. (1990). The neuromagnetic method in the study of the human auditory cortex. *Advances in Audiology, 6*(2), 222–282.

Hetland, L. (2000a). Learning to make music enhances spatial reasoning. *Journal of Aesthetic Education, 34*(3–4), 179–238.

Hetland, L. (2000b). Listening to music enhances spatial-temporal reasoning: Evidence for the "Mozart effect." *Journal of Aesthetic Education, 34*(3–4), 105–148.

Hodges, D. (1989). Why are we musical? Speculations on the evolutionary plausibility of musical behavior. *Bulletin of the Council for Research in Music Education, 99,* 7–22.

Hodges, D. (1996a). Human musicality. In D. Hodges (Ed.), *Handbook of music psychology* (2nd ed., pp. 29–68). University of Texas at San Antonio: IMR Press.

Hodges, D. (1996b). Neuromusical research: A review of the literature. In D. Hodges (Ed.), *Handbook of music psychology* (pp. 197–284). San Antonio, TX: Institute for Music Research.

Hodges, D. (2000). Why are we musical? Support for an evolutionary theory of human musicality. *Proceedings of the sixth International Conference on Music Perception and Cognition.*

Hubel, D. H., & Wiesel, T. N. (1970). The period of susceptibility to the physiological effects of unilateral eye closure in kittens. *Journal of Physiology, 206,* 419–436.

Ibatoullina, A. A., Vardaris, R. M., & Thompson, L. (1994). Genetic and environmental influences on the coherence of background and orienting response EEG in children. *Intelligence 19,* 65–78.

Imberty, M. (2000). The question of innate competencies in musical communication. In N. Wallin, B. Merker, & S. Brown (Eds.), *The origins of music* (pp. 449–462). Cambridge, MA: MIT Press.

Janowsky, J. S., & Carper, R. (1996). Is there a neural basis for cognitive transitions in school-age children? In A. J. Sameroff & M. M. Haith (Eds.), *The five to seven year shift: The age of reason and responsibility* (pp. 33–60). Chicago: University of Chicago Press.

Jensen, E. (1998). *Teaching with the brain in mind.* Alexandria, VA: Association for Supervision and Curriculum Development.

Johnson, J., & Ulatowska, H. (1995). The nature of the tune and text in the production of songs. In R. Pratt & R. Spintge (Eds.), *Music medicine: Vol. 2* (pp. 153–168). St. Louis, MO: MMB Music.

Juslin, P., & Sloboda, J. (Eds.). 2001. *Music and emotion: Theory and research.* New York: Oxford University Press.

Kaufmann, L., Curtis, S., Wang, J., & Williamson, S. (1991). Changes in cortical activity when subjects scan memory for tones. *Electroencephalography and Clinical Neurophysiology, 82,* 266–284.

Kimura, D. (1961). Cerebral dominance and the perception of verbal stimuli. *Canadian Journal of Psychology, 15,* 166–171.

Kimura, D. (1967). Functional asymmetry of the brain in dichotic listening. *Cortex, 3,* 163–178.

Krause, B. (1987). The niche hypothesis: How animals taught us to dance and sing [On-line]. Available: http://www.wildsanctuary.com.

Languis, M. K., & Miller, D. C. (1992). Luria's theory of brain functioning: A model for research in cognitive psychophysiology. *Educational Psychologist, 27,* 493–511.

Leng, X., & Shaw, G. L. (1991). Toward a neural theory of higher brain function using music as a window. *Concepts in Neuroscience, 2*(2), 229–258.

Leonhard, C., & House, R. (1972). *Foundations and principles of music education.* New York: McGraw-Hill.

Levitin, D., & Bellugi, U. (1998). Musical abilities in individuals with Williams syndrome. *Music Perception, 15*(4), 357–389.

McIntosh, G., Thaut, M., & Rice, R. (1996). Rhythmic auditory stimulation as an entrainment and therapy technique: Effects on gait of stroke and Parkinsonian's patients. In R. Pratt & R. Spintge, (Eds.), *Music medicine: Vol. 2* (pp. 145–152). St. Louis, MO: MMB Music.

Majkowski, J., Bochenek, Z., Bochenek, W., Knapik-Fijalkowska, D., & Kopec, J. (1971). Latency of averaged evoked potentials to contralateral and ipsilateral auditory stimulation in normal subjects. *Brain Research, 25,* 416–419.

Malyarenko, T. N., Kuraev, G. A., Malyarenko, Y. E., Khvatova, M. V., Romanova, N. G., & Gurina, V. I. (1996). The development of brain electric activity in 4-year-old children by long-term sensory stimulation with music. *Human Physiology, 22*(1) 76–81.

Marin, O., & Perry, D. (1999). Neurological aspects of music perception and performance. In D. Deutsch (Ed.), *The psychology of music* (2nd ed., pp. 653–724). New York: Academic Press.

Marler, P. (2000). Origins of music and speech: Insights from animals. In N. Wallin, B. Merker, & S. Brown (Eds.), *The origins of music* (pp. 31–48). Cambridge, MA: MIT Press.

Miller, D. C., & Flohr, J. W. (1995). Utilizing Quantitative EEG Techniques to evaluate processes elicited by music. In *Technological Directions in Music Education.* San Antonio: Institute for Music Research, University of Texas at San Antonio.

Miller, L. (1989). *Musical savants: Exceptional skill and mental retardation.* Hillsdale, NJ: Erlbaum.

Miller, R., Thaut, M., & Aunon, J. (1995). Event-related brain potentials in an auditory-motor synchronization task. In R. Pratt & R. Spintge (Eds.), *Music medicine: Vol. 2* (pp. 76–84). St. Louis, MO: MMB Music.

Moore, G. (1992). A computer-based portable keyboard monitor for studying timing performance in pianists. *Annals of the New York Academy of Sciences, 3,* 651–652.

Nakamura, S., Sadato, N., Oohashi, T., Hishina, E., Fuwamoto, Y., & Yonekura, Y. (1999). Analysis of music-brain interaction with simultaneous measurement of regional cerebral blood flow and electroencephalogram beta rhythm in human subjects. *Neuroscience Letters, 275,* 222–226.

Nelson, C. A., & Bloom, F. E. (1997). Child development and neuroscience. *Child Development, 68*(5), 970–987.

Paller, K., McCarthy, G., & Wood, C. (1992). Event-related potentials elicited by deviant endings to melodies. *Psychomusicology, 29*(2), 202–206.

Panksepp, J. (1998). *Affective neuroscience: The foundations of human and animal emotions.* New York: Oxford University Press.

Pantev, C., Oostenveld, R., Engelien, A., Ross, B., Roberts, L.

E., & Hoek, M. (1998). Increased auditory cortical representation. *Nature, 392,* 811–813.

Parsons, L. (2000, June). *Functional anatomy of pitch, rhythm, melody, and harmony.* Paper presented at Mapping Music in the Brain, a satellite symposium of the annual conference for Human Brain Mapping, San Antonio, Texas.

Parsons, L. (2001). Exploring the functional neuroanatomy of music performance, perception, and comprehension. In R. Zatorre & I. Peretz (Eds.), *The biological foundations of music* (pp. 211–230). Annals of the New York Academy of Sciences, vol. 930.

Parsons, L., & Fox, P. (1997). Sensory and cognitive tasks: The cerebellum and cognition. In J. D. Schmahmann (Ed.), *International review of neurobiology, cerebellum and cognitio* (pp. 255–272). San Diego: Academic Press.

Parsons, L., Fox, P., & Hodges, D. (1998, November). *Neural basis of the comprehension of musical melody, harmony, and rhythm.* Paper presented at Society for Neuroscience, Los Angeles.

Pascual-Leone, A., Dand, N., Cohen, L., Braskil-Neto, J., Cammarota, A., & Hallett, M. (1995). Modulation of muscle responses evoked by transcranial magnetic stimulation during the acquisition of new fine motor skills. *Journal of Neurophysiology, 74*(3), 1037–1045.

Paulus, W. (1988). Effect of musical modelling on late auditory evoked potentials. *European Archives of Psychiatry and Neurological Sciences, 237*(5), 307–311.

Payne, K. (2000). The progressively changing songs of humpbackwhales: A window on the creative process in a wild animal. In N. Wallin, B. Merker, & S. Brown (Eds.), *The origins of music* (pp. 135–150). Cambridge, MA: MIT Press.

Petsche, H., Lindner, K., Rappelsberger, P., & Gruber, G. (1988). The EEG: An adequate method to concretize brain processes elicited by music. *Music Perception, 6,* 133–159.

Piaget, J. (1950). *The psychology of intelligence.* London: Routledge and Kegan Paul.

Platel, H., Price, C., Baron, J. C., Wise, R., Lambert, J., Frackowiak, R., Lechevalier, B., & Eustache, F. (1997). The structural components of music perception: A functional anatomical study. *Brain, 20*(2), 229–243.

Posner, M., & Raichle, M. (1994). *Images of mind.* New York: Scientific American Library.

Pratt, R., & Spintge, R. (1996). *Music medicine: Vol. 2.* St. Louis, MO: MMB Music.

Raichle, M. 1994. Visualizing the mind. *Scientific American, 270*(4), 58–64.

Rauscher, F. H., Shaw, G. L., & Ky, K. N. (1993). Music and spatial task performance. *Nature, 365,* 611.

Rauscher, F. H., Shaw, G. L., Ky, K. N., & Wright, E. L. (1994, August). *Music and spatial task performance: A causal relationship.* Paper presented at the American Psychological Association 102nd annual convention, Los Angeles.

Reilly, M. (1999). Music: A cognitive behavioral intervention for anxiety and acute pain control in the elderly cataract patient. *Dissertation Abstracts International, 60*(07B), 3195.

Reimer, B. (1999). Facing the risks of the "Mozart effect." *Music Educators Journal, 86,* 37–43.

Restak, R. (1994). *The Modular Brain.* New York: Scribners.

Robinson, G., & Solomon, D. (1974). Rhythm is processed by the speech hemisphere. *Journal of Experimental Psychology, 102*(3), 508–511.

Sarnthein, J., vonStein, A., Rappelsberger, P., Petsche, H., Rauscher, F., & Shaw, G. (1997). Persistent patterns of brain activity: An EEG coherence study of the positive effect of music on spatial-temporal reasoning. *Neurological Research, 19,* 107–116.

Schlaug, G., Jäncke, L., Huang, Y., & Steinmetz, H. (1994). In vivo morphometry of interhemispheric asymmetry and connectivity in musicians. In I. Deliege (Ed.), *Proceedings of the third international conference for music perception and cognition* (pp. 417–418).

Schlaug, G., Jäncke, L., Huang, L., & Steinmetz, H. (1995). In vivo evidence of structural brain asymmetry in musicians. *Science, 267*(5198), 699–701.

Schlaug, G., Jänke, L., Huang, Y., Staiger, J. F., & Steinmetz, H. (1995). Increased corpus callosum size in musicians. *Neuropsychologia, 33,* 1047–1055.

Schwent, V., Snyder, E., & Hillyard, S. (1976). Auditory evoked potentials during multichannel selective listening: Role of pitch and localization cues. *Journal of Experimental Psychology: Human Perception and Performance 2*(3), 313–325.

Sergent, J. (1993). Mapping the musician brain. *Human Brain Mapping, 1*(1), 20–38.

Shaw, G. L. (2000). *Keeping Mozart in mind.* San Diego: Academic Press.

Slater, P. (2000). Birdsong repertoires: Their origins and use. In N. Wallin, B. Merker, & S. Brown (Eds.), *The origins of music* (pp. 49–64). Cambridge, MA: MIT Press.

Snowdon, D. A. (1997). Aging and Alzheimer's disease: Lessons from the nun study. *Gerontologist, 37*(2), 150–156.

Snowdon, D. (2001). *Aging with grace: What the nun study teaches us about leading longer, healthier, and more meaningful lives.* New York: Bantam Books.

Spintge, R., & Droh, R. (1992). *Music medicine.* St. Louis, MO: MMB Music.

Standley, J. (1998). Pre and perinatal growth and development: Implications of music benefits for premature infants. *International Journal of Music Education, 31,* 2–13.

Sylwester, R. (1995). *A celebration of neurons: An educator's guide to the human brain.* Alexandria, VA: Association for Supervision and Curriculum Development.

Thatcher, R. (1998, September 11). *EEG database guided neurotherapy: Practical applications.* Presentation at the annual conference of the Society for the Study of Neuronal Regulation.

Thaut, M., Brown, S., Benjamin, J., & Cooke, J. (1995). Rhythmic facilitation of movement sequencing: Effects on spatio-temporal control and sensory modality dependence. In R. Pratt & R. Spintge (Eds.), *Music medicine: Vol. 2* (pp. 104–112). St. Louis, MO: MMB Music.

Thaut, M., McIntosh, G., Prassas, S., & Rice, R. (1993). Effect of rhythmic cuing on temporal stride parameters and

EMG patterns in hemiparetic gait of stroke patients. *Journal of Neurologic Rehabilitation, 7,* 9–16.

Thulborn, K. R., Carpenter, P. A., & Just, M. A. (1999). Plasticity of language-related brain function during recovery from stroke. *Stroke, 30*(4), 749–754.

Trehub, S. (2000). Human processing predispositions and musical universals. In N. Wallin, B. Merker, & S. Brown (Eds.), *The origins of music* (pp. 428–448). Cambridge, MA: MIT Press.

Trehub, S., Bull, D., & Thorpe, L. (1984). Infants' perception of melodies: The role of melodic contour. *Child Development, 55,* 821–830.

Trehub, S., Schellenberg, E., & Hill, D. (1997). The origins of music perception and cognition: A developmental perspective. In I. Deliège & J. Sloboda (Eds.), *Perception and cognition of music* (pp. 103–128). East Sussex, England: Psychology Press.

Trehub, S., & Trainor, L. (1993). Listening strategies in infancy: The roots of language and musical development. In S. McAdams & E. Bigand (Eds.), *Thinking in sound: Cognitive perspectives on human audition* (pp. 278–327). New York: Oxford University Press.

van Baal, G. C. M., de Geus, E. J. C., & Boomsma, D. I. (1998). Genetic influences on EEG coherence in 5-year-old twins. *Behavior Genetics, 28*(1), 9–19.

Wallin, N., Merker, B., & Brown, S. (Eds). (2000). *The origins of music.* Cambridge, MA: MIT Press.

Warren, R. (1993). Perception of acoustic sequences: Global integration versus temporal resolution. In S. McAdams & E. Bigand (Eds.), *Thinking in sound: Cognitive perspectives on human audition* (pp. 37–68). New York: Oxford University Press.

Whaling, C. (2000). What's behind a song? The neural basis of song learning in birds. In N. Wallin, B. Merker, & S. Brown (Eds.), *The origins of music* (pp. 65–76). Cambridge, MA: MIT Press.

Williamson, S., & Kaufman, L. (1988). Auditory evoked magnetic fields. In A. Jahn & J. Santos-Sacchi (Eds.), *Physiology of the ear* (pp. 497–505). New York: Raven Press.

Wilson, F. (1986). *Tone deaf and all thumbs?* New York: Viking Press.

Wilson, F. (1988). Brain mechanisms in highly skilled movements. In F. Roehmann (Ed.), *The biology of music making* (pp. 92–99). St. Louis, MO: MMB Music.

Wilson, F. (1991). Music and the neurology of time. *Music Educators Journal, 77*(5), 26–30.

Wilson, F. (1992). Digitizing digital dexterity: A novel application for MIDI recordings of keyboard performance. *Psychomusicology, 11,* 79–95.

Wilson, F. (1998). *The hand.* New York: Vintage Books.

Wilson, F., & Roehmann, F. (1992). The study of biomechanical and physiological processes in relation to musical performance. In R. Colwell (Ed.), *Handbook of research on music teaching and learning* (pp. 509–524). New York: Schirmer Books.

Woodward, S., Fresen, J., Harrison, V. C., & Coley, N. (1996). The birth of musical language. *Proceedings of the seventh International Seminar of the Early Childhood Commission.*

Zatorre, R. (1994). Musical processing in the nonmusician's brain: Evidence for specialized neural networks. In I. Deliege (Ed.), *Proceedings of the third international conference for music perception and cognition* (pp. 39–40).

Zatorre, R., Evans, A., & Meyer, E. (1994). Neural mechanisms underlying melodic perception and memory for pitch. *Journal of Neuroscience, 14*(4), 1908–1919.

Zatorre, R., & Peretz, I. (2001). *The biological foundations of music.* Annals of the New York Academy of Sciences, vol. 930.

Zimmerman, M. P. (1971). *Musical characteristics of children.* Washington, DC: Music Educators National Conference.

Performing Arts Medicine

53

ALICE G. BRANDFONBRENER

RICHARD J. LEDERMAN

The Evolution of Performing Arts Medicine in the United States

Musicians have long recognized that music-making carries with it certain physical and psychological risks, the significance of which ranges from trivial annoyances to career-halting injuries. Since the publication of the first Handbook, an increased number of medical professionals themselves have acknowledged the existence of occupational injuries, as a consequence of which there is now a medical subspecialty, Performing Arts Medicine, sometimes referred to as "music medicine." This chapter will briefly review the recent history and current state of the field; its focus, limits, and potential. Most important, we will attempt to provide basic information for music educators so that they, together with medical practitioners and other researchers, can seek to limit the impact of these problems on musicians and especially attempt their prevention. A few preliminary disclaimers are in order. In spite of giant strides made in the past 15–20 years through clinical experience and accumulating epidemiologic data, much of the information about musicians' medical problems remains anecdotal. The symptoms with which musicians present are often nonspecific, with few if any objective physical findings and often without confirmatory diagnostic tests. Thus, treatment is also often nonspecific, directed more toward relief of symptoms than on understanding or eradicating their causes and more pragmatic than based on scientifically proven data. In summary, one should not expect more from this chapter than it can honestly supply, despite the combined experience of its authors of in excess of 50 years of providing medical care for musicians. Performing arts medicine remains in the year 2001 part art and part science.

In the early 1980s a number of events coincided in the United States that jump-started the interest of physicians and others in performing arts medicine. For one thing, two notable pianists went public about their inability to continue performing two-handed literature. Gary Graffman and Leon Fleisher, both with successful solo careers, both noted their painless loss of control at the keyboard of certain of their right hand fingers. After seeking many opinions and many diagnoses that proved to be false, they were both eventually diagnosed as having focal dystonia, a neurological movement disorder (discussed in more detail later). Unlike many other musicians with medical problems who choose to remain silent about them, these two men allowed the public in on their secrets. A flurry of media publicity about them not only piqued the curiosity of concert goers and music critics but also gave a sense of tacit permission to other musicians to acknowledge their own medical problems and, especially important, to seek professional advice for them.

At about the same time, groups of doctors, many who themselves had musical training or at least had strong interests in music, began to hold meetings about musicians' occupational medical problems and to organize clinical centers specializing in the care of performing artists. These clinics offer not only empathic care but care based on an understanding of the myriad of occupational medical issues of musicians. After difficulty finding understanding medical advice in the past, the availability of these clinics has been greeted positively by musicians in need of help (Chandler & Foster, 1999). Their existence, along with the widespread and generally helpful efforts of the press, has increased the level of awareness of musicians, educators, and music managements that music-making carries with it real health risks. Unfortunately, the increasing success of these

1009

clinics has been countered by the advent of managed care, with its efforts to limit access to specialized care of all sorts, performing arts medicine included. There remains a lack of recognition, including in medical circles, that even what appear to be minimal injuries in musicians may in fact be career threatening. It is assumed by the unenlightened that sports medicine specialists or general orthopedic surgeons can adequately provide for these medical needs. Furthermore, even with access to specialized care, selecting a qualified provider may still pose problems for musicians in need of advice. It is not unlike selecting a music teacher! Most physicians providing this care are dedicated and are doing so because of a deep and abiding interest in music and in helping musicians achieve and maintain good health. While this usually implies that the services provided will be of a certain quality, in and of itself this carries no guarantee of experience, knowledge, or judgment of individual practitioners. There is no requisite training program or certification process in performing arts medicine, so that achieving skill largely depends on individual experience and reliance on that of others, through reading and attendance at meetings.

In part because of the increased visibility of performing arts medicine but also because of their concern about the apparent increased incidence of injuries among students, many conservatories have made increased provisions for specialized medical care. Some institutions have added health-related courses, including on the Alexander Technique and the Feldenkrais Method.[1] Likewise, both abroad and in the United States, many orchestras and orchestra musicians have become actively engaged in seeking ways to improve the health of their members through better working conditions as well as in providing improved medical care.

Performing Arts Medicine Organizations, Texts, and Journals

In 1989, in order to promote performing arts medicine, facilitate communication among health practitioners nationally and internationally, and to encourage education and research initiatives, the Performing Arts Medicine Association (PAMA) was founded in the United States. While not large, the organization has grown and has sponsored annual meetings in Aspen, Colorado, as well as smaller sessions and workshops in other parts of the country. There are active organizations in many European countries, notably in Germany and Great Britain, both of which have sponsored major international congresses. During the October 2000 Eighth International Congress in Mainz, it was agreed to form an international organization for promoting music medicine to comprise representatives from the national bodies. The purposes of this group will be to

promote the exchange of scientific and clinic information and research and to integrate the subject matter of meetings held around the world.

The literature of performing arts medicine has grown along with the clinical specialty. In 1986 the first and only peer-reviewed quarterly medical journal devoted solely to health issues of performers, *The Medical Problems of Performing Artists (MPPA),* was founded by the publisher Hanley and Belfus. This journal, which is now the official journal of PAMA, is the major resource of information about musicians' medical problems and general arts medicine and contains articles from not only the United States but all over the world. Included are case reports, review articles, epidemiological data, and reports of current research in arts medicine. Other articles concerning musicians' health have occasionally appeared in some of the established medical specialty journals, including the *Journal of the American Medical Association* (Hochberg, Leffert, Heller, & Merriman, 1983), the *New England Journal of Medicine* (Lockwood, 1989), and the *British Journal of Rheumatology* (Lambert, 1992). In addition, many articles on health topics have been published in many music education journals and instrument-specific publications. Many medical journals can be accessed through *Index Medicus,* while *MPPA* is listed in *Current Contents/Arts and Humanities,* the *International Index to Music Periodicals,* the *Music Index,* and others. A number of internet sites are also maintained by performing arts medicine organizations and clinics, as well as some nonmedical arts health–related sites.

A number of medical texts have been published since the early 1990s and serve as useful references for teachers and medical therapists, including *Performing Arts Medicine* (Sataloff, Brandfonbrener, & Lederman, 1998), a German text (Blum, 1995), a British text, *The Musician's Hand: A Clinical Guide* (Winspur & Wynn Parry, 1998), and, also from Britain, *The Medical Problems of the Instrumentalist Musician* (Tubiana & Amadio, 2000). A plethora of other health advice books for musicians have been written by less medically traditional medical and nonmedical authors; some of these provide helpful information and advice based on medically sound ideas, while others offer formulas for good health based on scientifically unsubstantiated material, misinformation, or misinterpretations of medical information.

Research

In any new science it takes time to develop a significant body of information based on scientific research. Music medicine has faced many inevitable hurdles in its initial research efforts. In part this is because small compared to other medical subspecialties, but especially because it has arisen at a time when there is difficulty in obtaining funding for any medical research, let alone for research into non-life-threatening problems or those deemed economically unimportant.

Nevertheless, efforts have been underway for the past 20 or more years, and the quality and quantity of these projects has been steadily gaining. Unique to performing arts medicine is that a number of studies represent the joint work of scientifically and musically trained researchers. Most of the work that has been done concerning the medical problems of instrumental musicians can be divided into several categories: epidemiological and population studies, studies relating to the mechanics of performance, studies on performance anxiety, and studies of the causes and treatments of focal dystonias. Representatives of these kinds of studies will be cited.

A landmark study undertaken by the International Conference of Symphony and Opera Musicians (ICSOM) was conducted (Fishbein, Middlestadt, Ottati, Straus, & Ellis, 1988) among the 4,000-plus musicians in the 48 ICSOM member orchestras, of whom 2,212 completed the questionnaires, a response rate of almost 50%. Of these, 76% said they had had a medical problem affecting their playing. The information collected provided data on the relative frequency of problems among different sections of the orchestra, on gender- and age-associated risks, and on identification of the anatomic locations of musculoskeletal problems. While based on subjective information, this study nevertheless provided new insights into the extent of the health problems of musicians and gave impetus to many of the subsequent surveys performed on other musical populations. Although diverse groups have been studied, the results were generally confirmatory of the ICSOM study, with similarly high rates of injury being reported (Brown, 1997; Cayea & Manchester, 1998; Lederman, 1994; Zetterberg, Backlund, Karlsson, & Werner, 1998).

Several studies have attempted to better understand the origins of musical performance anxiety (MPA). One such investigation was done to determine the possible relation of learning style to MPA. It was found that cognitive flexibility was inversely related to musical performance anxiety in 70 elite orchestra players and was also associated with a generally improved performance level (Rife, Lapidus, & Shnek, 2000). Another study sought to understand levels of disability due to MPA and why some musicians are less subject to it. Seventy percent of a mixed population of 154 musicians (and 79% of the 42 keyboard players) admitted impairment and were also the group most subject to music-related physical complaints. Those less subject to injuries were also significantly less impaired by performance anxiety. The authors postulate a musical stress hardiness or resistance, perhaps due to more effective coping methods, that needs further investigation (Salmon, Shook, Lombart, & Berenson, 1995).

There has long been speculation among musicians regarding the possibility for increasing finger-spreading and hand span. A study of 210 cellists and classical guitarists determined that there was minimal if any effect of the span from such long-term physical stretching as occurs through playing these instruments (Kloeppel, 2000). Another study was concerned with developing an accurate measurement of wrist mobility and the relation of greater or lesser degrees of wrist flexibility to strain of wrist joints in 54 healthy musicians (Schuppert & Wagner, 1996). There are many physical factors affecting wrist mobility, but reduced mobility was associated with increased strain, and it was suggested that monitoring wrist mobility might be important in attempting to reduce wrist-related injuries.

There has been a remarkable surge of interest worldwide in the mechanism involved in focal and generalized dystonia, in part prompted by the availability of newer techniques for analyzing brain functions. Dystonia may be defined as a syndrome of intermittent or sustained muscular contraction, producing twisting or repetitive movements or abnormal postures. While much of the research is certainly relevant to the problems seen in musicians, the majority is not specifically directed toward this group. The interested and scientifically sophisticated reader might seek an overview in the neuroscience literature (Begardelli et al., 1998).

Some investigations related to the mechanism of dystonia have been carried out with musicians as the primary focus. Charness and colleagues have been interested in the relationship of nerve entrapment and dystonia. They have shown that patterns of muscle activity in patients with ulnar neuropathy may mimic those seen in focal dystonia, involving the ring and little fingers, and have found a high correlation (far higher, in fact, than others working in the field have been able to identify) between ulnar nerve entrapment and dystonia in a group of musicians (Charness, Ross, & Shefner, 1996; Ross, Charness, & Logigian, 1995).

Treatment of dystonia with botulinim toxin has been carefully studied by Hallett and coworkers. They found that most musicians have a favorable, if incomplete, response to botulinim toxin, but ultimately the benefits are found to be insufficient to justify the continued expense and difficulties inherent in obtaining such treatment (Cole, Cohen, & Hallett, 1991; Karp et al., 1994).

Understanding of the mechanisms involved in dystonia would be greatly enhanced by developing an animal model of the disorder. This has, to some extent, been accomplished by Byl and colleagues. They have produced a focal disorder of motor control in monkeys by subjecting the animals to repeated and prolonged hand activity and have demonstrated changes in the cortical representation of the hand in the appropriate portion of the brain. It remains to be seen whether this will ultimately lead to a clearer picture of the way focal dystonia develops in musicians, as well as others with repetitive hand use, and whether this will facilitate more effective treatment for the impaired motor control (Byl, Merzenich, & Jenkins, 1996).

Risk Factors

While one factor can play the primary role in the etiology of musicians' injuries, it is the rule rather than the exception that most are the result of the interaction of multiple risk factors and are typically cumulative over time. In order to accurately diagnose and appropriately treat musicians, it is essential for medical practitioners who diagnose and treat and musicians who teach to be similarly cognizant of the wide range of potential risk factors for injuries, including the impact of the musician's individual physical characteristics. Music teachers have a unique role to play both in their efforts to prevent injuries in their students and in knowing how best to aid in their rehabilitation if injured.

It is difficult to assign relative importance to the many risk factors. However, it is convenient to divide them into those intrinsic to the music-making itself and those stemming from the musicians. Characteristically, it is the interaction of the two that is responsible and is greater than the sum of either by itself, and it is frequently impossible to separate them.

First among risks is the instrument itself. It is well established that those instruments requiring the greatest number of repetitive finger/hand actions are associated with the highest incidence of musculoskeletal problems in all classes of musicians—students, professionals, and amateurs. Thus, most studies demonstrate the highest incidence in keyboard and string players (plucked and bowed), followed by percussion, woodwinds, and brass (Cayea & Manchester, 1998; Fishbein et al., 1988; Lederman, 1994). Although it has not been studied, it is interesting to speculate about the potential role of the early start of many string and keyboard players, both as a risk and a protection. Theoretically, the accumulated trauma to muscles, tendons, and joints might, over time, subject these tissues to greater risk of damage. On the other hand, perhaps starting at an age when there is greater ease of learning and less tension might make for a long-term reduced vulnerability. These are areas deserving future study.

Among string players there is a higher incidence of injuries as the instruments get progressively larger (Middlestadt & Fishbein, 1989). While numerically there are more injured violinists, because they are the largest group, there are proportionately greater numbers of affected cello and bass players. Violas are unique because of their large variation in size, not only in string length but in width and depth as well. Among violists, the incidence of injuries is greater the larger the viola, regardless of the musicians' gender (Blum & Ahlers, 1994). Hand size and span is an especially important risk factor for pianists, and injuries bear a relationship to the type of repertoire being played, with hand size being a major related factor and, therefore, gender as well (Donison, 2000). Woodwind and brass players are subject, although less frequently, to problems of the muscles, nerves, and joints of their hands, arms, shoulders, and spine, of the much smaller muscles of the embouchure, and of the teeth and jaws (Howard & Lovrovich, 1989) and, occasionally, to respiratory problems.

In addition to the problems that result directly from the manipulation of keys, bows, and strings are the physical positions, usually seated, required to support and play the instrument (Cailliet, 1990). While the support of the instrument is a property of its weight and requisite position, its impact is largely a function of the habits and technique of the player. Musicians come in assorted sizes and shapes; with few exceptions, instruments are less variable. The stature and build of the musician often affects technique. Relative disproportion of the arm length or upper versus lower arm segments, the hand span, or the relative finger lengths may impose limits on musicians' technique by determining how they must adapt with their own physical limitations to the instrument's requirements. Such compromises in how the instrument can be handled may put some musicians at greater risk than those with more favorable physiques. There is some evidence that chronic wrist strain resulting from biomechanical restrictions on wrist mobility may increase the risk of symptoms (Schuppert & Wagner, 1996). In addition, although there has been occasional controversy on the subject, most practitioners agree that excessive joint flexibility, especially in the fingers and wrists, can increase the risks of injuries, especially with certain instruments (Brandfonbrener, 2000; Hoppmann & Patrone, 1989; Larsson, Baum, Mudholkar, & Kollia, 1993). Thus the player whose fingers tend to collapse when putting pressure on strings or keys will tend to compensate by using greater muscle tension to stabilize the fingers.

Although great strength is rarely needed by musicians, endurance and stamina are requisite. This involves not only the muscle groups most directly involved in playing but also the more proximal and larger postural muscles of the back, neck, and shoulders. Many musicians lead sedentary lifestyles, due in part to the hours spent in practice and rehearsal, and habitually neglect conditioning their total bodies. Poor posture and inadequately supportive back and shoulder muscles may be reflected in greater stress being applied to the smaller and more distal muscle of the upper extremities. Weight training using small resistances and many repetitions will increase endurance. However, the use of heavy weights with fewer repetitions serves to produce large and well-defined muscles but fails to benefit most musicians and puts them at risk due to the relative inflexibility of such bulky musculature.

Stress

Perhaps the single greatest contributory risk factor for musicians increasing their vulnerability to physical injury is psychological stress (Middlestadt & Fishbein, 1988). While the following is an oversimplification of often complicated circumstances, the mechanism for these events is that muscle tension tends to be an unconscious reflection of an individual's emotional state. Exaggerated muscle tension increases the work of playing and consequently reduces endurance. It is also known that sudden increases in practice time, especially when associated with increased stress, as in anticipation of juries, competitions, and recitals, is associated with an increased incidence in medical problems for musicians in general and students in particular. Other contributory and closely related nonmusical risk factors include diet, general health, caffeine, alcohol, and lack of exercise and sleep.

One particular aspect of stress we have observed with some frequency, based on talks with students and teachers, are factors within the student-teacher relationship that appear to contribute to the risks for tension-related medical problems. It goes without saying that some teachers possess greater gifts of communication than others; likewise, there are students who are more challenging than others to teach. A corollary is that not every teacher is the best one for every student or can meet each student's needs, and vice versa. Certain students thrive working with a teacher with whom others fail. The relationship between studio teachers and students, at all levels, can be intense and has the potential for being both healthy and unhealthy for both student and teacher. However, the responsibility rests largely with the teacher to be watchful so that, whether the problem originates with the student or teacher if and when things go awry, the teacher can take prompt corrective measures to avert the development of medical symptomatology. As far as we are aware, there have been no studies examining student-teacher relationships and their bearing on the health of students—or, for that matter, on the health of teachers! We have no doubt that this would be an area for fruitful, albeit complicated, investigation.

Other Pedagogical Issues

The interface between musician and musical instrument represents an essential way to understand medical problems. It is in this context that the influence of technique and teaching on medical problems may be most productively examined. There have been few objective studies of the relative risk, if any, of different pedagogical techniques, and this will be an important area for investigation if there are to be significant advances in injury prevention. It seems obvious, given the complex and precise movements required in musical performance, that techniques requiring the least effort would also be the most effective in preventing problems. It would also seem logical that no single technique of playing a particular instrument will suffice for all players and that selection of repertoire, especially for students, should be individually determined. From a medical viewpoint, it seems clear that the choice of repertoire must in part be determined by the physical limitations and characteristics of the players rather than by their level of musical development or by a rote progression in difficulty of repertoire.

Incidental Injuries and Illnesses

It must be borne in mind that simply because one is a musician does not mean that is the only source of injuries. What are referred to as "activities of daily living" (ADLs) pose the same potential problems to musicians as to anyone else. Thus sports, household responsibilities, and even working out may be responsible or share in responsibility for what at first glance may appear to be a music-induced problem, and these may need to be treated differently because they have occurred in a musician (Dawson, 1990). Activities that are out of the ordinary or excessive, as in the "weekend warrior" who sporadically overindulges and is otherwise more sedentary, are particularly suspect.

Successful music-making is dependent on the general health status of the individual; thus both acute and chronic illness can affect the individual's performance ability. The treatment of these conditions may also have performance consequences, so these effects and possible treatment options should be explored by musicians with all treating physicians.

Finally, in any discussion of musicians and their injuries, there are always notable exceptions to any rule, in part because we are dealing with so many individual and interacting risk factors but especially because of inherent biological variability and unpredictability. We are dealing with human beings and not with machines. This must always be borne in mind in interpreting any generalizations and particularly when applying these generalizations to a specific musician.

Presenting Symptoms and Medical Assessment

The decision by a performer to seek medical consultation is often arrived at reluctantly. There are many possible reasons for this, including prior experience with similar symptoms that may have abated spontaneously, pressures of school or job, fear that the advice will be to stop playing, general distrust of physicians or previous unsatisfactory experience, or lack of medical insurance. Many will have exhausted their own resources, including consultation with peers, family, teachers, and other practitioners.

Despite the common misperception that pain is a necessary accompaniment of playing an instrument, it is usually pain that brings the musician to the medical practitioner. The pain may be highly localized, for instance, to a single joint or digit or one or both of the upper extremities, or it may be widespread or generalized. Some predictability for pain localization exists for certain instruments, such as the left arm and hand in violinists or violists, the right hand of oboists and clarinetists, and the right upper trunk and arm of the pianist. Instrumental musicians may couch their complaints in musical terms. While some might describe pain, numbness, or weakness, others may report impairment in facility or speed of fingering or tone articulation, alteration of finger or embouchure control, or loss of endurance and fatiguability of hand, arm, or lip. It is physicians' responsibility to translate these "musical symptoms," if necessary, into physiologic or medical terms that we can more readily interpret. With pain there may be localized soreness to touch. A description of "numbness" may on further inquiry be a loss of feeling or a spontaneous sensory experience (paraesthesia) such as pins and needles or prickling. What may be described as weakness may not actually represent loss of power. Impairment of control may translate to weakness, loss of speed or dexterity, involuntary movement (e.g., tremor), or incoordination.

At the time of medical consultation, the physician will attempt to define fully the reported symptoms. It is necessary to determine the time of onset and the circumstances in which the symptoms arose, the temporal progression, any accompanying features, and the impact of the symptoms on musical as well as nonmusical activities. These symptoms must further be placed in the context of the overall medical and musical health. It has been our common experience that this attempt at clarification sometimes forces instrumentalists to think about their symptoms in greater detail than before, and they may on occasion consider these attempts at clarification to be excessively intrusive. This is obviously not the purpose. A review of the musician's psychosocial history and musical background is also of clear importance.

The physical examination would include special attention to the skeletal and neuromuscular systems. Configuration and mobility of the spine and of the joints, along with assessment of posture and body motion, is often critical. Neurological examination includes assessment of strength, coordination, dexterity, sensation, and reflexes. The importance of observing the musician while performing with the instrument or singing cannot be overstated. For those of us with a special interest in this area, a piano has become a necessary piece of office equipment. Most other instruments can be brought to the appointment, with few exceptions. While the physician cannot be expected to be an expert in the technique involved in playing any, let alone all, instruments, it is often possible to observe postures, positions, and movements that may contribute to the origin of the symptoms. The disorder known as focal dystonia may only be observable during the playing of the instrument.

While most problems will not require additional testing, a variety of procedures are available, if necessary, to elucidate further the nature of the disorder. Blood tests, x-ray, electrodiagnostic studies, and several imaging procedures may be considered to supplement the history and examination, with the goal of arriving at a specific diagnosis.

Diagnosis

It should be self-evident that musicians are subject to the entire spectrum of health problems that might affect anyone else. It would be neither reasonable nor fruitful to survey the potential illnesses that might lead a musician to seek medical help. What we can do, however, is review briefly the major types of disorders that in some way have been brought on or aggravated by the musical activity and hence have a direct impact on the musician's ability to perform.

Pain Syndromes

Pain, primarily in the upper trunk and arms, is the most common reason for medical consultation, as already mentioned. We have all on occasion carried out some physical activity for which we were inadequately prepared, such as carrying a heavy object, shoveling snow, or engaging in an athletic endeavor too vigorously. The end result was a sore and tender muscle, which we probably characterized as a "strain." This painful condition generally subsided over a few days, and, since we knew exactly what we had done to cause it, it produced no particular concern or fear. Furthermore, since this was probably a one-time activity, the disability had a limited impact on our occupation or productivity. Most musicians can also recall times when they engaged in excessive playing (or singing), with a resulting strain that had a similar effect and course. It is only when this pain persists or spreads that the musician seeks medical help.

The terminology used to describe pain syndromes has been a source of controversy for many years, engendering a debate not limited to performing arts medicine (Dawson, Charness, Goode, Lederman, & Newmark, 1998). Space constraints prevent us from discussing the pros and cons of the various terms that may be utilized, including tendinitis, overuse, cumulative trauma disorder, and repetitive stress injury. Each of these may, in a particular situation, be appropriate, and each has its proponents. We have, in recent years, gravitated toward the least restrictive and specific term, "regional pain syndrome," which describes only the localization without implying a specific cause (e.g., overuse) or a specific affected tissue (e.g., tendon, muscle, or ligament). The pain may be very well localized to a specific digit or even a fingertip, to the hand and wrist, to the forearm, upper arm, or entire upper extremity, or to the neck and upper trunk. All of these would be characterized as regional pain syndromes; in each case, the health care practitioner is charged with the task of identifying the contributing factors and formulating a management program for relieving the symptoms.

On occasion, pain may be more widespread and even generalized. When this is accompanied by multiple areas of sensitivity to pressure, it may be characterized by the term "fibromyalgia." This disorder, which is itself controversial, is generally defined as a syndrome of widespread pain, with multifocal tenderness both above and below the waist, accompanied by fatiguability and disordered sleep. It is commonly considered a chronic ailment that may wax and wane; the cause is unknown, and treatment is aimed primarily at controlling the symptoms (Goldenberg, 1999).

Nerve Entrapments

Peripheral nerves are the structures that connect the central nervous system to the periphery and hence carry sensory and motor information to and from the brain and spinal cord. These nerves are potentially subjected to compression, or "pinching," as they traverse the pathway between their origin and termination. Although the specific symptoms and signs expected in a nerve entrapment syndrome depend on the particular nerve that is entrapped and the point along it where that occurs, there are some general features common to all entrapment neuropathies. These would include pain, commonly at the site of entrapment and distally (toward the periphery) along the pathway of the nerve, sensory symptoms such as tingling, pins and needles, or numbness in the area of the skin supplied by that nerve, and weakness, in some or all of the muscles supplied by the nerve.

The most common nerve entrapment in musicians and in the general population is carpal tunnel syndrome (CTS). The carpal tunnel is an anatomic channel through which the median nerve passes at the base of the palm. It is accompanied in this compartment by nine tendons that control flexion (curling) of the digits. The floor of the tunnel is formed by an arcade of wrist bones, and its roof consists of a dense ligament. Any thickening of this structure, in-

flammation or swelling of the tendons or their sheaths, or changes in the wrist bones may impinge on the already rather tight space and can produce nerve compression. In addition, extremes of both flexion and extension of the wrist further compromise this space.

The symptoms associated with CTS include pain, most commonly of the wrist and hand but also more proximally, even to the shoulder and neck. Numbness and tingling are characteristically reported in the thumb and index through ring fingers, which are supplied by the median nerve. Both the pain and the sensory symptoms characteristically occur at night and awaken the person from sleep but may also occur during the day, particularly with certain hand usage and position. Weakness and clumsiness or impaired dexterity may also be reported. Physical findings on examination may be minimal. There can be demonstrable loss of sensation on portions of the thumb, index, middle, and ring fingers, and less commonly there is weakness of the thumb. Tapping the palmar surface of the wrist overlying the median nerve may elicit an electrical sensation in the fingers, commonly called Tinel's sign. Flexing the wrist for 1 minute may produce or aggravate numbness in the fingers, a maneuver described as Phalen sign. Pressing the base of the palm for 1 minute may produce numbness and tingling by further compressing the nerve. Electrodiagnostic testing, in which transmission of electrical impulses along the median nerve through the carpal tunnel is assessed, can be extremely useful in confirming or excluding the diagnosis and yield abnormal results, if done with proper technique, in at least 95% of cases.

Many disorders can be confused with CTS. Compression of the median nerve fibers more proximally, even in the neck, as well as other sources of wrist and arm pain and hand numbness may be incorrectly diagnosed as CTS. Accurate diagnosis is obviously important for determining proper treatment.

Another common nerve entrapment among musicians is ulnar neuropathy at the elbow. The ulnar nerve traverses several potential compression sites, including a bony channel at the back of the elbow (the "funnybone") and a less obvious channel a short distance beyond that, where it dives between two portions of a muscle flexing the wrist. Symptoms in both cases are similar, again consisting of pain at the elbow and along the ulnar (little finger) side of the forearm, continuing into the hand and little and ring finger, and numbness or tingling that is confined to these two fingers and to the adjacent portion of the palm and back of the hand. Weakness can be minimal or very prominent and can affect all five digits. Both sites of entrapment at the elbow are further compromised by flexing of the elbow, obviously a position associated with the playing of many instruments, especially the bowed strings. Physical signs in ulnar neuropathy include loss of sensation on the little finger, the adjacent half of the ring finger, and the hand proximal to these two digits. Weakness can be identified in some patients, particularly involving the ability to spread and appose the fingers and to flex the tips of the index through small fingers. As with CTS, the ulnar nerve may be sensitive to tapping or pressing in the region of the elbow; fully flexing the elbow for 1 minute may produce numbness and tingling in the affected fingers, a maneuver equivalent to the Phalen sign mentioned earlier.

Electrodiagnostic testing can again be very helpful but is unfortunately less commonly abnormal than in CTS, a reflection of technical difficulties in the electrical assessment of conduction through the elbow region.

There are a number of other potential nerve entrapment syndromes producing symptoms and signs appropriate to the distribution of those nerves (Lederman, 1994). In addition to these well-documented and well-accepted nerve entrapment syndromes, there are several more controversial disorders that are thought to be related to compression of nerve. These may differ because of uncertainty or lack of specificity of clinical symptoms or difficulties in confirming the presence or absence of nerve entrapment by objective techniques such as electrodiagnosis. Among these is the thoracic outlet syndrome (TOS). This disorder is generally characterized by pain, which may again be anywhere from the neck and upper trunk down to the hand, and by sensory symptoms that may mimic those of ulnar neuropathy or may involve the forearm or other portions of the hand and arm. Symptoms are usually highly dependent on position, tending to occur with the arm held at shoulder level or above or in other provocative postures. Physical findings are variable, but objective signs of sensory or motor impairment are minimal or absent. Without clearly defined diagnostic criteria, determining the presence or absence of TOS is obviously difficult.

Focal Dystonia

The third general category of disorders frequently diagnosed among musicians are the motor control disorders, commonly known as focal dystonias. Although there are many different forms of dystonia, the disorder commonly seen among musicians affects the hand or arm involved in instrumental playing or, in brass and woodwind instrumentalists, the embouchure. Unlike most of the disorders previously discussed, pain is an unusual feature of dystonia. More commonly, the instrumentalist will note problems in control, coordination, or production of sound. Typically, at least early in the development of these disorders, the problem occurs only with playing of the instrument and in many cases it remains task specific. Thus, the pianist or violinist may be able to use that hand for any other activity, such as writing, typing, painting, or using utensils or tools. Only when the instrument is held or played does the disorder show itself. This may make rec-

ognition extremely difficult and obviously makes it mandatory to observe the instrumentalist while playing. Our understanding of these disorders remains quite rudimentary, despite having recognized them for well over 100 years. It is now generally acknowledged that they represent some disruption of the normal sensory and motor coordination integrated at the highest levels of brain function. For reasons that are not understood, men are much more likely to develop dystonia than women, and the disorder commonly begins in the third or fourth decade of life. It is entirely unknown why only a small percentage of instrumentalists develop this disorder, despite the fact that many more are subjected to the same physical and emotional stresses. Nonetheless, certain patterns of clinical involvement can be discerned, including the tendency for pianists to have problems with the right hand, often specifically the ring and little fingers, and for violinists and violists to have problems with the left fingers and hand. Brass instrumentalists seem to have a greater likelihood of developing dystonia of the embouchure, compared to woodwinds, although flutists are not uncommonly affected.

The difficulties with muscular control will often progress over several years and frequently reach a point at which it becomes impossible to play. The diagnosis is made by clinical assessment. As noted, since the problem may only be manifest with playing the instrument, the clinician must of necessity observe the instrumentalist while playing. There are no clinically useful diagnostic tests that confirm the diagnosis.

Treatment

In this section, we discuss in broad terms the general approach to playing-related disorders and particularly to the pain syndromes, which, as already noted, represent the large majority of problems for which medical consultation is sought. It is important to recognize that because, most commonly, multiple factors are contributing to the pain syndromes, a simple or single possible approach to management is rarely identifiable. In almost all cases, several therapeutic options exist, and these are usually not mutually exclusive. We will then briefly examine the treatment of nerve entrapment syndromes and focal dystonia.

The decision regarding treatment obviously depends on the diagnosis arrived at by the evaluation methods outlined previously. Once a specific diagnosis has been rendered, it is incumbent on the healthcare practitioner to present the therapeutic options as thoroughly and openly as possible. This must include a discussion of the potential risks and benefits of each of the approaches as well as the feasibility. At the same time, the musician has every right to expect that the healthcare practitioner will offer an opinion as to which options are favored in that particular situation. The practitioner may wish to seek therapeutic suggestions from other consultants, both medical and nonmedical, at times including a teacher, colleague, or other professional musician. The contribution of psychological factors, either to the cause of the clinical symptoms or to the musician's ability to cope with the symptoms, may indicate a need for involvement of a mental health consultant. These various therapeutic approaches may be undertaken simultaneously or sequentially, depending on circumstances and needs. Finally, it is important to point out that there is rarely if ever a "correct" recipe for treatment, to the exclusion of all others.

Nonsurgical Treatment Approaches

The cornerstone of treatment for acute localized or regional pain disorders has traditionally been to prescribe rest for the affected body part. This indeed is what most of us would do on our own without input from a healthcare practitioner and, in most cases, this will suffice to produce relief of pain, with or without the addition of over-the-counter analgesic medication. Most often, it is when these self-help measures have failed that consultation with a healthcare practitioner takes place.

A period of rest may also be a major component of the prescription for treatment by the medical practitioner. Most commonly this will involve a reduction in use of the painful body part but will not require complete immobilization. In our view, absolute rest is rarely necessary and often counterproductive if sustained for more than a few days. Similarly, antiinflammatory medications, either over the counter or those requiring prescriptions, are seldom indicated for more than a few days to several weeks. Since the vast majority of playing-related pain syndromes are not inflammatory in nature, such medications rarely help beyond the initial acute phase.

Involvement of a physical or occupational therapist is most commonly important in the treatment program. These practitioners are skilled at utilizing pain-relieving modalities such as icing or heat, ultrasound, electrical stimulation, and others. Furthermore, they are trained to assess and prescribe specific exercises that are effective in reducing the muscle spasm, or tightness contributing to the pain, and, once the pain subsides, additional exercises for strengthening, postural correction, and enhancing endurance.

Many, but by no means all, regional pain problems can be attributed, entirely or in part, to flaws in posture and technique. Improper or excessive practice habits may contribute significantly as well. The healthcare practitioner may be able to offer advice in this regard but often may wish to seek the help of a teacher or instrument-playing colleague. Indeed, some of our most rewarding therapeutic successes have been achieved by this collaboration between

the healthcare practitioner and the musician consultant. Modification of playing schedules, position, or technique and even adaptations of the instrument itself may prove dramatically helpful in reducing the stresses associated with playing and, as a result, a reduction in playing-related symptoms.

Symptoms of CTS may be ameliorated by splinting the wrist, which can prevent extremes of flexion or extension, just at night or through the day as well. This may of course interfere with normal hand activity. Many patients with CTS may improve simply by modifying or reducing hand activity; this may not be an option for the instrumental musician. Antiinflammatory medications are sometimes prescribed. Injection of a corticosteroid into the carpal tunnel is utilized by some practitioners and can temporarily or even permanently alleviate symptoms. Treatment of ulnar neuropathy again may consist of attempting to protect the nerve from compression by limiting flexion or by padding the area overlying the nerve, thereby reducing the tendency for compression from the outside. Most would agree that some form of physical therapy is the initial treatment of choice for TOS, but the exact form of this is still debated. While an extraordinary variety of therapeutic techniques have been utilized in attempting to control or reverse focal dystonia, the general experience is that these are ineffective. A lengthy and often tedious program of technical retraining, treating even the affected concert performer as a beginner, is required. Even this, however, does not guarantee success.

"Nontraditional" Treatment Approaches

A discussion of nonsurgical treatments, especially involving the health of musicians and other performing artists, would hardly be adequate without some consideration of what has previously been called "alternative" and now preferably "complementary" medicine. A satisfactory definition of complementary medicine has largely eluded those who have attempted to formulate one (Zollman & Vickers, 1999). It generally encompasses a broad range of therapeutic disciplines that are usually untaught in medical schools and unavailable in Western hospitals and medical centers. Surveys have suggested that between 30% to 50% of persons in the United States have utilized at least one form of complementary medicine, and probably, among performing artists, the actual percentage exceeds that (Eisenberg et al., 1998). The range of services classifiable as complementary is broad, and it would be unproductive to list any but the most commonly utilized. These would include acupressure and acupuncture, Alexander technique, chiropractic, Feldenkrais, herbal medicine, homeopathy, massotherapy, and therapeutic touch. A detailed discussion of any of these would be beyond the scope of this chapter and would fail to do justice to the topic. Many medical practitioners have argued that the one thing they all have in common is the lack of reliable scientific study as to efficacy and this represents a serious criticism. It can similarly be argued, however, that many "traditional" approaches in medicine have also failed to achieve proof of efficacy in scientifically conducted studies, yet continue to be utilized. There have recently been attempts made to develop methods for studying some of these alternative techniques, although the difficulties encountered have proven almost overwhelming (Angell & Kassirer, 1998).

Aside from the question of scientific credibility, other issues also relate to the use of complementary methods in treatment, particularly the economics. Suffice it to say that most complementary medical treatments are not covered by insurance plans, making many of them beyond the reach of many who might otherwise seek such help.

We believe that it behooves the traditional medical practitioner to remain open-minded about at least some of the complementary techniques. It should be obvious that traditional and nontraditional approaches may not be mutually exclusive but may indeed be utilized sequentially or simultaneously. Indeed this "integrative" approach has been advocated by at least some members of the "traditional" medical community.

Surgical Treatments

We have already mentioned that surgery is only occasionally required for playing-related problems. In almost all cases, it should be reserved for those who have failed to respond to nonsurgical or "conservative" approaches. There can, however, be occasions in which surgery may indeed prove more "conservative" than attempts to delay or avoid it entirely. It is generally acknowledged that surgical release of the median nerve is the definitive therapy for CTS if nonoperative measures have proven ineffective. The development of progressive sensory and motor impairment in a person with even recent onset CTS might well justify a decision for immediate surgical release rather than a trial of rest, splinting, physical therapy, and anti-inflammatory medication, during which program there may be additional and perhaps even irreversible damage to the median nerve. Similarly, in ulnar neuropathy, decompressing the nerve at the elbow, generally carried out only after failure of nonsurgical modalities, may be considered early in the face of progressing sensory or motor impairment. Surgical indications for TOS, like other aspects of this disorder, remain controversial.

There are also a number of musculoskeletal disorders that may ultimately require surgical intervention. The specific techniques utilized are obviously beyond the scope of this review (see Winspur, 2000). For disorders such as ganglion cysts, nonsurgical approaches usually suffice, but surgery may ultimately be required. For inflammatory tendon

disorders such as lateral epicondylitis ("tennis elbow") or deQuervain syndrome at the wrist, surgery may be dramatically helpful in those who have not responded to other forms of therapy.

Additional disorders, including trigger finger (a tendency for a finger to lock or fail to move smoothly in flexion or extension) and Dupuytren's contracture (a gradual restriction of movement of the digits, usually drawing them into a fixed flexion deformity), may be clear surgical indications. Degenerative arthritis, while always initially approached nonsurgically, may ultimately require either joint replacement or fixation. At the shoulder, rotator cuff injuries may need arthroscopic or open repair. As with any treatment approach, the options must be fully discussed along with risks and potential benefits and an informed decision made before proceeding.

Performance Anxiety

Definition

It has proven difficult to formulate an accurate and comprehensive definition of performance anxiety that might satisfy all with an interest in the subject. It should first be said that performance anxiety is a universal and normal phenomenon rather than a medical disorder. In the vast majority of situations, the performer learns how to control or minimize the manifestations of performance anxiety sufficiently to be able to function. It is only when a performer's own resources are insufficient to deal with the problem that it becomes a therapeutic issue.

While some authorities prefer the more restricted term "music or musical performance anxiety," we will use the broader designation, since it is common to all types of performers. The most easily recognized features are the physiological symptoms, including palpitations, shortness of breath, dizziness, sweating, tremor, numbness or tingling, difficulty swallowing or a choking sensation, abdominal symptoms such as queasiness, nausea, or vomiting, dry mouth, and a need to empty the bladder or bowel. Performance anxiety also includes behavioral and cognitive aspects. The former are manifest as changes in facial expression or body language before or during performance and even avoidance behaviors. Cognitive aspects may include rumination before and during performance, such as self-doubt, imagined criticisms or comments from the audience, and mental preoccupation with technical difficulties, potential for memory lapse, or the perceived consequences of a faulty performance.

Cause of Symptoms in Performance Anxiety

There is little agreement as to the actual cause of performance anxiety. As already indicated, it is nearly a universal

Table 53.1 Autonomic Nervous System

Target organ	Sympathetic	Parasympathetic
Heart	Rate, force	Rate, force
Bronchi	Dilate	Constrict
Gut	Motility	Motility
Bladder	Relax	Contract
Sweat glands	Secretion	—
Salivary glands	—	Secretion
Pupils	Dilate	Constrict

phenomenon, although young children appear to be relatively free of the problem and it seems to develop as one approaches adolescence. The basis for the physiological manifestations is quite well understood and is rooted in the "fight or flight" response mediated by the autonomic nervous system. This is a highly complex collection of nerve cells that is largely responsible for maintaining stability of the body's internal environment. It is composed of two components, the sympathetic and parasympathetic systems, which often have opposite effects on the targeted organ systems (as outlined in table 53.1). The physical manifestations of the performance anxiety syndrome can largely be attributed to overactivity of the sympathetic component or imbalance resulting from it. Thus, palpitations are related to increased rate and force of heart contraction, abdominal distress is due to effects on gastrointestinal motility, sweating is due to increased secretion, particularly of the facial, axillary, and palmar sweat glands, and dry mouth is due to diminished salivary secretion. The mechanism underlying tremor is less well understood but clearly relates to receptors in muscle. Even less well understood are the mechanisms underlying the behavioral and cognitive manifestations. Experts from various disciplines continue to debate the reasons for development of performance anxiety, but at least in some cases it may relate to the perceived need to achieve performance perfection.

Management of Performance Anxiety

As indicated, most performers will evolve their own personal method of controlling or coping with performance anxiety out of necessity. The strategies employed are extremely varied and individualized. Any attempt to catalogue these is guaranteed to leave some method unmentioned and disappoint one or many readers. Most would agree that adequate preparation is a critical component, but thisne clearly does not suffice in all cases.

Performers who are unable to develop a coping strategy will seek the help of colleagues, teachers, and a variety of amateur and professional practitioners. Physicians, including psychiatrists and medical practitioners, are likely to be last resorts, and this may well be appropriate. Pharmacologic approaches to performance anxiety have a long history of use by performers, including alcohol and various sedative medications, most recently the tranquilizers, that have been available since the 1950s. Since the 1970s, medical treatment of performance anxiety has largely focused on the still controversial use of what are called beta-blockers. The sympathetic nervous system achieves its effects through the mediation of adrenaline (epinephrine) and noradrenaline (norepinephrine), which are known to activate receptors on target organ cells. These receptors come in several forms, grouped as alpha- or beta-receptors. The latter are largely responsible for the physical manifestations of anxiety, and drugs that inhibit or prevent these effects are called beta(adrenergic)-blockers. A number of studies carried out during the 1970s set the stage for recommending that these pharmacologic agents, such as propranolol (e.g., Inderal) can be highly effective in blocking the destructive symptoms of performance anxiety, including sweating, tremor, and palpitations, without interfering with other physical or the emotional aspects of performance. There continues to be intense debate as to the wisdom, effectiveness, safety, and even ethics of this approach, and the interested reader can consult a variety of sources for further elaboration of these arguments (Lederman, 1999; Sataloff, Rosen, & Levy, 1999). We believe that the benefits far outweigh the risks when certain guidelines are followed, certain restrictions are placed on usage, and adequate medical supervision, at least initially, is in place.

Pharmacologic treatment of performance anxiety is meant to be used on an intermittent and occasional basis. For those with more consistent needs, it is far better to find alternative approaches, including an assessment of the possible underlying causes for the persisting problems with performance. A variety of psychotherapeutic and behavioral approaches have been utilized, and these can be dramatically helpful in allowing the performer to control not only the physical or somatic symptoms but also the cognitive and behavioral aspects of performance anxiety. This may include psychophysiological therapies such as systematic desensitization and relaxation/stress management techniques, cognitive therapies, and behavioral approaches. It should again be emphasized that professional help is sought primarily when all self-help methods have been found wanting. In most cases, attention to adequate rehearsal, sufficient advance planning regarding equipment and performance needs, adequate rest and general health measures prior to performance, selection of repertoire consistent with the performer's level of skill, experience, and preparation, and a realistic acceptance that all performances fall short of perfection will suffice.

Prevention of Musicians' Medical Problems

Based on what is known about the etiology of musicians' medical problems, there are logical means for preventing them: initial good teaching and avoidance of subsequent risk factors, especially over practice. While there have been numerous studies of various populations of musicians with convincing evidence for the relation of certain risk factors to the occurrence of injuries, there have been very few studies proving the efficacy of specific modes of prevention. This does not mean that there are not many opinions concerning how to avoid performance-related medical problems: almost every article written and talk presented on music medicine offers preventive strategies. It is simply that few have been tested.

One area of potentially preventive intervention for which the surface has barely been scratched has to do with altering the instrument. It is clear that the instrument is critical in the etiology of many injuries, that some instruments are more hazardous than others, and that instrumental adaptation to fit individual requirements represents a potentially fruitful area for investigation. While there has been a historic reluctance to alter traditional configurations of instruments, makers and medical personnel alike have been increasingly looking at the ergonomics aspects of music (Norris, 2000).

It may seem inappropriate for physicians to discuss teaching in the context of preventing injuries. However, after many years of evaluating and observing musicians in a clinical setting, it seems the essential place to start a consideration of preventive techniques. The fact is that most musicians seem to agree that with "proper teaching," whatever that may be, many problems would not arise later in their musical life. Certainly practice habits and musical technique both bear on how the individual musician approaches and interacts with the instrument. Therefore, in the context of injuries and their prevention, the discussion of technique and of music pedagogy should be understood as being from a physiologic point of view, which may well not always coincide with accepted and even proven teaching methods. Some useful questions to pose that are helpful in assessing playing from a medical standpoint are: Is the overall posture conducive to good body mechanics? Does the playing display an economy of motion, or is there wasted activity? Is the technique protective of joints, or is there excess pressure on joints, or are they used so as to exceed the normal range of motion? Is there evidence of excessive muscle tension, not only in the muscles directly involved but also, for instance, in the neck and back? Is there anything about the musician that suggests undue psychological stress? All of these are factors that tend to have a role in producing problems at all stages of musical careers, not just in students. Given the current in-

terest between both the medical and musical communities in musicians' medical problems, the time may have come for launching major research efforts into some of these questions. Historically accepted pedagogical methods need to be objectively tested for their short- and long-term implications in musical ease, health, and longevity. This will clearly be complex research that must be jointly undertaken by experts representing musical, medical, and biomechanical disciplines.

Few prevention studies have been conducted thus far. One of the more successful projects, if limited in its size, was that reported by Crispin Spaulding, a physician working at the Trondheim conservatory in Norway (Spaulding, 1988). With coworkers, she designed courses to teach music students about the body and its mechanics and prescribed specific exercise routines. She also worked with instrumental teachers at the school on posture and movement training and reported a significant reduction in the incidence of problems among those students for whom the curriculum was obligatory.

A larger scale prevention intervention project was undertaken by Brandfonbrener, Middlestadt, Shybut, and Brooks using 9 ICSOM orchestras, 6 as experimental subjects and 3 as controls (Brandfonbrener, 1997). The hypothesis was that with education through lectures and specific prescribed exercises, and warmups and cool-downs, the occurrence of injuries among professional orchestra members could be significantly reduced from the 76% reported in the ICSOM study. This experiment took place over a year, extending from the start of one orchestra season to the next. In recruiting the voluntary subjects it was emphasized that the study was for prevention, not treatment, and was especially targeting those without a history of medical problems. Initially approximately half of the members of each orchestra participated, but by the final and third visit, up to half had dropped out. The reason given in most cases was that the 15–20 minutes required to do the prescribed stretching or strengthening exercises given to each orchestra was more than was justified in the absence of medical problems. In spite of the failure to keep the subjects involved in the study, there was a general acknowledgment that the briefer warmup and cool-down exercises had been "helpful," and many thought they would continue doing these. Perhaps the most encouraging result of this effort was that the insurance rates of one of the participating orchestras was reduced because fewer claims were filed during the experimental period.

In general it is difficult to motivate patients to undertake proactive health measures. However, for musicians, despite their injuries being non-life-threatening, the stakes seem especially high in terms of long-term career risks and musical longevity. The behavior modification efforts that appear to be advisable seem rather common-sense and minimal, including the pacing of playing with frequent rests, participating in some form of regular exercise, watching one's posture, and so forth. New tactics need to be devised to motivate reluctant musicians, for which the first step may be to establish convincing evidence that these preventive strategies do in fact work, that they may ease the work of playing over time, and that the 76% of orchestra players in the ICSOM data who admitted to medical problems can be reduced by a significant percentage. Some conservatories have begun to make available either Feldenkrais or Alexander lessons, techniques to which musicians and other performers have long been attracted. There are no statistics regarding the effectiveness of such body disciplines for preventing injuries and stress-related problems, but even in the absence of data they appear to be useful, are unlikely to do any harm, and represent a move in the right direction.

Another place to start in attempting to prevent medical problems in musicians is in stress reduction. It is known that perceived stress among professional orchestra members is associated with an increase in musculoskeletal complaints (Middlestadt & Fishbein, 1988). Our own observations during some 30 years of seeing conservatory students is that there is a dramatic rise in their medical visits associated with juries, competitions, and recitals. Some of this can be explained by the increase in time spent playing, as cited by Manchester and others, as a precipitant for injuries (Manchester, 1997; Newmark & Lederman, 1987), but some of it appears to be the stress in and of itself. Studies of conservatory students associate times of competitions, auditions, and juries as times of increased injuries. Numerous other anecdotal reports support this association. However, in spite of what seems more than ample evidence of the relation of stress and injury, no one has actually studied stress reduction in order to document its effect on reducing medical problems among musicians. Further study of conservatory students with whom systematic stress reduction strategies have been introduced would offer invaluable evidence to serve as the impetus for institutional changes and, using conservatories as a model, could serve to bring about efforts towards stress reduction in the larger musical community.

NOTE

1. F. Matthias Alexander (1869–1955) originally developed the Alexander Technique as a method of vocal training for singers and actors in the 1890s. He realized that the basis for all successful vocal education was an efficiently and naturally functioning respiratory mechanism. Alexander focused primarily on helping the breathing mechanism to function more effectively. The helped him become "free from the throat and vocal trouble and from the respiratory and nasal difficulties with which I had been beset from birth" (Jones, 1976, p. 18). Basically, Alexander had evolved a method for learning how to consciously change maladaptive habits of coordination (including movement, posture, breathing, and tension patterns). Dr. Moshe Feldenkrais developed the Feldenkrais Method of Somatic Education that uses movement to help improve our capabilities to function in our daily lives. It is an educational system that develops a functional awareness of the self in the environment. The method utilizes the fact that the body is the primary vehicle for learning. The Feldenkrais Method is an approach to working with people that expands their repertoire of movements, enhances awareness, improves function, and enables people to express themselves more fully (Feldenkrais, 1981; 1985; Rywerant, 1983).

REFERENCES

Angell, M., & Kassirer, J. P. (1998). Alternative medicine: the risks of untested and unregulated remedies. *New England Journal of Medicine, 339,* 839–841.

Begardelli, A., Rothwell, J. C., Hallett, M., Thompson, P. D., Manfredi, M., & Marsden, C. D. (1998). The pathophysiology of primary dystonia. *Brain, 121,* 1195–1212.

Blum, J., & Ahlers, J. (1994). Ergonomic considerations in violists' left shoulder pain. *Medical Problems of Performing Artists, 9,* 25–29.

Blum, J. (Ed.). (1995). *Medizinische probleme bei musikern.* New York: Thieme Stuttgart.

Brandfonbrener, A. G. (1997). Orchestral injury prevention intervention study. *Medical Problems of Performing Artists, 12,* 9–14.

Brandfonbrener, A. G. (2000). Joint laxity and arm pain in musicians. *Medical Problems of Performing Artists, 15,* 72–74.

Brown, A. N. (1997). Musculoskeletal misuse among youth symphony string players. *Medical Problems of Performing Artists, 12,* 15–18.

Byl, N., Merzenich, M. M., & Jenkins, W. M. (1996). A primate genesis model of focal dystonia and repetitive strain injury: Learning-induced dedifferentiation of the representation of the hand in the primary somatosensory cortex in adult monkeys. *Neurology, 47,* 508–520.

Cailliet, R. (1990). Abnormalities of the sitting postures of musicians. *Medical Problems of Performing Artists, 4,* 131–135.

Cayea, D., & Manchester, R. (1998). Instrument-specific rates of upper extremity injuries in music students. *Medical Problems of Performing Artists, 13,* 19–25.

Chandler, P. A., & Foster, B. (1999). Health services to performing artists: What do they think? *Medical Problems of Performing Artists, 14,* 133–137.

Charness, M. E., Ross, M. H., & Shefner, J. M. (1996). Ulnar neuropathy and dystonic flexion of the fourth and fifth digits: Clinical correlation in musicians. *Muscle Nerve, 19,* 431–437.

Cole, R. A., Cohen, L. G., & Hallett, M. (1991). Treatment of musician's cramp with botulinim toxin. *Medical Problems of Performing Artists, 6,* 137–143.

Dawson, W. J. (1990). Upper extremity injuries in high-level instrumentalists: An end-result survey. *Medical Problems of Performing Artists, 5,* 109–112.

Dawson, W. J., Charness, M., Goode, D. L., Lederman, R. J., & Newmark, J. (1998). What's in a name? Terminologic issues in performing arts medicine. *Medical Problems of Performing Artists, 13,* 45–50.

Donison, C. (2000). Hand size vs. the Standard Piano Keyboard. *Medical Problems of Performing Artists, 15,* 111–114.

Eisenberg, D. M., Davis, R. B., Ettner, S. L., Appell, S., Wilkey, S., Van Rompay, M., & Kessler, R. C. (1998). Trends in alternative medicine use in the United States, 1990–1997. *Journal of the American Medical Association, 280,* 1569–1575.

Feldenkrais, M. (1981). *The elusive obvious.* Cupertino, CA: Meta.

Feldenkrais, M. (1985). *The potent self.* New York: Harper and Row.

Fishbein, M., Middlestadt, S. E., Ottati, V., Straus, S., & Ellis, A. (1988). Medical problems among ICSOM musicians: Overview of a national survey. *Medical Problems of Performing Artists, 3,* 1–6.

Goldenberg, D. L. (1999). Fibromyalgia syndrome a decade later: What have we learned? *Archives of Internal Medicine, 159,* 777–785.

Hochberg, F. H., Leffert, R. D., Heller, M. D., & Merriman, L. (1983). Hand difficulties among musicians. *Journal of the American Medical Association, 249,* 1869–1872.

Hoppmann, R. A., & Patrone, N. A. (1989). A review of musculoskeletal problems in instrumental musicians. *Seminars in Arthritis and Rheumatism, 19,* 117–126.

Howard, J. A., & Lovrovich, A. T. (1989). Wind instruments: Their inter-play with orofacial structures. *Medical Problems of Performing Artists, 1,* 20–23.

Jones, F. P. (1976). *Body awareness in action.* New York: Schocken Books.

Karp, B. L., Cole, R. A., Cohen, L. G., Grill, S., Lou, J. S., & Hallett, M. (1994). Long-term Botulinim toxin treatment of focal hand dystonia. *Neurology, 44,* 70–76.

Kloeppel, R. (2000). Do the "spreadability" and finger length of cellists and guitarists change due to practice? *Medical Problems of Performing Artists, 15,* 23–34.

Lambert, C. M. (1992). Hand and upper limb problems of instrumental musicians. *British Journal of Rheumatology, 31,* 265–271.

Larsson, L. G., Baum, J., Mudholkar, G. S., & Kollia, G. D. (1993). Benefits and disadvantages of joint hypermobility among musicians. *New England Journal of Medicine, 329,* 1078–1082.

Lederman, R. J. (1994). Neuromuscular problems in the performing arts. *Muscle and Nerve, 17,* 569–577.

Lederman, R. J. (1999). Medical treatment of performance anxiety: A statement in favor. *Medical Problems of Performing Artists, 14,* 117–121.

Lockwood, A. H. (1989). Medical problems of musicians. *New England Journal of Medicine, 320,* 221–227.

Manchester, R. A. (1997) Musculoskeletal problems of adolescent musicians. *Medical Problems of Performing Artists, 12,* 72–74.

Middlestadt, S. E., & Fishbein, M. (1988). Health and occupational correlates of perceived stress in symphony orchestra musicians. *Journal of Occupational Medicine, 30,* 687–692.

Middlestadt, S. E., & Fishbein, M. (1989). The prevalence of severe musculoskeletal problems among male and female symphony orchestra string players. *Medical Problems of Performing Artists, 4,* 41–48.

Newmark, J., & Lederman, R. J. (1987). Practice doesn't necessarily make perfect: Incidence in overuse syndromes in amateur musicians. *Medical Problems of Performing Artists, 2,* 142–144.

Norris, R. N. (2000). Applied ergonomics. In R. Tubiana & P. C. Amadio (Eds.), *Medical problems of the instrumentalist musician* (pp. 595–614). London: Dunitz.

Rife, N. A., Lapidus, L. B., & Shnek, Z. M. (2000). Musical performance anxiety, cognitive flexibility, and field independence in professional musicians. *Medical Problems of Performing Artists, 15,* 161–166.

Ross, M. H., Charness, M. E., & Logigian, E. L. (1995). Does ulnar neuropathy predispose to focal dystonia? *Muscle Nerve, 18,* 606–611.

Rywerant, Y. (1983). *The Feldenkrais method: Teaching by handling.* New York: Harper & Row.

Salmon, P., Shook, C. P., Lambert, K. G., & Berenson, G. (1995). Performance impairments, injuries, and stess hardiness in a sample of keyboard and other instrumentalists. *Medical Problems of Performing Artists, 10,* 140–145.

Sataloff, R. T., Brandfonbrener, A. G., & Lederman, R. J. (Eds.). (1998). *Performing arts medicine* (2nd ed.). San Diego: Singular.

Sataloff, R. J., Rosen, D. C., & Levy, S. (1999). Medical treatment of performance anxiety: A comprehensive approach. *Medical Problems of Performing Artists, 14,* 122–126.

Schuppert, M., & Wagner, C. (1996). Wrist symptoms in instrumental musicians: Due to biomechanical restrictions? *Medical Problems of Performing Artists, 11,* 37–42.

Spaulding, C. (1988). Before pathology: Prevention for performing artists. *Medical Problems of Performing Artists, 3,* 135–139.

Tubiana, R., & Amadio, P. C. (Eds.). (2000). *Medical problems of the instrumentalist musician.* London: Dunitz.

Winspur, I. (2000). Special techniques and planning issues in surgery. In R. Tubiana & P. C. Amadio (Eds.), *Medical problems of the instrumentalist musician* (pp. 433–451). London: Dunitz.

Winspur, I., & Wynn Parry, C. B. (1998). *The musician's hand.* London: Dunitz.

Zetterberg, C., Backlund, H., Karlsson, J., & Werner, H. (1998). Musculo-skeletal problems among male and female music students. *Medical Problems of Performing Artists, 13,* 160–166.

Zollman, C., & Vickers, A. (1999). What is complementary medicine? *British Medical Journal, 319,* 693–696.

Musicians' Health

54

KRIS CHESKY

GEORGE KONDRASKE

MIRIAM HENOCH

JOHN HIPPLE

BERNARD RUBIN

A dedicated group of physicians, audiologists, psychologists, and other healthcare professionals are seeking solutions to a variety of physical, psychological, and behavioral problems among musicians that can cause extreme hardship to the afflicted. The Performing Arts Medicine Association is recognized as the leader in this effort (see chap. 53). However, these dedicated healthcare professionals face obstacles when attempting to research musicians or to implement preventive education-based strategies because they primarily work in clinical settings. A major need exists within music education to acknowledge that these problems exist and to become involved in the development and implementation of music education–based prevention programs. Currently, there is little evidence that the field of music education acknowledges the medical risks involved with learning and performing music or that the field has defined an active role for music educators in efforts to prevent such problems. Not only are these actions necessary as a potentially effective preventative measure, the need for such actions is increased because the new 2001–2002 National Association of Schools of Music *Handbook* recommends, as a general standard for undergraduate and graduate programs in music, that institutions should assist students to acquire knowledge from qualified professionals regarding the prevention of performance injuries (NASM, 2001).

The purpose of this chapter is to critically review selected studies for the music education profession in order to highlight the need for further study. Following a brief introduction to occupational health, this chapter focuses on national surveys as one approach to help establish the magnitude and patterns of medical problems among musicians. Subsequent sections focus on human performance engineering as one approach to assist in the development of research strategies for assessing and modifying risk. Hearing loss and mental health issues will be summarized with suggestions for future research. Because any one area could easily constitute a whole chapter, the literature reviews are limited to selected studies that highlight the need for additional research and that offer novel investigative tactics.

Introduction

The cause-and-effect relationships between making music, including being a professional musician, and various occupational diseases are far from being fully understood. As with other occupational diseases, disease among musicians may be slow to develop and symptoms may be confused with changes resulting from the aging process. Not all individuals react in the same way to similar exposures and, in some cases, off-the-job exposures may contribute or be a primary cause of illness. Further complicating this issue, the World Health Organization (WHO, 1995) characterizes work related diseases as multifactorial to indicate that a number of risk factors, including the physical, work organizational, psychosocial, individual, and sociocultural, contribute to causing occupational diseases. There is much controversy and debate surrounding work-related disorders because of the disagreement regarding the relative importance of multiple and individual factors in the development of diseases. Perhaps this debate would increase in complexity if it is taken into consideration that musicians are typically exposed to the physical and psychosocial demands of music very early in life and long before entering the workforce.

In light of this multifactorial perspective, it is also important to highlight that musicians are misrepresented, underrepresented, or not represented in national strategies designed to collect and disseminate information regarding vocational patterns or occupational injuries. For instance, the routinely published national source of information about occupational injuries and illness among U.S. workers is the Annual Survey of Occupational Injuries and Illnesses (ASOII) conducted by the Bureau of Labor Statistics (BLS). This survey is a random sample of about 250,000 workers from the private sector and provides estimates of workplace injuries and illnesses based on information that employers provide. The information includes demographic information about the injured workers as well as the following characteristics of the injury or illness: (1) the nature of the injury or illness, such as noise-induced hearing loss or carpal tunnel syndrome; (2) the part of the body affected, such as the inner ear or wrist; (3) the source(s) that directly produced the condition, such as loud noise or a specific task; and (4) the event that describes the manner in which the injury or illness was inflicted, such as overexposure or repetitive motion. Such information about musicians would be very helpful, but this process was not intended for and is not used to collect information about musicians.

The primary method for tracking occupational patterns in the United States relies on household surveys administered by the U.S. Census Bureau and also contributes little to the understanding of musicians. Surveys include the Decennial Census of Population (DCP) and the Current Population Survey (CPS). The BLS and the National Endowment for the Arts (NEA) use these data sets to describe the occupational trends of artists at the national level. Since the inception of its Research Division in 1975, the NEA claims to be the principal research facilitator for understanding artist occupations (Ellis & Beresford, 1994). Unfortunately, the methodology used by the DCP and CPS is considered inadequate for understanding musician populations (NEA Research Division, 1998). Because of the way the surveys establish primary occupation, many musicians would not be acknowledged as musicians. Furthermore, if an individual does meet the inclusion criteria, he or she is grouped with all others into one *musician/composer* category, making it impossible to determine what group(s) of musicians impact economic trends or, more important, what group(s) are being employed and why. As declared by the NEA, this methodology also prohibits determining income from an artist's chosen occupation, versus a secondary or supplemental occupation (Bradshaw, 1996).

National Surveys

Without national data on either the occupational patterns or the associated occupational injuries, it is very difficult to identify the patterns and characteristics, let alone the causes, of particular diseases. Whereas a clinical approach is concerned with diagnosis, treatment, and education of an individual musician, an epidemiology approach often begins with descriptive data of the population and is concerned with identifying subgroups of the population at risk for particular diseases and for providing evidence for causal associations. In this type of research, the health "response" may be a discrete endpoint, such as the occurrence of a symptom (e.g., physical pain, ringing in the ears, low self-esteem) or disease diagnosis (e.g., carpal tunnel syndrome, sensory neural hearing loss, depression). Measures of "exposure" may be as crude as membership in an occupational group (e.g., musician) or subgroup (e.g., trumpeter) or based on stratification within a subgroup (e.g., lead big-band trumpeter) or as refined as the result of complex analytic techniques (e.g., the amount and direction of mouthpiece force against the lips during performance). Translating the concern for musicians' health into effective prevention strategies requires at least some acceptable inferences regarding possible causal relationships from the patterns of the associations that have been found. Although clinical and prevalence studies of musicians have been published, including some with music student populations, there are only two known musician health surveys intended to collect data on a national level.

The ICSOM Study

The first national study, conducted about 15 years ago, was completed with the support of the International Conference of Symphony Musicians (ICSOM) by professors at the University of Illinois at Champaign (Fishbein, Middlestadt, Ottati, Straus, & Ellis, 1988). This study is often referred to and described as the most extensive and reliable study to date (Brandfonbrener, 2000). Because of its size, relevance, and subsequent impact on the field of performing arts medicine, its importance cannot be overestimated.

A self-completed questionnaire was distributed to members of 48 ICSOM orchestras. In addition to general demographic and occupational questions, it included a list of 34 musculoskeletal locations, 25 nonmusculoskeletal problems, 9 musculoskeletal symptoms, 11 musculoskeletal diagnoses, and 32 medical treatments. Musicians were asked to circle all problems they had experienced. Further questions sought information regarding symptoms and treatments. Another question asked whether they considered the stress they experienced on the job to be more than, less than, or about the same as that experienced by other professional musicians.

The return rate for the questionnaire was 55% and resulted in a sample of 2,212 musicians who were performing on a regular basis with one or more of the ICSOM orchestras. The report indicated that a statistical weighting was used to adjust for nonresponses and imbalances with respect to gender, instrument group, and type of orchestra in order to project to the total population of ICSOM musicians within a 2% accuracy rate.

The main finding, or health "response," was that 82% of the musicians reported experiencing a medical problem and 76% indicated that at least one problem was severe in terms of its effects on performance. The authors also reported that the prevalence rates for medical problems differed according to gender, age, and instrument type. For instance, females were more likely than males to report at least one problem and at least one severe problem. String players were more likely to report at least one problem and at least one severe problem when compared to woodwind, brass, and other instrument groups.

Representing the whole group, regardless of instrument type, the percentage of subjects who indicated a specific problem at specific locations was reported. For instance, over 20% reported problems with individual sites, including the left and right lower back, neck, and shoulders. Similar percentages also were reported for the occurrence of some nonmusculoskeletal problems, including eyestrain and stage fright. Detailed analyses were presented for both stage fright and left hand. The left hand was mentioned as the site most mentioned by string players as a severe problem site, suggesting an instrument-specific etiology.

In the introduction to the article, the authors indicated that "the report only scratches the surface of the data . . . and illustrates the types of analyses which can be done with the survey data" (p. 1), suggesting that other analyses would be published. However, as can be determined, only two other articles were published (Middlestadt & Fishbein, 1988, 1989). The first examined perceived stress, whether it was perceived as different from other musician groups, and its relationship to prevalence rates for some musculoskeletal and nonmusculoskeletal problems. The second examined the prevalence of severe musculoskeletal problems among the orchestra string players. No detailed examinations of the non–string players have been found for either the musculoskeletal or nonmusculoskeletal problems. This data may have provided interesting details to suggest possible etiological relationships between affected part(s) of the body or nonmusculoskeletal problems and specific musical instruments.

The UNT-Musician Health Survey

The second national study, titled the University of North Texas Musician Health Survey (UNT-MHS), was conducted through the Texas Center for Music and Medicine and funded, in part, through a research grant from the National Academy of Recording Arts and Sciences. When conceiving this study, the researchers considered that, even though some factors among working symphony musicians may be common to non-symphony musicians, there may be important differences when compared to other musician groups. The variability may be most obvious when considering the physical "exposures" associated with nonorchestral instruments (e.g., acoustic folk guitar, drum set) or nonclassical musicians performing orchestral instruments (e.g., jazz trumpet, bluegrass fiddle, Latin percussion). In addition, there are notable differences in the work organizational factors. For instance, many nonorchestral musicians are not employed full-time, freelance, and or work for more than one employer.

A traditional mail-out survey was considered unreasonable in order to acquire a large, geographically diverse, heterogeneous sample of musicians within the United States. Furthermore, it was considered unrealistic, if not impossible, to identify and survey a representative sample of the whole population of musicians. Considering that the internet has been effective for conducting survey research (Bell & Kahn, 1996; Houston & Fiore, 1998), the UNT-MHS was developed as an online survey in order to generate a nonrandomized, recruited sample of musicians. Recruited samples are used for targeted populations in surveys that require more control over the makeup of the sample. The survey included questions and response options that were similar but modified to those used in the ISCOM survey (Corns, Edmond, & Wilson, 1996) and included the same lists of 34 musculoskeletal locations and 25 nonmusculoskeletal problems. Demographic and national distribution characteristics (Chesky, Corns, & Devroop, 2000) and socioeconomic profiles of the recruited sample of over 4,000 musicians have been reported (Chesky, Devroop, & Corns, 2001). Table 54.1 shows a basic profile of the subject population.

Ongoing analyses of these data have focused on particular subgroups based on the primary instrument of the musicians. The foci of the published reports have included clarinet (Thrasher & Chesky, 1998), saxophone (Thrasher & Chesky, 1999), flute (Spence, 2001) double reeds (Thrasher & Chesky, in press), piano (Pak & Chesky, 2001), strings (Chesky & Devroop, 2001), and brass instruments (Chesky, Devroop, & Ford, in press). Whereas data for specific musculoskeletal sites in the ICSOM study were reported for all musicians together, regardless of instrument, this approach focused on generating data specific

Table 54.1 Demographic profiles of total cohort from UNT-MHS

	n	Age M	Years of college music instruction M	Years as professional musician M
Gender				
Females	1659	31.0	3.6	8.5
Males	2216	36.5	3.3	12.8
Musician type[a]				
Folk/C&W	256	39	1.4	10.0
Rock/pop	267	30	1.3	18.0
Music educator	584	36	5.7	14.8
Classical	1587	31	4.2	9.8
Jazz/blues	449	33	2.5	11.5
Church	131	37	3.0	11.3
Total	4017	33.2	3.5	10.7

Note: Data are based on valid responses listwise. Totals represent the full cohort. M = mean.
[a]Subgroups include: Folk/C&W: Folk/country and western/bluegrass; Rock/Pop: rock/alternative/rhythm and blues/hiphop/Top 40/rap/pop; Classical: classical/opera; Church: church/gospel/contemporary Christian. College instruction refers to formal music instruction at the college level.

to the type of instrument played in order to identify possible relationships to biomechanical risks associated with certain instruments. The most successful example of this process is related to the findings from musicians reporting clarinet as their primary instrument (Thrasher & Chesky, 1998). This reported showed that 37.2% of 324 clarinetists reported problems with their right wrist. This figure was over 50% for females.

As with any study, there are limitations and concerns, especially considering that the internet was used to derive a recruited sample of musicians. Referring to the many forms of empirical research (Wilkenson, 2000), the American Psychological Association (APA) expressed concern that some researchers have the impression or have been taught to believe that some forms of data collection yield information that is more credible than others. The APA article pointed out that various methodologies are necessary for generating hypotheses, that they explore data to form or sharpen hypotheses about a population, while others are hypotheses testing and others are meta-analytic.

To help establish validity of the UNT-MHS data, prevalence rates from musicians reporting flute as their primary instrument were compared to a subsequent data set derived from a hard copy version of the UNT-MHS administered to volunteers during the 1999 National Flute Association's annual convention in Atlanta, Georgia (Spence, 2001). Results indicated no significant differences in the demographics of the populations and no significant differences in the prevalence rates for musculoskeletal problems between the two samples in all but one site. Among the 24 non-musculoskeletal problems, there were four problems statistically different between the two groups.

In addition to the lack of national data on musicians, there are only two studies (ICSOM and UNT-MHS) that

attempted to quantify, on a national level, the prevalence rates for medical problems among musicians. Although the ICSOM study provided insight into the problems experienced by orchestral musicians, it was completed 15 years ago, and no replication studies have been reported. Findings from the UNT-MHS, conducted online to recruit a heterogeneous sample of musicians, cannot be considered representative of all musicians. Furthermore, subject bias is a concern in all survey research. Although both studies provide evidence that many musicians experience medical problems, future and ongoing studies are desperately needed in order to fully understand these problems. Because almost every aspect of society is increasingly relying on the internet as a primary means of communication, we suggest that music education researchers continue to explore this tool. Although internet survey research is not appropriate for all populations and all projects, it provides definite cost and logistical advantages. Perhaps music educators can start by developing longitudinal research projects while training "early adopter" populations and by encouraging music students to participate via the internet while they are in school and later on when they enter the workplace.

Human Performance Engineering

This section introduces human performance engineering as one approach to assist in the development of research strategies for assessing and altering risk. Work-related musculoskeletal disorders are defined differently in assorted studies. Some restrict themselves to case definitions based on clinical pathology, some to the presence of symptoms, some to "objectively" demonstrable pathological processes, and some to work disability. However, the most common health outcome for these problems has been the occurrence of pain, which is assumed to be the precursor of more severe disease (Riihimaki, 1995). It also is common for a given discipline to view problems within that discipline as unique. For example, medical problems (and solutions) for musicians may be different from those of athletes and those may be different from those of heavy laborers, and so on. However, over the past several decades, there have been efforts to characterize these problems using more generalizable perspectives, thereby achieving at least the possibility for a common approach to problem conceptualization, research, and intervention strategies. In addition to epidemiology, one field that offers promise in this regard is human performance engineering (HPE). While musician health problems do have unique aspects, there are several specific risk factors (posture, force, repetition) that are common with those that affect the human system in many other occupational and recreational contexts.

The ultimate goal of HPE is the enhancement of performance and safety of humans in the execution of tasks (Kondraske, 2000). The dual nature of this goal deserves emphasis, in that it is the simultaneous combination of safety and performance within a specific musician that is of particular concern in music. The scope of definition applied to the term "human" in HPE not only encompasses individuals with capabilities who differ from those of a "typical" healthy individual (e.g., individuals who are disabled, injured, unusually endowed with regard to some aspect of performance, etc.) but also includes those who are "healthy" and "typical." HPE further encompasses the integration of cognitive, sensory, biomechanical, neuromuscular, cardiovascular, and other human subsystems. Consequently, one finds a wide range of problems in which HPE and associated methods are employed. In a generic view, all such problems involve one or more of the following: (1) a human, (2) a task(s), and (3) the interface of the human with the task(s). This generic view is useful in music education research because of the great variety encountered with regard to both humans and tasks. Given this, the goals of this section are to provide: (1) a basic conceptual framework for understanding the interface of the musician to tasks, (2) a general approach to address factors that relate to risk for injury and musical performance, and (3) a basis for evaluating the growing number of studies that pertain to such issues. Several representative studies are briefly overviewed as well.

The interface of a musician with tasks, or performing music, can be conceptualized using the elemental resource model (ERM), which attempts to provide a complete (i.e., incorporating all human subsystems), quantitative framework for describing the human system (at multiple hierarchical levels) and explaining the interface of any human

system with any task (Kondraske, 2000). The ERM consistently uses a resource construct to model all aspects of a system's performance; that is, the human system possesses "performance resources," or performance capacities. It also employs the nonlinear threshold effect, associated with resource economic mathematics, that governs system-task interfaces. This suggests the idea that the amount of performance resource availability must exceed the amount that is needed or demanded by a given task.

Since resource economic principles are common to both chemistry and the ERM, it is useful to think of the ERM as "chemistry" for human performance. Elements like carbon, hydrogen, and oxygen are combined in different amounts to obtain simple compounds. Simple compounds are combined in different amounts to obtain more complex substances. The ERM incorporates multiple hierarchical levels as well (basic element level, generic intermediate level, and "high" level). Performance resources at the "basic element level" are finite in number, as dictated by finite sets of human subsystems and their respective dimensions of performance. A basic element of performance (BEP) is identified by first identifying an elemental level system (e.g., index finger flexor) and one of its dimensions of performance (e.g., strength). At higher levels, new systems (e.g., car polishers, ball throwers, keyboard players, trumpet players, etc.) are readily created by reconfiguration of elemental level subsystems (i.e., different performance elements are drawn on in different combinations and amounts). The overall approach permits even the most abstract items, such as "motivation," "confidence," and "comfort" (i.e., the inverse of "pain"), to be considered using the same framework used for "strength" and "speed."

Considering the human–task interface, success in a given task requires that "performance resource availability" is equal to or exceeds the "performance resource demand" for each BEP involved in the task. In other words, the human system must have "enough" of each performance resource. The ERM concepts just noted provide a basis for understanding risk of injury in general terms. The concept of stressing a performance resource is defined quantitatively as the ratio of the amount of a performance resource utilized to the amount available. As this stress increases, the risk for injury increases. Note that stress and therefore risk is higher when either the amount utilized is high or the amount available is low. In a biomechanical context for work related musculoskeletal injuries, the important performance resources are related to the forces, postures, and repetitions used during the work-task. This conceptual approach is supported by experimentally based findings in the literature associated with nonmusicians who have biomechanically related injuries such as upper extremity cumulative trauma (Bernard, 1997).

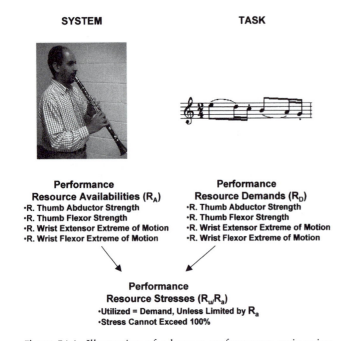

SYSTEM

TASK

**Performance
Resource Availabilities (R$_A$)**
·R. Thumb Abductor Strength
·R. Thumb Flexor Strength
·R. Wrist Extensor Extreme of Motion
·R. Wrist Flexor Extreme of Motion

**Performance
Resource Demands (R$_D$)**
·R. Thumb Abductor Strength
·R. Thumb Flexor Strength
·R. Wrist Extensor Extreme of Motion
·R. Wrist Flexor Extreme of Motion

**Performance
Resource Stresses (R$_u$/R$_a$)**
·Utilized = Demand, Unless Limited by R$_a$
·Stress Cannot Exceed 100%

Figure 54.1. Illustration of a human performance engineering perspective on the musician–musical task interface and key factors that influence and are affected by injuries.

Representative Applications to Biomechanical Problems in Music Performance

Several representative studies are summarized next that focus on clarinet and trumpet instruments. While these illustrate how the general ERM and risk determination concepts are applied in specific instances, they also demonstrate a number of other key attributes associated with the type of studies that lead to biomechanical insights. It is intended that these brief summaries will provide a basis for understanding and evaluating other studies that appear and will appear in the literature.

Clarinet

A number of musculoskeletal problems are associated with playing the clarinet. Fry (1988) reported that among 69 professional clarinetists affected by an overuse syndrome, 52% reported problems with the right hand and/or wrist in addition to problems with forearms and shoulders. Clarinet performance may lead to TMJ problems (Betz, 1989). The ICSOM study did not include prevalence rates for specific musculoskeletal problems among clarinetists. However, the findings from the UNT-MHS did show that 37% of 324 clarinetists reported problems with the right wrist (Thrasher & Chesky, 1998). Neck straps and other support devices to relieve the stress on the right hand and wrist have been recommended (Farmer, 1979; Mazzeo, 1989). However, no research has been found that investigates the

mechanisms of these injuries or the utility of preventative measures.

Based on the findings from the UNT-MHS, an initial study was conducted to characterize this problem by first focusing on which subsystems and which performance resources are utilized during clarinet performance (Chesky, Kondraske, & Rubin, 2000b). While determining which performance resources are likely to be stressed to the greatest degree, it was noted that only the right thumb remains stationary and statically loaded by the weight of the clarinet. These forces also steady the instrument during finger movements and generate and sustain a certain amount of force toward the performer's mouth. Depending on the exact posture used, the forces at the right thumb are probably produced by a combination of flexors and abductors of the carpometacarpal (CMC) joint in combination with abductors of the metacarpophalangeal (MCP) joint. In relation to the clarinet, a total or composite force (F$_C$) is generated from both a radial force (F$_R$), produced by mostly flexors of CMC and MCP, and an axial force (F$_A$) produced mostly by abductors of the CMC.

No studies were available that evaluated the forces against the right thumb of clarinetists or the influence of certain performance variables on these forces (e.g., fingerings required for various pitches). Therefore, it was necessary to design a special two-axis sensor to measure right thumb forces at the interface with the clarinet. This sensor measured axial thumb force (along the longitudinal axis of the clarinet generated primarily by thumb abductors) as well as radial force (along the radial axis of the clarinet, orthogonal to the axial axis, generated primarily by thumb flexors) for the right thumb.

Nine clarinetists were studied. It was found that as more keys were pressed, the composite forces increased and the composite angles decreased. A higher composite force angle represented an increase in the ratio of the axial force to radial force.

Next, a follow-up study (Chesky, Kondraske, & Rubin, 2000a) was conceived to evaluate the impact of using an elastic neck strap with the clarinet. One possible method for reducing risk for musculoskeletal problems is to reduce the amount of force by attaching an elastic neck strap to the clarinet. This practice was previously suggested as a possible means to reduce injuries (Farmer, 1979) and is often recommended by university-level clarinet instructors but rarely used in music education. An analytic scheme was designed to determine the influence of an elastic neck strap on forces against the thumb. Results showed that composite forces were reduced and force angles were also changed in ways that would lead to reduced stress on the maximally stressed right thumb subsystem. This, in turn, can be argued to reduce risk for occupationally related musculoskeletal injury. Furthermore, the elastic neck strap did not seem to hinder performance technique.

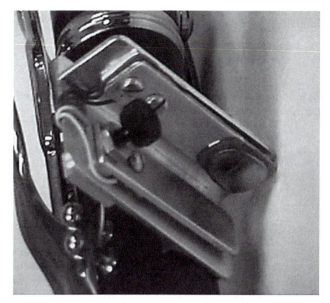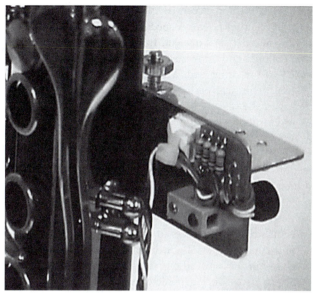

Figure 54.2. Special two-axis force sensor used to measure forces on the thumb while playing.

To further advance the understanding of problems in clarinetists, another prospective study was designed to investigate relationships between musician performance capacities (e.g., strength, extremes of motion, speed, etc.), playing style, and performance-related pain or injury (Kondraske, Chesky, & Rubin, in press). This study addresses more completely the full complexity of the situation. Forty-three clarinetists participated. Extensive musical history profile, anthropometric measures (e.g., hand size, wrist diameter, etc.) and musician resource availability measures (e.g., wrist flexor and extensor strengths, movement speeds, extremes of motion, etc.) were included. Other performance capacities that may indirectly reflect the presence of nerve compression, such as finger vibratory sensation and electrical current perception thresholds, were also measured. Subjects also performed special musical exercises while right thumb forces and acoustical recording were made. Although a full presentation is beyond the scope of this context, preliminary results from this study showed findings similar to those of previous reports, including prevalence rates for problems with the right wrist, forces generated against the right thumb, and the utility of an elastic neck strap to reduce forces during performance.

Trumpet

Performing a trumpet requires physical demands to hold and position the instrument, press the mouthpiece against the lips, produce and sustain blowing pressure, and press valves. It is assumed that these physical demands may contribute to potential performance-related medical problems.

Unlike the lack of reports related to specific medical problems of clarinetists, there are reports suggesting that blowing pressure during trumpet performance may cause increases in intraocular pressure and glaucomatous damage (Schuman, 2000), respiratory problems (Sataloff, Spiegel, & Hawkshaw, 1990), cardiac arrhythmias (Tucker, Faulkner, & Horvath, 1971), and orofacial dysfunction (Howard & Lovrovich, 1989). Injury to the orbicularis oris muscle (Papsin, Maaske, & McGrail, 1996) and other embouchure problems, including lip pain and limited flexibility (Brevig, 1991) as well as tooth displacement (Borchers, Gebert, & Young, 1995), are related to mouthpiece forces against the lips. In addition, medical problems linked to brass performance have included dermatitis (Fisher, 1999), hand and wrist problems (Lammers & Kruger, 1991; Manchester, 1988) and overuse syndromes (Fry, 1986; Fry, Ross, & Rutherford, 1988; Newmark & Lederman, 1987).

The trumpet is supported by the upper extremity musculoskeletal system to allow for proper interface with the musician's lips. Varying degrees of force are generated along the primary axis of the trumpet and are transmitted through the jaws and produce torques about the joints of the cervical spine that must be countered by neck/spinal musculature to maintain the proper interface with the instrument mouthpiece. In fact, the trumpet, head, neck, and shoulders form a "chain" within which forces are generated. Again, to gain further insight, it is desirable to quantitatively consider performance resource stresses, especially those associated with force and strength.

It is difficult to measure neck and upper extremity forces directly during musical performance. However, neck and upper extremity forces can be inferred if forces "through the trumpet" are known. A special three-axis force sensor was designed that has one end that fits onto the lead pipe of the trumpet and allows any standard mouthpiece to be inserted in the other end. Most important, the design is such that acoustical performance of the trumpet is unaffected with the sensor in place. The sensor produces voltages proportional to the force along the axis of the lead pipe as well as to forces along the two directions that are orthogonal to the lead pipe axis (i.e., Z, Y, and X-directions of a Cartesian coordinate system).

Other aspects of this project are analogous to those described for the clarinet study. Force data can be used with simple static biomechanical models to estimate the demands on strength resources of neck and upper extremity neuromuscular subsystems. Such demands can be expected to vary significantly based on playing style. In addition to measuring forces during predetermined performance exercises, the strength (i.e., performance resource availability) of neck and upper extremity muscles will be determined for each study subject. This combination of quantitative data representing demand and availability allows calculation of performance resource stress levels. It is hypothesized that subjects who exhibit high performance resource stresses (due to either low strength coupled with average levels of demand or high strength and high levels of demand) will also have the highest reports of pain and previous injury history.

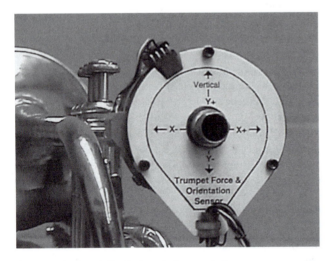

Figure 54.3. Specially designed three-axis force sensor used to study trumpet biomechanics during musical performance. The port on the near end fits onto the trumpet lead pipe. The unit also contains sensors to measure the angle at which the trumpet is held during playing. The sensor weighs 147 grams, which is approximately 13% of the weight of a typical trumpet with mouthpiece.

Guidelines for Research

The ERM described here provides a robust conceptual basis for studying the musician–instrument interface in any context. The following brief guidelines summarize how these concepts are applied in these contexts and are offered as a basis for planning new and evaluating existing studies.

1. Conduct a gross task analysis. Determine which performance resources are "involved" in the musical task(s) of interest; that is, make a list.
2. Refine the task analysis. Use findings from previous studies or defensible logical arguments to obtain a narrowed list of those performance resources that are likely to be stressed to the greatest degree (or maximally) by the musical task(s) of interest. Remember that stress involves the relative relationship between availability and demand; note that "availability" can differ widely in musician populations and may indeed be impacted by early effects of injury.
3. Determine measurement tools to be used for obtaining data related to the performance resources on the narrowed list. These will probably include sensors (that may need to be specially designed at present) that allow measurement of resource utilization (demand) during musical tasks. Tools will also be required that allow profiling of the musician subjects in terms of their performance resource availability profile.
4. Arrive at assessments by bringing demand and availability data together to determine "stress." Rank order resources by stress and focus concern on those performance resources (e.g., wrist flexor extreme of motion) with the highest stress levels.
5. Consider intervention alternatives. Two basic options are generally available: modify the task (e.g., use a neck strap with the clarinet; modify how the instrument is played, including changes in postures, force used, or length of performance time), or modify the musician (e.g., increase the availability of selected performance resources through use of focused strength, endurance, or joint mobility exercises).

For some contexts, measurement such as that highlighted in the preceding studies is not feasible. Another new approach, called nonlinear causal resource analysis (Kondraske, 2000; Kondraske & Beehler, 1994; Kondraske, Johnston, Pearson, & Tarbox, 1997), has been derived from performance theory and employed only thus far in nonmusician populations. It offers a potentially powerful alternative for determining task demands in quantitative terms. It requires only measurement of performance resource availability (e.g., strengths, extremes of motions, etc.) and some method of measuring or estimating overall task performance in the population of interest. With this method, demand is inferred using a special algorithm from the availability data.

Occupational Hearing Loss

The American College of Occupational and Environmental Medicine's Noise and Hearing Conservation Committee has defined noise-induced hearing loss as a slowly developing hearing loss resulting from exposure to continuous or intermittent loud noise (1987). Hearing loss is the most pervasive occupational health problem in America today and affects workers in manufacturing, construction, transportation, agriculture, and the military. According to OSHA, approximately 30 million workers are exposed to hazardous noise levels. At present, estimates show that one in four will develop a permanent hearing loss as a result of occupational exposure. Although the slow progression of this problem may be less dramatic than other occupational diseases, it is a very significant and permanent handicap for the afflicted individual, especially if the individual is a musician. Musicians have vocational hearing demands that are much greater than those required in other occupations. The demands require more than simply understanding speech and include the highly developed ability to accurately match frequencies over a broad range, including frequencies outside of the range for those required for speech comprehension. Musicians must be able to detect and manipulate changes in loudness levels, complex timbres, and blends. Even mild pitch distortion may make it difficult for a musician to perform in tune, and elevated high-frequency thresholds may lead to excessively loud, and therefore unacceptable, performances at higher pitches. Therefore, it is vital for the vocational viability of musicians, as an occupational group, to be educated about and protected from hearing loss.

Even though noise-induced occupational hearing loss is a major health issue in the United States, the research is inadequate to suggest the magnitude of the problem among musicians. Again, musicians are not included in the annual Survey of Occupational Injuries and Illnesses (ASOII) conducted by the BLS. The data from the two national musician health surveys do provide some evidence supporting a concern for this problem. The ICSOM study of symphony musicians indicated that 7% reported problems with earaches and 13% reported "other ear problems." There was no indication regarding the meaning of "other ear problems," and no comparisons were made across any subgroups. Suggestive of a major concern, over 21% of the total group responding to the UNT-MHS reported "problems with hearing loss" (Chesky & Henoch, 2000). These data also imply that problems with hearing loss may be related to the type of music or the type of instruments involved. For instance, rates of occurrence for problems with hearing loss across musician type ranged from as high as 32.8% among the rock/alternative/rhythm-and-blues musicians to 16.8% for church musicians. The magnitude

of variability was even higher across instrument type. The percentage reporting problems by primary instrument, regardless of musician type, ranged from 36.6% for electric bass to 3.8% for harp. When collapsing and comparing all nonclassical musicians to classical musicians across primary instruments, considerable differences were noted for many instrument groups. For example, 7.4% of classical acoustic bass musicians reported problems, compared to 27.8% for their nonclassical counterparts. Again, whereas 28.1% percent of classical trombonists reported problems, 44% of nonclassical trombonists reported problems. This trend was seen in several primary instrument groups, including trumpet, clarinet, acoustic guitar, and saxophone.

Although other studies have examined hearing loss in both the orchestra and rock venues (Axelsson, Eliasson, & Israelsson, 1995; Jerger & Jerger, 1970; Johnson, Sherman, Aldridge, & Lorraine, 1986; Karlsson, Lundquist, & Olaussen, 1983; Ostri, Eller, Dahlin, & Skylv, 1989; Reddell & Lebo, 1972; Schmidt, Verschuure, & Brocaar, 1994; Westmore & Eversden, 1981), they provided conflicting information relative to whether continued exposure to music played at high intensity levels, over the period of a musician's working life, can result in hearing loss, much less hearing loss that has the potential to threaten the musician's livelihood (Sataloff, 1991). Other than this research that focuses on amplified music performed primarily by rock groups, there is little information on either the risk factors or occurrence of hearing loss for nonclassical musician populations who perform nonamplified music. These nonclassical musicians perform in typical wind, concert, marching, studio, and jazz bands. Nonamplified groups usually include more brass and percussion instruments and represent the kind of music ensembles found in most public school, university, and community music education settings.

Assessing Hearing Loss

The studies noted here that examined the hearing of musicians utilized the standard subjective procedure for obtaining hearing threshold data, specifically, the pure tone audiogram. Although it is a proven reliable and valid method for establishing an individual's hearing thresholds, it is not clear that this traditional method can track small changes in hearing acuity over short periods of time. That is, the traditional hearing test might not be sensitive enough to detect minor changes in cochlear function and therefore perhaps not effective for identifying musicians who may be at greater risk for hearing loss.

Recent data has suggested that otoacoustic emissions (OAE), an objective method of evaluating the integrity of the cochlea, specifically the outer hair cells, is more sensitive to changes in hearing sensitivity than traditional audiometric testing (Hall & Lutman, 1999; Oeken, 1998).

Hall and Lutman (1998) found OAEs to be more reliable than pure tone audiometry for distinguishing small changes in cochlear function resulting from noise-induced hearing loss. Evans (1993) and Pick and Evans (1983) have suggested that frequency selectivity, a function specifically of outer hair cells (OHCs), may give earlier evidence of cochlear damage due to loud music, evidence that may be of more functional significance. On the basis of these indications, Hall and Lutman used Transient Evoked Otoacoustic Emissions to study OAE in 28 young adults and found differences in transiently evoked OAE sensitivity in subjects who had greater exposure to amplified music.

Because OAE testing is simple to perform and can be conducted simply and accurately, it is a test that can be easily conducted on very young musicians as they begin to learn to play an instrument. Monitoring the hearing of children throughout their music education would provide an effective means for identifying early changes in hearing sensitivity so that subsequent education and prevention controls could be implemented.

Assessing Risk in the Musical Setting

Studies attempting to establish the level of risk in a particular music context have used sound level meters and personal dosimeters to measure sound pressure levels. Measures at various positions within orchestra settings have shown that levels can exceed the permitted noise exposure of 90 dBA (Jansson & Karlsson, 1983; McBride et al., 1992; Royster, Royster, & Killion, 1991). However, as Sataloff (1991) has indicated, the results and the quality of studies that have examined noise exposure and exposure risk have been inconsistent. Procedures to measure sound levels within orchestral settings have varied from study to study. In some instances (McBride et al., 1992; Westmore & Eversden, 1981), sound measurements were made with one sound level meter placed in the center of the orchestra, a practice that does not give a true picture of sound exposure levels for individual musicians.

Only in one study, (Royster, Royster, & Killion, 1991) were a large number of individual dosimetry samples made (68 samples on 44 musicians) within an orchestra over a long period of time. In addition to the limitations of many of the studies that examine risk for hearing loss relative to exposure levels during musical performance, the majority of investigations related to the measurement of sound levels within musical ensembles have focused on orchestral musicians.

Some recent investigations have begun to examine risk factors associated with hearing loss in musicians with the ultimate goal of preventing problems that might be associated with those risks. These studies have included in situ measurements of sound spectra associated with individual musical instruments (Henoch & Chesky, 1999a); sound pressure levels produced by individual musicians as a function of seating position within musical ensembles (Henoch & Chesky, 2000b); a national survey of self-reports of hearing problems by music genre and age (Henoch & Chesky, 1999b); and the efficacy of using otoacoustic emissions testing for making a priori assumptions regarding the risk of hearing loss in musicians (Henoch & Chesky, 2000a).

Risk Factor Criteria

Little is known about when and under what conditions musicians are at risk for noise-induced hearing loss (NIHL), and the application of present risk criteria, developed for industry, may not function well in a music context. For example, a recent study of a college jazz band ensemble (Henoch & Chesky, 2000b) indicated that certain positions within the ensemble were more at risk than others, based on dosimeter measures. The lead trumpet, lead trombone, and lead alto saxophone players had the highest measured sound exposures, with each musician averaging over 90dBA. The lead alto saxophone player had the highest measured level of exposure, averaging more than 98 dBA for the 50-minute rehearsal period. These sound levels are above what is normally considered acceptable in an occupational environment. However, the present risk criteria for NIHL (Occupational Safety and Health Administration [OSHA], 1983) was developed for workers in industrial settings and incorporated a standard 8-hour day in the identification of risk. It has been suggested (Franks, Stevenson, & Merry, 1996), that for many workers, an 8-hour noise exposure period may not be appropriate. This would be the case with most musicians. All of the studies that have been conducted to investigate the risk of hearing loss in musicians have used the OSHA (1983) criteria when determining if the sound levels experienced by musicians placed them at risk for hearing loss. Musicians do not normally perform for an 8-hour period. They may rehearse alone for a period of time during the day, rehearse as part of a larger ensemble for another portion of a day, and perform in one or more concerts during the same day. In other words, the risk of hearing loss in the musician population cannot be reliably assessed on an 8-hours-per-day criterion.

Another method for assessing risk for hearing loss in workers who are exposed to a complex mixture of events has been suggested; this is the Task-Based Exposure Assessment (T-BEAM) concept (National Institute for Occupational Safety and Health [NIOSH], 1996), which uses work tasks as the central organizing principle for collecting descriptive information on variables used to assess the hearing risk for a worker. Theoretically, in the T-BEAM approach, an "expert" (e.g., perhaps a music educator) who is familiar with what is required of a musician in a particular ensemble would develop a list of "tasks" associated with performing within an ensemble. This would become the basis for developing a hazardous task inventory, for example, determining the times during the day, as well as the number of days per week, on average, that a musician rehearses and performs. Once these tasks have been identified, the information would be used to develop an approach for surveying the task, for example, making dosimeter measurements during each segment of time that the musician is actually rehearsing and performing. In this way it can be determined which of the tasks are potentially hazardous to hearing. If it is found that the musician is reaching levels of exposure considered hazardous, appropriate actions, for example, changes in rehearsal and performance scheduling or use of musician earplugs or engineering methods that reduce the sound, might then be put into place to protect the musician from possible loss of hearing.

There is much still to be learned about the risks to musicians of music-induced hearing loss, not only the levels of sound that can result in hearing loss but also the effects of music-induced hearing loss on a musician's ability to perceive and perform such attributes of sound as loudness, pitch, and timbre.

Psychological Issues Facing Musicians

Musicians at all levels and in all genres face a wide variety of social/emotional issues. In the popular arena Raeburn (1987a, 1987b, 1999, 2000) discusses the problems of emotional stress, anxiety, stage fright, substance abuse, highly competitive musical situations, perfectionism, unpredictable and unstable work opportunities, unhealthy working conditions, and transient social support systems as being of great importance. O'Conner and Dyce (1997) and Olson (1997) outline the importance of the interpersonal characteristics of musicians, especially those playing in groups. Butler (1995) in a study of college music students discussed the importance of internal and external stress in the survival of talented young people. Others such as Piparek (1981), Wilson (1984), Wills and Cooper (1988), Cooper and Wills (1989), and Parasuraman and Purohit (2000) have identified the issues of rigorous and long training requirements, unusual work schedules, competition, stage fright, boredom, lack of influence in selection of music, task difficulty, group social tension, and marital discord as existing in classical and other musical genres. Sternbach (1995), in a summary article, went on to identify the factors of time pressure, workload, insecurity and poor compensation, personal perfectionism, and

labor-management issues as high contributors to musician stress.

From a scientific rigor perspective, these studies have individual strengths and weaknesses. There is a lack of agreement on how stress is measured; some studies used questionnaires while others did in-depth, face-to-face interviews. There is also a wide variation of sample size. However, despite these technical variations, the conclusions are all quite similar. Musicians are challenged with various social/emotional stressors that have a negative impact on their personal as well as professional well-being.

Performance Anxiety

Performance anxiety or stage fright is a problem of concern to many music students as well as professional musicians (Brodsky, 1996). The ICSOM study found that 24% reported some episodes of stage fright and 13% reported instances of acute anxiety (Fishbein et al., 1988). Studies of university music majors have found similar rates (Wesner, Noyes, & Davis, 1990; Pratt, Jessup, & Nieman 1992). Shoup (1995) found that 55% of a high school sample reported that they had experienced performance anxiety, with 18% saying the anxiety was great enough to interfere with performance. European studies have reported even higher rates (Van Klemenade & Van Son, 1995). One trend is that women report a higher incidence than men (Wesner et al., 1990). From a research perspective, generalization of incidence rates is difficult because there was not a common thread of how performance anxiety was defined and some research subject survey response rates were low. In addition, one is hard-pressed to find research dealing with anxiety in musical genres other than classical.

Performance anxiety may depend on one's belief as to the nature of the situation. Deffenbacher (1980) contended that this type of anxiety was a combination of worry about the quality of the performance and the subsequent social implication of any failure as well as the somatic arousal that accompanied the emotionality. Wolverton and Salmon (1991) suggest that high anxious performers are more self-focused and less music-focused than low anxious performers. In addition, higher anxious musicians are more invested in audience approval than those who were more motivated by a desire to be involved in the music itself. Steptoe (1989) noted that career stress played a large part in anxiety. He went on to identify the impact of high performance quality demand and low decision involvement among classical musicians as important factors.

Implementing remedial processes may depend on the willingness of musicians to commit time and money to the process. Since many musicians, especially classical players and students, don't have much influence over conditions at the ensemble level, changes must be made at the individual practice level. Zaza (1994) suggested experimenting with practice warmups, pacing, taking breaks, varying content, relaxation, cognitive rehearsal, exercise, and breathing exercises as ways to reduce stress. Sataloff, Rosen, & Levy (1999) as well as a host of others (Fogle, 1982; Kendrick, Craig, Lawson, & Davidson, 1982; Nagel, Himle, & Papsdorf, 1989; Salmon, 1990), outline cognitive therapy approaches that may be helpful in changing the negative mindsets that are often a part of performance anxiety.

Niemann, Pratt, and Maughan (1993) discussed the use of biofeedback in situations of performance anxiety. He noted there was not a great deal of research connecting music-based performance anxiety and biofeedback. In his research with college students, which used 12 intervention sessions, a multifaceted treatment approach including more than biofeedback was most appropriate.

Many musicians, especially students, may be anxious because they are not adequately prepared by the time of a performance. For some, the anticipatory discomfort is so intense that it interferes with the preparatory process. For others the music selected or assigned is beyond their technical or musical ability. From the perspective of the music educator, students can benefit from an early discussion of performance anxiety that includes suggestions for dealing with the discomfort. Educators who actively involve their students in the selection of pieces may help to reduce anxiety. It is also important to clearly identify when anxiety reactions take place. Among students, performance anxiety may take place during lessons, juries, auditions, solo performances, or ensemble performances. The location of the disruption will have an impact on remediation. Referral to an outside consultant or psychotherapist is best done sooner rather than later in the disruptive process.

Alcohol and Other Drug Use Among Musicians

Use of alcohol and other chemicals by musicians representing a wide range of genres has been commented on by a number of authors. Raeburn (1987a, b) studied a small sample of rock musicians and reported that 80% were users. In the ICSOM study (Fishbein et al., 1988), 21% reported being worried about the use of alcohol. Regarding drug use, over one-third of the musicians participating in the UNT-MHS study (Chesky & Hipple, 1999) believed that substance use is widespread among musicians. Young and Hipple (1996) found that 10% of music students seeking assistance at a university counseling center were concerned about their chemical use. It is clear that alcohol consumption is an integral and even essential part of many musical venues. Musicians often perform in environments where alcohol, as well as other drugs, is easily available. Prevention of abuse is best based on early education ef-

forts; consequently, it is important for music educators to integrate alcohol and drug education and discussion within their lesson plans. For the addicted or alcoholic, a program of complete abstinence is best. However, for the abusing musician, a program focused on getting back into control with moderate use following a harm reduction approach may be possible (Fromme, Marlatt, Baer, & Kivlahan, 1994; Marlatt & Gordon, 1998).

Problems may be avoided if students have a realistic view of their future work world and basic information for dealing with the stress of performing in a hazardous environment that is very substance centered. Educational efforts should be based on an understanding of the developmental patterns of alcohol use and associated alcohol-related problems among music students. One study by Chesky and Hipple (1997) did assess alcohol-related problems of entering music students and compared the data to those for non-music majors. In this study, the music majors reported significantly less alcohol problems compared to the non-music majors. No studies have been found investigating alcohol-related patterns associated with the transition from college to the workplace.

Counseling Strategies for the Musician

Outside of the area of performance anxiety, very little has been written in regard to counseling with musicians. Ostwald (1987) overviewed the problems professional musicians presented at clinics that did outreach into the musician community. He concluded that among these samples, musicians presented psychological problems slightly below the rates for the population at large. Young and Hipple (1996) examined the problems presented at a university counseling center. Almost 50% of the students were classified as having depressive symptoms. In another study of counseling center clients (Young, Hipple, & Chesky, 1999), there were no differences between music majors and non-music majors as to the type of personal problems discussed with the counselor.

Ostwald (1987) identified a number of helping behaviors that can be utilized by music educators as they work with students in distress.

1. Provide undivided attention to the student. Use responsive listening techniques, provide good visual contact, live up to teacher/student contracts, and be sensitive to any separation issues.
2. Clarify the meaning of what is said or implied. Ask questions and seek more information whenever necessary.
3. Be willing to make suggestions and offer assistance in coming to understandings regarding personal and musical alternatives.

4. Be willing to integrate professional counseling with active teaching.

5. In a timely manner speak to specific issues of being a performer, and as a role model share performing experiences.

In the future, music educators as well as researchers should consider the practical skills of communication and problem solving. Most music is made in groups, and being able to fully communicate and deal with problems can be critical to successful performance (Rose, 1994). Accompanying these skills is the art of personal disclosure. Not only do musicians need to be able to discuss musical issues, but this can often be best accomplished when those involved know how each other stands in regard to stress and other personal issues (Dyce & O'Conner, 1992). As these factors are taught and practiced it will be easier for musicians to have an increased sense of inclusion and influence. Consequently, from a stress, and personal emotional issue perspective, individual and group emotional dissonance is reduced.

Summary and Future Directions

From the perspective of the literature cited in this review, there is a clear need for research documenting the occupational diseases in the population of musicians. The study of musicians offers overwhelming challenges, considering the lack of data that defines this population. To date, only two national studies have investigated the prevalence rates for medical problems of musicians. Results from both studies were based on surveys and therefore are representative of a biased population that chose to participate. The proportion of the ICSOM members that responded suggests that symphony musicians experience medical problems that negatively impact performance. From the UNT-MHS survey, findings indicate that nonclassical musicians also experience medical problems. Although the recruited sample was almost twice the size of the ICSOM study, the limitations associated with the internet-based research methodology of the UNT-MHS only allows for the generation of hypotheses and cannot be automatically applied to an individual or subgroup of individuals. However, such hypothesis-generating data is needed in order to identify risk factors for disease. Once risk factors have been isolated, protocols can be developed for measuring the risk factors and then used for intervention trials to determine what changes in the risk factor affect the incidence of a disease. This sequence of research activities has been observed in the series of studies regarding the medical problems among clarinetists. High prevalence rates for right wrist problems fostered the development of procedures to

measure forces at the right thumb and then the use of this procedure to determine the effectiveness of an elastic neck strap to alter risk.

This review introduced novel research strategies, including the use of the internet, applications of human performing engineering, otoacoustic emissions as an objective measure for hearing loss, and a task-based assessment and exposure method (T-BEAM) for organizing data for determining risk.

In addition to reviewing and offering possible research strategies for music educators, we desire to reaffirm and propagate our view that the most distinguishing feature of all diseases and injuries related to music is that they are preventable. In order to take advantage of this opportunity, it is important to reinforce that music educators are the primary professional group in a position to prevent problems. A major need exists within music education to acknowledge that these problems exist and to become involved in the development and implementation of music education–based prevention programs. Currently, there is little evidence that the field of music education acknowledges the medical risks involved with learning and performing music or that the field has defined an active role for music educators in efforts to prevent such problems. This may be due to the lack of research documenting the extent of these problems. Furthermore, since the beginning of music in public schools, music educators have cited the physical, mental, and spiritual benefits as major reasons for inclusion of music. In direct contrast to healthcare professionals, music educators teach about music and musicians, help select a musical instrument for a child, and then provide instruction on how to practice. In addition, music educators are in an ideal position to help prevent problems because they dictate the sequence and set the pace for musical learning and are in everyday contact with students before and during skill and potential problem development.

The Music Educators National Conference (MENC) has helped to raise awareness among music educators that these problems do occur by including information in this Handbook. A further step may be the formation of a special task force to be charged with developing appropriate health education programs for music educators. As research continues to develop specific recommendations, such as having all beginning clarinetists introduced to an elastic neck strap, these procedures can be utilized not only to efficiently educate music educators but also to quickly introduce important information in a timely manner. Hopefully, other associations will follow the lead of MENC and include specific goals and objectives that ensure that students are at least informed of the possibility of medical risk associated with music performance and music as a career choice. Funding agencies will, it is hoped, follow the lead of the National Academy of Recording Arts and Sciences by funding much-needed research projects specifically in this area.

In all decisions to influence policy within these national organizations, it must be considered that it is not always necessary to know every detail of the pathogenic mechanism to be able to prevent disease. Even though the available data suggests that a sizable percentage of musicians experience medical problems, the decisions to move forward with such policy changes should be considered even if only a very small percentage of musicians suffer from one or more of the problems cited in this chapter.

REFERENCES

American College of Occupational and Environmental Medicine Noise and Hearing Conservation Committee. (1987). Guidelines for the conduct of an occupational hearing conservation program. *Journal of Occupational Medicine, 29,* 981–989.

Axelsson, A., Eliasson, A., & Israelsson, B. (1995). Hearing in pop/rock musicians: A follow-up study. *Ear and Hearing, 16,* 245–253.

Bell, D. S., & Kahn, C. E. (1996). Health status assessment via the World Wide Web. In J. C. Cimino (Ed.), *Proceedings of the AMIA Annual Fall Symposium* (pp. 338–342). Philadelphia: Hanley and Belfus.

Betz, S. (1989). Are you a victim of TMJ disfunction? *The Clarinet, 16*(2), 44–47.

Bernard, B. (1997). *Musculoskeletal disorders and workplace factors: A critical review of epidemiologic evidence for work-related musculoskeletal disorders of the neck, upper-extremity, and low back.* Cincinnati: U.S. Department of Health and Human Services.

Borchers, L., Gebert, M., & Jung, T. (1995). Measurement of tooth displacements and mouthpiece forces during brass instrument playing. *Medical Engineering and Physics, 17*(8), 567–570.

Bradshaw, T. (1996, December). Counting artists [On-line]. In *National Endowment for the Arts.* Available: http://arts.endow.gov/Archive/Features8/Research.html [1998, June 26].

Brandfonbrener, A. G. (2000). Epidemiology and risk factors. In R. Tubiana & P. Camadio (Eds.), *Medical problems of the instrumentalist musician* (pp. 36–42). London: Dunitz.

Brevig, P. (1991). Losing one's lip and other problems of the embouchure. *Medical Problems of Performing Artists, 6*(3), 105–107.

Brodsky, W. (1996) Music performance anxiety reconceptualized: A critique of current research practices and findings. *Medical Problems of Performing Artists, 11*(3), 88–98.

Butler, C. (1995). Investigating the effects of stress on the success and failure of music conservatory students. *Medical Problems of Performing Artists, 10*(1), 24–31.

Chesky, K. S., Corns, J. S., & Devroop, K. (2000). *Population characteristics of an internet-based musician survey.* In K.

Chesky, P. Ellis, & D. Laufer (Eds.), *Kolner studien zur musik in erziehung und therapie* [Music as a medium: Applications and interventions] (pp. 39–51). Kleikamp, Germany: Druck und Bindung.

Chesky, K. S., & Devroop, K. (2001). *Medical problems of string instrumentalists: Prevalence rates for violin, viola, cello, and string bass.* Manuscript submitted for publication.

Chesky, K. S., Devroop, K., & Corns, J. S. (2001). *Income from performing music and college music instruction, age, and gender: Results from a national internet survey.* Manuscript submitted for publication.

Chesky, K. S., Devroop, K., & Ford, J. (in press). Medical problems of brass instrumentalists: Prevalence rates for trumpet, trombone, French horn and low brass. *Medical Problems of Performing Artists.*

Chesky, K. S., & Henoch, M. (2000). Instrument specific reports of hearing loss: Differences between classical and non-classical musicians. *Medical Problems of Performing Artists, 15*(1), 35–38.

Chesky, K. S., & Hipple, J. (1997). Performance anxiety, alcohol related problems, and social/emotional difficulties of college students: A comparative study between lower division music and non-music majors. *Medical Problems of Performing Artists, 12*(4), 126–132.

Chesky, K., & Hipple, J. (1999). Musicians' perceptions of widespread drug use among musicians. *Medical Problems of Performing Artists, 14*(4), 187–195.

Chesky, K. S., Kondraske, G. V., & Rubin, B. (2000a). Effect of elastic neck strap on right thumb force and force angle during clarinet performance. *Journal of Environmental and Occupational Medicine, 42*(8), 775–776.

Chesky, K. S., Kondraske, G. V., & Rubin, B. (2000b). The Texas Center for Music and Medicine explores the biomechanics of clarinet performance. *The Clarinet, 27*(2), 34–36.

Cooper, C., & Wills, G. (1989). Popular musicians under pressure. *Psychology of Music, 17,* 22–36.

Corns, S., Edmund, D., & Wilson, S. (1996). World Wide Web research in performing arts medicine: The University of North Texas Musician Health Survey. In K. S. Chesky & B. R. Rubin (Eds.), *Applications of medicine in music* (pp. 8–13). Denton: University of North Texas.

Deffenbacher, J. (1980). Worry and emotionality in test anxiety. In I. Sarason (Ed.), *Test anxiety: Theory, research, and applications.* Hillside, NJ: LEA Press.

Dyce, J., & O'Conner, B. (1992). Personality complementarity as a determinant of group cohesion in bar bands. *Small Group Research, 23*(2), 185–198.

Ellis, D. C., & Beresford, J. C. (1994). *Trends in artist occupations: 1970–1990.* (National Endowment for the Arts, Research Division Report No. 29). Washington, D.C.: Government Printing Office.

Evans, E. F. (1993). Basic physiology of the hearing mechanism. In *The Proceedings of AES Twelfth International Conference: Perceptions of Reproduced Sound* (pp. 11–21). New York: Audio Engineering Society.

Farmer, G. J. (1979, June). Use of the elastic neck strap. *Woodwind World-Brass and Percussion,* 8–9.

Fishbein, M., Middlestadt, S. E., Ottai, V., Straus, S., & Ellis, A. (1988). Medical problems among ICSOM musicians. *Medical Problems of Performing Artists, 3*(1), 1–8.

Fisher, A. A. (1999). Dermatitis in a musician: Part 4. Physiologic, emotional and infectious problems in musicians. *Cutis, 63*(1), 13–14.

Fogle, D. (1982). Toward effective treatment for music performance anxiety. *Psychotherapy: Theory, Research and Practice, 19*(3), 368–375.

Franks, J. R., Stephenson, M. R., & Merry, C. J. (Eds.). (1996). *Preventing occupational hearing loss.* Cincinnati: National Institute for Occupational Safety and Health.

Fromme, K., Marlatt, G., Baer, J., & Kivlahan, D. (1994). The alcohol skills training program: A group intervention of young adult drinkers. *Journal of Substance Abuse Treatment, 11*, 143–154.

Fry, H. J. H. (1984). Medical problems from clarinet playing. *Clarinet Scene, 8*(1), 9–11.

Fry, H. J. H. (1986). Incidence of overuse syndrome in the symphony orchestra. *Medical Problems of Performing Artists, 1*(2), 51–55.

Fry, H. J. H. (1987). Overuse syndrome in clarinetists. *The Clarinet, 14*(3), 48–50.

Fry, H. J. H. (1988). Patterns of over-use seen in 658 affected instrumental musicians. *International Journal of Music Education, 11*, 3–16.

Fry, H. J. H., Ross, P., & Rutherford, M. (1988). Music-related overuse in secondary schools. *Medical Problems of Performing Artists, 3*(4), 133–134.

Hall, A. J., & Lutman, M. E. (1999). Methods for early identification of noise-induced hearing loss. *Audiology, 38*, 277–280.

Henoch, M., & Chesky, K. S. (1999a). Ear canal resonance as a risk factor in music induced hearing loss. *Medical Problems of Performing Artists, 14*(3), 103–106.

Henoch, M., & Chesky, K. S. (1999b). Hearing loss and aging: Implications for the professional musician. *Medical Problems of Performing Artists, 14*(2), 76–79.

Henoch, M., & Chesky, K. S. (2000a). [Distortion product otoacoustic emissions: A more sensitive measure of changes in cochlea function related to music induced hearing loss]. Unpublished raw data.

Henoch, M., & Chesky, K. S. (2000b). Sound levels experienced by a college jazz band: Comparison to OSHA Standards. *Medical Problems of Performing Artists, 15*(1), 17–22.

Houston, J. D., & Fiore, D. C. (1998). Online medical surveys: Using the Internet as a research tool. *M.D. Computing, 15*(2), 116–120.

Howard, J. A., & Lovrovich, A. T. (1989, June). Wind instruments: Their interplay with orofacial structures. *Medical Problems of Performing Artists, 4*(2), 59–72.

Jansson, E., & Karlsson, K. (1983). Sound levels recorded within the symphony orchestra and risk criteria for hearing loss. *Scandinavian Audiology, 12*, 215–221.

Jerger, J., & Jerger, S. (1970). Temporary threshold shift in rock-and-roll musicians. *Journal of Speech and Hearing Research, 13*, 218–224.

Johnson, D. W., Sherman, R. E., Aldridge, J., & Lorraine, A. (1986). Effects of instrument type and orchestral position on hearing sensitivity for 0.25 to 20 kHz in the orchestral musician. *Scandinavian Audiology, 14*, 215–221.

Karlsson, K., Lundquist, P. G., & Olaussen, T. (1983). The hearing of symphony orchestra musicians. *Scandinavian Audiology, 12*, 257–264.

Kendrick, M., Craig, D., Lawson, D., & Davidson, P. (1982). Cognitive and behavioral therapy for musical-performance anxiety. *Journal of Consulting and Clinical Psychology, 50*(3), 353–362.

Kondraske, G. V. (2000). A working model for human system-task interfaces. In J. Bronzino (Ed.), *The biomedical engineering handbook* (2nd ed., pp. 147.1–147.17). Boca Raton, FL: CRC Press.

Kondraske, G. V., & Beehler, P. J. (1994). Applying general systems performance theory and the elemental resource model to gender-related issues in physical education and sport. *Women in Physical Education and Sport Journal, 3*(2), 1–19.

Kondraske, G. V., Chesky, K. S., & Rubin, B. (in press). Investigation of relationships between musician performance capacities, playing style, and performance related injuries in clarinetists. *Archives of Physical Medicine.*

Kondraske, G. V., Johnston, C., Pearson, A., & Tarbox, L. (1997). Performance prediction and limiting resource identification with nonlinear causal resource analysis. *Proceedings, Nineteenth Annual Engineering in Medicine and Biology Society Conference* (pp. 128–137).

Lammers, M., & Kruger, M. (1991). The right arm of trombonists: A pedagogical reference. *ITA Journal, 19*(3), 14–15.

Manchester, R. A. (1988). The incidence of hand problems in music students. *Medical Problems of Performing Artists, 3*(1), 15–18.

Mansfield, J. D., Baghurst, P. A., & Newton, V. E. (1999). Otoacoustic emissions in 28 young adults exposed to amplified music. *British Journal of Audiology, 33*, 211–222.

Marlatt, G., & Gordon, J. (1998). Treatment of comorbid addictive behaviors: Harm reduction as an alternative to abstinence. *In session: Psychotherapy in practice.* New York: Wiley.

Mazzeo, R. (1989). Mazzeo musings. *The Clarinet, 16*(2), 7–9.

McBride, D., Gill, G., Proops, D., Harrington, M., Gardiner, K., & Attwell, C. (1992). Noise and the classical musician. *British Medical Journal, 305*, 1561–1563.

Middlestadt, S. E., & Fishbein, M. (1988). Health and occupational correlates of perceived stress in symphony orchestra musicians. *Journal of Occupational Medicine, 30*(9), 687–692.

Middlestadt, S. E., & Fishbein, M. (1989). The prevalence of severe musculoskeletal problems among male and female symphony string players. *Medical Problems of Performing Artists, 4*(1), 41–48.

Nagel, J., Himle, D., & Papsdorf, H. (1989). Cognitive-behavioral treatment of musical performance anxiety. *Psychology of Music, 17*, 12–21.

National Association of Schools of Music. (2001). *Handbook.* Reston, VA: Author.

National Endowment for the Arts Research Division. (1998). Artist employment in America—1997. [On-line]. *National Endowment for the Arts.* Available: http://arts.endow.gov/Resource/Catalogue/RDN61.DOC [1998, June 26].

National Institute of Occupational Safety and Health. (1996). *Preventing Occupational Hearing Loss* (DHHS Publication No. 96-110).

Newmark, J., & Lederman, R. J. (1987). Practice doesn't necessarily make perfect: Incidence of overuse syndromes in amateur instrumentalists. *Medical Problems of Performing Artists, 2*(4), 142–144.

Niemann, B., Pratt, R., & Maughan, M. (1993). Bio-feedback training, selected coping strategies, and music relaxation interventions to reduce debilitative musical performance anxiety. *International Journal of Arts Medicine, 2,* 7–15.

Occupational Safety and Health Administration: Occupational noise exposure: Hearing conservation amendment. (1983). *Federal Register, 46,* 9738–9785.

O'Conner, B., & Dyce, J. (1997). Interpersonal rigidity, hostility, and complementarity in musical bands. *Journal of Personality and Social Psychology, 72*(2), 362–372.

Oeken, J. (1998). Topodiagnostic assessment of occupational noise-induced hearing loss using distortion-product otoacoustic emissions compared to the short increment sensitivity index test. *European Archives of Otorhinolaryngology, 256,* 115–121.

Olson, B. (1997). The social psychology of music education. In D. Hargreaves & A. North (Eds.), *The social psychology of music* (pp. 255–287). Oxford: Oxford University Press.

Ostri, B., Eller, N., Dahlin, E., & Skylv, G. (1989). Hearing impairment in orchestral musicians. *Scandinavian Audiology, 18,* 243–249.

Ostwald, P. (1987). Psychotherapeutic strategies in the treatment of performing artists. *Medical Problems of Performing Artists, 2*(4), 131–136.

Pak, C., & Chesky, K. (2001). Prevalence of hand, finger, and wrist musculoskeletal problems in keyboard instruments: The University of North Texas Musician Health Survey. *Medical Problems of Performing Artists, 16*(1), 17–23.

Papsin, B. C., Maaske, L. A., & McGrail, S. (1996). Orbicularis oris muscle injury in brass players. *Laryngoscope, 106,* 757–760.

Parasuraman, S., & Purohit, Y. (2000). Distress and boredom among orchestra musicians: The two faces of stress. *Journal of Occupational Health Psychology, 5*(1), 74–83.

Pick, G. F., & Evans, E. F. (1983). Dissociation between frequency resolution and hearing threshold. In R. Klinke & R. Hartmann (Eds.), *Hearing: Physiological bases and psychophysics* (pp. 393–398). Berlin: Springer-Verlag.

Piparek, M. (1981). Psychological stress and strain factors in the work of a symphony orchestra musician. In M. Piparek (Ed.), *Stress and music* (pp. 8–13). Vienna: Braumuller.

Pratt, R., Jessop, S., & Niemann, B. (1992). Performance-related disorders among music majors at Brigham Young University. *International Journal of Arts Medicine, 12,* 7–20.

Raeburn, S. (1987a). Occupational stress and coping in a sample of professional rock musicians: Part 1. *Medical Problems of Performing Artists, 2,* 41–48.

Raeburn, S. (1987b). Occupational stress and coping in a sample of professional rock musicians: Part 2. *Medical Problems of Performing Artists, 2,* 77–82.

Raeburn, S. (1999). Psychological issues and treatment strategies in popular musicians: A review: Part 1. *Medical Problems of Performing Artists, 14*(4), 171–179.

Raeburn S. (2000). Psychological issues and treatment strategies in popular musicians: A review: Part 2. *Medical Problems of Performing Artists, 15*(1), 6–17.

Reddell, R. C., & Lebo, C. P. (1972). Ototraumatic effects of hard rock music. *California Medicine, 116,* 1–4.

Riihimaki, H. (1995). Hands up or back to work: future challenges in epidemiologic research on musculoskeletal diseases. *Scandinavian Journal of Work, Environment, and Health, 21*(6), 401–403.

Rose, J. (1994). Communication challenges and roll functions of performing groups. *Small Group Research, 25*(3), 411–432.

Royster, J. D., Royster, L. H., & Killion, M. C. (1991). Sound exposures and hearing thresholds of symphony orchestra musicians. *Journal of the Acoustical Society of America, 89*(6), 2793–2803.

Salmon, P. G. (1990). A psychological perspective on musical performance anxiety: A review of the literature. *Medical Problems of Performing Aritsts, 5,* 1–11.

Sataloff, R., Rosen, D., & Levy, S. (1999). Medical treatment of performance anxiety. *Medical Problems of Performing Artists, 14*(3), 122–126.

Sataloff, R. T. (1991). Hearing loss in musicians. *American Journal of Otology, 12*(2), 122–127.

Sataloff, R. T., Spiegel, J. R., & Hawkshaw, M. (1990). The effects of respiratory dysfunction on instrumentalists. *Medical Problems of Performing Artists, 5*(2), 94–97.

Schmidt, J. M., Verschuure, J., & Brocaar, M. P. (1994). Hearing loss in students at a conservatory. *Audiology, 33,* 185–194.

Schuman, J. S., Massicotte, E. C., Connolly, S., Hertzmark, M. S., Mukherji, B., & Kunen, M. Z. (2000). Increased intraocular pressure and visual field defects in high resistance wind instrument players. *Ophthalmology, 107*(1), 127–133.

Shoup, D. (1995). Survey of performance-related problems among high school and junior high school musicians. *Medical Problems of Performing Artists, 10*(3), 100–105.

Spence, C. (2001). Prevalence rates for medical problems among flautists: A comparison of the UNT-Musican Health Survey and Flute Health Survey. *Medical Problems of Performing Artists, 16*(3), 99–101.

Steptoe, A. (1989). Stress, coping, and stage fright in professional musicians. *Psychology of Music, 17,* 3–11.

Sternbach, D. (1995). Musicians: A neglected working population in crisis. In S. Sauter & L. Murphy (Eds.), *Organizational risk factors for stress* (pp. 283–302). Washington, DC: American Psychological Association.

Taubenheim, A. M. (1999). Conducting survey research on the Internet: Use of the Internet to search for information on arthritis and musculoskeletal and skin diseases. Unpublished doctoral dissertation, University of Maryland, College Park.

Thrasher, M., & Chesky, K. S. (1998). Medical problems of clarinetists: Results from the UNT Musician Health Survey. *The Clarinet, 25*(4), 24–27.

Thrasher, M., & Chesky, K. S. (1999). Medical problems of saxophonists: A comparison of physical and psychological dysfunction among classical and non-classical performers. *Saxophone Symposium, 24,* 77–84.

Thrasher, M., & Chesky, K. S. (in press). Medical problems of double reed performers. *Medical Problems of Performing Artists.*

Tucker, A., Faulkner, M. E., & Horvath, S. M. (1971). Electrocardiography and lung function in brass instrument players. *Archives of Environmental Health, 23,* 327–334.

Van Klemenade, J., Van Son, M., & Van Heesch. N. (1995). Performance anxiety among professional musicians in symphonic orchestras: A self-report study. *Psychological Reports, 77,* 555–562.

Wesner, R., Noyes, R., & Davis, T. (1990). The occurrence of performance anxiety among musicians. *Journal of Affective Disorders, 18,* 177–185.

Westmore, G. A., & Eversden, I. D. (1981). Noise-induced hearing loss and orchestral musicians. *Archives of Otolaryngology, 107,* 761–764.

Wilkinson, L., & Task Force on Statistical Inference. (2000). Statistical methods in psychology journals: Guidelines and explanations. [On-line]. *American Psychological Association.* Available: http://www.apa.org/journals/amp/amp 548594.htm [2000, July 8].

Wills, G., & Cooper, C. (1988). *Pressure sensitive: Popular musicians under stress.* London: Sage.

Wilson, G. (1984). The personality of opera singers. *Personality and Individual Differences, 5,* 195–201.

Wolverton, D., & Salmon, P. (1991). Attention allocation and motivation in music performance anxiety. In G. Wilson (Ed.), *Psychology and performing arts* (pp. 231–237). Amsterdam: Zeitlinger and Swets.

World Health Organization. (1985). Identification and control of work-related diseases (Technical Report No. 174). Geneva: Author.

Young, J., & Hipple, J. (1996). Social/emotional problems of university music students seeking assistance at a student counseling center. *Medical Problems of Performing Artists, 11*(4), 123–126.

Young, J., Hipple, J., & Chesky, K. (1999). Do music major clients present different problems than non-music major clients? *Medical Problems of Performing Artists, 14*(3), 150–153.

Zaza, C. (1994). Research based prevention for musicians. *Medical Problems of Performing Artists, 9*(1), 3–6.

Part IX

OUTCOMES IN GENERAL EDUCATION

Michael L. Mark
Editor

Introduction

MICHAEL L. MARK

Music educators, like visual art, dance, and theater teachers, find themselves in a paradoxical age. Music education thrives in schools, performance standards continue to rise with each new generation of students, and the demand for new music teachers increases each year. The paradox is that, in this time of plenty, a belief in the nonmusical power of music education has spread throughout the country, persuading politicians, education policy-makers, and the general public that children who study music tend to perform better in other subjects. There is a research base that supports this belief. There is also a research base that contradicts it. In any case, the belief in nonmusical values of music instruction has added a new facet to music education, one that is good for the profession and that, ironically, threatens the core belief of many music educators who are adamant that the principal benefit of their profession lies in the development of aesthetic sensitivity to music.

Nonmusical values of music education have guided the profession throughout Western history. For well over 2,000 years, music education has played many roles, including supporting religious, intellectual, and physical aspects of life and promoting community, whether in the form of nationalism or ethnic society. Music educators have proven during this long history that music can indeed do these things. It was not until the 20th century, however, that the profession of music education began to argue that the true value of the study of music was in the music itself and how individuals respond to it. Regardless of what people believed, it was not until recently that research findings related to psychological and neurological responses have allowed music educators to offer a rationale based on solid scientific support.

The conviction that music education is to be valued for nonmusical purposes became a trend in the 1990s. Promoted by such music education advocates as the Music Educators National Conference and VH1 Save the Music, legislators and other policy-makers have adopted resolutions and policies and enacted laws that support music education, sometimes in conjunction with other arts disciplines. The most visible achievement of music education advocacy was the inclusion of the arts in the Goals 2000 Act of 1994. From that law came the National Education Standards of 1996, which served as a model for many states in developing their own standards.

The implementation of music education for its nonmusical values is often in the form of curricular integration, in which music is infused into the general education curriculum. The musically enriched curriculum is believed by many to elevate student achievement in other subjects, to increase standardized test scores, and to improve attendance and attitudes toward school. Curricular infusion is a goal of many state departments of education. A typical example is the Maryland Artist/Teacher Institute (MATI), sponsored each summer by the Maryland State Department of Education. Teams of educators from elementary schools, including the principals, classroom teachers, resource teachers, and arts specialists, spend a week digesting a philosophy of infusion and acquiring techniques and materials from artist educators. Similar programs are sponsored by other state departments of education and by private, not-for-profit organizations like the Galef Institute in Los Angeles. Galef supports arts-rich curricula in many states. The Galef Institute writes that it "helps compensate for cutbacks in art and music programs by placing the visual, performing, and literary arts at the heart of the curriculum. . . . [It] uses the visual arts, music, drama, dance, and literature, and hands-on approaches to learning as a key to open the door to all subject areas." A sampling of other initiatives, many supported by grants from the Annenberg Foundation, include the Center for Arts Education

Partnership Programs (New York City), Transforming Education Through the Arts (six regional consortia in California, Florida, Nebraska, Ohio, Tennessee, and Texas), several programs of the Lola and Rudy Perpich Minnesota Center for Arts Education, the Chicago Arts Partnerships in Education, and the A+ Schools Program (North Carolina). It is noteworthy that most preservice and in-service teacher training in arts integration comes from entities other than institutions of higher education. Some colleges and universities have addressed themselves to the subject, but most have not. The principal involvement of teacher education institutions has been in the research arena. As mentioned earlier, the myriad of research studies offers conflicting findings on the nonmusical values of music education.

The following three chapters cover the history of nonmusical values of music education, music education as an instrument for teaching nonmusical subjects, and research that advocates find relevant for their work with policymakers.

Nonmusical Outcomes of Music Education: Historical Considerations

55

MICHAEL L. MARK

Undoubtedly, people have always studied music in informal settings for the pleasure it has given them. For the purpose of this chapter, however, a distinction is made between informal and formal music education in order to focus on nonmusical outcomes of the study of music in formal education systems. In the context of this chapter, nonmusical outcomes are those that serve any purpose other than developing the learner's sensitivity to the aesthetic component of music.

The subject of nonmusical outcomes of formal music education is rich in historical roots, embracing the opinions and theories of educators, religious leaders, civic leaders, philosophers, psychologists, neuroscientists, and others. It has continually, for millennia, referred to behavioral conformity, effects on intelligence, skill development, and religiosity. The literature on this subject is so broad and embracing that one who is familiar with it might well ask what purpose music education serves other than nonmusical values. Although music educators have probably never been insensitive to the sheer joy of music, it was only in the second half of the twentieth century that a widespread philosophy of music education, based on extensive research and reflective thinking, recognized the value of music education as knowledge and appreciation of the music itself. That philosophy, aesthetic education, will be discussed later in this chapter.

For the Good of the Society: Intellectual, Moral, Physical

Generally, nonmusical outcomes of music education have always been expected to influence individuals in ways that would help them support the values of their communities or societies. This was to occur as the result of the intellectual, moral, and physical benefits of music study. These three benefits, stated in the 1838 report of the Boston School Committee, were the essence of the rationale for the committee's recommendation that music be included in the curriculum of the Boston schools: "There is a threefold standard, a sort of chemical test, by which education itself and every branch of education may be tried. Is it intellectual—is it moral—is it physical? Let vocal Music be examined by this standard" (p. 123). The lengthy examination, in the flowery journalistic language of the day, acknowledged that music satisfied the tripartite standard, and school music instruction was indeed implemented the following year. The three-pronged rationale serves as point of reference for examining and interpreting virtually every formal music education system throughout Western history, from the early Hebrews to contemporary music education. Other rationales, including community cohesiveness and professional training, appear at various times and places as well. Taken together, the rationales serve both the individual and the greater society that sponsors a formalized system of music instruction. I will examine and analyze some of the ways Western societies expected music education to produce the desired outcomes.

Who Spoke for Music Education?

To understand why music education was expected to instill nonmusical values, we must be aware of who actually spoke for music education throughout Western history. Those people who left writings about the role of music education, who explained to us why music education was important to their societies, were not music educators.

They were philosophers, religious leaders, aristocrats, civic officials, and others who were concerned with matters beyond who was to receive music instruction and who was to teach it. Their concerns usually were related to the preservation and advancement of their societies. A sampling of historical writings on music education that inform us about our professional history might include those of Plato, Aristotle, St. Augustine, Boethius, Charlemagne, Martin Luther, John Calvin, John Amos Comenius, John Locke, Johann Heinrich Pestalozzi, and Herbert Spencer, among others. These figures recognized that music education has some capacity to help achieve or maintain certain desirable societal characteristics, whether spiritual or communal (Mark, 1994).

The same phenomenon occurred in America. From colonial days, societal leaders continued the tradition of writing about music education. Thus we find written testimony for the teaching of music by Cotton Mather, the Boston School Committee, Horace Mann, and many others. By the 19th century, we begin to see more writings by music educators. The contributions of Lowell Mason and others began to form a new literary genre—the justification of music education necessary to maintain its support by the greater society. A fairly substantial body of literature had accumulated by the 20th century when the insights of Oscar Handlin, Will Earhart, Walter Damrosch, Karl Gehrkens, Horatio Parker, Osbourne McConathy, W. Otto Miessner, Hazel Nohavec Morgan, Russell V. Morgan, Frances Elliott Clark, and many others became available in publications and public addresses. Philosophers and psychologists were added to the list with the writings of John Dewey, Max Schoen, and James L. Mursell, and others. By the middle of the 20th century, there was a substantial body of literature that illuminated the benefits of music education and why it should be supported in the schools (Mark, 1999).

Music Education in Earlier Times

The Hebrews of the Old Testament provide an early example of music instruction for both religious and communal purposes. Moses could well have been the first music educator as we use the term today. He not only demonstrated the use of music but also composed and taught it (Deut. 31:13, 19, 22). As formalized religious rituals developed, everyone was expected to participate. Formal instruction developed later when community representatives traveled to Jerusalem, where they were taught music by Levites in a synagogue (Idelsohn, 1948). In a community that expected and depended on universal participation, the communal benefits of music education are obvious.

Ancient Greek society prized learning, and much of its education system was built on music. In Athens, choral singing was integral to religious ceremonies held by the city. They were sometimes accompanied by intertribal choral competitions, which, like present-day musical and athletic competitions, built community spirit. Boys learned music in the warrior city-state of Sparta to develop loyalty to the state, which was a Spartan version of community spirit. Plato's writings on music education are widely known. His idealized society depended on education to shape ideal citizens. Music and gymnastics were the basis of the formal education curriculum of his utopian society—music for the soul, gymnastics for the body (Idelsohn, 1948, pp. 9, 10). The soul, in this case, reflects the view that music affected moral development. Plato wrote in *The Republic:* "Education in music is most sovereign, because more than anything else rhythm and harmony find their way to the innermost soul and take strongest hold upon it, bringing with them and imparting grace, if one is rightly trained, and otherwise the contrary" (Plato, 1984, p. 322).

Centuries later, after the fall of Rome, the emperor Charlemagne recognized the value of music in education. Establishing a basic curriculum for the 9th-century Carolingian Empire, he wrote: "There should be schools for boys who can read. The Psalms, the notation, the chant, and arithmetic and grammar [ought to be taught] in all monasteries and episcopacies." The same decree required that clerics were to learn the Roman chant. With the unification of religious and civic authority in the Holy Roman Empire, music was a means of enhancing the religious experience, thereby reinforcing the authority of the state (Charlemagne, 1956, pp. 54–55). An ignominious example of the use of religious music education to control a population occurred when Cortes conquered Mexico in 1521. It was in the best interest of Spain, as both a civil and religious power, to convert the natives to Catholicism, thereby strengthening the Europeans' control and ensuring the loyalty of the natives. Cortes brought Pedro de Gante to Mexico in 1523 to teach the Indians the music of the church, which he did admirably well. Heller (1979) wrote:

> Fully 100 years before any sizeable colonization efforts were noticeable in North America, his [de Gante's] students in Mexico City were singing European music, copying Franco-Flemish polyphony, playing and building violins and organs, and composing and teaching music in the European style. (p. 2)

The cruel truth, however, is that the indigenous native culture was destroyed, the Indians were enslaved, and the theft of their gold and silver made Spain wealthy almost beyond imagination.

Formal music education for the purpose of training professional musicians began at some undefined time in the shadows of the past, but we know that as the church developed throughout the Middle Ages and the Renaissance there was always a need for choristers to participate in religious rituals. The nobility depended on professional musicians, and municipalities employed musicians for civic ceremonies and rituals. A career as musician was one of the few means by which musically capable people could escape a life of impoverished servitude. The Italian addiction to opera created an insatiable demand for singers and musicians. In Venice alone, where 1,200 new operas were performed in the 18th century, such composers as Monteverdi, Cavalli, Porpora, and Vivaldi composed music to help train students in charitable asylums, *conservatoria*, to become professional musicians in the opera houses (Mark & Gary, 1992, pp. 34–35).

In the realm of higher education, the medieval and Renaissance universities carried on the Roman tradition of the seven liberal arts. Students studied the quadrivium (arithmetic, geometry, astronomy, and music) to understand the physical and mystical world in which they lived. Kresteff (1962) wrote: "It [quadrivium] constituted the only way one could penetrate into the mysteries of physical and spiritual realities and gain knowledge of the ultimate reason and truth dwelling beyond them" (p. 19). The quadrivium "was the vehicle by which one could learn the secrets of the universe" (Mark & Gary, 1992, p. 19).

There are many other writings, too numerous to cite here, about nonmusical values of music education throughout the Renaissance and the centuries that followed. These writings, like those already discussed, indicate that morality was the principal goal of music education. Morality is a relative trait that varies from one society to another, but generally, children who were educated correctly and with the proper kinds of music were expected to become mature citizens whose lives were in harmony with their communities.

Across centuries and an ocean, in the British colonies in the New World, formal music education was introduced by singing masters. The quality of congregational singing suffered increasingly with each new generation of Americans, and many ministers complained about it. In 1721, Thomas Walter said:

> The tunes are now miserably tortured and twisted and quavered in our churches, into a horrid medly of confused and disorderly voices. Our tunes are left to the mercy of every unskilled throat to chop and alter, to twist and change, according to their infinitely diverse and no less odd humours and fancies. (Quoted in Fisher, 1918, p. 5)

The solution was the establishment of singing schools by singing masters, entrepreneurs who charged tuition for their classes, in which they taught the rudiments of music

and sight reading. The singing schools not only served a religious purpose but were also popular as social meeting places. They were an early example of American music education satisfying both religious and community needs.

The three-part rationale of the Boston School Committee was used by many school systems as they introduced music into their schools as a curricular subject throughout the 19th century and into the 20th. The committee's report also contained a statement that related music to quality of life and might even be considered a precursor to the philosophy of aesthetic education: "The defect of our present system, admirable as that system is, is this, that it aims to develop the intellectual part of man's nature solely, when for all the true purposes of life, it is of more importance, a hundred fold, to feel rightly, than to think profoundly" (Boston School Committee, 1838, p. 1). This remarkable insight is a historical connection between Plato and the late-20th-century music education philosophy of aesthetic education.

The statement about feeling rightly was echoed in 1897, when John Dewey also acknowledged Plato's view of music education: "We need to return more to the Greek conception, which defined education as the attaching of pleasure and pain to the right objects and ideals in the right way" (Dewey, 1897, pp. 329–330). Dewey's supposition was reflected in the introduction of one of the most popular basal series of the time, the *Progressive Music Series*:

> The general aim of education is to train the child to become a capable, useful, and contented member of society. The development of a fine character and of the desire to be of service to humanity are results that lie uppermost in the minds of the leaders of educational thought. . . . Music, because of its powerful influence upon the very innermost recesses of our subject life, because of its wonderfully stimulating effect upon our physical, mental, and spiritual nature . . . contributes directly to both of the fundamental purposes of education. (Parker, McConathy, & Miessner, 1916, p. 9)

The same motif was sometimes echoed by commercial interests. The publisher of *The Universal Series* asserted in a 1926 advertisement that its basal series "stimulates children's aesthetic interests through music and lyrics that are beautiful, satisfying and exalting and tend to enrich, refine and enoble their entire lives" (*Cultural! The Universal Series*, 1926, p. 27).

By the second decade of the 20th century, not only had music become an integral part of school programs throughout the country, but adult musical activities reflected school programs as well. Community singing was done by large gatherings of people both in public places and at private work sites. In 1913, 6 years after it was founded, the Music Supervisors National Conference

(MSNC; later MENC) established its Community Song Committee, and soon music teachers were taking their skills and talents beyond the schools as they led community sings using the MSNC book *Eighteen Songs for Community Singing*. The songs in that book, like "America," "Annie Laurie," "Auld Lang Syne," "Drink to Me Only with Thine Eyes," and others, were part of a common national music heritage with which many Americans could identify. The purpose of making them easily available in *Eighteen Songs* (5 cents per copy) was affirmed as follows:

> Of a much deeper significance than the mere singing of these few songs is . . . the spread of community feeling voiced in a better understanding, good-will—a real brotherhood. The singing in its larger significance is extended as a means of stimulating a feeling of solidarity which should exist in a community between man and man, for when a country becomes one in lifting its voice in singing the same good songs a note is struck for harmony of understanding, mutual good-will, and similar ideals. (*18 Songs for Community Singing*, 1913, p. 6)

There were even neighborhood sings in large cities:

> The street sing in all its roughness enriches the emotional life of many who never see the inside of a concert hall, seldom or never go to church, and who wouldn't know what you were talking about if you advertised a "community sing." It is a first step in reclaiming the desert places which have sprung up in the midst of our civilization. It sows a seed which, if properly nourished, will bear much fruit in the cause both of music and good citizenship. (Bartholomew & Lawrence, 1920, p. 89)

Community singing was a way for communities to celebrate together the seasons and national events, it was a means of selling bonds to finance wars, and it was also done for no particular reason other than that it was enjoyable and uplifting.

The Business of Music Education Helps Build Community Spirit

The 20th century presented many new opportunities for music publishers, manufacturers, and retailers, and it could be said that one of the nonmusical values of music education was its importance to industry—what's good for business is good for the country. Industry was largely responsible for the growth of instrumental music in schools, especially bands. The military bands of World War I had created a highly profitable market that needed to be replaced after the Armistice. Ingeniously, the music industry conceived and promoted the band contest movement. The contests solidified the place of bands in American schools and at the same time guaranteed a thriving market for

years to come for band instruments, music, uniforms, and paraphernalia. The band contests, like high school athletic teams, created strong and cohesive community spirit, especially for those communities fortunate enough to sponsor winning bands (Mark, 1992a). The experience of William D. Revelli demonstrates the extent of community support for a winning band. Revelli was director of the Hobart (Indiana) High School Band during the Great Depression. When the community was called on to sacrifice beyond reasonable expectations to keep its band going, it did so willingly. Having won the National Band Contest in 1930, the people of Hobart wanted to continue sponsoring a winner. Revelli recalled:

> The band's success was the source of what was probably the greatest community pride that Hobart ever developed. Hobart became famous and respected. The community responded by providing the moral and economic support necessary for the band to develop into and remain the best. The expense was great, and it is an indication of the community's pride that it supplied significant financial support for equipment, music, and travel during the Great Depression, when money for food was often scarce. (Mark, 1980, p. 9)

One year in the early 1930s, Hobart could not even afford to keep its schools open for the entire year. When they closed in the spring, Revelli was able to rehearse his band on a full-time basis, giving him much more time to prepare for the state, regional, and national contests (Mark, 1980, p. 10).

Aesthetic Education, Advocacy, and the Mozart Effect

American education began to undergo profound change in the early 1950s, when it became apparent that the schools were not equipped to prepare students adequately for the emerging technological age. This was during the Cold War, when the threat of a catastrophic military conflict with the Soviet Union loomed over the nation. Educators began to emphasize those subjects that would help the nation remain a world power. In 1959, both educators and scientists expressed concern for an unbalanced curriculum. The American Association of School Administrators (AASA) asserted:

> [W]e believe in a well-balanced school curriculum in which music, drama, painting, poetry, sculpture, architecture, and the like are included side by side with other important subjects such as mathematics, history, and science. It is important that pupils, as a part of general education, learn to appreciate, to understand, to create, and to criticize with discrimination those produces of the mind, the voice, the

hand, and the body which give dignity to the person and exalt the spirit of man. (American Association of School Administrators [AASA], 1959, pp. 248–249)

The National Education Association (NEA) spoke out for a balanced curriculum in a report calling for "fundamental understanding of the humanities and the arts, the social sciences and the natural sciences, and literature, music, and the visual arts" (Sand, 1963, p. 101). Scientists agreed with AASA and NEA. The White House Panel on Educational Research and Development said:

> Certain members of the Panel were convinced that there was a degree of correlation between excellence in scientific achievement and the breadth of an individual's human experience. The best scientists, it was thought, were not necessarily those who had devoted themselves singlemindedly to their own field; somehow, familiarity with the arts and humanities sharpened a good scientist's vision. (Lowens, 1971, p. E4)

Music education needed visionary leadership to make it an integral part of the dawning new curriculum, and its leaders began to discourage music educators from promoting the nonmusical benefits of music education, referring to them in their writings and addresses as "ancillary," "instrumental," and "utilitarian" values. Music educators began to support the position that the value of music education was to be found in the music itself. This clearly was part of the progression toward the development of the philosophy of aesthetic education. Charles Leonhard (1965) wrote:

> While reliance on statements of the nonmusical value of music may well have convinced some reluctant administrator to more fully support the music program, those values cannot stand close scrutiny, because they are not unique to music. In fact, many other areas of the curriculum are in a position to make a more powerful contribution to these values than is music. (p. 42)

Allen Britton (1958) agreed: "Many who seek to justify the present place of music in American schools tend to place too heavy a reliance upon ancillary values which music may certainly serve but which cannot, in the end, constitute its justification" (p. 195). A small group of music educators turned to the field of philosophy, studying the writings of such aestheticians as Leonard Meyer and Susanne Langer. They began the development of what would become known as aesthetic education. The 1970 publication of Bennett Reimer's book, *A Philosophy of Music Education,* provided a bible for the philosophy, and the publication of the second edition in 1989 indicates that the philosophy of aesthetic education remains influential. J. Terry Gates (2000) said in the Vision 2020 Symposium, "Bennett Reimer and his philosophical predecessors such

as Charles Leonhard, Harry Broudy, and James Mursell argue for a music-based rationale for music study, rather than a justification based on extramusical benefits. This . . . is a value that music teachers share" (p. 65).

At about the time that the aesthetic education movement was maturing, new developments in cognitive psychology and advocacy were also occurring (see Wolff, 1978). Howard Gardner, codirector of Project Zero at Harvard University, posed his theory of multiple intelligences, which has provided strong support for the unique value of arts education (Gardner, 1983). Gardner was followed by several others who also identified artistic intelligence as a unique way of knowing (Mark, 1996, pp. 653–654). The new theories of learning fueled the advocacy efforts of MENC, and the entry of neuroscientists into the study of the effects of music education helped stimulate public support for the profession to a degree that was unanticipated only a few years earlier. The MENC's advocacy efforts, drawn largely from research findings, have had a profound impact on public perception of music education. The study that was best known to the public and policy-makers and that music education advocates locked onto was Rauscher, Shaw, and Ky (1995). It was this study that made the public aware of the "Mozart effect," which indicated a relationship between listening to the music of Mozart and increased intelligence in children. Although this study has had little effect on music education practices and has been controversial among researchers, it triggered an even higher level of public interest in nonmusical outcomes of music education. Since that time there has been a virtual flood of research studies, many of which have been cited by MENC in its advocacy efforts to the public and to policy-makers, including the United States Congress. Research in nonmusical outcomes has become a focus of interest for the fields of cognitive sciences and behavioral neuroscience, in part because music is an entry point for study of the mind and body. A review of numerous Websites confirms that the subject has become a topic of central interest for many music educators, psychologists, and scientists of varying interests. MENC published in its book *Music Makes the Difference* (2000, pp. 134–144) an annotated bibliography of publications in scientific journals, professional journals, and the popular press and of websites; Liora Bresler describes some of these studies in her chapter entitled "Research in Advocacy Outcomes" in this book.

One result of the new scientific focus on music education is a flurry of studies on how music supports learning in other subjects. Music educators have made this claim for a long time; it surfaced in actual school situations and became controversial in the early 1970s when Congress reauthorized Title I of the Elementary and Secondary Education Act, making funds for music instruction dependent on its effectiveness in supporting instruction in reading, writing, and mathematics. Some school districts accepted this new challenge and found ways to justify the relationship between music and communication and computational skills (Mark, 1996, p. 6). Others, unable to prove such a claim, lost Title I funds for their music programs. This was the first time in the history of American music education that the federal government required school administrators to justify music programs on the basis of nonmusical objectives. Now it is a given among many educators that music supports instruction in other subjects. This relationship is explored in chapter 56, "Teaching Other Subjects Through Music," by Merryl Goldberg and Carol Kassner.

The new research has shown up in other venues as well. Some symphony orchestras, for example, acknowledge it in their education programs. The Baltimore Symphony Orchestra (2000), describing its education program, "Arts Excel" (similar to programs sponsored by other orchestras), says: "The program's goal is to introduce an arts-integrated curriculum into the schools using music and the other arts as tools to teach such core subjects as mathematics, social studies, science and language skills." Since the business of professional orchestras is to maintain audiences, it is curious that they would focus their education programs on teaching subjects other than music.

The music industry is equally enthusiastic, having jumped on the bandwagon to publicize the new data and information. The industry sponsors advertisements, displays at conventions, and television spots. One example is a booklet published by United Musical Instrument U.S.A., a coalition of six musical instrument manufacturers formed in 1985. The publication, *Spin-Offs: The Extra-Musical Advantages of a Musical Education* (Cutietta, Haman, & Walker, 1995), was written by three prominent music educators. There has also been significant foundation support for music and arts education related to research. For example, the GE Fund and the MacArthur Foundation sponsored a report, *Champions of Change: The Impact of the Arts on Learning* (President's Committee on the Arts and Humanities, 1999), which compiled seven research studies on the subject. The federal government participated as well, when Richard Riley, the U.S. secretary of education, wrote in the introduction that the findings "address ways that our nation's educational goals may be realized through enhanced arts learning" (p. vi). In a speech to the MENC, he discussed nonmusical values of arts education, thereby assuring music educators that their work had the support of the executive branch of the United States government (Riley, 2000). Following Riley's speech, President Clinton spoke for music education on national television. Nor was the executive branch the only one to speak out for arts education. In June 2000, the House of Representatives passed a resolution in support of music education.

The resolution, presented by Congressman David McIntosh (R-IN), read as follows:

> Music education has touched the lives of many young people. . . . It has taught them teamwork and discipline, while refining their cognitive and communications skills. Music education enables children with disabilities to participate more fully in school while motivating at-risk students to stay in school and become active participants in the educational process. (House of Representatives Concurrent Resolution 266 [2000])

MENC has framed the new research findings primarily in the form of advocacy for some time. It has, however, broadened its outlook, and its book *Music Makes the Difference: Music, Brain Development, and Learning* (2000) contains a section entitled "The Intrinsic Value of Music Education." In it is an adaptation of the rationale for music education originally published in its earlier book, *The School Music Program: Description and Standards* (Music Educators National Conference, 1987). The first of the 10 rationales says simply: "Music is worth knowing." The book's opening essay, "Talking Points," identifies four categories of benefits of music instruction and declares, regarding one, "success in society": "Perhaps the basic reason why every child must have an education in music is that music is a part of the fabric of our society . . . every human culture uses music to carry forward its ideas and ideals" (MENC, 2000, p. 3). Statements like this align current professional leadership with historic justifications for music education. They help broaden the views of educators, the public, and policy makers in regard to how music education serves society.

Conclusion

The history of nonmusical values of music education reaches back to the beginnings of Western culture. In return for society's sponsorship, music education has always been expected to serve particular communal needs in ways that go beyond the aesthetic component of music. At the turn of the 21st century, interest in the nonmusical values of music education remains strong. Public support and enthusiasm for music education continues to grow as educators and policy-makers seek new ways to increase student achievement in reading, writing, and computational skills. Although this brings economic and moral support to the profession, the reasons are somewhat disheartening to those who believe that the unique value of music education is rooted in the music itself and the ability of students to understand and respond to it. Diametrically opposite the nonmusical values that would make music a tool in teaching other subjects, the philosophy of aesthetic education remains a strong foundational belief of many music educators. The two views, one a rationale, the other a philosophy, exist ambiguously, side by side, and will probably continue to do so in the foreseeable future.

Perhaps it would be helpful to the contemporary music education profession to recognize that even the philosophy of aesthetic education can have a nonmusical outcome. As Plato said: "One who was properly educated in music . . . would praise beautiful things and take delight in them and receive them into his soul to foster its growth and become himself beautiful and good (1984, p. 643). The person who is properly educated in music, in other words, is a good citizen. If one agrees that good education leads to good citizenship, then Plato's statement might establish a connection between aesthetic development and good citizenship. And good citizenship, whether in the 5th century B.C. or the 21st century A.D., is a nonmusical value of music education.

Beyond the benefit of good citizenship, it is likely that music will continue to be justified on the basis of nonmusical outcomes, just as it has been throughout Western history. The tension between aesthetic and nonmusical outcomes is healthy for the profession because it stimulates music educators to think deeply about their profession and it strengthens the bond between the music education profession and the social and physical sciences that continually explore and analyze the effects of music on humans. As science develops, new thinking on the subject is bound to evolve. As yet it has had little effect on the teaching of music; in the future, however, it is quite possible that curricular developments will be based on the research of nonmusicians whose efforts illuminate the effects of music on humans.

REFERENCES

American Association for School Administrators. (1959). *Official report for the year 1958*. Washington, DC: American Association of School Administrators.

Baltimore Symphony Orchestra (2000, September 16–November 20). Arts excel reaches out. *Overture*.

Bartholomew, M. & Lawrence, R. (1920). *Music for everybody*. New York: Abingdon Press.

Boston School Committee. (1838, December 5, 12, 26). Report. *Boston Musical Gazette, 18*, p. 1.

Britton, A. (1958). Music in early American public education: A historical critique. In N. Henry (Ed.), *Basic Concepts in Music Education*. Chicago: National Society for the Study of Education.

Charlemagne. (1956). *Monumenta germania historica*. In G. Ellard, *Master Alcuin, liturgist*. Chicago: Loyola University Press.

Cultural! The Universal Series. (1926, March). *Music Supervisors Journal, 12*(4), 27.

Cutietta, R., Haman, D., & Walker, L. (1995). *Spin-offs: The extra-musical advantages of a musical education*. Elkhart, IN: United Musical Instruments, USA.

Dewey, J. (1897). The aesthetic element in education. In *Addresses and proceedings of the National Education Association*. Washington: National Education Association, 1897.

18 Song's [sic] for Community Singing. Boston: Birchard, 1913.

Fisher, W. A. (1918). *Notes on Music in Old Boston*. Boston: Ditson, 1918. Quoted in Birye, W. B. (1996). *History of public school music in the United States* (p. 5). Washington, DC: Music Educators National Conference.

Gardner, H. (1983). *Frames of mind: The theory of multiple intelligences*. New York: Basic Books.

Gates, J. T. (2000). Why study music? In C. Madsen (Ed.), *Vision 2020: The Housewright Symposium on the future of music education*. Reston, VA: Music Educators National Conference.

Heller, G. (1979). Fray Pedro de Gante, pioneer American music educator. *Journal of Research in Music Education, 27*, 23, 24.

Idelsohn, A. Z. (1948). *Jewish music in its historical development*. New York: Tudor.

Kresteff, A. D. (1962). Musical disciplina and musical sonora. *Journal of Research in Music Education, 10*, 13–29.

Leonhard, C. (1965). The philosophy of music education—past and future. In *Comprehensive musicianship: The foundation for college education in music*. Washington, DC: Music Educators National Conference.

Lowens, I. (1971, May 30). MUSIC: Juilliard Repertory Project and the schools. *The Sunday Star* [Washington, DC] p. E4.

Mark, M. L. (1980). William D. Revelli: Portrait of a distinguished career. *Journal of Band Research, 16*(1) 1–29.

Mark, M. L. (1992a). American music education in the national context, 1892–1992. In M. Fonder (Ed.), *The Ithaca conference on American music education: Centennial profiles*. Ithaca, NY: Ithaca College.

Mark, M. L. (1992b). *Source readings in music education history*. Charlottesville, VA: Lincoln-Rembrandt.

Mark, M. L. (1996). *Contemporary music education* (3rd ed). New York: Schirmer Books.

Mark, M. L. (1999). An historical interpretation of aesthetic education. *Journal of Aesthetic Education, 33*(4), 7–15.

Mark, M. L., & C. L. Gary. (1992). *A history of American music education* (2nd ed). Reston, VA: Music Educators National Conference.

Music Educators National Conference. (1987). *The school music program: Description and standards*. Reston, VA: Author.

Music makes the difference: Music, brain development, and learning. (2000). Reston, VA: Music Educators National Conference.

Parker, H., McConathy O., & Miessner, O. (1916). *The progressive music series. Teacher's manual: vol. 2*. Boston: Silver, Burdett.

Plato. (1984). *The collected dialogues of Plato* (E. Hamilton & H. Cairns, Eds.). Princeton: Princeton University Press.

President's Committee on the Arts and the Humanities. (1999). *Champions of change: The impact of the arts on learning.* Washington, DC: Council of Chief School Officers.

Rauscher, F., Shaw, G., & Ky, K. (1995). Listening to mozart enhances spatial-temporal reasoning. *Neuroscience Letters, 185,* 44–47.

Reimer, B. (1999). Facing the risks of the "Mozart effect." *Music Educators Journal, 86*(1), 37–43.

Reimer. (1989). *A philosophy of music education* (2nd ed.). Englewood Cliffs, NJ: Prentice-Hall.

Riley, R. W. (2000, March 9). Address to Music Educators National Conference, Washington, DC.

Sand, O. (1963, September). Current trends in curriculum planning. *Music Educators Journal, 50*(1), 128–131.

Sims, W. L., & Wilson, C. C. (2000). Annotated bibliography: Music, brain development, and learning. In *Music makes the difference: Music, brain development, and learning* (pp. 134–141). Reston, VA: Music Educators National Conference.

Wolff, K. (1978). The nonmusical outcomes of music education: A review of the literature. *Bulletin of the Council for Research in Music Education, 55,* 1–27.

Teaching Other Subjects Through Music

56

MERRYL GOLDBERG

CAROL SCOTT-KASSNER

Imagine a group of fourth graders listening to Gustav Holst's *The Planets*. They listen intently, contemplate, discuss in detail how the music represents the motion of the planets; and then the teacher poses the question to them: "How could we make a sound sculpture that would represent the orbital value of each planet?" In this chapter, we seek to uncover the issues and research related to teaching other subjects, like this science lesson, through music. In order to do so, we begin by offering an overview of historical, social/cultural, and theoretical perspectives. We then address the literature on classroom teachers and arts integration, including a discussion outlining the various ways teachers teach other subjects through music. A review of major studies in this area follows, and the chapter concludes with reflections and conclusions based on the research. In writing this chapter, we recognized that this topic brings with it considerable debate, and we embraced the controversies with interest and rigor.

Arts education in the United States is at a dynamic crossroads. For the past few decades music, visual art, drama, and dance have usually been taught as separate subjects in school, if they were taught at all (see Leonhard, 1991; National Endowment for the Arts [NEA], 1988). Of all the arts, music is the one most likely to be taught by a specialist teacher trained to teach that subject. This discipline-based model of music and arts education is fundamental to the education of children, giving them key skills and understandings through the sequential development of the tools needed to receive a basic education in each art form. A vision for student accomplishment in these disciplines is outlined in the National Standards for Arts Education (1994). Included in these standards is a call for the promotion of arts as a medium for integrating

learning across the curriculum within state and local planning efforts.

Historical Frame for Music in the Education of Humanity

Educational models are fluid and constantly changing. Integrated and interdisciplinary study is one model that educational reformers have embraced, or reembraced, as the history of educational reform reinvents itself. Though relatively new to the way music has been taught in U.S. classrooms for many years, integrating music with other subjects is not a new concept or debate in the historical, cultural, or global sense. According to James Hoffmann (1991), "music, a potent social instrument from earliest times, operates not merely in imitation of society but also in dynamic interaction with it" (p. 270). Music, in its many forms, has served as an educative tool throughout history, from disseminating information in the form of ballads to recounting events and emotions of history through song. Thus, a question musicologists have asked is: "Is there such a thing as autonomous music; a division between music and society?" The ideology of "autonomous art" is an important consideration (Leppert & McLary, 1987) in the debates concerning the role of music in society, history, and culture.

This dynamic relationship can be seen through an examination of the history of music in American public schools. The roles music has played have shifted with changes in society and with expectations for what it means to be an educated person. They have also shifted with changes in beliefs concerning the nature of children and

1053

how children learn. Initially, music in the schools was a reflection of the singing school movement, designed to create better singers to improve the hymn-singing in churches (Birge, 1928/1966). The theories of the European educators Johann Pestalozzi and Friedrich Froebel influenced American educators to establish a child-centered view of the curriculum and the importance of music and the emotion. The early 20th century brought the invention of recordings and radio, and a new focus on music listening. At the same time, societal trends in character or moral education resulted in the teaching of songs that included moral lessons. The progressive education movement of the 1930s viewed the child and curriculum holistically and music as an integral part of an overall education. In the 1950s and early 1960s, elementary music texts based their curriculum on the social studies model of Hilda Taba and were firmly rooted in a sense of being connected with the community.

Since the curriculum reform movement of the late 1950s and 1960s, prompted by the beginning of the Cold War and the advent of Sputnik, music and the other arts have been approached less from a child-centered or societal perspective and more as disciplines to be studied in their own right (Efland, 1990). The notion of a disciplinary approach to the curriculum largely came from the sciences, which looked at disciplines as "having an organized body of knowledge, specific methods of inquiry, and a community of scholars who generally agree on the fundamental ideas of their field" (Efland, 1990, p. 19). President John F. Kennedy's Panel on Educational Research and Development of the President's Science Advisory Committee suggested in 1963 that curriculum reform that had been developed in science education could be applied to arts education (Efland, 1990).

A number of private and federally funded initiatives of the 1960s challenged music educators to define the nature of their discipline, the processes they used to engage students, and the quality of the music that students performed (Mark & Gary, 1992). Perhaps the most important of these was the Tanglewood Symposium, held in 1967, during which music educators took stock of their field, asking how they might better serve the schools of America. This symposium anticipated many current practices, such as introducing students to music of diverse periods, styles, forms, and cultures. The primary tenet of Tanglewood was that "music serves best when its integrity as an art is maintained" (Mark & Gary, 1992, p. 312). Nonetheless, Tanglewood did call for the study of a wide variety of music from many cultures and traditions.

At virtually the same time in history, the philosophy of aesthetics began to permeate the field of music education in America and became a justification for music education in the schools. The focus of music education began to change to viewing music as an artistic discipline with the idea of music being taught "for its own sake" (see Reimer, 1970). This coincided with emphasis on conceptual teaching in all of the disciplines, based on the work of Jerome Bruner (1960). The result was a shift more and more to treating music as an object for study and contemplation. Analysis of music and its component parts and music as aesthetic object has been the prevailing philosophy in music education since that time. The primary role of music education became to help students achieve aesthetic experiences by studying all music, whether the "great works" of Western culture or non-Western music and popular music from an aesthetic perspective. (For a more complete discussion of this history, see Mark and Gary [1992] and Goble [1999].)

In the decade of the 1990s, many of the assumptions underlying this dominant theory have been called into question. Elliott (1995) calls for more of a praxial view of music that focuses on the development of student's cognition through the making and creating of music or "musicing" in addition to listening. Goble (1999) challenges music education to take a semiotic view of music as "socially situated psychosocially equilibrating behavior" (p. 367). This pragmatic view of music education strives to place music education more fully into serving a societal role, as well as a psychological and spiritual role in meeting the needs of a multicultural society.

Social and Cultural Perspectives

Some of what is driving these changes in music education is the expanded perspective that has come from the struggle in the postmodern period to move beyond a Western view of the world to a more global perspective. Ethnomusicologists and anthropologists have long known the powerful role that music and the arts play in culture. In many places throughout the world, music is intimately interwoven with cultural and social events and rituals. For example, according to Sutton (1992), within Javanese culture, " 'concerts' of gamelan music simply do not occur, at least not in anything like the circumstances of a concert of Western classical music" (p. 276). Rather, the musical events are "better understood as social events that involve gamelan music" (p. 276).

Merriam (1995, pp. 3–4) outlined the functions of music in society as follows:

1. Emotional expression: releasing of emotions and expression of feelings
2. Aesthetic enjoyment: using music for deep intellectual and emotional enjoyment, for experiencing beauty deeply
3. Entertainment: using music for diversion and amusement

4. Communication: conveying of feelings and emotions understood by people within a particular culture
5. Symbolic representation: expression of symbols in the texts of songs and cultural meaning of the music
6. Physical response: using music for dancing and other physical activity
7. Enforcement of conformity to social norms: using music to provide instructions or warnings
8. Validation of social institutions and religious rituals: using music on state occasions and in religious services
9. Contribution to the continuity and stability of culture: using music to pass on cultural values
10. Contribution to the integration of society: using music to bring people together

Contemporary writers might add therapy and healing to this extensive list of uses of music. These multiple uses of music can readily inform teachers as they view the many ways they might integrate music into the curriculum. Such societal expectations for music across all aspects of life may also have other positive effects. John Blacking, the British anthropologist, raises the provocative question of the relationship between musical ability and societal expectations, suggesting that those expectations are probably more powerful than a separate musical intelligence. The Venda people of Africa, described by Blacking (1990, p. 75), provide opportunities for every child to participate in music-making. In his observations Blacking described music as a part of normal social life and its performance as a necessary feature of most institutions. Children were encouraged to sing and dance by their peers, no less than by adults. Nobody was excluded from musical activity, since musicality was regarded as a part of the human condition.

At a time in which so much of educational reform is focused on the development of intelligent children and on testing, it is intriguing to consider what impact arts integration as a basic part of the life of schooling might have on that development. Perhaps the Venda experience has much to offer in terms of an educational approach with music integration as a key aspect toward learning throughout the day.

Theoretical Frame for Music Integration in Education

According to Burton, Horowitz, and Abeles (1999), "learning in arts is complex and multidimensional" (p. 43). The role of arts in schools can take many forms, from a disciplinary study to a tool for the understanding of mathematics or science. As a tool for the understanding or exploration of other subjects, arts in general and music specifically have been described as languages for learning (Gallas, 1994; Goldberg, 2001). In other words, consider

a child who is well versed at music but reticent toward discussing concepts or a child who is just learning English as a second language. Both may not be equipped to "tell" about a concept, but through their music, drawings, play-acting, or dancing might be able to "show" understanding. In this case the arts become a fundamental tool or language to demonstrate subject-matter understanding where verbal language serves as a barrier. In broadening the use of arts as a form of language, communication, or expression, teachers significantly widen their ability to reach all students, both in how they present complex material and how they assess their students' understandings of that material.

Inconsistent support for arts programs in the schools over the last 2 decades coupled with theoretical frameworks focused on reforms have led, in part, to this broadening role of arts in education. This has often left the classroom teacher responsible for arts education if the children are to receive any education in the arts. As of 1998, only the states of Arizona, California, Delaware, Mississippi, and Oregon required elementary teachers to take courses in the arts for certification, although individual colleges and universities may require such courses for their elementary education students (Council of Chief State School Officers [CCSSO], 1998).[1] Universities may also require courses in the arts as part of their liberal arts core. Frequently, however, a beginning classroom teacher enters teaching having taken only one or two general classes in the arts as a part of his or her college education. It is no wonder then, that the multiple-subject teacher might not feel equipped to teach about the arts.

A number of efforts have emerged to expand ways to bring the arts into education. Innovative arts centers and universities have devised several collaborative initiatives in keeping with educational reform efforts in an effort to ensure arts presence in education. The benefit for the arts institutions lies in their individual futures. Each is committed to building audiences/patrons of the future. In order to do so, they must establish a young, appreciative, and excited audience, banking on the notion that as adults they will want to attend performances and support the arts.

Key players in these reforms are community artists, community arts organizations, arts specialists, and schools. Partnerships between various individuals and organizations are dedicated to changing schools through the arts. These initiatives may happen on a school-by-school basis or across an entire state, as exemplified in the Kentucky Education Reform Act of 1990 (KERA), which calls for "sufficient grounding in the arts to enable each student to appreciate his or her cultural and historical heritage" (Remer, 1996, p. 23).

Theoretical frameworks for the integration of arts have been made in the areas of learning styles, multiple intelligences, meeting the needs of multicultural and multilingual student populations, and literacy. In the realm of the multiple intelligence (Gardner, 1983), the arts play a significant role as they are linked to linguistic, spatial, bodily-kinesthetic, and musical intelligences. It should be noted, however, that Gardner did not intend his work to be interpreted as suggesting that one subject area should be used to teach another area, rather that students should have the opportunity to learn through each of the intelligences. In grasping the importance of teaching in the multicultural and multilingual classroom, many teachers are broadening their teaching methods so that various forms of communication become opportunities for students (Goldberg, 2001).

In literacy pedagogy, language arts theorists are broadening their definition of what it means to be literate. This is due, in large part, to the infusion of technology into our lives and schooling. "If it were possible to define the mission of education," writes the New London Group (1996), an international assembly of literacy theorists and practitioners, "one could say that its fundamental purpose is to ensure that all students benefit from learning in ways that allow them to participate fully in public, community, and economic life" (p. 60). In order to do this, the authors argue for what they describe as "multiliteracies"—a much broader view of literacy that includes many forms of representation in addition to the written word. "Literacy pedagogy now must account for the burgeoning variety of text forms associated with information and multimedia technologies" (p. 61). This includes representational forms, such as visual images and musical symbols or representation.

The notion of multiliteracy perhaps parallels what musicians and some teachers describe when they talk of the arts as "languages" or "languages of learning" (Blecher & Jaffee, 1998; Gallas, 1994). Though it is true that a universal definition or agreement on music as "language" is yet to be agreed on, one can find use of the term "language" across the fields of performance, literacy, and elementary education.[2] As Igor Stravinsky discussed in his talks at Harvard, "art is by essence, constructive" (1942, p. 11). The "tone of a work like the Rite may have appeared arrogant, the *language* that it spoke may have seemed harsh in its newness, but that in no way implies that it is revolutionary" (p. 10). Mickey Hart (1991), one of the drummers with the Grateful Dead, describes music as a "reflection of our dreams, our lives, and it represents every fiber of our being. It's an aural soundscape, a *language* of our deepest emotions; it's what we sound like as people" (p. 7). Art Hodes, a jazz pianist who lived well into his nineties, wrote of the blues as a language. Hodes was well known for his playing with Louis Armstrong and Bessie Smith, performing standards—enduring jazz selections. Hodes describes an early experience in his career, before he learned the language, as he puts it, of the blues.

Many times they'd ask me to play. I was kidded plenty. Someone would holler, "Play the blues, Art," and when I would play they would laugh. That hurt, but I couldn't blame them. I hadn't as yet learned the idiom. I was entranced by their *language* but I hadn't learned to speak it yet. (Gottlieb, 1996, p. 62)

Classroom Teachers and Music Integration

Classroom teachers must often take on the role of introducing music if the students are to receive any instruction at all in music. In fact, historically, the Music Educators National Conference (MENC) was originally the Music Supervisors National Conference because music educators were responsible for supervising classroom teachers in teaching music. The name was changed in 1932 because more specialists were teaching music by that time (Mark & Gary, 1992). Unfortunately, in recent years, some parts of the country have seen a decline (severe in some cases, like California) in music specialists. According to Barbara McKean (2000),

today, the major responsibility for providing comprehensive arts education falls on the shoulders of the classroom teachers. A critical concern is how classroom teachers view this change and how they might be prepared to teach the arts in ways consistent with the vision provided in part by both national and state standards. (p. 3)

While some classroom teachers are prepared to teach music, others are more comfortable with integrating music into their already existing curriculum. This is true in spite of an ambivalence experienced by many that they feel excited by what the arts can do for children but little support for what it takes to integrate the arts (Bresler, 1995). An effective interdisciplinary curriculum creates connections while respecting the unique contributions of the disciplines combined (Jacobs, 1989). Doing this well requires both a commitment on the part of the teachers involved and broader administrative support. Drake (1993) identifies conditions for success in integration as: (1) time to plan together; (2) leadership and team stability; and (3) budgetary support for such things as field trips, in-service training, materials, and artists-in-residence.

Research by Bresler (1995) found that classroom teachers generally used one of four styles in integrating the arts into their curriculum. She names the first "subservient integration." This is the most prevalent style and involves spicing up other subjects by having children sing a song about the solar system or "Fifty Nifty United States" to learn the names of the states. Generally these activities are at a low cognitive level and do not develop specific artistic skills or encourage aesthetic growth. Such activities generally focus on the technical but do allow for the use of different ways of thinking other than verbal and mathematical.

The second she names "the co-equal, cognitive integration style." This was the least common approach observed in her study, though it is the one she described as most advocated in the literature on arts integration. This style was used by classroom teachers who had an extensive artistic background or worked in collaboration with arts specialists. This approach is suggested through some of the models that follow. It involves higher order cognitive skills such as perceiving, interpreting, analyzing, synthesizing, and evaluating.

The third approach, the "affective style" of integration, helped to set a mood or stimulate creativity. Music was used in the background to calm students down or expose children to particular styles. At times students were invited to create using different artistic media such as creating a drawing inspired by a piece of music. This style is open-ended, and imagination is encouraged. The arts are considered by teachers as vehicles for self-expression. This was most prevalent in grades K–2.

The final style, "social integration," complemented the academic curriculum by utilizing the arts as vehicles for creating community and making the social events of the school a success. This approach was generally promoted by the principals. When classroom teachers led these efforts without the help of specialists, the level of involvement was generally high but the quality of performance low. Emphasis was on getting all of the children involved in singing and dancing and some crafted art but not on educating the children or the audience in the arts. At the same time, the arts were present and appreciated.

A qualitative study by Wilson (1999) of the role of musical intelligence in grades K–3 in a multiple intelligence school showed that all of these uses of music were present, with the affective style predominant. Teachers believed that they were introducing children to a wide variety of music through playing it softly in the background while the children worked on other projects. Actual examination of the music played showed that it represented a very narrow selection. Children were able to sing a repertoire of songs that had been taught in conjunction with other subjects. In no instance was music treated as an intelligence to be developed, used to assess learning in other subjects, or assessed in its own right. Teachers reported a need for more training and increased support from their principals to gain understanding of how to teach to all of the intelligences.

Not surprisingly, much of what is labeled as music integration has been received with a certain cautiousness among music educators (see for example, Campbell, 1995; Veblen & Elliott, 2000; Wiggins & Wiggins, 1997). At the same time, many music educators have responded posi-

tively to the potential benefits of thoughtful integration of music and have developed materials and ideas to assist in this process (Anderson & Lawrence, 1992; Barrett, McCoy, & Veblen, 1997; Campbell & Scott-Kassner, 1995).

Another way of viewing the use of music in an integrated curriculum is by thinking of learning *with* music and learning *through* music (Goldberg, 2001). Learning *with* music occurs when already composed music becomes the source of some study. One of the most common examples and uses of music in this regard is the integration of history and music. In the study of historical events, music written at a specific time in history may be used as primary documents of history, aiding in an understanding of that time period. Music may also be integrated with other subjects, such as mathematics. Young children can study patterns by listening to and then analyzing the various forms music takes (ABA, ABABAB, rondo, etc.). By identifying musical concepts and forms they also identify specific patterns that can be related to patterning in their mathematics curriculum. A musical pattern such as ABA can turn into a pattern such as square-circle-square. A rondo might create a row of geometric shapes: square-circle-square-rectangle-square-triangle-square-rhombus-square, and so on.

Learning *through* music occurs when students actively engage in creating music to work with some idea. For example, students may write chants or raps describing photosynthesis or create a sound sculpture to better understand the movement of the planets. The following is an example of just that and a result of a collaboration between a professional musician and a classroom teacher from the SUAVE program, an interdisciplinary program in California (Goldberg, 2001).[3]

Sonic Solar System: A Musical Sculpture

Nancy Marron, fourth grade teacher

Subject areas: math, science, music

Materials: A variety (nine is ideal) of percussive or tonal instruments

Description: Students move desks to the sides of the room to create working space for the lesson. Students are seated on the floor. Students close their eyes and imagine themselves as an individual planet spinning in space. The lesson begins with a review of the order of the planets in our solar system. Students are told that they are going to be able to make a musical model of the solar system based on the orbital values of each planet—that is to say, the students will experience planetary movement based on how long it takes each planet to make one rotation around the sun. Students discuss the distance each planet is away from the sun and use a table that relates each planet's complete rotation (that planet's year) to a complete earth's year (one complete orbit around the sun). Using mental math, the students convert these numbers into gross orbital ratios.

- Mercury, closest to the sun, circles four times as fast as Earth, and is four quarter notes.
- Venus, further from the sun, is considered two half notes.
- Earth's rotation is considered a whole note.
- Mars fully rotates every two whole notes.
- Jupiter rotates one time for every five rotations of Mars.
- Saturn rotates one time for every two rotations of Jupiter.
- Uranus rotates once every three rotations of Saturn.
- Neptune rotates every two rotations of Uranus.
- Pluto would rotate every 15 rotations of Uranus, but we made it more frequent, 1:3, because this child would have to wait forever to participate in the event.

A child is picked for every planet and given a percussion instrument. They are then placed in their proper orbital position in relation to the sun. There is a visual aspect to the experience, but more important to the success of the project is that each child is next to the planet that their musical relationship is based on. Students are told that all music starts with silence. Just as in visual art, silence and emptiness are as important as sound or form. Pattern is key to this piece. What we are creating was once described as "music of the spheres."

Each student is instructed to play their instrument only at the point when their planet has completed its orbit and has returned to its point of origin. The rest is silence. As the students wait for their rotations to complete, the silence emphasizes the vast distances and varying lengths of time that cannot be conceived by long strings of numbers. Several students in the class assisted musicians with their counting, so for some, one instrument was "played" by two students. This "acoustic sculpture" demanded extreme concentration on the part of the students. Mistakes were discussed and several performances were done so that most students were able to participate.

Skills developed: mental math, listening skills, patterning, working cooperatively, self-restraint and patience, knowledge of musical notation, spatial knowledge is extended.

Assessment: Students could be assessed in their ability to round and to mentally manipulate numbers. Listening skills could be assessed. The success of this project depended on the understanding of musical notation and ratios when the piece was produced without error, then understanding is seen as class-wide. Students were assessed on their ability to work as a group towards a common goal.

Where to go from here: group mobiles, more patterning, xylophones, rounds, studying patterns in poems, making group poems with pre-established restrictions or structures, mosaics, exploring "noise" as music, looking at Fibonacci numbers.

This math/science/music lesson is a lesson that will not be easily forgotten. Learning about music is not sacrificed to the study of science or math, nor is the study of science or math sacrificed to music. The children were engaged in a meaningful musical process to better understand the concept of orbital value. While the teacher and musician described this lesson as quite successful, Karen Gallas reminds us that the processes of learning with and through the arts, much like the arts themselves, are uncertain. Gallas (1994) writes, "this process is full of uncertainty. Teachers who are committed to the importance of the creative process must live with a certain amount of ambiguity and tension, with disequilibrium in the Piagetian sense" (p. 118). They are processes, which limited research has shown can have a positive impact on learning in the subject areas, including the arts.

Review of Research on Teaching Other Subjects Through Music

While there are many articles written on the benefits and limitations of music integration, there are unfortunately few research studies that examine the effectiveness of such approaches. There are, broadly speaking, three different kinds of research in this area: research related to educational reform that integrates the arts; research related to the process of integration, focusing heavily on uncovering the role of professional development of teachers; and research related to student learning through music (ethnographic studies).

Research Related to Educational Reform That Integrates the Arts

The A+ Model from North Carolina. The A+ Schools Program from North Carolina is a school reform initiative begun in 1993 by the Kenan Institute for the Arts. It was funded outside of state government and planned by schools, school district personnel, and arts professionals in the community. After an 18-month period of development, 25 elementary schools were selected from a statewide application process to participate in the program. The institute is preparing the publication of a 4-year evaluation of the program.

The model is based on Gardner's multiple intelligences theory, with the arts playing a central role. Every school has full-time specialists in visual art, music, dance, and drama. Children have daily instruction in the arts as disciplines. In addition, arts specialists work with classroom teachers to help integrate the arts across the curriculum in meaningful ways. Teacher growth is supported in a variety of ways through workshops, summer school courses, the expertise of specialists, the establishment of a network of all of the A+ schools for the sharing of ideas, and partnerships with community organizations.

Since the founding of the program a number of schools have joined the A+ network, and more are in line to do so. Teacher workshops and planning efforts are ongoing. The state of North Carolina has also placed funding for these schools in the regular budget and approved them as an appropriate strategy for school reform.

Initial results show that student performance has improved to the state average. There were no low-performing schools by the end of the third year, whereas there had been five the previous year. Teachers reported that learning was more enjoyable for all students, including those who often struggle with learning via more traditional means. School attendance improved, as did both student self-confidence and sense of competence.[4]

The Leonard Bernstein Center.   A model for school reform called Artful Learning was begun with the support and involvement of Leonard Bernstein. It is based on the premises that children learn when they are engaged in learning; that they start to inquire when they are interested; that they start to love learning when they create something; and that they begin to master subjects when they reflect on what they have learned. These four dimensions—experience, inquire, create, and reflect—are at the center of the model. Lessons begin with the study of masterworks and continue through each of the four processes. Goals are to develop students who master the art of self-learning and to help develop effective teaching practices leading to these kinds of students.

K–12 schools that choose to adopt the model must have a majority of the faculty willing to buy into the model. All faculty members must go through two levels of teacher training over 3 years. A design team must be formed in each school to oversee the process. Faculty members receive 5- to 10-day training in summer institutes, support through networking, follow-up coaching, and help with assessment of the project in their school. Artists are also involved in programs in the schools. The Bernstein Center assists in fundraising for schools that wish to participate.

From 1992 to 1997, the Bernstein Center worked with the Northwest Regional Laboratory to conduct extensive research at 14 sites around the country. Two different controlled studies of the impact of Artful Learning on student achievement showed positive impact on student learning in reading, math, writing, science, and social studies. Other outcomes are higher levels of creativity and motivation for learning.

Arts Partnerships: Research Related to the Process of Music Integration and the Professional Development of Classroom Teachers

This section reviews literature related to the professional development of teachers learning to integrate music and other arts (often they are not separated) to meet the needs of education reform. Though limited in scope, the research does uncover many pros and cons of teacher learning in the realm of arts integration. The following initiatives are partnership programs linking professional artists and organizations with classroom teachers. The research tends to focus on the process of teacher learning and subsequent practice rather than the correlation between teacher-initiated lessons in music (and/or other arts) and student learning.

Larsen Research of a Chicago Project.   Larsen (2000) examined a 5-year project in one Chicago elementary school to determine the impact on teachers of incorporating the arts in the curriculum. She was particularly interested in viewing change through the arts in urban schools. Key elements of the success of this project were that it was site specific and long-term and involved collaborations with external partners. It was based on the belief that schools and teachers can change and that the school does not have to do it all—there is other expertise and funding. The realization of these beliefs engendered hope in the teachers and resulted in positive change.

The project occurred in three phases, which evolved organically rather than by plan.

1. Phase 1 was a top-down model, mandated by the principal, in which everyone in the school participated in teacher training through workshops and a concurrent college course in arts integration. All teachers were beneficiaries of cultural resources provided by a range of community arts organizations.
2. Phase 2 occurred in the second year as a result of pressure from the school district to affect test scores. Many teachers dropped out, and the focus was on the teachers who were committed to change through the arts. Smaller groups of teachers formed clusters and began to support each other. An outside person connected them with arts organizations and demonstrated ideas for them. The arts organizations were asked to develop programs that would integrate their offerings into the curriculum the teachers were required to teach. A number of these teachers also requested group guitar lessons once a week from the outside person so that they could

grow in their musical skills and utilize the guitar with children.

3. Phase 3 occurred in the final 2 years. The same groups of teachers developed a professional community, stimulated to a great extent by learning to play the guitar together. They began to attract their own arts resources to meet specific needs for projects they were doing in their classrooms. They felt confident and empowered, and the change became institutionalized.

SUAVE, CAPE.   Both SUAVE and CAPE are long-term professional development projects that have been rigorously documented and researched. While neither focuses solely on music integration, each delves into the subject and has important findings to report. SUAVE is a program designed to help teachers in multicultural and multilingual classrooms use the arts to teach the content areas of mathematics, science, language arts, and social studies. The program is a joint effort of California State University San Marcos, the California Center for the Arts in Escondido, and several school districts. (SUAVE is an acronym for Socios Unidos para Artes Via Educación, or United Community for Arts in Education.)

SUAVE began in 1994–95 with three schools and 30 elementary teachers in three districts and has grown to include all elementary schools in each of the original districts, as well as expanding to middle and high schools and other districts. Ten teachers per school work individually with an artist, who is referred to as a "coach," during school (with children in the classroom) for 1 hour a week for the period of 2 years. The artists as a group are multicultural and multilingual and represent many art forms, including music, drama, dance, visual arts, poetry, puppetry and mime.

The program is not an add-on. Rather, each coach works with individual teachers to develop strategies to teach core curriculum through the arts. The goal at the end of 2 years is that the teacher will have gained the strategies to continue teaching through the arts on his or her own. The artist/coaches are supported through weekly 2-hour meetings with each other and the program director where they brainstorm ideas concerning specific content and discuss effective strategies for working with individual teachers.

Teachers and artists/coaches attend five in-service days with teachers from all participating schools where they share curriculum, do arts-based activities, and meet with visiting artists who are performing at the Center for the Arts. For example, the teachers have had workshops with Peter Galk, a classical pianist, the Shakespeare Company, and Marcel Marceau. Teachers are also invited to attend subsidized performances, have some afterschool workshop opportunities, and present their work at the end of the school year at an annual curriculum fair.

Chicago Arts Partnerships in Education (CAPE) was founded in 1992 to revive arts programs in the Chicago schools through partnerships with teachers of all grades. When fully implemented, CAPE included 20 active school sites. Teacher-artist partnerships were created and (after a proposal competition) charged with "planning integrated instruction, joining instruction in an art form such as painting or music with specific instructional goals in other subjects such as reading or science" (Catterall & Waldorf, 1999, p.48). The CAPE program is similar to SUAVE in that artists and teachers are paired together to develop curriculum incorporating an art form with an academic teaching objective (Catterall & Waldorf, 1999).

A main difference between the projects is that SUAVE is ongoing (2 years' constant coaching and then support), whereas CAPE is based on specific units lasting on average 4 to 6 weeks. Both programs provide workshops outside of the classroom and connections to local arts agencies. Both programs were the object of a 3- or 4-year study (respectively) including regular surveys, classroom observations, interviews, focus groups, and case studies.

The SUAVE research looked at the changes in beliefs and practice of the teachers. The CAPE research focused on kinds of integration, such as which subjects were integrated the most, as well as which arts areas were utilized. They found that reading and social studies were the most likely subjects to be integrated, followed by science and math, respectively. The most integrated art form was visual arts (41%), followed by theater (25%), music (19%), dance (9%), and other (6%). Overall, the results of each study paint a picture that arts integration has a positive impact on teachers and students as well as the environment of learning. Teachers and artists learned to collaborate successfully, and the research has shown that they continue to integrate the arts after full-time coaching has ceased.

The SUAVE research revealed, among other things, that the artist-teacher relationship was successful even though there was no "recipe for success"; in other words, each relationship took a different form (Goldberg, Bennett, & Jacobs, 1999). Tension occurred in many of the relationships, but because of the structure of the program, including multiple environments for learning and the sustained partnerships of 2 years, tensions turned into significant learning experiences (Bennett et al., 1999; Jacobs, 2000). The SUAVE research also revealed that once teachers became comfortable integrating the arts as a methodology for the teaching of a subject, they became interested in the arts in and of themselves. This interest blossomed in two ways: (1) Teachers took classes in the arts to further their personal knowledge of an art form; (2) teachers were more motivated to include arts-based lessons as a part of their curriculum, with the belief that the arts are intrinsically valuable in the education of their students

(Jacobs, Goldberg, & Bennett, in press). Neither study, however, focuses solely on music, and even CAPE, while it reveals data concerning the ratio of music integration, shows that music is not the most popular art form to integrate. Both studies, however, point to positive aspects of arts integration.

Young Audiences. Young Audiences is a not-for-profit organization with chapters in more than 30 states. Young Audiences artists are brought to schools for workshops and performances intended to integrate the arts into the curriculum. A research project focusing on the professional development of teachers engaged in Young Audience programming in Arizona had more mixed results than those of SUAVE or CAPE. Barbara McKean (2000) followed a group of teachers as they participated in their district's arts partnership program, which involved artists giving workshops to teachers in an area of the performing arts. The workshops were to involve the teachers in the performing arts to allow them to better prepare their students for performances. They were also meant to prepare the teachers to integrate the art forms into their curriculum. The workshops and performances were by arts companies of different cultures.

The structure of the workshops, which were preplanned (as opposed to collaboratively constructed, as in the SUAVE and CAPE projects), caused some tensions. One teacher said, "I can't teach what I can't do. If I had the talent to do it, I would" (McKean, 2000, p. 6). McKean reported her concern that the presence of teaching artists reinforced a sense of inadequacy in the arts rather than building a sense of confidence, or knowledge. Her conclusions fell along the lines of conclusions others in professional development research have found concerning partnerships with the outside community. She identifies four key factors for success: "(1) collaboration; (2) identifying specific roles for the classroom teachers and outside professionals; (3) ensuring that the values, goals and objectives of the partners are consistent; and (4) maintaining a reciprocal relationship between all of the participants" (p. 17). These factors are consistent with the findings and recommendations in both SUAVE and CAPE.

Research Related to the Process of Student Learning

There are a few ethnographic studies concerning music and other subjects. These studies are rich in stories and descriptions of student learning when music becomes key to the curriculum. An example of an ethnographic study comes from Pamela Rossi (1997a, 1997b), who used ethnographic and arts-based methods to research and document

the processes involved in the composition, production, and performance of an opera in a first-grade bilingual classroom. This project involved collaboration among a teacher, artist-in-residence, students, and researcher. The aim of the project was to enhance students' abilities in the area of reading, writing, and interpretation. Rossi makes the point that literacy is more than reading and writing and that art is not a frill. Furthermore, she argues that opera is not inaccessible, even to first graders.

Sharon Blecher and Kathy Jaffee, in their book *Weaving in the Arts: Widening the Learning Circle* (1998), share the results of a 2-year project to immerse their first and second graders in the arts. Their daily schedule included what they called "creating a languages-rich environment with music and movement" (p. 16), along with writing and reading poetry and using art as a visual response to show understanding. In addition, music and art were treated in great depth as ways of knowing and creating. Reading and writing were integrated into workshops in the visual arts and music. Among other things, children created an opera. The authors share many insights into the benefits of this work. They found that "divisions between disciplines began to blur as children looked at learning from multiple perspectives" (p. 168). The practice of *bridging,* or using concepts and experiences from one learning situation in another, was particularly helpful to children who struggled with more traditional approaches to reading, writing, and thinking. Inclusion of the arts also helped to break down barriers between the school and the larger community. Blecher and Jaffee realized that they needed the expertise of community-based artists to help them succeed, and the presence of those artists forced the teachers to look through multiple lenses.

Karen Gallas (1994) has also published in the area of young children's learning through the arts. Gallas, however, does not limit her research to the area of music. As a teacher-researcher, she documents many aspects of her kindergarteners' and first graders' process of learning. For example, she writes of an early June afternoon when she and six of her students sat watching a butterfly struggle to emerge from its chrysalis. One student, Juan, is carefully sketching the scene. He has been sketching the progress of the butterfly since early May. The children become anxious, having been watching all morning wondering about the plight of the butterfly and if it will ever get out. Gallas writes: "Sophia smiles to herself and then begins to hum a tune. 'I'll sing it out,' she says. 'Yeah, let's sing it out!' agrees Matthew, and all the children begin to improvise a song."

This anecdote from her class can be viewed as simply a cute moment or a profound learning experience. The students are encouraged by Gallas to follow their exploration through improvising a song. The fact that they feel comfortable improvising and singing is significant in and of itself in terms of their music education and could be built on in terms of further music learning. The acceptance of music as a viable form of expression in this science observation indicates to the students that music is indeed a vehicle for expressing their anticipation and anxiousness concerning the emerging butterfly.

Programs to Watch

In this section we have listed major initiatives underway. Clearly there are many other initiatives and efforts that are not identified. There are also most certainly dedicated musicians and teachers engaged in meaningful collaborations to integrate music into the curriculum. It is our hope that many of these individuals, programs, reforms, initiatives, and partnerships will receive recognition and become available to researchers seeking to broaden the understanding of music integration.

The Galef Institute, founded in 1989, is a nonprofit educational organization dedicated to work in public schools focusing on the integration of history and social studies with literature and writing, math and science, and the arts. The institute has initiated many programs and research focusing on "Different Ways of Knowing." While their projects have not focused solely on music, they have several initiatives that research the role of arts in children's understandings. With a $13 million research and development grant from the U.S. Department of Education Office of Educational Research and Improvement (OERI), the Galef Institute is developing a model of comprehensive school reform for middle-level grades. The model will be implemented in fall 2001 and will no doubt provide rich data, including possibilities in the realm of music and learning.[5]

New York City public schools are involved in a long-term study of the impact of reinstating the arts in that school system after years of neglect. An initial grant from the Annenberg Foundation to the New York City Center for Arts Education resulted in annual funding for these programs being included in the budget for the schools, and there are arts programs at 200 different sites throughout the city. These programs are not sequential or based on an arts curriculum. They involve 13-week residencies cosponsored by cultural organizations throughout New York City. A number of universities are also involved as partners. The cultural organizations are quite realistic about the value of this, realizing that they are providing a short-term apprenticeship in their particular art form. Each school is responsible for assessing its own project. An overall assessment is being developed but is very complex because of all of the variables.[6]

The Chicago Annenberg Challenge is a 3-year program in three Chicago public schools reaching children from grades K to 8. The partnering agency is the Chicago Symphony Orchestra, which is committed to the integration of its resources into these schools. Teachers are given release time to learn from the symphony people and from each other. Support is given to them in their schools, and an effort is being made to create a community of teachers who can learn from each other.

Finally, three evolving projects to watch are the Minnesota Arts and Education Project, sponsored by the Perpich Foundation of Minneapolis and the Annenberg Foundation, the Learning Through Music initiative launched in spring 2000 at the New England Conservatory of Music in Boston, and the National Endowment for the Arts updated version of *Schools, Communities, and the Arts*, originally published in 1995. The compendium highlights many initiatives, including a few music programs. The new edition of this booklet, currently undergoing an update, is worth looking for.

What Do We Learn from This Research?

The research tells us there are many important educational reform and curriculum efforts devoted to learning through music and other arts. The research does not, however, offer significant data focused solely on music integration and its implications in terms of those reform or curriculum projects. Perhaps a common theme that could be culled from the research is that, in the words of Barbara McKean (2000), "Reciprocal Relationships" coupled with sustained efforts at integration whereby musicians and teachers collaborate together are highly effective. This is important to note if educational reform continues to embrace music integration. This essentially would mean a broadening of the role of the music teacher(s) in a school from a strictly disciplinary approach to include working with teachers to create integrated projects.

The CAPE project tells us that music has only a 19% probability of being integrated in comparison to other arts. The professional development research shows us that current projects focus on many arts and not music specifically. Is music more difficult for some reason, making it a less likely subject to integrate? It would be interesting to follow up on research projects like CAPE and SUAVE to investigate the perception of integrating music versus other arts disciplines.

It is important, as Bresler points out (1995), to be aware of the ways music is integrated. Music integration can be profound and have an impact on children's learning. It can also be, in her words, "subservient," as when a child learns a song in order to remember the names of all 50 states. Many music educators have responded positively to the movement to integrate music and have developed thoughtful materials to assist classroom teachers.

Questions for Further Research

There are many exciting programs and partnerships dedicated to bringing the arts to teachers and children and integrating music and the other arts across the curriculum. Initiatives abound, but clear results are often lacking. Pressures from the accountability movement to adopt reform programs that will lead directly to a rise in test scores may force people to ask the wrong kind of questions when looking at results of such initiatives. Discomfort on the part of many with using qualitative data to describe program success also has the potential of limiting what we say we can know and learn. Terry Baker (personal communication, January 19, 2001) of the Center for Arts Education in New York City suggests that often the wrong questions are asked by applying nationally normed measures to specific projects whose objectives may not be congruent with what is being tested. He also suggests that many projects are so poorly funded there is little available to bring in people who can do effective research. He encourages a kind of collaborative assessment where the focus is on learning what students can and do achieve. Such questions need to be specific to the goals of the project being assessed.

The following list is intended to be a stimulus for thinking about future research in this area of music and arts integration across the curriculum. Many of these questions have been addressed in individual studies, but there does not seem to be a body of collected research that speaks to these generally, across many settings and programs.

1. What conditions can be said to be the most effective for achieving teacher change in confidence and competence in using music and the other arts with children?
2. What is the long-term impact of such teacher change on student learning for *all* students?
3. What is the long-term impact of such teacher change on school climate?
4. What is the long-term impact of such teacher change on teacher retention?
5. What dimensions of student growth and attitude do such programs affect?
6. How can we measure student growth and attitudes in programs that integrate music and other arts?
7. How do we assess students' understandings of subject matter through music and other arts?
8. What are holistic ways that we can examine the kinds of changes that occur in environments that are so rich and complex?
9. What are the differences in the impact on student learning between programs where the arts are taught as disciplines by specialists as well as integrated into the classroom and programs where classroom teachers are responsible for integrating the arts?
10. Is there a difference between the kinds of programs that succeed in urban settings and those that succeed in more rural settings? In multilingual settings versus monolingual settings? In multicultural settings versus homogeneous cultural settings?
11. Can significant change occur without the buy-in from all of the teachers in a school? What is the nature of those changes on students as well as teachers?
12. Should new research efforts relate to advocacy aimed at invigorating arts into school reform efforts?

Conclusion

Music education history parallels the multiple roles of music in society. It is dynamic and complex in nature on the one hand and stable (sometimes even stodgy) on the other. The use of music to teach other subjects has a long history not only in schools but in cultures and religions as well. A relatively new debate in education circles concerning music as a specific discipline arose in the late 1950s and into the 1960s in response to subjects such as science gaining new eminence as a separate disciplinary approach. Prior to that, music education had a broader use in education that included religious training (hymn-singing), character and moral education, and an emphasis on music being important to child-centered learning. As the role of education turns toward meeting the needs of a multilingual, multicultural student body and addressing the importance of technology in our lives, as well as what it means to be literate, the role of music in education has shifted once again.

In most of the research studies reviewed, classroom teachers are coached or trained by professional musicians or music educators. The door has been opened. Learning subjects through music is an educational reality. While integrated music lessons (or learning subject matter through music) may not focus on learning music as a discipline, they do offer an opportunity to engage with music and musical concepts and in the making of music. If teachers are deliberate in using music terminology and highlighting musical concepts, students have a better chance to gain music knowledge while studying another subject through music.

The scope of research related to this issue is small. This is unfortunate because new research focusing on music integration and learning, as well as the development and implementation of models and their impact on students and teachers, could be extremely important and informative.

NOTES

1. In California, however, arts methods are not required at all. Students must take arts classes as part of their liberal

studies degree or test out of arts in order to qualify for an elementary credential program.

2. If the notion of "music as language" is of interest, we suggest investigating the works of Susanne K. Langer and R. G. Collingwood as a start.

3. This lesson was created by Nancy Marron.

4. Further information will be available and can be found at the website of the North Carolina Education and Law Project: http://www.aplus-schools.org.

5. For more information visit their website: http://www.dwoknet.galef.org.

6. Further information about these programs and what is happening at individual sites can be found at the website, www.cae-nyc.org.

REFERENCES

Anderson, W., & Lawrence, J. (1992). *Integrating music into the classroom*. Belmont, CA: Wadsworth.

Barrett, J. R., McCoy, C. W., & Veblen, K. K. (1997). *Sound ways of knowing: Music in the interdisciplinary curriculum*. New York: Schirmer Books.

Bennett, T. (1999, April). *The power of multiple learning environments in professional development*. Paper presented at the American Educational Research Association meeting, Montreal.

Birge, E. B. (1928/1966). *History of public school music in the United States*. Reston, VA: Music Educators National Conference. (Original work published 1928)

Blacking, J. Music in children's cognitive and affective development. (1990). In F. R. Wilson & F. L. Roehmann (Eds.), *Music and child development: The biology of music making*. St. Louis: MMB Music.

Blecher, S., & Jaffee, K. (1998). *Weaving in the arts: Widening the learning circle*. Portsmouth, NH: Heinemann.

Bresler, L. (1995). The subservient, co-equal, affective, and social integration styles and their implications for the arts. *Arts Education Policy Review, 96*(5), 31–37.

Bruner, J. S. (1960). *The process of education*. Cambridge, MA: Harvard University Press.

Burton, J., Horowitz, R., & Abeles, H. (1999). *Learning in and through the arts: Curriculum implications* (Champions of Change Report). The Arts Education Partnership and the President's Committee on the Arts and Humanities.

Campbell, M. R. (1995, September). Interdisciplinary projects in music. *Music Educators Journal, 82*(2), 37–44.

Campbell, P. S., & Scott-Kassner, C. (1995). *Music in childhood: From preschool through elementary years*. New York: Schirmer Books.

Catterall, J. & Waldorf, L. (1999). Chicago arts partnerships in education summary evaluation (Champions of Change Report). The Arts Education Partnership and the President's Committee on the Arts and Humanities.

Consortium of National Arts Education Associations. (1994). *What every young American should know and be able to do in the arts* [National Standards for Arts Education]. Reston, VA: Music Educators National Conference.

Council of Chief State School Officers. (1998). *Key state education policies on K–12 education: A 50-state report*. Washington, DC: Author.

Drake, S. M. (1993). *Planning the integrated curriculum: The call to adventure*. Alexandria, VA: Association for Supervision and Curriculum Development.

Efland, A. D. (1990). *A history of art education: Intellectual and social currents in teaching the visual arts*. New York: Teachers College Press.

Elliott, D. J. (1995). *Music matters: A new philosophy of music education*. New York: Oxford University Press.

Gallas, K. (1994). *Languages of learning: How children talk, write, dance, draw, and sing their understanding of the world*. New York: Teachers College Press.

Gardner, H. (1983). *Frames of mind: The theory of multiple intelligences*. New York: Basic Books.

Goble, J. S. (1999). *Ideologies of music education: A pragmatic, historical analysis of the concept "music" in music education in the United States*. Unpublished doctoral dissertation, University of Michigan, Ann Arbor.

Goldberg, M. (2001). *Arts and learning: An integrated approach to teaching and learning in multicultural and multilingual settings* (2nd ed.). New York: Longman.

Goldberg, M., Bennett, T., & Jacobs, V. (1999, April). *Artists in the classroom: A role in the professional development of classroom teachers*. Paper presented at the American Educational Research Association meeting, Montreal.

Gottlieb, R. (Ed.). (1996). *Reading jazz: A gathering of autobiography, reportage, and criticism from 1919 to now*. New York: Pantheon Books.

Hart, M. (1991). *Planet drum*. San Francisco: Harper.

Hoffmann, J. (1991). Computer aided music instruction. *Harvard Educational Review, 61*(3), 270–278.

Jacobs, H. H. (1989). *Interdisciplinary curriculum: Design and implementation*. Alexandria, VA: Association for Supervision and Curriculum Development.

Jacobs, V. (2000, April). *What happens when the artistic world and a teacher's world meet?* Paper presented at the American Educational Research Association meeting, New Orleans.

Jacobs, V., Goldberg, M., & Bennett, T. (in press). Uncovering artistic identity while learning to teach through the arts. In *Passion and pedagogy*. Lang.

Larsen, C. (2000). *Complex silences: Exploring the relationship between teacher change and staff development in the arts*. Unpublished doctoral dissertation, Northwestern University, Evanston, IL.

Leonhard, C. (1991). *Status of arts education: Summary and conclusions*. Urbana-Champaign, IL: Council for Research in Music Education.

Leppert, R., & McLary, S. (Eds.). (1987). *Music and society: The politics of composition, performance, and reception*. Cambridge, England: Cambridge University Press.

Mark, M. L., & Gary, C. L. (1999). *A history of American music education*. Reston, VA: Music Educators National Conference.

McKean, B. (2000, April). *Worries and considerations for teacher development in the arts.* Paper presented at the annual meeting of the American Educational Research Association, New Orleans.

Merriam, A. P. (1964). *The anthology of music.* Evanston, IL: Northwestern University Press.

National Endowment for the Arts. (1988). *Toward civilization: A report on arts education.* Washington, DC: Author.

National Standards for Arts Education. (1994). Reston, VA: Music Educators National Conference.

New London Group. (1996). A pedagogy of multiliteracies: Designing social futures. *Harvard Educational Review, 66,* 60–92.

Reimer, B. (1970). *A philosophy of music education.* Englewood Cliffs, NJ: Prentice-Hall.

Remer, J. (1996). *Beyond enrichment: Building effective arts partnerships with schools and your community.* New York: American Council for the Arts.

Rossi, P. (1997a, September). Having an experience in five acts: Multiple literacies through young children's opera. *Language Arts, 74*(5) 352–368.

Rossi, P. (1997b). *Having an experience: Multiple literacies through young children's opera.* Unpublished doctoral dissertation. University of Arizona, Tucson.

Stravinsky, I. (1942). *Poetics of music.* Cambridge: Harvard University Press.

Sutton, R. (1992). In J. T. Titon (Ed.), *Worlds of music* (2nd ed., pp. 216–317). New York: Schirmer.

Titon, J. T. (Ed.). (1992). *Worlds of music.* (2nd ed.). New York: Schirmer Books.

Veblen, K. K., & Elliott, D. J. (2000). Integration: For or against? *General Music Today, 14,* 4–8.

Wiggins, R., & Wiggins, J. (1997, January). Integrating through conceptual connections. *Music Educators Journal, 83*(4), 38–41.

Wilson, F. R., & Roehmann, F. L. (Eds.). (1990). *Music and child development: The biology of music making.* St. Louis, MO: MMB Music.

Wilson, S. L. (1999). *The role of musical intelligence in a multiple intelligences focused Central Florida elementary school.* Unpublished doctoral dissertation, University of Central Florida, Orlando.

57

Research: A Foundation for Arts Education Advocacy

LIORA BRESLER

The history of virtues (and vices) associated with the arts goes back a long way, to early myths, the Old Testament, and Greek philosophy. Music, for example, has been viewed throughout the last 26 centuries as an agent of affect, a mode of cognition, a sophisticated form, a symbol system, and a social and political force. These attributes reverberate in contemporary philosophy of music and the other arts, as well as in educational goals and practices of arts education. Of these wide-ranging attributes, cognitive aspects have assumed in the last decades a central place in advocacy outcomes of arts education, testimony to the enduring power of the cognitive revolution.

Elliot Eisner (1982) remarked that the kinds of nets we know how to weave determine the kinds of nets we cast, which, in turn, determine the kinds of fish we catch (p. 49). In the context of research and advocacy in arts education, our methodological tools often shape our research questions, reflecting the types of benefits we seek and the values that we espouse. This chapter presents research on outcomes associated with engagement in the arts, including: (1) metaanalyses of empirical studies examining connections between music and achievements in reading, math, spatial abilities, and creativity; (2) research focusing on the impact of music on the brain, searching for neurophysical impact of learning; and (3) holistic studies on the impact of music and other arts on students, investigating learning opportunities and exploring the long-term impact of arts instruction.[1] The discussion of the various criteria for advocacy research is directed toward its contribution to an enhanced understanding of the possibilities of arts education and toward the improvement of theory and practice.

The Era of Advocacy: From Federal Support to the Media Industry

Before the era of compulsory schooling, dating to antiquity, music, one of the classical subjects of study along with philosophy, mathematics, and Latin, enjoyed an elevated status. In contrast, the contemporary arena of school music[2] often resembles a battleground, concerned with survival. It is this perceived need to win the battle, I believe, that has prompted the framing of the arts as contributing directly to narrowly conceptualized utilitarian functions of a society.

The 1990s in particular witnessed a flurry of empirical research aimed to show connections between engagement with the arts and the results of intelligence test scores. Federal agencies have provided some support for the arts through their sponsorship of research on the impact of the arts on learning and their provisions of compilations of research studies on the subject.[3] In the trinity of policy, funding, and the need for accountability, the media were mobilized in the translation of arts education research to advocacy for administrators. Well-meaning advocates and the media, however, are sometimes quick to popularize research studies and in the process of transposing research to newspapers articles tend to oversimplify and overgeneralize. The format and style of newspaper and webpage headlines, such as "The arts make kids smarter" or "Children who study the arts in high school get higher SAT scores," shape the message. At best, it is uncalled-for extrapolation; at worst, distortion.

Because education is a normative, applied discipline (rather than a basic discipline like anthropology), the relationships between research and advocacy are inherently complex and rarely dichotomous. Still, the differences in styles in which research and advocacy are conducted and communicated are critical to the field. Researchers expect to refute their hypotheses and expectations in the inquiry process (see Hempel, 1966; Popper, 1969). Advocates aim to prove a priori notions of goodness.

In this climate, professional associations, too, representing both researcher and practitioner constituencies, juggle research and advocacy in a benevolent acceptance of each other's fundamentally different and often conflicting principles. Advocacy outcomes present a rare area of interaction, where advocacy-style claims of extramusical benefits (see, for example, MENC publications such as *Growing Up Complete* [1991] and *Music Makes the Difference* [1999]; Hinckley, 1999), are countered by cautions of scholars about the dangers of uncritical acceptance and decontextualization of studies highlighting extrinsic outcomes to the arts as a rationale for music education (Eisner, 1998; Reimer, 1999).[4]

Among the various constituents, the industry plays an important role. A representative example is the collaboration between the National Music Council, the Music Education Council, and the Music Industries Association in Great Britain. They have put forward an online article entitled *The Fourth R* (1998) (for rhythm). Like many others, this webpage presents short, selective summaries of empirical evidence from around the globe[5] associating the learning of music by children with significantly improved abilities in other subjects. The advocacy in the service of industry is explicit ("Learning music makes children part of a vibrant and fundamental sector of British industry"). Here, too, the issue is presented as the survival of the vulnerable music discipline, which "only recently secured its rightful place in the National Curriculum."[6]

The attempts to demonstrate a relationship between the arts and other areas of achievement, in particular those associated with economic success, are not unique to the United States but are raised internationally, especially in times of national curricular reforms (see Abbs, 1992; Best, 1992, 1995; Espeland, 1997; McPherson, 1995).[7] Especially in times of unemployment and economical problems, people tend to look to education to serve the needs of industry, reduce the number of unemployed, and increase the country's competitiveness in a global economy. The arts, as well as other disciplines, are then asked to place more emphasis on the skills that prepare students for employment. These skills can be narrow, but they can also be interpreted broadly, incorporating the cognitive, structural, communicative, and expressive aspects of the arts (see Abbs, 1992; Espeland, 1997; Livermore & McPherson, 1998; McPherson, 1995).

Quantitative Research on Transfer from the Arts to Academic Domains

Advocacies for the arts as promoting academic competencies must hinge on the notion of transfer. Transfer is defined as the effect of learning skills, knowledge, or attitudes on the later learning of other skills, knowledge, or attitudes and their application in *novel* settings (Tunks, 1992). Nineteenth-century theories of learning maintained that like physical faculties, the mental faculties of analysis, memory, and even judgment can be strengthened by the disciplinary activities of math and Latin. Transfer was assumed to occur automatically by strengthening the various mental faculties through certain activities. In the early 20th century, Thorndike (Thorndike, 1903; Thorndike & Woodward, 1901) published his groundbreaking theory of "identical elements," observing in controlled experiments that transfer occurs only in tasks sharing identical elements, or common features. The scientific investigation involving probing into the conditions of transfer brought about the recognition of important distinctions between different types of transfer. In particular, these include dichotomies between general and specific transfer; near and far transfer; and the "high road" and the "low road" to transfer (Tunks, 1992). These distinctions provide useful categories for advocacy research. An underlying issue at the root of transfer is the old debate on the nature of intelligence. Can intelligence be seen as one global property corresponding to a hierarchical model, or is it a community of separable intelligences that humans develop in distinct ways (see Gardner, 1983; Gruhn, 2000)?

Quantitative studies searching for transfer can be categorized into the following three types: correlation studies, "applied" experimental studies investigating the effects of engagement in the arts on academic learning, and "basic" experimental studies searching for anatomical and physiological evidence for the effects of engagement in the arts on brain structure and function. Correlation studies are the easiest to perform and therefore the most prevalent. However, they cannot prove a causal relationship between the arts and academic achievement and therefore can not establish transfer. Lack of correlation, however, would suffice to reject the existence of transfer. True experimental studies can establish a causal relationship but are hard to conduct, and researchers often use quasi-experimental methods instead. Finally, brain research offers the potential to determine underlying mechanisms for transfer, but, as discussed later, has thus far limited implications for actual transfer of cognitive faculties.

Empirical research concerning the transfer of music learning to other skills dating before 1990, reported by Tunks (1992) in the first edition of the *Handbook of Music*

Teaching and Learning, had mixed results. Tunks reports positive transfer of the Suzuki and Kodály methods of music instruction to spatial abilities for boys and positive transfer in special populations and neurologically impaired children but no transfer to verbal abilities. Tunks classifies most of the then current research on transfer as a simple correlation research, or descriptive comparisons of music participants with nonparticipants on some achievement or aptitude variable. Not surprisingly, Tunks concludes that there is a considerably larger transfer of music learning to music skills as compared to nonmusic skills.

Metaanalyses

The recent widespread decontextualized presentations of research in popular media combining fragmented statistical information with "headline" style has created the need for cautious metaanalyses of existing empirical research on the effects of arts education.

Metaanalysis is a way of synthesizing and explaining existing studies in terms of focused questions and a means of guiding the direction of future research (Winner & Hetland, 2000). The "method of choice for summarizing research and explaining what can and cannot be concluded, meta-analysis preserves the best features of a narrative review, but adds a quantitative synthesis by calculating an effect size for each study and then combining and comparing effect sizes across studies" (Winner & Hetland, 2000, p. 4). The significance of effects is further put in perspective by calculating measures of stability and robustness. These include, in addition to traditional measures such as confidence intervals, file drawer analysis. File drawer analysis attempts to address the possible bias in metaanalyses in favor of positive outcomes, due to lower preference given to the publication of "unsuccessful" research that found no evidence to reject the null hypothesis. Thus, this analysis reports on the number of hypothetical unpublished (i.e., lingering in file drawers) research reports that would be sufficient to render the effects found by metaanalysis insignificant.

In their Reviewing Education and the Arts Project (REAP) (Winner & Hetland, 2000), Winner and her colleagues at Harvard Project Zero investigated the relationship between learning in the major art forms of music, visual art, dance, and drama and learning in other areas of the curriculum.[8]

Winner and her colleagues coded for three designs: correlation, experimental-matched, and experimental-unmatched (quasi-experimental). Because the positive effect sizes that were found were based on correlation studies, Winner and her colleagues said that these studies do not allow them to conclude that arts education *causes* academic skills to improve.[9]

Winner and Cooper (2000) report on their analysis of research assessing the effects of more than one of the four major art forms, where the effects of specific arts forms could not be disentangled. They report that they were unable to find any experimental studies that provided a test of which causal mechanism might underlie academic improvement as a function of arts study. The research they reviewed tells them only: (a) whether there is a correlation between arts study and academic achievement and (b) whether academic achievement improves when students are exposed to the arts.[10]

Winner and Cooper say that their five metaanalyses converged to demonstrate that a positive relationship between studying the arts and academic achievement does exist. However, there is no evidence to suggest a causal relationship between arts study and verbal or math achievement. The finding that students in the United States who self-select into the arts are high academic achievers was shown by the authors' five metaanalyses to be extremely reliable. Two of the studies showed that even among poor, at-risk students, those who chose to study the arts did far better in school than those who did not choose to study the arts (Winner & Cooper, 2000, p. 58). This relationship, however, was tempered by a study from Britain showing that students who took several arts courses actually performed worse on their academic exams than those who did not concentrate in the arts.

Why, ask Winner and Cooper, have experimental studies been unable thus far to demonstrate that studying the arts leads to improved academic performance? They suggest two possible reasons. First, most of the experimental studies examine the effects of a year or so of arts study. In contrast, most of the correlation studies examine the effects of at least several years of studying the arts. For instance, the College Board findings showed that studying the arts for 4 years in high school is associated with higher SAT scores, compared to the SAT scores of students who study no arts. Catterall and his colleagues showed high academic performance in students who had remained immersed in the arts from eighth to twelfth grade (Winner & Cooper, 2000, p. 63). Winner and Cooper comment that one can hardly expect a brief exposure to the arts lasting a year or less to have strong academic transfer effects. A second reason for the failure to demonstrate a causal relationship may have to do with the kinds of outcomes that almost all the studies measured: multiple-choice test scores. The arts, Winner and Cooper write,

> are messy, they do not point to clear answers, and they call for multiple and conflicting interpretations. They are fundamentally divergent. Standardized tests call for right and wrong answers and convergent thinking. These are not measures where we should expect the arts to transfer. (p. 63)

This issue will be addressed in the discussion of alternative research methodologies.

Although the link between SAT scores and study of the arts is positive, Eisner (1999; also quoted in Vaughn & Winner, 2000) found an even stronger link between SAT scores and long-term study of academic subjects. Eisner has compared SAT scores of students taking 1, 2, 3, 4, and 4-plus years of English, math, science, history, and social science/foreign language, and arts and music. He found that in every case, students who take at least 4 years of a given academic subject score considerably higher on their SATs (in both math and verbal) than students who take only 1 year of this subject. Furthermore, the differences between scores of students with 1 versus 4 or more years of the subject is far smaller in the case of the arts and music than in the case of each of the other academic areas examined. Eisner concludes that these data suggest that students who focus on particular areas are high-achieving students: focusing on the arts is one indication of high academic achievement, but focusing on academic areas is an even stronger indication of high academic achievement (Vaughn & Winner, 2000, p. 87; Eisner, 1999).

Of the 1,000 records of research studies considered, only two studies followed a true experimental design, in which students were randomly assigned to arts versus control programs, and these two studies had extremely low effect size. Winner and Cooper conclude that there is no evidence that studying the arts has a causal effect on academic achievement. They caution that the existing research is limited in its exclusive focus on outcome rather than process, that is, studies (with one exception) have examined the outcome of academic achievement and have simply speculated on how such an outcome might be achieved. None of the empirical studies examined the effects of programs in which teachers taught for transfer (Winner & Cooper, 2000).[11] Winner and Cooper suggest that for transfer to occur, teachers must teach explicitly for transfer. (A related although much narrower conclusion might be drawn from experiments in brain research, as discussed hereafter.) For instance, to demonstrate transfer of learning from one domain to another, teachers must explicitly lay the groundwork and help students to see how learning in one area may be similar to learning in another area.

Music and Math

The intimate connection between music and math was established by Pythagoras in the 6th century B.C. and has been pursued through the past centuries by scientists like Kepler, Galilei, and Euler. The continuous interest in the relationship between math and music is echoed in contemporary books such as *Emblems of Mind: The Inner Life of Music and Mathematics* (Rothstein, 1995), *Pythagoras' Trousers: God, Physics, and the Gender Wars* (Wertheim,

1995) and *Godel, Escher, Bach* (Hofstadter, 1979). Rothstein comments that music and mathematics share not only the clarity of their expression but also their beauty and mystery:

> Our attempt to comprehend music and mathematics, to understand their workings and their purposes, is . . . a model for our coming to know at all—a model for our education, for the ways we make distinctions and connections.
>
> We begin with objects that look dissimilar. We compare, find patterns, analogies with what we already know. We step back and create abstractions, laws, systems, using transformations, mappings, and metaphors. This is how mathematics grows increasingly abstract and powerful; it is how music obtains much of its power, with grand structures growing out of small details. In music and mathematics, it may be just a modest, but mind-opening, step from the kindergarten to the cosmos.

Are these principles exhibited in test scores? Metaanalyses on studies centering on the effect of music instruction/exposure on school achievement in math were conducted by Vaughn (2000).[12] Correlation studies (including large sample studies from the College Board) demonstrated a small positive association between the voluntary study of music and mathematical achievement. Vaughn comments that though it is conceivable that the music education received by the students in these studies actually led to improvement in math performance, other explanations for this correlation (like stronger economic backgrounds of students or that music-rich schools may be stronger academically) cannot be ruled out.

The experimental studies showed that individuals exposed to a music curriculum in school (not voluntarily selected) show higher mathematical achievement (a small causal relationship) as a consequence of this music instruction. The experimental studies also showed that background music heard while thinking about math problems serves to enhance mathematical ability, at least during the music listening time, but the effect size found was trivially small. Even if such a conclusion could be drawn, Vaughn writes, we would need to examine the effect of soothing music on other kinds of academic performance in order to determine whether background music has a particularly enhancing effect on math or whether it enhances any academic task as a function of its relaxing effect.

Music and Reading

According to Butzlaff (2000), there are several possible reasons to hypothesize that instruction in music may help children acquire reading skills: (1) music and written text both involve formal notation that must be read from left to right, and in both cases, the written code maps onto a specific sound; (2) practice in reading music notation may make the reading of linguistic notation an easier task (Butzlaff, 2000); (3) experience in reading lyrics that are often repetitive may be helpful for reading texts.

Butzlaff identified for the metaanalyses 6 experimental and 24 correlation studies, 10 of which were of the College Board Studies (1988–98), where all reading performance by students with some music experience was compared to reading performance by students without music experience.[13] The metaanalysis demonstrates a strong and reliable association between the study of music and performance on standardized reading/verbal skills. Butzlaff comments that a causal relationship may exist but there are other possibilities, such as that students who are already strong in reading choose to study music. Students studying music do in fact have significantly higher scores on standardized reading tests (i.e., on the verbal portion of the Scholastic Achievement Test). The mean effect size, though small, was found to be more robust than that found for the experimental studies. The metaanalysis on experimental studies designed to test the hypotheses that music study enhances (or causes) reading improvement yielded no reliable effect.

Music and Spatial-Temporal Reasoning

One aspect of intelligence (i.e., a component of IQ tests) is the ability to perform on temporal tasks, defined as requiring "the ability to transform mental images in the absence of physical model" (Rauscher, Shaw, & Ky, 1993). The temporary enhancement of spatial-temporal reasoning following the listening to Mozart music (Rauscher, Shaw & Ky, 1993) (or the "Mozart effect," as it became known in both popular and scholarly circles) had dramatic presentation in the media. Studies related to visual-spatial abilities can be categorized into correlation, and experimental studies attempting to discover a physiologial model for the effects of music on cognitive impacts of nonmusical tasks (e.g., reading, math).

Rauscher and her colleagues found that college students' scores on spatial subtests of the Stanford-Binet IQ battery increased an equivalent of 8–10 points for 12 minutes after listening to about 10 minutes of the first movement of Mozart's Piano Sonata for Two Pianos (K. 448). The control group sat in silence or listened to a tape of relaxation instructions to lower blood pressure. The experiment was motivated by the "trion" model of the cortex, and the authors explained their result by the following model: columns of neurons in the cortex involved in musical processing (with three levels of activation, hence the term "trion") primed neurons used for spatial tasks (in Hetland, 2000b).

The "Mozart effect" contradicts prevailing views on two related topics: modularity and transfer (Hetland, 2000b, p. 105). Modularity is the theory that the mind comprises relatively separate units dedicated to particular kinds of information (Fodor, 1993; Gardner, 1983). Cognitive transfer, in which one kind of learning supports performance on other kinds of tasks, is difficult to achieve, especially when the transfer is "far"—between two different kinds of performances (e.g., Salomon & Perkins, 1989). Furthermore, results with similar size of the effect could not be replicated. Hetland (2000b) analyzed all available experiments, including unpublished ones (36 studies with 2,465 subjects using spatial-temporal measures and 31 studies with 2,089 subjects using spatial-temporal outcomes) to avoid "publication bias," as published studies are more likely to report positive results than unpublished ones.

Hetland concludes that the Mozart effect exists and not only when the comparison is between music and relaxation. The Mozart effect is not greater for women (who traditionally perform less well than males on measures of mental rotation). The effect is limited, however, to a specific type of spatial task that requires mental rotation in the absence of a physical model. It is a moderate effect, and it is robust. The enhancing effect is not limited to Mozart's music. Some kinds of music enhance, while other kinds do not. The properties of music that enhance spatial tasks have not yet been explicitly specified. It has been suggested that "complex" music or music possessing symmetry might activate the right hemisphere and hence enhance spatial tasks. It has also been suggested that, whatever type of music enhances, the enhancement is related to its rhythmic elements (Hetland, 2000a).[14]

The Search for Physiological Evidence for Transfer

The recent development and improvement of brain imaging techniques, such as functional MRI, which allow the localization of brain activation in space and time, have provided new and powerful tools to study brain function. These tools allow the design of studies on the internal effects of music on the brain and encourage the attempt to find support for transfer from music to other faculties at this most basic level. In contrast to empirical studies on *external effects*, such as transfer or stimulation by music for skills in other than musical domains, the study of internal brain effects has the potential to elucidate the mechanism that underlies such transfer. Such understanding might, in turn, be used to prescribe ways to maximize the transfer and take optimal advantage of it.

This situation is not unlike that in the development of treatments in medical science, where traditional research has initially involved correlation studies, then controlled trials to determine effects of proposed treatments and, most recently, fundamental studies at the molecular level to uncover disease mechanisms and the interactions of drugs with them.

That there is a relationship between the development of specific brain areas and musical activity has been demonstrated in various studies (see Rauscher, 1998). Similarly, real-time specific brain responses to musical stimulus have been observed. However, in view of the modular theory of brain function, it is not clear that such development has implications for extramusical brain faculties. Thus, a central question with respect to transfer is whether music stimulates brain areas other than those directly related to music, so that other cognitive functions are affected (Gruhn, 2000).

The research on this question appears to be at an early stage. As evidence of internal transfer, Gruhn (2000) reviews an experiment that demonstrated, by EEG activation measurements, the establishment of testing internal maps between motor and auditory areas in the brains of novice piano players in response to training in the performance of a musical piece. According to Gruhn, if we agree that this result can be interpreted as a transfer effect, then it is obvious that a special training effect is likely to be seen as an operant conditioning. Gruhn hypothesizes that the task establishes a synaptic link between synchronically stimulated areas, so that learning tends to develop a dense neuronal network of connections that enables corepresentations.

In view of the results of brain research, the answer to whether brain research supports the claim for transfer effects is not easily found. Some data confirm internal transfer, but effects of musical abilities on other cognitive domains are rare or missing. Gruhn (2000) concludes:

> There is little evidence for an inevitable external transfer effect from one intelligence to another, but there is strong evidence for internal correlation between different brain functions and brain activation areas that tempt us to believe in or hope for external transfer effects as well.

Gruhn quotes Gardner (in Gruhn, 2000): "We could know what every neuron does and we would not be one step closer to knowing how to educate our children."

This negative view of brain research should, however, be tempered with some useful lessons provided by the research already discussed. First, as far as transfer is concerned, results such as those in the Bangert experiment (cited in Gruhn, 2000) provide objective grounding for the recommendation voiced by authors of empirical metaanalyses (see Butzlaff, 2000; Hetland, 2000a,b; Winner & Cooper, 2000) that one should intentionally teach for transfer if transfer is to occur. Indeed, the linking of cortical maps of different domains (aural and motor) only occurred as a result of training that encouraged the for-

mation of a robust association between the two, with no such effects observed in the control group where such associations were prevented by the experimental conditions. Second, the localization of musical representation in the brain and the specificity of their activation by aural stimuli and the recognition that learning involves the development and incremental differentiation of mental representation together suggest a model for music instruction. Musical entities such as pulse, meter, tonality, intervals, motives, and contours can only be articulated in singing or playing if developed as mental representations. This calls for "teaching music musically" (see Gruhn, 2000). In a way that advances strategies and learning modes that promote the development of genuine musical representations by priming an aural-oral loop (Gruhn, 2000).

Finally, according to Gruhn (2000), genuine musical representations appear to contradict transfer effects. Music has a strong effect on the brain, but there is little evidence that music learning automatically affects other cognitive skills. The present state of brain research on the effects of music leads us to conclude that the prime, if not the only, goal of music education is to teach music for its inherent merit.

Methodological Issues

As noted by Tunks (1992) and Winner and Hetland (2000) as well as metaanalyses of other art disciplines such as dance (Keinanen, Hetland, & Winner, 2000), drama (Podolzny, 2000) and visual art (Moga, Burger, Hetland, & Winner, 2000), there are several methodological problems associated with the study of transfer. The first has to do with the measurement of transfer, which is conceptualized as a causal relationship. The media presents research findings as causal (e.g., the arts make you smarter). However, few studies were truly experimental. Almost all of the studies that were identified by the Harvard Project Zero group in the initial electronic search were nonempirical, advocacy articles arguing about the power of art but not researching it. In empirical studies, most studies that professed to address transfer were correlation studies or lacked the control needed to make valid conclusions about cause (e.g., not double-blind experiments, so experimenter expectancy effects cannot be ruled out) (see Hetland, 2000a, b; Tunks, 1992; Winner & Hetland, 2000).

The lack of appropriate comparison groups in so-called experimental studies is raised by all of the researchers who conducted metaanalyses (Winner & Cooper, 2000; Winner & Hetland, 2000; Vaughn & Winner, 2000). True experimental research with random assignment of students versus teachers to arts versus control classroom is difficult to carry out (Winner & Hetland, 2000, p. 5). Research then must revert to quasi-experimental methods. In order for clear conclusions to be drawn, the two programs in the experiment should have students matched in preexisting ability and other relevant background variables. In addition, as Winner and Hetland point out (2000), schools that grant the arts a special role may attract better teachers than do more traditional schools.

"Real" teaching is complex (as compared to "stimuli" like presenting a musical piece). Not only contents, but pedagogies and implicit messages about what is important, vary greatly across teachers. The climate of the environment in which the arts are presented can affect learning dramatically.

In her critique of Katie Overy's article, Janet Mills (1998) proposes another way of conceptualizing methodological problems. Mills highlights the distinction between the two questions "Can music really improve the mind?" and *"Does it?"* Like many other researchers, Overy is asking whether there are circumstances or conditions (e.g., a particular sort of music or a style of music teaching) under which music may improve the mind. They are not asking whether *any* sort of experience that could qualify under the general heading of "music" always improves the mind (Mills, 1998). As Mills points out, the answer to the second question is clearly negative. It takes only one counterexample to refute it. "Depending on our prejudices, we may need to look no further than the nearest . . . radio station, supermarket or crush bar for our counter-example" (Mills, 1998, p. 103). Mills refers to a Swiss study by Spychiger that found that children who did more music at school, at the expense of language and mathematics, became better at language and reading and no worse at mathematics. Mills points out that if we were to require that all schools give children more music at the expense of mathematics and English, we are likely to find counterexamples of schools where standards in mathematics and English dropped down, if only because the teachers would not have been persuaded that this experiment was likely to work. The operating mechanisms in Spychiger's effect are not understood. In the absence of control groups (for example, one can envision another classroom where physical education was increased at the cost of academics), one could envision a number of possible explanations that have nothing to do with music. We need detailed information that can help us understand the mechanisms at work and what could account for the effects.

Outcomes of Advocacy Research

It is the shaking of deeply held beliefs, our "folk theories" (Bruner, 1996), that makes headlines. In this case, it is the questioning of the disassociation, as old as Plato, of the arts from rationality (or their contemporary equivalents—the "hard-core" academic subjects and measurements of intelligence) that makes news.[15] Public interest creates a market for "headline information" that in turn further shapes public interest. Stake's (1997) discussion of a "headlines" frame of mind applies here: "We seek the quotable quote, the executive summary, the declining graphic, the bottom-line indicator, even the cartoon, to stand for Quality in each constantly moving, complex, and contextual evaluated" (p. 471). Form shapes content. The headlines communication of arts advocacy can easily distort findings, transforming research findings into simplistic advocacy. Advocacy can prompt action. The apparent ability to effect quick change with low budget is appealing to administrations. In music, for example, the Mozart effect research investigates the effects of *exposure* to music. Following the news on the impact of music on the brain, the state of Georgia distributed classical CDs to all mothers with newborns. School districts in different states established the practice of background listening to Mozart during recess. The principle behind these policies and practices is not new, fitting in with the use of music as background for supermarkets, telephones on hold, and hotel elevators to shape mood and behavior. In this practice, we are taught to "tune out," *not* to pay attention. It is a desensitizing rather than an intensifying and expansive experience.

These practices can be related to a narrow conceptualization of both academic subjects (reducing them to scores on standardized tests and IQs) and the arts (treated as subservient to academic subjects). We are doomed if the arts deliver and doomed if they don't. If research can't demonstrate students' progress in multiple choice test scores, the arts may be abandoned as quickly as they were adopted, in search of a new quick fix. Using the arts as background effect and as means to increase test scores and consequent outcomes sets a dangerous precedent in terms of the value of arts in education and the ways they are framed. In response to the problems involved in the narrow conceptualizations of the arts, the past 2 decades saw increasing research focus on the impact of the arts education as it relates to their actual offering, including the meanings of those involved with the artistic experiences. The next section discusses studies that include examination of the particular learning opportunities of arts programs and that explore participants' meanings of arts experiences.

Beyond Measurement

The scholarly world of educational research became sensitized to the limitation of measurement as an exclusive tool of inquiry in the 1960s and 1970s. The adage attributed to Albert Einstein that "not everything that can be counted counts, and not everything that counts can be counted" became widely acknowledged. In a similar vein, Theodore Sizer's statement about testing acknowledged a complex social and political world: "You can hide in a test. You can't hide in an inspection. Tests are an easy out. They have a facade of toughness and objectivity. Tests put no burden on the people who most often demand them—the politicians" (in Kantrowitz, 1999, p. 51).

Controlled experiments typically involve a specific, well-defined arts activity as an intervention (e.g., a particular piece of music, played for so many minutes). However, when it comes to "real," day-to-day arts curricula of the schools (or, for that matter, interactions with the arts in general), the manifestations of art are extremely diverse. Any attempt to connect "arts education" to specific results should specify what is meant by arts education, including the *context* for interactions with the arts. The careful, "thick" description of the context in which music and arts experiences take place is central to understanding their meaning and import for those involved. Thus, before we can extrapolate from lab studies to the real, complex world, researchers need to turn attention to the operational curriculum of arts programs.

These new directions call for corresponding methods and data sources. In the 1980s and 1990s the scope of research in music and arts education expanded to encompass a variety of qualitative methods (see Bresler & Stake, 1992, and chap. 61). The data sources of intensive observations of programs can convey qualities of music and art experience and the educational opportunities they provide. Open-ended, phenomenological interviews can capture how these experiences are interpreted by the participants and the meanings and values they construct.

Contexts of Learning

School Arts

Spychiger (1998) points out that the improvement of academic skills works similarly to Thorndike and Woodward's (1901) notion of identical elements. Not just any musical activity promotes extramusical capabilities; rather, the musical activity and the topic of extramusical improvement need to be similar. Music activities, for instance, learning to play an instrument, may increase concentration and good learning habits but do not necessarily improve creativity, expression, improvisation, or social skills if that has not been an explicit goal of performance. Studies that investigate programs can connect specific skills to specific learning opportunities. The particular contents, structures, and contexts in which learning takes place shape learning and its transfer to areas artistic, academic, and beyond.

Research findings indicated great variance in school offerings within and across schools. Contents, pedagogies, structures, and formats for arts education vary from rich and sophisticated to poor. Arts curricula range from a rote curriculum of dittos and low-level skills to producing stereotypical holiday craft to sophisticated work where students are taught skills of observation, production, and communication of ideas while reflecting, creating, interpreting, and thinking like artists (see Stake, Bresler, & Mabry, 1991). Within music, for example, there is tremendous diversity, from low-level skills of singing off-tune with little attention to dynamics or form to skillful, expressive singing and playing recorders. Clearly, to be told that students receive arts instruction, without a clear indication of contents and pedagogies, provides little information about the knowledge, skills, and sensitivities they actually develop.

Little can be known about arts practices in the schools without actively exploring them. The absence of national, state, and district-level prescriptions that are taken seriously and the fact that we have few widely accepted and respected arts education curricula and textbooks leave more room for diversity and open-endedness. The study of the operational curriculum of music and other arts requires intensive observations in naturalistic settings.

The context of the school is fundamental to the understanding of both the actual and possible impacts of arts education. Unlike the fine and popular arts, "school arts" function in contexts that are compulsory. School art in the United States evolved in educational settings of the 19th century with the expansion of mass education. The incorporation of the arts into the general curriculum was a struggle from the very beginning, never quite assuming equal status with the academic disciplines that have constituted the foundations of schooling.

There is an interesting interplay between the goals of school art and the larger goals of school reflecting society's values. During the 150 years of its existence, school art rode different ideological and pedagogical waves, assuming radically different advocacies: serving utilitarian goals to earn a living (e.g., by training in drawing skills); spiritual goals (e.g., singing to praise the Lord); humanistic goals (e.g., cultivating the mind); therapeutic goals (e.g., providing children with means of self-expression and emotional outlet); and public relations goals (representing the school in the community). Each of these goals generated different arts curricula, contents, pedagogies, and experiences, several of which can be traced to contemporary schooling (Bresler, 1998).

Thus, in addition to the *subservient* role of the arts to academics, some arts education fulfill a *complementary* role, highlighting affect and expression or celebrating the communal aspects of art (Bresler, 1995). The latter role matches teachers' and administrators' beliefs about the "real" educational value of the arts. In a school climate that is often perceived by teachers as increasingly rigid, the arts are regarded as providing those educational benefits that are seen to be missing from the academic curriculum (Bresler, 1994). This dual expectation of the arts (subservient and complementary) reflects a fundamental dilemma of whether the arts should mirror or expand school values.[16]

A project by Burton, Horowitz, and Abeles (1999) from Teachers College, Columbia University, examined the impact of learning opportunities in the art curriculum on students' learning and attitudes. Based on a study of 2,046 students attending public schools in grades 4–8, the researchers found significant relationships between rich in-school arts programs and the creative, cognitive, and personal competencies needed for academic success (Burton, Horowitz, & Abeles, 1999). Broad research questions included: What is arts learning? Does it extend to learning in other school subjects? What conditions in schools support this learning? The 2-year study encompassed 12 schools, four of which were sites for in-depth case study, in New York, Connecticut, Virginia, and South Carolina. Research design included qualitative and quantitative measures.[17]

The researchers found that students in "high-arts" groups performed better than those in "low-arts" groups on measures of creativity, fluency, originality, elaboration, and resistance to closure, capacities central to arts learning. Students in arts-intensive settings were also strong in their abilities to express thoughts and ideas, exercise their imagination, and take risks in learning. In addition, they were described by their teachers as more cooperative and willing to display their learning publicly. High-arts youngsters were far more likely than their low-arts counterparts to think of themselves as competent in academics. Importantly, the results of the study were more firmly tied to rich arts provision than high economic status.

The arts were found to be subjects where students could take risks in their thinking as they tried out new and unexplored arenas of learning. In the high-arts settings, researchers found considerable flexibility in curriculum design, with less emphasis on conformity, formalization, or centralization. The results show that teachers in arts-rich schools, which tended to favor change and experimentation, demonstrated more interest in their work, were more likely to become involved in professional development experiences, and were more likely to be innovative in their teaching.

Teachers spoke of the effects of the arts programs on students' different dimensions of ability, including expression of ideas and feelings openly and thoughtfully; the ability to imagine different vantage points of an idea or problem and work toward a solution; and the ability to focus perception on items of experience and sustain this focus over a period of time. The appearances of arts competencies in other disciplines was found in contexts where, for example, there was a need for students to figure out and elaborate on ideas on their own; when there was a need to structure and organize thinking in light of different kinds of experiences; and where learning involved task persistence, ownership, empathy, and collaboration with others. In subjects such as science, mathematics, and language, invitations to accommodate conflicting ideas, to formulate new and better ways of representing thoughts, and to take risks and leaps call forth a complex of cognitive and creative capacities. These capacities were typical of the arts learning in this study.

Burton and her colleagues conceptualize the competencies developed by the arts as "habits of mind" (rather than higher order thinking), interweaving intuitive, practical, and logical modes of thought that characterize arts learning. These habits of mind are accompanied by an array of personal dispositions such as risk-taking, task persistence, ownership of learning, and perceptions of academic accomplishment in school. The findings in this study address competencies and dispositions that cannot be observed in brain research in its present state.

A study with mixed findings is *Arts Education in Secondary Schools*, by Harland et al. (2000). Their 3-year study of the effects and effectiveness of arts education in English and Welsh secondary schools[18] aimed to (1) investigate the range of outcomes attributable to arts education in secondary schools, in particular the hypothesis that engagement in the arts can boost general academic performance, and (2) analyze the key factors and processes that may bring about these effects.[19]

Effects on students included a heightened sense of enjoyment, excitement, and fulfillment, and therapeutic release of tensions; an increase in the knowledge and skills associated with particular art forms; the development of social and cultural issues; the development of creativity and thinking skills; and effects that transfer to other contexts, such as learning in other subjects, the world of work, and cultural activities beyond school. From arts-oriented students in schools with strong arts programs, each art discipline generated different effects. Music, for example, tended to promote active listening skills; dance increased awareness of the body and movement; visual art promoted expressive skills; and drama promoted empathy. Gaps in outcomes noted by Harland include the development of metaawareness of the intellectual dimensions to artistic processes and the development of critical discrimination and aesthetic judgment–making.

From a larger and more representative sample of schools, there was no evidence to support the claim that the arts boost general academic performance at GCSE (Harland et al., 2000). From the case study schools, however, students volunteered accounts of arts-based learning that had transferred to other subjects, especially in visual art and drama and less so for music. Music, while benefiting from status similar to that of visual art, attracted the highest proportion of "no impact" responses, registered a limited range of outcomes compared with visual art and drama, and received lower levels of enjoyment in GCSE courses, with students commenting that relevance, creativity, and expressive dimensions were often absent. The research report concluded that individual teacher factors were probably more important determinants of effectiveness than whole-school factors.

Discipline-based Art Education and the Culture of Change

Not surprisingly, the quality of arts education impacts its effect on learners. What factors support a climate conducive to meaningful arts education? Aiming to improve the cognitive aspects of visual art education, the Getty Education Institute for the Arts funded six Regional Institute Grant (RIG) programs, which introduced the disciplined-based arts education (DBAE) approach, integrating (visual) art history, appreciation and aesthetics, and studio studies into elementary, middle, and high schools. Wilson (1997) conducted a 7-year study for the Getty Educational Institute of the six RIG programs. Data sources included observations in more than 100 schools in which DBAE programs were implemented. The study focused on the curricular and administrative levels but had direct implications for students' learning.

Wilson concluded that change initiatives succeeded when change was systemic—specifically, when school district leaders steer the initiative, change communities share ownership, and multiple reform efforts reinforce and enhance each other (Wilson, 1997).

Another Getty Center project, initiated in collaboration with the College Board, focused on the integration of the four arts into academic disciplines. This was a case study evaluation of five high schools supported by the Getty Center, chosen for their exemplary support for the arts by principals and teachers and for their diverse student populations (Bresler, 1997a). Methods of inquiry included intensive observations of the integrated arts/academic instruction (replacing traditional offerings); in-depth interviews with teachers, administrators, students and parents; and analysis of curricular materials and student work (Bresler, 1997a).

The study revealed that one impact of the arts curricula on those engaged in it was a change of roles for both students and teachers. For students, their emergent ownership of art and academic work was connected with issues of identity, voice, and pride in their ideas and creation. Observations of the operational arts curriculum revealed reflective and engaged discussions, coaching of individual students, and encouragement of academic excellence in the projects, as well as personal meanings of such work. Students' attitudes toward their learning and general school experiences as revealed in interviews were positive to enthusiastic. The curriculum—contents, assignments, evalu-

ation—encouraged students' higher level thinking and creativity. Students' communication of their work to a wider, interested audience of teachers and peers provided an additional incentive to excel.

Students' changes of role were directly related to the changed curricula. In these five high school settings, the integration of arts and academics was not technical but rather a transformative process. The integrated curricula emphasized personal and social relevance, connecting the past to the present and faraway cultures to that of contemporary United States. Teachers' evaluation strategies drew on portfolios and projects (instead of essays and tests), encouraging the presentation of concepts and ideas in a variety of modes of representation and learning styles.

The most obvious change of roles for participating teachers was a heightened movement toward *developing*, rather than just implementing, curricula: curriculum as an act of creation. In particular, teachers reported feeling expanded in the integration process, and these feelings of self-growth sustained them in their efforts and feelings of uncertainty. Teachers of academic subjects who participated in arts integration units moved away from reliance on textbooks towards the active identification of overarching themes and broad issues. Instead of feeling isolated, teachers became conscious of how their own curriculum fit and affected other subjects and how they could draw on other subjects.[20]

In studies focusing on programs of art education, measuring achievement and impact was important. Thus, the increased test scores in Brownsville High School in the College Board/Getty Center study on arts integration was a major event signifying success and legitimization. However, the intrinsic rewards were central: engaging and engaged teaching and learning where important intellectual and affective connections were made and where opportunities for creation, interpretation, and expression were provided. It is the understandings of what supports excellent arts programs and their relationships to students' achievements in the arts, and the repercussions in other areas, that allow us to make changes at the educational level.

Learning the Arts During Nonschool Hours: A Linguistic Ethnography

Heath and Roach (1999) conducted a decade-long study investigating effective learning sites that young people in economically disadvantaged communities choose for themselves in their nonschool hours. The motivation for the study was an "institutional gap," where the traditional institutions of school, family, and church no longer fully meet the needs of today's children and youth. The researchers were anthropologists examining learning and language development in 124 youth-based organizational environments for students likely to be labeled "at-risk" in their schools. These organizations centered around athletic-academic groups (sports teams that heavily integrated instruction in academic topics related to the sport being played) with sports activities; community service centers, where participants oriented their activities toward community services (e.g., ecological, religious, economic); or arts-based activities in a variety of media, including visual, technical, musical, and dramatic.[21]

Researchers spent time immersed, sometimes over several years, in each site, following the talk, work patterns, and interactions of youth members. In addition, researchers audio-recorded everyday language both within and outside the organizations, interviewed local residents and youth not linked to youth-based organizations, and supervised other young people in their keeping of daily logs and journals. A sample of youth organization members in non-school activities was compared on various features with a national sample of high school students.

The focus of data collection and analysis was the language that young people and their adult leaders used. Environments of arts organizations emerged as somewhat different from those of groups engaged primarily in community service or sports. In addition, the young people who belonged to arts programs exhibited more of certain attitudes and behaviors than those attending organizations of other types. Students said: "[Art] changes your perception of the world." "You can say really important things in a piece of art." "You center yourself and things pour out." "When I am actually doing my art, I feel like I'm in a different frame [of mind]."

Contexts of arts organizations were found to be rich linguistic and cognitive environments.[22] Heath and Young (1999) conclude that contexts of learning matter greatly in exploring what goes into creating and sustaining these contexts. They found that the communal aspects were central. Young people were expected to help to make rules, be able to try something new, take inspiration from various sources, and create. Adults in these organizations expected more than just problem solving. They ensured that students got extensive practice in looking ahead and figuring out where problems might arise down the road.

Ethnomusicological literature (see Blacking & Keali'nohomoku, 1979; Bjorkvold, 1989; Mans, 1997) is investigating the roles of music and dance as practiced in the community in developing complex cognitive skills. These studies include looking at music as a patterned event in a system of social interaction, as part of a process of conscious decision-making, expanding consciousness and influencing subsequent decision-making and cultural invention (see Blacking & Keali'nohomoku, 1979).[23]

Long-term Impact

The Development of Talent on Economically Disadvantaged Students

Questions about the nature and quality of students' experiences are assuming increasing prominence. In a study focusing on the development of talent and the impact of the arts on students from economically disadvantaged, low socioeconomic status backgrounds, Oreck, Baum, and Mc-Cartney (1999) focused on 23 students, aged 10–26, in three different stages of talent development in music and dance.[24] Research questions concerned the impact of serious arts involvement over an extended period of time on economically disadvantaged verbal students' lives and capacities and the external support and internal characteristics that helped them overcome those obstacles. Data sources consisted of extended interviews with the students, their parents and families, arts instructors, and current and former academic teachers; observations in both school and professional settings; and the collection of academic data.[25]

While the artistic, academic, and professional outcomes were different for each individual, many of the personal qualities and behavioral indicators that seemed to directly contribute to the students' success were common across cases and age groups. These qualities included the experience of resilience, the ability to bounce back from adverse experiences, and self-regulation, the general habits of practice, focus, and discipline that helped students progress in demanding instruction.

What was it about the arts environment (but not the regular classroom) that encouraged these and other important qualities? Self-regulation includes paying attention, using feedback, problem solving in a curricular context, self-initiating, asking questions, taking risks, cooperating, persevering, being prepared, setting goals (Baum, Owen, & Oreck, 1997). Baum, Owen and Oreck visited several classrooms to observe how a sample of students who were talented in dance, music, or theater used self-regulation in typical academic settings. Many of the students who were self-regulated during their arts lessons demonstrated few self-regulation skills in an academic environment.

Is this proof that self-regulation does not transfer from the arts to other academic subjects? Not necessarily. A closer look at contextual factors and complexities that might have been overlooked by a quantitative measurement study reveals otherwise. The research points out important differences between the environments of the arts and academic classes. Baum et al. (1997) describe the art classes they observed (but *not* the observed regular classrooms) as typically characterized by: (1) a physical and emotional climate conducive to active learning (e.g., arrangement of physical space for activity, individual small group participation, encouragement of unique individual answers, and the tolerance of some noise and chaos); (2) goal-setting (goals are set collaboratively by instructor and students, result in performance for an audience, are related to talents and interests, and involve real-world challenges); (3) instructional process (lessons require active participation and student leadership and offer opportunities to move around and confer, opportunities for students to ask questions, and opportunities for divergent thinking); and (4) teachers' expectations and feedback: high standards for all, frequent specific feedback (positive and negative), encouragement of student feedback to other students, and encouragement of regular self-evaluation. The "thick description" of arts instruction provided in this report can help educators understand how to make changes and how to transfer insights from arts learning to other areas of learning in a meaningful way.

Observations of students involved in arts classes and performances provide evidence of successful learning and reveal a wide range of self-regulatory behaviors at work. Although any learning situation can be used as a model to teach self-regulation, the arts processes can provide particularly rich and effective opportunities to enhance and develop these behaviors. On a broader scale, effective arts instruction (as manifested in these settings) encourages the development of unique individual strategies and multiple solutions to problems. Activities were performance-based, providing students with immediate feedback to evaluate their own learning. Because language was not the sole modality of instruction, a wide range of students, including those with limited English proficiency or special nonverbal skills, could learn and communicate what they knew in different ways. Once the stage is set to allow students' self-regulatory behaviors to emerge, teachers need instruction on recognizing and developing these in their students. And they also need guidance in planning their curricula to enhance the abilities of students to use their effective strategies and interests to master curricular topics.

The Impact of the Suzuki Method on Students' Lives

Of particular importance are long-term studies of students' experiences that reflect a perspective gained through time. A doctoral dissertation by Collier-Slone (1991) centered on students' lived experience, where participants define the categories. Using open-ended, phenomenological interviews, Collier-Slone explored students' and parents' experiences with the Suzuki method and its impact on their lifelong learning and attitudes. The 26 participants in her study had been involved in Suzuki method training from

their preschool or early elementary years through high school graduation. Their narratives highlighted the contribution of the Suzuki method in developing their self-esteem, attitudes, and values. Participants reported the ability to be fully present and to live in the here and now as one result of learning via the Suzuki method.

Students' experiences also included perceived self-discipline transferred to a later stage of maturation; involvement in the process of self-analysis and the development of self-regulation as a natural and positive force from the early days of study; the development of significant work habits and residual skills that impacted their current professional endeavors; and the ability to isolate difficult tasks and work repetitively in small segments until mastery, using building-block steps in approaching a project or new learning.

Criteria of Advocacy Research

A detailed discussion of qualitative criteria is provided in chapter 61. This section touches briefly on some criteria as related to previously mentioned studies. Stake's note on the changing criteria in evaluation applies here:

> Part of the educational evaluator's plight is that of being caught in a field losing its authority. I find it aesthetically pleasing and methodologically enabling to honor personal experience and postmodern insight, to recognize multiple realities and constructivist knowledge—but at such a cost! . . . Honoring personal construction of knowledge leads to denial that anything important can be known that is not value laden and advocative. (Stake, 1997, p. 470)

In the search for criteria compatible with a postmodern view of research and its goals, methods, assumptions, and styles of communication, the techniques suggested by Lincoln and Guba (1985) are useful in our considerations of the previously discussed research to make it more likely that credible findings and interpretations will be produced. *Prolonged engagement,* the investment of sufficient time to detect and take account of distortions that might otherwise creep into the data, is exemplified in ethnographic studies such as Heath's. *Persistent observation,* which provides depth by adding the dimension of salience to what might otherwise be little more than a mindless immersion, is manifested in Oreck, Baum, and McCartney's identification of the arts' impact on self-regulation, and resilience. *Triangulation* of sources and methods, as reflected in the multiple sources used by Burton, Horowitz, and Abeles, addresses the convergence of findings from different perspectives. *Member checking,* aiming to increase the likelihood that the rich multiple realities of participants are represented with integrity, is evident in Collier's study. In addition, ethical criteria are essential in a methodology that focuses on individuals in private and semiprivate settings (see Bresler, 1997b; Punch, 1994). Discussion of these criteria in publications takes space, and conventions of qualitative research often do not require it. Still, it is crucial that researchers explicitly address the criteria they follow.

Beyond techniques, the ability to provide fresh meanings is central to qualitative research. Exploratory studies that reveal unexpected effects of programs and teachers are invaluable. These kinds of studies typically opt for

> an epistemology of ambiguity that seeks out . . . meanings that are . . . tentative, incomplete, sometimes even contradictory, and originating from multiple vantage points. Such an epistemological stance seems appropriate to a project of educational inquiry whose role or purpose is the enhancement of meaning, rather than a reduction of uncertainty. (Barone, 2001, p. 161)

Unlike quantitative research on the one hand and advocacy on the other, qualitative studies seek to present complexity and multiple perspectives. Advocates may find the contextuality of the findings and the fact that they cannot be captured in headlines to be cumbersome and the lack of generalizability inherent in these methodologies to be problematic, but we know of no shortcuts.

In this quest for meaning, raising important questions about the nature of the educational process is as important as providing answers. For example, Spychiger's study (quoted in Mills, 1998) is interesting not because it is generalizable to all settings but because it "questions the educationally unquestionable," providing "plenty of food for thought" (Mills, 1998, p. 103). The studies discussed provide contextual findings, inviting us to think of texts of educational inquiry theoretically as well as pragmatically.

Research Toward the Expansion of Arts Education: Values and Cherishing

Both qualitative and quantitative inquiry contribute to our knowledge. Quantitative findings offer the promise of generalizability with the succinctness and the rigor that large numbers carry and, as such, provide a powerful tool for advocacy. Qualitative inquiry can explore phenomena in their complexity and their meanings for participants, providing enhanced meaning to quantitative results and grounding findings within institutional, sociological, and cultural contexts that have a central role in effecting learning.

The quantitative and qualitative studies discussed in this chapter engage us in important issues about the impact of arts education. What Oreck, Baum, and McCartney (1999)

discovered about their participants deepens our understanding about what enhances resilience and self-regulation. Likewise, Heath (1999) and Burton, Horowitz, and Abeles (1999) offer examples of arts education that can help us to design programs to help students who have talent and drive but few opportunities. Studies like Wilson (1997) and Bresler (1997a) help us to understand the mechanisms of successful curriculum reform. Effective reform is seldom born of goal-setting and standards-raising but rather of intensive analysis of successes and problems and careful delineation of areas susceptible to improvement. The careful examination, description, and interpretation of arts programs, of teachers' instruction and students' experience, deepen understanding and facilitate improvement of all teaching, in the arts as well as academics.

Given that education initiates the young into the knowledge, skills, values, and commitments common to the adult members of the society (see, for example, Egan, 1997) and that the central task of socialization is to inculcate a set of norms and beliefs of the adult society that the children will grow into, it is essential to reflect on what and whose values we advocate in arts education and in its research. To come back full circle to the opening issue of this chapter, at the core is what we value as a society, and how broadly. Clearly, the research we conduct reflects our cherishing—the kinds of knowledge and practices we would like to see expanded. Scholarly research in education is based on what kind of value system we want to promote, on our vision of the human beings we want to help shape. Clearly the arts can serve fundamentally diverse values and types of interpretation and expressivity and different aesthetics. We need a better understanding of the values embedded and communicated in current arts education and the educational goals they serve. As educational researchers who aim not just to understand what exists but ultimately to improve and expand it, we want to consider those aspects of arts education that are conducive to growth in its broadest sense rather than search for the magic potion for instant achievement.

The issue is not whether or not we advocate the anachronistic ideal of "arts for arts' sake" (see Catterall, 1998). I believe that educators are always concerned with "arts for *people's* sake." The question, of course, is how we define people's sake: what creates our well-being and success. Researchers recognize that meaningful interaction with music is more complex and richer than a short-term exposure to classical music; that the benefits of music are deeper and more rewarding than a temporary increase in IQ or improved test scores.[26] As the metaanalyses show, engagement in the arts, as measured in experiments, has not been proven to cause an improvement in academic achievement. Rather, it is the findings from qualitative studies that illuminate various types of learning (e.g., enhanced linguistic skills, self-regulation) and trace them to specific learning opportunities and the sociocultural contexts in which these qualities flourish. These learnings, central to the educational enterprise, cannot be located and measured in our brain, simply because our knowledge is far from being able to pinpoint which areas in the brain correspond to these complex, hard-to-isolate qualities.[27]

Clearly, test scores matter. Equally clearly, however, success is not defined only by test results as measured in mathematical or verbal scores (Eisner, 1982; Gardner, 1983). The narrow versus expanded view of intelligence shapes our educational practices, how we perceive the goals of arts education, and the research we do to evaluate it.

Informed advocacy is based on our understanding of the nature and role of the arts in education and the factors that contribute to current and excellent arts education practice. The ultimate value of ideas and knowledge generated by research will depend on the extent to which practitioners view them as speaking to their concrete concerns, as well as professional commitments, when the outcome is both theoretical and a form of action.

NOTES

Many thanks to Michael Mark, Richard Colwell, and David Myers for sharing with me important and interesting resources. I am indebted to Regina Murphy, Richard Colwell, Magne Espeland, Michael Mark, Gary McPherson, Joan Russell, and Peter Webster for their careful reading of this manuscript and insightful comments. Many thanks to Eunju Yun and Deb Fisher for their excellent editorial assistance.

1. I am reporting in this chapter on research pertinent to arts advocacy, not on research reporting on goals traditional to arts education or on the voluntary national standards. I also do not address literature regarding cultural humanistic cognitive values.

2. As part of school arts.

3. See, for example, in the publications of *Toward Civilization: A Report on Arts Education* (1988); *Schools, Communities, and the Arts: A Research Compendium* (1994); *Eloquent Evidence: Arts at the Core of Learning*; and *Priorities for Arts Education Research* (1997); and *Champions of Change* (President's Committee on the Arts and Humanities, 1999). In his introduction to the *Champions of Change*, Richard Riley, U.S. Secretary of Education, referred to the research findings, declaring that "[the findings] address ways that our nation's educational goals may be realized through enhanced arts learning" (p. vi).

4. An example of a thoughtful advocacy that draws on the complex philosophical and scholarly thinking is Fowler's *Can We Rescue the Arts for America's Children* (1988).

5. E.g., from research in Hungary in the 1950s to the most current brain research in Germany and the United States.

6. In Great Britain, music was part of the Education Reform Act of 1988, although the National Curriculum was not introduced in music (and some other subjects toward the end of the list) until 1992.

7. Research on advocacy outcomes is marginal to comparative (crossnational) achievement research (Espeland, e-mail communication, 2001).

8. The researchers reported searching seven electronic databases from their inception through 1998. These include: the Arts and Humanities Index (1988–98), Dissertation Abstracts International (1950–98), the Educational Resource Information Clearinghouse (1950–98), Language Linguistics Behavioral Abstracts (1973–98), Medline (1966–98), PsychLit/PsychINFO (1984–98), and the Social Science Index (1988–98). In addition, they conducted hand searches of 41 journals from 1950 to 1998 that publish articles in education, development, and the arts. They also sent requests to over 200 arts education researchers for unpublished data or manuscripts not yet published.

9. They say that it is possible that studying the arts leads to the development of cognitive skills that, in turn, lead to heightened achievement in academic areas. Similarly, studying the arts may lead to greater engagement in school, which in turn leads to greater academic achievement. Another possibility is that high academic achievers may choose to study the arts (Winner & Hetland, 2000).

10. None of the studies reported on competency in the art form (reflecting the current interests of the general public and the media).

11. The design of studies where teachers did teach for transfer (see, for example, Podolzny, 2000) violates the "double blind" expectancy of a truly experimental study.

12. Vaughn excluded correlation studies assessing whether individuals who have a high musical aptitude also have a high mathematical aptitude; studies in which music was used as a memory aid to teach math; and studies in which music was used as a reward for good performance in math.

13. Of all identified studies, Butzlaff retained for his meta-analysis only studies that met the following three criteria: standardized measure of reading ability was used as the dependent variable; a test of reading followed music instruction, excluding studies in which students read while listening to music; and statistical information was sufficient for the determination of effect size. He also excluded studies in which students were trained to read musical notation but received no other music instruction and studies where statistical information was insufficient to allow for the calculation of an effect size.

14. Researchers don't know why the effect occurs. Shaw (in Hetland, 2000a) hypothesized that music enhances spatial-temporal performance because it primes spatial processing areas in the cortex. Brain imaging studies showing that music and spatial-temporal tasks activate proximal brain regions provide support for this hypothesis (Hetland, 2000b, p. 137). Alternative mechanisms suggested include arousal that involves increased adrenalin in the brain. However, Hetland points out that arousal should enhance any kind of spatial performance, but her analysis shows that music enhances spatial-temporal tasks more than other types of spatial tasks. Second, although relaxation is thought to dampen arousal more than does silence, scores following relaxation and si-

lence conditions do not differ. There is also evidence that levels of arousal do not correlate with levels of spatial-temporal performance.

Some labs have found the "Mozart effect" more consistently than others. In 1998, Rauscher and Shaw reviewed the literature and attempted to explain the varied findings in relation to experimental designs and procedures. They acknowledged that there are many kinds of spatial abilities and, on the basis of the "trion" model, recommended the use of partial-temporal measures, which they defined as requiring the ability to transform mental images in the absence of a physical model (in Hetland, 2000a). With the new wave of replication efforts that followed the Rauscher and Shaw (1998) review, one hypothesis is that music listening produces an optimal level of adrenalin in the brain and thus elevates performance on cognitive tasks compared to performance following silence. According to this theory, cognitive performance following relaxation should be even lower than that following silence, since subjects should be least aroused following instructions to induce relaxation (Hetland, 2000a).

15. In studies of arts education in elementary schools, teachers have emphasized frequently that the arts allow success for students who are *not* successful in academic subjects (Stake, Bresler, & Mabry, 1991).

16. The same dilemma is reiterated at a metalevel: Should the school mirror the values of the society or expand them?

17. Quantitative measures included: (1) the Torrance Test of Creative Thinking, which measures creative thinking abilities (defined as a constellation of generalized mental abilities commonly presumed to be brought into play in creative achievements); (2) the Self-Description Questionnaire, which measures self-concept; (3) the School-level Environment Questionnaire as a tool for evaluating aspects of school climate; (4) the Teacher Perception Scale to measure teachers' judgments about qualities such as risk-taking and creativity on the part of individual children; (5) the Classroom Teacher Arts Inventory, assessing teachers' practices and attitudes regarding the arts; and (6) the Student Arts Background Questionnaire to determine how much in-school experience children had had with the arts. Qualitative data sources included interviews with school administrators and general classroom and specialist teachers in science, mathematics, and language; observations of classroom performances and exhibitions; the analysis of students' artwork and writing; and photo documentation of in-school activities.

18. Launched by the Royal Society for the encouragement of Arts, Manufactures and Commerce in 1997 and conducted by the National Foundation for Educational Research (NFER).

19. Research methods included questionnaires completed by 2,296 year 11 pupils in 22 schools, with related information on their GCSE results; case studies of five secondary schools with good reputations in the arts, including annual interviews with approximately 80 students each year who were performing well in the arts, interviews with school managers and arts teachers, and video observations of arts lessons; analyses of wider ranging information compiled through NFER's Qualitative Analysis for Self-Evaluation (QUASE) project, data on a total of 27,607 pupils from 152 schools in

three cohorts of year 11 pupils taking GCSEs in 1994–96; and interviews with a cross-section of 20 employers and some employees in 20 companies, including banks, advertising agencies, a large firm of accountants, and a computer software developer.

20. Another study of successful arts programs is the President's Committee of the Arts and the Humanities (see Heath & Roach, 1999). The study examines eight school districts selected on the basis of demographic and geographic considerations for site visits by a team that included one researcher and one superintendent of schools. The publication reports on a general set of findings as well as on specific strategies and excellent arts education practices found in the districts. According to the report, the single most critical factor in sustaining arts education is the active involvement of influential segments of the community in shaping and implementing the policies and the programs of the district. Supportive superintendents, school boards, and principals proved to be essential. Other factors for success include strong art education programs at the elementary level; a comprehensive vision and plan for arts education; and the identity and expertise of teachers as artists.

21. Sites ranged in location from Massachusetts to Hawaii and in character from urban to rural, including midsized cities.

22. Researchers report the high frequency of "what if" questions, mental stage verbs ("believe," "plan"), complexity of hypothetical proposals, and types of language uses that are rarely available to young people in any other setting. Older children and adolescents have relatively few occasions to work in a sustained way to plan and carry out a project with an adult or guiding expert. The research team recorded patterns of ordinary language interactions of young people in their nonschool hours *outside of youth-based organizations*. For students who did not attend organized nonschool activities and were not extensively involved in extracurricular activities at school, each week offered them at best only 15–20 minutes of interaction with adults in sustained conversations (defined here as conversations of at least 7 minutes duration) on a single topic that included planning.

23. Mans, for example, explores the role of mental templates or models relating to music/dance in Namibian cultures, aiming to establish connections to educational practices. A class is asked to chant and then clap an *epera* rhythmic pattern given by the teacher in the form of a mnemonic such as *pundu*. Learners direct their attention to the teacher's sounds. The auditory sound of the teacher's words is briefly memorized and then transformed by learners into spoken sounds, a process that requires inner verification in terms of the sequence of the sounds (orientation). This is repeated, thus enhancing the memory process. The pattern is then transformed again into a kinesthetic mode and clapped while the inner verification process continues to monitor the performance. Through repetition the clapping pattern can be formed into an automatism and stored in long-term memory. It is likely to be memorized with the association of the mnemonic pattern, which promotes recall.

24. The talent identification process, developed through a grant from the United States Department of Education, was

designed to be equitable to students who have no previous arts instruction and come from diverse cultural backgrounds. The programs strive to recognize and develop the outstanding talents of many students who would not be identified as gifted and talented through academic tests of other traditional means.

25. The students in the study were current or former participants in the Young Talent Program (YTP), provided by the Arts Connection Program in their elementary schools. The YTP program, begun in 1979, served at the time of the study approximately 400 students in grades 3 to 6 in eight New York City Public Schools by providing instruction in dance, music, or theater. The YTP offers introductory experiences for all students and more rigorous instruction for students who have been identified as potentially talented. The basic talent development program consists of weekly classes for 25 weeks between October and May for students in grades 4, 5, and 6, taught by a team of two professional teaching artists. An alumni program is offered at the Arts Connection's Center in midtown Manhattan for students graduating from the elementary school program. Advanced students attend five to ten classes per year at professional studios and cultural institutions around the city. The curriculum is designed to be challenging and broad in scope, to give students opportunities to learn a variety of styles and techniques, and to develop their skills to prepare them for further study in the art form.

26. In fact, scientific, well-designed research is careful to qualify its findings and to point at what needs to be done to enhance applicability and meaningfulness of research.

27. As Mills (1998) reminds us, we should not lose sight of the main reason we teach music: "Perhaps, it helps if teachers have a particular sort of commitment. Perhaps it helps if the teaching is particularly sequential. . . . Perhaps it helps if children are taught to perform from memory, or to sing at sight, or to try to refine their compositions through thought experiments, instead of always reaching for a keyboard. Doubtless there are a host of other possible factors. Perhaps we need just one of them to be in place. Perhaps we need them all. Once we know more we will need to establish whether these factors can be packaged in a music education that is excellent musically. If they cannot, then the investigation may have added to the sum of human knowledge, but will not be of educational value. Whatever the potential of music to improve the mind, the main purpose of teaching music in schools is excellence in music" (p. 103).

REFERENCES

Abbs, P. (1992). The generic community of the arts: Its historical development and educational value. *Journal of Art and Design Education, 11*(3), 265–285.

Barone, T. (2001). *Touching eternity: Life narratives and consequences of teaching.* New York: Teachers College Press.

Baum, S., Owen, S., & Oreck, B. (1997). Transferring individual self-regulation processes from arts to academics. *Arts Education Policy Review, 98*(4), 32–39.

Best, D. (1992). *The rationality of feeling: Understanding the arts in education.* London: Falmer Press.

Best, D. (1995). Collective, integrated arts: The expedient generic myth. *Arts Education Policy Review, 97*(1), 32–39.

Bjorkvold, J. (1989). *The muse within: Creativity and communication, song and play from childhood through maturity* (W. H. Halverson, Trans.). New York: Harper.

Blacking, J., & Keali'nohomoku, J. W. (Eds.). (1979). *The performing arts: Music and dance.* The Hague: Mouton Press.

Bresler, L. (1994). Imitative, complementary and expansive: The three roles of visual arts curricula. *Studies of Arts Education, 35*(2), 90–104.

Bresler, L. (1995). The subservient, co-equal, affective and social integration style of the arts. *Arts Education Policy Review, 96*(5), 31–37.

Bresler, L. (1997a). *General issues across sites: The role of the arts in unifying high school curriculum* (A Report for the College Board). Los Angeles: Getty Center for the Arts.

Bresler, L. (1997b). Towards the creation of a new code of ethics in qualitative research. *Council of Research in Music Education, 130,* 17–29.

Bresler, L. (1998). The genre of school music and its shaping by meso, micro, and macro contexts. *Research Studies in Music Education, 11,* 2–18.

Bresler, L., & Stake, B. (1992). Qualitative research methodology in music education. In R. Colwell (Ed.), *The handbook of research on music teaching and learning* (pp. 75–90). New York: Schirmer Books.

Bruner, J. (1996). *Culture of Education.* Cambridge: Harvard University Press.

Burton, J., Horowitz, R., & Abeles, H. (1999). Learning in and through the arts: Curriculum implications. In E. Fisk (Ed.), *Champions of change: The impact of the arts on learning* (pp. 35–46). Washington, DC: The Arts Education Partnership and the President's Committee on the Arts and the Humanities.

Butzlaff, R. (2000). Can music be used to teach reading? *Journal of Aesthetic Education, 34*(3–4), 167–178.

Catterall, J. (1998). Does experience in the arts boost academic achievement? A response to Eisner. *Art Education, 51*(4) 6–8.

Catterall, J., Chapleau, R., & Iwanaga, J. (1999). Involvement in the arts and human development. In E. Fisk (Ed.), *Champions of change: The impact of the arts on learning* (pp. 1–18). Washington, DC: The Arts Education Partnership and the President's Committee on the Arts and the Humanities.

Collier-Slone, K. (1991). *The psychology of humanistic life education: A longitudinal study.* Unpublished doctoral dissertation, Union Institute, Cincinnati.

Egan, K. (1997). *The educated mind.* Chicago: University of Chicago Press.

Einstein, A. [On-line]. Available: http://geocities.com/CapeCanaveral/Hangar/6469/quotes.htm.

Eisner, E. (1982). *Cognition and curriculum.* New York: Longman.

Eisner, E. (1998). Does experience in the arts boost academic achievement? *Art Education, 51*(1), 7–15.

Eisner, E. (1999). What justifies arts education: What research does not say. In M. McCarthy (Ed.), *Enlightened advocacy:*

Implications of research for arts education policy and practice (The 1999 Charles Fowler Colloquium on Innovation in Arts Education). College Park: University of Maryland.

Espeland, M. (1997) Once upon a time there was a minister: An unfinished story about reform in Norwegian arts education. *Arts Education Policy Review, 99*(1), 11–16.

Fodor, J. A. (1993). *The modularity of mind: An essay on faculty psychology.* Cambridge, MA: MIT Press.

The Fourth R. [On-line]. Available: http://www.mia.org.uk/mia/join/4thr.htm.

Fowler, C. (1988). Can we rescue the arts for America's children? Coming to our senses—10 years later. New York: American Council for the Arts.

Gardner, H. (1983). *Frames of mind: The theory of multiple intelligences.* New York: Basic Books.

Growing up complete: The imperative for music education. (1991). Reston, VA: Music Educators National Conference.

Gruhn, W. (2000). *Does brain research support the hope for musical transfer effects?* [On-line]. Available: http://www.mia.org.uk/mia/join/4thr.htm.

Harland, J., Kinder, K., Lord, P., Stott, A., Schagen, I., & Hayners, J. (2000). *Arts education in secondary schools: Effects and effectiveness.* Slough, UK: National Foundation for Educational Research.

Heath, S. B., & Roach, A. (1999). Imaginative actuality: Learning in the arts during nonschool hours. In E. Fisk (Ed.), *Champions of change: The impact of the arts on learning* (pp. 19–34). Washington, DC: The Arts Education Partnership and the President's Committee on the Arts and the Humanities.

Hempel, C. (1966). *Philosophy of natural sciences.* London: Prentice-Hall.

Hetland, L. (2000a). Learning to make music enhances spatial reasoning. *Journal of Aesthetic Education, 34*(3–4), 178–238.

Hetland, L. (2000b). Listening to music enhances spatial-temporal reasoning: Evidence for the "music effect." *Journal of Aesthetic Education, 34*(3–4), 105–148.

Hinckley, J. (1999). *Testimony on "Elementary and Secondary Education Act—Educating Diverse Populations" to the House Subcommittee on Early Childhood, Youth and Families (July 15, 1999).* Reston, VA: Music Educators National Conference.

Hofstadter, D. R. (1979). *Godel, Escher, Bach: An eternal golden braid.* New York: Basic Books.

Kantrowitz, B. (1999, September). Tests are an easy way out. *Newsweek,* 50–51.

Keinanen, M., Hetland, L., & Winner, E. (2000). Teaching cognitive skill through dance: Evidence for near but not far transfer. *Journal of Aesthetic Education, 34*(3–4), 295–306.

Lincoln, Y., & Guba, E. (1985). *Naturalistic inquiry.* Thousand Oaks, CA: Sage.

Livermore, J., & McPherson, G. (1998). Expanding the role of the arts in the curriculum: Some Australian initiatives. *Arts Education Policy Review, 99*(3), 10–15.

Mans, M. E. (1997). *Namibian music and dance as Ngoma in arts education.* Unpublished doctoral dissertation, University of Natal, Durban, South Africa.

McPherson, G. (1995). Integrating the arts into the general curriculum: An Australian perspective. *Arts Education Policy Review, 97*(1), 25–31.

Mills, J. (1998). Response to Katie Overy's paper "Can Music Really Improve the Mind?" *Psychology of Music, 26,* 102–103.

Moga, E., Burger, K., Hetland, L., & Winner, E. (2000). Does studying the arts endanger creative thinking? Evidence for near but not far transfer. *Journal of Aesthetic Education, 34*(3–4), 91–104.

Music makes the difference: Music, brain development, and learning (2000). Reston, VA: Music Educators National Conference.

Oreck, B., Baum, S., & McCartney, H. (1999). Artistic talent development for urban youth: The promise and the challenge. In E. Fisk (Ed.), *Champions of change: The impact of the arts on learning* (pp. 63–78). Washington, DC: The Arts Education Partnership and the President's Committee on the Arts and the Humanities.

Podolzny, A. (2000). Strengthening verbal skills through the use of classroom drama: A clear link. In *Journal of Aesthetic Education, 34*(3–4), 239–276.

Popper, K. (1969). *Conjectures and refutations.* London: Routledge and Kegan Paul.

President's Committee on the Arts and the Humanities (1999). *Champions of change: The impact of the arts on learning.* Washington, DC: Council of Chief School Officers.

President's Committee on the Arts and the Humanities & Arts Education Partnership. (1997). *Gaining the arts advantage: Lessons from school districts that value arts education* [On-line]. Available: http://www.pcah.gov/gaa.

Priorities for arts education research. (1997). Washington, DC: Goals 2000 Arts Education Partnership.

Punch, M. (1994). Politics and ethics in qualitative research. In N. Denzin & Y. Lincoln (Eds.), *The handbook of qualitative research* (pp. 83–98). Thousand Oaks, CA: Sage.

Rauscher, F. (1998). Response to Katie Overy's paper "Can Music Really Improve the Mind?" *Psychology of Music, 26,* 97–99.

Rauscher, F., & Shaw, G. (1998). Key components of the Mozart effect. *Perceptual and Motor Skills, 86,* 835–41.

Rauscher, F., Shaw, G., & Ky, K. (1993). Music and spatial task performance. *Nature, 365*(6447), 611.

Reimer, B. (1999). Facing the risks of the "Mozart Effect." *Phi Delta Kappan, 81*(4), 278–283.

Riley, W. (2000). Address to Music Educators National Conference, Washington, DC.

Rothstein, E. (1995). *Emblems of mind: The inner life of music and mathematics.* New York: Times Books.

Salomon, G., & Perkins, D. N. (1989). Rocky roads to transfer: Rethinking mechanisms of a neglected phenomenon. *Educational Researcher, 24*(2), 113–124.

Stake, R. (1997). Advocacy in evaluation: A necessary evil? In E. Chelimsky & W. Shadish (Eds.), *Evaluation for the twenty-first century: A handbook* (pp. 470–476). Thousand Oaks, CA: Sage.

Stake, R., Bresler, L., & Mabry, L. (1991). *Custom and cherishing: Arts education in the U.S.* Urbana, IL: Council for Research in Music Education.

Spychiger, M. (1998). Response to Katie Overy's paper "Music: Does It Improve the Mind?" *Psychology of Music, 26,* 199–201.

Thorndike, E. L. (1903). *Educational psychology.* New York: Lemcke and Buechner.

Thorndike, E. L., & Woodward, R. S. (1901). The influence of improvement in one mental function upon the efficiency of other functions. *Psychological Review, 8,* 247–261.

Toward civilization: A report on arts education. (1988). Washington, DC: National Endowment for the Arts.

Tunks, T. (1992). The transfer of music learning. In R. Colwell (Ed.), *The handbook of research on music teaching and learning* (pp. 437–447). New York: Schirmer Books.

Vaughn, K. (2000). Music and mathematics: Modest support for the oft-claimed relationship. *Journal of Aesthetic Education, 34*(3–4), 149–166.

Vaughn, K., & Winner, E. (2000). SAT scores of students who study the arts: What we can and cannot conclude about the association. *Journal of Aesthetic Education, 34*(3–4), 77–90.

Wertheim, M. (1995). *Pythagoras' trousers: God, physics, and the gender wars.* New York: Times Books.

Wilson, B. (1997). *The quiet evolution: Changing the face of arts education.* Los Angeles: Getty Education Institute for the Arts.

Winner, E., & Cooper, M. (2000). Mute those claims: No evidence (yet) for a causal link between arts study and academic achievement. *Journal of Aesthetic Education, 34*(3–4), 11–76.

Winner, E., & Hetland, L. (2000). The arts in education: Evaluating the evidence for a causal link. *Journal of Aesthetic Education, 34*(3–4), 3–10.

Part X

RESEARCH DESIGN, CRITICISM, AND ASSESSMENT IN MUSIC EDUCATION

Jack J. Heller

Nicholas DeCarbo

Editors

Introduction

Scholarly Inquiry and the Research Process

JACK J. HELLER

NICHOLAS DECARBO

The Handbook contains a variety of views about the research process in music education. While there is some disagreement about what should be called research, all agree that there are many ways to inform the profession about the teaching and learning process in music education. Scholarly inquiry of all sorts should be embraced.

There is a large body of research about music teaching and learning published in music education journals as well as in psychological, educational, acoustical, and neuroscience journals, but the quality of some of these reports is suspect. Yet, these studies often are cited to support a particular view or used as models for further study. Conclusions in such studies are sometimes not supported by evidence. And the external or ecological validity of many studies can be questioned, especially those carried out by researchers outside the field of music education.

Even though studies reported in most of the refereed journals in music education have improved over the years, there still seem to be published reports of research that should not be in print. Journal editorial boards need to be more stringent in decisions about the quality of articles accepted for publication, and the profession needs to exert the strongest effort to continue to raise the quality of music education research that is reported in our journals.

The chapters in this part and the rest of the Handbook provide an outstanding array of insights into important aspects of the research enterprise. Hopefully the profession will continue to move forward in its quest for verifiable answers to the myriad questions about music teaching and learning. Excellent scholarship and research can help to lead the way.

Maintaining Quality in Research and Reporting

58

JACK J. HELLER
EDWARD J. P. O'CONNOR

Scholarly Inquiry and a Research Perspective

What Is Research?

In order to evaluate competence in research, the evaluator must first have a clear conception of what constitutes research as opposed to other scholarly activities. There are many scholarly pursuits that may in a broad sense fall under the category "research." The word research (from the French *rechercher*, which means to travel through or survey) implies a going back to search for something. With respect to research in music education, however, that concept is too broad. We are concerned primarily with the systematic search for solutions to problems based on empirical observation. This is not meant to disparage scholarly endeavors that fall outside our more restricted definition. Of course, research searches for something. But that something should be very specific and it should be stated at the outset of any research report. The researcher must have a very clear idea of what the question is that will be investigated. The techniques and methodology used to search for an answer to a question should be appropriate to the question posed. Good research is that which provides as unbiased an answer as possible to a question supported by empirical evidence. "Empirical" here is meant to be viewed as "observations."

The view of the nature of observations has changed over time. Based on the seminal monograph of Campbell and Stanley (1963), research in education during the 1970s and 1980s was dominated by the methodological ideal represented by the premise expressed in that publication: that the "true" experiment was the model for educational researchers. That view was adopted by researchers in music education.

In recent times, however, research methodology became divided between quantitative and qualitative methodologies (see Fraenkel & Wallen, 2000; Grady, 1998). But the seeming dichotomy in current educational research literature between the value of qualitative and quantitative research is misguided. Once the researcher has identified a problem, appropriate means for addressing that problem should be decided. For most research questions, there are multiple techniques that can provide answers to the researcher's hypotheses. The issue should be which approach is appropriate for the question(s) asked.

The term "research" often is used to categorize precursors of the "scientific method." For example, data collection (going to a library to determine what others have written about a topic), taxonomy generation (generating well-thought-out lists), and "experimenting" (in the sense of seeking new experiences: "If I mix these sounds with that rhythm what will happen?") are all considered "research" in the popular use of the word. While these may be necessary activities, their importance is due to the part they play as tools in the total research process, not as research projects in themselves.

In order to seek answers to questions about music teaching or learning, researchers may use a method that has been labeled "historical" (e.g., which answers questions of past practice by examining original documents or artifacts); "descriptive" (e.g., determines the status or state of the art of a phenomenon such as examining process through surveys, case studies, trend studies); or "experimental" (e.g., applying or manipulating various conditions in controlled situations). All of these methods may use techniques that are qualitative or quantitative in nature to provide acceptable answers, depending on the nature of the question. The issue should be whether the answer to an educational question is defensible and persuasive to the informed reader.

Relationship of Theory to Practice and Research

Theory. The questions researchers seek to answer should not be unique to a given situation. Rather, research should be theory driven (see chap. 7 in this Handbook). In order to contribute anything useful to our knowledge about human behavior (musical or otherwise) research must have an underlying theory to test. However, theory does not develop in isolation. A theory should be based on a philosophical position supported by empirical evidence.

There are some that insist on adding "philosophical" to the methodologies of research. Philosophy is important; it can be scholarly; but it is not research. It is philosophy. Philosophical discourse is essential to a better understanding of music and music teaching and learning, but we do not consider philosophy research. (See Jorgensen, 1992.) Philosophy is a highly regarded scholarly activity.

Philosophical discourse (or, more precisely, model building) should lead to testable hypotheses that allow researchers to collect observations that support or refute a theory (or model). Theories about music teaching or learning can lead us to design research studies that may clarify practice in the music education enterprise. Price (1997) correctly points out that "all pursuits of knowledge inform all others. To ignore any is to be ignorant. Philosophical and historical inquiry uninformed by empirical evidence is very deep in a cave; conversely, empirical evidence without solid philosophical and historical foundation is a pursuit operating without illumination" (p. 4). Amen.

Practice. Practice in music education is driven by many factors: economics, political issues, religion, taxonomies of educational importance, philosophy of what it means to be "educated," and so on. Music educators encounter many pitfalls in their quest for clear and unambiguous answers to questions about the teaching/learning process in music. It is unlikely that the research enterprise, *as it is currently practiced,* will be able to inform the music education profession about the very complex process of becoming musically educated. This is because music education research often is fragmented, rarely led by theory, and too frequently supported by biased evidence.

Even though there are national standards, there is no united agreement among practicing music educators in the elementary, secondary, or tertiary schools in the United States about what it means to be musically educated. Curriculum specialists and philosophers have provided some help. They have generated the taxonomic framework and rationale for music education practice. The profession has had notable scholars who have provided guidance by using these important approaches. Herculean efforts have generated the national standards, goals and objectives, and assessment strategies for music education. But there seems to be little persuasive evidence *from research* that music teachers can use to help them become more successful teachers. While the profession has provided a number of journals (e.g., *The Journal of Research in Music Education, Council Bulletin, Psychology of Music, Update,* etc.) that do report some good research, teachers and professors do not always seem to read and take advantage of what is reported. Part of the reason for this gulf is the lack of substantial support in time and fiscal resources for research in music education.

Research. Examples of research fall into at least three general types: historical (mostly qualitative in technique), descriptive (qualitative or quantitative), and experimental (mostly quantitative). These categories are descriptions in a broad sense of the particular methodologies used to address a research question. They are not meant to exclude other divisions of the research process, or to exclude combinations of these three methodologies.

The nature of human learning in music is extremely complex. Many more carefully designed studies must be carried out in order to begin to understand how musical learning takes place. Psychologists, after more than a century of carefully constructed studies and huge amounts of funding, are only now beginning to understand the nature of human learning under very limited conditions. Even though good music teachers do generally understand the teaching/learning process, knowledge from research of the underlying processes might help improve current practice to a broader community.

Much of the reported research in music education continues to be the reworking of doctoral dissertations. Many of these studies represent a novice's efforts that usually contribute little to understanding the complex issues of music teaching and learning. Such studies do not add credibility to the music education research enterprise. This issue led to the birth of the *Bulletin of the Council for Research in Music Education* in 1963 under the able leadership of Richard Colwell (1969). One of the original purposes of this periodical was to offer critiques of doctoral dissertations in the hope that such critiques would improve future research, and ultimately, teaching practice. While the *Bulletin* certainly made the profession more acutely aware of the many problems that researchers faced and it did have a very positive effect on some subsequent research, the general problem of shoddy research still existed a quarter of a century after the *Bulletin* first was published (Colwell, 1988). Shoddy research still exists today. Doctoral advisers at too many universities are still not well equipped to direct research. University music schools and departments mostly give obeisance to research but do not give release time for faculty to develop their research skills and a research agenda. Teaching loads in music are typically extremely heavy and research funding is small compared to other social sciences, including education.

By contrast, psychologists, who are well-schooled in research techniques, have for many years carried out studies in music. Unfortunately, most of these studies seem to ask questions that are beside the point for music educators. Results of laboratory-type experiments in which computers generate stimuli often are generalized inappropriately to a musical situation. The Ann Arbor Symposium (Taylor, 1981) clearly demonstrated the lack of understanding by prominent psychologists of the issues concerning the music learning and teaching processes. This group of psychologists made it clear that they had no answers to the questions music educators raised. Their feeble attempts to address these questions showed their inability to provide answers, even tentative ones, for the music education profession.

More recently, psychology seems to have embraced music as a robust means to study human behavior. Organized conferences for and by psychologists have proliferated with music as the main topic. Most of the research reported at these meetings have excellent internal validity but questionable external validity. Generalizability to music education issues seems to be limited.

To expect that research in music education or psychology, as currently practiced, can tell music teachers how to improve their instruction is a figment of our collective imaginations. Until the field of music education can justify time release for music faculty to engage in meaningful research (including pre-K to college level teachers) and to provide reasonable funding for such research, not much hope for improvement can be expected. Even if the impairments of time and money were somehow magically removed, the generally low level of graduate research instruction in music still remains a serious problem.

Research is not considered here to be a panacea for the many problems and issues the music education profession faces. It is simply one more human activity that strives to answer perplexing, interesting problems inherent to music education. But good persuasive theorizing accompanied by good persuasive research may help to provide answers. Evidence to convince school boards and state departments of education to require music study as part of the basic school curriculum and to fund such programs properly must continue to be generated if high-quality music education programs are to become the norm rather than the exception.

The music education profession needs to raise the level of understanding about what good research means. And the necessary time must be allocated by administrators to encourage good systematic long-range research programs. University faculty development seminars should be offered for music education faculty so that they can update and

upgrade their research skills. If several years (maybe even decades) can be devoted to well-designed research studies in music teaching and learning, then there is hope for research to play a significant role in meeting some of the many lofty goals music educators have.

Distinguishing Research from Other Forms of Scholarly Inquiry

The following taxonomy is an attempt to establish an ordinal scale for written and oral scholarly pursuits.[1] Its purpose is to focus attention on a restricted definition of the term "research," applied here to one endpoint of a continuum. There are many scholarly pursuits, presented in various forms (performance, debate, etc.) that do not properly fall under this definition of research. These forms can be organized into a taxonomy. The reader should keep in mind the distinction between work that is based on empirical observation and that which is not, even though it may masquerade under the term "research."

Eisner (1997) takes the view that *all* forms that are used to "inform" should be called research. In defense of his definition of qualitative research he writes that,

> there is an intimate relationship between our conception of what the products of research are to look like and the way we go about doing research. What we think it means to do research has to do with our conception of meaning, our conception of cognition, and our beliefs about the forms of consciousness that we are willing to say advance human understanding—an aim, I take it, that defines the primary mission of research. What succeeds in deepening meaning, expanding awareness, and enlarging understanding is, in the end, a community decision. Conversation and publication are, in part, aimed at testing ideas in that community. (pp. 5–6)

What Eisner is talking about includes *all* human communication. The arts accomplish Eisner's notion of informing us about the world. Only in that broad sense are the arts then considered research. Eisner would probably call each of the categories that follow (i.e., Performance, Documentary, Position Paper, or Debates) research, as each can inform us about the world in some way. Yet, each of these categories misses some essential character of research. The essential character of research is that it must attempt to present unbiased evidence, with equal opportunity for an opposing point of view to be considered.

We do not accept Eisner's proposition. The many ways that may inform us about the education process are ubiquitous. They may tell us what the writer (or actor, or musician, or painter, etc.) believes, and they may be very powerful. But as the following taxonomy tries to show, these varied forms of human discourse or communication systems are not, by our definition, research. The taxonomy's purpose is to focus attention on a restricted definition of the term "research." If research, in this restricted sense, is carried out with care and systematic rigor, it hopefully will add a measure of knowledge about the music teaching/ learning process.

The Taxonomy

Performance (Dance, Plays, Poems, Music).   The first activity in the taxonomy is performance. A performance is complete or sufficient by itself. That is, there is (usually) no direct reference to other similar productions, although knowledge of the genre, style, and of the milieu from which it springs is usually necessary for the reader's, listener's, or viewer's understanding of the work. Judgment of the merits of the work is an external function (literary criticism), not part of the "performance."

One can argue successfully that good performing artists (musicians, dancers, and actors) follow the general guidelines set out in the "scientific method." For example, the performer often identifies a problem, defines the problem more specifically, sets up a question (what will happen if I do this or that?) or an hypothesis (I think this will happen if I do that), collects data (tries out a particular passage to see if the hypothesis is correct), and draws conclusions about the evidence that was collected. That process does follow the steps generally given for the "scientific method." But this entire activity usually *is not explicit* and not available to others than the performer. The judgment of the performance by listeners is much like literary criticism, not research.

Documentary (News Reports, Book Lists, Catalogues).   A documentary is an enumeration of data or a reporting of "events" (a list of musical scores collected, documentary coverage of a convention, an enumeration of a school's assets). Often a taxonomy is generated to help organize a list into categories (étude taxonomies, curriculum taxonomies). In all documentaries, the choice of the data to be included implies an editorial function. Accuracy and completeness may suffer even with unbiased authors. Judgment of the work is external and is usually accomplished by comparison with an alternative presentation. Isomorphism (having similar or identical structure or appearance) is usually the standard of comparison.

The person responsible for producing the documentary chooses the data to be reported. This is the editorial function. The reporter's enlightenment may be very important to the success of the finished product and the end result may be very elucidating. In fact, it may lead to someone carrying out a research project to try to verify an aspect of the documentary. The documentary may be very well crafted and be very useful, but it is not research in our restricted sense.

As Colwell (1988) rightly points out, "Too often journals present 'this is the way it is' articles; conventions and workshops offer sessions on 'how to do it,' and our professional lives become crowded with in-service education that is primarily observation of 'successful' techniques rather than enlightening dialogue about the theoretical rationale, the value, and the effect of practices" (p. 5). Such reports and activities are not research. They are either documentaries or position papers.

Position Paper (Political Speeches, Sales Promotions).   The position paper presents its case in the strongest possible terms using arguments that do not admit to any essential deficiencies. Examples are monographs or essays supporting a particular point of view or dogma (pro arguments), polemics rejecting a particular point of view or dogma (con arguments), political speeches, commercials, and so on. Unending varieties of persuasion are employed (hard sell, soft sell, reverse psychology, etc.). Judgment is external and can be directed toward the merits of the argument or toward the (internal) virtuosity of the author, depending on the critic's agreement with or opposition to the point of view expressed.

Some position papers may be regarded as fine examples of scholarly endeavor. But, again, they are not research. Strong, even elegant, arguments for or against an issue do not meet the essential requirements for research. The researcher must take a neutral position and must make a strong attempt to minimize bias. *This chapter should be considered a position paper.*

Competitive Debate (High School or College Debating Team Competition).   In a competitive debate the pro and con arguments are presented by two groups under rules of procedure designed to provide a "fair" competition. A third group, the judges, observes. The outcome is based on the relative virtuosity of the participants, each of whom presents a *position paper.* The merit of the position is not a consideration, as the sides of the argument are assigned to the participants on a chance basis. Judgment is accomplished within the context of the debate.

Formal Debate (Town Meeting, Courtroom Trial).   In a formal debate (often on a referendum at a town meeting, or a civil or criminal trial) opposing views concerning a specified issue are presented by two individuals or groups. A third group (judge, jury, or voters) determines the outcome of the debate. The judgment is based, ideally, on the merits of the position presented. However, the relative virtuosity of the advocates often carries more weight. The "right to counsel" in legal proceedings is an example of the attempt to diminish the difference in virtuosity between the prosecution and the defense. Judgment is accomplished within the context of the debate.

Research (Historical, Descriptive, Experimental, and So On). According to *Webster's Dictionary*, research is the "careful, systematic, patient study and investigation in some field of knowledge, undertaken to discover or establish facts or principles" (Agnes, 1999). This definition is somewhat naive. We prefer not to use "discover" in any definition of research. Research does not "discover or establish facts." "Facts" often change when new evidence is presented. Barzun and Graff (1992) assert, "The choice of facts and of relations is dictated by human interest as well as by nature. . . . [T]he facts, moreover, are seen through ideas (for example, the idea of a molecule) that are not immediately visible and ready to be noted down. They are searched for *with a purpose in mind*" [italics added] (p. 182). "Careful, systematic, patient study and investigation" (Agnes, 1999), nevertheless, must take place in research. Good research can verify principles and can address theory.

The researcher must develop arguments supported by careful observations that are clearly elucidated. These arguments should provide support for or against a particular theory that is being tested. The researcher acts as the prosecution, the defense, and as a preliminary judge. There is judgment (usually implicit, but sometimes explicit) of the methodology in terms of its appropriateness, sensitivity, and balance. With bias minimized or controlled, a natural balance is maintained, as both sides of the argument have the same advocate. The researcher in the statement of conclusions gives an initial critique of the merits of the issue under investigation. In addition, the researcher ties the research to the results and arguments of others through a careful presentation of references and bibliography, including opposing or contradictory points of view.

Interpretation of the Research Report

The *Bulletin of the Council for Research in Music Education* has since its inception in 1963 successfully provided critiques of doctoral dissertations (Colwell, 1969). Many of these critiques have demonstrated the lack of understanding in certain doctoral dissertations of what research means and what may appropriately be concluded from research reports.

Some of the criteria that should be used to determine the "goodness" of a particular research report are as follows.

1. Is there a theory or model that the research is designed to explore?
2. Is there a specific question or questions that the research will attempt to answer?
3. Does the research cite related research that seems appropriate to the study?
4. Are the techniques for data collection specified? These may be quantitative or qualitative in nature. Do these techniques seem appropriate to the questions asked?
5. If statistics are used, are the underlying assumptions for the statistical tests met?
6. Do the conclusions logically follow from the evidence collected?

Schneider and Cady (1967) provided an analysis of research in music education from 1930 to 1962. Their results showed that 273 research reports out of 1,818 analyzed (about 15%) could be considered "relevant and competent research" by their stated criteria for relevance and competence. Of course, the validity of these data is based on the authors' critical analyses. But whatever analytic techniques were used, their perception of competence in music education research was not very high.

While there have been other excellent content analyses of research in music education (e.g., Abeles, 1980; Hair, 2000; Standley, 1996; Yarbrough, 1984, 1996), these have not focused on the *competence* of the research cited. Grieshaber (1987) does provide a critical review but only in general terms does she note "many problems" with the cited research. Radocy and Boyle (1997) cite an extraordinary number and wide range of research topics in music education. While much of the research cited in their excellent book has been reported in prominent journals, the studies either tend to have poor external validity (to music) or the conclusions are not supported by reasonable evidence. Radocy and Boyle state that "much of it [music education experimental research] . . . lacks the rigorous control of the variables that would enable it to meet standards for research design in the behavioral sciences as delineated by Campbell and Stanley (1963), so interpretations must be made with caution" (p. 147).

In fact, many researchers cite related research without always selecting research reports that are exemplary in design and data collecting procedures. So, instead of building on the work of good previous research, often poorly designed studies are used as models. This practice seems to be fairly widespread in music education.

Often the conclusions reported in published research articles are not appropriate to the evidence provided. Some research reports generalize far beyond what the data analysis allows. In order to have confidence in any research, the reader must judge whether the research states a clear objective, follows an appropriate methodology, and draws reasonable conclusions.

The evaluator's first task is to attempt to reconstruct the research process from the report to determine if anything was missed or not carried out properly. (See the second section of this chapter.) Barzun and Graff (1992) have pointed out that one should recognize the difference between the research activity (developing hypotheses, collecting data, etc.) and the research report. They are two distinct activities. What viewers see in journals or hear in presentations is a summary of the research activity. All research reports are considered to be representations of the researcher's perspective. Barzun and Graff warn that, as unbiased as the researcher tries to be, the reader always should be on guard for unwarranted statements.

The overriding decisions about the "goodness" of a research report should adhere to the following guidelines. Whatever the research methodology or technique used, the researcher should have:

1. Clearly stated the purpose of the study (i.e., defined the problem).
2. Shown that she or he knows something about the area to be studied. This is generally accomplished by providing a section of related research. The related research should be assessed for its competence.
3. Clearly stated an hypothesis (or hypotheses) that points toward a solution to the problem and consequences that indicate what data should be collected.
4. Told the reader what techniques were used to gather evidence. This may range from studying artifacts or documents from an earlier century, to interviewing an artist, to giving a specific group a task oriented auditory stimulus tape, and so on.
5. Not generalized to situations other than what the evidence shows. Too often the author generalizes far beyond the data. For example, if musical scores of a particular composer demonstrate use of a specific harmonic technique, it may not be reasonable to generalize this information to other scores of that composer. The scores that were not examined may be quite different in the use of the harmonic technique. For an in-depth case study of an individual, it is not always proper to generalize to other individuals, even if the others seem to be similar to the case studied. There can, however, be one or more "principles" that the study has produced that can be generalizable.

   In an experimental study, if inferential statistics are not employed, the researcher should not generalize. In that situation, only the data from the sample(s) studied are all that should be discussed. Often, even when inferential statistics are employed, and the statistical tests turn out not to be significant, the author will point out that the data were almost significant. That is like being almost pregnant. If the statistical analysis from an inferential test is not significant, then there is no difference predicted in the population. The author may still discuss the data that were collected and their possible implications, but generalization beyond the sample data is not warranted or acceptable.
6. Decided whether or not a statistically significant difference between levels of a variable represents a meaningful or practical difference. Tunks (1978) suggested that a fairly straightforward procedure known as "Omega Squared" be used in order to estimate the strength of association between or among variables. He points out that traditional statistical tests that have been used in a "substantial portion of published music education research . . . yield . . . limited information" (p. 28). Tunks

(p. 33) gives the following suggestions for researchers and research readers:

- When reading research results, do not stop with statistical significance. If strength of association is reported, consider it; if not, calculate it.
- When reporting research, include a strength of association estimate, or at least calculate and consider it carefully before formulating conclusions that may be unfounded.
- If strength of association is not reported, include sufficient data for the reader to make the appropriate calculations.

Excellent discussions of other ways to address the issue of the magnitude of a statistically significant test in a research study can be found in Cohen (1994), Kirk (1996), Rosenthal (1991), Rostov and Rosenthal (1984), and Thompson (1996).

Cohen (1994) points out the "near-universal misrepresentation" of significant testing and suggests the use of graphs to describe effect size (p. 997). Without going into the details of the meaning of testing a null hypothesis here, suffice it to say that Cohen recommends that "we routinely report effect sizes in the form of confidence limits" (p. 1002). Cohen says the best way to reduce misinterpretation of a statistically significant result is to reduce the variance attributable to unreliable and invalid measurement. We agree that all observations (measurements) in a research study should be reliable and valid.

Kirk (1996) actually argues against null hypothesis testing. He asserts that there is only one way to know whether an effect size is due to chance sampling variability and that is to do a replication of the study (p. 756). He agrees with Cohen when he suggests utilizing confidence intervals for sample data.

Meta-analysis is described in great detail by Rosenthal (1991). This approach to estimating the magnitude of a relationship between two or more variables deals with quantification procedures for comparing and combining the results of a *series* of studies. That is, the researcher should not consider the results of *one* study to draw conclusions about the magnitude of an effect.

Rostov and Rosenthal (1984) discuss various ways to determine whether a statistical difference is a meaningful difference. The most straightforward is to define an effect size as "small," "medium," or "large" based on the correlation squared (r^2) among variables. They designate a correlation of .10 as small, .30 as medium, and .50 as large (p. 106).

Thompson (1996) argues that "many people who use statistical [significance] tests might not place such a premium on the tests if these individuals understood what the tests really do, and what the tests do not do" (p. 26).

Among the approaches suggested to determine effect size are adjusted R^2, eta^2, and $omega^2$ (see Tunks, 1978, discussed earlier). Thompson encourages authors "to (a) correctly interpret statistical tests, (b) always interpret effect sizes, and (c) always explore result replicability" (p. 29).

The six guidelines presented above are intended to point out some of the most egregious weaknesses to look for in research reports. No doubt there are others. Careful researchers (in the critique of their own research and the research of others) should always be on guard for unwarranted bias and generalization. There are numerous volumes that describe in great detail various methodologies and techniques that can help to minimize bias in research and to allow the researcher to generalize results. The reader is encouraged to seek out this expertise in order to improve his or her own research skills.

Evaluating the Research Process and Reports

Critiquing the Research Process

As a field of research develops, we expect it to become more mature and sophisticated with an increasingly higher quality of production. But, we cannot take that for granted. Ultimately, quality in research depends on the rigor with which each researcher practices the craft. Unfortunately, rigor is not a finite quality. We cannot set a goal by which we expect researchers to demonstrate at least an 80% level of rigor. What we can do is periodically to remind our colleagues—both the practitioners and the readers of research—of the criteria by which research of quality may be achieved. Each individual must apply these criteria conscientiously and with discipline; in other words, with all the rigor that can be mustered.

The process of evaluating research parallels that of doing research. The model for research says, "State assumptions"; the model for evaluation says, "Were assumptions stated?" The key in either case is the application of criteria to determine whether the statement is adequate. Our goal here is to make these criteria explicit, particularly from the perspective of the evaluator. To do so, we will look at each step in the research process.

Researchers follow models in the same way composers follow forms. All works called symphonies will have certain structural features in common. Beyond that, each work will have unique characteristics that derive from the composer's creative, problem-solving process. The person analyzing a composition will attempt to identify the features of the work and understand the process the composer executed. Along the way, the analyst may make certain judgments, for example, "The work lacks rhythmic variety." Similarly, the person evaluating research starts with the report and, because the format of the report differs

from the actual research process, attempts to reconstruct the steps the researcher took and to make some decisions about the adequacy of those steps.

We should note at this point that, if the evaluator is an advisor or member of an advisory committee, the evaluation will be an ongoing process as a student's research progresses. The same criteria will apply at each step.

Certain steps in the process must follow in a given order. It is impossible to define a research problem adequately if the subject has not been sufficiently delimited or is vaguely stated. Hypotheses cannot be identified if the problem is poorly conceived. Techniques for data gathering and analysis cannot be detailed if hypotheses do not point to the data that must be treated.

Other steps in the process occur whenever it is necessary to refine the study further. For example, assumptions may underlie the general topic, the specific subject, the research problem, or hypotheses. Similarly, terms must be defined whenever they arise. Concepts must be recognized and made explicit any time that it is necessary to be sure the reader understands what is being discussed. Limitations must be applied whenever it is essential to narrow the scope of the project further. It is the job of the evaluator to track these steps even if they are not made explicit in the report.

A couple of general observations may be useful. The art of research is the art of asking questions. The more questions that are asked, and the more incisive they are, the more likely the researcher is to uncover the pertinent variables of a study. The evaluator can judge whether sufficiently incisive questions have been asked. The science of research is the application of analysis and synthesis. Analysis does not occur only when the researcher has gathered data; it occurs at every step of the way. The general topic is analyzed to determine its major components and extract a specific subject; the subject is analyzed to identify something that is problematic; the problem is analyzed to discover relationships that may lead to hypotheses.

When the data have been analyzed, the process of synthesis begins. The data are categorized to show results; the results are examined to draw conclusions; the conclusions are placed in the context of the original topic. The research model should have a nice hourglass figure—broad at the level of the topic, narrow at the waist where individual points of data are identified, and again broad where the conclusions contribute some new insight to the field. The details of this process of questioning, analysis, and synthesis provide the framework for evaluating the research.

In his chapter, "Toward a Rational Critical Process," Gonzo (1992) presents several models for critiquing research, depending on the type of research or review. These models have a number of steps in common, differing primarily in the techniques for treating data. We will consider here the criteria for judging each of the common steps.

Topic or Theory. Gonzo's models begin with the terms "Introductory model" or "Introductory rationale." Other terms for this beginning phase found in the literature include "topic," "theory," or "general hypothesis" (sometimes "working hypothesis"). The point is that an individual study should be related to the field and should help advance our knowledge in regard to some general concern; in other words, it will be one tile in a mosaic of a broad idea (see the section on theory and practice earlier in this chapter).

Sometimes we encounter a very specific problem. A person comes around a bend on a wooded trail and is face-to-face with a mother bear and cubs. The problem is evident immediately. It may be difficult in that situation to place the problem into the general context of animal behavior and hypothesize whether to run, freeze, or jump and scream like a maniac. Likewise, in teaching, we may encounter a bear of a problem—a particular approach is just not working with an individual student. To avoid trial and error (or screaming like a maniac), it is useful to put the problem into the context of some form of learning theory. This allows the researcher to bring a substantial body of literature to bear on the problem.

The evaluator's first question, therefore, may be whether there is a clearly stated topic, theory, or rationale for the study. How does one recognize a theory? Ironically, "learning theory" is not a single theory; it is a collection of theories. There are theories about individual learning styles, about the relation of maturation to music learning, and about how people learn to identify intervals.

Let us turn to a specific example of a well-stated theory. In *Africa and the Blues,* Kubik (1999) said:

> We proceed from the notion that there is no such thing as "roots" of the blues, but that the American blues were a logical development that resulted from specific processes of cultural interaction among eighteenth- to nineteenth-century African descendants in the United States, under certain economic and social conditions. (p. 4)

Substitute the word "theory" for "notion." Note that the theory, or topic, is not stated as a title, for example, "The Origin of the Blues." It begins by denying a common perception, that there is some primordial root of the blues, like the taproot of a tree. Rather, the blues resulted from cultural interaction, and there was an identifiable process involved. The process can be examined. Also, blues did not emerge in isolation, the product of some individual's creativity in the studio, but under particular economic and social conditions. How does this theory relate to general concerns in the field? Kubik said,

> In respect to its earlier history, most authors agree that the blues is a tradition that developed in the Deep South at the end of the nineteenth century under specific circumstances,

molding together traits whose remote origins can be traced to distinctive African regions with other traits from Euro-American traditions, such as the use of ending rhymes in most of the lyrics, reference to I–IV–V degrees, strophic form, and certain Western musical instruments. The search for the blues' "African roots" has been a persistent concern in African-American studies. (pp. 3–4)

Following the previous statement of theory, Kubik posed questions: "Which African eighteenth- to nineteenth-century traditions preceded the blues, channeling experiences and energies into the formative processes of this music? And in which parts of Africa were these traditions established?" (p. 4). These questions form a general hypothesis establishing a direction for the research: to look for the origin of the blues in particular related African traditions and in specific African regions. To illustrate how the ending relates back to the theory, one of Kubik's conclusions was that ". . . most of the blues tradition in the rural areas of Mississippi has prevailed as a recognizable extension in the New World of a west central Sudanic style cluster" (p. 203).

Analysis of the Topic. The research report may go directly from the general theory to the specific subject of the study. However, in the process of identifying the subject, the researcher analyzes the topic quite thoroughly. The major components and subcomponents of the topic are determined, relationships between these components are examined, and a specific research subject is selected. The reason for identifying all of the components and subcomponents is to be sure that nothing that has bearing on the subject has been overlooked. If a researcher is primarily concerned with the learning activities in a classroom or rehearsal but has overlooked the impact of an administrative decision to shift to a block schedule, a major variable will have been missed.

In their large-scale study of the economics of the performing arts, Baumol and Bowen (1966, p. xv) began with three major components: the current state of affairs, the trends and their analysis, and sources of financial support. Each was further delineated. Under the current state of affairs they considered the organizations (in theater, opera, music, and dance); the cultural boom; the audience; the performer, composer, playwright, and choreographer; and the financial state of the organizations. In a work of this scope, each of these components became a chapter of the book. After a similar analysis of the other major components, they made the following statement: "The central purpose of this study is to explain the financial problems of the performing groups and to explore the implications of these problems for the future of the arts in the United States" (p. 4). This was professional research done over a few years with a large staff and substantial funding. A student project, starting with the same topic, might further subdivide the components to arrive at relationships between more specific aspects. The following subject might result: What effect would an expansion of advertising by the Hartford (CT) Symphony have on ticket sales for concerts, and would it be cost-effective?

Need.   It may seem self-evident that there should be a recognized need for a study, but in practice it is not that simple. The researcher must review the literature thoroughly to be certain that the need has not already been met. One student proposed to his advisor to do a dissertation on a specific aspect of orchestration, only to be gruffly rebuffed. Later he discovered that the advisor's dissertation had been on the same subject. (This is not meant to suggest that a replication of a study may not be appropriate. But if a student suggests a change in certain aspects of the original work, and that these changes may contribute to a better understanding of the underlying theory, the replication may be warranted.)

The evaluator of research, particularly an advisory committee member, will want to know whether the need for a study extends beyond a local situation. Will the results be generalizable, replicable, or disseminatable elsewhere? Is the subject of consequence or is it trivial? Will it contribute in some way to filling a gap in the literature or theory of the field? Even though there may be a legitimate need, can it be met at this time or are there intervening steps that must be taken first? Is there sufficient theory to back up the study; for example, if it involves some aspect of musical cognition, are there sufficient operational definitions of the cognition process to underlie the study?

There are at least two cautions that reviewers should bear in mind. First, was the need driven by expedience? Many researchers face the three-headed monster known as RPT (reappointment, promotion, and tenure). Was there a legitimate need for a particular study or was something rushed into print or onto a conference program in order for it to appear on a resume? Second, does the reviewer's own bias intervene? In response to a dissertation proposal in a graduate seminar, one class member blurted out, "Why in the world would anyone want to do that?" To him, the subject was a piece of meaningless minutia; to the proposer, it was an important missing link in his area of specialization. It is the responsibility of the researcher to state the need clearly and show its importance in the field; it is the responsibility of the reviewer to keep an open mind as to interests that may be different from his or her own.

Lomax presented a clear-cut example of a statement of need in *Folk Song Style and Culture* (1968) regarding his collection and analysis of folksongs and related cultural materials. "The work was filled with a sense of urgency. To a folklorist, the uprooting and destruction of traditional cultures and consequent gray-out or disappearance of the

human variety presents [a] serious . . . threat. . . . The folk, the primitive, the non-industrial societies account for most of the cultural values of the planet" (p. 4).

Needs may be identified through the researcher's own teaching and musical experience, through conflicts and gaps in the literature, and through the suggestions for further research found at the end of most research reports. Researchers should be cautious, however, to weigh carefully the merit of suggstions for further research.

Purpose.   The purpose of the study refers back to the "introductory rationale" but is somewhat more narrowly defined. It should point to the specific subject of the research after the topic has been analyzed and the need has been made explicit. It is important to distinguish between the need and the purpose. That is, it is not helpful to say, "There is a need to solve the problem. The purpose is to solve the problem." The purpose should be to apply and test new methodologies, make comparisons, derive principles, establish connections or correlations, and the like. To return to the Lomax example above, he stated:

Our study began with the perception that there are powerful stylistic models shaping the majority of song performances in large regions of the world. The goal of our research was, first, to devise a descriptive technique [later called *cantometrics*] that would locate these grand song-style patterns in the recorded data itself and, second, to find what cultural regularities underlie and are relevant to these far-ranging and powerfully formative styles. (1968, p. 13)

The reviewer will want to make sure that the purpose (goal, intent, and such synonyms) is appropriate to the scope of the study. A purpose that is too grandiose and does not point to a specific subject is not likely to be met. The reviewer also will want to know what the study is intended to accomplish because the conclusions should show that the purpose has been fulfilled. In general, there should be just one purpose to a study, otherwise it is likely to go in divergent directions and never be resolved.

Survey of the Literature.   While there may be a section or chapter in a dissertation or book titled Survey of Literature that reviews what the researcher has learned, in fact the process of reviewing literature is continuous throughout the study. Initially, the review helps the researcher select a topic and determine what is already known about it, including the theory on which it is based. It helps delimit the subject and identify variables having bearing on the subject. The literature will verify the existence of a problem.

To take a fairly simple example, one student wanted to determine whether beginning instrumental students will make better progress in groupings of like instruments (such as all single reeds) or unlike instruments. He found articles, four of which favored like instruments, four unlike, and four said the issue was inconclusive. Therefore, the problem remained. The literature should provide instruments for data-gathering or, at least, guidelines and models for the design of instruments or techniques. The researcher also will find appropriate quantitative tools. Finally, the literature will keep the researcher up-to-date in the field. The reviewer may ask several questions about the way in which the literature was treated. Does the researcher show a sufficiently broad knowledge of the field? Did the individual examine the literature critically by determining whether authors were writing from the point of view of a particular philosophy? Were biases in the literature accounted for? Did the researcher determine whether recent literature extends, contradicts, or confirms past conclusions? Did the researcher determine whether certain data-gathering or analytical techniques have been supplanted or rendered obsolete by recent developments? Does the researcher present both (or all) sides of an issue and treat issues without bias; or does the researcher stack the deck with literature supporting a particular point of view? In the report, has the writer padded the bibliography with items that are beyond the scope of the study? Has appropriate form been used for citations and references?

The Subject.   The convention of using the heading "Statement of the Problem" sometimes masks the need to distinguish between the research topic, the subject, and the problem. The topic is the broad field of interest, the subject is the specific phenomenon to be examined, and the problem is that which needs solution. Without the intervening step of defining the subject, the problem is likely to stay on too general a level to be resolved.

From a general topic, the researcher selects a specific subject to study. How specific should it be? The scope depends, in part, on the researcher's situation. A university faculty member may be engaged in a fairly large-scale, long-term project; a doctoral candidate will select a more limited subject that can come to completion probably within 1 to 3 years; a master's student will be wise to confine a thesis to a project that can be completed within the last year of study.

Regardless of scope, the rule of thumb is that a subject is adequately defined when all relevant questions about that subject have been asked within the scope of the study. For example, Landau (1960) wanted to know whether composers' compositional practices conform to the theories that they profess to follow. He selected Paul Hindemith, who had written about his theories in *The Craft of Musical Composition*. Because he could not answer all relevant questions about all of Hindemith's works, Landau selected chamber music extending over the composer's career and chose comparable sections to analyze, such as the first theme of sonata-allegro movements. So, the scope was

limited to one composer, one genre, and one segment of form. The subject, then, was the relation between theory and practice in selected chamber works of Paul Hindemith. Landau could reasonably expect to answer all relevant questions about that subject. Notice, however, that there is nothing problematic about that statement. Before reaching the level of the problem, he had to define theory in terms of specific compositional rules and practice according to particular examples in the music. The problem was to determine the extent to which the examples conformed to the rules.

The person evaluating research needs to determine whether the subject is too broad for all relevant questions to be answered or, conversely, whether it is too narrow, failing to account for certain relevant questions. Questions that may be related to the subject but not relevant to the problem are set aside as limitations.

Analysis of the Subject.   In order to arrive at a concrete problem that leads toward observable data, the subject must be analyzed. Proposals by some novice researchers smack of the following example:

Subject: A car

Problem: The car won't run.

Hypothesis: If the car is fixed, it will run.

Only after the hood is raised and the components of the mechanical system are identified—battery, wires, spark plugs, distributor, and so on—is it possible to begin to identify the problem.

The analysis of the subject may begin by asking the questions who, when, where, why, what, and how. If a subject statement contains an abstract term such as "teaching," the researcher can apply these questions: Who is the teacher (training, experience, duties)? When does teaching take place (schedule, use of time)? Where does it take place (use of space, relationships in space)? Why (philosophy, goals, objectives)? What is included (curriculum)? How is it administered (methods)? Relationships between these items may be examined to determine one or more research problems. In one school system, for example, administrative pressure for a performance-based program conflicted with the teachers' goal for a problem-solving approach.

At this point, other steps in the process may be applied to the analysis of the subject. Which elements are relevant and which may be set aside as limitations? Is it necessary to further clarify the meaning and characteristics of relevant items? Are there assumptions that need to be made explicit or questioned underlying the facts, explanations, and relations?

Literature can be of considerable help in analyzing the subject. For example, Buttram (1969) wanted to know what factors were involved in a person's ability to identify intervals correctly. Four factors were identified in the literature. This led to a problem in which the factors were compared to see which had the greatest influence on accuracy of interval identification.

The challenge for the person evaluating the research is not only to follow the researcher's analysis but also to determine whether any important steps are missing or misapplied.

Limitations. The application of limitations in a study serves important functions: It establishes the scope of the study, distinguishes the essential from the unessential, helps define steps in the process and determine pertinent variables, and informs both the reader and the researcher as to what is purposely being omitted. The report may contain a section in which limitations are listed. Or, they may be stated at any point in the text where it is necessary to inform the reader that something has been omitted. In either case, the researcher wants to anticipate the reader's concern, "But you didn't cover such-and-such point," by already having accounted for such points in the report as much as possible.

The evaluator will want to ask several questions about the limitations. Does the researcher have a rationale for the limitations? In Landau's study (1960), he did not discuss Hindemith's acoustical theories because they had no bearing on the rules for composition. In the study of groupings of instruments for lessons, the student eliminated the full ensemble because ensemble rehearsals tend to have different objectives than lessons. Has the researcher appropriately omitted items that would not lead toward observable data? Have certain limitations been set for expediency? Sometimes researchers want to limit the setting for a study to locations that are convenient, such as their own schools, when that might bias the sample by excluding certain ethnic groups, socioeconomic levels, and the like. It is possible to limit a study too narrowly. Has a sample been limited to a point that would affect the ability to generalize from the study? Has the researcher consulted literature that would help determine the appropriate size of a sample? Have any limitations been set that would cause relevant variables to be omitted? For example, if the participants in a study were limited to one grade level, it probably would eliminate maturation as a variable. Has the learning portion of a study omitted anything pertinent to the test? It is important for the evaluator to account for the fact that not all limitations are intentional or stated by the writer.

Definition of Terms and Concepts. The purpose of defining terms and concepts is to ensure that the researcher and reader have a common understanding, both in respect to the connotation of words and the perception of phenom-

ena. The researcher also has to be conscientious about definitions in order to advance through the project. Vague terms and ill-considered ideas are stumbling blocks. If there are a number of technical terms, they may be grouped together in the report under the heading Definition of Terms. Otherwise, terms are defined in the text as they are encountered, often illustrated by an example beginning "such as. . . ."

The researcher should consider the audience in order to judge whether it is necessary to refine a term. For an audience of musicians, it is unnecessary to define an orchestra as an ensemble of strings, brass, woodwinds, and percussion. But, if the subject is the development of orchestration for the early concerto grosso, then a precise accounting of instruments at given points in time would be essential.

Concepts are somewhat more elusive, more difficult to recognize and define than terms. Essentially, they tell how people, including the researcher, think about things. Merriam (1964), in *The Anthropology of Music*, identifies a number of concepts about the practice of music and its role in society (pp. 63–84). These may be summarized as questions. How does any culture distinguish between music and nonmusic? What constitutes musical talent? What is the purpose or function of music in the society? What is the nature and importance of song texts? What is the optimum size for the performing group? What are the sources of music? Is music an emotion-producer? Who owns music? To what extent is there a preference for vocal or instrumental music? The answers to these questions tell how people of a given culture conceptualize their music.

Differing concepts about how people perceive music are embodied in the terms psychoacoustics and psychomusicology. One says that people respond to acoustical signals. The other says that two people may respond to the same acoustical signals differently (in a performance jury, one judge responded "Weak tone," another judge said "Refined tone.")

The evaluator needs to determine whether the researcher has consistently informed the reader about the meaning of terms and concepts, identifying any point at which the reader might say, "What do you mean by that?" The reviewer also should determine whether the research has been in any way hindered because the researcher has taken certain terms and concepts for granted and failed to recognize the impact that might have on a study. A careless researcher might base a study on older concepts that have since been rendered obsolete.

Assumptions. Assumptions serve a number of purposes in a study. First, they state conclusions and understandings from previous research. It is not necessary for the researcher to repeat previous research; rather, she or he may assume the validity of conclusions that others have reached as a point from which to develop something new or extend the previous research. Of course, the previous conclusions must be verifiable. Buttram cited previous research based on the assumption that "[A] highly developed awareness and understanding of musical intervals is considered basic to good musicianship. Interval discrimination has been used as an indicator of musical aptitude in tests . . . indicat[ing] that a close relationship exists between skill in sightsinging and interval identification" (1969, p. 309). However, since few attempts had been made to verify these views experimentally, he felt that there was a need for further research.

Second, assumptions may summarize the current status of thought in a particular field. In the book cited earlier, Merriam gave four assumptions about the then relatively new field of ethnomusicology (1964, pp. 37–39). First, "that ethnomusicology aims to approximate the methods of science"; second, "that ethnomusicology is both a field and a laboratory discipline"; third, "that ethnomusicology has been concerned primarily with non-Western cultures and most specifically with nonliterate societies"; and fourth, "while field techniques must of necessity differ from society to society, field method remains essentially the same in overall structure no matter what society is being investigated."

Third, assumptions state a point of view. In proposing a computerized system of score analysis, Forte (1966) said that the musical event is represented by the symbols on the page. Someone might say, "Wait a minute. You're ignoring the performance as part of the musical event." But, Forte was implying that musicians start developing an interpretation of the music (the musical event) by studying a score. A computer could count the number of secondary dominants in a score faster and as accurately as a person could. As long as a reader recognizes Forte's assumption that the score represents the musical event, it is possible to follow the logic of his train of thought through the study.

Some assumptions are not just those of the researcher but express commonly held views in the field. Buttram began his article with the following statement (substitute "assumed to be" for "considered"): "The musical interval may be considered the basic unit of musical construction. With its two tones presented sequentially, the interval is the basic melodic unit; with the tones presented simultaneously, the unit is harmonic" (1969, p. 309).

Fourth, assumptions help advance the analysis of the study by contributing to the definition of the problem. Often, assumptions are derived from concepts. If we conceive of something in a particular way, then certain things will follow. Buttram found that there were four factors that influenced interval identification. Each factor has an associated concept and assumption that might be summarized in this way:

1. Concept: Each interval has a distinctive character (quale) by which it is recognized.
   Assumption: The interval should be recognized instantly (it does not require time to figure it out).
2. Concept: The distance between pitches in an interval may be judged by the listener.
   Assumption: It takes time (a few seconds) to judge the distance between pitches.
3. Concept: Intervals do not normally appear in isolation but within a tonal context.
   Assumption: Hearing the interval within a tonal context will help the listener to identify the interval.
4. Concept: Certain intervals are more distinctive to the listener.
   Assumption: There will be a hierarchy of intervals in terms of accuracy of identification.

These concepts and assumptions led to a problem statement in which each factor was compared to a control set of intervals to determine accuracy of identification with college students as subjects.

As with other steps in the research process, assumptions should not be used for the sake of expediency. One student said, "For the purpose of this study, I will assume that all teachers are good teachers." Hardly.

The evaluator needs to determine whether stated assumptions are verifiable in fact or are open to question. If the assumptions cannot be supported, the results of the study are open to challenge. Has the researcher presented assumptions as fact or truth? Are there assumptions implied in the report that the researcher has not recognized and stated? Although it was never stated explicitly, in one study it was clear that minority students were assumed to have lower self-esteem than majority students. (In fact, minority students scored higher than majority students on both the pretest and posttest of the Coopersmith Self-Esteem Inventory.) Have assumptions connected to the conclusions and interpretation of results been stated?

Problem. A research problem represents a recognized difficulty, omission, question, conflict, or inaccuracy discovered through the analysis of a subject. It may result from the need to extend, update, reinterpret, or validate earlier studies, or it may result from explorations in a new direction.

We encounter the term "problem" in three connotations, and this is a source of confusion to students. A student may say, "Scheduling classes, rehearsals, and lessons is a problem." No, it is a task, not a problem. The solution is already known. It may not be an easy task, it may be complicated to work out, but it is something teachers have been doing annually for decades. By contrast, if a teacher wanted to compare the effect of two or more scheduling patterns on the progress of beginning students, that might bear fruit as a problem. In other words, it is important to distinguish tasks from research problems.

Second is the connotation of a general "problem," in which the term is used synonymously with topic or subject (Statement of the Problem). Recognizing that teaching students to be creative is a problem in no way points toward a solution. At that level, it is not so much a problem as a general concern. By contrast, if we think of creativity as a process of weighing alternatives and seek to examine problem-solving skills, we are on the road to pinning down a concrete research problem.

A third connotation is the one we are concerned with at this stage of the research process. What is it, in concrete, explicit terms, that the analysis of the subject suggests needs to be solved? The following criteria may be applied to judge whether the problem has been adequately defined. Is it a specific problem? Does the statement contain abstract terms that require further definition? What variables have bearing on the problem? What variables may be accounted for by assumptions? Are any of the variables not relevant to the solution to the problem and, therefore, may be set aside as limitations? Does the problem lend itself to empirical observation? What relationships may be observed that would point toward the solution to the problem as stated in one or more hypotheses?

The more analysis the researcher can do to determine conditions related to the problem, the easier it will be to define hypotheses. Compare these examples:

Problem: Will beginning students progress faster in groups of like instruments or unlike instruments?

Problem: Will beginning students in groups of 6–8 show greater progress in classes of like or unlike instruments when taught by a single teacher using the Belwin Band Method for one semester as measured by the Watkins-Farnum Performance Scale?

If the problem has been well defined, the step to the hypothesis may be a short one.

Hypothesis.   There are many definitions of the hypothesis in the literature, but let us keep it simple. As the step that follows the problem, it is a suggested solution to the problem, not yet tested to determine whether that solution is accurate.

Problem: The car's engine turns over, but it won't fire.

Hypothesis: Perhaps there is a loose wire. (We have not yet looked at the wires.)

In a sense, the hypothesis is a specialized assumption. We assume a solution to the problem and then test to see if that assumption can be accepted.

In the example of the instrumental groupings, we might hypothesize that students would make faster progress in groups of like instruments because we assume that the techniques of the instruments are similar and the teacher can address the group rather than individuals. But we cannot be certain until we test. We must let the data speak for themselves.

A single hypothesis may not be sufficient, not allowing the researcher to account for multiple conditions and variables, nor for interaction between variables. Buttram (1969) used four hypotheses to test the four factors:

1. There is no difference in accuracy of identification of intervals between a control version and one designed to reveal the influence of interval quale.
2. [The same statement ending with pitch distance.]
3. [The same statement ending with tonal context.]
4. There is no difference between the relative distinctiveness of intervals as identified in a control version and in versions designed to reveal the influence of quale, pitch distance, tonal context, and melody. (p. 312)

The evaluator should apply the following questions to the statement of an hypothesis: Does it contain a specific solution to the problem? Is that solution observable? Testable? Is there a basis for the solution in known fact? What variables are related to the solution? What alternative solutions might there be? Are there ambiguous or imprecise terms in the hypothesis? Does it point to the facts that must be collected? Does the hypothesis have multiple aspects, each of which should be accounted for in separate hypotheses? Are there interactions between variables that should be accounted for in separate hypotheses?

Once an hypothesis has been tested, it is either confirmed or rejected. If an hypothesis is rejected, it does not invalidate the study; it simply means that a different solution was the correct one. (It was not a wire; it was the distributor.) It is best to think of the hypothesis as a tool, not a truth.

Consequences of the Hypothesis.   This step tends to be overlooked in research designs. The consequences tell what one would expect to observe if the hypothesis is confirmed. As such, it establishes the criteria for analysis of the data It is especially important to be aware that consequences are not conclusions (a source of confusion for students), because the data have not yet been collected and tested. The consequences tell what the researcher is going to look at to determine whether the hypothesis is confirmed. Virtually every statement of consequences should start with the phrase "We would expect to observe." To determine whether students in groups of like instruments made greater progress than those in the other groups, we would expect to observe greater accuracy in playing pitches, rhythms, dynamics, phrasing; better tone quality, and so on. These are the parameters of the test. Once the test has been scored, we can accept or reject the hypothesis.

Consequences must point to data that are observable and testable. The consequences must be logically implied by the hypotheses and must be stated precisely and unambiguously. The consequences should account for all relevant variables. They form the connection between the hypotheses and the test design—a smooth segue.

Guidelines for the Dissertation

The remainder of this chapter is addressed particularly to doctoral students and doctoral advisors. The discussion may seem at first glance to be almost self-evident, but, too often, a potentially important contribution to our knowledge about the teaching/learning process in music is missed, or a doctoral degree is not earned because some of the cautions suggested here are not followed.

Some graduate students look forward to the dissertation with the same anticipation they would to the gallows. However, it need not be that way. First, we suggest a practical perspective. A dissertation is not a magnum opus; it is the last practice in research of a person's student days. If eventually it leads to the publication of a book, fine, but that should not be the goal. The goal is to fulfill successfully a degree requirement. The primary audience is the doctoral committee. Once the dissertation is approved, the audience may expand to anyone who wishes to order it. A paper may be extracted from it for presentation at a meeting of a professional society or for publication in a journal, but those are eventualities and not a consideration for the dissertation itself.

It may help, also, to bear in mind that the dissertation is not of the magnitude of *War and Peace*. It is, in its series of chapters, a collection of short papers, not unlike those that students have written for various courses.

Length is not an important criterion for judging the quality of a dissertation. Papers that involve a good deal of description of data (case studies, musical analysis) will usually be longer than those in which quantitative data are presented in concise, graphic form.

Selection of the subject is a critical step in the research process. Close communication between the student and advisor is crucial. Some advisors feel that the student should work on something closely related to the advisor's own area of research so that the student may benefit from the advisor's expertise. The advisor may literally say, "I haven't gotten to this yet; do this." This has the additional advantage of immediately putting the student's work into the context of a theory-based field with a body of literature and perhaps some laboratory or field techniques already defined.

By contrast, the student may wish to pursue a field of interest that is outside the advisor's primary field. The advisor should have a sufficient knowledge of research procedures to be able to guide the student through the process in either case.

Ultimately, it is wise for the student to pick a subject in which she or he already has some professional expertise so that all of that prior knowledge may be brought to bear on the problem without having to master a new field. Would a particular subject require knowledge of a foreign language, and does the student have the time to learn the language sufficiently to deal with the literature? Is the subject likely to take the student into a related field that would require extensive study (for example, the subject of concept development in music could lead into a vast literature in psychology on concept development)? A further practical consideration is whether the student has the financial resources required to carry out the research, or whether there is a reasonable chance of obtaining a grant.

Other practical considerations in choosing a subject include the student's own personal circumstances. For example, does one really want to launch a longitudinal study if promotion, tenure, or salary increase are dependent on finishing the degree? The purist may say that these considerations are irrelevant to the research. But they are relevant to the quality of the research if such circumstances make the student feel pressured and therefore anxious and careless or inclined to take shortcuts.

There are some pitfalls for which both the student and advisor must be vigilant. One is the subject that is too broad. One student wrote a history of the string quartet. The paper was 1,500 pages long and took 5 years to complete. The doctoral studies office sent it back with the notation, "Since you did not use proper footnote form and will have to redo this, we suggest you do some drastic pruning." The advisor should never have approved such a broad subject.

At the opposite extreme is the trivial subject, either one that does not relate to general topics or theories in the field or is a confirmation of something already known by common experience of musicians and music educators. A couple of studies on the "discovery method" come to mind where children were left on their own to "discover" composition. As most teachers would predict, the studies simply confirmed that the children did not have the necessary skills to progress and, therefore, were soon frustrated.

A third pitfall is what we might call the "Messianic Concept." A person sets out to solve all of the problems of music education in one dissertation. That may sound facetious, but anyone who has sat through sessions of dissertation proposals will know exactly what we are talking about because this happens all too frequently. This concept results in a subject that is impossibly broad and is usually biased in tone.

A fourth pitfall is expedience. A person is the conductor of an ensemble and, therefore, chooses to do a study using his or her own ensemble. That may or may not prove to be feasible, and must be considered with great care. The possibilities of bias, inadequate sampling, and so on are strong.

In carrying out the research, following a well-established methodology is essential. Such methodologies are described elsewhere in this chapter, in these handbooks, and in the literature of various fields of study. For example, if a study involves a survey, there are textbooks on survey techniques.

Keeping up with the literature is critical to the dissertation. Not only does the literature tell about the history of the subject, but about current developments while the dissertation is in progress. One student's proposal was approved and he was well along in the design of a survey when, in the latest issue of *Dissertation Abstracts,* he discovered that someone else had completed a virtually identical study. Because replication did not seem appropriate in this case, he had to start over with a different subject. Journal articles tend to be more current than books, although for some journals there may be a backlog of as much as 2 years before an article appears in print. Presently, websites may have the most up-to-date information.

It is especially important for the student to look at the research literature critically. As mentioned previously, not all literature is of high quality. Have writers' assumptions and conclusions been verified, and were they theory-based? Was the methodology appropriate to the problem? Have certain errors been passed on from one writer to another? For example, one historian misidentified an early instrument. Several other writers who failed to verify his conclusion passed on his error.

As the dissertation progresses, ultimately it is the student's responsibility to see that all requirements are met. The first step is to check with the graduate school or doctoral studies office to obtain any printed regulations. These are likely to include the composition of the advisory committee, requirements for the oral examination, guidelines for form and style in the dissertation, and a series of deadlines that must be met. The student should start with the last deadline (when the final, approved copy must be submitted prior to commencement) and work backward to establish a calendar. It is wise to allow time for unanticipated delays. Also, an advisor or committee should not be expected to read and respond thoughtfully to a draft over night.

After the student and advisor agree on the subject of the study, it is time to establish the advisory committee. Procedures may differ from one institution to another. The committee usually has three to five members, one or two from the student's major field and others from related fields. The quality of the dissertation may depend in part on the constitution of the committee. For example, if the major advisor does not feel comfortable with guiding the

student through a particular form of analysis, someone else may serve as the dissertation advisor. If the study involves analysis of complex contemporary music, it may be wise to have someone from the music theory faculty as the principal advisor. Persons from outside the department may be required, or at least desirable, on the committee. If complex quantitative analysis is involved, perhaps there should be someone from the statistics department on the committee.

The next step usually is the approval of the dissertation proposal. This may take the form of an outline presented orally to the committee or a graduate seminar, or it may be a formal, written proposal presented to the doctoral committee or to a committee of the graduate school that reviews proposals university-wide. While the student will not yet have done the actual gathering and testing of data, the study should, at this stage, be completely defined. The review of literature will essentially be complete, the problem and hypotheses defined, data-gathering techniques identified, and procedures for data analysis justified. Instead of conclusions, the proposal will suggest anticipated outcomes. The more rigorously the proposal is defined, the better its chances of approval. That may sound obvious, but we all have seen proposals submitted with the attitude, "Let's run it up the flagpole and see if anyone salutes," usually resulting in its being shot down.

In the process of preparing the proposal, the student needs to anticipate the need for other types of approval. Any study using human subjects may require written approval from parents, a public school administrator, or a special university office designated for such purposes. Before a questionnaire is distributed, it may require approval by some officer of the university if the student is viewed as a representative of the university.

When the data have been analyzed and it is time to write the dissertation, the student should inquire as to whether the graduate school has a prescribed format for the report (some do) and a prescribed manual of style. If none is prescribed, there are several guides to writing theses and dissertations as well as several manuals of style (some serve as both). The latest editions should be consulted because conventions change, especially as technology changes. It might be well to consult journals in the student's field to determine which manuals are customarily used. In any case, the rule of thumb is to pick one manual and use it consistently.

In general, writing a dissertation is no different from writing papers. But a few observations are in order, based on some common errors we have seen. First, the student should be sure that his or her own thoughts are prominent in the report. Some reports seem to be strings of quotations untouched by the human mind. The writer should introduce the material, provide transitions, paraphrase some material, and give assessments and explanations of the material. The reader should be led through the study with a logical train of thought.

Second, the writer should try to anticipate readers' questions. As much as possible, no questions should be left unanswered for the reader. This depends entirely on the writer's ingenuity. But, the goal is for the reader to say, "I may not agree with everything, but I understand exactly what you mean." Having others read the draft will help bring out any questions that need clarification. If the writer is uncertain whether something is clear, it is best not to engage in wishful thinking—"Maybe I can get by with that." It never works; revisions are in order.

Third, once all of the data are in hand, the writer should try to find a block of time to write straight through. It is extremely difficult to write in piecemeal fashion. One loses continuity of thought. It is a good idea to take a Christmas vacation, spread the papers out on the ping-pong table, let someone else cook the meals and run errands while the writing receives exclusive attention. It will soon be finished.

The student and advisor should agree on how the manuscript is to be presented. Some advisors like to see each chapter as it is finished; others like to see the complete dissertation so they can follow the continuity.

In the end, the quality of the dissertation depends on the conscientiousness of the student and the diligence of the advisor. If they have done their work thoroughly, the review by the committee and the scrutiny in the oral examination should go quite smoothly.

The Oral Examination

It is important for the student to understand the purpose of the oral examination because that will be a guide to preparation. The purpose is for the student to demonstrate that the subject of the dissertation has been so well mastered that the student can talk about it as well as having written about it. The committee knows that the student can write because they have already read the report. Some of us can write about a particular subject, and days later it seems as though someone else had written it; it does not seem familiar at all. We have put together a sequence of statements and lost track of the overall themes. The student needs to have the continuity of the subject in mind, be able to describe the process of the research, and relate the material to other aspects of the field through an oral presentation.

To plan for the oral examination, the student should check with the graduate school to determine the necessary steps to complete this requirement in a timely way. For example, it may be necessary to submit a copy of the dissertation to the graduate school at a date well in advance of the examination so that anyone interested in attending can read the manuscript beforehand. The graduate school may want to be certain that its requirements for the dis-

sertation (from form and style to the bond of the paper) are met before the examination.

Usually, it is the student's responsibility to see that all procedures and requirements are met. It is up to the student to contact committee members, see that they have copies of the dissertation, and schedule the examination. Most institutions require that an announcement of the examination be published in a campus newspaper, or some other vehicle, at least 2 weeks before the scheduled time, so that interested persons may plan to attend. Oral examinations normally are open to the public. Other doctoral candidates are particularly interested in attending so that they may have a preview of what they will face.

The format of the oral examination will vary from one institution to another, but we can describe some general practices. First, the candidate may be asked to discuss how he or she arrived at the subject and then to talk through the research process. This not only shows the candidate's mastery of the material, but also provides a summary for guests who have not seen the report. The candidate is permitted to use notes, but the notes should be used sparingly. The individual should not read extensively from the notes because then it is no longer an oral examination.

It is acceptable to use handouts or projection, particularly when data may be presented in graphic form, such as the results of statistical treatments. Video may be used for the presentation of certain classroom activities or conducting situations. Audiotapes may be necessary for studies that test aural discrimination. When any audio-visual equipment is used, the student should check the equipment before the examination to be sure that it is working properly and have all taped examples cued up.

During the student's initial presentation, committee members may interrupt for clarification of certain points. However, the advisor should be sure that the discussion does not become sidetracked to the point that the student does not have an opportunity to finish the presentation.

Following the presentation, the committee members may ask questions. Some questions may be designed to test whether the student really understands the procedures that were used or was just blindly following prescribed procedures. A typical question might be, "What is meant by statistical significance?" Other questions may expose that which the candidate has taken for granted. One student's subject was orchestrational styles of two composers. The first question was, "What do you mean by style?" The student was stumped because he had taken for granted that everyone understood what that term meant. He had actually defined style in his analytical criteria, but was momentarily stunned by the question. Other questions may be designed to test the limits of a student's knowledge, deliberately going beyond what the student might reasonably be expected to know. It is all right for the student to say "I don't know" when faced with such a question, and the student should not consider that response to be a sign of failure.

A significant point is the fact that the student is expected to have knowledge beyond the subject of the dissertation. This is often overlooked in the preparation for an oral examination. For example, if the study deals with the works of a particular composer, questions may be asked as to how this composer's work relates to those who came before or after him, or to historical style trends. If the study has to do with individual learning styles, questions may arise as to how this relates to classroom management. While it is impossible for the student to anticipate all questions, it would be useful to consider the broader context of the subject and the definition of terms used in the study. It is a good idea to practice by giving a presentation to friends before facing the committee.

The results of an oral examination usually fall into one of three categories: no revisions, minor revisions, major revisions. The advisor is responsible for assuring that the appropriate forms are filled out and submitted to the graduate school with the results of the examination. If both the student and the advisor have been diligent and insured that committee members have reviewed the manuscript well in advance of the oral so that they could raise concerns and make suggestions, there should be no need for major revisions.

The Role of the Major Advisor

The term "advisor" seems self-explanatory, but, in fact, is not. Misunderstandings about the role and responsibilities of the advisor may lead to serious difficulties. The following guidelines should be considered.

First, it is well to check the university by-laws to determine whether the role and responsibilities of the advisor are defined. The by-laws may say that advising, including dissertation advising, is part of a faculty member's duties, but that final responsibility for meeting degree requirements rests with the student. Policy may vary from one institution to another. Because poor advising has been known to lead to litigation, the advisor should give serious thought to the nature of the duties. At the beginning of the dissertation process, the advisor and student should come to agreement as to the responsibilities of each in respect to such things as meeting deadlines, selecting the subject of the research, determining appropriate research procedures, editing the manuscript, and preparing for the defense of the dissertation.

Because a goal of the dissertation is to prepare the student to be an independent researcher on completion of the degree, the student should take as much initiative as possible at every step along the way. But because the student is a novice at research, the advisor should give close oversight. Extremes should be avoided. One advisor, trying to be accommodating, was overhead to say, "Oh, anything you want to do is fine with me." That gave the student no guidance at all. By contrast, an advisor may become too manipulative without thinking of the consequences. One student was preparing a performance edition of a folio of early music when he discovered that one of the tunes was the basis for a parody mass. The advisor insisted that he find every parody mass derived from that folio even though it was a tangent to the research problem. It proved to be an overwhelming task, but the advisor refused to relent. The student never finished, causing him to lose his job because he did not complete the degree in a specified time. Also, an advisor should not write the dissertation for the student. That seems almost too apparent to mention, but cases have been observed where a student struggles with the writing and the advisor, out of frustration and impatience, winds up writing most of the manuscript under the guise of editing. This leaves the student dependent rather than independent.

At the outset, the advisor should review with the student any guidelines and deadlines specified by the graduate school and establish a calendar by which the student will complete various steps in a timely manner. They also should review the student's personal situation to determine any limitations on time and resources. Will the student be working on the dissertation full-time, part-time, or piecemeal? Will the student be in residence at the institution or back on the job? Does the student have financial limitations? Is completion of the degree related to job retention?

The advisor should guide the student in the selection of a subject and help the student judge the appropriateness of the subject, both in terms of its relevance to the field and the student's capability to carry the study to completion.

The advisor is in a position to help the student select other committee members. Because of previous coursework, the student may feel comfortable or uncomfortable with certain faculty members. Or, the student may have had no contact with some who might contribute good advice to the study, especially persons from outside the department. Both student and advisor should be alert to when potential committee members will be on sabbatical. As much as possible, members should be chosen because their areas of expertise complement the subject and the methods of analysis. The student should determine with each committee member when that person wishes to be involved. All too often, the time for the oral examination arrives and a member of the advisory committee is asked to participate, having had almost no prior contact with the student and no opportunity to advise on the study.

If kept involved, the committee can perform a sometimes necessary function. An advisor and student may develop a close relationship, especially if the student is also the advisor's assistant. At times, this relationship can make it difficult for the advisor to remain objective or to say "No" when necessary. The committee provides a check on that happening. There have been times when members have had to say to the advisor, "Do you really want that study to represent you and this institution?" to which the advisor has usually responded, "No," and further work was in order.

The advisor should be sufficiently familiar with the research procedures and literature on the subject of the study to guide the student through the process with precision. Precision results primarily from the rigor with which the dissertation proposal is defined. If it is thoroughly and carefully defined, the rest of the project should be busy work, filling in the blanks, so to speak. Both the advisor and committee should feel that the study will be defensible at the time of the preliminary approval.

The advisor's role is critical in assuring that appropriate techniques are identified or designed for gathering and analyzing data. Many of these are described elsewhere in this Handbook and in other research literature, but it is the advisor's experience that should help point the student in the right direction. The advisor should be especially alert for the need to administer pilot versions of instruments with subsequent revisions. The advisor should take responsibility for informing the student of the need for approval of the use of human subjects, administration of questionnaires, and the like. This is especially true when the student is no longer in residence at the university and may not be in regular communication with the advisor. It is dismaying to discover that a student has sent out a poorly designed questionnaire under the name of the university without prior approval.

Some studies require more supervision than others. If a study involves primarily the analysis of music, and criteria for analysis have been agreed on, the student may work independently to complete the analysis and describe the results. But, if the study involves public school classroom activities where unanticipated turns of events may occur, it may be necessary for the student, advisor, and cooperating teachers to be in close communication throughout to account for any necessary adjustments.

When it comes time for the writing of the dissertation, the advisor and student should agree on how the material should be submitted: chapter by chapter or in larger segments. In either case, the advisor should take the responsibility to review the material promptly and thoroughly. One student who had turned in a draft was asked by a friend when she expected to finish. She replied, "Hopefully, within my lifetime." The advisor held the material for several months without responding. When reviewing the material, the advisor should watch for any evidence of plagiarism, intentional or unintentional.

Bearing in mind that the dissertation is still practice in research—still a learning experience—the advisor should not only critique the manuscript for content but also for form and style. It is not satisfactory for the advisor to say, "That's not good enough. Do it again." That provides no guidance. Perhaps it is helpful to remember that both the name of the advisor and the institution will appear in the dissertation and be eternally represented by that report.

The dissertation should be as polished as possible before the oral examination. The advisor should assure that all committee members have had ample time to review it and are satisfied with the results before the oral. (The same advice was given to the student. That avoids the possibility of each thinking the other had taken care of it.)

During the examination, the advisor serves as the moderator, gives instructions to the student, sees that the discussion stays on track, and may choose to invite questions from guests if there is time. It is especially important that the advisor not let the discussion deteriorate into a debate between faculty members, an all-too-frequent occurrence. At the conclusion of the oral, with the candidate and guests out of the room, the advisor chairs a meeting of the committee to determine the results of the oral and obtain the members' signatures on the appropriate form before informing the candidate of the results. Silly as it may seem to have to mention this—but it does happen—this meeting should not wander into unrelated discussions while the candidate suffers in the hallway.

The advisor's duties usually end with a signature on the approval page of the dissertation.

NOTE

We wish to acknowledge our former colleague, Professor Warren C. Campbell, in the development of this ordinal scale. Shared discussions over many years contributed to these ideas.

REFERENCES

Abeles, H. F. (1980). Responses to music. In D. A. Hodges (Ed.), *Handbook of music psychology* (pp. 105–140). Lawrence, KS: National Association for Music Therapy.

Agnes, M., Ed. in chief. (1999). *Webster's new world college dictionary* (4th ed.). Cleveland: Macmillan USA.

Barzun, J., & Graff, H. F. (1992). *The modern researcher* (5th ed.). New York: Harcourt Brace Jovanovich College Publishers.

Baumol, W. J., & Bowen, W. G. (1966). *Performing arts— The economic dilemma*. Cambridge, MA: MIT Press.

Buttram, J. B. (1969). The influence of selected factors on interval identification. *Journal of Research in Music Education, 17*(3), 309–315.

Campbell, D., & Stanley, J. (1963). *Experimental and quasi-*

experimental designs for research. Chicago: Rand Mc-Nally.

Cohen, J. (1994). The earth is round (*p* < .05). *American Psychologist, 49*(12), 997–1003.

Colwell, R. J. (1969). *A critique of research studies in music education, final report*. U.S. Office of Education Research Project 6-10-245, Arts and Humanities Branch, University of Illinois at Urbana-Champaign.

Colwell, R. J. (1988). Editor's remarks. *Bulletin of the Council for Research in Music Education, 97*(Summer), 1–15.

Eisner, E. W. (1997). The promise and perils of alternative forms of data representation. *Educational Researcher, 26*(6), 4–10.

Forte, A. (1966). A program for the analytic reading of scores. *Journal of Music Theory, 10*, 330–64.

Fraenkle, J. R., & Wallen, N. E. (2000). *How to design and evaluate research in education* (4th ed.). New York: McGraw-Hill.

Gonzo, C. (1992). Toward a rational critical process. In R. Colwell (Ed.), *Handbook of research on music teaching and learning* (pp. 218–226). New York: Schirmer.

Grady, M. P. (1998). *Qualitative and action research: A practitioner handbook*. Bloomington, IN: Phi Delta Kappa Educational Foundation.

Grieshaber, K. (1987). Children's rhythmic tapping: A critical review of research. *Bulletin of the Council for Research in Music Education, 90*, 73–82.

Hair, H. (2000). Children's descriptions of music: Overview of research. *Proceedings of the 18th International Research Seminar, International Society for Music Education Research Commission: University of Utah, Salt Lake City*, 128–141.

Jorgensen, E. R. (1992). On philosophical method. In R. Colwell (Ed.), *Handbook of research on music teaching and learning* (pp. 91–106). New York: Schirmer.

Kirk, R. E. (1996). Practical significance: a concept whose time has come. *Educational and Psychological Measurement, 56*(5), 746–759.

Kubik, G. (1999). *Africa and the blues*. Jackson: University Press of Mississippi.

Landau, V. (1960). Paul Hindemith: A case study in theory and practice. *The Music Review, 21*, 38–54.

Lomax, A. (1968). *Folk song style and culture*. Washington, DC: American Association for the Advancement of Science.

Merriam, A. (1964). *The anthropology of music*. Evanston, IL: Northwestern University Press.

Price, H. E. (1997). Forum. *Journal of Research in Music Education, 45*(1), 3–4.

Radocy, R., & Boyle, J. D. (1997). *Psychological foundations of musical behavior* (3rd ed.). Springfield, IL: Charles Thomas.

Rosenthal, R. (1991). *Meta-analytic procedures for social research* (rev. ed.). Newbury Park, CA: Sage Publications.

Rostov, R. L., & Rosenthal, R. (1984). *Understanding behavioral science*. New York: McGraw Hill.

Schneider, E. H., & Cady, H. L. (1967). Evaluation and synthesis of research studies relating to music education: 1930–62. *Bulletin of the Council for Research in Music Education, 9*(Spring), 3–16.

Standley, J. M. (1996). A meta-analysis on the effects of music as reinforcement for education/therapy objectives. *Journal of Research in Music Education, 44*(2), 105–133.

Taylor, R. G. (Ed.). (1981). *The documentary report of the Ann Arbor Symposium*. Reston, VA: Music Educators National Conference.

Thompson, B. (1996). AERA editorial policies regarding statistical significance testing: Three suggested reforms. *Educational Researcher, 25*(2), 26–30.

Tunks, T. (1978). The use of omega squared in interpreting statistical significance. *Bulletin of the Council for Research in Music Education, 57*(Winter), 28–34.

Yarbrough, C. (1984). A content analysis of the *Journal of Research in Music Education*, 1953–83. *Journal of Research in Music Education, 32*(Winter), 213–222.

Yarbrough, C. (1996). The future of scholarly inquiry in music education: 1996 senior researcher award acceptance address. *Journal of Research in Music Education, 44*(3), 190–203.

Trends in Data Acquisition and Knowledge Development

59

LEE R. BARTEL

RUDOLF E. RADOCY

Research is "a systematic process by which investigators gather information, organize it in a meaningful way, and analyze and interpret it" (Asmus & Radocy, 1992, p. 141). While this definition does not indicate why investigators gather and work with information, a clue is in "a meaningful way"—the research process should be meaningful. Organizing, analyzing, and interpreting is a process of developing knowledge. Another way to express this is to say that research is a systematic process of data acquisition and knowledge development. The terms "data acquisition" and "knowledge development" resonate clearly with the current computer lexicon (Knowledge Discovery in Databases or KDD). This is intentional because technology is one of the most influential forces affecting research in the past 30 years. We have selected these terms to serve as "lenses" with which to examine trends in research.

A trend is direction of movement, a course, an inclination. To identify a trend means to note change over time and then to project the "direction" and "movement" of the change into the future. We are not futurists. Nevertheless, we identify seven trends in research:

1. *Construct complexity*—researchers are taking into account more dimensions, facets, or connections as they construct research problems and build conceptual frameworks for studies;
2. *Ethical complexity*—recognizing and honoring the complexity of constructs such as teaching and learning takes the researcher into dimensions of students' lives that have strong ethical implications. This trend intersects with a growing attention to individual and human rights and requires compromise with traditional design principles;
3. *Methodological complexity*—the pursuit of satisfying answers to questions consisting of complex constructs requires greater diversity and multiplicity of method;

4. *Data complexity*—multivariate and multimethod studies result in complexity in data as a whole and within specific types of data such as video recordings;
5. *Analytical complexity*—data and construct complexity dictates analytical complexity in the process of fitting most appropriate analyses with specific questions and data, and developing knowledge through patterns, relationships, similarities and differences, and so on;
6. *Representation complexity*—technological developments are providing new and easier ways of presenting data, data reductions, and knowledge claims, while epistemological argument is redefining what counts as "knowledge," with the result that knowledge representation is becoming increasingly complex; and
7. *Dissemination complexity*—website postings, e-journals, teleconferences, video journals, CD-ROMs are current indicators of dissemination opportunity, choice, and complexity.

Perhaps there are two mega trends: the use of technology, and increasing complexity in all facets of the process. Due to constraints on length, our focus is principally on three of the areas in which complexity is increasing.

We draw attention to complexity because the natural function of research is to simplify. Complexity, a property of an object, idea, phenomenon, organism, or system, stems from "compoundness"—multiple parts, layers, or dimensions. In addition, complexity lies not only in an entity as multiple components but also in the interconnectedness or interwovenness of the parts, each of which may depend on or influence the other, neither of which is in a fixed relationship or quantity, nor is related to a fixed behavior. For example, learning is complex. Learning depends on the many attributes of the learner, the home, the teacher, the curriculum, the school, and the environment. Each of these in turn is complex, with related and dependent dimensions.

Considering learning without considering these interconnected dimensions would be to deny the essential nature of learning. Complexity, as a quality of being differentiated yet integrated, is commonly regarded as "the direction in which evolution proceeds" (Csikszentmihalyi, 1993, p. 157). Since we are looking at trends or changes in research, our perspective is a view over time.

Explanation of changes in complexity over time, or simply explanation of complexity itself is the focus of Complexity Theory. Although we are not making a direct application of Complexity Theory (or Chaos Theory), the implication of our observations and explanations may have some commonalities with it. An important assumption of Complexity Theory is its inherent dialectic of simplicity and complexity: "What looks incredibly complicated may have a simple origin, while surface simplicity may conceal something stunningly complex" (Briggs & Peat, 1999, p. 79). In its application in research, the most important premise of Complexity Theory is that complexity and simplicity are not so much "inherent in objects themselves, but in the way things interact with each other, and we, in turn, interact with them" (Briggs & Peat, 1999, p. 89).

To understand the seven trends more fully, we need to reconceptualize research in terms of "knowledge development" and "data acquisition." This may transcend the qualitative-quantitative division by focusing on essential processes of research.

Knowledge Development

Constructs as Knowledge

Graduate student Pierre plays with questions of creativity for a research study. He wonders whether it is an inherent potential or learned ability and then realizes he needs to clarify what he means by "creativity." Pierre reflects on instances when he was told he was especially creative. He remembers the feelings of anguish when he had to improvise in music class and the sense of euphoria when he crafted an exceptional poem. He describes the characteristics of some people he considers creative. He realizes the meaning "creativity" has in his mind is an accumulation of at least (1) personal experiences that were designated "creative," (2) demonstrations of others engaging in "creativity," (3) stories involving "creativity," and (4) the meanings of other words associated with creativity like spontaneous, artistic, novel, unique, and special. Pierre has constructed this set of meaning connections with creativity over many years. A complex construct relates to and depends on a multitude of other constructs; it constantly and continuously develops.

In research, the term "construct" generally means a defined concept, a formalized description of an informal notion, a distillation of an idea so that it can be operationalized with a "test" or checklist or categorical assignments. We use the term "construct" to reflect individuals' active mental involvement in building a definition, the engagement in a constructive process to give clear meaning to an idea. The mind selects some things, rejects some things, connects some things. For example, "creativity" as a commonly used term, clearly has a shared meaning that communicates something to many people in our culture. But, to study it in a formal research context, a researcher might define creativity in a way related to manipulation of materials, to certain procedures, or to observable products with defined characteristics; in other words, as an operational definition.

An infant's first recognitions of a violin and its associated sound, Pierre's association with "creativity," or the researcher's theoretical construct all share the feature of being a locus of meaning *constructed* by a mental process of selection and association from a host of "perceptual data." "Cronbach has concluded that all human action is constructed, not caused, and that to expect Newton-like generalizations describing human action, as Thorndike did, is to engage in a process akin to 'waiting for Godot' " (Donmoyer, 1990, p. 178, referring to Cronbach, 1982).

Various types and levels of constructs exist. The first level is descriptive—the denotative "noun" is one construct type at this level. Many constructs begin as object recognition in nonlinguistic modes. Others begin almost as dictionary linguistic descriptions but as such are essentially "empty" constructs (like web pages that have only one thing on them and with no further links). Connotations can be added to these basic constructs through verbal and visual connections, but active experience is what essentially develops the richness of the construct. Clearly, a parent or teacher cannot simply "transfer" a fully-formed construct to the child. The person must engage perceptual data and build (construct) or organize it into a mental structure. One level of constructs is the noun and verb level—they relate mostly to objects and actions, but they always have links to all modes of perception and sensation.

A second type at the basic level of constructs is one that is essentially abstract—adjectives and adverbs. These emerge as a locus of meaning from attributions or characterizations of other constructs related to objects and actions, and tend to take on values on a dichotomous continuum (e.g., hot–cold, excellent–mediocre, loud–soft). For example, "creative" is a construct that derives from generalized characterizations of observations of production and product.

A higher level construct is the "theory-making" or explanatory level. Kelly (1955) refers to this level in his *Psychology of Personal Constructs* and it is more recently described by Schema Theory. The person develops a mental structure that encompasses the links and relationships between constructs. This relational, explanatory construct can be seen as an hypothesis or, with development, a theory. It acts as a means of making predictions about the world. As the person experiences a stream of sensory data from any or all the bodily senses, these hypothesis constructs offer "explanations" of the data by allocating them to existing constructs and relationships among constructs previously experienced, or introduce "modifications" to existing constructs.

In most cases in this chapter, we refer to descriptive and explanatory level constructs simultaneously. Where necessary, we will differentiate by referring to schema-type constructs as "explanatory constructs." For example, knowledge is the sum of consciously and intentionally accessible constructs (in this case both descriptive and explanatory types). In addition, we assume that constructs exist not only linguistically as words meanings but also in relation to all perceptual modes (Phenomenal, Linguistic, Kinaesthetic, Affective, and Performance [Perlmutter & Perkins, 1982]) and to all forms of intelligence (Gardner, 1999).

Knowledge development and understanding is concerned with: (1) increasing the complexity of constructs (adding pages with more on them to the Website), (2) increasing the associations among constructs (creating more links between sites), (3) increasing the complexity of explanatory constructs, (4) increasing the extent of construct consciousness or clarity, (5) making associations more readily accessible, and (6) increasing facility at accessing and using the links, thereby (7) increasing the accuracy of explanatory constructs to anticipate and predict the future. The purpose of research is knowledge development.

Constructs in Research Design.   Fine (1998) asserts, "What science makes is knowledge, which includes concepts and theories, along with things and even facts" (p. 4). Research is about constructing knowledge. Especially in the social sciences, where most music education research is methodologically situated, research works with constructs. We rarely work with objects or matter, as physicists do, where only the most radical constructivists might argue properties do not exist apart from representations of them. The things that concern music educators are more likely theoretical constructs such as musicianship, creativity, aptitude, preferences, attitudes, abilities, effectiveness, competence, artistry, achievement, excellence, learning, response, or understanding, for which we normally use "indicators" or representations from which we infer what we can know. What our research efforts are aimed at, then, is to refine, elaborate, or clarify our constructs.

Research design is generally a data acquisition and analysis plan for the purpose of developing knowledge. It is possible to make a plan to acquire data without a clear view of what knowledge exactly will be developed, but in most cases, even in research trying to develop "grounded theory," the researcher has a prediction of the type of knowledge, the category of constructs, that will emerge. The way to acknowledge this prediction is in the form of a question. A real question, one without an already formulated answer, is the means to examining the nature and adequacy of constructs. A question demands a method of answering. The plan to secure an answer is the research design. The constructs a researcher will think to question, the kinds of questions, and the kinds of methods admissable as legitimate for answering those questions are culturally influenced—whether that is a religious, societal, or research culture.

A researcher may decide to further knowledge in a defined area, on one facet of a problem, or a simple construct, but must recognize that resulting "incompleteness" and, thus, the possible irrelevance of the knowledge to the holistic and complex essence of education and life. Simplifying a construct in research may clarify method and design but risks distortion. Imposing a favorite method or design on possible questions thereby eliminates potentially useful and important questions. In addition, exploring phenomena one or two unidimensional constructs at a time is a slow process within a changing context. Cronbach (1975) stresses this problem of social science research: "The trouble, as I see it, is that we cannot store up generalizations and constructs for ultimate assembly into a network. It is as if we needed a gross of dry cells to power an engine and could only make one a month. The energy would leak out of the first cells before we had half the battery completed. So it is with the potency of our generalizations" (p. 123).

Construct contemplation and analysis is of greatest importance as a step toward research design. The next step, deciding what data will provide the sources of information from which knowledge can be advanced is just as crucial. What cannot be overemphasized is that all that can be obtained is a "representation" of the construct under study. The number on an ability test is a representation (or estimate in statistical terms) of ability-related tasks as defined by a theory-driven testmaker. If a student is observed demonstrating behaviors that are physical, verbal, or musical representations one may infer something about that student's ability. An interview with a person will obtain a linguistic representation, as well as some gestural representation, of an internal state.

Researchers are concerned about construct validity, that is, the extent to which the data being obtained adequately represent the construct theorized. If we are studying creativity, data might be observations of the manipulation of materials, of certain procedures, or of observable products with defined characteristics. Such data, selected to relate to a theoretical construct, may well ignore many aspects of the "creative experience" like the creator's feelings, some of the thought process occurring during the process of creation, the kinesthetic abilities limiting realization of an idea, or the ideas rejected during the process. A serious concern for researchers of creativity is one of construct validity, that is, do the dimensions included in the "observables" or the "test" really match the richness of meaning we give the word creativity. The problem may be that a complex construct is simplified into a "theoretical construct" that is too one-dimensional, too reliant on the immediately evident, or too poorly understood by the researcher.

Theoretical construct validity depends both on how well one knows the "common" construct and on how faithful the selected representations are to the "reality" they are taken to represent. If the constructs are thoroughly known, questions can be anticipated and the research design improved. If the complexity entailed in a situation is not understood, or if the researcher believes there may be unanticipated questions from incomplete construct-awareness, the research may begin exploring the environment and attend to the constructs being "tweaked" by the incoming data. The researcher then is becoming aware of the constructs employed in classifying and filing incoming data. Whether through formal "instruments" or mentally analyzed informal observations, this is a process of data acquisition and knowledge development.

Constructs and Analysis.   Given that the data in a large database are of various types, a program to make sense of them must be flexible enough to accommodate the diversity. One way is to apply to software the concepts of Kelly's (1955) "Psychology of Personal Constructs." The fundamental principle holds that a person's psychological processes are directed by explanatory constructs. Kelly sees the main function of explanatory constructs (or schema) as creating personal predictions about the world. The person then tests the predictions, and the construct is reinforced or changed depending on how well the experiential reality matches the prediction. Data mining software begins with constructs of postulated relationships among data. These anticipatory constructs are then confirmed, altered, or mutated in an iterative process. Knowledge constructs are "discovered" in the database by the computer.

In a similar manner, the researcher conducting a case study of a classroom acquires a constant stream of "data." These data are processed with existing explanatory constructs—the result of all previous "learning" (knowledge development). As the researcher's explanatory constructs encounter data that cannot be accommodated by existing structures, new ones are created or existing ones modified. This process of the mind is essentially the same as that of

normal living that results in our "informal" knowledge or common sense. However, when the researcher makes the process conscious by making the construct structure conscious, it is clearly recognizable as an analysis process. Researchers gathering verbal, gestural, artistic, or emotive representations must be especially aware of the "data mining" nature of their analysis.

The quantitatively descriptive researcher engages in virtually the same process but in a slower and more linear manner. Data are representations, believed to have validity related to the constructs under study. The representations are analyzed with an existing construct and the degree to which they coincide with the construct is made conscious. The researcher then decides whether the basic construct or the anticipatory/explanatory construct is confirmed or requires modification.

Implication of Constructs for Method

If Cronbach (1982) is right in that all human action is constructed, not caused, and the explanations we have presented are plausible, then research method begins with and accounts for the nature of the constructs to be studied. Furthermore, method and analysis must acknowledge that in social science, the phenomena of interest are usually enmeshed with the construct structure of each individual in the study. That emphasizes the urgent need for attention to construct validity in any study and that validity probably rests to a great extent on the complexity of the representations as well as what Keeves (1997a) calls "band width" (range of manifestations) and "fidelity" (observational unidimensionality). To honor the complexity inherent in most constructs, researchers must plan for a program of research, multiple data types, multimethods, or close identification with a "family" of studies contributing to a shared knowledge.

Data Acquisition

A Basic Research Process

Without data, there is no research. The data employed in knowledge development may not be recent but nonetheless are data and should be recognized as such. The philosopher engaged in criticism of a praxial approach to music education may employ constructs acquired from Kant or Sparshott 10 years ago. The historian may have strong personal memories of participation in an organization she is now studying. The experimenter gathers his computer file of data. The anthropologist writes copious field notes, creates audio and video recordings, and gathers representative objects. Data acquisition is crucial in every case.

Types of Data

All data are representations. An achievement test score is a representation of the student's achievement (itself a theoretical construct). Numbers are not quantities, they are mental surrogates for quantities. The numeral "7" in and of itself is an indication of "sevenness" in whatever property to which it is applied. The words in the interview transcription are not the meanings and thoughts of the interviewee, they are surrogates for those meanings. Therefore, to understand the types of data, we must explore types of representations. (Just to clarify the obvious, we are assuming there is a reality apart from representations of it.)

Representations of knowledge are both internal (the way we represent images and concepts internally) and external (the way we represent our knowledge to communicate it to others). For example, through internal representation, we create a construct we label "up" by about kindergarten. It develops with every lift off the floor or climbing of the stair (kinesthetically), with tossing a toy or pointing to the sky (spatial), with making a vocal glissando (musical), with counting while building the block tower (mathematical), and with adding words to all these experiences (linguistic). We can communicate something about "up" to others through external representations—moving our hand upward (gestural), pointing upward (symbolic), drawing an arrow pointing to the "top" of the page (iconic), saying the word "up" (linguistic), saying a series of numbers representing increasing quantities (numeric), or making a sound increasing rapidly in pitch (musical). Representations fall at least into the areas of Gardner's (1999) basic intelligences: linguistic, logical-mathematical, musical, bodily-kinesthetic, spatial, and, probably, intra- and interpersonal, and possibly even naturalist and spiritual. Within each there are different expressions and forms. For example, linguistic representations may be a single word, a logical proposition, a poem, or a story. Bodily-kinesthetic representations may include symbolic gestures such as sign language, kinesthetic analogues, dance, or pantomine. The important conclusion here is that all forms of external representation can be regarded as "data" and therefore recorded and analyzed.

Roles of Data

Data, as knowledge representation, have distinct roles. Davis, Shrobe, and Szolovits (1993) identify five roles of a knowledge representation that are pertinent to artificial intelligence applications on computers. Three are particularly relevant here. The first and most obvious is the basic role of a knowledge representation as a surrogate—something that substitutes for the thing itself. The second role of data is as a "set of ontological commitments." External reality can be represented in various ways, and no representation is perfect. Each attempted representation captures some things but necessarily omits others. Therefore, every time researchers decide what they will focus on in the world and how they will represent it, they are "making a set of ontological commitments. The commitments are in effect a strong pair of glasses that determine what we can see, bringing some part of the world into sharp focus, at the expense of blurring other parts" (Davis, Shrobe, & Szolovits, 1993, p. 20).

A third role a knowledge representation fulfills is as a "medium of human expression." This is most important in research in terms of communicating knowledge developed in the research process. An important point here is that knowledge as a construct is generally complex, and the selection of a means of representing it again focuses on some facets and ignores others. Expression and communication are different. A person may choose a way to express knowledge and it may satisfy that person, but it may not communicate what was intended or meant. It is one thing to record video data of a conductor's gesture, analyze the gestures as knowledge representations, and reshape existing knowledge about musical problem solving, and quite another to appear in front of a research conference and demonstrate that knowledge only with gestures. Gesture may be needed to communicate aspects of knowledge that are not easily represented in words, but words are pragmatically useful. Anyone traveling in a country where his or her language is not understood knows how difficult gestural communication alone is. At the same time, in many contexts, seeing another's gestures enhances communication accuracy.

Data Acquisition Concerns

The primary requirement of data, of a representation as a surrogate, is that it is something out of which we can make meaning that is warranted and that the meaning it contributes is supported or at least not contradicted through multiple perspectives (i.e., it is valid). Although validity often appears to hinge on methodology (e.g., randomization and control in experiments, population and sampling in descriptive, triangulation in interpretivist), validity is primarily about credible, defensible meaning-making from the selected representation. Cronbach (1971) asserts, "One validates, not a test, but an interpretation of data arising from a specified procedure" (p. 447). Zeller (1997) explains, "it is not the indicant itself that is being validated, but rather it is the purpose for which the indicant is being used that is submitted to validation procedures" (p. 824). If a professor uses a highly "valid" music history examination as a measure of achievement in a musical acoustics class, there certainly would be indefensible meaning-making.

Because the constructs we deal with in social science are

complex, selecting any one representation from which we can credibly infer meaning is nearly impossible. Consequently, researchers concerned about validity may need to draw on several types of representations (complex data) and multiple methods. Zeller (1997) argues, "A valid inference occurs when there is no conflict between messages received as a result of the use of a variety of different methodological procedures" (p. 829).

Seven Trends

Trend 1: Construct Complexity

The most fundamental trend affecting the social and behavioral science dimensions of music education research is the growing recognition by researchers of complexity as a central characteristic of all constructs and phenomena and the increasing complexity of the constructs themselves. Constructs do not exist in external reality—only the sources for our constructs do. Constructs are mental creations and develop toward complexity. Complexity is characterized by "compoundness"—multiple parts, layers, or dimensions—and interconnectedness of the parts, each of which may depend on or influence the other, none of which are in a fixed relationship or quantity, nor are related to a fixed behavior. For example, the researcher today may acknowledge that "self-concept" as a research construct is more complex than researchers thought 15 years ago, but the self-concept construct in the typical research subject's mind may be more complex today than it was 25 years ago, because of an increase in comparative images from the media, peer comparisons through Internet chat lines, or societal standards resulting from cultural diversity.

The complexity problem was first described in relation to the problem of generalizability of specific research findings. The hope enunciated by E. L. Thorndike (1910) was to "tell every fact about everyone's intellect and character and behavior, . . . the cause of every change in human nature . . . the result which every educational force . . . would have" (p. 6). In 1957, Cronbach reiterated this hope, but argued that to accomplish this researchers would have to focus on the effects of interactions rather than the effects of treatments. Frustration from inconsistent findings from similar studies led Cronbach (1975) to conclude as we said on page 1109:

> Once we attend to interactions, we enter a hall of mirrors that extends to infinity. However far we carry our analysis—to third-order or fifth-order or any other—untested interactions of still higher order can be envisioned. (p. 119)

A major part of the problem seemed related to changing cultural context and the speed with which studies can be done. Cronbach concluded:

> The trouble, as I see it, is that we cannot store up generalizations and constructs for ultimate assembly into a network. It is as if we needed a gross [12 dozen] of dry cells to power an engine and could only make one a month. The energy would leak out of the first cells before we had half the battery completed. So it is with the potency of our generalizations. (1975, p. 123)

A problem for research is that we are dealing with complex constructs within a complex context that is evolving rapidly toward greater complexity. One social science reaction to this problem may be the rise of qualitative research. "Qualitative" researchers frequently point to the simplifying, linear approach of quantitative researchers as focusing on phenomena or constructs that have no relevance in the complicated real world. Quantitative researchers have been slow to respond with analytic techniques that can accommodate the complexity inherent in education or even to acknowledge the complexity. The arguments between the two groups have been so drenched in philosophic fundamentals of Cartesian reductionism, hermeneutics, epistemology, Realism, Relativism, Constructivism, and so on, that the more practical issues of construct complexity have been lost behind the smokescreen of the paradigm wars in educational research. Cziko (1989) observes that "the debate, centered on issues related to quantitative versus qualitative approaches to research, has at the very least raised serious questions. . . . There appears, however, to have been little discussion among educational researchers of what may be an even more basic issue, that is, the possibility that the phenomena studied in the social and behavioral sciences are essentially unpredictable and indeterminate [complex]" (p. 17). Evolution toward increasing complexity has not only affected the social sciences. Perhaps not yet openly perceived as a paradigm war in "hard science," limitations of the Newtonian Paradigm are showing and "a major fault line has developed in the episteme" (Hayles, 1991, p. 16). The wedge now driving open this fault is Complexity Theory.

Qualitative researchers reacted to the simplicity and linearity problem of traditional scientific research by abandoning formal measurement and calculation. Naturalistic contexts are inherently complex and make credible analysis and understanding difficult. Complexity-informed researchers in social science are responding now in several ways. One is to imitate the physical scientists in searching for "chaotic order in dynamic data sets measured across very large numbers of time points" (Byrne, 2000, p. 2) with statistically rigorous analysis of the dynamics of chaos in social science data. Another approach is the development through computer-based simulations "of very elegant graphical representations of the behavior of uninterpreted deterministic chaotic expressions" (Byrne, 2000, p. 3). This allows for the examination, for example, "of whole system properties corresponding exactly to Durkheim's conception of social facts, and allows for examination of their emergence and transformation over time" (Byrne, 2000, p. 3).

A third way complexity-informed social science researchers are changing is to look in a new way at both quantitative and qualitative approaches. In quantitative research, we either have or can envision large and complex data sets—of the sort acquired through national assessments, polls, census, market surveys, government revenue data, school evaluations, and so on. These data sets are complex because they contain varied data about individuals and groups in a time-series manner. Perhaps logistic regression and loglinear procedures are appropriate analysis techniques because of the possibility for handling interaction. However, Bryne (2000) says—and Cronbach (1975) might agree—"It has been unfortunate that the emergent complexity generated by interaction has so often been reduced to terms in linear equations. A way of thinking informed by complexity leads us to treat procedures which enable the identification of significant interaction as qualitative exploratory devices rather than as ways of establishing law-like models . . . Instead of generating models which seek to describe determinants of outcomes, and writing interactions as terms in those models, we can see interactions as signs of the presence of complexity in general" (Byrne, 2000, p. 4). In qualitative research, we are seeing a trend toward computer-assisted analysis. The influence of Complexity researchers will probably result in an emphasis on time-ordered data and analysis that looks for development and change.

Trend 2: Ethical Complexity

At least three factors have contributed to a trend of increasing ethical complexity in conducting music education research. The first is the increasing complexity of the constructs under study. No longer are rigorous researchers satisfied to administer a short paper-pencil test and claim, for example, it is a valid measure of self-concept. The acknowledgement of construct complexity means researchers are probing deeper into sensitive areas—psychological issues, home and private matters, relationships, roles and perceptions—all of which potentially can destabilize the participant's mental state or raise questions that provoke transformative reflection. Also, some constructs studied in music education are diversified and include topics that may touch on sensitive or confidential data, for example, mentoring (Lamb, 1997b, 1998, 1999), peak experience (Gabrielsson, 1991; Sundin, 1989), negative feedback (Cameron & Bartel, 2000; Jacques, 2000), or brainwave manipulating sounds (Bartel, 2000).

A second factor is the increasing complexity of the social environment within which music education takes place. In cosmopolitan cities, cultural diversity continues to increase. Not long ago, a researcher in Canada or the

United States could send a letter requesting permission written in English to parents with considerable confidence that it could be read and understood. Today in Toronto, for example, most schools have upwards of 30 language groups represented among the students and many of the families are recent immigrants. Although students are learning English, parental permission for research necessitates extensive translation of letters and further raises fears among many people of privacy invasion through student observation or questioning. Subject diversity of language, culture, or religion becomes a prominent issue in the interpretation of data representing most constructs. This is less of a problem with simple constructs but a serious problem in complex constructs. An ethical issue resides in the integrity of our interpretations—do we really understand and correctly represent what people know, believe, experience, perceive, or achieve.

A third factor increasing ethical complexity is "the rights revolution" (Ignatieff, 2000). Beginning with the 1948 Universal Declaration of Human Rights, the past 50+ years have seen a constant struggle for freedom, civil rights, equal rights, self-government, or human rights. Often the battle has been between individual rights versus special group rights. The development of an increasingly litigious culture has exacerbated the situation. One consequence of these struggles has been a climate where both subjects and researchers are much more aware, and ethical watch-dog agencies are much more cautious. As a result researchers must anticipate and clarify procedures and effects, communicate clearly and accurately to all touched by the research, and obtain legally defensible permissions for all research.

Trend 3: Methodological Complexity

Research methodology is the plan employed to acquire data and make meaning (develop knowledge) out of those data. It is an intentional process to reshape or confirm existing constructs (knowledge). In education, this process has always been relatively complex, because educational research is inherently multidisciplinary—the concerns of education draw on many disciplines. Historical and philosophical research have methodological traditions pursued in music education research. Psychology as a discipline developed in the past 120 years, and has two, at times competing, orientations—experimental and correlational (Cronbach, 1957; Shulman, 1988). Both psychological research orientations have been prominent in music education research. Musicology, in addition to its historical dimension, is an analytic approach, one that is applied in music education research. Sociological research in the past relied heavily on surveys—questionnaires and interviews. This is one of the most common approaches in music education research. Anthropology has had less application in music education research until recently, but ethnomethodology has been rising in popularity. Some disciplines, such as linguistics, economics, and demography, have had little effect on music education research.

Educational research is inherently multilevel—concerned about both individuals and groups. Educational research deals with problems that are inherently complex: "It is rare that a problem in educational research can be reduced in such a way that it can be viewed in terms of only two constructs or variables" (Keeves, 1997b, p. 278). Educational research often examines learning over time making multiple or repeated measures necessary.

As a result of being multidisciplinary, multilevel, and inherently complex, educational research is multimethod. However, the existence of many methods, if these were clearly differentiated but not integrated, would demonstrate diversity but only limited complexity. The growing acceptance of multiple epistomologies, however, adds another layer of real complexity.

The often heated paradigm wars in educational research that attempted to demonstrate the "rightness" of one paradigm over another, assumed that distinct paradigms existed and that, if so, only one could be "true." There are serious flaws in the concept of distinct paradigms (Walker & Evers, 1997), but as foundational theories for a specific set of research methodologies they do have utility. Walker and Evers (1997) explain:

> In offering a broader, three-way taxonomy of research to account for diversity in inquiry, Popkewitz (1984, p. 35) says: "the concept of paradigm provides a way to consider this divergence in vision, custom and tradition. It enables us to consider science as procedures and theories of social affairs." He assumes that "in educational sciences, three paradigms have emerged to give definition and structure to the practice of research." After the fashion of "critical theory" (Habermas, 1972), he identifies the paradigms as "empirical-analytic" (roughly equivalent to quantitative science), "symbolic" (qualitative and interpretive or hermeneutical inquiry), and "critical" (where political criteria relating to human betterment are applied in research). (Walker & Evers, 1997, p. 23)

The coexistence of these epistomological perspectives is important. They do not supersede each other as paradigms in the way natural sciences are assumed to do (although that is now in question as well), or as Lincoln and Guba (1984) seem to assume with their "paradigm eras."

Another facet of research methodology has greatly affected the overall complexity of knowledge development processes in the past 15 years—theoretical orientation. These orientations are differentiated in specific ways from each other, with common features between some, and selective discipline and paradigm acceptance among them. Babbie (1995) argues that these orientations coexist and

cocontribute to a complete view of social and behavioral phenomena because each "offers insights that others lack—but ignores aspects of social life that other[s] . . . reveal" (p. 41).

Babbie (1995) and Rothe (1993) identify the following as distinct theoretical orientations affecting methodological decisions: (1) Social Darwinism—research finding factors predicting or facilitating survival of the fittest (e.g., finding characteristics of band students most likely to succeed); (2) Conflict theory—questions related to class or group (e.g., how "ethnic minorities" are excluded from mainstream musical culture through the maintenance of "racial" stereotyping); (3) Symbolic interactionism—concerns about how the individual constructs an image of self through interactions with groups and individuals, is able to take on the perspective of the other, and then tailors communication in anticipation of the reaction of the "generalized other." For example, orchestra members may have a view that conductors are volatile, passionate, dictators. Consequently, they act cautiously, await instructions, and tolerate abusive behavior. The conductor sees them as musicians to be instructed, controlled, and manipulated, possibly by dramatized anger in order that they will play with adrenalin and passionate vigor. The interaction between the group and the individual is symbolic; (4) Role theory—examinations of how taking on a role restricts or permits certain behaviors, for example, the role of passionate conductor. Dolloff (1999) focuses on how music teachers have an image of "teacher" that sets behavioral expectations for themselves when they assume the role of teacher; (5) Ethnomethodology—examines a culture in context to make sense of how people live and what meaning they give to their reality, assuming that people's realities are constructed in cultural context. For example, a community choir can be a distinct culture and the researcher could "live" awhile in this culture to discover the realities experienced there; (6) Structural functionalism—organizations or societies are systematically structured like organisms—consisting of components that each contribute to the function of the whole (e.g., what distinguishes tenured professors from untenured professors from graduate students from undergraduate students by examining values, norms, community types, or individual roles); (7) Feminist theory—an orientation that has common features usually including a rejection of positivism, a ubiquitous concern with gender, stress on the value-ladeness of all research, the adoption of liberatory methodology, and the pursuit of nonhierarchical research relationships (Haig, 1997, pp. 180–181); (8) Exchange theory—examination of the rationality applied in weighing costs and benefits of all choices (Homans, 1974). A researcher might examine what constitutes music students' cost and benefit ledger related to time-intensive practice and the benefits of musical achievement; (9) Phenomenology—a focus on how people internalize the objective world into consciousness and negotiate its reality in order to make it livable and shareable, for example, what is it like being a musical child prodigy? (10) Conversational analysis—assumes conversation is central in interpersonal behavior. Particular interest is in status and power revealed in conversational structure, for example, through interruptions and overlaps. The "talk" between trumpet teacher and trumpet student might be the means of studying student/teacher relationship; (11) Social Ecology—assumes "physical properties of territory act as reference points for people's interactions with one another" (Rothe, 1993, p. 56). A field experiment manipulating music room environment would address its social ecology; (12) Action research—not so much a theory as an attitude with focus on improvement. A teacher might enlist the cooperation of a choir to record, in a reflective journal, responses to some innovative strategies to build a sense of community. Analysis of the students' and teacher's journals would serve as data to determine whether the innovations result in improvement.

Other discipline-related orientations are surely possible, but these serve to illustrate the complexity that develops as paradigm, discipline, and orientation interact in the creation of research method. Music education research does not reveal all of these orientations, but a basic trend is toward a greater emphasis on sociology of music, constructivism, and the social aspects of music making and learning, and with that will come specific social research orientations (McCarthy, 1997, 2000; Paul, 2000).

The relevance of discipline, paradigm, and orientations to research method is evident if one sees research method not simply as the data acquisition method but, rather, as an interaction among the question posed, the analysis required to answer the question, and the data appropriate for the analysis. An important role of the orientations is in influencing what questions will be asked, but they also influence who will be asked, how answers will be obtained, what will count as valued representations and as knowledge, and what analyses will be conducted.

We must make an important observation: The primary form of data (representation) in empirical-analytic research is the numeral, hence the common designation "quantitative." The primary form of data (representation) in symbolic and critical research is the word. Words allow for use of adjectives and adverbs, the description of qualities, and hence the designation "qualitative." We differentiate, however, among quantitative methods on the basis of: (1) How the data are acquired (by asking questions requiring ratings it could be survey, by asking questions on a "test" it could be an experiment or a correlational study, and by counting checkmarks on a list representing behaviors it could be an observational study); (2) from whom the data are acquired (random sample assigned to comparative groups could be an experiment, or a single group volunteer sample might

be a survey); (3) what happens between data acquisition efforts (if a planned treatment is administered it may be an experiment); and (4) what analysis is planned for the acquired data (if two sets of scores from a group of individuals are compared for relationship it is correlational, if the averages are compared it could be an experiment). The question(s) that motivate the research are directly answered by the analysis and so have an important defining role for methodology.

These four aspects of research: how the data are *acquired*, from *whom* the data are acquired, what *happens* between data acquisition efforts, and what *analysis* is planned for the acquired data, along with the defining role of the research questions and their explanatory intention, determine method. They do so in "quantitative" research and they do so in "qualitative" research. Consequently, the general category of qualitative research contains many specific methods. However, the definition of these methods may not be settled, because the field is still evolving.

The most direct way to methodological relatedness is in multimethod studies. Exploring complex constructs raises multiple questions that frequently demand multiple methods. In the past, these were most likely methods within a single epistomological paradigm, but researchers are beginning to combine "quantitative" and "qualitative" methods in a single study. Zeller (1997) asserts that "one method used in isolation does not provide compelling answers to many research problems. The reason for this is clear. Different techniques differ dramatically in their purposes, goals, objectives, tactics, strategies, strengths, and weaknesses. The original questions that prompt the research and the new questions that emerge from its results require a blending of methods" (p. 828). In the discussion of validity in research, Zeller argues further that "inferences about validity do not lend themselves to solely quantitative or statistical solutions. On the contrary, an interactive research strategy combining quantitative and qualitative is advocated. A valid inference occurs when there is no conflict between messages received as a result of the use of a variety of different methodological procedures" (Zeller, 1997, p. 829).

Trend 4: Data Complexity

All data are representations, intentionally acquired or captured for study. An achievement test score sets a fixed point, a freeze-frame of sorts, for the individual's ever developing achievement. A video recording of a piano lesson can later be viewed and reviewed. The image on the video screen is not the actual lesson—it is a representation of the lesson. It is selected for study and is fixed (selected, made stable, not repaired) to the extent that it can be repeatedly viewed.

The researcher's selection of the phenomenon or representation for study is one of the most important and urgent decisions in any research effort. In traditional empirical-analytic research, this is done early in the process, and study design is created accordingly. In interpretivist approaches, the researcher may decide that some aspect of teaching may be studied, commence video recording many episodes of teaching, and delay the decision on what specific phenomena or representations to describe or interpret. But, regardless of delay, or multiple viewings of a tape, eventually the researcher selects the words, actions, or gestures to include in the analytic and interpretive process.

Ways to fix representations for study include: (1) Audio recorded language (often transcribed into written form); (2) written language of various types; (3) audio recorded sound; (4) video recordings of the phenomena; (5) test scores; (6) verbal or numeric categorical assigments; (7) numeric rating or rank values; (8) graphic displays; (9) photographic or pictorial prints; (10) artifacts; and (11) symbols and symbolic notations. Obviously, categories and subcategories are possible. For example, audio recorded sound could have subcategories such as music, ambient room noise, subject's nonverbal sounds, and so on.

There is a simple to complex specificity range in fixed data. Consider the following: a checkmark in a category, the number on a rating scale, or the test score; an audio recording of an interview or a written narrative account; a video recording of an interpretive dance; or an artist's self-portrait. All hold meaning and can be interpreted; however, the layers, strands, connections, and interrelationships of meaning in the latter are considerably greater.

An important characteristic to note about different types of data is data depth. Certain types of data, such as categorical assignments or test scores, have a simple relationship with the construct they represent. Other data types, however, are more complex. The data fixed by a video recording of a band rehearsal can be subjected to various theoretical orientation "lenses" or to various research questions. Such data has "depth" that can be mined and refined repeatedly before its store is depleted. The more complex the data type is, the more depth it offers for data mining.

Trend 5: Analytical Complexity

Despite the increasing complexity of constructs, methodology, and data, analysis is essentially a process of simplification, a process of creating order within the represented reality that allows for meaning making (interpretation). Analysis is a process of clarification, a process of reducing unknowns. In a computer systems context, complexity is defined as "the existence of unknowns" (Kafre Systems International, 1998). The goal of research is to eliminate unknowns through the development of knowing, and it may do so by imposing a simplification system. It is in analysis

that the tension between complexity and simplification exists most obviously. In statistical analysis, the researcher lets a number represent a phenomenon, manipulates the collected numbers to reduce them to a number representing something new, and postulates an implication of the number for the original observed phenomenon. In qualitative analysis, the researcher frequently transcribes or notates the representations, categorizes and classifies these for further comparative examination, and postulates an explanation or interpretation about the observed phenomena. However, the phenomena and constructs of interest to music educators are complex and analyses leading to unidimensionality, simple linearity, or "stories that dissolve all complexity" (Shenk, 1997, p. 157), are no longer useful if progress in research is to be made.

General Responses to Complexity

In educational research, attendance to complexity can be seen as giving greater place to individual uniqueness and context, to multiple perspectives, and different representations. Several developments in research design, analysis, and measurement illustrate how these requirements can be accommodated.

Rasch Analysis. Rasch analysis recognizes the inevitable interaction of a measurement technique with the person being measured (Keeves, 1997a). The technique links qualitative analysis to quantitative methods by converting dichotomous and rating scale observations into linear measures. It is often misclassified under item response theory or logit-linear models. These describe data. "Rasch specifies how persons, probes, prompts, raters, test items, tasks, etc. *must* interact statistically for linear measures to be constructed from ordinal observations. Rasch implements stochastic Guttman ordering, conjoint additivity, Campbell concatenation, sufficiency and infinite divisibility" (Linacre, 1995).

Single-Case Design and Change Measurement. Recognizing complexity raises serious doubt about the generalizability of results from large samples. When researchers average results from groups of subjects, they omit considerable richness in the data (Sharpley, 1997, p. 451). Practitioners' concerns with individuals rather than aggregates mean that the scientific theory generalized from research actually has limited application in practice. "Even statistically significant findings from studies with huge, randomly selected samples cannot be applied directly to individuals in particular situations; skilled clinicians will always be required to determine whether a research generalization applies to a particular individual, whether the generalization needs to be adjusted to accommodate individual idiosyncrasy, or whether it needs to be abandoned entirely with certain individuals in certain situations" (Donmoyer, 1990, p. 181). As a result, research aimed at establishing the utility of specific interventions rather than at establishing scientific principles is finding single-case design particularly useful (Jutai, Knox, Rumney, Gates, Wit, & Bartel, 1997).

Single-case studies can have a macrofocus (Stake, Bresler, & Mabry, 1991) or a microfocus (Jutai et al., 1997) and can be designed to yield various types of data. For those generating numeric data, the measurement of change in the interrupted time series is the primary analytic task. In the past, there was debate between advocates of simple visual analysis of a graphic representation of research participants' change and advocates of statistical analysis. The problem was that graphic representation was easily distorted and that traditional statistical procedures were not properly applicable because simple pre and postcomparisons were not adequate. One of the concerns influencing analysis is both the within person change and the between person change. Least-squares regression analysis has been used for within person change and weighted least-squares regression analysis for between person change. However, recent developments have made change measurement more powerful, assuming the collection of considerable longitudinal data. High-quality analysis of within- and between-person models can be conducted with hierarchical linear modeling (Bryk & Raudenbush, 1992) or with covariance structure analysis (Willett & Sayer, 1994, 1995).

Meta-Analysis. Glass (1976) coined the term "meta-analysis" for an approach that allows the quantitative, analytic integration of the results from many studies on a particular phenomenon. Although the statistical procedure treats the studies selected for integration as being alike, in actual fact the meta-analysis merges multiple perspectives and varying definitions of constructs. It is then a form of analysis that simplifies the complexity inherent in research in a particular field. If "reality" is complex and any one study cannot adequately encompass that complexity to form an explanation of it, then integrating all attempts at such explanation in a meta-analysis may more adequately honor the complexity.

Integration of analyses from multiple independent studies had been done in some form before Glass (1976). Cotes (1722) describes how astronomers' observations were combined by using weighted averages. Pearson (1904) integrated five separate samples by averaging estimates of correlation. Birge (1932) attempted to integrate results in physics by weighting combinations of estimates; Cochran (1937) and Yates and Cochran (1938) did so with agricultural experiments. Tippett (1931) and Fisher (1932) proposed a method of combining probability values.

The use of meta-analysis has been increasing, especially in the past 15 years. Barrowman (1998), surveying of the use of meta-analysis in medical research, found two or three studies per year in the early 1980s, increasing to about 10 per year by the mid-1980s, and to 80 by the end of the 1980s. Egger and Smith (1997, p. 1) found this trend continued, with close to 800 meta-analysis studies reported in Medline by 1996. In music education, few meta-analysis studies have been done. A search of the major journals revealed two, Standley (1996) and the more sophisticated Hetland (2000). However, "meta-analysis seems well suited . . . to make a larger and larger contribution to the social and behavioral sciences, and to a broad range of policy-relevant research" (Wachter & Straf, 1990, p. 28).

The most common approach to meta-analysis is to calculate the effect size on each study selected for inclusion. Effect size is basically the mean of the treatment group minus the mean of the control group divided by the standard deviation of the control group (Light & Pillemer, 1984). The pattern of effect sizes can then be examined visually by plotting them on frequency distributions or funnel displays that plot effect size, for example, against sample size. Statistical procedures are used to calculate cumulative effects, for example, overall mean effect size (Glass, McGraw, & Smith, 1981; Hunter, Schmidt, & Jackson, 1982; Rosenthal, 1991).

Criticisms of meta-analysis focus primarily on three issues: independence, the "apples" and "oranges" problem, and the "file drawer" problem. When a single study consists of multiple "experiments," several effect-size estimates result. These cannot be used separately in a meta-analysis, because they may be drawn from the same sample and, consequently, are not independent. Glass et al. (1981) acknowledge the problem and suggest calculating an average effect for the study as a whole. As these individual study effects are mostly related to distinct variables, critics argue that averaging them is not an adequate solution (Chou, 1992). This is a criticism that focuses on the tension between the complexity of reality and the analytic drive to simplify for understanding. The "apples" and "oranges" problem is somewhat related. Critics point out that meta-analysis integrates effects from variables based on different theoretical constructs. Glass et al. (1981) argue that researchers constantly aggregate data from different individuals who are like "apples" and "oranges." The important consideration is that the meta-analysis concern must be about "fruit," and then "apples" and "oranges" can be included. The "file drawer" problem is based on the premise that researchers selecting studies for inclusion in a meta-analysis will favor published studies because of availability and that there is a publication bias: The selection process for publication tends to favor studies that show significance (the studies that do not reject the null hypothesis remain in the file drawer) (McGaw, 1997). Rosenthal (1991) argues this problem does not exist, but

Glass et al. (1981) show that effects from meta-analyses of theses and dissertations are weaker than effects from published studies.

Recent developments with Bayesian statistics have been applied to meta-analysis with considerable promise. DuMouchel (1990), Efron (1996), and Smith, Spiegelhalter, and Thomas (1995) demonstrate that Bayesian methods provide a framework for handling meta-analytic issues such as fixed-effects versus random-effects models, appropriate treatment of small studies, possible shapes of the population distribution, and how to include covariates (Barrowman, 1998).

Concept Mapping.   The concept map is familiar to most teachers as an efficient teaching strategy; it has more recently been used as a technique in interpretivist research. Specifically, it can be used to probe and visualize the complexity of constructs residing in a research participant's mind. Novak (1990) employed the concept map in research with elementary students as a means of facilitating analysis of interview data by applying this structural device for representing a student's understanding of a complex phenomenon. The visual, often hierarchical, display of ideas does clarify participants' understanding, but the common two-dimensionality of visualization may distort or at best inadequately represent the participants' knowledge. "The limitation [of concept mapping in a research context] is inherent in a hierarchical representation of knowledge in which complex concepts, or complexes of concepts, are established in a superordinate/subordinate relationship. The concept complexes situated in the subordinate positions are, however, multilevel entities whose constituent parts often relate in a complex manner to the focus concept" (Lawson, 1997, p. 294).

An alternative to the "hand-drawn," hierarchical, qualitative concept maps has been emerging. Particularly when a group of participants is involved, a method described by Trochim (1989a, 1989b) that draws on multivariate analysis can be used. The concept or domain to be mapped is focused for the group, statements are generated through brainstorming, the statements are placed on cards, each participant sorts the cards into piles that make sense to the person (not a forced distribution like Q-sort), statements are rated (e.g., on priority or preference), the cards in sorted piles are then analyzed through cluster analysis and nonmetric multidimensional scaling, and finally displayed in various maps for interpretation. Although this approach is described by Trochim (1989b) as "soft science or hard art," it is an indication of a trend in analysis of complex constructs—the use of statistical analysis with "qualitative" data and attention to complexity by statistical analysts.

Dual Scaling.   One of the most common analysis techniques of interpretivist research is the identification of "themes" in data—essentially a process dependent on the categorization of observations (verbal statements or descriptions of behavior). Computer programs now assist in categorization, or at least in tracking and retrieving, of text data for purposes of thematic analysis. Using the categorization for further analysis by doing numeric, statistical analysis on the categorical data, however, is not so common. A recent method designed to extract quantitative information from nonnumerical (qualitative) data is dual scaling (Nishisato, 1980, 1994; Nishisato & Nishisato, 1994). It addresses simultaneously in analysis a number of the characteristics of complex data—it is descriptive, optimal, multidimensional, and multivariate. For example, it will derive the most reliable scores for respondents from multiple-choice data, as well as provide all the necessary coordinates for multidimensional representation of data. It handles both incidence data and dominance data. Its potential for music education research is still to be explored.

Analysis Preceding Theory

Scientific research typically begins with theory. Growing out of philosophical inquiry, scientific method requires the researcher to begin by engaging in the essence of philosophical thinking, conceptual analysis. This process of examining and defining constructs culminates in the postulation of relationships and the design of a means of acquiring empirical data to test the theory. Analysis is driven by the theory under investigation. Now data-gathering techniques are such that researchers can be faced with databases so large and complex that analysis must begin without a coherent theory in place. The process of investigating data acquired and stored by a computer is now essentially the same as that of investigating the data acquired and stored by the mind—the sifting, sorting, categorizing, and classifying, with constructs that modify and mutate as the analysis proceeds.

Data Mining.   Data mining is, in a sense, a computer-based "grounded theory" analysis approach. Rather than the scientific, verification-based approach (establish theory and use analysis to verify it), it is a discovery approach to analysis (hence the use of the term Knowledge Discovery in Databases). "Data mining is a set of techniques used in an automated approach to exhaustively explore and bring to the surface complex relationships in very large datasets" (Moxon, 1996, p. 1). Although most frequently applied to largely tabular databases, "these techniques can be, have been, and will be applied to other data representations, including spatial data domains, text-based domains, and multimedia (image) domains" (Moxon, 1996, p. 1). The computer programs that do the data mining use algorithms that can examine many multidimensional data relationships concurrently and highlight dominant or exceptional ones. In nontechnical terms, the data mining computer programs employ a form of Kelly's (1955) Psychology of Personal Constructs. The computer begins with a set of rather simple predictor constructs. As it attempts to handle the flow of data with these constructs, anomalies reshape the constructs in the process. These newly mutated constructs are then tested against the data. In this way the computer "learns" and refines constructs very much as people do.

Data mining analysis focuses on a variety of possible productive courses to make sense of the data including: association, sequence, clustering, classification, estimation, case-based reasoning, fuzzy logic, genetic algorithms, and fractal-based transforms. Problems in data mining (Moxon, 1996, p. 4) stem from: (1) Its susceptibility to "dirty" data—database errors due to magnitude and multiple source input; (2) inability to "explain" results in human terms—do not fit simple if-then terms; and (3) the data representation gap—problems in combining data forms from different computers and database types.

Database sources of potential research value for music education are increasing. "Big Brother" governments, financial institutions, and Internet companies are collecting vast amounts of data potentially relevant to aspects of music in society. These include government census, national survey and assessment data (Burke, 1997), public and private institutional data banks and data archives (Anderson & Rosier, 1997), and commercial data. For example, Launch.com and other music websites offer their "free" service in exchange for user profile data and then track all music and music-video use. They invite users to create preference lists, to rate individual songs, and so on. This information is stored in a database (now called a data warehouse). Access to government census databases is relatively easy. Access to commercial data may be more difficult. However, the data acquisition is constant; knowledge development is the responsibility of researchers.

Exploratory Data Analysis. EDA, first defined by Tukey (1977), is, in a sense, a manual form of data mining. In the strict scientific method, all analyses are for verification, based on hypotheses articulated before data gathering. Scientific analysis takes its inferential validity from this approach. Consequently, " 'playing around' with data is not 'good' science, not replicable, and perhaps fraudulent. Many experienced researchers pay lip service to this view, while surreptitiously employing ad hoc exploratory procedures they have learned are essential to research" (Leinhardt & Leinhardt, 1997, p. 519). EDA is gaining greater

importance, because desktop computer analysis makes "snooping" easier, and there is more recognition that finding pattern in nature, the purpose of EDA, is inherently a subjective enterprise. "Exploratory analyses incorporate the wisdom, skill, and intuition of the investigator into the experiment" (Palmer, 2000, p. 2). As an analysis method, EDA blatantly recognizes the "constructive" dimension of scientific research—searching does go on in research. EDA is particularly necessary in educational research because often data is gathered on a hunch, intuition, or just because it can be gathered and might be useful.

The analyses deemed "exploratory" now often include various dimensional analyses (correspondence, canonical, principal components, smallest space, multidimensional scaling, configuration comparison, factor scoring, metric dimensional scaling) as well as nonhierarchical and hierarchical cluster analyses. All have a pretheory or theory formulation function. For statistically rigorous analysis, EDA cannot be combined with confirmatory analysis on the same data set. One way to accommodate this is to acquire a large enough data set to allow its division into an exploratory subset and a confirmatory subset.

Theory-Confirming Analysis

The current mind-set in research is increasingly accepting exploratory analysis as not only permissible but necessary. Confirmatory analysis, however, is the natural follow-up. Exploration leads to theory which then must be subjected to confirmatory procedures. Most traditional parametric and nonparametric statistical analyses serve this purpose (Asmus & Radocy, 1992). Statistical-based modeling is particularly powerful in theory confirmation and Asmus and Radocy (1992) identify path analysis and linear structural relations analysis (latent trait modeling) as important approaches. They observe that, "Many in the field of music have claimed that a variety of important musical concepts are simply unmeasurable. Latent trait modeling provides a means of accounting for these "unmeasurable" concepts in complex systems" (Asmus & Radocy, 1992, p. 165).

"A prominent theme in methodological criticism of educational research during the 1980s was the failure of many quantitative studies to attend to the hierarchical, multilevel character of much educational field research data . . . Perhaps more profound than such technical difficulties, however, is the impoverishment of conceptualization which single-level models encourage" (Raudenbush & Bryk, 1997, p. 549). An important analytic response to this problem is hierarchical linear modeling also referred to as multilevel linear models, random coefficient models, and complex covariance components models. Effective explanations of hierarchical linear modeling are given by Goldstein (1987), Bock (1989), Raudenbush and Willms (1991) and Bryk and Raudenbush (1992).

Exploration-Confirmation Dynamic

Although technically and ideally the analyses described under the previous two headings precede theory or confirm theory, most analysis realistically is a constructive, dynamic process in which there is some interplay between exploration and explanation, prediction and confirmation. An example of such an approach is *Q-methodology* (McKeon & Thomas, 1988). Although not strictly a form of analysis, it is a technique that has real potential for exploring intrapersonal relations and as such it is a "qualitative" technique. Q-methodology also lends itself easily to theory confirmation. As an analytic technique it drew serious criticism from strict statisticians, but its blending of qualitative and statistical aspects is causing a resurgence of use in preference-oriented research in political science and psychology.

Repertory Grid Technique is another approach that interacts with analysis to explore and explain. It is designed to carry out effectively the process of trying to find out how people view the world from their own perspective (analysis of the person's own internal representation of the world). A variety of mathematical analyses can be conducted (Fansella & Bannister, 1977), but recent developments in concept mapping and dual scaling have potential with repertory grids as well.

Event History Analysis, also known as survival analysis or hazard modeling, is an approach to exploring whether and when events occur. For example, a researcher might explore when a music student learns a particular skill or when people stop playing their band instruments. An analytic challenge is the problem that some people may not have developed the musical skill at the time the researcher is studying it or this skill may never develop. Event history analysis provides a sound mathematical basis for dealing with such anomalies through predictive modeling (Singer & Willett, 1991; Willett & Singer, 1991).

A battery of new techniques has developed for qualitative data analysis. Since qualitative research often focuses on a "grounded theory" approach, these analytic methods tend to contribute both to exploration and confirmation. Contingency Table Analysis, Correspondence Analysis, and Configural Frequency Analysis can be subsumed under Dual Scaling described above. Galois Lattice or G-lattice is a graphic method of examining and representing knowledge structures within small groups (Ander, Joó, and Merö, 1997). Social Network Analysis is an approach that allows for the examination of complex (multiplex, meaning multistranded) social relationship networks through mathematical models instead of simple sociograms (Scott, 1991).

Trend 6: Knowledge Representation Complexity

The earlier sections on Types of Data and Roles of Data explained many aspects of representation. Here, focus is primarily on the way knowledge is represented to others in a process of communicating the results of a research study. As a basic premise, research is the systematic development of knowledge. Knowledge, like intelligence, exists in multiple forms or types. Knowledge, therefore, must be represented in multiple forms. In the past, a particular type of knowledge has been favored by "research culture"—propositional written representations of the researcher's understanding. Even at conferences where oral presentations were made, the basic mode of presentation has been to "read the paper." Other forms of linguistic and nonlinguistic representation are now emerging as research presentations including the use of story (Barone, 1983), poetry or proestry (Andrews, 2000; Denton, 1996), drama (Goldstein, 2000; O'Toole, 1994; Reynolds, 1996), visual/photographic (Karsemeyer, 2000; Woolley, 2000), or combinations that take the form of documentaries or paper "performances" (Lamb, 1997a).

The trend in representation of research knowledge is clearly toward diversity and integration into multiple mode presentations. The later artistic and combination forms are particularly more complex because they are multirepresentational, have representational depth (multiple attempts to understand the representation may lead to different meanings), and are richer in meaning (inherently more construct links), with less specific, researcher controlled interpretation. This means the research communication act can no longer effectively be a one-way communication, a short 15-minute session, or definitive in meaning. The researcher now engages in a communication process that encounters the knowledge "recipient" and reflexively constructs meaning from research efforts.

Researcher bias is an important consideration in all forms of representation. The term "bias" itself is a problem. Traditional scientific researchers may take "bias" to mean an expression of the researcher's voice in the report, evidence of the researcher's personal construct-oriented interpretation, or research that involves data gathering through intentional experience. However, obscuring the researcher's voice may create bias: All research has someone's interpretation, and all research data gathering is done through a construct structure, regardless of the form of representation or the "fixing" method. Bias is more a matter of researcher integrity. Bias in representation is a form of error resulting from the researcher's misperception of phenomenal features due to existing construct rigidity, lack of fidelity to a consensus of perception, or a deliberate mis-"representation" of knowledge due to conscious or unconscious allegiance to a preexisting construct. Traditional scientific researchers believed that adherence to methodological formulae and descriptive propositional reporting of results would prevent bias. What was not recognized was that the "objective," "scientific," "truth" aura that clung to such reports could communicate a "bias" (an erroneous representation of knowledge) despite the researcher's best intentions. Furthermore, the limited range of questions that could be explored with these "scientific" methods indicated a bias through ontological commitment in the very choice of methodology. Since the possibility of misperception, misrepresentation, or failure to develop a broad enough consensus among instruments or perceivers, is inherent in all research, describing the intentionality of data acquisition, personalizing the knowledge claims, and acknowledging the interpretive act are essential criteria for researcher integrity.

The most researcher-controlled forms of representation of knowledge are the written expository essay and its oral presentation. Within the restricted range of knowledge communicated by propositional language and to the extent that language can encode meaning in the least ambiguous way, such research reports minimize potential misinterpretation and unrecognized bias. When the researcher chooses a form of representation that is less propositional, there is more complex meaning—more levels or layers of meaning drawing on more types of intelligence (more hot buttons on the website being accessed). The potential for misinterpretation (or the construction of a personal interpretation) rises as well, leaving those with an ontological commitment to objective "truth," that can be discovered through empirical evidence and logical reasoning, quite worried. If one recognizes that knowledge is constructed and personal, and that research is ultimately about knowledge development, then research-derived, knowledge representations that serve as stimuli to personal knowledge construction should be clear but potent. Multiple forms of representation have the best chance of altering the receiver's knowledge structure, because each form contributes a dimension the others lack.

Although multiple forms of representation contribute dimensions of meaning, the forms are not equal in communicative power. Marshall McLuhan gave us the concept of a hot medium (television) versus a cool medium (print). We recognized now that it is more than media. The anecdote (story) is a particularly powerful form. Shenk (1997) writes that "anecdotage is a particular problem in the context of today's media age. 'With the sophisticated mental apparatus we have used to build world eminence as a species,' Robert Cialdini says of this catch-22, 'we have created an environment so complex, fast-paced, and information-laden that we must increasingly deal with it in the fashion of the animals we long ago transcended'" (p. 159). According to Shenk, we deal with life's complexity by clinging to simple stories. Social psychologists show

how meeting a particular case (e.g., a brutal prison guard) can overshadow considerable statistical data about the general category (e.g., all prison guards) (Shenk, 1997, pp. 156–157). Researchers selecting story and other artistic forms of representation must be fully aware of the power of their selected communication medium, exercise caution, and demonstrate integrity in how they shape the meaning of the communication. Shenk (1997) expresses the caution: "Beware stories that dissolve all complexity" (p. 157).

Trend 7: Dissemination Complexity

Research dissemination is about facilitating knowledge development in others. Frequently researchers believe, or at least act as if, dissemination is about "putting the information out there" and others may read and try to understand if motivated. However, communication can be more active and more reflexive—researchers have a responsibility for developing knowledge in others.

There are two important issues related to dissemination of research-derived knowledge: In whom should knowledge be developed, and how. Until recently, new research-derived knowledge was primarily communicated to other academic researchers. Researchers have lamented the lack of application of research by practitioners, yet have lived in and perpetuated a system that does not value practical dissemination. Now practitioners and the general public are coming to expect that research findings may inform aspects of their daily lives from diet choices to what music they play for their babies.

In Whom Is Knowledge to Be Developed?   The groups to whom research knowledge should be communicated are now more numerous than they were even a decade ago. These now include: (1) researchers in music education; (2) researchers in other disciplines; (3) users of research—researchers and their university establishments must learn to value direct communication with teachers through in-service workshops, demonstrations, and the development of pedagogical resources, as highly as they value refereed publication; (4) advocacy groups; (5) the music industry—music education researchers may be uncomfortable with the industrial R&D approach, but often there is "product" development potential in research. Conflict may, of course, arise between research "objectivity" and desired outcomes in research intentionally conducted for advocacy groups or proprietary purposes; and (6) the public.

To communicate effectively with teachers, advocacy groups, the music industry, and the general public the researcher needs to take a "public relations" view. One important requirement is the elimination of jargon. Although we may be dealing with complex phenomena and ideas, understanding starts with simplification rather than complexification. This may be through a potent visual image, story, or specific case example. The temptation is to sensationalize and thereby distort as well as to allow bias to enter the communication. Although the researcher targets communication to specific groups, what is communicated must be the result of real research.

How Is Knowledge to Be Developed?   "How" to communicate research knowledge depends to some extent on "to whom" it is to be communicated, but today there are several ways to reach almost every target population. Three variables influence the choice of dissemination medium: time, cost, and form of representation required. The effect of electronic media on time is obvious. The need for face-to-face meeting and discussion versus electronic forms has the largest bearing on cost. The form the knowledge representation takes greatly affects the choice of medium for dissemination. When knowledge was represented only in static visual graphics or text, print publication was efficient. The recognition that knowledge exists in gesture, image, or sound requires alternative forms of knowledge communication. Knowledge performances require "in person" presentation or must be captured on video. Combining text, talk, music, and photographed or computer animated video images, can be done by the new media forms such as DVD, CD-ROM, or Internet-based Web productions. As there is a trend in music education research toward multiple forms of representation of research knowledge, more complex media will be employed in dissemination.

An example of the "public relations" approach to research dissemination is described in detail by Smithrim, Upitis, Meban, and Patteson (2000). The premise of the article is that researchers must go "public or perish." Efforts to communicate to their "publics" have included: reports at nine academic conferences, papers for refereed journals, interviews on morning radio, photographs in the university newspaper, a story for the local paper, an exhibit of children's art work from the project, articles in the participant research school newspapers, creation of a website, a video describing the project, and a glossy brochure to accompany press releases or for conference distribution. The researchers became advocates for their own research project.

Conclusion

This chapter has essentially been about ontology and epistemology, reality and knowledge, external and internal representation. We have argued that reality is complex but exists apart from representations of it, and that knowledge about reality is constructed through a process of prediction, verification, or accommodation. The mind is engaged in a process of acquiring data related to reality and, from

these data, constructing knowledge in a systematic way. Research is the same process, only formalized. Because all the senses provide data for the knowledge constructing process, knowledge exists in multiple forms. If knowledge exists internally in multiple forms, it is most accurately represented externally in multiple ways.

The general trend we have explored has a twofold manifestation: phenomena in which researchers are interested are increasing in complexity; and there is increasing recognition that all human behaviors and characteristics are inherently complex. We have argued this means that mental constructs associated with all human behavior and expression must be regarded as interrelated and multifaceted, and that theoretical research constructs must reflect this complexity. What follows from this is that data have multiple meanings and connections, yet do not represent fully the associated phenomena. To address complex constructs, given the limitation of data, a variety of research methods must be employed. Multiple data and varied method lead to complex analyses to accommodate multiple levels, hierarchical structures, nonlinear relations, and nonpropositional, nondiscursive data.

Although not directly applying complexity theory (chaos theory), we have purposefully aligned some of our rhetoric with it. One of the most important implications of complexity theory is that researchers will never be able to make a complete description and will never be able to completely predict phenomena. This is implied by Cronbach's (1975) "hall of mirrors" (p. 119) or empty "first cells before we had half the battery completed" (p. 123).

Can research exist without a drive to predict and control? Is research not about theory, theory not about predicting, and predicting not about controlling? The hope of researchers has been to find that "other elusive variable," another interaction, a more detailed path analysis. We know that students do not simply drop out of band because their aptitude is low and they are assigned to an instrument for which they do not like the timbre. But, we believe if we also account for intelligence, teacher behavior, home support, socioeconomic status, and early music experiences, we will be closer. And we assume one day we could account for 100% of the variance and predict who will stay and who will drop out.

The prospect of not being able to discover answers or even partial answers to many of our problems and challenges is probably frightening to music education researchers. As mentioned earlier, each researcher functions in a research culture. Ours is one influenced by the fact that we are musicians, educators, and researchers. Musicians in the Western European tradition are masters of replicative music making in which minute control of every muscle, pitch, rhythm, timbre, and nuance is practiced through hours and hours of repetitive, disciplined effort. Most challenges must be solved before a successful performance is realized. As educators, we function in a milieu where the normal need for class control is amplified by the noisiness of our art and our love of large group performance. The public performance pressure makes efficiency and learning management paramount. As researchers, we live in an era of rational science in which the central purpose is prediction and control.

So how can we respond to the challenge of complexity? We can draw on our unique strengths as music education researchers—persistence, discipline, and creative thinking. But, in addition, we need to be more rigorous in conceptual analysis to understand the constructs we encounter. We must be ingenious in identifying the form of data that most validly represent the phenomena we value. We must be flexible and open-minded in selecting methods to provide reliable observations. We must be disciplined in analysis to transcend the easy answer, the known analytic technique, or the simple solution. We must be daring, confident, and willing to engage the people who matter to music education in the development of knowledge.

In the face of complexity, we also must realize that we are not going to solve the whole puzzle and find every answer. As a result, we may ask different questions. Although we cannot manage the whole system, we are a part of the system and need to realize how we are connected to others. We may ask questions that help us understand another's perspective, another's plight, another's joy. Second, we can change from a perspective of only finding problems to which we can match solutions to one where we see beauty in life's chaos, and describe that beauty. Third, we must engage in "lateral thinking"—encountering the complexity to find imaginative new solutions. Fourth, we must believe in small, local efforts that can have global results. A common metaphor in chaos theory is the assertion that a butterfly flapping its wings in China can affect the weather in New York. Although our power is limited, we are in a dynamic system and we do have influence. Finally, we must learn to discover, attend to, and appreciate life's rich subtleties.

REFERENCES

Ander, C., Joó, A., & Merö, L. (1997). Galois Lattices. In J. P. Keeves (Ed.), *Educational research methodology, and measurement: An international handbook* (2nd ed., pp. 543–549). Tarrytown, NY: Pergamon Elsevier Science.

Anderson, J., & Rosier, M. J. (1997). Data banks and data archives. In J. P. Keeves (Ed.), *Educational research methodology, and measurement: An international handbook* (2nd ed., pp. 344–349). Tarrytown, NY: Pergamon Elsevier Science.

Andrews, B. (2000). Land of Shadows. *Language and literacy: A Canadian educational e-journal*, 2(1). Retrieved from http://educ.queensu.ca/~landl/

Asmus, E. P., & Radocy, R. E. (1992). Quantitative analysis. In R. Colwell (Ed.), *Handbook of research in music teaching and learning* (pp. 141–183). New York: Schirmer Books.

Babbie, E. R. (1995). *The practice of social research* (7th ed.). Belmont, CA: Wadsworth Publishing.

Barrowman, N. (1998). *A survey of meta-analysis: Dalhousie University*. Retrieved from www.mscs.dal.ca/~barrowma/ma.html

Bartel, L. (2000). A foundation for research in the effects of sound on brain and body functions. In H. Jørgensen (Ed.), *Challenges in music education research and practice for a new millennium* (pp. 58–64). Oslo, Norway: Norges musikkhogskole.

Barone, T. (1983). Things of use and things of beauty: The story of the Swain County High School Arts Program. *Daedalus*, 112(3), 1–28.

Birge, R. T. (1932). The calculation of errors by the method of least squares. *Physical Review, 40*, 207–227.

Bock, R. D. (Ed.) (1989). *Multilevel analysis of educational research*. New York: Academic Press.

Briggs, J., & Peat, D. (1999). *Seven life lessons of chaos*. New York: HarperCollins.

Bryk, A. S., & Raudenbush, S. W. (1992). *Hierarchical linear models: Applications and data-analysis methods*. Beverly Hills, CA: Sage.

Burke, G. (1997). Census and national survey data. In J. P. Keeves (Ed.), *Educational research methodology, and measurement: An international handbook* (2nd ed., pp. 323–327). Tarrytown, NY: Pergamon Elsevier Science.

Byrne, D. (2000). Complexity theory and social research. *Social Research Update, 18*, pp. 1–7. Retrieved from www.soc.surrey.ac.uk/sru/SRU18.html

Cameron, L., & Bartel, L. (2000). Engage or disengage: An inquiry into lasting response to music teaching. *Orbit, 31*(1), 22–25.

Chou, S. L. (1992). *Research methods in psychology: A primer*. Calgary, AB: Detselig Enterprises Ltd.

Cochran, W. G. (1937). Problems arising in analysis of a series of similar experiments. *Journal of the Royal Statistical Society (Supplement), 4*, 102–118.

Cotes, R. (1722). Aestimatio Errorum in Mixta Mathesi, per Variatones Partium Trianguli Plani et Sphaerici. Part of Cote's *Opera Miscellanea,* published with *Harmonia Mensurarum,* ed. R. Smith. Cambridge, MA: Harvard University Press.

Cronbach, L. (1957). The two disciplines of scientific psychology. *American Psychologist, 12*, 671–684.

Cronbach, L. (1971). Test validation. In R. L. Thorndike (Ed.), *Educational measurement* (2nd ed.). Washington, DC: American Council on Education.

Cronbach, L. (1975). Beyond the two disciplines of scientific psychology. *American Psychologist, 30*, 116–127.

Cronbach, L. (1982). Prudent aspirations for social inquiry. In W. Kruskal (Ed.), *The social sciences: Their nature and lines* (pp. 61–82). Chicago: University of Chicago Press.

Cziko, G. A. (1989). Unpredictability and indeterminism in human behavior: Arguments and implications for educational research. *Educational Researcher, 18*(3), 17–25.

Csikszentmihalyi, M. (1993). *The evolving self: A psychology for the third millennium.* New York: HarperCollins.

Davis, R., Shrobe, H., & Szolovits, P. (1993). What is a knowledge representation. *AI Magazine, 14*(1), 17–33.

Denton, D. (1996). In the tenderness of stone: A poetics of the heart. (Doctoral dissertation, Ontario Institute for Studies in Education, University of Toronto, 1996). *Dissertation Abstracts International, 58*(06), 2085.

Dolloff, L. (1999). Imagining ourselves as teachers: The development of teacher identity in music teacher education. *Music Education Research, 1*(2), 191–207.

Donmoyer, R. (1990). Generalizability and the single-case study. In E. W. Eisner & A. Peshkin (Eds.), *Qualitative inquiry in education: The continuing debate* (pp. 175–200). New York: Teachers College Press.

DuMouchel, W. (1990). Bayesian meta-analysis. In D. A. Berry (Ed.), *Statistical methodology in the pharmaceutical sciences.* New York: Dekker.

Efron, B. (1996). Empirical Bayes methods for combining likelihoods. *Journal of the American Statistical Association, 91,* 538–565.

Egger, M., & Smith G. D. (1997). Meta-analysis: Potentials and promise. *British Medical Journal, 315,* 1371–1374.

Fansella, F., & Bannister, D. (1977). *A manual for repertory grid techniques.* London: Academic Press.

Fine, A. (1998). Scientific realism and antirealism. In E. Craig (Ed.), *Routledge encyclopedia of philosophy online.* Retrieved from http://www.rep.routledge.com

Fisher, R. A. (1932). *Statistical methods for research workers* (4th ed.). London: Oliver and Boyd.

Gabrielsson, A. (1991). Experiencing music. *Canadian Journal of Research in Music Education, 33* (ISME Research Edition), 21–26.

Gardner, H. (1999). *Intelligence reframed.* New York: Basic Books.

Glass, G. V. (1976). Primary, secondary, and meta-analysis. *Educational Researcher, 5,* 3–8.

Glass, G. V., McGraw, B., & Smith, M. L. (1981). *Meta-analysis in social research.* Beverly Hills, CA: Sage.

Goldstein, H. (1987). *Multilevel models in educational and social research.* Oxford: Oxford University Press.

Goldstein, T. (2000). Program notes for "Hong Kong, Canada." University of Toronto.

Haig, B. D. (1997). Feminist research methodology. In J. P. Keeves (Ed.), *Educational research methodology, and measurement: An international handbook* (2nd ed., pp. 180–185). Tarrytown, NY: Pergamon Elsevier Science.

Hayles, N. K. (1991). *Chaos and order.* Chicago: University of Chicago Press.

Hetland, L. (2000). Listening to music enhances spatial-temporal reasoning: Evidence for the Mozart effect. *The Journal of Aesthetic Education, 34,* 3–4.

Homans, G. C. (1974). *Social behavior: Its elementary forms.* New York: Harcourt Brace Janovich.

Hunter, J. E., Schmidt, F. L., & Jackson, G. B. (1982). *Meta-analysis: Cumulating research findings across studies.* Beverly Hills, CA: Sage.

Ignatieff, M. (2000). *The rights revolution.* Toronto: House of Anansi Press Ltd.

Jacques, B. (2000). Abuse and persistence: Why do they do it? *Canadian Music Educator, 42*(2), 8–13.

Jutai, J., Knox, R., Rumney, P., Gates, R., Wit, V., & Bartel, L. (1997, May). *Musical training methods to improve recovery of attention and memory following head injury.* Paper presented at the Executive Function and Developmental Psychopathology: Theory and Application Conference, University of Toronto.

Kafre Systems International. (1998). On eliminating risk by managing complexity. *Technical Reports KSI-TN-100102.* Retrieved from http://www.ksiinc.com/onrisk

Karsemeyer, J. (2000). *Moved by the spirit: A narrative inquiry.* Unpublished doctoral dissertation, University of Toronto.

Keeves, J. P. (1997a). Introduction: Advances in measurement in education. In J. P. Keeves (Ed.), *Educational research methodology, and measurement: An international handbook* (2nd ed., pp. 705–712). Tarrytown, NY: Pergamon Elsevier Science.

Keeves, J. P. (1997b). Introduction: Methods and processes in educational research. In J. P. Keeves (Ed.), *Educational research methodology, and measurement: An international handbook* (2nd ed., pp. 277–285). Tarrytown, NY: Pergamon Elsevier Science.

Kelly, G. (1955). *The psychology of personal constructs.* 2 vols. New York: Norton.

Lamb, R. (1997a, February). *Dorothy troubles Musicland.* Paper presented at the Faculty of Music, University of Toronto.

Lamb, R. (1997b). Music trouble: Desire, discourse, and the pedagogy project. *Canadian University Music Review, 18*(1), 84–98.

Lamb, R. (1998, May). *Mentoring: Master teacher/student apprentice as pedagogy in music.* Paper presented at the Canadian University Music Society, University of Ottawa.

Lamb, R. (1999). "I never really thought about it": Master/ apprentice as pedagogy in music. In K. Armatage (Ed.), *Equity and how to get it: Rescuing graduate studies* (pp. 213–238). Toronto: Inanna Publications and Education.

Lawson, M. J. (1997). Concept mapping. In J. P. Keeves (Ed.), *Educational research methodology, and measurement: An international handbook* (2nd ed., pp. 290–296). Tarrytown, NY: Pergamon Elsevier Science.

Leinhardt, G., & Leinhardt S. (1997). Exploratory data analysis. In J. P. Keeves (Ed.), *Educational research methodology, and measurement: An international handbook* (2nd ed., pp. 519–528). Tarrytown, NY: Pergamon Elsevier Science.

Light, R. J., & Pillemer, D. B. (1984). *Summing up: The science of reviewing research.* Cambridge, MA: Harvard University Press.

Linacre, J. M. (1995). *Rasch measurement: Construct clear concepts and useful numbers!* University of Chicago. Retrieved from http://www.winsteps.com/

Lincoln, Y. S., & Guba, E. G. (1984). *Naturalistic inquiry.* Beverly Hills, CA: Sage.

McCarthy, M. (1997). The foundations of sociology in American music education, 1900–1935. In R. Rideout (Ed.), *On the sociology of music education* (pp. 71–80). Norman: School of Music, University of Oklahoma.

McCarthy, M. (2000). Music Matters: A philosophical foundation for a sociology of music education. *Bulletin of the Council for Research in Music Education, 144,* 3–9.

McGaw, B. (1997). Meta-analysis. In J. P. Keeves (Ed.), *Educational research methodology, and measurement: An international handbook* (2nd ed., pp. 371–380). Tarrytown, NY: Pergamon Elsevier Science.

McKeon, B., & Thomas, D. (1988). *Q-methodology.* Newbury Park, CA: Sage.

Moxon, B. (1996, August). The hows and whys of data mining, and how it differs from other analytical techniques. *DBMS Data Warehouse Supplement,* 1–3.

Nishisato, S. (1980). *Analysis of categorical data: Dual scaling and its applications.* Toronto: University of Toronto Press.

Nishisato, S. (1994). *Elements of dual scaling: An introduction to practical data analysis.* Hillsdale, NJ: Lawrence Erlbaum.

Nishisato, S., & Nishisato, I. (1994). *Dual scaling in a nutshell.* Toronto: MicroStats.

Novak, J. (1990). Concept mapping: A useful device for science education. *Journal of Research in Science Teaching, 27*(10), 937–949.

O'Toole, P. A. (1994). Redirecting the choral classroom: A feminist poststructural analysis of power relations within three choral classrooms. *Dissertation Abstracts International, 55*(07), 1864. (UMF No. AAT 9426965)

Palmer, M. (2000). *Hypothesis-driven and exploratory data analysis.* Retrieved from http://www.okstate.edu/artsci/botany/ordinate/motivate.htm

Paul, S. J. (2000). The sociological foundations of David Elliott's "Music Matters" philosophy. *Bulletin of the Council for Research in Music Education, 144,* 11–20.

Pearson, K. (1904). Report on certain enteric fever inoculations. *British Medical Journal, 2,* 1243–1246.

Perlmutter, M. L., & Perkins, D. N. (1982). A model of aesthetic response. In S. S. Madeja & D. N. Perkins (Eds.), *A model for aesthetic response in the arts* (pp. 1–29). St. Louis, MO: CEMREL, Inc.

Raudenbush, S. W., & Bryk, A. S. (1997). Hierarchical linear modeling. In J. P. Keeves (Ed.), *Educational research methodology, and measurement: An international handbook* (2nd ed., pp. 549–556). Tarrytown, NY: Pergamon Elsevier Science.

Raudenbush, S. W., & Willms, J. D. (1991). *Schools, classrooms, and pupils: International studies of schooling from a multilevel perspective.* New York: Academic Press.

Rosenthal, R. (1991). *Meta-analytic procedures for social research* (rev. ed.). Newbury Park, CA: Sage.

Reynolds, J. L. (1996). Wind and song: Sound and freedom in musical creativity. (Doctoral dissertation, University of Toronto, 1996). *Dissertation Abstracts International, 58*(06), 2127.

Rothe, J. P. (1993). *Qualitative research: A practical guide.* Toronto: PDE Publications.

Scott, J. (1991). *Social network analysis: A handbook.* Newbury Park, CA: Sage.

Sharpley, C. F. (1997). Single case research: Measuring change. In J. P. Keeves (Ed.), *Educational research methodology, and measurement: An international handbook* (2nd ed., pp. 451–455). Tarrytown, NY: Pergamon Elsevier Science.

Shenk, D. (1997). *Data fog: Surviving the information glut.* New York: Harper *Edge.*

Shulman, L. (1988). Disciplines of inquiry in education: An overview. In R. M. Jaeger (Ed.), *Complementary methods for research in education* (pp. 3–17). Washington, DC: American Educational Research Association.

Singer, J. D., & Willett, J. B. (1991). Modeling the days of our lives: Using survival analysis when designing and analyzing longitudinal studies of duration and the timing of events. *Psychological Bulletin, 110*(2), 268–298.

Smith, T. C., Spiegelhalter, D. J., & Thomas, A. (1995). Bayesian approaches to random-effects meta-analysis: a comparative study. *Statistics in Medicine, 14,* 2685–2699.

Smithrim, K., Upitis, R., Meban, M., & Patteson, A. (2000). Get public or perish. *Language and Literacy: A Canadian Educational E-Journal, 2*(1). Retrieved from http://educ.queensu.ca/~landl/

Stake, R., Bresler, L., & Mabry, L. (1991). *Custom and cherishing: The arts in elementary schools.* Urbana-Champaign, IL: Council for Research in Music Education.

Standley, J. M. (1996). A meta-analysis on the effects of music as reinforcement for education/therapy objectives. *Journal of Research in Music Education 44*(2), 105–133.

Sundin, B. (1989). Early music memories and socialization. *Canadian Journal of Research in Music Education, 30*(2), 154–161.

Thorndike, E. L. (1910). The contribution of psychology to education. *Journal of Educational Psychology, 1,* 5–12.

Tippett, L. H. C. (1931). *The methods of statistics.* London: Williams & Norgate.

Trochim, W. (1989a). An introduction to concept mapping for planning and evaluation. *Evaluation and Program Planning, 12,* 1–16.

Trochim, W. (1989b). Concept mapping: Soft science or hard art? *Evaluation and Program Planning, 12,* 87–110.

Tukey, J. W. (1977). *Exploratory data analysis.* Reading, MA: Addison-Wesley.

Wachter, K. W., & Straf, M. L. (Eds.). (1990). *The future of meta-analysis.* New York: Russell Sage Foundation.

Walker, J. C., & Evers, C. W. (1997). Research in education: Epistomological issues. In J. P. Keeves (Ed.), *Educational research methodology, and measurement: An international handbook* (2nd ed., pp. 22–31). Tarrytown, NY: Pergamon Elsevier Science.

Willett, J. B., & Sayer, A. G. (1994). Using covariance structure analysis to detect correlates and predictors of change. *Psychological Bulletin, 116,* 363–381.

Willett, J. B., & Sayer, A. G. (1995). Cross-domain analyses of change over time: Combing growth modeling and covariance structure analysis. In G. A. Marcoulides & R. E. Schumaker (Eds.), *Advanced structural equation modeling: Issues and techniques.* Hillsdale, NJ: Lawrence Erlbaum.

Willett, J. B., & Singer, J. D. (1991). From whether to when: New methods for studying student dropout and teacher attrition. *Review of Educational Research, 61*(4), 407–450.

Woolley, J. C. (2000). *Making connections: Pre-reading reader response and mother-research from one family's perspective.* Unpublished doctoral dissertation, University of Toronto.

Yates, F., & Cochran, W. G. (1938). The analysis of groups of experiments. *Journal of Agricultural Science, 28,* 556–580.

Zeller, R. A. (1997). Validity. In J. P. Keeves (Ed.), *Educational research methodology, and measurement: An international handbook* (2nd ed., pp. 822–829). Tarrytown, NY: Pergamon Elsevier Science.

60 Assessment's Potential in Music Education

RICHARD COLWELL

An entire section of the first *Handbook of Research on Music Teaching and Learning* was devoted to assessment. Those authors successfully summarized the history of assessment in music with chapters on assessment in five areas: teaching, creativity, program, general, and attitude. This chapter is an update on a few of the issues raised in the first *Handbook*.

In the 1990s, assessment is one of the more important issues in education. The priority of education in the United States has risen, and now education outweighs almost all other social issues—immigration, the homeless, welfare, national defense, and even foreign policy. Evaluation's importance is portrayed by its use in the struggle for power over the curriculum. Arts advocates welcome positive assessments, some of which are relatively marginal in value. The high public interest and greatly expanded funding for education, preschool through college, has brought to the playing field two assessment issues, standards and accountability. The definition of a standard is a description of how well or at what level a student is expected to perform, and accountability is the avenue for ascertaining that value for resources expended is attained. A few individuals have questioned whether assessment as the single means of establishing value is appropriate (Broadfoot, 2000). High-stakes evaluation has become the subject of educational and political debates, often so emotional as to complicate the resolution of the accompanying assessment issues. The U.S. Office for Civil Rights has entered the fray, publishing in December 2000 *The Use of Tests When Making High-Stakes Decisions for Students*. John Fremer (2000) suggests that the level of public debate about testing needs to be raised, as there is "so much uninformed and wrong-headed commentary." Good assessments provide data on the extent of success and failure but only hint at causes. Assessment, of course, has always been part of teaching and learning; what is new is its uses. One type of assessment, program evaluation, has become a major discipline that provides data on programs as diverse as welfare, the military, and education. In education, assessment is used to portray the success of society in enabling all students to attain high standards in multiple areas, with the additional role of determining the value of funding for administration, programs, and facilities—these in addition to its continued role in aiding teaching and learning.

The focus of the chapter is a description of selected recent developments in assessment in education and in music teaching and learning. It is written for the individual who already has a basic grasp of the principles of assessment. Not much space is devoted to such important admonitions as the following:

1. There must be a direct match between the curriculum and what the student is expected to know and do in the assessment. (Note: a major section is devoted to research in taxonomies, which is intended to assure a close relationship between the curriculum and any assessment.)
2. On-demand assessments should address important outcomes, not trivial items selected for ease of measurement.
3. Allowing students to answer three out of five question is inappropriate on high-stakes tests. All questions should be important; all questions must be answered to determine minimal competency.

The statement that what is tested is what is taught (often used pejoratively) does not indicate a fault of the assessment system; it arises when teachers and curriculum writers are insecure about the importance and priority of the goals of instruction. Assessors have a range of excellent devices to provide data on a variety of educational procedures and products, but in the hands of the inept one or more of these tools can be counterproductive to attaining the goals of schooling.

Overview

A number of issues cloud discussions about assessment. *High-stakes assessment* is the focus of wrangling about the value and use of assessments in education. The definition of *high-stakes* is not firm; it generally refers to situations where the assessment determines whether a student passes a grade level, graduates from secondary or tertiary school, is licensed to teach, or is denied renewal of licensure of accreditation based upon an assessment. An audition or interview can be high-stakes (for example, failure to qualify for the Boston Marathon), the height of the stake depending upon the importance placed on the task by the individual or the culture. Concern intensifies when a single assessment is used in these high-stakes events, although the definition of single assessment is also controversial. Does a battery of tests that encompasses many competencies constitute a single assessment? When one has several opportunities to pass an assessment, is this a "single assessment"? There are few, if any, high-stakes assessments in the pre-K–12 school music program, although selection for the madrigals may seem high-stakes to the auditioning singers. Arts advocates champion music as a basic subject without realizing that basic subjects are those subjects of sufficient importance to society that a high-stakes test may be required. Language arts and mathematical competence are the most common high-stakes subjects. High-stakes testing is a component of the standards movement, with most states developing such assessment in conjunction with their standards. The literature and discussion of high-stakes assessment are useful to music educators to the extent that improvements in its use aid development of better measures in music.

Evaluation and *assessment* are used interchangeably in this chapter. *Measurement* has traditionally referred to a single test, a test being the smallest unit in assessment. Individuals are measured in terms of height or weight but not in terms of personal characteristics. *Evaluation* is distinguished by the making of judgments based on the data derived from measurements and other procedures, while *assessment* refers to a considerable body of data that has the potential to diagnose and provide clues to causes. Assessment is then used to improve or judge instruction or do both.

Little distinction is made in this chapter between achievement and ability; the term *aptitude* is today seldom used in education and is not used here. *Achievement* customarily refers to short-term learning, *ability* to more long-term outcomes. No priority is assigned to the relative im-

portance of facts, knowledge, concepts, principles, understandings, creativity, critical thinking, metacognition, strategic knowledge, procedural knowledge, performance, and other worthwhile outcomes. Each outcome is appropriate at times. Also, no priority is assigned to types of assessments: auditions, rubrics, portfolios, videos, observations, demonstrations, exhibitions, fill-in-the-blanks, performances, interviews, essays, classroom discussion, research papers, and multiple-choice tests; each is situationally appropriate depending upon the task to be assessed and how instruction has been conducted.

Authentic assessment as a descriptor is avoided, as it is seldom related to assessment in music education. Almost all assessment in music is authentic. The more important concern is transfer of what has been learned. Critical reflection and self-assessment are also not addressed despite their presence in the educational literature. Self-assessment, especially of skills, is more complex than most realize; its importance is instructional. Reflection is also important. Experiencing music, however, is more important than talking *about* music, and an emphasis on reflection as an assessment technique could influence the objectives of instruction, an influence that should be avoided.

Rubrics is another hazy term; it refers to a tool for evaluation of performance in the areas of teaching, composing, conducting, improvising, singing, and playing. Such rubrics have seldom been subjected to the rigor required in assessment, and their misuse is potentially damaging to the assessment profession. They are most useful on items about which there is general consensus as to what constitutes excellence.

Organization

Eight areas have been selected as topics for the chapter. First, "Dependent Variables in Research" and "Recently Published Tests" describe the published research that relates to assessment since the publication of the first *Handbook* in 1992. Second, "Unpublished Measures" describes unpublished instruments that were systematically developed. Third is a brief discussion of the criteria for a rubric to be used as an assessment device and the rubric's limitations. Fourth, there is a brief description of the potential of program evaluation in music. Fifth, the various types of validity are defined; sixth, recent developments in educational taxonomies are outlined. Here the intent is to emphasize the importance of connecting instructional objectives and procedures with assessment. Seventh and eighth are the chapter's two concluding sections, one on the potential of technology in assessment, the other on what the future of assessment *may* be should the current reform movement result in systemic change in education. As the extent of change in education or in the music program is hypothetical, the future of assessment can be based only on current premises.

Assessment in Music Education

To achieve high standards for everyone requires an extensive assessment program to chart progress and to facilitate learning in a multitude of areas: facts, skills, understandings, self-esteem, metacognition, and interest in continuing to learn. Past assessment measures have not provided satisfactory answers; if those measures had been adequate, education would not be so impoverished, with many of the traditional assessment measures completely inadequate for any high-stakes evaluation. Educators and others have criticized assessment devices and procedures for not being valid, for being poorly connected to the competencies expected of students, and for failing to provide data needed for change. Assessment, however, is not an exact science; there will always be a certain amount of error, providing an opportunity not only for the politicization of assessment but also, more important, for the voicing of many viewpoints and interpretations.

It is difficult to suggest just how important assessment is to music education in the 21st century, as music education is not connected to education in the same manner as mathematics, language arts, science, or even social studies. Music education is not one of the subjects criticized for its lack of effectiveness; music's public issue has been an inadequate amount of instructional time due to its low priority in the eyes of most educational administrators, at the local and/or state level. Program evaluation is hampered by the existence of two (or more) independent music programs: required music education and elective music education, each with variations. Variations of required music programs include integrated course work, enhancement of other subjects, and recreation. Elective music—band, orchestra, choir, guitar, group piano, advanced placement theory, and more—is focused on skill development, and these experiences, traditionally defined, have few common outcomes. With such diversity, development of assessments of student competency in music has been impeded due to multiple *satisfactory* outcomes. It is likely, although not certain, that music would command higher priority on the school's resources if a music assessment were high-stakes—and high-stakes at every grade level. Any judgment about the importance of assessment must wrestle with the initial question of whether the purpose of assessment is aiding progress toward achieving "standards" or toward accountability, an important difference. The accountability movement currently appears to have more support than the standards movement. Use of assessment to improve instruction remains relevant.

Music educators may decide that their outcomes are not high-stakes and take a lower road toward assessment, but if so there will still be a need to rethink the role of assessment and music's relationship to basic subjects. Further, new curricula, new ways of teaching, new priorities require new forms of assessment. Ratings at contests and festivals and student satisfaction have been the primary assessment indicators in music; these do not reveal current program strengths and weaknesses and provide only partial answers in any assessment endeavor.

Evidence from learning psychology reveals that assessment properly conducted makes a major difference in student learning and, when incorrectly used, a corresponding negative effect. The current hype, however, has not produced much action in music education in the United States, Canada, or Great Britain. To many music educators, assessment is so much a part of instruction—especially in achieving goals in performance—that they do not believe more is needed. Other music educators believe that any assessment is inappropriate as either too quantitative or too mechanical. The literature commonly divides assessment by its purpose, summative assessment indicating degree of worth of the finished product, formative assessment indicating only feedback obtained in the process of moving toward the final goal or outcome. Assessment when embedded in music instruction is formative evaluation because its primary purpose is to improve the performance and, one would hope, the learning. Despite the desire of arts advocacy groups to have "hard" data on music learning, there has been little interest in summative evaluation of learning in required music instruction and only slightly more interest in outcomes of elective music experiences. The expensive 1997 arts assessment by NAEP (National Assessment of Educational Progress) had little effect on teaching priorities, and few teachers can relate the results or describe their programs in relation to these national outcomes. Pockets of interested officials, such as SCASS (State Collaborative on Assessment and Student Standards), are pondering arts assessment issues, but any connection with extant programs is unknown. FairTest, a nonprofit organization based in Cambridge, Massachusetts, is a national player in criticizing tests and how they are used. It looks for issues of equity in the instruments. Educational Testing Service, however, has promoted the use of evaluation devices for half a century and tends to be the natural target for barbs from FairTest. FairTest is not against all assessment (although its publications give that impression), tending to approve of portfolio assessments without addressing their equity or validity. The public generally accepts the idea of assessment as a source of data on teaching and learning, aware of its importance in describing outcomes in science and medicine. Licensing tests are accepted as routine, ranging from a license to operate a motor vehicle to a license to operate in a hospital whether with knives, machines, or on-the-couch questions. The testing of teachers prior to awarding a license has become accepted practice in 41 states, and the public currently supports an assessment to determine whether students deserve to graduate or even pass from one grade to another.

Dependent Variables in Research

With assessment in music consisting mainly of formative evaluation, a primary resource to identify devices used to assess outcomes is the body of research in the field. All research has independent and dependent variables (although those two sometimes hide under different names). The discussion that follows is a result of scrutinizing the 1990–2000 issues of the major relevant publications in the field: *Psychology of Music, Psychomusicology, Journal of Research in Music Education*, the *Bulletin of the Council for Research in Music Education, Research Studies in Music Education, Music Education Research*, the *British Journal of Music Education, and Dissertation Abstracts International*. The studies cited were selected to indicate *types* of assessment used, with no judgment of their appropriateness. Many of the studies have serious flaws in the research design or in the interpretation of results and would not be cited in a chapter on research.

Continuous Response Digital Interface

The paucity of use of valid and reliable measures as dependent variables is surprising, as is the frequent use of observation or description, these latter procedures unaccompanied by a description of their systematic development. A Continuous Response Digital Interface (CRDI) developed at Florida State University was the dependent measure in a large number of studies (Blocker, Greenwood, & Shellahamer, 1997; Brittin, 1996; Brittin & Duke, 1997; Brittin & Sheldon, 1995; Byrnes, 1997; Davis, 1998; DeNardo & Kantorski, 1995, 1998; W. Fredrickson, 1994, 1995, 1997, 1999; Geringer, 1995; Gregory, 1994; Johnson, 1996; Lychner, 1998; Madsen, 1997a, 1997b, 1998; Madsen, Brittin, & Capprella-Sheldon, 1993; Rentz, 1992; Sheldon, 1994; Sheldon & Gregory, 1997; Siebenaler, 1997; Skadsem, 1997). Initially this device was used only to report on one dimension of a subject's response to musical stimuli; by the end of the decade the device was sufficiently more sophisticated so that it could provide a reading on two responses. The reading is displayed on a dial, connected to a computer. The connection with the computer provides multiple readings per second and thus provides data that are reliable. The validity of the data remains unknown. The premise for its use is that there is a match between aesthetic response, the dial reading, and the place in the score at which the reading was taken. Should *reflection* be necessary to respond, the CRDI would mea-

sure an important *preaesthetic* point. The chief developer of the CRDI reports that the same information is obtained that one obtains from a paper-and-pencil test, a finding that is supportive of its concurrent validity (Madsen, 1997a, p. 64). A current criticism of assessments throughout education is that they are not authentic; that the evaluation is not "real-world" but an artificial, multiple-choice assessment. Authenticity is not a major issue in music research, as nearly every dependent variable involves some type of music performance. Assessment critics would fault the CRDI because manipulating a dial is artificial to the same extent as a multiple-choice test is. In defense of its partial authenticity, the CRDI has been used with recordings of accepted great music similar to the requirement of many multiple-choice tests.

Along with authentic assessment, reflection is promoted as an assessment tool. Requiring students to describe musical meaning and understanding is troublesome. Students with equal understanding are not equally verbal. Even the terms *higher* and *lower* are confusing to young music students (Hair, 1997); thus attempts to measure student reflections when the experience entails far more complex musical concepts calls into question the potential of student verbalization as an important assessment tool.

Observation

The most common dependent variable in the research studies examined was simple observation of student and teacher performance, either live or videotaped. No observation schedule provided data on its validity or reliability, whether a Likert scale or a professional description of the observation was used. A common study was one that modeled the observation form used in earlier research by Madsen and Yarbrough, but no statements were made that concerned the rigor of the form's development or the adaptation (Elkholm, 2000). An encouraging trend is an increase in the number of points on the Likert scales used, often 7 or 9; Yarbrough's observation of teaching videos used 10 criteria (Effective Teaching Response Form, [Yarbrough & Henley, 1999]). Curiously, no criteria for excellence in teaching exist. To avoid establishing criteria, Goolsby (1996) identified three levels of teaching: student teachers, first-year teachers, and experienced teachers, rough categories if teaching excellence is the research criterion.

The misconceptions about the validity of many of the dependent variables indicate the present naïveté of much music education research. The use of observation as a valid assessment tool is one of the most flagrant flaws. Observation is an extremely crude method of determining the extent of learning in music, as a little serious thought will reveal. Yet teachers are often evaluated solely on the basis of observation, a process that does not reveal their teaching capabilities and gives only minimal evidence of student learning that occurs as a result of the teaching intervention. A student performance, live or recorded, is perhaps a better assessment device, but any single performance provides only an approximation of musicianship, musical understanding, attitude toward learning music, knowledge of and about music, or ability to discriminate. A seminal article on the weaknesses of observation in music (Froelich, 1995) pointed up that observer agreement and precision of agreement reveal little about the validity and reliability of assessing the behavior of the teacher. Froelich argues that valid observations require: (1) that they be derived from a specific instructional theory; (2) that, once collected, they are examined within the context of that theory; and (3) accuracy, which depends upon not only the construct of interest to the researcher but also on the participants' agreement that what was observed reflected their own interpretation of the behavior under study (p. 188). Froelich's arguments begin to address the complexities of observing teaching and learning and the minimal requirements for generalizability, transfer, and assumption of task and attribute relationship. As in all research and evaluation, estimation of error is important, and without well-designed investigative procedures predicting the amount of error is extremely difficult.

Other Measures

On the few occasions where the semantic differential was used as an assessment measure, there was a consistent lack of the expected rigor, that is, of establishing the viability of the semantic differential, and a statement of the extent to which the three constructs that are the usual outcomes—evaluation, potency, and activity—related to the research question.

Music education researchers did use a few dependent measures from outside the field to assess basic knowledge, personality, or teacher competencies; those that were used were rarely employed more than once during the past decade. Thoe measures emphasized an affective component—Gregorc's *Style Delineator*, Eysenck's tests, and the Dunn, Dunn, and Price *Learning Indicator*. The competence devices used more than once included the *Wechsler PreSchool Test*, the *Developing Cognitive Abilities Test*, the *Watkins-Farnum Performance Scale*, the Ohio and Australian proficiency examination, the Asmus attitude scale (unpublished), and Gordon's *Primary Measures of Music Audiation*.

Summary

Inspection of the dependent variables in published research and doctoral dissertations reveals little change from past practice, that is, teacher/researcher/panel of judges deter-

mining treatment effect. Interjudge reliability is generally high except in judging musical compositions. This interjudge reliability is a correlation among judges, not between judge and dependent variable. Limited use was made of researcher-constructed instruments, only one of which was examined for reliability except as noted in "Recently Published Tests," later in this chapter. Researchers appeared to believe there was no need to determine reliability or validity of interviews, observations, and especially Likert scales.

Recently Published Tests

Edwin Gordon's Readiness Test

Only one new test was published during the past decade—Edwin Gordon's *Harmonic Improvisation Readiness Record* and *Rhythm Improvisation Readiness Record* (1998)—which is actually two tests, as the scores of the two parts are not combined. As the title suggests, this readiness test was not developed as an achievement test but more as a needs-assessment measure. Its use to measure improvisational competence has not been established, nor does the author suggest this as a use. These tests are important as they continue to emphasize Gordon's primary contribution to music education, which is the centrality of the *mental conception* of music, an ability he has termed audiation. One wonders why there has not been more emphasis placed on teaching audiation in music classrooms, as this competency is essential to attaining many of the goals of the complete musician. It may be that teachers relate audiation only to creating and improvising and believe, as Gordon states in the test manual, "neither improvisation nor creativity . . . can be taught" (p. 8). The test results are of interest, as the scores for students in third-grade general music do not differ significantly from those of high school students in selective ensembles. One of the author's explanations for the lack of difference is that little instructional effort has been exerted to attain the needed competencies.

Gordon describes three ways one can improvise (possible dependent variables): One may perform a variation of a melody, without giving attention to the underlying existent or implied harmony (p. 8); a melody may be performed over a series of harmonic patterns (harmonic progressions); and harmonic patterns may be improvised to an old or new melody (p. 9).

Technical Considerations. The manual has numerous typographical errors, making it difficult to be confident of any critique. The sample size used to establish the norms is more than 15,000 students, Grades 3–12 (p. 48); the Ns for Grades 3–6, 7–8, and 9–12 are not provided. The number of students by grade level is established, however, based on a study conducted in Gilbert, South Carolina (pp. 58–

59), where the total N was 918. In a second study, a clever strategy to establish validity was to have 95 fourth- and fifth-grade students in a parochial school listen to six recorded unfamiliar songs, performed twice, and ask the students to "sing a response that sounded like the song but was not an imitation of the song."

Gordon concludes that the harmony and rhythm tests are independent and that the rhythm test is more basic (p. 76). He asserts that students with scores of 22 and above are "ready." As a score of 20 can be obtained by chance (40 items with response of "same" or "not same"), additional research is necessary. Researchers interested in test development should study Tables 7 and 8 (pp. 52–53), Item Difficulty and Item Discrimination for Grades 3–12, as both indices are nearly the same for all 86 items for Grades 3–6, 7–8, and 9–12, one of the most impressive examples of item stability for any test battery.

Nonstandard Published Measures

One test published only on the computer, John Flohr's *Contemporary Rhythm Skills Assessment* (2000), is computer-administered. It is designed to assess steady beat and rhythm pattern competence of students ages 4–12. It can be accurate to a millisecond. Part 1 consists of a folk song played at five different tempi; the task is to supply the beat. In part 2, the testee must listen to and repeat 20 rhythm patterns by tapping on the computer's space bar. A critique is not possible due to the fact that the results from students of nine different age groups, 4–12, are combined, making the data difficult to interpret.

James Froseth and Molly Weaver published *Music Teacher Self-Assessment* (1996), but this is not an assessment tool. Its purpose is to train teachers in observation techniques. The authors made no attempt to establish any validity or reliability for the observation scales or to argue that the observations are focused on important teaching ventures. It is also not based on any observational research. The use of the word *assessment* in the title is misleading.

Unpublished Measures

Instrumental Music Assessment

Gary McPherson (1995) developed a five-part assessment for instrumental music as his doctoral dissertation and has since continued its development. McPherson's work is important because he addresses concerns of teachers—practice, technique, and improvisation. His test is appropriate for Australian music education, where there is more emphasis on aural skills, musicology, theory, listening, appraising music, and composing, a much broader program than found in instrumental music instruction in the United

States. The current tentative movement toward teaching more *music* in the rehearsal indicates the importance of a careful review of McPherson's assessment research. His contribution is more a think piece to the literature in assessment than a rigorously developed assessment instrument. McPherson's concern was instructional; the tests were his way of attempting to identify strategies that students use in performing. In a search for learning strategies, McPherson provides an excellent description of the process of learning to play an instrument, enabling the reader to make a decision on the content- and criterion-related validity of the assessment measures. McPherson's term is *convergent* validity. Test reliability is not addressed; data on the reliability of the judges are provided, but this reliability number is not informative about the tests themselves, their coverage, length, and other qualities that would be important should the test be considered as a high-stakes measure. McPherson's primary concern was assessment of the student's musical memory and ability to play by ear. His sample consisted of 101 clarinet and trumpet students who lived in New South Wales, Australia, and were preparing to take the Australian Music Examinations Board (AMEB), which assesses a student's ability to perform a repertoire of rehearsal music. As his interest was in high school students, he divided his sample into students 12–15 years of age and those 15–18. (Often test developers seek a disparate group, as reliability may be enhanced when students vary.) McPherson used the *Watkins-Farnum Performance Scale* as a measure of sight-reading and data from the 12-point rating scale of performance from the AMEB test. He then created three additional measures, one assessing the ability to perform from memory, one the ability to play by ear, and a third to improvise. McPherson established pitch, rhythm, and phrasing as the criteria and asked three judges to rate the performance on a 6-point scale: no attempt, very poor, fair, good, reasonably accurate, and no errors.

Playing by ear was defined as the ability to perform a melody shortly after hearing it, perform a piece held in long-term memory that was learned aurally, and transpose a piece learned under one of the two methods. It was necessary for McPherson to identify two well-known songs for which his subjects had never seen the notation.

McPherson constructed a two-part test, the first part requiring the students to play "Happy Birthday" in two keys, F and G, and "For He's a Jolly Good Fellow" in F and C. Part 2 consisted of four short melodies played by the same instrument as that of the student. The melodies were played four times, with a one-measure rest between each playing. After each melody, the subject was asked to play the melody twice in the original key and twice in the transposed key. The evaluation was, again, on a 6-point scale for both renditions.

The third test, on ability to improvise, consisted of

seven items. Items 1 and 2 required the student to formulate an answering phrase to a four-measure musical question. Item 3 required a rhythmic improvisation to a melody that used only the durations of a given rhythm pattern. Items 4 and 5 provided an opening phrase for an improvisation. In Item 6, students were given a recorded piano accompaniment and asked to improvise a melody. Item 7 was a free improvisation in any style.

Having an instrumental music test available other than the Watkins-Farnum may encourage teaching the competencies McPherson investigated. McPherson's interpretation of his results suggests that the study of piano is important; beginning instruction at a young age helps, as well as the more obviously important mental rehearsal and envisioning how one would perform a song or improvisation on one's instrument. The requirement for judges makes the test inconvenient to administer.

Cognitive-Affective Measure

Lee Bartel (1992) aided the research community by providing research data on the robustness of the semantic differential to provide a measure of cognitive and affective responses to music. His tool was appropriately named the Cognitive-Affective Response Test; it consisted of 18 semantic differential scales, 9 for each dimension. His premise is that meaning in music can be assessed using the ideas of Charles Osgood (1957) in measuring meaning in language. Bartel emphasized the importance of minimizing the *evaluative* component of the semantic differential (while retaining the cognitive and affective components) when listening to music—should meaning have a relationship to the evaluation component it would be a separate construct.

Bartel's research results indicate that careful selection of the adjectives is required before the semantic differential can be trusted as an assessment measure. If one is constructing a semantic tool (questionnaire, Likert-type scale, etc.), pilot studies are necessary. Reliability and validity are critical and must be reported. Bartel's task was to identify adjectives meaningful both to the music and to the cognitive and affective dimensions of linguistics. Bartel drew upon the philosophical position of Peter Kivy (1984), who had provided a tripartite framework of adjectives to describe music. Bartel's task was to use different musical styles (he began with classical and gospel) that loaded on his two constructs of *cognitive* and *affective* when subjected to factor analysis, as his goal was to construct a test that provided a single score of meaning. The test has not been published; this is unfortunate, as it and a study by Robert Miller (1979) are seminal works in multidimensional scaling and should be related to responses from the CRDI.

Computerized Adaptive Technology

In view of the widespread reliance on observation and professional judgment for the assessment of objectives in music, it is not surprising that little attention has been paid to capitalizing on advances in the field of measurement. Walter Vispoel (1992), an educational psychologist, applied computerized adaptive technology (CAT) to extant music aptitude tests, using item response theory (IRT). With IRT (CAT) the computer selects the next appropriate question based on the correctness of the last response. The difficulty level of the questions in the computer's item data bank must be known or estimated, as the task of the computer is to advance the competent student quickly to more demanding items (it selects easier items when a response is incorrect). Testing is begun with a question of average difficulty, and the computer takes over until the desired reliability criterion is met. The use of a computer adaptive test is particularly appealing for situations where students must listen acutely, and fatigue is an issue in obtaining reliable and valid scores. Vispoel's use of only 30 college students means that the results are tentative and considerable additional research is needed. He used the tonal memory section of Seashore's *Measures of Musical Talents*, and the musical memory subtest from the second edition of the Drake *Musical Aptitude Tests*, finding that 9 items were as reliable as 30; he estimated concurrent validity based upon student self-reports on measures used by Drake a half-century ago. As neither the Seashore nor the Drake is currently in use, Vispoel's research teases us to identify important outcomes and to construct IRT measures that cover a broad range of outcomes, including mastery, diagnostic, and grade-specific tools.

Auditory Skills and Other Efforts

Louise Buttsworth, Gerald Fogarty, and Peter Rorkle (1993) developed a test for tertiary students to replace individual auditions, using as the criterion a battery of tests given at the end of one semester of aural training. Fourteen tests were constructed, all dealing with auditory skills, most with low reliability. Their work, too complex to be summarized, is an excellent example of the difficulty of constructing even a skills assessment.

One doctoral student (McCurry, 1998) constructed a test battery based on the Voluntary National Standards to document the value of using hand chimes in fourth- and fifth-grade general music. She used 80 students divided into four groups: choral, instrumental, general music, and hand chime. Her dependent variable, a measure of achievement on the nine standards, is of interest, as it illustrates the perspective of a classroom teacher on appropriate tasks at this grade level.

Other research that involved test construction, this less rigorous, includes doctoral dissertations by Diane Hardy, The Construction and Validation of an Original Sight-Playing Test for Elementary Piano Students (1995); Claude Masear, The Development and Field Test of a Model for Evaluating Elementary String Programs (1999); Henry Mikle, The Development of an Individual Sight-Reading Inventory (1999); and Hong Wei, Development of a Melodic Achievement Test for Fourth Grades Taught by a Specific Music Learning Methodology (1995). There has been little interest in reestablishing the validity of extant tests, the one exception being a doctoral dissertation by Charles Norris (1998), who explored the relationship of the aural tonal memory section of aptitude tests to a student's ability to vocally reproduce short tonal patterns. With a (small) sample of 210 students across eight grade levels (5–12) he found a stable relationship and a correlation of .66 with the Seashore measures.

Building on her doctoral dissertation, Sheila Scott (2000) experimented with 7 students to determine if it was possible to obtain a measure of a student's understanding of the characteristics of melody through oral explanations that she called think alouds and whether the student's understanding matched 1980s learning outcomes (Biggs & Collis, 1982). Scott found the task extremely time-consuming; to create the test materials, she wrote 26 melodies that portrayed 13 different characteristics of melody. Students responded inconsistently, ranging from understanding Level 2 to Level 5 on her test. Understanding at Level 5 did not indicate understanding at Levels 1–4, raising validity and sequencing issues.

A Published but Unavailable Test

The major assessment effort of the decade was the music portion of the NAEP that assessed students in Grade 8 (Persky, Sandene, & Askew, 1998). The contribution of this assessment (other than elevating the status of music among school subjects) was the construction and scoring of open-response tasks. Students were asked to perform, to improvise, and to create, providing a comparison of student achievement on these tasks with the 1970 national assessment. The new assessment raised as many questions as it answered; for example, the final report says that no consistent pattern was found between frequency of instruction and student scores (p. 145).

Rubrics

Development and Definition

Because rubrics have become almost a separate assessment technique, a definition and a short discussion of them seem appropriate. As used for assessment, a rubric is generally a well-defined rule, guide, or standard. Teachers of composition often offer carefully worded rubrics as their sole assessment device for a classroom experience, the scoring of which is enormously time-consuming and subjective (Hickey, 1999). Rubrics are often associated with authentic assessment devices but in fact lead to standardization of responses rather than to divergent and original thought. However, rubrics can clarify performance objectives, as the student is able to understand in rather precise terms what is expected. Rubrics are highly effective in focusing student effort (narrowing it) and serve well as external motivation. The greatest use of rubrics has been in language arts, and it is clear that students can and will "write to the rubric." The appropriate research process in rubric development is to have a panel of judges evaluate a large number of musical compositions, place these in four or five categories according to worth, and then formulate rubrics that best describe the compositional attributes that distinguish each group. Once adequate research has been completed, additional student compositions can be evaluated against these rubrics.

The intent of those who believe in rubrics is to obtain a single score, often for use in high-stakes assessment. Unless the rubric becomes as detailed as a checklist, it is difficult to imagine a rubric providing feedback that would be helpful. Thomas Newkirk (2000) believes that the use of rubrics indicates a resurgence of "mechanized instruction" in writing (p. 41). He argues (in the case of English composition) that rubrics conceal or mystify the process of writing when process may be one of the objectives. Linda Mabry (1999) in an excellent treatment of rubrics and their effect on teaching argues that rubrics overwhelm the writing curriculum and that writing to the rubric is more powerful than teaching to the test. The use of rubrics has not only standardized scoring but also standardized writing. Rubric construction in music has not had any rigorous scrutiny and at present is usually an inappropriate evaluation measure. Acceptance in assessment has been based on the power of the descriptions and whether these descriptions appear to differentiate quality in products and tasks.

Use in Portfolios

Our understanding of rubrics in portfolios stems from research in language arts. Aschbacher (1999) conducted an extensive project with establishing rubrics for middle school language arts, beginning with six descriptor scales: type of assignment, type of content knowledge used, type of student response, type of choice students were given, grading dimensions used, and types of feedback provided, plus five 4-point evaluative scales: cognitive demands of the task, clarity of grading, alignment of the task with learning goals, alignment of grading criteria with learning goals, and overall task quality. The alignment between grading with rubrics and student learning was .65, not high. Teachers not only volunteered but also were paid to be interviewed and to allow the investigator to look at student work. Even experienced teachers have had insufficient preparation to use rubrics. The relationship between overall rating and grading clarity was .14, with goals/task .16 and with goals/grading .24 at the elementary school level, slightly higher for middle school. Teachers had difficulty articulating their goals for the students and had only a vague notion of the criteria they used in grading student work. Seldom were students given assignments that were both coherent and intellectually challenging, and one-third or less of the reading comprehension, draft writing, and project assignments provided any intellectual rigor. No assessment method can be successful unless there is excellent instruction.

Program Evaluation

Importance of Program Evaluation

Few examples can be found of program evaluation in music. Indeed, in the entire area of teacher education little attention is given to program evaluation. Why then is it the subject of discussion here? The answer lies in the fact that if music is to be considered as an equal subject, educators and the public will focus on the adequacy of the *program,* not the test scores of individual students enrolled in the program or the competence of ensembles. The few evaluators who have assessed music "programs" have assessed ad hoc activities such as those of composers in the schools, opera organizations, and interested groups, and activities sponsored by orchestras. Constance Gee's (1994) evaluation of the artist in the classroom accurately portrays a valid assessment of a partial program. Program evaluators, often advocates, have seldom looked at typical school programs and, when they have, have neglected to give consideration to the goals of the program.

At present, program evaluation is the dominant form of assessment in all areas affected by the federal government (and what area is today not affected by the federal government?). The Government Performance and Results Act of 1993 called for the use of performance measurement in virtually all federal agencies by the year 2000. This act has provided a major impetus to assessment of the large-scale social (and other) programs funded by the federal government (Richardson, 1992). Assessments have been conducted, for example, of programs designed to reduce smoking and alcohol use among adolescents, programs to eliminate drug usage, and programs to educate school-age

children about sexually transmitted diseases. Other programs evaluated are those that concern toxic waste, catastrophic illness, air safety, deterring insider trading, terrorism, health care costs, nuclear hazards, AIDS, industry competitiveness, the trade imbalance, the social underclass, and employment for welfare mothers. There are also program assessments of those after-school and extended-day programs that receive federal money.

Music education needs to establish its place in the nation's educational priorities, but it lacks quantitative data necessary for comparison purposes or for use by efficiency experts. Government leaders use program evaluation to make decisions, especially when the data match their beliefs. Resources are allocated on the basis of program evaluations. Program evaluations are conducted for a variety of purposes: to back up beliefs, monitor public opinion, obtain a sense of what occurs in a program, show the program's importance, and affect the power structure. Arts advocates appear to have a better sense of the potential use of program evaluation data than do music teachers. Advocates sense that the reform movement is a power struggle over the curriculum, and in that struggle data from program evaluation are important, especially when standards are used for program justification. The federal government has actively supported the standards movement and has initiated program assessment on the effectiveness of curricula in most basic subjects.

Philosophies of Program Evaluation

Several differing evaluation philosophies exist, arising from the varying possible political colors of program assessment. The sheer quantity of material—citing one point of view or the other—makes fair treatment of program assessment nearly impossible. Most people in the field agree that the text by Shadish, Cook, and Leviton (1991) is the basic source. This volume, titled *Foundations of Program Evaluation: Theories of Practice,* consists of the ideas of seven leading program evaluators, followed by a critique of the strengths and weaknesses of each. Each of these seven, plus others in the field, has named his own assessment technique, making it necessary for any discussant to wade through differences among adaptive, realistic, discrepancy, cost-benefit, utilitarian, connoisseurial, planned variation cross-validation, justice, pluralistic, program theory, goal-free, and many more program evaluation models.

Purpose

In defining the purpose of evaluation, Ernest R. House (1994) cites Michael Scriven, determining the merit or worth of something according to a set of criteria, with those criteria often (but not always) explicated and justified (p. 14). House suggests that the work of evaluation consists of collecting data, including relevant values and standards, resolving inconsistencies in the values, clarifying misunderstandings and misrepresentations, rectifying false facts and assumptions, distinguishing between wants and needs, identifying all relevant dimensions of merit, finding appropriate measures for these dimensions, weighting the dimensions, validating the standards, and arriving at an evaluative conclusion which requires a synthesis of all these considerations. (p. 86)

Program evaluation, although only one facet of evaluation, encompasses all these aspects of evaluation.

Programs and policies can be simultaneously good and bad, depending upon how the evaluation is conducted and the side effects incurred. The questions asked by the evaluator about the program and its policies would include: what are the uses, the foci, the audience, the training, what data must be collected, and so on. *Good* and *bad* are relative terms. The individuals involved in any single evaluation project will have different interests and will approach education with fairly clear but differing ideas about what are valid education and music education programs. Because these differences exist, clear statements of program purpose are required, as well as the ability on the part of the evaluator to understand the reasoning of those affected by the evaluation. Often the resources to fund program evaluation in education are inadequate for the length of time required for educational interventions to have any effect; thus the history of program evaluation in education appears to show that (most) interventions do not have a lasting effect on learning. Among the many types of program evaluation, two are distinctive. The first, associated with Scriven (1993, 1997), requires that the evaluator provide his or her interpretation of the data and make a judgment of the program's worth. Judgments and recommendations often require hard choices, and this type of evaluation brings evaluators close to or into the political arena of education. A second school of thought would have an external evaluator gather data, then put that data in the hands of the program manager for the stakeholders to interpret (Stake, 1991, 2000). Often this approach involves negotiating among all involved in the assessment to arrive at the meaning of the data and decisions to be made. This approach avoids, for the external evaluator, both the "summative" decision and the task of interpreting raw and derived scores, as well as establishing the significance of any differences.

Focus

Cronbach (1995) took issue with the general experimental model for gathering program evaluation data when he suggested that the primary purpose of an evaluator was to be a program *improver* (p. 27). He put the emphasis on formative rather than summative evaluation, suggesting that the primary purpose of evaluation might be to ascertain whether students can paraphrase, generate examples, use models, solve problems, identify the critical properties in a concept, give reasons why things are done, and as a final step synthesize complex arguments in favor of or against a relationship or concept. Cronbach's stance is that philosophical and conceptual beliefs are more powerful than lists of significant and nonsignificant differences; thus theories can be more successful in changing behaviors than lists of consequences for failure to change. Cronbach's thinking often does not satisfy the politician who wants to know why things are as they are—is there profiling, ineffective staffing, or incompetent teaching? To answer these questions the "hard" approach to assessment is needed. Often, however, the focus is not on whether success has been achieved but on providing documentation that there is equal participation and a proper allocation of resources. Equity concerns are addressed by gender, age, socioeconomic class, and race to ensure that no one group of individuals is disadvantaged due to, for example, physical handicaps, language, place of residence, or political affiliation.

Social Context

An important concept in program evaluation, especially that conducted through case studies and qualitative means, is putting all data into an appropriate context. Diversity issues prompt this concern, but other prompts stem from the recognition that there are major differences not only among individuals but also among classrooms, schools, and communities. In light of these differences, the question is raised as to whether all students and all teachers can or should be assessed through use of a single standard. Consideration of the social context allows educational outcomes to differ and still be equal. With the acceptance of different outcomes, the results of evaluation may need to be interpreted *relative* to floating standards. The support for relativity comes from constructivist philosophy. Humans can construct what is meant by *competent* and by *the good life*; as the goals of education are something society creates, society is free to construct various definitions of success.

Context influences outcomes. For the evaluator, established programs and their context increase the difficulty of conducting a meaningful assessment. If the school's band program has consistently won blue ribbons at marching band, jazz, and concert contests and festivals, ascertaining that the program does not meet the school's educational goals would require extremely compelling data. Even average programs are contextually influenced for evaluators of any persuasion. The constructivist would suggest that society values excellence arrived at through cooperative learning; thus the goals attained by the band are as valid as any goal the school's administration might propose. The connection between evaluation and the politics of education is most obvious in the assessment of long-established programs and those *perceived* by the public to be successful.

With knowledge of how the music program fits into the social, political, educational, and organizational context, a realistic look at its range of effects in each of the contexts is possible. The qualitative approach to program evaluation has advantages here: The evaluator can devote sufficient time on-site to become familiar with the local situation and its biases, traditions, and values, where liberal and conservative views are most likely to surface.

Another viable approach to program evaluation is to involve a limited number of external evaluators, perhaps only one, and to train the stakeholders to conduct a self-evaluation. Shadish and Cook (2000) suggest that communities differ in the way they construct reality, contributing to differences in how they perceive an evaluation, methods of observation, validations, reporting formats, and strategies for evaluation use (p. 45). Because of these differences, assessment training in self-evaluation situations is necessary; few teachers have had any systematic instruction in any form of evaluation. Robert Stake (1997) would like the stakeholders to discover for themselves what changes they wish to make—he believes if teachers have conducted or helped conduct the assessment, their personal investment will contribute to the possibility that the results will be used. Similar arguments are made by Fetterman (2001), who champions *empowerment evaluation,* where through the evaluation process the stakeholders are enabled (empowered) to make necessary changes and to defend the validity of current practices. How well a teacher or student should perform is a concept that is "constructed" by a school system or a teacher; thus multiple stakeholders must be involved in constructing or reconstructing the definition of acceptable performance if constructive use is to be made of the data collected.

Quantitative Versus Qualitative

During the 1990s and the first decade of the 21st century, program evaluation literature abounded with discussions about quantitative and qualitative assessment and the extent to which the two could be combined in a single assessment (House, 1994; Reichardt & Rallis, 1994; M. L. Smith, 1994). There are important differences between the two techniques, but these differences should not affect the actual evaluation. It appears that those empowered to make changes usually require *quantitative* data—there is a need to know the number of students who were successful as a result of an after-school program compared to the number of successful students who missed the offering.

Success can have any number of important *qualitative* definitions, but they are usually not relevant to the need of school board members focused on costs, the number of students who do not graduate, the number of music students who fail, or even the number of students who have quit smoking as a result of a requirement in the after-school program. Quantitative data report the success or lack of success of a program in the simplest terms, a summative evaluation. Summative evaluations are used in comparing schools, states, and various remedial or gifted programs. A rich description, no matter how deep, of a student's experience in the school or in a classroom is seldom sufficiently generalizable or definitive to warrant school board action. Rich descriptions are more useful in formative evaluation, an evaluation that aids in changing classroom practices and classroom methods.

The methodology to be used in any assessment depends upon the subject matter and what it is that one wants to know. Until the content to be assessed is known, discussions about whether one should use quantitative or qualitative methodology in an assessment are not productive. The *problem* is the deciding factor. Teachers generally are not concerned with issues related to summative evaluation—it was not teachers who inspired the reform movement in education and its attendant content and performance standards. Teachers did not demand graduation examinations and, historically, have not requested information on how their class compares with other classes in the state or nation.

Currently evaluations in music that supposedly address program concerns through employment of qualitative data outnumber those that employ quantitative data, but those with quantitative data appear to be the more influential assessments in support of music programs. These data are not based on *musical outcomes;* data on higher academic tests scores, graduation rates, college acceptances, fewer delinquency incidents, better work habits, and such are the data that resonate with school administrators, school boards, and music activists. Qualitative data are more compelling on *instructional issues,* quantitative data on policy questions about the *value* of the program. A few qualitative assessments do not actually evaluate but are important instructional tools.

A major objection to the quantitative approach is that it reminds individuals of the pass-fail examination and all its related anxiety. The criticism of the quantitative evaluation involves the difficulty in teasing out the causes for any improvement or deficiencies from a summative score. The reference is usually to the "black box," meaning that administering a standardized test like the PRAXIS II examination provides a pass-fail based on the "cut-score" established by the state department of education, but the score provides little information to the candidate or his or her school on how to build upon successes or correct any weaknesses. The black box is the test that reveals nothing about what *caused* the score, whereas qualitative techniques are designed to observe frequently and in enough depth to identify probable causes of program weaknesses. It is not clear that observation, no matter how skillful, can assess many of the competencies required to be a successful teacher, but program evaluation is designed to look at programs, *not* individuals.

A Model

The current model for program evaluation in the arts is John Harland's *Arts Education in Secondary Schools: Effects and Effectiveness* (2000). A number of concerns in Great Britain prompted this study, among which were the following: There were fewer advisory services from local school districts, a decline in the arts content of initial training courses for primary teachers, a relaxation in the curriculum requirements to allow more time on literacy and numeracy, a worry that out-of-school programs were being boosted to replace in-school programs, and the promotion of the arts for their contribution toward combating social exclusion (p. 3). Harland's charge was to document the range of effects and outcomes attributable to school-based arts education, to examine the relationship between these effects and the key factors and processes associated with arts provision in schools, to illuminate good practice in schools' provision of high-quality education experiences in the arts, and to study the extent to which high levels of institutional involvement in the arts correlate with the qualities known to be associated with successful school improvement and school effectiveness. A survey of pupils in their junior year was conducted with interviews of employers and employees. The questions centered on objectives comparable to those in the United States; critical discrimination, aesthetic judgment, techniques, and skills at the key stage that was the end of required instruction, furthering of thinking skills, and the capacity to use the arts in their social, artistic, and cultural contexts and to prepare for a cultural life. Students in Great Britain ranked music as the least favorite subject with the highest proportion of responses that the curriculum had no impact on their abilities or attitudes. The curriculum and the school were not as persuasive as the teacher, a conclusion that indicates the importance of selection and education of all teachers involved with music.

Validity

Three Traditional Types

Validity has long been the sine qua non of research and evaluation. The term has been so misused that its meaning

and even importance are subject to confusion. One can discuss validity only in relational terms; whereas a general statement that *results* were invalid might be quite appropriate. To establish validity, the gathering, interpreting, and reporting of data should be valid *in relation to* a concept or idea of importance. Traditionally, evaluators focused efforts to establish validity on one of three areas: content, criterion-related, or construct. *Content validity* indicates a match between the assessment techniques and the content of a course or program. High-stakes tests have been delayed in several states to ensure that the students have been taught the content that appears on the high-stakes examination. Students often recall an experience when there was little match between the content of classroom discussions and the final examination and when a legitimate complaint was lodged about the content validity of a test, especially tests that influenced the final grade in the course. *Criterion-related validity* matches the results of an assessment with an accepted measure of competence in the same domain. There should be a relationship between a medical student's passing "the boards" (a battery of tests) and his or her ability to diagnose standard illnesses. Criterion-referenced assessments are also expected to predict future performance. Some assessors separate predictive validity from validity established by a match between test results and current task competency. *Construct validity* has long been considered the most important validity check for many assessments in formal schooling. A construct is a trait or ability (like personality) that is difficult to assess directly. Observations should have construct validity. Musicality is a construct, a construct recognizable under special conditions but one whose fuzzy definition presents assessment problems. Musicality is currently assessed through an audition, through an improvisational or compositional task, by requiring one to distinguish a musical from a nonmusical event—seemingly different abilities.

More Recent Types

Other descriptors of validity better convey the value of an assessment, and additional types of validity are of concern. A common type is *consequential validity,* where one asks what are the consequences to students who succeed or fail on the assessment or the consequences to the school. The consequences of failing a high-stakes assessment can be greater than the consequences of passing it, although both scenarios have consequences.

Predictive validity has been teased out of criterion-related validity in many assessments due to the importance of admissions tests in many fields. For example, the question is regularly asked as to how well the SAT score predicts one's success in college.

Systemic validity is a concern in schools where it was decided to not just make minor revisions in a course but be bold and make systemic changes in how students are educated. Reducing the number of electives and increasing graduation requirements to 4 years of math, science, language arts, and social science is a systemic change in the philosophy of secondary education. The change from junior high to middle school was a systemic change. Multiple-intelligence schools see themselves as involved in systemic changes. Assessment of these changes requires systemic validity. The 1997 NAEP in music with its emphasis on creating and improvising along with a test of sight-reading ability could be judged on its systemic validity—to what extent did this new assessment capture a major change in the priority of objectives in the music curriculum?

The relationships between assessment and task in these types of validity are important because inferences on the meaning of the assessment results depend upon the strength of these validity relationships. If one were to find little relationship between the instruction in the high school band rehearsal and the tasks of the 1997 NAEP, a lack of instructional validity would be indicated. NAEP could have strong consequential validity should graduation from high school for these band members depend upon their NAEP scores. Strength and type of validity is a judgment call.

A Taxonomy of Objectives

The Cognitive Domain

In the mid-1950s, Benjamin J. Bloom published his taxonomy in the cognitive domain (1956). It was a carefully worked out delineation of the many aspects of cognition, the ways in which the various aspects related to one another, and a hierarchical ordering of the development of cognition through its various aspects. Book 1 of *Taxonomy of Educational Objectives, Cognitive Domain,* opened up to educators a way of establishing clear objectives, sequencing these objectives, and assessing the extent to which the objectives were attained. Although the taxonomy was ordered from simple to complex, Bloom did not suggest that his sequence should necessarily be followed in instruction; teachers were expected to be simultaneously using several levels of the taxonomy. A striking feature of the taxonomy was that it consisted of multiple-choice and open-ended questions that looked, walked, and quacked like an assessment tool. Bloom's taxonomy demonstrated the importance of connecting the objectives of cognitive development with assessment and the necessity for the objectives to be clear and specific. Tremendous insights were gained by applying Bloom's taxonomy to a musical experience and constructing a task for each of the taxonomy categories. Such an exercise could serve as a check on the breadth and appropriateness of goal levels within one ac-

ademic grade. The taxonomy was frustrating to music educators, as there was no accommodation for tasks that involved perceptual skills and knowledge. (Bloom's colleagues later constructed a taxonomy of the affective domain [Krathwohl, Bloom, & Masia, 1964, the second domain of learning], and independent researchers, especially Anita Harrow [1972] and Elizabeth Simpson [1966], constructed a taxonomy in the psychomotor domain, the third hypothesized dimension of learning. Krathwohl's major levels were receiving [attending], responding, valuing, organizing, and characterization by a value or value concept, while Simpson's levels were perception, set, guided response, mechanism, and complete overt response.)

A Holistic Approach

Recently, influenced by the ideas of Howard Gardner and Bennett Reimer, education (including music education) has been moving toward a greater emphasis on cognition and broader definitions of learning. This new emphasis has given rise to the need for a new taxonomy, one that would reflect the new knowledge about learning. In 1998 A. Dean Hauenstein published *A Conceptual Framework for Educational Objectives: A Holistic Approach to Traditional Taxonomies,* which was an effort to update taxonomies in the three domains, Bloom's cognitive, D. Krathwohl's affective, and Simpson's psychomotor. In addition to making suggestions that allowed for constructivist thought, Hauenstein posits that the 63 categories contained in the three taxonomies were too many for teachers to use in curriculum planning. He revised the three taxonomies and added a fourth "behavioral domain" taxonomy with five levels: acquisition, assimilation, adaptation, performance, and aspiration (containing 15 subcategories), for a total of 20 categories, rather than the 63 in the Bloom/Krathwohl/Simpson configuration. Hauenstein's revised categories are applicable to research, assessment, and thoughtful curriculum planning. The revised basic categories for the cognitive domain are conceptualization, comprehension, application, and synthesis; for psychomotor: perception, simulation, and conformation (short-term goals) and production and mastery (long-term goals). Psychomotor learning depends on the interrelationship of cognition and affect.

Hauenstein's retention of the affective domain (to the consternation of the pure cognitivists) is helpful to arts curriculum planning. He asserts that the affective domain is "equal to, if not more important than, the cognitive domain" (p. 59). The development of feelings, values, and beliefs and the development of lifelong interests, values, and appreciations such as for arts and music are crucial to the outcomes of education—knowledgeable, acculturated, and competent individuals (p. 60). The revised categories for the affective domain are: receiving, responding, valuing, believing, and behaving. These are organized similarly to the categories established by Krathwohl, as both have three subcategories for the first three categories and two each for believing and behaving. Believing and behaving replace Krathwohl's organization and characterization by value or value complex.

Other updates in the cognitive and psychomotor taxonomies better account for recent thinking about learning. The author was careful to ensure that the taxonomy was applicable and inclusive, that the categories were mutually exclusive, and that there were consistent "principles of order" for the categories (p. 31).

The purpose of this taxonomy is "for curriculum writers: no attempt is made to provide information on how to write objectives or measure achievement" (p. 123). The premise is that assessment takes its cue from the curriculum and that a profitable place to begin is with the taxonomies of the curriculum. The emphasis is on learning as a whole person. All three taxonomies are essential, with the fourth for curriculum research, and use of them makes education more organized. In the cognitive domain, conceptualization, comprehension, and application are short-term goals, evaluation and synthesis long-term. Taxonomies focus on objectives that enable students to explore, refine, or change prevailing dispositions, values, and beliefs as they form their own concepts. Education is dependent on the degree to which prescriptions and information/content are included in the curriculum for instruction. Space prohibits giving examples in music even for the 20 categories. Readers might wish to review the examples in my 1970 *Evaluation of Music Teaching and Learning* and write assessment exercises for the four Hauenstein taxonomies.

A Revision of Bloom's Taxonomy

A second new taxonomy appeared in 2001, written by a task force that included Krathwohl (*A Taxonomy for Learning, Teaching, and Assessing: A Revision of Bloom's Taxonomy of Educational Objectives*, edited by Lorin W. Anderson and David Krathwohl). It is an update of only the cognitive taxonomy and is two-dimensional: cognitive processes and knowledge. The revised cognitive processes are remembering, understanding, applying, analyzing, evaluating, and creating, premised on the assumption that these processes are linear in complexity. Knowledge consists of the factual, conceptual, procedural, and metacognitive, also arranged linearly, proceeding from concrete to abstract. The authors posit that use of the taxonomy provides a better understanding of objectives and of what is important in education (p. 6) and that a taxonomy helps one to plan, to select and design assessment instruments and procedures, and to thereby ensure that objectives, instruction, and assessment are consistent.

The alignment of objectives and assessment is basic to high-quality instruction. The different types of objectives that result not only from new knowledge but also from state and federal frameworks require different instructional approaches.

Another reason for revision is that Ralph Tyler's behaviors became confused with behaviorism, requiring that the word *behavior* be replaced with *cognitive processes* (Anderson & Krathwohl, 2001, p. 14).

The Marzano Taxonomy

A third new taxonomy of educational objectives, this one formulated by Robert J. Marzano (*Designing a New Taxonomy of Education Objectives* [2001]), reflects the philosophical shift to cognition and recognizes the role of new knowledge about how learning occurs. Marzano's taxonomy is a new guide to understanding cognitive development and a new way of appraising the appropriateness of objectives, curriculum, and assessment in education. It is a marked departure from the Bloom taxonomy and the two revisions, particularly in that it combines the cognitive and psychomotor domains. The foundation level of the taxonomy of educational objectives is knowledge, which is attained through three systems: a cognitive system, a metacognitive system, and a self-system. There is no allowance for an affective domain; emotion is subsumed under Level 6, Self-System. A further complication for music educators is the lack of clarity that concerns a possible perceptual domain. Reimer (1996) suggests that perception is a type of cognition, but this explanation only partially answers the question of how the attainment of perceptual skills fits into the music curriculum. Marzano concludes that *information* cannot be executed, an understandable argument if, and only if, perception is not considered. When musicians hear an unknown piece of music and mentally classify it to obtain deeper meaning, they are actually executing one type of information; their minds process the information and a response to the music so perceived occurs. Another concern of music educators will be the emphasis the cognitive approach places on verbalizing, for example, verbalizing about the music and the musical experience. A large part of the musical experience defies verbal description; one is reminded of Martha Graham's comment to the effect that "if I could describe it, I would not have to dance it."

For the researcher in music education this taxonomy offers a guide to exploring many aspects of the musical learning process that have not yet been considered. And although at first glance the taxonomy may seem beyond any practical application for the music teacher in the classroom, the taxonomy is in reality an excellent tool for *thinking* about the learning process, *planning* learning sequences, *recognizing* various kinds of learning not previously considered, and *helping* to ensure that assessment gets to the heart of the learnings the teacher deems of primary importance. The practicing music teacher may find the taxonomy initially formidable but with some small effort will be able to see the ways in which it opens up the nature and the facts of learning in a way that is applicable to the teacher's goals.

Levels. Knowledge consists of information, mental procedures, and psychomotor procedures; to obtain this knowledge it is necessary to consider the three systems: cognitive, metacognitive, and self. There are six levels to the taxonomy, four of them cognitive, plus the levels of *metacognition* and *self,* which are intact levels.

Level 1: Knowledge Retrieval
Level 2: Comprehension
Level 3: Analysis
Level 4: Knowledge Utilization
Level 5: Metacognition
Level 6: Self

The levels are not organized by complexity, as was the earlier Bloom and the two revised taxonomies; rather, they are based on how an individual processes the stimuli received. Although there are subcomponents to the systems of metacognition and self, there is no order to these subcomponents. There is, however, an implied order to the cognition system, beginning with Level 1 and advancing to Level 4. The numbering of the levels is confusing, as the first step in learning is to engage the *self*-system, followed by the *metacognition* system. The *cognitive* system is the last one to be engaged. This taxonomy, like the Anderson and Krathwohl, is a work-in-progress, with Marzano allowing that not every subcomponent of the six levels may be essential to all subjects.

Marzano's Taxonomy Applied to Music. In view of the uniqueness of music and the importance of perception in music, this taxonomy is not entirely satisfactory, because audiation, a subcompetence of perception, does not fit neatly into it. Music educators believe that a student should perceive chord changes, melodic motifs, and the extent to which performers are in tune with one another. If the student is a performer, the ability to sing chord tones or to play in tune can be observed, but performance is not essential to derive meaning from music. Music educators believe that there are degrees of perceptual ability; due to talent or learning, some individuals have a "Harry Begian ear," where the smallest deviation is perceived, while others are apparently satisfied with gross approximations of the tonality.

Subcomponents. Each of the six levels of the taxonomy has three subcomponents: information, mental procedures, and psychomotor procedures.

Information (sometimes called declarative knowledge) consists of (1) details and (2) organizing ideas. *Details* consist of vocabulary, facts, time sequences, cause/effect sequences, and episodes. Music vocabulary and facts are familiar to all of us. Less is done in music with the other components of information detail. A time sequence requires identifying important events that occur between two dates, such as 1792 and 1795, Haydn's period in London, when he wrote the *London* Symphonies. (We'll ignore 1792–1794, when he returned briefly to Vienna and took Beethoven as a pupil.) Cause/event sequences would require understanding the relationship between the valve for brass instruments and the change in brass music. An episode could be the riot created by the premier of Stravinsky's *Le Sacre du Printemps.* Details are not limited to information retrieval and Level 1 of the taxonomy. *Organizing ideas* consist of principles and generalizations. Principles can be either correlational, a change in one factor resulting in a change in another factor, or cause- and effect, where one factor *causes* a change in the other.

Mental Procedures (sometimes called procedural knowledge) consist of (1) processes and (2) skills. *Mental processes* could be organized into a simple hierarchy, as some are more complex than others. If all students were assigned to improvise on a theme or to compose a piece, the varying products could be assigned to a rough hierarchy, but an exact hierarchy is unlikely, as the improvisations would have different strengths. *Mental skills* consist of tactics, algorithms, and simple rules. Following a single rule would be the simplest mental process; the skills should be included in any rough hierarchy of mental processes.

Psychomotor Procedures consist of (1) processes, (2) skills, and (3) the same mental procedures. *Psychmotor processes* consist of complex combination procedures, such as performing one's part accurately and musically in a concert. *Psychomotor skills* are simple combination procedures and foundational procedures. A simple combination procedure would be double-tonguing, while a foundational procedure would be exhaling correctly.

For Bloom, knowledge was "little more than the remembering of the idea or phenomenon" (1956, pp. 28–29). Bloom's nine levels of knowledge were clear, but there was no provision for the mental operation that accompanied the behavior at each level. Marzano's argument is that there must be a process for retrieving and using the knowledge acquired. His stages indicate how the cognitive, metacognitive, and self-systems act upon the various knowledges. Declarative knowledge remains basic to learning, the taxonomy placing the emphasis on how vocabulary, facts, and criteria are used. To use knowledge requires attention to three kinds of memory: sensory memory, where we learn, briefly, from our senses; long-term memory which is the basis for knowing and understanding; and working memory, the memory used when focusing on a task.

Application to Assessment: Level 6, Self.   Although much of the emphasis in the music classroom is on the cognitive requirements, the new taxonomy allows one to inspect the entire learning sequence. *Level 6: Self* is the first consideration. Bloom's taxonomy did not consider the self system.

Level 6: Self consists of examining importance, examining efficacy, examining emotional response, and examining motivation. Examining student motivation reveals a summary of the student's beliefs about importance, efficacy, and emotion. These differ in relative weight and combine to produce motivation.

The self-system of thinking addresses the question of whether to engage in the learning, how much energy to expend, what will be attended to, and to what extent this effort will satisfy a basic need. Personal goals are important in the self-system, as goals have to be at the personal level before one learns. Students may join music ensembles to have or be with friends, rather than to learn. The self-system begins to address the major questions of the purpose of life and to what extent the individual will need to change his or her environment to attain new goals. Bandura, Maslow, Buber, and other educational psychologists stress the importance of the student's investment in his or her own education.

In the self-system, the process is the same across the three domains of information, mental procedures, and psychomotor procedures. (Examples in this chapter are given only for the self and metacognition levels, as these are apt to be the most unfamiliar to the teacher.)

Self-system: Examining importance. The student decides what specific information is important:

Information
• *Details.* How important is it for me to know the events that surrounded the beginning of opera? Why do I believe this and how logical is my thinking?
• *Organizing ideas.* How important is it to me to know the principles of bowing? Why would I need to know the principles; how valid is my thinking about this?

Mental procedures
• *Skills.* How important is it to audiate? Why is it important? How logical has my thinking been in establishing this importance?
• *Processes.* How important is the ability to compose? Why is composing important to me? How logical have I been in deriving this importance?

Psychomotor procedures
• *Skills.* How important is it to me to practice double-tonguing? Why would I want to double-tongue? How logical have I been in making this decision?
• *Process.* How important is it for me to be able to perform my part well in the chorus concert? Why do I want to be proficient? How valid is my thinking at ascertaining the importance of practicing with all the other things I have to do?

Self-system: Examining efficacy. The student must have the will (motivation) to change from not knowing to knowing. To what extent do I believe that I can improve my understanding or competence relative to this week's goals of the music class? (Determining efficacy likely does not generalize to all of the goals of the music experience.) Do I have the resources, the ability, the power to change my situation or the situation at school? What are the veridical or logical aspects that might demonstrate to me that I can accomplish the goals?

Information
• *Details.* How much can I increase my understanding of the conditions that surrounded the origin of the opera? What is my reasoning?
• *Organizing ideas.* How much can I improve my knowledge of the principles of bowing in different genres? Have I been logical and realistic in my reasoning?

Mental procedures
• *Skills.* To what extent will I be able to improve my ability to audiate? What is my reasoning and how logical is it that I can actually improve?
• *Processes.* To what extent will I be able to improve my skill at composing? How likely is it that this is possible?

Psychomotor procedures
• *Skills.* How much can I improve my double-tonguing and be able to perform the way I want to? How reasonable is this goal?
• *Processes.* How close can I come to getting everything right in next week's choral concert? How logical is my reasoning?

Self-system: Examining emotional response. Negative emotions dampen a student's motivation. Emotions, though we have limited control over them, can be powerful motivators. Many charismatic leaders appeal essentially to a person's emotions; patriotism and respect for the motherland are emotion-based reasons for action. Marzano suggests that the flow from emotion to cognition is stronger than the flow from cognition to emotion. The emotional response differs from other categories, as the objective is to understand the *pattern* of one's thinking. There is no basis for determining that one pattern is better than another or that change is in order.

Information
- *Details*. How do I feel about paying for music that I was able to get free from Napster? Why do I feel this way? How logical is this reaction? (What emotions do I have about the need to sell grapefruit in order for the school orchestra to have new music?)
- *Organizing ideas*. What feelings do I have about the time spent warming up in choral rehearsals? How did I arrive at this feeling about warming up?

Mental procedures
- *Skills*. Why do I get so upset when we are expected to audiate? Is this feeling logical? How and when did it begin?
- *Processes*. Why do I become so emotional about the music I compose? Why do I not want anything to be changed? How logical am I? What is my reasoning?

Psychomotor procedures
- *Skills*. Why do I believe that I can triple-tongue at MM = 142? Is this logical or just a feeling? What logic or reasoning did I use to believe I could improve that much?
- *Processes*. Why am I so emotional and sad after the final choral concert of the year? What reason do I have for making this so important yet so sad? Am I logical in behaving as I do?

Self-system: Examining motivation. Assessing the strength of motivation is identical to assessing the three components of the self-system of thinking. Students review their reaction to the importance of goals, to what extent they have the resources to meet the goals, and any emotional reaction that can interfere with accomplishment of these goals. The importance of the goal to the individual is usually the strongest motivator. It is useful, however, to have students reflect upon and write responses to the information, mental procedures, and psychomotor procedures involved in motivation even when the material draws solely from past reflections. (Space will not be taken here for examples, as motivation is a summary step.)

Application to Assessment: Level 5, Metacognition. *Taxonomy level 5: Metacognition* follows Level 6. It prepares the student to learn and assess the depth of interest and capacity for learning. Metacognition moves beyond cognition and consists of four categories: goal setting, process monitoring, monitoring clarity, and monitoring accuracy. Metacognition is a way of determining the functioning of the other types of thought. If there is a hierarchy, goal setting is the most important accompanied by three monitoring strategies.

Metacognition: Goal setting. For knowledge to occur,

there must be a clear objective, a rough but thoughtful time line to accomplish that goal, and a knowledge of the resources required to meet that goal. There must be a clear picture of what the final product will look like and the relationship of any experiences to that product. Just practicing is not enough; one has to have an objective for any practice or drill. Where the student is involved in self-systems and in metacognition, the role of the teacher is changed.

Information
- *Details*. What is a goal that you might have relating to the Voluntary National Standards? What would you have to do to accomplish this goal?
- *Organizing ideas*. What goal would you suggest for yourself to improve your musical creativity? How might you accomplish that goal?

Mental procedures
- *Skills*. What goal might you set for your ability to audiate? What instruction and practice plan will enable you to reach that goal?
- *Processes*. Based upon your current competence, what goal do you have to learn to improvise in the genre of country and western music? What does your plan to accomplish this goal look like?

Psychomotor procedures
- *Skills*. State a terminal and intermediate goal that you have to improve your vocal high register. What resources will be required for you to meet these goals?
- *Processes*. What are your goals for this week to improve your musical understanding of the music we are singing in chorus? What are the procedures for improving understanding and how long would that process take?

Metacognition: Process monitoring. The function of this stage of monitoring is to assess the effectiveness of the algorithms, tactics, or rules used in a task. The taxonomy does not include monitoring the information stage, as the monitoring is to be authentic, that is, monitored in actual minutes required to accomplish a task. Thus the concern for the mental imagery of classifying a piece of music; little time elapses, and some classifying becomes almost automatic. Information such as vocabulary, facts, and causal sequences can be remembered and recalled but not acted upon. In ignoring perception to some extent, this definition indicates that much of the thrust of cognitive-based education could be *about* music, not *of* music. The mental and psychomotor skills that involve performance are unquestionably musical goals; there can be a question, however, about the importance in a music class of the extensive verbalization and reflection.

The student is to think about what he or she is doing *while* doing it. In some subjects, a verbal protocol is possible as it is in some music activities, but there are other situations where the opportunity to respond must be contrived, conducted after the experience.

Mental procedures
- *Skills.* To what extent were you able to hear every pitch mentally before you sang it?
- *Processes.* To what extent were you able to envision your composition before you performed it and how well were you able to interpret and perform your composition?

Psychomotor procedures
- *Skills.* Demonstrate a proper vocal warm-up. How effective were you at becoming more relaxed in your upper torso and getting the vocal cords to respond?
- *Processes.* As the student conductor of the orchestra, describe your musical thoughts into the tape recorder as you conduct. Comment on your effectiveness from your perception. I shall also stop you occasionally and ask you to orally evaluate your effectiveness at that point.

Metacognition: Monitoring clarity. The monitoring process is designed to assess any ambiguity in the goal or in how well the goal is to be attained. Often students do not understand all of the subgoals required in learning a piece of music and that more is required than getting the notes and rhythms correct. Clarity assists in establishing a disposition for learning the required tasks.

Information
- *Details.* Identify those sections of the test about which you were confused. What do you think caused your confusion on those sections? Are they related in some way?
- *Organizing ideas.* What concepts about appropriate breathing don't you understand? Be specific about the places in the music where you have inadequate breath support, where your breath support does not support the tone, and where your tone lacks a center due to your breathing.

Mental procedures
- *Skills.* Identify the places in the music where the score was confusing. What do you think caused this confusion?
- *Processes.* Identify the places in the score where the orchestra was unable to follow you. What is it about the music, the performers, or the situation that confused you?

Psychomotor procedures
- *Skills.* Identify those places in today's bowing exercises where you lost concentration. What do you think caused your inattention?
- *Processes.* Identify where in today's concert you missed the bowing pattern and became confused and played in the rests. What caused this confusion? Were you at letter B? With a downbow?

Metacognition: Monitoring accuracy. Accuracy is important in all subjects but none more so than music where the notes, rhythm, intonation, articulation, diction, and so forth must be precise. The student is to self-monitor to verify his or her own accuracy.

Information
- *Details.* How do you know that your explanation of Bach and Handel being the culmination of the Baroque period is an accurate explanation? What evidence do you have?
- *Organizing ideas.* What evidence do you have that you followed the compositional practices that were prevalent during the Classical period? What evidence do you have to verify that your composition authentically matches music of the Classical period?

Mental procedures
- *Skills.* Identify those parts of today's sight-reading exercise where you were able to audiate your part. How can you check your accuracy in audiating?
- *Processes.* Identify those computer programs that you used to help you arrange the music in the style of Ravel. What evidence do you have that your use of the programs provided a valid representation?

Cognitive System Processes. The four levels of the cognitive system detail the most familiar objectives, although some of the expected knowledge will require time-consuming assessments.

Level 1: Knowledge retrieval. Knowledge retrieval is defined as the ability to move knowledge from one's long-term memory to working memory. The level of knowledge is not sophisticated, consisting of facts and the simple structure of the topic. Questions about the style or genre of a piece of music satisfy Level 1.

Level 2: Comprehension. This level is comparable to comprehension in the Bloom taxonomy, except it does not include Bloom's extrapolation level. Synthesis in the new taxonomy matches Bloom's "interpretation." Comprehension is the process of preparing the major components of knowledge for inclusion in long-term memory. Knowledge specific to an experience may not be retained if it is not generalizable. The two stages of comprehension are synthesis and representation.

Level 3: Analysis. The basis for conducting an analysis is generation of new knowledge or new understanding. There are five types of analysis: matching, classifying, error analysis, generalization, and specification. For Marzano, analysis is comparable to Piaget's accommodation (1971), rather than assimilation or the idea of restructuring (which follows accretion and tuning), a system of Rumelhart and Norman (1981).

Level 4: Knowledge utilization. Level 4 is more advanced, if not more complex, than the other levels of cognition in the new taxonomy. The general categories are: decision making, problem solving, experimental inquiry, and investigation.

Assessment Strategies with the Marzano Taxonomy. As indicated by the length of the task descriptions, if music education programs were to be based upon this learning process, the assessments would need to parallel the objectives, follow the format suggested, and be embedded in the instruction.

Although retrieval of information is critical, as demonstrated in knowledge utilization, the most efficient way to assess a student's recall competence is through open-ended questions, multiple-choice, and on-demand type items.

Music notation could be used in matching, classifying, and demonstrating that the student understood the symbols of literacy. This assessment measure would satisfy a portion of Level 2: Comprehension and two of the methods of Level 3: Analysis, those of matching and classification.

Essays and oral reports are appropriate for all of the levels of the taxonomy except retrieval of information. Traditional sampling would constitute such a major source of variance that one could not determine the student's depth of knowledge of facts, definitions, time sequences, episodes, and cause/effect sequences; hence, new assessment formats are required.

Observation by teacher, peers, or outsiders is an inefficient and inaccurate assessment tool, because the observer brings too much baggage to the scene. Observing a student perform provides limited evidence of the range of the student's performing ability and even less of his or her comprehensive musical knowledge and skills. Observation provides partial information on a student's comprehension at one particular time and may provide partial information on the student's ability to retrieve information. In the best situations, the measurement error is great.

Performance tasks provide the opportunity to assess not only the student's cognitive competence but the metacognition and self levels when the performance task is substantive and on material worth knowing. A library assignment to conduct research and write a paper on an artist would not be very informative in assessing any of the nine Voluntary National Standards or one's basic musicianship. Administering one on-demand performance task will seldom produce adequate information. Even a complex task, if performed only once, is subject to substantial measurement error, less than that for the onetime high-stakes multiple-choice examination but of concern with any high-stakes assessment.

Assessment to improve (formative) must consist of frequent performance tasks, each scheduled to provide im-

mediate feedback to the student and an opportunity to demonstrate that corrective action has been taken.

New Devices

The emphasis in this chapter is on assessment issues that will arise with new instructional modes and the appropriateness of both embedded and external assessments. The new knowledge about both thinking and learning, coupled with advances in technology, allows psychologists and educators to create truly diagnostic and adaptive systems in the areas of ability, learning, development, and achievement.

Some of these advances have resulted from new statistical techniques or new uses of old techniques that increase assessment efficiency or that better interpret the data. No effort is made here to explain the mathematical or statistical background of these techniques; the reader needs to seek statistical understanding elsewhere.

Processing and Strategy Skills

Snow and Lohman (1993) in editors Norman Frederiksen, Robert Mislevy, and Isaac Bejar's *Test Theory for a New Generation of Text* (1993) identify stimulus encoding, feature comparison, rule induction, rule application, and response justification as examples of processing skills that can now be identified in ability test performance. Most of these processes are assessed through the multicomponent latent trait approach that can arrange the factors being assessed to provide a powerful means of gathering data relevant to how and in what sequence certain concepts are understood. Most statistical techniques, however, contain assumptions that are less easily met in the real world than in the statistical laboratories where these programs are devised. Music educators need to know their students and their subject well in ascertaining whether the statistical assumptions apply to their teaching situation. With reasonable course requirements or electives in graduate programs for teachers, a new frontier in music education is possible. Should this new interest occur, it will represent a major change in the profession compared to past lack of serious interest in assessment. Student variations in self-regulation with respect to speed, accuracy, and sequence are three of the assumptions of computer testing about which little data are available on tasks in music. Widespread use of computer testing in music must await such data. The computer programs make assumptions about the problem-solving strategy being used, a strategy not dependent upon skill but on how one processes information, how one learns from responding to other test items, and whether one recognizes the characteristics of the test items. The research of Ippel and Beem (1987) and Kyllonen, Lohman, and Woltz (1984) is based on a computer-administered test that systematically manipulates strategy choices and strategy shifts based on student response. At issue in most of these computer-generated tests is an understanding of why an individual has difficulty with a particular item, as that understanding must be programmed into the machine. If this is a problem for language arts teachers, as it is, it will be a greater problem for music. The item analysis currently available from music achievement tests is spotty, and little analysis exists as to the effect of preceding and follow-up questions.

In aural perception, simple intervals, timbres, and patterns often have high difficulty indices, due perhaps to student expectation or experience, factors that have not been systematically investigated for even one style or genre of music. Cognitive psychologists believe that cognitive analyses can lead to computerized item generation that is more valid than items written by humans. If this process becomes a reality, the concerted effort of both humans and computers will be required to devise tests that can explain (measure) the "Aha!" in musical understanding that escapes verbalization. A major advantage of the computer is that it can alter the assumption about the test taker's basic ability and adjust accordingly, where humans have to assume that a single ability continuum underlies the various tasks to be solved. The computer can also accommodate additional distractors or sources of variation as they are identified during the test administration. Test theory depends upon the degree of focus or concentration required by a specific item and also must account for learning and responses that become automatic during the test taking. Some individuals use multiple strategies to solve problems, thus requiring computer programs based upon fluid reasoning to respond to students who grasp quickly the conceptual basis for the test. Cognitive psychology is gaining a better understanding of how various individuals learn; music educators may find this attention to learning unprecedented, but if they cooperate with educational psychologists, throughout the required trial-and-error process, music education assessment can arrive at a position to take advantage of "the possible."

Lohman (1988) suggests that our understanding of spatial ability tests has been superficial and that spatial abilities also involve multiple strategies, some of which are not at all "spatial." Research with spatial ability testing is pertinent to music education when arguments are made that experiences with music improve students' spatial and temporal-spatial abilities. In other areas also, questions are being raised as better descriptions are created about what occurs as students learn to perceive, memorize, reason, and solve problems. These descriptions are especially relevant to the use of portfolios where convergent and discrimina-

tion validity of contrasting portfolio scores can be established by computers through use of a set of structural equations and LISREL.

Reasoning and Understanding

Such advances have allowed educators such as Ann L. Brown and John C. Campione (1986) to conduct research on student reasoning and on transfer that has led to accepted principles in the field of education. Their ideas on the self-regulatory functions of planning, monitoring one's own progress, questioning, checking, and correcting errors are based upon research that used student responses. The promotion of teaching for understanding through semantic networks, schemata, scripts, prototypes, images, and mental models is also based upon recent advances in assessment that have provided a view of the acquisition and structure of knowledge different from that derived using data from multiple-choice tests only. The use of elaboration, chunking, connecting, restructuring, and similar basic ideas in connectionism arises from analyses of achievement, mainly in mathematics and science but increasingly applied to other basic subjects. Whether these instructional ideas apply to music education will depend upon the application of cognitive psychology and its assessment techniques to priority issues in the music curriculum. Accepting these methodologies without such assessment research is unwarranted. Some information on these techniques can be gained from interviews and teach-back procedures that should provide data on chunk size and some strategies on restructuring and elaboration. These mental processes are what humans use to reason, recall, reflect, and solve problems. Thus music educators must be cautious in suggesting that current curricular practices are efficient in aiding students in these various thinking and understanding strategies. Previous learning is critical in the research conducted in test development in other subjects, and music educators have little experience in collecting substantive data about previous learning. Mislevy (1993) argues that standard test theory failed to consider just how people know what they know and do what they do and the ways in which they increase these capacities. His ideas are supported by Snow and Lohman (1993), from whom I quote at some length:

Cognitive psychology is now teaching us that to understand a particular individual's performance on a particular task, one must delve more deeply into its constituents— the configurations of knowledge, skill, understanding, belief, and attitude that underline particular responses. A richer, denser, more sensitive description is especially needed if tests are to be designed for diagnosis and classification in guiding instruction, rather than for summary selection and evaluation purposes only. This would seem to require test theories that use multivariate categorical as well as interval scale indicators and that apply to time series, not just to single-point assessments. The design of test items, the methods by which they are organized into tests, and the rules by which scores are assigned to responses must be guided by the purposes of testing. Modern theories of cognition and learning have described new, potentially useful constructs for measurement. One of the more important challenges for a new test theory and design, then, is to explore the measurement properties of these new scores. (p. 13)

Research on New Assessments

Computers.   Much of the research on new assessment procedures is based upon a general probability model and a Bayesian approach to estimating the parameters of the student and of the content to be assessed (Mislevy, Almond, Yan, & Steinberg, 2000). Shum's (1994) evidentiary reasoning derived from his Portal Project is a fundamental construct as investigators manage belief about a student's knowledge and skill (even that which is not observable) based upon what students say and can do. Content evidence is obtained in the context of a task that allows the computer to construct individualized tests, adding new tasks to each student's item pool and measuring different students with different items. The investigator builds the task model by describing the important features of a task (these must be known with certainty) along with the specifications for the work environment, the tools that the testee may use, the work products, stimulus materials, and any interactions between the testee and the task.

The model describes the mixture of tasks that go into an operational assessment, either a fixed or a dynamic task, and the model is built based upon probability consistent with knowledge about the underlying problem and the data collection process. The "unobservables" are obtained from responses to a given task from a large number of examinees. The test is continually updated, new items added, and the estimate of general proficiency changed by the Monte Carlo Markov Chain of estimation procedures. This technique has been applied to present tests that include the Graduate Record Examination and the ASVAB, in which the computer constructs an individual examination at the student's level. The ERGO computer program (Noetic Systems, 1991) provides probabilities for each student on as many as five skills. Multiple skill testing in one test is possible only when, in the initial test design, there is a coherent design for all of the skills.

At the heart of the development of computer-assisted assessment are the new psychometric models of learning where the purpose of assessment is not to establish the presence or absence of specific behaviors but to infer the nature of students' understandings of particular phenomena. There is little interest in the computer's ability to score isolated bits of knowledge; the goal is to develop programs that provide a model of understanding by individual students. The task is to design a set of questions that will expose different levels of understanding of a concept based on student response to several related questions, questions selected to reveal inconsistencies as well as consistencies in thinking. Computer-assisted assessments are not designed to replace current assessment measures that are appropriate to assess student learning of a body of factual material necessary in music and for which a well-designed multiple-choice format can reveal deep comprehension (Carroll, 1993).

Terminology and Concepts

Schemas.   Cognitive psychologists who conduct research in learning suggest that schemas are one way to reflect the nature of the domain, the instruction, and the learner's knowledge about that domain. Schemas, however, are poorly defined in the literature; they are really just a collection of information organized like a story with a theme and characters. Individuals, based on their own experiences, use different schemas to solve the same problems. Individuals differ not only in the depth of each schema but also in their ability to search for the best schemas to solve new problems. With complex problems, individuals link several extant schemas, thus requiring a healthy long-term memory to solve substantive issues. The linking of schemas reveals the common elements that everyone uses in problem solving and is the value of schema theory (Marshall, 1993). (In computerized testing, each item contributes to the estimate of the contents of the schema and/or to its connecting links.) The data that can be provided to assessors is the extent to which students have acquired the schemas taught for problem solving, not whether students can produce the correct answer. Chomsky (1968) differentiated between competence and performance, competence being the knowledge of language and performance being the ability to use language. This distinction is followed by those who employ research in learning and assessment. Assessors are interested in the schema constructs (strategies, knowledge structure, and related components) as an indicator of competence and an indicator of the individual differences that are the student's span of abstract or general reasoning.

Latent Trait.   Latent trait models are the psychometric standard for measuring ability, with the latent trait a mathematical model of the probability that an examinee passes a specific item, the Bayes probability mentioned earlier. The model is not based on the linear model of classical test theory but is sensitive to the nonlinear relationship of the probability of solving an item to the individual's actual ability. The relationship of item solving to actual ability (Rasch latent trait model) is an S-shaped curve in which the probability of .50 is reached when ability equals item difficulty. Verification of this model is often based on scores from the paper-folding spatial ability test that has become familiar to music educators as the dependent variable in the research of Shaw and Rauscher (1993). Test and item reliability are not based on the variance among student responses as is reliability in classical test theory but can be estimated through probability for each student.

Item Response Theory. This theory is loosely related to latent trait theory (although some would argue that it is philosophically at the other end of the continuum) in that it demonstrates the relationship of ability to performance in a nonlinear learning situation. The change in probability between any two abilities depends upon their relative location on the item response curve. An assumption is that there is more information when high-ability students do well on a difficult item and when low-ability students perform well on items appropriate for their ability. Pre- and posttests based on IRT must be designed to measure the same construct if gain scores are of interest; otherwise change score data are difficult to interpret. This change, however, is not measured on the same scale for individuals of different ability levels, thus providing a spurious negative relationship between change score and pretest score. Item response theory applies to dichotomously scored items although it probably can be used with more complicated responses; further research is needed. Despite accounting for individual differences, IRT assumes that there is a "characteristic" curve for each item that represents ability on that item. What IRT does best is assign a single, unidimensional continuum scale value to the examinee.

Behavioral Scaling. Behavioral scaling is a technique used to establish construct validity and is often not related to issues of generalizability or external validity. Scaling can be applied only to well-constructed tests, of adequate length and reliability. The assumption is that the task being measured is unidimensional and that a series of tasks of varying levels of difficulty can be constructed to measure this single construct. Reading skill, for example, is considered to be based on a single construct. Music educators Robert Miller (1979) and Lee Bartel (1992) separately investigated the potential of scaling, but their primary interest was in establishing the presence of constructs and not in developing classroom tests. There is inadequate research at present to indicate the extent to which this technique will be useful.

Another type of behavior scaling is used to establish anchor points on large-scale tests. The anchor points are verbal descriptions of a level of competence designed to be parametric descriptions that are both clear and objective.

(Anchor points for the test developer need not be describable to the public, but the test developer must have a thorough acquaintance with the characteristics of the task, scale, or domain, in order to report any results or to use the results in further test development.) Anchor points were used to describe results of the music portion of the 1997 NAEP, but the data used to establish these were not provided.

Summary

The use of computers in assessment holds considerable potential should music educators devote some of their resources to gaining more information about what learning is important, the extent of current student competency, and the importance of the situation. Knowing how to interpret error remains one of the difficulties in several of the strategies used in computer-adapted testing. The assessment strategies being developed rely on a relationship between instruction, learning, and testing. The research results in fields such as mathematics indicate that deep understanding of complex subject matter is not easily attained and seldom present in today's students. To attain any such goal will require the systemic change in education emphasized in educational literature. That change could be a narrowing of the curriculum to allow for the needed time, a greatly extended school day or year, or the development of more effective teaching strategies than are known at present. A greater integration of subject matter is also an option, but one that has been fraught with outcomes of misunderstanding, wrong information, and a lack of constructs for further learning. Concepts that appear to be related in the classroom seldom have the same strong relationships in the real world. The solution to this problem, some argue, is to enable students to recognize that the goals of instruction and ordinary experience are the same; others argue that the schools need to change what today passes for ordinary experience. One cannot assess complex ideas without stimuli that build a framework equal in complexity to that of the ideas involved; in essay assessments, for example, a detailed question would be necessary to elicit the extent of a student's understanding. Subjects and connections that appear to be logical on the surface often are not learned in the same way, and students may use different schemas to solve problems in different subjects. Such issues require considerable more research before the premise that it is easy to integrate music into the teaming efforts of middle school teachers can be accepted.

Portfolios

The idea of a portfolio to better capture evidence of student learning appears in almost all contemporary educational literature. Assessment professionals recommend multiple measures to reduce the error that exists in any assessment, including scorer error in arriving at a composite score for a portfolio. The advantage of a portfolio in determining student competence is that it can contain evidence from multiple indicators; the portfolio is not the assessment tool, but it *contains* the results of valid and reliable assessments and enough information about the student and instructional goals to allow for interpretation of these materials. The rise of the portfolio challenged the testing establishment, with the result that Educational Testing Service, CRESST, and other large organizations have devoted major resources during the past decade to improving the portfolio and to investigating how it might be used in their programs (Gitomer & Dusch, 1994; Jones & Chittenden, 1995). The initial efforts to employ portfolios as assessment tools in state assessment plans such as those in Vermont, Kentucky, and California were too ambitious; the users did not understand the difficulties of scoring a group of items that were far from homogenous. Portfolios suffer from low reliability and questionable standards-based validity.

The California Learning Assessment System (CLAS) was modeled after the most current constructivist ideas in education, subjected to intense scrutiny by the public, and eventually vetoed by the governor, but not until extensive research had been conducted. CLAS was to be involved in making high-stakes decisions, those decisions requiring not only several types of validity but respectable (high) reliability for the indicators upon which these decisions are based. Percentiles are commonly used by the state or the school district to report assessment data to the public, as being in the upper half of a class is not only understandable but a reasonable generalization. American business leaders like to know that *all* high school graduates are competent but still need to know which students would make the "best" employees. Individuals opposed to assessment have effectively used the lack of stability in percentile scores on these state and national tests to attack their use. The argument, based upon test reliability, is impressive, usually computed at the 50th percentile, which allows portrayal of the most severe cases. (Large numbers of students are grouped in the middle, which means that a small change in a score can make a rather large difference in a student's rank or percentile standing among the total group of students being compared.) There is always error in teacher judgments, in observation, in classroom tests, in contest ratings, and in performances (an error that is greater in qualitative assessments). The user of assessment data of any kind needs to know the amount of this error, but reducing error is seldom the primary consideration in qualitative assessment. Could a student who has made noticeable progress over the course of a year actually obtain a lower percentile rank in the second year? According to Rogosa (1999), if a test had a reliability of .8, the probability of this occurring is .229 (20% of the time). A test needs to have a reliability of .9 to reduce this error to .133 and .95 to further reduce the error to .053. (These figures should be retained by the reader to assist in interpreting research results where the author reports a "satisfactory" reliability of .71!) Is it difficult to improve the reliability of assessments? Yes. To increase the reliability from .90 to .95 requires doubling the length of the test.

Portfolio scoring of the CLAS (Webb & Schlackman, 2000) enabled scorers to determine general competence, but the results were not adequate to justify inferences about individual student performance (p. 66). Portfolio data did, however, allow teachers and students to learn how the quality of student work related to California's dimensions of learning (dimensions of learning are similar to standards). Scoring of portfolios does not allow for comparisons or for obtaining a ranking or percentile, as portfolios contain both differing items and items produced under differing conditions for each student. The CLAS portfolios were in many respects models. They were not limited to exhibitions but contained multiple-choice test scores, performance tasks, and on-demand questions that were curricular embedded. Curriculum-embedded tasks in portfolios must provide evidence of the critical concepts of the discipline, as embedded tasks most often relate to the objectives mandated or expected by the community and state. On-demand tasks in a portfolio are more likely to reflect the priorities of the teacher and the school system.

Reliability of scoring of major portfolio items is improved when a larger number of competence levels is used. The American Council on the Training of Foreign Languages (1989) (Aschbaker, 1999) established 10 levels: novice-low, novice-mid, novice-high; intermediate-low, intermediate-mid, and intermediate-high; advanced, advanced-plus, superior, and distinguished. Ten levels in music are desirable. Though the often-recommended 3 levels are inadequate, some states are recommending only a 2-level (pass-fail), which invites serious assessment problems that extend beyond reliability, affecting student morale and beliefs. It is not unusual to find portfolio research that employs 3 or 4 levels and the investigator reporting reliability based on agreement and agreement within 1 level. With 3 levels, it should be obvious that chance will be a major factor in establishing "agreement" within 1 level!

The portfolio is not a simplistic and straightforward method of documenting student learning; a portfolio is to help students develop concepts, theories, strategies, practices, and beliefs that are consistent with the ways of knowing, arguing, and exploring. In music, material in a portfolio needs to conform to practices in learning, knowing, criticizing, discriminating, and exploring. Portfolios add additional ways of knowing but are not intended to replace extant methods. It is expected that students (as well as teachers) will be able to see changes in their understanding of music through the systematic and progressive change in conceptual structures displayed by the projects in the portfolio. Projects, therefore, cannot be randomly selected. Each student approaches his or her portfolio having a theory of how he or she comes to understand, a theory based upon the crucial concepts learned in and out of school. The teacher's task is to identify this theory and move that student toward theories that represent "best practices" in music. If this is done, the portfolio will eventually demonstrate to the student (he or she will discover) that the projects in the portfolio actually portray one or more ways of knowing and standards and practices in the field.

The projects in a portfolio might include demonstrations of competence in practiced performance ability, the ability to sight-read, to improvise, to compose, to write a reflective essay, to discuss the contributions of Stravinsky, and more, depending upon the extent of the instructional use of various frameworks and standards. An adjustment has to be made for each task to account for individual differences, as even the best student is not likely to be "best" in meeting each of the objectives currently espoused for music education. Thus instability—or lack of reliability—results not only from changes in the rater but also from the difficulty of establishing clear standards for the variety of tasks. It is not unusual for a rating to be based upon the student's improvement and/or the student's competence in relationship to his or her past competence and hypothesized ability. This basis is valuable but affects reliability. (Reliability can of course be improved when the most trivial tasks find their way into the portfolio as raters agree more easily on a level of competence in trivia.)

The New Standards Project

The New Standards Project, a partnership of 19 states and six urban school districts, has developed methods of assessment that are intended to function not as an "external" test but as integral elements within the system, thus increasing validity and reliability. The project recognizes that time requirements obviate the need to integrate assessment. The project's model for assessing understanding is derived from the military, where assessment practices effectively determine individual competence on problem solving, understanding, and ability to think. The success of the military is due to the clarity of their instructional goals and the acceptance that *every* soldier given a map and a compass and dropped into the middle of nowhere must be able to determine not only location but also the direction to the nearest mess hall. If public education is serious about all students reaching high standards, those standards and the

projects that demonstrate knowledge and understanding of those standards must be equally clear. The New Standards Project found that teacher scoring of portfolios ranged from a reliability of .28 to .60, too low for most uses (Resnick, 1996). To raise the reliability, the project found it necessary to have multiple-choice or other on-demand items in the portfolio that provided evidence that the work in the portfolio was the student's own. Even with this stability, raising the reliability to a range of from .6 to .75 required constructing a clear course syllabus, setting the questions, describing the criteria for different grades, and establishing a grading sample. L. Resnick avers that a much more explicit theory of situated cognition is needed before performance assessment, the kind of assessment upon which portfolios are based, can progress (1996, p. 17).

Portfolio Validity

Student performance is sensitive to the assessment format (the context in which students are asked to perform, the type of task, and the conditions under which they assemble their portfolios). Portfolios, although authentic in one sense, differ from other authentic measures. For example, two-thirds of the students who were classified as capable on the basis of their portfolios were deemed not competent on the basis of a direct writing prompt, also an authentic measure. Observing students in the laboratory does not predict competent performance on a laboratory simulation. A number of researchers (Dunbar, Koretz, & Hoover [1991]; Linn, Burton, De Stefano, & Hansen [1995]; Shavelson, Baxter, & Gao [1993]; Shavelson, Baxter, & Pine [1991]; and Shavelson, Mayberry, Li, & Webb [1990]) have established that 15 to 19 tasks are needed in a portfolio for *each* objective if a portfolio is to serve as an assessment with a reliability of .80. The inclusion of one musical composition would reveal little about a student's musical understanding or about any of the reasons for asking the student to compose. In Vermont the average classroom teacher spent an additional 17 hours a month just managing the portfolios, leading 90% of the reporting principals to conclude that portfolios were helpful but probably too burdensome (p. 29).

Myford and Mislevy (1995) report that if AP Studio Art were viewed only as portfolio assessment, it would be nothing short of depressing (p. 13). What is learned from a portfolio in visual arts is an opportunity to assess not only skills and knowledge but also what students and judges value. The value component is more a social phenomenon than one in measurement (p. 13). The portfolio's greatest value is not in assessment but in improving learning, which, of course, is a major purpose of assessment when not used for accountability.

The Future

The lack of interest in assessment in music education may stem from music's low priority in the school, or, just as likely, it may be that the public is satisfied with the current status of music education. Another explanation is that the public is unconcerned about the music education *curriculum* and believes that any proposed outcomes will be positive but unimportant. The efforts of arts advocacy groups indicate that the public is uninformed about the music program and the student competencies it fosters. This lack of knowledge of outcomes is difficult to explain, as the music program is often highly visible in the community. The important outcomes may be the obvious ones. Advocates of music education programs seldom, if ever, suggest improving or changing the program; the effort is totally on rallying the public to *support* music education in the schools. This support apparently does not include allocating additional instructional time, reducing the student-teacher ratio, increasing the music knowledge/skill base of the classroom teacher, or encouraging school boards and school administrators to place a higher priority on a quality music program. Rather, support means providing instruments for students or contributing to the fund-raising efforts required to maintain the current program. The objectives of the advocates do not easily fit into any of the taxonomies.

Without external pressure to demonstrate what students should know and be able to do on accepted objectives, little internal change will occur. This status quo situation is both positive and negative. The positive side is that music education comes to the reform table without any of the negative reports and baggage that accompany the basic subjects. Music education has no history of misusing multiple-choice and true-false tests; the primary assessment has been "evaluation" by friendly audiences. These evaluations have not been used diagnostically, needs assessment has not been conducted, and assessment data have not been used to justify the requests for resources. Teachers have not "taught to the test," and there are no national norms or competence standards. Parents do not expect grades in music, and if grades are given their meaning is obscure. Instrumental music may report student competence through chair placements that are then listed on the concert program, but few would accept this indicator as a measure of success of the music program, only that of the individual student. Music education has few leaders who champion any role for assessment. Charles Leonhard wrote a seminal article on evaluation in *Basic Concepts of Music Education* (1958), a book that initiated major changes in music education, but his chapter was ignored and Leonhard is remembered for other significant contributions but not for this effort.

Basic Music and Performance Programs

Music education can profit from the current interest in assessment only if the profession realizes that there are at least two distinct programs in the schools—a basic program and a performance program. These are so distinct that both the instructional and the assessment concepts differ, often substantially. Additional programs or variations on the programs may exist in various school systems, but both the performance and the basic program have a legitimate claim on curriculum resources. The basic or required program is a cognitive program (Phillips, 1995) and relates most closely to the educational reform movement. A third program, one focused on "instrumental" or nonmusical objectives, is not discussed in this chapter, despite its potential importance. Instrumental objectives include development of skills for lifelong learning and leisure activities, such skills as cooperation, responsibility, prioritizing, and numerous other worthwhile outcomes.

Although the two established music programs differ in significant ways, they are mutually supportive. Basic music that includes the required music program provides competencies that enhance the performance program; performance in turn can enhance understanding of some of the goals of the basic program. Mediocrity occurs when the priorities of the two programs are not observed and too much "overlap" is attempted. A school system may wish to support only a performance program *or* a basic program, and where this situation exists the difficulty of achieving challenging goals will be great. It is not realistic to accept goals when the resources to accomplish these goals do not exist. Music is a large and wonderful field, too broad for even the professional to feel competent in performance, musicology, composition, and music in general education.

Assessment and Educational Reform

The thrust of this chapter has been on assessment strategies for basic music, for music programs that match some of the programs in other basic subjects. Currently there are marked philosophical differences between the cognitivists and the situativists (Greeno, Collins, & Resnick, 1996), whether educational experiences are to be structured according to what we know about learning from the world of psychology and educational psychology or all learning is situated in a particular location, a particular time, and the sociocultural background of students and teachers. Eventually there will likely be some compromise; these substantive differences need not currently concern the music educator. Systemic reform in education is emphasizing learning strategies and issues of transfer rather than performance. Doing well on a standardized test is a performance, and although external assessment of performance is accepted by most educators, the current gathering and use of assessment data is for its potential in improving the learning process. Students who believe the purpose of education is to enable them to perform tend to select easy tasks they can do well; students who believe that education is for learning accept setbacks when they recognize that they are developing strategies, skills, and knowledges that move them toward worthwhile objectives. Education for these individuals is analogous to running a confidence course: If the course is too easy, it fails to build any lasting confidence. Confidence courses involve problem solving: The individual forms hypotheses of the best route and the best order of tasks and draws upon his or her extant knowledge and skills. With a cognitivist orientation, students will want to sing individually as well as offer individual reflections on a number of classroom experiences. The older behavioristic orientation adhered to outdated theories of motivation that emphasized the negative consequences of failure rather than what is now believed about motivation. There will never be adequate instructional time for the expected content and character of assessment unless the teacher changes his or her instructional procedures to include recording on a regular basis each student's competence in accordance with standards *and* that individual student's improvement. Even when embedded in instruction, such an assessment process will seem formidable to the teacher who is pressed for instructional time. The reform movement advocates that assessment be individualized to the extent possible, to record how well each student is learning in relationship to his or her sociocultural background as well as his or her competency on grade-level standards. Although the most extreme cognitivists or situativists (Anderson, Reder, & Simon, 1996) are fearful of the standards movement, all recognize the philosophical importance of educating all students to high standards. Standards require the assessing of students, individually and collectively, on developmentally appropriate grade-level goals. The assessment, however, is not for accountability but to assist the teacher and student in identifying what is yet to be accomplished. Teachers currently control grade-level objectives in the basic music program and can drastically reduce their goals to a manageable level. State and district curricula merely suggest. Textbooks for basic music, school district music curriculum guides, and state and national frameworks are not appropriate sources for establishing content validity of future assessments, as their suggestions for content do not take into account the resources available.

The instructional and assessment strategies recommended for the basic subjects are applicable to a basic music program that is focused on understanding music listened to in and out of class. Understanding music would enable a graduate of the program to listen to music with heightened aural abilities and knowledge of what is occurring in the music, to attend concerts, to be discriminating, and to use music in his or her daily life. The emphasis on cognition and problem solving means that students learn to identify musical problems, talk about musical issues, argue about the qualities of music, establish criteria for excellence in musical performance and in musical works, and be open to all quality music and musical experiences. The questions included in the Marzano taxonomy suggest the knowledge and skill that will be needed. The unsolved question is one of transfer. The expectation is that an understanding of the principles of music composition and performance will be an enabler for transfer. The ideas of Vygotsky imply that only if these principles are derived from the situation and the interaction with the music, individually and collectively, will transfer to different music in different situations be achieved (Brown & Farrar, 1985). New teachers in all subjects must think hard about these educational ideas and strategies and how they apply to their subject matter content, as educators are making these teaching suggestions based on face validity; they make sense in light of what we know today and in light of past failures. (Without past assessment, we do not know what aspects of the basic music program have failed; the only evidence is from the performance program.)

The basic music program will have to use all types of measurement devices. Low-level knowledge is required in sequential programs before high-level knowledge and its concomitant understandings can be attained at a level that makes transfer possible. Multiple-choice, single-answer, and matching tests will be part of instruction; equally necessary will be assessment of singing and perceptual skills—on a regular basis and recorded. Contemporary philosophy rejects the idea that instruction ceases for assessment and that all students take the same test at the same time. Individualized assessment requires more time, but if the skill or knowledge is worth teaching, it is worth each student's attaining that competence. Matching pitch and singing an arpeggio in tune is a low-level but necessary ability in most music programs. This low-level skill, however, must make sense to the student, or he or she will not be actively involved in the learning. Performance programs often involve passive learning; students seldom object to a class where little thinking is required. They are told what and how to perform, what to practice for the next lesson, and how well the lesson should be performed—a luxurious escape from the arduousness of active learning. Passive learning is less likely to transfer, thus making understandable the lack of transfer in many performance programs. A performance program will profit from tracking—not tracking by race, gender, or socioeconomic status but by competence. When all students have an equal chance to study, practice, and learn, tracking does not discriminate; it is not elitist. Excellent performance programs exist in all types of schools, from Phillips Exeter to Eisenhower High School.

The basic program can emphasize instruction where the historical and cultural factors of the community not only influence learning but also are indicators of the student's initial knowledge and the skills that are needed to participate in a community of practice. These classrooms emphasize the socially negotiated meaning to experiences (Eisenhart, Finkel, & Marion, 1996). The instruction is characterized by not only open demonstrations of perceptual abilities but also discussions about music that allow the teacher to identify misunderstanding, skipped sequences, and lack of competencies that will interfere with future learning. In traditional "general" music classes students do not develop the needed skills or knowledges and there is no provision for remedial work, resulting in an American population of musical illiterates.

Revising and correcting the traditional general music program will result in students' becoming engaged in learning in fundamentally new ways. The model would be the music critic; that is, the focus would be on hearing and understanding music. It is this discipline, not the discipline of the high school chorus, that provides the content and ways of "knowing" desired for all students. To assume that all students can learn music requires a new way of thinking on the part of both students and teachers. A large number of students (and adults) reject learning in music on the basis of lack of ability because the model presented to them has been an incorrect model. Self-assessment of knowledge in the constructive classroom is not only possible but also necessary. Self- and teacher assessments need not meet the same standards as published tests when they are frequent and used primarily to improve. Shepherd, in her hypothetical vision of the future, suggests that it is *possible* for teachers thinking systematically over time to develop highly accurate assessments of student learning (2001). The italics in the original indicate that this will not be easy even for the teacher with a small classroom.

The music critic is the suggested model as the emphasis is on understanding relationships—to other performance, to other musics, and to other times. This type of learning seldom occurs in a performance program, as it requires time for listening, researching, comparing, contrasting, and, most of all, discussing the *important* features of the music. The broader range of assessment tools required will likely also require attention to long-term musical and factual knowledge. It will necessitate students' recognizing and singing melodies, motives, unifying rhythmic patterns, and more. If this sounds ambitious, it is, but these competencies are only a few that involve higher order thinking and are prerequisite to problem solving. Identifying an incorrect note is a trivial event in problem solving and leads to more trivial problem solving (Leper, Drake, &

O'Donnell-Johnson, 1997). With younger children more informal assessments will be needed, but these can be observation-based individual performances and responses and even the retelling of the stories in and of music.

Research by Camp (1992) indicates that students can articulate and apply critical criteria if given practice in doing so. This practice is necessary with portfolios, where the advantage is in analyzing past work. Portfolio scholars have found that it might be necessary to maintain two portfolios, instructional and performance, a near-impossibility in most music-teaching situations. Shepherd indicates that whether portfolios can be productively used for these two purposes is highly controversial even in basic subjects (2001). She indicates that the use of rubrics, which often accompany portfolios, is likely inappropriate in classrooms with young children. Rubrics are objectionable to others because of their resemblance to positivistic modes of assessment (Wile & Tierney, 1996). Other future assessment concerns center on the prescriptive nature of the scoring in using rubrics (Wolf & Reardon, 1996). A major need is research on rubric development. Their current use in teacher evaluation is unwarranted. Assessments should occur in the classroom as a normal part of instruction to take advantage of the social situation advocated by Vygotsky and to make assessment seem a part of learning. This description of assessment is not so different from current teacher efforts but demands new procedures and instruments. Assessments should not just judge competence as correct or incorrect, in-tune or out-of-tune, as might be expected in a performance program, but should also aid students in learning to distinguish quality of ideas, whether remarks are clear and accurate, whether previous knowledge is used in formulating a comment or reflection, and whether reference is made to standards. Assessment must also show the importance of *thinking* that occurs in reacting to musical experiences.

Assessment is ineffective whenever students do not have a clear understanding of the criteria by which their work will be assessed (Frederiksen & Collins, 1989). When required to become involved with self- and peer assessment, students become extremely interested in the criteria for excellence (Klenowski, 1995).

A Final Word

The suggestions for systemically changing education brought on by education's response to the reform movement are an idealization; research and experience are needed to determine their potential, including that for assessment. Teachers with successful music programs should not assume that these futuristic suggestions will automatically help their programs. Research has provided us with few cues, and those few are not based on current philosophies of education. Changing the culture of the music classroom to meet the new frameworks will change music education as it is currently practiced. Teachers cannot continue to randomly add and subtract experiences and objectives, as teaching for musical understanding requires focus on fewer objectives, fewer musical selections, and fewer types of music. The effort to develop assessment tools and dependent measures for research will occupy music educators for the next decade as not only the reliability and validity of even embedded measures need to be ascertained but also the requirements and substance of tools for program evaluation. Research in assessment needs to verify that NAEP has indeed established a working framework for the profession and to ascertain what are the alternatives. The teacher's rewards lie in positive feedback and the knowledge that one's efforts are worthwhile. More than a few of the ideas about the "mindful" school will require teachers to reflect on not only their own musical beliefs but also what they believe is possible for students to know and understand and what knowledge will be available to students on demand when performing, hearing, thinking about, and discussing music, in and out of school.

REFERENCES

Anderson, J. R., Reder, L. M., & Simon, H. A. (1996). Situated learning and education. *Educational Researcher, 25,* 5–11.

Anderson, L. W., & Krathwohl, D. (Eds.). (2001). *A taxonomy for learning, teaching, and assessing: A revision of Bloom's taxonomy of educational objectives.* New York: Longman.

Aschbacher, P. (1999). Developing indicators of classroom practice to monitor and support school reform. (CSE Tech. Rep. No. 513). Los Angeles: UCLA CRESST.

Bartel, L. (1992). The development of the cognitive-affective response test-music. *Psychomusicology, 11*(1), 15–26.

Biggs, J. B., & Collis, K. F. (1982). *Evaluating the quality of learning: The SOLO taxonomy.* New York: Academic Press.

Blocker, L., Greenwood, R., & Shellahamer, B. (1997). Teaching behaviors of middle school and high school band directors in the rehearsal setting. *Journal of Research in Music Education, 45*(3), 457–469.

Bloom, B. J. (Ed.). (1956). *Taxonomy of educational objectives: Book 1. Cognitive domain.* New York: Longman.

Brittin, R. V., & Sheldon, D. A. (1995). Comparing continuous versus static measurements in music listeners' preferences. *Journal of Research in Music Education, 43,* 36–45.

Brittin, R. (1996). Listeners' preference for music of other cultures: Comparing response modes. *Journal of Research in Music Education, 44*(4), 328–340.

Brittin, R., & Duke, R. (1997). Continuous versus summative evaluations of musical intensity: A comparison of two methods for measuring overall effect. *Journal of Research in Music Education, 45*(2), 245–258.

Broadfoot, P. (2000). Preface. In A. Filer (Ed.), *Assessment: Social practice and social product.* London: Routledge Falmer.

Brown, A. L., & Campione, J. C. (1986). Psychological theory and the study of learning disabilities. *American Psychologist, 41,* 1059–1068.

Brown, A. L., & Farrar, R. A. (1985). Diagnosing zones of proximal development. In J. Weartsch (Ed.), *Culture, communication and cognition: Vygotskian perspectives* (pp. 273–305). Cambridge: Cambridge University Press.

Brynes, S. R. (1997). Different age and mentally handicapped listeners' response to Western art selections. *Journal of Research in Music Education, 44,* 569–579.

Buttsworth, L., Fogarty, G., & Rorke, P. (1993). Predicting aural performance in a tertiary music training programme. *Psychology of Music, 21*(2), 114–126.

Camp, R. (1992). Portfolio reflections in middle and secondary school classrooms. In K. B. Yancey (Ed.), *Portfolios in the writing classroom* (pp. 61–79). Urbana, IL: National Council Teachers of English.

Cantu, N. (2000). *The use of tests when making high-stake decisions for students: A resource guide for educators and policy makers.* Washington, DC: U.S. Department of Education, Office of Civil Rights.

Carroll, J. B. (1993). *Human cognitive abilities.* New York: Cambridge University Press.

Chelimsky, E. (1992). Expanding evaluation capabilities in the General Accounting Office. In C. Wye & R. Sonnichsen (Eds.), *New directions for program evaluation: Vol. 5.* San Francisco: Jossey-Bass.

Chomsky, N. (1968). *Language and mind.* New York: Harcourt Brace Jovanovich.

Colwell, R. (1970). *The evaluation of music teaching and learning.* Englewood Cliffs, NJ: Prentice Hall.

Cronbach, L. (1995). Emerging roles of evaluation in science education reform. In R. O'Sullivan (Ed.), *New directions for program evaluation: Vol. 65* (pp. 19–29). San Francisco: Jossey-Bass.

Davis, A. P. (1998). Performance achievement and analysis of teaching during choral rehearsals, *Journal of Research in Music Education, 46*(1), 496–509.

DeNardo, G., & Kantorski, V. (1995). A continuous response assessment of children's music cognition. *Bulletin of the Council for Research in Music Education, 126,* 42–52.

DeNardo, G. F., & Kantorski, V. J. (1998). A comparison of listeners' musical cognition using a continuous response assessment. *Journal of Research in Music Education, 46*(2), 320–331.

Dunbar, S. B., Koretz, D. M., & Hoover, H. D. (1991). Quality control in the development and use of performance assessment. *Applied Measures in Education, 4,* 298–303.

Eisenhart, M., Finkel, E., & Marion, S. F. (1996). Creating the conditions for scientific literacy: A re-examination. *American Educational Research Journal, 33,* 261–295.

Ekholm, E. (2000) The effect of singing mode and seating arrangement on choral blend and overall choral sound. *Journal of Research in Music Education, 48*(2), 123–135.

Fetterman, D. (2001). *Foundations of empowerment evaluation.* Thousand Oaks, CA: Sage.

Flohr, J. (2000). *A contemporary rhythm skills assessment.* Champaign, IL: Electronic Courseware Systems.

Frederiksen, J. R., & Collins, A. (1989). A systems approach to educational testing. *Educational Researcher, 18,* 27–32.

Frederiksen, N., Mislevy, R., & Bejar, I. (Eds.). (1993). *Test theory for a new generation of tests.* Hillsdale, NJ: Erlbaum.

Fredrickson, W. (1994). Band musicians' performance and eye contact as influenced by loss of a visual and/or aural stimulus. *Journal of Research in Music Education, 42*(4), 306–317.

Fredrickson, W. (1995). A comparison of perceived musical tension and aesthetic response. *Psychology of Music, 23*(1), 81–87.

Fredrickson, W. (1997). Elementary, middle, and high school student perceptions of tension in music. *Journal of Research in Music Education, 45*(4), 626–635.

Fredrickson, W. (1999). Effect of musical performance on perception of tension in Gustav Holt's First Suite in E-flat. *Journal of Research in Music Education, 47*(1), 44–52.

Fremer, J. (2000, December). A message from your president. *Newsletter,* National Council on Measurement in Education.

Froelich, H. (1995). Measurement dependability in the systematic observation of music instruction: A review, some questions, and possibilities for a (new?) approach. *Psychomusicology, 14,* 182–196.

Froseth, J., & Weaver, M. (1996). *Music teacher self-assessment.* Chicago: GIA.

Gee, C. (1994). Artists in the classrooms: The impact and consequences of the National Endowment for the Arts' artist resident program on K–12 arts education, parts 1 and 2. *Arts Education Policy Review, 95*(3), 14–29, (4), 8–31.

Geringer, J. (1995). Continuous loudness judgments of dynamics in recorded music excerpts. *Journal of Research in Music Education, 43*(1), 22–35.

Gitomer, D., & Duschl, R. (1995). *Moving toward a portfolio culture in science education* (Document 94-07). Princeton, NJ: Center for Performance Assessment.

Goolsby, T. W. (1996). Time use in instrumental rehearsals: A comparison of experienced, novice, and student teachers. *Journal of Research in Music Education, 44*(4), 286–303.

Gordon, E. (1998). *Harmonic improvisation readiness record and rhythm improvisation readiness record.* Chicago: GIA.

Greeno, J. G., Collins, A. M., & Resnick, L. B. (1996). Cognition and learning. In D. C. Berliner & R. C. Calfee (Eds.), *Handbook of educational psychology* (pp. 15–46). New York: Macmillan.

Gregory, D. (1994). Analysis of listening preferences of high school and college musicians. *Journal of Research in Music Education, 42,* 331–342.

Hair, H. (1997). Divergent research in children's musical development, *Psychomusicology, 16,* 26–39.

Hardy, D. (1995). *The construction and validation of an original sight-playing test for elementary piano students.* Unpublished doctoral dissertation, University of Oklahoma, Norman.

Harland, J., Kinder, K., Lord, P., Stoff, A., Schagen, I., & Haynes, J. (with Cusworth, L., White, R., & Paola, R.).

(2000). *Arts education in secondary schools: Effects and effectiveness.* Slough, UK: National Foundation for Education Research,

Harrow, A. (1972). *A taxonomy of the psychomotor domain.* New York: Longman.

Hauenstein, A. D. (1998). *A conceptual framework for educational objectives: A holistic approach to traditional taxonomies.* Lanham, MD: University Press of America.

Hickey, M. (1999, January). Assessment rubrics for music composition. *Music Educators Journal, 85*(4), 26–33.

House, E. R. (1994). Integrating the quantitative and qualitative. In C. Reichard & S. Rallis (Eds.), *New directions for program evaluation: Vol. 61. The qualitative–quantitative debate: New perspectives* (pp. 13–22). San Francisco: Jossey-Bass.

House, E. R. (1995a). Principled evaluation: A critique of the AEA guiding principles. In W. Shadish, D. Newman, M. A. Scheirer, & C. Wye (Eds.), *New directions for program evaluation: Vol. 66. Guiding principles for evaluators* (27–34). San Francisco: Jossey-Bass.

House, E. R. (1995b). Putting things together coherently: Logic and justice. In D. Fournier (Ed.), *New directions for program evaluation: Vol. 68. Reasoning in evaluation: Inferential links and leaps* (33–48). San Francisco: Jossey-Bass.

Ippel, M. J., & Beem, L. A. (1987). A theory of antagonistic strategies. In E. DeCorte, H. Lodewijks, R. Parmentier, & P. Span (Eds.), *Learning and instruction: European research in an international context* (Vol. 1, pp. 111–121). Oxford: Pergamon Press.

Johnson, C. (1996). Musicians' and nonmusicians' assessment of perceived rubato in musical performance. *Journal of Research in Music Education, 44*(1), 84–96.

Jones, J., & Chittenden, E. (1995). *Teachers' perceptions of rating an early literacy portfolio* (Document 95-01). Princeton, NJ: Center for Performance Assessment.

Kivy, P. (1984). *Sound and semblance: Reflections on musical representation.* Princeton, NJ: Princeton University Press.

Klenowski, V. (1995). Student self-evaluation process in student-centered teaching and learning contexts of Australia and England. *Assessment in Education, 2,* 145–163.

Krathwohl, D., Bloom, B., & Masia, B. (1964). *Taxonomy of educational objectives: The classification of educational objectives handbook II: Affective domain.* New York: Longman.

Kyllonen, P. C., Lohman, D. F., & Woltz, D. J. (1984). Componential modeling of alternative strategies for performing spatial tasks. *Journal of Educational Psychology, 76,* 1325–1345.

Leonhard, C. (1958). Evaluation in music education. In N. Henry (Ed.), *Basic concepts of music education* [57th Yearbook of the National Society for the Study of Education], part 1. Chicago: University of Chicago Press.

Leper, M. R., Drake, M. F., & O'Donnell-Johnson, T. (1997). Scaffolding techniques of expert human tutors. In K. Hogan & M. Pressley (Eds.), *Scaffolding student learning: Instructional approaches and issues* (pp. 108–144). Cambridge: Brookline Books.

Linn, R. L., Burton, E., DeStefano, L., & Hanson, M. (1995). Generalizability of new standards project 1993 pilot study tasks in mathematics (CSE Tech. Rep. 392). Los Angeles: UCLA CRESST.

Lohman, D. F. (1988). Spatial abilities as traits, processes, and knowledge. In R. J. Sternberg (Ed.), *Advances in the psychology of human intelligence* (Vol. 4, pp. 181–248). Hillsdale, NJ: Erlbaum.

Lychner, J. (1998). An empirical study concerning terminology relating to aesthetic response to music. *Journal of Research in Music Education, 46*(2), 303–319.

Mabry, L. (1999, May). Writing to the rubric: Lingering effects of traditional standardized testing on direct writing assessment. *Phi Delta Kappan, 80*(9), 673–679.

Madsen, C. (1997a). Emotional response to music. *Psychomusicology, 16,* 59–67.

Madsen, C. (1997b). Focus of attention and aesthetic response. *Journal of Research in Music Education, 45*(1), 80–89.

Madsen, C. (1998). Emotion versus tension in Haydn's Symphony no. 104 as measured by the two-dimensional continuous response digital interface. *Journal of Research in Music Education, 46*(4), 546–554.

Madsen, C., Brittin, R., & Capprella-Sheldon, D. (1993). An empirical investigation of the aesthetic response to music. *Journal of Research in Music Education, 41,* 57–69.

Madsen, C., Geringer, J., & Fredrickson, W. (1997). Focus of attention to musical elements in Haydn's Symphony # 104. *Bulletin of the Council for Research in Music Education, 133,* 57–63.

Marshall, S. (1993). Assessing schema knowledge. In N. Frederiksen, R. Mislevy, & I. Bejar (Eds.), *Test theory for a new generation of tests* (pp. 155–180). Hillsdale, NJ: Erlbaum.

Marzano, R. J. (2001). *Designing a new taxonomy of educational objectives.* Thousand Oaks, CA: Corwin.

Masear, C. (1999). *The development and field test of a model for evaluating elementary string programs.* Unpublished doctoral dissertation, Teachers College, Columbia University, New York City.

McCurry, M. (1998). *Hand-chime performance as a means of meeting selected standards in the national standards of music education.* Unpublished doctoral dissertation, University of Georgia, Athens.

McPherson, G. (1995). The assessment of musical performance: Development and validation of five new measures. *Psychology of Music, 23*(2), 142–161.

Mikle, H. (1999). *The development of an individual sight reading inventory.* Unpublished doctoral dissertation, University of Minnesota, Minneapolis.

Miller, R. (1979). *An analysis of musical perception through multidimensional scaling.* Unpublished doctoral dissertation, University of Illinois at Urbana-Champaign.

Mislevy, R. (1993). Introduction. In N. Fredrickson, R. Mislevy, & I. Bejar (Eds.), *Test theory for a new generation of tests* (pp. ix–xii). Hillsdale, NJ: Erlbaum.

Mislevy, R., Almond, R., Yan, D., & Steinberg, L. (2000) *Bayes Nets in educational assessment: Where do the numbers come from?* Los Angeles: Center for the Study of Evaluation.

Myford, C., & Mislevy, R. (1995). Monitoring and improving a portfolio assessment system (Document 94-05). Princeton, NJ: Center for Performance Assessment.

Newkirk, T. (2000). A manual for rubrics. *Education Week, 20*(2), 41.

Norris, C. (1998). *The relationship of tonal memory tests of recognition and tonal memory tests of reproduction.* Unpublished doctoral dissertation, University of Illinois at Urbana-Champaign.

Osgood, C., Suci, G., & Tannenbaum, P. (1957). *The measurement of meaning.* Urbana: University of Illinois Press.

Persky, H., Sandene, B. & Askew, J. (1998). *The NAEP 1997 arts report card.* Washington, DC: U.S. Department of Education.

Phillips, D. C. (1995). The good, the bad, and the ugly: The many faces of constructivism. *Educational Researcher, 24,* 5–12.

Piaget, J. (1971). *Genetic epistemology* (E. Duckworth, Trans.). New York: Norton.

Rauscher, F., Shaw, G., & Ky, K. (1993). Music and spatial task performance. *Nature, 365,* 611.

Reichardt, C., & Rallis, S. (1994). The relationship between qualitative and quantitative traditions. In C. Reichardt & S. Rallis (Eds.), *New directions for program evaluation: Vol. 61. The qualitative-quantitative debate: New perspectives* (5–12). San Francisco: Jossey-Bass.

Reimer, B. (1996). *Musical roles and musical minds: Beyond the theory of multiple intelligences.* Evanston, IL: Northwestern University Press.

Rentz, E. (1992). Musicians' and nonmusicians' aural perception of orchestral instrument families. *Journal of Research in Music Education, 40*(3), 185–192.

Resnick, L. (1996). Performance puzzles: Issues in measuring capabilities and certifying accomplishments (CSE Tech. Rep. 415). Los Angeles: UCLA CRESST.

Richardson, E. (1992). The value of evaluation in evaluation in the federal government: Changes, trends, and opportunities. In C. Wye & R. Sonnichsen (Eds.), *New directions for program evaluation: Vol. 55* (pp. 15–20). San Francisco: Jossey-Bass.

Rogosa, D. (1999). *Accuracy of Year 1, Year 2 comparisons using individual percentile rank scores: Classical test theory calculations.* Los Angeles: UCLA CRESST.

Rumelhart, D. E., & Norman, D. A. (1981). Accretion, tuning and restructuring: Three modes of learning. In J. W. Colton & R. Kaltzky (Eds.), *Semantic factors in cognition* (pp. 37–53). Hillsdale, NJ: Erlbaum.

Scott, S. (2000). An application of the SOLO taxonomy to classify the strategies used by grade 5 students to solve selected music-reading tasks. *Contributions to Music Education, 27*(2), 37–57.

Scriven, M. (1993). *New directions for program evaluation: Vol. 58. Hard won lessons in program evaluation.* San Francisco: Jossey-Bass.

Scriven, M. (1997). Truth and objectivity in evaluation. In E. Chelimsky & W. Shadish, *Evaluation for the 21st century: A handbook* (pp. 477–500). Thousand Oaks, CA: Sage.

Shadish, W., & Cook, T. (2000). As cited by M. Patton in

Overview: Language matters, in R. Hopson (Ed.), *New directions in evaluation: Vol. 86. How and why language matters* (pp. 5–16). San Francisco: Jossey-Bass

Shadish, W., Cook, T., & Leviton, L. (1991). *Foundations of program evaluation: Theories of practice*. Newbury Park, CA: Sage.

Shavelson, R. J., Baxter, G. P., & Gao, X. (1993). Sampling variability of performance assessments. *Journal of Educational Measurement, 30*, 215–232.

Shavelson, R. J., Baxter, G. P., & Pine, J. (1991). Performance assessment in science. *Applied Measurement in Education, 4*, 347–362.

Shavelson, R. J., Mayberry, P. W., Li, W.-C., & Webb, N. M. (1990). Generalizability of job performance measurements: Marine Corps riflemen. *Military Psychology, 2*, 129–144.

Sheldon, D. (1994). Effects of tempo, musical experience, and listening modes on tempo modulation perception. *Journal of Research in Music Education, 42*(2), 190–202.

Sheldon, D., & Gregory, D. (1997). Perception of tempo modulation by listeners of different levels of educational experience. *Journal of Research in Music Education, 45*(3), 367–379.

Shepherd, L. (2001). The role of classroom assessment in teaching and learning. In V. Richardson (Ed.), *Handbook of research on teaching* (4th ed.). Washington, DC: American Educational Research Association.

Shum, D. A. (1994). *The evidential foundational of probabilistic reasoning*. New York: Wiley.

Siebenaler, D. J. (1997). Analysis of teacher–student interactions in the piano lessons of adults and children. *Journal of Research in Music Education, 45*(1), 6–20.

Simpson, E. (1966). *The classification of educational objectives, psychomotor domain*. (OE 5-85-104). Washington, DC: U.S. Department of Health, Education and Welfare.

Skadsem, J. A. (1997). Effect of conductor verbalization, dynamic markings, conductor gesture, and choir dynamic level on singers' dynamic responses. *Journal of Research in Music Education, 45*(4), 509–520.

Smith, M. L. (1994). Qualitative plus/versus quantitative: The last word. In C. Reichardt & S. Rallis (Eds.), *New directions for program evaluation: Vol. 61. Approaches in evaluation studies* (pp. 37–44). San Francisco: Jossey-Bass.

Smith, N. (1992). Aspects of investigative inquiry. In N. Smith (Ed.), *New directions for program evaluation: Vol. 56. Varities of investigative evaluation* (pp. 3–14). San Francisco: Jossey-Bass.

Smith, N. (1995). The influence of societal games on the methodology of evaluative inquiry. In D. Fournier (Ed.), *New directions for program evaluation: Vol. 68. Reasoning in evaluation: Inferential links and leaps* (pp. 5–14). San Francisco: Jossey-Bass.

Snow, R. E., & Lohman, D. F. (1993). Cognitive psychology, new test design, and new test theory: An introduction. In N. Frederiksen, R. Mislevy & I. Bejar (Eds.), *Test theory for a new generation of tests* (pp. 37–44). Hillsdale, NJ: Erlbaum.

Stake, R. E. (1991). Responsive evaluation and qualitative methods. In W. R. Shadish, T. D. Cook, & L. C. Leviton (Eds.), *Foundations of program evaluation: Theories of practice* (270–314). Newbury Park, CA: Sage.

Stake, R. E. (1997). Advocacy in evaluation: A necessary evil. In E. Chelimsky & W. R. Skadish (Eds.), *Evaluation for the 21st century* (pp. 470–478). London: Sage.

Stake, R. E. (2000). A modest commitment to the promotion of democracy. In K. E. Ryan & L. DeStefano, *New directions for program evaluation: Vol. 85. Evaluation as a democratic process: Promoting inclusion, dialogue, and deliberation* (pp. 97–106). San Francisco: Jossey-Bass.

Vispoel, W. (1992).Improving the measurement of tonal memory with computerized adaptive tests. *Psychomusicology, 11*(1), 27–43.

Webb, N., & Schlackman, J. (2000). *The dependability and interchangeability of assessment methods in science* (CSE Tech. Rep. 515). Los Angeles: UCLA CRESST.

Wei, H. (1995). *Development of a melodic achievement test for fourth grades taught by a specific music learning methodology*. Unpublished doctoral dissertation, University of Illinois, Urbana.

Weiss, C. H. (1998). *Evaluation* (2nd ed.). Upper Saddle River, NJ: Prentice Hall.

Wile, J. M., & Tierney, R. J. (1996). Tensions in assessment: The battle over portfolios, curriculum, and control. In R. Calfee & P. Perfumo (Eds.), *Writing portfolios in the classroom: Policy and practice, promise, and peril* (pp. 203–215). Mahwah, NJ: Erlbaum.

Wolf, D. P., & Reardon, S. F. (1996). Access to excellence through new forms of student assessment. In J. B. Baron & D. P. Wolf (Eds.), *Performance-based student assessment: Challenges and possibilities* (pp. 1–31). Chicago: University of Chicago Press.

Yarbrough, C., & Henley, P. (1999). The effect of observation focus on evaluations of choral rehearsal excerpts. *Journal of Research in Music Education, 47*(4), 308–318.

Contemporary Issues in Qualitative Research and Music Education

DAVID J. FLINDERS

CAROL P. RICHARDSON

In the first edition of the *Handbook of Research on Music Teaching and Learning,* Donald Casey (1992) used the broad term "descriptive research" to include common forms of qualitative inquiry. In the introduction to his chapter, Casey said: "Despite some speculation to the contrary, descriptive research should by no means be conceived as any less vigorous, worthwhile, or useful than other research modes" (p. 115). Although battles over legitimacy continue, qualitative researchers today face less "speculation to the contrary." Funding agencies, leading journals, and book publishers give qualitative studies an increasingly high profile. Professional organizations, such as the American Educational Research Association, have institutionalized qualitative approaches as a viable alternative to large-sample, statistical studies, and research universities now provide expanded training in qualitative methods. Together with these opportunities, the number of qualitative researchers has multiplied. Their ranks have grown so quickly over the past decade that it is difficult to find a more prominent trend in the field of educational research. Who and what have contributed to this trend are among the questions raised in this chapter.

We will argue that the growth of qualitative research is more than simply a matter of numbers. Instead, recent developments revolve around large issues, as researchers rethink the questions of what counts as a rigorous, worthwhile, and useful study. To take one example, research methodologists have increasingly questioned the value of applying quantitative criteria to qualitative work. We no longer ask qualitative researchers for hypotheses stated specifically to test causal relationships. We no longer ask for independent and dependent variables, let alone that these variables be operationalized in a way that allows for objective measurement. Qualitative researchers do begin their work with what Malinowski (1922/1984) called "foreshadowed problems" (p. 9). They are also interested in the perceived antecedents of what they observe. Today, however, the distinctions between hypotheses and orienting questions, or between causes and perceived antecedents, are recognized more widely and regarded as more important than they once were.

This growing differentiation among genres of empirical research has been motivated partly by a proliferation of traditions and approaches within qualitative inquiry itself. Earlier qualitative work drew primarily on its parent disciplines in the social sciences. Thus, a qualitative study was often viewed as falling within the same family as its more quantitative siblings. Today qualitative researchers draw on a broader gene pool, so to speak. In addition to the social sciences, they look to the arts, the humanities, and a range of professional studies. As a result, many of the recent approaches represent more distant kin, relatives who live by different customs and different cultures. Having more voices around the table has presented both challenges and opportunities. In this chapter we also consider these challenges and opportunities.

One challenge worth mentioning is that researchers who now turn to qualitative inquiry face what may seem like a bewildering array of possibilities for how to conceptualize, carry out, and write up a qualitative study. These possibilities open the door to new research questions, thereby serving a critical function, but they also heighten the need for researchers to explicitly situate their work within the traditions of which it is a part. With more options, less can be taken for granted. One cannot assume, for example, that a qualitative study participates in ethnographic traditions simply because it employs qualitative methods (Eisner, 1998; Wolcott, 1982). It would be a categorical mistake to fault educational criticism, school portraiture, biographic case studies, narrative inquiry, and other non-ethnographic approaches because they do not adhere to the canons set down by the likes of Malinowski, Mead, or even Geertz.

For this reason, in this chapter we seek to acknowledge the variety of qualitative approaches now used in education. Overall, the chapter is divided into two sections. The first section surveys qualitative trends, approaches, and continuing dilemmas within the field of educational research at large. As such, the focus of our survey is necessarily broad. On all counts, however, it should not be viewed as comprehensive because the relevant literature is now so large that we have left out far more than we have included. In deciding what to include, our aim has been to highlight some of the major landmarks of qualitative inquiry as a field of methodological study. Where details are provided, we have done so largely to illustrate broader categories or characteristics of qualitative work. We have also limited our review to the period of the 1960s to the present. Although the disciplinary roots and contributions to qualitative research go back much further, qualitative work has made its most significant gains in the field of education only over the past 4 decades.

The second section of the chapter examines trends and issues in qualitative research that are specific to music education. Here the literature is less extensive, but qualitative research on music teaching and learning is often similar to as well as distinctive from the broader contours of educational research. In this context, both similarities and differences deserve close attention.

The Rise of Qualitative Research and Its Aftermath

The rise of qualitative research in education defies simple explanation. Its exact causes and extent are especially difficult to pin down for at least two reasons. First, we are referring not to a single trend but to multiple changes in how researchers think about and carry out their work. Patterns in the overall development of qualitative research run parallel and intersect at various points, forming a confluence of permutations around similar but not identical themes. Like the field itself, its development has been anything but monolithic.

Second, qualitative research has a range of different meanings. Even the name *qualitative* has been debated (Eisner, 1998, p. 5; Lincoln & Guba, 1985, p. 7). A few of its potential synonyms, for example, include *naturalistic, descriptive, interpretive, case study,* and *field-based re-*

search. We will use the term *qualitative* because it is currently the most common and inclusive way in which researchers describe this broad style, category, and means of inquiry. Deciding on a label, however, only begs the larger question: What is qualitative research? For our purposes, we define qualitative research as work that illustrates at least some of the following characteristics. First, qualitative studies are a systematic form of empirical inquiry that usually includes some type of fieldwork. Artifacts such as textbooks and curriculum materials may be the focus of study, but qualitative work is typically field based, so that researchers may attend to the context in which events unfold. Second, once in the field, qualitative researchers are expected to do more than mechanically record their observations. To put this another way, their ability to see and hear is regarded as an achievement rather than a task, and knowledge is viewed as something constructed rather than as something given, found, or solely existing independently of the researchers. Third, qualitative studies usually assume an interpretive focus. Researchers may seek to understand the meanings of educational experiences from the participants' perspective (the so-called emic view), with respect to theory (the etic view), or both. The point, however, is that qualitative research is designed to examine *meaning* as a social, psychological, or political phenomenon. Fourth, data analysis strategies in qualitative research are typically thematic and sometimes emergent throughout the course of a study. Fifth, qualitative researchers usually work with small samples of voluntary participants (see also Bogdan & Biklen, 1998, pp. 4–7; Eisner, 1998, pp. 27–41).

These five characteristics are typical but not strict criteria for doing qualitative research. Some qualitative researchers work with large-sample data sets, some collect data solely at their office computers via the internet (which is fieldwork of a different sort), and some researchers, those who do observational studies, do not work directly with participants at all. Our point is not to limit the definition of qualitative research by laying claim to a specific set of theories, techniques, or beliefs. Rather, as Wolcott (1992) writes,

> to claim competence in qualitative research is, at most, to claim general familiarity with what is currently being done, coupled perhaps, with experience in one or two particular facets (e.g., to "be good at" collecting and interpreting life histories, or to "be" a symbolic interactionist). (p. 4)

This lack of precise definitions and clear criteria is sometimes viewed as problematic, but it does not seem to have prevented qualitative research from gaining increased acceptance over the past four decades.

The 1960s: Germination

Our review begins with the 1960s, a decade that represents not so much growth per se as rather the germination of renewed interest in qualitative work. At that time, educational research remained largely in the embrace of what Cronbach and Suppes (1969, p. 45) called "the heyday of empiricism" and especially its legacy of quantification. The broader foundations of this legacy stretch back directly through Edward L. Thorndike and his aspirations for a "complete science of psychology." Such a science, Thorndike (1910) wrote, "would tell the cause of every change in human nature, would tell the result which every educational force . . . would have" (p. 6). Thorndike's analogies were with physics and chemistry, suggesting that psychological and educational research should strive toward similar aims. As already implied, the aims he specified were those of prediction and control.

Today his view is often regarded as naive, if not utopian in an ignoble sense. Forty years ago, however, most educational researchers still looked to experimental science and its underlying epistemology of logical positivism as the model for their work. Qualitative and interpretive studies were carried out, but these studies generally went unnoticed even when researchers dressed them up to appear more "scientific" than they actually were. Denzin and Lincoln (1994, p. 8) refer to this period as "the golden age of rigorous qualitative analysis," citing Becker, Geer, Hughes and Strauss's (1961) study of medical education, *Boys in White,* as a "canonical" text of the period. In part, such studies reflect an effort to align qualitative research with the type of conventional criteria outlined in Campbell and Stanley's popular 1963 monograph on experimental and quasi-experimental research designs. Qualitative studies also looked to minor but well-established traditions in the sociology of education (e.g., Waller's classic 1932 study *Sociology of Teaching*) and to the case study work of the Chicago School sociologists (Bogdan & Biklin, 1998, pp. 8–11).

Anthropological studies of education represent what was perhaps the only other home for qualitative work in the 1960s. In particular, George Spindler edited two volumes, *Education and Anthropology* (1955) and *Education and Culture* (1963), that helped provide the foundations for the ethnography of schooling, which would soon become a productive category of qualitative research. Looking back on the 1963 volume in a later work, Spindler and Spindler (1992) commented: "The fact that the commitment to direct observation is more apparent in the papers that deal with educational process in non-Western societies than those at home is an indication that anthropologists had only begun their work in our own society" (p. 57). Here the Spindlers were noting the beginnings of domestic anthropology, another trend that would also further op-

portunities for qualitative researchers in education. Nevertheless, ties with traditional anthropology in the 1960s remained important for establishing the legitimacy of qualitative research as a form of discipline-based inquiry.

Other sources (e.g., Vidich & Lyman, 1994) have reviewed the history of qualitative research in fields such as sociology and anthropology. In education, most of the early qualitative studies were conducted by researchers whose primary identifications were with their parent disciplines rather than with the field of education itself. Philip Jackson's classic study *Life in Classrooms* (1968) is in some ways an exception that proves the rule. Its significance was the rarity of an educational researcher spending a year observing classes in an actual school. Jackson's work also overlapped quantitative and qualitative traditions, but if nothing else his style suggested broader possibilities for educational research. As Eisner (1998) writes: "What resulted from Jackson's observations was an insightful, artistically crafted book remembered more for its metaphors and insight than for the nods Jackson gave to the quantitative data he presented in its second half" (p. 13).

The decade of the 1960s was not known for producing a wealth of exemplar qualitative studies in education, although as we have already noted, sociological and anthropological field-based research continued to build on earlier traditions. Probably more influential in educational circles were books outside the field suggesting alternative perspectives on the structure and processes of research at large. Two such books foreshadowed future debates. The first was Thomas Kuhn's book *The Structure of Scientific Revolutions* (1962). Kuhn's historical perspective on science popularized the notion that researchers conceptualize topics of study and carry out their work within broad theoretical frameworks represented by the paradigm of a field. Kuhn's work brought two assumptions into question: the logical progression of science and, because a priori paradigms help determine what count as data, the objectivity of science in deciding questions of fact (see also Donmoyer, 1990, pp. 179–181; Phillips, 1990, pp. 31–34). A second book was Barney Glaser and Anselm Strauss's *Discovery of Grounded Theory.* Glaser and Strauss's perspective emphasized the mutual interaction between theory and data. Although largely a technical approach, grounded theory served to broaden the conventional assumptions that the primary aims of research are restricted to theory testing or theory verification (see also Creswell, 1998). Instead, qualitative researchers could view their work as a means of generating theory through repeated observations and emergent themes.

The 1970s: Growth

Qualitative developments in education signaled both continuity and change during the 1970s. Continuation of discipline-based studies not only held steady but also embraced a wider range of research. In educational anthropology, the term *ethnography* found its way into the field, and the ethnography of schooling increasingly focused on individual cases (Spindler & Spindler, 1992, pp. 57–58). Moreover, these cases were closer to home than previous studies had been. Domestic ethnographies of this decade are illustrated by Harry Wolcott's book *The Man in the Principal's Office* (1973) and Alan Peshkin's *Growing Up American* (1978). Although Peshkin's title looks back to the work of Mead, his reference predates (as does his book eschew) the 1960s tendency to drape qualitative studies in the names and games of experimental science.

A more general break from this tendency is also found in Clifford Geertz's book *The Interpretation of Cultures* (1973). This widely read book is remembered for popularizing Gilbert Ryle's term "thick description." For Geertz, the point of thick description was not to produce an objective record of culture but to make sense of local setting through the process of writing. When confronted with a puzzling experience, ethnographers write, and writing was seen as a matter of interpretation rather than the discovery of scientific laws. Geertz's emphasis on thick description as a means to understand "local knowledge" (Geertz, 1983) served to further distinguish the aims of qualitative inquiry. Interpretation, in this respect, provided a point on which qualitative researchers could begin defining their own rules rather than trying to play by the rules of someone else's game.

Seeking alternatives to the language of experimental science, qualitative researchers found support and guidance at other fronts as well. Hermeneutic philosophers, for example, were in the midst of epistemological debates that questioned whether knowledge is somehow waiting to be discovered, independent of the discovery and its discoverers, or contingent on the history and context in which it is produced. In particular, qualitative researchers were drawn to the work of Jurgen Habermas (1971, 1975) and Hans-Georg Gadamer (1975), who to different degrees argued for the contingency of knowledge (Smith, 1993). Their arguments again lent increasing support to the interpretive dimensions of inquiry. "Hermeneutics has a practical bent," Noddings (1995) later wrote. "It tries to make sense out of history and contemporary contexts without tying either to a rigid theoretical foundation" (p. 71).

Qualitative research in education also received help from a closer and often unrecognized source; that is, quantitative researchers who were beginning to abandon Thorndike's aspirations for a "complete science" of education. Some of these researchers, once hard-nosed positivists, came to align themselves with constructivist views of knowledge. Lee Cronbach is the most prominent example in this category. In his 1974 address to the American Psychological Association, Cronbach (1975, p. 123) acknowl-

edged that the complexity and changeability of culture prevented the social sciences from accumulating the type of generalizations found in the natural sciences. Cronbach's stature as a psychometrician—who he was—no doubt put tremendous weight behind his concerns. He was not, however, the only leading figure to rethink his earlier beliefs with respect to quantitative and qualitative forms of research. In 1963, Donald Campbell and Julian Stanley described case studies as the least defensible design for social research. By the end of the 1970s, however, Campbell (1979, p. 52) had nearly reversed his position, arguing that when qualitative studies contradict quantitative results, "the quantitative results should be regarded as suspect until the reasons for the discrepancy are well understood" (quoted in Scholfield, 1990, p. 206).

These developments gave qualitative researchers the opportunity to promote their work as a distinctive genre of educational inquiry, and subsequent lines of scholarship have pursued this goal. At the close of the 1970s, however, some researchers had begun another trend by proposing approaches that departed not only from large-sample, quantitative research but also from the leading forms of discipline-based qualitative inquiry. Elliot Eisner, in *The Educational Imagination* (1979), proposed one of the first alternatives to conventional ethnographic and case study research. Two chapters in this book outline "educational criticism and connoisseurship," which Eisner describes as a qualitative form of educational inquiry and evaluation that "takes its lead from the work that critics have done in literature, theater, film, music and the visual arts" (p. 190). Drawing on Dewey's (1934) aesthetic philosophy, as well as the work of Susanne Langer (1957) and Rudolf Arnheim (1969), Eisner argued that the arts could powerfully inform the work of educators and researchers alike.

The 1980s: New Ventures

With the beginning of the 1980s, other writers looked to the arts and humanities as a basis for conceptualizing educational research. Sarah Lawrence Lightfoot's work exemplifies this trend. Like many other qualitative researchers of her generation, Lightfoot was originally trained in the conventions of disciplined social science. Her contributions, however, departed from these traditions as she sought to develop a form of case study research known as "school portraiture." Her book *The Good High School* (1983) includes both a methodological discussion of this approach and portraits of two urban, two suburban, and two elite high schools. Others in secondary education turned to both formal and informal qualitative fieldwork to inform books such as Theodore Sizer's *Horace's Compromise* (1984) and Arthur Powell, Eleanor Farrar, and David Cohen's *The Shopping Mall High School* (1985). Unlike Lightfoot, these authors did not set out specific approaches. However, they did use qualitative methods in novel ways. Sizer used composite descriptions, for example, and Powell, Farrar, and Cohen enlisted metaphors to extend the theoretical significance of their work. An even more decided departure from social science is found in the work of Madeleine Grumet (1980). Grumet combined phenomenological and autobiographical methods from literary traditions to use as models for studying curriculum, teaching, and teacher education.

While qualitative researchers were emphasizing the continuities between systematic inquiry and other fields, broader critiques of quantitative research were emphasizing the discontinuities between the rigors of science and its relevance for practice. In 1983, Donald Schön's book *The Reflective Practitioner* directly challenged the assumed relationship between scientific knowledge and "applied" fields ranging from medicine to music. Widely recognized in education, Schön's argument was that the products of science, such as generalizations based on statistical probabilities, neither readily transfer to professional practice nor find fertile ground in the conditions under which professionals work. Such generalizations address central tendencies and broad principles of how aspects of the social or physical word operate under controlled or ideal conditions. Practitioners, however, are concerned with individual cases under conditions, to use Schön's words, of "complexity, uncertainty, instability, uniqueness, and value-conflict" (1983, p. 39).

Similar concerns were also being raised by an increasing number of feminist scholars in the 1980s. Like Schön, these writers were concerned with the neglect of anomalies and the "detachment" of science as an epistemological ideal that lifts knowledge above the interests, desires, and histories of those who seek it. Evelyn Fox Keller's biography of Barbara McClintock, *A Feeling for the Organism* (1983), served as an example of how a researcher's attachment to the subject of her research could enhance rather than detract from science. In education, Belenky, Clinchy, Goldberger, and Tarule's *Women's Way of Knowing* (1986) reported the results of interviews with women college students and former college students. These researchers focused on their participants' conceptions of teaching, curriculum, and knowledge. The themes developed from their data again challenged traditional notions of objectivity and universal truth by suggesting that such notions often hid or disparaged the experience of women.

Feminist scholars who sought to redefine subjectivity were joined by others, including some anthropologists and educational ethnographers. Alan Peshkin (1982, 1988, 2000), for example, began a series of articles on the roles of subjectivity in qualitative research. Although he initially regarded his own subjectivity as an "affliction," Peshkin came to argue that researchers cannot and should not exorcise it from the processes of research. Instead, subjectiv-

ity should be pursued as a way for researchers to better understand their own accounts of research (see also Rosaldo, 1989).

What we are describing is a confluence of trends that served a dual purpose: to distinguish qualitative work as a separate genre of inquiry and to challenge the leading assumptions of conventional, quantitative research. Neither of these trends went unchallenged. On the contrary, debates in the 1980s were rife between the proponents of quantitative and qualitative research, and the more researchers began to view qualitative inquiry as a legitimate alternative, the more intense the debates became. The conflict was often played out in leading journals. In 1983, for example, a classic exchange between Denis Phillips and Elliot Eisner appeared in the *Educational Researcher*. Phillips's article, entitled "After the Wake: Postpositivistic Educational Thought," cautioned researchers against prematurely assuming the demise of what Phillips correctly predicted would be the continuing dominance of a more modest but by no means vanquished positivist tradition. Eisner (1983) responded in the same issue, arguing for pluralism in both our conceptions of knowledge and the means by which it is obtained.

The qualitative versus quantitative debates were increasingly fueled by researchers on both sides who viewed the two traditions as resting on incommensurable epistemologies. On the qualitative side, Yvonna Lincoln and Egon Guba (1985, 1989) exemplify leading researchers who defined the assumptions of qualitative research as a rejection of, or at least in direct opposition to, the foundations of quantitative work. Their widely cited book *Naturalistic Inquiry* (1985) drew loosely on Kuhn's perspective in framing the debate as a case of conflicting paradigms. The assumptions of what Lincoln and Guba labeled the *positivist paradigm* included the following: (1) Reality viewed as independent; (2) research aims defined as developing "nomothetic," cause-and-effect generalizations; and (3) the use of procedural objectivity as the criterion for validity. They characterized the *naturalistic paradigm* as focusing on multiple realities constructed by the researcher, the development of "ideographic" knowledge, and the value-laden nature of inquiry (pp. 37–38). In later work, Guba and Lincoln (1989) renamed the naturalistic perspective the *constructivist paradigm*. They also became increasingly insistent that qualitative researchers give up the search for concepts and criteria that would mirror quantitative research.

Not all researchers, however, accepted the incommensurability of the two perspectives. Some argued that quantitative traditions offered valuable standards or, at least, applicable criteria to inform qualitative studies. In their sourcebook *Qualitative Data Analysis* (1984), for example, Matthew Miles and Michael Huberman sought methodological sophistication over epistemological dualism.

Their work represented the strategy of making qualitative research more rigorous in the conventional sense by adapting some of the logic and design techniques of quantitative research. Other researchers found it readily possible to blend qualitative and quantitative approaches within the same study (e.g., Shuy, 1986). Miles and Huberman's work focused largely on issues of design and method, as did other books published during this period, including Bogdan and Biklen's *Qualitative Research in Education* (1982), Jaeger's *Complementary Methods for Research in Education* (1988), and Van Maane's *Tales of the Field* (1988).

Methods per se, however, were not at the center of this decade's debate. Rather, the arguments focused on epistemological questions regarding the validity of qualitative research and thus its legitimacy as a whole. The persistence of such basic concerns were reflected in a small conference on qualitative research hosted by the Graduate School of Education at Stanford University in 1988. The conference brought together such diverse scholars as Denis Phillips, Matthew Miles, Michael Apple, Yvonna Lincoln, Egon Guba, Henry Wolcott, Howard Becker, Madeleine Grumet, and Philip Jackson. Their conference papers were later published in *Qualitative Inquiry in Education: The Continuing Debate* (1990), a book edited by the conference organizers, Elliot Eisner and Alan Peshkin. Both the conference and book organized the study of qualitative inquiry around five topics: subjectivity and objectivity, validity, generalizability, ethics, and the uses of qualitative research. Although these topics encompassed a broad range of issues, epistemological questions remained the center of gravity and the main points of contention. For many qualitative researchers, the field was characterized by what Eisner and Peshkin's book title had suggested, a series of continuing debates.

Yet, regardless of unresolved tensions, developments in the 1980s anticipated future growth in qualitative research on two counts. First, researchers continued to emphasize issues and methods specific to qualitative research. Reflecting this trend, the first issue of the *International Journal of Qualitative Studies in Education* was published in 1986. Second, qualitative research had gained a modest but strong foothold in mainstream educational research. This trend represented integration, so to speak, rather than separately building the field from within an already established circle of researchers. The third edition of the *Handbook of Research on Teaching*, for example, included new chapters on both qualitative methods (Erickson, 1986) and the "cultures of teaching" (Feiman-Nemser & Floden, 1986). Earlier editions of the handbook had defined research on teaching almost exclusively in terms of a quantitative framework (Gage, 1963). Qualitative approaches also made their way into the field of program evaluation research, which, like research on teaching, had initially been established as the sole province of quantitative mea-

surement. That orientation changed with writers such as Michael Patton (1980) and Robert Stake (1986), both of whom saw qualitative methods as a means of increasing the relevance and impact of evaluation results. In short, qualitative research was being advanced on two scenes: both in publications devoted specifically to qualitative inquiry and side-by-side with quantitative studies across areas of specialization.

The 1990s: New Challenges

Developments continued on both of these venues throughout the 1990s. The number of publications devoted specifically to qualitative approaches and methods grew so quickly that efforts to survey the field became major undertakings. *The Handbook of Qualitative Research* (Denzin & Lincoln, 1994), for example, revealed a scope and body of scholarship that most would have considered presumptuous a mere 10 years earlier.

The integration of qualitative approaches into mainstream research progressed as well. By the 1990s, classic, multiple-edition textbooks on educational research were including one or more chapters on qualitative methods alongside their standard chapters on quasi-experimental and survey research design. Illustrating this trend, the sixth edition of Meredith Gall, Walter Borg, and Joyce Gall's introductory text *Educational Research* (1996) included two new chapters, one addressing case study methods and the other focusing on qualitative orientations. The latter chapter, entitled "Qualitative Research Traditions," represents an ambitious attempt to map what had by then become a broad terrain. The chapter identifies 17 separate traditions classified into three groups based on the type of phenomena each tradition investigates. In the first group, "Investigation of Lived Experience," the authors included traditions such as cognitive psychology, life history, and phenomenology. In the second group, "Investigation of Society and Culture," they included traditions such as cultural studies, ethnography, and symbolic interactionism. In the third group, "Investigation of Language and Communication," they included traditions such as hermeneutics and semiotics.

The Gall, Borg, and Gall survey was one of the most inclusive attempts to organize the qualitative work being done in the 1990s (see Creswell, 1998; Wolcott, 1992). Space was found for traditions that overlap with quantitative research, as in the case of cognitive psychology. However, such inclusions are useful in now recognizing the past contributions that leading psychologists made to qualitative studies. Jerome Bruner's work, for example, strongly supported interpretive inquiry. In *Acts of Meaning* (1990), Bruner argued that "to insist upon explanation in terms of *causes* simply bars us from trying to understand how human beings interpret their worlds and how *we* interpret *their* acts of interpretation" (p. xiii, emphasis in original). Overall, figures such as Bruner, the new inclusiveness of textbooks, and a growing list of publications all signaled the ongoing expansion of qualitative research.

Methodological work in the 1990s continued to draw on philosophical traditions as well, especially hermeneutics and phenomenology. Yet scholars in this group expressed their alliance to these traditions in ways that were significantly different from those followed by their predecessors. The more contemporary scholars were increasingly explicit in aligning methods with epistemological assumptions and less apologetic about emphasizing the postmodern elements of their work. Max Van Manen's *Researching Lived Experience* (1990), for example, proposed a "hermeneutic phenomenological approach to human science research." The approach not only drew on interpretive traditions but attempted to integrate research and writing as a means to illuminate the researcher's stance within the context of his or her own study. Steinar Kvale (1996), to cite another example, integrated similar philosophical assumptions with interview methods to reconceptualize data as meanings coconstructed between researcher and participant.

The postmodern in research both extended and broke with Continental philosophy by reasserting the partiality of all knowledge and the view that objectivity is in itself a form of bias. This view also came to emphasize multiple identities based on gender, race, class, and ethnicity. These identities implied multiple epistemologies as well (Donmoyer, 1996), raising challenges that we will return to in the next section. The postmodern also called attention to the constitutive functions of language (i.e., as we speak language, it speaks us), and this view more broadly came to be known as the "interpretive turn" in social research. Perhaps most significant, the partiality of knowledge meant that its production in both research and education was also an expression of power (Bowers & Flinders, 1990, pp. 157–191; Clough, 1992, p. 8).

Although these perspectives were not new, postmodernism gave critiques of all research a hard political edge. As Howard Becker (1993) wrote, "Attacks on qualitative research used to come exclusively from the methodological right, from the proponents of positivism and statistical and experimental rigor. But now the attack comes from the cultural studies left as well" (p. 218). To the extent that qualitative work had been accepted into educational research, its advocates found themselves in a new role, that of centrist. The irony of this position came from qualitative researchers soon finding themselves criticized for reasons similar to the ones they had recently been using against quantitative research (for a recent example, see English, 2000).

Qualitative researchers responded to their postmodern critics in a variety of ways. First, many researchers welcomed more focus on the sociology of knowledge and the politics of research, even if it meant shifting attention away from other issues. Those who had participated earlier in the "paradigm wars" were already accustomed to seeing definitions of knowledge as expressions of power. Elliot Eisner, best known as an advocate for epistemological pluralism, had long argued that established methods of inquiry represented the interest and investment of those who used them. In the introduction to *The Enlightened Eye* (1991), Eisner wrote: "Which particular forms of representation become acceptable in the educational research community is as much a political matter as an epistemological one" (p. 8). At least on this count, qualitative researchers and their postmodern critics were not entirely at odds.

Second, qualitative researchers responded by renewing their efforts to reflexively place themselves within their work. Petra Munro (1993, p. 164) describes research self-reflexivity as a means of "establishing collaborative and nonexploitive research relationships" that avoid an objectification of research participants. Munro and others (e.g., Glesne, 1999, pp. 102–105) turned to feminist scholarship to inform the complexities of what "nonexploitive research relations" should mean in the context of qualitative fieldwork and reporting. This scholarship, especially the work of Nel Noddings (1999), cast researcher-participant relations in ethical as well as political terms. On the ethical side, qualitative researchers struggled with notions of friendship, intimacy, and rapport. Interest in such issues represented a shift away from using the two great ethical systems of philosophy—utilitarianism and Kantian ethics—as the only source from which to draw moral guidance (Flinders, 1992). The shift to relational ethics, or what Noddings (1992) referred to as an "ethic of care," complemented conventional approaches in a powerful way. Rather than locate moral reasoning largely within an individual agent or actor, as had utilitarian and Kantian principles, an ethic of care emphasizes relationships and intersubjective perspectives. Among other implications, this view meant that researchers needed to negotiate much of their work with their participants.

An emphasis on relational approach is also reflected in action research, a third trend that was and continues to be influenced by postmodern ideas. Action research is a broad label for several forms of inquiry, most but not all of which employ qualitative methods. While action research developed earlier, renewed interest in the 1990s was characterized by a responsiveness to the local problems of research participants and a commitment to collaboration. Some forms (such as political action and emancipatory action research) focused specifically on problems related to the oppression of socially, economically, or educationally marginalized groups. Ernest Stringer (1993, 1996), for example, developed a form of action research from his work with Aboriginal groups in West Australia. Stringer called his approach "socially responsive educational research," grounding it in the work of scholars such as Paulo Freire (1970). The approach was characteristic of action research in several ways. First, it took a problem-solving orientation by focusing the outcomes of inquiry on plans, policies, or program services. Second, the methods of the approach were described in a nontechnical language, widely accessible to lay participants. Third, the approach placed particular emphasis on the words and stories of participants themselves throughout the planning, methods, analysis, and reporting of research.

As postmodernism challenged researchers to think broadly, more established trends in qualitative research continued as well. We noted earlier, for example, the ongoing popularity in traditional forms of ethnography. The 1990s were also a decade in which increasing numbers of qualitative researchers used personal computers to help them with tasks such as recording and sorting data (see Gahan & Hannibal, 1998; Weitzman & Miles, 1995). Across this range of developments, however, our overview has emphasized the recent proliferation of qualitative approaches and the rise of postmodern perspectives. These two developments are of special interest because they have set the stage for many of the field's contemporary and continuing dilemmas. We identify three such dilemmas here and suggest some of the challenges they currently pose for the theory and practice of research.

Continuing Dilemmas

The first dilemma stems from epistemological pluralism in general and specifically as it relates to categories such as race, class, gender, and ethnicity. If cultural experience and identities within these broad categories imply different epistemologies, what Noddings (1995, pp. 192–194) calls "standpoint" epistemologies, then researchers (and readers of research) within each group are in a privileged position to conduct and evaluate that research. This argument can lead to a number of tensions, one of which is in deciding who is appropriate to judge the usefulness and rigor of different types of research. To draw an analogy from schools of thought in psychology, for example, one could question whether a Skinnerian behaviorist is the appropriate person to evaluate a study based on psychoanalytic theories. From the perspective of standpoint epistemologies, a similar question could be raised about cultural groups. In either case, however, within-group variations are often large. As a result, standpoint epistemologies could be defined with ever-increasing specificity, leading to an infinite regress (Donmoyer, in press).

Another tension posed by standpoint epistemologies is that such a view of knowledge, as already noted, implies a privileged position for researchers within a given group. Pressing the point further, one could argue that only

women researchers should study gender oppression, that only black researchers should study the lived experience of black participants, and so forth. Such balkanization, however, would contradict the postmodern call for research to include multiple voices and perspectives, a prospect that defeats the purpose of having different standpoints in the first place (Noddings, 1995, p. 184). To avoid these tensions, researchers can view different standpoints as in some ways compatible. Yet this view only raises another question: Compatible on what basis? Because postmodernism itself offers little guidance on exactly this point, the potential fragmentation of epistemological perspectives remains a contemporary challenge.

A second dilemma stems from a contemporary skepticism of all epistemological claims. In some ways, postmodernism can be viewed as an antiepistemology in its rejection of Descartes' aloof knower, free choice, and the notion of an autonomous subject. This rejection has brought into focus the historical and situated inevitability of all research. As Noddings (1995, p. 75) points out, however, some feminists are concerned that philosophers are declaring the "death of the subject" at the very time that women and other marginalized groups are finally gaining recognition in areas that value autonomous achievement. Beyond the frustration of feeling like the rules have been changed in the middle of the game, the challenge for qualitative researchers is in reconciling the partiality of all knowledge with the trend toward conceptualizing research specifically as a means of empowerment.

A third dilemma stems from the increasing number of qualitative researchers who look to the arts and humanities rather than the social sciences as models for their work. Eisner (1997, 1999), for example, has recently argued that because science can be viewed as a subcategory of inquiry, we should not demand that all qualitative research in education be scientific. Responding to Eisner, Mayer (2000) objected to this view on the grounds that to admit nonscientific methods would "diminish the reputation of our field" (p. 38). One response to concerns over the field's reputation would be to demonstrate that nonscientific forms of inquiry can be just as rigorous and useful on the basis of other criteria. The challenge of identifying such criteria is in its wide disparity, compared with what researchers usually have come to expect, from forms of systematic inquiry. Ambiguity in the arts, for example, functions in critical ways to convey meanings that cannot be stated literally. Ambiguity keeps a work of art open to interpretation, which allows for and promotes meaningful engagement. If we admit ambiguity into research, however, by what criteria would it be assessed? Does it make sense to speak of "rigorous" ambiguity or of a rigorously ambiguous study?

Another area in which criteria may be difficult to pin down involves the persuasive functions of language. As qualitative researchers turn to more literary uses of meta-phor, narrative forms, and poetic transcriptions of data, skillful writing might readily subvert as well as enhance the aims of research. In discussing the "rhetoric of in-quiry," Henry St. Maurice (1993, pp. 202–204) argues that all types of educational research, both quantitative and qualitative, employ rhetorical forms and thus privilege those who know how to use the rules of the discourse to their advantage. The politics of this issue have a long his-tory with respect to artistic traditions. It was Plato, after all, who banished poets (even Homer) from his utopian republic because of their ability to incite emotions and thereby persuade the unsuspecting. For contemporary qualitative researchers, however, appropriate use of rep-resentational forms may be most pressing as an ethical rather than political concern. As such, researchers find scant guidance in conventional research ethics such as in-formed consent, avoidance of harm, and confidentiality. Qualitative researchers who have addressed stylistic issues (see, for example, Wolcott, 1990a, 1990b), imply the role of a different ethic, one that emphasizes craft, balance, fair-ness, and attention to detail. Working out criteria in these areas, nevertheless, remains a largely unfinished task.

Qualitative Research and Music Education

The remaining sections of this chapter will focus on qual-itative research in music education by highlighting the ways that the major issues surrounding qualitative research in education have played out in music education research. We will first address the context in which qualitative meth-odology came to be considered a viable research tool for studying music teaching and learning and offer an analysis of the critical issues that have impacted the quality of the qualitative research genre in music education and its cur-rent position within the discipline. Second, we will present a range of exemplary music education research studies that used a wide variety of qualitative methodologies. In con-clusion we will propose promising points of departure for future research in music education using qualitative meth-odology.

Issues in Context

The description of the development of qualitative research in education during the decades from 1960 through 1990 presented earlier in this chapter has, not surprisingly, par-allels with the important features of the development of qualitative research as a viable methodology for inquiry in music education. Greatly influenced by research trends of the time and dominated by the need to achieve mainstream stature, music education researchers of the late 1950s and 1960s engaged in studies that produced quantifiable out-

comes exemplified in the work of experimental psycholo-gists. In addition to these were curriculum studies (projects in which a year's worth of teaching content was organized into a dissertation-length document) and status studies (typically, an uncritical look at the music program of a particular school district and academic unit, focused not on learning outcomes or teacher satisfaction but on aspects such as number of participants and budget). (See Colwell [1967] for a more detailed description of this era.) During this period, while education researchers such as Philip Jackson went into classrooms as ethnographers, music ed-ucation researchers such as Ed Gordon and Richard Col-well developed psychometric tests to help practitioners quantify students' musical aptitude and achievement. With the invention of these measures, music education research entered the heyday of quasi-experimental, experimental, and descriptive studies designed to use the new psycho-metric measures of musical aptitude and achievement to quantify effects on dependent variables. Emboldened by Gordon and Colwell, many novice researchers were en-couraged by their doctoral advisors to develop their own purpose-built "measures" of whatever construct they wished to study, often without any specialized coursework or expertise in measurement and evaluation. Such tests and checklists were often the sole source of data in the disser-tation study, yet the measures themselves typically were unproven as valid or reliable measures of the construct un-der investigation. The tendency to look to psychometrics as the answer to many of the discipline's questions and to encourage novices to dabble in test construction during this era brought music education research under what Shir-ley Brice Heath has called "the punishing influence of psy-chology" (Heath, 1999, p. 204). She continues: "During the 1970s, the discipline of psychology, with its attendant concepts of controls, variables, and quantifiable indicators, increasingly dominated estimations of sound research."

The problem with this limited focus was that the typical doctoral dissertation project sampled too few students and offered treatments that were either not well designed and controlled or not administered over a period of time long enough to reflect measurable changes in students' skills or achievement. Alan Schoenfeld (1999) characterized the re-sults of this approach this way: "I do not think it overly harsh to say that the wholesale and inappropriate adoption of statistical methods into small-scale studies was, in large measure, a triumph of scientism over common sense" (p. 181). He continued: "There are few findings of any lasting significance emerging from such statistics-dominated small-scale work in education over more than the quarter-century from the 1950s and 1960s through the 1970s" (p. 182).

Music education research has always been a hybrid field, its practitioners relying on such widely flung disci-plines as education, psychology, sociology, anthropology, and even ethnomusicology for both methods of inquiry and organizing constructs, attempting to adapt and apply these methods to the study of music teaching and learning. The appropriation by music education researchers of the emerging qualitative methodology during the 1980s and 1990s followed the pattern of the earlier appropriation of the quantitative/experimental canon: Add the new topic (qualitative methodology) to the extant research course syllabus and then rely on crosscampus departments or schools (education, sociology, "ed psych") to give doctoral students further expertise in "the real thing." The underlying assumptions behind this approach, which continue to guide doctoral programs in the current century, are that the music education doctoral student can successfully adapt the "new" research method to the discipline of music education and that the same student, when transformed into a novice music education researcher upon achieving candidacy, can derive deep and meaningful insights from data gleaned through any of the multitude of qualitative methodologies mastered in a single three-hour survey course. The insertion of "music education" where "education" appears in the following quotation summarizes succinctly the result of predicating practice on this pair of faulty assumptions.

> Researchers in education who call their ad hoc attempts to make sense of dialogue "discourse analysis," are not only bad scholars: they are giving education a bad name. The same could be said for those who make cavalier use of "clinical interviews," "protocol analysis," and so on. (Schoenfeld, 1999, p. 180)

The current generation of senior faculty who train music education researchers were themselves trained during the heyday of positivism and may have never expanded their own research expertise beyond its confines nor have any reason or interest in doing so. It is no surprise, then, that the language used in major refereed research publications in music education still bears the trappings of the positivist paradigm exclusively: hypothesis, variables, and objective measurement have not been replaced by the "orienting questions" and "perceived antecedents for what's observed" described earlier in this chapter. Eisner's assertion (1997) that "which particular forms of representation become acceptable in the education research community is as much a political matter as an epistemological one" (p. 8) certainly applies to the way the leadership of the music education research community has regarded qualitative studies in our discipline. One might be tempted to think that the paradigm wars are over, at least in the greater education research community, for qualitative studies and their frameworks have assumed a position of equal prominence alongside the more positivist research methods

(as evidenced by a cursory read through the program of the annual meeting of the American Educational Research Association). However, the fallout from this particular war appears to be not unlike the aftermath of the Civil War in this country, with hostilities still being played out, however politely, more than 100 years later. Lagemann describes the current political climate thus: "Quantitative types challenge qualitative types, and the reverse; discipline-based scholars question the rigor of studies undertaken by education-based scholars, and education-based scholars query the relevance of studies done by their discipline-based colleagues" (Lagemann, 1999, p. 8). Such partisan wranglings are not absent from the music education research community, either. Qualitative research and its trappings have yet to be fully embraced. For example, the directives to editorial boards of the major refereed journals look much the same today as they did in 1967, using the language and criteria of the positivist paradigm to evaluate manuscripts for publication. When the manuscript is "qualitative," the reviewer might not find the requisite problem statement and research questions on first glance, or ever. There may be no apparent conclusions or implications but plenty of prose. The way qualitative researchers use language to create their research reports can be problematic, both for themselves and the editorial board members who are unschooled in the genre.

For many of those trained in the positivist era, the terminology of qualitative research can be a forbidding foreign country, requiring a new lexicon. Evidence of exactly how different and extensive this new research language is from the old can be found in Thomas Schwandt's 1997 book *Qualitative Inquiry: A Dictionary of Terms*. This important volume was conceived as "an inviting overview of critical terms in the discourses of qualitative inquiry" (p. ix). The 215 terms, ranging from "action research" to "Weltanschuung," are presented in short annotations that offer both the philosophical orientation and methodological explanation. Though not exhaustive, this text demystifies the qualitative research language in an intellectually inviting way that the current generation of doctoral advisors and their students might find enlightening.

The use of the term "qualitative research" as it has come to be used in the music education context is one of the critical issues that needs to be addressed here. In their very fine chapter on qualitative research methodology in the first *Handbook of Research on Music Teaching and Learning*, Bresler and Stake (1992) defined qualitative research as a

> general term to refer to several research strategies that share certain characteristics: (1) noninterventionist observation in natural settings; (2) emphasis on interpretation of both emic issues (those of the participants) and etic is-

sues (those of the writer); (3) highly contextual description of people and events; and (4) validation of information through triangulation. (p. 76)

They elaborate further, listing seven additional characteristics of qualitative research that refine their definition considerably: holistic, empirical, descriptive, interpretive, empathetic, formulated from the bottom up (grounded theory), and validated (p. 79). The composite definition is illustrative of the specific meanings the term carries in education research. However, the term's meaning within the music education research discipline is much broader. For many reasons, including lack of familiarity on the part of music education researchers, less distinction has been made when applying the term, and the operant definition has come to be "research that relies on some form of verbal data rather than numerical data," often but not always coupled with "research based on observation of a music classroom setting (field work)." This imprecision resulted from the confusion proliferated, in part, by thesis advisors challenged to keep abreast of methodological developments in qualitative inquiry. Hence, when applying Bresler and Stake's definition to qualitative music education studies that were undertaken in the last 10 years, many would be more appropriately labeled "descriptive." This is not a criticism of the discipline but rather a sign of the era in which we work: one where a proliferation of new knowledge, new research methods, and new forms of representation make the task of preparing new generations of researchers daunting. Schoenfeld (1999) describes our era this way: "There is no canon, there are no core methods, this is not a time of normal science, and there are myriad models of mentoring [young researchers], even among those especially talented in it" (p. 167).

Schoenfeld goes on to argue that the single most important research skill we can instill in the new generation of researchers is the ability to find and frame important problems to solve: problems that are more than just "interesting" because they go after the deeper meanings behind phenomena. A concomitant skill we would argue for is the ability to write in a voice that frees the reader to find the meaning of the qualitative research report. Laurel Richardson (1994) asks: "How do we put ourselves in our own texts, and with what consequences? How do we nurture our own individuality and at the same time lay claim to 'knowing' something? These are both philosophically and practically difficult problems" (p. 517). The best qualitative work brings the reader in close contact with the setting, the participants, and interactions among these. The very best writing is required in the qualitative genre, for the whole enterprise rests on the ability of the researcher to portray, illustrate, and explain. However, the typical graduate-level research methods survey class continues to

initiate novices in the use of the positivist paradigm's omniscient third person, rather than "I." It is no wonder that our research students' first efforts at reading and writing qualitative studies often leave them wondering, "Is this research?"

Music educator/researchers operate under the additional pressure to answer the pragmatic question: "What difference does this study make?" Because the qualitative genre asks the reader to make her or his own meaning from the study, as well as subsequently create her or his own application in the form of new music classroom or rehearsal practice, the answer to the pragmatic question is not immediate but rather comes to the reader upon further reflection. The reader's interpretation depends entirely on the researcher's ability to provide a rich, in-depth, accurate description of the phenomenon as experienced by the researcher, along with an indication of how the researcher made her or his interpretive choices. Alan Peshkin (2000) offers one way of portraying the interpretive process through a series of "metanarrative reflections" that describe what he terms "problematics": offset paragraphs, in the body of the prose narrative, that explain not only the interpretive choices that were made but also the options that were discarded. The result offers the reader a glimpse of the influence of the researcher's subjectivity at each decision-making step of the interpretive process. Peshkin emphasizes that "to be forthcoming and honest about how we work as researchers is to develop a reflective awareness that . . . contributes to enhancing the quality of our interpretive acts" (p. 9). Music education researchers may take another 10 years to become accustomed to the fact that qualitative studies often yield insights that have parallels with the insights gained from musical experiences, for both can be powerful, emotion-laden, and difficult to put into words.

Exemplars of Qualitative Research in Music Education

The qualitative studies in music education included in this section exemplify the broader operant definition of "qualitative" rather than the Bresler/Stake definition. They are included here to illustrate how various species of qualitative methodology have been used to study some aspects of music teaching and learning. Included in this summary are case studies, participant observation, action research, ethnography, and verbal protocol analyses.

Case Studies

The purpose of a case study, according to Stake (1994), is "not to represent the world, but to represent the case" (p.

246). Stake emphasizes the need to "optimize understanding of the case rather than generalization beyond" (p. 246). Stake describes three general categories for types of case studies: intrinsic, instrumental, and collective. The intrinsic case study is undertaken because the researcher has an intrinsic interest in a particular setting or teacher. In an instrumental case study, the particular case is less important than the insight it can provide into a specific issue of theory. A collective case study is an "instrumental case study expended to several cases" (p. 237). Collective cases are selected because of the researcher's belief that "understanding them will lead to better understanding, perhaps better theorizing, about a still larger collection of cases" (p. 237).

Two examples of case studies are included here: one is the work of a research team made up of experienced researchers, the other a doctoral dissertation. Both exemplify, to differing degrees, the qualitative genre's ability to enable the researcher to get closer to the subject under consideration.

Stake, Bresler, and Mabry's (1991) look at what actually happened in the arts in several school districts around the United States focused on one middle school and seven primary schools to get an "understanding of particular situations" in a variety of locations and quality of arts programs (p. 6). In what is described as a "constructivist case study," the findings are experiences that the researchers constructed in an attempt "not to minimize but to preserve interactions between researcher and phenomena" (p. 11). The following six research issues guided the observations (p. 9):

1. Is there attention to aesthetics, to beauty, to intellectual understanding of the arts?
2. Are teachers encouraged to meet arts education needs by integrating arts activities into the teaching of other subject matter?
3. When studying significant artists and their works, are popular and multicultural arts included?
4. Does the responsibility to achieve measurable goals diminish the attention given to arts events and experiences happening outside the classroom?
5. Are there advocates for more discipline-based arts education or other high-quality curricula to replace present custom?
6. What forms of arts education leadership are present and how do they match the needs for leadership?

Each of the research team members developed their own list of specific questions from this broad list and spent 9 to 12 days at individual sites. The resulting report presents lively portraits of practice; each site is portrayed in an individual chapter authored by a single research team member.

The findings were not particularly flattering. The arts existed on the margins of the school day, dominated by popular arts and crafts rather than fine art and a discipline-based approach. "The message from the community to the school was 'Keep art and music part of the curriculum; keep it modest and conventional; continue the traditional performances and exhibits' " (p. 342). No connections to facilitate arts education improvement were found between the observed teachers and the public advocates of music and art education, such as academics, authors of disciplinary journals, or professional organizations such as the Music Educators National Conference (MENC) (p. 345).

The second example of the case study genre is L'Hommedieu's (1992) observational case study of a master studio performance teacher. The purpose of this study was to develop a pedagogical profile of the factors that define extraordinary master teaching in the one-to-one instructional environment of the performance studio. L'Hommedieu looked specifically at four factors of studio teaching, cues, participation, reinforcement, and feedback/correctives, and then considered how these teacher moves were interpreted by the students and how well the students' interpretation matched the teacher's intent.

The study is an important example of a young researcher's shift from one paradigm to another as the result of using an observation schedule in the pilot study. L'Hommedieu found that his musical expertise and experience made the observation schedule checklist data categories seem trivial and found Eisner's "connoisseur" model a better lens through which to consider the master teachers. He then used field notes to record his impressions during the 17 hours of lessons he observed in the study. Other data sources included videotapes of the observed lessons and interviews with the master teachers and their students. The resulting portraits of the individual teachers, though focused on the four pedagogical constructs described earlier, show the rich variety of differences between them, as well as pointing out individual instances of excellent teaching.

Participant Observation

Participant observation studies involve the researcher in some sort of role in the setting that is the focus of the study. There are gradations of amount and type of participation within this definition, as well as of how transparent the researcher's role is to the participants (Atkinson & Hammersley, 1994, p. 249). Each of these variations influences the outcomes of the study and needs to be addressed at the outset when using participant observation.

Berg's (1997) study examined how students in two small high school chamber ensembles reached conclusions about musical interpretation through social interaction. Two questions guided this study: Do identifiable patterns of music thought and action exist within the ensembles? How do these patterns reveal ways that student interactions, tools, and social structures assist or constrain movement through Vygotsky's zone of proximal development toward increased music awareness? During a 5-month period Berg was a participant observer of the two string ensembles during 13 rehearsals, 16 coaching sessions, and 6 performances. Her data sources included video- and audiotapes, transcribed dialogue, 11 interviews with ensemble members and coaches, field notes, and other miscellaneous documents. Berg found that there were similarities (in both groups members challenged each other to clarify, elaborate, and justify the problem solution) and differences (members of the two groups exchanged roles differently and used unique rehearsal strategies) between the social interaction pattern of the two groups. Berg's well-written dissertation portrays collaborative learning in music as a multifaceted process that can both help and hinder the individual performer's musical growth.

Action Research

Action research in music teacher education includes studies in which teachers use their own classroom or rehearsal as a place to implement untried teaching strategies, solve specific teaching-related problems, or document their own reflections on what they do in the course of a school day. There is often an evaluative component to this type of work, with teachers documenting the changes resulting from the innovation. Action research has achieved a resurgence in recent years with the advent of school-university collaborative research partnerships. (See Burnaford, Fischer, & Hobson [1996] for a detailed look at one institution's implementation of action research projects within school communities.)

O'Toole's (1994) action research study of power dynamics in the choral rehearsal class addressed the question of why anyone would be willing to participate in the typical performance ensemble, in which the individual's opinions, thoughts, and feelings are subordinated in favor of the director's opinions, thoughts, and feelings. The research questions focused on replacing the traditional power relations of the choral music classroom with a series of three 8-week projects that implemented feminist pedagogy in three choral ensemble settings. Working in collaboration with two high school choral directors and her own choir, O'Toole used their classroom concerns to design projects that would give more voice to individual students' responses, musical decision-making, and input. O'Toole attempted to involve the students' feelings, needs, and reactions in the rehearsal setting through activities ranging from large group discussion of the poetic text, journal entries about the rehearsals, and student interviews about their experiences. The data included field notes, teacher interviews, student interviews, student-conducted interviews, and researcher journals.

O'Toole's dissertation is noteworthy for both its attempt to apply feminist pedagogical principles in the choral rehearsal and its experimentation with a "postmodern format." The narrative, in first person, is juxtaposed with tales (classroom events) and with critical commentary, nonlinear drama (five unrelated scenes documenting individual and group interview analysis), verbal "snapshots" of interesting moments from the classroom projects, "montages" (a series of images that play with the point of view established in the snapshots), and "slippage" (the author's admission of personal or philosophical contradiction). The result is a rich, thought-provoking example of a more artistic way to represent qualitative research findings.

Ethnography

A form of participant observation that typically explores a particular case in detail by gathering extensive field note and interview data, the ethnographic analysis focuses on the interpretation of "meaning and functions of human actions" and is usually in the form of verbal description and explanation (Atkinson & Hammersley, 1994, p. 248). The main requirement for the ethnographer is to ask the right questions, and skill at interviewing is the prerequisite for data gathering in an ethnographic study.

The process of transmission of traditional music in Ireland and the "nature of both stability and change as seen through the role of the traditional music teacher" was the subject of Veblen's 1991 ethnographic study (p. xii). Her research questions focused on the role of the teacher and the musical network and formal structures for transmission of Irish folk music and the perceptions of teachers and participants' judgments of Irish music traditions as active or passive.

Veblen's 9 months in Ireland allowed her to observe the teaching of two well-known instrumental teachers and interview them. She then corroborated or refuted their points of view via interviews with 13 other teachers of traditional Irish folk music from around the country and interviewed another 26 people representing Irish music organizations. Data included audiotaped interviews, lesson observation notes, field notes, publications of organizations, and videotaped materials and photos.

The format chosen for this work enhances Veblen's excellent writing. The extensive quotations, typical of ethnography, feature the participants' voices, woven together with contextual, interpretive prose that skillfully preserves the flavor and local color experienced by the researcher. Veblen offers the reader an unusually high level of interpretation through tables that tally the findings from each section, followed by a detailed prose summary. Veblen's major finding, that the traditional means of transmission has shifted from being an informal, home-based, individual pursuit to a more organized, classroom endeavor, is offered with some reservation, given the powerful indictment of institutionalized music instruction offered early in the work by one informant: " 'I was rejected by the music teachers as being the only person who didn't have a musical ear and I'm the only one who ever did anything with music out of the entire class' " (p. 61).

Verbal Protocol Analysis: "Think Alouds"

Verbal protocol analysis is a method of data gathering in music education research that relies on the informant's ability to tell the researcher everything he or she is thinking while engaged in some musical task. The authoritative text on "think alouds" is Ericsson and Simon's *Protocol Analysis: Verbal Reports as Data* (1993). The methodology is drawn from the tradition of experimental psychology, where the researcher gives scripted prompts at regular intervals and does not deviate from the procedure. The resulting verbal data or "protocols" are analyzed for patterns of cognitive processes.

Though verbal protocol analysis is clearly a positivist methodology, it has come to be known as a qualitative research method in music education because of its reliance on verbal data. There has been some confusion about the difference between interview data and think aloud data, with "think aloud" used in a cavalier fashion by researchers whose questions to informants were clearly interviews rather than invitations to "tell me what you're thinking" while engaged in a musical activity. The methodology is included here because of its potential to reveal not only the cognitive processes of informants but the meanings they create when engaged with music.

Richardson's work with Cambodian refugee children was part of a research program focused on the cognitive processes involved in the music listening experience (Richardson, 1988, 1994, 1995, 1996, 1998, 1999). Sixty children in grades 1 through 8, designated "new arrivals," as they had just arrived in Sydney from Thai refugee camps, were asked to "think aloud" while listening to four short recorded examples of music drawn from western European classical music and four examples of traditional Cambodian music. The transcripts of their verbalizations were analyzed for evidence of cognitive processes found to be present in an adult musical connoisseur and musically trained elementary-aged children in a Chicago suburb. The results showed that the refugee children exhibited the same cognitive processes as their musically sophisticated age-mates, leading the researcher to conclude that human beings appear to be "hard wired" with universal cognitive processes that operate regardless of culture or education.

More recently, Richardson (in press) took a "postposi-tivist" look at the same data as a source of insight into the way these children create meaning while listening to both familiar and unfamiliar music. Their individual stories were brought to words in the clinical setting of the "think aloud" procedure by listening to the music of their homeland. Their tales of growing up in a state of constant danger and of leaving the green countryside of Cambodia for urban Sydney are a powerful contrast to the "data" reported in the earlier study, revealing the potential of think alouds to offer a window on children's affective lives as well as their cognitive processes.

Points of Departure for Future Studies

What kinds of music teaching and learning issues could best be studied using qualitative methodologies? We conclude by proposing a few possibilities.

Case Studies

- Studies of exemplar teachers and conductors, particularly ensemble directors and private teachers: What are the "teaching moves" that these individual practitioners do that result in highly skilled and musically expressive performances?
- What patterns of development occur in music teacher education students? How do their skills and understandings develop during the junior year 2-semester methods sequence?
- Further investigation of classroom practice to learn what is involved in teaching music for enhanced understanding, "interweaving the empirical with the conceptual" (Ball, 1999, p. 374)

Observational/Ethnographic Studies

What musical learnings result from enrichment and entertainment programs, such as artists-in-the-schools programs?

Ethnographic Case Studies

How has "school music" integrated with "real life" music in various settings? What meanings do kids have about each?

Verbal Protocol Analysis

What kinds of music learning can best be enhanced with technology? How do learners make meaning from their encounters with technology? What musical learnings happen? How is this integrated with what they learn in the classroom or ensemble?

REFERENCES

Arnheim, R. (1969). *Visual thinking.* Berkeley: University of California Press.

Atkinson, P., & Hammersley, M. (1994). Ethnography and participant observation. In N. K. Denzin & Y. S. Lincoln (Eds.), *Handbook of qualitative research* (pp. 248–261). Thousand Oaks, CA: Sage.

Ball, D. L., & Lampert, M. (1999). Multiples of evidence, time, and perspective: Revising the study of teaching and learning. In E. C. Lagemann & L. S. Shulman (Eds.), *Issues in education research: Problems and possibilities* (pp. 371–398). San Francisco: Jossey-Bass.

Becker, H. S., Geer, B., Hughes, E. C., & Strauss, A. L. (1961). *Boys in white: Student culture in medical school.* Chicago: University of Chicago Press.

Becker, H. (1993). Theory: The necessary evil. In D. J. Flinders & G. E. Mills (Eds.), *Theory and concepts in qualitative research* (pp. 218–229). New York: Teachers College Press.

Belenky, M. F., Clinchy, B. M., Goldberger, N. R., & Tarule, J. M. (1986). *Women's ways of knowing.* New York: Basic Books.

Berg, M. H. (1997). *Social construction of musical experience in two high school chamber music ensembles.* Unpublished doctoral dissertation, Northwestern University, Evanston.

Bogdan, R. C., & Biklin, S. K. (1998). *Qualitative research for education* (3rd ed.). Boston: Allyn and Bacon.

Bogdan, R. C., & Biklin, S. K. (1982). *Qualitative research in education.* Boston: Allyn and Bacon.

Bowers, C. A., & Flinders, D. J. (1990). *Responsive teaching.* New York: Teachers College Press.

Bresler, L., & Stake, R. E. (1992). Qualitative research methodology in music education. In R. Colwell (Ed.), *Handbook of research on music teaching and learning* (pp. 75–90). New York: Schirmer Books.

Bruner, J. (1990). *Acts of meaning.* Cambridge, MA: Harvard University Press.

Burnaford, G., Fischer, J., & Hobson, D. (1996) *Teachers doing research: Practical possibilities.* Mahwah, NJ: Erlbaum.

Campbell, D. T. (1979). Degrees of freedom and the case study. In T. D. Cook & C. S. Reichardt (Eds.), *Qualitative and quantitative methods in evaluation research* (pp. 49–67). Beverly Hills, CA: Sage.

Campbell, D. T., & Stanley, J. C. (1963). *Experimental and quasi-experimental designs for research.* Chicago: Rand McNally.

Casey, D. E. (1992). Descriptive research: Techniques and procedures. In R. Colwell (Ed.), *Handbook of research on music teaching and learning* (pp. 115–123). New York: Schirmer Books.

Clough, P. T. (1992). *The end(s) of ethnography: From realism to social criticism.* Newbury Park, CA: Sage.

Colwell, R. J. (1967). Music education and experimental research. *Journal of Research in Music Education, 25*(1), 73–84.

Creswell, J. W. (1988). *Qualitative inquiry and research design.* Thousand Oaks, CA: Sage.

Cronbach, L. (1975). Beyond the two disciplines of scientific psychology. *American Psychologist, 30,* 116–127.

Cronbach, L., & Suppes, P. (Eds.). (1969). *Research for tomorrow's schools.* New York: Macmillan.

Denzin, N. K., & Lincoln, Y. S. (Eds.). (1994). *The handbook of qualitative research.* Thousand Oaks, CA: Sage.

Dewey, J. (1934). *Art as experience.* New York: Perigee Books.

Donmoyer, R. (1990). Generalizability and the single-case study. In E. W. Eisner & A. Peshlein (Eds.), *Qualitative inquiry in education* (pp. 175–200). New York: Teachers College Press.

Donmoyer, R. (1996). Educational research in an era of paradigm proliferation: What is a journal editor to do? *Educational Researcher, 25*(2), 19–35.

Donmoyer, R. (in press). Paradigm talk reconsidered. In V. Richardson (Ed.), *Handbook of research on teaching* (4th ed.). Commerce, GA: Baker & Taylor Books.

Eisner, E. W. (1979). *The educational imagination.* New York: Macmillan.

Eisner, E. W. (1983). Anastasia might still be alive, but the monarchy is dead. *Educational Researcher, 12*(5), 13–14, 23–24.

Eisner, E. W. (1991). *The enlightened eye.* New York: Macmillan.

Eisner, E. W. (1997). The promise and perils of alternative forms of data representation. *Educational Researcher, 26*(6), 4–10.

Eisner, E. W. (1999). Rejoinder: A response to Tom Knapp. *Educational Researcher, 28*(1), 19–20.

Eisner, E. W., & Peshkin, A. (Eds.). (1990). *Qualitative inquiry in education: The continuing debate.* New York: Teachers College Press.

English, F. W. (2000). A critical appraisal of Sara Lawrence Lightfoot's *portraiture* as a method of educational research. *Educational Researcher, 29*(7), 21–26.

Erickson, F. (1986). Qualitative methods in research on teaching. In M. C. Wittrock (Ed.), *Handbook of research on teaching* (3rd ed., pp. 119–161). New York: Macmillan.

Ericsson, K. A., & Simon, H. A. (1993). *Protocol analysis: Verbal reports as data* (rev. ed.). Cambridge, MA: MIT.

Feiman-Nemser, S., & Floden, R. E. (1986). The cultures of teaching. In M. C. Wittrock (Ed.), *Handbook of research on teaching* (3rd ed., pp. 505–526). New York: Macmillan.

Flinders, D. J. (1992). In search of ethical guidance. *International Journal of Qualitative Studies in Education, 5*(2), 101–115.

Freire, P. (1973). *Pedagogy of the oppressed.* New York: Seabury Press.

Gadamer, H. (1975). *Truth and method* (G. Bardon & J. Cumming, Trans. and Eds). New York: Seabury Press.

Gage, N. L. (1963). *Handbook of research on teaching.* Chicago: Rand McNally.

Gahan, C., & Hannibal, M. (1998). *Doing qualitative research using QSR NVB IST.* Thousand Oaks, CA: Sage.

Gall, M., Borg, W. R., & Gall, J. P. (1996). *Educational research: An introduction* (6th ed.). White Plains, NY: Longman.

Geertz, C. (1973). *The interpretation of cultures.* New York: Basic Books.

Geertz, C. (1983). *Local knowledge: Further essays in interpretive anthropology.* New York: Basic Books.

Glaser, B. G., & Strauss, A. L. (1967). *The discovery of grounded theory: Strategies for qualitative research.* Chicago: Aldine.

Glesne, C. (1999). *Becoming qualitative researchers* (2nd ed.). New York: Longman.

Grumet, M. (1980). Autobiography and reconceptualization. *Journal of Curriculum Theorizing, 2,* 155–158.

Guba, E., & Lincoln, Y. (1989). *Fourth generation evaluation.* Newbury Park, CA: Sage.

Habermas, J. (1971). *Knowledge and human interests* (J. Shapiro, Trans.). Boston: Beacon Press.

Habermas, J. (1975). *Legitimation crisis* (T. McCarthy, Trans.). Boston: Beacon Press.

Heath, S. B. (1999). Discipline and disciplines in education research: Elusive goals? In E. C. Lagemann & L. S. Shulman (Eds.), *Issues in education research: Problems and possibilities* (pp. 203–223). San Francisco: Jossey-Bass.

Jackson, P. W. (1968). *Life in classrooms.* New York: Holt, Rinehart and Winston.

Jaeger, R. M. (Ed.). (1988). *Complementary methods for research in education.* Washington, DC: American Educational Research Association.

Keller, E. F. (1983). *A feeling for the organism: The life and work of Barbara McClintock.* New York: Freeman.

Kuhn, T. (1962). *The structure of scientific revolutions.* Chicago: University of Chicago Press.

Kvale, S. (1996). *Interviews: An introduction to qualitative research interviewing.* Thousand Oaks, CA: Sage.

Lagemann, E. C. (1999). An auspicious moment for education research? In E. C. Lagemann & L. S. Shulman (Eds.), *Issues in education research: Problems and possibilities* (pp. 3–16). San Francisco: Jossey-Bass.

Langer, S. (1957). *Problems of art.* New York: Scribner's.

LeCompte, M. D., Millroy, W. L., & Preissle, J. (1992). *The handbook of qualitative research in education.* New York: Academic Press.

L'Hommedieu, R. L. (1992). *The management of selected educational process variables by master studio teachers in music performance.* Unpublished doctoral dissertation, Northwestern University, Evanston.

Lightfoot, S. L. (1983). *The good high school.* New York: Basic Books.

Lincoln, Y. S., & Guba, E. G. (1985). *Naturalistic inquiry.* Thousand Oaks, CA: Sage.

Malinowski, B. (1988). *Argonauts of the Western Pacific: An account of native enterprise and adventure in the archipelagoes of Melanesian New Guinea.* London: Routledge. (Original work published 1922)

Mayer, R. E. (2000). What is the place of science in educational research? *Educational Researcher, 29*(6), 38–39.

Miles, M. B., & Huberman, A. M. (1984). *Qualitative data analysis.* Beverly Hills, CA: Sage.

Munro, P. (1993). Continuing dilemmas in life history research. In D. J. Flinders & G. E. Mills (Eds.), *Theory and concepts in qualitative research* (pp. 163–177). New York: Teachers College Press.

Noddings, N. (1992). *The challenge to care in schools.* New York: Teachers College Press.

Noddings, N. (1995). *Philosophy of education.* Boulder, CO: Westview Press.

Noddings, N. (1999). Care, justice, and equity. In M. S. Katz, N. Noddings, & K. A. Strike (Eds.), *Justice and caring* (pp. 7–20). New York: Teachers College Press.

O'Toole, P. A. (1994). *Redirecting the choral classroom: A feminist poststructural analysis of power relations within three choral settings.* Unpublished doctoral dissertation, University of Wisconsin, Madison.

Patton, M. (1980). *Qualitative evaluation and research methods.* Newbury Park, CA: Sage.

Peshkin, A. (1978). *Growing up American.* Chicago: University of Chicago Press.

Peshkin, A. (1982). The researcher and subjectivity: Reflections on ethnography of school and community. In G. Spindler (Ed.), *Doing the ethnography of schooling* (pp. 20–47). New York: Holt, Rinehart and Winston.

Peshkin, A. (1988). In search of subjectivity of one's own. *Educational Researcher, 17*(7), 17–22.

Peshkin, A. (2000). The nature of interpretation in qualitative research. *Educational Researcher, 29*(9), 5–9.

Phillips, D. C. (1983). After the wake: Postpositivistic educational thought. *Educational Researcher, 12*(5), 4–12.

Phillips, D. C. (1990). Subjectivity and objectivity: An objective inquiry. In E. W. Eisner & A. Peshkin (Eds.), *Qualitative inquiry in education* (pp. 19–37). New York: Teachers College Press.

Powell, A. G., Farrar, E., & Cohen, D. K. (1985). *The shopping mall high school.* Boston: Houghton Mifflin.

Richardson, C. P. (1988). *Musical thinking as exemplified in music criticism.* Unpublished doctoral dissertation, University of Illinois, Urbana-Champaign.

Richardson, C. P. (1994). The music listening processes of the child connoisseur: A developmental model. *Proceedings of the Third International Conference for Music Perception and Cognition of the European Society for the Cognitive Sciences of Music, Liège, Belgium* (pp. 153–154). Liège: European Society for the Cognitive Sciences of Music.

Richardson, C. P. (1995, April). *Toward a global model of children's music listening processes.* Paper presented at the annual meeting of the American Educational Research Association, San Francisco.

Richardson, C. P. (1996, April). *Finding the voice within the data: Think alouds in music.* Paper presented at the annual meeting of the American Educational Research Association, New York City.

Richardson, C. P. (1998). The roles of the critical thinker in the music classroom. *Studies in Music, 17,* 107–120.

Richardson, C. P. (1999). The music listening processes of Cambodian refugee children. *Bulletin of the Council for Research in Music Education, 142,* 91.

Richardson, C. P. (in press). Eastern ears in Western classrooms: Cambodian refugee children in the general music class. In B. Hanley (Ed.), *Papers from the Symposium on Musical Understanding*.

Richardson, L. (1994). Writing: A method of inquiry. In N. K. Denzin & Y. S. Lincoln (Eds.), *Handbook of qualitative research* (pp. 516–529). Thousand Oaks, CA: Sage.

Rosaldo, R. (1989). *Culture and truth*. Boston: Beacon Press.

Schoenfeld, A. H. (1999). The core, the canon, and the development of research skills: Issues in the preparation of education researchers. In E. C. Lagemann & L. S. Shulman (Eds.), *Issues in education research: Problems and possibilities* (pp. 166–203). San Francisco: Jossey-Bass.

Schofield, J. W. (1990). Increasing the generalizability of qualitative research. In E. W. Eisner & Alan Peshkin (Eds.), *Qualitative inquiry in education* (pp. 201–232). New York: Teachers College Press.

Schön, D. (1983). *The reflective practitioner*. New York: Basic.

Schwandt, T. A. (1997). *Qualitative inquiry: A dictionary of terms*. Thousand Oaks, CA: Sage.

Sherman, R. R., & Webb, R. B. (1988). *Qualitative research in education: focus and methods*. New York: Falmer Press.

Shuy, R. (1986). Secretary Bennett's teaching. *Teaching and Teacher Education*, 2(4), 315–323.

Sizer, T. R. (1984). *Horace's compromise: The dilemma of the American high school*. Boston: Houghton Mifflin.

Smith, J. K. (1993). Hermeneutics and qualitative inquiry. In D. J. Flinders & G. E. Mills (Eds.), *Theory and concepts in qualitative research* (pp. 183–200). New York: Teachers College Press.

Spindler, G. (Ed.). (1955). *Education and anthropology*. Stanford, CA: Stanford University Press.

Spindler, G. (Ed.). (1963). *Education and culture: Anthropological approaches*. New York: Holt, Rinehart, and Winston.

Spindler, G., & Spindler, L. (1992). Cultural process and ethnography: An anthropological perspective. In M. D. LeCompte, W. L. Millroy, & J. Preissle (Eds.), *The handbook of qualitative research in education* (pp. 53–92). New York: Academic Press.

Stake, R. E. (1986, April). *Situational context as influence on evaluation and use*. Paper presented at the annual meeting of the American Educational Research Association, San Francisco.

Stake, R. (1994). Case studies. In N. K. Denzin & Y. S. Lincoln (Eds.), *Handbook of qualitative research* (pp. 516–529). Thousand Oaks, CA: Sage.

Stake, R., Bresler, L., & Mabry, L. (1991). *Custom and cherishing: The arts in elementary schools*. Urbana, IL: National Arts Education Research Center.

St. Maurice, H. (1993). The rhetorical return: The rhetoric of qualitative inquiry. In D. J. Flinders & G. E. Mills (Eds.), *Theory and concepts in qualitative research* (pp. 201–217). New York: Teachers College Press.

Stringer, E. T. (1993). Socially responsive educational research. In D. J. Flinders & G. E. Mills (Eds.), *Theory and concepts in qualitative research* (pp. 141–162). New York: Teachers College Press.

Stringer, E. T. (1996). *Action research: A handbook for practitioners*. Thousand Oaks, CA: Sage.

Thorndike, E. L. (1910). The contribution of psychology to education. *Journal of Educational Psychology*, 1, 5–12.

Van Maanen, J. (1988). *Tales of the field*. Chicago: University of Chicago Press.

Van Manen, M. (1990). *Researching lived experience*. Albany: State University of New York Press.

Veblen, K. K. (1991). *Perceptions of change and stability in the transmission of Irish traditional music: An examination of the music teacher's role*. Unpublished doctoral dissertation, University of Wisconsin, Madison.

Vidich, A. J., & Layman, S. M. (1994). Qualitative methods: Their history in sociology and anthropology. In N. K. Denzin & Y. S. Lincoln (Eds.), *Handbook of qualitative research* (pp. 23–59). Thousand Oaks, CA: Sage.

Waller, W. (1932). *Sociology of teaching*. New York: Wiley.

Weitzman, E., & Miles, M. (1995). *Computer programs for qualitative data analysis*. Thousand Oaks, CA: Sage.

Wolcott, H. F. (1973). *The man in the principal's office: An ethnography*. New York: Holt, Rinehart and Winston.

Wolcott, H. F. (1982). Differing styles of on-site research or, if it isn't ethnography, what is it? *Review Journal of Philosophy and Social Science*, 7(1,2), 154–169.

Wolcott, H. F. (1990a). On seeking—and rejecting—validity in qualitative research. In E. W. Eisner & A. Peshkin (Eds.), *Qualitative inquiry in education* (pp. 121–152). New York: Teachers College Press.

Wolcott, H. F. (1990b). *Writing up qualitative research*. Newbury Park, CA: Sage.

Wolcott, H. F. (1992). Posturing in qualitative research. In M. D. LeCompte, W. L. Milroy, & J. Preissle (Eds.), *The handbook of qualitative research in education* (pp. 3–52). New York: Academic Press.

Index